DATE DUE

DEMCO 38-296

International Dictionary of
BALLET

International Dictionary of

BALLET

VOLUME 2
L – Z

EDITOR
MARTHA BREMSER

ASSISTANT EDITOR
LARRAINE NICHOLAS

PICTURE EDITOR
LEANDA SHRIMPTON

St J

St James Press

Detroit   London   Washington DC

Front Cover–Alessandra Ferri as Juliet
(© Leslie Spatt)

Copyright © 1993 by ST JAMES PRESS

All rights reserved including the right of reproduction in whole or in part in any form. For information, write to:
ST JAMES PRESS
835 Penobscot Bldg.
Detroit, MI 48226-4094
or
PO Box 699
Cheriton House
North Way
Andover
Hants SP10 5YE

ST JAMES PRESS is an imprint of Gale Research Inc.

Library of Congress Cataloging-in-Publication Data
International dictionary of ballet / editor, Martha Bremser;
        picture editor, Leanda Shrimpton.
            p.   cm.
        Includes bibliographical references and index.
        Contents: Vol. 1. A-K — v. 2. L-Z.
        ISBN 1-55862-084-2 (set)
        ISBN 1-55862-157-1 (Volume 1)
        ISBN 1-55862-158-X (Volume 2)
        1. Ballet — Encyclopedias.   I. Bremser, Martha.
    GV1585.I57   1993
    792.8'03 — dc20   93-25051
                                                           CIP

A CIP catalogue record for this book is available from the British Library.

Printed in the United States of America.
Published simultaneously in the United Kingdom.

The paper used in this publication meets the minimum requirements of American National Standard for Information Sciences—Permanence Paper for printed Library Materials, ANSI Z39.48-1984. ∞™

CONTENTS

ENTRIES L–Z   *page* 799

COUNTRY INDEX   1575

PROFESSIONS AND INSTITUTIONS INDEX   1581

NOTES ON CONTRIBUTORS   1591

PICTURE ACKNOWLEDGEMENTS   1599

L

LACOTTE, Pierre

French dancer, choreographer, teacher, and ballet director. Born in Chatoux, 4 April 1932. Studied at the Paris Opéra School, pupil of Gustave Ricaux, Carlotta Zambelli, Serge Lifar, Lubov Egorova, Victor Gsovsky, Boris Kniaseff, 1942–46; also studied with Madame Rousanne and Nicolas Zverev, Paris, and with Antony Tudor, Pierre Vladimirov, Margaret Craske, Martha Graham, New York, and Marie Rambert, London. Married dancer Ghislaine Thesmar, 1968. Dancer, Paris Opéra Ballet, from 1946 becoming petit sujet from 1947, grand sujet from 1951, and premier danseur, 1952–55; premier danseur, Metropolitan Opera, New York, 1956–57; guest artist, including in concerts with Violette Verdy, London, 1961; founder and director, Le Ballet de la Tour Eiffel (also Les Ballets de la Tour Eiffel), 1955–60; choreographer, Berlin Festival, 1959; director, Ballet National Jeunesses Musicales de France (JMF), 1963–68; guest choreographer, Ballet Rambert, London, 1966; authority on Romantic ballet, staging reconstructions of nineteenth-century ballets for Paris Opéra Ballet from 1972, and also in Novosibirsk, Buenos Aires, Rio de Janeiro, Rome, Warsaw, Sofia, Prague, and Boston; guest choreographer, Kirov Ballet, Leningrad, 1979, Moscow Classical Ballet, 1980; choreographer and associate director, Ballets de Monte Carlo, 1985–88; artistic director, Ballet de Nancy, from 1991; also teacher: Professeur d'Adage, Conservatoire nationale supérieur de musique et de danse, from 1970, and Paris Opéra Ballet, from 1971. Recipient: Belgian Prix de la Meilleure Emission Télévisée de l'Année (for *La Nuit est une sorcière*), 1954; Chevalier des Arts et des Lettres, 1975; Officier des Arts et des Lettres, 1981.

ROLES

1950   L'Assassin (cr) in *Septuor* (Lifar), Paris Opéra Ballet, Paris

1951   The Prince in *Blanche-Neige* (Lifar), Paris Opéra Ballet, Paris

James in *La Sylphide* (after Bournonville), French television

Principal dancer in *Napoli* (divertissement; after Bournonville), French television

1952   The Persian, *Ballet des Fleurs* in *Les Indes galantes* (Aveline, Lifar, Lander), Paris Opéra Ballet, Paris

Soloist in *Études* (Lander), Paris Opéra Ballet, Paris

Un Nègre (cr) in *Les Caprices de Cupidon* (Lander), Paris Opéra Ballet, Paris

1952/   Principal dancer in *Suite en blanc* (Lifar), Paris Opéra
55   Ballet, Paris

Principal dancer in *Les Saisons* (Aveline), Paris Opéra Ballet, Paris

Title role in *Le Spectre de la rose* (Fokine), Paris Opéra Ballet, Paris

Second Movement in *Le Palais de cristal* (Balanchine), Paris Opéra Ballet, Paris

Ademar in *La Grande Jatte* (Aveline), Paris Opéra Ballet, Paris

1953   L'Esprit du mal in *Cinema* (Lifar), Paris Opéra Ballet, Paris

1954   Principal dancer in *Oberon* (Aveline, Lifar, Lander), Paris Opéra Ballet, Paris

Un Amoureux in *Printemps à Vienne* (Lander), Paris Opéra Ballet, Paris

1956   Principal dancer in *Ernani* (opera; mus. Verdi, chor. Solov), Metropolitan Opera, New York

1956/   Principal dancer in *Soirée musicale* (Solov), Metropoli-
57   tan Opera Ballet, New York

1962   The Bridegroom in *Les Noces* (Skibine), Aix-en-Provence Festival

1964   Principal dancer in *Fantaisie Choreique* (Schmucki), T.E.P., Paris

1974   Dr. Coppélius in *Coppélia* (also chor., after Saint-Léon), Paris Opéra Ballet, Paris

Other roles include: for Paris Opéra Ballet—Le Dieu de la vie in *Istar* (Lifar), Bluebird Pas de deux from *The Sleeping Beauty* (after Petipa), Fourth Movement in *Le Palais de cristal* (Balanchine), principal dancer in *Études* (Lander), principal dancer in *Pas et lignes* (Lifar), the Poet in *La Sonnambula* (Balanchine), principal dancer in *Les Sylphides* (Fokine), principal dancer in *Divertissement* (from *The Sleeping Beauty*; Lifar after Petipa), principal dancer in *Grand Pas* (Lifar); for Ballet JMF—Basil in *Don Quixote* (after Petipa), principal dancer in *Annabel Lee* (Skibine), Albrecht in *Giselle* (own staging, after Petipa, Coralli, Perrot), Prince Siegfried in *Swan Lake* (own staging, after Petipa, Ivanov); as guest artist or in concert performances—Prince in *The Nutcracker* (after Ivanov), the Devil in *Orphée* (van Dyk), Prince Désiré in *The Sleeping Beauty* (after Petipa), the danseur in *Grand Pas classique* (V. Gsovsky).

WORKS

1948   *Le Dieu bleu* (mus. Hahn), Danse et Culture, Paris

1949   *Exode* (mus. Tchaikovsky), Académie Choreographique de l'Opéra de Paris

Clair de lune (mus. Debussy), Académie chorégraphique de l'Opéra de Paris

Dernière Vision (mus. Wayenberg), Académie chorégraphique de l'Opéra de Paris

1953   *Chansons* (mus. Cosma, Piaf, and others), Théâtre de Paris, Gala

Pierre Lacotte's ballet *La Nuit est une sorcière*, as performed by the Ballets de Monte Carlo, 1985

Inspiration (mus. Spear), Gala, Paris
Vaincre (mus. Bach), Gala, Théâtre de Paris, Paris
Renonciation (mus. Bach), Gala, Théâtre de Paris, Paris
En bateau (mus. Debussy), Gala, Théâtre de Paris, Paris
1955 *La Nuit est une sorcière* (mus. Bechet), Ballet de la Tour Eiffel, Paris
Solstice (mus. Wayenberg), Ballet de la Tour Eiffel, Paris
Gosse de Paris (mus. Aznavour), Ballet de la Tour Eiffel, Paris
Tempo universel (mus. Albinoni), Ballet de la Tour Eiffel, Paris
Concertino (mus. Vivaldi), Ballet de la Tour Eiffel, Monte Carlo
Aiguillage (mus. Lasry), Ballet de la Tour Eiffel, Monte Carlo
1959 *Such Sweet Thunder* (mus. Ellington), Berlin Festival, Berlin
1962 *Simple Symphony* (mus. Britten), Ballet JMF, Paris
Hotel des étrangers (mus. Galli), Ballet JMF, Paris
1963 *La Péri* (mus. Dukas), Teatro Colón, Buenos Aires
Elégie (mus. Fauré), Ballet JMF, Paris
Bifurcation (mus. Geninagni), Ballet JMF, Paris
1964 *Hamlet* (mus. Walton), Ballet JMF, Paris

Penthesilée (mus. Semenoff), French television
Hippolyte et Arice (mus. Rameau), Ballet JMF, Paris
1965 *Intermèdes* (mus. Vivaldi), Ballet JMF, Paris
La Femme et sa fable (mus. Castarede), Ballet JMF, Paris
La Voix (mus. Leveillée), Ballet JMF, French television
1966 *Intermède* (mus. Vivaldi), Ballet Rambert, London
Numeros (jazz), Ballet Rambert, London
1967 *La Proie* (mus. Schoenberg), Ballet JMF, Paris
Passion future (mus. Lutoslawski), Ballet JMF, Paris
Caline (mus. Satie), Ballet JMF, Paris
Contre danse (mus. Galli), Ballet JMF, Paris
1968 *L'École des Pickpockets* (mus. Delaubre), Strasbourg
1970 *La Favorita* (pas de deux; mus. Donizetti), La Fenice, Venice
Allegro romantico (new production of *La Péri*; mus. Bergmüller), La Fenice, Venice
1971 *Gymnopédies* (mus. Satie), Brantôme Festival
1973 *Le Roi de la nuit* (mus. Damase), Nice Opéra Ballet, Nice
1974 *Tales of Hoffmann* (mus. Offenbach), French television
1976 *Menuetto* (mus. Stravinsky), Hungarian State Opera Ballet, Budapest
1977 *La Dame aux camélias* (mus. Verdi), French television

Platée (mus. Rameau), Opéra-Comique, Paris

1985   *Philippe Taglioni* (with Carla Fracci), Italian television
Te deum (mus. Bizet), Ballets de Monte Carlo, Monte Carlo
L'Apprenti Sorcier (mus. Dukas), Ballets de Monte Carlo, Monte Carlo
24 heures de la vie d'une femme (mus. Niquet), Ballets de Monte Carlo, Monte Carlo

1986   *La Dame aux camélias* (new production; mus. Verdi), Sofia Opera Ballet, Sofia

1988   *A Midsummer Night's Dream* (*Sono di una notte di mezza estate*; mus. Mendelssohn), Rome Opera Ballet, Rome

Also staged:

1972   *La Sylphide* (after Taglioni; mus. Schneitzhoeffer), French television (also staged Paris Opéra Ballet, 1972; Novosibirsk Ballet, 1973; Teatro Colón, Buenos Aires, 1973; Boston Ballet, 1976; Tokyo Ballet, 1978; Rome Opera Ballet, 1982; Prague Opera Ballet, 1986; Ballet Verona, 1987; Ballets de Monte Carlo, 1989; Ballet de Rio de Janeiro, 1990)

1973   *Coppélia* (after Saint-Léon; mus. Delibes), Paris Opéra Ballet, Paris

1976   *La Vivandière* Pas de six (after Saint-Léon; mus. Pugni), Opéra-Comique, Paris (staged Kirov Ballet, 1979; Ballets de Monte Carlo)
Swan Lake (after Petipa, Ivanov; mus. Tchaikovsky), Grand Theatre, Bordeaux
Le Papillon (after M. Taglioni; mus. Offenbach), Paris Opéra Ballet, Paris (also staged Rome Opera Ballet, Kirov Ballet)

1978   *La Fille de Danube* (after Taglioni; mus. Adam), Teatro Colón, Buenos Aires
Giselle (after Coralli, Perrot; mus. Adam), Ballet du Rhin, Strasbourg (also staged Ballet JMF)

1979   *La Cachucha* (after Elssler, as first danced in Coralli's *Le Diable boîteux*; mus. traditional), Kirov Ballet, Leningrad

1980   *Nathalie; ou, La Laitière suisse* (after Taglioni; mus. Gyrowetz), Moscow Classical Ballet, Moscow

1981   *Marco Spada* (after Mazilier; mus. Auber), Rome Opera Ballet, Rome
Le Papillon (after M. Taglioni; mus. Offenbach), Rome Opera Ballet, Rome

1984   *La Cracovienne* (after Mazilier, Elssler, as first danced in Mazilier's *La Gipsy*; mus. Benoist, Thomas, Aurelio), French television
Marco Spada (after Mazilier; mus. Auber), Paris Opéra Ballet, Paris (staged Ballets de Monte Carlo, 1986)

1987   *Robert le Diable* (after Taglioni; mus. Meyerbeer), Italian television

1991   *Giselle* (new production; reconstruction after Coralli, Perrot; mus. Adam), Ballet National de Nancy, Lorraine

PUBLICATIONS

By Lacotte:

"La Conservation du ballet", in Hofman, André, *Le Ballet*, Paris, 1982

"Looking for *La Sylphide*", *Dance and Dancers* (London), October 1982

Interview with Otis Stuart, "A Really Good School is International", *Ballett International* (Cologne), October 1984

About Lacotte:

Coquelle, Jean, "Choreography in France", *Ballet Today* (London), May 1957

Herf, Estelle, "Ballet Rambert", *Ballet Today* (London), January–February 1967

Diénis, Jean Claude, "Pierre Lacotte, un retour aux sources", *Danser* (Paris), March 1984

Koegler, Horst, "Forward into the Past?", *Ballett International* (Cologne), March 1986

Pastori, Jean-Pierre, *Pierre Lacotte: Tradition*, Lausanne, 1987

*   *   *

In a career spanning more than four decades, Pierre Lacotte has established himself as one of the most active and industrious figures in French ballet in the second half of the twentieth century. A product of the Paris Opéra Ballet school, Lacotte entered the Opéra corps de ballet in 1946. He had reached the rank of premier danseur before breaking away from the Opéra in 1955 to pursue an independent career as a choreographer and company director. After two decades of heading his own troupes, Lacotte emerged in the 1970s as France's leading authority on nineteenth-century dance through a series of highly praised restorations of ballets from the Romantic era and the Second Empire.

Lacotte entered the ballet school of the Paris Opéra at the age of ten, and his major teachers included Gustave Ricaux. He had his début with the company during its first seasons after World War II, building a repertory that included a major created role in the premiere of Serge Lifar's *Septuor*. A disagreement with the Opéra administration, however, over Lacotte's interest in opportunities to choreograph away from his home company led to his departure in 1955. He established the first of his own companies with dancer Josette Clavier, the Ballet de la Tour Eiffel, with the aim of establishing a venue for contemporary ballets such as his own *Gosse de Paris* and *La Nuit est une sorcière*. As director of a second company, Les Jeunesses Musicales de France (established in 1962), Lacotte created new ballets for the company that included *Hamlet* and *Combat de Tancredi* while also working as guest choreographer for companies such as Ballet Rambert, for whom he staged *Intermède* in 1966.

Through Les Jeunesses Musicales, Lacotte also introduced French audiences to ballerina Ghislaine Thesmar, who became his principal subject and wife. When Lacotte restaged the original Taglioni *La Sylphide* for the Paris Opéra Ballet in 1972, the production proved a milestone for both Thesmar and Lacotte. Thesmar's personal success in the title role made her one of the few dancers in Opéra history to be taken into the company as a result of popular acclaim, rather than through the traditional ranks of the Opéra school and company.

Lacotte's painstaking, impassioned research into the period, and his interest in retrieving both the letter and the spirit of the original choreography, initiated a new career for him as the leading authority on nineteenth-century French ballet. His services now in international demand, Lacotte has staged a series of restorations for the Opéra, as well as for several other European troupes and for various individual guest artists, with his productions including *Coppélia*, *Robert le Diable*, and *Marco Spada*. When Thesmar retired from the Opéra in 1983, she and Lacotte were invited by the royal family of Monaco to establish a new Ballets de Monte Carlo, with Thesmar as principal ballerina and Lacotte as resident choreographer.

Despite Lacotte's earlier flirtations with modern-orientated dance and jazz, the nineteenth century is undoubtedly his real artistic heritage. Indeed, the era has virtually become his own responsibility to the late twentieth-century ballet world, which looks to him for an authentic representation and interpretation of the nineteenth century. Lacotte is characteristically frank about this burden. "I feel now that I have assumed a responsibility and it is a great responsibility to carry alone," he said in 1984. "I would like very much to find a student, to find someone I can teach how to restore the ballets that have been lost. There are so many and, even if they cannot be restored in their entirety, they can at least be partially restored."

Recognizing that his role as an authority on earlier ballet has made him push aside his own choreographic ambitions, Lacotte still remains passionate about his historical mission. As the great ballerina Lubov Egorova said to Lacotte when he first began work on *La Sylphide*, "None of the people of your generation are interested in preserving the past. You are the only one who can do that. You must do that."

—Otis Stuart

THE LADY AND THE FOOL

Choreography: John Cranko
Music: Giuseppe Verdi (selections from operas, arranged by Charles Mackerras)
Design: Richard Beer (scenery and costumes)
First Production: Sadler's Wells Theatre Ballet, New Theatre, Oxford, 25 February 1954
Principal Dancers: Patricia Miller (La Capricciosa), Kenneth MacMillan (Moondog), Johaar Mosaval (Bootface)

Other productions include: Sadler's Wells Ballet (restaged and revised Cranko), with Beryl Grey (La Capricciosa), Philip Chatfield (Moondog), Ray Powell (Bootface); London, 9 June 1955. Stuttgart Ballet (restaged Cranko, design Werner Schachteli); Stuttgart, 8 November 1961. Australian Ballet (staged Ray Powell), with Marilyn Jones (La Capricciosa), Ray Powell (Bootface); Sydney, 14 December 1962. German Opera Ballet; Berlin, 3 May 1965. CAPAB Ballet; Capetown, December 1965. Royal Danish Ballet (restaged Cranko); Copenhagen, 1971. Houston Ballet (staged Georgette Tsingvirides); Houston, 21 September 1978.

PUBLICATIONS

Barnes, Clive, "*The Lady and the Fool*", *Dance and Dancers* (London), May 1954
Beaumont, Cyril, *Ballets Past and Present*, London, 1955
Barnes, Clive, "John Cranko", *About the House* (London), Christmas 1965
Brinson, Peter, and Crisp, Clement, *Ballet for All*, London, 1970
Percival, John, *Theatre in My Blood: A Biography of John Cranko*, London, 1983

*   *   *

By 1954, John Cranko was well established in his career as choreographer with the Sadler's Wells Theatre Ballet, and had already made one of his most popular and enduring ballets, *Pineapple Poll* (1951). He had clearly demonstrated his strong interest in theatre and matters theatrical—at times, one might argue, to the detriment of the choreography itself. Cranko had shown that his works tended not to be "subtle", but boldly drawn, often highly dramatic, even melodramatic, or comic. In this sense *The Lady and the Fool*, first staged in February 1954, was not typical of his work; the plot is straightforward, and events, apart from the Lady's rejection of all "eligible" suitors in favour of the despised clown, are not dramatic. However, the ballet did present two recurring threads in Cranko's work during his English career: the use of symbolism, with characters who represent particular ideas or aspects of a personality, and the exploration of the nature of love and its power to transform.

The ballet was staged in one act, as were all of Cranko's works until *The Prince of the Pagodas* in 1957. His leading ballerina was Patricia Miller, who had created leading roles in a number of his earlier works, such as *Beauty and the Beast* (1949) and *Harlequin in April* (1951). The central female role was that of La Capricciosa, the capricious masked heroine whose face is only revealed by the clown Moondog, her earlier suitors each only being able to remove one mask to display another underneath. Moondog's success in removing the mask symbolizes his ability to awaken true love in the lady's heart and thus transform the lives of both. Later interpreters of the role of La Capricciosa have included Beryl Grey; and Kenneth MacMillan—who, like Miller, had already created roles for Cranko—was the original Moondog, the tall clown whose love is returned by La Capricciosa. Bootface, the second clown, was first danced by Johaar Mosaval. The small clown's dog-like devotion to his friend provided both an extra thread in the web of relationships and also an added dimension to the exploration of genuinely disinterested love.

The nature of love and its capacity to transform people was a theme which Cranko returned to on many occasions during the English phase of his career, appearing later in extended form in *The Prince of the Pagodas*. The well-loved comedy ballet *Pineapple Poll* is an earlier example, but in *The Lady and the Fool* a more serious and subtle approach was adopted (although in the view of some critics it was merely sentimental). In the opinion of most critics, the quality of choreographic writing was variable. On more than one occasion during Cranko's early career, a critic would declare that Cranko had come infuriatingly close to producing a masterpiece, only to spoil it either by failing to discipline his ideas or by a sudden and inexplicable descent into ordinariness. Peter Williams made such a judgement of *The Lady and the Fool*, writing, "*The Lady and the Fool* . . . is one of those near misses. It has all the makings of a splendid work yet it remains dreadfully superficial." However, the ballet was also seen as containing much of great value choreographically; another critic explained that "There is a fine pas de quatre for the lady and her three suitors, where the lifts, although acrobatic, have beauty and grace. In the pas de deux for the tall clown and the lady similar lifts acquire a tender, passionate quality" (Joan Lawson). Interestingly, the ballet was generally more readily understood by the Russians (the influential Bolshoi visit to England came two years after the first performance of *The Lady and the Fool*); they, according to John Percival, recognized "important issues beneath an entertaining surface triviality".

Cranko's predilection for fairy-tale or *commedia dell'arte* characters is evident in this ballet, as is his practice of investing them with the particular personalities required for his work, in the way that he had done in earlier ballets, such as *Harlequin in April* and *Pineapple Poll*. John Percival quotes Frank Tait, a close associate of Cranko's, in suggesting that "something of John himself was to be found in all three of the leading characters". Perhaps, as was apparently the case in two earlier ballets, *Beauty and the Beast* (1949) and *The Shadow* (1953), the division of aspects of his own self between different characters helped to abstract the more personal factors and make them

The Lady and the Fool, with Margaret Barbieri and Stephen Wicks, Sadler's Wells Royal Ballet, London

more universal and accessible. The fact that the best choreographic writing was found in some of the dances for these three would seem to bear this out. The generally criticized corps de ballet work could have suffered from lack of time because of delays in completion due to Cranko's illness; but perhaps, also, his interest was less keenly involved.

The Lady and the Fool was considerably revised for a production in 1955 at Covent Garden, with the plot streamlined and more tightly focused, and the characterization and comedy developed. However, Joan Lawson, writing of this new version, declared that in fact much was lost, and that the ballet had become "merely a spectacle of exciting dance", with pathos sacrificed as a result. Certainly it may be said that an essentially intimate work such as this needs very careful staging in larger theatres, and needs, above all, sensitive interpretation on the part of the leading dancers in order to illuminate the subtleties of the theme.

—Rachel S. Richardson

THE LADY OF THE CAMELLIAS
(original German title: *Die Kameliendame*)

Choreography: John Neumeier
Music: Frederic Chopin
Design: Jürgen Rose (scenery and costumes)
Libretto: John Neumeier (after Alexandre Dumas *fils'* novel *La Dame aux camélias*, 1848)
First Production: Stuttgart Ballet, Württembergisches Staatstheater, 4 November 1978
Principal Dancers: Marcia Haydée (Marguerite Gautier), Egon Madsen (Armand Duval), Birgit Keil (Manon), Richard Cragun (Des Grieux)

Other productions include: Hamburg Ballet (revival; restaged Neumeier); Hamburg, 31 January 1981.

Other choreographic treatments of story: F. Termanini (Turin, 1857), John Taras (New York, 1946), Anton Dolin (Mexico City, 1947), Antony Tudor (New York, 1951 and motion picture), Tatiana Gsovsky (Berlin, 1957), Ruth Page (Chicago, 1957), Kirsten Ralov (Copenhagen, 1960), Frederick Ashton

The Lady of the Camellias, with Marcia Haydée and Egon Madsen, Stuttgart Ballet

(London, 1963), William Dollar (Paris, 1964 and television 1977), Alberto Mendez (Havana, 1971), John Jorge Lefebre (Charleroi, 1980), Domy Reiter-Soffer (Dublin, 1984).

PUBLICATIONS

Koegler, Horst, "John Neumeier: *Kameliendame* in Stuttgart", *Das Tanzarchiv* (Cologne), December 1978

Percival, John, "Lady with the Camellias", *Dance and Dancers* (London), March 1979

Dienis, Jean-Claude, "*La Dame aux Camellias*", *Les Saisons de la danse* (Paris), January 1980

Croce, Arlene, *Going to the Dance*, New York, 1982

Finkel, Anita, "*Kameliendame* with North German T.V.", *Ballett International* (Cologne), May 1987

*   *   *

John Neumeier's *The Lady of the Camellias*, or *Kameliendame*, is one of several ballets over the years to use Dumas *fils*' 1848 novel *La Dame aux camélias* as its source and inspiration. Neumeier gives his own version of the story a slow start, as befits its mood. Groups of people stand about in Marguerite's salon; someone picks up an ornament and examines it; furniture is moved about. The prologue is just like a scene in a play. As the ballet continues, there are more and more brief play-like sequences of a type familiar to those who know Cranko's choreography. These include the first meeting, for example: Marguerite sits on a settee, surrounded by admirers. People chat and flirt together. Gaston introduces Armand to her. She asks him to sit next to her; someone takes the chair from underneath him. He falls to the ground. Marguerite and the other guests laugh at his expense.

One feels the inner action, so to speak; and the various characters' reflections on their desperate states of mind might be considered as the material of theatre rather than ballet. And yet the piece is always moved along by dance. Neumeier achieves this effect in the first instance through the society which is portrayed so luxuriously: in both the first and third acts there are great ball scenes, in the third act to breath-taking écossaises and fast waltzes, virtually providing self-portraits in dance of the house guests—for example of Prudence in her seductive solo, or Gaston in his semi-character whip solo—and showing the games which are employed by such classes to pass the time away.

In the first act, Neumeier also finds new choreographic possibilities by including the characters of Manon and Des Grieux, as Marguerite and Armand watch a ballet based on *Manon Lescaut*: he brings both pairs into mirror-image positions and leads them into mutual interaction. Marguerite appears on stage immediately and forces the dancing pair apart, identifying herself on a visual level with them. After the applause there is a duet with Armand and Des Grieux, which culminates in a pas de trois with Manon. In Marguerite's feverish dreams at the end, she too dances a pas de trois, this time with Manon and Des Grieux.

The highlights of the piece are four pas de deux: Armand paying court after the ballet, the great mutual love in the country house, the last night of passion, and—not least—the short meeting between Marguerite and Armand's father.

In the later film version of the ballet, which Neumeier had already planned as a concept before the stage version (and which he directed himself), the flash-back technique is even more marked. In the film, since it is technically feasible, time past is referred to more often in the narrative present of Marguerite's salon than in the stage version. What is more, film brings out the relationships between the different characters more effectively, through close-ups, panning round, and cuts.

The ballet is either rejected by critics as sentimental, or is dearly loved. Some consider it one of the masterpieces of narrative ballet in the twentieth century, following in the footsteps of John Cranko—not least because of the interpretation of Marcia Haydée, for whom the ballet was created. There are only a few ballets in which dance has such self-evident independent meaning and at the same time a narrative role from beginning to end. The meeting between Monsieur Duval and Marguerite has the distinct character of a dialogue: her frozen posture in the armchair, her small arabesques piqués en avant directed straight towards him, her fluttering bourrées around him, and her stiffening of body and arms in the lifts are her aggressive, pleading, declining, and resigned arguments.

The choreographic intermingling of the protagonists with their mirror pair makes their spiritual bond extremely clear; at the end of the first pas de trois Manon soars high above the heads of her admirers in a giddy circular movement, her legs wrapped in the supporting arms—the unattainable, a goddess. Much of the choreography in these giddy movements has the desired effect and one could wish that Neumeier had worked out even more meaningful movements and characters in the same vein.

For Armand, the pas de deux often contain a "celebratory" vocabulary—small jumps, renversés, all kinds of quick, whirling turns which finish on the floor in honour of his beloved. For Marguerite/Haydée, Neumeier choreographed many low piqués and emboîtées en pointe, slow promenades with an escort, quickly swung round, a great deal of running, and unorthodox softly swimming arms, which Haydée herself suggested in rehearsal. In the many lifts Marguerite always seems to flow about her partner, her movements melting into a single, danced language of love, while her vocabulary also includes the very realistic caresses, kisses, and passionate embraces of human relationships.

There are few ballets where the music is so appropriate to the subject and so sensitively used in each individual scene: in the buzzing social gatherings, the boisterous country outing, or the romantic pas de deux, the music always embraces and shares the mood intended. This ballet is undeniably a "weepy" and even more so in the film version. But so is the literary source of 1848. In Dumas's work, Marguerite is the archetype of the excessive, generous Romantic woman, a sinner whose love is without bounds, a type who is idealized to become a heart-rending portrait of female love. A great deal of this nineteenth-century quality lives on with Neumeier and Haydée, translated into the language of dance in an outstanding way. And Haydée, herself just over 40 years old in the first performance, knew how to give the ballet a personal meaning; from the elements of a basic melodramatic society drama she presented us with the bitter-sweet story of a woman no longer in the flush of youth, truly in love for the first time.

—Malve Gradinger

LAERKESEN, Anna

Danish dancer and choreographer. Born in Copenhagen, 2 March 1942. Studied with Edite Frandsen, Copenhagen, and at the Royal Danish Ballet School. Début, while still a student, in *La Sylphide*; dancer, Royal Danish Ballet, from 1959, becoming solo dancer (principal), from 1964, and first solo dancer (ballerina), from 1966, touring internationally with company; also leading dancer with ensemble group of soloists directed by Inge Sand, touring United States, 1961; retired from the stage in 1984; début as choreographer, Royal Danish Ballet, 1988, returning to stage several ballets for the Copenhagen company. Recipient: Betty Hennings Award, 1962; Festival Prize, 1963; Läkerols Kulturprize, 1964; Present of Honour from I. Zeuthens Mindelegat, 1964; Tagea Brandts Award, 1968; Award, Balletmaster Albert Gaubiers Fond, 1990.

ROLES

1959   First sylph in *La Sylphide* (Bournonville), Royal Danish Ballet, Copenhagen
1961   Elida in *The Lady from the Sea* (Cullberg), Royal Danish Ballet, Copenhagen
       The Lonely Girl in *Solitaire* (MacMillan), Royal Danish Ballet, Copenhagen
       Principal dancer in *Døren* (K. Ralov), Royal Danish Ballet, Copenhagen
1962   Aurora in *Les Victoires de l'amour* (Lander), Royal Danish Ballet, Copenhagen
1963   Juliet in *Romeo and Juliet* (Ashton), Royal Danish Ballet, Copenhagen
       The Ballerina in *The Nutcracker* Pas de deux (Brenaa after Ivanov), Royal Danish Ballet, Copenhagen
       Anna Stein in *Irene Holm* (von Rosen), Royal Danish Ballet, Copenhagen
       Principal dancer in *Bourrée Fantasque* (Balanchine), Royal Danish Ballet, Copenhagen
       Second Movement in *Symphony in C* (Balanchine), Royal Danish Ballet, Copenhagen
       Principal dancer in *Symphonie Classique* (Bartholin), Royal Danish Ballet, Copenhagen
1964   Juliet in *Romeo and Juliet* (Ashton), Royal Danish Ballet, Copenhagen
       Luxuria in *Katharsis* (Cramér), Royal Danish Ballet, Copenhagen
       Odette/Odile in *Swan Lake* (Petipa, Ivanov), Royal Danish Ballet, Copenhagen
       Principal dancer in *Stemninger* (Brenaa), Royal Danish Ballet, Copenhagen
1965   Ali in *Moon Reindeer* (Cullberg), Royal Danish Ballet, Copenhagen
       Myrtha in *Giselle* (Petipa after Coralli, Perrot; staged Volinine), Royal Danish Ballet, Copenhagen
1966   Title role in *La Sylphide* (Bournonville), Royal Danish Ballet, Copenhagen
       The Sleepwalker in *Night Shadow* (*La Sonnambula*; Balanchine), Royal Danish Ballet, Copenhagen
       Terpsichore in *Apollon musagète* (*Apollo*; Balanchine), Royal Danish Ballet, Copenhagen
       The Pupil in *The Lesson* (Flindt), Royal Danish Ballet, Copenhagen
       Junior Girl in *Graduation Ball* (Lichine), Royal Danish Ballet, Copenhagen
1968   Title role in *Giselle* (Petipa after Coralli, Perrot; staged Volinine), Royal Danish Ballet, Copenhagen
       The Siren in *Prodigal Son* (Balanchine), Royal Danish Ballet, Copenhagen
       Elisa in *Konservatoriet* (Bournonville), Royal Danish Ballet, Copenhagen
       Principal dancer in *Serenade* (Balanchine), Royal Danish Ballet, Copenhagen
       Hilda in *A Folk Tale* (Bournonville), Royal Danish Ballet, Copenhagen

1970   Caroline in *Lilac Garden* (Tudor), Royal Danish Ballet, Copenhagen
       Principal dancer in *Opus I* (Cranko), Royal Danish Ballet, Copenhagen
       Principal dancer in *Études* (Lander), Royal Danish Ballet, Copenhagen
1972   Principal dancer in *Chopiniana* (*Les Sylphides*; Fokine), Royal Danish Ballet, Copenhagen
       Swanilda in *Coppélia* (Lander after Saint-Léon), Royal Danish Ballet, Copenhagen
1983   Louise in *The King's Lifeguards on Amager* (Bournonville), Royal Danish Ballet, Copenhagen

WORKS

1988   *When I am in the Air* (mus. Rachmaninov), Royal Danish Ballet, Copenhagen
1989   *Hommage à Bournonville* (mus. Løvenskjold), Royal Danish Ballet, Copenhagen
       Manhattan Abstraction (mus. Ruders), Royal Danish Ballet, Copenhagen
1990   *Partita* (mus. Bach), Royal Danish Ballet, Copenhagen
1991   *Sonate for Seven* (mus. Beethoven), Royal Danish Ballet, Copenhagen
1992   *Polacca* (mus. Chopin), Royal Danish Ballet, Copenhagen

PUBLICATIONS

Percival, John, and Barnes, Clive, "Danish Direction", *Dance and Dancers* (London), July 1963
Kragh-Jacobsen, Svend, *20 Solo Dancers of the Royal Danish Ballet*, Copenhagen, 1965
Moore, Lillian, "Dazzled by Danes", *Dancing Times* (London), February 1966

* * *

Anna Laerkesen is one of the few Danish ballerinas who was not brought up as a dancer at the Royal Theatre's Ballet School in Copenhagen. She received her initial ballet training in a private ballet school, from the esteemed Latvian-Danish ballet teacher Edite Frandsen.

When Anna Laerkesen became a member of the Royal Danish Ballet in 1959, at the age of seventeen, she was soon recognized as a rare talent. With a strong and sensitive artistic expression and a brilliant technique, she immediately made a great impression, even as a corps dancer.

Although Laerkesen was not brought up on the Bournonville style, she soon adopted its significant features, and made her début as the first sylphide in Bournonville's *La Sylphide*. She was quite obviously an outstanding dancer. The leading dance critic at the time, Svend Kragh-Jacobsen, wrote: "She is not born to dance in line, but steals the picture. Her tall, slender figure, with the head slightly forward, immediately marks her out, but it is the beautiful lines—the long arms' proud bearing, the secure balance on slender legs, the calm pirouettes and the lyrical style in her dance—that distinguish her".

Clive Barnes, critic at the *Daily Express*, singled out Anna Laerkesen in 1962 as one of the strongest candidates to become the leading European ballerina. In 1964, she was promoted to the rank of solo dancer (principal) of the Royal Danish Ballet, and in 1966 she was given the rare title of first solo dancer, or ballerina. The magnificent technique and the sensitive but strong psychological interpretation of her roles made a *New*

York Times critic in 1965 compare her with the young Ulanova. Anna Laerkesen had in fact been to the Bolshoi in 1964, where she trained with Galina Ulanova.

It was in the title role of *La Sylphide* that Anna Laerkesen became internationally known. She has danced *La Sylphide* with many partners, among others Erik Bruhn in 1970, Peter Martins in 1971, and Rudolf Nureyev in 1973. In the double role of Odette/Odile in *Swan Lake*, she also developed two magnificent portraits, revealing a deep understanding of the complicated psychology behind each of the roles.

For more than ten years, Laerkesen was a favourite with both the critics and the public. The dance critic Henrik Lundgren remembered her as a unique ballerina, saying, "she could transform prose to poetry, and reveal secrets of the figures she danced which one hardly knew they possessed". In the middle of the 1970s, illness forced the ballerina to give up leading roles and to dance less frequently. She left the theatre in 1984.

Only four years later, however, she made a comeback, this time in the role of choreographer. Laerkesen's success in this field has been impressive. Her source of inspiration is the music, and in four years she has created six ballets in a modern classical style. The ballets have no story, but are not totally "dance-ballets". They are poetic interpretations of complicated psychological patterns in modern behaviour. She combines poetic beauty and dramatic tension, seriousness and humour— and she shows a sensitivity in the creation of each role, which gives it a rich life. Anna Laerkesen is today one of the most talented Danish classical choreographers.

—Anne McClymont

———

LA FONTAINE (also de la Fontaine), **Mademoiselle**
French dancer. Born c. 1655. Training unknown. First appearance at L'Académie royale de musique (Paris Opéra) in *Le Triomphe de l'amour* (ballet; mus. Lully), 1681; one of the first female professional dancers at the Opéra, creating roles in the "noble" style; also choreographer, staging own dances for entrées; possibly retired c. 1692, returning to the stage in 1693; pensioner at Couvent des Religieuses de l'Assomption, 1692–96, thereafter living as guest of Marquise de la Chaise, and finally becoming resident at convent near Croix Rouge. Died in Paris, 1738.

ROLES

1681   La Reine de danse in *Le Triomphe de l'amour* (ballet; mus. Lully, chor. Beauchamps, Pécour), Opéra, Paris
1682   Éthiopienne (cr) in *Persée* (tragédie-lyrique; mus. Lully, chor. Beauchamps, Pécour), Opéra, Paris
1683   Dancer (cr) in *Phaéton* (tragédie-lyrique; mus. Lully, chor. Beauchamps), Versailles
1684   Dancer (cr) in *Amadis de Gaule* (tragédie-lyrique; mus. Lully, chor. Beauchamps), Opéra, Paris
1685   Dancer (cr) in *Roland* (tragédie-lyrique; mus. Lully, chor. Beauchamps), Versailles
        Une Bergère, Fille de Bretagne, Africaine (cr) in *Le Temple de la paix* (ballet; mus. Lully, chor. Beauchamps), Fontainebleau
1686   Dancer in *Armide et Rénaud* (tragédie-lyrique; mus. Lully, chor. Beauchamps), Opéra, Paris
        Dancer (cr) in *Acis et Galatée* (pastorale-héroïque; mus. Lully, chor. Beauchamps), for the Duc de Vendôme, Anet
1687   Dancer (cr) in *Achille et Polixène* (tragédie-lyrique; mus. Lully, Colasse; chor. Lestang, Pécour), Opéra, Paris
1689   Nymphe (cr) in *Le Palais de Flore* (ballet; mus. Lalande), Trianon
        Phrygienne, Néréide in *Atys* (tragédie-lyrique; mus. Lully), Opéra, Paris
1690/   Dancer in *Cadmus et Hermione* (tragédie-lyrique; mus.
91   Lully), Opéra, Paris
1691   Espagnolette, Potevine dansante in *Le Bourgeois Gentilhomme* (comédie-ballet by Moliére; mus. Lully), Versailles
1693   Dancer (cr) in "Peuples de Carthage" in *Didon* (tragédie-lyrique; mus. Desmarets), Opéra, Paris

Roles attributed to La Fontaine:
1688   Dancer (cr) in *Zéphire et Flore* (ballet; mus. Lully), Opéra, Paris
1689   Dancer (cr) in *Thétis et Pélée* (tragédie-lyrique; mus. Colasse), Opéra, Paris
1690   Dancer in *Orphée* (tragédie-lyrique; mus. Lully), Opéra, Paris
        Dancer (cr) in *Énée et Lavine* (tragédie-lyrique; mus. Colasse), Opéra, Paris
1691   Dancer (cr) in *Coronis* (pastorale-héroïque; mus. Théobalde), Opéra, Paris

PUBLICATIONS

Parfaict, Claude and François, *Dictionnaire des théâtres*, Paris, 1756
Fontenai, *Dictionnaire des artistes*, Paris, 1776
Lajarte, Théodore de, *Bibliothèque national du théâtre de l'Opéra*, Paris, 1878
Migel, Parmenia, *The Ballerinas*, New York, 1972

*   *   *

Mlle. La Fontaine, although little else is known about her, is today remembered as one of the first professional ballerinas to appear before the French public at the Académie royale de musique (or the Paris Opéra, as it is called today), but such a historical claim should take into account the fact that several female dancers, some of them apparently the daughters of famous dancing masters, were engaged to appear in private performances at court ballets many years before La Fontaine made her début in 1681. The French succinctly term La Fontaine "la première des premières danseuses", meaning the first female soloist to dance at the Paris Opéra, where female roles invariably had been taken by masked male dancers (as they often had been at court as well).

Nothing is known about La Fontaine's early life or training prior to her professional début, which was at age 25, if the traditionally attributed birth date (c. 1655) is taken as accurate. It is possible (though this is only speculation) that she was related to a violinist named La Fontaine, who was a member of the King's orchestra directed by Jean Baptiste Lully; this is not an unlikely supposition given that a substantial proportion of the earliest professional ballet dancers at the Opéra were evidently connected by blood or marriage to other theatrical families.

Du Tralage, La Fontaine's contemporary, related how the ballerina retired to a convent during the early summer of 1692. In September of that year and thereafter, Mlle. Marie-Thérèse Perdou de Subligny succeeded her in the leading roles, especially ones that called for the noble or heroic style of dancing. The next year, however, Mlle. La Fontaine briefly returned to the stage for an appearance in the opera *Didon* (11 September 1693), but this would seem to be the last time she was mentioned in any cast listing. She remained as a pensioner at a convent in Paris operated by the Religieuses de l'Assomption, and, since she chose not to take vows, she was free to come and go as she pleased. In 1696, according to the Parfaict brothers, Mme. la Marquise de la Chaise generously donated an apartment in her own home to the ballerina as well as food for Mlle. La Fontaine's table. This unusual invitation would suggest the high esteem in which her contemporaries held her and is perhaps an indication of some social standing on her part. After her hostess died, the former ballerina returned as pensioner to yet another convent, located near Croix Rouge, where she lived a pious life and remained until her death in 1738.

La Fontaine's decision to retire from dancing after what seems to have been a fairly short career, particularly in comparison with others who entered at approximately the same time she did, may have been influenced by the scandalous backstage conduct of other dancers and singers; it is impossible to know for sure. Early eighteenth-century historians certainly all agreed upon Mlle. La Fontaine's modest demeanour and great piety. They also extolled her talents in "danse noble" and her grace as the first solo danseuse of the Opéra. Du Tillet, who wrote when she was still living, considered her remarkable for her beauty and the nobility of her dancing, whereas the brothers Parfaict, writing well after her death, adjudged her "pretty enough", describing her as having expressive eyes and a well-proportioned build, and being of rather unusual height. These were all the physical attributes of a "noble" dancer, as it came to be so defined. In addition, the character of her dancing contributed to the effect of noblesse, due to her outstanding modesty, a virtue associated with femininity in the dance at that time. The one portrait extant of Mlle. La Fontaine as the goddess Ceres shows a danseuse with a willowy build and an enigmatic smile. Her draperies billow behind her while she plays the castanets.

Mlle. La Fontaine set high standards for the ballerinas who followed her, particularly as a model in Lully operas that were to be revived continually throughout the eighteenth century. Furthermore, she defined the prima ballerina as a modest and noble exponent of serious dance, a tradition followed by Mlles. Subligny and Sallé. All the same, how or why the great composer Lully knew to recruit her to dance at the Académie royale de musique has never been explained.

In 1681 Lully had sudden need of female dancers who would take the daring step of appearing in public for a performance of *Le Triomphe de l'amour*. Perhaps motivated out of nostalgia for the pleasures of his own youth, Louis XIV had earlier ordered Lully to prepare a court ballet to celebrate the wedding of the royal dauphin, heir to the throne, in which the bride and groom, as well as other members of noble families, were to be featured dancers. When Lully decided to remount the entire court production of *Le Triomphe de l'amour* at the Paris Opéra later that spring, he was forced to seek women dancers to replace the princesses of the blood and other nobles who appeared in the original ballet, since nobles would not deign to appear before a paying audience. Although no libretti of the time are known to list their names or their roles, the eighteenth-century historians François and Claude Parfaict claim that the dancers' ranks included La Fontaine, Carre, Pesan, and la petite Leclerq.

Mlle. La Fontaine's career took off from that point. All in all, she is listed as a leading ballerina in at least eighteen ballets and operas in the thirteen years that ran from 1681 to 1693, appearing in one or two different works per year. Her roles can be divided mainly into two types: exotic or mythological. She appeared as a "Spanish dancer", a "Woman of Carthage", a "Girl from Bretagne", and a "Phrygienne", and she was cast as a black character when she played an "Ethiopian", an "Egyptian", and an "African". Her Greek roles equalled in number her exotic ones: she played a nymph on several ons, she was naïad, grace, Ceres, Hamadryade, and Nereid. She did play, according to the surviving libretti in which her name is listed, two pantomine or comical roles: she was a pantomine dancer in *Le Bourgeois Gentilhomme* and a French harlequin pantomime dancer in *Ballet de la jeunesse*. The harlequin roles were usually apportioned to Mlle. Dufort, while La Fontaine espoused primarily the noble or *danse sérieux* genre, of which she was said to be the pre-eminent exponent.

La Fontaine became the ballerina of choice for Lully's operas, featured in many original productions, and added to the lists of the remountings of others (where she replaced men who had previously played the women's roles *en travesti*). Eventually La Fontaine made her way to the rank of soloist, an unusual appellation reserved for the likes of Pierre Beauchamps and Louis Pécour, ballet masters and choreographers for the Opéra. In a court production of *Le Bourgeois Gentilhomme*, she is listed as "Mlle. La Fontaine, *seule*", a designation seldom accorded even to Beauchamps and Pécour.

According to the Parfaict brothers, La Fontaine was also given the rare privilege of composing her own dances, expressly reserved for the ballet masters of the company and certainly a unique honour for any woman. Thus Mlle. La Fontaine ranks, albeit in a limited sense, as the first woman choreographer of the Paris Opéra. She worked primarily under the choreographer Beauchamps, by then a vigorous older man who could still perform the most complicated of turning jumps. In addition, she danced in several of Pécour's ballets. Her dancing partners included both Beauchamps and Pécour, although she most often appeared at the head of a female corps de ballet.

When she began her career in *Le Triomphe de l'amour*, only a handful of professional female dancers evidently could be found to appear on the Opéra stage, whereas by the time she retired, a dozen or so years later, the ballerina was considered a desirable necessity for the spectacle, and ten women consistently danced in the Paris Opéra ballets. One hundred years after her début, the same theatre boasted 44 men and 47 women as professional dancers in the opera productions. Once Mlle. La Fontaine and her immediate successors entered the ranks, it would seem that there was no going back.

—Maureen Needham Costonis

LAING, Hugh

British dancer. Born Hugh Skinner in Barbados, 6 June 1911. Studied with Margaret Craske and Marie Rambert, London, from 1932, and with Olga Preobrazhenska, Paris. Married dancer Diana Adams, 1947 (div. 1953). Soloist, Ballet Club (later Ballet Rambert), 1932–37, creating many early Tudor roles; dancer in recitals with Agnes de Mille, Mercury Theatre, 1937, and with (Tudor's) London Ballet, 1938–39; left England for the United States with Tudor, 1939: principal dancer, Ballet Theatre (later American Ballet Theatre), 1940–50, and 1954–56; dancer, New York City Ballet, 1950–53; also appeared in London revues, musicals, and plays, including *The Flying Trapeze* (Furber after Müller; chor. Ashton and Bradley, 1935) and *The Happy Hypocrite* (Dane after Beerbohm; chor. Tudor, 1936), and on Broadway, including in musical *The Day Before*

Hugh Laing with Diana Adams in *Undertow*, **1946**

Spring (mus. Loewe, chor. Tudor, 1945); also appeared in films, including as Harry Beaton in *Brigadoon* (dir. Minnelli, 1954); performed in Japan with Nora Kaye, 1956; retired from stage to become commercial photographer in New York; assisted Tudor in many restagings of his ballets, also contributing designs, including for Royal Danish Ballet productions of *Gala Performance*, 1970, and *The Judgment of Paris*, 1982. Died in New York, 11 May 1988.

ROLES

1932   Laeg (cr) in *Unbowed* (S. Patrick), Ballet Club (later Ballet Rambert), London

Florestan in *Carnaval* (Fokine), Ballet Club, London

1933   Vikram (cr) in *Atalanta of the East* (Tudor), Ballet Club, London

1934   Darius (cr) in *Paramour* (Tudor), danced scene in *Doctor Faustus* (play by Marlowe), Oxford University Dramatic Society (OUDS), Oxford (also staged Ballet Club, 1934)

A Young Man (cr) in *Mephisto Valse* (Ashton), Ballet Club, London

A Lover (cr) in *Alcina Suite* (Howard), Ballet Club, London

Mortal under Mars (cr) in *The Planets* (Tudor), Ballet Club, London

1935   Mercury (cr) in *The Descent of Hebe* (Tudor), Ballet Rambert, London

1936   The Lover (cr) in *Jardin aux lilas* (Tudor), Ballet Rambert, London

Faun in *L'Après-midi d'un faune* (Nijinsky; staged Woizikowsky), Ballet Rambert, London

1937   Fifth Song (cr) in *Dark Elegies* (Tudor), Ballet Rambert, London

A Hired Performer (cr) in *Gallant Assembly* (Tudor), Dance Theatre, Oxford

1938   Principal dancer (cr) in *Seven Intimate Dances* (Tudor), curtain-raiser to *Marriage* (play by Gogol), Westminster Theatre, London

The Waiter (cr) in *The Judgment of Paris* (Tudor), Westminster Theatre, London

Principal dancer (cr) in *Soirée musicale* (Tudor), Palladium Theatre, London

Cavalier (cr) in *Gala Performance* (Tudor), London Ballet, London

1940   Third Song in *Dark Elegies* (Tudor), Ballet Theatre, New York

Benno in *Swan Lake*, Act II (Dolin after Ivanov), Ballet Theatre, New York

Caballero (cr) in *Quintet* (Dolin), Ballet Theatre, New York

Young Man (cr) in *Goya Pastoral* (Tudor), Ballet Theatre, New York

1941   Title role in *Bluebeard* (Fokine), Ballet Theatre

1942   The Young Man from the House Opposite (cr) in *Pillar of Fire* (Tudor), Ballet Theatre, New York

Young Gypsy (cr) in *Aleko* (Massine), Ballet Theatre, Mexico City

Faun in *Afternoon of a Faun* (*L'Apres-midi d'un faune*; Lazovsky after Nijinsky), Ballet Theatre, New York

1943   Romeo (cr) in *The Tragedy of Romeo and Juliet* (Tudor), Ballet Theatre, New York

Principal dancer in *The Wanderer* (*Errante*; Balanchine), Ballet Theatre, New York

The Gentleman with Her (cr) in *Dim Lustre* (Tudor), Ballet Theatre, New York

1944   The Husband (cr) in *Tally-ho!; or, The Frail Quarry* (de Mille), Ballet Theatre, Los Angeles

1945   The Transgressor (cr) in *Undertow* (Tudor), Ballet Theatre, New York

Albrecht in *Giselle* (Petipa after Coralli, Perrot; staged Dolin), Ballet Theatre

1946   A Lover in *Les Patineurs* (Ashton), Ballet Theatre, New York

A Man in *Facsimile* (Robbins), Ballet Theatre, New York

1948   Principal dancer, "Six Idlers of the Bamboo Valley", "Conversation with Winepot and Bird", "Poem of the Guitar" (cr) in *Shadow of the Wind* (Tudor), Ballet Theatre, New York

1949   Principal dancer (cr) in *The Dear Departed* (Tudor), Jacob's Pillow Dance Festival, Lee, Massachusetts

1950   Dream-Beau (cr) in *Nimbus* (Tudor), Ballet Theatre, New York

The Poet in *Illuminations* (Ashton), New York City Ballet, New York

1951   Armand (cr) in *Lady of the Camellias* (Tudor), New York City Ballet, New York

The Mandarin (cr) in *The Miraculous Mandarin* (Bolender), New York City Ballet, New York

Title role in *Tyl Ulenspiegel* (Balanchine), New York City Ballet, New York

1952   Leaves and Flowers (cr) in *Bayou* (Balanchine), New York City Ballet, New York

Hippolytus and Laertes (cr) in *La Gloire* (Tudor), New York City Ballet, New York

1956   The Painter in *Offenbach in the Underworld* (Tudor), Ballet Theatre, New York

Other roles include: for Ballet Rambert—Constant in *Valentine's Eve* (Ashton), Pavane in *Capriol Suite* (Ashton), Prince in *Cinderella* (Howard), Juggler in *Our Lady's Juggler* (Salaman, Howard), Le Vieux Marcheur in *Bar aux Folies Bergère* (de Valois), Lancelot in *The Lady of Shalott* (Ashton), Husband in *Lysistrata* (Tudor), Death in *Death and the Maiden* (Howard), Mars in *Mars and Venus* (Ashton), Prince in *Mermaid* (Howard); for New York City Ballet—title role in *Prodigal Son* (Balanchine), principal dancer in *The Age of Anxiety* (Robbins).

PUBLICATIONS

Amberg, George, *Ballet in America*, New York, 1947

De Mille, Agnes, *Dance to the Piper*, New York, 1951

Chujoy, Anatole, *The New York City Ballet*, New York, 1953

Davidson, Gladys, *Ballet Biographies*, revised edition, London, 1954

Barzel, Ann, "Ballet's Matinee Idol", *Dance Magazine* (New York), December 1957

Clarke, Mary, *Dancers of Mercury: The Story of Ballet Rambert*, London, 1962

De Mille, Agnes, *Speak to Me, Dance With Me*, Boston, 1973

Reynolds, Nancy, *Repertory in Review*, New York, 1977

Denby, Edwin, *Dance Writings*, edited by Robert Cornfield and William Mackay, New York, 1986

Perlmutter, Donna, *Shadowplay: The Life of Antony Tudor*, London, 1991

*   *   *

Dancers who affix themselves to a single choreographer are not an unknown species. But Hugh Laing, muse and *doppelgänger* to Antony Tudor, made the category remarkable.

His career rose and fell with Tudor's. It began in the 1930s with the choreographer who was the British playwright of the dance, who himself took inspiration from the young art-student-turned-dancer. It ended two decades later when the choreographer's creative wellspring temporarily ran dry. During its peak, in ballets as diverse as *Jardin aux Lilas* and *Undertow*, Laing was the central figure in an art form dominated by ballerinas.

As could be expected with a dancer exemplifying the Tudor aesthetic, Laing brought an inestimable verismo and intensity to his stage characterizations—whether the ardent Lover in *Jardin*, the warring Martian mortal in *The Planets*, or the grief-torn peasant in *Dark Elegies*.

When, with Tudor, Laing came to America, other Ballet Theatre dancers were taken aback at the discovery of his limited ballet technique and physical brittleness. But all, including critics of the day, conceded that with his blazing handsomeness and charismatic presence he had the power to mesmerize audiences. Tudor came to rely on this, and on his dancer's profound instincts for illuminating character. As a result, he made a ballet based on Laing's scenario (*Judgment of Paris*) and even let him choreograph the famous hip-swivelling strut in *Pillar of Fire*.

In rehearsal the two men fought furiously—always over some choreographic detail that Laing insisted he remembered more clearly than Tudor. But the process, despite its appearance to others, did not seem to wear either of them down. In 1950, when the two left the declining Ballet Theatre for New York City Ballet (along with Diana Adams, to whom Laing was married briefly), Laing danced a number of roles in Balanchine ballets, the most successful being *Prodigal Son*. But the artistic arbiters at this bastion of neo-classicism accorded neither him nor Tudor much value. Within three years they had both departed.

In *Undertow*, the single central role Laing inspired Tudor to make, he had his tour de force. Here were the pathways of mental derangement to plumb, and he could boast all the requisite dramatic qualities for doing so. Moreover, each role that Tudor tailored to Laing had autobiographic elements of one and the other in merging personas. Romeo, for instance, was conceived not as the typically love-sick swain but a narcissistic character full of self-love and arrogance, with Juliet the target of his emotional outbursts.

This, and all of Laing's other portrayals in Tudor ballets, took an oblique turn from the predictable, two-dimensional model that choreographed narrative tends to follow. For the discriminating dance watcher there were, on a consistent basis, unique meanings to be gleaned from any role on which Hugh Laing put his whole-hearted stamp. Even the innocent spectator was caught up by his sheer magnetism on stage.

—Donna Perlmutter

LAMBERT, Constant

English composer. Born in London, 23 August 1905. Studied at the Royal College of Music, London (scholarship student from 1922), pupil of Ralph Vaughan Williams. Early stage composition for music-hall with *Prize Fight*, 1923; first ballet score, *Romeo and Juliet* (also the first work by a British composer for Diaghilev's Ballets Russes), 1926; appointed conductor of the Camargo Society, London, 1930; conductor and musical director, Vic-Wells Ballet (later the Sadler's Wells Ballet), 1931–47, becoming an artistic director of the same company, from 1948; also writer on music, publishing articles in the *Nation* and *Athenaeum* from 1930, and for the *Sunday Referee* from 1931; directed performance of Weill's *Die Sieben Todsünden* for the London season of Les Ballets 1933; associate conductor of the Proms, 1945 and 1946; composer for films, including for *Anna Karenina* (dir. Duvivier, 1947); also broadcaster, making over 50 broadcasts for the BBC Third Programme, 1946–51. Died in London, 21 August 1951.

WORKS (Ballets)

1926   *Romeo and Juliet* (chor. Nijinska, with entr'acte chor. Balanchine), Diaghilev's Ballets Russes, Monte Carlo
1927   *Pomona* (chor. Nijinska), Teatro Colón, Buenos Aires
1931   *A Day in a Southern Port* (*Rio Grande*; chor. Ashton), Camargo Society, London
1932   *Adam and Eve* (chor. Tudor), Camargo Society, London (using music from *Romeo and Juliet*)
1938   *Horoscope* (chor. Ashton), Vic-Wells Ballet, London
1951   *Tiresias* (chor. Ashton), Sadler's Wells Ballet, London

WORKS (arrangements of work by other composers)

1928   *Les Petits Riens* (arrangement of mus. by Mozart; chor. de Valois), Vic-Wells Ballet, London
1929   *Hommage aux Belles Viennoises* (arrangement of mus. by Schubert; chor. de Valois), Vic-Wells Ballet, London
   Mars and Venus (arrangement of mus. by Scarlatti; chor. Ashton), ballet in *Jew Süss* (play by Ashley Dukes), Opera House, Blackpool
1930   *"Follow Your Saint": The Passionate Pavane* (arrangement of mus. by Dowland; chor. Ashton), and *Dances on a Scotch Theme* (arrangement of mus. by Boyce; chor. Ashton), in *A Masque of Poetry and Music*, presented by Arnold Haskell, Arts Theatre Club, London
1933   *The Birthday of Oberon* (arrangement of mus. by Purcell; chor. de Valois), Vic-Wells Ballet, London
   Les Rendezvous (arrangement of mus. by Auber; chor. Ashton), Vic-Wells Ballet, London
1934   *Bar aux Folies-Bergère* (arrangement of mus. by Chabrier; chor. de Valois), Ballet Club (later Ballet Rambert), London
1936   *Apparitions* (arrangement of mus. by Liszt, orchestrated by Gordon Jacob; chor. Ashton), Vic-Wells Ballet, London
   Prometheus (arrangement of mus. by Beethoven; chor. de Valois), Vic-Wells Ballet, London
1937   *Harlequin in the Street* (arrangement of mus. by Couperin, orchestrated by Jacob; chor. Ashton), Arts Theatre, Cambridge
   Les Patineurs (arrangement of mus. by Meyerbeer; chor. Ashton), Vic-Wells Ballet, London
1940   *Dante Sonata* (orchestration of mus. by Liszt; chor. Ashton), Vic-Wells Ballet, London
   The Wise Virgins (arrangement of mus. by Bach, orchestrated by William Walton; chor. Ashton), Vic-Wells Ballet, London
   The Prospect Before Us (arrangement of mus. by Boyce; chor. de Valois), Vic-Wells Ballet, London
1942   *Comus* (arrangement of mus. by Purcell; chor. Helpmann), Sadler's Wells Ballet, London

The Prospect Before Us, choreographed by Ninette de Valois to an arrangement by Constant Lambert, 1951

1946   *The Fairy Queen* (arrangement of mus. by Purcell; chor. Ashton), Covent Garden Opera and Sadler's Wells Ballet, London
1950   *Ballabile* (arrangement of mus. by Chabrier, orchestrated by Chabrier; chor. Petit), Sadler's Wells Ballet, London

Other ballets using Lambert's music: *Pomona* (Ashton, 1930).

PUBLICATIONS

By Lambert:
Music Ho! A Study of Music in Decline, London, 1934

About Lambert:
Frank, A., "The Music of Constant Lambert", *Musical Times* (London), November 1937
Buckle, Richard, "Constant Lambert", *Ballet* (London), November 1951
Howes, F., "Constant Lambert", *Ballet Annual* (London), no. 6, 1952
Walton, William, "Constant Lambert", *The Music Magazine* (London), 1953
Clarke, Mary, *The Sadler's Wells Ballet*, London, 1955
Ayrton, Michael, "A Sketch for a Portrait of Constant Lambert", *Ballet Annual* (London), no. 10, 1956
De Valois, Ninette, *Come Dance with Me*, London, 1957

Shead, Richard, *Constant Lambert*, London, 1973
Vaughan, David, *Frederick Ashton and his Ballets*, London, 1977
Motion, Andrew, *The Lamberts: George, Constant and Kit*, London, 1986
Sorley Walker, Kathrine, *Ninette de Valois: Idealist without Illusion*, London, 1987

*   *   *

A musician whose talents ranged right across the board—he was a composer, conductor, musical director, and writer—Constant Lambert was also a vital part of the cultural life of London during his entire career. His output as a composer, always distinctive and stylish, was largely curtailed by his devotion to the ballet as a practising musical director, and his contribution to the development of Sadler's Wells Ballet as musical mentor, conductor, and at times pianist cannot be overemphasized.

The son of a distinguished sculptor, Constant Lambert was one of the most brilliant students of his time at the Royal College of Music in London, to which he won a scholarship in 1922. He was in no way academically narrow, however, and his musical tastes included a passion for jazz. The pianist Angus Morrison, a fellow scholar and lifelong friend, has written of this enthusiasm and of Lambert's preoccupation as a composer with the fusion and blending of jazz's "rhythmic inventions and subtleties into the texture of more serious music". This was obvious in scores like *Rio Grande* (written in 1927, and performed as a ballet in 1931). Lambert also became and remained a champion of all those composers he felt to be neglected, and this wide-ranging group included Purcell and William Boyce as well as Chabrier and Milhaud.

Lambert was a highly attractive and positive personality, and soon became one of the leading spirits in London's artistic life. Disabilities—he was deaf in his right ear, lame from childhood osteomyelitis, and latterly had undiagnosed diabetes—were overcome, although pain throughout his life led him to drink to excess. His friends in the late 1920s included William Walton and the Sitwells, and naturally he was among those excited by the post-war Diaghilev Ballet. His early compositions were recognized as having quality, and Diaghilev, always interested in young talent, asked the twenty-year-old musician to write a ballet for him. The music was used for *Romeo and Juliet*, choreographed by Nijinska in 1926; but the entire association was an unhappy one, ending in an insoluble disagreement between Lambert and Diaghilev.

Nevertheless, this brought Lambert firmly into the ballet world. He composed and conducted for the Camargo Society's performances, and in 1931 he accepted the post of conductor and musical director to the Vic-Wells Ballet, newly formed by the young Ninette de Valois. De Valois, like Lambert, believed in the Diaghilev policy of creating ballets that were a unity of the arts of choreography, music, and design, and Lambert was to prove of inestimable help to her over the years. His own compositions were choreographed by Frederick Ashton—*Rio Grande*, *Horoscope*, and *Tiresias*—but Lambert also proved to be a scintillating arranger of scores. Ballets like *Apparitions*, to music by Liszt, *Les Patineurs*, to Meyerbeer, and *The Prospect Before Us*, to Boyce, were models of their kind, while Lambert also prepared and edited with great dramatic and musical sensitivity the music for productions of *Swan Lake*, *The Sleeping Beauty*, and *Giselle*.

In addition, Lambert was a ballet conductor par excellence, one of the few capable of doing justice both to the score and to the dancers' needs. During World War II, at any time when Sadler's Wells Ballet had to manage without an orchestra, Lambert was one of the two pianists who accompanied performances, and he was very much a part of the organization, living and travelling with the company on tour.

Apart from his involvement in ballet, Lambert was for a short time a music critic and was also the author of a provocative book, *Music Ho!*, published in 1934. He extended his career as a conductor in Britain and other European countries after the war, and in 1945 and 1946 was an associate conductor for the Henry Wood Promenade Concerts in London. In 1946, he was also concerned with a project very dear to his heart—the production of Purcell's *The Fairy Queen* at the Royal Opera House, Covent Garden, with singers, actors, and dancers involved, and with magnificent designs by Michael Ayrton. Lambert made a stringently cut "acting edition" of the text, but sacrificed little of the music, achieving a felicitous and memorable result.

In 1947 Lambert resigned from his position with Sadler's Wells Ballet but soon after accepted the offer of an artistic directorship with the company, conducting their opening performances at the Metropolitan Opera House in New York. He composed for them the important but controversial score for *Tiresias*, which was staged to a disappointing critical reception in July 1951, shortly before his sudden death on the 21st of August, two days before his forty-sixth birthday.

—Kathrine Sorley Walker

LANDER, Harald

Danish/French dancer, choreographer, ballet director, and teacher. Born Alfred Bernhardt Stevnsborg in Copenhagen, 25 February 1905. Studied at the Royal Danish Ballet School, pupil of Christian Christiansen and Hans Beck, from 1913; later studied Russian folk dance in U.S.S.R., 1926–27, and ballet with Mikhail Fokine, Ivan Tarasoff, and Adolph Bolm, United States, 1927–29. Married (1) dancer Margot Florentz-Gerhardt, 1932 (div. 1950); (2) dancer Toni Pihl Petersen, 1950 (div. 1965); (3) Lise Lander. Dancer, Royal Danish Ballet, from 1923, with official début, 1925; dancer in Paramount–Public Circuit shows, U.S., 1927–29; returned to Royal Danish Ballet as solo dancer (principal), 1929; first choreography for Royal Danish Ballet, 1931; artistic director (Royal Ballet Master), Royal Danish Ballet, 1932–51; resident choreographer, Paris Opéra Ballet, from 1951, taking French citizenship in 1956; international guest choreographer, staging own works as well as Bournonville repertoire for companies including the Grand Ballet du Marquis de Cuevas, London Festival Ballet, American Ballet Theatre, and Ballet of La Scala, Milan; returned to Copenhagen, as guest choreographer, Royal Danish Ballet, 1962; also teacher: director, Royal Danish Ballet School, 1932–33, and Paris Opéra Ballet School, 1956–57, 1959–63. Recipient: Knight of the Order of Dannebrog, 1951; Chevalier of the Order of Vasa, Sweden; Chevalier of Royal Order, Belgium; Medal of Honour of the City of Paris. Died in Copenhagen, 14 September 1971.

WORKS

1931   *Gaucho* (mus. Reesen), Royal Danish Ballet, Copenhagen

1932   *Tata* (mus. Henriques), Royal Danish Ballet, Copenhagen

1933   *Gudindernes Strid* (*The Strife of the Goddesses*; mus. Reesen), Royal Danish Ballet, Copenhagen
        Fodbold (*Football*; mus. Poulenc), Royal Danish Ballet, Copenhagen
        Diana (mus. Poulenc), Royal Danish Ballet, Copenhagen

1934   *Zaporogerne* (*The Zaporogians*; mus. Reesen), Royal Danish Ballet, Copenhagen
        Bolero (mus. Ravel), Royal Danish Ballet, Copenhagen
        Shepherdess and Chimney Sweep (mus. Enna), Royal Danish Ballet, Copenhagen

1935   *Det Var en Aften* (*A Day at Tivoli*; mus. Reesen), Royal Danish Ballet, Copenhagen

1936   *Svinedrengen* (*The Swineherd*; mus. Hye-Knudsen), Royal Danish Ballet, Copenhagen
        Den Lille Havfrue (*The Little Mermaid*; mus. Henriques), Royal Danish Ballet, Copenhagen
        De Syv Dødssynder (*The Seven Deadly Sins*; mus. Weill), Royal Danish Ballet, Copenhagen

1938   *Thorvaldsen* (mus. Hye-Knudsen), Royal Danish Ballet, Copenhagen

1939   *Danmark-Balletten* (*The Denmark Ballet*; mus. Hye-Knudsen), Royal Danish Ballet, Copenhagen

1940   *La Valse* (mus. Ravel), Royal Danish Ballet, Copenhagen
        Troldmandens Laerling (*The Sorcerer's Apprentice*; mus. Dukas), Royal Danish Ballet, Copenhagen

1942   *Qarrtsiluni* (mus. Riisager), Royal Danish Ballet, Copenhagen
        Slaraffenland (*The Land of Milk and Honey*; mus. Riisager), Royal Danish Ballet, Copenhagen

Fest-Polonaise (mus. Svendsen), Royal Danish Ballet, Copenhagen

Vaaren (*Spring*; mus. Grieg, arranged Neilsen), Royal Danish Ballet, Copenhagen

1945   *Quasi una Fantasia* (mus. Beethoven), Royal Danish Ballet, Copenhagen

1946   *Rebild* (mus. Schrøder), Royal Danish Ballet, Copenhagen

Fugl Fønix (*The Phoenix*; mus. Riisager), Royal Danish Ballet, Copenhagen

1948   *Étude* (mus. Czerny, arranged Riisager), Royal Danish Ballet, Copenhagen (staged as *Études*, Paris Opéra Ballet, 1952)

1949   *Valse triste* (mus. Sibelius), Royal Danish Ballet, Copenhagen

Rhapsodie (mus. after Liszt), Royal Danish Ballet, Copenhagen

Morgen—Middag—Aften (*Morning—Noon—Night*; mus. Turina), Royal Danish Ballet, Copenhagen

Salut for August Bournonville (*Salute to August Bournonville*; mus. various, arranged Reesen), Royal Danish Ballet, Copenhagen

1952   *Les Fleurs* in *Les Indes galantes* (new production; chor. Aveline, Lander, Lifar; mus. Rameau), Paris Opéra Ballet, Paris

1953   *Hop Frog* (mus. Loucheur), Paris Opéra Ballet, Paris

1954   *Printemps à Vienne* (mus. Schubert), Paris Opéra Ballet, Paris

1956   *Concerto aux étoiles* (mus. Bartók), Paris Opéra Ballet, Paris

1959   *Vita Eterna* (mus. Dvořák), London Festival Ballet, London

1961   *Rendez-vous* (mus. Mozart), Versailles

1962   *Les Victoires de l'amour* (mus. Lully), Royal Danish Ballet, Copenhagen

Also staged:

1932   *Napoli* (with Borchsenius, after Bournonville; mus. Paulli, Helsted, Gade, Lumbye), Royal Danish Ballet, Copenhagen

1933   *Konservatoriet* (with Borchsenius, after Bournonville; mus. Paulli), Royal Danish Ballet, Copenhagen

1934   *Coppélia* (after Beck, Glasemann, Saint-Léon; mus. Delibes), Royal Danish Ballet, Copenhagen (also staged London Festival Ballet, London, 1956)

1935   *Far from Denmark* (after Bournonville; mus. Glaeser, Lumbye, Lincke), Royal Danish Ballet, Copenhagen

1938   *Swan Lake* (after Petipa, Ivanov; mus. Tchaikovsky), Royal Danish Ballet, Copenhagen

1939   *La Sylphide* (after Bournonville; mus Løvenskjold), Royal Danish Ballet, Copenhagen (also staged Grand Ballet du Marquis de Cuevas, Paris, 1953; La Scala, Milan, 1962; American Ballet Theatre, 1964)

1941   *A Folk Tale* (with Borchsenius, after Bournonville; mus. Gade, Hartmann), Royal Danish Ballet, Copenhagen

La Ventana (with Borchsenius, after Bournonville; mus. Lumbye, Holm), Royal Danish Ballet, Copenhagen

1943   *The Kermesse in Bruges* (two-act version; with Borchsenius, after Bournonville; mus. Paulli), Royal Danish Ballet, Copenhagen

1947   *The King's Lifeguards on Amager* (with Borchsenius, after Bournonville; mus. Holm), Royal Danish Ballet, Copenhagen

1952   *The Whims of Cupid and the Ballet Master* (after Galeotti; mus. Lolle), Paris Opéra Ballet, Paris

1954   *Napoli* (*Bournonville Divertissement*; after Bournonville; mus. Paulli, Helsted, Gade, Lumbye), London Festival Ballet, London (also staged as *Napoli Act III*, Finnish National Ballet, 1965)

Other works include: Dances in operas *Schwanda* (mus. Weinberger; 1933), *Maskeballet* (*Un Ballo in maschera*, mus. Verdi; 1935), *Madonnas Ansigt* (*Madonna's Face*, mus. Andersen; 1935), *Skaebnens Magt* (*La Forza del destino*, mus. Verdi; 1937), *Andrea Chenier* (mus. Giordano; 1938), *Saturnalia* (mus. Bentzon; 1944), *Julius Caesar* (mus. Handel; 1947), *Kirke og Orgel* (*Church and Organ*, mus. Hye-Knudsen; 1947), *La Vida breve* (mus. de Falla; 1950); also dances in *Darduse; Brylluppet i Peking* (*Darduse, or, The Wedding in Peking*, fairy-comedy by Jensen; chor. with Ørnberg; mus. Riisager; 1937), *Chas* (heroic drama by Soya, mus. Reesen; 1938), *Elverskud* (ballad for chorus and orchestra, mus. Gade; 1939), *Et Spil om en Vej, som til Himlen gaar* (*A Play of a Way that to Heaven Leads*, by Lindström, mus. Swedish folk music; 1944), *Ejendommen Mtr. Nr. 267, Østre Kvarter* (*The Estate, Land Registry No. 267, Østre Kvarter*, festival play by Abell; mus. Riisager; 1948).

PUBLICATIONS

By Lander:

Thi Kendes For Ret? Erindringer, Copenhagen 1951

Interview in "Avante-Premier: Harald Lander", *Les Saisons de la danse* (Paris), March 1976

About Lander:

Hastings, Baird, "The Royal Danish Ballet in Recent Years", *Dance Magazine* (New York), March 1948

Fridericia, Allan, *Harald Lander og hans balleter*, Copenhagen, 1951

Schønberg, Bent, *Harald Lander i Paris*, Copenhagen, 1952

"Personality of the Month: Harold Lander", *Dance and Dancers* (London), October 1954

Young, Daniel, "Disciplined Imagination", *Ballet Today* (London), October 1954

Beaumont, Cyril, *Ballets Past and Present*, London, 1955

Kragh-Jacobsen, Svend, *Royal Danish Ballet*, London, 1955

Goodman, Saul, "Meet Harald Lander", *Dance Magazine* (New York), December 1961

*   *   *

Harald Lander became artistic director of the Royal Danish Ballet in 1932 at a time when the company faced a serious decline in world status. It had become increasingly anachronistic, as stale reproductions of Bournonville works threatened to eclipse the talents of its dancers. Company policy proved to be short-sighted, failing to develop fresh choreographic talent at home while importing works by Fokine and Balanchine (the latter was never popular in Denmark) to fill the gap in the modern repertoire. As artistic enervation set in, Lander's appointment proved to be highly auspicious.

Lander possessed the rare qualifications needed for dynamic and imaginative leadership. He combined a strong aesthetic integrity with acute commercial sense. He was a gifted and musical performer, teacher, and choreographer, bringing his personal vision to all the responsibilities he inherited at the Royal Theatre—including that of directing the dance performed in operas and drama. The most daring undertaking of his new position involved unifying all functions of his command under one energetic and creative force, fulfilling the traditional requirements of "Ballet Master" that had been established by Bournonville himself.

A spectacular revival of the Danish Ballet's fortunes began to take place, with Lander using a two-fold strategy to achieve his aims. First, he restaged the traditional ballets with care and intelligence, collaborating with the best-known interpreter of Bournonville, Valborg Borchsenius, to produce vigorous new versions of *Napoli*, *La Sylphide*, *La Ventana*, and *Konservatoriet*, among others. Later in his career he also tackled classics such as *Coppélia*, and *Swan Lake*, strengthening their impact with his impressive mark of individuality.

Second, he changed the focus of the contemporary repertoire. He promoted his own talents in choreography, which quickly provided the bulk of new work for the company. He nurtured the gifts of specific dancers to provide himself with the creative raw material for his ballets. Ulla Poulsen, Else Hojgaard, Margot Lander (his first wife), Børge Ralov, Toni Lander (his second wife), and Erik Bruhn were amongst those dancers who flourished under his régime. He also worked closely with character artists: Frank Schaufuss, Poul Gnatt, Stanley Williams, and Fredbjørn Bjørnsson reaped lasting benefit from Lander's policy of developing home-grown potential. But while cultivating talent at a national level, Lander also marketed the company extensively outside Denmark. Under his all-embracing direction, and with fresh energy and commitment, the company strove for artistic and commercial success and, for the first time in years, achieved international recognition.

Lander reversed the introspective attitude of the company while strengthening its national character. But he himself had not always conformed to the image of dedicated traditionalist that appears to have equipped him for directorship. Trained at the Royal Danish Ballet School from 1913 to 1923, and joining the company immediately afterwards, he soon showed signs of restlessness. His own physical limitations may have contributed to his sense of frustration with the restrictions of the Bournonville technique. His figure was unsuited to the male lead roles of classical ballet, a fact of which he was acutely self-conscious. However, he *did* excel in character and comic roles (such as Gennaro in Bournonville's *Napoli* and Don Alvarez in *Far from Denmark*), and his empathy with the dramatic and non-classical elements of the dance prompted a constant search for new forms.

During a two-year leave of absence from the company (commencing in 1925), he extended his range and experience, studying in the United States and Mexico with Mikhail Fokine, Adolph Bolm, Ivan Tarasoff, and Juan de Beaucaire-y-Montalbo, where he added Russian classical style and various ethnic dance techniques to his repertoire. Early creations that established his reputation as a choreographer, such as *Gaucho*, *Tata* (a gypsy ballet), and *Zaporogerne* (a Cossack ballet), all express the influence of national styles acquired abroad.

The inspiration Lander found outside Denmark was to exert a profound and long-lasting effect on his work when he returned to the company in 1929. It set the tone for his progressive directorship, taken up three years later. Its new emphasis on looking out beyond Denmark also precipitated his search for fresh interpretations of the refined classical style of the Danish school. The neo-classical *Diana*, the expressionist *The Seven Deadly Sins*, and the reworkings of old Danish ballets such as *The Shepherdess and the Chimney Sweep* typify his early modernizations of the classical form. Developments in dramatic expression came with *Vaaren* and *The Phoenix*. But ultimately Lander's style moved towards the abstraction of the rhythmic study in *Qarrtsiluni* and *Études*, which gained international renown for himself and the company.

Lander's choreographic development moved in a cyclical pattern. Prompted initially by a dissatisfaction with the archaisms of Bournonville, he finally returned to a classical purism that celebrated the rigours of that very same technique.

But this was no capitulation to conservative forms. *Études* represents Lander's finest reinterpretation of the traditional school, in which he vigorously extended the company to demonstrate the full potential of a Bournonville training. In this work he finally raised classical dance to a universal level, unhampered by costume, scenario, or historical context, and presented his strongest conviction that "dance is visible music".

Music itself had always provided a fundamental motivation for Lander's artistic life. His concern to elevate its importance in the creation of dance characterized his unique achievement both as director and choreographer. Like his predecessors, Bournonville and Galeotti, he successfully collaborated with contemporary Danish composers. He created ballets with Knudåge Riisager (*Études*), Emil Reesen, Fini Henriques, and Johan Hye-Knudsen, proving his commitment to national musical life, as well as to the dance. He also found enriching partnerships with dramatists (such as Kjeld Abell, with whom he created *The Land of Milk and Honey*), and encouraged visiting choreographers such as Massine (*Le Beau Danube*, 1948, *Symphonie Fantastique*, new version), and Børge Ralov (*The Widow in the Mirror*, 1934).

In 1951 Lander left the company to join the Paris Opéra as ballet master. Given his strong command over the artistic and economic development of the Danish company, he was inevitably difficult to replace. Although he continued to choreograph in France, his work now consisted chiefly of historical revivals (*The Whims of Cupid and the Ballet Master*, after Galeotti). There can be no doubt that the major phase of his career concluded when he left Denmark. He enjoyed affection there to the end of his life, and his exceptional achievement continues to be measured by the special qualities that the Danish ballet has inherited from him. He was popular with the critics, but he was particularly sensitive to dance as a performing art and frequently emphasized the importance of reception in the creative process: "it is the audience who accept or reject a ballet". Harald Lander's oustanding influence on the Royal Danish Ballet resonates to this day as the company continues to enjoy international acclaim.

—Susan Jones

LANDER, Margot

Danish dancer. Born Margot Florentz-Gerhardt in Copenhagen, 2 August 1910. Studied at the Royal Danish Ballet School, Copenhagen, from 1917. Married (1) dancer and choreographer Harald Lander, 1932 (div. 1950); (2) Erik Nyholm. Dancer, Royal Danish Ballet, from 1928, becoming solo dancer (principal dancer) from 1933, and first solo dancer (prima ballerina; the first to be given the title in Denmark) from 1942; retired from the stage in 1950; also appeared in dramatic roles, including as an Elf in *A Midsummer Night's Dream* (Shakespeare; 1932), Gabriele in *Ole Lukøie* (after Hans Christian Andersen; 1942), and Anitra in *Peer Gynt* (Ibsen; 1944). Died in Copenhagen, 19 July 1961.

ROLES

1920   Amager Polka (cr) in *Bygone Days* (Walbom), Royal Danish Ballet, Copenhagen
1924   Star (cr) in *Tycho Brahe's Dream* (Jørgen-Jensen), Royal Danish Ballet, Copenhagen

Margot Lander (right) in *Konservatoriet* with the Royal Danish Ballet, Copenhagen, 1933

Cloth dance (cr) in *Pan Twardowsky* (Uhlendorff), Royal Danish Ballet, Copenhagen

1925 Street dancer in *Petruschka* (Fokine), Royal Danish Ballet, Copenhagen

Nocturne in *Chopiniana* (*Les Sylphides*; Fokine), Royal Danish Ballet, Copenhagen

Polovtsian Maiden in *Polovtsian Dances from Prince Igor* (Fokine), Royal Danish Ballet, Copenhagen

1926 Eskimo Dance in *Far from Denmark* (Bournonville), Royal Danish Ballet, Copenhagen

Solo dance in *Napoli* (Bournonville), Royal Danish Ballet, Copenhagen

Worker Bee (cr) in *Butterflies* (Uhlendorff), Royal Danish Ballet, Copenhagen

1927 Capriccio (cr) in *Play of Colours* (Uhlendorff), Royal Danish Ballet, Copenhagen

Oriental Dance in *The Kiss* (Jørgen-Jensen), Royal Danish Ballet, Copenhagen

Dancing Woman (cr) in *Danish Folk Dances* (Uhlendorff), Royal Danish Ballet, Copenhagen

Divertissement: "Faith, Hope, and Love" in *The Little Mermaid* (Beck), Royal Danish Ballet, Copenhagen

1928 Pierette in *Harlequin's Millions* (*Harlequinade*; Walbom), Royal Danish Ballet, Copenhagen

Polichinelle's Tarantella in *Dream Pictures* (Walbom), Royal Danish Ballet, Copenhagen

Caroline in *Kaerlighedens Aarstider* (*The Seasons of Love*; Uhlendorff), Royal Danish Ballet, Copenhagen

Enchanted Princess (cr) in *Firebird* (Smith), Royal Danish Ballet, Copenhagen

1929 Mazurka in *Chopiniana* (*Les Sylphides*; Fokine), Royal Danish Ballet, Copenhagen

Jota in *The Torreador* (Bournonville), Royal Danish Ballet, Copenhagen

Bride in *Wedding in Hardanger* (Bournonville), Royal Danish Ballet, Copenhagen

A Wise Virgin in *The Foolish Virgins* (Smith), Royal Danish Ballet, Copenhagen

Eskimo Dance (cr) in *Bournonvilleana* (new production; Smith after Bournonville), Royal Danish Ballet, Copenhagen

1930 Chinese Porcelain (cr) in *Potpourri* (Smith), Royal Danish Ballet, Copenhagen

Court Lady with a Harp (cr) in *Hybris* (Jørgen-Jensen), Royal Danish Ballet, Copenhagen

Butterfly in *Little Ida's Flowers* (Walbom), Royal Danish Ballet, Copenhagen

Sevillana in *The Three-Cornered Hat* (Massine, revised Balanchine), Royal Danish Ballet, Copenhagen

A Slave Girl in *Schéhérazade* (Fokine, revised Balanchine), Royal Danish Ballet, Copenhagen

A Can-Can dancer in *La Boutique fantasque* (Massine, revised Balanchine), Royal Danish Ballet, Copenhagen

Farandole in *Carmen* (opera; mus. Bizet, chor. Jørgen-Jensen), Royal Danish Opera and Ballet, Copenhagen

Peasant Girl (cr) in *Benzin* (Jørgen-Jensen), Royal Danish Ballet, Copenhagen

1931 Calliope in *Apollon musagète* (Balanchine), Royal

Danish Ballet, Copenhagen
A Slave Girl in *Josephs Legende* (*La Légende de Joseph*; Fokine, revised Balanchine), Royal Danish Ballet, Copenhagen
Polyhymnia in *Apollon musagète* (Balanchine), Royal Danish Ballet, Copenhagen
Solo in *La Sylphide* (Bournonville), Royal Danish Ballet, Copenhagen
Solo in *A Folk Tale* (Bournonville), Royal Danish Ballet, Copenhagen
Marinetta in *The Servant and Two Gentlemen* (Jørgen-Jensen), Royal Danish Ballet, Copenhagen
Bolero (cr) in *Gaucho* (Lander), Royal Danish Ballet, Copenhagen
Manuela in *Gaucho* (Lander), Royal Danish Ballet, Copenhagen
1932 Soloist in *Aida* (opera; mus. Verdi, chor. Lander), Royal Danish Opera and Ballet, Copenhagen
Play (cr) in *Strauss in Paris* (Jørgen-Jensen), Royal Ballet, London
Czardas (cr) in *Tata* (Lander), Royal Danish Ballet, Copenhagen
Title role in *Tata* (Lander), Royal Danish Ballet, Copenhagen
Principal dancer in *Two in a Glass House* (Lander after Walbom), Royal Danish Ballet, Copenhagen
Pas de six in *Napoli* (Bournonville), Royal Danish Ballet, Copenhagen
Jewel Dance (cr) in *Asra* (Jørgen-Jensen), Royal Danish Ballet, Copenhagen
1933 Sailors' Reel in *The King's Lifeguards on Amager* (Bournonville), Royal Danish Ballet, Copenhagen
Italian Serenade (cr) in *The Strife of the Goddesses* (Lander), Royal Danish Ballet, Copenhagen
Dancer in *Pierrette's Veil* (Lander after Beck), Royal Danish Ballet, Copenhagen
A Young Lady (cr) in *Football* (Lander), Royal Danish Ballet, Copenhagen
Victorine in *Konservatoriet* (Bournonville), Royal Danish Ballet, Copenhagen
French Dance in *The Whims of Cupid and the Ballet Master* (Galeotti), Royal Danish Ballet, Copenhagen
1934 Ganymedes (cr) in *Orpheus in the Underworld* (B. Ralov), Royal Danish Ballet, Copenhagen
Tartar Woman (cr) in *Zaporogerne* (Lander), Royal Danish Ballet, Copenhagen
Columbine in *Dream Pictures* (Walbom), Royal Danish Ballet, Copenhagen
Swanilda in *Coppélia* (Beck, Lander after Saint-Léon), Royal Danish Ballet, Copenhagen
Nocturne, Prelude in *Chopiniana* (*Les Sylphides*; Fokine), Royal Danish Ballet, Copenhagen
Pas de deux (cr) in *The Widow in the Mirror* (B. Ralov), Royal Danish Ballet, Copenhagen
Dancing Master's Sweetheart in *Maskarade* (opera; mus. Nielsen, chor. Beck), Royal Danish Opera and Ballet, Copenhagen
1935 Poul in *Far from Denmark* (Bournonville), Royal Danish Ballet, Copenhagen
A Young Girl in *A Day in Tivoli* (Lander), Royal Danish Ballet, Copenhagen
1936 Love and Life's Joy (cr) in *The Little Mermaid* (new production; Lander after Beck), Royal Danish Ballet, Copenhagen
Anna II (cr) in *The Seven Deadly Sins* (Lander), Royal Danish Ballet, Copenhagen
1937 Principal dancer (cr) in *Darduse* (fairy-comedy; chor.

Lander), Royal Danish Ballet, Copenhagen
Mazurka in *Chopiniana* (*Les Sylphides*; Fokine), Royal Danish Ballet, Copenhagen
1938 The Swan Queen in *Swan Lake* (one-act version; Lander after Petipa, Ivanov), Royal Danish Ballet, Copenhagen
The Woman (cr) in *The Circle* (Theilade), Royal Danish Ballet, Copenhagen
Tennis in *Sportsballet* (Lander), Royal Danish Ballet, Copenhagen
A Young Girl (cr) in *Thorvaldsen* (Lander), Royal Danish Ballet, Copenhagen
1939 Choleric (cr) in *The Four Temperaments* (Ralov), Royal Danish Ballet, Copenhagen
Dance of Mlle. Camargo (cr) in *La Malade imaginaire* (play by Molière; chor. Ralov), Royal Theatre, Copenhagen
Svava in *The Valkyrie* (Bournonville), Royal Danish Ballet, Copenhagen
Columbine in *H.C. Lumbye-Fantasy* (divertissement; Walbom and Lander), Royal Danish Ballet, Copenhagen
Rococo Serenade and Sport (cr) in *The Denmark-Ballet* (Lander), Royal Danish Ballet, Copenhagen
1940 First Broom (cr) in *The Sorcerer's Apprentice* (Lander), Royal Danish Ballet, Copenhagen
1941 Indian dance in *Holger Dansk* (opera; chor. Lander), Royal Danish Opera and Ballet, Copenhagen
Solo and Divertissement in *The Troubadour* (Ralov after Bournonville), Royal Danish Ballet, Copenhagen
Elisa in *Konservatoriet* (Bournonville), Royal Danish Ballet, Copenhagen
Senorita in *La Ventana* (Bournonville), Royal Danish Ballet, Copenhagen
1942 The Dessert (cr) in *The Land of Milk and Honey* (Lander), Royal Danish Ballet, Copenhagen
Young Woman (cr) in *Qarrtsiluni* (Lander), Royal Danish Ballet, Copenhagen
Woman in Couple (cr) in *Fest-Polonaise* (Lander), Royal Danish Ballet, Copenhagen
A Young Girl (cr) in *Vaaren* (*Spring*; Lander), Royal Danish Ballet, Copenhagen
1943 Pas de deux in *The Kermesse in Bruges* (Bournonville; staged Lander), Royal Danish Ballet, Copenhagen
Birthe in *A Folk Tale* (Bournonville), Royal Danish Ballet, Copenhagen
The Woman in *La Valse* (Lander), Royal Danish Ballet, Copenhagen
1944 Teresina in *Napoli* (Bournonville), Royal Danish Ballet, Copenhagen
1945 Rosita in *Far from Denmark* (Bournonville), Royal Danish Ballet, Copenhagen
1946 Title role (cr) in *The Phoenix* (Lander), Royal Danish Ballet, Copenhagen
Title role in *Giselle* (Petipa after Coralli, Perrot; staged Volinine), Royal Danish Ballet, Copenhagen
1948 Ballerina (cr) in *Étude* (Lander), Royal Danish Ballet, Copenhagen
Fandango in *The Marriage of Figaro* (Bournonville), Royal Danish Ballet, Copenhagen

PUBLICATIONS

Kragh-Jacobsen, Svend, *Margot Lander, en balletkunsters baggrund udvikling og blomstring*, Copenhagen, 1948

Kragh-Jacobsen, Svend, *Farvel til en sommerfugl*, Copenhagen, 1950

Poulson, Ulla, "Margot Lander's Farewell", *Dancing Times* (London), April 1950

Beaumont, Cyril, *Ballets of Today*, London, 1954

Kragh-Jacobsen, Svend, *The Royal Danish Ballet: An Old Tradition and a Living Present*, Copenhagen and London, 1955

Fridericia, Allan, "Margot Lander", *Dancing Times* (London), September 1961

"The Other Margot", *Dance and Dancers* (London), November 1983

* * *

Margot Lander was the most important Danish ballerina of the first half of the twentieth century, and the star around whom Harald Lander built the repertoire when he restored the Royal Danish Ballet and its ballets from the beginning of the 1930s. She grew up in a period when the Bournonville style and the Bournonville repertoire was all-important. Margot Lander danced the leading roles in almost all the Bournonville ballets, in which her piquant grace and quick allegro were good assets. She was a charming Teresina in *Napoli* and had a flashing erotic temperament as Birthe (the trollgirl) in *A Folk Tale*. She knew her Bournonville, but it was actually outside this repertoire that she was to gain her greatest victories.

Margot Lander was a modern dancer and, as such, drew much inspiration from the guest visits to Copenhagen of Mikhail Fokine in 1925 and especially of George Balanchine in 1930 and 1931. In his new repertory Harald Lander presented her as a modern girl in ballets like *Football*, *Tennis* (part of *Sportsballet*), and *Thorvaldsen*, and he turned her sparkling wit and humour to account in *The Sorcerer's Apprentice* and as the Dessert in his *The Land of Milk and Honey*. As early as 1934 she was given the part of Swanilda in *Coppélia*, and danced it all through her career with the charm of a mischievous girl who also had a heart. That heart of hers would take her a long way.

In 1938 she was the first Danish Swan Queen—in a one-act version—and endowed the part with a sad, melancholic poetry. The same poetry was the hallmark of her style when she danced *Les Sylphides* and the young girl in Lander's Grieg ballet *Vaaren* (*Spring*). The climax of her career was *Giselle*—she was the first in Denmark to dance the role this century—where soul and feeling were just as important as technique, and Giselle was possessed of both a serene and yet a pathetic beauty. The ballerina in Harald Lander's *Étude* was created for Margot Lander in 1948 and she danced the part a few times before generously passing it on to the young Toni Pihl (later Toni Lander).

Margot Lander was not a virtuoso dancer in the modern sense of the word, though her technique was impressive considering the schooling she had had. She was above all a dancer with a great personality and with deep human feelings. She held a very central position in the Danish ballet, and in many ways it was her influence which lay behind the popularity and respect that ballet gained as an art during the twenty years of her career.

—Erik Aschengreen

LANDER, Toni

Danish dancer and teacher. Born Toni Pihl Petersen in Copenhagen, 19 June 1931. Studied with Leif Ørnberg, 1937– 39, and at the Royal Danish Ballet School, Copenhagen, 1939–47; later studied with Olga Preobrazhenska, Lubov Egorova, Nora Kiss, and Alexandre Volinine, Paris. Married (1) dancer and choreographer Harald Lander, 1950 (div. 1965); (2) dancer Bruce Marks, 1966: three sons. Début, 1947; dancer, Royal Danish Ballet, from 1948, becoming soloist (principal dancer), 1950–51; guest ballerina, Original Ballet Russe, 1951–52, Paris Opéra Ballet, 1951–54; principal dancer, London Festival Ballet, 1954–59, Ballet Théâtre Français, 1958, and American Ballet Theatre, 1961–71; soloist and teacher, Royal Danish Ballet, 1971–76; also appeared on television, including in *The Nutcracker* Pas de deux (British television, 1953), and in films, including in *The Dancing Heart* (Berlin, 1953); teacher, Ballet West, Salt Lake City, Utah, 1976–85. Recipient: Title of Knight of Dannebrog, 1957. Died in Salt Lake City, 19 May 1985.

ROLES

1947   Sophie in *The King's Lifeguards on Amager* (Bournonville), Royal Danish Ballet, Copenhagen

1948   Principal dancer in *Études* (Lander), Royal Danish Ballet, Copenhagen
First Hand in *Le Beau Danube* (Massine), Royal Danish Ballet, Copenhagen

1949   A Maiden in *Pas de trois cousines* (Lander after Bournonville), Royal Danish Ballet, Copenhagen
Lilac Fairy in *Aurora's Wedding* (from *The Sleeping Beauty*; after Petipa), Royal Danish Ballet, Copenhagen
Pas de trois in *Swan Lake* (H. Lander after Petipa, Ivanov), Royal Danish Ballet, Copenhagen
Picador (cr) in *Morgen—Middag—Aften* (*Morning—Noon—Night*; H. Lander), Royal Danish Ballet, Copenhagen

1950   Soloist in *Concerto* (Thailade), Royal Danish Ballet, Copenhagen
Second Variation (cr) in *Symphonie Classique* (Bartholin), Royal Danish Ballet, Copenhagen
Juliet in *Romeo and Juliet* (Bartholin), Royal Danish Ballet, Copenhagen
Soloist in *La Vida Breve* (opera; mus. da Falla, chor. H. Lander), Royal Danish Ballet and Opera, Copenhagen
The Swan in *The Ugly Duckling* (Seldorf), Den Fynsk Ballet, Odense
Pas de deux from *The Nutcracker* (Brenaa after Ivanov), Royal Danish Ballet, Copenhagen

1952   Princess Aurora in *Aurora's Wedding* (from *The Sleeping Beauty*; after Petipa), Original Ballet Russe, London
Pas de deux from *The Nutcracker* (after Ivanov), Original Ballet Russe, London
The Sylph in *Graduation Ball* (Lichine), Original Ballet Russe, London

1954   Odette in *Swan Lake*, Act II (after Ivanov), London Festival Ballet, London
Prelude and Valse in *Les Sylphides* (Fokine), London Festival Ballet, London
Teresina in *Napoli* (excerpts; H. Lander after Bournonville), London Festival Ballet, London

1955   The Snow Queen in *The Nutcracker* (Dolin, Beriozoff), London Festival Ballet
Mazurka in *Les Sylphides* (Fokine), London Festival Ballet
Ballerina in *Don Quixote Pas de deux* (Dolin, Obukhov after Petipa), London Festival Ballet, London

Toni Lander, with Flemming Flindt and John Gilpin, in *Études*, London Festival Ballet, 1955

Title role in *La Esmeralda* (Beriozoff), London Festival Ballet

1956   Sugar Plum Fairy in *The Nutcracker* (Dolin, Beriozoff), London Festival Ballet

Swanilda in *Coppélia* (H. Lander after Saint-Léon), London Festival Ballet

Marie Taglioni in *Pas de quatre* (Dolin), London Festival Ballet

Principal dancer in *Concerti* (Lichine), London Festival Ballet

Principal dancer in *Bournonville Divertissements* (H. Lander after Bournonville), London Festival Ballet, London

Ballerina in *Raymonda Pas de deux* (Balanchine), London Festival Ballet, London

1958   The Young Woman (cr) in *Le Rendezvous manqué* (*The Broken Date*; Taras), Monte Carlo Opera House, Monte Carlo

1959   Principal dancer in *Vita Eterna* (H. Lander), London Festival Ballet, London

1960   An Episode in His Past in *Jardin aux lilas* (Tudor), American Ballet Theatre

Title role in *Miss Julie* (Cullberg), American Ballet Theatre

Principal dancer (lead couple) in *Theme and Variations* (Balanchine), American Ballet Theatre

1960/   Title role in *Giselle* (Petipa after Coralli, Perrot; staged
61   Romanoff), American Ballet Theatre

Odette in *Swan Lake*, Act II (Dolin after Ivanov), American Ballet Theatre

1961   "La Déesse de la danse" from Milan in *Gala Performance* (Tudor), American Ballet Theatre

Ballerina in *Grand Pas Glazunov* (Balanchine), American Ballet Theatre, New York

1962/   Caroline in *Jardin aux lilas* (Tudor), American Ballet
63   Theatre

1964   Title role in *La Sylphide* (H. Lander after Bournonville), American Ballet Theatre, San Antonio, Texas

1966/   Title role in *Helen of Troy* (Lichine), American Ballet
67   Theatre

Ali in *Moon Reindeer* (Cullberg), American Ballet Theatre

Cybele and Medusa in *Undertow* (Tudor), American Ballet Theatre

Eliza in *Konservatoriet* (Bournonville), Royal Danish Ballet, Copenhagen

1967   Principal dancer in *Concerto* (MacMillan), American Ballet Theatre, Jacksonville, Florida

Principal dancer in *Danses concertantes* (MacMillan), American Ballet Theatre, Pittsburgh

Odette/Odile in *Swan Lake* (Ivanov, Petipa; staged Blair), American Ballet Theatre, New York

1970   Glove Seller in *Gaité Parisienne* (Massine), American Ballet Theatre, Albuquerque

Desdemona in *The Moor's Pavane* (Limón), Royal Danish Ballet, Copenhagen

Other roles include: principal dancer in *Flower Festival at Genzano* (Bournonville; staged H. Lander), principal dancer in *Fest Polonaise* (H. Lander).

WORKS

Staged:
1985 *Abdallah* (reconstruction, with Bruce Marks and Flemming Ryberg, after Bournonville; mus. Paulli), Ballet West, Salt Lake City, Utah

Other works include: numerous stagings of *Études* (after H. Lander; mus. Czerny, Riisager) throughout the world.

PUBLICATIONS

By Lander:
"A Dancer's Thoughts: Fair New World", *Dance Scope* (New York), Spring 1971
Interview in Newman, Barbara, *Striking a Balance*, Boston, 1982

About Lander:
Young, Daniel, "Disciplined Imagination", *Ballet Today* (London), October 1954
"Dancer of the Year", *Dance and Dancers* (London), December 1955
Fridericia, Allan, "Ballet in Denmark", *Dancing Times* (London), February 1957
Vaughan, David, "A Danish Ballerina Far From Home", *Dance and Dancers* (London), February 1957
Roberts, Sonia, "Toni Lander", *Ballet Today* (London), April 1958
Goodman, Saul, "Brief Biographies: Toni Lander", *Dance Magazine* (New York), July 1958
Coffey, Babette, "Toni Lander and Bruce Marks: On and Off Stage", *Dance Magazine* (New York), August 1969
Vaughan, David, "Toni Lander", *Ballet Review* (New York), Spring 1986
Croce, Arlene, *Sight Lines*, New York, 1987

* * *

Toni Lander is the only female dancer from the Royal Danish Ballet thus far this century who has followed in the footsteps of the famous Lucile Grahn, leaving the Royal Danish Ballet to establish a successful international career on her own. But her leaving Denmark was more a result of circumstances than a deliberate decision to expand her career.

Toni Lander entered the Royal Danish Ballet School in 1939, at the age of eight, after two years of training with Leif Ørnberg. Her astounding talents were soon recognized and during her early school years she developed a fine and strong technique. In 1947 she made her début with the Royal Danish Ballet as Sophie in *The King's Lifeguards on Amager*, and the following year she was formally accepted into the company.

Lander's great breakthrough came the following year when she was given the role of the principal ballerina in *Études*. Harald Lander had created the role for his second wife, Margot Lander, but after a few performances the part was passed on to Toni Lander (at that time Toni Pihl Petersen), and it became hers. Harald Lander soon remodelled it to show off Lander's long lines and strong, Russian-influenced technique. *Études* became an important ballet in Lander's career. Throughout the rest of her career she danced and staged it all over the world.

And in the minds of many Danish critics, Toni Lander and *Études* have become an inseparable entity.

Technically Lander excelled in the Russian academic style, which Harald Lander had introduced as a supplement to Bournonville training in 1932, when he became director of the Royal Danish Ballet School. But Toni Lander also built up a solid foundation in the Bournonville technique. She belonged to the last generation of dancers taught, coached, and featured in the Bournonville stagings by Valborg Borchsenius, who with Hans Beck was one of Bournonville's last students. It was invaluable knowledge of which Lander later made great use, when she began teaching and staging the Bournonville ballets and technique.

In 1950 the nineteen-year-old Lander was appointed soloist (principal dancer), the youngest ever during Harald Lander's tenure as ballet master at the Royal Danish Ballet, and in the same year the two were married. However, she was just at the beginning of her career as a ballerina when a dispute with the company management forced Harald Lander to leave his position as ballet master in Copenhagen. Toni Lander chose to follow her husband abroad.

She first appeared as a guest artist with the Original Ballet Russe during its final season. She then joined the Paris Opéra Ballet, where Harald Lander was acting as guest choreographer. In 1954 she became a principal dancer with the London Festival Ballet, where she stayed until 1959. During these years she danced various parts in *Les Sylphides*, as well as Teresina in *Napoli*, the Snow Queen and the Sugar Plum Fairy in *The Nutcracker*, the title role in *La Esmeralda*, and Swanilda in *Coppélia*. Her repertoire covered an array of classical roles, in which she won great acclaim for her impeccable technique, but most critics called her interpretations cold. Tired from an exhausting performance schedule and from repeated criticism, Lander considered retirement. Instead, she left the classical ballet world for a year in order to create the leading role in John Taras's and Don Lurio's dramatic ballet *Le Rendezvous manqué*, based on a novel by François Sagan. It was a new challenge for Lander, because it was an acting role. While doing it, she felt that she lost some of her technique, but it made her realize that she also had a gift for acting, which gave her a new self-confidence. It added a new dramatic quality to her dance, so when she joined American Ballet Theatre as a principal dancer in 1960, she was instantly cast as Miss Julie in Birgit Cullberg's ballet of the same name.

During her years with the American company—she stayed until 1971—Lander reached the peak of her career, excelling in *Theme and Variations*, *Giselle*, *Jardin aux lilas*, *La Sylphide*, *Undertow*, and *Moon Reindeer*. In 1967 she danced Odette/Odile in American Ballet Theatre's first full-length version of *Swan Lake*. In this role she won much acclaim, and she was finally recognized as more than simply the cool, brilliant technician. During these years her dancing became more lyrical, and her strong temperament added colour and life to her interpretations. At ABT she was frequently partnered by Fernandes Royes and Bruce Marks, whom she married in 1966, and with whom she had three sons.

In 1971 Lander returned with Marks to the Royal Danish Ballet as principal dancer and teacher. For some time she had been thinking about adding modern dance to her classical repertoire, and she now felt that at the end of her career she was able to relax enough to take on roles without worrying about technique. Her dream was fulfilled when she was given the part of Desdemona in José Limón's *The Moor's Pavane*, and this was the last role she danced.

Lander was a highly esteemed teacher at the Royal Danish Ballet, and it was hoped that she would remain there permanently. But in 1976 Bruce Marks was appointed artistic director of Ballet West in Salt Lake City, and she chose to follow him. She became instructor and principal teacher of the company.

The last project Lander embarked on was the reconstruction of Bournonville's long-lost ballet, *Abdallah*, from 1855. She and Marks had bought the libretto at an auction in London, and together with Flemming Ryberg they set about reconstructing the ballet. Where steps were missing they created new choreography in keeping with the Bournonville style. The ballet had its premiere with Ballet West in Salt Lake City in 1985, shortly before Lander died.

Abdallah is part of Lander's artistic legacy. Her great understanding of and love for the Bournonville tradition, with which she grew up, was passed on to the American company which was to become her last home. But it also became a gift to her native Denmark, when the ballet entered the repertoire of the Royal Danish Ballet in 1986. This ballet therefore lives alongside the memory of a brilliant dancer, who performed all over the world and created memorable interpretations in a wide array of classical roles.

—Jeannette Andersen

LANNER, Katti

Austrian dancer, choreographer, ballet director, and teacher. Born Katharina Josefa Lanner in Vienna, 14 September 1829. Studied at the Ballet School of the Vienna Court Opera, pupil of Pietro Campilli. Married Johann Alfred Geraldini, 1864. Début in *Angelica*, Kärntnertor Theater, Vienna, 1845; dancer, Vienna Court Opera Ballet, 1845–56; débuts in Berlin, Munich, and Dresden, 1856, thereafter touring in Scandinavia and Russia; ballerina and ballet mistress (choreographer), State Theatre, Hamburg, 1862–63; leading dancer and director of own troupe, "Viennese Ballet Company", performing in Bordeaux, 1869, New York, 1870, and Lisbon, 1870–71; appeared in London, 1871, and Paris, 1872; ballerina and director, "Kathi Lanner Coreographic Connection" [sic], touring the U.S., 1873–75; ballet mistress, Her Majesty's Theatre, London, 1877–81, staging ballets for Italian Opera Company; also choreographer for Drury Lane and Crystal Palace pantomimes; ballet mistress (choreographer), Empire Theatre, London, 1887–97; director and teacher, National Training School of Dancing, London, from 1876. Died in London, 15 November 1908.

ROLES

1845 Pas de deux (cr) added to *Angelica* (Guerra), Kärntnertor Theater, Vienna
1846 Dancer in *La Esmeralda* (Perrot), Kärntnertor Theater, Vienna
      Dancer in *Le Diable à quatre* (Mazilier), Kärntnertor Theater, Vienna
1847 Fenella in *Die Stumme von Portici* (*La Muette de Portici*, opera; mus. Auber), Kärntnertor Theater, Vienna
      Title role in *Elina* (Bartholomin), Vienna
      Elisa in *Dilara; oder, Ein Europäisches Ballfest in Tunis* Vienna
1852 Myrtha in *Giselle* (after Coralli, Perrot), Vienna
1853 Countess in *Die Verwandelten Weiber* (*Le Diable à quatre*; Mazilier), Vienna
1854 Dancer in *The Toreador* (Bournonville), Vienna

1856 Title role in *Giselle* (after Coralli, Perrot), Berlin
1873 Dancer in *Azrael* (pantomime spectacle), Niblo's Garden, New York
1874 Helene in *Robert der Teufel* (opera; mus. Meyerbeer), New York
1875 Dancer in *Tom and Jerry* (pantomime), Niblo's Garden, New York
      Ballet Divertissement in *Ahmed* (pantomime spectacle), Grand Opera House, New York

WORKS

1862 *Uriella, der Dämon der Nacht*, State Theatre, Hamburg
      Die Rose von Sevilla; oder, Ein Abend bei Don Bartolo, State Theatre, Hamburg
1863 *Sitala, das Gaukler-Mädchen*, State Theatre, Hamburg
      Asmodeus; oder, Der Sohn des Teufels auf Reisen, State Theatre, Hamburg
1873 *The Butterflies*, Kathi Lanner Coreographic Connection, Pittsburgh and Cincinatti
      Dances in *A Midsummer Night's Dream* (play by Shakespeare), New York
1877 *Les Nymphes de la forêt*, Her Majesty's Theatre, London
      Une Fete de pêcheurs à Pausilippe, Her Majesty's Theatre, London
1878 *Les Papillons* (possibly a version of *The Butterflies*; mus. Hansen), Her Majesty's Theatre, London
1887 *Dilara* (mus. Hervé), Empire Theatre, London
      The Sports of England (mus. Hervé), Empire Theatre, London
1888 *Rose d'Amour* (mus. Hervé), Empire Theatre, London
      Diana (mus. Hervé), Empire Theatre, London
1889 *The Duel in the Snow* (with Martinetti; mus. Hervé), Empire Theatre, London
      Cleopatra (mus. Hervé), Empire Theatre, London
      The Paris Exhibition (mus. Hervé), Empire Theatre, London
      A Dream of Wrath (mus. Wenzel), Empire Theatre, London (revised version staged 1890)
1890 *Cécile* (mus. Wenzel), Empire Theatre, London
      Dolly (mus. Wenzel), Empire Theatre, London
1891 *Orfeo* (mus. Wenzel), Empire Theatre, London
      By the Sea (mus. Wenzel), Empire Theatre, London (revised version staged 1892)
      Nisita (mus. Wenzel), Empire Theatre, London
1892 *Versailles* (mus. Wenzel), Empire Theatre, London
      Round the Town (mus. Wenzel), Empire Theatre, London (revised version staged 1893)
1893 *Katrina* (mus. Wenzel), Empire Theatre, London
      The Girl I Left Behind Me (mus. Wenzel), Empire Theatre, London
1894 *La Frolique* (mus. Ford), Empire Theatre, London
      On Brighton Pier (mus. Ford), Empire Theatre, London
1895 *Faust* (mus. Lutz, Ford), Empire Theatre, London
1896 *La Danse* (mus. Ford), Empire Theatre, London
      Monte Cristo (mus. Wenzel), Empire Theatre, London
1897 *Under One Flag* (mus. Wenzel), Empire Theatre, London
1898 *The Press* (mus. Wenzel), Empire Theatre, London
      Alaska (mus. Wenzel), Empire Theatre, London
1899 *Round the Town Again* (mus. Wenzel), Empire Theatre, London (revised version staged 1900)
1900 *Sea-Side* (mus. Wenzel), Empire Theatre, London
1901 *Les Papillons* (new version; mus. Wenzel), Empire Theatre, London
      Old China (mus. Wenzel), Empire Theatre, London

1902 *Our Crown* (mus. Wenzel), Empire Theatre, London
1903 *The Milliner Duchess* (mus. Wenzel), Empire Theatre, London (revised version staged 1904)
       Vineland (mus. Wenzel), Empire Theatre, London
1904 *High Jinks* (mus. Wenzel), Empire Theatre, London
1905 *The Dancing Doll* (after Hassreiter's *Die Puppenfee*; mus. Bayer, Clarke), Empire Theatre, London (revised version staged later in same year)
1906 *The Débutante* (mus. Clarke, Glaser), Empire Theatre, London
1907 *Sir Roger de Coverly* (mus. Carr), Empire Theatre, London

PUBLICATIONS

Perugini, Mark, *A Pageant of the Dance and Ballet*, London, 1946
Beaumont, Cyril, *Complete Book of Ballets*, revised edition, London, 1951
Guest, Ivor, "An Early 'National' School: The Achievements of Katti Lanner", *Dancing Times* (London), November 1958
Guest, Ivor, *Adeline Genée: A Lifetime of Ballet under Six Reigns*, London, 1958
Guest, Ivor, *The Empire Ballet*, London, 1962

* * *

Katti Lanner's illustrious career spanned the lacklustre years between the golden age of the Romantic ballet and the vibrant Diaghilev era. After attending the Vienna Court Opera School, Lanner made her début in 1845 at the Kärntnertor Theater, home to most Viennese ballet performances. There she danced with both the Italian Fanny Cerrito and Vienna's own Fanny Elssler in numerous outstanding ballet productions, performing in *La Esmeralda* and *Le Diable à quatre* in 1846 alone.

After the death of her father, the famous waltz composer Joseph Lanner, Katti travelled extensively in Europe to further her dancing career, one of her most famous roles being the dumb girl Fenella in *La Muette de Portici* (sometimes known as *Masaniello*). A turning point in her career, however, was when she was engaged as ballet mistress in Hamburg for the 1862–63 season. There she proved to have a penchant for choreography, turning out ten successful ballets on various themes with ease and proficiency. After this productive stint, she resumed her dancing career with appearances in Scandinavia, Russia, and the United States, where she danced *Giselle* in 1870.

The later years of Lanner's career, which were spent in London, were the most memorable, since she made a major contribution to the revival of ballet in England. In 1776 the opera impresario James Mapleson had founded a National Training School for Dancing which he saw as the first step towards his dream of a new opera house. Lanner was placed in charge of the school and soon afterwards she became its sole owner. In the school's brochure Lanner declared that the school's goal was "the resuscitation of the faded glories of ballet, and to bring a thorough knowledge of the choreographic art within the range of those classes among whom talent most abounds, by the adoption of mutually advantageous terms". She was very supportive of English dancers and firmly believed that with good training and hard work, combined with natural English charm and good manners, the English could make excellent dancers. Lanner was an affectionate but stern disciplinarian to her young charges, who served a nine-year apprenticeship. But her belief in English dancers was well founded, for the standard of dancing improved substantially at the opera house, in the ever popular Christmas pantomimes, and in other stage productions.

In addition to her teaching responsibilities Lanner continued her career as a choreographer. From 1877 to 1881 she choreographed ballet divertissements for the opera seasons at Her Majesty's Theatre, and then in 1887 she was appointed ballet mistress at the Empire Theatre, where she continued to choreograph until shortly before her death. She loved her work and often claimed, "I could not live without working".

Lanner's task at the Empire was challenging. The theatre was primarily a music hall featuring a wide range of variety acts, but in Lanner's skilful hands ballet soon became the main attraction on each programme. Together with the designer C. Wilhelm and composer Leopold Wenzel, she created delightful ballets ranging from the fantasy ballet *Rose d'Amour*, depicting the loves and quarrels of flowerland, to the topical *By the Sea*, one of the earliest ballets on an up-to-date subject. She was also responsible for introducing Danish-born ballerina Adeline Genée to London audiences in her ballet *Monte Cristo* in 1896. In all, she created 34 ballets for the Empire Theatre; most of them were very popular and often ran for many months.

Lanner is a remarkable figure in ballet history, since she was one of the first women to choreograph regularly. Her ballets were consistent in quality and the corps work was especially skilful. Lanner had the rare gift of being able to take almost any subject and turn it into a successful ballet that still preserved the classical ballet tradition. In addition, she helped change the path of British ballet by turning out well-trained dancers who swelled the corps de ballet at the Empire and other theatres. Unfortunately, the popularity and brilliance of Diaghilev's Ballets Russes, which burst on the scene towards the end of Lanner's career, tended to obscure her remarkable accomplishments in keeping ballet alive in England.

—Mary Jane Warner

———

LARIONOV, Mikhail

Russian painter and designer. Born Mikhail Fedorovich Larionov in Tiraspol, Ukraine, 3 April (22 May old style) 1881. Studied at the Voskvesensky Institute, Moscow, and at the Academy of Fine Arts, pupil of S. Ivanov, L. Pasternak, V. Serov, Moscow, 1898. Married designer Natalia Gontcharova, 1955. Met impresario Serge Diaghilev in 1903, travelling with him to Paris, 1906: exhibitor at Union of Russian Artists, Salon d'Automne, Paris, 1906; participator in *Golden Fleece* exhibition, also organizing exhibition of French painting under auspices of *Golden Fleece*, Moscow; co-founder, "Jack of Diamonds" group, 1910; leading proponent, with Natalia Gontcharova, of so-called "Rayonist" movement in art, from 1910; exhibitor at Roger Fry's "Post-Impressionism" exhibition, London, 1912; designer for Diaghilev's Ballet Russes, beginning with collaboration on *Le Soleil de nuit*, 1915, and continuing until 1922; also designer of ballets for Serge Lifar and Léon Woizikowsky; organizer, with Gontcharova, of Diaghilev restrospective exhibition, 1930; naturalized as French citizen, 1938. Died in Fontenay-aux-Roses, 10 May 1964.

WORKS (Ballet design)

1915 *Histoires naturelles* (costumes and projections; mus. Ravel; not produced)

Le Soleil de nuit (chor. Massine), Diaghilev's Ballets
     Russes, Geneva
1916 *Kikimora* (later part of *Contes russes*; chor. Massine),
     Diaghilev's Ballets Russes, San Sebastián
1917 *Contes russes* (costumes, with Gontcharova; chor.
     Massine), Diaghilev's Ballets Russes, Paris
1918 *Contes russes* (expanded version; chor. Massine), Diagh-
     ilev's Ballets Russes, London
1921 *Chout* (or *Le Bouffon*; chor. Larionov, Slavinsky),
     Diaghilev's Ballets Russes, Paris
1922 *Le Renard* (chor. Nijinska), Diaghilev's Ballets Russes,
     Paris
1924 *Karaguez* (chor. Bolm), Allied Arts, Chicago (not
     produced)
1930 *La Symphonie classique* (chor. Slavinsky), Opéra Ballet
     de Michel Benois, Paris
1932 *Sur le Borystène* (with Gontcharova; chor. Lifar), Paris
     Opéra Ballet, Paris
1935 *Port Saïd* (chor. Woizikowsky), Les Ballets de Léon
     Woizikowsky, European tour

PUBLICATIONS

By Larionov:
Les Ballets Russes: Serge Diaghilew et la décoration théâtrale,
     with Natalia Gontcharova and Pierre Vorms, revised
     edition, Belvès Dordogne, 1955
Diaghilev et les Ballets Russes, Paris, 1970

About Larionov:
Eganbury, E., *Natalia Goncharova, Mikhail Larionov*, Moscow,
     1913
Apollinaire, Guillaume, "Goncharova et Larionov", *Soirées de
     Paris* (Paris), July/August 1914
Fry, Roger, "Larionov and the Russian Ballet", *Burlington
     Magazine* (London), March 1919
Parnack, V., *Gontcharova et Larionov: L'Art décoratif théâtrale
     moderne*, Paris, 1919
Sitwell, Edith, *Children's Tales*, London, 1920
Isarlov, George, "M.F. Larionov", *Jar-Ptitza* (Paris), 1923
Amberg, George, *Art in Modern Ballet*, London, 1946
Waldemar, George, *Michel Larionov*, Paris, 1966
Bowlt, John, *Russian Stage Design: Scenic Innovation 1900–
     1930*, Jackson, Mississippi, 1982
Mikhail Larionov: La Voie vers l'abstraction, Frankfurt, 1987
Schouvaloff, Alexander, *Set and Costume Design for Ballet and
     Theatre* (catalogue of the Thyssen–Bornemisza Collection),
     London, 1987
Baer, Nancy van Norman, *The Art of Enchantment: Diaghilev's
     Ballets Russes 1909–1929*, San Francisco, 1988

*   *   *

Mikhail Larionov is most celebrated in the world of dance for
the works he designed between 1915 and 1922 for Serge
Diaghilev's Ballets Russes. Larionov, in fact, remarked in 1963
that he could not help being attracted to dance because he
derived such pleasure from being able to add something new to
the art form. It was this interest in experimentation, and in
integrating art forms, which made Larionov especially suited to
designing for the Ballets Russes, particularly in that period
when Diaghilev began to look beyond the works of choreographers like Mikhail Fokine and designers like Léon Bakst
and Alexandre Benois.

Larionov first met Diaghilev in 1903, and Diaghilev played
an influential role in his life from the earliest days of their
association. It was at Diaghilev's invitation that Larionov
travelled to Paris in 1906 to exhibit his art at the exceptionally
successful Russian section of the Salon d'Automne. Following a
period of experimentation with various avant-garde art
movements in Russia, Larionov and his life-long companion
Natalia Gontcharova left Russia for Switzerland in 1915.
Larionov was to convalesce there following injuries sustained
after being mobilized into the Russian army. The two artists
were never to return to Russia and, meeting up with Diaghilev
and his circle in Switzerland, Larionov began his various
commissions for the Ballets Russes. These commissions began
in Lausanne in 1915 with the unrealized *Histoires naturelles*.
Then followed *Le Soleil de nuit*, *Kikimora*, *Contes russes*, *Chout*,
and *Le Renard*, with Larionov often acting not simply as
designer but involving himself with choreography and artistic
collaboration as well.

Larionov's close association with Gontcharova, which was
both private and professional, is reflected in his work for
Diaghilev. Gontcharova in fact contributed designs for many
works attributed to Larionov; the precise nature of the
collaboration and the extent of her contribution has never been
fully examined.

Of the avant-garde art movements with which Larionov was
associated in Russia, the two which made the greatest impact
on his designs for the Ballets Russes were neo-primitivism and
rayonism. The characteristic features of Russian neo-primitivism were a use of strong, bold colours, emphatic lines, and
stylized motifs reminiscent of Russian peasant arts and crafts,
the use of naïve proportions, and a distortion of traditional
form and perspective. Larionov made considerable use of the
characteristics of neo-primitivism in his costumes and sets. The
vitality and spontaneity of the movement is especially
noticeable in Larionov's work for ballets such as *Le Soleil de
nuit* and *Contes russes*, ballets which were firmly based in the
Russian folk tradition. Rayonism was a movement invented by
Larionov, in which the artist explored the visual effects of light
rays emitted by an object rather than the object itself. Many of
his sets reflect an abstraction and a dynamism which resulted
from his experimentation with rayonism.

However, to the formal means at his disposal, all of which he
used to challenge conventional approaches to art, Larionov
added a unique sense of humour and an ability to juxtapose
contrasting elements of design, often to produce a farcical
effect. This is particularly noticeable in his work for *Chout*, in
which an element of pantomime is demanded by the storyline.
Larionov was always concerned, as was his collaborator
Gontcharova, that theatrical design contribute to an understanding of the characters of a particular piece and to the
creation of atmosphere in it.

Larionov's costumes were frequently uncomfortable and
unwieldy to wear, even to the extent of interfering with the
dancers' ability to perform. On occasions they caused the
dancers to strike. His vibrant use of colour, especially in his
costumes for the works based on Russian folk dances, was
visually exciting, but a similar use of colour and motif in dance
costume had already been used by others, notably with great
success by Gontcharova in *Le Coq d'or* in 1914. However, his
ability to use juxtaposition of design elements to express farce
was an unconventional approach to costume design, and his
sets challenged traditional approaches to space, proportion,
and perspective. With such innovations, an interpretation of a
ballet which extended beyond its narrative content was
possible.

Despite his attraction to dance, Larionov himself always
stressed that he was first and foremost an artist. It is in this light
that his contribution to the Diaghilev repertoire must ultimately be gauged. His designs for the ballet reflect innovations

Chout, as designed by Mikhail Larionov, performed by Thadée Slavinsky and Lydia Sokolova of Diaghilev's Ballets Russes, 1921

which he had developed as an artist of the Russian avant-garde before coming to Europe. They were disseminated beyond Russia, even as far as Australia, where works such as *Le Soleil de nuit* and *Contes russes* were performed by the de Basil companies in the 1930s, expressing Larionov's theoretical, avant-garde standpoint on art.

—Michelle Potter

LARSEN, Niels Bjørn

Danish dancer, choreographer, teacher, and ballet director. Born in Copenhagen, 5 October 1913. Studied at the Royal Theatre Ballet School, Copenhagen, from 1920. Married pianist Elvi Clara Henriksen: daughter, dancer and ballet director Dinna Bjørn, b. 1947. Début, as a child, in *Coppélia*, 1922; official début in *The Strife of the Goddesses*, 1933; dancer, Royal Danish Ballet, from 1932, becoming solo dancer (principal), from 1942, and also appearing as guest artist (particularly in mime roles) throughout the world; dancer (while on leave from Royal Danish Ballet), Trudi Schoop Comic Ballet, various seasons of U.S. tour, 1935–39; founder and director, Niels Bjørn Ballet, touring Scandinavia, 1940–46; first choreography, *The Dethroned Lion Tamer*, 1944, continuing to choreograph for both ballet and opera performances at the Royal Theatre; also choreographer for musicals, plays, and films; temporary artistic director, Royal Danish Ballet, 1951, becoming ballet master, 1953–56, and artistic director, 1958–65; also artistic director, Tivoli Theatre, Copenhagen, 1956–80; teacher, Royal Theatre Ballet School, from 1946; company ballet instructor, Royal Theatre, from 1947. Recipient: Knight of the Dannebrog; Arts Award from the American–Scandinavian Foundation, New York, 1992.

ROLES

1922   Negro boy in *Coppélia* (Beck after Saint-Léon), Royal Danish Ballet, Copenhagen
1925   Kirghiz boy in *Polovtsian Dances from Prince Igor* (Fokine), Royal Danish Ballet, Copenhagen

1928 Kuno, a child, in *The Seasons of Love* (Uhlendorff), Royal Danish Ballet, Copenhagen

1930 Dog in *La Boutique fantasque* (Massine, revised Balanchine), Royal Danish Ballet, Copenhagen

Polovtsian warrior in *Polovtsian Dances from Prince Igor* (Fokine), Royal Danish Ballet, Copenhagen

Peasant (cr) in *Benzin* (Jørgen-Jensen), Royal Danish Ballet, Copenhagen

1931 Reel in *The King's Lifeguards on Amager* (Bournonville), Royal Danish Ballet, Copenhagen

Joseph's brother in *The Legend of Joseph* (Balanchine), Royal Danish Ballet, Copenhagen

Tarantella in *La Boutique fantasque* (Balanchine after Massine), Royal Danish Ballet, Copenhagen

Negro (cr) in *Gaucho* (Lander), Royal Danish Ballet, Copenhagen

1932 Negro dance (cr) in *Asra* (Jørgen-Jensen), Royal Danish Ballet, Copenhagen

1933 Sailor (cr) in *The Strife of the Goddesses* (Lander), Royal Danish Ballet, Copenhagen

Dog (cr) in *Diana* (Lander), Royal Danish Ballet, Copenhagen

Pas de deux (cr) in *Football* (Lander), Royal Danish Ballet, Copenhagen

1934 A Zaporog (cr) in *The Zaporogians* (Lander), Royal Danish Ballet, Copenhagen

Apache (cr) in *Bolero* (Lander), Royal Danish Ballet, Copenhagen

The Worker in *The Widow in the Mirror* (B. Ralov), Royal Danish Ballet, Copenhagen

1935 Reel (cr) in *It was an Evening* (Lander), Royal Danish Ballet, Copenhagen

1937 Negro in *The Whims of Cupid and the Ballet Master* (Galeotti), Royal Danish Ballet, Copenhagen

1938 Hunter in *Swan Lake* (Petipa, Ivanov; staged Lander), Royal Danish Ballet, Copenhagen

A Man (cr) in *The Circle* (Theilade), Royal Danish Ballet, Copenhagen

1939 School teacher in *Thorvaldsen* (Lander), Royal Danish Ballet, Copenhagen

Young man (cr) in *The Denmark Ballet* (Lander), Royal Danish Ballet, Copenhagen

1940 One of six men (cr) in *La Valse* (Lander), Royal Danish Ballet, Copenhagen

Angry wave (cr) in *The Sorcerer's Apprentice* (Lander), Royal Danish Ballet, Copenhagen

Young Coachman in *Petrushka* (Fokine), Royal Danish Ballet, Copenhagen

Isidor Brown in *Gaucho* (Lander), Royal Danish Ballet, Copenhagen

1941 Diderik in *A Folk Tale* (Bournonville), Royal Danish Ballet, Copenhagen

Ballabile and Tarantella in *Napoli* (Bournonville), Royal Danish Ballet, Copenhagen

Gypsy dance in *Il Trovatore* (opera; mus. Verdi, chor. Bournonville), Royal Danish Ballet, Copenhagen

1942 Popeye (cr) in *The Land of Milk and Honey* (Lander), Royal Danish Ballet, Copenhagen

Angakok (cr) in *Qarrtsiluni* (Lander), Royal Danish Ballet, Copenhagen

March (cr) in *Twelve by the Post* (B. Ralov), Royal Danish Ballet, Copenhagen

Dancer (cr) in *Fest-Polonaise* (Lander), Royal Danish Ballet, Copenhagen

1943 Van Hoëck in *The Kermesse in Bruges* (Bournonville), Royal Danish Ballet, Copenhagen

1945 Dr. Coppélius in *Coppélia* (Lander after Saint-Léon), Royal Danish Ballet, Copenhagen

The Apprentice in *The Sorcerer's Apprentice* (Lander), Royal Danish Ballet, Copenhagen

Peppo in *Napoli* (Bournonville), Royal Danish Ballet, Copenhagen

Steward in *Far from Denmark* (Bournonville), Royal Danish Ballet, Copenhagen

1946 Charlatan in *Petrushka* (Fokine), Royal Danish Ballet, Copenhagen

Hilarion in *Giselle* (Petipa after Coralli, Perrot; staged Volinine), Royal Danish Ballet, Copenhagen

1947 Kolingen (cr) in *Kolingen* (B. Ralov), Royal Danish Ballet, Copenhagen

Diplomat in *Visions* (Walbom), Royal Danish Ballet, Copenhagen

Edouard in *The King's Lifeguards on Amager* (Bournonville), Royal Danish Ballet, Copenhagen

1948 The Artist in *Episode of an Artist's Life* (Massine), Royal Danish Ballet, Copenhagen

1949 Polichinel in *Salute to August Bournonville* (Bournonville, staged Lander), The Royal Danish Ballet, Copenhagen

French dance in *The Whims of Cupid and the Ballet Master* (Galeotti), Royal Danish Ballet, Copenhagen

1950 Gurn in *La Sylphide* (Bournonville), Royal Danish Ballet, Copenhagen

1951 Sheikh in *Desire* (Larsen), Royal Danish Ballet, Copenhagen

1952 The Man in *Desire* (Larsen), Royal Danish Ballet, Copenhagen

1953 The Dancing Master (cr) in *The Courtesan* (B. Ralov), Royal Danish Ballet, Copenhagen

Elderly artist (cr) in *Parisiana* (Bartholin), Royal Danish Ballet, Copenhagen

1954 Galeotti (cr) in *Capricious Lucinda* (Larsen), Royal Danish Ballet, Copenhagen

1955 Tybalt (cr) in *Romeo and Juliet* (Ashton), Royal Danish Ballet, Copenhagen

1956 The Dancer (cr) in *The Soldier's Tale* (B. Ralov), Danish television

Madge in *La Sylphide* (Bournonville), Royal Danish Ballet, Copenhagen

1957 Gallison in *The Sleeping Beauty* (Petipa; staged Ashton), Royal Danish Ballet, Copenhagen

1958 Old Folks' dance in *The Whims of Cupid and the Ballet Master* (Galeotti), Royal Danish Ballet, Copenhagen

Leander in *Harlequinade* (*Les Millions d'Arlequin*; Walbom, Brenaa), Royal Danish Ballet, Copenhagen

Baron in *Night Shadow* (*La Sonnambula*; Balanchine), Royal Danish Ballet, Copenhagen

1960 Grandfather in *Peter and the Wolf* (Larsen), Royal Danish Ballet, Copenhagen

Notary (cr) in *The Shadow* (Bartholin), Royal Danish Ballet, Copenhagen

1961 Bank manager in *La Chaloupée* (Petit), Royal Danish Ballet, Copenhagen

Headmistress in *Graduation Ball* (Lichine), Royal Danish Ballet, Copenhagen

The Outsider in *The Burrow* (MacMillan), Royal Danish Ballet, Copenhagen

1962 Fernandez in *Far from Denmark* (Bournonville), Royal Danish Ballet, Copenhagen

Circus manager in *Le Beau Danube* (Massine), Royal Danish Ballet, Copenhagen

1963 The Curate in *Irene Holm* (von Rosen), Royal Danish Ballet, Copenhagen

1964 Mother Simone in *La Fille mal gardée* (Ashton), Royal

Danish Ballet, Copenhagen

Il Dottore (cr) in *The White Supper* (Bjørnsson), Danish television

1965 Grandfather (cr) in *The Young Man Must Marry* (television version; Flindt), Danish television

1966 Louis XIII in *The Three Musketeers* (Flindt), Royal Danish Ballet, Copenhagen

Mirewelt in *The Kermesse in Bruges* (Bournonville), Royal Danish Ballet, Copenhagen

1967 Grandfather in *The Young Man Must Marry* (Flindt), Royal Danish Ballet, Copenhagen

1969 The King in *The Swineherd* (Flindt), Royal Danish Ballet, Copenhagen

Greed (cr) in *The Seven Deadly Sins* (Cramér), Royal Danish Ballet, Copenhagen

1971 Drosselmeyer in *The Nutcracker* (Flindt), Royal Danish Ballet, Copenhagen

1972 Old Man in *Triumph of Death* (Flindt), Royal Danish Ballet, Copenhagen

The Grocer in *The Nutcracker* (Flindt), Royal Danish Ballet, Copenhagen

1974 The Confessor (cr) in *Chronicle* (Holm), Royal Danish Ballet, Copenhagen

1975 Pascarillo, the Street Singer, in *Napoli* (Bournonville), Royal Danish Ballet, Copenhagen

1978 José, the Innkeeper, in *The Toreador* (Bournonville; staged Flindt), Royal Danish Ballet, Copenhagen

Tønnes in *The King's Lifeguards on Amager* (Bournonville), Royal Danish Ballet, Copenhagen

1982 Fra Ambrosio in *Napoli* (Bournonville), Royal Danish Ballet, Copenhagen

Ben (cr) in *Dawn* (La Cour), Royal Danish Ballet, Copenhagen

1983 Lorenzo in *Don Quixote* (Gorsky after Petipa), Royal Danish Ballet, Copenhagen

1985 Lord Capulet in *Romeo and Juliet* (Ashton), London Festival Ballet, London

WORKS

1944 *The Dethroned Lion Tamer* (mus. Tarp), Royal Danish Ballet, Copenhagen

1948 *Sylvia* (mus. Delibes), Royal Danish Ballet, Copenhagen

1951 *Drift* (*Desire*; mus. Gershwin), Royal Danish Ballet, Copenhagen

1954 *Till Uglspil* (mus. Rosenberg), Tivoli Theatre, Copenhagen

Capricious Lucinda (mus. Jersild), Royal Danish Ballet, Copenhagen

1956 *Tinsel* (mus. Hogenhaven), Tivoli Theatre, Copenhagen

1957 *Vision* (mus. Britten), Royal Danish Ballet, Copenhagen

1958 *Columbine and the Duck Tail* (mus. Hogenhaven), Tivoli Theatre, Copenhagen

1959 *A Newspaper Proposal; or, The Ballet School* (adapted from Bournonville; mus. Paulli), Tivoli Theatre, Copenhagen

1960 *Peter and the Wolf* (mus. Prokofiev), Royal Danish Ballet, Copenhagen

1961 *The Wild West* (mus. Schmidt), Tivoli Theatre, Copenhagen

1962 *Tivoliana* (mus. Strauss, Waldteufel, Lumbye), Tivoli Theatre, Copenhagen

1965 *Mosaic of Old Memories* (mus. various, arranged London), Tivoli Theatre, Copenhagen

1967 *Jubilee Ballet 800* (mus. Bentzon), Tivoli Theatre, Copenhagen

1968 *Congratulations Tivoli* (with E. Bidsted; mus. Schultz), Tivoli Theatre, Copenhagen

1969 *Contrasts* (mus. Fihn), Tivoli Theatre, Copenhagen

1973 *Suite in Working Clothes* (mus. Schumann), Tivoli Theatre, Copenhagen

1974 *From Harlequin's Motley World* (mus. various, arranged Henriksen), Tivoli Theatre, Copenhagen

1977 *The Little Mermaid* (mus. Henriques), Tivoli Theatre, Copenhagen

Also staged:

1952 *A Folk Tale* (after Bournonville; mus. Gade, Hartmann), Royal Danish Ballet, Copenhagen

1956 *Far from Denmark* (with Brenaa, after Bournonville; mus. Glaeser, Lumbye, Lincke), Royal Danish Ballet, Copenhagen

1957 *The Kermesse in Bruges* (with Brenaa, after Bournonville; mus. Paulli), Royal Danish Ballet, Copenhagen

1979 *The Flower Festival in Genzano* (with Hans Brenaa, after Bournonville; mus. Helsted, Paulli), Tivoli Theatre, Copenhagen

Other works include: dances in operas *Porgy and Bess* (mus. Gershwin; 1943), *Im Weissen Rössel* (mus. Benatzky; 1943), *The Merry Widow* (mus. Léhar; 1944), *Die Teresina* (mus. O. Straus; 1945), *The Nightingale* (mus. Stravinsky; 1946), *Les Brigands* (mus. Offenbach; 1948), *Faust* (mus. Gounod; 1950), *Rosaura* (mus. Jeppesen; 1950), *Dido and Aeneas* (mus. Purcell; 1952), *Falstaff* (mus. Verdi; 1958), *The Bartered Bride* (mus. Smetana; 1958), *La Belle Hélène* (mus. Offenbach; 1958), *The Magic Flute* (mus. Mozart; 1959), *The Abduction from the Seraglio* (mus. Mozart; 1959), *Knickerbocker Holiday* (mus. Weill; 1960), *La Traviata* (mus. Verdi; 1966), *Don Giovanni* (mus. Mozart; 1969), *A Night in Venice* (mus. J. Strauss Jr.; 1969), *Eugene Onegin* (mus. Tchaikovsky; 1970 and 1984), *King and Marshal* (mus. Heise; 1972), *Mam'zelle Nitouche* (mus. Hervé; 1972), *Manon Lescaut* (mus. Puccini; 1973), *Il Turco in Italia* (mus. Rossini; 1974); also dances in stage productions *Les Mouches* (play by Sartre; 1946), *Les Voleurs de bal* (comedy by Anouilh; 1947), *Oklahoma!* (musical; mus. Rodgers; 1949), *Show Boat* (musical; mus. Kern; 1949), *Annie Get Your Gun* (musical; mus. Rodgers; 1950), *As You Like It* (play by Shakespeare; 1951), *A Midsummer Night's Dream* (play by Shakespeare; 1957), *The Entertainer* (play by Osborne; 1959), *Macbeth* (play by Shakespeare; 1961), *Rosencrantz and Guildenstern are Dead* (play by Stoppard; 1968), *Schweik* (play by Brecht; 1968), *Le Boulanger* (play by Anouilh; 1970), *The Suicide* (play by Erdman; 1972).

PUBLICATIONS

By Larsen:

Interview in Hering, Doris, "Actor in the House", *Dance Magazine* (New York), March 1957

Interview in Newman, Barbara, "Speaking of Dance: Niels Bjørn Larsen", *Dancing Times* (London), August 1985

About Larsen:

Mørk, Ebbe, *Bag mange masker*, Copenhagen, 1974

Cunningham, Katharine, "Niels Bjørn Larsen: A Life in Mime", *Ballet Review* (New York), Summer 1982

Acocella, Joan, "Ashton's Romeo", *Ballet Review* (New York), Fall 1985

*   *   *

A favourite tale of Niels Bjørn Larsen's is the story of how his mother brought him to the Royal Danish Ballet School in 1920, because she wanted her six-year-old son to be a well-mannered little boy, and because she wanted him to be able to retire with a pension.

Niels Bjørn Larsen literally grew up on the stage of the Royal Theatre, having landed his first one-line part in a Danish comedy, *The Dear Family*, only three days after his arrival, and thereafter being used in several plays, operas, and ballets throughout his childhood and youth.

The Royal Theatre's Ballet School was dominated in the 1920s by the Bournonville tradition, and later in his career Niels Bjørn Larsen was to interpret a wide range of eminent Bournonville characters. But the first genuine inspiration and challenge for his natural talent as a mime came when he met the Swiss mime Trudi Schoop, who was doing "grotesque" pantomimes to present social satire of a stylized and very original kind. On leave from the Royal Danish Ballet, he danced and toured with the Trudi Schoop Comic Ballet for several seasons between 1935 and 1939. This probably was one of the greatest influences on his career as one of the most outstanding mime and character dancers in Danish ballet history, comparable even to the best in the world.

Niels Bjørn Larsen returned to Copenhagen in 1940, and during a period of more than 40 years he created an incredible amount of different characters, ranging from the tap-dancing American Isidor Brown in *Gaucho*, to witty portaits of women such as Mother Simone in *La Fille mal gardée* or the Headmistress in *Graduation Ball*, to old men such as the lustful old man in *The Whims of Cupid and the Ballet Master* or the senile Grandfather in *The Young Man Must Marry*, to the mysterious and vibrant role of Angakok in the Eskimo ballet *Qarrtsiluni*. Niels Bjørn Larsen has often claimed Angakok to be the toughest role he has ever danced, involving a fourteen-minute solo danced with the knees in a continued deep bend and with a small stick held crosswise in the mouth.

Larsen's most celebrated roles are, however, his mysterious but touching Dr. Coppélius in *Coppélia* and his wicked and vindictive witch Madge in *La Sylphide*. In 1957 and 1959 he guested as Coppélius at the Greek Theatre in Los Angeles, and as Madge he has danced at the Paris Opéra, the Metropolitan in New York, in Vienna, and for the London Festival Ballet, in Peter Schaufuss's 1979 staging of *La Sylphide*, broadcast the following year by British television.

Niels Bjørn Larsen has shown himself to be a man of many talents. In the crucial period after Harald Lander had left the Royal Danish Ballet, Larsen was appointed temporary artistic director, officially appointed ballet master from 1953 to 1956, and once again appointed artistic director and ballet master two years later. During these difficult years he managed to reorganize and reunite a divided company, proving himself a humane leader capable of balancing numerous different points of view.

Niels Bjørn Larsen never made his mark as an important choreographer, even though he choreographed several minor ballets and a great deal of divertissements. His effort to bring foreign guest choreographers to Copenhagen to work with the Royal Danish Ballet has, however, been of enormous importance in terms of providing much-needed change and renewal to the repertory, and providing new inspiration and challenge to both dancers and audiences. Many interesting and famous choreographers visited Denmark in the 1950s and early 1960s, among them David Lichine, George Balanchine, Frederick Ashton, Roland Petit, and Birgit Cullberg. Niels Bjørn Larsen also continued Harald Lander's initiative of producing annual May Festivals; and he went on tours with the company, mainly to Scandinavia and Europe. He organized the London tour in

1953, and ended his stage career with a successful tour of the United States in 1965.

Throughout his whole life, Niels Bjørn Larsen has been a tremendously energetic and vital force. In 1940 he formed his own company, touring in Scandinavia until 1946. From the late 1950s he was also artistic director of the Tivoli Theatre, for which he created several small, colourful, and light-hearted ballets. At the same time, he was still dancing, still teaching, still directing, and still staging works at the Royal Theatre and everywhere else. He has choreographed and arranged dances for revues, musicals, dramas, operettas, operas, and films. During the 1960s and 1970s he promoted the knowledge of ballet by visiting schools, and in 1979 he was one of the men behind the Bournonville exhibition at the State Museum of Art.

As a ballet master and artistic director, Niels Bjørn Larsen has staged a countless number of ballet productions. In the mid-1950s, on his own initiative, he started to film the ballet repertoire of the Royal Danish Ballet, "to make it easier to restage", as he has often said. And today he is the owner of a private collection of ballet films of great historic value.

Niels Bjørn Larsen had his farewell performance with the Royal Danish Ballet on 11 April 1986, aged 72, as the witch Madge in *La Sylphide*. But since then he has appeared in the same role with several foreign companies, just as he has been coaching and assisting in staging Bournonville ballets outside Denmark. But that is not all; during the Bournonville Festival in the spring of 1992 he also actively took part in the Symposium at the Copenhagen University. He was responsible for the staging of *Far from Denmark*, and he performed the role of Pascarillo, the street singer in *Napoli* at the Bournonvilleana Gala Evening. In 1992 Niels Bjørn Larsen is still going strong with no evidence that he will ever "retire with a pension".

—Majbrit Simonsen

LAURENCIA

Choreography: Vakhtang Chabukiani
Music: Aleksandr Krein
Design: Simon Virsaladze (scenery and costumes)
Libretto: Yevgeny Mandelberg (after the play *Fuente Ovejuna* by Lope de Vega)
First Production: Kirov Ballet, Leningrad, 22 March 1939
Principal Dancers: Natalia Dudinskaya (Laurencia), Vakhtang Chabukiani (Frondoso), Elena Chikvaidze (Jacinta), Tanya Vecheslova (Pascuale)

Other productions include: Bolshoi Ballet (staged Chabukiani; scenery Vadim Ryndin), with Maya Plisetskaya, Vakhtang Chabukiani; Moscow, 19 February 1956. Royal Ballet (Pas de six only; staged Rudolf Nureyev after Chabukiani), with Nureyev, Christopher Gable, Graham Usher, Nadia Nerina, Antoinette Sibley, Merle Park; London, 24 March 1965. Hungarian State Opera Ballet (restaged Chabukiani), with Adél Orosz and Viktor Róna; Budapest, 22 March 1970.

Other choreographic treatments of story: Aleksandr Chekrygin (Moscow, 1931), Aleksei Chitchanadze (Moscow, 1955).

PUBLICATIONS

Lawson, Joan, "Another Soviet Ballet: 'Laurencia'", *Dancing Times* (London), October 1940

Laurencia **Pas de six, as performed by Maria Almeida and Vivana Durante, Royal Ballet, London**

Beaumont, Cyril, *Supplement to the Complete Book of Ballets*, London, 1942

Lawson, Joan, "A Short History of Soviet Ballet", *Dance Index* (New York), June/July, 1943

Kremshevskaya, Galina, *Natalia Dudinskaya*, Leningrad and Moscow, 1964

Krein, Y., and Rogozhina, H., *Aleksandr Krein*, Moscow, 1964

Roslavleva, Natalia, *Era of the Russian Ballet*, London, 1966

Swift, Mary Grace, *The Art of Dance in the Soviet Union*, Notre Dame, Indiana, 1968

*   *   *

The ballet *Laurencia* is based on the seventeenth-century play by Lope de Vega, *Fuente Ovejuna*, a tragedy which tells the story of a peasants' uprising in response to the local Castilian Commander's attempt to seduce the young girl Laurencia. When the villagers' petition to the King is ignored, Laurencia encourages the people to revolt, and the Commander is killed by her brother. In the resultant investigation of the killing, many of the peasants are tortured for information; but their answer, when asked who killed the Commander, is always "Fuente Ovejuna", the name of the village.

Chabukiani's ballet *Laurencia* belongs to the classical tradition of Russian ballet. Created at a time when "choreo-drama" was considered the only acceptable form of contemporary ballet, it harks back to the time of genuine dance drama, wherein movement was a vehicle for meaning, and dance could serve as divertissement as well as dramatic purpose. At the same time, the story of a peasant revolution was obviously the ideal subject for a Soviet ballet.

Chabukiani in this period differed markedly from his contemporaries in art. As a dancer, he was regarded as the "god of dance" of his time, and as a ballet master he thought in the language of dance in his first ballets, *The Heart of the Hills* and *Laurencia*. In these two ballets, and especially in *Laurencia*, Chabukiani asserted once and for all the importance of male dance as championed by Fokine, furthering in particular the notion of "heroic" male dance. Chabukiani was absolutely unique among the Soviet choreographers of his time in this regard.

Chabukiani was one of the first to create a new choreographic language by means of his own particular blend of folk dance and classical dance. Where he acquired his knowledge of Spanish dance is unimportant: as in the ballet *Don Quixote* or the Spanish dances that Lopukhov (who was greatly influenced by Fokine's *Jota Aragonese*) staged for the opera *Carmen*, he succeeded in creating an image of Spain by mixing Spanish and classical dance. And the result was entirely his own. As Lopukhov wrote, "Chabukiani created his image of Spain the same way Liszt created his *Hungarian Rhapsodies*, which have their roots in folk art, but are at the same time typically Liszt."

The "dance" with castanets in the first act is a good example. It is a "choreographic symphonette" (as Lopukhov called it), performed by Laurencia and Frondoso; the centre of the ballet is the adagio celebration of the marriage of these two leading characters. Leaning heavily on the classical ballet tradition of "pas d'action", Chabukiani created an extensive choreographic suite that paves the way for the dramatic culmination of the act (the arrival of the Commander). This pas d'action begins with the entrance of three pairs of dancers (Laurencia, Frondoso, and Laurencia's two friends, Pascuale and Jacinta, with their cavaliers). The pairs face off and begin their dance, which is created upon endless complex combinations of partnering and aerial lifts. In this adagio Chabukiani demonstrated once again the great possibilities of classical ballet.

Krasovskaya wrote: "The choreographer makes skilful use of the technique of the synchronic movement of three pairs and the sequential reiteration of choreographic passages ... without diminishing the leading role of the ballerina and the premier danseur. The leading pair is always in the centre ... and the choreographer persistently summons up the leitmotif of the premier danseur—a *croisé* pose with sharply bent knee— mirroring and strengthening it in the dance of the three ballerinas. ... The adagio of the three pairs asserts the theme of triumphant bravery and of proud and happy youth that does not yet know the agony of defeat."

Generously filling the first and second acts with an avalanche of dances, the choreographer somehow exhausted himself, and the third act (the return of the tormented Laurencia from the Commander's castle and her call to rebellion) pales by comparison. But to this day the public loves *Laurencia*, and the first performers of the ballet have also entered the history of Soviet dance. Dudinskaya as Laurencia, Chabukiani as Frondoso, and Vecheslova as Pascuale will be remembered not least of all for their participation in the original production of this important and popular ballet.

—Nina Alovert

LAVROVSKY, Leonid

Russian/Soviet dancer, choreographer, teacher, and ballet director.   Born Leonid Mikhailovich Ivanov in St. Petersburg, 18 June (5 June old style) 1905. Studied at the Petrograd (later Leningrad) Choreographic School, pupil of Vladimir Ponomarev, from 1916; graduated in 1922. Married (1) dancer Elena Chikvaidze: son, dancer Mikhail Lavrovsky; (2) dancer Natalia Chadson. Dancer, State Academic Theatre for Opera and Ballet (GATOB, later the Kirov Theatre), 1922–35, also performing with the Evenings of Young Ballet, under Georgi Balanchivadze (later Balanchine) and Vladimir Dmitriev; first choreography, 1928, thereafter staging several works for Leningrad Choreographic School; artistic director, Leningrad Maly Theatre, 1935–38, Kirov Ballet, Leningrad, 1938–44, and Spendiarov Theatre, Erevan, 1942–43; chief choreographer, Bolshoi Ballet, Moscow, 1944–56, "Ballet on Ice" Company, Moscow, 1959–64, and Bolshoi Ballet, 1960–64; also teacher, from 1922; teacher at the Choreographers' Faculty of the Institute of Theatrical Art, 1948–67, becoming professor from 1952; director, Moscow Choreographic School, 1964–67; also directed, with L. Arnshtam, film version of own ballet, *Romeo and Juliet* (1955). Recipient: State Prize of the USSR, 1946, 1947, 1950; People's Artist of the USSR, 1965. Died in Paris, 27 November 1967.

ROLES

1923   Principal dancer (cr) in *The Magnificence of the Universe* (also called *Dance Symphony*; Lopukhov), Young Ballet and Dancers of the State Academic Theatre for Opera and Ballet (GATOB), Leningrad

1925   Jean de Brienne in *Raymonda* (Petipa), GATOB, Leningrad

1925/   Prince Siegfried in *Swan Lake* (Petipa, Ivanov),
30   GATOB, Leningrad

      Principal dancer in *Chopiniana* (*Les Sylphides*; Fokine), GATOB, Leningrad

      Amoun in *Egyptian Nights* (Fokine), GATOB, Leningrad

      Conrad in *Le Corsaire* (Petipa), GATOB, Leningrad

      The Count in *Swan Lake* (Vaganova after Petipa, Ivanov), GATOB, Leningrad

1930   The Fascist (cr) in *The Golden Age* (Vainonen, Yakobson, Chesnokov), GATOB, Leningrad

1933   The Count in *Swan Lake* (Vaganova after Petipa, Ivanov), GATOB, Leningrad

WORKS

1928   *The Seasons* (mus. Tchaikovsky), Leningrad Choreographic School, Leningrad

1930   *Etudes Symphoniques* (mus. Schumann), Leningrad Choreographic School, Leningrad

1932   Creative Evening for Young Ballet, including *Spanish Capriccio* (mus. Rimsky-Korsakov), Philharmonic Hall, Leningrad

1934   *Fadetta* (mus. Delibes), Leningrad Choreographic School, Leningrad (also staged Maly Theatre, 1936, Bolshoi Ballet, 1952)

1935   *Katerina* (mus. Rubinstein, Adam), Leningrad Choreographic School, Leningrad (also staged Kirov Ballet, 1936)

1938   *The Prisoner of the Caucasus* (mus. Asafiev), Maly Theatre Ballet, Leningrad

1940   *Romeo and Juliet* (mus. Prokofiev), Kirov Ballet, Leningrad (also staged Bolshoi Ballet, 1946)

1949   *The Red Poppy* (mus. Glière), Bolshoi Ballet, Moscow

1954   *The Story of the Stone Flower* (mus. Prokofiev), Bolshoi Ballet, Moscow

1959   *A Winter Fantasy*, "Ballet on Ice" Company, Moscow

      The Snow Symphony, "Ballet on Ice" Company, Moscow

1960   *Paganini* (mus. Rachmaninov), Bolshoi Ballet, Moscow

1961   *Night City* (mus. Bartok), Bolshoi Ballet, Moscow

      Pages from a Life (mus. A. Balanchivadze), Bolshoi Ballet, Moscow

1964   *Bolero* (mus. Ravel), Moscow Choreographic School, Moscow

1966   *Classical Symphony* (mus. Prokofiev), Moscow Choreographic School, Moscow

      Walpurgis Night in *Faust* (opera; mus. Gounod), Bolshoi Theatre, Moscow

1967   *The Heart's Memory* (mus. A. Balanchivadze), Moscow Choreographic School, Moscow

Also staged:

1937   *Vain Precautions* (*La Fille mal gardée*, after Petipa, Ivanov; mus. Hertel), Maly Theatre Ballet, Leningrad

1944   *Giselle* (after Petipa, Coralli, Perrot; mus. Adam), Bolshoi Ballet, Moscow

1945   *Raymonda* (after Petipa, Gorsky; mus. Glazunov), Bolshoi Ballet, Moscow

PUBLICATIONS

By Lavrovsky:
"From My Reminiscences about Sergei Prokofiev", in Prokof-

iev, Sergei, *Materials, Documents, Reminiscences*, Moscow, 1956

"Paths and Destinies of Soviet Ballet", *Sovetskaya Kultura* (Moscow), 3 April, 8 April, 1968

About Lavrovsky:

Slonimsky, Yuri, *The Soviet Ballet*, Moscow and Leningrad, 1950

Cox, A.J., "The Aims of Soviet Choreography", *Dance and Dancers* (London), October 1956

Cox, A.J., "Leonid Lavrovsky", *Ballet Today* (London), December 1956

Lopukhov, Fedor, *Sixty Years in the Ballet*, Moscow, 1966

Roslavleva, Natalia, *Era of the Russian Ballet*, London, 1966

Swift, Mary Grace, *The Art of the Dance in the USSR*, Notre Dame, Indiana, 1968

Golovkina, S., "Leonid Mikhailovich Lavrovsky", *Teatr* (Moscow), no. 5, 1968

Demidov, Aleksandr, *The Russian Ballet Past and Present*, translated by Guy Daniels, London, 1978

Lavrovsky (various authors), Moscow, 1983

Andreev, A., Stukolkina, N., "The Aims of 'Young Ballet'", *Sovetsky Balet* (Moscow), no. 5, 1987

*   *   *

It has been unfortunate for most Westerners that the appreciation of works by the major Soviet choreographers has been drastically curtailed by the problems of East–West political relations. Although Leonid Lavrovsky, together with Yuri Grigorovich, is highly regarded as one of the USSR's finest choreographers, his reputation at large rests principally on report: and sadly, little of his work has been widely seen in the West (although the historic visit by the Bolshoi company to London in 1956 with Lavrovsky's *Romeo and Juliet* proved a watershed in the development of ballet in the West).

His choreography has been enormously influential in contemporary Russian ballet, however, and marks one of the most significant attempts since the decline of the imperial Petipa style to develop new forms in a classical idiom, which would expand the dramatic potential of dance while integrating within it an increasingly sophisticated psychological and theatrical awareness.

The son of a St. Petersburg industrial worker, Lavrovsky developed his career first as a dancer at the Maryinsky, where he was a notable exponent of several major classical roles—especially Siegfried (*Swan Lake*), Jean de Brienne (*Raymonda*), Amoun (*Egyptian Nights*), and the Poet (*Chopiniana*). This experience seems to have formed his deep-rooted attachment to the essential vocabulary of nineteenth-century classicism, though at the same time his interest in new choreographic possibilities was stimulated by membership of the avant-garde group Molodoi Balet ("Young Ballet"), founded by George Balanchine and Vladimir Dmitriev, and he also took part in both Lopukhov's controversial *The Magnificence of the Universe*, or *Dance Symphony* (1923) and Shostakovich's *The Golden Age* as the principal fascist. It was at this time that he also became convinced that a deep understanding of music was at the core of choreography, and he began to study the rudiments of composition and piano.

His first choreography, created on student casts to such works as Schumann's *Etudes Symphoniques* and Tchaikovsky's *The Seasons*, was followed by full-length works based on themes of Georges Sand's novel in *Fadette*, and on elements of the serf theatre in *Katerina*. Subsequent ballets, such as *La Fille mal gardée* (known in Russia as *Vain Precautions*) and *The Prisoner of the Caucasus* established him in a unique style, blending an expanded classical vocabulary with a high proportion of stylized mime—a characteristic in his work which has attracted the most attention from Western commentators, for whom the mimic element of dance has since become increasingly alien (and which also has led to charges of choreographic heaviness).

This interweaving of dance and mime reached its most developed expression in Lavrovsky's staging of the first Soviet production of Prokofiev's *Romeo and Juliet* (1940), generally considered to be his finest work and the only one to have been highly influential in the West. Elements of his thought and dance imagery have found their way into most subsequent productions, and it says much for his grasp of dramatic values that the normally intransigent Prokofiev was induced to make significant changes in the otherwise completed score, many of which are now regarded among its most characteristic sections (for example Romeo's energetic solo in the balcony pas de deux, Juliet's variation in the ballroom scene, her scene with Paris, or Tybalt's funeral procession).

After the war, Lavrovsky's style changed significantly and he moved gradually away from a concentration on dramatic story ballets to work more frequently with abstract conceptions like *Paganini* (Rachmaninov) and Ravel's *Bolero*, where an emotional narrative is implied without specific reference. As with many artists in Soviet ballet, Lavrovsky appears to have suffered the one-sided development created by political pressures in the USSR—suppressing much of the liberating influence set widely in motion by the Diaghilev circle's experiments in new styles of movement and content, while concentrating heavily on technique and prescribed "correctness" of artistic attitude. In effect it fell to Lavrovsky to work with the remnants of the Petipa tradition without the benefit of exposure to the new trends; and it says much for his stature that he achieved a style so distinctive and yet so true to his traditions.

—Geoffrey Baskerville

LAVROVSKY, Mikhail

Georgian/Soviet dancer, choreographer, and ballet director. Born Mikhail Leonidovich Lavrovsky in Tbilisi, Georgia, son of dancer and choreographer Leonid Lavrovsky, 29 October 1941. Studied at the Moscow Choreographic School, pupil of Nikolai Tarasov, E. Evdokimov; graduated in 1961; later coached by Aleksei Yermolaev, Bolshoi Theatre; also studied at State Institute of Theatrical Art (GITIS), Faculty of Choreography, under Rostislav Zakharov; graduated in 1979. Dancer, becoming principal dancer, Bolshoi Ballet, Moscow, 1961–88, partnering leading ballerinas Natalia Bessmertnova, Ludmila Semenyaka, and Nina Timofeyeva; guest choreographer and principal dancer, Tbilisi, various seasons from 1977; also appeared frequently on television, including in *The Soloists of the Bolshoi Theatre* (1978), and *Nina Sorokina and Mikhail Lavrovsky are Dancing* (1982); artistic director, Paliashvili Theatre (theatre of the Tbilisi Ballet), Tbilisi, 1983–85; has also staged ballets for Kirov Ballet in Leningrad, Atlanta Ballet, California Ballet, and Ballet Arizona in the United States, and for film-musical in Australia. Recipient: First Prize, International Ballet Competition, Varna, 1965; Lenin Prize (for performance in *Spartacus*), 1970; Nijinsky Prize, Paris, 1972; title of People's Artist of the USSR, 1976; State Prize of the USSR, 1977.

Mikhail Lavrovsky in *Spartacus*, Bolshoi Ballet, Moscow, 1974

ROLES

1961   Georgi's Son (cr) in *Pages from a Life* (L. Lavrovsky), Bolshoi Ballet, Moscow
1962   Philippe in *The Flames of Paris* (Vainonen), Bolshoi Ballet, Moscow
1963   The Prince in *Cinderella* (Zakharov), Bolshoi Ballet, Moscow
        Albrecht in *Giselle* (Petipa after Coralli, Perrot; staged L. Lavrovsky), Bolshoi Ballet, Moscow
        Bluebird in *The Sleeping Beauty* (Grigorovich after Petipa), Bolshoi Ballet, Moscow
        Vaslav in *The Fountain of Bakhchisarai* (Zakharov), Bolshoi Ballet, Moscow
1964   Frondoso in *Laurencia* (Chabukiani), Bolshoi Ballet, Moscow
1965   Basil in *Don Quixote* (Gorsky after Petipa), Bolshoi Ballet, Moscow
        Kais in *Leili and Medzhnun* (Goleizovsky), Bolshoi Ballet, Moscow
        Romeo in *Romeo and Juliet* (Lavrovsky), Bolshoi Ballet, Moscow
        Ferkhad in *The Legend of Love* (Grigorovich), Bolshoi Ballet, Moscow
1966   The Prince in *The Nutcracker* (Grogorovich), Bolshoi Ballet, Moscow
1968   Title role in *Spartacus* (Grigorovich), Bolshoi Ballet, Moscow
        Romeo (cr) in *Romeo and Juliet* (Ryzhenko, Smirnov-Golovanov), Bolshoi Ballet, Moscow

1972   Principal dancer in *White Nights* (mus. Schoenberg), Bolshoi Ballet, Moscow
1976   Victor (cr) in *Angara* (Grigorovich), Bolshoi Ballet, Moscow
1977   Principal dancer (cr) in *Mziri* (also chor.), Tbilisi Ballet, Tbilisi
1978   Title role in *Ivan the Terrible* (Grigorovich), Bolshoi Ballet, Moscow
1981   Principal dancer (cr) in *Prometheus* (also chor.), Tbilisi Ballet, Tbilisi
1983   Porgy (cr) in *Porgy and Bess* (also chor.), Tbilisi Ballet, Tbilisi
1986   Artinov (cr) in *Anyuta* (Bolshoi version; Vasiliev), Bolshoi Ballet, Moscow
        Principal dancer (cr) in *Choreographic Novel* (also chor.), Tbilisi Ballet, Tbilisi
1989   Principal dancer in *The Dreamer* (also chor.), Tbilisi Ballet, Tblisi

WORKS

1977   *Mziri* (mus. Toradze), Tbilisi Ballet, Tbilisi
1981   *Prometheus* (mus. Scriabin), Tbilisi Ballet, Tbilisi
1983   *Porgy and Bess* (mus. Gershwin), Tbilisi Ballet, Tbilisi
1986   *Choreographic Novel* (mus. various), Tbilisi Ballet, Tbilisi
1987   *Bach Suite No. 2 for Flute* (mus. Bach), Ballet Arizona, Arizona
1989   *The Dreamer* (mus. Gershwin), Tbilisi Ballet, Tbilisi
        Fantasy on the Theme of Cazanova (mus. Mozart), Atlanta Ballet, Atlanta, Georgia
1991   *Revelations* (mus. Kitka), Citizens Company, Moscow
1992   *Jazz Café* (mus. Gershwin), Moscow Theatre of Operetta, Moscow

Also staged:
1982   *Romeo and Juliet* (chor. L. Lavrovsky), Tbilisi Ballet, Tbilisi (also staged for Kirov Ballet, Leningrad, 1991)

PUBLICATIONS

René, Natalia, "Bolshoi Prince", *Dance and Dancers* (London), March 1968
Demidov, Aleksandr, "Mikhail Lavrovsky", *Teatr* (Moscow), no. 7, 1971
Niehaus, Max, *Ballett Faszination*, Munich, 1972
Bolshoi's Young Dancers, translated by Natalie Ward, Moscow, 1975
Greskovic, Robert, "The Grigorovich Factor and the Bolshoi", *Ballet Review* (Brooklyn, N.Y.), vol. 5, no. 2, 1975–76
Matheson, Katy, "Western Style, *Porgy and Bess*", *Dance Magazine* (New York), September 1984
Helpern, Alice, "Informal Meeting with Mikhail Lavrovsky", Society of Dance History Scholars, Proceedings of the 10th Annual Conference, 1987
Smith, Helen, C., "Reviews—Atlanta", *Dance Magazine* (New York), April 1989

*   *   *

Ancestral shadows are hard to escape: children of famous men and women who follow in their parents' fields have to overcome charges of trading on a famous name and must prove themselves as individuals. Mikhail Lavrovsky has lived under an unusually large shadow. His father, the late Leonid

Lavrovsky, was a renowned Soviet choreographer and long-time director of the Bolshoi Ballet.

Mikhail has said in interview that as a dancer he had always "strived to excel". He recalled self-assigned practice after lessons with his father, indicating unusual determination for a youngster. He competed with other children for acceptance at the Bolshoi (Moscow Choreographic) school, which he attended from age ten. He graduated at the top of his class and was invited to join the Bolshoi company, where he spent the greater part of his life.

The competitive spirit never lessened. He won first prize in the International Ballet Competition at Varna, and was awarded the Nijinsky Prize by the French Academy of Dance. At age 28, he was the youngest recipient of the Lenin Prize, one of only three dancers to be so honoured.

Lavrovsky rose quickly at the Bolshoi, moving from soloist to principal to effective premier danseur, through talent and no apparent favouritism. Western critics as well as the Soviets were impressed with his bravura performances, particularly in *Spartacus*, with which he was closely identified. In 1965, when Grigorovich's *Legend of Love* moved from the Kirov to the Bolshoi, Lavrovsky alternated in the lead role of Ferkhad (Ferhad) with Maris Liepa. The following year Natalia Roslavleva wrote in her *Era of Russian Ballet* that Lavrovsky "... appeared to be the ideal Ferhad, more earthy and temperamental". "As a dancer," Roslavleva concluded, "Lavrovsky belongs in the same category as Vasiliev; he expresses everything in dance and is made for strong and virile roles."

Lavrovsky fully established his independence when he became director of the Georgian Tbilisi Ballet following his father's death. The elder Lavrovsky had been relatively innovative. During his tenure at the Bolshoi, he restaged many of the nineteenth-century war-horses, substituting dance for the lengthy, boring mime sequences that had been abandoned in the West a generation before. His son then went further. He had his own theatre in Georgia where he dared to introduce non-narrative ballets, including Balanchine's. He also staged *Porgy and Bess* as a ballet. "We have opera theatre," he said of the venture. "Why should we not have dance theatre as well?"

Lavrovsky was also among the first to collaborate artistically with Westerners. In recent years, he has been a guest choreographer at Ballet Arizona, he has worked with the Atlanta Ballet, and he has choreographed a work for the California Ballet Company in San Diego.

After twenty years as a principal, a Soviet dancer may retire from the stage with a pension or continue to work under contract. Lavrovsky chose retirement, explaining, "I have had a basically good life, but I am interested in other things. I will not give up dance. I have been offered a theatre again, but I do not want to be dependent on what others suggest. I want freedom to work."

By 1989, he had returned to Atlanta Ballet to stage a new ballet, and then co-produced a film-musical in Australia. Both are far from the famous shadow that is his heritage.

—William E. Fark

THE LEAVES ARE FADING

Choreography: Antony Tudor
Music: Antonin Dvořák
Design: Ming Cho Lee (scenery), Patricia Zipprodt (costumes), Jennifer Tipton (lighting)

First Production: American Ballet Theatre, New York State Theater, New York, 17 July 1975
Principal Dancers: Gelsey Kirkland, Marianna Tcherkassky, Jonas Kåge, Kim Highton, Amy Blaisdell, Nanette Glushak, Linda Kuchera, Michael Owen, Charles Ward, Richard Schafer, Clark Tippet

PUBLICATIONS

Barnes, Clive, "Tudor's Most Personal Work", *New York Times* (New York), 3 August 1975
Barnes, Patricia, "*The Leaves Are Fading*", *Dance and Dancers* (London), January 1976
Gruen, John, Interview with Tudor in *People Who Dance*, Pennington, N.J., 1988
Chazin-Bennahum, Judith, "After Pillar of Fire", *Choreography and Dance*, vol. 1, part 2, 1989
Farkas, Mark, "Antony Tudor: The First Zen Institute", *Choreography and Dance*, vol. 1, part 2, 1989
Perlmutter, Donna, *Shadowplay: The Life of Antony Tudor*, London, 1991

*   *   *

The Leaves are Fading, with its plotless, rhapsodic expression of couples in love, re-established Antony Tudor's pre-eminent position as a great choreographer at American Ballet Theatre. Tudor erased signs of his "personal technique" so that the viewer could see the movement, the pure seemingly spontaneous action. Tudor himself described this ballet as "empty" rather than abstract.

In 1974, Tudor had returned to American Ballet Theatre as associate director with Nora Kaye after a hiatus of 24 years. Although Tudor had not made a ballet on a big ballet company since *Knight Errant* for the touring company of the Royal Ballet and *The Divine Horsemen* for the Australian Ballet, he did choreograph several "little ballets" for Juilliard in 1971 with a National Endowment for the Arts grant. His loving and wistful *Continuo*, his strange and disturbing *Cereus*, and his compelling *Sunflowers* were by no means negligible artistic projects.

For his *The Leaves are Fading* score, Tudor chose Dvořák's little-known *Cypresses*, together with the String Quintet Op. 77, the String Quartet Op. 80, and part of his Terzetto. Tudor said in 1975, "It's incredibly hard to make those pieces fit together because of the changes in tonality from key to key. Dvořák composed in too many of the wrong keys".

With a cast of fifteen dancers, the ballet presents a series of passionate pas de deux, though beginning and ending with a single young woman drifting on stage as if a catalyst for the ebb and tide of memory. Gradually eight women dressed in simple, leaf-like dresses fill the stage, dancing in patterns of four and three when two men fly into the group to initiate leaps and lifts. The men organize into a circle doing slow jumps, their legs spread far apart at the height of their leaps. At times, Tudor's choreography shows borrowings from an East European folk dance vocabulary suggested by the music. The first pas de deux emphasizes quick and exacting allegro steps. The woman is lifted in airy, carefree passes, and spins with low piqué arabesque turns. One particular jeté lift transports her far backwards as she faces the audience. When the first couple leaves, young men enter in a series, wending their way in jumps with both knees bent, as if doing a Russian folk dance. Six women return to execute very formalized technical steps with a Baroque flavor, dancing for the men who retreat to the corners of the stage.

In the second pas de deux, originally danced by Gelsey

The Leaves Are Fading, with Gelsey Kirkland and Kevin McKenzie (foreground), American Ballet Theatre, 1975

Kirkland and Jonas Kåge, the man's stolid and weighted steps contrast with the ballerina's willowy and delicately fluid movements. He whisks her into arabesque and drop lifts her to swing around him. She tantalizingly dances for him with her arms over her head, and he hurries her into a lift recalling the backwards jump of the first couple. She finishes sitting on his knee. Their duet seems to symbolize a yearning for an idealized love, for what might be imagined rather than what is.

Again several couples re-enter, breaking the intimacy of the lovers. The third duet reveals a more serene amour, less ecstatic and more tender. This woman has an elegant and smooth confidence. The couple moves as one; her clear connection to him emphasizes his powerful and stalwart qualities. He lifts her with one leg in front of his shoulder, the other behind. The last couple dances, nervous and fleeting with a burgeoning passion. Playful, excited and youthful, they quickly achieve perfect lines that are enhanced by their spontaneity and clarity.

The second couple returns in an outburst of pure, wind-swept movement. She is supported, falls backward with complete trust, is swept into a lift which flies joyously skyward, as a wafting breeze carries the leaf. He parades her high like a ship's prow; they rush back and forth across the stage. Once again all the couples return. There is a feeling of a garden as people stroll with a sense of leisure and love. Finally the single woman enters stage left with her hands behind her back. She crosses the stage and leaves from the side of her first steps.

Through the transmutation of sensation, Tudor, in his Proustian way, rediscovers the reality of different kinds of love: one breathless and impetuous, another wisful and longing, another mutually strong and assured, and the last an infatuation in full bloom. *The Leaves are Fading* continues to be performed by American Ballet Theatre, and was re-created in London and Paris.

—Judith Chazin-Bennahum

LECLERCQ, Tanaquil

American dancer and teacher.   Born in Paris, 2 October 1929. Studied at the King-Coit School, New York, with Mikhail Mordkin, and at the School of American Ballet (on scholarship), pupil of Anatole Obukhov, Muriel Stuart, Pierre Vladimirov, and George Balanchine, from 1941. Married George Balanchine, 1952 (div. 1969). Professional début at Jacob's Pillow Festival, Massachusetts, 1945; dancer, soon becoming soloist, Ballet Society (later New York City Ballet), from its inception in 1946; principal dancer, from 1948; also appeared on television, including as actress and dancer in *A Candle for St. Jude* (Studio One production; chor. Ruthanna

Tanaquil LeClercq in *Bourrée Fantasque*, New York City Ballet, 1950

Boris, 1952); toured Europe with New York City Ballet, 1956: contracted poliomyelitis while in Copenhagen, and subsequently retired from dancing; teacher, including for Dance Theatre of Harlem School, New York; also author of several books.

ROLES

1946   Princess (cr) in *The Spellbound Child* (new version of *L'Enfant et les sortilèges*; Balanchine), Ballet Society, New York

Choleric (cr) in *The Four Temperaments* (Balanchine), Ballet Society, New York

1947   Principal dancer (cr) in *Divertimento* (Balanchine), Ballet Society, New York

Ariadne (cr) in *The Minotaur* (Taras), Ballet Society, New York

A Bridesmaid (cr) in *Highland Fling* (Dollar), Ballet Society, New York

Preludes III and IV (cr) in *The Seasons* (Cunningham), Ballet Society, New York

Principal dancer (cr) in *Symphonie Concertante* (Balanchine), Ballet Society, New York

1948   Ariadne (cr) in *The Triumph of Bacchus and Ariadne* (Balanchine), Ballet Society, New York

Second Movement in *Symphony in C* (new production of *Palais de Cristal*; Balanchine), Ballet Society, New York

Principal dancer (cr) in *Élégie* (Balanchine), Ballet Society, New York

Leader of the Bacchantes (cr) in *Orpheus* (Balanchine), Ballet Society, New York

1949   High School Girl in *Time Table* (Tudor), New York City Ballet, New York

Title role (cr) in *Cinderella* (Balanchine), "Through the Crystal Ball" television programme, National Broadcasting Corporation (NBC)

Bourrée Fantasque (cr) in *Bourreé Fantasque* (Balanchine), New York City Ballet, New York

Title role (cr) in *Ondine* (Dollar), New York City Ballet, New York

1950   Principal dancer (cr) in *The Age of Anxiety* (Robbins), New York City Ballet, New York

Sacred Love (cr) in *Illuminations* (Ashton), New York City Ballet, New York

Rescue from Drowning (cr) in *Jones Beach* (Balanchine), New York City Ballet, New York

The Bride in *The Fairy's Kiss* (*Le Baiser de la fée*; Balanchine), New York City Ballet, New York

1951   Eighth Waltz, La Valse (cr) in *La Valse* (Balanchine), New York City Ballet, New York

Principal dancer (cr) in *Cakewalk* (Boris), New York City Ballet, New York

The Woman in His Past in *Lilac Garden* (*Jardin aux Lilas*; Tudor), New York City Ballet, New York

Polyhymnia in *Apollo, Leader of the Muses* (new production of *Apollon musagète*; Balanchine), New York City Ballet, New York

Principal dancer (cr) in *The Pied Piper* (Robbins), New York City Ballet, New York

1952   Principal dancer (cr) in *Ballade* (Robbins), New York City Ballet, New York

Principal dancer (cr) in *Caracole* (Balanchine), New York City Ballet, New York

Odette in *Swan Lake* (one-act version; Balanchine after Ivanov), New York City Ballet, New York

Principal dancer (cr) in *Metamorphoses* (Balanchine), New York City Ballet, New York

Principal dancer (cr) in *Concertino* (Balanchine), New York City Ballet, New York

1953   Principal dancer (cr) in *Valse Fantaisie* (Balanchine), New York City Ballet, New York

Principal dancer (cr) in *Afternoon of a Faun* (Robbins), New York City Ballet, New York

1954   Second Time (cr) in *Opus 34* (Balanchine), New York City Ballet, New York

Dewdrop Fairy (cr) in *The Nutcracker* (Balanchine), New York City Ballet, New York

Rondo (cr) in *Western Symphony* (Balanchine), New York City Ballet, New York

In the Inn (cr) in *Ivesiana* (Balanchine), New York City Ballet, New York

1955   Principal dancer (cr) in *Roma* (Balanchine), New York City Ballet, New York

The Doll in *Jeux d'enfants* (Balanchine, Milberg, Moncion), New York City Ballet, New York

1956   Principal dancer (cr) in *The Concert* (Robbins), New York City Ballet, New York

Fourth Variation (cr) in *Divertimento No. 15* (Balanchine), New York City Ballet, Stratford, Connecticut

Principal dancer (cr) in *A Musical Joke* (Balanchine), New York City Ballet, Stratford, Connecticut

Other roles include: Principal dancer in *Concerto Barocco* (Balanchine), principal dancer in *The Guests* (Robbins), Prélude in *Bourreé Fantasque* (Balanchine), The Novice in *The Cage* (Robbins), principal dancer in (*Glinka*) *Pas de Trois* (Balanchine), the Siren in *Prodigal Son* (Balanchine), principal dancer in *Serenade* (Balanchine).

PUBLICATIONS

By LeClercq:
Mourka: The Autobiography of a Cat, New York, 1964
The Ballet Cookbook, New York, 1967

About LeClercq:
Ballet Society Yearbook, New York, 1947
Owen, Walter E., "Tanaquil LeClercq", *Dance Magazine* (New York), March 1950
Chujoy, Anatole, *The New York City Ballet*, New York, 1953
Palatsky, Eugene, "Tanaquil LeClercq", *Dance Magazine* (New York), October 1957
Taper, Bernard, *Balanchine: A Biography*, New York and London, 1974; revised edition, New York, 1984
Reynolds, Nancy, *Repertory in Review*, New York, 1977
Lobenthal, Joel, "Tanaquil LeClercq", *Ballet Review* (New York), Fall 1984
Denby, Edwin, *Dance Writings*, edited by Robert Cornfield and William Mackay, New York, 1986

*   *   *

Despite the brevity of her career, Tanaquil LeClercq might easily be termed the quintessential twentieth-century ballerina. Her dancing in works like George Balanchine's *Swan Lake*, William Dollar's *Ondine*, and Sir Frederick Ashton's *Illuminations* proved that the restraint and dignity of the nineteenth-century tradition lay easily in her muscles and bones—and in her comprehension. And yet she possessed a quality, like champagne, which suited her to the world of glass façades, Nadelman sculpture, and existential philosophy.

It was a sophistication usually associated with a far more mature dancer. LeClercq began her career with the New York City Ballet in 1946 when she was only seventeen years old. Unlike most dancers, she did not enter the corps de ballet. She immediately became a principal and was assigned roles in an overwhelming range of choreographic styles. In her first five years with the company her secure training, coupled with unusual intelligence, saw her through roles as stylistically divergent as the innocently sensuous Ariadne in Balanchine's *Bacchus and Ariadne*, the smoothly singing second movement of his *Symphony in C*, the brash cocotte of Balanchine's *Bourrée Fantasque*, the lonely young woman of Jerome Robbins's *Age of Anxiety*, and the remote Sacred Love in Sir Frederick Ashton's *Illuminations*.

In its variety and quality her career was indeed any young ballerina's dream. It was also a ballerina's nightmare: her performing life was abruptly cut off in 1956 when she contracted polio on tour, and was thereafter confined to a wheelchair.

Of the approximately 40 roles which came her way during that brief ten-year span, only eight were not made specifically for Tanaquil LeClercq. And while she was at that time Balanchine's chosen ballerina (and eventually his wife), she figured prominently in the Jerome Robbins repertoire. Antony Tudor also found her sufficiently authoritative (and yet poetic) to portray The Woman in His Past in *Lilac Garden*.

A role to this day indelibly associated with LeClercq is the doom-eager young woman in Balanchine's *La Valse*. Staged to Maurice Ravel's *Valses Nobles et sentimentales* and *La Valse*, the ballet was a brilliant, swirling meditation on the fragility of life. LeClercq, clad in a white romantic tutu which resembled ballroom attire, waltzed eagerly with Nicholas Magallanes as her ardent suitor. But when Francisco Moncion as Death entered and presented her with black gloves, a black necklace, and a translucent black redingote, she glanced hungrily into his sinister hand mirror and then whirled with him to her destruction. The conclusion of *La Valse* was particularly effective with LeClercq's inert body held aloft and swirled counter-clockwise to the other dancers. When she was stricken with polio, Balanchine withdrew *La Valse* from the repertory and did not revive it for several years.

At the opposite end of the spectrum was LeClercq's portrayal of the silly young woman with the big hat in Jerome Robbins's *The Concert*. The piece had to do with the fantasies of a group of people listening to a recital of Chopin music. The role for LeClercq was essentially daffy, but it became momentarily introspective as she slowly walked to the strains of a mazurka. The dreamy quality as her feet seemingly drew little patterns on the floor was so intimately associated with her that Robbins removed the solo from the ballet when her career came to an end.

It is rare for a dancer to exercise such a potent effect not only on her audiences but on her choreographers. How would that effect have deepened as she matured?

Since her retirement, Tanaquil LeClercq has written two books. The first, called *Mourka*, wittily describes the daily life of the cat she shared with Balanchine. She was responsible for both text and photographs. Her second published effort was *The Ballet Cookbook*. She has also taught at the school of the Dance Theatre of Harlem.

—Doris Hering

———

LEE, Mary Ann
American dancer and teacher. Born in Philadelphia, probably in July 1824 (some sources say 1823). Studied with Paul Hazard, Philadelphia, 1830s, and with James Sylvain (Fanny Elssler's partner in America), New York, 1840; later studied with Jean Coralli, Paris, 1844; may also have studied with Paul Taglioni in America, 1839. Married a Mr. Van Hook on retiring in 1847. Début as child actress, Philadelphia, c. 1832; début as dancer, Chestnut Street Theatre, Philadelphia, 1837; leading dancer, Walnut Street Theatre, Philadelphia, 1838–39; New York début, Bowery Theatre, 1839, also performing at Vauxhall Gardens, New York, 1840, and in various cities including Pittsburgh, Baltimore, New Orleans, Mobile, and Boston, from 1840; ballerina, leading small touring company (including George Washington Smith), performing in eastern American cities, 1845–47; farewell performance, Philadelphia, May 1847, with occasional appearances afterwards, including with George Washington Smith in 1852; also actress and singer, with stage appearances in melodrama, pantomime, farce, and burlesque; teacher, directing own school in Philadelphia from 1860. Died in Philadelphia, 25 January 1899.

ROLES

1837   Fatima (cr) in *The Maid of Cashmere* (opera-ballet; after Taglioni's *Le Dieu et la bayadère*), Chestnut Street Theatre, Philadelphia

1838   "Little Pickle" (cr) in *The Spoiled Child* (comic farce), Chestnut Street Theatre, Philadelphia
       Flora (cr) in *The Dewdrop; or, La Sylphide* (after Taglioni's *La Sylphide*; staged R.C. Maywood), Chestnut Street Theatre, Philadelphia
       Queen Lily of the Silver Stream (cr) in *The Lily Queen* (prod. Wemyss; chor. Amherst), Walnut Street Theatre, Philadelphia
       Dancer in *Tambourine Dance* (divertissement), Walnut Street Theatre, Philadelphia
       Albert (acting role) in *William Tell*, Walnut Street Theatre, Philadelphia

1839   Zoloé (also called Zelica) in *La Bayadère* (*The Maid of Cashmere*; opera-ballet after Taglioni), Bowery Theatre, New York
       Fanny (cr) in *The Sisters* (ballet), Bowery Theatre, New York
       Dancer in *The Cachucha* (solo; staged Hazard), Bowery Theatre, New York

1840   Dancer in *La Cachucha* (solo; after Elssler), Vauxhall Gardens, New York

1842   Title role in *La Sylphide* (own staging; after Taglioni), Boston
       Soloe in *Buy it, Dear, 'Tis Made of Cashmere* (burlesque of *The Maid of Cashmere, or Le Dieu et la bayadère*), Boston
       Lisette (acting role) in *The Swiss Cottage*, Boston
       Dancer in Ballet of the Nuns from *Robert le Diable* (opera; mus. Meyerbeer), New York

1843   Julietta in *The Dumb Girl of Genoa* (after Auber's opera *La Muette de Portici*), New York

1845   Beatrix in *La Jolie Fille de Gand* (own staging, after Albert), Arch Street Theatre, Philadelphia
       Title role in *La Fleur des Champs* (own staging, after Taglioni's *La Fille du Danube*), Arch Street Theatre, Philadelphia

1846   Title role in *Giselle* (own staging, after Coralli, Perrot), Howard Atheneum, Boston

Mary Ann Lee in *La Smolenska*

1853   Dancer in *Pas de Quatre Nations* (divertissement), Chestnut Street Theatre, Philadelphia
Fenella in *Masaniello* (*La Muette de Portici*, opera; mus. Auber), Seguin Opera Troupe, Philadelphia

Other roles include: divertissements and solos—*La Cracovienne, Bolero, El Jaleo de Jeres, La Smolenska* (all after Elssler, as staged Sylvain); *Tyrolienne, Opium Dance* (in play *Life in China*), *Mazurka, Grand Pas Russe, Pas de Diane* and *Grand Pas de deux* (both from *La Jolie Fille de Gand*).

PUBLICATIONS

Ludlow, Noah Miller, "Miss Lee, Danseuse", in *Dramatic Life, as I Found It*, St. Louis, 1880
Brown, T. Allston, *History of the American Stage*, New York, 1909
Moore, Lillian, "Mary Ann Lee: First American Giselle", *Dance Index* (New York), May 1943; reprinted in Magriel, Paul (ed.), *Chronicles of the American Dance*, New York, 1948
Chaffee, George, "Three or Four Graces: A Centenary Salvo", *Dance Index* (New York), September–November 1944
Amberg, George, *Ballet in America*, New York, 1949
Moore, Lillian, "Some Early American Dancers", *Dancing Times* (London), August 1950
Todd, Arthur, "Four Centuries of American Dance", *Dance Magazine* (New York), September 1950
Stern, Madeleine, *We the Women*, New York, 1963
Migel, Parmenia, *The Ballerinas*, New York, 1972
Kirstein, Lincoln, *Dance: A Short History of Classical Theatrical Dancing*, New York, 1974
Moore, Lillian, *Echoes of American Ballet*, New York, 1976
Cohen, Selma Jean, "The Fourth of July, or the Independence of American Dance", *Dance Magazine* (New York), July 1976
Swift, Mary Grace, *Belles and Beaux on their Toes: Dancing Stars in Young America*, Washington, D.C., 1980
Barker, Barbara, *Ballet or Ballyhoo*, New York, 1984
Farrell, Rita Katz, "Star-Spangled Giselles", *Ballet News* (New York), September 1984

*   *   *

Mary Ann Lee was an American ballerina of the pre-Civil War era, popular for her sweet and modest personality, pretty face and figure, and charming stage presence. Although her technical level improved throughout her brief career (1837–47), she did not rival such ballerinas as Augusta Maywood or Julia Turnbull in ballet virtuosity. Nevertheless, she attained nationwide fame, and championed the art of the classical dance in the United States.

A native of Philadelphia and the daughter of minor stage performers, Lee performed as a child in order to support her mother after her father's death. Initially taking small acting roles, she began her dance career studying with Paul H. Hazard, a Paris Opéra dancer who ran a successful ballet school in Philadelphia. Hazard staged Lee's ballet premiere in *The Maid of Cashmere*, an American version of Auber's *Le Dieu et la bayadère*, which featured Augusta Maywood in the leading role, while Lee danced the part of Fatima. Intense rivalry between the two young dancers stimulated both to their best efforts, and Lee was widely admired, despite Maywood's technical superiority. While she pursued further ballet training with Hazard, Lee continued to act in the stock companies of various Philadelphia theatres, where her dancing was also featured. Her New York début was at the Bowery Theatre, a

center of ballet performance, where she danced the lead in *La Bayadère*. She also danced such divertissements as *La Cachucha* in a version staged by Hazard. At the Bowery, ballerina Julia Turnbull provided Lee with the competition that seemed to inspire her. During a highly successful summer season at New York's Vauxhall Gardens, Lee was able to further her training by studying with the accomplished Irish danseur James Sylvain, who was partner and ballet master to Fanny Elssler during her American tour. From Sylvain, she learned a number of Elssler's character divertissements, such as the *Bolero, El Jaleo de Jeres, La Smolenska, La Cracovienne*, and the renowned (Elssler) version of *La Cachucha*. However, the finishing touches to Lee's ballet schooling came in 1844, when she studied at the Paris Opéra with Jean Coralli. She returned to America with not only a far superior command of ballet technique, but also the ability to stage such current French ballets as *Giselle, La Fille du Danube*, and *La Jolie Fille de Gand*.

Lee's tours of the United States upon her return from France marked both the high point and the conclusion of her ballet career. She was the first to dance *Giselle* in America (partnered by George Washington Smith), when she presented the work in Boston in 1846. With Smith as her partner, she toured widely with a repertory consisting of such works as *Giselle, La Fleur des Champs* (*La Fille du Danube*), *La Sylphide, La Bayadère*, and numerous divertissements. She was enormously popular in Boston, and continued to dance regularly in Philadelphia and in New York. She also acted and even sang on occasion, if the need arose. Her fame as an artist of charming beauty, good taste, technical accomplishment, and convincing interpretation spread wherever she toured. While still young, she was overtaken by illness during a lengthy tour of the south and west. She was forced to withdraw from the stage in May 1847, after a farewell season in Philadelphia. She retired to her home city where she married a businessman. "Mrs. Van Hook, late Mary Ann Lee" had a benefit performance again in Philadelphia five years after her retirement, and made occasional stage appearances for one more year after that. She opened a school in Philadelphia in 1860.

Lee is most significant as an exponent of classical ballet during its pioneering period in the United States, before it attained the wildly popular extravagance of such late-nineteenth-century spectacles as *The Black Crook* and its many spin-offs. She brought important Romantic ballets to the American public, and her modesty, charm, and winning stage presence earned her—and thus, the art of ballet—respect among the American theatre-going public.

—Lynn Matluck Brooks

———

LEGAT, Nikolai (Nicholas)
Russian dancer, choreographer, and teacher.   Born Nikolai Gustavovich Legat, son of Moscow Theatre School teacher and dancer Gustav Legat, 27 December (15 old style) 1869; brother of dancer and choreographer Sergei Legat (1875–1905). Studied at the St. Petersburg Theatre School, pupil of Gustav Legat, Nikolai Volkov, Pavel Gerdt, Christian Johansson; graduated in 1888. Married (1) Olga Chumakova (common-law wife); (2) Maryinsky dancer Antonia Chumakova (dissolved 1919): one daughter, Maria; (3) Bolshoi dancer Nadezhda (Nadine) Nikolaeva. Début (while still a student), 1887; dancer, soon becoming soloist, Maryinsky Theatre, St. Petersburg, from 1888, becoming principal dancer and favoured partner to ballerinas Legnani, Pavlova, Kshesinskaya, Trefilova, Vagan-

ova; performed also in Paris, Berlin, Leipzig, Vienna, Prague, and Warsaw, from 1907; assistant ballet master, Maryinsky Theatre, 1902, becoming second ballet master, from 1905, and chief ballet master, from 1910; left the Maryinsky in 1914, continuing to produce ballets for the popular stage; toured music halls with Nadine Nikolaeva, Paris and London, 1914–15; also produced ballets at Norodny Dom, Petrograd, after 1915; also leading teacher, teaching at St. Petersburg Theatre School, 1896–1914, succeeding Johansson as teacher of Class of Perfection, Maryinsky Theatre, c.1905: pupils included Pavlova, Nijinsky, Karsavina, Vaganova, Lopukhov; teacher in private studios, Petrograd, from 1917, including Akim Volynsky's School of Russian Ballet; left Russia in 1922; ballet master to Diaghilev's company, 1925–26, and later teacher, Salle Wacker, Paris; teacher at own studio, London, from 1930 until death: pupils included Danilova, Zorina, Lopokova, de Valois, Markova, Dolin, Eglevsky, Fonteyn; also known as a caricaturist: published *Russian Ballet in Caricature* (1903) with brother Sergei Legat. Recipient: Gold Medal of St. Stanislav; Palm of the Académie Française; title of His Majesty's Soloist; Honoured Artist of the Imperial Theatres, 1914. Died in London, 24 January 1937.

ROLES

1888/ Bluebird in *The Sleeping Beauty* (Petipa), Maryinsky
89   Theatre, St. Petersburg
     The Fisherman (pas de deux) in *The King's Command* (Petipa), Maryinsky Theatre, St. Petersburg
1891 Olivier (cr) in *Kalkabrino* (Petipa), Maryinsky Theatre, St. Petersburg
1892 Title role (cr) in *The Nutcracker* (Ivanov), Maryinsky Theatre, St. Petersburg
1893 The Marquis (cr) in *The Magic Flute* (Ivanov), Maryinsky Theatre, St. Petersburg
1894 Prince Charming in *Cinderella* (Petipa, Cecchetti, Ivanov), Maryinsky Theatre, St. Petersburg
1895 Phoenix in *The Caprices of the Butterfly* (Petipa), Maryinsky Theatre, St. Petersburg
     Lettish Dance (cr) in *The Little Humpbacked Horse* (Petipa after Saint-Léon), Maryinsky Theatre, St. Petersburg
1895/ Prince Siegfried in *Swan Lake* (Petipa, Ivanov),
96   Maryinsky Theatre, St. Petersburg
1896 Zephyr in *The Awakening of Flora* (Petipa), Maryinsky Theatre, St. Petersburg
1897 Lucas in *The Magic Flute* (Ivanov), Maryinsky Theatre, St. Petersburg
1898 Colin in *Vain Precautions* (*La Fille mal gardée*; Petipa), Maryinsky Theatre, St. Petersburg
1899 Franz in *Coppélia* (Petipa, Cecchetti), Maryinsky Theatre, St. Petersburg
     Albrecht in *Giselle* (Petipa after Coralli, Perrot), Maryinsky Theatre, St. Petersburg
1900 Zephyr (cr) in *The Seasons* (Petipa), Hermitage Theatre, St. Petersburg
     Zephyr in *The Talisman* (Petipa), Maryinsky Theatre, St. Petersburg
     The Harlequin in *Harlequinade* (*Les Millions d'Arlequin*; Petipa), Maryinsky Theatre, St. Petersburg
1902 Basil (cr) in *Don Quixote* (new production, St. Petersburg version; Gorsky after Petipa), Maryinsky Theatre, St. Petersburg
1904 Gringoire in *Esmeralda* (Petipa after Perrot), Maryinsky Theatre, St. Petersburg
     Prince Désiré in *The Sleeping Beauty* (Petipa), Mar-

Nikolai Legat: self-caricature, 1931

yinsky Theatre, St. Petersburg
1906 Jean de Brienne in *Raymonda* (Petipa), Maryinsky Theatre, St. Petersburg
     Lord Wilson in *Pharaoh's Daughter* (Petipa), Maryinsky Theatre, St. Petersburg
     Soloist (pas de deux) in *Nero* (opera; mus. Rubinstein, chor. Legat), Maryinsky Theatre, St. Petersburg
1907 "Reverie" (cr) in *The Blood-Red Flower* (also chor.), Maryinsky Theatre, St. Petersburg
1909 Franz in *Coppélia* (Saint-Léon), Opéra, Paris
     Nurredin in *The Talisman* (also chor.; after Petipa), Maryinsky Theatre, St. Petersburg
1910 Mars in *Bluebeard* (also chor., after Petipa), Maryinsky Theatre, St. Petersburg
1915 The Butterfly (cr) in *The White Lily* (also chor.), Narodny Dom, Petrograd
     The Clown (cr) in *The Rose of Margitta* (also chor.), Narodny Dom, Petrograd
1925 The Shopkeeper in *Le Boutique fantasque* (Massine), Diaghilev's Ballets Russes
     Old Showman in *Petrushka* (Fokine), Diaghilev's Ballets Russes
     Pierrot in *Le Carnaval* (Fokine), Diaghilev's Ballets Russes

Other roles include: at the Maryinsky Theatre—the Count, Tanzmeister in *Le Diable á quatre* (*The Capricious Wife*; Petipa after Mazilier), Ilas in *Les Offrandes á l'amour* (Petipa), Mutcha in *The Little Humpbacked Horse* (Petipa after Saint-Léon), leading dancer in *The Daughter of Mikado* (Petipa), title role in *Petrushka* (Fokine).

WORKS

1901 *Waltz Caprice* (mus. Rubinstein), Creative Evening for
Marius Petipa, Maryinsky Theatre, St. Petersburg
1903 *The Fairy Doll* (with S. Legat; mus. Bayer), Hermitage
Theatre, St. Petersburg
1906 *Puss-in-Boots* (mus. Mikhailov), Maryinsky Theatre, St.
Petersburg
Dances in *Nero* (opera; mus. Rubinstein), Maryinsky
Theatre, St. Petersburg
1907 *Les Saisons* (after Petipa; mus. Glazunov), Maryinsky
Theatre, St. Petersburg
The Blood-Red Flower (mus. Hartmann), Maryinsky
Theatre, St. Petersburg (staged Bolshoi Theatre,
Moscow, 1911)
Dances in *Judith* (opera; mus. Serov), Maryinsky
Theatre, St. Petersburg
1909 *The Talisman* (after Petipa; mus. Drigo), Maryinsky
Theatre, St. Petersburg
1910 *Bluebeard* (after Petipa; mus. Schenk), Maryinsky
Theatre, St. Petersburg
1911 Dance of the Persian Girls in *Khovanshchina* (opera;
mus. Mussorgsky), Maryinsky Theatre, St.
Petersburg
1912 *The Leopard's Skin; or, The Wily Florento* (mus.
Asafiev), Miniature Theatre, St. Petersburg
1915 *The White Lily* (mus. Asafiev), Narodny Dom,
Petrograd
The Rose of Margitta (mus. Armsheimer), Narodny
Dom, Petrograd
1916 *The Prince's Enchanted Dream* (mus. Sokolov), Narodny
Dom, Petrograd

PUBLICATIONS

By Legat:
Rusky Balet v Karikaturakh (*Russian Ballet in Caricature*; with
S. Legat), Leningrad and Moscow, 1903
Various articles on dance history and technique, including—
"The Making of a Dancer and Ballet Master", *Dancing Times*
(London), March 1931
"Twenty Years with Marius Petipa and Christian Johansson",
Dancing Times (London), April 1931
"The Class of Perfection at the Imperial Ballet School",
Dancing Times (London), July 1931
"The Secret of the Pirouette", *Dancing Times* (London), 3 parts,
August, September, November 1932
The Story of the Russian School, translated by Sir Paul Dukes,
London, 1932
Ballet Russe: Memoirs of Nicholas Legat, translated by Sir Paul
Dukes, London, 1939
Heritage of a Ballet Master: Nicholas Legat, compiled and
edited by John Gregory, New York, 1977

About Legat:
"A Chapter in the History of Russian Ballet", *Dancing Times*
(London), June 1926
"Nicholas Legat and the Class of Perfection", *Dancing Times*
(London), February 1930
Karsavina, Tamara, "Nikolai Legat", *Dancing Times* (London), August 1964
Krasovskaya, Vera, *Russian Ballet Theatre in the First Half of
the Twentieth Century*, Leningrad, 1972
Gregory, John (ed.), with Eglevsky, André, *Heritage of a Ballet
Master: Nicholas Legat*, London, 1978

Gregory, John, "Legendary Dancers: Nikolai Legat", *Dancing
Times* (London), October 1987

* * *

Nikolai Legat (later known as Nicholas), who is often credited as the father of the Russian school and was certainly one of its greatest ballet masters, might well have secured a position of more lasting influence on the teaching systems of our time had not various circumstances conspired against him. Unlike his contemporary Enrico Cecchetti and his successor Agrippina Vaganova, Legat never found himself in a position to codify his pedagogic theories into a formal system. As a result, his contributions have been largely ignored—despite the fact that the Russian system of today was inherited from both Legat and Vaganova.

At the turn of the century, Legat was achieving fame as an outstanding example of the new generation of Russian dancers in which the supremacy of the ballerina was being challenged. His extensive repertoire encompassed roles from the profoundly romantic to the highly comic. Noted for sensitivity as well as strength, he partnered two generations of such great ballerinas as Carlotta Brianza, Pierina Legnani, Mathilde Kshesinskaya, and Vera Trefilova. He was a musician and painter as well, whose somewhat caustic wit manifested itself in a series of brilliantly drawn caricatures.

As a choreographer, Legat was frequently asked by Marius Petipa to set various men's solos and pas de deux and, with his brother Sergei, he contributed to new choreographic trends, particularly in the areas of male dancing and of daring and dramatic lifts in partnering. The brothers' greatest choreographic triumph was *The Fairy Doll* (*Die Puppenfee*), produced in 1903, with music by Joseph Bayer and, most notably, sets and costumes by Léon Bakst in his first work for ballet. Inspired by the Legats' Russian heritage and memories of childhood joys, this ballet represented a break from Petipa's long established tradition of rigid classicism and fairy-tale themes. However, the suicide of Sergei in 1905 seemed to bring an end to Nikolai's best creative output (although he continued to stage ballets for some years); and Nikolai was instead set on the path to becoming the guardian of the Russian academic ballet tradition.

From that time until 1914, Legat enjoyed unparalleled prestige and influence at the Maryinsky Theatre, simultaneously holding the positions of premier danseur, ballet master, and director of the Class of Perfection. The Class of Perfection was originally established by Legat's mentor Christian Johannson as a class for continuing the training of dancers who had already reached professional status. It was briefly directed by Evgenia Sokolova; but Legat conducted a highly successful campaign among the dancers to have himself appointed, secure in the belief that his status as Johannson's favourite pupil and eventual assistant mandated his appointment. Among his famous pupils were Agrippina Vaganova, Tamara Karsavina, Anna Pavlova, Vaslav Nijinsky, and Mikhail Fokine, who was ultimately to become his critic, opponent, and rival, accusing him of being a slave to tradition without creative initiative or critical approach.

Legat celebrated his jubilee of 25 years of service at the Maryinsky Theatre in January 1914 amid a state of crisis, a time which saw a lack of artistic leadership following the death of Marius Petipa, a stifling bureaucratic atmosphere within the Imperial Theatres, and great political unrest, foreshadowing the Revolution of 1917. Nevertheless, unlike so many others, Legat chose to remain in Russia, feeling that it was his destiny. But having undertaken a world tour immediately after his jubilee, he found it impossible to return to his homeland for several years due to the outbreak of World War I. When he finally did return in the aftermath of the Revolution, he made several unsuccessful attempts to claim the post of principal choreographer and ballet master of the Maryinsky Theatre. Evidently such a powerful figure in the Imperial order would have been resented in any position of authority within the new order so bent upon reform. There was little left to do other than to attempt to dance and teach independently; but the general conditions of deprivation and the uncertain future of ballet in the Soviet order made the situation untenable and, in 1922, Legat left Russia forever.

In time he settled in London to spend the last twelve years of his life teaching in Colet Gardens, this following a brief and stormy engagement as ballet master for Diaghilev's Ballets Russes. Along with dancers of international fame, many of England's finest young dancers—including Ninette de Valois, a powerful influence herself in the development of British ballet—came to him to partake of his unique knowledge. However, the opportunity to make use of Legat's exceptional capabilities was repeatedly overlooked by company directors of the time, many of whom may have been unable to accept the influence of a great teacher in a spirit of deference. Legat even tried to establish his own company on several occasions; but, despite a favourable reception by the press, his ventures were ultimately unsuccessful in the face of growing interest in the establishment of a national company for England.

Somewhat out of step with time and place, and with his health beginning to fail, Legat nevertheless maintained remarkable strength and humour, and taught with skill to the end of his life. His colleagues and pupils considered him a cheerful, interesting, and lovable man, a gifted and inspiring teacher whose classes were characterized by thoroughness, elegance, spontaneity, and rich variety of movement grounded in logic and simplicity. Yet, as a victim of the tide of change which flooded his homeland following the Revolution, Legat has been all but forgotten by Russia; and he was not long enough in the West to have perpetuated his name there.

—Kristin Beckwith

THE LEGEND OF LOVE
(original Russian title: *Legenda o Lyubvi*)

Choreography: Yuri Grigorovich
Music: Arif Melikov
Design: Simon Virsaladze (scenery and costumes)
Libretto: Nazim Hikmet
First Production: Kirov Ballet, Leningrad, 23 March 1961
Principal Dancers: Aleksandr Gribov (Ferkhad), Irina Kolpakova (Shirien), Olga Moiseyeva (Mekmene-Banu), Anatole Gridin (Vizir)

Other productions include: Bolshoi Ballet (restaged Grigorovich), with Maris Liepa (Ferkhad), Natalia Bessmertnova (Shirien), Maya Plisetskaya (Mekmene-Banu), and Aleksandr Lavrenyuk (Vizir); Moscow, 15 April 1965.

PUBLICATIONS

Karp, Poel, "*The Legend of Love*", *Teatr* (Moscow), no. 9, 1961
Haskell, Arnold, "Russian Logbook", *The Dancing Times* (London), 3 parts: June, July, September 1962
René, Natalia, "A Legend of Love", *Dance and Dancers* (London), November 1962
Lvov-Anokhin, B., "*The Legend of Love* at the Bolshoi Theatre", *Teatr* (Moscow), no. 9, 1965
Vanslov, V.V., *The Ballets of Yuri Grigorovich and the Problems of Choreography*, Moscow, 1971
Balanchine, George, with Mason, Francis, *Balanchine's Complete Stories of the Great Ballets*, Garden City, N.Y., 1977

* * *

The Legend of Love was a revolutionary development in the history of Soviet ballet, choreographed in the beginning of the 1960s by Yuri Grigorovich to the music of Arif Melikov. It was based on a very well-known play by the Turkish dramatist and revolutionary leader, Nazim Hikmet. The story is rich in ideas and images, and was not simply a thin plot around which to arrange unrelated dances; it is a tale of blood, love, torment, and sacrifice. In the story, the tsarina Mekmene-Banu is forced to give up her beauty in order to cure the fever of her favourite sister Shirien. But then, finding out about the hasty retreat of Shirien with her beloved artist Ferkhad, the enraged tsarina, who is hopelessly in love with Ferkhad herself, orders the fugitives to return. She commands Ferkhad to build a waterway across the mountains to deliver the people from suffering: only then can he become Shirien's husband. Shirien is in despair; but Ferkhad leaves his love in order to bring happiness to the people.

At the time when Grigorovich created *The Legend of Love*, the term choreographic drama, or "dram-ballet", had begun to be used pejoratively, as a way to refer to something routine, something old—the tradition, which had its beginnings in the experimental theatre of the 1920s and expanded to include all applications of "socialist realism" to the dance stage, had become so weak that the most naïve, weak plots were now being used as a basis for choreography. The concept of movement and dance fused with dramatic expression had degenerated into stylized miming, usually of the most unsatisfying and improbable stories. Now, Yuri Grigorovich decided to eliminate all kinds of mime, all sorts of explanation by use of gesture and exaggerated arm movements: here, everything was explained and done by means of classical dance alone, with a tinge of national colour.

Of course, not everybody accepted the ballet at first, especially the bureaucrats and government officials—it was said that the ballet was too bold, too unusual for the Kirov stage, that it did not take into consideration the old traditions of the Kirov Ballet. Of course this was all nonsense; the ballet, artistically speaking, was a triumph, and the dance critics and cultural historians began to write articles and books which presented the opinion, virtually unanimous, that this ballet was in essence a dissertation on the art of choreography. Everything was there; Grigorovich accomplished the exact combination of different elements to create a convincing and satisfying artistic whole.

One of the strongest features of the ballet is the group dancing, and Grigorovich's development of the corps de ballet is one of the major reasons why *The Legend of Love* is so important. The heroine, so to speak, has her chorus, as in Greek tragedy. In the story, Mekmene-Banu, who sacrifices her beauty to save her sister, is surrounded by women in red. Shirien herself, the younger sister, resembles a young goat in the mountains; she is always surrounded by her friends in white dresses. Then the people, the crowd surrounding Ferkhad, the hero whom both girls love, are all dressed in brown, and are always with Ferkhad. So it is the dancer and the corps de ballet—the hero and the chorus, the voice of the protagonist

The Legend of Love, with Maria Bylova and Yuri Vasyuchenko, Bolshoi Ballet, Moscow

and the answer of the crowd, the people.

Even such things as gold and jewellery, typical empty decoration in choreographic drama, were now turned into meaningful choreographic images and symbols. For example, the tsarina asks a magician what price he wants to heal her sister; being very naive, she suggests that he take as much gold as he wants. In Grigorovich's vision, this gold is not just a piece of metal, some sort of prop, but is a wonderful corps de ballet of girls whose arms and hands are covered with small coins on threads, twinkling constantly as they dance. The soloist at the centre of the corps performs double turns and fouettés in the middle of the swirling mass of gold, which eventually overpowers the whole stage. Another example is the treatment of dream. In traditional ballet, we usually think of dream in the sense of dreamy, ethereal scenes—as in *La Bayadère*, where the dancers are visions in white, images of an overall dreamlike kingdom. In *The Legend of Love*, Grigorovich uses dream in a much more immediate and striking way. Here, dream is linked with a strong image of blood, like the throbbing heart of the tsarina. Girls in red appear as her own thoughts, which are tormenting her, not giving her a minute of rest day or night. She dances her duet with Ferkhad with a background of corps de ballet girls in red who also dance, like a separate suite expressing the idea of a dream, of the impossibility of the two being together.

Another innovation, surprising for the time, was Grigorovich's lack of dependence on a large cast; in *The Legend of Love* there are just three leading characters. The history of Soviet choreographic drama in its later years is one of many unnecessary personages on stage, and this simple combination of a few soloists with a related corps de ballet was a wonderful innovation. The ballet, then, was almost like a manifesto: look back to Petipa, who understood how to create rich and beautiful ballets, let us follow his example in using the art of dance itself to its fullest. At this new period, in the middle of the twentieth century, we will explore and experiment and aim for something different, but we will do so by using the older tradition. Grigorovich showed how the past of classical ballet could be used, but on a new level and at a different time: he dared to state yet again that it is *dance* which can express everything of importance in ballet.

—Igor Stupnikov

LEGNANI, Pierina

Italian dancer. Born in 1863. Studied at the Imperial Academy (Ballet School of Teatro alla Scala), Milan, and with Caterina Beretta, Milan; later studied with Nikolai Legat and Christian Johansson, St. Petersburg. Dancer at La Scala, Milan, from 1880s, becoming prima ballerina from 1892; prima ballerina, Alhambra Theatre, London, various seasons from 1888; prima ballerina, Maryinsky Theatre, St. Petersburg, 1893–1901, creating numerous roles for Marius Petipa and earning title of prima ballerina assoluta; also guest ballerina, appearing in Paris and Madrid; returned to Italy after retiring from stage, later serving as adjudicator of La Scala examinations. Died in 1923.

ROLES

1888   Nunziatella (cr) in *Amadriade* (Danesi), La Scala, Milan
   Title role (cr) in *Irene* (Casati), Alhambra Theatre, London
1890   Title role (cr) in *Salandra* (Casati), Alhambra Theatre, London
   The Princess (cr) in *Sleeping Beauty* (mus. Jacobi, chor. Espinosa), Alhambra Theatre, London
1891   Title role (cr) in *Oriella* (Coppi), Alhambra Theatre, London
1892   Title role (cr) in *Rodope* (Grassi), La Scala, Milan
   Title role in *Bianca di Nevers* (Smeraldi after Pratesi), La Scala, Milan
   Zerlina (cr) in *Don Juan* (Coppi), Alhambra Theatre, London
   Princess (cr) in *Aladdin* (Coppi after Hollingshead scenario), Alhambra Theatre, London

Pierina Legnani in 1893

1893   Title role (cr) in *Cinderella* (Petipa), Maryinsky Theatre, St. Petersburg
1894   Alice (cr) in *Sita* (Casati), Alhambra Theatre, London
1895   Odette/Odile (cr) in *Swan Lake* (Petipa, Ivanov), Maryinsky Theatre, St. Petersburg
   Niriti in *The Talisman* (Petipa), Maryinsky Theatre, St. Petersburg
   Tsar-Maiden (cr) in *The Little Humpbacked Horse* (Petipa after Saint-Léon), Maryinsky Theatre, St. Petersburg
1896   Theresa (cr) in *Cavalry Halt* (Petipa), Maryinsky Theatre, St. Petersburg
   Leading role (cr) in *The Beautiful Pearl* (Petipa), Maryinsky Theatre, St. Petersburg
   Ysaure de Renoualle (cr) in *Bluebeard* (Petipa), Maryinsky Theatre, St. Petersburg
1897   Genius of Britain, May Queen (cr) in *Victoria and Merrie England* (Coppi), Alhambra Theatre, London
1898   Title role (cr) in *Raymonda* (Petipa), Maryinsky Theatre, St. Petersburg
1900   Principal dancer (cr) in *The Pupils of Monsieur Dupré* (new version of *The King's Decree*; Petipa), Maryinsky Theatre, St. Petersburg
   Isabelle (cr) in *The Trials of Damis* (*Les Ruses d'amour*; Petipa), Hermitage Theatre, St. Petersburg
   Swanilda in *Coppélia* (Petipa, Cecchetti after Saint-Léon), Maryinsky Theatre, St. Petersburg
1901   Title role (cr) in *La Camargo* (revised by Ivanov after Petipa), Maryinsky Theatre, St. Petersburg

Other roles include: title role in *Catarina* (Petipa).

PUBLICATIONS

Pleshcheev, Aleksandr, *Our Ballet*, St. Petersburg, 1899
Khudekov, Sergei, *A History of Dancing*, vol. 6, Petrograd, 1918
Karsavina, Tamara, *Les Ballets Russes*, Paris, 1931
Legat, Nikolai, *The Story of the Russian School*, London, 1932
Lifar, Serge, *Histoire du ballet russe*, Paris, 1950
Beaumont, Cyril, *Complete Book of Ballets*, revised edition, London, 1951
San-Francisco, P., "Tea-Time with Pierina Legnani", *Dance Magazine* (New York), November 1955
Guest, Ivor, *The Alhambra Ballets*, Dance Perspectives no. 4, New York, 1959
Fokine, Mikhail, *Memoirs of a Ballet Master*, London, 1961
Krasovskaya, Vera, *Russian Ballet Theatre of the Second Half of the Nineteenth Century*, Leningrad and Moscow, 1963
Roslavleva, Natalia, *Era of the Russian Ballet*, London, 1966
Migel, Parmenia, *The Ballerinas*, New York, 1972
Gregory, John, "Legendary Dancers: Pierina Legnani", *Dancing Times* (London), December 1987
Guest, Ivor, *Ballet in Leicester Square*, London, 1992

*   *   *

The most famous representative of the Italian virtuoso school, Pierina Legnani was one of the greatest dancers of the late nineteenth century, imitated by dancers in Russia and setting an example for pupils in Milan who knew her only by reputation. Already renowned all over Europe, she charmed the St. Petersburg public from her first performances in 1893, especially in her most famous created role, Odette/Odile in *Swan Lake*. The technical brilliance of her performances marked her as a unique dancer. At a time when ballet was rising to its apex in Russia, while yet falling into decline in

Europe, Legnani was able to combine the best of both schools. She was able to bring Italian virtuosity to classical choreography, while at the same time maintaining the fluid idiom of the body, demonstrating the plasticity and lyricism of the Russian school.

After studying at La Scala—the cradle of every great dancer of the day—Legnani completed her training with Caterina Beretta, a teacher who demanded constant effort during endless hours of drills. Legnani made her reputation in European capitals, although perhaps not as dramatically as fellow ballerinas whose fame was enhanced by scandals or by outstanding beauty. A brunette with sparkling eyes, who possessed a short and robust silhouette, Legnani excelled in variety shows, demonstrating feats such as the famous series of fouettés, recorded at the London Alhambra in the 1880s and repeated to great acclaim on the St. Petersburg stage in the following decade.

Legnani's engagement in Russia marked the beginning of the most rewarding period of her life. She became a permanent member of the Imperial Theatres in St. Petersburg for eight consecutive seasons, revered by balletomanes, arbiters of taste and trends, and loved by public and critics alike. She dazzled her audiences with her amazing technique, above all with her famous fouettés. Karsavina recalled that Legnani's exploits reminded her of circus tricks, demanding a pause before they began, but she conceded that Legnani's spirit and charm reduced the enemies of the Italian school to silence. Fokine describes himself as a pageboy applauding Legnani on the stage itself, a gesture for which he was reprimanded.

Light and artistically naïve as most of Legnani's ballets were (Petipa recreated many of his older, quainter works for her), her repertoire delighted the Russian aristocracy and sometimes served as an encomium for imperial ceremonies. In the case of the mise-en-scène for a Perrault fairy-tale, such as *Cinderella* or *Bluebeard* (promoted by Imperial Theatre director Ivan Vsevolozhsky), a fantastic Versailles was the suitable ambiance for a homage to the tsar. In any event, the expansion of the Maryinsky repertory was accompanied by an enrichment of the choreographic lexicon or, at least, by an improvement in execution—and reviews became increasingly detailed, as critics described the grands pirouettes, the relevées in *Catarina*, or the renversés in the second act of *Swan Lake*, or even criticized the ballerina for her lack of elevation.

In the successful 1895 version of *Swan Lake*, Legnani created not only the brilliant and technically demanding role of Odile but also that of Odette, evoking the image of a melancholy white swan and sharing Ivanov's lyrical choreographic vision. In the process of mastering the idiosyncrasies of the Russian school (she studied under the guidance of Nikolai Legat and Christian Johansson), Legnani also demonstrated her ability to perform popular dances in *The Little Humpbacked Horse* to a generally favourable reception.

Although the scores of Legnani's ballets were written for the most part by traditional composers such as Minkus or Drigo, there was a growing interest in a more symphonic music for ballet, stimulated by Tchaikovsky's success and resulting in such works as Glazunov's *Raymonda*, of which Legnani was the first interpreter. The new century also saw a shift from the Petipa era to a transitional period when Ivanov, for example, restaged Petipa's *La Camargo* for Legnani, featuring a new pas de deux created by her partner Sergei Legat. A series of photographs captures the dancers' acrobatic lifts, which seem unusually aerial for the time, particularly in view of Legnani's cumbersome costume (copied from Nicolas Lancret's painting dedicated to Camargo).

Thanks to her endearing personal qualities, Legnani never inspired real jealousy, except perhaps in Matilda Kshesins-

kaya, who shared with Legnani the title of "prima ballerina assoluta" and aspired to take over Legnani's place. The famous picture of the 32 fouettés performed on a single spot, though an overworn and simplistic description of Legnani's abilities, conveys to a non-dancing public the nature of Legnani's impressive achievement. She helped to improve the position of dancers both within the theatre and in society in general, and together with other Russian ballet artists of her day she heralded the contemporary image of the truly professional dancer.

After her return to Italy, prompted by her mother's serious illness, Legnani's only tie with the dance world was as adjudicator of the examinations at La Scala. Thus, in her country, her heritage as a great performer was but a memory of the past.

—Concetta Lo Iacono

LEPESHINSKAYA, Olga

Russian/Soviet dancer. Born Olga Vladimirova Lepeshinskaya in Kiev, 28 September 1916. Studied at the Moscow Choreographic School, pupil of Viktor Semenov; graduated in 1933. Ballerina, Bolshoi Ballet, 1933–63, also touring frequently, and performing concert pieces in Paris, Hungary, Czechoslovakia, Japan, China, and Mexico; began teaching upon retirement: ballet mistress and artistic adviser, Hungarian State Opera Ballet, Budapest, 1963–65, also teaching in Paris, Rome, Berlin, Stuttgart, and many other cities. Recipient: State Prize, 1941, 1946, 1947, 1950; title of Honoured Artist of the Russian Federation, 1942; People's Artist of the USSR, 1947.

ROLES

1933 Lise in *Vain Precautions* (*La Fille mal gardée*; Gorsky after Petipa, Ivanov), Bolshoi Ballet, Moscow

1935 Suok (cr) in *Three Fat Men* (Moiseyev), Bolshoi Ballet, Moscow

1936 Princess Aurora in *The Sleeping Beauty* (Messerer after Petipa), Bolshoi Ballet, Moscow

1938 Pauline in *The Prisoner of the Caucasus* (Zakharov), Bolshoi Ballet, Moscow

1939 Title role (cr) in *Svetlana* (Radunsky, Pospekhin, Popko), Bolshoi Ballet, Moscow

1940 Kitri in *Don Quixote* (Gorsky after Petipa), Bolshoi Ballet, Moscow
       Principal dancer (cr) in *Gypsies* (choreographic miniature; Yakobson), Bolshoi Ballet, Moscow

1941 Oksana (cr) in *Taras Bulba* (Zakharov), Bolshoi Ballet, Moscow
       Odette/Odile in *Swan Lake* (Gorsky after Petipa, Ivanov), Bolshoi Ballet, Moscow
       Principal dancer (cr) in *Blind Girl* (choreographic miniature; Yakobson), Bolshoi Ballet, Moscow

1943 Assol in *Crimson Sails* (Radunsky, Pospekhin, Popko), Bolshoi Ballet, Moscow

1945 Title role (cr) in *Cinderella* (Zakharov), Bolshoi Ballet, Moscow

1946 Lisa Muromskaya in *Mistress into Maid* (Zakharov), Bolshoi Ballet, Moscow

1947 Jeanne in *The Flames of Paris* (Vainonen), Bolshoi Ballet, Moscow

Olga Lepeshinskaya teaching dancers of the Stuttgart Ballet

Principal dancer (cr) in *Fantasia* (choreographic minia-
ture; Yakobson), Bolshoi Ballet, Moscow
Principal dancer (cr) in *A Shoe* (choreographic minia-
ture; Yakobson), Bolshoi Ballet, Moscow
1949   Parasha (cr) in *The Bronze Horseman* (Moscow version;
Zakharov), Bolshoi Ballet, Moscow
Tao-Hoa in *The Red Poppy* (Lavrovsky), Bolshoi Ballet,
Moscow
Title role (cr) in *Mirandolina* (Vainonen), Bolshoi Filial
Theatre, Moscow
1959   Sari (cr) in *Path of Thunder* (Moscow version; Sergeyev),
Bolshoi Ballet, Moscow

Other roles include: Masha in *The Nutcracker* (Vainonen),
Swanilda in *Coppélia* (Gorsky), principal dancer in various
"miniatures" of Leonid Yakobson.

PUBLICATIONS

By Lepeshinskaya:
"Life of a Soviet Ballerina", *Dance News* (New York), January
1946

About Lepeshinskaya:
"Four Russian Dancers of Today", *Dancing Times* (London),
October 1941

Volkov, Nikolai, "Distinguished Artists of the Moscow
Ballet", *Dancing Times* (London), October 1944
Morley, Iris, *Soviet Ballet*, London, 1945
Dolgopolov, Mikhail, "Olga Lepeshinskaya", in Slonimsky,
Yuri et al., *The Soviet Ballet*, New York, 1947, 1970
Slonimsky, Yuri, *The Bolshoi Theatre Ballet*, Moscow, 1956
"O.V. Lepeshinskaya", *Bolshoi Teatr* (Moscow), 1958
Roslavleva, Natalia, *Era of the Russian Ballet*, London, 1966

*   *   *

Olga Lepeshinskaya's career developed successfully from the
very first steps she took as a dancer of the Bolshoi Theatre. She
soon came to occupy a position from which no one could shake
her. She became the leading female dancer of the company,
thrusting the great ballerina Marina Semenova into second
place in the 1930s and successfully competing with the great
ballerina Galina Ulanova during the 1940s. The reason for such
a privileged position was to be found not only in Lepeshinskaya's connections with government circles and not only in her
membership of the Communist Party. The very art of
Lepeshinskaya conformed remarkably well to official norms.
Lepeshinskaya demonstrated all that was required of the Soviet
artist in the 1930s and 1940s: joyfulness, impetuous enthusiasm, high standards of technique (as regards turns and some
of the most effective jumps ever seen), a simplified conception
of life and of the soul, freedom from any psychological

complexity whatever—but also, an unquestionably infectious presence, stage charm, and in many cases, theatrical brilliance. One can even say that Lepeshinskaya, much more than many less talented film stars, created the ideal model of the Soviet actress; and, although the most discerning of balletomanes did not always respond greatly to her art (noticing the absence of a true academic style), the general spectator loved Lepeshinskaya, and her popularity was genuine and unshakeable.

Lepeshinskaya, by her mood and by the atmosphere of the piece in which she was appearing, brought to mind May Day celebrations, popular festivals, or summer sporting parades: joyful excitement was the watchword. For this reason what suited Lepeshinskaya most of all was roles in comedy ballets such as *La Fille mal gardée* or *Don Quixote*; indeed, Lise in *La Fille mal gardée* was her début role, and Lepeshinskaya danced this ballet with great success and ever-improving mastery throughout her whole career. Her other crowning role was Kitri in *Don Quixote*. Until the appearance of Plisetskaya, hers was the best Kitri in the Soviet Union and perhaps the best Kitri of the time. Lepeshinskaya conveyed remarkably well the festival and public-square spirit of this Russian/Spanish ballet, and her virtuoso technique enabled her literally to create wonders. When Lepeshinskaya was in form, her appearance in *Don Quixote* became a major event at the Bolshoi Theatre.

However, Lepeshinskaya's attempts to dance *Swan Lake* (which she did a few times) or *Giselle* (which she tried to do once) resulted in obvious creative failures. Romantic choreography was not her sphere, especially old-style *ballet blanc*. A dazzling performer in partnered variations, Lepeshinskaya did not appear to such good effect in lyric adage and responded poorly to the music of slow variations. Her element was the hurricane tempo of super-fast ballet allegro; and, although in appearance and style Lepeshinskaya did not call to mind the ballerinas of Balanchine, there is no doubt that in his tempestuous compositions she would have felt herself at home. Unfortunately not only Balanchine but all of the contemporary choreography of Western countries was never encountered in the repertoire of Lepeshinskaya. Instead of this, she danced in dubious and artistically empty ballets produced for her in the 1930s and 1940s—ballets long since forgotten, but suiting her own style. Such works, quickly fashioned and responding to the themes of the day, are therefore no basis on which to regard Lepeshinskaya as successful or unsuccessful, though one wonders if her gifts as an artist were fully realized.

—Vadim Gaevsky

———

LEPICQ (also Le Picq, Lepic), Charles
French dancer and choreographer. Born in Naples, son of dancer Charles Picq, in 1744 (some sources say in Strasburg, 1749). Also appears as Lepic, Pick, and Lepij. Studied under Jean-Georges Noverre in Stuttgart from c. 1760/61. Married (1) dancer Anna Binetti; (2) dancer Mme. (Gertrude or Margherita) Rossi by 1782: daughter, dancer Wilhelmine (performer in Russia). Début with Noverre's ballet troupe at Court Opera House, Stuttgart, November 1761, becoming danseur sérieux, 1762; dancer, in partnership with first wife, Anna Binetti, in Venice, 1764, also appearing under Franz Hilverding, Vienna, 1765; choreographer and first dancer, Teatro San Benedetto, Venice, 1769–72; joint ballet master, with Jean Favier, Teatro Regio Ducale, Milan, 1773; returned to Naples, staging Noverre's ballets at Teatro San Carlo, from

1773; dancer under Noverre in Paris, 1776; choreographer, Teatro San Benedetto, Venice, 1777–78; leading dancer, under ballet master Noverre, King's Theatre, London, 1782, returning to appear at King's Theatre various seasons 1782–85; also ballet master, King's Theatre, 1783 and 1785; invited to Russia by Catherine II: court ballet master, St. Petersburg, 1786–98. Died in St. Petersburg c. 1806.

ROLES

1762   A Wrestler (cr) in *La Mort d'Hercule* (Noverre), Noverre Company, Stuttgart

1763   Chevalier danois in *Renaud et Armide* (Noverre), Noverre Company, Stuttgart

Hate (cr) in *Medée et Jason* (Noverre), Noverre Company, Stuttgart

1776   Entrée in *Alceste* (tragédie-lyrique; mus. Gluck), Opéra, Paris

Entrée in *L'Union de l'Amour et des arts* (opera-ballet; mus. Floquet), Opéra, Paris

Shepherd in *Les Caprices de Galathée* (ballet; mus. Fontainebleau, chor. Noverre), Opéra, Paris

1782   Apollo (cr) in *Apollon et les muses* (Noverre), King's Theatre, London

Apelles in *Apelles et Campaspe; or, The Generosity of Alexander the Great* (revival; Noverre), King's Theatre, London

Dancer (cr) in *New Dance* (Noverre), King's Theatre, London

Dancer in *Passacaille* (solo added to *New Divertissement*; Simonet), King's Theatre, London

Romulus (cr) in *Il Ratto delle Sabine* (also chor.), King's Theatre, London

1783   Leading role, including Pas de trois, Pas de deux, Seguidillas (cr) in *Le Tuteur trompé; or, The Guardian Outwitted* (also chor.), King's Theatre, London

Tamas (cr) in *Les Épouses persanes* (also chor.), King's Theatre, London

"La Recrue par force" (cr; pas de deux) in *Il Riposo del campo; or, The Recreations of the Camp* (also chor.), King's Theatre, London

Minuet, Divertissement (cr) in *La Bégueule; or, She Wou'd and She Wou'd Not* (also chor.), King's Theatre, London

Leading role (cr) in *The Amours of Alexander and Roxane* (also chor.), King's Theatre, London

Minuet de la Cour (cr) in *Le Déjeuner Espagnol* (Simonet), King's Theatre, London

Dancer in *Les Ruses de l'amour* (Noverre), King's Theatre, London

Dancer (cr) in *The Pastimes of Terpsichore* (Dauberval), King's Theatre, London

Dancer (cr) in *Friendship Leads to Love* (Dauberval), King's Theatre, London

1784   Title role (cr) in *Orpheo* (Dauberval), King's Theatre, London

Manhood (cr) in *The Four Ages of Man* (Dauberval), King's Theatre, London

Dancer (cr) in *Pygmalion* (Dauberval), King's Theatre, London

Dancer (cr) in *New Divertissement* (Dauberval), King's Theatre, London

Title role (cr) in *Le Déserteur; ou, La Clémence royale* (Dauberval), King's Theatre, London

Arsaces (cr) in *Sémiramis* (also chor.), King's Theatre, London

Dancer (cr) in *Le Parti de chasse d'Henri IV* (also chor.), King's Theatre, London

1785 Dancer (cr) in *Il Convito degli dei* (also chor.), King's Theatre, London

Dancer (cr) in *Le Jugement de Pâris* (also chor.), King's Theatre, London

Dancer (cr) in *À la plus sage; ou, La Vertu récompensée* (M. Gardel), King's Theatre, London

Dancer (cr) in *Il Convitato di Pietra* (also chor.), King's Theatre, London

Title role (cr) in *Macbeth* (also chor.), King's Theatre, London

Minuet, Gavotte, and Pas de trois (cr) in *L'Amour soldat*, King's Theatre, London

Dancer (cr) in *Les Amours d'été* (also chor.), King's Theatre, London

Dancer (cr) in *New Divertissement* (Simonet), King's Theatre, London

WORKS

1770 *Orfeo e Euridice* (probably after Noverre), Teatro San Benedetto, Venice

Trionfi e vittorie d'Ercole, Teatro San Benedetto, Venice

Le Prove dei balli, Teatro San Benedetto, Venice

1771 *I Fatti d'Achille figlio di Peleo*, Teatro San Benedetto, Venice

Gli Amanti protetti dall'amore, Teatro San Benedetto, Venice

1772 *Il Sacrificio di Efigenia*, Teatro San Benedetto, Venice

Dances in *Lucio Silla* (opera; mus. Mozart), Teatro Regio Ducale, Milan

1773 *Armide* (after Noverre's *Renaud et Armide*), Teatro San Carlo, Naples

1774 *Adèle de Ponthieu* (after Noverre), Teatro San Carlo, Naples

La Felice Metamorfosi; o, Siano i Petimetter maitres burlati; Followers of Amore, ballets between acts of *Orfeo* (opera; mus. Gluck), Teatro San Carlo, Naples

Aminta e Clori, Teatro San Carlo, Naples

1775 *Hymenée et Cryseus* (after Noverre), Milan

Caccia di Enrico IV, Teatro San Carlo, Naples

1776 *Gli Orazi egli curiazi* (after Noverre), Teatro San Carlo, Naples

1777 *Telemaco nell'isola di Calipso*, Teatro San Benedetto, Venice

I Tre Orazi e i tre curiazi, Teatro San Benedetto, Venice

1782 *Apelles et Campaspe; or, The Generosity of Alexander the Great* (after Noverre), King's Theatre, London

Il Ratto delle Sabine (mus. Vincentio), King's Theatre, London

1783 *Le Tuteur trompé* (mus. Martini), King's Theatre, London

Les Épouses persanes, King's Theatre, London

Il Riposo del campo; or, The Recreations of the Camp (mus. Borghi), King's Theatre, London

La Bégueule; or, She Wou'd and She Wou'd Not (mus. Borghi), King's Theatre, London

The Amours of Alexander and Roxane (mus. Barthélemon), King's Theatre, London

La Dame bienfaisante (mus. Floquet), King's Theatre, London

The Four Nations, King's Theatre, London

1784 *Sémiramis*, King's Theatre, London

La Partie de chasse d'Henri IV, King's Theatre, London

1785 *Il Convito degli dei* (mus. Barthélemon), King's Theatre, London

Le Jugement de Pâris (mus. Barthélemon), King's Theatre, London

Il Convitato di Pietra (mus. Gluck), King's Theatre, London

Macbeth (mus. Locke, arranged Barthélemon), King's Theatre, London

Les Amours d'été, King's Theatre, London

Dances in *Orfeo* (opera; Gluck), King's Theatre, London

Don Juan; or, The Libertine Destroyed (possibly *Il Convitato di Pietra*), King's Theatre, London

1789 Dances for *Le Bourgeois Gentilhomme* (comédie-ballet by Molière), St. Petersburg

Médée et Jason (after Noverre), St. Petersburg

Le Déserteur (after Dauberval), St. Petersburg

1790 *Nachalnoe Utrablenie Olega* (mus. Sarti, Canobbio, Pashkevich), Hermitage Theatre, St. Petersburg

Bergère, St. Petersburg

1795 *Didona abandonata*, St. Petersburg

La Belle Arsène, St. Petersburg

Les Deux Savoyards, St. Petersburg

1798 *Les Amours de Bayard*, St. Petersburg

Tancrède (mus. Martin), St. Petersburg

Other works include: for St. Petersburg Imperial Theatres—*La Mort d'Hercule* (after Noverre), *Psyché et l'amour* (after Noverre; St. Petersburg), *Acis et Galatée* (after Noverre), *Annette et Lubin* (after Noverre).

PUBLICATIONS

Noverre, Jean-Georges, *Lettres sur la danse et sur les ballets*; Stuttgart and Lyon, 1760; as *Letters on Dancing and Ballets*, translated (from the enlarged 1803 edition) by Cyril Beaumont, London, 1930

Baron, M.A., *Lettres sur la danse*, Paris, 1825

Lifar, Serge, *Histoire du ballet russe*, Paris, 1950

Lynham, Deryck, *The Chevalier Noverre*, London, 1950

Guest, Ivor, *The Romantic Ballet in England*, London, 1954

Roslavleva, Natalia, *Era of the Russian Ballet*, London, 1966

Swift, Mary Grace, *A Loftier Flight: The Life and Accomplishments of Charles-Louis Didelot, Balletmaster*, Middletown, Connecticut, 1974

Winter, Marian Hannah, *The Pre-Romantic Ballet*, London, 1974

* * *

Charles LePicq, known in his own day as the "Apollo of Dance", is best known to us as the most loyal student and zealous promoter of the choreographic ideals and repertoire of Jean-Georges Noverre. However, LePicq had notable contacts outside Noverre's circle: he danced with one of the other great pioneers of the *ballet d'action*, Hilverding, he choreographed for the young Mozart, and he holds the distinction of having taught Valberg, the first Russian choreographer to make a name in history. Born into a family of dancers (his father appeared with John Rich's Covent Garden company in 1741–42, and ended his life as a court dancer in Vienna), LePicq already knew the international dance world by the time, still a teenager, he arrived in Stuttgart as "figurant" under Noverre. Noverre was building an exciting Stuttgart company, which included Jean Dauberval, Gaetan Vestris, and Nancy Levier, when LePicq was promoted out of the corps de ballet to be specially instructed by Noverre as "danseur sérieux" in 1762. He was to spend his life dancing among the first rank of European dancers.

There are a number of accounts extant of LePicq's dancing, many of which are more informative than most early descriptions of dance. In 1773 he went to Naples with his first wife, the dancer Anna Binetti, and staged *Armide*, among other Noverre ballets. Abbé Galliani wrote "One must admit that he is as good a dancer as Vestris and Dauberval", but he adds that LePicq had feared that the Neopolitans (who put a premium on shows of vigour and endurance in dance) would boo him off the stage, for "in a theatre as enormous . . . as ours [they] could not see that he was dancing since he did not jump". Clearly, his was the French courtly "terre à terre" style, and by the end of the century this was becoming old-fashioned. Didelot, another pupil of Noverre's and a younger colleague of LePicq's in St. Petersburg, characterized his dancing in a chance remark made in 1809: "Vestris the father, LePicq and my wife [Rose Paul, d. 1803] had neither strength nor extreme vivacity; they pirouetted little, with difficulty, because their genre would not permit it".

His genre, however, served him well. By 1771 he was regarded as an important choreographer in his own right and one of the greatest performers. In Milan he wrote ballet divertissements, performed between the acts, for Mozart's opera *Lucio Silla*, the first of which was *Le gelosie del Seraglio* (a theme which was to fascinate Mozart again in *Zaide* and in *Entführung aus dem Serail*). A description of the ballet survives in Noverre's *Lettres*: exotically set in a Turkish harem, it involved the jealousies and subsequent reconciliation of two of the Sultan's favourites. The plot gives ample scope for a *ballet d'action* in the Noverrian style: a pas de deux danced by the Sultan and his momentary favourite, a solo by the neglected one, a pas de deux danced by the two women cleverly underscoring their reconciliation and a "contredanse noble" to mark the celebratory ending. It is a nicely structured piece, with the careful counterpointing of the two significant pas de deux. Comically, the ballet includes a dance called "Reumatismo", probably a private joke of Mozart's at his father's expense (Leopold's letters of this period are full of complaints of his ailment). Clearly not all of LePicq's choreography for Mozart could have been "sérieux".

LePicq also danced at the Opéra during Noverre's stormy period as maître de ballet there. In a 1776 revival of Noverre's *Les Caprices de Galathée*, in which La Guimard danced Galathée, LePicq played the infatuated shepherd who is driven to near despair by her capricious behaviour. Baron von Grimm, one of the few in the audience who seems to have understood the avant-garde aspects of this work, speaks of LePicq as one of the leading interpreters of Noverre's experimental mixing of dance and mime. He writes of LePicq: "A charming face, the slenderest of waists, the easiest and lightest of movements, the purest and most vivacious and yet most natural style, such are the qualities which mark the talent of the new mime." After comparing LePicq favourably with Vestris and Gardel, he concludes, "His grace and lightness triumph above all in demi-caractère dancing and that is the genre of the new ballet". Aware that "the new mime" required dramatic as well as technical abilities, the baron was later to criticize the young Auguste Vestris as not having yet "acquired in this style all the sensibility and the flowing movement which LePicq displayed" when he created the same role.

LePicq was dancing with Noverre during the golden years of his brilliant company's performances in London, a period during which cast-lists read like catalogues of the greatest dancers of the day. Praise of LePicq reached new heights, if possible, especially when he danced opposite the newly arrived Gertrude Rossi, his second wife: "Rossi's Fainting Fit, her Agitation preceding it and her Revival from it; LePicq's hovering over Rossi, when in the Swoon, and in his Separation from her, were all told very expressively indeed. LePicq is the most graceful dancer in Europe, and excells every Competitor in the Narrative and Pathos of Gesticulation." (*Public Advertiser*, 3 May 1784).

This gives us a glimpse of the sentimental nature of late eighteenth-century ballet, and testifies once again to LePicq's extraordinary gifts in "the new mime". However, LePicq was experimenting with mime in his own ballets as well; in his 1785 ballet of *Macbeth* he took on the challenge of representing Shakespearean complexities in dance. The *Public Advertiser* seemed bemused at the attempt but conceded that "considering the narrow boundaries of their art, which is tongue-tied, they discoursed 'with most miraculous organs'".

So successful was LePicq in his London season that Catherine II of Russia requested her ambassador to engage him for St. Petersburg, but she had to wait two years before he was free of engagements. Perhaps because Russian taste ran to the mythological and the allegorical, LePicq's Russian period (1786–98) appears to have been a return to his roots. Here he revived a number of Noverre's ballets from his student days in Stuttgart (such as *La Mort d'Hercule* and *Medeé et Jason*), especially those with allegorical roles. At least one historian of Russian ballet has charged that LePicq's St. Petersburg revivals were superficial and unacknowledged. This seems unlikely, however, in view of the sensitivity of his highly acclaimed reworking of, for example, Noverre's *Apelles et Campaspe* for the King's Theatre in London (1782), in which LePicq's alterations of the libretto actually made for a much stronger ballet. Furthermore, eighteenth-century choreographers seem all to have reworked the perennially favourite mythological tales, and plagiarism becomes a moot point under such circumstances.

Didelot commented on this very point while defending himself from a charge of having plagiarized LePicq and Nivelon by stressing that the themes in question "belong to every poet, artist or composer who wishes to avail himself of them". That LePicq was deeply grateful to Noverre is evident in his having convinced the Tsar to subsidize a new edition of his *Lettres* (1803–04), and in his having obtained a pension for his former teacher, an act of gratitude that astonished Noverre, after a separation of nearly two decades. On the other side, Noverre's pride in his students was fierce; he said in an angry retort to Angiolini: "but I would have him know that whilst he was spelling out barbarous caricatures of dances . . ., I was forming Dauberval, [here follows a list of dancers including LePicq] . . . who have carried my name and my ballets" across Europe. None of these did more for Noverre's reputation than LePicq.

—Kathryn Kerby-Fulton

THE LESSON
(Original Danish title: *Enetime*)

Choreography: Flemming Flindt
Music: Georges Delerue
Design: Bernard Daydé (scenery and costume)
Libretto: Flemming Flindt (after Eugène Ionesco's play *La Leçon*)

First Production: Royal Danish Ballet, as a television ballet, filmed by Danish Television, 16 September 1963
Principal dancers: Flemming Flindt (The Teacher), Josette Amiel (The Pupil), Tsilla Chelton (The Pianist)

Other productions include: Royal Danish Ballet (first stage production; restaged Flindt), with Flemming Flindt (Teacher), Josette Amiel (Pupil), and Lyna Garden (Pianist); Paris, 6 April 1964. Chicago Opera Ballet, with Orrin Kayan (Teacher), Josette Amiel (Pupil), Vicki Fisera (Pianist); New York, 19 February 1966. Western Theatre Ballet, with Flemming Flindt (Teacher), Arlette van Boven (Pupil), Elaine McDonald (Pianist); London, 20 June 1967. City Center Joffrey Ballet; New York, 27 September 1968. Nureyev Festival, with Rudolf Nureyev (Teacher), Natalia Makarova (Pupil), Vivi Flindt (Pianist); London, 1977.

PUBLICATIONS

Anderson, Jack, "Introducing Flemming Flindt", *Dance Magazine* (New York), November 1965
Hering, Doris, "Royal Danish Ballet", *Dance Magazine* (New York), February 1966
Näslund, Erik, and Ståhle, Anna Greta, "Flemming Flindt: Dansaren, Balettchefen, Koreografen", *Dans* (Stockholm), May 1974
Balanchine, George, with Mason, Francis, *Balanchine's Complete Stories of the Great Ballets*, Garden City, N. Y., 1977
Kersley, Leo, and Sinclair, Janet, "Men, Mice and Mountains", *Dance and Dancers* (London), June 1988

* * *

While there are many ballets which have transferred from the stage to the screen or television, and quite a few which were made only for the camera, there are not many which have made the journey in reverse. Flemming Flindt has achieved this feat with remarkable success, and when it is considered that the dominant factor in *The Lesson* is the claustrophobic atmosphere of the ballet studio in which the action takes place, it is easy to see why.

Based on the play of the same name by Ionesco, but moved from a professor's study to the dance studio, *The Lesson* deals with the episode of a young female dance student who comes to take a ballet lesson from the teacher, whom she so aggravates that he finishes up by strangling her. On the face of it it seems an unlikely story, but on the stage, *The Lesson*—a mixture of melodrama, grand guignol, and silent film techniques (it falls into no easy balletic category)—has its own fascination, one which lies not least in the fact that one continues to think about it long after the curtain has fallen: and to how many ballets of the past 25 years does this apply? Moreover, the three roles give their interpreters an opportunity rare on the ballet stage today: the chance to create real, living—if eccentric—characters. Can the three characters—the Teacher, the Pianist, and the Pupil—be exactly what they seem? Has one dance student been murdered before the ballet opens and will a third be killed after its close, or are the characters simply caught up in some time-warp which compels them to perform the same actions over and over again for eternity, like Sartre's characters in *Huis Clos* or Priestley's man, wife, and lover in *I Have Been Here Before*?

What relationship is the Pianist to the Teacher? Is she his mother, sister, wife, or mistress? Or is she simply an innocent, trapped in her own admiration, love, or pity? Is the Teacher mad from the start, or does he become temporarily insane, owing to frustration with a potential talent and its typical

stupidity? Has some injustice or indifference sent him off his rocker, or is he a sex maniac? Flindt leaves it to our imagination to fathom out the reasons behind the actions we see on stage.

The Lesson, a remarkable first work by any standards, could certainly be described as Flindt's most successful ballet to date, and falls into that category (rare at the present time) of dance works which make the audience think, through a well-balanced mixture of clear and unfussy choreography, finely tuned dramatic timing, and great opportunity for interpretation by its performers. It is an admirable example of the good use of the unique characteristics peculiar to the dance form, in that it uses a story which can be understood from movement, without reference to a detailed programme note. Hence the choreographer can do without the exact definition of the spoken word and leave more to the imagination of his audience than can the dramatist, who risks being labelled "obscure" if his use of words is ambiguous. Here we have the best of both worlds, and in this case the worlds of Ionesco and Flindt are skilfully intermingled to make a work in which three characters alone hold the attention of the audience for 30 minutes or so—a feat rarely rivalled in any other ballet, ancient or modern.

—Janet Sinclair

LESTER, Keith

British dancer, choreographer, and teacher. Born in Guildford, England, 9 April 1904. Studied with Anton Dolin, Serafina Astafieva, Nikolai (Nicholas) Legat, and Mikhail Fokine. Début in Fokine's dances for *Hassan* at His Majesty's Theatre, London, 1923; dancer in concert tours, partnering Lydia Kyasht, Britain, 1924–26, Tamara Karsavina, Riga, Central Europe, and Britain, 1927–30, Nadine Nicolaeva, France, 1930, and Olga Spessivtseva, Buenos Aires, 1931; principal dancer in independent ballet companies and stage shows including Ida Rubinstein Company, Paris, 1934, Ernest Matray's Ballet Revue, North America, 1935, Markova-Dolin Ballet, 1935–37, London Ballet, 1939, Arts Theatre Ballet, 1940–41; choreographer, Markova-Dolin Ballet, 1935–37, and Regent's Park Open Air Theatre, 1938; founder, choreographer, and co-director (with Harold Turner), Arts Theatre Ballet, 1940–41; principal dancer and choreographer, London Windmill Theatre, 1945–64, staging over 150 shows; principal teacher and director, Teacher Training Course of the Royal Academy of Dancing, London, 1965–75; Fellow of the Royal Academy of Dancing, from 1974.

ROLES

1923   Dancer in *Hassan* (play by James Elroy Flecker; chor. Fokine), His Majesty's Theatre, London
1927   Pas de deux from *Raymonda* (after Petipa), Karsavina company, tour
1931   Principal dancer in *Les Sylphides* (Fokine), Olga Spessivtseva company, Teatro Colón, Buenos Aires
       Ivan Tsarevitch in *The Firebird* (Fokine), Olga Spessivtseva company, Teatro Colón, Buenos Aires
       The Golden Slave in *Schéhérazade* (Fokine), Olga Spessivtseva company, Teatro Colón, Buenos Aires
       Title role in *Le Spectre de la rose* (Fokine), Olga Spessivtseva company, Teatro Colón, Buenos Aires

1932   Principal dancer in *The Miracle* (mystery play by Volmöller; chor. Massine), Lyceum Theatre, London
The Knight and the Spielman in *The Miracle* (mystery play by Volmöller; chor. Massine), tour
1934   The Captain in *Sémiramis* (Fokine), Ida Rubinstein Company, Paris
Serviteur de Pluton and Triptoleme in *Persephone* (Jooss), Ida Rubinstein Company, Paris
Principal dancer in *Diane de Poitiers* (Fokine), Ida Rubinstein Company, Paris
Principal dancer in *La Valse* (Fokine), Ida Rubinstein Company, Paris
Principal dancer in *Bolero* (Fokine), Ida Rubinstein Company, Paris
1935   Saul (cr) in *David* (also chor.), Markova–Dolin Ballet, Newcastle
Count Garin of Beaucaire in *Aucassin and Nicolette* (Toye), Markova–Dolin Ballet, British tour
First entrée (cr) in *Grande Valse* (also chor.), Markova–Dolin Ballet, British tour
Prince of Courland in *Giselle* (Petipa after Coralli, Perrot; staged Sergeyev), Markova–Dolin Ballet, British tour
1936   Sailor in *Fore and Aft* (also chor.), Markova–Dolin Company, British tour
Von Rothbart in *Swan Lake* (after Petipa, Ivanov), Markova–Dolin Ballet, British tour
1937   An Admirer in *The Beloved One* (Nijinska), Markova–Dolin Ballet, British tour
Peasant in *Hungaria* (de Moroda), Markova–Dolin Ballet, British tour
Adagio in *Bach Suite* (also chor.), Markova–Dolin Ballet, British tour
Chanson dansée ("Athlete") in *The House Party* (*Les Biches*; Nijinska), Markova–Dolin Ballet, British tour
1938   Wood Sprite in *A Midsummer Night's Dream* (also chor.), Open Air Theatre, Regent's Park, London
Chorus in *Lysistrata* (also chor.), Open Air Theatre, Regent's Park, London
1939   Cavalier in *Gala Performance* (Tudor), London Ballet, London
Neptune in *The Planets* (Tudor), London Ballet, London
Pâris in *Pas de déesses* (also chor.), London Ballet, London
Second Song in *Dark Elegies* (Tudor), London Ballet, London
The Client in *The Judgment of Paris* (Tudor), London Ballet, London
The Man She Must Marry in *Jardin aux lilas* (Tudor), London Ballet, London
1940   Second Movement (cr) in *Concerto* (also chor.), Arts Theatre Ballet, London
Flash mess' John (cr) in *May Collin* (Turner), Arts Theatre Ballet, London
Iain (cr) in *The Glen* (also chor.), Arts Theatre Ballet, London
Huntsman and Siegfried in *Swan Lake*, Act II (after Ivanov), Arts Theatre Ballet, London
Trepak and Spanish Dance in *The Nutcracker* (after Ivanov), Arts Theatre Ballet, London
Apollo (cr) in *The Four Mountains* (also chor.), Arts Theatre Ballet, London
A Labourer (cr) in *De Profundis* (also chor.), Arts Theatre Ballet, London
1941   Benno in *Swan Lake*, Act II (after Ivanov), Arts Theatre Ballet, London

Bluebird pas de deux from *The Sleeping Beauty* (after Petipa), Arts Theatre Ballet, London

Other roles include: for Karsavina company tour—principal dancer in *Galop*—*Vif Argent*, *Eine Kleine Nachtmusic*, *Carnival de Venise*, Pas des fiancés from *Russe d'amour*, solo variation in *Caucasian Dance*, Pas de deux from *Sylvia*; for the Arts Theatre Ballet—Solo variations in *Andaluza*, and *Sicilienne*, Pas de deux in *Nocturne*, *Rose Adagio* (from *The Sleeping Beauty*; after Petipa), *Cimarosa*, *Pavane*, *Tyrolienne*, principal dancer in *A Tchaikovsky pas de trois*, Albrecht in *Giselle* (after Coralli, Perrot).

WORKS

1935   *David* (mus. Jacobson), Markova–Dolin Ballet, Newcastle
Grande Valse (mus. Tchaikovsky), Markova–Dolin Ballet, British tour
1936   *Pas de quatre* (mus. Pugni), Markova–Dolin Ballet, Manchester
Fore and Aft (mus. Coates), Markova–Dolin Ballet, British tour
Bach Suite No. 2 (mus. Bach), Markova–Dolin Ballet, British tour
1938   *Titania and the Tar* (mus. Mendelssohn), Ballet Intime, Bexhill (also staged for Markova–Dolin Ballet)
Valse fantaisie (mus. Glinka), Ballet Intime, Bexhill
1939   *Olympic Antics* (mus. Holst), Ballet Guild
Pas de déesses (mus. Pugni), London Ballet, London
1940   *Concerto* (mus. Mozart), Arts Theatre Ballet, London
The Glen (mus. Mendelssohn), Arts Theatre Ballet, London
Sylvia (mus. Delibes), Arts Theatre Ballet, London
Perseus (mus. Bate), Arts Theatre Ballet, London
The Four Mountains (mus. Holst), Arts Theatre Ballet, London
De Profundis (mus. Chopin, arranged Lucas), Arts Theatre Ballet, London (also staged for Markova–Dolin Ballet)
Rondo Capriccioso (mus. Saint-Saëns), Arts Theatre Ballet, London
Les Fées aux fleurs (with Molly Lake; mus. Pugni), Arts Theatre Ballet, London
1941   *The Dark Mirror* (mus. Weber), Ballet Guild, Bath
Black Étude (mus. Moussorgsky), Ballet Guild
Fantasy (mus. Chopin), Ballet Guild
Sawdust (mus. Lucas), Ballet Guild
1951   *Sylvia* (one act version; mus. Delibes), Continental Ballet
Les Ombres, Continental Ballet
1955   *Room for Three* (mus. Gillis), London Festival Ballet, London

Other works include: *The Four Elements* (mus. Pugni), *Faust* (mus. Gounod), *Death in Adagio*, *Cinderella's Dream*, *Sicilienne* (mus. Schubert).

PUBLICATIONS

By Lester:
"Choreographers at Work: A Method in their Madness", *Dancing Times* (London), February 1941
"Dancers at the Windmill", *Dancing Times* (London), November 1964

"Rubinstein Revisited", *Dance Research* (London), Autumn 1983

About Lester:
Noble, Peter, *British Ballet*, London, c.1950
Beaumont, Cyril, *Complete Book of Ballets*, revised edition, London, 1951
Van Damm, V., *Tonight and Every Night*, London, 1952
Karsavina, Tamara, "An English Partner: Keith Lester", *The Dancing Times* (London), December 1967
Benari, Naomi, *Vagabonds and Strolling Dancers*, London, 1990

*   *   *

A leading dancer of great ability and fine appearance, Keith Lester was in constant demand as a freelance artist from the time of his début in 1923, when he danced in the play *Hassan*, with choreography by Fokine. Lester had a sound background of training with Nicholas Legat and Serafina Astafieva, and because he was an excellent cavalier, he partnered Tamara Karsavina, Olga Spessivtseva, and Lydia Kyasht in tours and guest appearances. With Spessivtseva he was engaged for the Teatro Colón in Buenos Aires (when Fokine was ballet master), and he danced the leading roles in *Le Spectre de la rose*, *Schéhérazade*, and *The Firebird*. The variety of a roving life without tight contractual commitments appealed to him. He appeared in the celebrated Reinhardt production of *The Miracle* in 1932, and joined Ida Rubinstein's company in Paris, appearing in ballets by Fokine and Kurt Jooss. He also toured the United States in musicals and revues during the 1930s.

Tamara Karsavina has written about her European tour with Lester as partner, saying "I felt safe in his hands. He was alert to my slightest variation of movement". She found him not only an indefatigable worker, but "a highly intelligent student of dance", willing to experiment constantly with new steps and lifts in their rehearsals. Having both worked with Fokine, they had a great deal of common ground, as well as being able to share jokes on occasion. They appeared in the Baltic States, in Germany, Poland, and Czechoslovakia, in all sizes of locales, from opera houses to improvised board stages, dancing mostly divertissement programmes.

After his peripatetic and varied early career, Lester joined the first Markova–Dolin Ballet as dancer and choreographer, composing *David* in 1935. This was an impressive beginning to a creative career that was never fully consolidated. Originally planned as a solo for Anton Dolin, it was expanded into a six-episode dramatic ballet with a scenario by Poppaea Vanda, based on biblical history to a score composed by Maurice Jacobson. Lester looked towards Assyrian art for influences regarding pose and movement, and achieved a clear and powerful production in which Dolin danced David and Lester himself created Saul. For this company, with which he remained until it closed in 1937, Lester also choreographed a sensitive and charming reconstruction of the famous nineteenth-century *Pas de quatre*, which has been largely obscured in later years by a version staged by Anton Dolin in the United States.

Lester's next solid connection was with Antony Tudor's London Ballet after Tudor had gone to the States in 1939. Lester took over Tudor's leading roles in *Dark Elegies* and *Jardin aux lilas*, and choreographed *Pas de déesses*—a natural progression from the *Pas de quatre*. Then Lester was given the chance of forming a small ballet company of his own at the Arts Theatre in London. Under the difficult conditions of wartime, he assembled and created an excellent small-scale repertoire, for which he and Harold Turner were the principal choreographers, and a strong group of dancers with international

experience. The Arts Theatre Ballet closed in 1941 and Lester returned to a roving life, mounting two or three ballets for the Ballet Guild, choreographing musicals for Ivor Novello, and arranging dances for other stage productions. At the end of the war he joined the Windmill Theatre as choreographer and principal dancer, an association that lasted some twenty years and resulted in between 150 and 200 ballets.

Lester then returned to ballet as a teacher and educator, joining the Royal Academy of Dancing in 1965 as principal teacher and director of their Teachers' Training Course. He devised their Dance Education syllabus, a stringent one based on his regular classes with Karsavina and known as the Karsavina Syllabus, and taught boys' classes and pas de deux work. He was elected a Fellow of the RAD on his retirement in 1974.

—Kathrine Sorley Walker

LICHINE, David

Russian/American dancer, choreographer, and teacher. Born David (Deivid) Lichtenstein, son of composer Alkansky (or Olshansky; some sources give name as Mikhail Lichtenstein) in Rostov-on-Don, 25 October 1910. Left Russia as a child, settling in Paris via Constantinople and Sofia: studied with Lubov Egorova, Paris, from 1926; later studied with Bronislava Nijinska. Married (1) Lubov Rostova, 1933 (diss. 1935); (2) dancer Tatiana Riabouchinska, 1943. Dancer, Ida Rubinstein's Company, Paris, 1928, Anna Pavlova's Company, 1930, Nijinska company and Ballet de l'Opéra Russe à Paris, 1931–32, and La Scala, Milan, 1932; principal dancer, Ballets Russes de Monte Carlo (becoming de Basil's Ballets Russes and eventually the Original Ballet Russe), 1932–41; début as choreographer (*Nocturne*), 1933, continuing as choreographer, de Basil's Ballets Russes, until 1940; dancer and choreographer, Ballet Theatre (later American Ballet Theatre), from 1941; also performed with the Original Ballet Russe in 1946, London season, 1947, and Spain, 1948; choreographer and principal dancer, Teatro Colón, Buenos Aires, 1947, and Ballets des Champs-Elysées, Paris, 1948; also staged ballets for Grand Ballet du Marquis de Cuevas, 1948–49, London Festival Ballet, 1950, 1951, and 1952, and for Borovansky Ballet, German Opera, Berlin, and others; moved to Los Angeles, founding own company, 1953, performing in Europe as Le Ballet de la Ville des Anges, 1954; also choreographer for Broadway stage, staging dances in *Beat the Band* (musical comedy by Marion and Abbot, mus. Green; 1942) and *Rhapsody* (musical comedy by Levinson and Sudgaard, mus. Kreisler; 1944), and choreographer for films, including *Song of Russia* (dir. Ratoff, 1944), *The Unfinished Dance* (dir. Koster, 1947), *Tonight We Sing* (dir. Mitchell Leisen, 1953). Died in Los Angeles, 26 June 1972.

ROLES

1931   Principal dancer (cr) in *Capriccio Espagnole* (Nijinska), Nijinska Ballets, Paris
    Principal dancer (cr) in *Études* (Nijinska), Nijinska Ballets, Paris (also performed with Ballet de l'Opéra Russe à Paris)
    The Bohemian Dance in *Russalka* (opera; mus. Dargomizhsky), Ballet de l'Opéra Russe à Paris, Paris
1932   Dancer (cr) in *Belkis* (Massine), La Scala, Milan

David Lichine in *Choreartium*, Ballets Russes de Monte Carlo, 1934

The Traveller (cr) in *Jeux d'enfants* (Massine), Ballets Russes de Monte Carlo, Monte Carlo

The First Guest in "La Toilette" and "La Lanterne magique" (cr) in *Cotillon* (Balanchine), Ballets Russes de Monte Carlo, Monte Carlo

Cléonte (cr) in *Le Bourgeois Gentilhomme* (Balanchine), Ballets Russes de Monte Carlo, Monte Carlo

Tarantella (cr) in *Suites de danse* (Balanchine), Ballets Russes de Monte Carlo, Monte Carlo

Blackamoor in *Petrushka* (Fokine), Ballets Russes de Monte Carlo

Mazurka, Pas de deux in *Les Sylphides* (Fokine), Ballets Russes de Monte Carlo

1933　Passion, the Hero (cr) in *Les Présages* (Massine), Ballets Russes de Monte Carlo, Monte Carlo

The King of the Dandies (cr) in *Le Beau Danube* (Massine), Ballets Russes de Monte Carlo, Monte Carlo

Nereus, Handsome Swimmer (cr) in *Beach* (Massine), Ballets Russes de Monte Carlo, Monte Carlo

Puck (cr) in *Nocturne* (also chor.), Ballets Russes de Monte Carlo, Paris

Principal dancer, First and Fourth Movements (cr) in *Choreartium* (Massine), Ballets Russes de Monte Carlo, London

Third Sailor in *Les Matelots* (Massine), Ballets Russes de Monte Carlo

The Hussar in *Le Beau Danube* (Massine), Ballets Russes de Monte Carlo

The Prince in *Swan Lake*, Act II (after Ivanov), Ballets Russes de Monte Carlo

1934　The Governor in *Le Tricorne* (Massine), (de Basil's) Monte Carlo Ballet Russe, Chicago

The Surveyor of the Chinese Workmen (cr) in *Union Pacific* (Massine), (de Basil's) Monte Carlo Ballet Russe, Philadelphia

Kostchei in *The Firebird* (Fokine), de Basil's Ballets Russes

The Triangle (cr) in *Les Imaginaires* (also chor.), de Basil's Ballets Russes, Paris

1935　The Prince (cr) in *Les Cent Baisers* (Nijinska), de Basil's Ballets Russes, London

Title role in *Petrushka* (Fokine), de Basil's Ballets Russes

A Cossack Chief in *La Boutique fantasque* (Massine), de Basil's Ballets Russes

Can-Can Dancer in *La Boutique fantasque* (Massine), de Basil's Ballets Russes

The Spirit of the Rose in *Le Spectre de la rose* (Fokine), de Basil's Ballets Russes

1936　The Poet (cr) in *Le Pavillon* (also chor.), de Basil's Ballets Russes, London

Danse Tzigane in *Danses Slaves et Tziganes* (Nijinska), de Basil's Ballets Russes

The Prince in *Thamar* (Fokine), de Basil's Ballets Russes

The Faun in *L'Après-midi d'un faune* (Nijinsky), de Basil's Ballets Russes

Harlequin in *Carnaval* (Fokine), de Basil's Ballets Russes

1937　The Lion (cr) in *Le Lion amoureux* (also chor.), de Basil's Ballets Russes, London

Pas de deux in *Cimarosiana* (Massine), de Basil's Ballets Russes

Paolo in *Francesca da Rimini* (also chor.), de Basil's Ballets Russes

1938　Title role (cr) in *Protée* (also chor.), (de Basil's) Russian Ballet, London

The Prince (cr) in *Cendrillon* (Fokine), (de Basil's) Russian Ballet, London

1939　Title role in *The Prodigal Son* (also chor.), (de Basil's) Covent Garden Russian Ballet

1940　Junior Cadet, Perpetuum Mobile (cr) in *Graduation Ball* (also chor.), Original Ballet Russe, Sydney

The Hussar (cr) in *Le Danube bleu* (Lifar), Original Ballet Russe, Sydney

Other roles include: Bluebird in *Aurora's Wedding* (from *The Sleeping Beauty*; Petipa, with additional chor. Nijinska).

WORKS

1933　*Nocturne* (mus. Rameau, arranged Desormière), Ballets Russes de Monte Carlo, Paris

1934　*Les Imaginaires* (mus. Auric), de Basil's Ballets Russes

1936 *Le Pavillon* (mus. Borodin, arranged Dorati), de Basil's Ballets Russes, London

1937 *Francesca da Rimini* (mus. Tchaikovsky), de Basil's Ballets Russes, London

The Gods Go a-Begging (mus. Handel), de Basil's Ballets Russes, London

Le Lion amoureux (mus. Rathaus), de Basil's Ballets Russes, London

1938 *Protée* (mus. Debussy), (de Basil's) Russian Ballet, London

The Prodigal Son (mus. Prokofiev), (de Basil's) Covent Garden Russian Ballet, Sydney

1940 *Graduation Ball* (mus. Strauss, arranged Dorati), Original Ballet Russe, Sydney

1942 *Helen of Troy* (finishing Fokine's uncompleted ballet; mus. Offenbach), Ballet Theatre, Detroit

1943 *Fair at Sorochinsk* (mus. Mussorgsky), Ballet Theatre, New York

1946 *Cain and Abel* (mus. Wagner), Original Ballet Russe, Mexico City

1947 *Evolución del Movimiento* (mus. Franck), Teatro Colón, Buenos Aires

Sueño de Niña (mus. Strauss), Teatro Colón, Buenos Aires

1948 *La Création* (no music), Les Ballets des Champs-Elysées, London

La Rencontre, ou Oedipe et le Sphinx (mus. Sauget), Les Ballets des Champs-Elysées, Paris

Orpheus (mus. Stravinsky), Les Ballets des Champs-Elysées, Paris

Valse-caprice (mus. Fauré), Les Ballets des Champs-Elysées, Paris

1949 *Un Coeur de diamant* (mus. Hubeau), Grand Ballet de Monte Carlo (de Cuevas's), Monte Carlo

Le Moulin enchanté (mus. Schubert), Grand Ballet de Monte Carlo (de Cuevas's), Paris

1950 *Harlequinade* (mus. Drigo), London Festival Ballet, London

1951 *Symphonic Impressions* (mus. Bizet), London Festival Ballet, Monte Carlo

Ballet des parfums (mus. Taillefer), London Festival Ballet, Monte Carlo

1952 *Concerto grosso en ballet* (mus. Vivaldi), London Festival Ballet, Monte Carlo (revised as *Concerti*, 1957)

1954 *Divertissement vénitien no. 1* (mus. Marcello, Cambini), Ballet de Los Angeles, Cannes

Les Oiseaux d'or (mus. Tchaikovsky), Ballet de Los Angeles, Cannes

Combat de coqs (mus. Soler), Ballet de Los Angeles, Cannes

1956 *Corrida* (mus. Scarlatti, arranged Herweg), Borovansky Ballet, Sydney (originally performed at Lichine's studio, Los Angeles, 1952; restaged Grand Ballet du Marquis de Cuevas, 1957)

1957 *The Nutcracker* (mus. Tchaikovsky), London Festival Ballet, London

1959 *Vision of Chopin* (mus. Chopin), London Festival Ballet, Barcelona

1962 *Image chorégraphique* (mus. Prokofiev), German Opera Ballet, Berlin

PUBLICATIONS

By Lichine:
"Ballet Milestones", *Dancing Times* (London), September 1939

"Thoughts of a Choreographer", *Ballet* (London), September 1947

About Lichine:
Monahan, James, "David Lichine, Choreographer", *Dancing Times* (London), March 1938
Beaumont, Cyril, *Supplement to Complete Book of Ballets*, London, 1948
Beaumont, Cyril, *Complete Book of Ballets*, revised edition, London, 1951
Davidson, Gladys, *Ballet Biographies*, revised edition, London, 1954
Kochno, Boris, *Le Ballet*, Paris, 1954
Beaumont, Cyril, *Ballets Past and Present*, London, 1955
Sorley Walker, Kathrine, *De Basil's Ballets Russes*, London, 1982
García-Márquez, Vicente, *Les Ballets Russes*, New York, 1989

* * *

A demi-caractère dancer rather than a pure classicist, David Lichine had a captivating theatre personality, good looks, and an abundance of charm and spirit. He was also a choreographer of great ability, in many ways working ahead of his time.

Born at Rostov-On-Don, he was taken to Paris as a child, studying dancing there with Lubov Egorova and Bronislava Nijinska. He danced with Pavlova and with the Ida Rubinstein Ballet, but his career proper began when he joined the newly formed Ballets Russes de Monte Carlo in 1932. His talents exactly suited the repertoire that was built up under the direction of René Blum and Colonel de Basil. He created the Master of Ceremonies in Balanchine's *Cotillon* and, when Balanchine was succeeded by Massine as choreographer, Lichine was equally essential to the success of new ballets. His creations included the King of the Dandies in *Le Beau Danube* and the central part of The Hero in the exciting symphonic ballet, *Les Présages*. Truly versatile, he was as much at home in comedy as in serious work, and very soon he began to have choreographic ambitions of his own.

His first ballet, for the Ballets Russes de Monte Carlo in 1933, was *Nocturne*, a version of *A Midsummer Night's Dream* set to music by Rameau, in which Alexandra Danilova danced Titania with Massine as Oberon. Other works, good and bad, followed. Particularly attractive was *Protée*, an atmospheric piece about an encounter between three young girls and a sea god, set to Claude Debussy's *Danse sacrée et danse profane*, while one of his most substantial productions was *Francesca da Rimini* which featured the splendid Lubov Tchernicheva in the title role. A highly dramatic work, this had a scenario by Henry Clifford based on the tale of Paolo and Francesca, and under Clifford's guidance Lichine studied Florentine painting and sculpture. The music was Tchaikovsky's *Fantasy Overture*, and exquisite designs were provided by the young Oliver Messel. In 1938 an excellent version of *The Prodigal Son* by Lichine stood up well in comparison with the currently surviving version by Balanchine.

With his second wife Tatiana Riabouchinska, Lichine spent a number of years with Colonel de Basil's company and his most enduring ballet, *Graduation Ball*, was created for it in Australia in 1940. This endearing work about military cadets and the young ladies of a neighbouring seminary, set to melodies by Johann Strauss the Younger (arranged by Antal Dorati), is one of the best examples around of lighthearted choreographic wit.

After leaving de Basil, Lichine joined Ballet Theatre in America, for whom he completed *Helen of Troy*, the ballet on which Fokine was engaged at the time of his death. In Europe

Lichine worked with the Grand Ballet du Marquis de Cuevas and with London Festival Ballet, for whom he produced a memorably enjoyable production of *The Nutcracker*. For Les Ballets des Champs-Elysées in Paris he produced two interesting experimental works, *La Création*—one of the first ballets to be danced in silence—and *La Rencontre*, about Oedipus and the Sphinx. A. H. Franks wrote about *La Création* in 1954: ". . . inert bodies lie strewn about the floor, clay in the hands of the creator, the choreographer. As he adjusts them, at first with tentative, uncertain fingers, then with growing confidence, they come to life . . . All the movements are based on the classical technique but are mostly stretched and moulded into that acrobatic style in which the young French dancers appear to take delight. . . . I left the theatre firmly of the opinion that I had witnessed a major choreographic advance."

Unfortunately, Lichine never found a company with which he could settle and further develop his undoubted ability. In 1954 he and Riabouchinska decided to make their home in Los Angeles, opening a studio which she continued after his death in 1972, and for some time also running a performing group, the Los Angeles Ballet Theatre.

—Kathrine Sorley Walker

LIEBESLIEDER WALZER

Choreography: George Balanchine
Music: Johannes Brahms
Design: David Hayes (scenery), Barbara Karinska (costumes)
First Production: New York City Ballet, City Center, New York, 22 November 1960
Principal Dancers: Diana Adams, Bill Carter, Melissa Hayden, Jonathan Watts, Jillana, Conrad Ludlow, Violette Verdy, Nicholas Magallanes

Other productions include: Royal Ballet (staged Karin von Aroldingen, supervised by Balanchine); London, 19 April 1979. Vienna State Opera Ballet; Vienna, 28 May 1977. Zurich Ballet; Zurich, 21 March 1981.

PUBLICATIONS

Balanchine, George, with Mason, Francis, *Balanchine's Complete Stories of the Great Ballets*, Garden City, New York, 1977
Reynolds, Nancy, *Repertory in Review*, New York, 1977
Croce, Arlene, *Afterimages*, New York, 1979
Tobias, Tobi, "Balanchine's Love Songs: Remembering *Liebeslieder Walzer*", *Dance Magazine* (New York), May 1984
Taper, Bernard, *Balanchine: A Biography*, revised edition, New York, 1984
Croce, Arlene, *Sight Lines*, New York, 1987

*   *   *

Liebeslieder Walzer is one of the most romantic of George Balanchine's masterworks. It suggests a personal meditation on "changing aspects of love", in the choreographer's own description, and on his veneration of woman.

Furthermore, the ballet's very structure symbolizes Balanchine's belief in the power of classical ballet: divided by a pause into two sections representing the two sets of Brahms lieder to which it is set, it shows first "the real people that are dancing", as Balanchine put it, and then "their souls". This second, higher sphere is depicted with tulle tutus and pointe shoes, in contrast to the satin ballgowns and heeled slippers of the first part. According to the perceptive Violette Verdy, who originated the single most important role in this ballet of equals, the second part ". . . is Balanchine showing what he does to people, the transcendence of his work, changing something that is quite ordinary, you know, but with certain possibilities, into the sublime".

What happens in the ballet is simply, in Balanchine's words, "dancing and gesture and music". The intimate Brahms songs, in the tradition of music meant for performance at home, set the atmosphere for four couples (the men are in tails throughout), presumably all friends, who have apparently gathered in a sumptuous home in order to dance by candlelight. They are accompanied onstage by four singers and two pianists, dressed like the dancers.

The scene is a place where passion and etiquette meet. Dance becomes the equivalent of the old, flirtatious "language of the fan", but here it is a language that cannot lie, however much it may half-state. The dancers' elegant manners, their graciousness toward each other, their composure, are not merely cloaks for the deep feelings that one glimpses below the surface; their exquisite consideration for each other seems an essential part of their feelings.

What they do is waltz—but what waltzes, and with what variety within the three-quarter time! "These waltz forms begin to tell what they know", wrote Edwin Denby about the ballet. In spite of small flirtations that break out when an extra man occasionally joins a couple in a pas de trois, the pairs are monogamous. Every touch of a woman by a man's white-gloved hand is an act of homage; he never grasps her, but gently guides her or whisks her just above the ground, perhaps supporting her circumspectly on his outstretched wrists. Every change of direction and surge of movement seems a nuance of feeling; every decorous lift of a woman's satin-shrouded leg, a powerful gesture. The circling of the dancers around each other delineates their attachments. Over and over, the men kneel to their muses.

Small incidents take on great significance. A man (originally Nicholas Magallanes) suddenly averts his gaze from his partner (Verdy), shielding his eyes with one hand as they dance, as if at a thought too painful to contemplate; at the end of this pas de deux he bears her prone body, and later she swoons. These events are only part of the dance and yet in context they intimate mortality. Another couple (originally Diana Adams and William Carter) walks a slow diagonal, the man whispering to the woman first in one ear, then in the other. Another couple (Melissa Hayden and Jonathan Watts) seem more mercurial, more dare-devil in their dancing. A fourth woman (Jillana) seems subtly distant from her partner (Conrad Ludlow).

In the second part, the relationships become more abstract but deeper, much like the second set of songs of the more mature Brahms. The setting, now dominated by the night sky, becomes almost cosmic in feeling. Lifts soar as do the dancers' leaps; pulses quicken with the speed of pointe work. For the first time, couples are alone on stage, often for extended sections encompassing several songs. Occasionally they dance solo, but always for each other. The men's adoration and pursuit of the women becomes even more passionate.

Then, magically, the candles rekindle and we return to the real room. The dancers re-gather—the women again attired in their ballgowns—to listen quietly to a final song, the only one with words by Goethe. While Balanchine has chosen not to

Liebeslieder Walzer, with Patricia McBride and Joseph Duell, New York City Ballet, 1984

reflect the conventional words of the earlier songs, he emphasizes this one, which translates: "Now, Muses, enough! You try in vain to portray how misery and happiness alternate in a loving heart." The dancers applaud the musicians as the curtain falls.

Although Balanchine is often regarded as a choreographer for the young, this magical ballet tells of mature love, and it was made on women who were mature artists. While the men's role here is primarily to adore them, the women show complexity and mystery of feelings that come only with experience.

The 1960 *Liebeslieder Walzer* was the second of Balanchine's three varied and deeply expressive major waltz ballets, along with the apocalyptic 1951 *La Valse* and the sweeping 1977 *Vienna Waltzes*.

The 1984 revival of *Liebeslieder Walzer* by the New York City Ballet was a milestone for the company in the period after Balanchine's death. The ballet had not been performed for a number of years, partly due to the cost of good singers, but also because of the delicate problem of casting the eight roles properly. Furthermore, the intimate set by David Hays, which suited the City Center stage for which it was created, was overwhelmed by the scale of the New York State Theater when the company moved there. For the new production, a handsome set was commissioned from David Mitchell, based on a rococo salon in the Amalienburg pavilion in Munich in accordance with the wish Balanchine had expressed on seeing it in 1971. Karinska's costumes were recreated. The new production was supervised by Karin von Aroldingen, who had often danced in *Liebeslieder* and whose sense of German culture Balanchine appreciated. The first cast was considered a total success, consisting of Kyra Nichols (Verdy's role) and Joseph Duell; Suzanne Farrell (Adams) and Sean Lavery; Patricia McBride (Hayden) and Bart Cook; and Stephanie Saland (Jillana) and Ib Andersen.

—Marilyn Hunt

LIED VON DER ERDE *see* **SONG OF THE EARTH**

LIEPA, Andris

Russian/Soviet dancer. Born Andris Marisov Liepa, son of dancer Maris Liepa, in Moscow, 6 January 1962. Studied at the Moscow Choreographic School, pupil of Aleksandr Prokofiev, from 1971; graduated in 1981. Dancer, Bolshoi Ballet, from 1981, becoming soloist, from 1983, and principal dancer, from 1983; guest artist, New York City Ballet, 1988, and American Ballet Theatre, New York, 1988–89; principal dancer, Kirov Ballet, Leningrad, from 1989, and permanent guest artist, Bolshoi Ballet, Moscow, from 1990; has also performed with the Paris Opéra Ballet, La Scala (with Carla Fracci), Milan, 1990, and Béjart's Ballet du XXe Siècle, 1991; also collaborator, with Isabelle Fokine, in restoration of various Diaghilev/Fokine ballets for the Russian stage. Recipient: Gold Medal, Junior Division, Moscow International Ballet Competition, 1981; Silver Medal, Senior Division, Moscow International Ballet Competition, 1985; Grand Prix, International Ballet Competition, Jackson, Mississippi, 1986; title of Honoured Artist of the Russian Federation, 1986.

ROLES

1980 Franz in *Coppélia* (Gorsky; staged Golovkina), Bolshoi School Production, Palace of Congresses, Moscow
1983 Salieri in *Mozart and Salieri* (Boccadoro), Bolshoi Ballet, Moscow
Benedict in *Love for Love* (Boccadoro), Bolshoi Ballet, Moscow
Nerso in *Gayané* (Vainonen), Bolshoi Ballet, Moscow
Soloist (cr), in "Tango", *Biographical Fragments* (Vasiliev), in "Image of Ulanova" Evening, Moscow
1984 The Prince in *The Wooden Prince* (Petrov), Bolshoi Ballet, Moscow
The Prince in *The Nutcracker* (Grigorovich), Bolshoi Ballet, Moscow
1985 Egor in *Kalina Krasnaya* (Petrov), Bolshoi Ballet, Moscow
Kurbsky in *Ivan the Terrible* (Grigorovich), Bolshoi Ballet, Moscow
Albrecht in *Giselle* (Petipa after Coralli, Perrot; staged Grigorovich), Bolshoi Ballet, Kremlin Palace of Congress, Moscow
1986 Boris in *The Golden Age* (Grigorovich), Bolshoi Ballet, Paris
Jean de Brienne in *Raymonda* (Grigorovich after Petipa, Gorsky), Bolshoi Ballet, Paris
Prince Siegfried in *Swan Lake* (Grigorovich after Petipa, Ivanov), Bolshoi Ballet, Tbilisi
1987 Prince Désiré in *The Sleeping Beauty* (Grigorovich after Petipa), Bolshoi Ballet, Moscow
Romeo in *Romeo and Juliet* (Grigorovich), Bolshoi Ballet, Moscow
1988 Principal dancer in *Raymonda Variations* (Balanchine), New York City Ballet, New York
Principal dancer in *Symphony in C* (Balanchine), New York City Ballet, New York
Title role in *Apollo* (Balanchine), New York City Ballet, New York
Title role in *Le Spectre de la rose* (Fokine), Bolshoi Ballet, Moscow
Solor in "The Kingdom of the Shades" from *La Bayadère* (Petipa), Bolshoi Ballet, Moscow
Prince Siegfried in *Swan Lake* (Baryshnikov after Petipa, Ivanov), American Ballet Theatre, New York
Principal dancer in *Ballet Imperial* (Balanchine), American Ballet Theatre, New York
1989 Romeo in *Romeo and Juliet* (MacMillan), American Ballet Theatre, New York
Principal dancer in *Les Sylphides* (Fokine), American Ballet Theatre, New York
Principal dancer in *Violin Concerto* (Balanchine), American Ballet Theatre, New York
1990 Solor in *La Bayadère* (Petipa), Kirov Ballet, Leningrad
Title role (cr) in *Petrushka* (second version; Vinogradov), Kirov Ballet, Paris
Ali in *Le Corsaire* (Petipa), Kirov Ballet, Leningrad
Prince Siegfried in *Swan Lake* (Nureyev after Petipa, Ivanov), Opéra Ballet, Paris
Soloist in *Song of a Wayfarer* (Béjart), Ballet du XXe Siècle, Lausanne
Title role in *Macbeth* (revival; Vasiliev), Ballet Theatre of the Kremlin Palace of Congresses, Moscow
1991 Prince (cr) in *Cinderella* (Vasiliev), Ballet Theatre of the Kremlin Palace of Congresses, Moscow
Romeo in *Romeo and Juliet* (Lavrovsky; staged Baltacheev, Semenov, Utreskaya), Kirov Ballet, Leningrad

Andris Liepa in *Ivan The Terrible*, Bolshoi Ballet

PUBLICATIONS

"Le Jeune Garde, Bolshoi de Moscow", *Danser* (Paris), October 1986

Verdy, Violette, "Violette Verdy on the Bolshoi", *Ballet Review* (New York), Summer 1987

Flatow, Sheryl, "Ananiashvili and Liepa", *Dance Magazine* (New York), June 1988

Roth, Claudia Pierpont, "Clio's Revenge", *Ballet Review* (New York), Spring 1988

Cournand, Gilberte, "Andris Liepa: Un Parcours sans faute", *Les Saisons de la danse* (Paris), May 1990

"Travelling Men", *Dance and Dancers* (London), August 1990

Alovert, Nina, "Andris Liepa: Romeo . . .", *Dance Magazine* (New York), July 1992

* * *

Andris Liepa is a product of the famous Bolshoi academy, the Moscow Choreographic School, where he studied for eight years. On graduation, he became a member of the Bolshoi Ballet, working his way up from corps de ballet to leading roles. His soft, lyrical style, combined with his handsome looks and fine physique, have made him a natural choice for the classical roles. He has a light, sharp jeté, a well-placed high arabesque, an easy jump which ends in deep plié, and a generous and open port de bras. He is a solicitous partner, gentle but watchful, yet

also demonstrates a commanding presence on stage.

Liepa is recognized as a hard worker. His dedication, talent, and thoughtful approach to his roles are much sought-after and appreciated. He has appeared with many of the top ballet companies of the world, and has spent a year with the American Ballet Theatre as a company member, the first Soviet to win a contract abroad and still be able to return home.

Liepa's partnership with the beautiful and talented ballerina Nina Ananiashvili began in early schooldays and flourished for several seasons at the Bolshoi. On stage, their sparkling techniques and exciting, enthusiastic personalities complemented each other. They looked charming together—Nina a Georgian beauty, dark-haired and sophisticated, Andris a blonde and boyish Slav. This youthful romantic image sparked the imaginations of audiences and the two became a popular pair both at home and on tour. Together they entered several international competitions and won many prizes as a partnership.

In 1988, Liepa and Ananiashvili became the first Soviets to be given official permission to dance as guests with an American company. They were invited to New York by Peter Martins, co-director of the New York City Ballet, to perform three works by founder and compatriot, George Balanchine. In three weeks they had to absorb and assimilate a new dance vocabulary, one which used speed, precision footwork, and tricky off-balance poses in contrast to the expansive and lyrical style of their Russian heritage. Hard work and, perhaps more important, enthusiasm for the new, made the experience a success.

Six months later, Liepa made ballet history again by taking advantage of Mikhail Gorbachev's "glastnost" to seek new professional horizons outside his own country. He was given official permission to accept a contract with the American Ballet Theatre, whose director at that time was Mikhail Baryshnikov. In his season with ABT, Liepa found himself dancing more leading roles than he had done in seven years with the Bolshoi. This "leap" to freedom—to establish his own freelance career—enabled Liepa to work in the West yet return home to Russia whenever he pleased—unlike his earlier compatriots, Nureyev, Makarova, and Baryshnikov, who had to defect for the sake of their art.

On Liepa's return to Moscow in December 1989, he found that his old job at the Bolshoi was no longer available—due perhaps to the fear that his re-admission would encourage other dancers to leave for short-term careers in the West and thus deplete the ranks on the Bolshoi stage. Hence Liepa went to Leningrad and asked the artistic director of the Kirov Ballet, Oleg Vinogradov, for work as a guest artist. He immediately proved himself in a gala honouring the great dancer Vaslav Nijinsky, where he performed *Le Spectre de la rose* with Olga Likhovskaya. (A Soviet critic wrote of his performance: "Liepa was a miracle, the embodiment of the spirit of the evening—elegant, soft, airy, a wonderful partner.") He also danced two performances of *Giselle* with the company.

The move to Leningrad was another "first": previously dancers have gone the other way—from Kirov to Bolshoi—the most notable being Galina Ulanova. For the Kirov's French tour in the spring of 1990, Liepa was given the leading role in the premiere of Vinogradov's modern "perestroika" version of the Fokine ballet *Petrushka*, as well as leading classical roles. When the exotic and popular Tartar dancer Farukh Ruzimatov left the Kirov and followed Liepa's footsteps to ABT, the door was open for Liepa to be the superstar of the Kirov's 1990 British summer season.

He was subsequently invited by Maurice Béjart, founder and director of Le Ballet du XXe Siècle, to work with his company in Lausanne, Switzerland, with the understanding that Liepa would be able to continue working with the Bolshoi as a "permanent guest artist". Sadly, injury has prevented Liepa from fulfilling that and various other subsequent engagements. He remains active, however, as a producer, collaborating with Isabelle Fokine in restoring Diaghilev ballets for the Russian stage.

Andris Liepa was born into one of the Soviet Union's most famous theatrical families, which originally came from Latvia. His grandfather worked in the theatre, his father, Maris Liepa, was one of the Bolshoi's most famous dancers who won the Lenin Prize for his role as Crassus in *Spartacus*, and his mother, Margarita Zhigunova, is a celebrated repertory actress who performs regularly in films and at Moscow's Pushkin Theatre.

—Margaret Willis

LIEPA, Maris

Russian/Soviet dancer. Born Maris Rudolf Eduardovich Liepa in Riga, 27 July 1936. Studied at the Choreographic School in Riga, pupil of V. Blinov, 1947–50, and at the Moscow Choreographic School, pupil of Nikolai Tarasov, 1953–55. Married (1) Bolshoi ballerina Maya Plisetskaya; (2) actress Margarita Zhingunova: 2 children, Ilsa and dancer Andris Liepa, b. 1962. Soloist, Latvian Theatre of Opera and Ballet, Riga, 1955–56, Stanislavsky and Nemirovic–Danchenko Lyric Theatre Ballet, Moscow, 1956–60, Bolshoi Ballet, Moscow, 1960–77; also guest artist, Hungarian State Opera, Budapest, 1956; teacher, Moscow Choreographic School, 1963–80, artistic director, Theatre of Contemporary Musical Drama, Moscow, 1987–89; also appeared in several Soviet ballet films, including *Hamlet* (Moscow Central Television, 1969), *The Lion's Grave* (Byelorussian film; dir. Rubinchik, 1972), and *Galatea* (dir. Belinsky, 1977), and on video, including *Liepa Teaching* (1973) and *Spartacus* (Bolshoi Ballet, 1977); also choreographed *Music for a Birthday* for film (1980). Recipient: Title of People's Artist of the Russian Federation, 1969; Lenin Prize, 1970; title of Honoured Artist of the USSR, 1976; Nijinsky Prize, Paris, 1971; Marius Petipa Prize, Paris, 1977. Died in Moscow, 26 March 1989.

ROLES

1955   Tots in *Jewel of Liberty* (Changa), Theatre of Opera and Ballet, Riga

Soloist, "Grand Pas" from *Raymonda* (Petipa), Theatre of Opera and Ballet, Riga

Nikita in *Laima* (Tangieva-Beresnyak), Theatre of Opera and Ballet, Riga

1956   "Pas d'esclave" from *Le Corsaire* (Petipa), Theatre of Opera and Ballet, Riga

Prince Siegfried in *Swan Lake* (Messerer after Gorsky, Petipa, Ivanov), Festival of Hungarian–Russian Friendship, Hungarian Opera Theatre, Budapest

Vaslav in *The Fountain of Bakhchisarai* (Zakharov), Hungarian State Opera Ballet, Budapest

Phoebus in *Esmeralda* (Burmeister after Perrot, Petipa), Stanislavsky and Nemirovich–Danchenko Ballet, Moscow

1957   Lionel (cr) in *Joan of Arc* (Burmeister), Stanislavsky and Nemirovich–Danchenko Ballet, Moscow

Conrad (cr) in *Le Corsaire* (new production; Grishina after Petipa), Stanislavsky and Nemirovich–Danchenko Ballet, Moscow

1959   The Poet in *Straussiana* (Burmeister), Stanislavsky and Nemirovich–Danchenko Ballet, Moscow

Sinbad in *Schéhérazade* (Burmeister), Stanislavsky and Nemirovich–Danchenko Ballet, Moscow

1960   Chaban (cr) in *The Fairy of the Forest* (Chichinadze), Stanislavsky and Nemirovich–Danchenko Ballet, Moscow

Basil in *Don Quixote* (Gorsky after Petipa), Bolshoi Ballet, Moscow

Lenny in *The Path of Thunder* (Sergeyev), Bolshoi Ballet, Moscow

1961   The Youth (cr) in *Night City* (Lavrovsky), Bolshoi Ballet, Moscow

George (cr) in *Pages from a Life* (Lavrovsky), Bolshoi Ballet, Moscow

Vakh in *Walpurgis Night* (Lavrovsky), Bolshoi Ballet, Moscow

Albrecht in *Giselle* (Petipa after Coralli, Perrot, staged Lavrovsky), Bolshoi Ballet, Moscow

1962   Title role in *Spartacus* (Yakobson), Bolshoi Ballet, Moscow

Armen in *Gayané* (Vainonen), Bolshoi Ballet, Moscow

The Youth in *Chopiniana* (Geidenreich after Fokine), Bolshoi Ballet, Moscow

1963   Soloist (cr) in *Class Concert* (Messerer), Bolshoi Ballet, Moscow

Maris Liepa in *Spartacus* with Tatiana Golikova, Bolshoi Ballet, Moscow, 1974

The Prince in *Cinderella* (Zakharov), Bolshoi Ballet, Moscow

Jean de Brienne in *Raymonda* (Lavrovsky after Petipa, Gorsky), Bolshoi Ballet, Moscow

The Prince in *The Sleeping Beauty* (Grigorovich after Petipa), Bolshoi Ballet, Moscow

Romeo in *Romeo and Juliet* (Lavrovsky), Bolshoi Ballet, Moscow

1964   The Devil in *The Soldier's Tale* (Suve), Bolshoi Ballet, Moscow

1965   Farkhad (cr) in *The Legend of Love* (Moscow version; Grigorovich), Bolshoi Ballet, Moscow

1967   Vaslav in *The Fountain of Bakhchisarai* (Zakharov), Bolshoi Ballet, Moscow

Title role in *Le Spectre de la rose* (also chor., after Fokine), Bolshoi Ballet, Moscow

1968   Crassus (cr) in *Spartacus* (Grigorovich), Bolshoi Ballet, Moscow

1972   Vronsky (cr) in *Anna Karenina* (Plisetskaya, Ryzhenko, Smirnov-Golovanov), Bolshoi Ballet, Moscow

1974   Prince Désiré in *The Sleeping Beauty* (Grigorovich after Petipa), Bolshoi Ballet, Moscow

1976   Karenin in *Anna Karenina* (Plisetskaya, Ryzhenko, Smirnov-Golovanov), Bolshoi Ballet, Moscow

1977   Prince Lemon in *Chippolino* (Maiorov), Bolshoi Ballet, Moscow

WORKS

Staged:
1967   *Le Spectre de la rose* (after Fokine; mus. Weber), Bolshoi Ballet, Moscow

1971   Dances in *Antony and Cleopatra* (play by Shakespeare; dir. Simonov), Vachtangov Theatre, Moscow

1979   *Don Quixote* (after Petipa, Gorsky), Dnepropetrovsk Theatre, Dnepropetrovsk

PUBLICATIONS

By Liepa:
"Urge for Flight", *Moskva* (Moscow), no. 3, 1976

"News from Russia", *Dance Magazine* (New York), January 1976

"News from the Soviet Union", *Dance Magazine* (New York), August 1976

"A Word About the Teacher" in Tarasov, Nikolai, *Ballet Technique for the Male Dancer*, translated by Elizabeth Kraft, New York, 1985

Interview in Kokich, Kim, "A Conversation with the Liepas", *Ballet Review* (New York), Summer 1987

About Liepa:

Avdeenko, A., "Maris Liepa", *Dancing Times* (London), January 1973

Barnes, Patricia (text) and Mira (photographs), *Maris Liepa*, Brooklyn, N.Y., 1975

Roslavleva, Natalia, *Marius Liepa*, Moscow, 1978

Demidov, Alexander, *The Russian Ballet Past and Present*, translated by Guy Daniels, London, 1978

Parks, Gary, "Soviet Artist in New Works", *Dance Magazine* (New York), July 1987

* * *

When a man dies of a heart attack at the age of 52, it could be said that he burned himself out. If one takes a good look at Maris Liepa's creative life, starting from the time he was a schoolboy, one can see the best example there is of this type of self-immolation. Talent, energy, ambition, a rare capacity for work—everything melted in this fire.

Maris's father, Eduard Liepa, worked as a stage manager at the Riga Opera and sent his son to choreography school where, in addition to physically rigorous ballet lessons, the boy also took up swimming. Sports competitions brought victories and, with them, happiness. Three times while still an adolescent Maris Liepa broke the record in Latvia for long-distance free-style swimming.

At one of the matches he was spotted by a group of instructors from the Moscow School of Choreography, who remembered that they had seen him as one of the troubadours in the ballet *Romeo and Juliet* at the Riga Theatre, and they invited him to come to Moscow. Thus, in 1953, Maris Liepa became a student at the Moscow School under Nikolai Ivanovich Tarasov. At first the instructors had in mind to make Liepa a character dancer. But he worked hard, completed his studies as a classical dancer, and went right back to his native theatre in Riga.

A year later there was an unexpected invitation from Moscow to go to Budapest to dance in *Swan Lake* (which had been the dancer's dream since he was a schoolboy) with Maya Plisetskaya. Fate had it that Maris Liepa then danced four different versions of *Swan Lake* by four different choreographers: Messerer, Tangieva-Beresnyak, Burmeister, and Grigorovich. And in each new version of *Swan Lake* he brought a new interpretation of the Prince to the stage.

In 1956 Liepa became a premier danseur with the Stanislavsky and Nemirovich–Danchenko Lyric Theatre in Moscow. He said of this period in his artistic career, "I started to understand myself in art and to understand art when I got to the Stanislavsky and Nemirovich–Danchenko Theatre." In 1960 Liepa went to work at the Bolshoi Theatre. The time of study and self-discovery had come to an end, and this was the beginning of his artistic maturity and creative blossoming.

In the three years before he came to the theatre of the new chief ballet master, Yuri Grigorovich, Liepa had danced all of the most popular "choreodrama" roles and many roles from the classical repertoire. The role of Albrecht in *Giselle* came to be not only one of the favourites in the artist's repertoire but, along with Basil in *Don Quixote*, his most significant work in classical ballet.

He reached the pinnacle of his artistry in Yuri Grigorovich's ballets *The Legend of Love* and *Spartacus*. The ballet master had conceived of the ballet *The Legend of Love*, to the music of Melikov, for the company of the Kirov Theatre, and then brought it to the Bolshoi Theatre, taking the role of the artist Ferkhad and making it over for Liepa. Liepa's masculine and passionate Ferkhad was simultaneously a tragic man and a national hero.

The role of Crassus was born in the course of the choreographer's and the performer's work together. It was this role that revealed the extent of Liepa's ability to express himself in every nuance of physical beauty and to render every leap and every pirouette intelligible and expressive. Liepa's Crassus was undeniably magnetic, both in the scenes of his might and triumph, and in the scenes of his humiliation and base villainy. He was a genuine patrician and an outstanding individual, an almost romantic villain—a worthy opponent and foil to Spartacus.

The role of the Devil in Stravinsky's *Soldier's Tale* stands apart in Liepa's career. The extraordinary role of the Devil required nine reincarnations. Not only did Liepa manage to cope with the intricate, rhythmically complex music better than anyone else; in this difficult role he was even able to speak while dancing.

Work on a given repertoire, however, did not deplete all of Liepa's energy. He worked for six years on a revival of Fokine's ballet *Le Spectre de la rose*. While on tour abroad Liepa discussed Fokine's masterpiece with any and all performers (including Karsavina herself) who remembered it, comparing variations and analyzing various choreographic readings.

Several films were made of Liepa's performance in ballets, and he also appeared in action films and feature films. He appeared in ballet performances at the Boris Eifman Theatre in Leningrad and went on numerous concert tours throughout the Soviet Union and abroad. He was greatly loved in the West, especially in England and America, and he is remembered to this day.

Liepa's death and his departure from the stage—unjustly early in the ballet world—are an irreplaceable loss. But the artistry of every important performer lives on after his departure from the stage. A genuine creator, which is what Liepa was, perforce leaves his mark, his lustre, on all of the roles that he performed. That which Liepa discovered in the roles of Basil or Crassus, for example, will most assuredly continue to make its way into the performance of future generations of dancers at the Bolshoi Theatre. This is the way that artistic tradition develops, grows richer, and comes to perfection in ballet. And that is why it is unthinkable that the future of the Bolshoi Theatre will not somehow include the creative energy and artistic individuality of Maris Liepa.

—Nina Alovert

LIFAR, Serge

Russian/French dancer, choreographer, ballet director, and writer. Born in Kiev, 2 April 1905. Studied with Bronislava Nijinska in Kiev, 1921–23; later studied with Nikolai (Nicholas) Legat, Enrico Cecchetti, and Pierre Vladimirov. Dancer, corps de ballet, Diaghilev's Ballets Russes, 1923–24, becoming soloist from 1924, and premier danseur, 1925–29; first choreography Ballets Russes, 1929; premier danseur étoile, choreographer, and ballet director, Paris Opéra, 1929–44, also working as choreographer and dancer, Cochran's Revue, London, 1930, and guest artist, (Denham's) Ballet Russe de Monte Carlo, 1938–39; left Paris, 1944: premier danseur and choreographer, Nouveau Ballet de Monte Carlo, 1944–47; founder, Institute Chorégraphique de l'Opéra (later the Académie des Chorégraphies), 1947; director and premier danseur, Paris Opéra Ballet, 1947–58; guest choreographer and producer, restaging works worldwide including for Paris Opéra, 1962–63, Teatro Colón, Buenos Aires, 1962 and 1964, as well as in Finland, 1964 and 1965, Peru 1965, Sweden, 1967, Turkey, 1968, and Portugal, 1969; also prolific writer on dance and dance history, publishing over 25 books; founder, Université de la danse, 1957; Member of Académie des Beaux Arts, 1968. Recipient: Carina Ari Medal, 1974. Died in Lausanne, 15 December 1986.

ROLES

1924 Un policier (cr) in *Les Fâcheux* (Nijinska), Diaghilev's
        Ballets Russes, Monte Carlo
        A Gigolo (cr) in *Le Train bleu* (Nijinska), Diaghilev's
        Ballets Russes, Paris
        Shop Assistant in *La Boutique fantasque* (Massine),
        Diaghilev's Ballets Russes
        Dancer (cr) in *Cimarosiana* (Massine), Diaghilev's
        Ballets Russes, Monte Carlo
1925 Borée (cr) in *Zéphire et Flore* (Massine), Diaghilev's
        Ballets Russes, Monte Carlo
        A Sailor (cr) in *Les Matelots* (Massine), Diaghilev's
        Ballets Russes, Paris
        An Officer (cr) in *Barabau* (Balanchine), Diaghilev's
        Ballets Russes, London
1926 Romeo (cr) in *Romeo and Juliet* (Nijinska, Balanchine),
        Diaghilev's Ballets Russes, Monte Carlo
        Telegraph Boy (cr) in *Pastorale* (Balanchine), Diaghi-
        lev's Ballets Russes, Paris
        Tom Tug, A Sailor (cr) in *The Triumph of Neptune*
        (Balanchine), Diaghilev's Ballets Russes, London
        The Faun in *L'Après-midi d'un faune* (Nijinsky), Diaghi-
        lev's Ballets Russes, London
        Ivan Tsarevich in *L'Oiseau de feu* (Fokine), Diaghilev's
        Ballets Russes, London
        Prince Siegfried in *Swan Lake* (one-act version; Petipa,
        Ivanov; staged Fokine), Diaghilev's Ballets Russes,
        London
        Dancer (cr) in *Le Sacre du printemps* (Massine),
        Diaghilev's Ballets Russes, Paris
        Prince Désiré in *Le Mariage d'Aurore* (divertissement
        from *The Sleeping Beauty*; Petipa, Nijinska), Diaghi-
        lev's Ballets Russes
        Principal dancer ("The Poet") in *Les Sylphides* (Fo-
        kine), Diaghilev's Ballets Russes
1927 The Young Man (cr) in *La Chatte* (Balanchine),
        Diaghilev's Ballets Russes, Monte Carlo
        Principal dancer ("A Worker") (cr) in *Pas d'acier*
        (Massine), Diaghilev's Ballets Russes, Paris
1928 The Student (cr) in *Ode* (Massine), Diaghilev's Ballets
        Russes, Paris
        Apollo (cr) in *Apollon musagète* (Balanchine), Diaghi-
        lev's Ballets Russes, Paris
        The Moor in *Petrushka* (Fokine), Diaghilev's Ballets
        Russes
1929 Italian Entrée (cr) in *Le Bal* (Balanchine), Diaghilev's
        Ballets Russes, Monte Carlo
        Title role (cr) in *Le Fils prodigue* (Balanchine), Diaghi-
        lev's Ballets Russes, Paris
        Prometheus (cr) in *Les Créatures de Promethée* (also
        chor.), Paris Opéra Ballet, Paris
1930 The Six-armed Man (cr) in *Luna Park*, A Highlander
        (cr) in *Picadilly 1830*, The Lover (cr) in *Heaven* (all
        chor. Balanchine), Charles B. Cochran's 1930 Revue,
        London
        Principal dancer (cr) in *La Nuit* (also chor.), Charles B.
        Cochran's 1930 Revue, London

Serge Lifar as Apollo in *Apollon musagète*, Diaghilev's Ballets Russes, 1928

1931 Principal dancer (cr) in *Prélude dominical* (also chor.),
        Paris Opéra Ballet, Paris
        Principal dancer (cr) in *L'Orchestre en liberté* (also
        chor.), Paris Opéra Ballet, Paris
        Bacchus (cr) in *Bacchus et Ariadne* (also chor.), Paris
        Opéra Ballet, Paris
        Principal dancer (cr) in *Suite de danses* (also chor., after
        Clustine), Paris Opéra Ballet, Paris
        Title role (cr) in *Le Spectre de la rose* (also chor., after
        Fokine), Paris Opéra Ballet, Paris
1932 Albrecht in *Giselle* (Petipa after Coralli, Perrot; staged
        Lifar), Paris Opéra Ballet, Paris
        Bluebird Variation in *Divertissement* (from *The Sleeping
        Beauty*; also chor., after Petipa), Paris Opéra Ballet,
        Paris
        Principal dancer (cr) in *Sur le Borysthène* (also chor.),
        Paris Opéra Ballet, Paris
1933 Principal dancer (cr) in *Jeunesse* (also chor.), Paris
        Opéra Ballet, Paris
        Principal dancer (cr) in *Giration* (Lifar), Gala, Théâtre
        des Champs-Elysées, Paris

1934 Polichinelle (cr) in *La Vie de Polichinelle* (also chor.), Paris Opéra Ballet, Paris
Daphnis in *Daphnis et Chloé* (also chor., after Fokine), Paris Opéra Ballet, Paris

1935 Pulcinella (cr) in *Salade* (Lifar), Paris Opéra Ballet, Paris
Faune (cr) in *Prelude à l'après-midi d'un faune* (solo version; also chor.) Paris Opéra Ballet, Paris
Title role (cr) in *Icare* (also chor.), Paris Opéra Ballet, Paris

1936 Prince Siegfried in *Swan Lake* (Act II; also chor., after Ivanov), Paris Opéra Ballet, Paris
Principal dancer (cr) in *Jurupary* (also chor.), Gala, Salle Pleyel, Paris
Principal dancer (cr) in *Harnasie* (also chor.), Paris Opéra Ballet, Paris
Title role (cr) in *Le Roi nu* (also chor.), Paris Opéra Ballet, Paris
Principal dancer (cr) in *Promenades dans Rome* (also chor.), Paris Opéra Ballet, Paris

1937 Title role (cr) in *David triomphant* (also chor.), Paris Opéra Ballet, Paris
Title role (cr) in *Alexandre le Grand* (also chor.), Paris Opéra Ballet, Paris

1938 Prince (cr) in *Oriane et le Prince d'amour* (also chor.), Paris Opéra Ballet, Paris
Principal dancer (cr) in *Le Cantique des cantiques* (also chor.), Paris Opéra Ballet, Paris
Title role (cr) in *Ænéas* (also chor.), Paris Opéra Ballet, Paris
Principal dancer (cr) in *Adélaïde* (also chor.), Paris Opéra Ballet, Paris

1940 Apollo (cr) in *Entre deux rondes* (also chor.), Paris Opéra Ballet, Paris

1941 Aminta (cr) in *Sylvia* (also chor.), Paris Opéra Ballet, Paris
The Knight Errant (cr) in *Le Chevalier et la damoiselle* (also chor.), Paris Opéra Ballet, Paris
Principal dancer (cr) in *Boléro* (also chor.), Paris Opéra Ballet, Paris
Life (cr) in *Istar* (also chor.), Paris Opéra Ballet, Paris

1942 Title role (cr) in *Joan de Zarissa* (also chor.), Paris Opéra Ballet, Paris
Principal dancer (cr) in *Les Animaux modèles* (also chor.), Paris Opéra Ballet, Paris
Romeo (cr) in *Roméo et Juliette* (pas de deux; also chor.), Salle Pleyel, Paris

1943 The Ghost (cr) in *L'Amour sorcier* (also chor.), Paris Opéra Ballet, Paris
Principal dancer (cr) in *Le Jour* (also chor.), Paris Opéra Ballet, Paris
Principal dancer (cr) in *Suite en blanc* (also chor.), Paris Opéra Ballet, Zurich
Principal dancer (cr) in *Prière* (also chor.), Paris Opéra Ballet, Paris

1944 Guignol (cr) in *Guignol et Pandore* (also chor.), Paris Opéra Ballet, Paris

1946 The Hunter (cr) in *La Mort du cygne* (Lifar), Nouveau Ballet de Monte Carlo, Monte Carlo
Title role (cr) in *Chota Roustaveli* (also chor.), Nouveau Ballet de Monte Carlo, Monte Carlo
Principal dancer (cr) in *Dramma per musica* (also chor.), Nouveau Ballet de Monte Carlo, Monte Carlo

1949 Roméo (cr) in *Roméo et Juliette* (also chor.), Opéra, Paris
Premier danseur (cr) in *Ballet de cour* (also chor.), Versailles

1950 Principal dancer (cr) in *L'Inconnue* (also chor.), Paris Opéra Ballet, Paris
Title role (cr) in *Le Chevalier errant* (also chor.), Paris Opéra Ballet, Paris
Hippolytus (cr) in *Phèdre* (also chor.), Paris Opéra Ballet, Paris
Principal dancer (cr) in *Les Éléments* (also chor.), Paris Opéra Ballet, Paris

1951 The Huntsman (cr) in *Blanche-Neige* (also chor.), Paris Opéra Ballet, Paris

1952 Principal dancer (cr) in *Fourberies* (also chor.), Paris Opéra Ballet, Paris

1953 Charlot (cr) in *Cinéma* (also chor.), Paris Opéra Ballet, Paris

1954 Principal dancer (cr) in *L'Oiseau de feu* (also chor.), Paris Opéra Ballet, Paris
Pas de quatre (cr) in *Divertissement* (also chor.), Versailles

1955 Friar Laurence (cr) in *Roméo et Juliette* (also chor.), Paris Opéra Ballet, Paris
Principal dancer (cr) in *Tentation* (also chor.), Aix-les-Bains

1956 Louis XIV (cr) in *Divertissement à la cour* (also chor.), Paris Opéra Ballet, Monte Carlo

Other roles include: for Ballet Russe de Monte Carlo (guest artist)—leading roles in *Nobilissima Visione* (St. Francis; Massine), *Schéhérazade* (Fokine).

WORKS

1929 *Renard* (new version of Massine ballet; mus. Stravinsky), Diaghilev's Ballets Russes, Paris
Les Créatures de Promethée (mus. Beethoven), Paris Opéra Ballet, Paris

1930 *La Nuit* (mus. Sauguet), Charles B. Cochran's 1930 Revue, London

1931 *Prélude dominical* (mus. Ropartz), Paris Opéra Ballet, Paris
L'Orchestre en liberté (mus. Sauveplane), Paris Opéra Ballet, Paris
Bacchus et Ariadne (mus. Roussel), Paris Opéra Ballet, Paris
Le Spectre de la rose (after Fokine; mus. Weber), Paris Opéra Ballet, Paris

1932 *Sur le Borysthène* (mus. Prokofiev), Paris Opéra Ballet, Paris

1933 *Jeunesse* (mus. Ferroud), Paris Opéra Ballet, Paris
Giration (mus. Pierné), Gala, Théâtre des Champs-Elysées, Paris

1934 *La Vie de Polichinelle* (mus. Nabokov), Paris Opéra Ballet, Paris

1935 *Salade* (mus. Milhaud), Paris Opéra Ballet, Paris
Prélude à l'après-midi d'un faune (mus. Debussy), Paris Opéra Ballet, Paris
Icare (mus. Szyfer), Paris Opéra Ballet, Paris (restaged Ballet Russe de Monte Carlo, 1938)

1936 *Jurupary* (mus. Villa-Lobos), Gala, Salle Pleyel, Paris
Harnasie (mus. Szymanovsky), Paris Opéra Ballet, Paris
Le Roi nu (mus. Francaix), Paris Opéra Ballet, Paris
Promenades dans Rome (mus. Samuel-Rousseau), Paris Opéra Ballet, Paris

1937 *David triomphant* (mus. Rieti), Paris Opéra Ballet, Paris
Alexander le Grand (mus. Gaubert), Paris Opéra Ballet, Paris
La Mort du cygne (mus. Chopin), French film

1938   *Oriane et le Prince d'amour* (mus. Schmitt), Paris Opéra Ballet, Paris
    Le Cantique des cantiques (mus. Honegger), Paris Opéra Ballet, Paris
    Æneas (mus. Roussel), Paris Opéra Ballet, Paris
    Adélaïde (mus. Ravel), Paris Opéra Ballet, Paris

1940   *Entre deux rondes* (mus. Rousseau), Paris Opéra Ballet, Paris
    Pavane (new version of Massine's *Las Meninias*; mus. Fauré), Original Ballet Russe, Sydney

1941   *Sylvia* (mus. Delibes), Paris Opéra Ballet, Paris
    La Princesse au jardin (mus. Grovlez), Paris Opéra Ballet, Paris
    Le Chevalier et la damoiselle (mus. Gaubert), Paris Opéra Ballet, Paris
    Istar (mus. d'Indy), Paris Opéra Ballet, Paris
    Boléro (mus. Ravel), Paris Opéra Ballet, Paris

1942   *Joan de Zarissa* (mus. Egk), Paris Opéra Ballet, Paris
    Roméo et Juliette (pas de deux; mus. Tchaikovsky), Salle Pleyel, Paris
    Eugène Onéguine (mus. Tchaikovsky), Salle Pleyel, Paris
    Les Animaux modèles (mus. Poulenc), Paris Opéra Ballet, Paris

1943   *L'Amour sorcier* (mus. de Falla), Paris Opéra Ballet, Paris
    Le Jour (mus. Jaubert), Paris Opéra Ballet, Paris
    Suite en blanc (mus. Lalo), Paris Opéra Ballet, Zurich
    Persée (pas de deux; mus. Debussy), Gala, Paris

1944   *Guignol et Pandore* (mus. Jolivet), Paris Opéra Ballet, Paris
    Les Mirages (mus. Sauguet), Paris Opéra Ballet, Paris
    Syrinx (mus. Debussy), Gala, Paris

1945   *Mephisto Valse* (mus. Liszt), Gala, Paris

1946   *Aubade* (mus. Poulenc), Nouveau Ballet de Monte Carlo, Monte Carlo
    Salomé (mus. Strauss), Nouveau Ballet de Monte Carlo, Monte Carlo
    A la mémoire d'un héros (mus. Beethoven), Nouveau Ballet de Monte Carlo, Monte Carlo
    La Péri (mus. Dukas), Nouveau Ballet de Monte Carlo, Monte Carlo
    Dramma per musica (mus. Bach), Nouveau Ballet de Monte Carlo, Monte Carlo
    Chota Roustaveli (mus. Honegger), Nouveau Ballet de Monte Carlo, Monte Carlo
    Une Nuit sur le mont chauve (mus. Mussorgsky), Nouveau Ballet de Monte Carlo, Monte Carlo
    Prière (mus. Beethoven), Nouveau Ballet de Monte Carlo, Monte Carlo

1947   *Nautéos* (mus. Leleu), Nouveau Ballet de Monte Carlo, Monte Carlo
    Pygmalion (mus. Prokofiev), Nouveau Ballet de Monte Carlo
    Passion (mus. Franck), Nouveau Ballet de Monte Carlo, Monte Carlo
    Les Contes de Hoffman (divertissement; mus. Offenbach), Nouveau Ballet de Monte Carlo, Monte Carlo
    Pavane pour une infante défunte (mus. Ravel), Paris Opéra Ballet, Paris

1948   *L'Écuyère* (mus. Kosma), Gala, Salle Pleyel, Paris
    Alborada del Gracioso (mus. Ravel), Gala, Théâtre des Champs-Elysées, Paris
    Le Pas d'acier (mus. Prokofiev), Gala, Théâtre des Champs-Elysées, Paris
    Daphnis et Chloé (mus. Stravinsky), La Scala, Milan
    La Valse (mus. Ravel), La Scala, Milan

    L'Enfant et les sortilèges (with Zverev; mus. Ravel), La Scala, Milan
    Zadig (mus. Petit), Paris Opéra Ballet, Paris
    Escales (mus. Ibert), Paris Opéra Ballet, Paris
    Lucifer (mus. Delvincourt), Paris Opéra Ballet, Paris

1949   *Fête polonaise* (mus. Chabrier), Opéra, Cannes
    Ballet de cour (mus. Rameau), Versailles
    Naissance des couleurs (with I. Popard) (mus. Honneger), Paris Opéra Ballet, Paris
    Endymion (mus. Lequerney), Paris Opéra Ballet, Paris

1950   *Septuor* (mus. Lutèce), Paris Opéra Ballet, Paris
    L'Inconnue (mus. Jolivet), Paris Opéra Ballet, Paris
    Le Chevalier errant (mus. Ibert), Paris Opéra Ballet, Paris
    Phèdre (mus. Auric), Paris Opéra Ballet, Paris
    La Pierre enchantée (mus. Auric), Gala, Palais de Chaillot, Paris
    Les Éléments (mus. Rebel), Versailles
    Rapsodie norvégienne (mus. Lalo), Opéra, Cannes

1951   *L'Astrologue* (mus. Barraud), Paris Opéra Ballet, Paris
    Blanche-Neige (mus. Yvain), Paris Opéra Ballet, Paris
    Roméo et Juliette (pas de deux; mus. Prokofiev), Salle Pleyel, Paris

1952   *Fourberies* (mus. Rossini, Aubin), Paris Opéra Ballet, Paris
    Le Turc généreux and *Les Sauvages* in *Les Indes galantes* (Lifar, Aveline, Lander, after Fuzelier 1735 libretto; mus. Rameau), Paris Opéra Ballet, Paris
    Trésor et magie (mus. Sauguet), Gala, Paris

1953   *Passionnata* (mus. Blareau), Danse et Culture, Paris
    Suite en ré (mus. Bach), Gala, J.M.F., Salle Pleyel, Paris
    Cinéma (mus. Aubert), Paris Opéra Ballet, Paris
    Variations (mus. Schubert, Aubin), Paris Opéra Ballet, Paris
    Grand Pas (mus. Brahms, Aubin), Paris Opéra Ballet, Paris
    Tannhäuser (*Romance à l'étoile*; mus. Wagner), Sorbonne
    Vision russe (mus. Mussorgsky), Sorbonne, Paris
    Danseuses de Delphes (mus. Debussy), Sorbonne, Paris
    Claire de lune (mus. Beethoven), Salle Pleyel, Paris

1954   *L'Oiseau de feu* (mus. Stravinsky), Paris Opéra Ballet, Paris
    Rondo Capriccioso (mus. Saint-Saëns), Gala, Enghein
    Pas et lignes (mus. Debussy), Aix-les-Bains Festival
    Nautéos (revised version; mus. Leleu), Paris Opéra Ballet, Paris

1955   *Nuages et fêtes* (mus. Debussy), Ballet de Janine Charrat
    Les Noces fantastiques (mus. Delannoy), Paris Opéra Ballet, Paris
    L'Âme et la danse (mus. Valéry), Gala, J.M.F., Salle Pleyel, Paris
    Romeo et Juliette (new version; mus. Prokofiev), Paris Opéra Ballet, Paris
    Tentation (mus. Blareau), Aix-les-Bains

1956   *Apollon musagète* (mus. Stravinsky), La Scala, Milan
    Divertissement à la cour (mus. Handel, Aubin), Paris Opéra Ballet, Monte Carlo

1957   *L'Eternel Amour* (mus. Strauss), Gala, Monte Carlo
    L'Indécise (mus. Boieldieu), Enghien Festival
    Hamlet; ou, Le Noble Fou (mus. Delannoy), Enghien Festival
    Symphonie classique (mus. Prokofiev), Gala, Nervi
    Adagio (mus. Albinoni), Gala, Monte Carlo
    Chemin de lumière (mus. Auric), Paris Opéra Ballet, Paris
    Idylle et jeux (mus. Ibert), Gala, Les Mans

Le Bel Indifferent (mus. Blareau), Gala, Monte Carlo
L'Amour et son destin (with Parlić; mus. Tchaikovsky), Grand Ballet du Marquis de Cuevas, Vienna

1958   *Duetto* (mus. Liszt), Grand Ballet du Marquis de Cuevas, Paris
Daphnis et Chloé (new version; mus. Ravel), Paris Opéra Ballet, Brussels
Francesca da Rimini (mus. Tchaikovsky), Ballet de France de Janine Charrat
Toi et moi (mus. Blareau), Monte Carlo

1959   *La Mort d'Yseult* (mus. Wagner), "Hommage à Serge Lifar", Opéra royal de Liège
L'Âme de la danse (mus. Rachmaninov), Marseilles

1960   *Le Maure à Venise* (mus. Thiriet), Netherlands Ballet, Monte Carlo
Études chorégraphiques (mus. Schumann), Netherlands Ballet, Paris
Bonaparte à Nice (mus. Thiriet), London Festival Ballet, Nice Festival
La Dame de pique (mus. Tchaikovsky), Opéra de Monte Carlo, Monte Carlo

1961   *On ne badine pas avec l'amour*, Opéra de Nice, Nice

1963   *Les Arbes meurent aussi* (mus. Tchaikovsky), French television

1964   *Fêtes d'Hébé* (mus. Rameau), Lyon Festival

1965   *Parade* (mus. Satie), Messidor Theatre, Toulouse
Divertissement (mus. Rameau), St. Gobain

1966   *Métamorphoses* (mus. Strauss), Gala, Salle Pleyel, Paris
Clé de sol (with L. Mail), Gala, Lille

1967   *Les Paladins* (with F. Adret; mus. Rameau), Lyon Festival

1969   *Constellations* (mus. Liszt), Paris Opéra Ballet, Paris
Le Grand Cirque (mus. Khachaturian), Paris Opéra Ballet, Paris
Fête chez le roi soleil (mus. Rameau), Nervi Festival

Also staged:

1932   *Giselle* (after Petipa, Coralli, Perrot; mus. Adam), Paris Opéra Ballet, Paris (also staged Ballet Russe de Monte Carlo, 1938)
Divertissement (divertissement after Petipa's *The Sleeping Beauty*; mus. Tchaikovsky), Paris Opéra Ballet, Paris

1934   *Daphnis et Chloé* (after Fokine; mus. Ravel), Paris Opéra Ballet, Paris

1936   *Swan Lake* (Act II, after Ivanov; mus. Tchaikovsky), Paris Opéra Ballet, Paris

1940   *Le Danube bleu* (restaging of Massine's *Le Beau Danube*; mus. J., J., and E. Strauss), Original Ballet Russe, Sydney

1955   *La Sylphide* (extracts, after Bournonville; mus. Schneitzhoffer), Sorbonne, Paris

Other works include: for concerts, performances, and galas—
Réversibilité (after Baudelaire; 1941), *Les Pas, Abeilles, Sylphes* (pas de deux, 1942), *Avant le bal* (mus. Schubert; 1943), *Symphonie printanière* (1943), *Persée* (mus. Debussy; 1943), *Danse orientale* (mus. Tcherepnine; 1943), *Anges* (mus. Bach; 1943), *Danses japonaises* (mus. Tcherepnine; 1943), *Plain-Chant* (1943), *Le Ciel est par-dessus le toit* (after Verlaine; 1943), *La Danse* (1943), *Diane* (mus. Chénier), *Trois Danseuses* (mus. Rosand; 1943), *Symphonie pastorale* (fragments, mus. Beethoven; 1944), *Allégresse* (mus. Poulenc; 1944), *La Nuit* (mus. Chénier; 1944), *Sospiro* (mus. Liszt; 1944), *Les Petits Riens* (mus. Mozart; 1945), *Réveil* (mus. Beethoven; 1945), *Carnet de bal* (mus. Auric; 1945), *La Pastourelle* (mus. Mozart; 1945), *Sunlight* (mus. Gershwin; 1946), *Danse monégasque* (1947),
Scènes de la forêt (mus. Schumann; 1947), *Gayaneh* (*Danse du sabre*; mus. Khachaturian; 1947), *Marche au supplice* (mus. Berlioz; 1947), *Sonnet de Pétrarque* (mus. Liszt; 1947), *Impromptu* (mus. Debussy; 1947), *Sarabande* (mus. Debussy; 1947), *Vol du bourdon* (mus. Rimsky-Korsakov; 1949), *Ballade* (mus. Chopin; 1949), *Le Pas d'armes du roi Jean* (mus. Saint-Saëns; 1949), *La Joie* (Verhaeren; 1949), *Hommage à Chopin* (mus. Chopin; 1949), *Printemps* (mus. Liszt; 1950), *Les Quatre Saisons* (mus. Glazunov; 1951), *La Chatte* (mus. Sauget; 1951), *Trésor et magie* (mus. Sauget; 1952), *Napoli* (mus. Liszt; 1953), *Can-Can* (mus. Ibert; 1953), *Trois Chants* (mus. popular; 1953), *Danse russe* (mus. Mussorgsky; 1953), *Le Chevalier Bayard* (1953), *Mystère de la passion* (1954), *Atropos* (mus. Roussel; 1954), *La Tempête* (mus. Sauget; 1955), *Flocon de neige* (mus. Tchaikovsky; 1956), *Mozart* (mus. Hahn; 1957), *Fête chez Thérèse* (mus. Hahn; 1957), *A la barre* (mus. Schubert; 1957), *Les Petits Rats de l'Opéra* (1958), *Défilé* (mus. Gluck; 1958).

PUBLICATIONS

By Lifar:
Le Manifeste du chorégraphe, Paris, 1935
Du temps que j'avais faim, Paris, 1935
Troisième Fête de Pouchkine, Paris, 1937
La Danse, Paris, 1938
Carlotta Grisi, Paris, 1941
Giselle, Paris, 1942
Terpsichore dans le cortège des muses, Paris, 1943
. . . A l'Opéra, Paris, 1943
Pensées sur la danse, Paris, 1946
A l'aube de mon destin. Sept Ans aux Ballets Russes, Paris, 1948
Traité de danse académique, Paris, 1949
Histoire du ballet russe, Paris, 1950
Vestris, dieu de la danse, Paris, 1950
Traité de chorégraphie, Paris, 1952
Méditations sur la danse, Paris, 1952
Dix ans de l'Opéra, 1929–1939, Paris, 1953
Serge de Diaghilev, Paris, 1954
Le Livre de la danse, Paris, 1954
La Musique pour la danse, Paris, 1955
Les Trois Graces du XXe siècle, Paris, 1957
Au service de la danse, Paris, 1958
Ma vie, 1965
La Danse académique et l'art chorégraphique, 1965
Memoires d'Icare, 1989 (posthumous)

About Lifar:
Levinson, André, *Les Visages de la danse*, Paris, 1929
Levinson, André, *Serge Lifar: Destin d'un danseur*, Paris, 1934
Augsbourg, G., *Serge Lifar*, 1937
Augsbourg, G., *Serge Lifar à l'Opéra*, 1943
Saillat, L., *Les Ballets de l'Opéra de Paris*, 3 volumes; Paris, 1943, 1947, 1957
Schaikevitch, A., *Serge Lifar et le ballet contemporain*, 1950
Laurent, Jean, and Sazanova, Julie, *Serge Lifar: Rénovateur du ballet français*, Paris, 1960
Tassart, Maurice, "The Serge Lifar Story", *Ballet Annual* (London), vol. 14, 1960
"Hommage à Serge Lifar", *Les Saisons de la danse* (Paris), February 1970
Schaikevitch, A., *Serge Lifar et le destin de ballet de l'Opéra*, Paris, 1971
Gruen, John, "Serge Lifar" in *Private World of Ballet*, New York, 1975
"Hommage à Serge Lifar", *Les Saisons de la danse* (Paris), January 1987

Serge Lifar remains one of the most fascinating and controversial personalities of twentieth-century ballet. If his exceptional beauty and his dazzling stage presence made him a star,
he also proved that he had a lively intelligence and sound
choreographic skills, as well as talents as a keen organizer and
director. His infectious enthusiasm, his impulsive nature, and
his daring outbursts simultaneously attracted admiration,
longstanding friendships, and lasting enmity. Indifferent to
events in daily life, Lifar very early on dedicated his life to
dance. Throughout the events of a dazzling career prematurely
disrupted by the intrusions of the outside world of politics (he
was obliged to leave Paris for some years immediately
following the liberation), he continued to assert his vocation in
all the ways he could, finding expression through his presence
as a dancer, his interest in choreographic research, his
authority as a ballet master, his sense of artistic culture, and his
intense friendships with musicians, painters, sculptors, and
poets. He was also active as a lecturer, writer, collector, and
founder of the "Université de la danse". Paul Valéry said of
him: "He is filled with the soul of dance; he is too great an
artist, too sure a creator, not to possess the very essentials of his
art, from the most precise idea to the most general."

Although he first made a name for himself as a dancer,
emulator of the great Vestris and Nijinsky, Lifar actually
discovered ballet at quite a late stage, in Bronislava Nijinska's
studio in Kiev. He left Ukraine to join Diaghilev's corps de
ballet; Diaghilev overlooked his less-than-perfect technique,
appreciating the young dancer's other expressive talents. With
perfect proportions and placing, his body was an artistic
expression itself: it inspired the sculptor Maillol, who refined
his nose, accentuating the exotic strangeness of his expressive
face. Lifar's obsessive determination, together with his rapid
powers of learning and a spontaneous, youthful charm, allowed
him to perfect his style rapidly with Cecchetti, Trefilova,
Egorova, and Legat, and to become principal dancer of
Diaghilev's company.

Lifar's versatility as an interpreter of roles was soon obvious.
If his French sailor in Massine's *Matelots* had an urchin-like
casualness, then he was seduced by Karsavina's feminine
lyricism in Balanchine's *Romeo and Juliet*. Balanchine went on
to make the most of his athletic qualities in *La Chatte*, then to
extol his beauty in *Apollon musagète*—the antithesis to his
moving interpretation of *Les Fils prodigue*, a symbolic creation
since it marked the end of the Diaghilev era and the death of his
spiritual father. The example and influence of the latter did in
fact play a deciding role in the younger artist's future
development, giving rise to imitation and valuable lessons in
aesthetic response.

Fate led Lifar to combine his two careers of dance and
choreography very closely from then on. He had made a
tentative beginning in choreography with *Renard*, but with the
sudden illness of Balanchine, and at the request of Jacques
Rouché (administrator of the Paris Opéra), he took on the role
of both principal dancer and choreographer of *Les Créatures de
Prométhée*. He instinctively made the Titan the central role of
the work, whose outstanding success decided his future and led
him to revive with renewed enthusiasm the Ballet de l'Opéra,
the traditions of which had been passed on to Russia by
Didelot, Perrot, and Petipa, but which had been gradually
dying out in France despite short-lived attempts to keep them
going.

Although he was ballet master, Lifar owed his prestige
initially to his qualities as a dancer. He left behind the memory
of some exceptional performances, notably in *Giselle*—in
which his entrance at the beginning of Act II was the picture of
romantic nobility—and also in his very personal interpretation
of *L'Après-midi d'un faune* in which he danced a solo that was

marked with an animal sensuality. He danced *Swan Lake* with,
amongst others, Olga Spessivtseva, but in fact he preferred
Sylvia. However, it was his own choreography which gave him
the opportunity to establish his original character and to define
the "neo-classical" style which he had been developing in his
adage classes. He gradually remodelled the corps de ballet and
the principal dancers, infusing them with expressivity, passionate lyricism, and precision. He was always searching for
gestures which were expressive and significant, and a
stylization which would convey action and feeling without
having to fall back on conventional and out-dated mime. While
his language remained classical, he stretched and extended the
arabesque, defining the sixth and seventh positions.

Lifar's character encouraged him to interpret roles as diverse
as the humanitarian hero (*Icare, Don Quixote, Le Chevalier
errant*), the victorious hero (such as *David triomphant, Ænéas,
Alexandre*), or the evil anti-hero like *Joan de Zarissa*, whose
female counterpart is *Phèdre*. His sense of humour inspired the
Italian ballets *Salade* and *La Vie de Polichinelle* and the French
Fourberies, Les Animaux modèles, and *Guignol et Pandore*. In
medieval or romantic "fairytales" he was able to celebrate
undying love: *Romeo and Juliet, Le Chevalier et la damoiselle*
and *Les Noces fantastiques*. Intuitively, he juxtaposed "plastique" with metaphysical concepts in *Les Mirages*, splitting the
personality of the hero who has become androgynous. A teller
of tales rather than a precise designer, able to change a knight
into a dagger or a maiden into a doe, he nevertheless arranged
one major abstract ballet: *Suite en blanc*. He favoured soloists
rather than groups, taking full advantage of his various
dancers, choreographing spontaneously and excelling at revealing each dancer's talents.

If some of his works have been lost, sadly, through lack of
notation, others still form today, at the end of the twentieth
century, the heritage of the company which he brought back to
life. Public idol and tireless worker, Lifar knew how to
communicate his enthusiasm to a whole generation of dancers
and choreographers and to instigate the rebirth of ballet in
France. In addition to this, he also wanted to be a French writer
and a member of the Institute. More than his passionate
memoirs—the reflection of an era and of a personality—and
more than his historical studies, it is his controversial books
defending the pre-eminence of true "dance" in ballet, *Traité de
danse* and *Traité de chorégraphie*, which will remain as enduring
witnesses of a life solely dedicated to dance.

—Marie-Françoise Christout

THE LITTLE HUMPBACKED HORSE
(also *The Humpbacked Horse; or, The Tsar-Maiden*; original
Russian title *Konek-gorbunok*)

Choreography: Arthur Saint-Léon
Music: Cesare Pugni
Libretto: Arthur Saint-Léon (after popular Russian tale by Petr
Ershov)
First Production: Bolshoi Theatre, St. Petersburg, 15 December
(3 December old style) 1864
Principal Dancers: Marfa Muravieva (Tsar-Maiden), Nikolai
Troitsky (Ivanushka), Felix Kshesinsky (Khan)

Other productions include: Bolshoi Theatre (restaged Saint-
Léon), with Adele Grantzow (Tsar-Maiden) and Vassily
Geltser (Ivanushka); Moscow, 13 December (1 December old

The Little Humpbacked Horse, in a version by Aleksandr Radunsky, Bolshoi Ballet, 1971

style) 1866. Maryinsky Theatre (restaged and revised Marius Petipa), with Pierina Legnani (Tsar-Maiden), Aleksandr Shiryaev (Ivanushka); St Petersburg, 18 December (6 December old style) 1895. Bolshoi Ballet (new version, chor. Aleksandr Gorsky); Moscow, 7 December (25 November old style) 1901. Bolshoi Ballet (new version; chor. Aleksandr Gorsky, design Konstantin Korovin), with Ekaterina Geltser (Tsar-Maiden), Vladimir Ryabstev (Ivanushka), Mikhail Mordkin (Khan); Moscow, 14 December 1914.

Other choreographic treatments of story: Aleksandr Radunsky (Moscow, 1960), Igor Belsky (Leningrad, 1963).

PUBLICATIONS

Konek-gorbunok, Moscow, 1929
Beaumont, Cyril, *Complete Book of Ballets*, revised edition, London, 1951
Hall, Fernau, *World Dance*, New York, 1955
Barnes, Clive, and Williams, Peter, "Bolshoi Attitudes", *Dance and Dancers* (London), August 1963
Krasovskaya, Vera, *Russian Ballet Theatre of the Second Half of the Nineteenth Century*, Leningrad and Moscow, 1963
Roslavleva, Natalia, *Era of the Russian Ballet*, London, 1966
Kirstein, Lincoln, *Movement and Metaphor*, New York, 1970
Lawson, Joan, *A History of Ballet and its Makers*, London, 1976
Saint-Léon, Arthur, *Letters of a Ballet Master*, edited by Ivor Guest, New York, 1981
Wiley, Roland John, *A Century of Russian Ballet*, Oxford, 1990

The Little Humpbacked Horse is considered to be the first ballet to reflect a national character, although its ersatz qualities brought predictable criticism from the choreographer's contemporaries.

Arthur Saint-Léon was encouraged by his St. Petersburg friends to undertake this ballet, based on a popular Russian folk tale by Petr Ershov, at a time when interest in national art forms was manifesting itself and ballet audiences, disenchanted with Romanticism, were seeking such novelties as pseudo-national themes and styles. By 1864, when *The Little Humpbacked Horse* was first produced, St. Petersburg's Western orientation was being challenged by a movement in arts and letters to establish a native idiom for music, literature, and dance. The publication of Aleksandr Pushkin's poems at the beginning of the nineteenth century had awakened a Russian faith in native art forms, though the aristocratic audiences of St. Petersburg had rejected Pushkin's efforts to establish colloquial Russian as the basis for all drama and literature, as well as his desire to see a national style of music and dance for opera and ballet. Now the group of composers known as the "Mighty Little Heap" was beginning to attract attention for its efforts to establish a national musical style. But it was *The Little Humpbacked Horse* that finally won over the aristocratic audiences, despite the bitter criticism and satirical attacks of the progressive press.

With his characteristic flair for seizing the moment, Saint-Léon proceeded with a great deal of help from his friends. Not knowing the Russian language, he first needed to have the fairy tale translated and explained. The general concept of a grand divertissement of characteristic dances of the various nations comprising Russia was suggested by the balletomane Lopukhin. The score was provided by Cesare Pugni who, lacking sufficient knowledge of Russian melodies, composed a pastiche which even included some of Rossini's overture to *Tancredi*. Saint-Léon used his own fertile imagination combined with his brilliant use of what little knowledge he had of Russian folk dance elements to create a ballet with an essentially Russian theme expressed through long series of pseudo-national divertissements linked by brief, formulaic scenes d'action.

This absurd concoction was ultimately highly successful for one outstanding reason. In this magical tale—about the young Ivanushka who travels through air, water, and fire to find the Tsar-Maiden and the magic ring with which to wed her, thus destroying the power of the Khan—the Russian dancers found vivid characters to portray in a story known and loved by them all as part of their national heritage. As a result, Saint-Léon, who knew well how to display the unique talents of his Russian dancers to advantage, was able to entrust them with the task of providing an air of authenticity by virtue of their genuine Russian spirit, expressiveness, and movement quality. The first Tsar-Maiden, Marfa Muravieva, was particularly successful in bringing her character to life. The second Tsar-Maiden, Matilda Madayeva, asked Saint-Léon to introduce the "Slav Fantasy" dance into the last act, enhancing the role with additional national colour (this was the first of many interpolations to follow, resulting finally in a "Pugni" score which included eighteen composers). It was the Moscow production of 1866 which evidently transformed *The Little Humpbacked Horse* into a truly Russian ballet due to the fine acting of their first Ivanushka, Vassily Geltser, whose skill completely eclipsed the St. Petersburg Ivanushka, Nikolai Troitsky. Saint-Léon until that time had insisted that the choreography existed as a vehicle for the ballerina, ignoring friends and critics alike who said that Ivanushka was the ballet's central character.

Marius Petipa revised the ballet in 1895 and, in 1901, Aleksandr Gorsky created a new, highly realistic production. The Gorsky production is still in the repertoire of the Kirov today, while the Leningrad Maly Opera and the Bolshoi use the 1960 score of Rodion Shchedrin with choreography by Igor Belsky and Aleksander Radunsky respectively.

In the course of the ballet's long history, so many changes have occurred that little of the original production remains. However, all these changes improved on the original conception and brought about the eventual transformation of a pseudo-patriotic, pseudo-Russian ballet into an authentically national one.

—Kristin Beckwith

———

LILAC GARDEN *see* **JARDIN AUX LILAS**

———

LITTLEFIELD, Catherine

American dancer, choreographer, and ballet director. Born in Philadelphia, 1905 (some sources say 1908). Early training with mother, Caroline Littlefield, at her school in Philadelphia; later studied with Ivan Tarasoff and Luigi Albertieri, New York, and with Lubov Egorova and Leo Staats, Paris. Married Philip Leidy, 1933. Stage début in Ziegfeld show *Sally* (lib. Guy Bolton, mus. Herbert, Kern), 1921: dancer in New York stage shows, 1922–26, including in Ziegfeld Follies productions *Louis XIV*, *Annie Dear*, and *Kid Boots*; principal dancer and choreographer, Philadelphia Grand Opera, from 1926; concert dancer and choreographer, 1926–34; founder, principal dancer, and choreographer, Littlefield Ballet, Philadelphia, touring America and Europe as the Philadelphia Ballet, 1934–41, and becoming resident company at Chicago Civic Opera, 1938–39, and 1941; director, *American Jubilee*, dance production for New York World's Fair, 1940; also choreographer and director for musicals, including *Hold on to Your Hats* (lib. Guy Bolton, mus. Lane; 1940), *Crazy with the Heat* (lib. Werris, Sheekman, Davis, et al.; mus. Graham, Suesse, Revil; 1941), *Follow the Girls* (lib. Bolton and Davis, mus. Shapiro, Pascal, Chang; 1944), and *The Firebrand of Florence* (lib. Mayer and Gershwin, mus. Weill; 1945), for J.M. Barrie's *A Kiss for Cinderella*, 1942, and for ice shows, including Sonia Henie's Ice Revues, 1942–48. Recipient: Medaille de la Renaissance Française, 1937. Died in Chicago, 19 November 1951.

WORKS

1932　*H.P.* (mus. Chavez), Philadelphia Grand Opera, Philadelphia
1935　*The Fairy Doll* (mus. Bayer), Littlefield Ballet, Philadelphia
　　　The Minstrel (mus. Debussy), Littlefield Ballet, Haverford, Pennsylvania
　　　The Snow Queen (mus. Cutter), Littlefield Ballet, Philadelphia
　　　Daphnis and Chloë (mus. Ravel), Littlefield Ballet, Philadelphia
1936　*Bolero* (mus. Ravel), Littlefield Ballet, Philadelphia
　　　Fête Champêtre (mus. Lully, Grétry, Rameau), Littlefield Ballet, Philadelphia
　　　Moment Romantique (mus. Chopin), Littlefield Ballet, Philadelphia
　　　Romantic Variations (mus. Saint-Saëns), Littlefield Ballet, Philadelphia
　　　Viennese Waltz (mus. Strauss), Littlefield Ballet, Philadelphia
　　　Poème (mus. Ravel), Littlefield Ballet, Philadelphia
1937　*Barn Dance* (mus. Guion, Powell, Gottschalk), Littlefield Ballet, Philadelphia
　　　Terminal (mus. Kingsley, orchestrated Boss), Littlefield Ballet, Paris
　　　Classical Suite (mus. Bach), Littlefield Ballet, Philadelphia
　　　Let the Righteous be Glad (mus. Gospel songs), Littlefield Ballet, Philadelphia
　　　Parable in Blue (mus. Gabowitz), Littlefield Ballet, Philadelphia
　　　The Sleeping Beauty (mostly own version, incorporating some Petipa variations; mus. Tchaikovsky), Littlefield Ballet, Philadelphia
1938　*Café Society* (mus. Grofé), Littlefield Ballet, Chicago
　　　Ladies' Better Dresses (mus. Kingsley), Littlefield Ballet, Chicago
1939　*The Vacant Chair* (mus. Serly), Littlefield Ballet

Other works include: for the Philadelphia Grand Opera—dances in operas *Lakmé* (mus. Delibes), *Carmen* (mus. Bizet), *Aida* (mus. Verdi), *Tannhaüser* (mus. Wagner), *Faust* (mus. Gounod), *The Jewels of the Madonna* (mus. Wolf-Ferrari), *Samson and Delila* (mus. Saint-Saëns), *Thaïs* (mus. Massenet), *La Gioconda* (mus. Ponchielli), *Orfeo* (mus. Gluck), *The Pearl Fishers* (mus. Bizet).

Catherine Littlefield in *Daphnis and Chloë*, with Thomas Cannon, Philadelphia, 1936

PUBLICATIONS

Deakin, I., *Ballet Profile*, New York, 1936

Ware, L. "A Young Company Grows Up", *American Dancer Magazine* (New York), 1937

Haskell, Arnold, *Dancing Around the World*, London, 1937

"Philadelphia Ballet", *Time Magazine* (New York), 22 February 1937

Beaumont, Cyril, *Supplement to Complete Book of Ballets*, London, 1945

Barzel, Ann, "The Littlefields", *Dance Magazine* (New York), 2 parts: May, June 1945

Amberg, George, *Ballet in America*, New York, 1949

Brooks Schmitz, Nancy, "Catherine Littlefield and Anna Sokolow: Artists Reflecting Society of the 1930s", in Overby, Lynette, Humphrey, James H. (eds.), *Dance: Current Selected Research* (New York), vol. 1, 1989

*   *   *

Catherine Littlefield's career as dancer, choreographer, and ballet company director pointed the direction ballet in America would take. Throughout her work there was evidence of her fascination with classical ballet's "danse d'école". Together with this respect for tradition, there was her belief in the destiny of a uniquely American ballet. And to add to this there was her significant participation in various types of theatrical presentations that involved dance, showing her understanding of the latter's more popular appeal.

Her early dance training in Philadelphia—her native city—was superficial, but later study in New York with Ivan Tarasoff and Luigi Albertieri and many months in Paris with Lubov Egorova and Leo Staats instilled a knowledge of—and a dedication to—the so-called danse d'école. This was evident in her dancing, which was precise and correct. Her style was unmannered, with a simplicity that was tasteful and accurate in classical roles. It is noteworthy that half a century later, American critics seeking to define the accepted American classical style described it as "simple, precise, unmannered". But apart from classical purity, Littlefield also had a gift for comedy and was very witty when roles demanded humor.

As a choreographer, she was more than merely interested in the vocabulary of classical ballet. She researched manuals and acquired a broad inventory of steps, including the correct classical terminology. In her ballets she fully employed the heritage of the academic school, but within the technical framework, when inspiration dictated, she expanded the steps inventively—especially when they involved batterie or pirouettes, at which she was particularly adept. She appreciated and understood the theatrical potential of the ballet vocabulary alone, and used it in its pure form in classical works. However, in her many works that were dramatic, ethnic, or comic, she stretched and elaborated on her medium. In her *Barn Dance*, a bucolic festival set in nineteenth-century rural America, she took the grande pirouette—in classical variations a statement of the male dancer's virtuosity—and made it an expression of the joyful romping of American boys. The beautiful line exhibited by the ballerina in a grand adagio was utilized in her ballet *Terminal* to portray the posturing of a movie queen.

The repertoire created by Catherine Littlefield for the company known as the Littlefield Ballet in America (and as the Philadelphia Ballet for its European tour) had a broad range, from plotless, abstract works in the classical idiom, such as *Classical Suite* and *Moment Romantique*, through dramatic pieces, such as *Parable in Blue* and *Daphnis and Chloë*, to American theme-pieces with comic flavor—namely *Terminal*, *Ladies' Better Dresses*, and *Café Society*. The last category had American characters in American situations. In these, added to the classical vocabulary were movements inspired by everyday activities and gestures—all in the American gait, and all jovial, open, and exuberantly danced.

The choreographer referred to *Terminal*, *Ladies' Better Dresses*, and *Café Society* as ballet-cartoons. They were in revue form, in that there was no one dramatic plot but a number of incidents and various characters related to a central theme. *Terminal*, to a commissioned score by Herbert Kingsley, was set in a busy railroad station, where various types of travellers were lampooned—businessmen commuters, honeymooners, unhappy wives bound for Reno (the divorce Mecca), a Negro family immigrating from the south. And there were the station workers—an information clerk, porters, a newsboy. *Ladies' Better Dresses* was a hilarious scrutiny of the fashion industry, the saga of a too-popular design. *Café Society*, to a score by famous jazz composer Ferde Grofé, satirized the publicized social set of the era—débutantes, a dime-store heiress, gigolos, and athlete-heroes.

Together with all her attention to "new"-style ballets, there was a landmark production of the three-act Tchaikovsky classic, *The Sleeping Beauty*, in January 1937, the first in America. The sixty-member Littlefield Ballet was augmented to 100 dancers and there was a symphony orchestra. The grand adagio and variations of the third act and the Bluebird pas de deux were in the Petipa choreography transmitted via Lubov Egorova. The rest was original choreography by Catherine Littlefield, following closely the musical intentions of the score and Petipa's style.

The company listed several ballets by company members Alexis Dolinoff and Edward Caton, and by modern dance choreographer Lazar Galpern. The last-named created *Home Life of the Gods* to music by Satie and *Prodigal Son* to music by César Franck. The first satirized classical ballet: but classicist Littlefield not only presented it, but danced in it. The employment of modern dancers to make ballets for classical companies came decades later. Again, Catherine Littlefield was a first.

The dancers in the Littlefield Ballet were for the most part trained in the Philadelphia school founded and operated by Caroline Littlefield, Catherine's mother. Catherine was listed as premiere danseuse. Her younger sister Dorothie, the principal soloist, was the most talented virtuoso dancer in the troupe, a Paris-trained ballerina who had danced for several months with Ballet Russe de Monte Carlo in Europe. Carl, the youngest Littlefield, was an athlete who in the beginning avoided the family's ballet activities. He succumbed to its allure when the company was successful, studied intensively, and became an excellent classical dancer, a particularly good partner for Catherine.

Among the leading dancers were Karen Conrad and Miriam Golden (who later became principals of American Ballet Theatre), and Joan McCracken, an enchanting dancer who became a star on Broadway. The list of male dancers was headed by Alexis Dolinoff, who had danced with the Diaghilev Ballet and with the Nijinska-directed Ida Rubinstein company in the 1930s. A distinguished principal was Edward Caton, well known as dancer and choreographer with a number of ballet companies. There were also William Dollar, Douglas Coudy, and Jack Potteiger, all of whom later danced with Balanchine's first company in America. Catherine Littlefield's concept of American ballet included the presence of virile, athletic male dancers, and she recruited a number of athletes. If some lacked the niceties of perfect classical training, they made up for it in astounding elevation, brilliant pirouettes, and robust, animated stage presence.

Although the company was based in Philadelphia, it danced

in New York and made extensive tours of America. A high point in Littlefield Ballet history was a memorable European tour in the spring and summer of 1937, during which there was notable critical acclaim for *Barn Dance* and more generally for the spirited dancing of the company. In Paris, Catherine received the Medaille de la Renaissance Française from President LeBrun. In London, critic Arnold Haskell was another fan, whose support led to the extension of the engagement in the Hippodrome to three weeks.

Catherine Littlefield had begun her professional career in opera ballet, and she was involved in that branch of dance for most of her dancing days. She worked many seasons in the 1920s with the Philadelphia Grand Opera, and later for three seasons with the Chicago Civic Opera. Unlike many ballet directors, who considered the ballet passages in operas a trivial chore to be given short shrift, she gave the genre respect, attention, and imagination. She made an effort to learn about the ballet episodes presented by leading European opera companies by going for tutoring to Albertieri at La Scala in Milan and to Léo Staats at the Paris Opera. The opera ballets produced by Littlefield were not only integrated in the drama and style of each opera, but were imaginative episodes that livened the entire *mise-en-scène*.

In December 1941, when the United States entered World War II, most of the Littlefield Ballet's male dancers entered military service and the company was disbanded. Throughout her career Catherine had been involved in various theatre projects on the side—Broadway musicals, prologues to the films in movie theatres, pageants. Her services were in demand for major productions, such as *American Jubilee*, an elaborate pageant presented four times a day at the New York World's Fair. Littlefield also created numbers for an ice-dancing show in New York and after disbanding her company she became involved in directing and choreographing the large-scale ice show, featuring skating star Sonia Henie. It played in immense stadiums throughout the country. With experience, Littlefield absorbed a great deal about both the possibilities and the limitations of ice-dancing. The originality and humor she exhibited in ballet were transferred to ice-dancing—and, of course, elements of ballet, especially line and ports de bras, were introduced to the skating routines. Also much ballet music, like Tchaikovsky's *Swan Lake* or Stravinsky's Coach-men's Dance from *Petrushka*, was slyly introduced. Three decades later, journalists congratulated ballet choreographers for introducing the "new" idea of having choreographers from the ballet create works for ice-dancing.

Catherine Littlefield, in all her many and varied activities, was more than a pioneer. She was an artist, always seeking and doing. Her dream of rebuilding a Littlefield Ballet after the war vanished with her death from cancer in 1951. Her sister Dorothie Littlefield carried on in Chicago, directing the ice shows, and she also made an attempt to organize a chamber ballet group in Philadelphia. However, she died of heart failure in 1953. After his service in the air corps during the war, Carl Littlefield danced for some years in Broadway musicals, then settled in San Francisco. He died in 1976.

The National Museum of Dance in Saratoga Springs, New York, includes Catherine Littlefield among the major artists who have contributed to dance in America.

—Ann Barzel

LIVRY, Emma

French dancer. Born Emma-Marie Emarot in Paris, 24

September 1842. Studied at the school of the Paris Opéra, pupil of Madame Dominique; later studied with Marie Taglioni. Début, Paris Opéra (at age of sixteen), 1858: première danseuse, Paris Opéra, 1858–1862. Died in Neuilly, 26 July 1863.

ROLES

1858   Title role in *La Sylphide* (F. Taglioni), Opéra, Paris
1859   Erigone (cr) in Divertissement (chor. Mazilier) in *Herculaneum* (opera; mus. David), Opéra, Paris
1860   Farfalla (cr) in *Le Papillon* (M. Taglioni), Opéra, Paris
1862   Divertissement (cr) in *La Reine de Saba* (opera; mus. Gounod, chor. L. Petipa), Opéra, Paris

PUBLICATIONS

Gautier, Theophile, *Portraits contemporains*, Paris, 1874
Vieil abonné, Un [Paul Mahalin], *Ces Demoiselles de l'Opéra*, Paris, 1887
Gautier, Théophile, *The Romantic Ballet as Seen by Théophile Gautier*, translated by Cyril Beaumont, London, 1932
Beaumont, Cyril, *Three French Dancers of the Nineteenth Century*, London, 1935
Moore, Lillian, *Artists of the Dance*, New York, 1938
Moore, Lillian, "Emma Livry", *Dance Magazine* (New York), June 1952
Guest, Ivor, *The Ballet of the Second Empire 1858–70*, London, 1953
Guest, Ivor, "Centenary: Emma Livry, 1842–63", *Ballet Annual* (London), vol. 18, 1964
Gautier, Théophile, *Gautier on Dance*, edited by Ivor Guest, London, 1986

*   *   *

The short life of Emma Livry evokes the ephemeral, tragic qualities of the Romantic ballet itself, and in some ways she appears closer to legend than history. She interpreted only a handful of roles before her career was cut short; she died from burns received when her ballet dress caught fire in the gaslights at the Paris Opéra. She was not alone in meeting this manner of death, and in fact a safer new material had been invented before she died. Sadly, she had herself written to the Opéra's management delaying her use of the new material, saying that she feared it spoiled the effect of the costumes.

Livry came quickly to fame at her début, aged sixteen, for her audacious but successful interpretation of Marie Taglioni's most famous role, La Sylphide. The simplicity of her style, her modesty, grace, and lightness, her incorporeality, reminded many of Taglioni and she was a great success. *Harper's Weekly* declared that Livry was destined to fill the place then occupied by Cerrito, Taglioni, and Elssler. She had certainly begun to put an end to the contemporary myth that great dancers had to be Italian. Livry was the pupil of Madame Dominique, the former dancer Caroline Lassiat, who also taught Léontine Beaugrand, Adèle Grantzow, and Giuseppina Bozzacchi. After Livry's début Marie Taglioni came out of retirement to tutor her, recognizing in Livry aspects of her own style and ability. In itself Taglioni's involvement is indicative of Livry's talent and the hopes that were invested in her.

Livry's career developed rapidly and she soon ranked second only in importance to Carolina Rosati and Amalia Ferraris in the Opéra's hierarchy. Two years after Taglioni began to tutor her she was given her first and only important creation in *Le Papillon*, with choreography by Marie Taglioni and music by

remained an angel or phantom flitting across the desert of Romanticism's decaying spirit when her wings, being too light, caught fire. In a sense the timing of her birth as well as of her death may well have denied her significance beyond that of her talent. There can be little doubt that Livry was a dancer of the first rank, but she was being modelled into little more than a replica of Taglioni. Taglioni's talent had coincided with a great period in ballet history; Livry was not so fortunate, and whether or not she would have inspired a new flowering of the ballet is impossible to tell.

—Lesley-Anne Sayers

LONDON FESTIVAL BALLET see ENGLISH NATIONAL BALLET

LOPOKOVA, Lydia

Russian/English dancer and actress. Born Lidiya (Lydia) Vasilievna Lopukhova (Lopokova) in St. Petersburg, sister of choreographer Fedor Lopukhov, 21 October (9 October old style) 1891. Studied at the Imperial Theatre School, pupil of Mikhail Fokine; graduated in 1909. Married (1) Diaghilev manager Randolpho Barocchi (annulled 1925); (2) English economist Lord Maynard Keynes, 1925 (naturalized as British citizen on marriage). Début, when still a child, as a page in *The Sleeping Beauty*, 1901; dancer, Maryinsky Theatre, St. Petersburg, 1909–10; leading dancer Diaghilev's Ballets Russes, first seasons, 1909, 1910; went to United States, 1910–15, appearing with Gertrude Hoffmann's "All-Star Russian Imperial Ballet" (later directed by Mikhail Mordkin), performing at the Winter Garden Theatre with Alexandre Volinine, New York, 1911, and Mordkin, 1912; also performed in dramatic theatre and on popular stage, including in musical comedy *The Lady of the Slipper* (Herbert, Montgomery, and Stone; New York, 1912); rejoined Diaghilev's company in New York, 1916, performing in Boston, Albany, and many other American cities; principal dancer, Diaghilev's Ballet Russes, 1916–29, appearing with great success in London seasons, 1919–20; also performer with Massine company, Covent Garden, London, 1922, own group at London Coliseum, 1922, and Comte Etienne de Beaumont's Soirées de Paris, 1924; leading participant in founding of Camargo Society, London, performing in early productions by Frederick Ashton, 1930–31; also actress, appearing in Percy Wallace MacKaye's *The Antick* (New York, 1915), and musical comedy *Fads and Fancies* (New York, 1915); later appeared in revue *You'd Be Surprised* (Weston, Lee, Clayton, Waller; London, 1923), Noël Coward's play *The Young Idea* (London, 1924), and London productions of Shakespeare's *Twelfth Night* (1933), and Ibsen's *The Doll's House* (1934) and *The Master Builder* (1936); co-founder, with husband Keynes, in founding of the Arts Theatre, Cambridge, 1935. Died in Seaford, Sussex, 8 June 1981.

ROLES

1910 Title role in *L'Oiseau de feu* (Fokine), Diaghilev's Ballets Russes, Paris
Dancer in *Les Sylphides* (Fokine), Diaghilev's Ballets Russes, Paris
Columbine in *Le Carnaval* (Fokine), Diaghilev's Ballets Russes, Paris
1911 Favourite Slave in *Cléopâtre* (after Fokine), Winter

Emma Livry in *Le Papillon*, Paris, 1861

Offenbach. In the scenario, by Saint-Georges, we find a disturbing portent of what was to happen to Livry in real life. Her character, Farfalla, is held in the spell of an evil fairy who turns her into a butterfly who, after convoluted adventures, is attracted by a flame on which her wings shrivel, breaking the spell. The ballet was well received, though the plot was thought to be too artificial and complicated; and Livry had a great personal success. Some critics declared that her impression of soaring flight surpassed Taglioni's. The sculptor Barre was moved to model Livry in the role, placing her alongside his statuettes of Taglioni, Elssler, and Amany. She was, however, to dance in only one more opera, Gounod's *La Reine de Saba*, for it was while rehearsing the leading role of Fenella in *La Muette de Portici* that her dress caught fire.

Livry was renowned for her ideal lightness, classical correctness, and poetic quality in movement. Marie Taglioni, in creating *Le Papillon* for Livry, clearly tried to create a role to exploit these qualities as well as give Livry an image with which she would always be identified. Livry kindled the embers of the dying Romantic ballet and the spirit of Romanticism, but Le Papillon is a much less profound and significant creature than La Sylphide. Livry came to fame at a time when the Romantic ballet was decidedly in decline, when its eclectic aspects had become trivialized into sentimentality and theatrical spectacle.

To Serge Lifar, almost a century after her death, Livry

Lydia Lopokova with Stanislas Idzikowski in *Le Carnaval*, **Diaghilev's Ballets Russes**

Palace Garden, New York
1916   Ballerina in *Petrushka* (Fokine), Diaghilev's Ballets
Russes, New York
Young girl in *Le Spectre de la rose* (Fokine), Diaghilev's
Ballets Russes, U.S. tour
Ta-Hor in *Cléopâtre* (Fokine), Diaghilev's Ballets
Russes, U.S. tour
Princess Florine in *La Princesse enchantée* (Bluebird pas
de deux from *The Sleeping Beauty*; Petipa), Diaghi-
lev's Ballets Russes, U.S. tour
1917   Mariuccia (cr) in *The Good-Humoured Ladies* (Massine),
Diaghilev's Ballets Russes, Rome
Acrobat (cr) in *Parade* (Massine), Diaghilev's Ballets
Russes, Paris
1918   Young girl in *Les Papillons* (Fokine), Diaghilev's Ballets
Russes, London
Polovtsian Maid in *Polovtsian Dances from Prince Igor*
(Fokine), Diaghilev's Ballets Russes, London
Snow Maiden in *Le Soleil de nuit* (Massine), Diaghilev's
Ballets Russes, London
1919   Leading Can-Can Dancer (cr) in *Le Boutique fantasque*
(Massine), Diaghilev's Ballets Russes, London
1921   Lilac Fairy, Enchanted Princess (Bluebird pas de deux)
in *The Sleeping Princess* (Petipa; staged Sergeyev,
with additional dances Nijinska), Diaghilev's Ballets
Russes, London
Princess Aurora in *The Sleeping Princess* (Petipa; staged
Sergeyev, with additional dances Nijinska), Diaghi-
lev's Ballets Russes, London
1922   Principal dancer in *Czardas* (Massine), *Lezghinka*
(Massine), Massine company, Covent Garden,
London
Polka and Galop in *The Fanatics of Pleasure*, Massine
company, Covent Garden, London
Principal dancer in *Les Elégants* (Bowen), *The Masquer-
ade* (Bowen), Lopokova group, Coliseum, London
1927   Princess in *L'Histoire du soldat* (mus. Stravinsky), Arts
Theatre Club, London
1930   The Lassie (cr) in *Dances on a Scotch Theme* (later *The
Tartans*; Ashton), in The Masque presented by
Arnold Haskell, Arts Theatre Club, London
The Lady (cr) in *Follow Your Saint* (*The Passionate
Pavane*; Ashton), in The Masque presented by Arnold
Haskell, Arts Theatre Club, London (performed with
Camargo Society, 1931)
1931   Procris (cr) in *Cephalus and Procris* (de Valois),
Camargo Society, London
Jodelling Song, Tango, Tarantella (cr) in *Façade*
(Ashton), Camargo Society, London
The Queen of the Port (cr) in *A Day in a Southern Port*
(later *Rio Grande*; Ashton), Camargo Society, London
1933   Swanilda in *Coppélia*, Acts I and II (Sergeyev after
Ivanov), Vic-Wells Ballet, London

Other roles include: for Diaghilev's Ballets Russes—leading
roles in *Pulcinella* (Massine), Young girl in *Les Matelots*
(Massine); for Massine company—principal dancer in *Polka
Mazurka, Kuiawiak, Peking Too, Fougis* (divertissements,
attributed to Massine).

PUBLICATIONS

By Lopokova:
*Lydia and Maynard: Letters between Lydia Lopokova and
Maynard Keynes*, edited by Polly Hill, Richard Keynes,
London, 1989

About Lopokova:
Beaumont, Cyril, *Lydia Lopokova*, London, 1920
Beaumont, Cyril, *The Diaghilev Ballet in London*, London, 1940
Beaumont, Cyril, *Complete Book of Ballets*, revised edition,
London, 1951
Grigoriev, Serge, *The Diaghilev Ballet*, translated by Vera
Bowen, London, 1953
Clarke, Mary, *The Sadler's Wells Ballet*, London, 1955
Joffe, Lydia, "The Lopukhov Dynasty", *Dance Magazine* (New
York), January 1967
Macdonald, Nesta, *Diaghilev Observed by Critics in England and
the United States*, London and New York, 1975
Keynes, Milo (ed.), *Lydia Lopokova*, London, 1983
Garafola, Lynn, *Diaghilev's Ballets Russes*, New York, 1989
Pritchard, Jane, "London's Favourite Ballerina", *Dancing
Times* (London), December 1989

*   *   *

Every so often, and in every facet of the theatre, a performer
appears, blessed with such unforced, natural charm that
everybody falls in love with her; middle-aged members of the
audience imagine she is their daughter, children know she is
their friend, the old remember their youth, and all would like to
put her in a little box and take her home at the end of the show.
Such a one was Lydia Lopokova, and to those who saw her
perform in her heyday, she was the absolute paragon, to which
no subsequent performer could compare. And such was her
charm that she could walk away from the Diaghilev company
at a minute's notice, causing panic and problems to those trying
to fill the resultant gap, and then, at the end of her unexplained
absence, be welcomed back with open arms, not only by
Diaghilev himself, but by those who had suffered all the
difficulties and the extra work caused by her escapade.

Charm is a gift, which cannot be acquired through work or
wishing. What Lopokova also had was the fruits of her
Maryinsky training—a sound classical technique, gained
through the strict discipline of ballet class (which must
incidentally have stood her in good stead when faced with the
mockery, dislike, and rudeness of some of the "Bloomsbury
set"—one of whom, Maynard Keynes, she married in 1925).
Her dance technique was strong enough to qualify her to dance
both the Princess Aurora in *The Sleeping Princess* for Diaghilev
in 1921, and the difficult title role in Fokine's *L'Oiseau de feu*;
her personality was strong enough to make her a worthy foil to
Massine, her partner in the Can-Can of *La Boutique fantasque*.
She also had the invaluable gift not only of enjoying her roles,
but of conveying that enjoyment to her audience. Those
fortunate enough to have seen her perform will recall the sheer
delight of her entrance as Swanilda in *Coppélia*, for example,
when she ran straight to the footlights with no nonsense and
mimed the plot of the ballet, in a way which took the audience
into her confidence quite as personally as if she had been
whispering in their individual ears. Anyone who saw her dance
will also have the clearest mental picture possible of her
dazzling jumps, such as her brisés in the Danse Slav.

Serge Grigoriev, recalling Lopokova's welcome return to
Diaghilev in 1916, explained it by referring not only to
Lopokova's "enormous charm" but to her "remarkable
elevation", commenting that "both Diaghilev and the public
greatly preferred her". Marie Rambert remembered, "Lopokova's dancing in the Can-Can was *fantasque*. She rejoiced on the
stage, but she could be more romantic than anyone in *Les
Sylphides* . . .". Rambert went on:

She was so sensitive, and had a wonderful stage
technique and belonged to the great ones. She never,

however, underlined the technique, but just danced with an incredible, contagious gaiety. Besides this, she showed great poetry and musicality, and really she could have danced without music. She was a born dancer, a born mover, and such a romp.

And fellow Ballet Russe dancer Lydia Sokolova recalled Lopokova in her memoirs as kind to all, "never jealous and never coveting another dancer's roles". The charming Lopokova was always "hopping off somewhere", but the key to her enduring charm may well have been her independence, for importantly, "she never sold her soul to Diaghilev, fond of him as she was".

If Lopokova's second career as an actress never brought her anything like equal acclaim, she nevertheless appeared with modest success in Molière, Shakespeare, and Ibsen; in her marriage (her second) to Maynard Keynes, the devoted care which she gave to her husband won the grudging approval of even the more spiteful members of the Bloomsbury coterie of Virginia Woolf and co. (who otherwise rarely lost any opportunity to point out what an idiot, in their estimation, Maynard Keynes had married).

Lopokova did a great deal to assist at the birth of English ballet, and took a generous interest in young dancers: one remembers how, during a performance of *Les Sylphides* by the (then) Sadler's Wells Opera Ballet in Cambridge, she broke into applause at the end of the Waltz, was vigorously hushed by the audience (it was not done to applaud in the middle of this ballet at that time), and, turning to Ninette de Valois, exclaimed: "I don't care, I will clap! I know just how difficult it is!" The dancer was Nadia Nerina, making her début in that most tricky of all the *Sylphides* solos.

Lopokova survived her husband by nearly four decades, and died a recluse in 1981. Her particular brand of extrovert gaiety has never been matched, let alone surpassed, on the ballet stage, according to anyone who ever saw her dance.

—Leo Kersley

LOPUKHOV, Fedor

Russian/Soviet dancer, choreographer, and ballet director. Born Fedor Vasilevich Lopukhov, brother of dancer Lydia Lopokova, in St. Petersburg, 20 October (8 October old style) 1886. Studied at the St. Petersburg Theatre School, pupil of Nikolai Legat; graduated in 1905; also studied with Aleksandr Gorsky in Moscow. Soloist, Maryinsky Theatre, St. Petersburg/Petrograd, 1905–09, 1911–22, Bolshoi Theatre, Moscow, 1909–10, company of Sedova and Legat, performing in Europe, 1907, and Paris, 1909, and Anna Pavlova's company, touring U.S., 1910–11; first choreography, 1916, soon restaging several of the classics of Petipa and others; choreographer and artistic director, State Academic Theatre for Opera and Ballet (GATOB, later the Kirov), Petrograd/Leningrad, 1922–31, Bolshoi Theatre, Moscow, 1926, and later 1935–36, Maly Theatre Ballet, 1930–35, Kirov Ballet, Leningrad, 1944–46 and 1951–56; also director, Choreographers' Course, Leningrad Choreographic School, 1936–41; founder and director, Choreography Department, Leningrad Conservatory, 1962–73, becoming Professor from 1965: pupils included Boris Fenster, Konstantin Boyarsky, Aleksandr Aleksidze. Recipient: title of Honoured Ballet Master of the Russian Federation, 1927; People's Artist of the Russian Federation, 1956. Died in Leningrad, 28 January 1973.

WORKS

1916   *Mexican Saloon* (mus. Goncharov), Theatre of Musical Drama, Petrograd
1916/   *The Dream* (mus. Shcherbachev), Theatre of Musical
18   Drama, Petrograd
1921   *Firebird* (mus. Stravinsky), GATOB, Petrograd
1922   Lilac Fairy Variation (first created for Egorova, 1914), Aurora's Variation (Act II), Entr'acte: "The Dream", Gavotte, Passe-pied, and Rigadon (Act II), Sarabande, Entrée of Aurora and Prince (Act IV) in *The Sleeping Beauty* (Petipa; staged Lopukhov; mus. Tchaikovsky), State Academic Theatre for Opera and Ballet (GATOB), Petrograd
1923   Dances in *The Snow Maiden* (opera; mus. Rimsky-Korsakov), GATOB, Petrograd
        The Magnificence of the Universe (also called *Dance Symphony*; mus. Beethoven), Young Ballet (dancers of GATOB), Petrograd
        Dances in *Tannhäuser* (opera; mus. Wagner), GATOB, Petrograd
1924   *Night on Bald Mountain* (mus. Mussorgsky), GATOB, Leningrad
        The Red Whirlwind (*Bolsheviki*; mus. Deshevov), GATOB, Leningrad
        Dances in *Carmen* (opera; mus. Bizet), GATOB, Leningrad
1925   Dances in *Judith* (opera; mus. Serov), GATOB, Leningrad
1926   *Pulcinella* (mus. Stravinsky), GATOB, Leningrad
        Dances in *Khovanshchina* (opera; mus. Mussorgsky), GATOB, Leningrad
1927   *A Tale about the Fox, the Rooster, the Cat, and the Ram* (*Le Renard*; mus. Stravinsky), GATOB, Leningrad
        The Ice Maiden (mus. Grieg), GATOB, Leningrad
        Serf Ballerina (mus. Korchmarev), GATOB, Leningrad
1929   *The Nutcracker* (new version; mus. Tchaikovsky), GATOB, Leningrad
        The Red Poppy (with Ponomarev, Leontiev; mus. Glière), GATOB, Leningrad
1931   *Bolt* (mus. Shostakovich), GATOB, Leningrad
1933   *Harlequinade* (new version; mus. Drigo), Maly Theatre, Leningrad
        Dances in *Carmen* (opera; mus. Bizet), Maly Theatre, Leningrad
1934   *Coppélia* (mus. Delibes), Maly Theatre, Leningrad
1935   *The Bright Stream* (mus. Shostakovich), Maly Theatre, Leningrad
1938   *The Christmas Eve* (with Burmeister; mus. Asafiev), Moscow Art Ballet, Leningrad
1939   *Nightingale* (with Yermolaev; mus. Kroshner), Minsk Theatre, Minsk
1940   *Taras Bulba* (with Kovtunov; mus. Soloviev-Sedoy), Kirov Ballet, Leningrad
1943   *Akbilyak* (with Turgunbaeva, Kamilov; mus. Vasilenko), Navoi Theatre, Tashkent
1947   *Spring Fairy Tale* (mus. Tchaikovsky, arranged Asafiev), Kirov Ballet, Leningrad
1959   *Love Ballad* (mus. Tchaikovsky), Maly Theatre, Leningrad
1963   *Pictures from an Exhibition* (mus. Mussorgsky), Stanislavsky and Nemirovich–Danchenko Ballet, Moscow

Also staged:
1922   *The Sleeping Beauty* (after Petipa, with own additional chor.; mus. Tchaikovsky), GATOB, Petrograd

Fedor Lopukhov's *The Nutcracker*, Leningrad, 1929

Harlequinade (after Petipa; mus. Drigo), GATOB, Petrograd
Raymonda (after Petipa; mus. Glazunov), GATOB, Petrograd
The Little Humpbacked Horse (after Petipa; mus. Pugni), GATOB, Petrograd
1923 Egyptian Nights (after Fokine; mus. Rimsky-Korsakov), GATOB, Petrograd
Le Pavillon d'Armide (after Fokine; mus. Tcherepnin), GATOB, Petrograd
The Nutcracker (with Shiryaev, after Ivanov; mus. Tchaikovsky), GATOB, Petrograd
Don Quixote (after Petipa, Gorsky; mus. Minkus), GATOB, Petrograd
1944 La Fille mal gardée (after Dauberval; mus. Hertel), Maly Theatre Ballet, Chukalov (during World War II evacuation)
1945 Swan Lake (after Petipa, Ivanov; mus. Tchaikovsky), Kirov Ballet, Leningrad
1962 "Kingdom of the Shades" scene in La Bayadère (Petipa; mus. Minkus), Bolshoi Ballet, Moscow
Egyptian Nights (after Fokine; mus. Arensky), Kirov Ballet, Leningrad

Other works include: for GATOB, Petrograd/Leningrad—dances in operas *The Mermaid* (mus. Dargomizhsky), *The Eagle's Revolt* (mus. Pashenko), *The Master Singer of Nürnberg* (mus. Wagner).

PUBLICATIONS

By Lopukhov:
The Magnificence of the Universe, Petrograd, 1922
Choreographer's Paths, Berlin, 1925
"The Principles of Choreography in *Pulcinella*", in Asafiev, B.V., *Igor Stravinsky and his Ballet "Pulcinella"*, Leningrad, 1926
"Comedy in Dance", in *Harlequinade*, Leningrad, 1933

"The Ballet Production of *The Clear Brook*", in *The Clear Brook*, Leningrad
Sixty Years in Ballet: Reminiscences and Notes of a Choreographer, Moscow, 1966
Choreographic Confessions, Moscow, 1972

About Lopukhov:
Benois, A., "Piety or Blasphemy?", *The Weekly of the Petrograd State Theatres*, no. 11, 1922
Grigorovich, Yuri, "Fedor Lopukhov", *Teatr* (Moscow), no. 7, 1965
Gusev, Petr, "The Artist's Pride", *Sovetskaya Muzyka* (Moscow), no. 8, 1965
Slonimsky, Yuri, "The Roads of Choreographer Lopukhov", Introduction to Lopukhov, *Sixty Years in Ballet*, Moscow, 1966
Roslavleva, Natalia, *Era of the Russian Ballet*, London, 1966
Joffe, Lydia, "The Lopukhov Dynasty", *Dance Magazine* (New York), January 1967
Krasovskaya, Vera, *Essays on Ballet*, Leningrad, 1967
Dobrovolskaya, G., *Fedor Lopukhov*, Leningrad, 1976
Souritz, Elizabeth, *The Art of Choreography in the 1920s*, Moscow, 1979; as *Soviet Choreographers in the 1920s*, translated by Lynn Visson, Durham, N.C. and London, 1990
Devereux, Tony, "Legend of a Lost Choreographer", *Dancing Times* (London), 2 parts: January, February 1988
Alovert, Nina, "Lopukhov's Legacy", *Dance Magazine* (New York), March 1989

*   *   *

Fedor Lopukhov is a paradox, an eminent twentieth-century choreographer whose work survives in only one fragment: the Lilac Fairy variation from the prologue of *The Sleeping Beauty*. He was the eldest of four Lopukhov children who trained as dancers at the St. Petersburg Theatre School (now the Leningrad Choreographic, or Vaganova, School in Leningrad). His younger sister Lydia came to the West as a star of the Diaghilev company, and stayed in Britain where she assisted the young Sadler's Wells Ballet. Fedor also toured in the West, but returned to Russia, where he remained through and after the Revolution.

He was destined for an amazing career. The veteran ballet master Marius Petipa had been removed from his post fourteen years before the Revolution, but no one had ever emerged as his successor. The Revolution brought intense questioning of ballet's right to exist, many claiming that it was outdated, but when it re-asserted its position as the flagship of Russian culture, Lopukhov became Petipa's heir. He was appointed artistic director of what had been in pre-revolutionary times St. Petersburg's Imperial Maryinsky Theatre and was later to become known as the Kirov Theatre, Leningrad.

Lopukhov had the many-sided talent required for this challenging position. He rebuilt the artistic cadres following the flight abroad of Russia's best performers. He consolidated priceless traditions with new productions of the classics (*The Sleeping Beauty*, *Raymonda*, *The Nutcracker*). These productions inevitably provoked controversy, for his idea of proper "reconstruction" involved doing away with familiar sections of old productions, but the spirit in which Lopukhov sought to reinstate the original quality of performance is well recognized and appreciated now. At the same time, he reacted to the interest in ballets of the Diaghilev company (never destined to return to its native country) by producing home-bred versions of Stravinsky's *Firebird*, *Pulcinella*, and *Le Renard*. More important, Lopukhov responded to the demand for new, breakaway choreography reflecting the Revolutionary dynamic, as in *The Red Whirlwind* and *The Ice Maiden*, without giving up his debt to classicism. *The Red Whirlwind* was performed only once, and Lopukhov himself later called it his "greatest failure", but Soviet dance scholar Elizabeth Souritz has referred to it as "the first ballet about the October Revolution". In his ambitious blend of naturalism and abstract, metaphorical dance, Lopukhov "aspired to conquer heights", she writes, "that . . . had not even been fully mastered by drama, let alone the lyric theatre." As for *The Ice Maiden*, it was both an artistic and a popular success, and showed the choreographer's ability to fuse the new concerns of twentieth-century Soviet ballet with the traditional heritage of Petipa and others. Again, Souritz writes, "It reinstated the classical lexicon, while at the same time making it the language of modern art, and it was orientated toward the search for pure abstract dance."

Lopukhov had been deeply influenced by the "symphonic dance" initiated by Petipa and developed by Ivanov and Fokine, and wrote about its principles in the book *A Choreographer's Paths*. He briefly took the style to one of the highest pinnacles it has ever attained with his "Dance Symphony" *The Magnificence of the Universe*, to Beethoven's Fourth Symphony—performed only once but now legendary in Russia for its attempt to unite music and pure, non-dramatic dance.

All this was his work of the 1920s. At the end of the decade, sentiment at the Kirov swung against Lopukhov, perhaps because he had tried to go too far too fast. He was replaced by the more conservative Agrippina Vaganova. But his fall was only the prelude to a higher rise. The Leningrad party authorities decided that ballet was sufficiently popular to merit a second company. Thus the Leningrad Maly Ballet was founded under Lopukhov, and despite Vaganova's classic revivals, it soon became clear where the real centre of creativity lay.

Lopukhov began collaborating with Shostakovich. The first result was *Bolt*, a ballet about industrial unrest in which the "goodies" were young communists and the "baddies" drunkards, hooligans, and a bureaucrat in the form of a factory

manager. The second was *The Bright Stream*, about life on a collective farm. Its impact belied its seemingly innocuous subject. The ballet's tremendous initial success won for Lopukhov the appointment to direct the Bolshoi Ballet, but before he could take it up, disaster struck. The ballet transferred to Moscow, where the authorities took offence. A *Pravda* article in 1936 charged the ballet with formalism, and dashed the careers of its creators. Ahead of Lopukhov was a long haul back, helped by the change of sentiment produced by World War II. Eventually he recovered the position he had started with—artistic direction of the Kirov. His interest now lay in developing other Russian choreographers, rather than in his own choreography. One of his protégés was Grigorovich, who obtained the post that had eluded Lopukhov—chief ballet master of the Bolshoi.

Lopukhov's contribution to Russia's national art is effectively symbolized in Grigorovich's ballets, his own choreography having vanished during the years of official disapproval. But we read as early as 1966 that "Lopukhov at times succeeded in attaining great heights of plastic expression with the help of new movements" (Natalia Roslavleva). And now of course we have Elizabeth Souritz's excellent book, *Soviet Choreographers of the 1920s* (English translation, 1990), which deals extensively with the work of Lopukhov, reconstructing his lost ballets from contemporary reports, and essentially arguing for Lopukhov's position as one of the most innovative and forward-looking choreographers of his day. Recently, efforts have been made to recover Lopukhov's hugely ambitious symphonic ballet, *The Magnificence of the Universe*.

The Lilac Fairy variation was created before any of Lopukhov's professional appointments. No Petipa choreography existed for it because the role was always performed by Petipa's eldest daughter Maria, a striking beauty but not a dancer on points. Petipa had gone when Maria was succeeded by Egorova, who asked Lopukhov for a danced variation in keeping with the rest of the prologue.

Lopukhov was a prolific writer, and his autobiography *Sixty Years in Ballet* throws unique light on ballet in Russia before, during, and after the Revolution. Published by Iskusstvo in Moscow in 1966, with an introductory article by Slonimsky, it is the principal source for Lopukhov's life.

—Tony Devereux

LORING, Eugene

American dancer, choreographer, and teacher. Born LeRoy Kerpestein in Milwaukee, Wisconsin, 1911. Studied theatre and dance in Milwaukee; later studied ballet at the School of American Ballet, pupil of George Balanchine, Anatole Vilzak, Muriel Stuart, Pierre Vladimirov, and Ludmila Schollar, New York, from 1933. Early stage experience with Wisconsin Players, Milwaukee; professional stage début, Michel Fokine Ballet, New York, 1934; dancer, American Ballet, 1935–38; soloist, Lincoln Kirstein's Ballet Caravan, from 1936; soloist, Ballet Theatre (later American Ballet Theatre), 1940–41; also choreographer: first choreography (entr'acte for production of *Credentials*), Milwaukee; choreographer, Ballet Caravan, 1936–39, Ballet Theatre, from 1940; founder, choreographer, and principal dancer, Dance Players, 1941–42; also performed as actor/dancer on Broadway, including as Owen Webster in *The Beautiful People* (play by William Saroyan, 1941); also choreographer for Broadway, from 1943, and for Ice Capades, 1958; appeared in films, including in *National Velvet* (dir.

Brown, 1945), *Torch Song* (dir. Walters, 1953), and became film choreographer, including in collaboration with Fred Astaire for *Funny Face* (dir. Donen, 1956); founder and teacher, American School of Dance, 1948; chairman, Dance Department, University of California, Irvine, from 1965, also staging ballets for San Diego Ballet. Recipient: *Dance Magazine* Award, 1967. Died in Kingston, New York, 30 August 1982.

ROLES

1934   Pantalon in *Carnaval* (Fokine), Fokine Company, New York

1935   The Photographer (cr) in *Alma Mater* (first professional production; Balanchine), American Ballet, New York

   Brighella (cr) in *Reminiscence* (first professional production; Balanchine), American Ballet, New York

   Dancer (cr) in *Card Game* (Balanchine), American Ballet, New York

1936   Harlequin in *Harlequin for President* (also chor.), Ballet Caravan, Bennington, Vermont

   Satyr (cr) in *Promenade* (Dollar), Ballet Caravan, Bennington, Vermont

1937   The Farm Boy (cr) in *Yankee Clipper* (also chor.), Ballet Caravan, Saybrook, Connecticut

   Saltarello (cr) in *Folk Dance* (Coudy), Ballet Caravan, Saybrook, Connecticut

   Introduction, Pantomime, and Imitation (cr) in *Show Piece* (Hawkins), Ballet Caravan, Saybrook, Connecticut

1938   Ray, a Truck Driver (cr) in *Filling Station* (L. Christensen), Ballet Caravan, Hartford, Connecticut

   Title role (cr) in *Billy the Kid* (also chor.), Ballet Caravan, Chicago

1940   Title role (cr) in *The Great American Goof* (also chor.), Ballet Theatre, New York

   Peter (cr) in *Peter and the Wolf* (Bolm), Ballet Theatre, New York

1941   The Devil in *Three Virgins and a Devil* (de Mille), Ballet Theatre, New York

WORKS

1936   *Harlequin for President* (mus. Scarlatti), Ballet Caravan, Bennington, Vermont

1937   *Yankee Clipper* (mus. Bowles), Ballet Caravan, Saybrook, Connecticut

1938   *Billy the Kid* (mus. Copland), Ballet Caravan, Chicago

1939   *City Portrait* (mus. Brant), Ballet Caravan, New York

1940   *The Great American Goof* (mus. Brant), Ballet Theatre, New York

1942   *The Man from Midian* (mus. Wolpe), Dance Players, Washington, D.C.

   Prairie (mus. Dello Joio), Dance Players, Washington, D.C.

   The Duke of Sacramento or Hobo of the Hills (mus. Dello Joio), New Hope, Pennsylvania

1953   *Capital of the World* (mus. Antheil), "Omnibus", American television (also staged American Ballet Theatre, New York, 1953)

1961   *Portrait of a Woman*, Idyllwild Arts Foundation, Idyllwild, California

   Quotations, Idyllwild Arts Foundation, Idyllwild, California

1966   *The Sisters* (mus. Ruggles), San Diego Ballet, Jacob's Pillow Festival, Lee, Massachusetts

   These Three (mus. Steinman), City Center Joffrey Ballet, New York

1968   *Prisms, Pinions, Paradox*, Studio Theatre, University of California, Irvine

1969   *Catulli Carmina*, (mus. Orff), Crawford Hall, University of California, Irvine

1970   *Polyphonica*, (mus. Mendelssohn), University of California, Irvine

1971   *Folkdances of a Mythical Country*, (mus. Allard, Loring, Beaver, Krause), University of California, Irvine

1973   *Who am I? Where do I Come From? What am I Doing Here?*, (mus. Copland, Badings), University of California, Irvine

1976   *The Voice*, (mus. Crumb), University of California, Irvine

1978   *Celebration*, University of California, Irvine

   The Tender Land, (mus. Copland), Oakland Ballet, California

1979   *American Gothic*, (mus. Copland), University of California, Irvine

1980   *Time Unto Time*, (mus. Bartók), Oakland Ballet, California

Other works include: dances in musicals *Carmen Jones* (mus. after Bizet, 1943), *Three Wishes for Jamie* (mus. Blane, 1952), *Silk Stockings* (mus. Cole Porter, 1955); choreography for films *Yolanda and the Thief* (dir. Minnelli, 1945), *Ziegfeld Follies* (dir. Minnelli, 1946), *The Thrill of Brazil* (dir. Simon, 1946), *Something in the Wind* (dir. Pichel, 1947), *Fiesta* (dir. Thorpe, 1947), *Mexican Hayride* (dir. Barton, 1948), *Inspector General* (dir. Koster, 1949), *The Toast of New Orleans* (dir. Taurog, 1950), *Mark of the Renegade* (dir. Fregonese, 1951), *5000 Fingers of Dr. T.* (dir. Rowland, 1953), *The Golden Blade* (dir. Juran, 1953), *Deep in My Heart* (dir. Donen, 1954), *Meet Me in Las Vegas* (dir. Rowland, 1956), *Funny Face* (with Fred Astaire; dir. Donen, 1956), *Silk Stockings* (dir. Mamoulian, 1957), *Pepe* (dir. Sidney, 1960); for television—*Capital of the World* (1953).

PUBLICATIONS

By Loring:
"Eugene Loring Talks to Olga Maynard", *Dance Magazine* (New York), 2 parts: July, August 1966
Interview in Delamater, Jerome, *Dance in the Hollywood Musical*, Ann Arbor, 1981

About Loring:
Amberg, George, *Ballet in America*, New York, 1949
Chujoy, Anatole, *The New York City Ballet*, New York, 1953
Lloyd, Margaret, and Cohen, Selma Jeanne, "Eugene Loring's Very American School of Dance", *Dance Magazine* (New York), August 1956
Maynard, Olga, *The American Ballet*, Philadelphia, 1959
Reynolds, Nancy, *Repertory in Review*, New York, 1977
Payne, Charles, *American Ballet Theatre*, New York, 1978
Maynard, Olga, "Eugene Loring's American Classic: The Legend of *Billy the Kid*", *Dance Magazine* (New York), December 1979
Denby, Edwin, *Dance Writings*, edited by Robert Cornfield and William Mackay, New York, 1986
Philp, Richard, "*Billy the Kid* turns 50", *Dance Magazine* (New York), November 1988

*   *   *

Loring's ballet training and early performing career were associated with two major figures in twentieth-century ballet, Mikhail Fokine and George Balanchine, both of whom were Russian-born. As an American choreographer, Loring often employed American themes and an expressive movement vocabulary that embraced many styles to present the personalities, moods, and dramatic situations of the characters in his ballets.

Loring began his choreographic career immersed in the Americana ballet movement of the late 1930s and early 1940s, choreographing four ballets while a member of Ballet Caravan. Loring's first work for Ballet Caravan, *Harlequin for President*, was American by metaphor only, using the buffoonery of Italian *commedia dell'arte* characters and their selection of Harlequin as their president to comment on the American presidential election process. However, *Yankee Clipper*, *Billy the Kid*, and *City Portrait* all used recognizably American characters or concepts. *Yankee Clipper* had as its main character a young American farm boy who sails around the world; *Billy the Kid* focused its attention on the America of pioneers, cowboys, dance-hall girls, and gun fighters. *City Portrait* presented a contemporary subject: an American family torn apart by the poverty, overcrowding, and desolation of the New York neighbourhood in which they live. These works taken together, and the success of *Billy the Kid* in particular, established Loring's reputation as an important American ballet choreographer with a gift for choreographic characterization and expression. He was one of only two Americans to choreograph for Ballet Theatre's first season in 1940.

Loring's evocation of character, mood, and setting was a major element in his work. In *Billy the Kid*, the powerful movements of the pioneers, the exhausted gait of the housewives, the suggestive preening of the dance-hall girls, and the horseback riding of the cowboys clearly defined the characters, their lives, and the demands placed on them. The lives of the family in *City Portrait* were explored in several episodes of familial conflict and street life, with an underlying mood of hopelessness supporting nearly every scene in the libretto. *The Capital of the World*, based on a short story by Ernest Hemingway, employed Spanish-style dancing as well as bullfighting.

Loring began his performing career as an actor, and the narrative, expressive concerns of his work are revealed in the libretti that most of his works employed and in the episodic nature of much of his work. Many of his ballets are in several scenes, and the rendering of place and time is often accomplished by the use of several supporting characters or types that lend a human variety to his setting. His interest in extending the expressive material available to him can be seen in *The Great American Goof*, Loring's contribution to Ballet Theatre's first season. *The Great American Goof* used a libretto by William Saroyan and required the dancers to speak as well as dance, extending a concept employed briefly in *Billy the Kid*.

American themes and social commentary continued to be important to Loring's work even after Ballet Caravan. *Prairie* examined, through one character's journey, the movement from rural America to the cities; in the final scene, the principal character acknowledged her roots in a life dependent on the land. As late as 1966, Loring choreographed *These Three* for the City Center Joffrey Ballet; this ballet was inspired by the civil rights struggle, specifically, the murder of three young civil rights workers in Mississippi.

Once he began to choreograph for Hollywood films, Loring's creative energies went into that genre and into the American School of Dance, which he founded in Hollywood in 1948. The American School was a major West Coast school with an innovative approach. Loring's primary pedagogical concern

was to train what he called "the complete dancer", one who was well-versed in the different styles and genres of the contemporary dance scene. The school offered classes in ballet (which formed the core of Loring's complete dancer), jazz, various ethnic forms, and freestyle—an intentionally loose term which allowed for a combination of genres. He developed a method for teaching choreographic skills and for fostering creativity in his students. Courses in acting for the dancer, dance history, music, movement theory, technical theatre, and dance notation (including Loring's own notation system, Kineseography) were further components of the complete dancer's training. When Loring founded the Dance Department at the University of California at Irvine in 1965, he brought the American School's philosophy to university dance education.

As one of the first American choreographers to emerge from the efforts to establish ballet in the United States, Loring himself was a pioneer. His lasting choreography for *Billy the Kid*, his establishment of the American School of Dance, his work in film choreography, and his commitment to dance as an expressive art form define his life in dance.

—Mary E. Corey

THE LOVES OF MARS AND VENUS

Choreography: John Weaver
Music: Symonds and Firbank
Libretto: John Weaver (after classical myth)
First Production: Drury Lane Theatre, London, 2 March 1717
Principal Dancers: Louis Dupré (Mars), Hester Santlow (Venus), John Weaver (Vulcan)

Other productions include: Ballet for All (educational ensemble of the Royal Ballet; extracts reconstructed by Mary Skeaping); 1969.

PUBLICATIONS

Avery, Emmett, "Dancing and Pantomime on the English Stage 1700–1737", *Studies in Philology* (Chapel Hill), vol. 31, 1934

Fletcher, Ifan, et al., *Famed for Dance: Essays on the Theory and Practice of Theatrical Dancing in England, 1660–1740*, New York, 1960

Brinson, Peter, *A Background to European Ballet*, Leyden, 1966

Kirstein, Lincoln, *Movement and Metaphor: Four Centuries of Ballet*, New York, 1970

Cohen, Selma Jeanne, *Dance as a Theatre Art: Source Readings in Dance History*, New York, 1974

Winter, Marian Hannah, *The Pre-Romantic Ballet*, London, 1974

Ralph, Richard, *The Life and Works of John Weaver*, London, 1985

Foster, Susan Leigh, *Reading Dancing*, Berkeley, California, 1986

*   *   *

The Loves of Mars and Venus, with its simple mythological libretto portraying Vulcan's entrapment of his wife, Venus, and her lover Mars, was a self-conscious experiment in dance theatre, created to illustrate Weaver's sophisticated theories of the dramatic potential of dance. Weaver, one of the most articulate choreographers of the period, published a preface to the libretto, in which he acknowledged the experimental nature of the work, "which I have here attempted to revive from the Ancients, in Imitation of their Pantomimes: I call it an Attempt, or Essay, because this is the first Trial of this Nature that has been made since the Reign of Trajan". In reviving the methods of the classical pantomime, Weaver sought to make his dancers "Imitators of all things, as the Name Pantomime imports", not merely virtuoso performers of what his contemporary Thomas Betterton had called "unmeaning motion" in his criticism of visiting Opéra dancers.

Weaver's preface stresses that the true pantomime dancer "perform'd all by Gesture ... without making use of the Tongue", but he realized that, in view of the difficulties of such an undertaking, it was necessary to instruct both dancers and spectators "in the rules and expressions of Gesticulation". To this end he provided a detailed list of the passions and their representation in mime at appropriate points in the libretto (for instance, "Astonishment. Both hands are thrown up towards the Skies; the Eyes also lifted up, and the Body cast backwards"). The gestures now seem histrionic, but they accord with those used in theatres of the day by actors like Betterton, and later Garrick, who so influenced Noverre. In an age in which dance usually formed sporadic, short entertainments on theatre bills, its use as the main vehicle of a full-length drama was revolutionary. So, too, was the emphasis on facial expression.

Weaver expressed concern that his dancers were not equal to the dramatic aspects of their task. His casting of parts reflects this worry: the role of Vulcan, by far the most demanding dramatically, was played by Weaver himself, while the role of Mars, which required mainly courtly gallantry and set-piece virtuosity, was danced by the great French Opéra danseur, Dupré. Casanova's famous description of his stylized manner, and Noverre's comment that he "ne varioit pas sa danse, ... [il] étoit toujours Dupré" give a sense of Weaver's problem in choreographing for him. Fortunately, Weaver's Venus was supplied by a great early English ballerina, Hester Santlow, whose acting abilities were well known.

These skills were put to the test in Scene II, in which Venus and Vulcan must convey the emotional complexities of marital disenchantment. It was the mimic *tour de force* of the piece, as Weaver's detailed instructions for the scene indicate. The scene opens with Venus and her attendant Graces dancing a passacaille, a dance form often used in finales; presumably Weaver used it here to underscore the false sense of assurance and triumph in Venus, who plays the disdainful coquette, until humiliated by the entrapment. The happy scene terminates abruptly as Vulcan enters to "a wild rough air"; husband and wife then perform a dance "altogether of the Pantomimic kind" in which Vulcan expresses "Admiration; Jealousie; Anger; and Despite" while Venus expresses "Neglect, Coquetry; Contempt; and Disdain". Weaver details these emotional abstractions, but does not personify them, as one might expect in other choreographers of the period, and this is a significant departure (decades later even Noverre could be found still giving roles to characters named "Jealousy" and the like). Furthermore, as historian Richard Ralph has shown, Weaver discarded the didacticism of earlier treatments of the story: for example, even though Cupid still mischievously steals Mars's arms, Weaver's choreography does not stress what Motteux had called "the deformities of Effeminacy or Libertinism" which arise when a man lets down his guard.

The result is that Weaver's is a more naturalistic, less didactic and less anti-feminist handling of the tale, at the same time as it is a more refined one. Venus is still a coquette, but a more chaste one, and Vulcan is no longer the comic cuckold, but a wronged husband who holds the power to dispense both vengeance and mercy, and uses it. Weaver draws attention to this dramatically in some of his stage directions: for example, after Vulcan's argument with Venus, he moves up stage and "strikes at the Scene which opens to Vulcan's Shop", where the net will be forged to capture the illicit lovers. Weaver's characters are mythological, but they are real human characters, not the usual type characters of pre-Noverrian ballet.

It has been common to view Weaver's serious pantomimes, of which *Loves* was the first, as isolated instances or premature attempts to establish the *ballet d'action* before Noverre's time. Increasingly, however, we are coming to see Weaver as a member of an internationally connected avant-garde, a man aware of what other dancing masters were doing and one whose influence on later dancers and choreographers can be traced. If his genius was ahead of its time in anything, it was in his emphasis upon what later decades of the eighteenth-century would call "sentiment". Cultural history was on Noverre's side, for in the few decades between Weaver and the French choreographer interests shifted toward the sentimental, toward what Northrop Frye called the "Age of Sensibility", poised on the brink of romanticism. Although *Loves* was performed eighteen times in 1717, Weaver's audience did not really know what they were seeing. Reviewers were astonishingly literal-minded in their comments, while the rival theatre, Lincoln's Inn Fields, responded with a Harlequin-style parody ("Mars and Venus, or the Mouse Trap"). Weaver only tried one more such purist experiment in serious pantomime (his *Orpheus and Eurydice*) before capitulating to commercial pressures.

—Kathryn Kerby-Fulton

LUKOM, Elena

Russian/Soviet dancer and teacher. Born Elena Mikhailovna Lyukom (Lukom) in St. Petersburg, 5 May (23 April old style) 1891. Studied at the Imperial Theatre School, St. Petersburg, pupil of Mikhail Fokine; graduated in 1909. Dancer, Maryinsky Theatre, later the State Academic Theatre for Opera and Ballet (GATOB), and eventually the Kirov Ballet, St. Petersburg/Leningrad, 1909–41: soloist, from 1912, and ballerina, from 1920; also ballerina touring with Diaghilev's Ballets Russes abroad, 1910, and in concerts with partner Boris Shavrov in Estonia, Latvia, Germany, Denmark, and Sweden, 1922–23; also teacher, Class of Perfection, and répétiteur (rehearsal director), Kirov Ballet, Leningrad, 1953–65. Recipient: title of Honoured Artist of the Republic, 1925; Honoured Arts Worker of the Russian Federation, 1960. Died in Leningrad, 27 February 1968.

ROLES

1909   Skylark, Rose in *Les Saisons* (M. Mikhailov after Petipa), Imperial Theatre School Graduation Performance, St. Petersburg

1911   Cupid in *The Awakening of Flora* (Petipa), Maryinsky Theatre, St. Petersburg

Chinese Girl in *The Fairy Doll* (N. and L. Legat), Maryinsky Theatre, St. Petersburg

The Fairy of Gold in *The Sleeping Beauty* (Petipa), Maryinsky Theatre, St. Petersburg

1912   Latvian Dance in *The Little Humpbacked Horse* (Petipa after Saint-Léon), Maryinsky Theatre, St. Petersburg

Variation ("Work") in *Coppélia* (Petipa, Ivanov, Cecchetti), Maryinsky Theatre, St. Petersburg

Lise in *The Magic Flute* (Ivanov), Maryinsky Theatre, St. Petersburg (first performed in Krasno-Selo)

Pas de trois in *Paquita* (Petipa), Maryinsky Theatre, St. Petersburg

Guadalquivir in *La Fille du Pharaon* (Petipa), Maryinsky Theatre, St. Petersburg

Soloist (cr) in "Almei" Dance in *Judith* (opera; mus. Serov, chor. Fokine), Maryinsky Theatre, St. Petersburg

1914   The White Cat in *The Sleeping Beauty* (Petipa), Maryinsky Theatre, St. Petersburg

Pearl in *The Little Humpbacked Horse* (Petipa after Saint-Léon), Maryinsky Theatre, St. Petersburg

The Canary Fairy in *The Sleeping Beauty* (Petipa), Maryinsky Theatre, St. Petersburg

Flower Girl in *Don Quixote* (Gorsky after Petipa), Maryinsky Theatre, St. Petersburg

Prelude in *Chopiniana* (Fokine), Maryinsky Theatre, St. Petersburg

1915   Gulnara and Pas d'esclave in *Le Corsaire* (Petipa), Maryinsky Theatre, Petrograd

Arsinoya in *Egyptian Nights* (Fokine), Maryinsky Theatre, Petrograd

Pas de trois in *Swan Lake* (Petipa, Ivanov), Maryinsky Theatre, Petrograd

Amour in *Don Quixote* (Gorsky after Petipa), Maryinsky. Theatre, Petrograd

1916   Soloist (cr) in *Aragonese Jota* (Fokine), Maryinsky Theatre, Petrograd

Young Girl in *Eros* (Fokine), Maryinsky Theatre, Petrograd

Columbine in *Harlequinade* (Petipa), Maryinsky Theatre, Petrograd

The Bride (cr) in *Nenufar* (Andrianov), Maryinsky Theatre, Petrograd

Naiad in *Sylvia* (Andrianov after Ivanov, Gerdt), Maryinsky Theatre, Petrograd

Fisherwoman in *Pharaoh's Daughter* (Petipa), Maryinsky Theatre, Petrograd

1917   Pierrette in *Harlequinade* (Petipa), State Maryinsky Theatre, Petrograd

Henrietta in *Raymonda* (Petipa), State Maryinsky Theatre, Petrograd

Fleur-de-lis in *Esmeralda* (Petipa after Perrot), State Maryinsky Theatre, Petrograd

1918   Butterfly in *Carnaval* (Fokine), State Maryinsky Theatre, Petrograd

Henrietta in *Raymonda* (Gorsky after Petipa), State Maryinsky Theatre, Petrograd

Bébé in *The Fairy Doll* (N. and S. Legat), State Maryinsky Theatre, Petrograd

Grand Pas in *Paquita* (Petipa), State Maryinsky Theatre, Petrograd

Lise in *La Fille mal gardée* (Petipa, Ivanov), State Maryinsky Theatre, Petrograd

Swanilda in *Coppélia* (Petipa, Cecchetti), State Maryinsky Theatre, Petrograd

Butterfly in *The Caprices of the Butterfly* (Petipa), State Maryinsky Theatre, Petrograd

Marinetta in *The Trials of Damis* (Petipa), State Maryinsky Theatre, Petrograd

1919   Clemence in *Raymonda* (Petipa), State Maryinsky Theatre, Petrograd

Title role in *Graziella* (Saint-Léon), State Maryinsky Theatre, Petrograd

Thérèse in *Cavalry Halt* (Petipa), State Maryinsky Theatre, Petrograd

Nasturtium (cr) in *The Love of a Rose* (Chekrygin), State Maryinsky Theatre, Petrograd

Isora's friend in *Bluebeard* (Monakhov and Chekrygin after Petipa, Legat), State Maryinsky Theatre, Petrograd

Princess Florine in *The Sleeping Beauty* (Petipa), State Maryinsky Theatre, Petrograd

1920   Principal dancer in *Chopiniana* (Fokine), State Academic Theatre for Opera and Ballet (GATOB), Petrograd

Odette/Odile in *Swan Lake* (Petipa, Ivanov), GATOB, Petrograd

Title role in *Raymonda* (Petipa), GATOB, Petrograd

Ballerina in *Petrushka* (Fokine), GATOB, Petrograd

1921   Manou in *La Bayadère* (Petipa), GATOB, Petrograd

Medora in *Le Corsaire* (Petipa), GATOB, Petrograd

Title role (cr) in *Firebird* (Lopukhov), GATOB, Petrograd

Aspiccia in *Pharaoh's Daughter* (Petipa), GATOB, Petrograd

Title role in *Giselle* (Petipa after Coralli, Perrot), GATOB, Petrograd

1922   Tsar-Maiden in *The Little Humpbacked Horse* (Petipa after Saint-Léon; staged Lopukhov), GATOB, Petrograd

Title role in *Esmeralda* (Petipa after Perrot), GATOB, Petrograd

Berenice in *Egyptian Nights* (Fokine), GATOB, Petrograd

Title role in *Fiametta* (Petipa, Ivanov after Saint-Léon), GATOB, Petrograd

1923   Kitri in *Don Quixote* (Gorsky after Petipa; staged Lopukhov), GATOB, Petrograd

1924   Nikiya in *La Bayadère* (Petipa), GATOB, Leningrad

Ear of Corn in *The Seasons* (Petipa, staged Leontiev), GATOB, Leningrad

1925   Clytia in *King Candaulus* (Petipa, staged Leontiev), GATOB, Leningrad

1929   Tao-Hoa (cr) in *The Red Poppy* (Lopukhov, Ponomarev, Leontiev), GATOB, Leningrad

1930   Diva in *The Golden Age* (Vainonen, Yakobson, Chesnokov), GATOB, Leningrad

1934   Maria in *The Fountain of Bakhchisarai* (Zakharov), GATOB, Leningrad

1935   Title role in *Esmeralda* (Vaganova after Petipa), Kirov Ballet, Leningrad

1937   The Lady in White in *Partisan Days* (Vainonen), Kirov Ballet, Leningrad

Other roles include: Concert pieces—Swan in *The Dying Swan* (Fokine), Columbine in *Two Pierrots and Columbine* (pantomime), *Barcarolla* and *Polka* (Lopukhov), *Souvenir* (Lopukhov), *Adagio* (Lopukhov), *Etude* (Lopukhov), *Waltz* (Chekrygin), *Melody* (Chabukiani), *Bacchanal* (Monakhov), *Pierrette and Harlequin* (with Boris Shavrov).

PUBLICATIONS

By Lukom:
My Work in Ballet, Leningrad, 1940

About Lukom:
Brodersen, Yuri, *Elena Lyukom*, Leningrad, 1941

Elena Lukom

Krasovskaya, Vera, *Russian Ballet Theatre at the Beginning of the Twentieth Century*, volume 2: Leningrad, 1972

Chernova, Nina, *From Geltser to Ulanova*, Moscow, 1979

Rosanova, Olga, *Elena Lyukom*, Leningrad, 1983

Dzyuba, T., Shamina, L., "Pages of the Calendar: E.M. Lyukom", *Sovietsky Balet* (Moscow), no. 4, 1986

* * *

The Russian ballerina Elena Lukom represented, in a sense, the epitome of the St. Petersburg school. Trained at the turn of the century in the St. Petersburg Imperial Ballet style, Lukom danced all of the major roles in the classical repertoire as a young soloist before the revolution. She was one of the few leading dancers who did not leave Russia, even though she could easily have done so in 1916 or 1917. And perhaps fittingly, her farewell performance was given on the day that the Second World War in Russia was announced: it was the end of an era.

Blonde, petite, and naturally graceful, Lukom also had a lively personality and sense of humour; she was charming, both as a person and as a performer. Her appearances in Petrograd during the 1910s and 1920s were undoubtedly especially appreciated at a time when so many other Russian dancers had left the country, and conditions in the ballet theatre had become quite stagnant. Her stage partner, Boris Shavrov, was an excellent partner in pas de deux, and together the two dancers developed many new movements, such as high lifts or dramatic fishdives, which were quite a novelty at the time. Together they toured Russia and Scandinavia in 1922 and 1923, forever surprising and delighting audiences with their virtuosity and daring. Elena Lukom was also partnered by such outstanding Soviet male dancers as Vakhtang Chabukiani and Konstantin Sergeyev during her long career.

Lukom's repertoire covered the traditional ballets, where she was admired in particular for the spiritual quality of her dancing; but she also danced in new ballets, creating such roles as the title role in Fedor Lopukhov's *Firebird*, and Tao-Hoa in *The Red Poppy*. Lopukhov remembered: "The public loved her for her unique absorption in dance, which endowed her movements with joyful zeal. Lukom was the first Leningrad ballerina who was widely known by the Soviet spectator." Lukom's early study with Fokine was also an important part of her career, and Lopukhov again explained, "The inspiration and expressiveness developed in Lukom by Fokine became one of the chief characteristics of her own creativity." And the critic Akim Volynsky wrote of Lukom, "It is necessary to acknowledge her as the best artist of pure ballet on our stage. This means not a dramatic but a balletic artist, not speaking but at the same time speaking with all the languages of the plastic arts."

After the end of her performing career, Lukom became a coach with the Kirov Ballet, where she was well liked as a helpful and generous teacher. Her gift was in explaining the very *image* of dance as it should appear—what was important was not just the technique, as in how to point a foot or where to hold the arms, but the inner understanding of a step or a pose. She would often spend a long time with dancers explaining the meaning of a character, such as Nikiya in *La Bayadère*. She remained in this position for twelve years at the Kirov, and many young dancers benefited from her thoughtful and spirited teaching. Lukom died in Leningrad in 1968.

—Igor Stupnikov

LULLY, Jean-Baptiste

Italian/French composer and dancer. Born Giovanni Battista Lulli in Florence, 28 November 1632. Studied music as a child in Italy; later studied violin with Lazzarini, harpsichord with Nicolas Meru, and organ with François Roberdet. Married Madeleine Lambert, 1662. Moved to France, c.1644, emerging as violinist, guitarist, and dancer while in service of Mlle. de Montpensier, Paris; member of *Vingt-quatre violins du Roi*, from 1652; appointed *compositeur de la musique instrumentale du Roi*, 1653; dancer, alongside Louis XIV, in *Ballet de la nuit*, 1653; director of "petite bande" of violins, or Les Petits Violins, for ballet performances, from 1656; composer of music for *Ballet de l'amour malade*, 1657; recipient of French citizenship, 1661; *maître de la musique de la famille royale*, from 1662; composer of first important comédie-ballet to libretto by Molière, *Le Mariage forcé*, 1664; secured royal privilege to establish L'Académie royale de musique, forbidding performances of complete works without his prior permission, 1672; took over running of Palais Royal, 1673; secrétaire du Roi, from 1681. Died in Paris, 22 March 1687.

WORKS (Ballets and comédies-ballets)

1658 *Ballet Royal d'Alcidiane* (chor. Beauchamps), Versailles
1659 *Ballet de la raillerie*, Louvre, Paris
1660 *Ballet de Toulouze "au mariage du Roy"*, Paris
1661 *Ballet Royal de l'impatience* (chor. Beauchamps), Paris
       Ballet des Saisons, Fontainebleu
1663 *Ballet des arts* (chor. Beauchamps, Vertpré), Palais Royal, Versailles
       Les Noces de village, Château de Vincennes
       L'Impromptu de Versailles (comédie by Molière), Versailles
1664 *Le Mariage forcé* (comédie by Molière; chor. Beauchamps), Louvre, Paris
       Les Amours déguisés (ballet; chor. possibly Beauchamps), Palais Royal, Paris
       Les Plaisirs de l'île enchantée (comédie-ballet by Molière), Versailles
       La Princesse d'Elide (comédie-ballet by Molière), Versailles
       Le Petit Ballet de Fontainebleau (same music as for *Oedipe* by Corneille, below), Fontainebleau
1665 *La Naissance de Vénus* (ballet; chor. Beauchamps), Palais Royal, Paris
       L'Amour médecin (comédie by Molière), Versailles
1666 *Ballet de Créquy; ou, Le Triomphe de Bacchus dans les Indes*, Hôtel de Créquy, Paris
       Ballet des muses (chor. Beauchamps), Saint-Germain-en-Laye
1667 *La Pastorale comique* (pastorale by Molière), Saint-Germain-en-Laye
       Le Sicilien; ou, L'Amour peintre (comédie by Molière), Saint-Germain-en-Laye
1668 *Le Carnaval; ou, Mascarade de Versailles*, Louvre (some sources say Tuileries), Paris
       George Dandin (grand divertissement in comédie by Molière; chor. Beauchamps, Dolivet), Versailles
       La Grotte de Versailles (divertissement), Versailles (performed as *Eglogue de Versailles* at Opéra, Paris, 1685)
1669 *Ballet de Flore*, Grand Salon, Tuileries, Paris
       Divertissement de Chambord in *Monsieur de Pourceaugnac* (comédie by Molière), Chambord
1670 *Les Jeux Pythiens*, Saint-Germain
       Divertissement Royal in *Les Amants magnifiques* (comé-

Jean-Baptiste Lully's *Le Triomphe de l'amour*, 1681 (costume designs by Jean-Louis Berain)

die-ballet by Molière, Benserade; chor. Beauchamps,
Dolivet), Saint-Germain
Le Bourgeois Gentilhomme (comédie-ballet by Molière;
chor. Beauchamps), Chambord

1671   *Psyché* (tragédie-lyrique by Molière, Corneille, Quinault; chor. Beauchamps), Tuileries, Paris
Ballet des ballets in *La Comtesse d'Escarbagnas* (comédie
by Molière; mus. from various other Lully stage
works), Saint-Germain

1675   *Le Carnaval* (ballet; chor. Beauchamps), Opéra, Paris

1681   *Le Triomphe de l'amour* (ballet; chor. Beauchamps,
Pécour), Saint-Germain-en-Laye

1685   *Idylle sur la paix* (divertissement), Sceaux
Le Temple de la paix (ballet; chor. Beauchamps),
Fontainebleu

WORKS (written in collaboration with other composers or
inserted into other works)

1653   *Ballet de la nuit* (with de Cambefort, Boësset, Lambert;
also chor., with Chancy, Mollier, Manuel, Vertpré),
Salle de la Petit-Bourbon, Paris

1654   *Les Proverbes* (with other composers; music lost),
Louvre, Paris
Les Noces de Pelée et de Thétis (airs for ballet in opera by
Caprioli), Salle du Petit-Bourbon, Paris
Ballets du temps (with Mollier, Boësset), Louvre, Paris

1655   *Ballet des plaisirs* (with Boësset; chor. Beauchamps),
Louvre, Paris
Ballet des bienvenus (with other composers; music lost),
Compiègne

1656   *Ballet de Psyché* (*Psyché et la puissance de l'amour*; with
Boësset; chor. Beauchamps), Louvre, Paris
La Galanterie du temps (with other composers), Paris
Ballet de l'amour malade (entrées in *L'Amor malato* by
Marazzoli), Louvre, Paris

1657   *Les Plaisirs troublés* (ballet-mascarade; chor. Beauchamps), Louvre, Paris

1660   *Xerxes* (ballets intermèdes in opera by Cavalli), Louvre,
Paris

1662   *Hercule amoureux* (ballet in opera by Cavalli), Salle des
Machines des Tuileries, Paris

1664   *Oedipe* (entrées for tragédie by Corneille),
Fontainebleau
Mascarade du capitaine (with other composers; music
lost), Palais Royal, Paris

Other works include: *Le Révente des habits de ballet* (ballet; in
collaboration with other composers; c.1655), *Les Gardes*
(ballet; 1665), *La Jeunesse* (ballet; 1669); operas—*Les Fêtes de
l'Amour et de Bacchus* (pastorale pastiche; 1672), *Cadmus et
Hermione* (tragédie-lyrique; 1673), *Alceste; ou, Le Triomphe
d'Alcide* (tragédie-lyrique; 1674), *Thésée* (tragédie-lyrique;
1675), *Atys* (tragédie-lyrique; 1676), *Isis* (tragédie-lyrique;
1677), *Psyché* (tragédie-lyrique; 1678), *Bellérophon* (tragédie-

lyrique; 1679), *Proserpine* (tragédie-lyrique; 1680), *Persée* (tragédie-lyrique; 1682), *Phaëton* (tragédie-lyrique; 1683), *Amadis* (tragédie-lyrique; 1684), *Roland* (tragédie-lyrique; 1685), *Armide* (tragédie-lyrique; 1686), *Acis et Galatée* (pastorale-héroïque; 1686), *Achille et Polyxène* (tragédie-lyrique, with Colasse; 1687); numerous airs and parodies from operas, comédie-ballets, and ballets.

Other ballets using Lully's music: *Fête champêtre* (also incorporating mus. by Grétry, Rameau; Littlefield, 1936), *Le Bourgeois Gentilhomme* (W. Christensen, 1944), *Fête signalétique* (Béjart, 1988).

PUBLICATIONS

Pougin, A., *Jean-Baptiste Lully*, Paris, 1883

Radet, E., *Lully, homme d'affaires, propriétaire et musicien*, Paris, 1891

Prunières, Henry, and de la Laurencie, Lionel, *La Jeunesse de Lully*, Paris, 1909

Prunières, Henry, *Lully*, Paris, 1910

De la Laurencie, Lionel, *Lully*, Paris, 1911

Pellisson, M., *Les Comédies-Ballets de Molière*, Paris, 1914

Prunières, Henry, *La Vie illustre et libertine de J.B. Lully*, Paris, 1929

Silin, C. I., *Benserade and his Ballets de Cour*, Baltimore, 1940

Hussey, Dyneley, "J.B. Lully", *Dancing Times* (London), June–July, 1947

Borrel, Eugène, *Jean-Baptiste Lully: Le Cadre, la vie, la personnalité*, Paris, 1949

Mellers, Wilfred, "Jean-Baptiste Lully", *The Heritage of Music* (London), vol. 3, 1951

Christout, Marie-Françoise, *Le Ballet de cour de Louis XIV 1643–1672*, Paris, 1967

Ellis, Helen Meredith, *The Dances of J.B. Lully (1632–1687)*, Ph.D. dissertation, Stanford University, 1967

Scott, R.H.F., *Jean-Baptiste Lully*, London, 1973

Newman, Joyce, *Jean-Baptiste Lully and his Tragédies lyriques*, Ann Arbor, 1974

Heyer, John (ed.), *Jean Baptiste Lully and the Music of the French Baroque: Essays in Honour of James R. Anthony*, New York, 1989

Beaussant, Philippe, *Lully, ou le musicien du soleil*, Paris, 1992

* * *

Jean-Baptiste Lully was born Giovanni Battista Lulli at or near Florence in 1632. His father was Lorenzo di Maldo Lulli, a miller, though in his letters of naturalization in 1661 Lully described his father as "a Florentine gentleman". He received his early musical training from a local priest and, according to Pierre Rameau in his *Maître à danser*, he came to France at the age of nine, though more recent researchers put his age at nearer to twelve years. He was brought to France by the Chevalier de Guise to take up an appointment as *garçon de chambre* in the service of Mlle. de Montpensier (La Grande Mademoiselle) at a salary of 150 livres. His talents as a violinist were soon recognized, and he was promoted to a position in La Grande Mademoiselle's band of musicians, where he made the most of his advancement and was soon the leading violin. After the defeat of the Frondists, La Grande Mademoiselle was banished to her château at St. Targeau, and Lully, who had already come to the notice of the King, applied for release from her service, returning to Paris in 1652 to become a member of the famous "24 Violins" in Louis XIV's household. (He so impressed the King that Louis later established a small band,

Les Petits Violins, especially for him.) On the death of Lazzarini in March 1653 he was appointed *compositeur de la musique instrumentale du Roi*.

Lully was also noted for his dancing skill, and in February 1653 he composed his first ballet (along with several other composers) for Louis XIV, *Le Ballet de la nuit*, in which he himself danced with the King. From this time onwards, he composed numerous ballets and divertissements in which he also danced. In December 1661, he was granted his "Lettre de naturalisation", which established him as a French citizen, opening the way for him to rise higher in Court circles, and to win even more lucrative appointments. After his appointment as *maître de la musique de la famille royale*, he consolidated his position at court by marrying Madeleine Lambert (daughter of Michel Lambert, the *maître de musique de la cour*), who brought with her a dowry of 20,000 livres. In March 1672, by somewhat devious means, he became director of the Académie royale de musique, and from this time onwards he concentrated his attentions on producing an annual opera. During the next fifteen years, with the support of Louis XIV, Lully ruled the Opéra as a virtual dictator.

Jean-Baptiste Lully was a man of his time. In a flamboyant age he was a master of flamboyance. He was a wit, a mimic, and a highly talented dancer and musician. From a very early age he showed himself to be ambitious and selfish. He was quick, for example, to sever his connections with La Grande Mademoiselle when she fell into disgrace, and having already made an impression on Louis XIV, he made the most of this by applying for a post at Court as a member of the famous "24 Violins", or *Vingt-quatre violons du Roi*. Lully felt strongly that the existing technique of violin playing was dull. He objected to the heavy use of decoration and embellishment and to the fact that musicians often played from memory with disastrous results. He soon persuaded Louis to create a new smaller band especially for him, which he ruled with extreme strictness, writing out the parts for each instrument in order to leave nothing to chance, and introducing the delicate *point de broderie* style of ornamentation with strongly dotted rhythms.

In addition to composing and playing, Lully was increasingly in great demand as a dancer. At the age of 20 he had danced his leading role with the 14-year-old King in the *Ballet de la nuit*, and from this time on he wrote and performed in many other ballets with Louis, making the comedy role of M. de Pourceaugnac his own particular speciality. Between the years 1653 and 1672 he composed over 40 ballets and divertissements, in most of which he himself took part as dancer and comic actor. His talents in both fields confirmed him in the favour of the King and he exploited this preference unashamedly. The ballets Lully created during this period were initially for performance by or before the King. This meant that they received only one or two showings, and he realized that to attract a larger audience he needed a theatre in which they could be played before the general public. In 1672 there were disagreements between the directors of the Académie royale de musique, and with great astuteness and much underhand dealing, Lully bought from Pierre Perrin the privilège granted to him by the King in 1669 to establish a theatre open to the general public. He followed this up by arranging for the letters patent to be transferred to him, and obtaining the lease of Béquet's Jeu de paume in which to stage his compositions. Up to this time much of Lully's work had been the creation of ballets and light divertissements which were the King's favourite, but he was now in a position to stage works on a grander scale and transferred his interest to opera, though dancing still found a place in this.

It was at this point that Lully made a contract with the poet Quinault to provide him annually with an operatic libretto. The two worked together for the next fourteen years, producing some of the most graceful and charming works of the seventeenth century. Although the setting-up of the theatre cost Lully and his partner, the artist Vigarani, 20,000 livres, the popularity of opera at this time ensured that they soon made ample profits. For one thing there were the box-office takings. According to La Fontaine, "The officer and merchant gave up all their roast to afford the opera on Sunday, which of their earnings took most." Because of the limited audience capacity at the theatre, Lully was given permission to charge not only "all persons of rank and standing" but even the members of the King's household who normally were admitted without charge to Paris theatres. In addition to this income, there was the sale of the libretto which audiences liked to have to help them follow the plot and, in some cases, to sing with the chorus.

Lully was not popular among his contemporaries, being greedy for both fame and fortune and unscrupulous in his methods of obtaining both. It is difficult to comprehend how such an apparently unpleasant character could produce so much exquisite and witty music, but there is no doubt that he was a master of stagecraft with an instinct for the picturesque and the dramatic. He revolutionized the ballet de la cour, replacing many of the slow stately dances commonly employed in court ballets with lively rapid airs, and introducing female dancers to the stage, to the delight of his audiences.

In 1681 Lully was granted Lettres de Noblesse and appointed one of the Secrétaires du Roi, an honour normally attained only by the nobility. In January 1687, while conducting a Te Deum for the recovery of Louis from an illness, Lully accidentally struck his foot with the staff he used to conduct his orchestra. An abscess developed which became gangrenous, and he died on 22 March 1687, leaving a wife, three sons, and three daughters.

—Madeleine Inglehearn

M

MACDONALD, Brian

Canadian dancer, choreographer, and ballet director. Born in Montreal, 14 May 1928. Educated at McGill University, Montreal (B.A.); studied dance with Gerald Crevier and Elizabeth Leese. Married (1) dancer Olivia Wyatt (d. 1959); (2) dancer Annette Weidersheim-Paul, 1965. Early career as music critic; character dancer, National Ballet of Canada, 1951–53; founder, Montreal Theatre Ballet, 1956; choreographer, Les Grands Ballets Canadiens and Royal Winnipeg Ballet, from 1958; guest choreographer, Norwegian Ballet, Olso, 1963; director, Royal Swedish Ballet, Stockholm, 1964–65, Harkness Ballet, New York, 1967–68, and Batsheva Dance Company, Israel, 1971–72; resident choreographer, Les Grands Ballets Canadiens, Montreal, becoming artistic director, 1974; also choreographer for television, 1954–58, and for variety shows and musicals, Montreal, Quebec, and Winnipeg, including for *My Fur Lady* (variety version of *My Fair Lady*), *Guys and Dolls* (mus. Loesser), *Pajama Game* (mus. Adler, Ross), *Damn Yankees* (mus. Adler), *Carousel* (mus. Rodgers), and *Oklahoma!* (mus. Rodgers); choreographer and stage director for musicals, operetta, and opera, including for Stratford Festival, Ontario; has also acted as director, Summer Dance Programme, Banff Centre, Banff. Recipient: Choreography Award, Paris International Dance Festival, 1964.

WORKS

1958   *Cordes* (*Strings*; mus. Bartók), Les Grands Ballets Canadiens, Montreal
      The Darkling (mus. Britten), Royal Winnipeg Ballet, Winnipeg

1959   *Les Whoops-de-doo* (mus. Gillis), Royal Winnipeg Ballet, Manitoba

1961   *Prothalamion* (mus. Delius), Les Grands Ballets Canadiens, Montreal (staged Royal Winnipeg Ballet, 1962, and as *Hymne*, Norwegian Ballet, 1963)

1962   *Aimez-vous Bach?* (mus. Bach), Banff Festival, Banff (staged Royal Winnipeg Ballet, 1963)
      Capers (mus. Rieti), Joffrey Ballet, Leningrad

1963   *Time out of Mind* (mus. Creston), Joffrey Ballet, New York (staged Harkness Ballet, 1965)

1965   *While the Spider Slept* (mus. Karkoff), Royal Swedish Ballet, Stockholm
      Octet (mus. Schubert), Royal Swedish Ballet, Stockholm

1966   *Rose Latulippe* (mus. Freedman), Royal Winnipeg Ballet, Stratford, Ontario
      Skymning (mus. Strauss), Royal Swedish Ballet, Stockholm
      Ballet Russe (mus. Tchaikovsky), Royal Swedish Ballet, Stockholm

1967   *Tchaikovsky* (mus. Tchaikovsky), Harkness Ballet, Chicago
      Zealous Variations (mus. Schubert), Harkness Ballet, New York
      Firebird (mus. Stravinsky), Harkness Ballet, New York
      Canto Indio (mus. Chavez), Harkness Ballet, New York

1970   *Ballet High* (mus. "The Lighthouse"), Royal Winnipeg Ballet, Ottawa
      The Shining People of Leonard Cohen (mus. arranged Freedman; verse by Cohen), Royal Winnipeg Ballet, Winnipeg

1971   *Martha's Vineyard* (mus. Dello Joio), Batsheva Dance Company, Israel

1972   *Jeu de cartes* (mus. Stravinsky), Les Grands Ballets Canadiens, Montreal
      Several Occasions (mus. Freedman, Bach), Festival Canada Ballet, Ottawa
      Star-crossed (mus. Freedman; text Shakespeare), Festival Canada Ballet, Ottawa

1974   *The Lottery* (mus. Stravinsky, *Le Sacre du printemps*, revised orchestration Rudolf), Harkness Ballet, New York
      Diabelli Variations (mus. Beethoven), Paris Opéra Ballet, Paris (staged Les Grands Ballets Canadiens, 1975)
      Tam Ti Delam (mus. Vigneault), Les Grands Ballets Canadiens, Montreal

1975   *Rags*, Ballet-Théâtre Contemporain, Paris
      Pic-Bois (mus. Rivard, Bertrand, Dommage), Les Grands Ballets Canadiens, Montreal
      Romeo and Juliet (new version of *Star-crossed*; mus. Freedman), Les Grands Ballets Canadiens, Montreal

1976   *Cantata pour une joie* (mus. Mercure), Les Grands Ballets Canadiens, Montreal
      Offrande (mus. Bach), Les Grands Ballets Canadiens, Montreal
      Lignes et pointes (with Paige; mus. Mercure), Les Grands Ballets Canadiens, Montreal
      Tournoi (*Tournament*; also *Marathon*; mus. various), Les Grands Ballets Canadiens, Montreal
      Bawdy Variations (mus. Confrey), Les Grands Ballets Canadiens, Montreal

1978   *Double Quartet* (mus. Schumann, Schafer), Les Grands Ballets Canadiens, Montreal
      Fête Carignan (*Hangman's Reel*; mus. Carignan), Les Grands Ballets Canadiens, Montreal
      Remembranza (pas de deux; mus. Tchaikovsky, Arensky), International Ballet Festival, Havana
      Prologue pour une tragédie (mus. Bach), Ballet Nacional de Cuba, Havana

1979   *Adieu Robert Schumann* (mus. Schafer), Les Grands

Ballets Canadiens, Montreal
1980 *Newcomers* (mus. Prevost, Freedman, Weinzweig, Klein), National Ballet of Canada, Toronto
1982 *Étapes* (*Stages*; mus. Matton), Les Grands Ballets Canadiens, Montreal
1983 *Findings* (mus. Garant, Bach), Alberta Ballet and Banff Centre Students, Banff Festival, Banff
      Chant du roseau (*Reed Song*; mus. Freedman), Les Grands Ballets Canadiens
1987 *Breaks* (mus. Mozart, Freedman), Banff Festival, Banff

Other works include: *Hommage, Artist and Model* (mus. Auric), *Dangerous Games, Post-Script, Voices from a Far Place.*

PUBLICATIONS

By Macdonald:
"The Impact of British Ballet on the Canadian Dance Scene", *Dancing Times* (London), April 1963
"*Rose Latulippe*: A Canadian Legend and Ballet", *Dance News* (New York), December 1966
"The Countdown Begins", *Dance Magazine* (New York), October 1967
Interview in "Macdonald Speaks . . .", *Canadian Dance News* (Toronto), June 1981

About Macdonald:
Whittaker, Herbert, "Brian Macdonald", *Dance in Canada* (Toronto), Summer 1956
Cohen, Nathan, "TV Dance in Canada", *Dance Magazine* (New York), August 1957
"In the News", *Dance Magazine* (New York), December 1963
Barnes, Clive, "*Rose Latulippe*", *Dance and Dancers* (London), October 1966
Crabb, Michael, "Dance in Canada Today", *Dancing Times* (London), November 1976
Crabb, Michael, "Les Grands Ballets Canadiens", *Dancing Times* (London), July 1982
Stoop, Norma McLain, "The Canadian Cosmopolitan", *Dance Magazine* (New York), April 1984

*   *   *

Brian Macdonald holds a special place in the history of Canadian dance both as a staunch champion of indigenous creative talent and as the country's first choreographer of international repute. His theatrical understanding, exercised both on stage and in television, has also helped make him a very successful director of musical theatre and operas.

Theatricality is, in fact, a key to Macdonald's artistic sensibility. It is no accident that his first big hit was a popular Canadian review, *My Fur Lady*, which he staged in 1957. Much as he is concerned with the formal aspects of dance composition, as evident in such an assured neo-classical work as *Double Quartet*, Macdonald is also an entertainer. His ability to respond to the mood of the moment, to embrace the responsibility of a resident choreographer and provide material as needed that both extends and shows off his dancers, help explain Macdonald's success in a long and continuing career.

Although Macdonald's tough, uncompromising approach has sometimes made him a controversial figure, his contributions to the development of such Canadian institutions as the Royal Winnipeg Ballet, Les Grands Ballets Canadiens and, as a director of musicals and operettas, the Stratford Festival in Ontario, are indisputable.

When Macdonald's dancing career as a founding member of the National Ballet of Canada was cut short by injury, he turned his attention to teaching and choreographing, first for television and music halls. Early on, Macdonald proclaimed his belief in the potential of Canadian artists by founding the short-lived Montreal Theatre Ballet in 1956, dedicated to presenting Canadian choreography with Canadian music and designs.

Although Macdonald, with no company of his own to direct in Canada, worked internationally through the 1960s, he put his stamp on an important phase in the growth of the Royal Winnipeg Ballet after his *Aimez-vous Bach?* helped win the company an important invitation to Jacob's Pillow, the gateway to a busy period of international touring. In 1964 the same work won Macdonald the gold star for choreography at the Paris International Dance Festival. In 1966, using a folk story as his theme, Macdonald created *Rose Latulippe*, Canada's first evening-length ballet for the Winnipeg Company. Other popular works from this period include his *Time out of Mind* and *The Shining People of Leonard Cohen*, inspired by the romantic poetry of Canadian Leonard Cohen and set to Canadian composer Harry Freedman's original score.

As artistic director and, subsequently, resident choreographer of Montreal's Les Grands Ballets Canadiens, Macdonald similarly made his choreographic and theatrical imprint with works such as *Tam Ti Delam* and *Fête Carignan*, setting classical steps to music with strong French-Canadian folkloric appeal.

During the 1980s Macdonald, while continuing to play an influential role in Canadian ballet as head of the Banff Centre's summer professional dance programme, became increasingly well known internationally as a stage director of musical theatre and opera, in particular for his very popular series of Gilbert and Sullivan productions at Ontario's Stratford Festival.

However, despite his versatility and enormous creative output, Macdonald remains an individualistic choreographer without stylistic disciples. He has been more successful in creating a temporary image for the companies with which he has worked, often simultaneously improving the technical standard of their dancing, than in imparting a lasting and distinctive style. The very eclicticism of Macdonald's choreographic approach, while helping explain his successes, has perhaps also limited the enduring artistic impact of his work.

—Michael Crabb

—

MACLEARY, Donald
Scottish dancer and teacher. Born in Glasgow, 22 August 1937. Studied under Sheila Ross, 1950–51, and at Sadler's Wells Ballet School, London. Dancer, Sadler's Wells Theatre Ballet (later Royal Ballet Touring Company, and Royal Ballet New Group), 1954–75, becoming soloist from 1955; principal dancer, Royal Ballet (at Covent Garden), from 1959, often partnering Svetlana Beriosova; international guest artist, including in Paris, Stuttgart, Berlin, Helsinki, Durban, Zimbabwe; also appeared with Scottish Ballet and London City Ballet; ballet master, Royal Ballet, 1976–79; continues as coach and teacher.

ROLES

1955 Moon in *Blood Wedding* (Rodrigues), Sadler's Wells Theatre Ballet

Donald MacLeary rehearsing as Albrecht in *Giselle*, **London**

Mazurka ("Poet") in *Les Sylphides* (Fokine), Sadler's Wells Theatre Ballet

Eusebius in *Carnaval* (Fokine), Sadler's Wells Theatre Ballet

Pas de trois in *Café des sports* (Rodrigues), Sadler's Wells Theatre Ballet

Pas de deux in *Danses Concertantes* (MacMillan), Sadler's Wells Theatre Ballet, London

The King (cr) in *Saudades* (Rodrigues), Sadler's Wells Theatre Ballet, Liverpool

1956 Pas de deux (cr) in *Solitaire* (MacMillan), Sadler's Wells Theatre Ballet, London

1957 Bridegroom in *La Fête étrange* (Howard), Royal Ballet Touring Company, London

The Morbid (cr) in *The Angels* (Cranko), Royal Ballet Touring Company, London

Leonardo in *Blood Wedding* (Rodrigues), Royal Ballet Touring Company, London

Pas de deux (cr) in *A Blue Rose* (Wright), Royal Ballet Touring Company, London

Prince Siegfried in *Swan Lake*, Act II (after Ivanov), Royal Ballet Touring Company

The Mariner in *Ile des sirènes* (Rodrigues), Royal Ballet Touring Company

1958 Adolescent (cr) in *The Burrow* (MacMillan), Royal Ballet Touring Company, London

Pas de deux (cr) in *First Impressions* (Beale), Sunday Ballet Club, London

Albrecht in *Giselle* (Petipa after Coralli, Perrot; staged Sergeyev), Royal Ballet Touring Company, tour

1959 Haeman in *Antigone* (Cranko), Royal Ballet, London

Knight in *La Belle Dame sans merci* (Howard), Royal Ballet, London

Prince in *Cinderella* (Ashton), Royal Ballet, London

Prince Siegfried in *Swan Lake* (Petipa, Ivanov; staged de Valois, Ashton), Royal Ballet, London

Pas de deux in *Les Patineurs* (Ashton), Royal Ballet, London

Aminta in *Sylvia* (Ashton), Royal Ballet, London

1960 Young Man (cr) in *Le Baiser de la fée* (MacMillan), Royal Ballet, London

Prince Florimund in *The Sleeping Beauty* (Petipa; staged Sergeyev, Ashton, de Valois), Royal Ballet, London

1961 Principal dancer (cr) in *Diversions* (MacMillan), Royal Ballet, London

Colas in *La Fille mal gardée* (Ashton), Royal Ballet, London

Jabez (cr) in *Jabez and the Devil* (Rodrigues), Royal Ballet, London

Palemon in *Ondine* (Ashton), Royal Ballet, London

Mazurka in *Les Sylphides* (Fokine), Royal Ballet, London

1962 Cousin in *The Invitation* (MacMillan), Royal Ballet, London

Principal dancer in *Symphonic Variations* (Ashton), Royal Ballet, London

Pas de deux and variation (cr) from *Raymonda* (Ashton after Petipa), Royal Ballet, London

Principal dancer in *Don Quixote* Pas de deux (after Petipa), Royal Ballet Touring Company

1963 Principal dancer in *Ballet Imperial* (Balanchine), Royal Ballet, London

First Red Knight in *Checkmate* (de Valois), Royal Ballet, London

Country boy in *La Fête étrange* (Howard), Royal Ballet, London

The Secret Admirer (cr) in *Night Tryst* (Carter), Royal Ballet, London

Variation, Adagio of Lovers in *Les Rendezvous* (Ashton), Royal Ballet, London

Principal dancer (cr) in *Symphony* (MacMillan), Royal Ballet, London

1964 Solor in *La Bayadère* (Nureyev after Petipa), Royal Ballet, London

"When love begins to sicken" (cr) in *Images of Love* (MacMillan), Royal Ballet, London

"Two loves I have" in *Images of Love* (MacMillan), Royal Ballet, London

Friday's Child in *Jazz Calendar* (Ashton), Royal Ballet, London

Elihu in *Job* (de Valois), Royal Ballet, London

Principal dancer in *Serenade* (Balanchine), Royal Ballet, London

1965 Romeo in *Romeo and Juliet* (MacMillan), Royal Ballet, London

1966 Title role in *Apollo* (Balanchine), Royal Ballet, London

Chanson dansée ("Athlete") in *Les Biches* (Nijinska), Royal Ballet, London

Principal dancer (cr) in *Brandenburg Nos. 2 and 4* (Cranko), Royal Ballet, London

Principal dancer in *Flower Festival at Genzano* (Bournonville), Royal Ballet, London

First song in *Song of the Earth* (MacMillan), Royal Ballet, London

1968 The Lover in *Lilac Garden* (*Jardin aux lilas*; Tudor), Royal Ballet, London

Drosselmeyer/Prince in *The Nutcracker* (Nureyev), Royal Ballet, London

Jean de Brienne in *Raymonda*, Act III (Nureyev after Petipa), Royal Ballet, London

1970 Pas de deux in *Birthday Offering* (Ashton), Royal Ballet, London

The Man (cr) in *Checkpoint* (de Valois), Royal Ballet New Group, Manchester

1971 Principal dancer in *Dances at a Gathering* (Robbins), Royal Ballet, London

1972 Ivan Tsarevich in *The Firebird* (Fokine), Royal Ballet, London

Moondog in *The Lady and the Fool* (Cranko), Royal Ballet New Group, London

Principal dancer in *The Mirror Walkers* (pas de deux; Wright), Royal Ballet New Group

Pierrot (cr) in *The Poltroon* (MacMillan), Royal Ballet New Group, London

1973 Second Movement in *Concerto* (MacMillan), Royal Ballet, tour

Principal dancer in *In the Night* (Robbins), Royal Ballet, London

1974 Dancer (cr) in *Pas de deux* (untitled: MacMillan), Gala, Royal Opera House, London

Bethena Waltz (cr) in *Elite Syncopations* (MacMillan), Royal Ballet, London

1975 Winter (cr) in *The Four Seasons* (MacMillan), Royal Ballet, London

1977 Principal dancer in *La Valse* (Ashton), Royal Ballet, London

Principal dancer in *Pavane* (MacMillan), Royal Ballet, London

1979 Prince (cr) in *Cinderella* (Darrell), Scottish Ballet, Aberdeen

PUBLICATIONS

By MacLeary:

"Dressage for Dancers—Donald MacLeary talks to *Dance and Dancers*", *Dance and Dancers* (London), February 1976

Interview in Newman, Barbara, *Striking a Balance: Dancers Talk About Dancing*, Boston, 1982

About MacLeary:

"Dancer You Will Know: Donald MacLeary", *Dance and Dancers* (London), June 1955

"Cover Stories: Donald MacLeary", *Dance and Dancers* (London), June 1960

Goodman, Saul, "Donald MacLeary", *Dance Magazine* (New York), November 1960

"Verona Revisited", *Dance and Dancers* (London), January 1966

Thorpe, Edward, *Kenneth MacMillan: The Man and the Ballets*, London, 1985

Woodcock, Sarah, *The Sadler's Wells Royal Ballet*, London, 1991

*   *   *

Donald MacLeary was a partner and performer in the great danseur noble tradition. His work was characterized by an innate dignity, breeding, and elegance that made him a natural portrayer of ballet's princes. Above all, his skill and dependability as a partner made him much in demand both by the established ballerina and by the novice, in need of support for first appearance in the classics.

MacLeary's apprenticeship began in the last days of the Sadler's Wells Theatre Ballet; here he was first noticed as one of the boys in MacMillan's *Danses concertantes* and later, as one of the young lovers in the premiere of *The Burrow*. It was not until he moved to Covent Garden in 1959, when Svetlana Beriosova asked him to become her regular partner, that MacLeary began to be hailed for his qualities as a danseur noble. Ballerinas appreciated the attentive care that he lavished upon them, knowing that he provided the perfect setting for their qualities. Although his partners were to include Margot Fonteyn, Natalia Makarova, Nadia Nerina, Merle Park, Lynn Seymour, Antoinette Sibley, Doreen Wells, and Lesley Collier, it is the years with Beriosova that will principally be remembered. They were perfectly matched in temperament, physique, and looks, their limbs blending into one harmonious whole. It was a partnership appreciated not only in the major opera houses, but throughout the length and breadth of Britain, for during the 1960s they made innumerable appearances with the Royal Ballet Touring Company, helping to win new audiences and establishing a respect for the Royal Ballet and its achievements.

MacLeary's talents as a partner tended to make many undervalue his brilliant technique. Although he was a highly competitive dancer, his stage personality was essentially modest and self-effacing, which meant that he would never be a spectacular virtuoso; his bravura style, however, was more than equal to the demands of the classical solos. If technique was not something one thought of first in connection with MacLeary, that was, perhaps, an indication of his total success as a performer, since technique was always at the service of the role, rather than the role being a mere vehicle for the performer.

MacLeary brought to dramatic parts sincerity and conviction, rather than detailed character analysis. As the princes of classical ballet he was outstanding, bringing to them a natural aristocracy. Outside the classics, he will always be remembered for his moving portrayal of doomed humanity in MacMillan's *Song of the Earth*, in which his depth of feeling and interpretation was almost overwhelming.

MacLeary retired from dancing in 1975, to become ballet master to the Royal Ballet. Here he was able to pass on to a new generation the benefits of his experience, both as partner and as performer, and his understanding of the traditions of the Royal Ballet.

—Sarah C. Woodcock

————

MACMILLAN, Kenneth

British dancer, choreographer, and ballet director. Born in Dunfermline, Scotland, 11 December 1929. Studied with Phyllis Adams, Great Yarmouth, and at Sadler's Wells Ballet School (on scholarship), from 1945. Dancer, Sadler's Wells Theatre Ballet, 1946–48, and Sadler's Wells Ballet, 1948–52, returning to Sadler's Wells Theatre Ballet, 1952; choreographer, Sadler's Wells Theatre Ballet and Sadler's Wells Ballet, 1952–64; resident choreographer, Royal Ballet, 1965–66; director and chief choreographer, Berlin Opera Ballet, 1966–69; director, Royal Ballet, 1970–77, and resident choreographer, from 1977; also choreographed for Royal Ballet Touring Company, Stuttgart Ballet, and for television; artistic associate, American Ballet Theatre, New York, 1984–89, and Houston Ballet, 1989–92; also theatre director, including for productions of Ionesco's *The Chairs* and *The Lesson* (New Inn, Eagling, 1982), Strindberg's *Dance of Death* (Royal Exchange, Manchester, 1983), and Tennessee Williams's *Kingdom of the Earth* (Hampstead Theatre, London, 1984). Recipient: Honoris Causa, University of Edinburgh, 1975; *Evening Standard* Ballet Award, 1978; Queen Elizabeth II Coronation Award, Royal Academy of Dancing, 1979; Krug Award for Excellence for *Mayerling*, 1980; Society of West End Theatres Award for *Gloria*, 1980, and for *Requiem*, 1983; Knighthood, 1983. Died in London, 29 October 1992.

WORKS

1953 *Somnambulism* (mus. Kenton), Sadler's Wells Choreographic Group, London

   Fragment (mus. Kenton), Sadler's Wells Choreographic Group, London

1954 *Laiderette* (mus. Martin), Sadler's Wells Choreographic Group, London

1955 *Danses Concertantes* (mus. Stravinsky), Sadler's Wells Theatre Ballet, London

   The House of Birds (mus. Mompou, arranged Lanchbery), Sadler's Wells Theatre Ballet, London

1956 *Noctambules* (mus. Searle), Sadler's Wells Theatre Ballet, London

   Solitaire (mus. Arnold), Sadler's Wells Theatre Ballet, London

   Valse excentrique (mus. Ibert), Sadler's Wells Theatre Gala, London

1957 *Winter's Eve* (mus. Britten), American Ballet Theatre, Lisbon

   Journey (mus. Bartók), American Ballet Theatre Choreographic Group, New York

1958 *The Burrow* (mus. Martin), Royal Ballet Touring Group, London

   Agon (mus. Stravinsky), Royal Ballet, London

1960   *Le Baiser de la fée* (mus. Stravinsky), Royal Ballet, London

        The Invitation (mus. Seiber), Royal Ballet Touring Company, Oxford

1961   *The Seven Deadly Sins* (mus. Weill), Western Theatre Ballet, Edinburgh

        Diversions (mus. Bliss), Royal Ballet, London

1962   *The Rite of Spring* (mus. Stravinsky), Royal Ballet, London

        Dance Suite (mus. Milhaud), Royal Ballet School Performance, London

1963   *Symphony* (mus. Shostakovich), Royal Ballet, London

        Las Hermanas (mus. Martin), Stuttgart Ballet, Stuttgart

1964   *La Création du monde* (mus. Milhaud), Royal Ballet Touring Company, Stratford

        Images of Love (mus. Tranchell), Royal Ballet, London

1965   *Romeo and Juliet* (mus. Prokofiev), Royal Ballet, London

        Song of the Earth (mus. Mahler), Stuttgart Ballet, Stuttgart

1966   *Valses nobles et sentimentales* (mus. Ravel), German Opera Ballet, Berlin

        Concerto (mus. Shostakovich), German Opera Ballet, Berlin

1967   *Anastasia* (one-act version; mus. electronic, various), German Opera Ballet, Berlin

1968   *Olympiad* (mus. Stravinsky), German Opera Ballet, Berlin

        The Sphinx (mus. Milhaud), Stuttgart Ballet, Stuttgart

        Cain and Abel (Panufnik), German Opera Ballet, Berlin

1970   *Miss Julie* (mus. Panufnik), Stuttgart Ballet, Stuttgart

        Checkpoint (mus. Gerhardt), Royal Ballet New Group, Manchester

1971   *Anastasia* (three-act version; mus. Tchaikovsky, Martinů), Royal Ballet, London

        Triad (*Trio*; mus. Prokofiev), Royal Ballet, London

1972   *Ballade* (mus. Fauré), Royal Ballet New Group, Lisbon

        Side Show (mus. Stravinsky), Royal Ballet, Liverpool

        The Poltroon (mus. Maros), Royal Ballet New Group, London

1973   *Pavane* (mus. Fauré), Royal Ballet, London

        Seven Deadly Sins (new version; mus. Weill), Royal Ballet, London

1974   *Manon* (mus. Massenet, arranged by Lucas), Royal Ballet, London

        Elite Syncopations (mus. Joplin), Royal Ballet, London

1975   *The Four Seasons* (mus. Verdi), Royal Ballet, London

        Rituals (mus. Bartók), Royal Ballet, London

1976   *Requiem* (mus. Fauré), Stuttgart Ballet, Stuttgart

        Feux follets (mus. Liszt), John Curry skating solo

1977   *Gloriana* (mus. Britten), Royal Ballet, London

1978   *Mayerling* (mus. Liszt, arranged by Lanchbery), Royal Ballet, London

        My Brother, My Sisters (mus. Schoenberg, von Webern), Stuttgart Ballet, Stuttgart

        6.6.78 (*Homage to Ninette de Valois*) (mus. Barber), Sadler's Wells Royal Ballet, London

        Métaboles (mus. Dutilleux), Paris Opera Ballet, Paris

1979   *La Fin du jour* (mus. Ravel), Royal Ballet, London

        Playground (mus. Cross), Sadler's Wells Royal Ballet, Edinburgh

1980   *Gloria* (mus. Poulenc), Royal Ballet, London

1981   *Isadora* (mus. Bennett), Royal Ballet, London

        Wild Boy (mus. Cross), American Ballet Theatre, Washington, D.C.

1982   *Verdi Variations* (mus. Verdi), Aterballetto, Reggio-Emilia

        Quartet (mus. Verdi), Sadler's Wells Royal Ballet, Bristol

        Orpheus (mus. Stravinsky), Royal Ballet, London

1983   *Valley of Shadows* (mus. Martinů, Tchaikovsky), Royal Ballet, London

        The Seven Deadly Sins (new version; mus. Weill), British television

1984   *Different Drummer* (mus. von Webern), Royal Ballet, London

1986   *Le Baiser de la fée* (new version; mus. Stravinsky), Royal Ballet, London

1989   *The Prince of the Pagodas* (mus. Britten), Royal Ballet, London

1990   *Farewell* (later part of *Winter Dreams*; mus. Tchaikovsky), Royal Ballet, London

1991   *Winter Dreams* (mus. Tchaikovsky, arranged Gammon), Royal Ballet, London

1992   *The Judas Tree* (mus. Elias), Royal Ballet, London

PUBLICATIONS

By MacMillan:

Interview in "How a Ballet is Born", *Ballet Today* (London), May 1956

Interview in "Talking to Kenneth MacMillan", *About the House* (London), June 1966

Interview in "MacMillan Talks to Clement Crisp", *About the House* (London), Summer 1971

About MacMillan:

Barnes, Clive, "Choreography Flows from Him", *Dance and Dancers* (London), March 1955

Clarke, Mary, "Kenneth MacMillan", *Dance Magazine* (New York), September 1956

Crisp, Clement, "Romeo, Juliet, and Kenneth MacMillan", *Dancing Times* (London), February 1965

Goodwin, Noël, and Koegler, Horst, "To Earth and Other Places", *Dance and Dancers* (London), January 1966

Bland, Alexander, *The Royal Ballet: The First Fifty Years*, London, 1981

Dromgoole, Nicholas, "Spotlight on Kenneth MacMillan", *Dance and Dancers* (London), March 1983

Seymour, Lynn, *Lynn* (autobiography), London, 1984

Thorpe, Edward, *Kenneth MacMillan: The Man and his Ballets*, London, 1985

Kane, Angela, "Kenneth MacMillan: Rebel with a Cause", *Dancing Times* (London), November 1989

Koegler, Horst, "Kenneth MacMillan", *Ballett International* (Cologne), December 1989

McMahon, Deirdre, "MacMillan at Sixty", *Dance Theatre Journal* (London), February 1990

Woodcock, Sarah, *The Sadler's Wells Royal Ballet*, London, 1991

Hunt, Marilyn, "Kenneth MacMillan", *Dance Magazine* (New York), September 1991

*   *   *

One of the greatest and most important choreographers of the twentieth century, Kenneth MacMillan has made a major contribution to the art by removing it from the realms of fairyland and mere moving sculpture, to explore its potential as a powerfully expressive part of the theatre. To this end, his development of the full-length narrative ballet has pushed the parameters of the form as far as (and sometimes farther than) they will go.

Kenneth MacMillan rehearsing his *Le Baiser de la fée*, Royal Ballet, London

Even so, a catalogue of his sixty-odd works reveals ballets of every type and genre, a wider range than any other choreographer past or present—from purely plotless works, to experiments in expressionism, to elaborate explorations of psychological disorder and political oppression.

MacMillan became a distinguished classical dancer with both of the Sadler's Wells (later Royal) Ballet companies, but an invitation to join a newly-established choreographic group led to his discovering his real metier as a choreographer. His early works were all immediately successful but, although revealing a highly individual talent, were influenced somewhat by post-war French choreographers with their emphasis on symbolism and fantasy. Soon, however, as an avid theatre-goer (and film fan), MacMillan was fascinated by the work of the "new wave" of young British playwrights such as John Osborne, Harold Pinter, Arnold Wesker, and John Arden, and this inspired him to create a ballet that dealt with real flesh-and-blood characters in a world of harsh reality. That work was *The Burrow*, which concerned a group of refugees hiding in a garret from the secret police of a repressive regime. It was a theme which, 25 years later, came full circle with *Valley of Shadows*, a ballet which did not shrink from portraying the horror of Nazi concentration camps.

Two years after *The Burrow*, MacMillan created *The Invitation*, another innovative work, that dared to deal with the subject of rape—thereby pushing ballet even more violently into the arena of psycho-sexual exploration. The subject of the ballet was the involvement of two teenage cousins with an older, embittered married couple, the young man seduced by the older woman, the young girl brutally raped by the older man. Lynn Seymour's performance as the young girl established her as a dancer of unrivalled dramatic power, inaugurated a brief but brilliant partnership with Christopher Gable, and consolidated her as MacMillan's "muse". For the next two decades she was to inspire him to create a whole gallery of wonderful ballerina roles.

MacMillan's first full-length ballet was *Romeo and Juliet*, to the Prokofiev score. Working closely with Seymour and Gable, MacMillan developed his large-scale production away from the rigid construction and formal set-pieces of the nineteenth-century classics. Of course the ballet does have its several pas de deux for the two principals, its dances for the soloists and corps de ballet (the narrative delineated by the score), but MacMillan integrated them into the text in a much more natural, flowing, almost cinematic way. It was a technique he was to develop even further in his later full-length works.

In the same year that he produced *Romeo and Juliet*, MacMillan created the first of his three great masterpieces based on scores with vocal accompaniment, Mahler's *Song of the Earth* (created for the Stuttgart Ballet after the Royal Ballet's rejection of the idea). MacMillan wisely decided not to attempt a literal interpretation of the songs but relied on the mood evoked by the score for the impetus behind the movement. More importantly, he created three symbolic figures rather than "characters": these are a Man, a Woman, and a Messenger of Death, a figure who appears in almost every scene, sometimes supporting, sometimes menacing, finally effecting a heart-easing reunion between the Man and the Woman in the final moments of the ballet. This Messenger of Death was the first manifestation of a concern with death that began to show itself more and more in the choreographer's work, often taking its place alongside the figure of the "outsider", a figure of isolation that recurs in several of his ballets.

When John Cranko died prematurely in 1973, MacMillan wished to create a work dedicated to his friend. He was then artistic director of the Royal Ballet and proposed using Fauré's *Requiem* for the work. Once again the Board objected, this time on the grounds that to use such a score might offend audiences' religious sensibilities. Once again the ballet was offered to Stuttgart, where Marcia Haydée immediately accepted the proposal.

Like *Song of the Earth*, *Requiem*, as the ballet is simply entitled, was instantly hailed as a great work, full of marvellous choreographic invention which mirrors the lyrical beauties of the score, a poignant work that challenges the technique of a large cast and honours both its dedicatee and the composer.

The third great work using a vocal score is *Gloria*, based on that portion of the Catholic mass by Poulenc. The ballet was inspired by a literary work, Vera Brittain's *Testament of Youth*, which pays homage to a whole generation of young men slaughtered in the First World War. MacMillan wanted his dancers to appear like ghosts from the no-man's-land of the battlefield or, perhaps, from the unseen realms of death; their first entrance, therefore, is from behind a slope so that they appear to come over the top of a hill, both as soldiers emerging from the trenches and as spirits from their graves. Poulenc's score is divided into six sections—some fast, some slow, some elegiac, some exultant—and the ballet encapsulates many of the qualities and characteristics of MacMillan's whole creative canon: his belief in ballet as an expressive force, his concern with the human condition, and his marvellous ability to devise choreography that is full of beautiful and evocative imagery.

Other one-act works which reveal this extraordinary expressive range include *The Rite of Spring*, a large-scale interpretation of Stravinsky's great atavistic score; *My Brother, My Sisters*, a strange, haunting work exploring the psychological complexities of private games invented by adult siblings; *Playground*, the story of a young man who becomes obsessed with a girl in a mental asylum; *Different Drummer*, an expressionist ballet based on George Buchner's play *Woyzeck*; and *La Fin du jour*, a work which is inspired by the extravagant fashions of the 1930s, and is a valedictory gesture to an era that, though carefree on the surface, was shadowed with the approach of war.

These are but a few among MacMillan's exceptional output of one-act works, but his most innovative ballets are arguably the full-length ones. In 1971 MacMillan expanded his one-act version of *Anastasia* (based on the story of Anna Anderson, the woman who claimed to be the sole survivor of the Russian royal family), looking backward through three acts to the events leading to the murder of Tsar Nicholas II and his family. Apart from its interesting construction, it was remarkable for a ballet

to engage in a historical panorama. The next full-length work, *Manon*, reverted to fictional characters and is a romantic drama based on the novel by the Abbé Prévost; this work is particularly notable for the inventiveness of the pas de deux which chart the progress of the lovers, the eponymous Manon and the theological student Des Grieux.

With *Mayerling* MacMillan once again turned to real-life characters in the dramatic story of the double suicide of Crown Prince Rudolf of Austria-Hungary and his teenage mistress Mary Vetsera. The ballet ignored the sentimentalized versions of the tragedy and sought to expose the corruption and decadence of the imperial court. The role of Rudolf is the longest and most demanding ever created for a male dancer, and once again the work is notable for the extraordinary inventiveness of the many pas de deux it includes, here for Rudolf and the various women in his life.

With *Isadora*, based on the extraordinarily melodramatic life of Isadora Duncan, MacMillan pushed the capabilities of ballet as a narrative form to their ultimate limits, so much so that he decided to have the central role played by both a dancer and an actress speaking lines from Duncan's own autobiography. His sixth full-length ballet, *The Prince of the Pagodas*, a complete reworking of the original by Cranko, reverted to the fairy-tale form of the nineteenth century, but even so was full of the highly inventive and imaginative details which always informed MacMillan's work. His last two ballets, *Winter Dreams* and *The Judas Tree*, were as different as night and day and demonstrated yet again MacMillan's range and versatility as a choreographer. The former, built around a romantic pas de deux (first performed under the title *Farewell*) for his latest muse Darcey Bussell and her Russian partner Irek Mukhamedov, was based on Chekhov's *The Three Sisters*, danced to a montage of Tchaikovsky pieces, while the latter depicted a post-modern urban waste land wherein degradation, rape, and ultimately murder take place in a baffling and quite disturbing sequence. Reviews were mixed, but the choreographer's continued creativity was unquestioned.

MacMillan's unexpected death took place on the evening of 29 October 1992, during the Royal Ballet's opening night performance of *Mayerling*; a shocked Jeremy Isaacs, general director of the Royal Opera House, was forced to come on stage at the end of the performance to announce that MacMillan had collapsed and died of a heart attack backstage. As the ballet world mourned the departure of a "great master", as Isaacs called him, critics such as Mary Clarke acknowledged that "It is no exaggeration to say . . . that Kenneth MacMillan, through his choreography and through his choice of subject matter, [has] pushed back the frontiers of ballet." It is as a great pioneer and a great artist that MacMillan will be remembered.

—Edward Thorpe

MADEMOISELLE ANGOT *see* **MAM'ZELLE ANGOT**

MADSEN, Egon
Danish dancer, teacher, and ballet director. Born in Ringe, 24 August 1942. Studied with Thea Jolles, Aarhus, from 1951, and with Birger Bartholin and Edite Frandsen, Copenhagen, from 1957. Married dancer Lucia Isenring. Stage début, while

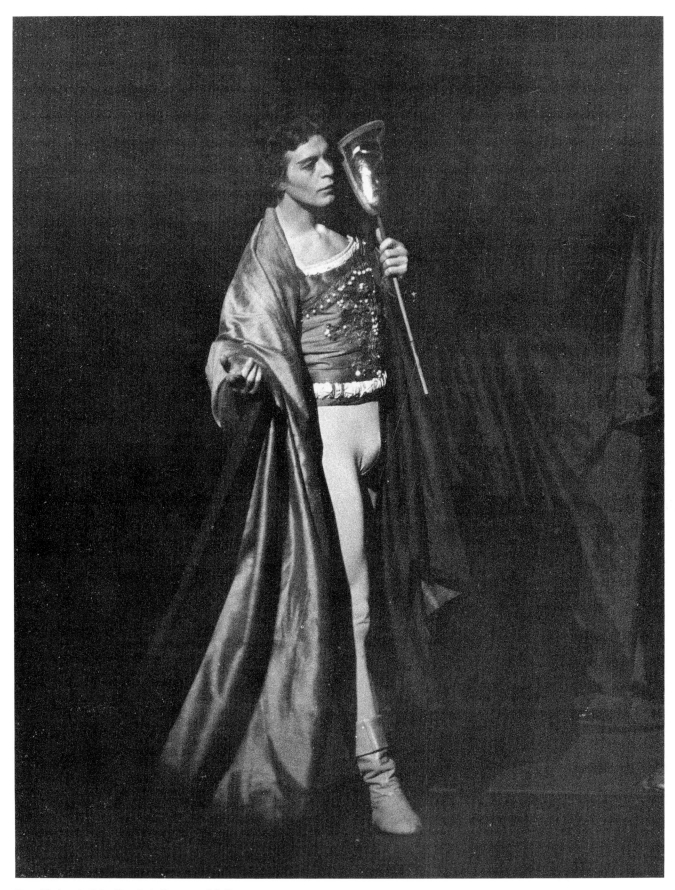

Egon Madsen in John Cranko's *Romeo and Juliet*

still a student, with performing group of Thea Jolles; dancer, Tivoli Theatre, Copenhagen, from 1958, and Elsa Marianne von Rosen's Scandinavian Ballet, from 1959; soloist, becoming principal dancer, Stuttgart Ballet, from 1961, creating many roles in ballets by John Cranko; artistic director, Frankfurt Ballet, 1981–84, Royal Swedish Ballet, 1984–86, Teatro Communale, Florence, 1986–88.

ROLES

1962 Paris (cr) in *Romeo and Juliet* (new version; Cranko), Stuttgart Ballet, Stuttgart
1963 Prince Siegfried in *Swan Lake* (Cranko after Petipa, Ivanov), Stuttgart Ballet, Stuttgart
1965 The Joker (cr) in *Jeu de cartes* (Cranko), Stuttgart Ballet, Stuttgart
       Lensky (cr) in *Onegin* (Cranko), Stuttgart Ballet, Stuttgart
       The Messenger of Death (cr) in *Song of the Earth* (MacMillan), Stuttgart Ballet, Stuttgart
1966 Principal dancer (cr) in *Pas de quatre* (Cranko), Stuttgart Ballet, Stuttgart
       The Prince in *The Nutcracker* (Cranko after Petipa), Stuttgart Ballet, Stuttgart
1967 Principal dancer (cr) in *The Interrogation* (Cranko), Stuttgart Ballet, Stuttgart
       Principal dancer (cr) in *Quatre Images* (Cranko), Stuttgart Ballet, Stuttgart
1968 A Man (cr) in *The Sphinx* (MacMillan), Stuttgart Ballet, Stuttgart
1969 Gremio (cr) in *The Taming of the Shrew* (Cranko), Stuttgart Ballet, Stuttgart
1970 Young Lover (cr) in *Poème de l'extase* (Cranko), Stuttgart Ballet, Stuttgart
       Principal dancer (cr) in *Brouillards* (Cranko), Stuttgart Ballet, Stuttgart
1971 Don José (cr) in *Carmen* (Cranko), Stuttgart Ballet, Stuttgart
1972 E. (= Egon) (cr) in *Initials R.B.M.E.* (Cranko), Stuttgart Ballet, Stuttgart
1973 Principal dancer (cr) in *Concerto* (MacMillan), Stuttgart Ballet, Stuttgart
       Principal dancer in *Arena* (Tetley), Stuttgart Ballet, Stuttgart
1974 Principal dancer in *Gemini* (Tetley), Stuttgart Ballet, Stuttgart
1975 Pan (cr) in *Daphnis and Chloe* (Tetley), Stuttgart Ballet, Stuttgart
       Pierrot in *Pierrot Lunaire* (Tetley), Stuttgart Ballet, Stuttgart
1976 The Double in *Songs of A Wayfarer* (Béjart), Stuttgart Ballet, Stuttgart
       Hamlet (cr) in *Der Fall Hamlet* (new version of *Hamlet Connotations*; Neumeier), Stuttgart Ballet, Stuttgart
       Principal dancer (cr) in *Requiem* (MacMillan), Stuttgart Ballet, Stuttgart
1977 The Prince in *The Nutcracker* (new production; Nijinska, Hightower after Petipa), Stuttgart Ballet, Stuttgart
       Principal dancer (cr) in *Innere Not* (Montagnon), Stuttgart Ballet, Stuttgart
1978 Principal dancer (cr) in *Therese* (Ursuliak), Stuttgart Ballet, Stuttgart
       Leading role (cr) in *Death and the Maiden* (Montagnon), Stuttgart Ballet, Stuttgart
       Armand Duval (cr) in *Lady of the Camellias* (Neumeier), Stuttgart Ballet, Stuttgart
1979 Principal dancer in *Symphony of Psalms* (Kylián), Stuttgart Ballet, Stuttgart
1980 Principal dancer (cr) in *Die Fenster* (Helliwell), Stuttgart Ballet, Stuttgart

Other roles include: Mercutio and Romeo in *Romeo and Juliet* (Cranko), principal dancer in *Nacht* (Neumeier), Daphnis in *Daphnis and Chloe* (Cranko), principal dancer in *Allegro Brillante* (Balanchine; staged Russell), principal dancer in *The Bitter Wierd* (de Mille).

PUBLICATIONS

By Madsen:
Interview in Stuart, Otis, "Form and Meaning: An Interview with Egon Madsen", *Ballett International* (Cologne), May 1984
Interview in Regitz, Hartmut, "Die Heimkehr des verlorenen Sohnes", *Ballett-Journal/Das Tanzarchiv* (Cologne), June 1990

About Madsen:
Goodman, Saul, "Egon Madsen and Susanne Hanke", *Dance Magazine* (New York), October 1969
Niehaus, Max, *Ballett Faszination*, Munich, 1972
Geitel, Klaus, "Egon Madsen, oder die Metamorphosen des Harlekin", *Ballett: Chronik und Bilanz des Ballettjahres* (Hanover), 1977

*   *   *

Egon Madsen's career has followed an unconventional pattern for a Danish dancer. Unlike so many of his successful compatriots, he did not train at the Royal Danish Ballet School in Copenhagen, thereafter to join the company as a matter of course. Instead, he worked from the age of nine with a private teacher, Thea Jolles, both at her school and with her small touring company in the summer vacations. When the Royal Danish School refused him entrance, remarking that he was "too skimpy", he continued undeterred with Mme. Jolles until the age of fifteen, at which point he went on to the eminent Pantomime Theatre of the Tivoli Gardens in Copenhagen under the direction of Niels Bjørn Larsen. During this period he continued his training with Birger Bartholin and Edite Frandsen privately in Copenhagen. In 1959 Madsen joined Elsa Marianne von Rosen's Scandinavian Ballet as a soloist and toured Sweden and Denmark for three years.

Madsen's early experience, gained outside the traditional fold of the Danish "star-system", cultivated his naturally ebullient spirit. His initial tours with Jolles's group had given him an invaluable taste of adventure, and the confidence to seek the right position even if it meant leaving his native country. That opportunity presented itself in 1961, when choreographer John Cranko became director of the Stuttgart Ballet in Germany, instigating a unique collaboration with a group of highly individual artists. Along with Marcia Haydée, Richard Cragun, and Birgit Keil, Madsen was invited by Cranko to join the quartet of dancers who formed the nucleus of the company. Cranko's venture proved to be an outstanding success. He built up a repertoire based on his own powerful versions of full-length works such as *Romeo and Juliet*, *Onegin*, and *The Taming of the Shrew*, specifically creating each ballet as a total piece of theatre and cultivating the dramatic powers of its interpreters. The first American tour in 1969 established the company's international popularity with huge box-office returns, ensuring a rosy future for all its dancers.

Madsen flourished in this environment. He created many roles in Cranko's productions, notably *Jeu de cartes, Onegin, The Nutcracker, The Taming of the Shrew,* and *Initials R.B.M.E..* He also worked with other choreographers, creating roles in MacMillan's *Song of the Earth,* Tetley's *Daphnis and Chloe,* and Neumeier's *The Lady of the Camellias.* He confronted technical and interpretative challenges with vigour, winning audiences with a captivating presence on stage, a strong dramatic gift, and an easy, convincing style. His comic talent shone through in such roles as Mercutio in *Romeo and Juliet.* With characteristic subtlety his biting wit sparkled in the banter between Romeo and Benvolio but added a touch of ironic poignancy to the death scene. He did not play the lead in the first season of *Romeo* in 1962, but when he eventually took on the part he conveyed passionate abandon, often credited for his "moonstruck romanticism" (as John Percival called it) in this role. His interpretation of Romeo matured over the years, and when he danced this part in his own staging of Cranko's production for the Frankfurt Ballet in 1982 he brought greater depth and refinement to the performance. Horst Koegler remarked on his deeper characterization, evident in the contrasting expression of balcony and bedroom pas de deux: ". . . the former full of romantic ardour, the latter charged with agonising despair".

Madsen remained in Stuttgart until Cranko's untimely death. Once again the lessons of his early years stood him in good stead, and he was prepared to move at the appropriate moment for his career. Having acquired a wealth of experience in dancing the classics, as well as dramatic and contemporary works, he turned his eye in 1981 to artistic direction, first with the Frankfurt Ballet, and susequently with the Royal Swedish Ballet and the Teatro Communale in Florence. His energetic personality and keen artistic and theatrical sense have guaranteed his valuable contribution to these new roles in his career.

—Susan Jones

MAGALLANES, Nicholas

Mexican/American dancer. Born in Camargo, Mexico, 27 November 1922. Studied at the School of American Ballet, pupil of George Balanchine, Pierre Vladimirov, Anatole Obukhov, and Muriel Stuart. Début, Lincoln Kirstein's Ballet Caravan, performing at New York World's Fair, 1940; dancer, American Ballet Caravan, touring South America, 1941; dancer, Littlefield Ballet, 1942, and Ballet Russe de Monte Carlo, 1943–46; principal dancer, Ballet Society (becoming the New York City Ballet), 1946–73. Died in North Merrick, Long Island, 1 May 1977.

ROLES

1940   Principal dancer (cr) in *A Thousand Times Neigh!* (Dollar), Ballet Caravan, World's Fair, Flushing Meadow, N.Y.

1941   Soloist (cr) in *Ballet Imperial* (later *Concerto No. 2*; Balanchine), American Ballet Caravan, Rio de Janeiro

Dancer (cr) in *Pastorela* (L. Christensen, Fernandez), American Ballet Caravan, Rio de Janeiro

Principal dancer (cr) in *Fantasia Brasileira* (Balan-

chine), American Ballet Caravan, Santiago de Chile

1944   Principal dancer (cr) in *Danses Concertantes* (Balanchine), Ballet Russe de Monte Carlo, New York

Cléonte (cr) in *Le Bourgeois Gentilhomme* (Balanchine), Ballet Russe de Monte Carlo, New York

Principal dancer (cr) in *Ballet Imperial* (Balanchine), Ballet Russe de Monte Carlo, Chicago

1945   Principal dancer in *Concerto Barocco* (Balanchine), Ballet Russe de Monte Carlo, New York

1946   The Poet (cr) in *Night Shadow* (*La Sonnambula*; Balanchine), Ballet Russe de Monte Carlo, New York

Jean de Brienne (cr) in *Raymonda* (new production; Balanchine, Danilova after Petipa), Ballet Russe de Monte Carlo, New York

1948   Bacchus (cr) in *The Triumph of Bacchus and Ariadne* (Balanchine), Ballet Society, New York

First Movement (cr) in *Symphony in C* (new version of *Le Palais de cristal*; Balanchine), Ballet Society, New York

Title role (cr) in *Orpheus* (Balanchine), Ballet Society, New York

1949   Principal dancer (cr) in *The Guests* (Robbins), New York City Ballet, New York

Prélude (cr) in *Bourreé Fantasque* (Balanchine), New York City Ballet, New York

1950   The Poet (cr) in *Illuminations* (Ashton), New York City Ballet, New York

"Rescue from Drowning" (cr) in *Jones Beach* (Balanchine), New York City Ballet, New York

Dancer (cr) in *Sylvia: Pas de deux* (Balanchine), New York City Ballet, New York

Bridegroom in *The Fairy's Kiss* (Balanchine), New York City Ballet, New York

1951   Eighth Waltz, La Valse (cr) in *La Valse* (Balanchine), New York City Ballet, New York

An Intruder (cr) in *The Cage* (Robbins), New York City Ballet, New York

Principal dancer (cr) in *The Pied Piper* (Robbins), New York City Ballet, New York

1952   Principal dancer (cr) in *Caracole* (Balanchine), New York City Ballet, New York

Principal dancer (cr) in *Metamorphoses* (Balanchine), New York City Ballet, New York

1953   Principal dancer (cr) in *Valse Fantaisie* (Balanchine), New York City Ballet, New York

The Stallion (cr) in *The Filly* (Bolender), New York City Ballet, New York

1954   "Second Time" (cr) in *Opus 34* (Balanchine), New York City Ballet, New York

The Cavalier (cr) in *The Nutcracker* (Balanchine), New York City Ballet, New York

Adagio (cr) in *Western Symphony* (Balanchine), New York City Ballet, New York

1956   Principal dancer (cr) in *Allegro Brillante* (Balanchine), New York City Ballet, New York

Principal dancer (cr) in *Divertimento No. 15* (Balanchine), New York City Ballet, Stratford, Connecticut

1957   The Poet (cr) in *The Unicorn, the Gorgon and the Manticore* (Butler), New York City Ballet, New York

Principal dancer (cr) in *Square Dance* (Balanchine), New York City Ballet, New York

1959   Principal dancer (cr) in *Episodes II* (Balanchine), New York City Ballet, New York

1960   Principal dancer (cr) in *Sinfonia No. 5* (Balanchine), in *Panamerica* (Balanchine, Contreras, Moncion, Taras, d'Amboise), New York City Ballet, New York

Duke of L'an L'ing (cr) in *The Figure in the Carpet*

(Balanchine), New York City Ballet, New York
Principal dancer, Fourth Couple (cr) in *Liebeslieder
Walzer* (Balanchine), New York City Ballet, New
York
1962 Lysander (cr) in *A Midsummer's Night's Dream* (Balanchine), New York City Ballet, New York
1965 Duke (cr) in *Don Quixote* (Balanchine), New York City Ballet, New York

Other roles include: Sanguinic in *The Four Temperaments* (Balanchine), Baron in *La Sonnambula* (Balanchine), principal dancer in *Serenade* (Balanchine).

PUBLICATIONS

Chujoy, Anatole, *The New York City Ballet*, New York, 1953
Reynolds, Nancy, *Repertory in Review*, New York, 1977
Croce, Arlene, *Going to the Dance*, New York, 1982

*   *   *

American-trained male dancers of the 1940s were not, on the whole, impressive technicians. This had nothing to do with talent, but with the comparative brevity of their training and with the paucity of professional outlets for their skills. Although born in Mexico, Nicholas Magallanes was an American-trained dancer. His longest company tenure before he entered the New York City Ballet (via its predecessor Ballet Society) was three years with the Ballet Russe de Monte Carlo. When he became part of the Lincoln Kirstein/George Balanchine organization in 1946, he was essentially the company's premier danseur, although company policy prevented the title from being conferred.

His style and technique were far from those of the male dancers who belonged to the company in the 1970s, when he retired. Magallanes was a boyish-looking dancer with a shock of dark hair that tended to fall beguilingly over his forehead. He lacked turnout. His energy flow tended to come from the hips and pelvis, rather than from the chest and back. This gave his dancing a certain softness, which motivated choreographers to cast him as a poet.

Magallanes was, for example, the lyre-playing poet in George Balanchine's *Orpheus*. He was Arthur Rimbaud in Sir Frederick Ashton's *Illuminations*. The ostracized poet in John Butler's *The Unicorn, the Gorgon and the Manticore* was created for him. And while the role was not created on him, he was for a long time identified with the equally ostracized poet in Balanchine's *La Sonnambula*.

Ballerinas enjoyed dancing with Magallanes because, as one of them rather prosaically declared, "Nicky's like a couch". By this she meant that he made the woman feel not only comfortable but entirely secure as they performed together. He was also charmingly self-effacing, always allowing his partner to shine as he stepped gallantly into her shadow. In this he somewhat resembled Michael Somes in his partnership with Dame Margot Fonteyn at the Royal Ballet, or Nikolai Fadeyechev, longtime partner of Galina Ulanova at the Bolshoi Ballet.

George Balanchine was a master at tailoring works to specific talents, and so he knew how to accentuate Magallanes's gentleness and to conceal his technical weaknesses. There was a touching nobility in his Orpheus as he led Eurydice from the underworld; there was tenderness in his lovesick cowboy in *Western Symphony*. As he pursued the Sleepwalker in *La Sonnambula*, he had the persevering fixation of the true artist. In *Liebeslieder Walzer* he was completely at home in the dreamy

Nicholas Magallanes as Orpheus

nineteenth-century ballroom atmosphere; the Brahms music also was well suited to him. Although Magallanes could not match Patricia Wilde's corruscating batterie in *Square Dance*, he displayed a casual boyishness that well suited the happy-go-lucky theme. And as he partnered Tanaquil LeClercq in *La Valse*, his mystified attentiveness seemed to indicate that he was preordained to lose her.

Gradually, beginning in the 1950s, the New York City Ballet began to acquire male principals with more impressive technique. The first of these was André Eglevsky, soon to be followed by Jacques d'Amboise, Edward Villella, Erik Bruhn (for a short time), Jean-Pierre Bonnefous, Helgi Tomasson, and Peter Martins. Although Magallanes was still given satisfying roles, notably the Cavalier in *The Nutcracker*, the second Intruder in Jerome Robbins' *The Cage*, and the Cavalier in Balanchine's *Allegro Brillante* and *Divertimento No. 15*, these began to dwindle in the 1960s. In ballets like Balanchine's *A Midsummer Night's Dream* and *Don Quixote*, he was relegated to essentially character roles.

But Magallanes could not make the transition, as had his contemporaries Francisco Moncion and Shaun O'Brien, to being a dance-actor. He lacked the versatility and perhaps the imagination. And so in 1973 Magallanes retired from the New York City Ballet, and only four years later, he died.

—Doris Hering

THE MAGIC FLUTE
(Original Russian title: *Volshebnaya fleita*)

Choreography: Lev Ivanov
Music: Riccardo Drigo
Libretto: Lev Ivanov
First Production: Imperial Theatre School, St. Petersburg, 3 April (22 March old style) 1893
Principal Dancers: Stanislava Belinskaya (Lise), Mikhail Fokine (Luke), Sergei Legat (Marquis), Agrippina Vaganova (The Farmer's Wife)

Other productions include: Maryinsky Theatre (restaged Ivanov), with Anna Johansson (Lise), Pavel Gerdt (Luke); St. Petersburg, 23 April 1893. Anna Pavlova Company (staged Enrico Cecchetti and Pavlova after Ivanov), with Anna Pavlova (Lise), Alexandre Volinine (Luke), Enrico Cecchetti (Marquis); London, 1913. School of American Ballet (new version, chor. Peter Martins); New York, 9 May 1981. New York City Ballet (restaged Martins), with Darci Kistler (Lise), Peter Martins (Luke); New York, 21 January 1982.

PUBLICATIONS

Beaumont, Cyril, *Complete Book of Ballets*, revised edition, London, 1951
Krassovskaya, Vera, *Russian Ballet Theatre of the Second Half of the Nineteenth Century*, Leningrad and Moscow, 1963
Drigo, Riccardo, "The Memoirs of Riccardo Drigo", excerpts edited by Roland John Wiley, part 2: *Dancing Times* (London), June 1982
Money, Keith, *Anna Pavlova: Her Life and her Art*, London, 1982
Ries, Frank W.D., "Rediscovering Pavlova's Dances", *Ballet Review* (New York), Winter 1984

*   *   *

The Magic Flute, a light, nineteenth-century story ballet by Lev Ivanov, has no connection either in music or in theme to Mozart's famous opera by the same name. Composed in 1893 by the Imperial Theatre's composer, Riccardo Drigo (reworking, on command, an older ballet by Bernadelli), the ballet score was choreographed by Lev Ivanov in his last years as assistant ballet master at the Maryinsky Theatre, St. Petersburg.

The story has many of the elements familiar to the comedy story-ballet, from the pre-Romantic *La Fille mal gardée* (wealthy lady farmer tries unsuccessfully to marry off wilful daughter to local squire), to Bournonville's *The Kermesse in Bruges* (a magical musical instrument makes everyone dance). The ballet tells the story of Lise and her sweetheart Luke (or Luc), whose hopes are thwarted by the ambitions of Lise's mother to marry her daughter off to the local Marquis. On a visit to the village the Marquis, in search of a suitable wife, has selected Lise—and despite the girl's original refusals, he has been encouraged by her mother.

Meanwhile, the discouraged Luke comes across a hermit, and in pity gives him a coin. The hermit subsequently hears Luke's tale of sorrow, and presents him with a magical flute whose tune will force all others around him to dance. As with Bournonville's *The Kermesse in Bruges*, the ensuing mayhem, when all the village is reduced to a craze of dancing, brings about the arrest of the young man (a slightly futile gesture, as the authorities themselves cannot help dancing, thereby losing their dignity). In the end, the true identity of the hermit is revealed as that of the great Oberon, who restores order, brings Lise and Luke together, and sanctions the proper celebration by the village of the young couple's marriage.

Ivanov's ballet was originally produced for the Imperial Theatre School of St. Petersburg, but it was performed by an eminent cast: Sergei Legat played the Marquis and Agrippina Vaganova the mother, while Luke was danced by Mikhail Fokine and Lise by the virtuoso ballerina Stanislava Belinskaya. Soon afterwards it transferred to the Maryinsky Theatre. Although little more than a playful, entertaining spectacle, the ballet was a success and was revived in 1901 for the rising young star of the Maryinsky, Anna Pavlova. It was by no means Ivanov's masterpiece, however, and Keith Money, Pavlova's biographer, calls the choice of *The Magic Flute* for a revival a questionable one, saying that "it was hardly representative of Ivanov's best work", being as it was "a light-hearted romp with an undue proportion of pantomimic gesture . . . [and] a familiar plot".

All the same, the ballet became a favourite touring piece of Anna Pavlova's once she had embarked on her independent career as an international star, and the ballet was restaged with her once again in the role of Lise, with Alexandre Volinine as Luke and veteran dancer/ballet master Enrico Cecchetti as the Marquis. Cecchetti assisted Pavlova in the staging.

The Magic Flute has not endured as well as some as Ivanov's other works, his greatest contribution to ballet being in the more lyrical vein of the "white acts" of *Swan Lake* or the Snow Scene and Grand Pas de deux of *The Nutcracker*. The ballet was recently rediscovered, however, by New York City Ballet dancer and ballet master Peter Martins, who staged his own version of the piece, rechoreographing it entirely but taking inspiration from the original libretto. Fittingly enough, it too was originally staged for the company's ballet school (the School of American Ballet), moving into the repertoire of the New York City Ballet the following year (1982). There, it brought success in particular to the delightful Darci Kistler, whose career as one of the company's most exquisite young dancers was just taking off.

—Virginia Christian

———

MAKAROVA, Natalia
Russian/American dancer, actress, and producer. Born Natalia Romanovna Makarova in Leningrad, 21 November 1940. Studied at the Leningrad Choreographic (Vaganova) School, from 1953, pupil of M. Mikhailov, Elena Shiripina; graduated in 1959. Married Edward Karkar, 1976: one son, André Michel, b. 1978. Début, while still a student, in graduation performance of Yuri Soloviev, 1958; dancer, soon becoming principal dancer, Kirov Ballet, 1959–70; defected from Soviet Union, 1970: principal dancer, American Ballet Theatre, from 1970, also performing as principal guest artist with Royal Ballet, London, from 1972, with other guest appearances including for Paris Opéra Ballet, La Scala, Milan, Stuttgart Ballet, Ballet du XXe Siècle, Hamburg Ballet, Roland Petit's Ballet National de Marseille, London Festival Ballet, and many others; also producer, staging Petipa classics for American Ballet Theatre and other companies; also actress: musical comedy début in *On Your Toes* (Rodgers and Hart; revival), 1983; guest artist, Kirov Ballet, London tour, 1988, appearing again with the Kirov, Leningrad, 1989; has also appeared in several ballet films and on television, including in "Live from Lincoln Center" broadcasts of *Swan Lake* (1976),

Natalia Makarova as Kitri in *Don Quixote* **Pas de Deux, London, 1972**

Giselle (1977), and *Romeo and Juliet* (1988), and in television specials *Assoluta* (1979), *Makarova* (1982), and *Makarova Returns* (1989); conceived and presented television series *Ballerina* (BBC, 1987). Recipient: Gold Medal, International Ballet Competition, Varna, 1965; title of Honoured Artist of the Russian Federation, 1970; Anna Pavlova Prize, Paris, 1970; Tony Award (Best Actress in a Musical), 1983; Laurence Olivier Award, 1984; *Evening Standard* Award, 1985.

ROLES

1958 Muse (cr) in *The Poet and his Muse* (Goleizovsky), Graduation Performance, Leningrad Choreographic School, Leningrad

Princess Florine in *Bluebird Pas de deux* (from *The Sleeping Beauty*; Petipa), Graduation Performance, Leningrad Choreographic School, Leningrad

1959 Title role in *Giselle* (Petipa after Coralli, Perrot), Kirov Ballet, Leningrad

Juanita (Flower Girl) in *Don Quixote* (Gorsky after Petipa), Kirov Ballet, Leningrad

Prelude, Mazurka in *Chopiniana* (Fokine), Kirov Ballet, Leningrad

1960/ Princess Florine in *The Sleeping Beauty* (full-length
62 ballet; Sergeyev after Petipa), Kirov Ballet, Leningrad

Pas de trois in *Swan Lake* (Sergeyev after Petipa, Ivanov), Kirov Ballet, Leningrad

Nina in *Masquerade* (Fenster), Kirov Ballet, Leningrad

1962 Zoya (cr) in *The Bedbug* (Yakobson), Kirov Ballet, Leningrad

1963 Title role in *The Distant Planet* (Sergeyev), Kirov Ballet, Leningrad

Soloist in (*Ravel's*) *Waltzes* (choreographic miniature; Yakobson), Kirov Ballet, Leningrad

1964 Juliet in *Romeo and Juliet* (Lavrovsky), Kirov Ballet, Leningrad

Krivliaka (cr) in *Cinderella* (Sergeyev), Kirov Ballet, Leningrad

Title role in *Cinderella* (Sergeyev), Kirov Ballet Tour, Chicago

Odette/Odile in *Swan Lake* (Sergeyev after Petipa, Ivanov), Kirov Ballet, Leningrad

Maria in *The Fountain of Bakhchisarai* (Zakharov), Kirov Ballet, Leningrad

1965 Love (cr) in *Man* (Lifshitz), Kirov Ballet, Leningrad

Title role in *The Pearl* (Boyarsky), Kirov Ballet, Leningrad

1967 Beautiful Maiden in *Land of Miracles* (Yakobson), Kirov Ballet, Leningrad

Title role in *A Passing Beauty* (Yakobson), Kirov Ballet, Leningrad

1968 Asiat (cr) in *Goryanka* (Vinogradov), Kirov Ballet, Leningrad

1968/69 Soloist (cr) in *Mozartiana* (Aleksidze), Kirov Ballet, Leningrad

Soloist (cr) in *Syrinx* (Aleksidze), Kirov Ballet, Leningrad

1970 Title role in *Raymonda* (Sergeyev after Petipa), Kirov Ballet, Leningrad

Princess Aurora in *The Sleeping Beauty* (Sergeyev after Petipa), Kirov Ballet, Leningrad

First Movement in *Symphony in C* (Balanchine; staged Dudinskaya), Leningrad Conservatory, Leningrad

Title role in *Giselle* (ABT début; Petipa after Coralli, Perrot; staged Blair), American Ballet Theatre, New York

1971 Caroline in *Jardin aux lilas* (Tudor), American Ballet Theatre

Title role in *La Sylphide* (Lander after Bournonville; staged Bruhn), American Ballet Theatre, New York

Lise in *La Fille mal gardée* (Romanoff after Dauberval), American Ballet Theatre, New York

Swanilda in *Coppélia* (Martinez after Saint-Léon), American Ballet Theatre, New York

Pas de deux (cr) added to *The River* (Ailey), American Ballet Theatre, New York

Juliet in *Romeo and Juliet* (Tudor), American Ballet Theatre, Washington, D.C.

The Girl (cr) in *The Miraculous Mandarin* (Ulf Gadd), American Ballet Theatre, New York

1972 Kitri in *Don Quixote* Pas de deux (after Petipa), Royal Ballet, London

Ballerina in *Theme and Variations* (Balanchine), American Ballet Theatre, Washington, D.C.

Hagar in *Pillar of Fire* (Tudor), American Ballet Theatre, New York

Chosen Maiden (cr) in *The Rite of Spring* (revised version; Taras), Ballet of La Scala, Milan

1973 Principal dancer (cr) in *I Vespri siciliani* (opera; mus. Verdi, staged Callas; chor. Lifar), Teatro Reggio, Turin

Princess Aurora in *The Sleeping Beauty* (MacMillan after Petipa), Royal Ballet, London

Juliet in *Romeo and Juliet* (MacMillan), Royal Ballet, London

Principal dancer in *Concerto* (MacMillan), Royal Ballet, London

1974 The Woman in *Song of the Earth* (MacMillan), Royal Ballet, London

Title role in *Manon* (MacMillan), Royal Ballet, London

Dancer (cr) in *Pas de deux* (untitled; MacMillan), Gala, Royal Opera House, London

1975 Title role in *Cinderella* (Ashton), Royal Ballet, London

Stop-Time Rag in *Elite Syncopations* (MacMillan), Royal Ballet, London

Principal dancer (cr) in *Epilogue* (pas de deux; Neumeier), American Ballet Theatre, New York

Adagietto ("La Garçonne") in *Les Biches* (Nijinska), Royal Ballet, London

Black Queen in *Checkmate* (de Valois), Royal Ballet Touring Company, London

1976 Principal dancer in *Serenade* (Balanchine), Royal Ballet, London

Puppet in *Rituals* (MacMillan), Royal Ballet, London

Principal dancer (cr) in *Other Dances* (pas de deux; Robbins), Gala, Metropolitan Opera House, New York

Principal dancer in *Le Sacre du printemps* (Tetley), American Ballet Theatre, New York

Principal dancer in *Voluntaries* (Tetley), Royal Ballet, London

Principal dancer in *Dances at a Gathering* (Robbins), Royal Ballet, London

Principal dancer in *Adagio Hammerklavier* (van Manen), Royal Ballet, London

1977 Clara in *The Nutcracker* (Baryshnikov), American Ballet Theatre, New York

Title role (cr) in *Firebird* (new production; C. Newton after Fokine), American Ballet Theatre, Los Angeles

Juliet in *Romeo and Juliet* (Chernichov), Maryland Ballet, Baltimore

The Pupil in *The Lesson* (Flindt), Nureyev and company, Coliseum, London

Pas de deux from *The Toreador* (Bournonville; staged Flindt), Nureyev and company, Coliseum, London

1978 Kitri in *Don Quixote* (*Kitri's Wedding*; Baryshnikov after Gorsky, Petipa), American Ballet Theatre, New York

1979 Principal dancer (cr) in *Contradances* (Tetley), American Ballet Theatre, New York

Tatiana in *Onegin* (Cranko), Stuttgart Ballet, New York

Principal dancer (cr) in *Mephisto Waltz* (Béjart), Ballet du XXe Siècle, Monte Carlo

1980 Nikiya (cr) in *La Bayadère* (also chor.; after Petipa), American Ballet Theatre, New York

Principal dancer (cr) in *Fantaisie sérieuse* (pas de deux; Lorca Massine), American Ballet Theatre, New York

Principal dancer in *Bach Sonate* (pas de deux; Béjart), Makarova and Company, New York

Principal dancer (cr) in *Ondine* (Moreland), Makarova and Company, New York

Principal dancer in *Vendetta* (Lorca Massine), Makarova and Company, New York

Ballerina in *Pas de dix* (from *Raymonda*; Balanchine), Makarova and Company, New York

Natalia in *A Month in the Country* (Ashton), Royal Ballet, London

Débutante in *Façade* (Ashton), Gala, Royal Royal Opera House, London

1981 Title dancing role (cr) in *Le Rossignol* (opera; mus. Stravinsky, chor. Ashton), Metropolitan Opera House, New York

The Woman (cr) in *The Wild Boy* (MacMillan), American Ballet Theatre, Washington, DC.

1981/82 Title role in *Carmen* (Petit), Ballet de Marseille, Paris

1983 Vera Baronova in *On Your Toes* (musical; mus. Rodgers, chor. Balanchine, staged Martins), Broadway, New York (preview at Kennedy Center, Washington, D.C., 1982)

Albertine in *Proust—Les Intermittences du coeur* (Petit), Ballet National de Marseille, North American tour

Esmeralda in *Notre Dame de Paris* (Petit), Ballet National de Marseille, North American tour

Death in *Le Jeune Homme et la mort* (Petit), Ballet National de Marseille, North American tour

1984   Title role in *Rosalinda* (Hynd), Ballet Nacional de Chile, Santiago
1985   Rosa (cr) in *The Blue Angel* (Petit), German Opera Ballet, Berlin
1987   The Woman in Ball Dress in *Apparitions* (Ashton), London Festival Ballet, London
1990   Principal dancer (cr) in *Lunar Romance* (Antonio), Gala Concert for "Spain in Dance", Kirov Theatre, Leningrad

Other roles include: for the Kirov Ballet—White Cat in *The Sleeping Beauty* (Sergeyev after Petipa), Tsar-Maiden in *The Little Humpbacked Horse* (Gorsky after Saint-Léon), Gamzatti in *La Bayadère* (Petipa), principal dancer in *The Kiss*, in *Triptych on Themes of Rodin* (*Choreographic Miniatures*; Yakobson), Ballerina in *Pas de quatre* (Dolin), Queen of the Ball in *The Bronze Horseman* (Zakharov); for American Ballet Theatre—pas de deux from *Le Corsaire* (after Petipa), principal dancer in *Dark Elegies* (Tudor), principal dancer in *Afternoon of a Faun* (Robbins), ballerina in *Études* (Lander), the Swan in *The Dying Swan* (after Fokine).

WORKS

Staged:
1974   "The Kingdom of the Shades" scene from *La Bayadère* (after Petipa, Chabukiani, Ponomarev; mus. Minkus), American Ballet Theatre, New York (staged National Ballet of Canada, 1984, London Festival Ballet, 1985)
1977   *Swan Lake*, Act II (after Ivanov; mus. Tchaikovsky), American Ballet Theatre, San Francisco
1980   *La Bayadère* (after Petipa, Chabukiani; mus. Minkus), American Ballet Theatre, New York (staged Royal Ballet, London, 1989, Royal Swedish Ballet, 1989, La Scala, Milan, 1992, Teatro Colón, Buenos Aires, 1992)
       Grand Divertissement from *Paquita* (after Petipa; mus Minkus), Makarova and Company, New York (also staged American Ballet Theatre, 1983, National Ballet of Canada, 1991)
1984   *Swan Lake* (after Petipa; mus. Tchaikovsky), London Festival Ballet, London

PUBLICATIONS

By Makarova:
"My Steps to Freedom", *The Daily Telegraph* (London), 20 September 1970
"My Struggle to Soviet Stardom", *The Daily Telegraph* (London), 27 September 1970
"Russian Ballet Behind the Glamour", *The Daily Telegraph* (London), 4 October 1970
Interview in Maynard, Olga, "Makarova: the Sublime Paradox", *Dance Magazine* (New York), April 1977
A Dance Autobiography, New York, 1979
Interview in Barnes, Patricia, "Conversation with Makarova", *Ballet News* (New York), March 1980

About Makarova:
Krasovskaya, Vera, *Natalia Makarova*, Leningrad, 1967
Clarke, Mary, "Guest Artist Makarova", *Dancing Times* (London), August 1973
Greskovic, Robert, "American Ballet Theatre: Dancers at a

Gathering", *Ballet Review* (Brooklyn, N.Y.), vol. 5, no. 1, 1975–76
Croce, Arlene, *Afterimages*, New York, 1977
Austin, Richard, *Natalia Makarova*, London, 1978
Maynard, Olga, "Giselle for Today", *Dance Magazine* (New York), August 1979
Hunt, Marilyn, "Recapitulation and Finale", *Dance Magazine* (New York), September 1980
Crisp, Clement, "The Art of Makarova", *Dance Chronicle* (New York), vol. 4, no. 2, 1981
Croce, Arlene, *Going to the Dance*, New York, 1982
Taub, Eric, "Back on her Toes", *Ballet News* (New York), July 1983
Alovert, Nina, *Baryshnikov in Russia*, New York, 1984
Smakov, Gennady, *The Great Russian Dancers*, New York, 1984
Gruen, John, "From Marlene to Makarova", *Dance Magazine* (New York), August 1985
Clark, Mary, and Crisp, Clement, *Ballerina* (to accompany 1987 BBC series), London, 1987
Croce, Arlene, *Sight Lines*, New York, 1987
Gruen, John, "Natalia Makarova: Off Her Toes", *Dance Magazine* (New York), January 1993
Zazulina, Natalia, *Natalia Makarova*, Moscow, 1993

*   *   *

Russian ballerina Natalia Makarova is undoubtedly the "first lady" of world ballet in the second half of the twentieth century. None of the new ballerinas who have come to the stage over the last decade, regardless of their youth or their talent, can be put on the same level as Makarova. She is somehow always more complete. She has an inherent perfection of line—a beautiful arabesque, lovely arms, an exquisitely arched spine—accompanied by an emotional spontaneity and intuitive artistry that are hers alone, and no one can duplicate her style.

Makarova possesses a remarkable gift, rare among performers: while different in every role, she remains, essentially, herself. For the 30 years that she has been on the stage, she has retained the capacity to be both a tomboy and Rafael's Madonna at the same time. In a sense, her pictorial charm resides in her amalgamation, in one style, of images of women from diverse epochs. All of Makarova's creations, even the most contemporary, possess a quality rare for a woman of the twentieth century—defencelessness. Makarova the performer has preserved this old-fashioned conception of women as captive. But the nervous energy of her tragic heroines and the angularity of her modern women clash with the poetic lyricism of the women of the past, and this creative contrast constitutes one of the most attractive features of her talent; it is one of her essential "artistic secrets".

Makarova retains her individuality in every image, but she has no one set role. There is, today, no more romantic Giselle than she, but at the same time Manon Lescaut is one of the most outstanding roles in her repertoire. Makarova is a genuinely tragic Juliet; but she has also captivated audiences in the role of Carmen, where she is an impenitent coquette, wilful and independent, seductively accessible and yet enigmatic at the same time.

Her Odette is tender, her Sylphide is incorporeal. A fugitive smile, a deliberate glide "through" poses (an art that only Ulanova possessed), and an astonishing sense of style in its purest sense all make Makarova an unsurpassed performer of the Romantic repertoire. Yet this ballerina won a Tony, the award for the best role on Broadway, for her performance of Vera in the musical *On Your Toes*. Vera is essentially a comic role.

On stage, Makarova the ballerina can be discarnate in the boldest of love scenes and sexually attractive in the most abstract and ethereal of ballets. It is most likely for this reason that there is no better performer of Béjart's *Sonate*.

Makarova's artistic and personal life are tightly interwoven, and could serve as the basis for a novel. She was born to a family of scientists, far removed from the theatre. She started ballet school later than is usually the case in Russia (at twelve instead of nine); she came by accident to the school and, as fate would have it, was accepted right away.

At the Kirov Theatre, Makarova was quickly given solo, and then principal, roles; but she was a "difficult child" in the artistic sphere. Beginning with her very first roles, she sought her own approach, challenging the traditional style of dancing for any given role. Upon her graduation performance of the adagio from *Giselle*, she became the unsurpassed "Leningrad Giselle". But there was no contemporary repertoire for her at the Kirov. It was only Leonid Yakobson who understood Makarova's gift of elasticity, and he created the role of Zoya in *The Bedbug* for her. It was in that role that Makarova's particular gift was made manifest, and critics noted her ability to "hear" music with her body, to respond elastically to the most subtle of musical nuances, to find inspiration in the first musical phrase.

Still, it was artistic starvation, the lack of any prospect of a creative future, and the impossibility of independence that pushed Makarova to her decision to pursue her career in the West. She did not return to Leningrad after the Kirov's London tour in 1970, but she chose to stay in England. In London she filmed *The Dying Swan* and the adagio from *Swan Lake* with Nureyev for the BBC, and was instantly invited to perform with the American Ballet Theatre (ABT).

In America Makarova made her debut in *Giselle* with ABT on the stage of the Metropolitan Opera House. Her professional mastery grew stronger and her talent undoubtedly developed in the West; but in all of her interviews, Makarova always said that it was thanks to the Russian school of ballet that she had become the ballerina she was. She made use of all of the opportunities that the Western world afforded her and she has danced ballets by all of the twentieth-century's leading choreographers—Balanchine, Béjart, Petit, Ashton, Cranko, Tudor, Robbins—yet her foundation remains the classicism of the Russian school. All the same, she is no cool virtuoso. From this wide world repertoire, Makarova prefers roles that have "drama", ballets in which she can project a complete image, such as Tatiana in *Onegin* or the title role in *Manon*.

The 1970 London tour did not change Makarova's future as a dancer—she was destined to become a great ballerina—but it did send her in the right direction, both personally and professionally. She has since married, has a son, and life has turned out happy. But in Russia her name was banned for many years.

It was only with the appearance of so-called "perestroika" that Makarova's fate took another turn. As early as 1987 Yuri Grigorovich had begun inviting Makarova to come to Moscow to perform in concert, but the ballerina wanted to go back to her native Leningrad. Her former ballet school classmate, Oleg Vinogradov, now the artistic director of the Kirov Ballet, went to great lengths to bring about her return to Russia. (Meanwhile she herself had played an important role in bringing the Kirov Ballet's latest hopefuls, Altynai Assylmuratova and Farukh Ruzimatov, to perform with a Western company for the first time in 1988.) Finally, in 1989, in the same London where Makarova had last appeared with the Kirov Ballet, she danced with that company again for the first time in eighteen years, performing the "White" pas de deux from *Swan Lake* with Konstantin Zaklinsky. In the winter of 1989–90 she was invited

to a showing of her film *Ballerina* at a film festival in Leningrad. There she saw her mother for the first time in more than eighteen years, was reunited with her friends, and, in February, danced again for the first time on the stage of the Kirov Theatre. She had come full circle. A talented girl who showed promise as a young dancer had returned to the stage of the Kirov, recognized by the world as the "ballerina assoluta".

—Nina Alovert

MAKHALINA, Yulia

Russian dancer. Born Yulia Viktorovna Makhalina in Leningrad, 23 June 1968. Studied at the Leningrad Choreographic (Vaganova) School, pupil of M. Vasilieva; graduated in 1985. Dancer, Kirov Ballet, from 1985, becoming principal artist, from 1988; has toured with the Kirov, performing in Canada, the U.S., Britain, and Japan; also guest artist, German Opera Ballet, Berlin, 1991. Recipient: Gold Medal, International Ballet Competition, Paris, 1990.

ROLES

1986   Myrtha in *Giselle* (Petipa after Coralli, Perrot), Kirov Ballet, Leningrad

Street dancer in *Don Quixote* (Gorsky after Petipa), Kirov Ballet, Leningrad

1987   Solo variation, Divertissement from *Paquita* (Petipa; staged Gusev), Kirov Ballet, Leningrad

Queen of the Dryads in *Don Quixote* (Gorsky after Petipa), Kirov Ballet, Leningrad

Medora in *Le Corsaire* (Petipa; staged Gusev), Kirov Ballet, Leningrad

Odette/Odile in *Swan Lake* (Petipa; staged Sergeyev), Kirov Ballet, Leningrad

1988   Gamzatti in *La Bayadère* (Petipa, Ponomarev, Chabukiani), Kirov Ballet, Leningrad

Mary Magdalen in *The Rehearsal* (Fodor), Kirov Ballet, Leningrad

1989   Kitri in *Don Quixote* (Gorsky after Petipa), Kirov Ballet, Leningrad

Grand Pas Classique (Gsovsky), International Ballet Gala, "Le Don des Étoiles", Montreal

Lilac Fairy in *The Sleeping Beauty* (Petipa, staged Sergeyev), Kirov Ballet, Leningrad

1990   Nikiya in *La Bayadère* (Petipa, Ponomarev, Chabukiani), Kirov Ballet, Leningrad

Ballerina in *Theme and Variations* (Balanchine, staged F. Russell), Kirov Ballet, Leningrad

1991   Soloist in *Apollo* (Balanchine), German Opera Ballet, Berlin

Dancer in *Tchaikovsky Pas de Deux* (Balanchine), German Opera Ballet, Berlin

Principal dancer in *Symphony in C* (Balanchine), German Opera Ballet, Berlin

Title role in *Giselle* (Petipa after Coralli, Perrot), German Opera Ballet, Berlin

PUBLICATIONS

By Makhalina:

Interview in Dunning, Jennifer, "Three Young Stars and their Paths to the Kirov", *The New York Times*, 14 July 1989

About Makhalina:
"Kirov Dancers You Should Know", *Dance and Dancers* (London), August 1990

* * *

The story of Yulia Makhalina is a rare example of theatrical fate and good fortune—the ballet school pupil who became a ballerina overnight. Her first role, that of Myrtha in *Giselle*, demonstrated that the young dancer possessed the gifts of a real ballerina. Breadth of movement and expression, originality, artistic intuition—all of these qualities were revealed from the very beginning. Makhalina's Myrtha was not just a merciless Queen of the Wilis; she was the human counterpart to Giselle. The fate of Makhalina's Myrtha is, perhaps, similar to that of Giselle—but, unlike Giselle, this Myrtha forgives nothing. On the contrary, she has become embittered and takes revenge on all men for her ruined life.

During her second season in the Kirov Theatre, Makhalina confirmed her right to be called a young star. She danced the role of Medora in *Le Corsaire*, a role for which her individual style of acting seemed to have been destined. She created an image of the character impressively close to that of the heroine of Byron's poem.

Makhalina works tirelessly from performance to performance. Sometimes the progress is slow and difficult, as was the case with her work on the contrasting images of Odette and Odile in *Swan Lake*. Slowly overcoming familiar moulds, and showing her own flexibility of approach, Makhalina has become one of the Kirov Theatre's best performers of *Swan Lake* today. Majestic calm, a sense of dignity yet a wealth of spirit—expressive arms, a fluid back, and lyrical arabesques—this is Makhalina's Odette. At the same time, the actress's sense of style and natural poise, performing the variation from *Paquita*, earned Makhalina the distinction of being called "a duchess at rest" by critic Clive Barnes.

Makhalina is a true St. Petersburg ballerina, in that she was trained in the tradition of the Russian classical school; but her style of performance is more similar to that of the West. Her graceful figure, beautiful line (including an unusually high *écarté*), and leaps that are modern in their extension and elevation, along with a visible energy of attack, are all good qualities for contemporary Western choreography. Vinogradov, sending Makhalina as a guest artist to dance with the German Opera Ballet in Berlin, has given her a great opportunity to try out her strengths in the ballets of Béjart and other Western choreographers.

Of all of the roles of the classical repertoire, Makhalina's undoubted greatest success has been in the role of Nikiya, and she is the company's best performer today of the Lilac Fairy. While the company was on tour in Washington the critic George Jackson wrote: "Makhalina is tall, but with such perfect proportions that she doesn't tower over her entourage. Classically proportioned, too, is her dancing. Legs extended so amply and arms making such generous sweeps could easily distort the body's harmony, but not in Makhalina's case. Instinctively she achieves balance. And, in her role, she's the good fairy of one's childhood now vividly visible even if one is afraid she mightn't be real to touch. . . . Yulia Makhalina, the Lilac Fairy, was like the Winged Victory and the Michelangelo madonna combined."

—Nina Alovert

MALY (Mussorgsky) THEATRE BALLET

Russian Ballet company based in Leningrad/St. Petersburg. Origins in small ballet company organized in Leningrad, under choreographer Fedor Lopukhov, in 1933, performing in theatre first known as the Imperial Mikhailovsky (or Mikhailovsky Court) Theatre (established 1915), later the Comic Opera Theatre, the Maly Opera Theatre, and finally the Maly Theatre of Opera and Ballet, 1963–89; has been known since as the Maly Theatre Ballet, the Maly Opera Ballet, or the Maly Ballet; named the official resident company of the Mussorgsky Theatre of Opera and Ballet, Leningrad/St. Petersburg, from 1989. Current artistic director: Nikolai Boyarchikov.

PUBLICATIONS

Roslavleva, Natalia, *Era of the Russian Ballet*, London, 1966
Swift, Mary Grace, *The Art of Dance in the USSR*, Notre Dame, Ind., 1968
The Leningrad Theatre of Opera and Ballet, 1918–1968, Leningrad, 1968
Degen, Arsen, and Stupnikov, Igor, *Ballet of the Young*, Leningrad, 1979
Degen, Arsen, *Leningrad Maly Ballet Company*, Leningrad, 1979
Degen, Arsen, and Stupnikov, Igor, *Leningrad Ballet, 1917–1987*, Leningrad, 1988
Alovert, Nina, "From St. Petersburg to Leningrad", *Dance Magazine* (New York), March 1989

* * *

The Mussorgsky Theatre of Opera and Ballet (the new name given to the Maly Theatre in 1989) is the second most important theatre in Leningrad/St. Petersburg after the Kirov (Maryinsky) Theatre, and its ballet company is one of the best in the country. The name of the theatre, located in the building of the former Mikhailovsky Court Theatre, has changed more than once: it has been called the Comic Opera, the Maly Opera Theatre, and the Maly Theatre of Opera and Ballet.

In 1933, a relatively small group of dancers who danced in operas and operettas organized a small ballet company. The head of the company was the ballet master Fedor Lopukhov, and he set himself the task of creating a company different from that of the Kirov Theatre. He turned to the genre, rare in contemporary ballet, of the lyrical comedy, employing scores from old ballets. Thus he set out to create an original version of Drigo's *Harlequinade*. The date of the premiere of that ballet—6 June 1933—has come to be considered the date of the ballet company's birth. Lopukhov then staged his own choreographic version of Delibes' *Coppélia* (1934) and of *The Bright Stream* (1935) to the music of Shostakovich. The latter ballet, on a contemporary theme, was immensely popular with the public, but at the time, the Soviet overseers of art subjected Shostakovich's music to decimating criticism. *The Bright Stream* was struck from the repertoire, and Lopukhov was dismissed.

But the theatre he had created continued to develop. Numerous young ballet masters began their artistic careers in that theatre, going on to become leading Soviet choreographers. Consequently, the theatre came to be known as a "laboratory of Soviet ballet". Lopukhov again headed the ballet company during the Second World War. In 1959, he staged his last ballet, *Ballad of Love*, to the music of Tchaikovsky's *The Seasons*.

After Lopukhov, Leonid Lavrovsky, one of the founders of the "dram-ballet" ("choreodrama") movement, became the

The Maly Theatre Ballet performing Tchernichov's *Antony and Cleopatra*, 1968 (Alla Osipenko, centre)

director of the theatre (1935–38). His ballet *Fadetta*, based on a short story by George Sand, and set to the music of Delibes' ballet *Sylvia*, was part of the theatre's repertoire for 30 years. Of the 22 ballet masters who have worked in this theatre, mention should also be made of Boris Fenster, one of Lopukhov's pupils, who led the company from 1945–65. His most important ballets were the lyrical comedy *An Imaginary Fiancé* (1946) and the heroic *Youth* (1949) to the music of Chulaki, and the children's ballet *Doctor "Ai-Bolit"* (1948, with ballerina Galina Isaeva, to the music of Morozov). Varkovitsky, another of Lopukhov's pupils, staged a brilliant comic ballet, *The Tale of the Priest and his Servant Baldel* (based on a Pushkin tale, to the music of Chulaki) in 1940.

In the 1950s and 1960s, ballets significant for the time appeared in the repertoire, such as Yakobson's *Solveig* (1952), Gusev's epic *Seven Beauties* (1953), and Boyarsky's *The Nobleman's Daughter and the Hooligan* (1962). The theatre also began reviving classical ballets. In 1955 Gusev revived, for the first time, Petipa's forgotten ballet *Le Corsaire*. In its revivals of such classics as *Swan Lake* in 1958 (Andrei Lopukhov and Boyarsky after Ivanov and Petipa) and *Giselle* in 1973 (Dolgushin after Petipa), the theatre strove to reconstruct as faithfully as possible the original productions of these ballets.

The years 1962–73, when former Kirov Ballet dancer and novice ballet master Igor Belsky was artistic director of the theatre, were an important stage in the theatre's development. "Exiled" to the Maly Theatre for his overly bold innovations, Belsky, like Lopukhov, continued developing the concept of symphonic dance, a concept first explored by his creative teacher Lopukhov, and followed in Belsky's own ballet to

Shostakovich's *Eleventh Symphony* (1966). He created an original version of Tchaikovsky's *The Nutcracker* (1969), attempting to bring the ballet and Hoffmann's tale closer together. In 1963 he also staged the brilliant comedy ballet, *The Little Humpbacked Horse*, based on Ershov's Russian fairy tale, to the music of Schedrin. During his years of directorship, Belsky also gave numerous novice ballet masters the chance to test their strength. Under him Nikolai Boyarchikov made his début as a ballet master, with the comic ballet *The Three Musketeers* (1964, to the music of Basner), as did Igor Chernyshev with *Antony and Cleopatra* (1968, to the music of Lazarev). The dancers Nikita Dolgushin and German Zamuel also made their débuts under his direction, and Boris Eifman created an original version of *Gayané* (1972).

Oleg Vinogradov also got his start at the Maly Theatre under Belsky. He staged his original rendition of *La Fille mal gardée* (1971, to Hérold's original music) and *Coppélia* (1973). The period 1973–77, when Vinogradov was the theatre's artistic director, was one of the most important periods in the life of the theatre. His ballets *Yaroslavna* (1974, to the music of Tischenko), *Educational Poem* (1977, Lebedev), and original productions of Prokofiev's *Cinderella* (1977) and *Romeo and Juliet* (1976) sparked the public's interest in the theatre. Also working here was Lebedev, one of the most talented of Leningrad's contemporary choreographers (co-author of the production of *Educational Poem* and, later, choreographer of Simakina's ballets *Dzhamkhukh—Son of the Reindeer*, *The Legend of the Bird Donenbai*, and others). Vinogradov strove not to duplicate the repertoire of the Kirov Ballet in reviving the classical heritage, but to explore them, in his own way. Petr

Gusev revived Petipa's minor masterpieces *Cavalry Halt* and *Harlequinade* (1975), and the Danish choreographer Elsa-Marianne von Rosen did a production of *La Sylphide* (1975) showing the way Bournonville's ballet is performed in Denmark.

In 1977, when Vinogradov left for the Kirov Theatre, Nikolai Boyarchikov became artistic director of the theatre. For seven years before that he had been successfully directing the ballet theatre in Perm, and he brought several of his ballets to the stage of the Maly Theatre—*Tsar Boris* (1978) and *A Servant of Two Masters* (1978)—and he staged new ballets: *Orpheus and Eurydice* (an opera ballet to the music of Gurbin), *Heracles* (1981, to the music of Martynov), *The Robbers* (1982, to the music of Minkov), *Macbeth* (1984, to the music of Kallosh), *The Wedding* (1986, to the music of Gurbin), *Romeo and Juliet* (1989, to the music of Prokofiev), and *And Quiet Flows the Don* (1987, to the music of Klinichev). He also revived *Swan Lake* (1980, after Petipa, Ivanov), and *Esmeralda* (1981, after Petipa and Vaganova, to the music of Pugni), with consultants Tanya Vecheslova and Petr Gusev. The theatre continues to be an active and vital force in Russian ballet today.

—Nina Alovert

MAM'ZELLE ANGOT
(originally *Mademoiselle Angot*)

Choreography: Léonide Massine
Music: Charles Lecocq (from his comic opera *La Fille de Madame Angot*), arranged by Efrem Kurtz and orchestrated by Richard Mohaupt
Design: Mstislav Dobuzhinsky
Libretto: Léonide Massine (based on opera libretto by Paul Siraudin, Louis-François Clairville, and Victor Koning, after A.F. Maillot)
First Production: Ballet Theatre, Metropolitan Opera House, New York, 10 October 1943
Principal Dancers: Nora Kaye (Soubrette), Léonide Massine (Barber), Rosella Hightower (Aristocrat), André Eglevsky (Artist)

Other productions include: Sadler's Wells Ballet (restaged Massine, mus. orchestrated Gordon Jacob, design André Derain), as *Mam'zelle Angot*, with Margot Fonteyn (Mam'zelle Angot), Alexander Grant (Barber), Moira Shearer (Aristocrat), Michael Somes (Caricaturist); London, 26 November 1947. Royal Ballet Touring Company, with Lucette Aldous (Mam'zelle Angot), Ronald Emblen (Barber), Shirley Grahame (Aristocrat), David Wall (Caricaturist); 31 January 1968. Australian Ballet (restaged Massine); with Lucette Aldous,

Mam'zelle Angot, with Lesley Collier and Wayne Sleep, Royal Ballet, London

Alan Alder, Kelvin Coe, Marilyn Jones; Melbourne, 9 December 1971.

PUBLICATIONS

Clarke, Mary, "Massine—In England and America", *Dance Magazine* (New York), April 1948
Beaumont, Cyril, *Ballets Past and Present*, London, 1955
Massine, Léonide, *My Life in Ballet*, New York, 1960
Williams, Peter, "The Case for Massine", *Dance and Dancers* (London), March 1968
Denby, Edwin, *Dance Writings*, edited by Robert Cornfield and William Mackay, New York, 1986

*   *   *

Mademoiselle Angot, originally produced by Léonide Massine in 1943 for Ballet Theatre in New York, was the last smash hit in a remarkably successful series of comedy ballets which the choreographer initiated in 1917 with *The Good-Humoured Ladies*, and which thus over more than a quarter of a century not only provided audiences with the welcome opportunity actually to laugh out loud at a ballet performance, but also influenced many imitators in the genre. The story was complicated in incident but simple in theme: boy loves girl who loves another boy who loves another girl. By the final curtain, boys get girls, to the general delight of the spectators—both on stage and in the audience.

At the first performance the roles of the Barber and the heroine Clairette (called on the original programme merely "Soubrette"), and of the Aristocrat and the Caricaturist (or "Artist") were taken by Massine himself, Nora Kaye, Rosella Hightower, and André Eglevsky, a casting which set the ballet off to a very good start indeed. When it was reproduced for the Sadler's Wells Ballet at Covent Garden in 1947, probably only the performance of Alexander Grant in the Massine role could bear any sort of comparison with the originals: Fonteyn was utterly miscast in the title role, though fortunately she was soon replaced by Farron and later Nerina—both of whom coped admirably with the character; Shearer looked pretty but in no way projected to the far reaches of the house; while nobody could ever have pretended that Somes had the charm with which Eglevsky invested the role of the Caricaturist. Be that as it may, however, the ballet produced some of Massine's most successful cameo roles, which in New York and London were given to enormous effect by several notable character dancers.

The choreographic fabric of the ballet follows the pattern of many of Massine's comedies; several strong contrasting personalities are immediately established through their characteristic gestures, clearly differentiated one from another, after which they are set in varying degrees of conflict with each other, ending up in an immensely complicated finale which leaves the dancers breathless, and the audience amazed and delighted, with the happy solution to everyone's problems.

Not all of the critics were delighted when the ballet was first performed, however. The American doyen of dance critics, Edwin Denby, felt that Massine had missed the mark drastically in a genre which usually suited his choreographic skills perfectly. "The trouble with *Mademoiselle Angot*," he wrote in 1943, "is simply that for all its constant commotion it seems endless and pointless; the successive dances seem to flounder around without either a steady subject or any consecutive form." Whereas the original operetta on which the ballet was based (*La Fille de Madame Angot*) had instilled human warmth and humour into the characters, Massine, in Denby's estimation, had now "passed over the human drama of the characterizations", providing mere "dance marionettes" instead of people.

But the ballet was still hugely successful, and remained a favourite with audiences. When it was transferred to England and staged for the Sadler's Wells Ballet (later the Royal Ballet), it remained in the Covent Garden repertory from 1947 until 1965, chalking up a total of 124 performances before being passed on to the Royal Ballet Touring Company, where it remained in the repertory until 1969. It would undoubtedly bear revival today, provided it had dancers of the wit and sparkle of the original cast to perform it.

—Janet Sinclair

————

MANEN, Hans van *see* **VAN MANEN, Hans**

————

MANON

Choreography: Kenneth MacMillan
Music: Jules Massenet (arranged and orchestrated by Leighton Lucas and Hilda Gaunt)
Design: Nicholas Georgiadis
Libretto: Kenneth MacMillan (after *L'Histoire du Chevalier des Grieux et de Manon Lescaut* by the Abbé Antoine François Prévost)
First Production: Royal Ballet, Royal Opera House, London, 7 March 1974
Principal Dancers: Antoinette Sibley (Manon), Anthony Dowell (Des Grieux), David Wall (Lescaut), Derek Rencher (Monsieur GM), Monica Mason (Lescaut's Mistress)

Other productions include: Swedish Royal Ballet (restaged MacMillan, with Anneli Alhanko and Weit Carlson); Stockholm, 22 November 1980. Paris Opéra Ballet, as *L'Histoire de Manon*, with Monique Loudières and Manuel Legris; Paris, 9 November 1990. Houston Ballet; Houston, 11 March 1992.

Other choreographic treatments of story: Jean Aumer (Paris, 1830), Giovanni Golinelli (Vienna, 1852).

PUBLICATIONS

Clarke, Mary, "Kenneth MacMillan's *Manon*", *Dancing Times* (London), April 1974
Lucas, L., "*Manon*" and Massenet's Music", *About the House* (London), Spring 1974
Maynard, Olga, "A Brief for *Manon*", *Dance Magazine* (New York), August 1974
Brinson, Peter, and Crisp, Clement, *Ballet and Dance: A Guide to the Repertory*, London, 1980
Thorpe, Edward, *Kenneth MacMillan: The Man and his Ballets*, London, 1985
Sulcas, Roslyn, "*Manon* Revisited", *Dance and Dancers* (London), February/March 1991

*   *   *

Abbé Prévost's *L'Histoire du Chevalier des Grieux et de Manon Lescaut*, published in 1733, inspired several nineteenth-century

Manon, with Antoinette Sibley and Anthony Dowell, Royal Ballet, London, 1974

stage productions. A ballet by Aumer (1830) and operas by Auber (1956), Massenet (1884), and Puccini (1893) were all based on Prévost's novel, but their scenarios strayed considerably from the original plot.

In 1974, Kenneth MacMillan returned to Prévost rather than to later interpretations of his ideas. Set in Regency-period Paris, *Manon* juxtaposes extremities of status and emotion. Sex, money, and corruption all conspire in the downfall of Prévost's main characters. Des Grieux is lured into crime by his obsessive love for Manon. He is described as "an ambiguous character, a mixture of virtues and vices". But Manon is the more mysterious character. Prévost's *histoire* is written in the first person—it is through Des Grieux's narration that Manon's identity and motivations are revealed. Thus, to the reader, she is always once removed.

In MacMillan's ballet, Manon is the central character. In his earlier *Romeo and Juliet* (1965), Juliet became the protagonist of Shakespeare's drama and in *Manon* MacMillan chose to focus again upon the heroine: through *her* actions, the drama unfolds. MacMillan discarded several of Prévost's secondary characters and concentrated his scenario on incidents occurring directly between Manon and Des Grieux. In this, Manon herself becomes more delineated, and the consequences of her actions command greater empathy. Prévost's Manon is uncompromising in her quest for prosperity, Des Grieux accepting that "it was no use counting on her in hard times. She was too fond of wealth and pleasure to give them up for me". In MacMillan's *Manon*, the power of money over love is challenged constantly. The climax of this three-act ballet occurs at the end of Act II, when Manon renounces forever her courtesan lifestyle. Des Grieux removes the furs and jewellery given to her by Monsieur GM. Initially, when Des Grieux unfastens her bracelet, she resists—the bracelet is Manon's last symbol of acquired wealth. From the moment she decides to relinquish it, her love for Des Grieux is confirmed. But their future together is doomed.

Like Act I, the closing scene of Act II is in Des Grieux's lodgings. In both acts, MacMillan contrasts the intimacy of second scene pas de deux with the bustle and interaction of public first scenes. (The first scene of Act I is set in the courtyard of an inn near Paris; the first scene of Act II is in a "hotel particulier"—a brothel.) Act III also alternates public and private scenes—from the port of New Orleans to the Penal Colony gaoler's room and, finally, to the swamps of Louisiana where, as Manon lies dying in Des Grieux's arms, associations from her past appear upstage.

In both Prévost's book and MacMillan's ballet, Manon is introduced as a sixteen-year old, en route to a convent. Immediately she steps out of her coach, Des Grieux is drawn to her. Instant—and fatal—attraction is his destiny. In Prévost's novel, Des Grieux describes his infatuation as "an overmastering passion" and, in MacMillan's opening scene, such singular attention towards Manon strikes a marked contrast with the collective activities of beggars, harlots, and aristocratic gentlemen who congregate in the courtyard. In the opening scene, too, MacMillan introduces the idea that Manon is capable of seduction. Her brother, Lescaut, instigates her meeting with the wealthy Monsieur GM. GM's money is Manon's passport to affluence and, though ostensibly virginal at this stage, she recognizes the advantages of a liaison with the old man.

Des Grieux describes Lescaut as "a coarse unprincipled scoundrel". MacMillan takes not only plot and characterization from Prévost but also the writer's interest in characters as types. The rogue, the besotted lover, the femme fatale—all are particularized. Their experiences transcend conventions of period or place and, like Romeo and Juliet, the sisters in *Las Hermanas*, or Anastasia and Isadora, temperament and destiny drive their actions. The maturation of Manon from adolescent to alluring courtesan, the ambiguity of her affections, Des Grieux's contradictions of character, Lescaut's ruthless manipulation of his sister for monetary gain—MacMillan makes these the cause and effect of the ballet's dénouement.

Manon's period style is provided by designer Nicholas Georgiadis. His set is one of the sparsest of MacMillan-Georgiadis collaborations. Large three-dimensional structures have been rejected in favour of simple properties and elaborate costumes. In *Manon*, Georgiadis uses cloth symbolically. Rags recur as leitmotif, their presence throughout a reminder of Regency "demi-monde" and of the poverty which haunts Manon.

MacMillan created *Manon* for Antoinette Sibley. (Sibley became ill during the rehearsal period and although she danced the role at the ballet's premiere, much of the choreography was created on the second-cast Manon, Jennifer Penney.) Initially, Anthony Dowell danced Des Grieux to David Wall's Lescaut but, at subsequent performances, the two dancers alternated roles.

In *Manon*, MacMillan continued his practice of creating a ballet around central pas de deux. There are four pas de deux for Manon and Des Grieux, and through each, MacMillan reveals the various stages of their relationship. From instant attraction to passionate fulfilment and, finally, death and desolation, the legato of gestures and lifts intensifies as their relationship deepens. In typical MacMillan style, grands rondes des jambes and développés are high. Manon is scooped steeply and enveloped around Des Grieux. Similar entwining is used to comic effect in a pas de deux for Lescaut and his mistress in the brothel scene. The drunken Lescaut is unable to synchronize his movements and partnering is fumbled. His mistress (Monica Mason in the original cast) totters in supported arabesques and slips ungracefully from his grasp.

Two of *Manon*'s most extended solos are also for Lescaut—in the ballet's courtyard and brothel scenes. These solos for David Wall augured MacMillan's next three-act ballet, *Mayerling* (1978). Rarely is a multi-act ballet created for a male dancer, but in *Mayerling* MacMillan focused the dramatic action on the demise of the Hapsburg heir, Crown Prince Rudolf. The role of Rudolf was created on Wall, four years after his impressive performances as both Lescaut and Des Grieux.

Similarities between *Manon* and other MacMillan ballets are also evident in terms of musical accompaniment. The scores of *Manon, Mayerling,* and *Isadora* (1981) are compilations of music culled from several sources. For *Manon*, MacMillan collaborated with the composer-conductor Leighton Lucas. Lucas selected music not from Jules Massenet's *Manon* but from several of his other operas and some of his songs and orchestral works. He arranged Massenet's music to complement the dramatic development of MacMillan's ballet. And by manipulating certain melodies, Lucas created signature tunes. The most significant is from Massenet's song *Crépuscule*, which becomes Manon's theme. It accompanies her first entrance—a series of forward steps en pointe, passing through fourth position. The upward emphasis of the step presents Manon as demure but also distant. In the courtyard, this suggests youthfulness. When the step is repeated in the brothel scene, amidst the harlots and other courtesans, it signals Manon's superior status as Monsieur GM's mistress.

Prévost's novel is a retrospective narration, by Des Grieux on his return from America. But MacMillan's *Manon* ends with tragedy rather than its aftermath. The plight of Prévost's lovers is the ballet's main focus and, fittingly, it culminates in a final death scene. The lovers' last pas de deux, in which Des Grieux tries unsuccessfully to revive the limp, dying Manon, is wrought with emotion. Love has triumphed over money but the chain of events which Manon's quest for wealth initiated has ultimately caught up with them. Only in death is the conflict resolved and Des Grieux's obsession quelled.

—Angela Kane

MARÉ, Rolf de *see* **DE MARÉ, Rolf**

MARGUERITE AND ARMAND

Choreography: Frederick Ashton

Music: Franz Liszt, orchestrated by Humphrey Searle

Design: Cecil Beaton (scenery and costumes)

Libretto: Frederick Ashton (after *La Dame aux camélias* by Alexandre Dumas fils)

First Production: Royal Ballet, Royal Opera House, London, 12 March 1963

Principal Dancers: Margot Fonteyn (Marguerite), Rudolf Nureyev (Armand), Michael Somes (His Father), Leslie Edwards (A Duke)

Other productions include: La Scala, with Nureyev and Fonteyn; Milan, 16 September 1966. Teatro Colón, with Nureyev and Fonteyn; Buenos Aires, 14 April 1967. Ballet de Rio de Janeiro, with Nureyev and Fonteyn; Rio de Janeiro, 25 April 1967. "An Evening with Fonteyn and Nureyev" (new costumes William Chappell from November 1975); Washington, D.C., 8 July 1975.

Other choreographic treatments of story: F. Termanini (Turin, 1857), John Taras (New York, 1946), Antony Tudor (New York, 1951), Ruth Page (Chicago, 1957), Tatiana Gsovsky (Berlin, 1957), Alberto Mendez (Havana, 1971), John Neumeier (Stuttgart, 1978: see *The Lady of the Camellias*), Jorge Lefèbre (Charlerois, 1980), André Prokovsky (London, 1990).

Marguerite and Armand, with Margot Fonteyn and Rudolf Nureyev

PUBLICATIONS

Franks, Arthur Henry, "*Marguerite and Armand*", *Dancing Times* (London), April 1963

Sherek, Henry, "Another View of *Marguerite and Armand*", *Dancing Times* (London), May 1963

Moore, Lillian, "Royal Ballet", *Dancing Times* (London), June 1963

Balanchine, George, with Mason, Francis, *Balanchine's Complete Stories of the Great Ballets*, Garden City, N.Y., 1977

Vaughan, David, *Frederick Ashton and his Ballets*, London, 1977

Bland, Alexander, *Fonteyn and Nureyev*, London, 1979

*   *   *

The novel by Alexandre Dumas fils, *La Dame aux camélias*, has inspired a very long list of ballets, not to mention operas, plays, and films, since its publication in 1848. Choreographers who have used the plot include Termanini, Taras, Dolin, Tudor, Page, Gsovsky, Mendez, Neumeier, and Lefèbre. Ashton's version tells the story in flashback from the perspective of his heroine's last illness, in order to concentrate its tragic force:

"the whole thing is digested down to a pill," Ashton himself remarked. The choreography in this treatment accordingly focuses all attention on Marguerite and Armand—the only other distinct character is Armand's father—and the other figures are deftly grouped and moved to set them off (Ashton's *Ondine* is a parallel case).

Ashton chose his subject for Margot Fonteyn, not so much as a vehicle for her and her new partner Rudolf Nureyev, but to extend her capacities as a dance actress. In the event, *Marguerite and Armand* was Ashton's last full ballet for Fonteyn, and it was, in David Vaughan's words, at once his "ultimate homage" to her and "a fable of her attainments and inevitable decline". Nobody has ever performed the roles apart from their original creators, so closely were they identified with them—and Fonteyn and Nureyev danced them frequently and to audiences in all corners of the world. Their performance is preserved in Pierre Jourdan's film about Nureyev, *I Am a Dancer*.

Ashton cast around for appropriate music, and by sheer chance heard Franz Liszt's B minor Piano Sonata on the radio: "almost immediately I could visualise the whole thing in it," he said. Cecil Beaton designed the semi-circular skeletal set, a great golden cage in which Marguerite is imprisoned by her lifestyle (he was also the designer of Ashton's earlier ballet to Liszt, *Apparitions* (1936), not to mention Taras's version of the Marguerite and Armand story, *Camille*, for Markova and Dolin). It was Beaton who described Ashton's moment of inspiration: "With *Marguerite and Armand* he heard this Liszt on the radio and it came to him like a vision. Each section of the music seems to mean a different phase in the story . . . and it was ideal. And when the music finished, he rang up the BBC to find exactly what it was they'd played. That was his moment of illumination". Liszt's sonata is in a cyclical form which had great appeal for Ashton.

The ballet is not a narrative—although a story emerges—but a dramatic series of five pas de deux (there is only one solo, for Armand in the Prologue); and the drama is built into the choreography. Each pas de deux reveals a development of Marguerite and Armand's relationship. Their first meeting is intense and passionate; once they are lovers, they become playful; but then, when Marguerite has decided to leave Armand, their dance is both desperate and erotic in mood, leading to a fierce and angry fourth pas de deux.

Marguerite and Armand moves frenetically, and the final, rawly uninhibited pas de deux has an intense romantic urgency; but it is counterpointed throughout, if not strictly underpinned, by Ashton's abiding sense of classical form. He had a keen sense of authority, perhaps most of all when he was challenging it. Marguerite's tragedy after all is that she was persuaded to observe and limit herself in an inhibiting set of rules.

—Martin Wright

MARKOVA, Alicia

British dancer, ballet director, and teacher. Born Lillian Alicia Marks in London, 1 December 1910. Studied at the Thorne Academy at Palmer's Green, then at School of Serafina Astafieva, London, from 1921; later studied under Enrico Cecchetti, Nikolai (Nicholas) Legat, Vincenzo Celli. Début, as child, in *Dick Whittington* (pantomime; George Shirley), London, 1920; dancer (performing as Alicia Markova), Diaghilev's Ballets Russes, 1925–29, becoming ballerina from

Alicia Markova as The Spirit of the Lake in *Where the Rainbow Ends*, London, c.1955

1926; performer in music halls and in individual concerts, London and Monte Carlo, from 1929; ballerina, Camargo Society, London, 1931, and Ballet Club (becoming Ballet Rambert), 1931–35, also performing with Vic-Wells Ballet, 1931–35; founder, with Anton Dolin, and prima ballerina, Markova–Dolin Ballet, performing in Britain, 1935–37; ballerina, Ballet Russe de Monte Carlo, 1938–41, and (American) Ballet Theatre, 1941–45, returning as guest ballerina, various seasons from 1945; founder and prima ballerina of re-formed Markova–Dolin Company in United States, 1945, touring Central America, 1945, and performing with Mexican Ballet, 1947; ballerina, partnered by Dolin, Gala Performances of Ballet, performing at Empress Hall, London, and on British tour, 1949: prima ballerina, London's Festival Ballet (growing out of previous Gala Performances), 1950–52; also performer in concert performances with Milorad Miskovitch, touring Europe and America, 1954, and with Alexis Rassine, touring Portugal, 1954; ballerina in stage show *Where the Rainbow Ends*, London, various seasons from 1954; international guest artist, including for Original Ballet Russe, 1946–47, Sadler's Wells Ballet (later Royal Ballet), 1948, 1953, and 1957, and for Grand Ballet du Marquis de Cuevas, Royal Winnipeg Ballet, Royal Danish Ballet, La Scala in Milan, and Chicago Opera Ballet; ballet director, Metropolitan Opera House, New York, 1963–69; visiting professor of dance, University of Cincinnatti, from 1970; Governor of the Royal Ballet, from 1973; President of London Festival Ballet (becoming English National Ballet), 1986. Recipient: *Dance Magazine* Award, 1957; title of Commander of the Order of the British Empire, 1958, and Dame of the Order of the British Empire, 1963; Queen Elizabeth II Award, Royal Academy of Dancing, 1963; Honorary Doctorate in Music, Leicester University, 1966.

ROLES

1925   Dancer (cr) in *Pizzicato Polka* (solo, also called *Variation*; Balanchine after Astafieva), Party of Princesse Héréditaire, Royal Palace, Monte Carlo
Dancer (cr) in *Valse Caprice* (solo; Balanchine), Party of Princesse Héréditaire, Monte Carlo
Red Riding Hood in *Aurora's Wedding* (divertissement from *The Sleeping Beauty*; Petipa, Nijinska), Diaghilev's Ballets Russes
Adagio in *Swan Lake* Act II (Petipa, Ivanov; staged, Fokine), Diaghilev's Ballets Russes
American Child in *La Boutique fantasque* (Massine), Diaghilev's Ballets Russes
Rich child in *Petrushka* (Fokine), Diaghilev's Ballets Russes
Papillon in *Carnaval* (Fokine), Diaghilev's Ballets Russes
Nightingale (cr) in *Le Chant du rossignol* (Balanchine), Diaghilev's Ballets Russes, Paris
1926   Ashes, A Squirrel in *L'Enfant et les sortilèges* (Balanchine), Diaghilev's Ballets Russes
Cygnet Pas de quatre in *Swan Lake*, Act II (Petipa, Ivanov; staged Fokine), Diaghilev's Ballets Russes
Ensemble in *Les Sylphides* (Fokine), Diaghilev's Ballets Russes
A Wedding Guest in *Les Noces* (Nijinska), Diaghilev's Ballets Russes
Ensemble in *The Triumph of Neptune* (Balanchine), Diaghilev's Ballets Russes
Ensemble in *Polovtsian Dances from Prince Igor* (Fokine), Diaghilev's Ballets Russes
1927   Title role in *La Chatte* (Balanchine), Diaghilev's Ballets

Russes
1928   Bluebird Pas de deux from *Aurora's Wedding* (divertissement from *The Sleeping Princess*; Petipa, Nijinska), Diaghilev's Ballets Russes, British tour
Pas de deux from *Cimarosiana* (Massine), Diaghilev's Ballets Russes, British tour
1930   Dancer (cr) in *Marriage à la mode* (play by Dryden; chor. Ashton), Lyric Theatre, London
1931   Procris (cr) in *Cephalus and Procris* (de Valois), Camargo Society, London
Title role (cr) in *La Péri* (Ashton), Ballet Club, London
Principal dancer (cr) in *The Dance of the Hours* (Fleming and Ashton (uncredited)), Regal Theatre, London
The Fox (cr) in *Foxhunting Ballet* (Ashton), Regal Theatre, London
Principal dancer (cr) in *Faust* (opera, excerpts; mus. Gounod, chor. Ashton (uncredited), Fleming), Regal Theatre, London
Polka (cr) in *Façade* (Ashton), Camargo Society, London
Tango, Finale in *Façade* (Ashton), Ballet Club, London
A Creole Girl (cr) in *A Day in a Southern Port* (also called *Rio Grande*; Ashton), Camargo Society, London
The Lassie in *Dances on a Scotch Theme* (originally part of Masque presented by Arnold Haskell; also called *The Tartans*; Ashton), Ballet Club, London
Katie Willows (cr) in *The Lord of Burleigh* (Ashton), Camargo Society, London
1932   Echo (cr) in *Narcissus and Echo* (de Valois), Vic-Wells Ballet, London
Myrrhina (cr) in *Lysistrata* (Tudor), Ballet Club, London
Psyche (cr) in *The Enchanted Grove* (Doone), Vic-Wells Ballet, London
The Princess (cr) in *Nursery Suite* (de Valois), Vic-Wells Ballet, London
Terpsichore (cr) in *The Origin of Design* (de Valois), Camargo Society, London
Terpsichore (formerly called Venus) in *Mercury* (Ashton), Camargo Society, London
Dancer in *Fête polonaise* (de Valois), Camargo Society, London
Violetta (cr) in *High Yellow* (Bradley, Ashton), Camargo Society, London
L'Étoile (cr) in *Foyer de danse* (Ashton), Ballet Club, London
Principal dancer (cr) in *The Ballet of Spring* in *A Kiss in Spring* (musical comedy; mus. Brammer, Grünwald; chor. Ashton), Alhambra Theatre, London
Swan Queen (Odette) in *Swan Lake*, Act II (after Ivanov), Vic-Wells Ballet, London
Principal dancer in *Scène de ballet* in *Faust* (opera; mus. Gounod, chor. de Valois), Vic-Wells Ballet and Opera, London
1933   Dancer (cr) in *Pas de deux* (Ashton), Coliseum, London
Leading dancer in *The Nightingale and the Rose* (Dolin), Coliseum, London
His Lady Friend (cr) in *Les Masques* (Ashton), Ballet Club, London
The Bride (cr) in *The Wise and Foolish Virgins* (de Valois), Vic-Wells Ballet, London
Adagio of Lovers, Variation (cr) in *Les Rendezvous* (Ashton), Vic-Wells Ballet, London
Bluebird Pas de deux from *The Sleeping Beauty*; after Petipa), Vic-Wells Ballet, London
Young girl in *Le Spectre de la rose* (Fokine), Vic-Wells Ballet, London

1934 Title role in *Giselle* (Petipa after Coralli, Perrot; staged Sergeyev), Vic-Wells Ballet, London
Sugar Plum Fairy in *The Nutcracker* (Sergeyev after Ivanov), Vic-Wells Ballet, London
Alicia (cr) in *The Haunted Ballroom* (de Valois), Vic-Wells Ballet, London
La Goulue (cr) in *Bar aux Folies-Bergère* (de Valois), Ballet Rambert, London
Marguerite (cr) in *Mephisto Waltz* (Ashton), Ballet Club, London
Columbine in *Carnaval* (Fokine), Ballet Club, London
Waltz, Mazurka in *Les Sylphides* (Fokine), Ballet Club, London
The Lady in *The Tartans* (*Dances on a Scotch Theme*; Ashton), Ballet Club, London
Principal dancer (cr) in *Pas de deux classique* (Ashton), Hippodrome, London
Odette/Odile in *Swan Lake* (Sergeyev after Petipa, Ivanov), Vic-Wells Ballet, London
1935 The Betrayed Girl (cr) in *The Rake's Progress* (de Valois), Vic-Wells Ballet, London
Rose Adagio from *The Sleeping Beauty* (after Petipa), Markova-Dolin Ballet, Newcastle
1936 Nicolette (cr) in *Aucassin and Nicolette* (Toye), Markova-Dolin Ballet, Liverpool
Principal dancer (cr) in *Bach Suite No. 2* (Lester), Markova-Dolin Ballet, British tour
Principal dancer in *Mother Goose* (pantomime), Hippodrome, London
1937 Adagietto ("La Garçonne") in *The House Party* (*Les Biches*; revival; Nijinska), Markova-Dolin Ballet, British tour
The Muse in *La Bien Aimée* (*The Beloved*; Nijinska), Markova-Dolin Ballet, London
Stenographer in *Death in Adagio* (Lester), Markova-Dolin Ballet
1938 The Sky (cr) in *The Seventh Symphony* (Massine), Ballet Russe de Monte Carlo, Monte Carlo
Chung-Yang in *L'Epreuve d'amour* (Fokine), Ballet Russe de Monte Carlo
Principal dancer in *Les Elfes* (Fokine), Ballet Russe de Monte Carlo
Swanilda in *Coppélia* (Sergeyev after Petipa, Cecchetti), Ballet Russe de Monte Carlo, U.S. tour
The Ballerina in *Petrushka* (Fokine), Ballet Russe de Monte Carlo, U.S. tour
1939 The Woman (cr) in *Rouge et noir* (Massine), Ballet Russe de Monte Carlo, Monte Carlo
Principal dancer in *Capriccio espagnol* (Massine), Ballet Russe de Monte Carlo
1940 Queen of Hearts (cr) in *Poker Game* (*Jeu de cartes*; Balanchine), Ballet Russe de Monte Carlo, New York
Entrée Chinoise (cr) in *Vienna—1814* (Massine), Ballet Russe de Monte Carlo, New York
1941 Marie Taglioni in *Pas de quatre* (Dolin), Ballet Theatre, New York
Caroline in *Jardin aux lilas* (Tudor), Ballet Theatre
Fioretta/Princess Hermilia (cr) in *Bluebeard* (Fokine), Ballet Theatre, Mexico City
The Swan in *The Dying Swan* (*Le Cygne*; after Fokine), Ballet Theatre, Boston
1942 Zemphira (cr) in *Aleko* (Massine), Ballet Theatre, Mexico City
Leonor (cr) in *Don Domingo de Don Blas* (Massine), Ballet Theatre, Mexico City
Elera, a Nymph (cr) in *Romantic Age* (Dolin), Ballet Theatre, New York

1943 Juliet (cr) in *Romeo and Juliet* (Tudor), Ballet Theatre, New York
1944 Ballerina (cr) in *Scènes de ballet* (Dolin) in *The Seven Lively Arts* (Billy Rose revue), Ziegfeld Theatre, New York
1945 Title role (cr) in *The Firebird* (Bolm), Ballet Theatre, New York
1946 Title role (cr) in *Camille* (Taras), Original Ballet Russe, New York
1947 Principal dancer (cr) in *Pas de trois* (Robbins), Original Ballet Russe, New York
Leading role (cr) in *Henry VIII* (Hightower), Markova-Dolin Company, Mexico City
Marguerite Gautier (cr) in *Lady of the Camellias* (Dolin), Markova-Dolin Company, Mexico City
1948 Kitri in *Don Quixote* Pas de deux (Obukhov after Petipa), Sadler's Wells Ballet, London
Princess Aurora in *The Sleeping Beauty* (Petipa; staged Sergeyev, Ashton, de Valois), Sadler's Wells Ballet, London
1951 Principal dancer (cr) in *Symphonic Impressions* (Lichine), London Festival Ballet, Monte Carlo
1953 Principal dancer (cr) in *Bolero 1830* (Ricarda), Concert Performance, Folkestone
Ballet Divertissement in *Die Fledermaus* (opera; mus. Strauss), Metropolitan Opera, New York
1955 The Widow in *Vilia* (*The Merry Widow*; Page), Chicago Opera Ballet, Chicago
Principal dancer in *Revanche* (Page), Chicago Opera Ballet, Chicago
1958 Ballet Divertissement in *Orfeo* (opera; mus. Gluck), Metropolitan Opera, New York

Other roles include: for "Gala Performances of Ballet" (precursor to London Festival Ballet)—principal dancer in *Chopiniana* (also chor., with Dolin, Cone), *Mr. Puppet* (Fonaroff), *Blue Mountain Ballads* (Sadler); for concert performances—dancer in *The Tyrolean* (pas de deux; also chor.).

PUBLICATIONS

By Markova:
Giselle and I, London, 1960
Markova Remembers, London, 1986

About Markova:
Beaumont, Cyril, *Alicia Markova*, London, 1935
Claydon, Humphrey, "The Art of Alicia Markova", *Dancing Times* (London), 3 parts: March, April, May 1938
Beaumont, Cyril, "Four Giselles", *Ballet* (London), March 1951
Anthony, Gordon, *Alicia Markova*, London, 1951
Dolin, Anton, *Alicia Markova: Her Life and Art*, New York, 1953
Davidson, Gladys, *Ballet Biographies*, revised edition, London, 1953
Fisher, Hugh, *Alicia Markova*, London, 1954
Clarke, Mary, *The Sadler's Wells Ballet*, London, 1955
"Thirty Years of Alicia Markova", *Dance and Dancers* (London), January 1955
Beaumont, Cyril, "Alicia Markova", *Ballet Annual* (London), vol. 10, 1956
Lidova, Irène, "Grandes Figures de la danse: Alicia Markova", *Les Saisons de la danse* (Paris), April 1975

Vaughan, David, *Frederick Ashton and his Ballets*, London, 1977

Bland, Alexander, *The Royal Ballet: The First Fifty Years*, London, 1981

Austin, Richard, *The Art of the Dancer*, London, 1982

Denby, Edwin, *Dance Writings*, edited by Robert Cornfield and William Mackay, New York, 1986

*   *   *

As with all great ballerinas, Dame Alicia Markova's career coincided with an exciting and formative period in ballet history. Lillian Alicia Marks started "fancy dancing" as a young child in London in the decade following the influencial appearances of the Russian ballet. The Russian dancers, who first arrived in London in 1910, had altered the public conception of ballet, raising it from the level of a music-hall spectacle to the status of a great, expressive art. Soon nicknamed "The Miniature Pavlova" herself, Markova in childhood performances showed a gift which led to classes with Serafina Astafieva, an ex-member of the Maryinsky Ballet and the Ballets Russes de Serge Diaghilev. Markova joined the Diaghilev company, at Astafieva's instigation, when she was only fourteen years of age. Other British dancers in the company then included Lydia Sokolova (Hilda Munnings), Ninette de Valois (Edris Stannus), and Anton Dolin (Patrick Healey-Kay).

Markova joined the Diaghilev company in its late phase, when its modernism had taken ballet to the forefront of the avant garde. Too small for the corps de ballet, Markova had solo parts as soon as she joined the company, including the role of the child in Massine's *La Boutique fantasque* and the title role in Balanchine's *Le Chant du rossignol*, which was created for her in 1925. At the time of Diaghilev's death in 1929, Markova's career had looked promising and certain within the company. With the loss of the great impresario, the troupe fragmented and Markova returned to London, a dancer without a home company in which to work. Fortunately, however, her needs were to coincide with those of other British artists who were working towards the emergence of British ballet.

The formative influences of Marie Rambert and de Valois were already in evidence in London, where their fledgeling companies were utilizing the rich talents of a young British choreographer, Frederick Ashton, amongst others. Markova quickly became a central vehicle for the development of early British ballet. She provided a first-rate model, in terms of both technique and artistry, for young dancers, and she brought status to her art at a time when the public in general thought that ballet was by definition a Russian art. The Camargo Society, Rambert's Ballet Club, and later the Vic-Wells Ballet made excellent use of Markova's abilities. She created roles in many early British ballets, including Ashton's *La Péri*, *Façade*, and *Les Rendezvous*, Antony Tudor's *Lysistrata*, and de Valois's *Bar au Folies-Bergère*, *The Haunted Ballroom*, and *The Rake's Progress*. Perhaps most importantly, Markova's technical strength allowed the Vic-Wells ballet to stage the nineteenth-century classical ballets, the notation for which had been brought to the West by Nicholas Sergeyev. Trained by both Cecchetti and Nikolai Legat, Markova had a strong classical technique, and quickly demonstrated that a British dancer and a first-class ballerina was not a contradiction in terms.

Yet the Vic-Wells could offer Markova little by way of financial reward, and she was perhaps in a sense already too established as an artist to fit happily within this young company. The rejection of Dolin, her partner from childhood years, in favour of Robert Helpmann was a deciding factor in Markova's decision to move on from the Vic-Wells company.

Like Pavlova before her, Markova chose to leave the structure and broad artistic environment of a ballet company proper to form a performing troupe that was primarily a vehicle for its star—or in this case, stars. The Markova–Dolin Company was formed in 1935, when the popularity of ballet in London was reaching an all-time high. By the time the company was disbanded in 1937, however, there was no real place for Markova in British ballet other than as a guest star. Her departure from the Vic-Wells had brought forward the career of the then very young dancer Margot Fonteyn, who was now performing Markova's roles within the company. It is ironic that, as a result of the timing of her career, and perhaps because of something in her own nature as well, Markova was always to be essentially a guest star in her native country, despite the fact that she was indeed the first British prima ballerina.

Markova joined the Ballet Russe de Monte Carlo in the late 1930s, when Massine created *Rouge et noir* for her and Igor Youskevitch, and she went with the company to America. Markova and Dolin both enjoyed enormous success in America and became stars of Ballet Theatre. Markova's work was much admired by the dance critic Edwin Denby, from whom we have many descriptions of her special qualities. Denby points particularly to her talent for phrasing and her musicality. He wrote, "As I watch her, Markova—like Duse in Ibsen—seems to be speaking poetry to the company's earnest prose." In 1944 Denby described Markova's Giselle as "Ballet Theatre's greatest glory". *Giselle* was clearly the ballet that Markova most valued and she became closely identified with the title role. In her autobiography, *Giselle and I*, she relates how she once threatened to jump off a balcony if the ballet was dropped from the repertory, and she had something of a pioneering zeal in taking this ballet to new audiences all over the world. She is renowned as one of the few truly great interpreters of Giselle; in particular, she was admired for her evocation of ethereal beauty in the second act. Throughout her career, critics pointed to Markova's lightness and ethereality as her major attributes. She had a precise as well as strong technique, and was renowned for the elegance and purity of her line.

During Markova's career, Ashton and Massine as choreographers both enabled the ballerina's versatility as an artist to be realized, and she demonstrated a gift for comedy as well as for the tragi-poetic. At an early age Markova had been exposed to the modernist trends of her day—to the choreography of Massine and Balanchine and to the music of Stravinsky for example—and during her career she originated roles in many new ballets by twentieth-century choreographers as various as Balanchine, Massine, Ashton, Tudor, and de Valois. Yet her real inspiration was in the idiom realized by Olga Spessivtseva in the roles of Giselle and Odette, and developed in the art of Anna Pavlova: increasingly Markova became essentially a ballerina in the romantic/classical mould. Her austere appearance, with sloping, romantic-style shoulders, and her qualities of incredible lightness and grace were ideally suited to this idiom. Like Pavlova before her, Markova adhered primarily to a romantic/classical conception of ballet and was instrumental in popularizing this form all over the world.

On their return to London in 1949, Markova and Dolin again assembled a company around themselves and this was to become London Festival Ballet. It toured extensively with a popular repertoire based on the classics and guest stars. Since her retirement in 1962, Markova has continued to teach and to influence the development of British ballet, becoming governor of the Royal Ballet School and President of the English National Ballet (the successor to London Festival Ballet). Overall, Markova's career forms a bridge between more endings and beginnings than perhaps any dancer before or after her. She saw no less than the demise of the great Diaghilev era and the beginnings of British and American ballet. She inherited the art of ballet in a time of flux when it could so easily have become, once more, an endangered form. Apart from becoming a great ballerina, Markova was to help the achievements of a past era take firm root in the present and come to fruition in a variety of places throughout the world.

—Lesley-Anne Sayers

———

MARTINS, Peter

Danish/American dancer, choreographer, teacher, and ballet director. Born in Copenhagen, 27 October 1946. Studied at the Royal Danish Ballet School, pupil of Stanley Williams, Vera Volkova, 1953–65; later studied with George Balanchine. Married (1) Danish dancer Lisa La Cour (div. 1973): one son, Nilas; (2) New York City Ballet dancer Darci Kistler, 1991. Dancer, Royal Danish Ballet, from 1965, becoming solo dancer (principal dancer), from 1967; guest artist, New York City Ballet, various seasons 1967–70; left Copenhagen in 1970: principal dancer, New York City Ballet, 1970–84; also international guest artist, including for London Festival Ballet, 1970 and 1972, Hartford Ballet, 1981, National Ballet of Canada, and Royal Ballet, London; début as choreographer, as director of Peter Martins and Company, Brooklyn, 1977, continuing as choreographer for New York City Ballet from 1978; joint Ballet Master, New York City Ballet, from 1981, becoming Ballet Master in Chief, with Jerome Robbins, New York City Ballet, from 1983, and sole Ballet Master in Chief, from 1989; also choreographer for musicals, including restaging of *On Your Toes* (mus. Rodgers; 1982), *Song and Dance* (1985), and *Carousel* (mus. Rodgers; 1986); teacher, School of American Ballet, New York, from 1975, and artistic advisor to Pennsylvania Ballet, from 1982. Recipient: *Dance Magazine* Award, 1977; *Cue*'s Golden Apple Award, 1977; Award for Arts and Culture, City of New York, 1981; title of Knight of the Order of Dannebrog, 1983; Award of Merit, Philadelphia Art Alliance, 1985; Liberty Award, 1986.

ROLES

1964 Principal dancer in *Garden Party* (Schaufuss), Royal Danish Ballet, Copenhagen
Principal dancer (cr) in *Moods* (Brenaa), Royal Danish Ballet, Copenhagen
1965 Leading role in *Moon Reindeer* (Cullberg), Royal Danish Ballet, San Diego
Principal dancer in *Konservatoriet* (Bournonville), Royal Danish Ballet, Copenhagen
Pas de six in *Napoli*, Act III (Bournonville), Royal Danish Ballet, Copenhagen
Leading role in *The Kermesse in Bruges* (Bournonville), Royal Danish Ballet, Copenhagen
Principal dancer in *Études* (Lander), Royal Danish Ballet, Copenhagen
Greek Dance in *The Whims of Cupid and the Ballet Master* (Galeotti), Royal Danish Ballet, Copenhagen
1966 Portos (cr) in *The Three Musketeers* (Flindt), Royal Danish Ballet, Copenhagen
Principal dancer in *Symphony in C* (Balanchine), Royal Danish Ballet, Copenhagen
Prince in *The Nutcracker* (after Ivanov), Royal Danish Ballet, Copenhagen

1967 Leading role in *The Miraculous Mandarin* (Flindt), Royal Danish Ballet, Copenhagen
Leading role in *The Young Man Must Marry* (Flindt), Royal Danish Ballet, Copenhagen
Principal dancer (cr) in *Gala Variations* (pas de deux; Flindt), Royal Danish Ballet, Copenhagen
Principal dancer in *Le Loup* (Petit), Royal Danish Ballet, Copenhagen
Title role in *Apollo* (Balanchine), New York City Ballet, Edinburgh
Prince in *Swan Lake* (Act II; Flindt after Ivanov), Royal Danish Ballet, Copenhagen
Cavalier in *The Nutcracker* (Balanchine), New York City Ballet, New York
1968 Principal dancer in *Jeu de cartes* (Cranko), Royal Danish Ballet, Copenhagen
Junior Cadet in *Graduation Ball* (Lichine), Royal Danish Ballet, Copenhagen
Principal dancer in *Aimez-vous Bach?* (Macdonald), Royal Danish Ballet, Copenhagen
Diamonds in *Jewels* (Balanchine), New York City Ballet, New York
First Movement in *Symphony in C* (Balanchine), New York City Ballet, New York
Prince Siegfried in *Swan Lake* (one-act version; Balanchine after Ivanov), New York City Ballet, New York
Principal dancer in *Liebeslieder Walzer* (Balanchine), New York City Ballet, New York
Second Movement in *Symphony in C* (Balanchine), New York City Ballet, New York
1969 Principal dancer in *Bagage* (Tomaszewski), Royal Danish Ballet, Copenhagen
Principal dancer (cr) in *Aspects* (Schaufuss), Royal Danish Ballet, Copenhagen
Moondog in *The Lady and the Fool* (Cranko), Royal Danish Ballet, Copenhagen
Principal dancer in *Cicatris* (Holm), Royal Danish Ballet, Copenhagen
Principal dancer in *Dances at a Gathering* (Robbins), New York City Ballet, New York
Principal dancer in *Ballet Imperial* (later called *Tchaikovsky Piano Concerto No. 2*; Balanchine), New York City Ballet, New York
1970 Principal dancer (cr) in *In the Night* (Robbins), New York City Ballet, New York
Principal dancer in *Divertimento No. 15* (Balanchine), New York City Ballet, New York
1971 Theme and Variations in *Tchaikovsky Suite No. 3* (Balanchine), New York City Ballet, New York
Oberon in *A Midsummer Night's Dream* (Balanchine), New York City Ballet, New York
Principal dancer in *(Tchaikovsky) Pas de deux* (Balanchine), New York City Ballet, New York
Principal dancer, Variations (cr) in *The Goldberg Variations* (Robbins), New York City Ballet, New York
Principal dancer in *Brahms–Schoenberg Quartet* (Balanchine), New York City Ballet, New York
1972 Principal dancer in *Chopiniana* (Danilova after Fokine), New York City Ballet, New York
Pas Classique Espagnol (cr) added to *Don Quixote* (Balanchine), New York City Ballet, New York
Toccata, Aria II (cr) in *Violin Concerto* (later *Stravinsky Violin Concerto*; Balanchine), New York City Ballet, New York
Prince Ivan in *Firebird* (Balanchine), New York City Ballet, New York

Peter Martins as Apollo, New York City Ballet

Principal dancer (cr) in *Symphony in E Flat* (Clifford), New York City Ballet, New York

Principal dancer (cr) in *Duo Concertant* (Balanchine), New York City Ballet, New York

Principal dancer (cr) in *Choral Variations on Bach's "Vom Himmel Hoch"* (Balanchine), New York City Ballet, New York

Principal dancer in *Scènes de Ballet* (Taras), New York City Ballet, New York

1973   Principal dancer (cr) in *Concerto No. 2* (new version of *Ballet Imperial*; Balanchine), New York City Ballet, New York

Third Waltz in *An Evening's Waltzes* (Robbins), New York City Ballet, New York

Principal dancer in *La Source* (pas de deux; Balanchine), New York City Ballet, New York

1974   Principal dancer in *Concerto Barocco* (Balanchine), New York City Ballet, New York

Principal dancer in *Bartók No. 3* (Clifford), New York City Ballet, New York

Pas de deux in *Agon* (Balanchine), New York City Ballet, New York

Principal dancer in *Who Cares?* (Balanchine), New York City Ballet, New York

Frantz in *Coppélia* (Balanchine, Danilova after Petipa), New York City Ballet, New York

Principal dancer in *Afternoon of a Faun* (Robbins), New York City Ballet, New York

1975   Principal dancer in *Raymonda Variations* (Balanchine), New York City Ballet, New York

Principal dancer (cr) in *Concerto in G* (later called *In G Major*; Robbins), New York City Ballet, New York

Daphnis (cr) in *Daphnis and Chloe* (Taras), New York City Ballet, New York

Principal dancer (cr) in *Tzigane* (Balanchine), New York City Ballet, New York

Classical Pas de deux in *Cortège Hongrois* (Balanchine), New York City Ballet, New York

Fourth Campaign ("El Capitan") in *Stars and Stripes* (Balanchine), New York City Ballet, New York

1976   Principal dancer (cr) in *Chaconne* (Balanchine), New York City Ballet, New York

Principal dancer in *Allegro Brillante* (Balanchine), New York City Ballet, New York

Menzies, Royal Navy (cr) in *Union Jack* (Balanchine), New York City Ballet, New York

Principal dancer in *Other Dances* (Robbins), New York City Ballet, New York

James in *La Sylphide* (Bournonville), Royal Danish Ballet, New York

1977   Pas de deux from *Flower Festival in Genzano* (Bournonville), in *Bournonville Divertissements* (staged Williams), New York City Ballet, New York

Gold and Silver Waltz (cr) in *Vienna Waltzes* (Balanchine), New York City Ballet, New York

1978   Principal dancer in *La Valse* (Balanchine), New York City Ballet, New York

Principal dancer (cr) in *Verdi Variations* (later part of *The Four Seasons*; Robbins), in *A Sketch Book* (works in progress; Robbins, Martins), New York City Ballet, New York

1979   Autumn in *The Four Seasons* (Robbins), New York City Ballet, New York

Principal dancer in *Fancy Free* (Robbins), New York City Ballet, New York

Principal dancer (cr) in *Gli Uccelli* (Weiss), Caramoor Music Festival

Title role in *Orpheus* (Balanchine), New York City Ballet, Saratoga Springs

Principal dancer in *Donizetti Variations* (Balanchine), New York City Ballet, New York

Junker Ove in *A Folk Tale* (Bournonville), Royal Danish Ballet

1980   Cleonte in *Le Bourgeois Gentilhomme* (Balanchine), New York City Ballet, New York

Principal dancer, Third Couple (cr) in *Robert Schumann's "Davidsbündlertänze"* (Balanchine), New York City Ballet, New York

Principal dancer in *Scotch Symphony* (Balanchine), New York City Ballet, New York

1981   Romeo (cr) in *Romeo and Juliet* (Uthoff), Hartford Ballet, Hartford

1982   Principal dancer in *Mozartiana* (Balanchine), New York City Ballet, New York

Lukes in *The Magic Flute* (also chor.), New York City Ballet, New York

1983   Principal dancer (cr) in *Ballet d'Isoline* (Tomasson), New York City Ballet, New York

Duet from *Lento* (Taylor), Paul Taylor Dance Company

Other roles include: for Danish television—leading roles in *Dream Pictures* (Walbom), *Helios* (von Rosen), *The Blade of Grass* (Theilade), *The Net* (Septimus), *The Dream* (von Rosen); for New York City Ballet—principal dancer in *Serenade* (Balanchine), Divertissement in *A Midsummer Night's Dream*

(Balanchine); as guest artist or in concert appearances—Prince Désiré in *The Sleeping Beauty* (after Petipa), principal dancer in *Concerto* (MacMillan), Albrecht in *Giselle* (Petipa after Coralli, Perrot), Prince Siegfried in *Swan Lake* (Bruhn after Petipa, Ivanov), pas de deux from *Le Corsaire* (after Petipa), pas de deux from *Paquita* (Danilova after Petipa), Waltz, Mazurka in *Les Sylphides* (Fokine).

WORKS

1977   *Calcium Light Night* (mus. Ives), Peter Martins and Company, Spokane, Washington

1978   *Tricolore* (with Jean-Pierre Bonnefous and Jerome Robbins; mus. Auric), New York City Ballet, New York

Rossini Pas de Deux (mus. Rossini) in *A Sketch Book* (with Jerome Robbins), New York City Ballet, New York

Tango-Tango (mus. Gade, Stravinsky), John Curry's "Ice Dancing", New York

1979   Dances in *Dido and Aeneas* (opera; mus. Purcell), New York City Opera, New York

Giardino di Scarlatti (later called *Sonate di Scarlatti*; mus. Scarlatti), New York City Ballet, Saratoga Springs (staged for Dutch National Ballet, 1981)

1980   *Eight Easy Pieces* (mus. Stravinsky), New York City Ballet, New York

Lille Suite (premiere as *Tivoli*; mus. Nielson), Tivoli Concert Hall, Tivoli (staged for New York City Ballet, 1980)

1981   *Suite from Histoire du Soldat* (mus. Stravinsky), New York City Ballet, New York

Capriccio Italien (mus. Tchaikovsky), School of American Ballet, New York (staged for New York City Ballet, 1981)

The Magic Flute (mus. Drigo), School of American Ballet, New York (staged for New York City Ballet, 1982)

Symphony No. 1 (mus. Tchaikovsky), New York City Ballet, New York

1982   *Delibes Divertissement* (mus. Delibes), School of American Ballet, New York (staged for New York City Ballet, 1983)

Piano Rag Music (mus. Stravinsky), New York City Ballet, New York

Concerto for Two Solo Pianos (mus. Stravinsky), New York City Ballet, New York

1983   *Waltzes* (mus. Schubert), Hartford Ballet, Hartford, Connecticut

Rossini Quartets (mus. Rossini), New York City Ballet, New York

Tango (mus. Stravinsky), New York City Ballet, New York

1984   *A Schubertiad* (mus. Schubert), New York City Ballet, New York

Rejouissance (mus. Bach), New York City Ballet, New York

Mozart Violin Concerto (mus. Mozart), Pennsylvania Ballet, Philadelphia

1985   *Poulenc Sonata* (mus. Poulenc), New York City Ballet, New York

We are the World (mus. popular), New York City Ballet, New York

Valse Triste (mus. Sibelius), New York City Ballet, New York

Eight More (mus. Stravinsky), New York City Ballet, New York

Eight Miniatures (mus. Stravinsky), New York City Ballet, New York

1986 *Songs of Auvergne* (mus. Cantaloube), New York City Ballet, New York

Four Gnossiennes (mus. Satie), School of American Ballet, New York (staged for New York City Ballet, 1990)

1987 *Les Petits Riens* (mus. Mozart), New York City Ballet, New York

Ecstatic Orange (mus. Torke), New York City Ballet, New York (second version staged later same year)

Les Gentilhommes (mus. Handel), New York City Ballet, New York

1988 *A Fool for You* (mus. Charles and others), New York City Ballet, New York

The Waltz Project (mus. various), New York City Ballet, New York

Barber Violin Concerto (mus. Barber), New York City Ballet, New York

Tanzspiel (mus. Zwilich), New York City Ballet, New York

Sophisticated Lady (mus. Ellington), New York City Ballet, New York

The Chairman Dances (mus. Adams), New York City Ballet, New York

Black and White (mus. Torke), New York City Ballet, New York

Tea Rose (mus. Gershwin), New York City Ballet, New York

1989 *Mozart Serenade* (mus. Mozart), New York City Ballet, New York

Beethoven Romance (mus. Beethoven), New York City Ballet, New York

Echo (mus. Torke), New York City Ballet, New York

1990 *Fearful Symmetries* (mus. Adams), New York City Ballet, New York

A Mass (*Missa Sicca*; with LaFosse; mus. Torke), New York City Ballet, New York

1991 *Ash* (mus. Torke), New York City Ballet, New York

A Musical Offering (mus. Bach), New York City Ballet, New York

1992 *Delight of the Muses* (mus. Wuorinen), New York City Ballet, New York

Jeu de Cartes (mus. Stravinsky), New York City Ballet, New York

Zakouski (pièce d'occasion; mus. various), New York City Ballet, New York

Also staged:

1985 *La Sylphide* (after Bournonville; mus. Løvenskjold), Pennsylvania Ballet, Philadelphia (also staged San Francisco Ballet, 1986)

1991 *The Sleeping Beauty* (after Petipa; mus. Tchaikovsky), New York City Ballet, New York

PUBLICATIONS

By Martins:

Interview in Gruen, John, *The Private World of Ballet,* New York, 1975

Far From Denmark (autobiography), Boston, 1982

Interview in Barnes, Patricia, "Something More than Dancing", *Dance and Dancers* (London), January 1982

Interview in Newman, Barbara, *Striking a Balance*, Boston, 1982

Interview in Gruen, John, "Peter Martins on Balanchine", *Dance Magazine* (New York), July 1983

Interview in Gruen, John, "Dancevision", *Dance Magazine* (New York), September 1983

Interview in Gruen, John, "Martins Talks Back", *Dance Magazine* (New York), November 1987

About Martins:

Swope, Martha (photographer), with Todd, Arthur, *Peter Martins*, New York, 1975

Tobias, Tobi, "Peter Martins", *Dance Magazine* (New York), June 1977

Barnes, Patricia, "Something More than Dancing", *Dance and Dancers* (London), January 1982

Croce, Arlene, *Going to the Dance*, New York, 1982

Greskovic, Robert, "Far From Denmark and Close to Home", *Ballet Review* (New York), Spring 1983

Gurewitsch, M., "Peter Martins", *Dance Magazine* (New York), February 1984

Caras, Steven, *Peter Martins: Prince of the Dance*, New York, 1986

Croce, Arlene, *Sight Lines*, New York, 1987

Paltrow, Scott, "Peter Martins, Off Balance", *Los Angeles Times Magazine*, 6 December 1992

* * *

As a performer, Peter Martins was one of the leading dance personalities of his generation. While still the most active presence at New York City Ballet, however, he has given only a few token performances since officially retiring in 1983, when he chose to devote his attention to his choreography and to his responsibilities as principal director ("Ballet Master in Chief") of the New York City Ballet.

Martins's bold features and striking good looks—he is tall, blond, powerful—enhanced a technique that was clean and strong, musical and intelligent, subdued but free. Born in Denmark, he trained from childhood in the school of the Royal Danish Ballet. There he responded particularly to the influence of teachers Stanley Williams and the Russian-born Vera Volkova, both of whom were not typical representatives of the Bournonville school. He was inspired early in his career by the examples of Erik Bruhn and Rudolf Nureyev. Despite a rebellious nature, he ascended rapidly through the ranks of the Royal Danish Ballet and was appointed the company's youngest principal in 1967.

At the same time, Martins was beginning to look outside Denmark for opportunities to grow as a dancer. Having recently learned the lead role in George Balanchine's *Apollo*, he was invited to be an emergency replacement for an injured Jacques d'Amboise at a performance at the Edinburgh Festival, where he first worked with and received the attention of Balanchine. He was soon invited to appear as a guest artist with the New York City Ballet, which he continued to do until 1970, when he officially joined the company. After some initially rocky times—he nearly abandoned the company to join American Ballet Theatre in 1972—his career in the company began to blossom. Balanchine, now assured of his dancer's commitment, began creating roles for him with *Duo Concertant* and *Violin Concerto*.

Martins mastered a large repertory of works by both Balanchine and Jerome Robbins. According to most observers, he became the "definitive" Apollo, embodying not only the godlike qualities that seemed natural for him, but the childlike aspects and gaucheries that were also part of the character.

Other notable interpretations ranged from the rigorous technical demands of the astringent *Agon*, through the virtuosic *Stars and Stripes* pas de deux, to the hieratic subtleties of *Orpheus*; he could embody the bravado of *Union Jack*, the elegance of *Vienna Waltzes*, the boyish charm of Frantz in *Coppélia*, or the cool passion of a lover in *Davidsbündlertänze*. He achieved a movement style that was both masculine and elegant, and could range from expansiveness to quick precision.

For Jerome Robbins, Martins performed created roles in *Goldberg Variations*, *In G Major*, and *In the Night*, and mastered the diversities of *Dances at a Gathering*, *Afternoon of a Faun*, and *Fancy Free*. Although never particularly interested in the nineteenth-century classics, he occasionally appeared in them as a guest with other companies, notably as James in *La Sylphide* with the Royal Danish Ballet during the New York City performances in 1976.

As a dancing partner, Martins was characterized by his self-effacement and tenderness, his early training in ballroom dancing apparently standing him in good stead. His partnership with Suzanne Farrell is considered one of the great partnerships of ballet, resulting in many sublime performances, particularly in the "Diamonds" section of *Jewels* and in *Chaconne*.

Martins began making dances in 1977 with *Calcium Light Night*, a series of abstract modernist studies to the music of Charles Ives which remains a critical favorite. Balanchine encouraged him from the beginning, and critics responded early on to his seeming promise as Balanchine's aesthetic heir. Martins created or staged nearly 50 works in his first fifteen years as a choreographer—but the critical consensus is that his works are not yet fulfilling his early promise. He seems still to be seeking his own voice, and this is no easy task in the face of such expectations. By his own admission he would not be listed among the top ten choreographers of his time.

His chief strengths include his musical sensitivity, his cleverness, and his willingness to try different styles (within a classical base). Although he does not have the inimitable musical background and expertise of Balanchine, he has a larger knowledge and surer instinct than many of his contemporaries in the field; the same musicality that informed his success as a performer sustains him as a choreographer. Martins has worked with many different types of music ranging from Bach, Beethoven, and Mozart to Ives and Stravinsky. He has commissioned scores from and collaborated several times with the avant-garde composer Michael Torke, most successfully perhaps in *Ecstatic Orange*.

Martins is capable of generating interesting steps and material, and has experimented with a considerable range of groupings and styles. Although his works are most frequently abstract, he looked at the dramas of relationships in *A Schubertiad* and created a full-length story ballet in *The Magic Flute*. In *Barber Violin Concerto*, he played with the interaction of ballet and modern dance (the original cast included two guest artists from Paul Taylor's Dance Company).

His cleverness, however, can be a hindrance as well as an asset. He is frequently accused of overchoreographing, of being too fussy or finicky. His attempts at humor sometimes seem forced, and the emotional distance that was his strength as a performer sometimes shows up as lack of involvement in his choreography. His ballets, for all their strengths, don't seem to add up to much or invite repeated viewing. His chief weakness is his apparent inability to explore the formal development of material in a coherent and cogent fashion. Critic Mindy Aloff has noted that he seems unable to think in terms of analogies or to sustain a continuous line of thematic development.

Martins has had varied success in his ability to explore the gifts of individual dancers. Arlene Croce has noted that he is one of a handful of choreographers who can choreograph for women on pointe. He has choreographed works for the young stars of his company—Kyra Nichols in *Poulenc Sonata* and Darci Kistler in *Delight of the Muses* and *Jeu de Cartes*—but in neither case really captured or stretched their abilities. His tributes to retiring ballerinas—*Sophisticated Lady* for Farrell and *Tea Rose* for Patricia McBride—were both gracious and graceful. Perhaps his most successful choreographies have been for Heather Watts in *Calcium Light Night* and *Ecstatic Orange*. Her eccentric body type and movement style gave his choreography in these works an equally eccentric quality. He has created works for younger dancers in his company (for example, the female trio of *Eight Easy Pieces*) and he has tried to increase the range and number of male roles, including the creation of all-male works such as *Eight More* and *Les Gentilhommes*. He has explored the possibilities in partnering, as well. Croce has noted that this is frequently the subject of his work, and Aloff has commented that Martins sometimes seems to be exploring the boundary between partnering and non-partnering.

As the principal director of New York City Ballet (he has served as Ballet Master in Chief since 1983, a title he shared until 1989) he has had the difficult responsibility of sustaining the company, maintaining the legacy of Balanchine, and infusing new life into the repertory. He attempted to seek fresh new material in the 1988 American Music Festival and the 1992 Diamond Project. His 1991 revival of *Sleeping Beauty* received critical praise for its respectful handling of a historic masterpiece. Although some of his policies have been controversial, Peter Martins undoubtedly continues to play a major role in the shaping of dance today.

—Katy Matheson

MASSINE, Léonide (Leonid)

Russian/American dancer, choreographer, teacher, and ballet director. Born Leonid (later changed to Léonide) Fedorovich Myasin (Massine) in Moscow, 8 August 1895. Studied at the Imperial Theatre School, Moscow, pupil of Aleksandr Gorsky; graduated in 1912; later studied with Enrico Cecchetti. Married (1) dancer Vera Savina; (2) dancer Eugenia Delarova; (3) Tatiana Orlova: son, dancer/choreographer Léonide (later changed to Lorca) Massine, b. 1944; daughter, dancer/choreographer Tatiana Massine. Dancer, corps de ballet, Bolshoi Theatre, from 1912; invited to join Diaghilev's Ballets Russes in 1913, creating lead role in Fokine's *Legend of Joseph*, Paris, 1914; début as choreographer (*Le Soleil de nuit*) in 1915: thereafter leading dancer and choreographer, Diaghilev's Ballets Russes, until 1921, and again 1925–28; left Diaghilev to tour independently, 1921, performing at Covent Garden with Lydia Lopokova, 1922, 1923; dancer and chief choreographer, Etienne de Beaumont's Soirées de Paris, 1924; also performer and choreographer of ballets for Cochran's Revue, London, 1925, 1926, and for Roxy Theater, New York, various seasons, 1927–30; choreographer, Ida Rubinstein's Company, Paris, 1928, 1931, and La Scala, Milan, 1932; choreographer, (Blum's and de Basil's) Ballets Russes de Monte Carlo, 1932, becoming chief ballet master, from 1933; broke with de Basil on division of company, 1938, becoming artistic director for (Blum's and Denham's) Ballet Russe de Monte Carlo, from 1938; moved to the U.S. in 1939: choreographer for (American) Ballet Theatre, New York, 1942–43, Ballet International, 1944, and own

Léonide Massine as the Chinese Conjuror in *Parade*, Diaghilev's Ballets Russes, 1917

company, "Ballet Russe Highlights", 1945–46; returned to Europe: staged and performed in revivals of own ballets for Sadler's Wells Ballet, London, 1946, 1951, also serving as choreographer for Ballets des Champs-Elysées, Paris, 1949, Opéra-Comique, 1951, Grand Ballet du Marquis de Cuevas, 1951, Rome Opera, 1954, and La Scala, Milan, various seasons from 1949, including 1953–54, 1959–60, 1966; founder and choreographer of Balletto Europeo for Nervi Festival, Genoa, 1960; guest choreographer and producer, staging or supervising revivals of own ballets throughout the world, including for Royal Danish Ballet, Teatro Colón in Buenos Aires, Teatro Municipal in Rio de Janeiro, Rome Opera, La Scala, Milan, and Joffrey Ballet; also worked in films, staging versions of own ballets and choreographing own dances in *The Red Shoes* (dir. Powell, chor. Helpmann, 1948), and *The Tales of Hoffmann* (dir. Powell, 1951); also teacher: opened own school in London, 1923: students include Frederick Ashton. Died in Weseke bei Borken, Germany, 15 March 1979.

ROLES

1914   Joseph (cr) in *The Legend of Joseph* (Fokine), Diaghilev's Ballets Russes, Paris

Night Watchman in *Petrushka* (Fokine), Diaghilev's Ballets Russes, Geneva

1915   Title role (cr) in *Le Soleil de nuit* (also chor.), Diaghilev's Ballets Russes, Geneva

1916   Courtier (cr) in *Las Meninas* (also chor.), Diaghilev's Ballets Russes, San Sebastián

Title role in *Petrushka* (Fokine), Diaghilev's Ballets Russes, U.S. tour

Eusebius in *Le Carnaval* (Fokine), Diaghilev's Ballets Russes, U.S. tour

Amoun in *Cléopâtre* (Fokine), Diaghilev's Ballets Russes, U.S. tour

Negro Slave in *Schéhérazade* (Fokine), Diaghilev's Ballets Russes, New York

1917 Leonardo (cr) in *Les Femmes de bonne humeur* (also chor.), Diaghilev's Ballets Russes, Rome

Bova Korolewitch (cr) in *Contes Russes* (also chor.), Diaghilev's Ballets Russes, Paris

Chinese Conjuror (cr) in *Parade* (also chor.), Diaghilev's Ballets Russes, Paris

1919 Can-Can Dancer (cr) in *La Boutique fantasque* (also chor.), Diaghilev's Ballets Russes, London

The Miller (cr) in *Le Tricorne* (also chor.), Diaghilev's Ballets Russes, London

1920 Title role (cr) in *Pulcinella* (also chor.), Diaghilev's Ballets Russes, Paris

1927 Principal dancer (cr) in *Le Pas d'acier* (also chor.), Diaghilev's Ballets Russes, Paris

1928 Principal dancer (cr) in *Ode* (also chor.), Diaghilev's Ballets Russes, Paris

1933 The Hussar (cr) in *Le Beau Danube bleu* (new version of *Le Beau Danube*; also chor.), Ballets Russes de Monte Carlo, Monte Carlo

Carlino (cr) in *Scuola di Ballo* (also chor.), Ballets Russes de Monte Carlo, Monte Carlo

The Hero in *Les Présages* (also chor.), Ballets Russes de Monte Carlo

1933/ First and Fourth Movements in *Choreartium* (also
35 chor.), Ballets Russes de Monte Carlo

1936 Young Musician (cr) in *Symphonie fantastique* (also chor.), de Basil's Ballets Russes, London

1938 The Peruvian (cr) in *Gaîté Parisienne* (also chor.), Ballet Russe de Monte Carlo, Monte Carlo

Francesco Bernadone (cr) in *Nobilissima Visione* (also chor.), Ballet Russe de Monte Carlo, London

1939 Gypsy Youth (cr) in *Capriccio Espagnole* (also chor.), Ballet Russe de Monte Carlo, Monte Carlo

1940 Entrée Chinoise (cr) in *Vienna 1814* (also chor.), Ballet Russe de Monte Carlo, New York

Timid Man (cr) in *The New Yorker* (also chor.), Ballet Russe de Monte Carlo, Monte Carlo

WORKS

1915 *Le Soleil de nuit* (mus. Rimsky-Korsakov), Diaghilev's Ballets Russes, Geneva

1916 *Las Meninas* (mus. Fauré), Diaghilev's Ballets Russes, San Sebastián

Kikimora (mus. Ljadov), Diaghilev's Ballets Russes, San Sebastián

1917 *Les Femmes de bonne humeur* (*The Good-Humoured Ladies*; mus. Scarlatti, arranged Tommasini), Diaghilev's Ballets Russes, Rome

Contes Russes (incorporating *Kikimora*; mus. Ljadov), Diaghilev's Ballets Russes, Paris

Parade (mus. Satie), Diaghilev's Ballets Russes, Paris

1919 *La Boutique fantasque* (mus. Rossini, arranged Respighi), Diaghilev's Ballets Russes, London

Le Tricorne (*The Three-Cornered Hat*; mus. de Falla), Diaghilev's Ballets Russes, London

1920 *Le Chant du rossignol* (new ballet version of opera; mus. Stravinsky), Diaghilev's Ballets Russes, Paris

Pulcinella (mus. Stravinsky after Pergolesi), Diaghilev's Ballets Russes, Paris

Dances in *Le Astuzie femminili* (opera; mus. Cimarosa, chor. Massine), Diaghilev's Ballets Russes, Paris

Le Sacre du printemps (new production; mus. Stravinsky), Diaghilev's Ballets Russes, Paris

Cimarosiana (suite of dances from *Le Astuzie femminili*; mus. Cimarosa), Diaghilev's Ballets Russes, Paris

1924 *Le Beau Danube* (mus. Strauss), de Beaumont's "Soirées de Paris", Paris (expanded and staged for Ballets Russes de Monte Carlo, 1933)

Salade (mus. Milhaud), de Beaumont's "Soirées de Paris", Paris

Mercure (mus. Satie), de Beaumont's "Soirées de Paris", Paris

1925 *Zéphyr et Flore* (mus. Dukelsky), Diaghilev's Ballets Russes, Monte Carlo

Les Matelots (mus. Auric), Diaghilev's Ballets Russes, Paris

1927 *Le Pas d'acier* (mus. Prokofiev), Diaghilev's Ballets Russes, Paris

1928 *Ode* (mus. Nabokov), Diaghilev's Ballets Russes, Paris

David (mus. Sauget), Ida Rubinstein's Company, Paris

1929 *Amphion* (mus. Honegger), Ida Rubinstein's Company, Paris

1930 *Le Sacre du printemps* (new version, for Martha Graham; mus. Stravinsky), Philadelphia Academy of Music, Philadelphia

1932 *Belkis* (mus. Respighi), La Scala, Milan

Jeux d'enfants (mus. Bizet), Ballets Russes de Monte Carlo, Monte Carlo

1933 *Les Présages* (mus. Tchaikovsky), Ballets Russes de Monte Carlo, Monte Carlo

Beach (mus. Françaix), Ballets Russes de Monte Carlo, Monte Carlo

Le Beau Danube bleu (new version of *Le Beau Danube*; mus. Strauss), Ballets Russes de Monte Carlo, Monte Carlo

Scuola di ballo (mus. Boccherini, arranged Françaix), Ballets Russes de Monte Carlo, Monte Carlo

Choreartium (mus. Brahms), Ballets Russes de Monte Carlo, London

1934 *Union Pacific* (mus. Nabokov), (de Basil's) Monte Carlo Ballet Russe, Philadelphia

1935 *Jardin public* (mus. Dukelsky), (de Basil's) Monte Carlo Ballet Russe, Chicago

1936 *Symphonie fantastique* (mus. Berlioz), de Basil's Ballets Russes, London

1938 *Gaîté Parisienne* (mus. Offenbach), Ballet Russe de Monte Carlo, Monte Carlo

Seventh Symphony (mus. Beethoven), Ballet Russe de Monte Carlo, Monte Carlo

Nobilissima Visione (also called *St. Francis*; mus. Hindemith), Ballet Russe de Monte Carlo, London

Bogatyri (mus. Borodin), Ballet Russe de Monte Carlo, New York

1939 *Capriccio Espagnol* (in collaboration with La Argentina; mus. Rimsky-Korsakov), Ballet Russe de Monte Carlo, Monte Carlo

Rouge et noir (also called *L'Étrange Farandole*; mus. Shostakovich), Ballet Russe de Monte Carlo, Monte Carlo

Bacchanale (mus. Wagner), Ballet Russe de Monte Carlo, New York

1940 *Vienna 1814* (mus. Weber), Ballet Russe de Monte Carlo, New York

The New Yorker (mus. Gershwin, orchestrated Raksin), Ballet Russe de Monte Carlo, Monte Carlo

1941 *Labyrinth* (mus. Schubert), Ballet Russe de Monte Carlo, New York

Saratoga (mus. Weinberger), Ballet Russe de Monte Carlo, New York

1942 *Aleko* (mus. Tchaikovsky), Ballet Theatre, Mexico City

Don Domingo (mus. Revueltas), Ballet Theatre, Mexico City

1943   *Mademoiselle Angot* (later called *Mam'zelle Angot*; mus. Lecocq), Ballet Theatre, New York

1944   *Moonlight Sonata* (mus. Beethoven), Ballet Theatre, Chicago

Mad Tristan (mus. Wagner), Ballet International, New York

1945   *Leningrad Symphony* (mus. Shostakovich), Ballet Russe Highlights, New York

1948   *Clock Symphony* (mus. Haydn), Sadler's Wells Ballet, London

Capriccio (mus. Stravinsky), La Scala, Milan

1949   *Quattro Stagioni* (mus. Vivaldi), La Scala, Milan

Le Peintre et son modèle (mus. Auric), Ballets des Champs-Elysées, Paris

1950   *La Valse* (new version; mus. Ravel), Opéra-Comique, Paris

Ballet du Pont du Nord (mus. Duport), Opéra-Comique, Paris

1951   *Symphonie allégorique* (mus. Sauget), Grand Ballet du Marquis de Cuevas, Bordeaux

Harold in Italy (mus. Berlioz), Ballet Russe de Monte Carlo, Boston

Donald of the Burthens (mus. Whyte), Sadler's Wells Ballet, London

1952   *Laudes Evangeli* (ancient mus. arranged Bucchi), Church of San Domenico, Perugia

1954   *Les Dryades* (mus. Chopin), Rome Opera Ballet, Rome

Mario e il mago (mus. Mannino), La Scala, Milan

Resurrezione e Vita (mus. various, arranged Mortari), Teatro Verde, Venice

1955   *Usher* (mus. Morillo), Teatro Colón, Buenos Aires

Hymne à la beauté (mus. Mignone), Teatro Municipal, Buenos Aires

1956   *Divertimento* (mus. Mannino), Janine Charrat's Company, Dublin

1959   *Don Giovanni* (mus. Gluck), La Scala, Milan

1960   *Fantasmi al Grand Hôtel* (mus. Chailly), La Scala, Milan

Ballo dei Ladri (*Bal des Voleurs*; mus. Auric), Balletto Europeo, Nervi Festival, Genoa

Il Barbiere di Siviglia (after the opera; mus. Rossini), Balletto Europeo, Nervi Festival, Genoa

Schéhérazade (new version; mus. Rimsky-Korsakov), Balletto Europeo, Nervi Festival, Genoa

La Commedia Umana (mus. ancient, orchestrated Arrieu), Ballet Europeo, Nervi Festival, Genoa

Other works include: for Massine/Lopokova season at Covent Garden (1922)—*Czardas, Lezghinka, Polka Mazurka, Kuiwiak, Peking Too, Fougis* (all divertissements, attributed to Massine); for revue *You'd be Surprised* (1923)—"Chinese Dance" (mus. Strauss); for Cochran's productions, London—dances in *On with the Dance* (1925), *Still Dancing* (1925), *Cochran's Revue* (1926), *Helen!* (after Offenbach's *La Belle Hélène*, 1932), *The Miracle* (Reinhardt, 1932); for Roxy Theatre, New York—*Rhythm*; for the Royal Theater, New York—dances in *Woof, Woof* (musical comedy by Hunt, Summers, and Wood; 1929); for La Scala, Milan—dances in operas *Carmen* (Bizet), *Khovanshchina* (Mussorgsky), *La Gioconda* (Ponchielli), *Ivan Susanin* (Glinka), *La Favorita* (Donizetti), *Guglielmo Tell* (Rossini), *Le Devin du village* (Rousseau); also dances in musical comedy *Bullet in the Ballet* (Edinburgh, 1946).

PUBLICATIONS

By Massine:
My Life in Ballet, London, 1960

Interview in *Dance and Dancers* (London), April 1971

Interview in Gruen, John, *The Private World of Ballet*, New York, 1975

Massine on Choreography, London, 1976

Interview in Hardin, Robert, "A Conversation with Leonid Massine", *Dance Magazine* (New York), December 1977

Interview in Gaye, Pamela, "Ballets Russes Celebration", *Dance Scope* (New York), vol. 13, no. 4, 1979

About Massine:
Moore, Lillian, *Artists of the Dance*, New York, 1938

Anthony, Gordon, *Massine*, London, 1939

Beaumont, Cyril, *Ballets Past and Present*, London, 1942

Denby, Edwin, *Looking at the Dance*, New York, 1949

Beaumont, Cyril, *Complete Book of Ballets*, revised edition, London, 1951

Grigoriev, Serge, *The Diaghilev Ballet*, translated by Vera Bowen, London, 1953

Sinclair, Janet, "Léonide Massine, Choreographer", *Ballet Today* (London), October 1960

Haskell, Arnold, "Leonid Massine: An Appreciation", *Dance Magazine* (New York), November 1969

Manchester, P.W., "Leonid Massine", *Dance Chronicle* (New York), vol. 3, no. 1, 1979

Anderson, Jack, *The One and Only: The Ballet Russe de Monte Carlo*, New York, 1981

Williams, Peter, "Twentieth-century Choreographers: Leonid Massine", *Dance Gazette* (London), October 1983

Garafola, Lynn, "The Making of Ballet Modernism", *Dance Research Journal* (New York), Winter 1989

Acocella, Joan, "Diaghilev Sits out World War II in Spain", *Dance Magazine* (New York), June 1989

Garafola, Lynn, *Diaghilev's Ballets Russes*, New York, 1989

García-Márquez, Vicente, *The Ballets Russes*, New York, 1990

*   *   *

If the word charisma did not exist, it would be necessary to invent it, in order to give present-day readers some idea of the effect which Léonide Massine had in his prime on ballet audiences, and indeed continued to do until the age of 60, at which time he was giving his final performances in Holland as the Miller in *Le Tricorne*. Massine's range as a dancer was enormous: the romantic hero of *Symphonie fantastique* would brush shoulders on the programme with the raffish Can-can Dancer of *La Boutique fantasque*; the Miller, most seductive of all his characters, might share the matinée with the dashing Hussar of *Le Beau Danube*, to be followed during the evening by the absolutely impersonal dancing of *Choreartium*. Nor was it solely in his own works that Massine could give a notable performance. His Petrushka was utterly real, his Prince Ivan in *Firebird* a model to every other dancer who attempted it, and his Eusebius in *Le Carnaval* the very essence of the romantic lover to be developed further when he came to set his role in *Symphonie fantastique*. All these infinitely varied characterizations and many more, though enhanced by costume, make-up, and situation, were achieved basically by his ability to alter his style of movement to fit in with the choreographic texture, whether his own or someone else's. He was the darling of the audience, fans often waiting at the stage door after the performance into the small hours simply to watch him walk past, without even asking for his autograph. This was the star personality at gale force; and Massine had intelligence to match.

Quite apart from his dancing, which could be relied upon in the 1930s to fill a London theatre on the hottest summer night, Massine's influence on twentieth-century ballet is considerable. It was Massine who first taught ballet to the young Ashton and subsequently recommended Marie Rambert's school as a good place to study; it was Massine whose influence on de Valois was so strong ("this man spells the word genius, not the genius of fiction but the genius of fact," she wrote in 1937) that the repertoire of the budding Vic-Wells Ballet under her direction in the 1930s followed his balletic principles. It was Massine who was the the biggest draw, as both dancer and choreographer, during the crucial period after Diaghilev's death, at which point the influence of the Ballets Russes spread through the Western world and laid the foundations which were later developed by the national ballet companies of so many countries under the tutelage of English expatriates. It was Massine who at times carried the entire responsibility of various Ballets Russes on his shoulders—dancing, choreographing, directing, and managing at a pitch not even Tudor attempted and only Jooss rivalled; while simultaneously he invented, developed and (eventually) abandoned the "symphonic" ballet, derivations from which dominate Western ballet stages today.

Massine's importance to the choreographic developments which have taken place in the twentieth century is three-fold. First, in the choreographic texture of all his works he went even further than Fokine (whom he revered) in eliminating all the superficialities which made the last years of the Romantic era in ballet so artificial and so devoid of any semblance of reality: never, in any ballet by Massine, did the corps stand about dressing the stage or dance in symmetrical rows, stretching from back to front, from wing to wing, like puppets, concerned only with moving in exactly the same alignment and at exactly the same moment as the rows next to them. No longer were these rows regarded as an inferior species, on stage solely to give the ballerina a breather. No longer was the male dancer unimportant in classical corps de ballet work, but the equal or even the dominant partner. Never, above all, were female dancers dressed in tutus, long or short, with pink pointe shoes and pink ribbons. Second, dance characters in his ballets became real, and could actually make people laugh out loud, a situation at odds with the precepts of Petipa, Ivanov, or indeed any other choreographer since pre-Romantic times. This treatment of ballet, which began with *Les Femmes de bonne humeur* (*The Good-Humoured Ladies*) in 1917, introduced an entirely novel trend into twentieth-century ballet and spawned dozens of imitations by choreographers from Lichine and Cranko to Hynd and Bintley, and ballet stages today are the more lively for it.

Massine's major influence, however, came with his development of "symphonic" or "abstract" ballet, which has been imitated on almost every ballet stage of the Western world since the 1933 productions of *Les Présages* and *Choreartium*. In these two works, though *Présages* was loosely tied to the theme of human destiny, the entirely novel spectacle was presented, to an immediately appreciative audience, of highly trained performers dancing, neither to show off their virtuosity nor to tell detailed stories but simply to present a series of movements, steps, and patterns which would parallel in value to the eye the value presented to the ear by the music in the orchestra pit. "Ballet music" as such, and sometimes ordered by the yard, was finally dead as the dodo: serious dancing to serious music would bring respect to the despised "art" of ballet dancing, to a degree in which it had never been respected in the past. Fokine's revolution was confirmed and extended by these two ballets.

Massine's theories and principles could have filled more than one book and it is a pity that, apart from the autobiography *My Life in Ballet*, his only other published work was *Massine on Choreography*, a densely written textbook, which requires intensive study before any of the examples in notation which

form the major part of the work can be comprehended. Throughout a long and productive life, which included study of the dances of American Indians and a teaching stint in choreography at the Royal Ballet School which strongly influenced many of the young students who attended the course, Massine never stopped thinking, theorizing, and clarifying his thoughts, and he remained active in the world of dance until his death. Perhaps his most important precept for any choreographer was, "Never begin a new work unless you have something different to say". This is a motto which should be written up above every ballet studio in the world, and if it were adhered to, how many pot-boilers and how much resultant boredom would the unfortunate ballet-goer have been spared in the past half-century?

—Janet Sinclair

MATISSE, Henri

French painter and stage designer. Born in Le Cateau-Cambrésis, 31 December 1869. Attended schools in St. Quentin; studied law at the Sorbonne, Paris, 1887–88; studied drawing at École Quentin de la Tour, 1890, also studying art under Bouguereau at the Académie Julian, Paris, 1892–93, with Gustave Moreau from 1893–97, and at the École des Beaux-Arts, from 1895; studied sculpture with Bourdelle, 1900–03. Married Amélie Noémie Alexandrine Parayre, 1898; one daughter, two sons. Exhibited at Salon d'Automne, 1905, becoming associated with group thereafter known as Fauves; director of art school, Paris, 1908–11; settled in Nice, 1917, living in both Nice and Paris from 1922; designer of stage and costume designs for Diaghilev ballet *Le Chant du rossignol*, 1920, returning to ballet design for Massine/Denham Ballet Russe de Monte Carlo with *Rouge et noir*, 1939; first "cutouts", 1938; designer and illustrator of books, including Mallarmé's *Poésies* and Joyce's *Ulysses*, 1930s–1940s; lived in Vence, 1943–48, decorating Dominican Chapel there, 1948–51; returned to Nice, working on large decorative commissions based on paper cutouts. Died in Nice, 3 November 1954.

WORKS (Ballet designs)

1920   *Le Chant du rossignol* (chor. Massine), Serge Diaghilev's Ballets Russes, Paris
1939   *Rouge et noir* (also known as *L'Étrange Farandole*; chor. Massine), Ballet Russe de Monte Carlo, Monte Carlo

PUBLICATIONS

Barr, Alfred H., *Matisse: His Art and His Public*, New York, 1951, 1975
Matisse: Dessins et sculpture (catalogue), Paris, 1975
Clarke, Mary, and Crisp, Clement, *Design for Ballet*, London, 1978
Schouvaloff, Alexander, "Stravinsky sur scène", *Connaissance des arts* (Paris), July/August 1982
Schneider, Pierre, *Matisse*, translated by N. Taylor and B.S. Romer, London, 1984
Watkins, Nicholas, *Matisse*, Oxford, 1984
Flam, Jack, D., *Matisse: The Man and his Art*, London, 1986
Baer, Nancy van Norman, *The Art of Enchantment: Diaghilev's Ballets Russes 1909–1929*, San Francisco, 1988

Flam, Jack D., *Matisse: A Retrospective*, New York, 1988

*   *   *

Henri Matisse is reputed to have preferred folk and popular dance to the ballet. He designed only two ballets during his lengthy and productive career as a visual artist: *Le Chant du rossignol*, first performed in Paris in 1920 by Serge Diaghilev's Ballets Russes, and *Rouge et noir*, staged in Monte Carlo in 1939 by the Ballet Russe de Monte Carlo. Both works had choreography by Léonide Massine, and a strong conceptual rapport can be detected between choreographer and designer.

Matisse was commissioned in 1919 to design sets, costumes, accessories, and drop curtain for *Le Chant du rossignol*, a ballet based on the Hans Christian Andersen fairytale *The Nightingale*. In executing the commission, Matisse used a restricted range of colours and a simplification of design which was unusual for the Ballets Russes, many of whose most successful productions had been designed in a rich profusion of decoration. Much later Matisse was highly critical of what he considered the excesses of colour employed by some of the more popular Ballets Russes designers. He singled out Bakst and his work for *Schéhérazade* in particular.

Le Chant du rossignol took place in an oriental land, although Matisse's designs reflected oriental restraint rather than exotic excess. The designs were generally not well received by contemporary critics or audiences. They appear, however, to have suited Massine's choreography well; in particular, the geometric patterns with which many of the costumes were decorated fitted well with Massine's arrangement of the dancers into pyramidal and vertical groupings.

Working on this ballet provided Matisse with the beginnings of a technique to which he was later to return with singular success in his work outside the theatre. The Russian scene painter Vladimir Polunin, who executed the sets to Matisse's design for *Le Chant du rossignol*, has recalled that Matisse had made no preliminary sketches, but began work by cutting out paper shapes and piecing and re-piecing them together to obtain the desired effect. This was an experimental technique for Matisse at that stage of his career, but foreshadowed his paper cut-out series of the 1940s and 1950s.

Le Chant du rossignol was revived by Diaghilev in 1925 with Matisse's designs, but with new choreography by George Balanchine. In this revival Matisse re-designed the costume for the Nightingale, this time dressing Alicia Markova in a startling and quite new unitard.

Rouge et noir was one of Massine's symphonic ballets, following in the footsteps of works such as *Les Présages* and *Choreartium*. Danced to the First Symphony of Shostakovitch, it concerned man's eternal struggle between spirituality and materialism, showing his eventual but inevitable yielding to his destiny. *Rouge et noir* was given a few performances in Paris with the revised, but temporary, name of *L'Étrange Farandole*. It was shown in New York in 1940 with its original name.

Matisse designed both sets and costumes for the work, accepting the commission in 1937. His backcloth looks back to one of his earlier non-theatrical commissions, a large mural to occupy three lunettes in a vaulted area of the Barnes Foundation building in Merion, near Philadelphia. In the lunettes, and against a background of flat planes of colour, Matisse executed groups of dancing figures. For the *Rouge et noir* backcloth, Matisse adapted the arrangement of arches and planes of colour of the Barnes mural, producing a backcloth with the look of a Gothic arcade. In front of this backcloth, Massine frequently grouped his dancers in sculptural poses, which in turn recalled Matisse's dancing figures from the lunettes.

Matisse dressed the dancers in *Rouge et noir* in unitards of various colours, corresponding to the forces they represented in the ballet. These he decorated with randomly placed, flame-like designs. In both form and decoration these costumes were sufficiently abstracted to suit the idea of a symphonic ballet; and the interaction between set, costume, and choreographic groupings achieved quite a startling coherence, both visually and in elucidating Massine's theme.

Matisse created numerous works outside the theatre which used dance as a subject, notably his monumental canvas *La Danse* and the related Barnes mural. They indicate a desire to explore the essence of dance, to portray the distillation of an idea. His sets and costumes for *Le Chant du rossignol* and *Rouge et noir*, with their restrained colours and simplified designs, fall within this same conceptual framework. Moreover, these works reflect a sympathy of purpose with certain ideas of Massine, especially his approach to choreographic groupings and his interest in developing the abstract qualities of the symphonic ballet.

—Michelle Potter

MATSUYAMA BALLET

Japanese ballet company based in Tokyo. Founded by Mikiko Matsuyama, 1948, with Masao Shimizu as director and with Mikiko Matsuyama as artistic director, choreographer, and ballerina (retired from the stage, 1978); early touring links with China, subsequently touring internationally; company repertoire and programming largely dominated by artistic director, Mikiko Matsuyama, principal choreographer, Tetsutaro Shimizu, and prima ballerina, Yoko Morishita. Official school associated with company, Matsuyama Ballet School, maintains 30 studios covering Tokyo. Current director of the Matsuyama Ballet: Mikiko Matsuyama.

PUBLICATIONS

Keene, Keiko, "The Matsuyama Ballet Company", *Dancing Times* (London), June 1985
Keene, Keiko, "Verve, Energy and Obsession", *Dance and Dancers* (London), July 1985
Percival, John, "Revelation from Japan", *Dance and Dancers* (London), October 1985
Kisselgoff, Anna, "This Troupe Transcends Family", *New York Times* (New York), 3 February 1991

*   *   *

The Matsuyama Ballet was formed by ballerina Mikiko Matsuyama in Tokyo in 1948. The company soon invited her husband Masao Shimizu to be the director, and she became artistic director. Now their son Tetsutaro Shimizu is the resident choreographer and his wife Yoko Morishita is the prima ballerina. These facts reveal the vital functioning of the company more than anything else.

As the director, Masao Shimizu was an ardent communist. The company established a good relationship with communist China, and was invited by the Chinese government to perform *The White-Haired Girl*, a revolutionary ballet with a Chinese theme, in 1958.

This was the first of the five tours the Matsuyama Ballet made to China, and the last was in 1984 with *Giselle*. The ballet

The Matsuyama Ballet performing *Swan Lake*

called *Gion Matsuri* (*Gion Festival*) was the most popular during those tours. This work was choreographed by Taneo Ishida, then resident choreographer, and dealt with the revolt of the citizens against the ruler of Kyoto in medieval Japan. The communist leader Mao Tse Tung highly praised this work, and held a special gala evening, inviting the entire diplomatic corps in Beijing. Now the company has discarded such political overtones, and has established a repertory consisting of standard classics, along with such modern works as Balanchine's *Allegro Brillante*.

The resident choreographer, Tetsutaro Shimizu, has not been content merely to stage and dance the Western classics; he wanted to introduce the Japanese cultural heritage to ballet, and with this aim he staged a new work, *Mandala*, in 1987. *Mandala* depicted the impossible love between a young girl denied the freedom to practise the Catholic faith to which she is devoted, and a young Buddhist artist. The ballet received several prizes, including the Art Festival prize of the Ministry of Education. It was also staged during Edinburgh Festival in 1988 with considerable success.

The company, performing this work among others, toured New York and Washington, D.C. during the 1990–91 season. In New York, the ballet capital of America, the Matsuyama Ballet was warmly received. *The New York Times* critic Anna Kisselgoff, reviewing the company's production of *Giselle*, wrote, "The Matsuyama Ballet . . . pays attention to stylistic refinement. The female corps has wonderful arms, with concern for use of the shoulders, and the toe work is

impressively centered, strong without an aggressive attack". Certainly, concluded Ms. Kisselgoff, "the company is not provincial, and its aspirations to international status are justified". The company has also danced in London as part of the Nureyev Festival, and toured Greece in 1985. At present, the Matsuyama Ballet is one of the major ballet companies in Japan, and enjoys great popularity with the Japanese ballet audience.

But, it must be remembered, this popularity is almost exclusively due to the popularity and reputation of the world-class ballerina Yoko Morishita. Further substantial development of the Matsuyama Ballet will require nothing less than a total break from arcane family-business practices, and the personality cult which has brought it this far.

—Kenji Usui

MAXIMOVA, Ekaterina

Russian/Soviet dancer. Born Ekaterina Sergeyevna Maksimova (Maximova) in Moscow, 1 February 1939. Studied at the Moscow Choreographic School, pupil of Elisaveta Gerdt, 1949–58; later coached by Galina Ulanova. Married Bolshoi soloist Vladimir Vasiliev. Dancer, soon becoming principal, Bolshoi Ballet, 1958–89; guest artist, Béjart's Ballet du XXe

Siècle, 1978, Moscow Classical Ballet, 1981, 1984, London Festival Ballet, 1989, Australian Ballet, National Ballet of Canada, 1990; has also performed on Soviet television and in many films, including *Galatea* (1978), *Old Tango* (1979), *Gigolo and Gigoletta* (dir. Vasiliev, 1980), *La Traviata* (dir. Zeffirelli, 1982), *Fouetté* (dir. Vasiliev, 1986), *Gappiniana* (1987), and *Volodia and Katia* (documentary; 1989); member, Board of Directors, Ballet Theatre of the Kremlin Palace of Congress, 1990. Recipient: Gold Medal, All-Soviet Ballet Competition, 1957, Festival of Youth Competition, Vienna, 1959, and International Ballet Competition, Varna, 1964, 1982; title of Honoured Arts Worker, Russian Federation, 1964; Anna Pavlova Prize, Paris, 1969; title of People's Artist of the Russian Federation, 1969; Marius Petipa Prize, France, 1972; Premium of Lenin Komsomol, 1972; title of People's Artist of the USSR, 1973.

ROLES

1957   Masha in *The Nutcracker* (Vainonen), Moscow Choreographic School Performance, Moscow

1958   Peasant Pas de deux in *Giselle* (Petipa after Coralli, Perrot), Bolshoi Ballet, Moscow

Four Cygnets in *Swan Lake* (Petipa, Ivanov, staged Messerer), Bolshoi Ballet, Moscow

1959   Katerina (cr) in *The Stone Flower* (Moscow version; Grigorovich), Bolshoi Ballet, Moscow

Waltz in *Chopiniana* (after Fokine), Bolshoi Ballet, Moscow

1960   Title role in *Giselle* (Petipa after Coralli, Perrot), Bolshoi Ballet, Moscow

Columbine in *The Bronze Horseman* (Zakharov), Bolshoi Ballet, Moscow

Lizzy in *The Path of Thunder* (Sergeyev), Bolshoi Ballet, Moscow

Nymph of the Water in *The Little Humpbacked Horse* (Radunsky after Gorsky), Bolshoi Ballet, Moscow

1961   Mavka in *Song of the Woods* (Lapauri), Bolshoi Ballet, Moscow

Jeanne in *The Flames of Paris* (Vainonen), Bolshoi Ballet, Moscow

1962   Masha in *The Nutcracker* (Vainonen), Bolshoi Ballet, Moscow

The Muse in *Paganini* (Lavrovsky), Bolshoi Ballet, Moscow

Maria in *The Fountain of Bakhchisarai* (Zakharov), Bolshoi Ballet, Moscow

A Nymph in *Spartacus* (Yakobson), Bolshoi Ballet, Moscow

A Bacchanalian in *Walpurgis Night* (Lavrovsky), Bolshoi Ballet, Moscow

Mazurka (cr) in *Skriabiinana* (Goleizovsky), Bolshoi Ballet, Moscow

1963   Princess Florine in *The Sleeping Beauty* (Grigorovich after Petipa), Bolshoi Ballet, Moscow

Principal dancer in *Class Concert* (Messerer), Bolshoi Ballet, Moscow

1964   Title role in *Cinderella* (Zakharov), Bolshoi Ballet, Moscow

Aurora in *The Sleeping Beauty* (Grigorovich after Petipa), Bolshoi Ballet, Moscow

Ballerina in *Petrushka* (Fokine, staged Boyarsky), Bolshoi Ballet, Moscow

1965   Kitri in *Don Quixote* (Gorsky after Petipa), Bolshoi Ballet, Moscow

1966   Masha (cr) in *The Nutcracker* (Grigorovich), Bolshoi Ballet, Moscow

1968   Odette/Odile in *Swan Lake* (Petipa, Ivanov, staged Messerer), Bolshoi Ballet, Moscow

Phrygia (cr) in *Spartacus* (Grigorovich), Bolshoi Ballet, Moscow

1971   The Girl in *Icarus* (Vasiliev), Bolshoi Ballet, Moscow

1973   Juliet in *Romeo and Juliet* (Lavrovsky), Bolshoi Ballet, Moscow

Princess Aurora (cr) in *The Sleeping Beauty* (new production; Grigorovich after Petipa), Bolshoi Ballet, Moscow

1976   Eola (cr) in *Icarus* (new production; Vasiliev), Bolshoi Ballet, Moscow

1978   Julia in *Romeo and Julia* (Béjart), Ballet du XXe Siècle, Brussels

Principal dancer (cr) in *These Charming Sounds* (Vasiliev), Bolshoi Ballet, Moscow

1980   Title role (cr) in *Natalie* (new production; Lacotte), Moscow Classical Ballet, Moscow

Shura Azarova in *Hussar Ballad* (Vinogradov, Briantsev), Moscow Classical Ballet, Moscow

1981   Juliet in *Romeo and Juliet* (Kasatkina, Vasiliev), Bolshoi Ballet, Moscow

1984   Eve in *The Creation of the World* (Kasatkina, Vasiliev), Moscow Classical Ballet, Moscow

1986   Title role (cr) in *Anyuta* (Vasiliev), Teatro San Carlos, Naples

1987   Rosa in *Blue Angel* (Petit), Ballet du Marseilles, Paris

1988   The Glove Seller in *Gaîté Parisienne* (Massine), Teatro San Carlo, Naples

1989   Principal dancer in *Russian Dance* (Goleizovsky), Bolshoi Ballet (Goleizovsky evening), Moscow

Romula in *Nijinsky Reminiscences* (Menegatti), Teatro San Carlo, Naples

Tatiana in *Onegin* (Cranko), English National Ballet, London

1990   "The Song of Solomon" (recitation; non-dancing role) in *The Bible* (dir. Alexander Parra), Moscow

PUBLICATIONS

By Maximova:

Interview, "Dancing is My Life" (reprint of Moscow interview), *Dance and Dancers* (London), August 1974

Interview, "Ekaterina Maximova et Vladimir Vassiliev," *Pour la danse* (Paris), no. 38, June–July–August 1977

About Maximova:

Arkina, N., "Ekaterina Maksimova", *Teatr* (Moscow), no. 1, 1972

Lvov-Anokhin, Boris, *Masters of the Bolshoi Theatre*, Moscow, 1976

Demidov, Alexander, *The Russian Ballet Past and Present*, translated by Guy Daniels, London, 1978

Gaevsky, Vadim, *Divertissement*, Moscow, 1981

Konstantinova, M., *Ekaterina Maksimova*, Moscow, 1982

Smakov, Gennady, *The Great Russian Dancers*, New York, 1984

Willis, Margaret, "Ballerina à la Russe", *Dance Magazine* (New York), October 1988

*   *   *

Ekaterina Maximova is a ballerina of lyrical purity and brilliant technical ability. To her roles she brings not only the

Ekaterina Maximova as the Girl in *Icarus***, Bolshoi Ballet, Moscow**

finest qualities of Russian classicism but an instinctive and fresh interpretation each time she performs. The combination of this inner understanding of her characters, the perception of the situation around her on stage, and her research and knowledge of the ballet enables Maximova to give performances of rarified dimension.

Maximova is a natural ballerina—petite and perfectly proportioned, with a sleek, tapered line and filigree technique. She possesses long slim legs, a gracious carriage, and loose, fluid arms which lift her so that to be on pointe seems more natural than walking. Added to these are superb technical skills—sharp, crisp footwork, confident pirouettes, and controlled correct placement—and both lyricism and pristine musicality. While a private person in real life, Maximova, once on stage, demonstrates an effervescence which shines through her dancing, bringing warmth and reality to fairy-tale roles. She is essentially feminine, coquettish, and often humorous.

Ekaterina Maximova was born in Moscow and always wanted to dance. She entered the Moscow Ballet School, where she trained for eight years, and graduated in 1958 under the tutelage of the great Russian teacher Elisaveta Gerdt, daughter of Pavel Gerdt (who had taught Anna Pavlova). During her years at school, Maximova often performed in in-house productions: it was at one of these school programmes, when she was ten, that she performed for the first time with fellow student Vladimir Vasiliev, her husband-to-be and long-term partner. She appeared in *Fadette* in 1951 and as Cupid in *Don Quixote* in 1952. Still a student, she took the role of Masha in *The Nutcracker* at the Bolshoi Theatre in 1957, a ballet she would perform many times in later years. In it, her wonderment and childlike expressions of anticipation and expectation conjured up the essential fairy-tale atmosphere.

Maximova has danced all the Russian ballerina roles—Aurora, Odette/Odile, Masha, Kitri, Giselle—bringing to each a sensitivity and an emotional commitment which reveals the "soul" of the Russian style. While still a teenager, she was coached for her début in *Giselle* by the legendary exponent of that role, Galina Ulanova. She won immediate recognition for her interpretation, which hinted at Ulanova's great dramatic and lyrical powers, yet remained essentially Maximova's own. She was the youngest ballerina to dance the role at the Bolshoi. Ulanova remained her coach for several years, preparing her for her major roles (which included Juliet, the role most associated with Ulanova) and handing down to her talented pupil the best of the Leningrad and Bolshoi classical traditions.

Maximova has also proved herself a fine performer of contemporary Soviet-style works, including those of Kasyan Goleizovsky and the somewhat block-buster ballets of the Bolshoi's artistic director, Yuri Grigorovich, where fast, non-stop, expansive movements rule the stage. A year after graduating, Maximova was given the leading role of Katerina in the Bolshoi's premiere of Grigorovich's ballet *The Stone Flower*. Her Danila was Vasiliev and the couple achieved tremendous success in the ballet both at home in the Bolshoi and on their first tour to America in 1959.

Maximova performs regularly as guest artist with the Moscow Classical Ballet, directed by Natalia Kasatkina and Vladimir Vasiliev. Here she dances roles often quite different from the Bolshoi's more traditional fare. As the innocent, waif-like Eve in Kasatkina and Vasiliev's *Creation of the World*, Maximova dispenses with tutu and classical line for a white, lycra unitard and fluid gymnastic form.

Together with her husband, Maximova has travelled the world, bringing success not only to herself but to Russian training and tradition. She has extended her repertoire and her style and has been given interesting, and often very different, work in recent years by various European companies. She has also made several ballet films—often under the direction of her husband, whose talents are many. But perhaps her most endearing film role was in *Galatea*, a balletic Pygmalion to the score from *My Fair Lady*. Her Professor Higgins, here a ballet master who wagers he can teach the street urchin girl to dance, was performed by Maris Liepa, as much a dapper aristocrat as Rex Harrison was in the musical. The performance of these two fine dancers in the film is quite impressive. Not only does Maximova convincingly present both the gawkiness and the graceful transformation of the main character, but she shows her ability to be a real comic.

Unlike many mature ballerinas whose careers are cut short by obvious technical failings, Maximova continues to face and to accept new challenges (indeed, her youthful appearance belies her actual age). She is a ballerina who has contributed much to ballet throughout the world.

—Margaret Willis

MAY, Pamela

British dancer and teacher.   Born in San Fernando, Trinidad, 30 May 1917. Studied with Freda Grant in London, Olga Preobrazhenska and Lubov Egorova in Paris, and with Ninette de Valois, Sadler's Wells Ballet School, from 1933. Dancer, corps de ballet, Vic-Wells Ballet, from 1934: first soloist role, November 1934, soon beoming leading dancer, and touring the U.S. and Canada with the Royal Ballet, 1949–50; named ballerina, 1952; guest artist, La Scala, Milan, 1950; also made several television appearances; teacher, Royal Ballet School, 1954–78; freelance teacher, including for Yorkshire Ballet Seminars, Ilkley, from 1980s; member of the Executive Committee, Royal Academy of Dancing, London.

ROLES

1933   Plant in *La Creation du monde* (de Valois), Vic-Wells Ballet, London
1934   Pas de trois in *Swan Lake* (Petipa, Ivanov; staged Sergeyev), Vic-Wells Ballet, London
Moyna (Solo, Wilis) in *Giselle* (Petipa after Coralli, Perrot; staged Sergeyev), Vic-Wells Ballet, London
1935   Creole Girl in *Rio Grande* (Ashton), Vic-Wells Ballet, London
Waltz in *Façade* (Ashton), Vic-Wells Ballet, London
A Woman of the Port in *Rio Grande* (Ashton), Vic-Wells Ballet, London
1936   The Fairy in *Le Baiser de la fée* (Ashton), Vic-Wells Ballet, London
The Serving Maid in *The Gods Go a-Begging* (de Valois), Vic-Wells Ballet, London
Alicia in *The Haunted Ballroom* (de Valois), Vic-Wells Ballet, London
Princess in *Nursery Suite* (de Valois), Vic-Wells Ballet, London
The Other Woman in *Prometheus* (de Valois), Vic-Wells Ballet, London
1937   Pas des patineuses (cr) in *Les Patineurs* (Ashton), Vic-Wells Ballet, London
The Woman in Ball Dress in *Apparitions* (Ashton), Vic-Wells Ballet, London
Violet (cr) in *A Wedding Bouquet* (Ashton), Vic-Wells Ballet, London

Pamela May with Alan Carter in *The Prospect Before Us*, Vic-Wells Ballet, 1940

The Red Queen (cr) in *Checkmate* (de Valois), Vic-Wells Ballet, Paris

Isabel in *The Lord of Burleigh* (Ashton), Vic-Wells Ballet, London

The Black Queen in *Checkmate* (de Valois), Vic-Wells Ballet, tour

Myrtha in *Giselle* (Petipa after Coralli, Perrot; staged Sergeyev), Vic-Wells Ballet, London

1938   The Moon (cr) in *Horoscope* (Ashton), Vic-Wells Ballet, London

The Empress in *Le Roi nu* (*The Emperor's New Clothes*; de Valois), Vic-Wells Ballet, London

1939   Rose Fairy, Diamond Fairy in *The Sleeping Princess* (Petipa; staged Sergeyev), Vic-Wells Ballet, London

1940   A Child of Light (cr) in *Dante Sonata* (Ashton), Vic-Wells Ballet, London

Foxtrot (cr; added) in *Façade* (Ashton), Vic-Wells Ballet, London

Variation "Dawn" in *Coppélia* (Petipa, Cecchetti; staged Sergeyev), Vic-Wells Ballet, London

Columbine in *Carnaval* (Fokine), Vic-Wells Ballet, London

La Superbe in *Harlequin in the Street* (Ashton), Vic-Wells Ballet, London

Odette in *Swan Lake*, Act II (Ivanov; staged Petipa), Vic-Wells Ballet, London

Mlle. Théodore (cr) in *The Prospect Before Us* (de Valois), Vic-Wells Ballet, London

Princess Florine (Bluebird pas de deux) in *The Sleeping Princess* (Petipa; staged Ivanov), Vic-Wells Ballet, London

1941   Lover (cr) in *The Wanderer* (new chor.; Ashton), Sadler's Wells Ballet, London

Odette/Odile in *Swan Lake* (Petipa, Ivanov; staged Sergeyev), Sadler's Wells Ballet, London

Lilac Fairy in *The Sleeping Princess* (Petipa; staged Sergeyev), Sadler's Wells Ballet, London

Princess Aurora in *The Sleeping Princess* (Petipa; staged Sergeyev), Sadler's Wells Ballet, London

Eurydice (cr) in *Orpheus and Eurydice* (de Valois), Sadler's Wells Ballet, London

1943   Rendezvous pas de deux in *Promenade* (de Valois), Sadler's Wells Ballet, London

1944   Young Girl (previously called "A Rich Girl") in *Nocturne* (Ashton), Sadler's Wells Ballet, London

Sugar Plum Fairy in *The Nutcracker* (Ivanov; staged Sergeyev), Sadler's Wells Ballet, London

1945   Swanilda in *Coppélia* (Petipa, Cecchetti; staged Sergeyev), Sadler's Wells Ballet, London

Variation, Adagio of Lovers in *Les Rendezvous* (Ashton), Sadler's Wells Ballet, London

1946   Principal dancer in *Symphonic Variations* (Ashton), Sadler's Wells Ballet, London

1947   Queen of Hearts in *La Boutique fantasque* (Massine), Sadler's Wells Ballet, London

Can-Can in *La Boutique fantasque* (Massine), Sadler's Wells Ballet, London

1948   Fairy Godmother (cr) in *Cinderella* (Ashton), Sadler's Wells Ballet, London

1950   Pas de deux in *Les Patineurs* (Ashton), Sadler's Wells Ballet, London

Shepherdess of the Golden Age (cr) in *Don Quixote* (de Valois), Sadler's Wells Ballet, London

1952   Mother (cr) in *Bonne-Bouche* (Cranko), Sadler's Wells Ballet, London

The Aristocrat in *Mam'zelle Angot* (Massine), Sadler's Wells Ballet, London

Other roles include: Prelude, Waltz, Mazurka in *Les Sylphides* (Fokine), Chiarina in *Carnaval* (Fokine), Princess-Mother in *Swan Lake* (Petipa, Ivanov; staged Sergeyev, de Valois).

PUBLICATIONS

By May:
"Across the USA with the 'Wells'", *Dancing Times* (London), December 1950

About May:
Gowing, Lawrence, "English Dancers in English Ballet", *Dancing Times* (London), January 1937
Percival, John, "Pamela May: A Study", *Ballet Today* (London), February 1952
Davison, Gladys, *Ballet Biographies*, revised edition, London, 1954
Clarke, Mary, *The Sadler's Wells Ballet*, London, 1955
Anthony, Gordon, "Pioneers of the Royal Ballet: Pamela May", *Dancing Times* (London), January 1971
Sinclair, Janet, "Thank you, Pamela May", *Dancing Times* (London), June 1982

*   *   *

A good argument can be made to support the theory that Pamela May was the most versatile ballerina ever to be a regular member of the Vic-Wells/Sadler's Wells/Royal Ballet. Not only did she dance all the leading roles in every classical ballet which was in the repertoire during her twenty years as a regular member of the company, excepting only *Giselle* (in which she gave an icily commanding performance as Myrtha), but she complemented her portrayals of Aurora, Odette/Odile, Swanilda, and the Sugar Plum Fairy with the supporting roles of the Lilac Fairy, the Bluebird, the pas de trois and leading Swan in *Swan Lake*, the Dawn solo in the last act of *Coppélia*, and a leading Wili in *Giselle* when not dancing Myrtha.

And beside all her work in the Russian classics, Pamela May was also equally at home in the Waltz, the Mazurka, and the Prelude of *Les Sylphides*: she danced Columbine in *Carnaval* and also Chiarina. Having first created the role of the Red Queen in *Checkmate*, she later appeared successfully in the entirely contrasting role of the Black Queen: she had no difficulty in taking over roles created for others (as in this case, and in the case of the role of the Rich Girl in Ashton's *Nocturne*) and always created her own version of the character, while avoiding any attempt to copy what had been achieved by the originator of the role.

Ninette de Valois's roles created for Pamela May displayed to perfection the individual qualities of the dancer—qualities which in the 1930s were sometimes at risk of being overshadowed by the poignant romanticism of her great friend Margot Fonteyn or by the luscious sex-appeal of her other great friend, June Brae. Yet May was versatile enough to take over Fonteyn's role as the Woman in Ball Dress in *Apparitions*—a role which Fonteyn had made completely her own—and to present a performance quite different in texture and emotion from that of Fonteyn, but equally valid; while similarly, when face-to-face with the role of the Black Queen, in which some, after her impressive performance as the Red Queen, expected her to be mis-cast, she was so successful that while the ballet remained in the original company's repertoire, only Beryl Grey performed it more often (apart, of course, from its creator, June Brae). The roles de Valois made for her, such as Mlle. Théodore (*The Prospect Before Us*), and Eurydice, and those de Valois roles she took over (*The Gods Go a-Begging*, *The Haunted*

Ballroom) would have led one to classify her as the "ideal de Valois dancer" were it not for the fact that she made an equally successful impression in Ashton's choreography—as the Moon in *Horoscope*, in *The Wanderer* and, of course, as one of the three ballerinas in *Symphonic Variations*.

May's technique was perfectly adequate, as her classical repertoire demonstrates, though she was never a virtuoso: in her day, it was sufficient to conceal technique, and use it not as an end in itself but as a means to the end—becoming not merely a dancer, but an artist as well. Though not classically perfect of feature, she effortlessly presented a picture of absolute radiance on stage, a radiance in which her beautiful legs and feet and serenity of carriage played an important part. She was remarkably successful when partnering Sasha Machov in the authentic Czech dances he mounted during the war for the Sadler's Wells Opera production of *The Bartered Bride*; and when she gave up the classical repertory, she embarked on a second career playing acting roles, where her elegant presence made a positive contribution in parts often given to an inexperienced novice.

She taught for some years at the Royal Ballet School, where her students adored her and gained enormously in strength and precision from her classes. It cannot have been easy for her to have been standing in Fonteyn's shadow throughout her dancing career, but the two remained great friends from the early 1930s. Pamela May was still teaching in the early 1990s, and her classes at the Yorkshire Ballet Seminars at Ilkley have been much sought-after, not only for the high standard of her teaching, but also for the kindness, sympathy, and understanding which she has extended to her students for over a quarter of a century.

—Janet Sinclair

MAYERLING

Choreography: Kenneth MacMillan
Music: Franz Liszt (arranged and orchestrated by John Lanchbery)
Design: Nicholas Georgiadis (scenery and costumes)
Libretto: Gillian Freeman (scenario after life story of Crown Prince Rudolf of Austria-Hungary)
First Production: Royal Ballet, Royal Opera House, London, 14 February 1978
Principal Dancers: David Wall (Crown Prince Rudolf), Lynn Seymour (Baroness Mary Vetsera), Wendy Ellis (Princess Stephanie), Merle Park (Countess Marie Larisch), Graham Fletcher (Bratfisch)

Other choreographic treatments of story: E. Bernhofer (Vienna, 1966).

PUBLICATIONS

Freeman, Gillian, "*Mayerling*", *About the House* (London), Christmas 1977
Freeman, Gillian, "The Scenario for *Mayerling*", *Dancing Times* (London), February 1978
Williams, Peter, "*Mayerling*", *Dance and Dancers*, March 1978
Clarke, Mary, "*Mayerling*", *Dancing Times*, March 1978
Clarke, Mary, "*Mayerling* Dancers", *Dancing Times* (London), April 1978
Clarke, Mary, "*Mayerling* Revisited", *Dancing Times* (London), February 1980
Brinson, Peter, and Crisp, Clement, *Ballet and Dance: A Guide to the Repertory*, London, 1980
Croce, Arlene, *Going to the Dance*, New York, 1982
Thorpe, Edward, *Kenneth MacMillan: The Man and his Ballets*, London, 1985
Crisp, Clement, "Kenneth MacMillan", *About the House* (London), Spring 1990

* * *

The story of Mayerling—the royal hunting lodge outside Vienna, where the Crown Prince Rudolf and his mistress Mary Vetsera ended their lives in a double suicide in 1889—has always held a peculiar fascination for historians and general observers alike, even some 100 years after the event. It is no surprise that Kenneth MacMillan, a choreographer instinctively drawn to themes of passion, violence, and death, should have been attracted to it. Drawing the essential facts of the case from a popular history and following up with extensive reading in the period, MacMillan from the start chose to ignore romanticized versions of the story (many of which had been featured in commercial films), and sought instead to dig into the reality, no matter how unpleasant, of Rudolf's sorry history. "What emerged from the history book", writes MacMillan's biographer Edward Thorpe of the ballet's genesis, "was not the lives of two people deeply in love, thwarted by political protocol, but a corrupt, depraved prince, a drug addict suffering from venereal disease and a precocious, social-climbing young woman ready to sacrifice herself for a romantic chimera." This was "ideal MacMillan material", writes Thorpe, pointing to the two main characters' positions as "outsiders" (a favourite MacMillan theme), and showing how their desperate entrapment in inescapable psychological and social circumstances was the very stuff of MacMillan's best ballet-dramas.

MacMillan's choice of collaborators was shrewd. The designer Nicholas Georgiadis, who had already successfully worked on several MacMillan ballets, was yet again able to combine historical accuracy with his own breed of imaginative symbolism (such as dummies placed about the stage during a court scene to suggest anonymous spies and listeners) to emphasize the corrupt and destructive milieu of the Crown Prince's existence, the disturbing underside of royal glamour and privilege. John Lanchbery arranged the score, an appropriate montage of works by Franz Liszt, and the writer Gillian Freeman dealt with the highly complicated task of compressing the tale and its relevant historical background into a comprehensible scenario. Despite Freeman's careful compression of the many and confusing events into a single story-line, however, *Mayerling* does remain a somewhat overwhelming and baffling ballet in terms of plot. Even the most enthusiastic of *Mayerling* fans have admitted that viewers are likely to be confused by the story, and one critic has even recommended background reading on the Austro-Hungarian Empire before seeing the ballet.

In keeping with MacMillan's primary interests in human psychology and motivation, the story was boiled down to Rudolf's most important individual relationships—mostly with women, as it happens—placed within the larger context of representative group scenes, be they court celebrations or gatherings in tawdry taverns. As a reviewer was later to point out, "MacMillan has never shown much interest in the minor characters of his ballets, in spite of his predilection for large subjects and three-act development." *Mayerling* is no exception, tracing Rudolf's downfall through a series of central

Mayerling, **with Lynn Seymour and David Wall, Royal Ballet, London, 1978**

individual relationships, starting with his new bride Princess Stephanie of Belgium (whom he frightens with a revolver on their wedding night), and going through to encounters with his mother, Empress Elisabeth, his ex-mistress and procuress Countess Larisch, his current mistress Mitzi Caspar, and last, his final lover and co-conspirator in downfall and death, Mary Vetsera. Through these many and varied relationships MacMillan expands and even inverts the art of the pas de deux, turning it from a highly ritualized courtly love-duet into a dance of passion, eroticism, love, hatred, and death.

MacMillan has always built his story ballets around a small number of central pas de deux, and *Mayerling* provided a phenomenal display of this genre in all its multiple and previously undiscovered possibilties. Although all showed Rudolf and his despair in new and different angles, perhaps the most powerful pas de deux were those with Mary Vetsera, played by the outstanding ballet actess Lynn Seymour, dancing opposite David Wall's superb Rudolf. As Clement Crisp and Peter Brinson write in *Ballet and Dance,* "In the duet for Rudolf and Mary, MacMillan is at his most persuasive as an erotic poet, exploring passion with images of dark beauty—the final coupling at Mayerling combining lust and despair."

Mayerling is considered by many critics to be one of

MacMillan's finest works, and is certainly thought to be his most successful story ballet. Critic John Percival, by no means a partisan MacMillan follower, wrote in 1978, "In spite of its faults I think *Mayerling* is MacMillan's best three-act ballet." Other critics followed in the same vein, claiming that *Mayerling* continued where other impressive efforts by the same choreographer, like *Manon* and *Anastasia,* left off, resulting in one of the classics of the twentieth-century canon. MacMillan's ability to distil the drama of a story into a series of powerful, searing moments of human encounter has been compared to cinematic technique, and his collaboration with Gillian Freeman in this case provided the perfect framework for the streamlined action, not so much a traditional narrative as a series of pointed, impressionistic moments. Crisp and Brinson go so far as to suggest that *Mayerling* could be called the twentieth-century *Swan Lake,* portraying for a modern sensibility the very same themes of "love in death, royal duty, [and] emotional instability".

Mayerling's success in 1978 was in no small measure a result of an excellent cast. Merle Park received much praise for her portrayal of Countess Larisch, a woman who is both dangerously manipulative and yet capable of sympathy towards Rudolf, understanding him where others do not; and

Lynn Seymour was of course in her element as a tortured, reckless young lover who appears willing to sacrifice anything for her flawed idea of love, passion, and personal advancement. But more than anything else the ballet at its premiere depended on the outstanding dramatic presence of David Wall, who made this hugely demanding role his own. The sheer dancing and partnering alone called for enormous reserves of strength on the part of the lead male dancer, and in addition to this Wall demonstrated superb skills as an actor, showing Rudolf in all his numerous moods as a man at once depraved, selfish, desperate and, ultimately, lost.

Other notable interpreters of the leading male role have been Stephen Jefferies, Wayne Eagling, and most recently, Russian star Irek Mukhamedov, for whom MacMillan revived the ballet shortly before his own death in 1992. MacMillan was at least able, as Mary Clarke later wrote, to see that his ballet was in safe hands before he died: indeed, he collapsed literally on the opening night of *Mayerling*'s 1992 revival. The fact that his death occured backstage at the Royal Opera House, while the dancers were on stage in the final scenes of his ballet, was seen by many as an appropriate exit for the choreographer of human passion, the master of high drama.

—Elizabeth Hudson

MAYWOOD, Augusta

American dancer. Born Augusta Williams in New York, 1825. Studied with Paul Hazard, Philadelphia, from 1836; later studied with Joseph Mazilier and Jean Coralli in Paris, 1838, and with Carlo Blasis at La Scala, Milan, from 1848. Married (1) dancer Charles Mabille (eloped 1840): one daughter, b. 1842; (2) Carlo Gardini, 1858. Début as "La Petite Augusta" at Chestnut Street Theatre, Philadelphia, 1837; première danseuse, Paris Opéra Ballet, Paris, 1839–40, leaving Paris in 1840; leading dancer (with husband Mabille), Marseille, 1841, Lyon, 1843, and Lisbon, 1843–45; ballerina (alternating with Fanny Elssler), Kärntnertor Theater, Vienna, 1845–47; prima ballerina and prima mima assoluta, La Scala, Milan, 1848–49, returning 1853; ballerina, touring Italy with own small troupe, 1850–58, with performances in Trieste, 1850, 1851–52, 1854–55, Padova, 1851, Ferrara and Ravenna, 1852, Genoa, 1853, Ancona, 1853 and 1856, and Turin, 1855–56; returned to Vienna, c.1858; choreographer, staging numerous dances in Vienna; teacher at own ballet school, Vienna, until 1873; retired to Lake Como. Died in Lemberg, Austrian Galicia (now Lvov, Poland), 3 November 1876.

ROLES

1837   Zelica (cr; later called Zoloé) in *The Maid of Cashmere* (opera-ballet; after Taglioni's *Le Dieu et la Bayadère*), Chestnut Street Theatre, Philadelphia

1838   Title role (cr) in *The Dew Drop; or, La Sylphide* (after Taglioni's *La Sylphide*; staged R.C. Maywood), Chestnut Street Theatre, Philadelphia

1839   Pas de deux (cr) added to *Le Diable boîteux* (Coralli), Opéra, Paris
       Solo in *La Tarentule* (Coralli), Opéra, Paris
       Dancer in *Nina* (Milon), Opéra, Paris
       Pas de trois in *Le Diable amoureux* (Mazilier), Opéra, Paris

1843/ Title role in *Giselle* (Mabille after Coralli, Perrot), Teatro São Carlos, Lisbon
44   Leading role (cr) in *Rolando e Morgana* (Carey), Teatro São Carlos, Lisbon
       Dancer in *Mascaras de Venesa* (divertissement; Carey), Teatro São Carlos, Lisbon
       Dancer in *Novo Azor* (divertissement; Carey), Teatro São Carlos, Lisbon
       Dancer in *A Aldeia polaca* (divertissement; Carey), Teatro São Carlos, Lisbon
       Zoloé in *La Bayadère* (ballet from *La Dieu et la Bayadère*; Carey after Taglioni), Teatro São Carlos, Lisbon

1845   Pas de deux (cr; chor. Mabille) added to *Der Mädchenraub in Venedig* (Guerra), Kärntnertor Theater, Vienna
       Principal dancer (cr) in *Es ist ein Scherz* (Guerra), Kärntnertor Theater, Vienna
       Principal dancer (cr) in *Manfred* (Guerra), Kärntnertor Theater, Vienna

1846   Principal dancer (cr) in *Die Hochzeit des Bacchus* (Guerra), Kärntnertor Theater, Vienna
       Principal dancer (cr) in *Die Zauberlampe* (Bartholomin), Kärntnertor Theater, Vienna
       Principal dancer (cr) in *Elina; oder, Die Rückkehr ins Dorf* (Bartholomin), Kärntnertor Theater, Vienna
       Principal dancer (cr) in *Ein Ländliches Fest* (Bartholomin), Kärntnertor Theater, Vienna

1847   Title role in *Katharina; oder, Die Töchter des Banditen* (after Perrot), Kärntnertor Theater, Vienna

1848   Principal dancer in *L'Assedio di Calais* (after Henry), La Scala, Milan
       Marguerite in *Faust* (Perrot), La Scala, Milan
       Leading dancer in *La Silfide* (Cortesi; staged Ronzani), La Scala, Milan

1849   Principal dancer in *La Orfana della Suleide* (Ronzani), La Scala, Milan

1850/ Title role in *La Esmeralda* (after Perrot), Maywood company, Italian tour
54   Beatrix in *La Jolie Fille de Gand* (after Taglioni), Maywood company, Italian tour
       Title role in *La Vivandiera* (after Saint-Léon), Maywood company, Italian tour
       Leading role in *La Sposa di Appenzello* (Ronzani), Maywood company, Italian tour
       Leading role in *Erta, la Regina dell'Elfride*, Maywood company, Italian tour
       Leading role in *Zelia; o, Il Velo magico* (after Guerra), Maywood company, Italian tour
       Margherita in *Mefistofele* (Lasiná after Perrot's *Faust*), Maywood company, Italian tour
       Principal dancer in *Una Festa di ballo* (Lasiná), Maywood company, Italian tour
       Divertissement from *Rigoletto* (opera; mus. Verdi), Maywood company, Italian tour
       Principal dancer in *I Suliotti* (Morosini), Maywood company, Italian tour

1852   Genevrella in *La Zingara* (Lasina), Teatro Comunitativo, Florence

1853   Lea (cr) in *L'Araba* (Battista, Lasiná), La Scala, Milan
       Eva (cr) in *Il Capenna di Zio Tom* (*Uncle Tom's Cabin*; Rota), Maywood company, Milan

1854   Principal dancer in *Das Goldene Pferd* (Ronzani), Vienna

1854/ Principal dancer in *Evellina di Lesormes* (Schiano), Carnival, Trieste
55

1855   Pas de deux in *Il Trionfo dell'innocenza* (Rota), Teatro

Augusta Maywood in *Rita Gauthier*, 1856

Argentina, Rome
1856   Title role (cr) in *La Fiorentina; ovvero Ginevra degli Albizzi* (Termanini), Teatro Comunitativo, Bologna
Title role (cr) in *Rita Gauthier* (Termanini), Italian tour
1858   Elena Douglas in *La Donna del lago* (Termanini), Teatro Vittorio Emanuele, Turin

PUBLICATIONS

Gautier, Théophile, *The Romantic Ballet as Seen by Théophile Gautier*, translated by Cyril Beaumont, London, 1932

Winter, Marian Hannah, "Augusta Maywood", *Dance Index* (New York), January–February 1943; reprinted in Magriel, Paul (ed.), *Chronicles of the American Dance*, New York, 1948

Michel, A., "Great American Ballerina", *Dance Magazine* (New York), November–December 1943

Amberg, George, *Ballet in America*, New York, 1949

Moore, Lillian, "Some Early American Dancers", *Dancing Times* (London), August 1950

Todd, Arthur, "Four Centuries of American Dance", *Dance Magazine* (New York), September 1950

Stern, Madeleine, *We the Women*, New York, 1963

Guest, Ivor, *The Romantic Ballet in Paris*, London, 1966; revised edition, 1980

"Augusta Maywood", *Portraits of the American Stage 1771–1971*, Washington, D.C., 1971

Migel, Parmenia, *The Ballerinas*, New York, 1972

Fabian, Monroe H., *On Stage: 200 Years of Great Theatrical Personalities*, New York, 1980

Farrell, Rita Katz, "Star-Spangled Giselles", *Ballet News* (New York), September 1984

*   *   *

Although Augusta Maywood is primarily remembered today as America's own first international ballerina, her career in Europe was considerably more substantial than that in her homeland, and she was widely recognized as one of the leading dancers of the Romantic ballet in Europe.

A child prodigy, Maywood knew success early, when she made her dancing début in Philadelphia at the age of twelve. Her two years of study with Paul Hazard endowed her with strength, grace, and dramatic ability. Although she could undoubtedly have pursued a successful career touring America, it was decided she should continue her training in Paris, where her talent was refined in the Paris Opéra classes of Joseph Mazilier and Jean Coralli. Reviewing her Paris Opéra début, Gautier compared her to Taglioni, Cerrito, and Grahn, stating: ". . . she has a style of her own, a very remarkable cachet of originality . . .".

Maywood's combined gifts of technique and dramatic interpretation allowed her to portray many of the major roles then popular. She was especially successful in *Giselle*, *Faust*, and *La Esmeralda*. In Italy, where she spent the greater part of her career, she acquired the rarely bestowed title of "prima ballerina assoluta" and created many roles in the epic narrative ballets such as *Rita Gauthier* (based on *La Dame aux camélias*) and *Uncle Tom's Cabin*, an Italian ballet version of the newly published American novel.

Maywood was probably the first dancer to have her own, albeit small, touring company: because of her constant tours throughout Italy, she decided that, rather than leave things to chance, she would travel with her own ballet master, dancing partner, supporting dancers, props, and costumes. She also made most of the business arrangements herself, a skill she might have acquired from her stepfather, Robert Maywood,

manager of Philadelphia's Chestnut Street Theatre.

For at least ten years following her retirement from the stage at the age of 34, Augusta Maywood was settled in Vienna and opened a successful ballet school which offered, in addition to the dance classes, a programme including courses in acting, art history, mythology, world history, French, and Italian. Maywood not only taught but also choreographed.

As Elssler had left her mark on America, and Cerrito had devoted many of her best years to Her Majesty's Theatre in London, Augusta Maywood's career flourished in Italy and Vienna. Despite her stepfather's promises to the American public, she never returned to dance in her native land, a fact which did not endear her to the American press.

However, despite the rejection by the Americans, acceptance of Maywood by the Italian public was complete. She was widely acknowledged as one of the glories of Italian ballet and was frequently identified with the Italian theatre. America's loss was Europe's gain. Her contributions were numerous, the most obvious being her success as a performer. Not to be forgotten, however, were her innovative ideas regarding touring companies and the education of a dancer. Unlike many of her contemporaries, her career did not end with her retirement but continued in the field of dance education for many years thereafter.

—Carol Egan

––––––––

MAZILIER, Joseph

French dancer and choreographer. Born Giulio Mazarini in Marseilles, 13 March 1797. Début as dancer in Bordeaux; dancer, Théâtre de la Porte-Saint-Martin, Paris, from 1822; début, Paris Opéra, in *La Fille mal gardée*, 1830; premier danseur de caractère, from 1833; also leading dancer, Covent Garden, London, 1836–37; choreographer, staging first Opéra work in 1838; maître de ballet, Paris Opéra, 1839–51, Imperial Theatres, St. Petersburg, 1851–52; premier maître de ballet, Paris Opéra, 1853–60, coming out of retirement to revive *Le Corsaire*, 1867. Died in Paris, 19 May 1868.

ROLES

1822   Mazurka in *Prisonniers de guerre* (melodrama), Théâtre de la Porte-Saint-Martin, Paris
1825   Dancer (cr) in *Jocko* (Blache), Théâtre de la Porte-Saint-Martin, Paris
Dancer (cr) in *Lisbell* (Coralli), Théâtre de la Porte-Saint-Martin, Paris
Dancer (cr) in *Les Ruses espagnoles* (Coralli), Théâtre de la Porte-Saint-Martin, Paris
1826   Dancer (cr) in *Monsieur de Pourceaugnac* (Coralli), Théâtre de la Porte-Saint-Martin, Paris
Dancer in *Gulliver* (Coralli), Théâtre de la Porte-Saint-Martin, Paris
Dancer (cr) in *La Visite à Bedlam* (Coralli), Théâtre de la Porte-Saint-Martin, Paris
1827   Dancer (cr) in *Le Mariage de raison* (Coralli), Théâtre de la Porte-Saint-Martin, Paris
Dancer (cr) in *La Neige* (Coralli), Théâtre de la Porte-Saint-Martin, Paris
1828   Dancer (cr) in *Les Hussards et les jeunes filles* (Coralli), Théâtre de la Porte-Saint-Martin, Paris

Dancer (cr) in *Léocadie* (Coralli), Théâtre de la Porte-Saint-Martin, Paris

1829   Dancer (cr) in *Les Artistes* (Coralli), Théâtre de la Porte-Saint-Martin, Paris

1830   Leading role in *La Fille mal gardée* (Dauberval), Opéra, Paris

Leading role in *Manon Lescaut* (Aumer), Opéra, Paris

1831   Don Carlos (cr) in *L'Orgie* (Coralli), Opéra, Paris

1832   James (cr) in *La Sylphide* (Taglioni), Opéra, Paris

The Hermit in *La Tentation* (opera-ballet; mus. Halévy, Gide, chor. Coralli), Opéra, Paris

Oswald (cr) in *Nathalie; ou, La Laitière suisse* (Taglioni), Opéra, Paris

1833   Ismaël (cr) in *La Révolte au sérail* (Taglioni), Opéra, Paris

Dancer (cr) in *Gustave* (opera; mus. Auber, chor. Taglioni), Opéra, Paris

1834   Fernando (cr) in *La Tempête; ou, L'Île des génies* (Coralli), Opéra, Paris

1835   Divertissement (cr) in *La Juive* (opera; mus. Halévy, chor. F. Taglioni), Opéra, Paris

Zamore (cr) in *Brézilia; ou, La Tribu des femmes* (F. Taglioni), Opéra, Paris

Octavio (cr) in *L'Île des pirates* (Henry), Opéra, Paris

1836   Cléophas (cr) in *Le Diable boîteux* (Coralli), Opéra, Paris

Rudolf (cr) in *La Fille du Danube* (F. Taglioni), Opéra, Paris

Divertissement (cr) in *Les Huguenots* (opera; mus. Meyerbeer, chor. F. Taglioni), Opéra, Paris

1837   Major Arwed (cr) in *Les Mohicans* (Guerra), Opéra, Paris

Oug-lou (cr) in *La Chatte métamorphosée en femme* (Coralli), Opéra, Paris

1838   Fernand (cr) in *La Volière; ou, Les Oiseaux de Boccace* (Thérèse Elssler), Opéra, Paris

Divertissement (cr) in *Guido et Ginevra* (opera; mus. Halévy, chor. Mazilier), Opéra, Paris

1839   Luidgi (cr) in *La Tarentule* (Coralli), Opéra, Paris

Stenio (cr) in *La Gipsy* (also chor.), Opéra, Paris

1840   Count Frédéric (cr) in *Le Diable amoureux* (also chor.), Opéra, Paris

1842   Father to Beatrix (cr) in *La Jolie Fille de Gand* (Albert), Opéra, Paris

1845   Mazourki (cr) in *Le Diable à quatre* (also chor.), Opéra, Paris

1846   The Landlord (cr) in *Betty* (also chor.), Opéra, Paris

1848   Leading role (cr) in *Griseldis; ou, Les Cinq Sens* (also chor.), Opéra, Paris

1853   Diego (cr) in *Jovita; ou, Les Boucaniers* (also chor.), Opéra, Paris

WORKS

1838   Dances in *Guido et Ginevra* (opera; mus. Halévy), Opéra, Paris

1839   *La Gipsy* (mus. Benoist, Thomas, Marliani), Opéra, Paris

1840   *Le Diable amoureux* (mus. Benoist, Réber), Opéra, Paris

1841   Dances in *Le Freichütz* (Opéra; mus. Weber), Opéra, Paris

1843   Dances in *Charles VI* (opera; mus. Halévy), Opéra, Paris

1844   *Lady Henriette; ou, La Servante de Greenwich* (mus. Burgmüller, Deldevez), Opéra, Paris

Dances in *Othello* (opera; mus. Rossini), Opéra, Paris

1845   *Le Diable à quatre* (mus. Adam), Opéra, Paris

1846   *Paquita* (mus. Deldevez), Opéra, Paris

Betty (mus. Thomas), Opéra, Paris

Dances in *Robert Bruce* (opera; mus. Rossini, arranged by Niedermeyer), Opéra, Paris

1847   Dances in *Jérusalem* (opera; mus. Verdi), Opéra, Paris

1848   *Griseldis; ou, Les Cinq Sens* (mus. Adam), Opéra, Paris

1851   Dances in *Zerline; ou, La Corbeille d'oranges* (mus. Auber), Opéra, Paris

Vert-Vert (mus. Deldevez, Tolbeque), Opéra, Paris

1852   *Orfa* (mus. Adam), Opéra, Paris

1853   *Aelia et Mysis; ou, L'Atellane* (mus. Potier), Opéra, Paris

Jovita; ou, Les Boucaniers (mus. Labarre), Opéra, Paris

1855   *La Fonti* (mus. Labarre), Opéra, Paris

Dances in *Sainte-Claire* (opera; mus. Ernst, Duke of Saxe-Coburg-Gotha), Opéra, Paris

1856   *Le Corsaire* (mus. Adam), Opéra, Paris

Les Elfes (mus. Gabrielli), Opéra, Paris

1857   *Marco Spada; ou, La Fille du bandit* (mus. Auber), Opéra, Paris

1858   Dances in *La Magicienne* (opera; mus. Halévy), Opéra, Paris

1859   Dances in *Herculaneum* (opera; mus. David), Opéra, Paris

Dances in *Roméo et Juliette* (opera; mus. Bellini, Vaccaj), Opéra, Paris

PUBLICATIONS

Géréon, Léonard de, *La Rampe et les coulisses*, Paris, 1832

Castil-Blaze, *L'Académie impériale de musique*, Paris, 1855

Gautier, Théophile, *The Romantic Ballet as seen by Théophile Gautier*, translated by Cyril Beaumont, London, 1932

Lifar, Serge, *L'Histoire du ballet russe*, Paris, 1950

Beaumont, Cyril, *The Complete Book of Ballets*, revised edition, London, 1951

Guest, Ivor, *The Romantic Ballet in Paris*, London, 1966

Guest, Ivor, *The Ballet of the Second Empire*, revised edition, London, 1974

*   *   *

Born in Marseilles and originally named Giulio Mazarini, Mazilier began his early career at the Théâtre de la Porte-Saint-Martin in Paris, where he worked until he received an appointment as a dancer at the Paris Opéra. It was not a time to try to make your mark as a performer if you were a man; this was an era when the Romantic ballerinas were coming to dominate audience interest. Mazilier successfully created leading roles in ballets such as *L'Orgie*, *Nathalie*, *La Sylphide* (he was the original James), *L'Ile des pirates*, *Le Diable boîteux*, and *Griseldis*, but critics rarely gave him more than passing mention. Those critics who did pause in their praise of the reigning Romantic star ballerinas—Taglioni, Elssler, Grisi, and so on—commended the manner in which Mazilier joined the skills of a fine dramatic performer with those of a good dancer. *Le Journal de Paris* wrote of his James that "with an attractive talent as a dancer, he possesses an extremely mobile and dramatic face ... there is drama in his dance". Romantic critic Jules Janin wrote that he showed himself a strong mime in *La Fille du Danube*, although he claimed that the role would be better played by a *danseuse*. But all the same, Mazilier's greatest impact was as a ballet master.

Joseph Mazilier was the third ballet master to play a significant role at the Opéra during the heyday of the Romantic ballet. Filippo Taglioni had come and gone (leaving *La Sylphide* as his legacy) and Coralli had been producing ballets

Joseph Mazilier's *Le Diable amoureux*, **with Pauline Leroux and Georges Elie, Paris, 1840**

at the Opéra for eight years when Mazilier presented *La Gipsy* in 1839. With his emphasis on dramatic action, he immediately proved himself to be an excellent balance to the spectacle-orientated Coralli. *La Gipsy* was a ballet in the mould of Noverre's *ballet d'action*, achieving something that not even Noverre himself could; it was intelligible without the use of a scenario, even though it told a complicated story. And apparently, it was not only his arrangement of the silent acting, the *action*, that contributed to the representation of events and passions, but his ability "to put ideas into the legs of his dancers". That is, rather than simply presenting dances that diverted the spectator at the expense of the progress of the action, he integrated them into the story. He was thus able to take full advantage of the romantic dancer's mastery of the expanded ballet vocabulary.

La Gipsy set the tone of Mazilier's works. Their impact was achieved by a powerful dramatic action, backed up by dancing and *mise en scène* that gave the action expressive depth and brilliance. Hippolyte Prévost describes a scene from Mazilier's second Opéra work, *Le Diable amoureux*, underlining the breadth of feeling the choreographer could depict through dance. "But what is most extraordinary in this choreographic composition ... is the second act devil dance in which Phoebée, fascinated by the page, disturbed, quivering with passion, abandons for an instant her erring senses to the convulsion of a delirium, to pleasure, to satanic bewilderment: a scene truly astonishing, without equal in the theatre, in which the two *danseuses* are admirably displayed, ... astonishingly truthful!" This dance was performed by Lise Noblet, a good dancer, but not a star, so the choreography had to stand up on its own merits.

Mazilier's imagination embraced the comic as well as the tragic. *Le Diable à quatre* was, according to the romantic poet and critic Gérard de Nerval, "an opéra-comique less the words; dance replaces the songs with advantage . . .". In a work which was often revived, the devil undertakes to teach a haughty lady humility by putting her in the place of a humble peasant girl. Ultimately, Mazilier's ability to unify the balletic elements and to use them to translate a dramatic scenario into action was a substantial attribute.

Ballets such as *Orfa*, *La Fonti*, and *Le Corsaire* maintained the high standard set by Mazilier's earlier works. During the 1850s the Italian ballerina Carolina Rosati proved an able interpreter of Mazilier's intensely dramatic choreography, performing dances such as the mad tarentella in *La Fonti*, danced in the depths of despair during the gaiety of carnival. His last work was *Marco Spada*, though he continued for three more years as premier maître de ballet at the Opéra.

Mazilier's retirement must have been an uneasy one as he watched the decline of the brilliance that he had helped to create during the great days of the Romantic ballet. More and more ballets became vehicles for the display of grand effects and ballerinas' figures. His departure from the Opéra in 1860 marked the end of a thirty-year tradition of choreographic brilliance.

—John Chapman

MAZZO, Kay

American dancer and teacher.   Born in Evanston, Illinois, 17 January 1946. Early training in Evanston; studied with Bernardene Hayes and at School of American Ballet, New York, pupil of Anatole Obukhov, Antonina Tumkovsky, Muriel Stuart, from 1959. Apprentice, New York City Ballet, 1961; professional début with (Jerome Robbins's) Ballets: USA., European tour, 1961; dancer, corps de ballet, New York City Ballet, from 1963, becoming soloist, from 1965, and principal dancer, from 1969; occasional guest artist, including for Mobile Civic Ballet, Alabama, the Tallchief/Fernandez company at Jacob's Pillow, Massachusetts, and Dallas Civic Opera Guild; also appeared on television, including for telecast of Ballets: USA's London and Berlin performances, 1961, and in *Hollywood Palace* television programme, 1965; teacher, School of American Ballet, from 1983.

ROLES

1961	Principal dancer in *Afternoon of a Faun* (Robbins), Ballets: USA, Paris
	Principal dancer in *Interplay* (Robbins), Ballets: USA, European tour
1963	Dancer in *The Creation of the World* (Bolender), New York City Ballet, New York
1964	Pas de deux in *Interplay* (Robbins), New York City Ballet, New York
	Eighth Waltz and La Valse in *La Valse* (Balanchine), New York City Ballet, New York
1965	Girl (cr) in *Shadow'd Ground* (Taras), New York City Ballet, New York
	Principal dancer in *Liebeslieder Walzer* (Balanchine), New York City Ballet, New York
	Courante Sicilienne (cr) in *Don Quixote* (Balanchine), New York City Ballet, New York
1966	Principal dancer in *Summerspace* (Cunningham), New York City Ballet, New York
1967	Emelia (cr) in *Prologue* (d'Amboise), New York City Ballet, New York
	Concerto in *Episodes* II (Balanchine), New York City Ballet, New York
	Sixth Variation in *La Guirlande de Campra* (Taras), New York City Ballet, New York
1968	Principal dancer (cr) in *Haydn Concerto* (Taras), New York City Ballet, New York
	Principal dancer (cr) in *Stravinsky: Symphony in C* (Clifford), New York City Ballet, New York
1969	Title role in *Firebird* (Balanchine), New York City Ballet, New York
	Principal dancer (cr) in *Fantasies* (Clifford), New York City Ballet, New York
	Diamonds in *Jewels* (Balanchine), New York City Ballet, New York
	Principal dancer (cr) in *Dances at a Gathering* (Robbins), New York City Ballet, New York
1969/ 71	Titania in *A Midsummer Night's Dream* (Balanchine), New York City Ballet, New York
	Principal dancer in *Serenade* (Balanchine), New York City Ballet, New York
	Second Movement in *Symphony in C* (Balanchine), New York City Ballet, New York
	Terpsichore in *Apollo* (Balanchine), New York City Ballet, New York
	Dulcinea in *Don Quixote* (Balanchine), New York City Ballet, New York
	Sugar Plum Fairy in *The Nutcracker* (Balanchine), New York City Ballet, New York
	The Sleepwalker in *La Sonnambula* (Balanchine), New York City Ballet, New York
	Allegro in *Brahms-Schoenberg Quartet* (Balanchine), New York City Ballet, New York

Principal dancer in *Who Cares?* (Balanchine), New
York City Ballet, New York

Pas de deux in *Agon* (Balanchine), New York City
Ballet, New York

First Movement in *Haydn Concerto* (Taras), New York
City Ballet, New York

1970 Principal dancer (cr) in *In the Night* (Robbins), New
York City Ballet, New York

Valse Mélancholique (cr) in *Suite No. 3* (later *Tchaikovsky Suite No. 3*; Balanchine), New York City Ballet,
New York

1971 Principal dancer in *Donizetti Variations* (Balanchine),
New York City Ballet, New York

Odette in *Swan Lake* (one-act version; Balanchine after
Ivanov), New York City Ballet, New York

Principal dancer (cr) in *PAMTGG* (Balanchine), New
York City Ballet, New York

1972 Principal dancer in *Chopiniana* (Danilova after Fokine),
New York City Ballet, New York

Toccata, Aria II (cr) in *Violin Concerto* (later *Stravinsky
Violin Concerto*; Balanchine), New York City Ballet,
New York

Principal dancer (cr) in *Scherzo à la Russe* (Balanchine),
New York City Ballet, New York

Principal dancer (cr) in *Duo Concertant* (pas de deux;
Balanchine), New York City Ballet, New York

1975 Principal dancer (cr) in *Schéhérazade* (Balanchine),
New York City Ballet, New York

1976 Dress MacDonald, Royal Navy (cr) in *Union Jack*
(Balanchine), New York City Ballet, New York

Principal dancer in *Square Dance* (Balanchine), New
York City Ballet, New York

1977 Gold and Silver Waltz (cr) in *Vienna Waltzes* (Balanchine), New York City Ballet, New York

1979 Principal dancer (cr) in *Gli Uccelli* (Weiss), Caramoor
Music Festival

1980 Principal dancer, Fourth couple (cr) in *Robert Schumann's "Davidsbündlertänze"* (Balanchine), New
York City Ballet, New York

Other roles include: Eurydice in *Orpheus* (Balanchine), princi-
pal dancer in *Scotch Symphony* (Balanchine), principal dancer
in *Monumentum pro Gesualdo* (Balanchine), principal dancer in
Raymonda Variations (Balanchine), principal dancer in *Bugaku*
(Balanchine), principal dancer in *Movements for Piano and
Orchestra* (Balanchine), The Lady with Him in *Dim Lustre*
(Tudor), Echo Figure in *Narkissos* (Villella), Emeralds in *Jewels*
(Balanchine), Second Movement in *Tchaikovsky Suite No. 2*
(d'Amboise), principal dancer in *La Source* (Balanchine),
Tema con Variazioni in *Tchaikovsky Suite No. 3* (Balanchine).

PUBLICATIONS

By Mazzo:
Interview in Gruen, John, *The Private World of Ballet*, New
York, 1975
Interview in Tracy, Robert, *Balanchine's Ballerinas*, New York,
1983

About Mazzo:
Goodman, Saul, "Kay Mazzo", *Dance Magazine* (New York),
New York, July 1966
Warren, Virginia Lee, and Fatt, Amelia, "Impressions of Kay
Mazzo", *Dance Magazine* (New York), January 1970
Goodman, Saul, "Spotlight on Kay Mazzo", *Ballet Today*
(London), May–June 1970

Niehaus, Max, *Ballett Faszination*, Munich, 1972
Boggs, William, "Kay Mazzo", *Dance News* (New York),
January 1973
Croce, Arlene, *Afterimages*, New York, 1979

* * *

Kay Mazzo was one of many girls whose physicians suggested
they study ballet to improve their health. By age thirteen, she
had moved from her native Chicago to study at the School of
American Ballet in New York. However, she deviated from the
direct path to the New York City Ballet. At the age of sixteen,
with George Balanchine's blessing, she danced with Jerome
Robbins's Ballets: USA in Europe and New York before
joining the New York City Ballet in 1962. With Ballets: USA
she received acclaim for her performance of *Afternoon of a
Faun*.

Mazzo's early years in NYCB were dominated by the rise of
Suzanne Farrell. But Mazzo carved her own little niche,
mastering a varied and increasingly demanding repertoire
(including Balanchine's *La Valse*, *Episodes*, *Liebeslieder
Walzer*, and Cunningham's *Summerspace*). She was praised for
her authoritative carriage and brisk, clean footwork. She
continued to perform in the Robbins repertoire, her lyrical gifts
used beautifully in the fluid romanticism of his *Dances at a
Gathering* and *In the Night*.

Mazzo's physique is comparable to Farrell's: she is tall (5'6"),
thin, and long-legged, with a small head and short torso. She
has dark hair and eyes. But her stage personality was quite
distinct from that of Farrell. There was a quiet reserve and a
great dignity to her dancing. She performed allegro smartly, but
also approached adagio with fine musicality, showing a strong,
defined line and generous warmth. She angled her head with a
particular nuance that gave her a look of both awareness and
vulnerability. When Farrell left NYCB in 1969, Mazzo
gracefully took on roles such as Titania in *A Midsummer Night's
Dream* and the Diamonds pas de deux in *Jewels*. She never
attempted to imitate Farrell but made each role her own. She
did not move with the same expansiveness or daring that
Farrell did, but she had a steely delicacy and discreet femininity
that revealed different aspects of the choreography.

When Alexandra Danilova set the controversial "no sets, no
costumes" *Chopiniana* (*Les Sylphides*) on the company in 1972,
Mazzo and Peter Martins alone received positive praise for
their understanding and performance of Fokine's choreography. Danilova had spoken of Mazzo as "a very mysterious
and most beautiful creature", saying, "she has a wonderful
ethereal quality". For the NYCB's Stravinsky Festival in 1972,
Balanchine created two particularly outstanding roles for
Mazzo. In both *Violin Concerto* and *Duo Concertant*, partnered
by Martins, Mazzo was able to expand on the most tender,
lyrical side of her dancing without forsaking her ease in quick,
quirky pointe work. The latter work, a pas de deux in which the
pianist and violinist share the stage with the dancers, was one
of Balanchine's more passionate, certainly most explicit,
examples of the depiction of the male dancer's worship of the
ballerina. For many viewers, the ballet became a metaphor for
Balanchine's adoration of his ballerinas, of ballet itself.
Particularly poignant was the use of spotlights to isolate
Mazzo's face and hands at the ballet's end. In *Violin Concerto*
Mazzo responded to the gentle touch of Martins' partnering
with a generous plasticity. They created a believable relationship on stage.

When Farrell returned to the company, she assumed her
position at head of the class. But Mazzo's place was secure and
she continued to dance major roles in revivals and new ballets.
In the revival of *Square Dance*, Mazzo unleashed the full power

Kay Mazzo with Arthur Mitchell in *Afternoon of A Faun*, New York City Ballet, early 1960s

of her fast footwork. Her range was very much in evidence. In the Gold and Silver Waltz of *Vienna Waltzes*, Balanchine gave Mazzo a very different kind of role. In a gorgeous black gown, a dramatically oversized black hat and a feather boa, she was a decidedly glamorous "Merry Widow". Her waltz with Martins was tinged throughout with a refined sexual tension. They pulled away, even as they were drawn together. In the final pose, their silhouettes implied the moment before an embrace.

Mazzo retired when she was still in top form. She was one of those supreme artists whose devotion to her work and consistency on stage made her a favorite of critics and audiences. She is currently on the faculty of the School of American Ballet.

—Rose Anne Thom

———

McBRIDE, Patricia

American dancer.   Born in Teaneck, New Jersey, 23 August 1942. Studied with Ruth A. Vernon, Teaneck, at the Sonia Doubrovinskaya School, New York, and at the School of American Ballet, New York, pupil of Anatole Obukhov, Pierre Vladimirov, Antonia Tumkovsky, Muriel Stuart, Felia Doubrovska. Married New York City Ballet dancer Jean-Pierre Bonnefous, 1973. Début with Eglevsky Ballet Company, 1958; dancer, corps de ballet, New York City Ballet, from 1959,

becoming soloist, from 1960, and principal dancer, from 1961; retired from the stage in 1989. Recipient: *Dance Magazine* Award, 1980.

ROLES

1960   Duchess of L'an L'ing (cr) in *The Figure in the Carpet* (Balanchine), New York City Ballet, New York
          Eve (cr) in *Creation of the World* (Bolender), New York City Ballet, New York
          Principal dancer (cr) in *Ebony Concerto* (Taras), New York City Ballet, New York
1962   Hermia (cr) in *A Midsummer Night's Dream* (Balanchine), New York City Ballet, New York
1963   Principal dancer (cr) in *Fantasy* (Taras), New York City Ballet, New York
1964   Principal dancer (cr) in *Tarantella* (pas de deux; Balanchine), New York City Ballet, New York
          The Lady with Him in *Dim Lustre* (Tudor), New York City Ballet, New York
1965   Columbine (cr) in *Harlequinade* (Balanchine), New York City Ballet, New York
          Ritornel (cr) in *Don Quixote* (Balanchine), New York City Ballet, New York
1966   Intermezzo (cr) in *Brahms–Schoenberg Quartet* (Balanchine), New York City Ballet, New York
          Echo Figure (cr) in *Narkissos* (Villella), New York City Ballet, New York

Patricia McBride with Edward Villella in *Dances at a Gathering*, New York City Ballet, 1969

1967 Rubies (cr) in *Jewels* (Balanchine), New York City Ballet, New York

Divertimento Brillante (cr) in *Glinkiana* (later *Valse Fantaisie*; Balanchine), New York City Ballet, New York

1968 Principal dancer (cr) in *Haydn Concerto* (Taras), New York City Ballet, New York

1969 Principal dancer (cr) in *Dances at a Gathering* (Robbins), New York City Ballet, New York

1970 Principal dancer (cr) in *In the Night* (Robbins), New York City Ballet, New York

"The Man I Love", "Fascinatin' Rhythm", "Clap yo' Hands" (cr) in *Who Cares?* (Balanchine), New York City Ballet, New York

1971 Variations II (cr) in *The Goldberg Variations* (Robbins), New York City Ballet, New York

1972 Principal dancer (cr) in *Divertimento from "Le Baiser de la Fée"* (Balanchine), New York City Ballet, New York

Principal dancer (cr) in *Scènes de Ballet* (Taras), New York City Ballet, New York

1973 Principal dancer (cr) in *Concerto No. 2* (new production of *Ballet Imperial*; Balanchine), New York City Ballet, New York

Principal dancer (cr) in *An Evening's Waltzes* (Robbins), New York City Ballet, New York

1974 Young Woman (cr) in *Dybbuk* (later *The Dubbuk Variations*; Robbins), New York City Ballet, New York

Swanilda (cr) in *Coppélia* (new production; Balanchine, Danilova after Petipa), New York City Ballet, Saratoga Springs, New York

1975 Principal dancer (cr) in *Introduction and Allegro for Harp* (Robbins), New York City Ballet, New York

Principal dancer (cr) in *Pavane* (solo; Balanchine), New York City Ballet, New York

Principal dancer (cr) in *Chansons Madécasses* (Robbins), New York City Ballet, New York

Principal dancer (cr) in *The Steadfast Tin Soldier* (Balanchine), New York City Ballet, Saratoga Springs, New York

1976 Pearly Queen (cr) in *Union Jack* (Balanchine), New York City Ballet, New York

1977 Aurora (cr) in *The Sleeping Beauty* (new production; Eglevsky after Petipa; Aurora's solo chor. Balanchine), Eglevsky Ballet, Hempstead, New York

Principal dancer (cr) in *Étude for Piano* (pas de deux; Balanchine), Spoleto Festival USA, Charleston, South Carolina

Voices of Spring (cr) in *Vienna Waltzes* (Balanchine), New York City Ballet, New York

1979 Lucille (cr) in *Le Bourgeois Gentilhomme* (Balanchine, with Robbins), New York City Opera, New York

1988 Principal dancer (cr) in *Tea-Rose* (Martins), New York City Ballet, New York

Other roles include: principal dancer in *Allegro Brillante* (Balanchine), First and Third Movements in *Symphony in C* (Balanchine), principal dancer in *Concerto Barocco* (Balanchine), Eighth Waltz and La Valse in *La Valse* (Balanchine), The Novice in *The Cage* (Robbins), principal dancer in *Scotch Symphony* (Balanchine), principal dancer in *Interplay* (Robbins), principal dancer in *Afternoon of a Faun* (Robbins), pas de deux in *Agon* (Balanchine), First and Fourth Campaign in *Stars and Stripes* (Balanchine), Five Pieces and Concerto in *Episodes II* (Balanchine), Sleepwalker in *La Sonnambula* (Balanchine), principal dancer in *Liebeslieder Walzer* (Balanchine), principal dancer in *Raymonda Variations* (Balanchine), principal dancer in *Sonatine* (Balanchine), Titania and Divertissement in *A Midsummer Night's Dream* (Balanchine), principal dancer in *Bugaku* (Balanchine), Queen of the Morphides in *Piège de Lumière* (Taras), principal dancer in *Trois Valses Romantiques* (Balanchine), ballerina in *(Tchaikovsky) Pas de Deux* (Balanchine), Tema con Variazioni in *Tchaikovsky Suite No. 3* (Balanchine).

PUBLICATIONS

By McBride:

Interview in Gruen, John, *The Private World of Ballet*, New York, 1975

Interview in Lyle, Cynthia, *Dancers on Dancing*, New York, 1977

Interview in Tracy, Robert, *Balanchine's Ballerinas*, New York, 1983

On McBride:

Goodman, Saul, "Brief Biographies: Patricia McBride", *Dance Magazine* (New York), February 1962

Bivona, Elena, "McBride", *Ballet Review* (Brooklyn, N.Y.), vol. 3, no. 3, 1970

Wentink, Andrew Mark, and Swope, Martha (photographer), *Patricia McBride*, Brooklyn, N.Y., 1975

Shaw, Alan, "McBride's Year", *Ballet Review* (Brooklyn, N.Y.), vol. 5, no. 1, 1975–76

Reynolds, Nancy, *Repertory in Review*, New York, 1977

Croce, Arlene, *Afterimages*, New York, 1977

Murphy, A., "The McBride Magic", *Ballet News* (New York), February 1981

Switzer, Ellen, *Dancers! Horizons in American Dance*, New York, 1982

Croce, Arlene, *Going to the Dance*, New York, 1982

Kaplan, Larry, "Dancing Balanchine's Legacy", *Ballet Review* (New York), Winter 1985

"Celebrating Patricia McBride", *Ballet Review* (New York), Spring 1989

* * *

Patricia McBride, one of the most beloved dancers in the history of the New York City Ballet, retired from performing in 1989. A star for three decades, McBride never quite fit the conventional image of a Balanchine ballerina. Equally adept at adagio and allegro, she danced the purest ballerina roles in the City Ballet repertory as well as those with a touch of the soubrette to them. One of her crowning achievements was *Coppélia*, which Balanchine co-staged for her with Alexandra Danilova; in it, McBride depicted Swanilda's hoydenish personality and resourcefulness as well as her innate classical elegance. Yet McBride was also possessed of a smouldering romantic presence that captivated audiences in *Brahms–Schoenberg Quartet* and *Who Cares?*, two other roles Balanchine choreographed for her. Her dazzling smile, glamorous presence, intense musicality, and huge eyes, which she utilized as an inherent part of adagio technique, all contributed to her allure.

Small and elegantly proportioned, McBride had a classical style which could be termed unorthodox, but she sailed through some of Balanchine's purest and most fiendishly difficult classical ballets (such as *Concerto No. 2*, *Allegro Brillante*, *Tchaikovsky Pas de Deux*, and the *Theme and Variations* section of *Tchaikovsky Suite No. 3*) to great acclaim. Never particularly associated with Balanchine's purest neo-classical style, she triumphed in *Rubies* and *Divertimento from "Le Baiser de la Fée"*. In some ways, McBride's great roles constituted her own private realm within the New York City Ballet repertory.

Some of the characteristic parts Balanchine made for McBride date from her great partnership in the 1960s with Edward Villella. In such works as *Tarantella* and *Harlequinade*, Balanchine made dances that gave this ballerina the opportunity to exhibit the ebullient, good-natured, teasing side of her personality. The choreography for *Tarantella* stressed speed and intricate combinations which McBride almost threw away with witty off-hand aplomb. In the role of Columbine in *Harlequinade*, Balanchine's recension of Petipa's *Les Millions d'Harlequin*, McBride created an adorable, entirely unforgettable character who was called upon to dance the strictest and most utterly refined classical choreography.

In the Rubies, section of *Jewels*, set to Stravinsky's *Capriccio for Piano and Orchestra*, Balanchine accompanied images of saucy Broadway showgirls with neo-classical dancing of breathtaking complexity, and came up with a fresh and wholly original role that seemed tailor-made for McBride. In *Who Cares?*, choreographed to a suite of George Gershwin songs, Balanchine further refined and somewhat softened this image of her into its most profoundly romantic and lustrous proportions. McBride's dancing in the pas de deux "The Man I Love" from this ballet produced a state of near rapture in her audience. Her dancing in the Intermezzo in *Brahms–Schoenberg Quartet* as well as in her pas de deux in the second section of *Liebesleider Walzer* induced a similar state of ecstasy. McBride's performances in these ballets summoned up for us the precarious nature of romantic love, and she seemed to represent to Balanchine not the unattainable ideal that he saw in some of his muses, but rather the human passion of youthful womanhood, the fulfillment that is possible on earth, if only temporarily. It was also this persona that Jerome Robbins tapped in his created roles for her in *Dances at a Gathering* and *Goldberg Variations*.

Throughout McBride's career, Balanchine presented the saucy, resilient dancer in such works as *The Steadfast Tin*

Soldier, the Costermonger pas de deux in *Union Jack*, and in the Voices of Spring in *Vienna Waltzes*. Yet alongside these roles, she left her mark on a full range of radiant Balanchine heroines in *Scotch Symphony*, *Raymonda Variations*, *La Valse*, *La Sonnambula*, *Donizetti Variations*, and *Cortège Hongrois*, to name just a few.

McBride could work on a large scale, and in *Scotch Symphony* she personified the historical image of the sylph that has come down to us from romantic ballet. But taking her cue from the formal elements in Balanchine's choreography and in Mendelssohn's music, which transcend the ballet's source material, she also breathed life into her character with full-bodied, highly articulated dancing that invited us to experience both aspects of a ballerina, the otherwordly and the flesh-and-blood. In *Sonatine*, a stylish, somewhat muted Balanchine pas de deux to Ravel, McBride scored her effects with just a partner and a pianist on the stage.

Lincoln Kirstein paid tribute to Patricia McBride as an artist who "has never failed to use steps as sparks that have kept [New York City Ballet] bright; there are times when she could be properly thanked for having kept our entire ensemble in focus".

Arlene Croce took up this cry, writing that the role of Swanilda in *Coppélia* was "a remarkable triumph for an artist whom the world knows as the flag-bearer of the New York City Ballet, the embodiment of its egoless-star ethic . . . The role comes as a climax to the present and most exciting phase of her career. The scale on which she has been dancing this year [1974] is a new development in her style, and to reach it she hasn't sacrificed any of her speed or sharp-edged rhythm or subtlety of intonation. And although the role of Swanilda gives her plenty of unaccustomed material (such as extended pantomime), she sweeps through it without ever once looking like anyone but herself. She persuades us Swanilda is Patricia McBride and always has been . . . she is a great dancer and a great star."

—Larry Kaplan

McDONALD, Elaine

British dancer. Born in Tadcaster, England, 2 May 1943. Studied with Olivia Morley, Louise Brown (on Royal Academy of Dancing scholarship), from 1954, and at the Royal Ballet School, London, from 1959. Dancer, Walter Gore's London Ballet, 1962–64; dancer, becoming principal dancer, Western Theatre Ballet (later Scottish Ballet), from 1964; principal dancer, New London Ballet (founders Galina Samsova and André Prokovsky), 1974, returning to Scottish Ballet, 1974/75; also international guest artist, including in Europe, United States, Canada, Mexico, Brazil, and Hong Kong; artistic controller, Scottish Ballet, 1988–89; associate artistic director, Northern Ballet Theatre, from 1991. Recipient: Order of the British Empire, 1983.

ROLES

1966   The Wife (cr) in *Sun into Darkness* (Darrell), Western Theatre Ballet, London
1967   The Pianist in *The Lesson* (Flindt), Western Theatre Ballet, London
         Chiarina in *Carnaval* (Fokine), Western Theatre Ballet, London

1968   Principal dancer (cr) in *Ephemeron* (Darrell), Western Theatre Ballet, London
1969   Andromache in *The Trojans* (opera; mus. Berlioz, chor. Meyer), Scottish Opera and Scottish Theatre Ballet, Glasgow
         Principal dancer (cr) in *Breakaway* (Lynne), Scottish Theatre Ballet, Glasgow
         A Sister (cr) in *Beauty and the Beast* (Darrell), Scottish Theatre Ballet, London
         Principal dancer (cr) in *Frontier* (Neumeier), Scottish Theatre Ballet, London
         The Señorita in *La Ventana* (Bournonville; staged Brenaa), Scottish Theatre Ballet, Perth
1970   Title role (cr) in *Herodias* (Darrell), Scottish Theatre Ballet, London
         Principal dancer (cr) in *Points of Contact* (Roope), Scottish Theatre Ballet, London
         Principal dancer in *Dances from William Tell* (Bournonville; staged Brenaa), Scottish Theatre Ballet, London
1971   Title role in *Giselle* (Petipa after Coralli, Perrot; staged Darrell, assisted Graeme), Scottish Theatre Ballet, Aberdeen
         The Chatelaine in *La Fête étrange* (Howard), Scottish Theatre Ballet, Glasgow
1972   Giulietta (cr) in *Tales of Hoffmann* (Darrell), Scottish Theatre Ballet, Edinburgh
         Principal dancer (cr) in *Some Bright Star* (Cazalet), Scottish Theatre Ballet, Glasgow
         The Older Woman in *Sonate à trois* (Béjart), Western Theatre Ballet
1973   Principal dancer (cr) in *Ways of Saying Bye-Bye* (van Schayk), Scottish Theatre Ballet, Glasgow
         The Woman (cr) in *Intimate Voices* (Moreland), New London Ballet, London
         Arabian Dance in *The Nutcracker* (Darrell), Scottish Ballet, Edinburgh
         Sugar Plum Fairy in *The Nutcracker* (Darrell), Scottish Ballet, Edinburgh
1974   Title role in *La Sylphide* (Bournonville; staged Brenaa), Scottish Ballet
1975   Principal dancer in *The Scarlet Pastorale* (Darrell), Scottish Ballet, Edinburgh
         Title role in *Paquita* (Petipa; staged Casenave), Scottish Ballet
1976   Title role (cr) in *Mary Queen of Scots* (Darrell), Scottish Ballet, Glasgow
         Desdemona in *Othello* (Darrell), Scottish Ballet, Ballet for Scotland tour
1977   Odette/Odile in *Swan Lake* (Darrell after Petipa, Ivanov), Scottish Ballet, Edinburgh
         Waltz, Mazurka in *Les Sylphides* (Fokine), Scottish Ballet, Glasgow
1978   Teresina in *Napoli* (Bournonville; staged Gnatt), Scottish Ballet, Edinburgh
         The Woman (cr) in *Five Rückert Songs* (Darrell), Scottish Ballet, Ballet for Scotland tour, Falkirk
1979   Title role (cr) in *Cinderella* (Darrell), Scottish Ballet, Aberdeen
         Lady Macbeth/Rita Hayworth (cr) in *Such Sweet Thunder* (Darrell), Scottish Ballet, Glasgow
1980   Lea in *Chéri* (Darrell), Scottish Ballet
1982   Juliet in *Romeo and Juliet* (Cranko), Scottish Ballet, Glasgow
1990   The Mother in *A Simple Man* (Lynne), Northern Ballet Theatre

Other roles include: for Western Theatre Ballet—Madeleine in

The Prisoners (Darrell), principal dancer in *Street Games* (Gore), the Girl in *The Web* (Meyer), Leading Mod in *Mods and Rockers* (Darrell), principal dancer in *Jeux* (Darrell); for Scottish Ballet—Youngest Sister in *Las Hermanas* (MacMillan), principal dancer in *The Water's Edge* (North), principal dancer in *Vespri* (divertissement; Prokovsky), principal dancer in *Belong* (pas de deux from *What to Do Until the Messiah Comes*; Vesak), leading role in *Francesca da Rimini* (Hulbert).

PUBLICATIONS

Scales, Roger, "Young Dancers 7: Elaine McDonald", *Dancing Times* (London), August 1967

Goodwin, Noël, *A Ballet for Scotland*, Edinburgh, 1979

Dixon, John S. (ed.), *Elaine McDonald*, Leeds, 1982

Goodwin, Noël, "Involved in the Whole", *Dance and Dancers* (London), March 1982

Oliver, Cordelia, "Elaine McDonald O.B.E.", *Dancing Times* (London), March 1983

Bowen, Christopher, "Company at a Crossroads", *Dance and Dancers* (London), January 1990

* * *

Elaine McDonald has established a reputation as one of the leading dramatic ballerinas of recent times, in close association with choreographer Peter Darrell, who created many of the principal female roles in his ballets for her. McDonald began her career under Darrell first as a leading dancer for pioneering Western Theatre Ballet and later as the prima ballerina for the Scottish Ballet (formerly Scottish Theatre Ballet), when the company changed its identity and moved north to become Scotland's national company in 1969.

The course of McDonald's career has been greatly influenced by her determination to remain within these companies, and by her close association with Darrell's work. To some extent, her reputation with a wider public has been constrained by having a base away from London and by the company's own difficulties (in recent years largely as a result of arts council policy) in mounting seasons of its work in larger capitals. It is in this context that Elaine McDonald has frequently been described as a world-class ballerina without a world audience.

McDonald's early career as a student at the Royal Ballet School was not marked by any of the promise which she rapidly showed after joining Darrell's Western Theatre ballet in 1964. At first principally a demi-caractère actress, she rapidly demonstrated an extraordinary and charismatic theatrical flair which deepened into the characteristic dramatic and psychological sensitivity which has since become her trademark.

The ballets Darrell was stimulated to created around McDonald's talents, especially in his earlier one-act narrative works, have frequently turned on the process and effects of sexual and psychological pressure—and in responding to these requirements McDonald has shown a great capacity for subtle and minutely shaded dramatic portrayals, in which the fleeting and ambiguous emotional responses of the characters are registered with great refinement. Her particularly fluid arm movements endow her dancing with extraordinary subtlety, and facilitate her capacity for conveying both pathos and tragedy to great effect. This is especially evident in two of her greatest roles, Lea in *Chéri*, and the Woman in *Five Rückert Songs*.

She has none the less developed a technical skill to command the major roles in the repertoire's great classical ballets, and has won respect for her *Giselle*, and for her Odette/Odile in Darrell's version of *Swan Lake*. The psychological complexity of the latter, in fact, frequently requires the ballerina to make clear to the audience which facet of the dual role she represents at any given moment to the ballet's other principal characters— even though she is involved in situations in which she is perceived differently by various characters present on stage at once. McDonald rose to this challenge, giving a powerful performance.

Though McDonald's characters are clearly drawn, they retain a capacity for suggesting unspoken depths within. Her performances create an impression that submerges technique, while concentrating on the finely shaded emotional world of adults as it might be experienced in straight theatre or the cinema, and distilling everyday human experiences into dance.

—Geoffrey Baskerville

McKENZIE, Kevin

American dancer, choreographer, and ballet director. Born in Burlington, Vermont, 29 April 1954. Studied at the Washington School of Ballet, pupil of Mary Day, 1967–72; also studied with Maggie Black, New York. Dancer, National Ballet of Washington, 1972–74; soloist, City Center Joffrey Ballet (now the Joffrey Ballet), 1974–78; guest artist, American Ballet Theatre, from March 1979, becoming principal dancer, 1979–1991; international guest artist, including for London Festival Ballet, Universal Ballet in Seoul, Ballet Nacional de Cuba, and Bolshoi Ballet, Moscow; also performed with Nureyev and Friends, 1988; permanent guest artist, Washington Ballet, from 1989, acting as artistic associate, 1990–91; also choreographer and associate artistic director, New Amsterdam Ballet, from 1984; artistic director, American Ballet Theatre, from 1992. Recipient: Silver medal, International Ballet Competition, Varna, Bulgaria, 1972.

ROLES

1974   Principal dancer (Trois Gymnopédies) in *Monotones* (Ashton), City Center Joffrey Ballet, New York

1976   Oberon in *The Dream* (Ashton), City Center Joffrey Ballet, New York

      Principal dancer in *Tchaikovsky Pas de deux* (Balanchine), Joffrey Ballet, New York

1977   Romeo in *Romeo and Juliet* (Araiz), City Center Joffrey Ballet, New York

1979   Principal dancer (lead couple) in *Theme and Variations* (Balanchine), American Ballet Theatre, Washington, D.C.

      Principal dancer in *Pas de deux Holberg* (Cranko), American Ballet Theatre, Chicago

1980   Principal dancer in *Les Sylphides* (Fokine), American Ballet Theatre, Washington, D.C.

      Her Lover in *Jardin aux lilas* (Tudor), American Ballet Theatre, Minneapolis

      Prince Siegfried in *Swan Lake* (Blair after Petipa, Ivanov), American Ballet Theatre, Minneapolis

      Champion Roper in *Rodeo* (de Mille), American Ballet Theatre

      Solor in *La Bayadère* ("Kingdom of the Shades"; Makarova after Petipa), American Ballet Theatre, Minneapolis

      Principal dancer in *Concert Waltzes* (Levans), American Ballet Theatre, New York

Solor in *La Bayadère* (full-length ballet; Makarova after
  Petipa), American Ballet Theatre, New York
Albrecht in *Giselle* (Petipa after Coralli, Perrot; staged
  Blair), American Ballet Theatre, New York
Second Song in *Dark Elegies* (Tudor), American Ballet
  Theatre
Principal dancer in *The Leaves are Fading* (Tudor),
  American Ballet Theatre
1981 Principal dancer in *Configurations* (Choo San Goh),
  American Ballet Theatre, Washington, D.C.
Young Man (cr) in *Wild Boy* (MacMillan), American
  Ballet Theatre, Washington, D.C.
Basil in *Don Quixote* (*Kitri's Wedding*) (Baryshnikov
  after Petipa), American Ballet Theatre
The Friend in *The Moor's Pavane* (Limón), American
  Ballet Theatre
Principal dancer in *Études* (Lander), American Ballet
  Theatre
1982 Principal dancer in *Torso* (pas de deux; Kylián),
  American Ballet Theatre, San Francisco
1983 James in *La Sylphide* (Lander after Bournonville),
  American Ballet Theatre
1984 The Prince in *Cinderella* (Baryshnikov, Anastos),
  American Ballet Theatre, Washington, D.C.
Amnon (cr) in *Amnon V'Tamar* (van Hamel), American
  Ballet Theatre, Miami
Principal dancer in *Other Dances* (pas de deux;
  Robbins), American Ballet Theatre, Chicago
Principal dancer in *Paquita* Grand Pas (Makarova after
  Petipa), American Ballet Theatre, Miami
Principal dancer in *Nine Sinatra Songs* (Tharp), Ameri-
  can Ballet Theatre
1985 Romeo in *Romeo and Juliet* (MacMillan), American
  Ballet Theatre, Washington, D.C.
Mercutio in *Romeo and Juliet* (MacMillan), American
  Ballet Theatre, Los Angeles
1987 Don José in *Carmen* (Petit), American Ballet Theatre,
  Washington, D.C.
The Gentleman with Her in *Dim Lustre* (Tudor),
  American Ballet Theatre, New York
Prince Désiré in *The Sleeping Beauty* (MacMillan after
  Petipa), American Ballet Theatre, Chicago
1988 Principal dancer in *The Garden of Villandry* (Clarke),
  American Ballet Theatre, New York
Principal dancer (cr) in *S.P.E.B.S.O.S.A.* (Tippet),
  American Ballet Theatre, New York
Principal dancer in *Song of a Wayfarer* (Béjart),
  Nureyev and Friends, tour
Principal dancer in *Two Brothers* (Parsons), Nureyev
  and Friends, tour

Other roles include: for Joffrey Ballet—principal dancer in
Interplay (Robbins); for American Ballet Theatre—The Friend
in *Pillar of Fire* (Tudor), Franz in *Coppélia* (Martinez after
Saint-Léon), principal dancer in *Sylvia Pas de deux*
(Balanchine).

WORKS

1984 *Groupo Zamboria* (mus. Milhaud), New Amsterdam
  Ballet, Santa Fe, California
1991 *Liszt Études* (mus. Liszt), New Amsterdam Ballet,
  Jacob's Pillow Dance Festival, Lee, Massachusetts
1992 *Lucy and the Court* (mus. Deak), Washington Ballet,
  Baltimore

PUBLICATIONS

Sinclair, Janet, and Gregory, John, "Two Views of Varna",
  Dancing Times (London), September 1972
Goldner, Nancy, "American Ballet Theatre, Metropolitan
  Opera House", *Dance News* (New York), June 1979
Croce, Arlene, *Going to the Dance*, New York, 1982
Croce, Arlene, *Sight Lines*, New York, 1987
Vaughan, David, "Dance on Camera", *Ballet Review* (New
  York), Summer 1988
Leivick, Laura, "McKenzie's Turn", *The New York Times
  Magazine* (New York), 27 December 1992

*   *   *

Even when still a very young dancer, Kevin McKenzie was
obviously a rare find, a male dancer of clean and natural
technique who was also handsome and *tall*. He was cut out for a
career dancing princely classical roles in the best "danseur
noble" tradition, and by the age of eighteen his promise was
assured when he won the silver medal at the International
Ballet Competition in Varna. By twenty, he was poised to
conquer the professional ballet world of New York, having had
two years of the best possible apprenticeship dancing with
Mary Day's National Ballet in Washington, D.C.

But McKenzie's potential fame, like that of several other
male dancers of his generation, was eclipsed by the sensational
arrival in the West of Mikhail Baryshnikov, the great Kirov
dancer who was to become McKenzie's boss and rival at
American Ballet Theatre. Indeed, as McKenzie later claimed,
it was his misfortune to turn up for audition at American Ballet
Theatre on the very day that the newly defected Baryshnikov
did. It is no wonder that he occasionally felt in the shadow.

Baryshnikov's impact on the American dance scene cannot
be underestimated, and his galvanizing effect on male dance in
particular is something that any American man pursuing a
career in ballet today can thank him for. But in retrospect one
can see the disadvantages, less obvious at the time, for those
homegrown talents whose careers Baryshnikov overshadowed.
McKenzie might not have been pushed into the arrogant
posturing, say, of another highly talented contemporary,
Fernando Bujones (who declared publicly that Baryshnikov
had the attention but he himself had the talent)—but
McKenzie's career ambitions were undoubtedly frustrated
during the height of Baryshnikovomania in the 1970s and
1980s. It is a supreme irony, therefore, that after Baryshnikov's
troubled departure from American Ballet Theatre in 1990, it
should be Kevin McKenzie succeeding him at the helm.

It must be remembered that McKenzie's career as a dancer
was far from uneventful itself, however. His four years with
Robert Joffrey's City Center company in New York (his first
professional engagement) won him much critical praise; in his
first year with the company, the doyenne of New York dance
criticism, Arlene Croce, was declaring him a "highly promising
newcomer"—and his successive years with the Joffrey showed
him more than living up to such promise. McKenzie's
repertoire after four years with this eclectic company was
considerable, and his talent and professionalism as a classical
dancer were such that he was invited by Lucia Chase to guest
with American Ballet Theatre in 1979. Soon afterwards
McKenzie was offered a permanent contract with the
company, becoming principal dancer in 1980, and remaining a
leading presence there until his unofficial retirement in 1989.

One of the factors in McKenzie's invitation to guest with
Ballet Theatre was ballerina Martine van Hamel, whose height
had always kept her on the lookout for suitable tall partners.
Van Hamel, as she later jokingly claimed, "ordered him up",

and her selection proved a good one. As a dancing partnership the two made a striking picture—tall, elegant, and perfectly balanced, they formed the very image of classical excellence; and in the full-length masterpieces of the Petipa canon in particular they were the ideal match. McKenzie performed with numerous other leading ballerinas, including with fellow American Cynthia Harvey, creating what one critic called a "most musical and romantic" partnership in *Cinderella*, and with French femme fatale Sylvie Guillem, another tall and leggy ballerina who specifically requested McKenzie as a partner.

Though declared by Arlene Croce in 1987 as one of American Ballet Theatre's "most authoritative performers of *danseur noble* roles", McKenzie's abilities were not just limited to the roles of fairytale princes. He also had outstanding success in twentieth-century dramatic roles, particularly in the dark and brooding ballets of Antony Tudor, whose work forms a substantial part of American Ballet Theatre's repertory. Here, McKenzie's somewhat overserious stage persona showed itself well suited to the introspection and dramatic depth of Tudor's characters, and the dancer revealed another, darker side to his talent as a dramatic performer.

However, a combination of injury, ill-health, and career frustration led to McKenzie's withdrawal from the ABT stage in 1989. He shifted his allegiances to the National Ballet in Washington, D.C. (the successor to Mary Day's Washington Ballet), where he acted as artistic associate, and also lent his services to Martine van Hamel's New Amsterdam Ballet, a small group for whom he choreographed a well-received chamber piece to the music of Liszt in 1991.

McKenzie's appointment to the directorship of American Ballet Theatre, particularly after the controversial, short-lived tenure of Baryshnikov successor Jane Hermann, was extremely popular with both company dancers and outside observers. He inherits a troubled company with huge debts, and a repertory which has undergone a fair number of artistic identity crises in recent years; but the will to succeed—both in McKenzie and in the dancers who take strength from the fact that their director comes from their own ranks—is almost enough to convince the onlooker of his capacity to do so.

—Virginia Christian

MÉRANTE, Louis

French dancer, choreographer, and ballet master.   Born into Italian family of dancers in Paris, 23 July 1828. Studied at the Paris Opéra School, pupil of Lucien Petipa. Married dancer Zinaïda Josefovna Richard, 1861. Début as child dancer (at the age of six) at Théâtre Royale, Liège; premier danseur, Marseilles, 1846, and La Scala, Milan, 1846–47; Paris Opéra début summer 1848, becoming premier danseur and leading partner at the Opéra; maître de ballet, Paris Opéra, from 1869; début as choreographer in 1873, staging ballets until last ballet in 1886. Died in Courbevoie, 17 July 1887.

ROLES

1852   Peasant Pas de deux in *Giselle* (Coralli, Perrot), Opéra, Paris
Aristec (cr) in *Les Abeilles* (divertissement; chor. Saint-Léon) in *Le Juif errant* (opera; mus. Halévy), Opéra, Paris

1853   Tigrane (cr) in *Aelia et Mysis*; *ou, L'Atellane* (Mazilier), Opéra, Paris
Don Altamirano (cr) in *Jovita; ou, Les Boucaniers* (Mazilier), Opéra, Paris
Divertissement (cr) in *La Fronde* (opera; mus. Niedermeyer, chor. L. Petipa), Opéra, Paris

1854   The Marquis of Santa-Croce (cr) in *Gemma* (Cerrito), Opéra, Paris
Divertissement (cr) in *La Nonne sanglante* (opera; mus. Gounod, chor. L. Petipa), Opéra, Paris

1855   Carlino (cr) in *Flore et Zéphyre* (divertissement) in *La Fonti* (Mazilier), Opéra, Paris

1857   Divertissement (cr) in *Il Trovatore* (opera; mus. Verdi, chor. L. Petipa), Opéra, Paris
Count Pepinelli (cr) in *Marco Spada* (Mazilier), Opéra, Paris
Divertissement (cr) in *Le Cheval de bronze* (opera; mus. Auber, chor. L. Petipa), Opéra, Paris

1858   Madhava (cr) in *Sacountala* (L. Petipa), Opéra, Paris
Principal dancer (cr) in *Les Échecs* (chor. Mazilier), in *La Magicienne* (opera; mus. Halévy), Opéra, Paris

1859   Divertissement (cr) in *Herculaneum* (opera; mus. F. David; chor. Mazilier), Opéra, Paris
Divertissement (cr) in *Roméo et Juliette* (opera; mus. Bellini and Vaccai; chor. L. Petipa), Opéra, Paris

1860   Endymion (cr) in *Les Amours de Diane* (chor. L. Petipa), divertissement in *Pierre de Médicis* (opera; mus. Poniatowski), Opéra, Paris
Prince Djalma (cr) in *Le Papillon* (Taglioni), Opéra, Paris

1861   Simon (cr) in *Le Marché des innocents* (M. Petipa), Opéra, Paris
Gianni (cr) in *L'Étoile de Messine* (Borri), Opéra, Paris

1863   Albrecht in *Giselle* (Coralli, Perrot), Opéra, Paris
Gennariello (cr) in *Diavolina* (Saint-Léon), Opéra, Paris

1864   Donato Rizzi (cr) in *La Maschera* (Rota), Opéra, Paris
Count Molder (cr) in *Néméa; ou, L'Amour vengé* (Saint-Léon), Opéra, Paris

1865   Jeannot (cr) in *Le Roi d'Yvetot* (L. Petipa), Opéra, Paris

1866   Djémil (cr) in *La Source* (Saint-Léon), Opéra, Paris

1867   Fisherman (cr) in *Le Ballet de la Reine: La Peregrina* (divertissement; chor. L. Petipa), in *Don Carlos* (opera; mus. Verdi), Opéra, Paris

1870   Principal dancer (cr) in *L'Invitation à la valse* (divertissement; mus. Berlioz, chor. Saint-Léon) in *Le Freychütz* (opera; mus. Weber), Opéra, Paris

1876   Amyntas (cr) in *Sylvia; ou, La Nymphe de Diane* (also chor.), Opéra, Paris

1879   Nori (cr) in *Yedda* (also chor.), Opéra, Paris

1880   Lilèz (cr) in *La Korrigane* (also chor.), Opéra, Paris

1882   Don Ottavio (cr) in *Namouna* (L. Petipa), Opéra, Paris

1886   First Gypsy (cr) in *Les Deux Pigeons* (also chor.), Opéra, Paris

WORKS

1873   *Gretna Green* (mus. E. Guiraud), Opéra, Paris

1876   *Sylvia; ou, La Nymphe de Diane* (mus. Delibes), Opéra, Paris

1877   *Le Fandango* (mus. Salvayre), Opéra, Paris

1879   *Yedda* (mus. O. Métra), Opéra, Paris

1880   *La Korrigane* (mus. Dubois), Opéra, Paris

1883   *La Farandole* (mus. Dubois), Opéra, Paris

1886   *Les Jumeaux de Bergame* (mus. Lajarte), Opéra, Paris
Les Deux Pigeons (mus. Messager), Opéra, Paris

Louis Mérante with Amelia Ferraris in *L'Etoile de Messine*, Paris Opera, 1861

PUBLICATIONS

Gautier, Théophile, *The Romantic Ballet as seen by Théophile Gautier*, translated by Cyril Beaumont, London, 1932

Beaumont, Cyril, *The Complete Book of Ballets*, revised edition, London, 1951

Guest, Ivor, "*Sylvia*: From Mérante to Ashton", *Ballet Annual*, (London), no. 8, 1954

Guest, Ivor, "*Les Deux Pigeons*: The History", *Dancing Times* (London), February 1961

Guest, Ivor, *The Ballet of the Second Empire*, revised edition, London, 1974

*   *   *

As principal dancer at the Paris Opéra from 1848, Louis Mérante partnered Emma Livry, Marfa Muravieva, Fanny Cerrito, and Amalia Ferraris, and created leading roles in ballets such as *Le Papillon*, *Diavolina*, and *La Source*. This tenure, however, paralleled the decline in the importance of the male dancer in French Romantic ballet.

The early nineteenth century had seen the ballerina enshrined as the embodiment of the Romantic ideal, a development encouraged by pointe work, which aided the dancer in her assumption of such characteristic Romantic roles as sylphs, fairies, and other ethereal beings. The male dancer, however, "tended more and more to become a mere *porteur*", according to Ivor Guest, until by the end of the century many male parts were being taken by ballerinas "en travestie".

Given this state of affairs, it is all the more interesting to read the contemporary critical assessments of Mérante's performances. Gautier, for instance, vividly describes the dancer's creation of the role of Santa-Croce in *Gemma*: "He knew how to assume a sinister and fatal expression by cleverly accentuating his delicate and youthful features, which are more suited to

express tender sentiments than ferocious passions. His gestures have authority; his look, fascination . . ." At the end of this ballet came a *coup de théâtre*: Santa-Croce's dramatic fall from a great height to his death, a fall much commented upon for Mérante's brilliant execution.

A few months later, an entirely different aspect of his talents captivated the Opéra audience, in the divertissement *Flore et Zéphyre*. Dressed as a woman, Mérante imitated a ballerina to great comic effect which brought the house down—an unusual achievement for a male dancer at the time.

The critic of *La France musicale*, on the occasion of the premiere of Saint-Léon's *La Source*, in which Mérante created the role of Djémil, describes him as a "conscientious artist . . . who knows how to invest his roles with the appropriate character and likeness"; and the critic Jouvin commented, on his appearance in a pas de deux inserted into the opera *Le Freychütz* in 1870, "Mérante is an intrepid and graceful dancer". When Mérante was made premier maître de ballet of the Opéra in 1869, Saint-Léon was equally commendatory: "He is an intelligent and able artist and a charming comrade."

So it was, then, a complete professional and admired colleague who succeeded to what had once been a most important position in the French ballet world. This importance, however, had as Guest explains ". . . declined as a result of a policy that often subordinated him to a guest choreographer from abroad. By 1870, the duties of the premier maître de ballet seemed to have shrunk to conducting the rehearsals of Saint-Léon's ballets during the great man's absence and devising divertissements for operas . . ."

Mérante's appointment coincided with the rehearsals of Saint-Léon's last work for the Opéra, *Coppélia*, in which the dancer appeared in a minor role as Lord of the Manor in the last act. His first choreographed work at the Opéra was *Gretna Green* in 1873, although it would seem that he had choreographed some minor pieces in the late 1840s at the San Carlo, Napoli, including a pas de trois inserted into the third act of *Paquita* in 1848.

Mérante's ballets, which were successful with contemporary audiences, were notable for the opportunities they gave their leading ballerinas to display their technical virtuosity (*Sylvia* and *Yedda* for Rita Sangalli, *La Korrigane* and *Les Deux Pigeons* for Rosita Mauri). In addition, their settings gave the theatre ample scope to provide the kind of sumptuous décor and stage spectacle that audiences had come to expect (the "exotic" Japanese setting of *Yedda*, the unusual use of a Breton milieu in *La Korrigane*).

Mérante was the thorough professional, much loved by his fellow dancers and respected for his expertise, an important member of the Paris ballet establishment. Degas, for instance, has left among his letters and journals a lively and evocative description of a dance examination at the Opéra with Mérante presiding, and occasionally refers to the premier maître in connection with various young dancers in whose careers the painter was interested. In fact, Mérante was one of the rare male figures to be seen in Degas' ballet paintings: he dominates the rehearsal in the 1872 *Foyer de danse à l'Opéra*, a painting now in the Musée d'Orsay, Paris.

Francois Coppée, the poet who devised the libretto of *La Korrigane* with Mérante, described the choreographer some eight years after his death as ". . . a very dignified man of simple and precise manners, who excelled in his art and who knew how to make himself loved and respected . . .".

—Louise Stein

MESSEL, Oliver

British painter and designer. Born in Cuckfield, 13 January 1905. Educated at Eton; studied art at the Slade School of Fine Arts, London. Designer of masks (some in collaboration with artist Rex Whistler), some of which used for Diaghilev's production of *Zéphyr et Flore*, 1925; invited to contribute stage designs to C.B. Cochran's revues, London, 1926, designing for Cochran 1928–33; designer for stage, opera, and ballet throughout 1930s and 1940s, working for Old Vic, Sadler's Wells, Covent Garden, and Glyndebourne, among others; also designer for films, including *The Scarlet Pimpernel* (dir. Korda, 1935), *Romeo and Juliet* (with Adrian and Gibbon; dir. Cukor, 1936), *The Thief of Baghdad* (costumes, with Armstrong, Vertès; dir. Powell, 1940), *The Winslow Boy* (costumes; dir. Asquith, 1948), and *Suddenly Last Summer* (dir. Mankiewicz, 1960). Recipient: Commander of the Order of the British Empire, 1958. Died in Bridgetown, Barbados, 13 July 1978.

WORKS (Ballet designs)

1925   *Zéphyr et Flore* (masks, added after Paris premiere; chor. Massine), Diaghilev's Ballets Russes, London
1937   *Francesca da Rimini* (chor. Lichine), de Basil's Ballets Russes, London
1942   *Comus* (chor. Helpmann), Sadler's Wells Ballet, London
1946   *The Sleeping Beauty* (chor. Petipa; staged Sergeyev, Ashton, de Valois), Sadler's Wells Ballet, London
1953   *Homage to the Queen* (chor. Ashton), Sadler's Wells Ballet, London
1960   *The Sleeping Beauty* (partly redesigned from 1946 production; chor. Petipa; staged Wright), Royal Ballet, London
1976   *The Sleeping Beauty* (partly redesigned from 1946 production; chor. Petipa; staged Skeaping), American Ballet Theatre, New York

PUBLICATIONS

By Messel:
Stage Designs and Costumes, London, 1934

About Messel:
Myerscough-Walker, R., *Stage and Film Décor*, London, 1948
Boyes, A., "Oliver Messel", *Harper's Bazaar* (New York), March 1950
Laver, James, *Drama: Its Costumes and Décor*, London, 1951
Pinkham, Roger (ed.), *Oliver Messel* (catalogue), London, 1983
Castle, Charles, *Oliver Messel*, London, 1986

*   *   *

The early twentieth century found English stage designers, inspired by the example of Edward Gordon Craig, in revolt against the excessive realism of the nineteenth-century theatre. They succeeded in transforming stage design from the province of the professional scene painter and costumier into a separate art, of equal importance to the actor and the play, thus establishing the professional status of the designer in the theatre. Youngest of these designers was Oliver Messel.

Messel brought back to the theatre spectacle of taste that recalled the great Stuart masques. His sense of rightness, flair, elegance, and taste enriched any period or setting, whether play, opera, ballet, musical, or film. He was not an innovative or theoretical designer like Craig but a pastiche-maker, with an especial feel for the eighteenth century and the Jacobean court masques. But he transcended his sources, filtering them through his own personal vision to create an unmistakable "Messel" look, at once poetic and nostalgic, mixing grandeur and romanticism in a particularly English way.

He began work with C. B. Cochran (who gave more young designers their first professional engagements than any other impresario this century), learning how to make an impact in the fast-moving world of smart revue. He soon revealed a special feeling for fantasy, which was to make him an excellent designer for opera and ballet. He had a well-defined sense of colour, with a clear understanding of the tones that would best enhance the sense of whatever epoch he was evoking; and he knew how to take the salient characteristics of a period or a style and to transform it into a costume for dancing. His first ballet, *Francesca da Rimini*, with its Renaissance setting, was notable for its rare combination of period feeling, beauty, and theatrically, while in *Comus* he perfectly evoked the English masque tradition. In *Homage to the Queen*, with its formal, courtly construction, he acknowledged his debt to the masque and Inigo Jones.

In the ballet world, however, Messel will always be remembered for the production of *The Sleeping Beauty* for the Sadler's Wells Ballet in 1946. His designs made such an impact upon the imagination of audiences that it became known as the "Messel" production, and, with modifications, it lasted over twenty years. Like Bakst in his 1921 designs for *The Sleeping Princess*, Messel approached the ballet via the Baroque architectural fantasies of the Bibienas; but while Bakst stressed the grandeur and Baroque splendour, Messel's vision was filtered through his own very English lyrical romanticism. He looked back to the seventeenth and eighteenth centuries, mixing touches of costume from various periods with panache and elegance, yet never sacrificing credibility of the overall stage picture. But the pervading atmosphere of fantasy was so strong that disbelief could be suspended totally and Messel's vision accepted as an authentic fairy-tale world. If he was shaky on architecture and perspective, and if some of the tutus were fussy in decoration and had to be streamlined over the years, the overall vision was so powerful that it has dominated the imagination of audiences ever since—such that it has bedevilled every subsequent attempt by the Royal Ballet to redesign it.

Messel was not just a visionary, but also a very practical and expert technician. His costume designs may have seemed vague, but he knew exactly what fabrics were to be used, how they would be cut, and how to make most of the decorative details himself. He could make head-dresses, jewellery, and masks (indeed, his first theatrical commission had been from Diaghilev to make the masks for *Zéphyr et Flore* in 1925); he created theatrical magic out of the most prosaic materials, like pipe cleaners, sponge, cellophane, mops, and tape. He experimented with fabrics, sometimes coating them with rubber so that they fell in huge stylized huge folds, sometimes painting them. He could make his own set models, which were miracles of the craft. He was always inventive, practical, and entirely theatrical.

It was a unique talent and a very personal vision that has, long after his death, continued to live in the imaginations of audiences fortunate enough to have witnessed his productions.

—Sarah C. Woodcock

Oliver Messel's set and costumes for Ashton's *Homage to the Queen*, Sadler's Wells Ballet, London, 1953

MESSERER, Asaf

Russian/Soviet dancer, choreographer, and teacher. Born Asaf Mikhailovich Messerer in Vilnius, 19 November (7 November old style) 1903. Married Bolshoi ballerina Irina Tikhomirnova; brother of ballerina (and stage partner) Sulamith Messerer, uncle of ballerina Maya Plisetskaya. First lessons in private studio of Mikhail Mordkin; studied at the Moscow Choreographic School from 1919, pupil of Aleksandr Gorsky and Vasily Tikhomirov; graduated in 1921. Dancer, Theatre of Working Youth, Moscow, before 1920; soloist, quickly becoming premier danseur, Bolshoi Ballet, Moscow, 1921–54, including tours of many cities outside the Soviet Union; début as choreographer, with own concert piece, 1924; also staged ballets for Bolshoi Filial (Experimental) Theatre, Bolshoi Ballet, Hungarian State Opera, Budapest, and Théâtre Royal de la Monnaie, Brussels; teacher, Bolshoi Ballet School, from 1923, directing Class of Perfection, from 1942; guest teacher, Ballet du XXe Siècle, Brussels, 1960–61, also acting as ballet master for foreign tours of the Bolshoi Ballet, 1956, 1958, 1962; author of two books on ballet technique. Recipient: title of Honoured Artist of the USSR, 1933; State Prize, 1941, 1947; title of People's Artist of the Russian Federation, 1951; People's Artist of the USSR, 1976. Died in Moscow, 7 March 1992.

ROLES

1921   Zephyr in *The Magic Mirror* (Gorsky), Bolshoi Ballet, Moscow

Colin in *Vain Precautions* (*La Fille mal gardée*; Gorsky after Petipa, Ivanov), Bolshoi Ballet, Moscow

1922   Prince Siegfried in *Swan Lake* (Gorsky after Petipa, Ivanov), Bolshoi Ballet, Moscow

The Prince in *The Nutcracker* (Gorsky), Bolshoi Ballet, Moscow

The Saracen Dance in *Raymonda* (Gorsky after Petipa), Bolshoi Ballet, Moscow

Bernard in *Raymonda* (Gorsky after Petipa), Bolshoi Ballet, Moscow

1923   The Moor in *Petrushka* (Fokine), Bolshoi Ballet, Moscow

Title role in *Petrushka* (Fokine), Bolshoi Ballet, Moscow

The Slave in *Le Corsaire* (Gorsky after Petipa), Bolshoi Ballet, Moscow

The Pirate in *Le Corsaire* (Gorsky after Petipa), Bolshoi Ballet, Moscow

Hindu dance in *La Bayadère* (Gorsky, Tikhomirov after Petipa), Bolshoi Ballet, Moscow

1924   Harlequin in *Harlequinade* (Petipa), Bolshoi Ballet, Moscow

The Slave in *The Little Humpbacked Horse* (Gorsky after Saint-Léon), Bolshoi Ballet, Moscow

Ocean in *The Little Humpbacked Horse* (Gorsky after Saint-Léon), Bolshoi Ballet, Moscow

Franz in *Coppélia* (Gorsky), Bolshoi Ballet, Moscow

1925   The Slave in *Joseph the Beautiful* (Goleizovsky), Bolshoi Ballet, Moscow

Title role in *Joseph the Beautiful* (Goleizovsky), Bolshoi Ballet, Moscow

Zephyr (cr) in *Teolinda* (Goleizovsky), Bolshoi Ballet, Moscow

1926   Zephyr (cr) in *La Esmeralda* (Tikhomirov), Bolshoi Ballet, Moscow

The Bluebird in *The Sleeping Beauty* (Tikhomirov after Petipa), Bolshoi Ballet, Moscow

1927   Idol in *The Red Poppy* (Tikhomirov, Lashchilin), Bolshoi Ballet, Moscow

Juggler, Japanese Sailor in *The Red Poppy* (Tikhomirov, Lashchilin), Bolshoi Ballet, Moscow

1928   Basil in *Don Quixote* (Gorsky), Bolshoi Ballet, Moscow

1930   The Cascade in *The Footballer* (Lashchilin, Moiseyev), Bolshoi Ballet Moscow

The Cat in *The Sleeping Beauty* (Tikhomirov after Petipa), Bolshoi Ballet, Moscow

1932   The fanatic in *Salammbô* (Moiseyev), Bolshoi Ballet, Moscow

Chief Signal Officer in *Salammbô* (Moiseyev), Bolshoi Ballet, Moscow

1933   Philippe in *The Flames of Paris* (Vainonen), Bolshoi Ballet, Moscow

1935   Balloon-seller (cr) in *Three Fat Men* (Moiseyev), Bolshoi Ballet, Moscow

Actor in *The Bright Stream* (Lopukhov), Bolshoi Ballet, Moscow

1936   Nur-Ali in *The Fountain of Bakhchisarai* (Zakharov), Bolshoi Ballet, Moscow

1938   The Figure Skater (cr) in *The Prisoner of the Causasus* (Zakharov), Bolshoi Ballet, Moscow

The Prince in *The Nutcracker* (Vainonen), Bolshoi Ballet, Moscow

1939   Cossack Dancer (cr) in *Svetlana* (Radunsky, Popko, Pospekhin), Bolshoi Ballet, Moscow

1942   Letika (cr) in *Crimson Sails* (Radunsky, Popko, Pospekhin), Bolshoi Ballet, Kuibyshev

1945   The Prince in *Cinderella* (Zakharov), Bolshoi Theatre, Moscow

1947   Philippe in *The Flames of Paris* (new version; Vainonen), Bolshoi Ballet, Moscow

1949   Franz in *Coppélia* (new version; Dolinsky, Radunsky after Gorsky), Bolshoi Ballet, Moscow

Other roles include: dancer in operas *The Huguenots* (mus. Meyerbeer), *Sadko* (mus. Rimsky-Korsakov), *Lakmé* (mus. Delibes); principal dancer in concert pieces *Gopak* (also chor.), *Waltz* (also chor.), *The Italian Beggar* (also chor.), *Pierrot and Pierette* (also chor.), *Saint Sebastian* (Goleizovsky), *Football Player* (also chor.), *Spanish Dance* (also chor.), *Russian Dance* (also chor.), *Melody* (also chor.), *Waltz* (Goleizovsky), *Spring Waters* (also chor.).

WORKS

1923   *Czardas* (concert piece; mus. Monti), Bolshoi Ballet School, Moscow

Waltz (concert piece; mus. Kreisler), Bolshoi Ballet School, Moscow

1924   *The Battle of Toys* (mus. Schumann), Lunarsky Theatre School, Moscow

Schumanniana (mus. Schumann), Lunarsky Theatre School, Moscow

1926   *The Fairy Doll* (mus. Bayer), Bolshoi Ballet School, Moscow

1953   *On the Sea Coast* (with Grivitskas, mus. Yuzelyunas), Theatre of Opera and Ballet, Vilnius

1960   *Ballet Class* (mus. Liadov, Glazunov, Shostakovich), Moscow Choreographic School, Moscow

1961   *Leçon de danse* (version of *Ballet Class*; mus. Liadov, Glazunov, Shostakovich), Ballet du XXe Siècle, Brussels

1963   *Class Concert* (also *Ballet Class* or *Ballet School*; mus. Liadov, Glazunov, Shostakovich), Bolshoi Ballet, Moscow

Asaf Messerer teaching company class, Bolshoi Ballet, Moscow

Also staged:
1926 *Le Corsaire* (after Petipa; mus. Adam et al.), Kharkov
       Opera Theatre, Kharkov
1930 *Vain Precautions* (*La Fille mal gardée*; with Moiseyev,
       after Petipa, Ivanov; mus. various), Bolshoi Filial
       Theatre, Moscow
1936 *The Sleeping Beauty* (after Petipa, with Chekrygin and
       Mordvinov; mus. Tchaikovsky), Bolshoi Ballet,
       Moscow
1937 *Swan Lake*, Act IV (production after Petipa, Ivanov;
       mus. Tchaikovsky), Bolshoi Ballet, Moscow
1944 *The Sleeping Beauty* (after Petipa; mus. Tchaikovsky),
       Bolshoi Ballet, Moscow
1951 *Swan Lake* (after Petipa, Ivanov, Gorsky; mus. Tchai-
       kovsky), Budapest Opera Ballet, Budapest
1952 *The Sleeping Beauty* (with Gabovich, after Petipa; mus.
       Tchaikovsky), Bolshoi Ballet, Moscow

Other works include: Concert pieces—*Melody* (mus. Gluck),
Spring Waters (mus. Rachmaninov), *Gopak* (mus. Niko-
laevsky), *Waltz* (mus. Moskovsky), *The Italian Beggar* (mus.

Saint-Saëns), *Pierrot et Pierette* (mus. Drigo), *Football Player*
(mus. Tsfasman), *Spanish Dance* (mus. Vasilenko), *Russian
Dance* (mus. various), *Waltz* (mus. Khachaturian).

PUBLICATIONS

By Messerer:
Interview with Janet and Leo Kersley in *Ballet Today*
   (London), November/December 1965
Lessons of Classical Dance, Moscow 1967; as *Classes in Classical
   Ballet*, translated by Oleg Briansky, New York, 1975
Interview in Robin, Sylvie, "Les Professeurs", *Pour la danse*
   (Paris), June/July/August 1977
Dance, Thought, Time, Moscow, 1979

About Messerer:
Morley, Iris, *Soviet Ballet*, London, 1945
Volkov, Nikolai, "Distinguished Artists of the Moscow
   Ballet", *Dancing Times* (London), October 1944
Slonimsky, Yuri (ed.), *The Soviet Ballet*, New York, 1947, 1970

Roslavleva, Natalia, *Era of the Russian Ballet*, London, 1966
Greskovic, Robert, "Ballet, Barre and Center, On the Bookshelf", *Ballet Review* (New York), vol.6, no. 2, 1977–78

*   *   *

An outstanding dancer himself, Soviet teacher Asaf Messerer belongs to a great artistic family. His elder brother Anzary is an actor of the Moscow Art Theatre, his sister Raisa a cinema actress and mother of Maya Plisetskaya, and his other sister Sulamith a ballerina and teacher who in the 1930s and 1940s danced leading roles at the Bolshoi Theatre, where she was often partnered by her brother. And finally, Asaf's son Boris is one of the best-known theatrical artists of Russia. In this way everything predestined Messerer to become an artist.

However, in his youth Messerer was interested not in the theatre but in sport. He came to ballet school at the unusually late age of sixteen. Still, genetic predisposition played its role, and Asaf Messerer acquired the secrets of his trade in just three years. Further, his short stay in the school gave him an advantage in that, as a young dancer, he was freer from academic stereotypes than his contemporaries, who had studied there seven or eight years. He was open to any new idea and to any theatrical experiment.

The year 1921, in which Messerer began his creative life, was the first year of the unprecedented (but not very long-lived) flowering of the Moscow Theatre, when Vakhtangov, Tairov, and Meyerhold were producing their famous stage works. All of Messerer's activities as a dancer, artist, and choreographer, especially in the beginning, were closely bound up with these searches for the so-called "left" theatre. As a producer of dances for the theatre he worked with Meyerhold. Nevertheless, he did not leave the Bolshoi Theatre and he continued to perfect his mastery of ballet. Very rapidly Messerer emerged as a classical virtuoso dancer, constantly developing the complexity of his dance movements and steps to sharpen their external line, and injecting into them an energy, swarthy strength, and sportive daring which showed how his youthful interest in sport had proven valuable to him in ballet. When he demonstrated his intricate jumps on stage he seemed a flying athlete.

At the same time, Messerer had a bright comic gift and an original, purely artistic sense of humour. Many of the roles in the old ballets were interpreted ironically by him, rather than fully seriously, and this tinge of irony was carried by Messerer throughout his whole life, successfully brought into one of his best roles, the Prince in Prokofiev's *Cinderella*. The ironic music of composers in the 1920s and 1930s was also close to his heart, and an especially important influence was Dmitri Shostakovich, with whom Messerer made friends and worked as a choreographer and producer.

Messerer began very early in the middle of the 1920s to test himself as a choreographer, and initially his choreographic compositions followed in the general course of the avant-garde theatre of those years. However, after the disintegration of the Soviet theatrical avant-garde, Messerer strove to carry on those principles which had been declaimed and from which had originated the so-called "dram-ballet", then triumphant on the ballet stage. Accordingly he attempted the new versions of the classical ballets *Swan Lake* and *The Sleeping Beauty*. However, this did not bring him great success. Having finished his artistic career, Messerer put all his energy and all his talent into the direction of teaching. It was here that Messerer found his second calling, and he obtained international fame conducting for many years the so-called Class of Perfection, the ballet class for leading professional dancers and ballerinas. Generalizing his method, Messerer wrote a book on dance technique and created an original ballet, *Class Concert*, inspired by his teaching (the idea of which, incidentally, was suggested by Harold Lander's *Études*). Such is the paradox of this life: a man, first entering into ballet class at the age of sixteen and studying for only three years, turns out to be the very greatest authority on classical dance in the Soviet Union and the living personification of academic traditions in ballet.

—Vadim Gaevsky

MEZENTSEVA, Galina

Russian dancer. Born Galina Sergeyevna Mezentseva in Stavropol, now Tolyatti, 8 November 1952. Studied at the Leningrad Choreographic (Vaganova) School, pupil of N.V. Belikova; graduated in 1970; later coached by Olga Moiseyeva. Dancer, becoming principal dancer, Kirov Ballet, from 1970–90, performing in numerous countries abroad during Kirov world tours; guest artist, Boris Eifman's Leningrad Theatre of Contemporary Ballet, 1987, Scottish Ballet, from 1990; also danced title role in Lebedev's television ballet *A Stranger* (dir. Belinsky, 1979). Recipient: Silver Medal, International Ballet Competition, Moscow, 1977, title of Honoured Artist of the Russian Federation, 1978; Gold Medal, International Ballet Competition, Osaka, Japan, 1980; State Prize of the Russian Federation, 1980; title of People's Artist of the Russian Federation, 1983,

ROLES

1972   Queen of the Dryads in *Don Quixote* (Gorsky after Petipa), Kirov Ballet, Leningrad
        Raymonda's Friend in *Raymonda* (Petipa; staged Sergeyev), Kirov Ballet, Leningrad
1973   Odette/Odile in *Swan Lake* (Petipa, Ivanov; staged Sergeyev), Kirov Ballet, Leningrad
        Lilac Fairy in *The Sleeping Beauty* (Petipa; staged Sergeyev), Kirov Ballet, Leningrad
1974   Nikiya in *La Bayadère* (Petipa, Ponomarev, Chabukiani), Kirov Ballet, Leningrad
1975   Title role in *Raymonda* (Petipa; staged Sergeyev), Kirov Ballet, Leningrad
        Mekhmeneh-Banu in *The Legend of Love* (Grigorovich), Kirov Ballet, Leningrad
        Zarema in *The Fountain of Bakhchisarai* (Zakharov), Kirov Ballet, Leningrad
1976   Aegina in *Spartacus* (Yakobson), Kirov Ballet, Leningrad
1977   Ballerina in *Pas de quatre* (Dolin), Kirov Ballet, Leningrad
1978   Esmeralda in *Notre-Dame de Paris* (Petit), Kirov Ballet, Leningrad
        Title role in *Giselle* (Petipa after Coralli, Perrot), Kirov Ballet, Leningrad
1979   Princess Aurora in *The Sleeping Beauty* (Petipa; staged Sergeyev), Kirov Ballet, Leningrad
1980   Kitri in *Don Quixote* (Gorsky after Petipa), Kirov Ballet, Leningrad
1981   Mistress of the Copper Mountain in *The Stone Flower* (Grigorovich), Kirov Ballet, Leningrad
        The Sylph in *La Sylphide* (Von Rosen after Bournonville), Kirov Ballet, Leningrad

Galina Mezentseva as Giselle

1982   The Girl in *Leningrad Symphony* (Belsky), Kirov Ballet,
       Leningrad
       Title role in *The Dying Swan* (Fokine), Kirov Ballet,
       Leningrad
1985   Nestan-Daredzhan (cr) in *The Knight in Tigerskin*
       (Vinogradov), Kirov Ballet, Leningrad
       Mazurka, Waltz in *Chopiniana* (Fokine), Kirov Ballet,
       Leningrad
1987   Margarita in *The Master and Margarita* (Eifman),
       Leningrad Theatre of Contemporary Ballet,
       Leningrad
1988   Medora (cr) in *Le Corsaire* (new production; Gusev),
       Kirov Ballet, Leningrad
1989   Principal dancer in *Scotch Symphony* (Balanchine;
       staged Farrell), Kirov Ballet, Leningrad
1990   Sugar Plum Fairy in *The Nutcracker* (Darrell), Scottish
       Ballet, Glasgow
1991   Title role in *Cinderella* (Darrell), Scottish Ballet,
       Glasgow
1992   Swanilda in *Coppélia* (Wright after Petipa, Cecchetti),
       Scottish Ballet, Glasgow

Principal dancer in *Who Cares?* (Balanchine; staged
   Neary), Scottish Ballet, Russian tour
Juliet in *Romeo and Juliet* (Cranko), Scottish Ballet,
   Glasgow

PUBLICATIONS

By Mezentseva:
"When the Soul has Wings", *Smena* (Leningrad), 3 September
   1978
"Only the True Feelings", *Leningradsky Rabochy*, 30 June 1979

About Mezentseva:
Degen, Arsen, "Where does Flying Begin?" *Leningradskaya
   Pravda*, 7 June 1980
Prokhorova V., "Time in Dance", *Sovetskaya Kultura* (Mos-
   cow), 30 April 1982
Greskovic, Robert, "Out of the Cradle", *Ballet News* (New
   York), September 1982
Parry, Jann, "Dancing Differently", *Dance and Dancers*

(London), September 1982

Yakovleva, E., "Galina Mezentseva", *Teatr* (Moscow), no. 6, 1983

Prokhorova, V., "Galina Mezentseva" (brochure), Leningrad, 1984

Krasovskaya, Vera, "The Knights of Modern Ballet", *Sovetsky Balet* (Moscow), no. 5, 1985

Kane, Angela, "Class Distinctions: First Sight of the Kirov Ballet", *Dancing Times* (London), October 1988

Pepys, Tom, "Curtain Up", *Dance and Dancers* (London), April 1991

* * *

From her very first steps on the stage, Galina Mezentseva managed to be original, but still remain true to the classical canons of the Leningrad ballet school. Unique personal advantages, such as long and graceful arms and legs, along with an appearance of fragility, seemed particularly to have designed Mezentseva for romantic roles; on top of that, she possessed a rare musicality and a unique talent for improvisation. Above all, Mezentseva revealed a strong dramatic instinct, rendering each choreographic phrase full of meaning and emotion whenever she danced.

Mezentseva is a dignified Lilac Fairy, a proud and passionate Odette, and a tragic, yet glamorous, Nikiya. A special role in her career has been Giselle, and in creating her own version of this part Mezentseva has followed a truly Russian tradition. Yet this ballerina is also convincing in the modern repertoire. Mekhmeneh-Banu, the heroine in *The Legend of Love* who sacrifices her beauty for the sake of her beloved sister, is a truly tragic role in Mezentseva's interpretation. Her charming but treacherous Aegina in *Spartacus* is another significant achievement. And the role of Esmeralda, which the ballerina prepared under Roland Petit for his *Notre-Dame de Paris*, was much lauded in the press. As for Vinogradov's 1985 ballet, *The Knight in Tigerskin*, Mezentseva created a Nestan-Daredzhan full of contrasts, revealing at once the passion of a lover and the fear of a woman in a forced marriage, expressing the frustration of a captive which ends, finally, with her a victim of sorcery. Vera Krasovskaya wrote about her performance in this work: "Mezentseva filled the Nestan-Daredzhan role with the poetry of her own outstanding personality, and by doing so she uncovered a whole world of feeling, well hidden inside the character's external 'plastique'. At once the movements are filled with the beat of a warm and noble heart, and each conventional gesture, each movement—a mere line in the involved pattern of dance—has turned into tenderness or chagrin, passion or wrath. The voice of a living soul can be heard in the character's dance 'monologues'."

In short, Mezentseva has been nothing less than a phenomenon in the Kirov Theatre. She is unusual in everything that she does; it is difficult to capture the essence of her dancing in words. Her every movement, her every arabesque, is in one way a repetition of a familiar pattern; yet she infuses everything she does with her own soul. In her more recent work, for example the adagio in Balanchine's *Scotch Symphony* (acquired in 1989 by the Kirov Ballet), she has shown even more the richness of her individual interpretations; she almost turns *Scotch Symphony* into a philosophical ballet. She creates something above the usual expectation of the audience; and those who watch her are mesmerized, only realizing afterwards that what they have seen is something great.

Since December 1990, when Mezentseva made her début as a guest artist with Scottish Ballet, British audiences have been able to witness and admire her great talents. Her range within a few years has been impressive: already she has danced in works by Peter Darrell, John Cranko, and George Balanchine. In the summer of 1991, in a curious twist of fate, Mezentseva was to be seen back in Russia, touring with a Scottish company, performing the supremely American Balanchine ballet, *Who Cares?*.

Mezentseva is in some ways a difficult artist; she has always been a private person, who avoids socializing with the company and who generally avoids crowds. Her passion for her art is obvious in her dedication to hard work. She was coached for many years by Olga Moiseyeva, who was like another mother to her from the days when the young dancer first came to Leningrad, a lonely and shy student from a rural town in the south. Today, Mezentseva's control and mastery on the stage is without question, and the example she has set for younger generations is great.

—Igor Stupnikov

A MIDSUMMER NIGHT'S DREAM

Choreography: George Balanchine
Music: Felix Mendelssohn
Design: David Hays (scenery and lighting), Barbara Karinska (costumes)
Libretto: based on the play by Shakespeare
First Production: New York City Ballet, City Center, 17 January 1962
Principal Dancers: Melissa Hayden (Titania), Edward Villella (Oberon), Arthur Mitchell (Puck), Patricia McBride (Hermia), Nicholas Magallanes (Lysander), Jillana (Helena), Bill Carter (Demetrius)

Other productions include: Zurich Opera Ballet (staged Patricia Neary); Zurich, 7 January 1979.

Other choreographic treatments of story: Marius Petipa (St. Petersburg, 1876), Mikhail Fokine (St. Petersburg, 1906), Frederick Ashton (London, 1964: see *The Dream*), Heinz Spoerli (Basel, 1975), John Neumeier (Hamburg, 1977), Robert de Warren (Manchester, 1981), Tom Schilling (Berlin, 1981).

PUBLICATIONS

Denby, Edwin, "*A Midsummer Night's Dream*: A Parent's View and a Fan's View", *Dance* (Brooklyn, N.Y.), vol. 42, 1963

Denby, Edwin, *Dancers, Buildings and People in the Streets*, New York, 1965

Balanchine, George, with Mason, Francis, *Balanchine's Complete Stories of the Great Ballets*, Garden City, N.Y., 1977

Reynolds, Nancy, *Repertory in Review*, New York, 1977

Swope, Martha (photographer), *A Midsummer Night's Dream*, New York, 1978

Croce, Arlene, *Going to the Dance*, New York, 1982

Cott, Jonathan, "Balanchine: Music and Dance", *Ballet Review* (New York), Fall 1983

Acocella, Joan, "Imagining Dance", *Dance Ink* (New York), December 1990

* * *

For his (and the United States') first original full-length balle
George Balanchine chose to divide the work into two act

A Midsummer Night's Dream, with Melissa Hayden as Titania, New York City Ballet, 1962

devoting the first to story-telling and the second to pure dance. The scheme serves a dramatic purpose as well as a practical one: the centerpiece of Act II is a pas de deux that, in its approaches and departures, its intertwining, and its formal conciliation, recapitulates in balletic terms the love story played out in Act I.

Approximately fifteen months earlier, Balanchine had used a two-part structure in a similar fashion for *Liebeslieder Walzer*. In that ballet, the choreographer placed the first set of waltzes in a nineteenth-century drawing room and had the women costumed in ballgowns and heeled slippers. When, after a short pause, the curtain rose for the second set, we saw the room open to the night sky, the women in tulle and pointe shoes, and the steps transformed into ecstatic variations on the waltzes of the earlier episode.

In *Dream*, too, there is a transition, this time from the prose of plot development to the poetry of balletic commentary. However, the ballet incorporates many more styles of movement and presentation than its predecessor. At the outset, Balanchine establishes a mood of innocence and a convention of fantasy by filling the stage with children costumed as fairies who dance steps suitable to their fledgling skills. The audience knows at once that no menace is to be taken seriously, and that everything will come right in the end. The rustics and the young lovers are characterized in broad, music-hall fashion—which helps make the story easy to follow—but the choreographer reminds us of a more noble, complex form of existence with a sweetly lyrical pas de deux for Titania and her Cavalier and a fiendishly virtuosic variation for Oberon.

Balanchine does not regard Bottom's transformation and the quarrel between the Fairy King and Queen as simple devices to forward the plot. In Bottom's speech, "The eye of man hath not heard, the ear of man hath not seen . . .", he found a reference to St. Paul: "The eye hath not seen, nor ear heard . . . the things which God hath prepared for them that love him". His Oberon, based more on the Germanic legend on which von Weber based his opera than on English folklore, is the personification of Autumn; Titania symbolizes Spring. After their reconciliation they leave the stage in opposite directions because, the choreographer explained, "They are married but they are not lovers . . . they are not human." Titania and Oberon may bless mortal marriage beds, but their own union was designed for preserving, not for begetting.

For Balanchine, as for Shakespeare, a quarrel between immortals disrupts the workings of the universe; the confusion as to who loves whom is not merely the result of Puck's mistake but the sign of a disordered world. Titania's pas de deux with her Cavalier reminds us that order and elegance will return in time, just as her duet with Bottom is a gentle, comic commentary on the failure of an ordained and necessary hierarchy. Puck, who serves as intermediary between the mortal and supernatural characters, has fairy powers—he is invisible to the lovers and the mechanicals—but is capable of errors and of overconfidence—his attempt to steal the changeling boy earns him a drubbing from Titania's followers.

The divertissement of the second act celebrates not only the triple wedding required by the plot (Balanchine dispenses with the play-within-a-play) but the restoration of universal order. Its formal structure contrasts with the informal comedy that dominates Act I, and its central pas de deux demonstrates the way courtship should be conducted: tenderly and with elegance. Dancers who play no characters but themselves surpass nobles, commoners, and even fairies in their representation of the ideal. In their disciplined movements, we see "the things which God hath prepared for them that love him": refinement, earthly (but not earthy) love, and the manifestation of beauty. The reappearance of the fairies and the joyous flying of Puck into the night sky disperse thoughts of solemnity and end the ballet, as it began, in cheerful fantasy.

However, Mendelssohn, even more powerfully than Shakespeare, presides over Balanchine's *Dream*. The bright, lyrical qualities of the music suggest joy and love, but its structure seems to evoke, for Balanchine, the ordering presence of the divine. When the dancers are entrusted entirely to it, rather than to the caprices of a dramatic plot, all quarrels and confusions are unmade and harmony and measure rule the world.

—Joseph H. Mazo

MILHAUD, Darius

French composer. Born in Aix-en-Provence, 4 September 1892. Studied violin and composition at the Paris Conservatoire, pupil of Xavier Leroux, Paul Dukas, André Gédalge, and Charles-Marie Widor. Composed first major work, incidental music to Paul Claudel's play *Protée*, 1913–19; first opera, *La Brebis égarée*, 1910–15 (produced 1923); secretary to poet and diplomat Paul Claudel, travelling to Rio de Janeiro, 1916; returned to Paris and became involved with "Les Six", group of French composers so named by Jean Cocteau, 1918; composed first ballet, *Le Homme et son désir*, 1918 (staged 1921), going on to compose several ballets for Jean Börlin and Les Ballets Suédois; visited London, 1920, and toured U.S., 1922; commissioned by Serge Diaghilev to compose ballet score for *Le Train bleu*, 1924; travelled extensively in Russia, Syria, Sardinia, Spain, and elsewhere during the 1920s and 1930s; left France for U.S., 1940, becoming lecturer in music, Mills College, Oakland, California; returned to France, 1947; appointed Professor of Composition at the Paris Conservatoire while retaining his post at Mills College until 1971; also composer of numerous operas, film scores, and radio scores; moved to Geneva due to ill health, 1971. Died in Geneva, 22 June 1974.

WORKS (Ballets)

1920 *Le Boeuf sur le toit* (pantomimic divertissement; dir. Cocteau), Fratellini Brothers, Paris
1921 *L'Homme et son désir* (chor. Börlin), Les Ballets Suédois, Paris
      Les Mariés de la Tour Eiffel (with other members of "Les Six": Auric, Honegger, Poulenc, and Tailleferre; chor. Börlin), Les Ballets Suédois, Paris
1923 *La Création du monde* (chor. Börlin), Les Ballets Suédois, Paris
1924 *Salade* (chor. Massine), (de Beaumont's) Soirées de Paris, Paris
      Le Train bleu (chor. Nijinska), Diaghilev's Ballets Russes, Paris
1926 *Jack-in-the-Box* (arrangement of mus. by Satie; chor. Balanchine), Diaghilev's Ballets Russes, Paris
1927 Polka in *L'Éventail de Jeanne* (with various composers; chor. Franck, Bourgat), Salon de Jeanne Dubost, Paris (staged Paris Opéra, 1929)
1928 *La Bien-aimée* (arrangement of mus. by Schubert and Liszt; chor. Nijinska), Ida Rubinstein Company, Paris
1933 *Les Songes* (chor. Balanchine), Les Ballets 1933, Paris
1944 *Imagined Wing* (chor. Graham), Martha Graham Dance Company, Washington D.C.
1946 *The Bells* (chor. Page), Chicago University Ballet, Chicago
1948 *'Adame Miroir* (chor. Charrat), Ballets de Paris, Paris
1957 *Mosé* (*Moïse*, composed 1940; chor. Milloss), Ballet of La Scala (Milan), Perugia
1958 *La Rose des vents* (chor. Petit), Ballets de Paris, Paris

Other ballets using Milhaud's music: *Saudades do Brasil* (Georgi, 1926; also Ashton, 1930), *La Création du monde* (new version; de Valois, 1931; also Bolender, 1960, MacMillan, 1964), *Le Train bleu* (new version; Georgi, 1931), *Salade* (new version; Lifar, 1935; also Darrell, 1961), *Black Ritual* (de Mille, 1940), *La Leçon apprise* (Toye, 1940), *The Maids* (Ross, 1957), *Concerto pour percussion et orchestre* (Béjart, 1957), *Chiaroscuro* (Darrell, 1959), *Scaramouche* (Petit, 1961), *Dance Suite* (MacMillan, 1962), *Carrefour* (Skibine, 1965), *Ephemeron* (Darrell, 1968), *The Sphinx* (MacMillan, 1968), *Lulu* (Carter, 1976), *Meadow of Proverbs* (Bintley, 1979).

PUBLICATIONS

By Milhaud:
Études, Paris, 1927
Notes sur Erik Satie, New York, 1946
Notes sans musique (autobiography), Paris, 1949; enlarged as *Ma vie heureuse*, Paris, 1974; as *Notes without Music*, New York, 1953

About Milhaud:
Collaer, Paul, *Darius Milhaud*, Paris, 1947; translated and edited by Jane Hohfeld, San Francisco, 1988
Beck, G., *Darius Milhaud: Étude suivie du catalogue chronologique complet de son oeuvre*, Paris, 1947
Roy, J., *Darius Milhaud*, Paris, 1968
Palmer, Christopher, *Milhaud*, London, 1976
Häger, Bengt, *Les Ballets Suédois*, translated by Ruth Sharman, London, 1950

*   *   *

In a brief essay about his composing, Darius Milhaud wrote, "A quartet is not written in the same way that a ballet is, or a film score like a sonata. The composer must adapt his tendencies, and remember that a ballet must be danced to, and must be subject to choreographic necessity . . .".

With well over 400 works to his credit, Darius Milhaud was unusually prolific for a twentieth-century composer. He wrote pieces in many different genres, explored many styles and forms, and is known for not only forging ahead of his contemporaries formally, but for letting his music forge ahead of himself, creating its own form and direction based on ideas and materials expressed in the beginning. This was especially true in the first half of his life, and it was during this early, fertile period that Milhaud wrote most of his ballets.

Milhaud's first three ballets, *L'Homme et son désir*, *Le Boeuf sur le toit*, and *La Création du monde*, are the ballets for which he is most widely known. Milhaud's dramatic works—the ballets and four operas written before 1926—gained him strong national recognition and marked the beginning of his international reputation.

Milhaud travelled widely and was constantly inspired by his surrounding environment. A variety of ethnic influences are particularly evident in his early music for dance. He spent two years in Brazil as secretary to the French minister Paul Claudel, also a poet and friend. This resulted in the strongly native, rhythmic influences in *L'Homme et son désir*, written in Brazil, and the two dance suites, *Saudades do Brasil*. *L'Homme et son désir* was first performed in Paris to the accompaniment of catcalls and guffaws, but with repeated performances it quickly gained the respect with which it is remembered today.

On his return to Paris, Milhaud became involved with Jean Cocteau's eclectic circle of artists and friends, and became one of the Satie-inspired "Les Six". Written at this time, *Le Boeuf sur le toit*, based on a popular Brazilian song, was originally conceived to accompany a Charlie Chaplin film. Full of brash energy, this popular work had its premiere in 1920 at the Théâtre Champs-Elysées, under the direction of Jean Cocteau, as a pantomime for acrobats and clowns.

During a brief trip to London in 1920 Milhaud became aquainted with jazz for the first time, an aquaintance that affected his music for the rest of his life. He steeped himself in as much jazz as he could find in Paris, and continued to do so when he went to America in 1922. The ballet *La Création du monde* was the first stunning result which showed the influence of Milhaud's exposure to jazz. In 1923 the premiere took place under the direction of Rolf de Maré with the Ballets Suédois. The scenario by Blaise Cendrars was drawn from African folklore, and Milhaud's score is imbued with the syncopated style of African rhythms, and with elements of American ragtime and blues. This is one of Milhaud's most significant works, a work which attracted many artists and cultural enthusiasts with its fresh forms, novel, seductive rhythms, and lyrical qualities. With *La Création du monde* Milhaud firmly established his international reputation as a collaborator and composer.

La Création du monde was immediately followed by two lighter ballets. With Jean Cocteau, Milhaud wrote *Salade* (choreographed by Massine), a work full of popular dance tunes including those of Rio. Written at the same time, *Le Train bleu* was commissioned by Diaghilev, and was essentially a light, frivolous, danced operetta.

During the Second World War, Milhaud and his family moved to the United States, settling in Oakland, California. After the war and until the end of his life, Milhaud shared his time between the U.S. and France, where he taught at Mills College and the Paris Conservatoire, respectively. His composing during this time consisted of many more purely instrumental works, symphonies, and chamber music. Milhaud finished his last ballet score in 1959.

Nearly all of Milhaud's works received premieres, and many of his ballets received numerous performances in Europe, the United States, and South America. Still, those for which he is most known today, and which made a significant impact on the culture of his time, are the early ballets, those written by 1923. In spite of the international influences on Milhaud's music, his personal style remained very French, a quality which shone through all of his music in its unpretentious lyricism.

—E. Amelia Rogers

———

MILLE, Agnes de *see* **DE MILLE, Agnes**

———

MILLOSS, Aurel (von)

Hungarian/Italian dancer, choreographer, and ballet director. Born Urel de Miholy in Ujozora, Hungary (now Uzdin, former Yugoslavia), 12 May 1906. Studied with Nicola Guerra, Budapest, and with Rodolf van Laban and Victor Gsovksy, Berlin; also studied with Enrico Cecchetti. Dancer, Berlin State Opera, from 1928, also performing in concerts and recitals in Germany; ballet master, Hagen, Duisburg, Breslau, Augsburg, and Düsseldorf, also returning to work in Budapest, 1930s; ballet master, Hungarian State Opera House, Budapest, 1936–38, Rome Opera, 1938–45 and 1966–69, Teatro alla Scala, Milan, 1946–50, Vienna State Opera, 1953–66 and 1971–74, and Cologne Municipal Theatres, 1960–63; also visiting choreographer for numerous opera houses in Italy, including in Naples, Palermo, Florence, and Venice; also staged ballets for Teatro Municipal in Rio de Janeiro, and for Ballets des Champs-Elysées, Paris; frequent collaborator with contemporary musicians and artists; settled in Rome, acquiring Italian nationality in 1960. Died in Rome, 21 September 1988.

WORKS

1932   *H. M. S. Royal Oak* (mus. E. Schulhoff), Opera House, Breslau

Zwölf Kammertanzwerke (mus. various), State Theatre, Augsburg

Der Besiegte Fakir (mus. various), State Theatre, Augsburg

1933   *Les Petits Riens* (after Noverre; mus. Mozart), State Theatre, Augsburg (restaged and revised Düsseldorf, 1935; Rome, 1945)

Der Feuervogel (*L'Oiseau de feu*; mus. Stravinsky), State Theatre, Augsburg

Die Puppenfee (mus. Bayer), State Theatre, Augsburg

Parkballett (mus. various), State Theatre, Augsburg

Don Morte (mus. Wilckens), State Theatre, Augsburg

Deutsche Tänze (mus. Schubert), State Theatre, Augsburg

Pulcinella (mus. Stravinsky after Pergolesi), State Theatre, Augsburg

Sonntagscsárdás (mus. Brahms), State Theatre, Augsburg

Die Josephslegende (mus. R. Strauss), Freilichtbühne am Roten Tor Theater, Augsburg

Der Zaubergeiger (mus. Grimm), Freilichtbühne am Roten Tor Theater, Augsburg

Die Geschöpfe des Prometheus (*Le Creature di Prometeo,* after Viganò; mus. Beethoven), State Theatre, Augsburg (also staged Rome Opera, 1940; La Scala, Milan, 1952; Vienna State Opera, 1963)

Don Juan (after Angiolini scenario; mus. Gluck), State Theatre, Augsburg

Carnaval (mus. Schumann), State Theatre, Augsburg

Petrushka (mus. Stravinsky), Hungarian State Opera House, Budapest

Das grosse Los (mus. J. Strauss jun.), State Theatre, Augsburg

1934 *Coppélia* (mus. Delibes), State Theatre, Augsburg

Der Dreispitz (*Le Tricorne*; mus. de Falla), State Theatre, Augsburg

Auf der Mondscheinredaktion (mus. various), Hotel Drei Mohren, Augsburg

Silvana (mus. Weber), State Theatre, Augsburg

Tod und Verklärung (mus. R. Strauss), State Theatre, Augsburg

Aufforderung zum Tanz (mus. Weber), State Theatre, Augsburg

Kleine Wiener Parade (mus. Schubert), State Theatre, Augsburg

Puszta-Zigeuner (mus. Liszt), State Theatre, Augsburg

Der Tanzgeist (mus. Weber), Opera House, Düsseldorf

Le Fils prodigue (mus. Prokofiev), Opera House, Düsseldorf

Das Zirkusliebchen (mus. Zillig), Opera House, Düsseldorf

1935 *Kuruc Mese* (*Karuc Fairytale*; with Brada; mus. Z. Kodály), Hungarian State Opera, Budapest

Antikes Tanzbild (mus. Handel), Opera House, Düsseldorf

Capriccio espagnol (mus. Rimsky-Korsakov), Opera House, Düsseldorf

Gaukelei (after Laban scenario; mus. Zillig), Opera House, Düsseldorf

Rosario la Tirana (mus. Juan Manén), Opera House, Düsseldorf

1937 *Aeneas* (mus. Roussel), Teatro San Carlo, Naples

Leggenda scandinava (mus. Sonzogno), Teatro San Carlo, Naples

1938 *A Csodofurulya* (*The Magic Pipe*; mus. Veress), Muvész Szinház, Budapest

1939 *La Bottega fantastica* (*La Boutique fantasque*; mus. Rossini, arranged Respighi), Rome Opera Ballet, Rome

Antiche danze ed arie (mus. Respighi), Rome Opera Ballet, Rome

La Giara (mus. Casella), Rome Opera Ballet, Rome

Le Donne di buon umore (*Les Femmes de bonne humeur*; mus. Scarlatti, arranged Tomassini), Rome Opera Ballet, Rome

1940 *Il Gallo d'oro* (mus. Rimsky-Korsakov), Rome Opera Ballet, Rome

Le Quattro Stagioni (mus. Verdi), Rome Opera Ballet, Rome

La Camera dei disegni (mus. Casella), Teatro delle Arti, Rome

1941 *Il Carillon magico* (mus. Pick-Mengiagelli), Rome Opera Ballet, Rome

Le Sacre du printemps (mus. Stravinsky), Rome Opera Ballet, Rome

Apollon musagète (mus. Stravinsky), Teatro delle Arti, Rome

Intermezzo ungherese (mus. Kodály), Teatro delle Arti, Rome

Tanz der Salome (*La Danza di Salome*; mus. R. Strauss), Rome Opera Ballet, Vienna

Danze Polovtsiane (mus. Borodin), Rome Opera Ballet, Vienna

Ungarische Romantik (mus. Liszt), Opera House, Breslau

1942 *La Tarantola* (mus. Picciolo), Rome Opera Ballet, Rome

Mavra (mus. Stravinsky), Rome Opera Ballet, Rome

Persefone (mus. Ferro), Rome Opera Ballet, Rome

Amphion (mus. Honegger), Ballet of La Scala, Milan

Il Mandarino meraviglioso (*The Miraculous Mandarin*; mus. Bartók), Ballet of La Scala, Milan

Coro di morti (mus. Petrassi), Rome Opera Ballet, Rome

Alomjáték (mus. Schumann), Hungarian State Opera, Budapest

1943 *Follia Viennese* (mus. J. Strauss jun.), Rome Opera Ballet, Rome

Visioni (mus. Pick-Mangiagalli after Chopin), Ballet of La Scala, Milan

La Rosa del sogno (mus. Casella), Rome Opera Ballet, Rome

Joan von Zarissa (mus. Egk), Rome Opera Ballet, Rome

Deliciae Populi (mus. Casella), Teatro delle Arti, Rome

Capricci alla Stravinsky (mus. Stravinsky), Teatro delle Arti, Rome

1944 *La Stella del circo* (mus. Stinco), Rome Opera Ballet, Rome

Bolero (mus. Ravel), Rome Opera Ballet, Rome

Il Meriggio di un fauno (*Le Après-midi d'un faune*; mus. Debussy), Rome Opera Ballet, Rome

Don Giovanni (mus. R. Strauss), Rome Opera Ballet, Rome

1945 *Visione nostalgica* (mus. Busoni), Rome Opera Ballet, Rome

Volti la laterna! (mus. Carabella), Rome Opera Ballet, Rome

Schéhérazade (mus. Rimsky-Korsakov), Terme di Caracalla, Rome

L'Isola eterna (mus. Bach), Balletti Romani di Milloss, Rome

La Dama delle camelie (mus. Vlad), Balletti Romani di Milloss, Rome

Allucinazioni (mus. Previtali), Balletti Romani di Milloss, Rome

L'Allegra piazzetta (mus. Mortari), Balletti Romani di Milloss, Rome

Danze di Galanta (mus. Kodály), Balletti Romani di Milloss, Rome

Lo Schiaccianoci (*The Nutcracker*; mus. Tchaikovsky), Balletti Romani di Milloss, Rome

1947 *La Follia di Orlando* (mus. Petrassi), Ballet of La Scala, Milan

Evocazioni (mus. Pick-Mangiagalli), Ballet of La Scala, Milan

Le Portrait de Don Quichotte (mus. G. Petrassi), Ballets des Champs-Elysées, Paris

1948 *Gioco di carte* (*Jeu de cartes*; mus. Stravinsky), Rome Opera Ballet, Rome

Il Galante Tiratore (mus. Veretti), Rome Opera Ballet, Rome

Rhapsody in Blue (mus. Gershwin), Rome Opera Ballet, Rome

Solsticio (mus. Ginastera), Teatro Rambla Sur, Mar del Plata

Orpheus (mus. Stravinsky), Rome Opera Ballet, Venice

La Ninfa di Diana (mus. Delibes), Rome Opera Ballet, Venice

Marsia (later *Marsyas*; mus. Dallapiccola), Roma Opera Ballet, Venice

1949   *Térszili Katicza* (*Katherine of Terszili*; mus. S. Veress), Opera, Stockholm

1950   *Chout* (mus. Prokofiev), Maggio Musicale Fiorentino, Florence

Il Principe di legno (*The Wooden Prince*; mus. Bartók), Balletti della Biennale, La Fenice, Venice

Ballata senza musica, Balletti della Biennale, La Fenice, Venice

La Boîte à joujoux (mus. Debussy), Rome Opera Ballet, Rome

1951   *La Soglia del tempo* (mus. Bartók), Rome Opera Ballet, Rome

Daphnis et Chloë (mus. Ravel), Rome Opera Ballet, Rome

Mystères (mus. Bartók), Théâtre National du Palais de Chaillot, Paris

Tirsi e Clori (mus. Monteverdi), Maggio Fiorentino, Teatro Comunale, Florence

Melos (mus. Préger), Casino Bellevue, Biarritz

1952   *Riflessi nell'oblio* (mus. Respighi), Ballet of La Scala, Milan

Coup de feu (mus. Auric), Grand Ballet du Marquis de Cuevas, Paris

1954   *Fantasia brasileira* (mus. Ibert), Ballet do IV Centenario de São Paulo, São Paulo

Passacaglia (mus. Bach), Ballet do IV Centenario de São Paulo, Rio de Janeiro

Indiscreçoes (mus. Ibert), Ballet do IV Centenario de São Paulo, Rio de Janeiro

No Vale da inocencia (mus. Mozart), Ballet do IV Centenario de São Paulo, Rio de Janeiro

Lenda do amor impossivel (no mus.), Ballet do IV Centenario de São Paulo, Rio de Janeiro

Loteria Viennese (mus. Strauss), Ballet do IV Centenario de São Paulo, Rio de Janeiro

Uirapúrú (mus. Villa-Lobos), Ballet do IV Centenario de São Paulo, Rio de Janeiro

O Guarda-chuva (mus. Mignone), Ballet do IV Centenario de São Paulo, Rio de Janeiro

Sonata de angustia (mus. Bartók), Ballet do IV Centenario de São Paulo, Rio de Janeiro

Cangaceira (mus. Guarnieri), Ballet do IV Centenario de São Paulo, Rio de Janeiro

1955   *Antiche iscrizioni* (mus. L. Rocca), Maggio Musicale Fiorentino, Teatro della Pergola, Florence

1956   *Ciaccona* (mus. J. S. Bach), Rome Opera Ballet, Rome

La Creazione del mondo (*La Creation du monde*; mus. Milhaud), Rome Opera Ballet, Rome

Hungarica (mus. Bartók), Rome Opera Ballet, Rome

Avventure di Pinocchio (mus. G. Marinuzzi, Sr. and jun.), Rome Opera Ballet, Rome

Idillio campestre (mus. Mozart), Rome Opera Ballet, Eliseo, Rome

Saltimbanchi (mus. Stravinsky), Rome Opera Ballet, Eliseo, Rome

Sogno romantico (*Rêverie romantique*; mus. Chopin), Rome Opera Ballet, Eliseo, Rome

1957   *Bacchus et Ariane* (mus. Roussel), Rome Opera Ballet, Rome

Estro Arguto (mus. Prokofiev), Rome Opera Ballet, Rome

Mirandolina (mus. V. Bucchi), Rome Opera Ballet, Rome

Vienna si diverte (mus. J. Strauss, arranged B. Rigacci), Maggio Fiorentino, Teatro Comunale, Florence

La Rappresentazione di Adamo ed Eva (mus. Rota), Ballet of La Scala (Milan), Perugia

Mosé (mus. Milhaud), Ballet of La Scala (Milan), Perugia

1958   *L'Enfant et les sortilèges* (mus. Ravel), Teatro Massimo, Palermo

Sei danze per Demetra (mus. A. Musco), Teatro Massimo, Palermo

Il Demone (mus. Hindemith), Maggio Musicale Fiorentino, Florence

La Volpe (*Renard*; mus. Stravinsky), Maggio Musicale Fiorentino, Florence

1959   *Memorie dall'Ignoto* (mus. Bartók), Rome Opera Ballet, Rome

Stasera la Bella Otero (mus. Rimsky-Korsakov), Rome Opera Ballet, Rome

Hellenikón (mus. Mulè), Teatro Massimo, Palermo

Petit Ballet en rose (mus. Petrassi), Teatro Massimo, Palermo

Danze e contradanze (mus. Beethoven), Teatro Massimo, Palermo

Allegrie brasiliane (mus. Milhaud), Teatro Massimo, Palermo (also staged Rome Opera Ballet)

I Sette Peccati (after A. Veretti), Teatro alla Pergola, Florence

1960   *Venezianisches Konzert* (mus. Vivaldi), Cologne State Opera Ballet, Cologne

Gezeiten (mus. Stravinsky), Cologne State Opera Ballet, Cologne

Danza sacra e profana (mus. Debussy), Rome Opera Ballet, Rome

Il Cimento dell'Allegria (mus. Poulenc), Rome Opera Ballet, Rome

Danze per i cinque cerchi (mus. Medin), Rome Opera Ballet, Rome

Dreizehn Stühle (mus. Stravinsky), Cologne State Opera Ballet, Cologne

Wandlungen (mus. Schoenberg), Cologne State Opera Ballet, Cologne

Der Mensch und sein Begehr (*L'Homme et son désir*, new version; mus. Milhaud), Cologne State Opera Ballet, Cologne

1961   *La Valse* (mus. Ravel), Cologne State Opera Ballet, Rotterdam

1962   *Die Wiederkehr* (mus. Vlad), Cologne State Opera Ballet, Cologne

Ballo per Antigona (mus. Traetta), Teatro Communale, Florence

1963   *Estro Barbarico* (mus. Bartók), Cologne State Opera Ballet, Cologne

Choreographische Paraphrase über Luigi Nono's "Polifonica-Monodia-Ritmica" (later called *Monodia*; mus. Nono), State Opera, Cologne

Salat (*Salade*; mus. Milhaud), Vienna State Opera Ballet, Vienna

1965   *Die Einöde* (mus. Varèse), Vienna State Opera Ballet, Vienna

Wiener Idylle (mus. Busoni), Vienna State Opera Ballet, Vienna

Les Jambes savantes (mus. Stravinsky), Vienna State Opera Ballet, Vienna

1966   *Orpheus Verliert Eurydike* (mus. Liszt), Vienna State Opera Ballet, Vienna

Les Noces (mus. Stravinsky), Vienna State Opera Ballet, Vienna

Alpbach-Quintett (mus. Krenek), Galerie Wiener Secession, Vienna

1967 *Variazione Corelliane* (mus. Corelli), Rome Opera Ballet, Rome

Divagando con brio (mus. Chedini), Rome Opera Ballet, Rome

Jeux (mus. Debussy), Rome Opera Ballet, Rome

1968 *Ricercare/Il Ritorno* (mus. Vlad), Rome Opera Ballet, Rome

Estri (mus. Petrassi), Festival of Two Worlds, Spoleto

1969 *La Pazzia senile* (mus. Banchieri), Rome Opera Ballet, Rome

Tautologos (mus. Ferrari), Rome Opera Ballet, Rome

1970 *Relâche* (mus. Satie), Maggio Musicale Fiorentino, Florence

Perséphone (mus. Stravinsky), Maggio Musicale Fiorentino, Florence

Hommage à Couperin (mus. Strauss after Couperin), Vienna State Opera Ballet, Vienna

1971 *Raremente* (mus. Bussotti), Maggio Musicale Fiorentino, Florence

Il Canto dell'usignolo (*Le Chant du rossignol*; mus. Stravinsky), Teatro della Pergola, Florence

Fantasia Indiana (mus. Busoni), Teatro della Pergola, Florence

1972 *An die Zeiten* (mus. Milhaud), Vienna State Opera Ballet, Vienna

Dedalo (mus. Turchi), Vienna State Opera Ballet, Florence

Panta Rhei (mus. Webern), Vienna State Opera Ballet, Florence

Wiener Operette (mus. J. Strauss jun.), Vienna State Opera Ballet, San Francisco

1973 *Tänze im Mirabellgarten* (mus. Mozart), Vienna State Opera Ballet, Vienna

Per Aspera (mus. Ligeti), Vienna State Opera Ballet, Vienna

Visage (mus. Berio), Maggio Musicale Fiorentino, Florence

1974 *Relazioni fragili* (mus. Carha), Vienna State Opera Ballet, Vienna

1977 *Rivolta di Sisifo* (mus. Petrassi), Ballet of La Scala, Milan

1980 *L'Ucello di fuoco* (*The Firebird*; new version; mus. Stravinsky), Rome Opera Ballet, Rome

Other works include: dances in operas *Rienza* (mus. Wagner; 1933), *Aida* (mus. Verdi; 1933), *La Giaconda* (mus. Ponchielli; 1935), *Tannhäuser* (mus. Wagner; 1938), *Oberon* (mus. von Weber; 1938), *L'Enfant et les sortilèges* (mus. Ravel; 1939), *Guglielmo Tell* (mus. Rossini; 1939), *Carmen* (mus. Bizet; 1939), *Sakuntala* (mus. Alfano; 1940), *La Favorita* (mus. Donizetti; 1940), *Turandot* (mus. Busoni; 1940), *Dido and Aeneas* (mus. Purcell; 1940), *Acis and Galatea* (mus. Handel; 1940), *L'Histoire du soldat* (mus. Stravinsky; 1940), *Armida* (mus. Gluck; 1941), *I capricci di Callot* (mus. Malipiero; 1942), *Kovanshchina* (mus. Mussorgsky; 1943), *Mefistofele* (mus. Boito; 1946), *Olimpia* (mus. Spontini; 1950), *Iphigenie in Aulide* (mus. Gluck; 1950), *Macbeth* (mus. Verdi; 1951), *Don Sebastiano* (mus. Donizetti; 1955), *Samson et Dalila* (mus. Saint-Saëns; 1955), *Gli Abenceragi* (mus. Cherubini; 1957), *La Traviata* (mus. Verdi; 1957).

PUBLICATIONS

By Milloss:

"Coresofia—corelogia—coregrafia: Breve introduzine accademica all'art della danza", *Musica* (Florence), vol. 1, 1942

Interview in *Chrysalis* (New York), vol. 3, nos. 5–6, 1950

"Das Ballett im eigenen Labyrinth", *Atlantis* (Zürich), November 1963

"Stravinsky und das Ballett", *Ballett-Journal/Das Tanzarchiv* (Cologne), vol. 30, no. 3, 1982

"La Lezione di Salvatore Vigano", *La Danza italiana* (Rome), Autumn 1984

Interview in Bentivoglio, Leonetta, "Aurel von Milloss", *Ballett International* (Cologne), May 1986

Interview in Tegeder, Ulrich, "Testaments from the Past", *Ballett International* (Cologne), November 1986

"Il Balletto nel propio labirinto: Confessioni di un coreografo", *Terzo occhio*, December 1988

About Milloss:

Zoete, Beryl de, "Aurel Milloss", *Ballet* (London), February 1948

Goth, Trudy, "Aurel von Milloss: Choreographer", *Dance Magazine* (New York), May 1953

Koegler, Horst, "Portrait of Aurel von Milloss", *Dance Magazine* (New York), May 1960

Agostini, Alfio, "Milloss: Coreografia è cultura", *Discoteca alta fedeltà* (Milan), July/August 1977

Il Balletto e l'opera di Aurelio M. Milloss al Maggio Musicale Fiorentino, Firenze, 1977

Carones, Laura, "Milloss e la critica anglosassone", *La Danza italiana* (Rome), Spring 1986

D'Amico de Carvalho, Caterina, "Le Stagioni romane di Aurelio Milloss", *La Danza italiana* (Rome), Spring 1986

"Aurel von Milloss", *Ballett-Journal/Das Tanzarchiv* (Cologne), December 1986

Veroli, Patrizia, "In Memoriam: Aurel Milloss", *La Danza italiana* (Rome), Spring 1989

Veroli, Patrizia, "The Choreography of Aurel Milloss", *Dance Chronicle* (New York), 4 parts: vol. 13, nos. 1–3, 1990; vol. 4, no. 1, 1991

*   *   *

Aurel (later Aurelio) Milloss made over 170 ballets; nevertheless, to celebrate his eightieth birthday in 1986, the Teatro dell'Opera in Rome—where his contribution had been crucial in earlier years—presented just a concert and an exhibition of photographs. Only Aterballetto, a touring company based in Regio Emilia, staged one of his ballets, *Estri* (1968), to mark the occasion. This abstract work, probably the best of those performed in the last two decades of the choreographer's life, has music by Goffredo Petrassi and scenery by Corrado Cagli. *Estri* was to be seen in Milloss's native Hungary for the first time in May 1990, when the State Opera Ballet in Budapest presented it, along with his *The Miraculous Mandarin*, to inaugurate the Spring Festival. *Estri* exemplifies the feature for which Milloss is best remembered, that of commissioning scores and scenery from well-known composers and designers of his adopted country, Italy.

He initiated this practice as early as 1942, when he commissioned scenery from Enrico Prampolini for his production (the first) of Bela Bartók's *The Miraculous Mandarin*. He personally knew his compatriot Bartók, who approved of his choreography. At that time Milloss was dancing the leading roles in all his ballets, which often had a male character as focus—Aeneas, Marsyas, or Orlando, for example. Photographs of Milloss in the role of the Mandarin show a striking and sinister figure. It may be that the ballet took on an extra dimension when he appeared in it himself; when he revived it decades later at the Teatro dell'Opera in Rome, it seemed unimpressive and lifeless.

Milloss's great achievement in Italy, apart from his championing of living composers and designers from his adopted country, was to ensure that ballet was taken seriously, and not just considered as a divertissement. Before his advent, evenings devoted to ballet alone were unheard of; Milloss instituted them and by all accounts brought about a notable improvement in the standards of performance, first in Rome and later at La Scala in Milan. Unfortunately, these improvements proved ephemeral, and apart from the fact that a few ballet programmes are now normally included in the opera house seasons, the theatres where he worked show little sign of his achievements, other than in their archives. This can be attributed in part to the deficiencies of the subscription system, which requires the preparation of new productions every season, with the concomitant wastage of previous ones. However, it is doubtful if that is the whole answer, since so very few ballets by Milloss have been revived, even during his lifetime.

In this century there has been no Italian choreographer of note, and the sparse visits by Diaghilev's Ballets Russes to Italy seem to have left little impression. Both these facts probably help to explain why it was not considered reprehensible for Milloss to make his own versions of several ballets from the Ballets Russes repertory, such as *Petrushka*, *Le Tricorne*, and *Les Noces* (the first of which, at least, was certainly far inferior to Fokine's original). And yet it was, apparently, seeing Karsavina and Nijinsky in *Le Spectre de la rose* that first fired Milloss's enthusiasm for ballet. Nothing in his intellectualized works would make one suspect a sympathy with romanticism. Rudolf von Laban, with whom Milloss worked later, would seem to have been a much stronger influence; although the two strands of Expressionism and classical ballet are interwoven in his choreography, he seemed to eschew the softer lines of many works in the classical mould.

In Italy Milloss was invariably referred to, and paid homage to, as "un uomo di cultura". He possessed a wide knowledge of painting and music (which he had studied), and there is no questioning either his varied academic background—which included philosophical studies with Bergson—or his wide culture. He was also very proud of his well-stocked dance library. It must have been partly his intellectual stature that made it possible for him to collaborate with composers and painters whose work did not always appeal to the less well-informed section of the general public. This is particularly so in the case of the music.

Apart from an engagement as director of the ballet company at the Vienna State Opera (like many Italian theatres, a home of lost glories so far as dance is concerned) and occasional commissions for ballets in a number of countries, Milloss worked in Italy, in nearly all the principal opera houses. The Ballets des Champs-Elysées was the only company of international importance for which he worked: in 1947, he made his Don Quixote ballet (*Le Portrait de Don Guichotte*) for Jean Babilée. The Maggio Musicale Fiorentino (Florence May Music Festival) staged several Milloss works over the years and later put on exhibitions of the often outstanding designs associated with those ballets.

Tall, with a distinguished but rather forbidding air, Milloss attended dance events in Rome quite frequently, and sometimes elsewhere in the country, but his habitual expression on these occasions denoted bitterness rather than enjoyment, at least in the last twenty years of his life. Possibly this represented the disappointment he felt at not being sufficiently appreciated, despite the respect that surrounded him in the Italian dance world. He was far too intelligent not to realize that a genuine

homage would have involved restaging some of his ballets. The sad fact is that while at the start of his career in Italy he had first-rate partners, such as Bianca Gallizia and Attilia Radice (a Cecchetti pupil, as Milloss was himself for a time), and while in Rome in the 1970s he may have been able to use artists of the calibre of Elisabetta Terabust and Alfredo Rainò, on the whole he worked with dancers who were not among the best. This may be another reason why his ballets failed to make such a strong impression in the 1970s.

While powerfully attracted to his adopted country by reason of its classical past and cultural heritage, Milloss had on the other hand to contend with very unsatisfactory conditions in the Italian dance world. However, he would have been less revered and fêted elsewhere, and he would probably not have enjoyed as many opportunities to call on leading composers and artists. That he should have been overrated in Italy was almost inevitable; that his works would suffer a total eclipse immediately after his death could hardly have been foreseen. The full extent of this sorry fate was demonstrated in May 1990, when the Verona Arena Ballet performed a new version (by its director, Giuseppe Carbone) of *La Follia di Orlando*, a ballet for which Milloss himself had originally commissioned the Goffredo Petrassi score.

—Freda Pitt

MINKUS, Léon

Austrian composer and violinist. Born Aloysius Ludwig Minkus (later took first names Léon Fedorovich) in Vienna, 23 March 1826. Probably studied in Vienna. Travelled to Russia in the 1850s; director, Prince Nikolai Yusupov's serf orchestra, St. Petersburg, 1853–56, also performing separately as concert soloist, Russia; soloist, Bolshoi Theatre, Moscow, 1861, and conductor, Bolshoi Theatre Orchestra, 1862–72; ballet composer, possibly collaborating with Edouard Delvedez on music for *Paquita*, performed in Paris, 1846; composer of several ballets for choreographer Arthur Saint-Léon, Paris Opéra, during 1860s; début as ballet composer in Russia, 1867; official ballet composer of the Imperial Theatres of St. Petersburg, in collaboration with ballet master Marius Petipa, 1872–86; also Inspector of the Orchestras to the Imperial Theatres, Moscow, from 1862, and teacher, Moscow Conservatory, from 1866; retired from Imperial Theatres, 1891, probably returning soon after to Vienna. Died in Vienna, 7 December 1917.

WORKS (Ballets)

1863　*Love's Flame; or, The Salamander* (chor. Saint-Léon), Bolshoi Theatre, Moscow (rechoreographed by Saint-Léon as *Fiametta; ou, L'Amour du Diable*, St. Petersburg, 1864, and as *Néméa; ou, L'Amour vengé*, Paris, 1864)

1866　*La Source* (with Delibes; chor. Saint-Léon), Opéra, Paris

1867　*Le Poisson doré* (chor. Saint-Léon), Bolshoi Theatre, St. Petersburg (Part I only first performed St. Petersburg, 1866)

1869　*Don Quixote* (chor. Petipa), Bolshoi Theatre, Moscow

1872　*La Camargo* (chor. Petipa), Bolshoi Theatre, St. Petersburg

1874　*Le Papillon* (chor. Petipa), Bolshoi Theatre, St. Petersburg

Léon Minkus's *La Bayadère*, Act IV, as performed by the Royal Ballet, London, 1963

1875   *The Bandits* (*Les Brigands*; chor. Petipa), Bolshoi Theatre, St. Petersburg
1876   *The Adventures of Peleus and Thétis* (with Delibes; chor. Petipa), Bolshoi Theatre, St. Petersburg
1877   *La Bayadère* (chor. Petipa), Bolshoi Theatre, St. Petersburg
1878   *Roxana; or, The Beauty of Montenegro* (chor. Petipa), Bolshoi Theatre, St. Petersburg
1879   *The Daughter of the Snows* (chor. Petipa), Bolshoi Theatre, St. Petersburg
       Frizak, the Barber; or, The Double Wedding (chor. Petipa), Bolshoi Theatre, St. Petersburg
       Mlada (chor. Petipa), Bolshoi Theatre, St. Petersburg (originally composed for unrealized 1872 production)
1881   Mazurka, Grand Pas added to *Paquita* (mus. Deldevez; chor. Petipa), Bolshoi Theatre, St. Petersburg
       Zoraya; or, The Lady Moor in Spain (chor. Petipa), Bolshoi Theatre, St. Petersburg
1883   *Night and Day* (chor. Petipa), Bolshoi Theatre, St. Petersburg
1886   *The Offerings to Love; or, The Pleasures of Loving* (*L'Offrande à l'amour*; chor. Petipa), Maryinsky Theatre, St. Petersburg
       The Magic Pill (chor. Petipa), Maryinsky Theatre, St. Petersburg

1891   *Kalkabrino* (chor. Petipa), Maryinsky Theatre, St. Petersburg

PUBLICATIONS

Drushkin, M., *Essays from the History of Dance Music*, Leningrad, 1936
Popova, L.S., "*Don Quixote*", *Bolshoi Teatr SSSR: Opera, balet*, Moscow, 1958
Krasovskaya, Vera, *Russian Ballet Theatre in the Second Half of the Nineteenth Century*, Moscow and Leningrad, 1963
Roslavleva, Natalia, *Era of the Russian Ballet*, London, 1966
Petipa, Marius, *Russian Ballet Master: The Memoirs of Marius Petipa*, edited by Lillian Moore, London, 1968
Marius Petipa: Materials, Recollections, Articles, Leningrad, 1971
Scherer, B. L., "Maligned Minstrel", *Ballet News* (New York), May 1980
Wiley, Roland John (ed. and trans.), *A Century of Russian Ballet: Documents and Accounts 1810–1910*, Oxford, 1990

*   *   *

Aloisius Ludwig Minkus, who took the first names Léon

Fedorovich in Russia, was closely associated in St. Petersburg with Marius Petipa, for whom he composed sixteen major ballet scores, from *Don Quixote* in 1869 to *Kalkabrino* in 1891. They include *La Bayadère* (1877) which, like *Don Quixote*, is still performed today in its entirety.

Minkus was born in Vienna, it is believed of Czech or Polish origin, and probably studied there; but almost nothing is known of his early years except that he acquired some skill as a violinist and some facility in composition and arrangement. Some sources credit him with a share in the music for Mazilier's ballet *Paquita* at Paris in 1846, for which the known composer was Edouard Deldevez; this may be a confusion with the substantial addition Minkus wrote for Petipa's version of *Paquita* in 1881.

By 1853 Minkus was certainly in Russia as first violin/conductor of a private serf orchestra belonging to Prince Nikolai Yusupov. He also taught the violin, and was next engaged as a violinist at the Bolshoi Theatre, Moscow, in 1861, becoming conductor the following year with the title "Inspector of the Orchestras". In the 1863–64 season he composed music for Saint-Léon's *Fiametta* (originally *Love's Flame*), of which a shortened version was given in Paris in 1864 as *Néméa*, and two years later there he shared with the younger Delibes the music for Saint-Léon's *La Source*, Minkus composing Act I and the second (final) scene of Act III.

Minkus had a major success in his music for Petipa's *Don Quixote*, first performed in Moscow in 1869. He used Spanish dance forms for narrative as well as decorative purposes, including the jota, seguidillas, and the fandango; the second pas de deux for Kitri and Basilio, with its lyrical violin solo in the Adagio, has long had a continued existence as a separate show piece for dancers, while the gypsy dances and those of the "Magic Garden" scene derive much from the character of the music written for them.

In 1872, Minkus succeeded Cesare Pugni as the staff Ballet Composer to the Imperial Theatres at St. Petersburg, a post he held until it was discontinued in 1886. During this time his music for other Petipa ballets included *La Camargo*, *La Bayadère*, and *Roxana*. In 1881 Petipa staged his own second version of the former Mazilier ballet *Paquita*, and for this Minkus now added a mazurka (for children of the Imperial Ballet School) and the whole of the Grand Pas (de dix) that has likewise survived in present-day performance, notably in versions edited by John Lanchbery for Rudolf Nureyev in London (1964) and for Natalia Makarova in New York (1980).

Renewed Western interest in *La Bayadère* as a ballet, by way of Nureyev and Makarova, has given Minkus new musical life in this context, and demonstrated most of his characteristic qualities and limitations. The orchestration always favours the violins, with limited interest in woodwind and brass; the rhythmic interest shows a preponderance of waltz-time, whatever the dancers represent (gypsies, bull-fighters, Oriental temple-dancers, ghosts, etc.); narrative music has often acquired disturbing overtones, to present-day listeners, of the silent cinema.

Against this should be counted an abundance of melodic charm and rhythmic verve, the ability to give emotional feeling to mood and situation without dominating it, and to show dancers to advantage, whether in the contrasting variations of a pas (as in the three solo Shades in *La Bayadère*), or in ensembles for the corps de ballet, in all of which a certain elegance of phrase often adds distinction. "Though it occasionally lapses into trite note-spinning," Lanchbery has observed of Minkus's music, "it possesses strongly the gift of making many a clumsy listener desperately want to dance"—and this may be thought a fair assessment of its intrinsic merit.

Some time after 1891 Minkus retired on a small pension from the Russian government and returned to Vienna, where he died.

—Noël Goodwin

THE MIRACULOUS MANDARIN
(Original Hungarian title: *A Csodálatos Mandarin*)

Staging: Hans Strobach
Music: Béla Bartók
Design: Hans Strobach
Libretto: Menyhert Lengyel
First Production: Municipal Theater, Cologne, as *Der Wunderbare Mandarin*, 28 November 1926
Principal Dancers: Wilma Aug (The Prostitute), Ernst Zeiller (The Mandarin)

Other productions include: Ballet of La Scala (new version; chor. Aurel Milloss, design Enrico Prampolini); Milan, 12 October 1942. Hungarian State Opera Ballet (new version: chor. Gyula Harangozó), as *A Csodálatos Mandarin*; Budapest, 9 December 1945. New York City Ballet (new version; chor. Todd Bolender, design Alvin Colt); New York, 6 September 1951. Teatro La Fenice (new version; chor. Jean-Jacques Etchevery, design Jean-Pierre Ponnelle), as *Le Mandarin merveilleux*; Venice, 13 September 1955 (restaged Théâtre de la Monnaie, Brussels, 2 December 1955). Sadler's Wells Ballet (new version; chor. Alfred Rodrigues, design Georges Wakhevitch), as *The Miraculous Mandarin*; Edinburgh, 27 August 1956. Belgrade State Opera Ballet (new version; chor. Dimitrije Parlic, design Dusan Ristic), as *A Csodálatos Mandarin*; Belgrade, 10 February 1957. Empire State Music Festival (new version; chor. Vera Pasztor and Erno Vasheggi); New York, 26 July 1957 (restaged for Netherlands Ballet as *De Wonderbaarlijke Mandarin*, May 1959). Vienna State Opera Ballet (new version; chor. Erika Hanka, design Georges Wakhevitch), as *Der Wunderbare Mandarin*; Vienna, 16 November 1957. Ballets de France de Janine Charrat (new version; chor. Ernö Vasheggi, design Max Rothisberger), as *Le Mandarin merveilleux*; Paris, 3 October 1958. Bavarian State Opera Ballet (new version; chor. Alan Carter, design Werner Schachteli), as *Der Wunderbare Mandarin*; Munich, 22 November 1960. Bolshoi Ballet (new version; chor. Leonid Lavrovsky), as *Night City*; Moscow, 21 May 1961. Metropolitan Opera Ballet (new version; chor. Joseph Lazzini, design Bernard Daydé); New York, 11 April 1965. Royal Danish Ballet (new version; chor. Flemming Flindt, design Preben Hornung), as *Den Forunderlige Mandarin*; Copenhagen, 28 January 1967. Opéra-Comique (new version; chor. Milko Sparemblek, design Roger Bernard); Paris, 4 May 1968. New Swedish Ballet (new version; chor. Ulf Gadd, design Herman Sichter); London, 9 September 1970 (restaged for American Ballet Theatre, New York, 29 July 1971). Hungarian State Opera Ballet (new version; chor. Laszlo Seregi); Budapest, 1971. Berlin State Opera Ballet (new version; chor. Conrad Drzewecki, design Krzysztof Pankiewicz); Berlin, 20 October 1974. Darmstadt Tanztheater (new version; chor. Gerhard Bohner), as *Der Wunderbare Mandarin*; Darmstadt, 1974. Ballet of La Scala (new version; chor. Roland Petit, design Josef Svoboda and Franca Squarciapino); Milan, 13 April 1980. Kolner Tanz-Forum (new version; chor. Jochen Ulrich), as *Der Wunderbare Mandarin*; Cologne, 30 November 1980. Ballet of La Scala (new version; chor. Mario Pistoni, design Eugenio Guglieminetti); Milan, 9

September 1986. Houston Ballet (new version; chor. Ben Stevenson); Washington, D.C., 28 January 1986. Les Ballets de Monte Carlo (new version; chor. and design Jean-Christophe Maillot); Monte Carlo, 1987.

PUBLICATIONS

Haskell, Arnold, "Shocking", *Dancing Times* (London), October 1956

Sabin, R., "Béla Bartók and the Dance", *Dance Magazine* (New York), April 1961

Barnes, Clive, "Bartók Country: Hungarian State Ballet at the Edinburgh Festival", *Dance and Dancers* (London), October 1963

Ståhle, Anna Greta, "Royal Danish Ballet has a Great Modern Work", *Dance News* (New York), March 1967

Balanchine, George, with Mason, Francis, *Balanchine's Complete Stories of the Great Ballets*, Garden City, N.Y., 1977

Kortvelyes, Geza, "Béla Bartók and the Hungarian Ballet", *Hungarian Dance News* (Budapest), nos. 1–2, 1981

Kortvelyes, Geza, "Der Wunderbare Mandarin", *Tanzblatter* (Vienna), March 1981

"Ballets de Bartók", *L'Avant scène: Ballet/Danse* (Paris), May/September 1981

Griffiths, Paul, *Bartók*, London, 1984

*   *   *

Styled by the composer as "a pantomime in one act", *The Miraculous Mandarin* is the third of Bartók's three closely related and almost contemporaneous works for the stage—alongside his one-act ballet *The Wooden Prince*, and the opera *Bluebeard's Castle*, also in one act. Though Bartók initially intended the first two works as a double bill, it seems that—on completion of *The Miraculous Mandarin*—he began to regard them as parts of one complete (if long) evening's performance, and although difficulties attending performances of the *Mandarin* prevented this during his lifetime, it is the context in which the works are now generally performed in his native country.

For a major score by a great composer, *The Miraculous Mandarin* has had a fraught and intermittent life in the theatre and, like Stravinsky's *Rite of Spring*, has fared far better in the concert hall than on the stage. Essentially a project of Bartók's own devising, the work shows him well ahead of his time in terms of theatrical realism and psychological awareness: it was outstandingly original for its day in its choice of theme, dealing frankly with sexual pathology and utilizing a seedy, urban, industrial milieu (complete with orchestral depiction of street noise and motor horns). In this it has claims to be the first truly twentieth-century ballet—preceding Prokofiev's "industrial" ballet *Le Pas d'acier* by nearly ten years. But although it has attracted several notable choreographers, none—by general critical agreement—has really succeeded with it, largely due to the difficulties inherent in trying to reconcile its depiction of basic taboos about human sexual motivation and its luridly bizarre and melodramatic action with audience acceptability.

The action is as follows: in a shabby room in the slums of a big city, three thugs force a young female prostitute to lure men up from the street to be robbed. A down-at-heel old roué and an inexperienced youth are found to have nothing worth taking and are thrown out. Their third victim is the unearthly Mandarin whose eerie impassiveness frightens the girl, though she tries to unfreeze his passions by dancing for him. When she finally succeeds, however, the force of his desire so terrifies her that she struggles to escape him. A wild dance of pursuit follows

The Miraculous Mandarin, in a version by Ulf Gadd, with Erik Bruhn and Natalia Makarova, 1971

and, as the Mandarin finally catches the girl, the thugs emerge from hiding to rob him of all his possessions. In their attempts to kill the Mandarin afterwards, they try at first to suffocate him, then to stab, and finally to hang him, but he remains alive, looking fixedly at the girl. His body begins to glow—it seems impossible for him to die. Only when the girl herself cuts him down and takes him in her arms do his wounds begin to bleed, and he finally dies.

The blatantly sexual theme evidently appealed greatly to Bartók's mood at that time, despite the externals of a plot which, given the moral climate of his day, he must have known from the outset would make the ballet unperformable on stage for many years. Drawing on his considerable technical resources—including his carefully cultivated understanding of folk music and its strong underlying dance movement—Bartók went on to produce what is arguably his most important orchestral score and one which paradoxically contains no intrinsically difficult musical problems for choreographers to handle. Though full of original and characteristic inner complexities, *The Miraculous Mandarin* has a clearly organized and thematically integrated structure of immense rhythmic drive, and displays enormous instrumental subtlety in the psychological depiction of its characters. It is this very psychological motivation, however, which has consistently revealed choreographers in disarray when handling the work.

Although completed in 1919, the ballet did not receive its first production until 1926 in Cologne, with Wilma Aug as the girl and Ernst Zeiller as the Mandarin. It was immediately banned on moral grounds by the then Lord Mayor of Cologne, Konrad Adenauer, and although it was briefly revived the following season in Prague, the work did not really enter the repertory until 1942 when it was produced by Milloss at La Scala, Milan. The first serious version in Hungary was choreographed by Gyula Harangozó (Sr.) in Budapest in 1945 (filmed in 1965) and remained in the repertory until Seregi's version replaced it in 1971. Both treatments rely on articulating and making acceptable the action, and in fighting shy of touching any deeper issues at the heart of the ballet's substance, thus remaining choreographically pallid.

In 1961 Lavrovsky made a version in Moscow for the Bolshoi, under the title of *Night City*, which—though moving in itself and containing a strong balance between effectively expressive movement and dramatic action—avoided the point of Bartók's "unpleasant" subject-matter entirely by dispensing with the Mandarin and his sexual proclivities. After a similar opening with two unsuitable victims, the story revolves around a genuine and redeeming love which develops between the girl and a young night-duty mechanic. The girl tries to protect him from her companions, especially a leading red-haired thug, but the latter manages eventually to kill the boy by throwing a knife. By the time police arrive the boy's body has vanished and the girl is seen dancing around her companions as at the beginning. The most theatrically effective version on Lengyel's original scenario is undoubtedly Flemming Flindt's for the Royal Danish Ballet in 1967, though even this refrains from engaging the full implications of Bartók's raw depiction of sex as an elemental force.

The stage history of *The Miraculous Mandarin* seems to indicate that audiences and choreographers alike would have preferred a composer of Bartók's obvious stature not to have presented the world with the uncompromising visions he chose for his dance projects, especially in this work. In all three of his stage works, however, he showed a Freudian frankness as contemporary as this ballet's setting, in regarding psycho-sexual pathology and sexual obsession as a basis for his subject-matter, and in the ballets, at least, commentators have been overly prudish in blaming the works' failures on inadequacies in plot construction or theme.

It is possible that Bartók may have had strong personal reasons for being attracted to such themes (it is now known that with his first marriage already under considerable strain, Bartók was deeply tormented at this time by his powerful but publicly inadmissible attraction to a young girl, then not quite 15 years old, whom he met on a folk-song collecting trip). But whether or not this is true, it remains significant to an adequate understanding of the ballet that he was a pioneer in bringing to dance (as well as to opera) hitherto taboo aspects of sexual relationships—"game-playing", struggles for control, the psychology of attraction, and exercise of destructive manipulation (as distinct from "love" as it was then popularly conceived)—and leaving them clearly revealed. In developing his treatment from the fairy-tale symbolism of *The Wooden Prince*, through the violence of *Bluebeard's Castle*, to the undisguised depiction of sex as an unassuageable life force in *The Miraculous Mandarin*, Bartók opened up areas still not easily approached in art, and his work still waits for a choreographer ready to acknowledge the brutal honesty of that vision.

—Geoffrey Baskerville

———

MISKOVITCH, Milorad

Yugoslavian/French dancer and teacher. Born in Voljevo, former Yugoslavia, 26 March 1928. Studied with Nina Kirsanova in Belgrade; later studied with Olga Preobraz-henska and Boris Kniaseff, Paris, from 1946. Dancer, corps de ballet, Belgrade State Opera House, 1945; soloist, Ballets des Champs-Elysées, 1946, (Mona Inglesby's) International Ballet, and (de Basil's) Original Ballet Russe, 1947, and Grand Ballet de Monte Carlo, 1948; principal dancer, Roland Petit's Ballets de Paris, 1949, Ballets Janine Charrat, 1952, Massine's Ballet Europeo, 1960, and Ruth Page's Chicago Opera Ballet, 1961; international guest artist, including with London Festival Ballet, 1952, Scandinavian Ballet, 1965; also appeared in concert performances partnering ballerinas Lycette Darsonval, Yvette Chauviré, 1950–51, Alicia Markova, 1954, and Collette Marchand, 1955; founder, with Irène Lidova, Les Ballets 1956, touring Europe, and becoming Les Ballets 1957, touring South America; choreographer, from 1962, staging works for companies in Italy, France, Yugoslavia, and America; guest choreographer, Dallas Ballet, 1972; guest teacher, especially in America; artistic advisor, UNESCO, Paris, from 1980; chairman, UNESCO's Conseil international de danse, from 1988.

ROLES

1947   The Land in *La Légende du bouleau* (new version of *Biroska*, also known as *The Silver Birch*; Kniaseff), Original Ballet Russe, London
1948   Albrecht in *Giselle* (after Petipa, Coralli, Perrot), Grand Ballet de Monte Carlo
        Colas in *La Fille mal gardée* (Nijinska; staged Balashova), Grand Ballet de Monte Carlo
        Roméo in *Roméo et Juliette* (Lifar), Grand Ballet de Monte Carlo
1949   Principal dancer (Tancredi) in *Le Combat* (Dollar), Ballets de Paris
        Principal dancer (cr) in *Pas d'action* (Petit), Ballets de Paris, London
        Sombre Seducer (cr) in *La Rêve de Léonor* (Ashton), Les Ballets de Paris, London
        Le Marin (cr) in *'Adame Miroir* (Charrat), Ballets de Paris, Paris
        A Bandit in *Carmen* (Petit), Ballets de Paris
        Hussar in *Le Beau Danube* (Massine), Ballets de Paris, Paris
        Principal dancer (cr) in *Thème et variations* (Charrat), Ballets de Paris, Paris
        Principal dancer in *Que le diable l'emporte* (Petit), Ballets de Paris
        Pas de deux from *The Sleeping Beauty* (after Petipa), Ballets de Paris
        Principal dancer (cr) in *Duet* (Cunningham), Garden Fête, Paris
        Principal dancer in *Bolero* (Ricarda), British television (with Markova)
        Grand Pas de deux from *The Nutcracker* (after Ivanov), British television (with Markova)
1951   Title role (cr) in *Orfeo* (Charrat), Venice Festival
        Principal dancer (cr) in *Melos* (Milloss), Gala, Biarritz
1952   The Young Man in *L'Écuyère* (Lifar), tour with Yvette Chauviré
        Principal dancer (cr) in *Les Fâcheux* (Berger), Ballet de Marigny
        Leading role (cr) in *Pour les enfants sages* (Chauviré), Ballet de Marigny

The Poet in *Les Sylphides* (Fokine), London's Festival
Ballet
1954   The Faun in *L'Après-midi d'un faune* (after Nijinsky),
tour with Markova, England
1955   The Prince (cr) in *La Dryad* (V. Gsovsky), Enghein
Festival
1956   Principal dancer (cr) in *Haute Voltage* (Béjart), Les
Ballets Charrat, Metz
Title role (cr) in *Prométhée* (first version; Béjart), Les
Ballets 1956, Lyons
Principal dancer (cr) in *Suite New-Yorkaise* (Taras), Les
Ballets 1956, Monte Carlo
Principal dancer (cr) in *Les Saisons* (Gore), Les Ballets
1956, Lyons
Principal dancer (cr) in *Entre cour et jardin* (later called
Le Rideau rouge; Taras), Les Ballets 1956, Monte
Carlo
1957   The Poet in *La Sonnambula* (Balanchine; staged Taras),
Le Ballet de Pâques, Monte Carlo
Principal dancer (cr) in *Soirée musicale* (pas de deux;
Taras), Le Ballet de Pâques, Monte Carlo
Principal dancer (cr) in *La Chaconne* (Parlić), Les
Ballets 1957
Pelléas (cr) in *Pelléas et Mélisande* (Skibine), Ballets
1957, Paris
The Stranger in *L'Échelle* (Sanders), Les Ballets 1957
Principal dancer (cr) in *Le Cycle* (Guélis), Ballets 1957,
Monte Carlo
1958   Leading role (cr) in *Le Poète assassiné* (Aul), Les Ballets
1958
The Knight (cr) in *La Belle Dame sans merci* (Howard),
Edinburgh International Ballet, Edinburgh
Guérin in *Les Algues* (Charrat), Ballets Charrat, Monte
Carlo
1959   Principal dancer (cr) in *Cache-Cache* (Aul), Monte
Carlo
Don Juan (cr) in *Señor de Mañara* (J. Carter), Enghein
Festival
Title role (cr) in *Le Cid* (Combes), Les Ballets 1959,
Enghein
Héros (cr) in *Héros et son miroir* (Sparemblek), Les
Ballets 1959
Principal dancer (cr) in *Le Sacre du printemps* (Béjart),
Théâtre de la Monnaie, Brussels
1960   Principal dancer (cr) in *Cherche partenaire* (Reich), Les
Ballets 1960, Enghein
Nastagio and The Prince (cr) in *La Commedia umana*
(Massine), Ballet Europeo, Nervi Festival, Genoa
1961   Title role (cr) in *Die Fledermaus* (Page), Ruth Page's
Chicago Opera Ballet, Rockford, Illinois
1963   Oberon (cr) in *Songe d'une nuit d'été* (Corelli), French
television
1964   The Prince in *Cinderella* (Orlikowsky), Raimondo de
Larrain Company, Paris
Title role (cr) in *Harold in Italy* (Corelli), French
television
Title role (cr) in *Pâris* (Charrat), Ballets de France, Paris
Title role in *Orpheus* (Lazzini), Marseilles Opera,
Marseilles
1965   Principal dancer (cr) in *Le Bal du destin* (Charrat),
Ballets de France, Nice
Leading role (cr) in *Jenny von Westphalen* (von Rosen),
Scandinavian Ballet, Aarhus
Romeo in *Romeo and Juliet* (Parlić), Marais Festival
1966   Principal dancer (cr) in *Le Cycle* (Charrat), Ballets de
France, Paris
Principal dancer (cr) in *Lélio* (Guélis), Bobino, Paris

Milorad Miskovitch in *Le Combat*

1968   Leading role (cr) in *La Mouette* (Gai), Siena Festival,
Italy
Title role (cr) in *Juan de Zarissa* (Parlic), Belgrade State
Opera Ballet, Belgrade
1971   Tancrède (cr) in *Le Combat de Tancrède* (also chor.),
Dubrovnik Festival, Dubrovnik

Other roles include: principal dancer in *Concerto* (pas de deux;
Charrat), Basil in *Don Quixote Pas de deux* (after Petipa).

WORKS

1962   *Guillaume Tell* (mus. Rossini), Venice
Le Jugement de Pâris (mus. Spontini), Ballet Parisien
Milorad Miskovitch, Spoleto Festival
Ce Soir (mus. Bernard), Ballet Parisien Milorad Miskovitch, Paris
1970   *The Creatures of Prometheus* (mus. Beethoven), Genoa
Opera, Genoa
1971   *Le Combat de Tancrede* (mus. Monteverdi), Dubrovnik
Festival, Dubrovnik
1972   *Le Cid* (mus. Massanet), Dallas Ballet, Dallas
1973   *Hommages romantiques* (mus. various), Florence

1975 *Hommage et sculptures musicales* (mus. Tynaire), Yugoslavia
1976 *La Figlia di Jorio* (mus. Hazon), Teatro di Vittoriale, Gardone
      The Nutcracker (mus. Tchaikovsky), Arena di Verona
1980 *Korak* (oratorio; mus. Hristic), Belgrade State Opera Ballet, Belgrade

Also staged:
1974 *Giselle* (after Petipa, Coralli, Perrot; mus. Adam), Arena di Verona
1976 *Swan Lake* (after Petipa, Ivanov), Florence

PUBLICATIONS

Lidova, Irène, *17 visages de la danse française*, Paris, 1953
Coquelle, Jean, "Men in Ballet", *Ballet Today* (London), January/February 1957
"Personality of the Month", *Dance and Dancers* (London), July 1958
Lidova, Irène, "Milorad Miskovitch", *Les Saisons de la danse* (Paris), June 1976
Lidova, Irène, "1957: Viaggio in Italia", *Ballettoggi* (Milan), May 1988
Lidova, Irène, "Da Spoleto à Verona", *Ballettoggi* (Milan), June 1988

* * *

Milorad Miskovitch started his life in dance as a member of the corps de ballet at the Belgrade Opera at the early age of seventeen. Since that time his career has spanned most areas of classical dance and dance production.

His early training with Preobrazhenska was to imbue him with the Russian nobility of style with which he would always be associated, and he was to become one of the finest European examples of the Russian school which included Toumanova, Skibine, and Golovine. He was to create a number of outstanding roles for such leading choreographers as Béjart, Howard, Massine, and Page.

During his late teens and early twenties Miskovitch gained valuable stage experience as a member of various companies which included the Ballets des Champs-Elysées, Mona Inglesby's International Ballet, de Basil's Original Ballet Russe, and the Grand Ballet de Monte Carlo. However, his international career really took off in France with Roland Petit's Ballets de Paris, from which he went on to join or to guest with other companies, including the London Festival Ballet. At the height of his career Miskovitch partnered some of the greatest ballerinas of the day, among them Alicia Markova, Yvette Chauviré, Janine Charrat, Carla Fracci, and Rosella Hightower.

His physique and demeanour, handsome face, and superb manners (both on and off stage) earned him praise and gratitude, and he was a much sought-after partner. It has been said that very few danseurs (excluding the late Erik Bruhn or Ivan Nagy) shared with Miskovitch that special quality of considerate and attentive partnering. While never self-effacing and a fine dancer himself, Miskovitch was always the "noble and gentle knight" and his ballerinas appreciated his skill and sensitivity as a partner.

In the 1950s Miskovitch went from strength to strength, winning prizes for best dancer of the year in polls taken in New York and Tokyo. The year 1956 brought a collaboration with Irène Lidova, when the two formed their own company, Les Ballet 1956, or Ballet des Étoiles de Paris, which toured the world and continued as Les Ballets 1957. Miskovitch continued to expand his experience with choreography and teaching, and in 1968 he returned to his native Yugoslavia, where he appeared in his own creations both in Belgrade and at the Dubrovnik Festival.

Inevitably the United States beckoned, and in 1973 Miskovitch went to Dallas to work with the company there, and thence to the Ballet of Alabama, but after a year he returned to Europe. On his return he was invited to mount *Giselle* for Carla Fracci at Verona and, probably as a result of that production's outstanding success, started a long-standing collaboration with Fracci and her partner Paolo Bortoluzzi, both in Italy and elsewhere. Those who were fortunate enough to have seen the Arena di Verona *Giselle* are unlikely ever to forget it.

A further high point came in 1975 when friend Maurice Béjart invited Miskovitch to take over the co-directorship of the Ballet du vingtième siècle tour of the U.S.A.. By this time Miskovitch was becoming more and more interested in production and the world of music and theatre as a whole, and in 1980 he became Artistic Advisor for UNESCO in Paris.

Since then he has organized some of the most important international events for that organization—a homage to Alicia Alonso, a gala in honour of Galina Ulanova and, to celebrate the fortieth anniversary of UNESCO, an evening at the Bolshoi in Moscow which included most of the étoiles of the dance world.

Miskovitch's talents, both artistic and administrative, eventually led to his appointment as President de conseil international de la danse (UNESCO) in 1988, succeeding Bengt Hager, the Swedish dance historian.

His aims at the Council are, of course, still artistic, but he is now a voice for dancers' rights, health, and welfare, and for the dissemination of dance information and education on all aspects of the art. The Video Dance Festival at Montpellier is developing strongly under his guidance, and folk and ethnic disciplines are part of his continuing international approach to the language of dance.

In Paris, Milorad Miskovitch remains the epitome of the "danseur noble", as elegant, handsome, and above all courteous a figure as ever. Young dancers would do well to take him as an example of all that a male dancer should be, and of what classical dance at the highest level represents.

—Sally Whyte

_____

MISS JULIE

Choreography: Birgit Cullberg
Music: Ture Rangström (arranged and orchestrated by Hans Grossman)
Design: Allan Fridericia (scenery and costumes)
Libretto: Birgit Cullberg (after August Strindberg's play *Fröken Julie*)
First Production: Riksteatern, Västerås, Sweden, 1 March 1950
Principal Dancers: Elsa Marianne von Rosen (Miss Julie), Julius Mengarelli (Jean, the Butler), Birgit Cullberg (Kristine)

Other productions include: Royal Swedish Ballet (restaged Cullberg; revised scenery by Sven Erixon), with von Rosen and Mengarelli; Stockholm, 7 September 1950. American Ballet Theatre (revised and restaged Cullberg), with Violette Verdy,

Miss Julie, with Cynthia Gregory and Erik Bruhn, American Ballet Theatre, c.1968

Erik Bruhn; New York, 18 September 1958. Royal Danish Ballet; Copenhagen, 18 December 1958. Ballet of the German Opera on the Rhine; Düsseldorf, 4 April 1965. German Opera Ballet; Berlin, 27 March 1979. Cullberg Ballet (television version; restaged Cullberg), with Galina Panova and Niklas Ek; Sveriges TV2, 1980. Ballet of La Scala; Milan, 12 February 1980. Pittsburg Ballet Theatre; 19 February 1982. Northern Ballet Theatre, with Evelyne Desutter and Rudolf Nureyev; London, 30 October 1987. Tani Ballet; Tokyo, 1989.

Other choreographic treatments of story: Kenneth MacMillan (Stuttgart, 1970).

PUBLICATIONS

Beaumont, Cyril, *Ballets of Today*, London, 1954

Regner, Otto Friedrich, *Reclams Balletführer*, Stuttgart 1972

Häger, Bengt, "*Fröken Julie, 25 ar*", *Dans* (Stockholm), February 1975

Balanchine, George, with Mason, Francis, *Balanchine's Complete Stories of the Great Ballets*, Garden City, N.Y., 1977

Näslund, Erik, *Birgit Cullberg*, Stockholm, 1978

Michel, Marcelle "Birgit Cullberg et l'Impressionisme Suédois", *Pour la danse* (Paris), June 1981

Engdahl, Horace, *Swedish Ballet and Dance: A Contemporary View*, Stockholm, 1984

*   *   *

"Västerås has been honoured. The town has been made the stage for a ballet premiere and it will go down in history." Perhaps it was hyperbole born out of local pride which inspired the newspaper critic of *Aftonbladets* to write up the first performance of Birgit Cullberg's *Miss Julie* in these terms, but there is some truth in the words. Since the premiere, some 40 years ago, it has become one of the most frequently staged of modern ballets, mounted on companies large and small not only in Scandinavia, where naturally its popularity is great, but all over America and Europe, and even in Tehran and Tokyo.

Miss Julie now belongs to the world, but it should not be forgotten that it saw the light of day on a regional Swedish tour by a small company, a group of highly talented individuals responding in part to current trends and national concerns.

Cullberg chose Strindberg's play as the theme for her new ballet at a time when Sweden had been celebrating the centenary of the playwright's birth. Out of this one-act play with only three characters, Cullberg fashioned a dramatic ballet in four scenes, enlarging the dramatis personae and using a small corps de ballet. Julie, the only offspring of an aristocratic house, rejects her fiancé, but tragically misjudges her seduction of the family butler, Jean. Unable to face the future as the mistress of a social inferior, she commits suicide, with a degree of complicity from him.

For Cullberg, this was not only a timely work for a Swedish tour, but the opportunity to choreograph a ballet built around a heroine with manifest sexual needs, as in the influential new work she had recently seen, Roland Petit's Carmen (1949).

Petit expressed Carmen's character through a modern use of classical technique; there is nothing ethereal about her presentation en pointe but rather an expression of will-power and the display of her considerable physical attractions. This came as a revelation to Cullberg at a time when she had begun to extend her Jooss–Leeder movement vocabulary through serious study of classical ballet.

In Miss Julie, Cullberg can be seen at the beginning of the process of finding a new and personal style that would draw on both techniques (as well as Graham technique later on). In this ballet, the characters are defined and separated by their movement styles. Julie's aristocracy is symbolized through the image of a ballerina. She makes use of the "danse d'école", she dances on pointe, and her riding habit costume in the first scene is based on the classical tutu shape. She is thus furnished from the start with all the latent sexuality of the ballerina, but without the ballerina's sexual decorum.

The servants and peasants move in a different way entirely. Their dance is vigorous and folk-based, their costumes close to everyday wear. They use deep, wide pliés in second position, raise their legs high with flexed feet, and lean their bodies forward in eagerness for scandal. Jean, the butler, exists in both worlds. While his dance can be as uninhibited as the other servants, he also knows his classical style. He snaps to attention in fifth position, arms in a rigorously rounded bras bas: this is his movement signature.

Social criticism is manifest through this hierarchy of styles. Julie's father and fiancé display a decadent version of classicism, reduced to nothing but aristocratic bearing and fussy steps. No wonder Julie gravitates towards Jean.

The title role will always be associated with its creator, Elsa Marianne von Rosen, ballerina of Oscarsteatern, a theatre in Stockholm supporting a ballet troupe. In some accounts of the genesis of the work, the initial idea is said to have come from the dancer's fiancé Allan Fridericia, designer of the first production, who was looking for a role to enhance von Rosen's reputation and advance her career. A vivacious blonde with a pronounced acting ability, she was also a genuine aristocrat in her own right, a fact which may have given an edge to her interpretation. Whether or not the initial idea came from Fridericia or Cullberg herself, the imprint of von Rosen, the ballerina-aristocrat, is clear.

For Cullberg and von Rosen, the ballet was to boost their international careers. Within months it was in the repertoire of the Royal Swedish Ballet, bringing them into the heart of the ballet establishment. Then came the numerous stagings and international guest appearances.

So much for the significance of Miss Julie in its original time, but how can we account for the continued success of this story, across many nations and for more than 40 years of the twentieth century? We should look first of all at the very nature of the story, for it faces two key issues of our time, sex and class, and condenses them into the essential power play in human relationships, a theme which maintains its contemporary relevance today.

Then, also, it continues to provide challenges for performers. The behaviour of Julie and Jean swings between the opposite poles of their obsessions, with a myriad of subtle gradations possible in between. They are both in turn seducer and seduced, slave and master, peasant and aristocrat. Miss Julie is quite simply a splendid work for principal dancers with a dramatic leaning.

Although it started out as a perfect vehicle for a new female ballet star, the most inspired performances of recent decades have been in the role of Jean. There is an affinity between Jean and the modern male stars who have fought their way out from behind the shadow of the ballerina. Erik Bruhn and Rudolf Nureyev were two of the role's most celebrated exponents. Bruhn's interpretation brought out all the hateful aspects of Jean's character, his manipulativeness and deceit, and yet allowed sympathy for his position as a man whose abilities had lifted him beyond his own class, while not allowing him access to that of his masters. Nureyev explored the complex aspects of Jean's nature—his sexual magnetism and peasant earthiness, combined with arrogance. As he walked away at the end of the ballet, it was clear that his act of collusion in Julie's suicide had freed him to be his own master.

Miss Julie continues to flourish in companies far and wide, because it is a potent dramatic narrative, with strongly defined characters, presented with psychological realism. Successful works of this nature are sadly very sparse on the ballet stage. Miss Julie remains a key work of the genre.

—Larraine Nicholas

———

MITCHELL, Arthur

American dancer, teacher, choreographer, and ballet director. Born in New York, 27 March 1934. Studied at the High School of Performing Arts, and at the School of American Ballet, New York. Stage début in Broadway musicals, also performing with modern dance companies of Donald McKayle and John Butler, 1953–55; dancer, New York City Ballet, from 1955, becoming soloist, from 1959, creating many Balanchine roles; also international guest artist, including for Munich Ballet Festival, 1963, Stuttgart Ballet, 1963, and National Ballet of Canada at Stratford, Connecticut, 1964; founding artistic director, Companhia Nacional de Brazil, Rio de Janeiro, 1966; founder and director, with Karel Shook, Dance Theatre of Harlem (and affiliated school), New York, from 1969, with professional début of company, 1971, touring domestically as well as London, various seasons from 1974, and Soviet Union, 1988; choreographer, staging works for Companhia Brasileira de Ballet, 1968, and Dance Theatre of Harlem, from 1969; teacher, Dance Theatre of Harlem, from 1969; also guest teacher, including for Katherine Dunham School and Jones-Hayward School of Ballet; member, National Council on the Arts, 1987. Recipient: Capezio Award, 1971; Dance Magazine Award, 1975; Lion of the Performing Arts, New York Public Library, 1985; Black History Makers Award, Association of Black Charities, 1985; Honorary Doctorate of Fine Arts, Williams College, 1985, and Princeton University, 1986; Honorary Doctorate of Art, Harvard University, 1987; Encore Award, 1987.

ROLES

1955   Attendant (cr) in Souvenirs (Bolender), New York City Ballet, New York

Arthur Mitchell in *Agon*, **New York City Ballet, 1957**

1956   Principal dancer (cr) in *Allegro Brillante* (Balanchine), New York City Ballet, New York
1957   The Unicorn (cr) in *The Unicorn, the Gorgon and the Manticore* (Butler), New York City Ballet, New York
       Pas de deux (cr) in *Agon* (Balanchine), New York City Ballet, New York
1960   Principal dancer (cr) in *Ocho por Radio* (Mexico; Contreras) in *Panamerica* (Balanchine, Contreras, Moncion, Taras, d'Amboise), New York City Ballet, New York
       The Oni of Ife (cr) in *The Figure in the Carpet* (Balanchine), New York City Ballet, New York
       Snake (cr) in *Creation of the World* (Bolender), New York City Ballet, New York
       Principal dancer (cr) in *Ebony Concerto* (Taras), part of *Jazz Concert*, New York City Ballet, New York
1961   Introduction (orchestra), Variant 3 (vibraharp), Variant 5 (quartet) (cr) in *Modern Jazz: Variants* (Balanchine), New York City Ballet, New York
       "In the Inn" in *Ivesiana* (four movements only; Balanchine), New York City Ballet, New York
1962   Puck (cr) in *A Midsummer Night's Dream* (Balanchine), New York City Ballet, New York
1963   A Dancer (cr) in *Arcade* (Taras), New York City Ballet, New York
1964   Warm-up (cr) in *Clarinade* (Balanchine), New York City Ballet, New York
       The Young Convict in *Piège de Lumière* (Taras), New York City Ballet, New York
1965   Rigaudon Flamenco (cr) in *Don Quixote* (Balanchine), New York City Ballet, New York
1966   Principal dancer in *Divertimento No. 15* (revival; Balanchine), New York City Ballet, New York
       Sixth Variation (cr) in *La Guirlande de Campra* (Taras), New York City Ballet, New York
1967   Othello (cr) in *Prologue* (d'Amboise), New York City Ballet, New York
       Dancer (cr) in *Ragtime* II (pas de deux; Balanchine), New York City Ballet, New York
       Principal dancer (cr) in *Trois Valses Romantiques* (Balanchine), New York City Ballet, New York
1968   Pas de deux in Pithoprakta (cr) in *Metastaseis and Pithoprakta* (Balanchine), New York City Ballet, New York
       Hoofer (cr) in *Slaughter on Tenth Avenue* (Balanchine), New York City Ballet, New York
       Principal dancer (cr) in *Requiem Canticles* (Balanchine; performed only once in honour of Martin Luther King), New York City Ballet, New York

Other roles include: Phlegmatic in *The Four Temperaments* (Balanchine), Dark Angel in *Orpheus* (Balanchine), Bourrée Fantasque in *Bourrée Fantasque* (Balanchine), second movement in *Interplay* (Robbins), principal dancer in *Afternoon of a Faun* (Robbins), Fourth Campaign in *Stars and Stripes* (Balanchine), Ricercata in *Episodes II* (Balanchine), Allegro and Rondo in *Western Symphony* (Balanchine), principal dancer in *Monumentum Pro Gesualdo* (Balanchine), principal dancer in *Bugaku* (Balanchine), Jason in *Medea* (Cullberg).

WORKS

1969   *Ode to Otis* (mus. Perkinson), Dance Theatre of Harlem, New York
1970   *Tones* (mus. Leon), Dance Theatre of Harlem, New York

Biostera (mus. Nobre), Dance Theatre of Harlem, New York
Fun and Games (mus. Piccioni), Dance Theatre of Harlem, New York
Holberg Suite (mus. Grieg), Dance Theatre of Harlem, New York
Spiritual Suite (mus. Perkinson), Dance Theatre of Harlem, New York
1971   *Rhythmetron* (mus. Nobre), Dance Theatre of Harlem, New York
       Fête Noire (mus. Shostakovich), Dance Theatre of Harlem, New York
       Concerto for Jazz Band and Orchestra (with Balanchine; mus. Lieberman), New York City Ballet and Dance Theatre of Harlem Gala, New York
1975   *Manifestations* (mus. Foutain), Dance Theatre of Harlem, Chicago
1976   "Dance in Praise of His Name" added to *Spiritual Suite* (mus. Perkinson), Dance Theatre of Harlem, Philadelphia
1977   *Breezin'* (mus. G. Benson), Dance Theatre of Harlem, New York
       The Greatest (mus. Messer), Dance Theatre of Harlem, New York
       El Mar (mus. G. Benson), Dance Theatre of Harlem, New York
1978   *Walk in the Light* (mus. Saunders), Dance Theatre of Harlem, Philadelphia
1987   *Phoenix Rising* (mus. Perkinson), Dance Theatre of Harlem, New York
1988   *John Henry* (mus. Rosenstock), Dance Theatre of Harlem, New York

PUBLICATIONS

By Mitchell:
Interview in "Dance Comes to Harlem", *Dance and Dancers* (London), October 1974
Interview in Gruen, John, *The Private World of Ballet*, New York, 1975
Interview in Goodwin, Noël, "Arthur Mitchell", *Dance Gazette* (London), October 1985
Interview in Newman, Barbara, "Speaking of Dance: Arthur Mitchell", *Dancing Times* (London), June 1986
Interview in Gruen, John, *People Who Dance*, New York, 1988

About Mitchell:
Goodman, Saul, "Brief Biographies: Arthur Mitchell", *Dance Magazine* (New York), December 1957
Maynard, Olga, "Arthur Mitchell and the Dance Theatre of Harlem", *Dance Magazine* (New York), March 1970
Siegel, Marcia B., *At the Vanishing Point*, New York, 1972
Tobias, Tobi, *Arthur Mitchell*, New York, 1975
Reynolds, Nancy, *Repertory in Review*, New York, 1977
Steinbrink, Mark, "Dream Factory", *Ballet News* (New York), February 1981
Maynard, Olga, "Arthur Mitchell and the Dance Theatre of Harlem", *Dance Magazine* (New York), January 1982

*   *   *

Arthur Mitchell was the first black dancer to reach principal rank in an American ballet company and the first black male classical dancer to achieve an international reputation. He went on to found and direct the Dance Theatre of Harlem, creating an opportunity for blacks to perform in the classical style. The key word is "classical"; when Mitchell joined the New York City Ballet in 1955, African-American artists were dancing with modern dance companies, on Broadway, and in specifically black troupes organized by pioneers such as Katherine Dunham. Ballet, in general, was closed to them. Mitchell was an established star of City Ballet, but commercial television stations in the southern United States refused to broadcast programs in which he danced with a white ballerina. During the formative years of Dance Theatre of Harlem, he sometimes pointed out that there were many black dancers who could perform ballet, but no companies in which they could do so. "We have to prove," he said in 1970, "that a black ballet school and a black ballet company are the equal of the best anywhere in the world."

As a dancer, Mitchell was both extraordinary talented and notably skilled. Commenting on his performance as Puck, the role George Balanchine made on him in *A Midsummer Night's Dream*, the critic Walter Terry wrote that he "leaps with the shimmer of a moonbeam". As an artistic director, he maintains equally high standards of performance and displays considerable political acumen. He is strikingly articulate, and his intense energy, considerable charm, clear intelligence, and remarkable determination have been invaluable instruments in promoting his company's survival.

After graduating from New York City's High School of Performing Arts, Mitchell was offered scholarships by Bennington College and by the School of American Ballet. Although his training until then had concentrated on modern dance and jazz, he chose the latter. In 1955, he made his début with the New York City Ballet in Balanchine's *Western Symphony*. He had already appeared on Broadway in the musical *House of Flowers*, and his modern dance credits included performances in the companies of John Butler and Donald McKayle.

During his fifteen years with NYCB, Mitchell danced many of the major male roles in the Balanchine repertory, including the "Phlegmatic" variation in *The Four Temperaments*, the Dark Angel in *Orpheus*, and the leading male part in *Bugaku*. Balanchine made the pas de deux in *Agon* on Mitchell and Diana Adams, and created the role of Puck for the dancer in 1962. Probably because of his early training, Mitchell was also called upon when Balanchine felt inspired to take on jazz or jazz-inspired music, as in *Jazz Concert*, to which three other choreographers contributed pieces, *Clarinade*, and the reworking of *Slaughter on Tenth Avenue* originally made for the musical *On Your Toes* in 1936. None of these experiments was notably successful, although *Slaughter* is enough of a crowd-pleaser to have been revived. Even so, Mitchell's dancing always was both elegant and energetic. His lithe body fitted itself easily around the stretchy steps of dances such as the *Agon* pas de deux; he could be cool, dignified, and weighted in neo-classic roles and playfully charming in lighter roles.

As early as 1960, Mitchell began to expand his career beyond NYCB. That year, at the invitation of Gian Carlo Menotti, he organized a company that performed at the Festival of Two Worlds in Spoleto, gaining his first experience as an artistic director. He appeared in musicals again; Terry described his dancing in one revue as being "sheathed in a beautiful combination of sexiness and elegance". In 1966, Mitchell was invited to become artistic director of Brazil's new Companhia Nacional de Ballet, and in 1968 he served as choreographer and teacher for the Companhia Brasileira de Ballet. He was in Rio de Janeiro when he learned of the assassination of Dr. Martin Luther King, Jr. and returned to New York with the intention of providing children in Harlem with training in the arts. The following year, with financial assistance from the Ford Foundation, Mitchell and Karel Shook founded Dance Theatre

of Harlem as a school and a professional company.

Mitchell contributed choreography to the company's repertory. His works include *Holberg Suite*, *Rhythmetron*, *Fête Noire*, and *Manifestations*. *Fête Noire* was described by Clive Barnes in *The New York Times* as "a very grand court ball set, say, in Liberia at the time of St. Petersburg". *Manifestations*, set to a jazz score by Primus Fountain, is a strongly theatrical version of the story of Adam and Eve, in which the juiciest role goes to the Snake, who enters by descending on a rope, head down. Mitchell's choreography was soundly crafted and intelligently constructed, but more competent than inspired. He drew on all the traditions he had absorbed during his dancing career to produce pieces that suited the vitality and honed style of a young company. As a teacher, Mitchell has a reputation for being both inspiring and demanding. He still teaches company class at DTH, although he stopped choreographing as his administrative duties increased.

—Joseph H. Mazo

MOISEYEV, Igor

Russian/Soviet dancer, choreographer, and company director. Born Igor Aleksandrovich Moiseev (Moiseyev) in Kiev, 21 January (8 January old style) 1906. Studied at the private ballet studio of Vera Mosolova, Moscow, from 1919, and at Moscow Choreographic School, pupil of Aleksandr Gorsky and Vasily Tikhomirov, 1921–24. Dancer, soon becoming soloist, Bolshoi Ballet, 1924–39, performing also at the Bolshoi Experimental Theatre, from 1925; choreographer, Bolshoi Ballet, from 1930; director, choreographic section, Moscow Theatre for Folk Art, 1936; founder and artistic director, USSR Folk Dance Ensemble, from 1937, touring USSR in 1947, and travelling abroad, with débuts in Paris, 1955, London, 1957, United States, 1958; founder, Choreographic Concert Ensemble (later called Young Ballet and Moscow Classical Ballet), 1966. Recipient: State Prize of the USSR, 1942, 1947, 1952; People's Artist of the USSR, 1953; Honorary Membership, Paris Academy of Dance, 1955; *Dance Magazine* Award, New York, 1960; Lenin Prize, 1967; title of Hero of Socialist Labour, 1976.

ROLES

1925   Raoul in *Teolinda* (Goleizovsky), Bolshoi Experimental Theatre, Moscow

Title role in *Joseph the Beautiful* (Goleizovsky), Bolshoi Experimental Theatre, Moscow

Slave in *Le Corsaire* (Gorsky, Petipa), Bolshoi Ballet, Moscow

1926   Phoenix in *The Red Poppy* (Tikhomirov, Laschilin), Bolshoi Ballet, Moscow

Slave in *La Bayadère* (Gorsky after Petipa), Bolshoi Ballet, Moscow

1930   Title role in *The Footballer* (also chor.), Bolshoi Ballet, Moscow

1932   Mato (cr) in *Salammbô* (also chor.), Bolshoi Ballet, Moscow

WORKS

1930   *The Footballer* (with Lashchilin; mus. Oransky), Bolshoi Ballet, Moscow

Vain Precautions (*La Fille mal gardée*; with Messerer; mus. various), Bolshoi Experimental Theatre, Moscow

Dances in *The Love for Three Oranges* (opera; mus. Prokofiev), Bolshoi Theatre, Moscow

1931   Dances in *Carmen* (opera; mus. Bizet), Bolshoi Theatre, Moscow

1932   *Salammbô* (mus. Arends), Bolshoi Filial Theatre, Moscow

1935   *Three Fat Men* (mus. Oransky), Bolshoi Ballet, Moscow

1958   *Spartacus* (mus. Khachaturian), Bolshoi Ballet, Moscow

Other works include: dances in *Turandot* (opera; mus. Puccini), *The Demon* (opera; mus. Rubinstein); concert pieces and folk dance cycles including—*Guerillas* (also known as *The Partisans*), *Moldovenskaya*, *A Street in a Collective Farm* (also known as *Kolhoz Street*), *Pictures from the Past, Soviet Pictures, Round the Globe, Dance of Fools, Poem from the Surroundings of Moscow, Tsam.*

PUBLICATIONS

By Moiseyev:
"Ballet and Reality", translated by Lyubov Solov, *Dance Magazine* (New York), May 1953
"Moiseyev Lecture" (excerpts), *Dance News* (New York), September 1958

About Moiseyev:
Lawson, Joan, "Soviet Ballet", *Ballet Annual*, no. 1, London, 1947
Soria, Georges, *Le Ballet Möisséiev*, Paris, 1955
Mason, Edward, "Dance Lectures: Moiseyev on Folk Dance as Theatre", *Dance and Dancers* (London), January 1956
Joel, Lydia, "The Moiseyev Dance Company", *Dance Magazine* (New York), June 1958
Moore, Lillian, "Class with Moiseyev", *Dance Magazine* (New York), August 1958
René, Natalia, "25 Years of Moiseyev", *Dance and Dancers* (London), May 1962
Moiseyev's Dance Company (in English and Russian), Moscow, 1966

*   *   *

An early curiosity about folk traditions, the opportunity to explore unspoiled rural areas of the Soviet Union, and a classical ballet foundation that proved too conservative: these were the ingredients in Igor Moiseyev's decision to found the Soviet Union's most famous folk dance troupe—the Moiseyev Dance Company, known in the Soviet Union as the State Academic Folk Dance Ensemble of the USSR.

Many paths led up to it. Igor Aleksandrovich Moiseyev was born in Kiev, in the Ukraine, in 1906. At the age of six, he was sent to live with his aunts in the country for four years. These relatives were relief school mistresses who travelled constantly from village to village, replacing teachers who were sick or called to other duties. They took the young Igor along with them and it was the different traditions and costumes of the people that he encountered on these journeys that made a lasting impression on him.

At the age of ten, Moiseyev left this unspoiled life and set off for Moscow, there to discover a more refined artistry. But even then, his love for exploring the country did not stop. He and his father, a keen hiker, set off whenever possible to trek over the Caucasus, the Crimea, the Urals, and Byelorussia. It was an

enriching childhood, in which the young boy discovered new traditions, absorbing the flavour and atmosphere of the varying cultures he saw.

After the Revolution, Moiseyev's father enrolled him in a small private ballet school run by Vera Mosolova. Moiseyev quickly showed an aptitude for dance, and in six months had accomplished the full three-year programme. His teacher took him to the Moscow Choreographic School (the Bolshoi academy) when Moiseyev was fourteen, and he was placed in the sixth class. Among his teachers were the distinguished dancers Aleksandr Gorsky and Vasily Tikhomirov. On graduation into the Bolshoi, Moiseyev soon became a soloist, dancing many character roles, including the title role in *Joseph the Beautiful*.

Of course, since the Revolution, the very existence of the Bolshoi was in jeopardy, as it was a reminder of Tsarist glories. An impassioned plea by Anatoli Lunacharsky, then First Commissar of Education, saved the theatre on the grounds that its productions could be used for propaganda. The democratization of choreography saw new works—not always successful, nor well received by the authorities—and it also saw the formation of the Bolshoi Experimental Theatre. But it was a period of uncertainty for many of the young dancers, including Moiseyev: resenting the conservatism of classical dance as it was upheld at the Bolshoi, and angered by what they believed was the stifling of creativity at the Bolshoi Theatre, they staged a mini-revolution. Moiseyev was made secretary of the group, with the duty of collecting signatures for a petition to the director. The result was inevitable—Moiseyev was seen to be the leader of the revolt and, along with several other dancers, was thrown out of the Bolshoi. However, the dancer fought for his cause, calling on the Minister of Culture. Fifteen minutes later, through the intervention of the minister, the company and the group were reinstated. Moiseyev was just nineteen. He was regarded by the "old guard" as an enemy, and, though he danced with the company for another twelve years, he found little artistic satisfaction in performing.

During this period Moiseyev choreographed many works, demonstrating a gift for humour and satire. Among them were *Salammbô*, *The Footballer* (*Futbolist*), and *Three Fat Men* (*Tri Tolstyaka*). Moiseyev also became, in 1936, the director of the choreographic section at the Moscow Theatre for Folk Art. Later, in 1958, he created his own version of *Spartacus*, and in 1966 he formed the classically oriented Choreographical Concert Ensemble (later called the Young Ballet and today known as the Moscow Classical Company). This ensemble took contemporary works around the Soviet Union, often to venues where there was no permanent ballet house.

In 1937, Moiseyev succeeded in convincing the authorities of the need to create a new group, to promote popular folk dance that drew on the rich cultural heritage of the USSR. Since nothing like it had ever been attempted, Moiseyev again had to use his persuasive powers, now to found a new school, create a specific repertoire, and search for authentic dances. Until this time, folk dancing had been considered an amateur activity only, featuring at festivals and celebrations. Now, Moiseyev requested a company of the highest professionalism and artistry. He set off, often on horseback with a pack on his back, into the interior regions of the Soviet Union. He brought back with him dancers from ballet schools, music-halls, and amateur stages, plus a fund of colourful costumes and dances for his new company. The dancers prepared for a whole year and the group won much success. When war interrupted normal life, Moiseyev took his troupe out of the theatres into the open air to perform for soldiers, factory workers, and children.

Moiseyev founded his school in 1943. Today, housed at the Tchaikovsky Hall in Moscow, it takes 40 students—20 boys, 20 girls—from the age of thirteen for a three-year course. Many are second- and third-generation folk dancers. Here, after an opening class of ballet, the students learn, often under the watchful eye of Moiseyev himself, to build up their skills for the squats, spinning turns, leaps, and gliding needed for the authentic dances. Moiseyev has taken his company, now past its half-century, all over the world. The company has changed over the years: from its initial total of 35 dancers it is now over a hundred strong, with an orchestra of 40. The artists today are polished and technically skilled, unlike the original amateurs who danced with more emotional commitment than technique.

Moiseyev has created many folk-dance cycles for his company, such as *Pictures from the Past*, *Tsam* (a Buryat pantomime), and *Regions of the World*. He has also taken themes from more contemporary life, such as *Soviet Pictures*, incorporating *Naval Suite* and *Partisans*, which glorify the Motherland; and there are dances set on a collective farm in *Kolhoz Street*. Through his work Moiseyev's diligence and keen observation of culture has uncovered the essence of people and their traditions. His company presents a rich panorama of the colourful and lively customs and traditions of the past. He has played a role, impossible to measure in historical terms, in the very preservation of Russian culture.

—Margaret Willis

MONCION, Francisco

American dancer and choreographer. Born in La Vega, Dominican Republic, 6 July 1922. Studied at the School of American Ballet, New York (on partial, and then full, scholarship), pupil of George Balanchine, Pierre Vladimirov, Anatole Obukhov, and Muriel Stuart, from 1938. Début, while still a student, New Opera Company, New York, 1942, appearing with American Concert Ballet, 1943; soloist, Marquis de Cuevas's Ballet International, New York, 1944, Original Ballet Russe, 1946–47; principal dancer, Ballet Society (precursor to New York City Ballet), 1946–48, New York City Ballet, 1948–86; also appeared in operetta and musical comedy, including in *The Chocolate Soldier* (mus. Strauss; chor. Balanchine, 1947); choreographer, staging works for New York City Ballet, from 1950, and for television; producer of Balanchine ballets for companies including Chicago Ballet and State Ballet of Missouri; also painter and private artist.

ROLES

1944   Title role (cr) in *Mad Tristan* (Massine), (de Cuevas's) Ballet International, New York
Title role (cr) in *Sebastian* (Caton), (de Cuevas's) Ballet International, New York
The Doctor (cr) in *The Mute Wife* (Cobos), (de Cuevas's) Ballet International, New York
Principal dancer (cr) in *Memories* (Semenoff), (de Cuevas's) Ballet International, New York
Principal dancer in *Brahms Variations* (Nijinska), (de Cuevas's) Ballet International, New York
1946   Theme (cr) in *The Four Temperaments* (Balanchine), Ballet Society, New York
1947   Principal dancer (cr) in *Divertimento* (Balanchine), Ballet Society, New York
1948   Midas (cr) in *The Triumph of Bacchus and Ariadne* (Balanchine), Ballet Society, New York
Second movement (cr) in *Symphony in C* (new version of *Le Palais de Cristal*; Balanchine), Ballet Society, New York
Moon (cr) in *Capricorn Concerto* (Bolender), Ballet Society, New York
Dark Angel (cr) in *Orpheus* (Balanchine), Ballet Society, New York
The Beast (cr) in *Mother Goose Suite* (Bolender), New York City Ballet, New York
Principal dancer in *Concerto Barocco* (Balanchine), New York City Ballet, New York
1949   Principal dancer (cr) in *The Guests* (Robbins), New York City Ballet, New York
Boyfriend in *Time Table* (Tudor), New York City Ballet, New York
Title role (cr) in *Jinx* (Robbins), New York City Ballet, New York
Prince Ivan (cr) in *Firebird* (Balanchine), New York City Ballet, New York
Matteo (cr) in *Ondine* (Dollar), New York City Ballet, New York
1950   Principal dancer (cr) *The Age of Anxiety* (Robbins), New York City Ballet, New York
The Lover (cr) in *The Witch* (Cranko), New York City Ballet, London
1951   La Valse (cr) in *La Valse* (Balanchine), New York City Ballet, New York
1952   Boy of the Bayou (cr) in *Bayou* (Balanchine), New York City Ballet, New York
Sextus Tarquinius and Hamlet's Stepfather (cr) in *La Celoise* (Tudor), New York City Ballet, New York
The Husband, King Mark (cr) in *Picnic at Tintagel* (Ashton), New York City Ballet, New York
Principal dancer (cr) in *Kaleidoscope* (Boris), New York City Ballet, New York
1953   Principal dancer (cr) in *Afternoon of a Faun* (Robbins), New York City Ballet, New York
1954   "Second Time" (cr) in *Opus 34* (Balanchine), New York City Ballet, New York
Coffee (Arabian Dance) (cr) in *The Nutcracker* (Balanchine), New York City Ballet, New York
"Central Park in the Dark" (cr) in *Ivesiana* (Balanchine), New York City Ballet, New York
1957   Principal dancer (cr) in *Pastorale* (also chor.), New York City Ballet, New York
1959   Ricercata (cr) in *Episodes* II (Balanchine), New York City Ballet, New York
1960   Principal dancer (cr) in *Sinfonia No. 5* (Balanchine) in *Panamerica* (Balanchine, Contreras, Moncion, Taras, d'Amboise), New York City Ballet, New York
Duke of Granada (cr) in *The Figure in the Carpet* (Balanchine), New York City Ballet, New York
1962   Theseus (cr) in *A Midsummer Night's Dream* (Balanchine), New York City Ballet, New York
1965   Merlin (cr) in *Don Quixote* (Balanchine), New York City Ballet, New York
1967   Emeralds (cr) in *Jewels* (Balanchine), New York City Ballet, New York
1969   Second Movement (cr) in *Tchaikovsky Suite* (No. 2) (d'Amboise), New York City Ballet, New York
1970   Principal dancer (cr) in *In the Night* (Robbins), New York City Ballet, New York
1972   The Emperor (cr) in *The Song of the Nightingale* (Taras), New York City Ballet, New York
Devil (cr) in *Pulcinella* (Balanchine, Robbins), New York City Ballet, New York

Francisco Moncion with Melissa Hayden in *The Cage*, New York City Ballet

1982   Principal dancer (cr) in *Noah and the Flood* (revised version; Balanchine with d'Amboise), New York City Ballet, New York

Other roles include: Melancholic and Phlegmatic in *The Four Temperaments* (Balanchine), Rooster in *Renard* (Balanchine), title role in *Prodigal Son* (Balanchine), principal dancer in *The Duel* (Dollar), an Intruder in *The Cage* (Robbins), Five Pieces in *Episodes* II (Balanchine), Baron in *La Sonnambula* (Balanchine), title role in *Don Quixote* (Balanchine), Othello in *Prologue* (d'Amboise), Theme in *The Goldberg Variations* (Robbins), Drosselmeyer in *The Nutcracker* (Balanchine).

WORKS

1950   *Passepied* in *Music and Dance* (with Balanchine and others; mus. various), New York City Ballet and School of American Ballet, Carnegie Hall, New York

1955   *Jeux d'enfants* (with Milberg, Balanchine; mus. Bizet), New York City Ballet, New York

1957   *Pastorale* (mus. Turner), New York City Ballet, New York

1959   *Choros No. 7* (Brazil; mus. Villa-Lobos) in *Panamerica* (Balanchine, Contreras, Moncion, Taras, d'Amboise), New York City Ballet, New York

1960   *Les Biches* (mus. Poulenc), part of *Jazz Concert*, New York City Ballet, New York

1964   *Songs of the Soul* (mus. Suriñach), U.S. television (CBS)

1966   *Night Song* (mus. Shapero), National Ballet of Washington, D.C.

PUBLICATIONS

By Moncion:
Contribution to *I Remember Balanchine*, edited by Francis Mason, New York, 1991

About Moncion:
Denby, Edwin, *Looking at the Dance*, New York, 1949
Owen, Walter, "Dancer of the Month: Francisco Moncion", *Dance Magazine* (New York), March 1951
Chujoy, Anatole, *The New York City Ballet*, New York, 1953
Boroff, David, "Group Portrait of a Ballet Dancer", *Dancing Times* (London), May 1957
Reynolds, Nancy, *Repertory in Review*, New York, 1977
Sandler, Ken, "In the Beginning", *Ballet News* (New York), June 1979
Hunt, Marilyn, "Balanchine's *Divertimento*: A New Life", *Ballet Review* (New York), Fall 1985

*   *   *

Francisco Moncion—dancer, painter, and choreographer—entered the New York City Ballet Company at its inception in 1948. When he retired without ceremony in 1986, his 38 years as a major artist within one company may well have set a record.

In 1944, dancing with the Marquis de Cuevas's Ballet International, Moncion had an opportunity to move quickly out of the corps by filling in for André Eglevsky in a new ballet, *Mad Tristan*, by Léonide Massine. A student of the School of American Ballet, he left Ballet International and joined Ballet Society, a small company which had been formed in 1938 by Lincoln Kirstein.

Clearly, there were male soloists with a stronger technique and others who could excel as "danseurs nobles". But Moncion, as he himself had stated, was valuable material both as a soloist and as a partner. What audiences saw at the beginning of his career, they continued to see throughout his career: a figure of commanding stage presence, of masculine solidity, whose features appeared almost mask-like under the stage lights—a dancer who, under different circumstances, might have entered the world of modern dance with equal success.

When the Balanchine/Stravinsky ballet, *Orpheus*, had its premiere in 1948, Moncion appeared as the Dark Angel, a role that was to be an embodiment of his stage persona and one he would continue to dance for more than 30 years. Moving from the outer world to the underworld, the Dark Angel is a figure that belongs to no world. Balanchine appropriated simple walking steps and arm movements for the Dark Angel, guiding the blinded Orpheus into Hades. Moncion's Dark Angel, an image of quiet control, became both a menace and a saviour, and brought an intensity and pictorial drama to this most delicate work.

In a later Ravel/Balanchine ballet, *La Valse*, the malevolent quality was intensified. Moncion, representing death, appeared in a crowded ballroom to tempt a young woman away from her lover. Accepting his offer to dance, she was swept into a dance with Death. Is it a cruel Death, taking an innocent life, or a Spirit again leading the guiltless to another world? Moncion, bringing his solemn and imposing presence to both the Dark Angel and the figure of Death, gave both ballets unusual theatrical substance.

Despite his commanding stage presence, Moncion did not seem to overshadow his partners. Maria Tallchief's triumph as the Firebird came first with his Prince Ivan. Attentive and bewildered, his Prince was mesmerized by the brilliant bird. Jerome Robbins created his version of *Afternoon of a Faun* on Moncion and Tanaquil LeClercq; Moncion's Faun moved with a languid narcissism as he supported LeClercq with ease and grace. Many years later, Robbins set Patricia McBride and Moncion together as the temperamental, quarrelling lovers in his Chopin Ballet, *In the Night*, which demanded virtuostic support in fast catches and lifts. Both works by Robbins, though opposites, displayed Moncion's masculine authority and partnering assurance. It was Balanchine again who used Moncion's simplicity and sense of calm to escort his partner through the Fauré section, Emeralds, of the *Jewels* ballet (1967).

Moncion's limitations in technique undoubtedly eliminated some of the fast-footed and nimble roles in the New York City Ballet repertory. However, within those undertaken, the range was great, from the lead in *The Prodigal Son* to Drosselmeyer in *The Nutcracker*. At the premiere of *The Nutcracker* in 1954, Moncion appeared in the Arab divertissement as Coffee, exotic in pantaloons and accepting an opium pipe from four dancing parrots. Moncion thought it was a delightful bit, but Balanchine had it changed shortly to a female dancer, apparently to pique the interest of the male parents in the audience. One of Moncion's major roles was taken late in his career, that of Don Quixote, an almost totally mimed part, in the three-act ballet by Balanchine.

Moncion, the creative artist on stage, was the creative artist off-stage as well. As a painter, he has had exhibitions in and around New York City, his subjects consistent with a person of the theatre: clowns, still-lifes, and architectural designs.

Moncion the choreographer mounted several short works for television and for the stage, including versions of Bizet's *Jeux* and Poulenc's *Les Biches*. His most successful was *Pastorale*, a ballet for City Ballet in 1957. Using Allegra Kent, Roy Robias, and himself, he created a sensitive and poetic work to the music of his contemporary, Charles Turner.

—Richard Rutledge

———

MONOTONES
(*Monotones I and II*)

Choreography: Frederick Ashton
Music: Erik Satie (orchestrated by John Lanchbery)
Design: Frederick Ashton (costumes)
First Production: Royal Ballet, Royal Opera House, London, 25 April 1966 (*Monotones II* alone, to *Trois Gymnopédies*, first performed for Royal Ballet Gala, 24 March 1965)
Principal Dancers: Vyvyan Lorrayne, Anthony Dowell, Robert Mead (*Trois Gymnopédies*); Antoinette Sibley, Georgina Parkinson, Brian Shaw (*Trois Gnossiennes*)

Other productions include: Royal Ballet Touring Company, with Doreen Wells, Lucette Aldous, David Wall (*Gnossiennes*), and Shirley Grahame, Hendrik Davel, Paul Clarke (*Gymnopédies*); Wiesbaden, 28 May 1968. German Opera Ballet (staged Robert Mead); Berlin, 20 June 1971. Chicago Ballet (staged Robert Mead; mus. original Satie piano score); Elgin, Illinois, 9 February 1974. City Center Joffrey Ballet (staged Faith Worth); New York, 11 October 1974. Australian Ballet (staged Robert Mead); Brisbane, 18 July 1975. San Francisco Ballet; San Francisco, 27 January 1981. Ballet West (staged John Hart); Salt Lake City, 1985. Scottish Ballet; Aberdeen, August 1990.

PUBLICATIONS

Monahan, James, "Two-Thirds of a Ballet: Ashton's *Monotones*", *Dancing Times* (London), June 1966

Williams, Peter, and Percival, John, "More Monotones", *Dance and Dancers* (London), June 1966

Hall, Fernau, "*Monotones*", *Ballet Today* (London), 2 parts, May–June, July–August 1966

Brinson, Peter, and Crisp, Clement, *Ballet for All*, London, 1970

Monotones, with Anthony Dowell, Vyvyan Lorrayne, and David Ashmole, Royal Ballet, London, 1975

Balanchine, George, with Mason, Francis, *Balanchine's Complete Stories of the Great Ballets*, Garden City, N.Y., 1977
Vaughan, David, *Frederick Ashton and his Ballets*, London, 1977

*   *   *

The second section of Ashton's *Monotones*, for two men and one woman in white, was composed the year before the first section, which was made for one man and two women all in green. Both sections are to music by Erik Satie, the first to *Trois Gnossiennes*, the second to *Trois Gymnopédies*, the score he published immediately before the *Gnossiennes*.

Monotones II was originally choreographed as a short pas de trois for the annual Royal Ballet Benevolent Fund gala. It was based on a simple, almost austere, idea of arabesques and attitudes, on which each *Gymnopédie* offers a variant. The movement in other words is deeply rooted in the danse d'école, but the overall impression is very contemporary. Just as in *Symphonic Variations* (1946) and *Scènes de ballet* (1948), Ashton's genius was to eliminate. As he said himself: "Usually as I work I just reject and reject, and I purify everything and get to the essence of what I really want".

Monotones II was an immediate success at the gala, but it was felt at the time that it was too short to stand as a repertory piece on its own: and accordingly Ashton composed *Monotones I* to precede it. *Monotones II* is other-worldly, calmly detached, as though (in David Vaughan's words) "Ashton thought of the dancers as celestial acrobats". By contrast, and a contrast typical of Ashton, *Monotones I* is more earthly, more tense, less serene. The music this time has a stronger pulse and Ashton accordingly made choreography more sharply accented than before. In both *Monotones I* and *II*, however, the emphasis is on the dancers' quality of line, perfectly matched to the clear, assured lines of Satie's music.

There is no scenario for *Monotones*. Ashton's subject is simply two groups of three dancers moving in relation to each other and to the space in which they find themselves. There are certainly "events" in the choreography, but they are the turning-points not of a narrative but of a formal, choreographic logic that nevertheless cannot be labelled simply abstract. Ashton's is a breathing geometry that quickens and frees the space that contains it. *Monotones* is a shifting pattern of reciprocities, complex and simple, symmetrical and asymmetrical, and potent beyond all the purity of its chaste means.

—Martin Wright

A MONTH IN THE COUNTRY

Choreography: Frederick Ashton
Music: Frédéric Chopin (arranged by John Lanchbery)
Design: Julia Trevelyan Oman (scenery and costumes)
Libretto: Frederick Ashton (after the play by Ivan Turgenev)
First Production: Royal Ballet, Royal Opera House, London, 12 February 1976
Principal Dancers: Lynn Seymour (Natalia Petrovna), Anthony Dowell (Beliaev), Wayne Sleep (Kolia), Denise Nunn (Vera)

PUBLICATIONS

"*A Month in the Country*", *About the House* (London), Spring 1976

Anderson, Jack, "Life, Literature, and the Royal Ballet", *Dance Magazine* (New York), August 1976
Balanchine, George, with Mason, Francis, *Balanchine's Complete Stories of the Great Ballets*, Garden City, N.Y., 1977
Vaughan, David, *Frederick Ashton and his Ballets*, London, 1977
Jordan, Stephanie, "*A Month in the Country*: The Organization of a Score", *Dance Research Journal* (New York), vol. 11, nos. 1 and 2, 1978–79
Brinson, Peter, and Crisp, Clement, *Ballet and Dance: A Guide to the Repertory*, London, 1980
Anderson, Jack, *Choreography Observed*, Iowa City, 1987

*   *   *

Ashton had cherished feelings of affection for Turgenev's play, *A Month in the Country*, from the 1930s, and in 1975 he began to consider it seriously as a possibility for a ballet. Julia Trevelyan Oman, the designer with whom he had worked on *Enigma Variations*, discussed it with him from the scenic point of view, and after much thought he decided on three early Chopin works for the music. These are the "*Là Ci Darem*" *Variations*, the *Fantasia on Polish Airs*, and the combined *Andante Spianato* and *Grande Polonaise in E Flat* for piano and orchestra, arranged by John Lanchbery.

An important feature of Ashton's choreography is that he used his originating dancers perfectly. In this case he cast the great actress-dancer Lynn Seymour as Natalia Petrovna, exploiting her ability for emotionally expressive movement in a role that extends classical dancing into conversational gesture. It is a subtle study of an older woman, surrounded by both a husband and a devoted admirer, who nevertheless falls in love with her son's young tutor. The tutor, Beliaev, was Anthony Dowell, whose dance range was exemplified in the contrasted pas de deux with Natalia, with her young ward Vera who becomes infatuated with him, and with the lively maid Katia. The other most developed role, choreographically, was that of Vera, created by Denise Nunn, an understanding study of first love expressed through enchaînements that are highly testing in their pace and precision. In Wayne Sleep, Ashton had an appropriate dancer for the boy Kolia and exploited his virtuosity—but this part, with its over-childish reactions, presents most dancers with serious problems. It has proven difficult for many dancers to perform the intricate steps without losing the boy-like characterization, while at the same time, over-exuberant interpretations of Kolia's childishness can look merely silly.

Two passages in particular exemplify Ashton's ingenuity over small ensembles. One is almost a mime passage the husband returns home to look for his keys, and gradually everyone on stage is involved in the search, blundering into each other, lifting each other out of the way, hunting under chairs and cushions, and eventually bringing them to light triumphantly. The other is a quartet for Natalia, Beliaev, Vera, and Kolia in which the dance style of each character is beautifully maintained.

A Month in the Country would have been improved by judicious cutting and tightening—there are longeurs that were barely noticeable with the original cast but sometimes show clearly in revivals. All in all, however, it is a superb example of Ashton's mastery of emotional dance and balletic portraiture.

—Kathrine Sorley Walker

A Month in the Country, with Lynn Seymour and Anthony Dowell, Royal Ballet, London, c.1976

MONUMENT FOR A DEAD BOY

(Original Dutch title: *Monument voor een gestorven jongen*)

Choreography: Rudi van Dantzig
Music: Jan Boerman
Design: Toer van Schayk (scenery and costumes)
Libretto: Rudi van Dantzig
First Production: Dutch National Ballet, Stadsschouwburg, Amsterdam, 19 June 1965
Principal Dancers: Toer van Schayk (The Boy), Christine Anthony and Danny Navon (The Parents), Benjamin Feliksdal (The Friend), Yvonne Vendrig (The Girl)

Other productions include: Harkness Ballet, with Lawrence Rhodes (The Boy); New York, 3 November 1967. American Ballet Theatre, with Ivan Nagy (The Boy); New York, 11 January 1973. German Opera Ballet; Berlin, 6 April 1976. Hungarian State Opera Ballet; Budapest, 20 November 1982.

PUBLICATIONS

Williams, Peter, "Controversial Subject: *Monument for a Dead Boy*", *Dance and Dancers* (London), May 1966
Goodwin, Noël, "Rudi van Dantzig", *About the House* (London), March 1970
Regner, Otto Friedrich, "*Monument voor een Gestorven Jongen*", *Reclams Ballettfuhrer* (Stuttgart), May 1972
Thom, Rose Anne, "A Case of Double Dutch?", *Dance Magazine* (New York), July 1975
Balanchine, George, with Mason, Francis, *Balanchine's Complete Stories of the Great Ballets*, Garden City, N.Y., 1977

*　　*　　*

Monument for a Dead Boy (*Monument voor een gestorven jongen*) is one of the ballets that marked Rudi van Dantzig as an important choreographer, and brought him to international attention. Its theme is the suppression and destruction of the life of a human being who does not adhere to the norms of the society in which he lives. The fact that *Monument* deals with the life of a young boy painfully discovering his own homosexuality makes the ballet very unusual, especially when one considers that it was created at a time when there were still very strict taboos about the subject. Just as courageous was its statement that heterosexual love is not always as beautiful as society wants us to believe: the boy has been conceived in a brutal sexual encounter that amounts to an act of rape of his mother by his drunken father.

The story is not told in a strict narrative way; reality is frequently mingled with fantasy and with images and emotions from the past. Clear characterizations are given to the parents,

Monument for a Dead Boy, with Toer van Schayk (left) and Rob van Woerkom, Dutch National Ballet, Amsterdam

the boy, his friend, his girlfriend. The ensemble of men confronts the boy in a violent, homo-erotic way. The group of women comment on the actions like the chorus in a Greek drama.

The ballet proved controversial: some critics protested against the frank treatment of the subject-matter, while others found it too literal, abrupt, and naïve in its choreographic treatment; but for the most part it was considered an impressive and fascinating work in which traditional classical dance was very successfully amalgamated with mime and elements from the Graham technique. Praise was unanimous for Toer van Schayk's expressive and touching interpretation of the boy. Other striking interpretations of this role were given later by Henny Jurriëns and by Rudolf Nureyev, for whom *Monument* represented the Russian dancer's first venture into "modern" ballet.

—Ine Rietstap

MORDKIN, Mikhail

Russian/American dancer, choreographer, teacher, and ballet director. Born Mikhail Mikhailovich Mordkin in Moscow, 21 December (9 December old style) 1880. Studied at the Moscow Theatre School, pupil of Vasily Tikhomirov; graduated in 1900. Married character dancer Bronislava Pozhitskaya (also known as Pojitska and Pojitskaya). Début (while still a student) in 1898, followed by success as Colin in *Vain Precautions* (*La Fille mal gardée*), 1899; soloist, soon becoming principal dancer, Bolshoi Theatre, Moscow, from 1900, with appointment to post of assistant ballet master, 1905; soloist, Diaghilev's Ballets Russes, Paris, 1909, leaving to tour with Anna Pavlova, including the U.S. and London, 1910, 1911; founder of own company, "All-Star Imperial Russian Ballet", U.S., 1911; returned to Russia as principal dancer, Bolshoi Theatre, 1912–18, also working with Moscow Art Theatre, 1913, Tairov's Kamerny Theatre, 1913–17, and performing and staging ballets in Kiev, 1919, Tbilisi, 1920, 1922, 1924, and Moscow, 1923; left Russia 1923, first for Lithuania and eventually the U.S.: performer, Greenwich Village Follies, New York, 1924, Morris Guest's company, touring 1924–26; founder and director, Mordkin Ballet Company (stemming from the Mikhail Mordkin Studio of Dance Arts, New York), 1926, touring the U.S. with Vera Nemchinova and Pierre Vladimirov, 1926–27; re-established Mordkin Ballet, the precursor to (American) Ballet Theatre, 1937, resigning soon afterwards; also teacher, with first teaching experience at Moscow Theatre School, 1905, and Moscow Art Theatre, from 1906; director and teacher of own school, Tbilisi, 1920–21; teacher, New York, from 1923 until his death; pupils included Patricia Bowman, Lucia Chase, Leon Danielian. Died in Millbrook, N.J., 15 July 1944.

ROLES

1898   Subaltern (while still a student) in *Cavalry Halt* (Petipa; staged Clustine), Bolshoi Theatre, Moscow
1899   Colin in *Vain Precautions* (*La Fille mal gardée*; Petipa, Ivanov; staged Mendez), Bolshoi Theatre, Moscow
1900   Espada (cr) in *Don Quixote* (Gorsky after Petipa), Bolshoi Theatre, Moscow
        Jean de Brienne (cr) in *Raymonda* (Gorsky after Petipa), Bolshoi Theatre, Moscow

1900/   Albert (Albrecht) in *Giselle* (Petipa after Coralli,
05   Perrot), Bolshoi Ballet, Moscow
        Basil in *Don Quixote* (Gorsky after Petipa), Bolshoi Ballet, Moscow
        Conrad in *Le Corsaire* (Petipa), Bolshoi Ballet, Moscow
1901   Prince Siegfried (cr) in *Swan Lake* (Gorsky, partly after Petipa, Ivanov), Bolshoi Ballet, Moscow
        Franz in *Clorinda, Queen of the Mountain Fairies* (Gorsky), Bolshoi Ballet, Moscow
1902   Phoebus (cr) in *Gudule's Daughter* (Gorsky), Bolshoi Ballet, Moscow
1904   Solor (cr) in *La Bayadère* (new production; Gorsky after Petipa), Bolshoi Theatre, Moscow
        Colin in *Vain Precautions* (*La Fille mal gardée*, new production; Gorsky after Petipa, Ivanov), Bolshoi Ballet, Moscow
1905   King Hitaris (cr) in *The Pharaoh's Daughter* (new production; Gorsky after Petipa), Bolshoi Ballet, Moscow
1906   Robert (cr) in *Robert and Bertram; or, the Two Thieves* (Gorsky after Mendez, Kshesinsky), Bolshoi Theatre, Moscow
1907   Albrecht (cr) in *Giselle* (new production; Gorsky, partly after Petipa, Coralli, Perrot), Bolshoi Ballet, Moscow
        Nur (cr) in *Nur and Anitra* (Gorsky), Bolshoi Ballet, Moscow
1909   Vicomte de Beaugency in *Le Pavillon d'Armide* (Fokine), Diaghilev's Ballets Russes, Paris
        Czardas (chor. Gorsky) in *Le Festin* (Fokine and others), Diaghilev's Ballets Russes, Paris
1910   Franz in *Coppélia* (after Petipa), Anna Pavlova's Company, Metropolitan Opera House, New York
        Pas de deux in *Les Sylphides* (Fokine), Anna Pavlova's Company, Metropolitan Opera House, New York
        Principal dancer (cr) in *Adagio* (also chor.), Anna Pavlova's Company, Metropolitan Opera House, New York
        Principal dancer (cr) in *Russian Dance* (also credited as chor.), Anna Pavlova's Company, Metropolitan Opera House, New York
        Principal dancer (cr) in *Bacchanale* (also credited as chor.), Anna Pavlova's Company, Metropolitan Opera House, New York
        Aziade (cr) in *The Legend of Aziade* (also chor.), Anna Pavlova's Company, U.S. tour
        Principal dancer in *Valse caprice* (pas de deux; Legat), Anna Pavlova's Company, London
        Mato (cr) in *Salammbô* (Gorsky), Bolshoi Ballet, Moscow
1911/   Prince Siegfried in *Swan Lake* (also chor., after Petipa,
12   Ivanov), All-Star Imperial Russian Ballet, U.S. tour
        Principal dancer in *Les Saisons* (after Petipa), All-Star Imperial Russian Ballet, U.S. tour
1913   Sonnewald (cr) in *Schubertiana* (Gorsky), Bolshoi Ballet, Moscow
        Norwegian Fisherman (cr) in *Love is Quick!* (Gorsky), Bolshoi Ballet, Moscow
1914   Khan (cr) in *The Little Humpbacked Horse* (new production; Gorsky after Petipa), Bolshoi Theatre, Moscow
1915   Petronius (cr) in *Eunice and Petronius* (Gorsky), Bolshoi Ballet, Moscow
1917   Solor (cr) in *La Bayadère* (new production; Gorsky after Petipa), Bolshoi Theatre, Moscow
1937   Old fisherman (cr) in *The Goldfish* (also chor.), Mordkin Ballet, New York

Mikhail Mordkin with Anna Pavlova, Palace Theatre, London, 1911

Devil (cr) in *Trepak* (also chor.), Mordkin Ballet, New York
1938   Widow Simone (cr) in *La Fille mal gardée* (also chor.; after Petipa, Ivanov), Mordkin Ballet, New York
General (cr) in *Voices of Spring* (also chor.), Mordkin Ballet, New York

Other roles include: concert miniatures and solos, including— *Bow and Arrow Dance* (also chor.), *Pas comique* (also chor.), *Valse caprice*, *Gypsy Dance*, *Greek Variations*.

WORKS

1910   *The Legend of Aziade* (mus. Bourgault-Ducoudray), Anna Pavlova's Company, Metropolitan Opera House, New York (staged for Moscow Circus, 1917)
Russian Dance, Anna Pavlova's Company, Metropolitan Opera House, New York
Bacchanale (mus. Glazunov), Anna Pavlova's Company, Metropolitan Opera House, New York
1914   *Kazachok* (mus. Rubinstein), *Mazurka* (mus. Vinyausky), *Matelot* (mus. Zolotarenko), Divertissement Programme, Bolshoi Ballet, Moscow
1917   Salomé's Dances in *Salomé* (with A. Koonen; mus. Hüttel), Tairov's Kamerny Theatre, Moscow
1922   *Le Carnaval* (mus. Schumann), Tbilisi Theatre, Tbilisi
The Flowers of Granada (mus. Moshkovsky), Tbilisi Theatre, Tbilisi
1924   *The Pearl of Seville* (mus. Pugni), Tbilisi Theatre, Tbilisi
1931   Dances in *Kovanshchina* (opera; mus. Mussorgsky), Mecca Temple, New York
1932   Dances in *Le Coq d'or* (opera; mus. Rimsky-Korsakov), Mecca Temple, New York
1934   Dances in *Revenge with Music* (musical comedy; Dietz and Schwartz), New Amsterdam Theatre, New York
1937   *The Goldfish* (mus. Tcherepnin), Mordkin Ballet, New York
Trepak (mus. Tcherepnin), Mordkin Ballet, New York
1938   *Voices of Spring* (mus. Strauss), Mordkin Ballet, New York
Dionysus (mus. Glazunov), Mordkin Ballet, New York

Also staged:
1911   *Swan Lake* (after Petipa, Ivanov; mus. Tchaikovsky), Covent Garden, London (also staged "All-Star Imperial Russian Ballet", New York, 1911)
1937   *Giselle* (after Petipa, Coralli, Perrot; mus. Adam), Mordkin Ballet, New York
The Sleeping Beauty (after Petipa; mus. Tchaikovsky), Mordkin Ballet, Waterbury, Connecticut
Swan Lake (one-act version; after Petipa, Ivanov; mus. Tchaikovsky), Mordkin Ballet, New York
1938   *La Fille mal gardée* (after Petipa, Ivanov; mus. Hertel), Mordkin Ballet, New York

Other works include: concert miniatures and solos, including— *Bow and Arrow Dance* (mus. Arends), *The Italian Beggar* (mus. Saint-Saëns), *Pas comique* (mus. Grieg).

PUBLICATIONS

Harvey, Alexander, "Mikhail Mordkin", *The Dance Magazine* (New York), November 1926
Amberg, George, *Ballet in America*, New York, 1949
Cross, Julia Vincent, "A Class with Mikhail Mordkin", *Dance Magazine* (New York), August 1956
Krasovskaya, Vera, *Russian Ballet Theatre at the Beginning of the Twentieth Century*, volume 2: Leningrad, 1972
Payne, Charles, *American Ballet Theatre*, London, 1978
Souritz, Elizabeth, *The Art of Choreography in the 1920s*, Moscow, 1979; as *Soviet Choreographers in the 1920s*, translated by Lynn Visson, Durham, N.C. and London, 1990
"In Pavlova's Shadow: Anna Pavlova's Partners", *Ballet News* (New York), January 1981
Money, Keith, *Anna Pavlova*, London, 1982
Smakov, Gennady, *The Great Russian Dancers*, New York, 1984

*   *   *

Russian choreographers Mikhail Fokine and Mikhail Mordkin were almost exact contemporaries, and yet their artistic visions were entirely opposed. Fokine, who was trained in St. Petersburg, had his eye on the future and created a dance style which used rounded forms and emphasized transition rather than pose. Mordkin was trained in Moscow. He was a traditionalist, expert in his use of turn-of-the-century ballet vocabulary.

For more than half his life Mordkin remained attached to the Bolshoi Ballet, where he made his début in 1898. Although he accepted dancing engagements abroad, he kept returning to his home company and continued to play an important role at the Bolshoi, particularly in the productions of Aleksandr Gorsky.

Despite prestigious positions staging ballets for various theatres, Mordkin's first love was not directing, nor was it teaching. He preferred to dance. And while he was not a bravura technician, his virility and expansive acting style had great appeal. When he toured as partner to Anna Pavlova in 1910, her delicacy and his athleticism contrasted most effectively, especially in the ballet *Bacchanale*, a hugely popular piece which Pavlova's biographer Keith Money refers to as "a display of finely tuned eroticism". During this tour Mordkin was also an audience favourite in his own solo, *Bow and Arrow Dance*, in which contemporary reviewers compared his physique to that of a Greek god. In fact, his popularity and subsequent demands for equal billing caused Pavlova to seek another partner.

In 1926, two years after he had settled permanently in the United States with his wife and son, Mordkin formed the first version of his Mordkin Ballet. But even though Pavlova and her little company were touring with enormous success, Mordkin and his wife Bronislava Pozhitskaya did not attract the same attention, nor did they have the funds to continue. They confined themselves to teaching in their New York studio, where Mordkin was known, among other things, for his unusual studio attire consisting of trousers and pajama top.

Gradually Mordkin began developing outstanding advanced students, among them Lucia Chase, Viola Essen, Leon Varkas, Leon Danielian, Patricia Bowman, and Dmitri Romanoff. Feeling the need to give these young artists a performing outlet, he made plans to reinstate the Mordkin Ballet in 1937. This time he could count on the financial assistance of Lucia Chase. Although Chase had started her ballet training very late, Mordkin made her the prima ballerina of his company.

Again Mordkin's timing proved wrong. His inexperienced ensemble, with its repertory of only seven ballets, was no competition for the Ballet Russe de Monte Carlo with its glamorous Russian stars and exotic repertory. The Mordkin Ballet sallied forth on tour with underpopulated versions of *Giselle*, *Swan Lake*, and *The Sleeping Beauty*. Its original works, all dramatic vignettes by Mordkin, were *The Goldfish*, *Trepak*, *Dionysus*, and *Voices of Spring*.

In 1940 the new American company, Ballet Theatre, sent up its first exciting shoots. Enticed by higher salaries and more interesting repertory, the Mordkin dancers joined the new company. Lucia Chase's wealth helped involve her in the early plans and eventually in the company's artistic direction. At the outset, she loyally included Mordkin's *Voices of Spring* with Mordkin himself portraying the gallant old general. But the progressive thinking rampant in this new company was too much for Mordkin. And so by the second season, he withdrew and returned to teaching. Four years later, in 1944, he was dead.

—Doris Hering

MORISHITA, Yoko

Japanese dancer. Born Yoko Shimizu in Hiroshima, Japan, 7 December 1948. Studied with Michiko Suwa and Akiko Tachibana, Tokyo, and at Matsuyama Ballet Company, pupil of Mikiko Matsuyama, from 1971; also studied with Igor Schwezoff, Tokyo, with Marika Besobrasova (scholarship from the Japanese Agency of Cultural Affairs), Monaco, 1975, and with Alexandra Danilova, New York. Married dancer Tetsutaro Shimizu, 1976. Dancer, while still a student, Tachibana Ballet, Tokyo; principal dancer, becoming company's prima ballerina, Matsuyama Ballet Company, Tokyo, from 1971; international guest artist, including for Margot Fonteyn World Tour, 1978 and 1979, American Ballet Theatre, New York, 1978 and 1980, Nureyev Festival, London, 1980, Paris Opéra Ballet, 1981, Ballet du XXe Siècle, 1982, Los Angeles Ballet, 1984, Vienna Opera Ballet, 1984 and 1985, and Zurich Ballet, 1986; has also appeared in concert tours, often partnered by Tetsutaro Shimizu and Rudolf Nureyev; judge for ballet competitions, including the Prix de Lausanne and the International Ballet Competitions at Jackson, Mississippi. Recipient: First Dance Critics Society Prize, 1969; Ministry of Education Arts Newcomer Award, 1970; Gold Medal, International Ballet Competition, Varna, 1974; Grand Award, Agency for Cultural Affairs Festival (with Tetsutaro Shimizu), 1975; Grand Prize of the Japanese Arts Festival, 1978; Tokyo Citizens Order of Merit, 1984; Japanese Arts Academy Prize, 1985; Laurence Olivier Award, 1985; Asahi Award, 1990.

ROLES

1975   Odette/Odile in *Swan Lake* (after Petipa, Ivanov), Matsuyama Ballet, Tokyo
1976   Princess Floride in *The Sleeping Beauty* (Petipa; staged Skeaping), American Ballet Theatre, New York
1977   Pas de deux from *Don Quixote* (Gorsky after Petipa), Queen's Silver Jubilee Gala, London
       Title role in *Giselle* (Shimizu after Petipa, Coralli, Perrot), Matsuyama Ballet, Tokyo
1980   Kitri in *Don Quixote* (Nureyev after Petipa), Nureyev Festival, London
1981   Marie Taglioni in *Pas de quatre* (Dolin), Paris Opera Ballet, Paris
       Title role in *Paquita* (after Petipa), Paris Opera Ballet, Paris
       Swanilda in *Coppélia* (after Saint-Léon), Monaco
1982   Principal dancer (cr) in *Light* (Béjart), Ballet du XXe Siècle, Brussels
1983   Sugar Plum Fairy in *The Nutcracker* Pas de deux (after

Ivanov), New Year's Eve Gala, Frankfurt Opera House, Frankfurt
1986   Title role in *Raymonda* (after Petipa), Monaco
1988   Moe (cr) in *Mandala* (Shimizu), Matsuyama Ballet, Edinburgh Festival, Edinburgh
1990   Title role in *Cinderella* (Shimizu), Matsuyama Ballet, Tokyo

PUBLICATIONS

By Morishita:
Wings of a Ballerina, Tokyo, 1976
A Ballerina's Obsession, Tokyo, 1984

About Morishita:
Maynard, Olga, "The Girl who Loves Jerome Robbins", *Dance Magazine* (New York), July 1970
Iijim, Atsushi (photographer), *Yoko Morishita: A World-Eminent Prima Ballerina*, Tokyo, 1976
Iijim, Atsushi (photographer), *Yoko Morishita's Ballets*, Tokyo, 1981
Shimizu, Masao, *A Prima Ballerina Came into the World*, Tokyo, 1982
Keene, Keiko, "Verve, Energy and Obsession", *Dance and Dancers* (London), July 1985
Dunning, Jennifer, "A Japanese Ballerina's Success Story", *The New York Times*, 22 January 1991

* * *

Yoko Morishita was born in Hiroshima in 1948: when the atomic bomb devastated the city, her family was living in central Hiroshima. Her grandfather died on the spot and her grandmother has suffered a long illness as a result. Yoko might have inherited some afflictions due to the atomic fall-out, for she was a weak child. Her parents sent her to a local ballet school to improve her health when she was three years old. As she grew older, she showed remarkable progress, and her teacher suggested she study in Tokyo. Every Saturday night, the ten-year-old Yoko took the night train from Hiroshima to Tokyo, reaching Tokyo early Sunday morning. She took a class or two, then caught the afternoon train from Tokyo to Hiroshima in order to be ready for school on Monday. She repeated this for two years, and after graduation from primary school, she moved to Tokyo and became the live-in apprentice of ballet mistress Akiko Tachibana.

Madame Tachibana studied classical ballet with the emigrée teacher Eliana Pavlova, and was one of the pioneers of ballet in Japan. She had somewhat peculiar theories about ballet education and taught tea ceremony, flower arrangement, and Japanese traditional dance along with classical ballet to young Morishita. Morishita realized later that that instruction helped her to become a full-fledged artist. During this period she also studied with Igor Schwezoff, who was the guest instructor there, and she trained with Alexandra Danilova during her visit to New York.

Morishita become the child prodigy of the Tachibana Ballet, and enjoyed immense popularity, but she moved to the Matsuyama Ballet in 1971. In 1974 she competed in the Varna International Competition and won the gold medal in the senior division, partnered by her future husband Tetsutaro Shimizu.

The following year, Morishita received a scholarship from the government, and spent one year at the school of Marika Besobrasova in Monte Carlo. Besobrasova was surprised to see the leg musculature of the young dancer. It had been distorted

Yoko Morishita as Giselle

and overdeveloped by the hard training of the Tachibana School. Morishita was subsequently taught how to use leg muscles properly under Besobrasova, and her technique has since been described as "rock solid" by leading Western critics. Besobrasova had shown the dancer how to make her legs look longer and straighter, like the legs of a Western dancer. Morishita realized her body was changing day by day under Besobrasova's care.

Gradually she became an internationally renowned ballerina. She acquired rare musicality: her dancing matched the music precisely but, within the realms of musical discipline, she found a floating and moving freedom. She also developed the technique of moving the hard tips of her pointe shoes softly, as if she were dancing with bare feet. Her feet, like sweeping feathers, barely brushed the dancing floor.

In 1978 and 1979, Morishita danced in a small group organized by Margot Fonteyn, and in 1978 and 1980 she was a guest artist with the American Ballet Theatre. Rudolf Nureyev again asked her to dance with him in a full-length *Don Quixote* in London for the Nureyev Festival in 1980. In 1981 she danced on the stage of Paris Opéra, an unprecedented honour for a Japanese dancer.

Morishita's fame was firmly established by this time, and the culmination of her international career was an offer from Maurice Béjart to dance the leading role in his new work, *Light*, in 1982. This was her first real encounter with modern ballet. She learned how to express herself without using traditional balletic mime. The ballet had its premiere in Brussels, and was a great success, especially for Morishita. Béjart said that he saw Japanese purity residing together with Western technique in Morishita, while critics and dancers alike recognized the remarkable change in her dancing after *Light*.

But it is as a classical ballerina of both technical brilliance and lyrical subtlety that Morishita has been most highly praised. Indeed, on a recent tour of the United States with the Matsuyama Ballet company, critics remarked on her continued improvement over the years. *New York Times* critic Anna Kisselgoff, who has referred to Morishita as "an exquisite dancer, perfect in her placement as a textbook example of classical style", pointed to the ballerina's venture into a highly dramatic role in *Mandala* and her ability to reveal "a full burst of passion" in the title role. Kisselgoff also remarked on the fact that ". . . over the years, she [has] infused her dancing with a naturalness that now has a profundity of its own". In the more traditional role of Giselle, the ballerina has impressed the critics by appearing to reveal greater depths in her portrayal each new time she performs the ballet.

Morishita has brought fame to Japan as a ballerina of international stature, but she also has contributed to the success and prominence of the company she leads, the Matsuyama Ballet. It is hoped that she leads the way for other Japanese ballerinas to follow in her footsteps.

—Kenji Usui

MORRICE, Norman

British dancer, choreographer, teacher, and ballet director. Born in Agua Dolce, Vera Cruz, Mexico, 10 September 1931. Studied at Ballet Rambert School, from 1952; also studied contemporary dance with Martha Graham (on Ford Foundation Scholarship), New York, 1961–62. Dancer, Ballet Rambert, from 1952; choreographer, Ballet Rambert, 1958, becoming principal choreographer on return from America,

1962; associate director, Ballet Rambert, from 1966, becoming co-director, 1970–74; freelance choreographer, including for Australian Dance Theatre, Batsheva Dance Company, and Contemporary Dancers Company, Winnipeg, various seasons 1974–77; artistic director, Royal Ballet, 1977–86; director, Royal Ballet Choreographic Group, from 1987; also teacher, including at York University in Toronto, Laban Centre, London, and Gulbenkian Summer School for Choreographers and Composers; director, Gulbenkian International Choreographic Summer School, 1971 and 1986; director of Choreographic Studies, Royal Ballet School, from 1987. Recipient: Queen Elizabeth II Coronation Award, Royal Academy of Dancing, 1973.

ROLES

1952   Huntsman, Courtier in *Giselle* (Petipa after Coralli, Perrot), Ballet Rambert, London
1953   Scotch Rhapsody in *Façade* (Ashton), Ballet Rambert, London
        Ensemble in *Plaisance* (Gore), Ballet Rambert, London
        Ensemble in *Winter Night* (Gore), Ballet Rambert, London
        Huntsman in *Swan Lake*, Act II (after Ivanov), Ballet Rambert, London
        Visions in *Czernyana* (Staff), Ballet Rambert, London
        A Friend in *Past Recalled* (Carter), Ballet Rambert, Windsor
        A Young Man in *Mephisto Waltz* (Ashton), Ballet Rambert, St. Ives
        Conductor in *Gala Performance* (Tudor), Ballet Rambert, Liverpool
        A Guest in *Lilac Garden* (Tudor), Ballet Rambert, Norwich
1954   A Sailor in *Mermaid* (Howard), Ballet Rambert, Scottish tour
        Ensemble in *The Life and Death of Lola Montez* (Carter), Ballet Rambert, Oxford
        Chorus (cr) in *Variations on a Theme* (Cranko), Ballet Rambert, London
        Dancer in *Simple Symphony* (Gore), Ballet Rambert, London
        A Gentleman (cr) in *Love Knots* (Carter), Ballet Rambert, London
        Grandpa in *Peter and the Wolf* (Staff), Ballet Rambert, Birmingham
        March in *Variations on a Theme* (Cranko), Ballet Rambert, Cambridge
1955   The Magistrate in *The Life and Death of Lola Montez* (Carter), Ballet Rambert, Morecombe
        A Shade (cr) in *Persephone* (Joffrey), Ballet Rambert, London
        A Guest in *Laiderette* (MacMillan), Ballet Rambert, London
1956   Hilarion in *Giselle* (Petipa after Coralli, Perrot), Ballet Rambert, London
        Pas de six in *Coppélia*, Act III (after Petipa, Cecchetti), Ballet Rambert, Cambridge
1957   Dr. Coppélius in *Coppélia* (after Petipa, Cecchetti), Ballet Rambert, tour
        Waiter in *The Judgment of Paris* (Tudor), Ballet Rambert, Nottingham
        A Cavalier in *Gala Performance* (Tudor), Ballet Rambert, Nottingham
        A Guest (cr) in *Mirror* (Yerrell), Ballet Rambert, Nottingham

Yodelling Song, Popular Song in *Façade* (Ashton), Ballet Rambert, Manchester

A Courtier (cr) in *Conte fantastique* (Howard), London

1958   Saint Leon in *Pas de déesses* (Joffrey), Ballet Rambert, Barking

His Brother in *Two Brothers* (also chor.), Ballet Rambert, Canterbury

1959   The Local Priest in *Hazaña* (also chor.), Ballet Rambert, London

The Man She Must Marry in *Lilac Garden* (Tudor), Ballet Rambert, London

Third Song in *Dark Elegies* (Tudor), Ballet Rambert, London

1960   Her Husband (later called "A gentleman Well-acquainted with Her") in *The Wise Monkeys* (also chor.), Ballet Rambert, Brighton

1961   James in *The Sylph* (*La Sylphide*; von Rosen after Bournonville), Ballet Rambert, York

The Poet in *Night Shadow* (Balanchine), Ballet Rambert, London

A Company Agent in *A Place in the Desert* (also chor.), Ballet Rambert, London

1962   Impresario, Duke of Barcelona in *Don Quixote* (Gorsky, Zakharov; staged Borkowski), Ballet Rambert, Liverpool

WORKS

1958   *Two Brothers* (mus. Dohnányi), Ballet Rambert, Canterbury

1959   *Hazaña* (mus. Surinach), Ballet Rambert, London

1960   *The Wise Monkeys* (mus. Shostakovich), Ballet Rambert, Brighton

1961   *A Place in the Desert* (mus. Surinach), Ballet Rambert, London

1962   *Conflicts* (mus. Bloch), Ballet Rambert, London

1963   *Travellers* (mus. Salzedo), Ballet Rambert, Spoleto Festival, Italy

1964   *Cul-de-sac* (mus. Whelen), Ballet Rambert, London

1965   *The Tribute* (mus. Sessions), Royal Ballet Touring Company, Stratford-upon-Avon

Realms of Choice (mus. Salzedo), Ballet Rambert, London

1966   *Side Show* (mus. Hindemith), Batsheva Dance Company, Israel

The Betrothal (mus. Ben Haim), Batsheva Dance Company, Israel

1967   *Hazard* (mus. Salzedo), Ballet Rambert, Bath

1968   *Rehearsal* (mus. Poulenc), Batsheva Dance Company, Israel

1-2-3 (mus. Orgad), Batsheva Dance Company, Israel

Them and Us (mus. Xenakis), Ballet Rambert, London

1969   *Pastorale Variée* (mus. Ben Haim), Ballet Rambert, London

Blind Sight (mus. Downes), Ballet Rambert, London

1970   *Percussion Concerto* (mus. Salzedo), Batsheva Dance Company, Israel

1971   *That is the Show* (mus. Berio), Ballet Rambert, London

Solo (mus. Downes), Ballet Rambert, London

1972   *Ladies, Ladies* (mus. Hymas), Ballet Rambert, London

1973   *Isolde* (mus. Lewis), Ballet Rambert, London

1974   *Spindrift* (mus. Lewis), Ballet Rambert, London

1975   *Trek* (mus. Lester), Batsheva Dance Company, Israel

1976   *Fragments from a Distant Past* (mus. Janáček), Contemporary Dancers Company, Winnipeg

The Sea Whisper'd Me (mus. Miranda), Ballet Rambert, London

1977   *Seven Songs* (mus. various, arranged Canteloube), Australian Dance Theatre, Adelaide (revised as *Songs for Contemporary Dancers*, Winnipeg)

Smiling Immortal (mus. Harvey), Ballet Rambert, London

Also staged:

1979   *Swan Lake* (after Petipa, Ivanov; mus. Tchaikovsky), Royal Ballet, London

1980   *Giselle* (after Petipa, Coralli, Perrot; mus. Adam), Royal Ballet, London

PUBLICATIONS

By Morrice:

"Morrice on the Town", *Dance and Dancers* (London), February 1962

Interview in "A Question of Time", *Dance and Dancers* (London), November 1966

Gow, Gordon, "Cheerfulness Breaks in", *Dancing Times* (London), December 1970

Interview in Williams, Peter, "Changing the Form, Preserving the Tradition", in Crisp, Clement, Sainsbury, Anya, and Williams, Peter (eds.), *Ballet Rambert: 50 Years and On*, revised edition, London, 1981

Interview in Garske, Rolf, "The Range of the Guard", *Ballett International* (Cologne), October 1983

"Pioneering In Beijing", *Dance and Dancers* (London), September 1987

About Morrice:

Todd, Arthur, "Norman Morrice, British Choreographer", *Dance Observer* (New York), February 1962

Palatsky, Eugene, "Norman Morrice", *Dance Magazine* (New York), March 1962

Brinson, Peter, and Crisp, Clement, *Ballet for All*, London, 1970

Davies, Richard, "Towards a Policy of Devolution", *Classical Music* (London), 30 September 1978

Stringer, Robin, "Ballet Battle of the Stars", *Telegraph Sunday Magazine*, 11 March 1979

Sorley Walker, Katherine, "Ballet Rambert", *Dance Gazette* (London), June 1980

Harris, Dale, "The Royal Command", *Ballet News* (New York), June 1981

Vaughan, David, "The Evolution of Ballet Rambert: from Ashton to Alston", *Dance Magazine* (New York), October 1982

*   *   *

The 1950s and 1960s were a period of great change in Britain; the post-war economic boom, the youth movement, and the growth of pop culture could be felt across all the arts. The dramatic theatre had experienced radical new developments in the work of Samuel Beckett and John Osborne, as well as the growth of "alternative theatre" with new playwrights such as Snoo Wilson, David Hare, and Howard Brenton. One of the ways that this new spirit manifested itself in dance was in the choreography of Norman Morrice, a member of Ballet Rambert. Morrice came to prominence early in his career with the success of his first ballet, *Two Brothers* (1958), and was anxious to pursue a new language with which to express new subject matter in ballet.

The desire for a contemporary spirit in ballet took Morrice towards a greater realism in ballet story lines. *Two Brothers* was one of the first serious attempts in British ballet to express realistically a contemporary social situation. The technique was classical but contemporary in style, with soft shoes and contemporary dress. Morrice's ballets were always intense, with a psychological, dramatic interest, in the mould of Antony Tudor. His themes—such as in *The Travellers*, concerning a group imprisoned behind the Iron Curtain—also displayed a social consciousness not seen in British ballet since Helpmann's *Miracle in the Gorbals* (1944). Critic Alexander Bland credited Morrice's ballet *Hazaña* (1959) with extending the expressive range of ballet. Most critics agreed, however, that the problem with many of Morrice's ballets was that his narratives could have been better explored in another medium, such as film or drama. His works promoted a great deal of comment about the unsuitability of realism to a medium like ballet.

Morrice was a prime mover in bringing the new spirit of his age into the ballet, and became a pivotal figure in the establishment of contemporary dance in Britain. In the early 1960s he had gone to America specifically to study the technique of Martha Graham, and his period with her was a great influence on his work. He was also greatly impressed by Balanchine's New York City Ballet. In 1966 he was made associate director of Ballet Rambert, with responsibility for a radical change in the company, moving it from a traditional ballet company to a smaller group of soloists seeking to incorporate contemporary techniques. Morrice sought to steer the company back to its former position as a leading producer of new works, and Netherlands Dance Theatre became his model. The corps de ballet was abandoned, and full-length classical works were no longer performed. The Tudor works were kept and Morrice invited Glen Tetley to work with the company. Tetley then became a great influence on the next generation of choreographers, such as Christopher Bruce. The company developed an exciting educational policy, and Morrice encouraged collaborations between novice choreographers in the company and new designers, and built up a fruitful relationship with the Central School of Art and Design—in particular with artist Ralph Koltai. Morrice brought Ballet Rambert from a state of financial collapse back to being a successful, innovative, and creative force in British Ballet.

In 1974, his work complete, Morrice left Ballet Rambert and worked for a time as a freelance choreographer in foreign companies, before returning to take over directorship of the Royal Ballet from Kenneth MacMillan. Here he is said to have increased company morale by cutting back on guest artists, and was also responsible for inviting Richard Alston to make his first ballet, *Midsummer* (1983), for the company.

—Lesley-Anne Sayers

MORRIS, Mark

American dancer, choreographer, and company director. Born in Seattle, Washington, 29 August 1956. Studied flamenco dance with Verla Flowers and ballet with Perry Brunson, Seattle; also studied flamenco dance in Madrid; studied ballet with Maggie Black, New York, from 1976. Dancer in semi-professional Balkan dance troupe, while still at school; dancer with companies of Eliot Feld, Lar Lubovitch, Twyla Tharp, Hannah Kahn, and Laura Dean, from 1976; founder, dancer, and choreographer, Mark Morris Dance Group, from 1980,

becoming resident company (Monnaie Dance Group/Mark Morris) of the Théâtre Royal de la Monnaie, Brussels, with Morris as Monnaie ballet director, 1988–91; also guest choreographer, staging works for modern dance, ballet, and opera companies, including for Joffrey Ballet, Boston Ballet, and American Ballet Theatre (commissioned by Mikhail Baryshnikov); co-founder, with Mikhail Baryshnikov, White Oak Dance Project, 1990. Recipient: New York Dance and Performance Award, 1984 and 1990; John Simon Guggenheim Memorial Foundation Fellowship, 1986; John D. and Catherine T. MacArthur Foundation Fellowship, 1991; *Dance Magazine* Award, 1991; "Genius" Award, MacArthur Foundation, 1991.

WORKS

1973 *Barstow* (mus. Partch), Students of Summer Dance Laboratory, Port Townsend, Washington

1974/ *Zenska* (mus. Bartok and traditional Bulgarian), First
75   Chamber Junior Company, Seattle

1978 *Brummagen* (mus. Beethoven), Pacific Northwest Ballet, Seattle

1980 *Rattlesnake Song* (mus. Jimmy Driftwood), Steffi Nossen Dance Company, Scarsdale, New York

Castor and Pollux (mus. Partch), Mark Morris Company, Merce Cunningham Studio, New York

Dad's Charts (mus. Buckner, Jacquet, Thompson), Mark Morris Dance Group, Merce Cunningham Studio, New York

1981 *Etudes Modernes* (mus. Nancarrow), Mark Morris Dance Group, Jersey City, New Jersey

Ten Suggestions (mus. Tcherepnin), Mark Morris Dance Group, Jersey City, New Jersey

I Love You Dearly (mus. traditional Romanian songs), Mark Morris Dance Group, Seattle

Gloria (mus. Vivaldi), Mark Morris Dance Group, New York

1982 *Canonic 3/4 Studies* (mus. various piano waltzes), Mark Morris Dance Group, Seattle

Junior High (mus. Nancarrow), Mark Morris Dance Group, Seattle

New Love Song Waltzes (mus. Brahms), Mark Morris Dance Group, New York

Not Goodbye (mus. traditional Tahitian), Mark Morris Dance Group, New York

Songs that Tell a Story (mus. Louvin Brothers), Kinetics Company, Seattle

1983 *Ponchielliana* (mus. Ponchielli), Mark Morris Dance Group, Becket, Massachusetts

Caryatids (mus. Budd), Mark Morris Dance Group, Seattle

Celestial Greetings (mus. popular Thai), Mark Morris Dance Group, Seattle

Deck of Cards (mus. Logsdon, Jones, Tyler), Mark Morris Dance Group, Seattle

Dogtown (mus. Yoko Ono), Mark Morris Dance Group, Seattle

Bijoux (mus. Satie), Mark Morris Dance Group, New York

The Death of Socrates (mus. Satie), Mark Morris Dance Group, New York

Minuet and Allegro in G (mus. Beethoven), Mark Morris Dance Group, New York

The "Tamil Film Songs in Stereo" Pas de Deux (mus. contemporary Indian), Mark Morris Dance Group, New York

Mark Morris (left) in *Pas de Poisson*, **with Penny Hutchinson and Mikhail Baryshnikov, New York, 1990**

1984   *Vestige* (mus. Shostakovich), Spokane Ballet, Spokane,
Washington

O Rangasayee (mus. Tyagaraja), Mark Morris Dance
Group, Montreal

Championship Wrestling after Roland Barthes (later
called *Championship Wrestling*, as part of *Mythologies*;
mus. Garfein), Mark Morris Dance Group, New
York

Love, You Have Won (mus. Vivaldi), Mark Morris
Dance Group, Seattle

My Party (mus. Françaix), Mark Morris Dance Group,
Seattle

Prelude and Prelude (mus. Cowell), Mark Morris Dance
Group, Seattle

She Came from There (mus. Dohnanyi), Mark Morris
Dance Group, Seattle

Forty Arms, Twenty Necks, One Wreathing (mus.
Garfein), Students of American Dance Festival,
Durham, North Carolina

Come on Home (mus. Lambret, Hendricks, and Ross),
Students of Jacob's Pillow Dance Project, Becket,
Massachusetts

Slugfest (no mus.), Mark Morris Dance Group, London

The Vacant Chair (mus. Root, Robach, Bond), Mark
Morris Dance Group, London

1985   *Marble Halls* (mus. J.S. Bach), Batsheva Dance Company, Jerusalem

Lovey (mus. Violent Femmes), Mark Morris Dance
Group, Seattle

Jealousy (mus. Handel), Mark Morris Dance Group,
Pittsburgh

Retreat from Madrid (mus. Boccerini), Mark Morris
Dance Group, Paris

Handel Choruses (mus. Handel), Mark Morris Dance
Group, New York

Frisson (mus. Stravinsky), Mark Morris Dance Group,
New York

One Charming Night (mus. Purcell), Mark Morris Dance
Group, New York

1986   *Mort Subite* (mus. Poulenc), Boston Ballet, Boston

Mythologies: Soap Powders and Detergents, Striptease,
and *Championship Wrestling* (all mus. Garfein), Mark
Morris Dance Group, Boston

Dances in *Salome* (opera; mus. R. Strauss), Seattle
Opera, Seattle

Ballabili (mus. Verdi), Mark Morris Dance Group,
Seattle

The Shepherd on the Rock (mus. Schubert), Mark Morris
Dance Group, Seattle

Esteemed Guests (mus. C.P.E. Bach), Joffrey Ballet, Los
Angeles

Pieces en Concert (mus. Couperin), Mark Morris Dance
Group, New York

Stabat Mater (mus. Pergolesi), Mark Morris Dance
Group, New York

1987   *Sonata for Clarinet and Piano* (mus. Poulenc), Mark
          Morris Dance Group, Seattle
        Strict Songs (mus. Harrison), Mark Morris Dance
          Group, Seattle
        The Fantasy (later incorporated into *Fugue and Fantasy*;
          mus. Mozart), Mark Morris Dance Group, Seattle
        Dances in *Nixon in China* (opera; mus. Adams),
          Houston Grand Opera, Houston
        Scarlatti Solos (mus. Scarlatti), Mark Morris Dance
          Group, Santa Barbara
1988   Dances in *Orphee et Eurydice* (opera; mus. Gluck),
          Seattle Opera, Seattle
        Offertorium (mus. Schubert), Mark Morris Dance
          Group, New York
        Dances in *Die Fledermaus* (opera; mus. Johann Strauss),
          Seattle Opera, Seattle
        Fugue and Fantasy (incorporating *The Fantasy*; mus.
          Mozart), Mark Morris Dance Group, New York
        Drink to Me Only with Thine Eyes (mus. V. Thomson),
          American Ballet Theatre, New York
        Dances in *Le Nozze de Figaro* (opera; mus. Mozart),
          Purchase, New York
        L'Allegro, Il Penseroso ed il Moderato (mus. Handel),
          Monnaie Dance Group/Mark Morris, Brussels
1989   *Dido and Aeneas* (mus. Purcell), Monnaie Dance
          Group/Mark Morris, Brussels
        Love Song Waltzes (mus. Brahms), Monnaie Dance
          Group/Mark Morris, Brussels
        Wonderland (mus. Schoenberg), Monnaie Dance
          Group/Mark Morris, Brussels
1990   *Behemoth* (no mus.), Monnaie Dance Group/Mark
          Morris, Brussels
        Going Away Party (mus. Bob Wills and his Texas
          Playboys), Monnaie Dance Group/Mark Morris,
          Brussels
        Ein Herz (mus. J.S. Bach), Paris Opéra Ballet, Paris
        Pas de Poisson (mus. Satie), Mark Morris Dance Group,
          New York
        Motorcade (mus. Saint-Saëns), White Oak Dance
          Project, Boston
1991   *The Hard Nut* (mus. Tchaikovsky), Monnaie Dance
          Group/Mark Morris, Brussels
        Dances in *The Death of Klinghoffer* (opera; mus.
          Adams), Théâtre de la Monnaie, Brussels
        A Lake (mus. Haydn), White Oak Dance Project,
          Vienna, Virginia
        Dances in *Le Nozze de Figaro* (opera; mus. Mozart),
          Théâtre de la Monnaie, Brussels
1992   *Paukenschlag* (mus. Haydn), Les Grands Ballets Cana-
          diens, Montreal
        Beautiful Day (mus. attributed to J.S. Bach or Hoffman),
          Mark Morris Dance Group, New York
        Polka (later part of *Grand Duo*; mus. Harrison), Mark
          Morris Dance Group, New York
        Three Preludes (mus. Gershwin), Mark Morris Dance
          Group, Boston
        Bedtime (mus. Schubert), Mark Morris Dance Group,
          Boston
        Excursion to Grenada: A Calypso Ballet (mus. Lionel
          Belasco and his Orchestra), Mark Morris Dance
          Group, Becket, Massachusetts
1993   *Grand Duo* (incorporating *Polka*; mus. Harrison), Mark
          Morris Dance Group, Amherst, Massachusetts
        Home (mus. Shocked, Wasserman), Mark Morris Dance
          Group, New York
        Mosaic and United (mus. Cowell), Mark Morris Dance
          Group, New York

PUBLICATIONS

By Morris:
Vaughan, David, "A Conversation with Mark Morris", *Ballet
  Review* (New York), vol. 14 no.2, Summer 1986
Interview in Sulcas, Roslyn, "Man on the Move", *Dance and
  Dancers* (London), January/February 1992

About Morris:
Gruen, John, "Mark Morris: He's Here", *Dance Magazine*
  (New York), September 1986
Barnes, Clive, "Mad About the Boy", *Dance and Dancers*
  (London), January 1987
Macaulay, Alastair, "Vivamus Atque Amemus", *The New
  Yorker* (New York), 20 June 1988
Acocella, Joan, "Morris Dances", *Art in America* (Marion,
  Ohio), October 1988
Garafola, Lynn, "Mark Morris and the Feminine Mystique",
  Ballet Review (New York), Fall 1988
Daniels, Don, "Alone Together", *Ballet Review* (New York),
  Winter 1988
Croce, Arlene, "Wise Guys", *The New Yorker* (New York), 31
  July 1989
Lawson, William James, "In the Monnaie", *Ballet Review*
  (New York), Summer 1989
Constanti, Sophie, "Mark Morris, Béjart Pulp, and Belgian
  Bores", *Dance Theatre Journal* (London), February 1990
Vaughan, David, "Two Leaders: Mark Morris and Garth
  Fagan", *Ballet Review* (New York), Summer 1990
Vaughan, David, "Mark Morris Here and There", *Ballet
  Review* (New York), Winter 1990–91

*   *   *

During the 1980s, Mark Morris became the most celebrated
young choreographer in America. Although his idiom was, for
the most part, modern dance, some critics went as far as to hail
him as a successor to Balanchine, because of his intense
musicality and his gift for using dancers in quasi-architectural,
quasi-mathematical formations. Like Balanchine's, his range is
enormous, from kitsch to classicism. He has explored the art of
striptease, in his *Mythologies*, based on essays by Roland
Barthes. And he has created heartbreakingly lovely works—
including *Love Song Waltzes* and *New Love Song Waltzes*, set to
the Brahms' Liebeslieder cycles—that unabashedly address the
human condition, what it is to live, love, believe, and die.

Morris fashions a movement vocabulary to fit each dance,
even borrowing from the American Sign Language used by the
deaf. If he has "signature" steps, they are the most basic—a
walk, skip, and run that he can manipulate seemingly endlessly.
In working with ballet companies, he is completely comfortable
in choreographing dances on pointe. His musical selections are
enormously varied. Known for works set to the baroque
repertory of Handel, Vivaldi, and Purcell, he has made
excursions into the romanticism of Brahms, twangy country
and western songs, and popular Thai music. In his 1990
Behemoth, he experimented with a dance to silence.

Morris's dance education was eclectic. As a child growing up
in Seattle, he saw a José Greco performance, and began
studying Spanish dance. He also studied ballet, played the
piano, and was involved in a church where both music and
ritual were important.

As a teenager, he joined a Balkan folk dance group, studied
flamenco in Madrid for six months, and then moved to New
York, where he performed in the dance companies of Eliot
Feld, Lar Lubovitch, Hannah Kahn, and Laura Dean. He did
not stay in any one company long enough to be greatly

influenced by another choreographer's style. The musical experience he acquired while dancing folk and flamenco was probably at least as important to his later work as his experience performing pieces by other modern choreographers.

In 1980 he started his own company in New York and for the next eight years his schedule combined rigorous touring, including one-night stands in college auditoriums, with rehearsal periods. His output was phenomenal.

An early, monumental piece was *Gloria*, set to the Vivaldi Gloria in D. Rather than riding along on the surface of the score, Morris plumbed its heart. Unafraid to appear awkward, he had one dancer lie on his stomach and inch along on the floor, and another stagger stiff-kneed. There are humpbacked leaps and a dancer who is tossed violently from the wings onto the stage. The effect is of people seeking grace and salvation. In the end, they find it, as a huge ring of spinning dancers collapse onto the floor, falling like dominoes, in an ecstasy of faith.

In addition to frank expressions of beauty and spirituality, though, Morris creates such works as *Lovey*, in which dancers molest baby dolls. Morris's universe is a wide one.

His own dancing veers between the luscious and the silly. In his wonderful solo *Ten Suggestions*, set to Tcherepnin's *Ten Bagatelles*, he romps in pink silk pajamas: he's a cross between Oscar Wilde and Tiny Tim. In his majestic treatment of Purcell's opera *Dido and Aeneas*, he plays both the Queen of Carthage and the Sorceress, and there isn't a whiff of camp in either part. He enjoys flaunting his thick, voluptuous body and opulently curving profile, though. The chiselled choreography of *Dido* gave him ample chance to sit in profile, and audiences ample chance to admire the sight.

Morris's company is not made up of Morris clones. He seeks out forceful individualists whose talents may not be immediately evident to others. His has been an unusually mature dance company, with dancers routinely continuing into their late 30s. Among his most striking company members have been Keith Sabado, Ruth Davidson, Penny Hutchinson, Tina Fehlandt, and Guillermo Resto. Morris, who is openly homosexual, is one of the few choreographers who creates equally well for both men and women, treating the sexes with a rare equality.

By the mid-1980s, Morris was beginning to get some of the recognition he deserved in America. His commissions included the large-scale trilogy, *Mythologies*, which had its premiere in Boston in 1986. But, exhausted by the round of one-night stands that made up the majority of his performing opportunities, Morris and his company were lured to Brussels in 1988 to replace Maurice Béjart's troupe as the resident company at the Théâtre Royal de la Monnaie. At the Monnaie he had the luxuries the U.S. could never provide: subsidy from the Belgian government, the use of a near-perfect theater, adequate rehearsal space, squads of technicians and seamstresses at his disposal, and, perhaps most important of all, live music. Most American choreographers make do with recorded sound, which was especially sad in the case of Morris, America's most musical young dance-maker.

Morris's three year stay in Brussels was controversial. He was resented by part of the Belgian public who missed Béjart, and often booed at curtain calls. Yet, while in Brussels, he did make masterpieces, including his first work there, to *L'Allegro, Il Penseroso, ed Il Moderato*, Handel's pastoral ode after poems by Milton. A two-and-a-half-hour work for 24 dancers, *L'Allegro* filled the stage with a potent emotional geometry.

While in Brussels, Morris continued to collaborate with Mikhail Baryshnikov. As director of American Ballet Theatre, Baryshnikov had hired Morris to make *Drink To Me Only With Thine Eyes*. After Baryshnikov quit ABT, in 1989, he went to Brussels to work with Morris on *Wonderland*, a dark, choppy ballet partly inspired by Alfred Hitchcock films and set to

Schoenberg's *Five Pieces for Orchestra* and *Accompaniment for a Film Score*.

In the fall of 1990, Baryshnikov and Morris embarked on a joint venture called The White Oak Project, a small group of modern and ballet dancers performing Morris's own choreography on an extensive U.S. tour.

—Christine Temin

MOZARTIANA

Choreography: George Balanchine
Music: Petr Ilyich Tchaikovsky
Design: Christian Bérard (costumes and design)
First Production: Les Ballets 1933, Théâtre des Champs-Elysées, Paris, 7 June 1933
Principal Dancers: Tamara Toumanova, Roman Jasinsky

Other productions include: Producing Company of the School of American Ballet dancers (restaged Balanchine); Hartford, Connecticut, 6 December 1934. American Ballet (restaged and revised Balanchine); New York, 1 March 1935. Ballet Russe de Monte Carlo (restaged Balanchine), with Alexandra Danilova, Frederic Franklin; New York, 7 March 1945. New York City Ballet (restaged and revised Balanchine, costumes Rouben Ter-Arutunian), with Suzanne Farrell, Ib Andersen; New York, 4 June 1981.

PUBLICATIONS

Balanchine, George, with Mason, Francis, *Balanchine's Complete Stories of the Great Ballets*, Garden City, N.Y., 1977
Reynolds, Nancy, *Repertory in Review*, New York, 1977
Croce, Arlene, *Going to the Dance*, New York, 1982
Taper, Bernard, *Balanchine: A Biography*, revised edition, New York, 1984
Macaulay, Alastair, "Balanchine's World" *Ballet Review* (New York), Spring 1984
Anastos, Peter, "A Conversation with Tamara Toumanova", *Ballet Review* (New York), Winter 1984
Maiorano, Robert, *Balanchine's Mozartiana: The Making of a Masterpiece*, New York, 1985
Pritchard, Jane, "Les Ballets 1933", *Ballet Review* (New York), Fall 1988

* * *

Of the two works that Balanchine made to the music of this name, the earlier *Mozartiana* of 1933 was his first full-fledged Tchaikovsky ballet, among the many that he was to choreograph in his career. The masterly 1981 ballet, on the other hand, was the choreographer's last major work before his death two years later. The score, an orchestration of several Mozart pieces, is Tchaikovsky's homage to Mozart as an inspiration for his own music. Tchaikovsky and Mozart were the composers that Balanchine admired most, along with Stravinsky (although he choreographed very few ballets to Mozart, feeling that Mozart's compositions were generally self-sufficient).

Like the 1981 *Mozartiana*, the 1933 ballet—made for Les Ballets 1933—was a primarily joyous suite of dances in classical style (the most classical piece in Les Ballets 1933's repertoire), and some of its Christian Bérard costumes suggested eight-

Mozartiana, with Suzanne Farrell and Ib Anderson, New York City Ballet, 1981

eenth-century versions of the *commedia dell'arte*. The atmosphere of the 1933 work must have been by far the more earthy of the two, however. It was set in the piazza of an Italian town (or, according to the company's Savoy Theatre program, was meant "to evoke the poetic sincerity of naive ballerinas in antique variety shows . . . against faded pantomime gardens that conjure up memories of Taglioni and Fanny Elssler"). It was an exuberant ballet containing gypsies, peasants, lovers, and a village eccentric. One of its most striking sections, however, was the *Preghiera, or Prayer*—based on Mozart's motet *Ave Verum Corpus*—for a mourning woman accompanied by two completely draped figures, perhaps suggesting an Italian funeral procession, although the woman was also described as a "lovelorn princess". Made for Balanchine's fourteen-year-old discovery Tamara Toumanova, partnered by Roman Jasinski, the ballet was later also danced briefly by Balanchine's first dancers in the United States and by Serge Denham's Ballet Russe, where it featured Alexandra Danilova and Frederic Franklin.

The 1981 *Mozartiana* is a late Balanchine masterpiece, showing eighteenth-century courtliness through a twentieth-century prism. Choreographed for an excellent cast led by a favorite Balanchine ballerina, Suzanne Farrell, it was pro-grammed as the first ballet in the New York City Ballet's 1981 Tchaikovsky Festival. Although on first viewing it may appear bewilderingly varied and "abstract"—a misleading term that, in Balanchine's case, should never be construed as "without meaning or humanity"—a key to the ballet is the fact that Balanchine took the rare step of changing the order of its score: the *Preghiera* became the first dance of the piece, and consequently of the Tchaikovsky Festival.

Here Farrell, with her lifted eyes and her gestures of devotion, suggests a Madonna praying for souls. She calls to mind the medieval Madonna of *Misericordia*, as her outstretched arms seem to shelter the four small student dancers who accompany her. With the ballet costumed predominantly in black and framed in black hangings, Balanchine clearly alludes to the untimely deaths of both Mozart and Tchaikovsky, and perhaps to the 77-year-old choreographer's own approaching death as well. (The festival closed with another memento mori, the *Adagio Lamentoso* from Symphony No. 6, the *Pathétique,* staged by Balanchine in reference to the Russian Orthodox liturgy for the dead, using angels with wings ten feet high as well as group movements recalling Laban movement choirs. Prostrate figures gave the impression of a huge cross heaving like a beating heart.)

The *Preghiera*'s tone of gentle elegy and spirituality reflects Balanchine's firm Christian faith. It makes a frame of reference for the remainder of the ballet, as if to show a joyous acceptance of life in all its fleetingness. Very relevant is a comment of Balanchine's: "I think that Mozart knew how to be happy . . . he knew that he did not have long to live. Perhaps that's why he tried to enjoy every moment."

Farrell's partner (in the *Tema con Variazione* that makes up the latter part of the ballet) is clearly meant to represent Mozart. The role was originated by the decidedly Mozartian Ib Andersen, a fine-boned dancer noted for his lightness and ease of execution, about whose performance of the role Balanchine is said to have commented, "Ib *is* Mozart!" Balanchine gave the role an inventively fresh and bounding virtuosity. Farrell, for her part, seems to represent Mozart's muse, as shown by Andersen's display of her in their courtly, processional first pas de deux, as well as their dazzling succession of solos and the quicker alternations in the later pas de deux. This artist-muse relationship, familiar in Balanchine's ballets, reflects Balanchine's ongoing inspiration from his ballerinas, and most especially Farrell herself. A second male role suggests a courtier or court entertainer with his quick, witty, and rather sassy *Gigue* solo. Four tall women, grown-up counterparts to the four small girls, complete the cast, which only comes together in the finale. Here, when the cast is finally assembled, they dance with hands joined in two lines, giving a sense of social unity.

With its turns of the wrist, its hand-to-hip gestures, and its elegance, the ballet embodies the score's eighteenth-century allusions, and yet just as Tchaikovsky made a modern gloss on the music, so does Balanchine. In *Mozartiana* the subtlety and joyousness of Balanchine's musicality are seen at full force as he plays with and syncopates the inner rhythms and voices of the music, especially in the Farrell and *Gigue* roles. The ballet offers a particularly vivid example of the way Balanchine made dance an illuminating partner to music, like a further voice or voices in the texture of the music, rather than a mere reflection of it. (The ballet offered an additional spice to Farrell in that the violin and clarinet cadenzas were, at least originally, played ad libitum by the musicans.) Balanchine's unflagging inventiveness within the classical vocabulary gave a remarkable freshness to this late ballet.

As the leading dancers of this ballet curtailed their dancing and retired, their roles were filled with notable success by Kyra Nichols and Damian Woetzel.

—Marilyn Hunt

MUKHAMEDOV, Irek

Russian dancer. Born Irek Dzhavdatovich Mukhamedov in Kazan, 8 March 1960. Studied at the Moscow Choreographic School, pupil of Aleksandr Prokofiev, 1970–78. Married Maria Leonidovna Zubkova, 1990: one daughter, Alexandra-Cholpon Mukhamedova. Soloist, Moscow Classical Ballet, 1978–81, also participating in world tours from 1978; principal dancer, Bolshoi Ballet, Moscow, 1981–90, Royal Ballet, London, from 1990. Recipient: Grand Prix, International Ballet Competition, Moscow, 1981; Honoured Artist of the Russian Federation, 1985; Hans Christian Andersen Prize "For the World's Best Dancer", Copenhagen, 1988.

PUBLICATIONS

Willis, Margaret, "Irek Mukhamedov: Superstar", *Dance Magazine* (New York), April 1987
Verdy, Violette, "Violette Verdy on the Bolshoi", *Ballet Review* (New York), Summer 1987
"The Participator" (profile of Mukhamedov), *Dance and Dancers* (London), October 1987
Clarke, Mary, "The Bolshoi Ballet: Part II", *Dancing Times* (London), September 1989
"Travelling Men", *Dance and Dancers* (London), August 1990
Clarke, Mary, "Romeos and Juliets at Covent Garden", *Dancing Times* (London), October 1992

ROLES

1978 Franz in *Coppélia* (Golovkina, Radunsky after Gorsky), Moscow Choreographic School, Moscow
Shepherd in *The Rite of Spring* (Kasatkina, Vasiliev), Moscow Choreographic School, Moscow
A Devil in *The Creation of the World* (Kasatkina, Vasiliev), Moscow Classical Ballet, Moscow
1978/ Tybalt in *Romeo and Juliet* (Kasatkina, Vasiliev),
81 Moscow Classical Ballet, Moscow
Romeo in *Romeo and Juliet* (Kasatkina, Vasiliev), Moscow Classical Ballet, Moscow
Armen in *Gayané* (Vainonen), Moscow Classical Ballet, Moscow
Pas de deux from *Carnival in Venice* (from *Santanilla*; Petipa), Moscow Classical Ballet, Moscow
"Diana and Acteon" Pas de deux (from *Esmeralda*; Petipa after Perrot), Moscow Classical Ballet, Moscow
Basil in *Don Quixote Pas de Deux* (Gorsky after Petipa), Moscow Classical Ballet, Moscow
Conrad in *Le Corsaire Pas de Deux* (after Petipa), Moscow Classical Ballet, Moscow
1980 Colin in *Lise and Colin; ou, La Fille mal gardée* (Vinogradov), Moscow Classical Ballet, Moscow
1981 Title role in *Spartacus* (Grigorovich), Bolshoi Ballet, Moscow
Basil in *Don Quixote* (Gorsky after Petipa), Bolshoi Ballet, Moscow
1982 Title role in *Ivan the Terrible* (Grigorovich), Bolshoi Ballet, Moscow
1983 Romeo in *Romeo and Juliet* (Grigorovich), Bolshoi Ballet, Moscow
1984 Boris (cr) in *The Golden Age* (Grigorovich), Bolshoi Ballet, Moscow
1985 Jean de Brienne in *Raymonda* (Grigorovich after Petipa), Bolshoi Ballet, Moscow
1988 Basil in *Don Quixote* (Nureyev), Royal Ballet of Flanders
Title role in *Cyrano de Bergerac* (Petit), Bolshoi Ballet, Moscow
1989 Prince in *The Sleeping Beauty* (Nureyev after Petipa), Opéra, Paris
1990 Title role in *Petrushka* (Fokine), Nijinsky Festival, Bolshoi Ballet, Moscow
Solor in *La Bayadère* (Makarova after Petipa), Royal Ballet, London
Principal dancer (cr) in *Farewell* (pas de deux; later incorporated into *Winter Dreams*; MacMillan), Royal Ballet, London
Prince in *The Nutcracker* (Wright), Royal Ballet, London

Irek Mukhamedov in *Spartacus*

1991 Des Grieux in *Manon* (MacMillan), Royal Ballet,
       London
       Lescaut in *Manon* (MacMillan), Royal Ballet, London
       Vershinin (cr) in *Winter Dreams* (MacMillan), Royal
       Ballet, London
       Jean de Brienne in *Raymonda* (Nureyev after Petipa),
       Royal Ballet, London
       Title role in *Cyrano de Bergerac* (Bintley), Royal Ballet,
       London
       Chanson Dansée (an "Athlete") in *Les Biches* (Nijin-
       ska), Royal Ballet, London
1992 Romeo in *Romeo and Juliet* (MacMillan), Royal Ballet,
       London

Irek Mukhamedov is one of the most exciting male dancers on
the world balletic scene. His "heroic" style of dancing and
forceful personality, evidenced in productions with the Bolshoi
Ballet, won him international acclaim. Yet at the very moment
of his greatest success, he abruptly left his country and the
Bolshoi, choosing to settle in England and to dance in the very
different style and repertoire of Britain's Royal Ballet.

It was at the fourth International Ballet Competition in
Moscow in 1981 that Mukhamedov's extraordinary talent was
first widely recognized. He had shown, as far back as his school
days, that he had a unique approach to dance. But at that time it
was not good enough to secure him a place in the Bolshoi Ballet.
Instead he went to the Moscow Classical Ballet, where for three

years he proved himself a strong dancer, working up from the corps de ballet to soloist roles.

Mukhamedov's career then took a dramatic turn, which led him from virtual obscurity to stardom, such that he is now called one of the greatest male dancers of our time. In 1981 he had entered the International Ballet Competition with 126 other dancers from 23 countries. He took the Bolshoi Theatre by storm with powerful performances which showed attack, drive, and an impressive mastery of technique. Mukhamedov was awarded the highest prize, the Grand Prix, by the international jury, thus receiving a personal invitation from Yuri Grigorovich, artistic director of the Bolshoi Ballet, to become a principal dancer with the company.

Irek Dzhavdatovich Mukhamedov was born in the Tartar Autonomous Republic, 500 miles east of Moscow, in the city of Kazan (once the stronghold of the Mongols and captured by Ivan the Terrible in 1552). A weak child, he was taken by his mother at the age of five to dance classes at the local Pioneer's Palace. He enjoyed the lessons and impressed his teachers; they suggested he try for admission into the Vaganova Choreographic School in Leningrad. He was not successful, but decided to audition for the Bolshoi School in Moscow (or the Moscow Choreographic School) and this time was given a place. At the age of ten he moved to Moscow to begin his training. His grades were not always good but his teacher, Aleksandr Prokofiev, believed in the young man and inspired him to strike out for individuality and expression beyond the expected classical male stereotype.

Not being offered a place on graduation at the Bolshoi, Mukhamedov readily joined the Moscow Classical Company, run by Natalia Kasatkina and Vladimir Vasiliev. Here he steadily worked his way up to roles which could make use of his unique athletic talent, such as the Shepherd in *The Rite of Spring*, Armen in *Gayané*, the pas de deux of *Diana and Acteon*, and leading roles in *Don Quixote* and *Le Corsaire*.

After his magnificent success at the Moscow competition, Mukhamedov joined the Bolshoi. For its artistic director this young dancer was a godsend. Grigorovich's own ballets are packed with bravura and require a specific type of hero, far removed from the refinements of the classical mould. Mukhamedov's début was the title role in Grigorovich's *Spartacus*. In it he stormed his way across the stage with an energy that gave the whole production an exciting new lease of life. There soon followed almost all the leading roles, and the part of Boris in *The Golden Age*, staged in 1984, was created by Grigorovich especially for Mukhamedov.

At the Bolshoi Mukhamedov danced constantly; he seemed tireless. His performances in the heroic ballets were electric, showing a reckless power that propelled the dancer into the air and across the stage in an endless blur of motion. His entrances catapulted him into jetés which spliced the air, pirouettes in which he spun like a whirling dervish on the spot, and barrel-turns which defied gravity and ended in a double twist. The audiences loved it.

Overseas tours began, and in 1986 he took London by storm. He was the epitome of the Soviet "heroic" danseur, the devil-may-care kind of performer that was not produced by the elegance of the British training. The Royal Opera House was packed each night. Dancers joined the Bolshoi class in the mornings to watch him at work. Companies sat up and took note of his style and approach. Later, his influence was seen on British stages.

Mukhamedov's physique is more that of a swimmer than a dancer—stocky with broad, powerful shoulders and well-developed muscles. Yet with all the fire and zest so often attributed to his Tartar background, he conveys a genuine innocence and simplicity on stage—suggesting in dramatic roles a natural unfolding of character rather than the static show of an actor repeating a well-turned role. Off-stage he is surprisingly unassuming, appearing genuinely grateful and modest when congratulated on his performance. His unique athletic style could have been used to present only one facet of dancing—that of the powerhouse. Yet Mukhamedov is also able to express unexpected freshness and ardour in the classical roles, bringing out different reactions from his ballerinas. His is a magnetic presence on stage which attracts even when in repose.

In 1988, Mukhamedov was invited to dance the role of Basil in *Don Quixote* with the Royal Ballet of Flanders, and in 1989 he danced Prince Désiré in the Paris Opéra's *Sleeping Beauty*. Obviously he liked the change from the Bolshoi style: suddenly in June 1990, after a tour to Spain, Mukhamedov and his wife, Maria Zubkova, decided not to return to the Soviet Union. Instead they flew to Britain, where Mukhamedov was offered an immediate contract with the Royal Ballet. Mukhamedov stated that his reasons for leaving were the stagnant situation in Soviet ballet and said also that he wanted his child (Alexandra Cholpon, born in August) to be brought up in the West.

Thus began a new chapter in Mukhamedov's life. He appeared almost immediately at the Queen Mother's 90th birthday gala in August, in a pas de deux hastily created by Sir Kenneth MacMillan for him and the Royal's delightful Darcey Bussell. (The work was later included in the one-act ballet *Winter Dreams*, an adaptation of Chekhov's *The Three Sisters* which was first performed in 1991.) Casting had already been publicized for the beginning of the Royal Ballet's season, so it was not until November 1990 that Mukhamedov began to dance in full productions, and his adaptation to the Royal Ballet style could be assessed. With less opportunity to launch himself into space in expansive Grigorovich ballets, he has had to rely on refining his technique, searching for interpretation through dramatic expression and grace rather than through the predictable heroics of the Bolshoi's productions. In his first season he danced, with variety and success, Solor in *La Bayadère*, the Prince in *The Nutcracker*, Des Grieux and Lescaut in *Manon*, Vershinin in *Winter Dreams*, *Raymonda*'s Jean de Brienne, Cyrano (de Bergerac), and an "Athlete" in *Les Biches*. After Mukhamedov's performance of Des Grieux in *Manon*, English critic Clement Crisp referred to the dancer as "uniquely gifted today as a dance-actor," saying, ". . . this was a magnificent, heart-searching view of Des Grieux, and one already to treasure." It is clear that Mukhamedov's artistry has only continued to develop, and his career is indeed a promising one.

—Margaret Willis

N

NÁDASI, Ferenc

Hungarian dancer, choreographer, and teacher. Born in Budapest, 16 October 1893. Studied with Jakab Holczer, Henrietta Spinzi, and Nicholas Guerra, Hungary, and with Enrico Cecchetti, St. Petersburg, 1910. Married (1) dancer Aranka Lieszkovszky (div.); (2) dancer Marcelle Vuillet-Baum. Dancer, while still a student, in dance group directed by Jakab Holczer, travelling to Russia, 1910; soloist, Budapest State Opera Ballet, 1913–14, returning there after army service, 1914–17; dancer, performing as independent artist on variety programmes with Marcelle Vuillet-Baum, European tours, 1921–36; teacher, directing own school in Budapest, and at Budapest State Opera Ballet, from 1936; teacher at newly founded State Ballet Institute, Budapest, from 1950; president of the Association of Dance Artists, 1955; artistic director, Budapest State Opera Ballet, 1959–61; head of a panel of teachers producing the book, *Method of Classical Dance*, 1963. Recipient: Title of Merited Artist, Hungarian National Republic, 1955; Kossuth Prize, 1958. Died in Budapest, 20 February 1966.

ROLES

1913   Arlequine in *The Games of Eros* (Guerra), Hungarian State Opera Ballet, Budapest

1914   Florestan in *The Veil of Pierette* (Guerra), Hungarian State Opera Ballet, Budapest

1917   Dwarf in *The Birthday of the Infanta* (Zobisch), Hungarian State Opera Ballet, Budapest

1918   Aminthas in *Sylvia* (Guerra), Hungarian State Opera Ballet, Budapest

       The Red Faun in *Prometheus* (Guerra), Hungarian State Opera Ballet, Budapest

       Title role in *Le Spectre de la rose* (Fokine), Hungarian State Opera Ballet, Budapest

1920   Principal dancer (cr) in *The Last Dream*, Hungarian State Opera Ballet, Budapest

WORKS

1943   *Sylvia* (mus. Delibes), Hungarian State Opera Ballet, Budapest

1948   *Le Spectre de la rose* (mus. Weber), Hungarian State Opera Ballet, Budapest

1959   *The Birthday of the Infanta* (mus. Carpenter), Hungarian State Opera Ballet, Budapest

Other works include: dances in operas *La Traviata* (mus. Verdi), *Un Ballo in Maschera* (mus. Verdi), *Carmen* (mus. Bizet), *Rigoletto* (mus. Verdi), *The Marriage of Figaro* (mus. Mozart).

PUBLICATIONS

By Nádasi:
Method of Classical Dance (in collaboration with various authors), Budapest, 1963; Berlin, 1964, 1978
Interview with Zoltan Imre in "Wayfaring Hungarian..", *Dance and Dancers* (London), February 1977

About Nádasi:
Various authors, *From the History of Hungarian Ballet* (in Hungarian), Budapest, n.d.
Szechy, Klari, "The Sensational Teaching of Ferenc Nadassy", *Ballet Today* (London), December 1953
Association of Dance Artists, *Dance Documents* (Budapest), 1980, 1984, 1986
Körtvélyes, Géza, *The Budapest Ballet*, translated by Lili Halápy and Elizabeth West, Budapest, 1981
Körtvélyes, Géza, "Remembering Ferenc Nádasi", *Hungarian Dance News* (Budapest), no. 5–6, 1983
Major, Rita, "Ferenc Nádasi the Teacher", *Hungarian Dance News* (Budapest), no. 1–2, 1984

*   *   *

The life story of Ferenc Nádasi reads like a true rags-to-riches tale. From the humblest beginnings he reached the summit of his profession and won the respect of both his peers and the younger generation which succeeded him.

Nádasi was an illegitimate child fostered by a peasant family, who was then brought up by a godmother who worked as a cleaning woman for the ballet master Jakab Holczer. One day Holczer discovered the boy outside the studio, imitating all the movements he had observed by watching the classes, and practising turns on the carpet. Master Holczer became Nádasi's first teacher, also acting as a sort of stepfather and mentor. The boy learned quickly, and at the age of twelve he had already performed a solo at the Operetta Theatre.

It was with Jakab Holczer's dance group that Nádasi went to Russia, where he took classes with Cecchetti: this was to be a profound influence on his whole career. He also had the opportunity to take classes alongside the great Russian dancers, including Vaslav Nijinsky. On his return from Russia he was engaged by the State Opera House in Budapest, becoming the very first male soloist that the company had ever had. He was an exceptional dancer with strong technique and a fiery temperament. He also excelled in emotional parts and mime, with one of his most memorable successes being in the role of the tragic dwarf in the ballet *The Birthday of the Infanta*.

Eventually, however, Nádasi became disillusioned with the leadership of the Opera House, and when his first marriage to the leading ballerina Aranka Lieszkovszky was dissolved, he left Hungary in search of a new partner and new engagements.

In Berlin, in the school of the Russian teacher Lubov Eduardova, he found Marcelle Vuillet-Baum, a boyish and shy young dancer who became his life-long partner on stage and in marriage. Together they toured the large variety theatres of Europe with classical ballet performances of the highest order. They refused to join any large permanent company because they felt that these were pioneering years for dance, with their greatest aim being to keep classical ballet alive by performing in as many places as possible. They felt they had to keep their independence in order to maintain their technical standard and their commitment to the classical style. Their partnership was ideal: Marcelle was a highly intelligent, well-read young woman, who had much to offer both in terms of choreography and costume design, and she had a great influence on Nádasi's natural instincts as a choreographer. Later, when they established their school in Budapest and choreographed together, all those qualities blended into a strong creative collaboration.

Nádasi earned his place in ballet history mainly through his teaching. When the touring days had ended he settled in his native Hungary, opened a dance studio, and was invited to take the post of ballet master at the State Opera. The private studio kept feeding the State Opera's ballet school with young students, and Nádasi soon emerged as an expert teacher, who was most responsible for establishing classical ballet in Hungary. According to his pupils—and judging by their own achievements—he was an extraordinarily gifted teacher. He not only taught his students the fundamentals of dance but he also passed on to them his fanatical love for the art. He had the ability to discern and develop the best qualities of a dancer; he could spot dancers' weaknesses and was able to help them to overcome their difficulties. Nobody knows exactly how he taught the art of turning, yet at every international festival his dancers were admired for their pirouettes. Nádasi absorbed many different styles in his teaching. The main influence was the grand Russian classical style, but he also passed on from his early Cecchetti training the lightness and speed of the Italian school. He was a passionate teacher, who loved his students but could also become infuriated by them. When angry he would jump up in the air (and even at an advanced age he could perform multiple tours en l'air ending in perfect position).

In the darkest days of the communist regime in the 1950s, Nádasi was forced to take a back-seat position, as only visiting Soviet ballet masters were entitled to prominence. When, however, these Soviet teachers and choreographers acknowledged the high standard of classical training in Hungary, and it became clear whose single-handed achievement it was, Nádasi was reinstated, eventually becoming artistic director of the State Opera Ballet Company. He was decorated with the most prestigious state awards and given the respect of the entire dance community. However, he did not enjoy the administrative side of running a company and retired from this position. But he still kept teaching, both at the Opera and at the State Ballet Institute, until his death.

In 1983, to commemorate the ninetieth anniversary of Nádasi's birth, a plaque with his portrait was placed by the entrance of the State Ballet Institute. The inscription says: "Love dance as much as I did". In Hungary, dancers address every ballet teacher as "Master", followed by the teacher's surname. While Nádasi was active, whenever people in the profession referred to *The Master* they meant Ferenc Nádasi.

—Myrtill Nádasi

NAPOLI
(subtitled *The Fisherman and his Bride*; original Danish title: *Napoli; eller, Fiskeren og hans Brud*)

Choreography: August Bournonville
Music: Holger Simon Paulli, Edvard Helsted, Niels Vilhelm Gade, and Hans Christian Lumbye
Design: C. F. Christensen
Libretto: August Bournonville
First Production: Royal Danish Ballet, Royal Theatre, Copenhagen, 29 March 1842
Principal Dancers: August Bournonville (Gennaro), Caroline Fjelsted (Teresina), Füssel (Golfo)

Other productions include: Vienna Hoftheater (restaged Bournonville); Vienna, 15 July 1854. Royal Danish Ballet (restaged and revised Hans Beck); Copenhagen, 1901 (restaged and revised by various subsequent choreographers including Beck, Harald Lander, Hans Brenaa, and Kirsten Ralov). London Festival Ballet (excerpts from Act III; staged Harald Lander); London, 30 August 1954. Royal Ballet (Divertissement; staged Eric Bruhn); London, 3 May 1962. Royal New Zealand Ballet (staged Kirsten Ralov); 7 July 1962. American Ballet Theatre (Divertissement; staged Toni Lander); Washington, D.C., 20 February 1963. Boston Ballet (Act III; staged Hans Brenaa); Boston, 17 January 1966. Göteborg Ballet (staged Elsa Marianne von Rosen, design Allan Fridericia); Sweden, 15 January 1971 (also staged for Royal Swedish Ballet). Paris Opéra Ballet (Divertissement; staged Hans Brenaa); Paris, 15 September 1976. New York City Ballet (Divertissement; staged Stanley Williams), as part of *Bournonville Divertissements*; New York, 3 February 1977. Scottish Ballet (staged Poul Gnatt); Glasgow, 2 August 1978. National Ballet of Canada (staged Peter Schaufuss); Toronto, 10 November 1981. Kirov Ballet (staged von Rosen); Leningrad, 24 March 1982. German Opera Ballet (Act III; staged von Rosen); Berlin, 30 January 1987. Teatro San Carlo (staged Peter Schaufuss); Naples, 9 December 1988.

PUBLICATIONS

Bournonville, August, *Mit Theater Liv* (autobiography), 3 parts: Copenhagen, 1848, 1865, 1877; as *My Theatre Life*, translated by Patricia McAndrew, Middletown, Connecticut, 1979

Beaumont, Cyril, *Supplement to the Complete Book of Ballets*, London, 1942

Kragh-Jacobsen, Svend, *The Royal Danish Ballet*, Copenhagen, 1955

Moore, Lillian, "The Bournonville Heritage", *Dance Magazine* (New York), September 1956

Bruhn, Erik and Moore, Lillian, *Bournonville and Ballet Technique*, London, 1961

Rosen, Elsa Marianne von, "Bournonville's Intentions for *Napoli*", *Dance and Dancers* (London), November 1971

Fridericia, Allan, "Bournonville's Ballet *Napoli*", (translated by L. Gold), *Theatre Research Studies* II, Copenhagen, 1972

Ralov, Kirsten (ed.), *The Bournonville School*, New York, 1979

Terry, Walter, *The King's Ballet Master*, New York, 1979

Fridericia, Allan, *Auguste Bournonville*, Copenhagen, 1979

McAndrew, Patricia (ed. and trans.), "The Ballet Poems of August Bournonville: The Complete Scenarios", *Dance Chronicle* (New York), vol. 3, no. 4, 1979–80

Aschengreen, Erik, Hallar, Marianne, and Heiner, Jorgen, *Perspektiv på Bournonville*, Copenhagen, 1980

Aschengreen, Erik, *Balletbogen*, Copenhagen, 1982

Napoli, Act III, as performed by the Royal Danish Ballet, Copenhagen, 1928

Croce, Arlene, *Going to the Dance*, New York, 1982
Macaulay, Alastair, "This World, and Others", *The New Yorker* (New York), 4 July 1988
Greskovic, Robert, "Romantic Ballet in Naples", *Dance Theatre Journal* (London), Autumn 1990
Hallar, Marianne, and Scavenius, Alette (eds.), *Bournonvilleana*, translated by Gaye Kynoch, Copenhagen, 1992

* * *

Napoli is the most famous of Bournonville's ballets. At its premiere in 1842, it was instantly popular, and since then it has been performed continuously by the Royal Danish Ballet in Copenhagen, on tour all over the world, and more recently by numerous other international companies. The third act alone, as a divertissement, has become a trademark of the Royal Danish Ballet. With its exuberant joy in life and dance, it epitomizes the essence of the Bournonville period in Danish ballet history.

Napoli belongs to what Bournonville termed his romantic ballets. In three acts, it tells the story of the young Italian couple Teresina and Gennaro, engaged to be married. Act I shows them on the quay of Santa Lucia in Naples. Teresina awaits the homecoming of Gennaro, who as a fisherman is out at sea. In the midst of the activity of the colourful Neapolitan street life her mother Veronica tries to marry Teresina off to the more wealthy street vendors Peppo and Giacomo. Teresina, how-ever, resists, thinking only of her beloved Gennaro. He finally arrives and Veronica gives the couple her blessing. After some intrigues the couple set out on a boat trip. A storm darkens the sky, and Gennaro is washed ashore alone. Everybody flees him, blaming him for the death of Teresina. The monk Fra Ambrosio finds him alone, in despair, and praying to the Madonna. He gives Gennaro an amulet with the Madonna's picture, and tells him to go and seek Teresina.

In the second act, Teresina finds herself in the realm of death in the grotto of Golfo, a sea spirit. He is enraptured by her beauty and turns her into a naïad. He makes advances to her, but she avoids him. Gennaro enters the grotto and is tempted by the naïads, but resists. He finds Teresina, but she does not recognize him. With the help of the picture of the Madonna, however, he manages to change her back to her human form. She pleads with Golfo, who eventually lets the couple leave, and endows them with many presents.

Thus endowed they return to the small fishing community, but everybody flees Gennaro, because they think that only with the help of evil has he managed to bring back Teresina and the riches. Fra Ambrosio, however, explains that it has all been due to Gennaro's and Teresina's faith in the Madonna. They get married and the rest of the act is one long dance of celebration.

Bournonville was inspired to make the ballet by a trip to Italy, where among other places he visited Naples and the Blue Grotto on Capri, where the ballet takes place. It reflects the contemporary interest in foreign countries and people, but the ballet also represents the core of Bournonville's philosophy of life. He was strongly influenced by the Romantics, who envisioned the world as divided between the spiritual—representing a higher order instituted by God—and the worldly, which was considered unharmonious and full of dangers, such as passion.

But Bournonville was not a true Romantic; he represents what the Danish dance scholar Erik Aschengreen calls "Danish Biedermeier". Bournonville depicts a world where idyll and harmony are prevailing forces. In *Napoli* there are no real dangers threatening Teresina and Gennaro. In the first act Gennaro flirts with another woman, but it is innocent, and he soon after seals his love for Teresina by giving her a ring. And Veronica is never serious in her efforts to marry off Teresina to the richer street vendors. The second act, which by many has been interpreted as a plunge into the subconscious, where passions are set free, is also devoid of real danger. When pursued by Golfo, Teresina has been transformed into a naïad and is therefore not her real self. Nevertheless, she rejects him and remains innocent and virtuous. Gennaro is tempted by the naïads, but he rejects them to pursue his true love, Teresina. In the end their faith overcomes all obstacles, and they are rewarded with riches and marriage.

As Bournonville was a strong believer in Christian morality, and throughout his life sought to create respectability for the profession of dance, he could not give the passions free play or even let them become threatening. Erotic urges are personified by supernatural beings existing outside society in a world of sea spirits and naïads.

When discussing a ballet of this age, the question of whether or not we today see the real Bournonville invariably arises. There is a distinct Bournonville style with its low rounded arms, low attitudes and arabesques, and minimal physical contact. But it is virtually impossible to say what exactly the ballets looked like during Bournonville's time.

Napoli has undergone a number of changes since its premiere. Hans Beck, who succeeded Bournonville as ballet master, restored some forgotten mime passages. He also reduced some of the other mime passages and increased the amount of pure dance, in order to adapt the choreography to the changing taste of the time. In the first act he put in some solos and music from *Abdallah* (1855), and he changed the third act pas de cinq to a pas de six. The third act as we see it today is basically due to Beck's hand. In the 1940s Harald Lander, with the help of Valborg Borchsenius (the Teresina to Hans Beck's Gennaro), restaged many of Bournonville's ballets. They further reduced the mimed scenes and made extensive deletions. Their work is the standard for the Royal Danish Ballet today. Brenaa later made some minor changes and the staging of the ballet today is in the hands of Kirsten Ralov, who has also choreographed the second act, for which the original Bournonville choreography has been entirely lost. The trend to reduce the mime and insert more dance has caused some scholars to complain that the focus has been shifted away from the conflicts to the light and entertaining aspects of the ballets.

Of the more controversial stagings there is Elsa Marianne von Rosen's in 1971, where she showed the scenes in a much more realistic way than is the tradition at the Royal Danish Ballet. And Peter Schaufuss, in his version for the National Ballet of Canada in 1981, re-choreographed the second act, so that it appeared as Gennaro's dream.

Today there are two approaches to the stagings of Bournonville's ballets. The first is a scholarly, purist approach in which it is argued that the stagings should be based on all the documentation existing about Bournonville and his ballets, in order to restore the ballets as closely as possibly to their original appearance. Then there is a dancerly approach, in which it is

claimed that Bournonville should be kept alive as a living tradition, that it is more important—as the Danish dancer Dinna Bjørn puts it—to recreate choreographically than actually to reconstruct, which means that the dancers should feel from the inside what they are dancing, instead of just repeating historically correct steps. So far the latter approach has been predominant at the Royal Danish Ballet.

Napoli is still very popular today. Maybe it is because its picturesque folklore is so appealing and, although it is a fairy-tale story with a happy ending, the ballet depicts common people with whom we can identify.

—Jeannette Andersen

NATIONAL BALLET OF CANADA

Canadian ballet company based in Toronto. Origins in founding committee formed after the Second Canadian Ballet Festival in Toronto, 1949; founded as an independent performing company, 1951, with first artistic director, Celia Franca, 1951–74, and artistic advisor, Kay Ambrose, 1952–61; celebrated directors have been Alexander Grant, 1976–83, and Erik Bruhn, 1983–86. Official school associated with company, the National Ballet School, founded by Celia Franca and Betty Oliphant, 1959; based in Toronto. Current artistic director of the National Ballet of Canada: Reid Anderson, from 1989.

PUBLICATIONS

Wittaker, Herbert, *Canada's National Ballet*, Toronto and Montreal, 1967

"Special Issue: Dance in Canada", *Dance Magazine* (New York), April 1971

Odom, Selma, and Doob, Penelope, "The National Ballet of Canada: Two Views from the Present", *Dance Magazine* (New York), March 1977

Franca, Celia, *The National Ballet of Canada: A Celebration*, Toronto, 1978

Crabb, Michael (ed.), *Visions: Ballet and its Future*, Proceedings of the National Ballet of Canada's 25th Anniversary Conference (Toronto, 1976), Toronto, 1978

Wyman, Max, *Dance Canada: An Illustrated History*, Vancouver and Toronto, 1989

*   *   *

The National Ballet of Canada was created in 1951, at a time when a number of groups in the country hoped to provide professional outlets for dancers trained in Canada and establish a Canadian tradition for the performing arts. The founding committee of interested citizens solicited advice from Dame Ninette de Valois and through her obtained the services of Celia Franca, whose energy and vision as artistic director shaped the company's first twenty-four years.

The young company had not only to develop its own dancers and theatrical personnel, but also to establish audience support in a vast but sparsely populated country. It did so by touring tirelessly in Canada and then in the United States, primarily to smaller centres and frequently under adverse conditions. Through its insistence on professional standards, whatever the circumstances, it quickly established itself as an important promoter of the art form on the continent. Its 1953 appearance at Ted Shawn's Jacob's Pillow Dance Festival in Lee,

The National Ballet of Canada in Rudolf Nureyev's staging of *The Sleeping Beauty*

Massachusetts, gave the company prominent critical exposure and laid the foundations for its growing North American reputation. With a group of dedicated dancers carefully schooled by Franca and Betty Oliphant, the first ballet mistress, the company performed a repertoire made up of the standard classics, of works by Tudor and Fokine, and a handful of new ballets by novice Canadian choreographers. The company became known for its team spirit and careful attention to stylistic detail and, for many observers these early years were among its most artistically satisfying.

Despite the frequent criticism that it modelled itself too closely on Britain's Royal Ballet, the company's dominant influences have come from elsewhere. Initially, Franca drew heavily on her Ballet Rambert connection with Antony Tudor. As the company expanded in the 1960s, Erik Bruhn, a friend from Franca's Metropolitan Ballet days, and John Cranko, later of the Stuttgart Ballet, provided major works appropriate to the larger theatres to which the company had graduated. Bruhn's *La Sylphide* and Cranko's *Romeo and Juliet*, neither of them works associated with the Royal Ballet, became staples in the company's repertoire. In 1972 Rudolf Nureyev's Kirov-inspired production of *The Sleeping Beauty* forced a major expansion in the company's size and activities and led it into touring on a new scale. The British influence of Tudor and Cranko, both of whom worked directly with the company, was thus balanced by that of Bruhn and Nureyev, who remained closely associated with it for many years.

Bruhn, who also mounted a controversial *Swan Lake* and more conventional productions of *Coppélia* and *Les Sylphides* for the National, remained in the background—as teacher and resident producer—during the next period of transition. When Franca resigned the artistic directorship in 1974, the post was taken up briefly by her associate David Haber, then in 1976 it

passed to Alexander Grant. Under Grant the company acquired a substantial Ashton repertoire, including *The Dream* and *La Fille mal gardée*, as well as the first complete North American *Napoli*, in the production by Peter Schaufuss. The company, which had enjoyed successes in its two London appearances at the Coliseum in 1972 and 1975, performed in Covent Garden in 1979 to a hostile reception. This setback, coupled with financial and artistic problems on the home front, led to a re-evaluation of the company's goals and a redefinition of its character. Bruhn, who had by this time retired as a dancer, accepted the position of artistic director following Grant. From 1983 until his death in 1986, Bruhn charted a new course which emphasized cooperation with Canadian choreographers from outside the company, exposure to the techniques of modern dance, and the creation of major works for the repertoire by Glen Tetley. The premiere of the first of these, *Alice*, took place just before Bruhn's death. Thereafter, Bruhn's associates Lynn Wallis and Valerie Wilder took over as the company's co-artistic directors and Tetley became its artistic associate. Under their influence, the company's emphasis shifted quietly but decisively away from the classical repertoire which had been its basis and towards a more modern look, with two further original works by Tetley and significant acquisitions by other modern choreographers. Reid Anderson, who became artistic director in 1989, took on a company whose reputation as an exponent of the classics rested on productions almost twenty years old, with dancers whose basic classical training had been modified by their exposure to modern dance and neoclassical style. The company's programming maintained the traditional emphasis on the classics, but its recent creative energies had gone in quite different directions. Its future character will depend on the successful reconciliation of these two impulses in a coherent artistic strategy.

The future will also depend on the company's ability to foster original choreography, an area in which its record is one of hopeful beginnings rather than significant achievement. Grant Strate and David Adams in its early period, Ann Ditchburn, James Kudelka, and Constantin Patsalas in the 1970s and 1980s and, more recently, David Allan and John Alleyne have emerged from the ranks of the company to become choreographers, but no single major choreographer has as yet made of the company a permanent, creative home. This fact may be attributed to the harsh exigencies of pioneering in the early days and to the emphasis, which has characterized it throughout its existence, on the company as a performing unit rather than as a seedbed for original creation. Without that emphasis, however, its real achievement of establishing classical ballet on the Canadian cultural horizon would not have been possible.

—James E. Neufeld

NATIONAL BALLET OF CHINA *see* **CENTRAL BALLET OF CHINA**

NEARY, Patricia

American dancer, ballet director, and teacher. Born in Miami, Florida, 27 October 1942. Studied with George Milenoff and Thomas Armour. Début, National Ballet of Canada, Toronto, 1956; dancer, New York City Ballet, from 1960, becoming soloist, 1962–68; ballet mistress, German Opera Ballet, Berlin, 1970–73; director, Geneva Ballet, 1973–78, and Zurich Ballet, 1978–85; ballet director, La Scala, Milan, 1986–87; artistic director, Ballet British Columbia, 1989–90; authority on the Balanchine repertoire, staging Balanchine ballets throughout the world, including in London, Paris, Geneva, Vienna, Berlin, Stuttgart, Rome, Amsterdam, Lisbon, Tokyo, and South Africa.

ROLES

1961   Principal dancer (cr) in *Valses et Variations* (later called *Raymonda Variations*; Balanchine), New York City Ballet, New York

1964   She Wore a Perfume in *Dim Lustre* (Tudor), New York City Ballet, New York
       Principal dancer in *Ballet Imperial* (later *Piano Concerto No. 2*; Balanchine), New York City Ballet, New York

1965   Danza della Caccia (cr) in *Don Quixote* (Balanchine), New York City Ballet, New York

1966   Principal dancer in *Summerspace* (Cunningham), New York City Ballet, New York
       Principal dancer (cr) in *Le Guirlande de Campra* (Taras), New York City Ballet, New York

1967   Rubies (cr) in *Jewels* (Balanchine), New York City Ballet, New York

Other roles include: for New York City Ballet—first pas de trois in *Agon* (Balanchine), principal dancer in *Concerto Barocco* (Balanchine), Choleric in *The Four Temperaments* (Balanchine), First Movement in *Symphony in C* (Balanchine), title role in *Firebird* (Balanchine), the Siren in *Prodigal Son*

(Balanchine), the Queen in *The Cage* (Robbins), principal dancer in *Scotch Symphony* (Balanchine), Five Pieces in *Episodes* II (Balanchine), Hippolyta in *A Midsummer Night's Dream* (Balanchine), Queen of the Morphides in *Piège de Lumière* (Taras), Polyhymnia in *Apollo* (Balanchine), principal dancer in *Divertimento No. 15* (Balanchine), principal dancer in *La Valse* (Balanchine), Allegro in *Western Symphony* (Balanchine), principal dancer in *Stars and Stripes* (Balanchine); as guest artist—Odette/Odile in *Swan Lake* (after Petipa, Ivanov), Myrtha in *Giselle* (after Petipa, Coralli, Perrot).

WORKS

1990   *Variations Concertantes* (mus. Ginastera), Ballet British Columbia, Vancouver

Also staged:
1970   *Agon* (chor. Balanchine; mus. Stravinsky), Stuttgart Ballet, Stuttgart
       (also staged Royal Ballet, 1973; Geneva Ballet, 1974; Dutch National Ballet, 1974; Paris Opéra Ballet, 1974; Hamburg Ballet, 1976; German Opera Ballet, Berlin, 1977; Zurich Ballet, 1978; Ater Balletto, 1981; Basle Ballet, 1987; Royal Danish Ballet, 1987; Frankfurt Ballet, 1991; Pennsylvania Ballet, 1992; San Francisco Ballet, 1992)
       The Four Temperaments (chor. Balanchine; mus. Hindemith), German Opera Ballet, Berlin
       (also staged Royal Ballet, 1973; Ballet Théâtre Contemporain, 1976; Zurich Ballet, 1978; Bavarian State Opera Ballet, Munich, 1980; CAPAB Ballet, 1983; Hamburg Ballet, 1983; Vienna State Opera Ballet, 1985; Teatro Colón, Buenos Aires, 1985; La Scala Ballet, 1987; Ballet de Nancy, 1988; Pennsylvania Ballet, 1991; Rome Opera Ballet, 1991)

1971   *Episodes* II (chor. Balanchine; mus. Webern), Geneva Ballet, Geneva
       (also staged Dutch National Ballet, 1973, 1992; Zurich Ballet, 1982)

1972   *Symphony in C* (chor. Balanchine; mus. Bizet), Vienna State Opera Ballet, Vienna
       (also staged Geneva Ballet, 1973; Stuttgart Ballet, 1976; Zurich Ballet, 1978; La Scala Ballet, Milan, 1987; Munich Ballet, 1991)

1973   *Allegro Brillante* (chor. Balanchine; mus. Tchaikovsky), Royal Ballet touring company, London
       (also staged Geneva Ballet, 1973; Norwegian Opera Ballet, 1975; Ater Balletto, 1979; Zurich Ballet, 1981; Matsuyama Ballet, 1981; Rome Opera Ballet, 1987; Royal Danish Ballet, 1992)
       Apollo (chor. Balanchine; mus. Stravinsky), Geneva Ballet, Geneva
       (also staged Rome Opera Ballet, 1973; Bavarian State Opera Ballet, Munich, 1974; Budapest, 1977; London Festival Ballet, 1988; Kirov Ballet, 1991; Royal Danish Ballet, 1992; Royal Ballet, 1993)
       Ballet Imperial (also *Tchaikovksy Piano Concerto No. 2*; chor. Balanchine; mus. Tchaikovsky), Geneva Ballet, Geneva
       (also staged Norwegian National Ballet, 1976; La Scala Ballet, 1986; PACT Ballet, 1989; American Ballet Theatre, 1991; Royal Danish Ballet, 1992; Royal Ballet, 1993; Dutch National Ballet, 1993)
       Serenade (chor. Balanchine; mus. Tchaikovsky), Geneva Ballet, Geneva
       (also staged Israeli Classical Ballet, 1975; Rome

Patricia Neary rehearsing *The Four Temperaments* with the Sadler's Wells Royal Ballet, London

Opera Ballet, 1976; Hungarian State Opera Ballet, 1977; Zurich Ballet, 1978; Matsuyama Ballet, 1982; Basle Ballet, 1982; CAPAB Ballet, 1983; Hamburg Ballet, 1983; German Opera Ballet, Berlin, 1984; German Opera Ballet on the Rhine, Düsseldorf, 1984; Warsaw Ballet, 1985; Teatro Colón, Buenos Aires, 1985; Royal Ballet, 1988; Royal Danish Ballet, 1991)

Tchaikovsky Pas de deux (chor. Balanchine; mus. Tchaikovsky), Geneva Ballet, Geneva
  (also staged Israeli Classical Ballet, 1979; La Scala Ballet, Milan, 1980; Belgrade Opera Ballet, 1980; Hamburg Ballet, 1983; Zurich Ballet, 1984; Ballet de Nancy, 1984; London Festival Ballet, 1985; Asami Maki Ballet, Tokyo, 1987)

1974 *Donizetti Variations* (chor. Balanchine; mus. Donizetti), Geneva Ballet, Geneva
  (also staged Dutch National Ballet, 1976; Ater Balletto, 1980; Pennsylvania Ballet, 1990)

1975 *Concerto Barocco* (chor. Balanchine; mus. Bach), Geneva Ballet, Geneva
  (also staged Royal Ballet touring company, 1977;

Zurich Ballet, 1978; Belgrade Opera Ballet, 1979; Ballet van Vlaanderen, 1982; Finnish National Ballet, 1984; German Opera Ballet on the Rhine, Düsseldorf, 1984; Basel Ballet, 1985; La Scala Ballet, 1986; Asami Maki Ballet, Tokyo, 1987; Sadler's Wells Royal Ballet, 1988; Scottish Ballet, 1991; Pennsylvania Ballet, 1991)

Scotch Symphony (chor. Balanchine; mus. Mendelssohn), Geneva Ballet, Geneva
  (also staged German Opera Ballet on the Rhine, Düsseldorf, 1983; Bern Ballet, 1987)

1976 *Divertimento No. 15* (chor. Balanchine; mus. Mozart), Geneva Ballet, Geneva
  (also staged Pennsylvania Ballet, 1991; Finnish National Ballet, 1992; Royal Danish Ballet, 1993)

La Valse (chor. Balanchine; mus. Ravel), Stuttgart Ballet, Stuttgart
  (also staged Geneva Ballet, 1974; German Opera Ballet, Berlin, 1976; Vienna State Opera Ballet, 1978; Zurich Ballet, 1978; Bavarian State Opera Ballet, Munich, 1982)

Western Symphony (chor. Balanchine; mus. Kay),

Geneva Ballet, Geneva
(also staged Zurich Ballet, 1978; Pennsylvania Ballet, 1990)

1977 *Coppélia* (after Petipa, Cecchetti; mus. Delibes), Geneva Ballet, Geneva

Prodigal Son (chor. Balanchine; mus. Prokofiev), Geneva Ballet, Geneva
(also staged Royal Ballet, 1993)

1979 *A Midsummer Night's Dream* (chor. Balanchine; mus. Mendelsohn), Zurich Ballet, Zurich

1980 *Who Cares?* (chor. Balanchine; mus. Gershwin), Zurich Ballet, Zurich
(also staged Basle Ballet, 1988; Malmo Ballet, Sweden, 1988; PACT Ballet, 1989; Ater Balletto, 1991; Scottish Ballet, 1992)

1983 *Sonatine* (chor. Balanchine; mus. Ravel), Zurich Ballet, Zurich

1985 *Pas de dix* (*Raymonda Pas de dix*; chor. Balanchine; mus. Glazunov), Reggio Emilia, Italy

1988 *Theme and Variations* (after Balanchine), National Ballet of Portugal, Lisbon
(also staged Sadler's Wells Royal Ballet, 1988; Matsuyama Ballet, 1988; Royal Danish Ballet, 1991; Ballet de Nancy, 1992)

Rubies (from *Jewels*; chor. Balanchine; mus. Stravinsky), PACT Ballet, Pretoria
(also staged Monte Carlo Ballet, 1990; Paris Opéra Ballet, 1990; Finnish National Ballet, 1992)

PUBLICATIONS

By Neary:
Reply to "Reader's Forum", *Dance Magazine* (New York), March 1985

About Neary:
Goodman, Saul, "Brief Biographies: Patricia Neary", *Dance Magazine* (New York), May 1964
Gruen, John "Close-up: Patricia Neary", *Dance Magazine* (New York), September 1975
Horosko, Marian, "Patricia Neary and the Zurich Ballet", *Dance Magazine* (New York), May 1983
Robertson, Allen, "At Home Abroad", *Ballet News* (New York), May 1983
Sorrell, Walter, "Watershedding the Arts", *Dance Magazine* (New York), December 1986
Wyman, Max, "Patricia Neary Feels at Home in Vancouver", *Dance Magazine* (New York), March 1990
Wyman, Max, "Patricia Neary says Farewell", *Dance Magazine* (New York), June 1990

*   *   *

Patricia Neary was certainly the model Balanchine dancer, or what the world of dance considered a Balanchine dancer to be: long-legged, loose-hipped, extraordinarily tall (the tallest ballerina of her generation), musically sensitive, and possessed with an exceptional speed in allegro, coupled with a clarity of attack—all the more unusual because of her height. Yet Balanchine created no role of importance for her in her eight years with his company. She danced exemplary performances of almost all the ballerina roles in the repertory of New York City Ballet, many learned literally at the last moment; but she had to contend with Balanchine's increasing fascination with Suzanne Farrell (as did every other ballerina in that company during the 1960s).

After Neary's years in the New York City Ballet, a series of guest appearances in the classical repertory largely proved unsatisfactory. Though she gave illuminating moments to such roles as Odette/Odile and Myrtha, and though her brilliant technique gave her the security to impose individual interpretations, artistically she was forced to draw on her own resources at a time when she should have been challenged with works made to expand her personality. When she *was* challenged, her technical feats were tempered by a seemingly endless legato, her attack by a vulnerable femininity, which made her performance both exciting and moving.

Another of her gifts, an almost photographic memory—which had stood her in such good stead when taking over a role a few minutes before the curtain rose—was to lead Neary into a new career. She has become one of the finest of the many official assistants sent around the world to stage Balanchine ballets. For, coupled with the literal reproduction of the steps, she imparts the shadings of musicality, the quality of movement, that elude so many of the other "ambassadors" of the Balanchine canon. One need only compare her staging of *The Four Temperaments* or *Concerto Barocco* with any other contemporary staging of the same ballets to realize how well Neary understands, and is capable of transmitting, the Balanchine legacy.

As a ballet director, Neary has had mixed success. Her dislike of compromise, her dissatisfaction with slow change, with working steadily toward a distant goal rather than expecting overnight results, have had varying results within the European theatre system. In Zurich she developed a solid company capable of giving performances at an international level. At La Scala in Milan, her approach had a catastrophic effect. She came face-to-face with theatre bureaucracy at its worst, and began to force changes in an effort to raise artistic standards. She did not succeed. In Vancouver, however, she seemed to have found the ideal situation: a young and enthusiastic company, anxious to profit from her experience. Sadly, Neary did not last there a year. Despite a successful season and favourable reviews (including of an original work choreographed by Neary), the new director was forced to resign after what one reporter called "an anti-Neary coup". She now continues on a freelance basis, and has recently staged works for the Pennsylvania Ballet, the Royal Danish Ballet, the Ballet de Nancy, and the Scottish Ballet.

—Richard Adama

NEGRI, Cesare

Milanese dancer, dancing master, choreographer, and theoretician. Born in Milan, c.1536. Studied under Pompeo Diabono. Dancing teacher in Milan, from c.1554, with students including numerous future dancing masters to royal households; dancer, appearing in masques and royal festivities; choreographer, from 1569, presenting mascarades and intermedios for royal courts; writer on dance, publishing major treatise, 1602 (reissued and retitled 1604). Died c. 1604.

PUBLICATIONS

By Negri:
Le Gratie d'Amore, di Cesare Negri Milanese, detto il Trombone, Milan, 1602; resissued as *Nuove Inventioni di Balli*, Bordone, 1604; reprinted New York, 1969

About Negri:

Reyna, Ferdinand, *Des Origines de la danse,* Paris, 1955

Verga, Ettore, *La Storia della Vita Milanese,* Milan, 1984

Kendall, Yvonne, "*Le Gratie d'Amore by Cesare Negri—Introduction and Translation,* Ann Arbor (University Microfilm), 1985

Mitchell, Bonner, *The Majesty of the State,* Florence, 1986

Daye, Anne, "The Professional Life of the Italian Dancing Master c.1550–1625", *Dancing Times* (London), February 1991

*   *   *

Little is known of Negri's life and works beyond what he himself says in his dance treatise, *Le Gratie d'Amore.* According to this source he was Milanese by birth and the father of a daughter named Margherita. He was a student of Pompeo Diabono until Diabono left Italy in 1554 to serve at the court of French king Henry II. At this point Negri began teaching in Milan, and in 1569 he began to present his original choreographies. Among his students were those who became dancing masters to Henry III of Poland and France, Philip II of Spain, and Emperor Rudolf II; various minor royalty of Europe; and those who ran schools in cities throughout Italy and Western Europe.

Negri himself served the several Spanish governors of Milan and in that capacity danced before the many crowned heads of Europe who passed through the city during his professional lifetime. In 1585, under order of Don Gabriello of Cueva, then governor of Milan, Negri travelled with the Count of Cifonte to the beseiged island of Malta to fight the Turks. The fact that Negri danced at numerous stops throughout the voyage gives a rather interesting picture of military travel in the sixteenth century.

On 29 July 1571 Negri danced at a masque held in Genoa for Don Juan of Austria and his two sons. Later, on 6 May 1574, he gave Don Juan dance lessons and in June of that year staged a grand masquerade in his honour. The November 1598 visit of Marguerite of Austria, Queen of Spain, to Milan provided a showcase for Negri and his students as they danced and performed staged combats and mattachins for the many noble guests assembled for the event. It was also to have set the stage for Negri's major work, the choreographies for the intermedio *Armenia Pastorale,* but the death of Philip II and subsequent mourning of the new queen delayed this production until July 1599, when Marguerite's cousin Albert and his new wife Isabelle, the Archduke and Archduchess of Austria, visited Milan. This performance was Negri's last recorded professional event.

Negri's 1574 grand masquerade in honour of Don Juan was performed on 26 June at the palace of Contessa Delia Angosciuola. Unlike the better known sixteenth-century "masque", that typically featured masked participants, the "masquerade", of which Negri's is a good example, was a parade of lavishly costumed, though non-masked, ladies and gentlemen representing allegorical characters. Following each of the 23 characters were musicians dressed as shepherds. Then came performers representing four kings and four queens carrying symbols of the four elements—earth, wind, fire, and water. These eight did a dance, after which there was a staged combat of sticks and shields and a mattachins, these last performed by dwarves and by dancers dressed as wild men, respectively. After numerous madrigals and clever verses identifying each noble participant came the *piece de resistance,* a choreography featuring 82 dancers. The dance for the kings and queens is included in the text of *Le Gratie,* but the choreography used for the dance for 82 is, unfortunately, not specified.

The performance of the 1599 intermedio featured a four-act comedy by Giovanni Battista Visconte, four intermedii written by Camillo Schiasenati, and dances choreographed by Negri. The ending dance, "Austria Felice", is included in *Le Gratie.* During this visit there was also an evening of dances performed by single-sex groups of noble ladies and gentlemen; two of those entrata choreographies are included: the "Ballo for Six Women" and the "Ballo for Six Men".

Negri's magnum opus, *Le Gratie d'Amore,* is the largest dance manual of the sixteenth century. It contains steps and choreographies for professionals as well as amateurs, and it includes a great deal of historical information that helps place dance in Italy into a historical and social perspective. Divided into three "treatises", *Le Gratie* gives a strong overview of dances and dance masters related in a witty and personal manner. The First Treatise is an extended introduction in which Negri discusses the importance of dancing in society, his reasons for writing the book and, in florid, falsely self-deprecating style, the reasons he is the best person to do it. He then launches into an annotated listing of famous Italian dancing masters, including the famous Fabritio Caroso, author of *Il Ballarino* (1598), Negri's teacher, Diabono, and several of Negri's more illustrious pupils (being always careful to list salaries and gifts they received, clearly an important part of a dance master's prestige). The next chapter of this treatise follows Negri's career from 1554, when he began teaching in Milan, through 1599, when he choreographed the Intermedio for Albert and Isabelle. Three events receiving special attention in this chapter are the above mentioned masquerade and intermedio, and the festivities surrounding the visit of Marguerite of Austria.

The Second Treatise is a collection of 54 instructions for deportment at dances and for the performance of steps, both simple—like the "riverenza grave", or opening bow—and complex—like the myriad gagliarda variations. These variations, some designated "very difficult" by Negri himself, often exceed the usual six-beat pattern of the gagliarda and include elaborate footwork. Another interesting and unique part of this Treatise is the tassel jumps, a series of virtuosic jumps, spins, and entrechats that end in the kicking of a tasselled rope suspended from the ceiling at shoulder height from the floor.

The Third Treatise contains the 43 choreographies, with their individual tunes in mensural notation for melody instruments and in lute tablature. Each choreography is dedicated to one of Negri's patronesses. There are dances for from one to four couples, for two men and one woman, and for as many as wish to dance. They come in six general formal types: the ballo, a simple repetitive dance normally serving an entrance function; the balletto, a multi-metered dance with choreographical and musical refrain; the bassa, a choreography that resembles the older bassa-danza in its stately forward-moving steps and quick triple-metered afterdance; the brando, the dance with both the greatest specified number of dancers and the most meter changes; the theme and variations dances, where steps and music become more complicated as the dance progresses; and the chain or country dances for unspecified number of dancers, these last generally serving as mixers. Towards the end of this Treatise is a brief description of the intermedio of 1599, giving the general plot of each of the intermedii along with the choreography for the final dance.

As the author of one of only four major treatises on dance in the sixteenth century, Negri's importance cannot be over-emphasized. In addition, his treatise provides information about historical events, levels of virtuosity, and theatrical productions that are not found in the *Orchésographie* (1589) of

Arbeau or the two treatises, *Il Ballarino* and *Nobilità di Dame* (1600) by Caroso. In fact, one of only two extant choreographies known to have been performed in an intermedio is found in Negri. The choreographies present formal and musical diversity. The multifaceted interest of the treatise makes it clear that Negri was correct when, speaking of Caroso, he said, "how very true it is that I could not add to his creations, but you will see in this work that the virtue of dancing has been considerably enriched since his time by my inventions . . .".

—Yvonne Kendall

———

NEMCHINOVA (Nemtchinova), **Vera**

Russian dancer and teacher.   Born Vera Nikolaevna Nemchinova (Nemtchinova) in Moscow, 26 August 1899. Studied at the ballet studio of Lydia Nelidova, Moscow, from 1911; also studied with Elisabeth Anderson, 1914, and later with Nikolai Legat, Enrico Cecchetti. Married (1) dancer Nikolai (Nicolas) Zverev; (2) dancer and ballet director Anatole Obukhov. Soloist, Diaghilev's Ballets Russes, 1915–26, becoming ballerina, from 1921; left Diaghilev to perform with Massine, Cochran Revue, London, 1926, also performing with Mikhail Mordkin's company, U.S. tour, 1926–27; founder, with Anton Dolin, Nemchinova–Dolin Ballet, performing in London and Europe, 1927–28; founder and ballerina, Ballets Russes de Vera Nemchinova, touring England and Europe, 1928–30; also toured Argentina with "Ballet Franco-Russe" of Leo Staats, 1930; guest ballerina, Riga, Latvia, 1930; guest artist, Ballet de l'Opéra Russe à Paris, 1931; prima ballerina, Lithuanian State Opera Ballet (or Lithuanian National Ballet), performing at the State Opera Theatre, Kaunas, and on tour, 1931–35; prima ballerina, René Blum's Ballets de Monte Carlo, from 1936, performing with Markova–Dolin Ballet, London, 1937, and de Basil's company (then called Covent Garden Russian Ballet), London, 1938; ballerina, touring Australia and U.S. with de Basil's Original Ballet Russe, 1939–40, returning as guest artist, 1940–41; moved to New York, 1941: guest ballerina, Ballet Theatre (later American Ballet Theatre), New York, 1943, and San Francisco Ballet, 1946; also teacher, Ballet Arts School, and at own studio, New York, from 1947. Died in New York, 22 July 1984.

ROLES

1916   Dancer in *Les Sylphides* (Fokine), Diaghilev's Ballets Russes
1919   Daughter, Queen of Hearts, Can-Can ensemble (cr) in *La Boutique fantasque* (Massine), Diaghilev's Ballets Russes, London
1920   Rosetta (cr) in *Pulcinella* (Massine), Diaghilev's Ballets Russes, Paris
         Principal dancer (cr) in *Le Astuzie femminili* (Massine), Diaghilev's Ballets Russes, Paris
1921   Princess Aurora in *The Sleeping Princess* (Petipa; staged Sergeyev, with additional dances Nijinska), Diaghilev's Ballets Russes, London
         Carnation Fairy, Columbine in *The Sleeping Princess* (Petipa; staged Sergeyev, with additional dances Nijinska), Diaghilev's Ballets Russes, London
1924   Shepherdess (cr) in *Les Tentations de la bergère; ou, L'Amour vainquer* (Nijinska), Diaghilev's Ballets Russes, Monte Carlo

Adagietto ("La Garçonne" or the Girl in Blue; cr) in *Les Biches* (Nijinska), Diaghilev's Ballets Russes, Monte Carlo
1925   Young girl (cr) in *Les Matelots* (Massine), Diaghilev's Ballets Russes, Paris
1926/   Title role in *Giselle* (after Petipa, Coralli, Perrot),
27   Mikhail Mordkin Ballet, U.S. tour
         Odette/Odile in *Swan Lake* (after Petipa, Ivanov), Mikhail Mordkin Ballet, U.S. tour
1927   Principal dancer (cr) in *The Nightingale and the Rose* (Dolin), Nemchinova–Dolin Ballet, London
1928   "Classic" (cr) in *Rhapsody in Blue* (Dolin), Nemchinova–Dolin Ballet, Paris
         Principal dancer (cr) in *Espagnol* (Dolin), Nemchinova–Dolin Ballet, Paris
1930   Diana (cr) in *Aubade* (Balanchine), Ballets Russes de Vera Nemchinova, Paris
1931   Ballerina in *Petrushka* (Woizikowsky after Fokine), Ballet de l'Opéra Russe à Paris, London
         Aurora in *Aurora Pas de deux* (after Petipa), Ballet de l'Opéra Russe à Paris, London
1935   Swanilda in *Coppélia* (after Petipa, Cecchetti), Lithuanian State Opera Ballet, London tour
         Title role in *Raymonda* (after Petipa), Lithuanian State Opera Ballet, London tour
         Principal dancer in *Islamey* (Zverev), Lithuanian State Opera Ballet, London tour
         Principal dancer in *Les Fiançailles* (Zverev), Lithuanian State Opera Ballet, London tour
         Principal dancer in *Rondo Capriccioso* (Dolin), Lithuanian State Opera Ballet, London tour
1936   Chung-Yang (cr) in *L'Epreuve d'amour* (Fokine), (René Blum's) Ballets de Monte Carlo, Monte Carlo
1943   Title role in *Princess Aurora* (suite of dances from *The Sleeping Beauty*; Dolin after Petipa), Ballet Theatre, New York

Other roles include: for Diaghilev's Ballets Russes—Acrobat in *Parade* (Massine).

PUBLICATIONS

By Nemchinova:
Interview in Horosko, Marian, "In the Shadow of Russian Tradition: Vera Nemtchinova", *Dance Magazine* (New York), February 1972

About Nemchinova:
Knight, Hadden, "A Lady of the Ballet", *Dance Magazine* (New York), October 1926
Haskell, Arnold, "The Younger Russian Dancers", *Dancing Times* (London), July 1928
Dolin, Anton, *Divertissement*, London, 1931
Grigoriev, Serge, *The Diaghilev Ballet*, translated by Vera Bowe, London, 1953
Moore, Lillian, "From Artist to Student", *Dance Magazine* (New York), May 1954
Anthony, Gordon, "Dancers to Remember: Vera Nemtchinova", *Dancing Times* (London), November 1976
Vaughan, David, "Balanchine's Ballerinas: 1925–1933", *Dance Magazine* (New York), January 1979

*   *   *

Vera Nemchinova was an Imperial Russian ballerina schooled in exile, a product of Diaghilev's vision and forethought, an

Vera Nemchinova in *Les Matelots*, Diaghilev's Ballets Russes, c.1925

enigmatic representative of a time of transition in the world of ballet.

In 1915, at the age of fifteen, she was recruited, along with her older sister Lydia, into the corps of Diaghilev's Ballets Russes by Serge Grigoriev, the company's régisseur, who had been sent to Moscow in search of dancers to fill the ballet's dwindling ranks. Unlike most of the company, she had not received her training through one of the Imperial theatres, but was coached privately for three years by Lydia Nelidova, a former Bolshoi soloist, and then by Elisabeth Anderson for a short three months. While this early training might have been a disadvantage for a less gifted dancer, the young Vera proved an eager and serious pupil.

Her career with Diaghilev spanned ten years, during which

time she studied and emulated the technique and manner of the outstanding dancers of the time—Lopokova, Pavlova, Karsavina, Spessivtseva, Egorova, and Nijinsky. By 1919, she began to take on solo and principal roles, rising to the rank of ballerina in 1921. In her final years with Diaghilev she reigned supreme as his prima ballerina assoluta. Nemchinova credited more than her apprenticeship to Diaghilev; in a 1936 London newspaper interview, she stated: "Spiritually, I am the child of Diaghilev, just as he was father to all young artists under his sway. To him nothing was too small to be important—even the correct dressing of one's hair was a point that must affect the dancer's work." This is a touching statement from a young woman who was both orphaned and exiled by the revolution in Russia.

Attention to detail was a hallmark of Nemchinova's dancing and, later, her teaching. She was heralded as a model of the grand classical manner, and much of her dancing career was devoted to the performance of the classical ballet repertory. Her most memorable role, however, was as the girl in blue in Bronislava Nijinska's 1924 ballet, *Les Biches*. Nemchinova later recalled her embarrassment when Diaghilev, prior to her opening-night entrance, cut away the skirt of her costume, leaving her legs "naked" except for tights and a short tunic-length of skirt—a scandalous costume for that day. Scandalous or not, this role established her as a legendary figure in the ballet world of the 1920s and 1930s.

Interviews, articles, and reviews from that era paint her as a small, dark-eyed beauty of considerable charm. She was a remarkable technician, noted for the steely strength of her legs (which were once insured for £30,000) and for her speed, clarity, and precision. She was also an exquisite example of the Imperial Russian style and excelled particularly as the Swan Queen in *Swan Lake* and as Princess Aurora in *The Sleeping Beauty*. She has told of a time when she decided to substitute 32 entrechat six for the usual 32 fouettés in *Swan Lake* because Diaghilev had told her, "Vera, you are not smart enough to do anything but turn." After hours of practice, she invited the great man to rehearsal and dazzled him with yet another astounding feat of her virtuosity.

Nemchinova and her first husband, Nicolas Zverev, left Diaghilev in 1926 to perform in London with Leonide Massine in the Cochran Revue—a move she bitterly regretted, since Diaghilev was unforgiving. In her words, "I wanted to go back so badly. Diaghilev would take you back if you left and returned yourself, but he would never invite you back. He would cry, but he would never ask you to come back." The split with Diaghilev began a period of short- and long-term engagements marked particularly by a partnership with Anton Dolin, with whom she had danced in Diaghilev's Ballets Russes. Critics found Nemchinova and Dolin "ideal partners", and for a year and a half they toured Britain and Europe with a company and repertory that featured their dancing partnership. Unfortunately, Dolin took great liberties with classical choreography in order to exploit Nemchinova's technical virtuosity, and the partnership ended.

In 1928, the Ballets Russes de Vera Nemchinova was established, an enterprise with Zverev and Anatole Obukhov, a new partner who was soon to become Nemchinova's mentor and second husband. This small company featured a varied repertory which included *Aubade*, a new ballet by the young George Balanchine. Some critics found Nemchinova unsuited to the harsh, angular Balanchine style, but the ballerina found this role challenging and artistically fulfilling.

The death of Diaghilev in 1929 shook the foundations of ballet in Europe and prompted Nemchinova and Obukhov to seek the security of an established company, and in 1931 they joined director Zverev at the National Opera Theatre in

Kaunas, in what was at that time the independent state of Lithuania. Here Nemchinova and Obukhov performed the classical repertory and, ironically, laid the foundation for the Russian ballet in Lithuania years before the country became a republic of the USSR.

During the latter half of the 1930s, the couple performed with a number of the Ballet Russe companies until they chose New York as their home. Nemchinova's final performances were with Ballet Theatre, where she once again distinguished herself as a supreme example of the grand manner.

From 1947 until her death in 1984, Nemchinova devoted herself to teaching. Here, too, she distinguished herself as a paragon of the Imperial Russian style. Her teaching was demanding, but human; she nurtured the individuality and personal strengths of her students, and encouraged the development of their artistry as well as their technical skills. She expected from her students not only clarity and control, but also, the spiritual essence of a dance rooted in tradition and grandeur. Long after she could fully execute the technique, her arms and upper body spoke eloquently and majestically of the art of the prima ballerina assoluta.

—Rosalind Pierson

NERINA, Nadia

South African dancer. Born Nadia Judd in Cape Town, South Africa, 21 October 1927. Studied with Eileen Keegan, Dorothy McNair in Durban; with Marie Rambert, Elsa Brunelleschi, Stanislas Idzikowski in London, 1945–46, and at Sadler's Wells Ballet School, 1946. Married Charles Gordon, 1956. Dancer, Sadler's Wells Opera Ballet (later Sadler's Wells Theatre Ballet), briefly appearing as Nadia Moore, 1946; soloist, Sadler's Wells Ballet (later Royal Ballet), from 1947, becoming ballerina from 1952; toured South Africa with Alexis Rassine, 1952, 1954, and Britain, 1956; guest artist, Bolshoi Ballet, Moscow, 1960, Kirov Ballet, Leningrad, 1960, and Western Theatre Ballet (later Scottish Ballet), 1965; also made numerous television appearances, especially in productions by Margaret Dale, 1957–62. Patron of the Cecchetti Society, London.

ROLES

1946   Sugar Plum Fairy in *The Nutcracker* (Ivanov; staged Sergeyev), Sadler's Wells Theatre Ballet
        Title role in *Khadra* (Franca), Sadler's Wells Theatre Ballet
        A Girl in Yellow in *Assembly Ball* (Howard), Sadler's Wells Ballet
        A Circus Dancer (cr) in *Mardi Gras* (Howard), Sadler's Wells Theatre Ballet, London
        Black Lady in *The Gods Go a-Begging* (de Valois), Sadler's Wells Theatre Ballet
        Vagabond girl in *The Vagabonds* (Burke), Sadler's Wells Theatre Ballet
1947   Columbine in *Carnaval* (Fokine), Sadler's Wells Theatre Ballet
        Young girl in *Le Spectre de la rose* (Fokine), Sadler's Wells Theatre Ballet, London
        Pas de trois in *Swan Lake* (Petipa, Ivanov; staged Sergeyev), Sadler's Wells Theatre Ballet, London
1948   The Fairy Spring (cr) in *Cinderella* (Ashton), Sadler's Wells Ballet, London

Nadia Nerina as the Firebird, 1956

Can-Can dancer in *La Boutique fantasque* (Massine), Sadler's Wells Ballet, London

Entrée ("Blue Girls") in *Les Patineurs* (Ashton), Sadler's Wells Ballet, London

Florestan's sister in *The Sleeping Beauty* (Petipa; staged Sergeyev, Ashton, de Valois), Sadler's Wells Ballet, London

1949   Polka in *Façade* (Ashton), Sadler's Wells Ballet, London

Principal dancer in *Scènes de ballet* (Ashton), Sadler's Wells Ballet, London

1950   Serving wench (cr) in *Don Quixote* (de Valois), Sadler's Wells Ballet, London

Débutante in *Façade* (Ashton), Sadler's Wells Ballet, London

Title role in *Mam'zelle Angot* (Massine), Sadler's Wells Ballet, London

Bride in *A Wedding Bouquet* (Ashton), Sadler's Wells Ballet, London

Odette in *Swan Lake*, Act II (Ivanov; staged Sergeyev), Sadler's Wells Theatre Ballet

1951   Title role in *Cinderella* (Ashton), Sadler's Wells Ballet, London

Swanilda in *Coppélia* (Petipa, Cecchetti; staged Sergeyev), Sadler's Wells Ballet, London

Neophyte in *Tiresias* (Ashton), Sadler's Wells Ballet, tour

Princess Florine (Bluebird pas de deux) in *The Sleeping Beauty* (Petipa; staged Sergeyev, de Valois, Ashton), Sadler's Wells Ballet, London

Princess Aurora in *The Sleeping Beauty* (Petipa; staged Sergeyev, de Valois, Ashton), Sadler's Wells Ballet, tour

1952   Title role in *Sylvia* (Ashton), Sadler's Wells Ballet, London

Daughter in *Bonne-Bouche* (Cranko), Sadler's Wells Ballet, London

Odette/Odile in *Swan Lake* (Petipa, Ivanov; staged Sergeyev, de Valois, Ashton), Sadler's Wells Ballet, London

1953   Lykanion in *Daphnis and Chloe* (Ashton), Sadler's Wells Ballet, London

Queen of the Earth (cr) in *Homage to the Queen* (Ashton), Sadler's Wells Ballet, London

1955   Principal dancer in *Variations on a Theme of Purcell* (Ashton), Sadler's Wells Ballet, London

Title role in *Giselle* (after Petipa, Coralli, Perrot), Ballet tour, Cape Town

1956   Principal dancer (cr) in *Birthday Offering* (Ashton), Royal Ballet, London

Title role in *The Firebird* (Fokine), Royal Ballet, London

The Faded Beauty (cr) in *Noctambules* (MacMillan), Royal Ballet, London

Principal dancer in *The Dragonfly* (after Pavlova), Charity Gala, Sadler's Wells Theatre, London

Principal dancer in *Don Quixote* pas de deux (after Petipa), Ballet tour (with Rassine)

Title role in *The Beloved* (Ashton), Ballet tour (with Rassine)

1957   Principal dancer in *Ballet Imperial* (Balanchine), Royal Ballet, London

The Ballerina in *Petrushka* (Fokine), Royal Ballet, London

1959   Variation/Adagio of Lovers in *Les Rendezvous* (Ashton), Royal Ballet, London

1960   Lise (cr) in *La Fille mal gardée* (Ashton), Royal Ballet, London

1962   Pas de deux in *Birthday Offering* (Ashton), Royal Ballet, London

Pas de deux from *Flower Festival at Genzano* (Bournonville), Royal Ballet, London

1963   Title role (cr) in *Elektra* (Helpmann), Royal Ballet, London

Principal dancer in *Grand Pas classique* (Gsovsky), Royal Ballet, London

1964   Title role in *Ondine* (Ashton), Royal Ballet, London

Dancer (cr) in *Images of Love* (MacMillan), Royal Ballet, London

1965   Principal dancer in *Laurencia* Pas de six (Nureyev after Chabukiani), Royal Ballet, London

The Girl (cr) in *Home* (Darrell), Western Theatre Ballet, Sunderland

Other roles include: for the Royal Ballet—Tango and Polka in *Façade* (Ashton), principal dancer in *Symphonic Variations* (Ashton), Papillon in *Carnaval* (Fokine), Peasant in *Bailemos* (Franca); for concert tours—Nymph in *L'Après-midi d'un faune* (shortened version; after Nijinsky).

PUBLICATIONS

By Nerina:

"Some Aspects of the Classical Technique", in *Ballet Annual* (London), vol. 14, 1960

"Visit to Russia", in *Ballet and Modern Dance*, London, 1974

Interview in Newman, Barbara, *Striking a Balance: Dancers Talk About Dancing*, Boston, 1982

About Nerina:

Austin, Richard, "Nadia Nerina", *Ballet Today* (London), June 1954

Swinson, Cyril, *Nadia Nerina*, London, 1957

"Dancer of the Year: Nadia Nerina", *Dance and Dancers* (London), January 1959

Kersley, Leo, "Ballerina of the Year", *Ballet Today* (London), November 1959

Clarke, Mary, "The Brink of Greatness", *Dancing Times* (London), March 1961

Crisp, Clement (ed.), *Ballerina: Portraits and Impressions of Nadia Nerina*, London, 1975

Grut, Marina, *The History of Ballet in South Africa*, Cape Town, 1981

*   *   *

Although Nadia Nerina created a number of roles by different choreographers, from that of the Circus Dancer in Andrée Howard's *Mardi Gras* to her part in Macmillan's *Noctambules* some ten years later, it was Frederick Ashton who fully explored the many different facets of Nerina's dancing—the lightness of her elevation and her sharp but delicate wrist movements in the Spring Fairy variation in *Cinderella*; her terre à terre work and springs on pointe for the Queen of the Earth in *Homage to the Queen*; her leaps and double *tours en l'air* for her spectacular *Birthday Offering* solo.

Yet nowhere did Ashton use both Nerina's formidable technical skills and her sunny, soubrette personality to greater effect than in *La Fille mal gardée*, in which she danced the lead role of Lise. Her partnership with David Blair in this ballet was one of the highlights of the Royal Ballet's performances in the 1960s. Both these dancers had continuously sought to extend the limits of their own technique and, in *La Fille mal gardée*, Ashton set about further developing this trend towards increased virtuosity.

Nerina attributes the underlying strength of her technique in large measure to her early training in the Cecchetti method. She is patron of the London-based Cecchetti Society and has stated categorically that any dancer who has mastered all the steps to be found in Cecchetti's enchainements will find that she can cope with all the movements she will encounter in performing the nineteenth-century classics.

Nerina's partnership with Alexis Rassine was particularly successful, if somewhat unusual, in that he was the more lyrical dancer whilst she excelled in high leaps and strong footwork. Both had trained originally in South Africa and their concert tours in that country in the 1950s not only gave them the opportunity of exploring a wider repertoire—including a condensed version of *L'après-midi d'un faune*—but also provided Nerina with her first opportunity to perform the role of Giselle.

Nerina's guest appearance with the Bolshoi Ballet in 1960, together with her creation of Lise at Covent Garden in the same year, established her as a prima ballerina of international standing. Her comparatively early retirement from performing was a great loss to the ballet world in general and to British ballet in particular: her outgoing personality and virtuoso technique were uncharacteristic of English ballet at that time and therefore added a different facet to the national company's style. Happily her legendary performance in *La fille mal gardée* has been preserved on film.

—Richard Glasstone

NETHERLANDS DANCE THEATRE
(Nederlands Dans Theater)

Dutch ballet and contemporary dance company based in The Hague. Founded by Benjamin Harkarvy with a splinter group from the Netherlands Ballet (Het Nederlands Ballet), including choreographer Hans van Manen, 1959; passed into direction of Glen Tetley and van Manen on Harkarvy's resignation, 1969; official home company of the Dans Theater aan't Spui, The Hague, from 1988; also incorporates small-scale training company, Nederlands Dans Theater 2 (NDT2), founded 1977. Current artistic director of the Netherlands Dance Theatre: Jiří Kylián, from 1975.

PUBLICATIONS

Dekker, K., *Hans van Manen and Modern Ballet in Nederland*, Amsterdam, 1981

Schaik, E. van, *Op gespannen voet: Geschiedenis van de Nederlandse theaterdans*, Haarlem, 1981

Monaghan, J., "Amsterdam and Kylián", *Dancing Times* (London), May 1984

Schaik, E. van, "Dutch Theatre Dance", *Ballett International* (Cologne), September 1987

Koegler, Horst, "Pledged to the Spirit of our Times: Nederlands Dans Theater 1959–1989", *Ballett International*, May 1989

"Spotlight on Jiří Kylián", *Dancing Times* (London), May 1991

* * *

The Netherlands Dance Theatre in Kylián's *Sweet Dreams*, The Hague, 1990

The Nederlands Dans Theater began life as a breakaway group from Sonia Gaskell's Nederlands Ballet. It aimed to offer dance which was radically different from that which had developed in the Netherlands in the post-war period. Dispensing with full-scale classical ballets, it presented new works by young living choreographers, using a group of dancers of equal status and a new dance technique which merged elements of the classical and the modern.

The company's first season, dominated choreographically by Benjamin Harkarvy and Hans van Manen, reflected these concerns. While classical duets were retained as reminders of the company's ballet roots, the focus was on new works created by either company-based or native Dutch choreographers, enhanced by the occasional contributions of American choreographers such as Anna Sokolow. Consequently the company rapidly gained critical acclaim for its contemporary freshness.

The American influence was one which grew with the company, the first in Europe to embrace the American modern dance techniques and to invite contributions from American choreographers. Indeed, together with van Manen, the American Glen Tetley was to make a vital impact on the character of the company during its first decade. Their work gave the company a broad choreographic scope derived from its initial constitution. While van Manen's work was musical and non-narrative, using pure dance and clarity of design, Tetley used dramatic characterization and bold theatrical effects. Both employed a fusion of modern and classical techniques and eliminated traditional ballet forms.

Following the departure of van Manen and Tetley, the company underwent a forced change. There was an influx of highly inventive American choreographers, including Falco and Keuter, and the emergence of new Dutch talent, Czarny, Flier, and Sanders. However, despite the experimental nature of their work their diversity meant that the company suffered a loss of clear identity and positive artistic direction.

Jiří Kylián, later to become company choreographer and director, also began to choreograph for Nederlands Dans Theater during this period. He enabled the Nederlands Dans Theater to establish a new company identity based on his own choreographic strengths—which included an inherent musicality, a fluent technique combining ballet with modern and folk dance, and articulate group work. Although Kylián was less innovative than his choreographic predecessors, the dominance of his ballets in the repertoire during the early years of his directorship brought the company international recognition for its exceptionally high dance standards, tightness of ensemble, and the international appeal of its well-crafted ballets.

Fears that the Nederlands Dans Theater might, as a one-choreographer company, stagnate from lack of inspiration were lessened by several new developments in the mid- to late 1980s. Kylián's policy to encourage young choreographers from within the ranks bore fruit in the work of Duato, Lightfoot, and Taylor. The NDT2, the junior company of the Nederlands Dans Theater, offered a training ground for such choreographers, as well as for the company's aspiring dancers. Van Manen's return as company choreographer in 1988 brought greater diversity and challenge to audience and dancers alike, and re-established historical, indigenous continuity. A new home was also secured for the company, the purpose-built Dans Theater aan't Spui in The Hague. The present-day company structure, unlike that of 1959—which provided the prototype for Ballet Rambert's classical to modern transformation—is one of two choreographers and two companies, with a permanent base and a multinational group of dancers. Despite the extra artistic and financial pressures which work on this scale entails, the 1990s look to be a period of consolidation and diversification for the rebellious company, which has gained

acceptance and recognition within the establishment it opposed.

—Kate King

———

NEUMEIER, John

American dancer, choreographer, and ballet director. Born in Milwaukee, Wisconsin, 24 February 1942. Educated at Marquette University, Milwaukee (B.A., 1961); studied ballet with Sheila Reilly, Milwaukee, with Bentley Stone and Walter Camryn, Stone-Camryn School, Chicago, 1957-62, at Royal Ballet School, London, 1962-63, and with Vera Volkova, Copenhagen; also studied modern dance with Sybil Shearer, Chicago, from 1957. Dancer, Sybil Shearer Company, Chicago, 1960-62; soloist, Stuttgart Ballet, 1963-69; first choreography as a student, with first major works in Stuttgart for Noverre Society performances, 1966; artistic director, Frankfurt Ballet, 1969-73; artistic director, Hamburg Ballet, from 1973; director, Hamburg Opera Ballet School, from 1978, and founder/director of Ballettzentrum Hamburg (housing company and school); international guest choreographer, including for Harkness Ballet, American Ballet Theatre, Royal Ballet in London, Royal Danish Ballet, National Ballet of Canada, Vienna State Opera Ballet, Paris Opéra Ballet, and Ballet du XXe Siècle; guest opera director, including for Bavarian State Opera (Munich Opera), Munich, and Hamburg State Opera; ballet director for films of own works, including *Rondo*, *Third Symphony of Gustav Mahler*, *Othello*, and *Lady of the Camellias*; also stage designer for many of own works. Recipient: Prix Italia (for film of *Rondo*), 1972; Golden Camera Award (for film of *Mahler* ballet), 1978; Knight of the Order of Dannebrog, Denmark; *Dance Magazine* Award, 1983; German (FDR) Cross of Merit, 1987; title of Professor from the City of Hamburg, 1987; German Dance Prize, 1988; Chevalier de l'Ordre des Arts et des Lettres, France, 1991.

WORKS

1960   *The Hound of Heaven* (mus. Prokofiev), Marquette University, Milwaukee
1961   *Ludus Coventriae* (mus. various), Marquette University, Milwaukee
       The Temptation of Eve (pas de deux), U.S. television (NBC), New York
1966   *Aria da Capo* (mus. Poulenc), Noverre Society (Stuttgart Ballet), Stuttgart
       Haiku (mus. Debussy), Noverre Society (Stuttgart Ballet), Stuttgart
1967   *Von Unschuld und Erfahrung* (mus. Honegger), Noverre Society (Stuttgart Ballet), Stuttgart
       Der Prinzessin Einziges Abenteuer (mus. Giuliani), Noverre Society (Stuttgart Ballet), Stuttgart
1968   *Separate Journeys* (mus. Barber), Stuttgart Ballet, Schwetzinger Festival
       Stages and Reflections (mus. Britten), Harkness Ballet, Monte Carlo
1969   *Frontier* (mus. Bliss), Scottish Theatre Ballet, London
1970   *Brandenburg 3* (mus. Bach, Carlos), Frankfurt Ballet, Frankfurt
       Der Feuervogel (mus. Stravinsky), Frankfurt Ballet, Frankfurt
       Unsichtbare Grenzen, including: *Frontier* (*Die Sperre*;

John Neumeier

mus. Bliss), *Aria da Capo* (mus. Poulenc), *Rondo* (mus. various), Frankfurt Ballet, Frankfurt

1971   *Romeo and Juliet* (mus. Prokofiev), Frankfurt Ballet, Frankfurt

Parade (mus. Satie), Frankfurt Ballet, Paris

Der Nussknacker (*The Nutcracker*; mus. Tchaikovsky), Frankfurt Ballet, Frankfurt

1972   *Der Kuss der Fee* (*The Fairy's Kiss*; mus. Stravinsky, Tchaikovsky), Frankfurt Ballet, Frankfurt

Daphnis und Chloe (mus. Ravel), Frankfurt Ballet, Frankfurt

Dämmern (*Twilight*; mus. Skriabin), Frankfurt Ballet, Frankfurt

Unterwegs (mus. Mussorgsky), Frankfurt Ballet, Frankfurt

Don Juan (mus. Gluck, de Victoria), Frankfurt Ballet, Frankfurt

Le Sacre (mus. Stravinsky), Frankfurt Ballet, Frankfurt

1973   *Trauma* (mus. Genzmer), Ballet-Théâtre Contemporain, Paris

Désir (pas de deux; mus. Skriabin), Hamburg Ballet, Hamburg

1974   *Meyerbeer—Schumann* (mus. Meyerbeer, Bialas, Schumann, Killmayer), Hamburg Ballet, Hamburg

Kinderszenen (mus. Schumann), Hamburg Ballet, Hamburg

Nacht (mus. Mahler), Stuttgart Ballet, Stuttgart

1975   *Die Stille* (mus. Crumb), Hamburg Ballet, Hamburg

Dritte Sinfonie von Gustave Mahler (mus. Mahler), Hamburg Ballet, Hamburg

Epilogue (pas de deux; mus. Mahler), American Ballet Theatre, New York

1976   *Hamlet—Connotations* (mus. Copland), American Ballet Theatre, New York

Der Fall Hamlet (mus. Copland), Stuttgart Ballet, Stuttgart

Illusionen—Wie Schwanensee (mus. Tchaikovsky), Hamburg Ballet, Hamburg

Rückert-Lieder (mus. Mahler), Hamburg Ballet, Hamburg

Petruschka-Variationen (mus. Stravinsky), Hamburg Ballet, Schwetzinger Festival

1977   *Josephs Legende* (mus. Strauss), Vienna State Opera Ballet, Vienna

The Fourth Symphony (mus. Mahler), Royal Ballet, London

Ein Sommernachtstraum (*A Midsummer Night's Dream*; mus. Mendelssohn-Bartholdy, Ligeti, traditional), Hamburg Ballet, Hamburg

Tanz für den Anfang (mus. Britten), Hamburg Ballet, Hamburg

Ariel (mus. Mozart), Nijinsky-Gala III, Hamburg Ballet, Hamburg

Tanz für den Schluss (mus. Vaughan Williams), Hamburg Ballet, Hamburg

Streichquintett C-Dur von Schubert (mus. Schubert), Hamburg Ballet, Hamburg

1978   *Elégie* (pas de deux; mus. Tchaikovsky), Nijinsky-Gala IV, Hamburg

Die Kameliendame (*Lady of the Camellias*; mus. Chopin), Stuttgart Ballet, Stuttgart

1979   *Don Quixote* (mus. Strauss), Hamburg Ballet, Hamburg

Vaslav (mus. Bach), Nijinsky-Gala V, Hamburg Ballet, Hamburg

Songfest (mus. Bernstein), Hamburg Ballet, Hamburg

The Age of Anxiety (mus. Bernstein), Hamburg Ballet, Hamburg

1980   *Liebe und Leid und Welt und Traum* (mus. Mahler), Ballet du XXe Siècle, Brussels

Bach Suite 2 (mus. Bach), State Opera Ballet, Munich

1981   *Matthäus-Passion* (*St. Matthew Passion*; mus. Bach), Hamburg Ballet, Hamburg

1982   *Vorläufer* (mus. Stravinsky), Hamburg Ballet, Hamburg

Unsere Schule (mus. Britten), School of the Hamburg Ballet, Hamburg

Igor S. (mus. Stravinsky), Nijinsky-Gala VIII, Hamburg Ballet, Hamburg

Petruschka (mus. Stravinsky), Nijinsky-Gala VIII, Hamburg Ballet, Hamburg

Artus-Sage (mus. Sibelius, Henze, and others), Hamburg Ballet, Hamburg

1983   *Der Feuervogel* (mus. Stravinsky), Vienna State Opera Ballet, Vienna

Regenlieder (mus. Brahms), Njinsky-Gala IX, Hamburg Ballet, Hamburg

Endstation Sehnsucht (*A Streetcar Named Desire*; mus. Prokofiev, Schnittke), Stuttgart Ballet, Stuttgart

1984   *Mozart 338* (mus. Mozart), Hamburg Ballet, Hamburg

Sechste Sinfonie von Gustav Mahler (mus. Mahler), Hamburg Ballet, Hamburg

1985   *Othello* (mus. Pärt, Schnittke, Vasconcelos, and others), Hamburg Ballet, Hamburg

Mozart und Themen aus "Wie Es Euch Gefallt" (*Mozart and Themes from "As You Like It"*; mus. Mozart), Hamburg Ballet, Hamburg

Amleth (*Hamlet*; mus. Tippett), Royal Danish Ballet, Copenhagen

Shakespeares Liebespare (mus. Prokofiev), Hamburg Ballet, Hamburg

1986   *Einhorn* (mus. Henze), German Opera Ballet, Berlin

Shall We Dance? (mus. Gershwin), Hamburg Ballet, Hamburg

Fratres (mus. Pärt), Stuttgart Ballet, Stuttgart

1987   *Magnificat* (mus. Bach), Paris Opéra Ballet, Avignon

1988   *Eine Reise Durch die Jahreszeiten* (mus. Glazunov), Hamburg Ballet, Hamburg

1989   *Peer Gynt* (mus. Schnittke), Hamburg Ballet, Hamburg

Le Spectre de la rose (mus. Berlioz), Hamburg Ballet, Hamburg

Seven Haiku of the Moon (mus. Schnittke, Bach), Tokyo Ballet, Tokyo

Des Knaben Wunderhorn Fünfte/Sinfonie von Gustav Mahler (mus. Mahler), Hamburg Ballet, Hamburg

1990   *Medea* (mus. Bartók, Schnittke, Bach, Galasso, and others), Stuttgart Ballet, Stuttgart

1991   *Fenster zu Mozart* (mus. Mozart, Reger, Beethoven, and others), Hamburg Ballet, Hamburg

Spring and Fall (mus. Dvořák), Hamburg Ballet, Hamburg

Requiem (mus. Mozart and Gregorian chants), Salzburg Festival, Salzburg

1992   *A Cinderella Story* (mus. Prokofiev), Hamburg Ballet, Hamburg

Also staged:

1978   *The Sleeping Beauty* (*Dornröschen*, chor. in addition to Petipa; mus. Tchaikovsky), Hamburg Ballet, Hamburg

1983   *Giselle* (chor. in addition to Petipa, Coralli, Perrot, and others; mus. Adam, Burgmüller), Hamburg Ballet, Hamburg

Other works include: dances in operas in *Moses und Aron* (mus. Schoenberg; Frankfurt, 1970), *Die Lustige Witwe* (mus. Lehár; Frankfurt, 1972), *Tannhauser* (mus. Wagner; Bayreuth, 1972), *De Temporum Fine Comoedia* (mus. Orff; Salzburg, 1973), Dances in *Falstaff* (mus. Verdi; Hamburg, 1974), *Khovanshchina* (mus. Mussorgsky; Hamburg, 1974), *Othello* (mus. Verdi; Munich, 1978), *Orpheus und Eurydike* (opera; mus. Gluck; Hamburg, 1978), *Aida* (opera; mus. Verdi; Salzburg, 1979); also choreography and staging of *West Side Story* (musical; mus. Bernstein; Hamburg, 1978), *On the Town* (musical; mus. Bernstein; Hamburg, 1991).

PUBLICATIONS

By Neumeier:

Interview in Garske, Rolf, "John Neumeier: A Vision of Continuity", *Ballett International* (Cologne), February 1983

Interview in Barzel, Ann, "Ten Years: John Neumeier and the Hamburg Ballet", *Dance Magazine* (New York), June 1984

Contribution to *Marcia Haydée* (various authors), Stuttgart, 1987

Interview in Merrett, Sue, "John Neumeier and the Hamburg Ballet", *Dancing Times* (London), October 1988

"Zum 'Weltballett' hin-tanzen", excerpts from interview with B. Beutler, *Ballett International* (Cologne), October 1989

About Neumeier:

Niehaus, Max, *Ballett Faszination*, Munich, 1972

John Neumeier Unterwegs (various authors), Frankfurt, 1972

Percival, John, "Neumeier's Ballets", *Dance and Dancers* (London), November 1972

Koegler, Horst, "John Neumeier: Success Story of the 70s?", *Dance Magazine* (New York), February 1973

Anderson, Jack, "Neumeier in Hamburg", *Dancing Times* (London), August 1975

John Neumeier und das Hamburger Ballett (various authors), Hamburg, 1977

Loney, Glenn, "Ballet's Freethinker: John Neumeier", *Dance Scope* (New York), Spring/Summer 1977

Como, William, "American Choreographer John Neumeier", *Dance Magazine* (New York), November 1980

John Neumeier: Traumwege, Hamburg, 1980

Albrecht, Christoph, *Zehn Jahre: John Neumeier und das Hamburger Ballett*, Hamburg, 1983

Dauber, Angela, *Matthäus-Passion*, Hamburg, 1983

Whitney, Mary, "John Neumeier's Passion", *Dance Magazine* (New York), March 1983

Anderson, Jack, *Choreography Observed*, Iowa City, 1987

Barzel, Ann, "Ballettzentrum Hamburg", *Dance Magazine* (New York), December 1990

*   *   *

John Neumeier is one of the most versatile internationally known choreographers in Germany. First and foremost, he is director and leading choreographer of the ballet company attached to the Hamburg Opera, known as the Hamburg Ballet, which under his leadership has developed into the second most important German ballet company after the Stuttgart Ballet. He has also been director of the Hamburg Opera Ballet School since its foundation in 1978—again, second only to the Stuttgart Ballet School, it is among the most important German dance training establishments attached to a ballet company.

Outside these official roles, however, John Neumeier has repeatedly engaged in other artistic activities, and continues to do so. Often he has not only choreographed but also designed the sets and costumes for his ballets, including *A Streetcar named Desire* (*Endstation Sehnsucht*) and *Medea*. He has on occasion produced operas at the state opera houses in Munich and Hamburg, and has produced two musicals by Leonard Bernstein, *West Side Story* and *On The Town*, with the Hamburg Ballet and guest artists. He also directed the film version of his narrative ballet *Die Kameliendame*. At the same time, Neumeier acts as critic and moderator of both the annual Hamburg Ballet "Nijinsky Gala" and the so-called ballet workshops mounted several times per season. Since his dance production of Johann Sebastian Bach's *St. Matthew Passion*, he has also returned to the stage as a dancer, occasionally in the role of Christ, or as partner to Marcia Haydée in the adaptation of Eugene Ionesco's *The Chairs* specially created for these two dancers by Maurice Béjart.

It was Marcia Haydée and Ray Barra, soloists in John Cranko's Stuttgart Ballet, who spotted John Neumeier as a student on a visit to London and the Royal Ballet School. They suggested that he come to Stuttgart as a soloist, and it was here that Neumeier began to dedicate his efforts to choreography, having made his first experiments in his home town, Milwaukee. He produced several works in quick succession for the Young Choreographers matinees run by the Stuttgart Noverre Society, followed by his first professional pieces for the Stuttgart Ballet itself, and then by works for the Harkness Ballet and the Scottish Theatre Ballet.

As director of ballet in Frankfurt, a position he took at the early age of 27, he made a name for himself throughout the region as a young, talented choreographer who was willing to experiment. In 1973 August Everding, then director of the Hamburg Opera, brought Neumeier to the Hanseatic town, where he not only consolidated his reputation as choreographer but also demonstrated his abilities as ballet director. His current contract with the Hamburg Opera runs until 1996. Since the establishment of the ambitious "Ballettzentrum Hamburg—John Neumeier", which provides facilities for the company and the school as well as boarding facilities for its pupils, Neumeier seems to have laid the foundations for a high level of ballet achievement, which should continue even after his departure. This is an achievement which should not be underestimated, especially in western Germany where dance has had no real centre to look to, but has created continually changing centres for itself through the commitment of prominent individuals.

John Neumeier's choreographic style is based on classical dance and follows the tradition of George Balanchine's neo-classicism. In many of his abstract pieces, one can see the influence of modern dance in the American mould. Neumeier's discoveries in movement show themselves through a highly developed sense of aesthetics and expressiveness. At the same time he gives free rein to his fondness for the American show style, particularly noticeable in the full-length production *Shall We Dance?*, set to a collage of George Gershwin pieces.

John Neumeier's choreographic oeuvre is exceptionally broad and varied. He is especially skilled in the creation of narrative ballet, in which he made his reputation with his early and important interpretations of *Romeo and Juliet* and *The Nutcracker*. These were followed by the productions *Illusionen—wie Schwanensee* (with the Bavarian King Ludwig II as central figure) and *The Sleeping Beauty*, both with a new dramatic slant. He developed his own style of narrative ballet, however, in the numerous multiple-act productions in which he did not feel duty-bound to follow a traditional choreographic pattern and create a "classical" ballet composition. Here, John Cranko's influence on John Neumeier as choreographer, dramatist, and librettist is unmistakable. Neumeier has tended to focus on works of internationally known literature, in particular William Shakespeare's plays, as the basis for his original dramatic ballets. These include *A Midsummer Night's Dream*, in which Neumeier pointedly contrasts the music of Felix Mendelssohn-Bartholdy with compositions by Gyorgy Ligeti, *Othello, Mozart and Themes from "As You Like It"* and *Hamlet*. Further prominent examples of Neumeier's narrative ballets are *Die Kameliendame* and *A Streetcar named Desire*, both of which were created for Marcia Haydée and the Stuttgart Ballet, *Artus-Sage*, and *Fenster zu Mozart*. His highest achievement so far in the field of narrative ballet, however, is *Peer Gynt*, his collaboration with the composer Alfred Schnittke and the designer Jürgen Rose, with whom he has often worked.

Neumeier has created his own versions of one-act narrative ballets, mostly from the era of Serge Diaghilev's Ballets Russes. He has also choreographed a multitude of non-narrative pieces, often to twentieth-century musical works, as well as interpretations of music originally written for a religious context. Most notably, he has worked intensively on Gustav Mahler's symphonies. This project began with *Nacht*, set to the fourth movement of the third symphony, which Neumeier created in Stuttgart in memory of John Cranko, and reached its as yet unchallenged high point in the complete choreographic production of the third symphony. John Neumeier's non-narrative works are rarely abstract, in the sense of setting out purely to give a portrait in dance of the musical composition. Moreover—and this is also true of the Mahler pieces—they visualize in Neumeier's interpretations a certain "programme" of composition; the choreography of these works is of a philosophical/theological nature and deals with basic experiences of human existence.

Horst Vollmer

———

NEW YORK CITY BALLET
American ballet company based in New York. Founded by Lincoln Kirstein and George Balanchine, with origins in first performances by the American Ballet, New York, 1935–38, joining with Ballet Caravan, a touring company organized by Kirstein, Lew Christensen, and Harold Christensen, 1936–40, to become American Ballet Caravan, touring South America, 1941; new organization, Ballet Society, founded 1946; became New York City Ballet (NYCB), official resident company of the New York City Center for Music and Drama, from 1948; has been resident company of New York State Theater, Lincoln Center, New York, from 1964. Official school associated with company, School of American Ballet (SAB), founded by Lincoln Kirstein and George Balanchine, Hartford, 1933, moving to New York, 1934; based in Lincoln Center (with the Juilliard School of Music), from 1970. Current artistic director of the New York City Ballet (succeeding George Balanchine): Peter Martins, from 1983.

PUBLICATIONS
Anderson, Jack, *The Ballet Society 1946–1947*, New York, 1947
Amberg, George, *Ballet in America*, New York, 1949
Chujoy, Anatole, *The New York City Ballet*, New York, 1953
Maynard, Olga, *The American Ballet*, Philadelphia, 1959
Goldner, Nancy, *The Stravinsky Festival of the New York City Ballet*, New York, 1973
Kirstein, Lincoln, *The New York City Ballet*, New York, 1973; revised as *30 Years: Lincoln Kirstein's The New York City Ballet*, New York, 1978
Taper, Bernard, *Balanchine: A Biography*, revised edition, New York, 1974
Mazo, Joseph H., *Dance is a Contact Sport*, New York, 1974
Croce, Arlene, *Afterimages*, New York, 1977
Reynolds, Nancy, *Repertory in Review: 40 Years of the New York City Ballet*, New York, 1977
Palmer, Winthrop, *Theatrical Dancing in America: The Development of Ballet from 1900*, revised edition, South Brunswick, New Jersey, and London, 1978
Croce, Arlene, *Going to the Dance*, New York, 1982
Parry, Jann et al., "Portrait of a Company: New York City Ballet", *Dance and Dancers* (London), November 1983
Croce, Arlene, *Sightlines*, New York, 1987
Barnes, Clive, "NYCB: State and Status", *Dance Magazine* (New York), April 1991

*   *   *

The New York City Ballet's formal history as an institution dates from 1948, but its true history began in 1934, when George Balanchine—having come to the United States at the invitation of the young writer and balletomane, Lincoln Kirstein—joined Kirstein to co-found the School of American Ballet (SAB). In 1935, the two established their first company together, the American Ballet, which drew on Balanchine's gifts as a choreographer and on a nucleus of dancers from SAB. (his famous *Serenade* was made for this group). This enterprise lasted about four years. Meanwhile, in 1936, Kirstein alone founded a chamber company called Ballet Caravan, as a showcase for the choreography of young Americans. In 1941, artistic forces from the American Ballet and Ballet Caravan—by then both moribund as such—united under the name of American Ballet Caravan, whose life as a company is principally associated with a five-month tour it took of South America, under the auspices of the U.S. State Department, and with *Concerto Barocco*, which Balanchine choreographed for that trip. At the end of the tour, the company disbanded. Balanchine continued to serve as the head of SAB and took on freelance choreographic assignments in New York and Hollywood. Kirstein founded the magazine *Dance Index* in 1942, and served as one of its editors. Then, in 1943 he joined the U.S. Army, and stayed with it until his discharge in 1945.

In 1949, *Dance Index* ceased publication: Kirstein had founded a new performing enterprise, Ballet Society, in 1946, and he could not sustain the publication as well. The first performance of Ballet Society on 20 November 1946, at the Central High School of Needle Trades in Manhattan, included the premiere of Balanchine's masterpiece, *The Four Temperaments*. The group performed infrequently, but the audiences were sophisticated, intellectual, and enthusiastic about Balanchine, who continued to produce impressive new work. In 1948, inspired by Balanchine's *Orpheus, Symphony in C,* and *Symphonie Concertante,* the lawyer Morton Baum arranged for Ballet Society to have a permanent home at the New York City Center for Music and Drama. The name of the enterprise was changed and the New York City Ballet was born.

The importance of this pre-history should not be underestimated. Since the founding of SAB, both Balanchine and Kirstein had passed from youth to middle age, and from idealism to weathered experience, with many formative disappointments along the way. Balanchine had been tested as a choreographer with concert groups, on Broadway, in the movies, and in opera houses. Kirstein had established a web of connections to the worlds of literature, the arts, and philanthropy. The New York City Ballet was founded with a clearly defined mission: to provide the highest quality of classical dancing at a price that everyone could afford. The false starts conditioned its founders to the practical realities of trying to keep a company going, as well as to the apparently irrational necessities of any art that tries to make magic with human beings as its basic material. The effort succeeded for many reasons, and one of them was that its founders knew how to take risks in the face of failure. Many veteran City Balletgoers remember the City Center years—when box office returns were often indifferent at best—as the company's golden age, both in terms of Balanchine's own work (which reached an astonishing intellectual peak with *Agon* and an emotional peak with *Liebeslieder Walzer*), and in terms of the variety, discipline, and individuality of the dancers, notably the ballerinas—among them, Tanaquil LeClercq, Maria Tallchief, Diana Adams, and Allegra Kent. Equally important was the presence of company associate Jerome Robbins, lighting designer Jean Rosenthal, and guest choreographers Frederick Ashton and Antony Tudor.

In terms of its stylistic development, however, this initial chapter in City Ballet's history as a theatrical entity did not end with *Agon* and *Liebeslieder Walzer* but rather with the move to a new permanent home: in 1964, the company moved to the New York State Theater at Lincoln Center, a facility designed to Balanchine's specification by Philip Johnson. The new house was much larger than the old one, and ballets which had looked electrifying on the old stage had to be re-scaled. Everything became bigger in order to project to all of the State Theater's 3,000 seats. Suzanne Farrell, a tall dancer who danced "large", taking enormous technical and musical risks, became a focal point for Balanchine and for his audiences.

Balanchine himself seemed to stretch in all sorts of ways, as did his colleague, co-ballet master Jerome Robbins. In 1965 Balanchine made the most personally revealing work of his life, the evening-length *Don Quixote*, with Farrell as its ballerina. In 1967, he choreographed *Jewels*, an evening-length plotless work to the music of Fauré, Stravinsky, and Tchaikovsky. In 1969, Robbins returned after a long absence to produce *Dances at a Gathering*, to an hour of Chopin. In 1972 both men participated, along with several other choreographers, in the Stravinsky Festival. In 1972 Robbins made *Watermill*, an hour-long work drawing on Japanese music and themes as well as on then-current avant-garde techniques; in 1971 he had produced *The Goldberg Variations* to Bach's complete score. The decade of the 1970s saw Balanchine's elaborately designed spectacles, *Union Jack* and *Vienna Waltzes*, a Ravel festival, an expansion in the number of dancers (there are now over 100), and an enviable growth in subscriptions. By the time of Balanchine's death in 1983, following a long illness, the company could be counted on to deliver what is debatedly the most exciting dancing in the world.

After Balanchine's death, the New York City Ballet's artistic directorship was shared by Jerome Robbins and Peter Martins, both of whom held the job-title "co-balletmaster-in-chief". Eventually, Robbins relinquished his position, and today Martins leads the company alone. In the past decade he has made many new ballets for the company, imported talented dancers (men primarily) from Europe, developed the careers of a few outstanding young female dancers, opened the repertory to edgy, outside choreographers (such as William Forsythe), and staged both a festival devoted to American music and a streamlined version of *The Sleeping Beauty*. By 1993 he was planning an ambitious Balanchine festival (73 works) to be presented in the spring of that year. Martins' tenure has suffered a number of problems, however, some of them of his own making.

What the company's fortunes will be at the turn of the second millenium is anybody's guess. What seems to be missing most today is the sense of urgency one felt when Balanchine was actively overseeing things—that feeling during a performance of something out-of-this-world happening, something right *here* and right *now*, when *you* are part of that moment.

—Mindy Aloff

NICHOLS, Kyra

American dancer.   Born in Berkeley, California, daughter of New York City Ballet dancer Sally Streets, 1959. Studied with mother, Sally Streets, with Alan Howard, Pacific Ballet, and at School of American Ballet, New York, from 1972. Married New York City Ballet dancer Daniel Duell. Apprentice to the New York City Ballet, Spring, 1974; dancer, corps de ballet, from Autumn 1974, becoming principal dancer, from 1979; has toured internationally with New York City Ballet; has also appeared on U.S. television, including on the Public Broadcasting Service (PBS) "Dance in America" series.

ROLES

1975   Sarabande (cr) in *Sarabande and Dance* (d'Amboise), New York City Ballet, New York
1976   Principal dancer (cr) in *Other Dances* (Robbins), New York City Ballet, New York
         Principal dancer in *Divertimento No. 15* (Balanchine), New York City Ballet, New York
1977   Variation from *La Ventana* (Bournonville) in *Bournonville Divertissements* (staged Williams), New York City Ballet, New York
1978   Rigaudon Flamenco in *Don Quixote* (Balanchine), New York City Ballet, New York

Principal dancer (cr) in *Verdi Variations* (later part of *The Four Seasons*; Robbins), in *A Sketch Book* (works in progress), New York City Ballet, New York

1979 Spring (cr) in *The Four Seasons* (incorporating *Verdi Variations*, 1978; Robbins), New York City Ballet, New York

Principal dancer in *Serenade* (Balanchine), New York City Ballet, New York

Principal dancer in *Concerto No. 2* (previously *Ballet Imperial*; Balanchine), New York City Ballet, New York

1979/ Sugar Plum Fairy in *The Nutcracker* (Balanchine), New
80 York City Ballet, New York

First Movement in *Symphony in C* (Balanchine), New York City Ballet, New York

1980 Polyhymnia in *Apollo* (Balanchine), New York City Ballet, New York

Principal dancer (cr) in *Rondo* (Robbins), New York City Ballet, New York

Ballerina in *Theme and Variations* (Balanchine), New York City Ballet, New York

Title role in *Firebird* (Balanchine), New York City Ballet, New York

1981 Principal dancer (cr) in *Suite from "Histoire du Soldat"* (Martins), New York City Ballet, New York

Principal dancer (cr) in *Concert Fantasy* (d'Amboise), New York City Ballet, New York

Principal dancer (cr) in *Valse-Scherzo* (Robbins) in *Tempo di Valse*, New York City Ballet, New York

Principal dancer (cr) in *Piano Pieces* (Robbins), New York City Ballet, New York

1982 Principal dancer (cr) in *Concerto for Piano and Wind Instruments* (Taras), New York City Ballet, New York

1983 Principal dancer (cr) in *Celebration* (d'Amboise), New York City Ballet, New York

Principal dancer (cr) in *I'm Old Fashioned* (Robbins), New York City Ballet, New York

1984 Ballerina in *Raymonda Variations* (Balanchine), New York City Ballet, New York

Principal dancer (cr) in *A Schubertiad* (Martins), New York City Ballet, New York

Principal dancer (cr) in *Brahms/Handel Variations* (Robbins, Tharp), New York City Ballet, New York

Principal dancer (cr) in *Antique Epigraphs* (Robbins), New York City Ballet, New York

Principal dancer (cr) in *Menuetto* (Tomasson), New York City Ballet, Saratoga Springs, New York

Principal dancer in *Liebeslieder Walzer* (Balanchine), New York City Ballet, New York

1985 Principal dancer (cr) in *Poulenc Sonata* (Martins), New York City Ballet, New York

Principal dancer (cr) in *Eight Lines* (Robbins), New York City Ballet, New York

Eighth Waltz, La Valse in *La Valse* (Balanchine), New York City Ballet, New York

1985/ Czardas in *Cortège Hongrois* (Balanchine), New York
86 City Ballet, New York

1986 Rondo alla Zingarese in *Brahms–Schoenberg Quartet* (Balanchine), New York City Ballet, New York

Allegro in *Brahms–Schoenberg Quartet* (Balanchine), New York City Ballet, New York

1988 Principal dancer (cr) in *Tanzspiel* (Martins), New York City Ballet, New York

Principal dancer (cr) in *Set of Seven* (Verdy), New York City Ballet, New York

Principal dancer (cr) in *The Bounding Line* (C. d'Am-boise), New York City Ballet, New York

1989 Principal dancer (cr) in *Beethoven Romance* (Martins), New York City Ballet, New York

Principal dancer in *In Memory of . . .* (Robbins), New York City Ballet, New York

1991 First Waltz (cr) in *Waltz Trilogy* (LaFosse), New York City Ballet, New York

Principal dancer in *Robert Schumann's "Davidsbündler-tänze"* (Balanchine), New York City Ballet, New York

Lilac Fairy (cr) in *The Sleeping Beauty* (Martins after Petipa), New York City Ballet, New York

Princess Aurora in *The Sleeping Beauty* (Martins after Petipa), New York City Ballet, New York

Principal dancer (cr) in *A Musical Offering* (Martins), New York City Ballet, New York

1992 Principal dancer (cr) in *Herman Schmerman* (Forsythe), New York City Ballet, New York

Other roles include: principal dancer in *Mozartiana* (Balanchine), Dewdrop Fairy in *The Nutcracker* (Balanchine), principal dancer in *Square Dance* (Balanchine), Fourth Campaign in *Stars and Stripes* (Balanchine), Emeralds in *Jewels* (Balanchine), Diamonds in *Jewels* (Balanchine), ballerina in *La Source* (Balanchine), principal dancer in *Vienna Waltzes* (Balanchine), principal dancer in *Union Jack* (Balanchine), principal dancer in *Walpurgisnacht Ballet* (Balanchine), principal dancer in *Tchaikovsky Pas de deux* (Balanchine), Hippolyta in *A Midsummer Night's Dream* (Balanchine), Sanguinic in *The Four Temperaments* (Balanchine), principal dancer in *Donizetti Variations* (Balanchine), principal dancer in *Ballo della Regina* (Balanchine), principal dancer in *Irish Fantasy* (d'Amboise).

PUBLICATIONS

Croce, Arlene, *Afterimages*, New York, 1977
Dupuis, Simone, "Profile: Kyra Nichols", *Les Saisons de la danse* (Paris), November 1980
Croce, Arlene, *Going to the Dance*, New York, 1982
Taub, Eric, *Ballet News* (New York), February 1982
Finkel, Anita, "In her True Center", *Ballet News* (New York), July 1985
Croce, Arlene, *Sight Lines*, New York, 1987
Kelly, Patrick, "Diamonds are Forever", *Dance Magazine* (New York), October 1988

*   *   *

Kyra Nichols is considered a New York City Ballet ballerina who especially suits British taste; on her introduction to London audiences during the company's 1979 visit, she was immediately likened to a Kirov ballerina. For her home audiences, she is not only the most classical of the company's ballerinas, but a prime bearer of George Balanchine's style and standards, especially since the choreographer's death in 1983 and Suzanne Farrell's gradual withdrawal from dancing in the 1980s. In an assessment of Nichols in 1986, critic Dale Harris wrote: "Of all the company's current dancers, she is the one most likely to help it make a successful transition from the age of Balanchine to that of his successors."

If Nichols exemplifies the Balanchine ideal of musicality and joyous energy, she also testifies to the individuality of Balanchine's ballerinas. "The way she dances is completely on her own," the choreographer said of her. "She's hard to explain."

It would be difficult to write in guarded terms about the ballerina whom the American critic Arlene Croce has characterized as a lioness and the Goddess of Reason in dancing Balanchine. To begin with, Nichols is blessed with ideal proportions: long, sleek limbs and neck, a richly flowing line, a lithe torso, and large, expressive green eyes in a small Botticelli classic-oval head.

Her dancing has a special amplitude, a large clarity of shape and a serene authority quite different from the loose-jointed, risk-taking style of a Farrell. Yet Nichols perfectly balances what Balanchine referred to as her "exactness of execution" with an impression of spontaneity and freedom; her musical impulse is always fresh, and she seems to discover each moment on stage as it happens.

Her Balanchine roles are naturally her most important. She matured slightly too late for Balanchine to have choreographed for her, though he cast her in many key roles and revised his *Firebird* for her in 1980, with a stunning new costume that seemed to apotheosize her as a statuesque golden apparition. Among the roles to which she has given her own stamp are several of Farrell's, such as the ultimate ballerinas of the Diamonds section of *Jewels* and *Mozartiana*. But her range in Balanchine roles also encompasses the mercurial and delicate Dewdrop in *The Nutcracker*, the frolicsome *Donizetti Variations*, and the speedy virtuosity of *Ballo della Regina*. In *Vienna Waltzes* she exemplifies youth; in *Liebeslieder Walzer*, tragic youth; in *Robert Schumann's Davidsbündlertänze*, tragic maturity. Her assumption of Violette Verdy's role in *Liebeslieder* was considered a key to its 1984 revival—an important success for the company the year after Balanchine's death.

Jerome Robbins has choreographed several lyrical roles for Nichols, as in *The Four Seasons* and *Piano Pieces*. She makes a heroic struggle of the role of the young woman claimed by Death in his *In Memory Of . . .* (another Farrell role). Peter Martins emphasized her dramatic side in *Poulenc Sonata* and her femininity in *A Schubertiad* and *Beethoven Romance*. Helgi Tomasson showed her as a regal muse in his *Menuetto*. But now, especially without Robbins or Tomasson on the scene, the company needs to find new frontiers for her artistry.

Nichols' technique has always been a "given". Her early training with former Ballet Russe dancer Alan Howard was rigorous and strengthening. She has in fact extended the realm of the possible in ballerina virtuosity. The poised security of her technique and placement, her centredness under any extreme of circumstance, allows her the most satisfying amplification and completion of any movement. She is mistress of controlled but active balances, majestic extensions, wide, soaring leaps, and perfect turning combinations.

She exemplifies the approach of Balanchine dancers to expression, which is achieved first of all through response to the music and its atmosphere—by variety of attack, phrasing, movement quality, and comportment. She revels in the music; at times it seems to emanate from the center of her body and ripple outward. Her dynamic range takes her from delicate to sharp, from brilliant allegro to the most fluid adagio, or any combination of qualities. Mercurial changes of direction contribute to an impression of movement wit and brilliance. But she also clearly enjoys roles that allow more room to savour the movement and to provide more overt drama.

For all Nichols' early polished Russian style and previous performing experience, she did not spring full-blown into prominence at New York City Ballet. "Too pretty", Balanchine commented on her dancing in the early days. Always an independent and self-motivated spirit, she worked out for herself her evolution into a Balanchine ballerina possessed of freedom and speed and joy. And she has never stopped evolving but has recently been working on enriching the use of the upper body in coordination with the legs.

Nichols' manner toward both partner and audience is at once gently confiding and that of an independent though gracious equal. She makes every movement and every detail meaningful, and she irradiates everything she does with integrity, taste, and a fresh glow. She has broadened the expressiveness of ballet technique and of classicism.

—Marilyn Hunt

———

NIGHT SHADOW *see* **SONNAMBULA, La**

———

NIJINSKA, Bronislava
Russian/American dancer, choreographer, teacher, and ballet director. Born Bronislava Fominichna Nizhinskaya (Nijinska), daughter of Polish dancers Eleanora Bereda and Foma Nizhinsky, sister of dancer Vaslav Nijinsky, in Minsk, 8 January 1891 (27 December 1890 old style). Studied at the Imperial Theatre School; graduated, with First Award, in 1908. Married (1) dancer Aleksandr Kochetovsky, 1911 (div. 1924): one daughter, Irina, b. 1913, and one son, Léon, b. 1919 (d. 1935); (2) dancer Nicholas Singaevsky, 1924. Dancer, Maryinsky Theatre, St. Petersburg, 1908–11, becoming coryphée, 1910; also performer in first seasons of Diaghilev's Ballets Russes, Paris, 1909, 1910; resigned from Imperial Theatres on brother Nijinsky's dismissal, 1911; dancer, becoming soloist, Diaghilev's Ballets Russes, 1911–13, 1914, resigning in 1914; returned to Russia during World War I: soloist, Petrograd Private Opera Theatre, 1915–16, and State Opera Theatre, Kiev, 1916–17; first choreography, Petrograd, 1915, presenting solo concerts in Petrograd, 1915 and 1919; rejoined Diaghilev, London, 1921: principal dancer, choreographer, and ballet mistress, Diaghilev's Ballets Russes, 1921–25: resigned, after disagreements with Diaghilev, 1925; founder and choreographer, Théâtre Chorégraphique Nijinska, touring England and Paris, 1925; choreographer, Paris Opéra, 1925, 1927; returned to Diaghilev, 1926; choreographer and principal dancer, Teatro Colón, Buenos Aires, 1926–27; choreographer, Ida Rubinstein's Company, Paris, 1928–29, and Anna Pavlova's Company, 1929; choreographer, Ballet de l'Opéra Russe à Paris, 1930–31, and Deutsches Theater, Berlin, 1932; founder and choreographer, Théâtre de la danse Nijinska, Paris, 1932–33, performing in Buenos Aires, 1933, Monte Carlo, 1934; artistic director and choreographer, Polish Ballet, touring Europe, 1937–38; also staged ballets for de Basil's Ballets Russes, 1935, Markova–Dolin Ballet, 1937 and 1947, Ballet Theatre, New York, 1940, 1945, and 1951, Denham's Ballet Russe de Monte Carlo, 1942–43, Ballet Repertory, Chicago, 1943, Teatro Colón, 1946, (Marquis de Cuevas) Grand Ballet de Monte Carlo, 1949 and 1952, Royal Ballet, London, 1964 and 1966; also choreographer for Hollywood film, *A Midsummer Night's Dream* (dir. M. Reinhardt, W. Dieterle), 1935; also teacher: opened first school, Kiev, 1915, later teaching for Diaghilev and for various Ballets Russes companies; founder and director, Bronislava Nijinska Hollywood Ballet School, 1941–50, and own studio in Beverly Hills, from 1951; guest teacher, various studios in Los Angeles, from 1955. Recipient: Medal of the Archives internationales de la danse, Paris, 1934. Died in Pacific Palisades, California, 21 February 1972.

Bronislava Nijinska with (from left to right) Robert Mead, Svetlana Beriosova, David Blair, Keith Rosson, and Georgina Parkinson during rehearsals for the Royal Ballet's revival of *Les Biches*, 1964

WORKS

1915   *La Poupée* (*La Tabatière*, solo; mus. Liadov), Narodny Dom, Petrograd
       Autumn Song (solo; mus. Tchaikovsky), Narodny Dom, Petrograd
1919   *Études* (solo; mus. Liszt), State Opera Theatre, Kiev
       Mephisto Waltz (solo; mus. Liszt), State Opera Theatre, Kiev
       Nocturne (solo; mus. Chopin), State Opera Theatre, Kiev
       Prélude (solo; mus. Chopin), State Opera Theatre, Kiev
       Fear (solo; no music), State Opera Theatre, Kiev

1920   *Twelfth Rhapsody* (mus. Liszt), State Opera Theatre, Kiev
       Mephisto (mus. Liszt), State Opera Theatre, Kiev
       Demons (mus. Tcherepnin), State Opera Theatre, Kiev
       Marche funèbre (mus. Chopin, orchestrated Metner), State Opera Theatre, Kiev
1921   Dances ("The Marquises", "Bluebeard", "Schéhérazade", "The Three Ivans", "Variation of Prince Charming") in *The Sleeping Princess* (Petipa; staged Sergeyev), Diaghilev's Ballets Russes, London
1922   *Le Mariage d'Aurore* (one-act version of *The Sleeping Beauty*; after Petipa), Diaghilev's Ballets Russes, Paris

Le Renard (mus. Stravinsky), Diaghilev's Ballets Russes, Paris

1923   *Polovtsian Dances from Prince Igor* (after Fokine, with additions; mus. Borodin), Diaghilev's Ballets Russes, Monte Carlo

Les Noces (mus. Stravinsky), Diaghilev's Ballets Russes, Paris

1924   *Les Tentations de la bergère: ou, L'Amour vainqueur* (mus. de Montéclair, arranged Casadesus), Diaghilev's Ballets Russes, Monte Carlo

Les Biches (mus. Poulenc), Diaghilev's Ballets Russes, Monte Carlo

Les Fâcheux (mus. Auric), Diaghilev's Ballets Russes, Monte Carlo

Night on Bald Mountain (*La Nuit sur le Mont Chauve*; mus. Mussorgsky), Diaghilev's Ballets Russes, Monte Carlo

Le Train bleu (mus. Milhaud), Diaghilev's Ballets Russes, Paris

1925   *Holy Études* (mus. Bach), Théâtre Chorégraphique Nijinska, Margate, England

The Sports and Touring Ballet Review (mus. Poulenc), Théâtre Chorégraphique Nijinska, Margate

Jazz (mus. Stravinsky), Théâtre Chorégraphique Nijinska, Margate

On the Road (mus. Lucas), Théâtre Chorégraphique Nijinska, Margate

The Puppet Show (*Le Guignol*; mus. Lanner), Théâtre Chorégraphique Nijinska, Margate

Les Rencontres (mus. Ibert), Paris Opéra Ballet, Paris

1926   *Romeo and Juliet* (mus. Lambert), Diaghilev's Ballets Russes, Monte Carlo

El Carillón Mágico (mus. Pick-Mangiagalli), Teatro Colón, Buenos Aires

Un Estudio Religioso (new version of *Holy Etudes*; mus. Bach), Teatro Colón, Buenos Aires

Cuadro Campestre (mus. Gaito), Teatro Colón, Buenos Aires

Intermedio Bailable (mus. Verdi), Teatro Colón, Buenos Aires

A Orillas del Mar (a version of *Le Train bleu*; mus. Milhaud), Teatro Colón, Buenos Aires

Las Amazonas (mus. Tcherepnin), Teatro Colón, Buenos Aires

1927   *Les Impressions de Music-Hall* (mus. Pierné), Paris Opéra Ballet, Paris

La Giara (mus. Casella), Teatro Colón, Buenos Aires

Petrushka (after Fokine; mus. Stravinsky), Teatro Colón, Buenos Aires (also staged Ballet de l'Opéra Russe à Paris, 1931)

Ala y Lolly (mus. Prokofiev), Teatro Colón, Buenos Aires

Daphnis y Chloé (after Fokine; mus. Ravel), Teatro Colón, Buenos Aires

Pomona (mus. Lambert), Teatro Colón, Buenos Aires

1928   *Les Noces de Psyché et de l'Amour* (mus. Bach, arranged Honneger), Ida Rubinstein's Company, Paris

La Bien Aimée (mus. Schubert and Liszt, arranged Milhaud), Ida Rubinstein's Company, Paris

Bolero (mus. Ravel), Ida Rubinstein's Company, Paris

Le Baiser de la fée (mus. Stravinsky), Ida Rubinstein's Company, Paris

Nocturne (mus. Borodin, orchestrated Tcherepnin), Ida Rubinstein's Company, Paris

La Princesse Cygne (after the opera *Tsar Sultan*; mus. Rimsky-Korsakov), Ida Rubinstein's Company, Paris

1929   *La Valse* (mus. Ravel), Ida Rubinstein's Company, Paris

1930   *Paysage enfantin* (for Olga Spessivtseva; mus. Krotoff), Coliseum, London

1931   *Capriccio Espagnole* (mus. Rimsky-Korsakov), Nijinska's Company, Paris

Étude (new version of *Un Estudio Religioso* and *Holy Études*; mus. Bach), Nijinska's Company, Paris

La Valse (new version; mus. Ravel), Ida Rubinstein's Company, Paris

1932   *Les Comédiens jaloux* (mus. Casella, after Scalatti), Théâtre de la danse Nijinska, Paris

Variations (mus. Beethoven, orchestrated Pohl), Théâtre de la danse Nijinska, Paris

Bolero (new version; mus. Ravel), Théâtre de la danse Nijinska, Paris

1934   *Hamlet* (mus. Liszt), Théâtre de la danse Nijinska, Paris

1935   *Les Cent Baisers* (mus. d'Erlanger), de Basil's Ballets Russes, London

Lezginka (mus. folk music), de Basil's Ballets Russes, London

1936   *Danses Slaves et Tsiganes* (divertissement from opera *Russalka*; mus. Dargomizhsky), de Basil's Ballets Russes, New York

1937   *Chopin Concerto* (mus. Chopin), Polish Ballet, Paris

La Légende de Cracovie (mus. Kondracki), Polish Ballet, Paris

Le Chant de la terre (mus. Palester), Polish Ballet, Paris

Le Rappel (mus. Woytowicz), Polish Ballet, Paris

Apollon et la belle (mus. Rozycki), Polish Ballet, Paris

1940   *La Fille mal gardée* (after Dauberval; mus. Hertel), Ballet Theatre, New York

1942   *The Snow Maiden* (mus. Glazunov), Ballet Russe de Monte Carlo, New York

1943   *Ancient Russia* (mus. Tchaikovsky), Ballet Russe de Monte Carlo, Cleveland

Vision (mus. Brahms, orchestrated Kondracki), Chicago Ballet Repertory, Chicago

Hitch Your Wagon to a Star (mus. Tchaikovsky), Chicago Ballet Repertory, Chicago

1944   *Brahms Variations* (mus. Brahms, orchestrated Boutnikov), Ballet International (du Marquis de Cuevas), New York

Pictures at an Exhibition (mus. Mussorgsky), Ballet International (du Marquis de Cuevas), New York

1945   *Harvest Time* (mus. Wieniawski, arranged Dorati), Ballet Theatre, New York

Rendezvous (mus. Rachmaninov, orchestrated Dorati), Ballet Theatre, New York

1947   *Fantasia* (mus. Schubert, Liszt), Markova-Dolin Ballet, Kingston, Jamaica

1949   *In Memoriam* (mus. Chopin, arranged Cloetz), Grand Ballet de Monte-Carlo (du Marquis de Cuevas), Paris

1951   *Schumann Concerto* (mus. Schumann), Ballet Theatre, New York

1952   *Rondo Capriccioso* (mus. Saint-Saëns), Grand Ballet de Monte Carlo (du Marquis de Cuevas)

Other works include: dances in operas *Mavra* (mus. Stravinsky; Paris, 1922), *Le Médecin malgré lui* (mus. Gounod, with additions Satie; Monte Carlo, 1924), *Sorochintsky Fair* (mus. Mussorgsky; Monte Carlo, 1924), *Manon* (mus. Massenet; Monte Carlo, 1924), *Romeo and Juliet* (mus. Gounod; Monte Carlo, 1924), *Prince Igor* (mus. Borodin; Monte Carlo, 1924), *Samson and Delila* (mus. Saint-Saëns; Monte Carlo, 1924), *Faust* (mus. Gounod; Monte Carlo, 1924), *La Damnation de Faust* (mus. Berlioz; Monte Carlo, 1924), *Mefistofèle* (mus.

Boito; Monte Carlo, 1924), *Aida* (mus. Verdi; Monte Carlo, 1924), *La Naissance de la lyre* (mus. Roussel; Paris, 1925), *Carmen* (mus. Bizet; Buenos Aires, 1926), *Hamlet* (mus. Thomas; Buenos Aires, 1926), *Nerón* (mus. Boito; Buenos Aires, 1926), *La Gioconda* (mus. Ponchielli; Buenos Aires, 1926), *Ollantai* (mus. Gaito; Buenos Aires, 1926), *Tannhäuser* (mus. Wagner; Buenos Aires, 1926), *Aida* (mus. Verdi; Buenos Aires, 1926), *La Traviata* (mus. Verdi; Buenos Aires, 1926), *Naïla* (mus. Gaubert; Paris, 1927), *Rigoletto* (mus. Verdi; Buenos Aires, 1927), *Le Rossignol* (mus. Stravinsky; Buenos Aires, 1927), *La Wally* (mus. Catalani; Buenos Aires, 1927), *Manon* (mus. Massenet; Buenos Aires, 1927), *Tsar Sultan* (mus. Rimsky-Korsakov; Buenos Aires, 1927), *Thaïs* (mus. Massenet; Buenos Aires, 1927), *Faust* (mus. Gounod; Buenos Aires, 1927), *Russlan and Ludmilla* (mus. Glinka; Paris, 1930), *Sadko* (mus. Rimsky-Korsakov; Paris, 1930), *Schwanda the Bagpiper* (mus. Weinberger; Vienna, 1930), *Russalka* (mus. Dargomizhsky; Paris, 1930), *Boris Godunov* (mus. Mussorgsky; Paris, 1931), *Prince Igor* (mus. Borodin; Paris, 1932), *The Tales of Hoffmann* (mus. Offenbach; Berlin, 1932), *Orfeo* (mus. Casalla; Brescia, 1933), *Andrea Chénier* (mus. Giordano; Buenos Aires, 1933), *Die Königskinder* (mus. Humperdinck; Buenos Aires, 1933), *Khovanshchina* (mus. Mussorgsky; Buenos Aires, 1933), *La Forza del Destino* (mus. Verdi; Buenos Aires, 1933), *La Vida Breve* (mus. de Falla; Buenos Aires, 1933), *Die Meistersinger von Nürnberg* (mus. Wagner; Buenos Aires, 1933), *Marouf* (mus. Rabaud; Buenos Aires, 1946), *Boris Godunov* (mus. Mussorgsky; Buenos Aires, 1946), *Mignon* (mus. Thomas; Buenos Aires, 1946), *Un Ballo in Maschera* (mus. Verdi; Buenos Aires, 1946).

PUBLICATIONS

By Nijinska:
Bronislava Nijinska: Early Memoirs, translated and edited by Irina Nijinska, New York, 1981

About Nijinska:
Beaumont, Cyril, *Complete Book of Ballets,* revised edition, London, 1951
Grigoriev, Serge, *The Diaghilev Ballet,* translated by Vera Bowen, London, 1953
Anderson, Jack, "The Fabulous Career of Bronislava Nijinska", *Dance Magazine* (New York), August 1963
Croce, Arlene, "Bronislava Nijinska", *Ballet Review* (New York), vol. 4, no. 2, 1972
Baer, Nancy Van Norman, *Bronislava Nijinska: A Dancer's Legacy,* San Francisco, 1986
Acocella, Joan, "Nijinska: The Survivor's Story", *Dance Magazine* (New York), April 1986
Severn, Margaret, "Dancing with Bronislava Nijinska and Ida Rubinstein", *Dance Chronicle* (New York), vol. 11, no. 3, 1988
Garafola, Lynn, *Diaghilev's Ballets Russes,* New York, 1989
Merrett, Sue, "Bronislava Nijinska Remembered", *Dancing Times* (London), May 1991
Meisner, Nadine, "The Making of a Choreographer", *Dance and Dancers* (London), June–July 1991

* * *

Bronislava Nijinska received some of the finest ballet training in the world and was given the First Award in her 1908 graduating class by the Imperial Theatre School; but as a dancer she was always overshadowed by her exceptional brother, Vaslav. While at the Maryinsky she performed minor roles, and even with the Ballets Russes, which she joined in 1909, she was a member of the corps de ballet. Although she was given larger roles in the company after 1911, it was while working with her brother on his controversial ballets that Nijinska began to formulate her own ideas on movement, which combined the classical tradition with choreographic innovation.

These concepts were furthered when she returned to Russia in March 1914, after she had resigned from the Ballets Russes in protest against her brother's dismissal. She stayed in Russia until 1921, and during this revolutionary period she formulated a credo which insisted on the importance of training, especially in the classical tradition (as opposed to Isadora Duncan and other modern dancers she had observed), but which also criticized the traditional ballet methodology that emphasized line and form and neglected the "melody" of dancing, since "movement constitutes the material of dance". During this period Nijinska was also heavily influenced by constructivist ideas: the concept of body as machine, movement as material, and other such analogies pervade her writings and influenced her choreography during this period.

In 1921, Diaghilev invited Nijinska back to the company both as principal dancer and to assist in the mounting of *The Sleeping Beauty* (retitled *The Sleeping Princess*). It was the changes she made to Petipa's choreography which made the impresario realize he had a choreographer worthy of following in her brother's footsteps. Many of these additions, such as the dance for the "Three Ivans" and the Pas de poisson added to the adagio of the final Grand Pas de deux, remain in many current productions. However, it was *Les Noces,* choreographed in 1923, which really established Nijinska's reputation and confirmed her Diaghilev-given title of "La Nijinska". *Les Noces* was a wedding stripped to its bare essentials, where pointe work was used not only to elongate the body, reminiscent of Russian icons, but to accentuate the anti-realist approach to this ritualistic ceremony. Many of the flattened gestures, parallel stances, and choreographic configurations were extensions and developments of her brother's modernist aesthetic.

In contrast, and demonstrating her versatility, was Nijinska's choreography for *Les Biches* in 1924. Often referred to as one of the first (if not the first) of "feminist" ballets, this ballet showed Nijinska giving women a freer style of movement, and actions that commented on the narcissism (often of the men) and lax morality which pervaded a certain stratum of society. Her own performance as the hostess of this gathering was a change for her, and gave the choreographer a chance to perform with abandon. She made further ironic observations on this society in *Le Train bleu,* although her relationship with the scenarist, Jean Cocteau, was strained, and precipitated her leaving the Ballets Russes. This ballet did, however, allow Nijinska to experiment with her neo-classical style on sports figures—again taking her brother's ideas (in this case *Jeux*) many steps further.

In 1925, Nijinska began her Théâtre Chorégraphique, a chamber ensemble of dancers which allowed her to experiment further with a repertoire of short ballets, each about ten minutes in length, to a variety of composers and in a wide range of styles. After 1925 Nijinska held a variety of jobs and continued to be in great demand as a choreographer, even in Hollywood, where she helped stage the dance sequences for Max Reinhardt's 1935 film *A Midsummer Night's Dream* (released by Warner Brothers). She was charmed by California and decided to settle there, even though she continued to spend much of her time travelling around the world. She trained many dancers in Los Angeles at her school and at other studios, and her influence on dancers on the American west coast has probably been underestimated.

As a choreographer, Nijinska and her work might have passed into oblivion if Sir Frederick Ashton, then director of the Royal Ballet, had not invited her to restage *Les Biches* in London in 1964 and then *Les Noces* in 1966. This helped reintroduce her work to a new generation of dancers and allowed historians and critics a chance to evaluate two of the most important works of the Ballets Russes. It is, however, only in recent years that Nijinska's importance and choreographic ability has been recognized, due in no small part to her daughter, Irina Nijinska, who continued to supervise stagings and reconstructions of her mother's works until her death in 1991. Nijinska's works outside the Ballets Russes, which have been the most neglected, may be even more experimental and innovative but, unhappily, have not survived for assessment. However, the publication of Nijinska's memoirs in 1981 and a comprehensive exhibition put together by the Fine Arts Museum of San Francisco in 1986 showed that many of her ideas were far ahead of their time, and indeed were forerunners of what we see today. Nijinska did not receive her proper due for such a long time probably because her ideas were so quickly assimilated by others, and because her work was, inevitably, overshadowed by her brother's legacy.

—Frank W. D. Ries

NIJINSKY, CLOWN DE DIEU

Choreography: Maurice Béjart
Music: Pierre Henry, with extracts from Peter Ilyich Tchaikovsky's *Symphonie Pathétique*
Design: Joëlle Roustan and Roger Bernard (scenery and costumes)
Libretto: Maurice Béjart
First Production: Ballet du XXe Siècle, Forêt Nationale, Brussels, 8 October 1971
Principal Dancers: Jorge Donn (The Clown of God), Paul Mejia (Spectre de la rose), Daniel Lommel (Golden Slave), Jorg Lanner (Faun), Micha Van Hoecke (Petrouchka), Suzanne Farrell (The Girl in Pink), Angele Albrecht (Nymph), Jaleh Kerendi (The Woman of the World), Cathérine Verneuil (The Ballerina), Hitomi Asakawa (The Doll), Pierre Dobreievich (Diaghilev)

PUBLICATIONS

Christout, Marie Françoise, "Béjart's *Nijinsky, Clown of God*", *Dance Magazine* (New York), December 1971
Phillip, Richard, "*Nijinsky, Clown of God*", *Dance Magazine* (New York), December 1972
Maynard, Olga, "Maurice Béjart on the Creative Process", *Dance Magazine* (New York), February 1973
Balanchine, George, with Mason, Francis, *Balanchine's Complete Stories of the Great Ballets*, Garden City, N.Y., 1977

*   *   *

Béjart, creator of the ballet *Nijinsky, Clown de Dieu*, first shown in Belgium in 1971, described his intent as not to create a biographical moment in Nijinsky's life, but to take instead ten isolated years, described in the dancer's diary, and to create on stage "an idealized, secret place where the heart can live".

Nijinsky is conceived in two parts which represent the fall of man from earthly paradise—envisioned as the Ballets Russes—into madness. The first act is entitled *Nijinsky of the Ballets Russes*; the second, *Nijinsky of God*, contains scenes which reflect the dancer's growing preoccupation with the ideas of Tolstoy on the nature of God in the universe, and which depict the beginnings of madness.

As a psychological study, the ballet illustrates Béjart's humanity as inspired by Nijinsky's diary. In fragments, using spoken excerpts from the diary as background narrative, it presents Nijinsky's quest for love, his vulnerability as a man, his ultimate fall from grace in the Russian ballet, and his search for God. Béjart's choice of subject was also an emotional quest; during the ballet's creation, he wore an orthodox cross and Russian peasant attire, immersing himself totally in the period.

As a ballet, *Nijinsky* reflects Béjart's choreographic style at its best, conceived almost entirely as a circus or literary collage. Its overtly theatrical form utilizes complex stage devices and scenic design, which include the use of masks to create the idea of "doubles", unusual interrelations of particular scenic effects, and skilful use of costume.

In *Nijinsky* the concept of the mask, or "other", represented by the clown persona, is introduced through the text of the diary ("I will introduce myself as a clown," wrote Nijinsky, "... to make myself better understood"). Béjart's professed intention in his portrait ballets is to awaken his audience, to make the viewer ask questions. In *Nijinsky* the double is both a literary and a theatrical device. Nijinsky's clown, or other self, is danced by another dancer; Diaghilev, has a magnificent *doppelgänger* made of wax and papier-maché. Nijinsky's companions, Petrouchka, the Golden Slave, the Spectre de la rose, and the Faun, also have, as their doubles, clowns (danced respectively by Robert Denvers as "Clown in Blue", Jean-Marie Limon as "Clown in Gold", Paul Mejia as "Clown in Rose", and Franco Romano as "Clown in Maroon") who people the dancer's world of fantasy and fear.

Béjart's choice of score juxtaposes the nineteenth-century music of Tchaikovsky (*Symphonie Pathétique*) and twentieth-century modern electronic pieces created by the French composer Pierre Henry. In the second half of the ballet the use of electronic sound and lighting vividly recreates Nijinsky's hallucinatory onset of madness and the loneliness with which he marked the stage with a cloak of black drapery, stretched to resemble the shape of a cross.

In *Nijinsky*, Béjart uses costume as an integral part of his collage. In the character of the Girl in Pink, danced by Suzanne Farrell, the disrobing which occurs throughout Act I represents the unmasking of artifice (in contrast with the masks, worn by the clowns, which suggest duality).

In Béjart's theatrical realm, the use of these effects as collage (as in the earlier *Baudelaire*), wherein a dreamlike assemblage of fragments forms images which are both exotic and banal through grotesque visions of costume, color, and sound, seems to make up for what, at times, is lacking in his choreography.

Whether Béjart's choreography measures up to his vision has been debated; nevertheless he gives to the dancer on stage a power previously undreamed of. Whereas in *Baudelaire* this power verged on the comic, enabling him "to sing *Swan Lake*", in *Nijinsky* it verges on the tragic, enabling him to evoke the brilliance of the Russian ballet set against the disturbing theme of madness.

The stage lighting ranged from vivid red to ochre hues, and projected on to a giant cross which stood at the base of the circular performance space. From this circle three ramps extended to form a triangle whose points signified Diaghilev, Woman, and Christ, and of which Nijinsky is the center.

Nijinsky Clown de Dieu was a showcase for the memorable

partnership of Suzanne Farrell and Jorge Donn; it also drew excellent performances from soloists such as Angele Albrecht, Cathérine Verneuil, and Paul Mejia. It revealed the interpretative genius of Jorge Donn who, in the role of Nijinsky, never left the stage. In spite of disputes concerning such matters as the suitability of such a spectacle for the ballet stage (its American premiere, fittingly for some, was at Madison Square Garden) and allegations of poor taste in its slogans and several of its choreographic images (such as a ballerina kissing the feet of a crucified dancer), Béjart's *Nijinsky* powerfully evokes the frenzy and despair of a life given to dance and to God.

—Pamela Gaye

NIJINSKY, Vaslav

Russian dancer and choreographer. Born Vaslav Fomich Nizhinsky (Nijinsky), son of Polish dancers Eleanora Bereda and Foma Nizhinsky, and brother of dancer/choreographer Bronislava Nijinska, in Kiev, 12 March (28 February old style) 1889 (some sources say 1888). Studied at the Imperial Theatre School, St. Petersburg, pupil of Nikolai and Sergei Legat, Mikhail Obukhov, from 1898; awarded Didelot scholarship, 1900; graduated in 1907; later studied with Enrico Cecchetti. Married Hungarian dancer Romola de Pulszky, 1913: two daughters, Kyra (b. 1914) and Tamara (b. 1920). Début, while still a student, Maryinsky Theatre, St. Petersburg, 1906; dancer, Maryinsky Theatre, from 1907; principal dancer and choreographer, Diaghilev's Ballets Russes, 1909–13: a leading performer in the Ballets Russes's first season, Paris, 1909, and subsequent seasons, 1910, 1911; dismissed from the Maryinsky Theatre, 1911, thereafter becoming permanent member of the Diaghilev company; first choreography, 1912, followed by three more major works for the Ballets Russes; dismissed by Diaghilev after marriage on South American tour, 1913; founder, choreographer, and leading dancer of own company, Palace Theatre, London, 1914 (closed after only fourteen days); returned to Ballets Russes as principal dancer, New York, 1916; later choreographer and director, U.S. tour (in absence of Diaghilev), 1916–17, also touring Spain, and South America with company, 1917; settled in Switzerland, 1918; entered Bellevue Sanatorium, Kreuzlingen, 1919; lived in Vienna, 1920, Budapest, 1921–23, Paris, 1924–29; returned to Bellevue Sanatorium, 1929–38; lived in Münsinger Hospital, Switzerland, 1938–40, Budapest, 1940–45, Vienna and western Austria, 1945–47, London, and eventually Sussex, 1947–50. Died in London, 8 April 1950; buried in Montmartre, Paris.

ROLES

1905   Dance of the Fauns (cr) in *Acis et Galatea* (Fokine), Imperial Theatre School Performance, St. Petersburg

Pas de deux (cr) in *The Parisian Market* (Kulichevskaya), Imperial Theatre School Performance, St. Petersburg

1906   Vol des Papillons (cr) in *A Midsummer Night's Dream* (Fokine after Petipa), Imperial Theatre School Performance, St. Petersburg

Pas de deux in *Divertissement—The Valse Fantasia* (Fokine), Imperial Theatre School Performance, St. Petersburg

Langurf (cr) in *The Gardener Prince* (Kulichevskaya), Imperial Theatre School Performance, St. Petersburg

Pas de huit added to *Don Giovanni* (opera; mus. Mozart), Maryinsky Theatre, St. Petersburg

1907   White Slave (cr) in *Eunice* (Fokine), Maryinsky Theatre, St. Petersburg

Rinaldo (cr) in *The Animated Gobelin* (later part of *Le Pavillon d'Armide*; Fokine), Imperial Theatre School Performance, Maryinsky Theatre, St. Petersburg

Prince Sing (cr) in *Salanga* (Kulichevskaya), Imperial Theatre School Performance, Maryinsky Theatre, St. Petersburg

Jeux des Papillons (cr; Kulichevskaya) added to *La Source* (Coppini after Saint-Léon), Maryinsky Theatre, St. Petersburg

Genie of the Forest in *The Enchanted Forest* (Ivanov), Maryinsky Theatre, St. Petersburg

Pas de deux in *Vain Precautions* (*La Fille mal gardée*; (Petipa, Ivanov), Maryinsky Theatre, St. Petersburg

Peasant pas de deux in *Giselle* (Petipa after Coralli, Perrot), Maryinsky Theatre, St. Petersburg

Colin in *Vain Precautions* (*La Fille mal gardée*; Petipa, Ivanov), Maryinsky Theatre, St. Petersburg

Bluebird Pas de deux in *The Sleeping Beauty* (Petipa), Maryinsky Theatre, St. Petersburg

Slave (cr) in *Le Pavillon d'Armide* (Fokine), Maryinsky Theatre, St. Petersburg

1908   The Poet in *Rêverie romantique: Ballet sur la musique de Chopin* (*Chopiniana*, second version; Fokine), Maryinsky Theatre, St. Petersburg

Slave (cr) in *Egyptian Nights* (later *Cléopâtre*; Fokine), Maryinsky Theatre, St. Petersburg

1909   Slave (cr) in *Cléopâtre* (new version of *Egyptian Nights*; Fokine), Diaghilev's Ballets Russes, Paris

Vaiyu (cr) in *Le Talisman* (Legat after Petipa), Maryinsky Theatre, St. Petersburg

Valse, Mazurka (cr) in *Les Sylphides* (new version of *Chopiniana*; Fokine), Diaghilev's Ballets Russes, Paris

1910   Principal dancer (cr) in *Danse Siamoise* (solo; Fokine), Maryinsky Theatre, St. Petersburg

Principal dancer (cr) in *Kobold* (solo; Fokine), Maryinsky Theatre, St. Petersburg

Golden Slave (cr) in *Schéhérazade* (Fokine), Diaghilev's Ballets Russes, Paris

Albrecht in *Giselle* (Petipa after Coralli, Perrot; staged Fokine), Diaghilev's Ballets Russes, Paris

1911   Spirit of the Rose (cr) in *Le Spectre de la rose* (Fokine), Diaghilev's Ballets Russes, Monte Carlo

Title role (cr) in *Narcisse* (Fokine), Diaghilev's Ballets Russes, Monte Carlo

Title role (cr) in *Petrushka* (Fokine), Diaghilev's Ballets Russes, Paris

Prince Siegfried in *Swan Lake* (two-act version; Petipa, Ivanov; staged Fokine), Diaghilev's Ballets Russes, Paris

1912   Title role (cr) in *Le Dieu bleu* (Fokine), Diaghilev's Ballets Russes, Paris

Faun (cr) in *L'Après-midi d'un faune* (also chor.), Diaghilev's Ballets Russes, Paris

Daphnis (cr) in *Daphnis et Chloé* (Fokine), Diaghilev's Ballets Russes, Paris

1913   Principal dancer (cr) in *Jeux* (also chor.), Diaghilev's Ballets Russes, Paris

1914   Principal dancer (cr) in *Les Sylphides* (also chor.; own version), Saison Nijinsky, Palace Theatre, London

1916   Title role (cr) in *Till Eulenspiegel* (also chor.), Diaghilev's Ballets Russes, New York

Vaslav Nijinsky as the Slave in *Le Pavillon d'Armide*, 1909 (left) and in the title role of *Le Dieu bleu*, 1912 (right)

WORKS

1912   *L'Après-midi d'un faune* (mus. Debussy), Diaghilev's Ballets Russes, Paris

1913   *Jeux* (mus. Debussy), Diaghilev's Ballets Russes, Paris
      Le Sacre du printemps (mus. Stravinsky), Diaghilev's Ballets Russes, Paris

1914   *Les Sylphides* (own version; mus. Chopin, orchestrated Ravel), Saison Nijinsky, Palace Theatre, London
      Danse Polovtsienne (mus. Borodin), Saison Nijinsky, Palace Theatre, London
      Danse Grecque (mus. probably Tcherepnin), Saison Nijinsky, Palace Theatre, London

1916   *Till Eulenspiegel* (mus. Strauss), Diaghilev's Ballets Russes, New York

PUBLICATIONS

By Nijinsky:
The Diaries of Vaslav Nijinsky, edited by Romola Nijinsky, London, 1933

About Nijinsky:
Beaumont, Cyril W., *Nijinsky*, London, 1932
Nijinsky, Romola, *Nijinsky*, London, 1933
Magriel, Paul (ed.), *Nijinsky: An Illustrated Monograph*, New York, 1946
Buckle, Richard, *Nijinsky*, London, 1971; revised edition, Harmondsworth, 1980

Krasovskaya, Vera, *Nijinsky*, Leningrad, 1974; translated by John E. Bowlt, New York, 1979
Kirstein, Lincoln, *Nijinsky Dancing*, New York, 1975
Buckle, Richard, *Diaghilev*, London, 1979
Nijinska, Bronislava, *Early Memoirs*, New York, 1981
de Meyer, Baron Adolf, et al., *L'Après-midi d'un faune: Vaslav Nijinsky 1912*, London, 1983
Hodson, Millicent, "Ritual Design in New Dance: Nijinsky's *Le Sacre du Printemps*, *Dance Research* (London), 2 parts: Summer 1985, Spring 1986
Hodson, Millicent, "Nijinsky's Choreographic Method", *Dance Research Journal* (New York), Winter 1986/87
Parker, Derek, *Nijinsky, God of the Dance*, Wellingborough, 1988
Garafola, Lynn, *Diaghilev's Ballets Russes*, New York, 1989
Guest, Ann Hutchinson, and Jeschke, Claudia, *Nijinsky's Faune Restored*, Philadelphia, 1991
Oswald, Peter, *Vaslav Nijinsky: A Leap into Madness*, New York, 1991
Nijinsky, Tamara, *Nijinsky and Romola*, London, 1991

*   *   *

The legends surrounding Nijinsky—the great dancer who became mad—have long clouded any rational assessment of this remarkable figure, who continues to haunt the imagination of those with even a casual interest in dance. When Serge Diaghilev first showed the achievement of Russian ballet to the West in Paris in 1909, the greatest surprise was the stunning range of male dancers. With the noble Mikhail Fokine and the "barbaric" Adolph Bolm, Vaslav Nijinsky's litheness and astonishing elevation helped re-establish a high standard of male virtuosity, providing a lasting example for generations of dancers and choreographers throughout the world. Under the tutelege of his lover/impresario Diaghilev, Nijinsky achieved world fame as the ethereal spirit of romance in *Le Spectre de la rose* (in which his leaps seemed to hang in mid-air), the voluptuous sexual animal of the Golden Slave in *Schéhérazade*, the dreamy poet of *Les Sylphides*, and the half-doll/half-human Petrushka, vainly struggling to achieve love and dignity. In each role he was different, seemingly transformed into the character.

On his graduation from the Imperial Theatre School in St. Petersburg in 1907, Nijinsky's rise in the ranks of the Imperial Ballet had been meteoric, with the dancer partnering the company's leading ballerinas in his first season. In 1911, after a scandal at the Maryinsky Theatre (perhaps engineered by Diaghilev), he was dismissed and became the star of Diaghilev's now permanently established Ballets Russes. Well-mannered but reserved, he was as unremarkable off-stage as he was electrifying when performing. The son of talented Polish dancers who never found a permanent home in the state or private theatres of the Russian empire, Nijinsky in his early twenties was nevertheless accepted by the leaders of the arts and society throughout Europe.

With the encouragement of Diaghilev and the great designer Léon Bakst, and aided by his remarkable sister Bronislava Nijinska, he now began his choreographic experiments, which over the next five years led to the creation of four remarkably different, but equally original ballets—a choreographic legacy only now becoming understood.

In *L'Après-midi d'un faune*, Nijinsky took Debussy's evocation of Mallarmé's poem about the sexual awakening of a young wild creature in a glade visited by nymphs, and placed it in an archaic Greece of the imagination. All movement was seen in profile, stylized in ways that emphasized shifts of weight and angular arm movements, thus negating all that he was famous for as a dancer. Roundness was replaced by movement on planes parallel to the front of the stage, even when reversing directions. Fokine had advocated that movement should be moulded into new forms to correspond with each new dramatic idea, on the theory that the entire body should be expressive, as exemplified in works as different as *Spectre*, *Schéhérazade*, and *Petrushka*. Nijinsky took these ideas further, showing the amoral innocence of the Faun—who awakens, eats, encounters a band of enticing and frightened nymphs, and captures the scarf of one as a trophy, with which he returns to his sleep and erotic dreams—as if carved in a frieze by an early Greek artist. The ballet created a sensation and a scandal, but has remained in the repertoire (the only one of his to do so) in versions of varying authenticity, including recent notable stagings from Nijinsky's own notation.

Each Nijinsky ballet approaches the question of movement in an entirely different fashion. The short-lived *Jeux* (only five performances despite a remarkable commissioned score by Debussy) used gestures derived from tennis and other popular sports to suggest the playful intertwinings of three young people (two women and a man) on a summer afternoon. Yet the same season saw *Le Sacre du printemps*, in which Stravinsky and Nicholas Roerich's vision of a primitive Russia, coming with wonder and terror to the rebirth of the fertile year and culminating in the sacrifice of a half-willing virgin, was matched by Nijinsky's total rethinking of movement. Knees, shoulders, and arms were turned in, not out as in classical ballet. Jumps were flat-footed, stressing weight and the difficulty of leaving the ground. Groups began by being scattered and asymmetrical, achieving symmetry only as the

sacrifice approached. The dancers were required to shudder, stamp, and jerk, while the Chosen Maiden's dance was convulsive. Following the stormy premiere, the work was given just seven more times (in Paris and London only) before Nijinsky left the company, but the Joffrey Ballet's remarkable conjectural reconstruction by Millicent Hodson and Kenneth Archer suggests the originality and power of the original choreography, matching Stravinsky's precedent-shattering score.

Till Eulenspiegel was Nijinsky's last completed ballet. Following his unexpected marriage in 1913 and subsequent dismissal from the Ballets Russes, he staged a few minor works in London before a tangle of events involving war, internment, and problems of touring brought a return to the Diaghilev company for a tour of the United States. Using Richard Strauss's jaunty, ironic score, *Till* presented a bustle of burghers and gentry jolted from complacency by an irrepressible spirit of mockery and independence. As Till, Nijinsky literally upset applecarts and thumbed his nose at pomposity, a truly immortal spirit of joy. Seen only in North America (and never by Diaghilev), it clearly exploited Nijinsky's virtuosity as his other ballets had not.

As performer and choreographer, Nijinsky resembled no one else. A slow worker who only gradually evolved principles from practice, his was a specifically "dance intelligence", as shown by his efforts to create a system of notation capable of capturing the nuances of his movement ideas—ideas he could not easily communicate to conventionally trained dancers. Yet in the need to make each work unique, inhabiting its own world of movement, scene, and sound, Nijinsky is among the pioneers of modernism, learning from such masters as Fokine, Bakst, Benois, and Debussy, yet going beyond them into uncharted territories.

What the unrealized projects—including ballets to music by J. S. Bach and Liszt's *Mephisto Waltz*—might have been remains unknowable. Torn by conflicting impulses, including the desires for marriage and a family yet also the need for the protection of a strong male like Diaghilev, Nijinsky gave his last performance (in January 1919 before an invited audience in a St. Moritz hotel ballroom) on strips of cloth forming a great cross, aiming to depict the sufferings of war. After that followed schizophrenia and silence. Yet the legend remains, supported by photographs, drawings, descriptions, his wife's sensationalistic biography, and the memories and memoirs of those who saw or worked with him. But with the work of such admirers as Lincoln Kirstein and Richard Buckle in seeking to find the reality behind the legend, the true originality of Nijinsky's conceptions and their realization on the stage is finally becoming widely accepted, some 40 years after his death.

—George Dorris

NIKITINA, Alice

Russian dancer and teacher. Born in St. Petersburg, c. 1904 (some sources say 1909). Studied at the Imperial Theatre School, St. Petersburg, pupil of Olga Preobrazhenskaya, Olga Ossipovna, Nikolai Legat, Lubov Egorova, Leonid Leontiev; left Russia during Revolution, thus failing to graduate; later studied with Enrico Cecchetti, from 1923. First performance (according to memoirs) in *The Fairy Doll*, Kislovodsk, before 1920; professional début, State Opera Ballet, Ljubljana (former Yugoslavia), 1920; performed with Lydia Kyasht, Vienna, thereafter joining Boris Romanov's Russian Romantic Ballet, Berlin, from 1921/22; engaged by Diaghilev for Ballets Russes, 1923: soloist, becoming ballerina, until 1929; performer in Cochran's revue, dancing in ballets by Lifar and Balanchine, London, 1930; ballerina, performing with Anatole Vilzak in own recitals, Brussels and Paris, 1932; leading dancer, Les Ballets Serge Lifar, London; returned to ballet stage to perform with de Basil's Ballet Russe, Covent Garden, London, 1937; début as singer, Palermo, 1938; founder and director of own ballet school in Paris, from 1949. Died in Monte Carlo, June 1978.

ROLES

1923   Soloist (cr) in *Chasse de Diane* (Romanov), Russian Romantic Ballet, Berlin

      A Maiden in *Polovtsian Dances from Prince Igor* (Fokine), Diaghilev's Ballets Russes, Monte Carlo

      Dancer in *Les Sylphides* (Fokine), Diaghilev's Ballets Russes, Monte Carlo

      Sister in "Florestan and his Sisters" Pas de trois in *Aurora's Wedding* (Petipa; staged Nijinska), Diaghilev's Ballets Russes

1924   A Baroness (cr) in *Les Tentations de la bergère* (Nijinska), Diaghilev's Ballets Russes, Monte Carlo

      Dancer ("Bridesmaid") in *Les Noces* (Nijinska), Diaghilev's Ballets Russes, Monte Carlo

      A Gossip (cr) in *Les Fâcheux* (Nijinska), Diaghilev's Ballets Russes, Monte Carlo

      Bluebird Pas de deux in *Aurora's Wedding* (Petipa; staged Nijinska), Diaghilev's Ballets Russes, London

1925   Flore (cr) in *Zéphyr et Flore* (Massine), Diaghilev's Ballets Russes, Monte Carlo

1926   Adagietto ("La Garçonne") in *Les Biches* (Nijinska), Diaghilev's Ballets Russes, Paris

      Juliet in *Romeo and Juliet* (Nijinska), Diaghilev's Ballets Russes, Paris

1927   Title role (cr; replacing Spessivtseva), in *La Chatte* (Balanchine), Diaghilev's Ballets Russes, Monte Carlo

      Dancer (cr) in *Le Pas d'acier* (Massine), Diaghilev's Ballets Russes, Paris

1928   Dancer (cr) in *Ode* (Massine), Diaghilev's Ballets Russes, Paris

      Terpsichore (cr) in *Apollon musagète* (Balanchine), Diaghilev's Ballets Russes, Paris

1929   The Lady (cr) in *Le Bal* (Balanchine), Diaghilev's Ballets Russes, Monte Carlo

1930   One-legged Woman (cr) in *Luna Park* (Lifar), The Lady in *La Nuit* (Balanchine), Wife (cr) in *Piccadilly 1813* (Balanchine), The Lady (cr) in *Heaven* (Balanchine), principal dancer (cr) in *Pas de deux* (Balanchine), Charles B. Cochran's 1930 Revue, London

1933   The Young Girl in *Le Spectre de la rose* (Fokine), Ballets Serge Lifar, London

      Principal dancer in *The Creatures of Prometheus* (Lifar), Ballets Serge Lifar, London

1937   The Queen (cr) in *Le Lion amoureux* (Lichine), de Basil's Ballet Russe, London

Other roles include: Estrella in *Le Carnaval* (Fokine), Doll in *La Boutique fantasque* (Massine), principal dancer in *Les Sylphides* (Fokine), Princess Aurora in *Aurora's Wedding* (Petipa; staged Nijinska), title role in *The Firebird* (Fokine), Dorotea in *The Good-Humoured Ladies* (Massine), Rosetta in *Pulcinella* (Massine), Pas de quatre in *Cimarosiana* (Massine).

Alice Nikitina in Massine's *Zéphyr et Flore*, Diaghilev's Ballets Russes, Monte Carlo, 1925

PUBLICATIONS

By Nikitina:
Nikitina By Herself, translated by Baroness Budberg, London, 1959

About Nikitina:
Haskell, Arnold, "The Younger Russian Dancers: Part 3", *Dancing Times* (London), June 1928
Dolin, Anton, *Divertissement*, London, 1931
Beaumont, Cyril, *The Diaghilev Ballet in London*, London, 1940
Grigoriev, Serge, *The Diaghilev Ballet*, translated by Vera Bowen, London, 1953
Vaughan, David, "Balanchine Ballerinas: 1925–1933", *Dance Magazine* (New York), January 1979

*   *   *

Alice Nikitina was a dancer for her time. Her brief but brilliant career was concentrated in a few years in the 1920s, when she was one of the leading dancers with the Diaghilev Ballets Russes. She was exceptionally well trained, her teachers having included Preobrazhenskaya, Egorova, Legat, and Cecchetti. She was graceful, with a notable jump and exceptional musicality, but her qualities as a dancer were less important than the fact that she epitomized a 1920s look, with her slim, almost boyish figure, sleek bobbed hair, and undeniable chic. Her exceptional "jolie laide" beauty and freshness made her a great favourite of audiences everywhere.

She came to prominence in the mid-1920s, partly through the patronage of Lord Rothermere, who backed several seasons for Diaghilev in which she was the star. Diaghilev himself, however, was fond of her, having early discerned her tremendous promise, although she later antagonized him by using influence to get more roles. Still, at this period, her technique did not measure up to her natural artistry, and there was a tendency to exploit her promise rather than her abilities.

Serge Grigoriev, Diaghilev's rehearsal director for many years, did not share in Diaghilev's apparent favouritism, as his memoirs (*The Diaghilev Ballet 1909-1929*) make clear. (Indeed, he even claims that Diaghilev did not like Nikitina, but knew the value of her appearance, as in, for example, her successful last-minute assumption of the title role in *La Chatte*.) Nikitina's emergence as a ballerina, he explains, was largely due to the departure of Vera Nemchinova in 1926, as was the young Alexandra Danilova's. But whereas "Danilova had made remarkable progress and was by this time fully capable of taking Nemchinova's place," he claims, "The same could not be said of Nikitina. Her technique was indifferent and the parts she could fill were fewer. But Nikitina possessed a most valuable endowment: self confidence, of which she command-ed an apparently boundless supply."

Nikitina's roles in the Diaghilev Ballet did suit her particular qualities perfectly, especially when she assumed the role of the icily remote, androgynous "Garçonne" in *Les Biches* and the title role in *La Chatte*, which she took over from Olga Spessiva (Spessivtseva): in this role the ballet's composer Henri Sauget described her as "the most cat-like cat, enigmatic, harmonious, capricious, silent, exquisite and delicate." Her major created role, Flore in *Zéphyr et Flore*, perfectly enshrined her qualities.

After Diaghilev's death, Nikitina appeared mainly in revue and concert performances, but in 1935 she began to train as an opera singer. In 1937 she returned to ballet to create the role of the Queen in Lichine's *Le Lion amoureux*, when it was noted that she had begun to acquire some of the mannerisms of the variety stage. The following year she made her début as an opera singer and temporarily abandoned ballet. She returned in the 1950s, dividing her time between opera and teaching, and eventually opened her own ballet school in the south of France.

—Sarah C. Woodcock

LES NOCES
(Russian title: *Svadebka*, or *Wedding*)

Choreography: Bronislava Nijinska
Music: Igor Stravinsky (dramatic cantata *Les Noces*)
Design: Natalia Gontcharova (scenery and costumes)
Libretto: song text by Igor Stravinsky
First Production: Diaghilev's Ballets Russes, Théâtre de la Gaîté-Lyrique, Paris, 13 June 1923
Principal Dancers: Felia Doubrovska (The Bride), Nicholas Semenov (uncredited: The Bridegroom), Léon Woizikowsky (uncredited: leading dancer, wedding guests), Lubov Tcher-nicheva (uncredited: leading dancer, wedding guests)

Other productions include: De Basil's Ballets Russes (restaged Nijinska), with Tamara Grigorieva (Bride), Roman Jasinsky (Bridegroom), Irina Baronova (leading female guest), Yurek Shabelevsky (leading male guest); New York, 20 April 1936. Royal Ballet (restaged Nijinska), with Svetlana Beriosova (Bride), Robert Mead (Bridegroom), Georgina Parkinson,

Anthony Dowell (Friends); London, 23 March 1966. Stuttgart Ballet (staged Irina Nijinska); Stuttgart, 1 June 1974. Paris Opéra Ballet (staged Irina Nijinska); Paris, 3 March 1976. Oakland Ballet (staged Irina Nijinska); Berkeley, California, 25 September 1981.

Metropolitan Opera House, League of American Composers (new version; chor. Elizaveta Anderson-Ivantzova, design Serge Soudekine); New York, 25 April 1929. La Scala Ballet (new version; chor. Tatjana Gsovsky); Milan, 28 January 1954 (staged Berlin, 1961). Les Ballets Chiriaeff (new version; chor. Ludmilla Chiriaeff, design Alexis Chiriaeff); Montreal, 1956. Ballet du XXe Siècle (new version; chor. Maurice Béjart); Salzburg, 1962 (revived Paris Opéra, 1965). American Ballet Theatre (new version; chor. Jerome Robbins, design Oliver Smith and Patricia Zipprodt), with Erin Martin (Bride), William Glassman (Bridegroom); New York, 30 March 1965 (revived Royal Swedish Ballet, 1969, Lar Lubovitch Company, 1976). Teatro alla Piccola Scala (new version; chor. Léonide Massine); Milan, 6 May 1966. Netherlands Dance Theater (new version; chor. Jiří Kylián, design John Macfarlane), as *Svadebka*; Scheveningen, Netherlands, 11 June 1982. Basle Ballet (new version; chor. and design Heinz Spoerli); Basel, 15 March 1989.

PUBLICATIONS

Belayev, Victor, *Stravinsky's "Les Noces": An Outline*, Oxford, 1928
Gontcharova, Natalia, "The Creation of *Les Noces*", *Ballet and Opera* (London), September 1949
Beaumont, Cyril, *Complete Book of Ballets*, revised edition, London, 1951
Anderson, Jack, "The Fabulous Career of Bronislava Nijin-ska", *Dance Magazine* (New York), August 1963
Kirstein, Lincoln, *Movement and Metaphor*, New York, 1970
Nijinska, Bronislava, "The Creation of *Les Noces*", *Dance Magazine* (New York), December 1974
Chamot, M., *Goncharova*, London, 1979
Weinstock, Stephen, "The Evolution of *Les Noces*", *Dance Magazine* (New York), April 1981
Como, William, "Kaleidoscope", *Dance Magazine* (New York), February 1982
Denby, Edwin, *Dance Writings*, edited by Robert Cornfield and William Mackay, New York, 1986
"Stravinsky's *Les Noces*" (various authors), *Dance Research Journal* (New York), Winter 1986-87
Johnson, Robert, "Ritual and Abstraction in Nijinska's *Les Noces*", *Dance Chronicle* (New York), vol. 10, no. 2, 1987
Baer, Nancy Van Norman, *Bronislava Nijinska: A Dancer's Legacy*, San Francisco, 1987
Garafola, Lynn, *Diaghilev's Ballets Russes*, New York, 1989
Meisner, Nadine, "Nijinska: The Making of a Choreo-grapher", *Dance and Dancers* (London), June-July 1991

*   *   *

Of its three collaborators, Nijinska came last to *Les Noces*. Stravinsky had written the music and Gontcharova had already produced her initial colourful designs by the time Diaghilev offered the choreography to Nijinska. Yet Nijinska was to be the determining force behind the final outcome of the ballet. Her success lies not only in the strength and innovation of her choreography, but also in that *Les Noces* excels the sum of its parts, reaching a synthesis and unity that puts it amongst the greatest of twentieth-century ballets.

Les Noces, **as performed by the Royal Ballet, London**

Thematically *Les Noces* is concerned with a wedding as a rite or ritual, a social/religious construct through which basic human drives are contained, channelled, and expressed in sublimated form. The choreography is powerfully driven by the thundering, relentless rhythms of the music. The focal figures of the Bride and Groom are anonymous and work paradoxically as background figures to the corps de ballet (a radical departure from the traditional use of the corps as decorative support to central individuals). Nijinska described *Les Noces* as the voice of the mass.

Yet it is in the dual meaning of the word "mass" that the complexity of the ballet is encapsulated. For there is both the liturgical theme of a religious celebration and, in the rhythms and dynamics, the qualities of mass movement. The sombre colours and austere setting of Gontcharova's final designs collude with the choreography's use of detached repetition to evoke the faceless impersonal crowd. The work points back to a primitive age of rites and ritual; it draws also, in its formality and incantations, on the spirit of the Russian church. But in its style and dynamics the work also encapsulates the spirit of the contemporary mass movements that stormed through Russia in the years immediately preceding this work. It is this rich complexity, so succinctly realized, that is the source of *Les Noces*'s power and brilliance.

Many critics have pointed to the important sense in which *Les Noces* realizes the essence of the peasant soul. It has been diversely interpreted as Marxist and as a nostalgic last look at Holy Russia. As Kirstein has said, however, "*Les Noces* praised the strength and quality of the Slavic peoples ... it made no decorative reference to a colourful past; it was not nostalgic over the loss of tsardom". Despite its vivid realization of elements of Holy Russia, this ballet clearly relates to Nijinska's experience of the new Russia. Nijinska undertook the choreography for *Les Noces* less than a year after she left Soviet Russia. She had lived and worked through the 1917 Revolution, having more direct experience of it than any of Diaghilev's other collaborators. She recalled in her recollections of the time of creating *Les Noces*, "I was still breathing the air of Russia. A Russia throbbing with excitement and intense feeling. All the vivid images of the harsh realities of the Revolution were still part of me and filled my whole being." Nijinska's vision was austere and elemental. While evoking the peasant soul of Holy Russia, her interpretation of Stravinsky's music evokes also the spirit of the rising proletariat. Curved, sickle-shaped arm movements combine with clenched fists and mass organized movement.

Both thematically and formally, *Les Noces* relates directly back to Stravinsky's earlier work, *Le Sacre du printemps* (1913), choreographed by Nijinska's brother, Nijinsky. In a wider context, however, the work relates to many diverse influences. The idea of a rite was a potent theme of the time. There was an artistic preoccupation with the idea of the primitive unconscious and a desire to recover the elements of a mythical pre-conscious period. This is a common thread running, for example, through the arcadia of Nijinsky's *L'Après-midi d'un faune* as well as through the abstract concerns of Kandinsky's paintings. There had been a revival of interest in folk art, in primitive rites, and in fertility myths. T.S. Eliot's seminal poem of the era, *The Waste Land* (1922), draws on similar themes. Stravinsky compared the songs of *Les Noces* to the use of conversation in Joyce's *Ulysses* (1922), as being "without the connecting thread of discourse". Nijinska's choreography realizes this haunting use of snatched, dislocated refererence by the outbreaks of simple movements, executed repeatedly by the women, that have the quality of childhood skipping routines, performed to the occasional nursery-rhyme rhythms of the music. The mechanistic qualities of the movement also relate to the influence of Futurism and Rayonism which had inspired the paintings of Gontcharova, as in *The Cyclist* (1913).

Part of the power and excitement of *Les Noces* is that it invites readings. The haunting chimes at the end, for example, are ambiguous. In tone they are high and celebratory, but their slow pacing brings them closer to a toll. Throughout the work the Bride and Groom move at a slower, seemingly more conscious, pace than the group. Their embraces at the end, set above the group's action, seem to transcend the more primitive and unconscious aspects of the ritual. In fact throughout the work Nijinska's use of stillness and groupings, such as in the pyramid of heads, counteracts the angst of the frenetic movement passages and could be seen to celebrate the strength and comradeship of the human being. Yet her groupings are also depersonalized and detached. The pile of heads appears as a bleak mass of anonymous bodies, brides of the past perhaps, or brides-to-be, upon which the bride of the moment doubtfully rests her head as if she is surrendering her individuality to the remorseless progress of fate.

Whatever the interpretation, it should not be forgotten that in terms of technique alone *Les Noces* is a seminal work. Nijinsky's ideas of banishing mime and replacing the "natura-listic" approach to technique with a language based on stylization and symbolic movement (realized in *Le Sacre du printemps*) had clearly been absorbed and understood by his younger sister. Nijinska was determined from the beginning that *Les Noces* should be performed on pointe. Kochno reports her as having said that this would "elongate the dancers' silhouettes and make them resemble the saints in Byzantine mosaics". Pointe work was associated, however, with the classical ballet repertoire—and thus one of the many revolu-tionary aspects of this landmark ballet is this use of pointe in such an otherwise "modernist" work. Instead of Romanticizing the body, the pointe work in *Les Noces* adds a frenetic, mechanistic quality to the movement range. Dancers mark time on pointe, contributing to the percussive power of the ballet's impact. The pointe work contrasts vividly and excitingly with the rounded backs, the stooping body postures, the curved arms and curled-in fingers, the clenched fists and turned-in legs. *Les Noces* represents a radical revitalization and extension of the classical technique.

—Lesley-Anne Sayers

NOIR ET BLANC *see* **SUITE EN BLANC**

NORTH, Robert

American dancer, choreographer, teacher, and company director.   Born Robert Dodson in Charleston, South Carolina, 1 June 1945. Studied art at the Central School of Art, London, 1963; studied ballet with Kathleen Crofton, and at the Royal Ballet School, London, 1965–67, also attending the London School of Contemporary Dance, from 1966; later studied with Martha Graham and Merce Cunningham, United States. Married dancer Janet Smith. Dancer, London Contemporary Dance Group, 1967, Martha Graham Company, 1968–69, and London Contemporary Dance Theatre, 1969; first choreo-graphy for London Festival Ballet Workshop; associate choreographer, London Contemporary Dance Theatre, 1975; guest choreographer for Ballet Rambert, Janet Smith and Dancers, and other companies including Stuttgart Ballet, Balleto di Toscana, Zurich Ballet, Zurich Dance Theatre, Hong Kong Ballet, Royal Danish Ballet, Geneva Ballet, and Ballet Jazzart, Paris; choreographer for stage shows, including *Carte Blanche* (revue, produced Tynan; London, 1975), and *Pilgrim* (rock musical; Edinburgh Festival, 1975); also choreographer for the film *Slow Dancing in the Big City* (dir. Avildsen; 1978), and for opera and stage plays; has appeared on television, including in the British (Granada) production of *The Seven Deadly Sins* (chor. MacMillan, 1984); contemporary dance teacher at Royal Ballet School, 1979–81, and international guest teacher; co-artistic director, London Contemporary Dance Theatre, 1981; artistic director Ballet Rambert, 1981–86; ballet director, Teatro Regio, Turin, 1990–91; artistic director, Göteborg Ballet, Sweden, from 1991. Recipient: Gold Prague Award, 1983.

WORKS

1967   *Death by Dimensions* (chor. as Robert Dodson; mus. Parsons), Ballet Rambert, London
        Out of Doors (mus. Bartók), Festival Ballet Workshop, London
        Pavane for a Dead Infanta (mus. Ravel), Balletmakers, London
1970   *Conversation Piece* (mus. Parsons), London Contempo-rary Dance Theatre, London
        One Was the Other (with Lapzeson; mus. Finnissy), London Contemporary Dance Theatre, London
        Brian (mus. Finnissy), London Contemporary Dance Theatre, Bath
1974   *Troy Game* (mus. Downes), London Contemporary Dance Theatre, Liverpool
        Dressed to Kill (mus. Miller, Smith), London Contempo-rary Dance Theatre, Southampton
1975   *Gladly, Badly, Madly, Sadly* (with Seymour; mus. Davis), London Contemporary Dance Theatre, London
        Running Figures (mus. Burgon), Ballet Rambert, Leeds
        David and Goliath (with Wayne Sleep; mus. C. Davis), London Contemporary Dance Theatre
        Still Life (mus. Downes), London Contemporary Dance Theatre
1976   *Just a Moment* (mus. Downes, Kool and the Gang), London Contemporary Dance Theatre
        Reflections (mus. Blake), Ballet Rambert, Horsham (later staged as pas de deux, and in new version for Janet Smith and Dancers)
1977   *Meeting and Parting* (mus. Blake), London Contempo-rary Dance Theatre
1978   *Scriabin Preludes and Studies* (mus. Scriabin), London Contemporary Dance Theatre (also staged in short-

ened version, Ballet Rambert)

Dreams with Silences (mus. Brahms), London Contemporary Dance Theatre

1979   *Reflections* (new version; mus. Blake), London Contemporary Dance Theatre

The Water's Edge (mus. Anderson, Palmer, Barre), Scottish Ballet, tour

January to June, New London Ballet

1980   *Death and the Maiden* (mus. Schubert), London Contemporary Dance Theatre

Lonely Town, Lonely Street (mus. Withers), Janet Smith and Dancers, Leicester (also staged as duet version, Ballet Rambert, 1981)

1981   *Songs and Dances* (mus. Schubert), London Contemporary Dance Theatre

1982   *Pribaoutki* (mus. Stravinsky), Ballet Rambert, Brighton

Electra (mus. Britten), Janet Smith and Dancers

1983   *For My Daughter* (mus. Janáček), Royal Danish Ballet, television production

Colour Moves (mus. Benstead), Ballet Rambert, Edinburgh Festival

On the Overgrown Path, Danish television

1984   *Entre dos Aguas* (mus. Paco de Lucia, arranged Rogers), Ballet Rambert, Manchester

Miniatures (mus. Stravinsky), Janet Smith and Dancers

1985   *Light and Shade* (mus. Stravinsky), Ballet Rambert, Brighton

Changing Shape (mus. Talking Heads), English Dance Theatre

Dances to Copland (mus. Copland), Batsheva Dance Company, Israel

Einsame Reise (mus. Schubert), Stuttgart Ballet, Stuttgart

1986   *Fool's Day* (mus. Renaissance songs), Janet Smith and Dancers

Der Schlaf der Vernunft (mus. Shostakovitch), Stuttgart Ballet, Stuttgart

1987   *Whip it to a Jelly* (mus. popular), Janet Smith and Dancers

Elvira Madigan (mus. Benstead, Shostakovich, Sibelius, Neilsen), Royal Danish Ballet, Copenhagen

1988   *Sebastian* (mus. Menotti), Balletto di Toscana

1990   *Romeo and Juliet* (mus. Prokofiev), Geneva Ballet, Geneva

Carmina Burana (mus. Orff), Göteborg Ballet, Sweden

1991   *Picasso and Matisse* (including revised version of *Miniatures*; mus. Stravinsky), Göteborg Ballet, Sweden

1992   *A Stranger I Came* (mus. Schubert), English National Ballet, Cambridge

The Heat (duet; mus. Gabriel), Covent Garden Gala, London

Other works include: for Spiral Dance—*Time after Time*; for Workcentrum—*Just a Moment*; for Extempory Dance—*Sometimes*.

PUBLICATIONS

By North:

Interview with Easton, Penelope, "North comes to the North-West", *Arts Alive Merseyside* (Liverpool), April 1981

"Trends in British Ballet: Discussion with Robert Cohan, Norman Morrice and Robert North", *Ballett International* (Cologne), October 1983

About North:

Goodwin, Noël, and Williams, Peter, "Rambert at the Roundhouse", *Dance and Dancers* (London), June 1975

Brinson, Peter, and Crisp, Clement, *The Pan Book of Ballet and Dance*, London, 1980

Cowan, John, "Rambert Rediscovered", *Dance and Dancers* (London), July 1982

Whitney, Mary, "Proud Export", *Ballet News* (New York), October 1982

Clarke, Mary, "Rambert at the Wells", *Dancing Times* (London), May 1984

Macaulay, Alastair, "The Rambertians", *Dancing Times* (London), May 1985

Constanti, Sophie, "Ballet Rambert", *Dance Theatre Journal* (London), Summer 1985

*   *   *

"I'm fed up with people explaining that their dance works are based on linear concepts or the quantum theory." There is nothing abstract about Robert North, dubbed "the thinking man's dancer". Hard-edged, unsentimental, sexy, eclectic, North is both a great performer and an accomplished choreographer. He has worked for the theatre—choreographing for the Royal Shakespeare Company and for the Prospect Theatre Company—and for the cinema, for example in the film *Slow Dancing in the Big City*. Three ballets from the 1980s—*Death and the Maiden*, *Pribaoutki*, and *Colour Moves*—show him at his best.

One of the most characteristic features of North's work is its musicality. He draws on both modern and classical composers, for example, Schubert (*Songs and Dances* and *Death and the Maiden*), Stravinsky (*Pribaoutki* and *Light and Shade*), Howard Blake (*Meeting and Parting*), Christopher Benstead (*Colour Moves*), and Bill Withers (*Lonely Town, Lonely Street*). What seems to attract North to the scores he uses is their *presence*: whether through dynamic qualities or instrumental textures, the music in his dances is never relegated to the background. In his more recent work, this has led North to use various forms of popular music, but always music that is rhythmically striking, adding tonal colour to his dances. North's background in theatre design (he was an art student before studying at the Royal Ballet School) is also evident in his pieces. In *Colour Moves*, North uses colour structures as designed by Bridget Riley in a series of exquisite cloths set against the sequence of the complementary and contrasting costumes of the dancers. The colours literally change on stage in front of the viewer's eyes through optical association. North has created a fast-flowing rationale of movement to reflect the structure. The dancing reflects the tonal colours of the music in a satisfying blend of light and movement. Collaboration with painters, film-makers, and other dancers (including Wayne Sleep and Lynn Seymour) is a hallmark of North's work.

Martha Graham once called North "the choreographer of the soul", attributing to him "the kind of searching choreography that was reminiscent of Antony Tudor's masterpieces". Astringent, disciplined, purposeful, North's choreography seems above all peculiarly and distinctively American. As Bryan Robertson says, "If much modern American prose comes from the Bible, mixed with the stresses and free-flow inflexions of jazz, then modern dance comes initially from a specifically American sense of movement—and of course a uniquely American sense of *space* and its occupancy". North himself claims: "In America more than here it is the thing to be aggressively energetic. It probably relates back to the American pioneering spirit symbolized by the male." Fluid and unrestrained, unerringly classical, the sharp energy of *Troy*

Game, or the raw aggressiveness of *Lonely Town, Lonely Street* are characteristic of the sometimes threateningly unmediated violent confrontations of North's work. "Dancing hits you visually, but primarily it has to hit you physically."

As a dancer, North is also an impressive actor, effortlessly assuming different personalities on stage. This chameleon quality is there in his choice of dance styles as well, which are surprisingly eclectic: jazz, tap-dance, flamenco, integrated with classical ballet and modern dance vocabulary. The characteristic "catwalks, heat, boogie rhythms and bomber jackets, the twilight urban beat, the stylized clichés, and the tender toughness" of *Lonely Town, Lonely Street* have led some critics to see North's choreography as "high-class disco" rather than real dance. But this is to misread North's elaborate thinking for the stage. There are few concessions behind the brilliant style, and none of the affectations of some kinds of modern choreography. Perhaps North himself should have the last word: "25 years ago some people came along and said we don't need music, we can just throw sticks on stage and crack eggs and hop around ... All art forms have gone through rarefied periods, but to revitalize themselves they must push back to the popular arena."

—C. Sandra Kemp

NOVERRE, Jean-Georges

French dancer, choreographer, ballet director, teacher, and theorist. Born in Paris, 29 April 1727. Studied with Marcel, from c.1740; later studied with Louis Dupré. Married actress Marie-Louise Sauveur (met in Strasbourg, c.1749). Début probably in company directed by Dupré and Jean-Barthélemy Lany, Opéra-Comique, Paris, 1743, appearing at Fontainebleau later the same year; dancer, under Lany, Berlin, 1944; ballet master at either Marseilles or Strasbourg, staging *Les Fêtes chinoises,* c.1748; principal dancer, Lyons, from 1750, staging pantomime ballet *Le Jugement de Pâris,* 1751; choreographer, Strasbourg, 1753–54, and Opéra-Comique, Paris, 1754–55; choreographer and director of own troupe, Drury Lane Theatre, London, seasons 1755–56 and 1756–57; ballet master, Opéra, Lyons, 1757–60, Württemberg Court, Stuttgart, 1760–66, Imperial Theatres, Vienna, 1767–74, and Teatro Reggio, Milan, 1774–76, returning to direct own troupe at Kärntnertor Theater, Vienna, 1776; ballet master, Opéra, Paris, 1776–81, supposedly resigning as result of political intrigues (organized by rivals Maximilian Gardel and Jean Dauberval), 1779; ballet master, directing own troupe of French dancers, King's Theatre, London, 1781–82; retired in 1782, returning to revive earlier works at Lyons, 1787, and London, 1787–89 and 1793–94; retired to St. Germain-en-Laye; writer and theorist on dance, publishing *Lettres sur la danse et sur les ballets,* 1760 (enlarged 1803), and numerous prefaces to own stage works. Died in St. Germain-en-Laye, 19 October 1810.

WORKS

c.1748 *Les Fêtes chinoises* (also called *Les Métamorphoses chinoises, Ballet chinois),* Marseilles or Strasbourg (staged Paris Opéra-Comique, 1954; Drury Lane, London, 1755)
1751 *Le Jugement de Pâris,* Opéra, Lyons (probably staged Marseilles, same year)

Jean-Georges Noverre, in a portrait by Jean-Baptiste Perronneau, 1764

1754 *Cythère assiégée* (in Favart's opera of same title; mus. Favart), Opéra-Comique, Paris
La Fontaine de jouvence, Opéra-Comique, Paris
1755 *Les Matelots,* Opéra-Comique, Paris
Les Réjouissances flamandes, Opéra-Comique, Paris
La Provencale (divertissement), Drury Lane, London
The Lilliputian Sailors (divertissement), Drury Lane, London
1758? *La Toilette de Vénus; ou, Les Ruses de l'amour* (mus. Granier), Opéra, Lyons
1758 *Les Caprices de Galathée* (mus. Granier), Opéra, Lyons
L'Impromptu du sentiment (mus. probably Granier), Opéra, Lyons
Les Jalousies; ou, Les Fêtes du serail (also *Les Cinq Soltanes;* mus. Granier), Opéra, Lyons
1758/ *L'Amour corsaire, ou, L'Embarquement pour Cythère* 59 (mus. Granier), Opéra, Lyons
1758/ *Le Bal paré,* Opéra, Lyons
60 *La Descente d'Orphée aux enfers,* Opéra, Lyons
Les Fêtes du Vauxhall, Opéra, Lyons
La Mariée du village, Opéra, Lyons
La Mort d'Ajax, Opéra, Lyons
Les Recrues prussiennes, Opéra, Lyons
Renaud et Armide, Opéra, Lyons (new versions 1761, 1775, 1782)
1759 *Le Jaloux sans rival,* Opéra, Lyons
1760/ *Alexandre* (mus. Deller), Hoftheater, Stuttgart
66 *Les Amours d'Enée et Didon,* Hoftheater, Stuttgart (probably revised, with music by Starzer, 1768/73, Burgtheater, Vienna)
Les Amours de Henry IV (also *Idée d'un ballet héroïque tiré de la Henriade),* Hoftheater, Stuttgart
Antoine et Cléopatre, Hoftheater, Stuttgart
Ballet hongrois, Hoftheater, Stuttgart

Don Quichotte, Hoftheater, Stuttgart (revised, with mus. Starzer, Vienna, 1768; probably revised, as *Die Aufnahme der Sancho Panza,* 1773)

Enée et Lavinie (mus. Deller), Hoftheater, Stuttgart

Pyrrhus et Polixène, Hoftheater, Stuttgart

Le Temple du bonheur, Hoftheater, Stuttgart

1761 *Admète et Alceste* (also *Alceste,* or *Le Triomphe de l'amour conjugal;* mus. Deller), Hoftheater, Stuttgart

Amors Sieg über die Kaltsinnigkeit (interpolated into Jomelli's *Isola disabitatta*), Ludwigsburg

Die Unverhoffte Zusammwnkunft (interpolated into Jomelli's *Isola disabitatta*), Ludwigsburg

1761/ *Diane et Endimion,* first staged either Hoftheater,
65   Stuttgart, or in Ludwigsburg

1762 *La mort d'Hercule* (*L'Apothéose d'Hercule;* mus. Rodolphe), Hoftheater, Stuttgart

Psyché et l'amour (mus. Rodolphe), Hoftheater, Stuttgart

Le Feste persiane (also *Balletto persiano,* or *L'Épouse persane;* mus. Rodolphe), Hoftheater, Stuttgart

1763 *Médée et Jason* (mus. Rodolphe), Hoftheater, Stuttgart

Orpheus und Eurydice (mus. Deller), Hoftheater, Stuttgart

Der Sieg des Neptuns (mus. Deller), Hoftheater, Stuttgart

Le Triomphe de l'amour (divertissement in Jommelli's opera by the same name), Palais de la Magnifique, Ludwigsburg

1764 *Hypermnestra* (*Les Danaïdes; ou, Hypermnestre;* mus. Rodolphe or Deller), Hoftheater, Stuttgart (restaged Ludwigsburg, 1765)

Der Tod des Lykomedes (mus. probably Deller), Hoftheater, Stuttgart

Atalanta ed Ippomene, Hoftheater, Stuttgart

1766 *Das Fest des Hymenäos* (*Les Fêtes de l'hymen;* mus. Deller), Ludwigsburg

Der Raub der Proserpina (*L'Enlèvement de Proserpine;* mus. Renaud), Ludwigsburg

1767 *Alceste* (opera by Gluck; grotesque ballet by Noverre), Burgtheater, Vienna

Pyramus und Thisbe (mus. Starzer), Burgtheater, Vienna

1767/ *Der Schiffbruch,* Vienna
68

1768 *Les Petits Riens* (mus. Aspelmayr), Kärntnertor-Theater, Vienna

Bagatelle, Vienna

Die Kleinen Weinleser, Vienna

Thelmire (possibly *Thémire*), Vienna

Die Wohltätige Fee (mus. Starzer), Burgtheater, Vienna

1768/ *Das Strassburghische Fest* (*Les Aventures champêtres;*
73   mus. Starzer), Burgtheater, Vienna

Les Grâces, Vienna

1768/ *Balla del amore* (mus. Starzer), Burgtheater, Vienna
74   (possibly revised as *Amore nascosto sotto i fiori,* Milan, 1776)

Castor et Pollux, Vienna

Flora (mus. Aspelmayr), Kärntnertor Theater, Vienna

La Foire du Caire, Vienna

1770 Ballets in *Paride ed Elena* (opera; mus. Gluck), Burgtheater, Vienna

Die Schnitter (*Les Moissonneurs*), Burgtheater, Vienna

1771/ *Der Gerächte Agamemnon* (*Agamemnon vengé;* mus.
72   Aspelmayr), Vienna

Die Wäscherinnen van Cythere (*La Lavandaras di Citera;* mus. Aspelmayr), Burgtheater, Vienna

Die Quelle der Schönheit und der Hässlichkeit, Burgtheater, Vienna

Roger et Bradamante (mus. Starzer), Burgtheater, Vienna

1772 *Iphigénie en Tauride* (mus. Aspelmayr), Vienna

Le Mariage double, Burgtheater, Vienna

La Statua animata (*Pygmalion;* mus. Starzer), Burgtheater, Vienna

Thésée; ou, La Noce précoce, Burgtheater, Vienna

Chinesische Hochzeitfeyerlichkeit auf der Redoute, Vienna

1773 *Vénus et Adonis,* Burgtheater, Vienna

Die Vestalin (mus. Starzer), Burgtheater, Vienna

Apelles et Campaspe; ou, Le Triomphe d'Alexandre (*La Generosité d'Alexandre;* mus. Aspelmayr), Vienna

Die Aufnahme der Sancho Panza in der Insel Barataria (probably a version of *Don Quichotte*), Kärntnertor Theater, Vienna

Adele de Ponthieu (mus. Starzer), Burgtheater, Vienna

Acis et Galathée (mus. Aspelmayr), Burgtheater, Vienna

Die Italienische Schaefer (mus. Starzer), Burgtheater, Vienna

Der Schaefer Gattung (*L'Union des bergères*), Burgtheater, Vienna

Das unterbrochene Gluck (*La Joie interrompue;* mus. Starzer), Burgtheater, Vienna

Les Amours de Vénus; ou, La Vengeance de Vulcain, Burgtheater, Vienna

Euthyme et Eucharis, Burgtheater, Vienna

1774 *Les Horaces et les Curiaces* (mus. Starzer), Kärntnertor Theater, Vienna

Ballo delle Pastorelle di Tempe, Teatro Regio, Milan (possibly revised as *Les Fêtes de Tempe,* 1788)

1775 *Festa di villaggio* (mus. L. de Baillou), Teatro Regio, Milan

Rinaldo e Armida (new version of *Renaud et Armide,* c.1760 and 1761), Teatro Regio, Milan

Le Premier Âge de l'innocence; ou, La Rosière de Salency (mus. de Baillou), Teatro Regio, Milan

Les Incidents: Conte (*Gl'incidente: Novella*), Teatro Regio, Milan

1776 *La Nuova Sposa persiana* (mus. de Baillou), Teatro Regio, Milan

Amore nascosto sotto i fiori (perhaps same ballet as *Ballo del amore*), Teatro Regio, Milan

Weiss und Rosenfarb, Kärntnertor Theater, Vienna

1777 Ballets (including *Les Jeux de la Grèce* and *La Fête d'Achille*) in *Iphigénie en Aulide* (opera; mus. Gluck), Opéra, Paris

Ballets in *Armide* (opera; mus. Gluck), Opéra, Paris

1778 Ballets in *Roland* (opera; mus. Piccini), Opéra, Paris

Annette et Lubin, Opéra, Paris

Les Petits Riens (mus. Mozart), Opéra, Paris

Les Fêtes de Tempe (revision of *Ballo delle pastorelle di Tempe,* 1774), Opéra, Paris

1779 Ballets (including *Danse de Scythes* and *Danse des Eumenides*) in *Iphigénie en Tauride* (opera; mus. Gluck), Opéra, Paris

Les Scythes enchaînés (mus. Gossec), Opéra, Paris (conclusion to *Iphigénie en Tauride*)

Ballets in *Echo et Narcisse* (opera; mus. Gluck), Opéra, Paris

1780 Ballets in *Le Seigneur bienfaisant* (opera; mus. Floquet), Opéra, Paris

Les Fêtes de Gamache (with Dauberval; mus. Montreuil), Opéra, Paris

1781 *Les Amans réunis,* King's Theatre, London

A Divertissement Dance, King's Theatre, London

1782 *The Prince of Wales Minuet, Quadrilles,* The Queen's

Allemande, The Emperor's Cossack, for Masked Ball at King's Theatre, London
Rinaldo and Armida (new version of *Renaud et Armide,* c. 1760; new mus. Le Brun), King's Theatre, London
Apollon et les muses, King's Theatre, London
New Dance, King's Theatre, London
1787 *Les Offrandes à l'amour* (mus. Mazzinghi), King's Theatre, London
1788 *L'Amour et Psyche* (new version of *Psyche et l'amour;* new mus. Mazzinghi), King's Theatre, London
New Dance, King's Theatre, London
Les Fêtes de Tempe (possibly new version of *Ballo delle pastorale di Tempe;* mus. Mazzinghi), King's Theatre, London
New Ballet, King's Theatre, London
1789 *Les Fêtes provençales,* King's Theatre, London
A New Divertissement, King's Theatre, London
Admete (new version of *Admete et Alceste;* new mus. Mazzinghi), King's Theatre, London
1793 *Les Époux du Tempe,* King's Theatre, London
Le Faune infidèle, King's Theatre, London
Iphigénia in Aulide; or, The Sacrifice of Iphigenia (mus. Miller), King's Theatre, London
1794 *A New Divertissement* (mus. Miller), King's Theatre, London
Adélaïde; ou, La Bergère des Alpes (mus. Miller), King's Theatre, London
Ballets in *Don Giovanni* (pasticcio; mus. Mozart, Gazzaniga), King's Theatre, London
New Divertissement, King's Theatre, London
Allegorical Ballet in *La Vittoria* (mus. Paisello), King's Theatre, London
Les Ruses de l'amour (after earlier production; new mus. Miller), King's Theatre, London
1795 *The Marriage of Peleus and Thetis,* for the marriage of the Prince and Princess of Wales

PUBLICATIONS

By Noverre:
Lettres sur la danse et sur les ballets, Lyons and Stuttgart, 1760
Introduction au Ballet des Horaces . . . ou Petite Réponse aux grands lettres du Sr. Angiolini, Vienna, 1774
Lettres sur la danse, sur les ballets et les arts, revised and enlarged edition of 1760 *Lettres,* St. Petersburg, 1803; as *Letters on Dancing and on Ballets,* translated by Cyril Beaumont, London, 1930
Lettres sur les arts imitateurs en général et sur la danse en particulier, Paris and La Haye, 1807

About Noverre:
Angiolini, Gaspero, *Lettere a Monsieur Noverre sopra i balli pantomimi,* Milan, 1773
Grimm, Diderot, et al., *Correspondence littéraire, philosophique et critique,* Paris, 1879
Campardon, Émile, *L'Académie royale de musique,* Paris, 1881
Kirstein, Lincoln, *Dance: A Short History of Classic Theatrical Dancing,* New York, 1935
Moore, Lillian, *Artists of the Dance,* New York, 1938
Lynham, Deryck, *The Chevalier Noverre: Father of Modern Ballet,* London, 1950
Tugal, P., *Jean-Georges Noverre der Grosse Reformator des Tanzes,* Berlin, 1959
Garrick, David, *Letters,* edited by D.M. Little and G.M. Kahrl, Cambridge, Massachusetts, 1963
Kirstein, Lincoln, *Movement and Metaphor: Four Centuries of Ballet,* New York, 1970
Winter, Marian Hannah, *The Pre-Romantic Ballet,* London, 1974
Sorrell, Walter, *Dance in its Time* New York, 1981
Chazin-Bennahum, Judith, "Cahusac, Diderot, and Noverre: Three Revolutionary Writers on the 18th-century Dance", *Theatre Journal* (Baltimore), May 1983
Carones, Laura, "Noverre and Angiolini: Polemical Letters", *Dance Research* (London), Spring 1987

* * *

Jean-Georges Noverre, author of *Lettres sur la danse* and choreographer of over 150 ballets, is often credited with the development of the *ballet en action* (*ballet d'action*), or pantomime ballet in France. He occupies a unique niche in the history of dance as the only choreographer whose works have not been performed for almost two centuries, yet whose fame amongst ballet lovers increases steadily. Noverre studied with the great Dupré, and, under his auspices, most likely made his stage début in Favart's *Le Coq au village* at the Opéra-Comique, making his court début at Fontainebleau, dancing a minuet. He danced in *Armino* at the Berlin opera in 1745 under Lany. His rather lacklustre career as a dancer was cut short several years later due to injury.

Noverre's choreographic career can be divided into three distinct creative periods. The first, dating from 1747 when he probably became ballet master at Marseilles, is characterized by experimentation. 1748 is the most likely year for the first staging of one of his most famous works, *Les Fêtes chinoises.* Noverre utilized lavish staging devices, and enchanted the audience with the rich creative imagination that was to mark his best theatrical works. He held appointments at Strasbourg and Lyons until he returned to the Opéra-Comique in Paris as ballet master. Noverre achieved great celebrity with *La Fontaine de jouvence,* in which processions of shepherds alternated with song and poetry until the final contredanse. Noverre anticipated the direction of his later *ballets en action* in a dramatic section where two old men grow youthful and "dance a pantomime".

The second phase began in London, where Noverre was engaged at the Drury Lane Theatre (1755–57). He was forced into hiding when rioting patrons sought to oust all French dancers, but he turned enforced idleness into a time to examine new possibilities for the dance. He had been impressed by the realism of English actors, in particular David Garrick, and he attempted to graft this model on to the French style of ballet. In his *Lettres sur la danse,* perhaps the most influential book about dance ever written, Noverre argued in favour of pantomime's pre-eminence as compared to dance divertissement. His book, couched in the form of fifteen letters on various themes, was translated and distributed throughout Europe only a few years after its publication date of 1760. Noverre advised aspiring choreographers to direct their dancers to "express an emotion or contribute to form a picture"; he urged dancers to abandon masks or cumbersome costumes, and "renounce *cabrioles, entrechats,* and over-complicated steps".

Noverre's ballets at this time dove-tail neatly with his theory of dramatic action achieved through expressive gestures and his advocacy of the heroic or tragic genres. An early example is *La Toilette de Vénus.* Here, the choreographer sharply delineates the pantomime and processions from the danced finale of a Chaconne. Only at the end of the ballet, as Grimm pointed out years later, would Noverre allow "dance for dancing's sake". His years at the Lyons Opera were highly productive: from 1757 to 1760, he produced thirteen original ballets.

Stuttgart was the scene of his most famous work, the tragic

Médée et Jason, which frightened audiences with its violence. Gaetano Vestris played Jason, and then staged the ballet at the Paris Opéra. Noverre's fame spread as dozens of his disciples (but never Dauberval) copied his ballets in Italy, Portugal, England, and Russia.

Some of Noverre's greatest triumphs came when he was appointed dancing master to the royal family and maître de ballet to the double opera houses of Vienna. From 1767–74, he staged 38 new ballets (notably *Agamemnon vengé* and *Apelles et Campaspe*), revived many others, and choreographed opera divertissements, including Gluck's *Alceste.*

The third phase of Noverre's career began around 1774 when he was engaged at the Teatro Reggio Ducal in Milan. He returned to writing in a series of exchanges with Angiolini, who challenged Noverre's position as originator of the *ballets en action.* Noverre eventually admitted insurmountable "barriers" to pantomime's dominant role as he first conceived it. Dance, he conceded, was the basis of ballet and should be honoured as such, even if it provides "mere" pleasure and diversion. His ballets, too, shifted focus. Noverre offered fewer tragic ballets, and choreographed pastorales or frolics. The Milanese audience stopped booing or laughing aloud at his works, and responded by praising Noverre's exquisite taste and imagination.

In 1776 Noverre achieved his life's ambition: Marie Antoinette became Queen of France and intervened to appoint her old teacher as the maître de ballet of the Paris Opéra. His contract reveals, however, the administration's concerns about his reputed extravagance, antagonistic attitudes, and intransigence. He was required to submit production plans for prior review, which were then turned down. His troubles multiplied as Gardel and Dauberval, to whom the post traditionally would have gone, joined together to force out the "foreigner". The handful of new ballets that Noverre then choreographed proved of little consequence, and were indifferently performed and received.

Noverre's appointment may have come too late: many reforms he advocated in his *Lettres* had already been accomplished. Even his famous *Médée and Jason* had been staged several times at the Opéra. Both Bournonville and Grimm testified that Noverre's ballets, especially the heroic and tragic, were outmoded; tastes had changed since his initial triumphs at the Opéra-Comique 25 years ago. What had been the long-dreamed-of day of vindication turned instead to one of mortifying failure, which Noverre excused by strident accusations of "poisoned arrows of jealousy and calumny".

Not long after his resignation was accepted in 1781 (he submitted it in 1779), Noverre left for London. The years in London at the King's Theatre were characterized by revivals or new entertainments that recalled earlier successes. His *Marriage of Peleus and Thetis,* perhaps his last ballet, was a court spectacle devised for the 1795 wedding of the Prince and Princess of Wales. It depicted heroic characters, such as Cupid and Terpsichore, who marched about the stage and formed beautiful poses. The final scene "is diversified by dancing, to celebrate a UNION on which the NATION's affection naturally rests". Noverre left soon after to return to France. He retired to prepare a new edition of his *Lettres,* which his devoted disciple Le Picq arranged to have published in St. Petersburg.

Noverre's choreographic genius was partially attributable to a highly visual imagination. His presentation was painterly in its use of graduated colours for costumes (rather than one shade for the entire corps) and clever use of perspective (so that small dancers were placed at the back of the stage rather than the front). It is not surprising that Grimm compared his work to that of Boucher or Tenniers, two great rococo painters of that time.

Noverre's actual ballets are forgotten today, but he is still extremely well known as a reformer of the ballet. He was a vociferous advocate of the *ballet en action,* although other choreographers, from Sallé to Hilverding, contributed to its emergence. Noverre, never one for false modesty, was more than aware of the importance of his contributions: "The glory of my art, my age, and my numerous brilliant successes, permit me to state that I have achieved a revolution in dancing as striking and as lasting as that achieved by Gluck in the realm of music." Far more influential than his choreography, Noverre's writings established a place of honour for dramatic ballet as a fully-fledged art form independent of its ancillary use as divertissement for opera.

—Maureen Needham Costonis

NUREYEV, Rudolf

Russian dancer, choreographer, and ballet director. Born Rudolf Hametovich Nureyev on trans-Siberian train, near Irkutsk, 17 March 1938. Studied folk dance and ballet in Ufa, and later at the Leningrad Choreographic School (now the Vaganova School), pupil of Aleksandr Pushkin, 1955–58. Dancer, corps de ballet, Ufa, 1955; début with Kirov Ballet while still a student; soloist, Kirov Ballet, 1958–61; defected to the West while in Paris, 1961: principal dancer, Grand Ballet du Marquis de Cuevas, 1961–62; permanent guest artist, Royal Ballet, London, 1962–77; international guest artist and choreographer, performing and staging ballets for companies including Vienna State Opera Ballet, Australian Ballet, London Festival Ballet, Ballet of La Scala in Milan, Royal Danish Ballet, Royal Swedish Ballet, Dutch National Ballet, Ballet du XXe Siècle, and many others; performer with several modern dance companies, including Paul Taylor Company and Martha Graham Company; return visit to Russia, performing at Kirov Theatre, 1989; appeared on television and in numerous films, including *An Evening with the Royal Ballet* (1963), *Romeo and Juliet* (chor. MacMillan; 1966), *Le Jeune Homme et la mort* (chor. Petit; 1966), *I am a Dancer* (1972), *Don Quixote* (own staging, after Petipa; 1972), and in acting roles in Hollywood films *Valentino* (dir. Russell, 1977) and *Exposed* (dir. Toback, 1983); director, principal dancer, and choreographer, "Nureyev and Friends", first performing on Broadway, New York, 1974–75; also stage actor, appearing in *The King and I* (musical by Rodgers and Hammerstein), U.S. tour 1989; artistic director, Paris Opéra Ballet, 1983–89; also made guest appearances as orchestral conductor, 1991. Recipient: *Dance Magazine* Award, 1973; Prix Marius Petipa, 1973; Medaille de Vermeil de la Ville de Paris, 1978; Queen Elizabeth II Coronation Award of the Royal Academy of Dancing, London, 1984; Chevalier de la Légion d'honneur, France, 1987; Commandeur de l'Ordre des Arts et des Lettres, France, 1991. Died in Paris, 6 January 1993.

ROLES

1957   The Prince in *The Nutcracker* (Vainonen), Kirov Ballet, Leningrad
        Pas de trois in *Swan Lake* (Petipa), Kirov Ballet, Leningrad
1958   Pas de deux from *Le Corsaire* (Chabukiani after Petipa), Moscow Ballet Competition, Moscow

Rudolf Nureyev as The Man in Roland Petit's *Paradise Lost*, **London, 1967**

"Diana and Acteon" Pas de deux from *Esmeralda* (Vaganova after Petipa), Moscow Ballet Competition, Moscow

Kurdish Dance from *Gayané* (Anisimova), Moscow Ballet Competition, Moscow

Frodoso in *Laurencia* (Chabukiani), Kirov Ballet, Leningrad

Pas de quatre in *The Red Poppy* (Zakharov), Kirov Ballet Leningrad

1959/ Basilio in *Don Quixote* (after Petipa, Gorsky), Kirov
60 Ballet, Leningrad

Albrecht in *Giselle* (Petipa after Coralli, Perrot), Kirov Ballet, Leningrad

Bluebird in *The Sleeping Beauty* (K. Sergeyev after Petipa), Kirov Ballet, Leningrad

Pas de quatre in *Raymonda* (K. Sergeyev after Petipa), Kirov Ballet, Leningrad

Armen in *Gayané* (Anisimova), Kirov Ballet, Leningrad

Principal dancer in *Muskovsky Waltz* (Vainonen), Kirov Ballet, Leningrad

1960/ Pas de deux from *The Flames of Paris* (Vainonen), Kirov
61 Ballet, Leningrad

Principal dancer (cr) in *Waltz* (Yakobson), Kirov Ballet, Leningrad

Prince Siegfried in *Swan Lake* (K. Sergeyev after Petipa, Ivanov), Kirov Ballet, Leningrad

Prince Désiré in *The Sleeping Beauty* (K. Sergeyev after Petipa), Kirov Ballet, Leningrad

1961 Title role in *Le Spectre de la rose* (after Fokine), television broadcast, Frankfurt

The Bluebird in *The Sleeping Beauty* (Nijinska, Helpmann after Petipa), Grand Ballet du Marquis de Cuevas, Paris

Principal dancer (cr) in *Poème tragique* (Ashton), Royal Academy of Dancing Gala, London

1962 Colas in *La Fille mal gardée* (Lazzini), Ballet de Marseille, Marseilles

Principal dancer (cr) in *Toccata and Fugue* (Bruhn), Nureyev/Bruhn Concert, Cannes

Principal dancer (cr) in *Fantaisie* (Bruhn), Nureyev/Bruhn Concert, Cannes

Principal dancer in *Dances from Raymonda* (also chor., after Petipa), Nureyev/Bruhn Concert, Cannes

Pas de deux from *Flower Festival at Genzano* (Bournonville; staged Bruhn), Nureyev/Bruhn Concert, Paris

The Poet in *Les Sylphides* (Fokine), Royal Ballet, London

Dancer in *Grand Pas classique* (V. Gsovsky), Stuttgart Ballet Gala, Stuttgart

Polovtsian Warrior in *Prince Igor* (opera; mus. Borodin, chor. Page, Martinez after Fokine), Chicago Opera and Ballet, Chicago

Danilo in *The Merry Widow* (Page), Chicago Opera Ballet, Chicago

Principal dancer in *Theme and Variations* (Balanchine), American Ballet Theatre, Chicago

1963 Etiocles in *Antigone* (Cranko), Royal Ballet, London

Principal dancer in *Diversions* (MacMillan), Royal Ballet, on tour

Armand (cr) in *Marguerite and Armand* (Ashton), Royal Ballet, London

Title role in *Petrushka* (Fokine), Royal Ballet, London

Solor in *La Bayadère* ("Kingdom of the Shades" scene; also chor., after Petipa), Royal Ballet, London

Principal dancer (cr) in *Fantasia in G Minor* (MacMillan), Royal Academy of Dancing Gala, London

Principal dancer in *Laurencia* Pas de six (also chor.,

after Chabukiani), British television

1964 "Two Loves I have" (cr) in *Images of Love* (MacMillan), Royal Ballet, London

Title role in *Hamlet* (Helpmann), Royal Ballet, London

Principal dancer (cr) in *Divertimento* (MacMillan), Western Theatre Ballet Gala

Jean de Brienne (cr) in *Raymonda* (new production; also chor., after Petipa), Royal Ballet Touring Company, Spoleto, Italy

Prince Siegfried (cr) in *Swan Lake* (new production; also chor., after Petipa, Ivanov), Vienna State Opera Ballet, Vienna

1965 James in *La Sylphide* (Bournonville; staged Bruhn), National Ballet of Canada, Toronto

Romeo (cr) in *Romeo and Juliet* (MacMillan), Royal Ballet, London

1966 Title role in *Tancredi* (also chor.), Vienna State Opera Ballet, Vienna

Messenger of Death in *Song of the Earth* (MacMillan), Royal Ballet, London

Prince Florimund (cr) in *The Sleeping Beauty* (new production; also chor., after Petipa), Ballet of La Scala, Milan

Basil (cr) in *Don Quixote* (new production; also chor., after Petipa, Gorsky), Vienna State Opera Ballet, Vienna

1967 The Man (cr) in *Paradise Lost* (Petit), Royal Ballet, London

Title role in *Apollo* (Balanchine), Vienna State Opera Ballet, Vienna

1968 Friday's Child (cr) in *Jazz Calendar* (Ashton), Royal Ballet, London

Pas de deux, Solo (cr; added) in *A Birthday Offering* (Ashton), Royal Ballet, London

Oberon in *The Dream* (Ashton), Royal Ballet Touring Company, European tour

Man (cr) in *L'Estasi* (Petit), Ballet of La Scala, Milan

The Boy in *Monument for a Dead Boy* (van Dantzig), Dutch National Ballet

1969 Pélléas in *Pélléas and Mélisande* (Petit), Royal Ballet, London

1970 The Traveller (cr) in *The Ropes of Time* (van Dantzig), Royal Ballet, London

Variation/Adagio of Lovers in *Les Rendezvous* (Ashton), Ashton Gala, Royal Ballet, London

The Poet in *Apparitions* (Ballroom Scene only; Ashton), Ashton Gala, Royal Ballet, London

Principal dancer in *Dances at a Gathering* (Robbins), Royal Ballet, London

Principal dancer (cr) in *Big Bertha* (pre-stage version; Taylor), Paul Taylor Dance Company, New York television

1971 Young man (cr) in *Song of a Wayfarer* (Béjart), Ballet du XXe Siècle, Brussels

The Chosen in *Le Sacre du printemps* (Béjart), Ballet du XXe Siècle, Brussels

Principal dancer in *Field Figures* (Tetley), Royal Ballet, London

First Red Knight in *Checkmate* (de Valois), Royal Ballet, London

1972 Principal dancer in *Afternoon of a Faun* (Robbins), Royal Ballet, London

Principal dancer in *Aureole* (Taylor), Paul Taylor Dance Company, Mexico City

Illuminations in *Book of Beasts* (Taylor), Paul Taylor Dance Company, Mexico City

Principal dancer (cr) in *Laborintus* (Tetley), Royal

Ballet, London

Principal dancer (cr) in *Sideshow* (MacMillan), Royal Ballet, Liverpool

The Moor in *Moor's Pavane* (Limón), National Ballet of Canada, Toronto

1973 Title role in *Prodigal Son* (Balanchine), Royal Ballet, London

Sarabande in *Agon* (Balanchine), Royal Ballet, London

1974 Title role in *Don Juan* (Neumeier), National Ballet of Canada, tour

Colas in *La Fille mal gardée* (Ashton), Royal Ballet, New York

Des Grieux in *Manon* (MacMillan), Royal Ballet, New York

Title role (cr) in *Tristan* (Tetley), Paris Opéra Ballet, Paris

1975 Franz in *Coppélia* (Bruhn after Saint-Léon), National Ballet of Canada, London

Title role (cr) in *Lucifer* (Graham), Martha Graham Dance Company, New York

Principal dancer (cr) in *Moments* (Louis), Scottish Ballet, Madrid

The Man in *Sonate à trois* (Béjart), Scottish Ballet, Madrid

The Teacher in *The Lesson* (Flindt), Scottish Ballet, Madrid

The Man (cr) in *Blown in a Gentle Wind* (van Dantzig), Amsterdam

The Revivalist in *Appalachian Spring* (Graham), Martha Graham Dance Company, New York

Oedipus in *Night Journey* (Graham), Martha Graham Dance Company, New York

Dimmesdale (cr) in *The Scarlet Letter* (Graham), Martha Graham Dance Company, New York

1976 Principal dancer in *Four Schumann Pieces* (van Manen), National Ballet of Canada, New York

1977 Title role in *Pierrot Lunaire* (Tetley), Royal Danish Ballet, Copenhagen

Title role in *El Penitente* (Graham), Martha Graham Dance Company, New York

Hamlet (cr) in *Hamlet Prelude* (Ashton), Silver Jubilee of Queen Elizabeth II, Covent Garden Gala, London

Romeo (cr) in *Romeo and Juliet* (also chor.), London Festival Ballet, London

Pas de deux from *The Toreador* (Bournonville staged Flindt), Nureyev and Company, London

1978 Title role (cr) in *Faun* (van Schayk), Dutch National Ballet, Amsterdam

Principal dancer (cr) in *About a Dark House* (van Dantzig), Dutch National Ballet, Amsterdam

Dancer (cr) in *Vivace* (solo; Louis), Nureyev Festival, New York

The Gentleman (cr) in *The Canarsie Venus* (also *The Brighton Venus*; Louis), Murray Louis Dance Company, New York

Principal dancer in *Conservatoire* (*Konservatoriet*; Bournonville; staged Vangsaae), London Festival Ballet, New York

The Golden Slave in *Schéhérazade* (Fokine), London Festival Ballet, New York

1979 Title role (cr) in *Ulysses* (van Dantzig), Vienna State Opera Ballet, Vienna

Cléonte (cr) in *Le Bourgeois Gentilhomme* (new version; Balanchine, Robbins), New York City Opera with students of School of American Ballet, New York

Faun in *L'Après-midi d'un faune* (after Nijinsky), Joffrey Ballet, New York

1980 Prince Myshkin in *The Idiot* (Panov), German Opera Ballet, Berlin

Jean, the Butler in *Miss Julie* (Cullberg), German Opera Ballet, Berlin

Principal dancer in *Five Tangos* (van Manen), German Opera Ballet, Berlin

1981 Title role (cr) in *Marco Spada* (Lacotte), Rome Opera Ballet, Rome

1982 The Ballet Master in *Konservatoriet* (Bournonville), Royal Ballet, London

Prospero in *The Tempest* (also chor.), Royal Ballet, London

1983 Quasimodo in *Notre-Dame de Paris* (Petit), Ballet de Marseille, New York

1984 Title role in *Harlequin, Magician of Love* (Cramér), Paris Opéra Ballet, Paris

Principal dancer in *Bach Suite* (also chor., with Lancelot), Paris Opéra Ballet, Paris

Principal dancer in *Le Sacre du printemps* (Taylor), Paris Opéra Ballet, Paris

Principal dancer in *Violin Concerto* (Balanchine), Paris Opéra Ballet, Paris

Mercutio in *Romeo and Juliet* (also chor.), Paris Opéra Ballet, Paris

Hippolytus in *Phaedra's Dream* (Graham), New York State Theater, New York

1985 Prince Siegfried in *Swan Lake* (also chor., after Petipa, Ivanov), Paris Opéra Ballet, Paris

L'Amour in *Quelques Pas graves de Baptiste* (Lancelot), Paris Opéra Ballet, Paris

Dr. Sloper (cr) in *Washington Square* (also chor.), Paris Opéra Ballet, Paris

Drosselmeyer in *The Nutcracker* (also chor.), Paris Opéra Ballet, Paris

1986 M. Duléger in *La Dansomanie* (Cramér, Skeaping after Gardel), Paris Opéra Ballet, Paris

Title role in *Manfred* (also chor.), Paris Opéra Ballet, Paris

The Producer (cr) in *Cendrillon* (*Cinderella*; also chor.), Paris Opéra Ballet, Paris

1987 Principal dancer (cr) in *Two Brothers* (Ezralow, Parsons), Paris Opéra Ballet, Paris

1988 Title role in *Orpheus* (Balanchine), New York City Ballet, New York

Rothbart in *Swan Lake* (also chor., after Petipa, Ivanov), Paris Opéra Ballet, New York

1989 Akaky Akakyevich (cr) in *The Overcoat* (Flindt), Maggio Musicale, Florence

1990 Mercutio in *Romeo and Juliet* (MacMillan), Royal Ballet, London

Dr. Coppélius in *Coppélia* (Nahat), Cleveland/San José Ballet, Edinburgh

1991 Aschenbach (cr) in *Death in Venice* (Flindt), Verona Opera Ballet, Verona

WORKS

1966 *Tancredi* (mus. Henze), Vienna State Opera Ballet, Vienna

1977 *Romeo and Juliet* (mus. Prokofiev), London Festival Ballet, London (also staged La Scala, Milan, 1980; Paris Opéra Ballet, 1984)

1979 *Manfred* (mus. Tchaikovsky), Paris Opéra Ballet (also staged Zurich Ballet, 1981)

1982 *The Tempest* (mus. Tchaikovsky), Royal Ballet, London (also staged Paris Opéra Ballet, 1984)

1984 *Bach Suite* (with Lancelot; mus. Bach), Paris Opéra Ballet, Paris
1985 *Washington Square* (mus. Ives), Paris Opéra Ballet, Paris
1986 *Cendrillon* (*Cinderella*; mus. Prokofiev), Paris Opéra Ballet, Paris

Also staged:
1962 *Le Corsaire* Pas de deux (after Petipa; mus. Drigo, Minkus), Bell Telephone television programme, New York
   Gayané Pas de deux (after Anisimova; mus. Khachaturian), American Ballet Theatre, New York
1963 *La Bayadère* ("Kingdom of the Shades" scene; after Petipa, Chabukiani; mus. Minkus), Royal Ballet, London (also staged Paris Opéra Ballet, 1974)
   The Flames of Paris Pas de deux (after Vainonen; mus. Asafiev), Royal Academy of Dancing Gala, London
1964 *Raymonda* (after Petipa; mus Glazunov), Royal Ballet Touring Company, Spoleto (also staged for Australian Ballet, 1965; Zurich Ballet, 1972; American Ballet Theatre, 1975; Paris Opéra Ballet, 1983)
   Swan Lake (after Petipa, Ivanov; mus. Tchaikovsky), Vienna State Opera Ballet, Vienna (including additions made to Royal Ballet productions, 1962, 1963; also staged Paris Opéra Ballet, 1984; La Scala, Milan, 1990)
   Paquita Grand Pas (after Petipa; mus. Minkus), Royal Academy of Dancing Gala, London (also staged Vienna State Opera Ballet, 1971; American Ballet Theatre, 1971)
1965 *Laurencia* Pas de six (after Chabukiani; mus. Krien), Royal Ballet, London (first staged for television, 1963)
1966 *The Sleeping Beauty* (after Petipa; mus. Tchaikovsky), Ballet of La Scala, Milan (also staged National Ballet of Canada, 1972; London Festival Ballet, 1975; Vienna State Opera Ballet, 1980; German Opera Ballet, Berlin, 1992)
   Don Quixote (after Petipa; mus. Minkus, arranged Lanchbery), Vienna State Opera Ballet, Vienna (also staged Australian Ballet, 1970; Zurich Ballet, 1979; Paris Opéra Ballet, 1981; Peking Opera Ballet, 1985; Matsuyama Ballet, 1985)
1967 *The Nutcracker* (after Ivanov, Vainonen; mus. Tchaikovsky), Royal Swedish Ballet, Stockholm (also staged Royal Ballet, 1968; Teatro Colón, Buenos Aires, 1971; La Scala, Milan, 1971; German Opera Ballet, Berlin, 1979; Paris Opéra Ballet, 1985)
1992 *La Bayadère* (with Kourgapkina, after Petipa; mus. Minkus), Paris Opéra Ballet, Paris

PUBLICATIONS

By Nureyev:
Nureyev: An Autobiography with Pictures, edited by Alexander Bland, London, 1962; New York, 1964
Interview in Cruikshank, Judith, "Nureyev Looks Forward", *Dance and Dancers* (London), June 1982

About Nureyev:
Kersley, Leo, and Sinclair, Janet, "Nureyev", *Ballet Today* (London), June 1962
Saal, H., "Tartar of the Dance", *Newsweek* (New York), 19 April 1965
Geitel, K., *Der Tanzer Rudolf Nurejew*, Verlag, 1967

Fonteyn, Margot, *Margot Fonteyn: An Autobiography*, London, 1975
Vollmer, Jurgen (photographs) and Devere, John (text), *Nureyev in Paris: Le Jeune Homme et la mort*, New York, 1975
Percival, John, *Nureyev*, New York, 1975; London, 1976
Bland, Alexander, *The Nureyev Image*, London and New York, 1976
Bland, Alexander, *Fonteyn and Nureyev: The Story of a Partnership*, London, 1979
Bland, Alexander, *The Royal Ballet: The First Fifty Years*, London, 1981
Dupuis, Simone, "Noureev, 20 ans en France", *Les Saisons de la danse* (Paris), November 1981
Deletraz, François, "Ce qu'ils pensent de lui", *Les Saisons de la danse* (Paris), November 1981
Barnes, Clive, *Nureyev*, New York, 1982
"Rudolf Noureev" (various authors), special issue, *L'Avant-scène: Ballet/Danse* (Paris), 1983
Smakov, Gennady, *The Great Russian Dancers*, New York, 1984
Gruen, John, "The Force Still with Us", *Dance Magazine* (New York), July 1986
Sklarevskaya, I., "Nureyev at the Kirov", translated by R. Johnson, *Dance Magazine* (New York), May 1990

*   *   *

The extent of Rudolf Nureyev's influence cannot be overestimated. Probably no-one in the history of ballet has had a wider concept of ballet and dance or a more complete experience of its scope and variety. In the eighteenth and nineteenth centuries the great ballet masters worked in many different countries, so that tracing the careers, for instance, of Jean-Georges Noverre or Marius Petipa is a geographical exploration—but Nureyev has gone further, not only as a world traveller but also in terms of working in and studying forms of modern dance as well as classical ballet.

An outstanding theatrical personality of our time and in his prime a superb and exciting dancer, Nureyev caught world headlines in 1961 when he claimed political asylum in Paris while on tour there with the Kirov Ballet. He had already made his mark in the Soviet Union. A Tartar from Ufa in the Ural Mountains, he was a late starter in ballet, taking his first lessons at the age of eleven, and being admitted to the Leningrad Kirov school at the unusually late age of seventeen. By his final year he was recognized as an outstanding virtuoso talent, and was able to choose between offers from the Kirov, the Bolshoi, and the Stanislavsky companies. He chose the Kirov and within a year was dancing leading roles in *Don Quixote* and *Giselle*.

Marked out, therefore, for an important career at home, Nureyev took a decision to stay in the West that was motivated purely by his hunger for artistic freedom, his desire to work in any way that appealed to him in the theatre. It is now obvious that his instincts were right—had he stayed in Russia he would have been the prisoner of a narrow and conventional repertoire instead of being able to respond to a wide diversity of challenges.

Nureyev's London début at a Royal Academy of Dancing Gala, organized by Margot Fonteyn, led to an invitation from Dame Ninette de Valois to appear with the Royal Ballet at Covent Garden with Fonteyn in *Giselle* in February 1962. It was one of ballet's historic occasions—the beginning of an acclaimed partnership and the obvious introduction of a lively and positive new element into the life of the Royal Ballet. In the years to come, in London as well as in every company with which he was associated, Nureyev acted as a major stimulus and catalytic force. He disturbed the smooth ripples of many organizations, forcing artists to think seriously about themselves, and providing a standard of performance for young male dancers to emulate.

As time went on, he entered the production field, staging his own, always thought-provoking, versions of familiar classics like *Swan Lake*, *The Sleeping Beauty*, and *The Nutcracker*, and less familiar ballets like the "Kingdom of the Shades" from *La Bayadère* (for the Royal Ballet) and *Don Quixote* (for Vienna, and then the Australian Ballet). He tested himself in ballets by Royal Ballet choreographers—Frederick Ashton, Kenneth MacMillan, John Cranko—and gradually widened his range to include works by Rudi van Dantzig, Jerome Robbins, Maurice Béjart, Paul Taylor, and Martha Graham. Illuminating interpretations resulted—treasured memories include his lightly humorous touch in *Dances at a Gathering* (Robbins), his depth of feeling in *Song of a Wayfarer* (Béjart), his range of reaction in Balanchine's *Prodigal Son*, and his delicately delineated and intensely passionate Des Grieux in MacMillan's *Manon*.

Difficulties in working with Nureyev always existed, but they primarily reflected his perfectionism both where he himself and others are concerned. As Marcia Haydée said (quoted by John Percival in his biography of Nureyev): "I love working with Rudolf. He has the reputation of being difficult and complicated, but I suppose all artists are complicated and most of us can be difficult at times. . . . Anyone who does not work hard he has no time for. He made me do all sorts of things I thought I could not do and he was so helpful." He certainly offered the dance world an example of drive, dedication, broadmindedness, and audacity. John Percival aptly wrote, "All through his career he . . . forced himself to attempt difficult things", pointing out that he constantly widened his range both within and outside classical dancing.

During the years from 1983 to 1989, when Nureyev was artistic director of the Paris Opéra Ballet, his influence gave the company a more catholic repertoire and a higher reputation in the international field. In his personal career, he successfully tackled the role of the King of Siam in *The King and I*, and at last came to terms with the years in roles like Dr. Coppélius in *Coppélia* and the leading role, a 50-year-old bank clerk, in Flemming Flindt's ballet *The Overcoat*, both of which he danced for the Cleveland San José Ballet.

When Nureyev died in January 1993, it was not a great surprise, as he had been visibly ill for some time—but it was nevertheless an event which stunned and saddened the ballet community the world over. As controversial as he may have been at times in his life, there was no controversy in what dance critics and historians stated at his death: he changed the face of twentieth-century ballet, and his influence will never be forgotten.

—Kathrine Sorley Walker

THE NUTCRACKER
(also *Casse-Noisette*)

Choreography: Lev Ivanov
Music: Petr Ilyich Tchaikovsky
Design: M.I. Bocharov, Konstantin Ivanov, Ivan Vsevolozhsky
Libretto: Marius Petipa (after E.T.A. Hoffmann's tale "The Nutcracker and the Mouse King", in version by Alexandre Dumas *père*)

First Production: Maryinsky Theatre, St. Petersburg, 18 December (6 December old style) 1892
Principal Dancers: Stanislava Belinskaya (Clara), Sergei Legat (The Nutcracker), Antonietta Dell'Era (The Sugar Plum Fairy), Pavel Gerdt (The Prince), Timofei Stukholkin (Drosselmeyer)

Other productions include: Bolshoi Ballet (new version; chor. Aleksandr Gorsky); Moscow, 21 May 1919. State Academic Theatre for Opera and Ballet (GATOB) (new version; chor. Fedor Lopukhov), with Elizaveta Gerdt (Sugar Plum Fairy), Mikhail Dudko (Prince); Petrograd, 1923. GATOB (new version; chor. Lopukhov), with Olga Mungalova (Masha), Petr Gusev (Nutcracker); Leningrad, 1929. Sadler's Wells Ballet (staged Nikolai Sergeyev after Ivanov), as *Casse-Noisette*, with Alicia Markova (Sugar Plum Fairy) and Stanley Judson (Prince); London, 30 January 1934. GATOB (later the Kirov Ballet; new version; chor. Vassily Vainonen), with Galina Ulanova (Masha), Konstantin Sergeyev (Prince); Leningrad, 18 February 1934. Ballet Russe de Monte Carlo (one-act version; staged Alexandra Fedorova after Ivanov), with Alicia Markova (Sugar Plum Fairy) and André Eglevsky (Prince); New York, 17 October 1940. San Francisco Ballet (staged Willam Christensen, partly after Ivanov), with Gisella Caccialanza (Sugar Plum Fairy), Willam Christensen (Her Cavalier); San Francisco, 24 December 1944. London Festival Ballet (staged Anton Dolin, Alicia Markova after Ivanov); London, 24 October 1950. Sadler's Wells Theatre Ballet (new version in two scenes; chor. Frederick Ashton partly after Ivanov), as *Casse-Noisette*, with Elaine Fifield (Sugar Plum Fairy), David Blair (The Nutcracker Prince); London, 11 September 1951. New York City Ballet (new version; chor. George Balanchine), with Maria Tallchief (Sugar Plum Fairy), Nicholas Magallanes (Cavalier), and Tanaquil LeClercq (Dewdrop Fairy); New York, 2 February 1954. London Festival Ballet (new version; chor. David Lichine); London, 24 December 1957. Bolshoi Ballet (new version; chor. Yuri Grigorovich), with Ekaterina Maximova (Masha), Vladimir Vasiliev (Prince); Moscow, 12 March 1966. Stuttgart Ballet (new version; chor. John Cranko); Stuttgart, 4 December 1966. Royal Swedish Ballet (new version; chor. Rudolf Nureyev partly after Vainonen, design Nicholas Georgiadis); Stockholm, 17 November 1967 (same version staged Royal Ballet, London, 29 February 1968). Royal Danish Ballet (new version; chor. Flemming Flindt); Copenhagen, 11 December 1971. Frankfurt Ballet (new version; chor. John Neumeier); Frankfurt, 21 October 1971. Scottish Ballet (new version; chor. Peter Darrell); Edinburgh, 19 December 1973. London Festival Ballet (new version; chor. Ronald Hynd); Liverpool, 9 November 1976. Ballet de Marseille (new version; chor. Roland Petit); Paris, December 1976. American Ballet Theatre (new version; chor. Mikhail Baryshnikov), with Marianna Tcherkassky (Clara), Baryshnikov (Nutcracker Prince); Washington, D.C., 21 December 1976. Royal Ballet (staged Peter Wright after Ivanov), with Lesley Collier (Sugar Plum Fairy) and Anthony Dowell (Prince); London, 20 December 1984. London Festival Ballet (new version; chor. Peter Schaufuss); London, 10 December 1986.

PUBLICATIONS

Dumas, Alexandre, *Histoire d'un Casse-Noisette*, Paris, 1895
Beaumont, Cyril, *Complete Book of Ballets*, revised edition, London, 1951
Chujoy, Anatole, "*The Nutcracker*, Then and Now", *Dance News* (New York), February 1954

The Nutcracker, Act I, as performed by the New York City Ballet, 1983

Barnes, Clive, "*The Nutcracker*", *Dance and Dancers* (London), December 1957

Petipa, Marius (translated by Joan Lawson), in Swinson, Cyril (ed.), *The Nutcracker*, London 1960

Anderson, Jack, "A New American Tradition", *Dance Magazine* (New York), December 1966

Guest, Ivor, "*Casse-Noisette*", *About the House* (London), Christmas 1967

Maynard, Olga, "*The Nutcracker*", *Dance Magazine* (New York), December 1973

Christout, Marie-Françoise, Goodwin, Noël, Williams, Peter, and Percival, John, "*The Nutcracker* in France and England", *Dance and Dancers* (London), March 1977

Anderson, Jack, *The Nutcracker Ballet*, New York, 1979

Maynard, Olga, "*The Nutcracker* History", *Dance Magazine* (New York), December 1982

Wiley, Roland John, "On Meaning in *The Nutcracker*", *Dance Research* (London), Autumn 1984

Lartigue, Pierre, "*Casse-Noisette*", *Opéra de Paris* (Paris), no. 33, December 1985

Wiley, Roland John, *Tchaikovsky's Ballets*, Oxford, 1985

Kennicott, P., "Dance Music: Notes on *The Nutcracker*", *Dance Magazine* (New York), December 1990

*   *   *

The Nutcracker is an acknowledged classic of the ballet repertory, and yet it has been remade continuously since it was first performed. Tchaikovsky's score has been expanded and shortened; the libretto has been variously adapted, taken back closer to E.T.A. Hoffmann's original story, "The Nutcracker and the Mouse King" of 1816 (Hynd, 1976), replaced (Cranko, 1966) and abandoned altogether (Ashton, 1951); scenery and costumes have ranged from the deliberately controversial and constructivist (Lopukhov, 1929) to the traditional and Christmassy (Balanchine, 1954; Lichine, 1957); and the choreography has sometimes tried to recreate Petipa and Ivanov's original steps (Sergeyev, 1934; Wright, 1984) and has sometimes jettisoned them altogether and jugglers, roller skaters, and acrobats have taken over (Beal, 1982). *The Nutcracker* has been presented with realistic detail and without the Sugar Plum Fairy (Gorsky, 1919), as a dream in which all the characters are figments of the young heroine's imagination (Grigorovich, 1966), and it has been set in the context of Tchaikovsky's biography (Schaufuss, 1986). The psychological aspects of the story have been developed (Vainonen in 1934, Nureyev in 1967, and Baryshnikov in 1976) and its internal symmetries exploited to create a ballet about ballet (Neumeier, 1971). There have been very many *Nutcrackers* and there will be many more.

The Nutcracker was originally planned as another ballet-féerie, a follow-up to the success of *The Sleeping Beauty* the year before; and it was originally part of a double bill (hence its comparative brevity) with Tchaikovsky's opera *Iolanta*. There were, however, problems from the first: Tchaikovsky was not happy with the scenario, itself an adaptation from a re-telling of Hoffmann's original by Alexandre Dumas *père*, and Petipa (who had given the composer precise instructions for both dances and mimed scenes) became ill, so that the choreography was made by his deputy, Lev Ivanov. Given *The Nutcracker*'s subsequent popularity (it has become, very probably because of box-office exploitation of its seasonal topicality, *the* ballet for children at Christmas), it is surprising that it received very few performances in its first years on the stage—indeed the first performance at the Bolshoi in Moscow was not until 1919, and the first full-length staging in the United States was as recent as 1944.

The many problems presented by *The Nutcracker* to its composer, to its original audience, and to a producer a century later, derive largely from the libretto. It falls too obviously into its two acts, the first all narrative and no dancing, the second all divertissement and no event. There is no real ballerina role—the Sugar Plum Fairy's contribution is glorious but brief—and Hoffmann's original, rich, and quirky fantasy has been thinned down to an innocuous pretext for a saccharine spectacle. As one early critic put it, "In The *Nutcracker* there is no subject whatever".

Tchaikovsky in fact worked wonders with what he was given, although *The Nutcracker* is shorter and on a smaller scale than either *Swan Lake* or *The Sleeping Beauty*. Faced with a largely incoherent libretto, he none the less produced a musical whole, symmetrically crafted in an arch-like pattern. The "real" B-flat world of the first-act Christmas party at the Stahlbaums is offset by the E minor of Drosselmeyer and his Kingdom of Sweets: the ordinary, as in Hoffmann, is literally and metaphorically in a different key from the fantastic which is characterised by unusual orchestral sounds—the celeste, a wordless choir, and flutes played frullato. The two worlds of

The Nutcracker are opposed but they are also complementary; the one informs the other and, as in the mysterious process of growing from child to adult (the fundamental basis of Hoffmann's story), fantasy is the first adumbration of, and is subsumed in, maturer realities. The spectacle and cuteness which bedevil productions of *The Nutcracker* obscure its essential truth.

Any production of *The Nutcracker* is a compromise between what is there in the 1892 original, what might have been there had Hoffmann's story been more faithfully adapted, and what dancers and audiences and indeed box-office managers would nowadays like to find there. If, as Roland John Wiley has argued, the center of the ballet is Drosselmeyer, the cause of the marvellous events, rather than the young heroine who merely participates in them, it is difficult to justify any enlargement of the ballerina role, much as this might satisfy dancers' hopes and audiences' expectations. Petipa's instructions to Tchaikovsky are so very precisely matched to the adaptation of Hoffmann's narrative that it is very difficult to deviate from it, even if the deviation is in fact a faithful return to the psychological strength of Hoffmann's original. But Hoffmann's disturbing and eerie and often erotically ambiguous story has also to be balanced against a desire to sell *The Nutcracker* as an essential Christmas present for children.

The popularity of *The Nutcracker* with audiences dates from the middle of this century, and is largely due to familiarity not with the full score but with the concert suite Tchaikovsky arranged of his music. Many heard it for the first time as the sound track to Walt Disney's animated film *Fantasia* (1941), in which, for instance, six inscrutable mushrooms are given the Chinese Dance. But whether the Arabian Dance is performed by a seductive white fish (Disney) or a belly dancer (Sergeyev), whether the Sugar Plum Fairy is used to display a brilliant talent like Markova's or to evoke memories of Tchaikovsky's diminutive niece Sasha who died in 1891, it is the music of the ballet that counts. It has been made to support all sorts of narratives, but it is the real pretext for and bedrock of any production. Whoever the choreographer, the designer, the dancer, whatever the style, the interpretation, the concept, *The Nutcracker* remains Tchaikovsky's ballet.

—Martin Wright

OBUKHOV (Oboukhoff), **Anatole**

Russian dancer and teacher. Born Anatoly Nikolaevich Obukhov in St. Petersburg, 15 January 1896. Studied at the St. Petersburg Theatre School, pupil of Samuil Andrianov, Nikolai Legat, (uncle) Mikhail Obukhov; graduated in 1913. Married dancer Vera Nemchinova. Dancer, Maryinsky Theatre, later the State Academic Theatre for Opera and Ballet (GATOB), Petrograd, 1913–19, becoming principal dancer from 1917; also partnered Anna Pavlova in her last Russian performances, 1914; left Russia in 1920: soloist, Romanian Opera, Bucharest, 1920–22; premier danseur, Russian Romantic Ballet (director Boris Romanov), 1922–25; dancing partner to Vera Nemchinova from 1928, performing with Latvian Opera Ballet, Riga, 1930, Ballet de l'Opéra Russe à Paris, 1931, Lithuanian National Opera Ballet (also serving as choreographer), Kaunas, 1931–35, de Basil's Ballets Russes, 1935–36, and René Blum's Ballets de Monte Carlo, 1936–37, Markova–Dolin Ballet, 1937, Original Ballet Russe (also acting as ballet master), 1939–40; teacher, School of American Ballet, New York, 1940–62. Died in New York, 25 February 1962.

ROLES

1916   Albrecht in *Giselle* (Petipa after Coralli, Perrot), Maryinsky Theatre, Petrograd
1913/   Prince Désiré in *The Sleeping Beauty* (Petipa), Mar-
19   yinsky Theatre, Petrograd
         Prince Whooping Cough in *The Nutcracker* (Ivanov), Maryinsky Theatre, Petrograd
         Prince Siegfried in *Swan Lake* (Petipa, Ivanov), Maryinsky Theatre, Petrograd
         Lucien in *Paquita* (Petipa), Maryinsky Theatre, Petrograd
         Gemil in *La Source* (Coppini after Saint-Léon), Maryinsky Theatre, Petrograd
         Zephyr in *The Awakening of Flora* (Petipa, Ivanov), Maryinsky Theatre, Petrograd
         The Slave in *Egyptian Nights* (Fokine), Maryinsky Theatre, Petrograd
         Companion Khan in *The Little Humpbacked Horse* (Gorsky after Saint-Léon), Maryinsky Theatre, Petrograd
         Ta-Hor in *Pharaoh's Daughter* (Petipa), Maryinsky Theatre, Petrograd
         Jean de Brienne in *Raymonda* (Petipa), Maryinsky Theatre, Petrograd
         Harlequin in *Harlequinade* (Petipa), Maryinsky Theatre, Petrograd
         Franz in *Coppélia* (Petipa after Saint-Léon), Maryinsky Theatre, Petrograd

         Raymond in *Bluebeard* (N. Legat after Petipa), Maryinsky Theatre, Petrograd
         Nureddin in *The Talisman* (N. and S. Legat), Maryinsky Theatre, Petrograd
         Gringoire in *Esmeralda* (Petipa after Perrot), Maryinsky Theatre, Petrograd
         Damis in *The Trial of Damis* (Petipa), Maryinsky Theatre, Petrograd
         Colin in *Vain Precautions* (*La Fille mal gardée*; Petipa, Ivanov), Maryinsky Theatre, Petrograd
         Basil in *Don Quixote* (Gorsky after Petipa), Maryinsky Theatre, Petrograd
         Phoenix in *Caprices of a Butterfly* (Petipa), Maryinsky Theatre, Petrograd
1922/   Principal dancer in *The Passion of Diana* (Petipa, staged
25   Romanov), Russian Romantic Ballet, Berlin
         Principal dancer in *Andalusiana* (Romanov), Russian Romantic Ballet, Berlin
         Principal dancer in *The Dancer and the Highwayman* (Romanov), Russian Romantic Ballet, Berlin
         Principal dancer in *The Sacrifice of Atoragi* (Romanov), Russian Romantic Ballet, Berlin
         Principal dancer in *Trapeze* (Romanov), Russian Romantic Ballet, Berlin
1928   Title role in *Petrushka* (Fokine), La Scala, Milan
1936   Ambassador (cr) in *L'Epreuve d'Amour* (Fokine), René Blum's Ballets de Monte Carlo, Monte Carlo

WORKS

Staged:
1940   *Coppélia* (after Petipa, Cecchetti; mus. Delibes), (de Basil's) Original Ballet Russe, Sydney
1944   *Don Quixote* Pas de Deux (after Gorsky), Ballet Theatre, New York

PUBLICATIONS

Moore, Lillian, "From Artist to Student", *Dance Magazine* (New York), May 1954
Krasovskaya, Vera, *Russian Ballet Theatre from the Beginning of the Twentieth Century*, vol. 2: Leningrad, 1962
Karsavina, Tamara, "My Partners at the Maryinsky", *Dancing Times* (London), December 1966
Nemchinova, Vera, "In the Shadow of Russian Tradition", *Dance Magazine* (New York), February 1972

* * *

Anatole Obukhov as Albrecht in *Giselle*

Anatole Obukhov was noticed by the critics as early as the graduation performance of his school, when he partnered Olga Spessivtseva in the ballet *A Tale of the White Night*. After Obukhov's first season on the stage of the Maryinsky Theatre, the venerable Akim Volynsky placed the novice "among the best dancers of the ballet company, with line of unusual clarity and assurance, tours en l'air distinguished by beauty, and ordinary pirouettes that were striking in their firmness. Sometimes Obukhov stopped after big jumps as if his leg were fixed to the floor." In the summer of the same year, 1914, Anna Pavlova herself chose Obukhov as her partner for her last tour in Russia. Soon, another critical authority in the capital, Andrei Levinson, noted the developing talent of the young artist: "Obukhov's variation . . . was irreproachable; a dancer with youthful features and a childish face, with genuine lightness and perfectly articulated gestures, he astounds with his casual indifference to the greatest difficulties."

Later, Obukhov succeeded more in lyrical roles than in others: the tender Zephyr, the sweet Lucien, the dreamy Désiré, the loving Siegfried, the elegant Damis, or the elegiac Youth in *Chopiniana* were all roles which suited his style. His dance was picturesque but flowing, and ballerinas valued him as partner. In 1917, only four years after his début, he was awarded the title of premier danseur.

Leaving his native country in February 1920, Obukhov remained the same elegant cavalier and superb classical dancer in varied roles on different stages. He danced as a soloist at the Romanian Opera in Bucharest, and then as premier danseur for the Russian Romantic Ballet in Berlin. Here his repertoire included *Harlequinade*, *Giselle*, and *The Passion of Diana*, as well as ballets by Boris Romanov, such as *Andalusiana*, *The Dancer and the Highwayman* and *Trapeze* to the music of Prokofiev. Some years later he became partner and husband to Vera Nemchinova, and together with her he appeared in a series of companies, including the Ballets Russes de Monte Carlo, the Markova–Dolin Ballet and the Original Ballet Russe. In 1940 he was invited by George Balanchine and Lincoln Kirstein to join the School of American Ballet in New York, where he was the leading men's teacher until his death in 1962.

—Arsen Degen

ODE

Choreography: Léonide Massine
Music: Nicolas Nabokov
Design: Pavel Tchelitchev (sets and costumes) and Pierre Charbonneau (projections)
Libretto: Boris Kochno
First Production: Diaghilev's Ballets Russes, Théâtre Sarah Bernhardt, Paris, 6 June 1928
Principal Dancers: Irina Beliankina (Nature), Serge Lifar (Student), Felia Doubrovska, Alice Nikitina, Léonide Massine

PUBLICATIONS

Evans, Edwin, "The New Ballets", *Dancing Times* (London), August 1928
Coton, A.V., *A Prejudice for Ballet*, London, 1933
Beaumont, Cyril, *The Diaghilev Ballet in London*, London, 1940
Nabokov, Nicolas, *Old Friends and New Music*, Boston, 1951
Grigoriev, Serge, *The Diaghilev Ballet*, translated by Vera Bowen, London, 1953
Massine, Léonide, *My Life in Ballet*, London, 1960
Kochno, Boris, *Diaghilev and the Ballets Russes*, New York, 1970
Tyler, Parker, *The Divine Comedy of Pavel Tchelitchew*, New York, 1971
Garafola, Lynn, *Diaghilev's Ballets Russes*, New York, 1989

*   *   *

Serge Diaghilev staged only two new works for the 1928 Paris season of the Ballets Russes: *Apollon musagète* and *Ode*. Both were ambitious, forward-looking ballets that dealt with cosmic themes rather than with style or modern life, as did so many of the Diaghilev projects of the 1920s. Yet while *Apollo*, as it is now called, went on to become a modern classic, *Ode*'s history was quite different.

In 1927 Nicolas Nabokov, a young Russian composer, approached Diaghilev about a "ballet-oratorio" he was writing based on a work by the eighteenth-century Russian court poet Mikhail Lomonosov, entitled "Ode to the Majesty of God on the Occasion of the Appearance of the Great Northern Lights". The poem was an allegory on the enthronement of the Empress Elizabeth, ruler of Russia from 1741 to 1762. Nabokov writes in his memoirs that Diaghilev liked the poem and was interested in the theme because he considered himself a descendant of Elizabeth. Diaghilev also was attracted to the idea of creating a Russian period piece and so asked Boris Kochno, his secretary, to create a libretto. In the scenario, a statue of Nature comes to life and shows a student the wonders she can perform. He is not satisfied, however, and demands to be given a feast in which he can take part. When he attempts to enter into the festivities, he destroys the harmony of the vision and Nature once more is transformed into a statue.

For years, Diaghilev had tried to convince the Russian artist Pavel Tchelitchev to create designs for a ballet. He finally agreed to do the sets and costumes for *Ode*. Kochno wanted George Balanchine to create the choreography, but he was already occupied with *Apollon musagète*, and so the project went to Léonide Massine.

The collaborators were at cross-purposes from the beginning. Nabokov's score was, in his own words, "essentially tender, gentle, and lyrical", reflecting the poet's love of nature and Nabokov's nostalgia for his native Russia. Diaghilev envisioned a court ballet, a grand pageant which was not much in keeping with the romanticism of Nabokov's music.

According to Kochno, Diaghilev wanted the décor to be based on eighteenth-century allegorical drawings and on engravings of court balls and the empress's coronation festivities. Tchelitchev had been trained in theatre design by the constructivist Alexandra Exter and had created a number of successful vanguard productions in Berlin. Since leaving Kiev in 1920, he had developed a highly personal vision associated with surrealism. Diaghilev was apparently dismayed at Tchelitchev's concept for the ballet, which included the use of such new technology as neon lights, film, and many special effects.

As for the choreography, Diaghilev and Massine had not seen eye to eye for years. Nabokov states that at one point Diaghilev complained to him that "what Massine is doing is modern, cold, angular stuff that has nothing to do with your music".

According to contemporary accounts, Diaghilev took little interest in *Ode* once it was under way. Grigoriev writes that Diaghilev considered Kochno his successor and wanted to give him the experience of leading a project. Nabokov, on the other

Ode, performed by Diaghilev's Ballets Russes, 1928

Alexandra Danilova (although she missed the Paris premiere because of illness). In a recent conversation Danilova recalled that during the duet, she and Massine held a slender horizontal pole from which two diaphanous strips of fabric hung. The fabric gave their dancing a now ghostly, now human quality as they moved in and out behind the gauze.

After seeing a performance of *Ode*, the British critic A.V. Coton wrote that "One's strongest remaining impression is of the unearthly beauty created in most of the scenes by a revolutionary use of light never before seen in any form of Theatre." Fade-outs that dematerialized objects, glittering mirror images, bursts and shafts of coloured light, and multiple projections conveyed the mystery and beauty of the aurora borealis.

Danilova says she felt the dances for *Ode* were limited because of the many props the dancers had to handle. But for Beaumont, "Massine's choreography showed the greatest invention and originality in the composition of his ever-changing groups, which were never symmetrical and yet always harmonious." Using a classical ballet vocabulary, Massine created patterns of Euclidean austerity which Beaumont saw as a laying bare of the human intelligence at work.

Ode, with its complex lighting, orchestra, and chorus was expensive to perform and never achieved great popularity. It remained in the repertory only briefly before being relegated to the pages of history and to the imaginations of those who continue to read about it.

—Gay Morris

hand, felt that Diaghilev was disappointed in the collaboration and so focused his attention elsewhere. What is certain is that the ballet was in disarray when the company reached Paris for final rehearsals. At the last moment, Diaghilev stepped in and took control, particularly of the complicated lighting, so that by opening night all went smoothly.

Those who saw *Ode* talked of its unearthly beauty and mystical quality. Tchelitchev's stage design was built around a mast-like structure to which white cords were attached. A series of dolls in crinolines were hung on two diagonal lines from this central structure, the dolls becoming progressively smaller as they neared the mast, so that the figures seemed to disappear into deep space. Part of the corps de ballet also were dressed in crinoline gowns, while other dancers wore leotards with mask-like helmets over their faces. The dancers manipulated the cords to form geometric patterns. Cyril Beaumont relates, "these strange figures, rendered impersonal by their masks, appeared like beings from another sphere, and gave a mystic Blake-like character to their sinuous movements and sculpturesque groupings".

Lifar, as the Student, was dressed in black eighteenth-century costume (the only hint of the original setting of Lomonosov's poem) and had little dancing to do, his major task being to interact with the stately Irina Beliankina in the mime role of Nature.

Massine set the central pas de deux for himself and

L'OISEAU DE FEU
(*The Firebird*; Russian title: *Zhar-ptitsa*)

Choreography: Mikhail Fokine
Music: Igor Stravinsky
Design: Aleksandr Golovin (scenery), Léon Bakst and Aleksandr Golovin (costumes)
Libretto: Mikhail Fokine
First Production: Diaghilev's Ballets Russes, Théâtre National de l'Opéra, Paris, 25 June 1910
Principal Dancers: Tamara Karsavina (Firebird), Mikhail Fokine (Ivan Tsarevich), Enrico Cecchetti (Köstchei), Vera Fokina (Tsarevna)

Other productions include: Diaghilev's Ballets Russes (restaged Fokine; new scenery and costumes Natalia Gontcharova); London, 25 November 1926. Teatro Colón (restaged Fokine), with Olga Spessivtseva (Firebird); Buenos Aires, 1930. De Basil's Ballets Russes, with Alexandra Danilova (Firebird), Léonide Massine (Ivan Tsarevich), David Lichine (Köstchei), Tamara Grigorieva (Tsarevna); Monte Carlo, 28 April 1934. Sadler's Wells Ballet (revival; staged Serge Grigoriev and Lubov Tchernicheva after Fokine), as *The Firebird*, with Margot Fonteyn (Firebird), Michael Somes (Ivan Tsarevich), Frederick Ashton (Köstchei), Svetlana Beriosova (Tsarevna); Edinburgh, 23 August 1954. Maly Theatre Ballet (staged Konstantin Boyarsky after Fokine); Leningrad, 26 March 1962. Bolshoi Ballet (staged Stanislas Vaslov, Anatoly Simachev after Fokine), with Maya Plisetskaya (Firebird); Moscow, 30 June 1964.

State Academic Theatre for Opera and Ballet (GATOB, later the Kirov; new version; chor. Fedor Lopukhov), with Elena

L'Oiseau de feu: costume design by Bakst for Tamara Karsavina as the Firebird, 1910

Lukom (Firebird); Petrograd, 2 October 1921. Ballet Theatre (new version; chor. Adolph Bolm, design Marc Chagall), with Alicia Markova (Firebird), Anton Dolin (Ivan Tsarevich), John Taras (Köstchei), Diana Adams (Tsarevna); New York, 24 October 1945. New York City Ballet (new version; chor. George Balanchine, design Marc Chagall), as *Firebird*, with Maria Tallchief (Firebird), Francisco Moncion (Prince Ivan), Edward Bigelow (Kostchei), Pat McBride (Prince's Bride); New York, 27 November 1949. Paris Opéra Ballet (new version; chor. Serge Lifar, design Georges Wakhévitch); Paris, 7 April 1954. Ballet du XXe Siècle (new version; chor. Maurice Béjart); Brussels, 1964 (staged Paris Opéra, 31 October 1970). German Opera Ballet (new version; chor. John Cranko); Stuttgart, 20 May 1964. Harkness Ballet (new version; chor. George Skibine); New York, 1965. Harkness Ballet (new version; chor. Brian Macdonald); New York, 1 November 1967. Frankfurt Ballet (new version; chor. John Neumeier); Frankfurt, 16 March 1970. New York City Ballet (new version; chor. Balanchine and Jerome Robbins), with Gelsey Kirkland (Firebird); New York, 28 May 1970. Royal Danish Ballet (new version; chor. Glen Tetley); Copenhagen, 12 December 1981. Dance Theatre of Harlem (new version; chor. John Taras); New York, 12 January 1982.

L'Oiseau de feu: Margot Fonteyn as the Firebird in the Sadler's Wells Ballet restaging (as *The Firebird*), 1956

PUBLICATIONS

Levinson, André, "Stravinsky and the Dance", *NBLA Theatre Arts* (New York), November 1924

Amberg, George, "Marc Chagall's Designs for *Aleko* and *The Firebird*", *Dance Index* (New York), November 1945

Beaumont, Cyril, *Complete Book of Ballets*, revised edition, London, 1951

Grigoriev, Serge, *The Diaghilev Ballet*, translated by Vera Bowen, London, 1953

Karsavina, Tamara, "Firebird", *Dancing Times* (London), May 1954

Evans, Edwin, "*L'Oiseau de feu*", *Dancing Times* (London), September 1954

Fokine, Michel, *Fokine: Memoirs of a Ballet Master*, translated by Vitale Fokine, London 1961

"Arena: Fokine", *Dance and Dancers* (London), 3 parts: January, February, March 1962

Barnes, Clive, "The Firebird", *Dance and Dancers* (London), 2 parts: April, May, 1963

Lester, Keith, "Fokine's *Firebird*", *Dancing Times* (London), April 1968

Stanovsky, Vladislav, *The Firebird*, London, 1969

Maynard, Olga, "*The Firebird*", *Dance Magazine* (New York), August 1970

Vaughan, David, "Fokine in the Contemporary Repertory", *Ballet Review* (New York), vol. 7, nos. 2–3, 1978–79

Taruskin, Richard, "From *Firebird* to *The Rite of Spring*", *Ballet Review* (New York), Summer 1982

Borovsky, Victor, and Schouvaloff, Alexander, *Stravinsky on Stage*, London, 1982

Horwitz, Dawn Lille, *Michel Fokine*, Boston, 1985

Garafola, Lynn, *Diaghilev's Ballets Russes*, New York, 1989

* * *

When Diaghilev returned to Paris in 1910, after his triumphant season of Russian opera and ballet the year before, the first new ballet to be created for his Ballets Russes (apart from the *Polovtsian Dances* in the opera *Prince Igor*) was *L'Oiseau de feu—The Firebird*. This one-act ballet bore the distinguishing marks of the early Diaghilev era: exotically beautiful designs, a distinctively Russian element in the choreography, and close collaboration between choreographer and composer. The ensemble dances were based on Russian folk dance, and Fokine made much use of mime in telling the story of the ballet, which was based on the Russian fairy tales "The Tale of Ivan Tsarevich" and "The Bird of Light and the Grey Wolf", incorporating the legend of the evil enchanter Köstchei, whose soul was contained in an egg. The Prince Ivan captures the mysterious Firebird, who persuades him to release her by giving him one of her plumes, which he can use to call upon her should he find himself in peril. In the second act Ivan meets and falls in love with the beautiful Tsarevna, and thereby falls into the power of Köstchei. As battle ensues between Ivan and Köstchei with his infernal followers, the Firebird appears as summoned, and forces the monsters to dance to exhaustion and death, thus enabling Ivan to find and smash the egg containing Köstchei's soul. With the death of the enchanter, Ivan and the Tsarevna are free to marry, the other princesses are freed from captivity, and the Firebird flies away.

It was perhaps the music, the first of three great ballet scores to be commissioned from Stravinsky by Diaghilev, that made the greatest initial impact in Paris and subsequently in London. The strangeness of the musical idiom, particularly to ballet audiences, was a challenge to critics; but early comparisons with other modern composers (for example Richard Strauss) developed into full-fledged acclaim for Stravinsky, and rapid fame in his own right. *The Sunday Times* critic described the score as "impressionistic", "advanced in its idiom, free and varied in its rhythm, and elaborately scored", commenting that while it was "hardly the sort of music that one would expect in alliance with the choreographic art, it fits the action of *L'Oiseau de Feu* like the proverbial glove, and seems to be very congenial to the dancers". In 1911 Stravinsky re-scored the music for a smaller ballet orchestra in the five-movement *Firebird Suite*, thereby ensuring its enduring accessibility to choreographers working on a smaller scale than Diaghilev offered Fokine.

In addition to securing lasting fame for Stravinsky, *The Firebird* was the ballet to make Karsavina's a household name in Europe. In her fantastical costume designed by Léon Bakst, her evocation of the terrified captive bird was the element in the ballet noted by all contemporary critics. *The Times* rather archly addressed itself to "the ornithologists", who would be interested to know of a newly discovered bird who "flew on to the stage at Covent Garden last night, disguised as Mme Karsavina": *The Sunday Times* four days later commented upon her "unforgettable" representation of the Firebird's "grace and fleetness of movement, and the suggestion of palpitating fear and violated purity". About the rest of the

choreography the English critics at least were less enthusiastic, *The Times* considering that "except for what the bird does there is little dancing of much choreographic merit in it".

The very Russian folkloric aspect of Fokine's ballet was emphasized by the original designs by Aleksandr Golovin, and by the later designs of Natalia Gontcharova. The Royal Ballet reconstructed this original ballet with the Gontcharova scenery and costumes in 1954, with Margot Fonteyn and Michael Somes (coached by Tamara Karsavina) in the principal roles. Later choreographers have interpreted the ballet rather differently. Balanchine, who made a version for the New York City Ballet in 1949 with Maria Tallchief in the title role, followed Fokine's libretto, but eliminated much of the mime and introduced more virtuoso choreography. This production of Balanchine's featured designs by Marc Chagall, created four years earlier for a version choreographed by Adolph Bolm for American Ballet Theatre. Maurice Béjart in his version altered the entire conception of the ballet and presented an allegory of revolution danced by men in dungarees, while John Neumeier in the same year placed his version in outer space, re-writing fairytale as science fiction. The extraordinary score continues to inspire choreographers, and the ballet in its various forms is an outstanding one in the ballet canon of the twentieth century.

—Penelope Jowitt

ONDINE

Choreography: Frederick Ashton
Music: Hans Werner Henze
Design: Lila de Nobili (scenery and costumes)
Libretto: Frederick Ashton (after the novel by Friedrich de la Motte Fouqué)
First Production: Royal Ballet, Covent Garden, London, 27 October 1958
Principal Dancers: Margot Fonteyn (Ondine), Michael Somes (Palemon), Julia Farron (Berta), Alexander Grant (Tirrenio)

Other productions include: Bavarian State Opera Ballet (new version; chor. Alan Carter); Munich, 25 January 1959. Berlin Ballet (new version; chor. Tatjana Gsovsky); Berlin, 22 September 1959. Wuppertal Ballet (new version; chor. Erich Walter); Wuppertal, 13 November 1962. Zurich State Opera Ballet (new version; chor. Nicholas Beriozoff); Zurich, 24 April 1965. Hungarian State Opera Ballet (new version; chor. Imre Eck); Budapest, 1969. Komische Oper (Comic Opera) Ballet (new version; chor. Tom Schilling); Berlin, 6 August 1970. Komische Opera (new version; chor. Arile Siegert); Berlin, 12 January 1992.

Other choreographic treatments of story: Louis Henry (Vienna, 1825), Paul Taglioni (Berlin, 1836, and London, 1847), Jules Perrot (London, 1843: see *Ondine; ou, La Naïade*).

PUBLICATIONS

Moore, Lillian, "Ondines of the Ballet", *Dance Magazine* (New York), May 1954

Henze, Hans Werner, *Undine: Tagebuch eines Balletts*, Munich, 1959

Guest, Ivor, "*Undine*: The Pure Gold of Romanticism", *Ballet Annual* (London), vol. 13, 1959

Ondine, **choreographed by Frederick Ashton, with Margot Fonteyn in the title role, London, 1958**

Barnes, Clive, "*Ondine*, Ashton and Fonteyn", *Dance Magazine* (New York), February 1959

Barnes, Clive, "*Ondine*", *Dance and Dancers* (London), 2 parts: December 1959, January 1960

Williams, Peter, "The Twenty-One Years that Changed British Ballet", *Dance and Dancers* (London), February 1971

Vaughan, David, *Frederick Ashton and his Ballets*, London, 1977

Clarke, Mary, "Ondine", *Dancing Times* (London), April 1988

Clarke, Mary, "*Ondine* Revisited", *Dancing Times* (London), June 1988

Harvey, Cynthia, "Working with Ashton", interview with David Vaughan, *Ballet Review* (New York), Fall 1989

*   *   *

Ondine was Ashton's fourth three-act ballet, but his first to a commissioned score composed to his own scenario. Ashton's starting point was the novel by Baron Friedrich de la Motte Fouqué, published in 1811, which quickly became a popular subject for Romantic choreographers. Most notable among Ashton's predecessors were Paul Taglioni, who produced two versions (as *Undine* for Berlin in 1836 and as *Coralia* with Carolina Rosati for London in 1847), and Jules Perrot, who devised his *Ondine* (London, 1843) with its famous "pas de l'ombre" for Fanny Cerrito. This Shadow Dance, in which the water nymph discovers, plays with, and tries to trap her shadow, was imitated by Ashton for Margot Fonteyn. *Ondine* in fact marks the high point of Ashton's writing for Fonteyn.

Ondine was a long time in preparation. Ashton considered ballets on *The Tempest* and *Macbeth* as well as *The Dybbuk* before he finally settled on *Ondine*. He had seen Jean Giraudoux's play *Ondine* in Paris in 1939, and had discussed the possibility of a one-act ballet on the subject with the play's designer, Ashton's friend Pavel Tchelitchev. Now in 1956 Ashton reconsidered the scheme, gained Fonteyn's approval, and on the recommendation of William Walton commissioned Hans Werner Henze for the score.

Henze's book *Undine: Tagebuch eines Balletts* maps the collaboration between Ashton and himself which began on holiday on the island of Ischia and continued from January 1957 in London. The designer Lila de Nobili, to whom Ashton wrote "I long for all three of us to make something beautiful and lasting", was also closely involved from an early stage. She actually painted some of the stage scenery herself to retain the delicate brushwork of her designs. Henze observed: "I could see Ashton and de Nobili worked very well together. Ashton admired her work enormously, as did I. My task was to try and adjust my music to the visual style that was being developed by the two of them." It must be added that during the rehearsal period the principal dancers themselves joined in the collaborative process.

Ashton read the scenarios for Taglioni's and Perrot's ballets but decided to go back to Fouqué's original tale (which he had known since childhood) and adapt it for himself. The libretto was revised extensively both before and during rehearsals. Ashton also studied Leonardo's drawings of water, as well as the sea itself. "I wanted the movement to be fluid like the rhythm of the sea rather than set ballet steps. In general, all the choreography has been inspired by the sea. I spent hours watching water move and have tried to give the choreography the surge and swell of waves. This is why I use the corps as an expressive instrument more fully than before." The texture of *Ondine* is freer and looser, and harks back to an earlier romantic tradition although its structure, as Ashton said, is firmly based on Petipa.

Essentially Ashton organized his ballet around the central role of Ondine, which is to say around Fonteyn's own genius in performance—and this has been seen as something of a limiting factor in the ballet's revival. Certainly *Ondine* dropped out of the repertory when Fonteyn felt she could no longer dance it; but the subsequent revival (in the late 1980s) suggested that, although the ballet remained a "concerto" rather than a "symphony", the real problem lay elsewhere. The difficulty, for both performers and audiences, is to accept Ashton's restatement of Romantic mythologies in terms of the conventions of Romantic ballet theatre. If one accepts the work's premise, the lure is there, in Ashton's choreography.

—Martin Wright

———

ONDINE; OU, LA NAÏADE

Choreography: Jules Perrot and Fanny Cerrito
Music: Cesare Pugni
Design: William Grieve
Libretto: Jules Perrot and Fanny Cerrito (after the novel by Friedrich de la Motte Fouqué)
First Production: Her Majesty's Theatre, London, 22 June 1843
Principal Dancers: Fanny Cerrito (Ondine), Jules Perrot (Matteo), Maria Guy-Stéphan (Giannina)

Other productions include: Bolshoi Theatre (restaged and revised Perrot), as *The Naïad and the Fisherman*, with Carlotta Grisi (Ondine, the Naïad); St. Petersburg, 6 February (25 January old style) 1851. Bolshoi Theatre (staged Marius Petipa after Perrot), as *The Naïad and the Fisherman*; St. Petersburg, 1874. Maryinsky Theatre (staged Aleksandr Shiryaev after Petipa, Perrot), as *The Naïad and the Fisherman*, with Anna Pavlova (Ondine); St. Petersburg, 7 December 1903.

Other choreographic treatments of story: Louis Henry (Vienna, 1825), Paul Taglioni (Berlin, 1836, and London, 1847), Frederick Ashton (London, 1958: see Ashton's *Ondine*).

PUBLICATIONS

Moore, Lillian, "Cerrito and *Ondine*", *Dancing Times* (London), June 1943

Beaumont, Cyril, *Complete Book of Ballets*, revised edition, London, 1951

Moore, Lillian, "Ondines of the Ballet", *Dance Magazine* (New York), May 1954

Au, Susan, "Ondine Depicted", *Dancing Times* (London), June 1977

Au, Susan, "The Shadow of Herself: Some Sources of Jules Perrot's *Ondine*", *Dance Chronicle* (New York), vol. 2, no. 3, 1978

Guest, Ivor, *Jules Perrot: Master of the Romantic Ballet*, London, 1984

Clarke, Mary, "*Ondine* Revived", *Dancing Times* (London), June 1988

Guest, Ivor, "Perrot and Bournonville", *Dancing Times* (London), November 1988

*   *   *

Ondine opens with the preparations for the Festival of the Madonna. Among the crowd are Matteo, a fisherman, and his

Ondine, choreographed by Jules Perrot, with Fanny Cerrito in the title role, London, 1843

ballet was brilliant, and the contrasted moods and episodes maintained the audience's interest throughout the ballet's hour-and-a-half duration. Part of Perrot's ingenuity lay in having the scenes performed before a drop curtain, thus allowing the action to continue while the more elaborate sets were constructed. Like *Alma*, the ballet was notable for its close collaboration between composer, scene painter, machinist, and choreographer to create a total illusion.

In common with most Romantic ballets, *Ondine* contrasted the reality of everyday people with the supernatural world into which man wished to escape. The ensembles were no mere padding, but served to establish the realism of the world against the insubstantial fantasy of the sea nymph. Perrot's brilliance in creating mood was shown in the bright and energetic tarantella, which is interrupted by a quiet pause for evening prayers (during which Ondine again tempts Matteo), before being resumed in all its exuberance. Such picturesque national dances were contrasted with the more formal classical choreography for Ondine and the naïads.

As Ondine, Cerrito continued to add to her reputation. The role did not call unduly upon her dramatic talents, which were always inferior to her dancing; Perrot skilfully created for her a role which, with its playful skittishness and changing moods, showed at once the lovable woman and ethereal spirit. So popular was *Ondine* that it even had an influence upon fashion, and stylish women were seen sporting white or pink stoles of "iris or zephyr gauze" over their evening dresses.

—Sarah C. Woodcock

betrothed, Giannina. The naïad Ondine has fallen in love with Matteo, and reveals herself to him, attempting to entice him away. She follows him to his cottage, and, jealous of his attentions to Giannina, again tries to fascinate him, but Giannina intervenes. Ondine reveals to him the beauty of the world beneath the sea. She is warned by Hydrola, Queen of the Waters, that mortal love is transient, and she is immortal, but Ondine cares for nothing so long as Matteo will love her. On the eve of the Festival of the Madonna, Ondine contrives to lure Giannina into the sea and takes her form. But mortality weighs heavy upon her and she becomes exhausted and weak. By the wedding she is almost dead when Hydrola intervenes, restores Giannina to life and to Matteo, and Ondine takes back her naïad form and returns to the sea.

Ondine was Perrot's first complete work as a choreographer and established his reputation as the leading choreographer of his day. The work was a model of balletic construction, and its completeness in blending music, design, and dance was an advance upon *Alma*, for which Perrot had been only partly responsible.

Continuing the development of dance as an expressive medium which Perrot had begun in the "pas de fascination" in *Alma*, *Ondine* was revolutionary in that all its episodes and dances grew naturally out of the action, and served to forward narrative or character and to build up the atmosphere of the whole. Thus Ondine's dance with her shadow was expressive of the character's playful wonderment and delight at this symbol of her mortality. In the "pas de la rose flétrie", Ondine's gradually weakening state was expressed in faltering steps contrasted with her brave attempts to reassure Matteo that all is well. Notable too was Perrot's growing mastery in establishing relationships and interplay between the characters, and his skilful blending of realism and fantasy. The construction of the

ONEGIN

Choreography: John Cranko
Music: Petr Ilyich Tchaikovsky
Design: Jürgen Rose (scenery and costumes)
Libretto: John Cranko (after the poem by Aleksandr Pushkin)
First Production: Stuttgart Ballet, Stuttgart, 13 April 1965
Principal Dancers: Ray Barra (Onegin), Marcia Haydée (Tatiana), Egon Madsen (Lensky), Ana Cardus (Olga)

Other productions include: Stuttgart Ballet (restaged and revised Cranko); Stuttgart, 27 October 1967. Bavarian State Opera Ballet; Munich, 20 June 1972. Royal Swedish Ballet; Stockholm, 1976. Australian Ballet (staged Anne Woolliams); 1976. London Festival Ballet (staged Georgette Tsinguirides); Manchester, 18 October 1983. Royal Danish Ballet; Copenhagen, 5 April 1991.

PUBLICATIONS

Barnes, Clive, "John Cranko", *About the House* (London), Christmas, 1965
Brinson, Peter, and Crisp, Clement, *Ballet for All*, London, 1970
Regner, Otto Friedrich, *Reclams Balletführer*, Stuttgart, 1972
Croce, Arlene, "John Cranko", *Ballet Review* (Brooklyn, N.Y.), vol. 4, no. 5, 1973
Kilian, Hannes, *Stuttgarter Ballett*, Weingarten, 1980
Percival, John, *Theatre in My Blood: A Biography of John Cranko*, London, 1983
Barnes, Clive, "Barnes on John Cranko", *Ballet News* (New York), September 1983

Onegin, with Marcia Haydée and Richard Cragun, Stuttgart Ballet

Russia's greatest poet, Aleksandr Pushkin (1799–1837), the author of the verse-novel *Eugene Onegin* which provides the scenario for John Cranko's ballet, was himself a great ballet-goer and had actually studied dance technique during his six secondary-school years. And like Lensky, the young poet in the novel, Pushkin died before his time and in an unnecessary duel. Pushkin's works inspired a whole host of operas and ballets, and it was in connection with the choreography for George Devine's production of Tchaikovsky's opera *Eugene Onegin* for the Sadler's Wells company (first performed on May 22, 1952) that Cranko first became interested in Pushkin's novel. The opera, like the ballet, has a large dance scene in each of its three acts, and Cranko's choreography was well received (one of his dancers, incidentally, was Kenneth MacMillan).

The Forgotten Room, also devised by Cranko in 1952, similarly points towards *Onegin* by virtue of its subject—a young woman who finds herself so absorbed in a book that she begins to live its events and is literally carried away by the fictional hero. This is very suggestive of Pushkin's bookish Tatiana and Cranko's later mirror pas de deux in *Onegin* itself.

Work on the ballet proper began in 1964. The immediate incentive was a Russian film of Tchaikovsky's opera which was released in the West that year. Cranko saw the film several times, taking with him members of his Stuttgart Ballet: Marcia Haydée (who was to be his first Tatiana), Ray Barra (his first Onegin), Egon Madsen (his first Lensky), and Richard Cragun (who eventually took over Onegin from Barra). Cranko said that the opera "struck me as being much more suitable for ballet". He explained that "the plot of the Pushkin poem is balletic—explainable in three different dance styles. The first act is a youthful peasant dance, the second is a bourgeois party, the third is an elegant St. Petersburg ball. And like a thread going through the labyrinth you have your soloists, with their problems, their stories." Cranko at first wanted to use an arrangement of the music from Tchaikovsky's opera, but the boards of directors at both the Royal Opera House (where there was talk of Cranko making the ballet for Fonteyn and Nureyev) and the Stuttgart Ballet would not countenance using opera music in this way. Accordingly there is no music from Tchaikovsky's opera in the ballet's score, though Cranko does follow the opera's adaptation of Pushkin's plot, working back in a good deal of what Tchaikovsky's librettist had omitted. Compare the opening of the opera, which starts with Olga offstage singing a mawkish poem by the seventeen-year-old Pushkin, with the ballet which, much closer to the mature Pushkin of the verse-novel itself, begins with Tatiana flat on her front, nose buried in a book—as unlyrical, unballetic a pose as you could ask for, but exactly right for Pushkin's provincial bookworm whom events turn into a tragic heroine.

The contrast (which Haydée played brilliantly to the limit) in the second scene of the first act between the child with the bedclothes over her head and the passionately sexual woman of the mirror pas de deux is as typical of Pushkin as it is of Cranko: in both men a sense of symmetry was closely matched by a keen feeling for the grotesque. Cranko in fact invented the mirror-sequence dream—in Pushkin Tatiana has a nightmare—but the dramatic function, to set fantasy against reality, is the same in each case.

Nobody would suggest that the success of a ballet is to be judged by its fidelity to its source; but to know that Pushkin's original is witty as well as romantic, self-consciously artistic as well as passionately direct, suggests aspects of Cranko's own style which contribute very much to his ballet's success, both its freedom and its formality. Pushkin and Cranko bring out the best in one another.

—Martin Wright

ORPHEUS

Choreography: George Balanchine
Music: Igor Stravinsky
Design: Isamu Noguchi (scenery and costumes)
First Production: Ballet Society, City Center, New York, 28 April 1948
Principal Dancers: Nicholas Magallanes (Orpheus), Maria Tallchief (Eurydice), Francisco Moncion (Dark Angel), Herbert Bliss (Apollo), Beatrice Tompkins (Leader of the Furies), Tanaquil LeClercq (Leader of the Bacchantes)

Other productions include: Rome Opera Ballet (new version; chor. Aurel Milloss); Venice, 9 September 1948. Théâtre des Champs-Elysées (new version; chor. Lichine, design Mayo); Paris, 16 November 1948. Wuppertal Opera Ballet (new version; chor. Erich Walter); Wuppertal, 31 October 1954. Frankfurt Ballet (new version; chor. Tatjana Gsovsky); Frankfurt, 12 November 1961. Maly Theatre Ballet (new version; chor. Konstantin Boyarsky); Leningrad, 26 March 1962. Stuttgart Ballet (new version; chor. John Cranko); Stuttgart, 6 June 1970. Vienna Ballet (new version; chor. Milloss), 15 March 1974. Dutch National Ballet (new version; chor. Rudi van Dantzig); London, 26 March 1974. Royal Ballet (new version; chor. Kenneth MacMillan), with Peter Schaufuss (guest artist: Orpheus); London, 11 June 1982. Paris Opéra Ballet (Balanchine version; staged John Taras); Paris, 13 March 1974. Australian Ballet (new version; chor. Glen Tetley); Melbourne, 19 February 1987.

Other choreographic treatments of story: Isadora Duncan (Munich, 1902), Leo Staats (Paris, 1926), Rudolf von Laban (1927), Ninette de Valois (London, 1941), Roland Petit (Paris, 1944), Janine Charrat (Venice, 1951), Yvonne Georgi (Hanover, 1955), Maurice Béjart (Liège, 1958), William Forsythe (Stuttgart, 1979), Heinz Spoerli (Basle, 1983).

PUBLICATIONS

Hussey, Dyneley, "Stravinsky's *Orpheus*", *Dancing Times* (London), April 1949
Beaumont, Cyril, *Ballets of Today*, London 1954
Kirstein, Lincoln, *Movement and Metaphor*, New York, 1970
Anderson, Jack, "A Hard-Headed Miracle", *Dance Magazine* (New York), September 1972
Balanchine, George, with Mason, Francis, *Balanchine's Complete Stories of the Great Ballets*, Garden City, N.Y., 1977
Reynolds, Nancy, *Repertory in Review*, New York, 1977
Graff, Ellen, "*The Four Temperaments* and *Orpheus*: Models of a Modern Classical Tradition", *Ballet Review* (New York), Fall 1985

*   *   *

Though not overtly autobiographical, George Balanchine's ballets often suggest profound statements of belief, and none more so than the 1948 *Orpheus*—a catechism of classicism, not in terms of ballet vocabulary but of classically restrained gesture and emotion, of dignified Greek poses of mourning, and of scenes with the compressed space and ritual distance of Greek friezes. The ballet's contemplative pace calls to mind opera, which Balanchine proposed to Stravinsky as the model for their undertaking. Stravinsky studied Monteverdi in preparation, though Stravinsky's spare, lucid score is very much his own. The ballet also recalls the restrained, contemplative grandeur of Greek tragedy and its ritual origins. Even a

Orpheus, with Nicholas Magallanes in the title role, in a New York City Ballet revival, 1972

chorus is present briefly at the beginning in the shape of three friends who come to console Orpheus.

Perhaps *Orpheus* represents another statement of Balanchine's belief as well: the archetypal artist Orpheus's relations to Eurydice and to the male figure called the Dark Angel parallel Balanchine's two most important artistic ties—with his dancers and his music, more specifically with a chosen ballerina and with Igor Stravinsky.

This idea is borne out by the history of the ballet's collaborative creation, Balanchine's closest ever with Stravinsky, excepting the later *Agon*. The subject was clearly a very personal choice for Balanchine. He had proposed it at Stravinsky's invitation when a score was commissioned from the composer by the Ballet Society (a forerunner of the New York City Ballet), even though Balanchine had previously choreographed and staged a complete version of Gluck's *Orpheus and Eurydice* (music to which he would later return) for the Metropolitan Opera in 1936.

Why would Balanchine want to deal with the myth afresh? Perhaps because of his belief that—as he said in an article in the anthology *Stravinsky in the Theatre* at about the time of the new *Orpheus*—"Stravinsky is himself an Orpheus of the twentieth century." "To music," Balanchine explained, "he

brings his own special eloquence of movement continuously felt and most completely expressed. . . . Today he shows us the humanist values that bind the past to the present. His new scores, grave and deliberate, suggest the discipline and the grandeur of the heroic human body."

Then, too, what more suitable representative of Balanchine himself, the choreographer for whom "ballet is woman", than Orpheus? He places his art at the service of woman, as he challenges Hades for his wife, Eurydice—originally danced by Maria Tallchief, then Balanchine's wife. The ballet's first-chosen designer, Pavel Tchelitchev, on the other hand, saw Orpheus as "symbolizing the power of the artist to create without the benefit of woman", according to Bernard Taper's Balanchine biography, and over this difference they parted company on the project. The lyre that Isamu Noguchi designed for the ballet reflected the circular emblem on Eurydice's abdomen—or womb—and it became the logo of the New York City Ballet's two later Stravinsky festivals.

The mysterious Dark Angel—related to Gluck's Amor and to Hermes, who guided souls to the underworld—was first suggested by Stravinsky. When one sees the Dark Angel clasp Orpheus's hand through the lyre or urge him to play his music, sustaining him and dancing with him in counterpoint, one can feel the closeness of choreographer and composer. The intimacy of their two arts is summed up in Orpheus and Eurydice's poignant pas de deux, at the moment when the music abruptly stops: Eurydice collapses, dead, because the dancer's "floor"—as Balanchine considered music to be—has been pulled from under her.

Noguchi's designs gave the ballet a non-specific, universal locale with elegant economy, while perhaps hinting at the ancient Minoan snake cult in the coiling patterns applied to many of the costumes. As Balanchine put it, "The time of the ballet seemed to me the period of the Greek earth legends, the time of sand and snakes." The beautiful white china silk curtain that descends at moments offered the possibility for Eurydice to disappear when she dies by being drawn under it, thus leaving Orpheus embracing empty space—a typically economical Balanchine idea and a psychologically resonant one.

Balanchine and Stravinsky planned *Orpheus* as the second of three Greek ballets, of which the first was *Apollo*, which takes a similarly spare approach to its mythological theme and whose score is related to *Orpheus* in its textural economy. (The third was to be *Agon*, which, however, has no suggestion of narrative, although the title refers to the Greek word for contest.) Stravinsky, who was present at rehearsals of *Orpheus*, conducted the warmly received premiere. While the original male leads, Nicholas Magallanes and Francisco Moncion, gave their onstage relationship a highly charged feeling, in the ballet's most successful revival (1979) Peter Martins and Adam Lüders maintained a more classical distance.

—Marilyn Hunt

OSATO, Sono

American dancer. Born in Omaha, Nebraska, 29 August 1919. Studied with Adolph Bolm, from 1930, and with Berenice Holmes, Chicago; later studied with Lubov Egorova, Edward Caton. Married Victor Elmaleh, 1943: two sons. Dancer, de Basil's Ballets Russes (also performing as the Monte Carlo Ballet Russe, the Covent Garden Russian Ballet, and eventually becoming the Original Ballet Russe), 1934–40: principal dancer, from 1936; principal dancer, Ballet Theatre, New York, 1940–42; also performed in Broadway stage musicals, including as the premiere danseuse in *One Touch of Venus* (mus. Weill, chor. de Mille; 1943), Ivy Smith in *On the Town* (mus. Bernstein, chor. Robbins; 1944), Cocaine Lil in *Willie the Weeper*, part of *Ballet Ballads* (mus. Moross 1948), in revues, including *Once Over Lightly* (New York, 1955), and in films, including in *The Kissing Bandit* (dir. Benedek, 1948); actress, appearing as Anitra in *Peer Gynt* (ANTA, 1951), and Vasantasana in *The Little Clay Cart* (1953); also teacher, Ruth Page's company, Chicago. Recipient: Donaldson Award for Best Dancer in a Musical, 1943.

ROLES

1934   Barman's Assistant (cr) in *Union Pacific* (Massine), de Basil's Ballets Russes (Monte Carlo Ballet Russe), Philadelphia
       Dancer in *Les Sylphides* (Fokine), de Basil's Ballets Russes, Barcelona
1935   A Maid-in-Waiting (cr) in *Les Cent Baisers* (Nijinska), de Basil's Ballets Russes, London

1935/   An Odalisque in *Schéhérazade* (Fokine), de Basil's
36   Ballets Russes, tour
1936   A Wedding Guest in *Les Noces* (Nijinska), de Basil's Ballets Russes, New York
       A Spirit of the Garden (cr) in *Pavillon* (Lichine), de Basil's Ballets Russes, London
       Dancer (cr) in *Symphonie fantastique* (Massine), de Basil's Ballets Russes, London
1937   Gypsy in *Petrushka* (Fokine), de Basil's Ballets Russes
       A Jewish Maiden in *Cleopatra* (Fokine), de Basil's Ballets Russes
       Tarantella in *Cimarosiana* (divertissement from *Le Astuzie femminili*; Massine), de Basil's Ballets Russes
       A Vision (cr) in *Le Coq d'or* (new version; Fokine), de Basil's Ballets Russes, London
       A Lady (cr) in *Les Deux mendiants* (new version; Lichine), de Basil's Ballets Russes, London
1938   A Maiden (cr) in *Protée* (Lichine), Russian Ballet of Educational Ballets, Ltd. (de Basil's Ballets Russes), London
1939   Principal dancer in *Choreartium* (Massine), Original Ballet Russe, Sydney
       The Siren in *The Prodigal Son* (Lichine), Original Ballet Russe, Sydney
       Guinevere in *Francesca da Rimini* (Lichine), Original Ballet Russe, Sydney
1940   Beauty (cr) in *La Lutte éternelle* (*The Eternal Struggle*; Schwezoff), Original Ballet Russe, Sydney
       Soloist in *Paganini* (Fokine), Original Ballet Russe, Sydney
1941   One of the Seven Variations in *Princess Aurora* (suite from *The Sleeping Beauty*; Dolin after Petipa), Ballet Theatre, Mexico City
       A Grisette in *The Beloved* (*La Bien-Aimée*; Nijinska), Ballet Theatre, Mexico City
       A Friend of Slavonika (cr) in *Slavonika* (Psota), Ballet Theatre, Mexico City
       Lilac Fairy in *Princess Aurora* (suite from *The Sleeping Beauty*; Dolin after Petipa), Ballet Theatre, New York
1942   A Lover-in-Experience (cr) in *Pillar of Fire* (Tudor), Ballet Theatre, New York
       A Muse (cr) in *Romantic Age* (Dolin), Ballet Theatre, New York
1943   Rosaline (cr) in *Romeo and Juliet* (Tudor), Ballet Theatre, New York

PUBLICATIONS

By Osato:
Interview in Gruen, John, *The Private World of Ballet*, New York, 1975
Distant Dances, New York, 1980
"My Trip to China", *Dance News* (New York), February 1981

About Osato:
Owen, Walter, "Sono Osato", *Dance Magazine* (New York), February 1945
Walker, Kathrine Sorley, "Sono Osato: A Certain Kind of Joy", *Dance Chronicle* (London), vol. 4, no. 2, 1981
Walker, Kathrine Sorley, *De Basil's Ballets Russes*, London, 1982

*   *   *

Sono Osato was the product of a difficult relationship between

Sono Osato as the Siren in *The Prodigal Son*, **Original Ballet Russe, 1939**

the French-Canadian/Irish Frances Fitzpatrick of Omaha and Shoji Osato of Akita, Japan. This resulted in an early childhood characterized by on-and-off separations between parents and numerous relocations. Her relationship with her mother remained at best ambivalent. Perhaps the aspect of their mother-child interaction with the least conflict was a shared interest in the arts. It was through their outing to see a version of *Cléopâtre* by Diaghilev's Ballet Russes in 1928 that Sono discovered dance. As in the stories of many of Osato's contemporaries, dance filled a void in a painful childhood. Upon returning to Chicago, Osato began her dance training under the influence of Adolph Bolm. Master teacher Berenice Holmes was to be her next teacher. The 1934 appearance of Wassily de Basil's Monte Carlo Ballet Russe in Chicago led to an audition, and Sono Osato became the youngest member of the company and the first Japanese dancer to perform with the Ballets Russes.

Osato's early career with the Ballet Russe de Monte Carlo was dominated by efforts to develop her technique and by experiments with ways to disguise her Oriental features. Her own writings on this phase of her life speak with an honest innocence about the power and significance of ballet in her life. *Distant Dances*, her autobiography, is a poignant account of the era, capturing many of the leading figures in dance without the long, romanticized descriptions that have dominated so much of the literature. Her own story with the ballet, however, is one of frustration and disappointment. Held captive in the role of dutiful corps member, Osato was rarely provided with opportunities for advancement. But she was observant, and she provides us with a detailed look at the company's history, such as Massine's departure from the Ballet Russe, and Fokine's re-entry, or the political struggles behind the creation of the short-lived Educational Ballet Limited, which reappeared as de Basil's Original Ballet Russe in the late 1930s.

While Osato was in awe of Kshesinskaya as a teacher, it was Bronislava Nijinska who pushed her towards the realization of her potential. Osato was a Maid-in-Waiting in *Les Cent Baisers*, and experienced for the first time the distinct movement vocabulary of Nijinska. The two were to work together again in the remounting of *Les Noces* at the Metropolitan Opera House in 1936. That year also marked another turning point. Sono Osato was finally given a soloist role, in the restaging of Massine's divertissement, *Cimarosiana*, performed the following year. She was coached by the originator of the role, Lydia Sokolova.

A tour of Australia and New Zealand in 1939 brought the opportunity to appear in Lichine's version of *The Prodigal Son*. As the Siren, Osato danced her first solo role which reflected full preparation. Soon afterwards, she achieved critical acclaim for her performance of the role in London, partnered by Lichine. She continued to fill a number of small solo roles in *Schéhérazade, Choreartium*, and *Le Coq d'or*. But it was the overwhelming number of other, smaller parts and chorus roles that led to her complete frustration. Faced with the prospect of being forever ignored by de Basil, she walked out on the company in 1940.

Anton Dolin brought Osato back to the classics in 1941, with *Princess Aurora* for Ballet Theatre. Sadly, her Ballet Theatre career spanned only two years. After Pearl Harbor, Osato temporarily changed her name to Fitzpatrick; she was not allowed to tour with the company internationally. Ruth Page provided her with an opportunity to teach in Chicago until the company's return. It was Antony Tudor who then ushered her into a new level of achievement. She was deeply affected by Tudor's *Pillar of Fire*, in which she created the role of Lover-in-Experience, and she was very successful in his *Romeo and Juliet* as Rosaline. "One of the most delightful things in Antony Tudor's *Romeo and Juliet*", wrote John Martin, "was Sono Osato as Rosaline. Though she had no more than two scenes... she made from them one of the best realized characters in the whole work." Shortly afterwards, however, Osato left the company to marry.

Agnes de Mille drew Osato back once more into the world of performance, serving both as mentor and choreographer. The Broadway musical *One Touch of Venus* finally brought Osato stardom, as well as an award for Best Dancer in a Musical. She remained with the show until 1944. Her colleague from Ballet Theatre, Jerome Robbins, cast her as Ivy Smith, the legendary "Miss Turnstiles" for the Broadway version of his ballet *Fancy Free*, retitled and expanded as *On the Town*. In spite of this dramatic shift in her career to national fame, Osato lived a simple, somewhat austere existence with her husband Victor, and she left *On the Town* in 1945 to start a family.

Her work on the stage brought Osato to Hollywood's attention. Her brief encounter with film, in *The Kissing Bandit* with Frank Sinatra, was neither an enjoyable nor a successful collaboration. Her performance in *Ballet Ballads* (by John La Touche and composer Jerome Moross), for the Off-Broadway Experimental Theatre in 1948, coincided with the release of the film. *Ballet Ballads* eventually moved to the Music Box Theatre, but the film got at best mixed reviews. Osato's subsequent appearance in the Broadway production of *Peer Gynt* was a failure.

Sono Osato's struggles and triumphs represent the legacy of the many changes and incarnations of the Ballets Russes from the 1930s onwards, and its impact on opportunities for dancers in America in the 1940s. Dancers like Osato were the pioneers of an emerging American ballet tradition, but they also contributed to another American success story in dance, the musical theatre on the Broadway stage, and on film.

—Susan Lee

OSIPENKO, Alla
Russian dancer and teacher. Born Alla Evgeneeva Osipenko in Leningrad, 16 June 1932. Studied at the Leningrad Choreographic School, pupil of Agrippina Vaganova; graduated in 1950. Married (1) Gennady Boropaev, 1962 (div.): one son, Ivan Boropaev; (2) Kirov soloist John Markovsky, 1967 (div.). Début, when still a student, in role especially created by Vakhtang Chabukiani, 1947; dancer, becoming soloist, Kirov Ballet, 1950–71; first appearance outside the USSR as guest artist, Stanislavsky and Nemirovich–Danchenko Ballet, Paris, 1956; soloist, Choreographic Miniatures company (dir. Leonid Yakobson), 1971–73, Leningrad Concert Organization, 1973–77, and Theatre of Contemporary Ballet (dir. Boris Eifman), 1977–82; teacher, Leningrad Choreographic School, 1966–70; guest coach and teacher, Italy and France, 1989–90; has also appeared frequently in dance films, including *The Kiss* (Yakobson; Leningrad television, 1961), *Antony and Cleopatra* (Chernyshov; Leningrad television, 1975); also actress, including in the films *The Voice* (dir. Averbach, 1981), and *Sorrowful Sympathy* (dir. Sokurov), 1986. Recipient: Prizes at International Festival of Youth and Students, Prague, 1950, and Moscow, 1957; Anna Pavlova Prize, Paris, 1956; titles of Honoured Artist of the Russian Federation, 1957, People's Artist of the Russian Federation, 1960.

Alla Osipenko as Cleopatra in Chernyshov's *Antony and Cleopatra*

ROLES

1947 Principal dancer (cr) in *Musical Moment* (Chabukiani), Leningrad Choreographic School, Leningrad

1948 Principal dancer (cr) in *Meditations* (Yakobson), Leningrad Choreographic School, Leningrad

1950 Masha in *The Nutcracker* (Vainonen), Graduation Performance, Leningrad Choreographic School, Kirov Theatre, Leningrad

1951 One of Two Swans in *Swan Lake* (Petipa, Ivanov), Kirov Ballet, Leningrad

Lilac Fairy in *The Sleeping Beauty* (Petipa), Kirov Ballet, Leningrad

Maria in *The Fountain of Bahkchisarai* (Zakharov), Kirov Ballet, Leningrad

Raymonda's Friend in *Raymonda* (Petipa; staged Sergeyev), Kirov Ballet, Leningrad

Queen of the Ball in *The Bronze Horseman* (Zakharov), Kirov Ballet, Leningrad

1952 Mona (soloist, Wilis) in *Giselle* (Petipa after Coralli, Perrot), Kirov Ballet, Leningrad

1953 Gamzatti in *La Bayadère* (Ponomarev, Chabukiani after Petipa), Kirov Ballet, Leningrad

Street Dancer in *Don Quixote* (Gorsky after Petipa), Kirov Ballet, Leningrad

1954 Nikiya in *La Bayadère* (Ponomarev, Chabukiani after Petipa), Kirov Ballet, Leningrad

Odette/Odile in *Swan Lake* (Petipa, Ivanov; staged Sergeyev), Kirov Ballet, Leningrad

The Summer Fairy in *Cinderella* (Sergeyev), Kirov Ballet, Leningrad

1955 Title role in *Raymonda* (Petipa; staged Sergeyev), Kirov Ballet, Leningrad

Vakchanka in *Walpurgis Night* (Lavrovsky), Kirov Ballet, Leningrad

Pannochka in *Taras Bulba* (Fenster), Kirov Ballet, Leningrad

1957 Mistress of the Copper Mountain (cr) in *The Stone Flower* (Grigorovich), Kirov Ballet, Leningrad

1958 The Eagle (cr) in *Prometheus* (choreographic miniature; Yakobson), Kirov Ballet, Leningrad

Principal dancer (cr) in *The Kiss* (choreographic miniature; Yakobson), Kirov Ballet, Leningrad

1959 The Beloved (cr; with Kolpakova) in *The Coast of Hope* (Belsky), Kirov Ballet, Leningrad

1960 Desdemona (cr) in *Othello* (Kirov production; Chabukiani), Kirov Ballet, Leningrad

Phrygia in *Spartacus* (Yakobson), Kirov Ballet, Leningrad

1961 Sari in *The Path of Thunder* (Sergeyev), Kirov Ballet, Leningrad

Mekhmene-Banu in *The Legend of Love* (Grigorovich), Kirov Ballet, Leningrad

Nina in *Masquerade* (Fenster), Kirov Ballet, Leningrad

1963 Sixth Waltz (cr) in (*Ravel's*) *Waltzes* (Yakobson), Kirov Ballet, Leningrad

1965 Title role (cr) in *The Pearl* (Boyarsky), Kirov Ballet, Leningrad

1966 Death (cr) in *Man* (Lifshits), Kirov Ballet, Leningrad

Principal dancer (cr) in *Syrinx* (Aleksidze), The Chamber Ballet (ensemble of Kirov dancers), Leningrad Philharmonic, Leningrad

1967 The Ugly Sister in *Cinderella* (Sergeyev), Kirov Ballet, Leningrad

1968 Cleopatra in *Antony and Cleopatra* (Chernyshov), Maly Theatre for Opera and Ballet, Leningrad

1971 Principal dancer (cr) in *Taglioni's Flight* and *The Minotaur and the Nymph* (choreographic miniatures; Yakobson), Yakobson's Choreographic Miniatures Company, Leningrad

Title role in *Firebird* (Yakobson), Yakobson's Choreographic Miniatures Company, Leningrad

1972 Principal dancer (cr) in *The Swan*, *Adagio: Duet and Tango*, and *Exercise XX* (Yakobson), Yakobson's Choreographic Miniatures Company, Leningrad

Principal dancer (cr) in *Brilliant Divertissement* (Yakobson), Yakobson's Choreographic Miniatures Company, Leningrad

1974 The Beauty (cr) in *Prodigal Son* (Murdmaa), Creative Evening for Mikhail Baryshnikov, Kirov Theatre, Leningrad

Juliet (cr) in *Romeo and Juliet* (pas de deux; Murdmaa), Concert Tour

Principal dancer in *Pas de Deux* (Markovsky), Concert Tour

1976 Soloist (cr) in *Rhapsody in the Style of Blues* (Azhuchanov), Guest Artist with the Young Ballet of Alma-Ata

Soloist (cr) in *Rondo Capriccioso* (Azhuchanov), Guest Artist with the Young Ballet of Alma-Ata

1977 The Song (cr) in *The Song Broken* (Eifman), New Ballet (dir. Eifman), Leningrad

Night Beauty (cr) in *Under Cover of Night* (Murdmaa), New Ballet, Leningrad

Soloist (cr) in *Bivocality* (Eifman), New Ballet, Leningrad

1978 Title role (cr) in *Firebird* (Eifman), New Ballet, Leningrad

1980 Nastasia (cr) in *The Idiot* (Eifman), Leningrad Ensemble Ballet (previously New Ballet), Leningrad

1981 Principal dancer (cr) in *Autographs* (Eifman), Leningrad Theatre of Contemporary Ballet (previously Leningrad Ensemble Ballet and New Ballet), Leningrad

Other roles include: for concert programmes—principal dancer in *Sarabanda* (Aleksidze), pas de deux from *The Talisman* (Petipa, staged Tiuntina), principal dancer in *Andante Sostenuto* (Dolgushin).

PUBLICATIONS

Krasovskaya, Vera, "Alla Osipenko", *Teatralnyi Leningrad* (Leningrad), no. 14, 1957

Lvov-Anokhin, Boris, "Alla Osipenko", *Muzykalnaya Zhizn* (Moscow), no. 12, 1962

Stupnikov, Igor, "Broken Dream", *Teatralnaya Zhizn* (Moscow), no. 9, 1967

Krasovskaya, Vera, "Alla Osipenko", *Teatr* (Moscow), no. 12, 1975

Zozulina, N., "Alla Osipenko", *Sovetsky Balet* (Moscow), no. 3, 1983

Alovert, Nina, *Baryshnikov in Russia*, New York, 1984

Smakov, Gennady, *The Great Russian Dancers*, New York, 1984

Zozulina, N., "Alla Osipenko", *Iskusstvo* (Leningrad), 1987

* * *

Alla Osipenko was an outstanding classical ballerina. She was distinguished by long and beautiful proportions, perfect line—

such as in a flawless attitude and arabesque—and an exact feeling for the nuances of dance, displayed in a style which combined precision and expressiveness. In the classical repertoire she was magnificent, excelling in such roles as the Lilac Fairy, Odette/Odile, and Raymonda. Here her technique and solid classical training (achieved under the great Vaganova) made her the ideal interpreter of the traditional nineteenth-century roles.

But Osipenko was also successful in the contemporary repertoire. The development of her own dramatic abilities, her pursuit of psychologically more complex roles, and her drive for creative challenge all coincided, fortunately, with a period of active interest in the new in choreographic art on the stage of the Kirov. Her encounter with the choreography of Yuri Grigorovich, and afterwards with that of Igor Belsky, was therefore timely, and provided the impetus for the ballerina's own discovery and development of her artistic individuality. The requirements of contemporary choreography matched her own special gifts, and allowed her to create her own dance style. Osipenko's work in *The Coast of Hope* was significant, but her crowning role was the Mistress of the Copper Mountain in *The Stone Flower*, created by Grigorovich in close collaboration with the dancer herself. Another of her great creative successes was as Mekhmene-Banu in *The Legend of Love*, in which she portrayed a queen simultaneously defenceless and wise, suffering and yet dignified.

Osipenko established herself as a significant force in contemporary ballet; she enjoyed a fruitful working relationship with Yuri Grigorovich, performing in some of his most important ballets, and she created leading roles in both of Belsky's ballets at the Kirov. Yet still she was dissatisfied. A woman of rather difficult temperament, Osipenko left the Kirov Theatre suddenly after twenty years. It was a complete mystery at first: why should such a dancer, at the height of her powers, choose to retire from the Kirov? In fact, Osipenko had been treated unfairly by the general director of the company, whose own personal favourite was Kaleria Fedicheva (a dancer who was referred to by some as "Madame Kshesinskaya", recalling the great and powerful ballerina who had been the lover of the Tsar). With Fedicheva virtually ruling ballet at the Kirov, Osipenko found conditions unworkable, and so eventually chose to leave with her (then) husband, John Markovsky. Together they went to work with Leonid Yakobson's company; and Osipenko says quite correctly that it was due to that outburst of feelings at the Kirov that she allowed herself to prolong, quite unwittingly, her artistic life for another ten or eleven years.

Thus it was that Osipenko, by departing from the stage of the Kirov, expanded her creative life, becoming a soloist with various contemporary ballet companies. With Yakobson's Choreographic Miniatures Company, she danced several powerful roles, assisting in the creation of such Yakobson ballets as *Exercise XX*. Later, at the Theatre of Contemporary Ballet, Boris Eifman created many roles for her—such as that of Nastasia in *The Idiot*, which was set to Tchaikovsky's music and later taken into the repertory of several European ballet companies. Osipenko's heroines always lived according to a complex inner life, searching for the answers to many questions, and acquiring wisdom and moral purity in the struggle—and it was through dance and her own uniquely expressive style of movement that Osipenko managed to convey the life of the inner self.

In the end, it is a matter of opinion whether or not this ballerina's great natural gifts and full potential were ever fully realized. Baryshnikov is said to have called Osipenko "the most modernistic, neo-classical classical ballerina". But some claim that, ultimately, in the world of Soviet ballet her talents were bound to be wasted. Others may disagree, but Osipenko's own originality as a dancer is indisputable.

—Igor Stupnikov

———

OTHELLO

Choreography: Vakhtang Chabukiani
Music: Aleksei Machavariani
Design: Simon Virsaladze (scenery and costumes)
Libretto: Vakhtang Chabukiani (after the play by Shakespeare)
First Production: Paliashvili Theatre of Opera and Ballet, Tbilisi, Georgia, 27 December 1957
Principal Dancers: Vakhtang Chabukiani (Othello), Vera Tsignadze (Desdemona), Zurab Kikaleishvili (Iago)

Other productions include: Kirov Ballet (restaged Chabukiani), with Chabukiani (Othello), Alla Osipenko (Desdemona), Svyatoslav Kuznetsov (Iago); Leningrad, 24 March 1960.

Other choreographic treatments of story: Salvatore Viganò (Milan, 1818), José Limón (New London, Connecticut, 1949), Erica Hanka (Vienna, 1955), Jiri Němeček (Prague, 1959), Serge Lifar (Monte Carlo, 1960), Jacques d'Amboise (New York, 1967), Peter Darrell (Trieste, 1971), John Butler (Ballet du Rhin, 1972).

PUBLICATIONS

Machavariani, Aleksei, *Othello*, Tbilisi, 1958
Entelis, L.A., *One Hundred Ballet Libretti*, Leningrad and Moscow, 1966
Smakov, Gennady, *The Great Russian Dancers*, New York, 1984

*   *   *

The brilliant Georgian dancer Vakhtang Chabukiani has rightly entered the ranks of Soviet and world dance history not only as a performer, but as a choreographer as well. A natural composer of dances, Chabukiani started staging concert pieces while still a student at ballet school. His extremely popular ballet, *Laurencia*, was staged for the Kirov Ballet in 1939. *Othello*, created in Tbilisi in 1957 and then produced for the Kirov in 1960, is one of his most significant productions.

Called the "god of dance" himself, Chabukiani was, for a long time, one of the most "dance-oriented" of Soviet ballet masters. He strove to express his ideas and to create images of heroes more through the language of choreography than through pantomime. Strangely enough, the ballet *Othello*, which he staged when "choreodrama" had virtually ceased to exist, is an archetypal "choreodrama"—but it must be emphasized that Chabukiani cannot be called a typical representative of that school.

The ballet derives from a detailed version of the libretto, retelling Shakespeare's tragedy. Unlike *Laurencia*, there are many pantomime scenes in this ballet, scenes in which the dancers convey the plot through gesture. But unlike other "choreodrama" ballet masters, in whose later works dance is virtually non-existent, Chabukiani, like a faithful knight, remains true to dance as the chief means of expression. Each of the heroes of his ballets has his own elastic language, and the climactic scenes of each production are resolved via dance and movement.

One of the most important of these scenes is the celebration in Cyprus after Othello's victory over the Turks. It is, first and foremost, a choreographic celebration—a device characteristic of Chabukiani. As in *Laurencia*, Chabukiani here used his experience of the classical heritage to create a divertissement typical of ballets of the past, that is, a dance suite in which the various parts are not directly related to the plot. The basic conflict of the plot is a hidden element in the two central dances of the suite—Othello's Mauritanean dance and the tarantella danced by Iago and Emilia. Chabukiani first staged the Mauritanean dance as an insert. But its tremendous success with the public gave him the idea of expanding Othello's dance and making it the centre of the suite (as later explained by Chabukiani's pupil, Igor Zelensky, a young premier danseur with the Kirov Ballet). The number was choreographed in the style of African dances; indeed, Othello's whole choreographic image was shaped in this style. Othello, radiant, arms extended, as if baring his soul to Desdemona, moved, spun, and danced yearningly. This radiant dance, especially in Chabukiani's own brilliant performance of it, was the choreographic embodiment of the Moor, a straightforward man, open and trusting.

Choreographically, the tarantella was the polar opposite of the Moor's dance. First of all, it is important to point to performance of Iago by Svyatoslav Kuznetsov in Leningrad. It was specifically because of this dancer's performances at the Kirov Ballet during the 1950s that the tarantella took on a special significance in the celebration divertissement. It can happen in the theatre that a particular performer so penetrates his role that he actually reveals hidden possibilities in the ballet. Iago's versatile role was choreographed on the basis of Georgian dance (the incorporation of Georgian classical dance was a favourite device in many of Chabukiani's ballets). While Georgian performers underscored the national colour of the role, Kuznetsov transformed the gait into the stealthy step of a man who wants to go unnoticed—a secretive, dangerous man. Kuznetsov stressed not the ascent, but the return to earth, heavily stomping into the floor of the stage with each step. The whole of Iago's dance was heavy, erotic, gloomy, and frenetic. Iago was rejoicing in anticipation of the success of his secret plan. Thus the choreographic juxtaposition of these two dances expressed the antagonism of the two main characters—the mainspring of the tragedy. (Later, Kuznetsov danced Othello, too, deepening the tragic aspect of that character's image.)

Also of interest was the way Chabukiani staged the scene in which Iago informs Othello of Desdemona's supposed infidelity. First Othello takes the lead, with Iago merely spinning around. Gradually Othello's dance becomes more mundane

Othello, with Svyatoslav Kuznetsov as Iago, Kirov Ballet, Leningrad

and Iago leaps up, his choreographic phrases growing ever longer—he has won. When the broken Moor falls unconscious to the floor, Iago stands on his chest, posing in "attitude", arms flung wide like a vulture over the body of his victim.

It is thanks to these and other well-staged scenes, and to the abilities of the original performers, that the ballet was successful with both public and critics, who recognized in Chabukiani's ballet a faithful and effective translation of Shakespeare into dance.

—Nina Alovert

PAGANINI

Choreography: Mikhail Fokine
Music: Sergei Rachmaninov
Design: Sergei Soudeikine (scenery and costumes)
Libretto: Mikhail Fokine and Sergei Rachmaninov
First Production: (de Basil's) Covent Garden Russian Ballet, London, 30 June 1939
Principal Dancers: Dmitri Rostov (Paganini), Irina Baronova (The Divine Genius), Tatiana Riabouchinska (A Florentine Beauty), Paul Petroff (A Florentine Youth)

Other productions include: Bolshoi Ballet (new version; chor. Leonid Lavrovsky), with Yaroslav Sekh (Paganini), Maria Kondratieva (Maria); Moscow, 7 April 1960 (revived Bolshoi Ballet, 1978). Tulsa Ballet Theatre (staged Vladimir Dokoudovsky after Fokine, assisted by Roman Jasinski); Tulsa, 8 February 1986.

PUBLICATIONS

Beaumont, Cyril, *Supplement to Complete Book of Ballets*, London, 1942
Fokine, Michel, *Fokine: Memoirs of a Ballet Master*, translated by Vitale Fokine, London, 1961
Buckle, Richard, *Buckle at the Ballet*, London, 1980
Sorley Walker, Kathrine, *De Basil's Ballets Russes*, London, 1982
Horwitz, Dawn Lille, *Michel Fokine*, Boston, 1985
Garafola, Lynn, "Fokine's *Paganini* Resurrected", *Ballet Review* (New York), Spring 1986
García-Márquez, Vicente, *Les Ballets Russes*, New York, 1990

*   *   *

Paganini, a ballet in three scenes choreographed by Mikhail Fokine to the *Rhapsody on a Theme of Paganini* by Sergei Rachmaninov, was first seen in 1939, danced by Colonel de Basil's Ballets Russes (then performing as the "Russian Ballet") at Covent Garden, London. It was a result of two years of collaboration between the choreographer and composer, old acquaintances and co-authors of the libretto. A psychological work, the ballet is based on the musical genius whose life was surrounded by myth and scandal, the strains of which interfered with his desire to achieve immortality.

Scene 1 shows Paganini in public on a concert platform, with an audience, through whose eyes he is seen. The devil appears in a goat mask, and dark figures seem to pluck at the strings of his violin. Gossip, Scandal, and Envy weave through the spectators (they actually came through the audience at the premiere), and ghosts and phantoms leap about as the light

fades. Scene 2 takes place in a mountain landscape above Florence. Here youths and maidens dance, and the focus is on a beautiful girl in a pink dress dancing with her lover. A gaunt figure (Paganini) enters carrying a guitar and begins to play music, to which the Florentine Beauty dances as if possessed, finally swooning in exhaustion at his feet. Scene 3, depicting his solitude, finds Paginini, old and ill, in his large dark study, with its single candle-lit table. He picks up his violin and begins to improvise, comforted and inspired by the Divine Genius. Then he has a nightmare in which his tormentors appear, led by Satan and all looking exactly like Paganini. When the spirits of Envy, Guile, and others appear, he beats them off with his bow. Finally, as death approaches, Divine Genius reappears with a group of Spirits and leads Paganini's soul up the staircase to heaven.

The letters between Fokine and Rachmaninov began in 1935, when Fokine wrote that he was trying to grant the composer's wish by creating a libretto for which Rachmaninov could write the music. In August 1937 the choreographer wrote about his continuing difficulty in finding a suitable subject, saying he needed a spark to set him off, and "often it is music . . .". Rachmaninov wrote back, suggesting a ballet based on the legend of Paganini "selling his soul to a dark spirit for perfection in art". By February of 1939, Fokine wrote that he was working on the ballet, but felt the second scene was too short and thus requested permission for a repetition of the twelfth variation, which the composer granted. Rachmaninov was injured in a fall and was unable to come to the opening, but his collaborator reported a flawless performance in which the music critics failed to notice that the special ending was a repeat of music heard earlier. In the original cast, the role of Paganini was, as Cyril Beaumont wrote, "admirably played" by Dmitri Rostov. "[He] does evoke for us that fantastic being described by Berlioz as 'a man with long black hair, piercing eyes, and wasted form—genius-haunted, a colossus among giants.'" The ballerinas Irina Baronova and Tatiana Riabouchinska performed the parts of "Divine Genius" and a "Florentine Beauty", respectively. The décor by Sergei Soudekeine was effective, if not outstanding.

The few excerpts from this ballet, on a black-and-white silent film made in 1946, show only the scene with the Florentine Beauty (Riabouchinska). The other maidens, wearing long dresses with empire waists, display flexible backs and soft, asymmetrical arms. The group movements are flowing in quality. The Beauty, wearing pointe shoes, performs a lovely solo that at first is softly romantic and employs an expressively arched back. The speed of movement then increases, as does the use of the floor, as she appears to be possessed by demons. One is reminded somewhat of Giselle.

Sono Osato, who was one of the maidens, says that during her hypnotic solo the body of the Florentine Beauty was in constant motion. She recalls that in the third scene a chain of Spirits performed slow, sustained arabesques around Paganini. Yurek Lazowsky recalls the role of Paganini as mainly mime, but otherwise there was much dancing in the work.

The ballet played to sold-out houses in London, where most critics considered it a perfect collaboration between composer and choreographer. In New York, Irving Kolodin called Fokine's realization of Paganini in terms of dance "superlative" and the blending of choreographic and theatrical elements "masterful". John Martin, although he found it better defined as theatre than as ballet, still termed the opening scene "deeply beautiful". Others found the philosophical ideas obscure and the ending, with the winged angels leading the soul, obsolete and sentimental.

The critical and popular success of *Paganini* spurred Fokine and Rachmaninov to plan another collaboration, but it never materialized. It was the last ballet Fokine created for de Basil.

—Dawn Lille Horwitz

PAGE, Ashley

British dancer and choreographer.   Born Ashley John Laverty in Rochester, England, 9 August 1956. Educated at St. Andrew's School, Rochester; studied dance at the Makinnon School of Dancing, Gillingham, and Royal Ballet Schools, London, 1968–75. Leading dancer, Ballet for All (of the Royal Ballet), 1975; dancer, Royal Ballet, from 1976, becoming principal dancer, from 1984, and touring with the Royal Ballet worldwide; choreographer, staging first work for Royal Ballet, 1984, and also choreographing for Rambert Dance Company, Dance Umbrella, Dutch National Ballet, and Istanbul State Ballet. Recipient: First Frederick Ashton Choreographic Award for Royal Ballet Choreographic Group, 1982; First Frederick Ashton Memorial Commission for Rambert Dance Company, 1990.

ROLES

1975   Gypsy Lover in *The Two Pigeons* (Ashton), Royal Ballet School Performance, London
       Albrecht in *The World of Giselle* (educational touring programme; chor. Petipa after Coralli, Perrot), Ballet for All
       Romeo in *Romeo and Juliet: Ballet and Play* (educational touring programme; chor. MacMillan), Ballet for All
       The Artist in *The Two Pigeons* (selections; chor. Ashton), in *Ashton and La Fille mal gardée* (educational touring programme), Ballet for All
1976   Dancer in *Voluntaries* (Tetley), Royal Ballet, London
1977   "Beginning" (cr) in *The Fourth Symphony* (Neumeier), Royal Ballet, London
       Principal dancer (Trois Gymnopédies) in *Monotones* (Ashton), Royal Ballet, London
       Dancer (cr) in *Gloriana* (MacMillan), Gala for Queen's Silver Jubilee, Royal Ballet, London
1978   Dancer in *Birthday Offering* (Ashton), Royal Ballet, London
       Popular Song in *Façade* (Ashton), Royal Ballet, London
       Saturday in *Jazz Calendar* (Ashton), Royal Ballet, London
       Dancer in *The Concert* (Robbins), Royal Ballet, London
       Hothouse Rag in *Elite Syncopations* (MacMillan), Royal Ballet, London

Spring in *The Four Seasons* (MacMillan), Royal Ballet, London
1979   Principal dancer in *Liebeslieder Walzer* (Balanchine), Royal Ballet, London
       Dancer in *Diversions* (MacMillan), Royal Ballet, London
       Chanson dansée ("Athlete") in *Les Biches* (Nijinska), Royal Ballet, London
1980   Third Song in *Dark Elegies* (Tudor), Royal Ballet, London
       Incroyable in *Mam'zelle Angot* (Massine), Royal Ballet, London
       An Angel (cr) in *Dances of Albion* (Tetley), Royal Ballet, London
       Soloist (cr) in *Rhapsody* (Ashton), Royal Ballet, London
       Principal dancer (lead couple) in *Rhapsody* (Ashton), Royal Ballet, London
       Pas de quatre (cr) in *Gloria* (MacMillan), Royal Ballet, London
       Dancer (cr) in *Love of Life* (Seymour), Royal Ballet Choreographic Group
       Principal dancer in *Troy Game* (North), Royal Ballet, London
1981   A Shepherd in *Daphnis and Chloe* (Ashton), Royal Ballet, London
       Principal dancer in *Afternoon of a Faun* (Robbins), Royal Ballet, London
       Tango Boy (cr) in *Isadora* (MacMillan), Royal Ballet, London
       The Poet in *Illuminations* (Ashton), Royal Ballet, London
       First Movement in *Concerto* (MacMillan), Royal Ballet, London
       Benvolio in *Romeo and Juliet* (MacMillan), Royal Ballet, London
1982   Angel of Light (cr) in *Orpheus* (MacMillan), Royal Ballet, London
       Ferdinand (cr) in *The Tempest* (Nureyev), Royal Ballet, London
       Title role in *The Prodigal Son* (Balanchine), Royal Ballet, London
       A Man in *Rite of Spring* (MacMillan), Royal Ballet, London
       Beliaev in *A Month in the Country* (Ashton), Royal Ballet, London
       Soloist in *Scènes de ballet* (Ashton), Royal Ballet, London
       Title song (cr) in *L'Invitation au voyage* (Corder), Royal Ballet, London
       The Brother in *My Brother, My Sisters* (MacMillan), Royal Ballet, London
       Dancer in *The Energy Between Us* (Burrows), Royal Ballet, London
1983   Principal dancer in *Requiem* (MacMillan), Royal Ballet, London
       Principal dancer (cr) in *Midsummer* (Alston), Royal Ballet, London
       Malnate (cr) in *Valley of Shadows* (MacMillan), Royal Ballet, London
       Grand Pas in *Raymonda, Act III* (Nureyev after Petipa), Royal Ballet, London
       Demetrius in *The Dream* (Ashton), Royal Ballet, London
       Paul in *A Wedding Bouquet* (Ashton), Royal Ballet, London
       Principal dancer in *Varii Capricci* (Ashton), Royal Ballet, London

Ashley Page's *Bloodlines*, **as performed by Darcey Bussell and Bruce Sansom, Royal Ballet, London, 1990**

1984   Dancer in *Song of the Earth* (MacMillan), Royal Ballet, London
Pas de quatre in *Raymonda*, Act III (Nureyev after Petipa), Royal Ballet, London
Sarabande in *Agon* (Balanchine), Royal Ballet, London
Romeo in *Romeo and Juliet* (MacMillan), Royal Ballet, London
Danse espagnole in *The Nutcracker* (Wright), Royal Ballet, London
1985   Hilarion in *Giselle* (Petipa after Coralli, Perrot; staged Wright), Royal Ballet, London
Principal dancer (cr) in *Half the House* (Jackson), Royal Ballet, London
Duamutef (cr) in *The Sons of Horus* (Bintley), Royal Ballet, London
1986   First Movement in *Young Apollo* (Bintley), Royal Ballet, London
Dancer in *Refurbished Behaviour* (also chor.), Dance Umbrella, London
Dancer (cr) in *Accident Ballroom* (also chor.), Dance Umbrella, London

1987   Spanish Dance in *Swan Lake* (Petipa, Ivanov; staged Dowell), Royal Ballet, London
Her Partner (cr) in *The Angel of Death is in my Bed Tonight* (also chor.), Dance Umbrella, London
1988   Lysander in *The Dream* (Ashton), Royal Ballet, London
Tirrenio in *Ondine* (Ashton), Royal Ballet, London
Principal dancer in *Fin du jour* (MacMillan), Royal Ballet, London
1989   King of the South (cr) in *The Prince of the Pagodas* (MacMillan), Royal Ballet, London
1990   Mars (cr) in *The Planets* (Bintley), Royal Ballet, London
1991   Pas de deux in *Danses concertantes* (MacMillan), Royal Ballet, London
Southern Cape Zebra in *Still Life at the Penguin Café* (Bintley), Royal Ballet, London
Valvert (cr) in *Cyrano* (Bintley), Royal Ballet, London

Other roles include: Gentleman, Lescaut in *Manon* (MacMillan), principal dancer in *Different Drummer* (MacMillan), Officer in *Mayerling* (MacMillan), Arthur Troyte Griffith (Troyte) in *Enigma Variations* (Ashton), Florestan in *The*

Sleeping Beauty (Petipa, Ashton; staged de Valois), Pas de quatre in *Swan Lake* (Petipa, Ivanov, Ashton), principal dancer in *Return to the Strange Land* (Kylián), principal dancer in *Four Schumann Pieces* (van Manen), Dr. Frankenstein in *Frankenstein, the Modern Prometheus* (Eagling), Friday Night in *Elite Syncopations* (MacMillan).

WORKS

1982 *Seven Sketches* (mus. Beethoven), Frederick Ashton Choreographic Award Performance, Bloomsbury Theatre, London

1983 *Apex Stretched Backwards* (text from *Four Plays for Dancers*, by W.B. Yeats), Dance Umbrella, London

1984 *Wanting, Running, Running* (mus. Bartók), Royal Ballet, London

Between Public Places (mus. Eric Pressly and others), Dance Umbrella, London

A Broken Set of Rules (mus. Nyman), Royal Ballet, London

1985 *This is What You Get* (mus. P.I.L.), Dance Umbrella, London

It Was, What, Where? (mus. Aiden Fisher), Dance Umbrella, London

Inevitable Geography (mus. Aiden Fisher), Dance Umbrella, London

Refurbished Behaviour (mus. P.I.L.), Laban Centre, London

Furnished Behaviour (no music), Chisenhale Dance Space, London

1986 *Carmen Arcadiae* (mus. Birtwistle), Ballet Rambert, London

The Organising Principle (mus. Aiden Fisher), Transitions '86, London

Accident Ballroom (mus. John-Marc Gowans), Dance Umbrella, London

1987 *Pursuit* (mus. Colin Matthews), Royal Ballet, London

The Angel of Death is in My Bed Tonight (mus. "This Heat"), Dance Umbrella, London

1988 *Soldat* (mus. Stravinsky), Rambert Dance Company, Canterbury

1989 *Piano* (mus. Beethoven), Royal Ballet, Plymouth

Savage Water (mus. Orlando Gough, Bruce Gilbert), "Dance on 4", British television (Channel 4)

1990 *Currulao* (mus. Orlando Gough), Rambert Dance Company, Mold

Bloodlines (mus. Bruce Gilbert), Royal Ballet, London

Slow Walk/Fast Talk (mus. Orlando Gough), Royal Ballet principals tour of North America

1991 *D. umb* (mus. Wire), Dance Umbrella Gala, London

Ballet of the Just Hatched Chicks (mus. Mussorgsky), Royal Ballet School students, London

1992 *Quartet* (mus. Liszt), Irek Mukhamedov and Company, British tour

Bisocosis Populi (mus. Nyman), London Studio Centre Images of Dance tour

Touch Your Coolness to my Fevered Brow (mus. Gough), Dutch National Ballet, Amsterdam

Heavenly Interior (mus. Tchaikovsky), Istanbul State Ballet, Istanbul

Slow Curve (solo; mus. Gilbert), Paris Ballet Competition, Paris

Other works include: *Early* (1981), *Twenty-five Hundred Hours* (1981), *Four Play* (mus. Purcell, 1983), *Bad, Bad, Baby Assolutas* (1985).

PUBLICATIONS

By Page:
Interview with Mackrell, Judith, in *Dance Theatre Journal* (London), Spring 1986

About Page:
"Dancer You Will Know", *Dance and Dancers* (London), January 1982

"Turning the Page", *Dance and Dancers* (London), July 1984

Macaulay, Alastair, "The Royal Ballet; The Next Choreographers", *Dance Theatre Journal* (London), Spring 1985

Mackrell, Judith, "Ashley Page", *Dance Theatre Journal* (London), Spring 1986

Shaw, Robert, "Fragmented Première", *Dance and Dancers* (London), October 1987

"The Royal Ballet: Biographies", *Ballet in London Year Book* (London), 1988/89, 1989/90

Macaulay, Alastair, "Almeida Rambert", *Dancing Times* (London), August 1989

Jordan, Stephanie, "Brittle and Disturbing", *Dance and Dancers* (London), December 1989

"Young Classical Choreographers", *Dancing Times* (London), January 1990

McHugh, Fionnulala, "Prize Performance", *Telegraph Weekend Magazine* (London), 10 March 1990

Craine, Deborah, "Deconstruction of the Classics by Royal Maverick", *The Times* (London), 28 November 1990

*   *   *

In his ambitious approach to ballet, Ashley Page brings to the form a strong understanding of what goes on beyond the dance world and a lively ironic eye upon what happens within. Perhaps he is still best known for his series of abstract ballets to ambitious musical scores, like *A Broken Set of Rules*, *Pursuit*, and *Piano* for the Royal Ballet, as well as *Carmen Arcadiae* for the Rambert Dance Company. But the works that Page has made outside of the established companies form a marked contrast. He undertook essays in simple, non-technical movement and contact-style improvization with the post-modern choreographer Gaby Agis in the early 1980s. More recently, there have been collages of rock, Gothic horror imagery, ballet, social and modern dance for Dance Umbrella Festivals and television.

Two other pieces for the Rambert company are loaded with references that go beyond the dance itself. *Soldat*, to Stravinsky's *Histoire du soldat* suite, has the clear narrative thread of a folk tale, but Page has pared down the story to essentials and made abstract the characters of devil, soldier, and princess. The choreography for this piece mixes cleverly with a multi-coloured set, overhead platform, ladder, and pillars by the sculptor Bruce McLean. *Currulao*, which was the first of Rambert Dance Company's Frederick Ashton Memorial Commissions, is explained by Page as a Colombian courtship dance that mixes Spanish and African influences. Clothed in big, bizarre costumes by the new-wave fashion designer John Galliano, and set to a blaring systems score by Orlando Gough, *Currulao* contains the inkling of a plot concerning two partner-swapping central couples.

Yet perhaps the most impressive Page is to be seen in his less narrative pieces. Here, he is primarily a symphonist, thinking in abstract terms across substantial time-spans and much like a musician. *Pursuit*, for instance, explores the possibility of dance pushing on at its own feverish energy, while it also has a classical structure, governed by principles of formal clarity. As much as the dancers exist in flurries of crazy counterpoint, they are tidied up at intervals into lines and blocks, and the work is paced to end with a slow, legible duet. In *Carmen*, there are similar points of rest for the attention, but order here is always at breaking point: tableaux of dancers teetering in imbalance or in counter-tension, the final stage picture a rough, ragged diagonal across which two women are caught diving towards each other.

Page's ambition for the language of his medium has led him towards a particular fusion of modern dance and ballet, with inversions and subversions of familiar classical behaviour. Ever since *A Broken Set of Rules*, the stability of classicism has been present in the line and curve of familiar positions solidly stated, but this has been set against discordant elements—isolated movements of body parts, the free use of the upper body to curve and tilt, jagged flexions, and sudden disregard for the traditional turned-out stance. Page's vocabulary is rich, and he gathers it into complex, convoluted phrases.

However, even Page's "pure dance" pieces always seem to be more than just that. There are hints of character and post-modern commentary—far less a question of movement style than an attitude. In *Piano*, Page eyes the polarities of ballet with irony, with opera-house monumentalism set against the traditional intimacies among leading protagonists. As well as his edgy answer to classical vocabulary, there is a sense of contrivance, the dancers appearing to "play at" their roles or else appearing to be played like marionettes. The effect is wry, witty, brittle, or even, at times, sinister. His seems to be a sceptical view of the balletic future.

Page has always been interested in collaborating with fine artists, commissioning designs, for example, from Deanna Petherbridge for *A Broken Set of Rules*, Jack Smith for *Carmen* and *Pursuit*, and Howard Hodgkin for *Piano*. And he has favoured new, or at least twentieth-century, music—most notably, Harrison Birtwistle for *Carmen*, Michael Nyman for *A Broken Set of Rules*, and Colin Matthews for *Pursuit*. Turning to a concert classic, Beethoven's Piano Concerto No. 1 for *Piano*, was an exceptional gesture.

One of the most promising aspects of Page's work is the energy that he produces from his dancers. Particularly refreshing in the context of the Royal Ballet is the forceful, no-nonsense spirit that his young casts bring to his ballets.

—Stephanie Jordan

PAGE, Ruth

American dancer, choreographer, and ballet director.   Born in Indianapolis, 22 March 1899 (some sources say 1900). Studied with Adolph Bolm, from 1917, Enrico Cecchetti, London, 1920, and Edna McRae; also studied modern dance with Harald Kreutzberg. Married (1) Thomas Hart Fisher, 1925 (d. 1959); (2) Andre Delfau, 1980. Dancer in revue (in choreography by Bolm), New York, 1917; dancer with Anna Pavlova company, South American tour, 1918–19; principal dancer, Adolph Bolm's Ballet Intime, U.S. tour, 1920–22; principal dancer, Irving Berlin's Music Box Revue, New York and on tour, 1922–24, and Adoph Bolm's Allied Arts Ballet, Chicago, 1924–27, also performing with Diaghilev's Ballets Russes, Monte Carlo, 1925; concert dancer on national and international solo tours from 1927, and on joint tours with partners including Harald Kreutzberg, 1933–34; dancer and choreographer in partnership with Bentley Stone, from 1935, becoming the Page–Stone Ballet, from 1938; ballet director and principal dancer for opera companies including Ravinia

Opera, from 1926, Metropolitan Opera Ballet, New York, 1927, Chicago Civic Opera, 1934–36, and Chicago Opera, 1941–42; co-director and principal dancer, Les Ballets Americains, Paris, 1950; choreographer and ballet director, Chicago Lyric Opera, 1954–69, at the same time developing an independent ballet company, Ruth Page's Chicago Opera Ballet (later known as Ruth Page's International Ballet, while touring); artistic director, Chicago Ballet, 1974–77; guest choreographer, including for Les Ballets des Champs-Elysées, London Festival Ballet, and (Massine's) Ballet Russe de Monte Carlo. Recipient: Honorary Doctorate, Colombia College, Chicago, 1974; *Dance Magazine* Award, 1980 and 1990; Illinois Gubernatorial award, 1985. Died in Chicago, 7 April 1991.

ROLES

1917   Dancer (cr) in *Falling Leaves* (*Poem Choreographic*; Bolm), in *Miss 1917* (Broadway revue), Century Theatre, New York

1919   Infanta (cr) in *The Birthday of the Infanta* (Bolm), Chicago Opera, Chicago

1922   Principal dancer (with Bolm) in *Danse Macabre* (first dance film with synchronized sound)

Premiere danseuse in *Music Box Revue* (Irving Berlin revue), Music Box Theatre, New York

1924   Premiere danseuse (cr) in *Foyer de la danse* (Bolm), Chicago Allied Arts Ballet, Chicago

1925   Principal dancer (cr) in *The Rivals* (Bolm), Chicago Allied Arts Ballet, Chicago

Polovtsian Maiden in *Polovtsian Dances from Prince Igor* (after Fokine), Chicago Allied Arts Ballet, Chicago

The Queen of Shemakhan in *Le Coq d'or* (Bolm), Teatro Colón, Buenos Aires

Principal dancer (cr) in *Étude* (Balanchine), Concert Performance, Monte Carlo

Dancer (cr) in *Polka mélancolique* (solo; Balanchine), Concert Performance, Monte Carlo

The Ballerina in *Petrushka* (after Fokine), Teatro Colón, Buenos Aires

Principal dancer (cr) in *Madragora* (Bolm), Chicago Allied Arts Ballet, Chicago

Principal dancer (cr) in *Bal de Marionettes* (Bolm), Chicago Allied Arts Ballet, Chicago

Principal dancer in *Elopement* (Bolm), Chicago Allied Arts Ballet, Chicago

1926   Principal dancer (cr) in *Parnassus au Montmartre* (Bolm), Chicago Allied Arts Ballet, Chicago

Principal dancer (cr) in *La Farce du Pont Neuf* (Bolm), Chicago Allied Arts Ballet, Chicago

Principal dancer (cr) in *Vision Mystique* (Bolm), Chicago Allied Arts Ballet, Chicago

The Flapper (cr) in *The Flapper and the Quarterback* (also chor.), Eighth Street Theatre, Chicago

1927   Dancer in *The Bartered Bride* (opera; mus. Smetana), Metropolitan Opera, New York

1928   Terpsichore (cr) in *Apollon musagète* (Bolm), Chamber Music Society, Washington, D.C.

WORKS

Solo dances or duets choreographed and performed by Page:

1921   *Girl with the Flaxen Hair*, *The Poisoned Flower* (mus. Hahn), *La Gitanette*, Apollo Theatre, New York

1922   *Chopin Mazurka* (mus. Chopin), Vassar College, Poughkeepsie, New York

Ruth Page in her own solo, *Pre-Raphaelite*, c.1930

1926 *Peter Pan and the Butterfly* (mus. Poldini), Goodman Theatre, Chicago
The Flapper and the Quarterback (mus. Loomis), Eighth Street Theatre, Chicago
1927 *Creole Dances* (also called *Bayou Ballads*, or *Negro Dances of New Orleans*; mus. traditional), Central High School, Madison, Wisconsin
1928 *Barnum and Bailey* (also called *Circus* or *Tightrope Walker*; mus. Smetana), *Coquette—1899* (mus. Joplin), Ravinia Park, Chicago
Blues (mus. Gershwin), Ravinia Park, Chicago
The Shadow of Death (mus. Mussorgsky), Imperial Theatre, Tokyo
Diana (mus. Mozart), Imperial Theatre, Tokyo
Ballet Scaffolding (mus. Prokofiev), Imperial Theatre, Tokyo
1929 *Japanese Print* (mus. arranged Goodman), *Oak Street Beach* (originally called *Sun Worshippers*; mus. Loomis), Ravinia Park, Chicago
Two Balinese Rhapsodies (mus. arranged Horst), *Gershwiniana* (also *Prelude No. 1*; mus. Gershwin), *St. Louis Blues* (mus. Handy), Women's Club, Chicago
Sentimental Melody (mus. Copland), Guild Theatre, New York
Indian Hill, Skokie School, Winnetka, Illinois
Étude op. 10 no. 3 (mus. Chopin), Guild Theatre, New York
1930 *Iberian Monotone* (also called *Bolero*; mus. Ravel), Ravinia Park, Chicago
Garçonette (mus. Poulenc), *Incantation* (mus. Albéniz), *Modern Diana* (sometimes performed with *Diana*, 1928, as *Evolution of a Goddess*; mus. Hindemith), *Pre-Raphaelite* (mus. Mompou), Nashville, Tennessee
1931 *Cinderella* (mus. Delannoy), Ravinia Park, Chicago
Pavane (mus. Ravel), *La Valse* (mus. Ravel), Booth Theatre, New York
1932 *Tropic* (mus. Scott), Amalgamated Centre, Chicago
Cuban Night (mus. Lecuona y Casado), *Lament* (mus. Tcherepnin), *Possessed* (mus. Villa-Lobos), *Vagabond* (mus. Vaughan Williams), State Normal University, Bloomington, Indiana
Three Humoresques (developed out of *Giddy Girl* solo, 1931; mus. Casella), State Normal University, Bloomington, Indiana
Largo (mus. Vinci), *Expanding Universe* (mus. Wolf), Fargo, North Dakota
1933 *Variations on Euclid* (mus. Mompou), Loyola University, Chicago
Morning in Spring (mus. Vaughan Williams), John Golden Theatre, New York
Country Dance (with Kreutzberg; mus. Wilckens), *Promenade* (with Kreutzberg; mus. Poulenc), Studebaker Theatre, Chicago
Jungle (mus. Scott), International House, Chicago
Mozart Waltzes (mus. Mozart), *My Sorrow is My Song* (mus. Milhaud), *Pendulum* (mus. Mompou), *Resurgence* (mus. Kodály), *Rustic Saint's Day* (mus. Respighi), *Shadow Dance—Homage to Taglioni* (mus. Mendelssohn), *Songs* (mus. Gershwin), International House, Chicago
1934 *Arabian Nights* (with Kreutzberg; mus. Satie), Shrine Temple, Peoria, Illinois
Bacchanale (with Kreutzberg; mus. Wilckens), Orchestra Hall, Chicago
1935 *Body in Sunlight* (mus. Wolf), Studebaker Theatre, Chicago
Fresh Fields (mus. Bartók), *Night Melody* (mus. Debussy), *Valse Mondaine* (mus. Castelnuovo-Tedesco), Studebaker Theatre, Chicago
Fugitive Visions (mus. Prokofiev), Carmel, New York
1936 *Hicks at the Country Fair* (with B. Stone; mus. Stravinsky), Chicago Women's Club, Chicago
1938 *Buenos Días, Señorita* (with B. Stone; mus. Villa-Lobos), *Gavotte* (with B. Stone; mus. Bach), Mt. Veron, Iowa
Delirious Delusion (mus. Mompou), Rogers Park Women's Club, Chicago
The Story of a Heart (mus. Casella), Chicago
1939 *Liebestod* (with B. Stone; mus. Wagner), *Night of the Poor* (with B. Stone; mus. Debussy), *Saudades* (with B. Stone; mus. Villa-Lobos), Civic Theatre, Chicago
Three Shakespearean Heroines (mus. Schubert, Liszt, Wilckens, Beethoven, arranged Schienfield), Civic Theatre, Chicago
Zephyr and Flora (mus. Liszt), Civic Theatre, Chicago
1940 *Songs of Carl Sandburg* (Sandburg recordings), Chicago
Catarina; or, The Daughter of the Bandit (mus. Drigo), Sociedad Pro-Arte Musical, Havana
1941 *Spanish Dance in Ballet Form* (mus. Albéniz), Goodman Theatre, Chicago
Garçonette (mus. Trench), Murrat, Indiana
Les Incroyables (with B. Stone; mus. Wolf-Ferrari), *Park Avenue Odalisque* (mus. Granados), Rainbow Room, New York
1948 *Harlequinade* (with B. Stone; mus. Casella), Maysville, Kentucky

WORKS

Ensemble and company productions:
1927 *The Snow is Dancing* (mus. Debussy), Hampden Theatre, New York
1928 *Moonlight Sailing* (mus. Zeckwer), Ravinia Park, Chicago
1933 *La Guiablesse* (mus. Still), Ruth Page and Dancers, Auditorium Theatre, Chicago
1934 *Hear Ye! Hear Ye!* (mus. Copland), Chicago Opera Ballet, Chicago
The Gold Standard (mus. Ibert), Chicago Opera Ballet, Chicago
1935 *Love Song* (mus. Schubert), Chicago Opera Ballet, Chicago (restaged and revised for Ballet Russe de Monte Carlo, Rochester, New York, 1948)
1936 *An American in Paris* (originally called *Americans in Paris*; mus. Gershwin), Cincinnati Opera Company, Cincinnati (restaged Les Ballets Americains, Paris, 1950)
1937 *An American Pattern* (with Bentley Stone; mus. Moross), Chicago City Opera Company, Chicago
1938 *Frankie and Johnny* (with Stone; mus. Moross), Federal Theatre Project, Chicago (Revived for Ballet Russe de Monte Carlo, Kansas City, 1945)
1939 *Guns and Castanets* (with Stone; mus. Bizet, arranged Moross), Page–Stone Ballet, Federal Theatre Project, Chicago
1946 *The Bells* (mus. Milhaud), Chicago University Ballet, Chicago (restaged for Ballet Russe de Monte Carlo, Jacob's Pillow, 1946)
Les Petits Riens (mus. Mozart), Ballet For America (Company), Montreal
Billy Sunday (text. Hunt; mus. Gassman), Chicago Opera Ballet, Chicago (restaged for Ballet Russe de Monte Carlo, York, Pennsylvania, 1948)
1949 *Beauty and the Beast* (mus. Tchaikovsky), Chicago

Grand Opera Ballet, Milwaukee, Wisconsin (originally performed as a pas de deux for Ruth Page and Bentley Stone, 1949)

Dance of the Hours (mus. Ponchielli), Chicago Grand Opera Ballet, Milwaukee, Wisconsin

1951   *Beethoven Sonata* (mus. Beethoven), Page–Stone–Camryn Ballet, Chicago

Impromptu aux bois (mus. Ibert), Les Ballets des Champs-Elysées, Freiburg im Breisgau, Germany

Revanche (also known as *Revenge*, after *Il Trovatore*; mus. Verdi), Ballets des Champs-Elysées, Paris

1952   *Salome—Daughter of Herodias* (pas de deux, also known as *Retribution*, and *Salome and Herod*; mus. Richard Strauss, arranged van Grove), Ruth Page and Bentley Stone Concert, Evansville, Indiana (staged Chicago Ballet Company, 1954)

1953   *Vilia* (later known as *The Merry Widow*; mus. Lehár), London Festival Ballet, Manchester

1954   *Triumph of Chastity* (mus. Ibert), Ballet Guild of Chicago, Chicago

El Amor Brujo (mus. de Falla), Ballet Guild of Chicago, Chicago

1956   *Susanna and the Barber* (after the opera *The Barber of Seville*; mus. Rossini), Chicago Opera Ballet, Chicago

1959   *Camille* (after the opera *La Traviata*; mus. Verdi), Chicago Opera Ballet, Columbia, Missouri

1960   *Carmen* (after the opera; mus. Bizet, arranged van Grove), Chicago Opera Ballet, Dubuque, Iowa

1961   *Concertino pour trois* (mus. Constant), Chicago Opera Ballet, Rockford, Illinois

Die Fledermaus (after the opera; mus. Johann Strauss), Chicago Opera Ballet, Rockford, Illinois

1963   *Mephistofela* (mus. Berlioz, Boito, Gounod), Chicago Opera Ballet, Park Ridge, Illinois

Pygmalion (pas de trois; mus. Suppé), Chicago Opera Ballet, Park Ridge, Illinois

Combinations (mus. van Grove), Ballet Guild of Chicago, Chicago

1965   *Bullets and Bonbons* (after the operetta *The Chocolate Soldier*; mus. J. Straus), Chicago Opera Ballet, Springfield, Illinois

Carmina Burana (mus. Orff), Chicago Opera Ballet and Lyric Opera of Chicago, Chicago

The Nutcracker (mus. Tchaikovsky), Ruth Page's International Ballet, Chicago

1968   *Bolero '68* (later *Bolero '69*; mus. Ravel), Ruth Page's International Ballet, LaCrosse, Wisconsin

1969   *Romeo and Juliet* (mus. Tchaikovsky), Ruth Page's International Ballet, Niles, Michigan

1970   *Alice in the Garden* (mus. van Grove), Jacob's Pillow School of the Dance, Lee, Massachusetts

1972   *Carmen and José* (revised version of *Carmen*; mus. Bizet), Dance Theatre of Harlem, Chicago

1978   *Alice in Wonderland; Alice through the Looking Glass* (full-length version of *Alice in the Garden*), Chicago

Other works include: *Dances with Words and Music* (solo dances to poetry and music, 1942–45)—*Anyone, Cambridge Ladies, Hist-wist* (all e.e. cummings), *Nocturne* (MacLeish), *Recuerdo* (Millay), *Eros in Time of War* (Turbyfill), *A Fairly Sad Tale, On Being a Woman, Unfortunate Coincidence* (all Parker), *The Sadness of the Moon* (Baudelaire), *Lucy Lake* (Nash), *Two Chinese Poems, The Little Peach* (Field), *I'll Go to Santiago* (García Lorca), *The Seven Spiritual Ages of Mrs. Marmaduke Moore* (Nash), *Rebecca, Who Slammed Doors for Fun and Perished Miserably* (Belloc), *Death in Harlem* (Hughes), *Lament for the Death of a Spanish Bullfighter* (Lorca).

PUBLICATIONS

By Page:

"Some Trends in American Choreography", in Sorrell, Walter, *The Dance Has Many Faces*, New York, 1951

Page by Page, Brooklyn, 1978

Class: Notes on Dance Classes Around the World, 1915–1980, Princeton, 1984

About Page:

Beaumont, Cyril, *Supplement to Complete Book of Ballets*, London, 1942

Amberg, George, *Ballet in America*, New York, 1949

Beaumont, Cyril, *Complete Book of Ballets*, revised edition, London, 1951

Maynard, Olga, *The American Ballet*, Philadelphia, 1959

Goodman, Saul, "Ruth Page, Cosmopolite of the Central Plains", *Dance Magazine* (New York), December 1961

Martin, John, *Ruth Page: An Intimate Biography*, New York, 1977

Wentink, Andrew Mark, "The Ruth Page Collection: An Introduction and Guide to Manuscript Materials through 1970", *Bulletin of Research in the Humanities* (New York), Spring 1980

Denby, Edwin, *Dance Writings*, edited by Robert Cornfield and William Mackay, New York, 1986

*   *   *

Ruth Page's long career as dancer, choreographer, and company director was marked by adventurousness. It may have been the eclecticism of her early dance experiences that made her realize dance can go in many directions, but it was also in her character to be open to new ideas. She was interested and involved in the avant garde of all the arts. She appreciated styles and forms of dance that were different from those in which she worked, and often ventured into them. For example, although basically a classical ballet dancer, she studied with German modern dancer Harald Kreutzberg and, appreciating the artistic verity of his style, formed a partnership with him, touring America and the Far East in 1933–34. Ruth Page's pioneering spirit was also evident in her 1933 ballet *La Guiablesse*, presented at a Chicago Opera program with an all-black cast (save Miss Page) in an era of racial separation. The piece, based on a Martinique legend, had a commissioned score by black composer William Grant Still.

From her beginnings Page was highly creative, choreographing scores of solos which she performed in concerts given during the first decades of her career in Chicago, where she lived, as well as on extensive tours. These dances showed a breadth of interests and more than a tangential acquaintance with music, literature, and painting. Along with abstract essays in classical ballet, often tinged with the romanticism to which ballet lends itself, there was an awareness of the times in dances that reflected contemporary life. There was the sport scene and "flaming youth of the '20s" in *The Flapper and the Quarterback*, or the jazz scene in *St. Louis Blues* and *Gershwiniana*, or the satire of "high society" in *Park Avenue Odalisque*. More than a nod to the Spanish Civil War, then raging, was her full-cast ballet *Guns and Castanets*, a 1939 version of *Carmen* in a different setting.

Page made a number of solo dances inspired by poetry—the works of García Lorca, e.e. cummings, Edna St. Vincent Millay, Baudelaire, Langston Hughes, and Dorothy Parker all inspired her in dance. In one suite of these dances she spoke the verses while dancing. Further adventures in literary dance were portrayals of Shakespearean characters—namely Katherine the Shrew, Juliet, and Lady Macbeth in *Three Shakespearian Heroines*. Edgar Allen Poe's long poem *The Bells* was the basis of a 1946 ballet for a full company, set to a commissioned score by Darius Milhaud with set and costumes by Isamu Noguchi. After a premiere in Chicago, *The Bells* was acquired by the Ballet Russe de Monte Carlo.

Music for Ruth Page's dances included the classics—Mozart (*Mozart Waltzes*), Chopin (*Mazurka* and *Étude*), Mendelssohn (*Shadow Dance*). Then there were contemporary composers—Hindemith (*Modern Diana*), Prokofiev (*Ballet Scaffolding*), Milhaud (*My Sorrow is My Song*). Often this original choreographer commissioned original music for her dances, such as that of Clarence Loomis for *Flapper and Quarterback* and *Sun Worshippers*, or Robert Wolf for *Expanding Universe* and *Body in Sunlight*). In the visual arts, the surrealism of Salvador Dali inspired *Delirious Delusion*, and the modern sculptures of Noguchi inspired *Expanding Universe*, for which Noguchi designed a shifting-shaped costume.

Partners are a necessity at some points in theater dance, and Ruth Page danced with prominent male dancers throughout her career. In the 1920s, when she was the premiere danseuse of Adolph Bolm's Ballet Intime and later a dancer with his Allied Arts Ballet, she was frequently partnered by Bolm himself in a number of pas de deux and longer ballets. When she launched her avant garde concert career, she invited a succession of well-known dancers to participate in her programmes, among them Blake Scott, Mark Turbyfill, Edwin Strawbridge, Jacques Cartier, Frank Parker, and Paul Draper. Although most of her large body of works—the solos, duets, and ballets for small groups and full companies—were choreographed entirely by herself, she sometimes had collaborators, usually her partners. Her partnership with Harald Kreutzberg included collaboration on duets, and this was followed by two decades—beginning in 1935 in Chicago—of working with Bentley Stone both as partner and choreographic collaborator. Together they staged and danced numerous pas de deux as well as ballets such as *Frankie and Johnny* and *An American Pattern*.

Ruth Page's travels and her broad range of friendships with artists in many fields are reflected in the cosmopolitan nature of some of her early solo dances, as well as in the sophisticated ballets of her later decades. During her summers as ballet director of the distinguished operas at Ravinia (a suburb of Chicago), she commissioned a score by French composer Marcel Delannoy for a one-act *Cinderella*, choreographed for a children's matinée. That was the first of a long list of collaborations with musicians and painters from all over the world. Musicians included Jacques Ibert, Darius Milhaud, Marius Constant, Aaron Copland and William Grant Still. The list of scenic and costume designers included Nicholas Remisoff, Antoni Clavé, Wakhevitch, Leonor Fini, Bernard Daydé, Isamu Noguchi, and André Delfau.

But underneath the cosmopolitanism of Ruth Page's art was an intrinsic Americanism, and a pioneer spirit which dictated that she incorporate American themes into her ballets. There were decidedly "American" solos, but Page went further into American themes for the one-act ballets for her company, made in an era when it was *chic* to be patriotic. The ballet *Hear Ye! Hear Ye!*, set in an American night club and in an American court at a murder trial, was innovative in more than subject-matter. The score by Aaron Copland was the first ballet score by that composer, who later composed music for Martha Graham, Agnes de Mille, and others. *An American Pattern*, choreographed with Stone, had an original score by Jerome Moross and a feminist theme about a rebellious woman searching for a mission in life other than housework.

Among Page's most notable works on American themes was *Frankie and Johnny* (based on a bawdy tavern ballad), made in

partnership with Stone to an original score by Jerome Moross. The piece became a success, and was the subject of some controversy when acquired by Ballet Russe de Monte Carlo. *An American in Paris* (to Gershwin) and *Oak Street Beach* (to Loomis) were early essays in Americana for large groups. Blatantly American, one could say loudly American, was *Billy Sunday*, an amusing ballet based on sermons of the famous revivalist Billy Sunday, who colored his diatribes with essays on the sins of biblical characters. Ruth Page made cartoon characters of King David, Samson, Delilah, and Bathsheba, and they spoke lines as they danced. When the ballet was presented by Ballet Russe de Monte Carlo, ballerina Alexandra Danilova created a sensation as Potiphar's chattering wife.

Until the mid-1950s, Ruth Page danced the principal roles in her own works and in the repertoire presented by the Page-Stone Ballet. From 1954 through to 1969, she limited her role to that of ballet director and choreographer for Chicago's Lyric Opera. She developed a company with excellent principal dancers who performed all the ballet roles in the operas as well as performed in the expanded dance company which, known as Ruth Page's Chicago Opera Ballet, had a repertoire of Page ballets and long independent touring seasons. The troupe was enhanced by a succession of world-famous stars which included Alicia Markova, Mia Slavenska, Erik Bruhn, George Skibine, Marjorie Tallchief, and Sonia Arova.

Opera ballet figured largely in Ruth Page's career, starting with her success in *The Bartered Bride* with New York's Metropolitan Opera in 1927. There were the summers with the Ravinia Opera and a number of seasons in the 1930s and 1940s with the Chicago Civic Opera, as well as a long tenure with the Lyric Opera. As ballet director for opera, Page became thoroughly familiar with the opera stories and opera music. In her adventurous manner she invented a different way of presenting this tradition-bound art. She converted a number of three- and four-hour popular operas into one-hour ballets. The stories were clarified, made logical, and presented in an accessible form with visual verity. (No portly, middle-aged lovers warbling in arm-length embraces.) The vocal music arranged tastefully for orchestra served the dance well. The repertoire of the company known as Ruth Page's Chicago Opera Ballet was seen coast to coast for 15 years and it included numerous familiar operas.

As a dancer, Ruth Page had personal beauty and natural talent. She was not a fine technician, but was expressive and had an attractive theatrical presence. Her professional career began in a period when dance with expansive movements in a limited vocabulary was acceptable. Page later confessed that she started to dance on stage long before she had acquired technical proficiency; however, with maturity, she appreciated the fine points of classicism and the danse d'école. (She took a daily ballet class until she was well into her eighties.) Her latter-day choreography, danced by highly trained dancers, utilized a broad and demanding balletic vocabulary alongside Page's own inventions in eclectic movement and gestural range.

—Ann Barzel

PALAIS DE CRISTAL *see* **SYMPHONY IN C**

Valery Panov in his own version of *Le Sacre du printemps*, Berlin, 1978

PANOV, Valery

Russian/Israeli dancer. Born Valery Matyevich Shulman (changed to Panov, 1958) in Vitebsk, 12 March 1938. Studied at the Leningrad Choreographic School, pupil of Abderakhman Kumisnikov, Mikhail Mikhailov, Igor Belsky, 1951–53, and 1956–57; graduated in 1957; also studied at the Vilnius Ballet School, pupil of Niola Taboraskaite, 1953–54, 1955–56, and at the Moscow Choreographic School, pupil of Petr Gusev, 1954; later coached by Simon Kaplan. Married (1) Maly Theatre dancer Liya Panova, 1958 (divorced); (2) Kirov ballerina Galina Ragozina. Professional début, when still a student, as soloist for Vilnius Ballet, from 1954; leading dancer, Maly Theatre Ballet, Leningrad, 1957–64, touring U.S., 1958; soloist, Kirov Ballet, 1963–72; also appeared on films, including as Bluebird in *The Sleeping Beauty* (Kirov film, 1965); expelled from Kirov (after application for exit visa to Israel), 1972, and briefly imprisoned, 1972; left USSR (with wife, Galina Panova) for Israel, 1974: guest artist, Batsheva Dance Company, and Bat-Dor Company, Tel-Aviv, 1974–77; guest choreographer and principal dancer, German Opera Ballet, Berlin, 1977, 1979, 1980, 1983; also staged ballets in San Francisco, 1976, Vienna, 1981, Stockholm, 1983, Oslo, 1984, for Royal Ballet of Flanders, Antwerp, 1985–86, and National Ballet of Chile, Santiago, 1990; artistic director, Royal Ballet of Flanders, 1984–86; freelance choreographer, based in Jerusalem from 1986; ballet director, State Opera, Bonn, from 1991. Recipient: Lenin Prize, 1969; title of Honoured Artist of the Russian Federation, 1970.

ROLES

1957   Faris in *Schéhérazade* (Anisimova), Maly Theatre Ballet, Leningrad

Principal dancer in *Ivushka* (Anisimova), Maly Theatre Ballet, Leningrad

Principal dancer in *Seven Beauties* (Gusev), Maly Theatre Ballet, Leningrad

Olaf in *Solveig* (Yakobson), Maly Theatre Ballet, Leningrad

1958   Pas de trois, Spanish dance, Hungarian czardas in *Swan Lake* (Petipa, Ivanov; staged Lopukhov, Boyarsky), Maly Theatre Ballet, Leningrad

Pas de deux from *Le Corsaire* (Petipa), Maly Theatre Ballet, U.S. tour

Pas de deux from *The Flames of Paris* (Vainonen), Maly Theatre Ballet, U.S. tour

1959   Principal dancer (cr) in *Ballad of Love* (Lopukhov), Maly Theatre Ballet, Leningrad

Title role in *Eros* (Boyarsky after Fokine), Maly Theatre Ballet, Leningrad

Paolo in *Francesca da Rimini* (Boyarsky), Maly Theatre Ballet, Leningrad

Siegfried in *Swan Lake* (Petipa, Ivanov; staged Lopukhov, Boyarsky), Maly Theatre Ballet, Leningrad

Slave solo in *To Freedom* (concert piece), Maly Theatre Ballet, Leningrad

Soloist in *Gopak* (concert piece), Maly Theatre Ballet, Leningrad

1960   Daphnis (cr) in *Daphnis and Chloë* (Davitashvili), Maly Theatre Ballet, Leningrad

Principal dancer (cr) in *Bolero* (Davitashvili), Maly Theatre Ballet, Leningrad

Shubin in *On the Eve* (Boyarsky), Maly Theatre Ballet, Leningrad

Principal dancer in *Paquita* Grand Pas (Petipa), Maly Theatre Ballet, Leningrad

1961   Title role (cr) in *Petrushka* (new production; Boyarsky after Fokine), Maly Theatre Ballet, Leningrad

Principal dancer in *Classical Symphony* (Boyarsky), Maly Theatre Ballet, Leningrad

Vadim in *The Strength of Love* (Varkovitsky), Maly Theatre Ballet, Leningrad

The Pilot in *Flowers* (Varkovitsky), Maly Theatre Ballet, Leningrad

1962   Title role (cr) in *Orpheus* (Boyarsky), Maly Theatre Ballet, Leningrad

Principal dancer in *Romantic Song* (Petrov), Maly Theatre Ballet, Leningrad

First Youth in *Meeting* (Boyarsky), Maly Theatre Ballet, Leningrad

The Hooligan (cr) in *The Lady and the Hooligan* (Boyarsky), Maly Theatre Ballet, Leningrad

1963   Basil in *Don Quixote* (Gorsky after Petipa), Kirov Ballet, Leningrad

Frondoso in *Laurencia* (Chabukiani), Kirov Ballet, Leningrad

Genie of the Waters in *The Little Humpbacked Horse* (Petipa after Saint-Léon), Kirov Ballet, Leningrad

1964   D'Artagnan (cr) in *The Three Musketeers* (Boyarchikov), Maly Theatre Ballet, Leningrad

Bluebird in *The Sleeping Beauty* (Petipa; staged Sergeyev), Kirov Ballet, Leningrad

Mercutio in *Romeo and Juliet* (Lavrovsky), Kirov Ballet, Leningrad

Solor in *La Bayadère* (Petipa, Ponomarev, Chabukiani), Kirov Ballet, Leningrad

The Man in *Distant Planet* (Sergeyev), Kirov Ballet, Leningrad

Philippe in *The Flames of Paris* (Vainonen), Kirov Ballet, Leningrad

Vaslav in *The Fountain of Bakhchisarai* (Zakharov), Kirov Ballet, Leningrad

Albrecht in *Giselle* (Petipa after Coralli, Perrot), Kirov Ballet, Leningrad

1965   Yevgeny in *The Bronze Horseman* (Zakharov), Kirov Ballet, Leningrad

1966   Harlequin in *Carnaval* (Fokine; staged Lopukhov), Kirov Ballet, Leningrad

Bacchus in *Walpurgis Night* (Lavrovsky), Kirov Ballet, Leningrad

Armen in *Gayané* (Anisimova), Kirov Ballet, Leningrad

Lenny in *Path of Thunder* (Sergeyev), Kirov Ballet, Leningrad

1967   Yasny Sokol (cr) in *Land of Miracles* (Yakobson), Kirov Ballet, Leningrad

1968   Osman (cr) in *Goryanka* (*Mountain Girl*; Vinogradov), Kirov Ballet, Leningrad

Pas de deux from *Harlequinade* (Petipa), "Class of Perfection" Performance, Kirov Theatre, Leningrad

1970   Title role (cr) in *Hamlet* (Sergeyev), Kirov Ballet, Leningrad

1971   The Devil (cr) in *The Creation of the World* (Kasatkina, Vasiliev), Kirov Ballet, Leningrad

1976   The Young Man (cr) in *Heart of the Mountain* (also chor.), San Francisco Ballet, San Francisco

1977   Prince (cr) in *Cinderella* (also chor.), German Opera Ballet, Berlin

1979   Rogozhin (cr) in *The Idiot* (also chor.), German Opera Ballet, Berlin

Other roles include: principal dancer in *Polovotsian Dances from Prince Igor* (after Fokine), Hilarion in *Giselle* (after Petipa,

Coralli, Perrot), principal dancer in *The Blind Girl* (Yakobson), principal dancer in *Belong* (pas de deux; Vesak).

WORKS

1976   *Heart of the Mountain* (mus. Kozhlayev), San Francisco Ballet, San Francisco

       Through the City Streets (after Boyarsky), Batsheva Dance Company, Tel Aviv

1977   *Cinderella* (mus. Prokofiev), German Opera Ballet, Berlin

       Le Sacre du printemps (mus. Stravinsky), German Opera Ballet, Berlin

1979   *The Idiot* (mus. Shostakovich), German Opera Ballet, Berlin (staged for the National Ballet of Chile, Santiago, 1990)

1980   *War and Peace* (mus. Tchaikovsky), German Opera Ballet, Berlin

1981   *Schéhérazade* (mus. Rimsky-Korsakov), Vienna State Opera Ballet, Vienna

       Petrushka (after Fokine; mus. Stravinsky), Vienna State Opera Ballet, Vienna

1983   *Ricardo W* (mus. Wagner, Liszt), German Opera Ballet, Berlin

       The Three Sisters (mus. Rachmaninov), Royal Swedish Ballet, Stockholm

1984   *Hamlet* (mus. Shostakovich), Norwegian Opera Ballet, Oslo

       Romeo and Juliet (mus. Prokofiev), Royal Ballet of Flanders, Antwerp

1985   *Panovaria* (mus. various), Concert of Panov choreography, Royal Ballet of Flanders, Antwerp

1986   *Moves* (mus. Glorieux), Royal Ballet of Flanders, Antwerp

1988   *Cléopâtre* (mus. Arensky), Istanbul Devlet Ballet, Turkey

Other works include: for concert performances and tours— *Albinoni Adagio* (pas de deux, with wife Galina Panova; mus. Albinoni), *Rachmaninov Dance Symphony* (solo; mus. Rachmaninov); for the Royal Ballet of Flanders—*Jacques Brel Songs* (mus. Brel).

PUBLICATIONS

By Panov:
To Dance (autobiography), New York, 1978
Interview in Barnes, Patricia, "The Russian Soul", *Ballet News* (New York), July 1980
Interview in Fanger, Iris, "Westernizing Russians", *Dance Magazine* (New York), July 1980
Interview in Whyte, Sally, "Walking the Tightrope", *Dance and Dancers* (London), September 1987

About Panov:
"Galina Panova and Valery Panov", *Tanzblätter* (Vienna), May 1979
Percival, John, "The Idiot", *Dance and Dancers* (London), August 1979
Williams, Peter, "The Grounded Panov", *Dance Magazine* (New York), June 1972
Williams, Peter, "A Modern Tragedy", *Dance and Dancers* (London), July 1975

*   *   *

Kirov Ballet dancer Valery Panov, in his prime acknowledged to be one of the greatest virtuoso dancers in Russia, became the object of an international "cause célèbre" when he applied for an exit visa to emigrate to Israel in 1972. He was summarily sacked from the Kirov overnight, imprisoned, ostracized, and not allowed to take class or use a studio for two years. His wife, Galina Ragozina, was also dismissed, but would have been allowed back if she had divorced her husband. It was only after intense world-wide protest, led by artists of the stature of Laurence Olivier and Paul Scofield, that, at the instigation of the then British Prime Minister Harold Wilson, the Soviet government gave in—and on the eve of the London performances of the Bolshoi Ballet, Panov was allowed to leave for Tel Aviv. Panov was never a "defector"—he had asked to leave legally—and this has always left him as something of an anomaly in relation to other Russian expatriate dancers—this, and the fact that he was a demi-caractère dancer as well as a virtuoso performer. He was, as has recently been recognized by Oleg Vinogradov, a "phenomenon", and was one of the most exciting dancers of his generation.

After Panov arrived in the West, he was thrown into the deep and murky waters of publicity "hype" and was sent on a world-wide tour with his wife as partner. That they could dance at all, let alone give the brilliant performances they did, was no small miracle; but this first tour gave the dancers no artistic breadth (and also provided a number of heartless critics, both in Britain and America, with the opportunity to pen some vicious notices). The public, however, loved Panov's infectious charm, and applauded his performances. Although Panov and his wife have their home in Israel, they have been unable to make their careers in a country which has only a tiny, if capable, ethic of classical dance. Panov has not been generally successful in the modern idiom since, like most Russians, he finds that his Kirov schooling does not really lend itself to what he considers (rightly or wrongly) a secondary dance form.

Panov's performances, even when subtle, are always strongly theatrical. He received the Lenin Prize in 1969, and was awarded the accolade of Honoured Artist of the Russian Federation for his Hamlet, which he created for choreographer Konstantin Sergeyev in 1970. He was, and still is, a silent actor with no equal. It is fair to say that Panov was not always subtle in his artistic approach, and this is true of his work as a choreographer, especially in his "Russian" work. Extremely well-versed in Russian literature and music, Panov is the creator of two widely seen choreographies, *War and Peace* and *The Idiot*, which have a colour and passion rarely seen outside the theatre. Panov fervently believes that art is a passionate business, and sees no reason to underplay the intensity of the written word simply because it is danced. When Dostoevsky's *The Idiot*, to a collage of some of Shostakovich's lesser-known and deeply felt pieces, was first performed at the German Opera in Berlin in 1979, the audience would not allow the curtain to come down for over forty minutes. The experience was to be repeated with *War and Peace*, set to a Tchaikovsky score.

For some reason Panov has never received general acclaim in the United Kingdom. His work has been called "old-fashioned" or "histrionic" (criticisms rarely levelled at other Russian dancers). These opinions may be justified by one or two choreographies in which he has ventured into unfamiliar territory. There was, for example, a fairly disastrous *Ricardo W* for the German Opera in Berlin, set to Richard Wagner (surely a risky undertaking for anybody), or *Brel Songs* for the Royal Ballet of Flanders, created during Panov's tenure as artistic director with that company between 1984 and 1987. And a delightful personality has not always been sufficient to disguise his own over-frank criticisms of other people's work.

All the same, since leaving performing to others, Panov has concentrated on choreography, working world-wide. From the start he was intensely musical; one of his first works was a duet for Galina and himself entitled *Albinoni Adagio*, which movingly and delicately followed the Death and the Maiden theme. He prefers to work with large companies, as a vast canvas is required for his most spectacular and major work. This has been true in Berlin, for example, where his first full-length ballet, *Cinderella*, was performed, to be followed by a controversial, highly primitive version of *Sacre du printemps*, or in Vienna, where Panov staged *Schéhérazade* and *Petrushka* for the State Opera.

A tour with the Berlin company to New York in 1980 with *The Idiot*, in which Panov danced the role of the depraved Rogozhin to his old classmate and rival Nureyev's saintly Prince Myshkin, produced duets to be cherished in the annals of ballet history. In 1988 *Cléopâtre* was created for the Istanbul Devlet Ballet in Turkey, with a cast of 200. However, one of Panov's greatest, most sought-after works has been *The Three Sisters*, almost a chamber ballet, set to a Rachmaninov vocal and piano score. Panov has also mounted *The Nutcracker* in Japan, and his own version of *Romeo and Juliet* has been performed by many companies, from Belgium to Israel. In 1990 he was invited to mount *The Idiot* for the National Ballet of Chile in Santiago.

Valery Panov, despite being educated and brought up within the strict discipline of a major artistic establishment, the Kirov, remains the non-conformist, always treading the path of the outsider, rightly convinced of his own artistic integrity yet able to recognize his own mistakes. Often dreaded by "the Establishment" of any kind, Panov is none the less admired and respected and often loved by dancers. He remains a maverick, yet an artist first and foremost, whose mastery of the dance-drama is unsurpassed, and whose soaring pas de deux can leave an audience breathless.

Panov remains an enigma, unaccountably disliked by individuals who have neither met him nor experienced much of his work. Always on the look-out for a challenge, he has even ventured into the territory of justice and anti-Semitism as subjects for ballet, feeling he is a world expert on such themes. Ironically, the West has almost given him too much freedom, committing him to a largely peripatetic life and career.

—Sally Whyte

LE PAPILLON

Choreography: Marie Taglioni
Music: Jacques Offenbach
Design: Martin, Edouard Despléchin, Nolau, Auguste Rubé, Charles-Antoine Cambon and Joseph Thierry (sets), Alfred Albert (costumes)
Libretto: Marie Taglioni and Vernoy de Saint-Georges
First Production: Théâtre Impérial de l'Opéra, Paris, 26 November 1860
Principal Dancers: Emma Livry (Farfalla), Louis Mérante (Prince Djalma), Louise Marquet (Fairy Hamza)

Other productions include: Göteborg Ballet (new ballet to score; chor. Elsa Marianne von Rosen), as *Utopia*; Göteborg, Sweden, 1974. Paris Opéra Ballet (chor. Pierre Lacotte after Taglioni); Paris, 23 December 1976. Houston Ballet (new version; chor. Ronald Hynd, mus. arranged John Lanchbery), as *Papillon*;

Houston, 8 February 1979 (same version staged Sadler's Wells Royal Ballet, 1980).

PUBLICATIONS

Beaumont, Cyril, *Complete Book of Ballets*, revised edition, London, 1951
Hill, Lorna, *La Sylphide: The Life of Marie Taglioni*, London, 1967
Guest, Ivor, *The Ballet of the Second Empire*, London, 1974
Levinson, André, *Marie Taglioni*, London, 1977
Hunt, Marilyn, "On the Wings of *Papillon*", *Dance Magazine* (New York), May 1979
Clarke, Mary, "*Papillon* for the Sadler's Wells Royal Ballet", *Dancing Times* (London), March 1980
Stoop, Norma McLain, "The Houston Ballet", *Dance Magazine* (New York), October 1981

* * *

Le Papillon, to quote André Levinson, Marie Taglioni's biographer, is "a Caucasus of fantasy, where ballet blanc alternated with oriental dances". The story concerns Farfalla, a beautiful young girl, who falls into the hands of the bad Fairy Hamza, who turns her into a butterfly. Before her metamorphosis she meets the Prince Djalma and they fall in love. But Hamza wants him for her own and this is why she casts her spell. Djalma captures a butterfly during a hunting party, and unknown to him, this beautiful creature is Farfalla (whose name in Italian means butterfly). He pins her to a tree and as he does so, the spell is temporarily broken and Farfalla is revealed to him as a sad and listless woman. He then demands that Hamza unravel her enchantment, which she does, but not without complications. In the end, it is revealed that Farfalla is the abducted daughter of the Emir to whom Djalma is bethrothed. They are reunited, but in a dream Djalma sees Farfalla as a butterfly who darts towards a burning torch that burns her wings. This burning restores her to her human form and Farfalla, the Princess, marries Djalma, while Hamza looks on, forever silenced by having been turned into a statue.

Le Papillon's significance is four-fold: it is the only ballet of which ballerina Marie Taglioni is part author, as well as the only ballet for which she composed choreography; it was the first ballet for which Jacques Offenbach composed music, and the ballet in which Emma Livry made her first great triumph. Taglioni created the ballet essentially as a showcase for Livry's own special capabilities; Livry was her protegée and pupil, and the only dancer who approximated "La Taglioni's" legendary style—one characterized by flowing grace and precision of line. Taglioni saw herself in Livry and doted on the young dancer like a second mother. Livry's triumphs were her own and she hand-picked her to be her successor on stage.

While attributed to Taglioni, the ballet was very much a collaborative effort. Saint-Georges had already completed the libretto before Taglioni contacted him. Monsieur Royer, then director of the Opéra, and Offenbach first approached Taglioni with the idea of doing the ballet. After contacting Saint-Georges she made her own revisions to the story, thus emerging as co-author. *Le Papillon* was nearly a year in the making, but when it made its glittering début, Taglioni, retired from the stage for thirteen years, had secured a successful comeback. More, Livry emerged a star dancing the role of Farfalla, a role she made her own. André Levinson noted that Livry had inherited her mentor's "imponderable lightness and silent flight". She even looked like Taglioni: "thin, almost emaciated, with a bony profile, Livry embodied in the extreme the physical type of the dancer of elevation as revealed by Taglioni".

The critical response at the time was adulatory. Paul de Saint-Victor, writing in *La Presse* on 2 December 1860, declared, "Mlle. Livry, launched by Mme. Taglioni into the rarefied air of the ideal dance, has raised herself among the stars." Paul Smith, writing in *Revue et gazette musicale de Paris* on the same day, corroborated. "First Emma Livry was elevated to the rank of Sylphide and now she passes to the state of butterfly. Did Mlle. Livry not exist, the Butterfly would not be possible. For this role, so ethereal and so diaphanous, an intangible artiste is imperative . . .".

Unfortunately for Livry, she was too much like the butterfly in the ballet. A year following her triumphant début in the role, she died of terrible burns after the muslin in her tutu caught fire at a rehearsal for Auber's opera *La Muerte de Portici*. As in art, as in real life: the butterfly was consumed by the candle-flame.

The ballet's success can measured by it being danced thirty times between November and May of its inaugural season. But following Livry's tragic death at the age of 21, Taglioni, almost 60, sadly renounced her position as "professeur de la classe de perfectionnement au conservatoire de danse de l'Opéra", and retired to her villa on Lake Como. *Le Papillon* was laid to rest and Taglioni died twenty years later in Marseilles without ever once returning to the dance.

The music for *Le Papillon* has been rechoreographed by Elsa Marianne von Rosen for her ballet called *Utopia* for Sweden's Göteborg Ballet in 1974, and most notably by Ronald Hynd, who produced his *Papillon*, a parody of nineteenth-century ballet conventions, for the Houston Ballet in 1979. John Lanchbery arranged and orchestrated the Offenbach score; scenery and costumes were by Peter Docherty. Hynd's ballet has three acts, with the libretto altered for his parodic purposes. The setting is transplanted to Persia and Hynd's heroine is renamed Papillon, her lover, Bijahn. They are studies in purity while Hamza and the Shah are pictures of pure evil. The ballet ends with Papillon and Bijahn both dying in the flame but living on in heaven in eternal love.

Hynd's version has had mixed reviews, with some critics calling it "a gentle Romantic burlesque", and others faulting Hynd for treating his subject with ridicule rather than affection. None the less, it is one of the most popular ballets in the Houston Ballet's repertory.

—Deirdre Kelly

PAQUITA

Choreography: Joseph Mazilier
Music: Edouard Marie Ernest Deldevez
Design: Humanité Philastre, Charles Cambon, Jules Diéterle, Charles Séchan, Edouard Despléchin, Hippolyte d'Orschwiller, Paul Lormier
Libretto: Joseph Mazilier and Paul Foucher
First Production: Théâtre de l'Académie royale de musique, (Paris Opéra), Paris, 1 April 1846
Principal Dancers: Carlotta Grisi (Paquita), Lucien Petipa (Comte d'Hervilly)

Other productions include: Drury Lane Theatre (staged James Silvain (formerly Sullivan) after Mazilier), with Grisi and Silvain; London, 3 June 1846. St. Petersburg Bolshoi Theatre (new version; chor. Marius Petipa and Frédéric after Mazilier), with Elena Andreyanova (Paquita) and Marius Petipa (Comte

d'Hervilly); St. Petersburg, 8 October (26 September old style) 1847. Moscow Bolshoi Theatre (staged Frédéric); Moscow, 5 October 1866. St. Petersburg Bolshoi Theatre (restaged Marius Petipa, with new Pas de trois, Mazurka, and Grand Pas; additional mus. Minkus), with Ekaterina Vazem (Paquita); St. Petersburg, 27 December 1881. Grand Ballet de Monte Carlo (du Marquis de Cuevas) (Pas de trois; chor. George Balanchine after Petipa), as *Pas de trois classique*; London, 9 August 1948 (restaged and revised as (*Minkus*) *Pas de trois*, New York City Ballet, 18 February 1951). Ballet Russe de Monte Carlo (one-act version; staged Alexandra Danilova after Petipa); New York, 20 September 1949. Maly Theatre Ballet (Grand Pas only; staged Konstantin Boyarsky after Petipa); Leningrad, 1957. Royal Academy of Dancing Gala at Drury Lane Theatre (staged Rudolf Nureyev after Petipa), with Margot Fonteyn and Rudolf Nureyev; London, 17 November 1964. London Festival Ballet (restaged Roland Casenave); Oxford, 9 February 1967. American Ballet Theatre (Nureyev version, restaged Marika Besobrasova) with Cynthia Gregory and Michael Denard; New York, 6 July 1971. Scottish Ballet (staged Roland Casenave after Petipa); Glasgow, 1975. Kirov Ballet (Divertissement and Grand Pas; staged Petr Gusev after Petipa); Leningrad, 1978. Sadler's Wells Royal Ballet (restaged Galina Samsova); Bournemouth, 17 April 1980. Natalia Makarova and Company (Grand Pas; staged Makarova after Petipa); New York, 7 October 1980 (staged American Ballet Theatre, Washington, D.C., 1983). Paris Opéra Ballet (staged Oleg Vinogradov after Petipa); Paris, 1980.

PUBLICATIONS

Pleshcheev, Aleksandr, *Our Ballet*, St. Petersburg, 1899

Borioglebsky, Mikhail (ed.), *Materials for the History of Russian Ballet*, Leningrad, 1937

Vazem, Ekaterina, *Reminiscences of a Ballerina of the St. Petersburg Bolshoi Theatre*, Moscow, 1937; as "Memoirs of a Ballerina", translated by Nina Dimitrievitch, *Dance Research* (London), 4 parts: Summer 1985, Spring 1986, Spring 1987, Autumn 1988

Beaumont, Cyril, *Complete Book of Ballets*, revised edition, London, 1951

Petipa, Marius, *Russian Ballet Master: The Memoirs of Marius Petipa*, translated by Helen Wittaker, edited by Lillian Moore, London, 1958

Krasovskaya, Vera, *Russian Ballet Theatre of the Second Half of the Nineteenth Century*, Leningrad and Moscow, 1963

Guest, Ivor, "*Paquita* Returns to Drury Lane", *Dancing Times* (London), December 1964

Guest, Ivor, *The Romantic Ballet in Paris*, London, 1966

Roslavleva, Natalia, *Era of the Russian Ballet*, London, 1966

Marks, Marcia, "American Ballet Theatre", *Dance Magazine* (New York), September 1971

Wiley, Roland John, *A Century of Russian Ballet: Documents and Accounts 1810–1910*, Oxford, 1990

*   *   *

Paquita was based on a successful pre-romantic model of sentimental ballet that centred on the trials of virtuous, brave, young maidens who overcome undeserved obstacles in their pursuit of justice for themselves and often their lovers. Louis Milon's *Nina* (1813) was one such ballet that enjoyed considerable success. What set *Paquita* apart from earlier ballets of this genre was its convincing re-creation of a romantic historical epoch and an equally romantic foreign culture. Set in Spain during the Napoleonic occupation, the story follows a pretty gypsy girl, Paquita (Carlotta Grisi), who saves a French officer, Lucien (Lucien Petipa), from an assassination plot engendered by the Spanish governor. The governor's plotting is eventually discovered and he is arrested. Meanwhile, Paquita's noble birth is discovered, which enables her to marry Lucien.

The critics found *Paquita*'s story somewhat disappointing. Fiorentino wrote that the plot, "as can be seen, is a mimodrame in all its naïve simplicity, and, we hasten to add, we do not like tragedies and dramas that are played with the feet". For him, as for many, the primary attraction was Carlotta Grisi, whose last dance alone was considered by some to be equal to the rest of the ballet. Romantic writer and critic Théophile Gautier divided his praise between Grisi's charms and the décor. "This ballet, in which the drama is perhaps a little too melodramatic, has succeeded perfectly. The richness and the singularity of the costumes of the Empire, the beauty of the décor, and especially the perfection of Carlotta's dancing, have carried away the success." Gautier's colleague, Jules Janin, was highly susceptible to the poetic images of distant places and times created by the romantic ballet. He writes: "This ballet-Empire has therefore shown the Imperial world in its splendour and joys. . . . In these happy salons of the Opéra, shine under their golden epaulettes the most beautiful army uniforms: the dragoon, the hussar, the ensign and the captain, the major of the guard and the lieutenant of the chasseurs." Costumes and sets were by a whole team of designers—Philastre, Cambon, Diéterle, Séchan, Despléchin, Lormier, and d'Orschwiller.

The ballet master, Mazilier, was generally known for the powerful dramatic impact of ballets such as *Le Corsaire* (1856).

His primary contribution to *Paquita*, however, was not his story-telling but his dances, which were "designed with the gracious picturesque quality that characterizes the talent of Mazilier". Authenticity, or at least apparent veracity, was an important feature of ballets during this period, when audiences sought to be swept away to foreign climes and bygone times. Not only were the costumes and sets based on the styles of the Empire, but Mazilier attempted to reconstruct the dance of the Napoleonic era for the grand ballroom scene. The composer, Ernest Deldevez, played his part as well, evoking "with art memories of the most popular contredanse and waltz timbres of the imperial epoque".

Marius Petipa produced *Paquita* for his St. Petersburg début in 1847. In 1881 he asked Minkus to compose new music for a Pas de trois and Grand Pas. *Paquita* is best known today through these two dances.

—John Chapman

The 1847 St. Petersburg production of *Paquita* was historic because in it, the French-born Marius Petipa made his Russian début both as dancer and as choreographer. Petipa's brother Lucien had danced the role of the Comte in Paris, and Marius now performed this role when he produced the ballet for his St. Petersburg début the following year. Ballet historian Vera

Petipa's *Paquita*, in a staging by Galina Samsova, performed by Sadler's Wells Royal Ballet, London

Mazilier's *Paquita*, as performed by Carlotta Grisi and James
Silvain, Drury Lane Theatre, London, 1846

Krasovskaya has explained, "Fifteen years divided *Paquita*
from *La Sylphide*, and only five years separated it from
Giselle—but the aesthetic principles of Romantic ballet, aiming
towards unity of dramatic action, music and dance, have been
deliberately discarded here. Deldevez's score consisted of a
number of disconnected, brilliant episodes. The demonstration
of spectacular technique was the dominant feature of solo and
ensemble dances alike, and character dances were nothing
more than concert pieces, with no connection to the plot."

This indicated the direction in which late nineteenth-century
ballet was heading; and in France, it was to slide into the
decadence of the Second Empire. In Russia, *Paquita* was to be
almost entirely forgotten, until it emerged again in a new 1881
staging by Petipa, now almost entirely the work of the St.
Petersburg ballet master. Ballerina Ekaterina Vazem, who
danced the leading role in the new production, recalled the
ballet in her memoirs. "For my benefit in 1881 Petipa revived
an old ballet by Mazilier, *Paquita*, which had not appeared on
our stage for quite some time," she writes. "The ballet, dating
from the 1840s, had a naïve melodramatic plot and a set of
larger-than-life 'evil' and 'virtuous' characters. From the
choreographic point of view there was not much to speak of and
it was completely out of date anyway. Petipa created new
choreography for all the dances and episodes, with the
exception of the corps de ballet's 'cloak dance', a curious
example of Parisian ensemble dancing, where men's parts are
danced by women *en travesti*. Petipa presented the last episode
as a grand celebration, with a newly choreographed Grand Pas
to the music of Minkus at its centre."

Vazem's comments are shrewd, and her estimation of Petipa
not always entirely complimentary. But her recognition of the
success of Petipa's new third act is fair. "In this scene", she
writes, "the prima ballerina and her partner appeared, as well
as several other soloists and a number of secondary dancers.
The Mazurka in the same act, performed by students of the
Theatre School, was also very popular, although there can
hardly be any logical explanation why that Polish national
dance should crop up in Saragossa, where *Paquita* is set."

In 1889, Petipa's production was transferred to the Bolshoi
Theatre in Moscow. In St. Petersburg, several other ballerinas
enjoyed success in the title role, including Virginia Zucchi,
Matilda Kshessinskaya, Carlotta Zambelli, Olga Preobrazhenskaya, and Anna Pavlova. By the 1910s, only the third act
of the ballet was being performed on the Maryinsky stage, with

the Grand Pas, which later became so famous, its obvious
central feature. By the 1920s the ballet seemed to have
disappeared for good; all one could see of it were isolated
variations performed at concerts given by the Leningrad
Choreographic School.

In 1957, however, Konstantin Boyarsky revived the Grand
Pas from Petipa's ballet at the Maly Theatre in Leningrad, and
from the 1970s onwards this was performed by companies all
over the Soviet Union. In the West, Russian expatriates like
George Balanchine and Alexandra Danilova kept alive their
memories of the Petipa Grand Pas, and in 1978 a divertissement from *Paquita*, featuring all of Petipa's 1881 pieces to the
music of Minkus, entered the permanent repertoire of the
Kirov Ballet.

—Arsen Degen

PARADE

Choreography: Léonide Massine
Music: Erik Satie
Design: Pablo Picasso (scenery and costumes)
Libretto: Jean Cocteau
First Production: Diaghilev's Ballets Russes, Théâtre du
   Châtelet, Paris, 18 May 1917
Principal Dancers: Léonide Massine (Chinese Conjuror), Lydia
   Lopokova, Nicholas Zverev (Acrobats), Maria Shabelska
   (American Girl), Léon Woizikowsky (The Manager in
   Evening Dress), M. Statkewicz (The Manager from New
   York)

Other productions include: Ballet du XXe Siècle (restaged and
revised Massine); Brussels, 19 February 1964. Joffrey Ballet
(revival; staged Robert Joffrey, with cooperation of Massine
and Picasso), with Gary Chryst (Chinese Conjuror), Eileen
Brady, Gregory Huffman (Acrobats), Donna Cowen (Little
American Girl), Robert Talmage (The Manager in Evening
Dress), Ted Nelson (The Manager from New York); New
York, 22 March 1973. London Festival Ballet (restaged
Massine), with Kerrison Cooke (Chinese Conjuror), Carole
Hill (Little American Girl); London, 22 May 1974. Zurich
Opera Ballet (staged Susy della Pietra after Massine); Zurich,
26 June 1981.

Les Ballets Modernes de Paris (new version; chor. Françoise
and Dominique Dupuy); Valence, 10 January 1962. Frankfurt
Ballet (new version; chor. John Neumeier); Paris, 9 March
1971. Metropolitan Opera Ballet (new version; chor. Gray
Veredon); New York, 1981.

PUBLICATIONS

Lieberman, William, "Picasso and the Ballet", *Dance Index*
   (New York), November–December 1946
Howe, Martin, "Erik Satie and his Ballets", *Ballet* (London), 2
   parts: August–September, October 1948
Beaumont, Cyril, *Complete Book of Ballets*, revised edition,
   London, 1951
Lieberman, William, "Picasso and the Dance", *Dance Maga-
   zine* (New York), September 1957
Massine, Léonide, *My Life in Ballet*, London, 1960
Kirstein, Lincoln, *Movement and Metaphor*, New York, 1970

Parade: Picasso's costumes for The New York Manager (left) and the Parisian Manager (right), 1917

Massine, Léonide, ["*Parade*"], *Dance Magazine* (New York), March 1973

Baker, Rob, "Joffrey's *Parade* ... 50 Years Later", *Dance Magazine* (New York), March 1973

Cooper, Douglas, "*Parade*", *Dance and Dancers* (London), June 1973

Balanchine, George, with Mason, Francis, *Balanchine's Festival of Ballet*, Garden City, N.Y., 1977

Gaye, Pamela, "A Conversation with Léonide Massine", *Dance Scope* (New York), vol. 13, no. 4, 1979

Cocteau, Jean, "A Season of the Ballets Russes", translated by Frank W.D. Ries, *Dance Scope* (New York), vol. 3, no. 4, 1979

Axsom, Richard, *"Parade": Cubism as Theatre*, New York, 1979

Schmoyer, L.M., "The Giant Jigsaw Puzzle: Robert Joffrey Reconstructs *Parade*", *The Drama Review* (Cambridge, Massachusetts), Fall 1984

Ries, Frank W.D., *The Dance Theatre of Jean Cocteau*, Ann Arbor, Michigan, 1986

Garafola, Lynn, *Diaghilev's Ballets Russes*, New York, 1989

Rothschild, Deborah M., *Picasso's "Parade"*, London, 1991

*   *   *

Parade was a landmark in the realization of Modernism in the theatre; although it has been rarely performed, its fame and influence have endured. In its time *Parade* was the most ambitious example of ballet as a collaborative art, fusing Picasso's Cubism, Satie's music, and Cocteau's script and ideas. Apollinaire hailed it in his programme notes as the marriage of painting and dance, the plastic and the mimetic, to form a new and more complete art. Yet dance critics have tended to see it rather differently, pointing to the domination of Picasso's Cubist designs and identifying a major flaw in the ballet in that choreography was of secondary importance.

Parade results from one of the rare periods in ballet history when dance was at the forefront of the avant garde, involving many leading artists. Cocteau had devised his idea in 1914, calling it *David*, and was a pivotal figure in *Parade*'s realization, even contributing sounds to the music. Satie's score was anti-impressionistic, having a collage method of construction that incorporated sounds from everyday life, including a typewriter and sirens as well as elements of ragtime and music hall. Similarly, Massine's concern was to make something new and representative of the time, incorporating jazz and cinematic techniques into balletic form. When Robert Joffrey reconstructed *Parade* in 1973 for the Joffrey Ballet, supervised by Massine, he referred to it as the first multi-media ballet.

Picasso's Cubist costume designs must be the most remarkable creations in theatre history. The ten-foot-high American Manager's costume for example, was a collage incorporating skyscrapers, pipes, and a megaphone within which the dancer moved. A satirical comment on commercialism was no doubt intended. Critics of both the 1917 production and its reconstructions have said that Picasso's designs dominate the ballet. Cyril Beaumont, who found the Cubist costume designs to be a distraction, gave one of the few reviews of the original production which reveals something of the nature of the work beyond its immediate visual and aural impact. Beaumont refers to the "incessant, purposeless activity" of the acrobats' movements and sees the work as a tragi-comedy as well as a satire.

The ballet appeared at a tense and crucial time in the progress of the First World War. John Berger has claimed that *Parade* was a "bourgeois palliative in its conscious triviality", and the simplicity of its subject matter has often been criticized. Lincoln Kirstein, however, replied to Berger's judgement by insisting that the ballet was an anti-German demonstration on an aesthetic level, with the figure of the Chinese Conjurer (danced by Massine) as representative of the indestructible creative spirit. Many interpretations of *Parade* are possible, but seen in its artistic context Berger's comment is perhaps misplaced. Cubism had been around in painting for approximately ten years as a radical rejection of Romanticism, the sensual qualities of Impressionism, and the decorative colour of Fauvism—but in 1917, *Parade* represented a radical and powerful departure for ballet theatre. *Parade* exploded the classical-Romantic aesthetics with which ballet was identified by blasting the contemporary world on to the stage, multi-faceted and fractured, in a stream of Modernist consciousness. It also amounted to the breaking of boundaries between popular and high art, bringing before an haut bourgeois audience images taken from circus, vaudeville, and everyday life.

It was called a "realist" ballet, and for Cocteau the ballet's simplicity, which was often thought of as its triviality, was its major source of importance. For Cocteau the ballet represented the "rehabilitation of the Commonplace". *Parade* was certainly a long way from ballets like *Giselle*, *Le Spectre de la rose*, *Les Sylphides* or *Schéhérazade*. It was not, however, the first ballet on contemporary themes: Nijinsky's *Jeux* (1913) predates it. But *Jeux*, despite its everyday costumes and theme, kept to the traditional classical vocabulary to a far greater extent than did the pedestrian movement of parts of *Parade*. Apollinaire's programme note stated that through *Parade* the audience would "come to know all the grace of modern movement, of which they have never dreamed. A magnificent music hall Chinese will release their imagination; the Young American Girl, as she cranks an imaginary car, will express the magic of their daily life, whose wordless rituals the Acrobat in blue and white tights celebrates with exquisite, amazing agility."

Larionov, one of Diaghilev's designers, wrote a Rayonist Manifesto in 1913 which foreshadowed the approach to images in *Parade*. Larionov wrote, "We declare the genius of our days to be trousers, jackets, shoes, tramways, buses, aeroplanes, railways, magnificent ships. . .". Cocteau envisaged his American girl in a similar stream of modern consciousness: "the little girl mounts a race-horse, rides a bicycle, quivers like movies on the screen, imitates Charlie Chaplin, chases a thief with a revolver, boxes, dances a rag-time, goes to sleep, is shipwrecked, rolls on the grass of an April morning, buys a Kodak, etc . . .".

In terms of the choreography, the most outstanding section is no doubt Massine's own solo as the Chinese Conjurer. In Joffrey's reconstruction, where the part was danced by Gary Chryst, we could appreciate Massine's wit and movement inventiveness. It was only Massine's third ballet, but his highly distinctive style was already clear. The contemporary balletomanes distrusted Diaghilev's increasing demand for novelty and spectacle, and were mostly out of sympathy with Modernist aesthetics. It was undoubtedly not an ideal model of ballet in that the choreography clearly took a secondary position, but *Parade* demonstrated that the Romantic-Classical aesthetics of ballet and ideals of Beauty need not be absolute criteria in the realization of the art form. It could be said that the ballet was ahead of its time, but today it is little more than a fascinating museum piece because it *was* so very much a part of its time. *Parade* needs to be understood in the context of its era, when shock was integral to the Modernist aesthetic and embodied an element of assault on contemporary values and tastes in art.

—Lesley-Anne Sayers

PARIS OPÉRA BALLET

French ballet company based in Paris. Origins in L'Académie royale de danse founded by Louis XIV, 1661, and L'Académie royale de l'Opéra (called Académie royale de musique after 1771), founded 1669; ballet generally part of opera performances until first complete evening of ballet, 1861; opera and ballet based at the Opera House, Palais Garnier (L'Opéra de Paris), from 1875; ballet company alone the official company of the Opéra Palais Garnier (opera having moved to the Opéra Bastille), from 1988; affiliated Groupe de Récherche Chorégraphique de l'Opéra de Paris (GRCOP), founded 1981. Official school associated with company, growing out of the Académie royale de musique, and with direct aim of preparing dancers for the Opéra stage, founded by royal edict, 1713; has since become known as the Paris Opéra Ballet School. Current artistic director of the Paris Opéra Ballet (succeeding Rudolf Nureyev): Patrick Dupond, from 1989.

PUBLICATIONS

Noverre, Jean-Georges, *Lettres sur la danse*, Paris and Stuttgart, 1760

Gautier, Théophile, et al., *Les Beautés de l'Opéra*, Paris, 1845

Royer, Alphonse, *Histoire de l'Opéra*, Paris, 1845

Campardon, Emile, *L'Académie royale de musique au XVIIe siècle*, Paris, 1884

Prod'homme, J.-G., *L'Opéra (1669–1925)*, Paris, 1925

Vaillat, L., *Ballets de l'Opéra de Paris*, Paris, 1947

Kochno, Boris, *Le Ballet*, Paris, 1954

Guest, Ivor, "An Introduction to the Paris Opera", *Ballet Annual* (London), no. 9, 1955

McGowan, Margaret, *L'Art du ballet de cour en France 1581–1643*, Paris, 1963

Guest, Ivor, *The Romantic Ballet in Paris*, London, 1966

Christout, Marie-Françoise, *Le Ballet de cour de Louis XIV*, Paris, 1967

Guest, Ivor, *The Ballet of the Second Empire*, London, 1974

Guest, Ivor, *Le Ballet de L'Opéra de Paris*, Paris, 1976

Hilton, Wendy, *Dance of Court and Theater: The French Noble Style 1690–1725*, Princeton, New Jersey, 1981

Guest, Ivor, "The Paris Opera Ballet: Its Historical Tradition", *Dancing Times* (London), July 1982

*   *   *

The Paris Opéra Ballet is the oldest national ballet company in the world. It developed from Louis XIV's Court ballets and was established by his founding L'Académie royale de danse in 1661 and L'Académie royale de l'Opéra in 1669. In 1672, in collaboration with Beauchamps, the first ballet-master of the Paris Opéra, and the designer Carlo Vigarani, Lully inaugurated a new form of opera with dance and elaborate spectacle. The day after Molière's death in 1673, Louis XIV allowed Lully to take over the Salle du Palais Royal from the actors, giving him the sole right to produce ballet.

At first noblemen were allowed to dance on the public stage without losing their rank, thus passing on the noble style of dance to the increasing number of professionals. Although there had been female professional dancers for many years, they were not officially permitted to dance at the Opéra until 1681 in *Le Triomphe de l'amour*, led by Mlle. de La Fontaine. During this time Beauchamps contributed considerably to the development of technique and virtuosity. After Lully's death in 1687, Beauchamps left the Opéra and was succeeded first by his pupil Louis Pécour, then by Michel Blondy in 1729.

In 1713 Louis XIV founded the school of dance affiliated to the Opéra in order to maintain and supervise standards and discipline. From this school emerged numerous famous dancers and teachers, including Françoise Prévost, Claude Ballon, Marie Sallé, and Marie-Anne de Cupis de Camargo, famous for her daring virtuosity, hitherto confined only to the male dancer.

Lully's tragédie-ballets, with their unity of plot, were gradually replaced by a new genre, the spectacular opera-ballet, often fragments loosely put together in which song and dance had little connection. Although many critics condemned the monotony of the choreography and the lack of dramatic interest, the dance was the most popular aspect of the opera-ballets. The French taste for dance inspired the composer Rameau to create dance tunes of an exceptional harmonic and rhythmic quality.

The publication in 1760 of Jean-Georges Noverre's famous *Lettres sur la danse* underlined the pressing need for drastic reforms, including unity of plot, tighter collaboration between spectacle, choreography, libretto, and music, and the discarding of masks and wigs so that dance could be more expressive. Noverre became ballet-master at the Paris Opéra in 1776 at the instigation of his former pupil, Queen Marie-Antoinette. Since it had hitherto been the policy of the Opéra to promote from within, and Noverre was an outsider, this caused serious antagonism. Hostile groups centred around the Gardel brothers and Marie-Madeleine Guimard. Noverre resigned in 1779, leaving in 1781, in favour of Maximilien Gardel and Jean Dauberval. Because of increasing friction, Dauberval resigned in 1783 and went to Bordeaux. On Maximilien's sudden death in 1787 he was succeeded by his brother Pierre, who led the Opéra officially until 1820 and unofficially until 1829, the longest period of office in the history of the Opéra. In spite of the spate of political upheavals caused by the Revolution—Directoire, Consulat, Empire, Restoration—he maintained discipline and upheld the rigorous standards of the leading company in Europe where the most famous nineteenth-century dancers, choreographers, and teachers were trained.

Despite the huge success of Charles-Louis Didelot's *Flore et Zéphyre* (1796) with wires enabling the dancers to fly, and Geneviève Gosselin's new feat of rising from half to full point, as well as the exciting innovation of gas lighting in 1822, the Opéra during the Restoration remained largely conservative. Jean Aumer, ballet master from 1820 to 1831, lacked imagination and the ability to integrate dance and action.

Following the Revolution of 1830, the Opéra took on a new lease of life. It became a private enterprise, run by Dr. Véron, an astute businessman who aimed to transform the Opéra into a fashionable meeting-place for the upper bourgeoisie. The foyer was opened to *abonnés*, season-ticket holders who could meet the ballerinas—a practice which led to much criticism of immoral relationships. He also abolished the traditional male distinction between noble, *demi-caractère*, and *caractère* roles. Véron offered Marie Taglioni a six-year contract, and with the Ballet of the Nuns in Meyerbeer's opera, *Robert le Diable* (1831), the Romantic movement entered the stage. Filippo Taglioni's *La Sylphide* (1832), created by him for his daughter, ensured the supremacy of the female dancer. Marie Taglioni's brilliant partner, Jules Perrot, resigned soon after. Véron invited Fanny Elssler, a sensuous and exotic dancer, to contrast with Taglioni's ethereal qualities. Elssler's voluptuous dancing was exploited fully by Jean Coralli in the famous Cachucha in *Le Diable boîteux* (1836). In 1841 Carlotta Grisi, partnered by Lucien Petipa, performed *Giselle*.

During the 1840s and 1850s the Paris Opéra Ballet attracted the best dancers and choreographers, but a decline set in by the end of the 1860s. The last masterpiece of Saint-Léon and Delibes was *Coppélia* in 1870. By this time male dancers were practically banished from the ballet, female dancers performing male roles *en travesti*.

In 1875 the company moved to the Palais Garnier, its present home, but it was barely tolerated. Ballet in Paris was at its lowest ebb, reduced to divertissements in operas. But with the advent of the Diaghilev seasons at the Opéra from 1910, ballet and the male dancer acquired a new status. On the eve of the 1914–18 war, Jacques Rouché became director of the Opéra until 1945. Despite the turmoils of two world wars, he managed to reform the ballet and bring back its prestige after a very long eclipse. However, this was achieved mainly by hosting guest dancers and choreographers such as Anna Pavlova, Mikhail and Vera Fokine, Ida Rubinstein, Olga Spessivtseva, Carlotta Zambelli, and Tamara Toumanova. The company had not found an individual identity.

The death of Diaghilev marked a turning point with the production in 1929 of *Les Créatures de Prométhée* by Serge Lifar, who became ballet master and leading dancer in 1930. He brought in stringent reforms and discipline, banishing the *abonnés* from the foyer. Soon entire evenings were devoted to ballet and a new generation of dancers began to emerge. In 1958 Lifar was succeeded by Georges Skibine. This was a period of transition during which foreign choreographers were engaged, eclipsing Skibine, who was succeeded in 1961 by Michel Descombey. Both Maurice Béjart and Roland Petit refused the post, which was taken successively by John Taras in 1969, Raymond Franchetti in 1971, Violette Verdy in 1977, Rosella Hightower in 1981, and Rudolf Nureyev in 1983. Nureyev's direction was too distant, as he was absorbed by his own career, and he was replaced in 1989 by Patrick Dupond, who trained with the company and who understands the internal problems.

Despite the lack of artistic and stylistic direction in the last two decades, a spectacular improvement can be seen in the general standard and the large number of international stars who have graduated from the school directed by Claude Bessy. In 1980 the rigid hierarchical star system was abolished, and since 1988 only ballet has been performed at the Opéra Garnier—opera having moved to the Opéra Bastille. The company is noted for its versatility and ability to perform ballets as diverse as classics such as *La Fille mal gardée* and contemporary works by Merce Cunningham or Twyla Tharp.

—Françoise Carter

PARK, Merle

British dancer and teacher.   Born in Salisbury, Rhodesia (now
Harare, Zimbabwe), 6 October 1937. Studied with Betty Lamb,
Rhodesia, Elmhurst School, England, from 1951, and at Royal
Ballet Upper School, from 1954. Married (1) dance critic James
Monahan, 1965 (div. 1969): one son, Anthony; (2) Sidney
Bloch, 1970. Dancer, Sadler's Wells Ballet (now Royal Ballet),
from 1954, becoming soloist, from 1958, and principal dancer,
from 1959; guest artist, Royal Ballet Touring Company, 1961;
also international guest artist, frequently performing abroad,
often partnered by Rudolf Nureyev; teacher, Royal Ballet
School, becoming director, from 1983. Recipient: titles of
Commander of the Order of the British Empire, 1974, Dame
Commander of the Order of the British Empire, 1986.

ROLES

1955   Ensemble (cr) in *Variations on a Theme of Purcell*
        (Ashton), Sadler's Wells Ballet, London
        Principal dancer in *Variations on a Theme of Purcell*
        (Ashton), Sadler's Wells Ballet, London
1955/   Milkmaid in *Façade* (Ashton), Sadler's Wells (becoming
57   Royal) Ballet, London
        Peasant Pas de deux in *Giselle* (Petipa after Coralli,
        Perrot; staged Sergeyev), Royal Ballet, London
        Spring Fairy in *Cinderella* (Ashton), Royal Ballet,
        London
        Pas de trois in *Les Rendezvous* (Ashton), Royal Ballet,
        London
        Street Dancer in *Petrushka* (Fokine), Royal Ballet,
        London
1956   Pas de deux in *Les Patineurs* (Ashton), Royal Ballet,
        London
        Bluebird in *The Sleeping Beauty* (Petipa; staged Ser-
        geyev, de Valois), Royal Ballet, London
1957   Entrée ("Blue Girls") in *Les Patineurs* (Ashton), Royal
        Ballet, London
        Variation in *Birthday Offering* (Ashton), Royal Ballet,
        London
1958   Waltz, Mazurka in *Les Sylphides* (Fokine), Royal Ballet,
        London
        Principal dancer in *Ballet Imperial* (Balanchine), Royal
        Ballet, London
        Principal dancer in *Agon* (MacMillan), Royal Ballet,
        London
        Swanilda in *Coppélia* (Petipa, Cecchetti; staged Ser-
        geyev, de Valois), Royal Ballet, London
        The Ballerina in *Petrushka* (Fokine), Royal Ballet,
        London
        Title role in *Mam'zelle Angot* (Massine), Royal Ballet,
        London
1959   Title role in *Pineapple Poll* (Cranko), Royal Ballet
        Touring Company
        Waltz, Polka in *Façade* (Ashton), Royal Ballet, London
1960   Principal dancer in *Ballabile* (Petit), Royal Ballet,
        London
        Lise in *La Fille mal gardée* (Ashton), Royal Ballet,
        London
        Variation, Adagio of Lovers in *Les Rendezvous* (Ash-
        ton), Royal Ballet, London
1961   Princess Aurora in *The Sleeping Beauty* (Petipa; staged
        Sergeyev, de Valois), Royal Ballet Touring Company
        The Fiancée in *Le Baiser de la fée* (MacMillan), Royal
        Ballet, London
1962   Mariuccia in *The Good-Humoured Ladies* (Massine),
        Royal Ballet, London

        Young Girl in *The Two Pigeons* (Ashton), Royal Ballet
        Touring Company
        Principal dancer in *Napoli* (Bournonville), Royal Ballet,
        London
1963   Principal dancer in *Flower Festival at Genzano* (Bour-
        nonville), Royal Ballet, London
1964   Titania in *The Dream* (Ashton), Royal Ballet, London
1965   Juliet in *Romeo and Juliet* (MacMillan), Royal Ballet,
        London
        Principal dancer in *Laurencia* Pas de six (Nureyev after
        Chabukiani), Royal Ballet, London
1966   Principal dancer (cr) in *Brandenburg nos. 2 and 4*
        (Cranko), Royal Ballet, London
1967   Title role in *Giselle* (Petipa after Coralli, Perrot; staged
        Ashton), Royal Ballet, London
        Celestial (cr) in *Shadowplay* (Tudor), Royal Ballet,
        London
        Principal dancer in *Symphonic Variations* (Ashton),
        Royal Ballet, London
1968   Nikiya in "Kingdom of the Shades" from *La Bayadère*
        (Nureyev after Petipa), Royal Ballet, London
        Tuesday (cr) in *Jazz Calendar* (Ashton), Royal Ballet,
        London
        Clara (cr) in *The Nutcracker* (Nureyev), Royal Ballet,
        London
1969   Title role in *Cinderella* (Ashton), Royal Ballet, London
        Chloe in *Daphnis and Chloe* (Ashton), Royal Ballet,
        London
1970   Pas de deux in *Birthday Offering* (Ashton), Royal Ballet,
        London
        Débutante in *Façade* (Ashton), Royal Ballet, London
1971   Mathilde Kschessinska in *Anastasia* (MacMillan), Roy-
        al Ballet, London
        Principal dancer in *Serenade* (Balanchine), Royal
        Ballet, London
        Principal dancer in *The Mirror Walkers* (pas de deux;
        Wright), Royal Ballet, London
1972   Tsarevna in *The Firebird* (Fokine), Royal Ballet,
        London
        The Girl in *Triad* (MacMillan), Royal Ballet, London
        Principal dancer (cr) in *Walk to the Paradise Garden*
        (Ashton), Royal Ballet, London
1973   Principal dancer in *Dances at a Gathering* (Robbins),
        Royal Ballet, London
        Principal dancer in *In the Night* (Robbins), Royal
        Ballet, London
        Title role in *The Firebird* (Fokine), Royal Ballet, London
        Odette/Odile in *Swan Lake* (Petipa, Ivanov; staged
        Sergeyev, de Valois), Royal Ballet, London
        Principal dancer in *Don Quixote* Pas de deux (after
        Petipa), Royal Ballet, tour
1974   Terpsichore in *Apollo* (Balanchine), Royal Ballet,
        London
        Stop-time Rag (cr) in *Elite Syncopations* (MacMillan),
        Royal Ballet, London
        Title role in *Manon* (MacMillan), Royal Ballet, tour
1975   Principal dancer (cr) in *Scène dansante* (pas de deux;
        Ashton), Artists of the Royal Ballet, Aldeburgh
1976   Title role (cr) in *Lulu* (J. Carter), Royal Ballet Touring
        Company, London
1977   Katherina in *The Taming of the Shrew* (Cranko), Royal
        Ballet, London
1978   Principal dancer in *The Concert* (Robbins), Royal Ballet
        Touring Company
        Countess Marie Larisch (cr) in *Mayerling* (MacMillan),
        Royal Ballet, London
1979   Principal dancer (cr) in *La Fin du jour* (MacMillan),

Merle Park as Isadora, 1981

Royal Ballet, London
Natalia Petrovna in *A Month in the Country* (Ashton),
Royal Ballet, tour
1980   Principal dancer (cr) in *Adieu* (Bintley), Royal Ballet,
London
1981   Title role (cr) in *Isadora* (MacMillan), Royal Ballet,
London
Principal dancer in *Voices of Spring* (from Strauss's *Die
Fledermaus*; Ashton), Royal Ballet, London
1982   Principal dancer (cr) in *Pas de deux Villa d'Este* (Deane),
Royal Ballet, London
Principal dancer (cr) in *Unsquare Dance* (Bintley),
Sadler's Wells Theatre Gala, London
Victorine in *Konservatoriet* (Bournonville), Royal Ballet,
London
1985   Principal dancer (cr) in *La Chatte métamorphosée en
femme* (solo; Ashton), Royal Ballet, London

Other roles include: Neapolitan Dance in *Swan Lake* (Petipa,
Ashton; staged Helpmann), Fire in *The Prince of the Pagodas*
(Cranko), Betrayed Girl in *The Rake's Progress* (de Valois),
Young Girl in *The Shadow* (Cranko), Bride in *A Wedding
Bouquet* (Ashton), principal dancer in *Scènes de ballet* (Ashton),
title role in *Raymonda*, Act III (Nureyev after Petipa).

PUBLICATIONS

By Park:
Interview in Gruen, John, *The Private World of Ballet*, New
York, 1975
Interview in Ferguson, Ian, "A New Role", *Dance and Dancers*
(London), April 1983

About Park:
"Dancer You Will Know: Merle Park", *Dance and Dancers*
(London), May 1955
Currie, Jean, "Merle Park and Nureyev", *Dancing Times*
(London), February 1967
Monahan, James, "Merle Park", *Dance Magazine* (New York),
May 1968
Kerensky, Oleg, *Ballet Today*, London, 1970
Crickmay, Anthony (photographer), and Manchester, P.W.,
Merle Park, Brooklyn, 1976
Bland, Alexander, *The Royal Ballet: The First Fifty Years*,
London, 1981

*   *   *

One of Merle Park's sharpest memories is of being taken as a
ballet student to see the Royal Ballet performing *Swan Lake*.
When asked after the performance what she had most enjoyed,
Park answered without hesitation: "the Neapolitan Dance". It
was a highly significant reply; in that production the
Neapolitan Dance, choreographed by Frederick Ashton, was a
fast show-stopping duet, exactly the sort of thing that, later in
her career, Park most enjoyed doing—a brilliant show-piece
that brought the house down. In her early years as a dancer with
the Royal Ballet Park's artistic philosophy was "get on, get off,
and get home".

Park was born in Rhodesia (now Zimbabwe), but came to
Britain in her teens to be a boarder at the Elmhurst Ballet
School in Surrey. Later she studied at the Royal Ballet Upper
School, entering the Royal Ballet in 1954, some two years
before Antoinette Sibley and three years before Lynn Seymour.
These three dancers were contemporaries of a particularly
talented generation, each of the three making their mark

through different but complementary qualities: Seymour was
the unrivalled dramatic dancer, Sibley the classical lyricist, and
Park the brilliant technician.

Park was made a soloist after two years in the corps de ballet,
and performed most of the solo variations in the classical and
Romantic repertoire, particularly the ones demanding a
virtuoso technique, such as the fairies in the Prologue to *The
Sleeping Beauty* and the Peasant Pas de deux in the first act of
Giselle. Her first full-length parts were Swanilda in *Coppélia*
and Lise in *La Fille mal gardée*. Both roles demand a diamond-
sharp brilliance of execution, charm and vivacity mixed with a
dash of pathos in the characterization, but nothing, perhaps,
very demanding in terms of dramatic expression. In those days
she was considered not much more than a soubrette, as Park
has said herself.

Park's first major ballerina roles in the classics came about
when she was guest artist with the Royal Ballet Touring
Company (now the Birmingham Royal Ballet) in 1961, and she
danced Princess Aurora in *The Sleeping Beauty*. Of all the big
classical roles it was probably the one most suited to her talents,
demanding continuous solo variations, a hugely daunting
supported adage—the Rose Adagio—and a final grand pas de
deux, with variations and a coda that represent the very
pinnacle of classical virtuosity. Park later danced the role many
times with the main company at Convent Garden, becoming,
arguably, the greatest exponent of the role of that generation.
She also frequently appeared in the other great virtuoso pas de
deux of *The Sleeping Beauty*, the Bluebird pas de deux.

Between the mid-1960s and mid-1970s Park gave more
performances of the title role of *Giselle* than any other Royal
Ballet ballerina, no doubt largely because of her ability to live
up to the exhausting technical demands of the second act. But
the first act requires considerable dramatic ability, and it was
in this Romantic classic that Park first gave serious thought to
her acting. To the surprise of many critics, Park not only
revealed an intelligent approach to her interpretation of the
role, but showed an ability to project that interpretation to the
audience with real dramatic power. It was a revelation that was
to make her one of the most satisfying interpreters of the great
dramatic roles devised by Kenneth MacMillan for his full-
length works, culminating in her performance of the tremendously taxing title role of *Isadora*.

Before that, however, the first role to be created on Park was
that of the Celestial in Antony Tudor's enigmatic *Shadowplay*,
a ballet partly based on Rudyard Kipling's *The Jungle Book*.
The role was that of a powerful goddess, a creature of glittering
sensuality; and, with such an acute, fastidious, and demanding
choreographer as Tudor in charge, it was no casual decision to
cast Park in the part. He had no doubt observed that both on
and off stage, Park epitomized feminine glamour and he saw
her potential as a seductress.

But it was in the full-length MacMillan ballets that Park
reached her full potential, combining virtuosity with a steadily
increasing theatrical expressiveness that had been not so much
absent as overlooked in the early years of her career. In 1965,
she was the fourth cast in *Romeo and Juliet*; she encompassed
the choreography with technical ease, without necessarily
reaching the emotional heights of Seymour and Fonteyn. Yet
over the years Park's conception of the role was presented with
greater clarity, as she learned to delineate more effectively the
development from rebellious girl to passionate woman.

The title role of *Manon*, that of the innocent girl turned
courtesan, torn between true love and a life of luxury, fitted
Park's glamorous on-stage personality like a glove. With her
glittering technique Park had always been able to project the
image of fascinating, desirable womanhood, and Manon,
emblazoned with jewels and richly dressed, gave her the

opportunity to project a sophisticated femme fatale with total conviction.

Two later MacMillan ballets enabled Park to bring her acting ability to full fruition, crowning her career with two memorable portraits of real-life characters. The first was Countess Larisch in *Mayerling*, the brilliant, conniving woman who had been Crown Prince Rudolf's mistress and who was responsible for bringing Rudolf into his suicidal alliance with the teenage Mary Vetsera. Park gave the role great depth—she was physically alluring, witty, cynical, yet still convincing as the only woman to understand the depraved Prince and his need for love.

The last great part created for Park was the title role of *Isadora*. Although MacMillan originally conceived the ballet for Seymour, she was not available when the ballet was finally created, and the choreographer then chose Park, whose svelte shape was hardly similar to Isadora Duncan's more voluptuous figure but whose technical ability and new-found authority as an actress gave her the range and presence for such a demanding role—one of the longest and toughest ever created for a ballerina. The choreography encompassed many styles of dance, from long, classically based pas de deux, to solos in the style of Duncan's own free-flowing form, to the tango and popular dances of the 1920s. The ballet was highly controversial and received mixed reviews, but most critics considered it a personal triumph for Park and a fitting pinnacle to a brilliant career—it was certainly a long way from being "just a soubrette".

—Edward Thorpe

PAS DE QUATRE

Choreography: Jules Perrot
Music: Cesare Pugni
Libretto: Jules Perrot
First Production: Her Majesty's Theatre, London, 12 July 1845
Principal Dancers: Marie Taglioni, Carlotta Grisi, Fanny Cerrito, Lucile Grahn

Other productions include: Her Majesty's Theatre (restaged Perrot), with Taglioni, Grisi, Cerrito, and Carolina Rosati; London, 1847. Markova–Dolin Ballet (reconstruction; chor. Keith Lester), with Molly Lake, Diana Gould, Prudence Hyman, and Kathleen Crofton; Manchester, 27 May 1936. American Ballet Theatre (chor. Anton Dolin after Lester), with Nana Gollner, Nina Stroganova, Alicia Alonso, and Katherine Sergava; New York, 16 February 1941.

PUBLICATIONS

Lumley, Benjamin, "The *Pas de Quatre* of 1845", *Dancing Times* (London), August 1939
Richardson, Philip J.S., "Centenary of the *Pas de Quatre*", *Dancing Times* (London), July 1945
Michel, Arthur, "*Pas de Quatre* 1845–1945", *Dance Magazine* (New York), July 1945
Guest, Ivor, "*The Pas de Quatre*", *Ballet* (London), August 1951
Beaumont, Cyril, *Complete Book of Ballets*, revised edition, London, 1951
Guest, Ivor, *The Romantic Ballet in England*, London, 1954
Maynard, Olga, "The History of *Pas de Quatre*", *Dance Magazine* (New York), April 1958
Guest, Ivor, *The Pas de Quatre*, London, 1968
Kirstein, Lincoln, *Movement and Metaphor: Four Centuries of Ballet*, New York, 1970
Guest, Ivor, *Jules Perrot: Master of the Romantic Ballet*, London, 1984
Cavers, J.K., "The Iconography of *Pas de Quatre*", *Dance Research* (London), Spring 1987

*   *   *

Performed in London at the height of Romanticism's frenzy, *Pas de quatre*, a culmination of eighteenth-century costume reforms, nineteenth-century stylistic developments, and on-going technical advances, celebrated the supremacy of the ballerina, who had become the embodiment of the Romantic ideal and satisfied a public obsession with spectacle. Marie Taglioni, Romantic ballet's grande dame; Fanny Cerrito, London's darling; Carlotta Grisi, a versatile star, and Lucile Grahn, the typification of the Bournonville ballerina—all were rival artists, but each was different in physical attributes, technical gifts, and temperament, and they united their talents in an unprecedented artistic collaboration with acclaimed dancer/choreographer Jules Perrot and composer Cesare Pugni.

The remarkably talented Perrot could recognize, extract, and transform dancers' capabilities into deftly constructed choreography. Required to create four unique variations, several non-competitive ensemble passages, and an ebullient finale which would flatter each dancer, favour none, and please the public, Perrot rose to the challenge admirably. He created an allegro variation to display Grahn's agility, vigour, and poetry, and a solo for Grisi which highlighted her adroit footwork, archness, and technical flexibility. He fashioned a short duet for Grisi and Cerrito, who was inspired by competition, and designed Cerrito's variation to show off her swiftness and elasticity. Taglioni appeared briefly with Grahn, then performed a variation exhibiting her unique lines and controlled technique.

Perrot's task was lightened by Pugni, a prolific composer with whom he frequently collaborated. Pugni innately understood choreographic needs. Willing to work in great haste and on demand, his scores tended to fluctuate in quality. However, *Pas de quatre*'s light, melodious score was composed at his artistic zenith, and is one of his outstanding works.

Artistic accomplishments aside, *Pas de quatre* was a skilful diplomatic stratagem and a slick marketing coup, a credit to Benjamin Lumley, manager of Her Majesty's Theatre, who manoeuvred the enterprise from conception to curtain. Ambitious, enthusiastic, and self-confident, Lumley had both a perception for commercial trends and exceptional managerial skills: with great tact, he commissioned the talents and appeased the egos of the rival foursome, and he understood the entertainment value of ballet, which then flourished in London as an imported novelty. Dedicated to enhancing his privately owned theatre, Lumley encouraged ballerina-mania, rousing public interest and inciting press coverage. He moulded history, perhaps literally.

Grahn, the least famous of the fabulous four, was coolly received at her London début. Lumley needed a star on par with Grisi, Cerrito, and Taglioni. Championing her career, he succeeded in boosting her box-office appeal and in proving his promotional talents.

The oft-told tale, excerpted from Lumley's memoirs, which recounts the pre-performance spat between Cerrito and Grisi over the right of succession may further attest to the manager's publicist instincts. The story, which exemplifies the quartet's

Pas de quatre, with (from left to right) Carlotta Grisi, Marie Taglioni, Lucile Grahn, and Fanny Cerrito, 1845

intrinsic rivalry, is plausible but melodramatic. An identical conflict arose in 1843, when Lumley, at Queen Victoria's request, negotiated a duet for Cerrito and Fanny Elssler. Considering the striking similarity between the arguments, Perrot's reported reaction to the repeated stunt seems over-dramatized. The credibility of the Cerrito–Grisi squabble—if it actually occurred—has been debated on other grounds, which challenge that the incident could not have happened on the performance day. Though not impossible, it seems unlikely that the ballet had never been run through sequentially and that consequently, at the final rehearsal, the score remained disjointed. Logically, the dispute should have surfaced earlier in the rehearsal process—which would, in the tale's retelling to the press, lessen the dramatic impact. The dancers did perform according to seniority. However, Grahn was two days, not two years, younger than Grisi, which suggests (if the truth were known), that the age ploy may have concealed a predetermined performance order, ranking the ballerinas by popularity, rather than by age or technical proficiency.

With *Pas de quatre*'s overwhelming success, Perrot, an advocate of the *ballet d'action*, ironically proved his choreographic expertise for pure dance choreography and brought into vogue a new genre of ballet, which satisfied the public's clamour for picturesque mindlessness. Although the divertissement solidified his choreographic reputation, Perrot believed that ballet should possess more substance and aesthetic merit than did this sparkling showpiece, produced according to Lumley's specifications.

Of Perrot's four all-star extravaganzas, *Pas de quatre* is unique. Attired in the standard ballet dress of the day (not unlike the generic leotard adopted a century later for pure dance works), the ballerinas performed non-narrative choreography constructed to compliment their techniques. Although the ballet was devoid of thematic elements, it unapologetically presented four luminaries as themselves. "Personality" with technique was *Pas de quatre*'s raison d'être and its key to success. Individuality and reputation superseded artistic components, a phenomenon of the plotless genre, a form which reveres choreography. Although *Pas de quatre* formulated the pattern for subsequent all-star divertissement, the initial fervour and anticipation incited by the premiere event remained unsurpassed.

Unfortunately, Perrot did not notate his choreography (though a century later several choreographers speculated on what might have been). A few evocative lithographs hint at some of Perrot's groupings. Newspaper accounts of the premiere provide little insight, demonstrating a better grasp of poetry than technique and no understanding of choreographic construction. Performed only six times in London and once in Milan, *Pas de quatre*'s lapse from the repertory was prompted by Perrot's departure from Her Majesty's Theatre and the absence of the superstars.

Orchestrated to assemble four rival celebrities at the pinnacles of their careers, *Pas de quatre* marked the climax of an era in which the ballerina reigned unchallenged. Perrot's masterful choreography served only as a vehicle to exhibit each star's individual technique and to appease her conceit as she presented herself to her admiring public. Consequently, without Taglioni, Cerrito, Grisi, and Grahn, whose personalities were the essence of *Pas de Quatre*, the divertissement lost its impact in addition to its meaning. Inseparable from its historical context, *Pas de Quatre* was an "event", sans pareil.

—Karen Dacko

LES PATINEURS
(*The Skaters*)

Choreography: Frederick Ashton
Music: Giacomo Meyerbeer, arranged by Constant Lambert
Design: William Chappell (scenery and costumes)
First Production: Vic-Wells Ballet, Sadler's Wells Theatre, London, 16 February 1937
Principal Dancers: Harold Turner (Variation "Blue Boy"), Margot Fonteyn and Robert Helpmann (Pas de deux), Pamela May, June Brae (Pas des patineuses), Mary Honor, Elizabeth Miller (Entrée "Blue Girls").

Other productions include: Ballet Theatre (scenery Cecil Beaton), with John Kriza (Variation), Nora Kaye and Hugh Laing (Pas de deux); New York, 2 October 1946. Sadler's Wells Theatre Ballet, with Donald Britton (Variation), Annette Page and David Poole (Pas de deux); London, 23 April 1955. State Ballet of Turkey (staged Ninette de Valois, Ann Parsons); Ankara, 15 January 1962. Royal Winnipeg Ballet (staged Miro Zolan); Winnipeg, 29 December 1966. Australian Ballet (staged Peggy van Praagh); Adelaide, 23 March 1970. Noverre Ballet (staged Robert Mead); Stuttgart, 6 May 1973. London City Ballet (staged Julie Lincoln); Edinburgh, 26 May 1992.

PUBLICATIONS

Coton, A.V., *A Prejudice for Ballet*, London, 1938
Beaumont, Cyril, *Complete Book of Ballets*, revised edition, 1951
Brinson, Peter, and Crisp, Clement, *Ballet for All*, London, 1970
Balanchine, George, with Mason, Francis, *Balanchine's Complete Stories of the Great Ballets*, Garden City, New York, 1977
Vaughan, David, *Frederick Ashton and his Ballets*, London, 1977

*   *   *

Few members of the audience who were present at the premiere of *Les Patineurs* at Sadler's Wells Theatre will ever forget the experience. Not only was it the first ballet created there by Frederick Ashton which could be described as choreographically quite flawless; but it was also a ballet which displayed every one of its performers at their very best, from star soloist to corps de ballet of four women and four men.

The idea of *Les Patineurs* was suggested first to Ninette de Valois by Constant Lambert, but the subject appealed to Ashton, who was familiar with the lithograph of Carolina Rosati and M. Charles in *Les Plaisirs de l'hiver; ou, Les Patineurs*, which hung in the boys' dressing-room at the Mercury Theatre. He met with no resistance when he suggested taking over the choreography. Although it seems strange that Ashton, so much in sympathy with what could perhaps be categorized as post-Wagner composers, felt attracted to the Meyerbeer score, this music nevertheless evoked one of his most perfectly constructed works. From the somewhat sketchy starting-point of commonplace daily events in a skating rink—Cyril Beaumont assures the reader that Ashton had never been to one—a ballet resulted, consistent in every aspect, which created a small unique world, a world in which Ashton had opportunity to invent the most delightful combinations of steps and patterns he had yet presented to the ballet public.

Despite the fact that *Les Patineurs* was a virtuoso tour de force danced by virtuoso performers, the ballet never became

Les Patineurs, **as performed by the Royal Ballet, London**

vulgar, which, given the unsubtle score, could all too easily have happened. The Blue Boy, biggest show-off of all, intersperses his more startling examples of technique for technique's sake with refreshing flashes of comedy, and the audience laughs with him, not at him. Even Ashton's touch of making the experienced dancers, Pamela May and June Brae, lose their balance and slip, instead of giving this to the "novices" Mary Honer and Elizabeth Miller, comments slyly on the relation between pride and fall; while the cool, flowing pas de deux for Margot Fonteyn and Robert Helpmann provides a restful interlude among the more energetic numbers surrounding it. Throughout the ballet one never stops being surprised and delighted by the ease and obvious pleasure with which the choreographer manoeuvres his cast of fifteen dancers in ingenious and inventive figures and patterns.

Les Patineurs has been performed by more companies outside the Vic-Wells/Royal organizations than has any other Ashton ballet (the runners-up are *Façade* and *La Fille mal gardée*), and this can only be due to the tight structure and logical choreographic development of the ballet, which makes faithful reproduction comparatively simple. If it has, in the half-century since the ballet's premiere, proved largely impossible to replace the combination of bravado, cheek, and virtuosity encapsulated in the Blue Boy of Harold Turner, nevertheless the opportunities given by the role have been seized upon with relish by every dancer attempting it—even Robert Helpmann, who took it on in a crisis and obviously enjoyed the chance to try to outdo, with even more cheek but a somewhat lighter technical equipment, his great rival of the 1930s.

—Leo Kersley

PAVANE, Lisa

Australian dancer. Born in New South Wales, Australia, 30 September 1961. Studied at Tessa Mounder Ballet School, 1965–77, and Australian Ballet School, from 1977. Married dancer Gregory Brian Horsman, 1988: one daughter, b. 1992. Dancer, Australian Ballet, from 1981, becoming soloist, 1983–85, senior soloist, 1985, and principal dancer from 1986, touring internationally with company including in Japan and China, 1987, London, Russia, Greece, 1988, Far East, 1989, United States, Italy, and London, 1992; guest artist, Boston Ballet, 1987, Kirov Ballet (now the St. Petersburg Ballet of the Maryinsky Theatre), Leningrad, 1989, Birmingham Royal Ballet, 1989; appeared at Sixth World Festival of Ballet, Tokyo, 1991. Recipient: Ballet Society Scholarship, 1983; Green Room Awards, Best Classical Dancer, 1986, 1987, 1988.

ROLES

1981   Principal dancer (Trois Gnossiennes) in *Monotones* (Ashton), Australian Ballet, Melbourne

      Girl in Pink in *Kettentanz* (Arpino), Australian Ballet, Melbourne

      My Fawny (cr) in *Poems* (Ray), Australian Ballet, Melbourne

1982   The Girl in *After Eden* (Butler), Australian Ballet, Sydney

      Principal dancer (cr) in *City Dances* (Ray), Australian Ballet, Sydney

      Principal dancer in *Our Waltzes* (Nebrada), Australian Ballet, Sydney

      Principal dancer in *Return to the Strange Land* (Kylián), Australian Ballet, Melbourne

      Clara in *The Nutcracker* (Kozlovs), Australian Ballet, Sydney

1983 Flavia in *Spartacus* (Seregi), Australian Ballet, Melbourne
Juliet in *Romeo and Juliet* (Cranko), Australian Ballet, Sydney
Antonia in *Tales of Hoffmann* (Darrell), Australian Ballet, Melbourne
Elisa in *Konservatoriet* (Bournonville), Australian Ballet, Sydney
1984 Lise in *La Fille mal gardée* (Ashton), Australian Ballet Sydney
Princess Aurora in *The Sleeping Beauty* (Petipa; staged Gielgud), Australian Ballet, Melbourne
Lilac Fairy in *The Sleeping Beauty* (Petipa; staged Gielgud), Australian Ballet, Melbourne
Flute, Pas de deux in *Suite en blanc* (Lifar), Australian Ballet, Melbourne
1985 Swanilda in *Coppélia* (Van Praagh after Petipa, Cecchetti), Australian Ballet, Melbourne
Odette/Odile in *Swan Lake* (Petipa, Ivanov; staged Woolliams), Australian Ballet, Melbourne
Title role in *La Sylphide* (Bournonville; staged Bruhn), Australian Ballet, Melbourne
Principal dancer in *In the Night* (Robbins), Australian Ballet, Sydney
Principal dancer in *Serenade* (Balanchine), Australian Ballet, Sydney
Doreen in *Sentimental Bloke* (Ray), Australian Ballet, Sydney
Pas de deux in *Aureole* (Taylor), Australian Ballet, Melbourne
1986 Kitri in *Don Quixote* (Nureyev after Petipa), Australian Ballet, Melbourne
Kate in *The Taming of the Shrew* (Cranko), Australian Ballet Melbourne
Title role in *Giselle* (Petipa after Coralli, Perrot; staged Gielgud), Australian Ballet, Ballarat
Myrtha in *Giselle* (Petipa after Coralli, Perrot; staged Gielgud), Australian Ballet, Adelaide
Prelude in *Les Sylphides* (Fokine), Australian Ballet, Sydney
Principal dancer in *Études* (Lander), Australian Ballet, Sydney
Black Queen in *Checkmate* (de Valois), Australian Ballet, Sydney
1987 Queen of France in *The Three Musketeers* (Prokovsky), Australian Ballet, Melbourne
Apparition (cr) in *Gallery* (Murphy), Australian Ballet, Melbourne
Carlotta Grisi in *Pas de quatre* (Dolin), Australian Ballet, Melbourne
Taglioni in *Pas de quatre* (Dolin), Australian Ballet, Melbourne
Nikiya in *La Bayadère* (Petipa; staged Popa), Australian Ballet, Sydney
Principal dancer in *The Concert* (Robbins), Australian Ballet, Sydney
Ballerina in *Raymonda* Grand Pas (Petipa; staged Nureyev), Australian Ballet, China tour
Young Girl in *Beyond Twelve* (Murphy), Australian Ballet, Melbourne
1988 Principal dancer (cr) in *Ballade* (Baynes), Australian Ballet, Melbourne
Milady in *The Three Musketeers* (Prokovsky), Australian Ballet, Sydney
Obelia in *Snugglepot and Cuddlepie* (Ashmole), Australian Ballet, Sydney
Principal dancer in *Forgotten Land* (Kylián), Australian Ballet, London
Ballerina in *Paquita* (Petipa; staged Valukin), Australian Ballet, Melbourne
1989 Principal dancer in *Birthday Offering* (Ashton), Australian Ballet, Canberra
Principal dancer in *Four Last Songs* (Béjart), Australian Ballet, Sydney
Tatiana in *Onegin* (Cranko), Australian Ballet, Perth
Ada in *Le Concours* (*The Competition*; Béjart), Australian Ballet, Melbourne
1990 Principal dancer (cr) in *Catalyst* (Baynes), Australian Ballet, Sydney
Hannah in *The Merry Widow* (Hynd; staged Helpmann), Australian Ballet, Melbourne
1991 Terpsichore in *Apollo* (Balanchine), Australian Ballet, Melbourne
Pas de deux from *La Favorita* (staged Ashmole), Australian Ballet, Tokyo
Principal dancer in *The Leaves are Fading* (Tudor), Australian Ballet, Melbourne
La Déesse de la danse from Milan in *Gala Performance* (Tudor), Australian Ballet, Melbourne
1992 Principal dancer in *Of Blessed memory* (Welch), Australian Ballet, Sydney
Mazurka in *Les Sylphides* (Fokine), Australian Ballet, Melbourne

PUBLICATIONS

Laughlin, Patricia, "Streamlined Beauty", *Dance Australia* (Keysborough), April/May 1988
Hough, David, "Character the Key", *Dance Australia* (Keysborough), December 1989–January 1990
Percival, John, "The Australian Ballet Today", *Dance and Dancers* (London), July 1992

* * *

It was evident from the beginning of Lisa Pavane's career that she had the potential to become a classical ballerina in the finest sense of the term. Indeed, so outstanding was her talent that her future was discussed with interest even while she was still a student at the Australian Ballet School. As each year passes, her development—technically, artistically, and interpretatively—fulfils all that early promise.

Pavane has a faultless technique. There is a diamond-cut quality to her dancing in virtuoso ballets such as *The Sleeping Beauty*, Act III of *Swan Lake*, or Serge Lifar's *Suite en blanc*. However, her range extends beyond mere virtuosity and, although she is always initially described as a pure classicist, she excels equally in romantic and dramatic roles.

Physically, Pavane is assisted by her strong, well-shaped legs, beautiful feet, long neck, and fine line. Technically, she has all the necessary attributes—such as secure turns, an excellent jump, and rock-solid balances. Maina Gielgud, artistic director of the Australian Ballet, has described Pavane as having "great stamina and extraordinary virtuosity" and commented that this degree of technical strength is not often associated with such beautiful feet.

As an interpretative artist, Pavane was initially somewhat bland, her characters tending to remain at the same level, for example, throughout the length of a three-act ballet. This apparent blandness was deceptive, however, as Pavane has always possessed a volatile temperament which, with increasing maturity, she is channelling into interpretations of greater depth.

Lisa Pavane as Aurora in *The Sleeping Beauty* for the Australian
Ballet

In romantic ballets such as *La Sylphide*, *Giselle*, and *Les
Sylphides*, Pavane's softly rounded arms and physique are
reminiscent of lithographs of Taglioni. She is intelligent and
has always had the good sense not to embellish her interpretations with fussy detail. From a simple, unmannered début in
such roles as Giselle, she has developed her characterizations as
her confidence and insight have grown. In 1988, she received
intensive coaching in *Giselle* from Galina Ulanova—one of the
greatest Giselles of all time—and the benefits of this were
immediately obvious in performance.

As Princess Aurora in *The Sleeping Beauty*, Pavane explores
every facet of the difficult role with ease and gives it exquisite
finish, whether it be her solos and the Rose Adagio in Act I, the
fluid beauty of line in Act II, or the regal pas de deux and
delicate solo in Act III. She appears to have been born and bred
for this role.

Other ballets to reveal Pavane's range have included Harald
Lander's *Études* and Nureyev's *Don Quixote*, both of which
display her ability to combine romanticism and virtuosity,
while she shows a steely strength and sensuous menace in the
role of the Black Queen in Ninette de Valois' *Checkmate*.

Pavane has a great affinity with the choreography of John
Cranko. She is a beautiful and tragic Juliet and a wonderful
Tatiana in *Onegin*, growing from a youthful beginning to a
tender and passionate mature woman. Perhaps more unusually,
she can also extend herself to the role of Kate in *The Taming of
the Shrew*, where her own fiery temper perhaps assists her
insight into the character.

Lisa Pavane's future should be boundless. She is still young,
but her natural physical attributes, musicality, sense of style,
technical strength, innate intelligence, and breadth of repertoire have already moulded her into an expressive dancer of the
highest international quality.

—Patricia Laughlin

LE PAVILLON D'ARMIDE

Choreography: Mikhail Fokine
Music: Nikolai Tcherepnin
Design: Alexandre Benois (scenery and costumes)
Libretto: Alexandre Benois (after *Omphale* by Théophile
  Gautier)
First Production: Maryinsky Theatre, St. Petersburg, 25
  November 1907
Principal Dancers: Anna Pavlova (Armide), Pavel Gerdt
  (Vicomte de Beaugency), Vaslav Nijinsky (Slave)

Other productions include: Imperial Theatre School (earlier
version; single scene) as *The Animated Gobelin*, with Vaslav
Nijinsky (Rinaldo), Elisaveta Gerdt (Armide); St. Petersburg,
28 April 1907. Diaghilev's Ballets Russes (restaged Fokine),
with Vera Karalli (Armide), Mikhail Mordkin (Vicomte),
Vaslav Nijinsky (Slave), Tamara Karsavina, Olga Fedorova
(Friends of Armide); Paris, 19 May 1909. State Academic
Theatre for Opera and Ballet (GATOB, later the Kirov; chor.
Fedor Lopukhov after Fokine), with Elisaveta Gerdt (Armide),
Mikhail Dudko (Vicomte); Petrograd, 6 May 1923. Latvian
Opera Ballet (staged Alexandra Fedorova-Fokine after Fo-
kine; design Ludolfs Liberts); Riga, 1931.

PUBLICATIONS

Beaumont, Cyril, *Michel Fokine and his Ballets*, London, 1935
Beaumont, Cyril, *Complete Book of Ballets*, revised edition,
  London, 1951
Fokine, Michel, *Fokine: Memoirs of a Ballet Master*, translated
  Vitale Fokine, London, 1961
Kirstein, Lincoln, *Movement and Metaphor*, New York, 1970
McDonald, Nesta, "London's First Sight of the Diaghilev
  Ballet", *Dancing Times* (London), June 1971
McDonald, Nesta, *Diaghilev Observed by Critics in England and
  the United States*, London, 1975
Horwitz, Dawn Lille, *Michel Fokine*, Boston, 1985
Garafola, Lynn, *Diaghilev's Ballets Russes*, New York, 1989

*   *   *

By 1901 Alexandre Benois had become artistic director and
producer for the Imperial Theatres. Inspired by Gautier's
novella *Omphale* and by a tapestry he had seen when collecting
items for what became the Exhibition of Russian Art, he
invited the young composer and Maryinsky conductor Nikolai
Tcherepnin to help write, design, and compose a ballet entitled
Le Pavillon d'Armide. The proposed libretto was as follows:

"The Vicomte de Beaugency sets out to visit his fiancée but is
caught in a storm. He seeks refuge in a mysterious castle, and
when he knocks is welcomed by the Marquis and invited to
spend the night in a pavilion containing the tapestry depicting
Armide and her court. As the Vicomte enters she seems to
beckon, and the tapestry starts to glow. At first afraid, he
gradually falls asleep; but on the stroke of midnight the
Marquis appears and orders the figures of Time and Love to
come from their niches and lead the Vicomte, Armide, and her
court into the dance. The Vicomte falls in love with Armide in a
passionate pas de deux, but as dawn breaks, Love and Time bid
all to disappear. The Vicomte falls senseless. As the sun warms
the earth, a shepherd passes with his sheep, and the Vicomte
comes to his senses. Was it a dream? He does not understand,
for Armide's scarf is in his hand."

The ballet was sent to Teliakovsky, the director, who rejected
it, saying that "there were not enough waltzes and no real dance

Le Pavillon d'Armide, with Tamara Karsavina as Armide, Diaghilev's Ballets Russes

music." But in 1907 he suggested to the new ballet master Fokine that it might be suitable for the graduation performance, as it contained many divertissements for all kinds of students, and the music had become popular at concerts. Fokine and Tcherepnin set out to cut down Benois's grandiose spectacle into three scenes, in which the choreographer set out to prove that the old-fashioned formulas of dance or mime should be developed further, to join in a continuous flow of meaningful movement. The students' performance was a success, so Teliakovsky invited Fokine to stage it for the Imperial Ballet. Benois had now returned from organizing his Exhibition and was angry to find that Fokine had reduced his ballet to three brief scenes. However, he quickly realized that *Le Pavillon d'Armide* marked an entirely new era in choreographic design, in which expressive dance meant more than all the stage effects and rich costumes worn by brilliant virtuoso soloists. He also noted the extreme stage artistry of Fokine himself as the Vicomte, Anna Pavlova as Armide, and Vaslav Nijinsky as the favourite slave. He also approved of the set and costumes by Léon Bakst. More interestingly, he commented on the intense involvement of the famous danseur noble, Pavel Gerdt, playing the purely dramatic role of the Marquis for the students.

In a letter Fokine acknowledged Gerdt's help in demonstrating and teaching his students how to feel that gesture could express the moods, emotions, and actions, particularly of the Vicomte and Armide as they danced. He described how Gerdt suggested and demonstrated typical gestures to weave into the choreography for courtiers, Jesters, Negroes, Pages, and the like, as well as those more formal gestures for the mythological characters necessary to signify the allegory of Love changing as time passes.

Le Pavillon d'Armide was included in the first Diaghilev season of Russian Ballet in Paris (1909), and created a great stir amongst the music critics, who realized, as Benois had done, that an entirely new approach was being made by Fokine to do away with the standard formulas of old court and opera ballets, to make expressive dance in tune with the music, without depending on virtuoso tricks. In this first Paris production Mikhail Mordkin played the Vicomte, Vera Karalli Armide, and Nijinsky the slave. It remained in the repertoire until Nijinsky left the company.

—Joan Lawson

PAVLOVA, Anna

Russian dancer, choreographer, producer, and teacher. Born Anna Matveyevna (later changed to Pavlovna) Pavlova in St. Petersburg, 12 February (31 January old style), 1881. Studied at the Imperial Theatre School, St. Petersburg, pupil of Aleksandr Oblakov, Nikolai Legat, Ekaterina Vazem, Pavel Gerdt; graduated in 1899; later studied under Caterina Beretta in Milan, from 1903, and Enrico Cecchetti, St. Petersburg, from 1905. Created first role in *Imaginary Dryads* (Gerdt), for graduation performance, 1899, with official début later in 1899; dancer, Maryinsky Theatre, 1899–1916: coryphée, from 1899, second soloist, 1902, first soloist, from 1903, ballerina, from 1905, and prima ballerina, 1906; first tour abroad, with dancers of the Maryinsky (dir. Adolph Bolm), 1908; début in Paris, with Diaghilev's Ballets Russes, 1909, performing also in Europe with Mikhail Mordkin, 1909; débuts in Berlin, New York, and London, 1910, touring the United States, 1911; last performance with Diaghilev's company, London 1911; founder

and principal dancer of own touring company, from 1911, performing at the Palace Theatre, London, seasons 1911, 1912, 1913, and touring cities around the world including (with Novikov as partner) in the British Isles, 1912, U.S. and Germany, 1913, and (with Volinine as partner), in Europe, 1914; performed U.S., Canada, and South America, various seasons, 1914–18, Mexico, 1918, Paris, Monte Carlo, 1919, London, 1920; toured the Far East, 1921; performed at Covent Garden, London, 1923, 1924; last U.S. tour, 1924–25, with final world tour, 1928–29, and last performance in England, 1930; also appeared in early dance films, including as Fenella in Hollywood silent film *The Dumb Girl of Portici*, 1915, and in test shots, made in 1924, put together to make *The Immortal Swan* (released 1956); also choreographer and producer, composing own solos for concert performances, and staging versions of the classics for her own company; teacher, based at Ivy House, London, her home from 1912. Recipient: Swedish Order of Merit, 1907; Palme Académique, Paris, 1909. Died in The Hague, 23 January 1931.

ROLES

1899   Soloist (cr) in *Imaginary Dryads* (Gerdt), Graduation Performance of the Imperial Theatre School, St. Petersburg

Pas de quatre (cr) added to *Cavalry Halt* (Petipa), Maryinsky Theatre, St. Petersburg

Pas de trois in *Vain Precautions* (*La Fille mal gardée*; Petipa, Ivanov), Maryinsky Theatre, St. Petersburg

Friend of Fleur-de-Lys in *Esmeralda* (Petipa after Perrot), Maryinsky Theatre, St. Petersburg

Pas de trois in *Paquita* (Petipa), Maryinsky Theatre, St. Petersburg

Zulme in *Giselle* (Petipa after Coralli, Perrot), Maryinsky Theatre, St. Petersburg

Candide Fairy in *The Sleeping Beauty* (Petipa), Maryinsky Theatre, St. Petersburg

Polka Folichonne (cr) in *Marcobomba* (Ivanov after Perrot), Maryinsky Theatre, St. Petersburg

1900   Dance of the Pearls in *The Beautiful Pearl* (Petipa), Maryinsky Theatre, St. Petersburg

Hoarfrost (cr) in *Les Saisons* (Petipa), Hermitage Theatre, St. Petersburg

La Serenade (cr) in *Harlequinade* (Petipa), Hermitage Theatre, St. Petersburg

Aurora in *The Awakening of Flora* (Petipa), Maryinsky Theatre, St. Petersburg

Flora in *The Awakening of Flora* (Petipa), Maryinsky Theatre, St. Petersburg

Anna and Venus in *Bluebeard* (Petipa), Maryinsky Theatre, St. Petersburg

Diana in *King Candaule* (Petipa), Maryinsky Theatre, St. Petersburg

Third Variation, "Kingdom of the Shades" in *La Bayadère* (Petipa), Maryinsky Theatre, St. Petersburg

1901   Snow variation in *Camargo* (Petipa), Maryinsky Theatre, St. Petersburg

Pas de six in *Markitantka* (*La Vivandière*; Petipa after Saint-Léon), Maryinsky Theatre, St. Petersburg

Henrietta in *Raymonda* (Petipa), Maryinsky Theatre, St. Petersburg

Katya in *Markitantka* (*La Vivandière*; Petipa after Saint-Léon), Maryinsky Theatre, St. Petersburg

Grand Pas Variation in *Paquita* (Petipa), Maryinsky Theatre, St. Petersburg

Anna Pavlova as the Dragonfly

Anna Pavlova with Laurent Novikoff in *Chopiniana*, c. 1926

Waltz of Gold in *The Nutcracker* (Ivanov), Maryinsky Theatre, St. Petersburg

Princess Florine in *The Sleeping Beauty* (Petipa), Maryinsky Theatre, St. Petersburg

Queen of the Naiads (cr) in *Sylvia* (Ivanov, Gerdt), Maryinsky Theatre, St. Petersburg

Lise in *The Magic Flute* (Ivanov), Maryinsky Theatre, St. Petersburg

1902 Juanita (cr) in *Don Quixote* (St. Petersburg version; Gorsky after Petipa), Maryinsky Theatre, St. Petersburg

Pierrette in *Harlequinade* (Petipa), Hermitage Theatre, St. Petersburg

Pas d'ensemble (cr) in *Javotte* (Gerdt), Hermitage Theatre, St. Petersburg

Nikiya in *La Bayadère* (Petipa), Maryinsky Theatre, St. Petersburg

Nereid in *The Little Humpbacked Horse* (Petipa after Saint-Léon), Maryinsky Theatre, St. Petersburg

Spanish Dance in *Swan Lake* (Petipa, Ivanov), Maryinsky Theatre, St. Petersburg

Pas de deux in *Graziella* (Ivanov), Maryinsky Theatre, St. Petersburg

Gulnare in *Le Corsaire* (Petipa), Maryinsky Theatre, St. Petersburg

Dance of the Ural Cossacks in *The Little Humpbacked Horse* (Petipa after Saint-Léon), Maryinsky Theatre, St. Petersburg

Pas de trois in *Le Corsaire* (Petipa), Maryinsky Theatre, St. Petersburg

Ephemerida (cr) in *La Source* (Coppini after Saint-Léon), Maryinsky Theatre, St. Petersburg

Lezghinka in *The Demon* (opera; mus. Rubinstein), Maryinsky Theatre, St. Petersburg

1903 Spanish Doll (cr) in *The Fairy Doll* (N. and S. Legat), Hermitage Theatre, St. Petersburg

Friend of the Princess (cr) in *The Magic Mirror* (Petipa), Maryinsky Theatre, St. Petersburg

Canary Fairy in *The Sleeping Beauty* (Petipa), Maryinsky Theatre, St. Petersburg

Title role in *Giselle* (Petipa after Coralli, Perrot), Maryinsky Theatre, St. Petersburg

Ramseya in *Pharaoh's Daughter* (Petipa), Maryinsky Theatre, St. Petersburg

Ondine in *The Naiad and the Fisherman* (Petipa after Perrot), Maryinsky Theatre, St. Petersburg

1904 Title role in *Paquita* (Petipa), Maryinsky Theatre, St. Petersburg

Carmen in *At the Crossroads* (Shiryaev), Maryinsky Theatre, St. Petersburg

A Bayadère in *The Talisman* (Petipa), Maryinsky Theatre, St. Petersburg

Medora in *Le Corsaire* (Petipa), Maryinsky Theatre, St. Petersburg

1905 Grand Pas in *Pharaoh's Daughter* (Petipa), Maryinsky Theatre, St. Petersburg

Kitri in *Don Quixote* (Gorsky after Petipa), Maryinsky Theatre, St. Petersburg

Swanilda's Friend in *Coppélia* (Petipa, Cecchetti), Maryinsky Theatre, St. Petersburg

Ilka in *The Enchanted Forest* (Ivanov), Maryinsky Theatre, St. Petersburg

Amour in *Fiametta* (Petipa after Saint-Léon), Maryinsky Theatre, St. Petersburg

1906 Bint-Anta in *Pharaoh's Daughter* (Gorsky after Petipa), Bolshoi Theatre, Moscow

Aspicia in *Pharaoh's Daughter* (Petipa), Maryinsky Theatre, St. Petersburg

Pas de deux (cr) in *The Vine* (Fokine), Maryinsky Theatre, St. Petersburg

Panaderos in *Raymonda* (Petipa), Maryinsky Theatre, St. Petersburg

1907 Cupid in *Fiametta* (Petipa after Saint-Léon), Maryinsky Theatre, St. Petersburg

Bacchante, "Autumn", in *Les Saisons* (Petipa; staged N. Legat), Maryinsky Theatre, St. Petersburg

Principal dancer (cr) in *Chopiniana* (first version; Fokine), Maryinsky Theatre, St. Petersburg

Atte (cr) in *Eunice* (Fokine), Maryinsky Theatre, St. Petersburg

Teresa in *Cavalry Halt* (Petipa), Maryinsky Theatre, St. Petersburg

Lise in *Vain Precautions* (*La Fille mal gardée*; Petipa, Ivanov), Hermitage Theatre, St. Petersburg

Swanilda in *Coppélia* (Petipa after Saint-Léon), Hermitage Theatre, Moscow

Butterfly in *The Caprices of the Butterfly* (Petipa), Maryinsky Theatre, St. Petersburg

Street Dancer and Mercedes in *Don Quixote* (Gorsky after Petipa), Maryinsky Theatre, St. Petersburg

Annunciata (cr) in *The Blood-Red Flower* (Legat), Maryinsky Theatre, St. Petersburg

Armide (cr) in *Le Pavillon d'Armide* (Fokine), Maryinsky Theatre, St. Petersburg

Title role (cr) in *The Dying Swan* (*Le Cygne*; Fokine), Hall of the Assembly of the Nobility, St. Petersburg (some sources say 1905)

1908 Lilac Fairy in *The Sleeping Beauty* (Petipa), Maryinsky Theatre, St. Petersburg

Princess Aurora in *The Sleeping Beauty* (Petipa), Maryinsky Theatre, St. Petersburg

Title role in *Eunice* (Fokine), Maryinsky Theatre, St. Petersburg

Nisia in *King Candaule* (Petipa), Maryinsky Theatre, St. Petersburg

Berenice (cr) in *Egyptian Nights* (*Une Nuit d'Egypte*; Fokine), Maryinsky Theatre, St. Petersburg

Principal dancer (cr) in *Reverie romantique* (second version of *Chopiniana*; Fokine), Maryinsky Theatre, St. Petersburg

Odette in *Swan Lake*, Act II (after Ivanov), Scandinavian and German tour

Columbine in *Carnaval* (Fokine), tour, Berlin

1909　Principal dancer (cr) in *Les Sylphides* (new version of *Chopiniana*; Fokine), Diaghilev's Ballets Russes, Paris

Ta-Hor (cr) in *Cléopâtre* (new version of *Egyptian Nights*; Fokine), Diaghilev's Ballets Russes, Paris

Pas de deux (from Gorsky's *Pharaoh's Daughter*) in *Le Festin* (Fokine), Diaghilev's Ballets Russes, Paris

Principal dancer (cr) in *Russian Dance* (Mordkin), Charity Gala, Opéra, Paris

Baby Doll in *The Fairy Doll* (S. and L. Legat), Maryinsky Theatre, St. Petersburg

Spanish Dancer in *The Nutcracker* (Ivanov), Maryinsky Theatre, St. Petersburg

1910　Pas de deux (cr) in *Bacchanale* (Fokine), Hall of the Assembly of the Nobility, St. Petersburg

Bluebird pas de deux (with Nijinsky), called *L'Oiseau d'or,* from *The Sleeping Beauty* (Petipa), Diaghilev's Ballets Russes, London

Diane in *Les Amours de Diane* (from *King Candaule*; Petipa), Palace Theatre, London

Principal dancer (cr) in *Valse Caprice* (pas de deux; Legat), Palace Theatre, London

Swanilda in *Coppélia* (Saracco after Saint-Léon), Metropolitan Opera House, New York

Principal dancer in *Le Papillon* (also chor.), Metropolitan Opera House, New York

Aziade (cr) in *The Legend of Aziade* (Mordkin), Metropolitan Opera House, New York

Principal dancer (cr) in *Bacchanale* (Mordkin), Metropolitan Opera House, New York

Dancer (cr) in *La Rose qui meurt* (later called *La Rose mourante*; also chor.), London

1911　Snowflake (cr) in *Snowflakes* (first version; also chor.), Pavlova Company, Palace Theatre, London

Dancer in *Danse espagnole* (Petipa), *Danse hongroise, Blue Danube* (also chor.), Pavlova Company, Palace Theatre, London

Title role in *Giselle* (Petipa after Coralli, Perrot; staged Fokine), Diaghilev's Ballets Russes, London

Columbine in *Le Carnaval* (Fokine), Diaghilev's Ballets Russes, London

Principal dancer (cr) in *Souvenir d'Espagna* (Chiriaeff), Pavlova Company, British tour

1912　Dancer in *Les Coquetteries de Colombine* (from *The Fairy Doll*; after N. and S. Legat), Pavlova Company, Palace Theatre, London

Paquita in *Grand Pas classique* (from *Paquita*; Cecchetti, Shiryaev after Petipa), Pavlova Company, Palace Theatre, London

Title role (cr) in *Amarilla* (Zaylich), Pavlova Company, Manhattan Opera Company, New York

Dancer in *En Orange* (pas de deux; Gorsky), Ivy House, London

Eliza (Lise) in *La Fille mal gardée* (shortened version; Shiryaev after Dauberval), Pavlova Company, Palace Theatre, London

Butterfly (cr) in *La Naissance du Papillon* (also chor., with Shiryaev), Pavlova Company, Palace Theatre, London

1913　Princess (cr) in *The Three Palms; or, The Seven Daughters of the Ghost King* (Fokine), Pavlova Company, Kroll Opera House, Berlin

Spirit of Love (cr) in *Les Preludes* (Fokine), Pavlova Company, Kroll Opera House, Berlin

Young Girl in *Invitation to the Dance* (Zaylich), Pavlova Company, Palace Theatre, London

Nymph in *Godard Pas de trois* (Clustine), Pavlova Company, London Opera House, London

Lise in *The Magic Flute* (after Ivanov, Cecchetti), Pavlova Company, London Opera House, London

Oriental Enchantress in *Oriental Fantasy* (Zajlich), Pavlova Company, London Opera House, London

Sylphide (cr) in *Une Soirée de Chopin* (later called *Chopiniana*; Clustine), Pavlova Company, London Opera House, London

Dancer (cr) in *Gavotte* (originally *Gavotte Directoire*; pas de deux; Clustine), Pavlova Company, Metropolitan Opera House, New York

1914　Principal dancer (cr) in *Petite Danse Russe* (Clustine), Pavlova Company, Palace Theatre, London

Principal dancer (cr) in *New Gavotte Pavlova* (Clustine), Pavlova Company, Bridgeport, Connecticut

Title role in *The Fairy Doll* (Clustine after N. and S. Legat), Pavlova Company, Metropolitan Opera House, New York

Helen of Troy (cr) in *Walpurguis Night* (from opera *Faust*; chor. Clustine), Pavlova Company, Metropolitan Opera House, New York

1915　Title role in *Raymonda* (Clustine after Petipa), Pavlova Company, Century Opera House, New York

Dancer (cr) in *Dragonfly* (solo; also chor.), Pavlova Company, Century Opera House, New York

Fenella in *The Dumb Girl of Portici* (opera; mus. Amber), Pavlova Company, Manhattan Opera House, New York

Dances in *The Love of Three Oranges* (opera; mus. Prokofiev), *Orfeo ed Euridice* (opera; mus. Gluck), *Carmen* (opera; mus. Bizet), *Madame Butterfly* (opera; mus. Puccini), *Aida* (opera; mus. Verdi), *Hansel and Gretel* (opera; mus. Humperdinck); Boston Grand Company and the Anna Pavlova Russian Ballet, Manhattan Opera House, New York

Queen of the Snow (cr) in *Snowflakes* (new version; Clustine), Pavlova Company, Chicago

1915/   Emilie (cr) in *L'École en Crinoline* (Hemmick, Clustine),
16　Pavlova Company, U.S. tour

1916　Dancer (cr) in *California Poppy* (solo; also chor.), Pavlova Company, U.S. tour

Princess Aurora in *The Sleeping Beauty* (Clustine after Petipa), Pavlova Company, Hippodrome, New York

Principal dancer (cr) in *Rondo* (solo; also chor.), Pavlova Company, U.S. tour

The Girl (cr) in *Christmas* (also chor.), Pavlova Company, U.S. tour

Priestess (cr) in *Egyptian Ballet,* Pavlova Company, U.S. tour

1917　Title role (cr) in *La Péri* (Clustine after Petipa), Pavlova Company, Teatro Colón, Buenos Aires

Mischievous Student (cr) in *Noir et blanc* (Clustine), Pavlova Company, Latin American tour

1918　Butterfly (cr) in *Danza de las Flores* (Clustine), Pavlova Company, Buenos Aires

Fiancée (cr) in *El Ultimo Canto* (Clustine), Pavlova Company, Buenos Aires

1919   The Girl (mime and dance role) in *Les Trois Pantins de bois* (mus. Maurice-Lévy), Pavlova Company, Théâtre de Champs-Elysées, Paris

Chrysanthemum (cr) in *Autumn Leaves* (also chor.), Pavlova Company, South American tour

1920   Mexican Girl (cr) in *Mexican Dances* (chor. traditional), Pavlova Company, Palace Theatre, London (possibly created 1919)

Young Girl (cr) in *Three Wooden Dolls* (also chor.), Pavlova Company, tour

1920/   Aurora (cr) in *Fairy Tales* (Clustine after Petipa),
21   Pavlova Company, U.S. tour

1921   Bacchante (cr) in *The Fauns* (Clustine), Fête de nuit a bagatelle, Paris

Principal dancer (cr) in *Russian Dance* (Clustine), Pavlova Company, Quebec

Priestess (cr) in *Dionysus* (Clustine), Pavlova Company, Manhattan Opera House, New York

Principal dancer (cr) in *A Polish Wedding* (Pianowski), Pavlova Company, U.S. tour

1923   Priestess (cr) in *Ajanta's Frescoes* (Clustine), Pavlova Company, Covent Garden, London

Principal dancer (cr) in *Oriental Impressions*, comprising: *Japanese Dances* (traditional), *Hindu Wedding* (Shankar), *Krishna and Radha* (Shankar), Pavlova Company, Covent Garden, London

Enchanted Bird Princess (cr) in *An Old Russian Folk Lore* (Novikov), Pavlova Company, Covent Garden, London

1924   Kitri in *Don Quixote* (new production; Novikov after Gorsky), Pavlova Company, Covent Garden, London

Isimkhab (cr) in *The Romances of a Mummy* (Clustine, Novikov), Pavlova Company, Covent Garden, London

1927   Principal dancer (cr) in *Au Bal* (divertissement; also called *Blue Mazurka*; Romanov), Pavlova Company, Covent Garden, London

1928   Tennis Player (cr) in *The Champions* (Romanov), Pavlova Company, Rio de Janeiro

Other roles include: Dancer in concert pieces *Egyptian Pas de deux* (Fokine, Clustine), *Danse Rustique* (Clustine), *Scène Dansante* (Clustine), *Anitra's Dance* (Clustine), *Czarina Waltz* (Clustine), *The Pavlovana* (Clustine), *Minuet* (Clustine), *Pizzicato* (from *Sylvia*; chor. Ivanov, Gerdt), *Farandole* (from *L'Arlésienne*; mus. Bizet), *Fandango* (from opera *Le Cid*; mus. Massenet), *Spring Waltz* (mus. Strauss), *Waltz* (mus. Sousa), *Assyrian Dance* (Clustine), *Valse Triste* (Clustine), *Minuet* (Clustine), *La Danse* (also chor.), *Serenade* (N. and S. Legat), *The Lorelei* (*The Ondines*; Clustine), *Tambourine* (Fokine, Clustine), *Thaïs* (mus. Massenet), *Ondine* (mus. Catalini), *Rondo* (mus. Beethoven), *Le Pavlova Polka* (mus. de Markoff), *Japanese Butterfly* (also chor.), *Masquerade* (also chor.), *Polka incroyable* (Clustine).

WORKS

1910   *Le Papillon* (mus. Minkus), Metropolitan Opera House, New York

La Rose qui meurt (later called *La Rose mourante*; mus. Drigo), London

1911   *Blue Danube* (mus. Strauss), Pavlova Company, Palace Theatre, London

Snowflakes (mus. Tchaikovsky), Pavlova Company, Palace Theatre, London

1912   *La Naissance du Papillon* (mus. Delibes), Pavlova Company, Palace Theatre, London

1913   *The Magic Flute* (after Ivanov, Cecchetti; mus. Drigo), Pavlova Company, London Opera House, London

1915   *Dragonfly* (solo; mus. Kreisler), Pavlova Company, Century Opera House, New York

1916   *California Poppy* (mus. Tchaikovsky), Pavlova Company, U.S. tour

Rondo (mus. Beethoven, Kreisler), Pavlova Company

Christmas (with Clustine; mus. Tchaikovsky), Pavlova Company, U.S. tour

1918   *La Danse* (mus. Kreisler), Pavlova Company, tour

1919   *Autumn Leaves* (mus. Chopin), Pavlova Company, South American tour

1920   *Three Wooden Dolls* (mus. Maurice-Lévy), Pavlova Company, tour

1923   *Japanese Butterfly* (mus. Grieg), Pavlova Company, tour

1926   *Masquerade* (mus. Wurmser), Pavlova Company, tour

PUBLICATIONS

Svetlov, Valerian, *Anna Pavlova*, London, 1930

Dandré, Victor, *Pavlova in Art and Life*, London, 1932

Beaumont, Cyril, *Anna Pavlova*, London, 1932

Magriel, Paul, *Pavlova*, New York, 1947

Franks, A.H. (ed.), *Pavlova: A Biography*, London, 1956

Lifar, Serge, *Les Trois Grâces du XXe Siècle*; as *The Three Graces*, translated by G. Hopkins, London, 1959

Krasovskaya, Vera, *Anna Pavlova*, Leningrad and Moscow, 1964

Krasovskaya, Vera, *Russian Ballet Theatre at the Beginning of the Twentieth Century*, vol. 2, Leningrad, 1972

Kerensky, Oleg, *Anna Pavlova*, London, 1973

Lazzarini, John and Roberta, *Pavlova: Repertoire of a Legend*, London, 1980

Money, Keith, *Anna Pavlova: Her Life and her Art*, London, 1982

*   *   *

In such a conservative enclave as the Tsar's Imperial Ballet School at the turn of the century, Anna Pavlova was a radical outsider by virtue of temperament and background. Her mother was a hard-working laundrywoman whose only child was most probably the illegitimate daughter of a young Jewish businessman, and although the central core of home life was a secure bond between mother and daughter, the circumstances were hard and, for the child, doubly disenfranchising. For much of her life this background, which she partially concealed, shaded her attitudes to all manner of things; only on stage did she seem an entirely free being.

The most important event in Pavlova's life was her first visit to a theatre, around the time of her ninth birthday, when her mother took her to the first production of *The Sleeping Beauty* at the Maryinsky. There was the novelty not only of the production but also Tchaikovsky's score, and the effect on a child who had probably never heard a full orchestra play before was entirely overwhelming. From that day she determined that dance would be the medium in which she would express herself, and it is a measure of her will that she overcame the doubts of her mother and, subsequently, the examiners at the school itself. She was of delicate build, seemingly at a disadvantage alongside the sort of robust ten-year-olds normally chosen for the prized entrance positions for the Imperial Ballet School, but there was a certain something about her, a gravity, that won over the doubters. She understood all too well what hard work was, and her student days were marked by an almost fierce sense of application. In her there burned a pride, not in herself exactly, as much as in what she was doing; the Dance itself was a form of religion for her, and from the outset she dedicated herself to it, above any other consideration.

Pavlova's drive kept her abreast of the more gifted of her fellow pupils, but such was the range of raw talent in the school that there was no possibility of her being more than one among several, though when she graduated in 1899, she had the unusual distinction of being posted as a coryphée; there was to be no apprenticeship in the corps. Thus she was the object of some attention from the start, in the theatre where first she had seen Princess Aurora dancing. The reality of company life was no fairy-tale; the depth of talent and the range of repertoire, both in Moscow and St. Petersburg, was such that even the most gifted exemplars of a role seldom got two performances of the same part in a given year, while throughout the Imperial school, hierarchical power saturated all decision-making, layer upon layer, to a suffocating degree. Senior-ranked dancers were not slow to encourage coteries to fight their particular cause, and for some, diplomatic techniques counted almost as much as classroom finesse. Pavlova, with no middle-class social connections, was at a distinct disadvantage in this form of power-brokering, and she was ill at ease with its ramifications; but she followed the general lead, and survived. Her idiosyncratic talent began to fascinate Marius Petipa at the very moment when his all-powerful reign was ending, and his fostering of Pavlova's cause was, in many ways, his own act of defiance against a system of vested power that was about to discard him. Although much of Pavlova's initial success had come in roles that exploited her knack in portraying vivacity and humour, Petipa could see in her a potentiality for pathos. This, and her marked aerial quality, led him in 1902 to cast her in one of prima ballerina Kchessinskaya's key roles, Nikiya in *La Bayadère,* an unprecedented advance for a coryphée, leading to much excited comment. Then, in 1903, at the very moment of his dismissal, Petipa cast Pavlova as Giselle. It was his final masterstroke, and he subtly reshaped some choreographic passages to exploit his young dancer's lightness and decorative line, reverting to the gossamer Romantic images pursued in his own youth. Pavlova's imprint on this ballet quickly became so inimitable that no one could remain entirely indifferent to her, and soon enough a group of fans, the *Pavlovtzi,* was rivalling the noise of the Kchessinskaya faction.

As she progressed, Pavlova's undeniable quality gave her real power within the school, but the ceaseless politicking seemed to get between her and the business in hand; increasingly, she viewed chances to tour as a desirable alternative. In 1908 she instigated a Baltic tour under the banner of the Tsar's Ballet, and extended the mission to Prague and Berlin. But for heavy pressure from Diaghilev, she might have launched Russian Ballet on Paris that summer; in the event she retreated, but went ahead with plans for a repeat tour the following year. Diaghilev, by comparison with Pavlova's relatively smooth progress, encountered nothing but difficulties in his attempts to harness the Imperial Ballet's talents under his own management. His great ideal was to pair Pavlova and Nijinsky in order to woo Paris. Pavlova tried to accommodate Diaghilev in many of these plans but was wise enough not to cancel any of her own contracts. As a result, she went into the famous 1909 Paris season late, but was a sensation when she did arrive.

The history of the antagonism between Pavlova and Diaghilev is very largely fiction as recorded in a number of books; most particularly, her supposed jealousy of Nijinsky's success is a nonsense, promulgated in some measure by the Karsavina/Romola Nijinsky school of memoirs. Karsavina was unaware that Diaghilev had never viewed her as his first choice to pair with his protégé. When Diaghilev muffed a further chance to present Pavlova and Nijinsky in 1910, in the process breaking a contract—which severely compromised Pavlova's own London contract—the pattern was established. By the time Pavlova made one final gesture to Diaghilev, dancing a handful of performances with Nijinsky during the 1911 season of Russian Ballet at Covent Garden, she was already a resident of London, and what is more, hugely famous on both sides of the Atlantic. As far as she was concerned, her appearance with Nijinsky in *Giselle* settled a debt of honour; at last she had been able to show herself to London in a full-scale dramatic work (her "signature" ballet, what is more) and, as it were, publicly reclaim her true base. It meant a great deal to her that people understood her framework; that her irridescent cameo roles in music hall programmes represented the sparkling tip of a serious iceberg.

In a span of twenty years' incessant global touring, pursuing itineraries that no present-day dancer could properly read, let alone emulate, Pavlova dismissed the comforts and financial safety of stardom in the great cities, and instead hit the trail to demonstrate her Russian heritage and her belief that the joy and wonder of *her* first sight of ballet could be recreated in some measure for children of all races—and indeed of all ages. In this pursuit she provided employment for an entire supporting company, many of whom were, like herself, exiled from the motherland by the circumstances of revolution and war. Her personality was distinctly manic, contained only by her indomitable sense of mission, and her life was subservient to the fragmented aspects of life she portrayed on stage. In the cameos—the swan, the dragonfly, the butterfly—she produced an electrifying intensity that burned an image in onlookers' memories. Despite her command of roles with pathos, it was Pavlova's depictions of human wit and gaiety that eclipsed everything. In her *Gavotte,* she could somehow invest Lincke's tea-room tune with an overlay of Mozartian wit and elegance, until even the sternest critic capitulated. Pavlova really burnt herself out in mid-flight, dead by 50. She could not imagine a life beyond dancing, and she was spared the discovery, but she left behind people all over the world who, suddenly, could not imagine life that did not contain some element of dance.

—Keith Money

PAVLOVA, Nadezhda

Russian dancer. Born Nadezhda Vasilievna Pavlova in Ufa, 15 May 1955. Studied at the Perm School of Choreography, pupil of Lyudmila Sakharova; graduated in 1974. Married Bolshoi soloist Vyacheslav Gordeyev (div.). Dancer, Tchaikovsky Opera and Ballet Theatre, Perm, while still a student; soloist, Bolshoi Ballet, from 1975; has also appeared in several ballet films, including television film *Juliet* (chor. Boyarchikov), Soviet-American film *The Blue Bird* (1976), and television film *Poem* (Baronovsky, Gordeyev, 1981). Recipient: Grand Prix and Gold Medal, Moscow International Ballet Competition, 1973; title of People's Artist of the USSR, 1984.

ROLES

1972   Juliet in *Romeo and Juliet* (Boyarchikov), Tchaikovsky Theatre of Opera and Ballet, Perm

Nadezhda Pavlova in *The Nutcracker*, **Bolshoi Ballet, Moscow, 1973**

1972/ Swanilda in *Coppélia* (after Petipa), Tchaikovsky
75   Theatre of Opera and Ballet, Perm
     Title role in *Giselle* (Petipa after Coralli, Perrot),
     Tchaikovsky Theatre of Opera and Ballet, Perm
1975 Title role in *Giselle* (Petipa after Coralli, Perrot), Bolshoi
     Ballet, Moscow
     Masha in *The Nutcracker* (Grigorovich), Bolshoi Ballet,
     Moscow
1976 Kitri in *Don Quixote* (Gorsky), Bolshoi Ballet, Moscow
     Hero in *Love for Love* (Boccadoro), Bolshoi Ballet,
     Moscow
1977 Phrygia in *Spartacus* (Grigorovich), Bolshoi Ballet,
     Moscow
     Princess Aurora in *The Sleeping Beauty* (Grigorovich
     after Petipa), Bolshoi Ballet, Moscow
     Valentina in *Angara* (Grigorovich), Bolshoi Ballet,
     Moscow
1978 Eola in *Icarus* (Vasiliev), Bolshoi Ballet, Moscow
1979 Juliet in *Romeo and Juliet* (Grigorovich), Bolshoi Ballet,
     Moscow
     Principal dancer in *These Enchanting Sounds* (Vasiliev),
     Bolshoi Ballet, Moscow
     Shirien in *The Legend of Love* (Grigorovich), Bolshoi
     Ballet, Moscow
1980 Nikiya in "The Kingdom of the Shades" from *La
     Bayadère* (Petipa), Bolshoi Ballet, Moscow
1981 Princess Florine in *The Sleeping Beauty* (Grigorovich
     after Petipa), Bolshoi Ballet, Moscow
     The Princess in *The Wooden Prince* (A. Petrov), Bolshoi
     Ballet, Moscow
1984 Odette/Odile in *Swan Lake* (Grigorovich after Petipa,
     Ivanov), Bolshoi Ballet, Moscow

Other roles include: dancer in concert pieces *Sonnet* (Boyarchikov), *A Girl and the Echo* (M. Gaziev), *The Little Ballerina* (Gaziev), *Naughty Girl* (Boyarchikov), *Hazy Vistas* (Maiorov), *Stenka Razin* (Baranovsky), *The Blind Girl* (Baranovsky).

PUBLICATIONS

By Pavlova:
Interview, "Take Me Back to Perm!", *Yunost*, no. 6, 1972
Interview, "I Love to Dance and This is My Happiness . . .",
   Kultura i Zhizn, no. 2, 1983
Interview, "A Romance of the Twentieth Century", *Literaturnaya Gazeta*, no. 6, 6 March 1985

About Pavlova:
Shumilova, Emma, and Chizhova, Aleksandra, "A Girl from
   Chuvashia", *Teatralnaya Zhizn* (Moscow), no. 20, 1972
Roslavleva, Natalia, "Nadezhda Pavlova", *Muzykalnaya
   Zhizn* (Moscow), no. 8, 1972
Lidova, Irène, "Jeune Vidage du Bolshoi: Nadejda Pavlova",
   Les Saisons de la danse (Paris), May 1977
Horosko, Marian, "Pavlova and Gordeyev: The New Generation of Bolshoi Dancers", *Dance Magazine* (New York),
   November 1979
Sandler, Ken, "Moscow's Favorites", *Ballet News* (New York),
   November 1979
Danilova, Galina, "On Behalf of a Generation", *Teatralnaya
   Zhizn* (Moscow), no. 24, 1980
Avdeev, Alexandr (text), and Makarov, A. et al. (photos),
   Nadezhda Pavlova is Dancing . . ., Perm, 1986
Danilova, Galina, "Nadezhda Pavlova", *Sovetsky Balet* (Moscow), no. 5, 1989

            *   *   *

Nadezhda Pavlova, ballerina of the Moscow Bolshoi Theatre, comes from Bashkiria, a small republic in the Ural mountains. She was born in Ufa, the capital of the republic, and it was there that she started to learn ballet dancing in a children's circle. There was no ballet school in Ufa, but the well-known ballet school in Perm had by then already established a tradition of selecting and training children from different places in the Urals. In Perm, Pavlova spent several years living in a boarding school. Her tutor was Lyudmila Sakharova, whose former students are now well-known dancers working in Moscow, Leningrad, and many other Soviet cities.

1972 was the year of the All-Union Ballet Competition in Moscow, for which Sakharova and Pavlova prepared a programme. The performance of the fifteen-year-old Perm schoolgirl was a sensation; she was given the top marks at the contest and the first prize was unanimously awarded to her.

A year later Pavlova won the Grand Prix and the Gold Medal at an international competition in Moscow. The girl demonstrated amazing confidence and a mastery of "adult" dance techniques: her développés were unbelievable (her leg being almost perpendicular to the floor) and there was a rare beauty about her pas de chat. She charmed both the public and the jury with her engaging childishness and freedom, and by showing the undisguised pleasure which dancing seemed to give her. There was a natural simplicity in her performance which won Pavlova the sympathy of the broad public alongside the appreciation of critics and experts. For some years she became the idol of the crowd, a "superstar". Her arrival was not just an event in ballet life but a general social phenomenon: everyone knew about the "girl from far-off Bashkiria", watched her on the television, and read articles about the "wonder-girl" in the popular youth and women's magazines.

In 1975 Pavlova was suggested to the Bolshoi Theatre as a possible new soloist of the company. It was tremendous luck for a student of a provincial ballet school brought up in far-away Perm. It meant a recognition of her all-Union fame. But the Bolshoi and its chief choreographer Yuri Grigorovich did not need her. Neither her physical appearance (Pavlova is very short) nor her artistic temperament (ingénue lyrique) suited the choreographer's purposes, since the company's repertoire largely consisted of his own productions and this determined his choice of cast. Most of Grigorovich's ballets were tailor-made for Natalia Bessmertnova as the leading ballerina, with her refined and romantic style. At the same time, Grigorovich tended to select tall, slender, and long-legged dancers for the corps de ballet, trying to bring the company closer to Western standards. Pavlova was an outsider in that company—in the literal as well as metaphorical sense of the word. It is impossible to say how the young ballerina would have coped had it not been for her Bolshoi tutor, Marina Semenova (formerly herself one of the greatest Soviet ballerinas). She supervised Pavlova's training for all the major classical parts, which, one after another, started to be included in her repertoire.

The first parts of this kind were Giselle and Masha in *The Nutcracker*. These were lucky choices. Pavlova was perfectly convincing both as the naive, sincere, loving peasant lass and as the little girl who, because of her selfless love for an ugly toy, becomes a fairy-tale princess. After that the ballerina's repertoire grew rapidly. By the beginning of the 1980s she was dancing leading roles in all the classical ballets and in some new productions. Her skills steadily developed; she learned to show her characters in a dynamic perspective and she revealed her own individual colours and details in performance.

However, none of the roles danced by Pavlova became a remarkable balletic event. And sadly, none of them revealed her creative potential to the full. For all the years that she has been a leading ballerina of the Bolshoi (and she is still formally attached to that company), it has proven an unfavourable environment for her. She was forever appearing in Grigorovich's productions only as the understudy of Natalia Bessmertnova—a dancer of a completely different, more aristocratic, elevated, and essentially "sylph-like" style. Nobody ever cared to stage revivals of the older classics that would so beautifully suit Pavlova's artistic personality, like *La Fille mal gardée* or *Coppélia*. Never did either Grigorovich himself or any of the visiting choreographers make a production especially for her, to help her reveal her personality, to show a special regard for her stronger and weaker points. Yet it is well known from the history of ballet that a dancer's talent is only revealed to its fullest when a choreographer creates new roles particularly for that dancer's special gifts. For example, a gift of comedy, which Pavlova had shown in some of the miniature pieces she danced in early years, was never given a chance to develop. And still, in some of her roles, Pavlova managed to prove herself a creative artist in her own right—as for instance, when she danced Juliet and produced an interpretation of the part which was strikingly different from that of Bessmertnova. She made her Juliet much more real and down-to-earth. Another of her achievements was the leading role in the "Shades" scene from *La Bayadère*, which she prepared under Marina Semenova, considered in her own time the best Nikiya of the Soviet stage.

Pavlova was successful during the Bolshoi's international tours, where she usually appeared together with Vyacheslav Gordeyev, for many years her husband and stage partner. However, in recent years she has been dancing on the stage less frequently.

—Irina Gruzdeva

PÉCOUR, Guillaume-Louis

French dancer, choreographer, and teacher. Born 10 August 1653 (according to most sources); possibly born before 13 April 1653. Studied with Pierre Beauchamps. First appearances as a dancer at Court Theatre, Tuileries, 1671; official Paris Opéra début probably in 1674, becoming leading Opéra danseur; also performed frequently and arranged dances for the court at Saint-Germain-en-Laye and Chantilly; dancing master to the King's pages (maître à danser des pages de la chambre), from 1680; maître de ballet (succeeding Beauchamps), L'Académie royale de musique (Paris Opéra), from 1687; official compositeur of ballets and King's pensioner, 1695; also a leading teacher, including with brother Louis-Alexandre, 1691–92, and as personal dancing master to the Duchess of Bourgogne; collaborator (composer of dances in) Feuillet's *Chorégraphie*, 1700. Died in Paris, 22 April 1729.

ROLES

1671 Zephyr (cr) in *Psyché* (tragédie-ballet by Molière, Corneille, Quinault; mus. Lully, chor. Beauchamps), Salle de Machines des Tuileries, Paris

1673 One of four Passions, Gardener's Boy, Disguised Person, Phantom, "Pastorelle" in *Sédécias* (tragédie), House of Monsieur Filz, Paris

Fury, Huntsman, Roman Captain, Armenian and "Hibérien" in *Zénobie* (tragédie), House of M. Filz, Paris

1675 Priestess, Sprite, Woman from Enchanted Isles, Slave (cr) in *Thésée* (tragédie-lyrique; mus. Lully, chor. Beauchamps), Saint-Germain-en-Laye

1676 Nymph, Phrygian, Agreeable dream, River god (cr) in *Atys* (tragédie-lyrique; mus. Lully, chor. Beauchamps), Saint-Germain-en-Laye

1677 One of seven liberal arts, Water god, Shepherd, People of Egypt (cr) in *Isis* (tragédie-lyrique; mus. Lully, chor. Beauchamps), Saint-Germain-en-Laye

1680 A follower of Bacchus, a Solyme, a Lord in *Bellérophon* (tragédie-lyrique; mus. Lully, chor. Beauchamps), Saint-Germain-en-Laye

A follower of Discord, Man from Sicily, Infernal Deity (cr) in *Proserpine* (tragédie-lyrique; mus. Lully, chor. Beauchamps), Saint-Germain-en-Laye

1681 Boreas, Indian, Follower of Pan (cr) in *Le Triomphe de l'amour* (ballet; mus. Lully, chor. Beauchamps and Pécour), Saint-Germain-en-Laye

1682 Courtier in Cephea's suite (cr) in *Persée* (tragédie-lyrique; mus. Lully, chor. Beauchamps), Opéra, Paris

1685 Shepherd, Basque, Breton, American, African (cr) in *La Temple de la paix* (ballet; mus. Lully, chor. Beauchamps), Fontainebleau

1686 Pantomime man, Moor, Man from Crete (cr) in *Ballet de la jeunesse* (divertissement; mus. Lalande, chor. Beauchamps), Versailles

Dancer (cr) in *Armide* (tragédie-lyrique; mus. Lully, chor. Beauchamps), Opéra, Paris

1688 Divertissement in *Le Jaloux* (play by Baron; additional text Duché), Marly

Divertissement in *L'Homme à bonnes fortunes* (play by Baron; additional text Duché), Marly

Faun, Egyptian, Danseur (cr) in *Orontée* (tragédie-lyrique; mus. Lorenzani, chor. Pécour), Chantilly

1689 Huntsman, Hero (cr) in *Le Palais de Flore* (ballet; mus. Lalande), Trianon

Spaniard, Harlequin in *Ballet des nations* (second entrée in *Le Bourgeois Gentilhomme*, comédie-ballet by Molière; mus. Lully, chor. Beauchamps), Opéra, Paris

Egyptian (solo) in *Atys* (tragédie-lyrique; mus. Lully), Opéra, Paris

1690 Peasant, Great Shadow, Solo in General Ballet in *Orphée* (ballet; also chor.), Collège Louis le Grand, Paris

1691 Dervish; Programme-giver in *Ballet des nations* in *Le Bourgeois gentilhomme* (comédie-ballet by Molière; mus. Lully, chor. Pécour), performed at court

Jason, Orpheus in *Ballet des passions* in *Idoménée* (tragédie; also chor.), Collège Louis le Grand, Paris

1695 Spaniard in *Ballet des saisons* (opéra-ballet; mus. Lully, Collasse, chor. Pécour), Opéra, Paris

1697 Faun, American in *Issé* (pastorale-héroïque; mus. Destouches, chor. Pécour), Trianon

1698 Morpheus in *Ballet de la paix* in *Charlemagne* (tragédie), Collège Louis-le-Grand, Paris

Faun, Egyptian in *Intermèdes de musique et de danse pour la comédie Mirtil et Mélicerte* (play by Molière; mus. Lalande), Fontainebleau

1699 Morpheus in *Les Songes* (ballet; also chor.) in *Joseph* (tragédie; verse by Father Le Jay), Collège Louis le Grand, Paris

Inhabitant of the Unknown Isle in *Intermèdes de la comédie des fées* (mus. Lalande), Fontainebleau

A Scythian in *Marthésie, reine des Amazones* (tragédie-lyrique; mus. Destouches, chor. Pécour), Opéra, Paris

1700 Harlequin (?cr; possibly danced by Ballon) in *Mascarade des Savoyards* (mus. Philidor), Marly

Spaniard in *Le Carnaval mascarade* (ballet; mus. Lully), Opéra, Paris

Harlequin in *Impromptu* (ballet-mascarade; also chor.), St. Maur

Prudence in *La Fortune*, ballet in *Moyse* (tragédie), Collège Louis le Grand, Paris

Fury in the guise of Pleasure (cr) in *Canente* (tragédie-lyrique; mus. Collasse, chor. Pécour), Opéra, Paris

Pleasure (cr) in *Hésione* (tragédie-lyrique; mus. Campra, chor. Pécour), Opéra, Paris

1701   Jason, solo in "People of Hesperis" in *Jason; ou, La Conquête de la toison d'or* (ballet; also chor.) in *Daniel* (tragédie; verse Father Le Jay), Collège Louis le Grand, Paris

Moor (cr) in *Omphale* (tragédie-lyrique; mus. Destouches, chor. Pécour), Opéra, Paris

1702   Ethiopian in *Phaëton* (tragédie-lyrique; mus. Lully, chor. Pécour), Opéra, Paris

Chief of the Nations (cr) in *L'Empire de l'imagination* (ballet; also chor.) in *Adonais* (tragédie), Collège Louis le Grand, Paris

WORKS

1687   "Entertainments", Shepherds' Dance in *Achille et Polyxène* (tragédie-lyrique; mus. Lully, Collasse), Opéra, Paris

1688   Dances in *Orontée* (tragédie-lyrique; mus. Lorenzani), Chantilly

1689   Dances in *Thétis et Pélée* (tragédie-lyrique; mus. Collasse), Opéra, Paris

1690   *Orphée* (for tragédie *Alexandre*), Collège Louis le Grand, Paris

1691   Dances in *Le Bourgeois Gentilhomme* (comédie-ballet by Molière; mus. Lully), performed at court

Ballet des Passions in *Idoménée* (tragédie), Collège Louis le Grand, Paris

1695   *Les Saisons* (opera-ballet; mus. Lully, Collasse), Opéra, Paris

1697   *L'Europe galante* (opera-ballet; mus. Campra), Opéra, Paris

Dances in *Vénus et Adonis* (tragédie-lyrique; mus. Desmarets), Opéra, Paris

Dances in *Issé* (pastorale-héroïque; mus. Destouches), Trianon

1699   *Le Carnaval de Venise* (opera-ballet; mus. Campra), Opéra, Paris

Dances in *Amadis de Grèce* (tragédie-lyrique; mus. Destouches), Opéra, Paris

Dances in *Marthésie, reine des Amazones* (tragédie-lyrique; mus. Destouches), Fontainebleau

Les Songes (ballet in tragédie *Joseph*; verse by Father Le Jay), Collège Louis-le-Grand, Paris

Dances in *Atys* (comédie-lyrique; mus. Lully), Opéra, Paris

Dances in *La Comédie des fées* (mus. Lalande), Fontainebleau

1700   *Le Carnaval mascarade* (ballet, revival; mus. Lully) Opéra, Paris

Dances in *Impromptu* (ballet-mascarade), St. Maur

Dances in *Canente* (tragédie-lyrique; mus. Collasse), Opéra, Paris

Dances in *Hésione* (tragédie-lyrique; mus. Campra), Opéra, Paris

1701   *Aréthuse* (ballet; mus. Campra), Opéra, Paris

Jason; ou, La Conquête de la toison d'or (ballet in tragédie *Daniel*; verse Father Le Jay), Collège Louis le Grand, Paris

Dances in *Omphale* (tragédie-lyrique; mus. Destouches), Opéra, Paris

1702   Dances in *Phaëton* (tragédie-lyrique; mus. Lully), Opéra, Paris

L'Empire de l'imagination (ballet), Collège Louis le Grand, Paris

Dances in *Médus, roi des Mèdes* (tragédie-lyrique; mus. Bouvard), Opéra, Paris

Les Fragments de Monsieur de Lully (ballet; mus. Lully, Campra), Opéra, Paris

Dances in *Tancrède* (tragédie-lyrique; mus. Campra), Opéra, Paris

1704   Dances in *Le Carnaval et la folie* (comédie-ballet; mus. Destouches), Opéra, Paris

Dances in *Iphigénie en Tauride* (tragédie-lyrique; mus. Desmarets, Campra), Opéra, Paris

Dances in *Le Prince de Cathay* (comédie-ballet; mus. Matho), for the Duchesse de Maine, Châtenay

Dances in *Télémaque* (tragédie-lyrique; mus. Campra et al), Opéra, Paris

1705   Dances in *Alcine* (tragédie-lyrique; mus. Campra), Opéra, Paris

Dances in *La Vénitienne* (comédie-ballet; mus. La Barre), Opéra, Paris

Dances in *La Tarantole* (comédie-ballet; mus. Matho), for the Duchesse de Maine, Chatenay

L'Empire du temps (ballet), Collège Louis le Grand, Paris

Dances in *Philomèle* (tragédie-lyrique; mus. Lacoste), Opéra, Paris

1706   Dances in *Alcione* (tragédie-lyrique; mus. Marais), Opéra, Paris

Dances in *Cassandre* (tragédie-lyrique; mus. Bertin, Bouvard), Opéra, Paris

Le Professeur et la folie (divertissement; mus. Gilliers), for the Duchesse de Maine, Chatenay

1707   Dances in *Bradamante* (tragédie-lyrique; mus. Lacoste), Opéra, Paris

Dances in *Monsieur de Pourceaugnac* (comédie-ballet by Molière; mus. Lully), Fontainebleau

1708   Dances in *Hippodamie* (tragédie-lyrique; mus. Campra), Opéra, Paris

1709   Dances in *Sémélé* (tragédie-lyrique; mus. Marais), Opéra, Paris

1710   *Les Fêtes vénitiennes* (opéra-ballet; mus. Campra), Opéra, Paris

Dances in *Diomède* (tragédie-lyrique; mus. Bertin), Opéra, Paris

1726   Dances in *Ajax* (tragédie-lyrique, revival; mus. Bertin), Opéra, Paris

Dances in *Pyrame et Thisbé* (tragédie-lyrique; mus. Rebel, Francoeur), Opéra, Paris

Other works include: Dances in revivals of *Persée* (tragédie-lyrique; mus. Lully), *Armide* (tragédie-lyrique; mus. Lully), *Isis* (tragédie-ballet; mus. Lully), *Acis et Galathée* (pastorale-héroïque; mus. Lully), *Didon* (tragédie-lyrique; mus. Desmarets), *Roland* (tragédie-lyrique; mus. Lully), *Alcide; ou, La Mort d'Hercule* (tragédie-lyrique; mus. L. Lully, Marais), *Le Triomphe de l'amour* (ballet; mus. Lully), *Alceste* (tragédie-lyrique; mus. Lully), *Thésée* (tragédie-lyrique; mus. Lully), *Le Bourgeois Gentilhomme* (comédie-ballet by Molière; mus. Lully), *Thétis et Pélée* (tragédie-lyrique; mus. Collasse); works probably by Pécour—Dances in *Cadmus et Hermione* (tragédie-lyrique; mus. Lully), *Le Ballet de Villeneuve St. Georges* (mus. Colasse).

Louis Pécour, c.1710

PUBLICATIONS

Feuillet, Raoul Auger, *Recueil de danses contenant un très grand nombre des meilleures entrées de M. Pécour*, Paris, 1704; reprinted 1970

Rameau, Pierre, *Le Maître à danser*, Paris, 1725

Parfaict, les frères (Claude et François), *Dictionnaire des théâtres*, Paris, 1756

Castil-Blaze, *L'Académie impériale de musique*, Paris, 1855

Jal, A., *Dictionnaire critique de biographie et d'histoire*, second edition, Paris, 1872

Jullien, Adolphe, *La Comédie à la cour*, Paris, c.1884

Moore, Lillian, "The Great Dupré", *Dance Magazine* (New York), June 1960

Guest, Ivor, *Le Ballet de l'Opéra de Paris*, Paris, 1976

Hilton, Wendy, *Dance of Court and Theater: The French Noble Style, 1690–1725*, Princeton, N.J., 1981

Witherell, Anne Louise, *Louis Pécour's 1700 "Recueil de Danses"*, Stanford University Ph.D., Stanford, California, 1981

de la Gorce, Jérôme, "Guillaume-Louis Pécour: A Biographical Essay", translated by Margaret McGowan, *Dance Research* (London), Autumn 1990

*   *   *

Louis Guillaume Pécour was almost certainly the premier choreographer in the French "noble" dance style of the late seventeenth and early eighteenth centuries. Prolific and highly inventive, Pécour demonstrated through his dances a wide range of choreographic and expressive possibilities which set high standards for other dancing masters working within the style. His much-admired compositions earned him an international reputation, and were performed in ballrooms and theatres not only in France, where he lived and worked, but also throughout Europe.

Pécour began his career as a dancer at the French court in 1671. He was recognized immediately as a gifted and promising dancer and subsequently assumed major roles in similar court productions. Pierre Rameau would later celebrate his dancing in the preface to *Le Maître à danser* (1725), citing Pécour as a model for all in the profession and describing the parts he danced as technical tours de force demanding precise footwork coupled with exceptional grace. Raoul Auger Feuillet called Pécour a perfect dancer in *Chorégraphie* (1700) and remarked further that other dancers could only hope to imitate him.

Only Pécour's subsequent fame as an excitingly imaginative choreographer exceeded his early renown for technical virtuosity. His rapid rise to prominence as a choreographer began in 1687 with the death of Lully and Pierre Beauchamps' concurrent retirement from his position as official composer of the King's ballets at the Académie royale de musique. Pécour was chosen as the successor, having already ably composed a number of ballets for the Court. Soon after assuming his new post, he demonstrated, according to Rameau, unusual talent as a choreographer both in new productions and in revivals of earlier Lully works.

Perhaps more than any other dancing master of the time, Pécour successfully collaborated with a number of prominent musical composers, such as André-Cardinal Destouches. His most fruitful collaboration, however, was with André Campra. Pécour composed the dances for Campra's first opéra-ballet, *L'Europe galante*, produced at the Paris Opéra in 1697. The two joined forces subsequently for other widely applauded productions including *Le Carnaval de Venise* (1699), *Hésione* (1700), *Tancrède* (1702), and *Les Fêtes vénitiennes* (1710).

Several of Pécour's dances for each of these productions survive in *Chorégraphie*, the eighteenth-century dance notation system, and can be found in Feuillet's and Gaudrau's collections of his dances published in 1704 and 1712 respectively. These collections demonstrate both Pécour's prowess as a choreographer for the theatre and the technical virtuosity of the professional dancers for whom he composed.

Pécour also choreographed many memorable dances for the ballroom throughout his distinguished career. His "danses à deux" brimmed with imaginative floor patterns creating, at times, poignant relationships between the partners. Dancers and observers alike, according to historian Wendy Hilton, "enjoyed [the dances] for their choreographic flow, their musicality, and their continuing originality within a highly systematized step vocabulary".

Many of Pécour's ballroom dances, like his theatre dances, were recorded in *Chorégraphie*, and together they make up the majority of the available notated baroque dance repertoire. His most popular danses à deux were republished numerous times through the mid-eighteenth century both in France and in other countries. The loure *Aimable Vainqueur* (1701), probably the best-loved and most frequently published of all his ballroom dances, appeared as *El Amable* in Pablo Minguet's *El Noble Arte de Danzar a la Francesa* (Madrid, 1758), and as late as 1765 in Magny's *Principes de chorégraphie* (Paris).

Pécour and his dances epitomized the French noble style. Although a number of his contemporaries also produced excellent dances for both the ballroom and the stage, Pécour's compositions became the standard against which the quality of these other dances was measured. Today his dances remain the finest examples of the baroque dance style.

—Susan F. Bindig

PENNEY, Jennifer

Canadian dancer. Born Jennifer Beverley Penney in British Columbia, Canada, 5 April 1946. Studied with Gweneth Lloyd and Betty Farrally, British Columbia, and at the Royal Ballet School, London, 1962–63. Married Philip Porter, 1983 (div. 1984). Dancer, Royal Ballet, 1963–88, becoming soloist, from 1966, and principal dancer, from 1970; also international guest artist, including for Hamburg Ballet, for Tokyo Ballet World Festival, 1979, and Canadian National Ballet, 1982. Recipient: *Evening Standard* Award for Outstanding Achievement in Ballet, London, 1980.

ROLES

1966 Third Song in *Song of the Earth* (MacMillan), Royal Ballet, London
      Ballerina in *Petrushka* (Fokine), Royal Ballet, London
      Bluebird in *The Sleeping Beauty* (Petipa; staged Sergeyev, de Valois, Ashton), Royal Ballet, London
      Titania in *The Dream* (Ashton), Royal Ballet, tour
1967 Principal dancer in *Symphonic Variations* (Ashton), Royal Ballet, London
1968 Princess Aurora in *The Sleeping Beauty* (Petipa, Ashton; staged Wright), Royal Ballet, London
      Clara in *The Nutcracker* (Nureyev), Royal Ballet, London
      Tuesday in *Jazz Calendar* (MacMillan), Royal Ballet, London
      Variation in *Birthday Offering* (Ashton), Royal Ballet, London
      Valse in *Les Sylphides* (Fokine), Royal Ballet, London
1969 The Bride in *A Wedding Bouquet* (Ashton), Royal Ballet, London
1970 Chloe in *Daphnis and Chloe* (Ashton), Royal Ballet, London
      Principal dancer in *Scènes de ballet* (Ashton), Royal Ballet, London
1971 Celestial in *Shadowplay* (Tudor), Royal Ballet, London
      Monday in *Jazz Calendar* (Ashton), Royal Ballet, London
      Principal dancer in *Dances at a Gathering* (Robbins), Royal Ballet, London
1972 Odette/Odile in *Swan Lake* (Petipa, Ivanov, Ashton; staged Helpmann), Royal Ballet, London
      Title role in *Cinderella* (Ashton), Royal Ballet, London
      Principal dancer in *Afternoon of a Faun* (Robbins), Royal Ballet, London
1973 Anna II in *The Seven Deadly Sins* (MacMillan), Royal Ballet, London
1974 Title role in *Manon* (MacMillan), Royal Ballet, London
      Golden Hours (cr) in *Elite Syncopations* (MacMillan), Royal Ballet, London
1975 Autumn (cr) in *Four Seasons* (MacMillan), Royal Ballet, London
      Mathilde Kschessinska in *Anastasia* (three-act version; MacMillan), Royal Ballet, London
      Principal dancer in *Four Schumann Pieces* (Van Manen), Royal Ballet
      Nikiya in "The Kingdom of the Shades" from *La Bayadère* (Nureyev after Petipa), Royal Ballet, London
      Mazurka in *Les Sylphides* (Fokine), Royal Ballet, London
1976 Principal dancer in *Adagio Hammerklavier* (van Manen), Royal Ballet, London
      Stop-time Rag in *Elite Syncopations* (MacMillan), Royal

Jennifer Penney in *Gloria*, Royal Ballet, London, 1980

Ballet, London
1977 Principal dancer (cr) in *Fourth Symphony* (Neumeier), Royal Ballet, London
      Puppet in *Rituals* (MacMillan), Royal Ballet, London
      The Girl in *Triad* (MacMillan), Royal Ballet, London
1978 Countess Marie Larisch in *Mayerling* (MacMillan), Royal Ballet, London
      Principal dancer in *Serenade* (Balanchine), Royal Ballet, London
1979 Principal dancer (cr) in *La Fin du jour* (MacMillan), Royal Ballet, London
      Principal dancer in *Liebeslieder Walzer* (Balanchine), Royal Ballet, London
      Adagietto ("La Garçonne") in *Les Biches* (Nijinska), Royal Ballet, London
1980 Leading role (cr) in *Gloria* (MacMillan), Royal Ballet, London
      First sister in *My Brother, My Sisters* (MacMillan), Royal Ballet, London
      Title role in *Giselle* (Petipa after Coralli, Perrot; staged Wright), Royal Ballet, London
1981 Juliet in *Romeo and Juliet* (MacMillan), Royal Ballet, London
      Sacred Love in *Illuminations* (Ashton), Royal Ballet, London

1982 Eurydice (cr) in *Orpheus* (MacMillan), Royal Ballet, London
1984 Baroness Mary Vetsera in *Mayerling* (MacMillan), Royal Ballet, London
1986 Principal dancer in *The Concert* (Robbins), Royal Ballet, London

PUBLICATIONS

By Penney:
Interview in Gruen, John, "Jennifer Penney", in *The Private World of Ballet*, New York, 1975
Interview with Steinbrink, Mark, *Ballet News* (New York), October 1981

About Penney:
Niehaus, Max, *Ballett Faszination*, Munich, 1972
Bland, Alexander, *The Royal Ballet: The First Fifty Years*, London, 1981
Rigby, Cormac, "The Dancer who Became Herself," *Dance and Dancers* (London), May 1988
Sorley Walker, Kathrine, "British Columbia's Jennifer Penney", *Vandance* (Vancouver), Summer 1988
"The Royal Ballet: The Biographies", *Ballet in London Yearbook* (London), 1988/89

* * *

Despite possessing superb technique, a gorgeous physique, and seductive musicality, Jennifer Penney was never a classical ballerina in the true sense. Her ultimate achievement was as a romantic dancer, and nowhere was that more evident than in the MacMillan ballets she made her own later on in her career. A beautiful dancer, with big eyes and a long neck, she was, unlike Margot Fonteyn, a performer who could not express herself facially. She had a tendency towards petulance and an aloofness in the classics which led critics to suggest that she was an insipid interpreter of the ballerina roles in *The Sleeping Beauty* and *Swan Lake* (roles which she confessed she never enjoyed anyway). Nor was she particularly acclaimed in Frederick Ashton's ballets. Yet Penney was a great Manon, an equally great Mary Vetsera, and a fine Juliet.

When Penney danced in MacMillan's works there was a thrilling dramatic intensity in the way she hurled her tiny frame into the expressive physicality of the choreography, letting the body speak for itself at moments of overwhelming passion and tragedy. As she showed so eloquently in *Mayerling*, for example, she was not afraid to take risks as a performer, abandoning herself to the demands of the choreographer with an unquestioning faith and seeming disregard for her own personal safety. Her Manon had a hard core, hinting right from her first entrance that the young convent girl was not as innocent as she looked and making her later transformation into a calculating seductress utterly convincing. At the other end of the scale, her Juliet was enchanting and tender. Always a glamorous presence on stage, Penney had effortless elegance and delicacy—qualities seen to glorious effect in *La Fin du jour*—matched by a natural seductiveness born of a sex appeal rare among Royal Ballet ballerinas. She was not embarrassed by the explicit sexual overtones of MacMillan's choreography and her partnership with Anthony Dowell in those ballets produced some ecstatic pas de deux.

Penney also had a flirtatious nature as a performer, sometimes daring the orchestra to stand still while she executed a spectacular long balance in the Rose Adagio scene. Surprisingly, to those who saw her as a romantic ballerina, she

was a born comedienne who excelled in Jerome Robbins's *The Concert*, where her sense of timing and cheeky flair were impeccable.

Her long association with the Royal was not always an easy one, her ups and downs owing partly to her own highly-strung nature, nervous disposition, and lack of self-confidence, especially in her younger years. The crowning glory of her professional career probably occurred during the Royal's 1987 tour of the Soviet Union, where she triumphed as Manon, prompting Bolshoi Ballet director Yuri Grigorovich to hail her as "the best ballerina from England that I have seen since Margot Fonteyn's visit over twenty years ago". Yet back in England, opportunities to perform at Covent Garden were rare.

Penney was a joy to watch in roles that came closest to her own personality or those which, like Gloria, utilized the limpid fluidity of her perfectly proportioned body with its exquisite legs and feet. She will be remembered by many as the definitive Manon. Perhaps her failing, though, was that she was too gifted; it just came too easily to her. It was once said of Penney that if she had been a little less naturally talented, and had needed to work at it a little harder, she could have been one of the greatest dancers of her day.

—Debra Craine

PERETTI, Serge
French dancer and teacher. Born in Venice, 28 January 1910. Studied at the Paris Opéra School, pupil of Gustave Ricaux, Albert Aveline, Carlotta Zambelli, and Nicola Guerra, from 1922. Début, Paris Opéra Ballet, while still a student, performing leading roles from 1925; named premier danseur in 1930, and étoile from 1931; guest artist and independent performer, touring South America with group of French dancers, 1946; also choreographer and ballet director, staging own ballet, 1945, and acting as provisional maître de ballet (on departure of Serge Lifar), Paris Opéra, 1945–46; also teacher: founder and director of own school of dance in Paris, 1948; professeur de danse à l'Opéra in charge of étoiles, 1963–70; retired from the Opéra in 1976.

ROLES

1923 Alfred (cr) in *La Nuit ensorcelée* (Staats), Paris Opéra Ballet, Paris
1924 Pitchung (cr) in *Siang-Sin* (Staats), Paris Opéra Ballet, Paris
Vision céleste (cr) in *Istar* (Staats), Paris Opéra Ballet, Paris
L'Ecuyer in *Giselle* (Petipa after Coralli, Perrot; staged Sergeyev), Paris Opéra Ballet, Paris
Le Jeune Homme (cr) in *Laurenza* (Staats), Paris Opéra Ballet, Paris
1925 Le Jeune Homme (cr) in *Les Rencontres* (Nijinska), Paris Opéra Ballet, Paris
Principal dancer in *Soir de fête* (Staats), Paris Opéra Ballet, Paris
Endymion in *Le Triomphe de l'amour* (Staats), Paris Opéra Ballet, Paris
1926 Morwach (cr) in *Prêtresse de Korydwen* (Staats), Paris Opéra Ballet, Paris

Principal dancer (cr) in *La Traviata* (opera; mus. Verdi, chor. Staats), Paris Opéra, Paris

Le Bourdon in *Les Abeilles* (Staats), Paris Opéra Ballet, Paris

Un Laquais in *Taglioni chez Musette* (Staats), Paris Opéra Ballet, Paris

1927   Dorkon in *Daphnis et Chloé* (Fokine), Paris Opéra Ballet, Paris

Le Dieu de feu (cr) in *Cyrca* (Guerra), Paris Opéra Ballet, Paris

Un Garçon (cr) in *Le Diable dans le beffroi* (Guerra), Paris Opéra Ballet, Paris

Un Clown (cr) in *Impressions de Music-Hall* (Nijinska), Paris Opéra Ballet, Paris

1928   Le Jeune Homme (cr) in *Rayon de lune* (Ari), Paris Opéra Ballet, Paris

1929   L'Homme (cr) in *Les Créatures de Promethée* (Lifar), Paris Opéra Ballet, Paris

Iskander in *La Péri* (Clustine), Paris Opéra Ballet, Paris

1930   Le Soleil in *Castor et Pollux* (Guerra), Paris Opéra Ballet, Paris

1931   Variations (cr) in *L'Orchestre en liberté* (Lifar), Paris Opéra Ballet, Paris

Bacchus (cr) in *Bacchus et Ariadne* (Lifar), Paris Opéra Ballet, Paris

Principal dancer in *Suite de danses* (Clustine), Paris Opéra Ballet, Paris

Achmet (cr) in *La Péri* (Staats), Paris Opéra Ballet, Paris

Le Jeune Homme (cr) in *Le Rustre impudent* (Staats), Paris Opéra Ballet, Paris

Principal dancer (cr) in *Prélude Dominical* (Lifar), Paris Opéra Ballet, Paris

1932   Pas de trois (cr) in *Divertissement* (from *The Sleeping Beauty*; Lifar after Petipa), Paris Opéra Ballet, Paris

1933   Le Corsaire (cr) in *Roselinde* (Staats), Paris Opéra Ballet, Paris

Variations (cr) in *Jeunesse* (Lifar), Paris Opéra Ballet, Paris

Lilez in *La Korrigane* (Mérante), Paris Opéra Ballet, Paris

Principal dancer (cr) in *Fête champêtre* (Aveline), Paris Opéra Ballet, Paris

1934   Principal dancer in *Soirée romantique* (Aveline), Paris Opéra Ballet, Paris

Arlequin (cr) in *La Vie de Polichinelle* (Lifar), Paris Opéra Ballet, Paris

1935   Jean in *Javotte* (Aveline), Paris Opéra Ballet, Paris

Don Ottavio in *Namouna* (Aveline), Paris Opéra Ballet, Paris

Cinzio (cr) in *Salade* (Lifar), Paris Opéra Ballet, Paris

Le Danseur in *La Grisi* (Aveline) Paris Opéra Ballet, Paris

1936   L'Anglais (cr) in *Promenades dans Rome* (Lifar), Paris Opéra Ballet, Paris

Saic (cr) in *Le Rouet d'Armor* (Staats), Paris Opéra Ballet, Paris

Principal dancer (cr) in *Ilean* (Staats), Paris Opéra Ballet, Paris

L'Esprit (cr) in *Un Baiser pour rien* (Aveline), Paris Opéra Ballet, Paris

1937   Le Jeune Homme en blanc (cr) in *Elvire* (Aveline), Paris Opéra Ballet, Paris

1938   Le Poète (cr) in *Oriane et le Prince d'amour* (Lifar), Paris Opéra Ballet, Paris

L'Aveugle (cr) in *Les Santons* (Aveline), Paris Opéra Ballet, Paris

Les Joies funestres (cr) in *Aneas* (Lifar), Paris Opéra Ballet, Paris

Principal dancer in *Ballet blanc* (Aveline), Paris Opéra Ballet, Paris

1939   Prince (cr) in *La Nuit venitienne* (Darsonval), Paris Opéra Ballet, Paris

Bacchanale in *Tannhaüser* (opera; mus. Wagner, chor. Aveline), Paris Opéra Ballet, Paris

1940   Statue in *Entre deux rondes* (Lifar), Paris Opéra Ballet, Paris

Styrax in *Cydalise et le chevre-pied* (Staats), Paris Opéra Ballet, Paris

1941   L'Iris noir (cr) in *La Princesse au jardin* (Lifar), Paris Opéra Ballet, Paris

Le Damoiseau bleu in *Le Chevalier et la demoiselle* (Lifar), Paris Opéra Ballet, Paris

Divertissement (cr) *El Cid* (Aveline), Paris Opéra Ballet, Paris

Spontano (cr) in *Bolero* (Lifar), Paris Opéra Ballet, Paris

Paganini in *La Nuit ensorcelée* (Staats), Paris Opéra Ballet, Paris

1942   Le Coq blanc (cr) in *Les Animaux modèles* (Lifar), Paris Opéra Ballet, Paris

King of the Gypsies (cr) in *Les Deux Pigeons* (Aveline after Mérante), Paris Opéra Ballet, Paris

Le Jeune Chevalier (cr) in *Joan de Zarissa* (Lifar), Paris Opéra Ballet, Paris

1944   Pandore (cr) in *Guignol et Pandore* (Lifar), Paris Opéra Ballet, Paris

Albrecht in *Giselle* (Lifar after Petipa, Coralli, Perrot), Paris Opéra Ballet, Paris

1945   Mac Guire in *L'Appel de la montagne* (also chor.), Paris Opéra Ballet, Paris

Principal dancer (cr) in *Castor et Pollux* (Guerra), Paris Opéra Ballet, Paris

1946   Prince Siegfried in *Swan Lake*, Act II (Gsovsky after Ivanov), Paris Opéra Ballet, Paris

Le Coq noir and Le Lion in *Les Animaux modèles* (Lifar), Paris Opéra Ballet, Paris

1949   Dorkon in *Daphnis et Chloé* (Fokine), Paris Opéra Ballet, Paris

1976   Charlatan in *Petrushka* (Fokine), Paris Opéra Ballet, Paris

Dr. Coppélius in *Coppélia* (Lacotte after Saint-Léon), Paris Opéra Ballet, Paris

WORKS

1945   *L'Appel de la montagne* (mus. Honegger), Paris Opéra Ballet, Paris

PUBLICATIONS

By Peretti:
Interview in Gruen, John, *The Private World of Ballet*, New York, 1975
Interview with Steinbrink, Mark, *Ballet News* (New York), October 1981
Interview in Llorens, Pilar, "Entrevista: Maestro Serge Peretti", *Monsalvat* (Barcelona), December 1989

About Peretti:
Vaillat, Léandre, "Serge Peretti", in *15 Danseurs et Danseuses*, Paris, 1948
Vaillat, Léandre, *La Danse à l'Opéra de Paris*, Paris, 1951
Guest, Ivor, *Le Ballet de l'Opéra de Paris*, Paris, 1976

Lerouvillois, Monique, "La Vie des cours de danse", *Pour la danse* (Marseille), March 1981

* * *

The French dancer and choreographer Serge Peretti was, in fact, born in Venice. He was the illegitimate child of a girl of sixteen, who abandoned him and went to Brazil. He was brought up by his grandmother, Civelari di Padua, and by his aunt Inez Bettini, who was the model and companion of the futurist painter Umberto Boccioni. Serge Peretti spent his childhood in Milan in an artistic atmosphere which influenced him for the rest of his life. Exceptionally talented as a dancer, he was also a gifted painter.

Peretti arrived in Paris in 1913 when he was eight, and was a lively, wilful child. Friends advised him to take up dancing. At the age of twelve he took it upon himself to go to the ballet school of the Opéra to enrol. He was past the normal age for enrolment, but he was most insistent and finally the director admitted him. Peretti was well-proportioned, of medium build, and possessed beautifully arched feet. He was a brilliant student and progressed quickly through the ranks. Albert Aveline and Gustave Ricaux were his first teachers, both of whom upheld the purity of style inherited from Beauchamps and Vestris. Gustave Ricaux was Olga Spessivtseva's favourite partner and an excellent teacher, and Serge Peretti was one of his most devoted students. Peretti also worked with the Italian ballerina Carlotta Zambelli and the Italian ballet master Nicola Guerra, from whom he learnt speed and virtuosity. It was at this time that the famous director of the Opéra, Jacques Rouché, turned towards Russia. He invited the Ballets Russes de Serge Diaghilev, Anna Pavlova, Ida Rubinstein and her company to perform, asked Mikhail Fokine and Bronislava Nijinska to choreograph ballets, and engaged Olga Spessivtseva. No other dancer of our time has had such a complete international training as Serge Peretti. As Ivor Guest wrote in *Le Ballet de l'Opéra de Paris*, "His faultless style puts him straightaway into the great tradition of *danseurs nobles*."

Serge Peretti was taken into the ballet in 1921 and made his first appearance in Fokine's production of *Daphnis and Chloe* (in later revivals he took the role of Dorkon). In 1924 Léo Staats choreographed *Siang-Sin*, in which Peretti was the brilliant partner of Camille Bos. In 1925 Bronislava Nijinska set the seal on his talent by choosing him to partner Olga Spessivtseva in *Les Rencontres*. He partnered her again in Léo Staats' *Soir de fête*, replacing Ricaux. Léo Staats, who was an excellent choreographer, set for him a dazzling variation of beats with a manège of coupés jétes, which is still part of the annual competition of the Opéra ballet.

From 1925 onwards, Serge Peretti took part in most of the ballets created by Léo Staats, Nicola Guerra, Aveline, and Serge Lifar, and in the revivals of other works in the repertory. He was made premier danseur in 1930 without having to take part in the usual competition at the same time that his partner, Suzanne Lorcia, was made premiere danseuse, following their sparkling performance of *La Péri*. 1937 saw the creation of a ballet by Aveline, *Elvire*, in which Peretti danced with Lycette Darsonval with great elegance and virtuosity. The "Tambourin de Rameau" was his chef d'oeuvre; in this court dance he made the most of his beats, his changements, his elegant ports de bras—in other words all the "jewels" of the danseur noble. In 1931 Peretti was promoted to étoile; he was the first dancer to be given this title (although Aveline was a premier danseur étoile). At the same time, he also began teaching, as Rouché had entrusted him with the senior boys after Ricaux left. It was he also who created the professional class for the étoiles.

In due course Peretti danced the roles of the princes in *Giselle* and *Swan Lake* with the greatest ballerinas, Lycette Darsonval and Yvette Chauviré, and shared Solange Schwarz's triumphs in Lifar's ballets. In 1945 Peretti was in charge of the choreography of *L'Appel de la montagne* to music by Arthur Honegger.

In 1946 he left the Opéra for a long tour in South America (Argentina, Uruguay, Colombia, Venezuela, Cuba, Costa Rica) with young dancers from the Opéra Roger Fenonjois (étoile), Marianne Ivanoff (première danseuse), Lolita Parent (sujet), Daniel Seillier, and the Russian pianist Constantinov.

Back in Paris in 1948, Peretti resumed teaching his boys' class at the Opéra and started classes of his own at the Studio Constant in Pigalle. Some of the best-known names in the dance world came to learn from him: Jean Babilée, Roland Petit, Michel Renault, Jean-Paul and Xavier Andreani, Serge Golovine, Cyril Atanasoff, Attilio Labis, Gilbert Mayer, Jean-Pierre Bonnefous, Zizi Jeanmaire, Yvette Chauviré, Christiane Vlassi, Christiane Vaussard, and Claude Bessy are some of the many who admired and revered him. She created a supplementary advanced class for him at the École de danse. The indefatigable Serge Peretti has also taught at Paul and Yvonne Goubé's Paris Dance Centre. Now in his eighties, Serge Peretti has not lost his biting wit, his youthfulness of heart, nor his love for dance.

—Gilberte Cournand

LA PÉRI

Choreography: Jean Coralli
Music: Friedrich Burgmüller
Design: Charles Séchan, Jules Diéterle, Édouard Despléchin, Humanité Philastre, Charles Cambon (sets), Paul Lormier (costumes)
Libretto: Théophile Gautier and Jean Coralli
First Production: Théâtre de l'Académie royale de musique (Paris Opéra), Paris, 22 February 1843
Principal Dancers: Carlotta Grisi (La Péri), Lucien Petipa (Achmet), Jean Coralli (Slave Dealer)

Other productions include: Theatre Royal, Drury Lane (staged Eugène Coralli after Jean Coralli), as *The Peri*, with Carlotta Grisi and Lucien Petipa; London, 30 September 1843. Bolshoi Theatre (staged Frédéric after Coralli), with Elena Andreyanova; St. Petersburg, 1 February (20 January old style) 1844. Bolshoi Theatre (staged Frédéric); Moscow, 26 November (14 November old style) 1844.

Other choreographic treatments: Filippo Taglioni (Milan, 1843), Ivan Clustine (Paris, 1912), Léo Staats (Paris, 1921), Frederick Ashton (London, 1931 and 1956), Serge Lifar (Monte Carlo, 1946), George Skibine (Paris, 1966), Darrell (London, 1973).

PUBLICATIONS

Moore, Lillian, "The Origin of Adagio in Ballet", *Dancing Times* (London), April 1936
Beaumont, Cyril, *Complete Book of Ballets*, revised edition, London, 1951
Guest, Ivor, *The Romantic Ballet in Paris*, London, 1966

La Péri, with Carlotta Grisi in the title role, from an 1843 lithograph

Joffe, Lydia, "*La Péri* 1843, *La Péri* 1912, *La Péri* 1967", *Dance Magazine* (London), April 1967

*   *   *

Achmet, bored with the sensuous life of an oriental lord, falls into a drug-induced sleep. Drifting through realms of fantasy he sees a group of exquisitely beautiful beings, the Péris. One falls. He awakens and catches her. So begins the oriental fantasy, *La Péri*, the vision of poet/critic Théophile Gautier, the production of ballet master Jean Coralli. They had collaborated before, on the ballet *Giselle*. And many of the elements that made *Giselle* a success were there in *La Péri*. There were bountiful opportunities for dancing and for the creation of poetic illusion. There was romance and the romantic. There was the theme of love between a mortal and a spirit. There was death, ambivalent and mysterious.

Gautier's tale tells of Achmet (Lucien Petipa) who falls in love with the Queen of the Péris (Carlotta Grisi). She sets out to test his feelings and in so doing causes the death of a beautiful slave girl and the near-death of Achmet himself. Critics recognized that Gautier had followed a formula, and as far as the dramatic action went, were not impressed with the result. Indeed, without the participation of playwright Saint-Georges, who had brought much-needed simplicity and unity to Gautier's *Giselle* scenario, *La Péri* showed more "imagination than good sense" and more complexity than was consistent with clarity. The ballet's appeal was not in overall artistic unity or dramatic intensity, but in the romantic imagery evoked by the dances, costumes, sets, music, and lighting. Thus one critic wrote: "It is not therefore M. Gautier, but M. Coralli who is the true magician of this fairy tale. M. Gautier has only repeated that which others have done; M. Coralli, himself, has imagined a thousand delicious groupings, a thousand charming dances! Honor to Mmes Grisi, Pauline Leroux, Sophie Dumilâtre et Marquet, and to M. Petipa, who have made the success of la Péri! The music of M. Burgmüller is pleasant. MM. Philastre, Cambon, Séchan, Diéterle and Despléchin are the authors of four or five charming and magnificent décors: what more could you want?"

Carlotta Grisi was, at a time when the ballerina reigned supreme, not surprisingly *La Péri*'s primary attraction. Her Act I "pas du songe", when she falls from a platform into Achmet's arms, and the sensuous Act II "pas de l'abeille" (dance of the bee) were the highlights. In the second dance a bee enters her clothing which she proceeds to remove with charmingly "modest embarrassment". Here, as elsewhere, ballet artists were not reluctant to foster sexual fantasy. Indeed, part of the allure of the Péris, Sylphs, Ondines, and Wilis was their freedom from the restrictive sexual mores of the real world. They could maintain their innocence in their sexuality.

It is to *La Péri* that one should go for understanding of the Romantic ballet. Even though many observers recognized that ballets during the Romantic period often made their most powerful statements through the poetic illusions they evoked, and not through their dramatic action, most ballet masters continued to emphasize complicated, confusing stories that detracted from the romantic images they so beautifully created. *La Péri* was a work praised for its depiction of fantastic places and beings, but it was at the same time criticized for being difficult to follow. This was ironic, for Théophile Gautier in his ballet reviews often wrote of the ideal response to ballet in which the viewer ignored the story in order to allow his fancy to drift through the beautiful pictures created on stage. The contrast between the beauty of *La Péri*'s stage illusion and the heaviness of its action make it a fine example of the Romantic ballet at its worst and best.

—John Chapman

PERROT, Jules

French dancer, choreographer, and ballet master. Born Jules Joseph Perrot into theatrical family, in Lyons, 18 August 1810. Studied in Lyons, from 1819; later studied with Auguste Vestris. One daughter, probably named Caronne Adèle Josephine Marie, by dancer Carlotta Grisi, b. 1837; married Russian dancer Capitoline Samovskaya, c. 1850: two daughters. Paris début (at the age of 13), 1823: comic mime, Théâtre de la Gaîté, 1823–25; joined ballet company of the Théâtre de la Porte-Saint-Martin (under ballet master Coralli), 1826, continuing as dancer until 1929; London début, King's Theatre, 1830, returning there to perform 1833–36, 1842; Paris Opéra début (in opera *Le Rossignol*), 1830; engaged as Opéra dancer, 1830–33; also performed in Naples, 1834, Munich and Vienna, 1836, Milan, 1838, and Lyons, 1840; first major choreography (*Le Nymphe et le papillon*) for the Kärntnertor Theater, Vienna, 1836, also choreographing in Venice 1838, and Naples, 1839; returned to Théâtre de la Renaissance, Paris (performing with Carlotta Grisi), 1840, and Paris Opéra, 1841; ballet master, King's Theatre, London, 1843–46, becoming joint ballet master with Paul Taglioni, 1846–48; choreographer, La Scala, Milan, 1848; ballet master, Imperial Theatres, St. Petersburg, 1851–59, staying in Russia until 1861; retired to Brittany. Died in Paramé, 24 August 1892.

ROLES

1823   Pulcinella in *Le Petit Carnaval de Venise* (after Milon), Théâtre des Celestins, Lyons
   Polichinelle in *Le Polichinelle avalé par la baleine* (pantomime; Lefebvre), Théâtre de la Gaîté, Paris
1824   Philps in *Le Rameau d'or* (folie-pantomime-féerie), Théâtre de la Gaîté, Paris
1825   Sapajou in *Sapajou; ou, Le Naufrage des singes* (folie-pantomime), Théâtre de la Gaîté, Paris
   Divertissement (chor. Lefebvre) in *L'Etrangère* (melodrama), Théâtre de la Gaîté, Paris
1828   Dancer (cr) in *Léocadie* (Coralli), Théâtre de la Porte-Saint-Martin, Paris
   Pas de trois (cr) in *Les Artistes* (Coralli), Théâtre de la Porte-Saint-Martin, Paris
   Divertissement (cr) in *Macbeth* (Anatole), Théâtre de la Porte-Saint-Martin, Paris
1830   Dancer in *Le Carnaval de Venise* (Milon), King's Theatre, London
   Pas de trois in *Guillaume Tell* (A. Léon), King's Theatre, London
   Pas de deux (chor. A. Vestris) added to *Le Rossignol* (opera; mus. Le Bruhn), Opéra, Paris
   Intermezzo in *La Muette de Portici* (opera; mus. Auber, chor. Aumer), Opéra, Paris
   Pas de deux in *Fernand Cortès* (opera; mus. Spontini, chor. P. Gardel), Opéra, Paris
1831   Zéphire in *Flore et Zéphire* (revival; Didelot, staged Aumer, Albert), Opéra, Paris
   Pas de deux (cr) in *L'Orgie* (Coralli), Opéra, Paris

Pas de cinq (cr) in *Robert le Diable* (opera; chor. F. Taglioni), Opéra, Paris

1832   Pas de deux (cr; also chor.) in *Moïse* (opera; mus. Rossini), Opéra, Paris

1833   Divertissement (cr) in *Ali-Baba* (opera; mus. Cherubini, additional mus. Halévy), Opéra, Paris

Pas du sylphe, Divertissement in *Faust* (Deshayes), King's Theatre, London

Pas de deux (cr) in *La Révolte au sérail* (F. Taglioni), Opéra, Paris

1834   Dancer (cr) in *Sire Huon* (F. Taglioni), King's Theatre, London

Dancer (cr) in *Armide* (T. Elssler), King's Theatre, London

James in *La Sylphide* (F. Taglioni), King's Theatre, London

1835   Divertissement in *Nina* (Deshayes), King's Theatre, London

Dancer in *Paul et Virginie* (Deshayes), King's Theatre, London

Dancer (cr) in *Zéphir berger* (Deshayes), King's Theatre, London

Pas de deux (cr) in *Mazilia* (F. Taglioni), King's Theatre, London

Dancer in *Tyrolienne* (divertissement), King's Theatre, London

Edmund in *La Somnambule* (Deshayes), King's Theatre, London

Zephyr in *Zeffiro* (after Didelot), Teatro San Carlo, Naples

1836   Principal dancer (cr) in *Il Ritorno di Ulisse* (after Didelot), Teatro San Carlo, Naples

Pas de deux (inserted) in *Le Rossignol* (Deshayes), King's Theatre, London

Principal dancer (cr) in *Tarantella* (also chor.), King's Theatre, London

Principal dancer (cr) in *Pas de deux* (also chor.), Théâtre Français, Paris

Sylph (cr) in *Die Nymphe und der Schmetterling* (also chor.), Hofoper, Vienna

Julien (cr) in *Das Stelldichein* (also chor.), Hofoper, Vienna

Pas de deux added to *Don Giovanni* (opera; mus. Mozart), Hofoper, Vienna

Pas de deux in *Liebe, Stärker als Zaubermacht* (Campilli), Hofoper, Vienna

1837   Principal dancer (cr) in *Pas de deux* (also chor.), Opéra-Comique, Paris

1838   Pietro (cr) in *Die Neapolitanischen Fischer* (also chor.), Hofoper, Vienna

Title role (cr) in *Der Kobold* (also chor.), Hofoper, Vienna

Pas de deux (cr; also chor.) added to *I Figli de Edoardo* (Cortesi), La Scala, Milan

1839   Pas de deux (cr; also chor.) added to *Il Rajah di Benares* (S. Taglioni), Teatro San Carlo, Naples

1840   Title role (cr) in *Zingaro* (opera; mus. Fortuna, chor. Perrot), Théâtre de la Renaissance, Paris

1841   Pas de deux (cr; also chor.) in *La Favorite* (opera; mus. Donizetti), Opéra, Paris

Pas de deux (cr; also chor.) in *Don Juan* (opera; mus. Mozart), Opéra, Paris

1842   Belfegor (cr) in *Alma; ou, La Fille de feu* (Deshayes, Perrot, Cerrito), Her Majesty's Theatre, London

Albrecht in *Giselle* (also chor., with Coralli), Her Majesty's Theatre, London

1843   Principal dancer (cr) in *L'Aurore* (divertissement; also

Jules Perrot in the title role of *Zingaro*, Paris, 1840

chor.), Her Majesty's Theatre, London

Matteo (cr) in *Ondine; ou, La Naïade* (also chor.), Her Majesty's Theatre, London

Stephano (cr) in *Le Délire d'un peintre* (also chor.), Her Majesty's Theatre, London

1844   Gringoire (cr) in *La Esmeralda* (also chor.), Her Majesty's Theatre, London

Principal dancer (cr) in *Polka* (also chor.), Her Majesty's Theatre, London

Pan (cr) in *Zélia; ou, La Nymphe de Diane* (also chor.), Her Majesty's Theatre, London

Principal dancer (cr) in *La Paysanne Grande Dame* (divertissement; also chor.), Her Majesty's Theatre, London

1845   Rübezahl (cr) in *Eoline; ou, La Dryade* (also chor.), Her
        Majesty's Theatre, London
        Principal dancer (cr) in *Kaya; ou, L'Amour voyageur*
        (also chor.), Her Majesty's Theatre, London
        Principal dancer (cr) in *La Bacchante* (divertissement;
        also chor.), Her Majesty's Theatre, London
        Endymion (cr) in *Diane* (also chor.), Her Majesty's
        Theatre, London
1846   Diavolino (cr) in *Catarina; ou, La Fille du bandit* (also
        chor.), Her Majesty's Theatre, London
        Principal dancer (cr) in *Pas de trois* (also chor.), Her
        Majesty's Theatre, London
        Fadladeen (cr) in *Lalla Rookh; or, The Rose of Lahore*
        (also chor.), Her Majesty's Theatre, London
        Mercury (cr) in *Le Jugement de Pâris* (also chor.), Her
        Majesty's Theatre, London
1847   Villon (cr) in *Odetta; ou, La Demenza di Carlo VI re di
        Francia* (also chor.), La Scala, Milan
        Principal dancer (cr) in *Pas de deux* (also chor.), Her
        Majesty's Theatre, London
1848   Mephistopholes (cr) in *Faust* (also chor.), La Scala,
        Milan
1849   Alain (cr) in *La Filleule des fées* (also chor.), Opéra, Paris
1851   Matteo (cr) in *The Naiad and the Fisherman* (also chor.),
        Bolshoi Theatre, St. Petersburg
        Principal dancer (cr) in *Les Tribulations d'un maître de
        ballet* (divertissement; also chor.), Bolshoi Theatre,
        St. Petersburg
1852   Kolo (cr) in *The War of the Women; or, The Amazons of
        the Ninth Century* (also chor.), Bolshoi Theatre, St.
        Petersburg
1853   Zingaro (cr) in *Gazelda; or, The Tsiganes* (also chor.),
        Bolshoi Theatre, St. Petersburg
1854   Title role (cr) in *Marcobomba* (also chor.), Bolshoi
        Theatre, St. Petersburg
1855   Gianneo (cr) in *Armida* (also chor.), Bolshoi Theatre, St.
        Petersburg
1856   Periphète in *La Fille de marbre* (saint-Léon, with new
        dances Perrot), Bolshoi Theatre, St. Petersburg
1857   The Ballet Master (cr) in *La Débutante* (also chor.),
        Bolshoi Theatre, St. Petersburg (originally staged
        Peterhof, 1856)
1858   Seyd Pasha (cr) in *Le Corsaire* (new production; also
        chor., after Mazilier), Bolshoi Theatre, St. Petersburg
        Rübezahl (cr) in *Eoline; ou, La Dryade* (new version;
        also chor.), Bolshoi Theatre, St. Petersburg

WORKS

1832   Pas de deux in *Moïse* (opera; mus. Rossini), Opéra,
        Paris
1835   Pas de deux added to *La Tempête* (ballet), Grand
        Theatre, Bordeaux
1836   *Tarantella* ("The Original Tarantella, as imported from
        Naples"), King's Theatre, London (possibly first
        staged in Naples, 1835/36)
        Pas de deux, Théâtre Français, Paris
        Die Nymphe und der Schmetterling (with ensemble chor.
        by Campilli), Hofoper, Vienna (restaged Munich,
        1838)
        Das Stelldichein (mus. Aigner), Hofoper, Vienna (re-
        staged Munich, 1838)
1837   *Pas de deux* (for Perrot and Grisi), Opéra-Comique,
        Paris
1838   *Die Neapolitanischen Fischer*, Hofoper, Vienna
        Der Kobold (mus. Reuling), Hofoper, Vienna

Pas de deux added to *I Figli di Edoardo* (ballet; Cortesı),
        La Scala, Milan
L'Appuntamento (new production of *Das Stelldichein*;
        mus. Aigner), Teatro Fondo, Naples
1839   Pas de deux added to *Il Rajah di Benares* (S. Taglioni),
        Teatro San Carlo, Naples
1840   Dances in *Zingaro* (opera; mus. Fortuna), Théâtre de la
        Renaissance, Paris
1841   Pas de deux added to *La Favorite* (opera; mus.
        Donizetti), Opéra, Paris
        Pas de deux added to *Don Juan* (opera; mus. Mozart),
        Opéra, Paris
        Giselle (with Jean Coralli; mus. Adam), Opéra, Paris
1842   *Le Pecheur napolitain* (new production of *Die Neapolitan-
        ischen Fischer*; mus. probably Auber), Her Majesty's
        Theatre, London
        Pas (with Cerrito) in *Alma; ou, La Fille du feu*
        (Deshayes; mus. Costa), Her Majesty's Theatre,
        London
        Une Soirée du carnaval (divertissement with other
        chors.), Her Majesty's Theatre, London
1843   *L'Aurore* (divertissement; mus. Pugni), Her Majesty's
        Theatre, London
        Un Bal sous Louis Quatorze (divertissement; mus.
        Nadaud), Her Majesty's Theatre, London ("Pas de
        Diane chasseresse" added later in 1843)
        Ondine; ou, La Naïade (mus. Pugni), Her Majesty's
        Theatre, London
        Le Délire d'un peintre (divertissement; mus. Pugni), Her
        Majesty's Theatre, London
1844   *La Esmeralda* (mus. Pugni), Her Majesty's Theatre,
        London (restaged by Perrot in Milan, 1844, and St.
        Petersburg, 1849)
        Polka (mus. Pugni), Her Majesty's Theatre, London
        Zélia; ou, La Nymphe de Diane (mus. Pugni), Her
        Majesty's Theatre, London
        La Paysanne Grande Dame (divertissement), Her Majes-
        ty's Theatre, London
1845   *Eoline; ou, La Dryade* (mus. Pugni), Her Majesty's
        Theatre, London
        Kaya; ou, L'Amour voyageur (mus. Pugni), Her Majes-
        ty's Theatre, London
        La Bacchante (divertissement; mus. Pugni), Her Majes-
        ty's Theatre, London
        Pas de quatre (mus. Pugni), Her Majesty's Theatre,
        London
        Diane (divertissement), Her Majesty's Theatre, London
1846   *Catarina; ou, La Fille du bandit* (mus. Pugni), Her
        Majesty's Theatre, London (restaged by Perrot in
        Milan, 1847, and St. Petersburg, 1849)
        Pas de trois, Her Majesty's Theatre, London
        Lalla Rookh; or, The Rose of Lahore (mus. Pugni), Her
        Majesty's Theatre, London
        Le Jugement de Pâris (mus. Pugni), Her Majesty's
        Theatre, London
1847   *Catarina* (expanded version; additional new mus.
        Bajetti), La Scala, Milan
        Odetta; ou, La Demenza di Carlo VI re di Francia (mus.
        Panizza), La Scala, Milan
        Pas de deux, Her Majesty's Theatre, London
        Les Éléments (divertissement; mus. Bajetti), Her Majes-
        ty's Theatre, London
1848   *Faust* (mus. Panizza, Costa, Bajetti), La Scala, Milan
        (restaged by Perrot in St. Petersburg, 1854)
        Les Quatre Saisons (divertissement; mus. Pugni), Her
        Majesty's Theatre, London
        "Grand Quintette Dansante" added to *La Esmeralda*

(1844), Her Majesty's Theatre, London

1849   *La Filleule des fées* (mus. Adam, de Saint-Julien), Opéra, Paris (restaged by Perrot in St. Petersburg)

1851   *The Naiad and the Fisherman* (mus. Pugni), Bolshoi Theatre, St. Petersburg

       Les Tribulations d'un maître de ballet (divertissement; mus. Pugni), Bolshoi Theatre, St. Petersburg

1852   *The War of the Women; or, The Amazons of the Ninth Century* (mus. Pugni), Bolshoi Theatre, St. Petersburg

1853   *Gazelda; or, The Tsiganes* (mus. Pugni), Bolshoi Theatre, St. Petersburg (restaged by Perrot in Milan, 1864)

1854   *Faust* (new production; additional mus. Pugni), Bolshoi Theatre, St. Petersburg

       Marcobomba (mus. Pugni), Bolshoi Theatre, St. Petersburg

1855   *Armida* (mus. Pugni), Bolshoi Theatre, St. Petersburg

       Dances added to *La Fille de marbre* (Saint-Léon), Bolshoi Theatre, St. Petersburg

1857   *La Débutante* (mus. Pugni), Bolshoi Theatre, St. Petersburg (originally staged Peterhof, 1856)

       La Petite Marchande de bouquets (choreographic interlude), Bolshoi Theatre, St. Petersburg

       Dances in *L'Île des muets* (comedy by Deligny; mus. Labarre, Pugni), Bolshoi Theatre, St. Petersburg

1858   *Eoline; ou, La Dryade* (new production; mus. Pugni), Bolshoi Theatre, St. Petersburg

1864   *Gazelda* (new production; additional mus. Giorza), La Scala, Milan

Also staged:

1857   *The Rose, the Violet and the Butterfly* (after Petipa; mus. Peter II, Grand Duke of Oldenburg), Bolshoi Theatre, St. Petersburg

1858   *Le Corsaire* (after Mazilier, with new dances by Perrot; mus. Adam, Pugni), Bolshoi Theatre, St. Petersburg

PUBLICATIONS

Gautier, Théophile, *Les Beautés de l'Opéra*, Paris, 1845

Saint-Léon, Arthur, *La Sténochorégraphie*, Paris, 1852

Gautier, Théophile, *The Romantic Ballet as Seen by Théophile Gautier*, translated by Cyril Beaumont, London, 1932

Moore, Lillian, *Artists of the Dance*, New York, 1938

Lifar, Serge, *Giselle*, Paris, 1942

Walker, Kathrine Sorley, "Perrot and his Lost Choreography", *Ballet* (London), April 1946

Beaumont, Cyril, *Complete Book of Ballets*, revised edition, London, 1951

Guest, Ivor, *The Romantic Ballet in England*, London, 1954

Guest, Ivor, *Fanny Cerrito*, London, 1956

Roslavleva, Natalia, *Era of the Russian Ballet*, London, 1966

Guest, Ivor, *The Romantic Ballet in Paris*, London, 1966

Guest, Ivor, *Fanny Elssler*, London, 1970

Guest, Ivor, *The Pas de Quatre*, London, 1970

Winter, Marian Hannah, *The Pre-Romantic Ballet*, London, 1974

Au, Susan, "The Bandit Ballerina: Some Sources of Jules Perrot's *Catarina*", *Dance Research Journal* (New York), vol. 10, no. 2, 1978

Au, Susan, "The Shadow of Herself: Some Sources of Jules Perrot's *Ondine*", *Dance Research Journal* (New York), vol. 2, 1978

Guest, Ivor, *Jules Perrot: Master of the Romantic Ballet*, London, 1984

Guest, Ivor, "Perrot and Bournonville", *Dancing Times* (London), November 1988

*   *   *

Son of a theatre machinist, Jules Perrot spent his youth as a dancer in two Parisian Boulevard theatres, the Gaîté and the Porte-Saint-Martin; he also studied ballet with one of the century's greatest teachers, Auguste Vestris, who included August Bournonville among his students. At the age of twenty he was accepted into the Paris Opéra company, where he became one of Marie Taglioni's principle partners, indeed almost a rival. He possessed exceptional strength and stamina, which imparted to his dancing an ease that made the most difficult technical feat appear totally natural. He possessed in common with Taglioni an aerial grace that simulated flight. Romantic critic Théophile Gautier described him as "Perrot the aerial, Perrot the sylph, the male Taglioni". Jules Janin, a self-confessed despiser of male dancers, referred to Perrot as ". . . that light male sylphide, that fine dancer for whom we have made so great a concession in allowing him to be a dancer". Perrot's style, in keeping with the Romantic vision, emphasized movement—that is, change, not the sharp-edged poses that characterized the classical approach to art. The essence of Romanticism was the vision of a universe in flux.

Perrot left the Opéra in 1833, the result of a contract dispute. He danced in London and Naples, where he met Carlotta Grisi in 1834. He became her teacher, partner, and lover, eventually introducing her to audiences in Paris and London. He probably choreographed her dances in *Giselle* (Paris, 1841). Though Perrot continued to dance into the 1840s (he partnered Grisi in the London production of *Giselle* in 1842) he was plagued by knee problems that seriously hampered his career as a performer.

Just as his dancing reflected the Romantic spirit, so Perrot's ballets encompassed a wide range of that era's preoccupations—mediaeval settings and human depravity in *La Esmeralda*, the supernatural in *Ondine* and *Eoline*, exotic orientalism in *Lalla Rookh*, and local colour in *Catarina*. Though his career embraced Vienna, Naples, Milan, Paris, Bordeaux, and St. Petersburg, his most prolific period was spent in London, where he was ballet master from 1843 to 1848. Here he infused his ballets with sympathy for the individual, successfully giving his characters human depth; they were not the archetypes of the neo-classical world view, but the unique individuals that were at the centre of the Romantic vision—Matteo, the fisherman in *Ondine*; Pierre Gringoire, the itinerant poet in *La Esmeralda*; and Esmeralda, the gypsy beggar-girl herself. Also Romantic was his concern to make his stage picture totally convincing. In crowd scenes, for example, he carefully attended to every performer's part, creating a completely coherent, unified stage illusion. Thus his ballets often relied as much on the effect of the ensemble as the soloists. Perrot was supported in the realization of his vision by the designers William Grieve and Charles Marshall, as well as by the composer Cesare Pugni (who joined Perrot in Russia in the 1850s). Pugni's descriptive music added much to the realization of a scene, for example his suggestion of the rippling of water in *Ondine*.

Perrot's greatest accomplishment, and that which contributed most to the intensity of his ballets, was his ability to use dancing directly to further the action. Traditionally, ballets represented stories through silent acting (pantomime), with dance playing a secondary role. With the expanded skills of dancers that appeared during the romantic period, Perrot made dance expressive of feeling. The integration was seamless: "Every portion of the action is danced," wrote an observer in

1844, "which avoids the tedious gesticulations and mimicry between the pas, which the public had formerly to endure, and avoids those sudden transitions that mar the illusion."

Perrot added to his keen dramatic sense a talent for the creation of dances that possessed purely abstract beauty, dances which were artistically valid in their own right. The Russian critic Fedor Koni, making a distinction between a ballet master and a choreographer, wrote: "... Perrot is not merely a ballet-master who produces dances, but a choreographer in the sense of a creator and interpreter of marvellous images that spring forth, one after the other, like shadowy pictures from his imagination." The most notable of such dances were the four divertissement ballets he produced as show pieces for the great ballerinas who visited London, *Pas de quatre*, *Le Jugement de Pâris*, *Les Éléments*, and *Les Quatre Saisons*. The most famous, *Pas de quatre*, was danced by Taglioni, Cerrito, Grisi, and Grahn, a formidable quartet indeed. The ballet could have easily become a circus piece featuring the virtuosity of the four contending ballerinas—audiences were certainly ready for such an approach, as they eagerly awaited the opportunity to cheer their particular favourite to victory. Given such an atmosphere, it is a testament to Perrot's genius that his dances were consistently commended for their intrinsic interest and beauty; many writers considered his contribution to the success of the pieces to have been as great as that of his interpreters. This is attested to by the *Morning Herald*, which reported, "Perrot ... certainly was entitled to a share in the honours. It was no easy matter to compose a 'pas' which should serve the curious purpose of developing simultaneously the executive powers of the four great European artists, without placing them in unpleasant antagonism. A beautiful effect seems to have been aimed at, and it has been accomplished; the 'ensemble' is literally perfect, for the combinations are fanciful and varied, and are constructed upon a principle of novelty as to form, which gives them recommendation and interest, independently of the piquant zest wound up in the competition of the dancers."

Though Paris snubbed Perrot, the Opéra only producing one of his works, *La Filleule des fées*, in 1849, St. Petersburg welcomed him as it had opened its arms to another Opéra exile half a century before, Charles-Louis Didelot. It was here that Perrot produced his last ballet in 1858.

Ultimately, Perrot's work was an eloquent statement for the power and versatility of dance as a means of artistic expression. What was unique about his work was the sense of life he brought to his romantic settings, characters, and touching stories. But his genius was not powerful enough to save an art that was so much a victim of the whims of fashion. When Perrot left London for the last time in 1848, ballet there was rapidly becoming an accessory to opera, and worse, a mere vehicle for the exhibition of feminine charms. It was a route that ballet would follow all over Europe during the next half-century. For the most part, Perrot's achievements were forgotten, and his works lost.

—John Chapman

PETIPA, Marius
French dancer, choreographer, and ballet master. Born in Marseilles, son of dancer and teacher Jean Antoine Petipa, and

brother of dancer and choreographer Lucien Petipa, 11 March 1818. Educated at the Grand College and Conservatoire, Brussels; studied dancing with father, Jean Petipa; later perfected training with Auguste Vestris. Married (1) dancer Maria Surovshchikova, 1854 (separated 1867): daughter, dancer Maria Mariusovna Petipa, b. 1857; (2) dancer Lyubov Savitskaya, 1882. Stage début with father's dancing company, Brussels, 1831, performing with same company in Bordeaux, from 1834; principal dancer, Nantes, 1838; toured America with family company, 1839; principal dancer at the Comédie-Française, Paris, and in Bordeaux; toured Spain, 1843–46; performed in Paris, 1847, and then as principal dancer of the Imperial Theatres, St. Petersburg, from 1847; choreographer, staging first ballets while performing as dancer in Nantes, 1838, and later acting as choreographer, Madrid, 1845; leading dancer, also staging works by Mazilier and Perrot, Bolshoi Theatre, St. Petersburg, from 1847; choreographer's assistant to Jules Perrot, rechoreographing part of "Scene of the Wilis" in 1850 revival of *Giselle* (restaging it completely in 1884); ballet master of the Imperial Theatres, from 1862, becoming chief ballet master, 1869; created over 50 ballets until retirement in 1903. Died in Gurzuf, Crimea, 14 July 1910.

ROLES

1831   A Savoyard in *La Dansomanie* (J. Petipa after Gardel), Théâtre de la Monnaie, Brussels
1834/ Colin in *La Fille mal gardée* (Dauberval), Grand
38   Theatre, Bordeaux
       Albrecht in *Giselle* (Coralli, Perrot), Grand Theatre, Bordeaux
       Leading dancer in *La Péri* (Coralli), Grand Theatre, Bordeaux
1847/ Lucien in *Paquita* (Mazilier), Bolshoi Theatre, St.
50   Petersburg
       Principal dancer in *Armida* (Perrot), Bolshoi Theatre, St. Petersburg
       Diavolino in *Catarina* (Perrot), Bolshoi Theatre, St. Petersburg
       Principal dancer in *La Esmeralda* (Perrot), Bolshoi Theatre, St. Petersburg
       Favio in *Satanella* (also chor., after Mazilier), Bolshoi Theatre, St. Petersburg
       Stefano in *Le Délire d'un peintre* (Perrot), Bolshoi Theatre, St. Petersburg
1852   Mitsislas (cr) in *The War of the Women; or, The Amazons of the Ninth Century* (Perrot), Bolshoi Theatre, St. Petersburg
1853   Karl (cr) in *Gazelda; or, The Tsiganes* (Perrot), Bolshoi Theatre, St. Petersburg
1854   Title role in *Faust* (Perrot), Bolshoi Theatre, St. Petersburg
       Leading dancer (cr) in *Marcobomba* (Perrot), Bolshoi Theatre, St. Petersburg
1855   Rinaldo (cr) in *Armida* (Perrot), Bolshoi Theatre, St. Petersburg
1857   The Marquis (cr) in *La Débutante* (Perrot), Bolshoi Theatre, St. Petersburg (originally staged Peterhof, 1856)
1858   Conrad in *Le Corsaire* (Perrot after Mazilier, with additions by Petipa), Bolshoi Theatre, St. Petersburg
1859   Simon (cr) in *Parisian Market* (also chor.), Bolshoi Theatre, St. Petersburg
1862   Lord Wilson (cr) in *Pharoah's Daughter* (also chor.), Bolshoi Theatre, St. Petersburg

WORKS

1838   *Le Droit du Seigneur*, Nantes
        La Petite Bohémienne, Nantes
        La Noce à Nantes, Nantes
1845   *Carmen et son toréro*, Teatro del Circo, Madrid
        La Perle de Séville, Teatro del Circo, Madrid
        L'Aventure d'une fille de Madrid, Teatro del Circo, Madrid
        La Fleur de Grenade, Teatro del Circo, Madrid
        Départ pour la course des taureaux, Teatro del Circo, Madrid
1847   *Catarina* (after Perrot; mus. Pugni), Bolshoi Theatre, St. Petersburg
        Paquita (with Frédéric, after Mazilier; mus. Deldevez), Bolshoi Theatre, St. Petersburg
1848   *Satanilla* (after Mazilier's *Le Diable amoureux*; mus. Réber, Benoist), Bolshoi Theatre, St. Petersburg
1849   *Lida; or, The Swiss Milkmaid* (with J. Petipa; mus. Pugni), Bolshoi Theatre, St. Petersburg
1850   Scene of the Wilis (with Perrot) in *Giselle* (Perrot), Bolshoi Theatre, St. Petersburg (later became the Grand Pas des Wilis in *Giselle*, 1884)
1855   *The Star of Granada* (mus. various), Bolshoi Theatre, St. Petersburg
1857   *The Rose, the Violet and the Butterfly* (mus. Oldenburg), Court Theatre, Tsarskoye Selo
1858   *Royal Marriage* (or *Un Mariage sous la régence*; mus. Pugni), Bolshoi Theatre, St. Petersburg
        Le Corsaire (revival; Perrot after Mazilier, with additional chor. Petipa; mus. Adam, Pugni), Bolshoi Theatre, St. Petersburg
1859   *Parisian Market* (*Le Marché de Paris*; mus. Pugni), Bolshoi Theatre, St. Petersburg (staged as *Le Marché des innocents*, Paris Opéra, 1861)
        La Somnambule (mus. Bellini), Bolshoi Theatre, St. Petersburg
        Venetian Carnaval (grand pas de deux; mus. Pugni), Bolshoi Theatre, St. Petersburg
1860   *The Blue Dahlia* (mus. Pugni), Bolshoi Theatre, St. Petersburg
1861   *Terpsichore* (mus. Pugni), Court Theatre, Tsarskoye Selo
1862   *Pharaoh's Daughter* (*La Fille du Pharaon*; mus. Pugni), Bolshoi Theatre, St. Petersburg
1863   *The Beauty of Lebanon; or, The Spirit of the Mountains* (mus. Pugni), Bolshoi Theatre, St. Petersburg
1865   *The Travelling Ballerina* (*La Danseuse en voyage*; mus. Pugni), Bolshoi Theatre, St. Petersburg
1866   *Titania* (mus. Pugni), Palace of the Grand Duchess Elena Pavlovna, St. Petersburg
        Florida (mus. Pugni), Bolshoi Theatre, St. Petersburg
1867   *Faust* (mus. Panica, Pugni), Bolshoi Theatre, St. Petersburg
1868   *Love, the Benefactor* (*L'Amour bienfaiteur*; mus. Pugni), Imperial Theatre School, St. Petersburg
        The Slave (divertissement; mus. Pugni), Court Theatre, Tsarskoye Selo
        Le Corsaire (after Mazilier, Perrot; mus. Adam, Pugni, Delibes), Bolshoi Theatre, St. Petersburg
        King Candaule (mus. Pugni), Bolshoi Theatre, St. Petersburg
1869   *Don Quixote* (mus. Minkus), Bolshoi Theatre, Moscow (staged St. Petersburg, 1871)
1870   *Trilby; or, the Devil at Home* (mus. Gerber), Bolshoi Theatre, Moscow
        Katerina, the Brigand's Daughter (after Perrot; mus. Pugni), Bolshoi Theatre, St. Petersburg

1871   *The Two Stars* (*Les Deux Étoiles*; mus. Pugni), Bolshoi Theatre, St. Petersburg
1872   *La Camargo* (mus. Minkus), Bolshoi Theatre, St. Petersburg
1874   *Le Papillon* (mus. Minkus), Bolshoi Theatre, St. Petersburg
        The Naïad and the Fisherman (after Perrot's *Ondine*; mus. Pugni), Bolshoi Theatre, St. Petersburg (Act I originally staged by Petipa 1871)
1875   *The Bandits* (*Les Brigands*; mus. Minkus), Bolshoi Theatre, St. Petersburg
1876   *The Adventures of Peleus and Thétis* (mus. Delibes, Minkus), Bolshoi Theatre, St. Petersburg
        A Midsummer Night's Dream (mus. Mendelssohn), Hermitage Theatre, St. Petersburg
1877   *La Bayadère* (mus. Minkus), Bolshoi Theatre, St. Petersburg
1878   *Roxanna; or, The Beauty of Montenegro* (mus. Minkus), Bolshoi Theatre, St. Petersburg
        Ariadne (mus. Gerber), Bolshoi Theatre, St. Petersburg
1879   *The Daughter of the Snows* (mus. Minkus), Bolshoi Theatre, St. Petersburg
        Frizak, the Barber; or, The Double Wedding (mus. Minkus), Bolshoi Theatre, St. Petersburg
        Mlada (mus. Minkus), Bolshoi Theatre, St. Petersburg
1880   *La Fille du Danube* (after Taglioni; mus. Adam), Bolshoi Theatre, St. Petersburg
1881   *Paquita* (after Mazilier, with own additional chor.; mus. Deldevez), Bolshoi Theatre, St. Petersburg
        Zoraya; or the Lady Moor in Spain (mus. Minkus), Bolshoi Theatre, St. Petersburg
        Markitantka (after Saint-Léon; mus. Pugni), Bolshoi Theatre, St. Petersburg
1882   *Paqueretta* (after Saint-Léon; mus. Benoist, Pugni, Minkus), Bolshoi Theatre, St. Petersburg
1883   *Night and Day* (mus. Minkus), Bolshoi Theatre, St. Petersburg
        Pygmalion (mus. Trubetskoy), Bolshoi Theatre, St. Petersburg
1884   *Coppélia* (after Saint-Léon; mus. Delibes), Bolshoi Theatre, St. Petersburg
        Giselle (after Coralli, Perrot; mus. Adam), Bolshoi Theatre, St. Petersburg
1885   *The Capricious Wife* (after Mazilier's *Le Diable à quatre*, also known as *The Devil to Pay*; mus. Adam), Maryinsky Theatre, St. Petersburg
        Vain Precautions (with Ivanov, after Dauberval's *La Fille mal gardée*; mus. Hertel), Bolshoi Theatre, St. Petersburg
1886   *The King's Command* (mus. Vizentini), Maryinsky Theatre, St. Petersburg
        The Offerings to Love; or, the Pleasures of Loving (mus. Minkus), Maryinsky Theatre, St. Petersburg
        The Magic Pills (mus. Minkus), Maryinsky Theatre, St. Petersburg
        Esmeralda (after Perrot, with own new pas de six; mus. Pugni), Maryinsky Theatre, St. Petersburg
1887   *Fiametta* (with Ivanov, after Saint-Léon; mus. Minkus), Maryinsky Theatre, St. Petersburg
        The Tulip of Haarlem (with Ivanov; mus. Fitinhof-Schel), Maryinsky Theatre, St. Petersburg
1888   *La Vestale* (mus. Ivanov), Maryinsky Theatre, St. Petersburg
1889   *The Talisman* (mus. Drigo), Maryinsky Theatre, St. Petersburg
        The Caprices of the Butterfly (also known as *The Grasshopper Musician*; mus. Krotkov), Maryinsky

Theatre, St. Petersburg
1890   *The Sleeping Beauty* (*La Belle au bois dormant*; mus. Tchaikovsky), Maryinsky Theatre, St. Petersburg
        Nenuphar (mus. Krotkov), Maryinsky Theatre, St. Petersburg
1891   *Kalkabrino* (mus. Minkus), Maryinsky Theatre, St. Petersburg
        A Fairy Tale (mus. Richter), Imperial Theatre School, St. Petersburg
1892   *La Sylphide* (after Coralli, Perrot; mus. Schneitzhoeffer and others), Maryinsky Theatre, St. Petersburg
        The Nutcracker (*Case-noisette*; scenario by Petipa; dances staged Ivanov; mus. Tchaikovsky), Maryinsky Theatre, St. Petersburg
1893   *Cinderella* (with Ivanov, Cecchetti; mus. Fitinhof-Schel), Maryinsky Theatre, St. Petersburg
1894   *The Awakening of Flora* (*Le Reveil de Flore*; with Ivanov; mus. Drigo), Maryinsky Theatre, St. Petersburg
1895   *Swan Lake* (*Le Lac des cygnes*; mus. Tchaikovsky), Maryinsky Theatre, St. Petersburg
        The Little Humpbacked Horse (after Saint-Léon; mus. Pugni), Maryinsky Theatre, St. Petersburg
1896   *Cavalry Halt* (*Halte de cavalerie*; mus. Armscheimer), Maryinsky Theatre, St. Petersburg
        The Beautiful Pearl (mus. Drigo), Bolshoi Theatre, Moscow (staged Maryinsky Theatre, St. Petersburg, 1900)
        Bluebeard (mus. Schenk), Maryinsky Theatre, St. Petersburg
1897   *Thetis and Peleus* (new version of *The Adventures of Peleus and Thetis*; mus. Minkus, Delibes), Maryinsky Theatre, St. Petersburg
1898   *Raymonda* (mus. Glazunov), Maryinsky Theatre, St. Petersburg
1899   *Le Corsaire* (completely new version; music of 1868 production, plus additional mus. Drigo), Maryinsky Theatre, St. Petersburg
1900   *Les Saisons* (mus. Glazunov), Hermitage Theatre, St. Petersburg
        The Trials of Damis (also known as *Les Ruses d'amour*; mus. Glazunov), Hermitage Theatre, St. Petersburg
        Harlequinade (*Les Millions d'Arlequin*; mus. Drigo), Hermitage Theatre, St. Petersburg (staged Maryinsky Theatre, St. Petersburg, same year)
        The Pupils of Monsieur Dupré (new version of *The King's Command*; mus. Vincentini, Delibes), Maryinsky Theatre, St. Petersburg
1902   *Le Coeur de la marquise* (pantomime; mus. Guiraud), Hermitage
1903   *The Magic Mirror* (mus. Koreshchenko), Maryinsky Theatre, St. Petersburg

Other works include: dances in operas *Alessandro Stradella* (mus. von Flotow; 1849), *Rusalka* (mus. Dargomizhsky; 1856), *Martha* (mus. von Flotow; 1859), *Orpheus and Eurydice* (mus. Gluck; 1868), *Hamlet* (mus. Thomas; 1872), *Tannhäuser* (mus. Wagner; 1874), *The Demon* (mus. Rubinstein; 1875), *Aida* (mus. Verdi; 1875), *Il Guarany* (mus. Gomes; 1879), *The Queen of Sheba* (mus. Goldmark; 1880), *Mefistofole* (mus. Boito; 1881), *The King of Lahore* (mus. Massenet; 1881), *Robert the Devil* (mus. Meyerbeer; 1882), *Carmen* (mus. Bizet; 1882), *Faust* (mus. Gounod; 1882), *Les Hugenots* (mus. Meyerbeer; 1882), *La Gioconda* (mus. Ponchielli; 1883), *The Captive of the Caucasus* (mus. Cui; 1883), *The North Star* (mus. Meyerbeer; 1883), *Richard III* (mus. Salvayre; 1883), *Philémon et Baucius* (mus. Gounod; 1883), *Lalla-Roukh* (mus. David; 1884), *Nero* (mus. Rubinstein; 1884), *Rogneda* (mus. Serov; 1884), *Aldona* (mus. Ponchielli; 1884), *Lakme* (mus. Delibes; 1884), *Manon* (mus. Massenet; 1885), *Tamara* (mus. Fitingof; 1886), *Ruslan and Ludmila* (mus. Glinka; 1886), *Pique Dame* (mus. Tchaikovsky; 1890), *Johann von Leyden* (mus. Meyerbeer; 1891), *Dubrovsky* (mus. Nápravník; 1895), *Hansel and Gretel* (mus. Humperdinck; 1897), *Fra Diavolo* (mus. Auber; 1897), *Don Giovanni* (mus. Mozart; 1898), *Feramors* (mus. Rubinstein; 1898).

PUBLICATIONS

By Petipa:
Russian Ballet Master: The Memoirs of Marius Petipa, edited by Lillian Moore, London, 1968
Mémoires, translated and edited by Galia Ackerman and Pierre Lorrain, Paris, 1990

About Petipa:
Leshkov, D.I., *Marius Petipa*, Petrograd, 1922
Yakovlev, M.A., *Ballet Master Marius Petipa*, Petrograd, 1924
Legat, Nikolai, "Twenty Years with Marius Petipa and Christian Johannsen: Pages from the Journal of Nikolai Legat", *Dancing Times* (London), April 1931
Legat, Nikolai, "Memories of Marius Petipa", *Dancing Times* (London), July 1939
Slonimsky, Yuri, "Marius Petipa", translated by Anatole Chujoy, *Dance Index* (New York), May–June 1947
Beaumont, Cyril, *Complete Book of Ballets*, revised edition, London, 1951
Krasovskaya, Vera, *Russian Ballet Theatre of the Second Half of the Nineteenth Century*, Leningrad and Moscow, 1963
Marius Petipa: Materials, Recollections, Articles, Leningrad, 1971
Krasovskaya, Vera, "Marius Petipa and *The Sleeping Beauty*", translated by Cynthia Read, *Dance Perspectives 49*, New York, 1972
Koegler, Horst, "Marius Petipa, A New Perspective", *Dance Magazine* (New York), September 1978
Vazem, Ekaterina, "Memoirs of a Ballerina of the St. Petersburg Bolshoi Theatre", translated by Nina Dimitrievitch, part 3: *Dance Research* (London), Spring 1987
Wiley, Roland John (ed. and trans.), *A Century of Russian Ballet: Documents and Accounts 1810–1910*, Oxford, 1990

*   *   *

Marius Petipa is, historically speaking, the earliest choreographer whose work has been preserved to the present. There were others before him, but it is hard to judge their importance, whereas to judge Petipa's importance we have only to ask what ballet would be like without *The Sleeping Beauty*, *Swan Lake*, or *Giselle*. The last-named reminds us that he not only created classics, but preserved the best of his predecessors' work in classic form, as a window on to an earlier age.

Arguably, Petipa merits a status second to none among the great choreographers, but the world has never been able to get his achievements into proper focus, for a variety of reasons. The setting for his life's work was St. Petersburg, founded on the Baltic scarcely 150 years before he arrived. The city was deliberately created as a "window on to Europe" through which western influences could flow into the culturally isolated Russian Empire. Petipa's engagement as a dancer with the Imperial Theatres was pursuant to this policy; St. Petersburg sucked in European artistes of every kind. Although a member of an eminent French dancing family, the 29-year-old recruit (sensibly pretending to be 25) was at first a subordinate figure, and for a long time, so remained.

It is ironic that after nearly 40 years of service as a dancer and choreographer, and nearing retirement age, he obeyed a summons to see his director, Vsevolozhsky, with no higher hope than a modest pension. Contrary to expectation, he came away with the title of chief ballet master and, as destiny was to reveal, the most brilliant phase of his career ahead of him. Although Petipa had produced *Paquita* and *Satanilla* in his first year in St. Petersburg, these were brought from Paris. It was his compatriot Jules Perrot who, arriving a year later, became the pre-eminent choreographer of St. Petersburg; Petipa mainly performed in Perrot's ballets.

He branched tentatively in other directions, as a teacher at the theatre school, and as a choreographer; but his creative opportunities were at first largely limited to divertissements for his wife, Maria Surovshchikova-Petipa. As a performer, he enjoyed a reputation for character dances, especially Spanish, and mime, but no acclaim as a classical dancer. He appeared on the stage for the last time as Conrad in *Le Corsaire* at the age of 50, opposite Ekaterina Vazem.

Eventually Perrot went, to be succeeded as principal choreographer by another Frenchman, Arthur Saint-Léon. It was during a temporary absence of Saint-Léon that Petipa had the chance to produce his first successful full-length ballet, *Pharaoh's Daughter*, with music by Cesare Pugni. Petipa claimed it was created in six weeks to provide a benefit for the ballerina Carlotta Rosati, but the eminent Russian writer Yuri Slonimsky says Petipa worked hard on its four acts for nearly two years. The ballet was not a classic, but survived most of Petipa's lifetime. It revealed his gift for massing dancers in orderly action, and it won him recognition as St. Peterburg's number two ballet master.

Russia was awakening to her own rich heritage of folklore and national dance, and Saint-Léon produced, with Petipa's assistance, the first and most famous ballet combining these elements, *The Little Humpbacked Horse*. A later version was entirely Petipa's (not the most recent version). *King Candaule*, again with Pugni's music, was the second of his successful full-length ballets, but owed its rapturous reception to the ballerina Henriette d'Or. Petipa later dismissed it as "a sin of my youth". However, it left him, following Saint-Léon's departure, as Russia's principal ballet master.

This was at the end of the 1860s. Petipa then entered on a busy period. From it came *Don Quixote* with music by Ludwig Minkus, now a mainstay of the modern Russian repertoire (though in Gorsky's revision rather than Petipa's original). In 1877 came another Minkus collaboration, *La Bayadère*, the first Petipa "classic". Only in recent years has it become familiar to Western audiences and critics, who are as yet far from perceiving that, having survived a century in defiance of all prediction, it may eventually come to rank, as Slonimsky suggests, on a level with *Swan Lake*. *Giselle*, in 1884, was in the tradition of Coralli and Perrot but is unquestionably a Petipa classic, today sharing with *Swan Lake* the distinction of being the most frequently produced ballet on world stages.

In the "Kingdom of the Shades" scene of *La Bayadère* and the second act of *Giselle*, Petipa gave ballet a new artistic direction. The union of music and dance became all-important, with the aim of creating an emotional or evocative atmosphere; narration of the story was secondary. This was the dawn of "symphonic dance", to use a term typical of Russian critics. It later developed in the second act of *Swan Lake* (by Ivanov) and *Les Sylphides* (by Fokine). The style went hand-in-hand with the late-nineteenth century's revived interest in the Romantic era, and subsequently attracted twentieth-century choreographers. Not least among them was Balanchine, who preferred to call it "story-less" ballet (it is also called "abstract").

The success of *Giselle* proved no invitation to rest on laurels. The septuagenarian choreographer soon had to beat off a challenge from the popular stage that was threatening to make the Imperial Theatres laughable. All accepted standards of performance were being swept away in an avalanche of dazzling acrobatics from the new Italian school. Petipa's response was *The Sleeping Beauty*, combining art with virtuosity in an encyclopaedia of classical ballet technique. This was his first collaboration with Tchaikovsky, in which he specified the musical requirements in advance.

The Sleeping Beauty, which is better preserved in the West than in Russia (thanks to the interest of the young Vic-Wells ballet, who in 1939 staged the ballet with the assistance of Nicolas Sergeyev's notations from Russia), exemplifies Petipa's main choreographic strength, the ability to create variations for female dancers. Frederick Ashton acknowledged the "finger variation" of its prologue (properly called Fairy Violante) as his favourite in all choreography. Two further Tchaikovsky classics followed, *The Nutcracker* and *Swan Lake*, the latter in revival after undistinguished choreography by Reisinger. Petipa's name is linked with both of them, but generous credit must be given to assistant ballet master Lev Ivanov. (The exact balance of the scales still remains undecided.)

It must be remembered that Petipa was not merely a principal choreographer delegating to a subordinate. He devised the overall creative approach; in other words, he was the artistic director. The charge is sometimes made that Petipa suppressed Ivanov's creativity in favour of his own, but it is not deserved. Fedor Lopukhov asserts that *Swan Lake* is the work of two equal choreographers, with its overall artistic unity counting as the achievement of Petipa.

Largely thanks to Petipa, ballet in St. Petersburg by the late-nineteenth century had long surpassed its Western counterpart. As an octogenarian he remained prolific. Collaboration with the composer Glazunov produced *Raymonda* and *Les Saisons*. But the four-act *Magic Mirror* (1903), with music by Koreshchenko, was a fiasco. It happened when Petipa was already out of favour with the new Director, Telyakovsky, and he was swiftly dismissed.

This unfortunate manner of departure unfairly blighted Petipa's reputation. In the West another adverse influence was the impact of Diaghilev's Ballets Russes; its creations, particularly Fokine's, were heralded as break-aways from Petipa's supposed stagnation. Meanwhile, in revolutionary Russia, ballet criticism deferred to dogma: it was necessary to regard everything pre-revolutionary as in some way inferior. It would have been better for Petipa if he had not been a Westerner and if he had worked in Moscow instead of St. Petersburg. Ultimately, however, it is the latter city that has done his reputation the most service: the principal source is the exhaustive compendium *Marius Petipa* published in Leningrad in 1971.

As the twentieth century draws to its close, it is the richer legacy of Petipa that is being discovered in the West. Full-length classics such as *La Bayadère* and *Raymonda* are being seen by ever-increasing audiences, while strangely enough, Fokine ballets often slip from the repertoire.

—Tony Devereux

PETIT, Roland

French dancer, choreographer, and teacher. Born in Ville-momble, 13 January 1924. Studied with Gustave Ricaux and Serge Lifar, and at Paris Opéra School, from 1934. Married dancer and music-hall artist Renée (Zizi) Jeanmaire; one daughter, Valentine. Début in corps de ballet, Paris Opéra Ballet, 1935: dancer, second quadrille, from 1940, becoming grand sujet, 1943–44; dancer in recitals with M. Bourgat and Janine Charrat, 1941–1943; dancer and choreographer, Vendredis de la danse, Théâtre Sarah-Bernhardt, from 1944; founder (with Boris Kochno and Irène Lidova), principal dancer, and choreographer, Ballets des Champs-Elysées, 1945–47; founder, principal dancer, and choreographer, Ballets de Paris, from 1948, and Revue des Ballets de Paris; choreographer, Ballet du Théâtre National Populaire, 1962–1963; owner/producer and director, Casino de Paris, 1970–75; dance director, Paris Opéra Ballet, February–June 1970; artistic director and chief choreographer, Ballet National de Marseille, from 1972; international guest choreographer, including for Royal Ballet in London, German Opera Ballet in Berlin, Hamburg Ballet, and La Scala, Milan; also choreographer for films, including for Hollywood films *Hans Christian Andersen* (dir. Vidor, 1952), *The Glass Slipper* (dir. Walters, 1954), *Daddy Long Legs* (dir. Negulesco, 1955), *Anything Goes* (dir. Lewis, 1956), French films *Charmant/Garçon* (1957) and *Les Collants noirs* (*Black Tights*; 1960), and for television. Recipient: Officer de l'ordre national du mérite des arts et des lettres, 1962; Chevalier de la Legion d'Honneur, 1974; Grand Prix National des arts et des lettres (for dance), 1979; Prix Bournonville, 1981.

ROLES

1942   Clown (cr) in *Saut du tremplin* (also chor.), Gala, Salle Pleyel, Paris

1943   Amant (cr) in *L'Amour sorcier* (Lifar), Paris Opéra Ballet, Paris

Paul (cr) in *Paul et Virginie* (also chor.), Gala, Salle Pleyel, Paris

1944   Albrecht in *Giselle* (extracts; after Petipa, Coralli, Perrot), Gala, Paris

Orphé (cr) in *Orphé et Eurydice* (also chor., with Charrat), Gala, Salle Pleyel, Paris

Le Jeune Homme (cr) in *La Jeune Fille endormie* (also chor., with Charrat), Gala, Salle Pleyel, Paris

Le Danseur (cr) in *Ballet blanc* (also chor.), Théâtre Sarah-Bernhardt, Paris

Le Poète (cr) in *Le Rossignol et la Rose* (also chor.), Théâtre Sarah-Bernhardt, Paris

Le Danseur noir in *Un Americain à Paris* (also chor.), Théâtre Sarah-Bernhardt, Paris

1945   Mephisto (cr) in *Mephisto Valse* (also chor.), Théâtre Champs-Elysees, Paris

Un Homme (cr) in *Guernica* (also chor.), Théâtre Champs-Elysees, Paris

The Ring Master (cr) in *Les Forains* (Petit), Théâtre Champs-Elysees, Paris

Le Jeune Homme (cr) in *Le Rendezvous* (also chor.), Théâtre Sarah-Bernhardt, Paris

Title role (cr) in *Le Poète* (also chor.), Théâtre Sarah-Bernhardt, Paris

Vagabond (cr) in *Le Déjeuner sur l'herbe* (also chor.), Ballets des Champs-Elysées, Paris

Le Diable (cr) in *La Fiancée du Diable* (also chor.), Ballets des Champs-Elysées, Paris

1946   Toreador in *Los Caprichos* (Nevada), Ballets des Champs-Elysées, Paris

The Swan, the Eagle, Jupiter (cr) in *Les Amours de Jupiter* (also chor.), Ballets des Champs-Elysées, Paris

Butcher Boy (cr) in *Le Bal des Blanchisseuses* (also chor.), Ballets des Champs-Elysées, Paris

Ace of Spades (cr) in *Jeu de cartes* (Charrat), Ballets des Champs-Elysées, Paris

James (cr) in *La Sylphide* (new production; Gsovsky after Taglioni), Ballets des Champs-Elysées, Paris

1947   Un Gilles (cr) in *Treize Danses* (also chor.), Ballets des Champs-Elysées, Paris

1948   Hussar in *Le Beau Danube* (Massine), Ballets de Paris, Paris

Sailor (cr) in *'adame Miroir* (Charrat), Ballets de Paris, Paris

Principal dancer (cr) in *Études symphoniques* (Kniaseff), Ballets de Paris, Paris

The Prince in *The Sleeping Beauty* (extracts; after Petipa), Ballets de Paris, Paris

Musician (cr) in *Les Demoiselles de la nuit* (also chor.), Ballets de Paris, Paris

1949   Le Chef (cr) in *L'Oeuf à la coque* (also chor.), Ballets de Paris, London

Don José (cr) in *Carmen* (also chor.), Ballets de Paris, London

1950   Principal dancer (cr) in *Chaises musicales* (also chor.), Ballets de Paris, Biarritz

Delivery Boy (cr) in *La Croqueuse de diamants* (also chor.), Ballets de Paris, Paris

1953   Cinema fan (cr) in *Cine-Bijou* (also chor.), Ballets de Paris, Paris

The Wolf (cr) in *Le Loup* (also chor.), Ballets de Paris, Paris

1956   Night's Advocate (cr) in *La Nuit* (also chor.), Revue des Ballets de Paris, Paris

Racing Cyclist (cr) in *Valentine; ou, Le Vélo magique* (also chor.), Revue des Ballets de Paris, Paris

1958   Sailor (cr) in *La Rose des vents* (also chor.), Ballets de Paris, Paris

Can-Can dancer (cr) in *La Dame dans la lune* (also chor.), Ballets de Paris, Paris

1959   Title role (cr) in *Cyrano de Bergerac* (also chor.), Ballets de Paris, Paris

1960   Principal dancer (cr) in *Ballet des electrons* (also chor.), Gala, Théâtre des Champs-Elysées, Paris

1962   Maldoror (cr) in *Les Chants de Maldoror* (also chor.), Ballets de Paris, Chaillot

1965   Quasimodo (cr) in *Notre-Dame de Paris* (also chor.), Paris Opéra Ballet, Paris

1971   Principal dancer (cr) in *Show Roland Petit* (also chor.), French television

1972   Maïakvsky (cr) in *Allumez les étoiles* (also chor.), Ballet National de Marseille, Marseilles

1975   Dr. Coppélius (cr) in *Coppélia* (also chor.), Ballet National de Marseille, Paris

1985   Professor Unrat (cr) in *Blue Angel* (also chor.), German Opera Ballet and Ballet de Marseille, Berlin

WORKS

1942   *Saut de tremplin* (text by de Banville), Gala Salle Pleyel, Paris

1943   *Paul et Virginie* (mus. Sauguet), Gala, Salle Pleyel, Paris

1944   *Orphé et Eurydice* (with Charrat; mus. Franck), Gala, Salle Pleyel, Paris

La Jeune Fille endormie (with Charrat; mus. Liszt), Gala, Salle Pleyel, Paris

Roland Petit with Renée (Zizi) Jeanmaire in *Carmen*, Paris, 1956

Ballet blanc (mus. Chopin), Théâtre Sarah-Bernhardt, Paris

Le Rossignol et la Rose (mus. Schumann), Théâtre Sarah-Bernhardt, Paris

Un Americain à Paris (mus. Gershwin), Théâtre Sarah-Bernhardt, Paris

1945 *Fables de La Fontaine* (mus. Hubeau), Gala, Théâtre des Champs-Elysées, Paris

Mephisto Valse (mus. Liszt), Gala, Théâtre des Champs-Elysées, Paris

Guernica (mus. Bonneau), Gala, Théâtre des Champs-Elysées, Paris

Les Forains (mus. Sauguet), Théâtre des Champs-Elysées, Paris

Le Rendezvous (mus. Kosma), Théâtre Sarah-Bernhardt, Paris

Le Poète (mus. Godard, Koechlin), Théâtre Sarah-Bernhardt, Paris

Le Déjeuner sur l'herbe (mus. Lanner, Tcherepnin), Ballets des Champs-Elysées, Paris

La Fiancée du Diable (mus. Paganini, Hubeau), Ballets des Champs-Elysées, Paris

1946 *Les Amours de Jupiter* (mus. Ibert), Ballets des Champs-Elysées, Paris

Le Jeune Homme et la mort (mus. Bach), Ballets des Champs-Elysées, Paris

Le Bal des blanchisseuses (mus. Duke), Ballets des Champs-Elysées, Paris

1947 *Treize Danses* (mus. Gretry), Ballets des Champs-Elysées, Paris

1948 *Les Demoiselles de la nuit* (mus. Françaix), Ballets de Paris, Paris

Que le Diable l'emporte (mus. eighteenth-century, and Rosenthal), Ballets de Paris, Paris

1949 *L'Oeuf à la coque* (mus. Thiriet), Ballets de Paris, London

Carmen (mus. Bizet), Ballets de Paris, London

Pas d'action (mus. Wagner), Ballets de Paris, London

1950 *Ballabile* (mus. Chabrier), Sadler's Wells Ballet, London

Chaises musicales (mus. Auric), Ballets de Paris, Biarritz

La Croqueuse de diamants (mus. Damase), Ballets de Paris, Paris

1953 *Le Loup* (mus. Dutilleux), Ballets de Paris, Paris

Cine-Bijou (mus. P. Petit), Ballets de Paris, Paris

Deuil en 24 heures (mus. Thiriet), Ballets de Paris, Paris
Lady in the Ice (mus. Damase), Ballets de Paris, London
Pas de deux (mus. Liszt), Ballets de Paris, Paris
La Belle au bois dormant (mus. Dutilleux), Ballets de Paris, London

1955 *Les Belles damnées* (mus. Legrand, Damase), Ballets de Paris, Paris
La Chambre (mus. Auric), Ballets de Paris, Paris

1956 *La Nuit* (mus. Ferre), Revue des Ballets de Paris, Paris
Valentine; ou, Le Vélo magique (mus. Legrand), Revue des Ballets de Paris, Paris
La Peur (mus. Constant), Revue des Ballets de Paris, Paris
La Fille aux yeux secs (mus. Legrand), Revue des Ballets de Paris, Paris

1957 *Zizi au Music-Hall* (mus. Beart, Legrand), Alhambra, Paris

1958 *Contrepointe* (mus. Constant), Ballets de Paris, Paris
La Rose des vents (mus. Milhaud), Ballets de Paris, Paris
La Dame dans la lune (mus. Français), Ballets de Paris, Paris

1959 *Cyrano de Bergerac* (mus. Constant), Ballets de Paris, Paris
Patron (operetta; mus. Beart), Théâtre Sarah-Bernhardt, Paris

1960 *Ballet des electrons* (mus. Cornu), Gala, Théâtre des Champs-Elysées, Paris
Rain (mus. Constant), "Zizi à London", London

1961 *La Chaloupée* (mus. Thiriet), Royal Danish Ballet, Copenhagen
Mon truc en plumes (mus. Constantin), Revue des Ballets de Paris, Lyon
España (mus. Chabrier), Revue des Ballets de Paris, Lyon
Scaramouche (mus. Milhaud), Revue des Ballets de Paris, Lyon
Tarantelle (mus. Rossini), Revue des Ballets de Paris, Lyon
Pas de trois (mus. Constant), Revue des Ballets de Paris, Lyon

1962 *Palais de Chaillot* (mus. Berlioz), Ballets de Paris, Paris
Les Chants de Maldoror (mus. Jarre), Ballets de Paris, Paris
Le Violon (mus. Paginini, Constant), Ballets de Paris, Paris
Rhapsodie espagnole (mus. Ravel), Ballets de Paris, Paris

1963 *Les Quatre Saisons* (mus. Vivaldi), Ballet of La Scala, Milan
La Silla, Gourmandises (mus. Mention), Revue des Ballets de Paris, Paris

1965 *Chemins de la creation* (mus. Damase), Ballets de Paris, French television
Notre-Dame de Paris (mus. Jarre), Paris Opéra Ballet, Paris
Adage et variations (mus. Poulenc, Français), Paris Opéra Ballet, Paris

1966 *Eloge de la folie* (mus. Constant), Ballets de Paris, Paris

1967 *Paradise Lost* (mus. Constant), Royal Ballet, London
24 Preludes (mus. Constant), Hamburg Ballet, Hamburg
Formes (pas de deux; mus. Constant), Paris Opéra Ballet, Montreal

1968 *La Voix humaine* (text by Cocteau), Zizi Jeanmaire solo, Florence
Turangalila (mus. Messiaen), Paris Opéra Ballet, Paris
L'Estasi (mus. Scriabin), Ballet of La Scala, Milan
Show Zizi (mus. Robrecht), Olympia, Paris

1969 *Quatre Études et une sonate* (mus. Chopin), Théâtre de Ville, Paris

Pelléas et Mélisande (mus. Schoenberg), Royal Ballet, London
Krannerg (mus. Xenakis), National Ballet of Canada, Ottawa

1970 *La Revue de Roland Petit*, Zizi et Les Danseurs du Casino, Casino de Paris
Pas de deux (mus. Verdier), Zizi Jeanmaire et Jean-Pierre Bonnefous, French television

1971 *Show Roland Petit* (mus. Pink Floyd, Gainsbourg, Marceau), French television
Pas de deux (mus. Kabelac), UNESCO Gala, Paris

1972 *Pink Floyd Ballet* (mus. Pink Floyd), Ballet National de Marseille, Marseilles
Zizi, je t'aime (mus. Drigo, Kreisler), Casino de Paris, Paris
Allumez les étoiles (mus. Prokofiev, Tchaikovsky, Mussorgsky), Ballet National de Marseille, Marseilles
Divertissement russe (popular Russian music), Ballet National de Marseille, Avignon

1973 *La Rose malade* (mus. Mahler), Ballet National de Marseille, Paris

1974 *Les Intermittences du coeur* (mus. various), Opéra de Monte Carlo, Monte Carlo
L'Arlésienne (mus. Bizet), Ballet National de Marseille, Marseilles
Jeux d'enfants (mus. Bizet), Ballet National de Marseille, Marseilles
Schéhérazade (mus. Ravel), Paris Opéra Ballet, Paris
Estudios y Preludios (mus. Villa-Lobos), Ballet National de Marseille, Marseilles
Top à Zizi (pas de deux; mus. Gainsbourg and others), French television
Et ils auront des rêves d'archange (mus. Papathanassiou), French television

1975 *La Symphonie fantastique* (mus. Berlioz), Paris Opéra Ballet, Paris
Coppélia (new version; mus. Delibes), Ballet National de Marseille, Paris
Une heure avec Roland Petit et Rudy Bryans, French television
Septentrion (mus. Constant), Ballet National de Marseille, Marseilles
Pas de deux (mus. Schubert), Paris Opéra Ballet, Paris
Variations chromatiques (mus. Bizet), Ballet National de Marseille, Paris (television version, 1978)

1976 *La Nuit transfigurée* (mus. Schoenberg), Paris Opéra Ballet, Paris
Nana (mus. Constant), Paris Opéra Ballet, Paris
Mouvances (mus. Verdi), Paris Opéra Ballet, Paris
Casse-Noisette (*The Nutcracker*; mus. Tchaikovsky), Ballet National de Marseille, Paris

1977 *Perfume Suite*, French television
Blues (solo; mus. S. Williams, M. Davies), Ballet National de Marseille, Marseilles
À la memoire d'un ange (mus. Berg), Ballet National de Marseille, Marseilles
Fascinating Rhythm (mus. Gershwin), Ballet National de Marseille, Marseilles
Zizi dans un Spectacle de Roland Petit, Bobino, Paris

1978 *Barres parallèles* (mus. M. Davies), French television
Variation (solo; mus. Hoffmann), Théâtre de Ville, Paris
Tango (mus. Stravinsky), Théâtre de Ville, Paris
Ragtime (mus. Stravinsky), Ballet National de Marseille, Marseilles
La Dame de pique (mus. Tchaikovsky), Ballet National de Marseille, Paris

1979 *Thême et variations* (mus. Tchaikovsky), Ballet National de Marseille, Paris

La Chauve-Souris (mus. Strauss), Ballet National de Marseille, Monte Carlo

Parisiana 25 (mus. various), Ballet National de Marseille, Marseilles

1980 *Le Fantôme de l'Opéra* (mus. Landowski), Paris Opéra Ballet, Paris

The Miraculous Mandarin (mus. Bartók), Ballet of La Scala, Milan

1981 *Les Amours de Frantz* (mus. Schubert), Ballet National de Marseille, Marseilles

Six Danses (mus. Chabrier), Ballet National de Marseille, Paris

Can-Can (musical; mus. Porter), Broadway, New York

Rosa (mus. York), Ballet National de Marseille, Marseilles

1982 *Les Contes d'Hoffmann* (mus. Offenbach), Ballet National de Marseille, Monte Carlo

Soirée Debussy (mus. Debussy), Ballet National de Marseille, Marseilles

Les Hauts de Hurlavent (mus. Landowski), Ballet National de Marseille, Paris

Sonate (mus. Franck), Moscow Classical Ballet, Moscow

Choros (mus. Villa-Lobos), Moscow Classical Ballet, Moscow

Pas de deux d'espace, de temps, de matière, de mouvement (mus. Landowski), Ballet National de Marseille, Paris

1983 *Divertissement* (mus. Pink Floyd), Piccolo Scala, Milan

La Danse du feu (mus. de Falla), Ballet National de Marseille, Monte Carlo

1984 *Marriage of Heaven and Hell* (mus. Art Zoyd), Ballet of La Scala, Milan

Pelléas et Mélisande (new production; mus. Debussy), Ballet National de Marseille, Marseilles

Symphonie (mus. Constant), Ballet National de Marseille, Marseilles

La Mer (mus. Debussy), Ballet National de Marseille, Marseilles

Children's Corner (mus. Debussy), Ballet National de Marseille, Marseilles

Hollywood Paradise (mus. Assous), Ballet National de Marseille, Marseilles

Les Quatre Saisons (mus. Vivaldi), Ballet National de Marseille, Venice

1985 *Le Chat botté* (mus. Tchaikovsky), Ballet National de Marseille, Paris

Blue Angel (mus. Constant), German Opera Ballet, Berlin

1986 *My Pavlova* (mus. various), Ballet National de Marseille, Barcelona

1988 *Tout Satie* (mus. Satie), Ballet National de Marseille, Marseilles

Valentine's Love Songs (mus. Art Zoyd), Ballet National de Marseille, Marseilles

Java for Ever (mus. various), Opéra-Comique, Paris

1989 *Le Diable amoureux* (mus. Yared), Ballet National de Marseille, Naples

Les Valses de Ravel (mus. Ravel), Ballet National de Marseille, Marseilles

1990 *Debussy pour sept danseurs* (mus. Debussy), Paris Opéra Ballet, Paris

1991 *Charlot parmi nous* (mus. Bach, Chaplin, Carpi), Ballet National de Marseille, Marseilles

1992 *La Valse triste* (mus. Sibelius), Rome Opera Ballet, Rome

Also staged:

1990 *La Belle au bois dormant* (*The Sleeping Beauty*; after Petipa; mus. Tchaikovsky), Ballet National de Marseille, Marseilles

PUBLICATIONS

By Petit:

Interview in *Dance Digest* (San José, California), November 1958

Interview in Vaughan, David, "Shop Talk with Roland Petit and Zizi", *Dance and Dancers* (London), December 1960

Interview in Dupis, Simone, "Roland Petit", *Les Saisons de la danse* (Paris), 10 February 1980

About Petit:

Michaut, Pierre, *Le Ballet contemporain*, Paris, 1950

Craig-Raymond, Peter, *Roland Petit*, Surbiton, Surrey, 1953

Lidova, Irène, *Dix-Sept Visages de la danse française*, Paris, 1953

Beaumont, Cyril, *Ballets of Today*, London, 1954

Lidova, Irène, *Roland Petit*, Paris, 1956

Lidova, Irène, "Roland Petit", *Les Saisons de la danse* (Paris), Summer 1968

Williams, Peter, "Roland Petit at Covent Garden", *About the House* (London), March 1976

Barnes, Clive, "Barnes on Roland Petit", *Ballet News* (New York), August 1980

Crisp, Clement, "A Talent to Amuse", *Ballet News* (New York), August 1980

Koenig, J.-F., *La Danse contemporaine*, Paris, 1980

Ballet National de Marseille, Paris, 1981

Croce, Arlene, *Going to the Dance*, New York, 1982

Mannoni, G., *L'avant-scène "Ballet danse" Special Roland Petit*, Paris, 1984

Mannoni, G., *Roland Petit: Un Choréographe et ses peintres*, Paris, 1990

Mannoni, G., *Petit: Un Choréographe et ses danseurs*, Paris, 1992

*　　*　　*

In a 1956 interview, Roland Petit described the three elements which he considered essential to a ballet: "The shock of music, the shock of steps and the shock of light". The desire to make his audiences sit up and take notice has been a constant factor throughout his career.

His career began at the School of the Paris Opéra but his external contacts with the French intelligentsia and the post-war world of art quickly made activities at the Opéra seem too narrowly contained, and he began to choreograph elsewhere with sufficient success to attract the attention of such figures as Boris Kochno, Irène Lidova, and Christian Bérard. When Petit became the main choreographer of the Ballets des Champs-Elysées, these three, especially Boris Kochno, performed the function of a Diaghilev, guiding the artistic format of his ballets, helping to form his style, and bringing him considerable success.

For most of his career Petit has constructed his ballets on the same principles. His ballets are rarely abstract. Each has a strong theme or a strong story-line, frequently an adaptation of a well-known literary or theatrical source, that will provide opportunities for strong characterizations and theatrical situations. His collaborators are chosen for the impact their work will have in the theatre; he has worked with designers such as Clave and Fini, and composers such as Françaix,

Dutilleux, and Constant. He has a notable record for commissioning scores, but also makes use of music already successfully used in the theatre, as in *Coppélia* and *Die Fledermaus*, or *La Chauve-Souris*. This is all very much part of his Diaghilev legacy, the creation of a balanced, well-constructed ballet that draws equal attention to all the various elements. There are other influences. The tradition of the music hall—its need to entertain, its nostalgia, and sentimentality—is also part of the Petit style. This is partly derived from Cocteau, with whom the choreographer collaborated on *Le Jeune Homme et la mort*. The philosophical movements current in his youth have also influenced him, especially existentialism. The idea that a person creates his own values by his actions and that each moment must be lived to the full are essential to the impulses that motivate the central characters of many of his ballets.

It is Petit's earlier ballets for the Ballets des Champs-Elysées or for his own early companies that have survived, notably *Carmen*, *Le Jeune Homme et la mort*, and *Le Loup*. The lighter, more entertaining works such as *La Croqueuse de diamants* have disappeared. Despite considerable success in their day, the choreographic content of these works has failed to outlive their essentially 1950s sense of chic. What today has become a rather stereotyped "French" allure is an essential ingredient of all his ballets of the period. Almost before Balanchine, he discovered the sexy appeal of the long-legged ballerina as exemplified by Colette Marchand and others.

The movement employed in Petit's early ballets is a lively mixture. The basic steps are simple and classical, but often executed from turned-in positions: indeed, the contrast between "turn-in" and "turn-out" is often what gives his ballets their provocative sexual quality. Such movements are contrasted with the more showy classical steps, such as fast turns and jumps. The inward-turned movement provides the character, while the classical steps provide the excitement. Put together in the same sequence this combination can result in a very heady theatrical experience, especially if performed by a Jeanmaire as Carmen or a Cragun in *Notre-Dame de Paris*. Petit also uses natural movement to heighten effect—kicks, rolls, and everyday gestures such as lighting a cigarette or washing hands often punctuate the ballet's action. Sound too is used for emphasis—for example rhythmical stamps, hand claps, or even the clatter of saucepan lids in *L'Oeuf à la coque*. Dancers break into song to increase the momentum and theatrical effect. In short, the theatrical effect is everything. In a Petit pas de deux, the movement is not necessarily interesting or inventive in terms of classical vocabulary, but given the right dancers it is sufficient to create a mood and to enable the dancers to build very positive characterizations.

Movement for the corps de ballet is less inventive and consists mostly of big, bold group movements in sweeping circles and lines. Together with the décor and lighting, the typical Petit corps de ballet is used to heighten tension, when the actual choreographic movement for them is often rather dull. Where he is obliged to provide divertissements in the later full-length ballets, these can often be rather forced. Obviously not a natural "ensemble" choreographer, Petit demands personality and an ability to project from all his dancers, and for this purpose has always been ready to find and promote fresh talent from the ranks.

Petit's earlier ballets were all in one act, but he was also one of the earliest choreographers to experiment with and tour full-length ballets. The first, *Cyrano de Bergerac*, proved to be difficult to stage convincingly. The basic idea of a love affair carried on by a substitute by letter was not easy to interpret by dance means alone, although Petit solved this rather ingeniously (if not altogether credibly), by means of a pas de trois. *Cyrano* was successful enough, however, to be mounted by

the Royal Danish Ballet, and at this point Petit's career was typically that of a successful visiting choreographer, his ballets being mounted by many international companies. How own companies tended to be intermittent and he returned to the Opéra to mount a second full-length ballet—a modern version of the old classic *La Esmeralda*, now called *Notre-Dame de Paris*—but he declined the offer to return as director. He did not settle until 1972, when he became director of the Ballet de Marseille. Until his arrival, the Ballet de Marseille was a typical European opera house company which had achieved little distinction. Since becoming its director, Petit has concentrated on full-evening ballets and by now has probably produced more full-length works than any other choreographer working today. His full-length works continue to be constructed with the same skills as his earlier one-act ballets: a good literary, familiar story-line, strong characters for the principal dancers, and theatrically effective (but still essentially weak) corps de ballet work. His collaborators in music and design have continued to make theatrical impact, as in Svodoba's moving scenery in *Le Chat botté* and the barracks by Frigerio at the opening of *Coppélia*. He is still at his most expressive in pas de deux, and at times he shown a greater lyricism, as in his *Les Amours de Frantz*. The full-length ballets have enabled him to build up a solid repertory and to attract and develop leading dancers who have the technique and powers of characterization to carry off such works successfully. Few of these later works, however, show signs of entering the general repertory in a period in which such works are in great demand throughout the world.

Roland Petit's "other" career has been spent in the light entertainment areas of the theatre and film, most successfully in the Parisian music halls. He owned the Casino de Paris for five years in the 1970s, staging lavish spectacles built around his wife Zizi Jeanmaire's saucy, gamine stage personality. These offered considerable scope for his ability to create theatrical spectacle, but interestingly also reflect his shortcomings as a choreographer. Such works tellingly do not translate well out of the theatre into other media: both video and film of the lighter works look superficial, appearing contrived and too obviously "French" in their rather dated, coy naughtiness.

Three of Petit's ballets have recently been revived at the Paris Opéra and have retained all their ability to surprise, if not shock, a new generation. His ballets tend to leave a series of arresting photographic images in the memory rather than a flow of movement. He is a Helpmann rather than an Ashton, but his prime asset of theatricality has made him one of the most enduring of twentieth-century choreographers.

—Peter Bassett

LES PETITS RIENS

Choreography: Jean-Georges Noverre
Music: Wolfgang Amadeus Mozart
First Production: Théâtre de l'Académie royale de musique (Paris Opéra), 11 June 1778
Principal Dancers: Marie-Madeleine Guimard, Marie Allard (Bergères), Auguste Vestris, Jean Dauberval

Other productions include: King's Theatre (restaged Noverre; new mus. Barthélemon); London, 11 November 1781. Pupils of Marie Rambert (new version, using parts of score; chor.

Les Petits Riens: an anonymous costume design for a "Berger Galant"

Frederick Ashton), as *Suite de danses*; London, 23 July 1927 (probably basis of *Nymphs and Shepherds*; London, 9 March 1928). Old Vic Theatre (new version; chor. Ninette de Valois, mus. arranged Lambert), as *Les Petits Riens*; London, 13 December 1928. Marie Rambert Dancers (later Ballet Club, and eventually Ballet Rambert; chor. Ashton, probably revision and expansion of previous versions), as *Dances from "Les Petits Riens"*; London, 25 February 1930. Vic-Wells Ballet (new version; chor. Ninette de Valois); London, 1931. Royal Ballet School (new version; chor. David Bintley); London, 20 July 1991.

PUBLICATIONS

Lynham, Deryck, *The Chevalier Noverre*, London, 1950

Beaumont, Cyril, *Complete Book of Ballets*, revised edition, London, 1951

Nettl, Paul, "Mozart: Man of Genius Who Loved the Dance", *Dance Magazine* (New York), January 1957

Nettl, Paul, *Mozart und der Tanz*, Zurich, 1960

Brinson, Peter, and Crisp, Clement, *Ballet for All*, London, 1970

Vaughan, David, *Frederick Ashton and his Ballets*, London, 1977

Osborne, Charles, *The Complete Operas of Mozart*, London, 1978

*   *   *

"Slight is the subject, but not the praise": Pope's verse might easily be applied to Mozart's only full-length score devoted purely to ballet. Mozart's delightful gift for lyric inspiration provoked by the slenderest of subjects is well demonstrated by his music for Noverre's little jeu d'esprit, *Les Petit Riens* (*The Little Trifles*). The original libretto has been lost, but descriptions survive in the *Journal de Paris* of 12 June 1778, and from the pen of Mozart's friend and ally in the foreign world of French music, Baron von Grimm. The baron describes it as a succession of unconnected anacreontic tableaux "of which the brush of a Boucher or a Watteau need not have been ashamed".

Cupid is caught in a net and put in a cage in the first scene, which was danced by Mlle. Guimard and Auguste Vestris; the second scene involved a game of blind man's buff, danced by Dauberval; however, the third scene is the one which attracted most comment, with its cheeky dénouement in which a shepherdess (Mlle. Asselin), disguised as a man, proves her gender by baring a breast to end a jealous dispute over her between two infatuated shepherdesses (Mlles. Guimard and Allard). The *Journal* noted that the scene was greeted by a mixture of protest and applause, and the baron, commenting that "decency still exercises a very strong hold on our stage", seemed surprised both by the event itself, and by the "modesty" of Mlle Asselin under the circumstances. Unfortunately, neither commented on the choreography, beyond lavish praise for the dancers (it was, after all, a star-studded cast).

We do not know how complex either the choreography or the libretto of *Les Petits Riens* were; the dramatic sophistication of much of Noverre's Paris work, and his tendency during this period to experiment with more difficult subjects for dance and pantomime, might lead one to suspect a piece as difficult as, for example, the similarly anacreontic *Les Caprices de Galathée*, a psychologically sophisticated ballet which deals with a flirtatious shepherdess and the subtleties of Cupid, probably demanding a good deal of mime. On the other hand, *Les Petits Riens*, coming shortly after Noverre's re-staging of *Caprices* (the same sets were used for both), found much more favour with its audience, and this suggests that it was less ambitious. Whether *Les Petits Riens* represented a relaxation of Noverre's ideals about the integration of dance and mime, and an attempt to produce a crowd-pleaser (as the bit of comic sensationalism suggests), or whether it simply represented a *relaxation*, as the name itself suggests, we may never know.

However, it is not for its choreography that *Les Petits Riens* is remembered today, but for its music. It comes from Mozart's unrewarding six-month stay in Paris, during which Noverre had befriended the young composer. They initially discussed a commission for an opera, which came to nothing, but in a letter to his father of 14 May 1778, Mozart suddenly mentions the prospect of a ballet, and then, as suddenly, reports its performance to his father in a letter of 9 July, the same letter in which he breaks the news of his mother's death six days before. This sad event may account for the disillusioned and dismissive tone in which he discusses the ballet: "As for Noverre's ballet, all that I ever told you was that he might perhaps design a new one . . . Six pieces in it are composed by others and are made up entirely of wretched old French airs, while the overture and contredanses, about twelve pieces in all, have been contributed by me. This ballet has already been performed four times with the greatest applause. But I am now determined not to compose anything more, unless I know beforehand what I am going to get for it".

In fact, Mozart was paid nothing for it, and even worse perhaps, in view of Leopold's persistent pressure on his son to achieve fame in Paris, Mozart's name did not even appear on the programme (in fact the ballet was only restored to the Mozart canon after its discovery in the Opéra library in 1872—hence its appearance in Köchel's Appendix, where it is No. 10). The off-hand fashion, however, in which Mozart describes all the pieces as "contredanses" is misleading, for the thirteen surviving pieces believed to be his are sharply distinctive, one from another, as dance music. Numbers 2, 6, 9 and 12 are all marked as gavottes, Number 11 as a passepied, and 10 is explicitly marked "Pantomime" (its character and position in the score suggest that it was for the flirtation scene of the deluded shepherdesses); Number 8, which is unmarked, has a lively gigue-like style. Folk tunes had long been a staple of such dance music and Mozart, in spite of his disparaging of the French airs used by the others, availed himself of a Czech folk song ("Let us go to Bethlehem", perhaps chosen for a playful association with shepherds) and a French folk song ("Charmante Gabrielle"). Indeed, he would be most unpleased today by musicologists' indecisiveness about exactly which of the tunes are his and which are those wretched French airs, but many of the pieces are unmistakably Mozart's. The Overture, scored, unlike the dances, for full orchestra, anticipates passages in *Die Entführung*, while the flute melodies of Number 3 recall *Die Zauberflöte*, and Number 5 echoes the last movement of the piano quartet in E flat (K. 493).

How Noverre felt about the score is unclear: when he revived the ballet in 1781 for the King's Theatre, London, he used a score by Barthélemon—but this may simply have been a reworking of Mozart's score. It is also possible that Mozart's score was not available to him, or, since Noverre had very specific views on ballet music, it may be that he was never satisfied with it: scholars have pointed out that Mozart's charming little pieces lack the cohesion and development of the ballet scores by Starzer and Rodolphe for Noverre, but these seem inappropriate comparisons in view of the disconnectedly casual series of tableaux for which Mozart had been asked to compose.

If Noverre was not pleased, later choreographers have been, notably Ninette de Valois, who chose Mozart's score for her first ballet, and Ashton, who returned to it more than once during his career. Inspired by a play about Mozart, Ashton created, with Rambert, his *Suite de danses*, first performed on 23 July 1927 to the music of *Les Petits Riens*. A fuller version was done in 1928 by the pupils of Rambert, and yet another version entitled *Dances from "Les Petits Riens"* was given in 1930. This was a period marked by a creative antiquarianism for Ashton, during which he did a great deal of choreography inspired by early music and dance, but it is fitting that as late as the 1960s he was again contemplating a ballet to Mozart's score, having already danced the role of Noverre in de Valois' ballet, *The Prospect Before Us*.

—Kathryn Kerby-Fulton

PETRUSHKA
(French title: *Petrouchka*)

Choreography: Mikhail Fokine
Music: Igor Stravinsky
Design: Alexandre Benois (scenery and costumes)
Libretto: Igor Stravinsky and Alexandre Benois
First Production: Diaghilev's Ballets Russes, Théâtre du Châtelet, Paris, 13 June 1911
Principal Dancers: Vaslav Nijinsky (Petrushka), Tamara Karsavina (The Ballerina), Alexandre Orlov (The Moor), Enrico Cecchetti (The Old Showman)

Other productions include: Metropolitan Opera House (staged Adolph Bolm after Fokine), with Bolm (Petrushka); New York, 1919. State Maryinsky Theatre (staged Leonid Leontiev after Fokine); with Leontiev (Petrushka), Elena Lukom (Ballerina), Vasily Vainonen (Moor); Petrograd, 20 November 1920. Royal Danish Ballet (restaged Fokine); Copenhagen, 21 October 1925. La Scala (staged Boris Romanov after Fokine), with Cia Fornaroli (Ballerina); Milan, 1925. Ballet de l'Opéra Russe à Paris (staged, with some alterations, Bronislava Nijinska after Fokine); Paris, January 1931. Ballet de l'Opéra Russe à Paris (staged Léon Woizikowsky after Fokine); London, 1931. Les Ballets Russes de Monte Carlo (staged Woizikowsky after Fokine); Monte Carlo, 19 April 1932. (René Blum's) Ballets de Monte Carlo (restaged Fokine), 1936. Original Ballet Russe (restaged Fokine), with Yurek Lazowski (Petrushka), Tamara Toumanova (The Ballerina), Alberto Alonso (The Moor); New York, 21 November 1940. (American) Ballet Theatre (restaged Fokine), with Yurek Lazowski (Petrushka), Irina Baronova (Ballerina), David Nillo (Blackamoor); Mexico City, 27 August 1942. Paris Opéra Ballet (staged Serge Lifar and Nicholas Zverev after Fokine); Paris, 7 April 1948. London Festival Ballet (staged Nicholas Beriozoff after Fokine), with Anton Dolin (Petrushka); Southsea, 15 August 1950. Royal Ballet (staged Serge Grigoriev, Lubov Tchernicheva after Fokine), with Alexander Grant (Petrushka), Margot Fonteyn (Ballerina), Peter Clegg (Blackamoor), Frederick Ashton (Showman); London, 26 March 1957. Maly Theatre Ballet (staged Konstantin Boyarsky after Fokine), with Valery Panov (Petrushka); Leningrad, 1961 (restaged Bolshoi Theatre, Moscow, 1964). Joffrey Ballet (staged Léonide Massine, Yurek Lazowski, Tatiana Massine after Fokine), with Edward Verso (Petrushka), Erika Goodman (Ballerina), Christian Holder (Blackamoor); New York, 12 March 1970.

Essen State Opera Ballet (new version; chor. Kurt Jooss, design

H. Heckroth); Essen, 1930. German State Opera Ballet (new version; chor. Tatjana Gsovsky, design W. Schmidt); Berlin, 1946. German Opera on the Rhine (new version; chor. Erich Walter); Düsseldorf, 30 April 1966. Ballet du XXe Siècle (new version; chor. Maurice Béjart); Brussels, 1977. Hamburg Ballet (new version; chor. John Neumeier); Nijinsky Gala, Hamburg, 26 June 1982. Scottish Ballet (new version; chor. Oleg Vinogradov); Glasgow, 23 March 1989 (revised version, Kirov Ballet, Leningrad, 1990).

PUBLICATIONS

Cocteau, Jean, *La Saison russe*, Paris, 1911
Beaumont, Cyril, *Petrouchka*, London, 1919
Beaumont, Cyril, *Michel Fokine and his Ballets*, London, 1935
Benois, Alexandre, *Reminiscences of the Russian Ballet*, London, 1941
Beaumont, Cyril, *Complete Book of Ballets*, revised edition, London, 1951
Grigoriev, Serge, *The Diaghilev Ballet*, translated by Vera Bowen, London, 1953
Barnes, Clive, "The Birth and Death of *Petrouchka*", *Dance Magazine* (New York), September 1957
Karsavina, Tamara, "Benois the Magician", *Ballet Annual* (London), vol. 15, 1961
Fokine, Michel, *Fokine: Memoirs of a Ballet Master*, translated by Vitale Fokine, London, 1961
Maynard, Olga, "*Petrouchka*", *Dance Magazine* (New York), February 1970
Vaughan, David, "Fokine in the Contemporary Repertory", *Ballet Review* (New York), vol. 7, no. 2–3, 1978–79
White, Eric Walter, *Stravinsky: The Composer and his Works*, Berkeley, Cal., 1979
Horwitz, Dawn Lille, *Michel Fokine*, Boston, 1985
Garafola, Lynn, *Diaghilev's Ballets Russes*, New York, 1989

* * *

Petrushka, the Fokine/Stravinsky/Benois ballet about the *commedia*-based puppet who turns out to be immortal, is considered by many to be the masterpiece of the Diaghilev Ballets Russes, a complete theatrical conception never again equalled, and a supreme example of story-telling in ballet. It was also the climax of the early Diaghilev period, of Fokine's association with him, and of the group's collective achievement.

The plot, revealed in four scenes with no interval, is set during the annual Butterweek Fair, the Russian version of Mardi Gras. The first scene opens on a square filled with diverse people—peasants, aristocrats, soldiers, gypsies, nursemaids, street performers, and vendors. Their varied and multiple activities are interrupted by the appearance of a bearded Showman, who presents his three puppets—the doll-like Ballerina, the opulent Moor, the sad Petrushka—performing a short mechanical dance. Scene 2 takes place in Petrushka's dark cell, dominated by a portrait of the Showman, and reveals the puppet's awkward and despairing love for the self-involved and uncomprehending Ballerina. Scene 3 shifts to the Moor's warm red room, where he plays with a coconut and allows the admiring Ballerina momentarily to distract him. His rage at Petrushka's entrance results in a chase. In the last scene, back at the fair, Petrushka runs out of the Showman's booth followed by the Moor, who kills him. The crowd is horrified, but the Showman picks up the limp puppet, proving to them that it is simply a doll. As the Fair ends, the ghost of Petrushka appears above the rooftop, both threatening and triumphant.

Petrushka: costume designs by Alexandre Benois for the Ballerina and Petrushka, Paris, 1911

None of these characters is new: Petrushka is the Russian version of Pierrot, the Ballerina is related to Columbine, and the Showman to the Doctor of the *commedia dell'arte*. The Moor can be traced back to earlier characters such as the Turk and the medieval wildman.

Choreographically, this is a remarkable ballet. Fokine dealt with solo elements, crowd scenes, and ensembles, and managed to blend them together in such a way that each element emerges and then returns seamlessly to the whole. This work, most particularly the solos, utilized all of his theories of expressive dance. It was created under the most difficult conditions in a hot, stuffy, carpeted basement in Rome.

The Ballerina and the Moor are obviously puppet dolls. His steps, on legs which are always turned out, are gauche, ponderous, and almost primitive. The Ballerina is gay and dainty; she dances on pointe in a very feminine way, but in her mechanical manner is never human. Petrushka, whose legs are always turned in, performs the most natural steps, although at times he is stiff and doll-like. His staccato movements reveal him as a puppet, but somehow his gestures indicate that, unlike the other two, there are human emotions inside him, which finally well up convulsively.

The ensemble dances are basically national in character, but they are the result of crowd action, not spectator divertissements as seen previously in ballets. Outstanding are the coachmen, the grooms, the wet nurses, and the street dancer. The crowd itself uses over 100 choreographic themes, and the eye goes many places at once. Fokine's adept handling of the crowd influenced many later choreographers.

Much of the impact of *Petrushka* was due to the talents and acting of the original cast: Tamara Karsavina as the Ballerina, Enrico Cecchetti as the Showman, Alexandre Orlov as the Moor, and Vaslav Nijinsky as Petrushka.

The influence of Alexandre Benois on the work was probably greater than is credited. As librettist and designer, it was he who created the story, filled with characters and vignettes, to music that had already been produced by a composer with his own definite ideas. In his memoirs, Benois says that he had been familiar with Petrushka since his childhood when he had seen travelling Punch and Judy shows. He added the Blackamoor because he recalled a separate intermezzo with two Blackamoors during these street performances. Not only did he design individual costumes for dozens of characters, making each a unique individual, but he also created, in the original version, a merry-go-round for children, windmills, a samovar, and gingerbread stalls, as well as buildings around the square, the Showman's booth, and assorted vendors' carts.

Igor Stravinsky's score is a popular masterpiece that is often presented on its own in the concert hall. It evokes the atmosphere, the sights, and the sounds of the Fair, as well as the despondent and spiritual side of Petrushka in his cell, the Ballerina waltzing in the Moor's cell, and the magic of the Showman, while integrating old Russian themes. In his autobiography, Stravinsky was very critical of Fokine's choreography in relation to the music, failing to remember that the work was created to a piano score. Others, however, have found Fokine's interpretation of the music accompanying the action in Petrushka's cell inadequate. Coming before *Sacre*, this score was, in many ways, just as avant garde, and many in the audience did not understand it.

Fokine points out that the creative process for this work was not a simultaneous mutual method; rather, each artist showed Petrushka's suffering in his own way. But with the blend of music, visual elements, and brilliant dancing, *Petrushka* was a great success in 1911 and, when carefully reconstructed, is still quite relevant.

—Dawn Lille Horwitz

PHARAOH'S DAUGHTER

(original Russian title: *Doch Faraona*; also known as *La Fille du Pharaon*)

Choreography: Marius Petipa
Music: Cesare Pugni
Design: A. Roller, G. Wagner (scenery), Kelwer and Stolyakov (costumes)
Libretto: Jules-Henri Vernoy de Saint-Georges and Marius Petipa (partly after Théophile Gautier's *Le Roman de la momie*)
First Production: Bolshoi Theatre, St. Petersburg, 30 January (18 January old style) 1862
Principal Dancers: Carolina Rosati (Mummy/Aspicia), Nicholas Goltz (Pharaoh), Marius Petipa (Ta-Hor), Lev Ivanov (Fisherman)

Other productions: Bolshoi Theatre (restaged Petipa), with Praskovia Lebedeva (Aspicia); Moscow, 29 November (17 November old style) 1864. Bolshoi Theatre (staged Aleksandr Gorsky after Petipa), with Vasily Tikhomirov (English Tourist), G. Grimaldi (Mummy/Bunt-Anta); Moscow, 27 November 1905.

PUBLICATIONS

Benois, Alexander, *Memoirs of the Russian Ballet*, London, 1941

Beaumont, Cyril, *Complete Book of Ballets*, revised edition, London, 1951

Petipa, Marius, *Russian Ballet Master: The Memoirs of Marius Petipa*, translated by Helen Wittaker, edited by Lillian Moore, London, 1958

Romanovsky-Krassinsky, S.A.S. La Princesse (Kshessinskaya, Mathilde), *Souvenirs de la Kschessinska*, Paris, 1960

Krasovskaya, Vera, *Russian Ballet Theatre of the Second Half of the Nineteenth Century*, Leningrad and Moscow, 1963

Roslavleva, Natalia, *Era of the Russian Ballet*, London, 1966

Kirstein, Lincoln, *Movement and Metaphor: Four Centuries of Ballet*, New York, 1970

Vazem, Ekaterina, *Reminiscences of a Ballerina of the St. Petersburg Bolshoi Theatre*, Moscow, 1937; as "Memoirs of a Ballerina . . .", translated by Nina Dimitrievitch, *Dance Research* (London), 4 parts: Summer 1985, Spring 1986, Spring 1987, Autumn 1988

Wiley, Roland John, *A Century of Russian Ballet: Documents and Accounts 1810–1910*, Oxford, 1990

*   *   *

Even if *Pharaoh's Daughter*, or *La Fille du Pharaon*, has not been in repertory since the beginning of this century, its importance lies in the fact that it was in this ballet that Carolina Rosati danced her farewell to Russia and it was the occasion for Petipa's appointment as second ballet master. It was also a product of the choreographic trend parallel to that of the grand opera in music, towards the ballet *à grand spectacle*, which lasted four hours and used different styles and techniques and a large number of people (about four hundred), with plots characterized by strong dramatic contrasts.

Interest in ancient Egypt was revived by archeological and political events—the discovery in 1851 by Auguste Mariette of the Serapeum at Memphis and the digging of the Suez Canal in 1859—and by the reports of the educated élite returning from the Grand Tour.

The ballet's literary source is *Le Roman de la momie* by Théophile Gautier, the exponent of literary exoticism which offered all sorts of romantic expedients: the passionate love story of the great priest's daughter Tahoser and the Pharaoh set in a Biblical Egypt which, however, disappeared in the ballet, and the Gothic taste for gloomy corridors and dark tombs. What the ballet retains of Gautier's world is the sense of the fantastic which accompanies the most earthly passions. A fragment of the past or a puff of opium—a familiar influence in the works and lives of contemporary artists, such as De Quincey—gave Gautier the possibility of adding a brighter aura to his characters by setting them on the borderline between life and death from which all Egyptian art took nourishment.

So as not to overwhelm his readers with terror, Gautier frequently appeals to irony, which has an anticlimactic effect. Irony serves the same function in the ballet, for example in the moment when Lord Wilson, the quintessence of Englishness, impassively attempts to sketch the scene of the desert disturbed by the simoom, or when Aspicia, the Pharaoh's daughter, after rising from the sarcophagus, looks into a mirror and is pleased to find herself as pretty as she was a few millennia before.

The plot of the ballet shows Lord Wilson and his servant John Bull, who have come to Egypt in search of antiquities, seeking shelter during a windstorm in a pyramid together with an Armenian caravan. After finding refuge near a niche containing a royal sarcophagus, they smoke a pipe of opium and fall into a deep sleep. The Pharaoh's daughter then comes back to life and the two Englishmen are transformed into the noble Ta-Hor and his slave Passifont.

Ta-Hor falls in love with Aspicia and, during a lion-hunt, rescues her. He is invited to the palace where the king of Nubia arrives and asks to marry Aspicia. The two lovers, pursued by the king, escape to the Nile and take refuge in a fisherman's hut. Aspicia, momentarily alone, is discovered by her royal suitor and is forced to throw herself into the waters. At the bottom of the river she is greeted by the Nile itself, who appears in a festival of the rivers, and she asks to be reunited with her beloved. At the very moment when Ta-Hor and Passifont are sentenced to death, Aspicia reappears and begs her father for mercy, stating that she is ready to die in the same way. Her father, moved, unites the two lovers and in a final apotheosis all the deities welcome Aspicia. Then the dream is over and Lord Wilson and his servant awaken.

The story called for an artist in the title role who had a special dramatic talent (as did Rosati), because of all the scenes of love, fear, and courage which culminated in Aspicia's attempt to cast herself onto a flower-basket hiding a snake, a classic gesture since Cleopatra's time. Twenty years later, Zucchi (less conventionally) portrayed an unusually humane princess, not as arrogant and voluptuous as that of her successor Kshessinskaya who, on the other hand, made it more of a virtuoso role.

Petipa's penchant for folklore enhanced the dance of unlikely bayadères and the pageant of the rivers—from

Guadalquivir to Neva—all dressed up in national costumes. But historical inaccuracy and mixing of styles raised—especially in Moscow—a few criticisms, in spite of the general taste for sets and costumes reinvented with a minimum of realism and a maximum of grandeur.

Once the thirst for knowledge about an increasingly familiar country was satisfied, the huge appeal of *The Pharaoh's Daughter* was diminished. Its decline could only have been delayed by actual artistic merit, both in choreography and music (as in Verdi's *Aida*), which would have allowed the ballet to continue to reign in Soviet Russia.

The mysterious and adventurous stories of Egyptian mummies, however, were taken up by a new medium—film—thus freeing the dance theatre from all Egyptiana (with a few exceptions, such as Fokine's *Cléopâtre*). As long as Petipa's and Pugni's work is kept hidden in archives, their Aspicia will remain mummified as well.

—Concetta Lo Iacono

<hr />

PHÈDRE
(*Phaedra*)

Choreography: Serge Lifar
Music: Georges Auric
Design: Jean Cocteau
Libretto: Jean Cocteau
First Production: Paris Opéra Ballet, Théâtre National de l'Opéra, 14 June 1950
Principal Dancers: Tamara Toumanova (Phaedra), Serge Lifar (Hippolytus), Lycette Darsonval (Oenone), Liane Daydé (Aricie), Roger Ritz (Theseus)

Other choreographic treatments of story: Gaspero Angiolini (Milan, 1788), Charles-Louis Didelot (St. Petersburg, 1825), Ferdinando Pulini (Turin, 1874), Françoise Adret (Amsterdam, 1956), Martha Graham (New York, 1962), Birgit Cullberg (Swedish television, 1966), Flemming Flindt (Dallas, 1987).

PUBLICATIONS

Cocteau, Jean, "*Phèdre*: tragédie chorégraphique", *L'Opéra de Paris* (Paris), no. 1, July 1950
Guest, Ivor, "Notes on the Paris Opéra Repertory", *Ballet* (London), September/October 1950
Beaumont, Cyril, *Ballets Past and Present*, London, 1955
Wildman, Carl, "Jean Cocteau and the Dance", *Dancing Times* (London), October 1973
Duverny, Anne, and Robin, Sylvie, "Hommage à Serge Lifar à L'Opéra de Paris", *Magazine pour la danse* (Paris), December 1977/January 1978
Ries, Frank W.D., *The Dance Theatre of Jean Cocteau*, Ann Arbor, Michigan, 1986
Aschengreen, Erik, *Jean Cocteau and the Dance*, translated by Patricia McAndrew and Per Avsum, Copenhagen, 1986
Glasstone, Richard, "Poet and Dancer", *Dancing Times* (London), December 1989

* * *

When the composer Georges Auric received a commission

from the Paris Opéra for a ballet, it was on his invitation that Jean Cocteau became involved in the project. When Auric consulted Cocteau about a theme for the piece the poet reportedly replied: "What is the height of every actress's ambition? Phèdre, of course! Why can't it be a ballet, too?". According to stories published at the time of the ballet's creation, the actress Greta Garbo was considered for the lead, but Cocteau was probably, in reality, interested in her for a film version of the story.

Cocteau based his *découpage* (the French term for film script) on Racine's version of the tragedy rather than on Euripides', and conveyed the story in episodic, almost cinematic, terms with each scene outlined in one or two sentences: "Phèdre forbids her women to adorn her . . . Phèdre tells Oenone of her love for Hippolytus", and other similar directions. Cocteau also designed the sets and costumes. He utilized the stage on two levels: the fore-stage was used for the "present" action, and a small Greek stage, set backstage centre, was used for the appearance of the gods and to show action happening elsewhere, depicted in "*tableaux vivants*". The costumes were in sn-baked colours and Phèdre was clothed in black with a long scarlet cloak (a colour and device Cocteau used in many of his ballets, films, and plays). He insisted this red cloak be used in parts of the choreography.

The choreographer for the ballet was Serge Lifar, recently returned as director of the Paris Opéra, and although he later claimed to have originated the idea for the ballet some years before, there was no connection between the Auric/Cocteau commission and Lifar's concept, especially since Lifar wanted to focus the ballet upon Hippolytus rather than Phèdre. Lifar agreed to Cocteau's suggestion that Tamara Toumanova play the lead, but he refused to consider Jean Babilée for Hippolytus, since he wanted to perform this role himself. Cocteau was never very happy about this, nor about Lifar's approach to the choreography, and he began to withdraw further and further from the production; he did not even attend the opening night.

Lifar felt that both the score and the *découpage* limited his choreographic ability but tried to forge a new choreographic style for the ballet. Many of the reviews commented on how little dancing "in the traditional sense" the ballet contained, although Cocteau said there was more dancing in it than he had originally intended. Many critics thought the corps de ballet was under-used, though Lifar felt justified in his minimal use of the corps since within the confines of a Greek tragedy—and as dictated by Cocteau's scenario—they would primarily be used as commentators on the protagonists.

In general, despite these comments, the ballet was very well received—especially the performance of Toumanova, which was a *tour de force* of both acting and dancing, and which, in many scenes, was very powerful in conveying the emotions inherent in the tragedy. Lifar's performance, however, was not as well received, and many critics felt that he was too old for Hippolytus, a feeling shared by Cocteau. Auric's music was lauded, as were Cocteau's sets and costumes, although the background projections Cocteau had created from photographs by Brassaï received much criticism and were cut from later performances, as well as revivals. Cocteau had wanted these pictures—Greek ruins as they appeared in 1950—to take the myth out of historical context and present it in a contemporary milieu. In the programme Cocteau wrote: "A myth is a myth because poets have breathed fresh life into it through the ages, thus ensuring its continuance." The methodology Cocteau was using here was the same with which he was experimenting in his plays and films that modernized Greek myths and legends.

The ballet was revived in 1959 and again at the Paris Opéra in 1977. At this last revival Marie-Françoise Christout said, "this choreographic tragedy reflects well on the auspicious conjunction of talents. Today no doubt we see better than then the importance of this or that part of a work which influenced an epoch." The ballet has never been taken on by other companies, however, and its influence outside France must be considered minimal.

—Frank W. D. Ries

PICASSO, Pablo

Spanish painter, sculptor, and set designer.   Born Pablo Ruiz Picasso de Blasco in Malaga, 25 October 1881. Studied art under his father at La Coruña, 1891, at School of Fine Arts, La Coruña, from 1892, and at School of Fine Arts, Barcelona, from 1895; left Barcelona to study at Royal Academy of San Fernando, 1897, returning to Barcelona, 1899. Married (1) dancer Olga Kokhlova, 1918: one son, Paulo, b. 1921; (2) Jacqueline Rocque: daughter, Paloma, b. 1949; also father of daughter Maya (by Marie-Thérèse Walter), b. 1935, and son (by Françoise Gilot), b. 1947. Art editor and illustrator of journal *Arte Joven*, Barcelona; moved to Paris, 1901, working there and in Barcelona, 1902–03; moved permanently to Paris, 1904; first exhibition on circus theme, 1905; Harlequin paintings, 1909, and beginning of Cubist style, 1911; met Jean Cocteau, 1915, and invited to design set and costumes for *Parade*, 1917; began collaboration with Serge Diaghilev, visiting Naples with Diaghilev, Cocteau, and Léonide Massine to plan designs for *Pulcinella*, staged 1920; designer of several more ballets for Diaghilev's Ballets Russes until 1924; also designer for Comte Etienne de Beaumont's Soirées de Paris, Roland Petit's Ballets des Champs-Elysées, and the Paris Opéra. Died in Mougins, 8 April 1973.

WORKS (Ballet designs)

1917   *Parade* (chor. Massine), Diaghilev's Ballets Russes, Paris
1919   *Le Tricorne* (*The Three-Cornered Hat*; chor. Massine), Diaghilev's Ballets Russes, London
1920   *Pulcinella* (chor. Massine), Diaghilev's Ballets Russes, Paris
1921   *Cuadro Flamenco* (chor. traditional), Diaghilev's Ballets Russes, Paris
1923/ 24   *Trepar* (chor. Nijinska), Diaghilev's Ballets Russes (not produced)
1924   *Mercure* (chor. Massine), Comte Etienne de Beaumont's Soirées de Paris, Paris
       Le Train bleu (drop curtain; chor. Nijinska), Diaghilev's Ballets Russes, Paris
1945   *Le Rendezvous* (drop curtain; chor. Petit), Les Ballets des Champs-Elysées, Paris
1962   *L'Après-midi d'un faune* (chor. Lifar; design proposals rejected)
       Icare (chor. Lifar), Paris Opéra, Paris

PUBLICATIONS

Lieberman, W.S., "Picasso and the Ballet", *Dance Index* (New York), November 1946
Grigoriev, Serge, *The Diaghilev Ballet 1909–29*, translated by Vera Bowen, London, 1953
Picasso et le théâtre (catalogue), Toulouse, 1965
Cooper, Douglas, *Picasso Theatre*, London, 1967
Migel, Parmenia (ed.), *Pablo Picasso: Designs for "The Three-Cornered Hat"*, New York, 1978
Axsom, Richard, *Parade: Cubism as Theater*, New York, 1979
Picasso and the Theatre (catalogue), Bracknell, 1982
Garafola, Lynn, *Diaghilev's Ballets Russes*, New York, 1989
Rothschild, Deborah Menaker, *Picasso's "Parade" From Street to Stage*, London, 1991
Genné, Beth, "Picasso and Ballet", *Dancing Times* (London), March 1992

*   *   *

Pablo Picasso's work in the theatre can be divided into two distinct phases: his early phase, beginning with his designs for *Parade* (1917) and concluding with his work for *Le Train bleu* (1924), and a later period, beginning in 1936 when he created a curtain for the play *Le 14 Juillet*, and finishing in 1962 with his designs for a version of Serge Lifar's ballet *Icare*. His most prolific period of creating for the ballet was during the first period, when he designed seven ballets—six for Serge Diaghilev's Ballets Russes and one, *Mercure* (1924), for the Comte Etienne de Beaumont's Soirées de Paris. His works during this first phase are distinguished by a great commitment to originality of design, as opposed to the recycling of existing works, a technique to which he resorted in many of his works during the later phase.

In conceptual terms, Picasso's most original work for the ballet was also his first: it was *Parade*, that famous collaboration among artists Jean Cocteau, Léonide Massine, Eric Satie, and Picasso. For *Parade*, Picasso designed a curtain, set, and costumes; however, his contribution extended beyond these designs. Although the original idea for *Parade* was Cocteau's, Picasso made fundamental changes to it by persuading Cocteau to add three extra characters—the Managers—to the ballet. The Managers stood in stark contrast to the other characters in the ballet, visually, choreographically, and in the role they assumed in the storyline; and they exerted a strong influence on how the other characters were perceived. By introducing them, Picasso also transformed the work from the original, slightly occult story to a street performance. In this way he brought to the work popular overtones which were in keeping with his cubist aesthetic, and which recalled his earlier interest in itinerant performers, whom he had depicted in many of his canvases.

With the actual designs for *Parade*, Picasso created a collage of elements which reflected his experiments with cubism and with the technique of collage itself. Picasso's curtain is full of intricate iconographic references, and is evocative of a romantic mood which is at odds both with the startlingly modern approach he adopted for setting and costumes and with the mood of the ballet itself. Behind the front curtain, the street setting is a townscape, executed as a series of flat planes and in muted colours, while the costumes for the Chinese Conjuror, the Little American Girl, and the Acrobats add dramatic colour accents. Against these elements are juxtaposed the overtly cubist-inspired costumes for the Managers, adding an element of modern commentary to the ballet. The overall effect is that of a three-dimensional moving collage of disparate styles.

Following *Parade*, which initially was not well received, Picasso continued to work with the Ballets Russes. His contacts with the ballet opened up a new life style to him, and these experiences are reflected in numerous sketches he made of artists from all fields who were members of Diaghilev's circle. In 1918 Picasso married one of Diaghilev's dancers, Olga Kokhlova, and she became the subject of various portraits. He

Pablo Picasso (wearing cap) and assistants painting the curtain for _Parade_, 1917

also enjoyed a creative working association with Massine, with whom he collaborated on _Le Tricorne_, _Pulcinella_, and _Mercure_.

Although formalistically Picasso's designs for the latter part of his first theatrical phase are sometimes in the same vein as _Parade_, in that they are frequently composed of a number of juxtaposed disparate elements, they never achieve the same level of innovation and creativity. Nevertheless, his designs for _Le Tricorne_ and _Cuadro Flamenco_ are distinguished by their traditionally Spanish flavour and imagery and luscious use of colour, while _Pulcinella_ looks with flair to the traditional forms of the Italian _commedia dell'arte_. However _Mercure_, as yet largely unexamined, may well in terms of innovation prove to be the successor to _Parade_. Essentially experimental, and revolving around a succession of episodes which depicted aspects of the personality of the god Mercury, it was composed of a series of _poses plastiques_. Picasso's designs, which included movable scenery that was manipulated by the dancers, created a furore—as had those for _Parade_—and, against the criticisms of the contemporary press, he was supported by leading avant-garde artists and critics of the day, including Georges Auric, André Breton, and Max Ernst.

The last of Picasso's works during his first theatrical phase was _Le Train bleu_, and in many respects it prefigured his second phase. Picasso designed a curtain for this work, which was an enlarged version of his 1922 gouache, _Women Running on the Beach_. During the second phase of his theatrical career, in which he was associated with only three ballets and in a much smaller way than before, Picasso continued to recycle works from his earlier oeuvre. His curtain for _Le Rendezvous_, designed in 1945 for Les Ballets des Champs-Elysées, was a reworking of a 1943 gouache, and his curtain for _Icare_ for Lifar's 1962 production of this ballet at the Paris Opéra was originally a design executed in 1960 as an illustration for a book about Lifar.

In her autobiography, _Theatre Street_, Tamara Karsarvina has referred to Picasso as having "an absolute sense of the stage and its requirements". With works from his first theatrical phase this appears to be a perceptive comment. At his most innovative Picasso was able to use both the form and content of his designs to extend the meaning of a work. In his second phase his works showed less commitment to the theatre; most probably it was only the Ballets Russes which, in his time, was able to provide the kind of climate in which his innovative approaches could be nurtured.

—Michelle Potter

PIERROT LUNAIRE

Choreography: Glen Tetley
Music: Arnold Schoenberg (song cycle set to poems by Albert Giraud)
Design: Rouben Ter-Arutunian
Scenario: Glen Tetley (loosely based on Giraud and on *commedia dell'arte* characters)
First Production: The Glen Tetley Company, Fashion Institute of Technology, New York, 5 May 1962
Principal Dancers: Glen Tetley, Linda Hodes, Robert Powell

Other productions include: Robert Joffrey Ballet Company (earlier version; chor. Robert Joffrey); New York, 24 March 1955. Netherlands Dance Theatre (restaged Tetley); The Hague, 23 October 1962. Ballet Rambert (restaged Tetley), with Christopher Bruce; Richmond, Surrey, 26 January 1967. Royal Danish Ballet, with Vivi Gelker, Niels Kehlet, Henning Kronstam; Copenhagen, 31 October 1968. Bavarian State Opera Ballet, with Ferenc Barbay; Munich, 12 December 1972. Stuttgart Ballet; Stuttgart, 29 November 1975. Basel Ballet (new version; chor. Heinz Spoerli); Basel, 15 September 1984.

PUBLICATIONS

Barnes, Clive, "Dutch Treat", *Dance and Dancers* (London), January 1964
Williams, Peter, Percival, John, and Goodwin, Noël, "Pierrot Lunaire", *Dance and Dancers* (London), March 1967
Brinson, Peter, and Crisp, Clement, *Ballet for All*, London, 1970
Percival, John, "Glen Tetley", in *Experimental Dance*, London, 1971
"Glen Tetley", *Tanzblatter* (Vienna), March 1980
Goodwin, Noël, "Alchemist . . . Choreographer Glen Tetley", *Ballet News* (New York), October 1982

*   *   *

Tetley's *Pierrot lunaire*, based on Schoenberg's song-cycle of the same name that is set to 21 poems by Albert Giraud, was first produced with the choreographer dancing the title role for his own new company, The Glen Tetley Company, in 1962. It is the only version to Schoenberg's work to have entered the repertory, although a previous version—now lost—was created by Robert Joffrey for his own company in 1955. Léonide Massine had wanted to choreograph the cycle in 1922, but with the vocal line transposed to an instrument, which Schoenberg refused to allow. Another version by John Cranko, proposed for the 1958 Edinburgh Festival, was forbidden by the Schoenberg Estate. Tetley's version, however, was an overnight sensation and was the first fruit of his many "cross-over" experiments in a variety of dance techniques. It was also Tetley's first major work, marking his emergence as a mature choreographer. After nearly 30 years it has remained one of his most enduring and potent creations.

Though at the time both choreographer and contemporary critics regarded such a fusion of techniques as both innovative and daring, *Pierrot lunaire* now occupies a significant place in ballet history as being the work in which Tetley crystallized the style of lean neo-classicism which came to define so much of the work of the 1960s and 1970s. It did much to revitalize the vocabulary of ballet during the period by incorporating many of the discoveries of American contemporary dance.

Tetley worked his setting around three traditional *commedia dell'arte* characters, though with some licence since, in the development of that form, various traditional characters rose and fell in popularity and did not actually overlap in theatre history. Therefore the combination of Pierrot, Columbine, and Brighella is not a truly historical one. However, the most important aspect is the use to which Tetley has put them, accurately described in his own note on the ballet: "In the antiquity of the Roman Theatre began the battle of the white clown of innocence and the dark clown of experience. Pierrot and Brighella are their lineal descendents and the Columbine their eternal pawn".

Much of Tetley's originality in creating *Pierrot lunaire* arises from his refusal to let the text suggest his dance invention, though there are moments when the movements' cumulative effect suggests the pictures conjured up by Giraud's imagery. So when the work opens, the still innocent Pierrot—swinging on the central scaffolding frame which is so essential to the action and which circumscribes his spiritual domain—suggests by his upward stetches and simple développés his yearning for the unattainable moon. The use of the tower is crucial throughout and the other characters' manner of climbing or swinging from it also defines their personalities and emotions. The sequences of the ballet demonstrate how the worldly influences of Brighella "The Intriguer" and Columbine "The Inamorata" destroy Pierrot's childlike innocence as they systematically bully, swindle, entice, and cheat him—finally robbing him of all he possesses except for his eternally renewable hope and capacity for forgiveness. (At the end he embraces them both and folds their heads on to his chest.)

The movement is graphic, rich, and potent throughout, with many references to the traditional situations of *commedia dell'arte* stories, but requiring the dancers—especially Columbine and Brighella—to define clearly how they are in reality as well as in the innocent Pierrot's eyes. Despite its potential for pessimism, much of the ballet's appeal lies in its final reconciliations and the creation of a dance language which admits many layers of emotion within a tightly organized compass.

—Geoffrey Baskerville

PILLAR OF FIRE

Choreography: Antony Tudor
Music: Arnold Schoenberg
Design: Jo Mielziner (scenery and costumes)
Libretto: Antony Tudor
First Production: Ballet Theatre, Metropolitan Opera House, New York, 8 April 1942
Principal Dancers: Nora Kaye (Hagar), Lucia Chase (Eldest Sister), Annabelle Lyon (Youngest Sister), Antony Tudor (The Friend), Hugh Laing (The Young Man from the House Opposite)

Other productions include: Royal Swedish Ballet (restaged Tudor), with Mariane Orlando, Conny Borg, Verner Klavsen; Stockholm, 30 December 1962. Vienna State Opera Ballet; Vienna, 26 May 1969. The Australian Ballet; 11 July 1969.

PUBLICATIONS

Schulman, Jennie, "Antony Tudor and the Modern Ballet", *Dance Observer*, February 1951

Pierrot lunaire, with Glen Tetley in the title role, New York, 1962

Pillar of Fire, with (from left to right) Annabelle Lyon, Antony Tudor, Lucia Chase, Nora Kaye, and Hugh Laing, Ballet Theatre, 1942

de Mille, Agnes, *And Promenade Home*, New York, 1952
Beaumont, Cyril, *Ballets Past and Present*, London, 1955
Menuhin, Diana, "The Varying Moods of Tudor", *Dance and Dancers* (London), July 1955
Cohen, Selma Jeanne, "The Years in America and After", *Dance Perspectives* (New York), no. 18, 1963
Anderson, Jack, "The View from the House Opposite", *Ballet Review* (New York), vol. 4, no. 6, 1974
Jordan, Stephanie, "Antony Tudor: His Use of Music and Movement", *Eddy* (New York), Spring–Summer 1976
Payne, Charles, *American Ballet Theatre*, New York, 1978
Siegel, Marcia, *The Shapes of Change*, Boston, 1979
Osterle, Hilary, "The Tudor Spirit", *Ballet News* (New York), April 1982
Szmyd, Linda, "Antony Tudor; Ballet Theatre Years", *Choreography and Dance*, vol. 1, part 2, 1989

*   *   *

The premiere of *Pillar of Fire* was a great success, receiving 30 curtain calls. John Martin wrote in *The New York Times* in 1942, "It was a great night at the Metropolitan Opera House last night, for the Ballet Theatre put on a program of unusual distinction with the world premiere of Antony Tudor's magnificent new work *Pillar of Fire* as its particular feature." He commented, "By the very artificiality of the ballet technique, and its constant contrast with sheer colloquialism of movement, Tudor achieves a sharp and vivid inner truth for his people and his theme . . .". The ballet catapulted Nora Kaye (Hagar) and Hugh Laing (The Man Opposite) into overnight stardom.

In *Dance Observer* in 1942 Robert Sabin wrote, "*Pillar of Fire* culminates in the situation pre-established in the Richard Dehmel poem which inspired Schoenberg, the confession of a woman to a man that she is going to bear another man's child and his answer that his love for her will embrace her child and make it their own". Tudor reworked the Schoenberg scenario in order to make a dance about sexuality and lust, a subject that interested him and that heretofore seemed decidedly unsuitable for ballet. Tudor said, ". . . Hagar, like Hagar in the Bible, was a lost soul. She thought she had lost a life of sexuality—and sexuality helps a lot of people out of their problems."

The set for the ballet includes a frame house stage to project a New England-like aura. According to Tudor, "The family lives in what was a very nice house at one time in the respected environs of a provincial town." The ballet opens with Hagar sitting on the steps of her house, her back and shoulders tensely held, her head lifted looking into the distance, perhaps imagining all the scenes that follow. People begin to enter, indicating their identities by their sparsely chosen gestures. The Eldest Sister, a spinster in long skirts, walks and moves purposefully, tautly, with necessity. The Youngest Sister in a childish short dress bounces, spins, flicks her wrists, and tilts her head. Hagar, like most middle sisters, is caught between them.

Then we meet the men in Hagar's life-dream: the Man Opposite, who looks like a bartender with vest and rolled shirt sleeves; he slinks, moving with jazzy syncopated steps, stereotypically sexy. The Friend (originally played by Tudor) who will be her savior, dressed in a suit and correct in his bearing, enters Hagar's house. Hagar, left out, remains outside of her own house, as well as outside of the bar in which people seem to be enjoying themselves. The Man Opposite appears and there is no question as to what he lewdly suggests, his body moving his leg that opens intentionally, his hands touching his thighs. A chorus of Lovers in Innocence, the women dressed like the Youngest Sister, the men dressed as male ballet dancers, briefly dance in unison. But Hagar is really the one puzzling and interesting person on stage and she is there, in front of the audience, for the entire ballet. In the next phrases of music Hagar's Youngest Sister dances with the Friend, both encouraging him to dance with Hagar and twisting him into her own fickle web of games. Hagar dances in this trio, but is distant and out of sorts. Her sister pushes her; she falls. In fact she falls often in the piece, a metaphor for what she is feeling and what is happening to her.

The first important duet then takes place between the Man Opposite and Hagar. She gives herself to him and spends the rest of the ballet feeling guilty. After this "fall" she is greeted by the Eldest Sister, who responds to Hagar's sin by looking at the heavens, her hands clasped, held high above her head and thrust up and down. Gradually, as others enter the stage, Hagar's fright and shame grow while the night darkens and a pause interrupts these whirling events.

The second scene of the ballet provides resolution. An awkward Hagar tries to imitate the Lovers in Innocence, but she is pathologically discontent and maladroit in her attempt to attract the Man Opposite, her seducer. When she is down, he drags her on the floor. Her second and brief duet with him leaves the viewer exhausted and Hagar beaten in this masochistic exercise. The entrance of the chorus, both Lovers in Innocence and Lovers in Experience, as well as the sisters, provides the scenic and metaphoric amplitude that lifts Hagar from her low state.

In the final romantic duet, sometimes criticized for its unconvincing happy ending, the Friend tenderly and consolingly helps Hagar to recover her balance and self-assurance. The couple quietly walk off stage holding each other's hands, looking not at one another but into the future.

Radical in its approach to human sensuality and innovative in its manner of psychological characterization, *Pillar of Fire* has become one of Tudor's most influential and powerful ballets. It remains Tudor's greatest achievement at Ballet Theatre, where it continues to be revived. It was also re-created in 1962 by the Royal Ballet in Sweden. A Swedish video of this production, starring Mariane Orlando, exists as well as a film of the Ballet Theatre production with Sallie Wilson.

—Judith Chazin-Bennahum

————

PINEAPPLE POLL

Choreography: John Cranko
Music: Arthur Sullivan (from various Gilbert and Sullivan operas) arranged by Charles Mackerras
Design: Osbert Lancaster (scenery and costumes)
Libretto: John Cranko (after William S. Gilbert's Bab Ballad, *The Bumboat Woman's Story*)
First Production: Sadler's Wells Theatre Ballet, Sadler's Wells Theatre, London, 13 March 1951
Principal Dancers: Elaine Fifield (Pineapple Poll), David Poole (Jasper), David Blair (Captain Belaye)

Other productions include: Borovansky Ballet (restaged Cranko), with Kathleen Gorham (Pineapple Poll); Melbourne, 1954. Royal Ballet (restaged and revised Cranko), with Merle Park (Pineapple Poll), Stanley Holden (Jasper), David Blair (Captain Belaye); London, 22 September 1959. Australian Ballet, with Elaine Fifield; Sydney, 1966. City Center Joffrey Ballet (staged Celia Franca); New York, 25 February 1970. Noverre Society (restaged Cranko); Stuttgart, 1972. Stuttgart Ballet; Stuttgart, 18 February 1974.

PUBLICATIONS

Lansdale, Nelson, "Accent on Youth: The Sadler's Wells Theatre Ballet", *Theatre Arts* (New York), October 1951
Beaumont, Cyril, *Ballets of Today*, London, 1954
Barnes, Clive, "*Pineapple Poll*", *Dance and Dancers* (London), April 1961
Brinson, Peter, and Crisp, Clement, *Ballet for All*, London, 1970
Balanchine, George, with Mason, Francis, *Balanchine's Complete Stories of the Great Ballets*, Garden City, N.Y., 1977
Taylor, Burton, "Preparing a Role", *Dance Magazine* (New York), January 1982
Percival, John, *Theatre in my Blood: A Biography of John Cranko*, London, 1983

*   *   *

Pineapple Poll has been one of the most successful ballets created by a British choreographer since the war; its popularity with public, press, and performers alike has probably only been surpassed by that of Ashton's *La Fille mal gardée*, created nearly a decade later. With *Pineapple Poll*, John Cranko has succeeded—as did Ashton in *Fille*—both in making his audience laugh and in arousing in them feelings of genuine sympathy with the predicament of his characters. In this ballet, Cranko has created three totally believable characters: Belaye, the handsome strutting peacock of a naval officer; Jasper, a pierrot-type figure who touches the audience's hearts with his unrequited love for Poll; and Poll herself, plucky, wilful, and totally besotted with the dashing Captain. The determination of Poll and the other young women in the port to be close to their hero leads them surreptitiously to board his ship disguised as sailors. The ensuing misunderstandings, and the retribution of their menfolk, are the stuff of pure farce. This is also true of the zany pas de trois between Belaye, his simpering fiancée Blanche, and her aunt, Mrs. Dimple. Both Blanche and Mrs. Dimple are cardboard cut-outs compared to Jasper and Poll, but their exaggerated, farcical behaviour helps point up the genuine humanity of the other two protagonists, while Belaye is the link between these two extremes.

Based on W.S. Gilbert's Bab Ballad, *The Bumboat Woman's Story*, Cranko's ballet captures the Englishness of Sullivan's

Pineapple Poll, as performed by Sadler's Wells Royal Ballet, London

theatrical style. Charles Mackerras, who arranged the score, took advantage of the lapse of copywright on Sullivan's music to plunder the wealth of tuneful, eminently danceable music to be found in his popular operettas. The result is one of the most successful of British ballet scores.

Osbert Lancaster's boldly humorous designs encapsulate Gilbert and Sullivan's England and Cranko brings the whole ballet to a perfect climax with a real coup de théâtre. In a trice Mrs. Dimple's parasol becomes a shield, as a trident is thrust into her hand and a Union Jack draped about her. Hoist aloft, the dotty aunt has been miraculously and instantaneously transformed into Britannia, as the curtain falls on a triumphant note of Land of Hope and Glory.

—Richard Glasstone

PLATEL, Elisabeth

French dancer.   Born Elisabeth Marie Geneviève Platel in Paris, 10 April 1959. Studied at the Conservatoire national supérieur de musique de Paris, 1971–75, and at the Paris Opéra School, pupil of Christiane Vaussard, Pierre Lacotte, Alexandre Kalioujny, 1975–76. Dancer, Paris Opéra Ballet, from 1976, becoming coryphée, 1977, sujet, 1978, première danseuse, 1979, and étoile from 1981; international guest artist, including with Royal Ballet, Royal Danish Ballet, Les Grands Ballets Canadiens, Royal New Zealand Ballet, Ballet du Nord, Municipal Theatre in Rio de Janeiro, Hamburg Ballet, and Bolshoi Ballet, Moscow; has also appeared in Vienna, Berlin, Chicago, and at Cuba Festival, 1985; has appeared on television, including in British (BBC) television series *Ballerina* (1987), and in French film *Le Spectre de la danse* (Delouche, 1982). Recipient: Prix à l'Unanimité, Conservatoire de Paris, 1975; Prix René Blum de l'université de la danse, 1977; Second Junior Prize, International Ballet Competition, Varna, 1979; Benson and Hedges Award for Outstanding Achievement of the Year in Ballet, 1982.

ROLES

1978   The Young Girl in *Le Spectre de la rose* (Fokine), Paris Opéra Ballet, Paris

Principal dancer in *Divertimento No. 15* (Balanchine), Paris Opéra Ballet, Paris

Third Theme in *The Four Temperaments* (Balanchine), Paris Opéra Ballet, Paris

1979   Principal dancer in *Life* (Béjart), Paris Opéra Ballet, Paris

Pas de deux in *Le Bourgeois Gentilhomme* (Balanchine), Paris Opéra Ballet, Paris

Principal dancer in *Serait-ce la mort?* (Béjart), Paris Opéra Ballet, Paris

Elisabeth Platel as Aurora in *The Sleeping Beauty*, **Paris Opéra Ballet**

Lilac Fairy in *The Sleeping Beauty* (Petipa; staged Alonso), Paris Opéra Ballet, Paris

1980 Principal dancer in *Schema* (Nikolais), Paris Opéra Ballet, Paris

The Chosen One in *Le Sacre du printemps* (Béjart), Paris Opéra Ballet, Paris

Myrtha in *Giselle* (Petipa after Coralli, Perrot; staged Alonso), Paris Opéra Ballet, Paris

1981 Title role in *La Sylphide* (Lacotte after Taglioni), Paris Opéra Ballet, Paris

Odette/Odile in *Swan Lake* (Burmeister after Petipa, Ivanov), Paris Opéra Ballet, Paris

Title role in *Giselle* (Petipa after Coralli, Perrot; staged Alonso), Paris Opéra Ballet, Paris

Title role in *Paquita* (Vinogradov after Petipa), Paris Opéra Ballet, Paris

Queen of the Dryads in *Don Quixote* (Nureyev after Petipa), Paris Opéra Ballet, Paris

Principal dancer in *Three Preludes* (Stevenson), Paris Opéra Ballet, Paris

The Nightingale in *Le Chant du rossignol* (L. Massine), La Fenice, Venice

1982 Princess Aurora in *The Sleeping Beauty* (Petipa, Nijinska; staged Hightower), Paris Opéra Ballet, Paris

Principal dancer in *Voluntaries* (Tetley), Paris Opéra Ballet, Paris

Principal dancer in *Serenade* (Balanchine), Paris Opéra Ballet, Paris

Lucille Grahn in *Pas de quatre* (Dolin), Paris Opéra Ballet, Paris

1983 Title role in *Raymonda*, Act III (Nureyev after Petipa), Paris Opéra Ballet, Paris

Kitri in *Don Quixote* (Nureyev after Petipa), Paris Opéra Ballet, Paris

Pas de deux in *Agon* (Balanchine), Paris Opéra Ballet, Paris

1984 Nikiya in *La Bayadère* ("Kingdom of the Shades" scene; Nureyev after Petipa), Royal Ballet, London

Marquise in *Marco Spada* (Lacotte after Mazilier), Paris Opéra Ballet, Paris

Principal dancer in *Violin Concerto* (Balanchine), Paris Opéra Ballet, Paris

Estrella in *Carnaval* (Fokine), Paris Opéra Ballet, Paris

Principal dancer (cr) in *Premier Orage* (Childs), Paris Opéra Ballet, Paris

1985 Swanilda in *Coppélia* (Skouratoff), Ballet de Bordeaux

Second Movement in *Le Palais de cristal* (*Symphony in C*; Balanchine), Paris Opéra Ballet, Paris

Principal dancer in *Concerto Barocco* (Balanchine), Paris Opéra Ballet, Paris

Odette/Odile in *Swan Lake* (Nureyev after Petipa, Ivanov), Paris Opéra Ballet, Paris

Principal dancer in *Before Nightfall* (Christie), Paris Opéra Ballet, Paris

Caroline in *Jardin aux lilas* (Tudor), Paris Opéra Ballet, Paris

Principal dancer in *Song of the Earth* (MacMillan), Paris Opéra Ballet, Paris

Title role in *La Sonnambula* (Balanchine), Ballet Théâtre Français de Nancy, Paris

1986 Principal dancer in *Sonate à trois* (Béjart), Paris Opéra Ballet, Paris

The Countess in *Manfred* (Nureyev), Paris Opéra Ballet, Paris

Title role in *Cendrillon* (*Cinderella*; Nureyev), Paris Opéra Ballet, Paris

Principal dancer in *Grosse Fugue* (van Manen), Paris Opéra Ballet, Paris

1987 Terpsichore in *Apollon musagète* (*Apollo*; Balanchine), Paris Opéra Ballet, Paris

Principal dancer in *Symphony in Three Movements* (Balanchine), Paris Opéra Ballet, Paris

Woman of the People (cr) in *Sans armes citoyens!* (van Dantzig), Paris Opéra Ballet, Paris

Principal dancer (cr) in *Magnificat* (Neumeier), Paris Opéra Ballet, Avignon

Principal dancer in *Suite en blanc* (Lifar), Paris Opéra Ballet, Paris

Principal dancer in *Four Last Songs* (van Dantzig), Paris Opéra Ballet, Paris

Principal dancer (cr) in *Les Anges ternis* (Armitage), Paris Opéra Ballet, Paris

1988 Principal dancer in *Études* (Lander), Paris Opéra Ballet, Paris

Principal dancer in *In the Middle, Somewhat Elevated* (Forsythe), Paris Opéra Ballet, Paris

Esmeralda in *Notre-Dame de Paris* (Petit), Paris Opéra Ballet, Paris

1989 Principal dancer in *Les Présages* (Massine), Paris Opéra Ballet, Paris

Principal dancer in *In the Night* (Robbins), Paris Opéra Ballet, Paris

The Siren in *Le Fils prodigue* (Balanchine), Paris Opéra Ballet, Paris

1990 Principal dancer in *Sinfonietta* (Kylián), Paris Opéra Ballet, Paris

Principal dancer in *Les Noces*, Paris Opéra Ballet, Paris

First variation in *Variations* (Lifar), Paris Opéra Ballet, Paris

1991 Titania in *A Midsummer Night's Dream* (Neumeier), Paris Opéra Ballet, Paris

Chanson dansée ("La Garçonne") in *Les Biches* (Nijinska), Paris Opéra Ballet, Paris

Principal dancer in *Glass Pieces* (Robbins), Paris Opéra Ballet, Paris

Principal dancer in *Dancers at a Gathering* (Robbins), Paris Opéra Ballet, Paris

1992 Marguerite in *La Dame aux camélias* (Neumeier), Hamburg Ballet, Hamburg

Gamzatti in *La Bayadère* (Nureyev after Petipa), Paris Opéra Ballet, Paris

Other roles include: principal dancer in *Chaconne* (Balanchine), *Tchaikovsky Pas de deux* (Balanchine), *Theme and Variations* (Balanchine), *Tzigane* (Balanchine), *Webern Opus V* (Béjart), *Vaslav* (Neumeier), *Adagietto* (Neumeier).

PUBLICATIONS

By Platel:

Interview in Pourrieux, Frédéric, "Elisabeth Platel: Instants de vérité", *Danser* (Paris), July/August 1984

About Platel:

Gourreau, Jean Marie, "*La Sylphide*", *Pour la danse* (Marseilles), April 1981

Mannoni, Gerard, *Les Étoiles de l'Opéra de Paris*, Paris, 1982

Mannoni, Gerard, "Elisabeth Platel", *Opéra de Paris* (Paris), September 1982

Finkel, Anita, "The Dancers of the Ballet de l'Opéra de Paris", *Ballett International* (Cologne), December 1986

Dienis, Jean Claude, "Elisabeth Platel: Le Manège d'une étoile", *Danser* (Paris), February 1987

*   *   *

Unusually for an étoile of the Paris Opéra Ballet, Elisabeth Platel is not a product of the Paris Opéra Ballet School, but trained at the Paris Conservatoire supérieur, where she gained first prize on her graduation in 1975. This honour enabled her to enter the so-called "pre ballet corps" of the Paris Opéra Ballet, where once again she passed all her exams with flying colours. It was only at the grade of première danseuse that competition became intense, when other outstanding young dancers from the Opéra Ballet school were also seeking entry to the topmost ranks of the company. But so gifted was Platel, with her flawless legs and feet, elegant line, high extensions, and easy jump, that a few weeks after her nomination as étoile virtually everyone—including her rivals—acknowledged that the jury was right to have nominated her.

It was Maurice Béjart who first gave the young dancer the chance to shine as a soloist, creating *Life* for her and veteran dancer Jean Babilée in 1979. Following this, Pierre Lacotte, one of Platel's former teachers at the Conservatoire, coached her for the title role of *La Sylphide*, in which she excelled as the perfect embodiment of the early nineteenth-century style. Platel then went on to dance in two further classics, *Swan Lake* and *Giselle*, for which she was praised as a worthy follower of French ballerinas Yvette Chauviré and Nina Vyroubova; critics commented on her virtuosity, lightness, and precision.

Platel's early partners were Jean-Pierre Franchetti, Michaël Denard, and Cyril Atanassoff. She was the first to dance the role of the Queen of the Dryads in Nureyev's staging of *Don Quixote* for the Paris Opéra Ballet in 1981, and from then onwards, leading ballerina roles in virtually all the three-act ballets came her way. Critic Freda Pitt, after viewing Platel's earliest performances in the role of Odette/Odile in *Swan Lake*, wrote, "Her dancing was meltingly lovely, with all challenges triumphantly met, and if only the right person could give her coaching in the interpretation, she could certainly become a great exponent of the role."

Platel has herself expressed a preference for ballets with an obvious story-line, but is equally at ease in abstract ballets, particularly those of George Balanchine. With her long legs and small head, she could have easily been a Balanchine ballerina. As Irène Lidova wrote in 1982 after Platel's promotion to étoile, "Platel is tall [and] long-limbed with a pure and clean profile. She is thought of as a Balanchine dancer. . . . Her style is brilliant and she has a splendid line."

In 1982 Platel visited London with the Paris Opéra Ballet and was so successful in *La Sylphide* that she received the "Benson and Hedges" trophy for the best foreign performance that year. Since then she has tackled ballets by Jerome Robbins, to which she brings a special lyrical quality, as well as works by Serge Lifar, Jiří Kylián, John Neumeier, and many others. Her recent partners have included the Opéra star Laurent Hilaire, with whom she has appeared in guest performances at the Royal Ballet in London.

British critic Mary Clarke perhaps put it best, calling Elisabeth Platel "a ballerina of great purity of style and clarity of line and execution". "The technique is strong and unforced, the extensions high and beautifully held at the end of a phrase," Clarke wrote, concluding, "She wears her ballerina title to the manner born, a lovely example of the best of French classical schooling."

—Monique Babsky

———

PLISETSKAYA, Maya

Russian/Soviet dancer, choreographer, and ballet director. Born Maya Mikhailovna Plisetskaya in Moscow, 20 November 1925. Studied at the Moscow Choreographic School, pupil of Elisaveta Gerdt, from 1934; graduated in 1943; later trained with M. Leontieva and Asaf Messerer. Married composer and conductor Rodion Shchedrin, 1958. Soloist, soon becoming leading principal dancer, Bolshoi Ballet, from 1943, with first U.S. tour, 1959; prima ballerina (on retirement of Galina Ulanova), from 1962; international guest artist, including for Paris Opéra, 1961, 1964, Ballet de Marseille, 1973, and Ballet du XXe Siècle, Brussels, 1975–76, and on U.S. tour, 1977; star guest artist (in "Hommage à Plisetskaya"), Boston, 1988; also choreographer, with first choreography (*Anna Karenina*), 1972; also ballet director, serving as guest director, Rome Opera Ballet, 1984–86, artistic director and guest artist, Ballet del Teatro Lirico Nacional, Madrid, 1987–90; has also appeared as dancer and actress on television and in numerous films, including in *Plisetskaya Dances* (Soviet television, 1966), *Anna Karenina* (acting role; Soviet film, 1968), film version of own ballet *Anna Karenina* (1974), and *Fantasy* (television film; 1976). Recipient: title of People's Artist of the USSR, 1959; Anna Pavlova Prize, 1962; Lenin Prize, 1964; *Dance Magazine Award*, 1965; title of Hero of Socialist Labour, 1985; Pegaso Prize, Spoleto Festival, 1989; Gold Medal, Spain, 1991.

ROLES

1937 The Cat (cr) in *The Little Stork* (Popko, Posepkin, Radunsky), School Performance of the Moscow Choreographic School, Bolshoi Theatre, Moscow

1941 Principal dancer in Grand Pas from *Paquita* (Petipa), Performance of Moscow Choreographic School, Moscow

1942 The Swan in *The Dying Swan* (*Le Cygne*; Fokine), Bolshoi Ballet, Moscow

1943 Pas de trois in *Swan Lake* (Gorsky after Petipa, Ivanov; staged Messerer) Bolshoi Ballet, Moscow

      Mazurka in *Chopiniana* (*Les Sylphides*; Fokine), Bolshoi Ballet, Moscow

1944 Myrtha in *Giselle* (Petipa after Coralli, Perrot), Bolshoi Ballet, Moscow

      Masha in *The Nutcracker* (Vainonen), Bolshoi Ballet, Moscow

      Lilac Fairy in *The Sleeping Beauty* (Petipa, staged Messerer), Bolshoi Ballet, Moscow

      Fairy Violante in *The Sleeping Beauty* (Petipa, staged Messerer), Bolshoi Ballet, Moscow

      Queen of the Dryads in *Don Quixote* (Gorsky after Petipa), Bolshoi Ballet, Moscow

1945 Title role in *Raymonda* (Lavrovsky after Petipa), Bolshoi Ballet, Moscow

      Autumn Fairy in *Cinderella* (Zakharov), Bolshoi Ballet, Moscow

1947 Odette/Odile in *Swan Lake* (Gorsky after Petipa, staged Messerer), Bolshoi Ballet, Moscow

      Tsar-Maiden in *The Little Humpbacked Horse* (Gorsky after Petipa, Saint-Léon), Bolshoi Ballet, Moscow

1948 Zarema in *The Fountain of Bakhchisarai* (Zakharov), Bolshoi Ballet, Moscow

1950 Kitri in *Don Quixote* (Gorsky after Petipa), Bolshoi Ballet, Moscow

1952 Princess Aurora in *The Sleeping Beauty* (Messerer after Petipa), Bolshoi Ballet, Moscow

1954 Mistress of the Copper Mountain (cr) in *The Story of the Stone Flower* (Lavrovsky), Bolshoi Ballet, Moscow

Maya Plisetskaya in *Don Quixote*, **Bolshoi Ballet, Moscow, 1968**

1955   Syumbike (cr) in *Shurale* (new version of *Ali-Batyr*;
        Yakobson), Bolshoi Ballet, Moscow
        Myrtha in *Giselle* (new production; Petipa after Coralli,
        Perrot; staged Lavrovsky), Bolshoi Ballet, Moscow
1956   Title role in *Laurencia* (revival; Chabukiani), Bolshoi
        Ballet, Moscow
1958   Aegina (cr) in *Spartacus* (Moiseyev), Bolshoi Ballet,
        Moscow
1959   Mistress of the Copper Mountain (cr) in *The Stone
        Flower* (Moscow version; Grigorovich), Bolshoi Bal-
        let, Moscow
1961   Juliet in *Romeo and Juliet* (Lavrovsky), Bolshoi Ballet,
        Moscow
1962   Phyrgia in *Spartacus* (Yakobson), Bolshoi Ballet,
        Moscow
1963   Princess Aurora (cr) in *The Sleeping Beauty* (new
        production; Grigorovich after Petipa), Bolshoi Ballct,
        Moscow
1964   Title role in *The Firebird* (Vlasov, Simachev, after
        Fokine), Bolshoi Ballet, Moscow

1965   Mekmene-Banu (cr) in *The Legend of Love* (Moscow
        version; Grigorovich), Bolshoi Ballet, Moscow
1967   Title role (cr) in *Carmen Suite* (*Carmen*; Alonso), Bolshoi
        Ballet, Moscow
1969   Tsar-maiden in *The Little Humpbacked Horse* (Ra-
        dunsky), Bolshoi Ballet, Moscow
1972   Title role (cr) in *Anna Karenina* (also chor., with
        Ryzhenko, Smirnov), Bolshoi Ballet, Moscow
1973   Principal dancer (cr) in *La Rose malade* (Petit), Ballet de
        Marseille, Paris
1976   Principal dancer in *Bolero* (Béjart), Ballet du XXe
        Siècle, Brussels
        Title role (cr) in *Isadora* (Béjart), Ballet du XXe Siècle,
        Monte Carlo
1979   Title role (cr) in *Leda* (second version; Béjart), Bolshoi
        Ballet, Paris
1980   Title role (cr) and Nina (cr) in *The Sea Gull* (also chor.),
        Bolshoi Ballet, Moscow
1985   Anna Sergeyevna (cr) in *Lady with a Lapdog* (also chor.),
        Bolshoi Ballet, Moscow
1988   Title role (cr) in *Maria Estuardo* (Granero), Ballet del
        Teatro Lirico Nacional, Madrid
1990   Principal dancer (cr) in *El Renedero* (Lopez), Teatro
        Colón, Buenos Aires

Other roles include: Autumn Fairy in *Cinderella* (Sergeyev),
principal dancer in *Bach Prelude* (Messerer), title role in *Phèdre*
(Lifar), Persian Captive in *Khovanshchina* (opera; mus.
Mussorgsky, chor. Koren), Bacchante in *Walpurgis Night* (chor.
Lavrovsky) in *Faust* (opera; mus. Gounod).

WORKS

1972   *Anna Karenina* (with Ryzhenko, Smirnov-Golovanov;
        mus. Shchedrin), Bolshoi Ballet, Moscow
1980   *The Seagull* (mus. Shchedrin), Bolshoi Ballet, Moscow
1985   *Lady with a Lapdog* (mus. Shchedrin), Bolshoi Ballet,
        Moscow

Also staged:
1984   *Raymonda* (after Petipa; mus. Glazunov), Rome Opera
        Ballet, Rome

PUBLICATIONS

By Plisetskaya:
Interview in Feiter, George, "Plisetskaya Portrait", in 5 parts,
Dance News (New York), November, December, 1971;
January, February, March, 1972
Interview in Plekhanova, N., "Talking to Plisetskaya",
Dancing Times (London), February 1972

About Plisetskaya:
Gaevsky, Vadim, "Maya Plisetskaya", *Teatr* (Moscow), no. 1,
1964
Roslavleva, Natalia, *Maya Plisetskaya*, Moscow, 1968
Baril, J., "Maya Plisetskaya", *Les Saisons de la danse* (Paris),
October 1968
Lvov-Anokhin, B., *Masters of the Bolshoi Ballet*, Moscow, 1976
Kapterova, Galina (ed.), *Maya Plisetskaya*, translated by
Kathleen Cook, Moscow, 1976
Demidov, Alexander, *The Russian Ballet Past and Present*,
translated by Guy Daniels, London, 1978
Atlas, Helen V., "Maya the Magnificent", *Ballet News* (New
York), April 1983

Smakov, Gennady, *The Great Russian Dancers*, New York, 1984

Horosko, Marian, "Plisetskaya Teaches", *Dance Magazine* (New York), October 1987

Macaulay, Alastair, "Grand Concerns", *The New Yorker* (New York), 11 April 1988

Barnes, Clive, and Kerensky, Oleg, "Another Bolshoi Ballet", *Dance and Dancers* (London), June 1988

Willis, Margaret, "Boston Bows to Plisetskaya", *Dance Magazine* (New York), July 1988

Messerer, Asaf, "Maya Plisetskaya: Childhood, Youth, and First Triumphs", *Dance Chronicle* (New York), vol. 12 no. 1, 1989

*   *   *

Maya Plisetskaya possesses the grand and buoyant technique of her Bolshoi ballet training. Her dramatic skills are respected for their poetic range and genuine intensity. Strength and confidence characterize her dancing.

Maya Plisetskaya is considered an ideal example of the Bolshoi style, and yet her perfectionism and her determined individual vision set her at odds with the Bolshoi management. Audience reaction to her début performances was so strong that, fearing her potential defection to the West, the Bolshoi determined not to send her on its first tour of the United States in 1956.

Plisetskaya could bring the house down when she danced *The Dying Swan*, originally choreographed by Mikhail Fokine for Anna Pavlova, and some consider her the only ballerina who could surpass the brilliance of its original interpreter. Performed for decades in what often became a double encore, *The Dying Swan* afforded us a glance at the lyrical, albeit struggling swan as impersonated by Plisetskaya. Relying on the superior fluidity and "plastique" of her bourrées across the stage, her miraculous arms took over, framing and shaping the magnificent neck and head of the once proud bird. For the time she was on stage, there was no doubt that she was a dying swan who loved life.

In an era that saw the appreciation of very tall, thin dancers, she was considered muscle-bound. She was one of the first ballerinas to take classes with the men, doing their combinations. She was not a light or fragile dancer. Hers was a light of quite a different sort, that of the thunderbolt; and she conveyed fragility by being vulnerable to love. She defied the earth's gravity with her famous arched-back, split attitude leap, imparted delicacy by understated suggestion, and used her characters' flaws as her own way of showing the true strengths within.

Her greatest triumphs were the tragic roles, where she could complement her technical acumen with her dramatic skills—roles such as Carmen, Anna Karenina, Odette/Odile, and the Dying Swan. These are the roles most often associated with her and they have each come under attack. The critic Margaret Willis complained about Plisetskaya's role in *Lady with a Lapdog* in a 1986 article, saying it was "too passionate, too full of turmoil". It was a role that did not boast refined balletic dance, and some critics and audiences see no point in going to a ballet that is more dramatic gesture than jet-propelled virtuosity.

Some roles suffered. In *Romeo and Juliet*, Plisetskaya was restricted by Lavrovsky's choreography, and the resultant emphasis on the struggle against parental will detracted from Romeo's place in the story.

Plisetskaya sees her maturity as an artistic asset, and refuses to be denied her place as an artist simply because she has somewhat diminished physical capacities. She has challenged everything in the world of ballet. She always took control of her roles, particularly the classical ones, in new ways that some found irritating; however, this was her gift to the audience, as she saw it—a new way of looking.

As she performs less and less, Plisetskaya has tried her talents at directing other ballet companies, such as the Spanish National Ballet and the Rome Opera Ballet.

Plisetskaya's most recent U.S. tour was generally well-received. Although in her sixties, she could still easily be mistaken for being decades younger. She has continued to have problems with the Bolshoi management for not giving her more control over the choice of dancers with whom she can tour; but she says that she will only stop fighting when she no longer has anything to offer.

—Kim Kokich

POLOVTSIAN DANCES FROM PRINCE IGOR *see* **PRINCE IGOR**

PONOMAREV, Vladimir

Russian dancer, choreographer, and teacher. Born Vladimir Ivanovich Ponomarev in St. Petersburg, 22 July (10 July old style) 1892. Studied at the St. Petersburg Theatre School; graduated in 1910. Dancer, performing roles while still a student, Maryinsky Theatre, from 1910, also performing with Diaghilev's Ballets Russes, 1911–12; soloist, State Academic Theatre for Opera and Ballet (GATOB), later the Kirov Ballet, 1912–51; teacher, St. Petersburg (Maryinsky) Theatre School, later Leningrad Choreographic School, from 1913; teacher, Class of Perfection, from 1931, and chief répétiteur, Kirov Theatre, 1944–51, coaching leading dancers including Galina Ulanova, Yuri Grigorovich, Leonid Yakobson, Vakhtang Chabukiani, Konstantin Sergeyev, Petr Gusev, Leonid Lavrovsky; assistant artistic director, Kirov Ballet, 1935–38, becoming acting artistic director, 1941–44; artistic director, Maly Theatre Ballet, Leningrad, 1938–39; also guest teacher, including in Budapest. Recipient: Honoured Artist of the Russian Federation, 1934. Died in Budapest, 21 March 1951.

ROLES

1920   Solor in *La Bayadère* (Ponomarev, Chabukiani after Petipa), State Academic Theatre for Opera and Ballet (GATOB), Petrograd
       Title role in *Petrushka* (Fokine), GATOB, Petrograd
1921   Ivan Tsarevich in *Firebird* (Fokine), GATOB, Petrograd
       The Fisherman in *Pharaoh's Daughter* (Petipa), GATOB, Petrograd
1922   Harlequin in *Harlequinade* (*Les Millions d'Arlequin*; Petipa), GATOB, Petrograd
       The Companion of the Khan and the Genie of the Waters in *The Little Humpbacked Horse* (Gorsky after Saint-Léon), GATOB, Petrograd
       Bluebird in *The Sleeping Beauty* (Petipa; staged Lopukhov), GATOB, Petrograd

The Troubador in *Raymonda* (Petipa; staged Lophu-
    kov), GATOB, Petrograd
Grasshopper in *Caprices of a Butterfly* (Petipa; staged
    Chekrygin), GATOB, Petrograd
1923 The Youth in *Chopiniana* (Vaganova after Fokine),
    GATOB, Petrograd
    Cleopatra's Slave in *Egyptian Nights* (Fokine),
    GATOB, Petrograd
    Colin in *Vain Precautions* (*La Fille mal gardée*; Petipa,
    Ivanov; staged Ponomarev), GATOB, Petrograd
1925 Satyr in *King Candaule* (Petipa; staged Leontiev),
    GATOB, Leningrad
1931 Seid-Pasha in *Le Corsaire* (Petipa; staged Vaganova),
    GATOB, Leningrad
1934 Drosselmeyer in *The Nutcracker* (Vainonen),
    GATOB, Leningrad
    Prince Adam (cr) in *The Fountain of Bakhchisarai*
    (Zakharov), GATOB, Leningrad
1935 Gringoire in *Esmeralda* (Vaganova after Petipa), Kirov
    Ballet, Leningrad
1940 Montague (cr) in *Romeo and Juliet* (Lavrovsky), Kirov
    Ballet, Leningrad
1943 Marcelline in *Vain Precautions* (*La Fille mal gardée*;
    own staging, after Petipa, Ivanov), Kirov Ballet,
    Leningrad

Other roles include: Peasant pas de deux in *Giselle* (Petipa after
Coralli, Perrot), Franz in *Coppélia* (Petipa), Prince Siegfried in
Swan Lake (Petipa, Ivanov), Soloist in *Aragonese Jota* (Fokine),
Harlequin in *Carnaval* (Fokine).

WORKS

1929 *The Red Poppy* (with Lopukhov, Leontiev; mus. Glière),
    GATOB, Leningrad

Also staged:
1922 *La Sylphide* (after Taglioni; mus. Schneitzhoeffer),
    Petrograd Choreographic School, Petrograd
1923 *Vain Precautions* (*La Fille mal gardée*, after Petipa,
    Ivanov; mus. various), GATOB, Petrograd (also
    Leningrad Choreographic School, 1933)
1924 *Sylvia* (after Ivanov; mus. Delibes), Leningrad Choreo-
    graphic School, Leningrad
1925 *La Source* (with Vaganova, after Petipa; mus. Minkus,
    Delibes), Leningrad Choreographic School,
    Leningrad
1926 *The Talisman* (after Petipa; mus. Drigo), Leningrad
    Choreographic School, Leningrad
1928 *Harlequinade* (after Petipa; mus. Drigo), Leningrad
    Choreographic School, Leningrad
1929 *The Seasons* (after Petipa, N. Legat; mus. Glazunov),
    Leningrad Choreographic School, Leningrad
1932 *The Fairy Doll* (after S. and N. Legat; mus. Bayer),
    Leningrad Choreographic School, Leningrad
1941 *La Bayadère* (with Chabukiani; after Petipa; mus.
    Minkus), Kirov Ballet, Leningrad
    Don Quixote (after Petipa, Gorsky; mus. Minkus),
    Kirov Ballet, Leningrad
    Giselle (after Petipa, Coralli, Perrot; mus. Adam), Kirov
    Ballet, Leningrad

PUBLICATIONS

Albert, G., "A Thousand Times Recreated in Children",

Sovetsky Balet (Moscow), no. 2, 1983

*   *   *

Vladimir Ponomarev was a master and a connoisseur of
classical dance. Besides being an important dancer of the pre-
revolutionary period in Russia, he was also an excellent and
influential teacher. He chose not to leave Russia but stayed
with the Maryinsky Theatre all his life, leaving behind him a
valuable legacy which is still felt today.

As a dancer, Ponomarev shone in such roles as the Grasshopper in Petipa's *Caprices of a Butterfly*, and Colin in *Vain
Precautions* (*La Fille mal gardée*), and he was an elegant Ivan
Tsarevich in *Firebird*. Great discipline, coupled with his love
for the art, helped him in the post-revolutionary years to master
many newly created roles in Soviet ballet. He was a good
partner, demonstrating strength, physical endurance, and
dexterity in his performance of pas de deux as well as in his
impressive solo roles.

The most fundamental of Ponomarev's contributions to
Soviet dance, however, was his teaching activity. A brilliant
"method" teacher, and the effective creator of the contemporary school of classical dancing, Ponomarev taught at the St.
Petersburg (later Leningrad) Choreographic School from 1913
to 1950. He was a typical teacher of the St. Petersburg school;
like Aleksandr Pushkin, he was a very mild and cultured man,
intelligent and perceptive, with piercing eyes that seemed to
notice everything that was going on at the Kirov. He was the
natural link between pre-revolutionary and post-revolutionary
ballet; and he actively instilled in dancers the idea that male
dance should be independent, a stronger tradition on its own
than it had been. Important pupils who were influenced by him
included Vakhtang Chabukiani, Nikolai Zubkovsky, Simon
Kaplan, and Aleksei Yermolaev—and he found a ready
response from male dancers willing to put his ideas into
practice. Ponomarev's pupils were always dancers of impeccable style, who had an understanding of the history of ballet;
and under his care, many became great dancers.

After the revolution, during the 1920s, Ponomarev was the
one responsible for preserving the classical heritage of the
Russian school; it was due to him that such ballets as *La
Bayadère*, *Swan Lake*, *The Sleeping Beauty*, and *The Nutcracker*,
as well as important sections from *Pharaoh's Daughter* (*La Fille
du Pharaon*), were remembered and passed on to a new
generation of dancers. He was also one of the more significant
choreographers of late-1920s Russia; *The Red Poppy*, about the
revolutionary movement in China, is probably his best-known
work. He coached Galina Ulanova, and many other ballerinas,
who performed the leading role in this ballet. In 1947 he staged,
along with Chabukiani, the new version of *La Bayadère*, and he
encouraged the young Chabukiani in every possible way to
reproduce the ballet faithfully on the Kirov stage. This is the
version which has remained in the Kirov repertoire to this day.

Later, in the 1950s, Ponomarev was eagerly welcomed by
companies abroad, for example in Budapest, where he was in
demand as the representative of the Russian classical ballet
school. He taught in Budapest in his final years, and he died
there; his body was brought back to Leningrad, where he is
buried. Ponomarev is fondly remembered by the Kirov
company; he, together with Pushkin, Aleksandr Chekrygin,
and Fedor Lopukhov, was the founder of Leningrad ballet as it
is known today.

—Igor Stupnikov

PONTOIS, Noëlla

French dancer and teacher.   Born in Vendôme, 24 December
1943. Studied at the Paris Opéra School, pupil of Janine
Schwarz, Huguette Devanel, Yves Brieux, Raymond Fran-
chetti, Serge Peretti, and Alexandre Kalioujny. Married dancer
Daini Kudo: one daughter, Miteki. Dancer, Paris Opéra
Ballet, from 1961, becoming coryphée from 1963, sujet from
1964, première danseuse from 1966 and étoile, 1968–83, also
touring internationally with Paris Opéra company including to
Russia, 1969; international guest artist, including for London
Festival Ballet, 1967, American Ballet Theatre, 1975, Ballet du
Rhin, 1976, Ballet de Wallonie, French tour, 1977, Ballet
Théâtre de Nancy, and La Scala, Milan, 1984; has also
appeared with Les Ballets de Pierre Lacotte, with Rudolf
Nureyev in various concert performances, and in galas in
London, Tokyo, Hamburg, Bologna, Venice, Stockholm, and
Moscow; has appeared on television, including in *Portrait d'une
étoile* (chor. Kudo, 1972), and in *Giselle* with Baryshnikov
(1981); also teacher, including for Paris Opéra Ballet, from
1988; member of jury of Prix de Lausanne, 1984; chairman of
Fourth Paris International Ballet Competition, 1990. Recipient: Prix René Blum, 1964; Prix Pavlova, 1969; Chevalier de
l'Ordre du Mérite, 1978; Chevalier de la Légion d'Honneur,
1984.

ROLES

1964   Principal dancer (cr) in *La Dame de carreau* (Ollivier),
        Gala, Théâtre de Paris
        Principal dancer (cr) in *Symphonic Metamorphoses*
        (Ollivier), Gala, Théâtre de Paris
        Ballerina in *Grand Pas d'Auber* (also *Grand Pas
        classique*; Gsovsky), Gala, Paris
        Pas de deux (cr) in *Bris* (Schmucki), Gala, Cité
        Universitaire
1965   Principal dancer (cr) in *Adage et variations* (Petit), Paris
        Opéra Ballet, Paris
        Pas de deux des Vendangeurs in *Giselle* (Descombey
        after Petipa, Coralli, Perrot), Opéra, Grenade
1966   Principal dancer (cr) in *Colin Maillard* (Boccadoro),
        French television
        Principal dancer (cr) in *Jazz Suite* (Descombey), Le
        Havre
        Principal dancer (cr) in *Zyklus* (Descombey), T.E.P.
        Principal dancer in *Arcades* (Labis), Paris Opéra Ballet,
        Paris
        Principal dancer in *Pas de trois* (Balanchine), Paris
        Opéra Ballet Gala, Le Havre
        Principal dancer (cr) in *Passepied* (Mayer), Gala
        Principal dancer (cr) in *Banque d'X* (Kudo), Gala,
        Tokyo
        Phryné in *Faust* (Aveline), Paris Opéra Ballet, Paris
1967   Pas de cinq in *Suite en blanc* (Lifar), Paris Opéra Ballet,
        Paris
        La Grisi in *Pas de quatre* (Dolin), Gala
        Princess Aurora in *The Sleeping Beauty* (Petipa),
        London Festival Ballet, London
1968   Principal dancer (cr) in *Sarabande* (Labis), Opéra-
        Comique, Paris
        Principal dancer (cr) in *Extase* (Petit), Paris Opéra
        Ballet, Paris
        Title role in *Giselle* (Descombey after Petipa, Coralli,
        Perrot), Paris Opéra Ballet, Paris
        Principal dancer in *Turangalila* (Petit), Paris Opéra
        Ballet, Paris
        Grand Pas de deux from *The Nutcracker* (Nureyev after

**Noëlla Pontois with Cyril Atanasoff in The Sleeping Beauty, Paris
Opéra Ballet, 1974**

        Ivanov), Paris Opéra Ballet, Paris
        The Young Girl in *Le Spectre de la rose* (Fokine), Gala
1969   Swanilda in *Coppélia* (Descombey), Paris Opéra Ballet,
        Chaillot
        Odette/Odile in *Swan Lake* (Burmeister after Petipa,
        Ivanov), Paris Opéra Ballet, Paris
        Chloé in *Daphnis et Chloé* (Skibine), Paris Opéra Ballet,
        Paris
        Waltz, Mazurka in *Les Sylphides* (Fokine), Paris Opéra
        Ballet, Paris
1970   Principal dancer in *Serenade* (Balanchine), Paris Opéra
        Ballet, Paris
        Principal dancer in *Concerto Barocco* (Balanchine),
        Paris Opéra Ballet, Paris
        Sanguinic in *The Four Temperaments* (Balanchine),
        Paris Opéra Ballet, Paris
        Principal dancer (cr) in *In Quarto* (Goubé), Gala,
        Maisons-Lafitte
        Second Movement in *Le Palais de cristal* (*Symphony in
        C*; Balanchine), Paris Opéra Ballet, Paris
1971   Terpsichore in *Apollon musagète* (Balanchine), Paris
        Opéra Ballet, Paris
        Princess Aurora in *The Sleeping Beauty* (Hightower
        after Petipa), Ballet de Marseille, Paris
        Principal dancer (cr) in *Pas de deux* (Labis), Blois
        Principal dancer (cr) in *Pas de deux* (Lacotte), Saint-
        Malo
        Principal dancer in *Études* (Lander), Paris Opéra Ballet,
        Paris
        Principal dancer in *Flower Festival at Genzano* (Bour-
        nonville), Paris Opéra Ballet, Paris
        Principal dancer in *Le Corsaire Pas de deux* (Petipa),
        Gala, Saint-Malo
1972   Title role in *La Sylphide* (Lacotte after Taglioni), Paris

Opéra Ballet, Paris

Esmeralda in *Notre-Dame de Paris* (Petit), Paris Opéra Ballet, Paris

1973   Principal dancer (cr) in *Onkou*, Gala, Nice

Principal dancer (cr) in *Jeux* (Flindt), Paris Opéra Ballet, Paris

La Grisi (cr) in *Pas de quatre* (Alonso), Paris Opéra Ballet, Paris

Principal dancer (cr) in *Spartacus* Pas de deux (Labis), Gala, Nice

Principal dancer (cr) in *Pulsion* (Kudo), Gala, Poissy

1974   Principal dancer in *Afternoon of a Faun* (Robbins), Paris Opéra Ballet, Paris

La Reine des abeilles (cr) in *Scherzo fantastique* (Robbins), Paris Opéra Ballet, Paris

Principal dancer (cr) in *Variations Diabelli* (Macdonald), Paris Opéra Ballet, Paris

Principal dancer in *Soir de fête* (Staats, Vaussard), Paris Opéra Ballet, Paris

Nikiya in *La Bayadère* ("Kingdom of the Shades" scene; Nureyev after Petipa), Paris Opéra Ballet, Paris

Swanilda in *Coppélia* (Lacotte after Saint-Léon), Paris Opéra Ballet, Paris

1975   La Jeune Fille in *Le Loup* (Petit), Paris Opéra Ballet, Paris

La Fille de Terpsichore from Paris in *Gala Performance* (Tudor), American Ballet Theatre, New York

1976   The Ballerina in *Petrushka* (Fokine; staged Golovine), Paris Opéra Ballet, Paris

Principal dancer (cr) in *Mouvances* (Petit), Paris Opéra Ballet, Paris

Anastasia in *Ivan the Terrible* (Grigorovich), Paris Opéra Ballet, Paris

Principal dancer in *Sonatine* (Balanchine), Paris Opéra Ballet, Paris

Lise in *La Fille mal gardée* (Romanoff), Ballet de Wallonie, Grenade

Principal dancer in *Delta T./L'Infini* (Schmucki), La Havane

Principal dancer in *Tchaikovsky Pas de deux* (Balanchine), Gala, Geneva

1977   L'Ombre in *Les Mirages* (Lifar), Paris Opéra Ballet, Paris

Marie in *The Nutcracker* (Petit), Ballet de Marseille, Paris

Juliet in *Romeo and Juliet* (Skibine), Ballet de Wallonie, Evry

1978   Autumn in *The Four Seasons* (MacMillan), Paris Opéra Ballet, Paris

Pas de deux (cr) in *La Naiade* (Schmucki), Créteil

1979   Principal dancer in *Serait-ce la mort?* (Béjart), Paris Opéra Ballet, Paris

Title role in *Sylvia* (Darsonval after Lifar), Paris Opéra Ballet, Paris

Lucile in *Le Bourgeois Gentilhomme* (Balanchine), Paris Opéra Ballet, Paris

1980   Title role in *Paquita* (Vinogradov after Petipa), Paris Opéra Ballet, Paris

Principal dancer in *Solstice d'eté* (Moreland), Paris Opéra Ballet, Paris

1981   Kitri in *Don Quixote* (Nureyev after Petipa), Paris Opéra Ballet, Paris

Lise in *La Fille mal gardée* (Spoerli), Paris Opéra Ballet, Créteil

Title role (cr) in *L'Oiseau de feu* (Van Dyk), Capitole, Toulouse

1982   Princess Aurora in *La Belle au bois dormant* (Hightower after Petipa), Paris Opéra Ballet, Paris

Sugar Plum Fairy in *The Nutcracker* (Hightower), Paris Opéra Ballet, Paris

Titania in *A Midsummer Night's Dream* (Neumeier), Paris Opéra Ballet, Paris

1983   Juliet in *Romeo and Juliet* (Cranko), Paris Opéra Ballet, Paris

Title role in *Raymonda* (Nureyev after Petipa), Paris Opéra Ballet, Paris

1984   Principal dancer (cr) in *Pulcinella* (Pendleton), Ballet Théâtre de Nancy, Nancy

PUBLICATIONS

By Pontois:
Interview in Lavolé, Jean-Pierre, "Noëlla Pontois", *Pour la danse* (Paris), April/May 1977

Interview in Pourrieux, Frédéric, "Noëlla Pontois", *Danser* (Paris), April 1983

About Pontois:
Niehaus, Max, *Ballett Faszination*, Munich, 1972

Dienis, J.-C., "Noëlla Pontois", *Les Saisons de la danse* (Paris), January 1973

Cournand, Gilbert, *Noëlla Pontois*, Paris, 1979

Mannoni, Gérard, *Les Étoiles de l'Opéra de Paris*, Paris, 1981

Gorlav, J.M., *Noëlla Pontois*, Paris, 1983

Dewez, Alexandre, *L'Étoile*, Paris, 1983

* * *

Noëlla Pontois' association with the Paris Opéra Ballet, lasting nearly a quarter century, saw her emerge as the brightest light of the post-Chauviré generation of French dancers, the first Opéra ballerina after Chauviré to achieve international stardom. Between the time she entered the Opéra ballet company in 1961 and her retirement in 1983 (in accordance with Opéra regulations, which require female dancers to retire at 40), Pontois became the company's de facto prima ballerina. Through guest performances with, among other companies, London Festival Ballet and American Ballet Theatre, she also achieved a level of lasting international visibility that eluded all other French ballerinas of her generation except Ghislaine Thesmar.

Pontois entered the ballet school of the Paris Opéra at the age of ten, and graduated into the company's corps de ballet in 1961. She was awarded the coveted Prix René Blum three years later and reached the rank of premiere danseuse in 1966. The following year Pontois appeared as guest artist with London Festival Ballet, partnered by Rudolf Nureyev. The next year she was elevated to the highest rank in the Opéra hierarchy, étoile.

Although Pontois eventually established her versatility in a wide-ranging repertory, including in works by twentieth-century choreographers Balanchine, Robbins, and Petit, her reputation was secured by her work in the standard nineteenth-century repertory. A slight, fleet, and classically precise dancer, Pontois was celebrated amongst her peers for the purity and refinement of her dancing. Her technical signatures embraced both the lightest, most sparkling of allegro techniques and rock-steady balances, but Pontois was more than the sum of her specialties. She was also, first and foremost, the Opéra's ranking classical artist. Her major triumphs were the ballerina roles in *Swan Lake*, *The Sleeping Beauty*, and *Giselle*. In 1972 she danced the first performance of Pierre Lacotte's highly regarded restaging of *La Sylphide*, after the Taglioni original. Once again her classical perfection and grace made her the ideal interpreter of this authentic return to the spirit of nineteenth-century ballet.

The achievements of Pontois have been recognized worldwide. British critic John Percival, for example, writing about the Paris Opéra Ballet's visit to London in 1982, singled out Pontois for special praise, calling her the best ballerina to live up to the role created by Violette Verdy in Balanchine's *Tchaikovsky Pas de deux*. "Only Pontois", he wrote, "can combine sparkling technique and superb musicianship as Verdy did." Percival goes on, "That gives you the clue what to expect from her: a brilliant virtuosity and control, combine with a very pure classical style. Pontois never imposes her own character on a part; she simply dances it as near perfectly as human nature allows, and lets the choreography shine through her movements."

Pontois married the dancer Daini Kudo, who has also choreographed several small pieces for the ballerina, in 1967. Their daughter, Miteki Kudo, is currently a member of the Paris Opéra corps de ballet. In 1984, the French government awarded Pontois the order of the Chevalier de la Légion d'Honneur.

—Otis Stuart

POULENC, Francis

French composer. Born Francis Jean Marcel Poulenc in Paris, 7 January 1899. Educated at the Lycée Condorcet, Paris; studied piano with mother from age of five; later studied piano with Ricardo Viñes, and with Charles Koechlin, Paris, 1921–24. Met Auric, Honegger, Milhaud, and Satie, 1917–18, becoming part of "Les Six", group of French composers associated with Jean Cocteau from 1918; first ballet score, collaboration on *Les Mariés de la tour Eiffel*, in 1921; commissioned by Serge Diaghilev to compose *Les Biches*, performed in 1924; also composer of incidental music for plays, including for Jean Cocteau, from 1921, and for film, from 1935; remained in France during World War II; first opera staged Opéra-Comique, Paris, 1947; made the first of several visits to the United States, 1948, going on American tour with Denise Duval, 1960. Died in Paris, 30 January 1963.

WORKS (Ballets)

1921   *Les Mariés de la Tour Eiffel* (with Auric, Honegger, Milhaud, Tailleferre; chor. Börlin), Les Ballets Suédois, Paris

1924   *Les Biches* (chor. Nijinska), Diaghilev's Ballets Russes, Monte Carlo

1927   Pastourelle in *L'Éventail de Jeanne* (with various composers; chor. Franck, Bourgat), Salon de Jeanne Dubost, Paris (staged Paris Opéra, 1929)

1929   *Aubade* (chor. Nijinska), Residence of the Vicomte de Noailles, Paris

1942   *Les Animaux modèles* (chor. Lifar), Paris Opéra Ballet, Paris

Other ballets using Poulenc's music: *Sculpture nègre* (Börlin, 1929), *Aubade* (Balanchine, 1930; also Lifar, 1946), *Les Masques* (Ashton, 1933), *Football* (Lander, 1933), *Diana* (Lander, 1933), *Paris-Soir* (Gore, 1939), *Hoops* (Gore, 1951),

Les Animaux modèles (Georgi, 1951), *Le Bal masqué* (Joffrey, 1954), *Les Biches* (Georgi, 1955; also Moncion, 1960, and Darrell, as *The Houseparty*, 1964), *The Masquers* (Bolender, 1957), *Secrets* (Cranko, 1958), *Les Joyeux* (Gore, 1961), *Summer's Night* (Wright, 1964), *Adage et variations* (Petit, 1965), *Aria da Capo* (Neumeier, 1966), *Desportistas* (Gore, 1969), *Gravité* (E. Walter, 1969), *In the Beginning* (Cauley, 1969), *Voluntaries* (Tetley, 1973), *Gloria* (Skibine, 1974; also MacMillan, 1980), *Poulenc Sonata* (Martins, 1985), *Sonata for Clarinet and Piano* (M. Morris, 1987).

PUBLICATIONS

By Poulenc:
Interview in "Entretien avec Francis Poulenc", *Guide de concert* (Paris), April–May 1929
Interview in "Francis Poulenc on his Ballets", *Ballet* (London), September 1946
Francis Poulenc: entretiens avec Claude Rostand, Paris, 1954
Emmanuel Chabrier, Paris, 1961
Moi et mes amis, Paris, 1963
Journal de mes Mélodies, Paris, 1964
Correspondance 1915–1963, edited by H. de Wendel, Paris, 1967

About Poulenc:
Cocteau, Jean, "*Les Biches* ... Notes de Monte Carlo", *Nouvelle Revue française* (Paris), no. 126, 1924
Milhaud, Darius, *Études*, Paris, 1927
Hell, Henri, *Francis Poulenc, musicien français*, Paris, 1958; translated by Lockspeiser, London, 1959
Myers, R.H., "Hommage à Poulenc", *Music and Musicians* (London), July 1963
Roy, J., *Francis Poulenc*, Paris, 1964
Amis, J., "In Search of Poulenc", *Music and Musicians* (London), March 1973
Bernac, P., *Francis Poulenc*, Paris, 1977

*   *   *

Francis Poulenc came to prominence as one of "Les Six", the group of Paris-based composers who began setting new trends in French music after World War I (the other five were Auric, Durey, Honegger, Milhaud, and Tailleferre). Poulenc's first major musical success was in 1924 with *Les Biches*, the ballet score by which he is best remembered, but three years previously he had collaborated with others of Les Six (excluding Durey) in a collective score for *Les Mariés de la Tour Eiffel*, the surrealist entertainment devised by Jean Cocteau and staged by Rolf de Maré's so-called Ballets Suédois.

Poulenc composed two of the ten musical numbers: a tiny, one-minute polka for two cornets that mocked a spoken "Discours du Général", and "La Baigneuse de Trouville" (subtitled "Carte postale en couleurs"), in which a slinky cabaret-type waltz for the bathing belle is framed by animated scene-setting music. The raffish, music-hall character of both pieces points towards the style of affectionate irony that became a frequent element in Poulenc's later music.

Les Biches was a commission from Diaghilev, supposedly for a kind of updated *Les Sylphides*, but Poulenc's own idea was for "a sort of contemporary version of the *fêtes galantes* in which, as in certain pictures by Watteau, anything one wishes may be seen or imagined". The form comprises an overture and eight dance movements, of which two—"Chansons dansées" and "Jeu"—originally had folk-song texts sung by a chorus offstage; but in 1947 the composer re-worked the score so these

Francis Poulenc's *Les Biches*, as performed by the Royal Ballet, London, 1991

could be performed without voices.

Notable passages include the strongly rhythmic "Rag-Mazurka", unusually combining elements of ragtime with the mazurka's triple metre, and the smoothly seductive "Adagietto", sometimes heard separately, for which Poulenc acknowledged a debt to a variation in Tchaikovsky's *The Sleeping Beauty*. The brisk "Final" includes at least one quotation from Mozart (from the finale of the "Prague" Symphony), and other overt influences include the Stravinsky of *Pulcinella* (1920) and the comic opera *Mavra* (1922).

Poulenc nevertheless wove from all this a distinctive style which contributed strongly to the success of Nijinska's original ballet, not least in the sudden, often unexpected modulations of harmony that may make the same phrase in close juxtaposition sound polite one moment and rakish the next. One dance number of elegant refinement will be followed by another of sharp allusiveness, and tender sensibility can suddenly seem coloured by a knowing awareness.

A charming "Pastourelle" was Poulenc's contribution to *L'Éventail de Jeanne*, another corporate effort devised by Cocteau as a ballet involving ten different composers, each of whom contributed one number, of which Poulenc's was the eighth. *Aubade*, for piano and eighteen instruments, subtitled "Concerto chorégraphique", was first choreographed by Nijinska (later by Balanchine and Lifar) and performed with Poulenc as piano soloist; its seven movements played without a break are the composer's counterpart to the *style galant* of the eighteenth-century "opera-ballets" of Rameau.

Les Animaux modèles was a response to a long-standing invitation from the Paris Opéra, a suite corresponding to six fables of La Fontaine first choreographed by Serge Lifar. The music was praised at the time for its richness of harmony and orchestration, as well as for its diversity of rhythmic character, ranging from up-tempo java to restrained adagio—but it has seldom been played since.

Much choreographic use has instead been made of Poulenc's other music, including ballets by Frederick Ashton, Geoffrey Cauley, Walter Gore, Erich Walter, and Peter Wright. An integral dance element has also been found in some of his sacred or quasi-religious music, as in Kenneth MacMillan's *Gloria* for the Royal Ballet (1980), with chorus and solo soprano, and Glen Tetley's *Voluntaries* (1973) in memory of John Cranko, to the Concerto for Organ, Strings, and Timpani.

—Noël Goodwin

———

PRAAGH, Peggy van *see* VAN PRAAGH, Peggy

———

PREOBRAZHENSKAYA (Preobrajenska), Olga

Russian dancer and teacher.   Born Olga Osipovna Preobraz-
henskaya (Preobrajenska) in St. Petersburg, 2 February (21
January old style) 1871. Studied at the Imperial Theatre School,
St. Petersburg, from 1879, pupil of Lev Ivanov, Marius Petipa,
Christian Johansson; graduated in 1889; later trained under
Enrico Cecchetti in St. Petersburg, Caterina Beretta in Milan,
Katti Lanner in London. Dancer of the corps de ballet,
Maryinsky Theatre, St. Petersburg, from 1889, becoming
soloist from 1896, and prima ballerina, 1900; named "Honoured Artist of His Majesty's Theatres", 1909; also guest artist,
touring numerous countries from 1895, including in Dresden
and Monte Carlo, Milan, 1904, Paris, 1909, London, 1910, and
South America, 1912; left Russia in 1921 for Berlin and
eventually Paris; also teacher, St. Petersburg Theatre School
(later Petrograd Choreographic School), 1901–02, 1914–17,
1919–21: students include Alexandra Danilova, Olga Mungalova, Agrippina Vaganova; teacher, Akim Volynsky's private
studio, Petrograd, 1917–21; teacher at own studio in Paris,
1923–60: students include Irina Baronova, Hugh Laing,
Milorad Miskovitch, Tamara Toumanova, Tatiana Riabou-
chinskaya, Nina Vyroubova, Ludmila Tcherina, Mia Slavenska, Igor Youskevich, Serge Golovine. Died in Paris, 27
December 1962.

ROLES

1889   Dancer in *Esmeralda*, Act II (Petipa after Perrot),
         Maryinsky Theatre, St. Petersburg
         Pas de trois in *The Pearl of Seville* (Saint-Léon),
         Maryinsky Theatre, St. Petersburg
1892   Columbine in *The Nutcracker* (Ivanov), Maryinsky
         Theatre, St. Petersburg
1895   The Fly (cr) in *The Caprices of the Butterfly* (Petipa),
         Maryinsky Theatre, St. Petersburg
1896   Imene in *Acis and Galatea* (Ivanov), Maryinsky Theatre,
         St. Petersburg
         Chloë in *Les Offrandes de l'amour* (Petipa), Maryinsky
         Theatre, St. Petersburg
         Anna (cr) in *Bluebeard* (Petipa), Maryinsky Theatre, St.
         Petersburg
1897   Fleur-de-lis in *Esmeralda* (Petipa after Perrot), Mar-
         yinsky Theatre, St. Petersburg
         Swanilda in *Coppélia* (Petipa, Cecchetti), Maryinsky
         Theatre, St. Petersburg
1898   Butterfly in *The Caprices of the Butterfly* (Petipa),
         Maryinsky Theatre, St. Petersburg
1899   Lise in *The Magic Flute* (Ivanov), Maryinsky Theatre,
         St. Petersburg
         Title role in *Giselle* (Petipa after Coralli, Perrot),
         Maryinsky Theatre, St. Petersburg
1900   Pierrette (cr) in *Harlequinade* (Petipa), Maryinsky
         Theatre, St. Petersburg
         Rose (cr) in *Les Saisons* (Petipa), Maryinsky Theatre, St.
         Petersburg
         Sugar Plum Fairy in *The Nutcracker* (Ivanov), Mar-
         yinsky Theatre, St. Petersburg
         Gamzatti in *La Bayadère* (Petipa), Maryinsky Theatre,
         St. Petersburg
1901   Title role (cr) in *Sylvia* (Ivanov, Gerdt), Maryinsky
         Theatre, St. Petersburg
1902   Title role (cr) in *Javotte* (Gerdt), Maryinsky Theatre, St.
         Petersburg
         Naïla (cr) in *La Source* (Coppini after Saint-Léon),
         Maryinsky Theatre, St. Petersburg
         Street dancer in *Don Quixote* (Gorsky after Petipa),

Olga Preobrazhenskaya

         Maryinsky Theatre, St. Petersburg
1903   Baby Doll (cr) in *The Fairy Doll* (N. and S. Legat),
         Maryinsky Theatre, St. Petersburg
         Title role in *Raymonda* (Petipa), Maryinsky Theatre, St.
         Petersburg
1904   Title role in *Paquita* (Petipa), Maryinsky Theatre, St.
         Petersburg
         Princess Aurora in *The Sleeping Beauty* (Petipa),
         Maryinsky Theatre, St. Petersburg
         Princess in *The Magic Mirror* (Petipa), Maryinsky
         Theatre, St. Petersburg
1906   Lise in *Vain Precautions* (*La Fille mal gardée*; Petipa),
         Maryinsky Theatre, St. Petersburg
1907   Angelika (cr) in *The Blood-Red Flower* (N. Legat),
         Maryinsky Theatre, St. Petersburg
         Corn in *Les Saisons* (Petipa; staged N. Legat), Mar-
         yinsky Theatre, St. Petersburg
1908   Solo variation (cr) in *The Night of Terpsichore* (Fokine),
         Maryinsky Theatre, St. Petersburg
         Dance with the Veil (cr) in *Egyptian Nights* (later
         Cléopâtre; Fokine), Maryinsky Theatre, St.
         Petersburg
         Prelude (cr) in *Rêverie romantique: Ballet sur la musique
         de Chopin* (*Chopiniana*, second version; Fokine),
         Maryinsky Theatre, St. Petersburg
1909   Niriti in *The Talisman* (Petipa; staged N. Legat),
         Maryinsky Theatre, St. Petersburg
1910   Odette/Odile in *Swan Lake* (shortened version; after
         Petipa, Ivanov), Hippodrome, London
1915   Gold Butterfly (cr) in *The White Lily* (N. Legat),
         Narodny Dom, Petrograd

Other roles include: at the Maryinsky Theatre—Emilia in *The Haarlem Tulip* (Petipa, Ivanov), Isabella in *The Trials of Damis* (Petipa), Mercedes in *Don Quixote* (Petipa), title role in *Camargo* (Ivanov after Petipa), Gotaru-Gime in *The Daughter of Mikado* (Ivanov), Medora in *Le Corsaire* (Petipa after Perrot), Marietta in *Kalkabrino* (Petipa), Berta in *A Wayward Wife* (Petipa after Mazilier's *Le Diable à quatre*), Aspicia in *La Fille du Pharaon* (Petipa), Dancer in *The Travelling Dancer* (Petipa), Armide in *La Pavillon d'Armide* (Fokine), and character dances, including Rhapsody in *The Little Hump-backed Horse* (Petipa after Saint-Léon), Mazurka in *A Life for the Tsar* (opera; mus. Glinka), Palotas in *Raymonda* (Petipa), Gopak in *Mlada* (Petipa); for Milan tour—leading role in *A Story of the Lace Yarn*.

PUBLICATIONS

Svetlov, Valerian, *Preobrazhenskaya*, St. Petersburg, 1902
Svetlov, Valerian, *Terpsichore*, St. Petersburg, 1906
Legat, Nikolai, "Famous Dancers I Have Known", *Dancing Times* (London), 2 parts: May, June, 1931
Dolin, Anton, "Preobrajenska—Great Ballerina and Teacher", *Dance and Dancers* (London), May 1953
Chandon, Laura, "Preobrajenska at Eighty-Six", *Dance Magazine* (New York), February 1958
Lopukhov, Fedor, *Sixty Years in Ballet*, Moscow, 1966
Krasovskaya, Vera, *The Russian Ballet Theatre of the Early Twentieth Century*, volume 2: Leningrad, 1972
Roné, Elvira, *Olga Preobrazhenska: A Portrait*, translated by Fernau Hall, New York, 1978
Finch, Tamara, "Les Ballets 1933", *Dancing Times* (London), March 1988

* * *

Both Preobrazhenskaya's contemporaries and those who studied her work in later years spoke quite explicitly of the special kind of talent she possessed. "Small in stature, with her calf-muscles bulging conspicuously, very plain-looking off stage and absolutely charming on the stage, Olga Preobrazhenskaya was uncommonly hard-working, and tried persistently to make her every movement expressive and her whole dance imaginative," wrote choreographer and critic Fedor Lopukhov. "She was best suited to lyrical-comic parts, but she could also perform dramatic roles, such as Raymonda and Isora, with real dignity." Preobrazhenskaya's greatest successes, as Lopukhov pointed out, were as Swanilda in *Coppélia*, Javotte, Lise in *Vain Precautions* (*La Fille mal gardée*), and finally, the Butterfly (*Caprices of the Butterfly*)—which, as Lopukhov put it, "the charm of her talent rendered irresistible".

"There is something sweet, playful, and arch about Mademoiselle Preobrazhenskaya's dancing, and when you watch her wayward Butterfly you understand its symbolism, and your heart follows all the events of this graceful love poem," wrote the famous ballet critic Valerian Svetlov. "The fire of her lyrical talent was not very bright, but it was constant and pure," is the way that the historian Vera Krasovskaya has put it. "Preobrazhenskaya's spectators would not shed tears or feel shaken very often—a reaction which Pavlova achieved without any effort. Yet, [Preobrazhenskaya] too was capable of acting with a strong and sincere emotion, even in the most sentimental drama."

"Her charm lies not in the beautiful shape of the body but in the clarity, precision and liveliness of her style, in the generous diversity of those invisible lines which her movements draw in the air. The beauty of her dance can be best described not in terms of painting or sculpture, but rather by comparing it to a drawing," is the way André Levinson described it. Or here is the writer Shebuev, commenting on the ballerina's accessibility to the more general audience, and to the untrained eye: "Preobrazhenskaya has made ballet a popular and democratic art. Of all our ballerinas she is the most accessible to the common public. She has taken the art of ballet from the theatre stage and moved it on to the concert arena. But for all this democratization, for all her success in life and in genre dancing, she has remained a sensitive and accurate artist, always lyrical and romantic, beautiful and stimulating."

Clearly, there has been no shortage of warm and complimentary descriptions of this ballerina. However, Preobrazhenskaya's fame as a dancer has been neither widespread nor long-lived. The reason for this, first and foremost, is the state of transition in which Russian ballet found itself at the turn of the century. During the 1890s, Preobrazhenskaya could not yet equal the sparkling talents of the Italian virtuoso Pierina Legnani, or the leading Russian ballerina of the day, Mathilde Kshesinskaya. On the other hand, during the first decade of the new century, when Preobrazhenskaya's own artistic personality had blossomed and matured, the time had come for a completely different form of expression. Preobrazhenskaya's mastery of ballet technique, her fine precision of line and execution, seemed outdated to Fokine and Diaghilev, who were ushering in the era of Anna Pavlova and Tamara Karsavina.

But Preobrazhenskaya was clearly one of the most outstanding ballerinas of the day, and it says much for her versatility that her best roles ranged not only from the romantic/tragic to the comic in the classical repertoire, but from the traditional to the avant-garde: she performed in several of the first choreographic productions of Fokine at the start of his career in Russia.

And it was Preobrazhenskaya's perfect technical mastery, combined with a sharp analytic understanding of various choreographic techniques—along with the ability to locate, and carefully remove, this or that defect—which led her to become a ballet teacher. In this field, she achieved greatness and indisputable success. While still in Russia, she taught at the St. Petersburg Theatre School, influencing in particular the dancer Agrippina Vaganova, who eventually became a great teacher herself. After leaving Russia and settling in Paris, Preobrazhenskaya (who became known as Preobrajenska) set up her own studio at the Salle Wacker. Among her students, virtually all of whom paid her tribute (either in words or in their own evidence of excellent training), were Diaghilev "baby ballerinas" Irina Baronova, Tamara Toumanova, and Tatiana Riabouchinska, along with such ballet stars as Ludmila Tcherina, Igor Youskevitch, and Serge Golovine. Madame Preobrazhenskaya taught at her studio at the Salle Wacker until 1960.

—Arsen Degen

LES PRÉSAGES

Choreography: Léonide Massine
Music: Petr Ilyich Tchaikovsky (Fifth Symphony)
Design: André Masson
Libretto: Léonide Massine
First Production: Ballets Russes de Monte Carlo, Monte Carlo, 13 April 1933

Les Présages, performed by Les Ballets Russes de Monte Carlo, 1933

Principal Dancers: Nina Verchinina (Action), Irina Baronova (Passion), David Lichine (Hero), Léon Woizikowsky (Fate), Tatiana Riabouchinska (Frivolity)

Other productions include: Teatro Municipal (revival; staged Massine, assisted by Tatiana Leskova); Rio de Janeiro, 16 October 1956. Paris Opéra Ballet (revival; staged Tatiana Leskova); Paris, 17 February 1989. Joffrey Ballet (staged Tatiana Leskova); Los Angeles, March 1992.

PUBLICATIONS

Goodman, G.E., "Décor at the Alhambra", *Dancing Times* (London), August 1933
Beaumont, Cyril, *Complete Book of Ballets*, revised edition, London, 1951
Massine, Léonide, *My Life in Ballet*, London, 1960
Sorley Walker, Kathrine, *De Basil's Ballets Russes*, London, 1982
Finch, Tamara, "*Les Présages* Revived", *Dancing Times* (London), April 1989
García-Márquez, Vicente, *Les Ballets Russes*, New York, 1990
Morris, Gay, "The Joffrey Ballet", *Dancing Times* (London), October 1992

*   *   *

"Ever since my visit to Sicily", Massine wrote in his autobiography, "I had been pondering over the problem of how one could create a correct ballet interpretation of a symphonic work. I had often listened to Tchaikovsky's Fifth Symphony and I felt now that its theme of man and his destiny could provide me with the right material on which to base my experiment." Massine's visit to Sicily took place in summer 1931: the ballet germinated in his mind for a year, and eventually came to the stage after almost another year, in the spring of 1933.

Massine's recollections of the origins of *Les Présages*, filling three pages in *My Life in Ballet*, make fascinating reading, but are too long to quote here. However, what emerges clearly from his account is the choreographer's serious attitude to his work: into the creation of *Présages* was concentrated all the erudition, experience, intellect, and inventiveness recognized and encouraged by Diaghilev some two decades previously, and consequently at the choreographer's command to the very end of his long life.

One of Massine's most brilliant gifts was his capacity to gear the style and content of each and every one of his ballets to the quality of the music he was using—and one of the most telling instances of this was his understanding of the fact that the Tchaikovsky score, in contrast to Brahms' Fourth Symphony to which he created his masterpiece *Choreartium* later in the same year, was basically "programme music", and therefore, when used as a balletic score, called if not for real characters, at least for idealizations, or personifications of ideas, in order to mesh with the ideas and ideals which inspired the composer when writing his symphony. (Tchaikovsky's use of leitmotiv in the score also gave the choreographer a peg on which to hang his own ideas, and must have provided landmarks towards which Massine could work, while wrestling with the creation of an entirely new genre of ballet.)

One of the unique features of *Les Présages* in the 1930s—and a feature equally distinctively on view when the ballet was triumphantly revived at the Paris Opéra more than half a century later—was the way in which Massine deliberately avoided the symmetrical, and eliminated also the "traditional formula of male and female partnering" so that the basic classical ballet was presented in a new form, without conventional "double-work" of the type familiar in the works of Petipa, Ivanov, and their contemporaries. In *Les Présages* there were no supported pirouettes, penché arabesques, or falls; in their place Massine used the contrasted characteristics and strengths of male and female, moving in their individual ways to complement each other, not for the sole purpose of female display. (In this context it is odd to think that in the ballet studio ever since, the now-common lift of the girl held over the man's head, both his arms stretched to their full extent, has been colloquially known for the past fifty years as "a *Présages*"). And in this ballet Massine abandoned completely the solo/pas-de-deux/pas-de-whatever form, which allows applause between short numbers, and breaks the continuity that is so imperative if ballet is to be an art, not merely a display of coquetry for the entertainment of tired businessmen.

Perhaps the most essential novelty of *Les Présages*, and something quite distinct from the technical novelties set out above, was the idea that a ballet which was basically just dancing, without any specified place, time, or story, and with no named characters, could be approached quite seriously by the dancers, and therefore by the audience as well. It was the first example of a ballet geared to nothing but the interest it generated by its movement, which gave its performers absolutely no chance to grin at the audience, or even to acknowledge that audience's presence. As such, *Les Présages*, together with its successor *Choreartium*, opened up an entirely new field to the choreographer, a field followed with great success by many other choreographers such as Ashton with his *Dante Sonata*, *The Wanderer*, *Symphonic Variations*, and other entirely serious dance works. This was in fact distancing classical ballet from the divertissement, in that it engaged the intellect, not merely the eye, in the way that serious music concentrates the mind, not the ear alone.

—Janet Sinclair

————

PRÉVOST, Françoise

French dancer and teacher.   Born (probably) in Paris, 1681. Studied under a Monsieur Thibaud, Paris. One daughter, by Alexandre Maximilien Balthazar de Gand, Comte de Middlebourg: Anne Auguste de Valjolly, b. 1718. Paris Opéra début unknown; probably first appeared in *Ballet des saisons*, 1695; official début, according to some sources, in 1699; began dancing solo roles (sharing with Opéra dancer Mlle. Guyot) after retirement of Mlle. Subligny, 1705; also choreographer of own dances, often in collaboration with composer Jean-Joseph Rebel, and including the famous *Les Caractères de la danse*, 1715; also staged entrées for other female dancers; teacher in Paris: pupils included Paris Opéra dancers Mlle. Richalet, Anne-Marie Cupis de Camargo, and Marie Sallé; retired from Opera, 1730. Died in Paris, 1741.

ROLES

1695   Dancer in *Le Ballet des saisons* (ballet; mus. Lully, Collase, chor. Pécour), Opéra, Paris

1699   Un Roisseau in *Atys* (tragédie-lyrique; mus. Lully, chor. Pécour), Opéra, Paris

1701   Une Petite Jardinière (cr) in *Aréthuse* (ballet; mus. Campra, chor. Pécour), Opéra, Paris

1702   Une Grecque in *Omphale* (tragédie-lyrique; mus. Destouches, chor. Pécour), Opéra, Paris
Entrée des bergers français (cr) in *Mèdus, roi des Mèdes* (tragédie-lyrique; mus. Bouvard, chor. Pécour), Opéra, Paris
Entrée des harlequins in *Cariselli*, divertissement from *Fragments de M. de Lully* (ballet; mus. Lully, Campra, chor. Pécour), Opéra, Paris
Une Suivante de la paix (cr) in *Tancrède* (tragédie-lyrique; mus. Campra, chor. Pécour), Opéra, Paris

1703   Une Grecque, Une Petite Fille in *Les Muses* (ballet; mus. Campra), Opéra, Paris
"Suite de la jeunesse", Bacchante (cr) in *Psyché* (tragédie-ballet; mus. Lully), Opéra, Paris

1704   Une Néréide (solo), Une Prêtresse, Une Grecque (cr) in *Iphigénie en Tauride* (tragédie-lyrique; mus. Desmarets, Campra, chor. Pécour), Opéra, Paris
Une Nymphe in *Didon* (tragédie-lyrique; mus. Desmarets, chor. Pécour), Opéra, Paris
"Suite de la félicité", "Feste marine", Une Bergère (cr) in *Télémaque* (tragédie-lyrique; mus. Campra et al., chor. Pécour), Opéra, Paris

1705   Une Néréide (cr) in *Alcine* (tragédie-lyrique; mus. Campra, chor. Pécour), Opéra, Paris
Une Fée, Peuples, Une Paysanne in *Roland* (tragédie-lyrique; mus. Lully, chor. Pécour), Opéra, Paris
Une Barquarolle, Une Arlequine in *La Vénitienne* (comédie-ballet; mus. La Barre, chor. Pécour), Opéra, Paris
Une Bergère, Une Athénienne, Courtisans de Térée, Une Bacchante, Une Matelotte (cr) in *Philomèle* (tragédie-lyrique; mus. Lacoste, chor. Pécour), Opéra, Paris
Une Bacchante, Une Prêtresse in *Bellérophon* (tragédie-lyrique; mus. Lully), Opéra, Paris

1706   Une Matelotte, Une Néréide (solo) (cr) in *Alcione* (tragédie-lyrique; mus. Marais, chor. Pécour), Opéra, Paris
Une Moresse, Une Sultane in *L'Europe galante* (mus. Campra), Opéra, Paris
Une Bergère (solo) (cr) in *Cassandre* (tragédie-lyrique; mus. Bouvard, Bertin, chor. Pécour), Opéra, Paris
La Danse (duet; cr) in *Le Professeur et la folie* (divertissement) in *Le Carnaval et la folie* (comédie-ballet; mus. Destouches, chor. Pécour), Opéra, Paris
Une Habitante de la Seine, Une Thracienne, Une Grâce, "Suite de Junon", Une Paysanne (cr) in

Polyxène et Pyrrhus (tragédie-lyrique; mus. Collasse), Opéra, Paris
Une Habitante de la Seine, Une Paysanne, Une Matelotte in *Alceste* (tragédie-lyrique; mus. Lully, chor. Pécour), Opéra, Paris

1707   Amans enchantées, Une Marseillaise (solo), Une Génie (cr) in *Bradamante* (tragédie-lyrique; mus. Lacoste, chor. Pécour), Opéra, Paris
"Suite de Cérés", Une Prêtresse, Une Grecque, Une Bergère, Une Divinité in "Suite de Minerve" in *Thésée* (tragédie-lyrique; mus. Lully, chor. Pécour), Opéra, Paris
Duet (cr) in *Mostellaria* (comédie-ballet), for Duchesse du Maine, Chatenay
Dancer in *Amadis de Gaule* (tragédie-lyrique; mus. Lully), Opéra, Paris

1708   Une Bergère (solo), Une Amante, Une Néréide, Une Prêtresse (cr) in *Hippodamie* (tragédie-lyrique; mus. Campra, chor. Pécour), Opéra, Paris
Une Hespéride, Une Chasseuse in *Issé* (pastorale; mus. Destouches), Opéra, Paris
Une Heure du jour, Une Néréide, L'Africaine (solo) in *Thétis et Pélée* (tragédie-lyrique; mus. Colasse, chor. Pécour), Opéra, Paris
Une Nymphe, Une Sarrazine, "Peuple de Palestine" in *Tancrède* (revival, tragédie-lyrique; mus. Campra), Opéra, Paris

1709   Une Aegipan, Peuples, Une Bergère, Une Thébaine (cr) in *Sémélé* (tragédie-lyrique; mus. Marais, chor. Pécour), Opéra, Paris
L'Italie (solo), Une Bergère (cr) in *Méléagre* (tragédie-lyrique; mus. Baptistin [Stuck]), Opéra, Paris

1710   Une Ethiopienne in *Phaéton* (tragédie-lyrique; mus. Lully, chor. Pécour), Opéra, Paris
Une Grecque (solo) (cr) in *Dioméde* (tragédie-lyrique; mus. Bertin), Opéra, Paris
Une Gondolière, Une Espagnolette, Une Matelotte, Une Bohémienne (cr) in *Les Fêtes venitiennes* (opéra-ballet; mus. Campra, chor. Pécour), Opéra, Paris
"Jeux junoniens", "Peuple de la suite de Céphée" in *Persée* (tragédie-lyrique; mus. Lully, chor. Pécour), Opéra, Paris

1711   Une Faune (cr) in *Manto, la fée* (opera; mus. Baptistin [Stuck]), Opéra, Paris
Une Bergère, Une Matelotte in *Amadis de Grèce* (tragédie-lyrique; mus. Destouches), Opéra, Paris
Une Crétoise, "Fête marine" in *Nouveaux Fragments* (fragments from various works; mus. Lully, Campra, Destouches, La Barre; chor. Pécour), Opéra, Paris

1712   Une Matelotte, Une Crétoise (cr) in *Idoménée* (tragédie-lyrique; mus. Campra), Opéra, Paris
Suivante (Fable de l'histoire), Une Athénienne, Une Bergère (cr) in *Créüse l'Athénienne* (tragédie-lyrique; mus. Lacoste), Opéra, Paris
Une Driade (cr) in *Callirhoé* (tragédie-lyrique; mus. Destouches), Opéra, Paris
Dancer (cr) in *Danse du Caprice* (solo; also chor.), Opéra, Paris

1713   Une Bergère (cr) in *Télèphe* (tragédie-lyrique; mus. Campra), Opéra, Paris
Amants contents, "Fête marine" (cr) in *Médée et Jason* (tragédie-lyrique; mus. Salomon), Opéra, Paris
Une Bergère, Un Habitant de Chypre (cr) in *Les Amours déguisés* (ballet; mus. Bourgeois), Opéra, Paris
Une Bergère, Une Amante fortunée in *Armide* (tragédie-lyrique; mus. Lully), Opéra, Paris

1714   Une Bergère, Une Néréide (solo) (cr) in *Arion* (tragédie;

mus. Matho), Opéra, Paris

La Mariée (cr) in *Les Fêtes de Thalie* (opéra-ballet; mus. Mouret, chor. Blondy), Opéra, Paris

Camilla (cr) in *Apollon et les muses* (divertissement after *Les Horaces*, play by Corneille; mus. Mouret, Lamotte, chor. Prévost, Ballon), for Duchesse du Maine, Sceaux

Lemnienne in *Les Amours déguisés* (revival, ballet; mus. Bourgeois), Opéra, Paris

1715 Une Ombre heureuse in *Proserpine* (tragédie-lyrique; mus. Lully), Opéra, Paris

Une Bergère (cr) in *Les Plaisirs de la paix* (ballet; mus. Bourgeois), Opéra, Paris

Pas seul (cr) in *Les Caractères de la danse* (ballet; mus. Rebel, chor. Prévost), Opéra, Paris

Une Prêtresse d'Apollon (cr) in *Théonoé* (tragédie-lyrique; mus. Salomon), Opéra, Paris

1716 Duet (with Guyot) in *Le Bourgeois Gentilhomme* (comédie-ballet by Molière; mus. Lully), Opéra, Paris

Une Marinière (cr) in *Les Fêtes de l'été* (ballet; mus. Montclair), Opéra, Paris

Une Matelotte, Une Bergère (cr) in *Hypermestre* (tragédie-lyrique; mus. Gervais), Opéra, Paris

1717 Une Crétoise (solo), Une Bergère dansante (cr) in *Ariadne* (tragédie-lyrique; mus. Mouret), Opéra, Paris

Une Grâce in *Vénus et Adonis* (tragédie-lyrique; mus. Desmarets), Opéra, Paris

1718 Une Bergère (cr) in *Le Jugement de Pâris* (pastorale-héroïque; mus. Bertin), Opéra, Paris

Une Masque, Fille du seigneur (cr) in *Les Âges* (opéra-ballet; mus. Campra), Opéra, Paris

Une Babylonienne, "Peuples élémentaires" (cr) in *Sémiramis* (tragédie-lyrique; mus. Destouches), Opéra, Paris

Sémiramis in *Sémélé* (revival, tragédie-lyrique; mus. Marais), Opéra, Paris

1719 Une Bergère (cr) in *Les Plaisirs de la campagne* (ballet; mus. Bertin), Opéra, Paris

1720 Une Matelotte, Une Thracienne (cr) in *Polydore* (tragédie-lyrique; mus. Baptistin [Stuck]), Opéra, Paris

Une Néréide (solo), Une Bergère (cr) in *Les Amours de Prothée* (ballet; mus. Gervais), Opéra, Paris

Une Bergère dansant seule, La Mariée (cr) in *L'Inconnu* (ballet; mus. Lalande, chor. Ballon), Opéra, Paris

Un Plaisir, "Quadrille d'Indiens", Une Bergère (cr) in *Les Folies de Cardénio* (ballet; mus. Lalande, chor. Ballon), Tuileries

1721 Une Néréide, l'Amérique (cr) in *Les Éléments* (ballet; mus. Lalande, Destouches; chor. Ballon), Tuileries, Paris

1722 Thalie, Dame de la cour en masque (cr) in *Le Ballet des vingt-quatre heures* (ballet; chor. Blondy), Château de Chantilly

1723 Un Songe inquiet (cr) in *Pirithoüs* (tragédie-lyrique; mus. Mouret), Opéra, Paris

Terpsichore (cr) in *Les Fêtes grecques et romaines* (ballet-héroïque; mus. de Blamont), Opéra, Paris

"Suite de Neptune", L'Amérique (solo) in *Thétis et Pélée* (revival, tragédie-lyrique; mus. Colasse), Opéra, Paris

1725 "Fête marine", "L'Inconstance" (solo) (cr) in *La Reine de Péris* (comédie; mus. Aubert), Opéra, Paris

Une Matelotte, Un Démon transformé en plaisir, Une Bergère (cr) in *Télégone* (tragédie-lyrique; mus. Lacoste), Opéra, Paris

Un Zéphir, "Suite de Pomone" in *Les Éléments* (ballet;

mus. Lalande, Destouches), Opéra, Paris

1726 Une Bergère (cr) in *Le Ballet sans titre* (?*Le Ballet des ballets*; mus. various), Opéra, Paris

Une Egyptienne, Une Bergère (cr) in *Pyrame et Thisbé* (tragédie-lyrique; mus. Rebel, Francoeur, chor. Pécour), Opéra, Paris

Une Troyenne, Une Esclave (cr) in *Les Stratagèmes de l'amour* (ballet; mus. Destouches), Opéra, Paris

1727 Une Bergère (cr) in *Les Amours des dieux* (ballet-héroïque; mus. Mouret), Opéra, Paris

Amants heureux in *Médée et Jason* (revival, tragédie-lyrique; mus. Salomon), Opéra, Paris

1728 Une Bergère (cr) in *La Princesse d'Elide* (ballet-héroïque; mus. Villeneuve, chor. Blondy), Opéra, Paris

"Suite de la sybille delphique", Une Bergère héroïque (cr) in *Tarsis et Zélie* (tragédie-lyrique; mus. Rebel, Francoeur), Opéra, Paris

Une Nymphe de Diane (cr) in *Orion* (tragédie-lyrique; mus. Lacoste), Opéra, Paris

Une Nymphe in *Alceste* (revival; tragédie-lyrique; mus. Lully), Opéra, Paris

1729 Duet in Prologue, Première Entrée (mus. Lully), Une Bergère in "Présent des Dieux", Troisième entrée (mus. Blamont) (cr) in *Le Parnasse* (fragments from various works; chor. Blondy), Versailles

WORKS

1712 *Danse du Caprice* (solo; mus. Rebel), Opéra, Paris

1714 Duet in *Apollon et les muses* (with Ballon; divertissement after *Les Horaces*, play by Corneille; mus. Mouret, Lamotte), for Duchesse du Maine, Sceaux

1715 *Les Caractères de la danse* (later *Les Caractères de l'amour*; mus. Rebel), Opéra, Paris

PUBLICATIONS

Bonnet, Jacques, *Histoire générale de la danse, sacrée et profane*, Paris, 1723

Rameau, Pierre, *Le Maître à danser*, Paris, 1725; as *The Dancing Master*, translated by Cyril Beaumont, London, 1931

Parfaict, les Frères (Claude et François), *Dictionnaire des Théâtres*, Paris, 1756

Noverre, Jean-Georges, *Lettres sur la danse et les ballets*, Stuttgart, Lyons, 1760; as *Letters in Dancing and Ballets*, translated by Cyril Beaumont, London, 1930

Nécrologies des hommes célèbres, Paris, 1771

Grégoir, *Des Gloires de l'Opéra et la musique à Paris*, Paris, 1878

Ces Demoiselles de l'Opéra, Paris, 1887

Dacier, Emile, *Mademoiselle Sallé, Une Danseuse de l'Opéra sour Louis XV*, Paris, 1909; reprinted Geneva, 1972

Daniels, Diana, "The First Ballerina?", *Dance Magazine* (New York), January 1960

Kirstein, Lincoln, *Movement and Metaphor: Four Centuries of Ballet*, New York, 1970

Migel, Parmenia, *The Ballerinas*, New York, 1972

Winter, Marian Hannah, *The Pre-Romantic Ballet*, London, 1974

* * *

Françoise Prévost was one of the earliest ballerinas. It was French composer and dancer Jean Baptiste Lully who first

Mlle. Prévost as a Bacchante, in a painting by Jean Raoux

introduced female dancers to the stage after his assumption of the directorship of the Académie royale de la musique (the Paris Opéra) in 1672, and two of the earliest of these were Mlles La Fontaine and Subligny. Prévost succeeded Subligny in 1705. Nothing is known of her origins, though there is a reference to a Prévost as "Intendent de la danse du roi" in 1646, so it may be that she was of a family of dancers.

According to the *Nécrologies des hommes célèbres*, when Camargo came to study in Paris in 1720/21, Prévost's "graces, vivacity and ear [for music] were already the delight of our Ballets". All her contemporaries emphasized her ability as a mime. Rameau spoke of her grace, lightness, and precision and described her as having "the same attributes as Proteus had in the fable. She takes at will all sorts of forms, with this difference that Proteus employed them often to frighten certain mortals who came to consult him; and she does it only to enchant the greedy eyes which look upon her." Both Cahusac (1754) and Gallini (1762) spoke of the effect that her performance in *Apollon et les muses* (*Les Horaces*) had upon her audience at Sceaux. At the point where the young Horace (danced by Claude Ballon) killed Camilla, Gallini said that "their dance painted it with all the energy and pathos of which it was susceptible", and Cahusac claimed the audience was in tears.

Both Marie Sallé and Marie-Anne Cupis de Camargo were Prévost's pupils. Sallé became her pupil in 1718, and in 1721, due to the illness of Prévost, *Le Mercure* reported that "a young person of 10 or 11 years" was allowed to dance an entrée. It is believed that this young person was Sallé. In 1727 Prévost was again taken ill before a performance of *Amours des dieux* and again Sallé stepped in. It seems, however, that Prévost did not get on quite so well with Camargo. According to the *Necrologies des hommes célèbres*, Prévost tried to keep Camargo in the corps de ballet. It is reported that one evening the dancer Dumoulin missed his cue and failed to appear on stage, whereupon Camargo sprang forward and danced "the entire steps of the absent dancer". This caused a quarrel between Prévost and Camargo with the result that Pécour and Blondy "on the refusal of Dlle Prévost took it upon themselves in future to choreograph and rehearse the various entrées that she [Camargo] had to dance."

In 1715, Jean Ferry Rebel composed a suite of dances for Prévost called *Les Caractères de la danse*. This piece began with a Prelude, followed by a suite of eleven dances in different rhythms, and concluded with a Sonata. The Prelude is introduced with a poem:

In his temple one day,
    Love
said to the mortals
who set up altars to him,
    Make your wishes,
    I want
to see if your inconstant souls
    can be content.
Take advantage, lovers, young beauties
of the gifts which you are given.

Each of the eleven dances then represented a different type of lover, ranging from the Courante—"An elderly lover, sighing for a young beauty, who laughs at him"—to the Musette—"A lover so perfectly happy that she has no request to make of Love". Prévost danced all these lovers, both male and female, herself, and mimed them according to the description given.

It is interesting to note that when Marie Sallé danced the suite in London in 1726, she interpreted it in the same way, illustrating the various characters in mime and dance, whereas Camargo in the same year performed it in Paris purely as a suite of dances and a vehicle for her virtuosity. This may be a clue to Prévost's relationship with her two pupils. There is no doubt that she had a strong technique as well as a very graceful and elegant style. *Les Caractères de la danse* suggests that she also had a sense of humour. Marie Sallé would seem to have inherited these qualities and was possibly temperamentally closer to her teacher than Camargo, for whom technique and virtuosity seem to have been all-important.

—Madeleine Inglehearn

PRINCE IGOR
(*Polovtsian Dances from Prince Igor*)

Choreography: Mikhail Fokine
Music: Aleksandr Borodin (from his opera *Prince Igor*, or *Knyaz Igor*)
Design: Nicholas Roerich
First Production: Diaghilev's Ballets Russes, Théâtre du Châtelet, Paris, 19 May 1909
Principal Dancers: Adolph Bolm (Chief Warrior), Sophie Fedorova (Polovtsian Maiden), Elena Smirnova (Oriental Slave)

Other productions include: Maryinsky Theatre (chor. Lev Ivanov, in original production of Borodin's opera *Prince Igor*); St. Petersburg, 4 November (23 October old style) 1890. Diaghilev's Ballets Russes (staged Bronislava Nijinska after Fokine); Monte Carlo, 24 April 1923. Royal Danish Ballet (restaged Fokine); Copenhagen, 21 October 1925. Opéra Privé de Paris (restaged Fokine); Paris, 26/27 January 1929. Latvian National Opera (restaged Fokine); Riga, 7 February 1929. Ballet de l'Opéra Russe à Paris (staged Nijinska after Fokine, design Ivan Bilibin); Paris, 1931. Teatro Colón (restaged Fokine); Buenos Aires, 1931. Les Ballets Russes de Monte Carlo (after Fokine); Monte Carlo, 11 February 1932. (René Blum's) Ballets de Monte Carlo (restaged Fokine), with Anatole Vilzak (Chief Warrior); London, 15 May 1936. International Ballet (staged Nicholas Sergeyev after Ivanov); Glasgow, 19 May 1941. Metropolitan Ballet (staged Nicholas Beriozoff after Fokine); Northampton, 15 April 1948. Paris Opéra Ballet (staged Serge Lifar, Nicholas Zverev after Fokine); Paris, 22 June 1949. London Festival Ballet (staged Beriozoff, Serge Grigoriev, Léon Woizikowsky after Fokine); 19 June 1951. Royal Ballet (staged Grigoriev and Lubov Tchernicheva after Fokine), with Rudolf Nureyev (Chief Warrior), London, 24 March 1965. London Festival Ballet (staged Vassilie Trunoff after Fokine); London, 19 June 1968.

PUBLICATIONS

Beaumont, Cyril, *Complete Book of Ballets*, revised edition, London, 1951

Grigoriev, Serge, *The Diaghilev Ballet*, translated by Vera Bowen, London, 1953

Barnes, Clive, "Prince Igor", *Dance and Dancers* (London), 2 parts: September, October 1958

Hering, Doris, "Against the Tide", *Dance Magazine* (New York), 2 parts: August, September 1961

Grigoriev, Serge, "*Polovtsian Dances from Prince Igor*", *About the House* (London), March 1964

Prince Igor (Polovtsian Dances) in a production by Nicholas Beriozoff

McDonald, Nesta, "London's First Sight of the Diaghilev Ballet", *Dancing Times* (London), June 1971

*   *   *

Fokine's *Polovtsian Dances from Prince Igor* was the first ballet made especially for Diaghilev's opening season of Ballets Russes at the Châtelet Theatre, Paris, in May 1909. At the close of the Diaghilev era, twenty years later, it was still in the repertoire. Apart from a couple of war-time seasons and for the period immediately following the 1921 débâcle of *The Sleeping Princess*, the *Polovtsian Dances from Prince Igor* held their place throughout—even during the later, more "modernistic" seasons of the company.

It was Diaghilev who came up with the idea of setting a series of dances to excerpts from Borodin's opera *Prince Igor* (which had originally been choreographed by Lev Ivanov in 1890)—and despite Fokine's initial hesitations about the project, his ballet was an instant success. Cyril Beaumont wrote, "No one who has seen this dance will deny its right to be acclaimed a masterpiece. Nothing could be more removed from the traditions of the Petipa epoch and nothing could be more

indicative of Fokine's genius as a choreographer. After its first performance it was greeted with a veritable tempest of spontaneous applause which seemed never-ending. There were no less than six curtain calls."

Fokine's own comments on the birth of this ballet, which eventually he acknowledged as his favourite of all his works, are illuminating. "While in *The Dying Swan*", he tells us, "I wanted to prove that a solo dance number could be expressive even with the most conventional costume, in the Polovetzian [sic] Dances I wished to illustrate the feasibility of the expressiveness of a group dance . . . . Now I reflected. What do I know of the dancing of the Polovtzy? Even history knows very little about these wild people. How can I, in my composition, give some feeling of authenticity, when there is so little known about them? What possible steps could be incorporated into the pattern of these dances? The absence of historic material, and my admiration for the music—which I so feared to ruin— embarrassed me to a degree . . .". But with encouragement from both Diaghilev and the designer, Nicholas Roerich, Fokine was able to overcome his doubts and begin work. "Where did I get my ideas? I should say: from the music alone . . . I visualised everything very clearly and I had faith in the fact that, if the Polovtzy did not actually dance in this way to the music of Borodin, that is exactly how they should have danced."

When one is lucky enough to see these dances of Fokine's performed at the conclusion of the second act of the opera, as given for example by members of the de Basil Ballets Russes at the Royal Opera House, Covent Garden in 1935, with solo singers, orchestra, and chorus combined, it is not difficult to agree with the choreographer that "that is exactly how they should have danced". The musical build-up to the dances, the dramatic situation between the Khan and his captive, the foretaste of the dance music in the score, and the wonderful Roerich set which clears the stage so that the dancers can spread themselves, could lead to nothing but a vast disappointment, were the choreography in any way turned out in a conventional mould, with virtuoso soloists, grinning ballerinas, or any of the pre-Fokine trappings of the accepted nineteenth-century opera ballet. Fortunately, Fokine threw all convention out of the window and produced a work full of steps which fit into the musical structure like a hand into a glove, presenting them in a stage pattern which makes them appear a perfectly natural occurrence, not a staged spectacle laid out simply to divert an audience. Of course at certain points the dancers move towards the footlights; but they are dancing for the Khan and his guest, not for us at all. We just happen to be watching by lucky chance. And even when these dances are presented independently of the opera, their construction still demands the concentration which only dancers not "dancing to the audience" can give.

To anyone who has experienced the Polovtsian Dances in the choreography of Ivanov, as, for example, was produced for the International Ballet of Mona Inglesby in 1941, the difference demonstrated between Fokine and pre-Fokine choreographers is remarkable for the fact that perhaps the actual steps given to the dancers do not always absolutely differ between the two versions; but the difference in presentation stands out vividly.

"My goal", Fokine tells us, "was to create an excitement-arousing dance for the *corps*." No one who has seen his choreography danced in sufficient space, danced with enthusiasm by dancers of passion and personality, could doubt that he achieved it.

—Leo Kersley

THE PRINCE OF THE PAGODAS

Choreography: John Cranko
Music: Benjamin Britten (commissioned)
Design: John Piper (scenery), Desmond Heely (costumes), William Bundy (lighting)
Libretto: John Cranko
First Production: Royal Ballet, Royal Opera House, London, 1 January 1957
Principal Dancers: Svetlana Beriosova (Princess Belle Rose), Julia Farron (Princess Belle Epine), David Blair (The Prince of the Pagodas), Leslie Edwards (The Emperor of the Middle Kingdom)

Other productions include: Ballet of La Scala (restaged Cranko); Milan, May 1957. Munich Opera Ballet (new version; chor. Alan Carter, design Fabius Gugel); Munich, March 1958. Stuttgart Ballet (restaged Cranko), as *Der Pagodenprinz*; Stuttgart, 6 November 1960. Basle Ballet (new version; chor.

Vaslav Orlikovsky), Basle, 1961. Kirov Ballet (new version; chor. Oleg Vinogradov), as *The Enchanted Prince*; Leningrad, 30 December 1972. Point Park Dance Company (new version; chor. Nicholas Petrov, design Boyd Ostroff); Pittsburgh, 2 December 1977. (Carla Fracci's) Compagnia Italiano di Balletto (new version; chor. Sallie Wilson, design Anna Annie), as *Il Principe delle Pagode*; Genoa, November 1979. Royal Danish Ballet (new version; chor. Richard Alston), as *Dances from the Kingdom of the Pagodas*; Copenhagen, 2 April 1982. Royal Ballet (new version; chor. Kenneth MacMillan, design Nicholas Georgiadis); London, 7 December 1989.

PUBLICATIONS

Gishford, Anthony, "The Prince of the Pagodas", Tempo (London), Winter 1956–57
Franks, Arthur Henry, "The Prince of the Pagodas", Dancing Times (London), February 1957
Haskell, Arnold, "Ballet: The Prince of the Pagodas", London Musical Events (London), February 1957
Barnes, Clive, Hunt, David, and Williams, Peter, "The Prince of the Pagodas", Dance and Dancers (London), February 1957
Percival, John, Theatre in My Blood: A Biography of John Cranko, London, 1983
Goodwin, Noël, "Britten and the 'Pagodas'", Dance and Dancers (London), December 1989
Percival, John, and Goodwin, Noël, "Opportunity Knocked", Dance and Dancers (London), February 1990

* * *

Asked by the Sadler's Wells organization to submit a scenario for a three-act ballet, John Cranko set out to devise a work which could be a vehicle for creative choreography rather than a mere pastiche of the traditional full-length nineteenth-century classics. Yet it was still essential for the ballet to have popular appeal. Cranko came to the conclusion that a fairy-tale would best serve both of these requirements, providing a framework for his vivid choreographic imagination as well as an entertainment with a format suited to the traditions of the Royal Opera House.

Cranko originally conceived the work as a series of images from various myths and fairy-tales, linked by a narrative thread which he regarded as of only limited importance. Although he chose to take Petipa as his model, he departed from nineteenth-century balletic convention in two important ways: there was to be no traditional mime, and the classical dance vocabulary would be supplemented, where appropriate, by elements of acrobatics or jazz dance. John Piper, the designer, had worked closely with Cranko on the original plan for the ballet. They had conceived the idea of scenery which moved in such a way as to become part of the choreography, rather than merely providing a static, illustrative element.

The final form of the work, however, was much influenced by the strength of Benjamin Britten's musical imagery. In the end, this tended to dominate many of Cranko's and Piper's original ideas. Britten's composition was based on a number of musical themes, some of them short enough to suit the relevant choreographic requirements, but his main concern was to weave these themes into a musically coherent whole. The result was a powerful score but one which departed too much from Cranko's conception of the ballet. Yet it was Cranko's original idea that held within it the seeds of the ballet's ultimate failure. The hotch-potch of fairy-tale themes comprising the scenario provided numerous choreographic opportunities but lacked the dramatic motivation which a simpler narrative thread would

The Prince of the Pagodas, in a version by Kenneth MacMillan, with Darcey Bussell and Jonathan Cope, Royal Ballet, London, 1989

have provided. Interesting though the music is, several passages were too long even for Cranko's seemingly limitless choreographic invention. There was much to admire but little to involve and move the audience in this spectacular but ultimately unsuccessful production. The struggle between good and evil which is the crux of the story remained a symbolic one, and was never really translated into characters or situations which fully engaged the audience's sympathy.

Cranko's *Pagodas* did not survive in the repertoire, but in 1989 Kenneth MacMillan produced a new version of this work for the Royal Ballet. Some ten years in gestation, the realization of MacMillan's *Pagodas* was several times delayed, partly through his own ill health, and partly because of difficulties in obtaining permission from Britten's estate to alter the relationship between the story-line and the music. In the event, his efforts to rationalize the scenario merely detracted from its fairy-tale flow, as did his attempts to provide the spectator with an insight into the darker, psychological aspects of the relationship between the princess and the four kings.

Departing to a considerable extent from the expressionistic style associated with so much of his work, MacMillan presented *Pagodas* in a classical/romantic manner, seeing it as a homage to the balletic tradition in which he was originally brought up. The ballet contains a torrent of dancing, but it certainly always moves the story forward—something which Cranko had not succeeded in doing. Particularly successful are some of the almost Ashtonian lyrical passages, such as the first-act pas de deux. Much of the other choreography is inventive, if the doublework is sometimes contrived, but the dancing for the corps de ballet borders on the trivial.

In composing *Pagodas* Britten had used the basic structure of a nineteenth-century score, but he transmuted this into a contemporary idiom. In the final analysis, it seems that both MacMillan and his designer, Georgiadis, failed to match this achievement in terms of choreography and décor.

—Richard Glasstone

The Prodigal Son, with Bryony Brind and Rudolf Nureyev, Royal Ballet, London

THE PRODIGAL SON
(original French title: *Le Fils prodigue*)

Choreography: George Balanchine
Music: Serge Prokofiev
Design: Georges Rouault
Libretto: Boris Kochno
First Production: Diaghilev's Ballets Russes, Théâtre Sarah Bernhardt, Paris, 21 May 1929
Principal Dancers: Serge Lifar (The Prodigal Son), Felia Doubrovska (The Siren), Michael Fedorov (The Father), Léon Woizikowsky, Anton Dolin (Friends of the Prodigal Son)

Other productions include: New York City Ballet (revival; restaged Balanchine), as *Prodigal Son*, with Jerome Robbins (Prodigal Son), Maria Tallchief (Siren), Michael Arshansky (Father), Frank Hobi, Herbert Bliss (Servants to the Prodigal Son); New York, 23 February 1950. Royal Danish Ballet (staged John Taras), with Flemming Flindt (Prodigal Son), Anna Laerkesen (Siren); Copenhagen, 31 October 1968. Royal Ballet (staged Taras), with Rudolf Nureyev (Prodigal Son), Deanne Bergsma (Siren), Adrian Grater (Father); London, 25 January 1973 (also staged Royal Ballet Touring Company, Tel Aviv, 8 August 1973). Paris Opéra Ballet (staged Taras); Paris, 29 November 1973. American Ballet Theatre (staged Taras), with Mikhail Baryshnikov (Prodigal Son); Washington, D.C., 10 December 1980. Les Grands Ballets Canadiens (staged Richard Tanner); Montreal, 27 October 1989.

Düsseldorf Ballet (new version; chor. Aurel Milloss), with Milloss (Prodigal Son), Attilia Radice (Siren); Düsseldorf, 10 November 1934. (De Basil's) Covent Garden Russian Ballet (new version; chor. David Lichine), with Anton Dolin (Prodigal Son), Tamara Grigorieva (Siren), Dimitri Rostov (Father); Sydney, 30 December 1938.

Other choreographic treatments of story: Kurt Jooss (Essen, 1931 and new version Bristol, 1939), Ivo Cramér (Stockholm, 1957), Barry Moreland ("Ragtime" version; London, 1974).

PUBLICATIONS

Beaumont, Cyril, *Complete Book of Ballets*, revised edition, London, 1951

Grigoriev, Serge, *The Diaghilev Ballet*, translated by Vera Bowen, London, 1953

Balanchine, George, with Mason, Francis, *Balanchine's Festival of Ballet*, Garden City, N.Y., 1977

Croce, Arlene, *Afterimages*, New York, 1977

Hunt, Marilyn, "George Balanchine's *Prodigal Son*", *Dance Magazine* (New York), May 1981

Croce, Arlene, *Going to the Dance*, New York, 1982

Hunt, Marilyn, "The Prodigal Son's Russian Roots", *Dance Chronicle* (New York), vol. 5, no. 1, 1982

Taper, Bernard, *Balanchine*, revised edition, New York, 1984

*   *   *

The Prodigal Son was the last work Balanchine made for Diaghilev's Ballets Russes in 1929; it was revived in 1950 by the New York City Ballet with Jerome Robbins in the role of the Prodigal Son. Since then many great male dancers have performed the ballet, including Edward Villella, the virile Prodigal of the 1960s, and Mikhail Baryshnikov in the early 1980s. Its music, by Prokofiev, was written for the ballet, and its costumes and décor were created by Rouault, making it a perfect example of the collaborative efforts among artists that produced some of the best works of the Diaghilev era.

The Prodigal Son offers one of the few great male dramatic roles in modern ballet; the demands it makes on its principal dancer are enormous. The first and last scenes of the ballet, which take place at the home of the Prodigal's Father and two sisters, must somehow be made to link with the central scene of profligacy, during which the Prodigal is made drunk, seduced, and robbed by a group of grotesque revellers and a long-legged Siren. In the first scene the Father, a huge figure in a cloak and elevator shoes who towers over the Son, tries to pull the Prodigal into a submissive family group. The Prodigal rebels (understandably enough, it seems) against this overwhelming paternal power and leaves home, leaping over the gate in haste and defiance. When he returns in the third section, however, pulling himself along on his knees with the aid of a staff, he is too weak even to open the gate, and finally must be carried in to where he prostrates himself at his Father's feet and begs for succour.

In comparison to this world of demeaning filial servitude, anything outside would seem to be preferable. But no, in this work Balanchine suggests that servitude is better than experience—given that experience is so horrible. The nine trogloditic revellers, clad in bald skull-caps, play patty-cake, lift each other by the crotch, and form an impenetrable wall that shoots out arms from all directions as the Prodigal arrives and attempts to make their aquaintance. Finally the Prodigal thinks he is getting along better with them, and has joined in their flat-footed leaps when the Siren arrives.

Perennially on pointe and elongated with a scarlet headdress to match her endless scarlet train, the Siren wraps the cape around her thighs, beats her breast and back in slow motion, and walks like a crab, dragging her cloak out behind her and then drawing it over her as she crouches in a turtle position. When the Prodigal pulls the cloak off she unfolds, dancing a twisting, sinuous solo like an Indian goddess come to life. The two of them form a four-armed deity. She slides down his back, forms a ring and slips down his legs to the floor, then sitting on his head; and the seduction ends with the Prodigal's head on her breast and her arm raised in triumph. Then follows the robbery: the revellers stamp on the Prodigal, slide him down the table (the multi-purpose piece of décor that serves as fence, table, and wall), then stand him up and run their feelers up and down his sides. His two companions hold him upside down and shake him; the Siren steals his jewel. The scene ends as the revellers form the oars of a ship (the table, once again flat on the floor) while the Siren's cloak becomes the sail.

Many of the individual details of this dance are unforgettable, from the swaying walk of the revellers to the Siren's stylized bumps and grinds. The music is a masterpiece in its own right, and the power of a great Prodigal can more than contain the piece's flirtation with camp (what many critics have sensed as the work's 1920s feel). Yet it may be that the bedrock situation of this piece is simply too far from the modern experience for it to speak to us as anything more than melodrama. For it seems to present a duality of, on one hand, a domestic situation that offers safety at the price of bowing to the iron will of a dominant father, and on the other a world of knowledge that is at the same time both terrible and destructive. Is there no alternative to these, no more gradual transition to adulthood? Or is it perhaps the case that the world really is like this?—can it be that this work is in fact the perfect expression of the modern age?

—Bruce Fleming

PROKOFIEV, Sergei

Ukrainian/Soviet composer.   Born Sergei Sergeevich Prokofiev in Sontsovka, Ukraine, 23 April (11 April old style) 1891.
First tutored by Reinhold Glière, from 1902; studied at the St.
Petersburg Conservatory (on advice of Aleksandr Glazunov),
1904–14, with graduation from composition course, 1908–09,
piano studies under Anna Esipova, from 1909, and conducting
course under Nikolai Tcherepnin. Married (1) singer Lina
Llubera, 1923: two sons, Svyatoslav (b. 1924) and Oleg (b.
1928); (2) Mira Mendelson. Début as composer-pianist, 1908;
travelled to London to meet Serge Diaghilev, 1914: first ballet,
Ala and Lolly, 1914 (though not performed until 1927);
performed New York, 1918, returning to tour the United
States, various seasons, 1919–22, and Paris, 1920, and more
regularly from 1922; after many years abroad, returned to the
Soviet Union as permanent resident, 1936; composed most
famous ballet, *Romeo and Juliet*, at request of the Kirov
Theatre, 1935–36 (official Leningrad premiere, with some
alterations, not until 1940); several early works banned by
Soviet government, 1948. Recipient: Rubinstein Prize, Petrograd, 1914; title of People's Artist of the Russian Federation,
1947. Died in Moscow, 5 March 1953.

WORKS (Ballets)

1914 *Ala and Lolly* (commissioned by Diaghilev, but not
      performed; later staged Terpis, Berlin, 1927)
1921 *Chout* (chor. Slavinsky, Larionov), Diaghilev's Ballets
      Russes, Paris
1925 *Trapeze* (chor. Romanov), Russian Romantic Ballet
      (Boris Romanov Company), Berlin
1927 *Le Pas d'acier* (*The Steel Dance*; chor. Massine),
      Diaghilev's Ballets Russes, Paris
1929 *Le Fils prodigue* (*The Prodigal Son*; chor. Balanchine),
      Diaghilev's Ballets Russes, Paris
1932 *Sur le Borysthène* (chor. Lifar), Paris Opéra Ballet, Paris
1938 *Romeo and Juliet* (chor. Psota), Brno, Czechoslovakia
1945 *Zolushka* (*Cinderella*; chor. Zakharov), Bolshoi Ballet,
      Moscow
1954 *The Story of the Stone Flower* (later staged as *The Stone
      Flower*; chor. Lavrovsky), Bolshoi Ballet, Moscow

Other ballets using Prokofiev's music: *Visions Fugitives* (Golei-
zovsky, 1922; also Sanders, 1973; van Manen, 1990), *Prodigal
Son* (new version; chor. Milloss, 1934; also Lichine, 1938), *Gala
Performance* (Tudor, 1938), *Peter and the Wolf* (Bolm, 1940; also
Staff, 1940; Cramér, 1950; Parlic, 1951), *Romeo and Juliet* (new
version, chor. Lavrovsky, 1940; also Cullberg, 1944, 1955, and
1969; Gsovsky, 1948; Parlić, 1949; Ashton, 1955; Lifar, 1955;
Cranko, 1958 and 1962; Staff, 1964; MacMillan, 1965;
Vinogradov, 1965; van Dantzig, 1967 and 1974; Neumeier,
1971; Boyarchikov, 1972; Smuin, 1976; Nureyev, 1977; Araiz,
1977; Panov, 1984; Seregi, 1985), *Russian Soldier* (Fokine,
1942), *Cinderella* (new version; chor. Sergeyev, 1946: also
Ashton, 1948; Gsovsky, 1950 and 1952; Orlikowsky, 1963;
Vinogradov, 1964; Adret and Staff, 1966; W. Christensen,
1967; Stevenson, 1970; L. Christensen and Smuin, 1973;
Panov, 1977), *Pygmalion* (Lifar, 1947), *Para la dó oriente*
(Cramér, 1948), *Stone Portal* (Cullberg, 1950), *Quartet* (Rob-
bins, 1954), *Le Retour* (Skibine, 1954), *Symphonie classique*
(Lifar, 1957; also Bolender, 1982), *The Stone Flower* (new
version; chor. Grigorovich, 1957; also Schilling, 1960; Orli-
kowsky, 1962; Walter, 1976), *Estro arguto* (Milloss, 1957), *The
Hound of Heaven* (Neumeier, 1960), *Prokofiev Waltzes* (L.
Christensen, 1961), *Image chorégraphique* (Lichine, 1962),
Fantasma (L. Christensen, 1963), *Lieutenant Kizhe* (Lapauri,

Tarasova, 1963), *Classical Symphony* (Lavrovsky, 1966), *Har-
binger* (Feld, 1967), *Aleksandr Nevsky* (Vinogradov, 1969),
Deuxième Concerto (Blaska, 1970), *Four Portraits* (Darrell,
1971), *Triad* (MacMillan, 1972), *An Evening's Waltzes* (Robbins, 1973), *Ivan the Terrible* (Grigorovich, 1975), *Tsar Boris*
(Boyarchikov, 1975), *Opus 19* (Robbins, 1979), *Piano Variations
II* (*Sarcasms*) (van Manen, 1981), *The Heart of the Matter*
(Kudelka, 1986), *Romeo and Juliet Before Parting* (Kudelka,
1990), *Violin Concerto* (*Misfits*) (Kudelka, 1990), *Désir* (Kudelka, 1991).

PUBLICATIONS

By Prokofiev:
Autobiography, edited by M.G. Kozlova, Moscow, 1973

About Prokofiev:
Sergei Prokofiev: Autobiography, Articles, Reminiscences (var-
     ious authors), Moscow, n.d.
Nesteva, Marina Izrailevna, *Prokofiev*, Moscow, 1957; trans-
     lated by Jonas, London, 1960; enlarged edition, 1973
Katanova, S., *The Ballets of Prokofiev*, Moscow, 1962
Hanson, L. and E., *Prokofiev*, London, 1964
Dorris, George, "Prokofiev and the Ballet", *Ballet Review*
     (New York), vol. 5, no. 6, 1974
Danko, L., *S.S. Prokofiev*, Moscow and Leningrad, 1966
Dorris, George, "Music for Spectacle", *Ballet Review* (Brook-
     lyn, N.Y.), vol. 6, no. 1, 1977
Goodwin, Noël, "Prokofiev and the Ballet", *Dance and Dancers*
     (London), January, 1983
Savkina, Natalia, *Prokofiev*; translated by Catherine Young,
     Neptune City, N.J., 1984
Robinson, Harlow, *Prokofiev: A Biography*, New York, 1987
Guttman, David, *Prokofiev*, London, 1988
Kennicott, P., "Dance Music: Sergei and Ivan", *Dance
     Magazine* (New York), October 1990
Goodwin, Noël, "The Prodigal's Return", *Dance and Dancers*
     (London), April 1991

*   *   *

With Prokofiev's music for *Romeo and Juliet* having stimulated
choreographic versions worldwide, he must be counted the
twentieth-century's leading ballet composer after Stravinsky.
His nine original scores for dance began with the abortive *Ala
and Lolly* (1914), invited by Diaghilev but then turned down
after a change of mind about the story to which it was
composed (the music was re-cast for concert performance as the
Scythian Suite, Op. 20), and perhaps because both story and
musical idiom were too reminiscent at the time of *The Rite of
Spring*.

Prokofiev and Diaghilev together then mapped out another
scenario for *Chout*, the name of a comic peasant character or
buffoon in Russian folk-tales. Its six scenes, linked by musical
entr'actes, alternate narrative passages with set dances in
closed forms. Principal characters are given folk-like themes,
although the melodic line may be caricatured in wide leaps and
the harmony distorted. Prokofiev himself conducted the Paris
premiere, and later made a concert suite of twelve numbers
from it.

Of his two further scores for Diaghilev, *Le Pas d'acier* (*The
Steel Dance*) in 1927 had its chosen "socialist realism" theme,
praising the virtues of factory work, reflected in pounding
ostinato rhythms and a toccata-like melodic fabric. The music
turned away from earlier chromaticism towards more diatonic
harmony, as did *The Prodigal Son*, on the Biblical parable, for

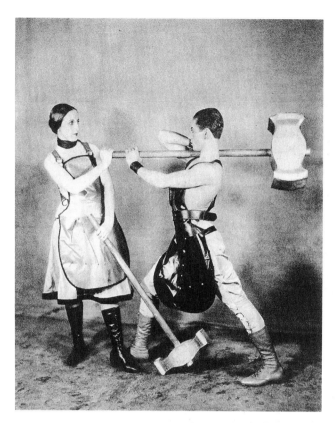

Prokofiev's *Le Pas d'acier*, with Lubov Tchernicheva and Serge Lifar, Diaghilev's Ballets Russes, Paris, 1927

which Balanchine's contrasts of mood and situation were skilfully matched by and to the music. Some of this foreshadowed the richer lyricism of Prokofiev's later three-act ballets, as the Siren's music is likewise a prototype for his later heroines: Juliet, Cinderella, and (in the opera *War and Peace*) Natasha.

The earlier *Trapeze* was a short-lived ballet on a circus theme for Boris Romanov, whose company could not afford an orchestra. It was accordingly composed for a quintet of oboe, clarinet, violin, viola, and double-bass, and with the idea of separate musical performance, for which Prokofiev later incorporated the music in his Quintet, Op.39. *Sur le Borysthène* (*On the Dnieper*) for Serge Lifar had music in a similar style to *Prodigal Son* but few performances; Prokofiev made an orchestral suite from it the next year, but even this has been seldom heard.

After many years in the West, Prokofiev returned permanently to the USSR in the mid-1930s, where he was asked by the Leningrad Kirov Theatre management for a *Romeo and Juliet* score that would meet the prevailing taste for three-act narrative ballets. Subsequent procrastination at Leningrad and Moscow (never fully explained) led to the premiere production at Brno (Czechoslovakia) instead (in 1938), as well as to Prokofiev's publication of three concert suites from the music. Various musical changes and additions were made for Leonid Lavrovsky's production at Leningrad (1940) and Moscow (1946), from which the ballet's wider success then stemmed.

In its definitive form the score provides a basis of illustrative musical strife against which the lyrical love-tragedy develops, and expresses the drama's force of destiny. Juliet's awakening from shyness to passion can be traced in the music, as can Romeo's change from impetuous youthfulness to ardent love and aggressive anger. Other characters are musically outlined

but not developed; the leading themes are flexibly varied, from particular personality to more general mood or situation, rather than rigidly applied.

For *Cinderella*, Prokofiev sought musical sophistication, taking older dance forms like the gavotte, pavane, and passepied, and opening them out into a narrative structure to give illustrative support to the dance movement. *The Stone Flower*, for which the Urals-based folk-tale was partly shaped by his second wife, Mira Mendelson-Prokofieva, makes some use of themes from earlier (non-ballet) works, and has a more folk-like flavour in the lyrical romantic musical tradition. On the day he finished revising the last-act pas de deux as the ballet was in its much-postponed rehearsal at Moscow, Prokofiev died without having heard or seen it performed (his death exactly coinciding with that of Stalin).

Prokofiev once defined five stylistic elements which appertain to his ballet music as much as to the rest: continuing use of a classical idiom; innovatory harmonies, especially in his youthful works; the often-favoured percussive "motor-rhythms"; the impulse to lyricism, most obvious in the later ballets; and the *scherzando* element of humour or caricature, first evident in *Chout* but to be found in the more romantic scores as well. His ear for striking instrumental colour plays an important part in the theatre success of his ballet music.

These elements have also meant that some of his concert works have been given a fruitful dance context, for example the Classical Symphony (No.1) in Antony Tudor's *Gala Performance* (1938), Violin Concerto No.1 for Kenneth MacMillan (*Triad*, 1972) and Jerome Robbins (*Opus 19*, 1979); various anthologies for Yuri Grigorovich (*Ivan the Terrible*, 1975) and Nikolai Boyarchikov (*Tsar Boris*, 1975), and ballets by a number of other choreographers.

—Noël Goodwin

PROKOVSKY, André

French dancer, choreographer, and ballet director. Born in Paris of Russian parents, 13 January 1939. Studied with Lubov Egorova, Nora Kiss, Serge Peretti, Nicholas Zverev, Paris. Married dancer Galina Samsova, 1972 (div. 1981). Début in Molière's *Les Amants magnifiques*, Comédie-Française, 1954; dancer, Les Ballets Janine Charrat, touring Spain, Portugal, France, and Italy, 1954; performed with Jean Babilée company, 1954, and Roland Petit's Ballets de Paris, 1956; dancer, London Festival Ballet, from 1957, becoming principal dancer in same year; principal dancer, Grand (International) Ballet du Marquis de Cuevas, 1960–61; principal dancer, New York City Ballet, 1963–66; international guest artist, including for Stuttgart Ballet, 1960, Rome Opera, Spoleto Festival, Belgrade and Zagreb Operas, various seasons, 1961–63, and in Zurich, Munich, Dallas, Washington, D.C., 1963–66; toured Far East with ensemble of French dancers, 1964; guest artist, PACT Ballet, South Africa, 1966 and 1967; principal dancer, London Festival Ballet, 1966–73; founder, principal dancer and co-director, with Galina Samsova, New London Ballet, 1972–77, and for brief season in 1979; artistic director, Rome Opera Ballet, 1977–78; guest choreographer, staging ballets for Australian Ballet, PACT Ballet, Northern Ballet Theatre, Turin Ballet, Nice Opera Ballet, Norwegian Ballet, London City Ballet, and others; freelance choreographer, from 1979. Recipient: Silver Medal, International Ballet Competition, Moscow Festival of Youth, 1957; Nijinsky Prize, Paris, 1967.

André Prokovsky with Galina Samsova in *Le Corsaire* Pas de deux

ROLES

1957 Variation (cr) in *Variations for Four* (Dolin), London Festival Ballet, London

Prince in *The Nutcracker* (Lichine), London Festival Ballet, London

1958 Gennaro in *Napoli* (Lander after Bournonville), London Festival Ballet, tour

Principal dancer in *Études* (Lander), London Festival Ballet

Drummer in *Graduation Ball* (Lichine), London Festival Ballet

Blackamoor in *Petrushka* (Fokine), London Festival Ballet

Prince in *Black Swan Pas de deux* (from *Swan Lake*; after Petipa), London Festival Ballet

1959 Dancer in *Don Quixote* Pas de deux (Dolin after Obukhov), London Festival Ballet

Chief Guardsman in *London Morning* (Carter), London Festival Ballet

Polovtsian Chief in *Polovtsian Dances from Prince Igor* (Fokine; staged Trunoff), London Festival Ballet

Principal dancer in *Vita Eterna* (Lander), London Festival Ballet, London

Prince in *Swan Lake*, Act II (after Petipa, Ivanov), London Festival Ballet

1960 Le Garçon (cr) in *Barbaresque* (Adret), London Festival Ballet, Nice

The Prince in *The Sleeping Beauty* (Petipa, Nijinska), Grand (International) Ballet du Marquis de Cuevas, Paris

Principal dancer in *Hommage à Garnier* (Lifar), Royal Academy of Dancing Gala, London

1962 Albrecht in *Giselle* (after Petipa, Coralli, Perrot), Grands Ballets de France, Paris

1963 Principal dancer in *Idylle* (Skibine), Bordeaux

First Movement in *Symphony in C* (Balanchine), New York City Ballet, New York

Principal dancer in *Scotch Symphony* (Balanchine), New York City Ballet, New York

Principal dancer in *Gounod Symphony* (Balanchine), New York City Ballet, New York

Fourth Campaign in *Stars and Stripes* (Balanchine), New York City Ballet, New York

Dancer in *Tchaikovsky Pas de deux* (Balanchine), New York City Ballet, New York

Principal dancer in *Raymonda Variations* (Balanchine), New York City Ballet, New York

Duke (cr) in *The Chase* (d'Amboise), New York City Ballet, New York

1964 Principal dancer (cr) in *Irish Fantasy* (d'Amboise), New York City Ballet, New York

Iphias in *Piège de lumière* (Taras), New York City Ballet, New York

1965 Principal dancer (cr) in *Pas de deux and Divertissement* (Balanchine), New York City Ballet, New York

1966 Allegro (cr) in *Brahms–Schoenberg Quartet* (Balanchine), New York City Ballet, New York

Prince Siegfried in *Swan Lake* (Carter after Petipa, Ivanov), London Festival Ballet, Southampton

The Marquis in *Beatrix* (Carter), London Festival Ballet, London

Pas de deux from *Le Corsaire* (Klavin), London Festival Ballet

Principal dancer in *Walpurgis Night* (Adams), London Festival Ballet, Venice

1967 The Prince in *The Nutcracker* (Carter), London Festival Ballet

Principal dancer in *Paquita* (Petipa; staged Casenave), London Festival Ballet, Oxford

Principal dancer (cr) in *Gluck Pas de deux* (Wright), London Festival Ballet, London

Bluebird in *The Sleeping Beauty* (Stevenson after Petipa), London Festival Ballet, London

Prince Florimund in *The Sleeping Beauty* (Stevenson after Petipa), London Festival Ballet, Bournemouth

1968 Principal dancer in *Minkus Pas de deux* (Balanchine; staged Prokovsky), London Festival Ballet, London

1969 The Young Convict in *Piège de lumière* (Taras), London Festival Ballet, Venice

Principal dancer in *Unknown Island* (Carter), London Festival Ballet, Rome

Principal dancer in *Spring Waters* (Messerer), London Festival Ballet

1970 Principal dancer in *Dvořák Variations* (Hynd), London Festival Ballet, Nottingham

Basil in *Don Quixote* (full-length version; Borkowski after Gorsky), London Festival Ballet, London

1971 Title role in *Petrushka* (Fokine; staged Beriozoff), London Festival Ballet, London

1972 Principal dancer in *Danscape* (Gore), London Festival Ballet, London

1973 Principal dancer in *Mozartiana* (Hynd), London Festival Ballet, London

Iskander in *La Péri* (Darrell), London Festival Ballet, London

Principal dancer in *Moses* (also chor.), New London Ballet, Trieste

Title role in *Othello* (Darrell), New London Ballet, Trieste

Principal dancer in *Laurencia Pas de six* (after Chabukiani), New London Ballet, Trieste

Principal dancer in *Tanka* (Uboldi), New London Ballet, Seville

Principal dancer (cr) in *Vespri* (also chor.), New London Ballet, La Coruña, Spain

1975 Principal dancer (cr) in *Elégie* (later called *Soft Blue Shadows*; also chor.), New London Ballet, Southsea

Principal dancer in *Faust Divertimento* (also chor., with Samsova), New London Ballet

1976 Pas de deux in *William Tell* (opera; mus. Rossini, chor.

Charrat), Rome Opera Ballet, Rome

1977 Jean de Brienne in *Raymonda*, Act III (Nureyev after Petipa), Sadler's Wells Royal Ballet, London

Other roles include: principal dancer in *Les Sylphides* (Fokine), principal dancer in *Allegro Brillante* (Balanchine), Sanguinic in *The Four Temperaments* (Balanchine).

WORKS

1971 *Moses* (mus. Rossini), Opera Ballet, Trieste

1972 *Scarlatti and Friends* (mus. Scarlatti, Fiorenza), New London Ballet, Cyprus

Bagatelles, Opus 126 (mus. Beethoven), New London Ballet (restaged and revised, Northern Ballet Theatre 1976)

1973 *Vespri* (mus. Verdi), New London Ballet, La Coruña, Spain

1974 *Piano Quartet No. 1* (mus. Beethoven), New London Ballet

Folk Songs (mus. Berio), New London Ballet

1975 *Simorgh* (mus. Tjeknavorian), New London Ballet, Birmingham

Élégie (later called, in expanded version, *Soft Blue Shadows*; mus. Fauré), New London Ballet, Southsea

Commedia I (mus. Bennett), New London Ballet, London

The Seven Deadly Sins (mus. Weill), PACT Ballet, Johannesburg

1976 *Faust Divertimento* (with Samsova; mus. Gounod), New London Ballet, tour

1977 "April", "October" in *Our Tchaikovsky* (various chors.), New London Ballet, British tour

Day Dreams (mus. arranged Riley), Northern Ballet Theatre, Manchester

1978 *Pantea* (mus. Malpiero), Turin Ballet, Turin

Sonata (mus. Bartók), Rome Opera Ballet, Rome

1979 *Anna Karenina* (mus. Tchaikovsky, arranged Woolfenden), Australian Ballet, Melbourne

Königsmark (mus. Tchaikovsky, arranged Grey), New London Ballet, York

1980 *The Three Musketeers* (mus. Verdi, arranged Woolfenden), Australian Ballet, Sydney

1981 *The Storm* (mus. Shostakovich, arranged Riley), London Festival Ballet, Southsea

Verdi Variations (mus. Verdi), London Festival Ballet, Norwich

The Nutcracker (mus. Tchaikovsky), Northern Ballet Theatre, Manchester

1983 *Brahms Love Songs* (mus. Brahms), Northern Ballet Theatre

Zhivago (mus. Rimsky-Korsakov, Borodin, arranged Tuffin), CAPAB Ballet, South Africa

1984 *That Certain Feeling* (originally *The Aquarium*; also *Fascinating Rhythm* and *Gershwin Songbook*; mus. Gershwin), London Festival Ballet, Dartford

Mathilde (mus. Wagner), London City Ballet, Swindon

Vocalise Opus 34 (mus. Rachmaninov), Sadler's Wells Royal Ballet, London

1985 *Romeo and Juliet* (mus. Berlioz, arranged Salzedo), London City Ballet, Kristiansand, Norway

Two Berio Pieces (mus. Berio), Teatro Communale, Florence

Ballet of the Nuns in *Robert le Diable* (opera; mus. Meyerbeer), Paris Opéra, Paris

1986 *Victoria*, Norwegian Ballet, Bergen, Norway

Two Electronic Pieces (mus. Marie), Nice Opera Ballet, Nice

1987 *The Great Gatsby* (mus. Schuller), Pittsburg Ballet, Pittsburgh

Bacchus et Arianne (mus. Roussel), Ballet du Nord

1988 *Dumky* (mus. Dvořák), Quicksilver Ballet, London

1989 *La Traviata* (mus. Verdi, arranged Woolfenden), London City Ballet, Stevenage

1991 *A Woman in Love* (mus. Schumann), Cincinnati Ballet, Cincinnati

Macbeth (mus. Earl), Santiago Ballet, Chile

1992 *Poema en forma de Canciones* (mus. Granados, Turina), Ballet du Nord, Roubaix

Also staged:

1978 *The Sleeping Beauty* (after Petipa; mus. Tchaikovsky), Rome Opera Ballet, Rome

1986 *Swan Lake* (after Petipa, Ivanov; mus. Tchaikovsky), Northern Ballet Theatre, Glyndebourne

PUBLICATIONS

By Prokovsky:

Interview in "The Prokovskys", *Dance and Dancers* (London), February 1977

About Prokovsky:

"Dancer You Will Know: André Prokovsky", *Dance and Dancers* (London), December 1957

Herf, Estelle, "André Prokovsky", *Dance Magazine* (New York), July 1962

Goodman, Saul, "Brief Biographies: André Prokovsky", *Dance Magazine* (New York), October 1963

Livio, Antoine, "D'Aventure en aventure: André Prokovsky", *Danser* (Paris), July/August 1984

*   *   *

In his dancing days André Prokovsky was an exciting performer to watch; virtuosity was his by-word. He acquired his strong technique after studying with Egorova, Kiss, Peretti, and Zverev, and his talents were first noticed after his display of dazzling technique won him the Silver Medal at the 1957 Youth Dance Festival in Moscow.

His potential was subsequently recognized by Anton Dolin who, ignoring those who questioned Prokovsky's range of ability, was instrumental in getting the young Parisian (born to Russian parents) to join the London Festival Ballet. While Prokovsky's physical build, inclining to stockiness (with a short neck and, by his own admission, a back "as stiff as a board") deceived many, Dolin's foresight was rewarded when Prokovsky made a terrific impact in the virtuoso divertissement, *Variations for Four*. Dolin created this exacting showcase for four male dancers (Prokovsky, Flindt, Godfrey, and Gilpin) for London Festival Ballet's Birthday gala in 1957, and even the choreographer is cited as having been "speechless with surprise" at Prokovsky's sensational rendering of the technically loaded first solo. Thus Prokovsky was freed from the corps, in which he always looked quite out of place, and his career took off.

His next significant break came when he was called upon, at short notice, to replace an injured Flemming Flindt in Lander's *Études*, and his success in this technically demanding work continued over many years. His multiple pirouettes were stunning and his leaps were astonishingly buoyant. He appeared to be tireless.

Not surprisingly, Prokovsky became associated with roles calling for bravura. He was also an excellent partner, however, being both utterly reliable and strong, and he muscled his way through the repertoire of show-stopping pas de deux—*Don Quixote, Le Corsaire, Spring Waters*—to great acclaim. He formed a much lauded partnership with Galina Samsova, and danced with her during the height of her career as Festival's leading ballerina.

Working with New York City Ballet for three years, Prokovsky created roles in several Balanchine ballets, but was never seriously rated as a Balanchine dancer. Similarly, he was not regarded as a great actor, being rarely given opportunities to demonstrate any real dramatic ability on stage. But his talent in this direction was most credibly realized in Peter Darrell's *Othello*.

With Samsova (his wife for some years), Prokovsky established in the early 1970s a group of dancers which grew into the New London Ballet. A classical company dedicated to performing ballets created by contemporary choreographers, it toured extensively both in Britain and overseas, until dire financial problems caused it to fold in 1977. It was during this period that Prokovsky started to choreograph, and he created ten ballets during New London Ballet's life, of which perhaps *Vespri* (despite one critic's references to its "meagre ... inventiveness") is best remembered.

After the demise of the New London Ballet, Prokovsky concentrated his energies entirely on choreography and production. His staging of *The Nutcracker*, for Northern Ballet Theatre, was happily free of any psychological underpinnings, and was hailed a success for its straightforward magical simplicity.

His own original choreographies have inspired mixed reviews. In *Anna Karenina* he appeared to have difficulties in maintaining a cohesive dramatic thread. As a result, his reading of the Russian saga of emotional pain and passion is too obviously padded out with non-incidents on stage, such that one often has the impression of characters just milling about waiting for the music to catch up with them. Act II is particularly thin in this respect.

Prokovsky employed a far better sense of theatrical awareness in *The Three Musketeers*, based on Alexandre Dumas's famous novel, and was also more inspired and varied in his choreographic creation. The ballet's characters are defined by different styles of choreography: robust and swashbuckling for the Musketeers, crisp and succinct for the conniving Milady, and dreamy and lush in the romantic pas de deux. However, the work sinks artistically by succumbing to too much coarse humour, and the rape scene is downright tawdry.

Generally speaking, Prokovsky appears to be happier, and is far more inventive, when working with a small group of dancers—or just a pair—than with a huge cast. In his treatment of love stories (exemplified in his *Romeo and Juliet* and *La Traviata*), he focuses the action more or less entirely on the two lovers, in a succession of sensual pas de deux, and brings in the rest of the cast almost as an obligation to decorate the stage rather than to advance the plot. After viewing several Prokovsky ballets, one is able to discern a predictable (but not unpleasing) stylistic flow in his case in stringing steps together.

Prokovsky's stubborness often exasperates his colleagues, and he will not have his artistic ideals compromised. In his recent *La Traviata*, for instance, he favoured lighting so dim that all the facial expressions of the performers were lost on stage. It took a clutch of terse, critical reviews to make him reconsider his extreme view. He has very definite ideas about who is to dance in his ballets, and will not tolerate a dancer he does not wish to use. As a choreographer and ballet director

Prokovsky has shown clarity of vision, well-structured, even methodical working methods, and a respect for hard work in the service of his art.

—Emma Manning

PUGNI, Cesare

Italian composer.   Born in Genoa, 31 May 1802. Studied with Rolla (violin) and Asioli (composition), Milan, 1815–22. Contributed to *Il Castello di Kenilworth* (chor. Gioia), 1823, for La Scala, Milan; début as a ballet composer with *Elerz e Zulmida* (chor. Henry), La Scala, 1826; *maestro al cembalo* and music director at La Scala, 1832–34; travelled to Paris, meeting choreographer Jules Perrot; first major collaboration with Perrot, *Ondine, ou La Naïade*, 1843; chief composer for Perrot at Her Majesty's Theatre, London, 1943–50, also collaborating with choreographers Arthur Saint-Léon and Paul Taglioni; moved to Russia: official composer to the Imperial Theatres, St. Petersburg, from 1851, creating numerous scores for choreographer Marius Petipa, from 1849; also music teacher, St. Petersburg Conservatory. Died in St. Petersburg, 26 January (14 January old style) 1870.

WORKS (Ballets)

1823 *Il Castello di Kenilworth* (with other composers; chor. Gioia), La Scala, Milan

1826 *Elerz e Zulmida* (chor. Henry), La Scala, Milan
      Le Fucine di Vulcano, Parma

1827 *L'Assedio di Calais* (chor. Henry), La Scala, Milan
      Pellia e Mileto (chor. S. Taglioni), La Scala, Milan
      Don Eutichio della castagna; ovvero, La Casa disabitata (chor. Galzerani), La Scala, Milan

1828 *Agamennone* (chor. Galzerani), La Scala, Milan

1829 *Adelaide di Francia* (chor. Henry), La Scala, Milan

1830 *Macbeth* (chor. Henry), La Scala, Milan

1843 *L'Aurore* (divertissement; chor. Perrot), Her Majesty's Theatre, London
      Ondine; ou, La Naïade (chor. Perrot, Cerrito), Her Majesty's Theatre, London
      Le Délire d'un peintre (chor. Perrot), Her Majesty's Theatre, London

1844 *La Esmeralda* (chor. Perrot), Her Majesty's Theatre, London
      La Vivandière (chor. Saint-Léon, Cerrito), Her Majesty's Theatre, London (also staged St. Petersburg, 1855)
      Zelia; ou, La Nymphe de Diane (chor. Perrot), Her Majesty's Theatre, London
      La Paysanne grande dame (chor. Perrot), Her Majesty's Theatre, London

1845 *Éoline; ou, La Dryade* (chor. Perrot), Her Majesty's Theatre, London
      Kaya; ou, L'Amour voyageur (chor. Perrot), Her Majesty's Theatre, London
      La Bacchante (chor. Perrot), Her Majesty's Theatre, London
      Rosida; ou, Les Mines de Syracuse (chor. Saint-Léon, Cerrito), Her Majesty's Theatre, London
      Pas de quatre (chor. Perrot), Her Majesty's Theatre, London
      Diane (chor. Perrot), Her Majesty's Theatre, London

1846 *Catarina; ou, La Fille du bandit* (chor. Perrot), Her Majesty's Theatre, London
      Lalla Rookh; or, The Rose of Lahore (chor. Perrot), Her Majesty's Theatre, London
      Le Jugement de Pâris (chor. Perrot), Her Majesty's Theatre, London (expanded as *Les Soucis du maitre de ballet*)

1847 *Coralia; ou, Le Chevalier inconstant* (chor. P. Taglioni), Her Majesty's Theatre, London
      Théa; ou, La Fée aux fleurs (chor. P. Taglioni), Her Majesty's Theatre, London
      Orithia; ou, Le Camp des Amazones (chor. P. Taglioni), Her Majesty's Theatre, London
      La Fille de marbre (mus. after Costa; chor. Saint-Léon, new version of *Alma*), Opéra, Paris
      Edoardo III; ossia, L'Assedio di Calais (chor. Hus), La Scala, Milan

1848 *Fiorita et la reine des Elfrides* (chor. P. Taglioni), Her Majesty's Theatre, London
      Tartini il violinista (with other composers; chor. Saint-Léon), La Fenice, Venice
      Les Quatre Saisons (mus. partly after Panizza; chor. Perrot), Her Majesty's Theatre, London

1849 *Lida; or The Swiss Milkmaid* (chor. J. and M. Petipa), Bolshoi Theatre, St. Petersburg
      Electra; ou, La Pleiade perdue (chor. P. Taglioni), Her Majesty's Theatre, London
      La Prima Ballerina; ou, l'Embuscade (chor. P. Taglioni), Her Majesty's Theatre, London
      Les Plaisirs de l'hiver; ou, Les Patineurs (chor. P. Taglioni), Her Majesty's Theatre, London

1850 *Stella; ou, Les Contrebandiers* (chor. Saint-Léon), Opéra, Paris
      Les Métamorphoses (chor. P. Taglioni), Her Majesty's Theatre, London
      Les Grâces (chor. P. Taglioni), Her Majesty's Theatre, London
      Les Délices du sérail (chor. Gosselin), Her Majesty's Theatre, London
      Pas de cinq inserted in *Giselle* (chor. Coralli, Perrot), Bolshoi Theatre, St. Petersburg

1851 *The Naiad and the Fisherman* (chor. Perrot), Bolshoi Theatre, St. Petersburg
      Les Tribulations d'un maître de ballet (chor. Perrot), Bolshoi Theatre, St. Petersburg

1852 *The War of the Women; or, The Amazones of the Ninth Century* (chor. Perrot), Bolshoi Theatre, St. Petersburg

1853 *Gazelda; or, The Tsiganes* (chor. Perrot), Bolshoi Theatre, St. Petersburg

1854 *Faust* (additions to 1848 score by Panizza, Costa, Bajetti; chor. Perrot), Bolshoi Theatre, St. Petersburg
      Marcobomba (arrangement of various composers; chor. Perrot), Bolshoi Ballet, St. Petersburg
      Saltarello (additions to 1854 score by Saint-Léon; chor. Saint-Léon), Bolshoi Theatre, St. Petersburg

1855 *Satanella; oder Metamorphosen* (new version; chor. P. Taglioni), Royal Opera House, Berlin
      Armida (chor. Perrot), Bolshoi Theatre, St. Petersburg

1856 *La Débutante* (arrangement of other and own music; chor. Perrot), Peterhof (staged Bolshoi Theatre, St. Petersburg, 1957)

1857 *La Petite Marchande de bouquets* (chor. Perrot), Bolshoi Theatre, St. Petersburg

1858 *Le Corsaire* (mus. added to 1856 score by Adam; chor. Perrot after Mazilier), Bolshoi Theatre, St. Petersburg
      Royal Marriage (or *Un Mariage sous la régence*; chor.

Petipa), Bolshoi Theatre, St. Petersburg

1859 *The Parisian Market* (or *Le Marché de Paris*; chor. Petipa), Bolshoi Theatre, St. Petersburg

1860 *The Blue Dahlia* (chor. Petipa), Bolshoi Theatre, St. Petersburg

Pâquerette (additions to 1851 score by Benoist; chor. Saint-Léon), Bolshoi Theatre, St. Petersburg

Graziella; ou Les Dépits amoureux (chor. Saint-Léon), Bolshoi Theatre, St. Petersburg

1861 *The Pearl of Seville* (chor. Saint-Léon), Bolshoi Theatre, St. Petersburg

Meteora (chor. Saint-Léon), Bolshoi Theatre, St. Petersburg (mus. not attributed to Pugni until Moscow, 1862)

Nymphes and satyre (chor. Saint-Léon), Bolshoi Theatre, St. Petersburg

Terpsichore (chor. Petipa), Court Theatre, Tsarskoye Selo

1862 *Pharaoh's Daughter* (chor. Petipa), Bolshoi Theatre, St. Petersburg

Theolinda, the Orphan; or, The Elf of the Valley (chor. Saint-Léon), Bolshoi Theatre, St. Petersburg

1863 *The Beauty of Lebanon; or, The Spirit of the Mountains* (chor. Petipa), Bolshoi Theatre, St. Petersburg

1864 *The Little Humpbacked Horse; or, The Tsar-Maiden* (chor. Saint-Léon), Bolshoi Theatre, St. Petersburg

1865 *Don Zeffiro* (chor. Saint-Léon), Theatre-Italien, Paris
The Travelling Ballerina (chor. Petipa), Bolshoi Theatre, St. Petersburg

1866 *Florida* (chor. Petipa), Bolshoi Theatre, St. Petersburg
Gli Elementi (chor. Saint-Léon), Théâtre-Italien, Paris
Titania (chor. Petipa), Palace of Grand Duchess Elena Pavlovna, St. Petersburg

1868 *Love, the Benefactor* (*L'Amour bienfaiteur*; chor. Petipa), Imperial Theatre School, St. Petersburg

The Slave (chor. Petipa), Court Theatre, Tsarskoye Selo
King Candaule (chor. Petipa), Bolshoi Ballet, St. Petersburg

1869 *Basilico* (additions to 1865 score by Graziani; chor. Saint-Léon), Bolshoi Theatre, St. Petersburg

1871 *The Two Stars* (chor. Petipa), Bolshoi Theatre, St. Petersburg

Other ballets using Pugni's music: *The Water Nymph* (Kyasht, 1912), *The Pearl of Seville* (new version; chor. Mordkin, 1924), *Russian Dance* (Yakobson, 1936); numerous twentieth-century restagings of surviving works by Perrot, Saint-Léon, and Petipa.

PUBLICATIONS

Beaumont, Cyril, *A History of Ballet in Russia*, London, 1930
Borioglebsky, M., *Materials for the History of Russian Ballet*, vol. 1, Leningrad, 1938
Chujoy, Anatole, "Russian Balletomane", *Dance Index* (New York), no. 7, 1948
Guest, Ivor, *The Romantic Ballet in England*, London, 1954
Krasovskaya, Vera, *Russian Ballet Theatre of the First Half of the Nineteenth Century*, Leningrad and Moscow, 1958
Krasovskaya, Vera, *Russian Ballet Theatre of the Second Half of the Nineteenth Century*, Leningrad and Moscow, 1963
Roslavleva, Natalia, *Era of the Russian Ballet*, London, 1966
Petipa, Marius, *Russian Ballet Master: The Memoirs of Marius Petipa*, edited by Lillian Moore, London, 1968
Guest, Ivor, "Cesare Pugni", *Dance Gazette* (London), no. 1, 1979
Guest, Ivor, "Cesare Pugni: A Plea for Justice", *Dance Research* (London), Spring 1983
Guest, Ivor, *Jules Perrot: Master of the Romantic Ballet*, London, 1984
Wiley, Roland John, *A Century of Russian Ballet: Documents and Accounts 1810–1910*, Oxford, 1990

* * *

Between 20 and 30 ballets composed by Cesare Pugni were published in piano score during his lifetime, but he is known to have composed many more, chiefly in Milan, London, and St. Petersburg, and to have contributed to literally dozens of others at a time when ballet music usually comprised a patchwork of arrangements mixed with new bits and pieces. He was taught the violin and composition at Milan (though not at the Conservatorio), contributed to *Il Castello di Kenilworth* (1823), a ballet by Gaetano Gioia at La Scala, and composed his first known full ballet at that house in 1826, as *Elerz e Zulmida* for Louis Henry.

Others were composed in Milan for Henry, for Salvatore Taglioni (brother to Filippo, Marie Taglioni's father), and for Giovanni Galzerani, as well as some operas and orchestral music, and in 1832 Pugni was appointed Director of Music and *maestro al cembalo* at La Scala. Two years later he left in disgrace, said to be caused by a weakness for gambling, and went with his family to Paris, where several years were spent in poverty alleviated only by music-copying tasks (including for the opera composer, Bellini) and some further composition for Henry, who died in 1836.

Nothing is known of Pugni in the next seven years, until he came to London in 1843 as ballet composer at Her Majesty's Theatre under Benjamin Lumley's management. Here he produced a stream of fluent compositions for ballets by Jules Perrot, Arthur Saint-Léon, and Paul Taglioni. The first for Perrot was *Ondine* (1843), where the music's rippling effects for underwater scenes were much admired, and specific dance forms such as tarantella and saltarello were given dramatic function in the narrative.

Other scores for Perrot included the celebrated *Pas de quatre* (1845) in which Cerrito, Grahn, Grisi, and Taglioni appeared together, and its successor, *Le Jugement de Pâris* (1846). Also composed for Perrot were *La Esmeralda* in 1844 (heard again edited by Geoffrey Corbett in Nicholas Beriozoff's staging for London Festival Ballet, 1954), *Catarina* (1846), where a "Valse à cinq temps" is the earliest known use of five-four time in the theatre, and *La Vivandière* (1844), from which a pas de six survived in Saint-Léon's own notation so that Pugni's music has been heard in present-day reconstructed performance.

It is thought likely that Perrot's appointment as ballet master at St. Petersburg in 1851 brought about Pugni's employment there as staff Ballet Composer to the Imperial Theatres. Pugni made his home there, and never returned to the West. For almost 20 years he composed to order, supplying additional music for revivals that needed extending, and writing new scores for Perrot, Saint-Léon, for whose *Konyok gorbunyok* (*The Little Humpbacked Horse*, 1864) he incorporated Russian folk-themes, and Petipa, for whom he composed *The Blue Dahlia* (1860), *Pharaoh's Daughter* (1862), *The Beauty of Lebanon* (1863), and *King Candaule* (1868).

Pugni also taught counterpoint at the St. Petersburg Conservatory, but seems to have succumbed to increasing alcohol addiction, which made him both professionally unreliable and domestically spendthrift. These were traits mentioned by Petipa in his memoirs, and also by Saint-Léon, who wrote in a letter in 1869 that he found Pugni desperately in debt, owing 5,800 roubles in all, and feeding eight children on the proceeds of a collection taken up for him by dancers of the Imperial Ballet. For some years he had seldom been sober, and by the following year he was dead. (Ivor Guest, the ballet historian, notes that a son, Nikolai, was a corps de ballet dancer at St. Petersburg, and a granddaughter, Leontina, was also a dancer who accompanied Pavlova on tour to Scandinavia and Germany in 1908–09.)

Pugni exemplified the category of journeyman-composer for ballet in the nineteenth century who wrote entirely to order, and supplied music of melodious grace and rhythm skilfully calculated to "lift" and support the dancers without obtruding on the visual spectacle. Apart from the few minor innovations mentioned, the music that survives shows a facility and expressive quality and an easygoing appeal in harmony and rhythm, qualities that remained a subservient but still essential element in the ballet of its time and its corresponding place in history.

—Noël Goodwin

PULCINELLA

Choreography: Léonide Massine
Music: Igor Stravinsky, after Giovanni Battista Pergolesi
Design: Pablo Picasso (scenery and costumes)
Libretto: Léonide Massine, after the *commedia dell'arte*
First Production: Diaghilev's Ballets Russes, Théâtre National de l'Opéra, Paris, 15 May 1920
Principal Dancers: Léonide Massine (Pulcinella), Tamara Karsavina (Pimpinella), Lubov Tchernicheva (Prudenza), Vera Nemchinova (Rosetta), Stanislas Idzikowski (Caviello), Nicholas Zverev (Florindo), Enrico Cecchetti (Il Dottore)

Other productions include: La Scala (revival; restaged and revised Massine); Milan, 10 December 1971. Joffrey Ballet (staged Robert Joffrey, after Massine's 1971 version); Wolf Trap, Virginia, 15 August 1974.

State Academic Theatre for Opera and Ballet (GATOB, later the Kirov; new version; chor. Fedor Lopukhov); Leningrad, 16 May 1926. Hanover Opera Ballet (new version; chor. Yvonne Georgi); Hanover, 1926 (revived 1963). Ballet de l'Opéra Russe à Paris (new version; chor. Boris Romanov), with Romanov (Pulcinella), Felia Doubrovska (Pimpinella); Paris, April 1931 (earlier version staged Teatro Colón, 1928). Ballets Russes de Monte Carlo (restaged Romanov), with Leon Woizikowsky (Pulcinella), Felia Doubrovska (Pimpinella); Monte Carlo, 30 April 1932. Folkwang Tanzbühne (new version; chor. Kurt Jooss); Essen, April 1932. Latvian Opera Ballet (new version; chor. Anatole Vilzak), design Romana Suta); Riga, 1933. Augsburg Theatre (new version; chor. Aurel Milloss), with Milloss (Pulcinella), Magda Karder (Pimpinella); Augsburg, 7 May 1933. Les Ballets Léon Woizikowsky (new version; chor. Woizikowsky), as *Les Deux Polchinelles*, with Woizikowsky (Pulcinella); London, 1935. Ballet Théâtre de Maurice Béjart (new version; chor. Béjart); Liège, 10 September 1957. American Ballet Theatre (new version; chor. Michael Smuin), as *Pulcinella Variations*; New York, 11 July 1968. New York City Ballet (new version; chor. George Balanchine and Jerome Robbins), with Edward Villella (Pulcinella), Violette Verdy (Girl); New York, 23 June 1972. Paris Opéra Ballet (new version; chor. Douglas Dunn); Paris, 1980. London Festival Ballet (new version; chor. Tetley); London, 12 June 1984.

Ballet Rambert (new version; chor. Richard Alston); Leeds, 13 January 1987.

PUBLICATIONS

Levinson, André, "Stravinsky and the Dance", *Theatre Arts* (New York), November 1924

Stravinsky, Igor, *Chronicle of My Life*, London, 1936

Beaumont, Cyril, *Complete Book of Ballets*, revised edition, London, 1951

Grigoriev, Serge, *The Diaghilev Ballet*, translated by Vera Bowen, London, 1953

Lieberman, William, "Picasso and the Dance", *Dance Magazine* (New York), September 1957

Massine, Léonide, *My Life in Ballet*, London, 1960

Cooper, Douglas, *Picasso, Theatre*, Paris, 1967

Kochno, Boris, *Diahilev and the Ballets Russes*, New York, 1970

Meeker, Marilyn, "Putting the Punch in *Pulcinella*", *Dance Magazine* (New York), April 1981

Borovsky, Victor, and Schouvaloff, Alexander, *Stravinsky on Stage*, London, 1982

Percival, John, "In and Out of Favour", *Dance and Dancers* (London), January 1989

Garafola, Lynn, *Diaghilev's Ballets Russes*, New York, 1989

*   *   *

After Russia, Italy was Serge Diaghilev's favourite country. Over the years he spent much time there, and during the First World War he began to conduct extensive research into the work of eighteenth-century Italian composers. *Pulcinella* was the second ballet to emerge from his studies; *Les Femmes de bonne humeur*, with music by Scarlatti, was produced in 1917.

Diaghilev chose the artistic collaborators for *Pulcinella* well. Léonide Massine, Pablo Picasso, and Igor Stravinsky were all personally interested in the project, respected each other, and worked together closely. Massine had been engaged in research into the *commedia dell'arte* since visiting Naples in 1917. It was he who discovered the story for *Pulcinella* after reading through numerous *commedia* plots in search of one appropriate for a ballet. He settled on *The Four Pulcinellas*, which focused on the wily Neapolitan whose misadventures made him one of the best known *commedia* characters.

This story involves Pulcinella in a series of encounters with two young women, Rosetta and Prudenza, who find him attractive. Pulcinella rebuffs one but is dancing gaily with the other when he is discovered by his mistress, Pimpinella, whom he appeases in an affectionate duet. Caviello and Florindo—Rosetta and Prudenza's suitors—are jealous of the attention Pulcinella is receiving and try to kill him. After several attempts they appear to succeed, and as Pulcinella lies dead, four little Pulcinellas come to mourn him. A magician appears, revives the corpse, and then reveals that the whole episode has been a hoax. Pulcinella did not die at all. The magician is Pulcinella and a friend has impersonated the corpse. The ballet ends happily with all the lovers united.

For the ballet's music, Diaghilev collected fragments of unfinished compositions by Pergolesi and then approached Igor Stravinsky to orchestrate them. In his memoirs of 1936, Stravinsky said that he was always "enchanted by Pergolesi's Neapolitan music". But Stravinsky was not content simply to string together the Pergolesi selections, and he created a juxtaposition between old and new that gave the composition a life of its own. Boris Kochno wrote in *Le Ballet*, "The ironic embellishments of the trombone and bassoon transformed the melodies of Pergolesi. There were perhaps not twelve bars of

Pulcinella: a costume design by Pablo Picasso for Pimpinella

music which were really by Stravinsky, yet it all bore his mark."

Diaghilev invited Picasso to create the designs for *Pulcinella*. Picasso had worked with the Ballets Russes with considerable success on *Parade* in 1916–17 and *Le Tricorne* in 1919. He also had an abiding interest in *commedia* and circus themes, which he had used throughout his career. Picasso told Douglas Cooper that he originally wanted to transpose the ballet from the eighteenth century into "modern terms", but Diaghilev rejected the idea. He also rejected Picasso's next concept, which was to create a theatre-within-a-theatre. A number of drawings survive which depict rows of theatre boxes and beyond them a proscenium arch giving on to a false stage, with a second décor showing the Bay of Naples and Mount Vesuvius. Picasso made several different versions of this design but Diaghilev was adamantly opposed to all of them. Picasso finally submitted a much simpler décor made up of panels reminiscent of the improvised screens of travelling players. The panels depicted several buildings in a flattened synthetic cubist style, leading down to a quay and a moon-drenched bay with Vesuvius in the background. The set was in tones of black, blue, and white, and the dancers performed on a white ground cloth, to suggest moonlight. Costumes were in an eighteenth-century style and brightly coloured, contrasting with the monochromatic set. Pulcinella, who was masked, wore his traditional baggy white costume with red underwear that showed at wrists, neck, and ankles.

One of the reasons Massine was attracted by the *commedia* style was "the importance of the expressive plasticity of the body, rendered imperative by the habitual use of masks". At the time, he was trying to extend the classical vocabulary and felt he might find a clue to accomplishing it in the *commedia* characters' expressive movement. While in Naples in 1917, he had bought a mask that once belonged to Antonio Petito, a great eighteenth-century *commedia dell'arte* actor and producer. Working with the mask, Massine discovered unaccustomed ways of moving which he incorporated into the ballet. "As I was unable to rely on facial expression because of my mask, I used every possible flourish, twist and turn to suggest the unscrupulousness and ambiguity of Pulcinella's character." *Pulcinella* remained in the Ballets Russes repertory until Diaghilev's death. The reasons for its success are suggested in Stravinsky's comment: "*Pulcinella* is one of those productions—and they are rare—where everything harmonizes, where all the elements—subject, music, dancing and artistic setting—form a coherent and homogeneous whole".

If the collaborators brought to *Pulcinella* a notable consistency of vision, they also found in it elements that played an important role in each of their individual careers. Picasso drew heavily on themes from the ballet for paintings and drawings of the period. For instance the oil, *Pulcinella with a Guitar in Front of a Curtain* from 1920 shows Massine taking a bow. The works of 1920 using *commedia* themes led directly to the two great masterpieces of synthetic cubism created in 1921, both called *Three Musicians*. In *Pulcinella*, Stravinsky discovered he could draw on music of the past to create works of the present, a practice he continued for the next 30 years. For Massine, *Pulcinella* formed part of his choreographic education, teaching him to make the entire body expressive. All the collaborators, with Diaghilev's urging, found ways to comment upon historical material by giving it modern form.

—Gay Morris

———

DIE PUPPENFEE
(*The Fairy Doll*)

Choreography: Joseph Hassreiter
Music: Josef Bayer
Design: Anton Brioschi (scenery), Franz Gaul (costumes)
Libretto: Joseph Hassreiter and Franz Gaul
First Production: Court Opera House, Vienna, 4 October 1888
Principal Dancers: Camilla Pagliero (Fairy Doll), Franciska Well (Drum Majorette), Otto Thieme (The Poet), Eduard Voitus van Hamme (Polichinelle), Louis Frappart (Shopkeeper), Joseph Hassreiter (Shopkeeper's Assistant).

Other productions include: Bolshoi Theatre (new version; chor. Joseph Mendez), as *Feya Kukol*, or *Fairy Doll*; Moscow, 4 March (20 February old style) 1897. Bolshoi Theatre (new version; staged Ivan Clustine); Moscow, 1901. Maryinsky Theatre (new version; chor. Sergei and Nikolai Legat, with additional mus. Tchaikovsky, Rubinstein, Drigo, costumes Léon Bakst), with Mathilde Kshesinsksaya (Fairy Doll), Olga Preobrazhenskaya (Baby Doll), Anna Pavlova (Spanish Doll), Pavel Gerdt (Shopkeeper); St. Petersburg, 28 February (16 February old style) 1903. Empire Theatre (new version; chor. Katti Lanner, mus. arranged Clarke), as *The Dancing Doll*, with Adeline Genée (Bébé); London, 3 January 1905. Anna Pavlova Company (restaged Ivan Clustine), with Anna Pavlova (Fairy Doll); U.S. tour, 1914. Ballet of La Scala (new version; chor. Heinrich Kröller), with Luisa Baldi (Fairy Doll); Milan, 1930. Littlefield Ballet (new version; chor. Catherine Littlefield, scenery A. Jarin, costumes P.T. Champ); Philadelphia, 1935. Vienna State Opera Ballet (staged and revised Willy Fränzl); Vienna, 1958. Vienna State Opera Ballet (reconstruction of original; staged Gerlinde Dill, Riki Raab after Hassreiter, design after Brioschi and Gaul); Vienna, 13 December 1983.

PUBLICATIONS

Baum, Vicki, *It Was All Quite Different*, New York, 1964

Jackson, George, "Notes on *Die Puppenfee*", *Washington Dance View* (Washington D.C.), October/November 1979

Schüller, Gunhild, and Oberzaucher, Alfred, "Josef Hassreiter: On the 40th Anniversary of his Death", *Tanzblätter* (Vienna), June 1980

Amort, Andrea, *Die Geschichte des Balletts der Wiener Hofoper 1918–1942*, Vienna, 1981

Matzinger, Ruth, *Die Geschichte des Balletts der Wiener Hofoper 1869–1918*, Vienna, 1982

Money, Keith, *Anna Pavlova: Her Life and Art*, London, 1982

Koegler, Horst, "Ein Beitrag zur Spurensicherung der Wiener Ballettkultur?", *Ballet: Chronik und Bilanz des Ballettjahres*, Zurich, 1984

Téri, Evelyn, "*Die Puppenfee*", *Ballett-Journal/Das Tanzarchiv* (Cologne), February 1984

Jackson, George, "Vienna", *Ballet News* (New York), April 1984

Koegler, Horst, "Three Hits in Vienna", *Dance and Dancers* (London), August 1984

Die Puppenfee (*The Fairy Doll*), a pantomimic divertissement in one act and two scenes, is the only nineteenth-century ballet from central Europe with a continuous performance tradition. First performed in 1888 by the Vienna (Court) Opera Ballet (following the three-act opera *Stradella* by Flotow), it is still in the repertory of the opera house (now the Vienna State Opera) in an edition that preserves not only the original's music and dances, but even the costumes and scenery.

Hassreiter's first version was a pantomime for amateurs, *In the Doll Shop* (*Im Puppenladen*), performed at a charity benefit organized by Princess Pauline Metternich in April 1888. The Princess had seen and liked a doll ballet by Mariquita in Paris, and thought doll roles would suit non-professional performers. Hassreiter complied at her bidding, and the result was such a success that he, a first dance soloist at the Vienna Opera, was asked to elaborate on the choreography for performance by that company. Some roles were developed technically and a huge ballabile was added at the end, but the seeming simplicity that so charmed viewers of the first version was preserved.

The ballet has a little bit for everyone. There is realism as well as social satire in depicting the daily routine of a doll shop and its staff and customers (including a boorish family of rich farmers and a prim family of English tourists). The mini-dances of the dolls on display are given variety by national, stylistic, or personality traits; they include a mechanical baby doll that says "Papa! Mamam!", a Poet rag doll, and dolls of varied nations and professions. As a climatic centre-piece, the shop-owner reluctantly displays his best piece, the Fairy Doll. Her role is crucial, though she hardly moves: the dancer portraying her must express beauty, a Coppélia-like wonder of waking to life, and at the same time a Myrtha-like willpower. The second scene takes place in the closed shop, as the Fairy Doll commands the other dolls to come to life. Their midnight revels (the ballabile with variations) wake the Shopkeeper. There is a horror-story ending, as he enters, sees only stillness and then, suddenly, sinks frightened to his knees as the Fairy Doll and hundreds of her subjects advance on him. The ballabile's manoeuvres include complex marching formations, a carousel formation, and a single classical variation (for the Drum Majorette) against a corps of Bunny Girls who do high kicks. A final piece of satire is the participation in the ballabile of audience members—they are dandies (portrayed by girls in travesty) who have come to ogle the dancers.

Die Puppenfee became the most popular work performed at the Vienna Opera, accumulating more performances than any other ballet or opera. It has been staged by over 100 theatres around the world (even in the Far East), sometimes in Hassreiter's choreography, often not. Other versions of note were those by Ivan Clustine for the Bolshoi Theatre in Moscow and later for Anna Pavlova's company (which toured the work widely in both hemispheres) and one by the Legat brothers for the Maryinsky Theatre in St. Petersburg—a pas de trois from which (to inserted music by Drigo) survived on Soviet highlights programmes through the twentieth century. For years, the late Vincenzo Celli taught Hassreiter's variation for the Drum Majorette in his classes.

However, between the two world wars, *Die Puppenfee* was somewhat eclipsed by Léonide Massine's similar *La Boutique fantasque*. In Vienna, the work was maintained by Hassreiter himself (who lived until 1940), Anton Birkmeyer, Willy Fränzl (who revised it in 1958), and Gerlinde Dill with Riki Raab, who restored the original choreography in 1983 for the Gerhard Brunner production. This recent production also revived the original sets and costumes, a crucial factor when we see how they create rainbow effects in motion. A screen version of Fränzl's altered staging was also shot by Wien Film. Susanne Kirnbauer dances the title role in the film, with Ully Wührer as the Drum Majorette, Karl Musil as the Poet, Paul Vondrak as Polichinelle, and Christl Zimmerl as the Spanish doll. The value of *Die Puppenfee* today is that it looks so different from the other nineteenth-century ballets we know.

—George Jackson

PUSH COMES TO SHOVE

Choreography: Twyla Tharp
Music: Franz Joseph Haydn and Joseph Lamb
Design: Santo Loquasto (costumes)
First Production: American Ballet Theatre, Uris Theatre, New York, 9 January 1976
Principal Dancers: Mikhail Baryshnikov, Marianna Tcherkassky, Martine van Hamel, Clark Tippet, Christopher Aponte

Other productions include: Paris Opéra Ballet (restaged Tharp); Paris, 1989.

PUBLICATIONS

Balanchine, George, with Mason, Francis, *Balanchine's Complete Stories of the Great Ballets*, Garden City, N.Y., 1977
Croce, Arlene, *Afterimages*, New York, 1977
Harris, Dale, "Twyla Tharp", *Contemporary Dance* (New York), 1978
Siegel, Marcia, *The Shapes of Change*, Boston, 1979
Taplin, Diana, *Dance Spectrum*, Waterloo, Ontario, 1982
Coe, Robert, *Dance in America*, New York, 1985
Tharp, Twyla, *Push Comes to Shove* (autobiography), New York, 1992

* * *

"It's like a giant Euclidean doodle," was Doris Hering's oft-quoted response to Twyla's Tharp's *Push Comes to Shove*, "with a firm undercurrent of pure ballet logic." Tharp's 1976 ballet stands as a milestone in the history of twentieth-century American dance; it marks the arrival of the wild child of modern choreography in the mainstream ballet world of American Ballet Theatre, and it holds a place as one of the very first Western pieces made on the newly defected Russian emigré, Mikhail Baryshnikov. As such, it could be said to symbolize the ultimate marriage of ballet and modern dance in a combination which seemed to typify the heady 1970s mood of the all-embracing "dance boom". But Twyla Tharp's "Euclidean doodle" is also a thoughtful, clever, and engaging contemplation of themes in movement; it is a deliberately teasing juxtaposition of old and new, serious and silly, imaginative and wickedly derivative. George Balanchine, in *Balanchine's Complete Stories of the Great Ballets*, stated it simply: "*Push Comes to Shove* displays the genius of the contemporary dancer in rare and droll combinations."

At the centre of the ballet is undoubtedly the male figure, so perfectly tailored around Baryshnikov's compact, energetic form and mercurial personality, who has been described as a sort of Chaplinesque hero (inseparable from a bowler hat), whose stage persona is a cross between a vaudeville star and a premier danseur. He alternates between a coy, stagey flirtation—whether with the audience or with the two leading ladies

on stage with him—and an apparently serious pursuit of the demands of classical ballet, displaying a breathtaking virtuosity punctuated by lapses into rehearsal-room behaviour (pauses, fiddles, fingers through hair: the sort of conscious unselfconsciousness of a dancer in practice mode which Tharp's choreography can mimic brilliantly). Tharpean trademarks, such as slinky, low-weighted, off-centre "jive" movement mixed with frenetic runs and changes in direction, is played off successfully against a balletic vocabulary that Tharp dips into frequently and irreverently. The music, which ranges from ragtime to Handel, emphasizes this free and easy flow between various disciplines.

In her 1992 autobiography, which (as is often the case with such personal records) frequently provides us with startlingly banal explanations for the writer's choreographic genius, Tharp describes her arrival at the structural bare bones of *Push Comes to Shove* (whose self-confessedly "trashy" title came later):

> I drafted a drama for the ballet. Misha [Baryshnikov] was the womanizer, and being perverse, I decided to give him his wish: every woman in the company. There would be his two principals, the little one, Marianna [Tcherkassky], and a big one who towered over him, capable of squashing him, a terrifying, dominating Marta-esque figure [Martine van Hamel] in juxtaposition to Marianna's lovely petite coquette."

A certain amount of the ballet's "action" can be conveyed by this description of the so-called characters and their interaction. But perhaps more illuminating is Tharp's later description of her approach to Baryshnikov himself, and her apparent contemplation of his position as the world's current "ballet star", newly arrived from Russia to live in the world of jazz and Hollywood and Broadway. She says that she set out to tackle the significance of the term "American Ballet Theatre", and within that seemingly narrow world she considered the play of American twentieth-century pop-culture—a world of kitsch which so obviously fascinated the newly arrived Russian ballet star—against the currents of higher art. As Tharp wittily perceived it, Baryshnikov's god was Astaire, not Apollo, and Tharp set out to show this. It goes without saying that Baryshnikov's own double passion for highbrow and lowbrow mirrored the eclectic tastes of that other god to both of them, George Balanchine. And so, as critics acknowledged at the time, Tharp followed in the great master's footsteps by showing a rare ability to blend the two cultural extremes successfully. "The synthesis", to quote Arlene Croce, "involves an amalgamation of high and popular art which no other choreographer except Balanchine has achieved in this country."

When *Push Comes to Shove* was unveiled for the public in 1976, it was instantly acclaimed. Audiences cheered wildly, critics grinned in spite of themselves, and *Time* magazine called it "the most important dance event of the year". With hindsight, the piece might perhaps look dated (although it was successfully staged in Paris over a decade later); certainly its huge popularity at its premiere says as much about its era—the mid 1970s—as about its potential greatness as a dance piece. Whether all the critics who proclaimed it a masterpiece in 1976 would still do so today is an open question. The most serious issue at the time—just how much the ballet rose above its simple external appearance as a witty, playful parody—would apply more than ever now, when critics increasingly wonder if Tharp herself seems to have become too clever for her own good. As much as her extremely inventive blend of influences and styles reminds the viewer of the choreographer's own admitted model, Balanchine, the cruel fact is that Twyla Tharp

Push Comes To Shove, with Mikhail Baryshnikov, American Ballet Theatre, 1976

is no George Balanchine. The dialectic, if it can be so labelled, of her dialogue in movement is not so finely balanced as Balanchine's, nor does her equally fluent use of allusions from numberless sources seem to add up to a balanced aesthetic of Balanchinean proportions.

Nevertheless, Tharp's musicality, originality, and sheer creative energy give this ballet an undisputed place in the twentieth-century canon. What can be said to save *Push Comes to Shove* from mere comic pastiche is the uncanny logic of its structure; in her use of patterns from the ballet classics—both revered and ridiculed—Tharp almost outdoes the originals themselves; she twists and toys with the ensemble to result in what Croce brilliantly termed "a space-filling geometrical composition in the style of a drunken Petipa". And in doing so Tharp does actually succeed in paying a witty, irreverent tribute to the art of ballet, which after all lies at the heart of her inspiration here. She created the perfect signature piece for a ballet company and a star, both of whom embodied the classical ideal, yet were ripe for influences from the popular culture around them. As such, *Push Comes to Shove*, like Balanchine, could only have happened in America, and is an important event in the history of dance in that country.

—Virginia Christian

PUSHKIN, Aleksandr

Russian/Soviet dancer and teacher.   Born Aleksandr Ivanovich Pushkin in Mikulino, in the province of Tverskaya, 7 September 1907. Early dance training at the private studio of Nikolai Legat; studied at the Leningrad Choreographic School, pupil of Aleksandr Shiryaev, Nikolai Ivanovsky, Aleksandr Monakhov, and Vladimir Ponomarev; graduated in 1925. Début in Saint-Léon's *La Source* with Marina Semenova; dancer, GATOB, later the Kirov Theatre, Leningrad, 1925–53; teacher, Leningrad Choreographic School, from 1932, directing the Class of Perfection from 1953, and becoming one of the most celebrated teachers of his time: pupils include Askold Makarov, Yuri Grigorovich, Nikita Dolgushin, Yuri Soloviev, Valery Panov, Rudolf Nureyev, and Mikhail Baryshnikov. Recipient: title of Honoured Artist of the Bashkirskaya ASSR, 1947; title of Honoured Artist of the Russian Federation, 1968. Died in Leningrad, 20 March 1970.

ROLES

1927   Asak in *The Ice Maiden* (Lopukhov), State Theatre for Opera and Ballet (GATOB), Leningrad
1932   Philippe (cr) in *The Flames of Paris* (Vainonen), GATOB, Leningrad
1934   The Youth, Vatslav in *The Fountain of Bakhchisarai* (Zakharov), GATOB, Leningrad
1936   The Poet (cr) in *Lost Illusions* (Zakharov), Kirov Ballet, Leningrad

Other roles include: Peasant Pas de Deux in *Giselle* (Petipa after Coralli, Perrot; staged Vaganova), Pas de Trois and the Prince in *Swan Lake* (Petipa, Ivanov; staged Vaganova), Companion of the Khan and Genie of the Waters in *The Little Humpbacked Horse* (Gorsky after Saint-Léon), The Bluebird and Puss-in-Boots in *The Sleeping Beauty* (Petipa; staged Lophukov), Phoenix in *The Red Poppy* (Lopukhov, Ponomarev, Leontiev), Frondoso in *Laurencia* (Chabukiani), Colin in *Vain Precautions* (*La Fille mal gardée*; Ponomarev after Petipa, Ivanov), Acteon

in *Esmeralda* (Vaganova after Petipa, Perrot), Nutcracker Prince in *The Nutcracker* (Vainonen), the Merchant in *Le Corsaire* (Petipa; staged Vaganova), Jerome and Louis XIV in *The Flames of Paris* (Vainonen), the Youth in *Chopiniana* (Fokine), the Cavalier in *Cinderella* (Sergeyev), the Negro of Peter the Great in *The Bronze Horseman* (Zakharov), the Troubadour in *Raymonda* (Vainonen), Pan in *Walpurgis Night* (from the opera *Faust*; chor. Chabukiani), the Troubadour in *Romeo and Juliet* (Lavrovsky).

PUBLICATIONS

Prokhorova, V., "The Applause of Severe Judges", *Teatralnaya Zhizn* (Moscow), no. 14, 1969
Baryshnikov, Mikhail, and France, Charles (ed.), *Baryshnikov at Work*, New York, 1976
Albert, G., "To Live Means to Teach Dance", *Sovetsky Balet* (Moscow), no. 6, 1983
Alovert, Nina, *Baryshnikov in Russia*, New York, 1984

*   *   *

The great Russian ballet teacher Aleksandr Pushkin has become nothing less than a legend in his native country, where his influence is still felt despite his death over twenty years ago. A mild-mannered, cultured, and intelligent man, he was a genius in the sphere of dance education. As a performer he created many roles, and he partnered many of the leading ballerinas of the day, but he was not a particularly outstanding dancer. As a teacher, however, he accomplished miracles. Among his pupils are practically all of the leading soloists of the Kirov Theatre from the 1940s, 1950s, and 1960s—and his students include the world-famous Rudolf Nureyev and Mikhail Baryshnikov. His lessons were fascinating, demonstrating great innovation and creativity. He worked closely with his pupils, slowly and carefully explaining everything in a quiet voice. Dancers enjoyed his classes; even such difficult and temperamental pupils as Nureyev were tamed by Pushkin's gentle character.

Pushkin began his dancing career in the mid-1920s at the State Academic Theatre for Opera and Ballet (GATOB), which was to become the Kirov. His début was with Marina Semenova in *La Source* (after Saint-Léon), and soon his roles covered a wide range in the classical repertoire. His gift for teaching was discovered early, and he began as a teacher at the Leningrad Choreographic School in 1932, at the age of 25; when he retired from the stage he taught the Kirov's Class of Perfection, from which many first-class male dancers were produced. Pushkin was also instrumental in rearing artists for the various republics of the USSR—the Tartar ASSR and the Bashkirskaya ASSR—and also for foreign countries, such as Czechoslovakia and Bulgaria.

Pushkin's achievements live on in the tradition of Leningrad/St. Petersburg ballet, and he is still remembered fondly by those at the Kirov. Indeed, once a year at the Kirov Theatre there is a special day during which class is dedicated to the memory of the great teacher; leading soloists come to the big hall at the Kirov and class is conducted in honour of Pushkin's special exercises and methods. This perhaps more than anything else is a testament to the man: the glory of Pushkin lives on through his pupils.

Perhaps the greatest tribute of all comes from Baryshnikov, who, in his book *Baryshnikov at Work*, pays homage to this "extraordinary man" who oversaw the young dancer's training from the age of fifteen. "Pushkin's influence was enormous," he writes:

His experience in the classroom was unmatched, and his authority unquestionable. A calm, serene man, he was not given to elaborate verbal instructions. His style was the simplest—quiet and direct, but never confining. He very often began by helping a dancer choose a line to pursue. That is, early on in his students' careers he would steer them in one direction or another: this one toward the romantic-lyrical route, that one toward the virtuoso. He taught in such a way that the dancer began to know himself more completely, and that, I believe, is the first key to serious work—to becoming an artist—to know oneself, one's gifts, one's limitations, as fully as possible. It is the only way.

Pushkin's great skill was in guiding, rather than driving, his students; his was an ideal of what Baryshnikov elsewhere has called "the idea of self-education". And undoubtedly many a dancer today who began under Pushkin would claim, along with Baryshnikov, "Everything he gave me is in one way or another the beginning—the solid beginning—of how I understand it all."

—Igor Stupnikov

————

LES QUATRE SAISONS

Choreography: Jules Perrot
Music: Cesare Pugni
Libretto: Jules Perrot
First Production: Her Majesty's Theatre, London, 13 June 1848
Principal Dancers: Fanny Cerrito (Spring), Carlotta Grisi (Summer), Carolina Rosati (Autumn), Marie Taglioni the younger (Winter)

Other choreographic treatments of theme: Lucien Petipa (London, 1856), Marius Petipa (St. Petersburg, 1900), Joseph Hassreiter (Vienna, 1911), Merce Cunningham (New York, 1947), Jack Carter (London, 1950), Erich Walter (Düsseldorf, 1970), André Prokovsky (London, 1973), Kenneth MacMillan (London, 1975), Jerome Robbins (New York, 1979).

PUBLICATIONS

Michel, Arthur, "Pas de Quatre 1845–1945", *Dance Magazine* (New York), July 1945
Beaumont, Cyril, *Complete Book of Ballets*, revised edition, London, 1951
Guest, Ivor, *The Romantic Ballet in England*, London, 1954
Guest, Ivor, *Jules Perrot: Master of the Romantic Ballet*, London, 1984

* * *

Les Quatre Saisons was the fourth and last of the great divertissement ballets created by Jules Perrot for Her Majesty's Theatre, London. Like its predecessors, *Pas de quatre* (1845), *Le Jugement de Pâris* (1846), and *Les Éléments* (1847), its main attraction was as a dancing contest between the star ballerinas present in London, in this case Fanny Cerrito, Carlotta Grisi, Carolina Rosati, and Marie Taglioni the younger. Indeed, *Les Quatre Saisons* followed what had become a formula. The seasons— Cerrito as Spring, Grisi as Summer, Rosati as Autumn, and Taglioni as Winter—enter in succession with their retinues of nymphs to execute group and solo dances, only to be driven after a time from the scene by the next season. Consulting contemporary reports, we find that Cerrito's "free, large, and joyous style" qualified her to dance Spring. Carlotta Grisi charmingly depicted the "gentle and poetical languor of 'Summer'". "The well-disciplined mechanism of Rosati" served her portrayal of Autumn well. Taglioni, the weakest of the quartet, capered "nimbly" as Winter. In the end the four seasons unite in a "Pas de l'Union des Saisons", "recognising one another's domain of choreography . . .". "A more charming almanak," wrote one observer, "we never contemplated—this is a living one of irresistible persuasion, in which there is nothing 'old style'." ("Old style" here refers to neo-classical *ballet d'action*. In fact, the idea of a divertissement ballet based on the four seasons went back to the eighteenth century.)

Enhancing the popularity of *Les Quatre Saisons*, as with Perrot's three other divertissement ballets, was the fact that the competitions it was based upon were as real off stage as on. Audience members, like sports fans, had their favourite performer, and arrived at the theatre eager to demonstrate their loyalty by rapturously cheering her efforts. And the performers themselves saw their sister dancers as rivals; each wanted to be the most popular, the most successful, the most adored. The result of their rivalry was invariably a triumph: "It is almost unnecessary to add that *Les Quatre Saisons* was quite as successful as any of the previous examples of the same kind, and that the 'stars' fought each other well with entrechats, rondes des jambes, and pirouettes. Each won her own victory— that is, each maintained her credit with her adherents without a shadow of reproach . . .".

It was a tribute to Perrot's genius that his dances were accepted as equal in importance to the overwhelmingly popular ballerinas. In fact, what saved *Les Quatre Saisons* from being a mere sporting event, a circus extravaganza, was Perrot's fine dance compositions. "This ballet of M. Perrot," wrote one critic, "is full, not only of poetry, but of the study of painting and sculpture, from the best models, and we had never even dreamt that choregraphy [sic] could attempt such things, still less succeed, as it did last night." The writer for the *Morning Herald* felt that "The 'variations', wherein each endeavors to out vie that which went before, produce a long series of eloquent gymnastics, and as step succeeds step with flashing rapidity, the spectators' eyes widen with interest, and he applauds with some sensations of the old fanaticism." That was the sad thing for ballet lovers. Already in 1848 people were aware that ballet had seen better days, had experienced greater triumphs, had known more fanatical audience support. Many knew that Perrot's exploration of a new balletic genre could not alter the tide of fashion that was flowing in favour of opera. *Les Quatre Saisons*, his last work in England, marked the end of an era.

—John Chapman

Les Quatre Saisons, **Her Majesty's Theatre, London, 1848**

RADUNSKY, Aleksandr

Russian/Soviet dancer, choreographer, and teacher. Born Aleksandr Ivanovich Radunsky in Moscow, 3 August (21 July old style) 1912. Studied at the Moscow Choreographic School; graduated 1930. Dancer, Bolshoi Ballet, 1930–35, becoming character soloist, 1935–62; training sessions choreographer, Aleksandrov Soviet Army Song and Dance Ensemble, 1949–62, becoming chief choreographer, 1962–65. Honoured Artist of the Russian Federation, 1958.

ROLES

1930 Magdavaya in *La Bayadère* (Gorsky after Petipa), Bolshoi Ballet, Moscow

Niquese (Alain) in *Vain Precautions* (*La Fille mal gardée*; Gorsky after Petipa, Ivanov), Bolshoi Ballet, Moscow

1932 Gallic Chief in *Salammbô* (Moiseyev), Bolshoi Ballet, Moscow

Merchant in *The Little Humpbacked Horse* (Gorsky after Saint-Léon), Bolshoi Ballet, Moscow

1933 Tutor in *Swan Lake* (Gorsky after Petipa, Ivanov), Bolshoi Ballet, Moscow

Khan in *The Little Humpbacked Horse* (Gorsky after Saint-Léon), Bolshoi Ballet, Moscow

1934 Squire in *Giselle* (Gorsky after Petipa, Coralli, Perrot), Bolshoi Ballet, Moscow

1935 Dr. Gaspard (cr) in *Three Fat Men* (Moiseyev), Bolshoi Ballet, Moscow

1936 Catalabutte in *The Sleeping Beauty* (Tikhomirov after Petipa), Bolshoi Ballet, Moscow

Maria's Father (cr) in *The Fountain of Bakhchisarai* (Moscow version; Zakharov), Bolshoi Ballet, Moscow

Modest Petrovich in *The Bright Stream* (Lopukhov), Bolshoi Ballet, Moscow

1938 Father of the Circassian Girl (cr) in *The Prisoner of the Caucasus* (Zakharov), Bolshoi Ballet, Moscow

1939 The King of Mice in *The Nutcracker* (Vainonen), Bolshoi Ballet, Moscow

1941 The Old Cossack (cr) in *Taras Bulba* (Zakharov), Bolshoi Ballet, Moscow

1942 Egle (cr) in *Crimson Sails* (also chor., with Popko, Pospekhin), Bolshoi Ballet, Kuibyshev

The Innkeeper in *Don Quixote* (Zakharov after Gorsky), Bolshoi Ballet, Moscow

1945 Master of Ceremonies (cr) in *Cinderella* (Zakharov), Bolshoi Ballet, Moscow

1946 Muromsky (cr) in *Mistress into Maid* (Zakharov), Bolshoi Ballet, Moscow

Lord Capulet in *Romeo and Juliet* (Lavrovsky), Bolshoi Ballet, Moscow

Friar Laurence in *Romeo and Juliet* (Lavrovsky), Bolshoi Ballet, Moscow

1948 Camel (cr) in *The Little Stork* (also chor., with Popko, Pospekhin), Bolshoi Ballet, Moscow

Dr. Coppélius in *Coppélia* (also chor., with Evgenia Dolinskaya; after Gorsky, Petipa, Ivanov), Bolshoi Ballet, Moscow

1949 Count Albafiorita (cr) in *Mirandolina* (Vainonen), Bolshoi Ballet, Moscow

Peter the Great (cr) in *The Bronze Horseman* (Moscow version; Zakharov), Bolshoi Ballet, Moscow

Captain (cr) in *The Red Poppy* (Lavrovsky), Bolshoi Ballet, Moscow

1952 Louis XVI in *The Flames of Paris* (Vainonen), Bolshoi Ballet, Moscow

1953 Count de Doris in *Raymonda* (Petipa, Gorsky; staged Lavrovsky), Bolshoi Ballet, Moscow

1954 The Landowner (cr) in *The Story of the Stone Flower* (Lavrovsky), Bolshoi Ballet, Moscow

1955 The Duke in *Giselle* (Petipa after Coralli, Perrot), Bolshoi Ballet, Moscow

1956 Father of Frondoso in *Laurencia* (Chabukiani), Bolshoi Ballet, Moscow

1958 Crassus (cr) in *Spartacus* (Moiseyev), Bolshoi Ballet, Moscow

1960 Tsar Gorokh (cr) in *The Little Humpbacked Horse* (also chor.), Bolshoi Ballet, Moscow

1961 Tamara's Father in *Pages from a Life* (Lavrovsky), Bolshoi Ballet, Moscow

Other roles include: Marcelina (Widow Simone) in *Vain Precautions* (*La Fille mal gardée*; Gorsky after Petipa, Ivanov); also many dances in Bolshoi Theatre opera productions.

WORKS

1937 *The Little Stork* (with Popko and Pospekhin; mus. Klebanov), Bolshoi Choreographic School Performance, Bolshoi Theatre, Moscow (staged Bolshoi Ballet, 1948)

1939 *Svetlana* (with Popko and Pospekhin; mus. Klebanov), Bolshoi Ballet, Moscow

1942 *Crimson Sails* (with Popko and Pospekhin; mus. Yurovsky), Bolshoi Ballet, Kuibyshev

1960 *The Little Humpbacked Horse* (mus. Shchedrin), Bolshoi Ballet, Moscow

Also staged:
1977 *Coppélia* (revival of Gorsky's production, after Petipa, Ivanov; mus. Delibes), Moscow Choreographic School, Moscow
1979 *Vain Precautions* (*La fille mal gardée*, after Gorsky; mus. Hertel and others), Moscow Choreographic School, Moscow

PUBLICATIONS

By Radunsky:
"Peace will Prevail over War", in *Aleksandr Yermolaev: Essays and Reminiscences*, Moscow, 1982

About Radunsky:
Aleksandr Ivanovich Radunsky, Moscow, 1953
Roslavleva, Natalia, *Era of the Russian Ballet*, London, 1966
Boguslavskaya, A., "Dancer, Choreographer, Teacher", *Teatr* (Moscow), no 5, 1978
Levashov, Vladimir, "Aleksandr Ivanovich Radunsky", *Bolshoi Theatre* (Moscow), Part 3, 1981
Iusim, M. "Aleksander Radunsky: In Connection with his 70th Birthday", *Sovetsky Balet*, no 5, 1982

*   *   *

Aleksandr Radunsky came from a family of circus actors. His father was a famous clown, known by his stage-name Bim. Radunsky junior was trained at the Moscow School of Choreography, where his talent for acting and mime was soon noticed. At that time the Bolshoi Ballet welcomed mime actors. This was partly because in Moscow, in contrast with St. Petersburg, there was a long tradition of close interaction between the opera, ballet, and drama companies. Moscow ballet had been famous for its character and mime dancers ever since the early nineteenth century. The style of the mime dancing in Moscow differed from that accepted in St. Petersburg in being less artificial and more improvisational.

The 1930s through to the 1950s were the heyday of the mime because a new type of ballet which was then prevalent was entirely based on it. This was the so-called "balletic drama" ("dram-ballet")—a multi-act performance, usually an adaptation of some well-known literary work, in which the characters expressed themselves through mime acting rather than through dancing. It was a good time for Radunsky to join the Bolshoi company. He had well-drawn and expressive movements together with a keen sense of humour and an ability to make spectators laugh—those qualities which had been worth inheriting from his circus predecessors. Even in his first years with the company, when he danced in corps de ballet, he stood out from the crowd because his performance was full of life and character. Very soon after the start of his career at the Bolshoi, he began to dance small individual roles with a strong mime element: the old fakir Magdavaya in *La Bayadère*, Khan and the Merchant in *The Little Humpbacked Horse*, the stupid fiancé Niquese (Alain) in *Vain Precautions* (*La Fille mal gardée*), and so on.

Still, a role in a new ballet is more exciting for an actor than anything else, particularly if it has been specially created for him. Such was one of Radunsky's first original roles, that of Doctor Gaspar in *Three Fat Men* (1935), choreographed by Igor Moiseyev: in this he played an old scholar, absent-minded, fussy, and unpractical but always taking the side of the good against the evil.

Radunsky danced many mime roles, ranging, thanks to his considerable gifts, from the intensely dramatic to the comic and

the grotesque. In Leonid Lavrovsky's production of *Romeo and Juliet* he outlined the character of Capulet, Juliet's father, through a sparing but convincing use of detail. His intuitive understanding of the epoch helped him to choose the right make-up and bearing, emphasizing his patrician arrogance and obstinate temper, enhanced by prejudice. (Radunsky's interpretation of this role can be seen in the film *Romeo and Juliet*, 1955, with Galina Ulanova as Juliet). In a similar way, Radunsky has been able to convey Peter the Great's iron-willed determination and short temper, as well as his tsar-like appearance, in Rostislav Zakharov's production of *The Bronze Horseman*. However, the comic roles were his native element. Among them can be listed Count Albafiorita in *Mirandolina* and numerous roles in the classical ballet productions—such as Marcelina (Widow Simone) in *Vain Precautions*, Dr. Coppélius in *Coppélia*, and many more.

Radunsky was also a choreographer. He staged four ballets in collaboration with Nikolai Popko and Lev Pospekhin: *The Little Stork*, *Svetlana*, *Crimson Sails*, and the ballet *The Little Humpbacked Horse* (with new music by Rodion Shchedrin). In all those ballets he danced himself. The role of Tsar Gorokh in *The Little Humpbacked Horse* was a particular success. The tsar in this humorous fairy-tale ballet is more like a clown or a jester than a proper ruler. This ridiculous figure is nevertheless quite real and true to life, a humbug who pretends to be a hearty old chap in order to get what he wants, yet ultimately is always caught in his own trap.

In more recent years, Radunsky has revived old ballet productions several times. Thus, the Moscow School of Choreography has invited him since 1977 to revive Gorsky's versions of *Coppélia* (with himself as Dr. Coppelius) and *Vain Precautions*.

—Irina Grusdeva

THE RAKE'S PROGRESS

Choreography: Ninette de Valois
Music: Gavin Gordon
Design: Rex Whistler (scenery and costumes)
Libretto: Gavin Gordon (after a series of paintings by William Hogarth)
First Production: Vic-Wells Ballet, Sadler's Wells Theatre, London, 20 May 1935
Principal Dancers: Walter Gore (The Rake), Alicia Markova (The Betrayed Girl), Ursula Moreton (The Dancer), Harold Turner (The Dancing Master and The Gentleman with a Rope)

Other productions include: Sadler's Wells Theatre Ballet (restaged de Valois), with Alexander Grant (The Rake), Shelagh O'Reilly (The Betrayed Girl); London, 18 June 1952. Turkish State Ballet (staged Claude Newman); April 1961. Bavarian State Opera Ballet (staged Peggy van Praagh); Munich, 18 May 1956. Vienna State Opera Ballet; Vienna, 1964. CAPAB Ballet; Capetown, October 1967. Ballet van Vlaanderen (staged Richard Glasstone); Antwerp, 1972.

PUBLICATIONS

Goodman, G.E., "Notes on Decor", *Dancing Times* (London), January 1936

The Rake's Progress, with Robert Helpmann as the Rake, Sadler's Wells Ballet, 1942

Howlett, Jasper, "The Betrayed Girl: A Note on *The Rake's Progress*", *Dancing Times* (London), July 1946

Lawson, Joan, *Job and the Rake's Progress*, London, 1949

Robertson, Marion, *The Rake's Progress and Checkmate*, London, 1949

Beaumont, Cyril, *The Complete Book of Ballets*, revised edition, London, 1951

Barnes, Clive, "*The Rake's Progress*", *Dance and Dancers* (London), April 1960

De Valois, Ninette, "*The Rake's Progress*", interview in *About the House* (London), Christmas 1967

Balanchine, George, with Mason, Francis, *Balanchine's Complete Stories of the Great Ballets*, Garden City, New York, 1977

Sorley Walker, Kathrine, *Ninette de Valois: Idealist without Illusions*, London, 1987

*   *   *

According to Kathrine Sorley Walker's biography of Dame Ninette de Valois, the original inspiration for *The Rake's Progress* came from Constant Lambert. Up to a point this may be true. However, considering the value which Ninette de Valois always put on Massine's work, it is hard to believe that she was ignorant of his production in 1925, in the Cochran revue *On with the Dance*, of a short ballet called *The Rake*, with music by Roger Quilter, décor by William Nicholson, and, according to Massine's autobiography, "based on Hogarth's drawings of The Rake's Progress". The work was successful enough to have been held over in a subsequent revue, *Still Dancing*. It is certainly unlikely that she was unaware of the Hogarth etchings, upon which both works were based.

But the Massine work is lost forever, while the de Valois ballet—if we were only allowed to see it—is still in the repertoire, and it is not hard to understand why it has held its place when other works have vanished. It was the result of a well matched collaboration between composer, designer, and choreographer. The literary/artistic basis of the work was very much in the genre in which de Valois's most successful ballets were made, and the ballet offered scope to dancers of varying ages and capabilities, taking care neither to overstrain nor to underexpose any of them. But most important of all, de Valois had the luck, or the judgement, to make the first "English" ballet, English in the sense that *Petrushka* is the first Russian ballet and *Billy the Kid* is the first American ballet. The essential Englishness of *The Rake* made the ballet unique in its time and set a standard for clear, simple, inventive choreography which is a model of how to tell a story in movement without cluttering it with inessentials. There are no virtuoso tricks in *The Rake*; they would be out of place, and de Valois never once (though the ballet is a long one) utilized any dance clichés as make-weight, either to fill a section of music arbitrarily, or because she could not find the right steps. The entire dance texture is free of choreographer's conventions and built up by means of movements which are technically simple, but call for intense commitment from the dancer. No one can afford to freewheel in this ballet: if the dancer's concentration were to slip for a moment the character inherent in the role, be it large or small, would be weakened, if not lost. The story of the Rake and how he achieves his own downfall, taken from Hogarth, is easy to follow: only one in the series of pictures—the Marriage—is omitted and the other scenes illustrate the progression downwards, which would fit the definition of tragedy were there not so much wry humour to be found along the way.

Quite beyond the highly personal choreographic language employed in this ballet, one cannot help but admire the absolute grasp of the rules of dramatic theatre displayed in the construction of *The Rake*. Each scene has its own individual style, clearly derived from the style of the Hogarth picture which inspired it, and the scene changes between them are deftly managed by means of a drop cloth, a device nowadays unfashionable but popular at the time when scene changes could not be relied upon to go quite so smoothly or so fast, perhaps, as they do today. Every character in the ballet is rapidly sketched in with a decisive, sure touch and, once established, developed with equal mastery to assume exactly the importance necessary to the balance of the ballet as a whole. In the scene in the Gambling House, the basic movements made by the dancers concerned could not be more simple, yet the timing, the arrangement of the scene so that everything is plainly visible, and the hypnotic repetition of simple movements combine with the relentless rhythm of the music to provide a riveting insight into the dreadful descending spiral of disaster in which the Rake has engaged himself. Some critics complained that the last scene in the madhouse was overlong. In fact, de Valois takes just enough time to demonstrate the boredom and mindless despair of those incarcerated in a lunatic asylum before bringing in the Betrayed Girl and the society visitors who provide a telling contrast to the misery of the inhabitants and an indictment of the callous attitude of society to the insane.

There could hardly have been a greater contrast in ballet at the time than that between the first two Rakes, Walter Gore (the creator of the role) and Robert Helpmann, or between the first Betrayed Girl of Markova and those of her immediate successors, Elizabeth Miller and Mary Honer. All turned in fine performances, and in subsequent years the following generations of dancers have been well served by the unconventional steps given to the performers of this ballet.

—Janet Sinclair

RALOV, Kirsten

Danish dancer, choreographer, teacher, and ballet director. Born Kirsten Laura Gnatt in Baden, Austria, 26 March 1922. Studied at the Royal Danish Ballet School, Copenhagen, pupil of Valborg Borchsenius, from 1929; later studied with Lubov Egorova, Anna Sevitzskaya, and Antony Tudor, Paris and London. Married (1) dancer Børge Ralov, 1944 (div. 1951); (2) dancer Fredbjørn Bjørnsson, 1954: 2 children. Stage début as a child, 1933; dancer, Royal Danish Ballet, from 1940, with official début in 1941, and becoming solo dancer (principal), 1942-62; also leading dancer on international tours with Inge Sand group, 1955, 1957-61, and with Royal Danish Ballet, 1956 and 1960; guest artist (performing Lady Capulet in *Romeo and Juliet*), London Festival Ballet, 1985-89; choreographer, Royal Danish Ballet, from 1960; international teacher and producer of Bournonville repertoire, from 1962, also restaging Bournonville ballets for Royal Danish Ballet, from 1975; associate artistic director, Royal Danish Ballet, 1978-88; managing director, Bournonville Centenary at the Royal Theatre, Copenhagen, 1979; director of the Hans Christian Andersen Award, 1988. Recipient: title of Knight of Dannebrog, 1953; Knight of Dannebrog, First Grade, 1978; Icelandic Order of the Falcon, 1981.

ROLES

1933   Fanny in *Konservatoriet* (Bournonville), Royal Danish Ballet, Copenhagen

1934   Shepherdess (cr) in *The Shepherdess and the Chimney-Sweep* (Lander), Royal Danish Ballet, Copenhagen

1935   The Child (cr) in *It was an Evening* (Lander), Royal Danish Ballet, Copenhagen

1936   The Princess (cr) in *The Swineherd* (Lander), Royal Danish Ballet, Copenhagen
Muse (cr) in *Psyche* (Theilade), Royal Danish Ballet, Copenhagen

1937   Butterfly in *The Widow in the Mirror* (B. Ralov), Royal Danish Ballet, Copenhagen
Persian woman in *Polovtsian Dances from Prince Igor* (Fokine), The Royal Danish Ballet, Copenhagen
Title role in *Coppélia* (Lander after Saint-Léon), Royal Danish Ballet, Copenhagen

1938   Lead Swan in *Swan Lake* (one-act version; Lander after Petipa), Royal Danish Ballet, Copenhagen
Earth (cr) in *The Circle* (Theilade), Royal Danish Ballet, Copenhagen
One of the Three Graces (cr) in *Thorvaldsen* (Lander), Royal Danish Ballet, Copenhagen

1939   Young Girl (cr) in *The Four Temperaments* (B. Ralov), Royal Danish Ballet, Copenhagen
Sylph solo, Act II, in *La Sylphide* (Bournonville), Royal Danish Ballet, Copenhagen
Valkyrie in *The Valkyrie* (Bournonville), Royal Danish Ballet, Copenhagen

1941   Nymph in *L'Apres-midi d'un faune* (Ralov after Nijinsky), Royal Danish Ballet, Copenhagen
Gypsy dance from *Il Trovatore* (opera; mus. Verdi, chor. Bournonville), Royal Danish Ballet, Copenhagen
Pas de six and Tarantella in *Napoli* (Bournonville), Royal Danish Ballet, Copenhagen
Pas de trois in *La Ventana* (Bournonville), Royal Danish Ballet, Copenhagen

1942   Snowdrop (cr) in *Twelve by the Post* (B. Ralov), Royal Danish Ballet, Copenhagen
Princess Sugarsweet (cr) in *The Land of Milk and Honey* (Lander), Royal Danish Ballet, Copenhagen
Ung woman in *Qarrtsiluni* (Lander), Royal Danish Ballet, Copenhagen
Dancer (cr) in *Festival Polonaise* (Lander), Royal Danish Ballet, Copenhagen
Sunbeam (cr) in *Spring* (Lander), Royal Danish Ballet, Copenhagen

1943   Slovanka in *The Kermesse in Bruges* (Bournonville), Royal Danish Ballet, Copenhagen
Victorine in *Konservatoriet* (Bournonville), Royal Danish Ballet, Copenhagen
Nocturne and Mazurka in *Les Sylphides* (Fokine; staged Lander), Royal Danish Ballet, Copenhagen

1944   Helena (cr) in *The Eternal Trio* (B. Ralov), Royal Danish Ballet, Copenhagen
The Fluttering (cr) in *Passiones* (B. Ralov), Royal Danish Ballet, Copenhagen

1945   Pas de trois in *Swan Lake* (one-act version; Lander after Petipa, Ivanov), Royal Danish Ballet, Copenhagen
Poul in *Far from Denmark* (Bournonville), Royal Danish Ballet, Copenhagen

1946   Ballerina in *Petrushka* (Fokine), Royal Danish Ballet, Copenhagen

1947   The Second Broom in *The Sorcerer's Apprentice* (Lander), Royal Danish Ballet, Copenhagen
The Girl (cr) in *Kolingen* (B. Ralov), Royal Danish Ballet, Copenhagen
Andrea in *The King's Lifeguards on Amager* (Bournonville), Royal Danish Ballet, Copenhagen

1948   Title role (cr) in *Sylvia* (Larsen), Royal Danish Ballet, Copenhagen

Kirsten Ralov with Frank Schaufuss in Ashton's *Romeo and Juliet*, Royal Danish Ballet, 1955

The Daughter in *Le Beau Danube* (Massine), Royal Danish Ballet, Copenhagen

Reverie in *Episode of an Artist's Life* (*Symphonie fantastique*; Massine), Royal Danish Ballet, Copenhagen

First Broom in *The Sorcerer's Apprentice* (Lander), Royal Danish Ballet, Copenhagen

Amelia in *Visions* (Walbom), Royal Danish Ballet, Copenhagen

1949 Myrtha in *Giselle* (Petipa after Coralli, Perrot; staged Volinin), Royal Danish Ballet, Copenhagen

Adagio-Bride in *The Widow in the Mirror* (B. Ralov), Royal Danish Ballet, Copenhagen

The Widow in *The Widow in the Mirror* (B. Ralov), Royal Danish Ballet, Copenhagen

The Woman in *Rhapsodie* (Lander), Royal Danish Ballet, Copenhagen

La Lithuanienne in *Salute to August Bournonville* (Lander after Bournonville), Royal Danish Ballet, Copenhagen

Princess Aurora in *Aurora's Wedding* (from *The Sleeping Beauty*; Brenaa after Petipa), Royal Danish Ballet, Copenhagen

1950 Odette in *Swan Lake* (one-act version; Lander after Petipa, Ivanov), Royal Danish Ballet, Copenhagen

Third Movement in *Symphonie classique* (Bartholin), Royal Danish Ballet, Copenhagen

Teresina in *Napoli* (Bournonville), Royal Danish Ballet, Copenhagen

The Woman (cr) in *Video* (B. Ralov), Danish television

1951 The Lonely Woman (cr) in *Desire* (Larsen), Royal Danish Ballet, Copenhagen

Columbine in *Visions* (Walbom), Royal Danish Ballet, Copenhagen

Title role (cr) in *Diana* (Lander), Royal Danish Ballet, Copenhagen

Eleonora in *The Kermesse in Bruges* (Bournonville), Royal Danish Ballet, Copenhagen

1952   Junior Girl in *Graduation Ball* (Lichine), Royal Danish Ballet, Copenhagen

Dancer in *Design with Strings* (Taras), Royal Danish Ballet, Copenhagen

Fourth movement in *Symphony in C* (Balanchine), Royal Danish Ballet, Copenhagen

1953   Title role (cr) in *The Courtesan* (B. Ralov), Royal Danish Ballet, Copenhagen

1954   Solo Dancer (cr) in *Behind the Curtain* (Bjørnsson), Royal Danish Ballet, Copenhagen

1955   Principal dancer in *Concerto Barocco* (Balanchine), Royal Danish Ballet, Copenhagen

Rosaline (cr) in *Romeo and Juliet* (Ashton), Royal Danish Ballet, Copenhagen

1956   Rosita in *Far from Denmark* (Bournonville), Royal Danish Ballet, Copenhagen

1957   Crystal Spring Fairy in *The Sleeping Beauty* (Petipa, Ashton), The Royal Danish Ballet, Copenhagen

Pas de trois in *The Sleeping Beauty* (Petipa, Ashton), Royal Danish Ballet, Copenhagen

Pas de deux from *Flower Festival at Genzano* (Bournonville), Royal Danish Ballet, Copenhagen

Principal dancer (cr) in *Roguery* (Bjørnsson), Tivoli Concert Hall, Copenhagen

1958   Amager Dance in *The Whims of Cupid and the Ballet Master* (Galeotti), Royal Danish Ballet, Copenhagen

Second Movement in *La Jeunesse* (Bartholin), Royal Danish Ballet, Copenhagen

The Good Fairy in *Harlequin's Millions* (Walbom), Royal Danish Ballet, Copenhagen

Bridge lady (cr) in *Happiness on Journey* (Bjørnsson), Royal Danish Ballet, Copenhagen

1959   Principal dancer (cr) in *Festa* (Bruhn), Royal Danish Ballet, Copenhagen

1960   Page (cr) in *The Shadow* (Bartholin), Royal Danish Ballet, Copenhagen

1961   Customer in *La Chaloupée* (Petit), Royal Danish Ballet, Copenhagen

1965   Solo dancer (cr) in *The Woman in the Mud Ditch* (Skov), Danish television

1966   Psyche's sister in *Psyche* (Theilade), Danish television

1985   Lady Capulet in *Romeo and Juliet* (Ashton), London Festival Ballet, London

WORKS

1960   *The Lady of the Camellias* (mus. Bjerre), Royal Danish Ballet, Copenhagen

1962   *The Door* (mus. Bentzon), Royal Danish Ballet, Copenhagen (television version, 1966)

1973   *Wednesday's School* (extracts from Bournonville syllabus; mus. Schmidt), Royal Danish Ballet, Copenhagen (also staged Boston Ballet, 1979)

Also staged:

1962   *Napoli* (after Bournonville; mus. Paulli, Helsted, Gade, Lumbye), New Zealand Ballet (also staged Royal Danish Ballet, 1975; Finnish National Ballet, 1986)

Flower Festival at Genzano Pas de deux (after Bournonville; mus. Helsted, Paulli), New Zealand Ballet (also staged Royal Ballet, 1982; Forth Worth Ballet, 1985; Bolshoi Ballet, 1989)

1968   *Napoli Divertissement* (excerpts, after Bournonville; mus. Paulli, Helsted, Gade, Lumbye), State Theatre, Bremen (also staged Royal Winnipeg Ballet; Basel Ballet, 1975; Royal Ballet, 1981; Forth Worth Ballet, 1985)

1979   *La Sylphide* (after Bournonville; mus. Schneitzhoffer), Bavarian State Opera Ballet, Munich (also staged Wielki Theatre, Poland, 1984)

A Folk Tale (after Bournonville; mus. Gade, Hartmann), Royal Danish Ballet, Copenhagen

1980   *La Ventana* (after Bournonville; mus. Lumbye), Pittsburg Ballet, Pennsylvania (staged Wielki Theatre, Poland, 1984; Forth Worth Ballet, 1985; Göteborg Ballet, 1988; Bolshoi Ballet, 1989)

1989   *Konservatoriet* (after Bournonville; mus. Paulli), Bolshoi Ballet, Moscow

The Kermesse in Bruges Pas de deux (after Bournonville; mus. Paulli), Bolshoi Ballet, Moscow

Other works include: dances in operas *The Cunning Little Vixen* (mus. Janáček; 1963), *Aida* (mus. Verdi; 1963), *Der Wildshütz* (mus. Lortzing; 1965), *Die Fledermaus* (mus. Strauss; 1973).

PUBLICATIONS

By Ralov:
The Bournonville School, New York, 1979
Interview in Terry, Walter, "The Bournonville School: An Interview with Kirsten Ralov", in *The Royal Danish Ballet and Bournonville*, Copenhagen, 1979

About Ralov:
Kragh-Jacobsen, Svend, *The Royal Danish Ballet*, Copenhagen and London, 1955
Fanger, Iris, "The Royal Danish Ballet's Kirsten Ralov", *Dance Magazine* (New York), November 1979

* * *

When Kirsten Ralov retired at the age of forty she left a legacy of performances which spanned the Fokine, Ashton, Petipa and, especially, Bournonville repertoires. She had not initially made her name as a Bournonville dancer, however. She joined the Royal Danish Ballet in 1940 and her first principal roles included those in *Petrushka* and *Les Sylphides*. But her early training with Valborg Borchsenius had guaranteed her place as one of the finest exponents of the Bournonville repertoire when she finally made her débuts in the leading roles of *Flower Festival at Genzano* and *Napoli*. She was always renowned for her musicality, and as one critic put it, for "her girlish gracefulness"—and these were attributes that she was able to pass on to others with her great natural gift for teaching.

From the age of six Ralov had never doubted her own abilities. She said, of the time when her mother brought her to audition for the Royal Danish Ballet School: "I was absolutely certain that I would be taken". She spoke with the same self-assurance off-stage that she showed on the stage throughout her career as a dancer. In a 1979 interview with *Dance Magazine* her responses were delivered swiftly and clearly, with a sincere confidence that reminds us of her exemplary execution of the Bournonville technique itself. Recalling that she had agreed to take three Bournonville pas de deux to America for the first time in 1955, she indicated that there had been no sense of trepidation at introducing an old style to the New World. She had promptly replied to the invitation, saying "Well, I would like to do it. I will do it, because I can".

There is nothing arrogant about Ralov's matter-of-fact self-awareness. One senses that her frank honesty about her own potential resided in an intensely pragmatic attitude to life. She met every challenge face-on, never missing a performance throughout her career (except for her pregnancies), and with stoic professionalism she danced through sickness and injury. Colleagues maintain that one of her finest performances of the punishing mazurka in *Les Sylphides* occured in South America when she was nearly prostrate with dysentry. Yet in spite of this unblemished performance record she possessed the wisdom and humility to step aside for younger dancers. She stopped dancing three years before the customary age for Danish ballerinas, explaining, "I retired because I felt it was time . . . I knew I would hardly get new parts . . . I had better get off now".

With her characteristic self-knowledge Ralov realized very early on that her talents lay equally with teaching, and she missed no opportunities in exploiting them. At the age of thirteen she assisted Harald Lander in the first revival of *The Shepherdess and the Chimney Sweep*, a work for children. In fact, she helped teach the part of the hero to her future second husband, Fredbjørn Bjørnsson (her first marriage was to the Danish dancer Børge Ralov). She found no difficulty in organizing the whole ballet for Lander, claiming that teaching was always "something natural" for her. Ralov continued to teach throughout her career as a dancer, but her significant role in the dissemination of the Bournonville technique, both at home and internationally, was established once she left the stage to concentrate on that side of her life.

This watershed in her career took place in 1962. It was marked by a memorable performance in which she danced her renowned interpretation of the pas de deux from Bournonville's *Flower Festival at Genzano* for the last time in the historic setting of the Royal Court Theatre in Christiansborg Castle, Copenhagen. The castle had been reconverted from a theatre museum to performance space in honour of Ralov's departure from the stage. This fitting location signified the importance of Ralov's role in the continuity of the Danish tradition, for it celebrated the transition from performer to full-time teacher at the very site of her predecessors' first contributions to Danish ballet.

The greatest interpreters of Bournonville had always transferred their expertise personally to the next generation, helping dancers to retain the technique's freshness and vitality. Ralov was no exception, first accepting the position of ballet mistress, and later associate artistic director at the Royal Danish Ballet, with the aim of preserving the Bournonville technique for posterity with accuracy and commitment.

She was aware of a great responsibility—that any Bournonville dancer should above all convey the "natural" quality of the traditional style. The uninitiated of the dance world often misinterpreted this brand of classicism, marring its simple effects with affectation and mannerisms. In the introduction to her book *The Bournonville School* (1979), Ralov complains that she had so often seen the teacher or the dancer trying to make it look "authentic—old-fashioned". That, says Ralov, "is a great, *fundamental mistake*". Her book goes a long way to rectify errors in interpretation. Her transcriptions of Bournonville's classes emphasize the musical phrasing and the natural logic of the master's enchaînements, the clean line and unfussy transitions between movements. These were the hallmarks of her own vivacious style as a performer, ones that ensured her successful and invaluable contribution to the world-famous tradition, both on stage and in the classroom.

—Susan Jones

RAMBERT DANCE COMPANY
(formerly Ballet Rambert)
English dance company based in London. Origins in ballet school founded by Marie Rambert, London, 1920, with first performances as the Marie Rambert Dancers, 1926; appeared as Ballet Club, based at the Mercury Theatre, London, from January 1931; performed as Ballet Rambert from 1935, with performances as joint Rambert–London Ballet at Arts Theatre Club, London, 1940–41; reorganized as full-scale touring company, performing as Ballet Rambert, from 1943; reorganized again as small-scale dance company, with increasing emphasis on modern dance, 1966; renamed Rambert Dance Company, 1987. Official school associated with the ballet company has foundations in Marie Rambert's School, founded 1920, becoming the Ballet Rambert School, based at the Mercury Theatre, London; Rambert Academy, set up in conjunction with London Institute of Higher Education, founded 1979: merged with the Rambert School, 1982. Artistic director of Rambert Dance Company (succeeding Richard Alston): Christopher Bruce, from 1994.

PUBLICATIONS

Haskell, Arnold, *The Marie Rambert Ballet*, London, 1930

Haskell, Arnold, *The Ballet in England*, London, 1932

Haskell, Arnold, "The Ballet Club: Marie Rambert's Laboratory", *The Bystander* (London), 9 March 1938

Rambert, Marie, "The Value of Intimate Ballet", *Dancing Times* (London), December 1940

Bradley, Lionel, *Sixteen Years of Ballet Rambert*, London, 1946

Noble, Peter (ed.), *British Ballet*, London, c.1950

de Mille, Agnes, *Dance to the Piper: Memoirs of the Ballet*, London, 1951

Anniversary Issue, *Dance and Dancers* (London), October 1955

Clarke, Mary, *Dancers of Mercury: The Story of Ballet Rambert*, London, 1962

Crisp, Clement, Sainsbury, Anya, and Williams, Peter (eds.), *Ballet Rambert: Fifty Years and On*, revised edition, London, 1981

Brinson, Peter, "To be Ahead", *Dance and Dancers* (London), June 1990

Kane, Angela, "Rambert Doubling Back to the Sixties", *Dance Theatre Journal* (London), Autumn 1990

Kane, Angela, "Moving Forward to the Seventies", *Dance Theatre Journal* (London), Spring 1991

* * *

British ballet found its foothold not through foresight and planning but through a series of singular developments. While the achievements of Ninette de Valois's company—today Britain's Royal Ballet and the country's "national" ballet institution—have been the more extensive, it is to Marie Rambert's endeavours that twentieth-century British ballet owes its beginnings. First to found a school, first to introduce British dancers to works by British choreographers, first to acknowledge the importance of both the Petipa and Ballets Russes legacies, and finally, first to obtain a permanent theatre to present seasons of ballet in London, Rambert took only a decade (1920–30) to establish a blueprint for the subsequent development of ballet in Britain.

Frederick Ashton's *A Tragedy of Fashion* established Rambert as choreographic alchemist. Her discovery and nurturing of talent during the 1930s was unrivalled. Initially known as the Marie Rambert Dancers, then from 1931 as the Ballet Club, and from the mid-1930s as Ballet Rambert, her company became the greatest creative force in British ballet. Rambert's optimism inspired both dancers and choreographers, many of whom would eventually leave her Mercury Theatre hot-house to seek more ambitious careers elswehere. As much through necessity as artistic policy, a continuous supply of "in-house" choreographers was produced. The emergence of Andrée Howard and Antony Tudor and, towards the end of the decade, of Walter Gore and Frank Staff, led to Rambert's ensemble being appropriately considered "a choreographers' company".

In the 1940s, the Ballet Rambert underwent two significant changes. During the war, after contractual disagreements with Harold Rubin at the Arts Theatre, the company was managed by CEMA (Council for the Encouragement of Music and the Arts), the government organization which was the forerunner of the Arts Council of Great Britain. For the first time since its inception, the company received financial support and thus began its transition from a privately owned London-based company (which toured occasionally) to a publicly funded touring company giving occasional London seasons. Performances at munitions factories, military bases, and theatres throughout England introduced ballet to new audiences. Under the CEMA/Arts Council, Ballet Rambert expanded in both personnel and repertory. Its most ambitious project—one which would initiate a new direction for the company—was the staging of *Giselle*, Act II, in 1945, followed by a complete staging in 1946. It was the company's first full-length ballet and, together with the success of Sadler's Wells Ballet's production of *The Sleeping Beauty*, the post-war trend thus became one of revivals of nineteenth-century classics alongside full-length ballets by British choreographers. (Howard's *The Sailor's Return* and Ashton's *Cinderella* followed in 1947 and 1948 respectively.)

Arts Council management of the company ceased in 1947, and in the same year Ballet Rambert embarked on a tour of Australia and New Zealand. After much success there, the company returned without several of its dancers and with little prospect of survival. An Arts Council grant of £500 enabled Ballet Rambert to begin again in 1949. The company acquired new dancers, began to tour extensively, and reclaimed its audience—but the quest to find a new choreographer met with many false starts. The 1950s were fallow years. Constant touring, the popular preference for full-length ballets and, for the first time in the company's existence, an inability to inspire talent from within the company meant that Ballet Rambert was no longer a company with an emphasis on creativity. More important, with the emergence of choreographers John Cranko and Kenneth MacMillan at Sadler's Wells, Ballet Rambert was no longer leading the way.

One of the most enduring characteristics of the Ballet Rambert has been its ability to survive. Resilience, resourcefulness, and an acute instinct for the times have enabled the company to anticipate change. Norman Morrice's first ballet, *Two Brothers* (1958), not only infused a new creative energy; it also presaged a new aesthetic. In the early 1960s, proposals to consolidate the company's classical tradition were rejected in favour of Morrice's plan to reform the company. The plan was a radical one, involving the reduction of the company to fewer than twenty dancers, the introduction of modern-dance training, and the creation of a repertory which reflected Ballet Rambert's own choreographic talents. Initially, the repertory included existing works by former Ballet Club choreographers, but after the company's reformation in 1966 it soon became apparent that Morrice's plan had initiated a more general desire to look forward. Just prior to this, choreographers from within the company, such as John Chesworth and Jonathan Taylor, had begun to present works on contemporary themes,

often introducing new music and design elements. Ralph Koltai, the designer of *Two Brothers*, and later Nadine Baylis and lighting designer John B. Read were not only to influence the visual environments of the reformed company's repertory but were also to inspire choreographers to incorporate new materials and effects into their works. The arrival of Glen Tetley in 1967 was also to exert considerable influence over the company's future development. The "new-look" Ballet Rambert once again led the way, in a development which in Britain came to be known as contemporary dance.

Since 1966, the company has continued to forge its style on modern-dance techniques. Tetley established a Graham-based tradition of emotive, theatrically charged works. It was a tradition which became evident in the works of Christopher Bruce in the early 1970s—and it was Bruce who became the company's next leading choreographer. In 1981, the London Contemporary Dance Theatre's Robert North was appointed as Ballet Rambert's new artistic director, and it was the first time the company had looked beyond its own dancers and choreographers for leadership. (John Chesworth, after succeeding Norman Morrice as artistic director in 1974, had left the company in 1980.) Working alongside Bruce and another ex-LCDT choreographer, Richard Alston, North established a directorship remembered for its eclecticism of styles and for its dynamic variety. It was North who introduced works by Merce Cunningham and Paul Taylor into the Rambert repertory and since 1986, when Alston became artistic director, it has been the Cunningham technique which has underpinned both training and selection of repertory. Alston's decision in 1987 to change the company's name to Rambert Dance Company reflected an attempt to encompass earlier Rambert traditions, but also aimed to allow scope for new ventures and forms. Under Alston, there has been a renewed emphasis on choreography. Although many American choreographers, such as Cunningham, David Gordon, Trisha Brown, and Lucinda Childs have been invited to work with the company, young British talent has also been encouraged. Under Alston, too, the Diaghilev concept of collaboration has received new impetus. Visual artists, fashion designers, and composers have been involved in many of Rambert's recent commissions. The present-day company reaffirms many of the values of its infancy. Thus, while administrative and technical aspects have become honed, the pioneering spirit of Marie Rambert lives on.

—Angela Kane

RAMBERT, Marie

Polish/British dancer, teacher, choreographer, and ballet director. Born Cyvia Rambam, known as Myriam Ramberg (also spelt Rambach), in Warsaw, 20 February 1888. Studied at the Sorbonne, Paris, from 1906; studied free-dance in Paris with Raymond Duncan, eurhythmics with Émile Jaques-Dalcroze, Geneva and Dresden, 1910–13, and ballet with Enrico Cecchetti, Margaret Craske, and Serafina Astafieva, London, from 1912. Married playwright Ashley Dukes, 1918; two daughters, dancer Angela Ellis (b. 1920), and dancer Lulu Dukes (b. 1923). Dancer and teacher of eurhythmics, Ballets Russes de Serge Diaghilev, 1913; solo dancer, teacher, and choreographer in Paris and London, from 1913, with first independent ballet staged in London, 1917; founder and director of Rambert Ballet School, London, from 1920, and of small performing group, Marie Rambert Dancers, from 1926; founder and director, Ballet Club (growing out of Marie

Rambert Dancers), 1931, becoming Ballet Rambert, from 1935; also co-founder, Camargo Society, London, 1930. Recipient: title of Commander of the Order of the British Empire, 1953; Queen Elizabeth Coronation Award, Royal Academy of Dancing, 1956; Chevalier, Legion d'Honour, France, 1957; Diploma of Associateship, College of Art, Manchester, 1960; title of Dame Commander of the Order of the British Empire, 1962; Doctorate of Literature, Sussex University, 1964; Jubilee Medal, 1977; Composers' Guild Award for Services to British Music, 1978; Gold Medal of the Order of Merit, Poland, 1979. Died in London, 12 June 1982.

ROLES

1913   Dancer in *Le Sacre du printemps* (Nijinsky), Ballets Russes de Serge Diaghilev, Paris
1917   Principal dancer (cr) in *La Pomme d'or* (Donnet), Stage Society, London
1918   Principal dancer (cr) in *Fêtes galantes* (Donnet, Rambert), Stage Society, London
1926   Orchidée (cr) in *A Tragedy of Fashion* (Ashton), in *Riverside Nights* (Revue), London
1930   Gavotte Sentimentale (cr) in *Dances from Les Petits Riens* (possibly a revision of *Nymphs and Shepherds*, 1928; Ashton), Marie Rambert Dancers, London
       The Virgin (cr) in *Our Lady's Juggler* (Salaman), Marie Rambert Dancers, London
       The Madonna (cr) in *A Florentine Picture* (Ashton), Marie Rambert Dancers, London

WORKS

1917   *La Pomme d'or* (with Vera Donnet; mus. Corelli), Stage Society, London
       Fêtes galantes (with Vera Donnet; mus. Rameau, Lully, Bach, Mozart), Stage Society, London
1918   *Ballet philosophique* (mus. Franck), Stage Society, London
1927   Dances in *The Fairy Queen* (with Frederick Ashton; mus. Purcell), Purcell Opera Society and Cambridge Amateur Dramatic Society, London
1928   *Leda* (with Frederick Aston; mus. Gluck), Marie Rambert Dancers, London

PUBLICATIONS

By Rambert:
"The Value of Intimate Ballet", *Dancing Times* (London), December 1940
"The Art of the Choreographer", *Journal of the Royal Society of Arts* (London), September 1962
Ulanova: Her Childhood and Schooldays, London, 1962
Quicksilver: An Autobiography, London, 1972
"Movement is my Element", Interview in Crisp, Clement, Sainsbury, Anya, and Williams, Peter (eds.), *Ballet Rambert: 50 Years and On*, revised edition, London, 1981

About Rambert:
Ashton, Frederick, "A Word about Choreography", *Dancing Times* (London), May 1930
Haskell, Arnold, *The Marie Rambert Ballet*, London, 1930
Haskell, Arnold, *The Ballet in England*, London, 1932
Haskell, Arnold, "The Ballet Club: Marie Rambert's Laboratory", *The Bystander* (London), 9 March 1938

Marie Rambert, c.1920

Bradley, Lionel, *Sixteen Years of Ballet Rambert*, London, 1946
Noble, Peter, *British Ballet*, London, c.1947
de Mille, Agnes, *Dance to the Piper: Memoirs of the Ballet*, London, 1951
Anniversary Issue, *Dance and Dancers*, October 1955
Bland, Alexander, "Marie Rambert", *Ballet Annual* (London), no. 9, 1955
Clarke, Mary, *Dancers of Mercury: The Story of Ballet Rambert*, London, 1962
"Marie Rambert", *Les Saisons de la danse* (Paris), November 1971
Robertshaw, U., "Marie Rambert Remembers Diaghilev", *Illustrated London News* (London), October 1972
Crisp, Clement, Sainsbury, Anya, and Williams, Peter (eds.), *Ballet Rambert: 50 Years and On*, revised edition, London, 1981
Nijinska, Bronislava, *Early Memoirs*, New York, 1981

*   *   *

Marie Rambert was a truly remarkable woman. She was cultivated, dynamic, witty, chic, and impassioned, and she was one of the prime instigators in the development of twentieth-century British ballet. Four years before Ninette de Valois, she established her own school in London from which, a decade later, her company emerged to give its first Hammersmith season in 1930 and its first West End season the following year. She was a woman of boundless energy and ravenous curiosity. Her unerring artistic instinct and innate sense of theatre led her to discover and encourage a whole catalogue of choreographers, dancers, designers, and eventually composers, all of great talent. For some, because of her determination, constant presence, and admitted lack of tact, Rambert might sometimes appear to be, in Agnes de Mille's words, "Madame Wasp"— but the majority of her students acknowledged their enormous debt to her as professional teacher and personal mentor, educating them in both art and life. Rambert's temperament was for artistic rather than business matters, and she turned to others for help in administration. She lacked vision and ambition in developing her company, but her openness of mind nevertheless enabled it, and her, to weather radical changes and rise phoenix-like from misfortune.

From the beginning she recognized that her Ballet Club (opened in 1931) should exist "to serve the twin purposes of tradition and experiment". Its creativity is well documented, and tradition and experiment continue to be the primary functions of the company that still bears her name. But Rambert's own skill was as a producer, and as such she not only made perceptive comments that guided her artists—Ashton maintained he "valued her opinions and appraisals beyond those of all, for her advice never failed to be just and to the point"—but she also contributed to the restaging of established works. It was because Rambert's pupils showed (in a lecture-demonstration in 1930) with such clarity and accuracy the differing styles used by the choreographers Marius Petipa and Michel Fokine that her venture gained the support of the influential writer and balletomane Arnold Haskell. The sheer quality of her early revivals of *Aurora's Wedding*, *Les Sylphides*, *Carnaval* and *L'Après-midi d'un faune* attracted the established ballet audience, and that same discerning and informed audience stayed to appreciate ballets by Ashton, Salaman, Tudor, Howard, Staff, Gore, and successive generations of choreographers.

Born in Warsaw and originally known as Myriam Ramberg, she early developed a life-long passion for movement and dance. She enjoyed social and folk dancing at school, although her first glimpse of ballet (a performance of *Swan Lake*) did not inspire her. A few years later she was overwhelmed by seeing Isadora Duncan and, after moving to Paris (to avoid getting involved in revolutionary activity at home and finding herself too young to begin studying medicine as she intended), dance became the central feature of her life. She worked with Raymond Duncan and took some basic ballet lessons from Madame Rat of the Opéra, but largely she worked alone, devising her own recital dances to perform at theatrical matinées and private soirées.

Crucial to the development of her career was the decision to attend a summer school in eurhythmics in Geneva given by Emile Jaques-Dalcroze. She remained with him through his school's move to Hellerau until December 1912 when she joined the Ballets Russes as Nijinsky's assistant to help the dancers with Stravinsky's score for *Le Sacre du printemps*. With Diaghilev, as with Jaques-Dalcroze, Rambert had opportunities to learn, teach, and perform (most of her performances with the Ballets Russes were given on the company's South American tour). More importantly, through Jaques-Dalcroze and Diaghilev, Rambert was exposed to innovative work by choreographers and skilled designers of sets, costumes, and lighting, as well as working with first-rate music. With Diaghilev she also acquired a passion for classical ballet, inspired in particular by watching Tamara Karsavina in class.

After settling in London, Rambert continued her training in classical ballet, taking classes from Serafina Astafieva and Enrico Cecchetti while continuing to dance in her own freer style. She performed for 25 years as an actress as well as a dancer, her vivacious personality delighting audiences. In London she worked initially in association with her friend, the

director Vera Donnet, for theatre clubs (most notably the Stage Society) and for prestigious impresarios including C.B. Cochran and Nigel Playfair. Through these performances and through her husband, the playwright Ashley Dukes, she built up important contacts so that when her school developed she and Dukes were able to operate as theatrical agents and to find commercial work for her students which subsidised their work for her. At the Ballet Club dancers were paid no more than expenses and choreographers and designers only received nominal fees. All Rambert's ballets were produced on a shoestring (she described it as "blessed poverty"), which demanded great ingenuity from her artists.

Rambert's last personal performances were in fact opportunities to show off her talented pupils, using their choreographic and dancing skills and enlisting the support of new designers (Fedorovitch, Chappell, Howard, Stevenson, and others) to decorate the works. At her school she always welcomed boys who wished to take class (de Valois's school was all-female until the mid-1930s), and consequently Rambert seldom needed to call on dancers from elsewhere to partner herself or her girls. Nevertheless she welcomed the support of stars to provide inspiration for her fledglings, and Karsavina, Léon Woizikowsky, Alicia Markova, and Rupert Doone were among those who appeared with her young company. Dancers who had begun with her would also return, usually to repeat roles they had created, and guests of the calibre of Margot Fonteyn and Robert Helpmann and later Nathalie Krassovska, Elsa Marianne von Rosen, and Flemming Flindt were warmly welcomed.

Rambert loved the Romantic ballet—she had first been introduced to *Giselle* with Diaghilev—and this was the first long work to enter her company's repertory in a production, carefully researched with the help of the dance historian Cyril Beaumont, which conveyed the very essence of its period. Even without star dancers in the leading roles, her productions of *Giselle* were always of the highest calibre and attracted great praise. Likewise when Fokine's ballets *Les Sylphides* and *Carnaval* were performed in the 1930s and 1940s, although her company was too small to complete the casts, Rambert's ability to capture the atmosphere of the ballets convinced audiences that they were watching faithful revivals.

Quality was the key to all Rambert's productions. They were noted for their style, wit, and poetry, elements so often lacking on other stages. She never allowed humour to be exaggerated, so that when ballets such as *Façade* and *Gala Performance* were danced by her company they were never vulgar or merely dull. Rambert productions were notably well lit, and design and music were almost always used to support and enhance. Rambert's observation on the BBC television programme *Monitor* (1960) that her company should be regarded as the equivalent, in the ballet world, of the Tate Gallery, as compared to the Royal Ballet's National Gallery, is both accurate and illuminating.

—Jane Pritchard

RAMEAU, Jean-Philippe

French composer. Born in Dijon; baptised 25 September 1683. Educated at Jesuit Collège des Godrans, leaving c. 1701 to study music in Milan, Avignon, and finally Paris. Married Marie-Louise Mangot, 1726. Organist for various cathedrals and abbeys, including Avignon Cathedral, then Clermont Cathedral, 1702, at Dijon (succeeding father), 1709, Lyons,

1713, and Clermont Cathedral, 1715–1723; settled in Paris, 1722/23; conductor of private orchestra, Le Riche de la Pouplinière, from 1733; first major tragic opera, *Hippolyte et Aricie* (performed privately, then by Paris Opéra), 1733; first opéra-ballet, the famous *Les Indes galantes*, staged Paris Opéra, 1735, followed by numerous opéra-ballets, often in collaboration with librettist Louis de Cahusac, from 1745; became embroiled in "guerre des bouffons", advocating own French-style music over Italian; named *Compositeur du Cabinet du Roi*, 1745; ennobled, 1763; also writer, publishing numerous works including influential *Traite de l'harmonie*, 1722, series of harpsichord books, 1724, 1728, and various theoretical works, from 1726. Died in Paris, 12 September 1763.

WORKS

1723   *L'Endriague* (opéra-comique), Foire-Saint-Germain, Paris
1726   *L'Enrôlement d'Arlequin*, Foire-Saint-Germain, Paris
1733   *Samson* (lib. Voltaire; not performed)
       Hippolyte et Aricie (tragédie-lyrique), La Pouplinière, Paris (later staged Opéra, Paris)
1735   *Les Indes galantes* (opéra-ballet; chor. probably Blondy and Sallé), including entrées *Le Turc généreux*, *Les Incas de Peru*, *Les Fleurs* (*Les Sauvages* added 1736), Opéra, Paris
1737   *Castor et Pollux* (tragédie-lyrique), Opéra, Paris
1739   *Les Fêtes d'Hébé; ou, Les Talents lyriques*; opéra-ballet), including entrées *La Poésie*, *La Musique*, *La Danse*, Opéra, Paris
       Dardanus (tragédie-lyrique), Opéra, Paris
1745   *La Princesse de Navarre* (comédie-ballet), Versailles
       Platée (comédie-lyrique), Versailles
       Les Fêtes de Polymnie (opéra-ballet), Opera, Paris
       La Temple de la gloire (opéra-ballet), Versailles
1747   *Les Fetes de l'hymen et de l'amour; ou, Les Dieux d'Egypte* (ballet-héroïque), Versailles
1748   *Zaïs* (ballet-héroïque), Opéra, Paris
       Pygmalion (acte de ballet), Opéra, Paris
       Les Surprises de l'amour (divertissement), Versailles
1749   *Naïs* (pastorale-héroïque), Opéra, Paris
       Zoroastre (tragédie-lyrique), Opéra, Paris
1751   *La Guirlande; ou, Les Fleurs enchantées* (acte de ballet), Opéra, Paris
       Acante et Céphise; ou, La Sympathie (pastorale-héroïque), Opéra, Paris
1752   *Linus* (tragédie; unperformed)
1753   *Daphnis et Eglé* (pastorale-héroïque), Fontainebleau
       Les Sybarites (acte de ballet), Fontainebleau
1754   *La Naissance d'Osiris* (acte de ballet), Fontainebleau
       Anacréon [i] (acte de ballet), Fontainebleau
1757   *Anacreon* [ii] (acte de ballet; revision of *Les Surprises de l'amour*), Opéra, Paris
1758   *Le Procureur dupé sans le savoir* (opéra-comique en vaudevilles), private performance
1760   *Les Paladins* (comédie-ballet), Opéra, Paris

Other works include: *Abaris; ou, Les Boréades* (tragédie-lyrique; unperformed), *Nélee et Myrthis* (acte de ballet; unperformed), *Zéphyre* (acte de ballet; unperformed), *Io* (acte de ballet; unperformed).

Other ballets using Rameau's music: *La Fête d'Hébé* (new version; chor. Bolm, 1912), *Castor und Pollux* (Gsovsky, 1950, 1952), *Les Indes galantes* (new version; chor. Aveline, Lander, Lifar, 1952).

PUBLICATIONS

By Rameau:
Traité de l'harmonie reduite à ses principes naturels, Paris, 1722; translated by P. Gossett, New York, 1971
Nouveau Système de musique théorique, Paris, 1726
Mémoire ou l'on expose les fondements du système de musique théorique et pratique de M. Rameau, Paris, 1749
Nouvelles réflexions de M. Rameau sur sa démonstration du principe de l'harmonie, Paris, 1752
Observations sur notre instinct pour la musique, Paris, 1754
Erreurs sur la musique dans l'Encyclopédie, Paris, 1755–56
Suite des erreurs sur la musique dans l'Encyclopédie, Paris, 1756
Prospectus, ou l'on propose au public, par voye de souscription, un code de musique pratique, composé de sept méthodes, Paris, 1757
Réponse de M. Rameau à MM. les editeurs de l'Encyclopédie, Paris, 1757
Nouvelles Réflexions sur le principe sonore, Paris, 1758–59
Code de musique pratique, ou Methodes pour apprendre la musique . . . avec de nouvelles réflexions sur le principe sonore, Paris, 1760
Lettre à M. de Alembert sur ses opinions en musique, Paris, 1760
Origine des sciences, suivie d'une controverse sur le même sujet, Paris, 1762
Vérités intéressantes (MS)
Complete Theoretical Writings, edited by E.R. Jacobi, Rome, 1967–72

About Rameau:
Cahusac, Louis de, *La Danse ancienne et moderne ou Traité historique de la danse*, Paris, 1754
Noverre, Jean-Georges, *Lettres sur la danse*, Paris, 1760; as *Letters on Dancing and Ballets*, translated by Cyril Beaumont (from 1803 edition), London, 1930
Pougin, A., *Rameau: Essai sur sa vie et ses oeuvres*, Paris, 1896
Masson, Paul-Marie, *L'Opéra de Rameau*, Paris, 1930
Kirstein, Lincoln, *Dance: A Short History of Classic Theatrical Dancing*, New York, 1935
Girdlestone, Cuthbert, *Jean-Philippe Rameau: His Life and Work*, London, 1957
Seefrid, Gisela, *Die Airs de danse in den Buhnenwerke von Jean-Philippe Rameau*, Wiesbaden, 1969
Anthony, J.R., "Some Uses of the Dance in the French Opéra-ballet", *Recherches sur la musique française classique* (Paris), ix, 1969
Kirstein, Lincoln, *Movement and Metaphor*, New York, 1970
Cyr, M., *Rameau's "Les Fêtes d'Hébé"* (dissertation), University of California, Berkeley, 1975
Sorrell, Walter, *Dance in its Time*, New York, 1981

* * *

Rameau's stage works, written in the middle of the eighteenth century, laid the foundations of modern ballet. Born two years before Bach and Handel, Rameau came to musical maturity at a time when the majestic Baroque formality of Lully was giving way to the "style galant", and when court entertainment, which had been shaped by Lully and his collaborators to show off Louis XIV's balletic talents, had changed with the introduction of professional dancers. Their technical skills evolved new steps, such as pirouettes and entrechats, beyond the abilities of even the most proficient amateur, and they used gesture and mime to portray character.

The most popular form of lyric theatre was the opéra-ballet, usually based on fantastic or pastoral themes. This contained as many as four acts, each act or entrée treating a different theme complete within itself, although all entrées were related to a vague overall idea. The other major theatrical form, closer in spirit to modern opera, was the tragédie-lyrique. This was based on a single theme, tragic or heroic, which would be developed through its five acts. Both forms contained singing and dancing; the tragédie-lyrique introduced dances as part of the dramatic action, while opéra-ballet was oriented towards dance, the singing serving as a means of explaining the action. Contemporary taste demanded elaborate and magnificent décor for both types of theatrical entertainment.

These were the theatrical forms Rameau inherited when he came to write his first dramatic work, the tragédie-lyrique *Hippolite et Aricie*, in 1733. At fifty, he was already well known for his *Traité de l'harmonie* (1722), a major theoretical work in which, using mathematical principles, he analyzed and classified chords, defining the major and minor scales. In addition, he had also published keyboard pieces and sacred music.

From his first dramatic work, Rameau showed a sympathetic instinct for the needs of the choreography. His music uses harmonic colour to shape the dramatic moment, while its precise rhythmic sense continually suggests specific gesture and movement. This strong rhythmic element undoubtedly suited the needs of the developing *danse haute*, with its increasing use of elevation. He employed all forms of contemporary dance, both of the court, such as the gavotte and minuet, and of the popular (tambourin, rigaudon). And he was a master of his orchestra, using its varied timbres for theatrical effect.

Rameau's first and most famous opéra-ballet, *Les Indes galantes* (1735), concerns the universality of love, presenting this theme formally in a Prologue, then illustrating it with the four succeeding entrées, each taking place in a different part of the globe: Turkey, Peru, Persia, and North America. These settings reflect the popular fascination with exotic and remote places of the world; the exotic—especially things Turkish—had long been a popular subject in the arts. The first opéra-ballet, Campra's 1697 *L'Europe galante*, had been set in Spain, Italy, and Turkey, and there are continuing examples through the centuries, for example Mozart's *Cosi Fan Tutte*, or Fokine's *Schéhérazade*.

Rameau, however, does not attempt to create an exotic sound to match the *Indes galantes* settings, but rather works within the contemporary musical palette. In addition to a wealth of variety in the dance music, there are striking examples of his ability to evoke the sounds of natural phenomena, whether the fury of storms or the lyricism of sunrise. The storm in the first entrée is a musical tempest of hurrying scales and dramatic tremolos. Even more spectacular is the earthquake depicted in *Les Incas*, the second entrée. Here too are scurrying scales, with a dramatic build-up of harmonic tension that then dies down to an ominous unison. The third entrée concludes with an extended dance sequence, *Les Fleurs*, in which the main role was taken by Mlle Sallé, fresh from her triumphs on the London stage. The work ends with a chaconne, the steps of which, it is said, had to be taught by the composer himself to the dancer Dupré.

Rameau not only brought new life to contemporary dance, but also developed the traditional slow–fast overture of Lully into something almost programmatic in nature. The music, often thematically related to the work itself, would describe the action or mood to follow.

Many of Rameau's contemporaries were critical of his music, finding his orchestration too complex or even noisy, and the amount of dancing excessive. Worst of all, he was accused of sacrificing melody to harmony. Popular taste turned against him with the arrival in Paris in 1752 of Pergolesi's *La Serva Padrona*, whose catchy tunes and down-to-earth plot swept the French public off its feet. Rameau's detractors, led by Rousseau in the so-called "guerre des bouffons", compared Rameau's music unfavourably with the *opera buffa*. Rameau's last works were composed for the enclosed circle of the Court.

Modern-day revivals of the stage works have once again brought to public attention Rameau's creative genius. His strong rhythmic sense, vivid harmonies, and fine orchestral timbres clearly demonstrate the musical sensibility that was able to advance the choreographic needs of dance, and set it on the road to the classical ballet of the nineteenth century.

—Louise Stein

RAMEAU, Pierre

French dancer, dancing master, and author. Born c.1674. Married (1) Elisabeth La Haye, 1705: one son, La Rochelle dancing master Jean Baptiste Rameau; (2) Catherine Muffat, 1709; (3) Marie-Anne Courbe, 1736. Dancer, Lyons Opéra, 1703–5, possibly also appearing at the Paris Opéra, c.1710–13; dancing master in Paris; official dancing master to the pages of the Queen of Spain, and also ordinary dancing master to the house of Louise Elisabeth de Montpensier (the second dowager Queen of Spain, widow of Louis I); author of dancing manual, *Le Maître à danser*, published in 1725. Died in Nanterre, 26 January 1748.

PUBLICATIONS

By Rameau:
Le Maître à danser, Paris, 1725, reprinted 1734, 1748; facsimile edition, New York, 1967; as *The Dancing-master*, translated by John Essex, London, 1728; as *The Dancing Master*, translated by Cyril Beaumont, London, 1931
Abrégé de la nouvelle méthode de l'art d'écrire ou de tracer toutes sortes de danses de ville, Paris, 1725–26; facsimile edition, London, 1972

About Rameau:
Derra de Moroda, Friderica, "A Spanish Book of 1758", *Dancing Times* (London), July 1931
Kirstein, Lincoln, *Dance: A Short History of Classic Theatrical Dancing*, New York, 1935
Winter, Marian Hannah, *The Pre-Romantic Ballet*, London, 1974
Hilton, Wendy, *Dance of Court and Theatre*, London, 1981
Marsh, Carol, "Essex the Dancing Master" in *French Court Dance in England 1706–1740, A Study of the Sources*, doctoral dissertation, 1985

*   *   *

Although so little is known about Rameau the man, his books are invaluable to our understanding of social dance in the early eighteenth century. From the mid-seventeenth century onwards, France had assumed the mantle formerly held by Italy as initiator and mentor of dance style and technique, and as Rameau himself says, "Nearly all foreigners, far from denying this, have for nearly a century come to admire our dances, teaching themselves through our performances and in our schools."

From the beginning of the eighteenth century these "foreigners" also had alternative ways of teaching themselves.

Pierre Rameau's *Le Maître à danser*, 1725: an illustration for a pirouette

In 1700 Raoul Feuillet published his book, *Chorégraphie ou l'art de décrire la danse*, which gave a detailed account of the dance notation invented by Louis XIV's dancing master Beauchamps. This notation made it possible for dancing masters throughout Europe to write down their choreographies and to exchange these by post or send them to students and colleagues. From this time onwards, therefore, we find the annual publication of new choreographies in both France and England.

Various attempts had been made about this time to invent a dance notation, but that of Beauchamps/Feuillet became the most widely used. It did, however, have certain shortcomings. Not only was it inadequate to express certain aspects of technique, for example which foot the dancer springs on in certain steps, but it was not always possible to make clear the timing of the step.

Until the invention of notation the most common formula for describing dance steps and dances was verbal. This was the method used by the Italians Caroso and Negri, and the Spaniards Esquivel and Jaques. Rameau reverts to this method with his book *Le Maître à danser*. Like Caroso and Negri, Rameau begins his treatise with instruction on manners and deportment in general—how to walk, how to bow and curtsey—together with details of the ceremonials to be employed at a court ball. He follows this with a detailed account of the most important ballroom dance of the time, the Minuet, describing its floor patterns and steps.

After this, he takes each of the basic dance steps of the period and analyzes its structure in detail, together with all its variants. This analysis is invaluable in clarifying the notation, as well as adding details such as the use of the arms. He also includes a number of engraved plates to illustrate his text because, as he says, "Rules aided by illustrations have more value than those deprived of such help". Rameau himself did

the art work, and while it is obvious that he is no great artist, the illustrations give us yet another guide to the interpretation of steps. He was well aware of his shortcomings as an artist, and with his illustration for the "elevation of the arms in dancing" he says, "I am not altogether happy with the attitude I have given my figures in the elevation of their arms; I consulted those who have more skill, not only in dancing but also in drawing, and they found that the drawings accorded with the rules."

Having completed his *Maître à danser* early in 1725, Rameau then set himself the task of refining the Beauchamps/Feuillet notation and in November 1925 he received his "Privelege" or authorization from the King to publish his second book, *Abrégé de la nouvelle méthode*. In this book he gives an analysis of his improved notation, which improvements take the form of adding certain symbols to show more precisely such detail as when the foot is lifted from the ground at the beginning of a movement, which foot a spring is taken on, whether a movement is slow or quick. He also changes some symbols, in particular those for turns, and simplifies the notating of entrechats by showing only one beat and then adding a number, 2, 4, etc., beside it. Rameau concludes with a paragraph on time and cadence in which he explains how certain steps should be fitted to the music. Finally he includes twelve dances by Pécour written in this new notation. It seems that Rameau's notation was not a great success, as most dancing masters continued to use the old form in writing out their choreographies.

Rameau's contribution to dance, mainly through his *Maître à danser*, was immensely valuable even in his own day, as witnessed by the number of translations and reprints produced at the time, and without it we would certainly have difficulty today recreating the exquisite dances of the eighteenth century.

—Madeleine Inglehearn

RAVEL, Maurice

French composer. Born Joseph Maurice Ravel in Ciboure, 7 March 1875. Studied at the Paris Conservatoire, 1889–1903, attending Fauré's composition classes as a student, from 1897, and as an "auditeur", from 1900. First ballet, *Ma Mère l'oye*, composed 1911 (expanded from piano piece of 1908–10); composed the more ambitious *Daphnis et Chloé*, to a commission from Diaghilev, 1909–12; arranger and orchestrator of own and others' music for balletic use; frequent traveller abroad, including tour of the United States, 1928; also composer for choreographer Ida Rubinstein, from 1928. Declined Légion d'honneur, 1920; recipient: Honorary Doctorate in Music, Oxford University, 1928. Died in Paris, 28 December 1937.

WORKS (Ballets)

1912 *Ma Mère l'oye* (expanded from piano piece; chor. Hugard), Théâtre des Arts, Paris
      Adelaide; ou, Le Langage des fleurs (orchestration of piano piece *Valse nobles et sentimentales*, 1911; chor. Clustine), Théâtre du Chatelet, Paris
      Daphnis et Chloé (chor. Fokine), Diaghilev's Ballet Russes, Paris
1920 *La Valse* (commissioned by Diaghilev but rejected; first performed as orchestral concert piece, 1920)
1927 Fanfare in *L'Éventail de Jeanne* (various composers;

Maurice Ravel (right) with Vaslav Nijinsky, looking over the score of *Daphnis et Chloé*

chor. Franck, Bourgat), Salon de Mme. Jeanne Dubost, Paris (staged Paris Opéra, 1929)

1928   *Boléro* (chor. Nijinska), Ida Rubinstein's Company, Paris

Other ballets using Ravel's music: *Ma Mère l'oye* (new version; chor. Staats, 1915; also Bolender, 1948; Robbins, 1975), *Le Tombeau de Couperin* (Börlin, 1920), *L'Enfant et les sortilèges* (*The Spellbound Child*, opera-ballet; chor. Balanchine 1925, and again 1947, 1975; also Descombey, 1960; Charrat, 1964; Kylián, 1984), *Pavane pour une infante défunte* (Bolm, 1928; also Ashton, 1933; Staff, 1941; Lifar, 1944; North, 1967), *The Mermaid* (Howard, 1934), *Bolero* (new version; chor. Fokine, 1935; also Lifar, 1941; Staff, 1950; Béjart, 1961; Lavrovsky, 1964), *La Valse* (chor. Korty, 1926; Nijinska, 1929; Fokine, 1935; Lander, 1940; Gsovsky, 1951; Balanchine, 1951; Ashton, 1958; W. Christensen, 1964; Hynd, 1975), *Poème* (Littlefield, 1936), *Daphnis and Chloe* (new version; chor. Littlefield, 1937; also Gsovsky, 1947; Ashton, 1951; Milloss, 1951; Lifar, 1958; Skibine, 1959; Cranko, 1962; Neumeier, 1972; Taras, 1972; Tetley, 1975), *Choreographic Étude* (Yakobson, 1942), *Alborada* (Yakobson, 1946), *Valse nobles et sentimentales* (Ashton, 1947; also MacMillan, 1966; van Manen, 1975; Hynd, 1975), *Alborada del gracioso* (Lifar, 1948), *Balada* (Cramér, 1948), *Beauty and the Beast* (Cranko, 1949),

Two Spanish Girls (Jakobson, 1950), *The Witch* (Cranko, 1950), *Western Wall* (Tetley, 1951), *Rhapsodie espagnole* (Petit, 1962), *Sea Shadow* (Arpino, 1962), *Love Novellas* (Yakobson, 1963), *Quatre Images* (Cranko, 1967), *Rêves* (Rusillo, 1973), *Schéhérazade* (Petit, 1974; Balanchine, 1975; G. Murphy, 1979), *Introduction and Allegro for Harp* (Robbins, 1975), *Concerto in G* (also called *In G Major*; Robbins, 1975), *Sonatine* (Balanchine, 1975), *Moment* (Louis, 1975), *La Fin du jour* (Macmillan, 1979).

PUBLICATIONS

By Ravel:

Ravel d'après Ravel, edited by Vlado Perlemuter and Hélène Jourdan-Morhange; as *Ravel According to Ravel*, translated by Frances Tanner, edited by Harold Taylor, London, 1988

About Ravel:

Roland-Manuel, *Maurice Ravel et son oeuvre*, Paris, 1914
Roland-Manuel, *Ravel et son oeuvre dramatique*, Paris, 1928
Calvocoressi, M.D., *Music and Ballet*, London, 1933
Roland-Manuel, *Maurice Ravel*, Paris, 1938; English translation (*Contemporary Composers* series) by Cynthia Jolly, London, 1947
Clarke, Mary, "*La Valse*", *Dancing Times* (London), May 1959

Myers, Rollo, *Ravel: Life and Works*, London, 1960
Dutronc, J.-L., "Maurice Ravel et le ballet", *Les Saisons de la danse* (Paris), November 1969
Stuckenschmidt, H.H., *Maurice Ravel: Variations on his Life and Work*, London, 1969
Orenstein, Arbie, *Ravel: Man and Musician*, New York, 1975
Balanchine, George, with Mason, George, *Balanchine's Complete Stories of the Great Ballets*, Garden City, N. Y., 1977
James, Burnett, *Ravel, His Life and Times*, New York, 1983
Nichols, Roger, *Ravel Remembered*, London, 1987
Kennicott, Philip, "Dance Music: Ravelation", *Dance Magazine* (New York), April 1990

*   *   *

Maurice Ravel was the first new composer Diaghilev approached for his Paris seasons with the Ballets Russes—even in advance of Stravinsky and his famous *The Firebird*—and *Daphnis et Chloé* (which became Ravel's magnum opus) was agreed between them, with Fokine as choreographer, as early as 1909. The fastidious composer, working on the largest musical scale he would ever attempt, took more than two years to finish the score.

By the time the ballet was produced, in 1912, two others to Ravel's music had had their premieres in that year. The first was *Ma Mère l'oye* (*Mother Goose*), staged to music that Ravel wrote in 1908 for a piano duet, and based on characters and illustrations in books of classic fairytales. To his original five pieces Ravel added a Prelude, a Spinning-wheel dance, and interludes to facilitate scene-changes.

For his own scenario, derived from the fairytales, Ravel used sparing instrumental means for a rich yet delicate tapestry of colour, a small orchestra supplemented by harp, percussion, and a few other extras. The music has simplicity of melody and timbre, reflecting Ravel's characteristic delight in miniaturism which hides a fascinating delicacy of detail; and it has attracted several later choreographers, including John Cranko (in *Beauty and the Beast*) and Jerome Robbins.

A similar adaptability is found for the *Valses nobles et sentimentales*, written for piano in 1911 and then orchestrated for *Adelaide; ou, Le Langage des fleurs* to be choreographed by Ivan Clustine for Natalia Trouhanova, again with a scenario by the composer. The seven waltzes and an epilogue were intended, Ravel said, to evoke the example of Schubert; but in orchestral form they become closer to Chabrier. They contain all the main elements of Ravel's musical personality in style and harmonic character, not least in flexibility of metre and displaced accents which challenge a choreographer's invention. Ravel himself conducted the premiere of Clustine's ballet, which had few performances, but among several later choreographers Frederick Ashton twice made use of it in his ballets.

Ravel defined *Daphnis et Chloé* as a "symphonie chorégraphique" and wrote that he "sought to compose a broad musical fresco, less concerned with archaic fidelity than with loyalty to the Greece of my dreams, resembling what French artists depicted in the latter part of the eighteenth century. The work is built symphonically, on a strict tonal plan, out of a small number of themes, the development of which ensures its homogeneity."

His orchestra is perhaps the largest ever required for a commissioned work for dance, with multiple instrumental groups and added exotica such as a wind-machine. The music corresponds to the ballet's three scenes, but played without a break. Descriptive themes are identified with characters and scenes; irregular rhythms abound, such as 7/4 in the opening scene and 5/4 for the final "danse générale"; a wordless chorus is woven into complex counterpoint (and Ravel publicly protested when Diaghilev dropped the chorus for his 1914 London season, though the composer provided an alternative organ part for "smaller centres").

La Valse in 1920 brought a permanent rift between Ravel and Diaghilev, who had asked for the score but found himself unable to stage it. The music, basically in D major, is a kind of apotheosis of the Viennese waltz in two well-defined sequences, each growing to a climax. The first waltz-chain is exuberant and cheerful in the Viennese manner, but the second is harsher and more turbulent, ending in discord, the brilliance of instrumental effect overshadowing subtleties of rhythm and harmony.

It was first choreographed (some nine years after its performance as an orchestral concert piece) by Bronislava Nijinska for Ida Rubinstein who, a few months previously, presented (also with Nijinska's choreography) the now-celebrated *Boléro* directly commissioned from Ravel. Although he said it was "vide de musique", its reiterated tune and relentless rhythm was a significant straw in the wind anticipating future musical trends. It still generates a strange sensory tension, suddenly released in the abrupt change of key near the end, which not even contemporary "pop" techniques have surpassed as a means of applied hysteria.

Much of Ravel's concert music has been used for dance, notably *Pavane pour une infante défunte*, *Le Tombeau de Couperin*, *Alborada del gracioso*, Piano Concerto in G, and other keyboard music; the opera, *L'Enfant et les sortilèges* (1925) requires substantial choreographic input and has on occasion been presented as a ballet with sung music.

—Noël Goodwin

————

RAYMONDA

Choreography: Marius Petipa
Music: Aleksandr Glazunov
Design: Orest Allegri, Konstantin Ivanov, Petr Lambin (sets), Ekaterina Ofizerova, Ivan Kaffi (costumes)
Libretto: Lydia Pashkova and Marius Petipa
First Production: Maryinsky Theatre, St. Petersburg, 19 January (7 January old style) 1898
Principal Dancers: Pierina Legnani (Raymonda), Sergei Legat (Jean de Brienne), Pavel Gerdt (Abderakhman, or "Abdérâme")

Other productions include: Bolshoi Theatre (staged Ivan Clustine and Aleksandr Gorsky after Petipa); Moscow, 23 January 1900. Bolshoi Theatre (new version; chor. Aleksandr Gorsky, design Aleksandr Golovin and Konstantin Korovin), with Ekaterina Geltser (Raymonda), Vasily Tikhomirov (Jean de Brienne); Moscow, 30 November 1908. Anna Pavlova Company (shortened version; staged Ivan Clustine after Petipa), with Pavlova (Raymonda); New York, 1914. State Academic Theatre for Opera and Ballet (GATOB) (staged Agrippina Vaganova after Petipa); Leningrad, 8 January 1931. National Opera Ballet of Lithuania (staged Nicolas Zverev, design Mstislav Dobuzhinsky), with Vera Nemchinova (Raymonda), Anatole Obukhov (Jean de Brienne); London, 18 February 1935. Kirov Ballet (new version; revised libretto Yuri Slonimsky and Vasily Vainonen, chor. Vainonen), with Galina Ulanova (Raymonda), Konstantin Sergeyev (Koloman); Leningrad, 22 March 1938. Bolshoi Ballet (staged Leonid Lavrovsky after Petipa, Gorsky) with Marina Semenova (Raymonda), Mikhail Gabovich (Jean de Brienne); Moscow, 7 April 1945. Ballet Russe de Monte Carlo (shortened version; staged George Balanchine and Alexandra Danilova after Petipa, design Alexandre Benois), with Alexandra Danilova (Raymonda) and Nicholas Magallanes (Jean de Brienne); New York, 12 March 1946. Kirov Ballet (staged Konstantin Sergeyev after Petipa, design Simon Virsaladze); Leningrad, 30 April 1948. Royal Ballet Touring Company (staged Rudolf Nureyev, design Beni Montresor), with Doreen Wells (Raymonda), Nureyev (Jean de Brienne); Spoleto Festival, 10 July 1964. Australian Ballet (restaged Nureyev), with Margot Fonteyn (Raymonda), Nureyev (Jean de Brienne); Birmingham, England, 6 November 1965. German Opera Ballet (staged Tatjana Gsovsky and Nicholas Beriozoff after Petipa), with Eva Evdokimova (Raymonda), Attilio Labis (Jean de Brienne); Berlin, 25 January 1975. American Ballet Theatre (restaged Nureyev, design Nicholas Georgiadis), with Cynthia Gregory (Raymonda), Nureyev (Jean de Brienne); Houston, 26 June 1975.

Other choreographic treatments: George Balanchine (*Pas de dix*, also known as *Raymonda Pas de dix*; New York, 1955; also *Valses et variations*, later renamed *Raymonda Variations*; New York, 1961; and *Cortège Hongrois*, New York, 1973).

PUBLICATIONS

Beaumont, Cyril, *Complete Book of Ballets*, revised edition, London, 1951

Glazunov, Aleksandr, *Musical Legacy*, vol. 1, Leningrad, 1959

Krasovskaya, Vera, *Russian Ballet Theatre of the Second Half of the Nineteenth Century*, Leningrad and Moscow, 1963

Guest, Ivor, "*Raymonda*'s History", *Dancing Times* (London), December 1965

Roslavleva, Natalia, *Era of the Russian Ballet*, London, 1966

Maynard, Olga, "*Raymonda*", *Dance Magazine* (New York), July 1975

"*Raymonda*" (Petipa's scenario), *Ballet Review* (Brooklyn, N.Y.), vol. 5, no. 2, 1975–76

Vaughan, David, "Nurreyev's *Raymonda*", *Ballet Review* (Brooklyn, N.Y.), vol. 5, no. 2, 1975–76

Balanchine, George, with Mason, Francis, *Balanchine's Complete Stories of the Great Ballets*, Garden City, N.Y., 1977

Molden, Peter, "Glazounov and the Ballet", *Dancing Times* (London), July 1987

Wiley, Roland John, *A Century of Russian Ballet: Documents and Accounts 1810–1910*, Oxford, 1990

*   *   *

Raymonda first came into being in 1895, when the society columnist and minor novelist Lydia Pashkova, writer of the scenario for *Cinderella*, submitted a scenario for *Raymonda* to Ivan Vsevolozhsky, director of the Imperial Theatres. From there it was sent, together with Vsevolozhsky's own substantial revisions, to Marius Petipa. The young composer Aleksandr Glazunov was commissioned to write the score (the elder statesman of ballet composition, Tchaikovsky, having died in 1893); and in fact the music has turned out to be one of the most satisfying features of a ballet otherwise acknowledged to be uneven.

The complete ballet was not performed until three years later, when it had its premiere at the Maryinsky Theatre in 1898 as a benefit evening in honour of the ballerina Pierina Legnani, creator of the role of Raymonda. Alongside her

danced Sergei Legat as Jean de Brienne, and Pavel Gerdt in the mimed role of Abderakhman. Pierina Legnani was one of the most brilliant technicians of her day (she was the creator of the famous fouttée sequence in *Swan Lake*, a feat with which many a modern ballerina still struggles today)—and for her Petipa created some of his most beautiful variations. Petipa was then 80 years old, but *Raymonda* is rich with invention, and the choreography, which has been handed down through various Russian stagings loyal to the original, has shown *Raymonda* to be, in pure dancing terms, the great choreographer's last true masterpiece.

The only flaw with this happy collaboration between composer and choreographer is the convoluted scenario, which is at best confusing and at worst simply "idiotic" (in the words of dance historians Clement Crisp and Peter Brinson). The somewhat ridiculous plot is constructed around a love story with a supernatural twist of events, much mime, and a final apotheosis to the three acts. It is set in medieval Hungary, where the noble Raymonda and her betrothed Jean de Brienne are deeply in love. Raymonda is also coveted by the Saracen knight Abderakhman, who hatches a plot to abduct her. His ruse fails, thanks to the intervention of the White Lady, a protecting spirit of Raymonda's family, and Abderakhman is slain by Jean de Brienne in combat. The third act, which has often been shown alone as a showpiece, is a celebratory spectacle in honour of the happy couple, now united—and it contains a grand Hungarian dance (the "Pas Classique Hongrois") and a concluding "galop final". The choreography in this ballet, again to quote Crisp and Brinson, can be "dazzling"—but it is understandable why some companies choose only to show extracts, and why twentieth-century versions of the full-length *Raymonda* have tended to veer from the original narrative line in an effort to even out the discrepancy between sublime choreography and absurd plot.

The history of *Raymonda* (and subsequent versions thereof), like so many of Petipa's ballets, is far from simple: but because it has scarcely left the Kirov's repertoire since its St. Petersburg beginnings we have a fairly sound idea of what its first performance was like. It was retained virtually in its original version in Leningrad all the way until the late 1930s, and then underwent several revisions, including one with a new libretto (by Slonimsky and Vainonen) performed in 1938 with Ulanova as Raymonda. Sergeyev's version for the Kirov (1948) had choreography that was somewhat closer to the original. Aleksandr Gorsky, who had danced in the St. Petersburg premiere, had reproduced (together with Ivan Clustine) Petipa's choreography and production in Moscow in 1900, and then Gorsky produced his own version at the Bolshoi in 1908. Subsequent Soviet productions are numerous and include one by Vainonen in 1938 and one by Lavrovsky in 1945.

Further variations on Petipa's theme include those for Diaghilev's company and later, by Balanchine. The "Grand Pas Hongrois" of Act III was incorporated into the opening programme of Diaghilev's first Paris season in 1909, with Nijinsky dancing in the now famous men's "Pas de quatre". Pavlova presented a version of the ballet in two acts by Clustine in 1914 and later presented the "Grand Pas" as a separate divertissement. In 1946 Alexandra Danilova and Balanchine created a version of Petipa's ballet for the Ballet Russe de Monte Carlo, and Balanchine subsequently used Glazunov's score to stage his own *Pas de Dix*, created for New York City Ballet in 1955, and later created *Cortège Hongrois* for Melissa Hayden in 1973. His *Raymonda Variations* (called at first *Valses et Variations*) was choreographed to a selection from the original music in 1961.

The music for *Raymonda* undoubtedly has much to do with its endurance. Glazunov has been described by the writer Peter

***Raymonda*, as performed by Sadler's Wells Royal Ballet (previously Royal Ballet Touring Company), London**

Molden as "not a composer of the first rank", but a composer in whose scores "over the years choreographers have seen the merit . . . and helped to keep the music alive". Glazunov's score for *Raymonda* was described by Balanchine as containing "some of the finest ballet music we have"—and Balanchine's own choreography to it is unabashed in its homage to the classicism of the original. In its reliance on technical excellence for success, *Raymonda* is quintessential Petipa. According to Balanchine in his *Festival of Ballet*, *Raymonda* was soon dismissed by the Russian balletomane Prince Lieven as having "everything but meaning"—but thanks to Petipa this has proven small hindrance to the ballet's longevity.

—Amanda Chisnell

THE RED DETACHMENT OF WOMEN

Choreography: Li Cheng-xiang, Jiang Zu-hui, Wang Xi-xian
Music: Wu Zu-qiang and Du Ming-xin
Design: Ma Yun-hong (set and costumes)
Principal dancers: Bai Shu-xiang (The Slave Girl, Wu Qing-hua), Liu Qing-tang (The Former Party Representative, Hong Chang-qing), Li Cheng-xiang (The Tyrant, Nan Ba-tian)

First Production: China Ballet Troupe (of the Central Opera and Ballet Theatre; later the Central Ballet of China), Beijing, 1 October 1964

Other productions include: China Ballet Troupe (revised version), with Xue Qing-hua (The Slave Girl); filmed in 1970. Matsuyuma Ballet (sometimes translated as *The Red Girls' Battalion*); Tokyo, 1973.

PUBLICATIONS

"Documents from China", *Drama Review* (New York), Spring 1971

Barnes, Clive, "The Ballet Nixon Saw In Peking", *New York Times*, 19 March 1972

Red Detachment of Women, Beijing (Foreign Language Press), 1972

Snow, Lois Wheeler, *China on Stage*, New York, 1972

Atlas, Helen, "China Dances to Revolutionary Tune", *Dance News* (New York), September 1972

Perris, Arnold, "Music as Propaganda: Art at the Command of Doctrine in the People's Republic of China", *Ethnomusicology* (Ann Arbor, Michigan), January 1983

Percival, John, "Dancing Their Own Way", *Dance and Dancers* (London), November 1986

*   *   *

The Red Detachment of Women performed by the Chinese Ballet Troupe (later the Central Ballet of China), Beijing, 1970

The Red Detachment of Women was the first Chinese "Revolutionary Model Ballet", performed in 1964 as a balletic celebration of the fiftieth anniversary of the founding of the People's Republic of China. Inspired by the late Chairman Mao's cultural policy—"Our literature and art should be created for the workers, peasants, and soldiers, and for their use"—and stimulated by the 1961 film by the same name (which won a prize at the Moscow Film Festival), the ballet represented a bold decision on the part of its creators to represent a revolutionary and thoroughly Chinese theme by means of a completely different, if not to say opposite, art form—that of the Western, classical, court-derived form of ballet. This naturally presented dancers and choreographers with a paradox, one which in a sense is faced by all contemporary ballet creators today: that is, how to blend new content and subject-matter with old forms and traditions (in this case, Chinese tradition as well as ballet tradition), without compromising the integrity of the whole. In short, the creators of *The Red Detachment of Women* had to remould themselves thoroughly in order to deal with these questions of conflicting ideals, aesthetic tastes, and movement vocabularies.

The story of the ballet takes place during the second Chinese Civil War of 1927–37, on the Hainan Island in Southern China. Wu Qing-hua, the slave girl of the local tyrant Nan Ba-tian, unable to put up with her master's inhuman treatment of her, tries repeatedly to run away, only to be beaten on her return. The Red Army leader Hong Chang-qing, disguised as a magnificent Chinese overseas merchant, meets Wu Qing-hua, sympathizes with her plight, and tells her to go to the liberated "Red Area", where she will find shelter and equality among others. In the "Red Area", she is warmly accepted into a branch of the Red Army known as "The Red Detachment of Women"; and through a series of blood-and-fire trials, she becomes a mature fighter and commander, eventually taking over Hong Chang-qing's post as the Communist Party Representative when he is killed by Nan Ba-tian.

The Red Detachment of Women was filmed in 1970 during the Cultural Revolution as one of the two so-called "Revolutionary Model Ballets" (the other was *The White-haired Girl*, also created in 1964), as an example for all major Chinese dance companies to follow—regardless of whether or not the dancers had training in pointe work. The film popularized ballet to a huge extent, making it the most important Chinese dance form of the day, and indeed resulting in various troupes of Chinese middle-school students attempting either *The Red Detachment of Women* or *The White-haired Girl* on pointe, without the benefit of professionally-made pointe shoes. (This proved that, technically speaking, Chinese revolutionary ballet was still underdeveloped, as no middle-school student in home-made pointe shoes and without proper training could ever have performed the full-length *Swan Lake*.)

In fact, many professional folk and classical Chinese dancers suffered as a result of this new enthusiasm: some were too old to acquire turn-out or pointe technique, and their own Eastern aesthetic ideals and movement skills were the exact opposite of those demanded by ballet. In any case, this embarrassing popular ballet "movement" lasted until 1976, when the Cultural Revolution officially ended. It is interesting to note that the film version of *The Red Detachment of Women*, which had done so much to popularize ballet in the 1970s, featured all the same cast as the stage version except for ballerina Bai Shu-xiang, who was replaced by the younger dancer Xue Qing-hua. Bai Shu-xiang, although only 31, had been sent to the country and deprived of the right to dance for five years, as a result of her having come from a supposed "exploiting-class" family; her failure to appreciate Jiang Qing's (Madame Mao's) favour evidently made her an "active counter-revolutionary". There

has been some confusion regarding the younger ballerina's role in the creation of the ballet; some believed that it was created especially for her, as she danced the central role in the film—but this was simply not true, and was only the impression that the younger dancer herself wanted to create.

The Red Detachment of Women has come to define the Central Ballet of China's image, both nationally and internationally, for several reasons. First, as already pointed out, it was a bold experiment in combining Western ballet with Chinese dance—both the peasant-based folk dance and the more formal classical dance of Chinese opera—in order to serve a contemporary national theme. It was an avant-garde step, and despite the use of ballet technique, the traditional fairy-like lightness and romanticism of traditional ballet style had to make way for the heavier, more realistic movement vocabulary of the peasant or the slave. Obviously, the typically "aristocratic" stance of the ballet dancer had to be discarded in favour of Chinese folk and classical movements, such as the "sparrow hawk's tilted turn" or the "black dragon twisting a pillar" used to depict the fighting spirit of the heroine Wu Qing-hua. Classical virtuosity for its own sake of course had no place here, and dance existed to develop the characters in the story.

Another important development in *The Red Detachment of Women* was the creation of enough male ensemble dancing to portray convincingly such groups as guerillas, Red Army soldiers, and Nan Ba-tian's militia-men. There were also several solos for the hero Hong Chang-qing (the last of which, taking place before the character's heroic death, lasts nearly ten minutes), and numerous pas de deux. Again, the traditional balletic pas de deux of classical or courtly love was not appropriate, as the movement theme of *The Red Detachment of Women* is life-or-death combat—and therefore, movement borrowed from the Chinese martial arts, as well as from acrobatics and Chinese opera, was employed to make thrilling, tense pas de deux.

Finally, the most noticeable departure from classical Western ballet was the use of the corps de ballet. As the representatives of the "Red Detachment of Women", the female dancers were made to move and behave in a "soldier-like" fashion, to give their movements more weight, and to find inspiration in the "labouring people's feeling". This last was perhaps the most difficult for the dancers to accomplish, as most of the ballerinas were from non-labouring families, and they did not have an understanding of the sort of life the ballet depicted, to say nothing of getting the "labouring people's feeling" across in their dancing. Moreover, being classically trained in Western technique, the dancers were used to aiming for lightness and weightlessness, rather than heaviness; but all the same, in preparation for the ballet they were brought to live with the people on Hainan Island, and made to join in with the soldiers in such activities as shooting, bayonet-fighting, and throwing hand-grenades.

The "Revolutionary Model Ballet" movement, led by *The Red Detachment of Women*, has proven to be the largest and most widely popularizing dance event in the entire 5,000-year history of Chinese dance. As a result of the widespread political enthusiasm during a certain period in history, it involved hundreds of thousands of professional and non-professional dancers in the art of ballet, and it showed millions the everlasting appeal of dance—not just as a platform for politics but as a way to show off the talents of the individual.

—Ou Jian-ping

THE RED POPPY
(Original Russian title: *Krasnyi Mak*)

Choreography: Lev Lashchilin and Vasily Tikhomirov
Music: Reinhold Glière
Design: Mikhail Kurilko
Libretto: Mikhail Kurilko
First Production: Bolshoi Ballet, Moscow, 14 June 1927
Principal Dancers: Ekaterina Geltser (Tao-Hoa), Aleksei Bulgatov (Captain)

Other productions include: State Academic Theatre for Opera and Ballet (GATOB) (new version; chor. Fedor Lopukhov, Vladimir Ponomarev, Leonid Leontiev, design Boris Erbstein), with Elena Lukom, Mikhail Dudko; 20 January 1929. Bolshoi Ballet (new version; chor. Leonid Lavrovsky, design Kurilko), with Galina Ulanova, Aleksandr Radunsky; Moscow, 12 December 1949. Kirov Ballet (new version; chor. Rostislav Zakharov); Leningrad, 26 December 1949. Bolshoi Ballet (new version; chor. Lavrovsky, with some of the original 1927 choreography), under the title *The Red Flower*; Moscow, 24 November 1957. Kirov Ballet (new version; chor. Aleksei Andreyev); Leningrad, 2 May 1958. Ballet Russe de Monte Carlo (shortened version; chor. Igor Schwezoff); Cleveland, Ohio, 9 October 1943.

PUBLICATIONS

Bogdanov-Berezovsky, Valerian, *The Red Poppy*, Leningrad, 1934
Schlee, Alfred, "The Dance in Soviet Russia", *Dance Index* (New York), June/July 1943
Slonimsky, Yuri, *Soviet Ballet*, Moscow and Leningrad, 1950
Beaumont, Cyril, *Complete Book of Ballets*, revised edition, London, 1951
Swift, Mary Grace, *The Art of Dance in the USSR*, Notre Dame, Indiana, 1968
Roslavleva, Natalia, *V.D. Tikhomirov: Artist, Balletmaster, Teacher*, Moscow, 1971
Souritz, Elizabeth, *The Art of Choreography in the 1920s*, Moscow, 1979; as *Soviet Choreographers in the 1920s*, translated by Lynn Visson, Durham, N.C. and London, 1990

*   *   *

The 1927 ballet, *The Red Poppy*, was the joint product of the Directorate of the Bolshoi Theatre, who commissioned the score (originally meant to be for a ballet entitled *The Daughter of the Port*, which never materialized), and who dictated the libretto and assigned the choreography to Vasily Tikhomirov, then chief ballet master of the Bolshoi. The choreographer for the first and third acts was Lev Lashchilin, though his name was not listed alongside Tikhomirov's and proper credit was not given to him for many years afterwards. Tikhomirov, a traditionalist and preserver of the classical school, and Ekaterina Geltser, his prima ballerina, were to be the chief artists in a ballet which was yet meant to be "modern" and to illustrate a revolutionary theme.

The action of *The Red Poppy* takes place in a Chinese port city. The Chinese dancer Tao-Hoa becomes enchanted with the Soviet captain of a cargo ship which has just docked, and gives him a red poppy. The exploitative Li Shan-Fu, her manager, plots to kill the captain by having Tao-Hoa bring him poisoned tea—but she refuses, and saves him. Later, during the coolies' uprising, she actually gives her life to save the captain, killed by Li Shan-Fu's bullet for her protection of the Soviet captain. The

red poppy, which she hands to a little Chinese girl as she dies, becomes a symbol of love and of the freedom of the oppressed. In the middle of this action is a dream sequence, and the second act is largely devoted to the opium-induced dreams of Tao-Hoa in which a Golden Buddha appears, ancient goddesses come to life, and bright visions of butterflies, birds, and dancing flowers crowd out the horrors of life.

The Red Poppy was an attempt to answer a demand from the Soviet government "to make art serve the purpose of educating the people", and so to make dance more easily accessible to the broad masses of the population. Avant-garde experiments, such as Kasyan Goleizovsky's *Joseph the Beautiful*, failed to answer such a purpose, for they were often difficult for the mass audience and demanded a certain cultural background of their viewers. What was needed was the kind of art which would in an easy and engaging way publicize state policies.

In the very situations of the libretto which was finally decided upon, there was a strong element of topicality. The opening of the ballet coincided with such events as the raid on the Soviet consulate in Canton, during which the consul and several of his employees were killed. On 7 June 1927, the Soviet ambassador P.L. Voikov was killed in Poland (an event which actually occasioned a special meeting at the Bolshoi Theatre). But the ballet's subject matter, for all its relevance, was cast in traditional dramatic forms: the action was developed in pantomime scenes punctuated by dance divertissements. In the first act the divertissement was the performance by the dancers at the port, and later, the various national dances of the sailors. In the second act there was the grand classical divertissement— the dream. In the third act there was a suite of Western dances at a ball given by a Chinese banker, and the performance of a Chinese opera.

Not surprisingly, *The Red Poppy* was a ballet full of contradictions. And, for all its ambitions from the very beginning, the ballet was born in an atmosphere of bitter quarrels and mistrust. There were few who believed, at the early stages, that there could be a successful re-working of the music and scenario of *The Daughter of the Port*—the ballet which had originally been envisioned—and there were even fewer who believed that a truly revolutionary ballet could be produced by such inveterate "academics" as Tikhomirov and Geltser. There were extraordinary demands on the various collaborators—from the composer Reinhold Glière, who had to create an authentic Dance of the Red Sailors in one act and classical ballet divertissement music in the next—to the chief choreographer Tikhomirov and the theatre's director, Aleksei Dikiy, who differed hugely on matters of staging.

In the end, *The Red Poppy* was a curious mixture of seemingly incongruous styles. In the so-called dream act, the "grand magic" of the nineteenth century was revived; at the ball, trendy Western ballroom dancing exhibited up-to-date fashions; in the story itself, one could have the combination of traditional melodrama, rather popular at the time (girl falls in love with captain, and then dies) and politics (the Chinese people fight against the British colonial powers). The resulting show was colourful, with plenty of dancing—undoubtedly lacking in taste, but still attractive to a wide public. And it was immensely successful: it was immediately transferred to other ballet theatres in the Soviet Union and for many years it was regarded as "the first Soviet ballet based on a modern story" (which was not exactly true, because it was the avant-garde choreographers who were truly "modern" in their aesthetic experiments).

The ballet had extremely mixed reviews, provoking everything from serious articles to satires and humorous verses. The academics praised it with certain reservations, mostly for the dream scene. The leftists outdid themselves with witty

The Red Poppy, in the original production by Lev Laschilin and Vasily Tikhomirov, Moscow, 1927

descriptions of the ballet's awkward moments, and poked vicious fun at its creators. The ballet's many examples of a not-entirely-convincing mixture of revolutionary and artificial balletic motifs gave Aleksandr Tcherepnin cause to write, "You don't make a statue of a Red Army officer out of whipped cream."

Yet in evaluating *The Red Poppy* now in the context of the developing art of the age, one can see that the ballet's authors keenly observed the events of life around them. Much in *The Red Poppy* now seems hopelessly dated, but it really began as quite a timely work. The archaic quality of the ballet is itself symptomatic. It was precisely in the late 1920s, when the wave of experimentalism began to subside, and a return to a more normative aesthetic began, that it became easier for the adherents of academicism to defend their positions. The form of *The Red Poppy* did seem traditional, even in comparision with the art of the pre-revolutionary period. But the recourse to tradition was not at all accidental and can be explained by more than mere apathy. *The Red Poppy* was created under the aegis of Ekaterina Geltser, for Ekaterina Geltser. Implacably opposed to the innovations of the choreographers of the younger generation, Geltser and Tikhomirov tried to prove that through the canonical forms of nineteenth-century ballet spectacle one can depict modern life, even revolution in China.

The Red Poppy, known in Russia as *The Red Flower* since 1957, has undergone numerous restagings and revisions; Fedor

Lopukhov, Vladimir Ponomarev, and Leonid Leontiev produced the ballet with their own choreography in Leningrad in 1929, and both Leonid Lavrovsky (Bolshoi Ballet) and Rostislav Zakharov (Kirov Ballet) choreographed their own versions in 1949.

—Elizabeth Souritz

———

REED, Janet

American dancer and teacher. Born in Tolo, Oregon, 15 September 1916. Studied with Eve Benson and Isadora Moldovan, Portland, Oregon, and Willam Christensen, Portland and San Francisco. Married Branson Erskine, 1946. Dancer, Willam Christensen Ballet, Portland, Oregon, 1935–36; dancer, becoming principal dancer, San Francisco Opera Ballet (later San Francisco Ballet), 1937–41, performing role of Odile in first full-length American production of *Swan Lake*, 1940; principal dancer, Eugene Loring's Dance Players, 1941–42; guest artist, Ballet Theatre (later American Ballet Theatre), 1943, becoming ballerina, 1943–46; temporarily retired, 1946, returning as principal dancer, New York City Ballet, 1949–60; also dancer in Broadway musicals, including in *Look Ma, I'm*

Dancin'! (chor. Robbins, 1947); also teacher: ballet mistress, New York City Ballet, 1959–64; dance teacher, Bard College, from 1965.

ROLES

1935   Principal dancer (cr) in *Chopinade* (W. Christensen after Fokine), Willam Christensen Ballet, Oakland, California

1936   Principal dancer (cr) in *Les Visions de Massenet* (W. Christensen), Willam Christensen Ballet, Portland, Oregon

Principal dancer (cr) in *Cour de glace* (W. Christensen), Willam Christensen Ballet, Portland

The Maiden (cr) in *L'Amant Rêve* (W. Christensen), Municipal Auditorium, Portland

1937   Principal dancer (cr) in *Encounter* (W. Christensen), San Francisco Opera Ballet, Oakland

1938   Principal dancer (cr) in *Sketches* (W. Christensen), San Francisco Opera Ballet, Santa Rosa

Juliet (cr) in *Romeo and Juliet* (W. Christensen), San Francisco Opera Ballet, Sacramento

Principal dancer (cr) in *Ballet Impromptu* (W. Christensen), San Francisco Opera Ballet, San Francisco

Principal dancer (cr) in *The Bartered Bride: Three Dances* (W. Christensen), San Francisco Opera Ballet, San Francisco

Titania (cr) in *A Midsummer Night's Dream* (L. Christensen), San Francisco Opera Ballet, Portland, Oregon

1939   Swanilda (cr) in *Coppélia* (new production; W. Christensen), San Francisco Opera Ballet, San Francisco

1940   Titania (cr) in *A Midsummer Night's Dream* (new production; W. Christensen), San Francisco Opera Ballet, San Francisco

Odile (cr) in *Swan Lake* (new production; W. Christensen after Petipa, Ivanov), San Francisco Opera Ballet, San Francisco

The Bride (cr) in *And Now the Brides* (new version of *American Interludes*; W. Christensen), San Francisco Opera Ballet, Burlingame, California

1942   Acrobat (cr) in *Jinx* (L. Christensen), Dance Players

Principal dancer (cr) in *The Man from Midian* (Loring), Dance Players, Washington, D.C.

Principal dancer (cr) in *Prairie* (Loring), Dance Players, New York

Principal dancer (cr) in *The Duke of Sacramento; or, Hobo of the Hills* (Loring), Dance Players, New Hope, Pennsylvania

Mother/Sweetheart in *Billy the Kid* (Loring), Dance Players

Principal dancer in *City Portrait* (Loring), Dance Players

1943   Candy Girl/The Cat (cr) in *Fair at Sorochinsk* (Lichine), Ballet Theatre, New York

Who Was She? (cr) in *Dim Lustre* (Tudor), Ballet Theatre, New York

1944   A Passerby (cr) in *Fancy Free* (Robbins), Ballet Theatre, New York

Pas de quatre (cr) in *Waltz Academy* (Balanchine), Ballet Theatre, Boston

1945   Hera (cr) in *Undertow* (Tudor), Ballet Theatre, New York

Pas de deux, ensemble (cr) in *Interplay* (Robbins), Billy Rose's "Concert Varieties", Ziegfeld Theater, New York (also performed with Ballet Theatre 1945)

Girl in Pink (cr) in *On Stage!* (Kidd), Ballet Theatre, Boston

1949   Fête Polonaise (cr) in *Bourrée Fantasque* (Balanchine), New York City Ballet, New York

1950   The Ballerina (cr) in *Pas de Deux Romantique* (Balanchine), New York City Ballet, New York

Principal dancer in *Mazurka from "A Life for the Tsar"* (Balanchine), New York City Ballet, New York

1951   Queen of Hearts in *The Card Game* (revival of *The Card Party*; Balanchine), New York City Ballet, New York

Queen of the Swamp Lilies (cr) in *Cakewalk* (R. Boris), New York City Ballet, New York

Principal dancer (cr) in *A la Françaix* (Balanchine), New York City Ballet, New York

Principal dancer (cr) in *The Pied Piper* (Robbins), New York City Ballet, New York

1952   Principal dancer (cr) in *Ballade* (Robbins), New York City Ballet, New York

Columbine in *Harlequinade Pas de deux* (Balanchine), New York City Ballet, New York

Pas de deux in *Interplay* (Robbins), New York City Ballet, New York

1953   Rich Girl in *Filling Station* (L. Christensen revival), New York City Ballet, New York

1954   Marzipan Shepherdess (cr) in *The Nutcracker* (Balanchine), New York City Ballet, New York

Adagio (cr) in *Western Symphony* (Balanchine), New York City Ballet, New York

"Central Park in the Dark" (cr) in *Ivesiana* (Balanchine), New York City Ballet, New York

1957   The Countess (cr) in *The Unicorn, the Gorgon and the Manticore* (Butler), New York City Ballet, New York

1960   Peaches (cr) in *Creation of the World* (Bolender), in *Jazz Concert*, New York City Ballet, New York

Other roles include: for Ballet Theatre—Youngest Sister in *Pillar of Fire* (Tudor), "La Fille de Terpsichore" from Paris in *Gala Performance* (Tudor), Fanny Cerrito in *Pas de quatre* (Dolin), the Lustful Virgin in *Three Virgins and a Devil* (de Mille), Angelo, a Page in *Bluebeard* (Fokine), Wife in *Tally-Ho!* (de Mille), Lise in *La Fille mal gardée* (Nijinska), Ballerina in *Petrushka* (Fokine), Variation and Bluebird Pas de deux in *Princess Aurora* (suite of divertissements from *The Sleeping Beauty*; Dolin after Petipa); leading roles in *The Judgment of Paris* (Tudor), *Mademoiselle Angot* (Massine), *Graduation Ball* (Lichine); for New York City Ballet—Young Girl in *Mother Goose Suite* (Bolender), Third Movement in *Symphony in C* (Balanchine), principal dancer in *Concerto Barocco* (Balanchine), the Lady in *Con Amore* (L. Christensen), principal dancer in *Serenade* (Balanchine).

PUBLICATIONS

By Reed:

Interview in Moor, R.A., "Five Foot Two, Eyes of Blue", *Dance Magazine* (New York), January 1946

Contribution to *I Remember Balanchine: Recollections of the Ballet Master by Those who Knew Him*, edited by Francis Mason, New York, 1991

About Reed:

Denby, Edwin, *Looking at the Dance*, New York, 1949

Reynolds, Nancy, *Repertory in Review*, New York, 1977

Tobias, Tobi, "Bringing Back Robbins's *Fancy*", *Dance Magazine* (New York), January 1980

Janet Reed

Steinberg, Cobbett, *San Francisco Ballet: The First Fifty Years*, San Francisco, 1983
Denby, Edwin, *Dance Writings*, edited by Robert Cornfield and William Mackay, New York, 1986

* * *

Born of pioneer descent in the state of Oregon, Janet Reed began her early ballet training with Willam Christensen. Anxious to have the thirteen-year-old girl as a student, Christensen invented a job as assistant for her at his studio to help pay for her tuition. At a time when ballet companies were stressing their Russian roots or connections and presenting glamorous, continental ballerinas, Janet Reed entered the San Francisco Ballet Company as an American red-haired, blue-eyed dancer, more the diminutive "girl next door" than a European exotic. Shortly after joining the company, she took part in a bit of ballet history—Willam Christensen choreographed and produced the first full-length *Swan Lake* to be given in the United States. With two dancers being used for the Swan Queen role, Reed was chosen to dance the Black Swan,

Odile. At that time she danced two other leading roles, both well-suited to her stage personality: Juliet and Swanilda from *Coppélia*, which was her favourite.

The World War II era was a difficult time for any professional dancer; the few companies that existed gave little assurance of steady employment. In 1941, Reed became a member of the "Dance Players", a group under the direction of Eugene Loring offering dance plays on American themes, where she was joined by fellow troupers Lew Christensen (brother of Willam), Michael Kidd, and Joan McCracken. During the war, Reed was enlisted by Ballet Theatre, where her special talents for comedy and character dancing were quickly utilized in *Fancy Free*, *Billy the Kid*, *La Fille mal gardée*, *Graduation Ball*, *Gala Performance*, in which she danced the French ballerina, and particularly *Tally Ho!*, in which she alternated with the choreographer, Agnes de Mille. Ballet Theatre gave Reed the opportunity to take on dramatic parts, such as the callous ballerina in *Petrushka* and the younger sister in *Pillar of Fire*. When she left Ballet Theatre for a Broadway musical, it was, not surprisingly, for a play about ballet dancers, *Look Ma, I'm Dancin'!*, with Harold Lang and Nancy Walker and directed by George Abbott. Her tenure with the New York City Ballet began in 1949 and was broken by retirement periods; Reed had married in 1946 and had a family to raise. "What's more," she confessed, "dancing is hard, touring brutal." In semi-retirement, she attended dramatic school and taught ballet classes. She was coaxed out of retirement to return to the company as ballet mistress, having already appeared in *The Unicorn, the Gorgon and the Manticore*, a new ballet by John Butler with a libretto by Gian Carlo Menotti.

Never an international star, Reed was none the less a polished dancer-actress; her characters could be delicate, vivacious, wistful, or sexy. Though never designated as a Balanchine ballerina, Reed danced in many of his ballets, among them the *Harlequinade Pas de deux* with André Eglevsky, the adagio of *Western Symphony*, *Ivesiana*, and *Serenade*—demonstrating a range that often found her dancing two or three times an evening. Other New York City ballets included Robbins's *The Pied Piper* and *Interplay*; the *Mother Goose Suite* by Todd Bolender had her playing Beauty opposite Jerome Robbins's Beast. From the City Ballet repertory came two roles that remained indisputedly Reed's: the tipsy débutante ("The Rich Girl") in Lew Christensen's *Filling Station*—where her performance of the comic adagio brought applause from the theatre's most severe critics, the stagehands in the wings—and in *Con Amore*, another Christensen ballet that matched Reed's ebullience as the coquettish wife with the spirit of Rossini's music. A ballet's success should not depend exclusively on one dancer's appearance, but Reed's persona brought life and vigour to many ballets that have, since her final retirement, disappeared from the stage.

—Richard Rutledge

REINHOLM, Gert
German dancer, teacher, and ballet director. Born Gerhard Schmidt in Chemnitz, Germany, 20 December 1926. Studied at Ballettschule Schork, Chemnitz, and at the Berlin State Opera Ballet School, pupil of Lizzie Maudrik, Lulu von Sachnowsky, from 1941; also studied with Tatjana Gsovsky, Berlin. Dancer, corps de ballet, Berlin State Opera (East Berlin), from 1942, becoming soloist from 1946; international guest artist, touring with Natasha Trofimova, West Germany, Italy, and Switzer-

land, 1946–50; principal dancer, Teatro Colón, Buenos Aires, 1951–53; also appeared with Yvette Chauviré in various concert programmes; soloist, Municipal (Städtische) Opera Ballet (later the Deutsche Oper, or German Opera Ballet), Berlin, from 1953; founder, with Tatjana Gsovsky, Berlin Ballet, 1955, touring Asia and North and South America; ballet director, German Opera Ballet (on merger of Berlin Ballet with German Opera Ballet), Berlin, 1961–66; ballet administrator, 1966–72, and artistic director, German Opera Ballet, 1972–89; also teacher: founder of ballet school, 1958, merging with Gsovsky's school to form Berliner Tanzakademie, 1967; lecturer, State High School of Music and the Performing Arts, Berlin, 1967–72. Recipient: German Critic's Prize, 1958; Art Prize of the City of Berlin, 1962; Golden Star, Théâtre des Nations, Paris, 1962; Diaghilev Prize, 1963; Cross of Merit of the German Federal Republic (Bundesverdienstkreuz), 1987.

ROLES

1946   Daphnis in *Daphnis und Chloe* (T. Gsovsky), Berlin State Opera Ballet, Berlin
St. Francis (cr) in *Nobilissima Visione* (T. Gsovsky), Berlin State Opera Ballet, Berlin
Title role in *Petrushka* (T. Gsovsky), Berlin State Opera Ballet, Berlin
1947   Principal dancer in *Die Nacht auf dem kahlen Berge* (T. Gsovsky), Berlin State Opera Ballet, Berlin
Principal dancer (cr) in *Goyescas* (T. Gsovsky), Berlin State Opera Ballet, Berlin
Faun in *Nachmittag eines Fauns* (T. Gsovsky), Berlin State Opera Ballet, Berlin
Harlequin (cr) in *Carnaval* (T. Gsovsky), Berlin State Opera Ballet, Berlin
1948   Romeo (cr) in *Romeo and Juliet* (T. Gsovsky), Berlin State Opera Ballet, Berlin
Title role in *Le Spectre de la rose* (T. Gsovsky after Fokine), Berlin State Opera Ballet, Berlin
1949   Principal dancer in *Prometheus-Ballett* (*Die Geschöpfe des Prometheus*; T. Gsovsky), Berlin State Opera Ballet, Berlin
The Prince in *The Sleeping Beauty* (T. Gsovsky after Petipa), Berlin State Opera Ballet, Berlin
1951   Title role (cr) in *Hamlet* (T. Gsovsky), Teatro Colón, Buenos Aires
Title role in *Apollon musagète* (*Apollo*; Balanchine), Teatro Colón, Buenos Aires
1953   Title role (cr) in *Hamlet* (new production; T. Gsovsky), German (Municipal) Opera Ballet, Berlin
1954   Pelléas (cr) in *Pelléas und Melisande* (T. Gsovsky), German (Municipal) Opera Ballet, Berlin
The Knight in *Die Dame und das Einhorn* (Rosen), German (Municipal) Opera Ballet, Berlin
Principal dancer (cr) in *Der rote Mantel* (T. Gsovsky), German (Municipal) Opera Ballet, Berlin
1955   Title role in *Orphée* (T. Gsovsky), Berlin Ballet, tour
The Signalman (cr) in *Signale* (T. Gsovsky), Berlin Ballet, tour
Title role in *Der Idiot* (T. Gsovsky), Berlin Ballet, tour
1956   Title role (cr) in *Der Mohr von Venedig* (T. Gsovsky), Berlin Ballet
Principal dancer (cr) in *Fleurenville* (T. Gsovsky), Berlin Ballet
1957   Armand (cr) in *Die Kameliendame* (T. Gsovsky), Berlin Ballet, Berlin
Title role (cr) in *Kain* (T. Gsovsky), Berlin Ballet

Title role in *Orpheus* (Walter), German (Municipal) Opera Ballet, Berlin
Theseus (cr) in *Labyrinth* (T. Gsovsky), Berlin Ballet
1958   Don Juan in *Joan von Zarissa* (T. Gsovsky), German (Municipal) Opera Ballet, Berlin
Title role in *Apollon musagète* (Gsovsky), German (Municipal) Opera Ballet, Berlin
Dr. Schön (cr) in *Menagerie* (T. Gsovsky), German (Municipal) Opera Ballet, Berlin
1959   Orest (cr) in *Schwarze Sonne* (T. Gsovsky), German (Municipal) Opera Ballet, Berlin
1962   Oedipus (cr) in *Rätsel der Sphinx* (T. Gsovsky), German Opera Ballet, Berlin
Principal dancer (cr) in *Vier Nachstück nach Goya* (T. Gsovsky), Berlin Ballet
Title role (cr) in *Raskolnikoff* (T. Gsovsky), Berlin Ballet
1963   Principal dancer in *Suite en blanc* (Lifar), German Opera Ballet, Berlin
Faust in *Abraxas* (T. Gsovsky), Teatro Colón, Buenos Aires
1965   Title role (cr) in *Tristan* (T. Gsovsky), German Opera Ballet, Berlin

WORKS

1958   *Amerikanischer Bilderbogen*, Kurfürstendamm Theater Free Company
1964   Dances in *Tannhauser* (opera; mus. Wagner), German Opera Ballet, Berlin
1970   *Romeo and Juliet* (mus. Prokofiev), El Paso, Texas

PUBLICATIONS

Koegler, Horst, "Report from Germany", *Dance Magazine* (New York), August 1956
Kellerman, H., *Gert Reinholm*, Berlin, 1957
Goléa, Antoine, "Pour son festival de 1959", *Musica Disques* (Paris), September 1959
Geitel, Klaus, "Gert Reinholm", *Ballett: Chronik und Bilanz des Ballettjahres*, Zurich, 1982

* * *

Gert Reinholm has devoted a lifetime to the promotion of classical dance in Germany. For most of his life the city of Berlin, and the state of Germany, have been the recipients of his devotion. Starting his performing career while still a student of fifteen, he entered the ranks of the ballet of the State Opera in Berlin during World War II. He has been in Berlin ever since, except for the years between 1951 and 1953 when he was invited to the Teatro Colón in Buenos Aires as a soloist. The longtime friend, partner, and early protegé of Tatjana Gsovsky, Gert Reinholm continued his career as artistic director of the German Opera Ballet, where his loyalty to his chosen art form has built up a company of international reputation.

Reinholm has always adhered to the classic concept in the arts, claiming that without adherence to beauty, dance loses its very *raison d'être*. As a performer himself, he epitomized the tradition of the danseur noble, creating roles which include St. Francis in *Nobilissima Visione*, Orestes, Tristan, Hamlet, and Romeo. With an exceptionally handsome face and perfect physical proportions, he literally embodied the nobility of every hero he danced. Reinholm had a sensitive acting style and great musicality, and it was a sad loss to the German performance world when he ceased dancing at a relatively early age. The loss for the audience, however, became a gain—albeit invisible at first—for the company, as he broadened the repertory by bringing in choreographers and performers from outside, many of whom were relative newcomers. His encouragement of artists such as John Cranko, Kenneth MacMillan, Maurice Béjart (who had his first major work performed in Berlin), Hans van Manen, Valery Panov, Eva Evdokimova, Lynn Seymour, and Galina Panova showed courage and a rare insight which were justly rewarded. Balanchine, Tudor, Ashton, and Lifar also all had works performed in Berlin.

Reinholm is not simply an administrator, but prefers getting involved in every aspect of ballet-making. The music, choreography, dramatic thrust, design, and style of a work all bear some mark of his influence. He is ballet master, teacher, and producer in the fullest sense of the word.

Reinholm founded the Berlin Dance Academy with Tatjana Gsovsky in 1967. While admitting the importance of modern dance and appreciating the influence of the early German modern dance pioneers on ballet, Reinholm none the less insists that "Art must be positive . . . people need Beauty". His artistic direction has been influenced by this philosophy.

—Sally Whyte

RENAULT, Michel

French dancer. Born in Paris, 15 December 1927. Studied at the Paris Opéra Ballet School, pupil of Mauricette Cébron, Serge Peretti, Robert Quinault, Albert Aveline, and Gustave Ricaux. Appeared in children's shows at Théâtre du Petit Monde; dancer, Paris Opéra Ballet, from 1944, becoming grand sujet, 1945, and danseur étoile, 1946–59; international guest artist, touring Europe and America, performing in Lisbon, 1949, and in Moscow and Leningrad, 1957–58; principal dancer in recitals with Jeunesses Musicales Françaises (J.M.F.), 1955, 1959, 1961, and in partnership with Liane Daydé; also appeared on television, including in *Tambourin* (1959), *La Place blanche* (1961), *Technicolor Valse* (1961); freelance choreographer for musicals, revues, and television; company teacher, Paris Opéra Ballet, from 1982; guest teacher, Skidmore College, Saratoga Springs, 1971, School of American Ballet, New York, 1973–74, Teatro San Carlo, Lisbon, 1981, Kyoto Ballet Academy in Japan, 1990, 1991, and various studios in Europe; teacher, Paris Opéra Ballet School, until 1990. Recipient: Médaille d'honneur de la ville de Paris, 1951; Prix Vaslav Nijinsky, 1957; Médaille d'argent de la ville de Paris, 1967; Chevalier des arts et des lettres, 1974; Chevalier de la Légion d'honneur, 1975; Prix Renaissance Descartes, Paris, 1991. Died in Paris, 29 January 1993.

ROLES

1944   Un gendarme (cr) in *Guignol et Pandore* (Lifar), Paris Opéra Ballet, Paris

1945   Principal dancer (cr) in *L'Appel de la montagne* (Peretti), Paris Opéra Ballet, Paris
    Principal dancer in *Divertissements d'Alceste* (Nijinska), Paris Opéra Ballet, Paris

1946   Aminta in *Sylvia* (Lifar after Mérante), Paris Opéra Ballet, Paris
    Un Chasseur in *Les Animaux modèles* (Lifar), Paris Opéra Ballet, Paris

Principal dancer in *Antar* (divertissement; V. Gsovsky), Paris Opéra Ballet, Paris

1947   Principal dancer in *Serenade* (Balanchine), Paris Opéra Ballet, Paris
    Apollo in *Apollon musagète* (Balanchine), Paris Opéra Ballet, Paris
    Third Movement (cr) in *Le Palais de cristal* (later called *Symphony in C*; Balanchine), Paris Opéra Ballet, Paris
    Chevalier in *Le Chevalier et la damoiselle* (Lifar), Paris Opéra Ballet, Paris
    Le Jeune Homme (cr) in *Les Mirages* (Lifar), Paris Opéra Ballet, Paris
    Spontano in *Boléro* (Lifar), Paris Opéra Ballet, Paris
    Daphnis in *Daphnis et Chloé* (Fokine), Paris Opéra Ballet, Paris

1948   Principal dancer (cr) in *L'Ecuyère* (Lifar), Salle Pleyel, Paris
    Title role in *Petrushka* (Fokine), Paris Opéra Ballet, Paris
    Guignol in *Guignol et Pandore* (Lifar), Paris Opéra Ballet, Paris
    Pas d'action (Rose Adagio) in *Divertissement* (from *The Sleeping Beauty*; Lifar after Petipa), Paris Opéra Ballet, Paris
    Pulcinella in *Salade* (Lifar), Paris Opéra Ballet, Paris
    Principal dancer (cr) in *Zadig* (Lifar), Paris Opéra Ballet, Paris
    Principal dancer (cr) in *Escales* (Lifar), Paris Opéra Ballet, Paris
    Principal dancer in *Suite en blanc* (Lifar), Paris Opéra Ballet, Paris
    Principal dancer in *Mort du cygne* (Lifar), Paris Opéra Ballet, Paris
    Archangel (cr) in *Lucifer* (Lifar), Paris Opéra Ballet, Paris

1949   Title role (cr) in *Endymion* (Lifar), Paris Opéra Ballet, Paris
    Principal dancer in *Divertissement des Paladins* (*Ballet de cour*; Lifar), Versailles
    Roméo in *Roméo et Juliette* (Lifar), Paris Opéra Ballet, Paris

1950   Young Soldier (cr) in *L'Inconnue* (Lifar), Paris Opéra Ballet, Paris
    Adhemar (cr) in *La Grande Jatte* (Aveline), Paris Opéra Ballet, Paris
    Un Animal (cr) in *Les Éléments* (Lifar), Versailles
    Bluebird in *The Sleeping Beauty* (Petipa), Paris Opéra Ballet, Paris

1951   Roméo in *Roméo et Juliette* (divertissement; Aveline), Paris Opéra Ballet, Paris

1952   White Cavalier in *Elvire* (Aveline), Paris Opéra Ballet, Paris
    Lelio (cr) in *Les Fourberies* (Lifar), Paris Opéra Ballet, Paris
    Tzigane in *Les Deux Pigeons* (Mérante, Aveline), Paris Opéra Ballet, Paris
    Zephyr (cr) in *Les Fleurs* (Lander), in *Les Indes galantes* (Aveline, Lifar, Lander), Paris Opéra Ballet, Paris
    Principal dancer in *Études* (Lander), Paris Opéra Ballet, Paris
    La Statue in *Entre deux rondes* (Lifar), Paris Opéra Ballet, Paris
    Principal dancer in *Printemps* (Lander), Salle Pleyel, Paris
    Pas de deux from *The Nutcracker* (after Ivanov), Paris Opéra Ballet, Paris

Leading role in *Castor et Pollux* (Guerra), Festival, Besançon

1953   Valentino (cr) in *Cinema* (Lifar), Paris Opéra Ballet, Paris

Principal dancer (cr) in *Grand Pas* (Lifar), Paris Opéra Ballet, Paris

1954   Prince Siegfried in *Swan Lake*, Act II (Ivanov), Paris Opéra Ballet, Paris

Title role (cr) in *Nautéos* (Lifar), Paris Opéra Ballet, Paris

1955   Paris (cr) in *La Belle Hélène* (Cranko), Paris Opéra Ballet, Paris

Roméo (cr) in *Roméo et Juliette* (new version; Lifar), Paris Opéra Ballet, Paris

1956   Principal dancer in *Soir de fête* (Staats), Paris Opéra Ballet, Paris

Maître de ballet (cr) in *Divertissement à la cour* (Lifar), Théâtre de Monte Carlo, Monte Carlo

Principal dancer (cr) in *Danse à Versailles* (Larrain), Celebration of Marriage of Prince Rainier of Monaco and Grace Kelly, Monte Carlo

1957   Albrecht in *Giselle* (Petipa after Coralli, Perrot; staged Lifar), Paris Opéra Ballet, Paris

1958   Principal dancer in *Pas et lignes* (Lifar), Paris Opéra Ballet, Paris

Principal dancer (cr) in *Symphonie classique* (Lifar), Paris Opéra Ballet, Paris

Principal dancer (cr) in *Isoline* (divertissement; Skibine), Opéra-Comique, Paris

1959   Le Chevalier in *La Dame à la licorne* (Rosen), Paris Opéra Ballet, Paris

1960   Principal dancer in *Passionnément* (Chabukiani), Enghien Festival

Principal dancer in *Songe d'une nuit d'été* (Stone), Cimiez, Nice

1961   Principal dancer (cr) in *Tendresse* (also chor.), J.M.F., Paris

Principal dancer (cr) in *Prière* (also chor.), J.M.F., Paris

1963   Principal dancer in *Le Triomphe de la paix* (Linval), Festival St. Ouen

1968   Principal dancer in *Temps de légende* (Conte), Gala, Théâtre Champs-Elysées, Paris

Other roles include: principal dancer ("The Poet") in *Les Sylphides* (Fokine), title role in *Le Spectre de la rose* (after Fokine), Polovtsian Warrior in *Polovtsian Dances from Prince Igor* (staged Zverev), principal dancer in *Suite de danses* (Clustine), Basil in *Don Quixote* Pas de deux (after Petipa).

WORKS

1961   *Tendresse* (mus. Schumann), J.M.F., Paris
       Prière (mus. Beethoven), J.M.F., Paris
1991   *Suite en blanc* (mus. Lalo), Kyoto Ballet Academy, Japan

Also staged:
1985   *Suite en blanc* (after Lifar; mus. Lalo), Teatro São Carlos, Lisbon
       Sylvia Pas de deux (after Mérante; mus. Delibes), Teatro São Carlos, Lisbon
1987   *Swan Lake* (after Petipa, Ivanov; mus. Tchaikovsky), Teatro São Carlos, Lisbon
1992   *Entre deux rondes* (after Lifar; mus. Samuel, Rousseau), École de danse de l'Opéra de Paris

PUBLICATIONS

By Renault:
"Mes Reflections sur la danse", Bon, S., *Les Grands Courants de danse,* Paris, 1954

About Renault:
Berlioz, Pierre, "Michel Renault", *15 Danseurs et Danseuses,* Paris, 1948
Lasky, G., "More about *Lucifer*", *Dancing Times* (London), March 1949
Lidova, Irène, *17 Visages de la danse,* Paris, 1953
Guest, Ivor, "Fair Exchange", *Dance and Dancers* (London), September 1954
Christout, Marie Françoise, "Nauteos", *Dance and Dancers* (London), October 1954
"Personality of the Month: Michel Renault", *Dance and Dancers* (London), November 1954
"Careers in Pictures: Michel Renault", *Ballet Today* (London), May 1959
Coquelle, J., "Michel Renault", *Ballet Today* (London), May 1959

*   *   *

Michel Renault's professional dancing career began in the 1940s when he was engaged by the Paris Opéra, joining the corps de ballet and rising quickly through the ranks of the company to become the youngest étoile in 1946 at the age of eighteen. This rapid success was due largely to two of his teachers, Gustave Ricaux and Serge Peretti, who equipped him with an excellent technique in which strength and grace were equally matched, his movements on stage appearing deceptively effortless.

Renault was at the peak of his performing career in the 1950s, dancing the male leads in a variety of ballets, and partnering the most celebrated ballerinas of the period—Lycette Darsonval, Tamara Toumanova, Liane Daydé, and Yvette Chauviré. He appeared with Daydé in *Roméo et Juliette* (divertissement by Aveline) in 1951, using his imagination and dramatic abilities to portray the romantic hero convincingly, executing each movement perfectly and with great feeling. Renault's appearances with Chauviré include the July 1954 production of *Nautéos* by Lifar, in which he portrayed the young fisherman of the title who falls in love and then proceeds to be unfaithful. The ballet gave him an opportunity to display his technical assurance as a soloist and adeptness as a partner, accompanying Chauviré in a pas de deux full of lyrical and sustained poses.

In the autumn of 1954 Renault's talents were appreciated by audiences in England, as part of a momentous occasion in the history of the Paris Opéra and Sadler's Wells ballet companies, when the two agreed to have an exchange, dancing in each other's theatres for a two-week period commencing at the end of September. Despite Renault's reputation in France, he was not particularly well known in England at the time, but this soon changed when his dancing on stage was warmly and enthusiastically received by audiences and dance critics alike, establishing him as a major international dancing star.

A London *Dance and Dancers* writer, covering this event, recalled a lady member of the audience declaring her disbelief at the programme notes, which listed Renault as dancing four principal roles during the same evening, a seemingly impossible task. However Renault was evidently more than capable of this feat, epitomizing to his English audience the French premier danseur who seemed to give more and have greater verve than male dancers of other dance backgrounds, jumping higher and turning faster than his British counterparts. "When characterization is called for," concluded this critic, "Renault . . . gives a performance which gets right under the skin of the role."

Other contemporary descriptions of Renault's performances confirm his high standing in the ballet world, highlighting the qualities which enabled the dancer to exert a commanding presence on stage. Renault's appearance in Lifar's *Les Mirages*, in which he danced the role of the young man, was legendary. British critic Peter Williams called Lifar's ballet unthinkable without Renault's excellent portrayal of the "alternatively arrogant and bewildered person" at the centre of the romantic fairy tale, while in the third movement of *Le Palais de cristal*, George Balanchine's abstract tribute to Bizet (later titled *Symphony in C*), Renault's energetic style and inexhaustible dancing were largely responsible for what contemporary reviewers called the ballet's "effervescent" quality. Balanchine had created this role for Renault in 1947, and during Balanchine's tenure as guest ballet master at the Paris Opéra the dancer also performed successfully in the classics *Serenade* and *Apollon musagète*.

In 1957 Renault was the first major French dance personality to be invited to tour Russia since Marius Petipa, who dominated the Russian ballet in the nineteenth century. Renault received a delirious welcome from ballet lovers and dignitaries, notably Nikita Kruschev. The press hailed Renault as the French ambassador of dance throughout the world, and the dancer himself commented favourably on his Russian experience, describing his ability to adjust easily to the Bolshoi's presentation of *Giselle*. As the Opéra and Bolshoi stagings of *Giselle* were quite similar, Renault found himself in unison with his fellow dancers in Russia, and dance proved an effective arena for cultural diplomacy. Indeed, the role of Albrecht was possibly one of Renault's finest. The expressive nature of his performance captured the hearts of his audience whenever he appeared in this role and inspired countless others to pursue the art of dance.

The desire to promote dance was always uppermost in Renault's ambitions and in attempting to popularize his art he ventured into choreography for the commercial theatre—musicals, night-clubs, revues (including the Folies Bergère), and television, including a dance programme shown on French television in 1959 featuring Brigitte Bardot, the Dinah Shore Show in America, and for the Israeli broadcasting service a production called *Tout va par deux* (1964). Through such media Renault was able to introduce dance to millions of spectators.

Renault also embarked on a successful teaching career in France, Portugal, and America, where he taught at Skidmore College, near Saratoga Springs, New York, and the School of American Ballet under the directorship of George Balanchine. His enduring passion for dance continued up until his death; he taught steadily at the Paris Opéra School, remaining in great favour with the Parisian public, and in 1991 was awarded the Prix Renaissance Descartes in the city of his birth, Paris, as recognition of the outstanding contribution he had made to the artistic and cultural life of his nation.

—Melanie Trifona Christoudia

LES RENDEZVOUS

Choreography: Frederick Ashton
Music: François Auber, arranged by Constant Lambert

Design: William Chappell (scenery and costumes)
First Production: Vic-Wells Ballet, Sadler's Wells Theatre, London, 5 December 1933
Principal Dancers: Alicia Markova and Stanislas Idzikowski (Adagio of Lovers), Ninette de Valois, Robert Helpmann, Stanley Judson (Pas de trois)

Other productions include: Sadler's Wells Theatre Ballet (restaged and revised Ashton, new scenery and costumes Chappell), with Elaine Fifield and Michael Boulton (Adagio des amoureux); London, 26 December 1947. National Ballet of Canada (staged Peggy van Praagh, scenery Kay Ambrose after Chappell); Hamilton, Ontario, 5 November 1956. Borovansky Ballet (staged van Praagh); Melbourne, 22 October 1960. Australian Ballet (staged van Praagh), with Marilyn Jones, Garth Welch (Adagio des amoureux); Sydney, 30 November 1962. PACT Ballet (staged John Hart), with Dawn Weller, Edgardo Hartley (Adagio des amoureux); Johannesburg, 3 September 1971. Bavarian State Opera Ballet (staged Ronald Hynd, Annette Page); Munich, 30 November 1972. American Ballet Theatre (staged Brian Shaw); Washington, D.C., 10 December 1980.

PUBLICATIONS

Barnes, Clive, Goodwin, Noël, and Williams, Peter, "*Les Rendezvous*", *Dance and Dancers* (London), July 1959
Croce, Arlene, *Going to the Dance*, New York, 1982
Vaughan, David, *Frederick Ashton and his Ballets*, London, 1977
Vaughan, David, "Birthday Offering", *Dance News* (New York), October 1979

*   *   *

This early ballet of Ashton's was his first to be made especially for the Vic-Wells Ballet, some eighteen months before he joined the company permanently as choreographer. Though brief and, in the choreographer's own estimation, relatively slight, it has proved enduringly popular and is now generally held to be, as David Vaughan puts it, "a seminal work in the Ashton canon". Although the details of production have undergone many changes, as have some aspects of the choreography, the broad outline of the ballet has remained as in Ashton's original "Ballet Divertissement": a group of young men and women meet in a park or garden, dance in various combinations, and disperse again. While the humour and variety of the choreography imparts a demi-caractère aspect to the ballet which adumbrates such later narrative ballets as *La Fille mal gardée* or *The Two Pigeons*, it is also an early statement of Ashton's classicism, as fulfilled so brilliantly in later ballets like *Symphonic Variations*. Its abstract classicism rather baffled its early critics; a review in *London Week* commented that "The possibilities of the square, and of its lively cousin the rhombus, have never, I am sure, been so adequately worked out."

However, comparison with such a ballet as *Les Sylphides* might have re-orientated this reviewer, and would not be wholly inappropriate, for all the light-heartedness of Ashton's ballet. *Les Rendezvous* uses the convention of threading together a number of classical divertissements and pas under a unifying title, and does so with the wit, musicality, and technical brio that have come to be the hallmarks of Ashton's style. The choreography of the ballet has undergone a number of revisions, not all of which are fully documented. The characters in the original production were the "Lovers" (later the "Amoureux"), danced by Alicia Markova and Stanislas

Les Rendezvous, with Alicia Markova and Stanislas Idzikowski, Vic-Wells Ballet, London, 1933

Idzikowski, an unnamed pas de trois danced by Ninette de Valois, Stanley Judson, and Robert Helpmann, and a corps de ballet of "Walkers Out" (later "Promeneurs") consisting of six women and six men, including Robert Helpmann. A year later a pas de quatre of "little girls" was added, one of whom was Margot Fonteyn, and much later again (1959) the touring section of the Royal Ballet expanded the "Promeneurs" to ten couples. The designs were also amended, and the costumes simplified (particularly the women's, from the grey decorated with roses and lilies-of-the-valley of the original production, to the present familiar white dresses trimmed with pink ribbons).

The choreography of the ballet seems to have settled into what might be considered a definitive account, based upon the revised version of 1947. A number of dance motifs are swiftly established—for example, the use of diagonals, with which the first groups enter and exit—which Ashton then develops and recapitulates throughout the ballet. Another theme is the exaggerated use of épaulement by the female soloist, which is echoed later by the pas de trois dancers; the female dancers (the pas de quatre and the soloist) also make recurrent twists and flicks of the wrists which the audience comes to recognize. In addition to his own movement motifs, specific to this ballet, Ashton makes witty reference to Petipa's very formal classical choreography, and also gives glimpses of certain movements which have since become familiar in Ashton ballets; in particular, the beautiful low supported lifts in which the woman seems to float across the stage.

The ballet does not set out to make any definitive statements; Ashton himself said at the time, with characteristic modesty, that "*Les Rendezvous* has no serious portent at all, it is simply a vehicle for the exquisite dancing of Idzikowski and Markova." However, while it remains true that *Les Rendezvous* is an unpretentious ballet, its real importance as an early demonstration of Ashton's capacity for pure classicism, leavened with wit, is too great to allow the choreographer the last word on this occasion.

—Penelope Jowitt

REQUIEM

Choreography: Kenneth MacMillan
Music: Gabriel Fauré
Design: Yolanda Sonnabend
First Production: Stuttgart Ballet, Stuttgart, 28 November 1976
Principal Dancers: Marcia Haydée (Sanctus, Pie Jesu), Birgit Keil (Agnus Dei), Richard Cragun (Sanctus), Egon Madsen, Reid Andersen

Other productions include: Royal Ballet (restaged MacMillan), with Marcia Haydée (guest artist; Sanctus, Pie Jesu), Bryony Brind (Agnus Dei), Wayne Eagling (Sanctus); London, 3 March 1983.

PUBLICATIONS

"MacMillan's *Requiem*: A Triumph in Stuttgart", *Dancing Times* (London), January 1977
Percival, John, "*Requiem*", *Dance and Dancers* (London), March 1977
Koegler, Horst, "Kenneth MacMillan's *Requiem*", *Dance Magazine* (New York), April 1977
Clarke, Mary, and Crisp, Clement, *The Ballet Goer's Guide*, London, 1981
Goodwin, Noël, "A Pilgrim's Progress", *Dance and Dancers* (London), May 1983
Thorpe, Edward, *Kenneth MacMillan: The Man and his Ballets*, London, 1985

* * *

Music for singers spurred Macmillan to some of his most profound choreography, and his response to Fauré's *Requiem* demonstrates the subtlety and intensity with which he could invent body positions and groupings that seem to convey an exact psychological equivalent in movement for the inner process of the music.

Requiem was created for the Stuttgart Ballet, and was dedicated to MacMillan's friend and exact contemporary John Cranko, the company's former artistic director who had died in 1973. It is worth recording that Macmillan's response to the German company had always been very strong, and drew from him some of his most significant choreography, including *Song of the Earth* in 1964, and *My Brother, My Sisters* in 1978.

It is generally well known that in composing his *Requiem*, Fauré chose to omit the customary *Dies Irae* section because he could not equate such a conception of divine anger and judgement with his own beliefs. He added an extra movement—the concluding *In Paradisum* section—instead. In consequence, his *Requiem* not only has a more outwardly elegiac tone but frequently achieves a greater intimacy, suggesting a personal trial and final liberation of the spirit rather than a public intercession in the face of damnation. In his realization of this quality, MacMillan penetrated beneath the gentle surface of the music to probe the tensions and agonies implied in the harmonies and by the text. This resulted in flights of invention that are often startling in their physical daring and complexity, but are none the less firmly rooted within the substance of the piece.

The ballet is abstract, and created for large forces which use at various times up to nine soloists and corps, though fined down in inner movements—notably the *Sanctus* and *Agnus Dei*. In particular, two female roles emerge from the large and skilfully handled ensembles as prominent vehicles for some of MacMillan's most delicately conceived renderings of purity in line, grace, and balance—especially one, as soloist, conveying radiant and ecstatic innocence in the *Pie Jesu*, the other as an agonized but soaring suppliant in the *Agnus Dei*. There are also some astonishingly acrobatic steps for the men, especially in relation to the décor's prominently sited off-centre column, which becomes the focus for a number of significantly placed leaps and difficult floor-rooted shoulder balances.

Requiem was an instant success on its first performance in 1976. Edward Thorpe, MacMillan's biographer, writes that the ballet "... had what can only be described as an ecstatic reception from audiences and critics—including some members of the British press who unhesitatingly called it Kenneth's best ballet for years". When the Stuttgart company performed the ballet in London during its 1978 tour, as Thorpe records, the work and the choreographer received a standing ovation from the audience at the London Coliseum. The critic for the *Financial Times* perhaps best summed up the effect of *Requiem* when he wrote:

What MacMillan has done in his realisation of the score is to match at every point Fauré's refinement and subtlety of means: without bombast or hysteria or penitential wallowing he finds images and streams of movement that treat with deepest sincerity of the hopes

Requiem, with Marcia Haydée and members of the Stuttgart Ballet

and fears we know in the face of death. *Requiem* is a ballet that needs almost to stand by itself in a programme, so deep are the feelings it engenders, so powerful the performances it inspires from its admirable cast.

Requiem was taken into the repertory of London's Royal Ballet in 1983.

—Geoffrey Baskerville

RIABOUCHINSKA, Tatiana

Russian/American dancer and teacher. Born Tatyana (Tatiana) Ryabushinskaya (Riabouchinska) in Moscow, 23 May 1917. Left Russia as a child: studied with Mathilde Kshesinskaya, Alexandre Volinine in Paris; later studied with George Balanchine and Pierre Vladimirov. Married dancer and choreographer David Lichine, 1943. Début, Nikita Balieff's "Chauve-Souris" revue, Paris, 1931; joined Blum's and de

Basil's Ballets Russes de Monte Carlo (becoming de Basil's Ballets Russes, and eventually the Original Ballet Russe), 1932, becoming ballerina, until 1942; also guest ballerina, Ballet Theatre, New York, 1942, and for various other companies, including Original Ballet Russe, the Ballet of Teatro Colón in Buenos Aires, Ballets des Champs-Elysées, Grand Ballet du Marquis de Cuevas, London Festival Ballet, and Los Angeles Ballet; also performer in musical comedies, including *The Waltz King* (chor. Lichine, 1943), *Polonaise* (chor. Lichine, 1945); also founder, with husband Lichine, of Los Angeles Ballet, 1953, and teacher, Beverly Hills, California, after retiring from the stage.

ROLES

1931   Diana in *Diana Hunts the Stag* (Devillier), "Chauve-Souris" revue, Paris
        The Ballerina in *The Romantic Adventures of an Italian Ballerina and a Marquis* (Romanov), "Chauve-Souris" revue, Paris
1932   The Child (cr) in *Jeux d'enfants* (Massine), Ballets Russes de Monte Carlo, Monte Carlo

A Girl (cr) in *La Concurrence* (Balanchine), Ballets Russes de Monte Carlo, Monte Carlo

Mistress of Ceremonies in *Cotillon* (Balanchine), Ballets Russes de Monte Carlo, Monte Carlo

Pas de sept (cr) in *Le Bourgeois Gentilhomme* (Balanchine), Ballets Russes de Monte Carlo, Monte Carlo

1933   Frivolity (cr) in *Les Présages* (Massine), Ballets Russes de Monte Carlo, Monte Carlo

The Eldest Daughter in *Le Beau Danube* (Massine), Ballets Russes de Monte Carlo, Monte Carlo

Cupid, Messenger (cr) in *Beach* (Massine), Ballets Russes de Monte Carlo, Monte Carlo

Rosina (cr) in *Scuola di Ballo* (Massine), Ballets Russes de Monte Carlo, Monte Carlo

Second Betrothed Pair (cr) in *Nocturne* (Lichine), Ballets Russes de Monte Carlo, Paris

Third and Fourth Movements (cr) in *Choreartium* (Massine), Ballets Russes de Monte Carlo, London

1934   The Circle (cr) in *Les Imaginaires* (Lichine), Ballets Russes de Monte Carlo, Paris

The Little Girl Lost in the Forest in *Contes Russes* (revival; Massine), de Basil's Ballets Russes, London

1936   The Chief Spirit (cr) in *Le Pavillon* (Lichine), de Basil's Ballets Russes, London

Reverie (cr) in *Symphonie Fantastique* (Massine), de Basil's Ballets Russes, London

1937   Angelic Apparition (cr) in *Francesca da Rimini* (Lichine), de Basil's Ballets Russes, London

The Golden Cockerel (cr) in *Le Coq d'or* (new ballet version; Fokine), de Basil's Ballets Russes, London

The Flower Girl (cr) in *Le Lion amoureux* (Lichine), de Basil's Ballets Russes, London

Principal dancer (cr) in *Orphée* (opera-ballet; chor. Lichine), de Basil's Ballets Russes, London

1938   Title role (cr) in *Cendrillon* (Fokine), (de Basil's) Russian Ballet, London

1939   The Florentine Beauty (cr) in *Paganini* (Fokine), (de Basil's) Covent Garden Ballet Russe, London

1940   The Romantic Girl (cr) in *Graduation Ball* (Lichine), Original Ballet Russe, Sydney

Swanilda in *Coppélia* (Obukhov after Petipa, Saint-Léon), Original Ballet Russe, Sydney

1947   The Romantic Girl (cr) in *Sueño de niña* (Lichine), Teatro Colón, Buenos Aires

Pathos (cr) in *The Evolution of Movement* (Lichine), Teatro Colón, Buenos Aires

1948   His Idea (cr) in *La Création* (Lichine), Ballets des Champs-Elysées, Paris

The Woman (cr) in *Valse Caprice* (Lichine), Ballets des Champs-Elysées, Paris

1949   Title role in *Giselle* (after Petipa, Coralli, Perrot), Grand Ballet du Marquis de Cuevas, London

1950   Principal dancer (cr) in *Harlequinade* (Lichine), London Festival Ballet, London

Principal dancer (cr) in *Symphonic Impressions* (Lichine), London Festival Ballet, London

1951   The Sugar Plum Fairy in *The Nutcracker* (Beriozoff, Lichine after Ivanov), London Festival Ballet, London

1952   Principal dancer (cr) in *Concerto Grosso* (Lichine), London Festival Ballet, Monte Carlo

1953   The Princess (cr) in *Les Oiseaux d'or* (Lichine), Los Angeles Ballet, Los Angeles

1960   Principal dancer (cr) in *Etude in E Major* (Lichine), Los Angeles Ballet, Los Angeles

Principal dancer (cr) in *New World Symphony* (Lichine), Los Angeles Ballet, Los Angeles

Tatiana Riabouchinska in *Les Imaginaires*, Ballets Russes de Monte Carlo, London, 1934

Other roles include: for de Basil's Ballets Russes—Bluebird pas de deux in *Aurora's Wedding* (from *The Sleeping Beauty*; after Petipa), the Girl in *Le Bal* (Massine), the Can-Can Dancer in *La Boutique fantasque* (Massine), Papillon and Columbine in *Le Carnaval* (Fokine), the Princess in *Les Cent baisers* (Nijinska), pas de deux in *Cimarosiana* (Massine), Favourite Slave in *Cléopâtre* (Fokine), Serving Maid in *Les Dieux Mendiants* (Lichine), Swan Queen (Odette) in *Swan Lake* (one-act version; after Ivanov), a Girl in *Les Matelots* (Massine), principal dancer in *Les Papillons* (Fokine), Ballerina in *Petrushka* (Fokine), Rosetta in *Pulcinella* (Romanov), the Girl in *Le Spectre de la rose* (Fokine), Prelude in *Les Sylphides* (Fokine); for Ballets des Champs-Elysées and Grand Ballet du Marquis de Cuevas—the Sylph in *La Sylphide* (after Taglioni); for Grand Ballet du Marquis de Cuevas—Mariuccia in *The Good-Humoured Ladies* (Massine).

PUBLICATIONS

Levinson, André, *Les Visages de la danse*, Paris, 1933

Haskell, Arnold, *Ballet Vignettes*, London, 1948

Davidson, Gladys, *Ballet Biographies*, revised edition, London, 1954

Swisher, Viola, "The Real Mirror: A Portrait of Tatiana Riabouchinska", *Dance Magazine* (New York), April 1972

Anthony, Gordon, "The Baby Ballerinas", *Dancing Times* (London), April 1973

Barnes, Clive, "Barnes on the Legendary Baby Ballerinas", *Ballet News* (New York), January 1982

Terry, Walter, "Baby Ballerinas", *Ballet News* (New York), January 1982

Sorley Walker, Kathrine, *De Basil's Ballets Russes*, London, 1982

Finch, Tamara, "The First Baby Ballerinas", *Dancing Times* (London), August 1985

García-Márquez, Vicente, *Les Ballets Russes*, New York, 1990

*   *   *

It was in London in 1931, while she was dancing for "Chauve-Souris", that George Balanchine discovered Tatiana Riabouchinska and signed her for the recently organized Ballets Russes de Monte Carlo. Although she was very young, her first roles for the Ballets Russes de Monte Carlo testified to those special stylistic and technical qualities that would characterize her dancing, and which were to be used to best advantage by Balanchine and Massine. From her first season, she was praised for her speed and quick footwork—James Monahan described her as "an embodied scherzo"—and for her elevation, which gave the illusion of her being frozen in mid-air, her lyrical arms, and her musicality and lightness. Her charismatic stage presence attracted the audience's attention the moment she came on stage, no matter how crowded with other dancers it was.

Between 1932 and 1933 Riabouchinska's creations with the Ballets Russes were milestones in her career. The Child in Massine's *Jeux d'enfants* was a vehicle for her speed, elevation, and whimsical interpretation; and of her Mistress of Ceremonies in Balanchine's *Cotillon* (she did not create the role, but Balanchine soon afterwards passed it on to her and she made it her own), André Levinson wrote: "Everything in this child is impetus, imperious will: the splendour of her clear face, the pure line of her profile. She is a little being of great race. As soon as she touches the ground after a fantastic flight, she parts again like an arrow, sparkling and minute like a hummingbird." Arnold Haskell gave tribute to her rare "sense of dramatic measure" that always pointed to the "essential contrast . . . of that magnificent choreographic poem . . . never stealing the limelight as the brilliant costume and the dancing involved gave her the opportunity of doing." As Frivolity in the third movement of Massine's *Les Présages*, she achieved maximum expression through her ethereal presence and, above all, through her ability to make the audience believe in her interpretation. She projected her character's gaiety across the footlights through her communication of musical mood and her feeling of spontaneity, creating what Haskell called "lightness of mind equal to lightness of dancing".

Riabouchinska reached artistic maturity while working with Fokine between 1937 and 1939. The roles that Fokine created for her included the Golden Cockerel, Cinderella, and the Florentine Beauty, and her work in these ballets was crucial to her artistic development. Her interpretation of the Florentine Beauty in *Paganini* has become her most renowned role among her creations. Beryl de Zoete wrote in London's *Daily Telegraph*: "She whirls and circles around him [Paganini] half dropping and recovering, and finally dropping prostrate at his feet. . . . The melody and lightness of her bending and fleeting body are indescribable." Haskell recalled her performance as "among the most moving" he had ever seen on the ballet stage.

Although she had danced other Fokine roles from the Diaghilev repertory, Riabouchinska's association with the choreographer now gave her the chance to be coached in those roles by Fokine himself. Her interpretation of the Prelude in *Les Sylphides* has become legendary for its lyric poetry as well as for its musical and fluid movement style. About this melodic quality in her dancing, de Zoete wrote: "It is the melody of her body which makes her line so perfect and so supple and gives it a quality of infinity."

When Riabouchinska's association with de Basil's Ballets Russes was interrupted in 1942, she appeared in the United States in musical comedies, danced in two Walt Disney films, and was a guest artist with American Ballet Theatre. After the war she and her husband, David Lichine, embarked on an international career as guest artists. She danced the classics as well as Fokine and Massine ballets, and any new creations by her were in works choreographed by her husband.

Riabouchinska will go into dance history as one of the most distinctive and individual of ballet artists. During her career critics regarded her as the most "unusual dancer of her generation". Throughout her career Riabouchinska was known for her intuitive capacity for unselfconscious immersion in her roles. This quality was so difficult to emulate that her colleagues seldom, if ever, attempted to essay roles she had created. Irving Deakin wrote: ". . . she gives to all her roles an aura that can only be called a Riabouchinska aura. Let any other dancer appear in any of her roles, and it becomes simply a dance done by someone wearing Riabouchinska's costume . . . [it] is so distinctly and individually hers that a role in her hands becomes hers and hers alone." For Haskell, the "characteristic of Riabouchinska is that she is able to convince her audience . . . that she is living what she dances, that to dance is as normal with her as breathing." The American critic Edwin Denby wrote: "Miss Riabouchinska . . . has so warm and true a presence, so clear a sense of musical enchantment that surrounds her, and so keen an instinct for natural characterization that one watches everything she does . . . with pleasure. . . . When you see her dancing with the happy absorption of a little girl, you wish other dancers in classic pieces would learn from her to believe in her imagination. . . . She creates a magic world around her—a very rare dancer indeed." Analyzing her dancing further, Denby added, ". . . when she dances she has a miraculous instinct for the atmosphere of a piece, so that her number fits naturally into the poetic illusion of it. Her dance makes sense in terms of the piece and it also makes natural sense as a dance. Her naturalness in action comes from the fact that she shows you so clearly the sustaining impetus, the dance impulse which carries her lightly through from beginning to end. Because the impetus is exactly right she strikes you as dancing her whole number on an impulse, spontaneously for the joy of it."

Since her retirement Riabouchinska and her husband have remained active in dance: they founded the first Los Angeles Ballet company and opened a dance academy in Beverly Hills, as well as founding several smaller performing groups.

—Vicente García-Márquez

RITE OF SPRING *see* **SACRE DU PRINTEMPS, Le**

ROBBINS, Jerome

American dancer, choreographer, and ballet director. Born Jerome Rabinowitz in New York, 11 October 1918. Educated at New York University, 1935–38; studied dance with Ella Dagonova, Helena Platova, Eugene Loring, and Antony Tudor; also studied modern dance with Sonia Robbins and

Jerome Robbins (second from right, front) rehearsing *Pulcinella* **with Balanchine and members of New York City Ballet, 1972**

Alice Bentley, and acting with Elia Kazan. Stage début, as actor, in 1937; début as dancer, Dance Center of Felia Sorel and Gluck-Sandor; dancer in Broadway stage musicals, 1938–40; dancer, corps de ballet, Ballet Theatre (later American Ballet Theatre), New York, 1940, becoming soloist, 1941–44; dancer, New York City Ballet, 1949–59; first major choreography, for Ballet Theatre, *Fancy Free*, 1944, thereafter also choreographing for Broadway stage musicals, beginning with *On the Town* (based on *Fancy Free*; 1945), and for film; staged first work for New York City Ballet, 1949, becoming associate artistic director, 1949–59; founder of own company, Ballets: USA, touring United States and Europe, 1958, regrouping for Spoleto Festival, 1961; founder (on recipient of government grant), American Theatre Lab, 1965; ballet master, New York City Ballet, 1969–83, becoming ballet master in chief (with Peter Martins), from 1983; also choreographer for television, from 1953, and producer and director for theatre and opera; Member, National Council on the Arts, 1974–80. Recipient: Donaldson Award, 1946, 1947, 1951, 1952, and 1954; Antoinette Perry (Tony) Award, 1947, 1958, 1965, 1989; *Dance Magazine* Award, 1950 and 1957; Emmy Award (for television production of *Peter Pan*), 1956; Academy Award (for *West Side Story*) for best direction, with special honorary award for best choreography, 1962; Chevalier de l'Ordre des arts et lettres, France, 1964; Capezio Award, 1976; Handel Medallion of the City of New York, 1976; Honorary Doctorate, City University of New York, 1980; Kennedy Center Award, 1981; Honorary Doctorate of Fine Arts, New York University, 1985; Hans Christian Andersen Award, Denmark, 1988.

ROLES

1941 Youth (cr) in *Three Virgins and a Devil* (new production; de Mille), Ballet Theatre, New York

Alfonso (cr) in *Bluebeard* (Fokine), Ballet Theatre, New York

1942 Hermes (cr) in *Helen of Troy* (Lichine), Ballet Theatre, Detroit

A Lover-in-Experience (cr) in *Pillar of Fire* (Tudor), Ballet Theatre, New York

1943 Benvolio (cr) in *Romeo and Juliet* (Tudor), Ballet Theatre, New York

Gypsy (cr) in *Fair at Sorochinsk* (Lichine), Ballet Theatre, New York

1944 Sailor (cr) in *Fancy Free* (also chor.), Ballet Theatre, New York

1945 Principal dancer (cr) in *Interplay* (also chor.), Ballet Theatre, New York

1946 Man (cr) in *Facsimile* (also chor.), Ballet Theatre, New York

1949 Bourreé Fantasque (cr) in *Bourrée Fantasque* (Balanchine), New York City Ballet, New York

Principal dancer in *The Guests* (also chor.), New York City Ballet, New York

1950 Title role in *Prodigal Son* (revival; Balanchine), New York City Ballet, New York

Principal dancer (cr) in *The Age of Anxiety* (also chor.), New York City Ballet, New York

"Hot Dogs" (cr) in *Jones Beach* (also chor., with

1951 Title role (cr) in *Tyl Ulenspiegel* (Balanchine), New York City Ballet, New York

Principal dancer (cr) in *The Pied Piper* (also chor.), New York City Ballet, New York

1952 Principal dancer (cr) in *Caracole* (Balanchine), New York City Ballet, New York

1972 Ring Master (cr) in *Circus Polka* (also chor.), Dancers of the School of American Ballet, New York

Beggar (cr) in *Pulcinella* (also chor., with Balanchine), New York City Ballet, New York

Other roles include: for Ballet Theatre—Peter in *Peter and the Wolf* (Bolm), Mercutio in *Romeo and Juliet* (Tudor), title role in *Petrushka* (Fokine), Alias in *Billy the Kid* (Loring), Devil in *Three Virgins and a Devil* (de Mille); for New York City Ballet—Hop o' My Thumb in *Mother Goose Suite* (Bolender), Third Movement in *Symphony in C* (Balanchine).

WORKS

1944 *Fancy Free* (mus. Bernstein), Ballet Theatre, New York

1945 *Interplay* (mus. Gould), "Concert Varieties", Ziegfeld Theater, New York (staged New York City Ballet, 1952)

1946 *Afterthought* (mus. Stravinsky), American Society for Russian Relief

Facsimile (mus. Bernstein), Ballet Theatre, New York

1947 *Summer Day* (pas de deux; mus. Prokofiev), Ballet Theatre, New York

1948 *Pas de Trois* (mus. Berlioz), Original Ballet Russe, New York

1949 *The Guests* (mus. Blitzstein), New York City Ballet, New York

1950 *The Age of Anxiety* (mus. Bernstein), New York City Ballet, New York

Jones Beach (with Balanchine; mus. Andriessen), New York City Ballet, New York

1951 *The Cage* (mus. Stravinsky), New York City Ballet, New York

The Pied Piper (mus. Copland), New York City Ballet, New York

Ballade (mus. Debussy), New York City Ballet, New York

1953 *Fanfare* (mus. Britten), New York City Ballet, New York

Afternoon of a Faun (mus. Debussy), New York City Ballet, New York

1954 *Quartet* (mus. Prokofiev), New York City Ballet, New York

1956 *The Concert* (mus. Chopin), New York City Ballet, New York

1958 *New York Export: Opus Jazz* (mus. Prince), Ballets: USA, Spoleto Festival

1959 *Moves* (no music), Ballets: USA, U.S. State Department tour

1961 *3 x 3* (mus. Auric), Ballets: USA, Spoleto Festival

Events (mus. Prince), Ballets: USA, Spoleto Festival

1965 *Les Noces* (mus. Stravinsky), American Ballet Theatre, New York

1969 *Dances at a Gathering* (mus. Chopin), New York City Ballet, New York

1970 *In the Night* (mus. Chopin), New York City Ballet, New York

Firebird (new production; with Balanchine), New York City Ballet, New York

1971 *The Goldberg Variations* (mus. Bach), New York City Ballet, New York

1972 *Watermill* (mus. Teiji Ito), New York City Ballet, New York

Scherzo Fantastique (mus. Stravinsky), New York City Ballet, New York

Circus Polka (mus. Stravinsky), New York City Ballet, New York

Dumbarton Oaks (mus. Stravinsky), New York City Ballet, New York

Pulcinella (with Balanchine; mus. Stravinsky), New York City Ballet, New York

Requiem Canticles (mus. Stravinsky), New York City Ballet, New York

1973 *A Beethoven Pas de deux* (later called *Four Bagatelles*; mus. Beethoven), New York City Ballet, New York

An Evening's Waltzes (mus. Prokofiev), New York City Ballet, New York

1974 *Dybbuk* (later called *The Dybbuk Variations*, and after 1980 *Suite of Dances*; mus. Bernstein), New York City Ballet, New York

1975 *Concerto in G* (later called *In G Major*; mus. Ravel), New York City Ballet, New York

Introduction and Allegro for Harp (mus. Ravel), New York City Ballet, New York

Ma Mère l'Oye (later called *Mother Goose*; mus. Ravel), New York City Ballet, New York

Une Barque sur l'Océan (mus. Ravel), New York City Ballet, New York

Chansons Madécasses (mus. Ravel), New York City Ballet, New York

1976 *Other Dances* (mus. Chopin), Gala for the Library of Performing Arts, New York

1978 *Tricolore* (with Martins, Bonnefous; mus. Auric), New York City Ballet, New York

A Sketch Book (with Martins; mus. various), New York City Ballet, New York

1979 *The Four Seasons* (mus. Verdi), New York City Ballet, New York

Opus 19: The Dreamer (mus. Prokofiev), New York City Ballet, New York

1981 *Rondo* (mus. Mozart), New York City Ballet, New York

Andantino (mus. Tchaikovsky), New York City Ballet, New York

Piano Pieces (mus. Tchaikovsky), New York City Ballet, New York

Pas de deux (mus. Tchaikovsky), New York City Ballet, New York

Allegro con Grazia (mus. Tchaikovsky), New York City Ballet, New York

1982 *Gershwin Concerto* (mus. Gershwin), New York City Ballet, New York

Four Chamber Works (mus. Stravinsky), New York City Ballet, New York

1983 *Glass Pieces* (mus. Glass), New York City Ballet, New York

I'm Old Fashioned (mus. Gould, after Kern), New York City Ballet, New York

1984 *Antique Epigraphs* (mus. Debussy), New York City Ballet, New York

Brahms/Handel (with Twyla Tharp; mus. Brahms), New York City Ballet, New York

1985 *Eight Lines* (mus. Reich), New York City Ballet, New York

In Memory of . . . (mus. Berg), New York City Ballet, New York

1986   *Quiet City* (mus. Copland), New York City Ballet, New York

Piccolo Balletto (mus. Stravinsky), New York City Ballet, New York

1988   *Ives, Songs* (mus. Ives), New York City Ballet, New York

1991   *Allegro con grazia* (mus. Tchaikovsky), New York City Ballet, New York

Other works include: choreography in stage musicals *On the Town* (mus. Bernstein, 1945), *Billion Dollar Baby* (mus. Gould, 1946), *High Button Shoes* (mus. Styne, 1947), *Look Ma, I'm Dancin'!* (also dir., with Abbott; mus. Martin, 1948), *Miss Liberty* (mus. Berlin, 1949), *Call Me Madam* (mus. Berlin; 1950), *The King and I* (mus. Rodgers, 1951; film version, dir. Lang, 1956), *Two's Company* (mus. Duke, 1952), *Peter Pan* (also dir.; mus. Charlap, 1954), *Bells are Ringing* (with Fosse; also dir.; mus. Styne, 1956), *West Side Story* (mus. Bernstein, 1957; film version, also dir., with Wise, 1961), *Gypsy* (also dir.; mus. Styne, Sondheim, 1959), *Fiddler on the Roof* (also dir., mus. Bock, 1964), *Jerome Robbins' Broadway* (also chor.; mus. various, 1989).

PUBLICATIONS

By Robbins:

"The Background of Ballets: USA", *Ballet Today* (London), October 1959

"The Evolution of the Modern Ballet: Some Observations", *World Theatre* (Brussels), vol. 8, no. 4, Winter 1959/60

Interview in Barnes, Clive, "Robbins Over Here", *Dance and Dancers* (London), March 1964

Interview in Tobias, Tobi, "Bringing Back Robbins' 'Fancy'", *Dance Magazine* (New York), January 1980

Interview in Barnes, Clive, "Ballet, Broadway, and a Birthday", *Dance and Dancers* (London), June 1989

About Robbins:

Beaumont, Cyril, *Ballets of Today*, London, 1954

Maynard, Olga, *The American Ballet*, Philadelphia, 1959

Lidova, Irène, "Jerome Robbins", *Les Saisons de la danse* (Paris), December 1969

Barnes, Clive, "Jerome Robbins, Choreographer", *The New York Times*, 9 February 1970

Barnes, Clive, "Jerome Robbins", *About the House* (London), Christmas 1972

Kirstein, Lincoln, *Thirty Years: The New York City Ballet*, New York, 1974

Mazo, Joseph, *Dance is a Contact Sport*, New York, 1974

Balanchine, George, and Mason, Francis, *Balanchine's Complete Book of the Great Ballets*, Garden City, N.Y., 1977

Howlett, John, "Prime Time for Robbins", *Ballet News* (New York), July 1980

Croce, Arlene, *Going to the Dance*, New York, 1982

Jowitt, Deborah, *The Dance in Mind*, Boston, 1985

Hering, Doris, "Jerry's Legacy", *Dance Magazine* (New York), April 1989

Schlundt, Christena, *Dance in the Musical Theater: Jerome Robbins and His Peers*, New York, 1989

*   *   *

The years surrounding his seventieth birthday were ones of artistic summation for Jerome Robbins. In 1989, he directed a Tony Award-winning Broadway production. Called *Jerome Robbins' Broadway*, it was a brilliant cavalcade of dances from

Robbins shows dating back to his first, *On the Town*. Although a narrator unified the material, *Jerome Robbins' Broadway* was essentially an all-dance show, one that made exceptional demands on its 62 performers.

They symbolized the demands that Robbins has made upon himself during his entire career. Whether his choreography is humorous (and he is a master at comic dance) or deeply serious, there has always been a perfection of detail and a dedicated attention to the shape and intent of the music.

In *Jerome Robbins' Broadway* it was a joy to revisit the Mack Sennett bathing beauty ballet from *High Button Shoes*. Called "On a Sunday by the Sea", it was a relentless chase along an Atlantic City Beach *circa* 1913: policemen careened through the crowd in search of their quarry, and the chase exploded in and out of a row of bathhouse doors. The episode was a miracle of theatrical timing. *Jerome Robbins' Broadway* also featured a suite of dances from *West Side Story*. Performed outside the original play's dramatic context, they took on almost symphonic proportions.

The eight other productions in *Jerome Robbins' Broadway* ranged in style and subject matter, from the Charleston antics of *Billion Dollar Baby*, to the Siamese dance-drama of *The King and I*; from the fantasy realm of *Peter Pan*, to the Russian Jewish exuberance of *Fiddler on the Roof*.

A similar range has always characterized Jerome Robbins's ballet choreography. This was amply displayed in the two-week festival of his ballets which highlighted the New York City Ballet's Spring 1990 season.

Robbins's first work for a ballet company was *Fancy Free*, created for Ballet Theatre when he was a young dancer in the company. Never has a first work received such universal acclaim—and it was deserved. His impudent yet wholly human vignette of three sailors pursuing girls during their brief time on shore was full of dance jokes, and yet created deft portraits of five young people in wartime. The Leonard Bernstein score spoke of its time as eloquently as the choreography.

Although typical of its period, *Fancy Free* has remained relevant throughout the ensuing years and changing casts. The same is true of Robbins's second ballet, *Interplay*, whose sequence of jazz dances revealed a young choreographer for whom succinctness and clarity were already second nature.

At this point Robbins began to experiment with psychologically oriented works, which did not endure. He also made a wise career decision. He asked George Balanchine if he could use him. Balanchine welcomed him to New York City Ballet as dancer and as choreographer. He also gave Robbins absolute choreographic freedom. It was the beginning of an ideal creative relationship between the two men.

Their work proved complementary. Balanchine's thinking was classical, and Robbins's was romantic. The latter's most enduring works of the 1950s were *The Cage* and *Afternoon of a Faun*. Both were poetic, with a touch of cynicism. In *The Cage* the novice in a swarm of female insects is taught how to destroy the males seeking to mate with her. In *Afternoon of a Faun*, a delicately fashioned reverie, two dancers prove more attracted to their own images in a studio mirror than they are to each other.

Robbins's most humorous ballet dates from this period. It is *The Concert*, in which a group of concert-goers act out their fantasies while listening to a sequence of Chopin piano pieces. This was the first of several Robbins ballets to the music of Chopin. The highlight is a female ensemble performing a "Mistake Waltz" in which someone is always out of step with the rest of the group. The humour comes from the totally unexpected timing of the errors and from the way in which they accumulate, until the audience begins to feel as frantic as the struggling dancers. Not many ballets elicit hearty laughter; *The*

Concert does.

By 1958 Robbins had decided to form his own dance company called Ballets: USA. He also accepted several important Broadway assignments, and, in order to devote himself to these projects, he took a leave from the New York City Ballet. Ballets: USA consisted of a hand-picked ensemble of versatile dance-actors. But its all-Robbins repertoire proved monochromatic. The company lasted only three years, and just one ballet endured. This is *Moves*, a purposeful abstract work danced in silence.

In 1965, Robbins staged a powerful version of Igor Stravinsky's *Les Noces* for American Ballet Theatre. That same year, the United States government launched the National Endowment for the Arts, and Robbins was among its first recipients. He received a two-year grant of $500,000 to form a project called the American Theatre Lab. Its intention was ". . . to provide a place for performing and creative artists to join together on ideas, create new works, extend and develop the musical theater into an art capable of poetically expressing the events, deep hopes, and needs of our lives".

Robbins derived much creative sustenance from this project. He returned to the New York City Ballet and in 1969 began a stream of distinguished works. The first one, *Dances at a Gathering*, was perhaps his most sensitive ballet to date. To a series of Chopin pieces lasting an hour, ten young people danced sometimes gently, sometimes with great sweep. They seemed to be experiencing a state of almost transcendent awareness—of each other, of their mood, and of the music. Another Chopin work called *In the Night* followed *Dances at a Gathering*. In a rather bittersweet way, it explored the deeper, more committed relationships of three couples. It was as though the participants in *Dances at a Gathering* were suddenly ten years older.

And then, as if to free himself from the romantic tendrils of Chopin, Robbins took on the monumental challenge of the Bach *Goldberg Variations*. It is a daring work, in which Robbins challenged himself to journey through the classical vocabulary as though he were turning a prism to reveal four centuries of evolving style.

With equal daring, Robbins then created *Watermill*, in which he challenged himself to manipulate stillness. He also drew upon some of the Japanese Noh studies which had taken place during the American Theatre Lab experiments. With Edward Villella as the pivotal character, the ballet was concerned with a mature man looking back on the events of his past. They went by in a procession so slow that they could be mirrored by the changes around the man as the seasons went their way.

The New York City Ballet's Stravinsky and Ravel Festivals required many works of Robbins. These included *Pulcinella*, a collaboration with Balanchine, in which both men also performed on one occasion.

The strain of romanticism so exquisitely handled in the Chopin works occasionally changed to sentimentality, especially in works like *Requiem Canticles*, *In G Major*, *In Memory of . . .*, and *Ives, Songs*. But in two works from this period, *Glass Pieces* and *Antique Epigraphs*, there was a return to the lucidity of structure which typifies Robbins at his most meaningful. In *Glass Pieces*, to music by the minimalist composer Philip Glass, the dancers engaged in variations on walking contrasted with a complex and yet equally objective pas de deux. And in *Antique Epigraphs*, Robbins seemed to create an analogy between ancient Greece and the roots of Western classical dance.

The Robbins Festival immediately preceded the choreographer's resignation as co-ballet master in chief of the New York City Ballet. Like the loss of George Balanchine, it marked the end of an important era. Together, Robbins and Balanchine had created the strongest repertoire of any contemporary ballet company. Without them, the company's future, while not uncertain, promised to be very different.

—Doris Hering

————

ROBERT SCHUMANN'S "DAVIDSBÜNDLERTÄNZE"
see DAVIDSBÜNDLERTÄNZE

————

RODEO
(subtitled *The Courting at Burnt Ranch*)

Choreography: Agnes de Mille
Music: Aaron Copland
Design: Oliver Smith (scenery), Kermit Love (costumes)
Libretto: Agnes de Mille
First Production: Ballet Russe de Monte Carlo, Metropolitan Opera House, New York, 16 October 1942
Principal Dancers: Agnes de Mille (Cowgirl), Frederic Franklin (Champion Roper), Casimir Kokitch (Head Wrangler), Milada Mladova (Ranch Owner's Daughter)

Other productions include: Ballet Theatre (restaged de Mille), with Allyn McLerie (Cowgirl), John Kriza (Champion Roper); Wiesbaden, Germany, 14 August 1950. San Francisco Ballet (staged Christine Sarry and Paul Sutherland); San Francisco, 2 February 1989.

PUBLICATIONS

Denby, Edwin, *Looking at the Dance*, New York, 1949
de Mille, Agnes, *Dance to the Piper*, Boston, 1952
Beaumont, Cyril, *Ballets of Today*, London, 1954
Maynard, Olga, *The American Ballet*, Philadelphia, 1959
Balanchine, George, with Mason, Francis, *Balanchine's Complete Stories of the Great Ballets*, Garden City, N.Y., 1977
Barnes, Clive, Interview with de Mille in *Inside American Ballet Theatre*, New York, 1977
Siegel, Marcia, *The Shapes of Change*, Boston, 1979
Barker, Barbara, "Agnes de Mille's Heroines of the 40s", *Proceedings* of the Society of Dance History Scholars, 12th Annual Convention, 1989
Goodwin, Noël, "Copland's Musical Americana", *Dance and Dancers* (London), November 1990

*   *   *

Rodeo, subtitled *The Courting at Burnt Ranch*, is Agnes de Mille's most popular ballet and is certainly the most frequently performed.

The ballet made dance history during the dark days of World War II with its exuberance, spirit, and recollections of happier times. It received 22 curtain calls on opening night at New York's Metropolitan Opera House, and led to de Mille's selection as choreographer for the landmark musical *Oklahoma!*

Against Oliver Smith's sun-drenched Western sky with its vast perspectives, a tomboy Cowgirl seeks to be one of the boys as they ride their horses in the corral with the bucking, prancing, and galloping movements for which de Mille is famous. The cowboys rebuff her, good-naturedly but firmly. She is crestfallen, since she had hoped to impress the Head Wrangler who has captured her heart. She may be a tomboy, but underneath her rough and ready garb and ways she is a girl on the threshold of womanhood.

City girls appear at the ranch. The cowboys are delighted with them, with their clothing, good looks, and refined ways, and anticipate a wonderful time at the dance that evening. They engage in a rousing rodeo in which the Cowgirl tries to take part on what appears to be a bucking bronco. Naturally, she is thrown. The city girls laugh, while the cowboys walk away in disgust.

The Head Wrangler, who has a date with one of the girls, walks past but turns back to talk to the Cowgirl. She is too shy to express her feelings and falls to the ground in despair as he shrugs and walks off. The Champion Roper, who does not see the Cowgirl, struts across the stage snapping his fingers and grinning at thoughts of the evening to come.

Rodeo's two scenes are separated by a running set of four couples and a Caller in front of a curtain decorated with galloping horses. When the curtain rises again the couples are paired and having a riotously good time, dancing and running in and out of the ranch house, now decorated for a Western hoedown. The Cowgirl in her daytime clothes sits alone on a bench, dejected and disconsolate. The Champion Roper, dressed to the nines in striped trousers and violet shirt, has been having marked success with the city girls. Out of sympathy, however, he asks the Cowgirl to dance, brushing off her clothes and wiping her face.

The Cowgirl is doing well, learning the intricacies of dancing, when the Head Wrangler shows up and all her yearnings resurface. Wrangler and Roper do battle, with the Cowgirl caught in the middle. At the end of the dispute the Cowgirl is again left to her devices, and she slumps back on her bench.

The Champion Roper returns and makes it clear that if the Cowgirl wants to be treated like a girl she should dress like one. The Cowgirl rushes out to return dressed in a parody costume, a garishly bright red dress and high button shoes. She looks gauche and acts it, but as the dance proceeds she becomes transformed. Not even the re-entry of the Head Wrangler, who now wants her, can impinge on her new-found love for the Champion Roper, and the ballet ends in a blaze of excitement.

There are few quiet moments in *Rodeo*. The work is packed with action, every movement segued into the next. *Rodeo* provides many opportunities for characterization and catches all the humor and contrasts of the Old West with its colorful and dramatic staging of a light-hearted, but moving, tale. In 1942, Edwin Denby expressed it perfectly, writing.

The effect of the ballet, as a friend of mine said, is like that of a pleasant comic strip. You watch a little coy and tear-jerky cowgirl-gets-her-cowboy story, and you don't get upset about it. What you are really recognizing is what people in general do together out West. Somehow the flavor of American domestic manners is especially clear in that particular desert landscape; and that is its fascination. The dance, the music, the décor . . . are drawn to that same local fact with affection; and so they have a mysterious unity of a touching kind. They also have a unity of being each one of superior workmanship. It is a modesty of the work that their relationship otherwise looks quite casual.

De Mille herself was the first Cowgirl and Frederic Franklin the first Champion Roper, with Casimir Kokitch as the original Head Wrangler. Other notable Cowgirls have been Bonnie Wyckoff and Christine Sarry.

—Joseph Gale

————

ROMANOV, Boris

Russian/American dancer, choreographer, and ballet director. Born Boris Georgievich Romanov (also known as Romanoff) in St. Petersburg, 22 March (10 March old style) 1891. Studied at the Imperial Theatre School, St. Petersburg, from 1900, pupil of Nikolai and Sergei Legat, Mikhail Obukhov, Aleksandr Shiryaev; graduated in 1909; also studied in the Class of Perfection under Mikhail Fokine. Married (1) dancer Elena Smirnova, 1920 (d. 1935); (2) Eugenie Romanov, 1938. Dancer, corps de ballet, Maryinsky Theatre, St. Petersburg, from 1909, becoming second dancer, 1912, and first dancer, excelling in character roles, from 1914; leading dancer with Diaghilev's Ballets Russes, seasons 1909–14, also partnering Anna Pavlova in Russia, 1914; first choreography for private stage, 1911/12; invited to stage dances for Maryinsky Theatre, St. Petersburg, 1914, becoming choreographer for the Imperial Theatres, 1914–17; also choreographer for Diaghilev's Ballets Russes, 1913, 1914, and for Letni Theatre of Miniatures (with future wife, Elena Smirnova, as ballerina), Petrograd, from 1914; elected director of Maryinsky Theatre, 1917; left Russia, 1921, first for Bucharest, then Berlin: founder, with Elsa Krüger, and director, Russian Romantic Ballet, touring England, Germany, Spain, France, 1921–25; choreographer, La Scala, Milan, 1925, and subsequent seasons from 1926; ballet master, Anna Pavlova's company, 1927; chief choreographer, Teatro Colón, Buenos Aires, 1928–34, also serving as ballet master to Opéra Privé of Paris, Yugoslavian tour, 1930–31, and Ballet de l'Opéra Russe à Paris, Monte Carlo and London, 1931, assisting in formation of de Basil's Ballets Russes de Monte Carlo, 1932; worked in Italy, including La Scala, Milan, and Teatro Reale, Rome, 1934–38; moved to U.S.: ballet master, Metropolitan Opera, New York, 1938–42, 1945–49; also choreographer for Marquis de Cuevas's International Ballet, the Foxhole Ballet, (Denham's) Ballet Russe de Monte Carlo, and Ballet for America; guest choreographer, Rome and Milan, various seasons after 1945; became naturalized American citizen, 1948. Member, Académie Chorégraphique, France, 1956. Died in New York, 30 January 1957.

ROLES

1909   Merchant in *The Little Humpbacked Horse* (Gorsky after Petipa), Maryinsky Theatre, St. Petersburg
        Buffoon (cr) in *Le Pavillon d'Armide* (Fokine), Diaghilev's Ballets Russes, Paris
        Jester (cr) in *Le Festin* (Fokine), Diaghilev's Ballets Russes, Paris
1910   Slave in *Eunice* (Fokine), Maryinsky Theatre, St. Petersburg
        Pierrot in *Carnaval* (Fokine), Maryinsky Theatre, St. Petersburg
1911   Coachman in *Petrushka* (Fokine), Diaghilev's Ballets Russes, Paris
1912   Young Lover (cr) in *Islamey* (Fokine), Maryinsky Theatre, St. Petersburg
1914   Pan (cr) in *Midas* (Fokine), Diaghilev's Ballets Russes, Paris

1915   Giovanni (cr) in *Francesca da Rimini* (Fokine), Maryinsky Theatre, St. Petersburg
Title role in *Stenka Razin* (Fokine), Maryinsky Theatre, St. Petersburg

Other roles include: Jester in *The Nutcracker* (Ivanov), Pierrot in *Papillons* (Fokine), Wandering Actor in *The Trials of Damis* (Petipa), Polovtsian Warrior in *Polovtsian Dances from Prince Igor* (Fokine), Satyr in *The Seasons* (Petipa).

WORKS

1911   *The Hand* (mime drama), Liteyny Theatre, St. Petersburg
1912   *The Prince Swineherd* (mus. Sats), St. Petersburg (staged Maryinsky Theatre, St. Petersburg, 1914/17)
Nocturne for the Blind Pierrot (mus. Chekrygin), Liteyny Theatre, St. Petersburg
Dances in *Carmen* (opera; mus. Bizet), Private Opera House, St. Petersburg
1913   *La Tragédie de Salomé* (mus. Schmitt), Diaghilev's Ballets Russes, Paris
Dance of the Persian Women in *Khovanschina* (opera; mus. Mussorgsky), Diaghilev's Ballets Russes, Paris
1914   *Le Rossignol* (opera-ballet; mus. Stravinsky), Diaghilev's Ballets Russes, Paris
Dances in *Aleko* (opera; mus. Rachmaninov), Maryinsky Theatre, St. Petersburg
Andalusiana (mus. Bizet), Maryinsky Theatre, St. Petersburg
"Lezghinka" in *Izmena* (opera; mus. Ipolitov-Ivanov), Maryinsky Theatre, St. Petersburg
1915/   Dances in *Carmen* (opera; mus. Bizet), Maryinsky
17   Theatre, St. Petersburg
Dances in *The Prophet* (opera; mus. Meyerbeer), Maryinsky Theatre, St. Petersburg
Dances in *The Demon* (opera; mus. Rubinstein), Maryinsky Theatre, St. Petersburg
Dances in *Samson and Dalila* (opera; mus. Saint-Saëns), Maryinsky Theatre, St. Petersburg
Solveig (mus. Grieg), Maryinsky Theatre, St. Petersburg
The Thief and the Ballerina (mus. Mozart), Maryinsky Theatre, St. Petersburg (staged Teatro Colón, Buenos Aires, 1925)
The Dream of Pierrot, Maryinsky Theatre, St. Petersburg
Tanek Satirov, Letni Theatre of Miniatures, Petrograd
Nocturne. . . . Pierrot, Letni Theatre of Miniatures, Petrograd
1922   *Prince Goudal's Festival* (mus. Rubinstein), Russian Romantic Ballet, Berlin
1925   *Petrushka* (after Fokine; mus. Stravinsky), La Scala, Milan
Francesco e Bianca (mus. Metzel), Teatro Colón, Buenos Aires
Grand Couture (*Ragtime*; mus. Satie), Teatro Colón, Buenos Aires
Trapeze (mus. Prokofiev), Russian Romantic Ballet, Berlin
1927   *The Champions* (mus. Milo), Anna Pavlova's company, tour
At a Ball (mus. Tchaikovsky), Anna Pavlova's company, tour
1928   *Pulcinella* (mus. Stravinsky), Teatro Colón, Buenos Aires

1929   *La Flor del Irupé* (mus. Mercante), Teatro Colón, Buenos Aires
El Amor brujo (mus. de Falla), Teatro Colón, Buenos Aires
La Valse (mus. Ravel), Teatro Colón, Buenos Aires
Thamar (mus. Balakirev), Teatro Colón, Buenos Aires
1930   *Chout* (mus. Prokofiev), Teatro Colón, Buenos Aires (staged for Ballet de l'Opéra Russe à Paris, 1931, and Ballets Russes de Monte Carlo, 1932)
1931   *L'Amour sorcier* (version of *El amor brujo*; mus. de Falla), Ballet de l'Opéra Russe à Paris, Monte Carlo (staged for Ballets Russes de Monte Carlo, 1932)
Le Rêve de Ratmir (scene from *Ruslan and Lyudmila*; mus. Stravinsky), Ballet de l'Opéra Russe à Paris, Monte Carlo
Pulcinella (after 1928 production; mus. Stravinsky), Ballet de l'Opéra Russe à Paris, Monte Carlo (staged for Ballets Russes de Monte Carlo, 1932)
Bacco in Toscana (mus. Castelnuovo-Tedesco), La Scala, Milan
Dances (probably after Nijinska) in *Rusalka* (opera; mus. Dargomizhsky), *Ruslan and Lyudmila* (opera; mus. Glinka), *Sadko* (opera; mus. Rimsky-Korsakov), Ballet de l'Opéra Russe à Paris, London
1932   *Bolero* (mus. Ravel), Teatro Colón, Buenos Aires
El Cometa (mus. Ortiz), Teatro Colón, Buenos Aires
Le Sacre du printemps (mus. Stravinsky), Teatro Colón, Buenos Aires
1934   *Homenaje a Schubert* (mus. Schubert, arranged Prokofiev), Teatro Colón, Buenos Aires
Histoire d'un pierrot (mus. Costa), Teatro Reale, Rome
Volti la lanterna (mus. Carabella), Teatro Reale, Rome
Madonna purità (mus. Bizzelli), Teatro Reale, Rome
1934/   Dances in *Tannhäuser* (opera; mus. Wagner), La Scala,
38   Milan
Dances in *The Damnation of Faust* (opera; mus. Berlioz), La Scala, Milan
1935   *Il Drago rosso* (mus. Savagnone), Teatro Reale, Rome
Balilla (mus. Guarino), Teatro Reale, Rome
Schéhérazade (mus. Rimsky-Korsakov), Teatro Arena, Verona
Dances in *Alceste* (opera; mus. Gluck), Musical May Festival, Florence
1936   *The Nutcracker* (mus. Tchaikovsky), Blum's Ballets de Monte Carlo, London
Madrigale (mus. Riete), Teatro Quirinetta, Rome
1937   *Gli Uccelli* (mus. Respighi), Teatro Reale, Rome
Lumawig e la saetta (mus. Lualdi), Teatro Reale, Rome
1945   *A Czech Village* (mus. Dvořák), Foxhole Ballet, U.S.
1949   *Orfeo* (mus. Monteverdi), Musical May Festival, Florence
Assedio di Corinto (mus. Rossini), Musical May Festival, Florence
Il Maestro di cappella (mus. Cimarosa), Musical May Festival, Florence
1955   *Prince Igor* (mus. Borodin), Teatro dell'Opera, Rome
Pisanella (mus. Pizzetti), Teatro dell'Opera, Rome
1956   *Harlequinade* (mus. Drigo), Ballet Russe de Monte Carlo, Chicago

Also staged:
1922   *Giselle* (after Petipa, Coralli; mus. Adam), Russian Romantic Ballet, Berlin (staged Paris, 1924)
1928   *Schéhérazade* (after Fokine; mus. Rimsky-Korsakov), Teatro Colón, Buenos Aires
The Firebird (after Fokine; mus. Stravinsky), Teatro Colón, Buenos Aires

1930 *Giselle* (after Petipa, Coralli, Perrot; mus. Adam),
     Teatro Colón, Buenos Aires
1937 *Swan Lake* (after Petipa, Ivanov; mus. Tchaikovsky),
     Teatro Reale, Rome

Other works include: *The Passion of Diana* (after Petipa), *The Dancer and the Highwayman, The Sacrifice of Atoragi, Voyage d'une danseuse* (mus. Mozart), *Walpurgis Night* (mus. Gounod), *A Midsummer Night's Dream, A Russian Wedding.*

PUBLICATIONS

By Romanov:
"Opera Ballet" in Chujoy, Anatole, *Ballet*, New York, 1936

About Romanov:
Lieven, Peter, *The Birth of the Ballets Russes*, New York, 1936
Moore, Lillian, *Artists of the Dance*, New York, 1938
Grigoriev, Serge, *The Diaghilev Ballet*, translated by Vera Bowen, London, 1953
Mara, T., "Boris Romanov", *Dance Magazine* (New York), March 1957
Krasovskaya, Vera, *Russian Ballet Theatre at the Beginning of the Twentieth Century*, volume 1: Leningrad, 1971
Sorley Walker, Kathrine, *De Basil's Ballets Russes*, London, 1982

*   *   *

Boris Romanov was one of the many great names to emerge from the St. Petersburg Imperial Theatre School, and one of the last ballet masters to have been trained in the Maryinsky-Diaghilev era. Having graduated from the Theatre's ballet school in 1909, he made his name as a leading character dancer at the Maryinsky Theatre during the early 1910s. While retaining his post at the Maryinsky, Romanov also performed in the first seasons of Diaghilev's Ballets Russes, creating several character parts in Fokine's first productions of *Le Pavillon d'Armide* and *Le Festin*, among others.

But Romanov also showed interest in choreography early in his career, staging several dances and "mime-dramas" for the private stage in St. Petersburg only two years after his graduation from the theatre school. On the basis of this experience, Romanov was invited to choreograph dances for opera productions at the Maryinsky Theatre in 1914, thereafter becoming official choreographer for the Imperial Theatres and staging the dances for eighteen operas, as well as several ballets, over the next several years.

Romanov's first choreography for Diaghilev's Ballets Russes was in 1913, with the staging of Florent Schmitt's *La Tragédie de Salomé*. This ballet had its première in Paris, and, despite the presence of Karsavina in the leading role, was judged more or less to be a failure—or at least to miss out on the attention and accolades won by other Diaghilev productions at this time. According to Serge Grigoriev, Diaghilev's régisseur (and the author of a detailed account of the Diaghilev years), the ballet's lack of success was not due to the choreography, but due to "a confused scenario and uninteresting scenery; for neither the music nor the choreography was by any means inferior". Prince Peter Lieven, another chronicler of the Diaghilev years, blames the fact that Romanov's ballet had its première in the same season as Nijinsky's notorious first choreographic efforts, *Le Sacre du printemps* and *Jeux*. Lieven, more outspoken about Diaghilev's dictatorial control of the company (and therefore, by implication, his favouritism), called Romanov "quite a talented choreographer", but claimed that "His comparative

lack of success in this instance can be explained by the fact that all the care and attention were devoted to the two ballets produced by Nijinsky." Whether or not this is true, it is perhaps more pertinent that once Nijinsky's ballets had been performed, the attention of the critics was almost entirely diverted from everything except the "scandale" created by Nijinsky's far more daring choreographic experiments.

Romanov was far from a traditional classicist himself, however (though later in his career he was to become something of a guardian and preserver of the classical tradition). A pupil of Fokine's, he was an advocate of the revolutionary ballet master's principles of choreography, and aimed (though perhaps in less dynamic ways) to subordinate mere technical display to higher artistic principles of unity of theme and dramatic purpose. Fokine's influence was to play an important role in Romanov's work as a choreographer, as was the more general influence of the "World of Art" movement in Russia previous to his work in the Diaghilev years. After his experience with the Diaghilev company Romanov worked as a choreographer for the experimental Letni Theatre of Miniatures, showing his interest in new and innovative forms of choreography and artistic expression.

Romanov choreographed another work for Diaghilev, to Stravinsky's opera *Le Rossignol*, in 1914—but his second work for the Ballets Russes was to receive an equally bland reception. Again, the cause may well have been bad timing, along with a failure of all the varied elements—scenario, music, design, choreography—to blend successfully together. Grigoriev writes:

> The chief appeal of *Le Rossignol* . . . was to lovers of the modern school of music. The general public remained puzzled by the lack of melody in the score. Moreover, neither the décor, in three scenes, designed by Benois in soft colours, nor the choreography by Romanov, which was similarly mild, in any way suited the stridencies of the composer. Stravinsky's new work provoked no scandal or incident. But neither did it make any great impression.

Taking into account Grigoriev's own personal prejudices, it still remains that the ballet, though competent, did not quite create a sensation. Interestingly enough, the designer, Alexandre Benois called the ballet "one of my most successful productions", complaining that after only a few performances the sets and costumes were left to moulder in storage, later to be partly destroyed during the war. Benois wrote that "Romanov, with rare sensitivity, understood precisely what I was aiming at", and paid tribute to the choreographer's understanding of the overall visual effect of staging and design together. Romanov's version of *Le Rossignol* was eventually eclipsed by Massine's reworking of the music for Diaghilev in 1920, for the far more successful *Le Chant du rossignol*.

If not one of the greatest names of the Diaghilev era, Romanov none the less remained an important representative of that important time in ballet history. As a choreographer, ballet director, and teacher Romanov brought both a pre-revolutionary Russian ballet background and an invaluable experience amongst the great avant-garde dance artists of the early twentieth century to many parts of the world. As the director of the Russian Romantic Ballet (based in Berlin but touring throughout Europe), he brought versions of the classics, as well as countless twentieth-century works (including his own), to many varied stages. As resident choreographer at the Teatro Colón in Buenos Aires (where Nijinska was choreographic director in the year immediately preceding), Romanov staged numerous Fokine works. He also brought his stagings of

Fokine's Diaghilev ballets to Italy, where he served as ballet director for the opera houses in both Milan and Rome in various seasons throughout the 1930s and 1940s. Romanov also worked briefly as ballet master to Anna Pavlova's company, for the Ballet de l'Opéra Russe à Paris, leading to the formation of de Basil's Ballets Russes de Monte Carlo, and the International Ballet of the Marquis de Cuevas.

Romanov eventually settled in the United States (becoming a naturalized American citizen in 1948), and spent several years as a respected choreographer and teacher for New York's Metropolitan Opera Ballet, among others. In the year of his death, 1957, Romanov had just completed his last ballet, *Harlequinade*, for the Ballet Russe de Monte Carlo. (Performed in Chicago in April, the ballet featured the great dancers Igor Youskevitch and Alicia Alonso in the leading roles.) As an artist whose career spanned nearly 50 years, and whose work joined two such distinct but hugely important eras in ballet history—those of pre-revolutionary Russian classicism and post-Diaghilev artistic experimentation in the West—Romanov held a special position, and his death marked the passing of a remarkable time in the growth and development of twentieth-century ballet.

—Elizabeth Hudson

ROMEO AND JULIET
(Original Danish title: *Romeo og Julie*)

Choreography: Frederick Ashton
Music: Sergei Prokofiev
Design: Peter Rice
Libretto: Frederick Ashton, after scenario by Sergei Prokofiev (based on the play by William Shakespeare)
First Production: Royal Danish Ballet, Köngelige Teater, Copenhagen, 19 May 1955
Principal Dancers: Henning Kronstram (Romeo), Mona Vangsaae (Juliet), Frank Schaufuss (Mercutio), Niels Bjørn Larsen (Tybalt), Flemming Flindt (Benvolio), Kjeld Noack (Paris)

Other productions include: London Festival Ballet (pas de deux only; restaged Ashton, with Niels Bjørn Larsen), with Peter Schaufuss (Romeo), Gaye Fulton (Juliet); London, 9 April 1973. London Festival Ballet (entire ballet; staged Larsen, supervised by Ashton); London, 23 July 1985. (see also other productions of Prokofiev score under *Romeo and Juliet*: Lavrovsky.)

PUBLICATIONS

Clarke, Mary, "*Romeo and Juliet*: Ashton's Contribution to the Royal Danish Ballet Festival", *Dancing Times* (London), July 1955
Clarke, Mary, "The Royal Danish Ballet", *Dance Magazine* (New York), July 1955
Williams, Peter, "*Romeo and Juliet*", *Dance and Dancers* (London), July 1955
Mason, Edward, "Festival in Copenhagen", *Dance and Dancers* (London), August 1957
"Homage to Ashton", *Ballet Annual* (London), no. 15, 1961
Young, B.A., and Williams, Peter, "*Romeo and Juliet*: The Origins of the Story, the Origins of the Ballet", *About the*

House (London), March 1965
Vaughan, David, *Frederick Ashton and his Ballets*, London, 1977
Vaughan, David, "Ashton's *Romeo and Juliet* Restored", *Dance Magazine* (New York), January 1986

*   *   *

Frederick Ashton's *Romeo and Juliet*, choreographed in 1955 to Prokofiev's magnificent score, has been perhaps overshadowed by other, more epic productions; after its ten years in the repertoire of the Royal Danish Ballet (for whom it was made), it was not seen again in its entirety until Ashton was persuaded to revive it for the London Festival Ballet 30 years later, in 1985. Ashton had proposed the ballet to Ninette de Valois, but it was felt at the time that one full-length Prokoviev ballet in the Sadler's Wells' repertoire, his 1948 *Cinderella*, was enough.

Ashton's version of *Romeo and Juliet* was made before the Lavrovsky staging—so influential on other choreographers since—had been seen in the West. The dynastic feuding and naturalistic Veronese street life, so prominent in the Lavrovsky and subsequent productions, are subordinate, in Ashton's reading, to the private tragedy of the young lovers. His Romeo and Juliet are passionately, physically in love, and this consuming passion is made the clear focus of the tragedy; they exchange kisses before dancing together, and the dance then seems a development of their mutual entrancement. Ashton was of course constrained by the intimate relation of the score to the Soviet libretto, allowing for only minor differences in broad outline; he also followed Shakespeare very closely (although in the revival in 1985 he made some adjustments among minor characters, for example losing Rosaline and adding Livia, a girlfriend for Mercutio). His interpretation of the score, however, shows the elegant understatement and innate lyricism which have become the hallmarks of his musicality. John Martin, writing in the *New York Times* of 27 September 1956, remarked that Ashton's solution to the problems inherent in choreographing to such overwhelmingly grand music was, characteristically, to approach it with humility. His choreography does not strive to compete with the score; by acknowledging the authority of Prokofiev's music, Ashton allows the dancers (and the audience) to inhabit its imaginative space, without recourse to the kind of realism that can so easily degenerate into blatant over-acting.

The Royal Danish Ballet in the 1950s, with its legacy of Bournonville ballets kept alive and polished by Harald Lander, and with such a background enhanced by the classical training of Vera Volkova, was able to provide Ashton with a formidable cast. His principals, the mature ballerina Mona Vangsaae and her much younger partner Henning Kronstam, were supported by a strong group of soloists and a unified corps de ballet, all schooled in a tradition of dramatically truthful ensemble playing. His version of the ballet was perhaps especially well suited to the intimate scale of the Köngelige Teater (Royal Theatre) in Copenhagen; some of the crowd scenes, and also the designs by Peter Rice (recreated for the Festival Ballet revival), seemed a little muted in the more spacious setting of the London Coliseum, although they fared better in some of the smaller provincial theatres visited on tour.

Ashton's choreography is distinguished by a poetic fluency, offset by a formal grandeur deriving from the best of Petipa, with touches of the sheer joy and bounce natural to dancers steeped in Bournonville repertoire. Exploiting the rich tradi-

Romeo and Juliet (Ashton) with (from left to right) Rafaelle Paganini, Matz Skoog, and Craig Randolph, London Festival Ballet

tion of mime and demi-caractère artistry among the ranks of the Royal Danish Ballet, Ashton had the ballet open with a brief mimed section introducing some of the principals (establishing, for example, the svelte feline character of Niels Bjørn Larsen's Tybalt). The several fights punctuating the libretto are less naturalistic, more choreographed and formalised than in some other productions, culminating in a swift and hair-raising duel between Romeo and Tybalt progressing up and down the steps and across the balcony, with Tybalt eventually rolling down the steps in his death-throes. Danish critic Erik Aschengreen, writing in the souvenir programme for the gala performance of the 1985 London revival, recalls that "The choreography was not built on high technical lifts or acrobatic virtuosity. The movements were poetic and gentle with a soft line and as wonderful a flow in the adagio dance as we had ever seen." Ashton's leitmotiv in the central balcony pas de deux is the arabesque; no choreographer understands the expressive range of that position better, whether it is Juliet doing exultant supported pirouettes into a penchée, the lovers skimming the stage in an estatic whirl of billowing lifts and runs, or the agonised parting embraces. These pas de deux find a macabre echo in Romeo's desperate attempts at reviving Juliet's "corpse" in the final scene of the ballet, where Ashton allows the pain of the lovers to break the constraints of formalism and emerge as raw emotion.

In a theatre where the tradition is for extreme audience restraint, the premiere of Ashton's *Romeo and Juliet* was greeted by nine curtain calls. Other productions are currently preferred, but this beautiful interpretation is an important chapter in the history of Shakespearean ballets, and deserves not to be forgotten.

—Penelope Jowitt

ROMEO AND JULIET
(Original German title: *Romeo und Julia*)

Choreography: John Cranko
Music: Sergei Prokofiev
Design: Jürgen Rose
Libretto: John Cranko, after scenario by Sergei Prokofiev (based on the play by William Shakespeare)
First Production: Stuttgart Ballet, Württemberg State Theater, Stuttgart, 2 December 1962
Principal Dancers: Marcia Haydée (Juliet), Ray Barra (Romeo), Egon Madsen (Paris), Ken Barlow (Tybalt), Hugo Delavalle (Mercutio)

Other productions include: Ballet of La Scala (earlier version; chor. Cranko, design Nicola Benois), with Carla Fracci

(Juliet); Milan, 26 July, 1958. National Ballet of Canada (restaged Cranko, design Rose), with Marcia Haydée (guest artist; Juliet; Toronto, 1964. Bavarian State Opera Ballet (restaged Cranko); Munich, 12 November 1968. Australian Ballet (staged Anne Woolliams); Sydney, 28 November 1974. Frankfurt Ballet (staged Georgette Tsinguirides, revised by Egon Madsen, with new design Elisabeth Dalton); Frankfurt, 17 October 1981. Scottish Ballet (staged Tsinguirides); Glasgow, 31 March 1982. Paris Opéra Ballet, with Noëlla Pontois (Juliet), Michaël Denard (Romeo); Paris, 30 April 1983. Joffrey Ballet; New York, 12 February 1984. (see also other productions of Prokofiev score under *Romeo and Juliet*: Lavrovsky.)

PUBLICATIONS

Paterson, Robert, "La Scala Premiere", *Ballet Today* (London), November 1958

West, Elizabeth, "Cranko's *Romeo and Juliet*: Success in Milan", *Dancing Times* (London), April 1959

Koegler, Horst, "Verona in Stuttgart", *Dance and Dancers* (London), February 1963

Höver, Fritz, "Ballet in Germany: Stuttgart", *Ballet Today* (London), March 1963

Koegler, Horst, "Canadian *Romeo and Juliet*", *Dance Magazine* (New York), June 1964

Kerensky, Oleg, "Cranko's Company: The Stuttgart Ballet Week", *Dancing Times* (London), July 1965

Balanchine, George, with Mason, Francis, *Balanchine's Complete Stories of the Great Ballets*, Garden City, N.Y., 1977

Percival, John, *Theatre in my Blood: A Biography of John Cranko*, London, 1983

Croce, Arlene, *Sight Lines*, New York, 1987

* * *

John Cranko's ballet version of the classic Shakespeare tale was first staged in Milan in 1958, but the 1962 Stuttgart version has become the standard Cranko *Romeo and Juliet*, later to join the repertories of the National Ballet of Canada, the State Opera Ballet in Munich, the Paris Opéra Ballet, Scottish Ballet, Frankfurt Ballet, Australian Ballet, and Joffrey Ballet. The Canadian version is particularly interesting because it preserves Jürgen Rose's original designs. Rose later slightly altered his sets and particularly revised his stunning costumes for the Capulets' Ball. At the rise of the curtain all the guests except Romeo, Mercutio, and Benvolio, appeared strikingly moving downstage in elegant black and gold costumes decorated with pearls. Rose's later costumes are more subtle, all in metallic tones of bronze, gold, copper—perhaps to set off the Capulets in their original gold, black, and pearl, perhaps to avoid the stagey uniform look of the originals, which the Canadian production retained. The La Scala version introduced Carla Fracci as Juliet; Marcia Haydée created the role in Stuttgart and Canada. A Canadian Broadcast Company television film by Norman Campbell exists with Veronica Tennant, Earl Kraul, and the National Ballet of Canada, while Margaret Dale filmed the Stuttgart Ballet production for the BBC, starring Marcia Haydée and Richard Cragun.

Cranko's is perhaps the most dramatically clear and effective of the many ballets choreographed to Prokofiev's magnificent score. But all succeeding versions made use of Leonid Lavrovsky's original (1940) ballet. The scenario (by Prokofiev, Radlov and Lavrovsky) is detailed in the music, and many of Lavrovsky's pantomime passages, gestures, and staging decisions show up intact in the versions by Cranko and Sir Kenneth

MacMillan, both of whom had seen Lavrovsky's when the Bolshoi Ballet introduced it at Covent Garden in 1956. Sir Frederick Ashton's *Romeo and Juliet* (for the Royal Danish Ballet), on the other hand, was created without seeing Lavrovsky's. Though it uses the Prokofiev music, Ashton's is a small-scale, lyrical ballet that does not attempt to recreate Shakespeare's sweeping drama. MacMillan's 1965 interpretation, clearly reflecting Cranko's, also balanced the male and female leading roles better than Lavrovsky's, which was dominated by the incomparable ballerina, Galina Ulanova.

Twenty *Romeo and Juliet* ballets (to various scores) preceded Cranko's. But these three—the seminal Lavrovsky's, Cranko's, and MacMillan's—became the models for many later ballets to the Prokofiev score, and Cranko's and MacMillan's remained rival versions in the repertory of several major companies worldwide.

As a choreographer of story-ballets, John Cranko did not display such compositional beauty as seen in Ashton's exquisite pas de deux in his *Romeo and Juliet*. Cranko's strength lay in his theatrical background and his genius for creating telling dramatic effects. His *Romeo and Juliet* has beautifully paced flow from scene to scene as it refines, clarifies, and makes more realistic many of Lavrovsky's operatic stagings and gestures. His pas de deux, and a pas de trois for Romeo, Mercutio, and Benvolio, are technically and theatrically impressive. His dances for the corps de ballet on the other hand, are rather more dramatically effective crowd scenes than memorable choreography.

The ballet is full of emotionally engaging touches. Especially imaginative and touching, for example, is Romeo's repeated gesture of playing with Juliet's hair. Act III opens with him awakening first in bed with Juliet and lazily lifting her long hair, then playfully letting it fall to the pillow. At her grave in the fourth act Romeo lies next to Juliet on her bier (the same structure as the bed, in the same spot on stage) and again lifts her hair with fond wonder and lets it fall as his final movement before rolling over and dying.

At the end of the balcony-scene pas de deux, he helps Juliet back up to her balcony, starts to leave, stops, raises himself, as in a chin-up exercise, to her level so that she can lean down to hold a kiss; then he drops quickly to the ground and, in one movement, picks up his cape and runs off with it flying behind him. At the end of the "Nightingale, not the lark" pas de deux in her chamber, he embraces Juliet from behind and places her facing stage right, in profile on pointes, her hands on her face. Then he picks up his cape in one hand and rushes off left, his upstage hand opening the richly embroidered curtain behind arches, pulling it open to reveal brilliant daylight as he exits, while Juliet she dutifully and fearfully faces away.

Cranko made few structural changes to Lavrovsky's scenario, but added many felicitous inventions. At the opening, for example, Rosalind, courted by Romeo, tosses him her fan. Lavrovsky's youngish Duke on horseback becomes a very old, fearsome Duke carried in by soldiers. Guests arrive in crimson cloaks, their rich costumes revealed only when the curtain opens on the ballroom scene. In front of the curtain, a showy, prankish dance by Romeo, Mercutio, and Benvolio precedes the ball. Romeo sees Rosalind and decides to follow her into the Capulets' ball. The clowns in the street scene have an acrobatic, comic set-piece, unlike the Bolshoi clowns' show-off athleticism. Juliet's fearful soliloquy about deciding to take the potion is dramatically explicit but internal, not virtuosic.

At the end of the ballet, Juliet's body is lowered by candelabra-carrying, black-caped mourners from the arched structure upstage to the tomb at floor-level, where dark hooded figures place her on the bier. Romeo encounters Paris in Juliet's tomb and stabs him almost in reflex action as mere obstacle to his reaching Juliet. Juliet awakes to embrace the still-warm Romeo on the bier with her, then finds nightmare in discovering him to be dead, also stumbling upon Paris's corpse. Romeo stabs himself; he does not take poison. Juliet uses the same dagger, then drags herself painfully to the base of the bier where he lies; she dies reaching up for his hand. No observers come in, as they do in Shakespeare and Lavrovsky. We end with a tableau of the two lovers lying dead, but still reaching to each other.

Sumptuously but impressionistically designed, this *Romeo and Juliet* is first-rate theatre as well as captivating dance.

—Herbert M. Simpson

ROMEO AND JULIET
(Original Russian title: *Romeo i Dzhulietta*)

Choreography: Leonid Lavrovsky
Music: Sergei Prokofiev
Design: Petr Williams
Libretto: Leonid Lavrovsky, after scenario by Sergei Prokofiev (based on the play by William Shakespeare)
First Production: Kirov Ballet, Leningrad, 11 January 1940
Principal Dancers: Galina Ulanova (Juliet), Konstantin Sergeyev (Romeo), Robert Gerbek (Tybalt), Andrei Lopukhov (Mercutio)

Other productions include: Brno State Theatre for Opera and Ballet (first production to Prokofiev's score; chor. Ivo Psota, design V. Skrušny), with Zora Semberová (Juliet), Ivo Psota (Romeo); Brno, Czechoslovakia, 30 December 1938. Cullberg Group (new version; chor. Birgit Cullberg); Stockholm, 1944 (new Cullberg versions staged 1955, 1969). Bolshoi Ballet (restaged Lavrovsky), with Ulanova (Juliet), Mikhail Gabovich (Romeo), Aleksei Yermolaev (Tybalt), Sergei Koren (Mercutio); Moscow, 28 December 1946. German State Opera Ballet (new version; chor. Tatjana Gsovsky); Berlin, 1948. Zagreb State Opera Ballet (new version; chor. Margarita Froman), with Sonia Kastl (Juliet), Nenad Lhotka (Romeo); Zagreb, 1949. Royal Danish Ballet (new version; chor. Frederick Ashton, design Peter Rice); Copenhagen, 19 May 1955 (see *Romeo and Juliet*: Ashton). Paris Opéra Ballet (new version; chor. Serge Lifar, design Georges Wakhevitch); Paris, 28 December 1955. Ballet of La Scala (new version; chor. John Cranko, design Nicola Benois); Venice, 26 July 1958 (restaged and heavily revised by Cranko for Stuttgart Ballet, 1962: see *Romeo and Juliet*: Cranko). CAPAB Ballet (new version; chor. Frank Staff); Cape Town, South Africa, 1964. Royal Ballet (new version; chor. Kenneth MacMillan, design Nicholas Georgiadis); London, 9 February 1965 (see *Romeo and Juliet*: MacMillan). Zürich State Opera Ballet (new version; chor. Nicholas Beriozoff, design Toni Businger); Zürich, 19 November 1966. Dutch National Ballet (new version; chor. Rudi van Dantzig); Amsterdam, 22 February 1967. Cullberg Ballet (new version; chor. Birgit Cullberg, design Eva Schaeffer), with Lena Wennergren (Juliet), Niklas Ek (Romeo); Stockholm, 28 September 1969. Frankfurt Ballet (new version; chor. John Neumeier, design F. Sanjust); Frankfurt, 14 February 1971 (staged Royal Danish Ballet, 1974). Perm Opera Ballet (new version; chor. Nikolai Boyarchikov); Perm, 1972 (staged German Opera Ballet, 1974). San Francisco Ballet (new version; chor. Michael Smuin, design William Pitkin); San Francisco, 27 January 1976. Maly Theatre Ballet (new version;

Romeo and Juliet (Lavrovsky) with Galina Ulanova and Konstantin Sergeyev, Kirov Ballet, Leningrad, 1940

chor. Oleg Vinogradov), with E. Alkanova (Juliet), Nikita Dolgushin (Romeo); Leningrad, 1976 (earlier version staged Novosibirsk, 1965). London Festival Ballet (new version; chor. Rudolf Nureyev, design Frigerio, Squarciapino), with Patricia Ruanne (Juliet), Rudolf Nureyev (Romeo); London, 2 June 1977 (staged La Scala Ballet, 1980, Paris Opéra Ballet, 1984). Joffrey Ballet (new version; chor. Oscar Araiz), 12 October 1977 (earlier version staged Buenos Aires, 1970). Bolshoi Ballet (new version; chor. Yuri Grigorovich, design Simon Virsaladze), with Natalia Bessmertnova (Juliet), Vatcheslav Gordeyev (Romeo); Moscow, 26 June 1979.

Other choreographic treatments of story (to scores other than Prokofiev): Vincenzo Galeotti (Copenhagen, 1811), Bronislava Nijinska (Monte Carlo, 1926), Willam Christensen (San Francisco, 1938), Gyula Harangozó (Budapest, 1939), Serge Lifar (Paris, 1942), Antony Tudor (New York, 1943; see *Romeo and Juliet*: Tudor), George Skibine (Monte Carlo, 1950; in collaboration with Serge Golovine, Vladimir Skouratoff, John Taras; Paris, 1955), Todd Bolender (New York, 1958), Erich Walter (Wuppertal, 1959), Maurice Béjart (Brussels, 1966), Ruth Page (Chicago, 1969), Jorge Lefèbre (Charleroi, 1980).

PUBLICATIONS

Lawson, Joan, "A New Soviet Ballet: *Romeo and Juliet*", *Dancing Times* (London), September 1940

Beaumont, Cyril, *Supplement to Complete Book of Ballets*, London, 1942

Morley, Iris, "*Romeo and Juliet* in Moscow", *Ballet* (London), August 1947

Roslavleva, Natalia, "The Soviet Ballet's Production of *Romeo and Juliet*", *Ballet Annual* (London), no. 2, 1948

Slonimsky, Yuri, *Soviet Ballet*, Leningrad and Moscow, 1950

Cox, A.J., "The Aims of Soviet Choreography", *Dance and Dancers* (London), October 1956

Barnes, Clive, Hunt, David, and Williams, Peter, "Bolshoi Ballet: *Romeo and Juliet*", *Dance and Dancers* (London), November 1956

S.S. Prokofiev: Materials, Documents, Reminiscences (various authors), Moscow, 1956

"The Bolshoi Ballet in London", *Dancing Times* (London), September 1963

Haskell, Arnold, "The Bolshoi Ballet at the Royal Opera House", *Ballet Annual* (London), no. 18, 1964

Young, B.A., and Williams, Peter, "*Romeo and Juliet*: The Origins of the Story, the Origins of the Ballet", *About the House* (London), March 1965

Vasilenko, S., *The Ballets of Prokofiev*, Leningrad and Moscow, 1965

Lopukhov, Fedor, *Sixty Years in Ballet*, Moscow, 1966

Roslavleva, Natalia, *Era of the Russian Ballet*, London, 1966

Lvov-Anokhin, Boris, *Galina Ulanova*, Moscow, 1970

Denby, Edwin, *Dance Writings*, edited by Robert Cornfield and William Mackay, New York, 1986

(See also publications under *Romeo and Juliet* (Ashton), *Romeo and Juliet* (Cranko), *Romeo and Juliet* (MacMillan), *Romeo and Juliet* (Tudor).)

* * *

Leonid Lavrosky's production of *Romeo and Juliet* was the first major ballet staging of Prokofiev's score, created a year after the very first production in Czechoslovakia. It not only is Lavrovsky's best ballet, but also represents the height of the development of "choreo-drama" in Soviet ballet.

Lavrovsky belongs to the group of ballet masters who began their search for a new era in the group known as the "Young Ballet". He was a talented successor to the choreographers of the past, especially Fokine. Fedor Lopukhov wrote about Lavrovsky's innovations, showing a sensitive understanding of the particulars of his choreographic style: "Lavrovsky demonstrated that he could create lyrical dance scenes and dramatic pantomime episodes, and also that he had a mastery of classical dance, and sought in it the means of giving his heroes imagistic characteristics and motivation for their relationships" (*Sixty Years in Ballet*). It is these qualities that helped the ballet master to create the choreographic drama that is, to this day, considered a classic of the twentieth-century repertoire.

Prokofiev's music was not offered to Lavrosky first. The composer had suggested that Lopukhov himself stage the work. Thoroughly delighted with the music, Lopukhov still thought that the love theme of the hero and heroine (in particular in the balcony scene) was insufficiently developed in the music. Prokofiev did not agree with him, and the music next went to Rostislav Zakharov and finally to Lavrovsky. Lavrovsky, too, suggested that he change the key and even the order of the musical episodes. Prokofiev, ultimately, relented.

In the opinion of Lopukhov, who ended up regarding Lavrovsky's production very highly, there were originally precious few dance numbers in the music—but Lavrovsky made use of every possibility for perfectly choreographed scenes. Thus, the famous "Cushion Dance", a powerful scene which grows into Juliet's tender dance, was developed by

Lavrovsky when there was no such specific scene designated by Prokofiev's music.

One of the high points of Lavrovsky's ballet is the wedding scene, constructed almost entirely on the theme of semi-arabesques. Not one of the subsequent choreographers of the music has managed to create as pure and as elevated an image of this sacred rite. Lavrovsky created memorable images of Tybalt and Mercutio, while the danced duel between them is one of most effective scenes in the ballet. The romantic deaths of these two characters demonstrate Lavrovsky's skill in creating moving and lasting images on stage.

Of course, Lavrovsky was also indebted to the first performer of the role of Juliet, Galina Ulanova, for the success of his ballet. Ulanova's understanding of the music was so sensitive, and she expressed the aesthetic and moral ideals of her time so thoroughly that, other than the talented and original ballerina Tatiana Vecheslova, no other subsequent performer in the role in either Leningrad or Moscow was ever able to do more than copy Ulanova's Juliet. Even in other twentieth-century choreographers' versions of Prokofiev's *Romeo and Juliet*, Ulanova has been a model to follow.

Other performers in the original Lavrovsky production have also become history in Soviet ballet: Konstantin Sergeyev is remembered as an outstanding Romeo, and Lopukhov as a powerful Mercutio, while both Robert Gerbek and Aleksei Yermolaev were notable Tybalts. More importantly, Lavrovsky's production was seen in the West, and had a profound effect on subsequent versions by Kenneth MacMillan and John Cranko.

Of the other significant productions of *Romeo and Juliet* in Russia which followed in the footsteps of Lavrovsky it is necessary to metion Oleg Vinogradov's version, employing the original libretto, which was first performed at the Novosibirsk Ballet in 1965, and later, in a new revised staging at the Maly Theatre in Leningrad in 1976. Another significant staging was that by Yuri Grigorovich (produced in Paris in 1978, and at the Bolshoi Theatre in 1979). Grigorovich staged the ballet to the original, unaltered score, which had been given to him by Zakharov, and tried to bring out the tragic character of the music as much as possible. The whole ballet is presented as an exclusively choreographic movement, devoid of pantomime episodes. In the third act, based on the old score, Grigorovich introduced the choreographic scenes "Juliet's Dream", "Paris prepares for the wedding", and the triple choreographic suite "In Mantua", which had been absent in Lavrovsky's production and in the ballets of his successors.

In Leningrad, the birthplace of Lavrovsky's *Romeo and Juliet*, the ballet has now been restored at the Kirov/Maryinsky Theatre.

—Nina Alovert

ROMEO AND JULIET

Choreography: Kenneth MacMillan
Music: Sergei Prokofiev
Design: Nicholas Georgiadis
Libretto: Kenneth MacMillan, after scenario by Sergei Prokofiev (based on the play by William Shakespeare)
First Production: Royal Ballet, Royal Opera House, London, 6 February 1965
Principal Dancers: Margot Fonteyn (Juliet; role created on Lynn Seymour), Rudolf Nureyev (Romeo; role created on

Romeo and Juliet (MacMillan) with Margot Fonteyn as Juliet, Royal Ballet, London, 1965

Christopher Gable), David Blair (Mercutio), Anthony Dowell (Benvolio)

Other productions include: Royal Swedish Ballet (restaged MacMillan), with Georgina Parkinson (Juliet), Jonas Kåge (Romeo); Stockholm, 5 December 1969. American Ballet Theatre (restaged MacMillan), with Leslie Browne (Juliet), Robert La Fosse (Romeo); Washington, D.C., 3 January 1985. (see also other productions of Prokofiev score under *Romeo and Juliet*: Lavrovsky.)

PUBLICATIONS

Crisp, Clement, "Romeo, Juliet, and Kenneth MacMillan", *Dancing Times* (London), February 1965

Goodwin, Noël, Barnes, Clive, and Williams, Peter, "*Romeo and Juliet*", *Dance and Dancers* (London), March 1965

Hall, Fernau, "The Royal Ballet: *Romeo and Juliet*", *Ballet Today* (London), March/April 1965

Barnes, Clive, "The Dancing in Verona", *Dance and Dancers* (London), April 1965

Crichton, Ronald, "Romeo's Designer: Nicholas Georgiadis", *Dancing Times* (London), April 1965

Hering, Doris, "Legends of Lovers", *Dance Magazine* (New York), July 1965

Goodwin, Noël, Percival, John, and Williams, Peter, "Verona Revisited", *Dance and Dancers* (London), January 1966

Monahan, James, and Clarke, Mary, "The Return of *Romeo and Juliet*", *Dancing Times* (London), January 1966

Anderson, Jack, "Ballets: Synthetic and Real", *Ballet Review* (Brooklyn, N.Y.), September/October 1968

Balanchine, George, with Mason, Francis, *Balanchine's Complete Book of the Great Ballets*, Garden City, N.Y., 1977

Buckle, Richard, *Buckle at the Ballet*, London, 1980

Thorpe, Edward, *Kenneth MacMillan: The Man and the Ballets*, London, 1985

Croce, Arlene, *Sight Lines*, New York, 1987

*   *   *

The closing couplet of Shakespeare's greatest love story is the crux of MacMillan's version of *Romeo and Juliet*:

> For never was a story of more woe
> Than this of Juliet and her Romeo.

MacMillan's adaptation centres on the play's "pair of star-cross'd lovers" with only sparse references to context or to secondary characters. Neither State (Prince Escalus) nor Church (Friar Laurence) feature prominently in his ballet, and the Montague/Capulet imbroglio is also under-played. There is no reconciliation of the two feuding families, unlike the resolution of Shakespeare's play. Thus, true love does not triumph. MacMillan's finale is one of tragedy—the lovers die, victims of fate and heaven's "stratagems".

Images of Love, choreographed by MacMillan in 1964, had used quotations from various Shakespeare texts in order to portray love in its many guises. Although the ballet was short-lived, it provided a stepping-stone for MacMillan in selecting certain lines from Shakespeare as the inspiration for his pared-down plot. Whereas Shakespeare's *Romeo and Juliet* is driven by its compressed time-span, MacMillan avoids any direct reference to Lord Capulet's decision to bring forward his daughter's arranged marriage. "Juliet and her Romeo" is MacMillan's focus. The urgency of Juliet's actions stems from her consuming love for Romeo. MacMillan presents her as more single-minded than Romeo; it is she who takes the initiative. Juliet, not Romeo, arranges their secret wedding, and once she has obtained the sleeping potion from Friar Laurence, it is her ill-timed ploy which speeds the ballet to its tragic conclusion.

Juliet's pas de deux with Romeo and Paris provide the most illuminating insights to MacMillan's perception of her character. With Romeo, Juliet is spontaneous and increasingly passionate, while with Paris, her initial reticence soon turns to determined resistance. MacMillan conveys Juliet's contrasting responses through leitmotiv. She dances two pas de deux with Paris, one before meeting Romeo and the other after their secret marriage. From Juliet's very first step, it is clear that between these two encounters with Paris, her perspective on love and filial duty has changed. Both pas de deux begin identically—with demi-ronde de jambe, posé into supported arabesque. The first is performed tentatively but in the second pas, Juliet (the pawn of Capulet's match-making) is manipulated by Paris throughout.

Conversely, with Romeo, Juliet dances unconditionally. An arc of emotion characterizes the lovers' four pas de deux. Following their "love at first sight" meeting in the Capulet ballroom, the balcony scene introduces more intimate partnering. MacMillan conveys escalating passion through breathless runs and soaring lifts. These are repeated in their next pas de deux in Juliet's bedroom but here, both body lines and lifts are more extreme. This pas de deux is the turning point. The intensity of the lovers' partnering emphasizes not only the peak of their relationship but also Juliet's despair at Romeo's imminent exile. In the final pas de deux in the Capulet crypt, Romeo attempts to revive the seemingly lifeless Juliet by taking her through many of the movements seen in their earlier dances together. Here though, the daring arches and angles are absent and, as Romeo lifts Juliet, she slumps limply in his arms.

Romeo and Juliet was MacMillan's first three-act ballet. One of the greatest challenges choreographically was the sustaining of narrative and dance action through the three-act form. Significantly, the lovers' pas de deux convey not only MacMillan's main theme; they also feature as structuring devices. They are the matrix around which he developed the choreography for other characters and, set against the ballet's other sections, the four pas de deux provide contrasts in light and shade.

It was in *Romeo and Juliet* that MacMillan mastered the interplay between large and small-scale perspectives. The action shifts smoothly from wide-canvas crowd scenes to the private liaisons of the duets. One pas de deux was the actual beginning of MacMillan's ballet: in 1964, he had been invited to choreograph a short ballet for Canadian television and, working with Lynn Seymour and Christopher Gable, he created the balcony scene pas de deux. In these two young dancers, MacMillan discovered the ideal dramatic combination for the two central characters in his full-length *Romeo and Juliet*. He drew upon their ideas and instincts. He encouraged them to study Shakespeare's play not only for its plot but, more importantly, in order to gain insights into the motivations of the two main characters.

Another important source for MacMillan's *Romeo and Juliet* was Sergei Prokofiev's music. The score's delineation of scenes and situations influenced MacMillan's progression (as it did earlier versions of the ballet by Leonid Lavrovsky and John Cranko, both of which MacMillan had seen). Musically, the lovers mature as the ballet progresses; introductory leitmotivs are simple and separate but as the relationship between Romeo and Juliet develops, more complex love themes identify their pas de deux. Prokofiev's score also reflects the ballet's shifts between large and small-scale settings. Full use is made of the orchestra to suggest the bustle of the market-place and the lavishness of the Capulet ballroom while more minimal instrumentation for the scenes in Juliet's bedroom and at Friar Laurence's cell highlights the increasing void between Juliet and her surroundings. The more involved she becomes with Romeo, the more alienated she is from her family and from their ordered, conventional world.

Curiously, it is the differences between MacMillan's choreography and Prokofiev's music which most distinguish this version of *Romeo and Juliet* from other productions. MacMillan's Romeo has far more *danced* action, made possible by re-arranging sections of Prokofiev's score. (An example of this is the dance for Romeo and a few of Juliet's friends interpolated by MacMillan in the ballroom scene. Originally, the music accompanied a group dance in the "Aubade" of Act III.) Conversely, although Juliet is MacMillan's dramatic protagonist, the majority of her dancing occurs during her pas de deux with Romeo and Paris. Rhythmically, too, there are crucial differences. In Juliet's bedroom, before she takes the sleeping potion, Prokofiev's music swells to reflect the magnitude of her dilemma. MacMillan's response, however, is for Juliet to do nothing. She sits motionless, the emotional energy of the music almost swallowing up this solitary figure to whom fate has dealt such an unfair hand.

Romeo and Juliet marked a watershed in MacMillan's career. Many of the structuring devices and the innovative pas de deux choreography influenced his subsequent three-act ballets. Also, the political manipulation of this ballet for the box-office (with Margot Fonteyn and Rudolf Nureyev as first-night casts both in London and New York despite the ballet being created on Gable and Seymour) forced MacMillan to re-think his career within the Royal Ballet. It was his last created work for the company until *Anastasia* in 1971 (his next three-act ballet, with Lynn Seymour once again his muse).

Romeo and Juliet is now a repertory favourite. It is viewed by many as MacMillan's greatest achievement. Watching the ballet today, we see that one of its marvels is just how fully MacMillan grasped the dramatic and movement possibilities of the three-act form at such a relatively early stage of his career. Subsequent generations of Royal Ballet choreographers have tried to emulate this rapid development but none have succeeded with such a sincere, individual signature.

—Angela Kane

ROMEO AND JULIET
(full title: *The Tragedy of Romeo and Juliet*)

Choreography: Antony Tudor
Music: Frederick Delius, arranged by Antal Dorati
Design: Eugene Berman
Libretto: Antony Tudor (after the play by William Shakespeare)
First Production: Ballet Theatre, New York, 6 April 1943 (incomplete); 10 April 1943 (complete)
Principal Dancers: Alicia Markova (Juliet), Hugh Laing (Romeo), Nicolas Orloff (Mercutio), Jerome Robbins (Benvolio), Antony Tudor (Tybalt), Richard Reed (Paris)

Other productions include: Royal Swedish Ballet (restaged Tudor); Stockholm, 30 December 1962.

PUBLICATIONS

Moore, Lillian, "*Romeo and Juliet* and *Helen of Troy*", *Dancing Times* (London), July 1943
Haskell, Arnold, "Ballet Theatre of New York at Covent Garden", *Ballet Annual* (London), no. 1, 1947
Severin, Reed, "Ballet Theatre in New York", *Dance Magazine* (New York), July 1947
Beaumont, Cyril, *Ballets Past and Present*, London, 1955
Menuhin, Diana, "The Varying Moods of Tudor", *Dance and Dancers* (London), July 1955
Barnes, Clive, "Tudor's Verona", *The New York Times*, 22 July 1971
Siegel, Marcia, *At the Vanishing Point*, New York, 1972
Tudor, Antony, Interview in Gruen, John, *The Private World of Ballet*, New York 1975
Balanchine, George, with Mason, Francis, *Balanchine's Complete Book of Great Ballets*, Garden City, N.Y., 1977
Payne, Charles, *American Ballet Theatre*, New York, 1978
Denby, Edwin, *Dance Writings*, edited by Robert Cornfield and William Mackay, New York, 1986
Perlmutter, Donna, *Shadowplay: The Life of Antony Tudor*, London, 1991

*   *   *

One of the more surprising facts about Tudor's *Romeo and Juliet* is the fact that Tudor could not finish this 45-minute epic by the date of the premiere. The impresario, Sol Hurok, insisted that the ballet go on even though the last two scenes were not choreographed. As Sono Osato later wrote in *Distant Dances*, "On opening night Tudor went before the audience to explain what they were and were not seeing. The stir caused by his unexpected announcement died down quickly with the first notes of the music. . . . When the curtain fell, we held our breaths. At first there was total silence, then a burst of thunderous applause. Tudor stepped out again to thank the audience and offer his apologies for such an unusual opening."

Interviewed by John Gruen about the birth of the ballet *Romeo and Juliet*, Tudor divulged, "I wanted it in the feel of the Shakespearean theatre—meaning, the feel of an open stage like the Globe. I felt that the gentle folk melodies that are sprinkled through the music of Delius were terribly reminiscent of a lot of Italian melodies, and I thought they also had the colors of the Italian painters of the period."

Tudor created a reverie, what might be called a meditation on the play of *Romeo and Juliet*. As Edwin Denby wrote, "Tudor's piece strikes me as a personal version of the story, a reverie on the subject, with muted and oppressed images. Shakespeare's openness is its foil. And it is precisely the private deformation Tudor has made which gives to the ballet its core of poetic reality, its odd spell." Tudor designed the scenario in ten scenes with no interruptions. Alicia Markova, his Juliet, said herself that she "purposely developed the role with a down-to-earth quality" equal to the desire and fervor of Romeo, played by the dramatic dancer, Hugh Laing. However Tudor did not create a realistic and physical ballet, where overwhelming passion leads to murder or where graphic scenes of love-making are depicted. Tudor prefered to distance us by means of poetic impressions and understatement.

It was important to Tudor, who studied character and period dancing, to create the mood of an era. In this case, he emphasized the Renaissance style with its push into the hips and tilt back for the gliding women, and its oppositional and erect stance for the men. Eight days after the complete version of *Romeo and Juliet* was presented, Tudor was honored by Ballet Theatre with a presentation of a laurel wreath and a parchment scroll including the signatures of every one of the dancers and staff in the company. Despite what seemed like minor setbacks at Ballet Theatre, Tudor was crowned King of Ballet Theatre not four years after his 1939 arrival in New York from London.

Romeo and Juliet was restaged in 1962 by the Royal Swedish Ballet and revised by Ballet Theatre in 1956 and 1971.

—Judith Chazin-Bennahum

RÓNA, Victor

Hungarian dancer, choreographer, and ballet director. Born in Budapest, 17 August 1936. Studied with Ferenc Nádasi at School of the Budapest State Opera House, 1945–50, and at Budapest State Ballet Institute; also studied with Aleksandr Pushkin, Naima Baltacheyeva, A. Kimishnikov, and Olga Lepeshinskaya, Leningrad, 1959. Dancer, Budapest State Opera Ballet, from 1950, becoming solo dancer (principal dancer) from 1957; international guest artist, including in China, Korea, and Vietnam, in Berlin and Nice, 1961, London and Washington, 1962, Paris, Moscow, and Geneva, 1963, Cuba, 1965–70; leading dancer, touring the U.S. with Janine Charrat, 1965, and also appearing in U.S., Germany, and France, various seasons 1965–72, also actor and dancer in films, including *Mischievous Students* (1966), *The Wooden Prince* (1968), *Ties* (dir. Máriássy, 1968), and on television, including Portrait film with Adel Orosz (Hungarian television, 1967), and *Portrait of Margot Fonteyn* (1968); ballet master, Norwegian National Ballet, 1974–80, Paris Opéra Ballet, 1980–83, La Scala, Milan, 1983–88; guest choreographer, Cologne,

1974, Venice, 1974–75, Cannes, from 1976, Nervi and Tokyo, 1983, Oslo, 1984, Stockholm, Oslo, Tokyo, 1986, Helsinki, Tokyo, Gothenburg, Bonn, Stockholm, West Berlin, 1989–90; choreographer for stage and television from 1975; deputy director, La Scala, Milan, 1984–85. Recipient: Third Prize, World Youth Meeting, 1955; First Prize, World Youth Meeting, 1959; Liszt Prize, 1961; Kossuth Prize, 1965; Knight of the White Rose, Finland, 1968; Merited Artist of the Hungarian National Republic, 1972; Outstanding Artist of the Hungarian National Republic, 1975; Béla Bartók Award, 1981.

ROLES

1950   Pas de trois in *The Nutcracker* (Vainonen), Hungarian State Opera Ballet, Budapest
         Drummer boy in *The Flames of Paris* (Vainonen), Hungarian State Opera Ballet, Budapest
1955   Prince in *The Nutcracker* (Vainonen), Hungarian State Opera Ballet, Budapest
1956   Mandarin (cr) in *The Miraculous Mandarin* (Harangozó), Hungarian State Opera Ballet, Budapest
1958   The Prince in *Swan Lake* (Messerer after Petipa, Ivanov), Hungarian State Opera Ballet, Budapest
         Albrecht in *Giselle* (Lavrovsky after Petipa, Coralli, Perrot), Hungarian State Opera Ballet, Budapest
         Title role in *The Wooden Prince* (Harangozó), Hungarian State Opera Ballet, Budapest
1959   Armen in *Gayané* (Anisimova), Hungarian State Opera Ballet, Budapest
1962   Mercutio in *Romeo and Juliet* (Lavrovsky), Hungarian State Opera Ballet, Budapest
1963   Principal dancer (cr) in *Tu auras nom . . . Tristan* (Charrat), Grand Theatre, Geneva
         The Prince (cr) in *Cendrillon* (*Cinderella*; Orlikowsky), Raimundo de Larrain Company, Paris
1967   Prince in *The Sleeping Beauty* (Gusev after Petipa), Hungarian State Opera Ballet, Budapest
1968   Title role in *Spartacus* (Seregi), Hungarian State Opera Ballet, Budapest
1969   Palemon (cr) in *Ondine* (Eck), Hungarian State Opera Ballet, Budapest
1970   Frondoso in *Laurencia* (Chabukiani), Hungarian State Opera Ballet, Budapest
1971   Colas in *La Fille mal gardée* (Ashton), Hungarian State Opera Ballet, Budapest
1972   Orion (cr) in *Sylvia* (Seregi), Hungarian State Opera Ballet, Budapest
1973   James in *La Sylphide* (Bournonville), Hungarian State Opera Ballet, Budapest

WORKS

1975   *The Nutcracker* (mus. Tchaikovsky), Norwegian National Ballet, Oslo

Also staged:
1991   *The Sleeping Beauty* (after Petipa; mus. Tchaikovsky), Hungarian State Opera Ballet, Budapest

PUBLICATIONS

"In the News", *Dance Magazine* (New York), January 1963

"Victor Róna", *Ballet Today* (London), August–September 1963

Näslund, Erik, "Rona i arbete: Viktor Rona at Work", *Dans* (Stockholm), December 1978

Kun, Zsuzsa, "Maître de Ballet—Victor Róna", *Hungarian Dance News* (Budapest), no. 5, 1980

* * *

Victor Róna was only fifteen years old when he became a member of the Hungarian State Opera's ballet company. He had been a weak boy with delicate health, but became a tall strong man who was the most popular leading dancer of his generation. In the beginning, his teachers at the State Ballet Institute believed there was no future for the boy; but Róna's teacher Ferenc Nádasi fought for his pupil: he knew the boy well and was aware of the special qualities that predestined him to be a dancer. A born artist, he absorbed the atmosphere of the theatre at an early age. His parents were actors; Victor was always with them, and from the age of two and a half he was on stage, reciting and acting. He developed a passionate interest in dancing, striving to overcome his physical limitations with an iron will. He led a Spartan life, constantly seeking to attain technical perfection.

Róna danced nearly all the roles in the classical repertoire. He formed an ideal partnership with his school contemporary, Adél Orosz; they danced and toured the world together. The great ballerinas of the world discovered the perfect partner in Victor and his greatest achievement was dancing with Margot Fonteyn in front of the British royal family and, at the invitation of President John F. Kennedy, in Washington. Later Róna partnered Galina Samsova, Alicia Alonso, Liane Daydé, Maina Gielgud, Jaqueline Rayet, and Ghislaine Thesmar. Ballerinas always felt safe in Róna's hands; his aim in a pas de deux was not just to show off his own technique, but to help his partner to give her artistic best too. His warm personality and humility as a performer was apparent not only to the great ballerinas, but to his audience as well.

Throughout his career Róna always remained faithful and grateful to his teachers. Having had an excellent basic training in Hungary, he also became familiar with the Russian ballet tradition during his visit to Leningrad. While in the Soviet Union he polished his interpretations of the Prince in *Swan Lake* and Albrecht in *Giselle*. He brought elegance and nobility to his roles; at the same time his temperament, which was typically Hungarian yet very much his own, always shone through. It proves his exceptional artistry that he created the role of the Miraculous Mandarin at the age of 20 with unbelievable maturity. In the leading role of Bartók's *The Wooden Prince*—recorded by Hungarian television—he struggled movingly to attain his desire. As Mercutio in Lavrovsky's *Romeo and Juliet* he portrayed a friend who sacrifices himself and goes to his death laughing. In Lászlo Seregi's *Spartacus* he exemplified the hero who gives everything for his ideals. He showed his sense of humour as Colas in Ashton's *La Fille mal gardée* and as Orion in Seregi's *Sylvia*. In another medium, the cinema, he played the dramatic lead in Félix Máriássy's film *Ties (Kotelekek)*.

Róna's foreign appearances were numerous. He performed and was applauded on the stages of nearly every city from East to West. The awards he received at home and abroad speak for his achievements.

When Róna felt that the time had come to pass on his experience to the younger generation, he started a new career as a ballet master and choreographer of classical ballets. He first tested himself in these roles in Oslo, while still a soloist. Then he became ballet master at the Paris Opéra with Rosella Hightower (with whom he still works closely), and subsequently became deputy director and ballet master at La Scala in Milan, again demonstrating the high standard of his professional skills. At present he works as guest ballet master with various leading classical companies.

In Victor Róna's own words, "It is not possible nor is it worth practising this profession without regular hard work; this takes a lot of sacrifice but brings great experiences and joy too." Róna lives according to these principles, setting an example for future generations.

—Agnes Roboz

ROSATI, Carolina

Italian dancer. Born Carolina Galletti in Bologna, 13 December 1826. Studied with Carlo Blasis, Giovanni Briol, and Antonia Torelli. Married Francesco Rosati. Début at age of seven; prima ballerina, Teatro dell'Apollo, Rome, 1841, performing in Trieste and Parma, 1843, and in partnership with husband Francesco Rosati, La Scala, Milan, 1846; ballerina, Her Majesty's Theatre, London, 1847–49, returning in seasons 1851, 1852, and 1856–58, and then performing at Paris Opéra, 1853–59, and Bolshoi Theatre, St. Petersburg, 1859–62; returned to Paris, eventually retiring in Cannes. Died in Cannes, May 1905.

ROLES

1846   Ballerina in *Pas de quatre* (Perrot; staged M. Taglioni), interpolated in *Le Diable à quatre*, La Scala, Milan
Dancer in *Manon Lescaut* (Casati), La Scala, Milan

1847   Title role (cr) in *Coralia* (P. Taglioni), Her Majesty's Theatre, London
Title role (cr) in *Théa; ou, La Fée aux fleurs* (P. Taglioni), Her Majesty's Theatre, London
Water (cr) in *Les Éléments* (divertissement; Perrot), Her Majesty's Theatre, London
Ballerina (Grahn's role) in *Pas de quatre* (Perrot), Her Majesty's Theatre, London
A Goddess in *Pas de déesses* (Perrot), Her Majesty's Theatre, London
Danseuse (cr) in *Pas de deux* (Perrot), Her Majesty's Theatre, London

1848   Title role (cr) in *Fiorita et la reine des Elfrides* (P. Taglioni), Her Majesty's Theatre, London
Autumn (cr) in *Les Quatre Saisons* (Perrot), Her Majesty's Theatre, London
Grand Quintette Dansante (cr) added to *Esmeralda* (Perrot), Her Majesty's Theatre, London

1849   Title role (cr) in *La Prima Ballerina* (P. Taglioni), Her Majesty's Theatre, London
"La Hussard" (cr) in *Les Plaisirs de l'hiver* (P. Taglioni), Her Majesty's Theatre, London

1851   Ariele in *La Tempesta* (opera; mus. Halévy), Théâtre Italien, Paris

1853   Title role (cr) in *Jovita; ou, Les Boucaniers* (Mazilier), Opéra, Paris

1855   Amalia (cr) in *La Fonti* (Mazilier), Opéra, Paris
Divertissement (cr) in *Saint-Claire* (opera; mus. Ernst, chor. Mazilier), Opéra, Paris

1856   Medora (cr) in *Le Corsaire* (Mazilier), Opéra, Paris

1857   Angela (cr) in *Marco Spada* (Mazilier), Opéra, Paris

Thérèse in *La Somnambule* (Aumer), Opéra, Paris

1859 Title role in *Jovita* (extended version; Saint-Léon after Mazilier), Bolshoi Theatre, St. Petersburg

1860 Title role in *Paquerette* (Saint-Léon), Bolshoi Theatre, St. Petersburg

Title role (cr) in *Graziella* (Saint-Léon), Bolshoi Theatre, St. Petersburg

1861 Title role (cr) in *The Pearl of Seville* (Saint-Léon), Bolshoi Theatre, St. Petersburg

1862 Aspicia (cr) in *Pharaoh's Daughter* (Petipa), Bolshoi Theatre, St. Petersburg

Title role in *Giselle* (Coralli, Perrot), Bolshoi Theatre, St. Petersburg

Tsar-Maiden in *The Little Humpbacked Horse* (Saint-Léon), Bolshoi Theatre, St. Petersburg

PUBLICATIONS

Lumley, Benjamin, *Reminiscences of the Opera*, London, 1864

Pleshcheev, Alexander, *Our Ballet*, St. Petersburg, 1899

Michel, Artur, "*Pas de Quatre, 1845–1945*", *Dance Magazine* (New York), July 1945

Beaumont, Cyril, *Complete Book of Ballets*, revised edition, London, 1951

Guest, Ivor, "Stars of the Second Empire", *Dance and Dancers* (London), December 1953

Guest, Ivor, *The Romantic Ballet in Paris*, London, 1966

Roslavleva, Natalia, *Era of the Russian Ballet*, London, 1966

Kirstein, Lincoln, *Movement and Metaphor: Four Centuries of Ballet*, New York, 1970

Migel, Parmenia, *The Ballerinas*, New York, 1972

Guest, Ivor, *The Ballet of the Second Empire*, revised edition, London, 1974

*   *   *

Carolina Rosati had already gained a reputation throughout Italy when she arrived in London in 1847, and from her first appearance critics singled out those special qualities that would place her at the forefront of her profession, both in London and later in Paris. From Benjamin Lumley, the impresario of Her Majesty's Theatre where Rosati made her début in Paul Taglioni's *Coralia*, we have a vivid description of the young dancer's outstanding qualities: "An easy rounded grace, combined with the requisite brilliancy of execution, constituted the merits of Rosati's style as a *danseuse*; as a pantomimist, she exhibited remarkable talent."

It is this "remarkable talent" that remained a constant throughout her career. From the first it was singled out for praise ("her pantomime [is] vivacious and impassioned", exclaimed contemporary reviews, complimenting "... the remarkable pantomimic powers of Rosati"), and it was this great asset that set her apart from her contemporaries, exciting critics and audiences alike. Ivor Guest has suggested that this talent for the dramatic was "stimulated by one of her teachers ... the celebrated mime Antonia Torelli".

Rosati, however, was not just a talented mime. *The Illustrated London News* pointed out the gracefulness of her movement, and *The Times* noted that "the easy execution of obvious difficulties marks Rosati". As her teacher, Carlo Blasis, pointed out, she was "all that the accomplished dancer, the model artiste, should be, because she is both dancer and mime at the same time", and it was as a dancer that London fêted her.

Rosati certainly must have been a fine dancer to have been entrusted by Perrot with Lucile Grahn's part in his *Pas de*

Carolina Rosati in *Thea; ou, La Fée aux fleurs*, London, 1847

quatre when the choreographer revived it in 1847, along with his *Pas de déesses* in which Rosati also appeared, dancing in both with the great Grisi and Cerrito, and also creating with the two prima ballerinas yet another of the divertissements with which Perrot had enthralled London: *Les Éléments*. And then 1848 saw a new Taglioni ballet, *Fiorita et la reine des Elfrides*, with Rosati's "remarkable pantomimic powers" again remarked upon, and a last Perrot creation for London, *Les Quatre Saisons*, in which Rosati danced Autumn.

Rosati had made her Paris début, as Ariele in Halévy's opera *La Tempesta*, in February 1851, but her début at the Paris Opéra did not come about until 1853. The ballet was *Jovita*, made for her by Mazilier, and it brought the plaudits of the Parisian critics. Gautier vividly described her precise pointe work and waxed lyrical about her dramatic powers, saying, "Her miming is clear, lively, impassioned, and always easily intelligible; she knows how to render her thoughts visible, and what is passing through her mind is at once reflected in her expression." Fiorentino noted her "sprightly vivacity ... the lightness of a bird skimming over the ground". Both critics were reminded of Fanny Elssler.

Rosati's performance in Mazilier's *La Fonti*, a little over a year later, brought new triumphs. Fiorentino, painting a vibrant picture of her death scene, felt her dramatic talent to be superior to Elssler's; and Blasis bestowed his highest praise upon her: "Her soul responds to every impression, which she can translate into the most eloquent and precise gestures."

Another new Mazilier ballet, *Le Corsaire*, followed in 1856.

This excited such praise—both for the production and for its prima ballerina—that the English impresario Lumley was determined to present it at Her Majesty's, despite an increasing lack of interest in the *ballet d'action* on the part of the London public. Once again the critics responded rapturously to Rosati's art. *The Illustrated London News* described her acting as having "an intelligence, grace and truthfulness which cannot be excelled—whose every look and gesture is instinct with meaning". And the *Sunday Times* described her lightness and speed in the great set-piece of the *pas d'eventail* as "the perfection of choreographic art".

Rosati's last original creation in Paris came in a unique partnership with the Opéra's other prima ballerina, Amelia Ferraris. Using the tale of Marco Spada because it boasted two equal roles for his female stars, Mazilier celebrated the best qualities of each dancer in his new ballet. If Rosati lacked Ferraris's elevation and *ballon*, her sense of the dramatic was superior. As Jouvin wrote, "La Rosati dances with her arms, with her body, with her features, with her intellect—in fact, with her all ... La Rosati is a *danseuse d'expression* ...".

Professional jealousy of what she saw as the Opéra's preferential treatment of Ferraris caused Rosati to break her contract with Paris in 1859. Like many of her contemporaries, she hoped for new triumphs on a new stage and set off for St. Petersburg, where she made her Russian début in *Jovita*. She remained in Russia for three years, her last created role being Aspicia in Marius Petipa's *Pharaoh's Daughter* (1862). At this stage in her career, Rosati was perhaps too heavy to produce the lightness and speed of which she had once been capable, but she could still appeal to an audience by the skill of her miming. This was praised, though otherwise she was found disappointing. Perhaps Petipa's style did not easily accommodate those dramatic powers and therefore did not show her off to advantage.

This was a distinguished career, with its triumphs in London, Paris, and St. Petersburg. At a time when the Romantic ballet was waning, Rosati, if not able to revive its glories, infused it with life by means of her remarkable dramatic abilities. Judging by the contemporary descriptions, she would have been at home in much of the late twentieth-century dramatic ballet repertoire.

—Louise Stein

ROSEN, Elsa Marianne von *see* **VON ROSEN, Elsa Marianne**

THE ROYAL BALLET

British ballet company based in London. Origins of company in group directed by Ninette de Valois, performing at the Victoria Theatre (the Old Vic), from 1926, becoming Vic-Wells Ballet, based at Sadler's Wells Theatre, from 1931; performed as Sadler's Wells Ballet, from 1941, becoming official resident company of the Royal Opera House, London, 1946; received Royal Charter, thereafter performing as the Royal Ballet, 1956. Official school associated with company has origins in Ninette de Valois's Academy of Choreographic Art, founded in London, 1926; became Sadler's Wells Ballet School, 1931, with establishment of Lower School (boarding and grammar school with ballet training) at White Lodge, Richmond Park, London,

1955; Upper and Lower Schools joined under title of Royal Ballet School, from 1956. Current artistic director of the Royal Ballet (succeeding Norman Morrice): Anthony Dowell, from 1986.

PUBLICATIONS

Beaumont, Cyril, *The Sadler's Wells Ballet*, revised edition, London, 1947
Noble, Peter (ed.), *British Ballet*, London, c.1950
Clarke, Mary, *The Sadler's Wells Ballet*, London, 1955
Haskell, Arnold (ed.), *Gala Performance*, London, 1955
Swinson, Cyril, *The Royal Ballet Today*, London, 1958
Bland, Alexander, *The Royal Ballet: The First 50 Years*, London, 1981
Vaughan, David, "Royal Ballet at 50: Entering a Golden Era", *Dance Magazine* (New York), June 1981
Sorley Walker, Kathrine, and Woodcock, Sarah, *The Royal Ballet: A Picture History*, revised edition, London, 1986
Sorley Walker, Kathrine, *Ninette de Valois: Idealist Without Illusions*, London, 1987

*   *   *

In laying the foundations of the Royal Ballet, Ninette de Valois had the foresight to begin with a school, thus ensuring a constant supply of dancers trained in the same style. Her sound theatrical understanding led her, in 1926, to ally her school to a repertory theatre, and she chose the Old Vic on London's unfashionable South Bank, run by the redoubtable Lilian Baylis and dedicated to the presentation of opera and Shakespeare for "the people" at low prices. Here, de Valois's pupils gained stage experience in the occasional short ballets and in opera ballets. In 1931 the company, known as the Vic-Wells Ballet, was installed at Sadler's Wells, and began to give regular ballet evenings.

Astutely, de Valois engaged as her ballerina Alicia Markova, often partnered by Anton Dolin, thus giving her young dancers role models to follow. As one of Britain's leading choreographers, de Valois produced most of the ballets, but in 1933 she contracted Frederick Ashton to share in the building of the repertory. In 1934 came the revivals of the great classical ballets *Giselle* and *Swan Lake* by Nicholas Sergeyev, former répétiteur of the St. Petersburg Imperial Ballet. De Valois realized that her dancers needed not only ballets built around their specific talents, but a yardstick against which they and their audience could measure progress; it was to be the combination of the classical style with her own and Ashton's that would build an unmistakably British style. She engaged Constant Lambert as musical director, and, among many talented young designers, Sophie Fedorovitch was to have great influence, especially upon Ashton.

When Markova left in 1935, de Valois determined to develop a successor from within—Margot Fonteyn. Through the late 1930s, Ashton made ballets, including *Apparitions*, *Nocturne*, and *Horoscope*, that exploited Fonteyn's particular qualities, and in the process developed the lyrical expressiveness that was to be a hallmark of the company's style. De Valois, using the supreme theatrical talents of Robert Helpmann in *The Rake's Progress* and *Checkmate*, demanded in *Job* a dramatic truth and interpretation which stretched the dancers as complete artists and not just as technicians. In 1939 Sergeyev produced the full-length *The Sleeping Beauty*, a challenge which the company was barely able to meet, artistically and financially.

The 1930s were spent out of the limelight at Sadler's Wells and touring the provinces. The company built up a faithful

The Vic-Wells Ballet, later to become the Royal Ballet, leaving London for a tour of Holland, 1940. From left to right: June Brae, Mary Honer, Robert Helpmann, Margot Fonteyn, Frederick Ashton, and Ninette de Valois

audience, but its existence was hardly recognized by the vociferous supporters of the Ballets Russes. The war changed everything. The company lost its first generation of male dancers, its orchestra, and its London home. As the Sadler's Wells Ballet, it toured incessantly throughout war-torn Britain, often dancing to two pianos, and replacing its men with boys from the School before they, too, were called up. Large audiences developed for ballet, especially in London for the company's seasons at the New Theatre—and it was now that the company became recognized as the undisputed, if unacknowledged, national ballet. The Fonteyn–Helpmann partnership became immensely popular, as did younger dancers like Beryl Grey and Moira Shearer. In Ashton's absence, Helpmann emerged as a talented choreographer of strong theatrical dance works, notably *Hamlet*.

With peace, the company returned to the Sadler's Wells Theatre, but in 1946 it took up residence at the Royal Opera House, opening with a brilliant new production of *The Sleeping Beauty*, which was to become its signature ballet. The company needed time to adapt to the larger theatre, and to produce works tailored to the larger stage (hence the importance of the classics); Ashton quickly proved himself master of the wider spaces in the luminously beautiful *Symphonic Variations*, using only six dancers. In contrast, in 1948 he produced *Cinderella*, the first full-evening ballet by a British choreographer. In 1949

the company appeared in New York and the huge success, especially of *The Sleeping Beauty* and Margot Fonteyn, established the company's international reputation and led to a series of exhausting, if profitable, North American tours. By the early 1950s de Valois had renounced choreography to devote herself to administration and future planning, but in her place emerged John Cranko, who in 1957 produced *The Prince of the Pagodas*. De Valois also paid her homage to other great contemporary choreographers, inviting Léonide Massine and George Balanchine to stage works.

In 1956, the company received the accolade of a Royal Charter and became the Royal Ballet. Now began its most influential period, as its dancers and choreographers took up posts all over the world, establishing schools and companies following the lines laid down by de Valois for the Royal Ballet.

De Valois's task was now to establish a line of succession; Frederick Ashton became assistant director with, as associate directors, Michael Somes, John Field (running the Touring Company), and John Hart. In 1963, de Valois relinquished the company to them and devoted herself to the School. The 1960s saw the company at its height. There were masterpieces by Ashton, notably *La Fille mal gardée*, *The Two Pigeons*, and *Monotones*, the developing talents of Kenneth MacMillan, and the revival of great works, including Nijinska's *Les Noces* and *Les Biches*. The appearance of the phenomenal Rudolf

Nureyev and his sensational partnership with Fonteyn brought a new popularity to ballet, providing example and challenge to the young dancers, especially the men. The decade also saw the development of the supreme English partnership of Antoinette Sibley and Anthony Dowell, the unique dramatic talents of Lynn Seymour, and the technically brilliant Merle Park.

In 1970 Ashton retired and Kenneth MacMillan became director. It was MacMillan who, stretching and developing the classical vocabulary, transformed the full-evening ballet into human dance dramas such as *Manon* and *Mayerling*. He also acknowledged the modern dance movement that had emerged during the 1960s in inviting Glen Tetley and Hans van Manen to work with the company. But the demands of administrator and creator proved too much, and MacMillan resigned as director in 1977 to concentrate on choreography. For the first time, the Royal Ballet looked outside its ranks for a leader and the choice fell upon Norman Morrice, who had overseen Ballet Rambert's transformation from a classical into a modern dance company. In place of the guest artists who had often appeared during the MacMillan years, Morrice concentrated upon the company's young dancers, but he lacked the mature artists to set the standards. Many performances, particularly of the classics, were lacklustre, and the company entered a difficult stage of transition.

In 1986 Anthony Dowell, brought up in the finest years of the Royal Ballet and the greatest of English male dancers himself, was appointed director. It was hoped that his experience would revitalize the company. He tried to return the classics to their original states, producing *Swan Lake* and bringing in Peter Wright to stage his highly acclaimed *Giselle*. He encouraged his young dancers, but also initiated a policy of foreign guest artists who, it was hoped, would provide a challenge and role models. The danger in that, however, was that too many guests from widely differing schools would devalue the company's unique qualities and diminish its individuality. Particularly disturbing was the substitution of technique for artistry, the seeming neglect of the rich existing repertory, and the lack of staff understanding Ashton's ballets and their importance to the company's particularly English style. It remains to be seen whether the Royal Ballet can maintain its particular identity under the pressure of increasing internationalism in dance style and choreography, and retain its characteristic mix of lyricism and dramatic eloquence in a world where technique and athleticism are valued at the expense of expressiveness.

—Sarah C. Woodcock

THE ROYAL DANISH BALLET

Danish ballet company based in Copenhagen. Origins in late sixteenth-century court spectacle, with dance established in the Lille Gronnegade Theatre, from 1722; dancing company established with the founding of the Royal Theatre, Copenhagen, 1784; both company and school dominated by ballet master August Bournonville, artistic director, 1829–77; first tours as the national ballet company of Denmark, during the 1940s, with company continuing as the official resident ballet company of the Royal Danish Theatre, Copenhagen. Official school associated with the company founded in 1771; still based at the Royal Theatre and known as the Ballet School of the Royal Theatre, Copenhagen. Artistic director (called Royal Ballet Master) of the Royal Danish Ballet: Frank Andersen, from 1985.

PUBLICATIONS

Lemkow, Lasse, "The Royal Danish Ballet", *American-Scandinavian Review* (New York), vol. 29, 1941

Hastings, Baird, "The Royal Danish Ballet in Recent Years", *Dance Magazine* (New York), March 1948

Bronsted, Henning, "The Royal Danish Ballet", *Dancing Times* (London), August 1953

Kragh-Jacobsen, Svend, *The Royal Danish Ballet*, London, 1955

Moore, Lillian, "Royal Danish Ballet Today", *American Scandinavian Review* (New York), September 1960

Fog, Dan, *The Royal Danish Ballet 1760–1958*, Copenhagen, 1961

Clarke, Mary, "Bournonville to Balanchine: A Look at the Royal Danish Ballet", *Dancing Times* (London), June 1963

Haven, Mogens von, *The Royal Danish Ballet*, Copenhagen, 1964

Veale, Tom, "Bournonville Preserved: The Story of Hans Beck", *Dance Magazine* (New York), August 1965

Moore, Lillian, *Bournonville's London Spring*, New York, 1965

Kerensky, Oleg, "The Royal Danish Ballet", *About the House* (London), August 1968

Anders, Georg, and Dyssegaard, Søren (eds.), "The Royal Danish Ballet and Bournonville", centenary edition of *Danish Journal* (Copenhagen), 1979

Fridericia, Allan, "Working Conditions for Dancers in Denmark", in Schønberg, Bent (ed.), *World Ballet and Dance 1989–90*, London, 1989

Guy, John, "Spotlight on Frank Andersen: Ballet Master to the Queen", *Dancing Times* (London), August 1991

* * *

There has always been dance at the Royal Danish Theatre. When the first Danish-language theatre opened in 1722 in Copenhagen, dance was an important part of the entertainment. In 1726 the French dancing master Jean-Baptiste Landé, later instrumental in the founding of the Imperial Ballet in St. Petersburg, was attached to the theatre. In 1771 the school, which to this day is the backbone of the Danish Ballet, was founded in Copenhagen, and the Italian Vincenzo Galeotti came to Copenhagen as artistic director four years later. He was responsible for the first major breakthrough period of the ballet in Denmark and he led the company up until his death in 1816.

Galeotti introduced the *ballet d'action* in which plot is integrated, expressed through (rather than separately from) dance and pantomime. Often he worked from literary inspiration, basing his ballets on the works of Voltaire and Shakespeare. He created the first Nordic ballet, *Lagertha*, which in 1801 ushered Romanticism into the Danish theatre. Of his 49 ballets, only *The Whims of Cupid and the Ballet Master* from 1786 has survived. This, however, is the world's oldest ballet that is still danced according to unbroken tradition.

The Danish Ballet's prominence in the international ballet scene is first and foremost due to August Bournonville, artistic director in Copenhagen from 1829 to 1877. He raised the Danish Ballet to an international standard of ability and at the same time gave it a unique national quality. He staged about 50 ballets. He was a sublime man of theatre and kept up to date with international theatrical developments.

Despite the strong influence of France and French Romanticism, Bournonville's ballets are very Danish, with a firm foundation in the Danish Biedermeier tradition. Bournonville maintained that art should be positive, its purpose to elevate us and make us harmonious human beings. The Bournonville

The Royal Danish Ballet in Bournonville's *Napoli*, c.1989

ballets comprise straightforward and uncomplicated idyllic ballets like *Far from Denmark* (1860) and *The King's Lifeguards on Amager* (1871). He created wonderful works based on folklore, such as the merry Flemish *Kermesse in Bruges* (1851) or the oriental *Abdallah* (1855), in addition to Norwegian, Italian, and Spanish ballets. In *The Valkyrie* (1861) and *The Lay of Thrym* (1868) he created ballets based on Nordic myths; but the major works, fortunately among the dozen or so ballets still performed, are *La Sylphide* (1836), *Napoli* (1842), and *A Folk Tale* (1854). These became treasures of the Danish ballet repertoire, and represent the essence of Bournonville's artistic outlook.

After August Bournonville, the Danish Ballet entered a quiet period. His successors tended the tradition, and first and foremost was Hans Beck, who in the 1890s gathered the practice steps and variations from the ballets in order to form the so-called Bournonville school which was the daily training programme of the Royal Danish Ballet for the next 30 to 40 years. Beck's artistic ideals were the same as Bournonville's, and with Beck's productions of the works of the Master began the so-called Bournonville tradition, with which all subsequent directors have had to wrestle.

The renewal of the Danish Ballet came about in this century. Visits by Mikhail Fokine and George Balanchine provided some inspiration, but it was thanks to Harald Lander that the ballet ceased to stagnate and entered a new and fertile period. At this time, the life nerve of the company was the rich contrast between a modern repertory on the one hand, forever absorbing new works, and a Bournonville repertory on the other hand, showing loyalty to a tradition which must never be abandoned but continually renewed, so that these works can come alive to us.

Together with Valborg Borchsenius, who was the Royal Theatre's leading ballerina around the year 1900, Lander staged eight Bournonville ballets, thus saving them for posterity. His adaptations often featured a special emphasis on dance, and a consequent curtailing of the mime passages which were thought to be too long. And the form the Bournonville ballets took in the 1940s, again based on Hans Beck, was decisive for productions of Bournonville at the Royal Theatre right up to our time, where the Lander–Borchsenius versions are still on the performance listings with smaller or larger revisions by Hans Brenaa and Kirsten Ralov.

Harald Lander was himself a choreographer, and with a repertory built up for the prima ballerina Margot Lander, he made the ballet extremely popular between 1932 and 1951. In fruitful cooperation with the composer Knudåge Riisager and the author Kjeld Abell, Lander understood how to use the ballet as a national rallying point during the years of occupation, and after the war he led an impressive company prepared to meet major international demands, from *Giselle* (1946) and *Aurora's Wedding* (1949) to the challenging works of Léonide Massine, the first guest choreographer (in 1948) of modern international stature. The highlight of Harald Lander's own creative activity was *Études* (1948), which later came to be the foundation for his own international fame. During the Lander period ballets by Nini Theilade, Børge Ralov, and Niels Bjørn Larsen were also significant and further confirmed that the Danish ballet had its own identity.

During the 1950s and 1960s a series of international

choreographers came to work with the Royal Danish Ballet—George Balanchine, Frederick Ashton (who created *Romeo and Juliet* in 1955), Roland Petit, and Birgit Cullberg among others. Niels Bjørn Larsen and for a few years Frank Schaufuss were directors in this period, when the Danish Ballet began regular touring, and Vera Volkova was chief pedagogue, responsible, together with Edite Frandsen, for polishing technical standards so that the dancers also could do the great classical Russian repertoire. A series of fine dancers resulted, including Børge Ralov, Kirsten Ralov, Mona Vangsaae, Margrethe Schanne, Erik Bruhn, Toni Lander, Stanley Williams, Inge Sand, Fredbjørn Bjørnsson, Flemming Flindt, Henning Kronstam, Kirsten Simone, and Niels Kehlet.

In 1966, Flemming Flindt took over the artistic leadership. He introduced modern dance with choreographers like Paul Taylor, Glen Tetley, and Murray Louis, and he himself produced modern works like *The Lesson* and *The Triumph of Death*, inspired by Eugène Ionesco, playwright of the absurd. Henning Kronstam was artistic director from 1978 to 1985 and became responsible for the Bournonville Festival in 1979, which brought international attention to the master one hundred years after his death.

Since 1985, Frank Andersen has been artistic director; brought up in the Bournonville tradition, he has renewed the historic repertoire with reconstructions like *Abdallah*, produced by Toni Lander, Flemming Ryberg, and Bruce Marks in 1986 (first performed in Salt Lake City in 1985), and *The Lay of Thrym*, recreated by Elsa Marianne von Rosen and Allan Fridericia in 1990. The Bournonville ballets and the Romantic tradition are today balanced with a modern repertory with works by choreographers like John Neumeier, Jiří Kylián, Hans van Manen, and Maurice Béjart.

—Erik Aschengreen

THE ROYAL SWEDISH BALLET

Swedish ballet company based in Stockholm. Origins in court ballets of the seventeenth century, with first court ballet in French style arranged by ballet master Antoine de Beaulieu, 1638; first professional company of the Opera, directed by ballet master Louis Gallodier, founded by Gustave III, 1773, and established at newly built Royal Opera House, 1773; company dominated by visiting foreign ballet masters, with first important Swedish director, Anders Selinder, appointed 1833; twentieth-century reputation as classical company distinguished by directorship of Antony Tudor, 1949–51, 1962–63, and Mary Skeaping, 1953–62, and by reconstructions of historical works at Drottningholm Court Theatre. Official school associated with company, the Royal Swedish Ballet School, founded 1773. Current artistic director of the Royal Swedish Ballet: Nils Ake-Häggbom, from 1986.

PUBLICATIONS

Häger, Bengt, "Swedish Ballet", *Dancing Times* (London), 2 parts: April 1947; May 1947
Robert, R., "Royal Swedish Ballet", *American Scandinavian Review* (New York), September 1961
Skeaping, Mary, "Ballet under Three Crowns: Royal Swedish Ballet, 1637–1792", *Dance Perspectives* (New York), Winter 1967
Svedin, Lulli, "Dance in Sweden", *Dance Magazine* (New York), May 1971
Ståhle, Anna Greta, "Mary Skeaping in Sweden", *Dancing Times* (London), April 1984
Engdahl, Horace, *Swedish Ballet and Dance: A Contemporary View* (in English), Stockholm, 1984
Koegler, Horst, "The Northern Heirs of Noverre", *Dance and Dancers* (London), February 1987
Merrett, Sue, "Royal Swedish Ballet", *Dancing Times* (London), October 1992

* * *

"He stamped his foot and out of the ground rose the Swedish Ballet." These are the words of André Levinson, the Russian critic based in Paris, describing the effect of Mikhail Fokine's engagement at the Stockholm Opera House and the subsequent inception of Les Ballets Suédois, the avant-garde group of mostly Swedish dancers who made their name in Paris under Jean Börlin. Levinson implies that the intrinsic condition of Sweden's state ballet was so impoverished that only an outside influence like Fokine could possibly account for the flowering of the wayward, exotic, and short-lived talent that was Jean Börlin; Swedish ballet in 1913 was a totally blank slate for Fokine to write upon.

There is a certain amount of truth in this. The troupe which Fokine discovered in 1913 was in a neglected state, but the same could be said of most opera ballets of Europe at this time, when the influence of the Ballets Russes was only just beginning. What reflected particularly badly on Stockholm was the poor level of its schooling, especially amongst male dancers, in comparison to its near neighbour, the Royal Danish Ballet. Perhaps it is even that proximity which inhibited Stockholm's development.

The long history of Swedish ballet had begun auspiciously under a succession of monarchs who lavished money on it. Court ballet was an import intended to bring French sophistication to the rather primitive northern court, during the minority of Queen Christina. Her expenditure on productions in later years was to scandalize many of her subjects. The Royal Opera, with its large ballet troupe, was founded by her famous successor Gustav III, the "Theatre King". Ironically, both monarchs were politically destabilized by their financial excesses, and the ballet in Sweden would rarely again have such wholehearted royal patronage.

Amongst the foreign ballet masters who continued to dominate the ballet in Stockholm in the late eighteenth and early nineteenth centuries were Antoine Bournonville, Filippo Taglioni, and August Bournonville, who staged a number of works for the company, including *Festival in Albano* (1857).

However, the trend for native-born talent to take itself elsewhere was established early on. Charles-Louis Didelot, born and bred in Stockholm (although the son of a French dancer), only danced at the Royal Opera between 1786 and 1787, and his main work was to be at St. Petersburg. Marie Taglioni, born in Stockholm, returned to perform there only once, in 1841. Per Christian Johansson, a Swedish dancer who regularly went to Copenhagen to study with Bournonville, came back to star in Stockholm only for a few years from 1837, until Taglioni whisked him away to Russia in 1841. These are circumstances to which Russian ballet has remained indebted; but we may only guess at what the outcome might have been if Johansson had remained at home. If his talent as a teacher had only been applied at home, it might have then been possible for the Royal Swedish Ballet to enter the twentieth century with some strong male dancers.

The outbreak of war in 1914 put paid to any plans for Fokine to become director. Standards dropped even lower between the wars, with the usual productions at the Royal Opera House consisting of reworkings of Massine and Fokine ballets adapted to the modest technical accomplishments of the dancers. Added to this was the general trend which favoured European modern dance at the expense of classical ballet.

The facts bear out the Levinson view that Swedish ballet was in an impoverished state in the first part of the early twentieth century. However, Bölin was only the first of a number of highly individual Swedish choreographers, and it has been the normal procedure for all of them to develop their work in companies of their own. Modern dance had a strong beginning in Sweden because ballet was so weak.

Things began to look up with the post-war directors. Antony Tudor set various improvements in motion, giving the company some of his works—*Lilac Garden, Gala Performance*, and his own staging of *Giselle*. Albert and Nina Koslovsky were put in charge of the school and set the training along Vaganova lines.

The turning-point came under Mary Skeaping, who directed the company from 1953 to 1962. Unlike most foreign directors, she gave the Royal Swedish Ballet her full-time attention. The repertoire became that of a national ballet company, with her own productions of *Swan Lake* (1953), *The Sleeping Beauty* (1955), and *Coppélia* playing a central role. For *The Sleeping Beauty*, she was able to offer four different Auroras, one of whom was Elsa Marianne von Rosen, a ballerina of international star quality. The company was also able to inspire a late flowering of Tudor's choreography, when he set *Echoing of Trumpets* on them in 1963.

Skeaping's other innovation was to bring into the repertoire some of the works of Sweden's modern choreographers—Birgit Cullberg's *Miss Julie*, Ivo Cramér's *The Prodigal Son*, and Birgit Åkesson's *Sisyphus*—beginning the fusion of interests between the classical and the modern which is typical of Swedish choreography as a whole.

Subsequent directors have kept the repertoire up to date. For Erik Bruhn in the late 1960s this meant Glen Tetley, Jerome Robbins, and Kenneth MacMillan. In the 1980s this has meant acquiring the works of Jiří Kylián and Hans van Manen. It has been suggested that it is in these works, the product of a modern and classical synthesis, that the Swedish dancers are most at home. Today's repertoire contains representative classics which any international company must perform, such as Natalia Makarova's *La Bayadère*, modern European works such as Kylián's *Stoolgame*, Maurice Béjart's *Le Sacre du Printemps*, and the works of Swedish choreographers, usually brought from outside the company—such as Ulf Gadd's *Gösta Berling's Saga*. While this shows a company of great breadth, there is still the lack of a body of works upon which a completely individual company style can be defined. The Royal Swedish Ballet still awaits its own Ashton.

If there is a national treasury of Swedish ballet, it must reside in the historical ballets, lovingly reconstructed at the eighteenth century court theatre of Drottningholm. The first was *Cupid out of his Humour*, produced by Mary Skeaping in 1956, after a scenario from 1649. While these works have celebrated the richness of the repertoire shared by all European countries in the early centuries of ballet, the artistic development of scholarly study in this way remains uniquely Swedish.

—Larraine Nicholas

ROYAL WINNIPEG BALLET

Canadian ballet company based in Winnipeg. Founded as Winnipeg Ballet Club by Gweneth Lloyd and Betty Farrally, 1938, with first performances as Winnipeg Ballet, 1939; remained semi-professional ensemble until first professional peformances, 1949; royal charter granted, 1953, thereafter performing under name of Royal Winnipeg Ballet; performances suspended as the result of fire damage, 1954–56; continues as resident company of Winnipeg, with tours in Canada and the United States. Official school associated with company, the Royal Winnipeg Ballet School, established in Winnipeg, 1970. Current artistic director of the Royal Winnipeg Ballet (succeeding Henny Jurriens): John Meehan, from 1990.

PUBLICATIONS

Wyman, Max, "The Royal Winnipeg Ballet: 35 Years of Pioneering", *Dance Magazine* (New York), September 1975
Wyman, Max, *The Royal Winnipeg Ballet: The First Forty Years*, New York, 1978
Windreich, Leland, "Out of the Prairies", *Dance and Dancers* (London), September 1982
Wyman, Max, *Dance Canada: An Illustrated History*, Vancouver and Toronto, 1989
Dafoe, Christopher, *Dancing Through Time: The First Fifty Years of Canada's Royal Winnipeg Ballet*, Winnipeg, 1991

*   *   *

The Royal Winnipeg Ballet, Canada's longest surviving dance troupe, has weathered more than a reasonable share of hardship and calamity to win a secure place in the affections of Canadian dance-lovers. Its popularity owes less perhaps to the quality of its diverse repertoire or the technical standards of its dancing than to an infectious good humour which, more than anything else, defines the company's stage personality.

Where the larger National Ballet of Canada, with its opulent productions of the classics, seems concerned to impress its audiences, the Royal Winnipeg Ballet clearly wants to communicate at a direct human level. Its exuberance and energy is distinctly North American.

The company's overt populism can be traced to the attitude of its English-born founders, Gweneth Lloyd and Betty Farrally. Lloyd wanted to rid ballet of what she perceived as its élitist image. As the troupe's principal choreographer for most of its early years, Lloyd carefully devised programmes of short works that balanced humour, romanticism, and drama with the aim of appealing to as many tastes as possible. Lloyd often used local composers and designers and embraced the spirit of her new home by dramatizing the hardship of the immigrant experience, as in *Shadow on the Prairie* (1952), and popular legends of the Wild West, as in *The Shooting of Dan McGrew* (1950).

Few of Lloyd's ballets survived a 1954 fire which devastated the company's home. However, when Arnold Spohr, a former company dancer, emerged as artistic director from the confused and desultory period of reconstruction that followed, he returned to Lloyd's basic populist approach. At the same time Spohr, who was to remain until 1988, continuously sought to develop the company's artistic range by searching out young and talented choreographers such as the Canadians Brian Macdonald and Norbert Vesak, and such foreigners as John Neumeier, Oscar Araiz, and Vicente Nebrada. Although this broadening of the company's choreographic base changed its earlier homespun character, it still provided a platform for such

The Royal Winnipeg Ballet in a production of Rudi van Dantzig's *Romeo and Juliet*

distinctly Canadian works as Macdonald's *The Shining People of Leonard Cohen* (1970) and Vesak's *The Ecstasy of Rita Joe* (1971), about a native Indian's tragic experience in a big-city environment.

The lack of a reliable stable of sound, classically trained dancers prompted Spohr in 1970 to institute a professional-level school under the direction of former principal dancer David Moroni. The result has been a continuous improvement in the dancing that has permitted the company to acquit itself creditably in pure classical work. Its style, particularly noticeable in the womens' arms and backs, clearly reflects Spohr and Moroni's allegiance to the Vaganova school.

When Evelyn Hart won the gold medal at Varna in 1980, Spohr finally had a home-bred ballerina of international repute and the opportunity to stage productions of such full-length classics as *Giselle* (1982) and *Swan Lake* (1987) around her unique talent, using students from the school as necessary to populate the female corps.

Despite this significant shift towards a more traditionally classical repertoire, the Royal Winnipeg Ballet has retained its broad appeal and under Spohr's successors, Henny Jurriens (1988–89) and John Meehan, it continues to mix such overtly popular works as Jacques Lemay's *The Big Top: A Circus Ballet* (1986) and *Anne of Green Gables* (1989), based on the famous children's story, with works by Balanchine, van Manen, and Kylián, among others.

By restricting its size and by offering such a diverse repertoire, the Royal Winnipeg Ballet has managed to remain affordably mobile in a time when many larger companies have costed themselves out of the international touring market. As a result, the company continues to be Canada's most travelled classical ballet troupe.

—Michael Crabb

RUBINSTEIN, Ida

Russian dancer, actress, and company director.   Born Lydiya (Ida) Lvovna Rubinshtein (Rubinstein) in Kharkov (some sources say St. Petersburg), 18 October (5 October old style) 1885. Studied music, dancing, and acting privately; also took private dance lessons with Mikhail Fokine, St. Petersburg, and drama lessons with Yuri Ozarovsky, director of the Aleksandrinsky Theatre, and A.K. Levsky. Married Vladimir Horwitz, c. 1907. Early career as independent actress and producer, staging *Antigone* (in collaboration with designer Léon Bakst) on the private stage, St. Petersburg, 1904, and staging and performing title role in Oscar Wilde's *Salomé* (chor. Fokine), 1908; artist, Diaghilev's Ballets Russes, 1909–11; founder and director of own company, Paris, 1911–13; actress and dancer, various Paris stages, including Paris Opéra, from 1917, reappearing with Diaghilev's Ballets Russes, Paris, 1920; founder and director of second company (with Bronislava Nijinska as choreographer), Paris, 1928–29, 1931, 1934; retired 1935, returning to the stage in 1938 and 1939. Recipient: title of Chevalier of the Légion d'Honneur, Paris, 1934. Died in Vence, southern France, 20 September 1960.

ROLES

1904   Title role in *Antigone* (staged Rubinstein after Sophocles), private stage, St. Petersburg

1908   Title role in *Salomé* (play by Oscar Wilde; chor. Fokine), Mikhailovsky Theatre, St. Petersburg

1909   Title role (cr) in *Cléopâtre* (Fokine), Diaghilev's Ballets Russes, Paris

1910   Zobéïde (cr) in *Schéhérazade* (Fokine), Diaghilev's Ballets Russes, Paris

1911   Saint Sébastien (cr) in *Le Martyre de Saint-Sébastien* (mystical play by d'Annunzio; chor. Fokine), Ida Rubinstein's Company, Paris (revived by Rubinstein at the Opéra, Paris, 1922)

Ida Rubinstein

1912   Title role (cr) in *Hélène de Sparte* (verse-play by Verhaeren), Ida Rubinstein's Company, Paris

Title role in *Salomé* (play by Wilde; chor. Fokine), Ida Rubinstein's Company, Paris

1913   Beggar Woman (cr) in *La Pisanelle* (play by d'Annunzio; chor. Fokine), Ida Rubinstein's Company, Paris

1917   Title role in *Phèdre* (Act IV of play by Racine), Opéra, Paris

1920   Salomé in *La Tragédie de Salomé* (Guerra), Gala Benefit, Opéra, Paris

Muse in *La Nuit de mai* (recitation of poem by de Musset), Opéra, Paris

Cléopâtre in *Antoine et Cléopâtre* (play by Shakespeare translated by Gide), Ida Rubinstein's Company, Paris

Title role (cr) in *Artémis troublée* (Guerra), Opéra, Paris

1923   Title role (cr) in *Phèdre* (play by d'Annunzio), Opéra, Paris

Marguerite Gautier in *La Dame aux camélias* (play after novel by Dumas), Théâtre Sarah Bernhardt, Paris

1924   The Sphinx (cr) in *Le Secret du Sphinx* (play by Rostand), Théâtre Sarah Bernhardt, Paris

Title role (cr) in *Istar* (Staats), Opéra, Paris

1925   Nastasia (cr) in *L'Idiot* (play by Bienstock and Nozière after Dostoyevsky), Théâtre de Vaudeville, Paris

Title role (cr) in *Orphée* (chor. Staats), Opéra, Paris

1927   Title role (cr) in *L'Impératrice aux rochers* (play by Bouhélier), Opéra, Paris

1928   Psyché (cr) in *Les Noces de Psyché et de l'Amour* (Nijinska), Ida Rubinstein's Company, Paris

Muse (cr) in *La Bien Aimée* (Nijinska), Ida Rubinstein's Company, Paris

Principal dancer (cr) in *Boléro* (Nijinska), Ida Rubinstein's Company, Paris

Fairy (cr) in *Le Baiser de la fée* (Nijinska), Ida Rubinstein's Company, Paris

Young Maiden (cr) in *Nocturne* (Nijinska), Ida Rubinstein's Company, Paris

Title role (cr) in *La Princess Cygne* (Nijinska), Ida Rubinstein's Company, Paris

Title role (cr) in *David* (Massine), Ida Rubinstein's Company, Paris

1929   Alcine (cr) in *Les Enchantements d'Alcine* (Massine), Ida Rubinstein's Company, Paris

Principal dancer (cr) in *La Valse* (Nijinska), Ida Rubinstein's Company, Monte Carlo

1931   Title role (cr) in *Amphion* (Massine), Ida Rubinstein's Company, Paris

1934   Title role (cr) in *Diane de Poitiers* (Fokine), Ida Rubinstein's Company, Paris

Title role (cr) in *Sémiramis* (Fokine), Ida Rubinstein's Company, Paris

1935 Clytemnestra in *Les Choéphores* (play by Aeschylus, translated by Claudel), Théâtre de la Monnaie, Brussels

1938 Title role (cr) in *Jeanne d'Arc au bûcher* (scenario by Claudel; mus. Honnegger), Basel

WORKS (as producer)

1904 *Antigone* (tragedy by Sophocles; staged Rubinstein), private stage, St. Petersburg

1908 *Salomé* (play by Oscar Wilde; mus. Glazunov; chor. Fokine; design Bakst), Mikhailovsky Theatre, St. Petersburg

1911 *Le Martyre de Saint-Sébastien* (mystical play by d'Annunzio; mus. Debussy; chor. Fokine), Ida Rubinstein's Company, Théâtre du Châtelet, Paris

1912 *Hélène de Sparte* (verse-play by Verhaeren; mus. Sévérac; design Bakst), Ida Rubinstein's Company, Théâtre du Châtelet, Paris

Salomé (play by Wilde; mus. Schmitt; chor. Fokine; design Bakst), Ida Rubinstein's Company, Théâtre du Châtelet, Paris

1913 *La Pisanelle; ou, La Mort parfumée* (play by d'Annunzio; mus. Pizzetti; chor. Fokine; design Bakst), Ida Rubinstein's Company, Théâtre du Châtelet, Paris

1920 *La Tragédie de Salomé* (ballet after poem by d'Humières; mus. Schmitt; chor. Guerra; design Plot), Gala Benefit, Opéra, Paris

Antoine et Cléopâtre (play by Shakespeare, translated by Gide; mus. Schmitt; design Drésa), Opéra, Paris

1922 *Artémis troublée* (libretto and design Bakst; after classical legend; mus. Paray; chor. Guerra), Opéra, Paris

1923 *Phèdre* (*Fedra*; play by d'Annunzio, translated by Doderet; mus. Pizzetti; design Bakst), Opéra, Paris

1924 *Istar* (mus. d'Indy; chor. Staats; design Bakst), Opéra, Paris

1926 *Phaedra* (new staging; play by d'Annunzio; new music Honegger), Teatro Costanzi, Rome

Orphée (mus. Ducasse; chor. Staats; design Allegri, Golovine), Opéra, Paris

1927 *L'Impératrice aux rochers* (play by Bouhélier; mus. Honegger; design Benois), Opéra, Paris

1928 *Les Noces de Psyché et de l'Amour* (mus. Bach; chor. Nijinska; design Benois), Ida Rubinstein's Company, Opéra, Paris

La Bien Aimée (mus. Schubert, Liszt, orchestrated Milhaud; chor. Nijinska; design Benois), Ida Rubinstein's Company, Opéra, Paris

Bolero (mus. Ravel; chor. Nijinska; design Benois), Ida Rubinstein's Company, Opéra, Paris

Le Baiser de la fée (mus. Stravinsky; chor. Nijinska; design Benois), Ida Rubinstein's Company, Opéra, Paris

Nocturne (mus. Borodin, orchestrated Tcherepnin; chor. Nijinska; design Benois), Ida Rubinstein's Company, Opéra, Paris

La Princess Cygne (mus. Rimsky-Korsakov; chor. Nijinska; design Benois), Ida Rubinstein's Company, Opéra, Paris

David (mus. Sauget; chor. Massine; design Doderet, Benois), Ida Rubinstein's Company, Opéra, Paris

1929 *Les Enchantements d'Alcine* (mus. Auric; chor. Massine; design Benois), Ida Rubinstein's Company, Opéra, Paris

La Valse (mus. Ravel; chor. Nijinska; design Benois), Ida Rubinstein's Company, Théâtre de Monte Carlo, Monte Carlo

1931 *La Valse* (mus. Ravel; new chor. Nijinska; new designs Benois), Ida Rubinstein's Company, Opéra, Paris

Amphion (ballet after poem by Valéry; mus. Honegger; chor. Massine, design Benois), Ida Rubinstein's Company, Opéra, Paris

1934 *Persephone* (melodrama by Gide; mus. Stravinsky; chor. Jooss, design Copeau, Barsacq), Ida Rubinstein's Company, Opéra, Paris

Diane de Poitiers (libretto de Gramont; mus. Ibert; chor. Fokine; design Benois), Ida Rubinstein's Company, Opéra, Paris

Sémiramis (libretto Valéry; mus. Honegger; chor. Fokine; design Benois), Ida Rubinstein's Company, Opéra, Paris

1935 *La Valse* (revised version; mus. Ravel, chor. Fokine), Ida Rubinstein's Company, Opéra, Paris

Bolero (revised version; mus. Ravel; chor. Fokine), Ida Rubinstein's Company, Opéra, Paris

1938 *Jeanne d'Arc au bûcher* (translation by H. Reinhardt; scenario Claudel; mus. Honegger), Basel

PUBLICATIONS

Nozierre, M., *Ida Rubinstein*, Paris, 1926

Schever, L. Franc, "The Rubinstein Ballets", *Dancing Times* (London), June 1934

Grigoriev, Serge, *The Diaghilev Ballet*, translated by Vera Bowen, London, 1953

Dumesnil, René, "Ida Rubinstein", *Journal Musical Français* (Paris), 15 November 1960

De Cossart, Michael, "Ida Rubinstein and Diaghilev: A One-Sided Rivalry", *Dance Research* (London), Autumn 1983

Lester, Keith, "Rubinstein Revisited", *Dance Research* (London), Autumn 1983

Baer, Nancy van Norman, *Bronislava Nijinska: A Dancer's Legacy*, San Francisco, 1986

De Cossart, Michael, *Ida Rubinstein: A Theatrical Life*, Liverpool, 1987

Severn, Margaret, "Dancing with Bronislava Nijinska and Ida Rubinstein", *Dance Chronicle* (New York), vol. 11, no. 3, 1988

Mayer, Charles, "Ida Rubinstein: A 20th-Century Cleopatra", *Dance Research Journal* (New York), Winter 1988

* * *

While the name of Ida Rubinstein has largely been forgotten except by dance historians, this Russian émigrée to the West should be counted among the unique women who contributed to the arts in the early twentieth century, gaining a reputation as a personality for her mystique as a stage performer as well as for her endeavours as a theatrical entrepreneur before and after World War I. Too often dismissed as an egotist or a dilettante, Rubinstein managed none the less to enchant the sophisticated Parisian audiences in her performances of two major roles with the Diaghilev Ballets Russes and in the central roles created for her in the spectacles she produced herself, with the help of the leading artists of the period. As the impresario of her own ballet company and an arts patron, she commissioned a number of important works in an era when women were rarely in charge in the theatre.

Rubinstein was born in Kharkov to a wealthy Jewish family. When her parents died, she was sent to live with her aunt in St. Petersburg, where she was introduced to the prominent artists of the city. Deciding on a theatrical career, although she did not have the requisite training, she made her début in the title role of *Antigone* in St. Petersburg, and then studied acting with the Moscow actor A.K. Levsky and with Yuri Ozarovsky of the Aleksandrinsky Theatre. She engaged Mikhail Fokine of the Imperial Ballet to give her ballet lessons and to provide the choreography for her production of *Salomé*, in which she took the leading role. *Salomé*, with music by Aleksandr Glazunov and costumes by Léon Bakst, was performed privately in November 1908 at the Mikhailovsky Theatre in St. Petersburg, and then (as *Dance of Salomé*) on a mixed programme on December 20 at the Petersburg Conservatory. Her *Salomé* (which created a scandal because Rubinstein as Salomé removed most of her veils) marked the first of Rubinstein's many collaborations with Bakst, who remained her friend until his death.

Rubinstein's next public appearance, as Cléopâtre in Fokine's ballet of the same name, created no less of a sensation. In her début role with the Diaghilev Ballets Russes in its first season in Paris, she made her first entrance as Cléopâtre in an ebony and gold coffin carried by six Nubian slaves, who lifted her out and unwrapped a dozen layers of swathing as she stood before the audience. She was hardly less exotic, in persona or character, in her next role with the company in the following year as Zobéïde, the favourite wife of the Sultan, in the Bakst-Fokine *Schéhérazade*. With her thin-limbed beauty, and indefinable stage presence, Rubinstein made no less of an impression than did the other stars of the Diaghilev troupe.

After 1911, Rubinstein began several decades of commissioning works that would feature her as central figure. Like Diaghilev, she chose a team of noted artists for each project, funded by her personal fortune. *Le Martyre de Saint-Sébastien* had its premiere at the Théâtre du Châtelet in 1911, causing a sensation because the Church banned the work. As the pale, wispy, androgynous Saint Sebastien, Rubinstein created another unforgettable character. In 1912, Rubinstein appeared in *Hélène de Sparte* by Emile Verhaeren, with music by Deodat de Severac and décors by Bakst, followed in 1913 by d'Annunzio's *La Pisanelle; ou, La Mort parfumée*.

Rubinstein was as adroit as Diaghilev in cultivating press notice, as often about her extravagant daily costumes as about her roles on stage. Her apparent romances, including the sizzling details of her relationships with d'Annunzio, Romaine Brooks, and Walter Guinness, also served to keep her in the public eye. After the war, Rubinstein staged a number of productions for the Paris Opéra, appeared as an actress in several plays, including in her adored friend Sarah Bernhardt's role in *La Dame aux camélias*, and then in 1928 formed her own ballet company. In the two seasons in which it flourished, Rubinstein commissioned a number of important works by the leading artists of the day: *Les Noces de Psyché et de l'Amour*, *La Bien Aimée*, and most notably *Boléro*. Other important works included Igor Stravinsky's *La Baiser de la feé*, and Ravel's *La Valse*, both staged by Nijinska, *David* and *Les Enchantements d'Alcine*, choreographed by Massine. Among the dancers in her company were Ludmilla Schollar, Anatole Vilzak, and two young men of promise, Frederick Ashton and David Lichine.

Two years later, in 1931, Rubinstein appeared in *Amphion*, followed in 1934 by a season of three works, *Persephone*, *Diane de Poitiers*, and *Sémiramis*. Her last stage appearance was as Joan of Arc in a production of the Claudel-Honegger play, *Jeanne d'Arc au bûcher*, presented in concert in Basel in 1938 and in Paris in 1939. She lived in London during World War II, then moved to the south of France, where she bought a villa outside the town of Vence. Her obituary in *The New York Times* did not appear until a month after her death in 1960. Rubinstein's memory lives on in several stunning photographs of her from the ballets of the Diaghilev Ballets Russes and anecdotes of her friendships with Bakst and d'Annunzio, but she must also be credited with stimulating some significant works of art that remain to our day.

—Iris M. Fanger

RUZIMATOV, Farukh

Uzbek/Soviet dancer. Born Farukh Sadullaevich Ruzimatov in Tashkent, 26 June 1963. Studied at the Leningrad Choreographic (Vaganova) School; pupil of Gennady Selyutsky, V. Ivanov; graduated in 1981. Dancer, soon becoming soloist, Kirov Ballet, from 1981; guest principal dancer, American Ballet Theatre, 1990, performing in Washington, D.C., New York, and London; returned to Leningrad, autumn 1990: principal dancer, Kirov Ballet, from 1990. Recipient: Silver Medal, International Ballet Competition, Varna, 1983; Special Diploma, Paris Academy of Dance, International Ballet Competition, Paris, 1984; title of Honoured Artist of Tadzhik SSR, 1988.

ROLES

1982   Peasant pas de deux in *Giselle* (Petipa after Coralli, Perrot), Kirov Ballet, Leningrad

1984   Basil in *Don Quixote* (Gorsky after Petipa), Kirov Ballet, Leningrad

        The Youth in *Chopiniana* (Fokine), Kirov Ballet, Leningrad

        The Youth (cr) in *Asiyat* (Vinogradov), Kirov Ballet, Leningrad

1985   Tariel (cr) in *The Knight in Tigerskin* (Vinogradov), Kirov Ballet, Leningrad

        Soloist in *Paquita* (Gusev after Petipa), Kirov Ballet, Leningrad

1986   Albrecht in *Giselle* (Petipa after Coralli, Perrot), Kirov Ballet, Leningrad

        James in *La Sylphide* (von Rosen after Bournonville), Kirov Ballet, Leningrad

1987   Ali (cr) in *Le Corsaire* (new production; Gusev after Petipa), Kirov Ballet, Leningrad

        Adam (cr) in *Adam and Eve* (Béjart), Kirov Ballet, Leningrad

        Prince Siegfried in *Swan Lake* (Sergeyev after Petipa, Ivanov), Kirov Ballet, Leningrad

        Principal dancer in *Bakhti* (Béjart), Kirov Ballet, Leningrad

1988   Christ (cr) in *A Rehearsal* (Fodor), Kirov Ballet, Leningrad

1989   Prince Désiré in *The Sleeping Beauty* (Sergeyev after Petipa), Kirov Ballet, Leningrad

        Principal dancer in *Adagio* (Eifman), Kirov Ballet, Leningrad

        Principal dancer in *Theme and Variations* (Balanchine, staged F. Russell), Kirov Ballet, Leningrad

        Title role in *Le Spectre de la rose* (Fokine), Creative Evening for Ruzimatov, Kirov Ballet, Leningrad

        Soloist (cr) in *The Wandering* (Timurshin), Creative Evening for Ruzimatov, Kirov Ballet, Leningrad

Farukh Ruzimatov as Basil in *Don Quixote*

Grand Pas from *Don Quixote* (Gorsky), Creative Evening for Ruzimatov, Kirov Ballet, Leningrad
1990   Albrecht in *Giselle* (Baryshnikov after Petipa, Coralli, Perrot), American Ballet Theatre, Washington D.C.
Solor in "The Kingdom of the Shades" from *La Bayadère* (Makarova after Petipa, Ponomarev, Chabukiani), American Ballet Theatre, Washington, D.C.
Romeo in *Romeo and Juliet* (MacMillan), American Ballet Theatre, New York
Soloist in *Violin Concerto* (Balanchine), American Ballet Theatre, New York
The Peruvian in *Gaité Parisienne* (Massine, staged Lorca Massine), American Ballet Theatre, New York
Prince in *The Sleeping Beauty* (MacMillan after Petipa), American Ballet Theatre, New York
1991   Soloist in *Choreographic Compositions* (Tagunov), Creative Evening for Ruzimatov, Kirov Ballet, Leningrad

Other roles include: for the Kirov Ballet—Indian Dance in *La Bayadère* (Petipa, Ponomarev, Chabukiani), Hungarian Dance in *Swan Lake* (Sergeyev after Petipa, Ivanov), Gypsy Dance in *Don Quixote* (Gorsky after Petipa).

PUBLICATIONS

By Ruzimatov:
Interview in Rozanova, Olga, "Farouk Came Back", *Sovetsky Balet* (Moscow), October 1990

About Ruzimatov:
Shmyrova, T., "Farukh Ruzimatov", *Sovetsky Balet* (Moscow), no. 5, 1985
Lidova, Irène, "Farukh Ruzimatov", *Balletoggi* (Milan), May 1988
Tobias, Tobi, "Flying Visit", *New York* (New York), 13 June 1988
Willis, Margaret, "Kiroviana: The Glasnost Difference", *Dance Magazine* (New York), July 1989
Garafola, Lynn, "Farouk Ruzimatov: Hero in a Golden Cage", *Dance Magazine* (New York), February 1990
Barnes, Clive, "Stars of American Ballet Theatre", *Dance and Dancers* (London), July 1990

* * *

A striking, often flamboyant dancer of the Kirov Ballet, Farukh Ruzimatov had already been noticed when he was a student at the Leningrad Choreographic School, impressing his teachers with his talent for both classical and character dance. Unlike many children, he worked hard and showed a determination to master all of the intricacies of classical technique and choreography. In this he was helped by his tutor Gennady Selyutsky, a talented teacher who shared the young Ruzimatov's aspirations.

When Ruzimatov joined the Kirov theatre, he soon began receiving offers of solo parts, which he prepared with enthusiasm, surprising the public every time with his technical prowess, often in extremely difficult combinations. He was lucky in retaining his old school instructor Selyutsky as his coach, so that the process of tuition continued in the new environment of the professional ballet company.

The name of Farukh Ruzimatov is now universally known in the world of ballet. Since the first performance of the youthful Leningrad dancer at the Paris competition, where he won the Special Diploma of the Dance Academy, his name has never disappeared from the pages of the Western press. At the final concert of the competition, Ruzimatov was the only participant whom the sophisticated Parisians asked to dance two encores (the variation from *Le Corsaire*). Influential French critics called him "the best dancer of the competition", and "the true diamond in the glittering crown of the contest".

Ruzimatov's first leading role, that of the barber Basil in *Don Quixote*, determined his future as a performer of all of the major male roles. Ruzimatov's performance of Basil was incomparable, and it overwhelmed the experienced Leningrad public with its daring and dazzling technique, including multiple turns that were both elegant and forceful. His dance glittered and sparkled. One combination merged into another, the pace grew faster and faster—and still the dancer's movements remained well-rounded, beautiful, and stylish.

Later Ruzimatov started dancing Solor in *La Bayadère*, a part which was consonant with his romantic temperament and dancing style. His performance of this role reflects the minutest changes of Solor's emotional life, the very throbbing impatience of his heart. His flowing movements are in harmony with the languid adagio of the first act, while his skill as a partner enables him to perform the extremely difficult duets in the second and third acts without any difficulty.

Ruzimatov's individuality reveals itself in a striking way in new ballets—as for example, in Oleg Vinogradov's *The Knight in Tigerskin*. The role of Tariel has become one of Ruzimatov's highest achievements. We see a youthful hero of exquisite beauty, as if descending to us straight from Shota Rustaveli's pages. His elaborate dance style, full of ornament, is itself like a poetic line. The message of Ruzimatov in this ballet is that of spiritual valour, the inseparability of love and self-sacrifice.

Ruzimatov's fifth season with the company was marked by his performance of Albrecht in *Giselle*. This character has been in perpetual change ever since, Ruzimatov finding in it some new aspect each time he performs. His interpretation is appealing both because of its artistic independence, and because of the obvious sincerity and seriousness of his approach. Exquisite arabesques and attitudes, with their exaggerated lines adding an emotional colouring to the movement, are interwoven with the choreographic compositions of the elegiac second act of *Giselle*. We observe the eye-opening experience of a Fortune's darling who only understands the true value and beauty of deep feeling at the cost of a great loss: such is the main underlying idea of Ruzimatov's interpretation.

Ruzimatov interprets the traditional parts of the classical repertoire through the eyes of his generation, giving them a modern touch. The young dancer breathes a new life into the classical masterpieces by establishing anew and developing the traditions of ballet which he worships. At the same time, he does not follow the recognized patterns slavishly but on the contrary, introduces his own understanding of a character according to his personal priorities. (This has not always pleased the critics, particularly in the West, where despite his ability to draw "stadium cheers" out of an audience he has been accused of unnecessary stylization and mannerism.)

Ruzimatov is obsessed with dancing, and he does not conceal his concentration on technical perfection—indeed, he keeps inventing new, ever more complex movements and combinations, which he practises tirelessly. This is how he achieves the freedom and confidence which are the basis of his artistic expression. Ruzimatov is a dancer first and foremost; he dances every single moment he spends on the stage, and in fact he finds it easier to perform an intricate choreographic exercise than to create a pause. Ruzimatov is still very young, and not all facets of his individuality have fully expressed themselves;

many powerful impulses in him have not so far taken shape. He needs more new roles, and this means new and varied choreographers. After a short and sadly unsuccessful season with American Ballet Theatre in New York, Ruzimatov has returned to his home company in Leningrad/St. Petersburg, and it will be interesting to see where his career takes him in the 1990s.

—Igor Stupnikov

RYOM, Heidi

Danish dancer. Born in Copenhagen, 26 August 1955. Studied at the Royal Danish Ballet School, Copenhagen, from 1964. Dancer, Royal Danish Ballet, from 1974, becoming solo dancer (principal), from 1982, also touring internationally with the company; also guest ballerina, in partnership with Julio Bocca, on international concert tours. Recipient: Tagea Brandt Award, Denmark, 1990.

ROLES

1977   Dancer in *Septet Extra* (van Manen), Royal Danish Ballet, Copenhagen

1978   Dancer in *The Toreador* (Flindt), Royal Danish Ballet, Copenhagen

1979   Principal dancer in *Divertimento No. 15* (Balanchine), Royal Danish Ballet, Copenhagen
Principal dancer in *La Ventana* (Bournonville), Royal Danish Ballet, Copenhagen
Elisa in *Konservatoriet* (Bournonville), Royal Danish Ballet, Copenhagen
Pas de deux from *Flower Festival at Genzano* (Bournonville), Royal Danish Ballet, Copenhagen

1980   Principal dancer in *William Tell* (opera; mus. Rossini, chor. Bournonville), Royal Danish Ballet, Copenhagen
Principal dancer in *Songs without Words* (van Manen), Royal Danish Ballet, Copenhagen
Helena in *A Midsummer Night's Dream* (Neumeier), Royal Danish Ballet, Copenhagen

1981   Swanilda in *Coppélia* (Lander after Saint-Léon), Royal Danish Ballet, Copenhagen
Principal dancer in *Memoria* (Ailey), Royal Danish Ballet, Copenhagen

1982   Principal dancer in *Concerto Barocco* (Balanchine), Royal Danish Ballet, Copenhagen
Hilda in *A Folk Tale* (Bournonville), Royal Danish Ballet, Copenhagen

1983   Princess in *The Nutcracker* (Flindt), Royal Danish Ballet, Copenhagen
Principal dancer in *Symphony in C* (Balanchine), Royal Danish Ballet, Copenhagen
Sanguinic in *The Four Temperaments* (Balanchine), Royal Danish Ballet, Copenhagen

1984   Principal dancer in *Études* (Lander), Royal Danish Ballet, Copenhagen
Principal dancer in *The Leaves are Fading* (Tudor), Royal Danish Ballet, Copenhagen

1985   Principal dancer in *Capriccio* (*Rubies* from *Jewels*; Balanchine), Royal Danish Ballet, Copenhagen

1986   Principal dancer in *The River* (Ailey), Royal Danish Ballet, Copenhagen

Principal dancer in *Troubadour Intermezzo*, Royal Danish Ballet, Copenhagen
Irma in *Abdallah* (Bournonville), Royal Danish Ballet, Copenhagen

1987   Juliet in *Romeo and Juliet* (Neumeier), Royal Danish Ballet, Copenhagen
Title role in *Elvira Madigan* (North), Royal Danish Ballet, Copenhagen

1988   Teresina in *Napoli* (Bournonville), Royal Danish Ballet, Copenhagen
Kitri in *Don Quixote* (Gorsky after Petipa), Royal Danish Ballet, Copenhagen
Ballerina in *Diana and Acteon* Pas de deux (from *Esmeralda*; Vaganova after Petipa), Royal Danish Ballet, Copenhagen

1989   Terpsichore in *Apollo* (Balanchine), Royal Danish Ballet, Copenhagen
Tatiana in *Onegin* (Cranko), Royal Danish Ballet, Copenhagen
Ali in *Moon Reindeer* (Cullberg), Royal Danish Ballet, Copenhagen
Principal dancer in *Fête galante* (Andersen), Royal Danish Ballet, Copenhagen

1990   Ballerina in *Tchaikovsky Pas de deux* (Balanchine), Royal Danish Ballet, Copenhagen
Sigyn in *The Lay of Thrym* (Bournonville), Royal Danish Ballet, Copenhagen
Title role in *Giselle* (Petipa after Coralli, Perrot), Royal Danish Ballet, Copenhagen
Principal dancer in *Concerto* (MacMillan), Royal Danish Ballet, Copenhagen
Principal dancer in *Pavane* (MacMillan), Royal Danish Ballet, Copenhagen
Principal dancer (lead couple) in *Theme and Variations* (Balanchine), Royal Danish Ballet, Copenhagen
Principal dancer in *Serait-ce la mort?* (Béjart), Royal Danish Ballet, Copenhagen
Principal dancer (cr) in *Birthday Dances* (Neumeier), Gala for Queen Margrethe II, Copenhagen

1991   Title role in *La Sylphide* (Bournonville), Royal Danish Ballet, Copenhagen

1992   Principal dancer in *Allegro Brillante* (Balanchine), Royal Danish Ballet, Copenhagen

*   *   *

Heidi Ryom was admitted to Copenhagen's Royal Theatre Ballet School in 1964, and became a member of the ballet company in 1974. In 1982, she was promoted to the rank of principal dancer. Her generation of dancers included many outstanding talents, and there were often more obvious choices for the leading roles than Ryom. Ryom's career therefore began with the more soubrette-like roles, which seemed more in her line, and she danced such roles as Swanilda in *Coppélia*, Helena in *A Midsummer Night's Dream*, and various lighthearted characters the Bournonville repertoire. But by persistently working on technical perfection, and then adding a mature artistry to the dramatic expression of her roles, Ryom worked her way to the top, and is today one of the leading principal dancers at the Royal Danish Ballet.

Ryom is a small and somewhat fragile dancer, with a technique characterized by speed and flexibility. Her dancing has been described as "sophisticated, poetic and strong". Since joining the company, Ryom has danced in most of the Bournonville repertory, including Hilda in *A Folk Tale*, Irma in *Abdallah*, and Teresina in *Napoli*. But she has also excelled in modern choreography, such as Balanchine's *Capriccio* (*Rubies* from *Jewels*) in which she was able to display her technical superiority.

It was in the role of Juliet in Neumeier's *Romeo and Juliet*, in 1987, that the range of Ryom's talent was fully recognized. Henning Kronstam was a great inspiration for her in the process of developing artistic expression and a dramatic approach to her interpretation of Juliet, which she has since danced with great success, particularly with Nikolaj Hübbe.

Since then Ryom has many times proven herself a first-class ballerina, with a special understanding of the classical female roles in ballet, such as Tatiana in *Onegin*—in which her interpretation has been described as intense and "detailed", showing the young innocent girl growing into a woman with exaggerated passions—as Kitri in *Don Quixote*, *Giselle*, and most recently, as Bournonville's Sylphide.

When American ballet star Julio Bocca visited the Royal Danish Ballet in 1988, he was immediately captivated by Ryom's charm and technique, and together they formed a partnership which brought out all the best qualities of Ryom's performance style. "She—the most modest of the Danish prima ballerinas—showed this evening that she could perform like a star. ... From the first *jétés passés* her dance had an extra boldness. Never has she been more witty and teasing in her pointe-work", wrote a leading Danish ballet critic. Bocca has since invited Ryom to partner him abroad, with great success for both.

In 1990 Heidi Ryom won the Tagea Brandt Award, which is given each year to a small number of outstanding Danish women in various professions. The citation for the award described Ryom's career as a line of artistic development in which she has shown ever more convincingly her ability to portray complicated psychological states of mind.

—Anne McClymont

LE SACRE DU PRINTEMPS
(*The Rite of Spring*)

Choreography: Vaslav Nijinsky
Music: Igor Stravinsky
Design: Nicholas Roerich (scenery and costumes)
Libretto: Igor Stravinsky and Nicholas Roerich
First Production: Diaghilev's Ballets Russes, Théâtre des Champs-Elysées, Paris, 29 May 1913
Principal Dancers: Marie Piltz (The Chosen Maiden)

Other productions include: Diaghilev's Ballets Russes (new version; chor. Léonide Massine), with Lydia Sokolova (The Chosen One); Paris, 15 December 1920. Philadelphia Academy of Music (new version; chor. Massine), with Martha Graham (The Chosen One); Philadelphia, 11 April 1930. Teatro Colón (new version; chor. Boris Romanov); Buenos Aires, 1932. Lester Horton Dance Group (new version; chor. Lester Horton); Los Angeles, 5 August 1937. Rome Opera (new version; chor. Aurel Milloss, design Nicola Benois), with Attilia Radice (The Chosen One); Rome, 27 March 1941. German Opera on the Rhine (new version; chor. Yvonne Georgi); Düsseldorf, 29 October 1953. Royal Swedish Ballet (restaged Massine); Stockholm, 30 May 1956 (also staged by Massine for La Scala, Milan, 1962). Berlin Municipal Opera (new version; chor. Mary Wigman, design Wilhelm Reinking); Berlin, 24 September 1957. Ballet du XXe Siècle (new version; chor. Maurice Béjart, design Pierre Caille); Brussels, 7 December 1959 (staged Paris Opéra, 1965). Warsaw Opera (new version; chor. Alfred Rodrigues); Warsaw, 1962. Royal Ballet (new version; chor. Kenneth MacMillan, design Sydney Nolan), as *Rite of Spring*, with Monica Mason (The Chosen Maiden); London, 3 May 1962. Bolshoi Ballet (new version; chor. Vladimir Vasiliev, Natalia Kasatkina), with Natalia Kasatkina; Moscow, 28 June 1965. German Opera on the Rhine (new version; chor. Erich Walter); Düsseldorf, 19 April 1970. Frankfurt Ballet (new version; chor. John Neumeier), as *Le Sacre*; Frankfurt, 25 November 1972. La Scala (new version; chor. John Taras, design Marino Marini), with Natalia Makarova (The Chosen One); Milan, 9 December 1972. Dutch National Ballet (new version; chor. Hans van Manen); Amsterdam, 16 June 1974. Bavarian State Opera Ballet (new version; chor. Glen Tetley, design Nadine Baylis); Munich, 17 April 1974 (staged American Ballet Theatre, New York, 1976). Harkness Ballet (new version; chor. Brian Macdonald), as *The Lottery*; New York, 1974. Wuppertal Dance Theatre (new version; chor. Pina Bausch); Wuppertal, 3 December 1975. German Opera Ballet (new version; chor. Valery Panov); Berlin, 5 November 1977. Paul Taylor Dance Company (new version; chor. Paul Taylor, to piano adaptation of score, design John Rawlings); New York, 15 April 1980. Ballet Rambert (new version; chor. Richard Alston, to piano adaptation of score); London, 6 March 1981. Martha Graham Dance Company (new version; chor. Martha Graham); New York, 28 February 1984. Joffrey Ballet (reconstruction: staged Millicent Hodson after Nijinsky, design Kenneth Archer after Roerich); Los Angeles, 30 September 1987.

PUBLICATIONS

Nijinsky, Vaslav, *The Diaries of Vaslav Nijinsky*, edited by Romola Nijinsky, London, 1933

Howe, Martin, "The Ballets of Nijinsky: A Summary", *Ballet* (London), May 1947

Beaumont, Cyril, *Complete Book of Ballets*, revised edition, London, 1951

Grigoriev, Serge, *The Diaghilev Ballet*, translated by Vera Bowen, London, 1953

Clarke, Mary, "MacMillan's *Rite of Spring*", *Dancing Times* (London), June 1962

Craft, R. (ed.), *The Rite of Spring: Sketches 1911–1913*, London and New York, 1969

Goodwin, Noël, "New Light on *Rite*", *Dance and Dancers* (London), July 1970

Kirstein, Lincoln, *Movement and Metaphor*, New York, 1970

Buckle, Richard, *Nijinsky*, London, 1971; revised edition, Harmondsworth, 1980

Krasovskaya, Vera, *Nijinsky*, Leningrad, 1974; translated by John E. Bowlt, New York, 1979

Rivière, Jacques, "*Le Sacre du Printemps*", in Copeland, Roger, and Cohen, Marshall (eds.), *What Is Dance?*, New York, 1983

"A Ballet that Changed History", *Dance and Dancers* (London), December 1984

Hodson, Millicent, "Nijinsky's Choreographic Method: Visual Sources from Roerich for *Le Sacre du printemps*", *Dance Research Journal* (New York), Winter 1986–87

Acocella, Joan, "In Search of *Sacre*", *Dance Magazine* (New York), November 1987

Berg, Shelley, *Le Sacre du Printemps: Seven Productions from Nijinsky to Martha Graham*, Ann Arbor, Michigan, 1988

Garafola, Lynn, *Diaghilev's Ballets Russes*, New York, 1989

* * *

The first performance of Vaslav Nijinsky's *Le Sacre du printemps* is almost as legendary as the work itself. The curtain had scarcely gone up on that May evening in 1913 at Paris's Théâtre des Champs-Elysées when the booing and catcalls started, drowning out the orchestra so the dancers could barely hear Igor Stravinsky's score. A full-scale riot broke out in the audience, with the conservative balletomanes shouting insults and the progressive intellectuals voicing their support of the

Le Sacre du printemps: "The Adolescents", Diaghilev's Ballets Russes, Paris, 1913

ballet. People threw fruit at the stage. A lady in the audience assaulted Jean Cocteau with a hat pin. On stage, Nijinsky stood in the wings calling out the counts while Serge Diaghilev—who had masterminded the collaboration for his Ballets Russes—held his head in his hands. At the end of the performance, the police were called in.

The reason for the uproar was Nijinsky's anti-balletic choreography and Stravinsky's complex, rhythmic score of clashing harmonies. The scenario involves a barbaric sacrifice. A virgin—the Chosen One—assists and leads the celebration of her own sacrifice and then dances herself to death. No one had ever seen or heard anything quite like it. Historically speaking, it was the most significant declaration of Modernism to appear up to that time in twentieth-century dance and music.

The basis of the ballet is Stravinsky's libretto, which describes an ancient Slavonic ritual. A 300-year-old woman consecrates the earth with a solemn kiss. Ritualistic dances confirm the Chosen One. The ballet climaxes with the "Sacrificial Dance" of the Chosen One. Stravinsky composed the driving, polyrhythmic score to evoke "the mystery and surge of the creative power of spring . . . like the whole earth cracking". Nijinsky, then 23 years old, described his dance as "the soul of nature expressed by movement. . . . It is the life of the stones and the trees . . . a thing of concrete masses, not of individual effects."

Nijinsky interpreted every note of the score. He mirrored the varying rhythms with small groups of celebrants stamping and shuffling in tight circles. In the final sacrifical dance, the Chosen One jumped repeatedly, straight up in the air, feet pulled together, and then landed heavily, giving in to the pull of gravity. The music pounded incessantly in accompaniment.

With *Le Sacre*, Nijinsky broke completely with classical ballet. Ballet had always aimed to conquer the air, emphasizing long lines, lyricism, and illusion. For *Le Sacre*, Nijinsky directed his dancers to move with their weight directed into the ground, to turn their feet inwards, and to stunt their arms by either cupping their hands or making fists. In this, he was inspired partly by Russian folk dances (his father was an accomplished Russian character dancer).

The dance was choreographed at the height of the Cubist movement in the visual arts, and many have said that Nijinsky unknowingly applied the principals of Cubism to his art. Just as Picasso did in his paintings, Nijinsky deliberately reordered and objectified the human figure. Facial expressions were non-existent. The dancers had to contort their bodies into unnatural poses—for instance, angling sideways and pitching their shoulders on a diagonal, or drawing their elbows back past their chests. Dancers from both the original 1913 production and the Joffrey Ballet's 1987 reconstruction complained of sore muscles they had never used before.

Though perhaps he did not realize it, Nijinsky was exploring "plastique", the form and line the body makes in space. According to Jacques Rivière, who attended the work's premiere, this was revolutionary, because for the first time dance was being stripped of all artifice to a point where the movement—however raw, crude, and even ugly—captured emotions in their purest forms. Nijinsky was reacting against the tradition of Mikhail Fokine, Diaghilev's former star choreographer, who revelled in the grace of formal ballet technique.

It should be noted that the impact of Stravinsky's magnificent score and the ballet's universal theme of the cycle of life, death, and rebirth has gone far beyond 1913. Over 20 choreographers—from Léonide Massine in 1929 to Martha Graham in 1984—have produced their own *Sacre du printemps*. Many have come up with a scenario similar to Nijinsky's, evoking a mass fertility rite (Maurice Béjart), an American Indian-influenced spring ritual (Lester Horton), and an Australian–African sacrificial rite (Kenneth MacMillan).

But others have taken a completely different approach.

Brian Macdonald based his dance on American author Shirley Jackson's short story "The Lottery". Bolshoi Ballet dancers Natalia Kasatkina and Vladimir Vasiliev threw in a love interest for the Chosen One, shifting the emphasis of the ballet from the ritualistic to the dramatic. Paul Taylor studied Nijinsky's original *Sacre*, and, like Nijinsky, employed a stylized movement vocabulary. But unlike Nijinsky's, Taylor's work is a product of twentieth-century dance developments. It is a combination dance company rehearsal/1930s cops-and-robbers melodrama, blending elements of vaudeville and cinema.

—Jody Leader

SADLER'S WELLS BALLET *see* **ROYAL BALLET**

SADLER'S WELLS ROYAL BALLET *see* **BIRMINGHAM ROYAL BALLET**

SAINT-LÉON, Arthur

French dancer, choreographer, teacher, and composer. Born Charles-Victor-Arthur Michel in Paris, 17 September 1821. Studied with father, Léon Michel (ballet master in Tuscany and Stuttgart), and later with Monsieur Albert (François Decombe), Paris, from 1837. Married dancer Fanny Cerrito, 1845 (sep. 1851). Début as violinist (at age of thirteen), Stockholm, 1834; début as dancer in Munich, 1835, performing thereafter throughout Europe, with début as premier danseur de demi-caractère, Brussels, 1838; first performance with Fanny Cerrito, Vienna, 1841; leading dancer in Italy, including at Teatro Regio, Turin, 1841–46, and La Scala, Milan, 1842; London début in 1843, continuing as leading dancer, Her Majesty's Theatre, 1843–48; performer in partnership with Cerrito on British tour, 1844, and in leading theatres in Rome, Venice, Florence, Turin, Hamburg, Berlin, Paris, Stockholm, and Madrid, until 1851; choreographer, staging first ballet in Rome, 1843, going on to stage own ballets (some in collaboration with Cerrito) in all major European cities except Milan; début as choreographer at Paris Opéra, 1847, staging several more ballets for Cerrito until 1851; also choreographer, Théâtre Lyrique, Paris, 1853, and, at Teatro de São Carlos, Lisbon, 1854–56; ballet master, Imperial Theatres, St. Petersburg (succeeding Perrot), 1859–69, returning to Paris Opéra, 1863–70, staging last and most successful work, *Coppélia*, in 1870; also teacher, including for Fanny Cerrito, and for classe de perfectionnement, Paris Opéra, 1851; writer of treatise on dance notation, 1852; composer of music for several of his own ballets. Died in Paris, 2 September, 1870.

ROLES

1835 Pas de deux in *Die Reisende Ballet-Gesellschaft* (Schneider), Munich

1838 Pas in *Robert le Diable* (opera; mus. Meyerbeer, chor. Albert), Théâtre de la Monnaie, Brussels
1839 Pirate in *Le Corsaire* (after Albert), Théâtre de la Monnaie, Brussels
1841 Pas de deux in *Le Diable boiteaux* (Aniel after Coralli), Théâtre de la Monnaie, Brussels
1843 Pas de deux (cr) in *Les Houris* (divertissement; Perrot), Her Majesty's Theatre, London
Principal dancer in *Pas Styrien* (divertissement), Her Majesty's Theatre, London
Pas de quatre in *Le Lac des fées* (Guerra), Her Majesty's Theatre, London
Matteo (cr) in *Ondine* (Perrot), Her Majesty's Theatre, London
Dancer in *L'Allieva d'amore* (Cerrito), Teatro Alibert, Rome
Passo a due Styriano (cr) in *La Vivandiera ed il Postiglione* (also chor., with Cerrito), Teatro Alibert, Rome
1844 Principal dancer (cr) in *La Manola* (also chor., with Cerrito), Her Majesty's Theatre, London
Phoebus (cr) in *La Esmeralda* (Perrot), Her Majesty's Theatre, London
Hans (cr) in *La Vivandière* (new production of *La Vivandiera* to new mus. Pugni; chor. Cerrito), Her Majesty's Theatre, London
Amyntas (cr) in *Zélia* (Perrot), Her Majesty's Theatre, London
1845 Alman (cr) in *Rosida; ou, Les Mines de Syracuse* (also chor., with Cerrito), Her Majesty's Theatre, London
1846 Leading role in *La Encantadora de Madrid* (Astolfi), Teatro Regio, Turin
Albrecht in *Giselle* (Hoguet after Coralli, Perrot), Berlin
Aliris, King of Bucharia/Feramorz (cr) in *Lalla Rookh; or, The Rose of Lahore* (Perrot), Her Majesty's Theatre, London
Pâris (cr) in *Le Jugement de Pâris* (Perrot), Her Majesty's Theatre, London
1847 Gringoire in *Esmeralda* (own staging, after Perrot), Königstheater, Berlin
James in *La Sylphide* (after F. Taglioni), Königstheater, Berlin
Principal dancer (cr) in *Das Blümenmädchen im Elsass* (also chor.), Königstheater, Berlin
Principal dancer in *Der Maskenball* (also chor., with Cerrito), Königstheater, Berlin
Manasses (cr) in *La Fille de marbre* (also chor.), Opéra, Paris
Principal dancer in *Giovanna Maillotte* (Galzerani), Teatro La Fenice, Venice
1848 Title role (cr) in *Tartini il violinista* (also chor.), Teatro La Fenice, Venice
Principal dancer (cr) in *L'Anti-Polkista ed i Polkamani* (also chor.), Teatro La Fenice, Venice
1849 Urbain (cr) in *Le Violon du diable* (new production of *Tartini il Violinista*; also chor.), Opéra, Paris
1850 Gennaro Vitelli (cr) in *Stella; ou, Les Contrenadiers* (also chor.), Opéra, Paris
1851 François (cr) in *Pâquerette* (also chor.), Opéra, Paris

WORKS

1843 *La Vivandiera ed il Postiglione* (with Cerrito; mus. Rolland), Teatro Alibert, Rome
1844 *La Vivandière* (new production of *La Vivandiera*; new mus. Pugni), Her Majesty's Theatre, London

Arthur Saint-Léon with Fanny Cerrito in *La Fille de marbre*, **Paris Opera, 1847**

1845   *Rosida; ou, Les Mines de Syracuse* (mus. Pugni), Her Majesty's Theatre, London
1846   *Der Maskenball* (with Cerrito), Königstheater, Berlin
1847   *Das Blümenmädchen im Elsass* (mus. Graziani, Conradi), Königstheater, Berlin
       La Fille de marbre (mus. Pugni after Costa), Opéra, Paris
1848   *Tartini il Violinista* (also mus., with Felis, Pugni), Teatro La Fenice, Venice
       L'Anti-Polkista ed i Polkamani, Teatro La Fenice, Venice
1849   *Le Violon du diable* (new production of *Tartini il Violinista*; mus. Pugni), Opéra, Paris
1850   *Stella; ou, Les Contrebandiers* (mus. Pugni), Opéra, Paris
       Menuet, Gavotte et Polka, ou Jadis et aujourd'hui, Grande Salle du Conservatoire, Paris
       Divertissement in *L'Enfant prodigue* (opera; mus. Auber), Opéra, Paris
1851   *Pâquerette* (mus. Benoist), Opéra, Paris
       Dances in *Les Nations* (cantata; mus. Adam), Opéra, Paris
1852   *Le Berger Aristée et les abeilles*, divertissement in *Le Juif errant* (opera; mus. Halévy), Opéra, Paris
1853   *Le Lutin de la vallée* (opéra-ballet; mus. Gautier), Théâtre Lyrique, Paris
       Le Danseur du roi (mus. Gautier), Théâtre Lyrique, Paris
1854   *La Rozière*, Teatro de São Carlos, Lisbon
       Saltarello; ou, O Maniaco po la dança (new version of *Le Danseur du roi*; also mus.), Teatro de São Carlos, Lisbon

Lia la bayadère, Teatro de São Carlos, Lisbon
1855   *O Ensaio geral; ou, As Afflicçóes de Zefferini* (also mus. arrangement), Teatro de São Carlos, Lisbon
       Bailados allegoricos, Teatro de São Carlos, Lisbon
1856   *O Triumvir amoroso; ou, Muitos espinhos e nenhuma rosa*, Teatro de São Carlos, Lisbon
       Os Saltimbancos; ou, Os processo do fandango (mus. orchestrated Santos Pinto), Teatro de São Carlos, Lisbon
       Meteora; ou, As estrellas cadentes (mus. Santos Pinto), Teatro de São Carlos, Lisbon
       Stradella; ou, O poder da musica, Teatro de São Carlos, Lisbon
1858   *Jahrmarkt zu Haarlem* (new production of *Os Saltimbancos*, 1856; also mus., with Pinto, Strebinger), Vienna
1859   *Jovita; ou, Les Boucaniers mexicains* (after Mazilier; mus. Labarre), Bolshoi Theatre, St. Petersburg
1860   *Graziella; ou, Les Dépits amoureux* (mus. Pugni), Bolshoi Theatre, St. Petersburg
1861   *Nymphes et Satyre* (mus. Pugni), Bolshoi Theatre, St. Petersburg
       La Perle de Séville (new production of *Os Saltimbancos*, 1856; also mus., with Pinto, Pugni), Bolshoi Theatre, St. Petersburg
1862   *Les Tribulations d'une répétition générale* (new production of *O Ensaio geral*, 1855; also mus., with Pinto), Bolshoi Theatre, St. Petersburg
       Théolinde l'orpheline; ou, Le Lutin de la vallée (mus. Pugni), Bolshoi Theatre, St. Petersburg
1863   *Diavolina* (based largely on *Graziella*, 1860; mus. Pugni), Opéra, Paris
       Plamya Lyubvi; ili, Salamandra (*Love's Flame; or, The Salamander*; mus. Minkus), Bolshoi Theatre, Moscow
1864   *Fiammetta; ou, L'Amour du Diable* (new version of *Plamya Lyubvi*, 1863; mus. Minkus), Bolshoi Theatre, St. Petersburg
       Néméa; ou, L'Amour vengé (new version of *Fiammetta*, 1864; mus. Minkus), Opéra, Paris
       Konek Gorbunok; ou, La Tsar-Dievitza (*The Little Humpbacked Horse; or, The Tsar-Maiden*; mus. Pugni), Bolshoi Theatre, St. Petersburg
1865   Dances in *L'Africaine* (opera; mus. Meyerbeer), Opéra, Paris
       Il Basilico (mus. Graziani), Théâtre Italien, Paris
       Don Zeffiro (new production of *Saltarello*, 1854), Théâtre Italien, Paris
1866   Dances in *Don Juan* (opera; mus. Mozart), Opéra, Paris
       La Fidanzata valacca (mus. Graziani, Mattiozzi), Théâtre Italien, Paris
       La Source (mus. Minkus, Delibes), Opéra, Paris
       Zolotaya rybka (*The Goldfish*; mus. Minkus), Bolshoi Theatre, St. Petersburg (Act I only; complete ballet performed Bolshoi Theatre, 1867)
1869   *Liliya* (*The Lily*; mus. Minkus), Bolshoi Theatre, St. Petersburg
1870   Divertissement in *Robert le Diable* (opera; mus. Meyerbeer), Opéra, Paris
       Divertissement (mus. Berlioz) in *Le Freychütz* (opera; mus. Weber), Opéra, Paris
       Coppélia; ou, La Fille aux yeux d'émail (mus. Delibes), Opéra, Paris

Other works include: stagings of *Ondine* (after Perrot, Cerrito), *Vincito al lotto* (after Cerrito), *L'Elève de l'amour* (after Cerrito), *Giselle* (after Coralli, Perrot), *Esmeralda* (after Perrot), *Pouvoir de l'art*, *Danses du Folletto*; dances in *Le Prophète* (opera; mus. Meyerbeer).

PUBLICATIONS

By Saint-Léon:

La Sténochorégraphie, ou Art d'écrire promptement la danse, Paris, 1852
De l'état actuel de la danse, Lisbon, 1856
Letters from a Ballet Master, edited by Ivor Guest, New York, 1981

About Saint-Léon:

Biographie de M. et Mme Fanny Cerrito Saint-Léon de l'Opéra, Paris, 1850
Moore, Lillian, *Artists of the Dance*, New York, 1938
Beaumont, Cyril, *Complete Book of Ballets*, revised edition, London, 1951
Guest, Ivor, *The Ballet of the Second Empire*, 2 volumes: London, 1953 and 1955; reprinted 1974
Guest, Ivor, *The Romantic Ballet in England*, London, 1954
Guest, Ivor, *Fanny Cerrito*, London, 1956
Guest, Ivor, "The Birth of *Coppélia*", *Dance Magazine* (New York), February 1958
Roslavleva, Natalia, *Era of the Russian Ballet*, London, 1966
Guest, Ivor, *Two Coppélias*, London, 1970
Guest, Anne Hutchinson, "Saint-Léon Revived", *Dancing Times* (London), November 1976
Hammond, Sandra Noll, "*La Sténographie* by Saint-Léon: A Link in Ballet's Technical History", Dance History Scholars, *Proceedings*, Fifth Annual Conference, February 1982
Christout, Marie-Françoise, "Revelations of the Choreographer of *Coppélia*", *Dance Chronicle* (New York), vol. 5, no. 3, 1983

*   *   *

A dominant choreographic force during the latter portion of the nineteenth century, Arthur Saint-Léon was something of a paradox: though inclined to compromise his artistry to achieve success, he was yet a man of perception, intelligence, and foresight, whose expansive and international career enabled him to explore many opportunities.

He is best remembered as a phenomenal performer for his time and as a choreographer of great popularity and influence. He was technically accomplished, energetic, and strong (despite a malformed shoulder), and possessed a light, easy jump, extraordinary elevation with the rare ability seemingly to pause mid-air, aesthetic port de bras, and solid balance, which facilitated controlled, cleanly finished multiple pirouettes. Criticized for acrobatic exhibitions and an Italian miming style, Saint-Léon as a partner subdued his ego, offering sturdy support to his ballerina. Younger than Jules Perrot, from whom he differed in style, the "danseur noble sérieux" Saint-Léon won accolades for his masculine grace, bravura, and artistry from a public which disdained male dancers. His acceptance may also be attributed to his adjunct career as a violinist, begun as a child prodigy.

During his lifetime Saint-Léon wrote over 70 pieces of music, predominantly for the violin. (Compared to dancer/composer Jean Baptiste Lully, Saint-Léon reportedly was the better dancer, but the less talented composer.) Performing in the salon circuit, he was seldom critically evaluated. A violinist "of the Paganini school", he was admired for his presentation, virtuosity, and ability to perform in mid-scene, without customary preparations, as demonstrated in *Tartini il Violinista*, in which he also danced.

Aided by his musicality and choreographic instincts, Saint-Léon adeptly created intricate and visually pleasing variations and divertissements, especially in his masterpiece, *Coppélia*.

His works, infused with tours de force and reflective of his technical prowess and tastes, brimmed with movement, which in a later era would have found greater appreciation. Especially talented at fashioning dances to display a ballerina's technical attributes, Saint-Léon created many successful vehicles for his wife, Fanny Cerrito, and for a succession of protégées, including his muse Adèle Grantzow.

Folk and national dances, an element of Romantic ballet, were Saint-Léon's specialty. Though criticized for undermining their national character and for unjustified interpolation, he popularized ethnic dances and influenced their incorporation into the classical repertory, assembled by his successor as ballet master of the Russian Imperial Theatres, Marius Petipa. Conversely, to compete with Petipa, his assistant and choreographic rival, Saint-Léon improved the quality of his crowd scenes, an area which he had previously ignored.

Saint-Léon's independently conceived scenarios were severely criticized, in France and Russia, for weak, illogical, and inane structure. Although mid-nineteenth century ballets subscribed to a story-formula, which challenged neither intellect nor emotions, Saint-Léon's neglect of dramatic sensibilities produced plots which were either blatantly trite (*Diavolina*) or convoluted (*Stella*). Saint-Léon was also charged with recycling his ballets (as in *Plamya Lyubvi/Fiammetta/Néméa*) and with piracy. However, in restaging his works for different ensembles in distant cities, he was no more guilty than other choreographers who have reworked their ballets, changed titles, imposed substitutions or interpolations, staged re-creations, and left assorted versions for posterity to argue over which is the "definitive" work.

Ironically enough, Saint-Léon's other major contribution to ballet history is as creator of a dance notation system and defender of a consistent "school" of ballet technique. An advocate of "serious" dance training, Saint-Léon was dissatisfied with ballet's undervalued position in France, consequently incurred from the ebbing popularity and influence of the Romantic ballet. Writing in 1856, he astutely blamed the discontinuance of dance training in general education as partially responsible for unappreciative audiences—a perception with ongoing relevance today. He theorized that Romanticism's dissipation could be offset by establishing professional dance conservatories. His ideal school, promoting concepts now generally accepted—specialized musical training, regimented classical technique, enforced daily practice, and sequential instruction—would elevate dance to an "art", produce well-rounded choreographers, and form disciplined corps de ballets. Although abandoning his prototype in Lisbon, he brought his expertise to St. Petersburg, where his technical knowledge added to the melting-pot of the "Russian" ballet.

Recognizing the fallibility of human memory, the evanescent nature of ballet, and the need for dance to find a written language, Saint-Léon invented a system of dance notation. Although several methods had been developed in the previous century, his visually-based stick figure technique, outlined in *La Sténochorégraphie, ou Art d'écrire promptement la danse* (1852), was the first to record upper-body movements instead of general floor-patterns.

Sténochorégraphie probably derives from the method created by Saint-Léon's teacher Albert (François Decombe), whose system combined the principles of telegraphy with those used in writing music. Advancing Albert's concepts with his own solid musical knowledge, Saint-Léon increased the horizontal staff to six lines, imposed above the music on the score. Positions of the legs and feet were drawn on the lower five lines, with the upper body allocated to the top line. The system, which recorded the dance from the audiences' perspective, was adequate for its time but was limited in its ability to notate technical intricacies.

Illustrating his treatise with traditional combinations, Saint-Léon captured for posterity his contemporary technical standard. These exercises, which in some form are still practised, serve as a direct link between the rudiments outlined by Italian dancing master Carlo Blasis and the advancements of the great Russian pedagogue Agrippina Vaganova.

Although Saint-Léon lamented the loss of his predecessors' ballets, he notated only a portion of *Giselle*'s "Peasant Pas de deux", the "Pas de quatre" from Antonio Guerra's *Le Lac des fées*, which was interpolated as a "Pas de six" into Fanny Cerrito's *La Vivandière*, and his *Il Basilico*. And thus the great irony that he left his major works unrecorded, presumably because of his busy lifestyle.

As a choreographer forever seeking innovations, Saint-Léon—who in his own productions masterfully employed stage effects—actually ventured into the avant-garde, without either critical success or directorial sanction. Although his anti-Romantic concepts—singers, musicians, bizarrely costumed dancers—were frequently eliminated during the pre-production negotiations, similar experiments would find outlets in a later era. Paradoxically, though he supported ballet as "art", he compromised inspiration to satisfy public tastes, to win directorial approval, and to advance his career, consequently stifling his choreographic potential and lowering his artistic status. Motivated by commercialism, not artistic vision, Saint-Léon was still a man ahead of his time.

—Karen Dacko

SALLÉ, Marie

French dancer and choreographer. Born into theatrical family of travelling players, 1707. Studied with Françoise Prévost, Paris, from 1718; possibly studied later with Claude Ballon. Child dancer, performing regularly at Foire Saint-Germain and Foire Saint-Laurent, Paris; engaged (at age 9) to perform at Lincoln's Inn Fields, London, 1716–17 season, returning to London for 1718–19 season; début at L'Académie royale de musique (Paris Opéra), replacing Prévost in *Les Fêtes vénitiennes*, 1721; also continued to perform with family troupe until 1725; leading dancer, Lincoln's Inn Fields seasons, 1725–27; première danseuse, Paris Opéra, 1727–30, leaving (after quarrel with management) to perform in London, 1730–31; returned to Opéra, August 1731–December 1731; leading dancer, Covent Garden, London, seasons 1733–35, Paris Opéra, 1735–40; also performed frequently at court, appearing regularly at Versailles, 1745–47, and Fontainebleau, 1752; choreographer of many of own dances, collaborating with composers Handel in London and Rameau in Paris; recipient of royal pension, 1740. Died in Paris, 27 July 1756.

ROLES

1716   Harlequiness in *Two Punchanellos, Two Harlequins, and Dame Ragonde*, Lincoln's Inn Fields, London
       Dancer (cr) in *Spanish Entrée*, Lincoln's Inn Fields, London
       Dancer in *Night Scene, Dutch Skipper* (divertissements), Lincoln's Inn Fields, London
       Dancer (cr) in *The Drunken Man* (also chor., with brother M. Sallé), Lincoln's Inn Fields, London
       Hermione, Andromache in *Andromache* (burlesque;

also chor., with brother, M. Sallé), Lincoln's Inn Fields, London
       Dancer (cr) in *Grand Comic Dance* (Moreau), Lincoln's Inn Fields, London
       Dancer (cr) in *Harlequin Executed; or, The Farmer Disappointed* ("Italian mimic scene"; also chor.), Lincoln's Inn Fields, London
1717   Dancer (cr) in *The Submission* (Tomlinson), Lincoln's Inn Fields, London
       Dancer (cr) in *La Folie* (Moreau), Lincoln's Inn Fields, London
       Columbine (cr) in *The Loves of Harlequin and Columbine*, Lincoln's Inn Fields, London
1718   Dancer in *La Princesse de Carisme* (opera; Lesage), Foire Saint-Laurent, Paris
1721   Entrée in *Les Fêtes vénitiennes* (revival; opéra-ballet, mus. Campra, chor. Blondy), Opéra, Paris
1722   A Grace in *Arlequin Deucalion* (mus. Piron), Foire Saint-Laurent, Paris
1724   A Peasant in *La Claperman* (mus. Piron), Foire Saint-Laurent, Paris
       A follower of Thesalus in *La Conquête de la toison d'or* (mus. Lesage, Orneval), Foire Saint-Laurent, Paris
       Divertissement in *Love's Last Shift* (comedy; Cibber), Lincoln's Inn Fields, London
1725   "The French Sailor and his Wife" in *Dance of Slaves* (divertissement), Lincoln's Inn Fields, London
       Dancer in *Shepherd and Shepherdess* (divertissement), Lincoln's Inn Fields, London
       The Danseuse in *Les Caractères de la danse* (mus. Rebel), Lincoln's Inn Fields, London
       Dancer in *Le Marrié* [sic] *ou le Mariage, Two Pierrots* (divertissements), Lincoln's Inn Fields, London
1726   Daphne, Flora in *Apollo and Daphne; or, The Burgomaster Trick'd* (pantomime; lib. Theobold), Lincoln's Inn Fields, London
       Dancer in *French Sailor* (also *The French Sailor and his Wife*; divertissement), Lincoln's Inn Fields, London
       Dancer in *Grand Dance* (divertissement), Lincoln's Inn Fields, London
1727   A Sylvan in *The Rape of Proserpine* (grand pantomime), Lincoln's Inn Fields, London
       Clemene in *The Loves of Damon and Clemene; or, The Metamorphosis of Leander*, Lincoln's Inn Fields, London
       Une Bergère, Pas de deux (cr) in *Les Amours des dieux* (ballet-héroïque; mus. Mouret), Opéra, Paris
       Entrée, Pas de deux in *Roland* (tragédie-lyrique; mus. Lully), Opéra, Paris
1728   Dancer (cr) in *The Beggar's Opera* (revival of ballad-opera by J. Gay; mus. arranged Pepusch), Lincoln's Inn Fields, London
       Pas de trois in *Hypermnestre* (tragédie-lyrique, revival; mus. Gervais, chor. Blondy), Opéra, Paris
       Dancer (cr) in *Orion* (tragédie-lyrique; mus. Lacoste), Opéra, Paris
       Divertissements in *Monsieur de Pourceaugnac* (comédie-ballet by Molière; mus. Lully), Versailles
       Dancer in *Bellérophon* (tragédie-lyrique; mus. Lully), Opéra, Paris
       Dancer (cr) in *La Princesse d'Élide* (ballet-héroïque; mus. Villeneuve, chor. Blondy), Opéra, Paris
       Dancer in *Les Amours de Protée* (ballet; mus. Gervais), Opéra, Paris
       Dancer (cr) in *Tarsis et Zélie* (tragédie-lyrique; mus. Rebel, Francoeur), Opéra, Paris
       Dancer in *Alceste* (tragédie-lyrique, revival; mus.

Marie Sallé, in an engraving after a painting by Lancret

Lully), Opéra, Paris

1729   The Danseuse in *Les Caractères de la danse* (as pas de deux; mus. Rebel), Opéra, Paris

Divertissement in *Tancrède* (tragédie-lyrique; mus. Campra), Opéra, Paris

Divertissement in *Le Bourgeois Gentilhomme* (comédie-ballet by Molière; mus. Lully), Versailles

Dancer (cr) in *Les Amours des déesses* (ballet-héroïque; mus. Quinault, chor. Blondy), Opéra, Paris

Dancer (cr) in *Le Parnasse* (fragments; chor. Blondy), Versailles

Dancer in *Hésione* (tragédie-lyrique; mus. Campra), Opéra, Paris

Dancer in *Thésée* (tragédie-lyrique; mus. Lully), Opéra, Paris

1730   Dancer in *Pastoral-héroïque* (mus. Rebel), celebration for the birth of the Dauphin, Versailles

Dancer in *Télémaque* (tragédie-lyrique; mus. Destouches), at court

Dancer in *Alcione* (tragédie-lyrique; mus. Marais), Opéra, Paris

Dancer (cr) in *Le Carnaval et la folie* (comédie-ballet; mus. Destouches), Opéra, Paris

Dancer in *Ballad*, Lincoln's Inn Fields, London

Dancer in *Tambourine*, Lincoln's Inn Fields, London

1731   Dancer in *Amadis de Gaule* (tragédie-lyrique; mus. Lully), Opéra, Paris

1732   Dancer (cr) in *Callirhoé* (tragédie-lyrique; new version; mus. Destouches, chor. Blondy), Opéra, Paris

Dancer (cr) in *Jephté* (tragédie-lyrique; mus. Montéclair), Opéra, Paris

Dancer (cr) in *Le Ballet des sens* (opéra-ballet; mus. Mouret, chor. Blondy), Opéra, Paris

Dancer (cr) in *Scylla* (tragédie-lyrique; revival; mus. Théobalde, chor. Blondy), Opéra, Paris

Dancer in *Biblis* (tragédie-lyrique; mus. Lacoste), Opéra, Paris

1734   The Statue of Venus (cr) in *Pigmalion* (also chor.), Covent Garden, London

Dancer in *A French Sailor and His Lass*, Covent Garden, London

Bridal Nymph (cr) in *Le Masque nuptial; ou, Les Triomphes de Cupidon et d'Hymen* (mus. Gaillard, chor. probably Sallé), Covent Garden, London

Ariadne (cr) in *Bacchus et Ariadne* (divertissement; also chor.) in *The Necromancer*, Covent Garden, London

Dancer in *Les Caractères de l'amour*, Benefit for Sallé, Covent Garden, London

Title role (cr) in *Terpsichore* (also chor.), Prologue to *Il Pastor fido* (opera; mus. Handel), King's Theatre, London

Dancer in *Orestes* (opera; mus. Handel), Covent Garden, London

1735 Divertissement (cr; also chor.) in *Ariodante* (opera; mus. Handel), Covent Garden, London

Dancer in *La Coquette Française*, Covent Garden, London

Cupid (cr) in *Alcina* (opera; mus. Handel, chor. Sallé), Covent Garden, London

Rose (cr) in *Ballet des fleurs* (probably also chor.) in *Les Indes galantes* (ballet-héroïque; mus. Rameau, chor. probably Blondy), Opéra, Paris

Dancer (cr) in *Scanderberg* (pantomime; mus. Rebel, Francoeur), Opéra, Paris

Dancer in *Les Fêtes de Thalie* (opéra-ballet; mus. Mouret), Opéra, Paris

1736 Dancer in *Thétis et Pélée* (tragédie-lyrique; mus. Collasse), Opéra, Paris

Divertissement (cr; also chor.) added to *L'Europe galante* (opéra-ballet; mus. Campra), Opéra, Paris

Une Sauvage (cr) in *Les Voyages de l'amour* (ballet; mus. Boismortier, chor. Blondy), Opéra, Paris

Dancer in *Les Romans* (ballet; mus. Cambini), Opéra, Paris

Dancer (cr) in *Les Génies* (opéra-ballet; mus. Mlle. Duval), Opéra, Paris

Dancer in *Médée et Jason* (tragédie-lyrique; mus. Salomon), Opéra, Paris

1737 Dancer in *Persée* (tragédie-lyrique; mus. Lully), Opéra, Paris

Dancer in *Le Triomphe de l'harmonie* (ballet-héroïque; mus. Grenet), Opéra, Paris

Dancer in *Cadmus et Hermione* (tragédie-lyrique; mus. Lully), Opéra, Paris

Dancer in *Les Éléments* (ballet; mus. Lalande, Destouches), Opéra, Paris

Hébé (cr) in *Castor et Pollux* (tragédie-lyrique; mus. Rameau), Opéra, Paris

1738 Dancer in *Atys* (tragédie-lyrique; mus. Lully), Opéra, Paris

Dancer (cr) in *Le Ballet de la paix* (tragédie-lyrique; mus. Rebel, Francoeur), Opéra, Paris

Dancer in *Tancrède* (tragédie-lyrique; mus. Campra), Opéra, Paris

1739 Dancer in *Les Plaisirs champêtres* (divertissement; mus. J.-F. Rebel), Opéra, Paris

Dancer (cr) in *Alceste* (tragédie-lyrique; mus. Lully, chor. Blondy), Opéra, Paris

Dancer in *Polydore* (tragédie-lyrique; mus. Baptistin [Stuck]), Opéra, Paris

Terpsichore (cr) in *Les Fêtes d'Hébé; ou, Les Talents lyriques* (ballet; mus. Rameau), Opéra, Paris

Dancer (cr) in *Zaïde, reine de Grenade* (ballet; mus. Royer), Opéra, Paris

Dancer (cr) in *Dardanus* (tragédie-lyrique; mus. Rameau), Opéra, Paris

1740 Dancer in *L'Oracle* (Laval), Versailles

Dancer in *Pyrame et Thisbé* (tragédie-lyrique; mus. Rebel, Francoeur), Opéra, Paris

1745 Divertissement (cr; also chor.) in *Platée* (ballet bouffon; mus. Rameau), Versailles

Dancer (cr) in *La Temple de la gloire* (ballet-"fête"; also chor., mus. Rameau), Versailles

1747 Dancer (also chor.) in *Persée* (tragédie-lyrique, revival; mus. Lully), Opéra, Paris

Dancer (cr; also chor.) in *Les Fêtes de l'hymen et de l'amour* (ballet-héroïque; mus. Rameau), Versailles

1752 Dancer in *Tyrcis et Doristée*, Fontainebleau

1753 Dancer in *Phaeton* (tragédie-lyrique; mus. Lully), Fontainebleau

WORKS

1734 *Pigmalion*, Covent Garden, London

Bacchus et Ariadne, Covent Garden, London

Terpsichore (Prologue to opera, *Il Pastor fido*; mus. Handel), King's Theatre, London

1735 Dances in *Ariodante* (opera; mus. Handel), Covent Garden, London

Dances in *Alcina* (opera; mus. Handel), Covent Garden, London

Ballet des fleurs (chor. probably Sallé) in *Les Indes galantes* (ballet-héroïque; mus. Rameau, chor. probably Blondy), Opéra, Paris

1736 Dances in *Atys* (tragédie-lyrique; revival; mus. Lully), Opéra, Paris

1737 Dances in *Castor et Pollux* (tragédie-lyrique; mus. Rameau), Opéra, Paris

1739 Dances in *Dardanus* (tragédie-lyrique; mus. Rameau), Opéra, Paris

1745 Dances in *Platée* (ballet bouffon; mus. Rameau), Versailles

Le Temple de la gloire (ballet-"fête"; mus. Rameau), Versailles

1747 Dances in *Persée* (tragédie-lyrique, revival; mus. Lully), Opéra, Paris

Les Fêtes de l'hymen et de l'amour (ballet-héroïque; mus. Rameau), Versailles

Other works include: at Lincoln's Inn Fields—stagings of divertissements *The Drunken Man* (with brother, M. Sallé), *Andromache* (burlesque, with M. Sallé), *Harlequin Executed; or, The Farmer Disappointed* ("Italian Mimic Scene").

PUBLICATIONS

Noverre, Jean-Georges, *Lettres sur la danse et les ballets*, Stuttgart and Lyon, 1760; as *Letters on Dancing and Ballets*, from 1803 edition, translated by Cyril Beaumont, London, 1930

Castil-Blaze, *La Danse et les ballets depuis Bacchus jusqu'à Mlle. Taglioni*, Paris, 1832

Castil-Blaze, *L'Académie impériale de musique*, Paris, 1855

Campardon, Émile, *Les Spectacles de la foire*, Paris, 1877

Campardon, Émile, *L'Académie royale de musique*, Paris, 1881

Dacier, Emile, *Mlle Sallé, Une Danseuse de l'Opéra sous Louis XV*, Paris, 1909; reprinted Geneva, 1972

"Mlle Sallé: A Handelian Ballerina", *Dancing Times* (London), June 1924

Gribble, Francis Henry, "A French Dancer in Gay's Opera", *Dancing Times* (London), May 1926

Avery, Emmet, "Dancing and Pantomime on the English Stage 1700–1737", *Studies in Philology* (Chapel Hill), vol. 31, no. 3, 1934

Beaumont, Cyril, *Three French Dancers of the Eighteenth Century*, London, 1934

Moore, Lillian, *Artists of the Dance*, New York, 1938

"The Portrait of Mlle Sallé", *Ballet Today* (London), August 1950

Vince, Stanley, "Marie Sallé, 1707–56", *Theatre Notebook*

(London), Autumn 1957

Daniels, Diana, "The First Ballerina?", *Dance Magazine* (New York), January 1960

Vince, Stanley, "Sallé in London", *Dance and Dancers* (London), May 1962

Migel, Parmenia, "Marie Sallé 1707–1756", *Ballet Review* (Brooklyn, N.Y.), vol. 4, no. 2, 1972

Murphy, Anne, "Rebel with a Cause", *Ballet News* (New York), June 1985

Prudhommeau, Germaine, "Camargo–Sallé: Duel au pied levé", *Danser* (Paris), March 1986

Semmens, Richard, "Terpsichore Reborn: The French Noble Style and Drama", Society of Dance History Scholars *Proceedings*, Tenth Annual Conference, 1987

*   *   *

Marie Sallé was born into a theatrical family, her father being a member of a travelling theatre company, directed by her uncle Francisque Moylin, which appeared frequently at the Foire Saint-Germain and the Foire Saint-Laurent in Paris. Brought up in this tough training school, Sallé learned adaptability from a very early age, and although her speciality seems to have always been dancing, there is no doubt that she learned the art of mime and drama from her family, and was taught not simply how to dance, but how to dance in character.

In 1715 Sallé's uncle Francisque visited England, and as a result of contacts made there, Marie and her brother were invited to appear at Lincoln's Inn Fields during the 1716–17 season. This visit coincided with the first performance of John Weaver's ballet *The Loves of Mars and Venus* in which Weaver first put into practice his revolutionary ideas of the *ballet d'action*. It is possible that the young Sallé saw this performance and remembered it in later years.

Sallé was a pupil of the great ballerina Françoise Prevost from 1718, and it is significant that when she came to England in 1725 she gave a performance of *Les Charactères de la danse*—a divertissement, to music by Rebel, originally created by Prévost for the Opéra, and first performed by her there in 1720. Prévost choreographed the piece as a series of character studies of different types of lover, and performed it as a solo. The published score is preceded by a brief summary of these characters. For example: "Bouree—An amourous shepherdess begs love to open the eyes of a shepherd who scorns her. Chaconne—A young man asks of love neither conquests, nor favours, but only the reputation of a man about town." Sallé followed her teacher's example, using her skills as a mime to portray the various characters. Later she was to perform it in Paris with a partner, M. Laval, but still as a character dance, whereas her contemporary and rival Marie-Anne Cupis de Camargo used the divertissement as a vehicle for showing her virtuosity and exceptional technical skill, without making any attempt at characterization.

It appears, therefore, that Sallé drew on a number of influences: first, her close family and their training in mime and gesture, then her teacher, Prévost, who herself made use of mime in her work, and finally, her contemporaries in England, in particular John Weaver and John Rich, famous for his portrayal of Harlequin. The culmination of all these influences came in January 1734 when Sallé presented her first choreography, *Pigmalion*, telling the classical story of the beautiful statue which comes to life and dances with her sculptor creator. A letter printed in *Le Mercure* in April 1734 describes the impact this ballet had on London audiences. "The statue begins gradually to come to life . . . she displays wonder at her new existence and all the things around her. Pigmalion dances before her to demonstrate, she copies with steps ranging from the simplest to the most complex . . .". Not only did Sallé link the arts of dance, mime, and drama in this piece, but she also revolutionized the dress of the dancer. Again in *Le Mercure* it was reported that "She dared to appear, without paniers, without skirt, without foundation, her hair loose and without a single ornament on her head; she was dressed, with corset and underskirt, only in a simple dress of muslin swathed in folds in the style of a greek statue."

1734 was the peak of Sallé's career in England. In the autumn she began to work with the composer Handel. Their collaboration produced such exquisite ballets as *Terpsichore* (the prelude to Handel's opera *Il Pastor Fido*) and suites of dances for the operas *Ariodante* and *Alcina*. For this latter ballet she cast herself in the role of Cupid, and as such she wore male dress. According to Dacier the costume did not suit her and displeased the audience. It is more probable, however, that Handel's rival, Porpora, had organized opposition. Whatever the cause, the capricious audience hissed and booed at her appearance, upsetting her so much that she never set foot on a London stage again.

On her return to Paris, Sallé's first major work for the Opéra was Rameau's ballet *Les Indes galantes*, in which she had ample scope for her superb dramatic qualities. The ballet represents a garden full of flowers, each one displaying different characteristics. The flowers dance together, led by the Rose (Sallé herself). A fierce wind interrupts the tranquility of the garden and attacks the flowers. Only the Rose withstands the fury of the wind with sweetness and dignity. Finally a Zephir arrives, bringing sunshine and reviving the flowers who pay homage to the tender Rose.

Although it was warmly received and Sallé went on to choreograph several more Rameau ballets, Parisian audiences were not yet ready for the advent of the *ballet d'action*. Sallé did, however, influence the development of ballet, for Jean Georges Noverre, who saw her work, acknowledged her artistry. "She replaced showiness by simple, touching graces; free from affectation, her features were refined, expressive and intelligent. It was not by means of leaps and jumps that she stirred the heart." Noverre is acknowledged as the foremost reformer of dance in the eighteenth century, with his advocacy of *ballet d'action*, or dramatic dancing; but his great admiration for Sallé suggests that she influenced many of his ideas. For Sallé dancing was clearly a means of expression rather than an end in itself.

—Madeleine Inglehearn

SAMSOVA, Galina

Russian/Canadian dancer and ballet director. Born Galina Martinovna Samtsova (Samsova) in Stalingrad, 17 March 1937. Studied at Kiev State Ballet School, pupil of Natalia Verekundova. Married (1) Canadian dancer Alexander Ursuliak, 1960; (2) French dancer André Prokovsky, 1972 (div. 1981). Dancer, becoming soloist, Kiev Ballet, 1956–60 (returning as guest artist, 1962); soloist, soon becoming principal dancer, National Ballet of Canada, 1961–64, also performing with Raymundo de Larrain company, 1963; guest artist, and then principal dancer, London Festival Ballet, 1964–73; founder and co-director, with André Prokovsky, as well as principal dancer, New London Ballet, 1973–77, and for brief season, 1979; international guest artist, from 1977, including for National Ballet of Canada, Marseilles Opera Ballet, Australian Ballet, Ballet West (U.S.), Louisville Ballet, Rome

Galina Samsova in *Paquita*

Opera Ballet, PACT Ballet (South Africa), Florence Opera Ballet, Hong Kong Ballet, Wiesbaden Ballet Company; principal dancer and teacher, Sadler's Wells Royal Ballet (now Birmingham Royal Ballet), 1980–90; guest artistic director, Scottish Ballet, 1990: artistic director, from 1991. Recipient: Gold Medal, Paris Festival, 1963; Prix Pavlova, Paris, 1963.

ROLES

1961   Pas de deux from *Le Corsaire* (after Petipa), National Ballet of Canada

Odette/Odile in *Swan Lake* (after Petipa, Ivanov), National Ballet of Canada, tour

1962   Title role in *Giselle* (Petipa after Coralli, Perrot; staged Franca), National Ballet of Canada, Hamilton, Ontario

Principal dancer in *Serenade* (Balanchine), National Ballet of Canada, Toronto

Principal dancer in *Concerto Barocco* (Balanchine), National Ballet of Canada, Toronto

An Episode in His Past in *The Lilac Garden* (Tudor), National Ballet of Canada, Toronto

1963   Title role (cr) in *Cendrillon* (Orlikowsky), Raymundo de Larrain company, Paris

1964   Juliet in *Romeo and Juliet* (Cranko), National Ballet of Canada, on tour

Dancer in *Spring Waters* (pas de deux; Messerer), London Festival Ballet

1965   Snow Queen and Sugar Plum Fairy in *The Nutcracker* (Carter, Howard, Trunoff, after Ivanov), London Festival Ballet, London

1967/   Princess Aurora in *The Sleeping Beauty* (Stevenson after
68   Petipa), Festival Ballet, tour

1969   Principal dancer (cr) in *The Unknown Island* (Carter), London Festival Ballet, London

1970   Principal dancer in *Dvořák Variations* (Hynd), London Festival Ballet, London

Kitri in *Don Quixote* (Borkowski, Gorsky), London Festival Ballet, London

1971   Desdemona (cr) in *Othello* (Darrell), New London Ballet, Trieste, Italy

Title role (cr) in *La Péri* (Darrell), London Festival Ballet, London

1973   Principal dancer (cr) in *Mozartiana* (Hynd), London Festival Ballet, London

Principal dancer (cr) in *Bagatelles* (Prokovsky), New London Ballet, London

Oracle of Delphi (cr) in *Pythoness Ascendant* (J. Carter), New London Ballet, Hong Kong

Principal dancer (cr) in *Vespri* (Prokovsky), New London Ballet, La Coruña, Spain

1974   Principal dancer (cr) in *Piano Quartet No. 1* (Prokovsky), New London Ballet, tour

1975   Principal dancer (cr) in *Elégie* (Prokovsky), New London Ballet, Southsea

Principal dancer (cr) in *Simorgh* (Prokovsky), New London Ballet, Birmingham

Anna (cr) in *The Seven Deadly Sins* (Prokovsky), PACT Ballet, Johannesburg

Principal dancer (cr) in *Valses nobles et sentimentales* (Hynd), New London Ballet, tour

1976   Lise in *La Fille mal gardée* (Ashton), Sadler's Wells Royal Ballet, Manchester

Principal dancer (cr) in *Faust Divertimento* (Samsova, Prokovsky), New London Ballet, tour

Pas de deux from *William Tell* (Bournonville), Florence Opera, Florence

1977   Title role in *Raymonda*, Act III (Nureyev after Petipa), Sadler's Wells Royal Ballet, tour

Venetian Songs in *Soft Blue Shadows* (expanded version of *Elégie*; Prokovsky), Salder's Wells Royal Ballet, London

1978   Title role in *La Sylphide* (Bruhn after Bournonville), National Ballet of Canada, Toronto

Title role in *Giselle* (Petipa after Coralli, Perrot; staged Wright), Sadler's Wells Royal Ballet

The Woman (cr) in *Intimate Letters* (Seymour), Sadler's Wells Royal Ballet, London

Eldest Sister in *Las Hermanas* (MacMillan), Sadler's Wells Royal Ballet, tour

Mazurka and Pas de deux in *Les Sylphides* (Fokine), Sadler's Wells Royal Ballet

Princess Aurora in *The Sleeping Beauty* (Prokovsky after Petipa), Rome Opera Ballet, Rome

1979   Title role in *Anna Karenina* (Prokovsky), Australian Ballet, Melbourne

Kitri in *Don Quixote* (Nureyev after Petipa), Australian Ballet

Sophie (cr) in *Königsmark* (Prokovsky), New London Ballet, York

Iseult in *Tristan and Iseult* (Darrell), New London Ballet

The Bride in *La Fête étrange* (Howard), Sadler's Wells Royal Ballet

1980   Lea (cr) in *Chéri* (Darrell), Scottish Ballet, Edinburgh

Title role (cr) in *Paquita* Grand Pas (new production; also chor., after Petipa), Sadler's Wells Royal Ballet, Bournemouth

Title role in *Papillon* (Hynd), Sadler's Wells Royal Ballet

Principal dancer in *Daydreams* (Prokovsky), Rome Opera Ballet, Rome

1981   Odette/Odile in *Swan Lake* (also chor., with Wright, after Petipa, Ivanov; mus. Tchaikovsky), Sadler's Wells Royal Ballet, Manchester

The Débutante in *Façade* (Ashton), Sadler's Wells Royal Ballet

1982   The Wife in *The Invitation* (MacMillan), Sadler's Wells Royal Ballet

Second Movement in *Concerto* (MacMillan), Sadler's Wells Royal Ballet

Second Movement (cr) in *Quartet* (MacMillan), Sadler's Wells Royal Ballet, Bristol

Principal dancer (cr) in *Adagio* (Wright), Sadler's Wells Theatre Gala, London

Title role in *Isadora* (MacMillan), Royal Ballet, Manchester

Principal dancer in *Allegro Brillante* (Balanchine), Louisville Ballet, Louisville, Kentucky

1984   Carabosse in *The Sleeping Beauty* (Wright after Petipa), Sadler's Wells Royal Ballet

Principal dancer (cr) in *Vocalise, Op. 34* (pas de deux; Prokovsky), Sadler's Wells Royal Ballet, London

1985   La Capricciosa in *The Lady and the Fool* (Cranko), Sadler's Wells Royal Ballet

1987   The Queen in *Gloriana* (Corder), Sadler's Wells Royal Ballet, London

Lady Henry Wotton (cr) in *The Picture of Dorian Grey* (Deane), Sadler's Wells Royal Ballet, Birmingham

The Older Woman (cr) in *Paramour* (Lustig), Sadler's Wells Royal Ballet, Birmingham

1988   Mary Magdalene in *Lazarus* (Cauley), Sadler's Wells Royal Ballet, London

Principal dancer (cr) in *Dumky* (Prokovsky), Quicksilver Ballet, Queen Elizabeth Hall, London

Elizabeth I (cr) in *Gloriana* (Corder), Sadler's Wells Royal Ballet

1990   Mrs. Stahlbaum in *The Nutcracker* (Wright), Sadler's Wells Royal Ballet, Birmingham

Other roles include: for London Festival Ballet—Barbara Allen in *The Witch Boy* (J. Carter), La Cigarette in *Noir et blanc* (Lifar), the Sleepwalker in *Night Shadow* (*La Sonnambula*; Balanchine), title role in *Phèdre* (Charrat), principal dancer in *Études* (Lander), a Butterfly in *Piège de lumière* (Taras), the Ballerina in *Petrushka* (Fokine).

WORKS

1976   *Faust Divertimento* (with Prokovsky; mus. Gounod), New London Ballet, tour

Walpurgis Night Pas de deux (mus. Gounod), London City Ballet

Also staged:

1963   *Laurencia* Pas de six (after Chabukiani; mus. Krien), National Ballet of Canada, Toronto (also staged New London Ballet, London City Ballet)

Le Corsaire Pas de deux (after Klavin; mus. Drigo) National Ballet of Canada, Toronto

1975   *La Bayadère* (after Petipa; mus. Minkus), Iranian National Ballet

1980   *Paquita* Grand Pas (after Petipa; mus. Deldevez, Minkus), Sadler's Wells Royal Ballet, Bournemouth

1981   *Swan Lake* (with Peter Wright; mus. Tchaikovsky), Sadler's Wells Royal Ballet, Manchester

1988   *Giselle* (after Petipa, Coralli, Perrot; mus. Adam), London City Ballet

1990   *Raymonda*, Act III (after Petipa; mus. Glazunov), Scottish Ballet

PUBLICATIONS

By Samsova:
Interview in "The Prokovskys: Reforming and Refreshing", *Dance and Dancers* (London), February 1977
Interview in *Dance and Dancers* (London), April 1981

About Samsova:
Cruikshank, Judith, "The Lady from Kiev", *Dance and*

Dancers (London), December 1961

Goodman, Saul, "Brief Biographies: Galina Samtsova", *Dance Magazine* (New York), April 1964

Herf, Estelle, "Galina Samtsova", *Ballet Today* (London), March/April 1966

Macaulay, Alastair, "In Quest of the Muse: The Sadler's Wells Royal Ballet", *Dancing Times* (London), November 1981

Newman, Barbara, and Spatt, Leslie, *Sadler's Wells Royal Ballet: Swan Lake*, London, 1983

* * *

In her prime, Galina Samsova was a true ballerina with a distinctive Russian style, who won acclaim at a time when few Soviet-trained dancers were performing in the West. She was radiant and musical with an expressive back and strong jump. She could be relied on to perform virtuoso pas de deux to add excitement and glamour to divertissement and mixed programmes—a notable asset when leading both London Festival Ballet's European tours and her own New London Ballet; and in André Prokovsky she found a partner whose style perfectly matched her own. More recently she has earned a reputation as an inspiring and considerate teacher, and as artistic director she has brought a new sense of purpose to Scottish Ballet.

Samsova's career began almost by chance. None of her family was involved with the arts but she accompanied a friend to dancing classes. She was offered a place at the Kiev Opera Ballet School but then had to win her parents' reluctant approval to accept it. She was appearing as a soloist with the Kiev Opera Ballet when in 1960 she met and married Alexander Ursuliak, a young, Canadian Ukranian teacher who was extending his experience of Russian dance. This was a period of improved relations between East and West, and Samsova was granted permission to leave the USSR with her husband. Even after Nureyev's defection she was invited to return and dance Odette/Odile with her old company in 1962.

Samsova's first years in the West were difficult; there were limited opportunities in Canada until she could be accepted as a soloist with the National Ballet of Canada. Here she was introduced to the work of Balanchine, Tudor, and Cranko—choreographers she would return to as artistic director of Scottish Ballet three decades later. Nevertheless, it was her appearance at the first International Festival of Dance in Paris in 1963 that transformed her into an international star. While taking class in London with Maria Fay, Samsova so impressed her new teacher that she recommended her to Raymundo de Larrain, who was casting his lavish new *Cinderella*. Her success in this production (for which she was awarded the Festival's gold medal) resulted in invitations to give guest performances with many companies, including the Marseilles Opera Ballet (where she met Prokovsky) and London Festival Ballet, whose leading ballerina she subsequently became for nearly a decade.

Applauded for her virtuosity in the pas de deux from *Le Corsaire* and *Spring Waters*, Samsova was also hailed as an interpretative artist of note. As Odette/Odile (which she performed in numerous different productions), she combined bravura technique with lyricism and pathos; her Kitri was noted as much for its femininity, charm, and wit as for its dazzling display of dancing; and her Giselle, a favourite role, was deeply moving. It was her perfect combination of dramatic ability and technical prowess that led choreographers to work with her repeatedly, and that sustained her career onstage through her forties. Her eagerness to create new roles and to commission ballets led to a richly varied performing career. Peter Wright, Ronald Hynd, and Jack Carter choreographed original works for her, the latter creating a powerful twenty-minute solo, *Pythoness Ascendant*, in which as the Delphic Sibyl

she grew from a simple woman to a visionary prophetess of awesome grandeur. Peter Darrell chose her for both the innocent Desdemona in *Othello* and the mature but still vibrantly passionate courtesan, Léa, in *Chéri*. Prokovsky in turn showed off her brilliant sense of comedy and timing in *Vespri* and her natural feel for drama and pathos as the tragic heroine of *Anna Karenina* (a role she shared with Marilyn Rowe) and as Sophie in *Königsmark*.

Early in her career in the West, Samsova began to stage divertissements she had learnt in Kiev, notably Chabukiani's show-piece pas de six from *Laurencia* for the National Ballet of Canada, and Klavin's version of the pas de deux from *Le Corsaire*, which became her signature piece. Understanding and sympathetic to the needs of her colleagues, she is ready to offer help and advice, and is acknowledged with gratitude and admiration for her ability to coach dancers in the style she herself perfected in nineteenth-century and other classical ballets.

—Jane Pritchard

SAND, Inge

Danish dancer, choreographer, and ballet director.   Born Inge Sand Sørensen in Copenhagen, 6 July 1928. Studied at the Royal Danish Ballet School, from 1936; later studied in Paris and London. Married (1) Niels Juul Bondo; (2) Paul Svarre; (3) Hans Jørgen Christensen. Début, Royal Theatre, Copenhagen, when still a student; dancer, Royal Danish Ballet, from 1947, becoming solo dancer (principal) from 1950; international guest artist, including for Original Ballet Russe, London, 1951–52; founder and director, group performing as Soloists of the Royal Danish Ballet, touring internationally, 1950s and 1960s; director, season of new choreography, New Theatre, Copenhagen, 1965; associate artistic director (under director Flemming Flindt), Royal Danish Ballet, from 1966; tour manager, Royal Danish Ballet, from 1971. Recipient: Order of Dannebrog. Died in Copenhagen, 9 February 1974.

ROLES

1937   Columbine in *The Shepherdess and the Chimney Sweep* (Lander), Royal Danish Ballet, Copenhagen

1940   Butterfly in *The Widow in the Mirror* (B. Ralov), Royal Danish Ballet, Copenhagen

1943   Persian Woman in *Polovtsian Dances from Prince Igor* (Fokine) Royal Danish Ballet, Copenhagen

1944   Horse in *The Dethroned Lion Tamer* (Larsen), Royal Danish Ballet, Copenhagen

1945   Friendly Wave in *The Sorcerer's Apprentice* (Lander), Royal Danish Ballet, Copenhagen

Sylph solo (Act II) in *La Sylphide* (Bournonville), Royal Danish Ballet, Copenhagen

Butterfly in *Spring* (Lander), Royal Danish Ballet, Copenhagen

1946   Woman in *The Phoenix* (Lander), Royal Danish Ballet, Copenhagen

Solo (Act II) in *Giselle* (Petipa after Coralli, Perrot; staged Volinine), Royal Danish Ballet, Copenhagen

1947   One of the Three Graces in *Thorvaldsen* (Lander), Royal Danish Ballet, Copenhagen

Trine in *The Lifeguards on Amager* (Bournonville), Royal Danish Ballet, Copenhagen

1948   Dragonfly in *Episode of an Artist's Life* (Massine), Royal

Danish Ballet, Copenhagen

Dancer (cr) in *Étude* (later *Études*; Lander), Royal Danish Ballet, Copenhagen

Hunting Nymph (cr) in *Sylvia* (Larsen), Royal Danish Ballet, Copenhagen

The Daughter in *Le Beau Danube* (Massine), Royal Danish Ballet, Copenhagen

First Broom in *The Sorcerer's Apprentice* (Lander), Royal Danish Ballet, Copenhagen

1949   One with gloves in *The Widow in the Mirror* (B. Ralov), Royal Danish Ballet, Copenhagen

Greek dance in *The Whims of Cupid* (Galeotti), Royal Danish Ballet, Copenhagen

Peasant girl (cr) in *Morning, Noon and Night* (Lander), Royal Danish Ballet, Copenhagen

Amager dance in *The Whims of Cupid and the Ballet Master* (Galeotti), Royal Danish Ballet, Copenhagen

Eskimo dance in *Salute to August Bournonville* (Lander after Bournonville), Royal Danish Ballet, Copenhagen

Flame Fairy in *Aurora's Wedding* (from *The Sleeping Beauty*; Brenaa after Petipa), Royal Danish Ballet, Copenhagen

1950   Zouay dance in *Visions* (Walbom), Royal Danish Ballet, Copenhagen

Snowdrop in *Twelve by the Post* (B. Ralov), Royal Danish Ballet, Copenhagen

Dancer (cr) in *Concerto* (Theilade), Royal Danish Ballet, Copenhagen

Bluebird Pas de deux in *Aurora's Wedding* (from *The Sleeping Beauty*; Brenaa after Petipa), Royal Danish Ballet, Copenhagen

1951   Swanilda in *Coppélia* (Lander after Saint-Léon), Royal Danish Ballet, Copenhagen

The Dancer (cr) in *Desire* (Larsen), Royal Danish Ballet, Copenhagen

The Florentine Beauty in *Paganini* (Fokine), Original Ballet Russe

The Cockerel in *Le Coq d'or* (Fokine), Original Ballet Russe

1952   First Junior Girl in *Graduation Ball* (Lichine), Royal Danish Ballet, Copenhagen

Principal dancer in *Designs with Strings* (Taras), Royal Danish Ballet, Copenhagen

Third Movement in *Symphony in C* (Balanchine), Royal Danish Ballet, Copenhagen

1953   Principal dancer (cr) in *Concertette* (Bruhn), Royal Danish Ballet, Copenhagen

1954   Black Swan in *Black Swan Pas de deux* (Bruhn after Petipa), Royal Danish Ballet, Copenhagen

Lucinda (cr) in *Capricious Lucinda* (Larsen), Royal Danish Ballet, Copenhagen

1955   Principal dancer in *Concerto Barocco* (Balanchine), Royal Danish Ballet, Copenhagen

Moor in *Night Shadow* (*La Sonnambula*; Balanchine), Royal Danish Ballet, Copenhagen

Leader of Polovtsian women in *Polovtsian Dances from Prince Igor* (Fokine), Royal Danish Ballet, Copenhagen

Fanny Cerrito in *Pas de quatre* (Dolin), Royal Danish Ballet, Copenhagen

1956   Nocturne and Mazurka in *Les Sylphides* (Fokine; staged Ralov), Royal Danish Ballet, Copenhagen

Poul in *Far from Denmark* (Bournonville), Royal Danish Ballet, Copenhagen

Rosaline in *Romeo and Juliet* (Ashton), Royal Danish Ballet, Copenhagen

Clarinet in *Fanfare* (Robbins), Royal Danish Ballet, Copenhagen

Pas de trois in *La Ventana* (Bournonville), Royal Danish Ballet, Copenhagen

1957   Principal dancer in *Serenade* (Balanchine), Royal Danish Ballet, Copenhagen

Fairy of the Golden Vine in *The Sleeping Beauty* (Petipa, Ashton), Royal Danish Ballet, Copenhagen

Pas de trois in *The Sleeping Beauty* (Petipa, Ashton), Royal Danish Ballet, Copenhagen

Pas de deux in *The Kermesse in Bruges* (Bournonville), Royal Danish Ballet, Copenhagen

Principal dancer (cr) in *Roguery* (Bjørnsson), Tivoli Concert Hall, Copenhagen

1959   Peasant Pas de deux in *Giselle* (Petipa after Coralli, Perrot; staged Bruhn), Royal Danish Ballet, Copenhagen

1960   Bandit in *Carmen* (Petit), Royal Danish Ballet, Copenhagen

Principal dancer in *Vivaldi Concerto* (Rodrigues), Royal Danish Ballet, Copenhagen

Olympe (cr) in *The Lady of the Camellias* (K. Ralov), Royal Danish Ballet, Copenhagen

1961   Dance for the Joy of Life in *The Little Mermaid* (Beck, Brenaa), Royal Danish Ballet, Copenhagen

Pas de six and Tarantella in *Napoli* (Bournonville), Royal Danish Ballet, Copenhagen

The Woman in *The Burrow* (MacMillan), Royal Danish Ballet, Copenhagen

1962   Dreams in *Les Victories de l'amour* (Lander), Royal Danish Ballet, Copenhagen

1963   First Movement in *Bourrée fantasque* (Balanchine), Royal Danish Ballet, Copenhagen

Lucille Grahn in *Pas de quatre* (Dolin), Royal Danish Ballet, Copenhagen

Principal dancer (cr) in *Garden Party* (Schaufuss), Royal Danish Ballet, Copenhagen

1964   Sagana in *Katharsis* (Cramér), Royal Danish Ballet, Copenhagen

Venetian dance in *Swan Lake* (Petipa, Ivanov), Royal Danish Ballet, Copenhagen

The Lion (cr) in *Tobias and the Angel* (Bartholin), Danish television

Columbine (cr) in *The White Supper* (Bjørnsson), Danish television

1965   Mother-in-law (cr) in *The Young Man Must Marry* (television version; Flindt), Danish television

Woman in *Sonate à trois* (Béjart), Copenhagen Ballet Theatre, New Theatre, Copenhagen

1966   Headmistress in *Graduation Ball* (Lichine), Royal Danish Ballet, Copenhagen

Mrs. van Everdingen in *The Kermesse in Bruges* (Bournonville), Royal Danish Ballet, Copenhagen

Principal dancer in *The Door* (television version; K. Ralov), Danish television

1967   Pianist in *The Lesson* (Flindt), Royal Danish Ballet, Copenhagen

Mother-in-law in *The Young Man Must Marry* (stage version; Flindt), Royal Danish Ballet, Copenhagen

Principal dancer (cr) in *Rendez-Vous* (Bjørnsson), Hotel d'Anleterre, Copenhagen

1969   Lady Kristine in *A Folk Tale* (Bournonville), Royal Danish Ballet, Copenhagen

Pride in *The Seven Deadly Sins* (Cramér), Royal Danish Ballet, Copenhagen

1972   Old Woman in *The Triumph of Death* (Flindt), Royal Danish Ballet, Copenhagen

WORKS

1964   *Life in the Togs* (mus. Glindemann), Tivoli Theatre, Copenhagen

PUBLICATIONS

Lawson, Joan, "The Royal Danish Ballet Festival", *Dancing Times* (London), July 1951

Hollander, Michael, "Walter Terry with Inge Sand and Fredbjørn Bjørnsson, *Dance Observer* (New York), December 1956

Hering, Doris, "Ten Young Dancers from the Royal Danish Ballet", *Dance Magazine* (New York), October 1961

"Inge Sand", *Dance News* (New York), May 1974

Sorley Walker, Kathrine, *De Basil's Ballets Russes*, London, 1982

*   *   *

One of Inge Sand's first major roles with the Royal Danish Ballet was in Harald Lander's *Spring*. She danced the role of the Butterfly. All those who ever saw her dance will now recognize the aptness of the symbol. Her dancing had a quick lightness, a joyousness, a fey fragility that recalled a butterfly's movements. (Like a butterfly's too, her life was tragically short: she died of cancer at the age of 45.)

Sand was a product of the Bournonville school, which promotes buoyancy among the female as well as the male students by stressing jumps and speed. The Danish tradition of mime had developed Sand's talent as an actress, and she excelled in dramatic roles.

During her engagement with the Original Ballet Russe, Sand was cast significantly in many of Tatiana Riabouchinska's roles: the Florentine Beauty in Fokine's *Paganini*, the Cockerel in *Coq d'or*, and one of the pigtailed Girls in Lichine's *Graduation Ball*—the sauciest and prettiest one, according to one critic. Obviously Serge Grigoriev and Lubov Tchernicheva, as régisseur and ballet mistress of the company, felt that Sand shared many of Riabouchinska's unusual qualities as a dancer.

Sand was an incomparable Swanilda, the greatest after Margot Lander among the Danish dancers. The role suited her admirably with her petite physique and her porcelain-pale colouring. She was a perfect soubrette, with her airy, witty style of dancing—not a ballerina in the grand manner.

A superb actress, Sand excelled in demi-caractère roles in Massine's *Le Beau Danube*, Bournonville's *Napoli*, Lander's *Sorcerer's Apprentice*, and Maurice Béjart's *Sonate à trois*, based on Sartre's *No Exit*. In this last ballet, her performance had an extraordinary intensity.

English and American critics in the 1950s were relatively unfamiliar with the Bournonville style of ballet, and some were critical of Sand's dancing, finding it unfluid and not etched sharply enough. This was particularly noticed at the Original Ballet Russe premiere in Wimbledon in 1951, when Sand's dancing stood out from the bravura style then favoured by the company.

All agreed, however, that Sand was a born organizer, who took pioneer groups of Royal Danish Ballet dancers on tour through Europe and North and South America. She organized the first Danish appearance at the Jacob's Pillow Festival in Massachusetts in 1954. From then until the late 1960s, the indefatigable Sand arranged an almost yearly tour beyond the confines of Denmark. Her enterprise and skill at managing these tours was undoubtedly responsible for making Danish ballet and the Bournonville technique known and appreciated throughout the world. In recognition for her service to dance, her country awarded Inge Sand the Order of Dannebrog.

—Alanna Matthew

———

SAN FRANCISCO BALLET

American ballet company based in San Francisco, California. Origins in the San Francisco Opera Ballet, formed by the San Francisco Opera Association, with Adolph Bolm as director, 1933; performed in operas and individual ballet evenings, War Memorial Opera House, with first independent ballet performances, 1937; performed as San Francisco Ballet, directed by Willam Christensen, from 1942. Official school associated with the company, founded in conjunction with the establishment of original company, 1933; independent San Francisco Ballet School, directed by Harold Christensen, founded 1942. Current artistic director of the San Francisco Ballet (succeeding Michael Smuin): Helgi Tomasson, from 1985.

PUBLICATIONS

Maynard, Olga, "The Christensen Brothers: An American Dance Dynasty", *Dance Magazine* (New York), June 1973

Buchau, S. von, "The Biggest Game in Town", *Ballet News* (New York), October 1980

Steinberg, Cobbett, *San Francisco Ballet: The First Fifty Years*, San Francisco, 1983

Ross, Janice, "New Signal: San Francisco Ballet", *Dance Magazine* (New York), August 1987

Wilkens-Veras, Jan, "Willam Christensen", *Dance Teacher Now* (West Sacramento), May 1989

Parish, Paul, "San Francisco Ballet", *Ballet Review* (New York), Summer 1990

Ross, Janice, "San Francisco Ballet: Helgi's Domain", *Dance Magazine* (New York), September 1991

Barnes, Clive, "San Francisco Ballet", *Dance and Dancers* (London), January/February 1992

Barnes, Clive, "San Francisco Ballet is on Point", *Performing Arts Magazine* (San Francisco), February 1992

*   *   *

The San Francisco Ballet is the oldest professional ballet company in the United States and the third largest. It is the resident ballet company at the San Francisco War Memorial Opera House, a home it shares with the San Francisco Opera. The company was established in 1933 by the Opera's founding director, Gaetano Merola, who wished to have a ballet company and school attached to the Opera. Adolph Bolm, star of the St. Petersburg Maryinsky Theatre and of Diaghilev's Ballets Russes, was the first ballet master, followed by Serge Oukrainsky in 1937. He was succeeded in 1938 by Willam Christensen, the oldest of the three Christensen brothers, all of whom became closely associated with San Francisco Ballet. The Christensens were well-trained classical dancers and their dedication to the basic tenets of classicism has marked the company and its style from the beginning.

Willam Christensen was an imaginative and determined director who built audiences and repertory and trained a number of important dancers including Janet Reed, Onna White, and Jocelyn Vollmar. He choreographed both abstract

San Francisco Ballet: Evelyn Cisneros in Helgi Tomasson's *The Sleeping Beauty*, 1990

and classical works, as well as his own full-length versions of *Swan Lake* (1940), *Coppélia* (1939), and *The Nutcracker* (1944).

In 1940 Harold Christensen and his wife Ruby Asquith, who had been dancing with Lincoln Kirstein's Ballet Caravan, joined the San Francisco company. In addition to performing, Harold became the director of the school, a position he held until his retirement in 1975. In 1942 the San Francisco Opera board decided it could no longer support the Ballet, and sold the school and company to Willam and Harold Christensen for $900. The company was renamed the San Francisco Ballet with William as director, and the school became the San Francisco Ballet School, directed by Harold.

Lew Christensen, who had been a principal dancer and then ballet master with several of the Lincoln Kirstein/George Balanchine companies, joined Willam as co-director in San Francisco in 1951. The next year Willam accepted a position on the University of Utah faculty, and Lew was named director. He built a strong, young company which danced primarily his own ballets, such as *Filling Station* and *Con Amore*, two of his best-known works. Lew Christensen also maintained close ties with George Balanchine, adding some twenty Balanchine ballets to the company's repertory over the years. In 1956, San Francisco Ballet made its début at the Jacob's Pillow Dance

Festival in Massachusetts, where it was reviewed enthusiastically by the national press. Three Department of State international tours followed in 1957 (Asia), 1958 (Latin America), and 1959 (the Middle East). During the 1950s, Lew Christensen also choreographed two full-length ballets: his own version of *The Nutcracker*, which remains in the repertory, and *Beauty and the Beast*. But during the 1960s the company saw many of its best dancers leave for New York. This, coupled with chronic financial difficulties and Lew Christensen's mounting health problems, caused the company to weaken considerably.

Then in 1973 Michael Smuin—a principal dancer with San Francisco Ballet before his move to American Ballet Theatre—returned as associate, and ultimately co-director, with Lew Christensen. The next decade was dominated by Smuin and was a period of vigorous growth. The company was reorganized after another financial crisis in 1974, and Richard E. LeBlond, Jr., a highly skilled administrator, was hired as president. He put San Francisco Ballet on a solid financial footing and initiated the building of a new permanent home for the company and school next to the Opera House.

Smuin brought new energy to the San Francisco Ballet and a new style that was highly theatrical. During his tenure he choreographed three full-length works, *Cinderella* (with Lew Christensen), *Romeo and Juliet*, and *The Tempest*, and added highly dramatic ballets to the repertory such as *Shinju* and *A Song for Dead Warriors*. He also increased the number of ballets by outside choreographers, including Frederick Ashton and Jerome Robbins, and developed choreographers from within the company who created works on a regular basis.

The company celebrated its fiftieth anniversary in 1983 in stronger condition than ever before. The next year Lew Christensen died, bringing to a close an era of the company's history that stretched back almost to its founding. Soon after, Smuin and the board had a falling out over artistic policies; Smuin left, and was replaced in 1985 by Helgi Tomasson, a leading dancer with Balanchine's New York City Ballet.

Tomasson's tenure has been marked by a return to classicism and a new level of dance artistry that has put San Francisco on an international footing. He has enlarged the company to 66 dancers and added his own stagings of the nineteenth-century classics *La Sylphide*, *Swan Lake*, and *The Sleeping Beauty*. His own choreography, in a lyrically classic idiom, is a main ingredient of the repertory. In addition, he has added classic works by Tudor, Robbins, Balanchine, and others, as well as giving a prominent place to ballets by newer choreographers David Bintley, James Kudelka, and William Forsythe. In 1992 Tomasson received the *Dance Magazine* Award for significant contributions to dance.

—Gay Morris

SATIE, Erik (Eric)

French composer. Born Eric-Alfred-Leslie Satie in Honfleur, 17 May 1866. Studied at the Paris Conservatoire, 1879–92, continuing with Taudou (harmony) and Mathias (piano), from 1885. Produced famous *Gymnopédies*, 1888, and *Gnossienes*, 1889; first dramatic work, ballet *Uspud*, completed 1892 (but not performed); pantomime *Jack-in-the-Box* composed 1899 (but only performed after his death); composer for Diaghilev's Ballets Russes, collaborating with Jean Cocteau, Pablo Picasso, and Léonide Massine for Diaghilev ballet *Parade*, Paris, 1917; composer of two more ballets, including for Les Ballets Suédois, 1924; composer of several other dramatic works, including incidental music, and opera for marionettes. Died in Paris, 1 July 1925.

WORKS

1892 *Uspud* (not performed)
1917 *Parade* (chor. Massine), Diaghilev's Ballets Russes, Paris
1924 *Mercure* (chor. Massine), Soirées de Paris, Paris (staged Diaghilev's Ballets Russes, 1927)
      Relâche (chor. Börlin), Les Ballets Suédois, Paris
1926 *Jack-in-the-Box* (orchestrated Milhaud, chor. Balanchine), Diaghilev's Ballets Russes, Paris (composed 1899; not staged until 1926)

Other ballets using Satie's music: *Mercury* (Ashton, 1931), *Croquis de Mercure* (Howard, 1938), *Idyllic Song* (Cunningham, 1944), *The Monkey Dances* (Cunningham, 1948), *Two Step* (Cunningham, 1949), *Waltz* (Cunningham, 1950), *Rag Time Parade* (Cunningham, 1950), *Septet* (Cunningham, 1953), *Nocturnes* (Cunningham, 1956), *Monotones* (Ashton, 1965,

1966), *Parade* (Neumeier, 1971), *Dark Voyage* (Moreland, 1973), *Danses de travers* (Petit, 1974), *Sports and Follies* (Taylor, 1974), *Piano Variations 3* (part of *Five Short Stories*; van Manen, 1982), *Bijoux* (Morris, 1983), *The Death of Socrates* (Morris, 1983), *Odalisque* (Tetley, 1983), *Four Gnossiennes* (Martins, 1986), *Pas de poisson* (Morris, 1986).

PUBLICATIONS

By Satie:
Satie Seen through his Letters, translated by Michael Bullock, London and New York, 1989

About Satie:
Jean-Aubry, *La Musique française d'aujourd'hui*, Paris, 1916
Cocteau, Jean, *Le Coq et l'arlequin: notes autour de la musique*, Paris, 1918
Coeuroy, *La Musique française moderne*, Paris, 1922
Milhaud, Darius, *Notes sans musique*, Paris, 1949
Myers, Rollo H., *Erik Satie*, New York, 1968
Templier, Pierre-Daniel, *Erik Satie*, translated by Elena and David French, Cambridge, Massachusetts, 1969
Harding, James, *Erik Satie*, New York, 1975
Bredel, Marc, *Erik Satie*, Paris, 1982
Gillmor, Alan, *Erik Satie*, Boston, 1988

*   *   *

Erik Satie was an artist whose eccentric, at times irascible and childlike personality was evident in all aspects of his life, including both his significant literary and musical outputs. Satie was never swayed by popular trends or opinions; he was strong-willed and stubborn, and his expressions, both verbal and otherwise, were brutally honest. As a composer he approached texts and scenarios in an uninhibited manner, and his music, especially the staged works, exhibits a spontaneity and freshness through a simplicity that was novel at the time.

Satie's early ballet, *Uspud* (composed in 1892, and sent to the Paris Opéra with no results) was followed by many works experimenting with popular song and dance forms, and by large works with unusual stage requirements. Satie's works for piano solo, piano four hands, and songs include minuettes, sarabandes, and many waltzes. The manuscript for *Jack-in-the-Box* (1899), written for pantomime and including three jigs, was misplaced by Satie, to be discovered only after his death, when it was finally performed in 1926, with orchestration by Darius Milhaud, sets and costumes by André Derain, and choreography by George Balanchine. Another significant work written by Satie at this time was *Geneviève de Brabant* (1900), a miniature opera for marionettes, marked by simplicity and charm. In their forms, rhythm, and melodies, both works bear the strong flavour of Satie's music-hall and cabaret experiences, which were to colour most of his music, including his ballets.

Although Satie entertained many ideas for ballets and wrote mostly dramatic works in many genres (including the work for which he is most acclaimed, *Socrate*, for four soprano voices and orchestra), his three major ballets were written only during the last ten years of his life. *Parade* is remarkable as one of the first truly experimental ballets, the first "cubist" ballet, as regards both its choreography and its music. Inspired by Jean Cocteau's scenario and Pablo Picasso's sets, Satie's music for *Parade* was particularly mechanistic: sometimes repetitive, sometimes shifting abruptly, it worked with precision to the steps of the dancers. This was in sharp contrast to the popular impressionist styles of the time. The music also strongly

Erik Satie's *Jack-in-the-Box*, with Alexandra Danilova and Stanislas Idzikowski, Diaghilev's Ballets Russes, 1926

demonstrated Satie's detached attitude toward his art, an attitude which regarded the emotional and the mechanical as equally valid, thereby allowing other aspects of the stage (sets, choreography, etc.) to flourish. The simplicity and directness with which this was achieved, while met with controversy among critics, proved to be inspiring to many other artists, including Diaghilev, Stravinsky, Milhaud, and Sauget. The music of *Parade* was significant also for its incorporation of the music of the streets—including everything from French music-hall to American rag-time—for the first time in a work which garnered obvious respect.

Mercure, "poses plastiques", and *Relâche*, "ballet instantanéiste", were conceived and created in the spirit of Dadaism. The score for *Mercure* is little known, largely due to its background quality. Satie is known for the development of what he termed "musique d'ameublement" (furnishing music), and in this score he appears to have been too successful for his own good, or at least for posterity.

Relâche, meaning "no performance", or "theatre closed", was Satie's last work. Unlike *Parade* and *Mercure*, which were written for Léonide Massine, this was for Jean Börlin of the Ballets Suédois, known in the 1920s for its very contemporary productions; and the scenario was by the flamboyant Francis Picabia, a lively Dadaist during that era's brief but pungent duration. René Clair, the future great film director, created a 22-minute film to be shown between the two acts of *Relâche*. This "Entr'acte" became the most successful aspect of the production in its expression of all the Dadaist fancies of the collaborators. Satie's functional score for this crazy, nonsensical film is now recognized as the earliest example of a technique for film scoring. Satie underscored the film's action as he did the dance in his ballets. Despite the nonsense scenario of the ballet itself, Satie's music is typically symmetrical, careful, and specific to the smallest detail. Again, as with *Parade*, Satie's most significant contribution was not so much the music itself, but in its example of a successful collaboration and its inspiration of possibilities outside of the traditional Germanic and French traditions in which so much ballet music had been steeped until that time.

—E. Amelia Rogers

SAUGET, Henri

French composer. Born Jean-Pierre Poupard near Bordeaux, 18 May 1901. Studied organ with Paul Combes, and composition with Joseph Canteloube and J.P. Vaubourgoin, Bordeaux. Founder, "Les Trois", a Bordeaux group modelled on Les Six; moved to Paris, becoming acquainted with Koechlin, Satie, and Poulenc, 1922/23; co-founder of l'École d'Arcueil, performing first concert at the Sorbonne, 1923; first ballet (and first major success), *Les Roses*, staged 1924; second ballet, *La Chatte*, commissioned by Diaghilev, 1927, and resulting in steady stream of commissions, culminating in *Les Forains*, 1945; composer for producer/dancer Ida Rubinstein and for choreographers George Balanchine, Serge Lifar, Leonide Massine, Roland Petit, and others; also composer of numerous operas and film scores, as well as incidental music for theatre, television, and radio. Elected to Académie des Beaux-Arts, 1975. Died in Paris, 22 June 1989.

WORKS (Ballets)

1924   *Les Roses* (chor. Massine), Les Soirées de Paris, Paris
1927   *La Chatte* (chor. Balanchine), Diaghilev's Ballets Russes, Monte Carlo
1928   *David* (chor. Massine), Ida Rubinstein's Company, Paris
1929   *Près du bal* (chor. Franck), private salon, Paris
1930   *La Nuit* (chor. Lifar), Charles B. Cochran Revue, London
1933   *Fastes* (chor. Balanchine), Les Ballets 1933, Paris
1941   *Cartes postales* (chor. Berezzi), Théâtre Hébertot, Paris
1943   *Paul et Virginie* (*Image à Paul et Virginie*; chor. Petit), Gala, Salle Pleyel, Paris
1945   *Les Forains* (chor. Petit), Théâtre de Champs-Elysées, Paris
1947   *Les Mirages* (chor. Lifar), Paris Opéra Ballet, Paris
1948   *La Rencontre; ou, Œdipe et le Sphinx* (chor. Lichine), Ballets des Champs-Elysées, Paris
         La Cigale et la fourmi (lib. Chesnais, La Fontaine; composed 1941), Marionettes del Buratonni de Maria Signorelli
1951   *Pas de deux classique* (chor. Guélis), Casino de Paris, Paris
         Les Saisons (based on Second Symphony, *Symphonie allegorique*, 1949; chor. Massine), International Music Festival, Grand Theatre, Bordeaux
1952   *Cordélia* (chor. Taras), Grand Ballet du Marquis de Cuevas, Paris
         Trésor et magie (chor. Lifar), Gala, Paris
         Le Cardinal aux chats (also lib.), Théâtre Marigny, Paris
1956   *Le Caméléopard* (chor. Babilée), Ballets Jean Babilée, Paris
1957   *La Dame aux camélias* (*Die Kameliendame*; chor. T. Gsovsky), Berlin Ballet, Berlin

1958 *La Solitude* (also lib.; not performed)
1960 *Les Cinq Étages* (chor. Orlikowsky), Basel Ballet, Basel
       L'As de coeur (chor. Lazzini), Marseilles Opera,
       Marseilles
1961 *Plus loin que la nuit et le jour* (cantata-ballet; chor.
       Etcheverry), Bordeaux Festival
1964 *Pâris* (chor. Charrat), Ballet Janine Charrat, Paris
1965 *Le Prince et le mendiant* (ballet-mimodrame; chor.
       Corelli), French television

Other ballets using Sauget's music: *Caprice* (chor. Balanchine,
1932). *Le Dernier Jugement* (chor. Charrat, 1951).

PUBLICATIONS

By Sauget:
La Musique, ma vie, Libraire Seguier, 1990

About Sauget:
Milhaud, Darius, *Études*, Paris, 1930
Brahms, Caryl, *A Seat at the Ballet*, London, 1951
Beaumont, Cyril, *Ballets of Today*, London, 1954
Schneider, Marcel, *Henri Sauget*, Paris, 1959
Massine, Léonide, *My Life in Ballet*, London, 1960
Bril, F.-Y., *Henri Sauget*, Paris, 1967
McDonald, Nesta, *Diaghilev Observed by Critics in England and
       the United States*, New York and London, 1975
Buckle, Richard, *Diaghilev*, London, 1979
Les Ballets 1933 (various authors), Royal Pavilion exhibition
       catalogue, Brighton, 1987
de Cossart, Michael, *Ida Rubinstein*, Liverpool, 1987
Roy, Jean, "Souvenirs d'en France", *Le Monde de la musique*
       (Paris), September 1989

*   *   *

During his long and prolific career, Henri Sauguet wrote the
scores for more than two dozen ballets, two of which stand as
important landmarks in the history of modern ballet: *La
Chatte*, with choreography by Balanchine, was commissioned
for the Ballets Russes by Diaghilev in 1927; and *Les Forains*
was the catalyst for the formation of Roland Petit's post-war
company, Les Ballets des Champs-Elysées.

Sauguet had moved to Paris in 1922 from his native
Bordeaux, and with several other young composers formed the
École d'Arcueil, their credo being as Arthur Hoérée puts it, "to
create music that was non-academic and unpretentious". The
success of their first concert resulted in an opera commission
for Sauguet. It was this opera, *Le Plumet du colonel* (1924), and
his earlier piano pieces *Trois Françaises*, that prompted
Diaghilev to ask Satie for an introduction to the young
composer, although a ballet commission did not immediately
follow. "At the beginning of 1927," Sauguet later wrote, "I set
out for Monte Carlo where the company was getting ready for
its season. I spent nearly three months there writing the music
for the ballet, royally welcomed by this quite extraordinary man
who treated his composers like princes . . .".

The success of *La Chatte*, which had its premiere in Monte
Carlo on 30 April 1927, was in large measure due to
Balanchine's choreography and the innovative Constructivist
set by Naum Gabo. Sauguet's score was criticized in some
quarters for its lack of corresponding modernity ("Critics were
disposed to blame Sauguet," wrote W.A. Propert, "because his
music didn't fit the spirit of this Talc-and-American-cloth
age"). But the score had its proponents, not least Alice
Nikitina, who danced the role of the Cat in Paris a month later,
learning the injured Spessivtseva's role in under two hours.
Nikitina described the music as "so melodious, so expressive
(that it) inspired me remarkably and was in such harmony with
the fairylike background of transparent and colourless
constructions".

From the solemn opening unison notes, played at opposite
ends of the scale, the score of *La Chatte* proclaims its classical
influences; the separate sections, for the most part, conform to
an A-B-A structure. When dissonance is used, it is quickly
resolved. The orchestration is deft and apt. The use of tonal
harmony, and the clear melodic lines in which can be heard
echoes of Gounod and even Delibes, suggest to the listener a
more straightforward and conventional telling of the plot than
the viewer in fact received.

There are lively dramatic contrasts, as for instance when the
vigorous "Jeux", with its staccato motive, gives way to the
"Invocation", a haunting threnody of melody introduced by the
flute. Indeed, this haunting little melody is reversed to form the
theme for the Adagio (whole tone rise on the upbeat, then four
downward notes of the scale). This is almost textbook stuff for
the classically trained composer. Melody follows melody until
the final chorale-like Hymn ends with a note played in unison
on brass. This quiet solemnity enhances the sense of ancient
ritual which Sauguet's clear classical style evokes, though there
is also a concomitant lack of danger, which perhaps inspired
Benois' dismissive description of the score as "drawing room
music".

La Chatte brought Sauguet a commission from Ida Rubinstein (*David*, 1928); and ballets for Balanchine and Lifar,
among others, followed. But it was Sauguet's collaboration with
Roland Petit on *Les Forains* which inspired his supreme
contribution to ballet music. During the winter of 1945,
Kochno and Petit approached Sauguet with the scenario of a
new ballet. "This scenario . . . seduced me completely," he
wrote. "(It) pleased me so much that I didn't hesitate to give my
agreement to complete the score. . . . Each day I met Roland
Petit in a studio he had rented. We agreed on the music, and his
choreography made me reconsider certain dances in order to fit
them musically to the characters he had devised." Thus, as
Sauguet himself explained it, the ballet was born of a "strict
collaboration between its choreographer and composer".

The score of *Les Forains* confirms Sauguet's talent for writing
music that sustains the mood of the choreography, and evokes
character and setting. Strong theatrical colours effortlessly
depict the tattered group of street entertainers of the title, the
gaiety and dedication of their performance, and the melancholy
ending when their audience melts away and the performers
must move on to their next port of call, dejected but not
defeated.

Inspired by memories of the fun-fairs he had been taken to
during his childhood, Sauguet wrote, as the *Dancing Times*
critic put it, "the kind of tunes that may be heard upon the
steam-organs of roundabouts". And haunting this score is the
enchantingly wistful waltz in a minor key, based on a pattern of
three descending notes with a little rise at the end of the phrase.
It accompanies the entrance of the performers, and echoes
throughout the ballet, suggesting, as Cyril Beaumont wrote,
"both the drudgery and the glamour of stage life".

The French word *spirituel*, meaning witty, was frequently
used to characterize Sauguet the man, while at the same time
this quality was contrasted with his *spiritualité*, a neat play on
words that would have delighted the composer himself, well-
known for his "mots" and mimicry. He was loved for his
vivacity and boundless curiosity—and yet at the same time his
music has been characterized as solitary and secret, "because
mystery, nuance, shadow were his preferences" (Jean Roy, *Le
Monde de la musique*).

This mixture of the witty and the mysterious in the man produced ballet music of great charm, highly responsive to the needs of choreographer and scenarist. What it lacks is an extra bite, a kind of danger, that might have taken the music beyond these immediate needs, and given it a longer life.

—Louise Stein

LA SCALA BALLET

Italian ballet company based in Milan. Established as the official dancing company of the Teatro alla Scala, opened 1778; theatre gained fame as host of great Romantic ballerinas, 1830s and 1840s, and celebrated ballet masters through the nineteenth century; resident company continues to be largely associated with the opera company which shares the Teatro alla Scala, Milan. Official school of La Scala Ballet, originally Imperial Academy of Dance (Imperial Regia Accademia), founded 1813: directed by ballet master Carlo Blasis, from 1838, becoming the leading centre of late nineteenth-century ballet technique; continues as associated school of Teatro alla Scala, Milan. Current artistic director of La Scala Ballet (succeeding Giuseppe Carbone): Robert de Warren, from 1988.

PUBLICATIONS

Carrieri, Raffaele, *La Danza in Italia 1600–1900*, Milan, 1946
Gatti, C., *Il Teatro alla Scala 1778–1963*, 2 volumes: Milan, 1964
Rossi, Luigi, *Il Balletto alla Scala*, Milan, 1972
Pitt, Freda, "Capriccio Italien", *Ballet News* (New York), July 1981

*   *   *

Although perhaps not considered one of the great capitals of ballet today, the city of Milan—and most especially the opera house of La Scala—has played an absolutely vital role in the history of ballet. No opera house was more important in the first half of the nineteenth century, apart from the Paris Opéra.

The Teatro alla Scala was opened in 1778, and, although ballet was by this time established at other theatres in Milan (particularly the Ducale), from this date onwards nearly all the most important performances took place on the stage of La Scala. At that time Angiolini, Noverre's great rival, was resident in the town; he later made a large number of ballets for the Scala. As was the practice throughout Europe, the Scala's programmes habitually followed an opera by one or more ballets—two on the occasion of the inauguration, after an opera by Salieri.

However, the theatre's balletic heyday arrived in the following century. The first of the great names was that of Salvatore Viganò, who made his Scala début—as a choreographer and not as a dancer—at the end of 1811, with a work he had already produced in Venice. In the following year, he reproduced other works he had previously staged in Vienna and elsewhere. In his 1813 reworking of his most famous ballet, *The Creatures of Prometheus*, he added music of his own as well as by Mozart and Haydn to the original Beethoven, adopting the abbreviated title of *Prometeo* for the expanded result. After his success with *Mirra* in 1817, Viganò attempted Othello and other grandiose dramatic subjects, in which mime took an all-

important place. Jean Coralli and Carlo Blasis were among the illustrious artists who appeared in his ballets.

While the Scala school (which still provides most of the dancers in the corps de ballet, and at which tuition is free) was founded in 1813, with the title Imperial Regia Accademia, it was with Blasis's appointment in 1838 that its golden age began. Blasis had earlier made his mark as a notable danseur noble, but a recurring foot injury put paid to his performing career. A list of his pupils would include the majority of the famous dancers of the Romantic age, including three of the ballerinas who took part in Perrot's 1845 London *Pas de quatre*: Carlotta Grisi, Fanny Cerrito, and Lucille Grahn. Giovanni Lepri, who in turn taught Enrico Cecchetti, was also a Blasis pupil.

In the nineteenth century the custom of producing, with new choreography, works made famous in their original versions elsewhere, was already established. For example, a few months before Marie Taglioni made her Scala début (1841), a version of *La Sylphide* by Antonio Cortesi—an active house choreographer of the time—was presented with Milan favourite Fanny Cerrito in the title role. *Giselle* was also first given in a version by Cortesi. However, Perrot himself reproduced and danced in his great London success, *Esmeralda*, with Fanny Elssler as the unfortunate gypsy girl. Other Perrot ballets were also given to general acclaim.

The imposing Scala stage has always invited the use of grandiose scenery, which Alessandro Sanquirico often supplied in the theatre's earlier years, especially for ballets by Viganò and Gioja. The decline in public taste in the later years of the nineteenth century, combining a passion for virtuosity with a weakness for spectacle, led to the popularity of the Marenco-Manzotti showpieces in the 1880s and 1890s, above all the triumph of *Excelsior*. Ballet sank back to the level of a mere divertissement, as it did throughout Europe. Thanks largely to the advent of Verdi, opera reigned supreme. Several great Italian ballerinas, such as Legnani and Zucchi, found greater satisfaction in Russia, although it is true that Carlotta Brianza danced in *Excelsior* in Russia as well as in *The Sleeping Beauty*, and she appeared in Milan and Paris after her creation of the role of Aurora in St. Petersburg.

When Arturo Toscanini called Enrico Cecchetti in to revive the Scala ballet in 1925, the great pedagogue's life was nearly over and he barely had the time to train a few gifted dancers, such as Vincenzo Celli, Attilia Radice, and Cia Fornaroli—who later became a choreographer and director of the school before moving to New York.

Diaghilev's Ballets Russes created no stir in Milan when they finally reached La Scala in 1927, because ballet as a serious art had become an unfamiliar concept. Of Diaghilev's choreographers, only Massine established a reputation at the Scala in later years, when he was living in Italy.

When Aurel Milloss was already well known and highly respected in Italy, he first staged his production of *The Miraculous Mandarin* for the Scala Ballet and then took over as ballet master in 1946. Unfortunately, like his successors, he was able to effect only short-term improvements, because he did not stay long enough to carry out lasting reforms. However, he invited some celebrated guests, thus affording the Milanese the opportunity to see important companies from abroad.

The Scala Ballet began to attract more attention when Carla Fracci, a product of the school, began to appear there, and particularly after her success in Harald Lander's production of *La Sylphide* in 1962, when Esmée Bulnes was in charge of the company and the school. In the mid-1960s the company began to give a brief season in September; it was at that time that Rudolf Nureyev staged his first production of *The Sleeping Beauty* (1966), with Fracci and himself in the leading roles.

Having first appeared at La Scala with Margot Fonteyn and the Royal Ballet (1965), Nureyev had a quite strong influence in Milan, where he frequently appeared as a guest and also staged four full-evening productions in all, spurring the dancers on to greater effort. In the early 1970s, when John Field was running the company, he appeared notably with Liliana Cosi, a striking classical dancer, in both *Giselle* and *The Sleeping Beauty*. Cosi left soon afterwards because of the limited opportunities offered. The management has frequently promised to upgrade the ballet, but these undertakings have not been fulfilled. The Scala remains very much an opera house, so proud of its worldwide reputation in that field that the ballet almost inevitably takes a poor second place. Largely for that reason, after Cosi, both Anna Razzi and Luciana Savignano (a very popular dancer in a different mould, and the Scala's Béjart specialist) danced more and more frequently with other companies even before they reached retiring age. Fracci continued to appear quite frequently, especially on first nights; but this left limited chances for younger dancers.

By 1990, when Robert de Warren had been the director for two years, the company was performing with greater frequency, but often in inferior Milan theatres, whereas at the Scala the dancers attracted most notice through appearing in the ballet set-pieces in the operas that inaugurated the season, such as *William Tell* and *I Vespri siciliani* (both with Fracci).

Several promising young dancers have been produced, but no choreographer of international stature. Probably the most active choreographer in the second half of the twentieth century was Mario Pistoni, Fracci's partner in the 1960s, whose most popular ballet was *La Strada*, based on the Fellini film.

The company (consisting of approximately 80 dancers) remains the best classical one in the country but still needs to acquire a regular repertory of its own.

—Freda Pitt

SCÈNES DE BALLET

Choreography: Frederick Ashton
Music: Igor Stravinsky
Design: André Beaurepaire (scenery and costumes)
First Production: Sadler's Wells Ballet, Royal Opera House, London, 11 February 1948
Principal Dancers: Margot Fonteyn, Michael Somes

Other productions include: Ziegfeld Theatre (first version to score; chor. Anton Dolin, scenery Norman Bel Geddes, costumes Paul Dupont), as part of Billy Rose revue, *The Seven Lively Arts*, with Anton Dolin, Alicia Markova; New York, 7 December 1944. German Opera Ballet (new version; chor. Gustav Blank, design Josef Fenneker); Berlin, 22 May 1952. Stuttgart Ballet (new version; chor. Robert Mayer, design Gerd Richter); Stuttgart, 1952. Hamburg Ballet (new version; chor. Peter van Dijk); Hamburg, 20 January 1962. Stuttgart Ballet (new version; chor. John Cranko); Stuttgart, 10 June 1962. German Opera Ballet (Ashton version; staged Monica Parker,

Scènes de Ballet, with Lesley Collier and Michael Coleman, Royal Ballet, London

Ray Barra; no designs); Berlin, 11 March 1968. New York City Ballet (new version; chor. John Taras), with Patricia McBride, Jean-Pierre Bonnefous; New York, 22 June 1972. Dutch National Ballet (Ashton version); Amsterdam, 21 March 1992.

PUBLICATIONS

Buckle, Richard, "The Adventures of a Ballet Critic", *Ballet* (London), May 1951

Balanchine, George, with Mason, Francis, *Balanchine's Complete Stories of the Great Ballets*, Garden City, N.Y., 1977

Vaughan, David, *Frederick Ashton and his Ballets*, London, 1977

* * *

Ashton's *Scènes de ballet* is the third of three post-war works—the others being *Symphonic Variations* (1946) and *Valses nobles et sentimentales* (1947)—that explore and re-affirm his allegiance to the classical tradition. Ashton himself called it "just an exercise in pure dancing".

Stravinsky was originally commissioned to write *Scènes de ballet* for a ballet in Billy Rose's revue *The Seven Lively Arts*. The leading dancers were Alicia Markova and Anton Dolin, and Dolin was responsible for the choreography. Stravinsky himself specified a cast of two soloists and a corps of four men and twelve women.

Ashton first heard the music on the radio while he was in the bath, and said later, "I was fascinated by the rhythm of it". He discussed the music with the ballet critic Richard Buckle, who provided a scenario and suggested André Beaurepaire as the designer; but in the end Ashton chose to follow Stravinsky's own sense of his score, each movement of which designates a specific dance. Stravinsky wrote: "This music is patterned after the forms of the classical dance, free of any given literary or dramatic argument. The parts follow each other as in a sonata or symphony, in contrasts or similarities."

Stravinsky's score is complex and subtle—its rhythms are broken, its time-signatures are inconsistent, its phrasing is fragmented—and Ashton needed to break the music down into its components. Accordingly, his approach was in part technical, astringent, and strictly mathematical. "I, who at school never got on with algebra or geometry, suddenly got fascinated with geometrical figures, and I used a lot of theorems as ground patterns for *Scènes de ballet*. I used to drive the girls mad trying to solve these theorems, moving them from one position to another. I also wanted to do a ballet that could be seen from any angle—anywhere could be front, so to speak. So I did these geometric figures that are not always facing front—if you saw *Scènes de ballet* from the wings you'd get a very different, but equally good picture. We would get into terrible tangles, but when it finally came out I used to say, QED!"

During rehearsals Ashton had his volume of Euclid in his hand, but the spirit of Petipa was in his heart: and *Scènes de ballet* is a deft and conscious homage. At the mid-point of the score comes the pas de deux, an adagio in C major, in which Ashton alludes repeatedly to the Rose Adagio in *The Sleeping Beauty*. Indeed, after the first entry of the corps, when they pass enchaînements from one line or group to the next, Ashton draws on a choreographic device characteristic of Petipa. *Scènes de ballet* as a whole recapitulates with both nostalgia and irony the executant hierarchy and the idealizing grandeur of the late nineteenth-century Russian manner.

Ashton's allegiance to classical techniques is the most fundamental feature of his choreography. "I always return to

Petipa. . . . People sometimes find me at a matinée of *The Sleeping Beauty*, which I have seen literally hundreds of times. And they ask me what I'm doing and I say 'having a private lesson'." *Scènes de ballet*, his "exercise in pure dancing", shows just how receptive and diligent and ingenious a student Ashton was.

—Martin Wright

———

SCHANNE, Margrethe

Danish dancer. Born Margrethe Marie Sophie Schanne in Copenhagen, 21 November 1921. Studied at the Royal Danish Ballet School, pupil of Valborg Borchsenius and Harald Lander, from 1930; later studied in London and Paris, pupil of Boris Kniaseff and Lubov Egorova, 1946–47. Married dancer Kjeld Noack. Dancer, Royal Danish Ballet, from 1940, becoming solo dancer (principal), from 1943; guest ballerina, Roland Petit's Ballets des Champs-Elysées, Paris, 1947, and Grand Ballet du Marquis de Cuevas, 1956, also touring the United States, 1956, 1960, and 1965, South Africa, 1958, Italy and Spain, 1957, 1961, 1962, and 1963, and London and Berlin, 1964; retired in 1966: teacher of dance and physical education in municipal schools, 1965–86. Recipient: Knight of Dannebrog, 1953; Theatre Trophy, 1955.

ROLES

1934   Butterfly (cr) in *The Widow in the Mirror* (B. Ralov), Royal Danish Ballet, Copenhagen

1937   Muse in *Psyche* (Theilade), Royal Danish Ballet, Copenhagen

Persian Woman in *Polovtsian Dances from Prince Igor* (Fokine), Royal Danish Ballet, Copenhagen

1938   Earth (cr) in *The Circle* (Theilade), Royal Danish Ballet Copenhagen

Muse (cr) in *Thorvaldsen* (Lander), Royal Danish Ballet, Copenhagen

1939   Young Girl in *The Four Temperaments* (B. Ralov), Royal Danish Ballet, Copenhagen

Sylph solo (Act II) in *La Sylphide* (Bournonville), Royal Danish Ballet, Copenhagen

Butterfly in *The Valkyrie* (Lander after Bournonville), Royal Danish Ballet, Copenhagen

1940   Female Painter in *Thorvaldsen* (Lander), Royal Danish Ballet, Copenhagen

Cobweb in *A Midsummer Night's Dream* (Ralov), Royal Theatre, Copenhagen

1941   Nymph in *L'Après-midi d'un faune* (Ralov after Nijinsky), Royal Danish Ballet, Copenhagen

The Young Girl in *Le Spectre de la rose* (Fokine), Royal Danish Ballet, Copenhagen

Gypsy dance from *Il Trovatore* (opera; mus. Verdi, chor. Bournonville), Royal Danish Ballet, Copenhagen

Pas de six in *Napoli* (Bournonville), Royal Danish Ballet, Copenhagen

Pas de trois in *La Ventana* (Bournonville), Royal Danish Ballet, Copenhagen

1942   May (cr) in *Twelve by the Post* (B. Ralov), Royal Danish Ballet, Copenhagen

Married Woman in *Qarrtsiluni* (Lander), Royal Danish Ballet, Copenhagen

Dessert in *The Land of Milk and Honey* (Lander), Royal

Margarethe Schanne with Børge Ralov in *Giselle*, Royal Danish Ballet, 1950s

Danish Ballet, Copenhagen
Dancer (cr) in *Festival Polonaise* (Lander), Royal Danish Ballet, Copenhagen
Butterfly (cr) in *Spring* (Lander), Royal Danish Ballet, Copenhagen
1943   Slovanka in *The Kermesse in Bruges* (Bournonville), Royal Danish Ballet, Copenhagen
Pas de deux in *The Kermesse in Bruges* (Bournonville), Royal Danish Ballet, Copenhagen
Nocturne and Prelude in *Les Sylphides* (Lander after Fokine), Royal Danish Ballet, Copenhagen
1944   The Circus Princess (cr) in *The Dethroned Lion Tamer* (Larsen), Royal Danish Ballet, Copenhagen
The Longing (cr) in *Passiones* (B. Ralov), Royal Danish Ballet, Copenhagen
1945   Swanilda's friend in *Coppélia* (Lander after Saint-Léon), Royal Danish Ballet, Copenhagen
Pas de trois in *Swan Lake* (one-act version; Lander after Petipa, Ivanov), Royal Danish Ballet, Copenhagen
Friendly Wave in *The Sorcerer's Apprentice* (Lander), Royal Danish Ballet, Copenhagen
Title role in *La Sylphide* (Bournonville), Royal Danish Ballet, Copenhagen
Edouard in *Far from Denmark* (Bournonville), Royal Danish Ballet, Copenhagen
1946   Princess (cr) in *The Soldier's Tale* (B. Ralov), Royal Danish Ballet, Copenhagen
1948   The Seamstress in *Le Beau Danube* (Massine), Royal Danish Ballet, Copenhagen
Columbine in *Visions* (Walbom), Royal Danish Ballet, Copenhagen
1949   She in *The Widow in the Mirror* (B. Ralov), Royal Danish Ballet, Copenhagen

The Woman (cr) in *Rhapsodie* (Lander), Royal Danish Ballet, Copenhagen
Elisa in *Konservatoriet* (Bournonville), Royal Danish Ballet, Copenhagen
Romantic night in *Salute to August Bournonville* (Lander after Bournonville), Royal Danish Ballet, Copenhagen
Pas de trois in *Aurora's Wedding* (from *The Sleeping Beauty*; Brenaa after Petipa), Royal Danish Ballet, Copenhagen
Bluebird Pas de deux in *Aurora's Wedding* (from *The Sleeping Beauty*; Brenaa after Petipa), Royal Danish Ballet, Copenhagen
1950   Ballerina in *Petrushka* (Fokine), Royal Danish Ballet, Copenhagen
Principal dancer (cr) in *Concerto* (Theilade), Royal Danish Ballet, Copenhagen
Second Movement (cr) in *Symphonie classique* (Bertholin), Royal Danish Ballet, Copenhagen
Señorita in *Morning—Noon—Night* (Lander), Royal Danish Ballet, Copenhagen
Odette in *Swan Lake* (one-act version; Lander after Petipa, Ivanov), Royal Danish Ballet, Copenhagen
1951   The Young Girl (cr) in *Desire* (Larsen), Royal Danish Ballet, Copenhagen
Title role in *Giselle* (Petipa after Coralli, Perrot; staged Volinin), Royal Danish Ballet, Copenhagen
Eleonora in *The Kermesse in Bruges* (Bournonville), Royal Danish Ballet, Copenhagen
1952   Pas de deux classique in *Graduation Ball* (Lichine), Royal Danish Ballet, Copenhagen
Principal dancer in *Designs with Strings* (Taras), Royal Danish Ballet, Copenhagen

First Movement in *Symphony in C* (Balanchine), Royal Danish Ballet, Copenhagen

1953   Victorine in *Konservatoriet* (Bournonville), Royal Danish Ballet, Copenhagen

The Parisienne (cr) in *Parisiana* (Bartholin), Royal Danish Ballet, Copenhagen

1955   The Sleepwalker in *Night Shadow* (*La Sonnambula*; Balanchine), Royal Danish Ballet, Copenhagen

Saltarello in Kjeld Abell's play *Andersen; or, The Tale of His Life* (Larsen), Royal Theatre, Copenhagen

Fandango in *The Marriage of Figaro* (opera; mus. Mozart, chor. Bournonville), Royal Theatre, Copenhagen

Marie Taglioni in *Pas de quatre* (Dolin), Royal Danish Ballet, Copenhagen

1956   Rosita in *Far from Denmark* (Bournonville), Royal Danish Ballet, Copenhagen

1957   Principal dancer in *Serenade* (Balanchine), Royal Danish Ballet, Copenhagen

Aurora in *The Sleeping Beauty* (Petipa, Ashton), Royal Danish Ballet, Copenhagen

1958   Principal dancer (cr) in *Opus 13* (Schaufuss), Royal Danish Ballet, Copenhagen

French Dance in *The Whims of Cupid and the Ballet Master* (Galeotti), Royal Danish Ballet, Copenhagen

Pierrette in *Harlequin's Millions* (Walbom), Royal Danish Ballet, Copenhagen

Bridge Lady (cr) in *Happiness on Journey* (Bjørnsson), Royal Danish Ballet, Copenhagen

1959   Title role in *Medea* (Cullberg), Royal Danish Ballet, Copenhagen

1960   Title role (cr) in *The Lady of the Camellias* (K. Ralov), Royal Danish Ballet, Copenhagen

1963   Principal dancer in *The Ballet Castle* (von Rosen), Danish television

Title role in *Irene Holm* (von Rosen), Royal Danish Ballet, Copenhagen

1964   The Experienced (cr) in *Moods* (Brenaa), Royal Danish Ballet, Copenhagen

Lady Karin in *The Virgin Spring* (von Rosen), Royal Danish Ballet, Copenhagen

Principal dancer in *Pas de deux italiano* (Dolin), Danish television

PUBLICATIONS

Roberts, Sonia, "Careers in Pictures: Margrethe Schanne", *Ballet Today* (London), October 1961

Roberts, Sonia, "Margrethe Schanne of the Royal Danish Ballet", *Ballet Today* (London), October 1961

Kragh-Jacobsen, Svend, *Twenty Solo Dancers of the Royal Danish Ballet*, Copenhagen, 1965

Moore, Lillian, "The Distant Flight of La Sylphide", *Dancing Times* (London), July 1965

Chujoy, Anatole, "Great Romantic Ballerina", *Dance News* (New York), February 1966

Kragh-Jacobsen, Svend, *Vor sidste Sylfide*, Copenhagen, 1966

*   *   *

Margrethe Schanne was trained at the Royal Danish Ballet School, and thus the Bournonville style was her native element. As early as 1945 she lent her poetic presence, heightened by exquisite dark eyes and an ethereal grace, to Bournonville's famous *La Sylphide*. Into this figure of evanescent beauty—which she brought to life more than 100 times up to her last performance in 1966—Schanne concentrated all the melancholy poetry of the Romantic concept of the woman as a purely spiritual being. This was the role which, more than any other, the ballerina made her own, her performances making what critics repeatedly called "an unforgettable impression" throughout her long career as one of the greatest exemplars of the Romantic and the Bournonville style.

Schanne's first "created" role was when she was still a student; like most students of Copenhagen's Royal Ballet School, she made early appearances on the stage of the Royal Theatre, and at the age of thirteen she performed the role of a butterfly in Borge Ralov's *The Widow in the Mirror*. Admitted officially into the company when still a teenager, Schanne soon developed into a ballerina of sensitivity and grace, and within five years was performing the role of the tragic sylph in the ballet which was to become her trademark. British critic Richard Buckle, writing in 1953, explained her effect, saying, "Margrethe Schanne is a light, delicate and whimsical sylph: no tragic heroine, but, more appropriately, a pathetic, capricious, devoted creature, loving as a butterfly might."

The tragedy of the sylph, who is a deadly threat to the man she loves, was developed further in Schanne's other great romantic role, Giselle. As the ghostly, other-worldly creature of Act II, Schanne was predictably delicate, graceful, and tragic—but as the innocent and light-hearted peasant girl in the first act she was equally convincing, and she performed the climactic mad scene with harrowing realism. Soulful and lyrical, Schanne also mastered the dreamlike poetry of Fokine's *Les Sylphides*, while as Marie Taglioni in Dolin's staging of *Pas de quatre* she added a subtle irony to the brilliant technique which, more and more through the 1950s, was to carry her confidently through the intensified technical demands of the international ballet world.

Margrethe Schanne performed most of the leading roles in the Bournonville repertoire, bringing her lovely presence and fine technique to such ballets as *The Kermesse in Bruges*, *Konservatoriet*, and *Far From Denmark*. But she was also successful in the Russian classical repertoire, performing both the Bluebird and Princess Aurora in *The Sleeping Beauty*, and Odette in the Royal Danish Ballet's one-act version of *Swan Lake*. In 1955, George Balanchine's *Night Shadow* (*La Sonnambula*) became another vehicle for Schanne's poetic qualities, and was a further culmination of her dramatic abilities. As the beautiful sleepwalker, Schanne bewitchingly combined dreamlike innocence and a glowing sensualism to suggest hidden danger as much as graceful beauty in her enchanting movements. On the other hand, in the title role of Elsa Marianne von Rosen's 1963 modern ballet, *Irene Holm*, Schanne gave a moving portrayal which showed the quiet tragedy of an anti-heroine of modern everyday life.

By the time of her retirement from the stage in 1966, Schanne had proven herself one of the great ballerinas of the twentieth century, whose perfection in the nineteenth-century repertoire made her the deserving recipient, alongside Alicia Markova, of the title "the last Romantic ballerina".

—Marie-Louise Kjølbye

SCHAUFUSS, Peter

Danish dancer, choreographer, and ballet director. Born in Copenhagen, Denmark, son of dancers Frank Schaufuss and Mona Vangsaae, 26 April 1949. Studied at the Royal Danish Ballet School, pupil of Stanley Williams and Hans Brenaa,

Peter Schaufuss as James in *La Sylphide*, London Festival Ballet, c.1979

from 1956. Married (1) dancer Maria Guerrero, 1971 (div.); (2) dancer Janette Mulligan, 1988. Début, Royal Theatre, Copenhagen, when still a child student; apprentice, Royal Danish Ballet, 1964, graduating into Royal Danish Ballet, 1965; dancer, National Ballet of Canada, 1967–68, Royal Danish Ballet, 1968–70; principal dancer, London Festival Ballet, 1970–74, New York City Ballet, 1974–77, and National Ballet of Canada, 1977–83; international guest artist, including for San Francisco Ballet, Pittsburgh Ballet, 1972–74, Kirov and Bolshoi Ballets, 1973, International Ballet, South Africa, American Ballet Theatre, and London Festival Ballet, various seasons, 1977–83, Paris Opéra Ballet, 1980, Aterballetto, Italy, 1982, Royal Ballet, 1982, Kirov Ballet, Leningrad and on tour, 1989–90; has also made guest appearances for Ballet National de Marseille, Royal Danish Ballet, Teatro San Carlo in Naples, Ballet of La Scala in Milan, German Opera Ballet, Berlin; has also appeared on film and on television, including in four-part television series *Dancer* (BBC television, 1984); choreographer, Royal Danish Ballet, 1969–70, and from 1979; artistic director, London Festival Ballet (now English National Ballet), 1984–90, German Opera (Deutsche Oper) Ballet, Berlin, from 1990. Recipient: Silver Medal, Second Moscow International Ballet Competition, 1973; *Evening Standard* Award, 1979; Society of West End Theatres Award (for *La Sylphide*), 1979; Knight of Dannebrog, 1988.

ROLES

1965   Principal dancer in *Don Quixote* Pas de deux (after Petipa), Royal Danish Ballet, Copenhagen

Pas de six in *Napoli* (Bournonville), Royal Danish Ballet, Copenhagen

Pas de sept in *A Folk Tale* (Bournonville), Royal Danish Ballet, Copenhagen

Porthos in *The Three Musketeers* (Flindt), Royal Danish Ballet, Copenhagen

Pas de trois in *Swan Lake* (Petipa, Ivanov), Royal Danish Ballet, Copenhagen

Soloist in *Konservatoriet* (Bournonville), Royal Danish Ballet, Copenhagen

1967   The Prince in *The Nutcracker* (Franca), National Ballet of Canada, Toronto

1968   Pas de deux from *Flower Festival at Genzano* (Bournonville), National Ballet of Canada, Toronto

1968/   Title role in *Homo* (also chor.), Royal Danish Ballet, 70   Copenhagen

Principal dancer in *Le Corsaire* Pas de deux (after Petipa), Royal Danish Ballet, Copenhagen

Drummer in *Graduation Ball* (Lichine), Royal Danish Ballet, Copenhagen

Romeo in *Romeo and Juliet* (Bartholin), Royal Danish

Ballet, Copenhagen

1970   Principal dancer ("Poet") in *Les Sylphides* (Fokine), London Festival Ballet, St. Juan de Luz

Principal dancer in *Études* (Lander), London Festival Ballet, San Sebastián

Bluebird in *The Sleeping Beauty* (Stevenson after Petipa), London Festival Ballet, London

Prince Florimund in *The Sleeping Beauty* (Stevenson after Petipa), London Festival Ballet, London

Principal dancer in *Dvořák Variations* (Hynd), London Festival Ballet, Manchester

Basilio in *Don Quixote* (Borkowski after Petipa), London Festival Ballet, Oxford

1971   The King of the Dandies in *Le Beau Danube* (Massine), London Festival Ballet, London

Albrecht in *Giselle* (Petipa after Coralli, Perrot; staged Skeaping), London Festival Ballet, London

Title role in *Petrushka* (Fokine), London Festival Ballet, London

Scotsman in *Graduation Ball* (Lichine), London Festival BalletBallet, London

The Poet in *Night Shadow* (*La Sonnambula*; Balanchine), London Festival Ballet, London

Flower Festival Pas de deux in *Bournonville Divertissement* (Bournonville; staged Vangsaae), London Festival Ballet, London

Second Movement in *Bourrée fantasque* (Balanchine), London Festival Ballet, London

Peasant Pas de deux from *Giselle* (Petipa after Coralli, Perrot; staged Skeaping), London Festival Ballet, Athens

1972   Pas de trois in *Swan Lake* (Petipa, Ivanov; staged Grey), London Festival Ballet, Eastbourne

Siegfried in *Swan Lake* (Petipa, Ivanov; staged Grey), London Festival Ballet, Eastbourne

Principal dancer in *Ebb and Flow* (Gadd), London Festival Ballet, London

Third Movement in *Mendelssohn Symphony* (Balanchine), London Festival Ballet, London

1973   Principal dancer in *Glazunov Pas de deux* (F. Schaufuss), London Festival Ballet, London

Balcony pas de deux from *Romeo and Juliet* (Ashton), London Festival Ballet, London

Principal dancer in *Noir et blanc* (Lifar), London Festival Ballet, Eastbourne

Solo dancer in *Conservatoire* (*Konservatoriet*; Vangsaae after Bournonville), London Festival Ballet, London

The Prince in *Cinderella* (Stevenson), London Festival Ballet, London

1974   Principal dancer in *Scotch Symphony* (Balanchine), New York City Ballet, New York

Third Movement in *Symphony in C* (Balanchine), New York City Ballet, New York

Principal dancer in *Raymonda Variations* (Balanchine), New York City Ballet, New York

Andante in *Brahms–Schoenberg Quartet* (Balanchine), New York City Ballet, New York

Tema con variazioni in *Tchaikovsky Suite No. 3* (Balanchine), New York City Ballet, New York

Pas de deux in *Cortège Hongroise* (Balanchine), New York City Ballet, New York

Principal dancer (second couple) in *An Evening's Waltzes* (Robbins), New York City Ballet, New York

Principal dancer in *Shéhérazade* (Balanchine), New York City Ballet, New York

Leader (cr) in *Daphnis and Chloe* (Taras), New York City Ballet, New York

1975   Principal dancer (cr) in *Rhapsodie Espagnole* (Balanchine), New York City Ballet, New York

The Soldier (cr) in *The Steadfast Tin Soldier* (Balanchine), New York City Ballet, Saratoga Springs, New York

Rubies in *Jewels* (Balanchine), New York City Ballet, New York

Principal dancer in *Bugaku* (Balanchine), New York City Ballet, New York

Principal dancer in *Stars and Stripes* (Balanchine), New York City Ballet, New York

Oberon in *A Midsummer Night's Dream* (Balanchine), New York City Ballet, New York

The Prince in *The Nutcracker* (Balanchine), New York City Ballet, New York

1977   Bluebird in *The Sleeping Beauty* (Nureyev after Petipa), London Festival Ballet

Romeo in *Romeo and Juliet* (Neumeier), Royal Danish Ballet, Copenhagen

Prince Siegfried in *Swan Lake* (Bruhn after Petipa, Ivanov), National Ballet of Canada, New York

Franz in *Coppélia* (Bruhn after Saint-Léon), National Ballet of Canada

Solor in *Bayaderka* ("Shades" scene from *La Bayadère*; Valukin after Petipa), National Ballet of Canada

James in *La Sylphide* (Bruhn after Bournonville), National Ballet of Canada

Karl in *The Nutcracker* (Hynd), London Festival Ballet, Cardiff

Principal dancer in *Greening* (Tetley), London Festival Ballet

1978   Romeo in *Romeo and Juliet* (Cranko), National Ballet of Canada, Toronto

Romeo in *Romeo and Juliet* (Nureyev), London Festival Ballet, Coventry

Blue Boy in *Les Patineurs* (Ashton), National Ballet of Canada

Hothouse Rag, Friday Night in *Elite Syncopations* (MacMillan), National Ballet of Canada

Franz in *Coppélia* (Petit), Ballet National de Marseille, Paris

Colas in *La Fille mal gardée* (Ashton), National Ballet of Canada

Alain in *La Fille mal gardée* (Ashton), National Ballet of Canada

Principal dancer in *The Toreador* (Flindt after Bournonville), Royal Danish Ballet, Copenhagen

1978/   Morris in *Washington Square* (Kudelka), National Ballet
79   of Canada

Oberon in *The Dream* (Ashton), National Ballet of Canada

1979   Oedipus in *The Sphinx* (Tetley), London Festival Ballet, Bristol

Johann in *Le Chauve-souris* (Petit), Ballet National de Marseille, Paris

James in *La Sylphide* (new production; own staging, after Bournonville), London Festival Ballet, London

1980   Title role (cr) in *La Fantôme de l'Opéra* (Petit), Paris Opéra Ballet, Paris

Principal dancer in *Les Intermittences du coeur* (Petit), Ballet National de Marseille, New York

1981   Don José in *Carmen* (Petit), Ballet National de Marseille

Gennario (cr) in *Napoli* (new production; own staging, after Bournonville), National Ballet of Canada, Toronto

1981/   Jean in *Miss Julie* (Cullberg), German Opera Ballet,
82   Berlin

1982   Title role (cr) in *Orpheus* (MacMillan), Royal Ballet, London
       Principal dancer (cr) in *Verdi Variations* (pas de deux; MacMillan), Aterballetto, Reggio Emilia
1983   Toreador in *Carmen* (Petit), Ballet National de Marseille
1985   Frédéri in *L'Arlésienne* (Petit), London Festival Ballet, Liverpool
       Franz (cr) in *Coppélia* (new production; Hynd after Petipa, Cecchetti), London Festival Ballet, London
       Romeo in *Romeo and Juliet* (Ashton), London Festival Ballet, London
       Principal dancer (cr) in *Le Chat botté* (Petit), Ballet National de Marseille, Paris
1986   The Poet in *Apparitions* (Ashton), London Festival Ballet, London
       Lenski in *Onegin* (Cranko), London Festival Ballet
       Lev/Cavalier in *The Nutcracker* (also chor.), London Festival Ballet, Plymouth
1991   Alberich in *Ring um den Ring* (Béjart), German Opera Ballet, Berlin

Other roles include: for Royal Danish Ballet—leading roles in *Jeu de cartes* (Cranko), *Cyrano de Bergerac* (Petit); Jester in *The Kermesse in Bruges* (Bournonville), Bandit in *The Miraculous Mandarin* (Flindt); for New York City Ballet—principal dancer in *Tchaikovsky Pas de deux* (Balanchine).

WORKS

1969   *Homo* (mus. popular), Royal Danish Ballet, Copenhagen
1986   *The Nutcracker* (mus. Tchaikovsky), London Festival Ballet, Plymouth (also staged German Opera Ballet, Berlin, 1992)

Also staged:
1979   *La Sylphide* (after Bournonville; mus. Løvenskjold), London Festival Ballet, London (also staged, assisted by Mona Vangsaae, Stuttgart Ballet, 1982, German Opera Ballet, Berlin, 1982; also staged Teatro Comunale, Florence, 1983; Vienna State Opera Ballet, 1990; Rome Opera Ballet, 1991; Ballet National de Marseille and Zurich Opera Ballet)
1981   *Napoli* (after Bournonville; mus. Paulli, Helsted, Gade, Lumbye), National Ballet of Canada, Toronto (also staged Teatro San Carlo, Naples, 1988; English National Ballet, 1989)
1983   *A Folk Tale* (after Bournonville; mus. Gade, Hartmann), German Opera Ballet, Berlin
       Dances from Napoli (extracts from *Napoli*, after Bournonville), London Festival Ballet, London (also staged, as *Bournonville*, for Aterballetto, 1984)
1991   *Giselle* (after Petipa, Coralli, Perrot; mus. Adam), German Opera Ballet, Berlin

PUBLICATIONS

By Schaufuss:
Interview in "All in the Danish Tradition", *Dance and Dancers* (London), July 1978
Interview in "Reviving and Revitalising Bournonville", in *Dance and Dancers* (London), December 1979
Interview in Bertozzi, Donatella, "Peter Schaufuss: Napoli a Napoli", *Ballettoggi* (Milan), February 1989

About Schaufuss:
Maynard, Olga, "Peter Schaufuss", *Dance Magazine* (New York), September 1974
Hodgson, M., "Peter Schaufuss Fulfils a Dream", *Dance News* (New York), February 1975
Taub, Eric, "A Life in the Theatre", *Ballet News* (New York), November 1981
Dodd, Craig, "Peter Schaufuss and the Festival Ballet", *Dancing Times* (London), October 1984
Bland, Alexander, and Percival, John, *Men Dancing*, London, 1984
Gruen, John, "Workhorse, Acrobat and Artist", *Dance Magazine* (New York), January 1985
Dodd, Craig, *Peter Schaufuss*, London, 1985
Clarke, Mary, and Crisp, Clement, *Men in Dance*, London 1985
Willis, Margaret, "The Two Sides of Peter Schaufuss", *Dance Magazine* (New York), December 1987
Kane, Angela, "Trading Places: LFB into ENB", *Dancing Times* (London), August 1989
Merrett, Sue, "Spotlight on Peter Schaufuss", *Dancing Times* (London), November 1991

*   *   *

Peter Schaufuss, a talented and distinguished soloist and an attentive, ardent partner, began his international career in his native Denmark. Since 1979 he has also made a name for himself as an arranger of nineteenth-century ballets for large and medium-scale companies; and as artistic director of London Festival Ballet from 1984 to 1990 and of Berlin's German Opera Ballet from 1990, he has earned a further reputation as a dynamic director and a visionary with the ability to make an old company new and exciting. His four-part television series, *Dancer*, introduced new audiences to ballet and opened their eyes to the history, function, and virtuosity of the male dancer.

Born into a family of dancers, Schaufuss appeared on stage as a child and attracted attention while still an apprentice with the Royal Danish Ballet. From the outset he resented the suggestion that his success might be the result of his connections and knew that he did not want to limit his career to performing in Denmark. For all his youthful ambition, however, his contracts with foreign companies were wisely negotiated to compensate for the loss of his secure job at home. At first Schaufuss's career was starry but directionless; but, after a decade familiarizing himself with the classics at the National Ballet of Canada and London Festival Ballet (where in effect he replaced John Gilpin as the company's male star), and after the further challenge of George Balanchine's choreography at New York City Ballet, Schaufuss began to appreciate where his real strengths lay. Winning the silver rather than the gold medal at the 1973 Moscow Competition and suffering a serious injury that halted his career for several months in 1975 led him to reassess his ambitions; and the chance opportunity to partner Natalia Makarova in *Giselle* for American Ballet Theatre in 1977 (Albrecht was always a key role for Schaufuss) finally made him aware that his talent was for romantic and dramatic works.

Schaufuss returned to the National Ballet of Canada on a flexible contract that allowed him to appear throughout the world, and again he became a regular guest with London Festival Ballet. Always a virtuoso, he used his powerful muscles to introduce individual tricks into his performances to impress his enthusiastic audiences. Schaufuss breathed life into showpieces like *Études* and *Le Corsaire* Pas de deux, although his emphasis on virtuosity rather distorted his approach to "The Kingdom of the Shades" from *La Bayadère*. His performances in the Bournonville repertory contributed to a revival of interest in the Danish choreographer's work outside his native land, and Schaufuss's forceful and dramatic interpretations of roles encouraged leading choreographers, including Roland Petit and Kenneth MacMillan, to create leading roles for him as a guest with the Ballet National de Marseille and the Royal Ballet respectively. Schaufuss's range as a performer is wide. He was the first dancer to alternate in the very different roles of Colas, the young hero, and the dim-witted Alain in Frederick Ashton's *La Fille mal gardée*, and he played Romeo in four very different productions of *Romeo and Juliet*, all to Sergei Prokofiev's score. The critic Mary Clarke once suggested that Schaufuss combined "the academic elegance of his compatriot Erik Bruhn with the temperamental ardour of Nureyev".

As an arranger of ballets, Schaufuss has shown particular sympathy in adapting Bournonville's works for large companies and big stages, shaping them to the taste of twentieth-century audiences. Helped by the Danish musicologist Ole Nørling, he has reinstated music that was cut from the ballets in Denmark and has used Bournonville's enchaînements and class-exercises to produce "new" choreography. He has maintained, with Niels Bjørn Larsen's help, the important mime roles in the ballets. *La Sylphide* and *A Folk Tale* have won critical acclaim and new audiences, but Schaufuss was less successful with his staging of *Napoli* (initially for the National Ballet of Canada), in which he transposed the supernatural elements of the Blue Grotto (Act II) into the hero Gennaro's dream and thus distorted Bournonville's intention of revealing the power of divine providence. Schaufuss's approach to other nineteenth-century ballets has been original, although he has a tendency to make scenes too busy and to include too many academic ideas. His *Nutcracker* for London Festival Ballet involved a close biographical study of Tchaikovsky's family and the more complicated elements of Hoffmann's original story which are usually overlooked. In *Giselle* for Berlin, all the peasants in the first act are individualized and personally named in the programme.

As an artistic director Schaufuss challenges his companies with a wide if sometimes uneven range of choreography, classical and contemporary, evidently determined by contacts made during his days as a performer. He has the ability to recognize and develop outstanding talent in young dancers; Katherine Healy, Trinidad Sevillano, Susan Hogard, and Lisa Cullum are among the young ballerinas he has promoted. Perhaps Schaufuss's biggest *coup* to date has been to arrange the successful reconstruction of Ashton's "lost" *Romeo and Juliet*, a ballet he had performed in as a child and one he had longed to return to the stage.

—Jane Pritchard

———

SCHAYK, Toer van *see* **VAN SCHAYK, Toer**

———

SCHÉHÉRAZADE

Choreography: Mikhail Fokine
Music: Nikolai Rimsky-Korsakov
Design: Léon Bakst (scenery and costumes)

Libretto: Alexandre Benois (from *The Thousand and One Nights*)
First Production: Diaghilev's Ballets Russes, Théâtre National de l'Opéra, Paris, 4 June 1910
Principal Dancers: Ida Rubinstein (Zobéïde), Vaslav Nijinsky (Favourite Slave), Alexis Bulgakov (Shahriyar), Enrico Cecchetti (Chief Eunuch), Sophie Fedorova (Odalisque)

Other productions include: Royal Danish Ballet (new version; chor. George Balanchine, design Kay Nielsen); Copenhagen, 12 October 1930. Teatro Colón (restaged Fokine); Buenos Aires, 1931. (De Basil's) Monte Carlo Ballet Russe (staged Serge Grigoriev after Fokine), with Lubov Tchernicheva (Zobéïde); Philadelphia, 16 February 1935. (René Blum's) Ballets de Monte Carlo (revival; supervised by Fokine), with Jeanette Lauret (Zobéïde), André Eglevsky ("The Negro"), Nicolas Zverev (Eunuch); Monte Carlo, 1936. Stanislavsky and Nemirovich–Danchenko Ballet (new version; chor. Vladimir Burmeister); Moscow, 31 December 1944. Maly Theatre Ballet (new version; chor. Nina Anisimova, design Simon Virsaladze); Leningrad, 17 June 1950. Paris Opéra ballet (staged Serge Lifar, Nicholas Zverev after Fokine); Paris, 25 April 1951. London Festival Ballet (staged Nicholas Beriozoff after Fokine); Monte Carlo, 19 January 1952. London Festival Ballet (staged Serge Grigoriev, Lubov Tchernicheva after Fokine); 6 January 1956. Paris Opéra Ballet (new version; chor. Roland Petit); Paris, 28 February 1974. Ballet Europeo, Nervi Festival (new version; staged Léonide Massine); Genoa, 27 June 1960. Vienna State Opera Ballet (new version; chor. Valery Panov); Vienna, 1981.

PUBLICATIONS

Beaumont, Cyril, *Complete Book of Ballets*, revised edition, London, 1951

Grigoriev, Serge, *The Diaghilev Ballet*, translated by Vera Bowen, London, 1953

Fokine, Michel, *Fokine: Memoirs of a Ballet Master*, translated by Vitale Fokine, London, 1961

Hering, Doris, "Against the Tide", *Dance Magazine* (New York), 2 parts: August, September 1961

"Arena: Fokine", *Dance and Dancers* (London), 3 parts: January, February, March 1962

Kirstein, Lincoln, *Movement and Metaphor: Four Centuries of Ballet*, New York, 1970

Spencer, Charles, *Leon Bakst*, New York, 1973

Balanchine, George, with Mason, Francis, *Balanchine's Complete Stories of the Great Ballets*, Garden City, N.Y., 1977

Vaughan, David, "Fokine in the Contemporary Repertory", *Ballet Review* (New York), vol. 7, no. 2–3, 1978–79

Horwitz, Dawn Lille, *Michel Fokine*, Boston, 1985

Pruzhan, Irina, *Léon Bakst*, translated by Arthur Shkarovski-Raffé, 1987

Garafola, Lynn, *Diaghilev's Ballets Russes*, New York, 1989

* * *

The St. Petersburg Imperial Theatre School, where Fokine was classically trained, became a microcosm for the political, social, and artistic issues which arose during the Russian Revolution in 1905. As a student strike leader at the age of 25, Fokine was both visionary and revolutionary. At that time, he wrote to the directors of the Imperial Theatres pleading for a break with the academic syntax of Russian ballet. He regarded it as an artifical, contained province which did not relate to time and place. Its purpose was to entertain audiences with a predictable

Schéhérazade: costume design by Léon Bakst for Alexis Bulgakov as Shahriyar, 1910

and recognizable spectacle, characterized by contrasts between drama and divertissement.

Only the use of prescribed gesture and mime language advanced the action. Technique was developed for technique's sake and was generally devoid of emotion. Styling of décor, costume, and movement was set in the Classical or Romantic tradition regardless of the content of the ballet. Music was generally composed to develop the story line. In response to this, Fokine developed his liberal ideas, which were soon reflected in both his choreographic process and the themes of his work. Often misunderstood and accused of annihilating the classical tradition of ballet, he envisioned dancing as interpretive and expressive. *Schéhérazade* was one of the most colourful and striking examples of Fokine's new aesthetic.

There had been other influences on Fokine's work besides the Russian Revolution. These include the philosophy of Jean Georges Noverre, referred to as the father of classical technique, who actually departed from the concept of ballet as mere divertissement, and introduced the idea of ballet as a vehicle for expressing a dramatic idea inspired by Nature. Fokine was also influenced by the resurgence of interest in Russian art during the late 1890s, and early 1900s, as demonstrated by the formation of a circle of brilliant and talented men who met to discuss the role of the arts, and published *Mir Iskusstva* (*The World of Art*), their collaborative journal, edited by Diaghilev, which espoused art for art's sake rather than art for humanity's sake. Though not a member of this group, Fokine later collaborated with Benois and Bakst, who were members. Finally, Fokine was undoubtedly influenced by Isadora Duncan's arrival in St. Petersburg in 1905. An opponent of traditional ballet, she was exploring in dance the use of the whole body, in order to find a greater freedom of movement and dramatic expression. Added to this is the fact that while travelling through Europe, and especially the eastern regions, Fokine had explored his interest in nativist themes, and studied man's use of ethnic dance to express life within a particular context of time and place. Extensive studies and acquired knowledge of drama, painting, and sculpture, in addition to his stature as a musician, provided a rich foundation for Fokine's approach to choreography.

Schéhérazade, sometimes labelled a choreographic or dance drama, seems to exemplify Fokine's commitment to exploring the concept and possibilities of total theatre. This involved a true integration and equal treatment of dance, music, décor, and costume, and suggested an inherent rebellion against Petipa's repetition of form, conventional approach to choreography, and use of stereotyped and set movements in the classical tradition. Under Diaghilev's guidance and through collaboration with other artists, Fokine was able to achieve a unique unity in this work which reflected his respect for pluralism.

Bakst's Oriental and exotic styling for both the décor and costuming of *Schéhérazade* were true to the history of the subject. Vibrant, intricate patterns and harem trousers were a testimony to this. Some authorities claim an influence of Impressionism in his work, while others see a synthesis of Persian, Turkish, and Moghul miniatures in his rich tapestry of dramatic and voluptuous colours and textures. While Fokine planned his ballets in minute detail, he departed from the traditional method of setting established steps on his dancers. Instead, he relied to some extent upon their own interpretation of a given part. Many of his contemporaries criticized this method of blocking choreography. Rather than featuring selected ballerinas and highlighting the virtuosity of their male counterparts, Fokine treated his male and female dancers, main characters and members of the corps de ballet, with equal attention and emphasis. The effect was an expansion of the expressiveness of a whole single body to that of an entire group. This subordination of personal values and goals for the benefit of an overall collaborative entity was reflective of larger social issues being addressed at the time.

The subject of adult sexuality in *Schéhérazade* was portrayed with a lusty realism, as seen in the serpentine, undulating movements Fokine devised for the orgy. Cyril Beaumont called it "the most voluptuous of all the ballets that were presented by the Diaghilev company". Heretofore, sexuality had been idealized and stylized in the classical tradition. According to his critics, Fokine also took liberties in adapting an existing musical work, with its own story, to his own choreographic idea. He eliminated Part III, used Part I for the overture, and Parts II and IV for the body of this one-act, uninterrupted ballet. Yet, despite the controversy raised over *Schéhérazade*, there were many who defended and supported Fokine's innovations.

The creation of *Schéhérazade* seems to express Fokine's personal and artistic philosophy. In his own words, "—if you are ready to challenge the struggle and sufferings confronting you, the elements do not frighten you, you do not require favourable weather, you do not have to inquire about favourable trade winds—you can boldly set your course against the tide."

—Laura H. Shucart

SCHOLLAR, Ludmila

Russian/American dancer and teacher. Born Lyudmila (Ludmila) Frantsevna Shollar (Schollar) in St. Peterburg, 15 March 1888. Studied at the Imperial Theatre School, from 1900, pupil of Mikhail Fokine, Klavdiya Kulichevskaya; graduated in 1906; later studied with Enrico Cecchetti. Married dancer and teacher Anatole Vilzak, 1921. Dancer, Maryinsky Theatre, St. Petersburg, 1906–14; performer in first season of Diaghilev's Ballets Russes, Paris, 1909, continuing as dancer for both Maryinsky Theatre and Diaghilev's company, 1909–14; served as Red Cross nurse during World War I; returned to Maryinsky (later the State Academic Theatre for Opera and Ballet, or GATOB), 1917–21; soloist, Diaghilev's Ballets Russes London season, Alhambra Theatre, 1921, continuing with company until 1925; travelled to Argentina with husband Anatole Vilzak, performing Teatro Colón, Buenos Aires, 1926–27; also leading dancer with Ida Rubinstein's company in Paris, 1928, Karsavina–Vilzak Company, London, and Bronislava's company, Paris and on tour; went to the U.S. with Vilzak in 1936: teacher, School of American Ballet, New York, from 1936, the Vilzak–Schollar School, New York, 1940–46, Ballet Theatre School, 1951–53, Washington School of Ballet, Washington, D.C., 1963–65, and San Francisco Ballet School, from 1965. Recipient: Medal of St. George, World War I. Died in Washington, D.C., 11 June 1978.

ROLES

1907 Actaea in *Eunice* (Fokine), Maryinsky Theatre, St. Petersburg
1908 Pas de deux from *Don Giovanni* (opera; mus. Mozart), Graduation Performance of the Imperial Theatre School, St. Petersburg
1909 Leading dancer (cr) in *Le Festin* (Fokine and others),

Ludmila Schollar (left) in *Jeux* with Vaslav Nijinksy and Tamara Karsavina, Diaghilev's Ballets Russes, 1913

Diaghilev's Ballets Russes, Paris
1909/   Soloist in *Polovtsian Dances from Prince Igor* (Fokine),
14   Diaghilev's Ballets Russes
          Dancer in *Les Sylphides* (Fokine), Diaghilev's Ballets
          Russes
          Queen of the Wilis in *Giselle* (Petipa after Coralli,
          Perrot; revised Fokine), Diaghilev's Ballets Russes
1910   Estrella (cr) in *Le Carnaval* (Fokine), Pavlova Hall, St.
          Petersburg
          An Odalisque (cr) in *Schéhérazade* (Fokine), Diaghilev's
          Ballets Russes, Paris
1911   Street dancer (cr) in *Petrushka* (Fokine), Diaghilev's
          Ballets Russes, Paris
1913   Principal dancer (cr) in *Jeux* (Nijinsky), Diaghilev's
          Ballets Russes, Paris
1914   Papillon (cr) in *Les Papillons* (Ballets Russes version;
          Fokine), Diaghilev's Ballets Russes, Monte Carlo
          Principal dancer (cr) in *Midas* (Fokine), Diaghilev's
          Ballets Russes, Paris
1921   White Cat in *The Sleeping Princess* (Petipa; staged
          Sergeyev, with additional dances Nijinska), Diaghi-
          lev's Ballets Russes, London
          Enchanted Princess (Bluebird pas de deux) in *The
          Sleeping Princess* (Petipa; staged Sergeyev, with
          additional dances Nijinska), Diaghilev's Ballets
          Russes, London
1924   A Gossip (cr) in *Les Fâcheux* (Nijinska), Diaghilev's
          Ballets Russes, Monte Carlo
          Ensemble (cr) in *Le Train bleu* (Nijinska), Diaghilev's
          Ballets Russes, Paris
1926   Columbine (cr) in *El Carillón magico* (Nijinska), Teatro
          Colón, Buenos Aires
          Young Girl in *Le Spectre de la rose* (Fokine), Teatro
          Colón, Buenos Aires
1928   Fiancée (cr) in *Le Baiser de la fée* (Nijinska), Ida
          Rubinstein's Company, Paris
          Dancer (cr) in *Les Noces de Psyché et de l'amour*
          (Nijinska), Ida Rubinstein's Company, Paris
1932   Clarisse (cr) in *Les Comédiens jaloux* (Nijinska), Théâtre
          de la danse Nijinska, Paris

Other roles include: for GATOB—Princess Florine in *The
Sleeping Beauty* (Petipa), Clemence in *Raymonda* (Petipa),
Pierrette in *Harlequinade* (Petipa), Waltz in *Chopiniana*
(Fokine), Papillon and Columbine in *Le Carnaval* (Fokine),

Gulnara in *Le Corsaire* (Petipa), Marinetta in *The Trials of
Damis* (*Les Ruses d'amour*; Petipa), pas de trois in *Swan Lake*
(Petipa, Ivanov).

WORKS

Staged:
1923   *Swan Lake* (shortened version, with Vilzak, after
          Petipa, Ivanov; mus. Tchaikovsky), Diaghilev's
          Ballets Russes, Monte Carlo

PUBLICATIONS

Haskell, Arnold, *Balletomania*, London, 1933
Lifar, Serge, *Serge de Diaghilew*, Paris, 1940
Barzel, Ann, "European Dance Teachers in the United States",
    Dance Index (New York), April–June 1944
Grigoriev, Serge, *The Diaghilev Ballet*, translated by Vera
    Bowen, London, 1953
Karsavina, Tamara, "Vilzak, Malcolm Sargent and Others",
    Dancing Times (London), May 1968
Krasovskaya, Vera, *Russian Ballet Theatre in the Early
    Twentieth Century*, volume 2: Leningrad, 1972
Horosko, Marian, "Teachers in the Russian Tradition", *Dance
    Magazine* (New York), part 2: April 1979
Garafola, Lynn, *Diaghilev's Ballets Russes*, New York, 1989

*   *   *

Ludmila Schollar was a dancer and teacher whose career
spanned from the traditional days of pre-war Maryinsky to the
experimentation of Diaghilev's Ballets Russes, and later, to the
opening of a successful ballet school in America with her
husband Anatole Vilzak. Her appearance in the graduation
performance of the Imperial Theatre School in 1908, when she
danced with the young Nijinsky, confirmed her an excellent
dancer, with special qualities of artistry that other colleagues
were quick to note. In recalling her early impressions of
Schollar, Tamara Karsavina said her appearance and style of
dancing were akin to a delicate Dresden china figure.
Furthermore, Schollar's knowledge of music, learned from her
father, who had been a conductor, and her sister, a harpist at
the Maryinsky, resulted in her being an extremely musical
dancer.

Such qualities prompted Fokine to select Schollar to be the
first Estrella in *Le Carnaval*, and Diaghilev to engage the
ballerina throughout the pre-war seasons given in Paris by the
Ballets Russes. For this company Schollar created roles in
Schéhérazade, *Petrushka*, and *Jeux*. In *Jeux*, Schollar worked
closely with Karsavina and Nijinsky, portraying one of the
tennis players and wearing a sports jumper, in keeping with the
ballet's depiction of a contemporary rather than a historical
scene.

The choreography for *Jeux* presented a challenge for
Schollar, since it drew on the modern vocabulary in contrast to
the classical technique she had been schooled in. Gestures were
split up rather than continuous, giving the impression of many
small movements, each limb performing a different motion and
following varying rhythms. The unusual look of the ballet met
with a mixed response, but for Schollar it proved a worthwhile
experience, expanding her capacities as a dancer and enabling
her to work thereafter in both the classical and modern idioms.

Unfortunately, the outbreak of World War I put a temporary
halt to Schollar's dancing career, as her artistic endeavours
gave way to duty and she returned home to serve as a nurse in

St. Petersburg. During this time Schollar was seriously wounded in the arm, but she showed great courage in continuing to carry out her duties nursing the soldiers, and was consequently rewarded with a medal.

After the war Schollar's dancing career resumed, and in 1921 Diaghilev invited her to rejoin his company in Paris along with dancer Anatole Vilzak, whom she married in Russia. Schollar was particularly pleased to receive the invitation, and accepted after learning that her old school friend Bronislava Nijinska was to be ballet mistress. Her friendship and admiration for Nijinsky's sister grew, and Schollar appeared in many ballets and dances choreographed by Nijinska for Diaghilev's company. For example, Schollar performed in Diaghilev's version of *The Sleeping Princess* (1921) in the role of the White Cat, and later she danced the Enchanted Princess in the Bluebird pas de deux, which featured additional dances created by Nijinska. She also performed in more experimental works entirely choreographed by her friend, such as *Les Fâcheux* and *Le Train bleu*, which satirized the fashionable community of the French Riviera.

The amiable relationship of these two women, however, contrasted with the less than cordial ending of Schollar's employment in Diaghilev's Ballets Russes. On the morning of 17 January 1925, a few hours before the company was due to give a gala performance attended by the royal family of Monaco and other dignitaries, the dancers threatened strike action unless their wages were increased. There had been considerable discontent on the part of the dancers concerning the amount of pay they were receiving, and Ludmila Schollar and her husband sympathized with the corps de ballet's grievance. Their association with the trouble led to their being dismissed from the Ballets Russes.

Nevertheless, Schollar's dancing abilities enabled her to gain employment performing in South America with her husband at the Teatro Colón in Buenos Aires. In 1928, her friend Nijinska was largely responsible for Schollar's recruitment into Ida Rubinstein's company, where she appeared in such works as *Les Noces de Psyché et de l'amour*, a sort of mythological tableau with Schollar portraying a baby in the heart of a cabbage. She also became involved in the formation of the Karsavina–Vilzak Company and danced Clarisse in *Les Comédiens Jaloux* by Nijinska, who had similarly ventured into setting up her own dance groups.

As with many dancers and choreographers formerly linked with Diaghilev, Schollar and Vilzak eventually settled in America, helping to lay the foundations for a thriving ballet culture in the United States. One of the most fruitful periods of Schollar's teaching career was during the 1940s, when the Vilzak–Schollar School was established in Steinway Hall in New York's 57th Street. In the classes Schollar taught technique and repertoire, emphasizing crisp pointework and graceful, expressive arms, and reflecting her training from Cecchetti and Fokine in her lyrical ports de bras. Her memory for variations and repertoire as performed by Mathilde Kchessinskaya and Karsavina was accurate to the last detail, enabling Schollar to pass on the Maryinsky traditions, together with innovations learned from her time spent in the Ballets Russes, to her students.

As a consequence, Schollar became a highly respected member of the dance community in America, called upon to train upcoming pupils at leading American dancing schools, including American Ballet Theatre School, the Washington School of Ballet, and the San Francisco Ballet School. It was at the San Francisco Ballet School that Schollar coached dancers in the Sugar Plum Fairy variation from *The Nutcracker*, forming part of a special project there to preserve classical dance works for future generations. The variation was notated as Schollar taught it by Laurencia Klaja and was later reproduced in *Dance Magazine*, a few months before the first anniversary of Schollar's death. It was a fitting tribute to the dancer/teacher who excelled both in demonstrating and in providing her students with a fine classical technique.

—Melanie Trifona Christoudia

SCHWARZ, Solange

French dancer and teacher. Born in Paris, daughter of dancer Jean Schwarz, 12 November 1910. Studied at the Paris Opéra School, pupil of Albert Aveline, Nicola Guerra, and Carlotta Zambelli, from 1921; also studied with Madame d'Alessandri, Lubov Egorova, and Madame Rousanne (Rousanne Sarkissian), Paris. Married Albert Sarrazin. Dancer, Paris Opéra Ballet, from 1924, becoming petit sujet from 1930; étoile, Opéra-Comique, 1932–37, returning to Paris Opéra Ballet, and becoming première danseuse, 1937, and étoile, from 1941; ballerina, Ballets des Champs-Elysees, 1945–47, also appearing with Grand Ballet du Marquis de Cuevas, and Bavarian State Opera, Munich; returned to Opéra-Comique, 1949–51; guest artist, Grand Ballet du Marquis de Cuevas, 1954, and Béjart's Ballet de l'Étoile de Paris; also appeared in films, including in *Symphonie en blanc*; teacher, including at Conservatoire de musique, Paris, 1957–77.

ROLES

1921   Le Petit Negrillon (cr) in *La Rêve de la marquise* (Fokine), Paris Opéra Ballet, Paris

1925   Dancer (cr) in *Les Rencontres* (Nijinska), Paris Opéra Ballet, Paris

La Jeunesse (cr) in *Le Triomphe de l'amour* (Staats), Paris Opéra Ballet, Paris

1931   Dancer (cr) in *Bacchus et Ariane* (Lifar), Paris Opéra Ballet, Paris

1932   Violet Fairy in *Divertissement* (from *The Sleeping Beauty*; Lifar after Petipa), Paris Opéra Ballet, Paris

Cendrillon (cr) in *La Pantoufle de vair* (Tcherkas), Opéra-Comique, Paris

1934   Principal dancer (cr) in *Printemps fleuri* (Tcherkas), Opéra-Comique, Paris

Principal dancer in *Nefertiti* (Tcherkas), Opéra-Comique, Paris

Principal dancer in *Reflets* (Quinault), Opéra-Comique, Paris

1935   Title role (cr) in *Le Cygne* (Tcherkas), Opéra-Comique, Paris

Odette in *Swan Lake*, Act II (after Ivanov), Opéra-Comique, Paris

1936   Ballerina (cr) in *La Rosière du village* (Tcherkas), Opéra-Comique, Paris

Principal dancer (cr) in *Jeux de couleur* (Ari), Opéra-Comique, Paris

1937   Swanilda in *Coppélia* (Larthe after Saint-Léon), Paris Opéra Ballet, Paris

Une Egyptienne (cr) in *Alexandre le Grand* (Lifar), Paris Opéra Ballet, Paris

1939   L'Ephémère (cr) in *Le Festin de l'araignée* (Aveline), Paris Opéra, Paris

1940   La Danseuse de Degas (cr) in *Entre deux rondes* (Lifar), Paris Opéra Ballet, Paris

          Principal dancer (cr) in *Un Jour d'été* (Tcherkas), Opéra-Comique, Paris

1941   La Damoiselle (cr) in *Le Chevalier et la damoiselle* (Lifar), Paris Opéra Ballet, Paris

          Title role in *Sylvia* (Lifar), Paris Opéra Ballet, Paris

          The Danseuse (cr) in *Reversibilité* (solo; Lifar), Gala, Paris

1942   La Plus Belle (cr) in *Joan de Zarissa* (Lifar), Paris Opéra Ballet, Paris

          La Poule et la Fourmi (cr) in *Les Animaux modèles* (Lifar), Paris Opéra Ballet, Paris

1943   La Cigarette and Pas de deux (cr) in *Suite en blanc* (Lifar), Paris Opéra Ballet, Zurich

          Principal dancer (cr) in *Exercices à la barre* (Lifar), Sorbonne

1945   Goddess (cr) in *Concert de danse* (Berge), Ballets des Champs-Elysées, Paris

1946   Europa (cr) in *Les Amours de Jupiter* (Petit), Ballets des Champs-Elysées, Paris

1947   La Petite Fille acrobate in *Les Forains* (Petit), Théâtre de Champs-Elysées, Paris

          Principal dancer *Le Déjeuner sur l'herbe* (Petit), Ballets des Champs-Elysées, Paris

          Bluebird Pas de deux from *The Sleeping Beauty* (Petipa), Ballets des Champs-Elysées, Paris

1948   Bellacastriga (cr) in *Abraxas* (Liupart), Bavarian State Opera Ballet, Munich

          La Danseuse in *La Boutique fantasque* (Massine), Opéra-Comique, Paris

          Rosine in *Le Precaution inutile* (Etchevery), Opéra-Comique, Paris

1949   Principal dancer (cr) in *Étude* (Etchevery), Opéra-Comique, Paris

          Le Soleil (cr) in *Les Heures* (Etchevery), Opéra-Comique, Paris

          Principal dancer (cr) in *Paris-Magie* (Etchevery), Opéra-Comique, Paris

          Principal dancer (cr) in *Bolero* (Etchevery), Opéra-Comique, Paris

          Principal dancer (cr) in *Hommage à Chopin* (Lifar), Chaillot, Paris

          Principal dancer (cr) in *Le Vol du bourdon* (Lifar), Gala, Paris

1950   Principal dancer (cr) in *Concerto* (Etchevery), Opéra-Comique, Paris

          Sugar Plum Fairy in *The Nutcracker* (excerpts; Etchevery after Ivanov), Opéra-Comique, Paris

          Lise in *La Fille mal gardée* (Balashova), Grand Ballet du Marquis de Cuevas

          Aurora in *La Forêt* (excerpts from *The Sleeping Beauty*; Gsovsky after Petipa), Théâtre de Champs-Elysées, Paris

          Nina (cr) in *La Valse* (Massine), Opéra-Comique, Paris

1954   Principal dancer (cr) in *La Lettre* (Béjart), Ballet de l'Etoile, Paris

          Grand Pas des déesses (cr) in *Le Jugement de Pâris* (Brieux), Ballets de l'Etoile, Paris

Other roles include: for the Paris Opéra—leading dancing roles in operas *Faust* (mus. Gounod), *Roméo et Juliette* (mus. Gounod), *Mârouf* (mus. Rabaud), *Samson et Dalila* (mus. Saint-Saëns), *Thaïs* (mus. Massenet); for galas and concert performances—principal dancer in *Impromptu* (Lifar), *Sarabande* (Lifar).

PUBLICATIONS

By Schwarz:
"Le neueu de Lully", *La Danse* (Paris), March 1957

About Schwarz:
Dolin, Anton, "Solange Schwarz: An Appreciation", *Dancing Times* (London), July 1938

Martin, L. L., *Les Demoiselles de l'Opéra*, Paris, 1940

Beaumont, Cyril, "Les Ballets des Champs-Elysées", in *Ballet* (London), June 1946

Laurent, Jean, "Solange Schwarz" in *15 Danseurs et danseuses*, Paris, 1948

Lidova, Irène, "Solange Schwarz", *La Danse* (Paris), no. 3, 1949

Vaillat, Léandre, *La Danse à l'Opéra de Paris*, Paris, 1951

Guest, Ivor, *Le Ballet de l'Opéra de Paris*, Paris, 1976

*   *   *

Solange Schwarz was born into a dancing family: nine members belonged to the ballet of the Paris Opéra. Her father Jean Schwarz (1884–1936) made his career at the Opéra; he married an actress, Nelly Nibert, and they had four daughters: Nelly, Solange, Janine, and Christiane. Jean Schwarz left the opera, acted for a while, opened a dancing school, and founded a dance magazine. When he and his wife divorced, his sister Jeanne Schwarz (herself a star at the Opéra) took on the education of the four girls.

Solange entered ballet school in 1921 and in 1924 became a member of the corps de ballet of the Opéra. Very artistic and industrious, Solange took classes with Carlotta Zambelli, Albert Aveline, and also with the Italian ballet master Nicola Guerra. Outside the Opéra she was taught by her aunt, Madame d'Alessandri, and Madame Egorova. Solange was small, blonde, and very pretty; her legs were wiry with very good extensions and strong pointes. She became Serge Lifar's partner and for her he created "les grands dégáges à la seconde en pivotante sur son axe" in the adage of *Le Chevalier et la damoiselle* (1941). This lyrical ballet is considered by dance historian Marie-Françoise Christout to be "the most important of the contemporary period. In turn mysterious, brilliant, and feminine, Solange Schwarz was able to embody the multiple aspects of a complex role."

In 1932 Solange Schwarz was appointed étoile of the Opéra-Comique, where her partner was Constantine Tcherkas, a former soloist with Diaghilev's Ballets Russes. Five years later the director of the Opéra, Jacques Rouché, invited her to dance Swanilda in *Coppélia*, a role which seemed to have been created for her, and she was made premiere danseuse. In 1940 Serge Lifar choreographed *Entre deux rondes* in which she took the role of Degas' little dancer and she was promoted to étoile the following year. (For the record, Edgar Degas' sculpture of a *petit rat* wears one of Solange Schwarz's tutus.)

The life of the national theatres was disrupted by the Second World War; in 1945 the Opéra ballet company was disbanded and Solange rejoined Roland Petit and Jean Babilée at the Ballets des Champs-Elysées. Between 1948 and 1951 she was reinstated at the Opéra-Comique and danced as guest artist with the Grand Ballet de Monte Carlo. In 1954 she toured with the Ballet de l'Étoile founded by Jean Laurent and Maurice Béjart and also danced as guest artist with the Grand Ballet du Marquis de Cuevas. Throughout her varied career Schwarz was always applauded not only for her virtuosity and brilliant, precise style, but for her dramatic gifts, and she excelled particularly in demi-caractère roles.

In January 1957 Schwarz danced her farewell on the stage of

the Opéra in the ballet of her greatest triumph, *Coppélia*. The same year, she became a teacher at the Paris Conservatoire, taking over from her aunt, Jeanne Schwarz. She kept this position for twenty years. Solange Schwarz lives in the south of France with her husband, Albert Sarrazin, a doctor well known in Paris. They have two daughters, Swanilda and Stella, neither of whom dance.

—Gilberte Cournand

———

SCHWEZOFF, Igor

Russian/American dancer, choreographer, and teacher. Born in St. Petersburg, nephew of Maryinsky ballerina Elena Lyukom (Lukom), 1904. Studied at the Private Studio of Baron Shickstaal, Petrograd, pupil of Snyetkova, from 1920, and at Leningrad Choreographic School, pupil of Vladimir Ponomarev, Leonid Leontiev, Aleksandr Monakhov, 1924/25; also studied in classes attached to Bolshoi Theatre, Moscow, and with Sophia Fedorova. Served in the U.S. Army, 1942–43 (naturalized as U.S. Citizen, 1945). First performances (while still a student), in corps de ballet of operetta company, touring Russian provinces, 1923; soloist, New Academic Theatre of the Ukraine, performing various opera houses in Kharkov, Kiev, Odessa, from 1926; first dancer and choreographer, Kiev, 1928, also performing for "Propaganda Studio Opera", provincial tours, Ukraine, 1928–29; performed in revues, China, 1930; principal dancer, Teatro Colón (under ballet director Bronislava Nijinska), Buenos Aires, from 1931; soloist, Théâtre de la danse Nijinska, Paris, and touring Italy and France, 1932; moved to Holland: choreographer and director of own company (growing out of own school), Amsterdam and The Hague, 1934–36; soloist, de Basil's Original Ballet Russe, 1939–41; moved to the U.S.: choreographer, New Opera Company, New York, 1941, and Ballet Russe de Monte Carlo, 1943, staging first U.S. version of *The Red Poppy*, Cleveland, Ohio, 1943; principal dancer, Teatro Municipal, Rio de Janeiro, 1945, also founding Ballet da Juventude in Rio de Janeiro, and serving as choreographer, 1945, 1947, and again in 1957; visiting choreographer, City Center Opera Company, New York, 1946; founder and director of own company, performing as Igor Schwezoff's Ballet Concerts (with Lupe Serrano as ballerina), touring South America, 1953; also teacher, directing own school in Amsterdam, 1934–37, London, 1935–39, and New York, from 1949; also teacher for Ballet Arts, New York, 1941, Ballet Russe de Monte Carlo, New York, from 1954, Ballet Theatre, New York, 1956–62, and private studios, including Igor Youskevitch's school, New York, from 1962; faculty director, School of the Washington Ballet (director Mary Day), Washington D.C., 1963–66; teacher, Metropolitan Opera Ballet, 1968–69. Died in New York, 28 October 1982.

ROLES

1926   Dancer in *Aida* (opera; mus. Verdi, chor. Messerer), Opera Theatre, Kharkhov

Title role in *Don Quixote* (Gorsky after Petipa), Opera Theatre, Kharkov

Slave, Pas de deux in Dream Scene in *Le Corsaire* (Riaptsev, Messerer after Petipa), Opera Theatre, Kharkov

1926/   Siegfried in *Swan Lake* (after Petipa, Ivanov), Opera
27   Theatre, Odessa

1931   Harlequin in *Le Carnaval* (Fokine), Teatro Colón, Buenos Aires

Polovtsian Warrior in *Polovtsian Dances from Prince Igor* (Fokine), Teatro Colón, Buenos Aires

Ivan Tsarevich in *Firebird* (Fokine), Teatro Colón, Buenos Aires

Harlequin in *The Adventures of Harlequin* (Fokine), Teatro Colón, Buenos Aires

Sorcerer in *The Sorcerer's Apprentice* (Fokine), Teatro Colón, Buenos Aires

1932   Chanson dansée ("Athlete") in *Les Biches* (Nijinska), Théâtre de la danse Nijinska, Paris

Principal dancer in *Bolero* (Nijinska), Théâtre de la danse Nijinska, Paris

1934/ Witch Doctor (cr) in *Emperor Jones* (also chor.),
35   Performing Group of Schwezoff's School, Netherlands

Leading role (cr) in *The Miracle* (also chor.), Performing Group of Schwezoff's School, Netherlands

1940   The Old General, Mazurka (cr) in *Graduation Ball* (Lichine), Original Ballet Russe, Sydney

WORKS

1933/ *Everyman*, Performing Group of Schwezoff's School,
35   Netherlands

Soirées en Granade, Performing Group of Schwezoff's School, Netherlands

Mouvement tragique, Performing Group of Schwezoff's School, Netherlands

Emperor Jones, Performing Group of Schwezoff's School, Netherlands

The Miracle, Performing Group of Schwezoff's School, Netherlands

Elckerlyc (mus. Schumann), Performing Group of Schwezoff's School, Netherlands

First Ball (mus. Lanner), Performing Group of Schwezoff's School, Netherlands

1940   *Eternal Struggle* (*La Lutte éternelle*; revision of *Elckerlyc*; mus. Schumann), Original Ballet Russe, Sydney

1941/ Dances in *Macbeth* (opera; mus. Verdi), New Opera
42   Company, New York

Dances in *La Dame Pique* (opera; mus. Tchaikovsky), New Opera Company, New York

Dances in *La Vie Parisienne* (opera; mus. Offenbach), New Opera Company, New York

1943   *The Red Poppy* (mus. Glière), Ballet Russe de Monte Carlo, Cleveland, Ohio

1945   *Concerto dansante* (mus. Saint-Saëns), Ballet da Juventude, Rio de Janeiro

Moonlight Sonata (mus. Beethoven), Ballet da Juventude, Rio de Janeiro

Bacchanale (mus. Wagner), Ballet da Juventude, Rio de Janeiro

Contes de Bouffon (Russian folk music), Ballet da Juventude, Rio de Janeiro

Drama Burgesa (mus. Lizst), Ballet da Juventude, Rio de Janeiro

1947   *Appricoes* (mus. Mussorgsky), Ballet da Juventude, Rio de Janeiro

Concerto tragico (mus. Addinsell), Ballet da Juventude, Rio de Janeiro

Valsas des Esquinas (mus. Mignone), Ballet da Juventude, Rio de Janeiro

Also staged:
1928   *Don Quixote* (after Gorsky, Petipa; mus. Minkus), Opera Theatre, Kiev

       Coppélia (after Petipa; mus. Delibes), Opera Theatre, Kiev

1945/ *Swan Lake* (after Petipa, Ivanov; mus. Tchaikovsky),
47   Teatro Municipal, Rio de Janeiro

       Les Sylphides (after Fokine; mus. Chopin), Teatro Municipal, Rio de Janeiro

PUBLICATIONS

By Schwezoff:
Borzoi (autobiography), London, 1935; as *Russian Somersault*, New York, 1936

About Schwezoff:
Russell, Nina, "Around the World with Igor Schwezoff", *Dance Magazine* (New York), June 1969
Anderson, Jack, *The One and Only: The Ballet Russe de Monte Carlo*, London, 1981

*   *   *

Igor Schwezoff was one of the many post-Revolutionary Russian émigrés who, fleeing for the West, led extraordinarily peripatetic careers (even by today's standards), but therefore played an important role in bringing Russian classical ballet to the West. Though Schwezoff eventually settled in the United States, where he became a well-known teacher, his influence through the 1930s and 1940s spread from Holland and England to South America, where among other things he was opera ballet director and founder of a youth ballet company in Brazil.

Schwezoff's training in Russia was not as orthodox as that of many. As he explains himself in his extremely readable autobiography, *Borzoi*, he did not attend dance class (apart from children's lessons with his aunt) until the age of sixteen. Then, as a pupil at Baron Shickstaal's private studio in Petrograd, he had to work unusually hard to develop his technique, and was not to gain entrance into the exclusive Theatre School (later the Leningrad Choreographic School) until he had taken the examination twice. Clearly, however, he was one of the beneficiaries of the excellent training provided by such outstanding teachers as Vladimir Ponomarev (whose other late-start pupils included the Georgian virtuoso Vakhtang Chabukiani). Furthermore, by this time Schwezoff was already performing, appearing with a touring operetta company in the provinces.

Unlike many Petersburg- or Moscow-trained dancers, who simply graduated into the company of their schools, Schwezoff therefore had his training largely "on stage". By the age of 24, he was first dancer and choreographer of the opera house in Kiev, having already spent two years performing at various theatres in the Ukraine. On the life of a touring artist in the farthest reaches of the Soviet Union, as well as on the strange and often awkward shift of ballet from an Imperial to a "Soviet" art in the 1920s, Schwezoff's autobiography makes fascinating reading. As an employee of a new organization called the "Propaganda Studio Opera", he was one of several entrusted with the task of bringing art (acceptable "socialist" art, of course) to the provinces. Travelling from city to city in the Ukraine, the young Schwezoff put up with ten-hour train journeys, and often quite basic living and working conditions, apparently as a matter of course. If the tone of his own memoirs is an accurate reflection of Schwezoff's character at the time, his incredible energy and enthusiasm for the art of dance were

by far the most operative factors, seeing him through an unusually varied apprenticeship, and taking him eventually over the border into Manchuria, in 1930, never to return to Russia again.

In the early 1930s, Schwezoff made his name mostly as a character dancer, performing in Fokine ballets at the Teatro Colón in Buenos Aires and for Nijinska in Paris. After having brought his training and knowledge to Holland, where he set up a school and company, and London, where he also ran his own school, Schwezoff returned to professional appearances with an international company, joining Colonel de Basil's Original Ballet Russe for two years. For this company he created the part of the Old General in Lichine's *Graduation Ball*, first performed in Sydney in 1940.

Having moved to the United States and served in the U.S. Army during the war, Schwezoff established his name further by staging (in 1943) the first American production of Glière's *The Red Poppy*. First created in 1927, this classic "socialist" ballet is perhaps better known as a fascinating historical relic of early Soviet propagandist art than for any particularly outstanding choreography; ever since the initial attempt by Tikhomirov and Laschilin in Moscow, several leading Soviet choreographers have tried to improve upon the unhappy blend of socialist theme and balletic medium. The original libretto centred upon the tale of a Chinese dancing girl, Tao-Hoa (oppressed worker), who is exploited by her manager, Li-Shan-Fu (crass capitalist), and eventually gives her life for a Russian sailor (honest socialist). In Schwezoff's version, made for the Ballet Russe de Monte Carlo, Li-Shan-Fu became a Japanese bar owner, and British and American sailors featured alongside the Russian ones—all reflecting the prevailing attitudes in wartime America. In his history of the Ballet Russe, Jack Anderson describes this production as "the season's closest thing to a hit" (and it did show off Alexandra Danilova, Frederic Franklin, and Igor Youskevitch in leading roles), but Anderson also quotes a New York critic's summation that it was "... timely and topical, and, as you may suspect, very corny indeed". George Anberg (in *Ballet in America*) put it more bluntly: "It was a workmanlike piece with an abundance of dramatic action but without artistic distinction".

During the 1940s, Schwezoff balanced his work as a choreographer (usually for opera) in New York with visits to Rio de Janeiro, where he served as a principal dancer and choreographer at the Teatro Municipal during various seasons from 1945. In his time there he also founded and created numerous works for the Ballet da Juventude, or the Youth Ballet. He was to return to South America in the 1950s when, with Chilean-born ballerina Lupe Serrano, he toured with the small touring group performing under the name of Igor Schwezoff Concerts. After this Schwezoff was to settle more or less permanently as a teacher in New York City. He served on the faculty of the School of American Ballet Theatre for six years, having also taught at the Ballet Russe de Monte Carlo, the Igor Youskevitch School, and the Metropolitan Opera Ballet. His classes were extremely popular, and his teaching principles—apparently based on a sound knowledge of and respect for the great eighteenth-century ballet master Noverre—were greatly admired.

"As a teacher," wrote Nina Russell in 1969, "Schwezoff was adored by his students." One of Schwezoff's discoveries, a dancer whom he taught himself in Japan and New York, was Japanese ballerina Yoko Morishita.

—Virginia Christian

SCOTTISH BALLET
(formerly Western Theatre Ballet)
British ballet company based in Glasgow.   Origins in Western Theatre Ballet, an English regional company founded by Elizabeth West and Peter Darrell, 1957, with Darrell continuing as director on death of West, 1962; moved to Scotland, 1969, performing first as Scottish Theatre Ballet, and establishing policy of regional touring, 1971; renamed Scottish Ballet, 1972, with official base in Glasgow. Official School associated with company, the Dance School of Scotland, based in Glasgow. Current artistic director of the Scottish Ballet (succeeding guest artistic director Nanette Glushak): Galina Samsova, from 1990.

PUBLICATIONS

Darrell, Peter, Interviews in *Dance and Dancers* (London), June 1963 and June 1979
Goodwin, Noël, *A Ballet for Scotland*, Edinburgh, 1979
Massie, Annette, "Elizabeth West and Western Theatre Ballet", *Dance Research* (London), Spring 1988
Bowen, Christopher, "Company at a Crossroads", *Dance and Dancers* (London), January 1990

*   *   *

Western Theatre Ballet occupies an important pioneering place in the history of post-war British ballet. Founded by Elizabeth West and Peter Darrell in 1957 and based initially in Bristol as a centre for its extensive touring operations, it was the first regionally-based ballet company in Britain and was set up in conscious reaction to the pressures and values of other, metropolitan-based, companies. It aimed, in particular, to create new audiences for dance by focusing on the most accessibly dramatic aspects of dance, and to achieve this it concentrated almost entirely on story ballets. In the choreographic work of Peter Darrell, who developed his influential principles on the contemporary portrayal of complex thematic material through providing its main body of works, Western Theatre Ballet became the main bastion of narrative dance in Britain and the driving force in its development during the period. In 1969 the company was invited by the Scottish Arts Council and Strathclyde Regional Council to move to Glasgow to form the basis of a national classical company for Scotland, originally renamed Scottish Theatre Ballet, though much of its original vigour was lost in subsequent attempts to reconcile its pioneering stance with national repertoire needs. Its present title, the Scottish Ballet, was assumed in 1972.

In its original form Western Theatre Ballet built up a considerable national and international reputation for the quality and inventiveness of its repertoire and, with Darrell as its principal choreographer (and sole director after West's death in 1962), was successful in demonstrating a rigorous concept of ballet theatre as its way of life, while retaining the basic essentials of classical technique. Until its move north it completely avoided the traditional repertory of the classics, concentrating entirely on the creation of new works and breaking extensive new ground in both subject matter and dramatic form.

Paralleling movements in British theatre and drawing on continental developments such as the French Nouvelle Vague film movement, Darrell's work for the company created a repertoire of mainly one-act story ballets on powerful, contemporary, and often controversial themes offering an immediate impact to the layman. Through his ballets, the company became the first to admit varied and subtle treatments of contemporary day-to-day life, with such topics as domestic drama, rape, homosexuality, murder—and sophisticated comedy (usually of a dark, Ortonesque kind)—as serious subjects for dance, while concentrating on psychological states in more traditional material as the principal mainspring for dramatic invention. In doing so it established broader, European, and to some extent more adult horizons for ballet, did much to break down social barriers and insularity in the world of post-war British dance, and helped force it to take account of developments in other forms.

Western Ballet Theatre also pioneered the use of playwrights and theatre producers to work with its choreographers and dancers to create higher standards of ensemble playing. In 1966 the company created the first full-evening British ballet with a contemporary setting with Darrell's *Sun into Darkness*, involving both these techniques. Through Darrell—who had allied the company's image to contemporary pop music to some extent through his television choreography for the then innovative pop programme *Cool for Cats*—Western Ballet Theatre also became the first company to make ballet especially for television (*The House Party*, to Poulenc's *Les Biches*), while the same interest in popular musical culture led to its innovative use in ballets such as *Mods and Rockers* (Darrell, to music by The Beatles) which caused an immediate sensation when it was produced in 1964.

—Geoffrey Baskerville

SEMENOVA, Marina
Russian/Soviet dancer and teacher. Born Marina Timofeevna Semenova (sometimes spelled Semynova) in St. Petersburg, 12 June (30 May old style) 1908. Studied at the Petrograd, later Leningrad, Choreographic School from 1919, pupil of Leonid Leontiev, Vladimir Ponomarev, Agrippina Vaganova; graduated in 1925. Married (1) dancer and teacher Viktor Semenov; (2) diplomat Kazokhan (died in the Gulag some time after 1936); (3) actor Aksenov: one daughter, Bolshoi dancer Ekaterina Aksenova. Soloist, State Theatre of Opera and Ballet (GATOB, later the Kirov Ballet), Leningrad, 1925–29; ballerina, Bolshoi Ballet, Moscow, 1930–52; guest ballerina, performing *Giselle* with Serge Lifar, Opéra, Paris, 1935, also returning as guest artist, Kirov Ballet, Leningrad, in the 1930s; teacher, Moscow Choreographic School, 1953–60, and répétiteur (rehearsal director), Bolshoi Ballet, from 1953: pupils include Maya Plisetskaya, Nina Timofeyeva, Natalia Bessmertnova, Nadezhda Pavlova; Professor, Choreographers' Faculty of the Institute of Theatrical Art, from 1960. Recipient: State Premium of the USSR, 1941; title of People's Artist of the USSR, 1975.

ROLES

1921   Lise in *The Magic Flute* (Ivanov), Petrograd Choreographic School, Petrograd
1925   Queen of the Dryads in *Don Quixote* (Gorsky after Petipa), State Theatre for Opera and Ballet (GATOB, later the Kirov Ballet), Leningrad
        Naila (cr) in *La Source* (Vaganova, Ponomarev after Saint-Léon), Graduation Performance of the Leningrad Choreographic School, GATOB, Leningrad
        Princess Florine in *The Sleeping Beauty* (Petipa), GATOB, Leningrad

Marina Semenova, Paris, 1937

1926   Odette/Odile in *Swan Lake* (Petipa, Ivanov), GATOB, Leningrad
Nikiya in *La Bayadère* (Petipa), GATOB, Leningrad
1927   Princess Aurora in *The Sleeping Beauty* (Petipa), GATOB, Leningrad
Avdotia (cr) in *Serf Ballerina* (Lopukhov), GATOB, Leningrad
1928   Aspicia in *Pharaoh's Daughter* (Petipa), GATOB, Leningrad
The Tsar Maiden in *The Little Humpbacked Horse* (Gorsky after Saint-Léon), GATOB, Leningrad
1929   Title role in *Raymonda* (Petipa; staged Lopukhov), GATOB, Leningrad
1930   Nikiya in *La Bayadère* (Gorsky after Petipa), Bolshoi Ballet, Moscow
1931   Concitta in *The Comedians* (Chekrygin), Bolshoi Ballet, Moscow
Kitri in *Don Quixote* (Gorsky after Petipa), Bolshoi Ballet, Moscow
1933   Mireille de Poitiers (cr) in *The Flames of Paris* (Moscow version; Vainonen), Bolshoi Ballet, Moscow
1934   Title role in *Esmeralda* (Tikhomirov after Petipa), Bolshoi Ballet, Moscow
Title role in *Giselle* (Petipa after Coralli, Perrot), Bolshoi Ballet, Moscow
1935   Leading dancer in *Chopiniana* (Fokine; staged Chekrygin), Bolshoi Ballet, Moscow

1937   Magic Maid in *Ruslan and Ludmila* (Zakharov), Bolshoi Ballet, Moscow
1938   Paulina (cr) in *The Prisoner of the Caucasus* (Zakharov), Bolshoi Ballet, Moscow
1939   Nymph in *Ivan Susanin* (opera; mus. Glinka, chor. Zakharov), Bolshoi Ballet, Moscow
Masha in *The Nutcracker* (Vainonen), Bolshoi Ballet, Moscow
1941   Persian Girl in *Khovanshchina* (Zakharov), Bolshoi Ballet, Moscow
Pannochka (cr) in *Taras Bulba* (Zakharov), Bolshoi Ballet, Moscow
1944   Street Dancer in *Don Quixote* (Gorsky after Petipa), Bolshoi Ballet, Moscow
1945   Waltz in *Ivan Susanin* (opera; mus. Glinka, chor. Zakharov), Bolshoi Ballet, Moscow
Title role (cr) in *Raymonda* (new production; Lavrovsky after Petipa, Gorsky), Bolshoi Ballet, Moscow
1946   Lisa (cr) in *Mistress into Maid* (Zakharov), Bolshoi Filial Theatre, Moscow
1947   Title role in *Cinderella* (Zakharov), Bolshoi Ballet, Moscow
1949   Title role in *Mirandolina* (Vainonen), Bolshoi Ballet, Moscow
The Queen of the Ball in *The Bronze Horseman* (Zakharov), Bolshoi Ballet, Moscow

Other roles include: Tao-Hoa in *The Red Poppy* (Laschilin, Tikhomirov).

PUBLICATIONS

Gvozdev, A., "Student Ballerina Semenova", *Zhizn Iskusstva* (Leningrad), no. 17, 1925
Raffé, Walter George, "Some Impressions from the Soviet Ballet: Agrippina Vaganova and Marina Semynova", *Dancing Times* (London), September 1936
Potapov, V., "Arabesques", *Teatr* (Moscow), no. 8, 1940
Morley, Iris, *Soviet Ballet*, London, 1945
Volkov, Nikolai, "Marina Semenova", in Slonimsky, Yuri, (ed.), *The Soviet Ballet* New York, 1947, 1970
Vaganova, Agrippina, *Collected Articles and Memoirs*, Leningrad, 1958
Ivanova, Svetlana, *Marina Semenova*, Moscow, 1965
Lopukhov, Fedor, *Sixty Years in Ballet*, Moscow, 1966
Gaevsky, Vadim, *Divertissement*, Moscow, 1981
Smakov, Gennady, *The Great Russian Dancers*, New York, 1984
Willis, Margaret, "Marina Semynova—The Vaganova Link", *Dance Magazine* (New York), February 1991

*   *   *

The name of Marina Semenova is not very widely known in the West, but in her native land it is surrounded by legend. All who saw her on the stage were convinced that they saw the greatest ballerina of the age. Her art was unreproduceable and her contribution to the history of Russian ballet theatre unusually great. She accomplished a virtual breakthrough into unknown spheres of classical ballet. Unusual, even super-human energy of movement, and an equally unusual sweep of gesture gave classical dance in Semenova's performance a new dimension, and demonstrated the emotional possibilities of the human soul in a completely new way. Her dancing extended the limits of virtuoso technique and even annihilated the very idea of such limits. At the same time Semenova was feminine in every movement on stage, in every step, in every gesture. In other words she was the ideal classical ballerina.

Ballerina roles in old ballets were the basis and support of Semenova's art, and she shone in them and felt herself most free in them. And above all, into these old ballets she injected that contemporary attitude which so many newer productions did not achieve. Semenova was an outstanding interpreter in particular of the ballets to the music of Tchaikovsky and Glazunov. Her interpretations struck one with their artistic radiance, dramatism, and depth. They were carefully thought out, but in them was some magical spontaneous strength. Semenova was a ballerina capable of high tragedy, although from nature she had received a comic gift—the gift of joyous dancing, the gift of laughter through dance. However, high tragedy attracted her more than anything else and she danced *Swan Lake* and *La Bayadère* in the noble tragic manner.

Sadly, the tragedy of life itself did not leave Semenova untouched. In 1936 her second husband was arrested, a victim of Stalin's great purge, and perished; consequently Semenova's position in the theatre collapsed, and a brilliantly promising theatrical life continued with difficulty, ending all too soon.

But severe trials did not break her. It seemed she had been prepared for them. It was not in vain that Semenova danced and acted and constantly carried within herself an unbreakable will to live. For this the spectators of Leningrad and Moscow loved her. For them she was more than just a phenomenally gifted ballerina. In her proud bearing were moral strength and the highest artistic beauty which returned to spectators their faith in humanity. In theatrical circles she was called Tsaritsa—the Queen—and this was the time when people were humiliated and insulted by the regime under which they lived. And it was no accident that Semenova's last role was the role of the Tsaritsa, or Queen of the Ball.

From that time on, and for nearly 40 years, Semenova conducted a class for the leading artists of the Bolshoi theatre, guiding the careers of such dancers as Maya Plisetskaya, Natalia Bessmertnova, and Nadezhda Pavlova.

—Vadim Gaevsky

———

SEMENYAKA, Ludmila

Russian/Soviet dancer. Born Lyudmila (Ludmila) Ivanovna Semenyaka in Leningrad, 16 January 1952. Studied at the Leningrad Choreographic School, pupil of Nina Belikova; graduated in 1970; later studied with Galina Ulanova, Marina Semenova. Married dancer Mikhail Lavrovsky (div). Dancer, corps de ballet, Kirov Ballet, Leningrad, 1970–72; principal dancer, Bolshoi Ballet, Moscow, from 1972, also appearing as guest ballerina, Maly Theatre Ballet, Leningrad; international guest artist, including for the Paris Opéra Ballet, Teatro Colón in Buenos Aires, Royal Swedish Ballet, Berlin State Opera Ballet, American Ballet Theatre, and Matsayuma Ballet, Japan; guest ballerina, Moscow City Ballet, touring England, 1991; also toured Japan with own concert group, 1991; principal dancer, English National Ballet, from 1991. Recipient: title of Honoured Artist of the Russian Federation, 1976; Bronze Medal, International Ballet Competition, Moscow, 1969; Silver Medal, All-Union Ballet Competition, 1972; Bronze Medal, International Ballet Competition, Varna, 1972; Lenin Komsomol Prize, 1975; Gold Medal, International Ballet Competition, Tokyo, 1976; State Prize of the USSR, 1977.

ROLES

1970/
72
Amour in *Don Quixote* (Gorsky after Petipa), Kirov Ballet, Leningrad

Colombine in *The Bronze Horseman* (Zakharov), Kirov Ballet, Leningrad

Princess Florine in *The Sleeping Beauty* (Petipa; staged Sergeyev), Kirov Ballet, Leningrad

1971
An Angel (cr) in *The Creation of the World* (Kasatkina, Soloviov), Kirov Ballet, Leningrad

1972
Odette/Odile in *Swan Lake* (Petipa, Ivanov; staged Messerer), Bolshoi Ballet, Kremlin Palace of Congresses, Moscow

1973/
74
Princess Aurora in *The Sleeping Beauty* (Grigorovich), Bolshoi Ballet, Moscow

Masha in *The Nutcracker* (Grigorovich), Bolshoi Ballet, Moscow

Shirien in *The Legend of Love* (Grigorovich), Bolshoi Ballet, Moscow

1974
Phrygia in *Spartacus* (Grigorovich), Bolshoi Ballet, Moscow

Title role in *Giselle* (Petipa after Coralli, Perrot), Bolshoi Ballet, Moscow

1975/
76
Valentina in *Angara* (Grigorovich), Bolshoi Ballet, Moscow

1976/
77
Anastasia in *Ivan the Terrible* (Grigorovich), Bolshoi Ballet, Moscow

Kitri in *Don Quixote* (Gorsky after Petipa), Bolshoi Ballet, Moscow

1978/
79
Katerina in *The Stone Flower* (Grigorovich), Bolshoi Ballet, Moscow

1979
Beatrice in *Love for Love* (Boccadero), Bolshoi Ballet, Moscow

1981
Lady Macbeth in *Macbeth* (Vasiliev), Bolshoi Ballet, Moscow

1982
Waltz, Mazurka in *Chopiniana* (*Les Sylphides*; Fokine), Bolshoi Ballet, Moscow

1983
Juliet in *Romeo and Juliet* (Grigorovich), Bolshoi Ballet, Moscow

Ballerina in *Petrushka* (Fokine), Bolshoi Ballet, Moscow

1984
Title role in *Raymonda* (Grigorovich after Petipa), Bolshoi Ballet, Moscow

1986
Rita in *The Golden Age* (Grigorovich), Bolshoi Ballet, Moscow

1988
Roxanne in *Cyrano de Bergerac* (Petit), Bolshoi Ballet, Moscow

1991
Sonia (cr) in *Crime and Punishment* (Murdmaa), Estonian Ballet, Tallin

Title role in *La Sylphide* (von Rosen after Bournonville), Maly Theatre Ballet, Leningrad

Sugar Plum Fairy in *The Nutcracker* (Stevenson), English National Ballet, London

1992
Red Waltz in *Our Waltzes* (Nebrada), English National Ballet, tour

Title role in *Cinderella* (Stevenson), English National Ballet

The Young Girl in *Le Spectre de la rose* (Fokine), English National Ballet

PUBLICATIONS

By Semenyaka:

Interview in Tobias, Tobi, "Bolshoi Profiles: Lyudmila Semenyaka", *Dance Magazine* (New York), August 1975

Ludmila Semenyaka as Princess Aurora in *The Sleeping Beauty*

About Semenyaka:
Gusev, Petr, "Lyudmila Semenyaka", *Teatr* (Moscow), no. 1, 1973
Greskovic, Robert, "The Grigorovich Factor and the Bolshoi", *Ballet Review* (Brooklyn, N.Y.), vol. 5, no. 2, 1975/76
Sakharova, O., "A Title with no Lofty Epithets", *Teatralnaya Zhizn* (Moscow), no. 9, 1978
Siemens, Reynold, "Bolshoi Here and There", *Dancing Times* (London), October 1987
Parry, Jann, "Russian Round-Up", *Dancing Times* (London), December 1991
"Literary Lady", in "Curtain Up", *Dance and Dancers* (London), March 1992

*   *   *

Ludmila Semenyaka, like the great Russian ballerinas Galina Ulanova and Marina Semenova before her, started her artistic career in Leningrad with the Kirov Ballet before moving south to Moscow to join the Bolshoi. Thus her Vaganova training of technical purity and refinement, with its neatness and precision, has been augmented by the dramatic and expansive style of the Bolshoi school. This careful blending of aristocracy and raw bravura has brought her much success worldwide. She has delighted audiences by taking risks with razor-sharp footwork and fearless execution of speedy multiple pirouettes. Yet, in spite of her dare-devilry, her dancing has never lost its sensitivity and elegance. Her performances reflect her love of artistic beauty in literature, art, and music and show a natural gift for acting which brings her sharply defined characters alive on stage.

Born in Leningrad of working parents, Semenyaka showed an early appreciation for music and an eagerness to dance. She was enrolled at the local palace of culture, where she started her first ballet classes. Her natural aptitude and grace were quickly noticed and at the age of ten, she was successfully entered for the examinations at the Leningrad Choreographic School. Although a shy child, she recalls that she always felt completely at ease when dancing and has found much pleasure in her work. She has nothing but praise for the Vaganova training which gently prepared her for her balletic career. As a student she would regularly watch rehearsals and performances by the Kirov company, gaining inspiration from such outstanding ballerinas as Alla Sizova, Irina Kolpakova, and Natalia Makarova. Her teacher was Nina Belikova, and her class-mate was Kirov dancer Galina Mezentseva.

As a student, Semenyaka danced many times with the Kirov Company in children's parts, and on graduation she was taken into the corps de ballet. Placed in the front line most of the time, she carefully observed the soloists and learned from them. She was given the roles of Amour in *Don Quixote*, Colombine in *The Bronze Horseman*, and Princess Florine in *Sleeping Beauty*, which she danced on her first trip to Japan. She was also one of the Angels in Kasatkina's and Vasiliov's *Creation of the World*, the ballet which saw Baryshnikov, Soloviev, Kolpakova, and Panov in its original cast. Semenyaka's dancing was coloured with a dramatic, open expressiveness that hinted of the Bolshoi style, so it was no surprise when, after eighteen months, she decided to move to Moscow. Her husband at that time was Mikhail Lavrovsky, one of the Bolshoi's finest male virtuosos at the peak of his career. Yuri Grigorovich, artistic director of the Bolshoi, who had also started his career in Leningrad and had noticed the young dancer's ability, offered her many of the Bolshoi's leading roles. However, Semenyaka arrived at a period when the company was bursting with talent: Bessmertnova, Maximova, Plisetskaya, and Sorokina were all in line in front of her, and she had to wait her turn. Her début was in

Swan Lake at the Kremlin Palace with Aleksandr Bogatyrev as her Prince. It is a ballet where the dual role of Odette/Odile gives her a perfect opportunity to show off her two schoolings—the purity and softness of one, the flashy attack of the other.

When Semenyaka joined the Bolshoi, Galina Ulanova took her under her wing to coach her in the nuances of the different roles. From Ulanova, Semenyaka learned to express a lyricism that flowed throughout her body, reaching beyond the tips of her fingers to melt into the next musical phrase. The legendary ballerina also carefully guided her young pupil into seeking and injecting her own individuality into her characters. Later, when Semenyaka was to dance Grigorovich's *Raymonda*, it was the gentle Marina Semenova who taught her the brilliant subtleties of that role.

Grigorovich gave Semenyaka the heroine roles in his ballets—Katerina (*The Stone Flower*), Anastasia (*Ivan the Terrible*), Juliet, Rita (*Golden Age*), Phrygia (*Spartacus*), Shirien (*Legend of Love*), Masha (*Nutcracker*), and Valentina in *Angara*, a dramatic role for which she received the USSR State Prize.

But it is with the fairy-tale roles that Semenyaka is most associated (though her own dream is to dance modern classics such as Cranko's *Onegin* and ballets by MacMillan, Ashton, and Petit to show a different facet of her talent). Her dainty frame and features, set off by grey, luminous eyes, give her an air of fragility and vulnerability, qualities needed for Giselle, Odette, Raymonda, and Aurora. Her porcelain-doll appearance belies her physical strength and stamina—she possesses strong feet and legs and has enormous energy.

During the 1979 Bolshoi tour of America, Alexander Godunov and the Kozlovs defected in a flurry of publicity—and Semenyaka lost one of her best partners. Godunov, tall, blond, and princely, set off her own dancing. The handsome partnership was exciting. His abrupt departure not only gave her the problem of finding new cavaliers—she has not had a regular one since—but the defections themselves caused such political reverberations that cultural events, including Bolshoi tours to America and Britain, were halted. This meant that during the peak years of Semenyaka's career, audiences in these countries were deprived of seeing her dance. It was only in 1986 and 1987 in Britain, and then in America, that Semenyaka was able to demonstrate again her sparkling technique.

Lyudmila Semenyaka has been on the committee of the USSR's Cultural Fund, organizing gala events to raise money for artistic and historic restoration. She has also worked for a period as artistic director to a new ballet company, directed by Boris Miagov from the region of Komi in Siberia. She coached the ballerinas, passing on some of her valuable expertise to the younger dancers. In late summer 1991, she returned to England to dance as a guest with the Moscow City Ballet, one of the new classical troupes springing up today in the Soviet Union's freer artistic society. Soon afterwards, she became a principal dancer with English National Ballet.

—Margaret Willis

SEREGI, László
Hungarian dancer, choreographer, and ballet director.   Born in Budapest, 12 December 1929. Studied dance while a member of the Hungarian Army Ensemble and with Marcella Nádasi, Ferenc Nádasi, and Gyula Harangozó, Budapest. Married dancer Katalin Seregi, 1953: one daughter, Katalin, and one

son, László. Dancer, Hungarian Army Ensemble, 1949–56; character dancer, Hungarian State Opera Ballet, from 1957; choreographer for opera, from 1965; first major ballet choreography, 1968, becoming chief choreographer, Hungarian State Opera Ballet, from 1974; artistic director, Budapest State Opera Ballet, 1977–84; has also choreographed and staged ballets in West Germany, Zurich, and Vienna; producer of films of own works, including *The Wooden Prince* (1970), and *The Cedar Tree* (1976). Recipient: title of Merited Artist of the Hungarian National Republic, 1972; Golden Cross of Culture, Austria, 1977; Kossuth Prize, Hungary, 1978; Golden Medal of the Hungarian State Republic, 1989.

WORKS

1963   *Electronic Love* (mus. Kozma), Hungarian State Opera Ballet, Budapest
1968   *Spartacus* (mus. Khachaturian), Hungarian State Opera Ballet, Budapest
1970   *The Wooden Prince* (mus. Bartók), Hungarian State Opera Ballet, Budapest
         The Miraculous Mandarin (mus. Bartók), Hungarian State Opera Ballet, Budapest
         Dances in *Bluebeard's Castle* (opera; mus. Bartók), Hungarian State Opera Ballet, Budapest
1972   *Sylvia* (mus. Delibes), Hungarian State Opera Ballet, Budapest
1975   *The Cedar Tree* (mus. Hidas), Hungarian State Opera Ballet, Budapest
1976   *Kammermusik No. 1* (mus. Hindemith), Hungarian State Opera Ballet, Budapest
1977   *Serenade* (mus. Bernstein), Hungarian State Opera Ballet, Budapest
         On the Town (mus. Bernstein), Hungarian State Opera Ballet, Budapest
         Air (pas de deux; mus. Bach), Hungarian State Opera Ballet, Budapest
1978   *Variation on a Nursery Song* (mus. Dohnanyi), Hungarian State Opera Ballet, Budapest
1982   *The Wooden Prince* (new version; mus. Bartók), Hungarian State Opera Ballet, Budapest
         The Miraculous Mandarin (new version; mus Bartók), Hungarian State Opera Ballet, Budapest
1985   *Romeo and Juliet* (mus. Prokofiev), Hungarian State Opera Ballet, Budapest
1989   *A Midsummer Night's Dream* (mus. Mendelssohn and others), Hungarian State Opera Ballet, Budapest

Other works include: *The Eternal Dance* (with Harangozó, Rábai; film featuring State Folk Ensemble and Hungarian State Opera Ballet); dances in numerous operas including *Walpurgisnacht* (from *Faust*; mus. Gounod).

PUBLICATIONS

By Seregi:
Interview in Maácz, László, "At Half-time . . . Conversation with László Seregi", *Hungarian Dance News* (Budapest), no. 5–6, 1982

About Seregi:
Körtvélyes, Géza, and Lörinzc, György, *The Budapest Ballet* (in English), Budapest, 1971
Koegler, Horst, "The Hungarian State Ballet", *Dance and Dancers* (London), September 1975
Percival, John, "The Inspiration from Traditions", *Dance and Dancers* (London), April 1977
Lörincz, György, "Hongrie", *Les Saisons de la danse* (Paris), October 1981
Lidova, Irène, "Le Ballet national de Hongrie", *Les Saisons de la danse* (Paris), November 1981
Clark, Mary, "Hungarian State Ballet", *Dancing Times* (London), April 1989

*   *   *

Dance cognoscenti, not only in Hungary but in the world, are of the opinion that László Seregi's 1968 version of *Spartacus*, the great dance-drama by Khachaturian, was a turning-point in the history of Hungarian ballet. This work was a summation of all that had gone before, bringing together the various elements of Harangozó's style and influence and making use both of the Soviet tradition of epic subjects and the heritage of Hungarian folk culture itself.

In 1970, the 25th anniversary of Béla Bartók's death, Seregi was invited by the Hungarian authorities to re-choreograph two major works—*The Miraculous Mandarin* and *The Wooden Prince*—together with the dances in Bartók's opera *Bluebeard's Castle*. The three pieces formed a trilogy, a homage to and an ongoing historical link with one of the world's greatest twentieth-century composers. *The Miraculous Mandarin*, a difficult work first staged in 1926, established itself in Seregi's version at the very forefront of the dance scene in Hungary, and despite a number of changes over the years, it is still today virtually the trademark work of the Hungarian State Ballet. *The Wooden Prince*, a fantasy/fairytale based on Hungarian folk legend, had been choreographed by numerous choreographers before Seregi, but found a definitive version in the 1970 staging.

The next major success for Seregi came in 1972 with a revival of Delibes's *Sylvia*. This work was in complete contrast to his previous work. *Sylvia*, first choreographed by Louis Mérante in 1876, is a light-hearted parody based on the ballet-within-a-ballet formula, incorporating in Seregi's version the elements of folk culture, classical Greece, and neo-classical dance. The ballet became an immediate hit with the public and remains so to this day; and it has been taken into the repertoire of a number of foreign companies.

In 1975, Seregi produced another, more serious, large-scale ballet, *The Cedar Tree*. The piece is strongly Hungarian in character and uses the music of Frigyes Hidas. It is based on a Hungarian turn-of-the-century figurative and symbolist painter Csontvary, following his oeuvre much as Mussorgsky did to compose his *Pictures at an Exhibition* in purely musical terms. This has not been an easy work for foreigners to come to terms with as it is so very national in character—but again, it has been a major success for Seregi at home.

In recent years, Seregi has travelled widely, and Western influences, as well as those from Russia, have started to mould the choreographer's style, taste, and techniques: the use of Leonard Bernstein's quintessentially American scores for his own versions of *On The Town* and *Serenade*, for example, show his openness to diverse influences.

Seregi is not an artist who creates his dance compositions with great speed; he has to be highly motivated by music and subject-matter, and he researches each work with meticulous attention to detail. One suspects that he is a true Romantic at heart and is also drawn to dramatic themes—certainly Shakespeare has been a major inspiration. Although rarely seen (if ever) outside Eastern Europe, Seregi's *Romeo and Juliet* can be called one of the most accurate, heartfelt, and truly "Shakespearean" versions of the tragedy to be seen in dance form. At the same time, Seregi's feel for romantic comedy is strong, and in 1989 he presented a delightful version of *A Midsummer Night's Dream* as part of the Christmas season in Budapest.

The name of László Seregi is not necessarily internationally well known outside the ballet world, but at home, he is among the most respected Hungarian artists of his generation. It has largely been his influence, both artistic and personal, as chief choreographer of the Budapest Ballet which has been responsible for the growing internationalism and continuing success of that company.

—Sally Whyte

SERENADE

Choreography: George Balanchine
Music: Petr Ilyich Tchaikovsky
Design: William Okie (costumes)
First Production: Students of the School of American Ballet, Avery Memorial Theatre, Hartford, Connecticut, 8 December 1934 (first performed privately at White Plains, New York, 9 June 1934)

Other productions include: American Ballet (restaged Balanchine, costumes Jean Lurçat), with Kathryn Mullowney, Heidi Vosseler, Charles Lasky; New York, 1 March 1935. Ballet Russe de Monte Carlo (restaged and revised Balanchine), with Igor Youskevitch, Frederic Franklin, Marie-Jeanne; New York, 17 October 1940. Paris Opéra Ballet (restaged Balanchine); Paris, 30 April 1947. San Francisco Ballet (costumes Russell Hartley), with Alexandra Danilova; San Francisco, 18 April 1952. Royal Danish Ballet; Copenhagen, 16 January 1957. La Scala Ballet; Milan, 1960. Hamburg Ballet; Hamburg 11 October 1960. National Ballet of Canada; Toronto, 25 February 1963. Royal Ballet; London, 7 May 1964. Bavarian State Opera Ballet; Munich, 8 May 1965. Vienna State Opera Ballet; Vienna, 18 May 1966. Geneva Ballet; Geneva, 23 January 1970. Australian Ballet; Adelaide, 23 March 1970. German Opera Ballet; Berlin, 7 October 1970. Royal Swedish Ballet; Stockholm, 10 November 1970. Frankfurt Ballet; Frankfurt, 21 April 1974. Hungarian State Opera Ballet; Budapest, 10 December 1977. Zurich Opera Ballet; Zurich, 9 September 1978. Dance Theatre of Harlem; New York, 27 February 1979. Matsuyama Ballet; Tokyo, 12 June 1982.

PUBLICATIONS

Barnes, Clive, "*Serenade*", *Dance and Dancers* (London), January 1959.
Daniels, Don, "Academy: The New World of *Serenade*", *Ballet Review* (Brooklyn, N.Y.), vol. 5, no. 1, 1975–76
Balanchine, George, with Mason, Francis, *Balanchine's Complete Stories of the Great Ballets*, Garden City, N.Y., 1977
Siegel, Marcia, *Two American Dance Classics*, Bronxville, N.Y., 1978
Siegel, Marcia, *The Shapes of Change*, Boston, 1979
Hunt, Marilyn, "Encounters with Poetry: *Serenade* at 50", *Dance Magazine* (New York), June 1985
Denby, Edwin, *Dance Writings*, edited by Robert Cornfield and William Mackay, New York, 1986
Croce, Arlene, *Sight Lines*, New York, 1987
Kaplan, Larry, "Corps Choreography by Balanchine", *Ballet Review* (New York), Winter 1988

*   *   *

Serenade holds a special place among the dance works of the twentieth century: both masterpiece and talisman, it is probably the most widely performed work of the century's greatest master; certainly it is the piece which is most immediately associated with his name. It is performed today by countless regional ballet companies across America and Europe, and is the "signature piece" of the New York City Ballet. Adding to the work's mystique is the fact that it formed part opart of the first program Balanchine presented in America, so that it is associated in the public mind with Balanchine's development, in America, of that brand of New World neo-classicism on which his reputation will certainly rest.

Set to the almost unnaturally tuneful *Serenade for Strings* of Tchaikovsky (with the order of the final two movements reversed), the piece is dominated by its women. This aspect has led the critic Arlene Croce to speak of the sense of "sisterhood of the corps" it produces; in any case this was the result as much of necessity as of volition, Balanchine's own company at the time being weak on men. The story is well-known too that Balanchine incorporated into the ballet two events that happened during rehearsals: a girl comes in late in the first movement, the Sonatina, and takes her place among the rows of girls facing downstage into the footlights; later on, another girl falls and is left on the stage, where she plays a role in the strange pas de trois of the piece's final movement, the Elegy.

As the curtain rises in the Sonatina, the stage is filled with women bathed in light and dressed in long white tutus with their feet together and their right arms outstretched, palms up as if to ward off an unseen danger. At an invisible signal they all crook their arms in unison, turning away their heads and touching their wrists to their temples as if expressing world-weariness, modesty, or existential headache. The pose dissolves as the women simultaneously open their feet into first position, and from then on begin to move across the stage. Indeed, the entire work is full of these strangely programmatic gestures (for which the spectator would like to develop the story, in each case merely hinted at), all embedded in so much pure dance of a technically predictable nature that the critic Edwin Denby saw in it a "graduation exercise".

The most dramatic of the movements, in this sense, is the last, the Elegy, which both begins and ends with images eerie enough to have been borrowed from a surrealistic poem—or at least, from the Romantic paintings of Caspar David Friedrich. As it opens a man appears, walking from upstage left on a diagonal to downstage right where lies a woman who has fallen, and he is followed and blindfolded by the hand of a woman who walks a step behind him. The pair becomes a pas de trois with the man supporting the fallen woman and turning her in an otherwise motionless arabesque, while the one who had both blinded and guided him makes great swooping motions behind him with her arms, evocative of a bird, or an angel.

At the end of the movement, with the pas de trois concluded and the man guided off once again by his muse/vampire/angel, a group of other men pick up the fallen girl who is once again sprawled on the stage, and carry her as a figurehead above them as they walk slowly in a kind of phalanx backstage right, into the light. The girl bends her upper body backwards as if in abnegation before a god to whom she is being carried as a sacrifice, and the curtain falls with one last luscious chord of the strings. A story? No; but we see the fragments of at least several stories, bits and pieces of enough myths and archetypes to keep

Serenade, **as performed by the students of the School of American Ballet, NewYork, 1989**

a psychoanalyst busy for years.

The cynical viewer might insist that *Serenade*'s popularity with dance companies is the result of its technical accessibility, and its popularity with audiences the result of its triumphant assertion in movement of Balanchine's famously quotable "ballet is woman". The motion is graceful; even the tutus are suitably like those of Fokine's *Sylphides* to make the scene on the stage palatable to even the most retrograde of contemporary audience tastes. It is Modernism without tears, in other words: if this is all neo-Classicism is about, why worry?

Yet if this work is still drenched in the Romanticism that some of Balanchine's later Stravinsky works seemed to have transcended, still it is a beautiful work, as much precisely because of its undigested fragments of plot as in spite of them. The dancing is symbiotic with the music, its graceful women the ideally appropriate equivalent of the music's dense string timbres; both music and dance are darkened with hints of tragedy and loss that never quite rise to the surface. *Serenade*, moreover, can be seen as a kind of essay on the uneasy balance of order and its destruction that seems the nature of all of our lives. The women, to be sure, execute many of their gestures in unison; yet individuals fall, or are late, or engage in other all too human actions. The man of the last movement is clearly involved with these two women, but how? As individuals or types? And all to what purpose? At the end, it all dissolves into the light and a sense of going somewhere unknown for a reason we cannot fathom.

Serenade is that all too rare object: an accessible masterpiece—which means that it is simultaneously profound and trivial, at once manipulative of its audience and fascinatingly beautiful. And for this reason, it seems, it will be performed as long as the classical ballet is alive.

—Bruce Fleming

SERGEYEV, Konstantin

Russian/Soviet dancer and choreographer. Born Konstantin Mikhailovich Sergeev (Sergeyev) in St. Petersburg, 5 March (20 February old style) 1910. Studied at the Leningrad Choreographic School, entering evening classes in 1924, pupil of M. Kozhukhova, E. Snetkova, V. Semenov; studied at the main school, pupil of Vladimir Ponomarev; graduated in 1930. Married (1) dancer Feya Balabina: one son, Kirov soloist Nikolai Sergeyev; (2) dancer Natalia Dudinskaya. Dancer, Iosif (Josef) Kshesinsky's touring company, 1928–29; dancer, becoming principal dancer, State Academic Theatre for Opera and Ballet (GATOB), later the Kirov Ballet, 1930–61; choreographer, 1946–51; chief choreographer and artistic director, Kirov Ballet, 1951–55, 1961–70; teacher, Leningrad Choreographic School, from 1931, becoming artistic director, 1938–40, 1973–82; also producer of several ballet films, including *Swan Lake* and *Sleeping Beauty*, and the television film *Don Juan*. Recipient: titles of Honoured Artist of the Russian Federation, 1939, People's Artist of the Russian Federation, 1951; State Prize of the USSR, 1946, 1947, 1949, 1951; title of People's Artist of the USSR, 1957; Honorary Award, Academy of Dance, Paris, 1965. Died in St. Petersburg (formerly Leningrad), 1 April 1992.

ROLES

1928/ Siegfried in *Swan Lake* (Petipa, Ivanov), Iosif Kshes-
29   insky's Company, Soviet tour

Albrecht in *Giselle* (Petipa after Coralli, Perrot), Iosif Kshesinsky's Company, Soviet tour

1930 Young Coolie in *The Red Poppy* (Lopukhov, Ponomarev, Leontiev), Graduation Performance, Leningrad Choreographic School, Leningrad

Phoenix in *The Red Poppy* (Lopukhov, Ponomarev, Leontiev), State Academic Theatre for Opera and Ballet (GATOB, later the Kirov), Leningrad

The Genie of the Waters in *The Little Humpbacked Horse* (Gorsky after Saint-Léon), GATOB, Leningrad

Sportsman (cr) in *The Golden Age* (Vainonen, Yakobson), GATOB, Leningrad

1931 Usbek (cr) in *The Bolt* (Lopukhov), GATOB, Leningrad

The Bluebird in *The Sleeping Beauty* (Petipa), GATOB, Leningrad

1932 Mistral (cr) in *The Flames of Paris* (Vainonen), GATOB, Leningrad

The Slave in *Egyptian Nights* (Fokine), GATOB, Leningrad

Prince Siegfried in *Swan Lake* (Petipa, Ivanov), GATOB, Leningrad

Prince Désiré in *The Sleeping Beauty* (Petipa), GATOB, Leningrad

Marseillese in *The Flames of Paris* (Vainonen), GATOB, Leningrad

1933 Count (cr) in *Swan Lake* (new production; Vaganova after Petipa, Ivanov), GATOB, Leningrad

1934 Vatslav (cr) in *The Fountain of Bakhchisarai* (Zakharov), GATOB, Leningrad

Nutcracker Prince (cr) in *The Nutcracker* (Vainonen), GATOB, Leningrad

1935 Lucien (cr) in *Lost Illusions* (Zakharov), Kirov Ballet, Leningrad

Acteon in *Esmeralda* (Vaganova after Perrot, Petipa), Kirov Ballet, Leningrad

1938 Koloman (cr) in *Raymonda* (new production; Vainonen after Petipa), Kirov Ballet, Leningrad

1939 Frondoso in *Laurencia* (Chabukiani), Kirov Ballet, Leningrad

1940 Romeo (cr) in *Romeo and Juliet* (Lavrovsky), Kirov Ballet, Leningrad

1941 Ostap (cr) in *Taras Bulba* (Zakharov), Bolshoi Ballet (guest artist), Moscow

1942 Armen (cr) in *Gayané* (Anisimova), Kirov Ballet, Perm

1945 Principal dancer (cr) in *Waltz* (choreographic miniature; Yakobson), Kirov Ballet, Leningrad

1946 Prince (cr) in *Cinderella* (also chor.), Kirov Ballet, Leningrad

1947 The Good Young Man (cr) in *Spring Fairytale* (Lopukhov), Kirov Ballet, Leningrad

Petro (cr) in *Militsa* (Vainonen), Kirov Ballet, Leningrad

Title role (cr) in *Pulcinella* (choreographic miniature; Yakobson), Kirov Ballet, Leningrad

Principal dancer (cr) in *Sentimental Waltz* (choreographic miniature; Yakobson), Kirov Ballet, Leningrad

1948 Jean de Brienne (cr) in *Raymonda* (new production; also chor., after Petipa), Kirov Ballet, Leningrad

1949 Evgeny (cr) in *The Bronze Horseman* (Zakharov), Kirov Ballet, Leningrad

1950 Title role (cr) in *Ali-Batyr* (later called *Shurale*; Yakobson), Kirov Ballet, Leningrad

Prince Siegfried in *Swan Lake* (new production; also chor., after Petipa and Ivanov), Kirov Ballet, Leningrad

1952 Prince Désiré in *The Sleeping Beauty* (new production; also chor., after Petipa), Kirov Ballet, Leningrad
1953 Andrei (cr) in *Native Fields* (Andreyev), Kirov Ballet, Leningrad
1955 Andrei (cr) in *Taras Bulba* (Fenster), Kirov Ballet, Leningrad
1957 Lenny (cr) in *Path of Thunder* (also chor.), Kirov Ballet, Leningrad

Other roles include: for Kshesinsky's touring company— Gringoire in *Esmeralda* (Vaganova after Petipa), Slave in *Le Corsaire* (Vaganova after Petipa), the Youth in *Chopiniana* (*Les Sylphides*; after Fokine); for the Kirov Ballet—Peasants' Pas de Deux in *Giselle* (Petipa after Coralli, Perrot), Prince's Friend and Pas de Trois in *Swan Lake* (Petipa, Ivanov), Philippe, Malbert, and Jerome in *The Flames of Paris* (Vainonen), the Slave in *Le Corsaire* (Petipa), various concert programmes, including choreographic miniatures by Yakobson and others.

WORKS

1946 *Cinderella* (mus. Prokofiev), Kirov Ballet, Leningrad
1957 *Path of Thunder* (mus. Karaev), Kirov Ballet, Leningrad (staged Bolshoi Ballet, Moscow, 1959)
1963 *Distant Planet* (mus. Maizel), Kirov Ballet, Leningrad
1964 *Cinderella* (new production; mus. Prokofiev), Kirov Ballet, Leningrad
1970 *Hamlet* (mus. Chervinsky), Kirov Ballet, Leningrad
1976 *Lefty* (mus. Aleksandrov), Kirov Ballet, Leningrad
1978 *Appassionata* (mus. Beethoven), Leningrad Choreographic School, Leningrad (restaged Leningrad, 1990)
1979 *The Legend of Joan of Arc* (mus. Peiko), Stanislavsky-Nemirovich-Danchenko Theatre, Moscow

Also staged:
1948 *Raymonda* (after Petipa; mus. Glazunov), Kirov Ballet, Leningrad
1950 *Swan Lake* (after Petipa and Ivanov; mus. Tchaikovsky), Kirov Ballet, Leningrad
1952 *The Sleeping Beauty* (after Petipa; mus. Tchaikovsky), Kirov Ballet, Leningrad (restaged, Kirov Ballet, 1989)
1973 *Le Corsaire* (after Petipa; mus. Adam and others), Kirov Ballet, Leningrad
1974 *The Seasons* (after Petipa; mus. Glazunov), Leningrad Choreographic School, Leningrad
1990 *The Fairy Doll* (after N. and S. Legat; mus. J. Bayer), Leningrad Choreographic School, Leningrad

PUBLICATIONS

By Sergeyev:
Interview in "A Friendly Visit: Lydia Joel Meets Natalia Dudinskaya and Konstantin Sergeyev", *Dance Magazine* (New York), November 1964
"Recollections" in *Lavrovsky* (various authors), Moscow, 1983
"My Path", *Teatr* (Moscow), no 6, 1983
"Living Tradition", *Sovetsky Balet* (Moscow), no. 4, 1984
"Choice for a Lifetime", *Sovetskaya Kultura* (Moscow), 24 April 1985

About Sergeyev:
Bogdanov-Berezovsky, Valerian, *K.M. Sergeev*, Leningrad, 1951
Hering, Doris, "Kirov Ballet—Endearing Anachronism",

Dance Magazine (New York), November 1961
Roslavleva, Natalia, *Era of the Russian Ballet*, London, 1966
Prokhorova, V., *Konstantin Sergeev*, Leningrad, 1974
Konstantin Sergeev: A Collection of Articles, Moscow, 1978
Smakov, Gennady, *The Great Russian Dancers*, New York, 1984
Maynard, Olga, "In the Moscow Tradition: *Swan Lake*", *Dance Magazine* (New York), May 1990

* * *

Konstantin Sergeyev has been called "the poet of dance" and "the king of the lyric phrase". The choreographer Fedor Lopukhov wrote of him, "In the person of Sergeyev we have a great dancer of the lyrical-romantic type. Today he is the best 'tenor' of Soviet ballet."

Sergeyev came to fame in the early days of post-Revolutionary Russian ballet. He graduated from the Leningrad Choreographic School in 1930, having performed already with the company of Josef Ksesinsky, and was soon dancing all of the most important male roles in the classical repertoire. What suited Sergeyev best was the theme of grand, ardent, and devoted love. He has rightly been regarded as the definitive Romeo of the Kirov stage in Leningrad, dancing in the original production opposite the incomparable Galina Ulanova, for whom the role of Juliet was created. His interpretation of all the male lyrical-romantic roles in the classical repertoire made him the very prototype of the "danseur noble".

But also, lyricism notwithstanding, Sergeyev asserted his continued, active relation to life, and was equally powerful in contemporary ballets. As Natalia Roslavleva has written, "His importance in the formative period of the ballet of the 1930s cannot be exaggerated." Sergeyev created numerous roles in Soviet works of the 1930s, 1940s, and 1950s, including Mistral in Vainonen's *The Flames of Paris*, Vatslav in Zakharov's *The Fountain of Bakhchisarai*, Evgeny in the same choreographer's *The Bronze Horseman*, and Andrei in *Taras Bulba* (Fenster).

In Sergeyev's first pre-war period of creativity, his major partner was the legendary Ulanova. "The carefully considered finish to every gesture and every moment on stage, particularly in dance movements, was what made Sergeyev a worthy partner to Ulanova," wrote Lopukhov. "They were created for one another . . . but alas, in the very flowering of their talents, circumstances broke up this partnership unprecedented in its formal and spiritual beauty."

After the war, Natalia Dudinskaya became Sergeyev's partner (they also married). The partnership of these two dancers was notable both for the technical accuracy of their dancing, and for their endless search for new shades of meaning and unexplored beauties in the roles they performed. Sergeyev was a romantic Siegfried, a poetic Désiré, and an ironic and comic Prince in *Cinderella* in a version of the classic fairy-tale which he choreographed himself (1946). One of his most interesting and compelling roles was as Albert (Albrecht) in *Giselle*, which he continued to perform with depth and incomparable lyricism for many years on the Kirov stage.

Sergeyev was also an active choreographer; following the success of his *Cinderella*, he staged new versions of *Raymonda* and *Swan Lake* for the Kirov Ballet (1948 and 1950), which have remained in the Kirov repertoire to this day. He created the three-act ballet, *Path of Thunder*, to music by Kara Karayev, in 1957; this work, about the tragic relationship between a white girl and a black teacher, is based on the novel of the same name by the South African author Peter Abrahams. The two leading parts, those of Sari and Lenny, were danced by Sergeyev and Dudinskaya. A version of *Hamlet*, to music by Chervinsky, was created in 1970, and the ballet *Lefty* in 1976.

Konstantin Sergeyev's *Path of Thunder*, with Alla Osipenko and Svyatoslav Kuznetsov, Kirov Ballet, 1960

Sergeyev has also staged definitive versions of the classics for the Kirov, not just those of Marius Petipa (*The Sleeping Beauty*, *Le Corsaire*, *The Seasons*), but such works as *The Fairy Doll*, after Nikolai and Sergei Legat.

Sergeyev's importance in twentieth-century Russian ballet is without question, and his great influence continues to be felt to this day—not just at the Kirov but throughout the Soviet Union and beyond; as "the master of the classic traditions of the [Kirov] repertoire", as Clement Crisp has described him, Konstantin Sergeyev has played an invaluable role in the preservation of the classical heritage by which the Kirov Ballet is known throughout the world today.

—Igor Stupnikov

————

SERGEYEV, Nicholas (Nikolai)
Russian dancer, teacher, and ballet director. Born Nikolai (later Nicholas) Grigorevich Sergeev (Sergeyev, or Sergueff) in St. Petersburg, 27 September (15 September old style) 1876. Studied at the Imperial Theatre School, St. Petersburg, pupil of Nikolai Volkov, Pavel Gerdt, Marius Petipa, Lev Ivanov, and Christian Johanssen; graduated in 1894. Married Evgenia Poplavska (d. 1950). Dancer, Maryinsky Theatre, St. Petersburg, from 1894, becoming soloist, from 1904; régisseur (stage and rehearsal director) in charge of notation, from 1903; régisseur general, from 1914; also teacher, Imperial Theatre School, 1897–1917; left Petrograd, bringing many of the

Maryinsky's ballet notations with him, in 1918: worked briefly in Moscow, settling in Paris, via Istanbul and Marseilles, 1920; staged Petipa's *The Sleeping Beauty* (as *The Sleeping Princess*) for Diaghilev's Ballets Russes, London, 1921; ballet master, staging nineteenth-century classics from notation for Latvian National Ballet, Riga, 1922–24; staged *Giselle* (for Russian ballerina Olga Spessivtseva) at the Paris Opéra, 1924; ballet master for Anna Pavlova's Company, 1927, and for Opéra Privé de Paris, travelling with company to South America, 1929; staged *Giselle* and *Swan Lake*, Act II, for Camargo Society, London, 1932; founder and director, Sergeyev's Russian Ballet, performing Britain, 1934; ballet master, staging full-length classics for Vic-Wells Ballet, 1933, 1934, 1939, Markova–Dolin Ballet, 1935, and (Blum's) Ballet Russe de Monte Carlo, 1938; also teacher, Vic-Wells Ballet, 1937–38; chief régisseur, (Mona Inglesby's) International Ballet, 1941–48. Died in Nice, 24 June 1951.

ROLES

1886   Dancer (as a student) in *Pygmalion* (Petipa), Maryinsky
        Theatre, St. Petersburg
1890   Waltz of the Flowers (cr) in *The Sleeping Beauty*
        (Petipa), Maryinsky Theatre, St. Petersburg
1894/ North Wind in *The Awakening of Flora* (Petipa),
1904   Maryinsky Theatre, St. Petersburg
        Nightingale in *The Caprices of the Butterfly* (Petipa),
        Maryinsky Theatre, St. Petersburg
        Jester's dance in *Mlada* (Petipa), Maryinsky Theatre, St.
        Petersburg

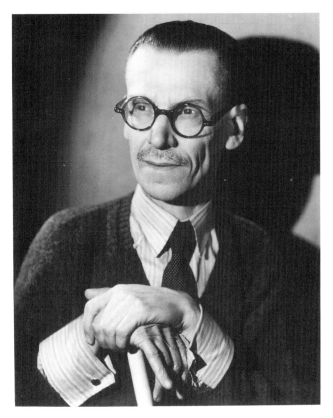

Nicholas Sergeyev

WORKS

Staged:

c.1904 *The Travelling Ballerina* (chor. Petipa), Maryinsky Theatre, St. Petersburg

c.1905 *King Candaule* (chor. Petipa), Maryinsky Theatre, St. Petersburg

c.1912 *Harlequinade* (chor. Petipa), Maryinsky Theatre, St. Petersburg

The Caprices of the Butterfly (chor. Petipa), Maryinsky Theatre, St. Petersburg

The Nutcracker (chor. Ivanov), Maryinsky Theatre, St. Petersburg

1921 *The Sleeping Princess* (*The Sleeping Beauty*; after Petipa, with additional dances Nijinska; mus. Tchaikovsky), Diaghilev's Ballets Russes, London

1922 *La Fille mal gardée* (after Petipa, Ivanov; mus. Hertel), Latvian National Ballet, Riga

Paquita (after Petipa; mus. Deldevez), Latvian National Ballet, Riga

1923 *La Bayadère* (one act, probably "The Kingdom of the Shades", after Petipa; mus. Minkus), Latvian National Ballet, Riga

The Magic Flute (after Ivanov; mus. Drigo), Latvian National Ballet, Riga

1924 *The Little Humpbacked Horse* (after Petipa, Saint-Léon; mus. Pugni), Latvian National Ballet, Riga

Esmeralda (after Perrot, Petipa; mus. Pugni), Latvian National Ballet, Riga

Gazelda (after Perrot; mus. Pugni), Latvian National Ballet, Riga

La Source (after Saint-Léon; mus. Minkus, Delibes), Latvian National Ballet, Riga

1924 *Giselle* (after Petipa, Coralli, Perrot; mus. Adam),

Opéra, Paris

1927 "Kingdom of the Shades" from *La Bayadère* (after Petipa; mus. Minkus), Anna Pavlova's Company (never performed)

1929 *Polovtsian Dances from Prince Igor* (opera; mus. Borodin, chor. after Ivanov), Opéra Privé de Paris, tour

Swan Lake, Act II (after Ivanov; mus Tchaikovsky), Opéra Privé de Paris, tour

Harlequinade Pas de deux (after Petipa; mus. Drigo), Opéra Privé de Paris, tour

Dances in *Tsar Sultan* (opera; mus. Rimsky-Korsakov), Opéra Privé de Paris, tour

Dances in *The Snow Maiden* (opera; mus. Rimsky-Korsakov), Opéra Privé de Paris, tour

Dances in *The Fair at Sorochinsk* (opera; mus. Mussorgsky), Opéra Privé de Paris, tour

Dances in *The Invisible City of Kitezh* (opera; mus. Rimsky-Korsakov), Opéra Privé de Paris, tour

1932 *Giselle* (after Petipa, Coralli, Perrot; mus. Adam), Camargo Society, London

Swan Lake (as *Lac des cygnes*), Act II (after Ivanov; mus. Tchaikovsky), Camargo Society, London

1933 *Coppélia* (after Saint-Léon, Petipa, Cecchetti; mus Delibes), Vic-Wells Ballet, London

1934 *Giselle* (after Petipa, Coralli, Perrot; mus. Adam), Vic-Wells Ballet, London

The Nutcracker (as *Casse-noisette*; after Ivanov; mus. Tchaikovsky), Vic-Wells Ballet, London

Swan Lake (as *Lac des cygnes*; after Petipa, Ivanov), Vic-Wells Ballet, London

"Bacchanal" from *Tannhäuser* (opera; mus. Wagner), Sergeyev's Russian Ballet, British tour

Swan Lake, Act II (after Ivanov; mus. Tchaikovsky), Sergeyev's Russian Ballet, British tour

The Rajah's Dream (after "The Kingdom of the Shades" from *La Bayadère* by Petipa; mus. Minkus), Sergeyev's Russian Ballet, British tour

Polovtsian Dances from Prince Igor (after Ivanov; mus. Borodin), Sergeyev's Russian Ballet, British tour

Les Rendezvous (divertissement; mus. Drigo, Polcinelli), Sergeyev's Russian Ballet, British tour

1935 *Giselle* (after Petipa, Coralli, Perrot; mus. Adam), Markova–Dolin Ballet, England

Swan Lake (two-act version; after Petipa, Ivanov; mus. Tchaikovsky), Markova–Dolin Ballet, England

Extracts from The Sleeping Beauty (after Petipa; mus. Tchaikovsky), Markova–Dolin Ballet, England

1938 *Coppélia* (after Saint-Léon, Petipa, Cecchetti; mus. Delibes), (Blum's) Ballet Russe de Monte Carlo, London

1939 *The Sleeping Princess* (after *The Sleeping Beauty* by Petipa; mus. Tchaikovsky), Vic-Wells Ballet, London

1941 *Swan Lake* (as *Le Lac des cygnes*), "Act I" [sic] (Lakeside act, after Ivanov; mus. Tchaikovsky), International Ballet

Polovtsian Dances from Prince Igor (after Ivanov; mus. Borodin), International Ballet

Aurora's Wedding (after *The Sleeping Beauty* by Petipa; mus. Tchaikovsky), International Ballet

1942 *Giselle* (after Petipa, Coralli, Perrot; mus. Adam), International Ballet

1944 *Coppélia* (after Saint-Léon, Petipa, Cecchetti; mus. Delibes), International Ballet

1947 *Swan Lake* (after Petipa, Ivanov; mus. Tchaikovsky), International Ballet

1948 *The Sleeping Beauty* (after Petipa; mus. Tchaikovsky), International Ballet

PUBLICATIONS

Raffé, Walter George, "Nicolai Sergueff", *Dance Magazine* (New York), July 1950

Beaumont, Cyril, "Nicholas Grigorievich Sergeyev", *Ballet Annual* (London), vol. 6, 1952

Davidson, Gladys, *Ballet Biographies*, revised edition, London, 1954

de Valois, Ninette, *Come Dance With Me*, London, 1957

Wiley, Roland John, "Dances from Russia: An Introduction to the Sergeyev Collection", *Harvard Library Bulletin* (Cambridge, Massachusetts), January 1976

Pritchard, Jane, "Bits of *Bayadère* in Britain", *Dancing Times* (London), September 1989

Telyakovsky, V.A., "Memoirs", translated by Nina Dmitrievitch, *Dance Research* (London), Spring 1991

*   *   *

Nicholas Sergeyev is sometimes regarded as the first professional dance notator of the twentieth century. He worked with Stepanov notation, and is remembered for the re-staging of ballets from their scores rather than for actually recording them; and as a matter of fact, some of the 22 notated scores he brought out of Russia were actually recorded by his assistants, Aleksandr Chekrygin and Victor Rakhmanov. The accuracy of his stagings, together with his real ability to read a notated score, has sometimes been called into question, but it must be remembered that he was reproducing works originally created for the Imperial Russian theatres and he generally had to adapt them for much smaller companies with more limited resources. Exiled Russians, including Serge Diaghilev and Anna Pavlova who remembered Marius Petipa's original productions, invited Sergeyev to mount *The Sleeping Princess* and part of *La Bayadère* for their respective companies. Diaghilev however (and later Ninette de Valois) realized that Sergeyev lacked the necessary sense of theatre, and once he had set the steps, they successfully remedied any shortcomings. Pavlova, without a producer of vision in her company, dropped the production of "The Kingdom of the Shades" before its premiere because it appeared so old-fashioned.

It is difficult to get a clear picture of Sergeyev, as his career was split into two equal halves, before and after the October Revolution. For the first part he was in Russia, where in some quarters he gained a reputation as an authoritarian villain; and as a result of his behaviour during the dancers' unsuccessful strike of 1905, he became known as "the Directorate's spy". For the second part of his career when he was in the West, most notably in France and England, he was regarded as the hero who enabled performances of the classics in complete form to take place, introducing and preserving a vitally important dance heritage. Analysis of Sergeyev's career is hampered further because, although he travelled widely in South America as well as in Europe, he was never a media figure who attracted attention in his own right. After he left St. Petersburg he was not employed with any one company for any length of time until, in 1941, he became Ballet Master for Mona Inglesby's International Ballet.

Sergeyev had begun his career as a performer with the Maryinsky Theatre. Although he reached the rank of soloist, there appears to be no evidence that he was a particularly good dancer. Nevertheless, his repertory did include the notoriously difficult Jester's dance in *Mlada*. More significantly for his subsequent career, he danced in the Waltz of the Flowers (the "Valse des fleurs", or Garland dance) at the premiere of *The Sleeping Beauty*, a ballet he subsequently staged several times. This particular dance in Act I he reproduced most memorably,

and probably most accurately, for International Ballet in 1948 when he had a full cast of 48 (16 men, 16 women and 16 children).

Sergeyev's interest in notation seems to have developed in about 1897, five years after Vladimir Ivanovich Stepanov's *L'Alphabet des mouvements du corps humaine* (1892) had been published in Paris, and a year after Stepanov (1866–96) had died. The notation system had been adopted for trial at the Imperial School in 1893 and the choreographer Aleksandr Gorsky took particular interest in it. Sergeyev began notation as Gorsky's assistant at the Maryinsky Theatre. When Gorsky returned to Moscow in 1900, Sergeyev took over his class in dance theory and notation. This led to his appointment as Régisseur in charge of notation from the 1903–04 season; he was promoted to Régisseur General a decade later.

At the Imperial Theatre, as later in his career, he was concerned only with the promotion of real talent and was not open to advancement through bribes. Notably he recognized talent in the young Olga Spessivtseva, to whom he gave principal roles early in her career, and he later worked with her on *The Sleeping Princess*, *Giselle*, and *Swan Lake* Act II in the West.

It has frequently been observed that Sergeyev was unmusical, and that when he mounted ballets he cut bars at random if the steps did not immediately fit. He became obsessed with traditional stage effects when more modern methods could have been used to achieve similar ends, and he craved the resources of a Maryinsky on which to stage the ballets he loved. He was generally out of sympathy with most twentieth-century developments in dance. Nevertheless, he gained pleasure working patiently with artists he admired, among them Spessivtseva, Lydia Lopokova, Alicia Markova, Mona Inglesby, and his wife Evgenia Poplavska. Poplavska, having been in the corps de ballet for *The Sleeping Princess*, danced soloist roles in Riga; and as a ballerina, partnered by Tanéeff, she performed for the Opéra Privé Russe de Paris in 1929 and for Sergeyev's Ballets Russes in 1934.

It was for the Opéra Privée and his own company that Sergeyev's productions were designed by Constantin Korovin. Some of these designs, for example those for the Polovtsian Dances from *Prince Igor* (with Ivanov's choreography), were re-used when the dances were mounted for International Ballet; they are lodged with the Sergeyev Papers now at Harvard University.

At the time of his death it was suggested that Sergeyev's notation would become useless, as he had not trained any successor. They have, however, provided material for recent productions, including Natalia Makarova's *La Bayadère* (1980) and Peter Wright's *The Nutcracker* (1984). The completeness of the records varies from one work to another, some limited simply to floor plans with noughts (O) and crosses (X) to represent women and men respectively with directional arrows to indicate the flow of movement. Nevertheless, the influence of Sergeyev's productions and records are likely to continue as the works of Ivanov and Petipa, and ballets such as *Giselle* and *Coppélia* which have passed down to us through Russian channels, maintain their position at the very heart of classical ballet.

—Jane Pritchard

SEYMOUR, Lynn

Canadian dancer, choreographer, and ballet director.   Born

Lynn Seymour as The Girl in *The Invitation*

Berta Lynn Springbett in Wainwright, Alberta, Canada, 8 March 1939. Married (1) Colin Jones, 1963 (div.); (2) Philip Pace, 1979 (div.); (3) Vanya Hackel, 1983 (div.). Studied with Jean Jepson and Nicholas Svetlanoff, Vancouver, and at Sadler's Wells Ballet School, pupil of Winifred Edwards, Pamela May, and Peggy van Praagh, London, from 1954. Dancer, Covent Garden Opera Ballet, 1956, and Royal Ballet Touring Company, 1957; soloist, Royal Ballet Touring Company, and Royal Ballet (at Covent Garden), from 1958, becoming principal dancer, Royal Ballet, 1959–66; prima ballerina, German Opera Ballet, Berlin, 1966–69; freelance artist, 1969–70, performing with National Ballet of Canada, London Festival Ballet, Les Ballets de Félix Blaska, and German Opera Ballet, Berlin; principal guest ballerina, Royal Ballet, 1971–78, also appearing with Alvin Ailey American Dance Theater, 1971, American Ballet Theatre, 1976, Chicago Ballet, London Contemporary Dance Theatre, and "Nureyev and Friends" season at the Coliseum, London; principal dancer and ballet director, Bavarian State Opera Ballet, Munich, 1978–80; retired from stage, returning as guest ballerina, London Festival Ballet (English National Ballet), 1988, 1989, and German Opera Ballet, Berlin, from 1990; other guest appearances include with the National Ballet of Canada, Stuttgart Ballet, Vienna State Opera Ballet, Hamburg Ballet, Western Theatre Ballet, and Ballet de Marseille; also choreographer, staging works for London Contemporary Dance Theatre, Sadler's Wells Royal Ballet, and Ballet Rambert. Recipient: *Evening Standard* Award, 1976; title of Commander of the Order of the British Empire, 1976.

ROLES

1958   Adolescent (cr) in *The Burrow* (MacMillan), Royal Ballet Touring Company, London

        Pas de deux (cr) in *First Impressions* (Beale), Sunday Ballet Club, London

        Dawn in *Coppélia* (Sergeyev after Petipa, Cecchetti; staged de Valois), Royal Ballet Touring Company

        Pas de trois in *Swan Lake* (Petipa, Ivanov; staged

Sergeyev, de Valois), Royal Ballet Touring Company

Waltz in *A Blue Rose* (Wright), Royal Ballet Touring Company

Odette/Odile in *Swan Lake* (Petipa, Ivanov; staged Sergeyev, de Valois, Ashton), Royal Ballet Touring Company, Australia/New Zealand tour

1958/ 59 Polka in *Façade* (Ashton), Royal Ballet Touring Company

Principal dancer in *Don Quixote* Pas de deux (after Petipa), Royal Ballet Touring Company

1959 Pas de deux in *Les Patineurs* (Ashton), Royal Ballet Touring Company

La Favorita in *Veneziana* (Howard), Royal Ballet Touring Company

1960 Fiancée (cr) in *Le Baiser de la fée* (MacMillan), Royal Ballet, London

Sixth variation in *A Birthday Offering* (Ashton), Royal Ballet, London

Title role in *Giselle* (Petipa after Coralli, Perrot; staged Sergeyev), Royal Ballet, London

The Girl in *Solitaire* (MacMillan), Royal Ballet Touring Company

The Girl (cr) in *The Invitation* (MacMillan), Royal Ballet Touring Company, Oxford

Title role in *Cinderella* (Ashton), Royal Ballet, London

Princess Aurora in *The Sleeping Beauty* (Petipa; staged Sergeyev, de Valois, Ashton), Royal Ballet Touring Company

1961 Pas de deux in *Danses concertantes* (MacMillan), Royal Ballet Touring Company

The Young Girl (cr) in *The Two Pigeons* (Ashton), Royal Ballet Touring Company, London

1962 Mariuccia in *The Good-Humoured Ladies* (Massine), Royal Ballet, London

Principal dancer in *Napoli Divertissement* (Bournonville), Royal Ballet, London

1963 The Bride in *La Fête étrange* (Howard), Royal Ballet, London

Principal dancer in *Symphony* (MacMillan), Royal Ballet, London

Tango in *Façade* (Ashton), Royal Ballet, London

1964 "Two Loves I Have" (cr) in *Images of Love* (MacMillan), Royal Ballet, London

Juliet in *Romeo and Juliet* (Cranko), Stuttgart Ballet, Stuttgart

Ophelia in *Hamlet* (Helpmann), Royal Ballet, London

Lilac Fairy in *The Sleeping Beauty* (Petipa; staged Sergeyev, de Valois, Ashton), Royal Ballet, London

1965 Juliet (cr; danced at premiere by Fonteyn) in *Romeo and Juliet* (MacMillan), Royal Ballet, London

The Sylph in *La Sylphide* (Bruhn after Bournonville), National Ballet of Canada, Toronto

1966 Two of Diamonds in *Card Game* (*Jeu de cartes*; Cranko), Royal Ballet, London

Second Song in *Song of the Earth* (MacMillan), Royal Ballet, London

Second Movement (cr) in *Concerto* (MacMillan), German Opera Ballet, Berlin

1966/ 67 La Reine de la danse from Moscow in *Gala Performance* (Tudor), German Opera Ballet, Berlin

1967 Anna Anderson (cr) in *Anastasia* (one-act version; MacMillan), German Opera Ballet, Berlin

Princess Aurora in *The Sleeping Beauty* (new production; MacMillan after Petipa), German Opera Ballet, Berlin

Eldest Sister in *Las Hermanas* (MacMillan), German Opera Ballet, Berlin

1968 Principal dancer (cr) in *Olympiad* (MacMillan), German Opera Ballet, Berlin

1969 Principal dancer (cr) in *Kraanerg* (Petit), National Ballet of Canada, Ottawa

Terpsichore in *Apollo* (Balanchine), German Opera Ballet, Berlin

Second Movement in *Symphony in C* (Balanchine), German Opera Ballet, Berlin

1970 Principal dancer (cr) in *Ballet pour tam-tam et percussion* (Blaska), Les Ballets de Félix Blaska

Principal dancer (cr) in *Pas d'action* (Blaska), Les Ballets de Félix Blaska

Pas de deux from *Walpurgisnacht* (after Sergeyev), London Festival Ballet

Principal dancer in *Dances at a Gathering* (Robbins), Royal Ballet, London

1971 The Artist (cr) in *Flowers* (Ailey), Alvin Ailey American Dance Theater

Grand Duchess Anastasia/Anna Anderson (cr) in *Anastasia* (three-act version; MacMillan), Royal Ballet, London

Title role in *Raymonda*, Act III (Nureyev after Petipa), Royal Ballet Touring Company

1972 Principal dancer in *Serenade* (Balanchine), Royal Ballet, London

Principal dancer (cr) in *Side Show* (MacMillan), Royal Ballet, Liverpool

Principal dancer (cr) in *Laborintus* (Tetley), Royal Ballet, London

1973 The Queen of the Cabaret (cr) in *The Seven Deadly Sins* (MacMillan), Royal Ballet, London

The Siren in *The Prodigal Son* (Balanchine), Royal Ballet Touring Company, Tel Aviv

1975 Principal dancer in *The Concert* (Robbins), Royal Ballet, London

Principal dancer in *Le Corsaire* Pas de trois (Nureyev after Petipa), Royal Ballet, London

Summer in *The Four Seasons* (MacMillan), Royal Ballet, London

Principal dancer in *Brahms-Waltz* (solo; chor. Ashton after Isadora Duncan), Nijinsky Gala, Hamburg Ballet, Hamburg

Principal dancer (cr) in *Gladly, Sadly, Badly, Madly* (also chor., with Robert North), London Contemporary Dance Theatre, London

The Mother (cr) in *Rituals* (MacMillan), Royal Ballet, London

1976 The Wife in *The Invitation* (MacMillan), Royal Ballet, London

Title role in *Manon* (MacMillan), Royal Ballet, London

Natalia Petrovna (cr) in *A Month in the Country* (Ashton), Royal Ballet, London

Principal dancer in *Twilight* (van Manen), Royal Ballet, London

Principal dancer in *Voluntaries* (Tetley), Royal Ballet, London

Solo (cr) in *Four Brahms Waltzes in the Manner of Isadora Duncan* (expanded version; Ashton), Royal Ballet, London

Hagar in *Pillar of Fire* (Tudor), American Ballet Theatre, New York

Juliet in *Romeo and Juliet* (Tudor), American Ballet Theatre, New York

1977 Principal dancer (cr) in *Fourth Symphony* (Neumeier), Royal Ballet, London

Katherina in *The Taming of the Shrew* (Cranko), Royal Ballet, London

Carabosse in *The Sleeping Beauty* (Petipa, Ashton; staged de Valois), Royal Ballet, London

1978   Baroness Mary Vetsera (cr) in *Mayerling* (MacMillan), Royal Ballet, London

Principal dancer (cr) in *Take Five* (Bintley), Sadler's Wells Royal Ballet, London

Principal dancer (cr) in *Mac and Polly* (also chor.), Commonwealth Dance Gala

1979   Principal dancer (cr) in *Tattoo* (also chor.), Bavarian State Opera Ballet, Munich

1980   The Dancer (cr) in *Famous Mothers Club* (solo; Forsythe), London

1987   Lowry's Mother (cr) in *A Simple Man* (Lynne), Northern Ballet Theatre

1988   Tatiana in *Onegin* (Cranko), London Festival Ballet, London

1989   Lady Capulet in *Romeo and Juliet* (Ashton), English National Ballet, Bradford

Veronica in *Napoli* (Schaufuss after Bournonville), English National Ballet (formerly London Festival Ballet), London

The Friend's Wife (Emilia) in *The Moor's Pavane* (Limón), English National Ballet, Athens

Sugar Plum Fairy in *The Nutcracker* (Schaufuss), English National Ballet, Manchester

Other roles include: Mazurka and pas de deux in *Les Sylphides* (Fokine), pas de deux from *Flower Festival at Genzano* (Bournonville), Can-Can dancer in *La Boutique fantasque* (Massine), the Girl in *Le Spectre de la rose* (Fokine); also for Nureyev and Friends—Pas de deux from *Le Corsaire* (Nureyev after Petipa), pas de deux in *Aureole* (Taylor), the Wife in *The Moor's Pavane* (Limón).

WORKS

1973   *Night Ride* (mus. Finnissy), Royal Ballet Choreographic Group, London

1974   *Breakthrough* (mus. Finissy), Royal Ballet Choreographic Group, London

1975   *Gladly, Sadly, Badly, Madly* (with Robert North; mus. Davis), London Contemporary Dance Theatre, London

1976   *Rashomon* (mus. Downes), Royal Ballet Touring Company, London (restaged Munich, 1979)

1977   *The Court of Love* (mus. Blake) Sadler's Wells Royal Ballet (previously Royal Ballet Touring Company), Bournemouth

1978   *Mac and Polly* (mus. Weill), Commonwealth Dance Gala

Leda and the Swan (text by W.B. Yeats; mus. Blake), British Broadcasting Corporation (BBC) Television

Intimate Letters (mus. Janáček, Downes), Sadler's Wells Royal Ballet, London (restaged Munich, 1978)

1979   *Tattoo* (mus. Weill), Bavarian State Opera Ballet, Munich

Tattooed Lady (new version of *Tattoo*; mus. Weill), Royal Festival Hall Gala, London

Boreas (mus. Blendinger), Bavarian State Opera Ballet, Munich

1980   *Love of Life* (mus. Goodings, Irwin), Royal Ballet Choreographic Group, London

1986   *Love is in the Air*, Choo San Gooh Company, Vancouver

1987   *Wolfie* (mus. Mozart), Ballet Rambert, London

Bastet (mus. Berkeley), Sadler's Wells Royal Ballet, Birmingham

Staged:

1991   *Five Brahms Waltzes* (in the manner of Isadora Duncan; after Ashton; mus. Brahms), Scottish Ballet, Forfar, Scotland

PUBLICATIONS

By Seymour:

Interview in Gruen, John, *The Private World of Ballet*, New York, 1975

Interview in Newman, Barbara, *Striking a Balance: Dancers Talk about Dancing*, Boston, 1982

Lynn (autobiography, in collaboration with Paul Gardner), London, 1984

Interview in Newman, Barbara, "Speaking of Dance: Lynn Seymour", *Dancing Times* (London), September 1987

About Seymour:

Clarke, Mary, "Lynn Seymour", *Dancing Times* (London), June 1959

Goodman, Saul, "Lynn Seymour", *Dance Magazine* (New York), June 1963

Gow, Gordon, "Lynn Seymour—Body and Mind", *The Dancing Times* (London), October 1975

Crisp, Clement, "Lynn Seymour", *Les Saisons de la danse* (Paris), May 1976

Crickmay, Anthony (photographer), *Lynn Seymour*, New York, 1976

Austin, Richard, *Lynn Seymour: An Authorised Biography*, London, 1980

Bland, Alexander, *The Royal Ballet: The First Fifty Years*, London, 1981

Thorpe, Edward, *Kenneth MacMillan: The Man and the Ballets*, London, 1985

* * *

Lynn Seymour is one of the greatest dramatic ballerinas of this century, combining an exquisite, deliquescent technique with a histrionic ability of unrivalled range and power. Much of her career was directly linked with that of Kenneth MacMillan, who created for her a whole gallery of important roles in which her interpretations remain the yardstick by which other dancers' performances are measured. Seymour's private life has often been as turbulent as some of the heroines she has portrayed on stage—and this is a factor which, with equal frequency, has affected the direction of her career.

She was born and brought up in Canada, where she first began studying ballet. It was one of her teachers there, Nicholas Svetlanoff, who first made Seymour aware that ballet was a dramatically expressive art, and this awareness was compounded by seeing a performance of *Coppélia* by the Ballet Russe de Monte Carlo, as well as the film *The Red Shoes*.

In 1953 the Sadler's Wells Ballet (now the Royal Ballet) visited Vancouver and held auditions. Seymour attended, watched by Frederick Ashton, and was accepted as a scholarship student to the Sadler's Wells Ballet School (later the Royal Ballet School) in the autumn of the following year. Leaving her family to live in cold, bleak digs in London, Seymour felt very homesick and alone, something of an outsider—and this was a feeling that never left her throughout her years as a student and, even later, as a principal dancer with the company.

At the end of her training Seymour joined the Covent Garden Opera Ballet and later joined the Royal Ballet Touring Company (now the Birmingham Royal Ballet). After several weeks in the corps de ballet Seymour was chosen by MacMillan as one of the young lovers in his new work, *The Burrow*, which depicted a group of characters hiding from the secret police of a repressive regime. Her performance in the harrowing work brought glowing notices from the critics, as did her interpretation of the Fiancée in a completely different MacMillan work, *Le Baiser de la fée*, to the music of Stravinsky. But the ballet which finally established her as a young dancer of unrivalled dramatic talent was *The Invitation*. MacMillan's sensational and disturbing work, in which two young cousins are emotionally involved with an older, embittered married couple, depicts two extraordinary events for the ballet stage: the seduction of the young man by the older woman, and the rape of the girl by the older man. Because of its subject matter the ballet achieved quite a bit of notoriety, but beyond this it also confirmed MacMillan as the most interesting and innovative of the new generation of choreographers—and Seymour's performance as the innocent girl traumatized, and left facing a frigid spinsterhood, was astounding. The ballet also initiated a brief but brilliant partnership between Seymour and Christopher Gable.

Throughout the next three years Seymour danced with both Royal Ballet companies, performing a wide range of roles both in the classics and in modern works, adding to her reputation as an artist of great dramatic sensibility. Then, when MacMillan created his first full-length ballet, *Romeo and Juliet*, it was natural that he would choose to build the roles of the leading characters upon Seymour and Gable, two dancers who not only worked well together but showed an instinctive understanding of MacMillan's style. Yet to Seymour's chagrin and undying bitterness, she found that the impresario Sol Hurok, who would be presenting the company on a forthcoming tour of the United States, insisted that the first-night cast should be Fonteyn and Nureyev. The decision reinforced her feeling of being an outsider with the company, a feeling which never left her, even during her greatest successes with the Royal Ballet.

When MacMillan was appointed director of the German Opera Ballet in Berlin, he took Seymour with him as his prima ballerina. The move resulted in more splendid roles built around her talents, particularly in the expressionistic one-act version of *Anastasia*. MacMillan's contract in Berlin expired in 1969, when he took up his appointment as director of the Royal Ballet. For the next eighteen months Seymour's career was in artistic limbo; she was a dancer without a company until, once more, she joined MacMillan in London. The next three years were golden years for Seymour, then at the height of her powers and receiving rapturous acclaim (although the actual number of appearances were relatively few, owing to the fact that the company had to accommodate no fewer than eleven ballerinas, plus Fonteyn as a frequent guest artist). Seymour could be prone to fits of depression; she put on weight which led to cancelled appearances, and this often led to more depression. But the following years were a kind of apotheosis of Seymour's career as a dancer: brilliant in the classics, equally strong in ballets by Ashton, MacMillan, or Tudor, she was beloved by audiences and critics.

In 1977 MacMillan decided to resign as director of the Royal Ballet in order to concentrate on choreography. He was replaced by Norman Morrice, who failed to respond to Seymour's plea to be used as much as possible during her last years as a ballerina, and her appearances with the company were rare. Her last great triumph was as Mary Vetsera in MacMillan's fourth great full-length work, *Mayerling*. A few seasons previously Seymour had choreographed her first work, *Rashomon*, for Sadler's Wells Royal Ballet, which was well received. A second work, *Intimate Letters*, was not so successful.

At this time Seymour was invited to become director of the Bavarian State Ballet in Munich, an invitation she saw as an interesting challenge, despite warnings that the company was riddled with factions, jealousies, intrigues, and restrictive policies. These reports of treachery and intrigue proved all too true, and Seymour's two years there proved a wretched experience. Her time in Munich coincided with MacMillan's creation of another innovative full-length work, *Isadora*, based on the dramatic career of the famous American dancer Isadora Duncan. MacMillan had intended to create the role around Seymour's talents, but her departure to Munich made this impossible.

Seymour's contract with Munich was terminated in 1980 and she returned, briefly, to the Royal Ballet. Despite being scheduled to dance in a number of roles ideally suited to her, she made the sudden decision to retire from her dancing career. For the next year or two she drifted happily, taking up various projects, some of which came to fruition, some not.

In 1987 Seymour appeared on stage again in Gillian Lynn's ballet *A Simple Man*, produced for Northern Ballet Theatre, directed by her old partner Christopher Gable. Soon afterwards she made a sensational return in a major role, that of Tatiana in Cranko's *Onegin*, produced for the London Festival Ballet (now the English National Ballet) which was directed at that time by Peter Schaufuss. When Schaufuss was peremptorily dismissed from the company in 1990, he immediately took up an appointment as director of the Opera Ballet in Berlin, taking Seymour with him. Included in the repertoire is MacMillan's one-act version of *Anastasia*, which Seymour first danced in Berlin in 1967—thus completing for Seymour one of the many interacting circles that have made up a distinguished and fascinating career.

—Edward Thorpe

SHABELEVSKY, Yurek

Polish/American dancer and ballet director. Born Jerzy Szabelevski (Shabelevsky) in Warsaw, 1911. Studied at the Warsaw Opera Ballet School, and with Bronislava Nijinska. Début, age nine, Teatr Wielki, Warsaw; dancer, Ida Rubinstein's company, Paris, 1928, also appearing with Olga Spessivtseva, London Coliseum, 1930, and with Ballets Russes de Boris Kniaseff, 1931; dancer, excelling in character roles, (de Basil's) Ballets Russes de Monte Carlo, 1932–38, becoming principal dancer from 1936, and touring Australia (with company performing as Covent Garden Russian Ballet), 1938; guest artist, Original Ballet Russe, 1941, 1943; guest artist, Ballet Theatre, New York, 1940; guest principal dancer, Teatro Colón, Buenos Aires, 1937, 1940, and various seasons 1942–47; guest artist and choreographer, La Scala Ballet, Milan, 1949–50; also founder and director of own touring groups, first in the U.S. and then South America, from the 1940s; ballet master, New Zealand, from 1967.

ROLES

1930   Principal dancer (cr; partnering Spessivtseva) in *Paysage enfantin* (Nijinska), Olga Spessivtseva's Company, Coliseum, London

1932   Second Tailor (cr) in *La Concurrence* (Balanchine), Ballets Russes de Monte Carlo, Monte Carlo

       Pas de trois, Turkish Divertissement (cr) in *Le Bourgeois*

Gentilhomme (Balanchine), Ballets Russes de Monte Carlo, Monte Carlo

Tarantella (cr) in *Suites de danse* (Balanchine), Ballets Russes de Monte Carlo, Monte Carlo

1933 Oarsman, "Airs from the Casino" (cr) in *Beach* (Massine), Ballets Russes de Monte Carlo, Monte Carlo

Philipino (cr) in *Scuola di Ballo* (Massine), Ballets Russes de Monte Carlo, Monte Carlo

The Second Betrothed Pair (cr; with Riabouchinska) in *Nocturne* (Lichine), Ballets Russes de Monte Carlo, Paris

Principal dancer, Third and Fourth Movements (cr) in *Choreartium* (Massine), Ballets Russes de Monte Carlo, London

1934 The Snob in *La Boutique fantasque* (revival; Massine), de Basil's Ballets Russes, London

Peasant dance in *Les Contes russes* (revival; Massine), de Basil's Ballets Russes, London

1935 The Poet (cr) in *Jardin public* (Massine), Monte Carlo Ballet Russe (de Basil's Ballets Russes), Chicago

The Bird Catcher (cr) in *Les Cent Baisers* (Nijinska), de Basil's Ballets Russes, London

Principal dancer (cr) in *Lezginka* (Nijinska), de Basil's Ballets Russes, London

Danse Tzigane in *Danses Slaves et Tziganes* (Nijinska), de Basil's Ballets Russes, London

1936 Leading male guest in *Les Noces* (Nijinska), de Basil's Ballets Russes, New York

The Jailer (cr) in *Symphonie fantastique* (Massine), de Basil's Ballets Russes, London

1937 The Shepherd (cr) in *Les Dieux mendiants* (Lichine), de Basil's Ballets Russes, London

Title role in *Petrushka* (Fokine), de Basil's Ballets Russes

1940 Colin (cr) in *La Fille mal gardée* (new production; chor. Nijinska), Ballet Theatre, New York

Eusebius in *Carnaval* (Fokine), Ballet Theatre, New York

Principal dancer (cr) in *Ode to Glory* (pas de deux; also chor.), Ballet Theatre, New York (first version staged Hartford, 1939)

"His Excellency the Incognito Prince" (cr) in *Offenbachiana* (Wallman), Teatro Colón, Buenos Aires

Guirhaú, the Warrior (cr) in *Panambi* (Wallman), Teatro Colón, Buenos Aires

The Faun in *L'Après-midi d'un faune* (after Nijinsky), Teatro Colón, Buenos Aires

1942 Adagio, Menueto (cr) in *Concierto de Mozart* (Balanchine), Teatro Colón, Buenos Aires

Apollo in *Apollon musagète* (Balanchine), Teatro Colón, Buenos Aires

Principal dancer (cr) in *Maruf* (*Mârouf*; opera by Rabaud; chor. Balanchine), Teatro Colón, Buenos Aires

1944 Apurimac Warrior (cr) in *Apurimac* (Wallman), Teatro Colón, Buenos Aires

Principal dancer (cr) in *La Ciudad de las puertas de oro* (Wallman), Teatro Colón, Buenos Aires

Other roles include: Favourite Slave in *Schéhérazade* (Fokine), Warrior Chief in *Polovtsian Dances from Prince Igor* (Fokine), King of the Dandies in *Le Beau Danube* (Massine), Young Musician in *Symphonie fantastique* (Massine), Gaoler in *Symphonie fantastique* (Massine), Vagabond in *La Concurrence* (Balanchine), the Traveller in *Jeux d'enfants* (Massine), Spanish Entrée in *Le Bal* (Massine), Hussar in *Le Beau Danube*

(Massine), Harlequin and Florestan in *Carnaval* (Fokine), Amoun in *Cléopâtre* (Fokine), Battista in *The Good-Humoured Ladies* (Massine), Midnight Sun in *Le Soleil de nuit* (Massine), Dandy in *Le Tricorne* (Massine), Chief Guest and Jailor in *Symphonie fantastique* (Massine).

WORKS

1940 *Ode to Glory* (pas de deux; mus. Chopin), Ballet Theatre, New York (originally staged Hartford, Connecticut, 1939)

Staged:
1949/ *The Firebird* (after Fokine; mus. Stravinsky), La Scala
50   Ballet, Milan

The Sleeping Beauty (after Petipa; mus. Tchaikovsky), La Scala Ballet, Milan

PUBLICATIONS

Hall, Fernau, "Men in Ballet: Yurek Shabelevsky", *Ballet Today* (London), October 1958

Anthony, Gordon, "Yurek Shabelevsky", *Dancing Times* (London), April 1976

Walker, Kathrine Sorley, *De Basil's Ballets Russes*, London, 1982

García-Márquez, Vicente, *Les Ballets Russes*, New York, 1990

*   *   *

Of all the great character dancers of the 1930s, none exuded more glamour than the Polish-born Yurek Shabelevsky. His natural assets of a handsome face and compact body were allied with an immaculate technique, set off by a prodigious jump, astonishing athleticism, and bounding vitality. It was a technique of great precision and clarity in which nothing was blurred or fudged. But he was no mere technician, and brought intelligence and artistry to a wide range of roles. During his great years with the de Basil company, he was one of the most popular dancers of his day.

He had a total understanding of the style of a work, from the "eccentric" rococo Massine style, through the neo-classicism of Nijinska and the classicism of Fokine. His astonishing vigour was best seen in the role of the Warrior in *Polovtsian Dances*, a performance in the great tradition of Bolm and Woizikowsky, in which he created an impression of unbridled savagery. In *Schéhérazade* he was electrifying—half-man, half-animal, calculating every move, like some wild creature stalking his prey. For a time he also executed the extraordinary head spin in the death scene, one of Nijinsky's very few successors to attempt this dangerous feat.

As the King of the Dandies in *Le Beau Danube* Shabelevsky also exuded charm and a stunning sense of style. Style, too, was predominant in *The Good-Humoured Ladies*, and he was unmatched as the Snob in *La Boutique fantasque* with its dandified, puppet-like precision, in which he was at once mechanical yet human. These urbane characterizations were contrasted with his wonderfully humorous Vagabond in *La Concurrence*, with its almost double-jointed contortions, or his naively boisterous Ivan in *Aurora's Wedding*. As *Petrushka* he confounded those who thought his talents were limited to vigorous technical display; his subtle artistry was revealed in countless small touches, which built a fine balance between the puppet and the aspiring human being with a soul.

His star in Europe shone briefly and brightly. For the rest of Shabelevsky's career, his gifts were at the service of a number of companies in America, South America, and Italy. Later, he was to work as ballet master and producer in New Zealand.

—Sarah C. Woodcock

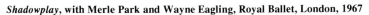

SHADOWPLAY

Choreography: Antony Tudor
Music: Charles Koechlin
Design: Michael Annals (scenery and costumes)
Libretto: Antony Tudor (after Koechlin's *Les Bandar-Log*, as inspired by Rudyard Kipling's *The Jungle Book*)
First Production: Royal Ballet, Royal Opera House, London, 25 January 1967
Principal Dancers: Anthony Dowell (The Boy with Matted Hair), Merle Park (Celestial), Derek Rencher (Terrestrial)

Other productions include: American Ballet Theatre, with Mikhail Baryshnikov (The Boy with Matted Hair), Gelsey Kirkland (Celestial), Jonas Kåge (Terrestrial); New York, 23 July 1975.

PUBLICATIONS

Cohen, Selma Jeanne, "Tudor and the Royal Ballet", *Saturday Review* (New York), 13 May 1967

Horsbrugh, Ian, "The Composer of *Shadowplay*: Charles Koechlin", *Dancing Times* (London), February 1967

Williams, Peter, Percival, John, and Goodwin, Noël, "*Shadowplay*: Mind Over Matter", *Dance and Dancers* (London), March 1967

Monahan, James, "*Shadowplay*", *Dancing Times* (London), May 1974

Balanchine, George, with Mason, Francis, *Balanchine's Complete Stories of the Great Ballets*, Garden City, N.Y., 1977

Brinson, Peter, and Crisp, Clement, *Ballet and Dance: A Guide to the Repertory*, London, 1980

Anderson, Jack, "The View from the House Opposite", *Choreography Observed*, Iowa City, 1987

Perlmutter, Donna, *Shadowplay: The Life of Antony Tudor*, London, 1991

*   *   *

Shadowplay, created for the Royal Ballet in London, does not resemble any of Tudor's other ballets and reinforces his own claim that he never liked to repeat himself. In it, he experimented with a movement vocabulary that seemed inimical to the cool, carefully positioned and fluid English style, thus testing his countrymen with a challenging scenario and a difficult technique.

Tudor told Selma Jeanne Cohen, "The ballet tells the story of

Shadowplay, with Merle Park and Wayne Eagling, Royal Ballet, London, 1967

a young boy's progression to a state of Nirvana beyond the distractions and irritations of the world. The young boy is beset by the menaces of the jungle (the world) and its creatures of the trees and of the air. His is confronted by a male figure (The Lord of the Jungle). He is successively charmed and threatened by the Celestial (a chaste goddess or a seductress). In the end he achieves peace (manhood) through an act of will (or the sexual act). Tudor agrees with any of the alternatives."

Tudor chose the main structure of his ballet from Koechlin's *Les Bandar-Log*. All of the original score is used, plus two interpolations derived from a much larger symphonic poem, *La Course du printemps*. Both compositions belong to Koechlin's vast fresco, *Le Livre de la jungle*, based upon Rudyard Kipling's *The Jungle Book*.

The ballet's major figure, the Boy with Matted Hair, has his origins in *The Jungle Book*'s Mowgli. But Tudor stretched this paradigm to be, as Mary Clarke wrote at the time, the "embodiment of all young manhood about to take his first steps". The Penumbra, the space of partial illuminations between the perfect shadow and the full light, is divided among the Arboreals, the Aerials, the Terrestrial, and the Celestials, "distractions that impede our deeper contemplation about life" (Peter Williams). The ballet begins with the Boy alone in the jungle. Contemplative balances and slow turns characterize this meditation. Suddenly tranquillity is interrupted as the Arboreals cavort, cajoling him. Bird-like Aerials with exotic plumage fly in dressed as Cambodian dancers and the imposing Terrestrial, a powerful man suggesting a Hindu deity, begins to joust with the Boy. The Arboreals return, menacing him until he hides in the trees. There a more terrifying threat descends. Celestial swoops over him in a passage that is full of sexual undertones, an elaborate adagio in which she inflames him by crouching on his back, then is supported in slow pirouettes, but three times is lifted away from him, only to return for more.

The major moment of the ballet occurs when all the creatures of the jungle unite to form a huge, snake-like structure. The Celestial Being as Peter Williams described it, ". . . is carried, her parted legs supported by two lines of Arboreals. The scorpion-like phalanx, with the Terrestrial as tail, approaches the Boy who dives into the tunnel they form." The Boy has achieved knowledge, be it sexual, or spiritual. Revitalized and re-empowered, the Boy then succeeds in forcing the others to leave the jungle, his place of conquest. Eventually the monkeys scramble back and the ballet ends with their acceptance of his quiet mastery.

Tudor's movement vocabulary in *Shadowplay* is subtle and suggests animal qualities rather than obvious pantomime. His introduction of poses and gestures from Hindu or Cambodian dancing is done with skill. The ballet fulfilled Tudor's hopes for a moderate and interesting success, "his Buddhist ballet in disguise", as he called it. The English critics delighted in the ballet and enjoyed deciphering the various scenes of confrontation. Mary Clarke thought it a minor but beautiful work. John Percival saw it as "richly suggestive, provoking ideas about the human condition". Richard Buckle also adored it, found it "just on the razor's edge, almost nonsense; Tudor hit it just right. The animal kingdom is with us for keeps."

Shadowplay had its début in America in 1967 when the Royal Ballet came to the Metropolitan Opera House in New York. Eight years later, the ballet was performed by Baryshnikov at the New York State Theatre, with Gelsey Kirkland as the Celestial and Jonas Kåge as the Terrestrial.

—Judith Chazin-Bennahum

SHEARER, Moira

British dancer and actress. Born Moira Shearer-King in Dunfermline, Scotland, 17 January 1926. First dance studies in Northern Rhodesia; studied in Britain with Flora Fairbairn, Nikolai and Nadine Legat, from 1936, and at Sadler's Wells Ballet School, from 1940. Married Ludovic Kennedy, 1950. Dancer, International Ballet, 1941, joining Vic-Wells Ballet (later Sadler's Wells Ballet), in 1941, and becoming principal dancer, 1944–52; guest artist, Ballets de Paris, 1950, Sadler's Wells Ballet, from 1952, and London Festival Ballet, 1954; film début as actress/dancer in *The Red Shoes* (dir. Powell and Pressburger), 1948, thereafter appearing as actress in films including *Tales of Hoffmann* (dir. Powell, chor. Helpmann, 1951), *The Story of Three Loves* (dir. Reinhardt, Minnelli, 1953), *The Man Who Loved Redheads* (dir. French, 1954), and *Black Tights* (chor. Petit, 1962); also stage actress, with roles including Titania in Shakespeare's *A Midsummer Night's Dream* (Edinburgh Festival, 1954), Sally Bowles in *I am a Camera* (play by Isherwood; Bournemouth, 1955), and title role in *Major Barbara* (play by Shaw; London, 1956); member of General Advisory Council of the British Broadcasting Corporation (BBC); director of Border Television, 1970s.

ROLES

1941   Fairy of the Song Birds in *Aurora's Wedding* (from *The Sleeping Beauty*; after Petipa), International Ballet, British tour
     Guardian Swallow (cr) *Planetomania* (Inglesby), International Ballet, Birmingham
     Pas de deux in *Orpheus and Eurydice* (de Valois), Vic-Wells Ballet, British tour
1942   The Serving Maid in *The Gods Go a-Begging* (de Valois), Sadler's Wells Ballet, London
     Pas de deux in *Les Patineurs* (Ashton), Sadler's Wells Ballet, London
1943   The Nightingale in *The Birds* (Helpmann), Sadler's Wells Ballet, London
     Pride (cr) in *The Quest* (Ashton), Sadler's Wells Ballet, London
     Pas de trois (cr) in *Promenade* (de Valois), Sadler's Wells Ballet, Edinburgh
     Rendezvous pas de deux in *Promenade* (de Valois), Sadler's Wells Ballet, London
1944   Polka in *Façade* (Ashton), Sadler's Wells Ballet, London
     The Butterfly (cr) in *Le Festin de l'araignée* (Howard), Sadler's Wells Ballet, London
     Young Girl in *Le Spectre de la rose* (Fokine), Sadler's Wells Ballet, tour
     Chiarina in *Le Carnaval* (Fokine), Sadler's Wells Ballet, London
     A Lover (cr) in *Miracle in the Gorbals* (Helpmann), Sadler's Wells Ballet, London
1945   Odile in *Swan Lake* (Petipa, Ivanov; staged Sergeyev), Sadler's Wells Ballet, tour
     Mlle. Théodore in *The Prospect Before Us* (de Valois), Sadler's Wells Ballet, London
     Lover in *The Wanderer* (Ashton), Sadler's Wells Ballet, London
     Countess Kitty in *Les Sirènes* (Ashton), Sadler's Wells Ballet, London
     The Dancer in *The Rake's Progress* (de Valois), Sadler's Wells Ballet, London
1946   Columbine in *Le Carnaval* (Fokine), Sadler's Wells Ballet, London
     Swanilda in *Coppélia* (Petipa, Cecchetti; staged Ser-

Moira Shearer in *The Red Shoes*, 1948

geyev), Sadler's Wells Ballet, London

Odcttc/Odile in *Swan Lake* (Petipa, Ivanov; staged Sergeyev), Sadler's Wells Ballet, London

Princess Aurora and Fairy of the Crystal Fountain in *The Sleeping Beauty* (Petipa; staged Sergeyev, Ashton, de Valois), Sadler's Wells Ballet, London

Dancer in *Symphonic Variations* (Ashton), Sadler's Wells Ballet, London

A Nymph, Attendant on Spring (cr) in *The Fairy Queen* (masque after Shakespeare; mus. Purcell, chor. Ashton), Covent Garden Opera and Sadler's Wells Ballet, London

1947   Can-Can dancer in *La Boutique fantasque* (Massine), Sadler's Wells Ballet, London

The Aristocrat in *Mam'zelle Angot* (Massine), Sadler's Wells Ballet, London

La Bolero in *Les Sirènes* (Ashton), Sadler's Wells Ballet, London

Jota in *The Three-Cornered Hat* (Massine), Sadler's Wells Ballet, London

1948   Princess (cr) in *Clock Symphony* (Massine), Sadler's Wells Ballet, London

Title role in *Giselle* (Petipa after Coralli, Perrot; staged Sergeyev), Sadler's Wells Ballet, London

Principal dancer in *Scènes de ballet* (Ashton), Sadler's Wells Ballet, London

Lilac Fairy in *The Sleeping Beauty* (Petipa; staged Sergeyev, Ashton, de Valois), Sadler's Wells Ballet, London

A Young Wife (cr) in *Don Juan* (Ashton), Sadler's Wells Ballet, London

Title role (cr) in *Cinderella* (Ashton), Sadler's Wells Ballet, London

1949   Débutante in *Façade* (Ashton), Sadler's Wells Ballet, London

Princess Florine (Bluebird Pas de deux) in *The Sleeping Beauty* (Petipa; staged Sergeyev, de Valois, Ashton), Sadler's Wells Ballet, London

Julia in *A Wedding Bouquet* (Ashton), Sadler's Wells Ballet, London

1950 Principal dancer in *Ballet Imperial* (Balanchine), Sadler's Wells Ballet, London
Title role in *Carmen* (Petit), Ballets de Paris, Paris
1987 Lowry's Mother (cr) in *A Simple Man* (Lynne), Northern Ballet Theatre, British television

PUBLICATIONS

By Shearer:
Interview in Newman, Barbara, *Striking a Balance: Dancers Talk About Dancing*, Boston, 1982
Balletmaster: A Dancer's View of George Balanchine, London, 1986
Interview in Gruen, John, *People who Dance*, Pennington, N.J., 1988

About Shearer:
Tenent, Rose, *Moira Shearer*, Edinburgh, 1947
Gibbon, Monk, *The Red Shoes Ballet*, London, 1948
Crowle, Pigeon, *Moira Shearer*, London, 1951
Fisher, Hugh, *Moira Shearer*, London, 1952
Craig-Raymond, Peter, "The Career of Moira Shearer", *Ballet Today* (London), December 1954
Davidson, Gladys, *Ballet Biographies*, revised edition, London, 1954
Barnes, Clive, "Moira Shearer Today", *Dance Magazine* (New York), May 1962
Nugent, Ann, "Moira Shearer", *Dance Gazette* (London), July 1985
McLean, Adrienne, "The Red Shoes Revisited", *Dance Chronicle* (New York), vol.11, no.1, 1988

*   *   *

In the archives of the Royal Opera House at Covent Garden is a typed press release, dated December 1967, announcing the return to the stage of ballerina Moira Shearer for a single performance. In this press release, or rather in an emendation to it, is exemplified the historical problem of Moira Shearer's theatrical career: following the opening words "Ballerina Moira Shearer" is the hand-written injunction to insert the phrase "famous star of the film *The Red Shoes*". Shearer the ballerina is forever being attached to the role she played in *The Red Shoes*, and this makes difficult any balanced discussion of her place in theatrical dance history. For although it is true that Shearer's professional work can be roughly divided into three parts, comprising careers in ballet, film, and theatre, the dance content of her films is not only of value historically but continues to influence, through continual dissemination in film theatres and on television, the formation of new dance audiences today. Shearer's prominence in the Sadler's Wells Ballet, over a fifteen-year period of immense importance to the development of British ballet in general, would alone have assured her a place in dance history; but it is as a ballet dancer in lavishly produced popular films such as *The Red Shoes, Tales of Hoffmann, The Story of Three Loves, The Man Who Loved Redheads*, and *Black Tights* that she is most widely known.

Particularly in her first three films, Shearer's dancing on the screen reflects well her concurrent progress and development as a theatrical dancer. But it was her very success in these films, which were greeted with enthusiasm by most of the public and with ambivalence often bordering on resentment by ballet critics, that contributed to Shearer's decision eventually to give up theatrical dancing to concentrate first on acting, and subsequently on her family. Certainly before *The Red Shoes* became a mass culture phenomenon, Shearer's career could be described as one of steady progress toward more or less standard ballet goals—dancing, with ever greater distinction, the leading roles in all the classic ballets, for example, while at the same time creating roles in important new works. That *The Red Shoes*, her first film and one she felt "pestered" into making, became a sleeper hit and acquired a devoted international (particularly American) cult following skewed her position within the Sadler's Wells, making her life there at best uncomfortable. No longer simply a talented rising dancer (she was only 22 when *The Red Shoes* was released) but a movie star as well, Shearer was forced to spend large amounts of time reiterating that she was still serious about her theatrical ballet career and well aware of her limitations therein.

Shearer's strengths as a dancer had always been of the sort that could also be perceived as shortcomings: her unusual beauty, her red hair and "pink-and-white" colouring, a slight physique that gave her appearance on stage an almost weightless quality, a steely intelligence, and a fine but restrained spirit. These same features were sometimes read as flashiness, as brittleness, or as a rather chilly reticence. Her dancing was always musically responsive and precisely executed, but against the warmth of personality and classical Markova-style appearance of Margot Fonteyn, Shearer appeared, to some British critics, to lack the emotional depth required by the great Romantic ballets. Nevertheless, Shearer arguably came closer than any other Sadler's Wells ballerina to challenging Fonteyn's position of solitary pre-eminence in that company in the 1940s. Shearer left the Sadler's Wells permanently in 1953 to concentrate on acting in the theatre, but continued to dance occasionally in films: in *The Man Who Loved Redheads* she performs the third-act pas de deux from *The Sleeping Beauty* with John Hart, and in Roland Petit's *Black Tights* she dances Roxanne to Petit's Cyrano. (She also did some jazz dancing in the 1960 Michael Powell horror film *Peeping Tom*.)

Looking backward to the critical success of her performances in abstract works such as Frederick Ashton's *Scènes de ballet* (1948) and Balanchine's *Ballet Imperial* (mounted on the Sadler's Wells in 1950), one muses whether Moira Shearer might simply have been in the proverbial wrong place at the wrong time. That is, she does not seem to be a typical British dancer "in the Fonteyn mould" but instead a very modern ballerina embodying modern values of technical brilliance, clarity, polish, and musicality. Indeed, the recognition that Shearer was somehow "unclassifiable", to use Caryl Brahms's term, goes far to explain her undiminished appeal across the decades. For in her films, Shearer continues to look contemporary; one can imagine her on stage today in a way that is not true of many other dancers whose work is preserved in popular films. It is interesting both that George Balanchine pointedly preferred Shearer to Fonteyn in *Ballet Imperial* and that Shearer was sufficiently influenced by her brief (four-day) association with Balanchine in 1950 to write a book about him in 1986.

—Adrienne McLean

SHÉHÉRAZADE *see* **SCHÉHÉRAZADE**

SHELEST, Alla

Russian/Soviet dancer and teacher.   Born Alla Yakovlevna Shelest in Smolensk, 29 February 1919. Studied at the Leningrad Choreographic School, pupil of Elisaveta Gerdt, Agrippina Vaganova; graduated in 1937. Married choreographer Yuri Grigorovich (div.). Dancer, becoming leading ballerina, Kirov Ballet, 1937–63, also performing in ballet films and on Soviet television, including in *Gayané* in *Masters of Soviet Ballet* (1952), and *Eternal Idol* (choreographic miniature by Yakobson; Soviet television, 1961); teacher, Leningrad Choreographic School, 1952–55; member of choreographers' faculty, Leningrad Conservatory, 1965–70; artistic director, Kuibyshev Ballet, 1970–73; coach, Kirov Ballet, 1977–79. Recipient: titles of Honoured Artist of the Russian Federation, 1953, and People's Artist of the Russian Federation, 1957; State Prize of the USSR, 1947, 1951.

ROLES

1936   Title role (cr) in *Katerina* (Lavrovsky), Kirov Ballet, Leningrad
1937/   Princess Florine in *The Sleeping Beauty* (Petipa; staged
  43   Lopukhov), Kirov Ballet, Leningrad
       Second Shade in *La Bayadère* (Petipa; staged Vaganova), Kirov Ballet, Leningrad
       Parasha in *The Bronze Horseman* (Zakharov), Kirov Ballet, Leningrad
1938   Natella (cr) in *The Heart of the Hills* (Chabukiani), Kirov Ballet, Leningrad
1939   Jacinta in *Laurencia* (Chabukiani), Kirov Ballet, Leningrad
1940   Oksana (cr) in *Taras Bulba* (Lopukhov), Kirov Ballet, Leningrad
1942   Russian dance (cr) in *Emelian Pugachev* (opera; mus. Koval, chor., Lopukhov), Kirov Opera and Ballet, Perm
1943   Soloist (cr) in *Barkarolla* (Yakobson), Concert Programme, Perm Theatre for Opera and Ballet, Perm
       Zarema in *The Fountain of Bakhchisarai* (Zakharov), Kirov Ballet, Perm
       Lilac Fairy in *The Sleeping Beauty* (Petipa; staged Lopukhov), Kirov Ballet, Perm
1944   Soloist (cr) in *Creole Dance* (choreographic miniature; Yakobson), Kirov Ballet, Leningrad
1945   Tsar-Maiden in *The Little Humpbacked Horse* (Lopukhov after Gorsky, Petipa), Kirov Ballet, Leningrad
1946   Zluka (Ugly Sister; cr) in *Cinderella* (Sergeyev), Kirov Ballet, Leningrad
1948   Diana in *Esmeralda* (Vaganova after Petipa), Kirov Ballet, Leningrad
1950   Syuimbike (cr) in *Shurale* (*Ali-Batyr*; Yakobson), Kirov Ballet, Leningrad
1955   Oksana (cr) in *Taras Bulba* (Fenster), Kirov Ballet, Leningrad
1956   Aegina (cr) in *Spartacus* (Yakobson), Kirov Ballet, Leningrad
1957   Katerina (cr) in *The Stone Flower* (Grigorovich), Kirov Ballet, Leningrad
1958   Soloist (cr) in *Eternal Idol* (choreographic miniature; Yakobson), Kirov Ballet, Leningrad
1960   Bianca (cr) in *Othello* (Chabukiani), Kirov Ballet, Leningrad
       Baroness Stral (cr) in *Masquerade* (Fenster), Kirov Ballet, Leningrad

Alla Shelest as Aegina in Yakobson's *Spartacus*, Leningrad, c.1956

Other roles include: Odette/Odile in *Swan Lake* (Sergeyev after Petipa, Ivanov), Aurora, Lilac Fairy in *The Sleeping Beauty* (Sergeyev after Petipa), Myrtha and title role in *Giselle* (Petipa after Coralli, Perrot), title role in *Raymonda* (Sergeyev after Petipa), Nikiya in *La Bayadère* (Petipa, Ponomarev, Chabukiani), title role in *Laurencia* (Chabukiani), title role in *Tatyana* (Burmeister), the Beauty in *Spring Fairytale* (Lopukhov), Mekhmeneh-Banu in *The Legend of Love* (Grigorovich), Street Dancer in *Don Quixote* (Gorsky after Petipa), Mistress of the Copper Mountain in *The Stone Flower* (Grigorovich), Juliet in *Romeo and Juliet* (Lavrovsky), title role in *Gayané* (Anisimova), Tsar-Maiden in *The Little Humpbacked Horse* (Lopukhov after Gorsky), Mireille de Poitiers in *The Flames of Paris* (Vainonen), Gulnara in *Le Corsaire* (Vaganova after Petipa), Cleopatra in *Eygptian Nights* (Lopukhov after Fokine), Prelude, Waltz in *Chopiniana* (Fokine), principal dancer in *The Kiss, The Blind Girl* (choreographic miniatures; Yakobson), Bacchante in *Walpurgis Night* (Lavrovsky).

WORKS

Staged:
1971   *Swan Lake* (with Vagabov, after Petipa, Ivanov; mus. Tchaikovsky), Kuibyshev Theatre, Kuibyshev
1972   *The Sleeping Beauty* (with Vagabov, after Petipa; mus. Tchaikovsky), Kuibyshev Theatre, Kuibyshev
1975   *Chopiniana* (after Fokine; mus. Chopin), Tartu Theatre, Tartu

PUBLICATIONS

By Shelest:
"Academy of Dance", *Sovietsky Balet* (Moscow), no. 3, 1941
"Shakespeare in My Life", *Teatr* (Moscow), no. 4, 1964

About Shelest:
Lvov-Anokhin, Boris, "Two Roles of Alla Shelest", *Neva* (Leningrad), no. 6, 1963
Lvov-Anokhin, Boris, *Alla Shelest*, Moscow, 1964
Lopukhov, Fedor, *Sixty Years in Ballet*, Moscow, 1966
Prokhorova, V., "In Honour of Alla Shelest", *Teatralnaya Zhizn* (Moscow), no. 20, 1983
Smakov, Gennady, *The Great Russian Dancers*, New York, 1984
Clarke, Mary, and Crisp, Clement, *Ballerina*, London, 1987

*   *   *

Alla Shelest was one of the leading classical ballerinas of the Soviet stage, excelling in romantic, heroic, and tragic roles. Fedor Lopukhov wrote of her: "Shelest is a typically heroic ballerina: nervous, fiery, wilful and strongly magnetic . . .". But, as Lopukhov pointed out, hardly any other ballerina was as unlucky in her career as Shelest. After studying with Elisaveta Gerdt for fifteen years, she ended up in the same class under Vaganova. The change in aesthetic and in teaching style was too severe, and caused great problems for the dancer. Even greater difficulties awaited Shelest in the theatre. For sixteen years she was relegated to performing as an understudy for the lead dancers in new roles. As Lopukhov put it, "What a tremendous amount of talent it takes not to lose confidence under such circumstances! And nevertheless, Shelest achieved a great deal."

Shelest's dancing remains something of a legend in the history of the Kirov Ballet, and to this day people speak of her with respect, even if they never actually saw her on stage. And she was not just a remarkable classical ballerina, one of the best performers ever of the Lilac Fairy in *The Sleeping Beauty* and of Nikiya in *La Bayadère*. Gerdt had instilled in her a highly cultured stage demeanor that distinguished her from many of her contemporaries. Her style of dance was open, aerial, and expansive. She was especially good at continuous, flowing movement, a sort of "cantilena" in dance. Her leaps were expansive and high, her poses were sculptured, and her every movement was well thought-out. In contemporary ballets she was similarly impressive. Her performance of Jacinta in *Laurencia* had no equal, and her performance in the title role has become part of the history of Leningrad ballet.

But only Leonid Yakobson really recognized the value of this marvellous ballerina. In addition to concert pieces, he created the role of Aegina in *Spartacus*, the beautiful but treacherous Roman courtesan, for her. This role represented the height of Shelest's accomplishment. She put the whole of her professionalism, her ability to feel, her sculptured line into this role, bringing to it the sense of "fateful doom" that she imparted to all her heroines.

Ulanova wrote of her: "Every ballet in which Shelest performed was remarkable not only for the ballerina's talent, but also for her mind and for the great inner level of culture that belongs to a genuine artist. The boldness and the innovation in her interpretation of each of her roles stunned me as an artist. . . . She is a tragic and inspired ballerina. You can always recognize Shelest by the perfection of the sketch, by the emotion, and by the dancer's self-abandon."

—Nina Alovert

SHOSTAKOVICH, Dmitri

Russian/Soviet composer. Born Dmitri Dmitrievich Shostakovich in St. Petersburg, 25 September 1906. Studied piano with mother; studied at the Petrograd Conservatory, pupil of Leonid Nikolaev (piano), Maximilian Shteinberg (composition), 1919–39: post-graduate student from 1925. First major composition, graduation piece (Symphony No. 1) acclaimed at 1926 premiere; first opera, *Nos* (*The Nose*), and first ballet, *The Golden Age*, both staged 1930; opera *Lady Macbeth of the Mtsensk District* attacked by *Pravda* newspaper, leading to difficulties with authorities; standing restored with composition of Symphony No. 5 in 1937; teacher, Leningrad Conservatory, 1937–39, 1945–48, 1961, and Moscow Conservatory, 1943–48; recipient of further attack from Communist Party, 1948; composer of numerous film scores, including *The Youth of Maksim* (1935), *The Return of Maksim* (1937), *The Vyborg Side* (1939), *The Man with a Gun* (1938), and *Hamlet* (1964). Recipient: Lenin Prize (for Symphony no. 5), 1940; titles of People's Artist of Russian Federation, 1948, People's Artist of the USSR, 1954, and Hero of Socialist Labour, 1966; Honorary Doctorates, Oxford University, 1958 and Académie des Beaux-Arts, 1975. Died in Moscow, 9 August 1975.

WORKS (Ballets)

1930   *The Golden Age* (chor. Kaplan, Vainonen, Tchesnakov, Yakobson), State Academic Theatre for Opera and Ballet (GATOB), Leningrad
1931   *Bolt* (chor. Lopukhov), State Academic Theatre for Opera and Ballet (GATOB), Leningrad
1935   *The Bright Stream* (or *The Limpid Stream*; chor. Lopukhov), Maly Theatre, Leningrad
1976   *The Dreamers* (based on *The Golden Age* and *Bolt*; chor. Ruzhenko), Stanislavsky and Nemirovich–Danchenko Theatre, Moscow

Other ballets using Shostakovich's music: *Physical Exercise* (Yakobson, 1931), *Three Bears* (Yakobson, 1936), *Rouge et noir* (Massine, 1939), *Leningrad Symphony* (Massine, 1945; also Belsky, 1961), *The Wise Monkeys* (Morrice, 1960), *The Catalyst* (Cranko, 1961), *The Lady and the Hooligan* (Boyarsky, 1962), *Symphony* (MacMillan, 1963), *Quatuor* (d'Amboise, 1964), *Ninth Symphony* (van Dyk, 1964), *Concerto* (MacMillan, 1966), *Eleventh Symphony* (Belsky, 1966), *Tenth Symphony* (Carter, 1967), *Concerto* (Staff, 1968), *Gaiety Girl and the Sailors* (Staff, 1968), *Jewish Wedding* (Yakobson, 1970), *Fête noire* (Mitchell, 1971), *Sacred Circles* (Drew, 1973), *The Bedbug* (Yakobson, 1974), *In Concert* (Mottram, 1974), *Elegia* (Kylián, 1976), *Epode* (Arpino, 1979), *The Idiot* (Panov, 1979), *Playhouse* (Kudelka, 1980), *The Storm* (Prokovsky, 1981), *Vestige* (Morris, 1984), *Hamlet* (Panpv, 1984), *Der Schlaf der Vernunft* (North, 1986), *Trois Études pour Alexandre* (Béjart, 1987).

PUBLICATIONS

By Shostakovich:
"My Creative Path", *Izvestiya*, 4 April 1935
"My Creative Answer", *Vechernyaya Moskva* (Moscow), 25 January 1938
"Thoughts about Tchaikovsky", in *Russian Symphony*, New York, 1947
"Concerning the Contemporary Artist", *Pravda*, 7 September 1960
"The Composer's Mission", *Pravda*, 17 January 1962
Forward to Barsova, I., *Gustave Mahler*, Moscow, 1964

The Power of Music (collection of essays), New York, 1968
Testimony: The Memoirs of Dmitri Shostakovich, edited by
    Solomon Volkov, translated by Antonina Bouis, New York,
    1979

About Shostakovich:
Rabinovich, D., *Dmitri Shostakovich, Composer*, Moscow and
    London, 1959
Roslavleva, Natalia, *Era of the Russian Ballet*, London, 1966
Swift, Mary Grace, *The Art of the Dance in the USSR*, Notre
    Dame, Indiana, 1968
Kay, Norman, *Shostakovich*, London, 1971
Seroff, V. (ed.) *Dmitri Shostakovich*, New York, 1979
Sollertinsky, Dmitri, *Pages from the Life of Dmitri Shostakovich*,
    New York, 1980
Roseberry, Eric, *Shostakovich: His Life and Times*, New York,
    1981
Noriss, Christopher, *Shostakovich: The Man and the Music*,
    London, 1982
Kennicott, P., "Dance Music: The Young Dmitri", *Dance
    Magazine* (New York), February 1990

* * *

Though one of the greatest composers of the twentieth century whose interest extended from purely musical forms to many aspects of theatre and film, Dmitri Shostakovich had relatively little involvement with ballet, his work limited to work on three commissioned scores whose highly critical reception by Soviet officials seems to have dimmed any further desire to write specifically for the dance stage.

None the less all three scores are important in the development of Soviet ballet in the 1930s, not only in revealing the significant early move towards contemporary subject-matter to reflect the realities of everyday life after the Revolution, but also in pointing out the beginning of change from an exuberant period of relative freedom and open expression in the 1920s to the barbaric restrictions of the Stalin era, which were to suppress so much artistic innovation in the Soviet Union for the next 40 years.

Shostakovich's first and most famous ballet, *The Golden Age*, centres on the conflict between workers in a capitalist city and players on a visiting Soviet football team, and ends with a reconciliation between the opponents in a dance symbolizing the joy of work. The result of a competition for new ballet librettos, and featuring the work of four different choreographers, the production also revealed the composer's efforts to introduce into dance some of the irony which was later to become a frequent feature of his orchestral music. It was criticized, however, for ideological destructiveness and for attempting to appease the conflicts of the class war—and it was quickly removed from the repertoire. Interestingly, it has been revived and toured abroad by the Bolshoi in recent years as an example of ballet influenced by the aesthetics of contemporary constructivist art.

Bolt, which Shostakovich wrote shortly afterwards for choreography by Lopukhov, was the first genuinely industrial ballet produced within the USSR (Prokofiev's *Le Pas d'acier* was produced in Paris for Diaghilev). It attempted to satirize the petty officialdom of the bourgeoisie, whose drunken representatives try to sabotage socialist progress by placing a bolt in a machine. The ballet was severely criticized for representing heroes of the revolution as anti-social primitives, and was likewise suppressed.

His third ballet, *The Bright Stream* (also known as *The Limpid Stream*), concerning amorous deception occasioned by the arrival of a group of artists on a collective farm, was taken off

directly as a result of Stalin's criticism that it used classical conventions to express contemporary Soviet society. After this, Shostakovich seems to have abandoned the ballet stage as such, though he subsequently produced six ballet suites. Most of the suites derive from these various scores, though the Fifth is based on entirely original material.

Musically, Shostakovich adopted a lighter approach to the material of his ballets than he did for his operas or for the many film scores which he produced around the same time. He has said himself that he wrote this music primarily to entertain and even to amuse, and it is a pity that political ideology should have cut off an aspect of his music which might not only have added to his own breadth of expression, but also established a new dimension in the development of dramatic ballet.

An integral dance element in some of the concert music of Shostakovich has given a number of his other works, however, a place in the Western repertoire—most notably by Massine with his *Leningrad Symphony*, Cranko with the First Piano Concerto (*The Catalyst*), and both MacMillan and Arthur Mitchell with the Second Piano Concerto (*Concerto* and *Fête noir*).

—Geoffrey Baskerville

SHURALE(H)

Choreography: Leonid Yakobson
Music: Farid Yarullin
Design: A. Ptushko, L. Milchin, I. Vano
Libretto: Leonid Yakobson (after Tartar folk tales)
First Production: (under title of *Ali-Batyr*) Kirov Ballet,
    Leningrad, 28 June 1950
Principal Dancers: Igor Belsky (Shurale), Natalia Dudinskaya
    and Alla Shelest (alternating as Syuimbike), Konstantin
    Sergeyev and Boris Bregvadze (alternating as Ali-Batyr)

Other productions include: Kazan Theatre for Opera and Ballet (original production to score; chor. Yakobson), Kazan, 12 March 1945. Bolshoi Ballet (restaged Yakobson), as *Shurale*, with Vladimir Levashev (Shurale), Maya Plisetskaya (Syuimbike), Yuri Kondratov (Ali-Batyr); Moscow, 29 January 1955.

PUBLICATIONS

Krasovskaya, Vera, "Ballet Performance of Lyricism and
    Drama", *Theatre and Life* (Leningrad and Moscow), 1957
Roslavleva, Natalia, *Era of the Russian Ballet*, London, 1966
Dyukina, E., "A Quarter-Century on the Stage", *Sovetskaya
    Muzyka* (Moscow), no. 3, 1970

* * *

After the Russian Revolution, ballet began to reach peoples in the heartland of Asia, and eastern cultures in return contributed to ballet. *Shurale* is the supreme example, created in the Tartar capital of Kazan about 600 miles east of Moscow on the eve of the Second World War. The national Tartar Theatre of Opera and Ballet had just been built. The ballet reached dress rehearsal, but got no further until after the war.

The libretto was based on Tartar folk stories and the music was by the Tartar composer Farid Yarullin. Choreography and production were by the Leningrad-trained Leonid Yakobson.

The ballet takes its name from a mythical wood-spirit reputed to look like the roots of a tree, and maliciously disposed towards travellers in forests. Formerly the title *Shurale* alternated with *Ali-Batyr* (or *Bityr*), the name of the hunter who is the hero, but public preference finally opted in favour of the villain for the title of the ballet.

The ballet is in three acts and four scenes. The action begins at night deep in the ancient forest, the realm of Shurale, master of all supernatural forest beings. The young hunter Ali-Batyr has lost his way. A bird is seen flitting; Ali-Batyr tightens his bowstring and follows.

A branch of an enormous tree shakes, and Shurale appears, surrounded by lesser wood-spirits who dance to please him. When the sun rises it drives the lesser spirits away, but Shurale resists. A flock of white birds appears high in the sky. Shurale conceals himself in a tree as the birds settle in a sun-bathed clearing. They cast off their snow-white plumage and become maidens. Among them is the beautiful Bird-Maiden, Syuimbike. Shurale steals her wings.

When the time comes for the other maidens to put on their wings and fly away, Syuimbike cannot follow. Suddenly Shurale appears before her and she is surrounded by his minions. At this moment Ali-Batyr appears. He defends Syuimbike, fighting and overcoming Shurale. She thanks him warmly, and he realizes how beautiful she is. She asks him to find her lost wings, and he escorts her out of the forest. Shurale then painfully rises and the forest shakes with his wrath as he threatens revenge.

The second act begins in Ali-Batyr's village, where everything is ready to celebrate his marriage to Syuimbike, who is borne in on a luxurious carpet. When the groom arrives, the bride is hidden according to custom and he must seek her out. At first the guests tease him with merry jokes and send him off on false trails, but eventually they let him find her. The marriage ritual is performed, and the guests enter the house to feast, leaving the couple alone.

Ali-Batyr sees that his bride is sad and guesses she is pining for her bird-companions. It grows darker, the feast ends, and the guests begin to go home. Suddenly Shurale enters, unable to resist the temptation to play jokes on people who have had plenty to drink. Syuimbike appears, gazing towards her companions in the sky. Shurale calls up black crow-like birds, who bring Syuimbike's wings. Shurale, unobserved, lays them before the dreamy Bird-Maiden. Her desire to return to her friends battles with her love for Ali-Batyr, and for the time being proves stronger. She puts on the wings and is immediately surrounded by the black birds who force her to fly to Shurale's lair. Children who see the black flock flying away with a white bird in its midst raise the alarm. Ali-Batyr goes in pursuit, and his father commands faithful friends to follow.

The third act returns to the forest clearing, where the flock alights with its captive. When Ali-Batyr approaches, all hide. In anger he sets fire to the forest. The supernatural creatures fling themselves upon him and hold him. Shurale prepares to throw Syuimbike's wings into the flames. Ali-Batyr breaks free, seizes the wings, and it is Shurale who is thrown in the flames.

Desperate for the safety of Syuimbike, Ali-Batyr enters the flames himself, finds her, and brings her into the clearing. But the flames surround them and Ali-Batyr offers her the wings as her only possible means of escape. Love triumphs and she flings the wings into the fire. At last, through a wall of flame, Ali-Batyr's friends appear and with their help he carries her to safety. The final scene is set in the village, where the people rejoice at the beautiful Syuimbike's return with her saviour.

Yakobson's *Shurale* was first shown to the public in Leningrad in 1950. It is not the only version, but it has been produced many times and is regarded as one of the ten or so ballets forming the "Golden Fund of Soviet Choreography" (of which *Spartacus* is the best known). In 1990, *Shurale* was receiving about twenty performances a year in the Soviet Union; outside the country, it has been seen in Outer Mongolia, Bulgaria, East Germany, and Czechoslovakia.

In his book *Sixty Years in Ballet*, Fedor Lopukhov writes at length about the ballet. Always a stern critic, he claims that it could have been still more thoroughly "Tartarised", but rates its artistic significance very highly. He was undoubtedly impressed, for within a few years his choice fell on Yakobson to create *Spartacus*.

—Tony Devereux

SIBLEY, Antoinette

British dancer. Born Antoinette Sibley Corbett in Bromley, England, 27 February 1939. Studied at Cone Ripman School, and at Sadler's Wells Ballet School (later the Royal Ballet School). Married (1) dancer Michael Somes, 1964 (div. 1969); (2) Panton Corbett, 1974: two children, Isambard Henry and Eloise Cleo. Dancer, Royal Ballet, from 1956, becoming soloist, from 1959, and principal dancer, from 1960, with international tours including to South Africa, United States, Canada, and the Soviet Union; also international guest artist, with appearances in the United States, Italy, Germany, Holland, Australia, and Monaco; retired officially from dancing in 1979, but returned to stage, various seasons, 1981–89; vice-president, Royal Academy of Dancing, from 1989, becoming president (on death of Margot Fonteyn), from 1991; has also appeared in films, including in *The Turning Point* (dir. Ross, 1977); patron, the Cecchetti Centre, 1983; governor, Elmhurst Ballet School; member of the panel of the *Evening Standard* Dance Awards. Recipient: title of Commander of the Order of the British Empire, 1973.

ROLES

1958 Bluebird in *The Sleeping Beauty* (Petipa; staged Sergeyev, de Valois, Ashton), Royal Ballet, London
1959 Principal dancer in *Ballet Imperial* (*Tchaikovsky Piano Concerto No. 2*; Balanchine), Royal Ballet, London
Swanilda in *Coppélia* (Sergeyev after Petipa, Cecchetti), Royal Ballet, London
Columbine in *Harlequin in April* (Cranko), Royal Ballet, London
Polka in *Façade* (Ashton), Royal Ballet, London
Odette/Odile in *Swan Lake* (Petipa, Ivanov; staged Sergeyev, de Valois), Royal Ballet, London
1960 Principal dancer in *Birthday Offering* (Ashton), Royal Ballet, London
Title role in *Giselle* (Petipa after Coralli, Perrot; staged Sergeyev), Royal Ballet Touring Company, Johannesburg
Princess Aurora in *The Sleeping Beauty* (Petipa; staged Sergeyev, de Valois, Ashton), Royal Ballet Touring Company, Johannesburg
1961 Fiancée in *Le Baiser de la fée* (MacMillan), Royal Ballet, London
Bride in *La Fête étrange* (Howard), Royal Ballet Touring Company
Mary (cr) in *Jabez and the Devil* (Rodrigues), Royal Ballet, London

Antoinette Sibley as Titania in *The Dream*, Royal Ballet, London, 1964

1962 Principal dancer in *Birthday Offering* (Ashton), Royal Ballet, London

Lise in *La Fille mal gardée* (Ashton), Royal Ballet Touring Company

Principal dancer in *Flower Festival at Genzano* (Bournonville), Royal Ballet, London

Mariuccia in *The Good-Humoured Ladies* (new production; Massine), Royal Ballet, London

Principal dancer in *Napoli* (Divertissement; Bournonville), Royal Ballet, London

Variation, Adagio of Lovers in *Les Rendezvous* (Ashton), Royal Ballet, London

1963 Principal dancer in *Symphony* (MacMillan), Royal Ballet, London

The Young Girl in *The Two Pigeons* (Ashton), Royal Ballet, London

The Betrayed Girl in *The Rake's Progress* (de Valois), Royal Ballet, London

1964 Titania (cr) in *The Dream* (Ashton), Royal Ballet, London

Ophelia in *Hamlet* (Helpmann), Royal Ballet, London

The Aristocrat in *Mam'zelle Angot* (Massine), Royal Ballet, London

Principal dancer in *Scènes de ballet* (Ashton), Royal Ballet, London

1965 Juliet in *Romeo and Juliet* (MacMillan), Royal Ballet, London

Principal dancer in *Laurencia* Pas de six (Nureyev after Chabukiani), Royal Ballet, London

1966 Principal dancer (cr) in *Brandenburg Nos. 2 and 4* (Cranko), Royal Ballet, London

Principal dancer (Trois Gnossiennes; cr) in *Monotones* (nos. 1 and 2; Ashton), Royal Ballet, London

Third Song in *Song of the Earth* (MacMillan), Royal Ballet, London

1967 Title role in *Cinderella* (Ashton), Royal Ballet, London

Principal dancer in *Symphonic Variations* (Ashton), Royal Ballet, London

1968 Friday (cr) in *Jazz Calendar* (Ashton), Royal Ballet, London

Nikiya in "Kingdom of the Shades" from *La Bayadère* (Nureyev after Petipa), Royal Ballet, London

Variation in *Birthday Offering* (Ashton), Royal Ballet, London

Dorabella (cr) in *Enigma Variations* (Ashton), Royal Ballet, London

Clara in *The Nutcracker* (Nureyev), Royal Ballet, London

Princess Aurora in *The Sleeping Beauty* (Petipa, Ashton; staged Wright), Royal Ballet, London

Caroline in *Lilac Garden* (*Jardin aux lilas*; Tudor), Royal Ballet, London

1969 Chloe in *Daphnis and Chloe* (Ashton), Royal Ballet, London

1970 Principal dancer in *Dances at a Gathering* (Robbins), Royal Ballet, London

Title role in *Giselle* (Petipa after Coralli, Perrot; staged Ashton), Royal Ballet, London

1971 Mathilde Kchessinska (cr) in *Anastasia* (three-act version; MacMillan), Royal Ballet, London

Title role in *Raymonda* (Nureyev after Petipa), Royal Ballet, tour

Principal dancer (cr) in Meditation from *Thaïs* (Ashton), Royal Ballet, London

Principal dancer in *Afternoon of a Faun* (Robbins), Royal Ballet, London

1972 Title role in *Firebird* (Fokine), Royal Ballet, London

The Girl (cr) in *Triad* (MacMillan), Royal Ballet, London

1973 Principal dancer in *In the Night* (Robbins), Royal Ballet, London

Princess Aurora in *The Sleeping Beauty* (new production; Petipa, staged MacMillan), Royal Ballet, London

Principal dancer (cr) in *Pavane* (MacMillan), Royal Ballet, London

1974 Title role (cr) in *Manon* (MacMillan), Royal Ballet, London

1980 Pas de deux (cr) in *Soupirs* (Ashton), Gala performance, London

1982 Principal dancer in *Minuet* (pas de deux; Corder), Gala performance, London

Principal dancer in *Impromptu* (pas de deux; Deane), Gala Performance, London

The Woman (cr) in *L'Invitation au voyage* (Corder), Royal Ballet, London

Elisa in *Konservatoriet* (Bournonville), Royal Ballet, London

1983 La Capricciosa (cr) in *Varii Capricci* (Ashton), Royal Ballet, New York

1984 Principal dancer (cr) in *Fleeting Figures* (Deane), Royal Ballet, London

1985 Natalia Petrovna in *A Month in the Country* (Ashton), Royal Ballet, Barcelona

Other roles include: Waltz and Mazurka in *Les Sylphides* (Fokine), Tango ("Débutante") in *Façade* (Ashton), Carlotta Grisi in *Pas de Quatre* (Dolin).

PUBLICATIONS

By Sibley:
Interview in Gruen, John, *The Private World of Ballet*, New York, 1975
Interview in Newman, Barbara, "Sibley Talks about Dancing", *Ballet Review* (Brooklyn), Summer 1981
Interview in Newman, Barbara, *Striking a Balance: Dancers Talk about Dancing*, Boston, 1982

About Sibley:
Goodman, Saul, "Antoinette Sibley", *Dance Magazine* (New York), September 1963
Maynard, Olga, "Pas de Deux Par Excellence", *Dance Magazine* (New York), April 1970
Crickmay, Anthony, *Antoinette Sibley*, Brooklyn, 1976
Spatt, Leslie (photographer), and Dromgoole, Nicholas, *Sibley and Dowell*, London, 1976
Hainsworth, Lois, "Antoinette Sibley", *Dance Gazette* (London), February 1980
Clarke, Mary, *Antoinette Sibley*, London, 1981
Macaulay, Alastair, "Antoinette Sibley", *Dance Theatre Journal* (London), Autumn 1985
Newman, Barbara, *Antoinette Sibley: Reflections of a Ballerina*, London, 1986

*   *   *

Like Anthony Dowell, with whom she developed an internationally famous partnership, Antoinette Sibley was a dancer with an impeccable classical line, displaying the unforced, limpid lyricism of the British style which owed much of its development to the choreography of Frederick Ashton.

Sibley's mother had trained as a dancer with Lea Espinosa,

and she placed her daughter, at the age of five, in the school run by the famous Cone sisters, Grace, Valerie, and Lillie, whose establishment was later to amalgamate with that of Olive Ripman's and become the Arts Educational Trust. Although she planned for a more general stage career (studying musical comedy, tap, mime, and acting), Sibley's balletic talent was so outstanding that her parents decided she should audition for the Sadler's Wells (later Royal) Ballet School. She was just nine years old when she was accepted.

Sibley joined the Sadler's Wells Ballet in 1956, shortly before it was granted a Royal Charter and became the Royal Ballet, and made her début in the corps de ballet of *Swan Lake*. Her rise through the ranks of the company was relatively rapid, and she danced her first Odette/Odile in 1959, after a mere two weeks' rehearsal period. She was coached in the role by Michael Somes (whom she married in 1964).

From the start it was clear that Sibley was one of the chosen few endowed with a wonderful natural facility, one which needs only the slightest regular honing. Beginning with perfect proportions between head, torso, and limbs, Sibley could make every pose and every movement, whether in a classroom enchainement or a full classical variation, appear like a textbook example—crystal clear, unforced, and ultimately shown to perfection in such roles as Aurora in *The Sleeping Beauty* and the leading ballerina in Ashton's *Scènes de ballet*.

The famous partnership with Anthony Dowell began when the two dancers were given the leading roles in Ashton's *The Dream*. The parts of Titania and Oberon were built around Sibley's and Dowell's fluent classicism and their perfect, complementary proportions. Their success together—particularly when the ballet was performed in New York—confirmed the work's place in the repertory, and helped define a masterpiece out of something that initially had been treated by the critics somewhat diffidently as a "pièce d'occasion".

Three months after the premiere of *The Dream*, Sibley succumbed to glandular fever (an illness to which dancers are particularly susceptible) and was forced to take a rest from the stage; this was the first of a number of major and minor illnesses and injuries which were to blight the rest of her career. In 1966 she was back with the company to dance her created role in Ashton's *Monotones*, a ballet perfectly suited to her cool, clear classical style. But less than a year later she was to undergo an operation on her left knee, which was to continue to give trouble, and this operation was followed by nervous collapse brought about by strain.

But in 1968 Sibley triumphed in two more Ashton works: *Jazz Calendar*, in which she danced a languorous pas de deux with Nureyev, and *Enigma Variations*, in which she created the role of the charming Dorabella. In 1970, MacMillan took over the direction of the Royal Ballet from Ashton, and one of the first works he introduced into the repertoire was Jerome Robbins's *Dances at a Gathering*, to music by Chopin. Sibley was one of an impressive cast which included Antony Dowell, Lynn Seymour, and Rudolf Nureyev. Sibley found working with the famous American choreographer an "absolute delight", and responded sensitively to the requirements of his choreography. On the night of her début as Giselle, Robbins informed her that he wanted her to partner Dowell in the London premiere of his *Afternoon of a Faun*—and this was another important success cementing the Dowell–Sibley partnership. Soon, Sibley was creating another role, that of the Girl in MacMillan's *Triad*, a ballet in which two brothers (Dowell and Wayne Eagling) compete for the attentions of a woman whose intrusion into their lives brings a bitter disaffection.

Following her success in *Triad*, Sibley once more succumbed to illness which prevented her from joining the Royal Ballet on

its American tour, but she was back on stage again in the autumn of 1973, dancing in Robbins's *In the Night*, a companion work to *Dances at a Gathering*. Not long afterwards, Sibley began work on her greatest created part, the title role of MacMillan's *Manon*. Following his usual custom, which is to begin with the most difficult and demanding sequences of a work, MacMillan began on the four great pas de deux which are the core of the ballet, delineating the progress of the lovers, Manon and the young theological student Des Grieux, whose obsession with her leads him into a life of dissolution, robbery and, finally, murder. Only the first duet was completed when Sibley once again fell ill, this time with an inflamed hip; the rest of the role was completed on Jennifer Penney.

Sibley recovered in time to dance at the premiere in 1974. The ballet received somewhat dismissive reviews, but the principal dancers were given a rapturous reception. The work has since proved to be one of the most popular and acclaimed works in the modern repertoire, and there is no doubt that it represents the pinnacle of the partnership between Sibley and Dowell.

Sibley retired officially in 1979, and the next year gave birth to a son, but in 1981 Ashton and Dowell persuaded her to come out of retirement and take part in the fiftieth birthday celebrations of the Royal Ballet. Ashton devised a witty role for her in a short, relatively light work, *Varii Capricci*, in which Dowell played a gigolo-ish character to Sibley's elegant, mature woman. Coaxed out of retirement, Sibley then continued to guest with the company for a few seasons, delighting audiences with performances in Ashton's *Scènes de ballet* and *The Dream* and MacMillan's *Manon*. She will be remembered as an exemplar of the British classical style, continuing the line established by the company's prima ballerina assoluta, Margot Fonteyn—and there can be no higher praise than that.

—Edward Thorpe

SIMONE, Kirsten

Danish dancer, choreographer, and teacher.   Born in Copenhagen, 1 July 1934. Studied at the Royal Danish Ballet School, Copenhagen, pupil of Vera Volkova, from 1945. Dancer, Royal Danish Ballet, from 1952, becoming solo dancer (principal) from 1956, and first soloist (ballerina) from 1966, touring London, United States, Italy, and Germany; also leading dancer with ensemble touring as Soloists of the Royal Danish Ballet; guest ballerina, appearing with various companies abroad including Edinburgh International Ballet, Ruth Page Company, American Ballet Theatre, and London Festival Ballet; teacher, Royal Theatre, Copenhagen, and Royal Danish Ballet School; international guest teacher, including in New York, Chicago, San Diego, Hawaii, and Hanover.

ROLES

1952 Hilda in *A Folk Tale* (Bournonville), Royal Danish Ballet, Copenhagen
      Sugar Plum Fairy in *The Nutcracker* (pas de deux; Brenaa after Ivanov), Royal Danish Ballet, Copenhagen
1955 Lucile Grahn in *Pas de quatre* (Dolin), Royal Danish Ballet, Copenhagen
      Pas de deux in *Les Sylphides* (Fokine), Royal Danish Ballet, Copenhagen

The Sleepwalker in *Night Shadow* (*La Sonnambula*; Balanchine), Royal Danish Ballet, Copenhagen

1956   Title role in *La Sylphide* (Bournonville), Royal Danish Ballet, Copenhagen

Principal dancer in *Konservatoriet* (Bournonville), Royal Danish Ballet, Copenhagen

Eurydice (cr) in *Myth* (Hansen), Royal Danish Ballet, Copenhagen

Amalie in *Dream Pictures* (Walbom), Royal Danish Ballet, Copenhagen

First Slave Girl in *Polovtsian Dances from Prince Igor* (Fokine), Royal Danish Ballet, Copenhagen

La Harpe in *Fanfare* (Robbins), Royal Danish Ballet, Copenhagen

1957   Princess Aurora in *The Sleeping Beauty* (Petipa; staged Ashton), Royal Danish Ballet, Copenhagen

Lilac Fairy in *The Sleeping Beauty* (Petipa; staged Ashton), Royal Danish Ballet, Copenhagen

Polyhymnia in *Apollon Musagète* (*Apollo*; Balanchine), Royal Danish Ballet, Copenhagen

Pas de trois in *Swan Lake* (Ivanov, Petipa; staged Lander), Royal Danish Ballet, Copenhagen

1958   The Girl in *Octet* (Taras), Edinburgh International Ballet, Edinburgh

The Sweet Young Thing (cr) in *Secrets* (Cranko), Edinburgh International Ballet, Edinburgh

The Fairy in *Harlequinade* (*Les Millions d'Arlequin*; Walbom, Brenaa after Petipa), Royal Danish Ballet, Copenhagen

Principal dancer in *Happy Journey* (Bjørnsson), Royal Danish Ballet, Copenhagen

Title role in *Miss Julie* (Cullberg), Royal Danish Ballet, Copenhagen

1959   Creusa in *Medea* (Cullberg), Royal Danish Ballet, Copenhagen

1960   Title role in *Carmen* (Petit), Royal Danish Ballet, Copenhagen

The Bride in *Blood Wedding* (Rodrigues), Royal Danish Ballet, Copenhagen

1961   Roxane in *Cyrano de Bergerac* (Petit), Royal Danish Ballet, Copenhagen

Principal dancer in *Danses concertantes* (MacMillan), Royal Danish Ballet, Copenhagen

Pas de deux from *Don Quixote* (Gorsky after Petipa), Royal Danish Ballet, Copenhagen

1962   Flora in *Les Victoires de l'amour* (Lander), Royal Danish Ballet, Copenhagen

1963   Principal dancer in *Flower Festival at Genzano* (Bournonville), Royal Danish Ballet, Copenhagen

Principal dancer in *The Merry Widow* (Balanchine), Ruth Page Company, Chicago

Third Movement in *The Four Temperaments* (Balanchine), Royal Danish Ballet, Copenhagen

Prélude in *Bourrée fantasque* (Balanchine), Royal Danish Ballet, Copenhagen

First Movement in *Symphony in C* (Balanchine), Royal Danish Ballet, Copenhagen

1964   Title role in *Giselle* (Petipa after Coralli, Perrot; staged Bruhn), Royal Danish Ballet, Copenhagen

La Capricciosa in *The Lady and the Fool* (Cranko), Royal Danish Ballet, Copenhagen

Odette/Odile in *Swan Lake* (Petipa, Ivanov; staged Anisimova), Royal Danish Ballet, Copenhagen

1965   Juliet in *Romeo and Juliet* (Ashton), Royal Danish Ballet, Copenhagen

1966   Milady in *The Three Musketeers* (Flindt), Royal Danish Ballet, Copenhagen

Principal dancer in *Afternoon of a Faun* (Robbins), Royal Danish Ballet, Copenhagen

Columbine in *Dream Pictures* (Walbom), Royal Danish Ballet, Copenhagen

1967   Tadea (cr) in *Don Juan* (von Rosen), Royal Danish Ballet, Copenhagen

Pas de deux in *Gala Variations* (Flindt), Royal Danish Ballet, Copenhagen

Teresina in *Napoli* (Bournonville), Royal Danish Ballet, Copenhagen

La Jeune Mariée in *Le Loup* (Petit), Royal Danish Ballet, Copenhagen

Señorita in *La Ventana* (Bournonville), Royal Danish Ballet, Copenhagen

1968   Principal dancer in *Donizetti Variations* (Balanchine), Royal Danish Ballet, Copenhagen

1969   Principal dancer in *Serenade* (Balanchine), Royal Danish Ballet, Copenhagen

1970   Principal dancer (cr) in *Fête polonaise* (Lander), Royal Danish Ballet, Copenhagen

Swanilda in *Coppélia* (Martinez after Petipa, Cecchetti), American Ballet Theatre, New York

1987   Lady Capulet in *Romeo and Juliet* (Ashton), London Festival Ballet

1990   Frigga in *The Lay of Thrym* (Bournonville), Royal Danish Ballet, Copenhagen

Other roles include: Madame in *The Kermesse in Bruges* (Bournonville), Madame in *The King's Lifeguards on Amager* (Bournonville).

PUBLICATIONS

"Careers in Pictures: Kirsten Simone", *Ballet Today* (London), May 1959

Goodman, Saul, "Brief Biographies: Kirsten Simone", *Dance Magazine* (New York), May 1963

Kragh-Jacobsen, Svend, *20 Solo Dancers of the Royal Danish Ballet*, Copenhagen, 1965

Aschengreen, Erik, "Kirsten Simone", *Les Saisons de la danse* (Paris), March 1971

Terry, Walter, "Royal Mime", *Ballet News* (New York), June 1980

Tobias, Tobi, "In Praise of Older Women", *Dance Magazine* (New York), November 1982

*   *   *

Kirsten Simone is one of the dancers of the Royal Danish Ballet whose career was crushed under Flemming Flindt's tenure as ballet master. When he took over this position (1966–78), she was at the prime of her career. She had danced the classical repertoire—Aurora and the Lilac Fairy in *The Sleeping Beauty*, the title role in *Giselle*, the Princess in *The Nutcracker*—and she was the one to dance Odette/Odile in the first Danish full-length production of *Swan Lake*. She had danced Bournonville, Balanchine, Ashton, Cullberg, Robbins, Petit, and MacMillan. She had been a soloist since 1956 and had had time to develop and mature into a ballerina repertory. In 1966 she was promoted to principal dancer and could look forward to perhaps ten more years as a leading dancer, during which time she could fill her roles with the deeper characterization of the mature dancer.

But Flindt stressed the modern repertory, and even though Simone was a principal dancer, she was hardly used. Her traditional classicism did not appeal to him or fit into the new repertory, especially his own modern ballets. In the 1973–74 season, for example, she only performed 21 times.

The audience and the critics, Danish as well as foreign, who in the mid-1960s had hailed Simone as "the most eminent Danish dramatic dancer", and had proclaimed her "at the peak of her career, ready to tackle new exacting tasks and able to dance the entire ballerina repertoire", were all painfully aware of this sad development, as was Simone herself. The audience showed their sympathy for her by applauding at every appearance she made, no matter how insignificant, and the critics never let any opportunity pass to comment that it was a shame that this brilliant principal dancer was not used more. Eventually, in 1973, she was so distressed that in an interview she blurted out: "Use me before I get afraid of the stage." And in 1980 she said in an interview with Walter Terry, "It is not easy . . . to know that your best years were lost. For twelve and a half years during Flindt's regime, the repertory was such that I was rarely assigned any roles . . . These would have been my best dancing years—from 32 to 42—but the classics were put away and there was very little Bournonville. I slowly died—a little every year—and in the end it was too late . . .". Although Simone made many successful guest appearances all over the world, it was a lost career.

It must have been a particularly bitter experience because Simone's success was not easily won in the first place. Apart from a few exceptions, all of her opening nights received modest or bad reviews—but after a few years, when she had grown into the parts, the critics raved about her. Of her first Carmen (one of the roles that really developed her as a dancer), the Danish critic Svend Kragh-Jacobsen wrote in 1960: "[Simone] does not possess the inner fire or drama this part demands." Five years later, he described her as "phenomenal" in the same role.

Simone also had to fight against many odds. The critics claimed that she was not a born dancer, that she was plump, with short arms and legs. But with an iron will she overcame these shortcomings and developed a very strong technique and clear classical style. Her determination to devote her life to dance was already apparent at the age of eleven, when she went to audition at the Royal Danish Ballet School all by herself—and was among the few who were admitted.

After 1976, Simone began her second career as a mime and character dancer in the Bournonville repertoire. This was somewhat ironic, given that she was always far better in the classical Russian style than in the Bournonville style.

One of Simone's latest appearances was as Frigga in the 1990 reconstruction of Bournonville's *The Lay of Thrym*, which had not been performed since 1905. When she is not performing at the Royal Danish Theatre, she is travelling all over the world giving guest performances and teaching.

—Jeannette Andersen

SINFONIETTA

Choreography: Jiří Kylián
Music: Leoš Janáček
Design: Walter Nobbe (scenery and costumes), Joop Caboort (lighting)
First Production: Netherlands Dance Theatre, Spoleto Festival U.S.A., Charleston, South Carolina, 9 June 1978
Principal dancers: Sabine Kupferberg, Leigh Matthews, Susan McKee, Ric McCullough, Eve Walstrum, Eric Hampton, Karen Tims, Gerald Tibbs, Arlette van Boven, Eric Newton, Roslyn Anderson, Michael Sanders, Alida Chase, Nils Christe.

Other productions include: Paris Opéra Ballet; Paris, 20 October 1989. American Ballet Theatre (staged Roslyn Anderson); New York, 26 April 1991.

PUBLICATIONS

Stoop, Norma McLain, "A New Chord in Dance", *Dance Magazine* (New York), September 1978
Tobias, Tobi, "Instant Recognition: Nederlands Dans Theater", *Dance Magazine* (New York), October 1979
Whitney, Mary, "Force of Nature", *Ballet News* (New York), July 1981

*　　*　　*

Sinfonietta was first performed at the American Spoleto Festival, in Charleston, South Carolina in June 1978, and, seven days later, at the Circustheater, Scheveningen, The Netherlands. The ballet was a breakthrough for the Netherlands Dance Theatre, and made Jiří Kylián world-famous.

Kylián's choreography drew its inspiration from music by his compatriot and favourite composer, Leoš Janáček, to whom the Spoleto Festival of 1978 was dedicated. Kylián left his native Czechoslovakia before the Warsaw Pact invasion in 1968 and was unable to return, or to visit his family there, until 1979, and *Sinfonietta* concerns his feelings about the country.

Janáček's music, *Sinfonietta*, was written in 1926, eight years after World War I had ended, and well before the outbreak of World War II. It expresses, in his own words, "the contemporary free man, his spiritual beauty and joy, his strength, courage and determination to fight for victory". It was composed for thirteen trumpets, two Wagner tubas, and a symphony orchestra, and is dominated by the fanfares of the brass section, which give the ballet such a glorious opening. Following the structure of the music, the ballet consists of five sections, and is the most classically based of Kylián's ballets.

The first production had a backdrop representing a typical Silesian countryside scene, and was painted by Walter Nobbe, who also created the costumes. These costumes consisted of white leotards and matching open shirts for the men, and mid-length, round-necked dresses, with blue and pink belts and soft shoes for the women. The lighting, designed by Joop Caboort, changed frequently during the five sections, creating effects of dawn, morning light, and full daylight.

The ballet, choreographed for seven couples, opens with an exhilarating series of leaps by the men, set to the celebratory opening fanfares. One dancer after another performs high elevation split jetés diagonally across the stage—an expression of joie de vivre. Then, couples twirl across the space in a continuous stream of movement. Kylián interweaves arabesques, lifts, and lyrical and classical steps elegantly with expressive movements and gestures derived from folk dance and modern dance. In contrast with the opening, the two couples in the middle section are subdued, using the space to circle around one another. Characteristic of Kylián's choreography is the next section, with its trio of one female dancer and two male dancers. In this, the men tenderly swing the woman, push her away from them, and draw her towards them in a pattern of flowing movements. At the end of the ballet the fanfare is heard again, and the dancers respond with high split jetés, this time with the women and men dancing together.

Rooted in the spirit of Janáček's score, Kylián's choreo-

Sinfonietta, **performed by Netherlands Dance Theatre, 1978**

graphy created a ballet celebrating the sheer exhilaration of life; he complemented the music to produce a joyous fusion of feelings of youthfulness, love, hope, and strength.

—Helma Klooss

SIZOVA, Alla

Russian/Soviet dancer. Born Alla Ivanova Sizova in Moscow, 22 September 1939. Studied at the Leningrad Choreographic School, pupil of Natalia Kamkova; graduated in 1958. Dancer, becoming ballerina, Kirov Ballet, 1958–88, touring internationally with the Kirov, including New York, 1961; also performed in films, including screen version of *The Sleeping Beauty* (Sergeyev, 1964), and the television film *Inspired Flight* (1969); teacher, Leningrad Choreographic School, from 1988, also teaching at the Universal Ballet Academy, Washington, D.C., from 1990. Recipient: Gold Medal, International Ballet Competition, Varna, 1964; Prix Anna Pavlova, Paris Academy of Dance, 1964; titles of Honoured Artist of the Russian Federation, 1966, People's Artist of the Russian Federation, 1972, People's Artist of the USSR, 1983.

ROLES

1958   Queen of the Dryads (while still a student) in *Don Quixote* (Gorsky after Petipa), Kirov Ballet, Leningrad

Pas de deux (with Nureyev) from *Le Corsaire* (Petipa), Graduation Performance of the Leningrad Choreographic School, Leningrad

1959/ Masha in *The Nutcracker* (Vainonen), Kirov Ballet,
60   Leningrad

1960   Principal dancer (cr) in *The Flying Waltz* (choreographic miniature; Yakobson), Kirov Ballet, Leningrad

Katerina in *The Stone Flower* (Grigorovich), Kirov Ballet, Leningrad

1961   The Girl (cr) in *Leningrad Symphony* (Belsky), Kirov Ballet, Leningrad

Princess Aurora in *The Sleeping Beauty* (Sergeyev after Petipa), Kirov Ballet Tour, Covent Garden, London

1963   Title role in *Giselle* (Petipa after Coralli, Perrot), Kirov Ballet, Leningrad

Queen of the Waters in *The Little Humpbacked Horse* (Gorsky after Saint-Léon), Kirov Ballet, Leningrad

1964   Title role in *Cinderella* (Sergeyev), Kirov Ballet, Leningrad

1965 Juliet in *Romeo and Juliet* (Lavrovsky), Kirov Ballet, Leningrad

1968 Maria in *The Fountain of Bakhchisarai* (Zakharov), Kirov Ballet, Leningrad

1969 Kitri in *Don Quixote* (Gorsky), Kirov Ballet, Leningrad

1970 Ophelia (cr) in *Hamlet* (Sergeyev), Kirov Ballet, Leningrad

1972 The Princess Rose (cr) in *The Enchanted Prince* (Vinogradov), Kirov Ballet, Leningrad

1979 Soloist (cr) in *Pas de Six* from *La Vivandière* (new production; Lacotte after Saint-Léon), Kirov Ballet, Leningrad

1980 The Fairy in *The Fairy of the Rond Mountains* (Vinogradov), Kirov Ballet, Leningrad

Other roles include: Princess Florine and the Gentle Fairy in *The Sleeping Beauty* (Petipa; staged Sergeyev), Myrtha in *Giselle* (Petipa after Coralli, Perrot), Waltz and Mazurka in *Chopiniana* (Vaganova after Fokine), Variation in *Paquita* (Petipa; staged Gusev), Maenada in *Spartacus* (Grigorovich), Parasha in *The Bronze Horseman* (Zakharov), Soloist in *Le Papillon* (Lacotte).

PUBLICATIONS

Barnes, Clive, "Kirov Ballet Backdrop", *Dance Magazine* (New York), September 1961

Hering, Doris, "Kirov Ballet—Endearing Anachronism", *Dance Magazine* (New York), November 1961

Goodman, Saul, "Meet Alla Sizova", *Dance Magazine* (New York), January 1962

Dudinskaya, Natalia, "A Generous Talent", *Smena* (Leningrad), 9 February 1966

Kiselev, Vadem, *The Leningrad Ballet Today*, Leningrad, 1968

Rachkova, T., "Alla Sizova", *Teatr* (Moscow), no. 6, 1983

* * *

Alla Sizova was above all a lyrical ballerina. She also always had a very high extension, and her leaps were both high and long, causing the critics to refer to her as "the flying Sizova". Sizova's repertoire was extensive; in effect, this ballerina mastered the entire wealth of classical choreography, in all its technical complexities and variances, in her years at the Kirov Theatre. Her dancing style can be described as austere, in the

Alla Sizova as Kitri in *Don Quixote*, Kirov Ballet, 1972

best sense of the word: she was graceful, elegant, and noble. Among the best features of her performance should be noted the sincerity of emotion in the dramatic roles she danced, coupled with a sense of joy and a true novelty and originality of vision.

Sizova was born in Moscow, but trained at the Leningrad Choreographic School, and graduated into the Kirov company in 1958. Fortunately for Sizova, as for many dancers of the Soviet Union at this time, graduation into the company took place during the period of the "New Era", the so-called thaw of Nikita Kruschev. Ballet companies within the Soviet Union, including of course the Kirov, began to tour abroad, and it was Sizova's fortune to start her career on the international stage.

Alla Sizova's first major classical role, and the one with which she came to be identified, was Aurora in *The Sleeping Beauty*. It was in this part that Sol Hurok, the American impresario, discovered Sizova and decided to present her to the American public for the first time, bringing her great success in 1961. She was quite a strong ballerina, coached by former Kirov ballerina Natalia Komkova; and her technique, particularly her jeté, was excellent. At the Kirov, Sizova danced several performances with Rudolf Nureyev, and it was a great—if brief—partnership, accentuating both dancers' strength and dynamism. The two were especially exciting to watch in the Bluebird pas de deux from *The Sleeping Beauty*, a choreographic gem which suited them both perfectly.

But Sizova is also a person of very mild, or gentle, temperament; in some senses she did not have enough stamina to be a real fighter in the world of ballet. She was without a doubt a top-quality dancer, but she was often in the shadow of stronger personalities—Irina Kolpakova, for example. Sizova was often in the second cast; for example she was the second Juliet when the Lavrovsky *Romeo and Juliet* was revived on the Kirov stage. She did not create many roles herself; but yet, as a second or third-cast dancer she was well-loved by the Leningrad public, and praised by the critics.

Sizova was inhibited by several difficulties, including a back injury; she was forced to take an absence from the stage to be in hospital for some time. She then came back to the stage, and virtually started her dance career and her dancing roles anew—with no less success than before. Among the stars of the Kirov, Sizova was indeed a special personality, whose individuality was continuously expressed in her dynamic technique and performance style; every image created by her in movement was unusual, unlike that of any other dancer. She always managed to put an additional touch on everything, and her splendid footwork, brilliant jeté, and impeccable pointe work made her a most exciting performer to watch.

Sizova was a dancer of a purely classical style: she never attempted anything in the modern repertoire. But in her sphere she was a truly first-rate ballerina. Her "comeback", when Pierre Lacotte came to Leningrad from France to stage part of *La Vivandière*, emphasized this. Lacotte's version of the famous pas de six from Saint-Léon's ballet was based on material discovered in a library at the Louvre, and was staged for the Kirov in 1979. Sizova appeared on the stage again as one of the *Vivandière* soloists, and was as vivacious as ever, an outstanding technician whose exquisite pointe work was admired once more.

Sizova retired fairly recently (1988), and has become a teacher at the Vaganova School, where she works with students of the middle school. Soon, no doubt, she will be teaching the graduation class, and passing on her valuable inheritance of the Russian classical tradition.

—Igor Stupnikov

SKEAPING, Mary

British dancer, choreographer, teacher, and ballet director. Born in Woodford, 15 December 1902. Studied with Francesca Zanfretta, Laurent Novikov, Léonide Massine, Seraphina Astafieva, Stanislas Idzikowski, Lubov Egorova, Vera Trefilova, and Margaret Craske, London. Dancer, Anna Pavlova Company, seasons 1925 and 1930–31, also performing with Nemchinova–Dolin Company, from c.1927, Ballet Club (later Ballet Rambert), and in cabaret and music hall; ballet mistress, Sadler's Wells Ballet, 1948–51; guest ballet mistress and producer of classical ballets for various companies in Canada and Cuba, 1952–54; guest ballet mistress, becoming ballet director, Royal Swedish Ballet, 1952–62; authority on early ballet, staging re-creations of court ballets, often in collaboration with Ivo Cramér, at Drottningholm Court Theatre, Sweden; freelance producer of classical ballets, staging works in Britain, United States, Canada, Finland, Sweden, and Cuba; participator in various Swedish and British television programmes on dance history as well as lecturer and authority on court ballet; author, publishing articles on various historical ballets and on history of the Royal Swedish Ballet, and translator of eighteenth-century treatise on dance. Recipient: Member of the Order of the British Empire, 1958; Order of Gustav Vasa, Sweden, 1961; C. Ari Medal, 1971; King's Own Medal, Sweden, 1980. Died in London, 9 February 1984.

WORKS

1956   *Cupid out of his Humour* (mus. Purcell), Royal Swedish Ballet, Drottningholm Court Theatre, Sweden

1964   *Atis and Camilla* (mus. Roman), Royal Swedish Ballet, Drottningholm Court Theatre, Sweden

1965   *The Return of Springtime* (after F. Taglioni libretto; mus. Bossi), Ballet for All, London (also staged Swedish Ballet, 1966)

1967   *The New Narcissus* (with Cramér; mus. Dupuy), Drottningholm Ballet, Sweden

1971   *The Fishermen; or, The Girl from the Archipelago* (with Cramér, after Antoine Bournonville libretto, 1789; mus. Kraus), Royal Swedish Ballet, Drottningholm

1976   *La Dansomanie* (with Cramér, after Gardel libretto, 1800; mus. Méhul, arranged Farncombe), Royal Swedish Ballet, Drottningholm

1980   *The False Phantom* (with Cramér, after Terrade libretto), Cramér Ballet, Drottningholm

1981   *Harlequin's Death* (with Cramér, after Terrade libretto; mus. anonymous), Royal Swedish Ballet, Drottningholm

Also staged:

1953   *Swan Lake* (after Petipa, Ivanov; mus. Tchaikovsky), Royal Swedish Ballet, Stockholm (also staged Finnish Opera Ballet, 1953; Ballet Alicia Alonso, 1954; Bavarian State Opera Ballet, 1959)

      Giselle (after Petipa, Coralli, Perrot; mus. Adam), Royal Swedish Ballet, Stockholm (also staged Ballet Alicia Alonso, 1954; Frankfurt Ballet, 1968; London Festival Ballet, 1971; Göteborg Ballet, 1977; West Australian Ballet, 1984)

1955   *The Sleeping Beauty* (after Petipa; mus. Tchaikovsky), Royal Swedish Ballet, Stockholm (also staged Finnish Opera Ballet, 1955; American Ballet Theatre, 1976; Malmo Ballet, 1982)

1958   *Coppélia* (after Petipa, Cecchetti; mus. Delibes); Royal Swedish Ballet, Stockholm

PUBLICATIONS

By Skeaping:
"Music with Movement", *Dancing Times* (London), March 1937
"The Restoration of *Giselle*", *Dancing Times* (London), January 1954
"The Training of Soviet Dancers", *Dancing Times* (London), January 1957
"Fokine in Sweden", *Dancing Times* (London), May 1957
Ballet under the Three Crowns 1637–1792, New York, 1967
Interview in Woodruff, Diane L., "On Composing a Period Ballet: A Chat with Mary Skeaping", *Dance Scope* (New York), Spring 1970
"*Giselle*" (on the occasion of her production for London Festival Ballet), *Dance and Dancers* (London), May 1971
Interview in Anastos, Peter, "A Conversation with Mary Skeaping", *Ballet Review* (New York), vol. 6, no. 1, 1977
Balett på Stockholmsoperan, with Anna Greta Ståhle, Stockholm, 1979
Den Svenska Hovbaletten, Stockholm, 1983
Translation, with Anne Ivanova and Irmgard Berry, of Magri, Gennaro, *Theoretical and Practical Treatise on Dancing* (1779), London, 1988

About Skeaping:
Hagman, Bertil, "The Royal Swedish Ballet", *Dancing Times* (London), August 1957
Ståhle, Anna Greta, "Drottningholm's New Ballet Attraction", *Dans* (Stockholm), October 1976
Guest, Ivor, "Mary Skeaping, M. B. E.", *Dance Chronicle* (New York), vol. 7, no. 4, 1984–85
Koegler, Horst, "The Northern Heirs of Noverre", *Dance and Dancers* (London), February 1987

*   *   *

Mary Skeaping is possibly unique in the dance world, having gained prominence in both performance and research. To her, the two were inseparable, with research leading to greater understanding and authenticity of performance.

Her own career as a dancer did not bring her particular fame, as her nature made her a technically competent but uninspired dancer. She studied with most of the great teachers of the period, including Zanfretta, Novikov, Massine, Astafieva, and Idzikowski, and became a leading exponent of the Cecchetti Method under the tutelage of Margaret Craske. After two seasons with Pavlova's company and three years with the Nemchinova–Dolin Ballet, her insatiable curiosity about all dance forms stood her in good stead in the 1930s when she appeared in pantomime, cabaret, and music hall, as well as maintaining her links with classical ballet through performances with the Ballet Club. Her willingness to try experimental dance made her the natural "muse" for Rupert Doone and the Group Theatre which was the starting point for such British artists as Christopher Isherwood, W.H. Auden, and Benjamin Britten.

The 1930s also saw Skeaping's first ventures into dance research and her lifelong obsession with the authentic performance of Early Dance, guided at first by Melusine Wood, founder of the Historical Dance Branch of the ISTD (Imperial Society of Teachers of Dancing). Skeaping was given the chance to combine research and performance in this field when, in 1952, after a few years as Ballet Mistress for the Sadler's Wells Ballet, she was appointed Guest Ballet Mistress and then Artistic Director of the Royal Swedish Ballet in Stockholm. The Ballet also performed at the Drottningholm

Court Theatre, the only eighteenth-century perspective theatre still in use, and Skeaping was asked to create ballets using the technique of the period. She choreographed three original works and staged several more in collaboration with Ivo Cramér, all based on ballet libretti and derived from techniques and steps described in treatises from the seventeenth to early nineteenth centuries, which she avidly collected. One such treatise delighted her so much that she was sponsored by the Calouste Gulbenkian Foundation and the Radcliffe Trust to make an English translation. The translation and preparation of Gennaro Magri's *Trattato teorico-prattico di ballo* (Naples, 1779) occupied her right up to the time of her death and was completed by her assistant (Irmgard Berry), being published in 1988.

Amongst her duties as Director of the Royal Swedish Ballet, which she transformed from an appendix to the Opera company into a company in its own right with an international repertoire, Skeaping found the time for research, making her the leading authority on Sweden's long, if somewhat erratic, dance history. Her findings were originally published in a Dance Perspectives monograph and later expanded into two books published in Sweden.

Her research into early dance formed the basis of the first two programmes, in the 1960s, of Ballet For All, the education section of England's Royal Ballet. These programmes, in turn, gave her the chance to experiment in recreating choreography for the "lost" sections of the original score of *Giselle* which she then interpolated into her various productions of *Giselle*, the definitive version of which is danced by English National Ballet (formerly the London Festival Ballet). Since its London premiere in 1971, it has been hailed as capturing the Romantic style and is probably the closest in content to the 1841 original. Rightly so, it brought her international acclaim with both audiences and scholars alike and remains a fitting tribute to her devotion to the dance.

—Irmgard E. Berry

SKIBINE, George

Russian/American dancer, choreographer, and director. Born Yuril (Yura) Borisovich Skibin (Skibine), son of dancer Boris Skibine, in Yasnia Poliana, Ukraine, 20 January 1920. Moved to Paris as a child: studied with Olga Preobrazhenska, Julie Sedova, Alexandre Volinine, and Serge Lifar, Paris; also studied with Anatole Obukhov, Anatole Vilzak, and Mikhail Fokine, New York, and with Lubov Egorova and Eugenia Eduardova. Married dancer Marjorie Tallchief: two (twin) sons, Georges and Alexandre, b. 1952. Served in the American Army, 1942–45. Début as can-can dancer, Bal Tabarin, Paris, 1936; dancer, Ballets de la Jeunesse, 1937, (Denham's) Ballet Russe de Monte Carlo (previously Les Ballets de Monte Carlo), 1938–39; soloist, Ballets Russes de Colonel de Basil, 1939–41, touring Australia as Original Ballet Russe; dancer, American Ballet Theatre, 1941–42; soloist, Markova–Dolin Ballet, New York and U.S. tour, 1946, performing with Original Ballet Russe (de Colonel de Basil), 1947; dancer, from 1947, and étoile and choreographer, Grand Ballet du Marquis de Cuevas, 1950–56; guest artist, Ruth Page's Chicago Opera Ballet, 1956 and 1958–59; danseur étoile and choreographer, from 1957, and maître de ballet, Paris Opéra Ballet, 1958–62; artistic director and choreographer, Harkness Ballet, 1964–66; freelance choreographer, United States, South America, and Europe, 1967–68; artistic director, Dallas Civic Ballet, from 1969; also

George Skibine with Rosella Hightower in the pas de deux from *Raymonda*

teacher: founder, Dallas Ballet Academy; visiting professor, North Texas University. Recipient: Medal, French Association des Critiques Lyriques et Choréographiques (for his ballet *Concerto*), 1958; Italia Prize, 1962; Prix Diaghileff Institute, Paris, 1964; title of Chevalier dans l'Ordre des Arts et des Lettres, 1967. Died in Dallas, Texas, 14 January 1981.

ROLES

1938   The Stag in *Seventh Symphony* (Massine), Ballet Russe de Monte Carlo, Monte Carlo
       Ensemble (cr) in *Nobilissima Visione* (Massine), Ballet Russe de Monte Carlo, London
1940   A Senior Cadet (cr) in *Graduation Ball* (Lichine), Original Ballet Russe, Sydney
       Principal dancer (cr) in *La Lutte éternelle* (*The Eternal Struggle*; Schwezoff), Original Ballet Russe, Sydney
       Dancer in *Pavane* (Lifar), Original Ballet Russe, Los Angeles
1941   Coachman in *Petrushka* (Fokine), Ballet Theatre
       Principal dancer in *Les Sylphides* (Fokine), Ballet Theatre
       Prince Siegfried in *Swan Lake*, Act II (Dolin after Ivanov), Ballet Theatre
       The Prince in *Aurora's Wedding* (divertissements from *The Sleeping Beauty*; Dolin after Petipa), Ballet Theatre
       Colin in *La Fille mal gardée* (also staged as *The Wayward Daughter*; Nijinska), Ballet Theatre
       Evil in *The Beloved* (*La Bien-Aimée*; Nijinska), Ballet Theatre, Mexico City
       Jan (cr) in *Slavonika* (Psota), Ballet Theatre, Mexico City
       Prince Sapphire (cr) in *Bluebeard* (Fokine), Ballet Theatre, Mexico City

1942   Hermit (cr) in *Aleko* (Massine), Ballet Theatre, Mexico City
       Title role in *Russian Soldier* (Fokine), Ballet Theatre
1946   The Prince in *The Nutcracker* Pas de deux (after Ivanov), Markova–Dolin Ballet, U.S. tour
       Albrecht in *Giselle* (Petipa after Coralli, Perrot; staged Dolin), Markova–Dolin Ballet, U.S. tour
       The Slave in *Sebastian* (Caton), Original Ballet Russe, New York
       Principal dancer in *The Mute Wife* (Cobos), Original Ballet Russe, New York
       Hilarion in *Giselle* (Petipa after Coralli, Perrot; staged Dolin), Original Ballet Russe, New York
1947   Actaeon in *Aubade* (Lifar), Grand Ballet de Monte Carlo (du Marquis de Cuevas), Paris
       Polotvsian Chief in *Polovstian Dances from Prince Igor* (Fokine), Grand Ballet de Monte Carlo (du Marquis de Cuevas)
       Spring in *Istar* (Lifar), Grand Ballet de Monte Carlo (du Marquis de Cuevas)
       Principal dancer in *Passion* (Lifar), Grand Ballet de Monte Carlo (du Marquis de Cuevas)
       Principal dancer in *Noir et blanc* (Lifar), Grand Ballet de Monte Carlo (du Marquis de Cuevas)
       Principal dancer in *Constantia* (Dollar), Grand Ballet de Monte Carlo (du Marquis de Cuevas)
       Chanson dansée ("Athlete") in *Les Biches* (Nijinska), Grand Ballet de Monte Carlo (du Marquis de Cuevas)
1948   Principal dancer in *Concerto Barocco* (Balanchine), Grand Ballet de Monte Carlo (du Marquis de Cuevas)
       The Poet in *La Sonnambula* (Balanchine), Grand Ballet de Monte Carlo (du Marquis de Cuevas), London
1949   Hussar in *Le Beau Danube* (Massine), Grand Ballet de Monte Carlo (du Marquis de Cuevas)
       Principal dancer (cr) in *Un Coeur de diamant* (Lichine), Grand Ballet de Monte Carlo (du Marquis de Cuevas), Monte Carlo
       El Torero (cr) in *Del Amor y de la Muerte* (Ricarda), Grand Ballet de Monte Carlo (du Marquis de Cuevas)
       Principal dancer in *Concerto* (Nijinska), Grand Ballet de Monte Carlo (du Marquis de Cuevas)
1950   Roméo (cr) in *Tragédie à Vérone* (also chor.), Grand Ballet de Monte Carlo (du Marquis de Cuevas), Monte Carlo
1951   Principal dancer (cr) in *Les Saisons* (*Symphonie allégorique*; Massine), Grand Ballet du Marquis de Cuevas, Bordeaux
       Title role (cr) in *Scaramouche* (Hightower), Grand Ballet du Marquis de Cuevas, Paris
       The Poet (cr) in *Annabel Lee* (also chor.), Grand Ballet du Marquis de Cuevas, Deauville
       The Russian Officer (cr) in *Le Prisonnier du Caucase* (also chor.), Grand Ballet du Marquis de Cuevas, Paris
1952   Don Pedro (cr) in *Doña Ines de Castro* (Ricarda), Grand Ballet du Marquis de Cuevas, Cannes
       Principal dancer (cr) in *Scherzo* (Taras), Grand Ballet du Marquis de Cuevas
       Principal dancer (cr) in *Rondo Capriccioso* (Nijinska), Grand Ballet du Marquis de Cuevas, Paris
       Emperor Hadrian (cr) in *Antinoüs* (V. Gsovsky), Grand Ballet du Marquis de Cuevas, Bordeaux
1953   The Prince in *Princesse Aurore* (Nijinska after Petipa), Grand Ballet du Marquis de Cuevas
       The Ghost of her Lover (cr) in *L'Ange gris* (also chor.), Grand Ballet du Marquis de Cuevas, Deauville
1954   He (Black Stallion) (cr) in *Idylle* (also chor.), Grand

Ballet du Marquis de Cuevas, Paris
The Young Man (cr) in *La Reine insolente* (also chor.), Grand Ballet du Marquis de Cuevas, Metz

1955 The Sheikh (cr) in *Le Prince du désert* (also chor.), Grand Ballet du Marquis de Cuevas
Roméo (cr) in *Roméo et Juliette* (also chor., with Golovine, Skouratoff, Taras), Grand Ballet du Marquis de Cuevas, Paris

1956 Principal dancer in *Revenge* (Page), Chicago Opera Ballet, Chicago
Principal dancer in *The Merry Widow* (Page), Chicago Opera Ballet, Chicago

1957 Prince Ivan in *L'Oiseau de feu* (Lifar), Paris Opéra Ballet, Paris
Principal dancer (cr) in *Concerto* (also chor.), Opéra de Strasbourg, Strasbourg

1959 Daphnis (cr) in *Daphnis et Chloé* (also chor.), Paris Opéra Ballet, Paris
Roger (cr) in *Conte cruel* (also chor.), Paris Opéra Ballet, Paris

1960 Des Grieux in *La Dame aux camélias* (T. Gsovsky), Paris Opéra Ballet, Paris

Other roles include: principal dancer in *Camille* (R. Page), Prince in *Black Swan Pas de deux* (after Petipa), Basil in *Don Quixote* Pas de deux (Petipa), the Faune in *L'Apres-midi d'un faune* (Nijinsky), principal dancer in *Le Palais de cristal* (Balanchine), Rose Adagio from *The Sleeping Beauty* (Petipa), Hippolytus in *Phèdre* (Lifar), title role in *Russian Soldier* (Fokine), principal dancer in *Designs with Strings* (Taras), Poet in *Les Sylphides* (Fokine), Pas de deux from *Raymonda* (Petipa staged Egorova).

WORKS

1950 *Tragédie à Vérone* (mus. Tchaikovsky), Grand Ballet de Monte Carlo (du Marquis de Cuevas), Monte Carlo

1951 *La Femme muette* (mus. Paganini), Grand Ballet du Marquis de Cuevas
Annabel Lee (mus. Schiffmann), Grand Ballet du Marquis de Cuevas, Deauville
Le Prisonnier du Caucase (mus. Khachaturian), Grand Ballet du Marquis de Cuevas, Paris

1953 *L'Ange gris* (mus. Debussy), Grand Ballet du Marquis de Cuevas, Deauville

1954 *Idylle* (mus. Serette), Grand Ballet du Marquis de Cuevas, Paris (staged Paris Opéra, 1958)
Le Retour (mus. Prokofiev), Grand Ballet du Marquis de Cuevas
La Reine insolente (mus. Seretta), Grand Ballet du Marquis de Cuevas, Metz

1955 *Achille* (mus. La Rochefoucauld), Grand Ballet du Marquis de Cuevas, Cannes
Roméo et Juliette (with Golovine, Skouratoff, Taras; mus. Berlioz), Grand Ballet du Marquis de Cuevas, Paris
Le Prince du désert (mus. Damase), Grand Ballet du Marquis de Cuevas, Paris

1956 *Pastorale* (mus. Couperin), Grand Ballet du Marquis de Cuevas, Paris

1957 *Concerto* (mus. Jolivet), Opéra de Strasbourg, Strasbourg

1958 *Les Fâcheuses Rencontres* (mus. Jarre), Edinburgh International Ballet, Edinburgh
L'Atlantide (with Lifar; mus. Tomasi), Paris Opéra Ballet, Paris
Symphonie de danses (mus. Lesur), Jeunesses Musicales Francaises (JMF), Salle Pleyel, Paris
Isoline (mus. Messager), Opéra-Comique, Paris

1959 *Daphnis et Chloé* (mus. Ravel), Paris Opéra Ballet, Paris
Conte cruel (mus. Delerue), Paris Opéra Ballet, Paris

1960 *Ombres lunaires* (mus. Jolivet), Opéra-Comique, Paris
Divertimento (mus. Rivier), Opéra de Strasbourg, Strasbourg

1961 *Marines* (mus. Jolivet), Opéra-Comique, Paris
Pastorale (mus. Couperin), Versailles, (staged Paris Opéra, 1961)
Metamorphoses (mus. Hindemith), Teatro Colón, Buenos Aires
Ophélie (mus. Bergmann), Opéra, Metz

1962 *Symboli Christiani*, Opéra, Nice

1963 *Le Proscrit* (mus. Kosma), Opéra, Nice
Danses breves (previously *Divertimento*; mus. Rivier), Opéra-Comique, Paris

1965 *Carrefour* (mus. Milhaud), Harkness Ballet, New York
Pas d'action (after Petipa; mus. Tchaikovsky), Harkness Ballet, New York

1966 *Sarabande* (mus. Couperin), Harkness Ballet, Temple, Arizona
Venta Quemada (mus. Surinach), Harkness Ballet, New York
La Péri (mus. Dukas), Paris Opéra Ballet, Paris

1967 *Four Moons* (with Hightower, Jasinsky, Terekoff), Oklahoma Festival
L'Oiseau de feu (mus. Stravinsky), French television
Suite Bergamasque (mus. Debussy), Louisville Civic Ballet
Roméo et Juliette (mus. Tchaikovsky), Louisville Civic Ballet

1968 *Aurora's Wedding* (from *The Sleeping Beauty*; mus. Tchaikovsky), Dallas Civic Ballet, Dallas
L'Oiseau de feu (mus. Stravinsky), Dallas Civic Ballet, Dallas

1969 *Les Bandar Log* (mus. Koechlin), Opéra-Comique, Paris
Le Soleil des eaux (mus. Boulez), Ballet Théâtre Contemporain, Amiens

1970 *La Légende des cerfs* (mus. Bartók), Ballet Théâtre Contemporain, Amiens

1974 *Gloria* (mus. Poulenc), Dallas Civic Ballet, Dallas

1975 *Schéhérazade* (mus. Hossein), Maison de la Culture, Rheims

1976 *Les Indes galantes* (with Guiliano; mus. Rameau), Ballet de Wallonie

1977 *Roméo et Juliette* (mus. Prokofiev), Ballet Royal de Wallonie

PUBLICATIONS

By Skibine:
"Joies et regrets", *La Danse* (Paris), January 1956
Interview in "An Interview with Marjorie Tallchief and George Skibine", *Dance Magazine* (New York), December 1956
Interview with Sonia Roberts, *Ballet Today* (London), November 1957
Anastos, Peter, "A Conversation with George Skibine", *Ballet Review* (New York), Spring 1982

About Skibine:
Manchester, P.W., "George Skibine", *Dancers and Critics*, London, 1950

Davidson, Gladys, *Ballet Biographies*, revised edition, London, 1954

Beaumont, Cyril, *Ballets Past and Present*, London, 1955

Glotz, Michel, *Georges Skibine*, Paris, 1955

Percival, John, "Accent on the Male: George Skibine", *Dance and Dancers* (London), January 1959

Lobet, M., *Le Ballet français d'aujourd'hui*, Brussels, 1959

Nemenchousky, Leon, *A Day with Marjorie Tallchief and George Skibine*, London, 1960

Lidova, Irène, "George Skibine", *Saisons de la danse*, 1970

Anastos, Peter, "George Skibine", *Ballet News* (New York), April 1981

*   *   *

One of the few romantic dancers of his time, George Skibine was the epitome of a fairy-tale "prince charming". Tall and elegant, with a handsome face lit by intense blue eyes, Skibine was most successful as the poet in *Les Sylphides*, the slave in *Sebastian*, the tragic king in *Doña Ines de Castro*, Romeo, Daphnis, and, above all, as the handsome stranger in *La Sonnambula*, a ballet which he stamped with his own personality, at once lyrical and virile.

The son of a dancer—his father, Boris, had been a member of the Ballets Russes—George (Yura to his friends) was brought up in Paris and made his début on stage at the age of sixteen, in the French can-can at the Bal Tabarin. His teachers were Julie Sedova, Olga Preobrazhenska, and Alexandre Volinine. His first success was in the role of the stag in Massine's famous ballet to Beethoven, *Seventh Symphony*. This was with the Ballet Russe de Monte Carlo, where Massine was ballet master. Skibine impressed audiences, not only with his physique but also with his expressive interpretation and his remarkable stage presence.

When war was declared, Skibine joined Colonel de Basil's company and went to Australia, then Latin America, ending up in New York where he became a soloist with Ballet Theatre (later American Ballet Theatre) in 1941. With Alicia Markova as his partner, he created *Aleko*, a ballet by Massine inspired by one of Pushkin's poems.

In 1942 Skibine joined the American army and in 1944 found himself back in Europe taking part in the invasion of Normandy. But 1947 saw the start of his brilliant European career as the leading dancer of a new company, Grand Ballet de Monte Carlo, directed by the Marquis George de Cuevas. For this company (also known as the Grand Ballet du Marquis de Cuevas, and much later as the International Ballet), Skibine danced many brilliant roles, and he married his partner, ballerina Marjorie Tallchief.

Georges Skibine began his choreographic career in 1950 with *Tragédie à Vérone*, a shortened version of the story of Romeo and Juliet, which he danced with Ethéry Pagava. This was followed by other works and gradually he became the chief choreographer of the company. Skibine was neither an innovator nor a revolutionary. The neoclassical style which he had inherited from his teachers—Lifar, Massine, and Fokine—formed the basis of his works, and he created colourful tableaux and poetic moods. His great success, *Les Prisonniers du Caucase*, was taken from Georgian folklore. His popular pas de trois, *Idylle*, was a triumph for his wife, Marjorie Tallchief, who danced the role of a flirtatious white filly torn between two handsome stallions.

In 1958 Skibine became maître de ballet of the Paris Opéra. While there his most successful ballets were *Daphnis et Chloé*, which he danced with Claude Bessy, and a more modern work, *Concerto* (originally staged in Strasbourg), to music by René Jolivet. In 1964 he accepted Rebekah Harkness's offer to create, with massive financial support, the Harkness Ballet, whose neo-modernist style would ultimately clash with the aesthetics of Skibine, its artistic director. He retired and became a freelance choreographer, working at the Teatro Colón de Buenos Aires, then in Belgium, and eventually leaving Europe for good in 1969 to settle in Dallas, Texas. He became director of a dance academy and worked for the ballet company, the Dallas Civic Ballet.

Skibine died prematurely in 1981. Although essentially Slav by nature and later an American citizen, Skibine nevertheless belonged to France, where he spent his childhood and experienced his first, and perhaps greatest, successes.

—Irène Lidova

SKOURATOFF, Vladimir

French dancer and teacher. Born in Paris, 12 March 1925. Studied with Olga Preobrazhenska, and later with Alexandre Volinine and Boris Kniasev. Early career as corps de ballet dancer at the Lido, Paris; performed with dancer Janine Charrat in recitals, Théâtre Sarah Bernhardt, and with Jeanmaire in Lifar ballets, Salle Pleyel, Paris, 1945; soloist, Nouveau Ballet de Monte Carlo, 1946; dancer, (de Basil's) Original Ballet Russe, London season, 1947, also appearing with concert groups including Les Étoiles de la danse and at Nijinsky Galas, London; dancer, Ballets de Paris, from 1948; leading dancer, touring with Tamara Toumanova and Yvette Chauviré, including at Maggio Musicale, Florence, 1950; leading dancer, Ballets des Champs-Elysées, 1951, Grand Ballet du Marquis de Cuevas, 1952–57; international guest artist, including for Ballet Théâtre Français, touring 1958, with London Festival Ballet, 1959, and with Scandinavian Ballet, 1960; also teacher, Geneva Opera, from 1963, and Strasbourg Opera, 1966–67; maître de ballet, Bordeaux Opera, 1970–90.

ROLES

1945	Principal dancer (cr) in *Mephisto Valse* (Lifar), Gala, Paris
	Dancer (cr) in *Reveil* (solo; Lifar), Gala, Paris
	Colas in *La Fille mal gardée* (extracts; Balashova), Salle Pleyel, Paris
1946	Acteon (cr) in *Aubade* (Lifar), Nouveau Ballet de Monte Carlo, Monte Carlo
	Principal dancer in *Noir et blanc* (Lifar), Nouveau Ballet de Monte Carlo, Monte Carlo
	Dancer in *Pygmalion* (Lifar), Nouveau Ballet de Monte Carlo, Monte Carlo
	Pas de deux (cr) in *La Péri* (Lifar), Nouveau Ballet de Monte Carlo, Monte Carlo
	Ensemble (cr) in *Nautéos* (Lifar), Nouveau Ballet de Monte Carlo, Monte Carlo
	Roméo in *Roméo et Juliette* (Lifar), Nouveau Ballet de Monte Carlo, Monte Carlo
	Principal dancer in *La Mort du cygne* (Lifar), Nouveau Ballet de Monte Carlo, Monte Carlo
	Principal dancer (cr) in *Dramma per musica* (Lifar), Nouveau Ballet de Monte Carlo, Monte Carlo
	Avtandil (cr) in *Chota Roustaveli* (Lifar), Nouveau Ballet de Monte Carlo, Monte Carlo
	Principal dancer (cr) in *Passion* (Lifar), Nouveau Ballet de Monte Carlo, Monte Carlo

Solo (cr) in *Gayanéh* (*Danse du sabre*; Lifar), Nouveau Ballet de Monte Carlo, Monte Carlo

1947 Variation in *Aurora's Wedding* (from *The Sleeping Beauty*; after Petipa), Original Ballet Russe

Principal dancer ("Poet") in *Les Sylphides* (Fokine), Original Ballet Russe

Slave in *Schéhérazade* (Fokine), Original Ballet Russe

1948 Principal dancer (cr) in *La Femme et son ombre* (Charrat), Ballets de Paris

Death (cr) in *'adame Miroir* (Charrat), Ballets de Paris, Paris

Principal dancer (cr) in *Que Le Diable l'emporte* (Petit), Ballets de Paris, Paris

Principal dancer (cr) in *Études symphoniques* (Kniaseff), Ballets de Paris, Paris

The Dandy in *Le Beau Danube* (Massine), Ballets de Paris

The Baron in *Les Demoiselles de la nuit* (Petit), Ballets de Paris

Pas de deux from *The Sleeping Beauty* (Petipa), Ballets de Paris

1949 A Chef (cr) in *L'Oeuf à la coque* (Petit), Ballets de Paris, London

Pas de deux from *The Nutcracker* (after Ivanov), Ballets de Paris

Tancredi in *Le Combat* (Dollar), Ballets de Paris

Pas de deux from *Swan Lake* (Petipa), Toumanova tour

Basil in *Don Quixote* Pas de deux (after Petipa), Toumanova tour

The Danseur (cr) in *Grand Pas classique* (*Grand Pas d'Auber*; pas de deux; V. Gsovsky), Ballets des Champs-Elysées, Paris

1950 Principal dancer in *Suite romantique*, Maggio Musicale Fiorentino, Florence

Prince in *L'Oiseau de feu* Pas de deux (Chauviré), Maggio Musicale Fiorentino, Florence

Principal dancer in *Balla senza musica* (Milloss), Venice Festival

Principal dancer in *Le Prince de bois* (Milloss), Venice Festival

1951 Principal dancer (cr) in *Romanza Romana* (Staff), Ballets des Champs-Elysées, Paris

Principal dancer (cr) in *Revanche* (R. Page), Ballets des Champs-Elysées, Paris

Oedipus in *Le Rencontre* (Lichine), Ballets des Champs-Elysées, Paris

Conjuror in *Les Forains* (Petit), Ballets des Champs-Elysées, Paris

The Young Man in *Le Rendezvous* (Petit), Ballets des Champs-Elysées, Paris

Gigolo (cr) in *Scaramouche* (Hightower), Grand Ballet du Marquis de Cuevas, Paris

1952 Principal dancer (cr) in *Coup de feu* (Milloss), Grand Ballet du Marquis de Cuevas, Paris

Principal dancer (cr) in *Une Nuit d'été* (Taras), Grand Ballet du Marquis de Cuevas, Paris

Principal dancer (cr) in *Scherzo* (Taras), Grand Ballet du Marquis de Cuevas, Paris

Le Jeune Bagnard (cr) in *Piège de lumière* (Taras), Grand Ballet du Marquis de Cuevas, Paris

Principal dancer (cr) in *La Tertulia* (Ricarda), Grand Ballet du Marquis de Cuevas, Paris

Principal dancer (cr) in *Antinoüs* (V. Gsovsky), Grand Ballet du Marquis de Cuevas, Bordeaux

1953 Principal dancer (cr) in *L'Aigrette* (Bartholin), Grand Ballet du Marquis de Cuevas, Cannes

1954 The Gypsy (cr) in *Saeta* (Ricarda), Grand Ballet du Marquis de Cuevas, Paris

"The Other" (The Circus Horse) (cr) in *Idylle* (Skibine), Grand Ballet du Marquis de Cuevas, Paris

Principal dancer (cr) in *Achille* (Skibine), Grand Ballet du Marquis de Cuevas, Cannes

Principal dancer (cr) in *Scarlattiana* (also chor.), Grand Ballet du Marquis de Cuevas, Paris

1956 A Lover (cr) in *Le Pont* (Starbuck), Grand Ballet du Marquis de Cuevas, Deauville

1957 Principal dancer (cr) in *Fiesta* (Martinez), Grand Ballet du Marquis de Cuevas, Paris

Emperor (cr) in *La Chanson de l'éternelle Tristesse* (Ricarda), Grand Ballet du Marquis de Cuevas, Paris

1958 Principal dancer (cr) in *Le Rendezvous manqué* (Taras, Lurio), Opéra de Monte Carlo, Monte Carlo

1959 Albrecht in *Giselle* (Petipa after Coralli, Perrot; staged Dolin), London Festival Ballet

Dancer in *La Tyrolienne* (pas de deux; Markova), London Festival Ballet

Other roles include: principal dancer in *Bolero* (Nijinska), Chief Warrior in *Polovtsian Dances from Prince Igor* (Fokine; staged Taras), Hussar in *Le Beau Danube* (Massine), principal dancer in *Constantia* (Dollar).

WORKS

1954 *Scarlattiana* (mus. Scarlatti), Grand Ballet du Marquis de Cuevas

1957 *Perlimplinade*, Grand Ballet de Marquis de Cuevas

1979 *Un Dimanche à l'Aube*, Grand Theatre, Bordeaux

PUBLICATIONS

Beaumont, Cyril, "Les Étoiles de la danse", *Ballet* (London), February 1948

Lidova, Irène, "Vladimir Skouratoff", *La Danse* (Paris), no. 3, 1949

Brunelleschi, Elsa, "Six Dancers of the Ballets des Champs-Elysées", *Ballet* (London), November 1951

Lidova, Irène, *16 Visages de la danse française*, Paris, 1953

Daguerre, P., *Le Marquis de Cuevas*, Paris, 1954

Percival, John, "Accent on the Male: Vladimir Skouratoff", *Dance and Dancers* (London), December 1959

* * *

Vladimir Skouratoff belongs to that generation of dancers which appeared so miraculously during the dark years of the Occupation in a cold and hungry Paris. Among his colleagues were Janine Charrat, Jean Babilée, Nina Vyroubova, Zizi Jeanmaire, and Alexandre Kalioujny. They all passed through the studio Wacker, where the great Olga Preobrazhenska reigned alongside Victor Gsovsky and Mme Roussane.

Skouratoff's childhood was full of hardship and he learned to dance largely in order to earn a living. While an adolescent he performed in Russian cabarets. Fiery, dynamic, and quick on his feet, he was ideally suited to Russian and Caucasian folk dances. This early work prevented him from achieving the absolute purity required of classical dance, but his virile temperament singled him out as a demi-caractère dancer. He never attempted the great romantic roles, the poet in *Les Sylphides*, or the princes in the full-length *Sleeping Beauty* or *Swan Lake*. He was much more a natural interpreter of the character ballets of Massine or of Fokine, or certain contemporary choreographers. It was his meeting with Zizi Jeanmaire in 1946 which set the seal on his career. He became her regular partner and went with her to Monte Carlo, where Serge Lifar was setting up a new company, the Nouveau Ballet de Monte Carlo.

The strong temperament and character of the young Skouratoff were revealed in *Aubade*, to music by Poulenc, in which he partnered Zizi Jeanmaire. He portrayed Acteon, seductive and spirited, at grips with a ravishing but cruel Diana. In Lifar's ballet *Chota Roustaveli* he gave a brilliant interpretation of the *lezginka* (a Georgian folk dance). In 1948, still as Jeanmaire's partner, he took part in the first season of Roland Petit's Ballets de Paris, creating leading roles in Petit's *Que le Diable l'emporte* and Charrat's *La Femme et son ombre*. He also joined Yvette Chauviré in a season of the Ballets des Champs-Elysées, creating with her Auber's *Grand Pas classique*, a demanding pas de deux which is still danced today by many stars. He was also the principal dancer in *Revanche*, the last production by the Ballets des Champs-Elysées choreographed by Ruth Page. The high point in Skouratoff's career, however, was his collaboration with the Grand Ballet du Marquis de Cuevas, which he joined in 1952. He created several roles, including *La Tertulia*, by Anna Ricarda, *Idylle*, by George Skibine, and most notably *Piège de lumière*, choreographed by John Taras to music by J.M. Damase, in which he portrayed an escaped convict who is captivated by the butterflies in a virgin forest and then goes mad. This ballet showed him to be an exceptionally talented dramatic dancer.

After leaving the Ballet du Marquis de Cuevas, Skouratoff became a freelance dancer. In 1958 he was one of the leading dancers in a ballet by Françoise Sagan, *Le Rendezvous manqué*, with choreography by John Taras for the Opéra de Monte-Carlo. His partner was Danish ballerina Toni Lander. In 1963 he settled in Geneva, and although he kept the title of "danseur étoile" he began a teaching career with the municipal opera. Later, he became a teacher in Strasbourg before finally settling down in Bordeaux, in 1970, at the Grand Theatre. He worked there for twenty years as ballet director and choreographer before retiring in 1990. Skouratoff's name seldom appeared in the press and he remained very much in the shadows, the ballets he choreographed for the theatre in Bordeaux being reworkings of his previous successes.

Skouratoff never achieved international fame as a dancer and yet he possessed a masculine charm and a spirited personality which made him a perfect demi-caractère dancer, something which is found less and less often nowadays in the theatre.

—Irène Lidova

Mia Slavenska, c.1950

SLAVENSKA, Mia

Yugoslavian/American dancer, teacher, choreographer, and ballet director. Born Mia Čorak in Brod-na-Savi (later Slavonski-Brod), Croatia (former Yugoslavia), 20 February 1916 (some sources say 1914). Studied at the Ballet School of the National Ballet Theatre, Zagreb, pupil of Josephine Weiss and Margarita Froman, 1921–34; studied ballet with Leopold (Leo) Dubois and free-dance with Gertrud Kraus, Vienna, 1928–30; also studied with Lubov Egorova, Mathilde Kshesinskaya, and Olga Preobrazhenska, Paris, from 1931, and with Vincenzo Celli, New York, from 1938. Married Kurt Neumann, 1946: one daughter, Maria, b. 1947. Début, when still a child, Zagreb, 1922; soloist, National Theatre (State Opera House), Zagreb, 1931–33, becoming prima ballerina, 1934–35; principal dancer, (Denham's) Ballet Russe de Monte Carlo, 1938–42, returning as guest artist, various seasons 1948–56; founder of own touring group, Slavenska, Tihmar and Company, 1944–45, and of Slavenska Ballet Variante, touring United States, Canada, and South America, various seasons 1947–52; co-founder (with Frederic Franklin), co-director, and choreographer, Slavenska-Franklin Ballet, 1952–55, touring North America and abroad, including Japan; guest ballerina, London Festival Ballet and Ballet Theatre (later American Ballet Theatre), 1951, Metropolitan Opera Ballet, New York, 1954–55; also guest artist for Ruth Page's Chicago Opera Ballet, Robert Joffrey Ballet, Cleveland Ballet, Jacob's Pillow Dance Festival, Boston Arts Festival; also appeared in film *La Mort du cygne* (U.S. title: *Ballerina*; Benoît-Levy, Epstein, 1937), in musical film *Song without Words* (California, 1945), and in musical *On Your Toes* (mus. Rodgers; Chicago, 1953); ballerina and guest director, Louisville Ballet, 1956–58; director, Fort Worth Civic Ballet, Texas, 1958–60; also teacher: founder and teacher of own studio, Hollywood, California, 1946–47; teacher, Virigina Self Dance Studio, Dallas, Texas, 1960; also teacher in New York, 1960s; member of faculty of dance, University of California at Los Angeles, and at School of Dance at California Institute of the Arts. Recipient: First Prize at Dance Olympics, Berlin, 1936; Plaque d'honneur, France, 1937.

ROLES

1934/ 36	Swanilda in *Coppélia* (Froman), State Opera House, Zagreb
	Title role in *Firebird* (Froman), State Opera House, Zagreb
	Zobéïde in *Schéhérazade* (Froman), State Opera House, Zagreb
	Columbine in *Carnaval* (Froman), State Opera House, Zagreb
	The Bride in *The Gingerbread Heart* (Froman), State Opera House, Zagreb
	The Young Girl in *Imbrek-with-the-Nose* (Froman), State Opera House, Zagreb
1936	Melchola (cr) in *David triomphant* (Lifar), Gala de la Maison internationale d'étudiants, Paris
1938	Bluebird Pas de deux from *The Sleeping Beauty* (Petipa), Gala performance (with Anton Dolin), London
	Glove-Seller in *Gaîté parisienne* (Massine), Ballet Russe de Monte Carlo, Monte Carlo
	Title role in *Giselle* (Petipa after Coralli, Perrot; staged Lifar), Ballet Russe de Monte Carlo, London
	Anastachiuska (cr) in *Bogatyri* (Massine), Ballet Russe de Monte Carlo, New York
1938/ 42	Odette in *Swan Lake*, Act II (after Ivanov), Ballet Russe de Monte Carlo
	Swanilda in *Coppélia* (Sergeyev after Petipa, Cecchetti), Ballet Russe de Monte Carlo
	Sugar Plum Fairy in The *Nutcracker* (Fedorova after Ivanov), Ballet Russe de Monte Carlo
	Columbine in *Carnaval* (Fokine), Ballet Russe de Monte Carlo
	The Young Girl in *Le Spectre de la rose* (Fokine), Ballet Russe de Monte Carlo
	Waltz, Mazurka in *Les Sylphides* (Fokine), Ballet Russe de Monte Carlo
	Zobéïde in *Schéhérazade* (Fokine), Ballet Russe de Monte Carlo
	Principal dancer in *Les Elfes* (Fokine), Ballet Russe de Monte Carlo
	Principal dancer in *Seventh Symphony* (Massine), Ballet Russe de Monte Carlo
1939	Gypsy Girl in *Capriccio espagnol* (Massine), Ballet Russe de Monte Carlo, London
	Eilley Orum (cr) in *Ghost Town* (Platoff), Ballet Russe de Monte Carlo, New York
1940	Fairy in *Le Baiser de la fée* (Balanchine), Ballet Russe de Monte Carlo
	Princess Lieven (cr) in *Vienna—1814* (Massine), Ballet Russe de Monte Carlo, New York
1948	Carlotta Grisi in *Pas de quatre* (Dolin), Ballet Russe de Monte Carlo, New York
1952	Blanche Dubois (cr) in *A Streetcar Named Desire* (Valerie Bettis), Slavenska-Franklin Ballet, Quebec
1955	Principal dancer (cr) in *Vittorio* (Solov), Metropolitan Opera Ballet, New York
1956	Title role (cr) in *Medea* (Weidman), Dance Festival, Louisville

WORKS

1944/ 45	*Symphonic Variations* (mus. Franck), Slavenska, Tihmar and Company, U.S. tour
	Trilogy (mus. Chopin), Slavenska, Tihmar and Company, U.S. tour
1947/ 52	*Concerto Romantique* (mus. Liszt), Slavenska Ballet Variante
	Settlers Sunday (mus. Byrns), Slavenska Ballet Variante
1953	*La Petite Danseuse à quatre ans* (mus. Dohnanyi), Slavenska-Franklin Ballet
1960	*Chiaroscuro* (mus. Saint-Saëns), Fort Worth Ballet Arts, Fort Worth, Texas

Other works include: for concert performances in Zagreb— *Harleguinade* (mus. Debussy), *Arabesque* (mus. Debussy), *La Plus que lente* (mus. Debussy), *En bateau* (mus. Debussy), *Sacre et profane* (mus. Debussy), *Ald Vienna Impressions* (mus. Strauss), *Iberia* (mus. Albeniz), *The Dear Story* (mus. Kunc), *L'Enfant s'endore* (mus. Schumann), *Pas d'action* (mus. Glazunov), *Salomé* (mus. Glazunov), *Suite de danse* (mus. Corelli), *La Folia* (mus. Corelli), *Funeral March* (mus. Beethoven), *Gypsy Airs* (mus. Sarasatte), *Poskocnica* (mus. Gotovac), *Balkan Sketches* (mus. Tajcevic), *Young Croatian Girl* (mus. Safranek-Kavec), *Perpetual Motion* (mus. Rimsky-Korsakov); for Louisville Ballet and Fort Worth Ballet companies—stagings of *Les Sylphides* (after Fokine; mus. Chopin), *Swan Lake*, Act II (after Ivanov; mus. Tchaikovsky), *Coppélia*, Act III (after Petipa, Cecchetti; mus. Delibes), *The Nutcracker* ("Kingdom of the Sweets", after Ivanov; mus. Tchaikovsky), *Pas de quatre* (after Dolin; mus. Pugni).

PUBLICATIONS

Pierre, Dorathi, "Mia Slavenska", *Dance Magazine* (New York), September 1942

Terry, Walter, *Invitation to the Dance*, New York, 1942

Denby, Edwin, *Looking at the Dance*, New York, 1949

Schnoor, Jack, "At Home with Mia Slavenska", *Dance Magazine* (New York), January 1955

Swisher, Viola, "Mia Slavenska: A Study in Contrasts", *Dance Magazine* (New York), March 1973

Anderson, Jack, *The One and Only: The Ballet Russe de Monte Carlo*, New York, 1981

Sorley Walker, Kathrine, *De Basil's Ballets Russes*, London, 1982

Tallmann, Margaret, "Dancescape", *Dance Magazine* (New York), August 1990

*   *   *

Mia Slavenska, known professionally in her early years as Mia Čorak, was famous as a child prodigy, and later became a ballerina of virtuoso "terre-à-terre" technique. She won equal recognition as company director, choreographer, and teacher. Born on the eve of World War I in Slavonski-Brod, Slavenska studied ballet in Zagreb with Josephine Weiss and Margarita Froman and later in Vienna, supplementing her studies in ballet with classes in modern dance with Gertrud Kraus and Lily von Weiden. Subsequently, in Paris, her teachers were the former Imperial Russian ballerinas, Kshesinksaya, Egorova, and Preobrazhenska. She praised her Vienna teacher Leo Dubois in particular for teaching her the meaning of classicism, whereas Godlewski she considered more of a circus acrobat than a dancer.

Slavenska danced with the Yugoslav State Opera at Zagreb as a ballerina, and then with the Opéra Russe in Paris. She won first prize at the 1936 Dance Olympics in Berlin, which led to guest appearances with Serge Lifar and Anton Dolin and a tour with her own group. She co-starred with Lifar, Yvette Chauviré, and Janine Charrat in J. Benoît-Levy's film *La Mort du cygne* (released in America as *Ballerina*), for which Lifar was choreographer. Mia Slavenska was ballerina with the Ballet Russe de Monte Carlo at its birth in 1938 from René Blum's Ballets de Monte Carlo, touring throughout the Western hemisphere. She settled permanently in the United States in the 1940s, eventually becoming an American citizen.

Slavenska's dancing had great clarity, energy, and stamina; her balances on pointe were legendary. With red-blonde hair and a well-shaped body (although perhaps somewhat short-legged by today's standards), she looked glamorous in the Ballet Russe editions of the classics and in works by choreographers Bronislava Nijinska, Léonide Massine, George Balanchine, and Serge Lifar. Gradually, however, she began to spend more time with her own touring groups, which included Slavenska and Company, Ballet Variante, and the Slavenska–Franklin Ballet, for which she was co-director, ballerina, and choreographer. Regular guest appearances continued with such big companies as Ballet Theatre, Festival Ballet (London), Ruth Page's Chicago Opera Ballet, and the Robert Joffrey Ballet (with André Eglevsky as partner). Considered suitable for worldly rather than spiritual roles at first, Slavenska matured into an actress and stylist of wide range. The hit of her last dancing years was Valerie Bettis's choreographic version of the Tennessee Williams play *A Streetcar Named Desire*, created in 1952 for the Slavenska–Franklin company. This was the ballet, more than any other, which confirmed Slavenska's talents as a dancer-actress, and critics applauded the "uncommon brilliance and dramatic force" (as Walter Terry put it) of her interpretation of the role of Blanche. In the late 1950s, for three seasons, Slavenska also became director of the Forth Worth Civic Ballet in Texas.

Slavenska's teaching career began in the 1960s, first in New York City—where she was a favorite ballet teacher to many modern and post-modern dancers of the time—and then in Los Angeles, especially at the University of California.

"She is a performer, rather than an interpreter or creator", wrote Walter Terry of Mia Slavenska, pointing to the ballerina's technique of presenting, "in handsome fashion", "her own personal beauty, her perfect technique, and all the outlines and some of the substance of the ballets in which she appears". Ballet Russe dancer Robert Lindgren remembered that "The one ballerina who occasionally added embellishments to the steps was Slavenska, who, being a virtuoso, liked to make steps harder." The magazine *Dance* in 1940 called Mia Slavenska, in terms of technique, the "strongest dancer" of the company, saying, "With exceptional aplomb, fine beats and turns, Slavenska is a dramatic dancer who delights any audience."

Slavenska, whose daughter Maria (Mrs. Joseph Ramos) is a historian, was in 1990 collaborating with her daughter on a book which is to be an autobiographical view of her life in ballet.

—George Jackson

THE SLEEPING BEAUTY
(*La Belle au bois dormant*; Russian title: *Spyashchaya Krasavitsa*)

Choreography: Marius Petipa
Music: Petr Ilyich Tchaikovsky
Design: Ivan Andreyev, Mikhail Bocharov, Konstantin Ivanov, Heinrich Levogt, Matvei Shishkov, and Ivan Vsevolozhsky
Libretto: Marius Petipa and Ivan Vsevolozhsky, after Charles Perrault
First Production: Maryinsky Theatre, St. Petersburg, 15 January (3 January old style) 1890
Principal Dancers: Carlotta Brianza (Princess Aurora), Pavel Gerdt (Prince Désiré), Marie Petipa (Lilac Fairy), Enrico Cecchetti (Carabosse and Bluebird), Varvara Nikitina (Princess Florine)

Other productions include: Teatro alla Scala (chor. Giorgio Saracco after Petipa), with Carlotta Brianza (Princess Aurora); Milan, 11 March 1896. Bolshoi Theatre (staged and revised Aleksandr Gorsky, design Anatoly Geltser and Karl Valts), with Lubov Roslavleva (Princess Aurora), Ivan Clustine (Désiré); Moscow, 29 January (17 January old style) 1899 (same version staged Maryinsky Theatre, 1914). Anna Pavlova Company (shortened version; staged Clustine after Petipa), with Pavlova (Princess Aurora); New York, 31 August 1916. Ballets Russes de Serge Diaghilev (restaged Nicholas Sergeyev after Petipa, with additional chor. Bronislava Nijinska, design Léon Bakst), as *The Sleeping Princess*, with Olga Spessivtseva (as Spessiva; Princess Aurora), Pierre Vladimirov (Prince Charming), Lydia Lopokova (Lilac Fairy and Bluebird, as "Enchanted Princess"), Carlotta Brianza (Carabosse), and Stanislas Idzikowski (Bluebird); London, 2 November 1921. State Academic Theatre for Opera and Ballet, or GATOB (staged and revised Fedor Lopukhov after Petipa), with Elisaveta Gerdt (Aurora), Mikhail Dudko (Prince Désiré); Petrograd, 8 October 1922. Bolshoi Theatre (staged Vasily Tikhomirov after Petipa), with Ekaterina Geltser (Princess Aurora), Tikhomirov (Prince Désiré); Moscow, 25 May 1924. Lithuanian National Opera Ballet (staged Nicholas Zverev after Petipa, design Mstislav Dobuzhinsky); Kaunas, 1934. Philadelphia Ballet (new version; chor. Catherine Littlefield partly after Petipa); Philadelphia, 12 February 1937. Mordkin Ballet (shortened version; staged Mikhail Mordkin after Petipa); Waterbury, Connecticut, 1937. Vic-Wells Ballet (staged Nicholas Sergeyev after Petipa, design Nadia Benois), with Margot Fonteyn (Princess Aurora), Robert Helpmann (Prince Charming), as *The Sleeping Princess*; London, 2 February 1939. Ballet Theatre (suite of divertissements from ballet; staged Anton Dolin after Petipa), as *Princess Aurora*, with Irina Baronova (Princess Aurora), Dolin (Prince Charming); Mexico City, 23 October 1941. Sadler's Wells Ballet (staged Nicholas Sergeyev after Petipa, with additional chor. Frederick Ashton and Ninette de Valois, design Oliver Messel), as *The Sleeping Beauty*; with Margot Fonteyn (Princess Aurora), Robert Helpmann (Prince Florimund), Beryl Grey (Lilac Fairy), Pamela May and Alexis Rassine (Bluebirds); London, 20 February 1946. International Ballet (staged Nicholas Sergeyev after Petipa); London, 24 May 1948. Kirov Ballet (staged Konstantin Sergeyev after Petipa), with Natalia Dudinskaya (Princess Aurora), Sergeyev (Désiré); Leningrad, 25 March 1952. Royal Swedish Ballet (staged Mary Skeaping after Petipa); Stockholm, 13 January 1955. Royal Danish Ballet (staged de Valois, Peggy van Praagh after Sergeyev); Copenhagen, 8 May 1957. Grand Ballet du Marquis de Cuevas (staged Robert Helpmann and Nijinska after

The Sleeping Beauty, as performed by the Kirov Ballet, Leningrad, 1965

Sergeyev); Paris, 25 October 1960. Bolshoi Ballet (staged Yuri Grigorovich after Petipa), with Maya Plisetskaya (Princess Aurora), Nikolai Fadeyechev (Prince Désiré); Moscow, 7 December 1963. Ballet of La Scala (staged and revised Rudolf Nureyev, design Nicholas Georgiadis); Milan, 22 September 1966 (also staged for National Ballet of Canada, 1972, and London Festival Ballet, 1975). German Opera Ballet (staged Kenneth MacMillan after Petipa, design Barry Kay); Berlin, 8 October 1967 (also staged for Royal Ballet, design Peter Farmer, 1973). Royal Ballet (new production; staged Peter Wright and Frederick Ashton after Petipa, design Henry Bardon, Lila de'Nobili and Rostislav Dobuzhinsky); London, 17 December 1968. Paris Opéra Ballet (staged Alicia Alonso after Petipa); Paris, 31 December 1974. American Ballet Theatre (staged Mary Skeaping after Petipa, design Oliver Messel), with Natalia Makarova (Princess Aurora), Mikhail Baryshnikov (Prince Florimund), Martine van Hamel (Lilac Fairy); New York, 15 June 1976. New York City Ballet (staged Peter Martins after Petipa), with Darci Kistler (Aurora), Ben Huys (Prince), Kyra Nichols (Lilac Fairy), Merrill Ashley (Carabosse); New York, 24 April 1991.

PUBLICATIONS

Beaumont, Cyril, *Complete Book of Ballets*, revised edition, London, 1951

Petipa, Marius, *Russian Ballet Master: The Memoirs of Marius Petipa*, translated by Helen Wittaker, edited by Lillian Moore, London, 1958

Barnes, Clive, "*The Sleeping Beauty*", *Dance and Dancers* (London), 2 parts: May, June 1961

Krasovskaya, Vera, *Russian Ballet Theatre of the Second Half of the Nineteenth Century*, Leningrad and Moscow, 1963

Roslavleva, Natalia, *Era of the Russian Ballet*, London, 1966

Anderson, Jack, "*The Sleeping Beauty*: A History of Her Perambulations", *Dance Magazine* (New York), June 1969

Kirstein, Lincoln, *Movement and Metaphor: Four Centuries of Ballet*, New York, 1970

Krassovskaya, Vera, *Marius Petipa and the Sleeping Beauty*, translated by Cynthia Read, New York, 1972

Maynard, Olga, "*The Sleeping Beauty*", *Dance Magazine* (New York), December 1972

Lopukhov, Fedor, and Asafiev, Boris, "Annals of *The Sleeping Beauty*", *Ballet Review* (Brooklyn, N.Y.), vol. 5, no. 4, 1975–76

Vaughan, David, "Aurora Awakened", *Ballet Review* (Brooklyn, N.Y.), vol. 6, no. 4, 1977–78

Wiley, Roland John, *Tchaikovsky's Ballets*, Oxford, 1985

Percival, John, "A Beauty Past Compare", *Dance and Dancers* (London), March 1990

Wiley, Roland John, *A Century of Russian Ballet: Documents and Accounts 1810–1910*, Oxford, 1990

Gruen, John, "Peter Martins Tackles *The Sleeping Beauty*", *Dance Magazine* (New York), April 1991

Scholl, Tim, "Anticipating a New *Sleeping Beauty*", *Ballet Review* (New York), Spring 1991

*   *   *

Modern writers on Petipa's *The Sleeping Beauty* tend to view the work as the summit of Marius Petipa's achievement and the chef d'oeuvre of nineteenth-century Russian ballet. Certainly, the work represents a high point in the career of the ballet master and Russian nineteenth-century choreography, but this view fails to acknowledge the work's importance for twentieth-century ballet or the significance of the work's homage to French dance of the seventeenth and eighteenth centuries. In anticipating the main trends in twentieth-century ballet as it cast a backward glance to the origins of the art form, *The Sleeping Beauty* summarized the Russian ballet's achievement in adapting and refining a foreign art form as it indicated a new direction for ballet in the coming decades.

From its inception, *The Sleeping Beauty* was planned as a

The Sleeping Beauty, **with Anthony Dowell and Antoinette Sibley, Royal Ballet, London, 1968**

tribute to the artistic culture of pre-revolutionary France—the culture that gave Russia its ballet in the eighteenth century. Ivan Vsevolozhsky, then the director of Russia's Imperial Theatres, suggested a ballet based on Perrault's *La Belle au bois dormant* to Petr Tchaikovsky in 1888. Vsevolozhsky himself designed the costumes in Louis XIV style, and suggested Lully and Rameau as models for his composer. Petipa, who played an active role in the authorship of the ballet's libretto as well as its choreography, had studied with Auguste Vestris and provided a tangible link to the traditions of the French ballet of the grand siècle. The resulting work borrowed liberally from the French court ballet of the seventeenth and eighteenth centuries. In addition to Vsevolozhsky's strict period costuming and Tchaikovsky's oblique musical references to grand siècle France, Vsevolozhsky and Petipa devised a libretto that used French flourishes to stylize the work, which bears structural similarities to the old *ballet à entrées* form. Court processionals begin the prologue and the third acts, effectively framing the ballet with *entrées*. The third act is comprised of the *entrées* of the fairy-tale characters.

The libretto of *The Sleeping Beauty* follows Perrault in the prologue, but the action of the remaining three acts is adapted to conform to the ballet structure that had evolved in Russia in the nineteenth century. The Romantic ballet's juxtaposition of the realistic and the fantastic—the material/spirit dichotomy of works such as *Giselle* and *La Sylphide*—remained an important compositional device in late nineteenth-century Russian ballet (well into the period of high literary realism). The fairy-tale setting of *The Sleeping Beauty* allowed for a more satisfactory adaptation of this plot structure than was the case in the majority of Petipa's *grands ballets*. The first act of the work (Princess Aurora's birthday party and début) is the most "real". Aurora is pricked on the finger with Carabosse's spindle and the resulting hundred years' sleep provide the transition to the "unreal" world of the Prince's vision in the second act. But in *The Sleeping Beauty* the narrative exigencies of the Romantic ballet are met in abstract rather than naturalistic terms. Aurora's "madness" is communicated by her deformation of classical enchaînements rather than the histrionics that signal Giselle's; the "walls" that separate Aurora and the Prince in the vision scene are never so literal or substantive as in *Giselle*, though they convey a similar sense of romantic hopelessness. Even the expected wedding celebration (Petipa's favourite finale to the romantic ballet's two-act formula) features characters from Perrault's tales rather than the usual national dances.

The coherence that characterized the narrative of *The Sleeping Beauty* was replicated in other aspects of the original production as well, even though the ballet's derivation from Perrault's fairy tale was a source of great concern among the cognoscenti of Petersburg's ballet world, who feared the incursion of the flashy, low-genre "ballet-féerie" on the imperial theatre stage. Petipa had borrowed from the féerie before, but *The Sleeping Beauty* was reputed to be the most expensive ballet the Imperial Theatres had ever produced. And although the astonishing success of the ballet's first production testified to its novelty as well as its innovation, the latter was not generally appreciated at the time of the work's premiere.

Even though the creators of *The Sleeping Beauty* mimicked the staging and production values of the foreign ballets-féeries, they produced a work that was hailed as a true balletic *Gesamtkunstwerk* by members of the next generation of workers in Russian ballet, those associated with Diaghilev's Ballets Russes. As Alexandre Benois and other Ballets Russes associates would later testify, the ballet showed the way to the Diaghilev "formula" of ballet production—essentially, the creation of the ballet as a *Gesamtkunstwerk*, or total art work, in which all elements (dance, music, décor, narrative) were designed to harmonize with one another. The meticulously planned production of *The Sleeping Beauty* was the first to approximate the Wagnerian ideal, though credit for this innovation usually goes to Diaghilev.

The Sleeping Beauty remains in the repertories of the world's great ballet companies because of the challenges and opportunities it presents to companies, dancers, and audiences. The choreography offers a complete syllabus of academic and character dance styles. The ballet charts the history of its art form in displaying a diapason of dancing that spans academic styles and the social dance forms from which the danse d'école developed. Its famous set pieces feature virtuoso academic variations (the fairies' variations in the prologue) as well as character dances (the fairy-tale characters' dances in the third act); the dances derived from social dancing forms include those practiced in the courts (in the second act) and dances of more democratic origins (the garland dance in the first act). The variety of these dances, and the hierarchy of the genres represented, suggests the complexity of ballet academy that had evolved in Russia at the end of the nineteenth century. *The Sleeping Beauty* is the work that best attests to that achievement.

—Tim Scholl

SMITH, George Washington

American dancer, ballet master, and teacher. Born in Philadelphia, c. 1820. Self-taught dancer, possibly also studying with Paul Hazard and Jules Martin, Philadelphia; later studied with James Sylvain (partner to Fanny Elssler on American tour). Married Mary Coffee, 1854: 10 children, including dancer Joseph Smith, b. 1875. Performer, including as clog-dancer, at Chestnut Street, Walnut Street, and other small theatres, Philadelphia, 1830s; début as dancer possibly in 1832; dancer with Fanny Elssler's company, beginning in Philadelphia from 1840, and touring United States and Cuba until 1842; partner to American ballerina Mary Anne Lee, from 1845, performing in first American *Giselle*, Boston, 1846, and reappearing with her in Philadelphia, 1852; first dancer and ballet master, Bowery Theatre, New York, from 1847; ballet master, Arch Street Theatre, Philadelphia, Autumn 1850; first dancer and ballet master, Brougham's Lyceum Theatre, New York, 1850–51; choreographer and dancing partner for Lola Montez, 1851–52, for Señorita (Pepita) Soto, touring United States, 1853–54, and for Louise Ducy-Barre, 1855–57; principal dancer in the opera and ballet company of Domenico Ronzani, 1859; ballet master, Theatre Comique, Boston, 1867–68; also ballet master for Fox's American (Variety) Theatre, Philadelphia; toured with Barnum's Roman Hippodrome, staging circus ballets, 1870s; also teacher throughout stage career, opening own school in Philadelphia, 1881–99; musician, arranging and probably composing scores for own ballets. Died in Philadelphia, 18 February 1899.

ROLES

1842   Sawbones in *Mazulme; or, The Black Raven of the Tombs* (also *The Night Owl*; traditional pantomime after the Ravels), Walnut Street Theatre, Philadelphia

1843   Flodoardo in *Mazulme; or The Black Raven of the Tombs* (also *The Night Owl*; traditional pantomime after the

George Washington Smith

Ravels), Walnut Street Theatre, Philadelphia

Fan-Fan La Julipe (cr) in *The Three Lovers; or, Mad as a March Hare* (ballet; Barnes), Walnut Street Theatre, Philadelphia

François (cr) in *Vol au Vent* (comic pantomime; Barnes), Walnut Street Theatre, Philadelphia

Leonardo (cr) in *Harlequin and the Ocean Imp* (comic pantomime; Barnes), Walnut Street Theatre, Philadelphia

1844   Dancer in *The Imp and the Elements* (pantomimic romance), Walnut Street Theatre, Philadelphia

Jemmy (cr) in *The Ladder of Love* (comic ballet), Walnut Street Theatre, Philadelphia

Bolero in *Gustave III* (opera; mus. Auber), Chesnut Street Theatre, Philadelphia

Pas de deux, Comic Pas, Comic Allemande (cr) in *A Night's Adventures* (ballet), Walnut Street Theatre, Philadelphia

Harlequin in *Mazulme; or, The Black Raven of the Tombs* (also *The Night Owl*; traditional pantomime after the Ravels), Walnut Street Theatre, Philadelphia

Hassan in *The Arabian Nights' Entertainment* (pantomime), Arch Street Theatre, Philadelphia

1845   Benedict in *La Jolie Fille de Gand* (Lee after Albert), Arch Street Theatre, Philadelphia

Rudolf in *Fleur des Champs* (after Taglioni's *La Fille du Danube*; staged Lee), Arch Street Theatre, Philadelphia

1846   Albrecht in *Giselle* (after Coralli, Perrot; staged Lee), Howard Atheneum, Boston

1847   Leading role in *Nathalie, la Laitière Suisse* (own staging, after Taglioni), Bowery Theatre, New York

1848   Lubin (cr) in *The Magic Flute* (probably also chor.), Bowery Theatre, New York

Endymion in *Diana and Endymion*, Bowery Theatre, New York

Roland (cr) in *The Abduction of Nina* (Neri), Bowery Theatre, New York

1849   Micos in *Eagle Eye* (equestrian drama), Bowery Theatre, New York

Principal dancer (cr) in *Les Jardinières* (Neri), Bowery Theatre, New York

Divertissement from *William Tell* (opera; mus. Rossini), Bowery Theatre, New York

Robin Red Breast in *Mother Bunch and her Magic Rooster* (pantomime; prod. Wood), National Amphitheatre, Philadelphia

Harlequin in *Mother Bunch and her Magic Rooster* (pantomime; prod. Wood), National Amphitheatre, Philadelphia

1851   Colin in *The Jolly Millers*, New York

Max Starner (cr) in *Betly, the Tyrolean* (also chor.), Broadway Theatre, New York

1852   Marco (cr) in *Un Jour de Carnaval à Seville* (also chor.), New York

1853   Jota Aragonesa, Pas de Matelot (cr) in *Carnival de Seville* (restaging of *Un Jour de Carnaval à Seville*; also chor.), Philadelphia

Leading role (cr) in *La Maja de Seville* (new production; also chor.), Philadelphia

King of the Tagus (cr) in *La Belle de l'Andalusia; or, The Daughter of the Tagus* (possibly after *La Fille du Danube*; also chor.), Chestnut Street Theatre, Philadelphia

1854   Grand Pas de deux (cr; also chor.) in *Semiramide* (opera; mus. Rossini), Academy of Music, New York

1855   Dancer (cr) in *L'Ecos del Tyrol* (pas de trois, divertissement), Boston

Pas de deux in *La Favorita* (opera; mus. Donizetti), Boston

Minuet in *Don Giovanni* (opera; mus. Mozart), Boston

Roucem, Chief of the Eunuchs (cr) in *La Péri* (probably own staging, after Coralli), Metropolitan Theatre, New York

Leading role (cr) in *Masaniello* (ballet version of *La Muette de Portici*; also chor.), Metropolitan Theatre, New York

Chevalier Bariano in *Mazulme* (traditional pantomime after the Ravels), National Theatre, New York

1856   Mazurka-Cracovienne (cr) added to *The Slave Actress* (play), Burton's New Theatre, New York

Pas de deux in *The Bottle Imp* ("legendary drama"), Burton's New Theatre, New York

Ivan (cr) in *Bluebelle* (after Mazilier's *Le Diable à quatre*), Burton's New Theatre, New York

1859   Gringoire in *Esmeralda* (Ronzani after Perrot), Ronzani Company, Philadelphia

Pierre in *La Bouquetière* (possibly ballet version of Adam's opera), Ronzani Company, Philadelphia

Teseo in *The Fountain of Love*, Ronzani Company, Boston

Fernandez in *Jocko* (traditional ballet-pantomime), Ronzani Company, Boston

Conrad in *The Corsair* (Ronzani after Mazilier), Ronzani Company, Boston

Ernest, a Duke in *Nathalie* (probably Ronzani), Ronzani Company, Boston

Grand Pastoral Divertissement (cr; also chor.) in *Faust and Marguerite* (play after Goethe), Walnut Street Theatre, Philadelphia

1861   Mazurka (cr; also chor.) in *Un Ballo in Maschera* (opera; mus. Verdi), Niblo's Garden, Philadelphia

1868   Henri (cr) in *La Doctor del Confusion* (also chor.), Boston Comique Ballet and Pantomime Troupe, New York

Other roles include: divertissements and solos—*Pas de Sabot* (solo), *Pas de Matelot* (solo), *Pas de Tambourine* (from American production of *Giselle*), *Pas de Deux*, *La Sicilienne*, *La Taquerette*, *La Manola*, *El Bolero de Cadiz* (probably after Elssler), *La Zingarella* (pas de deux), *Polka Nationale*, *Pas Styrien*, *The Spider Dance* (tarantella pas de deux with Montez).

WORKS

Staged:

1847   *Giselle* (after Coralli, Perrot; mus. Adam), Bowery Theatre, New York (restaged in 1867)

Nathalie, la Laitière Suisse (after Taglioni, as performed by Elssler), Bowery Theatre, New York

1848   *Fleur des Champs* (after Taglioni's *La Fille du Danube*), Bowery Theatre, New York

?The Magic Flute (mus. and libretto unknown; most likely choreographed by Smith), Bowery Theatre, New York

1851   *Betly, the Tyrolean* (mus. probably Adam), Broadway Theatre, New York

1852   *Un Jour de Carnaval à Seville* (mus. probably various), New York

Diana and her Nymphs, New York

1853   *Carnival de Seville* (restaging of *Un Jour de Carnaval à Seville*, with new Jota Aragonesa, Pas de Matelot; mus. probably various), Philadelphia

La Maja de Seville (new production), Philadelphia

La Belle de l'Andalusia; or, The Daughter of the Tagus (possibly after Taglioni's *La Fille du Danube*; mus. probably Adam), Chestnut Street Theatre, Philadelphia

1855   *La Péri* (after Coralli; mus. Burgmüller; probably staged by Smith), Metropolitan Theatre, New York

Masaniello (ballet version of *La Muette de Portici*; mus. Auber), Metropolitan Theatre, New York

1856   *?Les Lanciers Quadrille* (possibly staged by Smith), Burton's New Theatre, New York

?La Fille de l'Air (pas de deux; possibly staged by Smith), Burton's New Theatre, New York

?La Nymph des Bois (possibly restaging of *Diana and her Nymphs*; or version of new ballet, *The Nymph of the Chase*, described in notebooks), Burton's New Theatre, New York

1857   *Mose's Dream* (pantomimic ballet), Bowery Theatre, New York

1859   Grand Pastoral Divertissement, Final Scene in *Faust and Marguerite* (play after Goethe), Walnut Street Theatre, Philadelphia

1861   Mazurka in *Un Ballo in Maschera* (opera; mus. Verdi), Niblo's Garden, Philadelphia

The Seven Sisters ("extravaganza" previously produced by Laura Keene), Howard Atheneum, Boston

1867   Grand Turkish Ballet, Grand Transformation Scene in *The Forty Thieves* (pantomime), Theatre Comique, Boston

The Naiad Queen, Boston Theatre, Boston

1868   Divertissements in *The Devil's Auction*, Theatre Comique, Boston

La Doctor del Confusion, Boston Comique Ballet and Pantomime Troupe, New York

Dances and Marches in *The Black Crook*, Walnut Street Theatre, Philadelphia

Other works include: *Medora* (after *The Corsaire*; mus. Adam), restagings of *La Jolie Fille de Gand* (after Albert).

PUBLICATIONS

Clapp, William W., *A Record of the Boston Stage*, Boston, 1853; reprinted 1968

Tompkins, Eugene, *The History of the Boston Theatre 1854–1901*, New York, 1908; reprinted 1969

Brown, T. Allston, *History of the American Stage*, New York, 1909

O'Dell, George, *Annals of the New York Stage*, New York, 1927–49

Moore, Lillian, "George Washington Smith", *Dance Index* (New York), June-August 1945; reprinted in Magriel, Paul (ed.), *Chronicles of the American Dance*, New York, 1948

Moore, Lillian, "Some Early American Dancers", *Dancing Times* (London), August 1950

Todd, Arthur, "Four Centuries of American Dance", *Dance Magazine* (New York), September 1950

Cohen, Selma Jeanne, "The Fourth of July, or the Independence of American Dance", *Dance Magazine* (New York), July 1976

Barker, Barbara, *Ballet or Ballyhoo*, New York, 1984

*   *   *

George Washington Smith played an important role in the history of dance in the United States, establishing ballet as a popular dance form, bringing major Romantic ballets to the American stage, and setting high standards for ballet technique among male—as well as female—dancers. His many talents included classical dancing, pantomime, choreography, teaching ballet and social dancing, clowning, acting, and even singing for occasional roles. His stage career spanned over 45 years, making him the best-known American ballet dancer of his age, and giving him extensive experience on stage and in the studio.

Beginning his professional life as a stonemason in Philadelphia, Smith learned clog dancing by imitating other stage personalities, perhaps including John Durang, an earlier Philadelphia performer. It is likely that Smith took advantage of every opportunity to expand and polish his dance technique, probably studying with Paul H. Hazard, a Paris Opéra-trained dancer who taught several professional American dancers of this period. However, it was James Sylvain, the Irish ballet dancer and partner to Fanny Elssler during her American tour, who was Smith's chief teacher. Elssler hired Smith as one of her corps, probably during her September 1841 visit to Philadelphia, and he took advantage of Sylvain's knowledge not only of academic ballet technique, but also of the classical Harlequin tradition developed by James Byrne, which featured considerable dance virtuosity. It is also likely that Smith studied with Jules Martin of the Paris Opéra, who had been on Elssler's American tour and remained in Philadelphia after her return to Europe.

Elssler herself was probably the major artistic influence in

Smith's life, establishing a model of grace, technique, and taste by which Smith measured all dance and dancers in his continuing career. From Elssler, Smith also learned several important European ballets (*La Tarantule*, *La Sylphide*, *La Somnambule*, *La Gypsy*, *La Bayadère*, *Nathalie*), acquired a taste for Spanish-style divertissements, and learned partnering technique. This latter skill served him well, for he partnered nearly all the best American and European ballerinas dancing in the United States in the second half of the nineteenth century, including Mary Ann Lee, Julia Turnbull, Anna Walters, Giovanna Ciocca, Louise Ducy-Barre, Pepita Soto, Louise Lamoureaux, Annetta Galletti, Giuseppina Morlacchi, and Esmeralda Diani, in addition to Elssler herself. These dancers, trained by renowned teachers in Paris and Milan, valued Smith highly as a danseur, hired him to stage their ballets, and provided him with opportunities to demonstrate his own dancing skills. Clearly, both American and European ballet stars appreciated Smith, for such celebrated performers as Leon Espinosa and Mlle. Albertine volunteered to dance at his New York benefit, and Lola Montez hired him as her ballet master and partner during her 1851–52 tour of the United States. Even American newspaper critics, who then focused their commentary almost exclusively on the ballerina, felt moved to praise Smith's dancing and—on occasion—his stagings.

Although Smith may have studied in Paris, records are unclear on this point, and the French ballets which he restaged in America were learned from other dancers: from Elssler, the ballet *Nathalie*, and from Mary Ann Lee the ballets *Giselle*, *La Fille du Danube* (which he staged as *Fleur des Champs*), and *La Jolie Fille de Gand*. He also restaged divertissements learned from these and other artists, as well as creating works of his own such as *La Maja de Sevilla* and a "Pas de Sabot" (perhaps a version of his earlier clog dancing). He also did his own stagings of the popular extravaganza *The Black Crook*, and created the choreography for the pantomime spectacle, *Mose's Dream*. A devoted music-lover, Smith prepared many of the orchestral parts for the ballets he staged, and occasionally even wrote music for them.

Apart from his ballet work, Smith continued throughout his career to play various roles in the harlequinades then popular in the United States, particularly the long-lived *Mazulme*, in which he rose to play the lead. These pantomime roles often gave Smith an opportunity to show off his dancing skills, for such virtuosic steps as multiple pirouettes and turns en l'air were included in these works.

As a teacher, Smith was able to establish a regular school in Philadelphia shortly before his retirement from the stage in 1883, although previously he had taught whenever possible. His classes included not only academic ballet technique but also social dances and Spanish dancing, and he even made his pupils' ballet slippers for them. Two of his best-known students were his son, Joseph Smith, who inherited his father's versatility in ballet, pantomime, and social dance, and Bessie Clayton, a child vaudeville prodigy who in her day was compared with Adeline Genée.

Smith remained a peculiarly American performer. Although he briefly transformed his name to "Smythe" early in his career, he soon resumed the more straightforward spelling. He staged an American Indian dance for the drama *Eagle Eye*, and brought his dancing and his ballets to nearly every major city in the American Northeast and South. His eagerness to grasp every opportunity to perfect his technique, his skill in restaging established dance works to the best advantage of the ballerinas with whom he worked, his originality in creating new works as required by each dancer or each show, his versatility as a performer, and his loyalty to his home town of Philadelphia

further demonstrated his American ingenuity in this pioneering period of ballet in the United States.

—Lynn Matluck Brooks

SMITH, Oliver

American designer and company director. Born Oliver Lemuel Smith in Waupawn, Wisconsin, 13 February 1918. Studied at Pennsylvania State University, 1936–39. Freelance stage designer, New York, from 1941; co-director, with Lucia Chase, of Ballet Theatre (later American Ballet Theatre), New York, 1945–80, continuing as designer for Ballet Theatre, the Marquis de Cuevas International Ballet, and New York City Ballet, as well as for theatre and opera; leading designer (and occasional producer) of numerous Broadway stage musicals, including *Brigadoon* (chor. de Mille, 1947), *Gentlemen Prefer Blondes* (chor. de Mille, 1949), *On Your Toes* (ballet *Slaughter on Tenth Avenue*, chor. Balanchine, 1954), *My Fair Lady* (1956), *Candide* (1956), *West Side Story* (chor. Robbins, 1957), *Camelot* (1960), and *Hello Dolly!* (1964), and for films, including *Band Wagon* (dir. Minnelli, 1953), *Oklahoma!* (dir. Zinnemann, 1955), *Guys and Dolls* (dir. Mankiewicz, 1955), and *Porgy and Bess* (dir. Preminger, 1959); member of the National Council for the Arts, Washington, D.C., 1965–70; returned as co-director, American Ballet Theatre, New York, 1990. Recipient: Donaldson Award, New York, 1946, 1947, 1949, 1953; New York Drama Critics Award, 1956, 1957, 1959, 1960, 1964; Antoinette Perry ("Tony") Award, New York, 1960; Pennsylvania State University Distinguished Alumnus Award, 1962; Handel Medallion of the City of New York, 1975.

WORKS (Ballet designs)

1941   *Saratoga* (chor. Massine), Ballet Russe de Monte Carlo, New York

1942   *Rodeo* (chor. de Mille), Ballet Russe de Monte Carlo, New York

1944   *Fancy Free* (chor. Robbins), Ballet Theatre, New York
       Waltz Academy (scenery; chor. Balanchine), Ballet Theatre, Boston
       Sebastian (chor. Caton), (de Cuevas's) Ballet International, New York

1945   *Interplay* (scenery; chor. Robbins), Ballet Theatre, New York
       On Stage! (chor. Kidd), Ballet Theatre, Boston

1946   *Facsimile* (scenery; chor. Robbins), Ballet Theatre, New York

1948   *Fall River Legend* (chor. de Mille), Ballet Theatre, New York

1950   *The Age of Anxiety* (chor. Robbins), New York City Ballet, New York
       Nimbus (scenery; chor. Tudor), Ballet Theatre, New York

1961   *Points on Jazz* (chor. Krupska), American Ballet Theatre, Hartford, Connecticut

1965   *Les Noces* (chor. Robbins), New York City Ballet, New York

1967   *Swan Lake* (chor. Petipa, Ivanov; staged Blair), American Ballet Theatre, New York
       Harbinger (scenery; chor. Feld), American Ballet Theatre, Miami
       The Catherine Wheel (scenery; chor. Smuin), American

Ballet Theatre, Madison, Wisconsin
1968 *Giselle* (scenery; chor. Blair after Petipa, Coralli, Perrot), American Ballet Theatre, Washington, D.C.
1970 *Petrushka* (chor. Fokine; scenery and costumes adapted from Benois), American Ballet Theatre, New York
1974 *The Sleeping Beauty*, Act III (scenery; chor. Petipa, staged Blair), New York City Ballet, New York
1979 *Contredances* (chor. Tetley), American Ballet Theatre, New York

PUBLICATIONS

By Smith:
"Ballet Design", *Dance News Annual* (New York), 1953
American Ballet Theatre: 36 Years of Scenic and Costume Design (exhibition catalogue), New York, 1976

About Smith:
Amberg, George, *Art in Modern Ballet*, London, 1946
Barret, Dorothy, "Man Behind the Scenes", *Dance Magazine* (New York), March 1946
Fatt, Amelia, "Designers for the Dance", *Dance Magazine* (New York), 1967
Barsacq, Léon, *Le Décor de Film*, Paris, 1970; as *Caligari's Cabinet and Other Grand Illusions*, Boston, 1976
Maynard, Olga, "American Ballet Theatre: The Figure in the Prism", *Dance Magazine* (New York), January 1975
Clarke, Mary, and Crisp, Clement, *Design for Ballet*, London, 1978
Payne, Charles, *American Ballet Theatre*, New York, 1978
Hardy, Camille, "A Treasure in Transition: ABT", *Dance Magazine* (New York), May 1985
Denby, Edwin, *Dance Writings*, edited by Robert Cornfield and William Mackay, New York, 1986

*   *   *

Between 1945 and 1980, Lucia Chase was acknowledged as the director of American Ballet Theatre. She was involved in the daily operation of the company, in its financial and administrative affairs, and in dealings with the dancers and other personnel. But during this entire time the voice of her co-director Oliver Smith was heard along with hers in artistic decisions—in the choice of repertoire and in the choice of designers to enhance that repertoire.

Smith's was a self-assured voice. He knew his own taste, and he knew what he wanted to see on stage. Furthermore, he was the company's highly valued resident designer with about 30 ballet productions to his credit. As time went on, he also became the most sought-after designer on Broadway, with about 300 shows bearing his signature. He has also been a highly successful producer in that medium.

Chase and Smith both left American Ballet Theatre in 1980. But in 1990, when Jane Hermann succeeded Mikhail Baryshnikov at the helm, the company logo read, "Jane Hermann and Oliver Smith, directors". Smith's artistic judgment was again being called into play.

Oliver Smith's very first ballet production was Léonide Massine's *Saratoga*, created for the Ballet Russe de Monte Carlo in 1941. By the next year he had already evolved a "look" which is still associated with him today. This highly characteristic style was first seen in the drops for Agnes de Mille's *Rodeo*. One of these depicted a corral. It revealed Smith's predilection for the illusion of space as expressed through a receding perspective; the impression was one of endless flat land and equally endless open sky. Another Smith "trademark" was

evidenced in his drop depicting the ranch house parlor, where the final festivities of *Rodeo* took place. It consisted of a structure whose interior and surrounding landscape were simultaneously part of the action. Here Smith's architectural training came into play, as it was often to do in subsequent ballets. And, in his bold, clear colors united with the simplicity of his drawing, he seemed to be inspired by American painters like Edward Hopper and N.C. Wyeth.

In the Victorian house he designed in 1948 for Agnes de Mille's *Fall River Legend*, the architectural approach was especially impressive as well as integral to the dance action. It was as though part of this gloomy place had burned down, leaving the cramped living room with its three closely placed chairs for Lizzie Borden, her father, and her stepmother. There was an indoor staircase, and there was a door at the back of the room, but neither seemed to lead anywhere. The upper reaches of the house were a fragmented framework through which the sky could be seen. One of the timbers of the house also resembled the scaffold from which, in the final scene, the murderess would be hanged.

Oliver Smith is extremely sensitive to the spatial demands of dance. He is also responsive to its content. For Jerome Robbins's *Fancy Free* he seemed to shift from draftsman to cartoonist as he lightly outlined a bar-room and a tilted street-light outside. The playful set seemed almost to dance, and yet it created an environment as real as Robbins's sailors and their girls.

In his concept for Robbins's *Les Noces*, Smith juxtaposed intimacy and grandeur. The action of this Russian peasant wedding took place before small units more symbolical than literal, but the whole stage was unified by five huge, remote-looking icons. They elevated the ballet to the heroic dimension suggested by the Stravinsky score.

The décor of nineteenth-century ballets often tends to encumber the stage and dwarf the dancers. But even here, Smith has applied his deft hand. The *Swan Lake* he designed for David Blair's 1967 production emphasized the form but not the heaviness of the ballet's gothic environment—and so the lyricism of both the music and the choreography were underscored.

While in ballet he is consistently aware of the dancers, in his Broadway shows it is often the sets which do the moving. Smith makes imaginative use of turntables and other mechanical appurtenances. Here he also allows himself to be more lush, to give free rein to his penchant for drawing. Among his most memorable Broadway musicals are *Brigadoon*, *My Fair Lady*, *Candide*, *Camelot*, and *Hello, Dolly!* His designs for *West Side Story* stand apart from these. Because so much of the action in this production was devoted to dance, Smith returned to his spare, architectural look.

The variety in Oliver Smith's style also derives from his pleasure in functioning as part of a team. That may partially account for his long association with American Ballet Theatre.

—Doris Hering

SNOEK, Hans
Dutch dancer, choreographer, and ballet director. Born Johanna Snoek in Geertruidenberg, 29 December 1910. Studied with Kurt Jooss and Sigurd Leeder, Folkwangschule, Essen, 1929–31. Married producer Erik de Vries, 1951. Dancer, Folkwang Tanzbühne, Essen Opera (director Kurt Jooss), Essen, 1929–31, "Wagner Society", Amsterdam, Dutch Ballet

Company, and Yvonne Georgi company, Amsterdam and The Hague; teacher and organizer of small performing group, Amsterdam, World War II; founder, artistic director, and choreographer, Scapino Ballet, Amsterdam, 1945–70; co-founder, Scapino Academy, 1959, receiving official recognition from Dutch Ministry of Culture, 1968; co-founder, "Danscontact", educational dance and choreography programme; also choreographer for television, and producer of educational children's television programmes. Recipient: titles of Knight of the Orde van Oranje Nassau, 1960; Officer of the Orde van Oranje Nassau, 1970.

WORKS

1946 De Gouden Zwaan (The Golden Swan; mus. van Delden), Scapino Ballet, Amsterdam
Der Toverfluit (The Magic Flute; mus. Franken), Scapino Ballet, Amsterdam

1947 De Pasja en de Beer (The Pasha and the Bear; mus. van Delden), Scapino Ballet, Amsterdam
Het Papiernoodballet (The Paper-shortage Ballet; mus. Lankester), Scapino Ballet, Amsterdam

1948 Het Roversballet (The Robbers' Ballet; mus. Franken), Scapino Ballet, Amsterdam

1949 De Krekel en de mier (The Cricket and the Ant; mus. Schubert), Scapino Ballet, Amsterdam

1950 Dorp zonder Mannen (Village without Men; mus. Lankester), Scapino Ballet, Amsterdam

1951 De Tijgerprinses (The Tiger Princess; mus. Grovlez), Scapino Ballet, Amsterdam

1952 Er was eens . . . (Once Upon a Time . . ., with A. Mol; mus. van Erpen de Groot), Scapino Ballet, Amsterdam

1958 Op een regendag (On a Rainy Day, with J. Rebel, K. Poons; mus. van Erpen, Lankester), Scapino Ballet, Amsterdam

1959 Vadertje tijd neemt even rust (Father Time Takes a Rest; mus. Lankester), Scapino Ballet, Amsterdam

1960 De Wonderfluit (The Magic Flute, with Rebel; mus. van Zanten), Scapino Ballet, Amsterdam

1963 Moeke er staat een vrijer voor de deur (Mother, a Lover is Waiting Outside, with Rebel; mus. Nuyten), Scapino Ballet, Amsterdam

1964 In Lichterlaaie (On Fire, with Rebel; mus. van Erpen), Scapino Ballet, Amsterdam

1968 Waterballet (with Rebel; mus. Ittman), Scapino Ballet, Amsterdam
De Hollandse Bruiloft (Dutch Wedding; mus. Nuyten), Scapino Ballet, Amsterdam

1969 De Krant (The Newspaper; mus. Beuker), Scapino Ballet, Amsterdam
Mensen, Dieren en Dansen (People, Animals and Dance, with van Gulik, Wisden; mus. Mooten), Scapino Ballet, Amsterdam

1970 Op Schoolreis met een boek (A School Outing with a Book, with Ossoski, Wisden; mus. Geels), Scapino Ballet, Amsterdam

PUBLICATIONS

By Snoek:
Dance and Ballet, Amsterdam, 1956

About Snoek:
Voeten, Jessica, Scapino, Amsterdam, 1985

The Dutch dancer and choreographer Hans (Johanna) Snoek was born in the Netherlands in 1910, into a family that took a great interest in music and the theatre. As a child she studied Jacques-Dalcroze's Eurhythmics, which were to have a considerable influence on her dancing career. She was the first Dutch student to enrol in the Folkwangschule in Essen, where she studied dance, music, and drama between 1929 and 1931. She made her professional début with the Essen Opera ballet under the direction of Kurt Jooss, but returned to Amsterdam to dance with the "Wagner Society" and Yvonne Georgi. In 1940 she joined the Dutch Ballet Company in The Hague, leaving at the beginning of World War II when dancers were only allowed to perform in the Netherlands after signing an agreement with the German Occupation's "Chamber of Culture".

She illegally opened her own school in Amsterdam during the war, assembling other artists in the same circumstances as herself. Together they participated in so-called underground performances, in aid of artists working in the resistance movement. After the war, in 1945 and 1946, two performances were organized under the name "Op Vrije Voeten", for those dancers who had been unable to perform during the war.

During the war years, the idea of establishing a company to perform to children had emerged, and it was put into practice in 1945. The new company was called the Scapino Ballet, after the commedia dell'arte character Scapino, who explained what was happening on stage to the audience of children. The Scapino Ballet's first productions took place in Amsterdam's Theater Carr under the direction of Abraham van der Vries and were sponsored by the newspaper Parool. Initially the company suffered financial difficulties, but after five years the Dutch Ministry of Culture recognized the company's importance, and government subsidies to the company have increased ever since. Scapino Ballet continues to give free performances and visit schools in the Netherlands. Children are invited to contribute ideas, such as stage designs and ballet scenarios, which are then developed by professional artists and choreographers. There can be few members of the Dutch ballet-going public who did not receive their first impressions of dance from a Scapino Ballet performance.

In 1951 the Scapino Academy was founded under the direction of Karel Poons, former dancer-choreographer with the Scapino Ballet and Ballet-der-Lage-Landen. It was one of the first professional training schools in the Netherlands and was officially recognized by the Dutch Ministry of Education in 1968. Snoek insisted that there should be close cooperation between school and company, and still feels that every dance student should undergo the experience of performing for a young audience which may not appreciate brilliant technique but instinctively recognizes a dancer's stage presence and sincerity.

Snoek was also the co-founder of "Danscontact", an organization which, among other functions, invites guest teachers to give special tuition to talented Dutch dancers and encourage promising choreographers. Snoek herself choreographed nineteen ballets between 1945 and 1970, some specifically for children and others on topical subjects. She has also made dance-educational television programmes with and for children, and is a member of the children's television programming board for the Dutch television network NOS.

Snoek resigned as director of the Scapino Ballet in 1970, to be succeeded by Amando Navarro. In 1991 Navarro himself was succeeded by the Dutch choreographer Nils Christe.

Even now, Snoek retains her extraordinary energy and is full of ideas. She says, "Maybe if I had concentrated on just one or two subjects, I would have established more." However, it is this very multiplicity of approach that has brought about so much in the Dutch dance world, combined with her ability to find the right people to realize her ideas. She inspires a cooperative spirit that is rare in the ballet world, and from the earliest stages of her career she saw the need for designers, musicians, writers, and choreographers to work together as a team. Many choreographers began their careers with the Scapino Ballet and have found choreographing for children a valuable experience; it has taught them the importance of clarity.

—Jenny J. Veldhuis

SOKOLOVA, Evgenia (Eugenia)

Russian dancer and teacher. Born Evgeniya (Evgenia, or Eugenia) Pavlovna Sokolova in St. Petersburg, 1 December (19 November old style) 1850. Studied at the Imperial Theatre School, pupil of Lev Ivanov, Christian Johansson, Marius Petipa; graduated in 1868; also studied with Annunziata Ramaccini (wife of Carlo Blasis), Milan, and with Huguet. Married (1) Navy officer, 1871 (div.); (2) Edward Goer. First stage appearance, while still a student, in 1862, with official début, 1868; dancer, corps de ballet, Imperial Theatres, from 1869, leaving the stage to marry in 1871; returned, becoming prima ballerina of the Imperial Theatres, and creating many roles for ballet master Marius Petipa, 1874–86; also performed mime role in melodrama, *Yelva; ou, L'Orpheline russe*, 1886; invited to perform as guest ballerina by Paris Opéra, 1869, and by theatres in Milan and Florence, 1879, but permission denied by Imperial Theatres; teacher, Class of Perfection, Maryinsky Theatre, St. Petersburg, 1902–04: students included Mathilde Kshesinskaya, Lyubov Egorova, Anna Pavlova, Tamara Karsavina, Vera Trefilova; répétiteur (rehearsal supervisor) and coach, State Academic Theatre for Opera and Ballet (GATOB, previously the Maryinsky Theatre), Petrograd, 1920–23. Died in Leningrad, 2 August 1925.

ROLES

1862   Cupid in *The Pearl of Seville* (Saint-Léon), Bolshoi Theatre, St. Petersburg
1864   "Malarossian Dance" in *The Little Humpbacked Horse* (Saint-Léon), Bolshoi Theatre, St. Petersburg
1868   "Les Amours de Diane" (divertissement) in *King Candaule* (Petipa), Bolshoi Theatre (official début), St. Petersburg
       Amour (cr) in *L'Amour bienfaiteur* (Petipa), Graduation Performance of the Imperial Theatre School, St. Petersburg
1869   Pas de quatre in *Lilia* (Saint-Léon), Bolshoi Theatre, St. Petersburg
1870   Title role in *Esmeralda* (Perrot), Bolshoi Theatre, St. Petersburg
       Title role in *Fiametta* (Saint-Léon), Bolshoi Theatre, St. Petersburg
1874   Ondine in *The Naiad and the Fisherman* (Perrot), Bolshoi Theatre, St. Petersburg
       Kitri in *Don Quixote* (Petipa), Bolshoi Theatre, St. Petersburg
       Marguerita in *Faust* (Perrot), Bolshoi Theatre, St. Petersburg
1876   Thétis (cr) in *The Adventures of Peleus and Thétis* (Petipa), Bolshoi Theatre, St. Petersburg

Titania (cr) in *A Midsummer Night's Dream* (Petipa), Bolshoi Theatre, St. Petersburg
       A Star in *The Two Stars* (Petipa), Bolshoi Theatre, St. Petersburg
1878   Roxana (cr) in *Roxana; or, The Belle of Montenegro* (Petipa), Benefit for Sokolova, Bolshoi Theatre, St. Petersburg
1879   Title role in *La Camargo* (Petipa), Bolshoi Theatre, St. Petersburg
       Title role (cr) in *Mlada* (Petipa), Bolshoi Theatre, St. Petersburg
       Lise in *Vain Precautions* (*La Fille mal gardée*; Petipa), Bolshoi Theatre, St. Petersburg
1880   Medora in *Le Corsaire* (Petipa after Perrot, Mazilier), Bolshoi Theatre, St. Petersburg
       "La Sicilienne" (with Ivanov) in *Graziella* (Petipa after Saint-Léon), Bolshoi Theatre, St. Petersburg
1882   Title role in *Pâquerette* (revival; Saint-Léon), Bolshoi Theatre, St. Petersburg
1883   Queen of Night (cr) in *Night and Day* (Petipa), Coronation of Aleksandr III, Moscow
       Galatea (cr) in *Pygmalion* (Petipa), Bolshoi Theatre, St. Petersburg
1884   Title role in *Trilby* (Petipa), Bolshoi Theatre, St. Petersburg
1885   The Countess in *Le Diable à quatre* (revival; Mazilier), Bolshoi Theatre, St. Petersburg
       Aspicia in *Pharaoh's Daughter* (Petipa), Bolshoi Theatre, St. Petersburg
1886   Leading dancer (cr) in *The Magic Pills* (Petipa), Maryinsky Theatre, St. Petersburg
       Chloe (cr) in *Les Offrandes à l'amour* (Petipa), Maryinsky Theatre (farewell performance), St. Petersburg

Other roles include: at the Italian Opera, St. Petersburg— Fenella in *La Muette de Portici* (opera; mus. Auber), Elena in "Ballet of the Nuns" in *Robert le Diable* (opera; mus. Meyerbeer).

PUBLICATIONS

Plesheev, Aleksandr, *Our Ballet*, St. Petersburg, 1899
Borisoglebsky, M., *Materials on the History of Russian Ballet*, Leningrad, 1939
Krasovskaya, Vera, *Russian Ballet Theatre in the Second Half of the Nineteenth Century*, Moscow, 1963
Karsavina, Tamara, "Eugenia Sokolova: Family Album 4", *Dancing Times* (London), September 1964
Roslavleva, Natalia, *Era of the Russian Ballet*, London, 1966

* * *

The careers of Evgenia Sokolova and Ekaterina Vazem are similar in many respects: both were trained at the Imperial Theatre School in St. Petersburg, both became principal ballerinas with the Imperial Ballet in the Petipa years immediately following Saint-Léon's departure, and both taught at the Theatre School after retiring from the stage. As dancers, their strengths lay at opposite ends of the spectrum: Vazem was the cool technician; Sokolova was renowned for her grace and expressiveness.

These two ballerinas represent the evolution experienced by the Russian school during the tenure of Marius Petipa. Sokolova, although two years younger than Vazem, typified all that had been traditionally valued by Russian dancers and audiences. In the manner of the French school, Sokolova was a

Lydia Sokolova as the Ballerina in *Petrushka*, 1926

soft, lyrical dancer who was praised, as Natalia Roslavleva tells us, for her "rounded poses, her grace of body and enchanting personality". Sokolova's attributes were best displayed in ballets with a dramatic or Romantic theme. In contrast, Vazem represented the future of Russian ballet. Petipa made extensive use of her skills as his choreographic focus increasingly turned toward the invention of technically challenging variations.

Of the two ballerinas, Petipa favoured Vazem, but he also made frequent use of Sokolova's talents. While still a student, she made her début appearance in "Les Amours de Diane", a divertissement within Petipa's *King Candaule*. For her graduation performance, Petipa choreographed *L'Amour bienfaiteur*, in which she danced the lead role. She performed in several Petipa ballets during her career, including *A Midsummer Night's Dream*, *Don Quixote*, *Roxana; or, The Beauty of Montenegro*, *The Cyprus Statue* (*Pygmalion*), and *Mlada*. In 1883, Petipa choreographed *Night and Day*, a ballet featuring both Sokolova and Vazem. This work was created for the Gala celebrating the coronation of Tsar Aleksandr III, with Vazem as Queen of the Day contrasted with Sokolova as Queen of the Night.

Sokolova's lead roles were not restricted to Petipa ballets, as works by previous ballet masters often remained in the repertoire of the Imperial Theatre for many years. She performed in *Esmeralda* by Jules Perrot and in Saint-Léon's *Fiammetta* and *Pâquerette*. Preferring light-hearted roles over the dramatic or tragic, Sokolova particularly enjoyed dancing the role of Lise in *La Fille mal gardée* (known in Russia as *Vain Precautions*). Based on the ballet originally choreographed by Jean Dauberval, this production featured Sokolova as Lise in a Petipa restaging of the ballet.

In her memoirs, Vazem describes and comments on the strengths and weaknesses of several fellow dancers. Sokolova is credited with being "a fine dancer with a softness, grace and plasticity". The sentence concludes negatively: ". . . but technically, she was not strong." She also states that Sokolova "had no elevation". If we are to believe Vazem, Sokolova's considerable popularity hinged on her personal charm and "coyness". An excellent mime, she flirted with her audience and was a favourite with the public. Vazem implies that Sokolova's personality, not her dancing ability, was responsible for Petipa's casting her in ballets. (Conversely, we might surmise that Vazem's technical skills were more appealing to Petipa than her personality.) Petipa choreographed separately for Sokolova and Vazem throughout their careers. Their contrasting strengths precluded them from competing for the same roles. Still, there is little doubt that Sokolova and Vazem actively competed for the public's affection. Judging from the tone in Vazem's memoirs, it would appear that Sokolova enjoyed the upper hand in this regard.

In her teaching, Sokolova continued to represent and support those dancers whose talent lay more in expressiveness than in technical skill. According to Natalia Roslavleva, it was from Sokolova that "Anna Pavlova received her first blessing". Not surprisingly, Vazem did not share Sokolova's enthusiasm for this particular pupil. Sokolova's strength as a teacher lay in her ability to nurture artistry. Described by Tamara Karsavina as "a keeper of the Sylphic faith", Sokolova remained loyal to "the purity and fluency of the classical dance". Her allegiance to the past may also have been instrumental in her departure from the Theatre School. Upon Christian Johansson's retirement, Sokolova assumed control of the Class of Perfection. By this time, the young Russian dancers were intent on mastering the technical skills imported by the Italians, an aim Sokolova could not understand. Her class was poorly attended, and she was soon replaced by Nikolai Legat. Karsavina later studied privately with Sokolova, when she realized that technique

alone was insufficient for success in most roles. Ultimately, she too left Sokolova's tutelege to study with Enrico Cecchetti.

In each stage of her career, Evgenia Sokolova was constantly challenged by the ever-increasing emphasis placed on technical brilliance. It is to her credit that her artistry and personal charm enabled her not only to survive, but to earn lasting recognition. The respect and affection with which she was remembered was demonstrated by Serge Diaghilev, when he bestowed the name Lydia Sokolova upon Hilda Munnings. In explanation of his choice of name for the young English dancer, Diaghilev said "I hope you will live up to the name of Sokolova as it is that of a great dancer in Russia."

—Norma Sue Fisher-Stitt

SOKOLOVA, Lydia

British dancer. Born Hilda Munnings in Wanstead, 4 March 1896. Studied at Stedman's Academy, London, and with Anna Pavlova, Mikhail Mordkin, Aleksandr Shiryaev, Ivan Clustine, London; later studied with Enrico Cecchetti. Married Nicholas Kremnev, 1917: one daughter, Natasha (b. 1917). Début in corps de ballet, *Alice in Wonderland* (revue), London, 1910; dancer, Mikhail Mordkin's "Imperial Russian Ballet", U.S. tour, 1911, and Theodore Kosloff's company, European tour, 1912; dancer, Diaghilev's Ballets Russes, 1918–29, becoming soloist, 1925, and soon thereafter ballerina and leading character dancer; performer with Massine's company, 1922–23, including for revue *You'd Be Surprised* (Covent Garden), and in music halls with husband Kremnev, London, 1922–23; leading dancer with Léon Woizikowsky's company, London, 1935; also choreographer of dances for London musical, 1937, and Lydia Kyasht's Ballet de la Jeunesse Anglaise, 1939; returned to stage to perform in revival of *The Good-Humoured Ladies*, London, 1962. Died in Sevenoaks, 5 February 1974.

ROLES

1913/14 Polovtsian maid in *Polovtsian Dances from Prince Igor* (Fokine), Diaghilev's Ballets Russes, Monte Carlo
Dancer in *Les Sylphides* (Fokine), Diaghilev's Ballets Russes, Monte Carlo
Nymph in *L'Après-midi d'un faune* (Nijinsky), Diaghilev's Ballets Russes, Monte Carlo
1915 Papillon in *Le Carnaval* (Fokine), Diaghilev's Ballets Russes, Geneva
Dancer (cr) in *Le Soleil de nuit* (Massine), Diaghilev's Ballets Russes, Geneva
1916 Principal dancer (cr) in *Las Meninas* (Massine), Diaghilev's Ballets Russes, Saint Sebastien
1917 Ta-Hor in *Cléopâtre* (Fokine), Diaghilev's Ballets Russes, New York
Bacchante in *Narcisse* (Fokine), Diaghilev's Ballets Russes, New York
Kikimora (cr) in *Contes Russes* (Massine), Diaghilev's Ballets Russes, Paris
Apple Woman (cr) in *Til Eulenspiegel* (Nijinsky), Diaghilev's Ballets Russes, New York
Young Girl in *Le Spectre de la rose* (Nijinsky), Diaghilev's Ballets Russes, New York
1918 Felicita in *Les Femmes de bonne humeur* (Massine), Diaghilev's Ballets Russes, London

1919 Tarantella (cr) in *La Boutique fantasque* (Massine), Diaghilev's Ballets Russes, London
Variation, Finale (cr) in *Le Tricorne* (Massine), Diaghilev's Ballets Russes, London

1920 The Chosen Virgin (cr) in *Le Sacre du printemps* (Massine), Diaghilev's Ballets Russes, Paris
Death (cr) in *Le Chant du rossignol* (Massine), Diaghilev's Ballets Russes, Paris
Miller's Wife in *Le Tricorne* (Massine), Diaghilev's Ballets Russes, Paris
Character Pas de deux (cr) in *Le Astuzie femminili* (Massine), Diaghilev's Ballets Russes, Paris

1921 La Bouffonne (cr) in *Chout* (Larionov, Slavinsky), Diaghilev's Ballets Russes, Paris
Cherry Blossom Fairy, Red Riding Hood in *The Sleeping Princess* (Petipa; staged Sergeyev; additional dances Nijinska), Diaghilev's Ballets Russes, London

1923 Principal dancer (cr) in *You'd Be Surprised* (revue; chor. Massine), Covent Garden, London

1924 Chloé in *Daphnis et Chloé* (revival; Fokine, with additional dances Nijinska), Diaghilev's Ballets Russes, Monte Carlo
Chanson dansée ("Grey Girl") (cr) in *Les Biches* (Nijinska), Diaghilev's Ballets Russes, Monte Carlo
Sorceress (cr) in *Night on a Bald Mountain* (Nijinska), Diaghilev's Ballets Russes, Monte Carlo
Perlouse (cr) in *Le Train bleu* (Nijinska), Diaghilev's Ballets Russes, Paris
Principal dancer in *Les Sylphides* (Fokine), Diaghilev's Ballets Russes, Barcelona

1925 A Muse (cr) in *Zéphire et Flore* (Massine), Diaghilev's Ballets Russes, Monte Carlo
The Friend (cr) in *Les Matelots* (Massine), Diaghilev's Ballets Russes, Paris
Solo (chor. Nijinska) in *Polovtsian Dances from Prince Igor* (Fokine), Diaghilev's Ballets Russes, Marseilles

1926 Nurse (cr) in *Romeo and Juliet* (Nijinska), Diaghilev's Ballets Russes, Monte Carlo
Goddess (cr) in *The Triumph of Neptune* (Balanchine), Diaghilev's Ballets Russes, London

1929 Dancer (cr) in *Le Bal* (Balanchine), Diaghilev's Ballets Russes, Monte Carlo

1962 The Marquise Silvestra in *The Good-Humoured Ladies* (*Les Femmes de bonne humeur*; Massine), Royal Ballet, London

Other roles include: Peasant Woman in *Barabau* (Balanchine), Columbine in *Le Carnaval* (Fokine), Ballerina in *Petrushka* (Fokine), Pimpinella in *Pulcinella* (Massine), American Girl in *Parade* (Massine), Rag Mazurka ("The Hostess") in *Les Biches* (Nijinska).

WORKS

1922 *Phi-Phi* (uncredited), Pavilion, London
1937 Dances in *Crest of the Wave* (musical; libretto and mus. Ivor Novello), Drury Lane Theatre, London
1939 *Russki-Plasski*, Ballet de la Jeunesse Anglaise, Cambridge Theatre, London

PUBLICATIONS

By Sokolova:
"Early Days: My First Year with Diaghileff", *Dancing Times* (London), December 1938

Dancing for Diaghilev (memoirs, edited by Richard Buckle), London, 1960
"The Good-Humoured Ladies", *About the House* (London), November 1962

About Sokolova:
Grigoriev, Serge, *The Diaghilev Ballet*, translated by Vera Bowen, London, 1953
Buckle, Richard, *In Search of Diaghilev*, London, 1955
"Personality of the Month: Lydia Sokolova", *Dance and Dancers* (London), July 1960
Williams, Peter, "Lydia Sokolova Remembers", *Dance and Dancers* (London), November 1971
Buckle, Richard, *Nijinsky*, London, 1971
Buckle, Richard, "Lydia Sokolova", *About the House* (London), Spring 1974
Garafola, Lynn, *Diaghilev's Ballets Russes*, New York, 1989

* * *

Lydia Sokolova, born in England as Hilda Munnings, was among the first British dancers to be hired by Serge Diaghilev for his Ballets Russes. Munnings, who was given the name Lydia Sokolova by Diaghilev, joined the company in April 1913 at the salary of £30 a month, starting with the spring season in Monte Carlo. Her career spanned the history of the Ballets Russes from 1913 until Diaghilev's untimely death in August 1929. Sokolova became the quintessential Diaghilev dancer. In the sixteen years she performed with the Ballet Russes, she worked under the choreographers Fokine, Nijinsky, Massine, Nijinska, and Balanchine.

Sokolova/Munnings started her training at Stedman's Academy in England, where she perfected her elevation and technique. She made her professional début in 1910, in the corps de ballet of *Alice in Wonderland* at the Savoy Theatre, London.

After studying with the Moscow-trained Mikhail Mordkin, she was hired (at the age of fifteen) to join Mordkin's "Imperial Russian Ballet" for its 1911 tour of the United States. Although the dancer had performed in Mordkin's classical repertoire, she never felt that she excelled in the classics. She described herself as never very good at pirouettes on pointe (her best were always done to the left). It was while on tour that she mastered the Polish mazurka, thus expanding her range beyond the strictly classical. Upon her return to England in 1912, she studied with Anna Pavlova, and the Russian dancer and teacher Aleksandr Shiryaev. It was Shiryaev who encouraged Sokolova to concentrate on character dancing, and to learn as much as she could from the Russians.

Following this advice, she perfected her elevation along Russian lines. "What I always liked about the dancing of the Russians is the manner in which they jump. On stage I tried to do it their way. The secret is to travel 'through' the air, not 'up' into it. I learned that if one refuses to allow the body to sense any weight, lightness can become a habit," she wrote in her memoirs.

From Pavlova, Sokolova learned how the great ballerina controlled her arabesque and attitude. As soon as Pavlova took a position, she would start to concentrate: from the point of the toe which rested on the ground, she would think her way through the ankle to the calf, to the knee and all the way up to the head and the tips of the fingers; and when this controlling thought process was finished, it was time to move on.

Under the Diaghilev/Fokine Ballets Russes repertoire, Sokolova danced in *Cléopâtre* as the Slave Girl, in *Narcisse* as a Bacchante, in *Daphne et Chloé* as Chloé, and in *Petrushka* as the Ballerina. Under the (then) avant-garde theories of naturalism initiated by Fokine, Sokolova danced in bare feet for the first time, in the role of Chloé. She compared this to walking in public in a nightgown.

Under Nijinsky, Sokolova learned the Jaques-Dalcroze method of Eurhythmics as taught to the company by Marie Rambert. Sokolova was musical and had rhythmical sense; thus she understood Nijinsky's instructions to "walk between the bars of music and sense the rhythm which is implied" for his ballet *L'Après-midi d'un faune*. In the more complex *Le Sacre du printemps*, she danced as one of the corps de ballet, but in the later Massine version she shone as the Chosen One (or Chosen Virgin), and felt it was a more strenuous role than in Nijinsky's version. Although Nijinsky never created a role for Sokolova, she was one of the few dancers privileged to be his partner (in *Le Spectre de la rose*), and she danced in three Nijinsky ballets.

In 1917, the Léonide Massine period began for the Ballets Russes, reflecting artistically the diverse experiments of the Paris school. Sokolova always felt she was the perfect Massine dancer, and she became "première danseuse de caractère", as well as a leading ballet soloist. Massine bequeathed to her the roles of the Miller's Wife in *Le Tricorne*, Pimpinella in *Pulcinella*, Felicita in *Les Femmes de bonne humeur*, and The Chosen One in *Le Sacre du printemps*. She also danced the American Girl in *Parade*. The entrance and exit of the American Girl were extremely difficult; they consisted of sixteen bars of music, within which the dancer had to jump sixteen times with both feet straight out to the front, almost touching the toes with outstretched arms, while moving around the stage at full speed. In *Tricorne*, Sokolova mastered Spanish gypsy dancing, shaking her shoulders provocatively under Picasso's shawl.

With Bronislava Nijinska as Diaghilev's choreographer in the early 1920s, Sokolova danced many of the roles Nijinska herself had danced, as both were strong, had good elevation, and showed impressive endurance. Sokolova took over Nijinska's role of the Hostess in *Les Biches*, and created the role of the Bathing Beauty in *Le Train bleu*, dancing "Le Train bleu waltz" in a bathing costume designed by Chanel. The vigorous, forceful movements of Nijinska's *Les Noces* were Sokolova's forte as well.

In her comic character role in Massine's *Les Matelots*, Sokolova had to stand on stage with her back to the audience during intermission and stare at the drop curtain. (She learned that even with her back to the audience she could command attention simply by concentrating on the character of her role—her "feat of personality".) For Balanchine, Sokolova danced the clownish peasant woman in *Barabau*, and made a humorous picture in her unique stage make-up.

But it was as the Chosen One in Massine's *Sacre du printemps* that Sokolova had her greatest triumph. At the age of 24 she won great praise in this demanding role, and Stravinsky himself kissed her hand on stage. The movements were difficult, involving enormous sideways jumps that had to be performed very slowly, as well as big hammering steps around the stage, flinging the body from side to side. In the second scene, Sokolova had to stand absolutely still for twelve minutes, waiting for her part to begin, her left arm held across her body with its clenched fist in the air above her head. Her right hand was at her waist and her feet were turned inward. She came in with a crashing step and danced in a frenzy, with convulsive steps and spinning jumps.

Although she had to leave the company three times as a result of illness, Sokolova stated she could imagine no other life for herself than dancing for Diaghilev. She wrote in her memoirs, "I never have been and never could be a classical ballerina, but the fun I had in taking such different roles by choreographers of such varied genius, was more rewarding to my way of thinking,

than all the laurels and fortunes of Pavlova."

After the death of Diaghilev, Sokolova danced briefly with Léon Woizikowsky's company, and later taught in England. In 1962 she reappeared to play Marquise Silvestra in *The Good-Humoured Ladies* for the Royal Ballet.

—Rosaline George

SOLDIERS' MASS
(also known as *Field Mass*)

Choreography: Jiří Kylián
Music: Bohuslav Martinů (based on his composition *Polní Mše*)
Design: Jiří Kylián (scenery and costumes), Joop Caboort (lighting)
First Production: Netherlands Dance Theatre, Scheveningen, 13 June 1980
Principal Dancers: Patrick Dadey, Glen Eddy, Chris Jensen, Peter Lawrence, Gerard Lemaitre, Ric McCullogh, Eric Newton, Michael Sanders, Gerarld Tibbs, Tony Vandecasteele, James Vincent, Nils Christe

PUBLICATIONS

Whitney, Mary, "Force of Nature", *Ballet News* (New York), July 1981
Stoop, Norma McLain, "Netherlands Dance Theater", *Dance Magazine* (New York), November 1981
Clarke, Mary, and Crisp, Clement, *The Ballet Goer's Guide*, London, 1981

* * *

Soldiers' Mass, or *Field Mass*, was first produced by the Netherlands Dance Theatre in 1980, and was acclaimed as a masterpiece. The piece is built on a composition of the same name by Kylián's compatriot, the Czech composer Bohuslav Martinů (1890–1959). Martinů was staying in Paris when the Second World War broke out in 1939. He had to watch resignedly while his country was occupied, and he created, together with the poet Jiří Mucha, a mass. In the south of France at that time, an army of Czech volunteers was being trained for the liberation of its homeland. Martinů composed the mass for the young soldiers who would very soon be going into battle and for those who had already been killed. The mass had to be played in the open air and the instrumentation (woodwind, brass, percussion, portable piano, and harmonium) was chosen accordingly. The atmosphere of the piece is thus sombre and dramatic, and very Slavic due to the flexible rhythm of the choral parts. Mucha's text contained parts of Matthew's Gospel and a few psalms. The first part is an arrangement of the Lord's Prayer; then follows the prayer of the soldier, the prodigal son, who is far from home and wonders whether he can still be seen and whether his prayers will be answered. The words are moving, full of reminders of the motherland; thoughts about life and death; pleas for freedom; affirmations of the willingness to die. "Our death," they say, "is your life. . . .", and at the end there is a hopeful amen.

Kylián reveals the fear, impotence, and vulnerability of the soldiers with the poignant idiom of movement. Besides expressing the theme of the music, he wants to make a statement about the individual soldier: when he wears a

Soldiers' Mass, as performed by Netherlands Dance Theatre, 1980

uniform he loses his identity, he receives orders and must obey them; his own feelings count for nothing. Kylián also conveys the agonized and grieving soul of the individual soldier through movement.

The dancers were dressed in green shirts and trousers, with long socks reaching to their knees. The backdrop showed a curved horizon, accentuated by a red phosphorescent line, the upper part a glaring blue, the lower part black. Costumes and décor were created by Kylián, the lighting designed by Joop Caboort.

The twelve male dancers, representing a battalion of soldiers, stay on stage during the ballet, since soldiers spend day and night together. Their discipline is reflected in the rigidly structured form of the ballet: they move in straight lines, creating beautiful geometrical shapes, such as triangles and squares, by their complicated criss-crossing in groups. In these tide formations they hold hands or put their arms over each others' shoulders. But the powerful straight lines bend, and the rigid form suddenly softens, thus stressing even more effective-ly the anguish hidden beneath the military discipline of each individual soldier. The dancers twirl in a speedy tempo, fall down, get up again, sometimes moving on their knees. They hold their arms as birds hold their wings, or press them tightly to their bodies, or lift them high in the air. They clench their fists or hold their hands in front of their eyes.

One dancer after another leaves the group, expressing fear and emotion, until they all gather again in a heroic ensemble, dancing together. Then, to heavy drumbeats, the prodigal son leaves the group, exploring the space with large steps, whirling his upper torso around, back, and down to the floor, until three dancers lift him high, supporting him in his deep sorrow. During the last part of the dance, three groups of four dancers make quick changes of direction, creating beautiful strong lines. Then the chorus sings its last song and the soldiers, scattered over the stage, sing too, suddenly take off their shirts, throw them down, and hold their hands in front of their eyes, and fall down on the ground. Thus, symbolically, the soldiers regain their identities before facing death, in this moving final scene.

—Helma Klooss

SOLOVIEV, Yuri

Russian/Soviet dancer. Born Yuri Vladimirovich Soloviev in Leningrad, 10 August 1940. Studied at the Leningrad Choreo-graphic School, pupil of Boris Shavrov; graduated in 1958. Married Kirov soloist Tatyana Legat. Dancer, becoming principal dancer, Kirov Ballet, 1958–77, creating many leading roles; also appeared in films, including as the Prince in *The Sleeping Beauty* (Kirov film, 1965). Recipient: First Prize, International Festival of Youth and Students, Vienna, 1959; Nijinsky Prize, University of Dance, Paris, 1963; title of Honoured Artist of the Russian Federation, 1964; Gold Star Prize, International Festival of Dance, Paris, 1965; titles of People's Artist of the Russian Federation, 1967, and People's Artist of the USSR, 1973. Died in Leningrad, apparently by suicide, 12 January 1977.

ROLES

1961   The Youth (cr) in *Leningrad Symphony* (Belsky), Kirov Ballet, Leningrad
1963   Man (cr) in *The Distant Planet* (Sergeyev), Kirov Ballet, Leningrad
1965   Kino (cr) in *The Pearl* (Boyarsky), Kirov Ballet, Leningrad
1967   The Brave Warrior (cr) in *Land of Miracles* (Yakobson), Kirov Ballet, Leningrad
       Aitor (cr) in *Spanish Miniatures* (de Fonsea), Kirov Ballet, Leningrad
1968   Egisth (cr) in *Oresteya* (Aleksidze), Kirov Ballet, Leningrad
1969   Principal dancer (cr) in *Two* (Vinogradov), Creative Evening for Irina Kolpakova, Kirov Ballet, Leningrad
1971   God (cr) in *The Creation of the World* (Kasatkina and Vasiliev), Kirov Ballet, Leningrad
1974   Title role (cr) in *Icarus* (Belsky), Kirov Ballet, Leningrad

Other roles include: Prince Siegfried in *Swan Lake* (Petipa, Ivanov, staged Sergeyev), Prince Désiré, Bluebird in *The Sleeping Beauty* (Petipa; staged Sergeyev), Solor in *La Bayadère* (Petipa, Ponomarev, Chabukiani), Farkhad in *The Legend of Love* (Grigorovich), The Prince in *Cinderella* (Sergeyev), Fisherman in *The Coast of Hope* (Belsky), Danila in *The Stone Flower* (Grigorovich), The Nutcracker in *The Nutcracker* (Vainonen), Albrecht in *Giselle* (Petipa after Coralli, Perrot), Frondoso, Two Young Men in *Laurencia* (Chabukiani), Harlequin in *Carnaval* (Fokine), The Youth in *Chopiniana* (Vaganova after Fokine), Troubadour in *Raymonda* (Petipa; staged Sergeyev), The Genie of the Waters in *The Little Humpbacked Horse* (Gorsky after Saint-Léon), principal dancer in *The Skaters* (choreographic miniature; Yakobson).

PUBLICATIONS

Hering, Doris, "Kirov Ballet—Endearing Anachronism", *Dance Magazine* (New York), November 1961
Dobrovolskaya, G., "Yuri Soloviev", *Leningradskaya Pravda*, 26 April 1963
Prokhorova, V., "In Mid-Air", *Teatralnaya Zhizn* (Moscow), no. 9, 1965
Zemlemerov, V., "Another 'Cosmic Yuri'", *Muzykalnaya Zhizn* (Moscow), no. 12, 1965
Linkova, L., *Leningrad Ballet Today*, Leningrad, 1967
Stupnikov, Igor, *The Young Leningrad Ballet Dancers*, Leningrad, 1968
Krasovskaya, Vera, "Yuri Soloviov", *Sovetsky Balet* (Moscow), no. 3, 1983
Lopukhov, Fedor, "Yuri Soloviov", *Sovetsky Balet* (Moscow), no. 5, 1986

*   *   *

Yuri Soloviev

When Yuri Soloviev was found shot, apparently by suicide, at his dacha just outside Leningrad at the age of 37, the Soviet ballet world lost one of its finest talents. The purity of his technique and his phenomenal elevation made him one of the greatest virtuosos at the the Kirov Ballet during the 1960s.

Soloviev was cast from the same mould as Rudolf Nureyev, Mikhail Barishnikov, Natalia Makarova, and Valery Panov, all of whom trained at the Leningrad Choreographic School and danced with the Kirov Ballet Company at the same time. Had Soloviev, like these four, also fled to the West, he too might have become an international name. As it was, his untimely death came to be viewed by many as an "internal defection", a statement of his disappointment and despair within the political situation which ensnared him and his theatrical career, and gave him little hope of progressing. Even in the light of today's glasnost, the reasons for his death remain a mystery, and there is only speculation as to why he would leave his wife (Tatyana Legat) and child to go alone to end his life, when he still had so much to offer his art.

Yuri Soloviev was born in Leningrad a year before the city's 900-day siege by the Germans. He was admitted to the Leningrad ballet school, where he was seen to be a studious young boy, spontaneous and fearless. His young body was flexible and elastic, enabling him to execute difficult technical combinations with ease. But he did not at first show the aptitude for which he was to become famous. While his body was still developing and his muscles not yet strong, he often cried in despair because he could not jump as high as the other boys in his class. Nevertheless, with patience and perseverance, he came to possess what has been called "the greatest leap in the world". He would soar upwards, seemingly hovering in the air as though in a state of weightlessness, before returning gently to the ground in a soft, deep plié. Though later he had the well-developed thighs of a more athletic dancer, Soloviev incorporated in his build all the qualities of a danseur noble: tall, good, strong features, broad shoulders with long arms, and a regal bearing.

In 1958, Soloviev graduated from the Leningrad Choreographic School in the class of the respected teacher Boris Shavrov, amongst whose other pupils in previous years were Yuri Grigorovich, Igor Belsky, and Nikolai Boyarchikov. At the graduating concert, Soloviev danced the Bluebird pas de deux from *The Sleeping Beauty*, in a role which brought him immediate attention. He was compared to the great Nijinsky both for the quality of his elevation and "ballon", and for his physical appearance. In the testing virtuoso number, Soloviev demonstrated academically pure brisés, his feet tightly together, legs stretched and body arched, while his jumps soared and suspended him high in the air. His execution of this role was called by critics "one of the jewels in the crown of Russian classical ballet". (During a London tour in 1970, a petition was made by the gallery audiences of the Crystal Palace Sports Ground, where the Kirov was appearing, for Soloviev to dance the Bluebird on the last night of the tour. It was granted.)

Soloviev immediately joined the Kirov Ballet, along with Rudolf Nureyev, where he proved himself a brilliant all-round academic danseur, not only possessing an impeccable neatness of style, but also the skills of a caring partner. He was given most of the classical leading roles to dance, and created roles in many new ballets: God in the tongue-in-cheek *Creation of the World* by Kasatkina and Vasiliev, where, dressed in a long white nightshirt, he displayed a gift as a comic actor; the Youth in Belsky's *Leningrad Symphony*, a plotless work to Shostakovich's powerful score, which shows the heroics of the young people during the trials of the last war. Soloviev's forceful portrayal is said to have inspired many young Soviet soldiers. In Sergeyev's *The Distant Planet*, he was rightly cast as an astronaut whose celestial travels kept him quite literally "in flight".

In *Land of Miracles* by Leonid Yakobson, Soloviev danced the role of Yasny Sokol (the Brave Warrior)—an old Russian symbol of male strength. The ballet was vividly filled with national folk art, its visuals bringing to mind a traditional Russian painted lacquer-box, and the plot lay in the expected triumph of the Russian people over the forces of evil. Soloviev's ballerina was Natalia Makarova (as the Fair Maiden), whose impeccable musicality and technical virtuosity would later be hailed world-wide. Yet Soloviev, able to perform magnificently the demanding technical feats of the choreography, was not happy with the character's interpretation and after one performance refused to dance the ballet again. Some say he secretly preferred fishing to balletic experimentation.

—Margaret Willis

SOMES, Michael
British dancer and ballet director. Born in Horsley, 28 September 1917. Studied with Katherine Blott in Weston-super-Mare, Edouard Espinosa, and Phyllis Bedells; studied at the Vic-Wells School (on scholarship), pupil of Ninette de Valois, Vera Volkova, from 1934; also studied with Margaret Craske and Stanislas Idzikowski, London. Married (1) dancer Deirdre Dixon; (2) dancer Antoinette Sibley (div.); (3) Wendy Ellis. Served in the British forces during World War II. Dancer, Vic-Wells Ballet (later Sadler's Wells Ballet and eventually the Royal Ballet), from 1935, becoming principal dancer from 1938, and company's leading male dancer and chief partner to Margot Fonteyn; choreographer, Sadler's Wells Theatre Ballet, 1950; assistant director, Royal Ballet, 1963–70; principal teacher and répétiteur (rehearsal director), 1970–84, returning occasionally as coach; also guest ballet master, staging Ashton ballets internationally. Recipient: title of Commander of the Order of the British Empire, 1959.

ROLES

1936   Prince in *Nursery Suite* (de Valois), Vic-Wells Ballet, London

Vertumnus in *Pomona* (Ashton), Vic-Wells Ballet, tour

1937   Pas de huit (cr) in *Les Patineurs* (Ashton), Vic-Wells Ballet, London

Guy (cr) in *A Wedding Bouquet* (Ashton), Vic-Wells Ballet, London

A Black Knight (cr) in *Checkmate* (de Valois), Vic-Wells Ballet, Paris

1938   Young man (cr) in *Horoscope* (Ashton), Vic-Wells Ballet, London

Monseigneur (cr) in *Harlequin in the Street* (Ashton), Vic-Wells Ballet, London

Mazurka in *Les Sylphides* (Fokine), Vic-Wells Ballet, London

1939   First Red Knight in *Checkmate* (de Valois), Vic-Wells Ballet, tour

Pan (cr) in *Cupid and Psyche* (Ashton), Vic-Wells Ballet, London

Prince Siegfried in *Swan Lake*, Act II (Ivanov; staged Sergeyev), Vic-Wells Ballet, tour

The Emperor in *Le Roi nu* (*The Emperor's New Clothes*; de Valois), Vic-Wells Ballet, London

Bluebird in *The Sleeping Princess* (Petipa; staged Sergeyev), Vic-Wells Ballet, London

1940   A Child of Light (cr) in *Dante Sonata* (Ashton), Vic-Wells Ballet, London

The Bridegroom (cr) in *The Wise Virgins* (Ashton), Vic-Wells Ballet, London

A Lawyer (cr) in *The Prospect Before Us* (de Valois), Sadler's Wells Ballet, London

Popular Song in *Façade* (Ashton), Vic-Wells Ballet, London

Pas de deux in *Les Patineurs* (Ashton), Vic-Wells Ballet, tour

Variation, Adagio of Lovers in *Les Rendezvous* (Ashton), Vic-Wells Ballet, London

1941   Principal dancer ("Lover"; cr) in *The Wanderer* (Ashton), Sadler's Wells Ballet, London

Adagio in *Fête polonaise* (de Valois), Sadler's Wells Ballet, London

1945   Pierrot in *Carnaval* (Fokine), Sadler's Wells Ballet, London

Prince Siegfried in *Swan Lake* (Petipa, Ivanov; staged Sergeyev), Sadler's Wells Ballet, London

Young Man in *Nocturne* (Ashton), Sadler's Wells Ballet, London

St. George in *The Quest* (Ashton), Sadler's Wells Ballet, London

The Spirit of the Rose in *Le Spectre de la rose* (Fokine), Sadler's Wells Ballet, London

1946   Cavalier to the Lilac Fairy in *The Sleeping Beauty* (Petipa; staged Sergeyev, Ashton, de Valois), Sadler's Wells Ballet, London

The Stranger in *Miracle in the Gorbals* (Helpmann), Sadler's Wells Ballet, tour

Principal dancer (cr) in *Symphonic Variations* (Ashton), Sadler's Wells Ballet, London

Captain Bay Vavasour (cr) in *Les Sirènes* (Ashton), Sadler's Wells Ballet, London

Spirit of the Air (cr) in *The Fairy Queen* (masque; mus. Purcell, chor. Ashton), Covent Garden Opera and Sadler's Wells Ballet, London

1947   Albrecht in *Giselle* (Petipa after Coralli, Perrot; staged Sergeyev), Sadler's Wells Ballet, London

Title role in *Hamlet* (Helpmann), Sadler's Wells Ballet, London

The Caricaturist in *Mam'zelle Angot* (Massine), Sadler's Wells Ballet, London

Prince Florimund in *The Sleeping Beauty* (Petipa; staged Sergeyev, de Valois, Ashton), Sadler's Wells Ballet, London

1948   Principal dancer (cr) in *Scènes de ballet* (Ashton), Sadler's Wells Ballet, London

The Miller in *The Three-Cornered Hat* (Massine), Sadler's Wells Ballet, London

Genie of the Lighting (cr) in *Clock Symphony* (Massine), Sadler's Wells Ballet, London

The Prince (cr) in *Cinderella* (Ashton), Sadler's Wells Ballet, London

1950   Principal dancer in *Ballet Imperial* (Balanchine), Sadler's Wells Ballet, London

1951   Daphnis (cr) in *Daphnis and Chloe* (Ashton), Sadler's Wells Ballet, London

Title role (Tiresias as man; cr) in *Tiresias* (Ashton), Sadler's Wells Ballet, London

1952   The Poet in *Apparitions* (Ashton), Sadler's Wells Ballet, London

Aminta (cr) in *Sylvia* (Ashton), Sadler's Wells Ballet, London

1953   Consort to the Queen of Air (cr) in *Homage to the Queen* (Ashton), Sadler's Wells Ballet, London

1954   Ivan Tsarevitch in *The Firebird* (Fokine), Sadler's Wells Theatre Ballet, Edinburgh

1955   Rinaldo (cr) in *Rinaldo and Armida* (Ashton), Sadler's Wells Ballet, London

1956   Iskender (cr) in *La Péri* (Ashton), Sadler's Wells Ballet, London

Principal dancer (cr) in *Birthday Offering* (Ashton), Sadler's Wells Ballet, London

Mandarin (cr) in *The Miraculous Mandarin* (Rodrigues), Sadler's Wells Ballet, Edinburgh

1957   Creon (cr) in *Antigone* (Cranko), Royal Ballet, London

1958   Palemon (cr) in *Ondine* (Ashton), Royal Ballet, London

1959   Principal dancer (cr) in *Raymonda: Scène d'amour* (Ashton), Royal Academy of Dancing Gala, London

1963   The Father (cr) in *Marguerite and Armand* (Ashton), Royal Ballet, London

1965   Lord Capulet (cr) in *Romeo and Juliet* (MacMillan), Royal Ballet, London

1972   Tsar Nicholas I in *Anastasia* (MacMillan), Royal Ballet, tour

1978   Emperor Franz Joseph (cr) in *Mayerling* (MacMillan), Royal Ballet, London

Michael Somes with Margot Fonteyn in *Homage to the Queen*, 1953

WORKS

1950   *Summer Interlude* (mus. Respighi), Sadler's Wells Theatre Ballet, London

PUBLICATIONS

By Somes:

"Working with Frederick Ashton", in "Homage to Ashton", *Ballet Annual* (London), vol. 15, 1961

Interview in Gruen, John, *The Private World of Ballet*, New York, 1975

About Somes:

Davidson, Gladys, *Ballet Biographies*, revised edition, London, 1954

Fisher, Hugh, *Michael Somes*, London, 1955

Clarke, Mary, *The Sadler's Wells Ballet*, London, 1955

"Personality of the Month", *Dance and Dancers* (London), April 1958

Percival, John, "Accent on the Male: Michael Somes", *Dance and Dancers* (London), 2 parts: March, April 1959

"Personality of the Month", *Dance and Dancers* (London), October 1961

Anthony, Gordon, "Pioneers of the Royal Ballet: Michael Somes", *Dancing Times* (London), July 1971

Anthony, Gordon, *A Camera at the Ballet*, Newton Abbot, 1975

Fonteyn, Margot, *Margot Fonteyn: An Autobiography*, London, 1975

Monahan, James, "Michael Somes", *Dancing Times* (London), November 1984

Michael Somes was the first leading dancer to be developed by the Vic-Wells School, having been the first boy to be awarded a scholarship in 1934. By the end of the decade, he had established himself as one of the most promising of the younger soloists, and his particular qualities had already been discerned by Ashton, who created for him roles in *Horoscope* and *Dante Sonata* to show off the dancer's youthful virile lyricism, intensity of feeling, extraordinary jump, and exceptional musicality.

The war came at a crucial point in Somes's development, and the enforced break and subsequent injury were serious setbacks to his career in the late 1940s. However, as Robert Helpmann's interest in ballet diminished, Somes emerged as his obvious successor, both as leading dancer of the Sadler's Wells Ballet and as partner to Margot Fonteyn—a partnership whose possibilities Ashton had already perceived in *Horoscope* and now developed in a series of ballets, most notably *Daphnis and Chloe* and *Ondine*. Thus it was Somes who became Fonteyn's partner during the years of her great international triumphs; where Helpmann had been a goad to the young Fonteyn, Somes was now the perfect complement to her qualities at this stage of her development, attentive and self-effacing in the great danseur noble tradition, and an excellent foil. He also provided a role model for a new generation of male dancers, giving them leadership by example, and inspiring in them a group pride which had hitherto been lacking.

The break in his career and subsequent injury meant that Somes never achieved a virtuoso technique such as later became so prized, nor did he generate excitement through his dancing; instead, he evoked admiration for his quieter attributes. He proved, at a time when the male dancer was still regarded with suspicion, that it was possible to be strong yet sensitive, lyrical yet masculine. His particular forte was the area of the great classics and the Ashton repertory. His quality of noble self-effacement was seen at its best in the second movement of *Ballet Imperial*, where the solitary male dancer walks from the stage, the personification of nobility and aristocratic breeding.

Following his retirement from dancing in 1961, Somes took increasing responsibility for company rehearsals and especially for coaching the younger dancers. He was the principal architect of the Sibley–Dowell partnership, and his stern, unyielding drive towards perfection was undoubtedly a factor in developing the high Royal Ballet standards during what many regard as one of its greatest periods. His respect for tradition also made him a loving guardian of the Ballets Russes repertory, especially Nijinska's *Les Noces* and *Les Biches*, of which he took particular care, and the revivals by Grigoriev and Tchernicheva, particularly of *The Firebird*, in which he himself had been an outstanding Ivan Tsarevitch. But he was also keeper of the Ashton ballets, and the falling off in standards in later years, when these ballets were no longer in his care, was testimony itself to the quality he demanded and to his eye for detail. His understanding and devotion to Ashton's ballets ensured their high place in the repertory of the Royal Ballet, and he was also responsible for mounting several of them on companies abroad.

Somes dedicated his entire professional career to the Royal Ballet and did much, in performance and by example, to maintain the highest traditions of that company—traditions which he himself had helped to establish.

—Sarah C. Woodcock

SONG OF THE EARTH
(original German title: *Das Lied von der Erde*)

Choreography: Kenneth MacMillan
Music: Gustav Mahler (song cycle *Das Lied von der Erde*)
Libretto: Loosely based on text of Mahler's Song Cycle, translations of eighth-century poets of the T'ang Dynasty
First Production: Stuttgart Ballet, Staatstheater, Stuttgart, 7 November 1965
Principal Dancers: Egon Madsen (Der Ewige; later called "The Messenger of Death"), Marcia Haydée (Second and Sixth Songs; "The Woman"), Ray Barra (First, Fifth, and Sixth Songs; "The Man")

Other productions include: Royal Ballet (restaged MacMillan, design Nicholas Georgiadis), with Anthony Dowell (The Messenger of Death), Marcia Haydée (guest artist; "The Woman"), Donald MacLeary ("The Man"); London, 19 May 1966. Paris Opéra Ballet; Paris, 23 November 1978. Australian Ballet; Melbourne, 28 April 1987. National Ballet of Canada; Toronto, 1988.

PUBLICATIONS

Koegler, Horst, and Goodwin, Noël, "To Earth and Other Places", *Dance and Dancers* (London), January 1966

"Talking to Kenneth MacMillan", (interview), *About the House* (London), June 1966

Porter, Andrew, "The Song of the Earth", *About the House* (London), June 1966

Monahan, James, "*The Song of the Earth*: MacMillan's Masterpiece", *Dancing Times* (London), July 1966

Williams, Peter, and Goodwin, Noël, "*The Song of the Earth*", *Dance and Dancers* (London), July 1966

Crisp, Clement, "Grande-Bretagne", *Les Saisons de la danse* (Paris), April 1977

Balanchine, George, with Mason, Francis, *George Balanchine's Complete Stories of the Great Ballets*, Garden City, N.Y., 1977

Thorpe, Edward, *Kenneth MacMillan: The Man and the Ballets*, London, 1985

Crisp, Clement, "Kenneth MacMillan", *About the House* (London), Spring 1990

*   *   *

Kenneth MacMillan's intensely musical response to Mahler's song-symphony achieved what is widely regarded as one of his finest ballets and a great work by any standard. The music, which had earlier attracted Antony Tudor, another deeply musical choreographer (he choreographed *Shadow of the Wind* for American Ballet Theatre in 1948), was composed in Mahler's awareness that he was suffering from terminal heart disease, a man already shadowed by death. Although he completed *Das Lied von der Erde* in 1909, he died two years later without hearing it performed.

The work is a symphonic setting (for alternating tenor and alto soloists) of verses by Li-Tai Po and other eighth-century Chinese poets of the T'ang dynasty, in German translation. They express ideas akin to Mahler's own feelings about finding consolation against the threat of death in earthly beauty around him; his choice of poems reflects a range of emotional expression within an overall elegiac mood. There is consolation sought in wine; a sense of loneliness; wistful remembrances of the delights of youth and transient beauty; and finally, love and

Song of the Earth, with Marcia Haydée and Richard Cragun, Stuttgart Ballet, 1977

friendship linked to the irrevocable parting from life, but with the knowledge that life is ever renewed.

Each of the six symphonic movements embodies one poem except the last, "The Farewell", where Mahler incorporated two otherwise unrelated poems by different authors and added four lines of his own by way of coda:

Die liebe Erde allüberall

Blüht auf im Lenz und grünt aufs neu!

Allüberall und ewig blauen licht die Fernen!

Ewig . . . Ewig . . .

("Everywhere the dear earth/Blossoms in Spring and grows green again./Everywhere and forever the distance looks bright and blue!/Eternally . . . Eternally . . ."). These lines furnish the kernel of MacMillan's choreographic imagination, which is stimulated by the poetry without being closely tied to its detail—it is more a visual response to the moods expressed by the music. In his own words, "My interest was to create movements to describe the essence of the poems. Basically the theme of the ballet is quite simple: a man and a woman; Death takes the man; they both return to her and at the end of the ballet, in the last poem, we find that in Death there is the promise of renewal."

A slight shift of emphasis between music and ballet results in the second and fifth songs becoming part of the main choreographic theme, with the third and fourth ("Of Youth" and "Of Beauty") acting as intermezzi to the others. In all but one of the movements a half-masked male dancer shadows the principal Man and Woman: in German he is *Der Ewige*, who is not a threat but the inevitable companion to all life; a literal English equivalent such as "The Eternal One" would perhaps have been preferable to MacMillan's adoption of "The Messenger of Death" in the English cast listing.

In "The Drinking-song of Earth's Woe" (tenor), the Man and four other men celebrate mundane pleasures, leaping and turning, but with some heaviness of movement in deep pliés and turned-up feet that reflect underlying bitterness. The Messenger enters, shadowing the Man and mocking his steps, making him aware of his eternal omnipresence. Tights and tunics are plain and neutral, with the Messenger in black; the backcloth, originally sky-blue, was later changed to charcoal-grey silvered with light (not necessarily an improvement). At the end the Man is held high by the others, then dropped and caught by them on the final chord.

"Autumn Solitude" (alto) features the Woman with three other women, at first partnered by four men, but dancing with an underlying sense of melancholy. The Messenger returns and all leave except the principal Woman; a lyrical pas de deux between them begins at the line, "My heart is weary", with a particular poignancy when she droops over the Messenger's bent knee, ending with her kneeling alone in sorrowful melancholy.

"Of Youth" (tenor) has men and women in playful, springtime mood; one woman is given prominence and supported by the others as she spins. At the end, this female soloist jumps and is caught at waist-height by the Messenger in a sudden appearance; as the poem speaks of mirror-images in the surface of a quiet pool the dancers momentarily invert themselves on the stage.

"Of Beauty" (alto) opens and closes in silhouette, with seven women idyllically plucking imagined lotus-flowers at the water's edge, interrupted by seven male dancers in wide diagonal leaps suggesting the poem's riders on horse back. A woman soloist is attracted to one of the horsemen; they dance a brief passage of passion and yearning together, with oriental shaping of hands and arms.

Four men reel on tipsily for "The Drunkard in Spring" (tenor), seemingly in carefree carousal until it becomes apparent that one is the Messenger, despite his participation in all the illusory reeling and rolling. At the end, with the principal Man supported by his arms in a backward lift between the Messenger's legs, we understand that Death has claimed his victim.

"The Farewell" (alto) is a long (thirty-minute) sequence of dancing centred on the Man, Woman, and Messenger, the intensity of feeling in music and poetry matched by solo, duo, and trio dancing that defies verbal description. It assimilates the best of MacMillan's choreography from earlier works and subsumes it in fresh invention that is sublime in its eloquence and depth of spirit. After an ecstatic pas de deux to the music's non-vocal passage, the Messenger takes the man away to leave the Woman in bourrées of despair before they return, the Man now also half-masked. In the valedictory coda, to the singer's "Ewig . . . Ewig . . .", the three step slowly forward in line as the light brightens in hope of renewal and the curtain falls.

MacMillan had long contemplated a *Song of the Earth* ballet but was at first refused permission to stage it by the Board of Directors at the Royal Opera House, Covent Garden, who disapproved of using Mahler's work for dance. MacMillan offered the idea instead to John Cranko, who had invited him to create a work for the Stuttgart Ballet, where *Song of the Earth* eventually had its premiere. Its public and critical success at Stuttgart was such that a Royal Ballet production followed in London just over six months later, with the Paris Opéra Ballet following in 1978. The work has remained in the Royal Ballet repertory to general admiration which, despite some reservations in musical quarters, has only increased with time.

—Noël Goodwin

SONG OF A WAYFARER

(original French title: *Chant du compagnon errant*)

Choreography: Maurice Béjart
Music: Gustav Mahler (*Lieder eines fahrenden Gesellen*)
First Production: Ballet du XXe Siècle, Forêt Nationale, Brussels, 11 March 1971
Principal Dancers: Rudolf Nureyev (The Man), Paolo Bortoluzzi (His Double)

Other productions include: Stuttgart Ballet, as *Lieder eines fahrenden Gesellen*, with Richard Cragun and Egon Madsen; Stuttgart, 25 April 1976. Rudolf Nureyev and Friends, with Nureyev and Johnny Eliasen; New York, 1 March 1977. Frankfurt Ballet; Frankfurt, 10 December 1982. Ballet Théâtre Français de Nancy, with Nureyev and Patrick Armand; 8 February 1983. London Festival Ballet, as *Song of a Wayfarer*, with Darryl Norton and Craig Randolph; Eastbourne, 8 March 1985.

PUBLICATIONS

Percival, John, "Nureyev—Rites for the Traveller", *Dance and Dancers* (London), May 1971

Clarke, Mary, "The Gala and the Concert", *Dancing Times* (London), April 1975

Sorley Walker, Kathrine, "Béjart and the Ballet of the Twentieth Century", *Dance Gazette* (London), July 1982

Forzley, Richard, "Maurice Béjart: Contemporary Myth-Maker", *Ballet-Hoo* (Winnipeg), Winter 1984

Song of A Wayfarer, with Eric Vu-An and Richard Cragun

Como, William, "Maestro of Spectacle", *Dance Magazine* (New York), May 1987

* * *

Béjart's choreography has always provoked strong reactions: his concept of dance as "*un spectacle total*", with its theatricality, sensationalism, and above all, flamboyant use of the male physique and raw sexuality, has made him one of the most controversial figures in twentieth-century ballet. But there is another Béjart who is too often lost amidst the controversy. The son of a philosopher, Béjart has intellectual interests which include oriental spirituality, nineteenth-century Romantic thought, and an unusually serious study of literature. All these elements have been increasingly apparent in his work in the last two decades, and *Song of a Wayfarer* was created at the beginning of this period.

It is as if, in the creation of *Song*, Béjart the philosopher encountered Béjart the showman, and the philosopher prevailed. It is not that this short, introspective portrait of individual suffering is not highly theatrical; rather, it is because the kind of theatre it creates is not the infamous Béjartian kind. In contrast to so much of his choreography, *Song* is eked out of a stark, empty stage. Two figures, one in white and the other in dark clothing, dance a pas de deux to Mahler's *Lieder eines fahrenden Gesellen*. Its drama comes from its music, from the power of the two male roles in dialogue (originally danced by Nureyev and Béjart's own Bortoluzzi, but revived for many pairs since), and from the Romanticism it explores.

In 1974 Béjart wrote of the stage as "the last refuge in our world where a man can discover the exact measure of his own soul". Nothing could better describe the course Béjart charted for the key figure in *Song* (the dancer in white). Mahler's lyrics, however, which he wrote at the age of 23 in a state of lovelorn despair, are not ostensibly about self-knowledge. They are not precisely about love lost either, but rather about a love never found. The suffering, while poignant, is never personalized in the songs; the images are the universal images of love poetry (birdsongs, fields, blossoms), and what is portrayed is therefore the universal experience of mourning an impossible happiness known only by intimation. It is from this Platonic sense of premature loss that Béjart's choreography takes its cue, not from the overt and highly conventional love theme. His two figures are not lovers, but they are, in some obscure way, companions (the French title, *Chant du compagnon errant*, makes explicit what Mahler's German title leaves ambiguous, by stressing the notion of a wayfaring *companion*, a concept which is lost in the English title). On the basis of this slender linguistic suggestion, Béjart seems to have constructed a dialogue out of Mahler's monologue.

The figure in white has the most expressive role: his features and his dancing convey violent passions, while the dark figure remains calm and methodical, even when they are both executing the same movements. For example, there is a poignant moment (captured from the original performance in one of Lido's striking photographs) when, expressing extreme exhaustion, Nureyev leans on Bortoluzzi's shoulder, clasping his hand, but Bortoluzzi, mirroring his position in all but the leaning head, is disarmingly placed with his back to Nureyev—does the dark figure represent an unseen, comforting pillar of support? Or is he meant to seem silent and unresponsive? The choreography is strewn with such poses, almost embryonic tableaux which hint at an allegorical significance. The dark figure often gives such support to the desperate struggles of the white figure; at other times he lingers just behind the white figure, often mirroring or shadowing his position in some slightly altered way. Sometimes the dark figure seems to block

his companion, but the white figure remains the centre of dramatic attention. Cruciform poses and poses of dependency add to the sense of pain which the Mahler lyrics convey, even in their cheerful moments.

Interpretations of the relation between these two figures vary widely: the dark figure has been described as the white figure's destiny, his double, his conscience, or his hopes and fears. Given the late-Romantic qualities of the songs, another possibility is that the passionate nature of the white figure and the sustaining, circumscribing force of the dark suggest the imagination and reason in dichotomy, or, in an even older allegorical tradition, the will and the reason, or the soul and its *imago dei* (image of God within).

Whatever the two figures represent, the choreography, like the songs themselves, is not narrative, but lyrical. It creates meaning through bursts of feeling and imagery, rather than through a story. There is perhaps a hint of narrative in the ending, in which the choreography parallels the song in a sense of acquiescence and of having achieved serenity at last. Mahler's lover finds peace in an obliterating sleep ("Under the linden tree, whose blossoms fell gently down and covered me . . ."), one of many hints of the Romantic preoccupation with death. The songs have, through their use of the recurring image of the prematurely nipped blossom, already anticipated this theme, and so has Béjart, with his recurring cruciform motif.

Béjart's choreography, like the late-Romantic poets and musicians he so admires, betrays just such a fascination with death: "Death directs the strange carnival we call life", he said of his *Malraux*, a piece in which death is personified in a number of ways. Béjart's literary capabilities are especially evident in *Song*, where he draws out what is only implicit in Mahler's lyrics, and reshapes the *Lieder* into an allegory of the soul in passion ("There is a glowing dagger, a dagger which stabs my breast"); of the soul in exile ("And I must bid farewell alas to all that I hold dear"); and of the soul in acquiescence ("Under the linden tree. . . ."). What remains impressed upon the mind after watching a performance of *Song* is that the soul is calmed and guided by something—precisely what is only perceived darkly (here the costume colours offer support for reading the dark figure as an *imago dei*), but perceived none the less.

—Kathryn Kerby-Fulton

————

LA SONNAMBULA
(*Night Shadow*)

Choreography: George Balanchine
Music: Vicenzo Bellini, orchestrated and arranged by Vittorio Rieti
Design: Dorothea Tanning
Libretto: Vittorio Rieti
First Production: Ballet Russe de Monte Carlo (as *Night Shadow*), New York, 27 February 1946
Principal Dancers: Alexandra Danilova (The Sleepwalker), Nicholas Magallanes (The Poet), Maria Tallchief (The Coquette), Michel Katcharoff (The Host)

Other productions include: Grand Ballet du Marquis de Cuevas (restaged Balanchine; design Jean Robier), with Ethéry Pagava, George Skibine, Marjorie Tallchief; London, 26 August 1948. Royal Danish Ballet (staged John Taras, design André Delfau); with Margrethe Schanne, Henning Kronstram,

La Sonnambula, with Allegra Kent as the Sleepwalker, New York City Ballet, c.1960

Mona Vangsaae; Copenhagen, 9 January 1955. New York City Ballet (restaged Balanchine; scenery Esteban Francés, costumes André Levasseur), as *La Sonnambula*, with Allegra Kent, Erik Bruhn, Jillana, John Taras; New York, 6 January 1960. Ballet Rambert (design Alix Stone); London, 18 July 1961. London Festival Ballet (staged Taras, design Peter Farmer), with June Sandbrook, Norman Morrice, Lucette Aldous; Venice, 20 March 1967. American Ballet Theatre (staged Taras, scenery Zack Brown, costumes David Elliott); New York, 26 May 1981.

PUBLICATIONS

Beaumont, Cyril, "Grand Ballet du Marquis de Cuevas", *Ballet* (London), October 1948

Bland, Alexander, "Le Grand Ballet du Marquis de Cuevas", *Ballet* (London), December 1951

Beaumont, Cyril, *Ballets of Today*, London, 1954

Barnes, Clive, "*Night Shadow*", *Dance and Dancers* (London), December 1960

Balanchine, George, with Mason, Francis, *Balanchine's Festival of Ballet*, Garden City, N.Y., 1977

Anderson, Jack, *The One and Only: The Ballet Russe de Monte Carlo*, London, 1981

Ostlere, Hilary, "Rieti and Balanchine", *Ballet Review* (Brooklyn), Spring 1982

Shaw, Alan, "Balanchine's Angelic Messenger", *Ballet Review* (New York), Winter 1990

* * *

La Sonnambula (*Night Shadow*), one of George Balanchine's few dramatic ballets, was first presented by the Ballet Russe de Monte Carlo in 1946. Based on a scenario by Vittorio Rieti and using operatic themes from Bellini operas, the ballet sets forth nineteenth-century intrigues of murder, jealousy, and revenge against a background of a masked ball in the garden of a baronial estate. Its appeal lies in the fascination of a Romantic-Gothic plot and in the long pas de deux that is the centrepiece of the work.

Comparisons are often made with two other Balanchine works, *Cotillon* and *La Valse*, both ballroom ballets, both inhabited by societies that reveal subdued cruelties behind the pursuit of their pleasures. But the musical colours provided by the two French composers, Chabrier and Ravel, for *Cotillon* and *La Valse* create a far different world from the Bel Canto hues of Bellini.

La Sonnambula, as *Night Shadow* came to be known after the 1960 production by the New York City Ballet, bears no relation to the operatic plot. Rieti's scenario concerns the actions of four main characters: a Coquette, the Host, who is enamoured of the Coquette, a young man called the Poet, and a young woman, the Sleepwalker, who may or may not be the wife of the Host and who remains in a deep trance. Jealousy propels the action and consumes both the Host in his desire for the Coquette and the Coquette herself, as she fails to attract the attentions of the Poet. When the Poet, fascinated by the Sleepwalker, finds he is unable to wake her, he follows her into the private chambers. The Coquette informs the Host, who rushes off to murder the Poet.

Rieti's story, operatic in tone and texture, might not have been taken seriously if Balanchine had not elaborated and decorated it with spectacular choreographic invention. It is a dance piece that entertains and provides a chance for the viewers to see beautiful dancing. Remembered foremost for the final sleepwalking scene, *Night Shadow*, nevertheless, also contains solos and ensemble groupings. Within the masked ball mise-en-scene comes the opportunity for a variety of dances; these divertissements often change with each particular production, but usually include a dance for Shepherds, Acrobats, Blackamoors, and a Harlequin. Reminiscent of the nineteenth-century three-act ballets, the ballet allows extraneous diversions to interrupt the ballroom drama and to entertain the guests. But *Night Shadow* choreographically renders a darker and more sinister atmosphere. No bright bluebirds fly at this party; rather, the Harlequin ends his routine on a downbeat, with a painful strain.

The Coquette's attraction to the Poet is shown as their pas de deux develops. She circles, moves in and about her partner, closing the circle in possessiveness, demanding attention; but the Poet is indifferent to her advances. The second and longer pas de deux for the Poet and the Sleepwalker is an exercise in bourrée for the ballerina. The Sleepwalker enters en pointe, candle in hand, moves in every direction while still en pointe, and eludes every gesture of the Poet to wake her.

Rieti and Balanchine filled the whole ballet with odd and theatrical details—for example, a strange light descends for the Sleepwalker's entrance and reverses direction at her exit. And no more bizarre moment in dramatic dance occurs than when the lifeless body of the Poet is lifted into the outstretched arms of the still-sleeping young woman, who effortlessly backs away and disappears.

The role of the Sleepwalker has always been an attraction to dancers—Alexandra Danilova in the original Ballet Russe, and Marjorie Tallchief, Allegra Kent, and Darci Kistler in later productions; the Byronic Poet, a perfect role for Eric Bruhn, was also interpreted by Mikhail Baryshnikov and Ib Anderson in a solemn and elegant manner.

—Richard Rutledge

LA SOURCE

Choreography: Arthur Saint-Léon

Music: Aloisius Ludwig (Léon) Minkus and (Clément Philbert) Léo Delibes

Design: Edouard Despléchin, Jean-Baptiste Lavastre, Auguste Rubé, Chaperon (sets), Paul Lormier (costumes)

Libretto: Charles Nuitter and Arthur Saint-Léon

First Production: Théâtre Impérial de l'Opéra, Paris, 12 November 1866

Principal Dancers: Guglielmina Salvioni (Naïla), Eugénie Fiocre (Nouredda), Louis Mérante (Djémil)

Other productions include: Bolshoi Theatre (new version; chor. Saint-Léon), as *Le Lys*, with Adèle Grantzow; St. Petersburg, 2 November (21 October old style) 1869. Teatro alla Scala (chor. Cesare Marzagora after Saint-Léon), as *La Sorgente*; Milan, 1875/76. Vienna Court Opera (restaged Saint-Léon), as *Naïla*; Vienna, 1878. Maryinsky Theatre (chor. Achille Coppini after Saint-Léon), as *Ruchei* (The Stream), with Olga Preobrazhenska (Naïla); St. Petersburg, 8 December 1902. State Academic Theatre for Opera and Ballet (GATOB) (staged Agrippina Vaganova and Vladimir Ponomarev after Saint-Léon), with Marina Semenova (Naïla); Leningrad, 12 April 1925. Paris Opéra Ballet (new version; chor. Léo Staats, design Valdo Barbey), as *Soir de Fête*, with Olga Spessivtseva; Paris, 30 June 1925. Stuttgart Ballet (pas de deux only; new version, chor. John Cranko); Stuttgart, 30 May 1964. New

La Source: title-page of piano score, 1866

York City Ballet (pas de deux only; new version, chor. George Balanchine), with Violette Verdy and John Prinz; New York, 23 November 1968 (restaged Balanchine, with additional ensemble, New York, 1969).

PUBLICATIONS

Beaumont, Cyril, *Complete Book of Ballets*, revised edition, London, 1951

Guest, Ivor, *The Ballet of the Second Empire*, London, 1955

Krasovskaya, Vera, *Russian Ballet Theatre of the Second Half of the Nineteenth Century*, Leningrad and Moscow, 1963

Dunn, Thomas, "Delibes and *La Source*: Some Manuscripts and Documents", *Dance Chronicle* (New York), vol. 4, no. 1, 1981

Saint-Léon, Arthur, *Letters from a Ballet Master*, edited by Ivor Guest, New York, 1981

* * *

Arthur Saint-Léon's *La Source,* more noteworthy for its Second Empire mediocrity than for artistic merit, was produced in Paris after ballet-mania had peaked and plunged. The first grand ballet to have its premiere at the Paris Opéra in a half-decade, *La Source* adhered to shopworn Romantic principles, attempting to reproduce the formula's success. Motivated by box-office potential instead of artistic compulsion, the ballet offered applause-winning scenic delights and a praiseworthy score, but lacked the creative vision that separates art from diversion.

La Source's score, a collaboration between Léon Minkus, who understood choreographic demands and public tastes, and Léo Delibes, a neophyte then testing his balletic composition talents, accurately captured the dramatic essence of each act and provided a flattering musical contrast. Although Minkus's first scene was criticized for thinness, his music, always danceable and consistent, echoed the languidness and melancholy depicted in the ballet's opening and finale. Delibes's composition (scenes two and three), though conspicuously dependent upon Mendelssohn's *A Midsummer Night's Dream*, was acclaimed as the more melodious, lively, rhythmic, and artistically complex contribution. Significantly, Delibes's success with *La Source* brought him the commission for his masterwork—*Coppélia*.

Because Saint-Léon was a notoriously inept scenarist, Charles Nuitter, the Paris Opéra's archivist, was hired by the management to devise *La Source*'s story (a convoluted tale about Naïla, Spirit of the Spring, who is protected by the hunter Djemil and therefore helps him to win his love, Nouredda). However, Nuitter's non-artistic contribution to the ballet was greater than his creative output. As a correspondent to Saint-Léon, employed in Russia and unable to conduct the ballet's pre-performance rehearsals, Nuitter acted as a reporter to, and liaison for, the absent choreographer, disseminating instructions, decisions, and corrections to the Paris Opéra's manager Emile Perrin, to Delibes, and to the artistic staff and dancers. As Saint-Léon's artistic lifeline, Nuitter was instrumental in *La Source*'s production and in building the trust, friendship, and team spirit that would later spawn an unequivocal masterpiece—*Coppélia*, the ballet which would crown his success as a scenarist.

Saint-Léon, who was gifted with musicality, was reputed for filling his ballets with well-structured variations and dances, exemplified in *La Source* by Léontine Beaugrand's dainty Act II solo and the charming "Guzla Dance" performed by Eugénie Fiocre. Also noted for his penchant for stage effects, along with a skill in utilizing national dances and an ability to stage crowd scenes, Saint-Léon was particularly adept at creating choreography to display his dancers' talents. *La Source*, conceived for his muse Adèle Grantzow, was specifically designed to show off her lightness, delicacy, and technical attributes.

With Grantzow incapacitated by injury, however, the role of Naïla was inherited by the Milan-trained ballerina Guglielmina Salvioni, renowned for her technical virtuosity, strength, and solid pointe work. Although somewhat graceless, the tall and harsh-featured Salvioni compensated for her deficiencies with elegance and dramatic sensibility. Stylistically opposed to Grantzow, Salvioni was a gifted tragédienne who presented a successful interpretation of Naïla, adeptly applying her miming talents to the acclaimed death scene. Although criticized for errors in timing, along with lack of fluidity and an indistinctive style, she gave an adequate performance—but she was probably unable to punctuate the choreography artistically. Grantzow, who rightfully assumed her role in 1867, by contrast imbued Naïla with the required suppleness, grace, softness, and artistic shading.

Djémil was created by stout-legged Louis Mérante, who despite his physique was a capable, versatile performer and a partner preferred by numerous ballerinas. Although he originated many roles at the Paris Opéra, his talent was unappreciated by the public, which was prejudiced against male danseurs. Consequently, he attracted scant critical notice. Graceful, dignified, and intelligent, he innately employed facial expressions and gestures to colour his characterizations, skills used to his advantage in *La Source*.

Although *La Source* won accolades for its staging, spectacle, dancing, and music, the ballet failed to exert lasting impact.

The substitution of Salvioni for Grantzow may have contributed to its mixed reception. However, after Grantzow successfully re-created the leading role, the ballet did not achieve greatness. Saint-Léon's absence during the initial refining process inevitably deterred tightening the action and polishing the choreography, which gleaned little critical attention.

Although helpful reviewers suggested structural improvements, the ballet's scenario, common to the era's declining standards, was hopelessly inconsistent, a defect blatantly demonstrated by the plot's faulty dramatic impetus: Djémil prevents the gypsy Morgab from polluting Naïla's spring, only to cause its ultimate evaporation and ensuing ecological destruction with his own inconsideration. Although nymph/mortal relationships are predestined for doom by Romanticism's dictates, Djémil never proves himself worthy of Naïla's sacrifice. He is initially inspired by Morgab's spell to pursue the indifferent Nouredda, then is fired by revenge, and finally, in the last scene, is motivated by self-gratification—knowingly placing the fulfilment of his desire before Naïla's life. Nouredda, as a conspirator with Morgab and Mozdock, is an unsympathetic character. She deceives Djémil and repeatedly imperils his life. Although Djémil's disloyalty towards Naïla equates with Nouredda's betrayal of him, proving their compatibility, the story's only purpose is to unite two people, who without magical intervention, would not have chosen each other.

Despite its inherent failings, *La Source* has been reworked by other choreographers, probably drawn to the music's appeal. Saint-Léon's later version, which partially resurfaced in *Le Lys* (1869), a vehicle for Grantzow, has vanished. Although *La Source* imparted little to dance history, the ballet served as an artistic "dress rehearsal", assembling the three talents—Delibes, Nuitter, and Saint-Léon—who would produce the Second Empire's last and greatest success, *Coppélia*.

—Karen Dacko

SPARTACUS
(original Russian title: *Spartak*)

Choreography: Yuri Grigorovich
Music: Aram Khachaturian
Design: Simon Virsaladze (scenery and costumes)
Libretto: Nikolai Volkov
First Production: Bolshoi Ballet, Moscow, 9 April 1968
Principal Dancers: Vladimir Vasiliev (Spartacus), Ekaterina Maximova (Phrygia), Nina Timofeyeva (Aegina), Maris Liepa (Crassus)

Other productions include: Kirov Ballet (original production to score; chor. Leonid Yakobson, design Konstantin Khodasevich), with Askold Makarov (Spartacus), Inna Zubkovskaya (Phrygia), Alla Shelest (Aegina), Robert Gerbek (Crassus); Leningrad, 27 December 1956. Bolshoi Ballet (new version; chor. Igor Moiseyev, design A. Konstantinovsky), with D. E. Begak (Spartacus), Natalia Ryuzhenko (Phrygia), Maya Plisetskaya (Aegina), Nikolai Fadeyechev (Garmodius); Moscow, 11 March 1958. Bolshoi Ballet (restaged Yakobson), with Begak (Spartacus), Plisetskaya (Phrygia), Ryuzhenko (Aegina), Aleksandr Radunsky (Crassus); Moscow, 4 April 1962. Hungarian State Opera Ballet (new version; chor. László Seregi), with Viktor Fülöp (Spartacus), Zsuzsa Kun (Flavia);

Budapest, 18 May 1968. Australian Ballet (restaged Seregi); Melbourne, 26 October 1978.

PUBLICATIONS

About the Yakobson production:
Haskell, Arnold, "Russian Logbook", *Dancing Times* (London), 3 parts: June, July, September 1962
Parker, Ralph, "*Spartacus* and Plisetskaya", *Dance Magazine* (New York), September 1962

About the Grigorovich production:
"The Bolshoi's New Hit", *Dance Magazine* (New York), May 1969
Roslavleva, Natalia, "The Bolshoi's *Spartacus*", *Dancing Times* (London), June 1969
Goodwin, Noël, "Grigorovich's *Spartacus*", *Dance News* (New York), September 1969
Vanslav, Viktor, *The Ballets of Grigorovich and the Problems of Choreography*, Moscow, 1971
Greskovic, Robert, "The Grigorovich Factor and the Bolshoi", *Ballet Review* (Brooklyn, N.Y.), vol 5, no. 2, 1975–76
Balanchine, George, and Mason, Francis, *Balanchine's Complete Stories of the Great Ballets*, Garden City, N.Y., 1977
Alovert, Nina, "The Soviet Dance Theatre of Yuri Grigorovich", *Dance Magazine* (New York), December 1987

*   *   *

The ballet of *Spartacus* is based on a libretto by Nikolai Volkov, who studied works by Plutarch and Appian for authentic background while also inventing new characters and imaginary situations. The ballet tells the story of the slave revolt against Roman oppressors in the first century A.D. The leader of the slaves is Spartacus, who sets his rebel army against the powerful Crassus and his legions. He is killed, but his heroism lives on. For his version of the ballet, Leonid Yakobson studied Greek and Roman culture, taking images from sculpture, vases, bas-reliefs, and pictures to evoke the era. His ballerinas danced on three-quarter point in sandals rather than on their toes, and the choreography was fresco-like. (The Bolshoi's present artistic director and choreographer of the version performed today, Yuri Grigorovich, danced as a soloist in this version in Leningrad.) Igor Moiseyev's version had strong elements of colourful ensemble dance, springing from his background as head of the famous folk dance troupe; but the ballet survived only six performances due to its lack of action.

Yuri Grigorovich's *Spartacus* is a heroic spectacle, notable for its virile, non-stop displays of virtuosity. It is considered by many to be his finest ballet—it is certainly his most famous—finding huge success both at home in Moscow and abroad. It is pure Bolshoi in style—big, bold, and boisterous; it has been likened to a Hollywood "blockbuster" for its impact and energetic presentation. It is also a true "Soviet" ballet, in that Grigorovich also uses the story to fit the approved social theme of the common man triumphing over oppression.

The ballet follows the framework of the large Soviet productions, such as Leonid Lavrovsky's *Romeo and Juliet*, which swept the Soviet stage during the 1940s and 1950s. Yet Grigorovich uses a different formula. He breaks the mould of tradition by using four soloists—one pair good, the other villainous—rather than the more conventional two (a principal ballerina with her male partner). *Spartacus* requires full-fledged artistry and technical ability from every member of the ensemble, no matter how small the role, to support (though never rival) the leading dancers. Most importantly, *Spartacus*

Spartacus, **as choreographed by Yuri Grigorovich, performed by the Bolshoi Ballet, Moscow**

focuses—and depends—on the strength and stamina of its men. Grigorovich turns the spotlight away from the ballerina on to the male dancer, making him a dynamic force.

Scenes are filled with contrasts: the virile, heroic slave and the cruel, narcissistic Roman general; the love of Spartacus's devoted wife, Phrygia, and the sensualism of the concubine Aegina; the despair of the slaves seeking freedom and the orgies of the decadent Romans.

Grigorovich unfolds his story through a montage of tableaux in which massed action is punctuated with solos and duets. Danced "monologues" reveal the characters' innermost thoughts. These show Grigorovich's talent for lucidly exchanging words for movement without losing impact. He paints his stage with huge images of male supremacy and athleticism. Waves of movement bear the men up and over the set's canvas, with an overriding sense of commitment and competition which make the overall performance seem an Olympic contest. Ballerinas, freed from classical fragility, become human, with expansive but elegant mannerisms. The ballet relies on 100% execution from all—there are no back lines in which to hide.

Grigorovich's successful choreography for the ballet sets patterns which are found in his subsequent works: the crowd scatters to make a diagonal "flight-pattern" for the hero's soaring, bravura entrance in a spectacular series of leaps across the stage; there are daring lifts and acrobatic tricks in the pas de deux; the whole ballet is charged with energy, and is danced flat out. There are many theatrical moments—the fight to the death between two masked slave gladiators for the sport of the Romans; the spontaneous, jubilant dance of the shepherds who join the rebel army; the licentious Aegina inciting the rebel soldiers to forget their oath to their leader; Spartacus

"crucified" and thrust aloft by the spears of the Romans; and the chilling opening moments of the ballet where the cruel Crassus, astride his chariot and gripping an eagle-headed staff of authority, sets off with his goose-stepping legionnaires to conquer the world. Set to Aram Khachaturian's rousing, yet often lyrical score, the ballet has followed some of the Roman army's footsteps.

Vladimir Vasiliev first performed in the role of Spartacus, a role considered to be his finest. His portrayal of a proud leader caught in tragic circumstances combined passion in his powerful bravura dancing with an elegant manliness and sincerity in his acting. Mikhail Lavrovsky's character was a more athletic and impulsive leader, while Vyacheslav Gordeyev demonstrated pure, classical virtuoso dancing. The most recent star interpreter, Irek Mukhamedov, catapulting across the stage with unleashed energy, offered a charismatic characterization and forceful images which have been hard to replace since Mukhamedov's departure from the Bolshoi.

The role of Crassus will forever be associated with Maris Liepa, whose brilliant interpretation clearly showed the weaknesses and self-love of the arrogant and cunning general. His gifts as an actor and his aristocratic appearance made an unforgettable impact, which is still remembered today, and which in many ways has contributed to the ballet's lasting appeal.

—Margaret Willis

Le Spectre de la rose, **with Elisabetta Terabust and Patrice Bart, London Festival Ballet**

LE SPECTRE DE LA ROSE

Choreography: Mikhail Fokine
Music Music: Carl Maria von Weber (*Invitation to the Dance*), orchestrated by Hector Berlioz
Design: Léon Bakst (scenery and costumes)
Libretto: Jean-Louis Vaudoyer (after Théophile Gautier)
First Production: Diaghilev's Ballets Russes, Théâtre de Monte Carlo, 19 April 1911
Principal Dancers: Tamara Karsavina (Young Girl), Vaslav Nijinsky (Spirit of the Rose)

Other productions include: Saison Nijinsky (staged Vaslav Nijinsky), with Bronislava Nijinska, Vaslav Nijinsky; London, 23 February 1914. Marie Rambert's Dancers (staged Tamara Karsavina), with Karsavina, Harold Turner; London, 30 June 1930. Paris Opéra Ballet (revival, after Fokine); Paris, 31 December 1931. Vic-Wells Ballet (staged Anton Dolin after Fokine), with Ninette de Valois, Dolin; London, 4 March 1932. De Basil's Ballets Russes (staged Serge Grigoriev after Fokine), with Irina Baronova, Paul Petrov; London, 23 August 1935. (René Blum's) Ballets de Monte Carlo (revival, supervised by Fokine), with Maria Ruanova, André Eglevsky; Monte Carlo, 1936. Ballet Theatre (restaged Fokine), with Annabelle Lyon, Ian Gibson; Mexico City, 31 October 1941. Les Ballets Champs-Elysées (staged Roland Petit after Fokine); Paris, 1946. Metropolitan Ballet (after Fokine), with Svetlana Beriosova, Erik Bruhn; 1947. Sadler's Wells Ballet (staged Karsavina after Fokine; design Rex Whistler), with Margot Fonteyn, Alexis Rassine; London, 1 February 1944. Sadler's Wells Opera Ballet (staged Karsavina), with June Brae, Leo Kersley; London, 6 May 1946. London Festival Ballet (staged Dolin, Karsavina after Fokine; design Benn Toff after Bakst); 6 December 1950 (restaged Karsavina, with design Delaney, 21 April 1962). Bolshoi Ballet (staged Maris Liepa after Fokine), with Natalia Bessmertnova and Maris Liepa; Moscow, 3 June 1967. Pittsburgh Ballet Theatre (staged Vitale Fokine after Fokine, design after Bakst); Pittsburgh, 2 March 1973. Joffrey Ballet (revival; after Dolin, Karsavina staging), with Rudolf Nureyev; 6 March 1979. Hamburg Ballet (new version; chor. John Neumeier); Hamburg, 25 June 1986.

PUBLICATIONS

Cocteau, Jean, *La Saison russe*, Paris, 1911

Beaumont, Cyril, *Complete Book of Ballets*, revised edition, London, 1951

Grigoriev, Serge, *The Diaghilev Ballet*, translated by Vera Bowen, London, 1953

Barnes, Clive, "*Le Spectre de la rose*", *Dance and Dancers* (London), July 1959

Fokine, Michel, *Fokine: Memoirs of a Ballet Master*, translated by Vitale Fokine, London, 1961

Hering, Doris, "Against the Tide", *Dance Magazine* (New York), 2 parts: August, September 1961

Balanchine, George, with Mason, Francis, *Balanchine's Festival of Ballet*, Garden City, N.Y., 1977

Vaughan, David, "Fokine in the Contemporary Repertory", *Ballet Review* (New York), vol. 7, no. 2–3, 1978–79

"What Nijinsky Did", *Dance and Dancers* (London), October 1987

Garafola, Lynn, *Diaghilev's Ballets Russes*, New York, 1989

*   *   *

"About the composition of *Le Spectre de la rose*," Mikhail

Fokine wrote in his *Memoirs of a Ballet Master*, "I should like to say that, while I utilized all the resources of the classic ballet, I still considered this work as belonging to the classification of 'new ballet'. It contained no dances staged to display technique . . . and the dances were expressive at all times. . . . In none of the movements of the Spectre could one find any trace of dancing variations for the pleasure of the audience . . . he is in no circumstances a 'cavalier', a ballerina's partner."

This miniature ballet, flawless in a way in which only a miniature can be, employed only two dancers—but those among the greatest, if not *the* greatest, of the century, Tamara Karsavina and Vaslav Nijinsky. Based on the poem by Gautier, brought to Fokine's attention by the French poet Jean-Louis Vaudoyer, and set to Weber's *Invitation to the Dance*, the ballet was danced in the setting of (to quote Fokine again) "a tiny room, the two walls of which meet together in an upstage corner, leaving but little room for dancing. The difficulty lay in confining the dance to such a small space." Fokine further compounded his problems by using an armchair, in which the Young Girl falls asleep to dream of the Rose, which remains prominently on stage throughout, curtailing still further the available dancing space. However, in no art is the maxim "Necessity is the mother of invention" more valid than in the sphere of choreography, and it could well have been exactly the limitations set by the minimal cast, the reduced stage area, and the brief, already extant score which concentrated Fokine's mind to a point where he could produce an absolute masterpiece—a masterpiece marred only in performance by those stupid members of the audience who break into loud applause after the male dancer's final exit, killing the Young Girl's magical moment of awakening, when she realizes that she has been asleep and dreaming.

Le Spectre de la rose was, together with *Le Carnaval*, the *Polovtsian Dances*, *Le Pavillon d'Armide*, *Les Sylphides*, and the exotica *Schéhérazade* and *Cléopâtre*, one of the ballets which took London by storm in 1911, just as Paris had been taken by storm in 1909 and 1910. Not only were the Ballets Russes and the Russian dancers the toast of fashionable society, but writers such as Marcel Proust, Arnold Bennett, H. G. Wells, and Bernard Shaw attended performances regularly, and discussed the Russian Ballet with their friends into the small hours. *Le Spectre de la rose*, short as it was, encompassed (perhaps subconsciously, so far as the choreographer was concerned) two ideas novel at the time. First, instead of following the ideals of the Romantic period, with the male in pursuit of the elusive woman of his dreams, in this case it is the woman who is pursuing her ideal figure, the Spirit of the Rose. Second, the ballet could not help but recall the fact that Freud had recently published his theories on the meaning of dreams, and the psychology of those who have them. Both these revolutionary points of view as expressed in a wildly popular art form must have provided material for discussion by those who flocked to the performances: we can only imagine how fascinating it must have been to Proust to see a whole world opened up to the Young Girl by the scent of a rose, when he himself was about to astonish the reading public with his great novel, which evolves from the memories evoked in the narrator by the famous taste of the madeleine dipped in tea.

Le Spectre de la rose held its place in Diaghilev's repertoire from the date of its premiere, and was still there during the final season in 1929 (the other two survivors were *Les Sylphides* and the *Polovtsian Dances*.) Today *Le Spectre* is less popular, or rather, it has to work harder to make anything approaching the stir it made at its premiere: many (who never saw the original cast) affirm that without Karsavina and Nijinsky the ballet is not worth watching. Nevertheless, it has been revived times without number (nearly 150 performances by the various Royal

Ballet organizations alone) and its roles hold an undying fascination for those lucky enough to get the chance to dance them.

It is perhaps interesting in this connection to point out that although today the role of the Rose is generally accepted to be one of the heaviest in the male repertoire, at the time of its creation Nijinsky would frequently appear in other ballets (such as *Le Carnaval, Petrushka, Les Sylphides*—none of them sinecures) on the same evening. Few male dancers today would embark upon such a programme, and the fact that Fokine, the choreographer of each of these entirely different works, based Nijinsky's role in each one upon a different facet of the dancer's varied acting talents and distinctive physique must not obscure the fact that, though we hear on all sides that technique today is so much better than it used to be, there are few dancers at the present time who could dance three of these ballets on one programme. Indeed it might be possible to advance the argument that only a dancer who has performed all or some of these roles, with quite remarkable difficulties to be overcome, both technically and in interpretation, and—more difficult still—concealed from the audience, can appreciate fully the unique talents of the originator of the Rose, Vaslav Nijinsky.

—Leo Kersley

SPESSIVTSEVA (Spessiva), Olga

Russian dancer. Born Olga Aleksandrovna Spesivtseva (Spessivtseva) in Rostov-on-Don, 18 July (6 July old style) 1895. Studied at the St. Petersburg Theatre School, pupil of Klavdiya Kulichevskaya, graduated in 1913; also trained later under Ekaterina Vazem and Agrippina Vaganova. Married Russian/French dancer and choreographer Boris Kniaseff. Dancer, Maryinsky Theatre (later the State Academic Theatre for Opera and Ballet, or GATOB), St. Petersburg/Petrograd, 1913–24, becoming soloist from 1916, and ballerina from 1918; ballerina with Diaghilev's Ballets Russes, appearing in United States, 1916–17, and London, 1921–22; ballerina, Ballet de l'Opéra, Paris, 1924–32, also appearing with Diaghilev company in Monte Carlo, 1927, and Paris, 1929; performed in Buenos Aires, 1931, with the Camargo Society, London, 1932, with Viktor Landré and Alexander Levitov Ballet, 1934, and Opéra Comique, Paris, 1935; went to the U.S. in 1939: adviser to Ballet Theatre, New York, until nervous breakdown, 1943. Died in New York State, 16 September 1991.

ROLES

1913 Snow in *The Seasons* (N. Legat after Petipa), Maryinsky Theatre, St. Petersburg
Queen of the White Night in *Le Conte d'une nuit blanche* (Kulichevskaya), Maryinsky Theatre, St. Petersburg
1914/ Pas de trois in *Swan Lake* (Petipa, Ivanov), Maryinsky
15 Theatre, Petrograd
1915 Diamond Fairy in *The Sleeping Beauty* (Petipa), Maryinsky Theatre, Petrograd
Odette/Odile in *Swan Lake* (Petipa, Ivanov), Maryinsky Theatre, Petrograd
1916 Pierrette in *Harlequinade* (*Les Millions d'Arlequin*; Petipa), Maryinsky Theatre, Petrograd
Title role in *Giselle* (Petipa after Coralli, Perrot), Maryinsky Theatre, Petrograd

The Girl in *Le Spectre de la rose* (Fokine), Diaghilev's Ballets Russes, New York
1918 Sugar Plum Fairy in *The Nutcracker* (Ivanov), State Academic Theatre for Opera and Ballet (GATOB), Petrograd
Grand pas in *Paquita* (Petipa), GATOB, Petrograd
Title role in *Esmeralda* (Petipa after Perrot), GATOB, Petrograd
Mazurka, Waltz, Prelude in *Chopiniana* (Fokine), GATOB, Petrograd
Aspicia in *La Fille du Pharaon* (Petipa), GATOB, Petrograd
Title role in *Raymonda* (Petipa), GATOB, Petrograd
1920 Nikiya in *La Bayadère* (Petipa), GATOB, Petrograd
Medora in *Le Corsaire* (Petipa), GATOB, Petrograd
1921 Princess Aurora in *The Sleeping Princess* (Petipa; staged Sergeyev, with additional dances Nijinska), Diaghilev's Ballets Russes, London
1923 Kitri in *Don Quixote* (Petipa), GATOB, Petrograd
Title role in *Esmeralda* (Petipa; staged Mendez), GATOB, Petrograd
1924 Title role in *Giselle* (Petipa after Coralli, Perrot; staged Sergeyev), Opéra, Paris
1925 Soloist (cr) in *Les Rencontres* (Nijinska), Opéra, Paris
Soloist in *Suite de danses* (Clustine), Opéra, Paris
1926 Title role in *La Péri* (Staats), Opéra, Paris
Soloist in *Les Abeilles* (Staats), Opéra, Paris
1927 Title role (cr; though replaced by Nikitina at premiere) in *La Chatte* (Balanchine), Diaghilev's Ballets Russes, Monte Carlo
Title role in *L'Oiseau de Feu* (Fokine), Diaghilev's Ballets Russes, Monte Carlo
Flore in *Zéphire et Flore* (Massine), Diaghilev's Ballets Russes, Monte Carlo
Juliet in *Romeo and Juliet* (Nijinska), Diaghilev's Ballets Russes, Monte Carlo
1928 Butterfly (cr) in *Les Caprices de Papillon* (Kniaseff), Théâtre des Champs-Élysées, Paris
Salomé in *La Tragédie de Salomé* (N. Guerra), Opéra, Paris
1929 Odette in *Swan Lake*, Act II (Ivanov), Diaghilev's Ballets Russes, London
Soloist (cr) in *Les Créatures de Prométhée* (Lifar, Balanchine), Opéra, Paris
1931 Ariane (cr) in *Bacchus et Ariane* (Lifar), Opéra, Paris
1932 Title role in *Giselle* (Petipa after Coralli, Perrot), Camargo Society, London
1935 Title role (cr) in *Psyche* (Fokine), Opéra-Comique, Paris
Principal dancer (cr) in *Mephisto Waltz* (Fokine), Opéra-Comique, Paris

PUBLICATIONS

By Spessivtseva:
The Technique for the Ballet Artiste, London, 1967

About Spessivtseva:
Vaillat, Léandre, *Olga Spessivtseva*, Paris, 1944
Shaikevich, A., *Olga Spessivtseva*, Paris, 1954
Ilyin, Eugene, "Tragedy of a living 'Giselle'", *Dance Magazine* (New York), June 1954
Lifar, Serge, *Les Trois Graces de XX Siecle*, Paris, 1957
Kniaseff, Boris, "Reminiscences . . . in the Footsteps of Olga Spessivtseva", *Ballet Today* (London), 3 parts: July, August-September, October, 1957

Fern, Dale, "Spessivtseva", *Dance Magazine* (New York), 3 parts: April, May, July, 1960

Dolin, Anton, *The Sleeping Ballerina*, London, 1966

Bogdanov-Berezovsky, Valerian, "Spessivtseva", in *The People I Met*, Moscow, 1967

Krasovskaya, Vera, *Russian Ballet Theatre of the Early Twentieth Century*, vol. 2: Leningrad, 1972

Austin, Richard, *The Art of the Dancer*, London, 1982

Smakov, Gennady, *The Great Russian Dancers*, New York, 1984

* * *

Few personalities in the history of St. Petersburg ballet have won recognition as quickly and as easily as Olga Spessivtseva did. Three years after the start of her career she was already a soloist (1916), and two years later she effectively became the theatre's prima ballerina. In fact, she had been noticed by ballet critics as far back as her school years. The champion of classical choreography, Akim Volynsky, wrote about the young dancer in 1912: "Well proportioned and slim, with highly arched feet, she has a dreamy and slightly over-refined style of dancing, redolent of Taglioni." The lovely "bud" soon turned into a unique flower which combined the fragrance of the classical tradition with a disarming spirit of modernity.

Of all Spessivtseva's endowments her beauty was the first to strike the eye. Fedor Lopukhov later recollected: "A shapely body, a wonderful build, subtle movements of the arms, legs ideally formed, a cameo face with enormous eyes that were full of fire, a beautiful high and long leap—such were the diverse gifts bestowed on Spessivtseva by nature; whatever part she danced, the public always saw her as an incarnation of Beauty, and identified her with ideals, which might be trampled underfoot but still remained ideals." Later critics commented more on the nature of Spessivtseva's talent and her style of dancing than on the pictorial image: "Spessivtseva belongs to a rare category of 'Ethereal' dancers with her long legs and tendons; she reminds one of that sea-bird from Baudelaire's sonnet which could only fly because its over-long wings would not allow it to walk. Similarly, Spessivtseva's native element is the airy fantastic ballet, the soaring spirits of *Giselle* and *La Bayadère*" (André Levinson). Yuri Slonimsky wrote, "For Spessivtseva, the art of dancing became a kind of religion. She appeared on the stage like a believer entering a church, elevated and prepared to sacrifice all she had, even her life. Through her dance, Spessivtseva expressed her attitude not so much to the collisions of the plot as to the central questions of human existence that stood behind them. Beauty became, in Spessivtseva's interpretation, the centre of a dramatic discourse and one of the most vital ethical problems. This approach manifested itself to the full in *Giselle*. Like her great predecessors, Spessivtseva interpreted the main theme as that of betrayed trust. But in contrast with her Giselle the world appeared more than unjust—it was inhuman."

The part of Giselle became part and parcel of Spessivtseva's artistic career: she danced that role for nearly twenty years. Even back in her motherland, Volynsky called her Giselle "a spirit bemoaning its native bourns", but later Spessivtseva's interpretation of the character became ever more poignant and tragic, so that some contemporaries described her dancing as Expressionist, despite its remaining totally within the traditional limits of classical ballet.

However, there were other interpretations of Spessivtseva's dancing. Thus, Serge Diaghilev, whose praise of his ballerinas had never been prolific, wrote in 1927: "I have always thought that one only gets a limited 'portion' of joy to last through one's lifetime: only one generation has the privilege of admiring the

Olga Spessivtseva with Serge Lifar in *Swan Lake*, Paris, late 1920s

unique Taglioni or hearing the unique Patti. When I saw Pavlova in the days of her youth, and mine, I was sure that she was 'the Taglioni of my lifetime'. So it was really a great surprise to me when I met Spessivtseva, who is a finer and purer being than Pavlova. Earlier this winter I heard our great maestro Cecchetti saying 'There was an apple in the world that was cut in two halves. One of the two became Pavlova, the other Spessivtseva'. I can only add that to me Spessivtseva has always been the side of the apple which is turned towards the sun."

Thus Diaghilev engaged Spessitseva (who sometimes appeared as Spessiva) as a ballerina for his U.S. tour, and she had her American début in New York in 1916, where among other roles she performed *Le Spectre de la rose* with Nijinsky. Spessivtseva danced the role of Princess Aurora in Diaghilev's London staging of *The Sleeping Princess* in 1921–22 where despite the financial failure of the production she won great acclaim. She also performed the title role in Balanchine's *La Chatte* in 1927, and in 1929, Odette in *Swan Lake*, Act II. Later she made concert tours of Argentina, Australia, and Europe. In 1932 she danced in London again, and in 1935 she danced the main roles in Fokine's ballets at the Opéra Comique in Paris. Spessivtseva gave her last performance in 1939 in Buenos

Aires. Her career had a strangely unfocused quality to it by then, and her life of wandering came to an end in 1943, when she entered an asylum. The years 1943–63 were spent in mental institutions; from 1963 until her death she lived in a New York suburb, at a farm belonging to the Tolstoy Foundation.

Sadly, there was not much happiness in this ballerina's life. With the years, her tragic gift as a dancer, enhanced by various external and internal circumstances, had merged more and more into a personal drama, and she had begun to suffer from serious depression. The crisis came to a head with the end of her theatrical career (although signs of mental illness had been detected from her early performing days), and the ballerina virtually sank into a "slumber" for decades—ironically like the Princess Aurora, the Sleeping Beauty. This legendary figure lived until the age of 96, the only survivor of all the great Russian pre-Revolutionary ballerinas, and died in 1991.

—Arsen Degen

SPOERLI, Heinz

Swiss dancer, choreographer, and teacher. Born in Basel, 8 July 1941. Studied with Walter Kleiber, Basel, 1957–60; also studied at American Ballet Center (Joffrey Ballet School), School of American Ballet, London Dance Centre, and with Martha Graham, New York. Soloist, Basel Ballet, 1960–63, Cologne Ballet, 1963–66, Royal Winnipeg Ballet, 1966–67, Les Grands Ballets Canadiens, 1967–71; choreographer, staging first work in Geneva, 1971: choreographer and soloist, Geneva Ballet, 1971–73; ballet director and choreographer, Basel Ballet, 1973–91; artistic director and choreographer, German Opera on the Rhine, Düsseldorf, from 1991; also guest teacher and choreographer, People's Republic of China, 1984, and international guest choreographer, including in Tel Aviv, Berlin, Helsinki, Stockholm, Stuttgart, Paris, Düsseldorf, Vienna, Milan, and Zurich; founder, Open Air Festival, "Basel tanzt", mounted 1986, 1987, 1988, 1990; also choreographer for television and film. Recipient: Hans Reinhart-Ring, Swiss Organization of the Düsseldorf Ballet, 1982; Ehrespahlebärglemer, 1987; Cultural Prize of the City of Basel.

WORKS

1971   *Le Chemin* (mus. Gaudibert), Geneva Ballet, Geneva (restaged Basel Ballet, 1973)
1973   *Rendez-Vous* (mus. Haydn), Basel Ballet, Basel
      Der Feuervogel (mus. Stravinsky), Basel Ballet, Basel
1974   *Phantasien* (mus. Bartók), Basel Ballet, Basel
      Inventionen (mus. Bach), Basel Ballet, Basel
      Lamentoso (mus. Kabelac), Basel Ballet, Basel
      Hommage à Pauline (mus. Schumann), Basel Ballet, Basel
      Petrushka (mus. Stravinsky), Basel Ballet, Basel
1975   *Flowing Landscapes* (mus. Ives), Basel Ballet, Basel
      Opus 6 (mus. Webern), Basel Ballet, Basel
      Trois Gnossiennes (mus. Satie), Basel Ballet, Basel
      Concerto (mus. Vivaldi), Basel Ballet, Basel
      L'Amfiparnasso (mus. Vecchi), Basel Ballet, Basel
      Labyrinth (mus. Rachmaninov), Basel Ballet, Basel
1976   *Ein Sommernachtstraum* (mus. Mendelssohn), Basel Ballet, Basel
1977   *Sonate für Tänzer* (mus. Rossini), Basel Ballet, Basel
      War Poem (mus. Bram), Basel Ballet, Basel

      Drei Intermezzi (mus. Brahms), Basel Ballet, Basel
      "Wir Waren . . ." (mus. Bauer, Brecht), Basel Ballet, Basel
      Opus 35 (mus. Shostakovich), Basel Ballet, Basel
      Time Between (mus. Ligeti), Basel Ballet, Basel
      Vor dem Beginn (mus. Mendelssohn-Bartholdy), Basel Ballet, Basel
      Ein Faschingsschwank (mus. Schumann), Basel Ballet, Basel
      Romeo und Julia (mus. Prokofiev), Basel Ballet, Basel
1978   *Don Quixote* (mus. Mozart), Stuttgart Ballet, Ludwigsburg
      Chäs (mus. Bär), Basel Ballet, Basel
      Undine (mus. Henze), Basel Ballet, Basel
1979   *Catulli Carmina* (mus. Orff), Basel Ballet, Basel
      Wendung (mus. Mahler), Basel Ballet, Basel
      Der Nussknacker (*The Nutcracker*; mus. Tchaikovsky), Basel Ballet, Basel
      Tundermove (mus. Gruntz), Basel Ballet, Berlin
1980   *Le Mal du pays* (mus. Liszt), Basel Ballet, Basel
      Träume (mus. Wagner), Basel Ballet, Basel
      Der Rote Mantel (mus. Nono), Basel Ballet, Basel
      Die Weisse Rose (mus. Fortner), Basel Ballet, Basel
      Vier Gesänge (mus. Brahms), Basel Ballet, Basel
      Zwei Zigeunerlieder (mus. Brahms), Basel Ballet, Basel
      Hochzeitslieder (mus. Reutter), Basel Ballet, Basel
      Pulcinella (mus. Stravinsky), Basel Ballet, Basel
      Till Eulenspiegel (mus. Strauss), Basel Ballet, Basel
1981   *Opus 3 Nr. 6* (mus. Vivaldi), Basel Ballet, Ludwigsburg
      Backstage (mus. Honegger), Basel Ballet, Basel
      Der Narziss (mus. Ringger), Zurich Ballet, Zurich
      La Fille mal gardée (mus. Herold, Hertel), Paris Opéra Ballet, Paris
      Childe Harold (mus. Berlioz), German Opera Ballet, Berlin
1982   *Preludes* (mus. Rachmaninov), Basel Ballet, Basel
      Oktett (mus. Reich), Basel Ballet, Basel
      L'Estro armonico (mus. Vivaldi), Basel Ballet, Basel
      Sackgasse (also *Dead End*; mus. Stravinsky), Stuttgart Ballet, Stuttgart
      Die Hochzeit der Figaro—Harmoniemusik (mus. Mozart), Basel Ballet, Ludwigsburg
      Verklärte Nacht (mus. Schoenberg), Basel Ballet, Basel
1983   *Orpheus und Eurydike* (mus. Gluck), Basel Ballet, Basel
      Fantasien (mus. Brahms), Basel Ballet, Ludwigsburg
      Ballade (mus. Brahms), Basel Ballet, Interlaken
1984   *Coppélia* (mus. Delibes), Basel Ballet, Basel
      Igor (mus. Stravinsky), Basel Ballet, Basel
      Pierrot Lunaire (mus. Schoenberg), Basel Ballet, Ludwigsburg
      John Falstaff (mus. Jahn), Basel Ballet, Basel
1985   *Concitato* (mus. Bloch), Basel Ballet, Basel
      Die Nacht aus Blei (mus. von Bose), Basel Ballet, Basel
      Abschied (mus. Berg), Stuttgart Ballet, Stuttgart (restaged Basel Ballet, 1986)
1986   *Der Junge Törless* (mus. Henze), Basel Ballet, Ludwigsburg
      Miniaturen (mus. Henze), Basel Ballet, Ludwigsburg
1987   *Grid* (mus. Shostakovich), Basel Ballet, Basel
      Der Wunderbare Mandarin (mus. Bartók), Basel Ballet, Basel
      Bluelight (mus. Pärt), Basel Ballet, Basel
      Rendez-Vous (mus. Pärt), Basel Ballet, Basel
      Stabat Mater (mus. Pärt), Basel Ballet, Basel
      La Belle Vie (mus. Offenbach), Basel Ballet, Basel
1988   *Patently Unclear* (mus. Glass), Basel Ballet, Basel
      Orpheus (mus. Henze), Basel Ballet, Basel

Heinz Spoerli's _Träume_, with Birgit Keil (centre)

Einhundertdreiundzwanzig + 2 (mus. Zytynska, Heiniger), Basel Ballet, Basel

Der Nussknacker (new version; mus. Tchaikovsky), Ballet of the German Opera on the Rhine, Düsseldorf

1989   _Pas de deux von Romeo—Bluelight_ (mus. various), Basel Ballet, Basel

Loops (mus. Adams), Basel Ballet, Basel

Settings (mus. Bach), Basel Ballet, Basel

Les Noces (mus. Stravinsky), Basel Ballet, Basel

1990   _Miniaturen_ (mus. Stravinsky), Basel Ballet, Basel

1991   _Fondue_ (mus. Adams, Bach, Bär, Molnar), Basel Ballet, Basel

1992   _Josephslegende_ (mus. Strauss), Ballet of the German Opera on the Rhine, Düsseldorf

1993   _Goldberg-Variationen_ (mus. Bach), Ballet of the German Opera on the Rhine, Düsseldorf

Also staged:

1974   _Suite Raymonda_ (after Petipa; mus. Glazunov), Basel Ballet, Basel

1976   _Giselle_ (after Petipa, Coralli, Perrot; mus. Adam), Basel Ballet, Basel

1986   _Swan Lake_ (after Petipa, Ivanov; mus. Tchaikovsky), Basel Ballet, Basel

1989   _Don Quixote_ (after Petipa; mus. Minkus, Ravel, Arp), Basel Ballet, Basel

1991   _Swan Lake_ (after Petipa, Ivanov; mus. Tchaikovsky), German Opera Ballet, Berlin

1993   _Giselle_ (new version; mus. Adam), Ballet of the German Opera on the Rhine, Düsseldorf

PUBLICATIONS

By Spoerli:

Interview in Sorrell, Walter, "Heinz Spoerli Talks of Swiss Ballet", _Dance News_ (New York), November 1977

Interview in Dupuis, Simone, "Je suis un homme heureux", _Les Saisons de la danse_ (Paris), May 1981

About Spoerli:

Koegler, Horst, "Switzerland: Helvetian Ascent", _Dance and Dancers_ (London), July 1976

Como, William, "Heinz Spoerli and the Basel Ballet", _Dance_

Magazine (New York), January 1983

Robertson, Allen, "Perfect Timing", *Ballet News* (New York), January 1983

Flury, Philipp, and Kaufmann, Peter, *Heinz Spoerli: Ballett-Faszination*, Zurich, 1983

Livio, Antoine, "Heinz Spoerli, l'enfant de Bâle", *Danser* (Paris), May 1985

Como, William, "Back in the USA: Big Times for Basel", *Dance Magazine* (New York), February 1989

Eckert, Heinz, *Heinz Spoerlis Basler Ballett*, Basel, 1991

*   *   *

Heinz Spoerli had already made a name for himself in European and Canadian ballet companies when he came to Geneva in 1971. As a member of the Grand Theatre Ballet, which was dedicated at that time to the work of Balanchine under the directorship of Alfonso Catà (Balanchine acted as "artistic adviser" to the company), Spoerli devoted himself to choreography. His short ballet *Le Chemin*, created in Geneva and recorded by Swiss television, was reason enough for the Basel Theatre director Werner Duggelin to entrust Heinz Spoerli with the management of the ballet at the Basel Stadttheater from 1973. Out of this developed the longest and most fruitful ballet directorship to appear in the short history of dance on stage in Switzerland.

In the eighteen years in which Spoerli headed his home town's ballet company (he took over as director of the German Opera on the Rhine Ballet in Düsseldorf in 1991), he led the company to the forefront of Swiss ballet. Under his leadership, ballet in Basel enjoyed a boom whose effect was felt in the whole of Switzerland, and which can only be compared to the great success it enjoyed in the 1950s and 1960s under Vaslav Olikowsky's directorship. Together with ballet master Peter Appel, Spoerli turned the Basel Ballet into a company of outstanding technical standard. Its excellence—both artistic and academic—found international recognition again and again in numerous foreign tours across Europe, Asia, and the United States.

The Basel Ballet's repertoire under Spoerli was dominated by his own works. He created some 80 pieces for his company, about 60 of which were one-act ballets. At the same time Hans van Manen produced several of his pieces for the Basel Ballet. Other works in the ensemble's repertoire came from George Balanchine, John Cranko, Maurice Béjart, Paul Taylor, and Nacho Duato.

Heinz Spoerli had incorporated into the company a small, but not professional, training establishment for dancers. He took on more and more young dancers of all nationalities for the ensemble, however, who could gain valuable experience in Basel. Ruth Weber, Rudy Bryans, Sylviane Bayard, Weit Carlsson, Mikko Nissinen, Martin Schlaepfer, Chris Jensen, and Gilma Bustillo were among the dance personalities who made their mark on the Basel Ballet's profile through lengthy engagements with the company. Guests who have worked repeatedly with the Basel Ballet and Heinz Spoerli include Eva Evdokimova, Birgit Keil, Lynne Charles, Jonas Kåge, and Eric Vu-An. At the same time, Heinz Spoerli himself is one of the most sought-after guest choreographers of our time, and he has already worked with the great ballet companies in Stuttgart, Vienna, Paris, Berlin (the German Opera), Helsinki, Stockholm, and Beijing. Many of his ballets were shown on German, Swiss, and Czechoslovakian television. Others, such as *Die Nacht aus Blei*, were produced specifically for the screen.

The stylistic foundation of Heinz Spoerli's choreography is classical dance. From the beginning, however, he made an effort to give the classical a contemporary form. Spoerli's admiration for George Balanchine's neo-classicism was just as decisive in this respect as his interest in the modern dance of the United States. Not surprisingly, Spoerli is also an admirer of contemporary visual art. However, at the same time many of his ballets bear the stamp of an expressiveness deeply rooted in the European dance tradition, and live through the characteristic combination and mutual pervasion of abstract and concrete expression.

Recently (since the 1988 *Patently Unclear*), Spoerli's ballets have been based on his own maxim of "stylistic renewal". In his early works, the ballets with a narrative or at least anecdotal content outnumbered the purely abstract pieces. The relationship now appears to be reversing. Even in earlier works, Heinz Spoerli's choreography was given over to the portrayal of a mood rather than to narrative content, the most significant instance being the moving *Vier Gesänge*. At any rate, the ballets of that time created an atmosphere of profound gravity, and a cautiously displayed, yet overwhelmingly traditional, vocabulary of movement. Now dance itself stands at the core of his works, where an emphatically modernistic control of movement and a certain self-conscious irony are not to be overlooked. Certain elements of the dramatic conception of the work can be felt or suspected rather than directly named. Pure desire to move in an abstract form and at overwhelmingly breathless speeds are the new characteristics.

Spoerli's most telling works, however, are the dramatic full-length ballets. Here the extent of his choreographic mastery, narrative talent, and feel for intuitive characterization are best seen. Spoerli has produced versions of the traditional full-length repertoire as they have been handed down (for example *Giselle*), but also as completely reworked versions, in both dramatic and choreographic terms. The most brilliant example of this (and of his great sense of humour, which also runs throughout his repertoire of short ballets) is his production of *La Fille mal gardée*. Created in 1981 for the Paris Opéra Ballet, and subsequently performed across Europe, Spoerli's *Fille* is the most successful new version of the work since Ashton's 1966 production.

Along with a duty to the classics, Spoerli is also aware of the need to extend the limited repertoire of full-length ballets with new works. Examples of this are his ambitious and artistically extravagant production of *John Falstaff*, and *La Belle Vie*, which takes the theme of a French family tragedy at the time of the Second Empire. For the first time Spoerli used stylistic elements which can be traced back to the influence of German dance theatre. Following an initial, still predominately traditional, production of *The Nutcracker* in 1979, Spoerli created a radically modern and starkly psychological new interpretation of the same work for the Düsseldorf company. It bears reluctant witness to a dwindling trust in choreography faithful to the old recipe of story-telling. Since then it has been fair to speak of a "stylistic renewal" in the domain of Spoerli's full-length ballets as well.

—Horst Vollmer

SQUARE DANCE

Choreography: George Balanchine

Music: Arcangelo Corelli, Antonio Vivaldi

First Production: New York City Ballet, City Center, New York, 21 November 1957

Principal Dancers: Patricia Wilde, Nicholas Magallanes

Square Dance, **as performed by the Dance Theatre of Harlem, New York**

Other productions include: City Center Joffrey Ballet; New York, 12 March 1971. Ballet West; Salt Lake City, 1973. New York City Ballet (restaged and revised Balanchine), with Kay Mazzo and Bart Cook; New York, 20 May 1976. Pacific Northwest Ballet; Seattle, March 1981. Pennsylvania Ballet, 1981. Ballet Chicago; Chicago, April 1990.

PUBLICATIONS

Hering, Doris, "New York City Ballet", *Dance Magazine* (New York), January 1958

Balanchine, George, with Mason, Francis, *Balanchine's Complete Stories of the Great Ballets*, Garden City, N.Y., 1977

Reynolds, Nancy, *Repertory in Review*, New York, 1977

Kirstein, Lincoln, *Thirty Years: The New York City Ballet*, New York, 1978

Acocella, Joan, "Imagining Dance", *Dance Ink* (New York), December 1990

*   *   *

In the 1957–58 New York City Ballet season, George Balanchine presented the premieres of four different ballets which attested to the breadth and scope of his range as a choreographer. These ballets—*Square Dance, Agon, Stars and Stripes*, and *Gounod Symphony*—were all major achievements, each one demonstrating the fecundity and flexibility of Balanchine's classicism and the ability of his style to absorb various modes of music and dance to show how these forms are interconnected.

Agon was immediately hailed as a neo-classical masterpiece. It has taken its place as one of the most important twentieth-century ballets and its impact is still being felt today. *Stars and Stripes* and *Gounod Symphony* were large ensemble works in strictly classical idiom in which distinctive national performing styles and mannerisms had been absorbed. *Stars and Stripes*, one of the most popular ballets in the New York City Ballet repertory, invokes in gently parodic manner the patriotism and "razzmatazz" of American marching bands and military dress parades. *Gounod Symphony* is a conscious homage to and imaginative meditation on the Paris Opéra Ballet in the nineteenth century. This ballet passed out of the repertory soon after its premiere and was restaged for the City Ballet in 1984, the year after Balanchine's death.

Square Dance also dropped out of the active City Ballet repertory, a casualty of the company's move in 1964 from the City Center to the New York State Theater at Lincoln Center. Balanchine then revised and revived the ballet in 1976, and it has remained a favorite with his audiences ever since. The ballet is one of Balanchine's most beautifully wrought creations, an intricate, ebullient, even moving, suite of dances to Antonio Vivaldi's *Concerto Grossi, Op. 3, Nos. 10* (complete) and *12* (first movement), and Arcangelo Corelli's *Sarabanda, Badinerie*, and *Giga* (second and third movements).

Square Dance was choreographed for a leading couple and six demi-soloist couples, and these dancers are called upon to perform a profusion of rich, complex, and elegant steps that display Balanchine's unwavering fidelity to academic classicism. But the choreography also consciously refers not only to the social dances of the American West but to the salon and folk-dances of the eighteenth century from which such dances derived. Nancy Reynolds has written in *Repertory In Review* that ". . . whatever its other virtues, *Square Dance* offered more steps per minute than any other show in town".

The ballet is a great challenge for its cast. The ballerina in *Square Dance* must show herself mistress of adagio dancing as well as be able to jump and turn in a profusion of bravura sequences, and the man must match her at every turn. The soloist couples perform a veritable lexicon of classical steps from petit allegro combinations to partnering of the most sophisticated nature. Although in its present version the elements of old-time promenades, hoe-downs, and square dancing itself are not as pronounced as they were in 1957 when the ballet was performed with both a string orchestra and a genuine square dance caller on stage, they are nevertheless an integral part of the piece, most especially in the finale and in the sections in which the ballerina and the leading man dance their solos. And along the way all the dancers strike informal poses at the sides of the stage and pretend to be chatting as they might at any social gathering.

At its premiere, *Square Dance* was greeted as something of a novelty by most of the critics, even as they were aware that the ballet, in the words of John Martin in *The New York Times*, was "a genuine jewel, inventive, vivacious and rich in the comment of a witty and creative mind". Patricia Wilde and Nicholas Magallanes danced the leads in *Square Dance* at the time of its premiere, and the accompaniment to some of the dances for themselves and the soloists consisted not of music alone, but also of actual square dance calls, written and performed by Elisha C. Keeler. ("Do-si-do in mountain style / Under the arch, give her a smile / Down the center, lonesome gal / Now she's waiting for her pal . . ." is a small example of the inventive calls which accompanied the dancers.)

In the 1976 re-staging, which did away with the caller and returned the orchestra to the pit, Balanchine created a beautiful, introspective solo for Bart Cook, who danced the lead opposite Kay Mazzo. Cook had scored a notable success in the Melancholic variation in Balanchine's *The Four Temperaments* the year before and some of the arching backbends of that piece worked their way into the new choreography. Reynolds commented that without the orchestra on stage and without the caller, the dancing expanded, and this was pretty much the case.

The ballet opens with with bright allegro dances for the leads and ensemble followed by a tender, grave pas de deux which moves without a break into a fast paced conclusion. What follows are essentially two solo dances, first for the man and then another for the woman, each backed by the ensemble. The new solo for the man then leads into a finale in which the ballerina performs filigree footwork that requires the most astonishing technical dexterity.

Anna Kisselgoff in the *New York Times* called the revival "anything but rehash. The correct word is renewal. Originally Mr. Balanchine had found inspiration in the fact that this eighteenth-century music had been derived from folk-dance forms that were later refined. Now, it seems, he has chosen to emphasize the refinement." Balanchine wrote in his *Complete Stories of the Great Ballets*, "Anna Kisselgoff noted that while in the first version, you would have heard a call by Mr. Keeler and the music would repeat with the dancers performing the step, now the lead dancer calls the tune by dancing to it and the others follow him. 'He is the caller, but he uses movements instead of words,' she wrote."

Lincoln Kirstein compared *Square Dance* to *Le Tombeau de Couperin*, which Balanchine created for the 1975 Ravel Festival. The works are similar in style, but Kirstein saw "a world of difference between the optimistic urgency and driving impetus of the eighteenth century and the melancholy ripeness

of Ravel's twentieth-century fragmented recension of the rococo. *Le Tombeau* has its own deliberation, but its split diagonals and fractured quarterings are imbued with a courtesy and mutual attention for which the headlong insistence and high spirits of *Square Dance* had no time."

Merrill Ashley took over the ballerina role opposite Bart Cook in many performances of *Square Dance* and, like Cook, established a standard of performance that nearly every other interpreter has since aimed to emulate. Kyra Nichols also made a favorable impression in the part. In recent performances, Peter Boal, a young New York City Ballet principal, has danced the male role with particular distinction.

—Larry Kaplan

STAATS, Léo

French dancer, choreographer, ballet director, and teacher. Born in Paris, 26 November 1877. Studied at the Ballet School of the Paris Opéra, pupil of Louis Mérante and Joseph Hansen. Served in the French Army, World War I. Début on stage of Paris Opéra, when still a child, c. 1887; premier danseur, Paris Opéra Ballet, partnering ballerina Carlotta Zambelli, from 1893; choreographer, with first works created (when only sixteen) for own students, 1893; also producer of classical ballets, including works by Lucien Petipa and Louis Mérante; maître de ballet (succeeding Joseph Hansen), Paris Opéra, 1907–09, 1915–36; artistic director, Théâtre des Arts (dir. Jacques Rouché), Paris, 1910–14, returning to Paris Opéra, 1915; creator of "Défilé du corps de ballet", traditional programme featuring dancers of Paris Opéra school and company, 1926; also choreographer for music hall, revue, and various private companies; choreographer, "Roxy" Music Hall, New York, 1926; also teacher: founder and director of own school in Paris, from 1890s, and teacher, Paris Opéra School, from 1899; guest teacher, John Murray Anderson and Robert Milton Theatre School, and teacher at own studio, New York, 1926. Died in Paris, 20 February 1952.

WORKS

1893   *Ici l'on danse* (divertissement), Pupils of Léo Staats, Paris

1908   *Namouna* (mus. Lalo), Paris Opéra Ballet, Paris

1909   *Javotte* (mus. Saint-Saëns), Paris Opéra Ballet, Paris

1911   *España* (with Mauri; mus. Chabrier), Paris Opéra Ballet, Paris

1913   *Le Festin de l'araignée* (mus. Roussel), Théâtre des Artes, Paris

1915   *Ma Mère l'oye* (mus. Ravel), Théâtre Trocadero, Paris
        Offrande à la liberté (mus. Gossec), Théâtre Trocadero, Paris
        Mademoiselle de Nantes (mus. Lully, Charpentier), Théâtre Trocadero, Paris

1917   *Les Abeilles* (mus. Stravinsky), Paris Opéra Ballet, Paris

1920   *Taglioni chez Musette* (mus. Auber, Boieldieu, Meyerbeer, Weckerlin), Paris Opéra Ballet, Paris

1921   *Antar* (mus. Dupont), Paris Opéra Ballet, Paris
        Maïmouna (mus. Gérard), Paris Opéra Ballet, Paris
        La Péri (mus. Dukas), Paris Opéra Ballet, Paris

1922   *Frivolant* (mus. Poueigh), Paris Opéra Ballet, Paris

1923   *Cydalise et le chèvre-pied* (mus. Pierné), Paris Opéra
       Ballet, Paris
       La Nuit ensorcelée (mus. Chopin), Paris Opéra Ballet,
       Paris
1924   *Siang-Sin* (mus. Huë), Paris Opéra Ballet, Paris
       Istar (mus. d'Indy), Paris Opéra Ballet, Paris
1925   *Soir de fête* (mus. Delibes), Paris Opéra Ballet, Paris
1926   *Orphée* (mus. Ducasse), Paris Opéra Ballet, Paris
       La Pretresse de Korydwen (mus. Ladmirault), Paris
       Opéra Ballet, Paris
1929   *L'Écran des jeunes filles* (mus. Roland-Manuel), Paris
       Opéra Ballet, Paris
1931   *Le Rustre imprudent* (mus. Fouret), Paris Opéra Ballet,
       Paris
1933   *Roselinde* (mus. Hirschmann), Paris Opéra Ballet, Paris
1935   *Images* (mus. Pierné), Paris Opéra Ballet, Paris
1936   *Le Rouet d'armor* (mus. Piriou), Paris Opéra Ballet, Paris
       Iléana (mus. Bertrand), Paris Opéra Ballet, Paris

Also staged:
1909   *Namouna* (after L. Petipa; mus. Lalo), Paris Opéra
       Ballet, Paris
1919   *Sylvia* (after Mérante; mus. Delibes), Paris Opéra
       Ballet, Paris
1925   *Le Triomphe de l'amour* (opéra-ballet, after lib. by
       Benserade, Quinault; mus. Lully), Paris Opéra, Paris

Other works include: *Hommage à la Belgique* (1915), *Les Virtuosi de Mazarin* (1916), *Le Roman d'Estelle* (1916), *La Légende de Saint Christophe* (1920); dances in operas *Les Troyens* (mus. Berlioz), *Khovanshchina* (mus. Mussorgsky), *Falstaff* (mus. Verdi), *Esclarmonde* (mus. Massenet), *Padmâvatî* (mus. Roussel), *La Damnation de Faust* (mus. Berlioz).

PUBLICATIONS

Laloy, L., *Cinquante ans de musique française*, Paris, 1926
Beaumont, Cyril, *Complete Book of Ballets*, revised edition, London, 1951
Brillant, M., *Du Romantisme à Jacques Rouché*, Paris, 1952
Dumesnil, R., "La Danse à l'Opéra depuis 1900", in *L'Art du ballet dès origines à nos jours*, Paris, 1952
Guest, Ivor, "Carlotta Zambelli", *Dance Magazine* (New York), 2 parts: February, March 1974
Guest, Ivor, *Le Ballet de l'Opéra de Paris*, Paris, 1976

*   *   *

Léo Staats was one of the most important figures of the Paris Opéra at the turn of the century, for many years a prominent dancer and maître de ballet who was responsible for the production of ballets and dances in the operatic repertoire. His contemporaries considered him one of the most colourful and talented figures in Paris ballet.

Studying with Louis Mérante, a dancer at the Opéra, he made his début at ten years of age. In 1893, he was made premier danseur at the age of sixteen. Staats danced many roles with the Paris Opéra, and was probably best known for his interpretation of Jean in *Javotte*.

But it is Staats as choreographer whom we remember today. Records indicate *Ici l'on danse* as his first ballet, followed by *La Péri*, *Taglioni chez Musette*, and in 1923, his most famous work, *Cydalise et le chèvre-pied*, with music by Pierné and first danced by Carlotta Zambelli and Albert Aveline. Another well-known ballet was *Soir de fête*, a plotless, classical work which the Paris

Opéra Ballet performed when they visited the United States and Canada in 1948 (and seen again in 1988, when the Paris Opéra School of Ballet sent their young dancers to New York for a weekend of performances). *Soir de fête* served as an excellent example of the Opéra style. George Balanchine, who was well acquainted with Staats's work, seems to have been influenced by the Frenchman's ballets. As critic Anna Kisselgoff has pointed out, the Staats oeuvre, known for its purity and elegance, served as models for Balanchine, particularly in the French ballets *Symphony in C* (Bizet) and *La Source* (Delibes).

For the Paris Opéra itself, Staats composed or revived dances for *Les Troyens*, *Khovanshchina*, and *Esclarmonde* during the 1920s. Additionally, it was said that almost every music hall in Paris had dances with a Staats arrangement.

It was in his role as a teacher that Staats was most beloved. In his later years, he opened his own school in the rue Saulnier, behind the Folies-Bergère. Yvonne Daunt, a former étoile of the Paris Opéra Ballet, had this to say about him: "To anyone privileged to have been a pupil of Leo Staats during the 1914–22 period, his name brings back many wonderful memories. Born of Hungarian origin, Staats had a marvellous sense of rhythm and a dramatic sense that made all that he undertook colourful and exciting. As a person he was lovable and generous to a fault."

During World War I, most of the great dancers of that era gathered in Léo Staats's school in the rue Saulnier. Once again, according to Yvonne Daunt, "there was a period when Staats was serving in the Army and used to come to Paris on leave, and not take time to change into mufti, but give a class in uniform without bothering to take off his heavy boots. His brilliant batterie and elevation were always a joy to watch."

In 1926, as ballet master of the Paris Opéra, Staats came to New York. He taught for a short time at the John Murray Anderson and Robert Milton Theatre School and then opened a school of his own, where classic, tap, and ballet dancing were taught. In addition, Staats was in charge of the ballets for the Roxy Music Hall when in New York.

Pupils' memories of Staats were always fond ones. "He would execute feathery light and faultless brisées de Telemaque. His pupils never ceased to wonder how he managed to make his feet twinkle despite the weight of his Army boots. He had an amazing elevation and literally flew through the air in grands jétés."

Staats danced in many of the ballets he arranged, such as *La Péri*, *Frivolant*, and *Sylvia*. Indeed, it was said that he would have danced more often if he had not been handicapped with myopia; and he was unable to wear glasses on stage. ("Once," remembers Daunt, "during a rehearsal of *Frivolant*, in which he danced the role of the Wind, he misjudged the space near the footlights and jumped across the prompter's box right into the orchestra pit, landing in a perfect attitude, but frightening the wits out of the first violinist.")

In the 1920s, Staats dabbled in ballroom dancing and opened a "Dancing" School in the MacMahon Palace, close to the Étoile. He was also invited by the British Royal Academy of Dancing to produce the dances for a production of *La Damnation de Faust* at Covent Garden.

As late as 1937, Staats was still actively engaged at the Paris Opéra and taught daily in the rue Saulnier. After an active career that spanned 65 years, Leo Staats died in Paris in February 1952.

—Richard Rutledge

STAFF, Frank
South African dancer, choreographer, and ballet director. Born in Kimberley, South Africa, 15 June 1918. Studied with Helen Webb and Maude Lloyd in Cape Town, and with Marie Rambert, Antony Tudor, and Stanislas Idzikowski in London from 1933. Served as a Captain, Argyle and Sutherland Highlanders Regiment, during World War II. Married (1) dancer Elisabeth Schooling; (2) dancer Jaqueline St. Clere; (3) actress Heather Lloyd-Jones; (4) dancer Veronica Paeper. Dancer, Ballet Club (later Ballet Rambert), 1933–45, Vic-Wells Ballet, 1934–35, 1938–39, London Ballet, 1940; also appeared in Herbert Farjeon's revue *Spread it Abroad* (mus. Walker, chor. Walter Gore; 1936); first choreography (for Ballet Rambert), 1938, thereafter creating works for Ballet Rambert, 1938–41, South African National Ballet in Cape Town, 1946, Metropolitan Ballet, London, 1947, 1948, Les Ballets des Champs-Elysées, 1951, and San Francisco Ballet, 1952; also choreographer for London and Broadway musicals; ballet master and choreographer, Empire Theatre, London, 1949–50; returned to South Africa, 1953: founder and director, South African Ballet, 1955–58, and choreographer, UCT/CAPAB (University Cape Town/Cape Performing Arts Board) Ballet, Cape Town, 1963, becoming resident choreographer from 1964; choreographer, PACT (Performing Arts Council of the Transvaal) Ballet, Johannesburg 1965–68; director, PACOFS (Performing Arts Council of the Orange Free State) Ballet, Bloemfontein, 1969–71. Died in Bloemfontein, 10 May 1971.

ROLES

1934   A Young Man (cr) in *Mephisto Waltz* (Ashton), Ballet Club (later Ballet Rambert), London
1935   François (cr) in *Valentine's Eve* (Ashton), Ballet Rambert, London
        The Hornblower (cr) in *The Rake's Progress* (de Valois), Vic-Wells Ballet, London
        Boxing Kangaroo and Trapezist (cr) in *Circus Wings* (Salaman), Ballet Rambert, London
        Sir Plume (cr) in *The Rape of the Lock* (A. Howard), Ballet Rambert, London
        Stevedore in *Rio Grande* (*A Day in a Southern Port*; Ashton), Vic-Wells Ballet, London
        Brer Rabbit in *Uncle Remus* (S. Patrick), Vic-Wells Ballet, London
1936   The Virtuoso (cr) in *La Muse s'amuse* (Howard), Ballet Rambert, London
1937   Sir Andrew Aguecheek (cr) in *Cross-Garter'd* (W. Toye) Ballet Rambert, London
1938   Principal dancer (cr) in *The Tartans* (also chor.), Ballet Rambert, London
        Danse de tendresse (cr) in *Croquis de Mercure* (Howard), Ballet Rambert, London
        Mercury in *Croquis de Mercure* (Howard), Ballet Rambert, London
        Iskender (cr) in *La Péri* (also chor.), Ballet Rambert, London
        Bread Boy (cr) in *Harlequin in the Streets* (Ashton), Vic-Wells Ballet, London
1939   Cavalier to the Fairy of Song Birds, Fourth Prince, Wolf in *The Sleeping Princess* (Petipa; staged Sergeyev), Vic-Wells Ballet, London
        The Anarchist (cr) in *Paris-Soir* (Gore), Ballet Rambert, London
        Cupid (cr) in *Cupid and Psyche* (Ashton), Vic-Wells Ballet, London

Improvisation (cr) in *Czernyana* (also chor.), Ballet Rambert, London
1940   Summer (cr) in *The Seasons* (also chor.), London Ballet, London
        Julien (cr) in *La Fête étrange* (Howard), London Ballet, London
        Principal dancer in *Enigma Variations* (also chor.), Ballet Rambert, Cambridge
1941   Se habla Español (cr) in *Czerny 2* (also chor.), Ballet Rambert, London

Other roles include: for Ballet Rambert—The Lover in *Alcina Suite* (Howard), the Faun in *L'Après-midi d'un faune* (Nijinsky; staged Woizikowsky), Bluebird in *Dances from Aurora's Wedding* (after Petipa), Valentin and Vieux Marcheur in *Bar aux Folies-Bergère* (de Valois), the American Boxer in *Le Boxing* (Salaman), Harlequin in *Carnaval* (Fokine), the Prince, Court Hairdresser in *Cinderella* (Howard), Batsman, Umpire in *Le Cricket* (Salaman), Visions in *Czerny 2* (also chor.), principal dancer (Second, Third, and Fifth Song) in *Dark Elegies* (Tudor), Death in *Death and the Maiden* (Howard), Mercury and Hercules in *The Descent of Hebe* (Tudor), Popular Song and Tango in *Façade* (Ashton), Maître de ballet in *Foyer de danse* (Ashton), Cavalier in *Gala Performance* (Tudor), Hilarion in *Giselle*, Act II (after Petipa, Coralli, Perrot), Lover in *Le Jardin aux lilas* (Tudor), Client in *The Judgment of Paris* (Tudor), Prince Siegfried in *Swan Lake*, Act II (after Ivanov), Huntsman in *Lady into Fox* (Howard), Lover and Sir Lancelot in *The Lady of Shalott* (Ashton), Lysistrata's Husband in *Lysistrata* (Tudor), Personage and Lover in *Les Masques* (Ashton), Faust and Mephisto in *Mephisto Waltz* (Ashton), Prince in *Mermaid* (Howard, Salaman), Juggler in *Our Lady's Juggler* (Howard), Grandfather and Huntsman in *Peter and the Wolf* (also chor.), Mercury and Mortal under Venus in *The Planets* (Tudor), The Baron and Umbriel in *The Rape of the Lock* (Howard), The Player in *Le Rugby* (Salaman), Tarantella in *Soirée musicale* (Tudor), Spirit of the Rose in *Le Spectre de la rose* (Fokine), Mazurka in *Les Sylphides* (Fokine).

WORKS

1938   *The Tartans* (mus. Boyce), Ballet Rambert, London
        La Péri (mus. Dukas), Ballet Rambert, London
1939   *Czernyana* (mus. Czerny), Ballet Rambert, London
1940   *The Seasons* (mus. Glazunov), London Ballet, London
        Peter and the Wolf (mus. Prokofiev), Ballet Rambert, Cambridge
        Enigma Variations (mus. Elgar), Ballet Rambert, Cambridge
1941   *Czerny 2* (mus. Czerny), Ballet Rambert, London
        Pavane pour une infante défunte (mus. Ravel), Ballet Rambert, London
1945   *Un Songe* (mus. Lekeu), Ballet Rambert, Norwich
1946   *Romeo and Juliet* (mus. Tchaikovsky), South African National Ballet, Cape Town
        Variations on a Theme by Haydn (mus. Haydn), South African National Ballet, Cape Town
1947   *The Lover's Gallery* (mus. L. Berkeley), Metropolitan Ballet, London
1948   *Fanciulla delle Rose* (mus. Arensky), Metropolitan Ballet, London
1949   *Yester-year* (mus. various), Empire Theatre Ballet, London
        Amphytryon 50 (mus. Bach), Empire Theatre Ballet, London
1950   *Punch* (mus. Moross), Empire Theatre Ballet, London

Showboat Time (mus. Moross), Empire Theatre Ballet, London

Frankie and Johnny (mus. Moross), Empire Theatre Ballet, London

Bolero (mus. Ravel), Empire Theatre Ballet, London

1951 *Romanza Romana* (mus. Petit), Les Ballets des Champs-Elysées, Paris

1955 *Don Juan* (mus. Rachmaninov), South African Ballet

L'Atelier de Monsieur X (mus. Prokofiev), South African Ballet

Symphony for Sylphs (mus. Bizet), South African Ballet

Divertimento (mus. Ibert), South African Ballet

Transfigured Night (mus. Schoenberg), South African Ballet

1957 *The Judgment of Paris* (mus. Gould), South African Ballet

The Impresario, South African Ballet

Apollo 57 (mus. Britten), South African Ballet

The Birthday (mus. Grétry), South African Ballet

Ballade, South African Ballet

Lizzie Borden (mus. Gould), South African Ballet

1958 *Romantic Encounter*, South African Ballet

The Legend of Frankie and Johnny (mus. Moross), South African Ballet

Toccata and Fugue (mus. Bach), South African Ballet

Jamaican Rhumba (mus. Benjamin), South African Ballet

1959 *The Swan of Tuonela* (mus. Sibelius), South African Ballet

1964 *Romeo and Juliet* (mus. Prokofiev), UCT/CAPAB Ballet, Cape Town

1965 *The Five Faces of Eurydice* (mus. O'Reilly), PACT Ballet, Johannesburg

Soirée musicale (mus. Britten, Rossini), NAPAC Ballet, Durban

Apollo 65 (mus. Britten), NAPAC Ballet, Durban

1966 *Czernyana III* (mus. Czerny), PACT Ballet, Johannesburg

Spanish Encounter (mus. Rodrigo), PACT Ballet, Johannesburg

Cinderella (with Françoise Adret; mus. Prokofiev), PACT Ballet, Johannesburg

1967 *Le Coq d'or* (mus. Rimsky-Korsakov), PACT Ballet, Johannesburg

Raka (mus. G. Newcater), PACT Ballet, Johannesburg

Symphony 29 (mus. Mozart), PACT Ballet, Johannesburg

1968 *Concerto* (mus. Shostakovich), PACT Ballet, Johannesburg

Episodes (mus. Tchaikovsky), PACT Ballet

Soirée (mus. Rossini, Britten), PACT Ballet

Gaiety Girl and the Sailors (mus. Shostakovich), PACT Ballet

1970 *Mantis Moon* (mus. H. Maske), PACOFS Ballet, Bloemfontein

The Séance (mus. Britten), PACOFS, Bloemfontein

The Collection (mus. Stam), PACOFS, Bloemfontein

Kaleidoscope (mus. Cannon, Rowley), PACOFS, Bloemfontein

Comment? (mus. Arnold), PACOFS, Bloemfontein

1971 *The Rain Queen* (incomplete at Staff's death; mus. G. Newcater), PACOFS Ballet, Bloemfontein

Also staged:

1946 *L'Après-midi d'un faune* (after Nijinsky; mus. Debussy), South African National Ballet, Cape Town

Death and the Maiden (after A. Howard; mus. Schu-

Frank Staff in *La Muse s'amuse*, **Ballet Rambert, London, 1936**

bert), South African National Ballet, Cape Town

1966 *Don Quixote* pas de deux (after Petipa; mus. Minkus), PACT Ballet

PUBLICATIONS

Beaumont, Cyril, *Supplement to Complete Book of Ballets*, London, 1942

Holdes, Tarquin, "Born Under Mercury", *Ballet* (London), July 1946

Davidson, Gladys, *Ballet Biographies*, revised edition, London, 1954

Clarke, Mary, *Dancers of Mercury: The Story of Ballet Rambert*, London, 1962

Kersley, Leo, "Frank Staff", *Dancing Times* (London), June 1971

Grut, Marina, *The History of Ballet in South Africa*, Cape Town, 1981

* * *

Frank Staff was one of the most physically gifted dancers ever to appear on the English ballet stage. He was the only person one can remember to perform triple turns in the air on stage without strain or hesitation. With a good plié, well-stretched feet, first-rate turnout, and pleasant proportions, his only disadvantage lay in the fact that he did not use his face, preserving instead a reserved immobility of features, whether he was dancing serious or comic roles. At a time when he was competing on the one hand with Hugh Laing, and on the other with Robert Helpmann, both a decade older (as was Turner, his main competitor in the realms of classical technique), this did not help him establish a substantial rapport with a public already nurtured on the vivid characters brought on stage at that time by Laing and Helpmann.

Staff came to England from South Africa, where he had studied with Maude Lloyd, to study and dance with Rambert, with whose company he continued to work until his career was interrupted by war service. He also spent two short periods with the Vic-Wells Ballet, where he created a small role in *The Rake's Progress* and the male lead in Ashton's ill-fated *Cupid and Psyche*. His background was a musical one: his father was a music critic, also an amateur pianist, and Staff (whose financial circumstances were perhaps a little easier than were those of the majority working at the Ballet Club before the war) was in a position not only to listen for hours to gramophone records, but also to buy them. Respect for other artists was an important feature of Staff's make-up, and he would express himself forcibly, when the occasion arose, on the unacceptability of altering the work of other choreographers, dead or alive.

Staff was an extremely inventive choreographer whose potential was apparently discovered by Rambert during a rehearsal in which he was asked to improvise. Susan Salaman, rehearsing *Le Cricket* for a revival of *Sporting Sketches* for television, needed a batsman and the original steps had been forgotten. As Mary Clarke later described it, "Staff improvised brilliantly; his movements were full of vigour and significance and he created the role afresh throughout the entire sketch. People did laugh and Rambert immediately declared 'but you have a *talent* for arranging steps; you must try a ballet.'" *The Tartans*, "a completely delightful suite of dances ... distinguished by their wit and the easy flow of the movement", followed not long afterwards.

In a long career—Staff made nearly 50 ballets before his premature death in 1971 (not including those monthly stints embarked upon for the Empire Ballet in 1949 and 1950)—he became one of the very few choreographers of this century who never spent time tinkering with the classics, but concentrated solely on original works, and his continued creativity was impressive.

Staff was never satisfied with the mere combination of conventional classical steps into classical enchainements, and his inventive gifts were perhaps best displayed, so far as his work in England was concerned, by the enduringly memorable *Fanciulla delle Rose*, which he created for the radiant fifteen-year-old Svetlana Beriosova with the Metropolitan Ballet in 1948. His comedy, or character, ballets such as *Czernyana*, inspired by the playing of Angus Morrison, or *Czerny 2* and *Peter and the Wolf*, called a "comic masterpiece" by more than one critic, were funny through movement rather than through situation, and his outstanding classical technique enabled him to make roles which proved not only immensely challenging, but equally immensely rewarding to his casts, and those who had to follow him in his own ballets.

—Leo Kersley

————

THE STONE FLOWER
(original Russian title: *Kamennyi Tsvetok*)

Choreography: Yuri Grigorovich
Music: Sergei Prokofiev
Design: Simon Virsaladze
Libretto: Mira Prokofieva, with revisions by Yuri Grigorovich (after the story *The Malachite Casket* by Pavel Bashov)
First Production: Kirov Ballet, Leningrad, 25 April 1957
Principal Dancers: Irina Kolpakova (Katerina), Aleksandr Gribov (Danila), Alla Osipenko (Mistress of the Copper Mountain)

Other productions include: Bolshoi Ballet (original production to score; chor. Leonid Lavrovsky, design Tatyana Starzhenetskaya), as *The Story of the Stone Flower*, with Galina Ulanova (Katerina), Vladimir Preobrazhensky (Danila), Maya Plisetskaya (Mistress of the Copper Mountain); Moscow, 12 February 1954. Bolshoi Ballet (1957 version, restaged Grigorovich), with Ekaterina Maximova (Katerina), Vladimir Vasiliev (Danila), Maya Plisetskaya (Mistress of the Copper Mountain); Moscow, 7 March 1959. Royal Swedish Ballet (restaged Grigorovich); Stockholm, 1962. Wuppertal Ballet (new version; chor. Ivan Sertić); Wuppertal, 20 October 1972. Teatro Comunale (new version; chor. Loris Gai); Bologna, 8 March 1973 (restaged La Scala, Milan, 1973). German Opera on the Rhine (new version; chor. Erich Walter); Düsseldorf, 22 May 1976.

PUBLICATIONS

Terry, Walter, "The Bolshoi in Retrospect", *New York Herald Tribune* (New York), 24 May 1959
Franks, Arthur Henry, "Leningrad State Kirov Ballet", *Dancing Times* (London), July 1961
Karp, P., and Levin, C., *The Stone Flower by Prokofiev*, Leningrad, 1963
Lopukhov, Fedor, *Sixty Years in Ballet*, Moscow, 1966
Slonimsky, Yuri, *In Honour of Dance*, Moscow, 1968
Vanslov, Viktor, *The Ballets of Grigorovich and the Problems of Choreography*, Moscow, 1971
Balanchine, George, and Mason, Francis, *Balanchine's Complete Stories of the Great Ballets*, Garden City, N.Y., 1977
Percival, John, "Grigorovich of the Bolshoi", *Dance and Dancers* (London), September 1989

*   *   *

The story of *The Stone Flower* concerns Danila, a master stoneworker in the Urals, who dreams of creating a malachite goblet of unprecedented beauty. The universally detested steward, Severyan, rudely demands the goblet for himself, but the master stonecutter refuses to part with the unfinished work, and, when Severyan threatens him, he is defended by his beloved Katerina. Later, while Danila is dreaming alone of finding the secret of the beauty of stone, the Mistress of the Copper Mountain appears to him, causing the goblet momentarily to come alive, and then disappears. Danila follows her and is led into her kingdom, where delicately sculpted stone forms a magic flower of stone. Danila remains in the subterranean kingdom and continues to carve his goblet.

Katerina, left without her suitor, is forced to run away from the unwelcome attentions of Severyan and goes off in search of her loved one. She encounters Severyan again but he is distracted by the beckoning of an unknown woman, who is eventually revealed as the Mistress of the Copper Mountain herself. He begs for mercy, but in vain: the earth opens and swallows him up.

In the subterranean kingdom Danila, having attained the secret of mastery, asks that he should be released back to the world of people, but the Mistress has fallen in love with him and implores him not to leave her. Danila is unshakeable: he must bring to the people the secret he has learned of beauty. The Mistress, in order to keep him, turns him into stone. But Katerina appears, and, not fearing the threatening Mistress, she implores her to return her betrothed. The Mistress offers the choice to Danila, who throws himself into the embraces of Katerina. The Mistress then releases the master, understanding that in his soul the master can never forget his loved one. The people then welcome their master stonecutter returned home with his bride. Ahead of Danila are the new trials of creation, as the symbol of which there flowers over him the fabled Stone Flower, where, in the centre, is seen the Mistress of the Copper Mountain.

The Stone Flower was Sergei Prokofiev's last ballet; indeed, it is known that up to a few hours before his death the composer was still working on the score. However, its first production at the Bolshoi Theatre—the brilliant company of performers notwithstanding—was not a success. The cause of this was far from simply the music alone. The ballet's original choreographer, Leonid Lavrovsky, had conceived of it as not just a simple social ballet, but as one which, in keeping with the canons of Stalinist ideology, accused pre-Revolutionary landlords of mercilessly oppressing the talent of the Russian people. The ballet, then, was asked to illustrate this stale idea. "Unfortunately Lavrovsky the producer underlined the mistakes of Lavrovsky the scenarist: the anti-balletic scenario led to the anti-balletic nature of the whole stage performance. The ballet fell into two different parts; mime strove to tell the story and dance to adorn it. We had before us a typical mime drama with dances, that is to say something very far from the contemporary understanding of true ballet," wrote Yuri Slonimsky. Lavrovsky's *The Story of the Stone Flower* ingloriously brought to a close the era which had seen the decline of choreodrama in Soviet ballet. Yuri Grigorovich's *The Stone Flower*, recognized now as the definitive version, became the pioneer of the "new wave" in Russian national choreography.

"It was not by accident that Grigorovich removed the word 'story' from the name of the ballet. Its fundamental character seemed to undergo some change," is the way Demidov put it. "The choreographer turned to the music and understood it not as a stylized tale of epic dimensions, but as a tension-charged, lyrical-fantastic chronicle, filled with sharp conflicts and character clashes, requiring expression in a danced dramaturgy and controlled by the laws of poetic logic."

The choreographer Fedor Lopukhov wrote, "Grigorovich's service lay in the fact that he restored symphonic chronicling, in which actions, conditions, moods, lyrical thoughts, and patterns of nature all come to together in a complex picture. Therefore in particular the scene of betrothal is not a matrimonial ethnographic image but an image of Katerina herself, of her spiritual qualities, moods, and dreams—and such an approach exists with Grigorovich everywhere."

The principal idea of the ballet is that an artist can find the true beauty of art in life itself, in the service of his people. But the course of the creator towards his ideal is not simple. He passes through the temptations of the magic Mistress of the Copper Mountain, who promises to open to him the secret of stone. And the master workman's fate is tragic; the world of creation closed away from people is fruitless, but outside this world the artist cannot be happy. All of the personages in the ballet are living concrete people, with characters that are far from simple. At the same time, all of them—Katerina, the Mistress of the Copper Mountain, and even the openly wheedling and creeping Severyan or the Young Gypsy, thoughtless in his ecstatic carousing—reflect various facets of the soul of the artist-creator.

The Stone Flower became the first example of the unique creative union of the choreographer Grigorovich and the artist Simon Virsaladze, a collaboration which was to last decades. Grigorovich's ballet then enjoyed a fortunate creative destiny. It is preserved in the repertoire of the Moscow and Leningrad Theatres, notably in Leningrad, where the ballet has received more than 180 performances. As Dmitri Shostakovich put it, "The harmonic union of the music, the choreography, and the décor determine the success of the new production of *The Stone Flower*. Everything in it is wonderfully integrated, and all is created by a single creative will."

—Arsen Degen

STRAVINSKY, Igor

Russian/French/American composer. Born Igor Fedorovich Stravinsky, son of opera singer Fedor Stravinsky, in Oranienbaum, 17 June (5 June old style) 1882. Educated in law at St. Petersburg University, from 1901; studied piano with Leokadia Kashperova, harmony with Vassily Kalafaty, St. Petersburg; also pupil and friend of composer Nikolai Rimsky-Korsakov. First commissioned by Serge Diaghilev to orchestrate others' music for 1909 Ballets Russes Paris season; first ballet, *L'Oiseau de feu*, staged for 1910 season, leading to series of other commissions from Diaghilev until 1923; toured with Ballets Russes, also appearing as conductor/pianist; opera composer under aegis of Diaghilev, including *Le Rossignol* (chor. Bolm, 1914; later restaged as ballet *Le Chant du rossignol*, 1920), *Mavra* (1922), and *Œdipus Rex* (1927); composer for dancer/producer Ida Rubinstein, Paris, from 1928; became French citizen, 1934; settled in the United States (Hollywood), 1939, taking on U.S. nationality, 1945; artistic collaborator with choreographer George Balanchine, New York, from 1937, with many of his concert pieces thereafter choreographed by Balanchine; received by Krushchev on tour to Russia, 1962. Died in New York, 6 April 1971; buried (near Diaghilev's grave) in Venice.

WORKS (Ballets)

1910   *L'Oiseau de feu* (chor. Fokine), Diaghilev's Ballets Russes, Paris

1911   *Petrushka* (*Pétrouchka*; chor. Fokine), Diaghilev's Ballets Russes, Paris

1913   *Le Sacre du printemps* (chor. Nijinsky), Diaghilev's Ballets Russes, Paris

1918   *L'Histoire du soldat* (work to be read, played, and danced; G. Pitoeff), Lausanne

1920   *Le Chant du rossignol* (originally symphonic poem based on opera, *Le Rossignol*; chor. Massine), Diaghilev's Ballets Russes, Paris

      Pulcinella (after Pergolesi; chor. Massine), Diaghilev's Ballets Russes, Paris

1922   *Le Renard* (histoire burlesque chantée et jouée; chor. Nijinska), Diaghilev's Ballets Russes, Paris

1923   *Les Noces* (Russian title, *Svadebka*; chor. Nijinska), Diaghilev's Ballets Russes, Paris

1928 *Apollon musagète* (chor. Bolm), Chamber Music Society, Library of Congress, Washington

Le Baiser de la fée (chor. Nijinska), Ida Rubinstein's company, Paris

1934 *Perséphone* (melodrama; chor. Jooss), Ida Rubinstein's company, Paris

1937 *Jeu de cartes* (chor. Balanchine), American Ballet, New York

1942 *Circus Polka* (ballet for elephants; chor. Balanchine), Barnum and Bailey Circus, New York

1948 *Scènes de ballet* (divertissement for revue *The Seven Lively Arts*; chor. Dolin), Ziegfeld Theatre, New York

Orpheus (chor. Balanchine), Ballet Society, New York

1957 *Agon* (chor. Balanchine), New York City Ballet, New York

Other ballets using Stravinsky's music: *Petrushka* (new version; chor. Bolm, 1919; also T. Gsovsky, 1946; Walter, 1966; Neumeier, 1976; Béjart, 1977), *Le Sacre du Printemps* (new version; chor. Massine, 1920; also Milloss, 1941; Béjart, 1959; MacMillan, 1962; Eck, 1963; Flindt, 1968; Neumeier, 1972; van Manen, 1974; Kudelka, 1987), *L'Oiseau de feu* (*Firebird*: new version, chor. Lopukhov, 1921; also Bolm, 1945; Balanchine 1949 and with Robbins 1970; Georgi, 1951; Lifar, 1954; Béjart, 1964 and 1970; Cranko, 1964; Skibine, 1965; W. Christensen, 1967; Neumeier, 1970; Gore, 1972; Tetley, 1981; Taras, 1982), *Le Rossignol* (opera-ballet: new version: chor. Balanchine, 1925; also Cranko, 1968), *Pulcinella* (new version; chor. Lopukhov, 1925; also Georgi, 1926; Jooss, 1932; Woizikowsky, 1935; Béjart, 1957; Balanchine and Robbins, 1972), *Apollon musagète* (also *Apollo*: new version; chor. Balanchine, 1928 and various revisions; also Milloss, 1941; T. Gsovsky, 1951; Georgi, 1955; Lifar, 1956), *Renard* (new version; chor. Lifar, 1929; also Balanchine, 1947; Béjart, 1965), *Le Rêve de Ratmir* (Romanov, 1931), *Le Baiser de la fée* (new version; chor. Ashton, 1935; also Balanchine, 1937; Macmillan, 1960 and 1986; Hynd, 1968; Neumeier, 1972; Béjart, 1985), *Balustrade* (Balanchine, 1941), *Danses concertantes* (Balanchine, 1944 and 1972; also MacMillan, 1955; Blaska, 1968), *Le Histoire du soldat* (new version; chor. Cranko, 1944; also Béjart 1966 and 1982; Babilée, 1967; Gielgud, 1980; Martins, 1980; Kylián, 1986), *Jeu de cartes* (new version; chor. Charrat, 1945; also Cranko, 1965), *Elégie* (Balanchine, 1947), *Orpheus* (new version; chor. Lichine, 1948; also Milloss, 1948; Walter, 1954; Cranko, 1970; van Dantzig, 1974; MacMillan, 1982), *Scènes de ballet* (new version; chor. Ashton, 1948; also Blank, 1952; Taras, 1954; Cranko, 1962), *The Cage* (Robbins, 1951), *Agon* (new version; chor. MacMillan, 1958; also T. Gsovsky, 1958), *Monumentum pro Gesualdo* (Balanchine, 1960), *Ebony Concerto* (Taras, 1960; also Cranko, 1970; van Manen, 1976), *Jazz Concert: Ragtime* (Balanchine, 1960), *Ode* (Darrell, 1961), *Perséphone* (Ashton, 1961), *Les Noces* (new version; chor. Béjart, 1962; also Robbins, 1965), *Symphony in Three Movements* (van Manen, 1963), *Arcade* (Taras, 1963), *Movements for Piano and Orchestra* (Balanchine, 1963), *Meditation* (Balanchine, 1963), *Les Jambes savantes* (Milloss, 1965), *Variations* (Balanchine, 1966), *Jewels* ("Rubies" section, also performed as *Capriccio*, Balanchine, 1967), *Olympiad* (MacMillan, 1968), *Requiem Canticles* (Balanchine, 1968), *Symphony in C* (Clifford, 1968), *Tilt* (van Manen, 1972), *Side Show* (MacMillan, 1972), *Choral Variations on Bach's 'Vom Himmel Hoch'*, *Danses concertantes*, *Divertimento from "Le Baiser de la Fée"*, *Duo concertant*, *Scherzo à la Russe*, *Sonata*, *Symphony in E Flat*, *Symphony in Three Movements*, *Violin Concerto* (all Balanchine; Stravinsky Festival, 1972), *Circus Polka*, *Dumbarton Oaks*, *Requiem Canticles*, *Scherzo fantastique* (all Robbins;

Stravinsky Festival, 1972), *Serenade in A* (Bolender; Stravinsky Festival, 1972), *Concerto for Piano and Winds*, *Scènes de ballet*, *The Song of the Nightingale* (all Taras; Stravinsky Festival, 1972), *Ragtime* (Petit, 1978), *Eight Easy Pieces* (Martins, 1980), *Forgotten Land* (Kylián, 1981), *Pribaoutki* (North, 1982), *Concerto for Two Solo Pianos* (Martins, 1982), *Tango* (Martins, 1983), *Frisson* (Morris, 1984), *Eight Miniatures* (Martins, 1985), *Eight More* (Martins, 1985), *Picasso and Matisse* (North, 1991).

PUBLICATIONS

By Stravinsky:
Chronicle of My Life, London, 1936
Conversations with Igor Stravinsky (with Robert Craft), New York and London, 1959
Memories and Commentaries (with Robert Craft), New York and London, 1960
Expositions and Developments (with Robert Craft), New York and London, 1962
Dialogues and a Diary (with Robert Craft), New York, 1963
Themes and Episodes (with Robert Craft), New York and London, 1966
Selected Correspondence, edited by Robert Craft, New York, 1982

About Stravinsky:
Lederman, M., *Stravinsky in the Theatre*, New York, 1949
Stravinsky and the Dance (catalogue), New York Public Library, 1962
Erhardt, L., *The Ballets of Stravinsky*, Kraków, 1962
Vershinina, I., *The Early Ballets of Stravinsky*, Moscow, 1967
Portfolio on Stravinsky, *Dance Magazine* (New York), June 1972
Goldner, Nancy, *The Stravinsky Festival of the New York City Ballet*, New York, 1973
MacDonald, Nesta, *Diaghilev Observed by Critics in England and the United States 1911–1929*, New York, 1975
Reynolds, Nancy, *Repertory in Review*, New York, 1977
Vlad, Roman, *Stravinsky*, translated by Frederick Fuller, London and New York, 1979
White, Eric Walter, *Stravinsky: The Composer and His Works*, revised edition, Berkeley and London, 1979
Taras, John (ed.), "Comments and Quotations: Stravinsky on Art and Artists", *Dance Magazine* (New York), April 1981
Borovsky, Victor and Schouvaloff, Alexander, *Stravinsky on Stage*, London, 1982
Taper, Bernard, *Balanchine*, revised edition, New York, 1984
Boucourechliev, André, *Stravinsky*, translated by Martin Cooper, New York and London, 1987
Buckle, Richard, with Taras, John, *George Balanchine: Ballet Master*, New York, 1988
Garafola, Lynn, *Diaghilev's Ballets Russes*, New York, 1989

*   *   *

Throughout a long creative career, Igor Stravinsky's music continuously invigorated the dance repertory, changing for all time our perception of music's relationship to dance. He was a genius with the extraordinary faculty for growing younger in creative imagination as his body grew older, from the romantic pictorial style of his early works, through the neo-classical, to his late adoption of serial (note-row) technique. His music stimulated an extension of dance technique as well as a new awareness of music's function as an organic element in dance.

He was 28 years old when he first won international acclaim with *L'Oiseau de feu* (*The Firebird*, 1910), having been

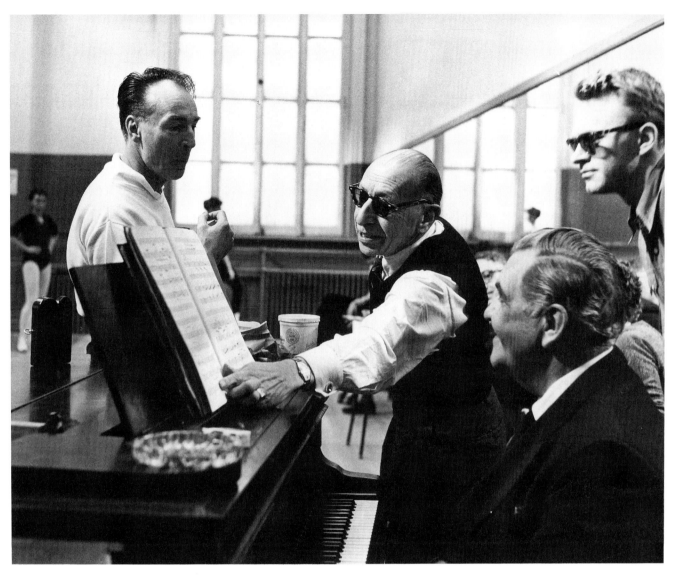

Igor Stravinsky (centre) with George Balanchine (left), New York, 1957

Diaghilev's second choice after Anatol Lyadov proved too dilatory with the original commission. Stravinsky composed to a previously devised scenario and, although it involved pictorial music of a kind he later said he had not wanted to write, it had immediate success in the context of Fokine's ballet. It became the single work of Stravinsky's that was most often performed, to the extent that he was once accosted in public by a stranger as "Mr Fireberg".

From his composition teacher, Rimsky-Korsakov (to whom the *Firebird* music is dedicated), Stravinsky borrowed the device of associating diatonic harmonies (including the quotation of two folk themes) with the ballet's human characters, and chromatic figuration based on the tritone (an augmented fourth) for all the magical elements. For *Petrushka*, first conceived as a concert work with solo piano, he used clashes of bitonality (two different keys heard simultaneously) for structural purposes and impressionistic effect, with further use of folk themes cunningly woven into the fabric.

Le Sacre du printemps (*The Rite of Spring*) first entered the composer's mind as a fleeting vision of a solemn pagan ritual while he was finishing *The Firebird*. The finished score begins with a Lithuanian folk theme (the only one in it not

Stravinsky's own), but the musical germ-cell, starting the "Augurs of Spring" section after the Introduction, is a chord of conflicting tonalities that cancel themselves out. This denies any pull towards a key-centre, restricting the conventional effect of melody and harmony and asserting instead a dominance of rhythm that had far-reaching consequences in music generally (as well as demanding extended musical responsiveness from dancers).

Of this seminal score Stravinsky was later to write: "I was guided by no system whatever. I heard, and I wrote what I heard. I am the vessel through which *Le Sacre* passed". Together with the irregular rhythms and accents, and the boldness of instrumentation (later twice revised, in 1921 and 1943), *The Rite of Spring* became a touchstone of orchestral virtuosity in the latter half of the twentieth century, as well as a continuing challenge to choreographers in the theatre.

While self-exiled in Switzerland during World War I, Stravinsky and C.F. Ramuz initiated the idea of what later came to be called "multi-media", with the combination of dance, singing, mime, and narration variously found in *Le Renard* and *Le Histoire du soldat* (*The Soldier's Tale*). *Le Rossignol* (*The Nightingale*), first staged by Diaghilev in 1914 as an opera-ballet (singers in the pit, dancers on stage) was independently re-cast by the composer as a symphonic poem before being taken by Diaghilev for a ballet in Massine's choreography; in 1925 it marked the inception of the epochal association of Stravinsky with Balanchine.

Meanwhile, the Diaghilev–Massine project for a *commedia dell'arte* ballet to follow their *Les Femmes de bonne humeur* (*The Good-humoured Ladies*) brought a choice of eighteenth-century music attributed to Pergolesi to Stravinsky to orchestrate, and this became what Stravinsky called "my discovery of the past— the epiphany through which the whole of my late work became possible". He did not simply orchestrate, but composed *on the* printed music, effectively re-working it in terms of his own personality so that the finished ballet score of *Pulcinella* is rather more than half "original Stravinsky".

During the 1920s there followed *Les Noces* (*The Wedding*), a choral cantata of which the "black-and-white" instrumentation for four pianos and percussion in Nijinska's celebrated ballet was the outcome of ten years searching for the right musical character on Stravinsky's part. *Le Baiser de la fée* (*The Fairy's Kiss*; choreographed by Nijinska for Ida Rubinstein) was Stravinsky's overt homage to Tchaikovsky (whose *Sleeping Beauty* he praised enthusiastically when Diaghilev first brought it to the West in 1921), with multiple use of Tchaikovsky themes in the music. In the same year his composition of *Apollon musagète* produced one of the century's most sheerly beautiful scores for strings alone, as a commission originally from Elizabeth Sprague Coolidge for the Library of Congress in Washington, D.C.

Jeu de cartes (*A Game of Cards*), in a continuing vein of neo-classicism for Balanchine (1937), is of lesser musical import except in the number and variety of allusions to works by classical composers and by Stravinsky himself. *Scènes de ballet*, for one of variously assorted elements in a Broadway revue, had an unexpected link with the past in being structured on almost identical lines to that of a Petipa ballet finale, its arch-like form of introduction balanced by apotheosis enclosing pas de deux with variations.

Orpheus in 1948 and *Agon* a decade later completed the trio of "Greek" ballets begun with *Apollo*. The former makes a virtue of modal harmonies and instrumental colours to express a scenario worked out between Stravinsky and Balanchine. *Agon* is a musical hybrid: it was begun as a diatonic composition but became overtaken by Stravinsky's increasing concern with serial technique, which reaches its strictest form at the climactic pas de deux. In association with Balanchine's original ballet, the result is widely regarded as the deepest inter-penetration of music and dance this century, sound and movement becoming an extension of each other to be heard with the eyes and viewed with the ears.

Balanchine largely pioneered the fruitful association of choreography with Stravinsky's other music, beginning with the ballet *Balustrade* (1941) to the Violin Concerto; the composer considered this one of the best visual realizations of his non-dance music. *Danses concertantes* (first performed in concert in 1942, and staged as a ballet in 1944), though not composed with choreography in mind, has been prominent among the plethora of Stravinsky ballets since created. These reached a famous climax in 1972 when Balanchine's New York City Ballet staged a Stravinsky Festival embracing 31 ballets to his music within ten days, of which 21 were newly choreographed for the occasion. Another fourteen ballets by the same company were created for a Centenary Festival in New York ten years later.

Concert suites were made by Stravinsky from several of the early scores which have in turn become a basis for choreography; he also made instrumental revisions in the interests of more practicable performance by smaller musical forces than the original orchestrations. His entire works have been recorded, including a series of recordings with himself as conductor.

—Noël Goodwin

STRAVINSKY VIOLIN CONCERTO *see* **VIOLIN CONCERTO**

STRUCHKOVA, Raisa
Russian dancer, teacher, and critic. Born Raisa Stepanovna Struchkova in Moscow, 5 October 1925. Studied at the Moscow Choreographic School, pupil of Elisaveta Gerdt; graduated in 1944. Married Bolshoi dancer Aleksandr Lapauri (d. 1975). Début (in *The Little Stork*, 1937) while still a student; dancer, soon becoming ballerina, Bolshoi Ballet, 1944–78; has also appeared on film, including as title role in *Cinderella* (Bolshoi film, 1961) and in *Thy Name* (dir. Lapauri); teacher, State Institute of Theatrical Art (GITIS), from 1967; also ballet writer and editor: editor-in-chief, *Sovetsky Balet* magazine (Moscow), from 1981. Recipient: title of People's Artist of the USSR, 1959.

ROLES

1937 Title role in *The Little Stork* (Popko, Pospekhin, Radunsky), Bolshoi Ballet, Moscow
1944 Little Red Riding Hood in *The Sleeping Beauty* (Messerer, Chekrygin after Petipa), Bolshoi Ballet, Moscow
1945 Dance with the Little Bells in *The Fountain of Bakhchisarai* (Zakharov), Bolshoi Ballet, Moscow
Spring in *Cinderella* (Zakharov), Bolshoi Ballet, Moscow
Three Oranges in *Cinderella* (Zakharov), Bolshoi Ballet, Moscow
1946 Prelude in *Chopiniana* (Fokine), Bolshoi Ballet, Moscow
Lise in *Vain Precautions* (*La Fille mal gardée*; Gorsky), Bolshoi Ballet, Moscow
1947 Title role (cr) in *Cinderella* (Zakharov), Bolshoi Ballet, Moscow
1948 Olya in *The Little Stork* (Radunsky, Pospekhin, Popko), Bolshoi Ballet, Moscow
Pas de trois in *Swan Lake* (Petipa, Ivanov; staged Gorsky, Messerer), Bolshoi Ballet, Moscow
The Pearl in *The Little Humpbacked Horse* (Gorsky after Saint-Léon), Bolshoi Ballet, Moscow
Maria in *The Fountain of Bakhchisarai* (Zakharov), Bolshoi Ballet, Moscow
1949 Parasha in *The Bronze Horseman* (Moscow version; Zakharov), Bolshoi Ballet, Moscow
Dawn in *Coppélia* (Gorsky), Bolshoi Ballet, Moscow
1950 Jeanne in *The Flames of Paris* (Vainonen), Bolshoi Ballet, Moscow
1951 Odette/Odile in *Swan Lake* (Petipa, Ivanov; staged Gorsky, Messerer), Bolshoi Ballet, Moscow
1952 Princess Aurora in *The Sleeping Beauty* (Petipa; staged Gabovich, Messerer), Bolshoi Ballet, Moscow

Tao-Hoa in *The Red Poppy* (Zakharov), Bolshoi Ballet, Moscow

1953 Juliet in *Romeo and Juliet* (Lavrovsky), Bolshoi Ballet, Moscow

1954 Katerina in *The Stone Flower* (Lavrovsky), Bolshoi Ballet, Moscow

1955 Title role in *Fadetta* (Lavrovsky), Bolshoi Ballet, Moscow

Title role in *Giselle* (Petipa after Coralli, Perrot; staged Lavrovsky), Bolshoi Ballet, Moscow

1956 Pascuale in *Laurencia* (Chabukiani), Bolshoi Ballet, Moscow

1957 Title role (cr) in *Gayané* (Vainonen), Bolshoi Ballet, Moscow

1958 Title role in *Mirandolina* (Vainonen), Bolshoi Ballet, Moscow

1959 Kitri in *Don Quixote* (Gorsky), Bolshoi Ballet, Moscow

1961 Tamara (cr) in *Pages from a Life* (Lavrovsky), Bolshoi Ballet, Moscow

Mavka (cr) in *Song of the Woods* (Tarasova, Lapauri), Bolshoi Ballet, Moscow

1963 Maid of Honour (cr) in *Lieutenant Kizhe* (Tarasova, Lapauri), Bolshoi Ballet, Moscow

1964 Leili (cr) in *Leili and Medzhnun* (Goleizovsky), Bolshoi Ballet, Moscow

Other roles include: principal dancer in concert pieces—*Étude* (Lapauri), *Waltz* (Lapauri), *Nocturne* (Yakobson), *Gavotte* (Vainonen), *Moszkovsky Waltz* (Vainonen).

PUBLICATIONS

By Struchkova:
Numerous interviews and articles on dance, including—
"How to Judge Terpsichore", *Zhurnalist*, no. 1, 1969
"Lofty Thoughts", *Sovetskaya Kultura* (Moscow), 25 July 1980
"What a Full and Noble Life", *Sovetsky Balet* (Moscow), no. 1, 1982
"Everyone's Duty", *Sovetsky Balet* (Moscow), no. 3, 1985
"School of the Heart", *Sovetsky Ballet* (Moscow), no. 6, 1990

About Struchkova:
Dolgopolov, Mikhail, "Raisa Struchkova", *Dancing Times* (London), September 1949
Fradkin, Herman, *Raisa Struchkova* (in English), Moscow, 1956
Sinclair, Janet, "An Appreciation of Raisa Struchkova", *Ballet Today* (London), November 1963
Roslavleva, Natalia, "Raisa Struchkova", *Muzykalnaya Zhizn* (Moscow), no. 2, 1975
Bogolubskaya, M., "The Wings of Dance", *Sovetskaya Musyka* (Moscow), no. 5, 1976
Vladimirova, A., "Raisa Struchkova", *Teatr* (Moscow), no. 3, 1976
Zviagina, S., "The Many Facets of Talent", *Teatralnaya Zhizn* (Moscow), no. 21, 1984

* * *

Raisa Struchkova studied at the Moscow Ballet School, but her tutor came from St. Petersburg. Moreover, her tutor was one of the most "academic" of the St. Petersburg dancers, Elisaveta Gerdt, who as a teacher was always the most ardent champion of the true St. Petersburg dancing tradition. That is why Struchkova was trained at a higher standard of artistry than many a dancer who, like her, had started a career in Moscow in

Raisa Struchkova as Giselle, Moscow, 1956

the 1930s. Elisaveta Gerdt's own style of performance was marked by exquisite technique (as well as by a certain coldness). And she demanded from her students a high degree of precision, an ideal clarity to every step—a harmony of dance. Struchkova was Gerdt's favourite student, but in spite of that she did not become a mere copy of her instructor.

Struchkova was remarkably well equipped for her profession. As early as her school performances and immediately afterwards, in 1944, when she started to perform as an understudy for the Bolshoi ballerinas, she attracted attention with the light, slender outline of her figure, the naturalness with which she seemed to handle the technical complexities of choreography, and with her sincerity and charm. She was particularly noted for her performance in a piece called *The Spring* to music by Grieg: her airily graceful dance, its melancholy easily turning into playfulness, seemed to convey the theme of the piece with great precision. *La Fille mal gardée* was the first major performance Struchkova danced at the Bolshoi and in it she showed that she possessed a good deal of cheerfulness, a sense of humour as well as a sense of lyricism. She also demonstrated her excellent technique. Elisaveta Gerdt had taught her how to achieve perfect dancing skills through a subtle gracefulness rather than the aggressive, showy, even vulgar "virtuoso" style which could sometimes be observed in the Moscow tradition of dancing.

However, Struchkova first came to be regarded a leading soloist of the Bolshoi after she had performed in Rostislav

Zakharov's *Cinderella*. Before her, the part of Cinderella had been danced by three famous ballerinas of the Bolshoi—Galina Ulanova, Olga Lepeshinskaya, and Marina Semenova. Each of them had interpreted the role in her own way. Struchkova's Cinderella was neither tremulously dramatic like Ulanova's, nor regal like Semenova's, nor playfully roguish like Lepeshinskaya's: it possessed a character of its own—a certain sweet homeliness, a poetic simplicity. She was neither a princess who accidentally finds herself in a humble forester's home, nor an abstract dream of a young prince's mind. She was a shy and gentle girl, skilled with a broom, who feels at home near a smoky hearth. She is not ashamed of her darned frock and she can turn the prose of life into poetry.

These very same qualities explain Struchkova's great success as Parasha in *The Bronze Horseman*. This ballet was based on Pushkin's long poem of the same title, and it has essentially two central characters. The first is the Tsar Peter the Great, whose equestrian statue ("The Bronze Horseman") stands on the embankment as a reminder that it was on his orders that St. Petersburg was built; and the other is the humble clerk, Evgeny, who loses the only dear thing in his life when his beloved Parasha is drowned in one of the city's great floods. When he learns of her death, Evgeny loses his mind, but in vain does he in his delusion threaten the bronze Tsar: the city will still stand, because such was the will of Peter the Great. Parasha symbolizes a simple, everyday happiness, which the humble man is striving to achieve and which is being taken from him. She is a naïve and touching dream of Evgeny's, a dream which is never to come true. This is exactly how Struchkova was in the ballet—simple-hearted, loving, and joyful; in her happiness of the moment she is unsuspecting of imminent tragedy.

Parasha was followed by the leading roles in the classical ballet repertoire: *Swan Lake*, *The Sleeping Beauty*, *Giselle*. Sometimes Struchkova allowed her lyrical colours to come to the fore, as in the slightly anaemic role of Maria in *The Fountain of Bakhchisarai*. In other cases, it was her extraordinary technique—for example, as Kitri in *Don Quixote* or in many of her concert pieces (staged by Struchkova's husband Aleksandr Lapauri)—which shone the most. Struchkova and Lapauri, who had studied together from the very first year at ballet school, and were married immediately after graduation, were regular partners on the stage. Lapauri was chiefly known for his skill in duets, particularly in support techniques. He was exceptionally fit and strong, while Struchkova was petite, very light, and quite fearless in her dancing—and this made it possible for them to perform all kinds of acrobatic stunts. Most of their concert pieces were based on striking supports in pas de deux. This could suit quite lyrical pieces, like *Étude* (to the music of Grieg), in which Lapauri carried Struchkova on to the stage on one arm over his head, and danced with her as if she were not a real live woman but a dream—unattainable, elusive, hovering in the air, and devoid of any materiality. However, most of their duets, like the *Waltz* to the music by Dunaevsky, were of a joyous, positive mood. After a swift run, Struchkova flung herself into her partner's arms, recklessly happy: he threw her up into the air and she flew into his arms and then up again, doing it all with gusto, as if enjoying the breathtaking pace of the music, and completely disregarding the danger.

Lapauri also staged, together with Olga Tarasova, a ballet for Struchkova in which she had an exciting role which was quite untypical of her. The ballet was *Lieutenant Kizhe* to music by Sergei Prokofiev. It was a fantastic satire depicting the grotesque court of the mad Tsar Paul I, who reigned from 1796 to 1801. The Maid of Honour who, on the tsar's orders, is being married to the non-existent Lieutenant Kizhe, is a clever intriguer and comedienne. She is coquettish and flirtatious in the scenes of her advances to the Tsar; she is also resourceful and unabashed in her dealings with her numerous suitors, and she skilfully plays the part of an unconsolable mourner at the "funeral" of her non-existent husband. Struchkova in this role proved herself a remarkable comic actress. Her dramatic gift also showed in a balletic film *Thy Name*, which was also directed by Lapauri and in which the verse of the French poet Paul Eluard was turned into dance.

Having left the stage in 1978, Struchkova continued her work as a rehearsal supervisor at the Bolshoi. In 1981, when the first ballet magazine in the USSR (*Sovetsky Balet*) was launched, Struchkova became its editor-in-chief.

—Irina Gruzdeva

STUTTGART BALLET

German ballet company based in Stuttgart. Origins in Württemberg court ballets of the seventeenth century, leading to establishment of professional company of the court theatre; era of "Sing-Ballette", under direction of balletmaster Jacques Courcelles, 1684–1709; dancing group directed by ballet master Jean-Georges Noverre, 1760–66, evolved into smaller ensemble of the court theatre, largely for the purposes of opera production; twentieth-century theatre renamed Württemburg State Theatre, with Ballet of the Württemburg State Theatre becoming known as the Stuttgart Ballet, achieving international recognition under directorship of John Cranko, 1961–73; small performing ensemble, the Noverre Ballet, established 1970, but absorbed into main company, 1973. First school associated with Stuttgart company, the Ducal Ballet School, operated 1771–94; ballet school affiliated with company, Stuttgart Ballet School, founded 1958, with affiliated boarding school set up in 1971; renamed the John Cranko School, 1974. Current artistic director of the Stuttgart Ballet (succeeding Glen Tetley): Marcia Haydée, from 1976.

PUBLICATIONS

Von Schraisbuon, C.A., *Das Königliche Hoftheater in Stuttgart von 1811 bis zur neuren Zeit*, Stuttgart, 1878

Lynham, Deryck, *The Chevalier Noverre*, London, 1950

Krüger, M., *Jean-Georges Noverre und sein Einfluss auf die Ballettgestaltung*, Emsdetten, 1963

Winter, Marian Hannah, *The Pre-Romantic Ballet*, London, 1974

Winkler-Betzendahl, Madeline, and Dominic, Zoë (photographer), *John Cranko und das Stuttgarter Ballett*, Pfullingen, 1975

Koegler, Horst, *Stuttgart Ballet*, London, 1978

Kilian, Hannes, *Stuttgarter Ballett*, Weingarten, 1980

Percival, John, *Theatre in my Blood: A Biography of John Cranko*, London, 1983

Schmidt, Jochen, "The Guardians of Cranko's Legacy", *Ballett International* (Cologne), October 1986

*   *   *

Of all the German theatres to emerge from the system of court theatre, Stuttgart, in terms of ballet, is at the forefront. This is accounted for not only by its ballet tradition, which goes back as far as 1609, but also by the fact that it has consistently attracted the best choreographers. Shortly after the birth of the "danse d'école" at the court of Louis XIV, Stuttgart had its first high point under the direction of the court ballet master Jacques Courcelles (1684–1709). He produced, among other ballets, *Le rendez-vous des plaisirs*.

In 1760 Prince Carl Eugen brought to Stuttgart the already renowned Jean-Georges Noverre, who choreographed twenty ballets for Stuttgart and Ludwigsburg. This Parisian dancer, choreographer, and theoretician, who set about reforming dance, condemned mere divertissements and self-seeking technique and promoted the dramatic narrative ballet. Although most of his works were performed between acts of an opera, they were, nevertheless, independent ballets. He extended the company to fourteen principal dancers, with 42 corps de ballet dancers. The most famous dancers, from Gaetano Vestris and Gardel through to Dauberval, Heinel, Saveur, and Miss Nancy Levier, made guest appearances during his term of office.

After Noverre made his way back to Vienna in 1766, Louis Dauvigny became responsible for the fate of a further reduced company. In the period 1771–94 there was a ballet school supported by the prince. Between 1824 and 1828 Filippo Taglioni came to Stuttgart with his daughter Marie; as a guest choreographer, he had already staged his ballet *Das Erwachen der Venus* there in 1824, and in 1826 *Jocko or the Brazilian Ape* was first performed in Stuttgart, with Marie in the leading role of Danina. The ballet was a great success and became part of the repertoire of theatres across Europe.

For a time, Stuttgart had to make do with dance as part of an opera interlude, or at best, a platform for guest artists. Then August Bruhl's *Puppenfee* became a great success, performed for seven weeks running in 1891. The Max Reinhardt productions of Richard Strauss's *Bürger als Edelmann* and *Ariadne auf Naxos*, choreographed by Fritz Scharf, also became known throughout the region. Stuttgart regained prominence as well through the architect Oskar Schlemmer's ballet *Triadisches Ballett*, which dressed its dancers in outsize cuboid and spherical costumes.

From 1927 to 1939 the Munich-born Lina Gerzer was consecutively ballet mistress, prima ballerina, and state ballet mistress (the title for ballet director). She choreographed, among other ballets, Gluck's *Don Juan*, Beethoven's *Die Geschöpfe des Prometheus*, Bayer's *Die Puppenfee*, Strauss's *Josephslegende*, Stravinsky's *Petrushka*, and de Falla's *Dreispitz*. She even wrote her own libretti for *Sonne und Erde, Der tapfere Zinnsoldat, Tanzsuite*, and *Tanzsuiten*.

There followed six more ballet directors until the engagement of the renowned Lithuanian-English dancer and choreographer Nicholas Beriozoff in 1957. Beriozoff, with his experiences with the Ballet Russe de Monte Carlo, the Marquis de Cuevas Ballet International, and other companies, mounted versions of the classics in Stuttgart—*The Sleeping Beauty, Giselle, The Nutcracker*, and *Swan Lake*. He also brought in the most important ballerinas of the time as guest artists, including the Parisian étoile Yvette Chauviré, the Cuban Dulce Anaya, his daughter Svetlana Beriosova, Margrethe Schanne, and Marjorie Tallchief. In so doing, he built a foundation upon which John Cranko could later build.

Cranko had created pieces for the troupe from 1946 onwards while a member of the London Sadler's Wells Ballet. Beriozoff himself invited Cranko to Stuttgart with his ballet *The Prince of the Pagodas* (created in 1957 for the Royal Ballet). On the strength of this work, theatre director Walter Erich Schäfer offered Cranko the post of ballet director. With Cranko's assumption of the post in 1961 began what came to be known as the Stuttgart ballet miracle.

John Cranko, who had already shown evidence of his gifts during his time in London, developed into a director of genius. He had a feeling for the talents of others which he then fully

exploited. The most striking example was Marcia Haydée, in no way technically brilliant, but transformed into a prima ballerina by Cranko, becoming one of the greatest dramatic ballerinas of this century. She gave to her roles and Cranko's ballets a specific, dramatically convincing character. Some excellent examples of this quality were her roles in *Romeo and Juliet* (1962), *Onegin* (1965), *Présence* (1968), *The Taming of the Shrew* (1969), and *Carmen* (1971). With such discoveries as Birgit Keil, Silvia Kesselheim, Kenneth Barlow, Bernd Berg, Richard Cragun, Dennis Griffith, Egon Madsen, John Neumeier, Jan Stripling, and David Sutherland (the soloists of the early years), he formed an excellent troupe. The soloists taken on from Beriozoff's days also became Cranko's lead dancers, such as Ray Barra, Hugo Delavalle, and Helga Heinrich. In later years it became more and more apparent that Cranko combined the precious gifts of the choreographic artist with a human warmth and concern for his dancers. A sense of belonging reigned more strongly in the Stuttgart company than in any other, a feeling which has helped them through difficult times since Cranko's early death in 1973.

In the 1960s, the Stuttgart ensemble became the best in Germany thanks to Cranko's many-faceted repertoire of the highest choreographic quality, and the town became a recognized centre for ballet. With his fresh look at the classics, and with the literary narrative ballets in particular (in which dance and drama are synthesised in a revolutionary fashion), he laid the foundations of Stuttgart's fame. As a result of the development of the repertoire, an exceptionally versatile type of dancer emerged in Stuttgart. Cranko did, it is true, have teachers as excellent as Anne Woolliams working with the company, but it is not possible to speak of a Stuttgart "school", as one can with the Royal, the Kirov, or the Bolshoi Ballets. For that very reason, a Stuttgart dancer is at home both in a neo-classical concert piece or a modern creation, in a classical as well as in a strongly dramatic ballet. Consequently, for the Stuttgart ensemble, personality comes before technique or school of style. With Cranko, the style came from a choreography sympathetic to the potential of whichever dancer he was working with. His works, and those of guest choreographers, always had a strong human element which immediately touched the spectator. Out of this immediacy developed a highly loyal following for the Stuttgart Ballet.

Also important to the company has been the Noverre Society, founded in 1958 by a few Stuttgart citizens interested in dance, which has developed increasingly into a platform for up-and-coming choreographers through its recitals and lecture demonstrations. Ashley Killar, John Neumeier, Jan Stripling, Gray Veredon, and Jiří Kylián all made their first choreographic sorties in Noverre Society matinées. In the 1970s, William Forsythe, Rosemary Helliwell, Patrice Montagnon, and Uwe Scholz did the same. No other German ensemble has attracted so much talent or brought on so many future choreographers, a fact which has given the ensemble a great advantage: for while numerous German municipal theatres were desperately seeking choreographers, they were all streaming to Stuttgart. They included world-famous choreographers such as Maurice Béjart, who gave Stuttgart works such as *Divine, Wien, Wien, nur du allein*, and *Die Stühle*. John Neumeier and Hans van Manen complete the trio who regularly stock the Stuttgart repertoire.

Through her artistic and personal qualities, ballerina and current director Marcia Haydée has attracted to Stuttgart choreographers who create new works nowhere else. An example is Glen Tetley. His fruitful but difficult directorship lasted only from 1974 to 1976. Tetley produced *Voluntaries, Daphnis and Chloë*, and *Greening*. He also broadened the company's horizons through his widely rejected but self-reflective style of work and his modern bent. Haydée, who concerned herself initially with existing works, compared Tetley's pieces, as she did those of other choreographers, with Cranko's legacy. In the meantime, she herself had also begun to choreograph.

The members of the ensemble still enjoy the reputation of being extremely talented dancers. But a range of soloists like those in Cranko's time has yet to emerge.

—Malve Gradinger

———————

SUBLIGNY, Marie-Thérèse

French dancer. Born Marie-Thérèse Perdou de Subligny in 1666. Début, Académie royale de musique (Paris Opéra 1688, performing in revival of Lully's *Atys*, 1689; soon succeeded Mlle. LaFontaine as premiere danseuse, dancing mostly in opéra-ballets by Lully and Campra; guest ballerina, performing in England (first professional French dancer to do so), 1700–1702; retired from the Opéra in 1707. Died in 1735.

ROLES

1689   Une Nymphe de Flore, Une Phrygienne, Une Neréide in *Atys* (tragédie-lyrique; mus. Lully), Opéra, Paris
1690   Une Bergère in *Cadmus et Hermione* (tragédie-lyrique; mus. Lully, chor. probably Pécour), Opéra, Paris
1692   Une Bergère (cr) in *Le Ballet de Villeneuve Saint-Georges* (ballet; mus. Collasse, chor. probably Pécour), Opéra, Paris
1693   Une Nymphe, Une Femme du peuple de Carthage (cr) in *Didon* (tragédie-lyrique; mus. Desmarets), Opéra, Paris
1695   Une Suivante du Printemps, La Femme du Seigneur (cr) in *Les Saisons* (ballet; mus. L. Lully, Collasse, chor. Pécour), Opéra, Paris
1697   Une Moresse, Une Sultane (cr) in *L'Europe galante* (opéra-ballet; mus. Campra, chor. Pécour), Opéra, Paris
        Une Hésperide, Une Bergère, Une Egyptienne (cr) in *Issé* (pastorale-héroïque; mus. Destouches, chor. Pécour), Opéra, Paris
1699   Une Bergère (cr) in *Amadis de Grèce* (tragédie-lyrique; mus. Destouches, chor. Pécour), Opéra, Paris
        Une Ombre heureuse in *Proserpine* (tragédie-lyrique; mus. Lully), Opéra, Paris
        Une Amazone, Une Bohémienne, Une Grâce (cr) in *Marthésie, reine des Amazones* (tragédie-lyrique; mus. Destouches, chor. Pécour), Opéra, Paris
1700   Diane, nymphe des fontaines, Un Faune (cr) in *Canente* (tragédie-lyrique; mus. Collasse, chor. Pécour), Opéra, Paris
        Une Bergère dansante, Une Espagnolette in *Le Carnaval* (mascarade; mus. Lully), Opéra, Paris
        Une Prêtresse de Junon, Une Héroine (cr) in *Hésione* (tragédie-lyrique; mus. Campra, chor. Pécour), Opéra, Paris
1701   Une Nymphe de Diane (cr) in *Aréthuse; ou, La Vengeance de l'Amour* (ballet; mus. Campra, chor. Pécour), Opéra, Paris
        Une Héroine in *Amadis de Gaule* (tragédie-lyrique; mus. Lully), Opéra, Paris
        Un Plaisir, Une Mégarienne (cr) in *Scylla* (tragédie-lyrique; mus. Théobalde), Opéra, Paris

Marie-Thérèse Subligny

        Dancer (cr) in *Omphale* (tragédie-lyrique; mus. Destouches), Opéra, Paris
1702   Une Suivante de Thomiris (cr) in *Médus, roi des Mèdes* (tragédie-lyrique; mus. Bouvard, chor. Pécour), Opéra, Paris
        Dancer (cr) in *Tancrède* (tragédie-lyrique; mus. Campra, chor. Pécour), Opéra, Paris
        Une Bergère, Une Suivante de Neptune in *Acis et Galathée* (pastorale-héroïque; mus. Lully), Opéra, Paris
        Une Matelotte, Une Bergère (cr) in *Les Fragments de Monsieur de Lully* (ballet; mus. Campra, chor. Pécour), Opéra, Paris
1703   Un Génie sous la forme d'un jeu et d'un plaisir (cr) in *Ulysse* (tragédie-lyrique; mus. J.-F. Rebel), Opéra, Paris
        Un Jeu junonien, Une Matelote in *Persée* (tragédie-lyrique; mus. Lully, chor. Pécour), Opéra, Paris
        Une Suivante de Flore, Une Scaramouchette in *Psyché* (tragédie-lyrique; mus. Lully), Opéra, Paris
        Une Bergère (cr) in *Les Muses* (opéra-ballet; mus. Campra), Opéra, Paris
        Une Habitante champêtre, Une Amante fortunée in *Armide* (tragédie-lyrique; mus. Lully, chor. Pécour), Opéra, Paris
1704   Une Suivante de Plutus, La Danse, Un Masque (cr) in *Le Carnaval et la folie* (comédie-ballet; mus. Destouches, chor. Pécour), Opéra, Paris

Une Nymphe (cr) in *Iphigénie en Tauride* (tragédie-lyrique; mus. Desmarets, chor. Pécour), Opéra, Paris
Une Suivante de la jeunesse in *Isis* (tragédie-lyrique; mus. Lully, chor. Pécour), Opéra, Paris
Une Suivante de Vénus, Une Danseuse dans une fête marine (cr) in *Télémaque* (tragédie-lyrique; mus. various arr. Campra, chor. Pécour), Opéra, Paris
1705 Flore (cr) in *Alcine* (tragédie-lyrique; mus. Campra, chor. Pécour), Opéra, Paris
Une Femme du peuple, La Mariée in *Roland* (tragédie-lyrique; mus. Lully, chor. Pécour), Opéra, Paris
Flore in *Alcide; ou, La Mort d'Hercule* (tragédie-lyrique; mus. L. Lully, Marais, chor. Pécour), Opéra, Paris
Une Bacchante, Une Danseuse dans une fête marine (cr) in *Philomèle* (tragédie-lyrique; mus. Lacoste, chor. Pécour), Opéra, Paris
Une Nymphe de Diane, Flore in *Le Triomphe de l'amour* (ballet; mus. Lully, revised by Campra, chor. Pécour), Opéra, Paris
1706 Une Matelote (cr) in *Alcione* (tragédie-lyrique; mus. Marais, chor. Pécour), Opéra, Paris
1707 Une Suivante de la paix, Une Sarrasine de la suite de Clorinde in *Tancrède* (tragédie-lyrique; mus. Campra), Opéra, Paris

PUBLICATIONS

Feuillet, Raoul-Auger, *Recueil de dances ... de Mr. Pécour*, Paris, 1704; reprinted 1972
Parfaict, Les Frères (Claude et François), *Dictionnaire des théâtres*, Paris, 1756
Jal, A., *Dictionnaire critique de biographie et d'histoire*, second edition, Paris, 1872
Campardon, Emile, *L'Académie royale de musique au XVIIIe siècle*, Paris, 1884
Ces Demoiselles de l'Opéra, Paris, 1887
Migel, Parmenia, *The Ballerinas*, New York, 1972
Winter, Marian Hannah, *The Pre-Romantic Ballet*, London, 1974
Hilton, Wendy, *Dance of Court and Theatre: The French Noble Style 1690–1725*, London, 1981

* * *

One of the earliest prima ballerinas of the Paris Opéra, Mlle. Subligny made her début in 1688, only seven years after the first professional dancer, Mlle. de LaFontaine, had appeared on stage. Subligny's nineteen-year career spanned an exciting time in dance history. Stage ballet, which for many years had been a kind of handmaiden to opera, now began to assert itself, and the presence of women on stage contributed much to its growing popularity. Women entered the profession in increasing numbers—many, especially in England, inspired by Subligny herself. Although England had seen women dance on the popular stage some twenty years before they appeared at the Paris Opéra, it was not until the arrival of Subligny in 1700 (imported along with L'Abbé and Ballon by the enterprising actor-manager of the Lincoln's Inn Fields Theatre, Thomas Betterton) that they saw their first professional ballerina in the modern sense.

Predictably, there were some reactionary opinions to Subligny's stage appearance (one critic referred to her as "a surprising monster"), but many were charmed, and by 1702 she had inspired four English women to become professionals. Campra, who with Lully and Pécour set most of the ballets in which Subligny performed, had already seen the potential of ballet as an art form in its own right when he remarked that the only way of making opera more popular was to lengthen the dances and shorten the ballerinas' skirts. Women dancers were still burdened with heavy full-length costumes and heeled shoes, as surviving portraits of Subligny on stage show. Whether Campra's remark was meant seriously or not, we do know that Mlle. des Mastins shortened her skirts and Mlle. Maupin appeared occasionally in male attire (both were contemporaries of Subligny's). The fact that the only surviving comment on Subligny's technique is the criticism that her knees and feet were not turned out enough suggests that she too must have performed at times in other than full-length costume. She apparently had expressive eyes and a pretty figure, and, along with her partner, Claude Ballon, her virtuosity was often praised. However, like Ballon, who was criticized by the English dancing master John Weaver for not striving to represent anything dramatically beyond "modulated motion", Subligny was primarily a product of the "danse noble" tradition of the Opéra. It is unlikely that she was a dramatic dancer in our modern sense; only in the eighteenth century did this become an important part of a dancer's training.

The French school was characterized by grace, charm, and elegance; steps involving elevation, such as Italian dancing of the day demanded, were rarely used. However, the vocabulary and many of the steps of modern ballet were already in use, and the technique was demanding in its own way. It necessitated practice and development of the muscles of the legs and instep over many years, with the goal of maintaining grace and equilibrium during demanding sequences of footwork. Adding to the pressures for professional dancers of both sexes was the fact that theatre ballet still shared many steps with court dancing, and therefore many members of the Opéra audience were likely to be well-informed. Thanks to Raoul-Auger Feuillet, who first published in dance notation the choreography of Pécour in 1700, we have a detailed knowledge of many of the pieces which Subligny performed. In Feuillet's 1704 edition of Pécour's *Recueil de dances*, we see Subligny and her partners (often Ballon) performing a minuet, or a passacaille, a sarabande or a bourrée, in operas like *Persée* (a tragédie-lyrique by Lully) or *Hésione* (by Campra), or in real ballets like *Ballet des Fragments de Monsieur de Lully*.

The same edition contains notation for a "Gigue pour une femme / Dancée par Mlle Subligny en Angleterre". The gigue, the dance for which she became famous in England, would actually have been a French or Italian "giga" (folk-dance), but the English confused it with native jigs and the result was a cross-fertilization of dance forms. We can get some sense of the character of Subligny's gigue from the description in Mlle. Prevost's *Les Caractères de la danse*, a piece containing twelve dance types in dramatic situations meant to characterize each dance. The libretto for the "Gigue" reads "a mad young thing, sweeping up all hearts that come her way, asks Amour for a lovable shepherd who won't get worn out dancing with her". The comic edge in the description accounts for Subligny's association in England with popular entertainment, as in a playbill of 1703, which promises that "The Devonshire Girl" will dance "in Imitation of Madamoiselle Subligni" in an evening of farce and acrobatics.

Of Subligny's personal life we know very little. She was apparently illiterate (in spite of her father's having been a man of letters), but she seems to have enjoyed the company of intellectuals none the less. She brought letters of introduction from two important authors, Dubos and Fontenelle, to John Locke, who offered to look after her business affairs while she was in England. This may seem an odd event in the life of the ill and ageing philosopher, but she had (unusually for an Opéra ballerina) a reputation for modesty and expressiveness, and the encounter is surely a tribute to the truth of the French courtly view of dance as the ultimate expression of all that is noble and civilized. She was also about to make English history; it is no wonder that Locke found her engaging.

—Kathryn Kerby-Fulton

SUITE EN BLANC
(also *Noir et blanc*)

Choreography: Serge Lifar
Music: Édouard Lalo (*Namouna*)
Design: André Dignimont
First Production: Paris Opéra Ballet, Zürich, 19 June 1943
Principal Dancers: Solange Schwarz, Yvette Chauviré, Lycette Darsonval, Serge Lifar

Other productions include: Nouveau Ballet de Monte Carlo (restaged Lifar), as *Noir et blanc*; Monte Carlo, 1946 (later becoming part of repertoire of company's successor, Grand Ballet du Marquis de Cuevas). Ballet Janine Charrat, as *Suite en blanc*, 1951/52. London Festival Ballet (staged Roland Casenave, design Norman McDowell), as *Noir et blanc*; London, 15 September 1966. Ballet du Rhin (staged Casenave), as *Suite en blanc*, 1977. Australian Ballet, as *Suite en blanc*, 1981.

PUBLICATIONS

Beaumont, Cyril, "Grand Ballet de Monte Carlo", *Ballet* (London), October 1948

Diénis, Jean Claude, "Le Retour de Lifar", *Les Saisons de la danse* (Paris), November 1977

Brinson, Peter, and Crisp, Clement, *Ballet and Dance*, Newton Abbot, 1980

Hommage à Serge Lifar, Paris, 1988

Hersin, André Philippe, "Hommage à Serge Lifar", *Les Saisons de la danse* (Paris), November 1990

* * *

Suite en blanc is known to many audiences as *Noir et blanc*, and is a rare example of Serge Lifar's "pure dance" style. It is a one-act ballet with many demanding technical passages, and calls for a strong classical company, well served with first-class principal dancers. Originally presented as a showcase for the étoiles of the Paris Opéra Ballet, it has served a similar purpose for many other companies.

In 1930 Lifar took over the moribund Ballet of the Opéra in Paris. He was a young, exciting dancer and had served his apprenticeship as Diaghilev's last male star. The formidable task of returning the Opéra Ballet to its former eminence was a daunting task which Lifar accomplished with panache. Maintaining his position during the difficult time of the Nazi occupation and the inevitable whisperings of "collaborator", he was on a creative peak when he choreographed *Suite en blanc*

Suite en blanc, as performed by the Australian Ballet

in 1943. The ballet is, in many ways, a vindication of his policy of continuing to build the strength of his company during the War.

Lifar selected the music for *Suite en blanc* from Édouard Lalo's *Namouna*, a short-lived two-act ballet choreographed by Lucien Petipa in 1882. Audiences had been enchanted by the beautiful score but had declared the ballet and its silly plot a failure. However, a curious connection remains between the plotless *Suite en blanc* and its ill-fated predecessor; the titles of the original musical numbers remain. Many bemused members of the public have attempted to make a connection between the display of pure classical dance they were witnessing and the titles "Cigarette, Siesta, Flute and Serenade", which made reference to the plot of the earlier ballet.

The original *Suite en blanc*, as the title suggests, was performed in simple white costumes—white tutus for the women and white tights and shirts for the men. When the ballet was revived for the Nouveau Ballet de Monte Carlo in 1946, the men wore black tights—hence *Noir et blanc*. The designs by Norman McDowell for the 1966 London Festival Ballet revival also included black bolero jackets with white trimming.

The curtain rises on a tableau of the entire company, arranged in parallel geometrical patterns against a stage dressed in black, with a raised section at the back of the stage reached by two staircases from the direction of the wings. The performers promenade slowly and precisely, displaying elegant ports de bras. This opening sequence can be stunning if performed in the appropriate grand manner, and calls for confident artists who understand the original Parisian "chic" style.

The corps de ballet act as a link to the various sections of the work as well as an accompaniment to the principals. The opening leads into two pas de trois numbers which are followed by a ballerina solo and a pas de cinq. These are succeeded by the "Cigarette" ballerina solo and a solo "Mazurka" for the premier danseur. The pas de deux which follows is the only part of the score not in its original form, since Lifar put it together from various parts of the original *Namouna*. The pas de deux leads into the final ballerina solo, "Flute", and the conclusion of the ballet again involves the entire company in a final tableau.

The correct performing style of *Suite en blanc* is extremely elusive. Lifar's particular requirements regarding the placement of feet, slightly exaggerated ports de bras, and insistence on an almost staccato brilliance in footwork have been met with varying levels of success. The Australian Ballet perform the piece with exhilarating bravura and technical assurance but fail to capture the French style. London Festival Ballet opened their Twentieth Anniversary season at the Coliseum with the piece (originally mounted in 1966 by Roland Casenave) in 1969, and performed the piece with impeccable style, although failing to match the technical level later reached by the Australians. As a display of classical ballet in a refined and elegant style *Suite en blanc* has few peers.

—Mike Dixon

SWAN LAKE
(also *Le Lac de cygnes*; Russian title *Lebedinoe Ozero*)

Choreography: Marius Petipa (Acts I and III) and Lev Ivanov (Acts II and IV)
Music: Petr Ilyich Tchaikovsky (edited by Riccardo Drigo)

Design: Mikhail Bocharov and Heinrich Levogt
Libretto: V. P. Begichev and Vasily Geltser
Production: Maryinsky Theatre, St. Petersburg, 27 January (15 January old style) 1895
Principal Dancers: Pierina Legnani (Odette/Odile), Pavel Gerdt (Prince Siegfried), Mikhail Bulgakov (von Rothbart)

Other productions include: Bolshoi Theatre (first production to Tchaikovsky's score; chor. Julius Reisinger, design H. Shangin, Karl Valts, H. Gropius), with Pelageya Karpakova (Odette/Odile), A.K. Gillert (Siegfried); Moscow, 4 March (20 February old style) 1877. Bolshoi Theatre (staged Joseph Hansen after Reisinger); Moscow, 1880 (restaged 1882). Maryinsky Theatre (Act II, later incorporated into 1895 version, chor. Lev Ivanov), with Pierina Legnani (Odette); St. Petersburg, 1 March (17 February old style) 1894. Bolshoi Theatre (staged Aleksandr Gorsky after Petipa and Ivanov), with Adelina Dzhuri (Odette/Odile), Mikhail Mordkin (Siegfried); Moscow, 5 February (24 January old style) 1901. London Hippodrome (two-act version; staged Mikhail Fokine after Petipa, Ivanov), with Olga Preobrazhenska (Odette/Odile); London, 16 May 1910. Diaghilev's Ballets Russes (two-act version; staged and revised Mikhail Fokine, design Konstantin Korovin and Aleksandr Golovin), with Mathilde Kshessinskaya (Odette/Odile), Vaslav Nijinsky (Siegfried); London, 30 November 1911. Mikhail Mordkin's "All-Star Imperial Russian Ballet" (staged Mikhail Mordkin after Petipa, Ivanov); New York, 19 December 1911. Bolshoi Ballet (staged Aleksandr Gorsky); Moscow, 29 February 1920. (De Basil's) Ballets Russes de Monte Carlo (one-act version; staged after Ivanov); Monte Carlo, 21 April 1932. Kirov Ballet (staged Agrippina Vaganova after Petipa, Ivanov), with Galina Ulanova (Odette), Olga Jordan (Odile), Konstantin Sergeyev (Siegfried); Leningrad, 13 April 1933. Vic-Wells Ballet (full-length production; staged Nicholas Sergeyev after Petipa and Ivanov, design Hugh Stevenson), with Alicia Markova (Odette/Odile), Robert Helpmann (Siegfried); London, 20 November 1934. Paris Opéra Ballet (extracts; staged Serge Lifar after Petipa, Ivanov), with Marina Semenova (Odette/Odile), Lifar (Siegfried); Paris, 22 January 1936. Royal Danish Ballet (one-act version; staged Harald Lander after Ivanov), with Margot Lander (Odette); Copenhagen, 8 February 1938. Ballet Theatre (Act II only; staged Anton Dolin after Ivanov), with Patricia Bowman (Odette), Dolin (Siegfried); New York, 16 January 1940. San Francisco Ballet (staged Willam Christensen after Petipa, Ivanov), with Jacquelin Martin (Odette), Janet Reed (Odile), Lew Christensen (Siegfried); San Francisco, 27 September 1940. Kirov Ballet (staged Fedor Lopukhov after Petipa, Ivanov), with Natalia Dudinskaya (Odette/Odile), Konstantin Sergeyev (Siegfried); Leningrad, 1945. New York City Ballet (one-act version; staged George Balanchine after Ivanov, design Cecil Beaton), with Maria Tallchief (Odette), André Eglevsky (Siegfried); New York, 20 November 1951. Stanislavsky and Nemirovich-Danchenko Theatre (staged Vladimir Burmeister, largely based on Lopukhov version; design Anatole Lushin and Archangelskaya), with Violetta Bovt (Odette/Odile), Oleg Chichinadze (Siegfried); Moscow, 25 April 1953. Paris Opéra Ballet (first full-length production; staged Burmeister, design Dimitri Bouchène), with Josette Amiel (Odette/Odile), Peter van Dijk (Siegfried); 21 December 1960. Stuttgart Ballet (staged John Cranko, design Jürgen Rose), with Marcia Haydée (Odette/Odile), Rudolf Nureyev (Siegfried); Stuttgart, 14 November 1963. Royal Ballet (staged Robert Helpmann, with additional chor. Frederick Ashton, design Carl Toms), with Margot Fonteyn (Odette/Odile), David Blair (Siegfried); London, 12 December 1963. Vienna State Opera Ballet (staged with additional chor.

Rudolf Nureyev, design Nicholas Georgiadis), with Margot Fonteyn (Odette/Odile), Rudolf Nureyev (Siegfried); Vienna, 15 October 1964. American Ballet Theatre (staged David Blair, design Freddy Wittop and Oliver Smith), with Nadia Nerina (Odette/Odile), Royes Fernandes (Siegfried); Chicago, 16 February 1967. National Ballet of Canada (staged Erik Bruhn, design Desmond Heeley), with Lois Smith (Odette/Odile), Earl Kraul (Siegfried); Toronto, 27 March 1967. Bolshoi Ballet (staged Yuri Grigorovich, design Simon Virsaladze), with Natalia Bessmertnova (Odette/Odile), Nikolai Fadeyechev (Siegfried); Moscow, 25 December 1969. Hamburg Ballet (staged John Neumeier); Hamburg, 2 May 1976. American Ballet Theatre (staged Mikhail Baryshnikov), with Martine van Hamel (Odette/Odile), Kevin McKenzie (Siegfried); Washington, D.C., 27 March 1981. Northern Ballet Theatre (new version; staged Christopher Gable); Leeds, 11 February 1992.

PUBLICATIONS

Beaumont, Cyril, "The Characters in *Swan Lake*", *Ballet* (London), March 1950

Beaumont, Cyril, *Complete Book of Ballets*, revised edition, London, 1951

Beaumont, Cyril, *The Ballet Called Swan Lake*, London, 1952

Slonimsky, Yuri, *Tchaikovsky and the Ballet Theatre of his Time*, Moscow, 1956

Slonimsky, Yuri, *Swan Lake*, Leningrad, 1962

Krassovskaya, Vera, *Russian Ballet Theatre of the Second Half of the Nineteenth Century*, Leningrad and Moscow, 1963

Lanchbery, John, "Tchaikovsky's *Swan Lake*", *Dancing Times* (London), December 1963

Guest, Ivor, "*Swan Lake*", *About the House* (London), Christmas 1963

Barnes, Clive, "Swan Lake", *Dance and Dancers* (London), 2 parts: December 1963, January 1964

Kirstein, Lincoln, *Movement and Metaphor: Four Centuries of Ballet*, New York, 1970

Samachson, Dorothy, *The Russian Ballet and Three of its Masterpieces*, New York, 1971

Dorris, George, "Once More to the Lake", *Ballet Review* (Brooklyn, N.Y.), vol. 6, no. 4, 1977–78

Percival, John, "What Happens in *Swan Lake*?", *Dance and Dancers* (London), October 1982

Brown, David, "Tchaikovsky and *Swan Lake*", *Ballet Review* (New York), Spring 1983

Wiley, Roland John, *Tchaikovsky's Ballets*, Oxford, 1985

Wiley, Roland John, "The Revival of *Swan Lake*", *Dancing Times* (London), March 1987

Barnes, Clive, "Some Ballet Called *Swan Lake*", *Dance Magazine* (New York), May 1989

Ross, Janice (ed.), *Why a Swan?*, San Francisco, 1989

Wiley, Roland John, *A Century of Russian Ballet: Documents and Accounts 1810–1910*, Oxford, 1990

*   *   *

Nearly one in ten of all ballet performances in Russia is of *Swan Lake*. While the frequency of performances may vary from country to country, there can be no doubt that *Swan Lake* everywhere occupies a unique place in the repertoire. As performed by the world's leading companies, it is virtually a sacred experience for the balletomane, and a measure of the company's status in the ballet world.

But there are now innumerable versions, and given such profusion it is inevitable that many of them have little,

artistically speaking, to recommend them. The linking factor between all productions is the music, but even this often suffers from extensive rearrangement and interpolation. Consequently the ballet's continuing survival is in spite of adverse factors. The curious fact is that this has been true from the first production, which was by no means distinguished: this took place at Moscow's Bolshoi Theatre in 1877. At that time, what was remarkable to the great majority of the public was that a composer with such an eminent reputation as Tchaikovsky should bother himself with ballet music, which was regarded as an inferior genre. Fortunately, Tchaikovsky saw its possibilities sufficiently well to put up with the tedium, and not infrequently the irritation, of collaborating with producers and choreographers.

Little remains on record of the original choreography by Reisinger (a Czech), or of the Odette/Odile created by Pelageya Karpakova. Both were considered uninspired. The choreography was soon revised by Joseph Hansen, and Karpakova was succeeded by other ballerinas. In this way the ballet remained in the repertoire at the Bolshoi through more than 40 performances up to 1883. By the standards of the day, this was a considerable success, probably owing chiefly to the music. Karpakova is credited with performing both as Odette and Odile, but the first Hansen production introduced different ballerinas for the roles, a fact which suggests that the choreography already provided technical contrast.

Tchaikovsky composed two further ballets, *The Sleeping Beauty* and *The Nutcracker*, but these were for the Imperial Maryinsky Theatre in St. Petersburg, where the artistic standards were far in advance of Moscow. In many respects these later ballets showed Tchaikovsky's increasing ability as a ballet composer. However, following his premature death in 1893, and in the realization of the tremendous loss to Russian culture, a memorial concert was planned in St Petersburg: and for this occasion the wistful, elegiac music of *Swan Lake* Act II best expressed the public mood. This act was chosen to be performed with new choreography by Lev Ivanov, second ballet master of the Imperial Theatres.

Ivanov's lakeside act led to the revival of the complete ballet under the artistic direction of chief ballet master Marius Petipa, who provided the first and third acts, while Ivanov added the fourth act (also lakeside). The Italian ballerina Pierina Legnani performed Odette and Odile with vividly contrasting technique, the role ever to be remembered for its 32 fouettés.

This 1895 staging was the production destined to make *Swan Lake* the international centrepiece of balletic art. It travelled down the years and across the continents by varied routes. The second act was seen outside Russia before the First World War, on both sides of the Atlantic, and the Diaghilev company toured a two-act *Swan Lake*. In Russia itself, war and revolution combined to create acute difficulties which at first prevented revival in Leningrad (the former St. Petersburg). The Bolshoi Theatre in Moscow preserved continuity with the original in productions by Gorsky, introducing Petipa–Ivanov elements, both before and after the Revolution.

A Leningrad revival eventually transpired in the early 1930s, in a version by Agrippina Vaganova, with Galina Ulanova as Odette and Olga Jordan as Odile. At about the same time the recently formed Vic-Wells Ballet made the first complete revival in the West, with Alicia Markova in the dual Odette/Odile role. The latter version was more artistically significant, in that it was produced with the help of Nicholas Sergeyev, former régisseur of the Imperial Maryinsky, and attempted to be as faithful as possible, while the Vaganova version reflected the baleful influence of current Soviet artistic ideology.

Swan Lake, as performed by Sadler's Wells Royal Ballet, London, 1981

After World War II came a resurgence of interest in ballet in general and *Swan Lake* in particular. Cultural integrity was being restored after years of barbarism, and *Swan Lake* appealed as an allegory of noble struggle against evil. Better stagings were sought, introducing greater authenticity and drawing on artists' inspiration.

This process began in Leningrad, in 1945, where Fedor Lopukhov had regained authority following pre-war political persecution. Lopukhov, so long deprived of recognition, was in fact the principal architect of ballet in Russia after 1917. His new production of *Swan Lake* at the Kirov, the former Imperial Maryinsky, became in turn a basis of Vladimir Burmeister of the Stanislavsky and Nemirovich-Danchenko Theatre, which possessed the second ballet company in Moscow after the Bolshoi. The Lopukhov–Burmeister version reached the West when Burmeister was invited to produce *Swan Lake* at the Paris Opéra in 1960. This production became its gateway to the rest of the world, influencing, for example, the Royal Ballet production of 1963.

Among the distinctive features of this version is the andante solo for the Prince which precedes his first encounter with Odette. Another is the structuring of the third act around a fantasy-style entrance by Rothbart, Odile, and their retinue (the retinue proceeds to perform the national dances), and their climactic fantasy-departure after the Prince has realized his deception by Odile. Both these features, now regarded as integral to the ballet, are owed, according to the eminent critic and historian Yuri Slonimsky, to Lopukhov.

The most notable development of recent years has come through the study of original Russian sources in Leningrad and Moscow by the American musicologist Roland John Wiley, author of *Tchaikovsky's Ballets* (1985). Wiley's work has been utilized extensively by the Royal Ballet in a production of *Swan Lake* which is probably more musically authentic than anything that has preceded it in the West. It is not an uncontroversial development, but this is in keeping with the ballet's tradition.

Swan Lake survives in spite of controversy. It does so primarily because of the eternal appeal of the Romantic era which it recreates in Act II. Remarkably, Hansen, who re-choreographed the Bolshoi production following Reisinger, showed a version of the lakeside scenes in London only seven years after the Moscow premiere, but without Tchaikovsky's music. Evidently the concept alone has magic, but it is the alliance with Tchaikovsky that makes *Swan Lake* irresistible.

—Tony Devereux

───────

LA SYLPHIDE

Choreography: Filippo Taglioni
Music: Jean Schneitzhoeffer
Design: Pierre Ciceri and Eugène Lami
Libretto: Adolphe Nourrit
First Production: Théatre de l'Académie royale de musique (Paris Opéra), Paris, 12 March 1832
Principal Dancers: Marie Taglioni (La Sylphide), Lise Noblet (Effie), Joseph Mazilier (James)

Other productions include: Covent Garden Theatre (restaged Taglioni), with Marie Taglioni; London, 26 July 1832. St. Petersburg Bolshoi Theatre (staged Antoine Titus after

La Sylphide, with Marie Taglioni in the title role, 1834

Taglioni); St. Petersburg, 9 April (28 May old style) 1835. Bolshoi Theatre (restaged Taglioni), with Marie Taglioni; St. Petersburg, 18 September (6 September old style) 1837. Park Theatre (staged Paul Taglioni); New York, 22 May 1839. Teatro alla Scala (staged Antonio Cortesi after Taglioni, design B. Cavallotti and D. Menozzi), with Fanny Cerrito (La Sylphide), Francesco Mérante (James); Milan, 27 January 1841. Moscow Bolshoi Theatre (staged Théodor Guérinau), with Aleksandra Voronina-Ivanova (La Sylphide); Moscow, 1844. Maryinsky Theatre (staged and revised Marius Petipa after Taglioni, with additional mus. Riccardo Drigo), with Vavara Nikitina (La Sylphide); St. Petersburg, 19 January (7 January old style) 1892. State Academic Theatre for Opera and Ballet, or GATOB (staged Vladimir Ponomarev after Petipa); Petrograd, 9 April 1922. Bolshoi Ballet (staged Vasily Tikhomirov after Petipa), with Ekaterina Geltser (La Sylphide), Tikhomirov (James); Moscow, 2 February 1925. Ballet des Champs-Elysées (chor. Victor Gsovsky after Taglioni, design A. Serebriakov and Christian Bérard), with Nina Vyroubova (La Sylphide), Roland Petit (James); Paris, 15 June 1946. Paris Opéra Ballet (chor. Pierre Lacotte after Taglioni), with Ghislaine Thesmar (La Sylphide), Michaël Denard (James); French television, 1 January 1972 (staged Paris Opéra Ballet, with Noëlla Pontois and Cyril Atanasoff, 7 June 1972).

Royal Danish Ballet (new version; chor. August Bournonville, mus. Herman Løvenskjold, design Christian Christensen), as *Sylfiden*, with Lucile Grahn (Sylfiden), August Bournonville (James); Copenhagen, 28 November 1836. Royal Swedish Ballet (restaged Bournonville, design F. Ahlgrensson); Stockholm, 1 April 1862. Grand (International) Ballet du Marquis de Cuevas (staged Harald Lander after Bournonville, design Bernard Daydé), as *La Sylphide*, with Rosella Hightower (La Sylphide), Serge Golovine (James); Paris, 9 December 1953. Scandinavian Ballet (staged Elsa Marianne von Rosen after Bournonville, reconstructed with assistance of Ellen Price de Plane, design Elvin Gay); Växjöe, 2 February 1960. Ballet Rambert (staged von Rosen after Bournonville, design Robin and Christopher Ironside), with von Rosen (La Sylphide), Flemming Flindt (James); London, 20 July 1960. American Ballet Theatre (staged Harald Lander after Bournonville, design Robert O'Hearn), with Toni Lander (La Sylphide), Royes Fernandez (James); San Antonio, Texas, 11 November 1964 (production restaged and revised by Erik Bruhn, American Ballet Theatre, 1971). National Ballet of Canada (staged Erik Bruhn after Bournonville, design Robert Prévost), with Lois Smith (La Sylphide), Erik Bruhn (James); Toronto, 31 December 1964. Royal Danish Ballet (staged Hans Brenaa and Flemming Flindt after Bournonville, design S. Frandsen); Copenhagen, 15 August 1967. Kirov Ballet (staged Elsa Marianne von Rosen after Bournonville, design Oleg Vinogradov); Leningrad, 29 June 1975. London Festival Ballet (staged Peter Schaufuss after Bournonville, design David Walker); London, 22 August 1979. Stuttgart Ballet (staged Peter Schaufuss, Mona Vangsaae after Bournonville, design David Walker); Stuttgart, 6 April 1982 (also staged German Opera Ballet, Berlin, 14 May 1982). Australian Ballet (staged Erik Bruhn after Bournonville, design Anne Fraser); Melbourne, 15 October 1985. San Francisco Ballet (staged Peter Martins, Solveig Østergard after Bournonville, design Susan Tammany); San Francisco, 8 February 1986. Vienna State Opera Ballet (staged Peter Schaufuss after Bournonville); Vienna, 16 February 1990.

PUBLICATIONS

Levinson, André, *Marie Taglioni*, Paris, 1929

Gautier, Théophile, *The Romantic Ballet as seen by Théophile Gautier*, collected and translated by Cyril Beaumont, London, 1932

Guest, Ivor, "*La Sylphide* in London", *Ballet* (London), December 1948

Beaumont, Cyril, *Complete Book of Ballets*, revised edition, London, 1951

Barnes, Clive, "*La Sylphide*", *Dance and Dancers* (London), August 1960

Moore, Lillian, "*La Sylphide*: Epitome of the Romantic Ballet", *Dance Magazine* (New York), March 1965

Moore, Lillian, "The Distant Flights of *La Sylphide*", *Dancing Times* (London), July 1965

Kirstein, Lincoln, *Movement and Metaphor: Four Centuries of Ballet*, New York, 1970

Aschengreen, Erik, "Ballet, Biedermeier and French Romanticism", *Theatre Research Studies* (Copenhagen), no. 2, 1972

Friderica, Allan, "Sylphiden", *Dans* (Stockholm), November 1974

Aschengreen, Erik, *Farlige Sylfider*, Copenhagen, 1975

Chapman, John, "An Unromantic View of 19th-century Romanticism", *York Dance Review* (Toronto), Spring 1978

Guest, Ivor, *The Romantic Ballet in Paris*, revised edition, London, 1980

Murphy, Anne, "Age of Enchantment", *Ballet News* (New York), March 1982

La Sylphide, with Carla Fracci and Erik Bruhn, American Ballet Theatre, c.1967

Lacotte, Pierre, "Looking for *La Sylphide*", *Dance and Dancers* (London), October 1982

McAndrew, Patricia (ed. and trans.), "The Ballet Poems of August Bournonville: The Complete Scenarios", *Dance Chronicle* (New York), vol. 6, no. 1, 1983

Macaulay, Alastair, "The Author of *La Sylphide*, Adolphe Nourrit", *Dancing Times* (London), November 1989

Hallar, Marianne, and Scavenius, Alette (eds.), *Bournonvilleana*, translated by Gaye Kynoch, Copenhagen, 1992

*   *   *

La Sylphide was heralded as the dawn of a new era by those who witnessed its premiere at the Paris Opéra on the 12th of March, 1832. Its impact was achieved through the intensity with which all elements—dancing, sets, costumes, lights, and story—joined together to create a unified, totally convincing poetic illusion. Ballets as far back as the early century had dealt with romantic subjects, but not until *La Sylphide* did a ballet master's approach fully embrace and enhance romantic ideas. During the decade prior to the premiere of *La Sylphide*, ballet masters such as Jean Aumer produced long multi-act works within which dance and story were separate. Dancing supplied the spectacle; pantomime (silent acting) furthered the dramatic action. *La Sylphide* surprised and delighted audiences because dance became an integral part of the story, and the ballet itself a convincing depiction of the lands of their dreams.

In the story, James, a Scots peasant, forsakes his fiancée Effie for a beautiful Sylphide, who has visited him in his dreams and entices him into an enchanted forest. However, the intervention of the evil witch Madge brings about the death of the Sylphide, and James is left grieving alone as Effie marries his rival Gurn.

Foremost amongst the dancers who contributed to *La Sylphide*'s impact was ballerina Marie Taglioni, who depicted character and atmosphere not through pantomime, but through dance. Her ability virtually to "become" the Sylphide of the title was due to developments in technique, training, and choreography which had occupied dancers, teachers, and ballet masters ever since the beginnings of the French Revolution—men such as Auguste Vestris, Pierre Gardel, Monsieur Albert, and Filippo Taglioni, the creator of *La Sylphide*. The strength and endurance emphasized in training imparted an ease and naturalness in performance that made it possible for dancers of Marie Taglioni's generation to transform themselves on stage from mere mortals into supernatural beings. Taglioni's dancing prowess was central to the creation of a totally convincing illusion, a poetic vision so real that audiences seemed to witness a dream transformed into reality. Important, too, was ballet master Filippo Taglioni's skilful use of his dancers to give depth to his choreographic conception. His dances for soloists and corps de ballet painted a picture, first of a rural Scottish manor, then of a spirit-filled forest.

Dance was not alone in its contribution to the depiction of

the poet's fantasy. Costumes, sets, lighting, and libretto all played an integral part in the stimulation of romantic sensibilities. With the exception of the latter, each was used in a way only seen once before, in the "Ballet of the Nuns" in Meyerbeer's *Robert le Diable* (1831). There, in a mouldering gothic graveyard, the inspiration of the brilliant designer Ciceri, Marie Taglioni, had danced as a ghostly nun. Eugène Lami's long white dresses, the spectral gas light, Taglioni's supernatural airiness, enhanced by her effortless jumps and pointe work, were a revelation. Those dresses—soft, billowing, light as air—became the uniform of the supernatural ballet, of the *ballet blanc*. The tendency of the fabric to drift on after movement had stopped blurred the edges of poses and steps, contributing to a sense of mystery. The pale flickering gas jets which had first cast their supernatural pallor on the gothic graveyard of *Robert le Diable* fell, in *La Sylphide*, upon Ciceri's evocation of the cold, spartan interior of a Scottish manor house, as rough as the heathland and forests around it. Ciceri's Act II forest appeared to have been planted by the chaotic hand of forces beyond the comprehension of man.

The "Ballet of the Nuns" from *Robert le Diable* so deeply inspired Adolphe Nourrit, the Robert of the opera, that he wrote the scenario for *La Sylphide*. His story had much in common with Charles Nodier's very popular story, "Trilby ou le lutin d'Argail" (1822). They shared a common setting, the Scottish highlands, a land of remote and rugged mountains and valleys, the natural haunt of supernatural beings such as the aerial Trilby, and the ethereal Sylph. They shared the theme of love between mortal and faery, between man and his ideal.

La Sylphide was enormously popular and was staged throughout Europe, including in London (1832), Berlin (1832), St. Petersburg (1837), and Milan (1841), by Filippo Taglioni for his daughter Maria. Other ballet masters staged their own version of Taglioni's original, including Antonio Cortesi, whose 1841 version at La Scala in Milan for ballerina Fanny Cerrito preceded the Taglionis' own appearance at the same theatre by some five months. The most important restaging, however, was that by August Bournonville for the Royal Danish Theatre in Copenhagen, produced four-and-a-half years after the first *La Sylphide* in Paris. Bournonville brought back to Denmark his own memories of the Paris production, and applied Taglioni's scenario to his own choreography and to a new score by Herman Løvenskjold. It is on this production, maintained in the repertory of the Royal Danish Ballet to this day, that modern stagings are based, for the Taglioni ballet was revived at the Opéra only until 1860, and then lost.

In truth, little of the original *La Sylphide* lives on in modern productions, not only because they are based upon August Bournonville's 1836 version, but because audiences and the art of dance have changed. Nevertheless, *La Sylphide* had an enormous influence on the development of ballet during the romantic period, supplying a model that was to be followed in many subsequent masterpieces, *Giselle* (1841) among them.

—John Chapman

LES SYLPHIDES
(also *Chopiniana*)

Choreography: Mikhail Fokine
Music: Frederic Chopin, orchestrated by Aleksandr Glazunov, Igor Stravinsky, Aleksandr Taneyev
Design: Alexandre Benois (scenery and costumes)

First Production: Diaghilev's Ballets Russes, Théâtre de Châtelet, Paris, 2 June 1909
Principal Dancers: Anna Pavlova, Tamara Karsavina, Alexandra Baldina, Vaslav Nijinsky

Other productions include: Maryinsky Theatre (first version of ballet; chor. Fokine, costumes Léon Bakst and others), as *Chopiniana*, with Anna Pavlova, Mikhail Obukhov, Aleksis Bulgakov, Yulia (Julie) Sedova, Vera Fokine; St. Petersburg, 10 February 1907. Maryinsky Theatre Benefit (second version of ballet; chor. Fokine, costumes Léon Bakst and Vera Fokina), as *Danses sur la musique de Chopin*, with Anna Pavlova, Tamara Karsavina, Mikhail Fokine; St. Petersburg, 16 February 1908. Maryinsky Theatre Benefit (third version, and basis for *Les Sylphides*; costumes Oreste Allegri, Léon Bakst), as *Rêverie romantique: Ballet sur la musique de Chopin* with Anna Pavlova, Olga Preobrazhenskaya, Tamara Karsavina, Vaslav Nijinsky; St. Petersburg, 8 March 1908. Anna Pavlova Company (staged Ivan Clustine after Fokine); London, 6 October 1913. Saison Nijinsky at the Palace Theatre (new version; chor. Vaslav Nijinsky); London, 2 March 1914. Gertrude Hoffman Company (restaged Fokine); New York, 25 December 1922. Royal Danish Ballet (restaged Fokine), as *Chopiniana*; Copenhagen, 14 October 1925. Marie Rambert's Dancers (Ballet Club, later Ballet Rambert; staged Tamara Karsavina after Fokine, with no décor); London, 23 June 1930. Bolshoi Ballet (staged Aleksandr Chekrygin after Fokine), as *Chopiniana*; Moscow, 24 January 1932. (De Basil's) Ballets Russes de Monte Carlo (revival; mus. orchestrated Vittorio Rieti, design Vladimir Polunin), with Valentina Blinova, Tamara Toumanova, Tatiana Riabouchinska; Monte Carlo, 12 April 1932. Vic-Wells Ballet (staged Alicia Markova after Fokine); London, 8 March 1932. (René Blum's) Ballets de Monte Carlo (restaged and revised Fokine, design "after Corot"); 1936. Markova–Dolin Ballet (staged Bronislava Nijinska after Fokine); 1936. San Francisco Ballet (Willam Christensen after Fokine), as *Chopinade*; San Francisco, 12 January 1939 (originally staged Seattle, 1935). Kirov Ballet (staged Agrippina Vaganova after Fokine), as *Chopiniana*; Leningrad, 1938. Ballet Theatre (restaged Fokine, design Augustus Vincent Tack), with Karen Conrad, Nina Stroganova, Lucia Chase, William Dollar; New York, 11 January 1940. Metropolitan Opera Ballet (staged Markova after Fokine); New York, 21 November 1964. New York City Ballet (staged Alexandra Danilova after Fokine, no design), as *Chopiniana*, with Kay Mazzo, Karin von Aroldingen, Susan Hendl, Peter Martins; New York, 20 January 1972.

PUBLICATIONS

Evans, Edwin, "The Music of *Les Sylphides*", *Dancing Times* (London), October 1939

Beaumont, Cyril, *Complete Book of Ballets*, revised edition, London, 1951

Grigoriev, Serge, *The Diaghilev Ballet*, translated by Vera Bowen, London, 1953

Barnes, Clive, "*Les Sylphides*", *Dance and Dancers* (London), 2 parts: September, October 1957

Fokine, Michel, *Fokine: Memoirs of a Ballet Master*, translated by Vitale Fokine, London, 1961

Monahan, James, "*Les Sylphides*", *Dancing Times* (London), February 1963

Dodge, Roger, "Tradition in Ballet: *Les Sylphides*", *Dancing Times* (London), January 1964

Kirstein, Lincoln, *Movement and Metaphor*, New York, 1970

Les Sylphides, as performed by Diaghilev's Ballets Russes, London, 1911

Les Sylphides, as performed by the Birmingham Royal Ballet, c.1990

Maynard, Olga, "*Les Sylphides*", *Dance Magazine* (New York), December 1971

Balanchine, George, with Mason, Francis, *Balanchine's Complete Stories of the Great Ballets*, Garden City, N.Y., 1977

Horwi Horwitz, Dawn Lille, *Michel Fokine*, Boston, 1985

Gregory, John, *Les Sylphides—Chopiniana*, Wales, 1989

Goodwin, Noël, "Fokine and Chopin", *Dance and Dancers* (London), November 1991

* * *

Mikhail Fokine's first essay at creating in contemporary abstract terms a ballet on the theme of the Sylph—inspired by the Gothic romanticism of the poet Heine, and immortalized by Maria Taglioni—was improvised very quickly as a Suite of social dances to present at a Charity Matinée in St. Petersburg in 1907. It later evolved into a purely classical work, and was again created very quickly, in a matter of days. Fokine was inspired by the influence of Isadora Duncan, but he did not dote upon her style or her Greek tunic; she was the spark that illumined the way towards a new freedom of movement. Fokine was immersed in the romantic period; he doted upon Taglioni, the first Sylph, and upon Carlotta Grisi, the first *Giselle*. They had created the image of classical beauty in its most ethereal form. The white tutu became the symbol of purity, spirituality, and well-being.

Fokine was intrigued to resurrect the spirit of the Sylph in modern abstract terms, without a literal story-line, but rather as an evocation of pure music expressed in mood, feeling, and the expressive flow of movement. To assist his objective there came to hand the rich orchestration by Glazunov of Chopin's melodious Mazurkas, Preludes, and Waltzes. It was the coming together of vital elements that endowed Fokine with an infallible touch and engendered originality; but those first essays were to some extent impromptu sketches that had to be refined and polished and in some instances remoulded. With time new and more subtle orchestrations emerged. The ballet evolved.

Diaghilev saw the possibilities of *Chopiniana* and when he brought the Imperial Russian Ballet to Europe, he wanted this work as an opening ballet in the Paris season of 1909. It was he who felt the need for more simple orchestration, and who renamed the ballet *Les Sylphides*, at first against the wishes of Fokine. Its success in that Paris season was sensational. Critics went into ecstasies of extravagant praise. They extolled the ballet as sheer poetry of movement, ethereal in mood yet human, spiritual yet sensuous; a communion of exceptional harmony.

Fokine once said: "No synopsis is needed for my ballets. My ballets unfold their stories on the stage. There is never any doubt as to what they say." However, some descriptions by the master himself to a pupil, Ann Barzel, divulge the secrets of his intentions and establish the essence of his intentions, his motif and characterization. First, the Waltz girl was music incarnate; music was inside her, and in her movement all her gestures expressed a giving-forth from the music of her heart. Second, the Mazurka girl was moon-struck, ecstatic—flying like moonbeams, radiating with joy. Third, the Prelude girl was enraptured by the sound of music, lost in a reverie. Not merely listening with her hand to her ear, she was more like an enchanted being entwined with the melody. And finally, the solitary Poet (the most daring and original of all Fokine's creations) expressed the soul of Chopin—a romantic love and yearning for the Polish soil.

Those bare thoughts or indications illustrate how Fokine's choreographic powers were motivated. They were the genes or stimulus for a totally articulate and expressive movement. His ballet communicated the essence and soul of the music; it was a unity of creative effulgence that has never been surpassed.

Fokine averred that he never changed a step in the numerous productions he master-minded in Europe and America, but one sees slight differences of step and style in almost every production, and even changes of tempo—some too quick, others too slow. When perfection is achieved it is something of a miracle. De Basil's company gave it a wondrous atmosphere, but a certain careless untidiness (not, however, when Fokine was around). Inevitably productions vary and alas, sometimes deteriorate: so much depends upon the taste and discipline and the sensitivity of the répétiteur. The Royal Ballet had a very authentic and beautiful version, and the American Ballet Theatre inherited from Fokine himself a superb production. The Kirov and the Bolshoi companies have brought forth some exquisite productions which are performed under the original title of *Chopiniana*, but sometimes these presentations have strayed beyond the boundaries of simplicity and naturalism which Fokine laid down. At times these productions have lost their freshness; in the process of refining they have become over-stylized and unnatural.

Les Sylphides might be said to be the supreme test of a classical dancer's abilities, to be able to dance with perfection of line, musicality, and feeling. Many try, but few succeed in attaining the perfection of unity that the ballet demands. Lydia Sokolova in her memoirs, *Dancing For Diaghilev*, wrote of this ballet: "Endless pains were always taken with this lovely work, and every performance of it had to be an absolute perfect unity. Every girl who danced in that ballet was chosen, not only for her grace, but also for her ability to move in unison with her fellow artists."

Les Sylphides/Chopiniana is a visual meditation of beauty and a reverie of the soul. Its appeal to the emotional responses of human beings is irresistible. It is loved and treasured by young and old; it may be seen again and again, and it does not weary. Fokine during his long creative life tried to make other Sylph ballets, but no other classical works of his ever achieved the spontaneous perfection or the sublime grace of his original work. If he had never choreographed another step however, this ballet would have established him forever, as indeed he is, a genius of the dance.

—John Gregory

SYLVIA
(*ou, La Nymphe de Diane*)

Choreography: Louis Mérante

Music: Léo Delibes

Design: Jules Chéret, August Rubé, Philippe M. Chaperon, Eugène Lacoste

Libretto: Jules Barbier and Baron de Reinach (after Torquato Tasso's *Aminta*)

First Production: Théâtre de l'Opéra, Paris, 14 June 1876

Principal Dancers: Rita Sangalli (Sylvia), Louise Marquet (Diana), Marie Sanlaville (Eros), Louis Mérante (Aminta)

Other productions include: Teatro alla Scala (staged Giorgio Saracco after Mérante), with Carlotta Brianza (Sylvia); Milan, 26 January 1896. Maryinsky Theatre (new version; chor. Lev Ivanov, completed by Pavel Gerdt), with Olga Preobrazhenska (Sylvia); St Petersburg, 15 December (2 December old style) 1901. Empire Theatre (new one-act version; chor. Fred Farren, mus. arranged Cuthbert Clarke, libretto revised C. Wilhelm), with Lydia Kyasht (Sylvia), Phyllis Bedells (Ianthe), Fred Farren (Pan), Unity More (Eros), Carlotta Mosetti (Amyntas); London, 18 May 1911. Paris Opéra Ballet (staged Léo Staats after Mérante, design Maxime Dethomas), with Carlotta Zambelli (Sylvia), Albert Aveline (Aminta), Léo Staats (Orion); Paris, 19 December 1919. Paris Opéra Ballet (new version; chor. Serge Lifar, design Brianchon); Paris, 12 February 1941 (revived by Lycette Darsonval, Paris Opéra Ballet, 1979). New York City Ballet (pas de deux version; chor. George Balanchine, costumes Barbara Karinska), with Maria Tallchief, Nicholas Magallanes; New York, 1 December 1950. Sadler's Wells Ballet (new version; chor. and revised libretto Frederick Ashton, design Robin and Christopher Ironside), with Margot Fonteyn (Sylvia), Michael Somes (Aminta), John Hart (Orion), Alexander Grant (Eros); London, 3 September 1952.

PUBLICATIONS

Beaumont, Cyril, *Complete Book of Ballets*, revised edition, London, 1951

Cooper, Martin, "The Historical Case for *Sylvia*", *The Daily Telegraph* (London), 20 September 1952

Guest, Ivor, "*Sylvia*: from Mérante to Ashton", *Ballet Annual* (London), no. 8, 1954

Haskell, Arnold, "*Sylvia*", *Ballet Annual* (London), no. 8, 1954

Balanchine, George, with Mason, Francis, *Balanchine's Complete Stories of the Great Ballets*, Garden City, N.Y., 1977

Vaughan, David, *Frederick Ashton and his Ballets*, London, 1977

Buckle, Richard, *Buckle at the Ballet*, London, 1980

McDonald, Nesta, "Hijacked", *Dance and Dancers* (London), January–February 1992

*   *   *

Mérante's *Sylvia*, the first new ballet to be staged at the Palais Garnier, Paris's recently built opera house, was an immediate success with its public. This was in no small measure due to the music composed for it by Léo Delibes, fresh from the success of his first ballet score, *Coppélia*. *Sylvia* provided a virtuoso part for the prima ballerina and gave ample scope for the kind of elaborate staging demanded by Parisian audiences. But the work lacked sufficient dramatic interest, its character essentially one-dimensional and its choreography undistinguished, and its continued life is owed purely to its outstanding score. Delibes is credited with being the first composer of talent to take seriously the writing of ballet music, and his symphonic treatment of it is considered to have been a strong influence on Tchaikovsky.

Delibes was involved in the making of the work from the beginning. "The first rehearsal took place on 15 August 1875, when Delibes had only completed the music for the first act," writes Ivor Guest of the ballet's genesis. "Mérante had already indicated to the composer a scheme on which to work, and Rita Sangalli, who was to play the leading role, was consulted almost from the start. . . . Delibes showed himself . . . obliging, and never took amiss the suggestions of the choreographer and the dancer. Most of the numbers were written three to four times before complete satisfaction was obtained. . . . Often Mérante would ask for so many more bars of music so that he could fit in the *enchaînements* he had in mind . . ."

This close collaboration between composer, choreographer, and prima ballerina, coupled with Delibes's own beguiling melodic invention, evocative orchestration, and harmonic

mastery, produced a score that gives the ballet continued life, whether in revivals at the Paris Opéra, in a one-act version by Fred Farren produced in London in 1911, or in Ashton's revival for the Sadler's Wells in 1952.

Some sense of the score's flavour can be demonstrated by a few pertinent examples. In the third scene of Act I, the movement "Les Chasseresses" announces the entry of Diana's nymphs, to a tuneful horn call in a dotted 6/8 rhythm, with punctuations on the timpani and an agitated string accompaniment. A playful middle section, built on a skipping motive with strings and woodwinds competing, follows, and then the hunting call returns. The effect is to depict most eloquently "the pleasures of the hunt" and the nymphs' "defiance of Eros in the name of their chaste goddess", as the scenario puts it. This is followed by Sylvia's first solo, the Valse lente called "L'Escarpolette", in which a little melody built on three rising notes played by the violins and punctuated by the harp is echoed by the horn, vividly evoking the sense of Sylvia lightly swinging on the trees' intertwined branches in the moonlight.

Act III contains the famous Pizzicati solo for Sylvia, a delightful tune that, as *Punch* described it in 1952, "for half a century past has snapped merrily from the violins in places where champagne corks popped", consisting of spritely plucking strings in E-flat major, contrasting with a wistful middle section played by flute and clarinet in A-flat major. This divertissement makes a contrast with the languid Barcarolle which preceeds it. A haunting melody on alto saxophone, accompanying Eros as he sails to the coast, it seems to echo Aminta's longing for Sylvia.

Delibes, influenced by Wagner, incorporates the use of *leitmotif* in his music—on a very limited scale perhaps, but it is there none the less, a striking example being the plaintive flute solo which introduced Aminta in Act I, and re-appears several times through the ballet to remind us of the shepherd's love-sickness.

Louis Mérante is not remembered as one of the greatest of Opéra choreographers, but he provided the Paris audience with the spectacle they loved and expected. The story, telling of the nymph Sylvia and the love for her by the shepherd Aminta, provided an engaging love story, a fanciful pseudo-Greek scenario, and much opportunity for background ensembles consisting, as Cyril Beaumont describes it in his reproduction of the scenario, of "Sylvans, Satyrs, Dryads, Nymphs, Shepherds, Shepherdesses, Villagers, Bacchantes, Priests of Bacchus, Slaves, Sailors, etc.". The story, based on the Tasso pastoral *Aminta*, tells of Sylvia's initial rejection of Aminta, who then sets out to rescue her when she is captured by the huntsman Orion. In Orion's grotto, Sylvia makes the huntsman drunk on wine, and then escapes with the help of Eros, who has been guiding the fortune of both Sylvia and Aminta. In the final act, Sylvia confesses her love for Aminta to her mistress Diana, who at first is unbending, but at the intervention of Eros blesses the union of the nymph and her shepherd.

In Mérante's production of *Sylvia*, Italian ballerina Rita Sangalli in the title role was given much opportunity to show off her technique, while various peripheral characters filled the stage at moments when grand late nineteenth-century Opéra spectacle was called for. The days of the great Romantic ballet in France were over, and *Sylvia* is generally considered to come at the end of a decline in ballet at the Paris Opéra, where the principles of a unified dramatic work of art had given way to a demand for sheer virtuosity and stage bravura. But largely due to the enduring quality of Delibes's score, *Sylvia* was a success and has continued to capture the imagination of choreographers who succeeded Mérante.

Ashton's 1952 version was based on the original scenario, using the Delibes score. Although the critics welcomed the

Sylvia, **as choreographed by Frederick Ashton, with Margot Fonteyn and Attilio Labis, London, 1965**

creation of a new three-act ballet—unusual for that time—there was much carping that, until the third act, Ashton's powers of invention were hampered by the weak nineteenth-century plot. As Martin Cooper noted, ". . . The characters in *Sylvia* are dolls, and it fell to Ashton to . . . animate them. . . . In this he succeeded, but within the limits set by the plot and the music, limits too narrow for those who are accustomed to look for far more in a ballet than ever entered the heads of French choreographers, composers or dancers 80 years ago."

Ashton certainly intended to re-animate the work of Delibes and Mérante. Mary Drage, who danced one of the huntresses in 1952, recalls: "We well knew that it was an old ballet we were using, the old score and old plot, because every now and then, very mild fun would be made of it."

The first scene, with its entrances of Naiads, Dryads, and Sylvains, bore the brunt of the critical drubbing. *Punch* called it "tepid"; Cyril Beaumont noted: ". . . the dances are not particularly attractive nor do they radiate a befitting immortality". Mary Drage agrees: ". . . There wasn't a lot of invention, but having given himself quite a lot of bodies to move about, I'm not sure what Ashton could have done with it. It was very pretty but there was no drama anywhere."

None of this is surprising. If the first act got off to a slow start, "it is because neither artists nor public in 1876 demanded immediately striking dramatic tensions in a ballet, which was . . . first and last a feast for the eye" (Martin Cooper). The solemn setting of a remote, sylvan age, with movement dictated by the undramatic opening numbers, was all that Ashton could achieve. Still, the choreographer, echoing his predecessor, made a loving gift of the role of Sylvia to Fonteyn, creating dances, as *The Times* critic wrote, "that display her virtuosity, her beauty and her expressiveness in worthy fashion", and in the great third act pas de deux, she was said to have swept away the audience "in a great gust of passion".

On the other hand, though Michael Somes danced Aminta with style and partnered admirably, there was disappointment with the role's lacklustre quality. Again, however, Ashton was hampered by his inheritance. Mérante, aged 48 in 1876, had choreographed the role for himself, doubtless giving himself as little strenuous dancing as possible, and the Delibes music would have suited that design. But Ashton's Aminta is eventually rewarded, as one critic put it, for "patiently dividing his time between porterage and the impersonation of the hapless lover" with a fine Act III solo.

In general it was this third act, with its Bacchic revels and splendid pas de deux, that won critical plaudits. The décor for the ballet, by Christopher and Robin Ironside, carried through the sense of mythological Greece as seen through nineteenth-century eyes: a "dreamy perspective of vast melancholy woods . . . and fantastic golden sky-scape combine the elements of several romanticisms: the swooning ecstasy of a Conder fan-painting, the Arcadian Rococo of Fragonard and Hubert Robert, the intricate splendour of the Second Empire . . ." was how *The Observer* described it.

This juxtaposition of the Ancient as seen by the nineteenth-century and then experienced through a twentieth-century perspective occasionally provided the uneasy feeling in the audience that perhaps events on stage were not meant to be taken entirely seriously. "The chief trouble," wrote Richard Buckle, "is that the original librettists, to whom Ashton has been faithful, were uncertain whether to take the mythology seriously or not." Mary Drage agrees: "This very close following of the score and the entrances and exists and so on: Ashton felt himself bound by it, I think. But sometimes [the audience] didn't know whether they were meant to be laughing. They *weren't*—you were meant to take it straight, as a sort of magical evening."

This sense of discomfort was particularly true of the god Eros. The original had been danced *en travestie* by the charming Marie Sanlaville. Ashton's Eros, created by Alexander Grant, "although not above dressing up as a comic witch, obviously expects to be worshipped occasionally" commented Buckle. "It is awkward to have a Figaro who is also a god. Until it has been decided whether *Sylvia* is a comedy or not, the choreographer does not know what effects to aim at producing."

In comparison to those "wholly Ashton" works that are so familiar now in the Royal Ballet's repertoire, Ashton's *Sylvia* might seem to have been a failure kept alive by its music. But if we accept Arnold Haskell's criteria, perhaps we must think again: Ashton's problem, he wrote, was "to create a ballet in the classic manner . . . but not a ballet that would be nothing but *pastiche*. He must make us believe that the movements imposed by him were inevitable and had always belonged to the music."

Keeping this dictat in mind when reading the contemporary accounts of Ashton's version, one would have to conclude that for his audiences he succeeded, within his own imposed limitations, in creating that magical world of the Ancients, where moonlight is magic and all conflict ends easily in sunny apotheosis.

—Louise Stein

SYMPHONIC VARIATIONS

Choreography: Frederick Ashton
Music: César Franck
Design: Sophie Fedorovitch (scenery and costumes)
First Production: Sadler's Wells Ballet, Royal Opera House, London, 24 April 1946
Principal Dancers: Margot Fonteyn, Pamela May, Moira Shearer, Michael Somes, Henry Danton, Brian Shaw

Other productions include: Royal Ballet Touring Company, with Antoinette Sibley, Jennifer Penney, Laura Connor, Anthony Dowell, Robert Mead, Michael Coleman; Nottingham, 9 November 1970. Dutch National Ballet (staged Michael Somes, with Wendy Ellis); Amsterdam, 2 November 1979. American Ballet Theatre (staged Michael Somes, with Wendy Ellis); Chicago, 20 March 1992.

PUBLICATIONS

Haskell, Arnold, "*Symphonic Variations* by Cesar Franck", *Ballet Annual* (London), vol. 1, 1947
Barnes, Clive, "*Symphonic Variations*", *Dance and Dancers* (London), March 1963
Clarke, Mary, "Return of a Masterpiece", *Dancing Times* (London), January 1968
Vaughan, David, *Frederick Ashton and his Ballets*, London, 1977
"Years of Achievement: Ashton's *Symphonic Variations*", *Dance and Dancers* (London), October 1986
Greskovic, Robert, "An Earthly Paradise", *Dance and Dancers* (London), September/October 1992

* * *

Symphonic Variations was Ashton's first new ballet after the Second World War (during which he had served in the Royal Air Force), and it was the first he had choreographed for the large stage of the Royal Opera House, the new post-war home of the Sadler's Wells Ballet. Ashton was literally exploring a new space, but emotionally he was staking out new ground as well. *Symphonic Variations* is a plotless ballet which develops directly from its score, but it has an economy of means and an intensity of feeling quite new in Ashton's work. He called it "a kind of testament".

Symphonic Variations can be read in terms of Ashton's personal circumstances and his creative response to them. He explained: "My mother died in 1939, just before the war . . . . Almost as soon as the war started I had to go into the RAF. Everyone was being called up—all the dancers and everyone I knew in the theatre—and I wanted, I suppose, to share their agony. I must say, I thought it was the end of everything . . . . The importance of the war was that it gave me a period to think and read a good deal and also, because I was rather unhappy, I went in for mysticism. I read St. John of the Cross and lots of books about mystics and mysticism." Ashton also discovered the music of César Franck which attracted him ". . . because he was also very mystical and very religious".

Ashton's first conception of *Symphonic Variations* as "a kind of mystic marriage" was by his own admission over-elaborate: "I was interested in the idea of 'dedication' and absorption in divine love . . . . But perhaps the dominant theme of the ballet was the seasons. At the beginning I meant it to be winter with the three women moving alone, unfertilized. When the man begins to dance he introduces the spring; and the last part of the ballet represents to a certain extent the fullness of summer and the plenty of harvest . . .'. This programme may have been the springboard for Ashton's imagination, but virtually no trace of it is visible in the final ballet.

If *Symphonic Variations* is a testament, it is one of Ashton's belief in the continuing viability of the classical vocabulary. It is also a statement of the qualities Ashton wanted associated with British ballet: musicality, perfect but unflashy technique, a serene lyric grace at once natural and elegant. It is worth remembering that in 1946 Sadler's Wells Ballet was on the brink of becoming an international company: *Symphonic Variations* was its manifesto.

Ashton's creative process was one of careful paring away of inessentials: as he said, "I had to do a lot of experimenting to find the sort of movement that I wanted". The end result was an

Symphonic Variations, with (from left to right, front) Moira Shearer, Margot Fonteyn, and Pamela May, Sadler's Wells Ballet, London, 1946

absolute economy of expression, with no narrative, no mime, not even a real pas de deux. There are no exits, no entrances. The form is cyclic, and at the final curtain the six dancers return to the meditative poses from which they originally started. The sheer spaciousness of their dancing, enhanced by Sophie Fedorovitch's majestically chaste backcloth, is an ebb and flow of movement and stillness, a weaving and unweaving of physical images which are heroic and splendid and elementally simple.

—Martin Wright

SYMPHONIE FANTASTIQUE

Choreography: Léonide Massine
Music: Hector Berlioz
Design: Christian Bérard
Libretto: after Hector Berlioz
First Production: de Basil's Ballets Russes, Covent Garden, London, 24 July 1936
Principal Dancers: Léonide Massine (A Young Musician), Tamara Toumanova (The Beloved), Marc Platov (The Old Shepherd), George Zorich (The Young Shepherd), Alexis Koslov (The Deer), Yurek Shabelevsky (The Jailer)

Other productions include: Teatro Colón (restaged Massine); Buenos Aires, 1948. Royal Danish Ballet (restaged and revised Massine), as *Episode from the Life of an Artist*; Copenhagen, 1 April 1948. Borovansky Ballet (staged Edouard Borovansky, design William Constable); Melbourne, January 1954. Paris Opéra Ballet (restaged Massine); Paris, 17 April 1957. Paris Opéra Ballet (new version; chor. Roland Petit, design Svoboda), with Zizi Jeanmaire, Michel Denard; Paris, 18 March 1975.

PUBLICATIONS

Goodman, G.E., "Notes on Décor", *Dancing Times* (London), September 1936

Haskell, Arnold, "Massine and Berlioz", *Dancing Times* (London), September 1936

Haskell, Arnold, "*Symphonie Fantastique*", *Dancing Times* (London), October 1936

Coton, A.V., *A Prejudice for Ballet*, London, 1938

Beaumont, Cyril, *Complete Book of Ballets*, revised edition, London, 1951

Massine, Léonide, *My Life in Ballet*, London, 1961

Sorley Walker, Kathrine, *De Basil's Ballets Russes*, London, 1982

García-Márquez, Vicente, *Les Ballets Russes*, New York, 1990

* * *

Massine tells us in his autobiography that he first began to think about a ballet to Berlioz's *Symphonie fantastique* during the period in which he was choreographing *Jardin public*, a work which had its premiere in America in 1935. The romantic themes of the Berlioz "libretto" for the symphony were much in fashion at the time, and indeed, Lambert's coincidental suggestion to Ashton that he use the Berlioz story for *Apparitions* must have been made at roughly the same moment at which Massine was visited by the idea of using the Berlioz score for a new "symphonic" work, to follow up the success of *Les Présages* and *Choreartium*. Though critics and others made a field day of the coincidence at the time, there was really no comparison, save that each choreographer was using the same story. The David-and-Goliath fable always holds a special fascination for those in sympathy with the underdog, but in this case David could not compete; Goliath had vastly more experience and he also had a bigger stage, a better orchestra, and a larger collection of brilliant dancers at his disposal. With all this, Massine could tell the story of the Musician unsuccessfully pursuing his Beloved through the course of several dreams and dying romantically at the ballet's conclusion with all his customary grasp of the essentials of balletic composition.

At the time of its premiere, *Symphonie fantastique* had an audience which fell into three categories. There was the first, more vocal group, composed of those who had disapproved passionately of Massine's attempts to create a genre of "symphonic" ballet to the abstract music of Brahms in *Choreartium*, and who hailed the new work as a welcome change from his assaults on "serious" composers. After all, Berlioz could hardly object, even had he still been present to do so, to the attempts of a choreographer to put on stage what the composer had had in mind when composing the score. The second group was smaller (comprised mainly of the critic A. V. Coton), and considered that Massine had betrayed the ideals he had exemplified on stage with his "symphonic" ballets; this group believed that the Berlioz ballet was a retrograde step. The third, and by far the largest group, was not concerned with making points of any kind whatsoever but simply went to the Royal Opera House to enjoy the new ballet, and in the event did so thoroughly.

Whether *Symphonie fantastique* represented a retrograde step or not, in fact Massine, when choreographing this work, gave himself an easier (if not a shorter) task than he had set himself with the previous "symphonic" works to Tchaikovsky and Brahms. The structure of the Berlioz libretto falls into five quite distinct parts, the only ingredient common to all being the figures of the protagonist and his feminine ideal. Consequently the ballet itself displays five quite different styles, of which only the last, with its posturing monks and devils, is not perhaps entirely successful. As anyone who has ever experimented with choreography will confirm, it is much easier to produce a long work which falls clearly into separate categories than to produce one not so defined. The first movement, with the figure of the Musician and his romantic despair dominating the action, offered Massine the chance to redevelop some of the extraordinary designs and spatial patterns he first worked with in *Les Présages*, without offending any musical purists in the process. To separate the Musician from the other dancers effortlessly created the necessary impression of an artist alienated by drugs or poison from the real world, which contrasted effectively with the strictly formal steps and movements of the dancers at the Ball of the second scene. With the pastoral scene of the third movement, a moment of rest in the Musician's fevered saga, the style changed again, creating a little island of serenity which at last gave way to one of Massine's most effective dramatic conceptions, linked to the

violent rhythms of the March to the Scaffold. Only in the closing fifth movement did his invention falter, as—one might feel justified in maintaining—did that of the composer: confrontations between monks and devils in this day and age are hard to take seriously, however dramatically presented.

The choreographic texture of the ballet in every scene was worked out to the high standard adhered to by Massine in all his ballets; nothing sloppy or careless, absolute attention to detail, and every facet of the production taken into account. No musician could fault his treatment of the score, for he had obviously listened to it with his usual meticulous attention before embarking on the choreography: the designs by Christian Bérard added just as much to the success of the work as did Beaton's to the Ashton *Apparitions*, and if the figure of the Musician dominated the work, putting his Beloved in the shade, such treatment is in line with the romantic ideal of the Eternal Feminine, never completely revealed to the lover, to the artist, or to the audience.

Symphonie fantastique also at its premiere showed to the audience yet a further unfamiliar aspect of Massine the performer, that of a hero of the romantic era—never overstated, always credible, and always able to hold the eye and the attention of the audience, whether in motion or in repose. His immediate successor in the role, Marc Platov, made a strong impression, having the intelligence not to try to copy Massine in any way, and performing the role in a much younger, more unsophisticated manner. As the Beloved, Tamara Toumanova was the more striking figure, but she could not bring to the role the qualities of sweetness and tenderness shown by Irina Baronova.

—Janet Sinclair

SYMPHONY IN C
(original title: *Le Palais de cristal*)

Choreography: George Balanchine
Music: Georges Bizet
Design: Léonor Fini (scenery and costumes)
First Production: Paris Opéra Ballet, Théâtre National de l'Opéra, Paris, 28 July 1947
Principal Dancers: Lycette Darsonval and Alexandre Kalioujny (First Movement), Tamara Toumanova and Roger Ritz (Second Movement), Micheline Bardin and Michel Renault (Third Movement), Madeleine Lafon and Max Bozzoni (Fourth Movement).

Other productions include: Ballet Society (precursor to New York City Ballet; restaged Balanchine), as *Symphony in C*, with Maria Tallchief and Nicholas Magallanes (First Movement), Tanaquil LeClercq and Francisco Moncion (Second Movement), Beatrice Tompkins and Herbert Bliss (Third Movement), Elise Reiman and Lew Christensen (Fourth Movement); New York, 22 March 1948. Royal Danish Ballet (staged Vida Brown); Copenhagen, 4 October 1952. La Scala Ballet; Milan, 1955. Royal Swedish Ballet; Stockholm, 1960. San Francisco Ballet; San Francisco, 17 March 1961. Dutch National Ballet; Amsterdam, 18 June 1962. Hamburg Ballet; Hamburg, 8 February 1965. German Opera Ballet (staging supervised Balanchine), with guest artists of New York City Ballet; Berlin, 31 October 1969. Geneva Ballet; Geneva, 17 March 1970. Rome Opera Ballet; Rome, 1972. Stuttgart Ballet (staged Patricia Neary); Stuttgart, 14 April 1976. Hungarian

Symphony in C, as performed by Matz Skoog (centre) and members of London Festival Ballet

State Opera Ballet; Budapest, 10 December 1977. Zurich Opera Ballet (staged Neary); Zurich, 9 September 1978. Royal Ballet (staged Victoria Simon and John Taras); London, 20 November 1991. Houston Ballet; Houston, 10 September 1992.

PUBLICATIONS

Hussey, Dyneley, "Bizet's *Symphony in C*", *Dancing Times* (London), July 1951

Balanchine, George, with Mason, Francis, *Balanchine's Complete Stories of the Great Ballets*, Garden City, N.Y., 1977

Reynolds, Nancy, *Repertory in Review*, New York, 1977

Kaplan, Larry, "Corps Choreography by Balanchine", *Ballet Review* (New York), Winter 1988

Kelly, Patrick, "Masterpiece Theatre", *Dance Magazine* (New York), November 1988

* * *

The enduring appeal of George Balanchine's exhilarating *Symphony in C* stems first of all from its dialogue between choreography and score. It combines the youthful vigour and the classical discipline of the seventeen-year-old Georges Bizet's first symphony to produce an effect much like light shining and refracting through grand architecture, thus making the original title, *Le Palais de cristal*, singularly apt.

Balanchine choreographed the work for the Paris Opéra Ballet while he was guest ballet master there. As a tribute to the Parisian company, he chose the French composer's long-unpublished score, which had only recently been discovered. The excitement of discovery seems to echo through the ballet.

The original designs by Léonor Fini included an ornate surrealist backdrop—an architectural fantasia of baroque columns and balconies. The costumes provided a different jewel-like colour scheme for each movement, an idea that Balanchine later returned to in his full-length abstract ballet, *Jewels*.

In the year following the ballet's creation, Balanchine staged it under the title *Symphony in C* for his own company (at that point called Ballet Society) with the women now all in white. It has remained a pillar of New York City Ballet's repertoire, as well as one of Balanchine's most widely produced works.

The four movements have separate casts of dancers—because, Balanchine pointed out, each of the sections develops different musical material. But in each the plan is the same, with a principal couple, two demi-soloist couples, and a small female corps. The finale brings all the dancers together. Throughout, the geometry of their deployment with the principals tightly framed suggests the grand symmetry of French public architecture and of traditional classical ballet, although the different ranks also interact, weaving in and out. As a French critic, Maurice Purchet, recognized at the time of the premiere, "Balanchine knows how to make a work both coherent and well structured—in a word, solid—under its appearance of lightness and ease."

Lightness and ease characterize the three sunny, quick sections. Here is a prime demonstration of the need for speed when dancing Balanchine, in order to allow the music its proper tempo. The first movement is led by a pair of virtuoso dancers—demon turners—while the third movement couple takes to the air by leaps and bounds. The fourth begins with yet another set of dancers, but soon these troops are replaced by those from the first movement—and then the second—and then the third. Finally the whole cast fills the stage, as the corps offers a box-like frame for the soloists while the music rises and rises in key. Wave on wave they advance, until a whole forest of legs is dancing in full-out, unison batterie, making a charming Balanchine applause-winning finale.

The ballet's renowned second movement has another tonality altogether. Its moonlit reverie to a broad, haunting melody—led by a melancholy oboe—hints at the doom-laden heroes and swooning heroines of romanticism. However, this being Balanchine, the ballerina asserts her own will. She *decides* to submit to her partner. In one of the ballet's most piercingly beautiful moments, as if on a suspended breath, she stretches upward unsupported in profile as the music swells, arms en couronne, and then releases herself backwards to fall into a *Swan Lake* swoon over the waiting arm of her cavalier. Having repeated this twice more, she dives forward into an arabesque penché with an actively circling port de bras that finishes in a swan's windswept pose.

The section contains some of Balanchine's most beautiful and difficult partnering, in which at full arms' length, linked only by their hands, the man must help the woman to maintain her balance in quick shifts of direction; she looks at once immensely heroic and fragile. In Suzanne Farrell's autobiography, *Holding On to the Air*, she calls the role, which she made very much her own, "one of the most revealing, vulnerable, and ecstatic parts he ever choreographed for a woman".

It was created for Tamara Toumanova, who was a guest with the Paris Opéra Ballet at the time, and it recalls her formidable prowess in balancing. But one can also surmise that Balanchine's reunion with a ballerina who had earlier been, like Farrell, an object of his personal as well as artistic interest may have influenced what Toumanova herself has called the adagio's "mood of complete silence". At that time, however (to judge by the Paris Opéra Ballet's recent revival of the ballet), the section seems to have lacked its more nostalgic, swooning movements.

The Paris Opéra has revived the ballet a number of times. In the late 1960s, while John Taras was ballet master of the company, he staged the New York City Ballet production, rather than deal with a certain vagueness about memories of the original (still called *Le Palais de cristal*)—but the original was the version the company returned to, and took to the U.S. on its 1986 tour. On this occasion, although Fini's backdrop was omitted, the ballet had costumes based on her colourful designs, creating a fantastic kaleidoscope effect in the finale. *Le Palais de cristal* aroused doubts in the U.S. as to its faithfulness to Balanchine's original. It may, however, be fairly close to the company's performing tradition, since they reportedly changed some steps soon after Balanchine left (adding the first movement ballerina's fouettés, for example), and Balanchine also made changes at the New York City Ballet. The Paris Opéra version has a more orthodox classicism than City Ballet's, but in some respects demands even greater virtuosity.

—Marilyn Hunt

T

TAGLIONI, Filippo

Italian dancer and choreographer. Born in Milan, 5 November 1777. Studied in Italy, and with Jean-François Coulon, Paris, from 1799. Married Edwige Sofia Karsten, Stockholm. Child dancer (performing female roles), Pisa, 1794; first dancer, Livorno, Florence, and Venice, also performing in Turin and La Scala, Milan, 1795 and 1798, and Paris, 1799; first dancer and ballet master (at invitation of Swedish court), Stockholm, 1802; début as choreographer in Vienna, 1805, thereafter working in theatres in Vienna, Cassel, Munich, Milan, Turin, Stuttgart, Paris, Berlin, St. Petersburg, and Warsaw; Paris début as choreographer, Opéra, 1830, staging famous La Sylphide, 1832; visiting ballet master, accompanying Marie as ballerina, Imperial Theatres, St. Petersburg, 1837–42, King's Theatre, London (under ballet master Antonio Guerra), 1840, 1841, and La Scala, Milan, 1841, 1842, 1846; also teacher: chief ballet teacher of daughter, ballerina Marie Taglioni, from 1821. Died in Como, 11 February 1871.

WORKS

1805   *Atalante und Hippomenes* (divertissement), Hoftheater, Vienna

1821   *Das Schweizer Milchmädchen* (mus. Gyrowetz), Hoftheater, Vienna
        Lodoiska (mus. Umlauff and Gyrowetz), Hoftheater, Vienna
        Jaconde (after Vestris), Vienna

1822   *Margarete, Königin von Catanea* (mus. Graf von Gallenberg), Hoftheater, Vienna
        La Réception d'une jeune nymph à la cour de Terpsichore, Hoftheater, Vienna

1826   *Danina; oder, Jocko der brasilianische Affe* (mus. Von Lindpaintner), Royal Theatre, Stuttgart

1830   *Le Dieu et la Bayadère* (opera-ballet; mus. Auber), Opéra, Paris

1831   *Ballet of the Nuns* in *Robert le Diable* (opera; mus. Meyerbeer), Opéra, Paris

1832   *La Sylphide* (mus. Schneitzhoeffer), Opéra, Paris
        Nathalie; ou, La Laitière suisse (mus. Gyrowetz, Carafa), Opéra, Paris

1833   Dances in *Gustave* (opera; mus. Auber), Opéra, Paris
        La Révolte au sérail (mus. Labarre), Opéra, Paris

1834   *Sire Huon* (mus. Costa), King's Theatre, London
        La Chasse des nymphes (divertissement), King's Theatre, London
        Le Pouvoir de la danse (divertissement), King's Theatre, London

1835   Dances in *La Juive* (opera; mus. Halévy), Opéra, Paris
        Brézilia; ou, La Tribu des femmes (mus. von Gallenberg), Opéra, Paris
        Mazilia (new production of *Brézilia*; mus. Nahaud), King's Theatre, London

1836   Dances in *Les Huguenots* (mus. Meyerbeer), Opéra, Paris
        La Fille du Danube (mus. Adam), Opéra, Paris

1838   *Miranda* (mus. Auber, Rossini), Bolshoi Theatre, St. Petersburg
        La Gitana (mus. Schmidt, Auber), Bolshoi Theatre, St. Petersburg

1839   *L'Ombre* (mus. Maurer), Bolshoi Theatre, St. Petersburg,

1840   *L'Ecumeur de mer* (mus. Adam), Bolshoi Theatre, St. Petersburg

1841   *Aglaë; ou, L'Eléve d'amour* (mus. Keller), Bolshoi Theatre, St. Petersburg
        Daya, Bolshoi Theatre, St. Petersburg

1842   *Gerta, Queen of the Elfrides*, Bolshoi Theatre, St. Petersburg

1843   *La Péri* (mus. Panizza), La Scala, Milan

1846   *La Ombra* (new production of *L'Ombre*; mus. Viviani), La Scala, Milan

PUBLICATIONS

[Véron, Louis Désiré], "Behind the Scenes at the Opéra in Marie Taglioni's Day", extracts from the memoirs of Dr. Véron, translated by Cyril Beaumont, *Dancing Times* (London), January 1924

Gribble, Francis, "Taglioni", *Dancing Times* (London), September 1928

Tugal, Pierre, "Notes sur la famille des Taglioni", 3 parts: *Archives internationales de la danse* (Paris), January, April, and October 1933

Michel, Artur, "Les Ballets de Philippe Taglioni", *Archives internationales de la danse* (Paris), October 1934

Beaumont, Cyril, *Complete Book of Ballets*, revised edition, London, 1951

Moore, Lillian, "La Sylphide: Epitome of the Romantic Ballet", *Dance Magazine* (New York), March 1965

Guest, Ivor, *The Romantic Ballet in Paris*, London, 1966

Winter, Marian Hannah, *The Pre-Romantic Ballet*, London, 1974

Pudetek, Janina, "The Warsaw Ballet under . . . Maurice Pion and Filippo Taglioni", *Dance Chronicle* (New York), vol. 11, no. 2, 1988

Wiley, Roland John, *A Century of Russian Ballet: Documents and Accounts*, Oxford, 1990

* * *

The Taglioni dynasty is recorded from the time of Carlo

Taglioni, a dancer and ballet master who practised in Turin and other Italian cities during the middle of the eighteenth century. Two of his sons have a prominent place in dance history: Salvatore, born in 1789, was for many years ballet master and principal dancer in Naples, where he founded a ballet school and staged over 200 ballets, and Filippo, born in 1777, was one of the leaders of the Romantic movement in ballet, who as teacher and choreographer launched his daughter Marie into a career as one of the most famous ballerinas of all time.

Filippo made his dancing début in Pisa in 1794, and then went to Paris to study with French ballet master Jean-François Coulon. He accepted an engagement in Stockholm, as principal dancer and ballet master, and it was there that he married and started a family, and his daughter Marie was born in 1804. It is to Marie that his fame as a choreographer is due—his ability to compose ballets that displayed her very special talents made his name celebrated, and ensured him engagements throughout Europe. His son Paul also had an eminent career as dancer and ballet master, spending many years in Berlin.

In writing of Filippo Taglioni's ballets, his contemporaries concentrated almost totally on detailed descriptions of Marie's exceptional performances—and, as none of his choreography has been handed down in the direct line, it is almost impossible to assess his ability. It seems improbable, however, that it had as few merits as some accounts suggest, particularly as he seems to have aroused much jealousy and enmity, leading to journalistic campaigns against him. A great dancer can do much to make a ballet memorable, but Filippo's arrangement of dances for Marie must have been ideally suited to her aerial quality and light-footed speed. In his book Marie Taglioni André Levinson describes Filippo Taglioni as an excellent dancer himself, who made a mark in ballets like Les Noces de Gamache, choreographed in 1801 by Louis Milon, and Le Retour de Zéphire, staged by Pierre Gardel in 1802. For the triumph of La Sylphide in 1832, however, Taglioni was never greatly credited, and his contributions to other ballets—in particular his libretti for them—came in for harsh criticism. Levinson defends him, pointing out that to perceive such a talent as his daughter's, and to reveal it in terms of dance, was no mean feat. It seems incontrovertible that inspired by his daughter's attributes, Taglioni did in fact enlarge the scope of ballet by introducing a less sensual and more poetic approach, so that the ballerina became an ideal to be admired rather than a seductive sex symbol to be coveted for herself.

Apart from La Sylphide, Taglioni's best known productions were Le Dieu et la Bayadère (an opera-ballet of 1830, in no way linked to Petipa's La Bayadère), Nathalie; ou, La Laitière suisse, La Révolte au sérail, in which he deployed a very large corps de ballet of women in spectacular balletic military manoeuvres, La Fille du Danube, which set Marie's ethereality and grace against lively and effective ensembles of nobles and villagers, La Gitana, which again contrasted fiery gypsy dances and formal ballroom quadrilles, and L'Ombre. The last of these contained a solo for Marie, the celebrated "Pas de l'ombre", whose description by Théophile Gautier in La Presse, 1 July 1844, shows to a large extent how cunningly Filippo Taglioni sustained by his choreography his daughter's special style: "The 'Pas de l'ombre' is one of the most charming choreographic compositions we have seen. And, what is rare in pas, it has a theme; the poses do not succeed one another at random and without reason . . . Mlle Taglioni evaporates, condenses in the form of mist, glides over the lake like a wreath of fog blown by the wind . . ."

Filippo Taglioni did not retire until 1852, five years after his daughter, when he settled in a villa on Lake Como with his wife (who died in 1862). His detractors always implied that his

daughter's straitened circumstances in her retirement were caused by his profligate handling of her earnings, but this is insufficiently proved. Whatever his faults or limitations, Taglioni—both as father and as choreographer—gave ballet one of its most illustrious artists.

—Kathrine Sorley Walker

TAGLIONI, Marie

Italian dancer. Born in Stockholm, daughter of choreographer Filippo Taglioni, sister of dancer and choreographer Paul Taglioni, 23 April 1804. Studied with Jean-François Coulon, Paris, from 1812, and with father Filippo Taglioni, first in Vienna, then in Cassel, from 1821. Married Comte Gilbert de Voisins, 1832 (sep. 1835, div. 1844): one daughter, Eugénie-Marie-Edwige (b. 1836), and one son, Georges Gilbert de Voisins (b. 1842). Début (in divertissement by Filippo Taglioni), Hoftheater, Vienna, 1822, thereafter performing in Vienna, Munich, and Stuttgart; Paris Opéra début, 1827, thereafter receiving contract as "remplaçant" of the Opéra, 1828–29, and premier sujet, from 1829; début in Bordeaux, 1828, and London, King's Theatre, 1830, continuing as premier sujet, Paris Opéra, until 1837, creating most famous role in La Sylphide in 1832; ballerina, Imperial Theatres, St. Petersburg (accompanied by father as ballet master), 1837–42, with performances also in London, 1838, Vienna, 1839, Paris, 1840, 1843, Stockholm, and Milan, 1841; retired to Lake Como, 1847, but returned to Paris, 1858: Inspectrice de la danse, Paris Opéra, 1859–70; choreographer, Le Papillon (for dancer Emma Livry), Paris Opéra, 1860. Died in Marseilles, 22 April 1884.

ROLES

1822　Dancer (cr) in La Réception d'une jeune nymphe à la cour de Terpsichore (F. Taglioni), Hoftheater, Vienna
　　　Dancer in La Belle Arsène (Rozier), Hoftheater, Vienna
　　　Dancer in Pas de châle (Shawl Dance; divertissement), Hoftheater, Vienna
　　　Dancer in Folies d'Espagne (divertissement), Hoftheater, Vienna
　　　An Amazon in Les Amazons (Henry), Hoftheater, Vienna
　　　Dancer in La Feé et le chevalier (Armand Vestris), Hoftheater, Vienna
1823　Dancer in Le Triomphe de la fidélité; ou, La Rose la plus belle (Henry), Hoftheater, Vienna
1824　Venus in Psyche (Armand Vestris after P. Gardel), Hoftheater, Vienna
1825　Dancer in Zemire et Azor (divertissement; with brother Paul), Royal Theatre, Stuttgart
1826　Danina (cr) in Danina; oder, Jocko der brasilianische Affe (F. Taglioni), Royal Theatre, Stuttgart
1827　Pas de deux added to Le Sicilièn; ou, L'Amour peintre (A. Petit), Opéra, Paris
　　　Pas de deux in Mars et Vénus; ou, Les Filets de Vulcain (Blache), Opéra, Paris
　　　Dancer in Le Prix de la danse (divertissement) in La Vestale (opera; mus. Spontini), Opéra, Paris
　　　Dancer in Le Carnaval de Venise (Milon), Opéra, Paris
1828　Title role (cr) in Lydie (revision of La Coquette soumise; Aumer), Opéra, Paris
　　　Vénus in Mars et Vénus (Blache), Opéra, Paris

Title role in *Cendrillon* (Albert), Opéra, Paris
1829 Naiad (cr) in *La Belle au bois dormant* (Aumer), Opéra, Paris
Title role in *Psyche* (P. Gardel), Opéra, Paris
Tyrolienne (cr) in *Guillaume Tell* (opera; mus. Rossini, chor. Aumer), Opéra, Paris
1830 Niuka (cr) in *Manon Lescaut* (Aumer; Taglioni's dances chor. F. Taglioni), Opéra, Paris
Zoloé (cr) in *Le Dieu et la Bayadère* (opera-ballet; mus. Aumer, chor. F. Taglioni), Opéra, Paris
Pas de deux (with Perrot) in *Fernand Cortès* (opera; mus. Spontini), Opéra, Paris
Flore in *Flore et Zéphire* (revival; Didelot), King's Theatre, London
1831 Flore in *Flore et Zéphire* (Albert, Aumer after Didelot), Opéra, Paris
Title role in *La Naïade*, King's Theatre, London
Title role in *La Bayadère* (Deshayes after Auber's opera-ballet *Le Dieu et la Bayadère*), King's Theatre, London
The Abbess Héléna (cr) in *Ballet of the Nuns*, (divertissement) in *Robert le Diable* (opera; mus. Meyerbeer, chor. F. Taglioni), Opéra, Paris
1832 Title role (cr) in *La Sylphide* (F. Taglioni), Opéra, Paris
Title role (cr) in *Nathalie; ou, La Laitière suisse* (F. Taglioni), Opéra, Paris
1833 Divertissement (cr) in *Ines de Castro* (Cortesi), King's Theatre, London
Zulma (cr) in *La Révolte au sérail* (F. Taglioni), Opéra, Paris
1834 Leading role (cr) in *Sire Huon* (F. Taglioni), King's Theatre, London
Principal dancer (cr) in *La Chasse des nymphes* (F. Taglioni), King's Theatre, London
1835 Dancer, Minuet and Gavotte, in *La Romanesca* (divertissement), Opéra, Paris
Brezilia (cr) in *Brezilia; ou, La Tribu des femmes* (F. Taglioni), Opéra, Paris
1836 Fleur-des-Champs (cr) in *La Fille du Danube* (F. Taglioni), Opéra, Paris
1838 Title role (cr) in *Miranda* (F. Taglioni), Bolshoi Theatre, St. Petersburg
Title role (cr) in *La Gitana* (F. Taglioni), Bolshoi Theatre, St. Petersburg
Dancer in *La Parisianna* (Mazurka, later known as *Le Pas de diamants*), King's Theatre, London
1839 Angela (cr) in *L'Ombre* (F. Taglioni), Bolshoi Theatre, St. Petersburg
1840 Leading role (cr) in *L'Ecumeur de mer* (F. Taglioni), Bolshoi Theatre, St. Petersburg
1841 Title role (cr) in *Aglaë; ou, L'Élève d'amour* (F. Taglioni), Bolshoi Theatre, St. Petersburg
Leading role (cr) in *Daya* (F. Taglioni), Bolshoi Theatre, St. Petersburg
1842 Title role (cr) in *Gerta, Queen of the Elfrides* (F. Taglioni), Bolshoi Theatre, St. Petersburg
1843 Title role (cr) in *La Peri* (F. Taglioni), La Scala, Milan
1845 Ballerina (cr) in *Pas de quatre* (Perrot), Her Majesty's Theatre, London
1846 Venus (cr) in *Le Jugement de Pâris* (Perrot), Her Majesty's Theatre, London

WORKS

1860 *Le Papillon* (mus. Offenbach), Opéra, Paris

PUBLICATIONS

Castil-Blaze, *La Danse et les ballets depuis Bacchus jusqu'à Mlle Taglioni*, Paris, 1832
Gautier, Théophile, *Les Beautés de l'Opéra*, Paris, 1844
Levinson, André, *Marie Taglioni*, translated by Cyril Beaumont, London, 1930; reprinted London, 1977
Moore, Lillian, *Artists of the Dance*, New York, 1938
Vaillat, Léandre, *La Taglioni, ou La Vie d'une danseuse*, Paris, 1942
Beaumont, Cyril, *Complete Book of Ballets*, revised edition, London, 1951
Clarke, Mary, *Six Great Dancers*, London, 1957
Daniels, Diana, "Marie Taglioni in England", *Dancing Times* (London), July 1957
Moore, Lillian, "*La Sylphide*: Epitome of the Romantic Ballet", *Dance Magazine* (New York), March 1965
Hill, Lorna, *La Sylphide: The Life of Marie Taglioni*, London, 1967
Migel, Parmenia, *The Ballerinas*, New York, 1972
Migel, Parmenia, "Marie Taglioni, 1804–1884", *Dance Magazine* (New York), September 1972
Heiberg, Johanne Luise, "Memories of Taglioni and Elssler", translated from the author's memoirs by Patricia McAndrew, *Dance Chronicle* (New York), vol. 4, no. 1, 1981
Harris, Dale, "Passion and Pathos", *Ballet News* (New York), September 1984
Woodcock, Sarah, "Margaret Rolfe's Memoirs of Marie Taglioni", *Dance Research* (London), Spring and Autumn 1989
Lecomte, Nathalie, "Marie Taglioni alla Scala", *La Danza italiana* (Rome), Winter 1990
Wiley, Roland John, *A Century of Russian Ballet: Documents and Accounts*, Oxford 1990

* * *

In 1822 a proud father presented his eighteen-year-old daughter in a dance début at the Vienna Hoftheater in a divertissement called *La Réception d'une jeune nymphe à la cour de Terpsichore*. The début was a success, and no doubt in later years, when the young men of Vienna would unhitch the horses from the ballerina's carriage and pull her vehicle through the streets themselves, many of that original audience boasted of their first glimpse of Marie Taglioni.

She was to become the great legend of the century. Rival factions would prefer other great ballerinas to her—particularly Fanny Elssler—but Taglioni's place was secure for ever as the creator of *La Sylphide*, the balletic embodiment of the supernatural enchantress, the unattainable ideal of the Romantic era.

In reality, of course, Taglioni was as hard-working, realistic, and dedicated as any other successful dancer: she came from a family of them. Her father, Filippo, was one of the most famous international ballet masters of his time, and her grandfather a well-known dancer in Italy. Her uncle Salvatore became ballet master in Naples, and her brother Paul settled in Berlin where he choreographed many ballets.

Taglioni first appeared at the Paris Opéra in 1827, dancing in *Le Sicilièn*, and she was immediately recognized as offering a style of dancing marked by an ethereal beauty rather than the more usual seductive or provocative qualities. She was placed under contract from the following April, when she became a "remplaçant", and soon afterwards she was made a premier sujet. Didelot's famous ballet *Flore et Zéphire* was to be revived for her in 1831, and, since she was allowed to appear abroad, she made her London début in that ballet first at the King's

Marie Taglioni in *La Bayadère*, King's Theatre, London, 1831

Theatre in June 1830. In October of that year her father created dances for her in *Le Dieu et la Bayadère*. This was an opera-ballet in which singers and dancers were both involved. The dancers sometimes had to mime replies to sung questions, and Théophile Gautier wrote admiringly (in 1844) of the way Taglioni coped with this situation: "By the expressive and touching play of her features ... she links herself with the action that forsakes her and demonstrates that she understands every word the actors say, although they do not speak the same tongue."

By 1830 Filippo Taglioni was already fully aware of his daughter's exceptional grace and lightness, her aerial qualities, and the illusion of otherworldly charm that she could create on stage. He recognized her as being ideally suited to reflect in ballet the Romantic movement which had just begun to sweep Europe in literature and art. ("Her début will open a new epoch," the perceptive critic of *Le Figaro* had written in 1827, "It is Romanticism applied to the dance.") Filippo Taglioni put this idea into operation to some extent in the *Ballet of the Nuns*, ballet's first venture into Romantic supernaturalism, in the opera *Robert le Diable* in 1831. The following year, he revolutionized balletic taste entirely with *La Sylphide*.

This ballet, and its star Marie Taglioni, completely conquered Paris. New fashions in dress and ornaments became the rage throughout Parisian society. At the Opéra, all previous works suddenly looked old-fashioned, and for several years subsequently, productions were dominated by themes taken from fairy-tales and legends. Marie Taglioni's fame rapidly spread throughout Europe. She travelled widely and was acclaimed in every capital city, returning year after year to favoured capitals like London or St. Petersburg, and becoming a household name wherever she went. Her name was applied to all manner of things, from hair-styles to caramels and cakes— not, as would be the case today, for "promotional" reasons, but as a simple recognition of the ballerina's popularity. In London in 1832, the critic of *The Times* (as quoted by Cyril Beaumont in 1937), wrote that Taglioni "convinces the most fastidious critic that dancing is an art worthy to rank with poetry and painting", and one of the dancer's earliest and most fervent admirers was the young princess who became Queen Victoria in 1837.

Marie Taglioni's success was not limited to *La Sylphide*. Other great victories were in *La Fille du Danube* (1836), a story about an orphan girl who drowns herself for love and is followed into the Danube by her lover, and *L'Ombre* (1839), in which she danced the ghost of a murdered woman. "None but Taglioni could have embodied this idea", wrote the critic of *The Times* in 1840. "She was wafted in all directions—she became a spiritual ubiquity, peering through every tree—a pure being with still a gentle love for earth." Entirely different, however, was *La Gitana* (1838), a romantic tale about a Duke's daughter abducted by the gypsies, who is eventually restored happily to her parents. In this her acting was outstanding, and her allegro dancing excited immense admiration.

One of the most famous episodes in Taglioni's later career came in 1845, when the manager of Her Majesty's Theatre in London arranged for the staging of the now-famous divertissement, *Pas de quatre*, choreographed by Jules Perrot for four of the greatest ballerinas of the time—Taglioni, Carlotta Grisi, Fanny Cerrito, and Lucile Grahn. Perrot cunningly paid tribute to the individual style of each dancer, and Taglioni's solo showed the grace and dignity, as well as the bounding leaps, which made her exceptional.

In 1847 Taglioni retired from dancing, but although she had acquired money and jewels during her career, her resources were soon depleted—rumour suggested, as a result of her ageing father's speculations. She returned to Paris in 1858, coaching the promising young dancer Emma Livry and creating the

ballet *Le Papillon* for her in 1860. Livry had a triumph, made poignant by her tragic death after an accident by fire in 1862. Taglioni remained as an "Inspectrice de la danse" in Paris until 1870, and then lived in London, teaching dance and deportment. In 1880 she joined her son in Marseilles—she had married Comte Gilbert de Voisins in 1832 and had a son and daughter, separating from her husband in 1835—and died there four years later.

—Kathrine Sorley Walker

TAGLIONI, Paul (Paolo)

German dancer and ballet master. Born in Vienna, son of dancer and choreographer Filippo Taglioni, and sister of dancer Marie Taglioni, 12 January 1808. Studied with his father, Filippo Taglioni, and with Jean-François Coulon in Paris. Married Amalia (also known as Anna) Galster, 1829: 3 children. Début in pas de deux with sister, Marie Taglioni, Stuttgart, 1825; solo guest dancer, Vienna, 1826–29; dancer, touring America with Amalia Galster, 1839; choreographer, staging first work in Berlin c.1831, and becoming ballet master to Berlin Court Opera; ballet master, Her Majesty's Theatre, London, 1847–51, 1856 and 1857; regular guest ballet master, Vienna, various seasons 1853–74; ballet master, Naples, 1853–56, Berlin Court Opera, 1856–83, La Scala, Milan, 1861–62. Died in Berlin, 6 January 1884.

WORKS

1831 *La Nouvelle Amazône*, Hofoper, Berlin
1832 *Les Jeunes Pensionnaires*, Hofoper, Berlin
1835 *Amors Triumph* (mus. Schmidt), Hofoper, Berlin
1836 *Der arme Fischer* (mus. Schmidt), Hofoper, Berlin
      Undine, die Wassernymphe (mus. Schmidt), Hofoper, Berlin
1838 *La Fille aux roses*, Hofoper, Berlin
1839 *Don Quixote* (mus. Gährich), Hofoper, Berlin
1847 *Thea; ou, La Fée aux fleurs* (mus. Pugni), Her Majesty's Theatre, London (also staged Berlin, 1847)
      Coralia; or, The Inconstant Knight (new version of *Undine*; mus. Pugni), Her Majesty's Theatre, London
1848 *Fiorita et la reine des Elfrides* (mus. Pugni), Her Majesty's Theatre, London
1849 *Electra; ou, La Pléiade perdue* (mus. Pugni), Her Majesty's Theatre, London
      La Prima Ballerina; ou, L'Embuscade (mus. Pugni), Her Majesty's Theatre, London
      Les Plaisirs de l'hiver (mus. Pugni), Her Majesty's Theatre, London
1850 *Les Métamorphoses* (mus. Pugni), Her Majesty's Theatre, London
      Les Grâces (mus. Pugni), Her Majesty's Theatre, London
1851 *L'Île des amours* (mus. Nadaud), Her Majesty's Theatre, London
1852 *Santanella, oder Metamorphosen* (new version of *Les Métamorphoses*; mus. Hertel), Hofoper, Berlin
1854 *Die Lustigen Musketiere* (mus. Hertel), Hoftheater, Vienna
      Alphea (mus. Hertel), Hoftheater, Vienna (restaged London, 1856)

1855 *Ballanda* (mus. Hertel), Hoftheater, Vienna (restaged Berlin, 1857, and Milan, 1863)

1856 *La Bouquetière*, Her Majesty's Theatre, London (possibly first staged London, 1852)

1857 *Die Insel der Liebe* (new production; mus. Strebinger), Hoftheater, Vienna

1858 *Flick und Flocks Abenteuer* (mus. Hertel), Hofoper, Berlin (restaged Milan, 1862, and Vienna, 1865)

1860 *Morgano* (mus. Hertel), La Scala, Milan

1861 *Ellinor; ossia, Vedi Napoli e poi mori* (mus. Hertel), La Scala, Milan

1862 *Le Stelle* (mus. Hertel), La Scala, Milan

1863 *I Due Soci* (mus. Hertel), La Scala, Milan

   Il Ratto di Proserpina (mus. Hertel), La Scala, Milan

   Ercole secondo (mus. Hertel), La Scala, Milan

1864 *La Fille mal gardée* (after Dauberval; new mus. Hertel), Berlin

1865 *Leonilda; o, La Fidanzata del filibustiere* (mus. Giorza), La Scala, Milan

   Sardanapal (mus. Hertel), Hofoper, Berlin (restaged Vienna, 1869)

1867 *Thea; o, La Fata dei Fiori* (new version; mus. Dall'Argine), La Scala, Milan

   Sardanapalo re d'Assiria (mus. Hertel), La Scala, Milan

1869 *Don Parasol* (mus. Hertel), La Scala, Milan

   Fantasca (mus. Hertel), Hofoper, Berlin

1872 *Militaria* (mus. Hertel), Hofoper, Berlin

PUBLICATIONS

Moore, Lillian, "A Dancer's Odyssey", *The American Dancer* (Los Angeles), March 1942

Beaumont, Cyril, *Complete Book of Ballets*, revised edition, London, 1951

Guest, Ivor, *The Romantic Ballet in England*, London, 1954

Beaumont, Cyril, "Taglioni Treasures", *Dancing Times* (London), September 1966

Mezzanotte, Riccardo (ed.), *Il Balletto: Repertorio del teatro di danza dal 1581*, Milan, 1979; as *Phaidon Book of Ballet*, translated by Olive Ordish, London, 1981

*   *   *

Perhaps overshadowed by those of his father and sister, Paul Taglioni's talents were nevertheless typical of the illustrious Taglioni family. He studied dancing with his father, Filippo Taglioni, and with the French dancer Coulon, during the Taglioni company's visit to Paris; and he made his début in *Zemire et Azor*, a pas de deux with his sister, Marie Taglioni, in Stuttgart in 1825. He was to partner her for several years, appearing in Vienna, Munich, Paris, and Berlin with great success.

In 1829 Paul married the ballerina Amalia Galster in Berlin, a city in which he had received a particularly warm welcome. He settled permanently in Germany, although he was to make many guest visits throughout Europe, whether as a dancer or choreographer, and was even to tour America with his wife in 1839. With Berlin more or less as his base, Taglioni served various appointments as ballet master to leading opera houses in Vienna, London, Naples, and Milan. In 1856 he became ballet master of the Berlin Court Opera, and remained in Berlin until his death, nearly 30 years later.

Paul Taglioni was undoubtedly a talented choreographer, whose entirely respectable but non-brilliant career may have suffered simply from the fact that he was not born a generation earlier. Unlike his father and his sister, who came to fame during the very heyday of the Romantic ballet (and indeed are often jointly credited with creating the genre), Paul was at the height of his powers when ballet in general was in a decline, and when audiences required increasingly banal spectacle. For example, when Paul arrived as ballet master at Her Majesty's Theatre in London, he could only seem a pale successor to his great predecessor Jules Perrot. Where Perrot had enjoyed fanatical ballet audiences, generous budgeting (from theatre manager Benjamin Lumley), and some of the world's greatest ballerinas as subjects (Cerrito, Grisi, Taglioni, Essler, Grahn), Paul Taglioni had altogether sparser resources. Thus, as Ivor Guest has written, "Paul Taglioni . . . was a choreographer of outstanding qualities, but he was unfortunate to lack those advantages which had assisted Perrot in his first years at Her Majesty's. . . . Paul Taglioni had to be content with working on a smaller scale, and with a somewhat less brilliant palette."

Paul Taglioni answered the demands of the day by adjusting his ballets to the changing tastes. Mime, the art of silent acting which had been so highly valued in opera and ballet of the earlier nineteenth century, was to make way for a greater emphasis on dance and dance technique. Audiences were no longer interested in dramatic or "pantomime" ballets, and in London anyway, Paul Taglioni's ballets became increasingly plotless, to the point where lengthy divertissement, pure and simple, was the substance—as in the extremely popular 1849 *Les Plaisirs de l'hiver*, which made no pretence at having a story-line, and was simply a series of enchanting scenes, like moving tableaux.

He also responded to audiences' needs for other stage effects to heighten the spectacle. Among the 40 or so ballets that Paul Taglioni composed, *Electra* and *Les Plaisirs de l'hiver* stand out as examples of his penchant for new technical devices. *Electra* featured electric lighting; according to one critic, "the audience was mute with astonishment at this startling sight". In *Les Plaisirs de l'hiver*, incongruously staged during a summer heatwave, the dancers imitated the feats of ice-skaters on roller skates to "constant laughter and applause", though the use of electric lighting appears to have been rather less successful in this production.

Until 1866 Taglioni's daughter Marie took the leading ballerina role in most of her father's ballets; an extremely successful dancer in her own right, she is often confused with her more illustrious aunt of the same name. Paul Taglioni's younger daughter, Augusta, became an actress, while his son, Charles, broke with family tradition by entering the diplomatic service.

Paul Taglioni retired from the Berlin Opera on 1 October 1883. He died on 6 January 1884, a successful ballet master at a time when the stage art of ballet was in transition.

—Jessica Griffin

TAGLIONI, Salvatore

Italian dancer, choreographer, and teacher. Born in Palermo, 1789. Studied probably with father, Carlo Taglioni, and later with Jean-François Coulon, Paris, 1806. Married dancer Adélaide Perraud. Dancer, performing in Lyons and Bordeaux, c.1806; returned to Italy, performing in various Italian cities including Turin, often with wife Adélaide Perraud; founder (with Louis Henry) and teacher, Ballet School of the Teatro San Carlo, Naples, from 1812; ballet master, Teatro San Carlo, Naples, also working at La Scala, Milan, Teatro Regio, Turin, and several other Italian theatres; choreographed over 200 ballets. Died in Naples, 1868.

WORKS

1817 *Atalanta ed Ippomene* (mus. Gallenberg), Teatro San Carlo, Naples

Il Principe fortunio; ossia, Le Tre Melarance, La Scala, Milan

1819 *La Conquista di Malacca; ossia, I Portoghesi nell'Indie* (mus. Gallenberg, Mercadante), Teatro San Carlo, Naples

1820 *Castore e Polluce* (mus. Brambilla), La Scala, Milan

Otranto liberata (mus. Raimondi, Carlini), Teatro San Carlo, Naples

Il Narciso corretto (mus. various), Teatro San Carlo, Naples

1822 *Il Natale di Venere* (mus. Carlini), Teatro San Carlo, Naples

Il Seduttore, Teatro San Carlo, Naples

La Promessa mantenuta (mus. Raimondi), Teatro San Carlo, Naples

1823 *Sesostri* (mus. Carlini), Teatro San Carlo, Naples

Attide e Cloe (mus. Carlini), Teatro San Carlo, Naples

Tippoo-Saeb (mus. Carlini), Teatro San Carlo, Naples

1824 *Bianca di Messina* (mus. Brambilla), Teatro San Carlo, Naples

1826 *L'Ira di Achille* (mus. Gallenberg), La Scala, Milan

1827 *Ines de Castro; ossia, Pietro di Portogallo* (mus. Mandacini), La Scala, Milan

Pelia e Mileto (mus. Pugni), La Scala, Milan

Eutichio della Castagna; ossia, La casa disabitata (mus. Pugni), La Scala, Milan

1827/ *Il Paria* (mus. Brambilla), La Scala, Milan
28

1828 *Il Flauto incantato* (mus. Mercadante), La Scala, Milan

Amore filosofo (mus. Mandanici), Teatro Fondo, Naples

Il Serto alloro (mus. Mandanici), Teatro Fondo, Naples

1829 *Le Montagne russe*, Teatro Fondo, Naples

1830 *La Prigione di Guido; ossia, Pelia e Mileto* (mus. various), Teatro Fondo, Naples (restaged as *Prigioni scatenati, La Prigionia di Dario, Prigioniere, I Prigioniere d'amore, Prigioniere di Cipro, Prigionieri usciti in libertà*)

1831 *Le Convulsioni musicali*, Teatro Regio, Turin

1832 *La Festa di ballo in maschera* (mus. Mercadante), Teatro Regio, Turin

Il Collegiale in vacanza, Teatro Regio, Turin

Romanow (mus. Mandanici), Teatro San Carlo, Naples

1833 *L'Ombra di Tsi-Ven; ossia, La Costanza premiata* (mus. Mandanici), Teatro San Carlo, Naples

1834 *I Saraceni in Sicilia* (mus. Mandanici), Teatro Fondo, Naples

1836 *Il Ritorno di Ulisse* (mus. Romani), Teatro San Carlo, Naples

I Promessi sposi, La Scala, Milan

1837 *Amore e Psiche* (mus. Romani), Teatro San Carlo, Naples

1838 *Le Nozze campestri*, Teatro San Carlo, Naples

La Notte di un proscritto; ossia, L'Ospitalità scozzese (mus. Gallenberg), Teatro San Carlo, Naples

Faust (mus. Gallenberg, Aspa), Teatro San Carlo, Naples

1839 *Il Perdono* (mus. Rossini's *Guglielmo Tell*), Teatro San Carlo, Naples

Amore alla prova (mus. Gabrielli), Teatro San Carlo, Naples

1840 *L'Assedio di Sciraz; ossia, L'Amor materno* (mus. Gabrielli), La Scala, Milan

Il Duca di Ravenna (mus. Gabrielli), Teatro San Carlo, Naples

Basilio III Demetriovitz (mus. Gabrielli), Teatro San Carlo, Naples

Un Episodio della campagna di Costantina (mus. various), Teatro San Carlo, Naples

1841 *Marco Visconti* (mus. various), Teatro San Carlo, Naples

La Foresta d'Hermanstadt (mus. various), Teatro San Carlo, Naples

1841/ *La Nozze di Romanow* (after d'Amore), Teatro Concordia, Cremona
42

1842 *La Zingara* (mus. Gabrielli), Teatro San Carlo, Naples

1843/ *Le Avventure di Don Chisciotte*, Teatro Regio, Turin
44

1846 *Guglielmo di Provenza* (mus. Graviller), Teatro Fondo, Naples

Margherita Pusterla (mus. Fornesini), Teatro San Carlo, Naples

L'Eroe cinese; ossia, Fedeltà e clemenza (mus. Fornesini), Teatro San Carlo, Naples

1849 *Bradamante e Russiero* (mus. Gabrielli), Teatro San Carlo, Naples

I Candiano (mus. Gabrielli), Teatro San Carlo, Naples

1850 *Il Ritorno di Alfonso d'Aragona dalla guerra d'Otranto* (mus. Fornesino), Teatro San Carlo, Naples

La Fedeltà premiata (mus. Gabrielli), Teatro San Carlo, Naples

1851 *La Stella del marinaio* (mus. Gabrielli), Teatro San Carlo, Naples

1852 *Bassora; ossia, Il Fantasma d'Arafat* (mus. Giaquinto), Teatro San Carlo, Naples

1853 *Olfa* (mus. Giaquinto), Teatro San Carlo, Naples

1854 *Hulda* (with A. Fuchs; mus. Giaquinto), Teatro San Carlo, Naples

L'Araba (mus. Giaquinto), Teatro San Carlo, Naples (staged Teatro Pergole, Florence, 1857/58)

1855 *Noama* (mus. Giaquinto), Teatro San Carlo, Naples

Zilmè; o, La Dea delle dovizie (mus. Giaquinto), Teatro San Carlo, Naples

1856 *Isaura; ossia, La Protetta delle Fate* (after Perrot's *La Belle au bois dormant*), Teatro San Carlo, Naples

Lady Enrichetta; o, La Fantesca di Greenwich (mus. Giaquinto), Teatro San Carlo, Naples

1860 *Rita* (mus. Giaquinto), Teatro San Carlo, Naples

1861 *Il Figlio dello Shak* (mus. Giaquinto), Teatro San Carlo, Naples

PUBLICATIONS

Croce, Benedetto, *I Teatri di Napoli—Secolo XV–XVIII*, Naples, 1891

Carrieri, Raffaele, *La Danza in Italia 1600–1900*, Milan, 1946

Gatti, Carlo, *Il Teatro alla Scala 1778–1963*, Milan, 1964

Winter, Marian Hannah, *The Pre-Romantic Ballet*, London, 1974

*   *   *

The career of Salvatore Taglioni is notable today for two major reasons: first, he was one of the leading members of the great Taglioni ballet dynasty, which produced choreographers Filippo and Paul Taglioni and the great ballerina Marie Taglioni; and second, he was one of history's most prolific choreographers, staging well over 200 ballets during his active career as a ballet master.

Salvatore Taglioni's career was concentrated almost entirely in Naples, one of the most important artistic centres of Europe during the eighteenth and nineteenth centuries. The Teatro San Carlo, internationally famous as an opera house, was the home of Salvatore Taglioni's ballet company and school (founded in 1812), and while ballet has remained a poor cousin to opera in Italy up until this day, it reached perhaps its greatest heights in Naples during Salvatore Taglioni's reign. His choreography was highly acclaimed in his adopted city (he was actually born in Palermo), and the Teatro San Carlo was to play an important role in the international careers of many other dancers—in particular, the ballerina Carlotta Grisi, whose career began in Naples.

Salvatore Taglioni had been a successful dancer himself, performing in partnership with his wife, Adélaide Perraud, often in Turin. Like his brother Filippo, Salvatore had trained with the great teacher Coulon when the Taglioni family was in Paris, and he brought his knowledge of the French school to Naples when he became director of the school as well as chief ballet master at the theatre.

Most of Salvatore Taglioni's ballets took their inspiration from historical or literary subjects, a notable example being the ballet based on Alessandro Manzoni's novel I Promessi sposi. Mythological subjects, in keeping with popular stage subject-matter of the day, figured prominently, but were undoubtedly treated with the originality and creativity with which Salvatore is credited today. Although ballet masters throughout Europe inevitably borrowed one another's ideas and plots for ballets, it is unlikely that Salvatore was the "inveterate plagiarizer" (to quote Marian Hannah Winter) that his brother Filippo was said to be.

Salvatore Taglioni staged works in Milan, Turin, and Florence as well as Naples, and continued choreographing up until his seventies, dying at the ripe old age of 79. Sadly, he is said to have died in misery: he was shot by mistake during the political upheavals of 1848, and then suffered further injury from a fall down the stairs, thereby never able to return to his active post at the Teatro San Carlo. His children carried on the Taglioni name, however; his daughter Luisa Taglioni became a dancer at the Paris Opéra, and his son Fernando Taglioni was a successful composer.

—Elizabeth Hudson

TALLCHIEF, Maria

American dancer, teacher, and ballet director. Born in Fairfax, Oklahoma, 24 January 1925. Studied with Ernest Belcher, Bronislava Nijinska, and David Lichine, California; also studied at the School of American Ballet, New York. Married (1) choreographer George Balanchine, 1946 (annulled 1951); (2) Henry Paschen, 1957: one daughter. Dancer, becoming soloist, Ballet Russe de Monte Carlo, 1942–47; guest artist, Paris Opéra Ballet, Summer 1947; leading ballerina, Ballet Society (later New York City Ballet), 1947–65, creating numerous Balanchine roles; also guest ballerina, (American) Ballet Theatre, 1949, 1960–61, Ballet Russe de Monte Carlo, 1954–55, Hamburg Ballet, 1965; also appeared in films, including in Hollywood film Million Dollar Mermaid (dir. Le Roy, 1952); artistic director and teacher, Chicago Lyric Opera Ballet, from 1975; founder and artistic director, Chicago City Ballet, 1981–87. Recipient: Achievement Award, Women's National Press Club, 1953; Title of Honorary Princess, Osage Tribe, 1953; Dance Magazine Award, 1960; Capezio Award, 1965; Distinguished Service Award, University of Oklahoma, 1972.

ROLES

1942   Ensemble in *Chopin Concerto* (Nijinska), Ballet Russe de Monte Carlo

1943   Principal dancer in *Étude* (Nijinska), Ballet Russe de Monte Carlo, Cleveland

Ensemble (cr) in *The Cuckold's Fair* (Lopez), Ballet Russe de Monte Carlo, Cleveland

Ensemble (cr) in *Ancient Russia* (Nijinska), Ballet Russe de Monte Carlo, Cleveland

1944   Variation IV (cr) in *Danses Concertantes* (Balanchine), Ballet Russe de Monte Carlo, New York

Danse indienne (cr) in *Le Bourgeois Gentilhomme* (Balanchine), Ballet Russe de Monte Carlo, New York

Principal dancer in *Ballet Imperial* (Balanchine), Ballet Russe de Monte Carlo, Cleveland

1946   Fairy in *Le Baiser de la fée* (Balanchine), Ballet Russe de Monte Carlo, New York

Lead Can-Can dancer in *Gaîté Parisienne* (Massine), Ballet Russe de Monte Carlo

Coquette (cr) in *Night Shadow* (*La Sonnambula*; Balanchine), Ballet Russe de Monte Carlo, New York

Pas classique hongrois (cr) in *Raymonda* (new production; Balanchine, Danilova after Petipa), Ballet Russe de Monte Carlo, New York

1947   Ballerina in *Divertimento* (Balanchine), Ballet Society, New York

Principal dancer (cr) in *Symphonie Concertante* (Balanchine), Ballet Society, New York

1948   First Movement (cr) in *Symphony in C* (new production of *Le Palais de cristal*; Balanchine), Ballet Society, New York

Earth (cr) in *Capricorn Concerto* (Bolender), Ballet Society, New York

Eurydice (cr) in *Orpheus* (Balanchine), Ballet Society, New York

Sanguinic in *The Four Temperaments* (Balanchine), New York City Ballet, New York

1949   Bluebird in *Princess Aurora* (divertissements from *The Sleeping Beauty*; Petipa, staged Balanchine), Ballet Theatre, Chicago

Kitri in *Don Quixote Pas de deux* (after Petipa), Ballet Theatre, tour

Black Swan Pas de deux from *Swan Lake* (Petipa), Ballet Theatre, tour

An Episode in His Past in *Lilac Garden* (Tudor), Ballet Theatre, tour

Principal dancer (lead couple) in *Theme and Variations* (Balanchine), Ballet Theatre, New York

Principal dancer (cr) in *The Guests* (Robbins), New York City Ballet, New York

Title role (cr) in *Firebird* (Balanchine), New York City Ballet, New York

Prélude (cr) in *Bourreé Fantasque* (Balanchine), New York City Ballet, New York

1950   The Siren in *Prodigal Son* (Balanchine), New York City Ballet, New York

"Hot Dogs" (cr) in *Jones Beach* (Balanchine), New York City Ballet, New York

Ballerina (cr) in *Sylvia: Pas de Deux* (Balanchine), New York City Ballet, New York

1951   Waltz from *Naïla* in *Music and Dance* (Balanchine), New York City Ballet and School of American Ballet, Carnegie Hall, New York

Principal dancer (cr) in (*Minkus*) *Pas de Trois* (Balanchine), New York City Ballet, New York

Maria Tallchief as the Firebird, 1949

Principal dancer (cr) in *Capriccio Brillante* (Balanchine), New York City Ballet, New York

Principal dancer (cr) in *A la Françaix* (Balanchine), New York City Ballet, New York

Terpsichore in *Apollo, Leader of the Muses* (revised staging of *Apollon musagète*; Balanchine), New York City Ballet, New York

Odette, Queen of the Swans (cr) in *Swan Lake* (new production, one-act version; Balanchine after Ivanov), New York City Ballet, New York

1952   Principal dancer (cr) in *Caracole* (Balanchine), New York City Ballet, New York

Principal dancer (cr) in *Scotch Symphony* (Balanchine), New York City Ballet, New York

Columbine (cr) in *Harlequinade Pas de Deux* (Balanchine), New York City Ballet, New York

1953   Title role (cr) in *The Filly* (Bolender), New York City Ballet, New York

1954   Sugar Plum Fairy (cr) in *The Nutcracker* (Balanchine), New York City Ballet, New York

1955   Principal dancer (cr) in *Pas de Dix* (Balanchine), New York City Ballet, New York

1956   Principal dancer (cr) in *Allegro Brillante* (Balanchine), New York City Ballet, New York

1958   Principal dancer (cr) in *Gounod Symphony* (Balanchine), New York City Ballet, New York

1960   Danzas Sinfónicas (cr; chor. Balanchine) in *Panamerica* (Balanchine, Contreras, Moncion, Taras, d'Amboise), New York City Ballet, New York

Title role in *Miss Julie* (Cullberg), American Ballet Theatre

Caroline in *Jardin aux lilas* (Tudor), American Ballet Theatre

Ellida in *Lady from the Sea* (Cullberg), American Ballet Theatre

1961   Principal dancer in *Études* (Lander), American Ballet Theatre

1964   Queen of the Morphides in *Piège de Lumière* (Taras), New York City Ballet, New York

Other roles include: for Ballet Russe de Monte Carlo—Zobéïde in *Schéhérazade* (Fokine), Waltz, Mazurka in *Les Sylphides* (Fokine), principal dancer in *Serenade* (Balanchine), leading roles in *The Snow Maiden* (Nijinska), *Virginia Sampler* (Bettis); for New York City Opera—Tavern Ballet in *Carmen* (opera; mus. Bizet, chor. Balanchine), Triumphal Ballet in *Aïda* (opera; mus. Verdi, chor. Balanchine); for New York City Ballet—Sacred Love in *Illuminations* (Ashton), Eighth Waltz and La Valse in *La Valse* (Balanchine).

PUBLICATIONS

By Tallchief:

Interview in Tracy, Robert, *Balanchine's Ballerinas*, New York, 1983

Interview in Gruen, John, "Tallchief and the Chicago City Ballet", *Dance Magazine* (New York), December 1984

About Tallchief:

Owen, Walter, "The Dancing Tallchiefs—Maria and Marjorie", *Dance Magazine* (New York), September 1945

Chujoy, Anatole, *The New York City Ballet*, New York, 1953

Davidson, Gladys, *Ballet Biographies*, revised edition, London, 1954

Crowle, Pigeon, "Ballerina and American Princess", *Ballet Today* (London), March 1955

Crowle, Pigeon, "Maria Tallchief: Her Early Years", *Dance Magazine* (New York), February 1956

Maynard, Olga, *The American Ballet*, Philadelphia, 1959

Taper, Bernard, *Balanchine*, New York, 1960

Maynard, Olga, *Bird of Fire: The Story of Maria Tallchief*, New York, 1961

Terry, Walter, "Maria Tallchief and the Maryinsky Tradition", *Theatre Arts* (New York), September 1961

Meyers, E., *Maria Tallchief*, New York, 1966

Reynolds, Nancy, *Repertory in Review*, New York, 1977

Anderson, Jack, *The One and Only: The Ballet Russe de Monte Carlo*, London, 1981

Denby, Edwin, *Dance Writings*, edited by Robert Cornfield and William Mackay, New York, 1986

*   *   *

Maria Tallchief was born on an Indian reservation; her father was an American Indian of the Osage tribe, and her mother was Scotch-Irish. In her early childhood the family re-located to Los Angeles, where the children started dance and piano lessons. It was in Los Angeles that she discovered the ballet teacher who was to mould her into one of America's most well-known prima ballerinas. With five full years of study, Bronislava Nijinska prepared the young dancer for her early career with Serge Denham's Ballet Russe de Monte Carlo. With the Ballet Russe she achieved soloist status, dancing *Serenade*, *Le Baiser de la fée*, *Gaîté Parisienne*, and *Schéhérazade*.

The artist most closely linked with Tallchief's exceptional development was, of course, George Balanchine, whom she married in 1946. For many years she was his muse. With her incomparable technique and musicality, she was given many choreographic gifts by Balanchine, including *Symphonie Concertante*, *Sylvia: Pas de deux*, *Orpheus*, *Night Shadow*, *The Four Temperaments*, *The Nutcracker*, *Scotch Symphony*, and *Firebird*.

Tallchief had been noticed by Balanchine while performing in New York with the Ballet Russe; they then worked together at the Paris Opéra as guests during the summer of 1947. Tallchief was offered a position with Ballet Society, Balanchine's young company which was to become the New York City Ballet. It was a very special era in the life of the company, and Balanchine was in full glory choreographically. The young New York City Ballet was small, and a principal dancer was in great demand, performing up to eight ballets in a week. Such conditions not only developed the ballerina's impressive versatility, but also contributed to Tallchief's rise as a popular figure in the dance. Tallchief was a model of dedication to her form; her life revolved around her classes and performances. She was given the great ballet roles and was partnered by many of the great male dancers of twentieth-century classical ballet. Her distinguished partners included André Eglevsky in numerous Balanchine ballets, Nicholas Magallanes in *Orpheus*, Erik Bruhn in *Miss Julie*, and Frank Moncion in *Firebird*.

Firebird became Tallchief's signature ballet internationally. Her stamina, attack, and musicality made her ideal for the tremendously demanding role that Balanchine created for her. It was a significant development for the choreographer and his ballerina, and had the additional bonus of enjoying popular appeal. Critical acclaim was equally enthusiastic. Dance critic Walter Terry put it simply, saying, "Tallchief gave a performance of historical proportions." John Martin, reviewing the first performances of *Firebird*, wrote, "Undoubtedly Tallchief has been [Balanchine's] inspiration. Hers is the key role, and he has built for her astonishing virtuosity almost as if he were challenging it." The ballet was obviously one of powerful artistic collaboration between choreographer and ballerina, and Martin goes on to explain,

> Yet there is nothing of the circus about it; there are fabulous acrobatic tricks in it, but they are invariably justified by the fact that the role is that of a magic bird who has been captured and is struggling for her freedom. Tallchief keeps this always before us, and as she gives us each of the choreographer's inventions, he is ready with another for her, as if he were actually feeding creatively on her performance. Certainly we have never seen a Firebird performed and choreographed with such uncanny unity.

Firebird was followed some five years later by another New York City Ballet classic, *The Nutcracker*, in which Tallchief, as a poised and commanding Sugar Plum Fairy (partnered by Nicholas Magallanes), contributed as much to the financial as to the artistic success of Balanchine's version of this classic Christmas ballet, for it was to become one of the most reliable box-office successes of the fledgling New York City Ballet.

For Tallchief, experiencing Balanchine's shift in artistic infatuation was undoubtedly painful. She had dedicated herself completely to working with him and performing the many works of his that had become her signature pieces; and she had shown absolute, unquestioning faith in his decisions. He had reshaped her style and execution, crafting the magnificent technique associated with her performance of the Balanchine repertoire, and she was considered the perfect embodiment of his neo-classical style. Part of Balanchine's genius was in allowing each ballerina to do what she did best, thus developing a personal style and range of roles. He knew how to capitalize on the individuality of his ballerinas, and to make them look wonderful. The choreographer's shift in attention to Tanaquil Le Clerq meant the end of a steady stream of ballets for Maria Tallchief, although she continued to create various Balanchine roles until 1960.

In 1955 and 1956, she was a guest artist with the Ballet Russe de Monte Carlo, reportedly receiving the highest salary in ballet history. In 1956 she remarried, taking a maternity leave in 1958—her only leave from the rigours of a professional ballet career. Two years later, Tallchief joined American Ballet Theatre. While with that company she danced *Miss Julie*, *Jardin aux lilas*, and others, joining them for both a tour of the USSR and the United States.

Maria Tallchief had no desire to dance beyond her prime, so she retired from her performing career in 1966. She returned to Chicago, and out of her association with the Lyric Opera Ballet attempted to craft an enterprise in the image of the New York City Ballet. Perhaps the most unfortunate decision of her professional career was the creation of the ill-fated Chicago City Ballet. While strong as a teacher and coach, she lacked the temperament and skills required of an artistic director. Eventually Paul Mejia became resident choreographer, but in spite of tremendous support from the critics in the early years, the company collapsed in 1987. Ms. Tallchief has since renewed her alliance with Lyric Opera Ballet School.

—Susan Lee
with Virginia Christian

TALLCHIEF, Marjorie

American dancer and ballet director. Born in Denver, Colorado, 19 October 1926. Studied with Bronislava Nijinska and David Lichine, Los Angeles; later studied with Olga Preobrazhenska, Paris. Married dancer and choreographer George Skibine, 1947: two (twin) sons, Georges and Alexandre b. 1952. Dancer, Ballet Theatre (later American Ballet Theatre), 1944–46, and Original Ballet Russe, 1946–47; soloist, becoming ballerina, Grand Ballet de Monte Carlo (later Grand Ballet du Marquis de Cuevas), 1947–57; guest ballerina, Ruth Page's Chicago Opera Ballet, 1956, 1958; première danseuse étoile, Paris Opéra Ballet, 1957–62; guest ballerina, Teatro Colón, Buenos Aires, 1961; ballerina, Harkness Ballet, 1964–66; associate director, Dallas Ballet, 1967–81; also teacher: director, ballet school of the Chicago City Ballet, 1981–88; artistic director, Harid Conservatory, Boca Raton, Florida, from 1989. Recipient: Title of Chevalier du Nicham-Iftikar.

ROLES

1944	Foutté competition in *Graduation Ball* (Lichine), Ballet Theatre, Montreal
	Nurse in *Romeo and Juliet* (Tudor), Ballet Theatre, Montreal
	Myrtha, Queen of the Wilis in *Giselle* (Petipa after Coralli, Perrot; staged Dolin), Ballet Theatre, Boston
1945	A Peasant Girl (cr) in *Harvest Time* (Nijinska), Ballet Theatre, New York
	A Bacchante (cr) in *Undertow* (Tudor), Ballet Theatre, New York
	Hairdresser/Christmas Shopper (cr) in *Gift of the Magi* (Semenoff), Ballet Theatre, Boston
	Medusa in *Undertow* (Tudor), Ballet Theatre
1945/46	Jitterbug in *On Stage!* (Kidd), Ballet Theatre
1946	Carlotta Grisi in *Pas de Quatre* (Dolin), Original Ballet Russe
	Dancer in *Constantia* (Dollar), Original Ballet Russe
1947	Pas de cinq in *Noir et blanc* (Lifar), Grand Ballet de Monte Carlo, Monte Carlo
	Mazurka, Pas de deux in *Les Sylphides* (Fokine), Grand Ballet de Monte Carlo, Paris
	Psyche in *Brahms Variations* (Nijinska), Grand Ballet de Monte Carlo, Paris
	Adagietto ("La Garçonne") in *Les Biches* (Nijinska), Grand Ballet de Monte Carlo, Paris
	Diana in *Aubade* (Lifar), Grand Ballet de Monte Carlo, Paris
	Principal dancer in *Pictures at an Exhibition* (Nijinska), Grand Ballet de Monte Carlo, Paris
1947/48	Prince's Sister in *Sebastian* (Caton), Grand Ballet de Monte Carlo, Monte Carlo
1948	Principal dancer in *Concerto Barocco* (Balanchine), Grand Ballet de Monte Carlo, Monte Carlo
	The Coquette in *La Sonnambula* (*Night Shadow*; Balanchine), Grand Ballet de Monte Carlo, London
	Principal dancer (cr) in *Pas de trois classique* (Balanchine), Grand Ballet de Monte Carlo, London
1949	Principal dancer in *Designs with Strings* (Taras), Grand Ballet de Monte Carlo, Cairo
	La Chimière in *Tristan fou* (Massine), Grand Ballet de Monte Carlo, Barcelona
	Pas de deux from *Don Quixote* (Obukhov after Petipa), Grand Ballet de Monte Carlo, Festival of Holland
1950	Princess Aurora in *Aurora's Wedding* (from *The Sleeping Beauty*; after Petipa), Grand Ballet du Marquis de Cuevas, Monte Carlo
	The Duchess in *Del Amor e la muerte* (Ricarda), Grand

Ballet de Monte Carlo, Barcelona
Constanza in *The Good-Humoured Ladies* (Massine),
Grand Ballet de Monte Carlo, Edinburgh
The Ballerina in *Petrushka* (Fokine), Grand Ballet de
Monte Carlo, Edinburgh
1951   The Sleepwalker in *La Sonnambula* (*Night Shadow*;
Balanchine), Grand Ballet de Monte Carlo, Cannes
Principal dancer in *Bal des jeunes filles* (Taras), Grand
Ballet de Monte Carlo, Cannes
Title role (cr) in *Annabel Lee* (Skibine), Grand Ballet du
Marquis de Cuevas, Deauville
Circassian Girl (cr) in *Le Prisonnier du Caucase*
(Skibine), Grand Ballet du Marquis de Cuevas, Paris
Odette in *Swan Lake*, Act II (after Ivanov), Grand
Ballet du Marquis de Cuevas
1953   The Duchess (cr) in *L'Ange gris* (Skibine), Grand Ballet
du Marquis de Cuevas, Deauville
1954   "She" (The White Mare) in *Idylle* (Skibine), Grand
Ballet du Marquis de Cuevas, Paris
Principal dancer in *Concerto de Chopin* (Nijinska),
Grand Ballet du Marquis de Cuevas, Deauville
Title role in *Giselle* (Petipa after Coralli, Perrot), Grand
Ballet du Marquis de Cuevas, Biarritz
Principal dancer in *Bolero* (Nijinska), Grand Ballet du
Marquis de Cuevas, Paris
L'Amour (cr) in *La Reine insolente* (Skibine), Grand
Ballet du Marquis de Cuevas, Metz
1955   Juliette (cr) in *Roméo et Juliette* (Skibine, Skouratoff,
Taras, Golovine), Grand Ballet du Marquis de
Cuevas, Paris
Sheila (cr) in *Le Prince du désert* (Skibine), Grand Ballet
du Marquis de Cuevas, Paris
1956   Title role in *The Merry Widow* (Page), Chicago Opera
Ballet, Chicago
Principal dancer in *Revenge* (Page), Chicago Opera
Ballet, Chicago
1957   The Bride in *Les Noces fantastiques* (Lifar), Paris Opéra
Ballet, Paris
Title role in *L'Oiseau de feu* (Lifar), Paris Opéra Ballet,
Paris
Principal dancer (cr) in *Concerto* (Skibine), Opéra de
Strasbourg, Strasbourg
1958   Estelle (cr) in *Les Fâcheuses Rencontres* (Skibine),
Edinburgh International Ballet, Edinburgh
1959   Title role (cr) in *Camille* (Page), Chicago Opera Ballet,
Columbia, Missouri
Vera (cr) in *Conte cruel* (Skibine), Paris Opéra Ballet,
Paris
1960   Principal dancer in *Études* (Lander), Paris Opéra Ballet,
Paris
Title role in *Giselle* (Petipa after Coralli, Perrot; staged
Lifar), Paris Opéra Ballet, Paris
1961   Ballerina in *Pastorale* (Skibine), Paris Opéra Ballet,
Paris
Principal dancer (cr) in *Metamorphoses* (Skibine),
Teatro Colón, Buenos Aires
1965   Principal dancer (cr) in *Scottish Fantasy* (Bruhn),
Harkness Ballet, Cannes
Title role (cr) in *Ariadne* (Ailey), Harkness Ballet, Paris
1966   Principal dancer (cr) in *Sarabande* (Skibine), Harkness
Ballet, Temple, Arizona

PUBLICATIONS

By Tallchief:
Interview in "An Interview with Marjorie Tallchief and

George Skibine", *Dance Magazine* (New York), December
1956

About Tallchief:
Owen, Walter, "The Dancing Tallchiefs—Maria and Mar-
jorie", *Dance Magazine* (New York), September 1945
Beaumont, Cyril, "Grand Ballet de Monte Carlo", *Ballet*
(London), October 1948
Amberg, George, *Ballet in America*, New York, 1949
Austin, Richard, "Marjorie Tallchief", *Ballet Today* (London),
March 1954
Davidson, Gladys, *Ballet Biographies*, revised edition, London,
1954
Glotz, Michel, *Marjorie Tallchief*, Paris, 1955
Skibine, George, "Joies et ... regrets", *La Danse* (Paris),
January 1956
Nemenschousky, L., *A Day with Marjorie Tallchief and George
Skibine*, London, 1960
Roberts, Sonia, "The Career of Marjorie Tallchief", *Ballet
Today* (London), April 1962
"The New Harkness Ballet", *Dancing Times* (London), April
1965

*   *   *

Marjorie Tallchief, younger sister of New York City Ballet
ballerina (and former Balanchine wife) Maria Tallchief, is
perhaps not as well known in America as her elder sister; but in
her time she enjoyed great popularity and critical acclaim in
Europe, where she performed as a leading dancer with the
glamorous company of the flamboyant Chilean-born impresario, the Marquis George de Cuevas. The Grand Ballet de
Monte Carlo, which eventually took the name of its director
and chief supporter to become Le Grand Ballet du Marquis de
Cuevas, performed regularly in its original base in Monaco, but
also toured throughout France, Europe, South America, and
the United States. After a ten-year career with this company
(which disbanded a few years later in 1962), Tallchief was
invited to join the Paris Opéra Ballet as "étoile", the first
American to be so honoured. It was a tribute to her position as
an honorary European as much as to her impressive technique
and artistry.

In the early days of her career, Tallchief had performed as a
soloist with the newly formed Ballet Theatre. A few important
roles came her way, such as the fouetté dancer in David
Lichine's *Graduation Ball* (high-speed fouettés, such as in the
famous Black Swan solo, became something of a trademark for
Tallchief). She also performed in ballets by Antony Tudor and
by her one-time teacher Bronislava Nijinska; but her greatest
breakthrough came with her performance, while still in her
teens, in the role of Myrtha, Queen of the Wilis in *Giselle*.
Although she was later to perform the central role of Giselle,
considered by many to be the pinnacle of a ballerina's career,
Tallchief herself admitted that Giselle was not her best role: the
imperious poise and dramatic presence of Myrtha, rather than
the frail, ethereal delicacy of Giselle, was much more of a
natural role for a "statuesque" dancer like Tallchief, as she
herself wisely saw.

After leaving Ballet Theatre, Tallchief danced briefly with
de Basil's Original Ballet Russe, but it was only when she joined
the Grand Ballet de Monte Carlo that her position as a bona
fide ballerina was established. She danced successfully in
Lifar's *Noir et blanc* and in Fokine's *Les Sylphides* in her first
year; and she attracted much positive critical attention with

her performance as "La Garçonne" in Nijinska's witty and enigmatic drawing-room ballet, *Les Biches*. Already on her way to becoming a virtuoso, Tallchief also had a capacity to perform with a certain air of cool detachment, and this, combined with her easy control of Nijinska's tricky choreography, suited the central role of *Les Biches* perfectly.

In 1948, George Balanchine came to Monte Carlo to restage two of his ballets for the de Cuevas company, and to create a new work, *Pas de trois classique*, which had its premiere in London some months later. Marjorie Tallchief danced a ballerina role in *Concerto Barocco*, took over what had been her sister's part (the "Coquette") in *La Sonnambula*, and created one of the two ballerina roles in Balanchine's Petipa-inspired tribute to Minkus, the *Pas de trois classique*. Two other technical wizards, Rosella Hightower and André Eglevsky, danced alongside Tallchief in this exciting display piece, which drew on Petipa's pas de trois from *Paquita*. New York critics, seeing the piece performed by the New York City Ballet some years later, called it "a spectacular tour de force", and its inspiration undoubtedly came as much from the outstanding virtuosity of its three original performers as from the Petipa original. Tallchief was to follow this with impressive performances in other strong classical roles, such as Odile, Kitri in the *Don Quixote* Pas de deux, and Aurora.

In some ways, Tallchief's virtuosity might almost be considered her greatest obstacle as well as her greatest strength, for she was frequently criticized for being too much of a technician, and not much else. British critic Cyril Beaumont, while commenting on Tallchief's elevation, strength, and brilliant pointe-work, found her style "cold and impersonal", while American critic Edwin Denby complained as early as 1945 about the dancer's "insistent self-assertiveness". But Tallchief undoubtedly improved her style, developing greater dramatic awareness and lyrical grace. She moved successfully from the Coquette to the far more ethereal role of the Sleepwalker in *La Sonnambula*, and she gave a moving interpretation of the role of Juliet in a 1955 version of the Shakespeare story. Indeed, Arnold Haskell was later to declare Marjorie Tallchief as ". . . to my mind one of the most lyrical of American dancers".

A significant factor in the development of Marjorie Tallchief's career was the presence of dancer and choreographer George Skibine, whom she married soon after joining the de Cuevas company in 1947. For his wife Skibine choreographed some of his more memorable works, such as *Annabel Lee*, a pas de deux based on the Edgar Allan Poe poem, and *Idylle*, a touching pas de trois telling the story of a white mare who temporarily leaves her black stallion partner to run off with a deceptively dressed-up circus horse. She performed in numerous other Skibine works including his *Le Prisonnier du Caucase*, *L'Ange gris*, *Le Prince du désert*, and *Roméo et Juliette*, choreographed in collaboration with a group of other de Cuevas choreographers.

After giving birth to twins in 1952, Tallchief—encouraged by her old teacher Nijinska—made an impressive comeback, and continued to dance for another fifteen years. She and her husband, who together excelled in dramatic and showy pas de deux, were joint étoiles at the Paris Opéra in the late 1950s, and then joined the newly formed (but short-lived) Harkness Ballet in New York. Important guest appearances included several seasons with Ruth Page's Chicago Opera Ballet. Tallchief has since made a successful career as a teacher.

—Virginia Christian

THE TAMING OF THE SHREW

Choreography: John Cranko
Music: Kurt-Heinz Stolze, in arrangement after Domenico Scarlatti
Design: Elisabeth Dalton (scenery and costumes)
Libretto: John Cranko, after William Shakespeare's play *The Taming of the Shrew*
First Production: Stuttgart Ballet, Württembergische Staatstheater, Stuttgart, 16 March 1969
Principal Dancers: Marcia Haydée (Katherina), Richard Cragun (Petruchio), Egon Madsen (Gremio), John Neumeier (Hortensio), Heinz Clauss (Lucentio)

Other productions include: Bavarian State Opera Ballet (design Jürgen Rose); Munich, 24 March 1976. Royal Ballet (design Elisabeth Dalton), with Merle Park (Katherina), David Wall (Petruchio); London, 16 February 1977. Ballet of La Scala (staged Georgette Tsinguirides), with Luciana Savignano (Katherina), Richard Cragun (guest artist; Petruchio); Milan, 1980. Sadler's Wells Royal Ballet, with Marion Tait (Katherina), Stephen Jefferies (Petruchio); 16 December 1980. Joffrey Ballet; New York, 23 October 1981. Australian Ballet (staged Anne Woolliams); Melbourne, 28 October 1986. Rome Opera Ballet; Rome, March 1989. English National Ballet (previously London Festival Ballet); Southampton, 16 April 1991. National Ballet of Canada (new designs Susan Blane); Toronto, February 1992.

Other choreographic treatments of story: Maurice Béjart (Paris, 1954), Vera Untermullerova (Liberec, 1961), Louis Falco (1980).

PUBLICATIONS

Wilson, G.B.L., "*The Shrew* in Stuttgart", *Dancing Times* (London), June 1969

Percival, John, "*The Taming of the Shrew*", *Dance and Dancers* (London), July 1969

Manchester, P.W., "The Season in Review", *Dance News* (New York), September 1969

Fischer, S., *John Cranko, Uber dan Tanze*, Frankfurt, 1974

Dalton, Elisabeth, "Making a Ballet—A Designer Speaks", *The Dancing Times* (London), February 1975

Cranko, John, Interview in Gruen, John, *The Private World of Ballet*, New York, 1975

Brinson, Peter, and Crisp, Clement, *Ballet and Dance*, Newton Abbot, 1980

Percival, John, *Theatre in my Blood: A Biography of John Cranko*, London, 1983

*   *   *

Cranko's *Taming of the Shrew* is a magnificent achievement on many scores: not only did it prove his rare capacity (hinted at in *Pineapple Poll*) for the creation of a full-length, emotionally charged comic ballet, but it revitalized for modern audiences a deeply problematic Shakespearean story, giving it warmth and contemporary resonance. Shakespeare's *Shrew*, even before the advent of modern feminism, must have disturbed its audiences with its ruthless parallels, both in imagery and in action, between the taming of wild creatures and the subjugation of wives. Shakespeare's Petruchio, who woos and subdues a wealthy but shrewish woman into sweet-tempered submission, speaks at one point like a falconer of breaking the spirit of his proud bride through starvation, vowing "To make her come

The Taming of the Shrew, with Richard Cragun as Petruchio and members of the Stuttgart Ballet

and know her keeper's call". While maintaining the same plot (even the sinister starvation scene), Cranko's sympathetic treatment of both Petruchio and Kate (brilliantly created by Richard Cragun and Marcia Haydée) brings the story roundly into the twentieth century.

Unlike Shakespeare's Kate, whose shrewishness seems largely unmotivated, Cranko's Kate is an intelligent nonconformist who disdains the pallid (and ultimately superficial) sweetness of her sister's winning ways as much as she disdains the suitors stupid enough to fall for them; this is apparent in the opening scene in which the intrepid Kate interrupts the ardours of Bianca's suitors by overturning a chamberpot upon them. Her shrewishness, in its comic moments, is clearly prompted by sibling rivalry, but in its more serious moments, it reflects the dilemma of the woman unwilling to play the conventional courtship game, for whom antisocial behviour is the only line of defense. Kate's eventual acquiescence in Cranko's version is not the subjugation of mind and body so darkly hinted at in Shakespeare, but rather the discovery of a soul-mate in her former adversary. Moreover, Cranko's Petruchio, every bit as psychologically complex, is high-spirited, fun-loving, and eager to take up the challenge of Kate, who clearly fascinates him at least as much as her money does. By the fourth scene of Act II, all sense of the imperious tamer has disappeared and there is an almost quixotic element in his insistence, for example, that Kate dutifully agree that a bystander is a water pump because he says so. Kate catches the spirit and Cranko transforms what seemed an absurd and whimsical test of her submissiveness in Shakespeare into a moment of fun as she enters into his imaginative world by gamely trying to extract water from the peasant's arm.

The subtlety and the warmth of Cranko's Shrew are the result of a number of magical ingredients: his gift for story-telling, his vibrantly natural choreography, Haydée's dramatic intensity, and Cragun's towering, spirited presence. Cranko was first attracted to Shrew because he found it "so visual". He had an unerring sense of what makes a good story: not only did he eliminate the Christopher Sly escapade and the staging of the actual Shrew story as a play within a play; he then structured the two acts (five scenes apiece) around three bravura duets for Haydée and Cragun—the first, a knockabout sparring session portraying Kate as a force to be reckoned with; the second, proving that in Petruchio she has met her match; and the third (Cranko's most powerful departure from Shakespeare) celebrating the strengths and energies of both equally. The troublesome closing speech, in which the converted Kate browbeats the other wives into submission is replaced by Kate's comic manhandling of the unfortunate women and the final virtuoso duet with its dreamlike range of fun-loving sparring and romanticism. Here the balletic conventions for happy endings, in which the lovers perform a celebratory pas de deux punctuated by alternating virtuoso solos, offered Cranko the possibility of a more equalitarian and humane ending to the story, which he adeptly took up.

Cranko once said that he liked "making ballets about real people . . . like Tatiana [in Onegin] and Kate", and his success can be measured by the way critics speak of Kate and Petruchio as if they were indeed real ("This marriage is not going to be dull", wrote one New York critic fervently). The secret to his success lies in his use of naturally expressive gestures and naturally expressive choreography. Frank Augustyn once said of Cranko's style, "Like most dancers who like [his] choreography, I am grateful for the naturalism . . . The movement is more like the movement you find in life, only it flows more smoothly, and this means that the drama becomes more important." Cranko, who had been deeply influenced by the Russian acrobatic style, which he first saw when the Bolshoi came to

London in 1956, pulled out all the stops in his choreography for Haydée and Cragun, and it is full of horizontal rolls, impossible catches, leaps, high lifts, and comically unballetic thuds to the floor.

Cranko seems to have known exactly what his dancers were capable of; as Marcia Haydée has said, "he can dream up steps that are absolutely dazzling. I mean, he will ask you to do things that you know are impossible to execute. But, miraculously, you can do them. And it always looks right." On the other side, Shrew could hardly have been created as we know it today had Cranko not had, in 1969, the outstanding dramatic virtuosity of Haydée and the formidable range of the young Cragun, whose triple tours en l'air in this role were performed with astonishing ease. Cranko wanted very much to change "the image of the ballerina as a perpetual virgin and the male dancer as a sort of romantic coat hanger", and in The Taming of the Shrew he did.

—Kathryn Kerby-Fulton

TARAS, John

American dancer, choreographer, teacher, and ballet director. Born in New York, 18 April 1919. Studied with Mikhail Fokine, Anatole Vilzak, Ludmilla Schollar, and Elisabeth Anderson-Ivantzova from 1936, and at School of American Ballet, New York. Dancer, (Catherine Littlefield's) Philadelphia Ballet, 1939–41, Ballet Caravan, New York World's Fair, 1940, and American Ballet Caravan, South American tour, 1941; dancer, becoming soloist, choreographer, and ballet master, Ballet Theatre (later American Ballet Theatre), 1942–46; choreographer, Markova–Dolin Ballet, Chicago, 1946, and (de Basil's) Original Ballet Russe, 1946, acting as dancer and ballet master for European tour, 1947; choreographer, Ballet Society, 1947, Metropolitan Ballet, 1948, San Francisco Ballet, 1948, Les Ballets des Champs-Elysées, 1949; principal choreographer and ballet master, Grand Ballet du Marquis de Cuevas (originally the Grand Ballet de Monte Carlo, and also performing as the International Ballet du Marquis de Cuevas), 1948–53; ballet master (assistant to Balanchine), New York City Ballet, from 1959; ballet master, Paris Opéra Ballet, 1969–70; ballet director, German Opera Ballet, Berlin, 1971–72; joint ballet master (with Balanchine and Robbins), New York City Ballet, 1972–83; associate director, American Ballet Theatre, from 1984; international guest choreographer, staging own and other (particularly Balanchine) works for companies including Monte Carlo Opera, Les Ballets 1956, Royal Danish Ballet, Netherlands Ballet, Geneva Ballet, André Eglevsky's Petit Ballet, National Ballet of Chile, Royal Ballet, London, Geneva Ballet, Dance Theatre of Harlem, Pittsburgh Ballet, and Bolshoi Ballet, Moscow; Honorary Chairman, International New York City Ballet Committee, from 1982. Recipient: Title of Officier de l'Ordre des Artes et des Lettres, France; International Dance Festival Merit Award, Chicago, 1989.

WORKS

1945   Graziana (mus. Mozart), Ballet Theatre, New York
1946   Tchaikovsky Waltz (mus. Tchaikovsky), Markova–Dolin Ballet, Chicago
       Camille (mus. Schubert, arranged Rieti), Original Ballet Russe, New York
1947   The Minotaur (mus. Carter), Ballet Society, New York

John Taras rehearsing *Arcade* **with Arthur Mitchell and Suzanne Farrell, New York, c. 1963**

1948 *Designs with Strings* (also *Design for Strings*; mus. Tchaikovsky), Metropolitan Ballet, Edinburgh
Élégie (mus. Chopin), (de Cuevas) Grand Ballet de Monte Carlo, Paris
Persephone (mus. Schumann), San Francisco Ballet, San Francisco (staged Grand Ballet de Monte Carlo, 1950)

1949 *D'Amour et d'eau fraîche* (mus. Rivier), Les Ballets des Champs-Elysées, Paris
Devoirs de vacances (mus. Walton), Les Ballets des Champs-Elysées, Paris
Le Réparateur de radio (mus. Rivier), Les Ballets des Champs-Elysées, Paris

1950 *Bal de jeunes filles* (mus. Mozart), (de Cuevas) Grand Ballet de Monte Carlo, Paris

1951 *Tarasiana* (mus. Mozart), Grand Ballet du Marquis de Cuevas, Paris

1952 *Cordélia* (mus. Sauget), Grand Ballet du Marquis de Cuevas, Paris
Scherzo (mus. Tchaikovsky), Grand Ballet du Marquis de Cuevas, Paris
Une Nuit de été (mus. Mendelssohn), Grand Ballet du Marquis de Cuevas, Paris

Piège de lumière (mus. Damase), Grand Ballet du Marquis de Cuevas, Paris (staged New York City Ballet, 1964)

1954 *Scènes de ballet* (mus. Stravinsky), Netherlands Ballet, The Hague

1955 *Le Forêt romantique* (mus. Glazunov), Monte Carlo Opera, Monte Carlo
Fanfares pour un prince (mus. Corelli, Vivaldi), Monte Carlo Opera, Monte Carlo
Suite New Yorkaise (mus. de Manfred), Monte Carlo Opera, Monte Carlo
Les Baladins (mus. Damase), Les Ballets de Pâques, Monte Carlo Opera, Monte Carlo
Roméo et Juliette (with Skibine, Skouratoff, Golovine; mus. Berlioz), Grand Ballet de Monte Carlo, Monte Carlo

1956 *Entre cour et jardin* (later called *Le Rideau Rouge*; mus. Blareau), Les Ballets 1956, Monte Carlo
Les Griffes, Les Ballets 1956, Monte Carlo

1957 *Le Rendezvous manqué* (*The Broken Date*; Acts I and III; scenario Françoise Sagan; mus. Magne), Monte Carlo Opera, Monte Carlo
Soirée musicale (mus. Rossini, arranged Britten), Grand

Ballet du Marquis de Cuevas, Paris
1958 *Octet* (mus. Wooldridge), Edinburgh International Ballet, Edinburgh Festival
1960 *Variaciones Concertantes* (mus. Ginastera) in *Pan America* (Balanchine, Contreras, Moncion, Taras, d'Amboise), New York City Ballet, New York
Ebony Concerto (part of *Jazz Concert*; mus. Stravinsky), New York City Ballet, New York
1963 *Arcade* (mus. Stravinsky), New York City Ballet, New York
Fantasy (mus. Schubert), New York City Ballet, New York
1965 *Shadow'd Ground* (mus. Copland), New York City Ballet, New York
1966 *Jeux* (mus. Debussy), New York City Ballet, New York
La Guirlande de Campra (mus. various, on a theme by Campra), New York City Ballet, New York
1968 *Haydn Concerto* (mus. Haydn), New York City Ballet, New York
1971 *Dolly Suite* (mus. Fauré), Boston Ballet, Boston
1972 *Concerto for Piano and Winds* (mus. Stravinsky), New York City Ballet, New York
The Song of the Nightingale (mus. Stravinsky), New York City Ballet, New York
Scènes de ballet (new version; mus. Stravinsky), New York City Ballet, New York
1973 *The Rite of Spring* (new version; mus. Stravinsky), La Scala, Milan
1974 *Dohnanyi Suite* (mus. Dohnanyi), Pittsburg Ballet, Pittsburg
1975 *Daphnis and Chloë* (mus. Ravel), New York City Ballet, New York
1981 *Souvenir de Florence* (mus. Tchaikovsky), New York City Ballet, New York
1982 *Concerto for Piano and Wind Instruments* (mus. Stravinsky), New York City Ballet, New York
Firebird (mus. Stravinsky), Dance Theatre of Harlem, New York
1986 *Francesca da Rimini* (mus. Tchaikovsky), American Ballet Theatre, Miami
1991 *Trio* (mus. Tchaikovsky), Pittsburgh Ballet, Pittsburgh

Also staged:
1948 *Les Sylphides* (after Fokine; mus. Chopin), San Francisco Ballet, San Francisco (also staged Dutch National Ballet, 1979; Ballets de Monte Carlo, 1985)
1955 *La Sonnambula* (*Night Shadow*; chor. Balanchine; mus. Bellini), Royal Danish Ballet, Copenhagen (also staged Ballet Rambert, 1961; London Festival Ballet, 1967; Ballet de Nancy; Ballet du Nord; Dallas Ballet; San Francisco Ballet; Ballet de Turin; American Ballet Theatre, 1981; Teatro Colón, Buenos Aires)
Concerto Barocco (chor. Balanchine; mus. Bach), Royal Danish Ballet, Copenhagen
1966 *Apollo* (chor. Balanchine; mus. Stravinsky), Royal Ballet, London (also staged Dutch National Ballet, 1966; German Opera Ballet, Berlin, 1969; Düsseldorf Ballet, 1971; Paris Opéra Ballet and Ballet du Nord)
1968 *Donizetti Variations* (chor. Balanchine; mus. Donizetti), Royal Danish Ballet, Copenhagen
1973 *Petrushka* (after Fokine; mus. Stravinsky), Royal Ballet, London (also staged Geneva Ballet, 1977)
1974 *Orpheus* (chor. Balanchine; mus. Stravinsky), Paris Opéra Ballet, Paris
Capriccio (*Rubies* from *Jewels*; mus. Stravinsky), Paris Opéra Ballet, Paris
1966 *Prodigal Son* (chor. Balanchine; mus. Stravinsky),

Dutch National Ballet, Amsterdam (also staged National Ballet, Washington, D.C., 1967; Royal Danish Ballet, 1968; Pacific Northwest Ballet; Royal Ballet, London, 1973; Paris Opéra Ballet, 1973; Dallas Ballet; American Ballet Theatre, 1980; Ballets de Monte Carlo, Bolshoi Ballet, 1991)
1980 *Illuminations* (Ashton; mus. Britten), Joffrey Ballet, New York (also staged Royal Ballet, London, 1981)

Other works include: Dances in operas *The Merry Widow* (mus. Lehár), *The Student Prince* (mus. Romberg), *Mireille* (mus. Gounod), *Don Giovanni* (mus. Mozart), *Le Nozze de Figaro* (mus. Mozart), *Carmen* (mus. Bizet), *Platée* (mus. Rameau), *Le Nozze di Figaro* (mus. Mozart), *Orpheus and Eurydice* (mus. Gluck).

PUBLICATIONS

By Taras:
"Stravinsky on Art and Artists" (editor), *Dance Magazine* (New York), April 1981
Interview in Davies, R., "A Man with a View", *Dance and Dancers* (London), April 1982
"Marie-Jeanne", *Ballet Review* (New York), Winter 1985
"Balanchine's Mozart Violin Concerto", *Ballet Review* (New York), Summer 1987
"Nora Kaye: A Tribute", *Ballet Review* (New York), Winter 1987
George Balanchine, Ballet Master: A Biography, in collaboration with Richard Buckle, London, 1988
Interview in Gruen, John, *People Who Dance*, Pennington, New Jersey, 1988
"American Ballet Theatre: The First Fifty Years", in *American Ballet Theatre*, 50th Anniversary issue, New York, 1989

About Taras:
Barzel, Ann, "Bright Young Men", *Dance Magazine* (New York), April 1946
Beaumont, Cyril, *Ballets of Today*, London, 1954
"Personality of the Month: John Taras", *Dance and Dancers* (London), June 1957
Croce, Arlene, "Ballets without Choreography", *Ballet Review* (Brooklyn, N.Y.), vol. 2, no. 1, 1967
Reynolds, Nancy, *Repertory in Review*, New York, 1977
Garske, Rolf, "John Taras: Energy and Freedom", *Ballett International* (Koln), September 1983
Gruen, John, "Balletmaster, John Taras", *Dance Magazine* (New York), October 1984

* * *

Choreographer and dancer John Taras was born in New York City to parents of Ukrainian stock. He had his first performing experience with a local Ukrainian folk dance company as a young boy. He started ballet study in his late teens with Mikhail Fokine. He had not had any previous ballet training but Fokine made no allowances, and expected Taras to keep up. He gained stage experience when he appeared in "Operas on Tour", a company for which Fokine arranged the dance sequences. Subsequently, Taras went back to learn the basics at the School of American Ballet.

In short order he danced with a number of companies, including a troupe at the New York World's Fair, which presented William Dollar's ballet *A Thousand Times Neigh* in the Ford Motor Car pavilion, telling the story of transportation from horse and buggy days to the introduction of the 1940 models. He appeared briefly with the Littlefield Ballet, joined American Ballet Caravan for a six-month tour of South America, and spent five years with Ballet Theatre (later American Ballet Theatre), rising to the level of soloist.

From the untrained tyro he had been while studying with Fokine, Taras progressed to the stage where he expressed a desire to teach, and began supervising ensemble rehearsals for several of the company's ballets. He created his first ballet, *Graziana*, to Mozart's Violin Concerto in G Minor, and critics remarked on a Balanchine influence. The desire to continue a choreographic career led him to leave Ballet Theatre to choreograph for a series of companies in the United States and Europe.

For the Original Ballet Russe, Taras produced a contrasting work, *Camille*, that examined the life of the consumptive courtesan. Far from the plotless work that *Graziana* was, it was totally developed with a clear plot-line. For his entire career, Taras moved back and forth between the two types of ballets.

Perhaps his best-known work was done for the relatively short-lived Metropolitan Ballet in Edinburgh. The piece was originally titled *Design for Strings*, possibly reflecting the scoring of the Tchaikovsky trio from which Taras selected the second movement. Later he renamed it *Designs with Strings*, thereby gaining a second, metaphorical implication that there were limiting conditions to the relations between the two men and four women in the piece.

While the work clearly announced that its choreographer had seen and admired the work of Balanchine, it had a cool individuality that made its own statement. The first company to acquire performing rights to it in the United States was Ballet Theatre, two years after its premiere. Since that time companies throughout the world have mounted productions of the work.

It develops with the dancers outlined in silhouette, devoid of any personality but linked by held hands. During the course of the piece, which slips rapidly and cleverly from one unsuccessful encounter to another, Taras keeps his characters in constant but inconclusive motion.

The theme of volatile human attachments was one which Taras explored throughout his career. In 1959, when he rejoined New York City Ballet (growing out of the American Ballet Caravan) after a decade abroad, he began an association (with occasional leaves-of-absence) that would last until Balanchine's death in 1983. The silhouette lighting that was so effective in *Designs With Strings* was used again to open his *Ebony Concerto*, a witty, jazzy ballet that had as its subject fleeting relationships.

Taras was the first choreographer to highlight the skills of Suzanne Farrell. *Arcade*, which was set in a cloister-like enclosure, revealed for the first time the growing talents of the dancer who was to become Balanchine's muse-in-residence until his death in 1983.

Looking back at ballet history, Taras decided to re-do in a contemporary setting Nijinsky's *Jeux*. Using the same Debussy score, he examined the relations of an inherently unstable trio of two women and a man. Emotional attachments flickered fitfully and unpredictably between the three.

Frequently asked by Balanchine to stage his works on companies throughout the world, Taras continued to do so, after Balanchine's death, for American Ballet Theatre, which he re-joined after an absence of nearly four decades. He continued to teach and stressed placement as he had throughout his career.

—Don McDonagh

LA TARENTULE

Choreography: Jean Coralli
Music: Casimir Gide
Design: Charles Séchan, Jules Diéterle, Edouard Despléchin, Feuchères (scenery), Paul Lormier (costumes)
Libretto: Eugène Scribe
First Production: Théâtre de l'Académie royale de musique (Paris Opéra), 24 June, 1839
Principal Dancers: Fanny Elssler (Lauretta), Joseph Mazilier (Luidgi), Jean-Baptiste Barrez (Dr. Omeopatico), Caroline Forster (Clorinde)

Other productions include: Her Majesty's Theatre (staged Barrez after Coralli), with Fanny Elssler (Lauretta); London, 21 March 1840.

PUBLICATIONS

Gautier, Théophile, *The Romantic Ballet as seen by Théophile Gautier*, edited and translated by Cyril Beaumont, London, 1932
Beaumont, Cyril, *Complete Book of Ballets*, revised edition, London, 1951
Guest, Ivor, *The Romantic Ballet in England*, London, 1954
Guest, Ivor, *The Romantic Ballet in Paris*, London, 1966, 1980
Guest, Ivor, *Fanny Elssler*, London, 1970

*   *   *

La Tarentule was one of the very few comedy ballets produced during the Romantic period at the Paris Opéra. Romanticism concerned itself more with deep passion than with laughter, more with poetic ideals than with the comic. But Eugène Scribe, *La Tarentule*'s author, had little sympathy for the excesses of Romanticism and there must have been many who shared his view, for he was an extremely successful author of some 300 works for the stage, and creator of the "well-made play", a formula that became the model for its day.

Scribe's forte as a ballet writer was within the sentimental genre, a pre-romantic idiom—innocent young girl is wrongly condemned for lack of virtue, but is vindicated in the end. This was the theme of his most popular ballet, *La Somnambule* (choreographed by Aumer in 1827) as well as his *L'Orgie* (choreographed by Coralli in 1831). Lauretta, the heroine of *La Tarentule*, was a girl of a different sort. Her tormentor, the lecherous Dr. Omeopatico, is almost as much her victim as she is his, for, she is not so innocent and naïve as to be powerless against his plotting. Thus the audience can laugh with her, rather than pitying and feeling moral indignation at her undeserved persecution. In *La Tarentule*, Lauretta's problems begin when her lover Luidgi is bitten by a tarantula. Dr. Omeopatico agrees to save his life only if Lauretta promises to marry him. She does so, but dupes the doctor, and in the process turns the whole village against him. In the end, the arrival of Omeopatico's wife releases Lauretta from her promise.

Several critics found the story too trivial for the Opéra. But the general reception was positive and the ballet's success was a testament to the skills of its leading performers, who prevented the piece from degenerating into a crude farce. Joseph Mazilier (who had just created the highly successful dramatic ballet, *La Gipsy*, in January of 1839) brought grace and pathos to his depiction of Luidgi. Jean-Baptiste Barrez (who would produce *La Tarentule* in London in 1840) as Dr. Omeopatico was comical without being offensive to the refined tastes of the audience. Gautier wrote he "managed to stop short at exaggeration . . .". But it was Fanny Elssler who stole the show with her eloquent silent acting, and with her latest character dance, the tarentella.

La Tarentule was a fine vehicle for Fanny Elssler's enormous pantomimic prowess, offering her the chance to display her wit, as well as her fiery charm and youthful grace. She was the high-spirited ingenue with whom audiences readily identified. "Fanny Elssler," wrote one critic, "is not only an alluring but a true actress . . ." Another commented: "I do not know a great actress who has rendered theatrical situations with such verve . . ." Unhappily for Parisians who had enjoyed her silent eloquence and her passionate dancing since her first appearance at the Opéra in 1834, this was to be her last ballet in Paris. She departed at the end of the 1839 season, leaving behind a standard of excellence in mime which others could only emulate.

Jean Coralli's role as ballet master was to create the dances and set the action. Coralli was a versatile artist who excelled in works of grandeur where a rapid succession of monumental scenes overwhelmed audience sensibilities (*La Tempête*, 1834) as well as in works that spoke through their poignant dramatic action (*Giselle*, 1841). *La Tarentule* offered him neither the human drama nor the vastness of scale to give full force to his creative vision. He was successful enough to avoid complaints in the press about lack of story clarity, but he did not draw significant praise in his own right. The composer, Casimir Gide, on the other hand, was commended for the taste and intelligence with which he chose and arranged popular music for the ballet. Commented one critic, "it is a collection of delicious airs from many sources, distributed and united to each other by a sure and talented hand; in this mixture . . . Gide has thrown original sections of his own composition which seem to be of the same family as those borrowed by him . . ." *La Tarentule* was staged in London in 1840, again with Fanny Elssler in the leading role.

—John Chapman

TAYLOR, Paul

American dancer, choreographer, and company director. Born in Alleghany County, Pennsylvania, 29 July 1930. Educated at Syracuse University; studied modern dance with Martha Graham, Doris Humphrey, José Limón, and Merce Cunningham; also studied ballet at Metropolitan Opera Ballet School and Juilliard School, New York, pupil of Antony Tudor and Margaret Craske. Dancer with various modern companies, including those of Merce Cunningham, 1953–54, Pearl Lang, 1955, and Martha Graham, 1955–62; guest artist, New York City Ballet, creating role in *Episodes* (Balanchine and Graham), 1959; first choreography in 1953: founder, director, and choreographer, Paul Taylor Dance Company, from 1954, touring throughout United States and the world, including Mexico City, Paris, London, and Spoleto; guest choreographer, including for Netherlands Ballet, 1960; has been featured on television with company, including for numerous "Dance in America" PBS (Public Broadcasting Service) Series; retired from dancing, 1974, continuing actively as company director and choreographer. Recipient: Best Choreographer Award, Théâtre des Nations Dance Festival, Paris, 1962; Premio de la Critica, Chile, 1965; Capezio Dance Award, 1967; title of Chevalier de l'Ordre des Arts et des Lettres, France, 1969; *Dance Magazine* Award, 1980; titles of Officier de l'Ordre des Arts et des Lettres, France, 1984, and Commandeur de l'Ordre

des Arts et des Lettres, France, 1990; Emmy Award (for television production of *Speaking in Tongues*, 1991); Kennedy Center Award, Washington, D.C., 1992.

WORKS

1953   *Jack and the Beanstalk* (mus. Gubernick), Dance Associates, New York

1955   *Circus Polka* (solo; mus. Stravinsky; restaged as *Little Circusy*), Paul Taylor Dance Company, New York

1956   *The Least Flycatcher* (mus. Rauschenberg), Paul Taylor Dance Company, New York

        4 Epitaphs (later *3 Epitaphs*, mus. early New Orleans jazz), Paul Taylor Dance Company, New York

        Untitled Duet (no mus.), Paul Taylor Dance Company, New York

        Tropes (mus. Rauschenberg), Paul Taylor Dance Company, New York

1957   *The Tower* (mus. Cooper), Paul Taylor Dance Company, New York

        Seven New Dances: Epic, Events I, Resemblance, Panorama, Duet, Events II, Opportunity (mus. Cage and various sounds), Paul Taylor Dance Company, New York

1958   *Rebus* (mus. Hollister), Paul Taylor Dance Company, New York

        Images and Reflections (mus. Feldman), Paul Taylor Dance Company, New York

1960   *Option* (mus. Maxfield), Paul Taylor Dance Company, New York

        Meridian (duet, mus. Boulez; ensemble, mus. Feldman), Paul Taylor Dance Company, Festival of Two Worlds, Spoleto

        Tablet (mus. Hollister), Paul Taylor Dance Company, Festival of Two Worlds, Spoleto

        The White Salamander (mus. Stockermans), Netherlands Ballet, Amsterdam

        Fibers (mus. Schoenberg), Paul Taylor Dance Company, New York

1961   *Insects and Heroes* (mus. McDowell), Paul Taylor Dance Company, American Dance Festival, New London, Connecticut

        Junction (mus. Bach), Paul Taylor Dance Company, New York

1962   *Tracer* (mus. Tenny), Paul Taylor Dance Company, Théâtre des Nations Festival, Paris

        Aureole (mus. Handel), Paul Taylor Dance Company, American Dance Festival, New London, Connecticut

        Piece Period (mus. Vivaldi and others), Paul Taylor Dance Company, New York

1963   *Poetry in Motion* (mus. L. Mozart), Paul Taylor Dance Company, New York

        La Negra (Mexican folk music), Paul Taylor Dance Company, Mexico City

        Scudorama (mus. Jackson), Paul Taylor Dance Company, American Dance Festival, New London, Connecticut

        Party Mix (mus. Haief), Paul Taylor Dance Company, New York

        The Red Room (mus. Schuller), Paul Taylor Dance Company, Festival of Two Worlds, Spoleto

1964   *Duet* (mus. Haydn), Paul Taylor Dance Company, Paris

        Nine Dances with Music by Corelli (mus. Corelli), Paul Taylor Dance Company, New York

1965   *Post Meridian* (new version of *The Red Room*; mus. Lohoeffer), Paul Taylor Dance Company, New York

Paul Taylor in *Aureole*, c. 1962

From Sea to Shining Sea (mus. McDowell), Paul Taylor Dance Company, New York

1966   *Orbs* (mus. Beethoven), Paul Taylor Dance Company, Holland Festival, Amsterdam

1967   *Agathe's Tale* (mus. Surinach), Paul Taylor Dance Company, American Dance Festival, New London, Connecticut

Lento (mus. Haydn), Paul Taylor Dance Company, Chicago

1968   *Public Domain* (mus. McDowell), Paul Taylor Dance Company, New York

1969   *Private Domain* (mus. Xenakis), Paul Taylor Dance Company, New York

Duets (mus. medieval), Paul Taylor Dance Company, American Dance Festival, New London, Connecticut

Churchyard (mus. Savage), Paul Taylor Dance Company, New York

1970   *Foreign Exchange* (mus. Subotnick), Paul Taylor Dance Company, New York

Big Bertha (mus. arranged McDowell), Paul Taylor Dance Company, New York (duet version for television, mus. Bacharach, also 1970)

1971   *Book of Beasts* (mus. de Falla), Paul Taylor Dance Company, American Dance Festival, New London, Connecticut

Fêtes (mus. Debussy), Paul Taylor Dance Company, Lake Placid, New York

1972   *Guests of May* (mus. Debussy), Paul Taylor Dance Company, Lake Placid, New York

So Long Eden (mus. Fahey), Paul Taylor Dance Company, Philadelphia

West of Eden (mus. Martinů), Paul Taylor Dance Company

1973   *American Genesis*: *Before Eden* (mus. Habdel), *So Long Eden* (mus. Fahey), *West of Eden* (mus. Martinů), *Noah's Minstrels* (mus. Gottschalk), Paul Taylor Dance Company, Philadelphia

1974   *Sports and Follies* (mus. Satie), Paul Taylor Dance Company, Lake Placid, New York

Untitled Quartet (mus. Stravinsky), Paul Taylor Dance Company, Lake Placid, New York

1975   *Esplanade* (mus. Bach), Paul Taylor Dance Company, Washington, D.C.

Runes (mus. Busby), Paul Taylor Dance Company, New York

1976   *Cloven Kingdom* (mus. Corelli, Cowell), Paul Taylor Dance Company, New York

Polaris (mus. York), Paul Taylor Dance Company, Lake Placid, New York

1977   *Images* (mus. Debussy), Paul Taylor Dance Company, New York

Dust (mus. Poulenc), Paul Taylor Dance Company, New York

Aphrodisiamania (mus. various), Paul Taylor Dance Company

1978   *Airs* (mus. Handel), Paul Taylor Dance Company

Diggity (mus. York), Paul Taylor Dance Company, Hempstead, New York

1979   *Nightshade* (mus. Scriabin), Paul Taylor Dance Company, New York

Profiles (mus. Radzynski), Paul Taylor Dance Company, Durham, North Carolina

1980   *Le Sacre du Printemps* (*The Rehearsal*) (mus. Stravinsky), Paul Taylor Dance Company, New York

1981   *Arden Court* (mus. Boyce), Paul Taylor Dance Company, New York

House of Cards (mus. Milhaud), Paul Taylor Dance Company, Brooklyn, New York

1982   *Lost, Found and Lost* ("wallpaper" muzak, orchestrated York), Paul Taylor Dance Company, New York

Mercuric Tidings (mus. Schubert), Paul Taylor Dance Company, New York

1983   *Musette* (mus. Handel), Paul Taylor Dance Company, New York

Sunset (mus. Elgar), Paul Taylor Dance Company, New York

Snow White (mus. York), Paul Taylor Dance Company, New York

Equinox (mus. Brahms), Paul Taylor Dance Company, Washington, D.C.

1984   *Byzantium* (mus. Varese), Paul Taylor Dance Company, New York

1985   *Last Look* (mus. York), Paul Taylor Dance Company, New York

Roses (mus. Wagner, Baermann), Paul Taylor Dance Company, New York

1986   *Musical Offering* (mus. Bach), Paul Taylor Dance Company, New York

Ab Ovo Usque ad Mala (mus. Bach), Paul Taylor Dance Company, New York

1987   *Kith and Kin* (mus. Mozart), Paul Taylor Dance Company, New York

Syzygy (mus. York), Paul Taylor Dance Company, New York (revised version staged 1989)

1988   *Brandenburgs* (mus. Bach), Paul Taylor Dance Company, New York

Counterswarm (mus. Ligeti), Paul Taylor Dance Company, New York

Danbury Mix (mus. Ives), New York City Ballet, New York

Speaking in Tongues (mus. Patton), Paul Taylor Dance Company, Philadelphia

1989   *Minikin Fair* (mus. Koblitz, Weiselman, Spae), Paul Taylor Dance Company, New York

1990   *The Sorcerer's Sofa* (mus. Dukas), Paul Taylor Dance Company, Washington, D.C.

Of Bright & Blue Birds & The Gala Sun (mus. York), Paul Taylor Dance Company, New York

1991   *Fact & Fancy* (mus. early New Orleans jazz, reggae), Paul Taylor Dance Company, New York

Company B (mus. The Andrews Sisters), Houston Ballet, Washington, D.C.

1992   *Oz* (mus. Horvitz), Paul Taylor Dance Company, New York (originally created for White Oak Dance Project)

PUBLICATIONS

By Taylor:

"Down with Choreography", in *Modern Dance*, Middletown, Connecticut, 1965

Private Domain (autobiography), New York, 1987

About Taylor:

Cohen, Selma Jeanne, "Avant-Garde Choreography", *Dance Magazine* (New York), 3 parts: June, July, August 1962

McDonagh, Don, *The Rise and Fall of Modern Dance*, New York, 1970

Baril, J., "Paul Taylor", *Les Saisons de la danse* (Paris), July 1973

Stern, L.E., "Paul Taylor, Gentle Giant of Modern Dance", *Dance Magazine* (New York), February 1976

Croce, Arlene, *Afterimages*, New York, 1977

Mazo, Joseph, *Prime Movers: The Makers of Modern Dance in America*, New York, 1977

Anderson, Jack, "Choreographic Fox: Paul Taylor", *Dance Magazine* (New York), April 1980

Croce, Arlene, *Going to the Dance*, New York, 1982

Siegel, Marcia, *The Shapes of Change*, Berkeley, 1985

Lobenthal, Joel, "Christopher Gillis: Dancing for Paul Taylor", *Ballet Review* (New York), Summer 1985

Denby, Edwin, *Dance Writings*, edited by Robert Cornfield and William Mackay, New York, 1986

Sorens, Ina, "Taylor Reconstructs Balanchine", *Ballet Review* (New York), Summer 1986

Anderson, Jack, *Choreography Observed*, Iowa City, 1987

Croce, Arlene, *Sightlines*, New York, 1987

Macaulay, Alastair, "The Music Man", *The New Yorker* (New York), 2 May 1988

Jacobson, Daniel, "Private Domains in Public Spaces", *Ballet Review* (New York), Spring 1989

Dalva, Nancy, "Paul Taylor: A Very Appealing Genius", *Dance Magazine* (New York), October 1991

*   *   *

Paul Taylor is one of the most respected and popular of American modern dance choreographers. Since the 1950s, when he began choreographing, Taylor has drawn on both modern dance and ballet vocabularies, incorporating everyday gesture, vernacular dance, popular entertainment traditions and, more recently, gymnastic movement to create an individual, readily recognizable style. Consistently transcending the split between ballet and modern dance that has characterized American dance in the past, Taylor's work has been commissioned by ballet and modern dance companies alike, and appeals not only to modern dance devotees, but also to balletomanes, experts and novices alike.

Taylor's widespread popularity may be due partly to the eclectic nature of his early training. He began dancing at Syracuse University, where he was an art student and scholarship swimmer, and spent a summer at the American Dance Festival, studying Graham technique and Humphrey and Horst composition, and dancing in several of Doris Humphrey's dances. It was there that he first met Martha Graham, whose dramatic choreography particularly attracted him. After coming to New York in 1952, Taylor studied ballet with Antony Tudor and Margaret Craske at the Juilliard School and the Metropolitan Opera Ballet School. At the same time, he took classes at the Graham school and with Merce Cunningham, whose fledgling company he danced with from 1953 to 1954. He joined Martha Graham's company on its Oriental tour in 1955 and was a principal dancer with the company until 1962. In 1959, George Balanchine created a solo for Taylor in the Balanchine–Graham collaboration, *Episodes*.

As a young choreographer, Taylor was associated with the idiosyncratic, often whimsical modern dance avant-garde dancemakers of the mid-1950s who performed under the auspices of James Waring's Dance Associates. During this period Taylor met artists Robert Rauschenberg and Jasper Johns, who designed sets for Taylor's dances through the early 1960s. Rather like Rauschenberg's creation of paintings out of found objects, Taylor attempted to make dances from a movement alphabet grounded in everyday gesture, anticipating the later works of the Judson Dance Theater. He also experimented with posture and stillness. Taylor's notorious 1957 concert, *Seven New Dances*, contained so little movement of any kind that Louis Horst, editor of *Dance Observer*, gave it a blank space in his review column. Under the influence of Merce Cunningham, Taylor also briefly tried choreographing by chance methods.

Through these attempts Taylor began to position himself in the choreographic experimentation of the time. Even in chance-derived dances he discerned the choreographer's individual stamp, and so he embraced a more conventional, active role in shaping his dances. In contrast to many artists and choreographers of the time who seemed either to reject drama or to cultivate mystery, Taylor found new sources of expressive power in the most mundane gestures and spatial interactions. After critics failed to comprehend his *Seven Dances* concert, he learned that he wanted to communicate with his audience. He broke decisively with the more mystical or individualistic branches of the avant-garde, and began to make his work more accessible. While critics have waxed enthusiastic over his big movement phrases and the engaging, open quality of his pieces, such evaluations are both astute and incomplete. For his seemingly genial dances are often fraught with contradictory movement information, spare understatements and brutal hyperboles, sly undercuttings and disavowals. Meaning is frequently tentative or qualified, yet almost always viscerally compelling.

By the 1960s Taylor's work seemed out of step with the newer experimental choreography of the Judson Church and the post-moderns. In fact, Taylor's work has continued the classic modern dance lineage of Graham, Doris Humphrey, Charles Weidman, and José Limón. But it also shares many sensibilities with experimental choreography of the 1960s and 1970s. Taylor has continued to work with everyday gesture, and has relied heavily on the individual characteristics of his dancers. He often choreographs under the influence of one piece of music, then adopts a different accompaniment for the dance as performed. His work is frequently tinged by a sense of the absurd that characterized avant-garde theatre of the 1960s. And like much experimental American dance of the period, his dances are concerned with community.

Thus, Taylor's dances may be sketches of a particular time and place, portraits of social mores, swipes at icons of American culture. They may also simply be tributes to the community of dancers in his own company. In any case, the socialness of Taylor's works distinguishes them from the essentially psychological emphasis of Martha Graham's dances, and manifests itself in his emphasis on ensemble choreography, as well as in his use of the open upper body, presentational demeanour, and clear, large-scale design often associated with ballet. Unlike Graham's mythic psychodramas, Taylor's dances enact a broad range of moods with, generally speaking, a lighter touch and frequent irreverence. Expansive humour characterizes many of his pieces, from cartoonish spoofs to barbed satires to lilting, sunny celebrations. But his humour can also run in a black stream, producing dances that are vitriolic or devastatingly, deliberately vulgar.

Taylor's range of expression is rooted in his choreography. His rather spare vocabulary owes much to Graham technique, but in contrast to the bound, percussive, earth-driven quality of classic Graham movement, Taylor's vocabulary is more buoyant. Weight is a crucial dimension of his dances, but he plays with a wider range of weight possibilities for expressive purposes than Graham did, using everything from airborne leaps and lifts to lurches, staggers, dives, and slides. Even his most balletic duets must be weighted.

Whereas the percussiveness of Graham's technique tends to isolate each movement, the trademark of Taylor's craft is an ongoing choreographic momentum, both in each dancer's phrasing, and in group choreography. Taylor obtains many of his expressive results by choosing dancers whose physical attributes can ring subtle changes on the quality of that flow, making it silky or jerky, sticky or rubbery. Not surprisingly, these colourings of the choreographic flow also make visible Taylor's enormous sensitivity to the music he uses. Other than Balanchine, Taylor is the contemporary choreographer most frequently associated with musicality, but unlike Balanchine, Taylor's musicality is not so much structural as an interplay with the expressive qualities and colours of the music. It is instructive to compare Balanchine's *Concerto Barocco* (1941) with Taylor's *Esplanade* (1975), both to Bach's "Two Violin Concerto", and also to look at *Polaris* (1976) in which the same movement is performed twice with different music and lighting, creating radically different moods.

Taylor is known for the quality and range of his choreography for men. For much of his career, this has been less a matter of displaying conventional male virtuosity than it has been of creating a broad vocabulary of expression on male bodies (perhaps a reaction to Graham's stiff, dynamically monochromatic heroes). Taylor—tall himself—has tended to work with men who are larger or more heavily-muscled than the average male dancer. Playing upon the effort and control required for a bulky man to perform fast, precise, intricate footwork, or a delicate, sustained adagio full of balances, Taylor has made dances that speak eloquently of courage, endurance, tenderness, and the struggle against the innate flaws of humankind. In doing so, he has set new standards for male virtuosity. More recently, Taylor has occasionally highlighted more conventional male virtuosity, as in his 1981 *Arden Court*.

Taylor's company has spawned a number of dancers who have gone on to make their names as choreographers, notably Twyla Tharp, Senta Driver, Dan Waggoner, Toby Armour, Victoria Uris, David Parsons, and the New Zealander Douglas Wright. His dances are in the repertory of the Royal Danish Ballet, American Ballet Theatre, the Joffrey Ballet, Paris Opéra Ballet, London Contemporary Dance Theatre, Ballet Rambert, and Les Grands Ballets Canadiens.

—Judith F. Burns

TCHAIKOVSKY, Petr

Russian composer. Born Petr Ilyich Chaikovsky (Tchaikovsky) in Kamsko-Votkinsk, 7 May (25 April old style) 1840. Educated at Schmelling School, 1848–49, and at the School of Jurisprudence, St. Petersburg, 1950–59; studied piano with Maria Palchikova, Kamsko-Votkinsk, and with Rudolf Kündinger, from 1855; studied at the Russian Musical Society (becoming the St. Petersburg Conservatory), 1861–63 (part-time), and 1863–65 (full-time), pupil of Nikolai Zaremba and Anton Rubinstein. Married Antonina Milyukova, 1877. Clerk, Ministry of Justice, 1859–63, resigning to devote full time to music; début as conductor of own overture at Conservatory, 1865; teacher, Moscow Conservatory, 1866–78; first ballet, *Swan Lake* (based on music composed in 1871), commissioned by Imperial Theatres in Moscow: performed, unsuccessfully, with interpolations by Pugni, 1877 (restaged far more successfully by Petipa and Ivanov, 1895); moved to outskirts of Moscow, 1885; appeared as conductor in Russia and on several European tours; composed greatest ballet, *The Sleeping Beauty*, 1888 (staged 1890); on returning from United States, composed *The Nutcracker*, 1891, extracting famous "suite" from it, 1892; also composer of numerous operas. Recipient: Order of St. Vladimir, 1884; Nomination as Member of Académie Fran-

caise, 1892; Honorary Doctorate in Music, Cambridge University, 1893. Died in St. Petersburg, 6 November (25 October old style) 1893.

WORKS (Ballets)

1877   *Swan Lake* (with interpolations; chor. Reisinger), Bolshoi Theatre, Moscow (rearranged version, chor. Petipa and Ivanov, Maryinsky Theatre, St. Petersburg, 1895)

1890   *The Sleeping Beauty* (chor. M. Petipa), Maryinsky Theatre, St. Petersburg

1892   *The Nutcracker* (chor. Ivanov), Maryinsky Theatre, St. Petersburg

Other ballets using Tchaikovsky's music: *The Four Seasons* (Fokine, 1908), *The Reaper's Dream* (Kyasht, 1913), *Autumn Song* (Nijinska, 1915), *Eros, Francesca da Rimini, Prelude, Romance* (all Fokine, 1915), *Andantino* (Fokine, 1916), *At a Ball* (Romanov, 1927), *The Seasons* (Lavrosky, 1928), *Mozartiana* (Balanchine, 1933), *Les Présages* (Massine, 1933), *Serenade* (Balanchine, 1934), *Kittens* (Yakobson, 1936), *Romeo and Juliet* (Bartholin, 1937), *Francesca da Rimini* (Lichine, 1937; also Lifar, 1958), *Meditations* (Yakobson, 1938), *Impromptu* (Yakobson, 1938), *Romeo and Juliet* (W. Christensen, 1938; also Lifar, 1942; Yakobson, 1944; Skibine, 1950), *Ballet Imperial* (Balanchine, 1941), *Aleko* (Massine, 1942), *Hamlet* (Helpmann, 1942), *Ancient Russia* (Nijinska, 1943), *Tchaikovsky Waltz* (Taras, 1946), *Theme and Variations* (Balanchine, 1947), *Spring Fairy Tale* (Lopukhov, 1947), *Designs with Strings* (Taras, 1948), *Parures* (Burke, 1948), *Waltz* (Yakobson, 1948), *Joke and Youth* (Yakobson, 1949), *Tragédie à Verone* (Skibine, 1950), *Youth Suite* (Yakobson, 1950), *Les Oiseaux d'or* (Lichine, 1954), *Eugene Onegin* (V. Gsovsky, 1954), *Allegro Brillante* (Balanchine, 1957), *L'Amour et son destin* (Lifar, 1957), *Concerto* (Ross, 1958), *Waltz Scherzo* (Balanchine, 1958), *Beauty and the Beast* (L. Christensen, 1958), *Love Ballad* (Lopukhov, 1959), *Pas de Deux* (Balanchine, 1960), *La Dame de pique* (Lifar, 1960; also Petit, 1978), *Snow Maiden* (Bourmeister, 1961), *Mirror Walkers* (P. Wright, 1963), *Onegin* (Cranko, 1965), *Episodes* (Staff, 1967), *Jewels* ("Diamonds" section; Balanchine, 1967), *Ni Fleurs ni couronnes* (Béjart, 1968), *Tchaikovsky Suite No. 2* (d'Amboise, 1969), *Reveries* (later *Tchaikovsky Suite No. 1*; Clifford, 1969), *Suite No. 3* (Balanchine, 1970), *Anastasia* (MacMillan, 1971), *Nijinsky, Clown de Dieu* (Béjart, 1971), *Reflections* (Arpino, 1971), *Elegie* (pas de deux; Neumeier, 1978), *War and Peace* (Panov, 1980), *Souvenir de Florence* (Taras, 1981), *Capriccio Italien, Symphony No. 1* (both Martins; Tchaikovsky Festival, 1981), *Andantino, Piano Pieces, Pas de deux, Allegro con Gracia* (all Robbins; Tchaikovsky Festival, 1981), *Family Portraits* (Cullberg, 1985), *La Chatte botté* (Petit, 1985), *Battleship Potemkin* (Vinogradov, 1986), *Winter Dreams* (MacMillan, 1991), *The Hard Nut* (Morris, 1991); numerous twentieth-century restagings of *Swan Lake*, *The Sleeping Beauty*, and *The Nutcracker*.

PUBLICATIONS

By Tchaikovsky:
Tchaikovsky's Letters, translated by von Meck, New York, 1973

About Tchaikovsky:
Slonimsky, Yuri, *Masters of the Ballet in the Nineteenth Century*, Leningrad and Moscow, 1937
Bogdanov-Berezovsky, Valerian, *The Operas and Ballets of*

Tchaikovsky, Leningrad and Moscow, 1940

Hussey, Dyneley, "The Composer of *The Sleeping Beauty*", *Dancing Times* (London), 2 parts: April, May 1946

Zhitomirsky, D.V., *Tchaikovsky's Ballets*, Moscow and Leningrad, 1950

Slonimsky, Yuri, *Tchaikovsky and the Ballet Theatre of his Time*, Moscow, 1956

Roslavleva, Natalia, *Era of the Russian Ballet*, London, 1966

Garden, E., *Tchaikovsky*, London, 1973

Warrack, J., *Tchaikovsky*, London, 1973

Brown, David, *Tchaikovsky: A Biographical and Critical Study*, 4 volumes: London and New York, 1978, 1982, 1986, and 1991

Warrack, J., *Tchaikovsky Ballet Music*, London, 1979

Acocella, Joan, "Mystery, Magic and the Majesty of Tchaikovsky and the Ballet", *Dance Magazine* (New York), June 1981

Volkov, Solomon, *Balanchine's Tchaikovsky*, translated by Antonina Bovis, New York, 1985

Wiley, Roland John, *Tchaikovsky's Ballets*, New York, 1985

Kendall, Alan, *Tchaikovsky: A Biography*, London, 1988

* * *

Tchaikovsky was annoyed when his fellow-composer Sergei Taneyev rebuked him for allowing "the flavour of ballet music" into his Fourth Symphony (1878). "I can never understand why the expression 'ballet music' should be something disapproving," he replied, "The music of a ballet is not invariably bad." By then he might have instanced his own *Swan Lake*, first staged at Moscow the previous year: with *The Sleeping Beauty* (1890) and *The Nutcracker* (1892), it comprises a trilogy of scores for classical ballet that set new standards for ballet music, and have remained unsurpassed.

Throughout his career Tchaikovsky's instinct was for theatrical music. Opera was his first ambition (he finished nine and started several others) and, alone among composers for the Russian Imperial Theatres of his time, he believed ballet deserved as much musical imagination as that which brought to opera. That he had to defend himself in this respect is testified by letters to Taneyev, Rimsky-Korsakov, and others, for whom it was anathema to submit to a ballet master's established prerogatives in requiring musical modifications to suit choreographic intentions.

The composer's first known mention of the genre, in 1870, is of "a huge four-act ballet" on *Cinderella* which he was supposed to be composing for Moscow. Nothing evidently came of this, and the next year brought the family entertainment on a "Lake of Swans" theme which he helped to devise and composed while staying with his married sister in Ukraine—a piece which may have led to or influenced his first ballet subject. Meanwhile, he had discovered Bizet's *Carmen* on a Paris visit in 1875 as well as Delibes, whose *Sylvia* and *Coppélia* music he greatly admired.

The Moscow commission for *Swan Lake* occupied Tchaikovsky for much of 1875 until April the next year. A scenario of sorts probably had his collaboration, and the music was composed virtually as a four-part tone-poem, as carefully structured as any symphony. A central key (B, major or minor) relates to Odette, Siegfried, and the Swans. Around it circulate mainly flat keys for the forces of evil and bewitchment and sharp keys for character dances and divertissements, so that conflict is reflected by opposite ends of the tonal spectrum. Themes are used for reference and reminiscence, rhythm to achieve contrast and variety.

An extra "Russian Dance" was quickly added for Pelagia Karpakova, the first Odette/Odile, and a new pas de deux for a more senior ballerina, Anna Sobeshchanskaya, at the fifth

Tchaikovsky's *Swan Lake*: title-page from the printed score, Moscow, 1890

performance, both in Act III (the ballroom scene). The music generally disconcerted orchestra and dancers alike at first, and was adversely reviewed (by non-musicians) as noisy and undanceable. Detrimental musical changes were made for three successive productions in under six years (more than 40 performances), but the music's virtues soon became more apparent, leading in due course to the historic Petipa/Ivanov production after Tchaikovsky's death.

The composer returned to ballet in 1888 at the invitation of the Director of the Imperial Theatres in St. Petersburg, who in 1886 abolished the post of staff ballet composer (then held by Minkus) and wanted to improve the standard of ballet music. Ivan Vsevolozhsky proposed *The Sleeping Beauty* to Tchaikovsky in an outline he had himself written, and secured the latter's consent ("I could not want anything better than to write the music for it") on condition that he and Marius Petipa were closely involved from the outset.

The prologue and three acts were composed to Petipa's detailed breakdown of each planned episode and each dance, the music for the second act (Hunt-Vision-Awakening) being composed after the rest and in something of a hurry; this accounts for the more spasmodic sequence towards the end, and its overburdening by an entr'acte (almost a mini-concerto intended for the violinist Leopold Auer) which had to be cut during rehearsals. The key relationships of *Swan Lake* are replaced by a different means to musical unity.

The prologue and each of the three acts begin and end with narrative music, enclosing dance numbers that also carry the story forward, while these in turn surround the non-narrative divertissement dances that occupy a central place in each act. The underlying conflict of good and evil is adumbrated in the Introduction, where an angry theme associated with the wicked

Carabosse is overcome by the more graceful melody of the Lilac Fairy.

Princess Aurora is associated throughout with waltz-rhythms, and often with a solo violin. These and other solos for cello, flute, oboe, and clarinet demand playing of concerto standard. Among abundant musical highlights are the six-part violins for the entry of the Prologue Fairies, the "Rose Adagio" in 12/8 time as the first part of a linked sequence of dances, the cello melody in the Vision scene (almost identical to one in the Fifth Symphony) played at different speeds to indicate contrasting aspects of Aurora, the descriptive Panorama's rhythmic subtlety, with its 6/8 metre propelling a melody seemingly in 3/4 time, and the 5/4 metre of the "Sapphire" variation in the Act III Jewel Fairies variations.

Divertissement dances have no less an imaginative musical character, depicting different qualities of the Fairies bringing their gifts in the Prologue, for instance, or the graphic illustration of mewing cats and the hovering flight of the Bluebird in the wedding celebration. At the very end, Tchaikovsky makes his only quotation of other music in the old French song, "Vive Henri quatre" (this monarch was the grandfather of Louis XIV), still capable of provoking wonder at the unusual effect of reaching a "happy-ever-after" resolution in a minor key.

Folk themes from Germany, France, and Georgia are woven into the music for *The Nutcracker*, commissioned by Vsevolozhsky as a two-act ballet to share a double-bill with a one-act opera (*Iolanta*), both by Tchaikovsky. Again a scenario was mapped out with Petipa, Tchaikovsky at first disliking the subject but becoming more reconciled as he worked on it. His despair at picturing a Sugar Plum Fairy in music was lifted when he heard in Paris the bell-like tones of Victor Mustel's newly invented celeste, which he had sent to him in Russia in strict secrecy so that he would be the first to use it.

Whether or not because of this, Tchaikovsky took the unusual step, for his time, of letting the ballet's music be heard in a suite, extracted for concert performance in St. Petersburg some nine months before the stage production. This comprised the Overture (with its toy-like character of no bass-register instruments) and March, plus six dances from the Act II divertissement, and almost every number was encored. This *Nutcracker Suite* later became so popular that the ballet is still sometimes thought to be a confection arranged to this alone, whereas the suite consists of less than a quarter of the full score, a score composed with a direct intention of exploiting musical charm more than expressive tension.

All three ballets have had later musical modifications which are more properly the subject of productions that brought them about, but full scores are available in definitive editions from the Russian State publishers as part of the collected works. Many other choreographers have made use of Tchaikovsky's concert music since Fokine in 1915 (*Eros* to the Serenade for Strings, this music later a signature-work of Balanchine in the United States from 1934), including all six Symphonies, beginning with Massine in *Les Présages* (1933, Fifth Symphony). In 1981 a Tchaikovsky Festival by New York City Ballet featured 25 ballets to his music in 15 programmes, including 12 works newly choreographed for the occasion.

—Noël Goodwin

———

TCHELITCHEV (Tchelitchew), **Pavel**
Russian/American stage designer and painter. Born in Moscow, 21 September (9 September old style) 1898. Educated privately; studied art at Moscow University, 1916–18, also taking private lessons in drawing and costume design with Bolshoi Theatre designer K. Korasne, Moscow, 1917; studied at Kiev Academy, pupil of Alexander Exeter, 1918–20. First stage designs for Ivan Caryll's operetta *The Geisha*, Kiev, 1919 (but this never staged, due to events of the Revolution); left Russia: designer of ballet sets for Boris Kniaseff, Sofia, and Viktor Zimin, Istanbul, 1920/21; lived in Berlin, 1921–23, working for Der Blaue Vogel Cabaret Theatre, Koenigsbratzerstrasse Theater, Russian Romantic Theatre, and Berlin Staatsoper; met Serge Diaghilev, early 1920s; moved to Paris, 1923, and continued as stage designer for productions in Paris, New York, London, and Monte Carlo, 1923–42; first Ballets Russes collaboration in *Ode* (chor. Léonide Massine), Paris, 1928; began association with George Balanchine, New York, 1933, settled in America, 1934: became U.S. citizen in 1952. Died in Rome, 31 July 1957.

WORKS (Ballet design)

1919 *The Geisha* (operetta; Ivan Caryll), Mardzhanov's Theatre, Kiev (never performed)
1921 Ballets for Weekly programmes of Viktor Zimin's Ballet Company, Istanbul
1922 Series of tableaux for Der Blaue Vogel Cabaret, Berlin
      The Wedding Feast of the Boyar (chor. Romanov), Russian Romantic Ballet, Berlin
      The Sacrifice of Atoraga (chor. Romanov), Russian Romantic Ballet, Berlin
1923 *Savonarola* (tragedy after Gobineau), Koenigsbratzerstrasse Theater, Berlin
      Le Coq d'or (opera-ballet; mus. Rimsky-Korsakov), Staatsoper, Berlin
1928 *Ode* (chor. Massine), Diaghilev's Ballets Russes, Paris
1933 *L'Errante* (chor. Balanchine), Les Ballets 1933, Paris
1936 *Serenata: Magic* (chor. Balanchine), Avery Memorial Theatre, Hartford, Connecticut
      Orpheus and Eurydice (opera; mus. Gluck, chor. Balanchine), Metropolitan Opera House, New York
1938 *Noblissima Visione* (*Saint Francis*; chor. Massine), Le Ballet Russe de Monte Carlo, London
1939 *Ondine* (play; Jean Giraudoux), presented by Louis Jouvet, Paris
1941 *Balustrade* (chor. Balanchine), Original Ballet Russe, New York
      The Cave of Sleep (chor. Balanchine), American Ballet Caravan (never produced)
1942 *Apollon musagète* (new production; chor. Balanchine), Teatro Colón, Buenos Aires
      Concierto de Mozart (chor. Balanchine), Teatro Colón, Buenos Aires

PUBLICATIONS

Kirstein, Lincoln, "The Position of Pavel Tchelitchew", *View* (New York), May 1942
Windham, Donald, "The Stage and Ballet Designs of Pavel Tchelitchev", *Dance Index* (New York), January/February 1944
Amberg, George, *Art in Modern Ballet*, London, 1946
Kirstein, Lincoln, "The Interior Landscapes of Pavel Tchelitchew", *The Magazine of Art* (New York), February 1948
Chujoy, Anatole, *The New York City Ballet*, New York, 1953

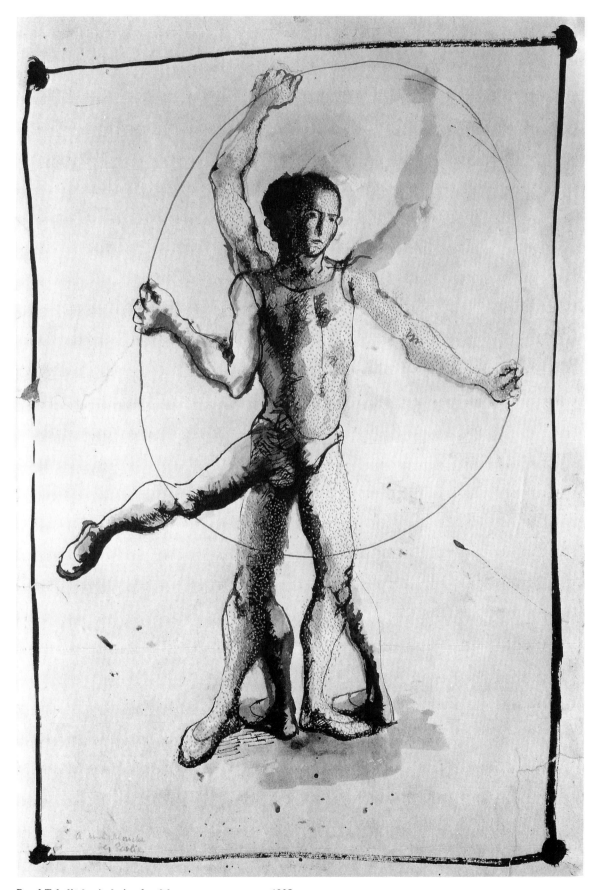

Pavel Tchelitchev's design for *Ode* programme cover, c.1928

Tyler, Parker, *The Divine Comedy of Pavel Tchelitchev*, New York, 1967
Pavel Tchelitchew: A Selection of Gouaches, Drawings and Paintings (catalogue), London, 1972
Nathanson, Richard, *Pavel Tchelitchew: A Collection of Fifty-four Theatre Designs c. 1919–1923*, London, 1976
Bowlt, John E., *Russian Stage Design: Scenic Innovation 1900–1930*, Jackson, Mississippi, 1982
Lassalle, Nancy, "Beyond Les Ballets 1933", *Ballet Review* (New York), vol. 16 no. 3, Fall 1988

*   *   *

Pavel Tchelitchev was a painter and designer whose vivid imagination led him to design some of the most exciting décors ever produced for ballet. He adapted many traditional devices, such as the wires for aerial ballets of the romantic period and the manipulation of lights first explored by Loie Fuller, and combined these with new innovations using fabrics and natural products, such as dead birch branches or various metals. These were often constructed according to a spiral or circular scheme and employed exotic colours, the designs generating an extraordinary sense of movement.

Throughout his life Tchelitchev travelled to many countries, including Germany and France, cultivating his interests in the occult and astrology. He was inspired by the burgeoning artistic movements in both locations, namely Constructivism and Surrealism. In this context it is not surprising that during his career Tchelitchev was to become involved with two of the most prominent figures in twentieth-century dance, Serge Diaghilev and George Balanchine.

In 1922 Diaghilev had been impressed by Tchelitchev's designs for the ballet *The Wedding Feast of the Boyar* (choreographed by Boris Romanov) and thus commissioned him to design for the Ballet Russes. However, it was not until six years later that Tchelitchev agreed, his reluctance in part due to his fascination for painting on canvas. His association with Diaghilev resulted in the revolutionary ballet *Ode* (choreographed by Léonide Massine) which employed the use of film, neon lighting, and phosphorescent costumes. Illumination came from on stage, where the lights were placed behind a pale blue cinema screen which diffused and dispersed them. Mannequins hung in space to create a false perspective and the dancers held cords and pulled them, creating geometrical diagrams in space.

The designs for *Ode* were indicative of Tchelitchev's approach to dance, for he regarded the dancers as an integral part of the overall design for a ballet, and attempted not only to dictate the costumes and sets, but also to influence the actual movements of the dancers. Such an approach has direct parallels with the work of choreographer/designer Alwin Nikolais some 40 years later, whose use of body extensions define the dancer as an abstract object. Thus in many ways Tchelitchev was a pioneer whose work was to have a lasting influence.

Indeed, the dance critic and historian Anatole Chujoy noted in 1953 that the influence of Tchelitchev on the development of American ballet could not be overestimated, for he helped shape the aesthetic tastes of George Balanchine and Lincoln Kirstein, founders of one of the world's great ballet companies—the New York City Ballet. When Tchelitchev discussed the images he had in mind for a ballet, Balanchine would listen spellbound, while Kirstein, for his part, collected Tchelitchev's paintings and organized exhibitions of his work. Many of these paintings are on display in the Museum of Modern Art in New York.

Tchelitchev's association with Balanchine began in 1933 when the two men were working on the ballet *L'Errante*, which symbolized the existence of man on earth after his creation. In it Tchelitchev further experimented with the use of transparency, using sheer fabrics and light to create, as Donald Windham wrote in 1944, "a visual image as compact as the reflection in a drop of water". Their next project was the ballet *Magic* (1936). Here Tchelitchev hung furniture from cheese-cloth walls so that it appeared to float in air, and in the side-walls, doors were constructed to provide false panels of a magician's box, in and out of which articles would appear and disappear. Such designs often bewildered audiences, for they were far ahead of their time; and as a consequence, some of Tchelitchev's work was never actually mounted on stage, including the 1938 work for *The Cave of Sleep*, intended to be performed by Balanchine's recently formed American Ballet Caravan. In preparation for this work, Tchelitchev sketched a series of costumes inspired by the four support systems of the human anatomy—the bone structure, and the lymphatic, nervous, and muscular systems. The composer of the score, Hindemith, was dissatisfied with Tchelitchev's sketches, feeling that the visual presentation offered him, however beautiful, was quite overwhelming and went far beyond his concept of the work. However, their artistic merit has since been more readily appreciated and the sketches are now in the Department of Theatre Arts of the Museum of Modern Art.

In contrast with Hindemith's reluctance to have Tchelitchev's designs used in a ballet for which he composed a score, Stravinsky's reaction was quite enthusiastic. Stravinsky's music was used for George Balanchine's *Balustrade* (1940) and of Tchelitchev's splendid scenery, dominated by the white balustrade from which the ballet takes its name, Stravinsky said that it was "one of the most satisfactory visualisations of any of my theatre works".

Certainly Tchelitchev received the recognition his designs deserved when the editor of the periodical *Dance Index* decided to devote an entire edition to him. (This appeared in the January/February 1944 issue and is a key text for anyone wishing to research his designs.) More recently a collection of 54 of Tchelitchev's theatre designs, covering the period 1919–23, was exhibited at the Alpine Club, South Audley Street, London, in December 1976. In the introductory catalogue which accompanied this event, its organizer Richard Nathanson wrote that Tchelitchev should be considered an important innovator of stage design, commenting that the collection "with its originality, vitality, humour and richness is a homage to the magic of true theatre". There can surely be no more fitting a tribute for this artist, whose visions extended the boundaries of design for ballet.

—Melanie Trifona Christoudia

TCHERINA, Ludmila
French dancer, artist, and comedienne.   Born Monika (Monique) Avenirova Tchemerzina in Paris, 10 October 1924. Studied with Blanche d'Alessandri, Olga Preobrazhenska, Paris; later studied with Ivan Clustine, Gustave Ricaux, Boris Kniaseff, and Paul Goubé. Married (1) dancer Edmund Audran (d. 1951); (2) Raymond Roi. Début at the age of eight, later performing as dancer, Maison de la Chimie, 1938, and in recital at École Normale de Musique, 1939; étoile, Opéra de Marseille, 1940, and Ballets de Monte Carlo, 1942; Paris début with Serge Lifar in *Romeo and Juliet*, 1942; principal dancer (performing as Tcherina), Ballets des Champs-Elysées, 1945,

and in recitals with Edmond Audran; ballerina, Opéra de Marseille, also performing with Nouveaux Ballets de Monte Carlo and Ballets de Paris, 1945; international guest artist, including at Metropolitan Opera, New York, 1950, La Scala, Milan, 1954, Paris Opéra Ballet, 1957, Bolshoi and Kirov Ballets, Russia, 1959, Ballet du XXe Siècle, 1961; founder and ballerina of own ensemble, touring France, Britain, and Italy, 1958, and performing at the Théâtre Sarah-Bernhardt, 1959; producer and principal dancer, Teatro San Carlo, Naples, 1960; also appeared in films, including in *Les Rendezvous* (dir. Jacque), *The Red Shoes* (dir. Powell, 1948) and *Tales of Hoffmann* (dir. Powell, 1951); also artist, exhibiting own paintings in Paris, 1962, 1973, 1975, and 1978, and sculpture at Seville International Fair and Strasbourg, 1992; author of two novels on dance. Recipient: Academy Award ("Oscar", for her role in *Tales of Hoffmann*), 1952; Prix de la Meilleure Interpretation Feminin au Referendum de Vichy; Premier Prix d'Interpretation du Film sur la danse à Buenos Aires, 1952; Leonardo da Vinci Prize, 1971; Prix International du Gemail, 1973; Grand Prix for *La Reine de Sabra*, 1975; Trophy de l'Année Européenne du Cinema et de la Télévision, 1988.

ROLES

1942   Ballerina in *Petrushka* (Fokine), Ballets de Monte Carlo, Monte Carlo
       Zobéïde in *Shéhérazade* (Fokine), Ballets de Monte Carlo, Monte Carlo
       Juliet (cr) in *Romeo and Juliet* (Lifar), Salle Pleyel, Paris
1945   La Belle Endormie in *Les Forains* (Petit), Les Ballets des Champs-Elysées, Paris
       Pas de deux from *The Sleeping Beauty* (after Petipa), Ballets des Champs-Elysées, Paris
       Pas de deux from *Swan Lake* (after Ivanov), Ballets des Champs-Elysées, Paris
       Principal dancer (cr) in *Mephisto Waltz* (Lifar), Gala, Salle Pleyel, Paris
1946   Young Bonaparte in *A la mémoire d'un héros* (Lifar), Nouveaux Ballets de Monte Carlo
       Principal dancer (cr) in *Madame La Lune* (Audran), Gala
1948   Principal dancer (cr) in *Alborado del Gracioso* (Lifar), Gala, Théâtre des Champs-Elysées, Paris
1954   Title role in *Giselle* (after Petipa, Coralli, Perrot), Ballet of La Scala, Milan
       The Swan in *Le Mort du cygne* (after Fokine), La Scala, Milan
1955   Antinea in *L'Atlantide* (opera; mus. Tomasi), Casino de Enghien
1957   Sébastien (cr) in *Le Martyre de Saint-Sébastien* (Lifar), Paris Opéra Ballet, Paris
       Antinea (cr) in *L'Atlantide* (Goubé), Ballets Tcherina, tour
1959   Principal dancer (cr) in *Les Amants de Teruel* (Sparemblek), Ballets de Ludmila Tcherina, Paris (also filmed 1962)
       Principal dancer (cr) in *Feu aux poudres* (Goubé), Ballets de Ludmila Tcherina
1961   Principal dancer (cr) in *Gala* (Béjart), Ballet du XXe Siècle, Venice
1967   Principal dancer in *The Miraculous Mandarin* (Lazzini), Metropolitan Opera Ballet, New York (also filmed 1967)
1968   Principal dancer (cr) in *Excelsior* (dell'Ara), Maggio Musicale Fiorentino, Florence

Ludmila Tcherina

1972   Fenella in *La Muette de Portici* (opera; mus. Auber), Palermo

Other roles include: television appearances in *Bonaparte* (chor. Lifar; 1968), *Jeanne au Bucher* (1970), *Salomé* (1972), *La Dame aux camélias* (1974), *La Passion d'Anna Karina* (play by Chekhov; French television, 1975), *La Reine de Saba* (1975), *La Création feminine* (1976), *Tcherina en masculin* (1979); film appearances in *La Belle que voilà*, *Clara de Montargis*, *Fandango Espagnol*, *La Figli de Mata Hari*, *Grand Gala*, *Lune de miel*, *La Nuit s'achève*, *Parsifal*, *Revenant*, *Sign of the Pagan*, *Spartaco*.

PUBLICATIONS

By Tcherina:
L'Amour au miroir, 1983
La Femme à l'envers, 1986 (also script for film)

About Tcherina:
The Red Shoes Book, London, 1948
The Tales of Hoffmann Book, London, 1951
Lidova, Irène, *17 Visages de la danse française*, Paris, 1953
Hirsch, Nicole, *Ludmila Tcherina*, Paris, 1958
"Personality of the Month: Ludmila Tcherina", *Dance and Dancers* (London), April 1959
Lido, S., *Ludmila Tcherina, tragédienne de la danse*, Paris, 1967
Garaudy, Roger, *Ludmila Tcherina, erotisme et mystique*, Paris, 1975

*   *   *

Ludmila Tcherina was the first of a new type of star ballerina in France. Not prepared to make do with the life of self-denial of a classical dancer, she decided to popularize her name through the cinema, television, and fashionable life. She had an infallible weapon at her disposal for the advancement of her career: her radiant beauty. Born of a Georgian father and French mother, Monique Tchemerzina (her real name) experienced poverty as a child. She led the life of a child prodigy, appearing in galas and dancing in fashionable salons. She astonished all with her maturity and physique, already blossoming. Her tutor, the Italian Blanche d'Alessandri, brought out a precocious stamina and virtuosity. Tcherina has always been a quick-footed, finely balanced dancer with expressive arms. She would astonish her contemporaries by staying in arabesque on pointe for several minutes without faltering.

When war was declared, she settled in Marseilles with her mother, where at the age of sixteen she made her début as danseuse étoile at the town opera. Having been taken on at Monte Carlo with her partner Edmond Audran, who later became her husband, she was discovered by Serge Lifar who gave the dancer her big chance by presenting her in Paris at the Salle Pleyel in his new ballet *Romeo and Juliet*, in which he himself was her partner. Lifar named her Ludmila Tcherina and her career took off. In 1945 she took part in the first season of the Ballets des Champs-Elysées, taking up the role of Nina Vyroubova in *Les Forains* by Roland Petit. The next year she was one of the stars of the Nouveaux Ballets de Monte Carlo directed by Serge Lifar, who mounted a production of *A la mémoire d'un héros*, in which Tcherina personified the young Bonaparte, a role which she particularly liked and which she danced often thereafter in television recitals.

Tcherina was now continuing her dance training with Paul Goubé, a dancer at the Opéra, but she was already a stranger to the world of dance and dedicated her efforts increasingly to the cinema. After her first film, *Le Rendezvous* by Christian Jacque, she danced in Michael Powell's famous films, *The Red Shoes* and *Tales of Hoffmann*. The tragic end of her young husband in an accident was devastating, but she continued to go through life with aplomb and ambition. She remarried a rich industrialist, and formed her own company in 1959 at the Théâtre Sarah-Bernhardt, where she danced *Les Amants de Teruel*, a dramatic ballet by Raymond Rouleau with choreography by Milko Sparemblek. This ballet became a full-length film, and Tcherina was proclaimed "the tragic actress of dance".

Tcherina was also a success at the Paris Opéra, where she was invited to play the young adolescent of *The Martyrdom of Saint Sebastian*. Her last new role as a dancer was a ballet by Salvador Dali and Maurice Béjart, *Gala*, first performed in Venice and later in Brussels and Paris.

In 1967, Tcherina made a television film of *The Miraculous Mandarin*, a piece choreographed by Joseph Lazzini. Her appearances on television became more and more frequent, although her acting lacks spontaneity, and some might claim that it is her beauty which most dominates her appearances on the screen. None the less, all her shows are widely discussed in the Parisian press. She has many talents, presenting her own art works in fashionable galleries, where she exploits erotic themes, often with great daring. She is also a writer, and has published two novels based on the tragedy of a dancer. She is to be seen in spectacular form at theatre premieres and fashionable galas, still beautiful and elegantly dressed by the great Parisian couturiers. Tcherina, it is obvious, will not easily relinquish her position as a true "star".

—Irène Lidova

TCHERKASSKY, Marianna

American dancer. Born in Glen Cove, New York, daughter of dancer Lillian Oka, 28 October 1952. Studied with mother, and at Washington (D.C.) School of Ballet, pupil of Mary Day and Edward Caton, from 1965; Ford Foundation Scholar, School of American Ballet, New York, from 1967. Married American Ballet Theatre ballet master Terence Orr, 1980. Professional début, André Eglevsky Ballet, Long Island, New York, 1968; dancer, American Ballet Theatre, from 1970, becoming soloist, 1972, and principal dancer, from 1976; guest artist, appearing at Aspen Festival, Colorado, 1982, and with Rudolf Nureyev and Friends on tour, 1988; has also appeared on national television, including for Public Broadcasting Service (PBS) series *In Performance at Wolf Trap*, in *On Stage America*, and in *Die Fledermaus* (opera; mus. Strauss, chor. Ruth Page).

ROLES

1971   Principal dancer (cr) in *Mendelssohn Symphony* (Nahat), American Ballet Theatre, New York
   Solo variation in *Paquita* (Nureyev after Petipa), American Ballet Theatre, New York
   Principal dancer (cr) in *Eccentrique* (Feld), American Ballet Theatre, Washington, D.C.

1972/   Prayer in *Coppélia* (Martinez after Saint-Léon), Ameri-
74   can Ballet Theatre
   Sweetheart/Mother in *Billy the Kid* (Loring), American Ballet Theatre
   Ballerina in *Petrushka* (Fokine), American Ballet Theatre
   Pas de deux in *At Midnight* (Feld), American Ballet Theatre
   "Giggling Rapids" in *The River* (Ailey), American Ballet Theatre
   Fouetté Competition in *Graduation Ball* (Lichine), American Ballet Theatre
   Princess Florine (Bluebird) in *The Sleeping Beauty* (Petipa), American Ballet Theatre
   Prelude in *Les Sylphides* (Fokine), American Ballet Theatre
   Peasant Pas de deux in *Giselle* (Petipa after Coralli, Perrot; staged Blair), American Ballet Theatre

1973   The White Girl in *Monument for a Dead Boy* (van Dantzig), American Ballet Theatre, Washington, D.C.
   Vision Pas de trois in *The Tales of Hoffmann* (Darrell), American Ballet Theatre, New York

1974   The Bride in *Le Baiser de la fée* (Neumeier), American Ballet Theatre, New York
   Principal dancer in *Napoli Variations* (Bournonville; staged Lander), American Ballet Theatre, New York

1975   Principal dancer (cr) in *The Leaves are Fading* (Tudor), American Ballet Theatre, New York

1976   Principal dancer (cr) in *Push Comes to Shove* (Tharp), American Ballet Theatre, New York
   Fairy of the Woodland Glades in *The Sleeping Beauty* (new production; Petipa; staged Skeaping), American Ballet Theatre, New York
   Nikiya in "The Kingdom of the Shades" from *La Bayadère* (Makarova after Petipa), American Ballet Theatre, New York
   Title role in *Giselle* (Petipa after Coralli, Perrot; staged Blair), American Ballet Theatre, New York
   Clara (cr) in *The Nutcracker* (Baryshnikov), American Ballet Theatre, Washington, D.C.

Marianna Tcherkassky as Giselle, American Ballet Theatre, New York

1979   Principal dancer in *Dark Elegies* (Tudor), American Ballet Theatre
1980   Nikiya in *La Bayadère* (full-length production; Makarova after Petipa), American Ballet Theatre, New York
Principal dancer in *Concert Waltzes* (Levans), American Ballet Theatre, New York
Variation and Adagio in *Les Rendezvous* (Ashton), American Ballet Theatre
1981   Pas de deux (Act I) from *La Fille mal gardée* (Joffe after Petipa), American Ballet Theatre
Principal dancer (cr) in *Configurations* (Choo San Goh), American Ballet Theatre, Washington, D.C.
1982   Principal dancer in *Great Galloping Gottschalk* (Taylor-Corbett), American Ballet Theatre
1983   Principal dancer in *Interludes* (McFall), American Ballet Theatre, San Francisco
Title role in *La Sylphide* (new production; Bruhn after Bournonville), American Ballet Theatre, New York
1984   Principal dancer (cr) in *In a Country Garden* (new version of *Elssler Pas de deux*; Vernon), American Ballet Theatre, Miami
Title role in *Cinderella* (Baryshnikov, Anastos), American Ballet Theatre, New York

Principal dancer in *Donizetti Variations* (Balanchine), American Ballet Theatre, Washington, D.C.
1985   Ballerina (cr) in *Grand Pas Romantique* (Bujones), American Ballet Theatre, Miami
Juliet in *Romeo and Juliet* (MacMillan), American Ballet Theatre, Washington, D.C.
1988   Principal dancer in *Bruch Violin Concerto No. 1* (Tippet), American Ballet Theatre
Glove-Seller in *Gaîté Parisienne* (Massine), American Ballet Theatre
1989   Ballerina in *Birthday Offering* (Ashton), American Ballet Theatre
1990   Principal dancer in *Nine Sinatra Songs* (Tharp), American Ballet Theatre

Other roles include: The Young Girl in *Le Spectre de la rose* (Fokine), principal dancer in *Concerto* (MacMillan), title role in *Firebird* (Fokine; staged Newton), Swanilda in *Coppélia* (Martinez after Saint-Léon), Kitri in *Don Quixote: Kitri's Wedding* (Baryshnikov after Petipa), principal dancer in *Études* (Lander), title role in *Paquita* (Grand Pas; Nureyev after Petipa), Bride in *Les Noces* (Robbins), Grand Pas Hongrois in *Raymonda* (Nureyev after Petipa).

PUBLICATIONS

By Tcherkassky:
Interview with Jennifer Dunning, *The New York Times*, 13 June 1980

About Tcherkassky:
Cunningham, Katharine, "Billy and the Virgins", *Dance and Dancers* (London), November 1973
Greskovic, Robert, "ABT: Dancers at a Gathering", *Ballet Review* (Brooklyn, N.Y.), vol. 5, no. 1, 1975-76
Gruen, John, "Robert La Fosse, Marianna Tcherkassky, George de la Pena", *Dance Magazine* (New York), September 1981
Greskovic, Robert, "The Past, the Present and the Ballet", *Ballet Review* (New York), Summer 1986

*   *   *

When Marianne Tcherkassky as a young girl made the statement that there was never any question what she would do, she was referring, of course, to a career in ballet—a career that was saluted in the spring of 1990 on her twentieth anniversary with the American Ballet Theatre.

If there is artistic heredity, Tcherkassky comes well enriched. Both parents were performing artists with widely diversified backgrounds; her mother of Japanese heritage appeared with the Grand Ballet du Marquis de Cuevas and the Markova-Dolin Ballet, and her father was an opera and concert singer of Russian descent. The Tcherkassky schooling at the barre was first-rate, including studies with Mary Day, Oleg Briansky, and André Eglevsky. As with many students of the School of American Ballet in New York City, she attracted many admirers at her graduation who then watched with interest her development from corps to principal dancer with American Ballet Theatre.

The eclecticism of that company allowed Tcherkassky to demonstrate a wide range of styles; contemporary choreographers have happily provided her with a variety of roles within works by Ashton, Ailey, and Feld. The particular Tcherkassky style, however, was apparent from the beginning—that of the nineteenth-century Romantic ballerina, technically assured, presenting a picture of charm and delicacy. As repertory enlarged, new ballets expanded her technique and made more demands, but the characteristics of Romanticism were pre-eminent. Standards such as *Swan Lake*, *Les Sylphides*, *Coppélia*, and *La Bayadère* were taken on with great confidence, but it was with her *Giselle* début in 1976 that she began one of the most celebrated artist-role identifications in twentieth-century ballet.

The ingredients for a very fine Giselle had been evident in earlier roles, particularly that of the young girl in *Le Spectre de la rose*. For the first-act Giselle, Tcherkassky appeared innocent, delicate, and vulnerable; whereas the dancer's second-act Giselle added the necessary steel to a figure incorporeal, yet determined to protect her prince. Tcherkassky's technique seems ideally suited to both acts, airy with an ethereal quality founded in a precise placement in attitude and fluid port de bras, all executed without artificiality.

The American Ballet Theatre's production of *Giselle* during the mid-1970s had had two outstanding ballerinas in Natalia Makarova and Gelsey Kirkland. When Marianne Tcherkassky followed them with her début *Giselle*, she made an immediate impact, but it was not until she had developed in the characterization a few years later that the total kinetic authority displayed itself, and her *Giselle* performances took on an artistic distinction that may well have exceeded that of her colleagues. Of all her many predecessors, Tcherkassky's rendering is probably most reminiscent of Alicia Markova, whose buoyancy and gossamer effects are part of history. Markova was often described as being "pulled from the air" by her partner—a phrase that could be applied to Tcherkassky as well.

With Sir Kenneth MacMillan's *Romeo and Juliet*, Tcherkassky undertook a role that could, once again, demonstrate the unique qualities that distinguished her Giselle. She was able to present a character of humanity; her Juliet was sweet and charming without being cloying. Both Juliet and Giselle challenged her in narrative detail and dance execution, and Tcherkassky more than met those challenges. Perhaps a similar challenge was not found in other roles such as those in Tharp's *Push Comes to Shove* and Ailey's *The River*—for these parts, though dutifully danced, could not be called definitive. Undoubtedly, Tcherkassky's small stature and medium proportions helped define and at times limit her choice of roles. Those roles that employ virtuosic fireworks or call for a demonstration of extreme extensions and balletic strengths do not comprise a large part of her repertory, though Lander's *Études* and *Firebird* were once found in her ballet treasure chest.

—Richard Rutledge

———

TCHERNICHEVA, Lubov

Russian/British dancer and teacher.   Born Lyubov (Lubov) Pavlovna Chernitseva (Tchernicheva) in St. Petersburg, 17 September 1890. Studied at the Imperial Theatre School, pupil of Mikhail Fokine; graduated in 1908; later studied with Enrico Cecchetti. Married ballet régisseur (stage and rehearsal director) Serge Grigoriev, 1909. Dancer, Maryinsky Theatre, St. Petersburg, 1908-11; joined Diaghilev's Ballets Russes (with husband Grigoriev) in 1911, becoming leading dancer, and touring South America with company, 1913; ballet mistress, Diaghilev's Ballets Russes, 1926-29, and Ballets Russes de Monte Carlo, from 1932; retired from dancing, but returned to stage occasionally, including for *Francesca da Rimini*, 1937; ballet mistress, de Basil's Ballets Russes (becoming Original Ballet Russe), 1937-52, also staging Fokine ballets for companies including Sadler's Wells Ballet (later the Royal Ballet), London, 1954, 1955, 1957, London Festival Ballet, 1956, and La Scala, Milan. Died in Richmond, Surrey, 1 March 1976.

ROLES

1911   A Princess in *Sadko* (Fokine), Diaghilev's Ballets Russes, Paris
1913   Nymph in *L'Après-midi d'un faune* (Fokine), Diaghilev's Ballets Russes, London
1916   Zobéïde in *Schéhérazade* (Fokine), Diaghilev's Ballets Russes, Madrid
1917   Costanza (cr) in *Les Femmes de bonne humeur* (Massine), Diaghilev's Ballets Russes, Rome
         Swan Princess (cr) in *Contes Russes* (Massine), Diaghilev's Ballets Russes, Paris
         A Young Girl in *Les Papillons* (Fokine), Diaghilev's Ballets Russes, London
         Tsarevna in *Sadko* (Bolm), Diaghilev's Ballets Russes, Madrid
1919   Queen of Clubs (cr) in *La Boutique fantasque* (Massine),

Lubov Tchernicheva as Cléopâtre, 1937

Diaghilev's Ballets Russes, London
Tsarevna in *L'Oiseau de feu* (Fokine), Diaghilev's Ballets Russes, London
1920 Prudenza (cr) in *Pulcinella* (Massine), Diaghilev's Ballets Russes, Paris
Principal dancer (cr) in *Le Astuzie femminili* (Massine), Diaghilev's Ballets Russes, Paris
1921 Mountain Ash Fairy, Countess, Ariana in *The Sleeping Princess* (Petipa; staged Sergeyev, with additional chor. Nijinska), Diaghilev's Ballets Russes, London
1923 Villager (cr) in *Les Noces* (Nijinska), Diaghilev's Ballets Russes, Paris
1924 Dancer in *Cimarosiana* (divertissement from *Le Astuzie femminili*; Massine), Diaghilev's Ballets Russes, Monte Carlo
Echo in *Narcisse* (revival; Fokine), Diaghilev's Ballets Russes, Monte Carlo
Aphrodite (cr) in *Les Tentations de la bergère* (Nijinska), Diaghilev's Ballets Russes, Monte Carlo
Chanson dansée ("Grey Girl"; cr) in *Les Biches* (Nijinska), Diaghilev's Ballets Russes, Monte Carlo
Orphise (cr) in *Les Fâcheux* (Nijinska), Diaghilev's Ballets Russes, Monte Carlo
1925 Lezghinka (cr) in *Le Démon* (opera; mus. Rubinstein, chor. Balanchine), Diaghilev's Ballets Russes, Monte Carlo (also performed as part of *Suite de danses*, Monte Carlo, 1925)
A Muse (cr) in *Zéphire et Flore* (Massine), Diaghilev's Ballets Russes, Monte Carlo
1926 Principal dancer (cr) in *Hamlet* (*La Fête du Printemps de Hamlet*, from the opera by Thomas; Balanchine), Diaghilev's Ballets Russes, Monte Carlo
A dancer (cr) in *Jack-in-the-Box* (Balanchine), Diaghilev's Ballets Russes, Paris
Emerald Fairy, Sylph (cr) in *The Triumph of Neptune* (Balanchine), Diaghilev's Ballets Russes, London
1927 Principal dancer (cr) in *Le Pas d'acier* (Massine), Diaghilev's Ballets Russes, Paris
1928 Calliope (cr) in *Apollon musagète* (Balanchine), Diaghilev's Ballets Russes, Paris
One of Two Ladies (cr) in *The Gods go a-Begging* (Balanchine), Diaghilev's Ballets Russes, London
1937 Francesca (cr) in *Francesca da Rimini* (Lichine), de Basil's Ballets Russes, London

Other roles include: Chiarina in *Le Carnaval* (Fokine), the Girl in *Le Spectre de la rose* (Fokine), title role in *Cléopâtre* (Fokine), principal dancer in *Les Sylphides* (Fokine), title role in *Thamar* (Fokine), the Miller's Wife in *Le Tricorne* (Massine), Flore in *Zéphire et Flore* (Massine).

WORKS

Staged:
1954 *The Firebird* (with Grigoriev, after Fokine; mus. Stravinsky), Sadler's Wells Ballet, Edinburgh
1955 *Les Sylphides* (with Grigoriev, after Fokine; mus. Chopin), Sadler's Wells Ballet, London
1956 *Petrushka* (with Grigoriev, after Fokine; mus. Stravinsky), London Festival Ballet, London (staged for Royal Ballet, London, 1957)

PUBLICATIONS

Beaumont, Cyril, *The Art of Lubov Tchernicheva*, London, 1921

Haskell, Arnold, *Balletomania*, London, 1934
Lifar, Serge, *Serge Diaghilew*, New York, 1940
Grigoriev, Serge, *The Diaghilev Ballet*, translated by Vera Bowen, London, 1953
Clarke, Mary, *The Sadler's Wells Ballet*, London, 1955
Johns, Eric, "Serge Grigoriev and Lubov Tchernicheva", *Dancing Times* (London), February 1964
Anthony, Gordon, "Lubov Tchernicheva", *Dancing Times* (London), February 1976
Vaughan, David, "Balanchine's Ballerinas", *Dance Magazine* (New York), January 1979

*   *   *

Lubov Tchernicheva was one of Diaghilev's most faithful dancers, staying with him from 1911, when she was a member of the corps de ballet, until the end in 1929, when she was not only ballet mistress but one of the finest character dancers and mimes in the company.

She came to prominence on the South American tour of 1913, and within a few years had inherited many of Karsavina's great roles, notably Zobéïde in *Schéhérazade* and the title roles in *Thamar* and *Cléopâtre*. If she lacked Karsavina's warmth and voluptuousness, she made up for it with an aristocratic elegance and icy sadism, enigmatic and controlled. She had an extraordinary theatrical power, which could fill the largest theatre with her very stillness, exuding a very Russian exotic glamour and personal magnetism. She was not a great classical technician, but she was a notable exponent of *Les Sylphides*, attaining what Cyril Beaumont called "the sweet melancholy which is the keynote of the ballet".

Tchernicheva was a distinguished interpreter of the work of many choreographers. She was a langorous, dreamy Constanza in Massine's *Les Femmes de bonne humeur* and an elegant Calliope in Balanchine's *Apollon musagète*, as well as illuminating in a wide range of roles in such ballets as *Pulcinella*, *Les Noces*, *Les Biches*, and *Les Fâcheux*. But it was in the Fokine repertory, with its particular combination of dance and drama, that she particularly excelled, and it was these interpretations of Zobéïde, Thamar, and Cléopâtre that she took up again in the 1930s when she was already at the age at which, in those days, most dancers had long retired. To the balletomanes of the time she was known as "Auntie Luba", a sign of the affection and respect in which they held her, besides being a delicate allusion to her age.

As Zobéïde she had lost none of her power to hold an audience, nor her exotic remoteness that combined so thrillingly with her icily erotic persona. As Thamar, she was alluring and sensual with a hair-raising menace. She also took on the role of the Miller's Wife in *Le Tricorne*—her age did not matter and, if she was a little too aristocratic for the earthy Wife, she could flirt with the best, using her beautiful eyes to full effect. At this time, too, she created a new role, the young Francesca in Lichine's *Francesca da Rimini*. Her years seemed to slip away, and she was the perfect realization of a young Renaissance girl in love, superbly dignified and expressive; her personification of youthful beauty contributed much to the success of the ballet. It also gave her the opportunity for one of her famous death scenes as, following the death of Paolo, she tore open her bodice to bare her breast to the sword of Malatesta.

In 1926, Tchernicheva took over the duties of ballet mistress to the Diaghilev Ballet, a position she was later to fill with equal success for the de Basil Ballets Russes throughout its life. She was a strict disciplinarian, upholding the traditions of the Imperial Russian Ballet School in which she had trained; but she is also remembered with affection by a generation of young dancers upon whose careers she had a great influence, as both teacher and coach. She helped them with interpretation and passed on to them something of her own exceptional understanding of the creation of character through movement. She maintained the highest possible standards, no mean achievement considering the nomadic life of the various Ballets Russes companies with which she worked.

In later life, when she and her husband, Serge Grigoriev, revived Diaghilev ballets for various companies, she had lost none of her touch, and the combination of her husband's phenomenal memory with her own coaching ability contributed especially to the famous revivals for the Royal Ballet of *The Firebird*, *Petrushka*, and *Les Sylphides*.

Tchernicheva was a woman of great personal beauty, with magnificent topaz eyes that could flash, melt, or flirt, and dominate the farthest recesses of the largest theatre. Allied to this was an aristocratic profile and natural elegance. She exuded breeding both in dance and mime, and her subtly economic gestures were a model to younger dancers. All the companies for which she worked owed her a debt, not only for her magnificent example, but for the care and attention that she lavished upon revivals.

—Sarah C. Woodcock

TENNANT, Veronica

Canadian dancer. Born in London, England, 15 January 1947. Studied at the Cone-Ripman School, London, 1952–55, and National Ballet of Canada School, Toronto, pupil of Betty Oliphant, 1956–64. Married Dr. John Wright, 1969: one daughter. Principal dancer, National Ballet of Canada, from 1965, touring extensively with company including in Paris, London, Stuttgart, Amsterdam, and Japan; featured ballerina on National Ballet of Canada's first London appearance, 1972, with Rudolf Nureyev on company's New York Metropolitan Opera début, 1973, and with Mikhail Baryshnikov immediately following his defection, 1974; guest artist, including for Jacob's Pillow Dance Festival at Lee, Massachusetts, New Orleans Ballet, Royal Winnipeg Ballet, Les Grands Ballets Canadiens, Nervi Festival, Italy, American Ballet Theatre, and on tour with ensemble of National Ballet of Canada soloists, Italy, 1985; has also appeared frequently on Canadian television, including in *Cinderella* (CBC, 1967; Emmy Award), *The Sleeping Beauty* (CBC/PBS, 1972; Emmy Award), and in documentaries *Veronica Tennant: A Dancer of Distinction* (CBC, 1983) and *Veronica: Completing the Circle* (CBC, 1989); also guest speaker, lecturer, broadcaster, and occasional actress; retired from the ballet stage, with farewell performance as Juliet, 1989. Recipient: Title of Officer of the Order of Canada, 1975; Toronto Arts Award for the Performing Arts, 1984; Honorary Doctorates from Brock University, 1985, York University, 1987, and University of Toronto, 1992.

ROLES

1965   Juliet in *Romeo and Juliet* (Cranko), National Ballet of Canada, Toronto
       Snow Queen in *The Nutcracker* (Franca), National Ballet of Canada, Toronto
       Sugar Plum Fairy in *The Nutcracker* (Franca), National Ballet of Canada, Toronto

Veronica Tennant as Aurora in *The Sleeping Beauty*, National Ballet of Canada, 1972

1966   Kitri in *Don Quixote* Pas de deux (after Petipa), National Ballet of Canada, Mexico City
1967   Odette/Odile in *Swan Lake* (Bruhn after Petipa, Ivanov), National Ballet of Canada, Toronto
       The Pupil in *The Lesson* (Flindt), National Ballet of Canada, Toronto
       The Visiting Operetta Star in *Offenbach in the Underworld* (Tudor), National Ballet of Canada, Toronto
1968   Title role in *Cinderella* (Franca), National Ballet of Canada, Toronto
1969   Principal dancer (cr) in *Kraanerg* (Petit), National Ballet of Canada, Ottawa
       The Bride in *Le Loup* (Petit), National Ballet of Canada, Toronto
1971   Principal dancer in *Original Pas de deux* (Kirby), Jacob's Pillow Festival, Lee, Massachusetts
1972   Title role in *La Sylphide* (Bruhn after Bournonville), National Ballet of Canada, London
       Princess Aurora in *The Sleeping Beauty* (Nureyev after Petipa), National Ballet of Canada, Ottawa
       Principal dancer in *Intermezzo* (Feld), National Ballet of Canada, Toronto
1973   Mazurka and Pas de deux in *Les Sylphides* (Fokine; staged Franca, Bruhn), National Ballet of Canada, Toronto
       Pas de deux in *Kettentanz* (Arpino), National Ballet of Canada, tour
1974   Title role in *Giselle* (Petipa after Coralli, Perrot; staged Wright), National Ballet of Canada, New York

Principal dancer (cr) in *Apples* (Kudelka), National Ballet of Canada, Niagara-on-the-Lake, Ontario

1975 Swanilda (cr) in *Coppélia* (new production; Bruhn after Saint-Léon), National Ballet of Canada, Toronto

The Ballerina in *Petrushka* (Fokine), Columbus Ballet, Columbus, Ohio

The Woman (cr) in *Whispers and Darkness* (Vesak), National Ballet of Canada, Toronto

1976 The Hostess (cr) in *The Party* (Kudelka), National Ballet of Canada, Toronto

1977 Lise in *La Fille mal gardée* (Ashton), National Ballet of Canada, Toronto

1978 Catherine (cr) in *Washington Square* (Kudelka), National Ballet of Canada, Toronto

Marie Taglioni in *Pas de quatre* (Dolin), Les Grands Ballets Canadiens, Montreal

1979 Isabelle-Marie (cr) in *Mad Shadows* (Ditchburn), National Ballet of Canada, film

1980 Pas de deux from *Le Corsaire* (after Petipa), Nervi Festival, Italy

Principal dancer (cr) in *Newcomers* (Macdonald), National Ballet of Canada, Toronto

Principal dancer (cr) in *Paranda Criolla* (Patsalas), National Ballet of Canada, Toronto

Principal dancer in *Four Schumann Pieces* (van Manen), National Ballet of Canada, Toronto

1981 Principal dancer (cr) in *All Night Wonder* (Kudelka), National Ballet of Canada, Toronto

Teresina in *Napoli* (Schaufuss after Bournonville), National Ballet of Canada, Toronto

Titania in *The Dream* (Ashton), National Ballet of Canada, Toronto

Pas de deux from *Flower Festival at Genzano* (after Bournonville), National Ballet of Canada, Toronto

Principal dancer in *Études* (Lander), National Ballet of Canada, Toronto

The dancer (cr) in *Bolero* (solo; Patsalas), National Arts Centre, Ottawa

1982 Dona Anna in *Don Juan* (Neumeier), National Ballet of Canada, Toronto

Thea (cr) in *Hedda* (Kudelka), National Ballet of Canada, Toronto

The Woman (cr) in *Portrait of Love and Death* (Nebrada), National Ballet of Canada, Toronto

Principal dancer (cr) in *Liebestod* (Patsalas), L'Aquila Festival, Italy

Kitri in *Don Quixote* (Beriozoff after Gorsky, Petipa), National Ballet of Canada, Toronto

1983 Principal dancer (cr) in *Canciones* (Patsalas), National Ballet of Canada, Toronto

Pas de trois in *Mobile* (Rudd), National Ballet of Canada, Toronto

1985 Tatiana in *Onegin* (Cranko), National Ballet of Canada, Ottawa

Principal dancer (cr) in *Etc!* (Allan), National Ballet of Canada, Toronto

1986 Solo (cr) in *Villanella* (Allan), National Ballet of Canada, New York

Hanna in *The Merry Widow* (Hynd), National Ballet of Canada, Toronto

Principal dancer (cr) in *Khachaturian Pas de deux* (Allan), National Ballet of Canada, Toronto

Principal dancer (cr) in *Capriccio* (Allan), National Ballet of Canada, Toronto

1987 Principal dancer in *Serenade* (Balanchine), National Ballet of Canada, London

Principal dancer (cr) in *Masada* (Allan), National Ballet of Canada, Toronto

Dancer in *Tchaikovsky Pas de deux* (Balanchine), Royal Winnipeg Ballet, tour

Principal dancer in *Four Last Songs* (van Dantzig), Royal Winnipeg Ballet, tour

1988 Principal dancer in *Forgotten Land* (Kylián), National Ballet of Canada, Toronto

Principal dancer (cr) in *Rendezvous des coeurs* (Allan), Gala, Toronto

Pas de deux (cr) in *Botticelli Pictures* (Allan), Ontario Place Forum, Toronto

1992 Ivy Smith/Miss Turnstiles in *On the Town* (musical; mus. Bernstein, chor. Moore after Robbins), Shaw Festival, Niagara-on-the Lake, Canada

PUBLICATIONS

By Tennant:
On Stage Please (novel), Toronto, 1977
The Nutcracker, Toronto, 1985

About Tennant:
Maynard, Olga, "Veronica Tennant: A Canadian Ballerina", *Dance Magazine* (New York), May 1972
Percival, John, "Travelling Hopefully in Canada", *Dance Magazine* (New York), February 1977
Odom, Selma, "Spotlight on Veronica Tennant", *Dance Magazine* (New York), March 1977
Mews, Ellen Shearer, "Schaufuss and Tennant", *Performing Arts in Canada* (Toronto), Summer 1978
Citron, Paula, "A Life in Dance: Veronica Tennant", *Vandance* (Vancouver), Spring 1989
Howard, Sebastian, "Veronica Tennant: A Dancer of Distinction", *Dance in Canada* (Toronto), Autumn 1989
Campbell, Donald, in "Dancescape", *Dance Magazine* (New York), November 1989
Kelly, Deirdre, "Dancing on the Town", *Performing Arts in Canada* (Toronto), Summer 1992

*   *   *

Veronica Tennant, like her younger colleague Karen Kain, was of a generation of Canadian dancers who saw the possibility of having a fully rounded career without having to join a more illustrious company abroad. Indeed, Tennant's extraordinary loyalty to the National Ballet of Canada over a 25-year career was a significant factor in the company's own artistic development. Tennant set a model of professionalism, artistic integrity, and dedication which influenced many of the dancers around her.

Although she did not possess an ideally proportioned body, Tennant showed a steely technique and a pronounced gift for dramatic portrayal which, combined with ambition and determination, quickly established her as a star at the National Ballet of Canada. She entered the company as a principal in 1965 to dance the lead in Cranko's *Romeo and Juliet* and was immediately acknowledged as a dancer-actress of smouldering intensity and outstanding potential.

With the retirement of former leading ballerina Lois Smith, and the departure of such dancers as Galina Samsova and Martine van Hamel, Tennant effectively became the company's major star, a position later shared with Karen Kain. She quickly assumed almost all the major full-length roles and received favourable international exposure through Emmy Award-winning television productions of *Cinderella* and *The Sleeping Beauty*.

Tennant was among several National Ballet dancers to benefit from Rudolf Nureyev's association with the company, but it was more especially Frederick Ashton's interest, during Alexander Grant's artistic directorship, which significantly affected Tennant's dancing. Although her well-crafted performances had always been admirable for their classical rigour and intelligence, the experience of dancing a range of Ashton ballets seemed to introduce a new element of emotional freedom and expressive spontaneity into Tennant's dancing, particularly evident in memorable performances of *The Dream*, partnered by guest artist Anthony Dowell.

While she performed a wide-ranging repertoire within the National Ballet, some of Tennant's greatest successes were in Romantic works, such as *La Sylphide* and *Giselle*, in which her musicality and sensitivity to style were fully apparent, or in dramatic ballets such as Cranko's *Onegin*, where her intensity was given full rein. At the same time, Tennant was always eager to encourage choreographers developing within the National Ballet, and gave memorable performances of created roles in works by James Kudelka, Constantin Patsalas, and David Allan.

Tennant's commitment to dancing had a potent communicative strength which made her an enduring favourite of audiences, and her farewell performances as Juliet in February 1989, followed by a special retirement gala nine months later, saw an unprecedented public outpouring of affection and appreciation.

Apart from her dance career, Tennant has also written two successful children's books and established a promising career as a television presenter.

—Michael Crabb

TERABUST, Elisabetta

Italian dancer. Born in Varese, Italy, 5 August 1946. Studied at Rome Opera Ballet School, pupil of Attilia Radice, 1955–63. Dancer, Rome Opera Ballet, from 1964, becoming prima ballerina, 1966–74; principal dancer, Ballet de Marseille, 1974–77; principal guest artist, London Festival Ballet, from 1973, becoming permanent company member, 1977, and associate artist, 1984–87; principal guest artist, Ballet of La Scala, Milan, from 1975, touring with company in South America, 1983; international guest artist, including for National Ballet of Canada, Ballet of German Opera on the Rhine in Düsseldorf, Makarova and Company, Aterballetto of Reggio Emilia, and Maggiodanza, Forence; has also appeared frequently on television, including in two Italian programmes (1981) and in *Dancer* (BBC, 1983); artistic director, Rome Opera Ballet, from 1990; director, Rome Opera Ballet School, from 1990. Recipient: Premio Positano, 1969; Le Noci d'oro, Lecce, 1970.

ROLES

1967　Dancer in *La Rosa del sogno* (Milloss), Rome Opera Ballet, Rome
　　　Dancer in *La Follia di Orlando* (Milloss), Rome Opera Ballet, Rome
　　　Dancer in *Follia Viennese* (Milloss), Rome Opera Ballet, Rome
　　　The Girl (cr) in *Jeux* (Milloss), Rome Opera Ballet, Rome

1967/　Myrtha in *Giselle* (Petipa after Coralli, Perrot; staged
68　　　Prebil), Rome Opera Ballet, Rome
1968　Waltz, Mazurka in *Les Sylphides* (Fokine), Rome Opera Ballet, Rome
　　　Kitri in *Don Quixote* Pas de deux (after Petipa), Rome Opera Ballet, Rome
　　　Principal dancer (cr) in *Estri* (pas de trois; Milloss), Festival of Two Worlds, Spoleto
1969　Columbine in *Carnaval* (Fokine), Rome Opera Ballet, Rome
　　　Principal dancer (cr) in *La Pazzia senile* (Milloss), Rome Opera Ballet, Rome
　　　Adagietto ("La Garçonne") in *Les Biches* (Nijinska), Rome Opera Ballet, Rome
1971　Title role (cr) in *Cinderella* (Prebil), Rome Opera Ballet, Rome
1972　Second Movement in *Symphony in C* (Balanchine), Rome Opera Ballet, Rome
　　　Title role in *Giselle* (Petipa after Coralli, Perrot; staged Prebil), Rome Opera Ballet, Rome
1973　Masha in *The Nutcracker* (Prebil), Rome Opera Ballet, Rome
　　　Terpsichore in *Apollon musagète* (Balanchine), Rome Opera Ballet, Rome
　　　Soloist, Ballet of the Seasons (chor. Lifar) in *I Vespri siciliani* (opera; mus. Verdi), Teatro Regio, Turin
　　　Title role in *La Sylphide* (Bruhn after Bournonville), Rome Opera Ballet, Rome
　　　The Young Girl in *Le Loup* (Petit), Ballet de Marseille, Monte Carlo
　　　Sugar Plum Fairy in *The Nutcracker* (Carter), London Festival Ballet
　　　Princess Aurora in *The Sleeping Beauty* (Stevenson after Petipa), London Festival Ballet, Leeds
1974　Swanilda in *Coppélia* (Carter after Petipa, Cecchetti), London Festival Ballet, London
　　　Title role in *Giselle* (Petipa after Coralli, Perrot; staged Skeaping), London Festival Ballet, Brussels
　　　Principal dancer (cr) in *Mozart Pas de deux* (Hynd), London Festival Ballet, St. Juan de Luz
　　　Esmeralda in *Notre-Dame de Paris* (Petit), Ballet de Marseille, Nervi Festival
　　　Title role in *Carmen* (Petit), Ballet de Marseille, Nervi Festival
1975　Principal dancer in *Dances from Napoli* (Vangsaae after Bournonville), London Festival Ballet, London
　　　Kitri in *Don Quixote* (Borkowski, Gorsky after Petipa), London Festival Ballet, Manchester
1976　The Girl in *Le Spectre de la rose* (Fokine), London Festival Ballet, London
　　　Marie (cr) in *The Nutcracker* (Petit), Ballet de Marseille, Marseilles
1977　Juliet in *Romeo and Juliet* (Nureyev), London Festival Ballet, Adelaide, Australia
　　　The Sleepwalker in *Night Shadow* (La Sonnambula; Balanchine), London Festival Ballet, London
　　　Louise in *The Nutcracker* (Hynd), London Festival Ballet, Cardiff
　　　Odette/Odile in *Swan Lake* (Petipa, Ivanov; staged Grey), London Festival Ballet, Newcastle
1978　Principal dancer in *Conservatoire* (Konservatoriet; Bournonville), London Festival Ballet, Bristol
　　　Principal dancer in *Greening* (Tetley), London Festival Ballet, Oxford
　　　A Girl (cr) in *La Chatte* (Hynd), London Festival Ballet, London
　　　Principal dancer (cr) in *Fantaisie* (Moreland), Festival

Elisabeth Terabust in *La Sylphide*, London Festival Ballet, c.1976

of Two Worlds, Spoleto
1979 Juliet in *Romeo and Juliet* (Walter), Ballet of the
      German Opera on the Rhine (Düsseldorf), Paris
      Ballerina in *Petrushka* (Fokine), London Festival Ballet,
      London
      Title role in *Rosalinda* (Hynd), London Festival Ballet,
      Cardiff
      Title role in *La Sylphide* (Schaufuss after Bournonville),
      London Festival Ballet, London
      Ballerina in *Études* (Lander), London Festival Ballet,
      Liverpool
      Title role in *Sphinx* (Tetley), London Festival Ballet,
      Bristol
1980 Principal dancer in *Dvořák Variations* (Hynd), London
      Festival Ballet, London
      Ballerina in *Paquita* Act III (Makarova after Petipa),
      Makarova and Company, New York
1981 Principal dancer in *Allegro Brillante* (Balanchine),
      Aterballetto, Regio Emilia
      Teresina in *Napoli* (Bournonville), National Ballet of
      Canada, Toronto
1982 Principal dancer (cr) in *Verdi Variations* (pas de deux;
      MacMillan), Aterballetto, Reggio Emilia
      Title role in *Cinderella* (Stevenson), London Festival
      Ballet, Bristol
1983 Principal dancer (cr) in *Afternoon of a Faun* (Amodio),
      Aterballetto, Reggio Emilia
1984 Pimpinella (cr) in *Pulcinella* (Tetley), London Festival
      Ballet, London
1985 Juliet in *Romeo and Juliet* (Ashton), London Festival
      Ballet, Bristol
      Ballerina in *Tchaikovsky Pas de deux* (Balanchine),
      London Festival Ballet
      Nikiya in "Kingdom of the Shades" from *La Bayadère*
      (Makarova after Petipa), London Festival Ballet,
      London
1986 Principal dancer in *Land* (Bruce), London Festival
      Ballet, Bath
      Principal dancer in *Necessarily So* (Christie), London
      Festival Ballet, Bath
      Tatiana in *Onegin* (Cranko), London Festival Ballet,
      London
      Alexandra/Sugar Plum Fairy (cr) in *The Nutcracker*
      (Schaufuss), London Festival Ballet, Plymouth
1989 Principal dancer in *Cheek to Cheek* (Petit), Gala,
      Fiesole, Italy
1992 Elisabeth, Empress of Austria (cr) in *La Valse triste*
      (Petit), Rome Opera Ballet, Rome
      Principal dancer (cr) in *Charlot danse avec nous* (Petit),
      Ballet de Marseille, Marseilles

Other roles include: Dawn in *Coppélia* (after Petipa, Cecchetti),
Swanilda in *Coppélia* (Petit), principal dancer in *Summer
Solstice* (Moreland), principal dancer in *Agon* (Balanchine),
principal dancer in *The River* (Ailey), principal dancer in
Artifact 2 (Forsythe), Juliet in *Romeo and Juliet* (Amodio).

PUBLICATIONS

Niehaus, Max, *Ballett Faszination*, Munich, 1972
Lidova, Irene, "Elisabetta Terabust", *Les Saisons de la danse*
    (Paris), December 1974
Ottolenghi, Vittorio, "Elisabetta, La Nostra Stella", *Balletto
    Oggi* (Milan), March–May 1981
Calvetti, Paola, "Elisabetta Terabust", *Pour la danse* (Paris),
    June 1981
Agostini, Alfio, "Elisabetta, Giulietta e Figlio prodigo",
    Balletto Oggi (Milan), February 1987
Ottolenghi, Vittorio, "Lo, Oggi, Elisabetta Terabust", *Balletto
    oggi* (Milan), February 1987
"London Festival Ballet: the Biographies", *Ballet in London
    Year Book 1988/89*, London, 1988

*   *   *

Elisabetta Terabust had the good fortune to attend the Rome
Opera Ballet School when it was directed by Attilia Radice, a
Cecchetti pupil who, as a result of her own excellent training,
inculcated all her students with an understanding of the
importance of the positions of the arms and head.

Her progress as a dancer was delayed by the programming of
the Rome Opera, which allowed for only a minimal number of
ballet programmes per season (rarely more than two). Despite
this, and despite the hierarchical system which virtually
prevented anyone except an officially titled principal dancer
from performing leading roles, Terabust was eventually moved
from comparatively small solo roles (such as Dawn in *Coppélia*)
to leading roles in a number of Balanchine ballets, including
Symphony in C and *Apollo*. She was also featured in a series of
reworkings of the classics by Yugoslav choreographer Zarko
Prebil. Terabust progressed from Myrtha, Queen of the Wilis in
Giselle (a role in which she excelled, in spite of her lack of
height), to the title role. However, the opportunities were still
far too limited to satisfy a dancer of talent and ambition, and
thus Terabust became the first Italian ballerina to become a
permanent company member—as opposed to a visiting guest
artist—of a company abroad, and the first of many Italians to
work with Roland Petit's Marseilles company.

Dancing in a highly disciplined group whose choreographer
was regularly present to observe and criticize (Petit is known to
be a hard task-master) strengthened Terabust's technical
powers. At the same time, performing roles that required great
expressiveness—such as Esmeralda in *Notre-Dame de Paris* or
Swanilda in Petit's reworked *Coppélia*—helped to increase the
ballerina's powers of interpretation.

With the (then) London Festival Ballet, Terabust alternated
over the years between being a member of the company and a
guest artist. In both capacities she was able to dance not only in
the nineteenth-century classics but also in ballets by a number
of twentieth-century choreographers. Later, she also made
important contact with the work of Bournonville when Peter
Schaufuss staged *La Sylphide* for the company. Terabust also
had success dancing in the works of Glen Tetley, who gave her
the title role of *Sphinx* and also cast her in *Greening*. When
Terabust first joined London Festival Ballet, Beryl Grey (who
had been responsible for inviting Schaufuss to stage the
Bournonville classic) had been director; the advent of John
Field in 1979 brought John Cranko's *Onegin* into the repertory
some four years later giving Terabust the opportunity to dance
Tatiana. The arrival of Peter Schaufuss in 1984 led in general to
a shift of emphasis to the male dancer, but Terabust
maintained a pre-eminent position notwithstanding this. In
particular, she appeared as the Sylphide, a role which she
repeated, with Schaufuss as her partner, in various Italian
towns as well. She dramatized the death scene more than could
be considered acceptable by lovers of pure Bournonville style,
lacking the inner lightness possessed by her colleague Eva
Evdokimova—but she danced the role well, and her approach
was more likely to be admired by Italians, who in general have
a weakness for full-blooded theatricality. Later on in her career,
Terabust widened her Bournonville experience—again with
Schaufuss at her side, and in his production—by appearing as
Teresina in *Napoli*, first in Toronto with the National Ballet of

Canada and later in Naples, where the ballet had not been seen before.

Despite her international career, Terabust had always been reluctant to stay away from Italy for too long. In the late 1980s she increasingly restricted her appearances elsewhere, touring extensively round her own country with the Reggio Emilia-based Aterballetto, adding lustre to it with her presence and dancing most often with Alessandro Molin, back from his stint as a member of London Festival Ballet. In previous years, Terabust had already appeared often with the company, dancing with a series of partners, the most important of whom was Peter Schaufuss. Kenneth MacMillan made a pas de deux for them to a movement from Verdi's String Quartet, and they also danced together in Schaufuss's excellent Bournonville potpourri, *Bournonvilleana*, as well as in Tetley's *Sphinx*. Terabust also danced in Balanchine's *Agon*, Alvin Ailey's *The River*, and, one of her most taxing roles, in William Forsythe's *Artifact 2*.

When, in 1989, Terabust began to spend more time with Aterballetto, its repertory was limited almost exclusively to works by its director, Amedeo Amodio, who made a version of *Romeo and Juliet* for her, using the Berlioz score. This Juliet is dramatic rather than lyrically romantic, in accordance with Terabust's temperament. Although she has appeared in so many classical and Romantic ballets, she lacks a certain softness that is an essential for those roles. She has, therefore, been at her best in neo-classical and modern ballets.

Terabust is a perfectionist and constantly worries over possible technical faults. She has also been dogged by injury and pain, and on occasion the tension she evidently felt in a work such as *Agon* became uncomfortably visible in her features.

In the early years Terabust had to struggle for recognition because of the power of the Fracci legend, according to which, for example, it was almost *lèse-majesté* for another Italian ballerina to dance the role of Giselle. From that point of view, her career abroad was something of a liberation, not to mention the fact that the fame that she accrued there strengthened her position in her homeland.

Terabust's position at the head of the Rome Opera Ballet's school (from 1990) has provided her with fresh obstacles to overcome, for there is a very great deal to be done to restore the standards that obtained when Terabust studied with Radice. With luck and great determination, perhaps she will be able to supply Rome (which is often mistakenly thought of as her birthplace) with a true, home-trained classical ballerina.

—Freda Pitt

TETLEY, Glen

American dancer, choreographer, and company director. Born Glenford Andrew Tetley, Jr., in Cleveland, Ohio, 3 February 1926. Educated at Franklin and Marshall College, 1944–46, and New York University 1946–48 (B.Sc.); studied modern dance with Hanya Holm and Martha Graham, New York; studied ballet with Margaret Craske, Antony Tudor, and at the School of American Ballet, New York. Served in the United States Navy, 1944–46. Dancer and director's assistant, Hanya Holm's company, 1946–51, also performing in musicals in New York; first dancer, New York City Opera, 1952–54; dancer, John Butler company, from 1953, including for European tour, 1955; guest artist, Joffrey Ballet, 1956–57; dancer, Martha Graham Dance Company, 1958, American

Ballet Theatre, 1960–61, and Jerome Robbins's Ballets: USA; director, Glen Tetley Dance Company, New York, 1962–69; dancer and choreographer, soon becoming co-director, Netherlands Dance Theater, The Hague, 1969–71; director (succeeding John Cranko), Stuttgart Ballet, Stuttgart, 1974–76; artistic associate, National Ballet of Canada, Toronto, 1987–89; has also served as director, Gulbenkian Choreographic Conference, London, and Australian Choreographic Conference, Melbourne, 1984; international guest choreographer, including for Ballet Rambert, Hamburg Ballet, Bavarian State Opera Ballet in Munich, Royal Danish Ballet, American Ballet Theatre, and Royal Ballet, London. Recepient: Die Feder German Critics Award, 1969; Queen Elizabeth II Coronation Award, Royal Academy of Dancing, 1981; Prix-Italia Rai Prize, 1982; Tennant-Caledonian Award, Edinburgh Festival, 1983; Ohioana Career Medal, 1986; New York University Achievement Award, 1988.

ROLES

1946   A Sailor in *On the Town* (musical; mus. Bernstein, chor. Robbins), Adelphi Theatre, New York

Dancer (cr) in *Walt Whitman Suite, Windows* (chor. Holm), Hanya Holm Company, Colorado Springs, Colorado

1947   Barber (cr) in *The Great Campaign* (musical; chor. Sokolow), Princess Theatre, New York

Dancer (cr) in *The Insect Comedy* (Holm), Hanya Holm Company, Colorado Springs, Colorado

1948   Xochi PiLi (cr) in *Ozark Suite* (Holm), Hanya Holm Company, Colorado Springs, Colorado

Harlequin (cr) in *Kiss Me Kate* (musical; mus. Cole Porter, chor. Holm), Century Theater, New York

1949   Principal dancer (cr) in *Baroque Concerto* (Holm), Pauline Koner Company, New York

Principal dancer in *Atavisms* (Weidman), Charles Weidman Company, New York

1950   Adonis (cr) in *Out of this World* (musical; mus. Porter, chor. Holm), Century Theater, New York

1951   Dancer in *Gentlemen Prefer Blondes* (musical; mus. Styne, Robbin, chor. de Mille) Ziegfeld Theater, New York

Dancer (cr) in *Amahl and the Night Visitors* (opera; mus. Menotti), New York City Opera, U.S. television (NBC)

1952   Principal dancer (cr) in *Rites* (Lang), Pearl Lang Company, New York

Principal dancer (cr) in *And Joy is My Witness* (Lang), Pearl Lang Company, New York

1953   Principal dancer (cr) in *Malocchio* (Butler), John Butler Dance Company, New York

Principal dancer (cr) in *Masque of the Wild Man* (Butler), John Butler Dance Company, New York

Principal dancer (cr) in *Three Promenades with the Lord* (Butler), John Butler Dance Company, New York

1954   Principal dancer (cr) in *Brass World* (Butler), John Butler Dance Company, New York

Principal dancer in *Long-Legged Jig* (Butler), John Butler Dance Company, New York

Principal dancer in *Triad* (Butler), John Butler Dance Company, New York

1956   Principal dancer in *Pas des Deésses* (Joffrey), Robert Joffrey Ballet, New York

1957   Principal dancer in *Passacaglia* (Humphrey), Doris Humphrey Company, New London, Connecticut

Glen Tetley, c.1983

1958   Iago in *The Moor's Pavane* (Limón), José Limón
         Company, New York
       The Stranger (cr) in *Embattled Garden* (Graham),
         Martha Graham Company, New York
       Apollo (cr) in *Clytymnestra* (Graham), Martha Graham
         Company, New York
1959   Slip-Jig in *Juno* (musical; mus. Blitzstein, chor. de
         Mille), Ziegfeld Theater, New York
       Principal dancer (cr) in *Carmina Burana* (opera; mus.
         Orff, chor. Butler), New York City Opera, New York
       Principal dancer (cr) in *Serenade for Seven Dancers* (H.
         Ross), Spoleto Festival, Charleston, South Carolina
       Principal dancer (cr) in *The Sybil* (Butler), Spoleto
         Festival, Charleston, South Carolina
1960   The Friend in *Pillar of Fire* (Tudor), American Ballet
         Theatre, New York
       The Lover in *Jardin aux Lilas* (Tudor), American Ballet
         Theatre, New York
       Jean in *Miss Julie* (Cullberg), American Ballet Theatre,
         New York
       Title role in *Bluebeard* (Fokine), American Ballet
         Theatre, New York
       Wangel in *Lady from the Sea* (Cullberg), American
         Ballet Theatre, New York

       The Sailor in *Lady from the Sea* (Cullberg), American
         Ballet Theatre, New York
       Alias in *Billy the Kid* (Loring), American Ballet Theatre,
         New York
1961   Principal dancer in *Afternoon of a Faun* (Robbins),
         Ballets: USA, European tour
       Husband in *The Concert* (Robbins), Ballets: USA,
         European tour
       The Intruder in *The Cage* (Robbins), Ballets: USA,
         European tour
       Principal dancer (cr) in *Events* (Robbins), Ballets: USA,
         Spoleto Festival, Italy
       Pas de deux in *Moves* (Robbins), Ballets: USA,
         European tour
1962   Title role (cr) in *Pierrot Lunaire* (also chor.), Glen Tetley
         and Dancers, New York

WORKS

1946   *Richard Cory* (text by E.A. Robinson), Colorado College
         Summer Dance, Colorado College
1948   *The Canary* (mus. Berg), Cherry Lane Theater, New
         York

Triptych (mus. Wilson), Humphrey-Weidman Studio Theater, New York

1951 *Daylight's Dauphin* (mus. Debussy), Brooklyn High School Concert Series, Brooklyn, New York

Hootin' Blues (mus. Reilly), Brooklyn High School Concert Series, Brooklyn, New York

Western Wall (mus. Ravel), Brooklyn High School Concert Series, Brooklyn, New York

1959 *Mountain Way Chant* (mus. Chavez), Alvin Ailey American Dance Theater, New York

1961 *Ballet Ballads: The Eccentricities of Davy Crockett* (mus. Moss), East 74th Street Theater, New York

1962 *Birds of Sorrow* (mus. Hartman), Glen Tetley and Company, New York

Gleams in the Bone House (mus. Shapero), Glen Tetley and Company, New York

How Many Miles to Babylon? (mus. Surinach), Glen Tetley and Company, New York

Pierrot Lunaire (mus. Schoenberg), Glen Tetley and Company, New York

1963 *Harpsichord Concerto* (mus. de Falla), Glen Tetley Dance Company, Jacob's Pillow Dance Festival, Lee, Massachusetts

1964 *The Anatomy Lesson* (mus. Landowski), Netherlands Dance Theatre, The Hague

Sargasso (mus. Křenek), Netherlands Dance Theatre, The Hague

1965 *Fieldmass* (mus. Martinů), Netherlands Dance Theatre, Amsterdam

The Game of Noah (mus. Stravinsky), Netherlands Dance Theatre, The Hague

Mythical Hunters (mus. Partos-Hezionot), Batsheva Dance Company, Tel-Aviv

1966 *Chronochromie* (mus. Messiaen), Glen Tetley Dance Company, Jacob's Pillow Dance Festival, Lee, Massachusetts

Lovers (mus. Rorem), Glen Tetley Dance Company, New York

Psalms (mus. Partos-Tehilim), Batsheva Dance Company, Tel-Aviv

Ricercare (mus. Seter), American Ballet Theatre, New York

1967 *Dithyramb* (mus. Henze), Glen Tetley and Company, New York

Freefall (mus. Schubel), Repertory Dance Theatre, University of Utah, Salt Lake City

The Seven Deadly Sins (mus. Weill), Glen Tetley Dance Company, Vancouver

Ziggurat (mus. Stockhausen), Ballet Rambert, London

1968 *Circles* (mus. Berio), Netherlands Dance Theatre, The Hague

Embrace Tiger and Return to Mountain (mus. Subotnick), Ballet Rambert, London

1969 *Arena* (mus. Subotnick), Netherlands Dance Theatre, The Hague

1970 *Field Figures* (mus. Stockhausen), Royal Ballet, Nottingham

Imaginary Film (mus. Schoenberg), Netherlands Dance Theatre, Scheveningen

Mutations (mus. Stockhausen), Netherlands Dance Theatre, Scheveningen

1971 *Rag Dances* (mus. Hymas), Ballet Rambert, London

1972 *Laborintus* (mus. Berio), Royal Ballet, London

Small Parades (mus. Varèse), Netherlands Dance Theatre, The Hague

Strophe-Antistrophe (mus. Bussotti), Batsheva Dance Company, Tel-Aviv

Threshold (mus. Berg), Hamburg State Opera Ballet, Hamburg

1973 *Gemini* (mus. Henze), Australian Ballet, Sydney

Moveable Garden (mus. Foss), Tanz Forum, Cologne

Rite of Spring (mus. Stravinsky), Bavarian State Opera Ballet, Munich

Stationary Flying (mus. Crumb), Utah Repertory Dance Theater, University of Utah, Salt Lake City

Voluntaries (mus. Poulenc), Stuttgart Ballet, Stuttgart

1975 *Alegrías* (mus. Chavez), Stuttgart Ballet, Stuttgart

Daphnis und Chloe (mus. Ravel), Stuttgart Ballet, Stuttgart

Greening (mus. Nordheim), Stuttgart Ballet, Stuttgart

Strender (mus. Nordheim), Norwegian National Ballet, Oslo

Tristan (mus. Henze), Paris Opéra Ballet, Paris

1977 *Poème Nocturne* (mus. Scriabin), Spoleto Festival, Charleston, South Carolina

Sphinx (mus. Martinů), American Ballet Theatre, Washington, D.C.

1978 *Praeludium* (mus. Webern), Ballet Rambert, Manchester

1979 *Contredances* (mus. Webern), American Ballet Theatre, New York

The Tempest (mus. Nordheim), Ballet Rambert, Schwetzingen

1980 *Dances of Albion* (mus. Britten), Royal Ballet, London

Summer's End (mus. Dutilleux), Netherlands Dance Theatre, The Hague

1981 *The Firebird* (mus. Stravinsky), Royal Danish Ballet, Copenhagen

1983 *Murderer Hope of Women* (mus. percussion, arranged Tyrrell), Ballet Rambert, Edinburgh

Odalisque (mus. Satie), National Ballet School Gala, Toronto

1984 *Pulcinelle* (mus. Stravinsky), London Festival Ballet, London

Revelation and Fall (mus. Maxwell), Australian Dance Theatre, Adelaide

1985 *Dream Walk of the Shaman* (mus. Křenek), Aterballetto, Reggio Emilia, Italy

1986 *Alice* (mus. del Tredici), National Ballet of Canada, Toronto

1987 *Orpheus* (mus. Stravinsky), Australian Ballet, Melbourne

La Ronde (mus. Korngold), National Ballet of Canada, Toronto

1989 *Tagore* (mus. Zemlinsky), National Ballet of Canada, Toronto

PUBLICATIONS

By Tetley:

Interview in "American Dancer", *Dance Magazine* (New York), February 1963

"Pierrot in Two Worlds", *Dance and Dancers* (London), December 1967

"Tai-chi and the Dance", *Dance and Dancers* (London), November 1968

"Dutch Mutations", *Dance Magazine* (New York), February 1971

Interview in Robertson, Allen, "Talking with Tetley", *Dance Magazine* (New York), October 1971

Interview in Garske, Rolf, "Creativity or Craft", *Das Ballett und die Künste*, Cologne, 1972

Interview in Gruen, John, *The Private World of Ballet*, New York, 1975

Interview in "Prospero's Island", *Dance and Dancers* (London), May 1979

Interview in Rogosin, Elinor, *The Dance Makers: Conversations*, New York, 1980

About Tetley:

Duncan, Donald, "One Dancer, Many Faces", *Dance Magazine* (New York), October 1960

Anderson, Jack, "A Gallery of American Ballet Theatre Choreographers", *Dance Magazine* (New York), January 1966

Percival, John, "Tetley All the Way", *Dance and Dancers* (London), September 1969

Percival, John, "Glen Tetley", *Experimental Dance*, London, 1971

McDonagh, Don, *Complete Guide to Modern Dance*, New York, 1976

"Glen Tetley", *Tanzblätter* (Vienna), March 1980

Croce, Arlene, *Going to the Dance*, London, 1982

Crabb, Michael, "Tetley Makes La Ronde go 'round", *Dance Magazine* (New York), July 1988

* * *

The diversity of Glen Tetley's dance training and performance augured an extremely broad choreographic palette. Both as a dancer and a choreographer, he worked first in modern dance and then in classical ballet; and it was Tetley's synthesis of these two idioms which came to characterize his choreography. He absorbed many of the physical and expressive emphases of the early American modern dancers and, in working with Hanya Holm and Martha Graham, he experienced first-hand their instinctive sense of theatricality. Parallels with Graham's work—particularly her use of three-dimensional structures, of metals, plastics, and cloth—are evident in many Tetley works.

In 1961, Graham had commissioned Rouben Ter-Arutunian to design the set for *Visionary Recital* (later revised as *Samson Agonistes*), and it was with Ter-Arutunian that Tetley collaborated when creating *Pierrot Lunaire* the following year. *Pierrot Lunaire* was the first of many Tetley–Arutunian works, and it was the work which launched Tetley's choreographic career. Tetley himself danced the title role, and two Martha Graham dancers, Linda Hodes and Robert Powell, were Columbine and Brighella. Previously, Tetley had created and performed several solos, and in 1959 he had choreographed *Mountain Way Chant* for the Alvin Ailey American Dance Theater. *Pierrot Lunaire* probes the physchological interplay of three *commedia dell'arte* characters and, like many of Tetley's subsequent works, its structure is episodic. The emphasis is on danced events rather than on narrative, although undertones of conflict, and the individual's search for identity—themes later developed in works such as *Sphinx* and *Alice*—are alluded to.

Throughout his career, Tetley has sought new sources of movement to supplement his dance vocabulary. In *Pierrot Lunaire*, Ter-Arutunian's scaffold structure is both support and fulcrum for much of the choreography; *Freefall* explores the physical laws of weight and gravity, while *Embrace Tiger and Return to Mountain* incorporates ideas and stances from T'ai Chi. In the early 1970s, Tetley returned to elements of his classical ballet training. For the Royal Ballet, he created *Field Figures* and *Laborintus*. Uncompromisingly modern in dance vocabulary and musical accompaniment (Stockhausen and Berio, respectively), these ballets signalled the first of several repertory reforms by the company's new artistic director, Kenneth MacMillan.

Laborintus was choreographed in 1972, the year Tetley created the virtuoso *Small Parades* and the lyrical *Threshold*, and it was from this time that new interests and invention became evident in his work. The emphasis of classical ballet on muscular control, on contour, and on complexity of movement, began to co-exist with Tetley's former preference for torso-focused choreography. In 1973, he created *Voluntaries* as a memorial to John Cranko, who died earlier that year, and created a dance epitaph of solemn, purged movement. Working with the Stuttgart Ballet for the first time, Tetley continued his association with the company the following year when he succeeded Cranko as artistic director of the German company.

Internationally, Tetley has been an important choreographic influence. As a freelance choreographer and in his work with such companies as Netherlands Dance Theatre, Stuttgart Ballet, and, more recently, the National Ballet of Canada, he has helped to mould both policy and repertory. He has been responsible for introducing modern dance to many classically trained companies. His works for them revealed new approaches to and initiated new ways of thinking about choreography. In breaking down barriers, opening up attitudes to movement, music, and design, Tetley has contributed to a new choreographic consciousness.

—Angela Kane

THARP, Twyla

American dancer, choreographer, and company director. Born in Portland, Indiana, 1 July 1941. Educated in art history at Barnard College, New York; studied ballet with Igor Schwezoff, American Ballet Theatre School, and with Richard Thomas and Margaret Craske, New York; studied modern dance with Martha Graham, Merce Cunningham, and Alwin Nikolais, and jazz dance with Luigi and Matt Mattox. Married Robert Huot (div.): one son, b. 1971. Début with Paul Taylor Dance Company, 1965; founder, dancer, and choreographer of own company, 1965, becoming Twyla Tharp Dance Foundation from 1973; company disbanded (with some dancers taken into American Ballet Theatre), 1988; international guest choreographer, including for Joffrey Ballet, American Ballet Theatre, John Curry (Olympic ice skater), and Paris Opéra Ballet; choreographer for films, including *Hair* (dir. Forman, 1979), *Ragtime* (dir. Forman, 1981), and *White Nights* (dir. Hackford, 1985); also choreographer and director of Broadway musical (based on the film), *Singin' in the Rain* (1985); artistic associate, American Ballet Theatre, 1988–90. Recipient: *Dance Magazine* Award, 1981.

WORKS

1965   *Tank Dive*, Hunter College Art Department, New York
       Stage Show, New York World's Fair, New York
       Cede Blue Lake, Hunter College Art Department, New York
       Unprocessed, Hunter College Art Department, New York
1966   *Re-Moves*, Judson Memorial Church, New York
       Yancey Dance, Judson Memorial Church, New York
1967   *One Two Three*, Kunstverein Museum, Stuttgart
       Jam, Stedelijk Museum, Amsterdam

Twyla Tharp rehearsing *Push Comes to Shove* **with Mikhail Baryshnikov and Marianna Tcherkassky, 1976**

Disperse, Richmond Professional Institute, Richmond, Virginia

Three Page Sonata for Four, State University of New York, Potsdam, New York

Forevermore, Midsummer Inc., Southampton, New York

1968   *Generation*, Wagner College Gymnasium, Staten Island, New York

One Way, Wagner College Gymnasium, Staten Island, New York

Excess, Idle, Surplus, Notre Dame University, South Bend, Indiana

1969   *After "Suite"*, Billy Rose Theatre, New York

Group Activities, Brooklyn Academy of Music, New York

Medley, American Dance Festival, Connecticut College, New London, Connecticut

Dancing in the Streets of London and Paris, Continued in Stockholm and Sometimes Madrid, Wadsworth Atheneum, Hartford, Connecticut

1970   *Pymffyppmfynm Ypf*, Sullins College, Bristol, Virginia

The Fugue, University of Massachusetts, Amherst, Massachusetts

Rose's Cross Country, University of Massachusetts, Amherst, Massachusetts

The One Hundreds, University of Massachusetts, Amherst, Massachusetts

1971   *The History of Up and Down, I and II*, Oberlin College, Oberlin, Ohio

Eight Jelly Rolls (mus. Jelly Roll Morton and The Red Hot Peppers), Oberlin College, Oberlin, Ohio

Mozart Sonata, K. 545, The Mall, Washington, D.C.

Torelli (mus. Torelli), Fort Tyron Park, New York

The Bix Pieces (mus. Beiderbecke), International Festival of Dance, Paris

1972   *The Raggedy Dances* (mus. Joplin, Mozart), ANTA Theatre, New York

1973   *Deuce Coupe* (mus. The Beach Boys), Joffrey Ballet with Twyla Tharp Dancers, Chicago

As Time Goes By (mus. Haydn), Joffrey Ballet, New York

1974   *In the Beginnings* (mus. Moss), Twyla Tharp Dance, Minneapolis, Minnesota

All About Eggs (mus. Bach), Twyla Tharp Dance, public television (WGBH), Boston

The Bach Duet (mus. Bach), Twyla Tharp Dance, New York

1975   *Deuce Coupe II* (revised version of *Deuce Coupe*; mus. The Beach Boys), Joffrey Ballet, St. Louis, Missouri

Sue's Leg (mus. Fats Waller), Twyla Tharp Dance, St Paul, Minnesota

The Double Cross (mus. various), Twyla Tharp Dance, St Paul, Minnesota

Ocean's Motion (mus. Chuck Berry), Twyla Tharp Dance, Festival of Two Worlds, Spoleto

1976   *Push Comes to Shove* (mus. Lamb, Haydn), American Ballet Theatre, New York

Give and Take (mus. various), Twyla Tharp Dance, Brooklyn, New York

Once More, Frank (mus. Sinatra), American Ballet Theatre, New York

Country Dances (mus. traditional American country, arranged Peaslee), Twyla Tharp Dance, Edinburgh

Happily Ever After (mus. traditional American country, arranged Peaslee), Joffrey Ballet, New York

After All (mus. Albinoni), for ice skater John Curry, Madison Square Garden, New York

1977   *Mud* (mus. Mozart), Twyla Tharp Dance, Brooklyn, New York

Simon Medley (mus. P. Simon), Twyla Tharp Dance, Brooklyn, New York

Cacklin' Hen (mus. traditional American country, arranged Peaslee), Twyla Tharp Dance, Brooklyn, New York

1979   *1903* (mus. Newman), solo for Tharp, Brooklyn, New York

Chapters & Verses (mus. various), Twyla Tharp Dance, Brooklyn, New York

Baker's Dozen (mus. Willie Smith), Twyla Tharp Dance, Brooklyn, New York

1980   *Three Fanfares*, for ice skater John Curry, Winter Olympics, Lake Placid, New York

Brahms' Paganini (mus. Brahms), Twyla Tharp Dance, New York

When We Were Very Young (mus. J. Simon), Twyla Tharp Dance, New York

Assorted Quartets (mus. traditional), Twyla Tharp Dance, Saratoga, New York

Short Stories (mus. Supertramp, Springsteen), Twyla Tharp Dance, Ghent, Belgium

Third Suite (mus. Bach), Twyla Tharp Dance, Paris

1981   *Uncle Edgar Dyed His Hair Red* (mus. Sebouh), Twyla Tharp Dance, New York

The Catherine Wheel (mus. Byrne), Twyla Tharp Dance, New Dance, New York

1982   *Nine Sinatra Songs* (mus. Sinatra recordings), Twyla Tharp Dance, Vancouver (staged American Ballet Theatre, 1990)

Bad Smells (mus. Branca), Twyla Tharp Dance, Vancouver

1983   *Once upon a Time* (later *The Little Ballet*; mus. Glazunov), American Ballet Theatre, Minneapolis

Bach Partita (mus. Bach), American Ballet Theatre, Washington, D.C.

Fait Accompli (mus. Van Tieghem), Twyla Tharp Dance, Austin, Texas

Telemann (mus. Telemann), Twyla Tharp Dance, Austin, Texas

1984   *Brahms/Handel* (with J. Robbins; mus. Brahms), New York City Ballet, New York

Sorrow Floats (mus. Bizet), Twyla Tharp Dance, American Dance Festival, Durham, Massachusetts

Sinatra Suite (mus. Schlager, Sinatra), American Ballet Theatre, Washington, D.C.

1986   *In the Upper Room* (mus. Glass), Twyla Tharp Dance, Highland Park, Illinois

Ballare (mus. Mozart), Twyla Tharp Dance, Highland Park, Illinois

1989   *Quartet* (mus. Riley), American Ballet Theatre, Miami Beach

Bum's Rush (mus. Hyman), American Ballet Theatre, Chicago, Illinois

Rules of the Game (mus. Bach, orchestrated Colombier), Paris Opéra Ballet, Paris

Everlast (mus. Kern), American Ballet Theatre, San Francisco

1990   *Brief Fling* (mus. Colombier, Grainger), American Ballet Theatre, San Francisco

1991   *Grand Pas: Rhythm of the Saints* (pas de deux; mus. P. Simon), Paris Opéra Ballet, Paris

The Men's Piece, Ohio State University, Columbus, Ohio

Octet (mus. Meyer), Ohio State University, Columbus, Ohio

1992   *Sextet* (mus. Telson), Twyla Tharp and Dancers, New
        York

Other works include: *The Willie Smith Series* (videotape, 1971),
Sue's Leg, Remembering the Thirties (for public television, 1976),
Making Television Dance (videotape for public television, 1977),
Confessions of a Cornermaker (videotaped compilation for
public television, 1981), *Scrapbook Tape* ("video anthology" of
works for public television, 1982).

PUBLICATIONS

By Tharp:
Interview in "Space, Jazz, Pop ...", *Dance and Dancers*
    (London), May 1974
Interview in Well, Suzanne, *Contemporary Dance*, New York,
    1978
Interview in Rogosin, Elinor, *The Dance Makers: Conversations
    with American Choreographers*, New York, 1980
Interview in Jowitt, Deborah, "The Choreographer and the
    World", *Ballett International* (Cologne), June/July 1984
Push Comes to Shove (autobiography), New York, 1992

About Tharp:
McDonagh, Don, *Complete Guide to Modern Dance*, New York,
    1976
Croce, Arlene, *Afterimages*, New York, 1977
Harris, Dale, *Contemporary Dance*, New York, 1978
Siegel, Marcia, *The Shapes of Change*, Boston, 1979
Robertson, Allen, "Tharp comes to Shove", *Ballet News* (New
    York), March 1980
Robertson, Michael, "Fifteen Years: Twyla Tharp", *Dance
    Magazine* (New York), March 1980
Croce, Arlene, *Going to the Dance*, New York, 1982
Vaughan, David, "Twyla Tharp: Launching a New Classi-
    cism", *Dance Magazine* (New York), May 1984
Macaulay, Alastair, "Twyla Tharp Dance", *Dancing Times*
    (London), August 1984
Jowitt, Deborah, *The Dance in Mind*, New York, 1985
Albert, Steven, "Utopia Lost—and Found?", *Ballet Review*
    (New York), Spring 1986
Barnes, Clive, "Twyla Tharp and the Modern Classicism",
    Dance and Dancers (London), September 1987
Croce, Arlene, *Sight Lines*, New York, 1987
Barnes, Clive, "Daring, Newness and Occasion", *Dance and
    Dancers* (London), September 1989
Acocella, Joan, "Balancing Act", *Dance Magazine* (New
    York), October 1990
Zuck, Barbara, "Tharp Moves", *Dance Magazine* (New York),
    January 1992

*   *   *

Twyla Tharp graduated from Barnard College with a degree in
art history. She spent a single season with the Paul Taylor
Dance Company before setting out on a career as an
independent artist in 1965. Like other choreographic rebels
emerging in the 1960s, such as Trisha Brown, Lucinda Childs,
and Meredith Monk, Tharp explored alternatives to traditional
theatre spaces, both out of doors and in gymnasiums as well as
art galleries. Like them, she too began with a female company,
though in Tharp's case she maintains this was for practical
rather than political reasons. During these early years Tharp
rejected the notion of establishing a repertoire. Instead, she
would work with a piece until she felt she had got what she
needed from it and then abandon it for the next project.

Creatively stimulating though this notion proved, it is not a
practical way in which to promote an ongoing company. The
earliest work she has kept is the rigorously structured trio *The
Fugue*.

A turning point in her career came when Robert Joffrey
invited Tharp to work with his company. *Deuce Coupe*, set to a
collage of tunes by The Beach Boys, and jointly danced by both
the Joffrey and Tharp's own company, proved a phenomenal
success. It became one of the icons of the era, and marked a new
way for a mainstream company to approach ballet. Tharp's
loose-limbed, seemingly nonchalant movement style, filled
with slouches, squiggles, and quotations from popular dance in
conjunction with classical ballet technique, captured a carefree
spirit which seemed to be vanishing as the 1970s generation
found itself caught up in the aftermath of the Vietnam war and
growing urban disillusion.

Tharp's joyous jazz suites, ranging from *The Bix Pieces* and
Eight Jelly Rolls through *Sue's Leg* and *Baker's Dozen*,
culminated with *Nine Sinatra Songs*. She said she chose Sinatra
because his songs symbolize the last time when innocently
falling in love was still possible. By mixing all kinds of dance
and allowing each style equal value Tharp created a synthesis of
American cultural attitudes.

Twyla Tharp, however, is far from being a Pollyanna. In
contrast to these pieces she created a pair of hard-hitting,
purposefully unpleasant evening-length shows for Broadway.
The chaotic *When We Were Very Young* led on to the much
more satisfactory *The Catherine Wheel*. Both focus on a typical
American family in the process of bickering self-destruction.
The latter features a dazzling, pyrotechnical finale known as
The Golden Section. This is one of Tharp's most celebratory
creations and has often been performed as a separate one-act
piece. With these works her movement takes on a supersonic
velocity that is as threateningly aggressive as it is high-flying
and inventive. Tharp gloriously combines these two threads of
her career in a suite to the music of Philip Glass called *In the
Upper Room*.

Tharp's work with ballet companies in the 1970s and 1980s
has frequently been regarded as the most innovative ballet
choreography of its era. Her American Ballet Theatre début,
Push Comes to Shove, became ABT's biggest-ever hit and a
signature work for Mikhail Baryshnikov. Only Jerome Robbins's *Fancy Free* (1944) can rival its continuing popularity in
the American repertory. Tharp went on to create several more
ballets for Baryshnikov, including the charmingly neo-classical
The Little Ballet (originally *Once upon a Time*), as well as the
choreography for Baryshnikov and Gregory Hines in the film
White Nights. She put her own company on ice in order to take
up a position as an artistic associate with American Ballet
Theatre. That company mounted several works from the Tharp
repertory, such as *Nine Sinatra Songs* and *In The Upper Room*, as
well as new pieces, notably *Brief Fling*.

American Ballet Theatre is not the only company to benefit
from Tharp's determination to revivify classical dance. Her
first European work was for the Paris Opéra Ballet. In 1989 she
staged *As Time Goes By*, initially done for the Joffrey Ballet,
and created *Rules of the Game* which cleverly capitalizes on that
company's narcissistic love of individual display. Here, as so
often in her work, Tharp creates images of contemporary,
obviously sexual women without reducing them to sluttish
harridans. Her ability to choreograph for real women, rather
than fairy-tale visions, has always been one of her most striking
gifts.

Tharp's major film choreography to date has been for the
musical *Hair*. In 1985, she directed and choreographed a
Broadway version of the Hollywood classic *Singin' in the Rain*.
Tharp's interest in video goes back to the earliest days of her

career, and has led to a number of important works for camera, both original and adapted from the stage.

—Allen Robertson

———

THEME AND VARIATIONS

Choreography: George Balanchine
Music: Petr Ilyich Tchaikovsky
Design: Woodman Thompson (scenery and costumes)
First Production: Ballet Theatre, City Center, New York, 26 November 1947
Principal Dancers: Alicia Alonso, Igor Youskevitch

Other productions include: Ballet Theatre (new costumes André Levasseur), with Violette Verdy and Royes Fernandez; New York, 17 September 1958. New York City Ballet (restaged Balanchine, costumes Barbara Karinska), with Violette Verdy and Edward Villella; New York, 5 February 1960 (restaged by Balanchine as Fourth Movement, or "Tema con Variazioni", in *Tchaikovsky Suite No. 3*, 3 December 1970). Les Grands Ballets Canadiens; Montreal, 17 March 1968. Dutch National Ballet; Amsterdam, 24 December 1981. Sadler's Wells Royal Ballet (staged Patricia Neary); Birmingham, 10 October 1988. Kirov Ballet (staged Francia Russell); Leningrad, 1989. Royal Danish Ballet (staged Neary); Copenhagen, 26 April 1991.

PUBLICATIONS

Hering, Doris, "New York City Ballet", *Dance Magazine* (New York), March 1960
Reynolds, Nancy, *Repertory in Review*, New York, 1977
Balanchine, George, with Mason, Francis, *Balanchine's Complete Stories of the Great Ballets*, Garden City, N.Y., 1977
Payne, Charles, *American Ballet Theatre*, New York, 1978

Theme and Variations **as performed by Miyako Yoshida and Petter Jacobsson, Sadler's Wells Royal Ballet, London**

Croce, Arlene, *Going to the Dance*, New York, 1982
Pierpont, Claudia Roth, "Clio's Revenge", *Ballet Review* (New York), Spring 1988

* * *

With its elegant pair of principals in a chandeliered ballroom, framed by demi-soloists and corps, *Theme and Variations* is one of George Balanchine's grandest and most succinct tributes to his alma mater, the Imperial Russian Ballet. But it is very much his own American gloss on his heritage, streamlined and speeded up, with linking steps removed, and introducing new variants of classical steps with a supreme and subtle musicality.

Significantly, Ballet Theatre commissioned the ballet for its great danseur noble, Igor Youskevitch, a Russian expatriate trained in the Maryinsky tradition. The ballet reflects the dual qualities of his Old World/New World style and of his partnership with the Cuban Alicia Alonso, whose more eclectic training nevertheless featured Russian influence. It also embodies their strongly contrasting masculine and feminine qualities.

Set to Tchaikovsky's "musique dansante", as Balanchine characterized highly danceable music, the ballet's formal beauty reflects the formality of the theme and variations structure and the grand simplicity of the musical theme—which Balanchine characterized as "so elegant and restrained—sheer Mozart!"

The principal roles are abstract homages to the great princes and princesses of classical ballet, most of all *The Sleeping Beauty*. The courtly pas de deux, with its challenges to control in elaborate promenades, looks like an amalgam of the Rose Adagio and the Grand Pas de deux in one. The corps has decorative hands-linked groupings à la Petipa (though their weaving in and out is Balanchinian), and the ballet ends with a great polonaise for the whole cast in best fairytale manner, with a last pose in which corps salute the ballerina held aloft by her partner.

The ballet can also be seen as a sophisticated microcosm of classical ballet schooling. It opens with tendu combinations with port de bras and quick changes of épaulement by the principals, standing in front of the corps as if setting the example for them. These "themes"—the extension of the leg and the quick facings, basic building-blocks of ballet vocabulary—are repeated and expanded upon as the ballet progresses. Similarly, the quick pas de chat separated by détournés in the ballerina's first solo become the more challenging pas de chat and pirouette combination of her second (or even incorporating a gargouillade and pirouette combination in the New York City Ballet's performances). The ballet's climax in a grand pas de deux is the ultimate test of academic schooling.

Tendu combinations had originally also featured in the danseur's second variation, but Youskevitch felt that the result was too low-key; when Balanchine happened to catch sight of him practicing ronds de jambe sautés in the studio, he quickly arranged the variation that is still a challenge to male dancers, using in Petipa-fashion just a few such steps, repeated. Most notoriously, the variation contains a series of double tours en l'air separated only by single pirouettes—most difficult coming at the end of the variation, and reflecting Youskevitch's impeccable technique and placement. Small changes in the man's choreography have been made from time to time for various dancers, notably with tours alternating to right and left in the New York City Ballet.

The ballet, an immediate success, was a milestone in the acceptance of Balanchine by critics and public, at a time when he did not have an active company of his own (his Ballet Society was giving performances only four times a year). For Ballet Theatre, the work was significant in developing its corps de ballet as well as in establishing one of its most popular works, especially while Youskevitch was on hand to dance it. He and Alonso brought to it a romantic interpretation that Balanchine disagreed with at the time, although he later relented. When the ballet entered the repertoire of Balanchine's own New York City Ballet, however, it was danced more impersonally. In 1970 Balanchine choreographed the three previous sections of Tchaikovsky's *Suite No. 3*, representing a kind of "haunted ballroom" sequence—and most interesting is the "Elégie", danced barefoot, in which a poet finds and loses his love/muse among a group of Russian maidens with loose hair.

Theme and Variations is now danced by a number of companies, including the Birmingham Royal Ballet and the Kirov Ballet. One of the Kirov's first two Balanchine acquisitions, it is appropriately danced against a background representing the Kirov (Maryinsky) Theatre itself, and serves as a challenge to the dancers to work on musical sensitivity, speed, and footwork.

—Marilyn Hunt

THÉODORE, Mlle.

French dancer. Born Maris-Madeleine de Crespé (also Crespi, or Crépé) in Paris, 6 October 1760. Studied with Jean-Barthélemy Lany, Paris. Married dancer and choreographer Jean Dauberval (Jean Bercher), 1783. Dancer, corps de ballet of L'Académie royale de musique (Paris Opéra), 1776, leaving to study with Lany; returned for official début in *Myrtil et Lycoris*, 1777; performed in Brussels, 1781; leading dancer, King's Theatre, London, 1781-84; imprisoned for eighteen days, for allegedly breaking contract with Opéra, 1783; premiere danseuse, Grand Théâtre, Bordeaux (under ballet master Dauberval), 1785-90, creating leading role in first production of *La Fille mal gardée* (*Le Ballet de la paille*), 1789; leading dancer, Pantheon Theatre (with husband Dauberval as ballet master), London, 1791-92, and Haymarket Theatre, London, 1792. Died in Audenge, 9 September 1796.

ROLES

1777 Dancer in *Myrtil et Lycoris* (pastorale; mus. Désormery), Opéra, Paris
1778 Dancer (cr) in *Phaon* (opéra-lyrique; mus. Piccini, chor. M. Gardel), Court Theatre, Choisy
1779 Dancer (cr) in *Mirza* (M. Gardel), Opéra, Paris
1780 A Corinthian in *Médée et Jason* (first Opéra version; Noverre), Opéra, Paris
      Dancer (cr) in *Andromaque* (tragédie-lyrique; mus. Grétry, chor. Dauberval), Opéra, Paris
      Dancer (cr) in *Laura et Pétrarque* (pastorale; mus. Candeille), Opéra, Paris
      Dancer (cr) in *Le Seigneur bienfaisant* (comédie-lyrique; mus. Floquet, chor. Dauberval, Noverre, M. Gardel), Opéra, Paris
1781 Dancer (cr) in *La Fête de Mirza* (M. Gardel), Opéra, Paris
      Principal dancer (cr) in *A Divertissement Dance* (Noverre), King's Theatre, London
      Principal dancer (cr) in *Les Amans réunis* (Noverre), King's Theatre, London

Principal dancer in *Les Petits Riens* (Noverre), King's Theatre, London
1782   Hébé (cr) in *Le Triomphe de l'amour conjugal* (Noverre), King's Theatre, London
Dancer (cr) in *The Emperor's Cossac[k]* (Noverre), King's Theatre, London
Chaconne in *New Divertissement Dance* (Simonet), King's Theatre, London
Armida (cr) in *Rinaldo and Armida* (Noverre), King's Theatre, London
Minuet (cr) in *La Contadina in Corte* (opera; mus. Sacchini), Benefit for Mlle. Théodore, King's Theatre, London
Clitandre in *La Rosière de Salency* (Noverre), King's Theatre, London
Medea in *Medea and Jason* (Noverre), King's Theatre, London
Muse (cr) in *Apollon et les muses* (Noverre), King's Theatre, London
Leading role (cr) in *Apelles and Campaspe; or, The Generosity of Alexander the Great* (Noverre), King's Theatre, London
Pas seul (cr) added to *New Divertissement* (Simonet), King's Theatre, London
Leading role (cr) in *Il Ratto delle Sabine* (Le Picq), King's Theatre, London
1783   Pas de basque (cr) in *Le Tuteur trompé; or, The Guardian Outwitted* (Le Picq), King's Theatre, London
Pas de Lapons (cr) added to *Le Tuteur trompé* (Le Picq), King's Theatre, London
Grand Allemande, Pas de deux (cr) in *Pastoral Ballet*, King's Theatre, London
Principal dancer (cr) in *Les Épouses Persanes; or, The Persian Wives* (Le Picq), King's Theatre, London
Principal dancer (cr) in *Il Riposo del campo; or, The Recreations of the Camp* (Le Picq), King's Theatre, London
Principal dancer (cr) in *The Amours of Alexander and Roxana* (Le Picq), King's Theatre, London
Gavotte (cr) in *Le Dejeuner Espagnol* (Simonet), King's Theatre, London
Pas de deux in *Les Ruses de l'amour* (Noverre), King's Theatre, London
Minuet and Gavotte (cr; also chor.), added to *Les Ruses de l'amour* (Noverre), King's Theatre, London
Principal dancer (cr) in *La Dame bienfaisante* (Le Picq), King's Theatre, London
Terpsichore (cr) in *The Pastimes of Terpsichore* (Dauberval), King's Theatre, London
Principal dancer in *Friendship Leads to Love* (Dauberval), King's Theatre, London
1784   Principal dancer (cr) in *Le Réveil du bonheur* (Dauberval), King's Theatre, London
Principal dancer (cr) in *Divertissement* (Dauberval), King's Theatre, London
Pastoral Minuet (cr) in *Le Coq du village; ou, La Loterie ingénieuse* (Dauberval), King's Theatre, London
Eglé (cr) in *Orpheo* (Dauberval), King's Theatre, London
Principal dancer (cr) in *Le Magnifique* (Dauberval), King's Theatre, London
Youth (cr) in *The Four Ages of Man* (Dauberval), King's Theatre, London
The Statue (cr) in *Pygmalion* (Dauberval), King's Theatre, London
Pas de deux, Pas seul (cr) added to *Le Tuteur trompé* (revival; Le Picq), King's Theatre, London

Louisa (cr) in *Le Déserteur; ou, La Clémence royale* (Dauberval), King's Theatre, London
Principal dancer in *Sémiramis* (Le Picq), King's Theatre, London
1785   Leading role in *L'Epreuve villageoise* (Dauberval), Grand Theatre, Bordeaux
1787   Leading role (cr) in *Le Page inconstant* (Dauberval; probably featuring Mlle. Théodore), Grand Theatre, Bordeaux
1789   Lison (cr; later called Lise) in *La Fille mal gardée* (originally performed as *Le Ballet de la paille*; Dauberval), Grand Theatre, Bordeaux
1791   Thalie, Muse de la comédie (cr) in *Amphion et Thalie; ou, Le Éléve des muses* (Dauberval), Pantheon, London
Eucharis (cr) in *Telemachus in the Island of Calypso* (Dauberval), Pantheon, London
Calysto (cr) in *La Siège de Cythère* (Dauberval), Pantheon, London
Principal dancer (cr) in *La Fête villageoise* (Dauberval), Pantheon, London
1792   Principal dancer (cr) in *Le Volage fixé* (Dauberval), Haymarket, London

PUBLICATIONS

Noverre, Jean-Georges, *Lettres sur la danse et les ballets*, Stuttgart and Lyons, 1760; as *Letters on Dancing and Ballets*, translated by Cyril Beaumont (from 1803 edition), London, 1930
Castil-Blaze, *L'Académie impériale de musique*, Paris, 1855
Ces Demoiselles de l'Opéra, second edition, Paris, 1887
Du Bois, A., *Une Page de la vie d'une danseuse française au XVIIIe siècle, Mlle Théodore*, Brussels, 1896
Lynham, Derek, *The Chevalier Noverre*, London, 1950
Migel, Parmenia, *The Ballerinas*, New York, 1972
Percival, John, "The Well-Guarded Daughter", *Dance and Dancers* (London), June 1992

*   *   *

Although today enjoying nothing like the fame of better known ballerinas of earlier centuries, such as Subligny, Camargo, or Taglioni, Mlle. Théodore is yet the object of some fascination for even the more casual of ballet historians. Creator of the great role of Lise in *La Fille mal gardée*, wife of the outstanding choreographer Jean Dauberval, and apparently quite a colourful personality in her own right, Mlle. Théodore occupies a special place in the history of ballet.

She had her apprenticeship with L'Académie royale de musique (the Paris Opéra), as was typical of stage danseuses of her day, when still a mere sixteen or seventeen years of age; her official début was a "1er remplacement" in 1777 in a pastoral by Désormery. Within five years, she was testing her wings abroad, performing in Brussels and London in 1781 and apparently enraging the Opéra authorities by violating her contract with them. At this point, a sense of Mlle. Théodore's reportedly "spirited" character emerges, for her difference with the Opéra (undoubtedly fuelled by her own degree of intransigence) resulted in her being imprisoned at La Force for eighteen days in 1783. Mlle. Théodore's career with the Opéra was not to endure much longer in any case, for she was to leave the Paris Opéra, accompanied by her new husband Dauberval (himself a victim of Opéra politics), for good in the same year. Obviously no retiring rose, Mlle. Théodore is also said to have been involved in a duel with a certain Mlle. Beaumesnil of the Opéra (fortunately both pistols misfired), and to be a reader of the philosophy of Jean-Jacques Rousseau in her spare time.

While she had been admired in her early years at the Opéra (she did not stay long enough to reach the rank of premiere danseuse), Mlle. Dauberval's first real triumphs were in London in the 1781–82 season, where the great choreographer Noverre had assembled a company at the King's Theatre that included Charles-Louis Didelot, Charles Le Picq, Pierre Gardel, and Giovanni Baccelli. The season was a huge success ("With such a company," writes Ivor Guest of that illustrious era, "it was hardly surprising that ballet should have attained an importance it had never had before in London.") Mlle. Théodore performed in a number of Noverre's *ballets d'action*, in which dramatic ability was as important as dancing skill. In 1782, she performed Medea in the famous *Medea and Jason*, a ballet which the London audiences had already seen, but which was appreciated even more now that Mlle. Théodore was the chief attraction. *The Public Advertiser* reported, "The ballet of Medea and Jason is too well known to need any particular mention; we shall only observe that the dance, as it now stands, *gains* some advantage over the last year's performance of it, by the introduction of Mlle. Théodore . . ."

In 1783 Mlle. Théodore married Dauberval. In 1785 they moved to Bordeaux, where Dauberval was engaged as ballet master, with his wife as premiere danseuse. It was in Bordeaux some four years later that Dauberval created his most famous and enduring work, *La Fille mal gardée* (performed originally under the title of *Le Ballet de la paille*). Staged on the very eve of the French Revolution, it nevertheless reflects a gentle, pastoral world of a previous era, depicting with lighthearted humour and a certain amount of irony the country life of provincial French farmers during the eighteenth century. The engaging heroine of this ballet, Lise (or Lison, in the original) is the character who holds the entire piece together, and considering the instant success of *Fille*, we can imagine the qualities of Mlle. Thédore's dancing which helped bring about this happy collaboration between dancer and choreographer.

Interestingly, it is only recently that historians could state with assurance that Mlle. Théodore was indeed the creator of the role of Lise. It was known that she performed the role in 1791, when Dauberval restaged the ballet in London; but it was only with Ivor Guest's discovery of the scenario in manuscript that Mlle. Théodore's original participation in the ballet could be confirmed. And, as John Percival has stated, "Madame [sic] Théodore must have been a marvellous dancer. Apart from guessing as much from the role she created, we have the word of the great Noverre that she was 'the image of Terpsichore'. He praised her fluidity, facility and brilliance, and said 'her ballon made her dancing seem so light that, even when she was not jumping, one was convinced, from the mere elasticity of her insteps, that she was not touching the ground'."

It was to the Pantheon that Mlle. Théodore (who also performed as Madame Dauberval, or Madame Théodore) returned with her husband in 1791 (the King's Theatre having burned down), and here *La Fille mal gardée* was staged with the great danseurs Charles Didelot and Salvatore Viganò in the leading roles opposite her Lise. She also performed in restagings of such Dauberval ballets as *Le Déserteur* and in his new ballets *Amphion et Thalie*, *Telemachus in the Island of Calypso*, and *La Siège de Cythère*. Mlle. Théodore died in 1796, when she was only 35 years old, leaving behind a forlorn Dauberval, whose notorious philandering was said to have come to an end with his marriage to a dancer whom he adored.

—Elizabeth Hudson

THREE-CORNERED HAT, The *see* TRICORNE, Le

TIKHOMIROV, Vasily

Russian dancer, teacher, and choreographer. Born Vasily Dmitrievich Tikhomirov in Moscow, 29 March (17 March old style) 1876. Studied at the Ballet Department of the Moscow Theatrical College, pupil of Ivan Ermolov, Platon Karsavin, Aleksandr Shiryaev, 1886–91; studied in the Class of Perfection under Pavel Gerdt, St. Petersburg, 1891–93. Married (1) dancer Ekaterina Geltser, c. 1900–08; (2) Lidy Abrikosovoi. First performances, while still a student, in children's roles, also performing in operas and dramatic spectacles at the Moscow Little Theatre; dancer of the Bolshoi Theatre, Moscow, from 1893, becoming premier danseur, from 1899; leading dancer at the Alhambra Theatre, London, 1911, and for Anna Pavlova's company during her world tour, 1913; also teacher at the Moscow Theatrical College, from 1896; assistant ballet master, Bolshoi Theatre, from 1908; manager of ballet company and director of ballet department, Moscow Theatrical College, from 1917; member of the Directorate of the Bolshoi Theatre, from 1919; ballet director, Bolshoi Theatre, from 1925; awarded pension from 1934. Recipient: titles of Honoured Artist, 1924, National Artist of the Republic, 1934. Died in Moscow, 20 June 1956.

ROLES

1894 Mario in *Cendrillon* (Bogdanov), Bolshoi Theatre, Moscow

1895 Lucien in *Paquita* (Petipa), Bolshoi Theatre, Moscow

1896 Colin (Colas) in *Vain Precautions* (*La Fille mal gardée*; Petipa), Bolshoi Theatre, Moscow

1897 Franz in *Coppélia* (after Saint-Léon), Bolshoi Theatre, Moscow

Mars in *The Stars* (Clustine), Bolshoi Theatre, Moscow

1898 The Poet in *Fee Dolly* (Mendez), Bolshoi Theatre, Moscow

Akhmed-Pasha in *La Péri* (after Coralli), Bolshoi Theatre, Moscow

Matteo in *The Naïad and the Fisherman* (*Ondine*; Perrot), Bolshoi Theatre, Moscow

Bacchus in *Fantasia* (Mendez), Bolshoi Theatre, Moscow

Luke in *The Magic Flute* (Clustine after Ivanov), Bolshoi Theatre, Moscow

The Prince in *Cinderella* (Ivanov), Bolshoi Theatre, Moscow

Pierre in *Cavalry Halt* (Petipa), Bolshoi Theatre, Moscow

1899 The Month of May in *Magical Reveries* (Clustine), Bolshoi Theatre, Moscow

Bluebird in *The Sleeping Beauty* (Petipa), Bolshoi Theatre, Moscow

Prince Désiré in *The Sleeping Beauty* (Petipa), Bolshoi Theatre, Moscow

1900 Bernard in *Raymonda* (Petipa), Bolshoi Theatre, Moscow

Jean de Brienne in *Raymonda* (Petipa), Bolshoi Theatre, Moscow

Albrecht in *Giselle* (Petipa after Coralli, Perrot), Bolshoi Theatre, Moscow

Basil (cr) in *Don Quixote* (Gorsky), Bolshoi Theatre, Moscow
1901   Prince Siegfried in *Swan Lake* (Gorsky after Petipa, Ivanov), Bolshoi Theatre, Moscow
1903   Waltz and Adagio (cr) in *The Goldfish* (Gorsky), Bolshoi Theatre, Moscow
1904   Solor in *La Bayadère* (Petipa), Bolshoi Theatre, Moscow
1905   Prince (cr) in *The Magic Mirror* (Gorsky), Bolshoi Theatre, Moscow
        English Tourist (cr) in *Pharaoh's Daughter* (new version; Gorsky after Petipa), Bolshoi Theatre, Moscow
1907   Harlequin in *Harlequinade* (Petipa), Bolshoi Theatre, Moscow
1911   Nar-Avas (cr) in *Salammbô* (Gorsky), Bolshoi Theatre, Moscow
        Principal dancer (cr) in *Dance Dream* (Gorsky), Alhambra Theatre, London
1912   Conrad (cr) in *Le Corsaire* (new version; Gorsky), Bolshoi Theatre, Moscow
1916   Petronius (cr) in *Eunice and Petronius* (Gorsky), Bolshoi Theatre, Moscow
1924   James (cr) in *La Sylphide*, Act II (also chor.; after Petipa), Bolshoi Theatre, Moscow
1926   Phoebus (cr) in *La Esmeralda* (also chor.), Bolshoi Theatre, Moscow
1927   The Captain (cr) in *The Red Poppy* (also chor., with Lashchilin), Bolshoi Theatre, Moscow

WORKS

1899   *Lively Flowers* (mus. Simon), Artists of the Bolshoi Theatre at the Noble Assembly, Moscow
1913   Individual dances in *Carnaval* (divertissement; with Gorsky; mus. various), Bolshoi Theatre, Moscow
1914   Individual dances in *Dances of Nations* (with Gorsky; mus. various), Bolshoi Theatre, Moscow
1926   *La Esmeralda* (mus. Pugni, Glière), Bolshoi Theatre, Moscow
1927   *The Red Poppy* (with Lashchilin; mus. Glière), Bolshoi Theatre, Moscow

Also staged:
1923   "The Kingdom of the Shades" scene in *La Bayadère* (Gorsky after Petipa; mus. Minkus), Bolshoi Theatre, Moscow
1924   *The Sleeping Beauty* (after Petipa; mus. Tchaikovsky), Bolshoi Theatre, Moscow
        La Sylphide, Act II (after Petipa; mus. Schneitzhoeffer), Bolshoi Theatre, Moscow

Other productions include: stagings of dances in operas *The Night Before Christmas* and *Sadko* (mus. Rimsky-Korsakov).

PUBLICATIONS

Roslavleva, Natalia (ed.), *V. D. Tikhomirov: Artist, Ballet Master, Teacher*, Moscow, 1971
Krasovskaya, Vera, *Russian Ballet Theatre at the Beginning of the Twentieth Century*, Leningrad, 1972
Chernova, Natalia, *From Geltser to Ulanova*, Moscow, 1979
Souritz, Elizabeth, *The Art of Choreography in the 1920s*, Moscow, 1979; as *Soviet Choreographers in the 1920s*, translated by Lynn Visson, Durham, N.C. and London, 1990
Smakov, Gennady, *The Great Russian Dancers*, New York, 1984

* * *

Vasily Tikhomirov was one of the most influential figures in Moscow ballet during the first third of the twentieth century. By the 1890s, ballet in Moscow had found itself in a crisis, significantly inferior to that in St. Petersburg. Its rise began when, at the turn of the century, the Bolshoi Theatre began to turn out talented dancers, and the troupe came under the direction of ballet master Aleksandr Gorsky. Gorsky came to Moscow from St. Petersburg soon after leading ballerina Ekaterina Geltser and first dancer Vasily Tikhomirov had joined the company. However, despite their joint efforts to achieve the rebirth of ballet at the Bolshoi Theatre, their views on art did not coincide and they were not always in agreement. In certain instances, Geltser and especially Tikhomirov sharply opposed Gorsky. Tikhomirov based his principles on the St. Petersburg academic system and brought them to life in his educational work. He stood for the preservation and inviolability of Petipa's form of "grand ballet" and classical dance. Gorsky, on the other hand, was a reformer and worked towards performance of a new type.

When Tikhomirov first appeared on the stage of the Bolshoi Theatre, the ballets of Joseph Mendez and the first productions of Ivan Clustine were being performed. In 1899 Gorsky transferred, with their original choreography, Petipa's ballets *The Sleeping Beauty* and *Raymonda* to Moscow. Tikhomirov could only welcome this. However, with Gorsky's next choreographic ventures, such as an adaptation of Petipa's *Don Quixote* (1900), and even more with his own ballets, beginning with *Gudule's Daughter*, it became clear that Gorsky was a supporter of a different type of performance—a realistic presentation, wherein the subject would be uncovered through pantomine and dance, and would be distinguished by historical and psychological authenticity. Accordingly, he demanded from the cast expressive mime and the ability to undergo a virtual transformation on stage, while the technical complexities of dance were considered a quality of second order; he preferred dancer-actors to dancer-virtuosos.

Tikhomirov, for all his virtues, could not please Gorsky. Here was classical dance par excellence; Tikhomirov was a dancer of noble bearing, classical purity, and superior technique. All the reviews noted the quickness of his rotations, the precision of his lifts, the power of his jumps, and especially his masterful control of grand pirouettes, that apogée of virtuoso male dance. At the same time, even in the prime of his youth, critics pointed to an excessively "statuesque" quality in Tikhomirov's figure (with age it became simply heavy) and to his limited acting ability.

Blind devotion to tradition is perhaps the basic trait of Tikhomirov's creativity. In the conditions of ballet's development in Moscow during the 1920s, this had both negative and positive aspects. On the one hand, his conviction of the unshakeability of certain canons and his defence of old forms of ballet helped to preserve a heritage which, with Gorsky's efforts, would have irrevocably vanished. On the other hand, Tikhomirov's conservatism was a serious obstacle to anything new, especially when he began to occupy administrative posts (and Tikhomirov was in a troupe of like-minded people, united under the flag of academic conservatism).

Tikhomirov appeared chiefly in ballets of the old repertoire. He danced Basil in *Don Quixote*, demonstrating a mastery of the most difficult pas de deux movements in the final act. In the role of Genie in *The Little Humpbacked Horse* he crossed the stage with powerful leaps; his Jean de Brienne in *Raymonda* preserved a statuesque strength even in the heat of battle. But in Gorsky's productions, such as *Gudule's Daughter*, *Salammbô*, and *Schubertiana*, Tikhomirov either did not participate or took roles especially adapted to his own abilities (such as Nar-Avas in *Salammbô*). Tikhomirov's greatest success was the role of

Conrad in *Le Corsaire*. Gorsky presented this ballet in an entirely new production (1912) and created for Tikhomirov a part which magnificently demonstrated his gifts. By this time, Tikhomirov had been forced to transfer to pantomime roles. His mighty figure in picturesque costumes by Konstantine Korovin had an extraordinary effect on audiences. Such a Corsaire could only command attention, and indeed, inspire quite a thrill. Tikhomirov's skill in supporting the ballerina was utilized through choreography, too: he lifted and carried Geltser as Medora as if she were a feather. His powerful arms would touch her delicately and with precision.

After the October Revolution (1917), Tikhomirov was the head of ballet at the Bolshoi Theatre for a number of years. He continued to defend the stability of tradition, constantly appearing in conflict with choreographers who suggested innovation. Thus he did not approve of Gorsky's presentation of *The Nutcracker* in 1919 and decisively objected to that choreographer's entirely new version of *Swan Lake* in 1920. At the same time Tikhomirov revived on the Bolshoi stage a number of nineteenth-century productions (for example, *La Bayadère*), and with particular stubbornness he opposed the innovation of Kasyan Goleizovsky in his ballet *Joseph the Beautiful* (1925). This resulted in a protest by the younger part of the troupe (the so-called "youth revolt") who refused to recognize the authority of Tikhomirov and his associates.

In 1926 Tikhomirov presented the ballet *La Esmeralda* at the Bolshoi. The famous 1927 ballet *The Red Poppy*, under Tikhomirov's initiative, gave the heroine's role to Ekaterina Geltser. Tikhomirov and Geltser aspired to create a production aimed at the fashionable revolution theme (the struggle of the Chinese under English colonizers), but utilizing the form of the "old grand ballet" through variations, pas de deux, and grand pas in classical ensembles during "The Dream" act, where flowers and birds danced. They wanted to show that in the contemporary world, one could, and indeed needed, to speak the language of traditional classical dance.

The ballet, which provoked a negative response from the critics (who then propagandized modern taste), was none the less greeted with delight by the mass audience and had a significantly greater success than the productions of more innovative choreographers. Tikhomirov was understood by the uninitiated. The success of *The Red Poppy* was a weighty victory for the conservative wing in Soviet ballet, striking a blow to many experimental undertakings. It is impossible to deny that Tikhomirov's defence of classical dance in the 1920s was opportune, since this is when many were choosing to move away from it.

Tikhomirov's most significant contribution was pedagogical. He was for many years the primary teacher of classical dance in the Moscow School—all of the well-known male dancers at the Bolshoi Theatre (and also many of the female ones) had him as their teacher. His can be considered the chief tendency of the Moscow style of male dancer, which called for a masculinity in execution, and valued force, strength, and open displays of virtuosity. Among his pupils were Mikhail Mordkin, Aleksandr Volinine, Vecheslav Svoboda, Lavrenty Novikov, and many others.

—Elizabeth Souritz

TIMOFEYEVA, Nina

Russian/Soviet dancer. Born Nina Vladimirovna Timofeeva (Timofeyeva) in Leningrad, 2 June 1935. Studied at the Leningrad Choreographic School, pupil of Natalia Kamkova; graduated in 1953. Married composer Kirily Molchanov (died 1982): one daughter. Début (while still a student) as Masha in *The Nutcracker*, 1952 with official début in 1953; dancer, Kirov Ballet, Leningrad, 1953–56; soloist, becoming leading ballerina, Bolshoi Ballet, Moscow, 1956–88. Recipient: title of People's Artist of the USSR, 1969; Order of the Red Banner of Labour, 1971.

ROLES

1956 Odette/Odile in *Swan Lake* (Gorsky after Petipa, Ivanov; staged Messerer), Bolshoi Ballet, Moscow

1957 Myrtha in *Giselle* (Petipa after Coralli, Perrot; staged Lavrovsky), Bolshoi Ballet, Moscow

Title role in *Laurencia* (Chabukiani), Bolshoi Ballet, Moscow

Miriam in *Gayané* (Vainonen), Bolshoi Ballet, Moscow

1958 Phrygia in *Spartacus* (Moiseyev), Bolshoi Ballet, Moscow

Street Dancer in *Don Quixote* (Gorsky), Bolshoi Ballet, Moscow

Bacchante in *Faust* (opera; music Gounod, chor. Lavrovsky), Bolshoi Ballet, Moscow

1959 Mistress of the Copper Mountain in *The Stone Flower* (Grigorovich), Bolshoi Ballet, Moscow

Kitri in *Don Quixote* (Gorsky), Bolshoi Ballet, Moscow

1960 One of the Three Swans in *Swan Lake* (Gorsky after Petipa, Ivanov; staged Messerer), Bolshoi Ballet, Moscow

1961 The Young Girl (cr) in *Night City* (Lavrovsky), Bolshoi Ballet, Moscow

Title role (cr) in *Gayané* (Vainonen), Bolshoi Ballet, Moscow

1963 Title role in *Raymonda* (Petipa, Gorsky; staged Lavrovsky), Bolshoi Ballet, Moscow

1964 Princess Aurora in *The Sleeping Beauty* (Grigorovich after Petipa), Bolshoi Ballet, Moscow

1965 Title role in *Giselle* (Petipa after Coralli, Perrot; staged Lavrovsky), Bolshoi Ballet, Moscow

Mekhmene-Banu in *The Legend of Love* (Grigorovich), Bolshoi Ballet, Moscow

Leili in *Leili and Medzhnun* (Goleizovsky), Bolshoi Ballet, Moscow

1967 Title role (cr) in *Asel* (Vinogradov), Bolshoi Ballet, Moscow

1968 Aegina (cr) in *Spartacus* (Grigorovich), Bolshoi Ballet, Moscow

1970 Odette/Odile in *Swan Lake* (Petipa, Ivanov; staged Grigorovich), Bolshoi Ballet, Moscow

1976 Beatrice (cr) in *Love after Love* (Boccadoro), Bolshoi Ballet, Moscow

1977 Lilac Fairy in *The Sleeping Beauty* (Grigorovich after Petipa), Bolshoi Ballet, Moscow

Nikiya in "The Kingdom of the Shades" from *La Bayadère* (Petipa), Bolshoi Ballet, Moscow

1980 Principal dancer in *These Charming Sounds* (Vasiliev), Bolshoi Ballet, Moscow

Lady Macbeth (cr) in *Macbeth* (Vasiliev), Bolshoi Ballet, Moscow

1981 Bakhor (cr) in *An Indian Legend* (Scott, Papko), Bolshoi Ballet, Moscow

Other roles include: leading roles in television ballets *White Nights* (mus. Schoenberg), *Fedra* (mus. Lokshin), *Moscow*

Fantasia (chor. Ryzhenko, Smirnov-Golovanov), *Three Cards* chor. Baranovsky).

PUBLICATIONS

By Timofeyeva:
Interview in V. Golubin, "Nina Timofeyevna", *Teatralnaya Zhizn* (Moscow), no. 10, 1973
Interview in "Macbeth on the Ballet Stage", *Soviet Literature* (Birmingham, Alabama), no. 12, 1980
Interview in Belova, E., "By One's Own Laws", *Television Broadcasting* (Moscow), no. 11, 1983
"Two out of Twelve", *Sovetsky Balet* (Moscow), no. 6, 1988
Interview in Chabukiani, V., "Confession in Love", *Ogonyot*, no. 16, 1989

About Timofeyeva:
Lvov-Anokhin, Boris, "Nina Timofeyeva of the Bolshoi Ballet", *Ballet Today* (London), July 1960
Lvov-Anokhin, Boris, *Masters of the Bolshoi Theatre*, Moscow, 1971
Demidov, Alexander, *The Russian Ballet Past and Present*, translated by Guy Daniels, London, 1978
Turin, Y., "Expression and Thought", in *Teatralnaya Zhizn* (Moscow), no. 5, 1983

*   *   *

Nina Timofeyeva, Leningrad dancer and graduate of the Leningrad school, found herself in Moscow by chance. The reason for her move from the Kirov to the Bolshoi was that the Bolshoi went to England in 1956 with *Swan Lake*; the best Odette/Odile, Maya Plisetskaya, was in disfavour with the officials at the Ministry of Culture, and a search for a replacement had found little success. Hurriedly, Timofeyeva was transferred to the Bolshoi.

In the early days of her Moscow career, Timofeyeva was not well liked by Muscovites. Everyone recognized that she had strong technique, but the opinion was that she "worked" rather than "danced"; her style was abrupt and somewhat coarse. But Timofeyeva stubbornly perfected her technique, displaying great force in her high jumps, quick pirouettes, and strong pointe work.

Then came the moment when Timofeyeva's virtuosity ceased to be perceived as an end in itself and became a means to convey her own vital being. At first she danced in traditional ballets—*The Sleeping Beauty*, *Raymonda*, *Don Quixote*—constructions of pure dance as it existed in the nineteenth century, now slightly modernized, but only in the sense of incorporating more complex technique. And in these roles, danced by hundreds of predecessors, Timofeyeva suddenly managed to bring something from within herself, creating a unique dramatic effect, especially in her powerful entrances.

Then Timofeyeva began to make her mark in modern ballet. The first role created especially for her was the Young Girl in the ballet *Night City*. This was a somewhat questionable work; the choreographer Leonid Lavrovsky had wanted to present Béla Bartók's *The Miraculous Mandarin*, but knew that he was not allowed to show any ballet which whimsically combined erotica (an officially designated taboo) with the fantastic. He therefore devised a new topic. In his own original libretto, a group of bandits force a young woman to lure passers-by, whom they then rob; but she comes across a young worker who defends her from the bandits. Love arises between the two, but the bandits kill the worker. The role of the young woman was secured by Timofeyeva, and was characteristic of her special

Nina Timofeyeva in *Spartacus*, Bolshoi Ballet, Moscow, 1970

dynamism. The power and expression of her dancing allowed her to create an image of great tragic force, exposing the contradictions in the human soul.

In Yuri Grigorovich's *The Legend of Love*, Mekhmene-Banu is a woman who gives up her beauty in order to save her sister's life, only to find that her beloved then chooses her sister. This was another role which Timofeyeva performed with astonishing expressive power. In 1965, the role of Asel in the ballet of the same name was created by Oleg Vinogradov especially for her. With great sincerity, Timofeyeva played a modern woman so passionately in love that her husband's betrayal becomes an irreparable tragedy for her. She leaves home, loses interest in life, and is saved only by meeting another man who is even more unhappy than she. Then also for Timofeyeva, Grigorovich created the role of Aegina in *Spartacus*, devising a courtesan who entices others for the purpose of destroying them; she is cynical and coldly calculating, deriving strength from her own very lack of principles. And finally, Timofeyeva's most significant role, also created for her, was that of Lady

Macbeth in *Macbeth*—the music of which was written by her husband Kirily Molchanov, with the choreography created by Vladimir Vasiliev. Timofeyeva's Lady Macbeth was a study of cruel ambition, showing a woman who tramples fearlessly on the laws of morality. She and her supporters forcefully and heartlessly take Macbeth, who is capable of hesitation and doubt, to his goal—which is actually his death.

Timofeyeva was not the favourite of those spectators and critics who went to the ballet for external beauty. She spoke about disharmony in the world, where evil and ugliness get the upper hand; yet her art was calling simultaneously for this evil to be fought.

—Irina Gruzdeva

THE TOKYO BALLET

Japanese ballet company based in Tokyo. Origins in the performing group of the Tokyo Ballet Gakko (Tokyo's first classical ballet school), based on Soviet teaching and founded by Koichi Hayashi, 1960, first performing as the Tchaikovsky Memorial Ballet; taken over, after bankruptcy, by impresario Tadatsugu Sasaki, 1964, with base in Tokyo but extensive tours in Japan and abroad; first visit to the Soviet Union in 1966, and to Europe in 1970. Artistic director of the Tokyo Ballet: Tadatsugu Sasaki.

PUBLICATIONS

Ogura, S., "Ballet in Japan", *Ballet Today* (London), March/April 1970

Téri, Evelyn, "Tokyo Ballet", *Ballett Journal/Das Tanzarchiv* (Cologne), December 1989

Agostini, Alfio, "Tokyo Ballet", *Balletto Oggi* (Milan), January–February 1990

* * *

The original Tokyo Ballet was the performing group of the Tokyo ballet school. The school opened in 1960, and was the first school in Japan to teach the Russian method of classical dance, with a faculty of Soviet teachers. It went bankrupt in 1964, and impresario Tadatsugu Sasaki took it over. The début performance of the company was in *Swan Lake*, which it took on a provincial tour through Japan.

In 1966 Olga Tarasova of the Bolshoi Ballet was invited to stage *Giselle* and *Ala and Lolly*. The company toured Soviet Russia later in the year with those two ballets, as well as *Marimo*, a ballet from the repertoire of the original Tokyo Ballet.

Guest choreographers from abroad have played an important part in the building of a repertoire. In 1969 the company staged two ballets by French choreographer Michel Descombey: *Mandala*, to music by Mayuzumi, and *Saracenia*, to music by Bartók. The Cuban Alberto Alonso then staged his *Carmen* for the company in 1972.

The Tokyo Ballet toured Europe extensively in 1975, visiting 40 cities in eight countries, with 87 performances in total. It was the first Japanese ballet company to tour Europe on such a scale. The following year, the company held its first world ballet festival. It was a gala affair, with the aim of gathering and showing off the prominent ballet personalities of the world. This first time, the long list of the participants was headed by

Margot Fonteyn, Alicia Alonso, and Maya Plisetskaya. Since then, the festival has been held every third year.

The company has shown firm growth since that time, and is now considered to be one of the most successful ballet companies in Japan. It has surely become the most well-known Japanese ballet company in Europe, largely a result of its many tours (in 1976, 1982, 1986, and 1988).

Apart from the standard classics, the Tokyo Ballet possesses a modern repertory including Hind's *Marco Polo* (1977, to music by Xenakis), Varlamov's *Princess Kaguya* (1978, to music by Meerovich), Béjart's *Kabuki* (1986, to music by Mayuzumi), and Neumeier's *Haiku* (1989, to music by Pert and Bach). The company also has an impressive roster of guest artists. Stars who have performed with the company include Natalia Bessmertnova, Nikolai Fadeyechev, Noëlla Pontois, Ekaterina Maximova, Vladimir Vasiliev, Carla Fracci, Rudolf Nureyev, and Sylvie Guillem. Guest teachers have included Galina Ulanova and Vakhtang Chabukiani.

What the Tokyo Ballet now lacks is the vision to establish a truly Japanese ballet company, performing works by Japanese choreographers. Of course Japan is proud of the Tokyo Ballet's success, but it is sad and somewhat ironic to see the company's fatal lack of confidence in Japanese artistry. To see a *Kabuki* by the French Béjart, or a *Haiku* by the American Neumeier is, in some ways, insulting. To relegate or throw away Japan's very own ancient culture is only to promote stereotypes, and continue the misconception that the Japanese are creative followers, rather than creative leaders.

—Kenji Usui

TOMASSON, Helgi

Icelandic/American dancer. Born in Reykjavik, Iceland, 8 October 1942. Studied with Erik and Lisa Bidsted, National Theatre, Reykjavik, and later in Copenhagen; also studied with Vera Volkova, Copenhagen, and at the School of American Ballet, pupil of Pierre Vladimirov, Anatole Obukhov, and Stanley Williams, New York, 1960. Married dancer Marlene Rizzo, 1965: two sons. Dancer, corps de ballet, Tivoli Theatre, Copenhagen, 1958–60; dancer, Robert Joffrey Theatre Ballet, 1962–64; dancer, becoming principal dancer, Harkness Ballet, 1964–70; principal dancer, New York City Ballet, 1970–85; guest artist, American Ballet Theatre, January 1977; occasional guest artist with regional American companies, including Atlanta Ballet, Maryland Ballet, and Georgia Dance Theatre; has also appeared on television, including "Bournonville Dances", programme in the Public Broadcasting Service (PBS) "Dance in America" series; also choreographer, with first full work staged for School of American Ballet, 1982; also staged ballets for Houston Ballet; artistic director, San Francisco Ballet, from 1985; guest teacher, Bartholin International Ballet Seminar, Denmark, 1986. Recipient: Silver Medal, International Ballet Competition, Moscow, 1969; titles of Knight of the Order of the Falcon, Iceland, 1974, Commander of the Order of the Falcon, Iceland, 1990; *Dance Magazine* Award, 1992.

ROLES

1962   Principal dancer in *Con Amore* (chor. L. Christensen), Robert Joffrey Theatre Ballet

Principal dancer in *Ropes* (Arpino), Robert Joffrey Theatre Ballet

Pas de deux from *Flower Festival at Genzano* (after Bournonville), Robert Joffrey Theatre Ballet

1963 Dancer (cr) in *Gamelan* (Joffrey), Robert Joffrey Theatre Ballet, Leningrad

1965 Daphnis in *Daphnis and Chloë* (Skibine), Harkness Ballet, New York

1967 Principal dancer (cr) in *Night Song* (Walker), Harkness Ballet, tour

Principal dancer (cr) in *A Season in Hell* (Butler), Harkness Ballet, New York

Mercutio in *Romeo and Juliet* (Tchernichov), Maryland Ballet, Baltimore

1968 Harlequin (cr) in *Stages and Reflections* (Neumeier), Harkness Ballet, Monte Carlo

1969 Principal dancer (cr) in *La Favorita* (Harkarvy), Harkness Ballet, New York

Title role (cr) in *Romeo Alone* (Walker), International Ballet Competition, Moscow

1970 Third Movement in *Symphony in C* (Balanchine), New York City Ballet, New York

Principal dancer in *Tchaikovsky Pas de deux* (Balanchine), New York City Ballet, New York

1971 Variations II (cr) in *The Goldberg Variations* (Robbins), New York City Ballet, New York

1971/ Principal dancer in *Donizetti Variations* (Balanchine),
72 New York City Ballet, New York

Emeralds in *Jewels* (Balanchine), New York City Ballet, New York

Fourth Campaign in *Stars and Stripes* (Balanchine), New York City Ballet, New York

Tema con Variazioni in *Tchaikovsky Suite No. 3* (Balanchine), New York City Ballet, New York

1972 Principal dancer (cr) in *Symphony in Three Movements* (Balanchine), New York City Ballet, New York

Principal dancer (cr) in *Divertimento from "Le Baiser de la fée"* (Balanchine), New York City Ballet, New York

1974 The Young Man (cr) in *Dybbuk* (later *The Dybbuk Variations*; Robbins), New York City Ballet, New York

Franz (cr) in *Coppélia* (new production; Balanchine, Danilova after Petipa), New York City Ballet, Saratoga Springs, New York

Title role in *The Prodigal Son* (Balanchine), New York City Ballet, New York

1975 Principal dancer (cr) in *Introduction and Allegro for Harp* (Robbins), New York City Ballet, New York

Principal dancer (cr) *Chansons Madécasses* (Robbins), New York City Ballet, New York

1976 Lennox (cr) in *Union Jack* (Balanchine), New York City Ballet, New York

1977 Albrecht in *Giselle* (Petipa after Coralli, Perrot; staged Blair), American Ballet Theatre

Voices of Spring (cr) in *Vienna Waltzes* (Balanchine), New York City Ballet, New York

1979 Harlequin in *Harlequinade* (Balanchine), New York City Ballet, New York

1982 Principal dancer (cr) in *The Magic Flute* (Martins), New York City Ballet, New York

Principal dancer in *Norwegian Moods* (L. Christensen), New York City Ballet, New York

Other roles include: for Harkness Ballet—the Boy in *Monument for a Dead Boy* (van Dantzig), Pas de deux from *Le Diable à Quatre* (Harkarvy); principal dancer in *Feast of Ashes* (Ailey),

Helgi Tomasson

Time Out of Mind (Macdonald), *Canto Indio* (Macdonald), *Abyss* (Hodes), *Madrigalesco* (Harkarvy), *Grand Pas Espagnol* (Harkarvy); for New York City Ballet—principal dancer in *Afternoon of a Faun* (Robbins), principal dancer in *Raymonda Variations* (Balanchine), Oberon and Divertissement in *A Midsummer Night's Dream* (Balanchine), principal dancer in *Tarantella* (Balanchine), First Movement in *Tchaikovsky Suite No. 2* (d'Amboise), principal dancer in *La Source* (Balanchine), principal dancer in *Dances at a Gathering* (Robbins), principal dancer in *Four Bagatelles* (Robbins).

WORKS

1982 *Theme with Variations, Polonaise, Op. 65* (mus. Giuliani), School of American Ballet Workshop Performance, New York

1983 *Ballet d'Isoline* (mus. Messager), School of American Ballet Workshop Performance, New York (later staged New York City Ballet)

1984 *Menuetto* (mus. Mozart) New York City Ballet, Saratoga Springs, New York

     Contredances (mus. Beethoven), Finis Jhung's Chamber Ballet USA

1985 *Valse* (mus. Coates), School of American Ballet Gala, New York

     Beads of Memory (mus. Tchaikovsky), Houston Ballet, Houston

1986 *Confidencias* (mus. Nazareth), San Francisco Ballet, San Francisco

     Concerto in D: Poulenc (mus. Poulenc), San Francisco Ballet, San Francisco

1987 *Intimate Voices* (mus. Gades), San Francisco Ballet, San Francisco

     Bizet Pas de Deux (mus. Bizet), San Francisco Ballet, San Francisco

1988 *Polonaise Defile* (mus. Dvorak), San Francisco Ballet, San Francisco

1989 *Handel—A Celebration* (mus. Handel), San Francisco Ballet, San Francisco

     Reflection of St. Joan (mus. Dello Joio), San Francisco Ballet, San Francisco

1990 *Con Brio* (mus. Drigo), San Francisco Ballet, San Francisco

     Valses Poeticos (*Love Letters*) (mus. Granados), San Francisco Ballet, San Francisco

1991 *Aurora Polaris* (mus. Bach, piano transcriptions Busoni), San Francisco Ballet, San Francisco

     "Haffner" Symphony (mus. Mozart), San Francisco Ballet, San Francisco

     Meistens Mozart (mus. Mozart and others), San Francisco Ballet, San Francisco

1992 *Forever More* (mus. Dvorak), San Francisco Ballet, San Francisco

     Two Plus Two (mus. Rossini), San Francisco Ballet, San Francisco

     Le Quattro Stagioni (*The Four Seasons*; mus. Vivaldi), San Francisco Ballet, San Francisco

Also staged:

1986 *The Nutcracker* (Lew Christensen, with additions by W. Christensen and Tomasson; mus. Tchaikovsky), San Francisco Ballet, San Francisco

1988 *Swan Lake* (after Petipa, Ivanov; mus. Tchaikovsky), San Francisco Ballet, San Francisco

1990 *The Sleeping Beauty* (after Petipa; mus. Tchaikovsky), San Francisco Ballet, San Francisco

     Flower Festival at Genzano (pas de deux; after Bournonville; mus. Paulli), San Francisco Ballet, San Francisco

PUBLICATIONS

By Tomasson:

Contributor to "The Male Image", *Dance Perspectives* (New York), no. 40, 1969

Interview in Gruen, John, *The Private World of Ballet*, New York, 1975

About Tomasson:

Goodman, Saul, "Helgi Tomasson", *Dance Magazine* (New York), February 1966

Daniels, Don, "Boutique Items and Risky Business", *Ballet Review* (New York), Summer 1985

Ross, Janice, "Back to Basics", *Dance Magazine* (New York), August 1987

Parish, Paul, "San Francisco's *Sleeping Beauty*", *Ballet Review* (New York), Summer 1990

Ross, Janice, "San Francisco Ballet: Helgi's Domain", *Dance Magazine* (New York), September 1991

* * *

When Helgi Tomasson took his final bow as a performer in 1985, after nearly fifteen years with the New York City Ballet, his achievement was writ large in dance history.

"With his outstanding technique and elegance," wrote Anna Kisselgoff of *The New York Times*, "Mr. Tomasson was the epitome of the classical male dancer. As the quintessential Robbins dancer, he knew how to filter the emotional through a crystal-clear classical prism. As the model of a Balanchine dancer, he enabled Balanchine, who had never before had dancers of Mr. Tomasson's caliber, to show off his own choreography for men at its most classical." Though Tomasson is once again prominent in dance, this time as choreographer, teacher, and artistic director of the San Francisco Ballet, it is as a performer that he will most be remembered.

Tomasson, like Peter Martins, was strongly influenced as a youth by the Danish teacher Stanley Williams, who stressed an ultra-pure Franco-Danish style. Later, in New York, Tomasson assimilated Balanchine's Russo-American ideas and technique. New York critics repeatedly described Tomasson's figure as elegant and dignified yet decidedly modest. Compared to the feral intensity of Mikhail Baryshnikov's Romeo, "you couldn't help seeing through [Tomasson's Mercutio] to Baryshnikov", wrote Arlene Croce. (It is telling that the one role Tomasson says he wishes he had performed is Romeo.) Tomasson's style, Croce continued, "has about it an almost moral tenacity".

Another kind of testimony to Tomasson's stature as a performer are the many dances created for him, not only by Balanchine and Robbins but by Alvin Ailey, Anna Sokolov, Brian Macdonald, Norman Walker, and Gerald Arpino. Of course, it is Tomasson's performances in no fewer than 24 of Balanchine's ballets that has forever linked his name with that of the choreographer's; in particular, the *Divertimento from Le Baiser de la fée* has served as Tomasson's signature piece. As for Robbins's works, Tomasson danced in the premieres of *Dybbuk* and *Goldberg Variations*, and frequently danced them thereafter.

The jury is still out, so to speak, on Tomasson's choreography. If *Ballet d'Isoline* relied too much on Balanchine's body language, the plotless, neo-classical *Menuetto* won high critical praise. Kisselgoff judged it a "first-class ballet", the sign of "a major new ballet choreographer". *Contredances* likewise has an "intense musicality", along with "precise footwork and the disciplined control necessary for flowing movements".

Then, in 1989, Tomasson tried his hand at narrative dance. Marcia Segal of *The Los Angeles Times* judged Tomasson's *Reflection of St. Joan* "stuffy mime pageant with no life or originality". And *Handel—A Celebration* was his "most predictable and least musical achievement ... glittering vulgarity".

But as a teacher and artistic director Tomasson has received consistently high marks. In San Francisco he focused first on the corps' technique and after four years' hard work achieved what Kisselgoff called a "stunning improvement". Tomasson stressed the extended line, heightened buoyancy, and calibrated smoothness of classical style.

Not surprisingly, Tomasson's biggest triumph to date with San Francisco's repertoire has been his revival of Balanchine's *Serenade*. And he has explored other styles with great success: a new *Sleeping Beauty*, Segal wrote, was superior to any by the

Kirov and Bolshoi Ballets or by American Ballet Theatre, dramatizing "how long it takes for goodness to vanquish evil". Tomasson's baroque *Swan Lake*, on the other hand, was not without problems: it achieved "its impact through sets and costumes more than its principals", wrote Kisselgoff.

Yet even as critics debate Tomasson's strengths as a choreographer and artistic director his reputation as one of the century's leading classical dancers remains secure.

—Lee Lourdeaux

TOUMANOVA, Tamara

Russian/American dancer. Born Tamara Vladimirovna Tumanova (Toumanova) in Tyumen, 2 March 1919. Left Russia as child: studied with Olga Preobrazhenskaya in Paris; later studied with George Balanchine and Bronislava Nijinska. Married screenwriter and producer Case Robinson. Stage début as child for Anna Pavlova gala, Paris, 1925, with Paris Opéra début, 1929; dancer, Ballets Russes de Monte Carlo (becoming de Basil's Ballets Russes and eventually the Original Ballet Russe), from company's inception, 1932, becoming ballerina until 1937, and again 1939–41; also ballerina, Balanchine's "Les Ballets 1933", and Denham's Ballet Russe de Monte Carlo, 1938; guest artist for numerous companies, including Ballet Theatre, New York, 1944–45, Paris Opéra Ballet, 1947 and 1950, Grand Ballet du Marquis de Cuevas, 1948–49, La Scala, Milan, 1951 and 1952, and London Festival Ballet, 1952 and 1954; also appeared at Teatro Colón in Buenos Aires, Teatro Municipal in Santiago de Chile, and Teatro Municipal in Rio de Janeiro; ballerina in individual concert performances, often with partner Vladimir Okhtomsky, from 1959; also appeared on popular stage, including for Broadway musical *Stars in Your Eyes* (lib. Fields, mus. Schwartz, 1939) and in films, including *Days of Glory* (dir. Tourneur, 1944), *Tonight We Sing* (dir. Leisen, 1953), *Invitation to the Dance* (dir. Kelly, 1954), *Deep in My Heart* (dir. Donen, 1954), *Torn Curtain* (dir. Hitchcock, 1966), *The Private Life of Sherlock Holmes* (dir. Wilder). Recipient: Grand Prix de Giselle, Paris, 1949.

ROLES

1929   Dancer in *L'Éventail de Jeanne* (Franck, Bourgat), Opéra, Paris

1932   The Young Girl (cr) in *Cotillon* (Balanchine), Ballets Russes de Monte Carlo, Monte Carlo
        The Girl (cr) in *La Concurrence* (Balanchine), Ballets Russes de Monte Carlo, Monte Carlo
        Lucille (cr) in *Le Bourgeois Gentilhomme* (Balanchine), Ballets Russes de Monte Carlo, Monte Carlo
        Tarantella (cr) in *Suites de danse* (Balanchine), Ballets Russes de Monte Carlo, Monte Carlo
        The Top (cr) in *Jeux d'enfants* (Massine), Ballets Russes de Monte Carlo, Monte Carlo

1933   Tema con variazioni (cr) in *Mozartiana* (Balanchine), Les Ballets 1933, Paris
        The Ballerina (cr) in *Les Songes* (Balanchine), Les Ballets 1933, Paris
        The Young Girl (cr) in *Fastes* (Balanchine), Les Ballets 1933, Paris
        First and Fourth Movements (cr) in *Choreartium* (Massine), Ballets Russes de Monte Carlo, London

1934   The Comet (cr) in *Les Imaginaires* (Lichine), de Basil's Ballets Russes, London
        Tarantella in *La Boutique fantasque* (revival; Massine), de Basil's Ballets Russes, London
        The Miller's Wife in *Le Tricorne* (Massine), (de Basil's) Monte Carlo Ballet Russe, Chicago
        The Mexican Girl (cr) in *Union Pacific* (Massine), (de Basil's) Monte Carlo Ballet Russe, Philadelphia

1935   The Poor Couple (cr) in *Jardin public* (Massine), (de Basil's) Monte Carlo Ballet Russe, Chicago
        Principal dancer (cr) in *Le Bal* (Massine), (de Basil's) Monte Carlo Ballet, Chicago

1936   The Beloved (cr) in *Symphonie fantastique* (Massine), de Basil's Ballets Russes, London

1938   Title role in *Giselle* (after Petipa, Coralli, Perrot), (Denham's) Ballet Russe de Monte Carlo, London

1940   Illusion (cr) in *La Lutte éternelle* (Schwezoff), Original Ballet Russe, Sydney
        Swanilda in *Coppélia* (Obukhov after Petipa, Saint-Léon), Original Ballet Russe, Sydney

1941   Third and Fourth Movements (cr) in *Balustrade* (Balanchine), Original Ballet Russe, New York
        Ariadne (cr) in *Labyrinth* (Massine), Denham's Ballet Russe de Monte Carlo, New York
        The Cakewalk (cr) in *Saratoga* (Massine), Denham's Ballet Russe de Monte Carlo, New York

1944   The Girl (cr) in *Moonlight Sonata* (Massine), Ballet Theatre, New York
        Principal dancer (cr) in *Harvest Time* (Nijinska), Ballet Theatre, New York
        Kitri in *Don Quixote Pas de Deux* (Obukhov after Petipa), Ballet Theatre, New York

1944/   Sugar Plum Fairy in *The Nutcracker* Pas de deux (Dolin
45   after Ivanov), Ballet Theatre, New York
        Odile in *Black Swan* Pas de deux (*Swan Lake*, Act III; Dolin after Petipa), Ballet Theatre, New York

1947   Second Movement (cr) in *Palais de cristal* (later called *Symphony in C*; Balanchine), Paris Opéra Ballet, Paris
        Title role in *Giselle* (Sergeyev after Petipa, Coralli, Perrot), Paris Opéra Ballet, Paris

1949   The Duchess (cr) in *Del Amor y de la muerte* (Ricarda), Grand Ballet du Marquis de Cuevas, Paris
        The Infanta (cr) in *Le Coeur de diamond* (Lichine), Grand Ballet du Marquis de Cuevas, Monte Carlo

1950   Title role (cr) in *Phèdre* (Lifar), Paris Opéra Ballet, Paris
        Principal dancer (cr) in *L'Inconnue* (Lifar), Paris Opéra Ballet, Paris
        Principal dancer (cr) in *La Fée d'Aibée* (Aveline), Paris Opéra Ballet, Versailles
        Principal dancer (cr) in *La Pierre enchantée* (Lifar), Paris Opéra Ballet, Paris

1951   Potiphar's Wife (cr) in *Leggenda di Giuseppe* (*The Legend of Joseph*; Wallmann), La Scala, Milan
        Principal dancer (cr) in *La Vita dell'uomo* (Wallmann), La Scala, Milan

1952   Principal dancer (cr) in *Rêve* (pas de deux; Dolin), London Festival Ballet, London

1956   Principal dancer (cr) in *The Seven Deadly Sins* (Charrat), La Scala, Milan
        The Dance of the Seven Veils (cr) in *Salomé* (opera; mus. Strauss, chor. Toumanova), La Scala, Milan
        Principal dancer (cr) in *Epoque romantique* (also chor.), Piccola Scala, Milan
        The Princess (cr) in *Le Fanfare pour le Prince* (Taras), Celebration of the Marriage of Prince Rainier and Grace Kelly, Monte Carlo

Tamara Toumanova in *Choreartium*, Ballets Russes de Monte Carlo, 1933

Other roles include: for de Basil's Ballets Russes—Princess Aurora in *Aurora's Wedding* (from *The Sleeping Beauty*; after Petipa), Eldest Daughter in *Le Beau Danube* (Massine), Columbine in *Le Carnaval* (Fokine), Princess in *Les Cent Baisers* (Nijinska), pas de deux in *Cimarosiana* (Massine), Ballerina in *Petrushka* (Fokine), title role in *The Firebird* (Fokine), Young Girl in *Le Pavillon* (Lichine), Passion in *Les Présages* (Massine), Tartar Girl in *Polovtsian Dances from Prince Igor* (Fokine), Prudenza in *Pulcinella* (Romanov), Swan Queen (Odette) in *Swan Lake* (one-act version; after Ivanov), Mazurka in *Les Sylphides* (Fokine), the Girl in *Le Spectre de la rose* (Fokine); dances (chor. Balanchine) in operas *Patrie* (mus. Paladilhe), *Turandot* (mus. Puccini), *Fay-yen-Fah* (mus. Redding), *Une Nuit à Venise* (mus. Strauss); for Denham's Ballet Russe de Monte Carlo—principal dancer in *Les Elfes* (Fokine), Chung-Yang in *L'Epreuve d'amour* (Fokine), the Queen of Hearts in *Jeu de cartes* (Balanchine), the Woman in White in *Rouge et noir* (Massine), principal dancer in *Serenade* (Balanchine), second movement in *Seventh Symphony* (Massine); for the Paris Opéra Ballet—Bride in *Le Baiser de la fée* (Balanchine), principal dancer in *Suite en blanc* (Lifar), the Swan in *Le Cygne* (*The Dying Swan*; after Fokine).

WORKS

1956   "Dance of the Seven Veils" in *Salomé* (opera; mus. Strauss), La Scala, Milan
       Epoque romantique, Piccola Scala, Milan

Other works include: individual works for concert tours—*Gamayoun*, *Le Chevalier et la princesse*, *Eternal Love*, *La Spiritualitè et la force*, *Florinda and Angelino*, *La Tragédie sicilienne*.

PUBLICATIONS

By Toumanova:
Interview with Philip Scheuer in *Dance Magazine* (New York), October 1946
Contributor to Beaudu, E., and Kogan, A. (eds.), *Dance, Art, Beauty*, Paris, 1947
"Toumanova on Balanchine", *Dance Magazine* (New York), July 1983
Interview, "A Conversation with Toumanova", *Ballet Review* (New York), Winter 1984

About Toumanova:
Levinson, André, *Les Visages de la danse*, Paris, 1933
Haskell, Arnold, *Ballet Vignettes*, London, 1948
Swisher, Viola, "Tamara Toumanova", *Dance Magazine* (New York), September 1970
Anthony, Gordon, "The Baby Ballerinas", *Dancing Times* (London), April 1973
Vaughan, David, "Balanchine Ballerinas", *Dance Magazine* (New York), January 1979
Terry, Walter, "Baby Ballerinas", *Ballet News* (New York), January 1982
Sorley Walker, Kathrine, *De Basil's Ballets Russes*, London, 1982
Finch, Tamara, "The First Baby Ballerinas", *Dancing Times* (London), August 1985
Finch, Tamara, "Les Ballets 1933", *Dancing Times* (London), March 1988
García-Márquez, Vicente, *Les Ballets Russes*, New York, 1990

*   *   *

The 1930s re-established the predominant role in Western ballet of the ballerina, who had been overshadowed by Diaghilev's emphasis on the male dancer. With the advent of the new decade, a new type of modern classical ballerina appeared, possessing a wide stylistic and interpretive range, and excelling in both the classical and the contemporary repertories. Tamara Toumanova is not only considered one of the great ballerinas; she is also important for having had a profound impact on twentieth-century ballet on an international level.

Toumanova made her stage début when she was six years old, in a benefit given by Anna Pavlova for the Red Cross in Paris in 1925. Four years later she appeared at the Paris Opéra in the one-act ballet, *L'Éventail de Jeanne*, and caused a sensation with her charismatic stage presence and technical virtuosity. André Levinson wrote at the time: "Tamara Toumanova, prodigious child of only ten years of age, accomplishes such feats of virtuosity as fouettés in tournant, doubles tours sur la pointe, relevés en arabesque with a precocious assurance and a personality that are not of her age. It is astounding and also frightening." In 1931, Balanchine recruited her for the newly organized Ballets Russes de Monte Carlo, and during the company's début season in the spring of 1932 she created an array of leading roles in ballets choreographed by Balanchine and Massine. From Monte Carlo the company came to Paris, where the young ballerina's series of grandes pirouettes and fouettés in *Cotillon*, *La Concurrence*, and *Jeux d'enfants* caused another sensation. Again, Levinson wrote: "Tamara, who carries the same first name as her illustrious predecessor, Karsavina, shares with her a certain Oriental languor and that rare poetic gift that penetrates each of her movements with a fluid elegiac lyricism. But . . . her large eyes, filled with a stupefying melancholy, hide a perfect and vigorous mechanism that was not possessed by any of the 'Imperial' Sylphides of 1909."

From the beginning of her career she was closely associated with Balanchine, and became an inspiration for many of his works. In 1937 Balanchine declared that Toumanova was the "greatest dancer and the greatest actress anywhere in the world". During the 1930s and 1940s he created eleven ballets for her. Anatole Chujoy remarked that Toumanova's work in *Balustrade* showed that "she, perhaps more than any other dancer I can think of, is the perfect exponent of Balanchine's choreographic inventions".

Although Toumanova was also a major exponent of Massine's ground-breaking abstract symphonic ballet, *Choreartium*, her long association with Massine exposed her to roles that required a wide range of dramatic interpretation, from the satirical comedy of the Miller's Wife in *Le Tricorne* to her own creation of the Beloved in *Symphonie fantastique*. Grace Robert wrote of Toumanova's Beloved: "Detached and beautiful through four movements, she was changed in the fifth into a fury whose like has not been seen on the stage since the grand manner passed away."

After her tenure with de Basil's Ballets Russes and Denham's Ballet Russe de Monte Carlo in the 1930s and early 1940s, Toumanova embarked on a career as one of ballet's true international superstars. Besides new creations for American Ballet Theatre, the Paris Opéra Ballet, La Scala Ballet, the Marquis de Cuevas Ballet, and London Festival Ballet, she especially excelled in the classics: *Swan Lake*, *The Nutcracker*, and *Coppélia* were her ballets, and she was particularly praised for her Giselle. After her first Giselle at Covent Garden in 1938, the *Daily Telegraph* wrote: "Toumanova's performance of *Giselle* . . . was probably the most satisfying seen in London. Her exquisite grace and astonishing balance, the lyrical quality of all her steps and her air of tragedy made a most moving experience ...". Arnold Haskell hailed her interpretation of Giselle as "a masterly combination of genuine emotion and theatrical artifice". In Paris, Léandre Vaillat stated that between "1900 and 1950 there had been three Giselles; Pavlova, Spessitseva and then Tamara Toumanova". In 1949, the ballerina was awarded Le Grand Prix de Giselle in Paris by Le Cercle des Journalistes et Critiques de la Danse.

A turning point in her career came in 1950 when Jean Cocteau created *Phèdre* at the Paris Opéra for her. He considered her "a great dancer and a great tragedienne", and in her interpretation of Phèdre, Toumanova brought to fruition her formidable qualities as an exceptional dramatic actress. Klaus Geitel, reviewing one of her last performances of *Phèdre* in Berlin in 1963, had this to say of her interpretation:

> With clawlike fingers she tears fate upon herself. She possesses the spell, the compelling gesture of the silent film divas ... With her the tragedy runs wild in the most exuberant manner—a ballerina in a world different from ours: a magnificent woman who becomes possessed when she loses herself in the role that she is impersonating. It is the part of an actress who knows how to dance ... She grasps the style of the work with utmost precision, remaining elegant even in the strongest emotional outburst. Her line stays beautiful—even in death. She is Madame La Mort of Cocteau's film *Orphée* transplanted to the stage.

Toumanova's career was exceptionally prolific and was blessed by an impressive history of important collaborations with some of the greatest artists of this century: choreographers such as Balanchine, Massine, Nijinska, Lichine, and Lifar; composers such as Stravinsky and Auric; and painters of the calibre of Miró, Derain, Bérard, and Tchelitchev. Called the "Black Pearl of the Russian Ballet", she embodied, as Kathrine Sorley Walker wrote, "everyone's idea of a Russian ballerina. Exotic in appearance ... with large eyes, raven wings of hair and magnolia skin, she combined lyricism and virtuosity to a remarkable degree."

Throughout her career she appeared in numerous films and in musical comedies and plays. During the early years with de Basil's Ballets Russes de Monte Carlo, Toumanova—along with Irina Baronova and Tatiana Riabouchinska—was internationally known as one of the "Baby Ballerinas", but her career carried her long beyond that legendary early beginning.

—Vicente García-Márquez

LE TRAIN BLEU

Choreography: Bronislava Nijinska
Music: Darius Milhaud
Design: Henri Laurens (scenery), Coco Chanel (costumes), Pablo Picasso (curtain)
Libretto: Jean Cocteau
First Production: Diaghilev's Ballets Russes, Théâtre des Champs-Elysées, Paris, 20 June 1924
Principal Dancers: Bronislava Nijinska (La Championne de Tennis), Lydia Sokolova (Perlouse), Anton Dolin (Beau Gosse), Léon Woizikowsky (Le Joueur de Golf)

Other productions include: Oakland Ballet (reconstructed by Frank W.D. Ries, supervised by Irina Nijinska); Oakland, California, 10 November 1989. Paris Opéra Ballet (restaged Ries); Paris, 11 March 1992.

PUBLICATIONS

Lieberman, William, "Picasso and the Ballet", *Dance Index* (New York), November–December 1946
Beaumont, Cyril, *Complete Book of Ballets*, revised edition, London, 1951
Grigoriev, Serge, *The Diaghilev Ballet*, translated by Vera Bowen, London, 1953
Lieberman, William, "Picasso and the Dance", *Dance Magazine* (New York), September 1957
Wildman, Carl, "Jean Cocteau and the Ballet", *Dancing Times* (London), October 1973
Baer, Nancy van Norman, *Bronislava Nijinska: A Dancer's Legacy*, San Francisco, 1986
Ries, Frank W.D., *The Dance Theatre of Jean Cocteau*, Ann Arbor, Michigan, 1986
Aschengreen, Erik, *Jean Cocteau and the Dance*, translated by Patricia McAndrew and Per Avsum, Copenhagen, 1986
Garafola, Lynn, *Diaghilev's Ballets Russes*, New York, 1989
Garafola, Lynn, "Reconstructing the Past: Tracking Down *Le Train bleu*", *Dance Magazine* (New York), April 1990
Hellman, Eric, "A Conversation with Frank W.D. Ries", *Ballet Review* (New York), Spring 1990
Hellman, Eric, "Shock of the 'Blue'?", *Ballet Review* (New York), Spring 1990

* * *

Jean Cocteau had originally devised the scenario for *Le Train bleu* after seeing the young Anton Dolin practice his gymnastics in a rehearsal studio in Monte Carlo. Cocteau was also inspired by the recent publicity on the Olympics, the rage for "sporting activities", and two important influences from the United States: silent movies and jazz music. Diaghilev was enthusiastic about the scenario, but the progress from text to stage was not smooth. Diaghilev made the Rumanian sculptor Henri Laurens re-design the set three times before it met with his approval. Gabrielle "Coco" Chanel's all-wool bathing suits were difficult to dance in and had to be adjusted and changed many times, both in Paris and for the London performances. Pablo Picasso had designed a front curtain for the Ballets Russes to use for the entire 1924 season, but Diaghilev decided to use it as the front curtain for *Le Train bleu*—to impress an audience that might not be won over by the balletic cavortings of the idle rich on the Riviera. The impresario was even nervous about the music Darius Milhaud wrote for the ballet, and in a programme note stated, "The music is composed by Darius Milhaud, but it has nothing in common with the music which we associate with Darius Milhaud."

Bronislava Nijinska, who had been assigned the choreography, was not entirely comfortable with Cocteau's scenario and the particular milieu it dealt with. To encourage her Cocteau introduced her, through newsreels, to the balletic tennis style of the American Suzanne Lenglen, which was transformed into the part of the champion tennis player, performed by "La Nijinska" herself. He also showed her films of the Prince of Wales (later Edward VIII and, subsequently, the Duke of Windsor) playing golf, which became Léon Woizikowsky's part of the golf player. The ballroom exhibition team of Marjorie Moss and Georges Fontana was the inspiration for the famous "Blue Train Waltz", danced by Lydia Sokolova as Perlouse with Woizikowsky. Dolin's unique acrobatic ability, combined with his theatrical flair (bordering

Le Train bleu, with (from left to right) Lydia Sokolova, Anton Dolin, Bronislava Nijinska, and Léon Woizikowsky, Diaghilev's Ballets Russes, Paris, 1924

on the narcissistic), was moulded by Nijinska into the vain swimming champion, Beau Gosse. Nijinska was quite knowledgeable about gymnastics and acrobatics since she had, even as a little girl, been interested in circus performers and had studied many of their tricks.

Nijinska's work went fairly smoothly until Cocteau returned during the final dress rehearsals and insisted that many changes needed to be made. Most of these changes dealt with the detailed scenario Cocteau had written, which Nijinska had discarded. Mime scenes were added and Dolin's part was expanded. Diaghilev backed Cocteau in this matter, and this was one of the major causes of the rift between Diaghilev and Nijinska, who left the company in 1925.

Despite all these problems in bringing *Le Train bleu* to the stage, the performances were a great success, even more so when the ballet was taken to London, and papers reported on how difficult it was to obtain even a single ticket for any performance. Further changes were made before the London premiere, including a special entrance for Dolin that incorporated more complicated gymnastics, cuts in some of the chorus sections, and substantial editing to some of the more complicated lifts in the swimmer–golfer duet as a result of problems with Sokolova's wool bathing costume. Approximately six minutes of music was deleted from the ballet.

The ballet did continue in the repertoire after Nijinska left the company, and Tamara Geva took over her part for several performances in Monte Carlo in 1925, but when Dolin left the company at the end of that season Diaghilev could not find a replacement. Serge Lifar began learning the part but could not cope with the gymnastics and acrobatics, so the ballet was dropped.

Although Nijinska's brother had dealt with a sports theme in 1913 in *Jeux*, there were not the acrobatics or contemporary references to well-known personalities that were incorporated into *Le Train bleu*. This ballet must certainly be considered an interesting precursor to the gymnastic choreography which has become a part of many contemporary ballets; the concept of dancer as athlete is one of the aesthetic legacies of this ballet which can still be seen today.

Anton Dolin tried for many years to revive this ballet, though with little success. He staged a brief sequence of solos on Kevin Haigen in 1979, although the correct order of the steps was altered. The first complete revival of the ballet took place in 1989, as performed by the Oakland Ballet. The production was staged with the use of notes and choreography learned from Dolin, as well as extensive interviews with former cast members, the original annotated music score, and Irina Nijinska's expert supervision, assisted by her extensive archives on her mother.

—Frank W. D. Ries

TREFILOVA, Vera

Russian dancer and teacher. Born Vera Aleksandrovna Trefilova in Vladikavkaz, 8 October (29 September old style) 1875. Studied at the Imperial Theatre School, St. Petersburg, pupil of Ekaterina Vazem; graduated in 1894; later studied with Caterina Beretta, Milan, Rosita Maura, Paris, and Eugenia Sokolova, Nikolai Legat, and Enrico Cecchetti, St. Petersburg. Married (1) Aleksandr Boutler; (2) Nikolai Soloviev (d. 1915); (3) ballet critic Valerian Svetlov. Dancer, corps de ballet, Maryinsky Theatre, from 1894, dancing solo roles from 1898, and becoming soloist, from 1901, prima

ballerina, from 1906; also dancer with company under Fokine, 1907; retired prematurely from Maryinsky Theatre (according to some sources, due to intrigues initiated by reigning ballerina Matilda Kshesinskaya), 1910; acting début, Mikhailovsky Theatre, St. Petersburg, 1915; left Russia for Paris, 1917; returned to stage, at Diaghilev's invitation, with Ballets Russes in London, 1921, performing also in Paris, 1922, and Monte Carlo, 1924; final performance at His Majesty's Theatre, London, 1926; also teacher in Paris, from 1916; pupils include Nina Vyroubova, Marina Svetlova. Died in Paris, 11 July 1943.

ROLES

1896   Amour (cr) in *Acis and Galatea* (Ivanov), Maryinsky Theatre, St. Petersburg
1899   Flower Seller in *Marco Bomba* (Perrot), Maryinsky Theatre, St. Petersburg
1899/ Teresa in *Cavalry Halt* (Petipa), Maryinsky Theatre, St.
1900   Petersburg
1900   Title role in *Graziella*, Act I (Saint-Léon), Maryinsky Theatre, St. Petersburg
1900/ The River Congo in *Pharaoh's Daughter* (Petipa),
06   Maryinsky Theatre, St. Petersburg
       Gulnara in *Le Corsaire* (Petipa), Maryinsky Theatre, St. Petersburg
       Canary Fairy in *The Sleeping Beauty* (Petipa), Maryinsky Theatre, St. Petersburg
       White Cat in *The Sleeping Beauty* (Petipa), Maryinsky Theatre, St. Petersburg
       Pierrette in *Harlequinade* (Petipa), Maryinsky Theatre, St. Petersburg
       Columbine in *The Nutcracker* (Ivanov), Maryinsky Theatre, St. Petersburg
1902   Title role in *Javotte* (Gerdt), Maryinsky Theatre, St. Petersburg
1902/ Naïla in *La Source* (Saint-Léon; staged Coppini),
03   Maryinsky Theatre, St. Petersburg
       Swanilda in *Coppélia* (Petipa, Cecchetti), Maryinsky Theatre, St. Petersburg
1903   Giannina in *The Naïad and the Fisherman* (Petipa after Perrot), Maryinsky Theatre, St. Petersburg
       Japanese Doll (cr) in *The Fairy Doll* (N. and S. Legat), Maryinsky Theatre, St. Petersburg
       Emma in *The Tulip of Haarlem* (Petipa, Ivanov; staged Shiryaev), Maryinsky Theatre, St. Petersburg
1904   Princess Aurora in *The Sleeping Beauty* (Petipa), Maryinsky Theatre, St. Petersburg
       Tsar-Maiden in *The Little Humpbacked Horse* (Petipa after Saint-Léon), Maryinsky Theatre, St. Petersburg
1906   Kitri in *Don Quixote* (Petipa), Maryinsky Theatre, St. Petersburg
       Odette/Odile in *Swan Lake* (Petipa, Ivanov), Maryinsky Theatre, St. Petersburg
       Princess Clementine in *Puss-in-Boots* (N. Legat), Maryinsky Theatre, St. Petersburg
1907   Title role in *Paquita* (Petipa), Maryinsky Theatre, St. Petersburg
       Hail in *Les Saisons* (Petipa; staged N. Legat), Maryinsky Theatre, St. Petersburg
       Flaminia (cr) in *The Blood-Red Flower* (N. Legat), Maryinsky Theatre, St. Petersburg
       Solo variation (cr) in *The Night of Terpsichore* (Fokine), Maryinsky Theatre, St. Petersburg
1921   Princess Aurora in *The Sleeping Princess* (Petipa; staged Sergeyev, with additional dances Nijinska), Diaghilev's Ballets Russes, Alhambra Theatre, London

Vera Trefilova as Swanilda in *Coppélia*, **St. Petersburg, c. 1903**

1922 Aurora in *The Marriage of Aurora* (from *The Sleeping Beauty*; Petipa; staged Nijinska), Diaghilev's Ballets Russes, Paris

The Girl in *Le Spectre de la rose* (Fokine), Diaghilev's Ballets Russes, Paris

1924 Odette/Odile in *Swan Lake* (Petipa, Ivanov), Diaghilev's Ballets Russes, Monte Carlo

Other roles include: for the Maryinsky Theatre—Flora in *The Awakening of Flora* (Petipa), Tyrolean Pas de Trois in *The Magic Mirror* (Petipa).

PUBLICATIONS

Haskell, Arnold, *Vera Trefilova: A Study in Classicism*, London, 1928

Ivchenko, Valerian, "The Recent Creations of Vera Trefilova", *Dancing Times* (London), 2 parts: December 1928, January 1929

Haskell, Arnold, *Balletomania*, London, 1934

Borisoglebsky, Mikhail, *Materials for the History of Russian Ballet*, Leningrad, 1939

Beaumont, Cyril, *The Diaghilev Ballet in London*, London, 1940; revised, 1951

Lifar, Serge, *Histoire du Ballet Russe*, Paris, 1950

Grigoriev, Serge, *The Diaghilev Ballet*, translated by Vera Bowen, London, 1953

Krasovskaya, Vera, *Russian Ballet Theatre of the Early Twentieth Century*, volume 2: Leningrad, 1972

Smakov, Gennady, *The Great Russian Dancers*, New York, 1984

* * *

Vera Aleksandrovna Trefilova was the illegitimate daughter of an actress by the name of Natalia Trefilova. In 1884, she entered the St. Petersburg Imperial Theatre School and studied under Ekaterina Vazem, graduating into the ballet company of the Maryinsky Theatre in 1894. Trefilova had inherited from Vazem the basic teachings of the classical school, shown in clear and masterly dancing. But at the time of her appearance at the Maryinsky, the stage was dominated by the brilliant dancing of Italian ballerina Pierina Legnani, the early triumphs of Matilda Kshesinskaya, and the appearance of Olga Preobrazhenskaya, who was steadily proving her right to perform the leading parts of the classical repertoire. In addition, two excellent Moscow ballerinas—Lubov Roslavleva and Ekaterina Geltser—often visited as the guest stars of the Russian capital's ballet theatre.

For several years Trefilova danced only in the corps de ballet. Then, as she explained in an interview in 1910, she began to attend the private class of Enrico Cecchetti, travelled to Milan and Paris to take lessons with Caterina Beretta and Rosita Mauri respectively, and, back in St. Petersburg, studied with Eugenia Sokolova and Nikolai Legat. This hard work obviously had visible results: soon Trefilova was being given such leading parts in the repertoire as Odette/Odile (*Swan Lake*), the Naïad (*The Naïad and the Fisherman*), and Naïla, Spirit of the Spring (*La Source*). In 1902, the ballet critic of the gazette *Novoe Vremia* wrote that Trefilova was "the best Aurora in *The Sleeping Beauty* since Carlotta Brianza" (the ballerina who created the role in 1890). The sparkling virtuosity of Kshesinskaya, or the lace-like grace of Preobrazhenskaya, paled by comparison to the sculptured beauty of Trefilova's poses and the noble cantilena of her adagio.

In 1910 Trefilova unexpectedly left the stage. It used to be said that this happened because her second husband insisted on her going. Stories of intrigues caused by the powerful prima ballerina Kshensinskaya have a certain amount of credence too. But probably the real cause was her disappointment with the direction in which the art of ballet was developing. On 23 January 1910, a writer for the *Peterburgskaya Gazeta* asked her if she liked the new trends in ballet. "I do not like the so-called Duncan trend," she said. "I do not see any art in running about the stage bare-foot." And when he questioned her about Mikhail Fokine's works, she firmly answered: "I have seen only *Egyptian Nights* and thought about it that everyone has his own way of making fun."

In 1917, Trefilova and her husband Svetlov left revolutionary Russia for the West and she opened a ballet school in Paris. In 1921 Diaghilev invited her to dance Princess Aurora in his London production of *The Sleeping Princess*. She alternated in this role with Lubov Egorova, Lydia Lopokova, and Olga Spessivtseva. The régisseur of the company, Sergei Grigoriev, wrote in his diary, ". . . the ballerina who had the most success in the part of Aurora was Trefilova, a true exponent of the Petipa tradition". In 1924, nearly 50 years old, and after fifteen years off the stage, Trefilova danced the role of Odette/Odile in the Monte Carlo sojourn of Diaghilev's Ballets Russes. Trefilova's turns were evidently one of her strong points, and Sergei Grigoriev wrote of her performance then, "She amazed everyone at Monte Carlo with her extraordinary fouettés". To her pupils, among whom was Nina Vyroubova, Trefilova passed on the perfect principles of Russian classical dance.

—Vera Krasovskaya

LE TRICORNE
(*The Three-cornered Hat*)

Choreography: Léonide Massine
Music: Manuel de Falla
Design: Pablo Picasso (scenery, costumes, and curtain)
Libretto: Gregorio Martinez Sierra (after Pedro Antonio de Alarcón's *El Sombrero de tres picos*)
First Production: Diaghilev's Ballets Russes, Alhambra Theatre, London, 22 July 1919
Principal Dancers: Léonide Massine (The Miller), Tamara Karsavina (The Miller's Wife), Léon Woizikowsky (The Corregidor), Stanislas Idzikowski (The Dandy)

Other productions include: Monte Carlo Ballet Russe (de Basil's Ballets Russes; restaged Massine), with Massine (Miller), Tamara Toumanova (Miller's Wife), David Lichine (Governor), Yurek Shabalevsky (Dandy); Chicago, 20 February 1934. Ballet Theatre (restaged Massine), as *The Three-Cornered Hat*, with Massine (Miller), La Argentinita (Miller's Wife), Simon Semenoff (Governor), Michael Kidd (Dandy); New York, 11 April 1943. Sadler's Wells Ballet (restaged Massine), as *The Three-Cornered Hat*, with Massine (Miller), Margot Fonteyn (Miller's Wife), John Hart (Corregidor) Alexander Grant (Dandy); London, 6 February 1947. Royal Swedish Ballet (restaged Massine); Stockholm, 4 June 1956. Joffrey Ballet (staged Tatiana Massine and Yurek Lazowsky, under supervision of Léonide Massine; Picasso designs reconstructed by William Pitkin), with Luis Fuente (Miller), Barbara Remington (Miller's Wife), Basil Thompson (Corregidor), Frank Bays (Dandy); New York, 25 September 1969. London Festival Ballet (restaged Massine); Eastbourne, 12 March 1973.

Le Tricorne, with (from left to right) Léonide Massine, Moira Shearer, and Beryl Grey, Sadler's Wells Ballet, London, 1947

PUBLICATIONS

Lieberman, William, "Picasso and the Ballet", *Dance Index* (New York), November–December 1946

Hussey, Dyneley, "Manuel de Falla", *Dancing Times* (London), 2 parts: March, April 1947

Beaumont, Cyril, *Complete Book of Ballets*, revised edition, London, 1951

Grigoriev, Serge, *The Diaghilev Ballet*, translated by Vera Bowen, London, 1953

Lieberman, William, "Picasso and the Dance", *Dance Magazine* (New York), September 1957

Massine, Léonide, *My Life in Ballet*, London, 1960

Karsavina, Tamara, "Dancers of the Twenties", *Dancing Times* (London), February 1967

Joel, Lydia, (ed.), "The Making of *The Three-Cornered Hat*" (excerpts from the memoirs of Massine, Sokolova, Karsavina, Grigoriev), *Dance Magazine* (New York), September 1969

Anderson, Jack, "Legends in the Flesh", *Ballet Review* (Brooklyn, N.Y.), vol. 3, no. 2, 1969

Garafola, Lynn, *Diaghilev's Ballets Russes*, New York, 1989

* * *

What makes a masterpiece of ballet? Some would say that any definition should specify an equally balanced partnership between choreographer, musician, and designer. Some would feel that the work ought to tell the audience something about human nature of which they had not perhaps been previously conscious. Others would say that above all a masterpiece must display an original approach and not be in any aspect a copy of any other work. To these theories it could also be added that to be a masterpiece, a ballet must survive changes of cast, and though subsequent performers may to some never be quite up to the standard of the originals, they should still be able to contribute their own individual versions, without destroying the ballet.

If these specifications are considered in connection with *Le Tricorne*, the obvious conclusion is that Massine's work falls painlessly into the category of masterpiece. In fact, it is among no more than half a dozen great works created for the Diaghilev ballet, and stands among the top dozen created in ballet in the twentieth century. First, as regards the question of equal partnership: in the case of *Le Tricorne*, the combination of de Falla, Massine, and Picasso can only be equalled during the two decades of Diaghilev's company by the combination of Stravinsky, Fokine, and Benois which resulted in *Petrushka*, and the team of Prokofiev, Balanchine, and Rouault which produced *Le Fils prodigue*. With *Le Tricorne*, the artists concerned were perfectly matched and perfectly in harmony, working together to produce a ballet which would amuse, entertain, please both eye and ear, and comment on human nature in a very down-to-earth fashion—a fashion aeons removed from the two-dimensional stereotyping of nineteenth-century romantic ballet, and even, to some extent, from ballets produced for Diaghilev's company up to that date. *Le Tricorne* was perfectly original in its theme and treatment. It is a simple story of the Miller and of his bored and jealous Wife, who attracts the attention of the aged Corregidor, leads him on in order to teach her husband a lesson, finds she has bitten off more than she can chew, and at last has to push the old boy into the river to escape his unwanted embraces. This cautionary tale could ring a bell in many a head. In addition, so thoroughly had Massine studied the dances of northern Spain, and so well had he translated them into coherent stage patterns, that even aficionados of authentic Spanish folk-dancing had to take him and his ballet seriously. And as for performers, if no one has ever equalled the choreographer himself as the Miller, yet the role has provided opportunities for success to some most apparently unlikely people, as well as some apparently cut out to dance it.

Difficult as it may be to grasp now, until Massine began with *The Good-Humoured Ladies* in 1917 to create an entirely novel genre of ballet, the comedy/character work, there had been no really funny ballets made—or at any rate, none surviving—since Galeotti's *Les Caprices de Cupidon* in 1786. Ballet was serious, dramatic, romantic, exciting, supernatural—anything you like except funny. Moreover, it rarely dealt with real people; or if it did, then it usually incorporated supernatural elements as well. With *The Good-Humoured Ladies*, *Le Tricorne*, and *Pulcinella* (1920), Massine initiated a completely new trend in twentieth-century ballet, a trend which was immediately popular with audiences everywhere, and of which both he and his imitators were to produce numerous examples during the following half century.

Le Tricorne is now out the contemporary repertoire, but let us hope that if dancers of the calibre of Massine and Karsavina ever appear on the ballet stage again, the work can be revived. It certainly should not be lost, for it is a unique piece of stagecraft, which added a new dimension to the ballet theatre.

—Janet Sinclair

TRINITY

Choreography: Gerald Arpino
Music: Alan Raph and Lee Holdridge (conductor Walter Hagen, rock group *Virgin Wool*)
First Production: City Center Joffrey Ballet, City Center, New York, 9 October 1969
Principal Dancers: Christian Holder, Gary Chryst, Rebecca Wright, Dermot Burke, Donna Cowen, Starr Danias, James Dunne

PUBLICATIONS

Siegel, Marcia, *At the Vanishing Point,* New York, 1972
Maskey, J., "The Dance", *High Fidelity* (New York), January 1971
McDermott, "From the Wonderful Folk", *Dance Magazine* (New York), October 1971
Maynard, Olga, "Arpino and the Berkeley Ballets", *Dance Magazine* (New York), September 1973
Croce, Arlene, *Afterimages,* New York, 1979

*   *   *

Trinity, a rock ballet in three movements, was born of Gerald

Arpino's experiences with the Joffrey company at the University of California at Berkeley, where he observed student peace demonstrations in protest to the Vietnam War. He identified the youths as "alienated from their families", attempting to find unity in so-called "love-ins". He witnessed how they focused attention on ecology by carrying flowers even as they were "beaten and pushed around" by government officials.

Though plotless, *Trinity* contains within it lyric ideas taken from this kind of reality. The presence of a live rock band in the pit was something of a novelty. Audiences didn't expect electronic music at the ballet, and it made them realize that young dancers are no different from young people. The elitist barrier between artist and ordinary citizen broke down further with *Trinity*, compounding the Joffrey Ballet's popular image as a vibrant, energetic troupe alive to its times.

At the conclusion of the Berkeley premiere, there was total silence. Then, a shouting of "Peace! Peace!" filled the auditorium, instead of cries of "bravo". When the Joffrey performed *Trinity* in Moscow in 1974, the audience cheered for over an hour on closing night and brought the company on stage for 42 curtain calls. *Trinity* was the Joffrey's signature ballet for eight years.

Arpino choreographed the ballet initially by working with the dancers as collaborators in improvisations. Some burned incense and brought flowers to the early rehearsals. They responded to the rock music as they might at an outdoor public concert or in a club, dancing with their hips gyrating and heads freely jerking. Arpino later formalized the work.

In the first movement, "Sunday" (to music by Alan Raph), a fanfare of trumpets and a steady drum-pulse summon the dancers to the stage. A man in daffodil yellow, sleeveless T-shirt, and blue tights (Chryst) executes a grand jeté. Changing direction at the top of the arc, he lands facing the opposite side. He runs forward, leaps, and turns mid-air. Then he runs forward, leaps, and changes direction. The other dancers follow his mesmerizing course, until the stage space appears to slosh rhythmically from side to side, much as water in a bowl that is being carried.

The sound of organ music brings a sense of ritualistic order. A row of dancers, their arms seeming to bear invisible flowers, comes from each side of the stage. They lay the "flowers" down before the audience. Their mood is reverential and, catching one another's eyes, they bond in a tight cluster. At its center, a tall black dancer (originally Holder, and traditionally maintained as a black role), disperses the group with arms waving in a gospel-sermonlike frenzy.

The second movement, "Summerland" (music by Holdridge), is distinguished by a boys' choir in the orchestra. The pure innocence of their voices is matched by the dancers pairing off in heterosexual couples. In a pas de deux, lovers roost with their heads curled together, and they walk tenderly hand in hand. The ballet's logic seems sometimes hormonally driven; transitions are passively abrupt and mood-swings evident. Other couples surround the principal pair; the women dive on top of their prone mates, pressing hips to hips in a brief, heated, sexual moment.

Still, the ballet's principal message is about hope rising from common humanity. In what is perhaps the ballet's most memorable image, the women are lifted high over the men's heads, their feminine, ribbon-thin torsos splayed belly-up to the sky and one leg diving forward to the ground. They look firm and determined and brilliant, like meteoric projectiles scorching trails through the dark.

The ballet's conclusion, "Saturday" (music by Raph), reiterates the back-and-forth grand jeté theme from the first movement. The space vibrates with calculated dashing around

Trinity, with (from left to right) Gary Chryst, Christian Holder, and Dermot Burke, Joffrey Ballet, New York, 1969

and is stilled only when the lights go out, the drums subside, and the dancers appear with votive candles. They individually deposit the candles on the floor and walk out: in a theatricalized moratorium.

—Sasha Anawalt

———

THE TRIUMPH OF DEATH
(Original Danish title: *Dodens Triumf*)

Choreography: Flemming Flindt
Music: Thomas Koppel
Design: Poul Arnt Thomsen (scenery and costumes), Jorgen Mydtskov (lighting)
Libretto: Flemming Flindt, after Eugène Ionesco's play *Le Jeu de massacre*
First Production: Danish Television, 23 May 1971
Principal Dancers: Flemming Flindt, Frank Shaufuss, Johnny Eliasen, Vivi Flindt

Other productions include: Royal Danish Ballet (first stage production; restaged Flindt); Copenhagen, 19 February 1972.

PUBLICATIONS

Percival, John, "Revivals and Creations in Copenhagen: *The Triumph of Death* . . .", *Dance and Dancers* (London), April 1972
Ståhle, Anna Greta, "Flemming Flindt's *Triumph of Death* Premiered", *Dance News* (New York), April 1972
Percival, John, "Triumph of Tradition and Death", *Dance and Dancers* (London), June 1974
Croce, Arlene, *Afterimages*, New York, 1977
Buckle, Richard, *Buckle at the Ballet*, London, 1980

* * *

Flemming Flindt's dance drama *The Triumph of Death* was first performed in 1971, but its content and presentation closely reflected popular themes associated with the previous decade. According to Arlene Croce, seeing the Danish ballet in New York, this ballet had little to do with a faithful adaptation of its dramatic source, Eugène Ionesco's *Le Jeu de massacre*. Flindt's main preoccupation, Croce remarked icily, was to restage "a series of freak-outs in the manner of the Broadway and Off-Broadway acid-rock musicals of the sixties".

Nevertheless, Flindt clearly intended to invoke the apocalyptic resonances of Ionesco's play about the demise of decadent societies. Poul Arnt Thomsen's scenery and costumes conveyed the appropriate end-of-the-world imagery with his towers of scaffolding, sinister cages, and mounds of plague victims, while Thomas Koppel's harsh and strident score, recorded by a Danish rock group (The Savage Rose) provided the aural equivalent. The tone of Flindt's work was didactic, a contemporary critique of corruption and the destructive forces underlying the ethos of materialism. Flindt converted Ionesco's rhetorical aims, designed to awaken the conscience of his audience, into a visual message, a social commentary in dance, in the tradition of Kurt Jooss's *The Green Table*.

The Triumph of Death, however, did not receive such great acclaim as Jooss's seminal work of the 1930s. The success of *The Green Table* had resided in the simplicity of Jooss's expression. But contemporary critics saw Flindt's attempts at shock tactics as tasteless rather than persuasive. The ballet consisted of a series of anecdotes designed to create a tapestry of social ills, ranging from pollution to tyranny, and culminating in a notorious nude scene. Here the choreographer himself appeared, stripped and sprayed with pink disinfectant. Richard Buckle's comment on the author's personal appearance in his work is particularly scathing, as he describes Flindt as "Flemming the Divine, a candidate well endowed for streaking". Buckle, writing in 1974, suggests in his flippancy the view of many that Flindt's outrageous "coup de théâtre" lacked the gravitas implied by the central theme of the piece.

In spite of the acerbic response to *The Triumph of Death* by the established critics of the day, the ballet remains a cultural document of interest. It contributed to a widespread artistic movement that was not often expressed in balletic form. The mid-century dissatisfaction with capitalist ideology amongst the young was much more frequently articulated through the popular media—subversive or "alternative" cultures that rejected any association with well-known institutions. The fact that this work was sponsored and first performed on stage by the Royal Danish Ballet—until then the bastion of ballet tradition—reflects the progressive and liberal artistic policy of that company under Flindt, and shows the radical influence that Flindt exerted on Danish ballet at that time.

—Susan Jones

TUDOR, Antony

British dancer, choreographer, and teacher. Born William Cook in London, 4 April 1909 (some sources say 1908). Studied with Marie Rambert, London, from 1928; also studied with Pearl Argyle, Harold Turner, and Margaret Craske. Dancer, Ballet Club, from 1930 (serving also as assistant and secretary to Rambert); dancer and choreographer, Ballet Club (becoming Ballet Rambert), 1930–37; founder and choreographer, London Ballet, 1937–40; resident choreographer, Ballet Theatre (later American Ballet Theatre), New York, 1939–50; also worked as international guest choreographer, including in Munich, Berlin, Oslo, Sydney, and Japan; artistic director, Royal Swedish Ballet, 1962–64; associate director, American Ballet Theatre, from 1974; also teacher: head of faculty, Metropolitan Opera Ballet School, New York, from 1950; ballet director, 1957–63, and teacher, Juilliard School, New York. Recipient: Carina Ari Gold Medal, 1973; *Dance Magazine* Award, 1974; Queen Elizabeth II Coronation Award, Royal Academy of Dancing, 1985; Handel Medallion of the City of New York, 1986; Capezio Dance Award, 1987; Kennedy Center Honors List; honorary doctorate, Oxford University. Died in New York, 19 April 1987.

ROLES

1930 The Bowler (cr) in *Le Cricket* (Salaman), Marie Rambert Dancers, London
1931 The Trainer (cr) in *Le Boxing* (Salaman), Ballet Club, London
Malvolio (cr) in *Cross-Garter'd* (also chor.), Ballet Club, London
1932 Husband to Lysistrata (cr) in *Lysistrata* (also chor.), Ballet Club, London
Cuchulain (cr) in *Unbowed* (Patrick), Ballet Club, London
Serpent (cr) in *Adam and Eve* (also chor.), Camargo Society, London
1933 King (cr) in *Atalanta of the East* (also chor.), Ballet Club, London
1934 A Lover (cr) in *Alcina Suite* (Howard), Ballet Club, London
Neptune (cr) in *The Planets* (also chor.), Ballet Club, London
1935 Hercules (cr) in *The Descent of Hebe* (also chor.), Ballet Rambert, London
Ringmaster (cr) in *Circus Wings* (Salaman), Ballet Rambert, London
The Baron (cr) in *The Rape of the Lock* (Howard), Ballet Rambert, London
1936 The Man She Must Marry (cr) in *Jardin aux lilas* (also chor.), Ballet Rambert, London
1937 Second Song (cr) in *Dark Elegies* (also chor.), Ballet Rambert, London
Aristocrat (cr) in *Gallant Assembly* (also chor.), Dance Theatre, Oxford
1938 Principal dancer (cr) in *Seven Intimate Dances* (also chor.), Westminster Theatre, London
Client (cr) in *The Judgment of Paris* (also chor.), Westminster Theatre, London
Tirolese (cr) in *Soirée musicale* (also chor.), Palladium Theatre, London
Cavalier (cr) in *Gala Performance* (also chor.), London Ballet, London
1940 Nobleman (cr) in *Goya Pastorale* (also chor.), Ballet Theatre, New York
1942 The Friend (cr) in *Pillar of Fire* (also chor.), Ballet Theatre, New York
1943 Tybalt (cr) in *The Tragedy of Romeo and Juliet* (also chor.), Ballet Theatre, New York
He Wore a White Tie (cr) in *Dim Lustre* (also chor.), Ballet Theatre, New York

WORKS

1931 *Cross-Garter'd* (mus. Frescobaldi), Ballet Club, London
1932 *Mr. Roll's Quadrilles* (mus. Roll), Ballet Club, London
Constanza's Lament (mus. Scarlatti), Ballet Club, London
Lysistrata (mus. Prokofiev), Ballet Club, London
Adam and Eve (mus. Lambert), Camargo Society, London
1933 *Pavane pour une infante défunte* (mus. Ravel), Ballet Club, London
Atalanta of the East (mus. arranged Szántó, Seelig), Ballet Club, London
1934 Dances in *Doctor Faustus* (play by Marlowe; mus. Boyce, arranged Lambert), Oxford University Dramatic Society (OUDS), Oxford (later performed by Ballet Club/Ballet Rambert as *Paramour*)

Antony Tudor

The Legend of Dick Whittington (danced interlude in *The Rock* by T.S. Eliot; mus. Shaw), Sadler's Wells Theatre, London

The Planets (mus. Holst), Ballet Club, London

1935 *The Descent of Hebe* (mus. Bloch), Ballet Rambert, London

1936 *Jardin aux lilas* (*Lilac Garden*; mus. Chausson), Ballet Rambert, London

1937 *Dark Elegies* (mus. Mahler), Ballet Rambert, London

Gallant Assembly (mus. Tartini), Dance Theatre, Oxford

1938 *Seven Intimate Dances* (with de Mille; mus. various), curtain raiser to *Marriage* (play by Gogol), Westminster Theatre, London

The Judgment of Paris (mus. Weill), Westminster Theatre, London

Soirée musicale (mus. Rossini, Britten), Palladium Theatre, London

Gala Performance (mus. Prokofiev), London Ballet, London

1940 *Goya Pastorale* (mus. Granados, orchestrated Byrns), Ballet Theatre, New York

1941 *Time Table* (mus. Copland), American Ballet Caravan, New York

1942 *Pillar of Fire* (mus. Schoenberg), Ballet Theatre, New York

1943 *The Tragedy of Romeo and Juliet* (mus. Delius, arranged Dorati), Ballet Theatre, New York

Dim Lustre (mus. Strauss), Ballet Theatre, New York

1945 *Undertow* (mus. W. Schuman), Ballet Theatre, New York

1948 *Shadow of the Wind* (mus. Mahler), Ballet Theatre, New York

1949 *The Dear Departed* (mus. Ravel), Jacob's Pillow Dance Festival, Massachusetts

1950 *Nimbus* (mus. Gruenberg), Ballet Theatre, New York

1951 *Lady of the Camellias* (mus. Verdi), New York City Ballet, New York

Les Mains gauches (mus. Ibert), Resident Company, Jacob's Pillow, Massachusetts

La Ronde du Printemps (mus. Satie), Resident Company, Jacob's Pillow, Massachusetts

1952 *La Gloire* (mus. Beethoven), New York City Ballet, New York

Trio con Brio (mus. Glinka), Resident Company, Jacob's Pillow, Massachusetts

1953 *Exercise Piece* (mus. Ariaga y Balzola), Juilliard School, New York

Little Improvisations (mus. Schumann), Resident Company, Jacob's Pillow, Massachusetts

Elizabethan Dances and Music (mus. various), Juilliard

School, New York
Britannia Triumphans (masque by Inigo Jones and William D'Avenant; mus. Lawes), Juilliard School, New York

1954 *Offenbach in the Underworld* (*Le Bar du can-can*; mus. Offenbach), Philadelphia Ballet Company, Philadelphia

1958 *La Leyenda de José* (*The Legend of Joseph*; mus. Strauss), Teatró Colon, Buenos Aires

1959 *Hail and Farewell* (mus. Strauss), Metropolitan Opera Ballet, New York

1960 *A Choreographer Comments* (mus. Schubert), Juilliard Dance Ensemble, New York

1962 Dance Studies in *Gradus ad Parnassum* (mus. various), Juilliard Dance Ensemble, New York

1963 *Fandango* (mus. Soler), Metropolitan Opera Ballet, New York
Echoing of Trumpets (mus. Martinů), Royal Swedish Ballet, Stockholm

1966 *Concerning Oracles* (mus. Ibert), Metropolitan Opera Ballet, New York

1967 *Shadowplay* (mus. Koechlin), Royal Ballet, London

1968 *Knight Errant* (mus. Strauss), Royal Ballet Touring Company, Manchester

1969 *The Divine Horsemen* (mus. Egk), Australian Ballet, Sydney

1971 *Sunflowers* (mus. Janáček), Juilliard School, New York
Cereus (mus. Grey), Juilliard School, New York
Continuo (mus. Pachelbel), Juilliard School, New York

1975 *The Leaves are Fading* (mus. Dvořák), American Ballet Theatre, New York

1978 *The Tiller in the Fields* (mus. Dvořák), American Ballet Theatre, Washington, D.C.

PUBLICATIONS

By Tudor:
Introduction to Etting, Emlen, *Drawing the Ballet*, New York, 1944
Interview with Anderson, Jack, in *Dance Magazine* (New York), May 1966
"Movement in Opera", in Nadel, Myron Howard (ed.), *The Dance Experience*, New York, 1970
Contribution to "Rambert Remembered", *Ballet Review* (New York), September 1983
Interview in Gruen, John, *People Who Dance*, Pennington, N.J., 1988

About Tudor:
Beaumont, Cyril, *The Complete Book of Ballets*, revised edition, London, 1951
Beaumont, Cyril, *Ballets of Today*, London, 1954
Davidson, Gladys, *Ballet Biographies*, revised edition, London, 1954
Percival, John, and Cohen, Selma Jeanne, "Antony Tudor", *Dance Perspectives* (New York), nos. 17–18, 1963
Ames, Suzanne, "Antony Tudor", *Dance Magazine* (New York), October 1973
van Praagh, Peggy, "Working with Antony Tudor", *Dance Research* (London), Summer 1984
Topaz, Muriel, "Notating and Reconstructing for Antony Tudor", *Dance Notation Journal* (New York), Spring 1986
Hunt, Marilyn, "Antony Tudor: Master Provocateur", *Dancing Times* (London), May 1987
Sinclair, Janet, "The Changes of Time", *Dance and Dancers* (London), January 1989
"Antony Tudor: The American Years", *Choreography and Dance* (New York), vol. 1, pt. 2, 1989
Chazin-Bennahum, Judith, "After *Pillar of Fire*", *Choreography and Dance* (New York), vol. 1, pt. 2, 1989
Perlmutter, Donna, *Shadowplay: The Life of Antony Tudor*, London, 1991

* * *

He plotted the intricacies of contemporary yearning in his landmark ballets, but, by Antony Tudor's own account of himself, he was "a solitary man", uneasy with the world he discovered and with his place in it. That assessment figured prominently into both process and aesthetic of an oeuvre depicting the emotional lives of ordinary people, as opposed to courtly characters and fairy-tale creatures. It enabled the choreographer to stand back and turn his observing eye on the specifics of pride and lust, shame and fear, tenderness and resignation. It also separated him from his titanic peers—Ashton and Balanchine—who did not typically approach choreography along the lines of a Stendhal or a Proust.

Tudor did. And it was that instinct—to create ballets in his autobiographic image—that yielded startling innovation as well as controversy. After all, he grew up in the wake of Freud and Diaghilev. It is not hard to explain why his powers of expression would lead to unimagined interiors of narrative. Seizing the existing ballet vocabulary, he forged a new and provocative language from which clichés were banished. Nor was music merely a rhythmic grid to which he applied steps, thus finding form for them. With his symphonist's frame of reference he composed in long phrases, taking a score like Schoenberg's *Verklarte Nacht*, for instance, and setting it to sweeping movement as the dramatic situation dictated; or to inward, seemingly motionless dancescapes that honoured the music's aura.

In *Jardin aux lilas*, his first enduring masterpiece, he conceived for himself the role of The Man She Must Marry. At once this figure was aggressively domineering and stern. He took arrogant pleasure in depriving Caroline of her lover, mirroring aspects of Tudor's off-stage personality. But the choreographer also found himself represented by the heroine, who must sacrifice her heart's desire for the sake of societal-familial pressures. And, not least, he refocused the original storyline so that it implied, perhaps inadvertently, the taboo of homosexuality in his real-life situation. Because he was on close terms with the characters' precise anguish he was able to mould truth in their images—a truth that he could apparently acknowledge nowhere else but in his art.

Often, with the other ballets, Tudor redeemed himself by taking on the attributes of a wise, caring patriarch: the Friend, for instance, in *Pillar of Fire*, who not only was there for Hagar, despite her initial disbelief that he would be, but also accepted the child she would bear as the result of a shameful encounter. Occasionally, however, he turned away from typecasting and allowed himself to be a victim—as the drunk Client in *Judgment of Paris* (not his own scenario, in this case, but one by Hugh Laing)—and an outright villain, the Serpent, in *Adam and Eve*, who seduces his Guardian Angel (Laing).

But mostly the leading roles he created fell to the heroine, a similarity he shared with other choreographers whose work defines the motto, "Ballet is Woman". Indeed, Caroline and Hagar are the rare first-name characters he used; typically the roles were given generic names, names of universal value. Whether his dancers were male or female, though, mattered far less than how they lent themselves to his inspiration. To do so successfully involved a degree of self-exposure some found abhorrent. But for those dancers not frightened away by the strange taskmaster who invariably "saw through to the quick", as many would say, there were the deepest rewards.

Tudor composed ballets from the fibres of vulnerability. He needed to touch it and sense it in others in order to create steps and gestures that conveyed the palpable human condition. He was referred to as the "playwright of the dance"—to that extent did his works derive from interaction between people. And nothing delighted him more than watching encounters in the studio, to have, right in his midst, the lightning rod for both choreography and performance of it.

It was this very narrative that informed the movements in his ballets—movements often as difficult and uncomfortable as the emotional tone they implied—and made them distinctively Tudorian. Even in *The Leaves Are Fading*, considered to be an abstract work, one can trace the psychological threads of relationships. However, this dappled remembrance of romantic things past also bears a clear imprint—allowing that inviolate space between partners, a space crowded with unspoken words, with downcast eyes and shoulders that reach out gently telling of quiet sorrows mingled with joys. It also luxuriates in movements of windswept abandon, inspired by Gelsey Kirkland. Beyond that, he ultimately left his mark on the way dancers approached such dramatic staples as *Giselle*.

Partly because he did not rely on format, as was the case in the abstract neo-classical ballets that flourished in his time, he waged a perpetual struggle to find new scenarios and to complement them with the appropriate means of expression. At his most successful he could turn from a nocturnal garden party's stifled passion, with bare-shouldered women wearing plumes in their hair (*Jardin*), to a paean plain with peasants locking arms and circling some untold grief as if to exorcise it (*Dark Elegies*) to the surreal nightmare of a matricidal anti-hero (*Undertow*).

Whether focusing on a sophisticated satire like *Knight Errant*, a mysterious parable like *Shadowplay*, or the reverie of a time-memory lapse like *Dim Lustre*, Tudor found his nub of interest in the primary couple. What transpired between the two dancers nearly always took into account the changing balance of power and engagement.

He championed the then rarely-heard music of Mahler and welcomed the influences of Mary Wigman and Kurt Jooss. At times, he set himself projects too unwieldy to even contemplate, much less carry out, and consequently met defeat.

But over the course of his troubled life, one from which he took little self-satisfaction, Antony Tudor gave the world a handful of luminous ballets—no less refutable as gems than a universally loved work like *Swan Lake*.

—Donna Perlmutter

TURNER, Harold

British dancer, choreographer, and teacher. Born in Manchester, 2 December 1909. Married (1) dancer Mary Honer; (2) dancer Gerd Larsen. Served in the Royal Air Force during World War II. Studied with Alfred Haines, Manchester, and at the Rambert School, London, from 1927. Début in the Haines English Ballet, 1927; dancer, soon becoming leading soloist, Marie Rambert Dancers (later Ballet Club, eventually Ballet Rambert), 1928–32; principal dancer, Vic-Wells Ballet, 1935–40, Arts Theatre Ballet, London, 1940, and (Mona Inglesby's) International Ballet, 1941–42; returned to Sadler's Wells Ballet, 1945–51; also guest artist with Anton Dolin and Tamara Karsavina, and Vic-Wells Ballet, London, 1930; choreo-

grapher, Arts Theatre Ballet, 1940, International Ballet, 1941, Anglo-Russian Merry-Go-Round, 1944; retired from the stage, 1951, becoming teacher, Sadler's Wells Ballet School and Covent Garden Opera Ballet, London. Died in London, 2 July 1962.

ROLES

1928 Gavotte joyeuse, Courante (cr) in *Nymphs and Shepherds* (Ashton), Marie Rambert Dancers, London
      Hermes (cr) in *Leda* (Ashton, Rambert), Marie Rambert Dancers, London
1929 A Satyr (cr) in *The Picnic* (later *The Faun*; de Valois), Old Vic Theatre, London
      Mars (cr) in *Mars and Venus*, ballet in *Jew Süss* (play by Ashley Dukes; chor. Ashton), Opera House, Blackpool
1930 Entrée de Cupidon (cr) in *Dances from Les Petits Riens* (probably revision of *Nymphs and Shepherds*; Ashton), Marie Rambert Dancers, London
      A Zephyr (cr) in *Leda and the Swan* (new production of *Leda*; Ashton), Marie Rambert Dancers, London
      Juggler (cr) in *Our Lady's Juggler* (Salaman), Marie Rambert Dancers, London
      Tordion, Mattachins (cr) in *Capriol Suite* (Ashton), Marie Rambert Dancers, London
      Gavotte, Sarabande, and Gigue (cr) in *Suite of Dances* (de Valois), Old Vic Theatre, London
      The Player (cr) in *Le Rugby* (Salaman), Marie Rambert Dancers, London
      A Suitor (cr) in *Follow Your Saint: The Passionate Pavane* (Ashton), in the Masque presented by Arnold L. Haskell, Arts Theatre Club, London
      A Lad (cr) in *Dances on a Scotch Theme* (Ashton), in the Masque presented by Arnold L. Haskell, Arts Theatre Club, London
      The Spirit of the Rose in *Le Spectre de la rose* (Fokine), Marie Rambert Dancers, London
1931 Cephalus (cr) in *Cephalus and Procris* (de Valois), Old Vic Theatre, London
1932 Principal dancer (cr) in *The Ballet of Spring* in *A Kiss in Spring* (musical comedy; chor. Ashton), Alhambra Theatre, London
1933 The Cactus (cr) in *The Orchid and the Cactus* (Ashton), and A Dancer (cr) in *Wall Street* (Ashton), in *After Dark* (revue; chor. Ashton and Bradley), Vaudeville Theatre, London
1935 The Dancing Master, The Gentleman with a Rope (cr) in *The Rake's Progress* (de Valois), Vic-Wells Ballet, London
      The Young Man (cr) in *Le Baiser de la fée* (Ashton), Vic-Wells Ballet, London
      Harlequin in *Carnaval* (Fokine), Vic-Wells Ballet, London
      The Nutcracker Prince in *The Nutcracker* (Sergeyev after Ivanov), Vic-Wells Ballet, London
      Franz in *Coppélia* (two-act version; Petipa, Cecchetti; staged Sergeyev), Vic-Wells Ballet, London
      Popular Song in *Façade* (Ashton), Vic-Wells Ballet, London
      Adagio, pas de deux in *Fête polonaise* (de Valois), Vic-Wells Ballet, London
      Variation, Adagio of lovers in *Les Rendezvous* (Ashton), Vic-Wells Ballet, London
      Stevedore in *Rio Grande* (Ashton), Vic-Wells Ballet, London

Harold Turner as the First Red Knight in *Checkmate*, Vic-Wells Ballet

Mazurka in *Les Sylphides* (Fokine), Vic-Wells Ballet, London

1936   The Hussar (cr) in *Apparitions* (Ashton), Vic-Wells Ballet, London

Title role (cr) in *Barabau* (de Valois), Vic-Wells Ballet, London

Cook's Man in *Douanes* (de Valois), Vic-Wells Ballet, London

Title role in *Prometheus* (de Valois), Vic-Wells Ballet, London

Prince in *The Sleeping Princess*, Act III (*Aurora Pas de deux*; after Petipa), Vic-Wells Ballet, London

1937   First Red Knight (cr) in *Checkmate* (de Valois), Vic-Wells Ballet, Paris

Variation ("Blue Boy"; cr) in *Les Patineurs* (Ashton), Vic-Wells Ballet, London

Paul (cr) in *A Wedding Bouquet* (Ashton), Vic-Wells Ballet, London

1938   The Empress's Lover (cr) in *Le Roi nu* (*The Emperor's New Clothes*; de Valois), Vic-Wells Ballet, London

1939   Satan in *Job* (de Valois), Vic-Wells Ballet, London

Bluebird in *The Sleeping Princess* (Petipa; staged Sergeyev), Vic-Wells Ballet, London

1941   Scientist (cr) in *Planetomania* (Inglesby), International Ballet

Polovtsian Warrior in *Polovtsian Dances from Prince Igor* (Sergeyev after Ivanov), International Ballet

Principal dancer (cr) in *Fête Bohème* (also chor.), International Ballet

1943   Death (cr) in *Everyman* (Inglesby), International Ballet, London

1946   Gravedigger in *Hamlet* (Helpmann), Sadler's Wells Ballet, London

The Rake in *The Rake's Progress* (de Valois), Sadler's Wells Ballet, London

King Hihat of Agpar in *Les Sirènes* (Ashton), Sadler's Wells Ballet, London

Bluebird in *The Sleeping Beauty* (Petipa; staged Sergeyev, de Valois, Ashton), Sadler's Wells Ballet, London

1947   Can-Can dancer in *La Boutique fantasque* (Massine), Sadler's Wells Ballet, London

1948   The Miller in *The Three-Cornered Hat* (Massine), Sadler's Wells Ballet, London

The Baron (cr) in *Clock Symphony* (Massine), Sadler's Wells Ballet, London

1950   The Travelling Barber (cr) in *Don Quixote* (de Valois), Sadler's Wells Ballet, London

1951   Orlando, the Marmalade Cat (cr) in *Orlando's Silver Wedding* (Howard), Festival of Britain Celebration, Battersea Park, London

Other roles include: for Ballet Club/Ballet Rambert—Harlequin in *Carnaval* (Fokine), Lover in *Jardin aux lilas* (Tudor), Cinesias in *Lysistrata* (Tudor), Mortal under Mars in *The Planets* (Tudor), Umbriel in *The Rape of the Lock* (Howard); for Sadler's Wells Ballet—Peasant Pas de deux in *Giselle* (Petipa after Coralli, Perrot; staged Sergeyev).

WORKS

1940 *May Collin* (mus. Bax), Arts Theatre Ballet, London
      Serenade (mus. Wolf), Arts Theatre Ballet, London
1941 *Fête Bohème* (mus. Dvořák), International Ballet, Glasgow

PUBLICATIONS

By Turner:
"Ballet in Opera", *Dancing Times* (London), April 1958

About Turner:
Davidson, Gladys, *Ballet Biographies*, revised edition, London, 1954
Clarke, Mary, *The Sadler's Wells Ballet*, London, 1955
Clarke, Mary, *Dancers of Mercury: The Story of Ballet Rambert*, London, 1962
Anthony, Gordon, "Pioneers of the Royal Ballet: Harold Turner", *Dancing Times* (London), August 1971
Anthony, Gordon, *A Camera at the Ballet*, 1975
Vaughan, David, *Frederick Ashton and his Ballets*, London, 1977

*   *   *

The career of Harold Turner is of considerable importance to the history of English ballet in the twentieth century, since he was the first great English virtuoso male dancer of the period who was discovered, encouraged, and developed entirely within the ballet scene of his own country. He began dancing at the age of sixteen in his home town of Manchester, and through the efforts of Alfred Haines, his first teacher, and Léonide Massine, Anton Dolin, and Marie Rambert, he was by the age of twenty ably partnering Karsavina in *Le Spectre de la rose*. Though he was only with the Rambert organization for a few years, he gained through his Ballet Club experience an ability which he held in common with many Rambert dancers—that of winding himself up for several weeks before a first night and giving a performance never to be to forgotten, and probably never to be repeated either.

An outstanding technician when he joined the Vic-Wells Ballet in 1935, Turner wasted no time in making his mark. He remained with the company, apart from a period spent with Mona Inglesby's International Ballet and time in war service, until he died, still active both as teacher and as performer.

In the mid-1930s, when Turner joined the Vic-Wells company and began to dance in such ballets as *Les Rendezvous*, *Le Baiser de la fée*, the Bluebird pas de deux from *The Sleeping Princess* (as the ballet was then called), or the Dancing Master and the Gentleman with a Rope in *The Rake's Progress*, he was the virtuoso pure and simple, the dancer who only wished to make a success of dancing and who attempted to put little more into a role than was called for by the actual steps involved. It would sound unkind to say he barged his way through everything given to him, but it would be true. When he danced the "Peasant" pas de deux in Act I of *Giselle*, he crashed to the ground with such enthusiasm after a double turn in the air that one sometimes feared he would break through the floorboards with his knee. His partnering could be on occasion less than gallant: it was as though he resented the passive "porteur" role of the male in classical ballet and could not wait to get on to the important part of the evening—that is, the man's solo, pirouettes, double turns, and all. There was little of the danseur noble about Turner at this period—just an exuberance, a technical flair and drive which could make most others on the stage look pale by comparison. For this reason his most successful role for the company in the 1930s was that of the "Blue Boy" in *Les Patineurs*, a part in which he was free to show off his technical prowess to its fullest extent, while not at any time having to take second place behind some female on pointe. In fact he was no actor, and when required to act, he was apt to do so with such dogged determination that some members of his audience wished he would abandon the attempt altogether. To Turner the dancing was all, and to attempt to get a subtle performance from him was waste of choreographer's time. It was simply not his line, and all one could do was to sit back and enjoy the dancing, without courting disappointment by looking for characterization in his performance.

It was both Turner's good luck and his misfortune that he was at his peak as a dancer at a period when choreographers were mainly interested in story and character, for few choreographers gave him original parts to create; yet when he was dancing his style stood out in vast contrast to the less confident dancing (as opposed to acting) performances around him. He would have been a lot better off had he been born 30 years later, for his technique and physique would have not been in any way inferior to that of post-war dancers, and he would not have been hampered by trying to make attempts to act, which were by and large very unconvincing.

With maturity and experience, however, Turner learned how to pace himself and how, too, to consider the importance of characterization once youth has gone and physical exuberance must be replaced by other qualities. Nobody in 1935 would have considered that Turner would be anything but laughable, were he to attempt to move from the roles of the Dancing Master and the Gentleman with a Rope to that of the Rake himself. But between 1946 and 1950 he turned in 34 performances of this part with real success, while at roughly the same period he followed that master of characterization, Léonide Massine, in his greatest role, that of the Miller in *Le Tricorne*, with a real understanding of the subtleties and sly humour inherent in the character.

Turner was only 53 years of age when he died, in the course of rehearsals for the revival of Massine's *The Good-Humoured Ladies*. Those who had followed his career right through from exuberant technical virtuoso to thoughtful, mature artist felt it would be hard to replace him and indeed, in the roles he made his own, the Blue Boy, the Red Knight, and the Gentleman with a Rope, it has not been easy so to do.

—Leo Kersley

THE TWO PIGEONS
(original title: *Les Deux Pigeons*)

Choreography: Frederick Ashton
Music: André Messager, arranged by John Lanchbery
Design: Jacques Dupont
Libretto: Frederick Ashton (after the fable by La Fontaine)
First Production: Royal Ballet Touring Company, Royal Opera House, London, 14 February 1961
Principal Dancers: Lynn Seymour (The Young Girl), Christopher Gable (The Young Man), Elizabeth Anderton (A Gypsy Girl), Robert Mead (Her Lover), Johaar Mosaval (A Gypsy Boy)

Other productions include: Paris Opéra (original production to Messager's score; chor. Louis Mérante); Paris, 18 October 1886

The Two Pigeons, with Doreen Wells and David Wall, Royal Ballet, London, c.1970

(see *Les Deux Pigeons*). Royal Ballet (restaged Ashton), with Seymour and Gable; London, 16 October 1962. CAPAB Ballet (staged Faith Worth; design Peter Rice); Bellville, South Africa, 19 October 1968. Australian Ballet (staged Robert Mead, design Dupont), with Lucette Aldous (The Girl), Kelvin Coe (The Boy), Marilyn Rowe (A Gypsy Girl), Jonathan Kelly (Her Lover), Paul Saliba (A Gypsy Boy); Sydney, 30 April 1975. National Ballet of Canada; Toronto, 28 February 1979. Teatro Regio Ballet (staged Faith Worth); Turin, January 1992.

PUBLICATIONS

Monahan, James, "A Gentle Charmer", *Dancing Times* (London), March 1961

Barnes, Clive, Goodwin, Noël, and Williams, Peter, "*Les Deux Pigeons*", *Dance and Dancers* (London), April 1961

Williams, Peter, "The 21 Years that Changed British Ballet", Part V, *Dance and Dancers* (London), April 1971

Balanchine, George, with Mason, Francis, *Balanchine's Complete Stories of the Great Ballets*, Garden City, N.Y., 1977

Vaughan, David, *Frederick Ashton and his Ballets*, London, 1977

Brinson, Peter, and Crisp, Clement, *Ballet and Dance: A Guide to the Repertory*, London, 1980

*   *   *

Ashton choreographed *The Two Pigeons* for the Touring Company of the Royal Ballet in the year after he had made *La Fille mal gardée* for the resident company at the Royal Opera House; and the two works respectively display the best qualities of the two companies. Both ballets are in two acts and both show a mastery of the form, which Ashton came to prefer after his fourth three-act ballet *Ondine* in 1958 (as he wryly admitted, "By the end of the second act the story has usually petered out anyway").

As with *Fille*, Ashton worked on the score of *The Two Pigeons* with John Lanchbery. The music had originally been written for *Les Deux Pigeons*, choreographed by Louis Mérante and first seen at the Paris Opéra on 18 October 1886. Messager prepared a shorter version of his score for a revival of the ballet at the Royal Opera House, where he had been musical director. The choreography was by François Ambroisiny and it was first performed on 21 June 1906. Messager's revised score was rediscovered while Ashton and Lanchbery were working on their own adaptation.

The scenario for *The Two Pigeons* finds its pretext—it is hardly an adaptation—in the fable by La Fontaine, which Ashton updated to the Bohemian Paris of the original ballet's composition. Ashton's real debt to his source is not its narrative but the pigeon imagery that pervades the ballet. In this respect, although the tone of the two works is different, *The Two Pigeons* bears comparison with Ivanov's swan imagery that informs *Swan Lake*.

The choreography is in the same vein of lyrical bravura that Ashton first tapped in *La Fille mal gardée*, and both character and situation are embodied in movement. The bored fidgets of the Young Woman in the first scene, wriggling about while she sits for her portrait, are danced and not just acted; and the scene that follows is a swiftly executed series of vivid dance-images based on naturalistic gesture. By contrast, the Young Man's solo after he has been thrown out of the gypsy camp is devised from classical steps matched with gestures of contrition, pleading, and hope. Two further examples of the way Ashton tells his story through movement occur in the first act: one is the pas de trois, danced by the Gypsy Girl full of voluptuous promise, the Young Man all panting expectation, and the Gypsy Lover all resentful pride; and other is the moment when the Young Woman puts her hands on her hips and fans her elbows in a bird movement (subsequently taken up by the corps), while the Young Man first watches in amused indulgence and then joins in her fluttering lovers' game. The good humour and high-spirited gaiety of *The Two Pigeons* is remarkable, as are its passages of brilliant technical display— shown by the soloists of course, notably in the dance "duel", but also by the corps, particularly in the exciting and spectacular gypsy dances of the second act.

Anna Pavlova, as Ashton himself repeatedly acknowledged, was his inspiration throughout his life; indeed, Robert Helpmann reports him as saying "I think of her when I'm working all the time". Ashton thought that Lynn Seymour, on whom the Young Woman in *The Two Pigeons* was created, had feet as naturally beautiful as Pavlova's and he showed her how Pavlova had showed them off to best advantage. Seymour's partner was to have been Donald Britton, but on the day of the dress rehearsal he was injured and his understudy Christopher Gable took over. Britton was 31, Gable 21; and so at its first performance the ballet told the story of a young man learning with remorse a lesson about true love (again, there is a parallel with *Swan Lake*, however accidental), rather than telling of an older man settling gratefully for the true affection of innocence after an ill-advised adventure with heartless Bohemian experience. So well-made is the ballet, however, that it works in either case. Ashton's comedy is charming and lyric and full of sentiment; it is also profound.

—Martin Wright

U

ULANOVA, Galina

Russian/Soviet dancer and teacher. Born Galina Sergeyevna Ulanova in St. Petersburg, daughter of dancers and teachers Serge Ulanov and Maria Romanova, 8 January 1910. Studied at the Petrograd, later Leningrad, Choreographic School, pupil of mother, Maria Romanova, 1919–25, and Agrippina Vaganova; also studied with Aleksandr Monakhov; graduated in 1928. Married (1) stage director Y. Zavadsky; (2) designer Vadim Ryndin. Soloist, soon becoming leading ballerina, State Academic Theatre for Opera and Ballet (GATOB, later the Kirov Theatre), Leningrad, from 1928, performing in Perm (World War II evacuation), 1941–42, and Alma-Ata, 1942–43; ballerina, Bolshoi Ballet, Moscow, 1944–60; also toured various cities in the world with both Kirov and Bolshoi Ballets, with first Western performance in Vienna, 1945, then appearing in Rome, 1949, Florence and Vienna, 1951, London, 1956, Paris, 1958, and New York, 1959; farewell performance in 1962; also teacher: ballet mistress and coach, Bolshoi Ballet, Moscow, from 1959: students include Nina Timofeyeva, Ekaterina Maximova, Ludmila Semenyaka, Nina Semizorova; also appeared in numerous films, including *Stars of the Ballet* (1946), *Ballerina* (1947), *Trio Ballet* (1953), *Romeo and Juliet* (1954), and *The Bolshoi Ballet* (British film, 1957); Chairman of the Jury, International Ballet Competitions, Varna, Bulgaria, 1964–72. Recipient: titles of Honoured Artist of the Russian Federation, 1939, National Artist of the Russian Federation, 1940; State Prize, 1941, 1946, 1947, 1950; title of People's Artist of the Russian Federation, 1951; Lenin Prize, 1957; Hero of Socialist Labour, 1974, 1980.

ROLES

1928 Waltz, Mazurka in *Chopiniana* (Fokine), Graduation Performance, Leningrad Choreographic School, Leningrad

Sugar Plum Fairy in Adagio from *The Nutcracker* (Ivanov), Graduation Performance, Leningrad Choreographic School, Leningrad

Pas d'esclave in *Le Corsaire* (Petipa), State Academic Theatre for Opera and Ballet (GATOB), Leningrad

Princess Florine in *The Sleeping Beauty* (Petipa), GATOB, Leningrad

1929 Odette/Odile in *Swan Lake* (Petipa, Ivanov), GATOB, Leningrad

Princess Aurora in *The Sleeping Beauty* (Petipa), GATOB, Leningrad

1930 Komsomolka (cr) in *The Golden Age* (Vainonen, Yakobson, Chesnokov), GATOB, Leningrad

1931 Title role in *Raymonda* (Petipa), GATOB, Leningrad

Solveig in *The Snow Maiden* (Lopukhov), GATOB, Leningrad

Pas de deux from *Le Corsaire* (Petipa), Concert Performance, Moscow

1932 Mireille de Poitiers in *The Flames of Paris* (Vainonen), GATOB, Leningrad

Tsar-Maiden in *The Little Humpbacked Horse* (Gorsky after Petipa; staged Lopukhov), GATOB, Leningrad

Title role in *Giselle* (Petipa after Coralli, Perrot), GATOB, Leningrad

The Swan in *The Dying Swan* (Fokine; staged Vaganova), GATOB, Leningrad

1933 Odette (cr) in *Swan Lake* (new production; Vaganova after Petipa, Ivanov), GATOB, Leningrad

1934 Maria (cr) in *The Fountain of Bakhchisarai* (Zakharov), GATOB, Leningrad

Masha (cr) in *The Nutcracker* (Vainonen), GATOB, Leningrad

1935 Odette/Odile in *Swan Lake* (Gorsky after Petipa, Ivanov), Bolshoi Ballet, Moscow

Title role in *Giselle* (Petipa after Coralli, Perrot), Bolshoi Ballet, Moscow

Diana (cr) in *Esmeralda* (new production; Vaganova after Perrot, Petipa), Kirov Ballet, Leningrad

1936 Coralie (cr) in *Lost Illusions* (Zakharov), Kirov Ballet, Leningrad

1938 Title role (cr) in *Raymonda* (new production; Vainonen after Petipa), Kirov Ballet, Leningrad

1940 Juliet (cr) in *Romeo and Juliet* (Lavrovsky), Kirov Ballet, Leningrad

1941 Nikiya in *La Bayadère* (Petipa; staged Vaganova), Kirov Ballet, Perm

1945 Title role (cr) in *Cinderella* (Zakharov), Bolshoi Ballet, Moscow

1946 Juliet in *Romeo and Juliet* (revival; Lavrovsky), Bolshoi Ballet, Moscow

1949 Tao-Hoa (cr) in *The Red Poppy* (Lavrovsky), Bolshoi Ballet, Moscow

Parasha in *The Bronze Horseman* (Zakharov), Kirov Ballet, Leningrad

1954 Katerina (cr) in *The Story of the Stone Flower* (Lavrovsky), Bolshoi Ballet, Moscow

Other roles include: leading dancer in concert pieces *Elegy* (Goleizovsky), *The Dove of Peace* (Chabukiani), *Waltz* (Zakharov), *Liebestraum* (Shuitsky), *Russian Dance* (Petipa).

PUBLICATIONS

By Ulanova:

"Ballerina's School", *Novy Mir* (Moscow), no. 3, 1954

Ulanova, Moiseyev and Zakharov on Soviet Ballet, translated by E. Fox, D. Fry, edited by Peter Brinson, London, 1954

"The Author of my Favourite Ballets", in *Prokofiev: Autobiography, Articles, Reminiscences* (in English), Moscow, 1956

"Notes from my London Diary", *Ballet Today* (London), 3 parts: June, July, August/September 1957

"The Making of a Ballerina", in *The Bolshoi Ballet Story*, New York, 1959

"On Ballet in Russia Today", *Dance Magazine* (New York), December 1974

Interview in Gould, Susan, "Talking with Galina Ulanova", *Dance Scope* (New York), vol. 14, no. 3, 1980

Interview in Gregory, John, "A Talk with Ulanova", *Dancing Times* (London), August 1983

About Ulanova:

Golubov, Vladimir, *Galina Ulanova's Dance*, Leningrad, 1948

Bogdanov-Berezovsky, Valerian, *Ulanova and the Development of Soviet Ballet*, translated by S. Garry and J. Lawson, London, 1952

Lvov-Anokhin, Boris, *Ulanova*, Moscow, 1954; English edition, Moscow, 1956

Slonimsky, Yuri, *The Bolshoi Theatre Ballet*, Moscow, 1956

Bogdanov-Berezovsky, Valerian, *Galina Sergeevna Ulanova*, 2nd edition, Moscow, 1961

Kahn, Albert, *Days with Ulanova*, London and New York, 1962

Sizova, M., *Ulanova: Her Childhood and Schooldays*, translated by M. Rambert, London, 1962

Roslavleva, Natalia, *Era of the Russian Ballet*, London, 1966

* * *

Galina Ulanova as Cinderella, Moscow, c.1945

In the dance of Spain there is a special quality called *duende*: it seeks to plumb the human soul and reveal its full depth; it is unafraid of sadness and can look at death. In Russia there is a similar expression, simply "dusha", or "soul".

The great Soviet ballerina Galina Ulanova brought such a quality to classical ballet. With unfailing taste she used it to colour her abstract as well as her dramatic roles.

In 1934, when Ulanova first performed the role of Maria, the captive Polish princess in Rostislav Zakharov's *The Fountain of Bakhchisarai*, the ballet critic Natalia Roslavleva wrote, "Ulanova's Maria was imbued with an elegaic sorrow close to the spirit of Pushkin." To convey this, Ulanova had prepared the role in the manner of the great stage director Konstantin Stanislavsky. She had analyzed it carefully and had found analogies within her own sensitive nature. She was, as she described it, "tapping the internal melody".

The role did not demand technical display. One of its leitmotifs was a low arabesque which gave the illusion of gentle upward flight—of a yearning for freedom. The most poignant moment of the entire ballet was also its most quiet: leaning against a pillar, the dying Maria slowly sank to the floor, her arm gradually falling away from the pillar like the tendril of a vine relinquishing its sustaining wall.

Zakharov had created *The Fountain of Bakhchisarai* with Ulanova in mind. Six years later, Leonid Lavrovsky made his full-length *Romeo and Juliet* with the same ballerina as his inspiration. And here, too, the most poignant moments were sometimes the simplest: Juliet running, as though borne by the wind, from her home to that of Friar Lawrence; or Juliet held high in Romeo's arms and rapturously gazing down into his eyes.

Composer Sergei Prokofiev was also inspired by Ulanova when he wrote the scores for *Romeo and Juliet*, *Cinderella*, and *The Stone Flower*. For him it was not only her psychological penetration but her encompassing grasp of the musical intent. She often stated that dance made music visible.

Two important elements helped give Galina Ulanova the confidence to experiment with the choreographic materials assigned to her. First, there was her fine classical training. She began as a child in Leningrad at the school of the Kirov Ballet. Its basic approach was more concerned with finesse and delicacy than the more spectacular Bolshoi curriculum in Moscow. Furthermore, her first teacher was her mother, Maria Romanova, who knew the right balance of firmness and gentleness to apply to a child as yet unconvinced that dance was for her. The concluding years of Ulanova's education were entrusted to the celebrated Agrippina Vaganova, who, among other things, developed her strength and endurance.

Equally important to her artistic development was Ulanova's keen mind. From early on, even the simplest waltz in Mikhail Fokine's *Chopiniana* (*Les Sylphides*) took on a special nuance when expressed through her body.

By the time she was 24 and had danced in *The Fountain of Bakhchisarai*, Ulanova realized that traditional roles like Princess Aurora in *The Sleeping Beauty* and Raymonda no longer held interest for her, because they contained little or no opportunity for character development. She began to eliminate them from her repertoire, while to other traditional roles like Odette in *Swan Lake* and Giselle she brought a fresh viewpoint.

Unlike most Soviet artists, Ulanova first danced with the Kirov Ballet and then moved to the Bolshoi Ballet, where she remained until her retirement in 1962. Since then, in addition to serving on many important artistic committees and juries, she has been an indefatigable mentor for younger ballerinas, notably the radiant Ekaterina Maximova, who owes much to her.

—Doris Hering

————

UNDERTOW

Choreography: Antony Tudor
Music: William Schuman
Design: Raymond Breinin (scenery and costumes)
Libretto: Antony Tudor (after a suggestion by John van Druten)
First Production: Ballet Theatre, Metropolitan Opera House, New York, 10 April 1945
Principal Dancers: Hugh Laing (The Transgressor), Diana Adams (Cybele), John Kriza (Pollux), Shirley Eckl (Volupia), Lucia Chase (Polyhymnia), Alicia Alonso (Ate), Patricia Barker (Aganippe)

PUBLICATIONS

Barrett, Dorothy, "Understanding Antony Tudor", *Dance Magazine* (New York), June 1945
Denby, Edwin, *Looking at the Dance*, New York, 1949
Cohen, Selma Jeanne, "The Years in America and After", *Dance Perspectives* (New York), no. 18, 1963
Gruen, John, *The Private World of Ballet* (New York), Viking, 1973
Anderson, Jack, "The View from the House Opposite", *Ballet Review*, vol. 4, no. 6, 1974
Balanchine, George, with Mason, Francis, *Balanchine's Complete Stories of the Great Ballets*, Garden City, N. Y., 1977
Schuman, William, "Toasting Tudor", *Ballet Review* (New York), Fall 1986
Chazin-Bennahum, Judith, "After Pillar of Fire", *Choreography and Dance*, 1989
Perlmutter, Donna, *Shadowplay: The Life of Antony Tudor*, London, 1991

*   *   *

With *Undertow* Antony Tudor presented a metaphor for the time. Modern warfare, urban poverty, and moral revulsion at the loss of life in Europe and Asia, were the realities of the day which set the tone and psychological backdrop for a unique ballet which dealt with the destruction of a young man's

Undertow, with Diana Adams, John Kriza, and Hugh Laing, Ballet Theatre, 1946

psyche. William Schuman, the only composer ever commissioned by Tudor to create music for a ballet, praised Tudor for his sophisticated and precise instructions on the specific emotional climate he hoped the music would produce.

When Tudor arrived in London in 1946, he told the English critic Fernau Hall that *Undertow* would be a flop for the critics as it had been in the States, saying, "They can't take the sex". "He was right about the critics," said Hall, "but the audience reception was quite astonishing".

The shock for all audiences in watching *Undertow* was the Transgressor's murder of the prostitute during the sexual act. Tudor developed it as though it were an anatomy lesson, as if he had read about a particular homicide in the newspaper, and then traced the murder back through its Freudian meanings. His psychoanalytic approach attempted to establish the unconscious memory which impelled the murderer to action, as in a case study. The action seems to take place in the mind of the Transgressor, while the scenery and symbology remove his anti-hero from realistic situations. The characters in the ballet, except for the protagonist, have Greek or Roman names that point to sexual contexts.

In the Prologue, the goddess mother Cybele gives birth to the Transgressor, and then rejects him, in a quite sexually specific dance-pantomime. Afterwards, the boy retreats into the shadows while Cybele remains on stage and dances a quiet solo, with piqué arabesques and balances before she departs, leaving him seduced but unrequited.

The scene becomes a street in the slums of a Central European city. Volupia, "the personification of sensual pleasure", places herself in the same spot where Cybele danced. Volupia's movements resemble Cybele's, though they are more lewd and suggestive. The Transgressor, now a young man, enters with Aganippe, a little girl mincingly tripping along on her toes. "She is the virtuous nymph who inspires all who drink from her fountain". The Transgressor moves toward Volupia, who looks at him contemptuously. The Satyrisci, young worshippers of Dionysus, strut and preen; Volupia lures an old man to her side. At one point the Transgressor, clearly an outsider, walks around the stage, his head dropped, and his feet dragging. Polyhymnia, the muse of sacred music, enters dressed in a Salvation Army cape and hat and collects an audience for a prayer meeting. Then the beautiful but hideous Ate, who leads men into evil, appears as a volunteer for prayer. One immediately focuses upon her obscene gestures and salacious expressions. An idyllic-looking wedding couple (Hera and Hymen) bounce across the stage with light, jumpy steps, but their bliss is short-lived in this corrupt environment. Unappetizing Bacchantes in aprons and high-button shoes shoot lascivious glances in all directions; a young girl flirtatiously taunts four men who then rape her. These unsavoury characters have given the anti-hero his "sentimental education".

When Ate re-enters, the Transgressor accosts her and tries to choke her, but Ate wrenches herself away from him. Finally Medusa enters, the mythical woman who "petrifies" those who look upon her. As a rule, she is danced by the same ballerina as Cybele, the Transgressor's mother. The Transgressor partners her; others enter and look on, for in this ballet, someone is almost always watching someone else. While moving together, they cross nervously back and forth on diagonals; she pirouettes; he stealthily catches her. They both fall to the ground and repeat the movements that he and Cybele performed in the Prologue. Alone with a woman for the first time and with their bodies entwined, he suddenly chokes her to death during the sexual act.

The scene changes. The Transgressor, terrified and alone, begins a long solo, in which he realizes the depth of his horrific experience where sex, evil, and death have come together. City people stroll past indifferently. He glances at Aganippe playing with a balloon and smilingly moves towards her; but she points fiercely at him and releases the balloon from her grip. The other characters join her and point at him. Condemned, he walks slowly off the stage.

The dancing in *Undertow*, with many hints of modern dance, takes on a new range with the theatrical power of gesture. Almost every critic remarked that the ballet was shocking. Some found the movements and the direction of the ballet at odds with the psychology of the protagonist. Edwin Denby complained, "Because *Undertow* lacks such a physical release of opposing forces, it remains intellectual in its effect, like a case history, and does not quite become a drama of physical movement." The ballet was revived in 1968 by American Ballet Theatre, the same company which had first performed it, and it proved a work that has remained both powerful and disturbing.

—Judith Chazin-Bennahum

———

VAGANOVA, Agrippina

Russian/Soviet dancer, teacher, and ballet director. Born Agrippina Yakovlevna Vaganova in St. Petersburg, 26 June (14 June old style) 1879. Studied at the Imperial Theatre School, St. Petersburg, pupil of Lev Ivanov, Ekaterina Vazem, Pavel Gerdt, Nikolai Legat, Christian Johansson; graduated in 1897; later studied with Olga Preobrazhenskaya. Dancer, Maryinsky Theatre, St. Petersburg, 1897–1916, becoming soloist, from 1905, and ballerina from 1915, also performing in Paris, 1912; teacher, Miklos Ballet School, Petrograd, 1917, Volynsky School of Russian Ballet, from 1920; teacher of beginners' classes, Petrograd Theatre School, later Leningrad Choreographic School, 1920–22, becoming teacher of graduation class, 1922–51: students include Marina Semenova, Galina Ulanova, Tatyana Vecheslova, Olga Mungalova, Olga Iordan, Natalia Dudinskaya, Nina Anisimova, Alla Shelest, Olga Moiseyeva, Alla Osipenko, and Irina Kolpakova; teacher (Class of Perfection) and coach, State Academic Theatre for Opera and Ballet (GATOB, later the Kirov), 1917–51; artistic director, Kirov Ballet, 1931–37; Head of the Teachers' Department of the Leningrad Choreographic School, 1934–41; member, Choreographers' Faculty, Leningrad Choreographic School at the Conservatory, from 1943, becoming professor, from 1946, and director, 1946–51; also teacher of Class of Perfection, Bolshoi Theatre, Moscow, 1943–44. Recipient: title of People's Artist of the Russian Federation, 1934; State Prize of the USSR, 1946; Leningrad Choreographic School named after Vaganova in 1957. Died in Leningrad, 5 November 1951.

ROLES

1897/ Queen of the Dryads in *The Daughter of Mikado*
1916   (Ivanov), Maryinsky Theatre, St. Petersburg
       Work (Variation) in *Coppélia* (Petipa, Cecchetti), Maryinsky Theatre, St. Petersburg
       Queen of the Dryads in *Don Quixote* (Gorsky after Petipa), Maryinsky Theatre, St. Petersburg
       Diamond Fairy, Canary Fairy in *The Sleeping Beauty* (Petipa), Maryinsky Theatre, St. Petersburg
       Clemence, Henrietta in *Raymonda* (Petipa), Maryinsky Theatre, St. Petersburg
       Empress of the Waters in *The Little Humpbacked Horse* (Petipa after Saint-Léon), Maryinsky Theatre, St. Petersburg
       Nerilia in *The Talisman* (Petipa), Maryinsky Theatre, St. Petersburg
       Butterfly in *Le Carnaval* (Fokine), Maryinsky Theatre, St. Petersburg
       Solo variation, "Kingdom of the Shades" in *La Bayadère* (Petipa), Maryinsky Theatre, St. Petersburg

1900   Hebe in *The Awakening of Flora* (Ivanov, Petipa), Maryinsky Theatre, St. Petersburg
1903   The Chinese Doll (cr) in *The Fairy Doll* (N. and S. Legat), Maryinsky Theatre, St. Petersburg
1907   Thaw in *The Seasons* (Petipa; staged N. Legat), Maryinsky Theatre, St. Petersburg
1910   Mazurka in *Chopiniana* (Fokine), Maryinsky Theatre, St. Petersburg
       Principal dancer (cr) in *The Whisper of Flowers* (solo; N. Legat), Maryinsky Theatre, St. Petersburg
1911   Naïla in *La Source* (Coppini after Saint-Léon), Maryinsky Theatre, St. Petersburg
       Title role in *The Pearl* (Petipa), Maryinsky Theatre, St. Petersburg
1913   Odette/Odile in *Swan Lake* (Petipa, Ivanov), Maryinsky Theatre, St. Petersburg
1915   Tsar-Maiden in *The Little Humpbacked Horse* (Petipa after Saint-Léon), Maryinsky Theatre, Petrograd
1916   Title role in *Giselle* (Petipa after Coralli, Perrot), Maryinsky Theatre (Benefit for Vaganova), Petrograd

WORKS

Staged:
1925   *La Source* (with Ponomarev, after Saint-Léon; mus. Minkus, Delibes), State Academic Theatre for Opera and Ballet (GATOB, later the Kirov), Leningrad
1933   *Swan Lake* (after Petipa, Ivanov; mus. Tchaikovsky), GATOB, Leningrad
1935   *Esmeralda* (after Petipa, Perrot; mus. Pugni), Kirov Ballet, Leningrad
1938   *Chopiniana* (*Les Sylphides*, after Fokine; mus. Chopin), Kirov Ballet, Leningrad
1948   *Esmeralda* (new version; after Petipa, Perrot; mus. Pugni), Kirov Ballet, Leningrad

PUBLICATIONS

By Vaganova:
Fundamentals of the Classic Dance, Leningrad, 1934; translated by Anatole Chujoy (also translated as *Basic Principles of Classical Ballet*), New York, 1937

About Vaganova:
Raffé, Walter George, "Some Impressions from the Soviet Ballet: Agrippina Vaganova and Marina Semenova", *Dancing Times* (London), September 1936
A.Y. Vaganova, Leningrad, 1940

Frangopulo, M., *Vaganova: Fifty Years in Ballet*, Leningrad, 1948

Bogdanov-Berezovsky, Valerian, *Vaganova*, Leningrad, 1958

René, Natalia, "She Linked the Generations", *Dance and Dancers* (London), January 1962

Litvinoff, Valentina, "Vaganova", *Dance Magazine* (New York), 2 parts: July, August, 1964

Greskovic, Robert, "Ballet, Barre and Center, on the Bookshelf", *Ballet Review* (Brooklyn, N.Y.), vol. 6, no. 2, 1977/1978

Ivzhina, Kamila, "Agrippina Vaganova and the Art of Teaching", *Dance Magazine* (New York), November 1979

Kremshevskaya, G., *Agrippina Vaganova*, Leningrad, 1981

Krasovskaya, Vera, *Vaganova*, Leningrad, 1989

*   *   *

Agrippina Vaganova could not have suspected how far-reaching her influence would be when, in the aftermath of the Russian Revolution, she set about systematizing the teaching of ballet for the new era of Soviet dance. A priceless legacy has evolved, in part a result of Vaganova's disillusionment with her own artistic career and her dissatisfaction with the old system of teaching which stimulated her desire for change.

Graduating into the Maryinsky company from its school in 1897, Vaganova displayed unequalled elevation and batterie. She performed leading roles in *La Source*, *Swan Lake*, *The Little Humpbacked Horse*, and *The Pearl*. Among other important solos there were the Mazurka in Mikhail Fokine's *Chopiniana* and a variation in "The Shades" scene in *La Bayadère* which is known at the Kirov ballet as the "Vaganova variation" even today. Despite her eminence as "the Queen of Variations", Vaganova did not receive the title of ballerina until the year before her farewell benefit performance in 1916, dancing for most of her career in the shadow of her contemporaries Anna Pavlova, Tamara Karsavina, Olga Preobrazhenskaya, and Matilda Kshesinskaya. She possessed neither good looks nor influential friends, and both were important for progress on the Imperial stage. The inadequacies which this self-critical and demanding ballerina found in her own technique brought her ultimately to question herself and the current system of teaching.

Vaganova had already begun a critical assimilation of the experiences of her teachers and contemporaries in her search for a personal approach to ballet by the time of her early retirement. Her first conclusions were drawn from a comparison of the French and Italian schools which were dominant at the end of the nineteenth century. The French school—represented by her teachers Christian Johannson, Pavel Gerdt, Nikolai Legat, and Ekaterina Vazem—cultivated a soft and graceful, but highly artificial, manner of performance which lacked energy and therefore restricted balletic virtuosity. The Italian school—represented by Enrico Cecchetti and such ballerinas as Pierina Legnani, Carlotta Brianza, and Antonietta Dell'Era—differed markedly, often lacking in poetry and harmony but developing reliable stability, dynamic turns, and strength and endurance, especially of the legs and feet. A national style of dancing had been developing over an extended period of time, as Russian dancers creatively assimilated the diverse influences of their own choreographers and teachers along with those of the representatives of the French and Italian schools. An expressive poetry and spirituality came to characterize the Russian style of performing, but little had been done to consolidate the collective experience into a formal system of teaching. This became Vaganova's life's work.

She began this second phase of her career immediately after the Revolution, first accepting a teaching position at the privately-owned School of Russian Ballet directed by the ballet critic and advocate Akim Volynsky. Three years later, when it became evident that skilled teachers were desperately needed for the new school being established by the Soviet ballet, she accepted an invitation to teach in the Leningrad Choreographic School. Her analytical skills and interest in the scientific aspects of ballet, and her enthusiasm and energy, brought her quickly to the forefront.

Vaganova's method evolved during the difficult period of the 1920s when the Soviet ballet's classical heritage was under constant attack, and both the ballet and its school were being accused of conservatism and creative impotence, in need of total reform. However, as one after another superb ballerina on whom Vaganova had formulated her teaching method began to appear on the Soviet stage, critical demands for reform subsided and the new Soviet school was born. Vaganova's attitude was one of openness to innovation without rejecting the best of the classical tradition. As a result, her system reflected to some degree the requirements of contemporary choreography as well. She was strongly influenced by the more naturalistic and poetic use of arms introduced in Fokine's ballets, for example, and by the strength of legs and feet developed by Cecchetti; and she sought to combine these elements in a complete and harmonious coordination of the whole body.

The efforts of choreographers in the 1930s were directed towards finding significant historical themes, dramatically well-developed plots, and artistically portrayed but realistic characters. Vaganova herself, as head of the State Academic Theatre of Opera and Ballet (the former Maryinsky) from 1931 to 1937, choreographed among other works a completely new and realistic version of *Swan Lake* which even included blood on the wounded Odette. She continued to champion the classical tradition, maintaining that even the theatricalized acrobatics which Fedor Lopukhov had boldly introduced into his new ballets should be based on the classical exercises. She felt that classical dance as a movement form should originate from and be expressive of human emotion and behaviour.

Between 1922 and 1951, Vaganova produced an unprecedented number of ballerinas: Marina Semenova, Natalia Kamkova, Galina Ulanova, Olga Mungalova, Tatyana Vecheslova, Irina Kolpakova, Olga Lepeshinskaya, Olga Iordan, Feya Balabina, and Natalia Dudinskaya (who inherited all of Vaganova's classes upon the premature death of her teacher in 1951). Her influence extended as well to the style of male dancing since her book, *Basic Principles of Classical Ballet*, first published in 1934, eventually became the basis of all Soviet ballet training.

The Russian school which emerged under Vaganova's powerful influence features rigorously planned classes directed at the creation of a virtuoso technique and a conscious awareness of the approach required by each movement. Careful training of the trunk of the body for strength and suppleness develops stability and allows movement of great complexity, diversity, amplitude, and speed. A pure classical line is emphasized from the earliest training with poised and expressive use of head, port de bras, and épaulement. The arms have dual importance—to express the dance and to assist it—by providing stability, force for tours, lift for big jumps, extension in the air, and design of the various poses.

A kind, helpful, and encouraging teacher, Vaganova demanded from her pupils that which she demanded of herself: exactness and attention to every detail, total concentration and dedicated hard work, honesty of expression, and the open-mindedness to learn from the ever-changing facets of life and art. She became one of the greatest ballet pedagogues of all time, possessing the credentials of ballerina, professor of choreography, instructor in the Leningrad State Ballet, or Choreographic, School (which bears her name now), People's Artist of the Russian Soviet Federation, author, and founder of the Russian system of ballet education now universally accepted and admired.

—Kristin Beckwith

VAINONEN, Vasily

Russian/Soviet dancer and choreographer. Born Vasily Ivanovich Vainonen in St. Petersburg, 21 February (8 February old style) 1901. Studied at the Petrograd Theatre School, pupil of Leonid Leontiev, Aleksandr Shiryaev, Vladimir Ponomarev; graduated in 1919. Married dancer and teacher Klavdia Armashevskaya. Dancer, excelling in character roles, State Academic Theatre for Opera and Ballet (GATOB), later the Kirov Ballet, 1919–38; choreographer, staging first work for Balanchine's Young Ballet group, early 1920s, and producing first full-length work, *The Golden Age*, 1930; guest choreographer producing ballets for Byelorussian Theatre of Opera and Ballet, Minsk, 1945, Hungarian State Opera Ballet, Budapest, 1950–51, Theatre of Opera and Ballet, Novosibirsk, 1952, and Bolshoi Theatre, Moscow, 1957; ballet master and choreographer, Bolshoi Ballet, Moscow, 1946–50, 1954–58. Recipient: title of Honoured Artist of the Russian Federation, 1939; State Prize of the USSR, 1945, 1947. Died in Moscow, 24 March 1964.

ROLES

1919/ The Faun in *The Seasons of the Year* (Leontiev), State
38   Academic Theatre of Opera and Ballet (GATOB, later the Kirov), Leningrad
     The Blackamoor in *Petrushka* (Fokine), GATOB/Kirov Ballet, Leningrad
     Puss in Boots in *The Sleeping Beauty* (Petipa), GATOB/Kirov Ballet, Leningrad
     The Youth in *Pulcinella* (Lopukhov), GATOB/Kirov Ballet, Leningrad
1924 Satyr in *The Seasons* (Petipa, staged Leontiev), GATOB, Leningrad
1927 The Ram (cr) in *A Tale about the Fox, the Rooster, the Cat, and the Ram* (*Le Renard*; Lopukhov), GATOB, Leningrad

WORKS

1920s *Moszkovsky Waltz* (pas de deux; mus. Moszkovsky), Evenings of Young Ballet, Leningrad (staged GATOB, Leningrad, 1930)
1930 *The Golden Age* (with Chesnakov and Yakobson; mus. Shostakovich), GATOB, Leningrad
1932 *The Flames of Paris* (mus. Asafiev), GATOB, Leningrad
1934 *The Nutcracker* (mus. Tchaikovsky), GATOB, Leningrad (staged again by Vainonen, Moscow 1939, 1947)
1936 *Partisan Days* (mus. Asafiev), Kirov Ballet, Leningrad
1947 *Militsa* (mus. Asafiev), Kirov Ballet, Leningrad
1949 *Mirandolina* (mus. Vasilenko), Bolshoi Ballet, Moscow
1952 *The Coast of Happiness* (mus. Spadavecchia), Theatre of Opera and Ballet, Novosibirsk
1957 *Gayané* (mus. Khachaturian), Bolshoi Ballet, Moscow

Also staged:
1938 *Raymonda* (after Petipa; mus. Glazunov), Kirov Ballet, Leningrad
1945 *Harlequinade* (after Petipa; mus. Drigo), Byelorussian Theatre of Opera and Ballet, Minsk
1952 *The Sleeping Beauty* (after Petipa; mus. Tchaikovsky), Theatre of Opera and Ballet, Novosibirsk

Other works include: Concert pieces—*Slackers and Idlers, Vyatskaya Toy, Finnish Polka, Anitra's Dance, Spanish Suite.*

PUBLICATIONS

By Vainonen:
"A Producer in his Work" in *Raymonda*, Leningrad, 1938

About Vainonen:
Lopukhov, Fedor, *Sixty Years in Ballet*, Moscow, 1966
Mikhailov, Mikhail, *Life in Ballet*, Leningrad and Moscow, 1966
Roslavleva, Natalia, *Era of the Russian Ballet*, London, 1966
Armashevskaya, Klavdia, and Vainonen, Nikita, *Balletmaster Vainonen*, Moscow, 1971

          *   *   *

An outstanding character dancer of the 1920s and 1930s, Vasily Vainonen had his early beginnings as a choreographer in dances on the popular stage. As Fedor Lopukhov wrote, "He loved sketches from life and possessed a genuine sense of humour. . . . It was enough to see the productions of Vainonen to realize that in him was a talented poet of dance. To portray real people in real situations is the most difficult thing of all for ballet masters to achieve."

Indeed, the genre of "dance from nature" is characteristic of both the many stage miniatures by Vainonen (*Slackers and Idlers, Vyatskaya Toy,* and *Finnish Polka*), and the theatrically pioneering work *The Golden Age*. Quite another thing was the four-act *The Flames of Paris*, inspired by the great French Revolution. Later the ballet theoretician Poél Karp noted, "The merit of the creators lay in that, having chosen an important popular revolutionary theme, they did not fear an epic resolution, but actually were able to find it in the scenario and in the music, and to embody it successfully in the choreography. For this reason the ballet *The Flames of Paris* survived on the stage for more than quarter of a century. Its second and third acts stand among the highest achievements of Soviet choreography."

Vainonen's *The Nutcracker* enjoyed an even longer existence, continuing to be revived 30 years after the premiere, and sustaining more than 400 subsequent productions; even today, it is seen on the stage of the Kirov Theatre as a presentation by the Leningrad Choreographic School. In Vainonen's treatment, the ballet represents an episode in the life of a bourgeois family (the Stallbaums), living, as Yuri Slonimsky puts it, "within the closed confines of their existence, where the parents are limited in their possibilities and the children can escape from these limited horizons only in dreams."

The two following works of the ballet master were in many ways experimental, and each had quite a different and short stage life. The first was *Partisan Days*, a unique example of a ballet wholly constructed on character dances (in this the dancer Nina Anisimova was exceptional) and pantomime. The successful scenes were those in which the choreographer departed from simply copying folklore, and created patterns in dance for the heroes of the Civil War. As for the second,

Raymonda, and the idea behind its revival, the authors of its new libretto, Vainonen and Slonimsky, wrote thus: "The first production of *Raymonda*, notwithstanding remarkable pages of music by Glazunov and the treasures of individual dances by Marius Petipa, was theatrically of little value. The reason for this was chiefly the libretto. We declined the attempt to improve the scenario by tidying up and correcting separate situations. At the centre of our production is Raymonda, the young woman of the Middle Ages who is shielded from the hardships of life by the wall of upbringing and prejudice and therefore idealizes her suitor, his world of knights, and the aim of the Crusades. The development and action bring Raymonda into collision with real life. In a captive negro she finds greater human human feelings than in the knights who surround her." The attempt had little success, and this was instructive. The new theme in many ways contradicted the music. The classicism of Petipa which remained in the piece was in too strong a contrast with Vainonen's style and approach.

Of the post-war works of the ballet master, noteworthy are the clearly comic Moscow ballet *Mirandolina*, after a piece by Goldoni, in which Olga Lepeshinskaya and Aleksei Yermolaev shone as Mirandolina and her cavalier, Ripafrata. The last of the creative initiatives of Vainonen was a new *Little Humpbacked Horse*, with music by Shchedrin. Vainonen succeeded only in working out the scenario of the ballet; however, his production was realized by others.

—Arsen Degen

VALBERGH (Valberkh), Ivan

Russian dancer, choreographer, and teacher. Born Ivan Lessogorov (said to be given name Ivan Ivanovich Valberkh, or Valbergh, by Catherine II, in 1786) in Moscow, 14 July (3 July old style) 1766. Studied at the Imperial Theatre School, St. Petersburg, pupil of Gasparo Angiolini, Giuseppe Canziani; graduated in 1786; also studied in Paris, 1802. Married dancer Sofia Petrovna Dentz; many children, including famous dramatic actress Maria Valberkhova. Premier danseur, Bolshoi Theatre, St. Petersburg, from 1786; ballet inspector of the ballet company of the Bolshoi Theatre, from 1794; first major choreography, 1795, followed by over 36 ballets and divertissements; worked with French ballet master Charles Didelot, Bolshoi Theatre, St. Petersburg, from 1801, succeeding him as ballet master (upon Didelot's departure), 1811; also teacher, Bolshoi Theatre, from 1794: students included Eugenia Kolosova, Anastasia Berilova, Isaak Abletz; teacher (sent by the Imperial Theatres to improve standards), Bolshoi Theatre, Moscow, 1808; also writer and translator of French plays into Russian. Died in St. Petersburg, 26 July (14 July old style) 1819.

WORKS

1795   *The Happy Contrition* (mus. unknown), Bolshoi Theatre, St. Petersburg
1799   *The New Werther* (mus. Titov), Bolshoi Theatre, St. Petersburg
1803   *Blanca; or, A Marriage of Vengeance* (mus. Titov), Bolshoi Theatre, St. Petersburg
1804   *The Count of Castelli; or, A Murderous Brother* (mus. various), Bolshoi Theatre, St. Petersburg
1806   *Clara; or, A Return to Virtue* (mus. Veigle), Bolshoi Theatre, St. Petersburg

1807   *The Triumph of Eugenia*, Bolshoi Theatre, St. Petersburg
      Raoul, Barbe-Bleu; or, The Dangers of Curiosity (mus. Gretry, Cavos), Bolshoi Theatre, St. Petersburg
1808   *Orpheus and Eurydice* (mus. Gluck), Bolshoi Theatre, St. Petersburg
1809   *Romeo and Juliet* (tragic ballet with choruses), Bolshoi Theatre, St. Petersburg
1811   *The New Heroine; or, The Woman Cossack*, Bolshoi Theatre, St. Petersburg
1812   *The People's Volunteer Corps; or, Love for the Motherland*, Bolshoi Theatre, St. Petersburg
      Festival in a Russian Village, Bolshoi Theatre, St. Petersburg
1813   *The Russians in Germany; or, What Comes of Love for the Motherland* (with August; mus. Cavos), Bolshoi Theatre, St. Petersburg
      Cossack in London, Bolshoi Theatre, St. Petersburg
      Festival in the Allied Armies' Camp at Montmartre, Bolshoi Theatre, St. Petersburg
1814   *The American Heroine; or, Perfidy Punished*, Bolshoi Theatre, St. Petersburg
      Russian Victory; or, The Russians in Paris, Bolshoi Theatre, St. Petersburg
1815   *The Amazons; or, The Destruction of the Magic Castle* (mus. various), Bolshoi Theatre, St. Petersburg
      Cinderella (mus. Steinbelt), Bolshoi Theatre, St. Petersburg
1816   *Henry IV; or, The Rewards of Virtue*, Bolshoi Theatre, St. Petersburg

Other works include: restagings of various earlier French ballets including *Le Déserteur* (after Dauberval).

PUBLICATIONS

By Valbergh:
From the Archives of the Ballet Master: Diaries, Correspondence, Libretti, edited and prefaced by Yuri Slonimsky, Leningrad and Moscow, 1948

About Valbergh:
Krasovskaya, Vera, *Russian Ballet Theatre from the Beginning to the Middle of the Nineteenth Century*, Moscow, 1958
Slonimsky, Yuri, "Sergei Titov's Ballet *The New Werther*", *Proceedings of the State Research Institute for Theatre, Music and Cinematography*, Leningrad, 1958
Gozenpud, A., *Musical Theatre in Russia, from its Appearance up to Glinka's Time: An Essay*, Leningrad, 1959
Roslavleva, Natalia, *Era of the Russian Ballet*, London, 1966
Swift, Mary Grace, *A Loftier Flight: The Life and Accomplishments of Charles-Louis Didelot, Balletmaster*, Middletown, Connecticut, and London, 1974
Winter, Marian Hannah, *The Pre-Romantic Ballet*, London, 1974

*   *   *

Russia's "first choreographer" Ivan Ivanovich Valbergh was born in Moscow in 1766, and trained at St. Petersburg's Imperial Theatre School under Angiolini and Canziani. He graduated in 1786 into the ballet company of St. Petersburg's Bolshoi Theatre, soon becoming a leading dancer and mime. Before long Valbergh was appointed ballet inspector of the company and teacher at the School. His most prominent pupils were Eugenia Kolosova (1780–1865), Anastasia Berilova (1766–1804), and Isaak Abletz (1778–1829). Among his many leading roles was Igor in *The Commencement of Oleg's Reign*, a spectacle with a libretto by Catherine the Great, based on a theme from Russian history and performed with drama, music, and ballet, along with Ivan in *The Russians in Germany; or, What Comes of Love for the Motherland*, Jason in *Medea and Jason*, Alexis in *Le Déserteur*, Raoul in *Raoul, Barbe-Bleu*, and many others. A well-educated man, he translated an impressive amount of French melodramas into Russian, in versions which remained in the repertory of the Russian dramatic theatre for years. In 1802 he visited Paris and recorded some shrewd remarks in his diary about French ballet and its tendencies towards frivolous dancing. In 1808 he was sent to Moscow's Bolshoi Theatre in order to raise the standards of that city's ballet.

Valbergh was the first native Russian ballet master and choreographer. He reconstructed ten ballets of the old masters, composed 36 original ballets and ballet divertissements based on themes from Russian folklore, and composed many dances for operas and dramas in the repertoire of the Imperial Theatres. The title of his first ballet—*The Happy Contrition* (1795)—indicates the major trend of his art. Placed as it was in between the conventions of eighteenth-century Classicism and the birth of Romanticism, Valbergh's art professed the ideals of sentimental moralism and proclaimed the necessity of a didactic treatment of subjects. The pantomime ballets of Valbergh, usually in four or five acts, praised virtue and condemned vice. Such were *Clara; or, A Return to Virtue, The Triumph of Eugenia, Raoul, Barbe-Blue; or, The Dangers of Curiosity, The American Heroine; or, Perfidy Punished*, and *Henry IV; or, The Rewards of Virtue*. Pantomime usually predominated in his ballets, while dance took the form of divertissement, appearing at feasts, weddings, and so on. Such a ballet, for instance, was *Blanca; or, A Marriage of Vengeance*, based on a subject from Le Sage, with music by Aleksei Titov.

From 1810 to 1814, Valbergh, under the influence of the war with Napoleon, staged ballets and divertissements on patriotic subjects, such as *The New Heroine; or, The Woman Cossack*, based on the story of a real girl, Nadezhda Durova, who was the heroine of the war; *The People's Volunteer Corps; or, Love for the Motherland*; the above-mentioned *Russians in Germany*; *Festival in a Russian Village*; *Cossack in London*; *Festival in the Allied Armies' Camp at Montmartre*; and *Russian Victory; or, The Russians in Paris*.

In accordance with the sentimental style of his art, Valbergh presented real people out of ordinary life, but coloured the action with strong melodramatic effects. In this fashion he created his outstanding ballet, *The New Werther*, with music by Sergei Titov, a work which occupies a notable place in the history of Russian theatre. Up to the last minute it was believed that Valbergh borrowed the subject from Goethe's famous novel, which was translated and made popular in Russia in 1781. But Valbergh insisted that his ballet was "founded on a real incident, which happened in Moscow".

This brings one to the novel by Alexander Klushin, *The Unlucky M—v*, published in 1793. The prototype for the novel's hero was a certain Maslov, who commited suicide because of an unhappy love affair. Later, in 1815, Valbergh wrote: "When I dared to make the ballet *The New Werther*, Oh! how the sham wits and connoisseurs attacked me! What? A ballet where they are going to dance in tail-coats? I thought that I was finished: but real connoisseurs appeared and the moral ballet was a success. Still, when I undertook another moral ballet, I dared not use tail-coats, but dressed myself and others in Spanish costume." He could be proud of *The New Werther*, for throughout the nineteenth century, Russian choreographers carefully eluded themes from contemporary life.

In 1801, Valbergh met a strong rival in Charles-Louis Didelot. But soon he modestly recognized the superior talent of the French choreographer and worked in harmony with him. And Didelot said publicly that Valbergh was "justly esteemed as a distinguished artist in several genres, as well as a good father, an upright man and an excellent comrade."

—Vera Krasovskaya

VALOIS, Ninette de *see* DE VALOIS, Ninette

LA VALSE

Choreography: Bronislava Nijinska
Music: Maurice Ravel
Design: Alexandre Benois (scenery and costumes)
First Production: Ida Rubinstein Company, Théâtre de Monte Carlo, Monte Carlo, 12 January 1929
Principal Dancers: Ida Rubinstein and Anatole Vilzak

Other productions include: Royal Flemish Opera Ballet (first production to Ravel's score, chor. Sonia Korty); 1926. Ida Rubinstein Company (restaged and revised Nijinska, with new designs Alexandre Benois); Paris, 22 June 1931. Ida Rubinstein Company (new version; chor. Mikhail Fokine); Paris, 1935. Royal Danish Ballet (new version; chor. Harald Lander); Copenhagen, 25 January 1940. Opéra-Comique (new version; chor. Léonide Massine, lib. after Lermontov, design André Derain); Paris, 17 May 1950. New York City Ballet (new version; chor. George Balanchine, costumes Barbara Karinska), with Tanaquil LeClercq, Nicholas Magallanes and Francisco Moncion; New York, 20 February 1951. Les Ballets Janine Charrat (new version; chor. Charrat); Santander, 13 August 1955. La Scala Ballet (new version; chor. Frederick Ashton, design André Levasseur); Milan, 31 January 1958 (restaged Royal Ballet, London, 10 March 1959). Finnish Opera Ballet (new version; chor. George Gé); Helsinki, 6 March 1958.

PUBLICATIONS

Beaumont, Cyril, *Complete Book of Ballets*, revised edition, London, 1951
Clarke, Mary, "*La Valse*", *Dancing Times* (London), May 1959
Balanchine, George, with Mason, Francis, *Balanchine's Complete Stories of the Great Ballets*, Garden City, N.Y., 1977
Vaughan, David, *Frederick Ashton and his Ballets*, London, 1977
Baer, Nancy van Norman, *Bronislava Nijinska: A Dancer's Legacy*, San Francisco, 1986
De Cossart, Michael, *Ida Rubinstein*, Liverpool, 1987
Kahane, M., *Les Artistes et l'Opéra de Paris: Dessins et Costumes*, Paris, 1987

* * *

"Ravel, it is a masterpiece . . . but it is not a ballet. . . . It is the portrait of the ballet." With these words in 1920 Diaghilev rejected *La Valse*, a score he had commissioned for his Ballets

La Valse, in a version by Frederick Ashton, performed by the Royal Ballet, London

Russes the previous year. Diaghilev had in mind that José Maria Sert would design the ballet, but the proposed choreographer, Léonide Massine, already seems to have planned to use a Lermontov story for the scenario and wanted André Derain to design the piece. The Massine–Derain version was eventually staged at the Opéra-Comique in 1950, but their narrative was too complex for so short a score. It also went against Ravel's intention that the stage should brighten as the ballet progressed: Massine plunged it into darkness as the climax of his murder-mystery approached.

Given Diaghilev's observation, a remarkable array of choreographers have taken up the challenge of Ravel's music. Its first staging was by the Royal Flemish Opera Ballet in 1926 with choreography by Sonia Korty, but it really entered the established ballet repertoire with Bronislava Nijinska's production for Ida Rubinstein's Company in 1929, first seen during the company's visit to Monte Carlo. As with most of Rubinstein's productions, *La Valse* had few performances in its original form, and Nijinska and her designer Alexandre Benois were pursuaded to revise the work completely two years later, bringing it back much closer to the composer's original intentions.

At the head of his score Ravel had sketched a synopsis: "Drifting clouds offer glimpses, through openings, of waltzing couples. The clouds gradually scatter, and one can distinguish an immense hall, filled with a swirling crowd. The scene becomes progressively more illuminated, until, finally, the light of the chandeliers bursts forth. An Imperial Court around 1855."

In 1929 Nijinska had ignored these directions, and within Benois's marbled hall, draped with blue velvet and hung with crystal chandeliers, Nijinska's ensemble of dancers wore uniform gold lamé tunics and closely fitting caps. They performed angular, impersonal movements with groupings that Ashton, who danced in the production, later recalled as being "somewhat reminiscent of *Les Noces*". In 1931 the ballet was set in a crimson and gold ballroom lined with mirrors and lit by candelabra. At the back a second ballroom opened out in which, for a while, the dancing provided a choreographic counterpoint to the movement on the main stage. This version reflected Ravel's working title for the ballet *Wien* (Vienna) with the ladies in crinolines and the men in dress uniform. It was all much closer to Benois' own taste. It began (as do so many versions of *La Valse*) behind a scrim to diffuse the image and present the dancers as if seen through clouds or mist. The number of waltzing couples builds, multiplied yet further by reflections in enormous mirrors. Fokine revised the choreography further for Rubinstein's 1935 revival.

Of the many subsequent productions, Ashton's 1958 *La Valse* is the one that follows the composer's intentions more closely. Indeed, after its premiere in Milan, Francis Poulenc (who had been present when the score was first played to Diaghilev) told the choreographer that it was the first time he had seen a successful realization of the music. Ashton created his version for the large stage of La Scala as part of an evening of Ravel's works. Using 21 couples, he built up to the ballet's climaxes by flooding the stage with dancers; but at quieter moments three individual couples have the ballroom to themselves. There is no story as such, but Ashton nevertheless introduced some stereotyped images such as dancers blindly seeking their partners, their hands covering their own eyes. It is not one of Ashton's greatest works, but *La Valse* remains a useful company ballet—despite the fact that it looks cramped on stage at Covent Garden where it was mounted on the Royal Ballet.

Productions like Ashton's confirm how well Diaghilev understood the music. Choreographers seem unable to enhance Ravel's score further. At best they simply reflect the music and its atmosphere of impending doom. It *is* self-sufficient.

In 1951 George Balanchine treated *La Valse* differently, combining it with Ravel's earlier *Valse nobles et sentimentales* (which itself has also attracted numerous choreographers). He took as his starting point Ravel's comment in his notes on the ballet to Comte de Salavandy: "We are dancing on the edge of a volcano". The eight *Valse nobles et sentimentales* (the first used as overture) establish a mood of wistful but disquieting gaiety as small groups and couples meet and part. Impending catastophe is hinted at when a figure in black appears. Then, for *La Valse* itself, the stage opens up to become a ballroom of waltzing couples. The man in black, Death, returns presenting the lure of the unknown to a mesmerised young girl in white. He gives her black jewels, dresses her in black and, unheeded by the whirling crowd, dances her to death. In *La Valse* Balanchine returned to the neo-romantic quality that had characterized much of his choreography in the early 1930s, drawing ideas and material from such ballets as *Cotillon* (1932) with its similar ominous foreboding within party revels.

—Jane Pritchard

VAN DANTZIG, Rudi

Dutch dancer, choreographer, and ballet director. Born in Amsterdam, 4 August 1933. Studied with Ann Sybranda, Sonia Gaskell, Amsterdam; later studied with Martha Graham. Dancer, Sonia Gaskell's Ballet Recital, 1952–54; dancer, Netherlands Ballet (successor to Ballet Recital), 1954–56, becoming soloist, 1956–59; first choreography, Netherlands Ballet, 1955; founder member, Nederlands Dans Theater, 1959–60, returning to Netherlands Ballet 1960, and becoming resident choreographer, Dutch National Ballet (resulting from amalgamation of Netherlands Ballet and Amsterdam Ballet), 1961–69; international guest choreographer, including for Ballet Rambert, Harkness Ballet, Royal Ballet, Royal Danish Ballet, American Ballet Theatre, Bat-Dor Dance Company, and Paris Opéra Ballet; associate artistic director, to Sonia Gaskell, Dutch National Ballet, from 1965, becoming co-director, with Robert Kaesen, from 1969, and sole artistic director, 1971–91; has also appeared on television and film, including in film *Rudi van Dantzig: Portrait of a Choreographer* (dir. Vrijman, 1972); also the author of several fiction and non-fiction books. Recipient: Critics Prize, Paris, 1961; Knight of the Orde van Oranje Nassau, 1969; Choreography Prize of the City of Amsterdam, 1956, 1970; Cross of Merit of the German Federal Republic, 1982; Sonia Gaskell Prize, 1985; Choreography Prize of the Society of Theatre and Concert-Hall Directors, 1987; Officer of the Orde van Oranje Nassau, 1991.

WORKS

1955   *Nachteiland* (*Night Island*; mus. Debussy), Netherlands Ballet, The Hague

1956   *Tij en Ontij* (*Tide and un-tide*; mus. van Delden), Netherlands Ballet, Amsterdam

1957   *Mozart Symphony* (mus. Mozart), Netherlands Ballet, Amsterdam

1958   *The Family Circle* (mus. Bartók), Netherlands Ballet, The Hague

1959   *Klein Avondspel* (mus. Gluck), Netherlands Ballet, The Hague
       Giovinezza (mus. Vivaldi), Nederlands Dans Theater, Ostend

1960   *Vergezicht* (mus. Schumann), Nederlands Dans Theater, Scheveningen

1961   *Jungle* (mus. Badings), Dutch National Ballet, Amsterdam

1963   *Ombres* (*Shadows*; mus. de Leeuw), Dutch National Ballet, Amsterdam

1964   *Een Finse Auto* (*A Finnish Car*; mus. Schat), Dutch National Ballet, Amsterdam

1965   *Monument voor een Gestorven Jongen* (*Monument for a Dead Boy*; mus. Boerman), Dutch National Ballet, Amsterdam

1967   *Romeo en Julia* (*Romeo and Juliet*; mus. Prokofiev), Dutch National Ballet, Amsterdam

1968   *Ogenblikken* (*Moments*; mus. Webern), Dutch National Ballet, Amsterdam
       Images (mus. Ives), Bat-Dor Dance Company, Tel Aviv

1969   *Epitaaf* (*Epitaph*; mus. Ligeti), Dutch National Ballet, Amsterdam
       Astral (mus. Webern), Dutch National Ballet, Amsterdam

1970   *Onderweg* (*On the Way*; mus. Yun), Dutch National Ballet, Amsterdam
       The Ropes of Time (mus. Boerman), Royal Ballet, London

1971   *Geverfde Vogels* (*Coloured Birds*; mus. Gastiglioni, Bach), Dutch National Ballet, Amsterdam

1972   *Are Friends Delight or Pain?* (*Après Visage*; mus. Berio), Dutch National Ballet, Amsterdam

1973   *Hier rust, een Zomerdag* (*Here Rests a Summer Day*; mus. Schubert), Dutch National Ballet, Amsterdam
       Ramifications (mus. Ligeti, Purcell), Dutch National Ballet, Amsterdam

1974   *Orpheus* (mus. Stravinsky), Dutch National Ballet, Amsterdam
       Couples (mus. Avni), Bat-Dor Dance Company, Tel Aviv
       Movements in a Rocky Landscape (mus. Ligeti), Bat-Dor Dance Company, Tel Aviv

1975   *Collective Symphony* (with van Manen and van Schayk; mus. Stravinsky), Dutch National Ballet, Amsterdam
       Blown in a Gentle Wind (mus. R.Strauss), Dutch National Ballet, Amsterdam
       Suite for Young Dancers (mus. Chopin), Nel-Roos Ballet Academy, Amsterdam

1976   *Ginastera* (mus. Ginastera), Dutch National Ballet, Amsterdam
       Isadora (mus. Brahms), Dutch National Ballet, Amsterdam

1977   *Vier Letzte Lieder* (*Four Last Songs*; mus. R. Strauss), Dutch National Ballet, Amsterdam
       Gesänge der Jünglinge (*Songs of the Youngsters*; mus. Stockhausen, Chopin), Dutch National Ballet, Amsterdam

1978   *Over een Donker Huis* (*About a Dark House*; mus. Haubenstock, Chopin), Dutch National Ballet, Amsterdam

1979   *Life* (with van Schayk; mus. Ives, de Victoria, Bowie),

Rudi van Dantzig's *Bend or Break*, performed by the Dutch National Ballet, Amsterdam, 1987

Dutch National Ballet, Amsterdam

Ulysses (mus. Raubenstock-Ramati), Vienna State Opera Ballet, Vienna

Voorbijgegaan (*Passed By*; mus. Chopin), Dutch National Ballet, Amsterdam

1980   *Antwoord gevend* (*Answering*; mus. Webern), Dutch National Ballet, Amsterdam

1981   *Onder mijne Voeten* (*Under my Feet*; mus. Schat), Dutch National Ballet, Amsterdam

1982   *Room at the Top* (mus. Berg), Dutch National Ballet, Amsterdam

1983   *Niemandsland* (*No Man's Land*; mus. Smit), Dutch National Ballet, Amsterdam

Ik hou gewoon mijn Adem in (*I Just Hold my Breath*; mus. Tarenskeen, van den Eyden, Strategier), Dutch National Ballet, Amsterdam

De Lof der Zotheid (*In Praise of Folly*; mus. Sibelius, Stravinsky, Eno), Dutch National Ballet, Amsterdam

1984   *Autumn Haze* (mus. Barber), National Ballet School of Canada, Toronto

Petits Pas pour petits rats (mus. Haydn), Nel-Roos Ballet Academy, Amsterdam

1985   *Want wij weten niet wat wij doen* (*For we do not know what we are doing*; mus. Meijering, Haydn, Purcell, Ivanovitchi, from the film *Best Boy*), Dutch National Ballet, Amsterdam

1986   *Afzien* (*Renounce*; mus. Bach), Dutch National Ballet, Amsterdam

1987   *Buigen of Barsten* (*Bend or Break*; mus. Meijering), Dutch National Ballet, Amsterdam

Sans armes, citoyens! (mus. Berlioz), Paris Opéra Ballet, Paris

1990   *Aartsengelen slachten de hemel rood* (*Archangels Butcher the Heavens Red*; mus. Kancheli), Dutch National Ballet, Amsterdam

Also staged:

1988   *Swan Lake* (after Petipa, Ivanov; mus. Tchaikovsky), Dutch National Ballet, Amsterdam

PUBLICATIONS

By van Dantzig:

Interview in *Dance and Dancers* (London), May 1966

Interview in Loney, Glenn, "Evolution of an Ensemble: Rudi van Dantzig on the National Ballet of Holland", *Dance Magazine* (New York), March 1974

Interview in "Democratic Direction", *Dance and Dancers* (London), September 1974

Ballet and Modern Dance, 1975

Nureyev: A Biography, 1975

The Cry of the Firebird, 1977

Olga de Haas; een herinnering, Amsterdam, 1981

Voor een Verloren Soldaat (novel), Amsterdam, 1986; as *For a Lost Soldier*, London, 1991

Interview in van Schaik, Eva, "Rudi van Dantzig", *Ballett International* (Cologne), November 1989

About van Dantzig:

Barnes, Clive, "Those Two Dutch Masters", *The New York Times* (New York), 2 August 1966

Dodd, Craig, "Keeping the Wrong Company", *Dancing Times* (London), January 1970

Goodwin, Noël, and Williams, Peter, "Two Rudis", *Dance and Dancers* (London), February 1970

Goodwin, Noël, "Rudi van Dantzig", *About the House* (London), March 1970

Niehaus, Max, *Ballett Faszination*, Munich, 1972

Villaruz, Basilio, "Emerging Europeans", *Eddy* (New York), Winter Solstice, 1974

"Farewell to a Choreographer", *Dance and Dancers* (London), June/July 1991

*   *   *

From his first choreography as a young dancer barely in his twenties, Rudi van Dantzig has been inspired by the moral struggle in human life between good and evil. His *Nachteiland* (*Night Island*), made in 1955, can be seen as the basis from which all his ballets were developed. Its theme was the purity of youth and the loss of innocence when it is confronted by a grown-up darker world. That theme, along with the everlasting hope that mankind can learn and find a way to create a better, peaceful world, is always present in van Dantzig's ballets, although it has been given different accents.

In *Onder mijne Voeten* (*Under my Feet*, a phrase from a children's song) and in *Wij weten niet wat wij doen* (*For we do not know what we are doing*), it is the individual who is crushed in the effort to escape the destructive power of a society governed by egoism, lust for power, and lack of tolerance. In *Life*, *Geverfde Vogels* (*Coloured Birds*), and *Buigen of Barsten* (*Bend or Break*), Van Dantzig wants to show us that not only the powerless suffer under tyranny and from the aggressive pursuit of gain; the world itself, an ever-growing consumer society, is left bereft as it drains its natural sources. In most of these works, a strict story line is never followed; rather, the ballets contain fragments of distinct anecdotal nature to state their theme.

Several of van Dantzig's works, like *Monument voor een Gestorven Jongen* (*Monument for a Dead Boy*) and *Gesänge der Jünglinge* (*Songs of the Youngsters*), refer boldly to homosexual relations and society's reactions to them. At the same time, alongside these highly dramatic ballets van Dantzig has made several abstract and poetic ballets; however, though plotless they are often full of melancholy and sadness, as in *Ramifications*, *Voorbijgegaan* (*Passed By*), and *Vier Letzte Lieder* (*Four Last Songs*), considered by many to be his masterpiece.

Van Dantzig uses a dance language that blends classical technique with elements from Graham-based modern dance. His movements often have an explosive emotional content, expressed, for example, by contracted bodies and a strong, complex use of reaching arms. He has a special talent for using large groups of people, moving quickly in different unexpected space patterns. Van Dantzig regularly uses music by Dutch composers such as Henk Badings, Lex van Delden, Ton de Leeuw, Peter Schat, and Chiel Meijering, and he is often inspired by poems. Phrases from poetry are often chosen for the titles of his ballets, or serve as epigrams for his programme notes.

Van Dantzig has staged two full-length ballets: *Romeo en Julia*, created in 1967, and revived and reworked several times since, and *Het Zwanenmeer* (*Swan Lake*) in 1988, based on the original Petipa/Ivanov version but with many personal inventions. Nearly all his ballets have been designed and costumed by Toer van Schayk.

Rudi van Dantzig was the first choreographer to offer Rudolf Nureyev a "modern" dance role, that of the lead in *Monument for a Dead Boy*. He also created three new ballets for Nureyev: *The Ropes of Time*, *Blown in a Gentle Wind*, and *About a Dark House*. Several of his works have been taken into the repertoire of foreign companies.

Apart from being a company director and choreographer of note, Rudi van Dantzig has presented himself as an author of impressive range. In 1986 his first novel *Voor een Verloren Soldaat* (*For a Lost Soldier*) was published and honoured with two literary awards. In its autobiographal story can be found the source of the main themes of his choreography.

—Ine Rietstap

————————

VANGSAAE, Mona

Danish dancer, choreographer, and teacher. Born in Copenhagen, 29 April 1920. Studied at the Royal Danish Ballet School, pupil of Valborg Borchsenius and Harald Lander, from 1926; later studied in Paris and London. Married dancer Frank Schaufuss (div.): son, dancer and ballet director Peter Schaufuss (b. 1949). Début as child in *The Whims of Cupid and the Ballet Master*, 1927; dancer, Royal Danish Ballet, from 1938, becoming solo dancer (principal), 1942–62; début as choreographer for Royal Danish Ballet with *Spectrum*, 1958; guest artist, National Ballet of Canada, 1968; co-founder and co-director, with Frank Schaufuss, Danish Ballet Academy, Copenhagen, with affiliated performing group, Danish Ballet Theatre, 1969–74; international guest teacher, including for Royal Ballet School, London, 1982–83. Recipient: Knight of Dannebrog. Died in Copenhagen, 17 May 1983.

ROLES

1938   The Street Dancer in *Petrushka* (Fokine), Royal Danish Ballet, Copenhagen

Imprisoned woman in *Polovtsian Dances from Prince Igor* (Lander after Fokine), Royal Danish Ballet, Copenhagen

Ethics (cr) in *The Circle* (Theilade), Royal Danish Ballet, Copenhagen

Dancer in *Les Sylphides* (Fokine), Royal Danish Ballet, Copenhagen

Valkyrie and Greek Woman in *The Valkyrie* (Bournonville), Royal Danish Ballet, Copenhagen

One of the Three Graces (cr) in *Thorvaldsen* (Lander), Royal Danish Ballet, Copenhagen

1939   Sylph (Act II) in *La Sylphide* (Bournonville), Royal Danish Ballet, Copenhagen

Amalie in *H. C. Lumbye—Fantasies* (Walbom, Lander), Royal Danish Ballet, Copenhagen

1940   Adagio-bride in *The Widow in the Mirror* (Ralov), Royal Danish Ballet, Copenhagen

Muse in *Psyche* (Theilade), Royal Danish Ballet, Copenhagen

Friendly Wave in *The Sorcerer's Apprentice* (Lander), Royal Danish Ballet, Copenhagen

Waltz in *Swan Lake* (Lander after Petipa, Ivanov), Royal Danish Ballet, Copenhagen

Girl in *The Four Temperaments* (Ralov), Royal Danish Ballet, Copenhagen

1941 Soloist in *Konservatoriet* (Bournonville), Royal Danish Ballet, Copenhagen

Soloist in *Napoli* (Bournonville), Royal Danish Ballet, Copenhagen

1942 Fairy (cr) in *The Land of Milk and Honey* (Lander), Royal Danish Ballet, Copenhagen

Young Woman in *Qarrtsiluni* (Lander), Royal Danish Ballet, Copenhagen

Amelie in *Visions* (Walbom), Royal Danish Ballet, Copenhagen

Pas de deux in *Festival Polonaise* (Lander), Royal Danish Ballet, Copenhagen

Sunbeam and Elf in *Spring* (Lander), Royal Danish Ballet, Copenhagen

1944 Title role in *Spring* (Lander), Royal Danish Ballet, Copenhagen

The Lonely One (cr) in *Passiones* (Ralov), Royal Danish Ballet, Copenhagen

The Woman in *Bolero* (Lander), Royal Danish Ballet, Copenhagen

Mrs. June in *Twelve by the Post* (Ralov), The Royal Danish Ballet, Copenhagen

1945 The Woman in the Dream (cr) in *Quasi una fantasia* (Lander), Royal Danish Ballet, Copenhagen

Czardas in *Coppélia* (Lander after Saint-Léon), Royal Danish Ballet, Copenhagen

1946 Hope in *The Phoenix* (Lander), Royal Danish Ballet, Copenhagen

Myrtha in *Giselle* (Petipa after Coralli, Perrot; staged Volinin), Royal Danish Ballet, Copenhagen

Elisa in *Konservatoriet* (Bournonville), Royal Danish Ballet, Copenhagen

Venus in *Maskarade* (opera; mus. Nielsen, chor. Beck), Royal Danish Ballet, Copenhagen

Genius of the Waltz in *La Valse* (Lander), Royal Danish Ballet, Copenhagen

1947 Sophie in *The Lifeguards on Amager* (Bournonville), Royal Danish Ballet, Copenhagen

1948 The Second Broom in *The Sorcerer's Apprentice* (Lander), Royal Danish Ballet, Copenhagen

Pas de six in *Napoli* (Bournonville), Royal Danish Ballet, Copenhagen

Street Dancer in *Le Beau Danube* (Massine), Royal Danish Ballet, Copenhagen

The Lover in *Episode of an Artist's Life* (*Symphonie fantastique*; Massine), Royal Danish Ballet, Copenhagen

Diana (cr) in *Sylvia* (Larsen), Royal Danish Ballet, Copenhagen

1949 Fandango and *Flower Festival* Pas de deux in *Salute to August Bournonville* (Lander after Bournville), Royal Danish Ballet, Copenhagen

The Bluebird Pas de deux and Pas de trois in *Aurora's Wedding* (From *The Sleeping Beauty*; Brenaa after Petipa), Royal Danish Ballet, Copenhagen

1950 Princess Aurora in *Aurora's Wedding* (from *The Sleeping Beauty*; Brenaa after Petipa), Royal Danish Ballet, Copenhagen

Teresina in *Napoli* (Bournonville), Royal Danish Ballet,

Mona Vangsaae rehearsing Birgit Keil in *La Sylphide*, Stuttgart Ballet, c.1982

Copenhagen

Woman (cr) in *Metaphor* (Theilade), Royal Danish Ballet, Copenhagen

Odette in *Swan Lake* (Lander after Petipa, Ivanov), Royal Danish Ballet, Copenhagen

Juliet (cr) in *Romeo and Juliet* (Bartholin), Royal Danish Ballet, Copenhagen

1951 Nocturne and Waltz in *Chopiniana* (*Les Sylphides*; Bartholin after Fokine), Royal Danish Ballet, Copenhagen

Pas de deux in *The Kermesse in Bruges* (Bournonville), Royal Danish Ballet, Copenhagen

1952 Young Girl (cr) in *Desire* (Larsen), Royal Danish Ballet, Copenhagen

Dancer in *Designs with Strings* (Taras), Royal Danish Ballet, Copenhagen

Second Junior Girl in *Graduation Ball* (Lichine), Royal Danish Ballet, Copenhagen

Second Movement in *Symphony in C* (Balanchine), Royal Danish Ballet, Copenhagen

Pothos (cr) in *Idolon* (Schaufuss), Royal Danish Ballet, Copenhagen

1954 Najade (cr) in *Capricious Lucinda* (Larsen), Royal Danish Ballet, Copenhagen

Black Swan (Odile) in *Black Swan Pas de deux* (Bruhn after Petipa), Royal Danish Ballet, Copenhagen

1955 Coquette in *Night Shadow* (*La Sonnambula*; Balanchine), Royal Danish Ballet, Copenhagen

Juliet (cr) in *Romeo and Juliet* (Ashton), Royal Danish Ballet, Copenhagen

Marie Taglioni in *Pas de quatre* (Dolin), Royal Danish Ballet, Copenhagen

1956   Persephone (cr) in *Myth* (Hansen), Royal Danish Ballet, Copenhagen

Señorita in *La Ventana* (Bournonville), Royal Danish Ballet, Copenhagen

1957   Soloist in *Serenade* (Balanchine), Royal Danish Ballet, Copenhagen

The Mother (cr) in *Vision* (Larsen), Royal Danish Ballet, Copenhagen

Aili (cr) in *Moon Reindeer* (Cullberg), Royal Danish Ballet, Copenhagen

Soloist in *Le Quatre Stagioni* (Skov), Charlottenborg, Copenhagen

1958   First Movement in *La Jeunesse* (Bartholin), Royal Danish Ballet, Copenhagen

Quaker in *The Whims of Cupid and the Ballet Master* (Galeotti), Royal Danish Ballet, Copenhagen

Columbine in *Harlequinade* (*Les Millions d'Arlequin*; Walbom after Petipa), Royal Danish Ballet, Copenhagen

Maria Theresia (cr) in *A Note Page* (also chor.), Charlottenborg, Copenhagen

1959   Title role in *Miss Julie* (Cullberg), Royal Danish Ballet, Copenhagen

Pas de deux in *As You Like It* (play by Shakespeare; chor. Schaufuss), Royal Danish Ballet on tour, Maribo

1960   The Princess (cr) in *The Shadow* (Bartholin), Royal Danish Ballet, Copenhagen

Gypsy dance in *Once Upon a Time* (play by Drachman; chor. Schaufuss), Royal Danish Ballet on tour, Maribo

1961   Dance for the Joy of Life in *The Little Mermaid* (Beck, Brenaa) Royal Danish Ballet, Copenhagen

1964   Fish (cr) in *Tobias and the Angel* (Bartholin), Danish television

1966   Psyche's sister in *Psyche* (Theilade), TV-ballet, Danish television

1968   Pas de deux from *Flower Festival at Genzano* (Bournonville), National Ballet of Canada, Toronto

Other roles include: title role in *Giselle* (after Petipa, Coralli, Perrot).

WORKS

1958   *Spectrum* (mus. Scriabin), Royal Danish Ballet, Copenhagen

A Note Page (mus. Mozart), Charlottemborg, Copenhagen

Also staged:
1971   *A Napoli Divertissement* (after Bournonville; mus. Paulli, Helsted, Gade, Lumbye), London Festival Ballet, London

1973   *Conservatoire* (*Konservatoriet*; after Bournonville; mus. arranged Paulli), London Festival Ballet, London

1982   *La Sylphide* (with Peter Schaufuss, after Bournonville; mus. Løvenskjold), Stuttgart Ballet, Stuttgart (also staged German Opera Ballet, Berlin, 1982)

PUBLICATIONS

Kragh-Jacobsen, Svend, and Krugh, Torben, *Den Kongelige Danske Ballet*, Copenhagen, 1952

"Peter Schaufuss: Far from Denmark", *Dance Magazine* (New York), September 1974

Vaughan, David, *Frederick Ashton and His Ballets*, London, 1977

*   *   *

Although Mona Vangsaae retired from the Royal Danish Ballet in 1962, she actually gave the last performance of her career five years later. Her son, Peter Schaufuss, then with the National Ballet of Canada, partnered her in the Pas de deux from August Bournonville's *Flower Festival at Genzano*.

Like her Royal Danish Ballet contemporaries Kirsten Ralov and Margrethe Schanne, Vangsaae was outstanding in the technical intricacies of the Bournonville repertoire. She brought great buoyancy and sparkle to ballets like his *Konservatoriet*, *La Ventana*, *Napoli*, and *The Kermesse in Bruges*. At the same time her arms and head were used with the utmost calm and delicacy. Despite this technical command, she approached each characterization with an endearing naturalness, as though batterie were as simple as a smile.

To a greater degree than Ralov and Schanne, Mona Vangsaae also displayed exceptional range beyond the Bournonville repertoire. The guest choreographers who were invited to expand the Royal Danish repertoire in the 1950s enjoyed setting new roles on her. When Sir Frederick Ashton created his *Romeo and Juliet* in 1955, it was Vangsaae whom he chose as Juliet. Ashton's ballet was not only an exquisite realization of the Prokofiev score; it also remained close to the atmosphere of Shakespeare's verse, conveying passion along with the gentle reticence characteristic of the British temperament and certainly characteristic of Ashton. Vangsaae gave herself to these qualities so completely that at times her Juliet seemed almost translucent in its poetic awareness.

In 1957, Swedish choreographer Birgit Cullberg was invited to Denmark to set her *Moon Reindeer*. She, too, selected Mona Vangsaae to portray her leading character, this time the mysteriously touching Girl Reindeer. Nine years earlier, a role vividly associated with the Russian–American ballerina Alexandra Danilova had also become Vangsaae's. It was the vivacious and seductive Street Dancer in Léonide Massine's *Le Beau Danube*.

During her career, the Royal Danish Ballet did not yet have a strong repertoire of ballets by George Balanchine. But Mona Vangsaae did perform the Coquette in *La Sonnambula*, and she was a soloist in *Serenade*.

In the romantic repertoire, ballerinas noted for their portrayal of the gentle peasant girl Giselle are not usually associated with the imperious Myrtha, Queen of the Wilis. Mona Vangsaae, however, danced both with distinction. This was also true of her melancholy Odette and her malevolent Odile in the Petipa–Ivanov *Swan Lake*.

When she retired, Vangsaae turned with great success to coaching and to teaching the Bournonville technique. At the time of her death, she was also about to open a private studio with her former husband, Frank Schaufuss.

—Doris Hering

VAN HAMEL, Martine

Dutch dancer, choreographer, and ballet director. Born in Brussels, 16 November 1945. Studied with Edith Dam in Copenhagen, from 1949, Henry Danton in Caracas, Venezuela, 1955–58, and at the National Ballet School of Canada, pupil of

Betty Oliphant, Toronto, 1958–62; has also studied with Maggie Black, New York. Soloist, National Ballet of Canada, Toronto, 1963–65, becoming principal dancer, from 1965; soloist, Joffrey Ballet, New York, 1970; dancer, corps de ballet, American Ballet Theatre, New York, 1970, becoming soloist, from 1971, and principal dancer, from 1973; international guest artist, including with Ballet Nacional de Cuba in Havana, Pennsylvania Ballet, and Royal Swedish Ballet; principal dancer, Netherlands Dance Theatre 3, 1992–93; début as choreographer, Jacob's Pillow Festival, Massachusetts, 1976, staging new work for American Ballet Theatre, 1984; also director and choreographer for own company, New Amsterdam Ballet, from 1984; has also appeared on national television, including Public Broadcasting Service (PBS) "Dance in America" series, and "Live from Lincoln Center", and on film, including in *The Turning Point* (dir. Ross, 1977). Recipient: Gold Medal and Prix de Varna, International Ballet Competition in Varna, Bulgaria, 1966; *Cue* Magazine Award, New York, 1976; *Dance Magazine* Award, 1983; Dance Educators of America Award, 1983.

ROLES

1962 Sugar Plum Fairy in *The Nutcracker* (after Ivanov), National Ballet of Canada, Toronto

1963 Myrtha in *Giselle* (Petipa after Coralli, Perrot; staged Franca), National Ballet of Canada, Toronto

1966 The Girl in *Solitaire* (excerpt; MacMillan), International Ballet Competition, Varna, Bulgaria

1966/ The Sylph in *La Sylphide* (Bruhn after Bournonville),
67   National Ballet of Canada, Toronto
      Odette/Odile in *Swan Lake* (Bruhn after Petipa, Ivanov), National Ballet of Canada, Toronto

1971 The Nurse in *Romeo and Juliet* (Tudor), American Ballet Theatre, New York
      Principal dancer in *Octageny* (Nahat), American Ballet Theatre, New York
      The Ballerina in *Theme and Variations* (Balanchine), American Ballet Theatre

1972 Principal dancer (cr) in *Some Times* (Nahat), American Ballet Theatre, New York

1973 Odette/Odile in *Swan Lake* (Blair after Petipa, Ivanov), American Ballet Theatre

1974 Solo Shadow (cr) in "Kingdom of the Shades" from *La Bayadère* (new production; Makarova after Petipa), American Ballet Theatre, New York
      Nikiya in "Kingdom of the Shades" from *La Bayadère* (Makarova after Petipa), American Ballet Theatre, New York
      Calliope in *Apollo* (Balanchine), American Ballet Theatre, New York

1975 Principal dancer in *Gemini* (Tetley), American Ballet Theatre, New York
      Clemence in *Raymonda* (Nureyev after Petipa), American Ballet Theatre, Houston
      The Girl in *Solitaire* (excerpts; MacMillan), American Ballet Theatre, Washington, D.C.

1976 Principal dancer (cr) in *Push Comes to Shove* (Tharp), American Ballet Theatre, New York
      Destino in *Carmen* (Alonso), American Ballet Theatre, New York
      Principal dancer in *Le Sacre du Printemps* (Tetley), American Ballet Theatre, New York
      Lilac Fairy in *The Sleeping Beauty* (Petipa; staged Skeaping), American Ballet Theatre, New York

Princess Aurora in *The Sleeping Beauty* (Petipa; staged Skeaping), American Ballet Theatre
      Ballerina in *Raymonda Variations* (Balanchine), Pennsylvania Ballet, New York

1976/ Mazurka in *Les Sylphides* (Fokine), American Ballet
77   Theatre, New York
      Swanilda in *Coppélia* (Martinez after Saint-Léon), American Ballet Theatre, New York
      Title role in *Giselle* (Petipa after Coralli, Perrot; staged Blair), American Ballet Theatre, New York

1977 Principal dancer in *Voluntaries* (Tetley), American Ballet Theatre, Cleveland, Ohio
      Title role (cr) in *Sphinx* (Tetley), American Ballet Theatre, Washington, D.C.

1979 Title role in *Firebird* (Fokine), American Ballet Theatre, New York

1980 Gamzatti (cr) in *La Bayadère* (new production; Makarova after Petipa), American Ballet Theatre, New York
      Nikiya in *La Bayadère* (new production; Makarova after Petipa), American Ballet Theatre, New York
      Desdemona in *The Moor's Pavane* (Limón), American Ballet Theatre
      The Siren in *The Prodigal Son* (Balanchine; staged Taras), American Ballet Theatre

1981 Principal dancer in *Configurations* (San Goh), American Ballet Theatre, Washington, D.C.
      Bourrée fantasque in *Bourrée fantasque* (Balanchine), American Ballet Theatre, Washington, D.C.

1982 Principal dancer in *Torso* (pas de deux; Kylián), American Ballet Theatre, San Francisco

1983 Viola in *Symphonie Concertante* (Balanchine), American Ballet Theatre, Washington, D.C.
      Principal dancer (cr) in *Estuary* (Taylor-Corbett), American Ballet Theatre, Miami

1984 Title role in *Paquita* (Makarova after Petipa), American Ballet Theatre
      Principal dancer in *Sylvia Pas de deux* (Balanchine), American Ballet Theatre
      Bathsheba (cr) in *Amnon V'Tamar* (also chor.), American Ballet Theatre, Miami
      Principal dancer (cr) in *Bach Partita* (Tharp), American Ballet Theatre, New York
      Ballerina (cr) in *Field, Chair and Mountain* (Gordon), American Ballet Theatre, Washington, D.C.
      Principal dancer (cr) in *Odalisque* (solo; Tetley), National Ballet of Canada School Gala, Toronto

1985 Title role in *Anastasia* (MacMillan), American Ballet Theatre, Los Angeles

1986 Principal dancer (cr) in *Walk this Way* (pas de deux; Parsons), American Ballet Theatre, Washington, D.C.

1988 First Aria in *Stravinsky Violin Concerto* (Balanchine), American Ballet Theatre, New York
      La Reine de la danse from Moscow in *Gala Performance* (Tudor), American Ballet Theatre
      Principal dancer (cr) in *Drink to Me Only with Thine eyes* (Morris), American Ballet Theatre, New York

1989 Pioneering Woman in *Appalachian Spring* (Graham), "In the American Grain" Gala, American Ballet Theatre and Martha Graham Company, New York
      Principal dancer in *Birthday Offering* (Ashton), American Ballet Theatre, New York

1990 Principal dancer in *Nine Sinatra Songs* (Tharp), American Ballet Theatre

1991 The Accused in *Fall River Legend* (de Mille), American Ballet Theatre, New York

Martine van Hamel as Nikiya in *La Bayadère*

1992/ Principal dancer in *Made in France* (Marin), Nether-
93   lands Dance Theatre 3, tour
        Principal dancer in *No Sleep till Dawn of Day* (Kylián),
        Netherlands Dance Theatre 3, tour
        Principal dancer in *Journey* (M. Ek), Netherlands
        Dance Theatre 3, tour

Other roles include: Pas de deux from *Le Corsaire* (Nureyev after Petipa), First and Second Song in *Dark Elegies* (Tudor), Kitri in *Don Quixote: Kitri's Wedding* (Baryshnikov after Petipa), principal dancer in *Études* (Lander), principal dancer in *The Garden of Villandry* (Martha Clarke), an Episode in His Past in *Jardin aux lilas* (Tudor), Solo Variation, "Grand Pas Hongrois" in *Raymonda* (Nureyev after Petipa), title role in *Miss Julie* (Cullberg), Lady Capulet in *Romeo and Juliet* (MacMillan).

WORKS

1976 *Trio à deux* (mus. Beethoven), Jacob's Pillow Festival, Massachusetts
1984 *Chansons Madecasses* (mus. Ravel), New Amsterdam Ballet, Santa Fe, New Mexico
      Amnon V'Tamar (mus. Calusdian), American Ballet Theatre, Miami
1991 *Water Nymph* (mus. Schoenberg), New Amsterdam Ballet
1992 *Elements* (mus. Bach), Milwaukee Ballet

PUBLICATIONS

By van Hamel:
Interview in Lyle, Cynthia, *Dancers on Dancing*, New York, 1977

About van Hamel:
Goodman, Saul, "Martine van Hamel", *Dance Magazine* (New York), February 1969
Tobias, Tobi, "Martine van Hamel", *Dance Magazine* (New York), October 1975
Greskovic, Robert, "Dancers at a Gathering", *Ballet Review* (Brooklyn, N.Y.), vol. 5, no. 1, 1975–76
Croce, Arlene, *Afterimages*, New York, 1977
Croce, Arlene, *Going to the Dance*, New York, 1982
Reiter, Susan, "Going Strong", *Ballet News* (New York), May 1984
Jowitt, Deborah, *The Dance in Mind*, New York, 1985
Croce, Arlene, *Sightlines*, New York, 1987
Tharp, Twyla, *Push Comes to Shove*, New York, 1992

*   *   *

Dutch ballerina Martine van Hamel came to prominence in America in an era when the thin, leggy ballerina was the accepted ideal, when ballet students starved themselves to look like Suzanne Farrell or Gelsey Kirkland, and when much contemporary choreography, following the lead of the great neo-classicist George Balanchine, made use of the female body as an abstract slender line instead of as a curved or rounded form. Van Hamel, at 5'7", is no frail sylph. Her body shape is more voluptuous than twiggy, her ribcage is large, and her stance is firm. In van Hamel's case, however, these are not shortcomings to conquer: rather, they are assets which the dancer has turned to her great advantage, earning such epithets

as "majestic", "commanding", "powerful", and "statuesque" whenever she performs.

Van Hamel's rise to fame, again rather unlike that of baby ballerinas Kirkland or Farrell, was relatively slow and not without its frustrations. Having established herself as a leading principal dancer with the National Ballet of Canada, where she performed as the Sugar Plum Fairy, Odette/Odile, and Myrtha in *Giselle* (later to become a signature role), van Hamel was forced to go backwards when she came to the United States to widen her career prospects. She was taken on as a soloist at the Joffrey Ballet, and then soon afterwards was offered only a corps de ballet contract with American Ballet Theatre (and this after having won the gold medal at the Varna International Ballet Competition).

Slowly, however, van Hamel won the attention of critics and audiences alike, and began her steady ascent to the position of ballerina. American Ballet Theatre choreographer Dennis Nahat picked out van Hamel for the cast of two of his ballets in the early 1970s, and then in 1973 van Hamel was given the chance to perform the double lead of Odette/Odile in *Swan Lake*. Her triumph in this was virtually undisputed, and since then she has established herself as one of the finest modern exponents of the nineteenth-century classical style. She has performed the ballerina role in just about every full-length classic at American Ballet Theatre, from tragic-romantic to showy bravura, and critics have bestowed on her the honour— rare outside Russia—of being called exemplar and protector of the pure Petipa style. Her technique is clean and precise, and her strength is at times awe-inspiring; yet she is no simple virtuoso, and her capacity for delicate lyricism and grace is remarkable. Her use of port de bras is particularly rich and expressive, and her upper body, reminiscent of ballerinas trained in the best Kirov tradition, moves in harmony with, rather than apart from, the rest of her body.

In the role of Nikiya—arguably one of her best roles—van Hamel has repeatedly been praised for her "majestic" and "grand-scale classicism" (Lewis Segal), "resplendent form" (Clive Barnes), and "magnificent performance" (Arlene Croce). "Martine van Hamel made of Nikiya the purest emblem of classical ballet," wrote Jennifer Dunning of *The New York Times* in 1987, "stated from her first movements on stage, through her expressive upper torso and sheer physical eloquence, and in dancing notable for its clarity, powerful simplicity and musicality." Perhaps more important than this, Dunning discerned the inner power of the ballerina's interpretations, pointing to the "cool white heat" which makes van Hamel's dancing what it is.

Besides her success in the classical roles, van Hamel has made use of her gifts as a dramatic dancer in the modern repertoire, particularly in the ballets of Antony Tudor. She has danced in Tudor's *Jardin aux lilas* and *Dark Elegies* and in Birgit Cullberg's 1950 classic, *Miss Julie*, and recently as "The Accused" in the revival of Agnes de Mille's compellingly ghoulish melodrama about Lizzie Borden, *Fall River Legend*. She is also at home in contemporary choreography, having won notice early on in works by Glen Tetley (she created the title role of his *Sphinx* in 1977), as well as in the offbeat Twyla Tharp 1976 classic, *Push Comes to Shove*. Indeed, in her autobiography, Tharp pays tribute to van Hamel's role in this ballet with a description that could be said to sum up the ballerina's best qualities: "She was a gloriously expansive and still very feminine beauty, extraordinarily strong on pointe and capable of enveloping space in a way that ordinarily requires a masculine drive."

As perhaps the final testament to her versatility, van Hamel has tackled Balanchine, showing an instinctive sensitivity to a style which one would not automatically assume would come naturally to her. Again, critic Jennifer Dunning pointed out astutely that while the ballerina was "capable, in other roles, of limpid delicacy and musicality", she was able to dance Balanchine's *Stravinsky Violin Concerto* "with a fierce and biting attack". "Like Balanchine", wrote this critic, "Miss van Hamel demonstrates ... the intensity and complexity of passion that can be generated by sheer movement."

Now in her forties, van Hamel shows no sign of diminishing strength or artistry. She has ventured into choreography and artistic direction, running a small concert group by the name of New Amsterdam Ballet, and making various guest appearances on tour. A divine goddess on stage, and a straightforward, utterly unfussy personality off the stage, Martine van Hamel remains one of America's most popular ballerinas.

—Virginia Christian

VAN MANEN, Hans

Dutch dancer, choreographer, and ballet director. Born in Nieuwer Amstel, the Netherlands, 11 July 1932. Studied with Sonia Gaskell, Françoise Adret, and Nora Kiss, from 1951. Dancer, Sonia Gaskell's Ballet Recital, 1951, Amsterdam Opera Ballet, 1952–58, and Roland Petit's Ballets de Paris, 1959; dancer and choreographer, Nederlands Dans Theater (Netherlands Dance Theatre), from 1960, becoming joint artistic director, 1961–70, first with Benjamin Harkavy, later with Glen Tetley; resigned from Nederlands Dans Theater, becoming freelance choreographer from 1970, including for Stuttgart Ballet and Royal Ballet, London; choreographer and ballet master, Dutch National Ballet, from 1973; also professional photographer, with exhibitions including *Dance Has Many Faces* (Nederlands Theater Institut, Amsterdam, and Centre Pompidou, Paris, 1985). Recipient: Officer of the Orde van Oranje Nassau, 1969; Dutch Theatre Critics' Prize, 1974 and 1991; Hendrik-Jan-Reinink Medal, 1976; Sonia Gaskell Prize in Choreography, 1991.

WORKS

1956 *Swing* (mus. Kenton, arranged de Hass), Scapino Ballet, Amsterdam

1957 *Feestgericht* (mus. Ponse), Amsterdam Opera Ballet, Amsterdam

1958 *Pastorale d'été* (mus. Honegger), Amsterdam Opera Ballet, Amsterdam

Mouvements symphoniques (mus. Haydn), Amsterdam Opera Ballet, Amsterdam

1959 *De Maan in de Trapeze* (mus. Britten), Nederlands Dans Theater, Ostend

1960 *Klaar af* (mus. Ellington), Nederlands Dans Theater, Etten

1961 *Concertino* (mus. Blacher), Nederlands Dans Theater, Scheveningen

Kain en Abel (mus. Jacobs, Martini), Nederlands Dans Theater, Hilversum

1962 *Eurydice* (mus. Frid), Nederlands Dans Theater, Amsterdam

Voet bij stuk (mus. Brubeck), Nederlands Dans Theater, The Hague

1963 *Symphony in Three Movements* (mus. Stravinsky), Nederlands Dans Theater, The Hague

1964 *Omnibus* (mus. Sauter, Getz, Sibelius), Nederlands Dans Theater, Amsterdam

Opus 12 (mus. Bartók), Nederlands Dans Theater, The Hague

1965 *Repetitie* (mus. Andriessen), Nederlands Dans Theater, The Hague

Essay in der Stille (mus. Messaien), Nederlands Dans Theater, The Hague

Metaforen (mus. Lesur), Nederlands Dans Theater, The Hague

1966 *Terugblik op Morgen* (mus. Barraud), Nederlands Dans Theater, Amsterdam

Point of No Return (mus. Pijper, Stockhausen, Henry), Nederlands Dans Theater, The Hague

Vij Schetsen (*Five Sketches*; mus. Hindemith), Nederlands Dans Theater, The Hague

1967 *Ready Made* (mus. various popular), Nederlands Dans Theater, The Hague

Dualis (mus. Bartók), Nederland Dans Theater, Scheveningen

1968 *Untitled* (mus. Lutoslawski), Nederlands Dans Theater, Amsterdam

Variomatic (mus. Berkeley), Nederlands Dans Theater, The Hague

Three Pieces (mus. Bacewicz), Nederlands Dans Theater, The Hague

Solo for Voice 1 (mus. Cage), Nederlands Dans Theater, Scheveningen

1969 *Squares* (mus. Satie), Nederlands Dans Theater, Paris

1970 *Situation* (mus. sound-collage), Nederlands Dans Theater, Scheveningen

Mutations (with Tetley; mus. Stockhausen), Nederlands Dans Theater, Scheveningen

Snippers (mus. Riley), Scapino Ballet, Amsterdam

Twice (mus. popular), Nederlands Dans Theater, London

1971 *Grosse Fuge* (mus. Beethoven), Nederlands Dans Theater, Scheveningen

Keep Going (mus. Berio), German Opera on the Rhine, Düsseldorf

Ajaka-Boembie (mus. Chopin), Scapino Ballet, The Hague

1972 *Tilt* (mus. Stravinsky), Nederlands Dans Theater, Scheveningen

Twighlight (mus. Cage), Dutch National Ballet, Rotterdam

Opus Lemaitre (mus. Bach), Nederlands Dans Theater, Paris

Daphnis und Chloe (mus. Ravel), Dutch National Ballet, Amsterdam

1973 *Septet Extra* (mus. Saint-Saens), Nederlands Dans Theater, Scheveningen

Adagio Hammerklavier (mus. Beethoven), Dutch National Ballet, Amsterdam

Assortimento (mus. Debussy), Scapino Ballet, Amsterdam

1974 *Le Sacre du printemps* (mus. Stravinsky), Dutch National Ballet, Amsterdam

Kwintet (mus. Mozart), Dutch National Ballet, Amsterdam

1975 *Four Schumann Pieces* (mus. Schumann), Royal Ballet, London

Noble et sentimentale (mus. Ravel), Nederlands Dans Theater, Amsterdam

Collective Symphony (with van Dantzig and van Schayk; mus. Stravinsky), Dutch National Ballet, Amsterdam

1976 *Ebony Concerto and Tango* (mus. Stravinsky), Dutch National Ballet, Amsterdam

Hans van Manen rehearsing Richard Cragun and Marcia Haydée in *Twilight*, **Stuttgart, 1972**

1977 *Octet Opus 20* (mus. Mendelssohn), Dutch National Ballet, Amsterdam
      Lieder ohne Worte (*Songs Without Words*; mus. Mendelssohn), Nederlands Dans Theater, Scheveningen
      Five Tangos (mus. Piazzola), Dutch National Ballet, Amsterdam
1978 *Dumbarton Oaks* (mus. Stravinsky), Dutch National Ballet, Amsterdam
      Unisono (mus. Haydn), students of the Royal Conservatory, The Hague
      Grand Trio (mus. Schubert), Vienna State Opera Ballet, Vienna
1979 *Memories of the Body* (mus. various), Nederlands Dans Theater, Scheveningen
      Live (mus. Liszt), Dutch National Ballet, Amsterdam
      Concerto for Piano and Wind Instruments (mus. Stravinsky), Nederlands Dans Theater, Scheveningen
1980 *Einlage* (mus. J. Strauss jun.), Dutch National Ballet, Amsterdam
      Klavier Variationen I (mus. Bach, Dallapiccola), Dutch National Ballet, Amsterdam
1981 *Klavier Variationen II* (*Sarkasmen*) (mus. Prokofiev), Dutch National Ballet, Amsterdam

1982 *Five Short Stories* (mus. Stravinsky and others), Dutch National Ballet, Amsterdam
      Klavier Variationen III (*Trois Gnossienes,* part of *Five Short Stories*; mus. Satie), Dutch National Ballet, Amsterdam
      Klavier Variationen IV (*Pose*; mus. Debussy), Dutch National Ballet, Amsterdam
1983 *Portrait* (mus. Satie), Dansproduktie Rotterdam, performing in Amsterdam
      In and Out (mus. Anderson), Dutch National Ballet, Amsterdam
1984 *Klavier Variationen V* (*Exposed*; mus. Debussy), Dutch National Ballet, Amsterdam
      Bits and Pieces (mus. Byrne, Eno, Mendelssohn), Dutch National Ballet, Amsterdam
1985 *Ballet Scenes* (mus. Stravinsky), Nederlands Dans Theater, Scheveningen
      Corps (mus. Berg), Stuttgart Ballet, Stuttgart
1986 *In Concert* (mus. de Wit), Dansproduktie Rotterdam, performing in Utrecht
      Opening (mus. Hindemith), Dutch National Ballet, Amsterdam
      In the Future (mus. Byrne), Scapino Ballet, Amsterdam

1987 *Symphonieen der Nederlanden* (mus. Andriessen), Dutch
National Ballet, Amsterdam
Wet Desert (mus. Reich), NDT2, The Hague
Shaker Loops (mus. Adams), Stuttgart Ballet, Stuttgart
1988 *The Sound of Music* (mus. van Baaren, Schumann,
Mozart), Stuttgart Ballet and students of John Cranko
Balettschule, Stuttgart
Pas de Crackkkk (section of *The Sound of Music*; mus.
Schumann), Stuttgart Ballet, Stuttgart
1989 *Black Cake* (mus. various composers), Nederlands Dans
Theater, The Hague
Brainstorm (mus. Honneger), Nederlands Dans Theater,
The Hague
1990 *Visions Fugitives* (mus. Prokofiev), Nederlands Dans
Theater, The Hague
Intermezzo voor Musici en Dansers (mus. Verdi), Neder-
lands Dans Theater and Nederlands Balletorkest,
Amsterdam
Two (mus. Busoni), Nederlands Dans Theater, The
Hague
1991 *Theme* (part of *True Colour,* other sections chor. Daniels,
Brandsen, Post; mus. de Wit), Nationaal Fonds,
Haarlem
Andante (mus. Mozart), Nederlands Dans Theater, The
Hague
Evergreens (mus. Saint-Saens, Peyronnin, Villa-Lobos),
NDT3, The Hague

PUBLICATIONS

By van Manen:
Interview in *Dance and Dancers* (London), May 1967
"Attitude Becomes Form", *Dance and Dancers* (London), June
1969
Interview in Koegler, Horst, "Hans van Manen", *Ballett
International* (Cologne), May 1982
Interview in van Schaik, Eva, "Hans van Manen: Movement
and Form", *Ballett International* (Cologne), January 1984

About van Manen:
Loney, Glen, "Hans van Manen: Setting the Record Straight
on Netherlands Dance Theatre", *Dance Magazine* (New
York), February 1974
Gow, Gordon, "Meeting of the Minds", *Dancing Times*
(London), March 1975
Percival, John, "Three Choreographers", *About the House*
(London), Christmas 1976
Brinson, Peter, and Crisp, Clement, *Ballet and Dance: A Guide
to the Repertory,* London, 1980
Dekker, Keso, *Hans van Manen and Modern Ballet in
Nederland,* Amsterdam, 1981
"Choreographer with a Difference", *Dance and Dancers*
(London), June 1984
Schmidt, Jochen, *Der Zeitgenosse als Klassiker uber den
Hollandischen choreographen Hans van Manen,* Cologne, 1987

*   *   *

Although Hans van Manen began his dance training late in life,
his first opportunity to make an impact as a choreographer
came comparatively quickly when, having created occasional
ballets for the existing Dutch ballet companies, he joined the
newly formed Nederlands Dans Theater just one year after its
foundation. With this company van Manen was able to
experiment with various dance genres and eventually to

consolidate his own personal choreographic style. The company aimed to combine American modern dance techniques,
primarily Graham work, with a balletic tradition—and van
Manen was keen to exploit this amalgamation. Further
influences on his early work added to this eclecticism. Van
Manen had seen and greatly admired the work of Jerome
Robbins and accordingly, *Klaar af* and *Voet bij stuk*, two of his
early ballets, purveyed elements of Robbins's casual American
jazz style. Balanchine's musicality and clarity of movement also
made a great impression on the young van Manen. Consequently his newly evolving oeuvre comprised ballets which
were usually non-narrative, musically based, clear in structure,
and concerned with the dancers' individuality. Such work
became inextricably linked with the qualities that characterized the young and innovative Dutch company. Ideas explored
during this period by van Manen were refined and matured
during the time he spent with the Dutch National Ballet and in
ballets created after his departure from the administration of
the Nederlands Dans Theater.

Van Manen has stated that he is not interested in relating
ballet and literature—he does not wish to use the narrative
form, portray dramatic characters, or recite anecdotes in
movement. However, that is not to say that his ballets are
without ideas or themes. There is always a keen concern with
the individual dancer and his or her partnership with fellow
individuals. Even within a group of dancers, identifiable
personalities emerge and van Manen builds upon the passions
and frictions which result from these distinctions. His primary
occupation is with the relationship between the sexes, and the
duet form has proven to be the hub of these investigations.
Early duets such as *De Maan in de Trapeze* illustrate this
fascination, followed by *Twilight* and more recent works such as
Sarkasmen and *Trois Gnossiennes* (*Klavier Variationen II* and
III). Fraught and occasionally erotic or violent relationships
may emerge between men and women, which are explored and,
wherever possible, peaceably resolved. When van Manen
interpolates all male and all female duets into a ballet
(*Metaforen* and *Situation*) or alternatively pitches an uneven
number of men against women (*Pose, Klavier Variationen IV*),
the complexity of such relationships is increased but the
preference for agreeable resolution remains undiminished.

Clarity and uncluttered logic are further characteristics of his
ballets. These are seen in terms of the relationship of dance
form to musical form. The selection of music is wide-ranging—
from Bach to Beethoven, Cage to Debussy. All are treated with
equal respect and are used to formulate the structure of the
dance. Choreographic form is also clear. Van Manen is
particularly skilled in making convincing transitions between
sections in a dance, using entrances and exits, making the
seams of his choreography virtually invisible. Similarly the
blending of modern and balletic techniques is a convincing one.
The only intrusive movements are the very human gestures
which are scattered throughout even his most classical ballets—
as with the brush back of the hair in *Four Schumann Pieces*—
together with a selection of personal choreographic quirks—
such as a distinctive way of carrying the arms and fingers—
which recur in many of his ballets.

Throughout his career van Manen has concentrated on the
one-act ballet form. Only later in his choreographic development has he investigated creating longer works in the guise of
the series of *Klavier Variationen* (1980–1984). These five works,
while having individual identities, share a common theme of
male/female encounter and are non-narrative, contemporary,
and artistically complementary. Therefore they fuse into a
cohesive whole in an innovative departure from the traditional
three-act narrative ballet.

Van Manen sees dance as being about dancers and the dance

itself, and thus his affinity with his dancers is essential to the integrity of his work. His choice of dancers has often been surprising, as he sees a particularly appealing quality in a dancer which is applicable to his own personal visions. A number of his earlier successes were created for Gerard Lemaitre, Han Ebbelaar, and Alexandra Radius, while later muses include Coleen Davis and Clint Farha, all of whom have sympathy with his intentions.

Design for van Manen's work is important for the emphasis it gives to space and dancers. Linear, geometric designs are favoured, particularly by his frequent collaborator, Jean Paul Vroom. Film and video screens have been utilised on several occasions in works such as *Twice*, *Live*, and *Brainstorm*. This interest in film and visual images is carried through into van Manen's hobby, photography. His photographs reveal the same themes which are integral to his dance—a fascination with men and women and a clarity of vision and intent.

Van Manen's ballets were viewed as remarkably radical during his first decade with the innovative Nederlands Dans Theater. While his more recent choreography can not be credited with the same qualities of invention, his concern with male and female, his clarity of concept and execution, and his ultimate focus on both the dancer and the dance enable the best of his work to remain both contemporary and timeless and to provide new and personal challenges to later generations of dancers.

—Kate King

VAN PRAAGH, Peggy

British dancer, teacher, and director. Born in London, 1 September 1910. Studied with Aimee Phipps, London, from c.1920; later studied with Margaret Craske, Lydia Sokolova, Vera Volkova, Agnes de Mille, and Tamara Karsavina. Début with Anton Dolin's company, London Coliseum, 1929; dancer, Marie Rambert Dancers (later Ballet Club, and eventually Ballet Rambert), becoming soloist, 1933–38; also performed with Camargo Society, 1932; dancer, (Antony Tudor's) London Ballet, 1938; joint director (with Maude Lloyd), London Ballet, 1939–40; member of directing committee, London-Rambert Ballet, 1940–41; principal dancer, Player's Theatre, 1941, and Sadler's Wells Ballet, 1941–46; ballet mistress, Sadler's Wells Opera Ballet (later Sadler's Wells Theatre Ballet), from 1946, becoming assistant director, 1951–56; also ballet producer, British Broadcasting Corporation (BBC) television, 1949–58; director, Norsk (Norwegian) Ballet, Oslo, 1957–58; director, Edinburgh International Ballet, Edinburgh Festival, 1958; artistic director, Borovansky Ballet, Australia, season 1959–60; invited to return to Australia: artistic director, Australian Ballet, 1962–65, and joint director (with Robert Helpmann), 1965–74, 1978–79; freelance ballet producer, staging ballets for numerous companies around the world; also teacher: examiner and member of London Committee of the Cecchetti Society, from 1935; teacher, Royal Ballet School, 1959, 1974–78; resident teacher, Grand Ballet du Marquis de Cuevas, 1961; international guest teacher, including for Jacob's Pillow Dance Festival, 1959, American Cecchetti Society, and Australian Ballet School, 1975–82; lecturer and writer on dance and dance technique. Recipient: Queen Elizabeth II Coronation Award, Royal Academy of Dancing, 1965; titles of Officer of the Order of the British Empire, 1966, and Dame Commander of the British Empire, 1970; Honorary Doctorates, University of New England, 1974, University of New South Wales,

Peggy van Praagh in *Dark Elegies*, Ballet Rambert, 1937

Armidale, 1974, Melbourne University, 1981; Distinguished Artist Award of Australian Art Circle, 1975. Died in Melbourne, 15 January 1990.

ROLES

1930   Tordion in *Capriol Suite* (Ashton), Marie Rambert Dancers, London
         Pavane in *Capriol Suite* (Ashton), Marie Rambert Dancers, London
         Madonna in *A Florentine Picture* (Ashton), Marie Rambert Dancers, London
         Prelude and Mazurka in *Les Sylphides* (Fokine), Marie Rambert Dancers, London

1931   Waltz in *Façade* (Ashton), Ballet Club, London
         Milkmaid in *Façade* (Ashton), Ballet Club, London
         Scotch Rhapsody in *Façade* (Ashton), Ballet Club, London
         Reflection in *The Lady of Shalott* (Ashton), Ballet Club, London

1932   Ensemble in *Foyer de danse* (Ashton), Ballet Club, London
         Lampito in *Lysistrata* (Tudor), Ballet Club, London

1933   One of Two Young Girls in *Les Masques* (Ashton), Ballet Club, London

1934   Ensemble in *Mephisto Valse* (Ashton), Ballet Club, London
         His Bride in *Mermaid* (Howard, Salaman), Ballet Club, London

The Planet Mars (cr) in *The Planets* (Tudor), Ballet Club, London

1935   The Tattooed Lady (cr) in *Circus Wings* (Salaman), Ballet Rambert, London

First Guest in *Cinderella* (Howard), Ballet Rambert, London

Night in *The Descent of Hebe* (Tudor), Ballet Rambert, London

1936   An Episode in His Past (cr) in *Jardin aux lilas* (Tudor), Ballet Rambert, London

Caroline in *Jardin aux lilas* (Tudor), Ballet Rambert, London

1937   First Song (cr) in *Dark Elegies* (Tudor), Ballet Rambert, London

Second Song in *Dark Elegies* (Tudor), Ballet Rambert, London

An Aristocrat in Love (cr) in *Gallant Assembly* (Tudor), Dance Theatre, Oxford

1938   Bolero (cr) in *Soirée musicale* (Tudor), London Ballet, London

La Reine de la danse from Moscow (cr) in *Gala Performance* (Tudor), London Ballet, London

Venus in *The Judgment of Paris* (Tudor), Ballet Rambert, London

1939   Mortal Born under Mercury (cr) added to *The Planets* (Tudor), London Ballet, London

Mortal Born under Neptune in *The Planets* (Tudor), Ballet Rambert, London

Juno (cr) in *Les Pas des déesses* (Lester), London Ballet, London

1940   Winter (cr) in *The Seasons* (Staff), London Ballet, London

First Daughter (cr) in *La Leçon apprise* (Toye), London Ballet, London

Cat in *Peter and the Wolf* (Staff), Ballet Rambert, London

Peter in *Peter and the Wolf* (Staff), Ballet Rambert, London

The Young Chatelaine in *La Fête étrange* (Howard), Ballet Rambert, London

Vivandière in *Cap Over Mill* (Gore), Ballet Rambert, London

1941   Waltz in *Les Sylphides* (Fokine), Sadler's Wells Ballet, London

Czardas in *Swan Lake* (Petipa, Ivanov; staged Sergeyev), Sadler's Wells Ballet, London

Cygnet in *Swan Lake* (Petipa, Ivanov; staged Sergeyev), Sadler's Wells Ballet, London

A Blue Girl in *Les Patineurs* (Ashton), Sadler's Wells Ballet, London

Pas de quatre in *Les Rendezvous* (Ashton), Sadler's Wells Ballet, London

Violet Fairy in *The Sleeping Beauty* (Petipa; staged Sergeyev), Sadler's Wells Ballet, London

Canary Fairy in *The Sleeping Beauty* (Petipa; staged Sergeyev), Sadler's Wells Ballet, London

1942   Swanilda in *Coppélia* (Sergeyev after Petipa, Cecchetti), Sadler's Wells Ballet, London

1943   Peasant in *Promenade* (de Valois), Sadler's Wells Ballet, London

WORKS

Staged:

1946   *Les Sylphides* (after Fokine; mus. Chopin), Sadler's Wells Theatre Ballet, London (also staged Australian Ballet, 1962)

1947   *Le Carnaval* (after Fokine; mus. Schumann), Sadler's Wells Theatre Ballet, London (also staged Norsk Ballet, 1957; Australian Ballet, 1964)

Swan Lake Pas de trois (after Petipa; mus. Tchaikovsky), Sadler's Wells Theatre Ballet, London

Les Rendezvous (chor. Ashton; mus. Auber), Sadler's Wells Theatre Ballet, London (also staged National Ballet of Canada, 1956; Borovansky Ballet, 1960; Australian Ballet, 1962)

1948   *Giselle* Peasant Pas de deux (Act I, after Petipa, Coralli, Perrot; mus. Adam), Sadler's Wells Theatre Ballet, London

Swan Lake, Act II (after Ivanov, Sergeyev; mus. Tchaikovsky), Sadler's Wells Theatre Ballet, London

Bluebird Pas de deux (after Petipa; mus. Tchaikovsky), Sadler's Wells Theatre Ballet, London

Coppélia (after Petipa, Cecchetti, Sergeyev; mus. Delibes), Sadler's Wells Theatre Ballet, London

Les Patineurs (chor. Ashton; mus. Meyerbeer), Sadler's Wells Theatre Ballet, London

1956   *The Rake's Progress* (chor. de Valois; mus. Gordon), Bavarian State Opera Ballet, Munich

1957   *The Sleeping Beauty* (after Petipa; mus. Tchaikovsky), Royal Danish Ballet, Copenhagen (also staged, with Helpmann, for Australian Ballet, 1973)

Gala Performance (chor. Tudor; mus. Prokofiev), Royal Swedish Ballet, Stockholm

Soirée musicale (chor. Tudor; mus. Rossini and Britten), Norsk Ballet, Oslo

The Judgment of Paris (chor. Tudor; mus. Weill), Norsk Ballet, Oslo

1960   *Coppélia* (new production; after Petipa, Cecchetti, Sergeyev; mus. Delibes), Borovansky Ballet, Melbourne (also staged Australian Ballet, 1962 and 1979)

1962   *Swan Lake* (new production; after Petipa, Ivanov; mus. Tchaikovsky), Australian Ballet, Sydney

1964   *Aurora's Wedding* (from *The Sleeping Beauty*; Petipa; mus. Tchaikovsky), Australian Ballet, Adelaide

1965   *Giselle* (after Coralli, Perrot; mus. Adam and Burgmüller), Australian Ballet, British tour

PUBLICATIONS

By van Praagh:

"Training a Classical Dancer", *Dancing Times* (London), 7 parts: May–November 1948

How I Became a Ballet Dancer, London and New York, 1954

"Experiences as a Travelling Ballet Teacher and Producer", *Ballet Annual* (London), no. 13, 1959

"Dancers and Companies of the Commonwealth", *Ballet Annual* (London), no. 16, 1962

The Choreographic Art, with Peter Brinson, London and New York, 1963

"Australian Test", *Dance and Dancers* (London), March 1963

Ballet in Australia, Melbourne, 1965

"Working with Antony Tudor", *Dance Research* (London), Summer 1984

About van Praagh:

Hall, Fernau, *Modern English Ballet*, London, 1950

Davidson, Gladys, *Ballet Biographies*, London, 1952

Clarke, Mary, *The Sadler's Wells Ballet*, London, 1955

Corathiel, Elisabeth, "Spreading the Prestige of British Ballet", *Ballet Today* (London), July 1957

Palatsky, Eugene, "Meet Peggy van Praagh", *Dance Magazine* (New York), November 1959

Dean, Beth, "A Year of Accomplishment", *Dance Magazine* (New York), August 1963

Sorley Walker, Kathrine, "About Peggy van Praagh", *Dancing Times* (London), December 1974

Sexton, Christopher, *Peggy van Praagh: A Life of Dance*, South Melbourne, 1985

Pelly, Noel, "A Tribute to Dame Peggy", *Dance Australia* (Keysborough), April–May 1990

*   *   *

Peggy van Praagh's career in England spanned a period of over a quarter of a century, from the pioneering days of British ballet's infancy to the full flowering of the Sadler's Wells and Royal Ballet companies. From humble beginnings in balletic interludes arranged by Anton Dolin for revues at the London Coliseum, her professional career as a performer progressed via increasingly important roles with the Camargo Society and Rambert's Ballet Club, to her position as one of the principal dancers in Antony Tudor's London Ballet (1938) and as a member of the Sadler's Wells Ballet in the early 1940s. In spite of a somewhat difficult physique, van Praagh was a very strong technician as well as an expressive artist of great distinction. The breadth of her dramatic range as a dancer is exemplified by two of the very contrasting roles for which she is particularly remembered: An Episode in His Past, in Tudor's *Jardin aux lilas*—a study in emotional conflict—and Swanilda, in *Coppélia*—a sunny soubrette of a role, requiring a virtuoso technique.

Even before securing her first engagement as a professional performer in 1929, Peggy van Praagh had acquired a considerable amount of teaching experience. This early interest in teaching was further fostered by her studies (in the 1930s) with Margaret Craske, from whom she learned the Cecchetti method. She was to specialize in this method, becoming one of the first dozen dancers to pass the Advanced examination set by the Cecchetti Society; later, she was appointed as one of its senior examiners. Her teaching of the Cecchetti method was characterized by her approach to this work as part of a living, theatrical tradition, rather than merely as a rigid academic discipline. But it was first as ballet mistress, and eventually as assistant director of the Sadler's Wells Theatre Ballet company, that Peggy van Praagh was to make her greatest contribution to British ballet.

The performances given by the Sadler's Wells Theatre Ballet under van Praagh, in the early 1950s, represent one of the artistic high points of English ballet. The company's rich repertoire included important revivals of key British works such as *The Rake's Progress* and *La Fête étrange*, as well as selected ballets from the Diaghilev repertoire (notably a superb restaging of *Les Sylphides*). Under van Praagh's sensitive artistic direction this repertoire provided both the historical context and the artistic example necessary for the nurturing of new choreographers, such as the young John Cranko. Her theatrical flair and musicality, combined with her pedagogic skills, ensured the emergence of a whole generation of fine dancers, including Elaine Fifield, Maryon Lane, Patricia Miller, David Blair, Pirmin Trecu, and David Poole. For those who were fortunate enough to have seen the Sadler's Wells Theatre Ballet under Peggy van Praagh, the artistic standards she achieved have remained a touchstone by which to assess later developments in British ballet. Barbara Fewster, who was to succeed van Praagh as the company ballet mistress and who then went on to direct the Royal Ballet School for many years, claims that it was from her that she learned both how to teach and how to direct dancers; thus, for many years after van Praagh had herself left England and the Sadler's Wells Ballet, her methods as well as her high artistic standards continued to be handed on through Fewster to another generation of British dancers.

Peggy van Praagh's departure from the British ballet scene was to become Australia's gain. Indeed, after a few years as guest producer with various theatres, and an all-too-brief spell directing the choreographically innovative but short-lived Edinburgh International Ballet (1958), van Praagh was eventually to settle permanently in Australia, where she became the first director of the newly formed Australian Ballet. Her achievement in Australia was no less significant than her contribution to the Sadler's Wells Theatre Ballet, although the emphasis was inevitably different. The artistic climate in England in the late 1940s and early 1950s had been particularly conducive to choreographic creativity. Although van Praagh strived to foster new choreographic talent in Australia (a task in which she was later helped significantly by Robert Helpmann, following his appointment as her co-director from 1965), her greatest achievement in that country was probably in the development of international standards of performance from the Australian Ballet in her restaging of the nineteenth century classics.

Peggy van Praagh's wide understanding of the art of ballet in all its many facets is exemplified by two of the books she wrote. The first, *How I Became a Ballet Dancer*, is a lucid exposition of the requirements and problems of a dancer's career, as well as an historically important first-hand account of the early days of British ballet. The second, *The Choreographic Art* (with Peter Brinson) is an exhaustive study of all aspects of choreography, written with enormous insight and drawing on her uniquely varied experience: it remains one of the most important and definitive works ever written on this subject.

—Richard Glasstone

————

VAN SCHAYK, Toer

Dutch dancer, choreographer, and stage designer. Born in Amsterdam, 28 September 1936. Studied with Iraïl Godeskov, Sonia Gaskell, Amsterdam; also studied and practised as a sculptor and painter in the Hague, Antwerp, and Greece, 1959–66. Dancer, Netherlands Ballet, 1955–59; soloist and designer, Dutch National Ballet, 1966–76; first choreography, 1971, also designing for own choreography and for Rudi van Dantzig; resident choreographer, Dutch National Ballet, from 1976; also guest choreographer, including for Scottish Ballet, National Ballet of Norway, Werkcentrum Dans; independent artist, exhibiting art works in London, New York, Amsterdam, and Athens. Recipient: Knight of the Orde van Oranje Nassau, 1979; Prize for Choreography from the Society of Theatre and Concert Hall Directors, 1987.

WORKS

1971   *Onvoltooid Verleden tijd* (*Past Imperfect*; mus. Ligeti), Dutch National Ballet, Amsterdam

1972   *Voor, Tijdens en na het Feest* (*Before, During and After the Party*; mus. van Bergeijk), Dutch National Ballet, Amsterdam

1973   *Ways of Saying Bye-Bye* (mus. Purcell, Poptie), Scottish Theatre Ballet, Glasgow

Toer van Schayk rehearsing *Mozart Requiem* with the Dutch National Ballet, 1990

1974   *Pyrrhische Dansen* (mus. Gey), Dutch National Ballet, Amsterdam

1975   *8 Madrigalen* (mus. Gesualdo), Dutch National Ballet, Amsterdam

1976   *Eerste Lugtige Plaatsing* (*First Light Placement*; mus. Spohr), Dutch National Ballet, Amsterdam

1977   *Jeux* (mus. Debussy), Dutch National Ballet, Amsterdam

        Pyrrhische Dansen II (mus. Lully, Danican-Philidor, Couperin), Dutch National Ballet, Amsterdam

1978   *Faun* (mus. Debussy), Dutch National Ballet, Amsterdam

1979   *Life* (with van Dantzig; mus. various), Dutch National Ballet, Amsterdam

        Een Verwaarloosde Tuin (*Neglected Garden*; mus. Mozart), National Ballet of Norway, Oslo

1980   *Pyrrhische Dansen III* (mus. Berg), Dutch National Ballet, Amsterdam

        Chiaro-scuro (mus. Gesualdo, van Vlymen), Dutch National Ballet, Amsterdam

1981   *I Hate You Too, Johnny* (mus. Weiss, Mozart), Dutch National Ballet, Amsterdam

        Strandquintet-Duinkerken (mus. Johnston), Werkcentrum Dans, Rotterdam

1982   *Landschap* (*Landscape*; mus. various), Dutch National Ballet, Amsterdam

1983   *Dodeneiland* (*Island of Death*; mus. Rachmaninov), Dutch National Ballet, Amsterdam

        Confectiespassen (*Steps Ready-made*; mus. Wagemans), Dutch National Ballet, Amsterdam

1984   *Rijmloos* (*Rhymeless*; mus. Müller-Siemens), Dutch National Ballet, Amsterdam

1985   *Sanitair Solitair* (mus. de Ruiter, Mayering, de Vries, Part), Dutch National Ballet, Amsterdam

1986   *Seventh Symphony* (mus. Beethoven), Dutch National Ballet, Amsterdam

        Zoals Orpheus (mus. Stravinsky, Gluck, Vamvarkaris), Dutch National Ballet, Amsterdam

1987   *In de Nacht Kans op Omwer* (*The Chance of Thunder in the Night*; mus. Mozart), Dutch National Ballet, Amsterdam

        Het Mythisch Voorwendsel (*The Mythical Pretence*; mus. Bartók), Dutch National Ballet, Amsterdam

1988   *Verschuiven van Tonelen* (*Shifting of Scenes*; mus. Zappa, Hamburg, Berlioz), Dutch National Ballet, Amsterdam

        Verbruik (*Consumption/Wastage/Expenditure*; mus. Bach, Liberda), Reflex Dance Company, Amsterdam

1990   *Mozart Requiem* (mus. Mozart), Dutch National Ballet, Amsterdam

1991   *Pyrrhische Dansen IV* (mus. Furrer, Liberda), Dutch National Ballet, Amsterdam

1992 *Stilleven wit plein* (mus. Schoenberg), Dutch National Ballet, Amsterdam

PUBLICATIONS

By van Schayk:
Interview with Nieuwpoort, Marcel Armand van, "Toer van Schayk", *Dansbulletin* (The Hague), vol. 10, no. 1/2, 1978

About van Schayk:
Percival, John, "Blown in a Gentle Wind", *Dance and Dancers* (London), January 1976
Percival, John, "The Dutch National Ballet", *Dance Magazine* (New York), November 1976
van Schaik, Eva, "Toer van Schayk", *Ballett International* (Cologne), June/July 1988
van Schaik, Eva, "Rudi van Dantzig" (interview), *Ballett International* (Cologne), November 1989

*   *   *

Toer van Schayk is an artist in whose work three disciplines are combined—those of dance, painting, and sculpture. As a dancer, he proved himself to be an expressive interpreter of strong emotional works, dancing them with great honesty, subtlety, and depth of feeling. His most impressive role was undoubtedly that of the lead in Rudi van Dantzig's *Monument for a Dead Boy*, the powerful physchological study of tormented homosexuality created for his talents in 1965. As a choreographer, he has distinguished himself by the way he uses movement like the delicate strokes of a paintbrush. As a painter and sculptor, he is known in Amsterdam, London, New York, and Athens—but his greatest fame in this field has come from his many simple and elegant set and costume designs, created for dance works by both van Dantzig and himself.

Van Schayk's ballets, almost all created for the Dutch National Ballet (Het Nationale Ballet), have a strong similarity to those of van Dantzig in their choice of theme; both choreographers show a deep concern for such issues as the destruction of the world's natural resources, the threat of war, the helplessness of the underprivileged, the lack of communication among human beings. *Voor, Tijdens en na het Feest* (*Before, During, and After the Party*), *Life* (made in collaboration with van Dantzig), and the full-length *Landschap* (*Landscape*) are striking examples.

Van Schayk's works differ from van Dantzig's in his measured view of life and the dry, ironic sense of humour which can pop up suddenly in even his most dramatic ballets. *Een Verwaarloosde Tuin* (*Neglected Garden*), *8 Madrigalen*, and *Dodeneiland* (*Island of Death*) have a distinctive melancholic undertone and yet a soft colouring of movement and gesture.

Another recurring element in van Schayk's choreography is the use of folk dance motifs and floor patterns, as in *Life*, *Pyrrhische Dansen I, II,* and *III*, and his surprisingly joyful *Seventh Symphony*. Several of his creations are inspired by events in dance history, such as the discovery and development of pointe-work, incorporated into *Eerste Lugtige Plaatsing* (*First Light Placement*), or the Diaghilev era, seen in references to the famous Nijinsky ballets *Jeux* and *L'Après-midi d'un faune* in van Schayk's *Jeux* and *Faun*.

Van Schayk's ballets are not "easy"; they leave a great deal to the imagination of the spectator, and they never tread comfortable, predictable paths. The dance vocabulary is often complicated, making use of unusually bent bodies, broken lines, and fast, unorthodox movements. At the same time, there is often a definite sculptural quality to the movement and a

delicate use of mine. Several of Van Schayk's ballets have been taken into the repertories of international companies.

—Ine Rietstap

———

VASILIEV, Vladimir

Russian/Soviet dancer, choreographer, and director. Born Vladimir Victorovich Vasiliev in Moscow, 18 April 1940. Studied at the Moscow Choreographic School, pupil of Mikhail Gabovich, 1948–58. Married Bolshoi ballerina Ekaterina Maximova. Dancer, Bolshoi Ballet, from 1958, becoming principal dancer, from 1959; first choreography for Bolshoi Theatre (*Icarus*), 1971, producing own ballets for Bolshoi and other Moscow theatres, various seasons, 1971–90; guest choreographer, Berlin, 1985, Budapest, Naples, Riga, 1986, Chelyabinsk, 1987, Kasyan, 1989; member, Board of Directors, Ballet Theatre of the Kremlin Palace of Congress, from 1990; international guest artist, often in concert tours with Ekaterina Maximova, and also appearing with Ballet du XXe Sièle, Ballet de Marseille, and Teatro San Carlo, Naples; has also appeared in and directed several ballet films, including *Narcissus* (1971), *Duet* (also dir., 1972), *Spartacus* (1976), *Gigolo and Gigoletta* (also dir., 1980), *The World of Ulanova* (also dir., 1981), *These Charming Sounds* (also dir., 1981), *La Traviata* (dir. Zeffirelli, 1982), *Aniuta* (also dir., 1982), *Dom u Dorogi* (also dir., 1984), *"I Want to Dance": Fragments of a Biography* (also dir., 1985), *Fouetté* (also dir., 1986), *Katia and Volodia* (French documentary, 1989); has also directed *"... And there Remains, as Always, Something else"* (1990). Recipient: Gold Medal, Festival of Youth, Vienna, 1959; Gold Medal, International Ballet Competition, Varna, 1964; Nijinsky Prize, Paris, 1964; title of Honoured Artist of the Russian Federation, 1964; Lenin Prize, 1970; Marius Petipa Prize, France, 1972; State Prize of the USSR, 1977; title of Professor, State Institute of Theatrical Art (GITIS), 1989.

ROLES

1958 Pan in *Walpurgis Night* (Lavrovsky), Bolshoi Ballet, Moscow
1959 Danila (cr) in *The Stone Flower* (Moscow version; Grigorovich), Bolshoi Ballet, Moscow
1960 Ivanushka (cr) in *The Little Humpbacked Horse* (Radunsky), Bolshoi Ballet, Moscow
       Benvolio in *Romeo and Juliet* (Lavrovsky), Bolshoi Ballet, Moscow
       The Prince in *Cinderella* (Zakharov), Bolshoi Ballet, Moscow
       Ali-Batyr in *Shuraleh* (Yakobson), Bolshoi Ballet, Moscow
1961 Likash (cr) in *Song of the Woods* (Lapauri, Tarasova), Bolshoi Ballet, Moscow
       Andrei (cr) in *Pages from a Life* (Lavrovsky), Bolshoi Ballet, Moscow
       Basil in *Don Quixote* (Gorsky), Bolshoi Ballet, Moscow
1962 Title role in *Paganini* (Lavrovsky), Bolshoi Ballet, Moscow
       Slave in *Spartacus* (Yakobson), Bolshoi Ballet, Moscow
1963 Bluebird in *The Sleeping Beauty* (Grigorovich after Petipa), Bolshoi Ballet, Moscow

Vladimir Vasiliev in *Icarus*, Bolshoi Ballet, 1971

The Prince in *The Nutcracker* (Vainonen), Bolshoi Ballet, Moscow

Principal dancer in *Class Concert* (Messerer), Bolshoi Ballet, Moscow

1964   Title role in *Petrushka* (Fokine; staged Boyarsky), Bolshoi Ballet, Moscow

Frondoso in *Laurencia* (Chabukiani), Bolshoi Ballet, Moscow

Medzhnun (cr) in *Leili and Medzhnun* (Goleizovsky), Bolshoi Ballet, Moscow

Albrecht in *Giselle* (Petipa after Coralli, Perrot), Bolshoi Ballet, Moscow

1966   The Prince (cr) in *The Nutcracker* (Grigorovich), Bolshoi Ballet, Moscow

1968   Title role (cr) in *Spartacus* (Grigorovich), Bolshoi Ballet, Moscow

1971   Title role in *Icarus* (also chor.), Bolshoi Ballet, Kremlin Palace of Congress, Moscow

1973   Romeo in *Romeo and Juliet* (Lavrovsky), Bolshoi Ballet, Moscow

Prince Désiré (cr) in *The Sleeping Beauty* (new production; Grigorovich after Petipa), Bolshoi Ballet, Moscow

1975   Title role in *Ivan the Terrible* (Grigorovich), Bolshoi Ballet, Moscow

1976   Title role in *Icarus* (new production; also chor.), Bolshoi Ballet, Kremlin Palace of Congress, Moscow

Sergei (cr) in *Angara* (Grigorovich), Bolshoi Ballet, Moscow

1977   Title role (cr) in *Petrushka* (Béjart), Ballet du XXe Siècle, Brussels

1979   Romeo in *Romeo and Julia* (Béjart), Ballet du XXe Siècle, Brussels

1980   Title role (cr) in *Macbeth* (also chor.), Bolshoi Ballet, Moscow

1986   Peotr Leontevich (cr) in *Anyuta* (also chor.), Teatro San Carlos, Naples

1987   Professor Ratt in *Blue Angel* (Petit), Ballet de Marseille, Paris

1988   Title role in *Pulcinella* (Massine), Teatro San Carlo, Naples

The Baron in *Gaîté Parisienne* (Massine), Teatro San Carlo, Naples

Title role in *Zorba the Greek* (Lorca Massine), Ballet dell'Arena di Verona, Verona

1989   Nijinsky in *Nijinsky Reminiscences* (Menegatti), Teatro San Carlo, Naples

1991   Stepmother (cr) in *Cinderella* (also chor.), Ballet Theatre of the Kremlin Palace of Congress, Moscow

WORKS

1971   *Icarus* (mus. Slonimsky), Bolshoi Ballet, Moscow (restaged 1976)

1978   *These Charming Sounds* (mus. Rameau, Mozart, and others), Bolshoi Ballet, Moscow

1980   *Macbeth* (mus. Molchanov), Bolshoi Ballet, Moscow (also staged Novosibirsk, 1982, Berlin, 1985, Budapest, 1986)

1981   *Juno and Avos* (mus. Rybnikov), Leninsky Kosomol, Moscow

1986   *Anyuta* (mus. Gavrillyn), Teatro San Carlo, Naples (also staged Moscow, 1986, Riga, 1986, Chelyabinsk, 1987, Kazan, 1989)

1990   *Romeo and Juliet* (mus. Prokofiev), Stanislavsky and Nemirovich–Danchenko Theatre, Moscow

Also staged:

1991   *Don Quixote* (after Petipa, Gorsky; mus. Minkus), American Ballet Theatre tour, Chicago

Cinderella (mus. Prokofiev), Ballet Theatre of the Kremlin Palace of Congress, Moscow

PUBLICATIONS

By Vasiliev:

Interview in Lavole, Jean-Pierre, "Ekaterina Maximova and Vladimir Vasiliev", *Pour la danse* (Paris), December 1977–January 1978

Interview in Garafola, Lynn, "Vladimir Vasiliev: Champion of Perestroika", *Dance Magazine* (New York), November 1990

About Vasiliev:

Iloupina, A., "Vasiliev", *Les Saisons de la danse* (Paris), June 1970

Tobias, Tobi, "Bolshoi Profiles: Vladimir Vasiliev", *Dance Magazine* (New York), June 1975

Avaliani, N., and Zhdanov, L., *Bolshoi's Young Dancers*, translated by Natalie Ward, Moscow and London, 1975

Cameron, Judy, *The Bolshoi Ballet*, New York, 1975

Kisselgoff, Anna, *Vladimir Vasiliev* (Dance Horizons Spotlight Series), New York, 1975

Lvov-Anokhin, Boris, *Masters of the Bolshoi Ballet*, Moscow, 1976

Demidov, Alexander, *The Russian Ballet Past and Present*, translated by Guy Daniels, London, 1978

Percival, John, "The Gift of Greatness", *Dance and Dancers* (London), October 1983

Smakov, Gennady, *The Great Russian Dancers*, New York, 1984

Garafola, Lynn, "Vladimir Vasiliev", *Dance Magazine* (New York), December 1990

*   *   *

In 1970, the Soviet choreographer Kasyan Goleizovsky wrote: "Vladimir Vasiliev is not simply a dancer of rare talent, he is literally an outstanding phenomenon in the history of ballet."

Indeed, Vasiliev has been proving these words over the past three decades, delighting audiences with his remarkable talent, which is a unique blend of Russian refinement and detail with raw Soviet bravura. He has earned himself the right to be called one of the greatest male dancers of this era. His virtuosity reaches from superb technical ability to an inner understanding of both role and music, and his dramatic presence is both thoughtful and exciting. He possesses an artistry that commands attention whenever he is on stage, even when he is not in the spotlight.

The son of a Moscow workman, Vasiliev first appeared on the Bolshoi stage as a very young student in the Bolshoi school's production of *Chapayev's Soldiers*. At eighteen, he was chosen for the part of Giotto in *Francesca da Rimini* at the school's graduation concert, and proved himself to be not only technically proficient but a master of dramatic expression. He joined the Bolshoi company at a time when the image of the male dancer was undergoing a tremendous change. No longer just a partner, the male was becoming a force to take equal billing with the ballerina. In Yuri Grigorovich's ballets, Vasiliev was to become the main focus.

In 1959, Vasiliev was made a principal dancer and given his first leading role, in Grigorovich's *The Stone Flower*. As Danila, he danced with lyricism and refreshing vitality, catching the elements of Danila's quintessentially "Russian" nature in both manner and dancing style. His success led to leading roles in both the classics and the ballets of Grigorovich. Into the tapestry of each one of these new roles Vasiliev wove a blend of colourful characterization with individual and fresh interpretation, convincingly transposing himself into his part through ingenious uses of movement. In the classics he was a romantic and gallant presence, manly, yet refined. In contemporary works, he charged his roles with fire and passion, powerfully conveying the inner fervour of the character through outward action.

Vasiliev's most famous role is that of Spartacus. His outstanding portrayal of the rebel slave won him the coveted Lenin Prize and took his career to even greater heights. His lucid interpretation presented the slave as a noble character, imbued with the highest moral qualities. Exceptional acting, virtuoso dancing, and tremendous physical strength combined to create a complex hero. The ballet is also considered to be Grigorovich's finest creation, for it cleverly contrasts scenes of mass male action with "soliloquies", or quiet moments of reflection, for the soloist. For Vasiliev, this format was ideal. He had an opportunity to display both his physical skills—breath-taking leaps, rapid spins, and powerful jetés—and his dramatic prowess, shown through impassioned acting which depicted Spartacus's innermost torments.

In the classical sphere, Vasiliev will be long remembered for his Albrecht in *Giselle*. He first danced the role in 1964, coached by the legendary ballerina Galina Ulanova and the great dramatic dancer Aleksei Yermolaev. Over the years, Vasiliev's count has never lost his romance, nor his nobility. *Giselle*, whenever danced by Vasiliev and Ekaterina Maximova, has taken on a magical, highly romantic quality. In May 1990, they performed the ballet, billed as their last performance in these roles together, with the American Ballet Theatre: the evening showed the depth and understanding that their years of dancing together have produced. The two, so familiar with each other's moods and movements, became one on stage, mirroring one another in lyricism and plasticity. Together their dancing flowed: Vasiliev constantly aware of the nuances of Maximova's balance, she so completely assured in his support of her. While some of his former elevation had disappeared, Vasiliev still presented intense and classically pure technique, and gave a compassionate and commanding interpretation. He once said that his Albrecht was the first truly to love Giselle.

After speaking out against Bolshoi policies at the end of the 1980s, Vasiliev and Maximova were no longer invited to dance regularly with the main Bolshoi company. They still give a few token performances in the Bolshoi Theatre, usually when the main bulk of the company is on tour. As a consequence, they travel extensively abroad, especially to Europe, where they perform as guests with many leading companies, often in interesting new roles and styles. In recent years, Vasiliev has become something of a cultural envoy for Russian, rather than Soviet, ballet. He seeks ways to promote it, not just as a dancer but also as an accomplished choreographer, director of ballet, film director, and spokesman for the arts. Feeling that the present trends of athleticism and pyrotechnics, evidenced at the Bolshoi and elsewhere, are stifling the very roots and traditions of the Russian ballet, he campaigns constantly to preserve ballet's purity and heritage. In the early 1980s he took a group of young Bolshoi stars to France to display this pure technique, and in 1989, he toured America with a group of dancers from several Soviet republics who epitomized the Russian style.

Vasiliev has also had much success as a choreographer, creating several works in differing styles. His first ballet, *Ikar* (*Icarus*), showed a clear understanding of characterization and included a long evocative adagio which began as two monologues. The plotless ballet *These Charming Sounds* was an exquisite set of pure classical cameos danced joyfully to the music of Mozart, Corelli, Rameau, and others, while his *Macbeth* returned to Bolshoi bravura and grandeur with emphasis on male dancing. Vasiliev offered an imaginative interpretation of Shakespeare's text—male witches on pointe and, for the ghosts of Macbeth's victims, stacked shoes and Kabuki masks. More recently he has transposed *Anyuta*, a Chekhov story, into a popular and successful ballet. As a film director, Vasiliev showed ingenuity and sensitivity, with touches of Fellini-type imagery, in the film *Fouetté*. Sadly, Vasiliev's most recent choreographic effort, *Cinderella* (1991), has not been as successful.

—Margaret Willis

————

VAZEM, Ekaterina

Russian dancer and teacher. Born Ekaterina Ottovna (also known as Matilda) Vazem in Moscow, 25 January (13 January old style) 1848. Studied at the Imperial Theatre School, St. Petersburg, pupil of Lev Ivanov, Aleksei Bogdanov; graduated in 1867; later studied with Eugene Huguet, Class of Perfection, and Marius Petipa. Married (1) balletomane Grinev, 1871 (d. 1883); (2) ballet critic Ivan Nosilov, 1896: one son, Nikolai Nosilov. First major appearance, while still a student, in pas de deux from *Teolinda* (Saint-Léon); official début as Ondine in *The Naïad and the Fisherman*, 1867; dancer, becoming ballerina, Bolshoi Theatre, St. Petersburg, creating many roles for ballet master Marius Petipa, 1867–84; visited Paris Opéra School (but unable to accept Opéra contract offered by Galantier), 1880; guest artist, Bolshoi Theatre, Moscow, 1883; teacher, St. Petersburg Theatre School, 1886–96: pupils included Agrippina Vaganova, Olga Preobrazhenskaya, Matilda Kshesinskaya, and Anna Pavlova; taught privately after 1917. Died in Leningrad, 14 December 1937.

ROLES

1867 Ondine in *The Naïad and the Fisherman* (*Ondine*; Perrot), Bolshoi Theatre, St. Petersburg

Elena in *Robert le Diable* (opera; mus. Meyerbeer, chor. Taglioni), Bolshoi Theatre, St. Petersburg

1868 Pas de Eventails (cr) in *Le Corsaire* (Petipa, Perrot after Mazilier), Bolshoi Theatre, St. Petersburg

Pas de deux in *Jovita*; *ou, Les Boucaniers* (Saint-Léon after Mazilier), Bolshoi Theatre, Moscow

Tsar-Maiden in *The Little Humpbacked Horse* (Saint-Léon), Bolshoi Theatre, Moscow

Galya in *The Goldfish* (Saint-Léon), Bolshoi Theatre, St. Petersburg

Medora in *Le Corsaire* (Petipa, Perrot after Mazilier), Bolshoi Theatre, St. Petersburg

1870 Kathi in *La Vivandière* (Saint-Léon), Bolshoi Theatre, St. Petersburg

1871 First Star (cr) in *Two Stars* (Petipa), Bolshoi Theatre, St. Petersburg

Betlie in *Trilby* (Saint-Léon), Bolshoi Theatre, St. Petersburg

1872 Catarina in *Catarina*; *ou, La Fille du bandit* (Perrot), Bolshoi Theatre, St. Petersburg

1873 Title role in *La Camargo* (Petipa), Bolshoi Theatre, St. Petersburg

1874 Farfalla (cr) in *Le Papillon* (Petipa), Bolshoi Theatre, St. Petersburg

Aspicia in *Pharaoh's Daughter* (Petipa), Bolshoi Theatre, St. Petersburg

1875 Angela (cr) in *The Bandits* (Petipa), Bolshoi Theatre, St. Petersburg

Nisia in *King Candaule* (Petipa), Bolshoi Theatre, St. Petersburg

1876 Fenella in *La Muette de Portici* (opera; mus. Auber, chor. Petipa) Bolshoi Theatre, St. Petersburg

1877 Nikiya (cr) in *La Bayadère* (Petipa), Bolshoi Theatre, St. Petersburg

1878 Title role in *Giselle* (Petipa after Coralli, Perrot), Bolshoi Theatre, Moscow

1879 Title role (cr) in *The Daughter of the Snows* (Petipa), Bolshoi Theatre, Moscow

1880 Fleur des Champs in *La Fille du Danube* (Petipa after Taglioni), Bolshoi Theatre, St. Petersburg

Kitri in *Don Quixote* (Petipa), Bolshoi Theatre, St. Petersburg

1881 Title role (cr) in *Zoraya; or, The Lady Moor in Spain* (Petipa), Bolshoi Theatre, St. Petersburg

Title role and Grand Pas (cr) in *Paquita* (new version; Petipa), Bolshoi Theatre, St. Petersburg

Kathi (cr) in *Markitantka* (new production of *La Vivandière*; Petipa after Saint-Léon), Bolshoi Theatre, St. Petersburg

1883 Queen of the Day (cr) in *Night and Day* (Petipa), Bolshoi Theatre, Moscow (on the occasion of the coronation of Alexander II)

Other roles include: Title role in *Teolinda* (also called *The Spirit of the Valley*; Saint-Léon), title role in *Meteor* (Saint-Léon), Pas de deux in *Le Carnaval de Venise* (Petipa), Titania in *A Midsummer Night's Dream* (Petipa), Roxana in *Roxana; or, The Beauty of Montenegro* (Petipa).

PUBLICATIONS

By Vazem:
Memoirs of a Ballerina of the St. Petersburg Bolshoi Theatre, Leningrad and Moscow, 1937
"Memoirs of a Ballerina of the St. Petersburg Bolshoi Theatre", translated by Nina Dimitrievitch, *Dance Research* (London), 4 parts: Summer 1985, Spring 1986, Spring 1987, Autumn 1988

About Vazem:
Pleshcheev, Aleksandr, *Our Ballet*, St. Petersburg, 1899
Borisoglebsky, Mikhail, (ed.), *Materials for the History of Russian Ballet*, Leningrad, 1939
Moore, Lillian (ed.), *Russian Ballet Master: The Memoirs of Marius Petipa*, translated by Helen Whittaker, London, 1958
Krasovskaya, Vera, *Russian Ballet Theatre of the Second Half of the Nineteenth Century*, Leningrad and Moscow, 1963
Roslavleva, Natalia, *Era of the Russian Ballet*, London, 1966
Wiley, Roland John (ed. and trans.), *A Century of Russian Ballet: Documents and Accounts, 1810–1910*, Oxford, 1990

* * *

From the time of her graduation from the Imperial Theatre School in St. Petersburg in 1867, until her retirement from the St. Petersburg Bolshoi Theatre in 1884, Ekaterina Vazem enjoyed the status of being Marius Petipa's favourite Russian ballerina. He created many roles on her, Vazem's personal favourite being Nikiya in *La Bayadère* (1877). A cool technician noted for her academic precision, Vazem described herself in her memoirs as "a terre à terre ballerina, an expert in technically difficult virtuoso dancing, and not endowed with an ability to 'fly'." Among her strengths were balances, quick batterie movements, pirouettes, and steel-like pointes. In *Le Papillon*, the first ballet created for her by Petipa (*Le Corsaire*, in which she danced the role of Medora in 1868, was originally choreographed by Mazilier in 1856), Vazem was given the opportunity to display her considerable abilities. One variation concluded with a series of hops on one foot, executed en pointe. This was an extremely unusual feat at this time; Vazem claims that it was "something never previously attempted by a ballerina". Whether this claim is an exaggeration is of little consequence; of greater importance is the realization that Vazem was able to rival the virtuosity for which the Italian dancers were famed.

Despite Petipa's support throughout her career, Vazem expressed little respect for his choreography. In her memoirs, she describes Petipa as "totally wanting in musicality", and calls most of his variations "monotonous". Her criticisms of Petipa are tempered, however, by a modicum of understanding for the conditions under which he laboured. She recognizes the considerable achievement of consistently mounting at least two major ballets each season, and gives him credit for incorporating new developments and trends within his ballets. Most significantly for her, he enthusiastically embraced the technical skills imported by the Italians. It was this aspect of Petipa's choreography that led him to make extensive use of Vazem.

Interestingly, Vazem herself was not a proponent of the Italian style, with that she described as "its leg-breaking tricks". She preferred the choreography of Saint-Léon, with its "small 'seed pearl' steps" and "careful filigree work". Vazem's negative attitude toward Italian virtuosity was likely the majority opinion held by Russian dancers at that time. Vazem's own reputation was built on her technical abilities, but she disapproved of technical prowess for its own sake. It would be the next generation of Russian dancers, including such dancers as Tamara Karsavina, who would resolve to challenge the supremacy of the Italians by equalling, and then surpassing, their technical skills.

Vazem taught the intermediate girls at the Imperial Ballet School in St. Petersburg from 1886 to 1896. Her memoirs are valuable for the information they provide on class content in the late nineteenth century. Even then, pointe work was restricted to the senior class. It was not permitted at the intermediate level, where the students ranged in age from twelve to fifteen years. When teaching, Vazem emphasized the use of the feet and the development of stamina. To combat the tendency of students to mimic mindlessly the actions of their teachers, she nurtured true understanding through the analysis of exercises and body positions, including use of the back, arms, and épaulement. Considerable attention also was paid to plié exercises. Vazem considered softness and plasticity to be the primary qualities of classical dancing, and believed they could be achieved through proper use of the plié. She did not equate softness with weakness, and appears to have favoured those students who were technically strong. According to Natalia Roslavleva, Anna Pavlova was one student who fell short of Vazem's standards. Vazem feared that Pavlova's lack of strength jeopardized her future. Nevertheless, Pavlova holds the distinction of being one of the few former pupils mentioned by Vazem in her memoirs; Agrippina Vaganova is another.

Vazem left the employ of the Theatre School in 1896, citing frustration with the bureaucracy. Despite being granted a generous amount of academic freedom within her classes, she found it increasingly difficult to work with administrators who knew little to nothing about dance. She taught privately for many years, and ended her days in a Home for the Veterans of the Stage in Leningrad.

Ekaterina Vazem's most intriguing contribution to dance history lies in her memoirs. Compiled by her son, N.I. Nosilov, they were published in Leningrad in 1937. Her writings offer a glimpse into the world and personalities of the Imperial Theatre in the latter half of the nineteenth century, seen through the eyes of an opinionated woman. Information on the dancers, choreographers, and ballets is frequently enlightening and always fascinating, coloured by personal bias. Although less concrete, her legacy as a teacher is also substantial. Teachers' reputations are built on the achievements of their pupils, and many of Russia's future ballerinas passed through Vazem's intermediate class. Vazem was a traditionalist, but her teaching approach nurtured the skills and understanding which allowed her students later to take risks and expand the boundaries of ballet. Finally, Vazem is justifiably remembered as one of the first Russian ballerinas whose technique rivalled that of the Italians. Her abilities made her a favourite of Petipa and she recognized the benefits of his esteem. Despite her criticisms of his work, Vazem conceded that "the artistic results of [their] partnership were highly positive". Each one helped further the other's career: Petipa provided Vazem with roles that displayed her talent; Vazem provided Petipa with the opportunity to develop the skills he needed as his choreography increasingly focused on expression through technique. Both played important roles in the development of ballet in Russia.

—Norma Sue Fisher-Stitt

Tatiana Vecheslova as Esmeralda, Leningrad, 1930s

VECHESLOVA, Tatyana

Russian/Soviet dancer, teacher, and ballet mistress. Born Tatyana Mikhailovna Vecheslova, daughter of ballerina Yevgenia Snetkova, in St. Petersburg, 25 February 1910. Studied at the Leningrad Choreographic School, pupil of Maria Romanova and Agrippina Vaganova; graduated in 1928. Married dancer Svyatoslav Kuznetsov, 1950 (div. 1955): son, dancer and choreographer Andrei Kuznetsov. Début, in first created role, while still a student, 1924; ballerina, State Academic Theatre for Opera and Ballet (GATOB), later the Kirov Theatre, 1928–53, becoming first Soviet ballerina to tour abroad (with Chabukiani), United States, 1934; teacher, 1950–70, and artistic director, 1952–54, Leningrad Choreographic School; répétiteur (rehearsal director), Kirov Ballet, 1954–71; also dance writer, having published over 50 articles on dance and choreography, and several books. Recipient: title of Honoured Artist of the Russian Federation, 1939; State Prize of the USSR, 1947; title of Honoured Worker of Arts of the Russian Federation, 1957. Died in Leningrad, July 1991.

ROLES

1924 Soloist (cr) in *Waltz* (Vaganova), Leningrad Choreographic School, Leningrad
1928 Gulnara in *Le Corsaire* (Petipa), State Academic Theatre for Opera and Ballet (GATOB), Leningrad
1929 Tao-Hoa in *The Red Poppy* (Lopukhov, Leontiev, Ponomarev), GATOB, Leningrad

      Canary Fairy in *The Sleeping Beauty* (Petipa), GATOB, Leningrad
      Masha in *The Nutcracker* (Lopukhov), GATOB, Leningrad
1930 Odette/Odile in *Swan Lake* (Petipa, Ivanov), GATOB, Leningrad
      White Pussycat in *The Sleeping Beauty* (Petipa), GATOB, Leningrad
      Title role in *Esmeralda* (Petipa after Perrot), GATOB, Leningrad
1931 The Komsomol Girl in *Bolt* (Lopukhov), GATOB, Leningrad
      Princess Aurora in *The Sleeping Beauty* (Petipa), GATOB, Leningrad
      Columbine in *Le Carnaval* (Fokine), GATOB, Leningrad
      Kitri in *Don Quixote* (Gorsky after Petipa), Paliashvili Theatre, Paliashvili
1932 Jeanne in *The Flames of Paris* (Vainonen), Kirov Ballet, Leningrad
      Kitri in *Don Quixote* (Gorsky after Petipa), Kirov Ballet, Leningrad
1933 Odile in *Swan Lake* (new production; Vaganova after Petipa, Ivanov), Kirov Ballet, Leningrad
1934 Zarema in *The Fountain of Bakhchisarai* (Zakharov), Kirov Ballet, Leningrad

1935 Title role (cr) in *Esmeralda* (Vaganova after Petipa), Kirov Ballet, Leningrad

1936 Florine (cr) in *Lost Illusions* (Zakharov), Kirov Ballet, Leningrad

1938 Manizhe (cr) in *Heart of the Hills* (Chabukiani), Kirov Ballet, Leningrad

1939 Pascuale (cr) in *Laurencia* (Chabukiani), Kirov Ballet, Leningrad

Medora in *Le Corsaire* (Petipa), Kirov Ballet, Leningrad

1940 Oksana in *Taras Bulba* (Lopukhov), Kirov Ballet, Leningrad

1941 Nikiya in *La Bayadère* (Ponomarev, Chabukiani after Petipa), Kirov Ballet, Leningrad

1942 Nuné (cr) in *Gayané* (Anisimova), Kirov Ballet, Perm

1943 Lise in *Vain Precautions* (*La Fille mal gardée*; Ponomarev after Petipa, Ivanov), Kirov Ballet, Perm

1946 Makeface (Ugly Sister; cr) in *Cinderella* (Sergeyev), Kirov Ballet, Leningrad

1947 Title role (cr) in *Tatyana* (Burmeister), Kirov Ballet, Leningrad

Other roles include: Title role in *Cinderella* (Sergeyev), Juliet in *Romeo and Juliet* (Lavrovsky), title role in *Giselle* (Petipa after Coralli, Perrot; staged Vaganova), title role in *Laurencia* (Chabukiani), Pannochka in *Taras Bulba* (Lopukhov), Parasha in *The Bronze Horseman* (Zakharov), Waltz and Mazurka in *Chopiniana* (Vaganova after Fokine), Bacchante in *Faust* (opera; mus. Gounod, chor. Chabukiani), Waltz in *Ivan Susanin* (opera; mus. Glinka, chor. Lopukhov, Koren).

PUBLICATIONS

By Vecheslova:

I am a Dancer, Leningrad and Moscow, 1964

Editor, textbook by Serebrennikov, N.N., *Support Techniques in Choreographic Duets*, Leningrad, 1969; second edition, 1979

Of the Things I Value Most, Leningrad, 1984

About Vecheslova:

Graham, Rockwell, "Harbingers of the New Russian", *The American Dancer* (Los Angeles), February 1934

Brodersen, Y., "Tatyana Vecheslova", *Rabotchy i Teatr* (Leningrad), no. 18, 1936

Krasovskaya, Vera, "The Pride of the Leningrad Ballet", *Vetcherni Leningrad* (Leningrad), 11 July 1947

Kremshevskaya, Galina, *The Honoured Artist of the Russian Federation, Tatyana Mikhailovna Vecheslova*, Leningrad, 1951

Kremshevskaya, Galina, "Ballerina Tatyana Vecheslova", *Vecherni Leningrad* (Leningrad), 24 June 1953

Karp, Poel, "Life Goes On", *Teatralnaya Zhizn* (Moscow), no. 23, 1961

Kremshevskaya, Galina, "Tatyana Vecheslova," *Teatr* (Moscow), no. 9, 1971

Chernova, Natalia, *From Geltser to Ulanova*, Moscow, 1979

Kremshevskaya, Galina, "Tatyana Vecheslova", *Sovetsky Balet* (Moscow), no. 3, 1983

*   *   *

Tatyana Vecheslova was one of the most outstanding Soviet ballerinas and actresses to appear on the Kirov stage. Her dancing demonstrated perfect classical technique, and she showed exceptional gracefulness on pointe. But she was more than a mere technician. Vecheslova was referred to as "one of the most exciting dramatic actresses among all Soviet ballerinas". She took an active part in virtually all the new ballet productions of her time, joining in the artistic quests and choreographic experiments of Fedor Lopukhov, Rostislav Zakharov, Leonid Lavrovsky, and Vakhtang Chabukiani. The characters she performed ranged from deeply tragic figures to comic types, and in each she was able to demonstrate the depth and range of her artistic gift. She had no equal either in comic roles, like that of the White Pussycat in *The Sleeping Beauty*, or in highly dramatic roles, like Tao-Hoa and Esmeralda. The only lyric-romantic role she liked to perform was that of Juliet, creating her own, original version of this role, rather than imitating Galina Ulanova, as so many other Russian ballerinas have done.

Vecheslova came to the Kirov Theatre when the artistic director of the ballet company was Fedor Lopukhov, who liked and promoted young performers. He immediately appreciated the young dancer's unusual gift: only seven days after the beginning of the season, Vecheslova was named to the second cast for the lead role in the ballet *The Red Poppy*, which Lopukhov was then staging. But she made her début unexpectedly on 9 September 1928, after only one rehearsal, in the role of Gulnara in *Le Corsaire*. A superb ballet "memory", a high level of professional training, and a natural dramatic responsiveness helped her to perform the role with only one rehearsal, and it became a permanent part of her repertoire.

Two years later, Vecheslova, almost in the same impromptu manner, made her appearance in one of her best roles—Esmeralda. According to the recollections of her contemporaries, Vecheslova was, and remained, the best of all the most famous performers in this role. She was capable of enhancing any choreographic movement with vital feeling. At once cunning and tender, loving and suffering, she seemed to bring to the stage the pain of all those who are defenceless, and so have been deeply injured. As Esmeralda, Vecheslova brought together all the emotions and experiences which her character's story demonstrated, and it was with the role of Esmeralda that Vecheslova was most often identified.

Being a serious, exacting artist, Vecheslova gave up her stage career when she was still in her prime. Her farewell performance, which took place on 24 June 1953, was a celebration of her unwithering talent and artistic courage. Near the end of her performing career, Vecheslova had begun teaching at the Leningrad Choreographic School, and after retirement from the stage she became a répétiteur for the Kirov company. As a rehearsal supervisor for the dancers of the Kirov Ballet she encouraged new ideas, and she openly supported every bright initiative on the part of young choreographers and dancers. In particular she showed a strong interest in the exciting work of the young Yuri Grigorovich, especially in his work on *The Stone Flower* (1957). She always showed an intelligent approach to dance, and proved this in her own writing; she was the author of several books and numerous articles on ballet.

The ballerina Ninel Petrova wrote of Vecheslova: "A whole generation of actors is indebted to her for comprehending the concept of their profession. . . . I don't know anyone who lived so passionately, so young, who took everything around her so much to heart, who would give herself so thoroughly to any cause. . . . Vecheslova has genuine talent, and it shows, one way or another, in everything she does."

—Igor Stupnikov
with Nina Alovert

LA VENTANA
(*The Window*)

Choreography: August Bournonville
Music: Hans Christian Lumbye, Wilhelm Christian Holm
Libretto: August Bournonville
First Production: Casino Theatre, Copenhagen, 19 June 1854
Principal Dancers: Juliette Price (Señorita), the Price family

Other productions include: Royal Danish Ballet (restaged and revised August Bournonville); Copenhagen, 6 October 1856. Royal Swedish Ballet (restaged Bournonville); Stockholm, 15 June 1858. Bonn Opera Ballet (staged Hans Brenaa after Bournonville); Bonn, 1973. American Ballet Theatre (pas de trois only; staged Erik Bruhn after Bournonville), with Bruhn, Cynthia Gregory, Rudolf Nureyev; New York, 28 July 1975. New York City Ballet (pas de trois only; staged Stanley Williams after Bournonville), as part of *Bournonville Divertissements*; New York, 3 February 1977. Pittsburgh Ballet Theatre (staged Kirsten Ralov after Bournonville, design Henry Heymann); Pittsburgh, 3 October 1980. Royal New Zealand Ballet (staged Harry Haythorne after Brenaa, design David Taylor); 27 June 1981. Bolshoi Ballet (staged Kirsten Ralov

after Bournonville, design Jens-Jacob Worsaae); Moscow, 10 May 1989.

PUBLICATIONS

Bournonville, August, *Mit Theater Liv* (autobiography), 3 parts: Copenhagen, 1848, 1865, 1877; as *My Theatre Life*, translated by Patricia McAndrew, Middletown, Connecticut, 1979
Fridericia, Allan, *August Bournonville*, Copenhagen, 1979
Terry, Walter, *The King's Ballet Master*, New York, 1979
McAndrew, Patricia (ed. and trans.), "The Ballet Poems of August Bournonville: The Complete Scenarios", *Dance Chronicle* (New York), vol. 6, no. 1, 1983
Hallar, Marianne, and Scavenius, Alette (eds.), *Bournonvilleana*, translated by Gaye Kynoch, Copenhagen, 1992

* * *

La Ventana's world premiere was in 1854 at the Casino Theatre, Copenhagen, but it was revised by Bournonville himself in 1856 for the Royal Danish Ballet at the Royal Theatre,

La Ventana, with Grethe Ditlevsen, Copenhagen, 1908

Copenhagen. The expanded version featured a sequidilla which Bournonville admittedly stole from Paul Taglioni and a thrilling pas de trois that some say is Bournonville's most perfect creation.

The story, which is scant, concerns a beautiful Señorita who dreams of the handsome man she has just met at Mass or on the Alameda. She gazes at herself in the mirror, dancing before her image (in the ballet the reflection is danced by another). She soon tires of this game and, sitting on the bed, she hears the melodies of her young man outside her window as he serenades her. She picks up her castanets and plays along and then, opening the window, tosses her lover a bow from her dress. In the second scene, later added by Bournonville, the Señorita's bedroom is transformed into a garden with a terrace where the Señor dances with his friends while showing off his love token. The Señorita enters the scene masked by her mantilla; she eventually reveals herself, and together she and her man dance joyously in celebration of his marriage proposal.

Bournonville created *La Ventana*, a divertissement with a Spanish flavour, in response to the craze for Spanish dance that was sweeping nineteenth-century Europe. In his memoirs (*My Theatre Life*), Bournonville writes that while attracted to the "pretty and romantic qualities to be found in the Spanish character", he was loath to repeat the showy excesses of the popular Spanish style which he deemed vulgar. His first venture into Spanish territory produced the highly successful *The Torreador* (1840). *La Ventana*, his second and last foray in this direction, was created, he says, "... to show how, without depriving the picture of its national physiognomy, one could idealize it and draw it into the dramatic sphere".

Bournonville also created *La Ventana* as a star vehicle for his favourite ballerina Juliette Price, a member of the famous English circus family which resettled in Copenhagen in the late eighteenth century. Bournonville revered Price, calling her "... one of those high priestesses of Terpsichore, after Marie Taglioni and Carlotta Grisi, who came nearest to my ideal of a female dancer".

One of Bournonville's shortest works, *La Ventana* is noteworthy for the quality of its choreography. The whole ballet revolves around an old trick, known as far back as the *commedia dell'arte*, called the Mirror Dance, in which the illusion of a reflection is created by another dancer performing in exact unison with the first. Bournonville's predecessor, Galeotti, had already surprised Danish audiences with this effect as early as 1802, though some critics credit Bournonville as the innovator. This dance dominates the first scene and in the second the sequidilla, pas de trois, and the seductive solo for the Señorita draw the ballet to a lively conclusion.

Best described as a choreographic curiosity, *La Ventana* asks its dancers to be vigorous while staying within the small-boned refinement of the Franco-Danish dancing mould. It stands as an example of an unusually pure and refined style of dance and beyond its title is as Spanish as the Little Mermaid. In all regards, it is a Danish ballet shot through with Bournonville's subtle touch. Easeful but zestful, *La Ventana* is full of airy "ballon" and fleet-footed bourrées, a character executed with rippling speed and an eye for elegance in motion.

La Ventana was revived by Frank Schaufuss and Hans Brenaa for the Royal Danish Ballet in 1941, and has been a staple of the company's repertoire ever since. The pas de trois from *La Ventana* was staged by Erik Bruhn for American Ballet Theatre in 1975, and by Stanley Williams for the New York City Ballet in 1977 as the third section of *Bournonville Divertissements*.

—Deirdre Kelly

VERDY, Violette

French dancer and ballet director. Born Nelly Guillerm in Pont-l'Abbé, Brittany, 1 December 1933. Studied with Madame Rousanne (Rousanne Sarkissian) and Victor Gsovsky, Paris. Début with Ballets des Champs-Elysées, Paris, 1945; dancer, (Roland Petit's) Ballets de Paris, 1950, performing with Maggio Musicale Fiorentino, 1951; principal dancer, Ballet Marigny, 1952, Ballets de Paris, 1953–54, and London Festival Ballet, 1954–55, also performing at La Scala, Milan, and in various festivals and galas; guest ballerina, American Ballet Theatre, 1957–58; principal dancer, New York City Ballet, 1958–76; also frequent guest artist, with appearances for Metropolitan Opera in New York, National Ballet in Washington, D.C., San Francisco Ballet, Boston Ballet, Stuttgart Ballet, and Bavarian State Opera Ballet, Munich; also actress, including with company of Madeleine Renaud and Jean-Louis Barrault, and in films, including in film *Ballerina* (released in United States as *Dream Ballerina*; dir. Berger, chor. Georgi, 1950), and *The Glass Slipper* (dir. Walters, chor. Petit, 1954); also made frequent appearances on American television; artistic director, Paris Opéra Ballet, 1977–80; associate director, Boston Ballet, 1980–84; teaching associate, New York City Ballet, from 1984; also frequent guest teacher and artistic adviser. Recipient: *Dance Magazine* Award, 1968; Doctor of Humane Letters, Skidmore College, 1971; title of Chevalier de l'Ordre des Arts et Lettres, France, 1971; Doctor of Arts, Goucher College, 1987.

ROLES

1945   Little Girl in *Le Poète* (Petit), Ballet des Champs-Elysées, Paris
1947   Young girl in *Le Déjeuner sur l'herbe* (Petit), Ballet des Champs-Elysées
       Child in Love in *Le Rendez-vous* (Petit), Ballet des Champs-Elysées
       Nymph in *Les Amours de Jupiter* (Petit), Ballet des Champs-Elysées
       August (cr) in *Treize danses* (Petit), Ballet des Champs-Elysées, Paris
1948   Follower of the Devil in *La Fiancée du Diable* (Petit), Ballet des Champs-Elysées, Cairo
       Soloist in *Fête galante* (Gsovsky), Ballet des Champs-Elysées, European tour
       Acrobat in *Les Forains* (Petit), Ballet des Champs-Elysées, European tour
       Soloist (cr) in *La Création* (Lichine), Ballet des Champs-Elysées, London
       Waltz in *Les Sylphides* (Fokine), Ballet des Champs-Elysées, Paris
       Son of William Tell in *Mascarade* (Gsovsky), Ballet des Champs-Elysées, Paris
       Eurydice in *Orpheus* (Lichine), Ballet des Champs-Elysées, Paris
       Servant (cr) in *La Rencontre* (Lichine), Ballet des Champs-Elysées, Paris
1950   Principal dancer (cr) in *Musical Chairs* (Petit), Les Ballets de Paris de Roland Petit, Biarritz
1951   Rosetta in *Scarlattiana* (Milloss), Maggio Musicale Fiorentino, Italy
       Spirit of the Air in *I Vespri Siciliani* (Milloss), Maggio Musicale Fiorentino, Italy
       Soloist in *Macbeth* (Milloss), Maggio Musicale Fiorentino, Italy
       Nymph of Clori in *Tirsi et Clori* (Milloss), Maggio Musicale Fiorentino, Italy

Violette Verdy in *Allegro Brillante,* **1968**

The Maid in *Nocturne* (Gsovsky), Maggio Musicale
    Fiorentino, Italy
Young Girl (cr) in *Romanza Romana* (Staff), Ballet des
    Champs-Elysées, Paris
Queen of Hearts in *Jeu de cartes* (Charrat), Ballet des
    Champs-Elysées, Paris
Principal dancer in *Les Amours de Jupiter* (Petit), Ballet
    des Champs-Elysées, Paris

1952 Principal in *La Lettre* (Rousane), Gala, Brussels
Princess in *L'Histoire du soldat* (Lemoine), International
    Jeunesses Musicales de France (JMF)
Juliet in *Romeo and Juliet* (Lifar), National Federation
    of War Invalids
Sugar Plum Fairy in *The Nutcracker* pas de deux (after
    Ivanov), Dance and Culture gala
Ballerina in *Grand pas classique* (pas de deux; Gsovsky),
    Gala, Brussels
Kitri in *Don Quixote* Pas de deux (after Petipa),
    National Federation of War Invalids
Mazurka in *Les Sylphides* (Fokine), Ballets de Marigny,
    Paris
Columbine in *Arlequinade* (Volinine), Ballets de Mar-
    igny, Paris
Orphise (cr) in *Les Fâcheux* (Berger), Ballets de
    Marigny, Paris
Soloist in *Pour les enfants sages* (Chauviré), Ballets de
    Marigny, Paris
Principal dancer (cr) in *Le Rendezvous sentimental*
    (Chauviré), Ballets de Marigny, Paris

Swanilda in *Coppélia,* Act II (after Petipa), Amsterdam
    Opera Ballet, Monte Carlo
Fiancée (cr) in *Le Loup* (Petit), Ballets de Paris, Paris
Title role (cr) in *La Perle* (Gsovsky), Ballets de Paris,
    Paris
Princess Aurora in *The Sleeping Beauty,* Act III
    (Petipa), Gala, Bordeaux
Widow in *Deuil en 24 heures* (Petit), Ballets de Paris,
    Paris
Princess Florine (Bluebird Pas de deux) in *Aurora's
    Wedding* (from *The Sleeping Beauty*; Petipa), Ballets
    de Paris, London

1954 Title role in *Carmen* (Petit), Ballets de Paris, New York
Snow Queen in *The Nutcracker* (pas de deux; Dolin after
    Ivanov), London Festival Ballet, Manchester
Odette in *Swan Lake* (Act II; Dolin after Ivanov),
    London Festival Ballet, Manchester
Fleur-de-Lys in *Esmeralda* (Beriozoff), London Festival
    Ballet, Detroit
Nocturne and Waltz in *Les Sylphides* (Fokine), London
    Festival Ballet, U.S. tour
Marguerite in *Vision of Marguerite* (Ashton), London
    Festival Ballet, Chicago

1955 Soloist in *Balance à trois* (Babilée), Gala, Enghien
Principal dancer (cr) in *Orpheus and Eurydice* (opera;
    mus. Gluck, chor. Taras), Aix-en-Provence Festival
Juliet (cr) in *Romeo and Juliet* (Rodrigues), Ballet of La
    Scala (Milan), Verona
Title role (cr) in *Cinderella* (Rodrigues), Ballet of La
    Scala, Milan

1956 Principal in *Les Belles Damnées* (Petit), Ballets de Paris,
    European tour

1957 Paramour (cr) in *Conte fantastique* (Howard), Ballet
    Rambert, London
Title role in *Giselle* (after Petipa, Coralli, Perrot), Ballet
    Rambert, London
Solo in *Designs with Strings* (Taras), American Ballet
    Theatre, tour
Clorinda in *Le Combat* (Dollar), American Ballet
    Theatre, tour
Operetta Star in *Offenbach in the Underworld* (Tudor),
    American Ballet Theatre, Portland
Ballerina in *Theme and Variations* (Balanchine), Ameri-
    can Ballet Theatre, Berkeley

1958 "Girl in White" in *Les Patineurs* (Ashton), American
    Ballet Theatre, tour
Principal dancer in *Paean* (Ross), American Ballet
    Theatre, Brussels
Title role in *Miss Julie* (Cullberg), American Ballet
    Theatre, New York
La Fille de Terpsichore from Paris in *Gala Performance*
    (Tudor), American Ballet Theatre, New York
Title role in *Helen of Troy* (Lichine), American Ballet
    Theatre, New York
Carlotta Grisi in *Pas de Quatre* (Dolin), American Ballet
    Theatre, New York
Fourth variation in *Divertimento No. 15* (Balanchine),
    New York City Ballet, New York
Creusa in *Medea* (Cullberg), New York City Ballet,
    New York
Third Campaign ("Rifle Regiment") in *Stars and
    Stripes* (Balanchine), New York City Ballet, New
    York
First movement in *Symphony in C* (Balanchine), New
    York City Ballet, New York
Title role (cr) in *The Princess* (Jo Anna), Palm Beach
    Ballet, Florida

First movement in *Western Symphony* (Balanchine),
New York City Ballet, New York

1959   Polyhymnia in *Apollo* (Balanchine), New York City
Ballet, New York

Symphony (cr) in *Episodes* II (Balanchine), New York
City Ballet, New York

Principal dancer in (*Glinka*) *Pas de trois* (Balanchine),
New York City Ballet, New York

Title role in *Medea* (Cullberg), New York City Ballet,
New York

Fourth Campaign ("Liberty Bell") in *Stars and Stripes*
(Balanchine), New York City Ballet, New York

Third Movement in *Symphony in C* (Balanchine), New
York City Ballet, New York

Ballerina in *Gounod Symphony* (Balanchine), New York
City Ballet, New York

Captain of the Amazons in *Con Amore* (Christensen),
New York City Ballet, New York

Snowbird in *A Fantasy of Japanese Birds* (de Larrain),
Embassy Ball Charity Gala

Court dancer in *The Gypsy Baron* (Danilova), Metropolitan Opera Ballet, New York

Dewdrop Fairy in *The Nutcracker* (Balanchine), New
York City Ballet, New York

1960   Second Pas de trois: Bransle Gay in *Agon* (Balanchine),
New York City Ballet, New York

Principal dancer in *Argentina* (Taras), New York City
Ballet, New York

Principal dancer (cr) in *Choros* (*Brazil*; Moncion),
Variaciones Concertantes (*Argentina*; Taras), *Sinfonia*
(*Uruguay*; d'Amboise) in *Panamerica* (Balanchine,
Contreras, Moncion, Taras, d'Amboise), New York
City Ballet, New York

The Sands of the Desert (cr) in *The Figure in the Carpet*
(Balanchine), New York City Ballet, New York

Title role in *Firebird* (Balanchine), New York City
Ballet, New York

Sleepwalker in *Night Shadow* (*La Sonnambula*; Balanchine), New York City Ballet, New York

Principal dancer (cr) in (*Tchaikovsky*) *Pas de Deux*
(Balanchine), New York City Ballet, New York

Principal dancer in *Donizetti Variations* (Balanchine),
New York City Ballet, New York

Principal dancer, Fourth Couple in *Liebeslieder Walzer*
(Balanchine), New York City Ballet, New York

Principal dancer in *Serenade* (Balanchine), New York
City Ballet, New York

1961   Odile in *Swan Lake*, Act III (Black Swan Pas de deux;
after Petipa), Columbia, North Carolina

Principal dancer (cr) in *Electronics* (Balanchine), New
York City Ballet, New York

1962   Principal dancer in *Orfeo* (opera; mus. Gluck, chor.
Taras), Metropolitan Opera Ballet, New York

Divertissement (cr) in *A Midsummer Night's Dream*
(Balanchine), New York City Ballet, New York

Hippolyta in *A Midsummer Night's Dream* (Balanchine),
New York City Ballet, New York

1963   Principal dancer in *The Still Point* (Bolender), America
Dances Touring Program

Chloe in *Daphnis and Chloe* (Cranko), Stuttgart Ballet,
Stuttgart

Title role in *Firebird* (Rosen), Bavarian State Opera
Ballet, Munich

Juliet in *Romeo and Juliet* (Cranko), Stuttgart Ballet,
Stuttgart

Principal dancer in *Ballet Imperial* (Balanchine), Royal
Ballet, New York

1966   Second Variation (cr) in *La Guirlande de Campra*
(Taras), New York City Ballet, New York

1967   Principal dancer in *Allegro Brillante* (Balanchine), New
York City Ballet, New York

Emeralds (cr) in *Jewels* (Balanchine), New York City
Ballet, New York

Soloist in *Grand Pas Classique* (Maule), Jacob's Pillow
Festival, Massachusetts

Title role in *The Snow Maiden* (Burmeister), Jacob's
Pillow Festival, Massachusetts

Polka (cr) in *Glinkiana* (later *Valse Fantaisie*; Balanchine), New York City Ballet, New York

1968   Principal in *Haydn Concerto* (Taras), New York City
Ballet

Ballerina in *Tarantella* (Balanchine), Miami Beach
Symphony, Miami

Ballerina (cr) in *La Source* (pas de deux; Balanchine),
New York City Ballet, New York

1969   Principal dancer (cr) in *Dances at a Gathering* (Robbins),
New York City Ballet, New York

Title role in *La Sylphide* (Bournonville), National Ballet,
Washington, D.C.

Solo in *La Lithuanienne* (Lefebvre), Boston Ballet,
Boston

Principal dancer in *Raymonda Variations* (Balanchine),
New York City Ballet, New York

1970   Principal dancer (cr) in *In the Night* (Robbins), New
York City Ballet, New York

Danse (cr) in *Sarabande and Dance* (Clifford), New
York City Ballet, New York

1971   Ballerina in *Airs de Ballet* (Christensen), San Francisco
Ballet, San Francisco

Court dancer in *La Périchole* (opera; mus. Offenbach,
chor. Saddler), Metropolitan Opera Ballet, New York

Odette/Odile in *Swan Lake* (Petipa, Ivanov), Miami
Ballet, Miami

1972   Principal dancer (cr) in *Printemps* (Lorca Massine),
New York City Ballet, New York

Principal dancer in *Scènes de Ballet* (Petrov), Pittsburgh
Ballet Theatre

The Girl (cr) in *Pulcinella* (Balanchine, Robbins), New
York City Ballet, New York

Solo in *The Concert* (Robbins), New York City Ballet,
New York

Louisa in *The Nutcracker* (Neumeier), Royal Winnipeg
Ballet

Principal dancer (cr) in *Choral Variations on Bach's
"Vom Himmel Hoch"* (Balanchine), New York City
Ballet, New York

1973   Principal dancer (cr) in *A Beethoven Pas de Deux*
(Robbins), New York City Ballet, New York

Principal dancer (cr) in *Sonatina* (Balanchine), New
York City Ballet, New York

1974   First movement in *Brahms–Schoenberg Quartet* (Balanchine), New York City Ballet, New York

Principal dancer in *Scotch Symphony* (Balanchine),
New York City Ballet, New York

1975   Principal dancer (cr) in *Sonatina* (Balanchine), New
York City Ballet, New York

Other roles include: Second movement in *Symphony in C*
(Balanchine), principal dancer in *Concerto Barocco* (Balan-
chine), Choleric in *The Four Temperaments* (Balanchine), the
Siren in *Prodigal Son* (Balanchine), the Queen in *The Cage*
(Robbins), Queen of the Morphides in *Piège de Lumière*
(Taras).

PUBLICATIONS

By Verdy:
Giselle, New York, 1970
Interview in Lyle, Cynthia, *Dancers on Dancing*, New York, 1977
Giselle: A Role for a Lifetime, New York, 1977
Interview in Lavole, Jean-Pierre, "Violette Verdy", *Pour la danse* (Paris), October 1977
Merrill, Bruce, "Violette Verdy Talks About Her Years at the Paris Opera", *Dance Magazine* (New York), November 1978
Interview in Tracy, Robert, *Balanchine's Ballerinas*, New York, 1983
"The Paris Opera", *Ballet Review* (New York), Fall 1986
"Violette Verdy on the Bolshoi", *Ballet Review* (New York), Summer 1987

About Verdy:
Lidova, Irène, "Une Visage de la Danse Française: Violette Verdy", *Ballet Annual* (London), vol. 9, 1955
Goodman, Saul, "Brief Biographies: Violette Verdy", *Dance Magazine* (New York), April 1958
"Profile: Violette Verdy", *Dancing Times* (London), November 1963
Marks, Marcia, "Violette", *Dance Magazine* (New York), February 1972
Swope, Martha (photographer), *Violette Verdy*, Brooklyn, 1975
Reynolds, Nancy, *Repertory in Review*, New York, 1977
Huckenpahler, Victoria, *Ballerina: A Biography of Violette Verdy*, New York, 1978
Croce, Arlene, *Afterimages*, New York, 1978

*   *   *

Violette Verdy's dancing sparkled with energy; it was the kind of energy which could well have made her seem competitive. But she did not use it that way. She made it an adjunct to her keen theatrical judgment and to her need to make everything she danced into a clearly formed artistic statement. Her dancing, no matter how ebullient, seemed always in quest of a life philosophy. Beneath the radiant exterior was the soul-searching typical of her Breton ancestry.

What were the statements she made? Sometimes they were about the music, as in George Balanchine's *Episodes*, about which she later said, with regard to the Anton Webern accompaniment, "The one thing that disconcerted me at first was to dance with so little sound coming from the pit, but then I realized that we had to imprint on top of the musical line. It was making its own time. . . . the sound came then as a kind of reward, rather than the expected motivation." Sometimes her statement was about the sheer fun of showing off, as when she led the Third Campaign ("Rifle Regiment") of Balanchine's *Stars and Stripes* as though she were the dance embodiment of Donizetti's saucy Daughter of the Regiment. Or her statement could embody the pain of betrayal, as in Birgit Cullberg's *Miss Julie*.

In his *Gala Performance*, choreographer Antony Tudor caricatured the typical French ballerina. She was flighty, coquettish, a bit malicious, and empty-headed. Violette Verdy was often called "typically French" in the delicious wit she brought to many of her interpretations. But she embodied the ideal French temperament. It was characterized by careful attention to detail, intellect (coupled with a formal education superior to that of most ballet dancers), and independence of artistic viewpoint.

Verdy's education was not formal in the institutional sense. She was guided into copious reading by her mother, who had been a teacher. And so, early in her career, when she prepared roles like Carmen or the Fiancée in Roland Petit's *Le Loup*, both of which she danced as a member of his Ballets de Paris, there was much imagery she could draw upon. She later prepared her classical roles with equal awareness of their roots. Of one of these, Giselle, she also wrote a book.

Violette Verdy was an unusual dancer to be taken into the New York City Ballet, for although a deeply serious artist, she had her own idiosyncratic way of accenting the music. This might not have appealed to the company's highly musical director, George Balanchine. As it was, she joined the company in 1958, and within two years had six roles created especially for her. Perhaps the most cognizant of her French "esprit" was Balanchine's *Pas de Deux* to the music of Tchaikovsky. But it was in his *Liebeslieder Walzer* that she was challenged to find her way into the same reverie which held all of the couples in its thrall. She did so with depth and intuition.

In 1967, when she performed the "Emeralds" section of Balanchine's *Jewels*, Verdy met still another challenge. Here the Fauré music required extended legato dance phrases. Verdy executed them with silken aplomb.

As she matured, Verdy sought outlets in addition to New York City Ballet. Among them were the Royal Ballet, Stuttgart Ballet, Paris Opéra Ballet, Boston Ballet, Miami Ballet, Royal Winnipeg Ballet, San Francisco Ballet, National Ballet of Washington, and Pittsburgh Ballet Theatre. In these settings she usually performed nineteenth-century ballet heroines. They complemented her New York City Ballet repertoire.

In 1976 she retired from dancing and in 1977 was offered the directorship of the Paris Opéra Ballet. She remained until 1980 and then became associate director of the Boston Ballet; but when the director, E. Virginia Williams, died in 1984, Verdy decided not to advance to her position.

The same restless nature which had sparked her performing has led Violette Verdy into many other facets of dance. Although she is a teaching associate with the New York City Ballet, she is a much sought-after guest teacher and choreographer for regional and college companies, and she has functioned as a perceptive artistic consultant for the Royal and San Francisco Ballet Companies, as well as for their schools.

—Doris Hering

VESTRIS, Auguste

French dancer and teacher. Born Marie Jean Augustin Vestris in Paris, 27 March 1760, son of Opéra dancers Gaetano (Gaëtan) Vestris and Marie Allard. Studied with father, Gaetano Vestris. Married (1) dancer Anne Catherine Augier, 1795 (d. 1809): one son, Armand; (2) Jeanne-Marie Thuillier, 1823. Opéra debut (at the age of 12), in *La Cinquantaine*, 1772; soloist ("danseur seul et en double"), Paris Opéra, from 1776; becoming premier danseur from 1778, and premier sujet de la danse, 1780; leading dancer, King's Theatre, London, 1780–81, 1783–84, 1785–86, 1788, 1791, 1815; retired from the Opéra, 1816; imprisoned for debt, 1819; came out of retirement to perform (at the age of 75) with Marie Taglioni, Paris Opéra, 1835; also a leading teacher for dancers of the Paris Opéra: pupils include Charles Didelot, August Bournonville, Jules Perrot, Fanny Elssler, Marie Taglioni. Died in Paris, 5 December 1842.

ROLES

1772   Dancer in *La Cinquantaine* (pastorale; mus. Laborde), Opéra, Paris

1773   L'Amour (cr) in *Endymion* (ballet; G. Vestris), Opéra, Paris

1775   Dancer in *Sabinus* (tragédie-lyrique; mus. Gossec), Opéra, Paris
       Dancer (cr) in *Céphale et Procris* (tragédie-lyrique; mus. Grétry), Opéra, Paris
       Dancer in *La Provençale* (act from *Les Fêtes de Thalie* ballet; mus. Mouret), Opéra, Paris
       Dancer (cr) in *Philémon et Baucis* (ballet; mus. Gossec), Opéra, Paris

1778   Dancer (cr) in *Les Petits Riens* (ballet, first Opéra production; Noverre), Opéra, Paris

1779   Dancer in *Alceste* (tragédie-lyrique; mus. Gluck, chor. Noverre), Opéra, Paris
       Le Berger (cr) in *Echo et Narcisse* (pastorale; mus. Gluck), Opéra, Paris

1780   Acis, Amant de Galathée (cr) in *Les Caprices de Galathée* (Noverre), Opéra, Paris
       Grand Chaconne in *Grand Serious Ballet* (Simonet), King's Theatre, London
       Leading Dancer in *Les Amants surpris* (Simonet), King's Theatre, London

1781   Leading dancer in *The Nymphs of Diana* (also chor.), King's Theatre, London
       Dancer in *The Rural Sports* (Simonet), King's Theatre, London
       Leading dancer in *Ninette à la cour* (G. Vestris after M. Gardel), King's Theatre, London
       Prince (cr) in *Medée et Jason* (new production; G. Vestris after Noverre), King's Theatre, London

1782   Zéphyr (cr) in *L'Embarras de richesses* (opéra-comique; mus. Grétry), Opéra, Paris
       Dancer in *Thésée* (tragédie-lyrique; new mus. Gossec), Opéra, Paris

1783   Dancer (cr) in *Atys* (tragédie-lyrique; new mus. Piccini), Opéra, Paris
       L'Eveillé in *La Chercheuse d'esprit* (ballet; M. Gardel), Opéra, Paris
       Dancer (cr) in *Péronne sauvée* (opera; Dézaides), Opéra, Paris
       Un Berger (cr) in *Renaud* (tragédie-lyrique; mus. Sacchini), Opéra, Paris
       Le Surveillant (cr) in *La Rosière* (ballet; M. Gardel), Opéra, Paris
       "Allegorical Ballet" (cr) in *The Pastimes of Terpsichore* (Dauberval), King's Theatre, London
       Dancer (cr) in *Friendship Leads to Love* (Dauberval), King's Theatre, London
       Pas de deux (cr; with Mlle. Theodore) in *New Divertissement*, King's Theatre, London

1784   Dancer (cr) in *Le Réveil du bonheur* (Dauberval), King's Theatre, London
       Cossack (cr) in *Divertissement* (Dauberval), King's Theatre, London
       Pastoral Minuet (cr) in *Le Coq au village; ou, La Lotterie ingénieuse* (Dauberval), King's Theatre, London
       Adonis (cr) in *Orpheo* (Dauberval), King's Theatre, London
       Dancer (cr) in *Le Magnifique* (Dauberval), King's Theatre, London
       Manhood (cr; pas de trois) in *The Four Ages of Man* (Dauberval), King's Theatre, London

Auguste Vestris, 1781

       Dancer (cr) in *Pygmalion* (Dauberval), King's Theatre, London
       Dancer (cr) in *Le Déserteur; ou, La Clémence royale* (Dauberval), King's Theatre, London
       Dancer (cr) in *Sémiramis* (Le Picq), King's Theatre, London

1785   Daphnis (cr) in *Le Premier Navigateur; ou, Le Pouvoir de l'amour* (ballet; M. Gardel), Opéra, Paris
       Dancer in *Divertissement villageois* (D'Egville), King's Theatre, London

1786   Acis in *Acis and Galatea* (Giroux), King's Theatre, London
       Daphnis (cr) in *Le Premier Navigateur; ou, La Force de l'amour* (also chor., after M. Gardel), King's Theatre, London
       Leading dancer (cr) in *L'Amour jardinier* (D'Egville), King's Theatre, London
       Pas de trois from *L'Épreuve villageoise* (opera; mus. Grétry, chor. A. Vestris), King's Theatre, London
       Dancer in *Iphigénie en Aulide* (tragédie-lyrique; mus. Gluck), Opéra, Paris
       Dancer (cr) in *Panurge dans l'île des lanternes* (opera; mus. Grétry, chor. M. Gardel), Opéra, Paris
       Dancer (cr) in *Pénélope* (tragédie-lyrique; mus. Piccini), Opéra, Paris
       Dancer (cr) in *Pizarre* (tragédie-lyrique; mus. Candeille), Opéra, Paris
       Dancer (cr) in *Phèdre* (tragédie-lyrique; mus. Lemoyne, chor. M. Gardel), Opéra, Paris
       Dancer (cr) in *Les Sauvages* (ballet; M. and P. Gardel), Opéra, Paris

1787   Dancer (cr) in *Alcindor* (opera; mus. Dézaides), Opéra, Paris
       Le Garçon (cr) in *Le Coq au village* (ballet; M. Gardel), Opéra, Paris
       Dancer (cr) in *Oedipe à Colone* (tragédie-lyrique; mus. Sacchini), Opéra, Paris
       Dancer (cr) in *Les Offrandes á l'Amour* (Noverre), King's Theatre, London

1788   Dancer (cr) in *Amphitryon* (opera; mus. Grétry, chor. P. Gardel), Opéra, Paris

Dancer in *Arvire et Evelina* (opera; mus. Sacchini), Opéra, Paris

Dancer (cr) in *Démophon* (tragédie-lyrique; mus. Cherubini, chor. P. Gardel), Opéra, Paris

Dancer (cr) in *The Military Dance* (Chevalier), King's Theatre, London

L'Amour (cr) in *Psyche et L'Amour* (new version; Noverre), King's Theatre, London

Euthyme (cr) in *Euthyme et Eucharis* (revival; Noverre), King's Theatre, London

Dancer in *Adèle de Ponthieu* (Noverre), King's Theatre, London

Dancer (cr) in *New Ballet* (Noverre), King's Theatre, London

Dancer (cr) in *La Bonté du Seigneur* (Didelot), King's Theatre, London

1789   Dancer (cr) in *Aspasie* (opera; mus. Grétry, chor. P. Gardel), Opéra, Paris

Dancer (cr) in *Démophon* (tragédie-lyrique; mus. Vogel), Opéra, Paris

Dancer (cr) in *Les Prétendus* (opera; Lemoyne), Opéra, Paris

1790   Dancer (cr) in *Les Pommiers et le moulin* (opera; Lemoyne), Opéra, Paris

1791   Provençal (cr) in *La Fête des matelots et des provençaux*, King's Theatre, London

Amant d'Amadriade (cr) in *L'Amadriade; ou, La Nimphe des bois* (G. Vestris), King's Theatre, London

Pas de trois (cr) in *Les Folies d'Espagne* (also chor.), King's Theatre, London

Colin (cr) in *La Fête du Seigneur* (G. Vestris), King's Theatre, London

1808   Antonio (cr) in *Les Amours d'Antoine et de Cléopâtre* (Aumer), Opéra, Paris

1816   Dancer in *L'Enfant prodige* (P. Gardel), Opéra, Paris

1826   Domingo in *Paul et Virginie* (P. Gardel), Opéra, Paris

Saint-Léger in *La Dansomanie* (P. Gardel), Opéra, Paris

WORKS

1781   *The Nymphs of Diana*, King's Theatre, London

1786   *Le Premier Navigateur; ou, La Force de l'amour* (after M. Gardel), King's Theatre, London

Dances in *L'Epreuve villageoise* (opera; mus. Grétry), King's Theatre, London

1791   *Les Folies d'Espagne*, King's Theatre, London

PUBLICATIONS

Noverre, Jean-Georges, *Lettres sur la danse et les ballets*, Stuttgart and Lyons, 1760; as *Letters on Dancing and Ballets*, translated by Cyril Beaumont (from 1803 edition), London, 1930

Campardon, Émile, *L'Académie royale de musique*, Paris, 1881

Capon, Gastron, *Les Vestris: Le Dieu de la danse et sa famille*, Paris, 1908

Beaumont, Cyril, "Auguste Vestris", *Ballet* (London), August 1947

Beaumont, Cyril, "Gaetano and Auguste Vestris in English Caricature", *Ballet* (London), March 1948

Lifar, Serge, *Auguste Vestris, Le Dieu de la danse*, Paris, 1950

Guest, Ivor, *The Romantic Ballet in England*, London, 1954

Reyna, Ferdinando, "Un dio della danza", *La Scala* (Milan), August/September 1960

Guest, Ivor, *The Romantic Ballet in Paris*, London, 1966

Winter, Marian Hannah, *The Pre-Romantic Ballet*, London, 1974

Fenner, Theodore, "Ballet in Early Nineteenth-century London", *Dance Chronicle* (New York), vol. 1, no. 2, 1978

Chapman, John, "Auguste Vestris and the Expansion of Technique", *Dance Research Journal* (London), Summer 1987

*   *   *

In an era when performers were national status symbols, and when ballets told stories that represented a nation's aspirations, the dancer Auguste Vestris reigned supreme. He was so valued as a national asset that Napoleon refused him permission to leave Paris in 1807 with the words: "Foreigners must come to Paris to see Vestris dance". The Emperor must have had a special regard for the dancer, for Vestris often played characters with whom he identified. As Ulysses, for example, Vestris depicted the warlike virtues fostered by Bonaparte—bravery, nobility, loyalty, and self-sacrifice. It was an age in which people and events seemed larger than life, when allusions to the monumental deeds of men such as Alexander, Achilles, and Mark Antony were not vain affectations but accurate metaphors of modern times.

Enthusiasm for Vestris was not exaggerated. The brilliance of his athletic style set a standard that led dance away from the values of the court into those of the bourgeois theatre. Whereas his father Gaétan (Gaetano) had been venerated for the dignity, nobility, restraint, and ease of his dancing, Auguste was applauded for his big jumps, rapid footwork, and multiple pirouettes. Even the great Jean-Georges Noverre recognized Vestris as "the most astonishing dancer in Europe". But he knew that the art was being changed irrevocably. Vestris was drawing material from all three of the genres—the *sérieux*, *demi-caractère*, and *comique*—that traditionally determined what dancers could do by body type and style. Noverre wrote that Vestris had caused "the three well-known and distinct genres to disappear; he has moulded them together . . . he has formed a new style . . .". Thus Vestris expanded enormously what the single performer could achieve on stage, both in terms of physical virtuosity and expressiveness.

Though Noverre had reservations about the direction in which Vestris was leading ballet, most critics and audiences showered him with praise. And the younger generation of dancers paid him the supreme compliment, almost without exception, of attempting to imitate him. Their failures to approach his mastery underlined Vestris's genius. Dancers in his day trained in a method within which strength of limb and lung, as well as the extreme muscular dexterity necessary to the successful execution of tours de force such as Vestris performed, were not considered important. Where Vestris transcended the limitations of eighteenth-century training, others stumbled, fell behind the music, and heaved their bodies in such an awkward manner that critics complained almost ceaselessly from 1800 to 1830. By 1830, teaching practice, thanks to the efforts of Vestris himself as well as men such as Filippo Taglioni and Monsieur Albert, had caught up with dancers' ambitions—Marie Taglioni, Jules Perrot, and Fanny Elssler were among those who reaped the harvest of excellence in dance training.

One dancer did manage to disturb Vestris's reign during the early nineteenth century. Louis Duport, in a "duel of dance" in 1804—Vestris was 44, Duport in his early 20s—appears to have at least equalled the old master in the area of athleticism. But as

Noverre pointed out, Duport was no match for Vestris when it came to dramatic expression. August Bournonville, who studied with Vestris in the 1820s, and captured the older dancer's style in the Bournonville syllabus, wrote: "Even in his old age, when during classes he rehearsed some scenes [from Gardel's *L'Enfant prodigue*] . . . he often allowed himself to be so carried away that the illusion became complete, and we imagined that we saw before us in the flesh a youth of nineteen, with all of his follies and aberrations."

Vestris's teaching career was as distinguished as his performing. Two of the most important ballet artists of the century were his pupils, Jules Perrot and Bournonville. To prepare dancers for the demands of the new style, daily classes were introduced as well as exercises intended to strengthen the heart, lungs, legs, feet, and torso.

Noverre said of Vestris that "he is, in all respects, the first dancer of the Opéra and Europe. As long as he has the ability to move, he will be the inimitable model for his art." For more than 40 years on the Opéra stage, he inspired dancers to imitate and audiences to cheer him, and in so doing did much to change his art.

—John Chapman

VESTRIS, Gaetano (Gaétan)

Italian/French dancer, choreographer, and ballet master. Born Gaetano Apolline Baldassare Vestris in Florence, into famous Italian-French dancing family, 18 April 1729. Studied probably with family, and at various Italian and German opera houses when engaged as a dancer; also trained with Louis Dupré in Paris. Married German dancer Anna Heinel, 1792; one son, Adolphe, by Heinel, b. 1791; also one son, dancer Auguste Vestris, by dancer Marie Allard, b. 1760. Early career in Italy: dancer in various opera houses including in Bologna, Venice, and Genoa; premier danseur, Vienna and Dresden, c.1740s; début at L'Académie royale de musique (Paris Opéra), 1748, becoming premier danseur (replacing Dupré), from 1751; left Opéra, 1754–56, appearing as leading dancer, Berlin, 1754, and ballet master, Turin, 1755; also performed under Jean-Georges Noverre, Stuttgart, from 1761; on return to Paris Opéra, made assistant maître de ballet to Jean-Barthélemy Lany, 1761, becoming chief maître de ballet, 1770–76; guest dancer, with son Auguste, King's Theatre, London, 1781; retired as premier danseur, 1782, reappearing at King's Theatre, London, 1788, 1791, and Paris Opéra, for the début of grandson Armand-Auguste Vestris, 1800; also director, ballet school of the Paris Opéra: pupils included son, Auguste Vestris, premier danseur of the Paris Opéra, and Charles-Louis Didelot. Died in Paris, 27 September 1808.

ROLES

1748 Un Matelot in *Le Carnaval et la folie* (comédie-ballet; mus. Destouches), Opéra, Paris

1750 Un Masque galant in *Les Fêtes vénitiennes* (opera-ballet; mus. Campra), Opéra, Paris

Un Turc (cr) in *Almasis* (ballet; mus. Royer), Opéra, Paris

Un Faune in *Ismène* (pastorale; mus. Rebel, Francoeur), Opéra, Paris

Un Romaine (cr) in *Léandre et Héro* (tragédie-lyrique; mus. Brassac), Opéra, Paris

Un Guerrier, Un Homme du peuple de la Palestine in *Tancrède* (tragédie-lyrique; mus. Campra), Opéra, Paris

Un Triton, Un Scythe in *Thétis et Pélée* (tragédie-lyrique; mus. Collasse), Opéra, Paris

1751 Un Génie suivant Oroès, Un Esprit cruel (cr) in *Acanthe et Céphise* (pastorale-héroïque; mus. Rameau), Opéra, Paris

Un Berger in *Le Ballet des sens* (opéra-ballet; mus. Mouret), Opéra, Paris

Un Suivant de la fortune (cr) in *Eglé* (ballet; mus. Lagarde), Opéra, Paris

Un Berger (cr) in *La Guirlande ; ou, Les Fleurs enchantées* (opéra-ballet; mus. Rameau), Opéra, Paris

Borée in *Les Indes galantes* (ballet-héroïque; mus. Rameau), Opéra, Paris

1752 Un Suivant de Polyphème in *Acis et Galathée* (pastorale-héroïque; mus. Lully), Opéra, Paris

Un Ombre d'amant heureux (cr) in *Les Amours de Tempé* (ballet; mus. Dauvergne), Opéra, Paris

Un Lydien, Un Grec, Un Magicien in *Omphale* (tragédie-lyrique; mus. Destouches), Opéra, Paris

1753 Un Pantomime en chasseur (cr) in *Le Devin du village* (intermède; mus. Rousseau), Opéra, Paris

Un Jeu et un Plaisir, un Chasseur in *Les Fêtes de Polymnie* (ballet; mus. Rameau), Opéra, Paris

Le Chef de la danse, Un Berger, Un Lutteur in *Les Fêtes grecques et romaines* (ballet-héroïque; mus. de Blâmont), Opéra, Paris

Un Jardinier (cr) in *La Gouvernante rusée* (opera; mus. Cocchi), Opéra, Paris

Un Plaisir, Un Jeu et un Ris (cr) in *Titon et l'aurore* (pastorale; mus. Mondonville), Opéra, Paris

Dancer in *Le Magnifique* (intermède; mus. Rebel, Francoeur, chor. Laval), Court Theatre, Fontainebleau

1754 Un Gladiateur, Un Génie qui préside aux planètes in *Castor et Pollux* (tragédie-lyrique; mus. Rameau), Opéra, Paris

Un Satyre in *Platée* (ballet; mus. Rameau), Opéra, Paris

Dancer in *Anacréon* (ballet-héroïque; mus. Rameau, chor. Laval), court theatre, Fontainebleau

1755 Pas seul, pas de deux (with Thérèse Vestris) in *Roland* (tragédie-lyrique; mus. Lully), Opéra, Paris

Dancer in *Giuoco di Contadini* (ballet; also chor.), Teatro di Torino, Turin

Dancer in *Coronazione di Apollo e Dafne* (ballet; also chor.), Teatro di Torino, Turin

Dancer in *Di Popoli orientali* (ballet; also chor.), Teatro di Torino, Turin

Dancer in *Cacci del cingliale Calidonia fatto de Meleagro, ed Atlante* (ballet; also chor.), Teatro di Torino, Turin

Dancer in *Combattimento navale di Spagnuioli e Cossari cotta vittoria de' primi* (ballet; also chor.), Teatro di Torino, Turin

Dancer in *Feste di Bacco* (ballet; also chor.), Teatro di Torino, Turin

1757 Endymion (cr) in *Les Surprises de l'amour* (ballet; mus. Rameau), Opéra, Paris

Un Sybarite (cr) in *Les Sybarites* (ballet; mus. Rameau), Opéra, Paris

1758 Dancer in *Alceste* (tragédie-lyrique; mus. Lully), Opéra, Paris

Dancer in *Proserpine* (tragédie-lyrique; mus. Lully), Opéra, Paris

1759 Dancer in *Amadis de Gaule* (tragédie-lyrique; mus. Lully), Opéra, Paris

1760 Dancer in *Canente* (tragédie-lyrique; new mus. Dau-

Gaetano Vestris with Giovanna Baccelli and Mme. Simonet in Medee et Jason, 1781

vergne), Opéra, Paris

Dancer in *Dardanus* (tragédie-lyrique; mus. Rameau), Opéra, Paris

Dancer (cr) in *Le Prince de Noisy* (ballet; mus. Rebel, Francoeur), Opéra, Paris

1761 Dancer in *Armide* (tragédie-lyrique; mus. Lully), Opéra, Paris

Dancer in *Zaïs* (ballet-héroïque; mus. Rameau), Opéra, Paris

Renaud in *Renaud et Armide* (ballet; mus. Rodolphe, chor. Noverre), Hoftheater, Stuttgart

Admète (cr) in *Admète et Alceste* (ballet; mus. Deller, chor. Noverre), Hoftheater, Stuttgart

1762 Dancer in *Iphigénie en Tauride* (tragédie-lyrique; mus. Desmarets, Campra, Berton), Opéra, Paris

Dancer in *Arueris* (intermède; mus. Rameau, chor. Laval, father and son), Court Theatre, Choisy

Hercules (cr) in *La Mort d'Hercule* (ballet; mus. Rodolphe, chor. Noverre), Hoftheater, Stuttgart

1763 Jason (cr) in *Medée et Jason* (ballet; mus. Rodolphe, chor. Noverre), Hoftheater, Stuttgart

Orpheus (cr) in *Orpheus und Eurydice* (ballet; mus. Deller, chor. Noverre), Hoftheater, Stuttgart

Neptune (cr) in *Le Triomphe de Neptune* (*Der Sieg des Neptuns*, ballet; mus. Deller, chor. Noverre), Hoftheater, Stuttgart

1764 Dancer in *Les Fêtes d'Hébé; ou, Les Talents lyriques* (ballet; mus. Rameau), Opéra, Paris

Dancer in *Naïs, opéra pour la paix* (ballet-héroïque; mus. Rameau), Opéra, Paris

1765 Dancer in *Les Fêtes de l'Hymen et de l'Amour* (ballet-héroïque; mus. Rameau), Opéra, Paris

Dancer in *La Femme* (act from *Les Fêtes de Thalie*, opera-ballet; mus. Mouret), Opéra, Paris

Un Argien in *Hypermnestre* (tragédie-lyrique; mus. Gervais), Opéra, Paris

Un More in *L'Italie* (act from *L'Europe galante*, opera-ballet; mus. Campra), Opéra, Paris

Dancer in *Erosine* (pastorale-héroïque; mus. Berton, chor. Laval, father and son), Court Theatre, Fontainebleau

Dancer in *Sylvie* (opéra-ballet; mus. Berton and Trial, chor. Laval, father and son), Court Theatre, Fontainebleau

Dancer in *Thétis et Pelée* (tragédie-lyrique; mus. Collasse, chor. Laval, father and son), Court Theatre, Fontainebleau

Dancer in *La Fée Urgèle* (opéra-comique; mus. Duni, chor. Laval, father and son), Court Theatre, Fontainebleau

Dancer in *Palmire* (ballet; chor. Laval, father and son), Court Theatre, Fontainebleau

Dancer in *Zénis et Almasie* (ballet-héroïque; mus. Laborde, Bury, chor. Laval, father and son), Court Theatre, Fontainebleau

Dancer in *Thésée* (tragédie-lyrique; mus. Mondonville, chor. Laval, father and son), Court Theatre, Fontainebleau

Dancer in *Le Ballet d'Eglé* (ballet; mus. Dauvergne, chor. Laval, father and son), Court Theatre, Fontainebleau

1766 Dancer in *Les Fêtes lyriques* (fragments from various works), Opéra, Paris

Dancer (cr) in *Sylvie* (opéra-ballet; mus. Berton, Trial), Opéra, Paris

1767 Dancer (cr) in *Ernelinde* (tragédie-lyrique; mus. Philidor), Opéra, Paris

1769 Dancer in *Enée et Lavinie* (tragédie-lyrique; new mus. Dauvergne), Opéra, Paris

Dancer in *Erigone* (act from *Les Fêtes de Paphos*, ballet; mus. Mondonville), Opéra, Paris

Dancer (cr) in *Hippomène et Atalante* (ballet; mus. Vachon), Opéra, Paris

1770 Dancer in *Ajax* (tragédie-lyrique; mus. Bertin), Opéra, Paris

Jason (cr) in *Médée et Jason* (ballet, new production; also chor., after Noverre), Opéra, Paris

Dancer in *Zoroastre* (tragédie-lyrique; mus. Rameau), Opéra, Paris

Dancer in *Aeglé* (ballet-héroïque; mus. Lagarde, chor. Laval), Court Theatre, Fontainebleau

Dancer in *Zaïde* (ballet; mus. Royer), Opéra, Paris

1771 Dancer in *Alcione* (tragédie-lyrique; mus. Marais), Opéra, Paris

Dancer (cr) in *Le Prix de la valeur* (ballet; mus. Dauvergne, chor. Vestris), Opéra, Paris

Dancer in *Pyrame et Thisbé* (tragédie-lyrique; mus. Rebel, Francoeur), Opéra, Paris

1772 Dancer in *Aline, reine de Golconde* (ballet-héroïque; mus. Monsigny), Opéra, Paris

Dancer in *L'Amour et Psyché* (ballet; mus. Mondonville), Opéra, Paris

1773 Dancer in *Le Feu* (act from *Les Éléments*, ballet; mus. Destouches), Opéra, Paris

Title role (cr) in *Endymion* (also chor.), Opéra, Paris

Dancer (cr) in *L'Union de l'amour et des arts* (opéra-ballet; mus. Floquet), Opéra, Paris

Dancer in *Zélindor, roi des sylphes* (ballet; mus. Rebel, Francoeur), Opéra, Paris

1774 Bacchus (cr) in *Azolan; ou, Le Serment indiscret* (ballet-héroïque; mus. Floquet), Opéra, Paris

Dancer in *Le Carnaval du Parnasse* (opéra-ballet; mus. Mondonville), Opéra, Paris

Dancer (cr) in *Iphigénie en Aulide* (tragédie-lyrique; mus. Gluck), Opéra, Paris

Dancer (cr) in *Orphée et Eurydice* (tragédie-lyrique; mus. Gluck), Opéra, Paris

Dancer (cr) in *Sabinus* (tragédie-lyrique; mus. Gossec), Opéra, Paris

1775 Dancer (cr) in *Alexis et Daphné* (pastorale; mus. Gossec), Opéra, Paris

Dancer (cr) in *Cythère assiégée* (ballet; mus. Gluck), Opéra, Paris

Dancer in *La Turquie* (act from *L'Europe galante*, opera-ballet; mus. Campra), Opéra, Paris

Dancer in *La Provencale* (act from *Les Fêtes de Thalie* (ballet; mus. Mouret), Opéra, Paris

Jason in *Médée et Jason* (ballet; mus. Rodolphe, additional music Berton, chor. Noverre), Opéra, Paris

1776 Apelles in *Apelles et Campaspe* (ballet; Noverre), Opéra, Paris

1777 Dancer (cr) in *Les Horaces* (ballet; Noverre), Opéra, Paris

Dancer (cr) in *Myrtil et Lycoris* (pastorale; mus. Desormery), Opéra, Paris

1778 Dancer in *Phaon* (lyric opera; mus. Piccini, chor. M. Gardel), Court Theatre, Choisy

1779 Dancer in *Alceste* (tragédie-lyrique; mus. Gluck), Opéra, Paris

Dancer (cr) in *Amadis de Gaule* (tragédie-lyrique; new mus. J.C. Bach), Opéra, Paris

Dancer (cr) in *Mirza et Lindor* (ballet; M. Gardel), Opéra, Paris

Dancer in *Echo et Narcisse* (pastorale; mus. Gluck, chor. probably M. Gardel), Opéra, Paris

1781 Prince in *Ninette à la cour* (ballet; chor. Vestris after M. Gardel), King's Theatre, London

Pas seul and pas de deux in *Grand Serious Ballet*, King's Theatre, London

Dancer (cr) in *Les Caprices de Galathée* (ballet anacréontique; also chor. after Noverre), King's Theatre, London

Jason (cr) in *Médée et Jason* (new production; also chor., after Noverre), King's Theatre, London

Dancer (cr) in *Gavotte de Vestris* (also chor.), King's Theatre, London

Divertissement (cr) in *L'Omaggio* (opera; mus. Bianchi, Rauzzini, Giordani, chor. Vestris), King's Theatre, London

Dancer in *Devonshire Minuet*, King's Theatre, London

1786 Dancer (cr) in *Le Nid d'oiseau* (ballet; also chor.), Opéra, Paris

1791 Hercules (cr) in *La Mort d'Hercule, and his Apotheosis* (also chor., after Noverre), King's Theatre, London

Minuet de la cour (cr) in *L'Amadriade; ou, La Nimphe des bois* (also chor.), King's Theatre, London

The Devonshire Minuet (cr) in *La Capricieuse* (also chor.), King's Theatre, London

Le Seigneur (cr) in *La Fête du Seigneur* (also chor.), King's Theatre, London

WORKS

1755 *Giuoco di Contadini*, Teatro di Torino, Turin

Coronazione di Apollo e Dafne, Teatro di Torino, Turin

Di Popoli orientali, Teatro di Torino, Turin

Cacci del cingliale Calidonia fatto de Meleagro, ed Atlante, Teatro di Torino, Turin

Combattimento navale di Spagnuioli e Cossari cotta vittoria de' primi, Teatro di Torino, Turin

Feste di Bacco, Teatro di Torino, Turin
1767   *Médée et Jason* (after Noverre), Burgtheater, Vienna
1770   *Médée et Jason* (after Noverre; new mus. de la Borde), Opéra, Paris (revived Paris Opéra, with new mus. Rodolphe and Berton, 1775)
1771   *Le Prix de la valeur* (mus. Dauvergne), Opéra, Paris
1773   *Endymion*, Opéra, Paris
1781   *Ninette à la cour* (after M. Gardel), King's Theatre, London
       Les Caprices de Galathée (ballet anacréontique; chor. after Noverre), King's Theatre, London
       Médée et Jason (new production; after Noverre, but unacknowledged; mus. Nosieri, Gluck), King's Theatre, London
       Gavotte de Vestris, King's Theatre, London
       Dances in *L'Omaggio* (opera; mus. Bianchi, Rauzzini, Giordani), King's Theatre, London
1786   *Le Nid d'oiseau*, Opéra, Paris
1791   *La Mort d'Hercule, and his Apotheosis* (after Noverre; mus. von Esch), King's Theatre, London
       L'Amadriade; ou, La Nimphe des bois, King's Theatre, London
       La Capricieuse, King's Theatre, London
       La Fête du Seigneur, King's Theatre, London

PUBLICATIONS

Noverre, Jean-Georges, *Lettres sur la danse et les ballets*, Stuttgart and Lyons, 1760; as *Letters on Dancing and Ballets*, translated by Cyril Beaumont (from 1803 edition), London, 1932
Berchoux, Joseph de, *La Danse ou les dieux de l'opéra*, Paris, 1806
Castil-Blaze, *La Danse et les ballets depuis Bacchus jusqu'à Mlle. Taglioni*, Paris, 1832
Castil-Blaze, *L'Académie impériale de musique*, Paris, 1855
Campardon, Émile, *L'Académie royale de musique*, Paris, 1881
Capon, Gaston, *Les Vestris: Le Dieu de la danse et sa famille*, Paris, 1908
Lichy, L.A., "Les Vestris: Gaétan, le 'dieu de la danse'", *Archives internationales de la danse* (Paris), July 1935
Moore, Lillian, *Artists of the Dance*, New York, 1938
Beaumont, Cyril, "Gaetano and Auguste Vestris in English Caricature", *Ballet* (London), March 1948
Lifar, Serge, *Auguste Vestris, Le Dieu de la danse*, Paris, 1950
Guest, Ivor, *The Romantic Ballet in England*, London, 1954
Winter, Marian Hannah, *The Pre-Romantic Ballet*, London, 1974
Guest, Ivor, *Le Ballet de L'Opéra de Paris*, Paris, 1976
Hammond, Sandra Neil, "The Gavotte de Vestris", Society of Dance History Scholars *Proceedings*, 1984

*   *   *

Gaetano Vestris was known as "Le Dieu de la danse"—the god of dance—at first jocularly and later as a serious tribute to his extraordinary talents as a dancer. Tall, well-formed, and "irresistibly charming", as Grimm termed him, Vestris was premier danseur at the Paris Opéra for over 30 years, and excelled in the style of dance known as "noble" or heroic. Over and over, contemporaries chose the word "perfect" to describe his dancing. Lebrun, for example, asserted that Vestris was "perfect in the *danse noble*" and related in precise detail how elegantly the dancer performed the graceful gesture of doffing his hat. The *Gavotte de Vestris* was often associated with his

name; he and his son performed it in London in 1781, and it remained popular into the early twentieth century.

Little is known about Vestris's early career in Italy. He worked his way up the peninsula, beginning with Naples and Palermo. He danced briefly at opera houses in Bologna, Venice, and Genoa en route to Vienna and Dresden, where he was engaged as premier danseur. In 1746 his family moved to Paris, where he began training with Dupré to remove deficiencies in his turn-out. Vestris made his Opéra debut as a sailor in the ballet of *Le Carnaval et la folie* (1748), and was appointed premier danseur in 1751, replacing Dupré. According to Noverre, Vestris equalled his master in the perfection of his style, but surpassed him in the versatility and in the taste with which he performed. The *Mercure de France* praised his "ease and nobility, lightness and precision".

In 1754 Vestris was imprisoned after he challenged the balletmaster Lany to a duel, affronted because his sister Thérèse was displeased with her assigned roles. Soon afterwards, he and his sister left for Berlin. In Turin (1755), he was engaged as ballet master and choreographed six ballets of the heroic genre. His tour ended back in Paris, and audiences greeted him with enthusiasm. In his entire Parisian career (1748 to 1782), Vestris danced leading roles in over 70 ballets and operas.

Vestris was greatly influenced by Jean-Georges Noverre when he danced in Stuttgart, from 1761 onwards. Following Noverre's example, he jettisoned the mask behind which he had always hidden his expressive features; furthermore, he may have sharpened his pantomimic skills on annual leaves spent at Stuttgart. Perhaps due to Noverre's suggestion, Vestris somewhat simplified his mode of dress over the years, moving away from his former preference for elaborate costumes. In 1754, for example, he wore an absurdly lavish peasant's outfit: it was made of white taffeta with chenille roses scattered about it, bestrewn with rose-coloured ribbons and garlands of flowers.

Vestris danced a leading role in the famous heroic ballet *Médée et Jason*, and was so impressed with this early example of a *ballet d'action* "that he mounted it at the Vienna court theatre (8 February 1767), at the Paris Opéra (11 December 1770), and in London (1781). There he also presented Noverre's *Les Caprices de Galathée*, another pantomime-ballet.

Vestris introduced the newly fashionable *ballet d'action* to the Paris Opéra after he was appointed its ballet master in 1770. He mounted *Médée et Jason*, which Grimm criticized for blurring Noverre's original distinction between the dramatic pantomime and its danced finale. Later, he composed *Endymion* (1773), termed an heroic "pantomime-ballet". Vestris's son Auguste made one of his earliest public appearances as Cupid (L'Amour), in a vehicle designed to display the boy's talents as much as the choreographer's own. In the ballet, Cupid is lost in the woods, but Nymphs discover him and become enraptured with the little god. Endymion (played by Vestris) enters, enslaved by love, and Cupid promises him victory over the cold-hearted Diane (Mlle. Guimard). The ballet concludes with a celebration of the Triumph of Love—Diane and Endymion pledge their love and Nymphs pair off with Fawns while Cupid is beguiled by Graces, Games, and Pleasures. Vestris also choreographed *Le Nid d'oiseau* (1786). Both ballets were said to be strikingly mediocre in concept, and were not retained in the repertoire.

Vestris was eminently successful, by contrast, as director of the Opéra school of dance. His most famous pupil was his son Auguste; the latter's greatness was due, he proudly boasted, to the boy's good fortune in having such a great teacher as himself. Other students included Charles-Louis Didelot and his wife Mlle. Rose.

Gaetano Vestris was the first and most famous performer

from a close-knit but large family of theatrical dancers, who dominated European stages for over a century. He retired in 1782, but returned to the Opéra in 1800 so that three generations of Vestris could dance a minuet together on the occasion of the four-year-old Armand's début. Baron, in his *Lettres à Sophie sur la danse*, suggested that confusion would be minimized if the various members of the Vestris clan were to append numbers behind their names, as kings do.

The man's vanity appeared to equal his accomplishments as a performer. Vestris was a favourite subject of contemporary anecdotes that touted his pretentious arrogance, such as reports of his boast that there existed only three great men in all of Europe: Frederick the Great, Voltaire, and himself. Or, when his son was imprisoned for refusing to dance at the Queen's express command, Vestris lamented, with real tears in his eyes, "Alas! This is the first quarrel of the house of Vestris with the Bourbon family."

—Maureen Needham Costonis

VIENNA WALTZES

Choreography: George Balanchine
Music: Johann Strauss jun., Franz Lehár, Richard Strauss
Design: Rouben Ter-Arutunian (scenery), Barbara Karinska (costumes)
First Production: New York City Ballet (as *Wiener Waltzer*), New York State Theatre, New York, 23 June 1977
Principal Dancers: Karin von Aroldingen, Sean Lavery (Tales of the Vienna Woods), Patricia McBride, and Helgi Tomasson (Voices of Spring), Bart Cook and Sara Leland (Explosion Polka), Kay Mazzo and Peter Martins (Gold and Silver Waltz), Suzanne Farrell and Jorge Donn ("Der Rosenkavalier")

PUBLICATIONS

Reynolds, Nancy, *Repertory in Review*, New York, 1977
Kirstein, Lincoln, *Thirty Years: The New York City Ballet*, New York, 1978
Croce, Arlene, *Going to the Dance*, New York, 1982

* * *

George Balanchine's *Vienna Waltzes*, called *Wiener Waltzer* during its 1977 premiere season, immediately became about as popular with the public as had his 1967 *Jewels*. While the new work was about an hour's worth of dancing, as opposed to a full evening's worth, it made for a spectacle even larger than that of *Jewels*. The five sections of this suite of waltzes take the audience on a grand Viennese circuit. With excellent assistance from Rouben Ter-Arutunian's fluidly changeable set and Barbara Karinska's lavish costumes, *Vienna Waltzes* starts out in dappled clearings of the Vienna woods and passes through an ornate, art nouveau café interior before arriving in a grand, stately, mirrored Secessionist ballroom.

Balanchine's choreographic programme carefully treads a fine line between the presentation of fresh ballet spectacle and the evocation of multitudinous personal images, conjured up in the presence of such beloved and familiar old world waltz music. The score's material includes, in order, "Tales from the Vienna Woods", "Explosion Polka", "Voices of Spring" (all by

Johann Strauss the Younger), "Gold and Silver Waltz", from *The Merry Widow* (by Franz Lehár), and a suite of waltzes from "Der Rosenkavalier" (by Richard Strauss).

The first section, originally led by Karin von Aroldingen and Sean Lavery, presents a decorous dalliance for young women in blush-pink ball dresses and dapper young officers in smart uniforms trimmed in braid and buckram. Though the leading dancers are central here, their moves and manners are delicately echoed by ten similarly costumed couples.

The scene changes slightly for the second waltz—two of the setting's central trees, about which the "Vienna Woods" couples have been innocently flirtatious, disappear, and into this bigger clearing comes a group of sprites (nine women, one principal dancer, and eight corps dancers). With the women dressed in tulle ballet dresses of rose and green, and in pointe shoes (for the only section that is danced on pointe), the mood of the "Voices of Spring" is one of windswept delicacy. Leading these smilingly sweet revels is a prominent wood nymph and her elegant rustic swain (originally performed by Patricia McBride and Helgi Tomasson). Their dance is airborne and friendly, more than impassioned and interwoven.

The "Explosion Polka" is the suite's wild card, both musically and dramatically. Its four couples (originally led by Sara Leland and Bart Cook) romp, by way of polka steps, through the woods, with the women in abbreviated bustled frocks and the men in tight and vibrant "incroyable" get-ups. Particularly with the men's hair swept up in fulsome coxcombs and their waists framed by pointy tail-coats, the frolicsome twosomes look as if they all scooted out of the local brothel for a little night air.

A major scenery change occurs for the "Gold and Silver" section. This site, a turn-of-the-century café frequented by officers and fancily dressed ladies, is framed in golden, tendrilled, art nouveau scroll-work. The central action here concerns a mysterious woman in black (originally performed by Kay Mazzo) and a dashing young officer in scarlet and cream (originally Peter Martins). The fascination she holds for all the men is made evident in the course of this waltz, and the special interest she has for the most elegant officer is equally pronounced. Amid the toasts and the sometimes decorous, sometimes seductive social dancing, a drama builds. In the end the officer and the "merry widow" are caught in silhouetted embrace. (In addition to adjusting the precise configuration of the ending, Balanchine also had the "widow's" costume revised a number of times.)

The fanfare introduction to the Richard Strauss mini-suite signals the ballet's final scene change. Eventually the stage is at its most grand and glacial: a wall of two-storey mirrors and stark white tree-trunk roots, serving as chandeliers, turn the stage into a chill, silvery ballroom. At first elegant strolling couples cross the space on isolated diagonals. Eventually into the midst of the empty ballroom comes a lone woman (Suzanne Farrell, originally), dressed in a carefully draped and cut white satin gown that bares her back. Initially her presence is one of private reverie, as she is seen dancing her way into Strauss's building waltz. An adoring partner enters like a phantom lover and supports her without disturbing her privacy. After a swirl of like couples chains on and ebbs off, the waltz ends with the lone woman's exit. Her deep and almost staggering back-bend cues the ballet's finale. The space becomes ablaze with light: the chandeliers come on all at once, sparkling with golden stars of brightness.

From here, as Strauss's waltz surges and subsides, and surges some more, the stage becomes awash with waltzing couples. As the women hold out their white satin trains, the black-clad men whirl them around in a frenzy both dizzying and precise, perfectly in tune with Strauss's music. The scene is one of

Vienna Waltzes, New York City Ballet, 1977

exciting depth and both austere and opulent movement. We see twenty corps-de-ballet couples skimming around the five principal couples—all the leading dancers from the other four waltzes return here, now also dressed in shiny black or white—and the mirrored stage appears peopled by 50 individuals all reacting to a common throbbing, driving pulse.

This finale, one seemingly frenetic and yet pointedly inevitable, is musically and dramatically fitting for Balanchine's *Vienna Waltzes*. But in tone and emotion it relates directly to at least two former waltz renderings by the choreographer: *Cotillon* (1932) and *La Valse* (1951).

—Robert Greskovic

VIGANÒ, Salvatore

Italian dancer, choreographer, and teacher. Born in Naples, son of choreographer Onorato Viganò and ballerina Maria Ester (née Boccherini), 25 March 1769. Studied composition with uncle, Luigi Boccherini, as well as painting and dancing; later studied with Jean Dauberval, Bordeaux and London, from 1789. Married Spanish dancer Maria Medina, 1789 (sep. c.1799). Stage début as dancer in female roles, 1783; appeared in Rome, 1786, and moved to Venice, 1788; guest performer in Spain, appearing in coronation festivities of Charles IV, 1789; met Dauberval in Spain: dancer, Grand Théâtre, Bordeaux (under ballet master Dauberval), 1789–90, travelling to London with Dauberval company to perform at King's Theatre, London, 1791; returned to Venice: début as choreographer, Teatro San Samuele, Venice, 1791, staging own version of Dauberval's famous *La Fille mal gardée* at Teatro La Fenice, 1792; leading dancer, Vienna, from 1793, touring central Europe with wife, including Prague, Dresden, Berlin, and Hamburg, 1795–98; choreographer, Hoftheater, Vienna, 1799–1804, staging *The Creatures of Prometheus*, 1801; returned to Italy: dancer and choreographer, including in Milan, 1804–05, Rome, 1807, Padua, and Venice, 1809; choreographer, Teatro alla Scala, Milan, 1811–21. Died in Milan, 10 August 1821.

WORKS

1791   *Raul Signore di Crequi; ossia, La Tirannida repressa* (ballo tragicomico; also mus.), Teatro San Samuele, Venice

I Divertimenti di Amore (mus. G. Viganò), Teatri San Samuele, Venice
1792 *La Figlia mal custodita* (*La Fille mal gardée*; after Dauberval), Teatro La Fenice, Venice
1793 *Diana und Endymion* (after Muzzarelli), Hoftheater, Vienna
Die Tochter der Luft, oder: Die Erhöhung der Semiramis, Hoftheater, Vienna
1794 *Die Lupercalien* (divertissement), Hoftheater, Vienna
Die Liebe Galateens (divertissement), Hoftheater, Vienna
1795 *Richard Löwenherz, König von England* (*Riccardo Cuor di Leone*; mus. Weigl), Kärntnertortheater, Vienna
Das gefundene Veilchen, Vienna
1798 *I Serviani*, Teatro San Benedetto, Venice
Giorgio Principe della Servia (mus. Trento), La Fenice, Venice
Divertimento, La Fenice, Venice
1799 *Clothilde, Hergzogin von Salerno* (after Gozzi), Hoftheater, Vienna
1800 *Mazilli und Orisko*, Hoftheater, Vienna
1801 *Die Geschöpfe des Prometeus* (*The Creatures of Prometheus*; mus. Beethoven), Burgtheater, Vienna
1802 *Il Noce di Benevento*, Kärntnertortheater, Vienna
Spanier auf der Insel Christina (*Gli Spagnoli nell'Isola Cristina*), Kärntnertortheater, Vienna
1803 *I Giuochi Istmici* (mus. Weigl), Kärntnertortheater, Vienna
1804 *Divertimento campestre*, Carcano, Milan
Cajo Marzio Coriolano (after Shakespeare; mus. Weigl), Carcano, Milan
1805 *Sammette e Tamiri*, for Coronation of Napoleon Bonaparte, Carcano, Milan
La Prepotenza vinta dall'egoismo (after Beaumarchais), Milan
1807 *Principessa nel bosco*, Rome
1809 *Ippotoo Vendicato*, Festa del Santo, Padua
Gli Strelizzi (mus. various), Teatro La Fenice, Venice
1810 *Il Semplice e la Vanarella*, Teatro Imperiale, Turin
Il Barbiere di Villafranca, Teatro Imperiale, Turin
1811/ *Un Equivoco*, La Scala, Milan
12
1812 *La Pastorella fortunata*, La Scala, Milan
Le Due Case attigue, La Scala, Milan
Il Noce di Benevento (expanded version; mus. Süssmayr), La Scala, Milan
Le Villanelle bizzarre, La Scala, Milan
1813 *Prometeo* (mus. Beethoven, Mozart, Haydn, Weigl, Viganò), La Scala, Milan
Il Diavolo alla vendemmia, La Scala, Milan
Samandria liberata; ossia, I Serviani (new version of *I Serviani*), La Scala, Milan
Il Nuovo Pigmalione, La Scala, Milan
1814 *Gli Ussiti sotto a Naumburgo*, La Scala, Milan
Il Sindaco vigilante, La Scala, Milan
1815 *Numa Pompilio*, La Scala, Milan
1817 *Mirra; o sia, La Vendetta di Venere*, La Scala, Milan
Psammi, re d'Egitto, La Scala, Milan
Le Tre Melarance, La Scala, Milan
Le Nozze del villaggio, La Scala, Milan
Dedalo (mus. Lichenthal and various), La Scala, Milan
La Scuola del villaggio, La Scala, Milan
1818 *Otello; o sia, Il Moro di Venice* (after Shakespeare; mus. various), La Scala, Milan
La Spada di Kenneth, La Scala, Milan
La Vestale (mus. various), La Scala, Milan
1819 *Bianca; o sia, Il Perdono per sorpresa* (mus. Ayblinger), La Scala, Milan
I Titani (mus. Ayblinger, Viganò), La Scala, Milan
Il Calzolaia di Mompellieri, La Scala, Milan
Cimene (mus. Lichtenthal), La Scala, Milan
1820 *Alessandro nell'Indie* (mus. Ayblinger), La Scala, Milan
Giovanna d'Arco (mus. Ayblinger, Brambilla), La Scala, Milan
Le Sabine in Roma (mus. Ayblinger), La Scala, Milan
1821 *Didone* (mus. Ayblinger), La Scala, Milan

PUBLICATIONS

Ritorni, Carlo, *Commentaria della vita e delle opera coreodrammatiche di Salvatore Viganò*, Milan, 1838
Saint-Léon, Arthur, *La Sténochorégraphie, ou Art d'écrire promptement la danse*, Paris, 1852
Regli, Francesco (ed.), *Dizionario biografico dei piu celebri poeti ed artisti melodrammatici . . . che fiorirono in Italia dal 1800 al 1860*, Turin, 1860
Prunières, Henri, "Le Ballet au XIXe siècle", *La Revue musicale* (Paris), December 1921
Levinson, André, "Le Ballet de *Prométhée*: Beethoven and Viganò", *La Revue musicale* (Paris), April 1927
Kirstein, Lincoln, *Dance: A Short History of Classic Theatrical Dancing*, New York, 1935
Beaumont, Cyril, *Complete Book of Ballets*, revised edition, London, 1951
Gatti, Carlo, *La Scala nella storia e nell'arte 1778–1963*, Milan, 1964
Howes, Frank, "Prometheus: Creator—Beethoven", *Dancing Times* (London), January 1971
Winter, Marian Hannah, *The Pre-Romantic Ballet*, London, 1974
Il Balletto: Reperterio del teatro di danza dal 1581, Milan, 1979; as *Phaidon Book of the Ballet*, translated by Olive Ordish, London, 1980
Raimondi, Ezio, *Il Sogno del coreodramma*, Reggio Emilia, 1984
Ferrero, Mercedes Viale, "Costume designs by Alessandro Sanquirico and others for ballets performed at the Teatro alla Scala, Milan 1820–1824", *Dance Research* (London), Summer 1984
Terzian, Elizabeth, "Salvatore Viganò: His Ballets at the Teatro La Scala (1811–1821)", Master's thesis, University of California, Riverside, 1986

* * *

Salvatore Viganò was considered by his contemporaries the only choreographer of his time to possess all the qualities required for a composer of ballet, as defined by the Greek author Lucian: he was poet, composer, musician, and actor.

Viganò's critics compared him to Shakespeare in his poetic treatment of the drama. His personal genius lay in his ability to use pantomime effectively in his ballets. He incorporated dances into the action of the ballet, according to the precepts taught by his teacher Dauberval. He made use of the dance steps of the time in his dance numbers such as the Furlana in Act I of *Otello*, the Sicilian dance of *Bianca*, and the sacred dance of the vestals in Act I of *La Vestale*. In the latter, the dancers raised their arms and lifted their eyes to the heavens, assuming the residence of the deities in the sky. Viganò called for new ways of acting and dancing. The last act of *Otello* shows all the gradations of feelings that succeed one after the other in Otello's soul: anger, tears, disdainful and mocking laughter, curious glances of suspicion, bitter moanings, prostration of

Salvatore Viganò with his wife Maria Medina, 1790

grief, violence, and finally fury and murder.

A "mute poet", Viganò was also an artist in painting and sculpture in the way he composed his picturesque tableaux. His group scenes resemble works by famous artists: *Prometeo* is said to be worthy of the brush of Raphael and of Francesco Albani. Several scenes in *La Vestale* are based on statues by Antonio Canova. Extant etchings of scenographic designs for the ballets and of iconography determine the postures of the dancers and give a more concrete sense of the style than any written description. The etchings represent actual groupings in the ballets. Viganò's figures have the quality of mosaics and the linear designs of an engraving. The silhouettes, the lines, the drapery folds—all indicate motion and levitation. Viganò used the groups and crowds creatively. In his ballets, the crowds acted as protagonists rather than serving merely as a decorative background.

Scenic design was an important element in Viganò's ballets. The famous Paolo Landriani, Giovanni Perego, and Alessandro Sanquirico designed the scenes of his Milanese ballets. The splendour of the painted and sculpted designs increased the lavishness of the ballets. The elaborate costumes further explain the strong theatricality of Viganò's works. At La Scala, 1,085 dresses were made for one ballet, with Viganò himself supervising the costume designs. He directed the distribution of colours in *Mirra*'s costumes, which were magnificent, varied, and harmonious.

In music, Viganò selected the best pieces by contemporary composers and arranged them according to the needs of the action in the ballet. The practice of using a patchwork of musical pieces, most of it drawn from operas, was common at the time. In *La Vestale*, Viganò used excerpts from Rossini's *La Gazza ladra* and Spontini's *La Vestale*. His earlier works include eighteenth-century dances such as the minuet in *Die*

Lupercalien and the chaconne and gigue in *Raul Signore di Crequi*. The music of his later works marks an important development in ballet music as related to the drama. It is descriptive and charged with atmosphere. Action and music support each other harmoniously; movements are carefully studied in their relationship to the music; and the melodies of most of the numbers are memorable and appealing. They are characterized by variations and repeats of the motifs.

Viganò's catholicity in all art forms essentially determines the vast scope of his choreographic composition. His ballets can be divided generally into two main categories: the serious ballets in five or six acts, with themes of chivalry, heroism, dignity, and grandeur; and the comic ballets in two acts, marked by farce and comedy.

Viganò drew upon a wide variety of European sources for his subject material. His sources included authors such as Virgil, Shakespeare, Corneille, Metastasio, Alfieri, and Schiller. Historical events appealed to him. The tragedy of *La Vestale* has its roots in ancient Rome. *Gli Strelizzi* deals with Peter the Great's repression of the strelizzi. He also used Greek and Roman mythology in *Prometeo, Il Noce di Benevento, Mirra, Dedalo, I Titani*.

Viganò knew how to adapt his artistic concepts according to the needs of a particular ballet. His emphasis on progressive action, used in historical ballets, was not necessarily followed in his mythological ones. Another mode of presentation was needed in the latter, a succession of magnificent tableaux as in *Prometeo*, and not continuous action.

Viganò emphasized authenticity in his ballets. In *La Vestale* he recreated scenes of Roman life, such as the chariot races, the celebrations for the feast of Ceres, and the sacrifices to the gods. The accuracy of detail was such that the audience felt transported to life within the walls of ancient Rome. In *Psammi*, Viganò maintained the Egyptian style of varied movement and of beautiful tableaux.

Viganò's accuracy in historical matters is also valid in his portrayal of passions. In *Mirra*, he depicted passions with truthfulness of expression; in *Gli Ussiti sotto au Naumburgo*, he expressed love for the family and the homeland; in *Otello*, he represented the Moor literally dancing mad with jealousy.

At each performance, one could discover new beauties in Viganò's ballets, for he had touched the limit of perfection. The audience shed tears of compassion during the performances of his ballets. Three thousand people attended the first performance of *Prometeo*. They all paid tribute to the choreographer by their applause, waving handkerchieves as a sign of their ardent fervour. Two eulogistic odes were written, one for *Otello*, and the other for *La Vestale*.

Viganò's works consisted of a cumulative theatrical experience and of a perfect fusion of all the arts. His principles of composition are summarized in the *Dizionario biografico*: "Morality, erudition, idealism, unity, variety, order, ceremony, expression, evidence of the dramatic arts, grace, the sublime, the wonderful, and the comic. Viganò's art embraced the principles of Aesthetics, defined by the German philosopher Alexander Gottlieb Baumgarten as the sensory recognition of perfection."

—Elizabeth Terzian

VILLELLA, Edward

American dancer. Born in Bayside (Long Island), New York, 10 January 1936. Studied at the School of American Ballet,

New York (scholarship student), pupil of Anatole Obukhov, Pierre Vladimirov, Muriel Stuart, Felia Doubrovska, from 1946; also studied dance at the High School of Performing Arts; attended New York State Maritime College, Fort Schuyler, 1951–55; resumed ballet training, Ballet Arts school, New York, and School of American Ballet, from 1955; received B.A., 1959. Married dancer Janet Greschler, 1962 (div.). Dancer, soon becoming soloist, New York City Ballet, from 1957; principal dancer, from 1960; international guest artist, including for Royal Danish Ballet, Copenhagen; also appeared in Broadway musicals, including *Brigadoon* (mus. Loewe, chor. de Mille; 1962), and on television, including in documentary about his career, *Man Who Dances* (NBC television, 1968), and in Public Broadcasting Service (PBS) "Dance in America" series; also choreographer, staging numerous small concert pieces, with first full-scale ballet, *Narkissos*, staged 1966, and television ballet for children (CBS television), staged 1976; artistic coordinator of Eglevsky Ballet, from 1979, also serving as chairman, New York Commission for Cultural Affairs; director, Miami City Ballet, Miami, Florida, from 1986. Recipient: *Dance Magazine* Award, 1965; Emmy Award for Television, 1976; Capezio Dance Award, 1989.

ROLES

1958   Principal dancer (cr) in *Octet* (W. Christensen), New York City Ballet, New York

1958/   Principal dancer in *Interplay* (Robbins), New York City
60   Ballet, New York

Third Movement in *Symphony in C* (Balanchine), New York City Ballet, New York

First pas de trois in *Agon* (Balanchine), New York City Ballet, New York

Scherzo in *Western Symphony* (Balanchine), New York City Ballet, New York

1959   Title role in *Prodigal Son* (Balanchine), New York City Ballet, New York

1960   Harlequin in *Night Shadow* (*La Sonnambula*; Balanchine), New York City Ballet, New York

Principal dancer (cr) in *Variaciones Concertantes* (*Argentina*; Taras) in *Panamerica* (Balanchine, Contreras, Moncion, Taras, d'Amboise), New York City Ballet, New York

Principal dancer in *Theme and Variations* (Balanchine), New York City Ballet, New York

Prince of Lorraine (cr) in *The Figure in the Carpet* (Balanchine), New York City Ballet, New York

Sweep (cr) in *Creation of the World* (Bolender), New York City Ballet, New York

1961   Principal dancer (cr) in *Electronics* (Balanchine), New York City Ballet, New York

1962   Oberon (cr) in *A Midsummer Night's Dream* (Balanchine), New York City Ballet, New York

1963   Principal dancer (cr) in *Bugaku* (Balanchine), New York City Ballet, New York

Principal dancer (cr) in *Fantasy* (Taras), New York City Ballet, New York

1964   Principal dancer (cr) in *Tarantella* (pas de deux; Balanchine), New York City Ballet, New York

The Gentleman with Her in *Dim Lustre* (Tudor), New York City Ballet, New York

Title role in *Apollo* (Balanchine), New York City Ballet, New York

1965   Harlequin (cr) in *Harlequinade* (Balanchine), New York City Ballet, New York

1966   Andante (cr) in *Brahms–Schoenberg Quartet* (Balan-

chine), New York City Ballet, New York

Young man (cr) in *Jeux* (Taras), New York City Ballet, New York

Title role (cr) in *Narkissos* (also chor.), New York City Ballet, New York

1967   Rubies (cr) in *Jewels* (Balanchine), New York City Ballet, New York

Divertimento Brillante (cr) in *Glinkiana* (later *Valse Fantaisie*; Balanchine), New York City Ballet, New York

1969   Principal dancer (cr) in *Dances at a Gathering* (Robbins), New York City Ballet, New York

1970   Tema con Variazioni (cr) in *Suite No. 3* (later *Tchaikovsky Suite No. 3*; Balanchine), New York City Ballet, New York

1972   Principal dancer (cr) in *Watermill* (Robbins), New York City Ballet, New York

Principal dancer (cr) in *Symphony in Three Movements* (Balanchine), New York City Ballet, New York

Title role (cr) in *Pulcinella* (Balanchine, Robbins), New York City Ballet, New York

1975   Principal dancer (cr) in *Schéhérazade* (Balanchine), New York City Ballet, New York

Other roles include: principal dancer in *Scotch Symphony* (Balanchine), principal dancer in *Afternoon of a Faun* (Robbins), principal dancer in *Gounod Symphony* (Balanchine), First and Fourth Campaign in *Stars and Stripes* (Balanchine), principal dancer in *Waltz-Scherzo* (Balanchine), principal dancer in *Native Dancers* (Balanchine), principal dancer in *Raymonda Variations* (Balanchine), principal dancer in *Pas de Deux and Divertissement* (Balanchine), principal dancer in *La Source* (Balanchine).

WORKS

1966   *Narkissos* (mus. Prince), New York City Ballet, Saratoga Springs, New York

1976   *Harlequin* (children's ballet), CBS television

PUBLICATIONS

By Villella:

Interview in Maynard, Olga, "Edward Villella Talks to Olga Maynard", *Dance Magazine* (New York), May 1966

Contribution to Youskevitch, Igor, and others, *The Male Image*, New York, 1969

Interview in Gruen, John, *The Private World of Ballet*, New York, 1975

Interview in Shapiro, Brett, "One Ballet Dancer: Edward Villella", *Dance Scope* (New York), vol. 15, no. 1, 1981

"Villella Speaks on Balanchine", *Dance Teacher Now* (Davis, California), March 1985

Prodigal Son (autobiography), in collaboration with Larry Kaplan, New York, 1992

About Villella:

Goodman, Saul, "Brief Biographies: Edward Villella", *Dance Magazine* (New York), March 1959

Moore, Lillian, "Villella as Choreographer", *Dancing Times* (London), February 1967

Maynard, Olga, "A Dancer's Phases: Villella in '72", *Dance Magazine* (New York), December 1972

Edward Villella

Niehaus, Max, *Ballett Faszination*, Munich, 1972
Reynolds, Nancy, *Repertory in Review*, New York, 1977
Terry, Walter, *Great Male Dancers of the Ballet*, New York, 1978
Horn, Laurie, "Taking Care of the Roles: Villella", *Dance Magazine* (New York), November 1989
Barnes, Clive, "Edward Villella", *Dance Magazine* (New York), November 1989

*   *   *

Edward Villella will always be America's first major male ballet star, due both to his prodigious talent and, partly, to the dawning era of dance on television. Edward Villella was the first American male dancer ever to be asked to perform an encore at the Bolshoi Theatre in Moscow. His dance performances revealed an explosive spirit that, when released in a high leap or whirling pirouette, could vivify an entire audience, within the theatre as well as in front of the screen. He is internationally respected as one of the best male dancers in the world.

Villella belongs to a generation of ballet students who attended the School of American Ballet during its fledgling decade of the 1940s, when the teachers were direct links to the last Tsar's Maryinsky Theatre in St. Petersburg and to the Italian master there, Enrico Cecchetti. Villella's sister attended ballet class, and he was brought along to stay off the streets. At the school's urging he auditioned and was immediately accepted and put on scholarship. He has said that the intense beauty of extreme physical grace and control, juxtaposed with the power of music, overwhelmed him. When his sister decided to leave ballet, it was a blow to Villella because his parents wanted him to leave as well.

His father wanted him to finish college, so his training was thus interrupted during a crucial period in a dancer's development—the middle and late teen years. This hurt Villella physically when later he returned and tried to pack four years of lost time into the first year of performing.

It did not take long for Villella to discover that Balanchine was the wrong teacher for him. He never doubted Balanchine's genius as a choreographer, but he quarrelled with the master's methods of increasing speed, stamina, and control in company class for his generally lanky and loose female dancers. He observed that when the body is rushed, it tenses. Villella's stocky, muscle-bound body became overworked and cramped as a result.

He argued that his was not a problem of speed and control, for he had those skills naturally; his concern was stretching out—releasing the compression that the choreography often caused in his muscles. For this he turned to Danish teacher and School of American Ballet faculty member Stanley Williams, whom Villella credits with guiding him safely through the rest of his career of dancing for Balanchine.

Unforgettable in roles he originated, such as the boy in Jerome Robbins's *Afternoon of a Faun* (first performed by Moncion but inspired by Villella), or the bridegroom in *Bugaku*, Villella showed that his facial expressions were as powerful and as memorable as his leaps and turns. His style was regarded by some as too brash and earthy, but his handsome looks and charismatic presence made him very popular.

Villella's athleticism and attractiveness also made him an excellent partner. Here was a man who shone as beautifully as the women with whom he was paired (Patricia McBride, Allegra Kent, and Violette Verdy danced frequently with him). Others he partnered seemed even more lovely in his presence. The Villella and McBride partnership was a perfect match, for both obviously loved the allegro work Balanchine designed especially for them and which they could do as no one else.

Later, in the mid-1970s, Villella won accolades and awards for his work as a producer and director on the CBS television production *Harlequin*, and on the Public Broadcasting System series, "Dance in America".

Villella's compact physique, with its sharply defined proportions, lent its lines beautifully to the geometry of Balanchine's choreography. In roles of cavaliers and princes, Villella was the essence of the gentleman—but the gentleman who understands the potential passion within the tender romance.

Villella created roles in nearly a dozen Balanchine works that span the 1960s and 1970s, and he was cast in countless other works. Two great roles he inherited were Apollo and the Prodigal Son, which was revived for him in 1959. He achieved great distinction as Apollo, and his Prodigal Son was cited in a Capezio Award presentation as "one of ballet's most memorable".

Although Villella has choreographed a number of concert works, choreography is not his strong talent. When it became clear in 1979 that he would no longer be able to dance because of chronic injury, he bridged the transition from stage life to backstage life very well.

From the beginning of his career, Villella used his business instincts to build upon his assets, investing in non-dancerly things like real estate. He fought for recognition as a professional and demanded that his salary reflect that. He also capitalized on an innate talent for speaking about dance to the general public. After retiring from performing, he was artistic director for the small Eglevsky Ballet company and then briefly artistic director for Ballet Oklahoma. He has achieved outstanding success with his young Miami City Ballet company, which he began in 1986. In all his efforts what is constant is his passionate love of ballet.

—Kim Kokich

VILZAK, Anatole

Russian/American dancer and teacher. Born Anatole Iosifovich Viltzak (Vilzak) in Vilna, Lithuania, 29 August 1896. Studied at the Petrograd Theatre School, pupil of Leonid Leontiev; graduated in 1915. Married dancer Ludmila Schollar, 1921. Stage début as child performer, including with Bolshoi Circus of Chinizelli; dancer, Maryinsky Theatre, later the State Academic Theatre for Opera and Ballet (GATOB), Petrograd, 1915–21, becoming soloist from 1917; leading dancer, Diaghilev's Ballets Russes, from 1917, also staging *Swan Lake* (with wife, Schollar), for Ballets Russes, 1923; principal dancer, under ballet director Bronislava Nijinska, Teatro Colón, Buenos Aires, from 1926, and with Ida Rubinstein's Company, 1928–29, 1931, 1934; principal dancer and ballet master, State Opera, Riga (Latvia), from 1932; also leading performer with Théâtre de la danse Nijinska, 1932, Ballets Russes de Paris, 1935, René Blum's Ballets de Monte Carlo, 1936, and American Ballet Ensemble (under George Balanchine), Metropolitan Opera House, New York, 1935–37; teacher, School of American Ballet, New York, 1940, and at own studio, Vilzak-Schollar School, 1940–46: students include Maria Tallchief, Rosella Hightower; also teacher, Ballet Russe de Monte Carlo School, New York, 1949–51, American Ballet Theatre School, 1951–63, Washington School of Ballet, 1963–65, and San Francisco Ballet School, 1965–86.

Anatole Vilzak with Lubov Egorova in *The Sleeping Princess*, Diaghilev's Ballets Russes, London, 1921

ROLES

1915   The Youth (cr) in *Eros* (Fokine), Maryinsky Theatre,
        Petrograd
        Leading role in *Pharaoh's Daughter* (Petipa), Maryinsky
        Theatre, Petrograd
1915/ The Harlequin in *Harlequinade* (*Les Millions d'Arlequin*;
21   Petipa), Maryinsky Theatre, later State Academic
        Theatre for Opera and Ballet (GATOB), Petrograd
        Bluebird in *The Sleeping Beauty* (Petipa), GATOB,
        Petrograd
        Prince Désiré in *The Sleeping Beauty* (Petipa), GATOB,
        Petrograd
        The Youth in *Chopiniana* (Fokine), GATOB, Petrograd
        Pierrot in *The Fairy Doll* (N. and S. Legat), GATOB,
        Petrograd
        Phoebus in *Esmeralda* (Petipa after Perrot), GATOB,
        Petrograd
        Conrad in *Le Corsaire* (Petipa), GATOB, Petrograd
        Damis in *The Trials of Damis* (Petipa), GATOB,
        Petrograd
        Albrecht in *Giselle* (Petipa after Coralli, Perrot),
        GATOB, Petrograd
        Prince Siegfried in *Swan Lake* (Petipa, Ivanov),
        GATOB, Petrograd
        René in *Le Pavillon d'Armide* (Fokine), GATOB,
        Petrograd
        The Niger in *Islamé* (Fokine), GATOB, Petrograd
        Basil in *Don Quixote* (Petipa), GATOB, Petrograd
1920   Amoun in *Egyptian Nights* (Fokine), GATOB,
        Petrograd
        Solor in *La Bayadère* (Petipa), GATOB, Petrograd
1921   Spanish Prince, Harlequin (cr) in *The Sleeping Princess*
        (new production; Petipa, staged Sergeyev, with
        additional dances Nijinska), Diaghilev's Ballets
        Russes, London
        Prince Charming in *The Sleeping Princess* (Petipa,
        staged Sergeyev, with additional dances Nijinska),
        Diaghilev's Ballets Russes, London
1923   Principal dancer in *Danses Russes* (Fokine), Diaghilev's
        Ballets Russes, Monte Carlo
1924   King (cr) in *Les Tantations de la Bergère; ou, L'Amour
        vainqueur* (Nijinska), Diaghilev's Ballets Russes,
        Monte Carlo
        Chanson dansée ("Athelete") (cr) in *Les Biches* (Nijin-
        ska), Diaghilev's Ballets Russes, Monte Carlo
        Principal dancer (cr) in *Ballet de l'Astuce Féminine*
        (Massine), Diaghilev's Ballets Russes, Monte Carlo
        Eraste (cr) in *Les Fàcheux* (Nijinska), Diaghilev's
        Ballets Russes, Monte Carlo
1926   Harlequin (cr) in *El Carillón* (Nijinska), Teatro Colón,
        Buenos Aires
        Principal dancer (cr) in *Cuadro Campestre* (Nijinska),
        Teatro Colón, Buenos Aires
1928   Amour (cr) in *Les Noces de Psyché et de l'Amour*
        (Nijinska), Ida Rubinstein's Company, New York
        The Poet (cr) in *La Bien-Aimée* (Nijinska), Ida Rubin-
        stein's Company, Paris
        Principal dancer (cr) in *Boléro* (Nijinska), Ida Rubin-
        stein's Company, Paris
        Young Man (cr) in *Le Baiser de la fée* (Nijinska), Ida
        Rubinstein's Company, Paris
        Fiancé in *Nocturne* (Nijinska), Ida Rubinstein's Com-
        pany, Paris
        Guidon (cr) in *La Princesse Cygne* (Nijinska), Ida
        Rubinstein's Company, Paris
1929   Principal dancer (cr) in *La Valse* (Nijinska), Ida

Rubinstein's Company, Monte Carlo
1931   Principal dancer (cr) in *La Valse* (new version;
        Nijinska), Ida Rubinstein's Company, Paris
        The Premier Danseur (cr) in *Orphée aux Enfers* (opera;
        mus. Offenbach, chor. Balanchine), Théâtre Moga-
        dor, Paris
1932   Flavio (cr) in *Les Comédiens Jaloux* (Nijinska), Théâtre
        de la danse Nijinska, Opéra-Comique, Paris
        Idomène (cr) in *Variations* (Nijinska), Théâtre de la
        danse Nijinska, Opéra-Comique, Paris
1934   Principal dancer (cr) in *Persephone* (Jooss), Ida Rubin-
        stein's Company, Paris
        Henry II (cr) in *Diane de Poitiers* (Fokine), Ida
        Rubinstein's Company, Paris
1936   Death (cr) in *La Juive* (opera; mus. Halévy, chor.
        Balanchine), Metropolitan Opera and American
        Ballet Ensemble, New York
        Dance of the Comedians (cr) in *The Bartered Bride*
        (opera; mus. Smetana, chor. Balanchine), Metropoli-
        tan Opera and American Ballet Ensemble, New York
        Title role (cr) in *Don Juan* (Fokine), (Blum's) Ballets de
        Monte Carlo, London
        Chief Warrior in *Polovtsian Dances from Prince Igor*
        (Fokine), (Blum's) Ballets de Monte Carlo, London
1937   Day (cr) in *La Gioconda* (opera; mus. Ponchiella, chor.
        Balanchine), Metropolitan Opera and American
        Ballet Ensemble, New York

Other roles include: for American Ballet (Ensemble) at the
Metropolitan Opera—leading dancing roles (chor. Balanchine)
in operas *La Traviata* (mus. Verdi), *Tannhäuser* (mus. Wagner),
Carmen (mus. Bizet).

WORKS

Staged:
1923   *Swan Lake* (shortened version, with L. Schollar, after
        Petipa, Ivanov; mus. Tchaikovsky), Diaghilev's
        Ballets Russes, Monte Carlo
1982   *Vilzak Variations* (after Petipa), San Francisco Ballet
        School, San Francisco

PUBLICATIONS

By Vilzak:
Interview in Newman, Barbara, *Striking a Balance: Dancers
    Talk about Dancing*, Boston, 1982
Contributor to Klaja, Laurencia, *A Ballerina Prepares*, Classi-
    cal Ballet Variations for the Female Dancer as taught by
    Ludmilla Shollar [sic] and Anatole Vilzak, Garden City,
    N.J., 1982

About Vilzak:
Maynard, Olga, *The American Ballet*, Philadelphia, 1959
Karsavina, Tamara, "Vilzak, Dolin, Malcolm Sargent and
    Others", *Dancing Times* (London), May 1968
Horosko, Marian, "Teachers in the Russian Tradition", *Dance
    Magazine* (New York), part 2: April 1979
Heymont, George, "A Real Charmer", *Ballet News* (New
    York), February 1983
Steinberg, Cobbett, *The San Francisco Ballet: The First Fifty
    Years*, San Francisco, 1983
Ross, Janice, "Vilzak Variations", *Dance Magazine* (New
    York), July 1988

                        *   *   *

Anatole Vilzak was a talented classical dancer and a first-class cavalier and mime actor. His noble carriage and handsome figure made him a marvellous performer in the roles of classical princes in the nineteenth-century ballets. But his scope was broad, and his heroes were not only romantic but also masculine, and genuinely passionate. He was a brilliant partner, and was acknowledged to be a favoured partner of the great ballerina Olga Spessivtseva, among others.

Upon finishing school at the famous Imperial Theatre School of St. Petersburg (then called Petrograd), Vilzak was accepted into the corps de ballet of the Maryinsky Theatre. During his first year at the theatre, the all-powerful Mathilde Kshesinskaya noticed him and, at her behest, he was given his first leading role in the ballet *Pharaoh's Daughter*, dancing opposite Olga Spessivtseva. In 1921 Vilzak married the ballerina Ludmila Schollar, with whom he spent the rest of his life until her death in the late 1970s. They performed together, travelled throughout the world, and, ultimately, took up teaching careers in the United States.

But before they came to America they had established firm reputations in Europe as leading representatives of the great Russian Imperial style. No sooner had they left their own country, having sustained themselves (like many other Russian émigrés of that time) with what Vilzak later called "our concert performances of little pas de deux in Europe", than Serge Diaghilev invited the two dancers to join his now-famous troupe, the Ballets Russes. From Berlin in 1921 they went on to Paris, where they both danced major roles with the company, jointly staging the 1923 Ballets Russes production of *Swan Lake* as well.

The most important period of Vilzak's artistic life, after the Maryinsky Theatre, came in the 1920s and 1930s, when he worked not only with Diaghilev but with choreographer Bronislava Nijinska and with the Ida Rubinstein company. He travelled to Buenos Aires to work with Nijinska at the Teatro Colón, and he also served as principal dancer under Nijinska for Ida Rubinstein's company in Paris. Vilzak always acknowledged Nijinska, along with Mikhail Fokine, as one of the greatest influences in his life. Both Nijinska and Fokine were extremely exacting and demanding—as teachers and choreographers—and they inspired a similar devotion from their dancers. From Fokine in Russia Vilzak had gained his first true sense of theatre, not just learning technical detail but developing a strong sense of the inner dramatic motivation behind dance and mime. In Nijinska Vilzak admired, and attained for himself, precision and a certain spiritual toughness which inspired a fierce dedication to the art. Of his time performing with Nijinska's company, Vilzak later said, "The company held our Russian banner high and proud. It made Europe aware of our Russian art and duly acknowledged and respected it in its highest and purest form."

Vilzak was an impressive technician, well-trained and classically correct, but his understanding of character roles was especially notable. The role of Harlequin in Fokine's *Carnaval* was one of the roles most identified with him; and of his creation of the title role in Fokine's *Don Juan* in 1936, British critic Cyril Beaumont wrote that it was ". . . a portrait so fascinating in its combination of noble grace, bravado and polished will, as to induce strong sympathy for the villain".

In 1935, Vilzak and his wife came to America and, at Balanchine's invitation, he became first dancer with the American Ballet at the Metropolitan Opera House. But for both Vilzak and Schollar, as for many others of their artistic class who had left Europe for the "new world", their performing life was essentially over, due to the lack of high-calibre companies in the United States at that time. As Marian Horosko wrote in 1979, "The Vilzaks, like so many artists who came to America

and taught, never danced again in a company although they were in the prime of their powers and at the height of their fame. . . . But no pupil will ever forget any of them, so strong have they been in their tradition, and so disciplined in a country that could not yet appreciate them or their art."

Vilzak and Schollar began teaching at Balanchine's School of American Ballet in 1940, and they later opened the Vilzak-Schollar School of Ballet in New York City, where they attracted such dancers as Maria Tallchief, Rosella Hightower, and Michael Kidd. Horosko recalled that Vilzak was famed for both the technical speed and the brain-twisting demands of his classes. His entrances into the studio at the Vilzak–Schollar School, to a fanfare on the piano from *Swan Lake*, were dramatic and memorable: in he walked, "the Prince of Teachers, the most debonair, sophisticated, musical, and sarcastic of them all, Anatole Vilzak".

Eventually Vilzak and his wife went to San Francisco to join the faculty of the San Francisco Ballet School, becoming permanent and popular fixtures there. Schollar died in 1978, and Vilzak only stopped teaching full-time in the late 1980s. Writing recently on Vilzak's influence on the west-coast company, Janice Ross wrote, "He is rightly held to be a man who conveys a sense of tradition to the company, as well as grace, etiquette of stage deportment, and the techniques for convincing character portrayal." A true professional in every sense of the word, Anatole Vilzak brought that professionalism and artistry to countless generations of American dancers. From the Maryinsky Theatre in St. Petersburg, through the capitals of Europe and America and eventually to the west coast of the United States, Vilzak has undoubtedly been one of the strongest and most important links between Russian and Western ballet, between an old tradition and a new. As Horosko wrote of Vilzak and Schollar together, "They set an example, defining the professional dancer for a nation just discovering their profession. . . . They gave us their history that we might make it our own."

—Nina Alovert

VINOGRADOV, Oleg

Russian/Soviet dancer, choreographer, and ballet director. Born Oleg Mikhailovich Vinogradov in Leningrad, 1 August 1937. Studied at the Leningrad (Vaganova) Choreographic School, pupil of Aleksandr Pushkin; graduated in 1958; graduated from State Institute of Theatrical Art (GITIS), Moscow, in 1965. Artist, dancing character roles, and then assistant ballet master, Novosibirsk Ballet, 1958–65; choreographer, Kirov Ballet, 1968–72, becoming member of artistic collegium from 1971; artistic director and ballet master, Maly Theatre Ballet, Leningrad, 1973–77; artistic director and chief ballet master, Kirov Ballet, Leningrad, from 1977, with company becoming St. Petersburg Ballet of the Maryinsky Theatre, from 1992; also director, Universal Ballet Academy, Washington D.C., from 1990. Recipient: title of Honoured Artist of the Daghestan ASSR, 1969; State Prize of the Russian Federation, 1970; title of Honoured Artist of the Russian Federation, 1976; Petipa Prize, Academy of Dance, Paris, 1979; Order of People's Friendship, USSR, 1981; title of Honoured Artist of the USSR, 1983; Picasso Golden Dancer Prize, Paris, 1987; Chevalier and Order of the Cross of the French Republic, 1990; Nijinsky Prize, Warsaw, 1991; Lumier Prize, Paris, 1991.

WORKS

1964   *Cinderella* (mus. Prokofiev), Novosibirsk Ballet, Novosibirsk (staged Maly Theatre Ballet, Leningrad, 1977)
1965   *Romeo and Juliet* (mus. Prokofiev), Novosibirsk Ballet, Novosibirsk (staged Maly Theatre Ballet, Leningrad, 1976)
1967   *Asel* (mus. Vaslov), Bolshoi Ballet, Moscow
1968   *Goryanka* (*Mountain Girl*; mus. Kazhlayev), Kirov Ballet, Leningrad
1969   *Aleksandr Nevsky* (mus. Prokofiev), Kirov Ballet, Leningrad
   Two (mus. Melikova), Choreographic Evening for Irina Kolpakova, Kirov Ballet, Leningrad
1971   *Lise and Colin; or, La Fille mal gardée* (mus. Hérold), Maly Theatre Ballet, Leningrad (staged Odessa, 1973, Berlin, 1974, Riga, 1976, Minsk, 1979)
1972   *The Enchanted Prince* (mus. Britten), Kirov Ballet, Leningrad
1973   *Coppélia* (mus. Delibes), Maly Theatre Ballet, Leningrad
1974   *Yaroslavna* (mus. Tishenko), Maly Theatre Ballet, Leningrad
1977   *Educational Poem* (with Lebedev; mus. Lebedev), Maly Theatre Ballet, Leningrad
1979   *The Hussar Ballad* (with Bryantsev; mus. Khrenikov), Kirov Ballet, Leningrad
1980   *The Fairy of the Rond Mountain* (mus. Grieg), Kirov Ballet, Leningrad
   The Government Inspector (mus. A. Tchaikovsky), Kirov Ballet, Leningrad
1983   *Testaments of Past Times* (mus. various), Kirov Ballet, Bicentenary Celebration, Leningrad
1984   *Asiyat* (new version of *Goryanka*; mus. Kazhlayev), Kirov Ballet, Leningrad
1985   *The Knight in Tigerskin* (mus. Machavarian), Kirov Ballet, Leningrad
1986   *Battleship Potemkin* (mus. Tchaikovsky), Kirov Ballet, Leningrad
1989   *Petrushka* (mus. Stravinsky), Scottish Ballet, Glasgow
1990   *Petrushka* (revised version; mus. Stravinsky), Kirov Ballet, Opéra, Paris
1991   *Adagio* (mus. S. Barber), Kirov Ballet, Leningrad

PUBLICATIONS

By Vinogradov:
Dialogue with G.V. Tomson, in *Music and Choreography of Modern Ballet* (first edition), Leningrad, 1974
"The Union of Music and Dance" (with S. Slonimsky), in *Music and Choreography of Modern Ballet* (second edition), Leningrad, 1977
Interview in Gregory, John, "Vinogradov's Testament", *Dancing Times* (London), August 1982
Interview in Degen, Arsen, "The Pride of Native Choreography", *Sovetsky Balet* (Moscow), no. 3, 1983
Interview in Alovert, Nina, "An Interview with Oleg Vinogradov", *Dance Magazine* (New York), July 1989
Oleg Vinogradov: Portrait of a Contemporary Classicist (booklet; Universal Ballet Academy), Washington, D.C., 1990

About Vinogradov:
René, Natalia, "The Cause of Controversy: Oleg Vinogradov", *Dance and Dancers* (London), November 1967
Bohlin, Peter, "Oleg Vinogradov", *Dans* (Stockholm), March 1976

Krasovskaya, Vera, *Soviet Ballet Theatre*, Moscow, 1976
Stupnikov, Igor, *Oleg Vinogradov* (booklet), Leningrad, 1984
Krasovskaya, Vera, "Knights of Contemporary Ballet", *Sovetsky Balet* (Moscow), no. 5, 1985
Gaevsky, Vadim, "The Monologue of Corps de Ballet", *Teatr* (Moscow), no. 12, 1986
Degen, Arsen, "Two from the Kirov", *Dance Magazine* (New York), July 1989
Clarke, Mary, "Vinogradov's *Petrushka*", *Dancing Times* (London), March 1989
Krekhov, V., "Why *Petrushka* Went to Paris", *Sovetskaya Kultura* (Moscow), 17 March 1990
Kendall, Elizabeth, "Reflections: The Kirov", *The New Yorker* (New York), 8 June 1992

*   *   *

Oleg Vinogradov is a dominant figure in the history of Soviet ballet. Not only is he one of the best Russian choreographers of the later twentieth century, he is also (after Fedor Lopukhov) the most progressive director the Leningrad/St. Petersburg ballet has ever had. He has, furthermore, done much to join and consolidate the forces of Russian and Western ballet.

Vinogradov began creating dances while still a student at the Leningrad School of Choreography. He made his first piece, to Chopin's *Nocturne*, in the late 1950s for his classmate Natasha Makarova. Upon finishing his studies, Vinogradov left for the Novosibirsk Theatre of Opera and Ballet, which was at the time under the direction of Petr Gusev, then gathering a group of young enthusiasts at the Novosibirsk Theatre. Vinogradov danced character roles for eight years, also becoming assistant ballet master to Gusev, staging dances for operas and dramatic performances. Then Gusev proposed that Vinogradov stage Sergei Prokofiev's *Cinderella*.

It was after the premiere of *Cinderella* that Vinogradov became famous throughout the world of ballet in Russia. His choreography was fresh and expressive. It was a theme unusual for the time, a fable portraying two attitudes to life. Against the consumerist mentality of those possessed by vanity and triviality he counterposed the attitude and life-philosophy of people with creativity and talent. Vinogradov displayed great boldness in selecting Prokofiev's music for his début—there was nothing in Soviet music that could compare with Prokofiev's score in both complexity and dramatic content. Venerable choreographers (Rastislav Zakharov and Leonid Lavrovsky) had already staged ballets to this music in Moscow and Leningrad, but Vinogradov's move immediately set the creative tenor of much of his future work: he liked novelty, and one of the most central themes of his ballets (*Cinderella, Romeo and Juliet*, and *Goryanka*) was to be the struggle against the power of prejudice.

These first productions suggested other particulars of the ballet master's future work as well. His work was to continue a tradition begun in Russian ballet at the beginning of the century, in which ballet productions are a union of music, choreography, and visual art—the latter including set design, costumes, unusual lighting, and even the elements of modern technology.

Vinogradov remained faithful to this principle in his productions of ballets of every genre: romantic (*The Fairy of the Rond Mountain*), allegorical (*Battleship Potemkin*), comic (*The Hussar Ballad*), grotesque fairy-tale (*The Government Inspector*), social parable (*Petrushka*), and epic (*The Knight in Tigerskin*). With time, Vinogradov's ballets became increasingly his own creations. Not only did he himself write the librettos, devise the choreography, and make suggestions to the artists as to how to realize their roles, he also took an active part in the composition

Oleg Vinogradov

of the music when this was specially commissioned for the work.

Choreography is not an end in itself for Vinogradov. He conceives of dance as the boldest conjunction of ideas and images. In dance Vinogradov seeks, via the language of modern movement, expressive symbolism and metaphor. Classical dance lies at the base of his choreography, but it is freely interpreted. "In my choreography," he writes, "I am trying to enhance the expressiveness of pure dance by employing the enormous potential of the elasticity of the human body. I love the abundance of complex coordination, leaps, and complicated risky situations. My choreography is a synthesis of free elasticity and the possibilities of the Russian school of male dance." *Battleship Potemkin* is an example of this "male dance": a ballet about life and death, about man's struggle for freedom. The complex polyphony of the music reflects that of the choreography, in which the main "char-

acter" is a male corps de ballet of 32 men. Vinogradov tries to use the form of the ballet to express the essence of the production. For example, he created the ballet *The Knight in Tigerskin* as a kind of dance fresco; the qualities of monumentality and expressiveness he injected into it reflected the almost epic nature of the theme with its celebration of life and beauty.

One of the characteristic features of Vinogradov's choreography is the linking of classical dance and national folk dance; he uses Georgian and Indian dance in *The Knight in Tigerskin*, for instance, and Russian folk dance in *Petrushka*. The latter is one of Vinogradov's most original creations, the parable of an enslaved people and of the hero who can free them. Vinogradov portrays the clash and opposition of these two by juxtaposing two forms of Russian dance. The dance of the people and of their leaders, who have forgotten Russian culture and no longer know how to dance Russian folk dances, is sterile and hideous, while Petrushka's dance is constructed on ancient Russian folk-dance steps in conjunction with acrobatics and other elements of contemporary male dance. Petrushka's choreographic solos are harmonic and buoyant because he is the vehicle of the Russian soul. Such experimentation has been controversial, and Western critics in particular objected to Vinogradov's unexpected separation of the familiar Stravinsky score from all other elements which have come to be associated with the famous Diaghilev ballet.

However, experimentation and originality are ruling forces in Vinogradov's art. When, for example, he moved to Leningrad and became the artistic director of the ballet troupe of the Maly Theatre, Vinogradov, in a few short years, restored to this company its distinction and former fame as an experimental theatre. He made his début in Leningrad with the ballet *Vain Precautions* (*La Fille mal gardée*). His completely original choreographic version of this work, a firework display of classical and character dance, was based on an old Dauberval libretto and early music by Hérold. It was also at the Maly Theatre that Vinogradov created one of his most original ballets, *Yaroslavna*.

In 1977, the government issued a decree on the incompetence of the directorship of the Kirov Theatre, which was undergoing a period of serious creative decline. Vinogradov was virtually forced to abandon the Maly Theatre and become the artistic director of the Kirov Ballet. He fired the pensioners who made up 60% of the company, collected a corps de ballet of young dancers, restored the former number of dancers in corps de ballet numbers, and worked hard on the accent and the intonation of the theatre's performance style to overcome the eclectic and stylized manner that had resulted from the uncreative atmosphere of the previous regime. Legitimizing more contemporary styles of performance, Vinogradov reanimated the corps de ballet. He promoted new soloists from the ranks of the new dancers and invited top dancers from other cities. And the Kirov Theatre now has the most interesting and creative roster of virtually any company.

Respectful of the beautiful traditions of the Kirov Theatre, where the classical ballets of Marius Petipa are preserved, Vinogradov not only cleansed Petipa's masterpiece, *The Sleeping Beauty*, of the distortions to which it had been subjected, but together with Gusev revived the ballet *Le Corsaire* (keeping as close as possible to the lost original) and incorporated the ballets of Bournonville into the repertoire. Aware of just how long the Kirov Ballet had been out of touch with the world, Vinogradov made contact with the leading choreographers of the twentieth century in the West, Roland Petit and Maurice Béjart. He also managed to get George Balanchine's ballets *Theme and Variations* and *Scotch Symphony* (1989) included in the theatre's repertoire.

Directing the theatre is as artistic and bold an experiment for Vinogradov as staging a ballet. He strives to strengthen the ties between Russian and Western ballet with the same inexhaustible energy that pervades all of his work. He was appointed director of the Universal Ballet Academy in Washington, where all the instructors are Russian. His plans include opening similar schools in other countries and even creating a special theatre with a Russian company in America.

Vinogradov's art as a choreographer and his theoretical and aesthetic views are constantly developing. His constant attempts at experimentation and his careful artistry, multiplied by his talent and mastery, lead one to expect his creative biography to repeat itself.

—Nina Alovert

VIOLIN CONCERTO
(later called *Stravinsky Violin Concerto*)

Choreography: George Balanchine
Music: Igor Stravinsky
First Production: New York City Ballet, New York State Theatre, 18 June 1972
Principal Dancers: Karin von Aroldingen, Kay Mazzo, Peter Martins, Jean-Pierre Bonnefous

Other productions include: Original Ballet Russe (first production to Stravinsky score; chor. Balanchine, design Pavel Tchelitchev), as *Balustrade*; New York, 22 January 1941. New York City Ballet (restaged and revised Balanchine), as *Stravinsky Violin Concerto* (title since 1973); "Dance in America" telecast, Public Broadcasting Service (PBS), 1977. Paris Opéra Ballet, with Michaël Denard, Elisabeth Platel; Paris, 26 November 1989. Royal Ballet; London, 29 November 1990.

PUBLICATIONS

Anderson, Jack, "Stravinsky Celebrations", *Dancing Times* (London), August 1972
Anderson, Jack, "Hard-headed Miracle", *Dance Magazine* (New York), September 1972
Balanchine, George, with Mason, Francis, *Balanchine's Complete Stories of the Great Ballets*, Garden City, N.Y., 1977
Reynolds, Nancy, *Repertory in Review*, New York, 1977

*   *   *

One of three important works that Balanchine made for the New York City Ballet's Stravinsky Festival of 1972, *Violin Concerto* is a haunting ballet of contrasting moods and components—it is both Russian and American, as is its score, with very private and very public moments; it is tightly structured and symmetrical, and yet is at times spiky and unbuttoned in its movements. One of Balanchine's Stravinsky leotard works, it is perhaps closest to *Agon*.

Violin Concerto, uncharacteristically for Balanchine, features two equal (though quite different) couples. Of its four sections, the two outer ones, with eight women and eight men in addition to the principals, have an almost manic, prancing energy like their music. A formal schema dominates the first section, marked Toccata in the score. Each principal is introduced in turn, dancing with four attendants who frame or surround the dancer; the attendants to each principal are first of the opposite sex, and then a second time around consist of four dancers of the same sex. The closing section, the Capriccio, with its Russian folk dance motifs, its bobbing bodies and interweaving sashays, has a double-exposure look, like Russians kicking up their heels on a wild Saturday night in the western United States. Yet the celebrants never move very far from their own spots of turf, and they present themselves constantly and frankly to the audience's inspection.

At the heart of the ballet, two highly contrasting pas de deux follow one immediately after the other. The first, to Aria I, is for an athletic couple, originally Karin von Aroldingen and Jean-Pierre Bonnefous (soon after, on his early retirement, replaced by Bart Cook, who appears in the *Dance in America* videotape of the work). It is set to eerie music, featuring the insinuating glissandos and jumpy pizzicatos of the violin. The couple carry on an intimate struggle, twining and straining as if for psychological dominance. The woman seems to have the edge through her independent contortions, as she makes a

Violin Concerto, with Jean-Pierre Bonnefous and Karin von Aroldingen, New York City Ballet, 1972

bridge of her body or does a handstand to escape the man's embrace. Their gropings contain echoes of Balanchine's earlier ballet to the same score, the surrealist 1941 *Balustrade* (with designs by the painter Pavel Tchelitchev), which, as one can see from a bit of surviving film, had a similar strangeness, with its non-human, insect-like world of slithering creatures. Similarly, for the later *Violin Concerto*, Balanchine told von Aroldingen she was to be like a snake, "a bit sneaky". Then, too, a sudden image of her as an idol with four arms recalls exoticisms in *Balustrade*. The section ends with the woman in a backbend, the exhausted man lying at her feet.

Made for a more classical pair, Kay Mazzo and Peter Martins, Aria II is the most haunting part of *Violin Concerto*. (For the Danish-trained Martins, the ballet's creation was a breakthrough in assimilating the Balanchine style.) The music's tender and plaintive lyricism is paralleled by a pas de deux retaining Aria I's twining motif and angularity, now transmuted into a modern romanticism. It is based on the contrast of Mazzo's long, slender, fragile-looking body—made more so by being almost constantly poised on the narrow base of her long pointes—with the power of Martins' solid body and sense of authority. As he gently moulds her limbs and she hooks an arm or leg around him in order to achieve wildly off-balance

positions, she is a pliant and yet active participant in some benign process of love or art—ballerina material to Martins' choreographer-figure.

Mysterious images from Aria II stay in the mind: twice in the course of the duet, on a poignant outcry in the music, the dancers pose face to face, each forming a an "X" with his or her spread limbs. Then suddenly he lunges to kneel at her feet and make her knees buckle inward—or does he save her from falling? It is an image that is worshipful and perhaps manipulative at the same time. As the pas de deux nears its end, he extends his arm over her shoulder, as if indicating something to her with his extended palm. Perhaps it is the music, because they then bow—in acknowledgement, Balanchine said, of Stravinsky, who had died the year before the ballet was made. In a final gesture, tender but dominating, the man places his hand over the woman's eyes and, as he kneels behind her, draws her into a backbend, very different from the athletic one that ended Aria I.

A later exponent of Martins' role, Joseph Duell, said of the pas de deux, "When I dance it, I know that the shapes I'm making are strong things. ... At the core of Balanchine's genius was his ability to make something beautifully expressive and inventive happen between a man and a woman on stage that wasn't shocking or sentimental, but love as expressed by the hard edge of beauty". This perceptive remark makes a lasting commentary on the essence of one of Balanchine's great ballets.

—Marilyn Hunt

VIRSALADZE, Simon

Georgian/Soviet theatrical designer. Born Simon (Soliko) Bagratovich Virsaladze in Tbilisi, 13 January 1909. Studied at the Academy of Art, Tbilisi, 1926–27, All-Union Technical Art Institute (VHUTEIN), pupil of J. Rabinovich, Moscow, 1928–30, and Academy of Art, pupil of M. Bobyshev, Leningrad, 1930–31. First theatre designs for Theatre of Working Youth, Georgia, 1927; chief designer, Paliashvili Theatre for Opera and Ballet, Tbilisi, 1932–36; designer, Kirov Ballet, Leningrad, from 1937, becoming chief designer, 1940, 1942, 1962, and also designing for Maly Theatre Ballet and Novosibirsk Theatre; chief designer, Bolshoi Ballet, Moscow, 1964–90, working with ballet director Yuri Grigorovich on every production from 1957; also designer of sets and costumes for numerous plays, operas, and films, and for the Georgian Folk Dance Ensemble. Recipient: State Prize of the USSR, 1949, 1950, 1977; title of People's Designer of the USSR, 1976; Lenin Prize, 1970; Membership of the Academy of Arts from 1975. Died in Tbilisi, 7 February 1990.

WORKS (Ballet designs)

1933   Le Corsaire (chor. Kononovich after Petipa), Paliashvili Theatre, Tbilisi

1935   Swan Lake (chor. Iorkin after Petipa, Ivanov), Paliashvili Theatre, Tbilisi

1938   The Heart of the Hills (chor. Chabukiani), Kirov Ballet, Leningrad

1939   Laurencia (chor. Chabukiani), Kirov Ballet, Leningrad

1940   Ashik Kerib (chor. Fenster), Maly Theatre Ballet, Leningrad

1942   Don Quixote (chor. Chabukiani after Petipa, Gorsky), Paliashvili Theatre, Tbilisi

1943   Chopiniana (chor. Chabukiani after Fokine), Paliashvili Theatre, Tbilisi

Giselle (chor. Chabukiani after Petipa, Coralli, Perrot), Paliashvili Theatre, Tbilisi

1947   Spring Fairytale (chor. Lopukhov), Kirov Ballet, Leningrad

1948   Raymonda (chor. Sergeyev after Petipa), Kirov Ballet, Leningrad

1950   Schéhérazade (chor. Anisimova), Maly Theatre Ballet, Leningrad

Swan Lake (chor. Sergeyev after Petipa, Ivanov), Kirov Ballet, Leningrad

1952   The Sleeping Beauty (chor. Sergeyev after Petipa), Kirov Ballet, Leningrad

1953   The Seven Beauties (chor. Gusev), Maly Theatre Ballet, Leningrad

Le Corsaire (chor. Gusev after Petipa), Maly Theatre Ballet, Leningrad

1954   The Nutcracker (chor. Vainonen), Kirov Ballet, Leningrad

1956   Swan Lake (chor. Messerer after Petipa, Ivanov), Bolshoi Ballet, Moscow

1957   The Stone Flower (chor. Grigorovich), Kirov Ballet, Leningrad (staged Bolshoi Ballet, Moscow, 1959)

1959   Ballad of Love (chor. Lopukhov), Maly Theatre Ballet, Leningrad

1961   The Legend of Love (chor. Grigorovich), Kirov Ballet, Leningrad (staged Bolshoi Ballet, Moscow, 1965)

1963   The Sleeping Beauty (chor. Grigorovich after Petipa), Bolshoi Ballet, Moscow

The Seven Beauties (chor. Gusev), Novosibirsk Theatre, Novosibirsk

1966   The Nutcracker (chor. Grigorovich), Bolshoi Ballet, Moscow

1968   Spartacus (chor. Grigorovich), Bolshoi Ballet, Moscow

1969   Swan Lake (chor. Grigorovich after Petipa, Ivanov), Bolshoi Ballet, Moscow

1975   Ivan the Terrible (chor. Grigorovich), Bolshoi Ballet, Moscow

1976   Angara (chor. Grigorovich), Bolshoi Ballet, Moscow

1979   Romeo and Juliet (chor. Grigorovich), Bolshoi Ballet, Moscow

1982   The Golden Age (chor. Grigorovich), Bolshoi Ballet, Moscow

1984   Raymonda (chor. Grigorovich after Petipa), Bolshoi Ballet, Moscow

PUBLICATIONS

Vanslov, Viktor, Simon Virsaladze, Moscow, 1969

* * *

In the development of Russian ballet at the middle and end of the twentieth century, the theatrical artist Simon Virsaladze played a role similar to that once played by Benois, Bakst, or Korovin. A man of enormous talent, culture, and erudition, he worked with various ballet masters, inevitably serving as their first consultant in any given project, and knowing instinctively how to give direction to a choreographer's thought. Virsaladze is a direct descendent of the "World of Art" ("Mir Iskusstva") artists, whose ideas he developed artistically while retaining an entirely distinctive style of his own.

Virsaladze developed a love for the ballet and for painting early in his childhood while still a student in Tbilisi, where he attended two studios at the same time: a ballet studio and an art studio. In Moscow and Leningrad, Virsaladze studied with the leading theatrical artists of the beginning of the century. He staged his first performance, Mardzhanov's production of Rossini's opera William Tell, in Tbilisi. Over the course of his life, Virsaladze staged many operas and dramatic productions, but it was the ballet that was to become his main sphere of activity.

After successful work with the choreographer Vakhtang Chabukiani on the ballets The Heart of the Hills and Laurencia, the Kirov Theatre and the Maly Theatre in Leningrad became, for many years, Virsaladze's permanent place of work. In 1957, he created the sets for the then avant-garde Yuri Grigorovich's production of Prokofiev's The Stone Flower. The forward-looking choreography and equally daring sets of this production precipitated a real revolution in Soviet ballet. With the premiere of The Stone Flower, a new period began not only in the history of Soviet ballet, but also in the creative life of the artist himself. After 1957, Virsaladze and Grigorovich became inseparable friends, and the artist could well be called the choreographer's co-author in his creation of a new trend in ballet. Virsaladze moved with Grigorovich to Moscow, where he remained Grigorovich's only set director until his death in

1990. The year 1957 marked the end of the artist's period of assimilating the aesthetic values and devices needed for creating sets; the main principle of Virsaladze's work, "artistic symphonism", reached its consummation in his work on Grigorovich's ballets.

Virsaladze did not simply sketch out the sets and the costumes for a ballet; his conception reached to the whole image of the performance and he sought, above all, a device that would set the tenor for the whole production. In *The Stone Flower*, the device was a malachite box, within which the action of the ballet took place; in *The Legend of Love*, it was a set of screens depicting an oriental market-place theatre that opened up like a book, revealing the characters of the ballet. In creating his sets, Virsaladze made use of both construction and painting. From the era of constructivism in set design, Virsaladze gleaned the ability to create an enriched image for a given ballet.

Virsaladze's sets are marked by an astounding beauty and a subtle juxtaposition of colours. He liked to use black in conjunction with other colours, and to incorporate gold and silver in his palette, creating an enchanted romantic world and uniting, through his colours, the music, choreography, and drama of the ballet. And his sets are unthinkable without his costumes. Constructing his set designs on a certain combination of hues, he carefully executed the costumes in that same range of colours. He felt and understood the style of the choreography of each production so thoroughly that he virtually saw in advance how each of his costumes would dance, how it would leap and turn. Each of his costumes was an image in itself, a character. Were one of his costumes to disappear, an important aspect of the dance itself would in effect disappear as well.

Once he had sketched his designs, Virsaladze continued working in the workshops of the theatre to the end, directing the creation of sets and costumes. He participated in the creation of every detail, demanding numerous revisions until a given concept was rendered artistically incarnate.

"Virsaladze's work has unique value for the culture of our nation," said Grigorovich; "[it is] a rare example of the union of a great gift with brilliant mastery, imagination, and astounding erudition, [as seen] in both profundity of thought and sophisticated taste." Virsaladze's contribution to Soviet ballet will not soon be forgotten.

—Nina Alovert

LA VIVANDIÈRE

Choreography: Arthur Saint-Léon and Fanny Cerrito
Music: Cesare Pugni
Design: Edouard Despléchin, Charles Séchan, Jules Diéterle
Libretto: Arthur Saint-Léon
First Production: Her Majesty's Theatre, London, 23 May 1844
Principal Dancers: Fanny Cerrito (Kathi), Arthur Saint-Léon (Hans)

Other productions include: Teatro Alibert (earlier version; staged Saint-Léon and Cerrito, mus. Enrico Roland), as *La Vivandiera ed il Postiglione*; Rome, 26 November 1843. Teatro Comunitativo (restaged Saint-Léon, Cerrito); Bologna, November 1844. Paris Opéra (restaged Saint-Léon and Cerrito); Paris, 20 October 1848. Bolshoi Theatre (restaged Jules Perrot), with Fanny Cerrito; St. Petersburg, 13 December 1855. Bolshoi

Theatre (staged Marius Petipa after Saint-Léon), as *Marki-tantka*; St. Petersburg, 8 October 1881. Kirov Ballet (Pas de six only; reconstruction by Pierre Lacotte after Saint-Léon); Leningrad, 1979. Sadler's Wells Royal Ballet (Pas de six only; reconstruction by Ann Hutchinson Guest after Saint-Léon); London, 2 March 1982.

PUBLICATIONS

Beaumont, Cyril, *Complete Book of Ballets*, revised edition, London, 1951
Guest, Ivor, *The Romantic Ballet in England*, London, 1954
Guest, Ivor, *Fanny Cerrito*, London, 1956
Guest, Ann Hutchinson, "*Vivandière* for the Sadler's Wells Royal Ballet", *Dancing Times* (London), March 1982

*   *   *

La Vivandière was a small "toy-like" ballet of a single act that achieved its success through the evocation of a foreign culture and its dances. Arthur Saint-Léon and Fanny Cerrito first presented their *La Vivandière* in Rome in 1843. The 1844 version in London (credited to Cerrito) became famous for its introduction of the "Redowa, or Original Polka of Bohemia". Set in a little Hungarian village, the ballet is about Kathi, a camp-follower, who loves a tavern-keeper's son, Hans. However, the Burgomaster and Baron both have their eyes on Kathi, who must go through the typical trials and tribulations before the final unification with her lover.

The story was based on a work by Pierre-Jean de Beranger, whose considerable fame rested on poems that evoked the glory of the Napoleonic Empire. It was of the sentimental, pre-romantic type that supplied the model for innumerable ballets and theatre pieces, Jean Dauberval's *La Fille mal gardée* (1789) among them. Hence, it was not particularly romantic in anything other than its reliance on local colour.

The work had its premiere at the Paris Opéra in 1848 (when it was credited to Saint-Léon), where it was recognized that the story was secondary to the dancing. The critic for *Le Moniteur* wrote that "All that is asked, is that it be well danced." *Le Charivari* considered that the story was simply a vehicle for the dancing of Cerrito and Saint-Léon and that the latter's performance was so strong that he might rehabilitate masculine dancing which had fallen from fashion. Cerrito was an established favourite. "Pretty, alert, dazzling, elegant," wrote Jules Janin, ". . . she dances with so much joy and with such a lively foot, and a heart so gay, and with such a satisfied glance . . .". *Le Constitutionnel* enjoyed her portrayal of Kathi, calling her character "ravishing with malice, with gaiety, and with petulance. Not for a long time have we seen a *danseuse* at the Opéra obtain such a deserved success."

Saint-Léon's and Cerrito's choreography possessed merit as well. "The manner in which M. Saint-Léon composes his dance steps," commented *L'Illustration*, "spreads a continual animation. His steps have in effect something special, and are worthy of being pointed out, for instead of being, like so many other dances, a collection of incoherent jumps, pointes, entrechats, pirouettes, etc.; they are small tableaux full of expression, and, through the ingenious use of the mimic art, their meaning is always clear, pleasing, interesting or piquant according to the situation. The dance of the 'Vivandiere', for example, depicts all the episodes of military life with the most acute realism." The use of dance as a tool to enhance the depiction of character and atmosphere, though it was a feature of the best works of the romantic era, was not a skill many ballet masters consistently mastered. Cesare Pugni's arrange-

La Vivandière, with Fanny Cerrito as Kathi

ment of well-known music was generally found to be appropriate, rich, and harmonious.

La Vivandière has the distinction of being the only ballet from its period to have been partially notated. In 1852 Saint-Léon wrote *La Sténochorégraphie*, in which he publicised his own system of dance notation. It was here that he wrote down many of the dances from *La Vivandière*. The dances, when reconstructed, exude vivacity from flurries of small, brilliant steps and carefully delineated corps de ballet patterns. The expansive extension of body and movement through and into space that characterizes ballet of the latter twentieth century are absent. Energy, precision, speed, and lightness give the dances an intimate, conversational quality that must have appealed to audience members, many of whom aspired in real life to intimacy with the performers.

—John Chapman

VLADIMIROV, Pierre

Russian/American dancer. Born Petr (later Pierre) Nikolaevich Nikolaev (later changed to Vladimirov, or Vladimiroff) in Gatchina, near St. Petersburg, 1 February (according to some sources) 1893. Studied at the Imperial Theatre School, St. Petersburg, pupil of Sergei Legat, Samuil Andrianov, Anatole Obukhov, Mikhail Fokine; graduated in 1911. Married dancer Felia Doubrovska (Dluzhnevska) in 1922. Dancer, Maryinsky

Theatre (later State Academic Theatre for Opera and Ballet, or GATOB), St. Petersburg/Petrograd, 1911–19, becoming principal dancer, from 1915; leading performer with Diaghilev's Ballets Russes, seasons 1912, 1914; also dancing partner (at the ballerina's request) to Mathilde Kshesinskaya; left Russia, 1919, appearing as premier danseur, Diaghilev's Ballets Russes, 1921–22, 1925; independent artist, touring with wife Felia Doubrovska, 1922, and performing with Tamara Karsavina, New York, 1924; dancer with Mikhail Mordkin Ballet, U.S., 1925–27; premier danseur and leading partner, Anna Pavlova's company, touring South America, Europe, Egypt, India, 1928–31; settled in the U.S.: teacher, School of American Ballet, New York, 1934–67: students include Todd Bolender, William Dollar, William Christensen, Ruthanna Boris, Tanaquil LeClercq, Maria Tallchief. Died in New York, 25 November 1970.

ROLES

1911   Pas de trois in *Swan Lake* (Petipa, Ivanov), Maryinsky Theatre, St. Petersburg
1912   Pas de trois in *Paquita* (Petipa), Maryinsky Theatre, St. Petersburg
       Slave in *Cléopâtre* (Fokine), Maryinsky Theatre, St. Petersburg
       Slave in *Le Pavillon d'Armide* (Fokine), Maryinsky Theatre, St. Petersburg
1913   Prince Siegfried in *Swan Lake* (Petipa, Ivanov), Maryinsky Theatre, St. Petersburg
1914   Albrecht in *Giselle* (Petipa after Coralli, Perrot), Maryinsky Theatre, St. Petersburg
       Merchant in *Le Corsaire* (Petipa), Maryinsky Theatre, St. Petersburg
       Slave in *Le Corsaire* (Petipa), Maryinsky Theatre, St. Petersburg
       Harlequin in *Harlequinade* (Petipa), Maryinsky Theatre, St. Petersburg
       Vaiyu in *The Talisman* (Petipa), Maryinsky Theatre, St. Petersburg
       Warrior Chief in *Polovtsian Dances from Prince Igor* (Fokine), Diaghilev's Ballets Russes
       Slave in *Cléopâtre* (Fokine), Diaghilev's Ballets Russes
1915   Title role (cr) in *Eros* (Fokine), Maryinsky Theatre, Petrograd
       Paolo (cr) in *Francesca da Rimini* (Fokine), Maryinsky Theatre, Petrograd
1916   Harlequin in *Le Carnaval* (Fokine), Maryinsky Theatre, St. Petersburg
1921   Ivan Tsarevich in *The Firebird* (Fokine), Diaghilev's Ballets Russes, London
       Prince Charming (cr) in *The Sleeping Princess* (new production; Petipa, staged Sergeyev, with additional dances Nijinska), Diaghilev's Ballets Russes, London
1928/ Principal dancer in *Dionysus* (Clustine), Anna Pavlova's
31   Company, tour
       Principal dancer in *The Fairy Doll* (Clustine after N. and S. Legat), Anna Pavlova's Company, tour
       Principal dancer in *Dance of the Hours* (Clustine), Anna Pavlova's Company, tour

Other roles include: for the Maryinsky Theatre/State Academic Theatre for Opera and Ballet (GATOB)—Solor in *La Bayadère* (Petipa), Youth in *Chopiniana* (Fokine), Bluebird in *The Sleeping Beauty* (Petipa), Conrad in *Le Corsaire* (Petipa), Abderakhman and Jean de Brienne in *Raymonda* (Petipa), Arthur in *Bluebeard* (Petipa).

Pierre Vladimirov teaching class, New York

PUBLICATIONS

Dolin, Anton, *Divertissement*, London, 1929

Kyasht, Lydia, *Romantic Recollections*, London, 1929

Dandré, Victor, *Anna Pavlova in Art and Life*, London, 1932

Barzel, Ann, "European Dance Teachers in the U.S.", *Dance Index* (New York), April–June 1944

Karsavine, Tamara, "Touring with Vladimirov", *Dancing Times* (London), June 1967

Doubrovska, Felia (as told to Marian Horosko), "Pierre Vladimiroff", *Dance Magazine* (New York), February 1971

Horosko, Marian, "In the Shadow of Russian Tradition", *Dance Magazine* (New York), February 1971

Krasovskaya, Vera, *Russian Ballet Theatre of the Early Twentieth Century*, volume 2, Leningrad, 1972

Relkin, Abbie, "In Pavlova's Shadow", *Ballet News* (New York), January 1981

Money, Keith, *Anna Pavlova*, London, 1982

Smakov, Gennady, *The Great Russian Dancers*, New York, 1984

*   *   *

Pierre Vladimirov was one of the most exciting and gifted dancers of his generation, according to many of those who saw him perform in his heyday at the Maryinsky Theatre—and, although not one of the most famous names of Diaghilev's Ballets Russes, for whom he appeared in various seasons from 1912 to 1921, Vladimirov had sufficient presence to create a sensation when he was seen amongst that illustrious company.

He graduated from the Imperial Theatre School at a time when the Russian ballet was making a name for itself abroad under the aegis of impresario Serge Diaghilev, and the male dancer causing the greatest stir, both at home and abroad, was Vaslav Nijinsky. Some critics and historians have claimed that Vladimirov was spurred on by a sense of competition with Nijinsky (with whom the young Vladimirov's first performances had apparently been compared), but in fact his stage presence was of a different style altogether. Unlike the slightly boyish, androgynous Nijinsky, Vladimirov instantly communicated a strong sense of masculine strength; his stage persona was more along the lines of Mikhail Mordkin or Adolf Bolm, dancers who thrilled early twentieth-century audiences with the athletic power and attack of their dancing.

Vladimirov was evidently well known for his temper and for his rebellious attitude, which instantly set him on a path different from that of the traditional "danseur noble". He rejected what he did not like (such as boring roles), and evidently added what he did like—including his own variations on the choreography of the classical ballets. Felia Doubrovska, who married Vladimirov in 1922, remembered, "Not only did Pierre create a sensation with *Swan Lake*. He . . . planned a new entrance to the male variation in the coda of the Black Swan Pas de Deux. Legat entered to centre stage for this variation, but Pierre was the first to enter with a grand jeté from the wings after the music had begun. Everyone now thinks it was in the original choreography."

Vladimirov's profile was not especially high at the Maryinsky until he had performed abroad with Diaghilev in 1912, and he then returned home again to much bigger roles in full-length classics like *Giselle* and *Swan Lake*. (It cannot have hurt that Nijinsky had now left the Maryinsky in order to perform exclusively with Diaghilev's company.) Doubrovska tells us that it was Fokine who encouraged Vladimirov to go back to St. Petersburg after his first appearances with Diaghilev, saying that the dancer needed to be seen in ballets other than Fokine's in order to prove that he was a strong classical dancer. In the years from 1912 until 1919, when he left Russia, Vladimirov triumphed in a series of great male roles in the classical repertoire, thereby distinguishing himself in exactly the way that Fokine had predicted. His leaps were especially admired, not only for their elevation but for the way the dancer could cover vast distances on the stage in a matter of a few steps. Such was Vladimirov's reputation that he was asked to partner the grande dame of the Imperial Russian ballet, Mathilde Kshesinskaya, performing for the tsar and touring through Russia before the Revolution.

Vladimirov was not a failure in the more modern repertoire, nor would he have failed to emerge as a leading Ballets Russes dancer had he chosen to stay with Diaghilev throughout the era of Diaghilev's Ballets Russes. Indeed, he was the one who replaced Nijinsky in the famous slave variation in Fokine's *Cléopâtre*, inspiring the company's régisseur, Serge Grigoriev, to write later, ". . . that performance of *Cléopâtre* [in 1914] remains in my memory for the extraordinarily brilliant dancing of Vladimirov, in Nijinsky's old part of the Negro slave". On the other hand, his performances in some of Fokine's other works were not always unanimously admired; André Levinson complained that Vladimirov's performance in *Carnaval* was misdirected. "His exaggerated briskness and inappropriate high jumps were at odds with Fokine's picturesque vignette", he wrote in 1916. Diaghilev, therefore, was shrewd to invite Vladimirov some years later to perform the more straight-forward classical leading role of Prince Charming in the company's 1921 production of *The Sleeping Princess*. Here, according to Cyril Beaumont, "Vladimirov brought style and nobility to his Prince Charming and was particularly good in his scenes with the Lilac Fairy and in the grand pas de deux in the last act."

Vladimirov stayed on stubbornly in Russia even after the Revolution—not necessarily because he supported the new regime, but simply because, as Doubrovska later said, "He just liked Russia". But eventually it was Doubrovksa who found a way to leave the country, and the two escaped on skis, via Finland, in 1919. From this point on, Vladimirov, like so many Russian expatriate dancers, had a largely peripatetic, freelance career. He performed, mostly in touring concert performances, with his wife Felia Doubrovska, and partnered Tamara Karsavina in New York in 1924; he also danced with Mikhail Mordkin's company in the 1920s. As Anna Pavlova's leading partner from 1928 onwards, he travelled around the world with her company, performing from South America to India. When he finally settled in the United States, he was taken on by Balanchine as a teacher for his newly formed School of American Ballet; he remained there for over thirty years,

helping to produce some of the finest American dancers of that era.

Vladimirov died of a stroke in 1970. Doubrovska, interviewed soon after his death, said, "Pierre Vladimirov was the Nureyev of his day. But not in America. Here his career ended and his teaching began." Whether remembered as a great virtuoso dancer or as one of the most important teachers during the formative days of American ballet, Pierre Vladimirov is undoubtedly a memorable figure in the history of twentieth-century ballet.

—Elizabeth Hudson

———

VOLININE, (Volinin) **Alexandre**

Russian/French dancer and teacher. Born Aleksandr Emelyanovich Volinin (Volinine) in Moscow, 16 September (4 September old style) 1882. Studied at the Moscow Imperial Theatre School, pupil of Vasily Tikhomirov, Aleksandr Gorsky; graduated in 1901. Dancer, Bolshoi Theatre, Moscow, 1901–10, becoming principal dancer from 1903; performer with Diaghilev's Ballets Russes (partnering Ekaterina Geltser), Paris season, 1910; leading dancer in partnership with Lydia Lopokova, U.S. tour, 1910–11; premier danseur, Gertrude Hoffmann's "Ballets Russes", Winter Garden Theatre, New York, 1911, and Mordkin's "All-Star Imperial Russian Ballet", 1911–12; partnered Adeline Genée, U.S., Australian, and New Zealand tour, 1912–13, and Lydia Kyasht, Empire Theatre, London, 1913; premier danseur and leading partner, Anna Pavlova's company, world tours, 1914–25; teacher after retirement from stage, founding own school in Paris, 1926: students included André Eglevsky, David Lichine, Jean Babilée, Berger Bartholin; also guest ballet master for Royal Danish Ballet, 1943. Died in Paris, 3 July 1955.

ROLES

1894   Soloist in *The Gypsy* (after Mazilier), Bolshoi Theatre, Moscow
       Soloist in *The Goldfish* (after Saint-Léon), Bolshoi Theatre, Moscow
1903/ Prince Désiré in *The Sleeping Beauty* (Petipa), Bolshoi
10   Theatre, Moscow
       Prince Siegfried in *Swan Lake* (Gorsky after Petipa, Ivanov), Bolshoi Theatre, Moscow
       Pierre in *Cavalry Halt* (Petipa; staged Clustine), Bolshoi Theatre, Moscow
       Colin in *Vain Precautions* (*La Fille mal gardée*; Gorsky after Petipa Ivanov), Bolshoi Theatre, Moscow
       Miamun in *The Pharaoh's Daughter* (Gorsky after Petipa), Bolshoi Theatre, Moscow
1906   Candine (cr) in *Robert and Bertram; or, The Two Thieves* (Gorsky), Bolshoi Theatre, Moscow
1907   Spirit (cr) in *Nur and Anitra* (Gorsky), Bolshoi Theatre, Moscow
       Prince in *The Magic Mirror* (Gorsky after Petipa), Bolshoi Theatre, Moscow
       Franz in *Coppélia* (Gorsky after Petipa, Saint-Léon), Bolshoi Theatre, Moscow
1910   Principal dancer in *Les Sylphides* (Fokine), Diaghilev's Ballets Russes, Paris
       Principal dancer (cr) in *Les Orientales* (Fokine), Diaghilev's Ballets Russes, Paris

Alexandre Volonine in the *Bow and Arrow Dance*

1911   Slave in *Cléopâtre* (Fokine), Winter Garden Theater, New York

Beno, Spanish Dance in *Swan Lake* (one-act version; Mordkin after Petipa, Ivanov), All-Star Imperial Russian Ballet, Washington, D.C.

1911/   Franz in *Coppélia* (after Petipa, Ivanov, Cecchetti), All-
12   Star Imperial Russian Ballet, U.S. tour

1912   Polka Comique in *Les Millions d'Harlequin* (after Petipa), All-Star Imperial Russian Ballet, U.S. tour

Vestris in *La Camargo* (Petipa), Adeline Genée tour

Principal dancer (cr) in *La Danse*, Adeline Genée tour, New York

Robert in "Ballet of the Nuns" from *Robert le Diable* (opera; mus. Meyerbeer), Adeline Genée tour

Divertissements: *Bow and Arrow Dance*, *Sad Pierrot*, *Variation Brillante* (also chor.), Adeline Genée tour, Australia

Dmitri (cr) in *First Love* (Kyasht), Empire Theatre, London

1914   Zephyr in *The Awakening of Flora* (after Petipa), Palace Theatre, London

Slave to Helen (cr) in *Walpurgis Night* (from opera *Faust*; chor. Clustine), Anna Pavlova's Company, Chicago

Prince Charmant in *The Fairy Doll* (Clustine after S. and N. Legat), Anna Pavlova's Company, Chicago

1914/   Principal dancer in *Pierrot* (own solo; also chor.), Anna
15   Pavlova's Company, Australian tour

1915   Jean de Brienne in *Raymonda* (Clustine after Petipa), Anna Pavlova's Company, New York

Principal dancer in *Hebrew Dance* (pas de deux; mus. Saint-Saëns), Anna Pavlova's Company, New York

Pas de deux in *The Hours* (Clustine), Anna Pavlova's Company, U.S. tour

1916   Principal dancer in *Gavotte* (after Clustine), Anna Pavlova's Company, tour

Pas de deux in *Land of the Golden Fleece* (mus. Sousa), Anna Pavlova's Company, tour

Prince Désiré in *The Sleeping Beauty* (Clustine after Petipa), Anna Pavlova's Company, Hippodrome, New York

1918   Romeo (cr) in *Romeo and Juliet* (also known as *Juliet's Dream*; mus. Gounod), Anna Pavlova's Company, Buenos Aires

El Sol (cr) in *Danza de las Flores* (Clustine), Anna Pavlova's Company, Buenos Aires

1919   A Young Poet (cr) in *Autumn Leaves* (Pavlova), Anna Pavlova's Company, South American tour

1920   Luc in *The Magic Flute* (after Ivanov, Cecchetti), Anna Pavlova's Company, tour

Principal Cavalier (cr) in *Christmas* (Clustine), Anna Pavlova's Company, tour

1924   Espada in *Don Quixote* (Novikov after Gorsky), Anna Pavlova's Company, tour

Other roles include: for Anna Pavlova's Company—Cavalier in "Snowflakes" scene from *The Nutcracker* (Pavlova after Ivanov), Albrecht in *Giselle* (after Petipa, Coralli, Perrot), Prince Hassan in *The King's Daughter* (*The Three Palms*; Fokine), Amarilla's Brother in *Amarilla* (Clustine), principal dancer in *Chopiniana* (Clustine), Colin in *La Fille mal gardée* (after Petipa), and leading roles in *Coquetterie de Colombine* (from *The Fairy Doll*; after N. and S. Legat), *Valse caprice* (Legat), *Les Ondines*, *Suite dansante* (Clustine), *Valse triste*, *Bacchanal*, *Slave Dance*.

WORKS

1912   *Arabian Nights*, Adeline Genée's Imperial Russian Company, Australia

Staged:
1912   *Les Sylphides* (after Fokine; mus. Chopin), Adeline Genée's Imperial Russian Company, Australia

1946   *Giselle* (after Petipa, Coralli, Perrot; mus. Adam), Royal Danish Ballet, Copenhagen

1950   *Harlequinade Pas de deux* (after Petipa; mus. Drigo), London Festival Ballet

PUBLICATIONS

By Volinine:
"My Dance of Life", (in collaboration with A.R. Pirie), *The Dance* (New York), 4 parts: January, February, March, April 1930

"In Memory of Anna Pavlova", fragments from an unfinished book, *Dancing Times* (London), January 1937

About Volinine:
Cross, V.J., "A Volinine Vignette", *Dance Magazine* (New York), February 1952

Lazzanini, John and Roberta, *Pavlova: Repertoire of a Legend*, London, 1980
Money, Keith, *Anna Pavlova*, London, 1982

*   *   *

Moscow-born Russian dancer Alexandre Volinine was a noted classical dancer of handsome appearance who played a significant role in pioneering classical ballet in the West. In demand as a skilled, strong partner, he worked with many major ballerinas, including Geltser, Karalli, Genée, and Pavlova. More elegant than most of the muscular danseurs from Moscow, Volinine had excellent elevation and batterie. He was regarded by Pavlova's companion and administrator, Victor Dandré, as the best male dancer of his generation after Vaslav Nijinsky. After a decade and a half of continual touring, Volinine settled in Paris (becoming a French citizen in 1937) and opened an important school.

Coming from a family of engineers, Volinine owed his introduction to dance to a chance acquaintance with the dancer Litavkin, who recognized that the young Volinine had the potential to become a dancer, as he had a remarkable natural jump. Litavkin encouraged Volinine's father to enter his son for the Imperial School in Moscow, where the boy soon made his dancing début in *The Gypsy* at the age of twelve. At the school his principal teacher was Vasily Tikhomirov, who moulded so many Bolshoi male dancers, and after graduation Volinine was quickly promoted to premier danseur. At the Bolshoi his repertoire included *Coppélia*, *Swan Lake*, and *The Pharaoh's Daughter*.

Serge Diaghilev invited Volinine to the West in 1910 as Geltser's partner for the divertissement *Les Orientales*. The dancer then appeared with Diaghilev's company in Germany and Paris, where Charles Frohman signed him, together with Lydia Lopokova and her brother Fedor Lupukhov, for a nation-wide tour of the United States—and here began his years of taking classical ballet to audiences who had never seen dancing of such calibre. Agreement to Frohman's tour, however, meant that Volinine extended his leave from the Imperial Theatre beyond the agreed period, and so he never returned to Russia.

For the next couple of years Volinine worked in America, following the Frohman tour with an engagement in Gertrude Hoffman's pirated "Ballets Russes" in New York (he danced the poet in *Les Sylphides*). He then rescued the tour of the All-Star Imperial Russian Ballet (1911–12), taking over the role of Franz in *Coppélia* when Mikhail Mordkin was hospitalized with appendicitis, and later enabling the tour to continue when Mordkin left for a more lucrative and comfortable engagement in New York. Ever the pioneer, Volinine accompanied Adeline Genée to Australia with a self-styled Imperial Russian Company, the repertoire of which combined new Russian ballets like *Les Sylphides* with standard works from Genée's repertoire, such as *Robert the Devil*. From Genée Volinine moved to her successor at London's Empire Theatre, Lydia Kyasht, whom he partnered in the trifle *First Love* before receiving an invitation to partner Anna Pavlova when her then partner, Novikov, returned to Moscow on doctor's orders.

Volinine partnered Pavlova primarily in classical roles, and was regarded by many as Pavlova's most able partner. He worked with her until his retirement from the stage in 1925. Volinine could be temperamental, but not without reason, as most of his outbursts related to poor working conditions (draughty theatres, the lack of changing facilities on tour) or the difficulty of performing in weighty costumes (such as those designed by Bakst for the New York *Sleeping Beauty*). However, he had the ability to calm Pavlova when she was under similar stress. He worked with Pavlova in North and South America, on Far Eastern tours, and in Europe, partnering her in her company's adaptations of *Raymonda*, "Snowflakes" from *The Nutcracker*, *Giselle*, *The Fairy Doll*, *Walpurgis Night*, and *Gavotte*. Inevitably, Volinine's involvement with Pavlova's company limited his opportunities for more innovative work, but there seems to be nothing to suggest that he might have preferred to perform in more experimental ballets.

Volinine opened his Parisian school with support from Madame Tamara d'Erlanger. At a time when most of the émigré teachers in Paris were women, he attracted rising and established male dancers to his studio. Among those who acknowledge their debt to him were David Lichine, André Eglevsky, Berger Bartholin, and Jean Babilée, as well as visiting British dancers Anton Dolin, Michael Somes, and John Field. Volinine's classes were athletic and drew on his Bolshoi heritage. His pupils learned to dance with vigour and grace, and he passed on his own attributes of skilled partnering, strength, and a smooth-flowing quality of movement.

Not only did Volinine teach class, but he also occasionally mounted works from the Russian repertoire for his pupils and their companies. For example, he taught John Gilpin the pas de deux from *Harlequinade*, performed by London Festival Ballet in the years 1950–62, and in 1946 he staged a full production of *Giselle* for the Royal Danish Ballet.

—Jane Pritchard

VOLKOVA, Vera

Russian/British dancer, choreographer, and teacher. Born in St. Petersburg, 7 June 1904. Studied at the Russian Choreographic School (founder Akim Volynsky), pupil of Maria Romanova and Agrippina Vaganova, Petrograd/Leningrad, 1920–25. Married architect Hugh Finch Williams, 1937. Dancer, State Academic Theatre for Opera and Ballet (GATOB; later the Kirov Ballet), 1925–29; dancer, touring Japan and China with small ensemble, remaining in Shanghai, 1929: dancer and teacher, Georgi Goncharov's Russian ballet school and company, Shanghai, from 1929; founder and teacher of own school, Hong Kong, 1932; moved to England: founder and teacher of own studio, West Street, London, from 1936; teacher, Sadler's Wells Ballet School and company, 1943–50; teacher and artistic adviser, La Scala, Milan, 1950; guest teacher, Royal Danish Ballet, Copenhagen, 1951, becoming permanent teacher and artistic adviser, 1952–75; also international guest teacher, including for Kurt Jooss's Folkwang Schule, New York City Ballet, and Harkness Ballet, New York. Recipient: title of Knight of Dannebrog, 1956; Carlsberg Memorial Legacy, 1974. Died in Copenhagen, 5 May 1975.

PUBLICATIONS

By Volkova:
"Agrippina Vaganova", *Ballet Annual* (London), no. 7, 1953
Interview with Svend Kragh-Jacobsen, *Ballet Review* (Brooklyn, N.Y.), vol. 5, no. 4, 1975–76

About Volkova:
Zoete, Beryl de, "Vera Volkova", *Ballet* (London), January/February 1951

Wilson, G.B.L., "The Living Tradition in Denmark", *Ballet Annual* (London), no. 7, 1953

Clarke, Mary, *The Sadler's Wells Ballet*, London, 1955

Hering, Doris, "America Meets Vera Volkova", *Dance Magazine* (New York), September 1959

Aschengreen, Erik, "Hommage à Vera Volkova", *Les Saisons de la danse* (Paris), June 1975

Boscawen, Penelope, "Remembering Vera Volkova", *Dancing Times* (London), October 1985

* * *

Vera Volkova, daughter of a Russian Army officer, attended the Smolny Institute for Young Girls in St. Petersburg, and then studied as a private pupil at the Russian Choreographic School, owned and run by the influential ballet critic Akim Volynsky. Among her most important teachers were Maria Romanova (mother of the great Soviet ballerina Galina Ulanova) and Agrippina Vaganova, later to become one of the most important pedagogues in the history of Russian ballet.

Although herself a late starter, Vera Volkova eventually became a member of GATOB (the State Academic Theatre for Opera and Ballet), formerly the Maryinsky Theatre, later to become known as the Kirov Ballet. In 1929, while in Shanghai, she defected with the intention of joining Diaghilev's Ballets Russes. However, on hearing of Diaghilev's death and on meeting her future husband, Hugh Finch Williams, Volkova decided to stay on in Shanghai, where she began teaching for the local "Russian" company, directed by her compatriot Georgi Goncharov.

Opening her own studios, Volkova continued teaching, first in Hong Kong, and later in London. She adapted to her own purposes Vaganova's happy synthesis of a number of styles, adjusted to twentieth-century demands; these principles became the foundation of Volkova's own teaching. In these early years she taught company classes, but her true interest lay with special coaching and with preparing dancers for specific roles—the work joining classroom to stage.

A growing reputation, along with recommendations from Margot Fonteyn, whom Volkova had first taught as a child in Shanghai, induced ballet director Ninette de Valois to invite Volkova to teach at Sadler's Wells and Covent Garden in London. Much of the style of the famous post-war Sadler's Wells Ballet production of *The Sleeping Beauty*—as well as the success of Fonteyn's portrayal of the leading role—came from Volkova's own efforts. As a guest teacher, Volkova taught for Kurt Jooss's school and for the ballet school and company of La Scala in Milan, where her influence was great.

In 1952, following an engagement as guest teacher to the company, Vera Volkova was appointed artistic adviser to the Royal Danish Ballet in Copenhagen. Over the years she carved a permanent reputation as one of the company's greatest teachers, and became rightly credited as the one who lifted the Danish company out of its somewhat narrow preoccupation with the Romantic Bournonville style of movement and gave it a more forceful, contemporary style. This style, moreover, did not obliterate but complemented the company's heritage, remembering its obligation to a tradition which Volkova herself regarded as the most important in Europe.

One of Volkova's achievements in redirecting the destiny of the Royal Danish Ballet was to bring in guest choreographers such as Sir Frederick Ashton, who created his famous *Romeo and Juliet* on the company. Another result of Volkova's new techniques was to change the face of Bournonville dancing: the ballerinas danced more on pointe, the men ventured more virtuoso pirouettes, and so on. Volkova also suggested dancers for specific roles, as well as presenting her own ideas for cuts and changes in works being created. Thus she inspired choreographers and the guardians of the repertoire to continue to provide challenge and education, while continuing herself to guide her pupils. Among her pupils were Kirsten Simone, Erik Bruhn, Henning Kronstam, Peter Martins, Peter Schaufuss, Margot Fonteyn, Rudolf Nureyev, John Neumeier, John Cranko, and Stanley Williams, all people who were themselves to go on and influence the direction of ballet history.

The Volkova influence on Western and, in particular, Danish ballet has been immense. Her service to the dance was in shaping the creative lives of others. She saw herself not only as a pedagogue, but as a link between past and future in the continuity of dance. "Dance historians are preoccupied with yesterday," she said. "I care about the future."

—Alexander Meinertz

VOLUNTARIES

Choreography: Glen Tetley
Music: Francis Poulenc
Design: Rouben Ter-Arutunian (scenery and costumes)
First Production: Stuttgart Ballet, Württembergische Staatstheater, Stuttgart, 22 December 1973
Principal Dancers: Marcia Haydée, Richard Cragun, Birgit Keil, Reid Anderson, Jan Stripling

Other productions include: Royal Ballet, with Lynn Seymour, David Wall, Vergie Derman, Wayne Eagling, Mark Silver; London, 18 November 1976. American Ballet Theatre, with Cynthia Gregory, Charles Ward, Martine van Hamel, Michael Owen, Richard Schafer; Cleveland, 4 February 1977. Royal Danish Ballet, with Linda Hindberg, Arne Villumsen; Copenhagen, 13 December 1978. Paris Opéra Ballet, with Elisabeth Platel, Jean Guizerix; Paris, 24 May 1982. Australian Ballet, with Christine Walsh, Dale Baker; 16 April 1984. National Ballet of Canada; Toronto, 28 April 1988.

PUBLICATIONS

Balanchine, George, with Mason, Francis, *Balanchine's Complete Stories of the Great Ballets*, Garden City, N.Y., 1977

Rogosin, Elinor, *The Dance Makers*, New York, 1980

* * *

Glen Tetley had already been asked to create a work for the Stuttgart Ballet when its director, choreographer John Cranko, died unexpectedly in 1973. *Voluntaries* became the ballet he produced in December of that year, and was specifically conceived "in memoriam" for Cranko, to whom the work is dedicated. Its stature, even among Tetley's oeuvre, and the rapport which it created between choreographer and company, also ushered in a brief period during which Tetley was invited to assume the company's creative direction—bridging the enormous gap left by Cranko while it recovered from the blow—before internal friction led to his resuming a freelance international career two years later.

In his choice of Poulenc's *Concerto for Organ, Strings and Timpani* Tetley selected one of several highly personal concert works by the composer, in which an integral dance element—very much part of his own musical identity—is conspicuously

Voluntaries, **as performed by the Stuttgart Ballet**

close to the surface. (The music had already attracted the attention of other choreographers, notably Erich Walter for *Gravité* in 1969.) Its highly individual atmosphere, as well as its musical structure, is well suited to Tetley's purpose: the organ is used for solemn declamation throughout much of the work, as well as for sections of ruminative meditation, while the absence of brass or woodwind allows the strings to assume glistening transparent contrasts as the timpani provide both dramatic emphasis and rhythmic drive. Its progression from dark seriousness to lighter exuberance and release of energy not only mirrors Poulenc's own balance between intense spirituality and frank earthiness but provides Tetley with an apt vehicle in which to express progression—appropriate in a personal tribute—from serious inward devotion to a soaring and uplifting optimism.

Instead of the usual three-movement concerto form, the piece is constructed more in the manner of seventeenth-century baroque organ fantasias, which were conceived like divertimenti in a succession of contrasting sections. Tetley made effective cumulative use of the concerto's seven short sections, which are played without a break and are unified by a recurring theme heard at the opening and subsequently treated to substantial musical variation. There is an overall progression in the dancing from manipulation of tight, inwardly-focused groupings—frequently highlighting a characteristic posture of the body that suggests preparation for flight—towards free-

ranging and widely spaced leaps at the end, into which Tetley has poured some of his most inventive and arresting choreography. The designs and lighting are intimately related to one another and essentially keep the whole stage-space free, but there is also a relation between the subdued atmosphere created by a back-projected disc (reminiscent of a pointilliste cathedral rose window) to the discreet mottling of the dancers' otherwise white body-tights.

The choreographer's own note for the ballet is worth recording: "*Voluntaries*—by musical definition—are free-ranging organ improvizations, often played before, during and after religious service. The Latin root of the word can also connote flight or desire, and the ballet is conceived as a series of linked voluntaries."

With its five leading roles originally created by Marcia Haydée, Richard Cragun, Birgit Keil, Reid Anderson, and Jan Stripling, *Voluntaries*—and Tetley's subsequent experience at Stuttgart—marks a significant reintegration of classical technique into the choreographer's widely eclectic style. This followed a previous decade of widely varied experimentation in a variety of movement forms, which had followed Tetley's emergence as a major choreographer with *Pierrot Lunaire*.

—Geoffrey Baskerville

VON AROLDINGEN, Karin

German/American dancer.   Born in Greiz, East Germany, 9 September 1941. Studied with Tatjana Gsovsky (Gsovska), Berlin, from 1951; later studied with George Balanchine, New York. Married Morton Gewirts, 1965: one daughter. Dancer, American Festival Ballet, Bremen, 1958; soloist, Frankfurt Ballet, 1959–60, performing lead in Balanchine's *Seven Deadly Sins*, Frankfurt, 1959; invited by Balanchine to come to the United States: dancer, corps de ballet, New York City Ballet, from 1962, becoming soloist, from 1967, and principal dancer, from 1972; has also appeared on television, including for Public Broadcasting Service (PBS) "Dance in America" series, 1977; retired from the stage in 1984; teacher, children's classes at the School of American Ballet, New York; has also staged Balanchine works for other companies.

ROLES

1960   Anna I in *The Seven Deadly Sins* (Balanchine; staged T. Gsovsky), Frankfurt Ballet, Frankfurt
1963   The Lady in *Con Amore* (Christensen), New York City Ballet, New York
       Leto in *Apollo* (Balanchine), New York City Ballet, New York
       Soloist in *Raymonda Variations* (Balanchine), New York City Ballet, New York
1967/ Principal dancer in *Serenade* (Balanchine), New York
69   City Ballet, New York
       Principal dancer in *Scotch Symphony* (Balanchine), New York City Ballet, New York
       Young girl in *Jeux* (Taras), New York City Ballet, New York
       Principal dancer in *La Guirlande de Campra* (Taras), New York City Ballet, New York
       Principal dancer in *Movements for Piano and Orchestra* (Balanchine), New York City Ballet, New York
       Rondo in *Western Symphony* (Balanchine), New York City Ballet, New York
       Third Campaign in *Stars and Stripes* (Balanchine), New York City Ballet, New York
       Principal dancer in *Liebeslieder Walzer* (Balanchine), New York City Ballet, New York
1970   "I'll Build a Stairway to Paradise", "Who Cares?", "Clap yo' Hands" (cr) in *Who Cares?* (Balanchine), New York City Ballet, New York
       Élégie (cr) in *Suite No. 3* (later *Tchaikovsky Suite No. 3*; Balanchine), New York City Ballet, New York
1971   Variations, II (cr) in *The Goldberg Variations* (Robbins), New York City Ballet, New York
       Principal dancer (cr) in *PAMTGG* (Balanchine), New York City Ballet, New York
1972   Principal dancer in *Chopiniana* (Danilova after Fokine), New York City Ballet, New York
       Toccata and Aria I (cr) in *Violin Concerto* (later *Stravinsky Violin Concerto*; Balanchine), New York City Ballet, New York
       Principal dancer (cr) in *Scherzo à la Russe* (Balanchine), New York City Ballet, New York
       Principal dancer (cr) in *Choral Variations on Bach's "Vom Himmel Hoch"* (Balanchine), New York City Ballet, New York
1973   Character Pas de deux (cr) in *Cortège Hongroise* (Balanchine), New York City Ballet, New York
       The Siren in *The Prodigal Son* (Balanchine), New York City Ballet, New York
1974   Principal dancer (cr) in *Variations pour une Porte et un Soupir* (pas de deux; Balanchine), New York City Ballet, New York
1975   Lyceion (cr) in *Daphnis and Chloe* (Taras), New York City Ballet, New York
       Le Gibet (cr) in *Gaspard de la Nuit* (Balanchine), New York City Ballet, New York
       Principal dancer (cr) in *Rhapsodie Espagnole* (Balanchine), New York City Ballet, New York
1976   MacDonald of Sleat, Royal Navy (cr) in *Union Jack* (Balanchine), New York City Ballet, New York
1977   Tales from the Vienna Woods (cr) in *Vienna Waltzes* (Balanchine), New York City Ballet, New York
1978   Principal dancer (cr) in *Kammermusik No. 2* (Balanchine), New York City Ballet, New York
       Majorette (cr) in *Tricolore* (Martins, Bonnefous, Robbins), New York City Ballet, New York
1980   Principal dancer, first couple (cr) in *Robert Schumann's "Davidsbündlertänze"* (Balanchine), New York City Ballet, New York
       Eurydice in *Orpheus* (Balanchine), New York City Ballet, New York
1981   Fire (cr) in *The Spellbound Child* (*L'Enfant et les Sortilèges*, new production; Balanchine), "Dance in America" television series of the Public Broadcasting Service (PBS)
       Principal dancer (cr) in *Hungarian Gypsy Airs* (Balanchine), New York City Ballet, New York
       Adagio Lamentoso (cr) in *Symphony No. 6—Pathétique* (Balanchine), New York City Ballet, New York
1982   Principal dancer (cr) in *Tango* (pas de deux; Balanchine), New York City Ballet, New York
       Spirit of Perséphone (cr) in *Perséphone* (Balanchine, with Taras, Zorina), New York City Ballet, New York

Other roles include: Principal dancer in *Concerto Barocco* (Balanchine), First and Third Movements in *Symphony in C* (Balanchine), title role in *Firebird* (Balanchine, Robbins), Profane Love in *Illuminations* (Ashton), Second Pas de trois in *Agon* (Balanchine), Five Pieces in *Episodes* II (Balanchine), the Coquette in *La Sonnambula* (Balanchine), Helena and Titania in *A Midsummer Night's Dream* (Balanchine), principal dancer in *Movements for Piano and Orchestra* (Balanchine), The Lady with Him in *Dim Lustre* (Tudor), Pas classique Espagnol in *Don Quixote* (Balanchine), Allegro and Rondo in *Brahms–Schoenberg Quartet* (Balanchine), Emeralds and Rubies in *Jewels* (Balanchine), principal dancer in *Stravinsky: Symphony in C* (Clifford).

PUBLICATIONS

By von Aroldingen:
"Thoughts of a Dancer", *Dance Scope* (New York), Spring/Summer 1972
Interview in Gruen, John, "Karin von Aroldingen", *The Private World of Ballet*, New York, 1975
Interview in Tracy, Robert, *Balanchine's Ballerinas*, New York, 1983

About von Aroldingen:
Niehaus, Max, *Ballett Faszination*, Munich, 1972
Croce, Arlene, *Afterimages*, New York, 1978
Croce, Arlene, *Going to the Dance*, New York, 1982
Reiter, Susan, "Such a Gift", *Ballet News* (New York), February 1983

Karin von Aroldingen as The Siren in *The Prodigal Son*, New York City Ballet

Mason, Francis, "Forewords and Afterwards", *Ballet Review* (New York), Summer 1984
Croce, Arlene, *Sight Lines*, New York, 1987

*   *   *

At New York City Ballet, Karin von Aroldingen may well have been the strongest Balanchine ballerina of her generation. Tall, with square shoulders, square jaw, and extremely well-defined muscular form, she described herself once as a horse who had to race. Indeed, gymnastics training in her early childhood seemed to prepare her well for the kind of choreographic racing George Balanchine favored.

Her ballet training began at age eleven in her native Germany under the tutelage of Tatjana Gsovsky (Gsovska), who is considered one of the most influential teachers in the development of ballet in postwar Germany. After passing the state exam in dance history and technique, von Aroldingen joined the American Festival Ballet for six months before signing on as a first soloist at the Frankfurt Ballet. Her former teacher, Gsovsky, was its new ballet mistress and von Aroldingen performed in several of her ballets during the 1959–60 season.

It was at that time that Gsovsky remounted *The Seven Deadly Sins* by Bertolt Brecht, Kurt Weill, and George Balanchine, and she cast von Aroldingen as the dancing Anna ("Anna I") to complement Lotte Lenya's Singing Anna ("Anna II"). Lenya was impressed by the dancer's expressive performance and arranged for her to audition for Balanchine.

In an interview with Susan Reiter, von Aroldingen confessed that the audition did not go well. "I had on terrible shoes—they were clunky and noisy. I was so frightened and nervous. I fell all over. I was really awful. But later he told me that he could see through it."

At first the choreographer was not able to take her into his company, but nearly two months after the audition he offered von Aroldingen a place in the corps de ballet. She finished her season with the Frankfurt company and moved to New York, where she joined NYCB for their 1962 season. She stayed there until her retirement in 1984.

Hers was not a meteoric rise to principal status. Although she was a very busy dancer, whom Balanchine often cast in solo roles, von Aroldingen spent five years in the corps de ballet before being officially promoted to soloist. Those first years were difficult for her. Not only was she one of the older members of the corps, but von Aroldingen also spoke no

English and was unused to Balanchine's demands for speed and extension. She worked on her own, with little verbal encouragement from Balanchine, but her dedication and diligence greatly mattered to him.

It took an additional five years for Balanchine to make her a principal dancer. In that year, 1972, Balanchine was choreographing a dizzying array of new ballets for the Stravinsky Festival at Lincoln Center and von Aroldingen created lead roles in a number of these. One, *Stravinsky Violin Concerto*, was her most stunning success. No one has yet been able to match her wiry fluidity or pin-point precision in the Aria I pas de deux.

She was at her best in roles that challenged her masterful command of allegro technique. Her talents included excellent flexibility and balance, a marvelous jump, split-second phrasing, and outstanding stamina. Her chiseled facial features made her remarkably goddess-like, but a goddess such as Athena, not Venus. As it happened, it was as the goddess Leto, mother of Apollo, that critics first began to notice her.

Von Aroldingen was not universally admired, partly because she did not quite fit the traditional ballerina mold. She was aggressive and ambitious rather than ethereal and delicate. She bit into each role with great hunger and attack. Her dramatic range, however, was considerable. She could dance the lyrical *Vienna Waltzes* with great poignance and sensitivity, but could also be a most brutal seductress as the Siren in Prodigal Son.

Karin von Aroldingen never missed a performance during her entire dancing career, even when pregnant with her daughter in 1965. She possessed great dignity and had a reputation for being loyal, gentle, and kind. Throughout her career she had maintained her family life, and Balanchine became a close family friend. After retiring, she continued her association with the company and its School of American Ballet by teaching children's classes and acting as a scout for potential students. She has also staged selected Balanchine works for other companies. When Balanchine died in 1983, he designated her an heir to a portion of his estate, which included the rights to several ballets.

—Kim Kokich

VON ROSEN, Elsa Marianne

Swedish dancer, choreographer, ballet director, and teacher. Born in Stockholm, 21 April 1924. Studied with Vera Alexandrova, Otto Thorensen, Albert Koslovsky, and Jenny Hasselquist, Stockholm, and at the Royal Danish Ballet School, Copenhagen, 1945–47. Married dance critic and designer Allan Fridericia, 1950. Stage début in independent dance recitals, with professional début in 1941; soloist, Oscarsteatern, Stockholm, 1947–50; dancer, Original Ballet Russe, 1948–49; principal dancer, Royal Swedish Ballet, 1951–59; international guest artist, including for Metropolitan Ballet, (de Basil's) Original Ballet Russe, and Ballet Rambert; founder, principal dancer, and choreographer, Scandinavian Ballet, 1960–61, reassembled for additional performances in 1965; choreographer and artistic director, Göteborg (Gothenburg) Ballet, 1970–76, and Malmö Ballet, 1980–87; collaborator, with Fridericia, on authentic stagings of Bournonville ballets, acting as guest producer for stagings throughout the world, including in Europe, Russia, and South America; also teacher: founder and teacher at own school in Copenhagen. Recipient: Carina Ari Medal, 1962.

ROLES

1938   The Young Girl in *Le Spectre de la rose* (Fokine), University Auditorium, Oslo

1939   Dancer in *Slavisk Dans* (solo; Thoresen), Dance Evening, Konserthuset, Stockholm

1940   Title role in *Törnrosa* (*Sleeping Beauty*; Thoresen), Christmas Matinée, Stockholm

       Title role in *Askungen*, Christmas Matinée, Stockholm

1941   Dancer in *Flickan och Solen* (solo; Gé), *Romance* (also chor.), Dance Evening, Konserthuset, Stockholm

       Ballet Divertissement in *Sol över Stan* (revue; chor. Gé), Royal Theatre, Stockholm

1942   Dancer in *Trollblomman* (solo; Gé), *Lola* (solo; Gé), Konserthuset, Stockholm

1943   Principal dancer in *Adagio* (pas de trois; Gé), *Valse triste* (pas de deux; Gé), *Kamarinskaja* (also chor.), Konserthuset, Stockholm

       Ulla Winblad in *Bellmansspelen* (Gé), Tivoli, Stockholm

       Ballet Divertissement in *Tre Valser* (operetta; mus. Strauss, chor. Gé), Oscarsteatern, Stockholm

1944   Dancer in *Soy Sevillana* (Spanish solo; Lander), *Yota* (Spanish solo; Lander), *Zigenardans* (*Gypsy Dance*; Gaubier), *Prudence* (pas de trois from *Swan Lake*; Lander after Petipa), *Adagio* (solo; also chor.), Konserthuset, Stockholm

1945   Prélude and Valse from *La Sylphide* (Fokine; staged Lander), Konserthuset, Göteborg

       Girl in *Midsommarvaka* (*Midsummer Night*; Cassel), International Choreography Competition, Konserthuset, Stockholm

       The Bird in *Peter och Vargen* (*Peter and the Wolf*; Svedin), International Choreography Competition, Konserthuset, Stockholm

       Soloist, Divertissement in *Blomstervalsen* (Bartholin), Gala Performance, Copenhagen

1946   Three Interludes (chor. Lander), in *Jean de France* (Holberg), Århus Theatre, Århus

       Solo in *Grevinnan Maritza* (operetta; mus. Hubay), Århus Theatre, Århus

1947   Principal dancer in *Chopiniana* (Koslovsky after Fokine), Liseberg, Göteborg

       Dulcinea-Aldonza in *Don Quixote* (Koslovsky after Petipa), Oscarsteatern, Stockholm

       Soloist, Brides' Dance in *Brigadoon* (musical; mus. Loewe, chor. Koslovsky), Oscarsteatern, Stockholm

       Girl in *Les Préludes* (Dombrovska), Oscarsteatern, Stockholm

1948   Soloist, Spanish Divertissement in *Ökensången* (Koslovsky), Oscarsteatern, Stockholm

       Four Solos from *Napoli* (Bournonville), Oscarsteatern, Stockholm

       Odette/Odile in *Swan Lake* (Koslovsky after Petipa, Ivanov), Oscarsteatern, Stockholm

       The Sylphide in *Graduation Ball* (Lichine), Original Ballet Russe, Spain

1949   Kitri in *Don Quixote* Pas de deux (after Petipa), Palais de Chaillot, Paris

       Pas de deux from *Flower Festival at Genzano* (Bournonville), Palais de Chaillot, Paris

       Principal dancer in *Études* (Lander), "Stars of the Ballet", Prince's Theatre, London

       Principal dancer in *Suite en blanc* (Lifar), "Stars of the Ballet", Prince's Theatre, London

       Soloist dancer in *Annie Get Your Gun* (musical; mus. Berlin, chor. Larsen), Oscarsteatern, Stockholm

       Terpsichore in *Apollon musagète* (excerpts; Balanchine),

Royal Theatre, Stockholm

Ballerina in *Black Swan Pas de deux* (from *Swan Lake*; Koslovsky after Petipa), Royal Theatre, Stockholm

1950   Title role (cr) in *Fröken Julie* (*Miss Julie*; Cullberg), Riksteatern, Västerås, Sweden

The Woman in *Rhapsodi* (Lander), Riksteatern, Västerås, Sweden

Rose Marie in *A Day in Paris*, Ballet in *Rose Marie* (operetta; mus. Friml, chor. Kruuse), Oscarsteatern, Stockholm

1951   Title role in *Medea* (Cullberg), Swedish Ballet, Prince's Theatre, London

Principal dancer in *Pas de deux* (Cullberg), Swedish Ballet, Prince's Theatre, London

Principal dancer in *Variations de ballet* (Holmgren), Royal Theatre, Copenhagen

Ballet Student in *La Répétition au violin* (Béjart), Royal Theatre, Copenhagen

Dancer in *Polka 1845* (solo; Hasselquist), Royal Theatre, Copenhagen

Title role in *Stumsfilmsstjärnan* (*Silent Film Star*; Béjart), Royal Theatre, Copenhagen

The Swan in *Doënde Svanen* (*The Dying Swan*; solo after Fokine), Danish Ballet Club, Copenhagen

Mazurka, Pas de deux in *Les Sylphides* (Fokine), Royal Swedish Ballet, Stockholm

1952   Principal dancer in *Ungdom* (*Youth*; Béjart), State Theatre, Uppsala

The Angel in *Paganini* (Olsson-Ahrberg), Royal Swedish Ballet, Stockholm

First Princess (cr) in *Ungersvennen och de Sex Prinsessorna* (*A Swain and Six Princesses*; Cullberg), Royal Swedish Ballet, Stockholm

Principal dancer in *Grand Pas classique hongrois* (Koslovsky), Royal Swedish Ballet, Stockholm

The Girl in Red in *Serenade* (Cullberg), Royal Swedish Ballet, Stockholm

Pas de cinq in *Suite classique* (Holmgren), Royal Swedish Ballet, Stockholm

Dancer in *La Lithuanienne* (solo; Lefebvre), Royal Swedish Ballet, Stockholm

1953   Odette/Odile in *Swan Lake* (new production; Skeaping after Petipa, Ivanov), Royal Swedish Ballet, Stockholm

Title role in *Medea* (revised version; Cullberg), Royal Swedish Ballet, Stockholm

Milady in *The Three Musketeers* (Cullberg), Royal Swedish Ballet, Eskilstuna

1955   Princess Aurora in *The Sleeping Beauty* (Skeaping after Petipa), Royal Swedish Ballet, Stockholm

1956   The Glove Seller in *Gaité Parisienne* (Massine), Royal Swedish Ballet, Stockholm

The Miller's Wife in *Le Tricorne* (Massine), Royal Swedish Ballet, Stockholm

Venus (cr) in *Cupid out of his Humour* (Skeaping), Royal Swedish Ballet, Drottningholm

1957   The Queen of Araby (cr) in *The Prodigal Son* (Cramér), Royal Swedish Ballet, Stockholm

1958   The Young Woman (cr) in *Prometheus* (also chor.; mus. Beethoven), Stockholm Philharmonic Orchestra Commission, Stockholm

Principal dancer (cr) in *Midsummer's Vigil* (Holmgren), Edinburgh International Ballet, Edinburgh

1960   Title role in *La Sylphide* (own staging, after Bournonville), Scandinavian Ballet

Principal dancer (cr) in *Teenagers* (also chor.), Scandinavian Ballet, Kalmar

1965   Title role (cr) in *Jenny von Westphalen* (also chor.), Scandinavian Ballet, Århus

WORKS

1958   *Prometheus* (mus. Beethoven), Stockholm Philharmonic Orchestra Commission, Stockholm

1960   *Irene Holm* (mus. Lumbye), Scandinavian Ballet, Växjö (also staged Royal Danish Ballet, Copenhagen)

Helios (mus. Nielsen), Scandinavian Ballet, Copenhagen

1961   *Teenagers* (mus. Bach), Scandinavian Ballet, Kalmar

1964   *Labyrintlek* (mus. Roman), Göteborg Ballet, Göteborg

1965   *Jomfrukilden* (*The Virgin Spring*; mus. Alfven), Royal Danish Ballet, Copenhagen

Klassiskt spel (mus. Hambraeus), Scandinavian Ballet, Århus

Friskt Mod (mus. Buxtehude), Scandinavian Ballet, Århus

Jenny von Westphalen (mus. Bentzon), Scandinavian Ballet, Århus

1967   *Don Juan* (mus. Gluck), Royal Danish Ballet, Copenhagen

1972   *Pictures at an Exhibition* (mus. Moussorgsky, arranged Emerson, Lake, and Palmer), Göteborg Ballet, Göteborg

Romeo and Juliet (mus. Prokofiev), Göteborg Ballet, Göteborg

1974   *Utopia* (mus. Offenbach), Göteborg Ballet, Göteborg

1975   *A Girl's Story* (mus. Emerson, Lake, and Palmer), Göteborg Ballet, Göteborg

1981   *Johannesnatten* (mus. de Frumerie), Malmö Ballet, Malmö

1984   *Faust* (mus. Liszt, Berlioz), Malmö Ballet, Malmö

Also staged:

1957   *Flower Festival at Genzano* (after Bournonville; mus. Helsted, Paulli), Royal Swedish Ballet, Stockholm (also staged Ostgötaballetten, Sweden, 1974; Maly Theatre Ballet, Leningrad, 1975; Ballet Nacional de Cuba, 1978)

1960   *La Sylphide* (after Bournonville; mus. Løvensjold), Scandinavian Ballet, Växjö, Sweden (also staged Ballet Rambert, 1960; Teatro Municipal de Santiago de Chile, 1963; Monte Carlo Opera, 1967; Washington Ballet, 1969; Göteborg Ballet, 1974; Kirov Ballet, 1975; Ballet of the Opera on the Rhine, Düsseldorf, 1978)

1961   *The Festival in Albano* (after Bournonville), Scandinavian Ballet

1969   *Konservatoriet* (after Bournonville; mus. Paulli), Ballet for All, England (also staged Göteborg Ballet, 1972)

1970   *The Whims of Cupid and the Ballet Master* (after Galeotti; mus. Lolle), Drottningholm Court Theatre, Drottningholm

1971   *Napoli* (after Bournonville, Lander, Borchsenius; mus. Paulli, Helsted, Gade, Lumbye), Göteborg Ballet, Göteborg (also staged Malmö Ballet, 1982; Kirov Ballet, 1982; Royal Swedish Ballet, 1986)

1972   *Swan Lake* (after Petipa, Ivanov; mus. Tchaikovsky), Göteborg Ballet

1987   *Napoli*, Act III (after Bournonville; mus. Paulli et al.), German Opera Ballet, Berlin

1990   *The Lay of Thrym* (after Bournonville; mus. Hartmann), Royal Danish Ballet, Copenhagen

Other works include: solos in early dance concerts—*Romance* (mus. Sibelius; 1941), *Kamarinskaja* (mus. Ferraris; 1943), *Adagio* (mus. Bach; 1944).

PUBLICATIONS

By von Rosen:
"Bournonville's Intentions for *Napoli*", *Dance and Dancers* (London), November 1971
Interview in Lidova, Irène, "Une heure avec Elsa Marianne von Rosen", *Les Saisons de la danse* (Paris), December 1976

About von Rosen:
Idestam-Almquist, Bengt, *Svensk Ballett* (with Swedish and English text), Malmö, 1951
Fridericia, Allan, *Elsa Marianne von Rosen: En Svensk Ballerina*, Stockholm, 1953
Percival, John, "Danish Tarantella in Sweden", *Dance and Dancers* (London), April 1971
Näslund, Erik, "Elsa Marianne von Rosen och Göteborgsballetten", *Dans* (Stockholm), November 1974

*   *   *

In the 1930s it was not unique for a dancer to begin as did Elsa Marianne von Rosen, as a privately trained, independent artist, rather than in the structured hierarchy of a ballet company and school. In her early recitals in Stockholm she sometimes performed her own compositions, but also amongst the choreographers she worked with during this period was Harald Lander, then director of the Royal Danish Ballet. At his instigation she was admitted to the company's school as guest pupil in 1945.

Von Rosen's technique had already been shaped in Stockholm by the Russian dancer Vera Alexandrova, and by the Cecchetti technique as taught by Otto Thorensen. The Copenhagen experience would not only add a powerful third strand to her personal style, but also was to lay the foundation for the international reputation she would later enjoy for her own stagings of Bournonville ballets.

But it was still as a dancer with a wide-ranging style that von Rosen returned to Sweden after two years. As ballerina at Oscarsteatern, under the ballet direction of Albert Koslovsky, she featured in operettas and musicals (*Brigadoon, Annie Get Your Gun*), as well as Koslovsky's versions of *Don Quixote* and *Swan Lake*.

Other crucial alliances were made at this period. Allan Fridericia, the Danish critic, designer, and Bournonville scholar who became von Rosen's husband in 1950, was tirelessly to promote her development as an artist, becoming her collaborator in some important stagings of Bournonville works, and designing for several of her own choreographies.

It was Fridericia who designed Birgit Cullberg's seminal 1950 work, *Miss Julie*. Indeed, the alliance among these three was a significant part of a revival in Swedish ballet which began in the 1950s. Von Rosen's portrayal of the sexual dilemma confronting the heroine of *Miss Julie*, a character both seducing and being seduced by the butler Jean, revealed her as a powerful dramatic dancer. This was to become her signature role, with guest appearances with the Royal Swedish Ballet the same year, and international performances in the role for many years afterwards.

Von Rosen had established herself in Sweden as a popular performer in a wide range of styles, from classical set-pieces like the *Don Quixote* Pas de deux, to intense psychological modern roles, such as those in *Miss Julie* and in Cullberg's later

work, *Medea*. She was also a dancer of great personality and wit in lighter works. The eclecticism of her style, however, tended to be an obstacle against her becoming a permanent member of the Royal Swedish Ballet. The administration finally bowed to public and private pressure, engaging von Rosen as principal dancer in November 1951.

It was with the challenge of the major nineteenth-century roles—Odette/Odile and Aurora—that she achieved a balance between strong technique and deep interpretation, making her a true ballerina in every sense. Her début as Aurora in 1955 confirmed her position as a classical ballerina, but perhaps also reaffirmed her strength in roles demanding a light touch, and a warm personality. A critic saw her as "an ideal type for the Princess Aurora, young, gay, sprightly, full of glittering charm and loveableness". The next year she found another ideal outlet for her vivacious demi-charactère quality, as the Glove Seller in Massine's revival of *Gaîté Parisienne*.

Not content to remain in the environment of the Royal Swedish Ballet, however, von Rosen founded a company with Fridericia called the Scandinavian Ballet, which featured a number of her own ballets as well as stagings of Bournonville. *La Sylphide*, successfully remounted for many other companies since, was a revelation of romantic style in countries like Britain, where the work was hardly known. In attempting to get closer to Bournonville's original, von Rosen and Fridericia received help from the 82-year-old Danish dancer Ellen Price de Plane, who suggested some sequences that were no longer to be seen in the Danish version.

Von Rosen's own choreography may be of uneven quality, but her topics are wide and she does not shrink from difficult subjects. She ranges from *Johannesnatten* (1981), a version of the biblical story of Salomé, in the style of Swedish peasant wall-painting, to *Teenagers* (1961), a ballet dressed in contemporary fashion, to the music of Bach. Following the precedent of Cullberg, she has been concerned to make ballets about the condition of women. *Jenny von Westphalen* is about Karl Marx's wife; *Irene Holm* is based on the novel by Herman Bang; *A Girl's Story* (1975), with a pop score by Emerson, Lake, and Palmer, shows the heroine defying the conventional role which her husband and society expect her to fulfil. Although not altogether successful, it stimulated discussion of feminist views in Göteborg (Gothenburg) where it was first performed, and no one could doubt the choreographer's confidence and commitment in making such a subject the basis of a three-act ballet.

Von Rosen's respect for Bournonville's original intentions contrasts with the modernity in her own works. In her version of *Napoli*, originally staged for the Göteborg Ballet in 1971, she returned to Bournonville's notes, and unlike the version then current in Copenhagen, she returned to the full length of the score, filling the choreographic gaps with Bournonville choreography from other works, or from the daily classes, or with stylistically appropriate choreography of her own. Her *Napoli* was acclaimed for the dramatic integrity she brought to a full-length ballet, chiefly known only for its joyous final-act divertissement.

Less successful was *The Lay of Thrym* (1990) for the Royal Danish Ballet. This attempt to reconstruct one of Bournonville's serious ballets was hampered by its own ponderous structure and convoluted mythological plot. Clearly Bournonville's heirs had not always been wrong in cutting or even neglecting some of his works. Nevertheless, it could not be denied that von Rosen and Fridericia had made available a new perspective on Bournonville through their three-year reconstruction project.

Deeply underlying von Rosen's success both as dancer and choreographer/reconstructor is a great relish for the act of theatrical communication through dance. Dance should be a sensual experience both for audience and dancer. Most revealingly she says: "You cannot dance Bournonville well and not be happy. . . . It's a very elementary, direct pleasure. For me, it's like the feeling, when you are a little girl, of having a new dress to put on, or of getting into bed between crisp, clean sheets."

—Larraine Nicholas

VYROUBOVA, Nina

Russian/French dancer and teacher. Born in Gurzof, Crimea, 4 June 1921. Studied with mother, then with Vera Trefilova, Olga Preobrazhenska, Boris Kniaseff, Lubov Egorova, Victor Gsovsky, Yves Brieux, and Serge Lifar, Paris. Married (1) dancer Vladimir Ignatoff; (2) Arcady Kniazeff: one son, dancer Youra Kniazeff, b.1951; (3) Luis Carriedo. Début with Opera Russe d'Agreniaff, Caen, 1937; dancer in revue, La Chauve-Souris, Paris, also performing in London with Belaiev company, 1938; dancer, Ballets Polonais, 1939, and Ballets Russes de Paris, 1940; soloist in recitals, including at Salle Pleyel, and in "Vendredis de danse", 1941–44; principal dancer, Les Ballets des Champs-Elysées, 1945–47 and 1949, and Les Ballets de Paris, 1949; étoile, Paris Opéra Ballet, 1949–56; ballerina, Grand Ballet du Marquis de Cuevas, 1957–62; also guest ballerina, including for La Scala, Milan, 1956, John Taras's Ballets de Pâques, 1957, Enghein Festival, 1957, Festival des Baux de Provence, Hamburg Opera Ballet, Grand Ballet de France, and Rome Opera Ballet; also appeared in films, including in Le Calvaire de Cimiez (1932), Le Spectre de la danse (chor. Lifar; 1960), Adage (1965); teacher, Troyes Conservatoire, from 1983; founder and teacher of own studio (now retired). Recipient: Prix Pavlova, 1957; Prize, Una vita per la danza, Positano, 1980.

ROLES

1937   Swanilda in Coppélia (after Saint-Léon), Opéra Russe d'Agreniaff, Caen
1940   Polovtsian Maiden in Polovtsian Dances from Prince Igor (Fokine), Ballets Russes de Paris, Paris
         Dancer in Forêt de Vienne, Les Ballets Russes de Paris, Paris
1944   Dancer (cr) in Ballet blanc (Petit), Théâtre Sarah Bernhardt, Paris
         Dancer (cr) in Le Rossignol et la rose (Petit), Théâtre Sarah Bernhardt, Paris
         Principal dancer (cr) in Un Americain à Paris (Petit), Théâtre Sarah Bernhardt, Paris
         Peasant Pas de deux from Giselle (after Petipa, Coralli, Perrot), Théâtre Sarah Bernhardt, Paris
1945   The Sleeping Beauty (cr) in Les Forains (Petit), Théâtre Champs-Elysées, Paris
1946   Title role (cr) in La Sylphide (new production; V. Gsovsky after Taglioni), Ballets des Champs-Elysées, Paris
1947   Le Papillon d'amour (cr) in Treize Danses (Petit), Ballets des Champs-Elysées, Paris
1949   A Chicken (cr) in L'Oeuf à la coque (Petit), Ballets de Paris, London
         Princess Aurora in Divertissement d'Aurore (Lifar after Petipa), Paris Opéra Ballet, Paris

La Cigarette in Suite en blanc (Lifar), Paris Opéra Ballet, Paris
L'Ombre in Les Mirages (Lifar), Paris Opéra Ballet, Paris
The Swan in La Mort du cygne (Lifar), Paris Opéra Ballet, Paris
Odette in Swan Lake, Act II (Ivanov), Paris Opéra Ballet, Paris
1950   La Dame in Dramma per musica (Lifar), Paris Opéra Ballet, Paris
         Title role in Giselle (Petipa after Coralli, Perrot; staged Lifar), Paris Opéra Ballet, Paris
         Oenone in Phèdre (Lifar), Paris Opéra Ballet, Paris
         Title role in Phèdre (Lifar), Paris Opéra Ballet, Paris
1951   The Queen (cr) in Blanche-Neige (Lifar), Paris Opéra Ballet, Paris
         Juliet (cr) in Romeo and Juliet Pas de deux (Lifar), Salle Pleyel, Paris
1952   Arzigogola (cr) in Fourberies (Lifar), Paris Opéra Ballet, Paris
         Ballet des Incas (cr; chor. Lifar) in Les Indes galantes (Aveline, Lifar, Lander), Paris Opéra Ballet, Paris
1953   The Divine (Greta Garbo) (cr) in Cinema (Lifar), Paris Opéra Ballet, Paris
         Violet (cr) in Variations (Lifar), Paris Opéra Ballet, Paris
         Principal dancer (cr) in Tannhäuser (Lifar), Sorbonne, Paris
         Principal dancer (cr) in Vision russe (Lifar), Sorbonne, Paris
         Principal dancer (cr) in Danseuses de Delphes (Lifar), Sorbonne, Paris
         Principal dancer (cr) in Clair de lune (Lifar), Salle Pleyel, Paris
1954   Roxane (cr) in Oberon, Act III (opera; mus. Weber, chor. Lifar), Paris Opéra Ballet, Paris
         Title role (cr) in L'Oiseau de feu (Lifar), Paris Opéra Ballet, Paris
1955   La Fiancée (cr) in Les Noces fantasiques (Lifar), Paris Opéra Ballet, Paris
         Principal dancer (cr) in Divertissements (Zvereff), Vevey Festival
         Principal dancer (cr) in L'Âme et la danse (Lifar), Gala, Salle Pleyel, Paris
1956   Terpsichore (cr) in Apollon musagète (Lifar), La Scala, Milan
         La Favorite (cr) in Divertissement à la cour (Lifar), Paris Opéra Ballet, Monte Carlo
1957   Juliette in Romeo et Juliette (Lifar), Ballets de Pâques, Monte Carlo
         The Sleepwalker in La Somnambule (Balanchine), Ballets de Pâques, Monte Carlo
         Ballerina in La Forêt romantique (Taras), Ballets de Pâques, Monte Carlo
         Title role (cr) in Hamlet (Lifar), Enghein Festival, Enghein
         Yang-Kuei-Fei, Chinese Princess (cr) in La Chanson de l'éternelle tristesse (Ricarda), Grand Ballet du Marquis de Cuevas, Paris
         The Woman (cr) in L'Amour et son destin (Lifar, Parlic), Grand Ballet du Marquis de Cuevas, Vienna
         Title role in Doña Ines de Castro (Ricarda), Grand Ballet du Marquis de Cuevas
         Title role in La Péri (Lifar), Grand Ballet du Marquis de Cuevas
1958   His reflection (cr) in La Morte de Narcisse (Golovine), Grand Ballet du Marquis de Cuevas, Paris
         Pas de deux in Le Mal de siècle (Starbuck), Grand Ballet

Nina Vyroubova in *Blanche-Neige* with Serge Lifar, Paris Opera, 1951

du Marquis de Cuevas, Paris
Principal dancer in *Constantia* (Dollar), Grand Ballet du
  Marquis de Cuevas
Rosaria in *La Lampara* (dell'Ara), Grand Ballet du
  Marquis de Cuevas, Paris
Principal dancer (cr) in *Duetto* (pas de deux; Lifar),
  Grand Ballet du Marquis de Cuevas, Paris
Principal dancer in *Tarasiana* (Taras), Grand Ballet du
  Marquis de Cuevas, Paris
1960 Princess Aurora in *The Sleeping Beauty* (Nijinska,
  Helpmann after Petipa), Grand (International) Ballet
  du Marquis de Cuevas, Paris
1964 Principal dancer (cr) in *Le Corbeau* (Olivier), Gala,
  Théâtre de Paris, Paris
1965 Leading role (cr) in *Abraxas* (van Dyk), Hamburg
  Ballet, Hamburg

Other roles include: Kitri in *Don Quixote* Pas de deux (Petipa),

ballerina in *Pas de quatre* (Dolin), principal dancer in *Pas de
trois classique* (Balanchine); principal roles in *Salade* (Lifar),
Danses orientales (Lifar), *Ça bardait* (Lifar), *À la barre* (Lifar).

PUBLICATIONS

Laurent, Jean, "Nina Vyroubova in *Giselle* at the Paris Opéra",
  Ballet Today (London), April–May 1950
Michaut, Pierre, "Nina Vyroubova", in Swinson, Cyril (ed.),
  Dancers and Critics, London, 1950
Lidova, Irène, "Quatre Visages de la danse française", *Ballet
  Annual* (London), vol. 4, 1950
Lidova, Irène, *Dix-sept Visages de la danse française*, Paris, 1953
Guest, Ivor, "Fair Exchange: The Stars of the Paris Opéra",
  Dance and Dancers (London), September 1954
Williams, Peter, "Riviera Rendezvous", *Dance and Dancers*
  (London), 2 parts: June, July 1957

Laurent, Jean, *Nina Vyroubova et ses visages*, Paris, 1958

Zürner, Inge, "Nina Vyroubova", *Ballet Today* (London), January/February 1964

Livio, Antoine (ed.), *Étoiles et Ballerines*, Brenne, 1965

Dorvanne, Jeanine, "Hommage à Nina Vyroubova", *Les Saisons de la danse* (Paris), November 1980

Denby, Edwin, *Dance Writings*, edited by Robert Cornfield and William Mackay, New York, 1986

*   *   *

Nina Vyroubova belongs to the generation of Parisian children of Russian emigrés which came to the fore after the Second World War, and which contributed to the sudden renaissance of French ballet. Her difficult childhood years were spent in suburban mediocrity in Meudon, Paris. Her first dance classes took place under the iron rule of her mother, who had been a little-known dancer, and whose ambition it was to make her daughter a star. Vyroubova possessed the physique of a true Slav dancer; she had a strange face with an exotic air, a smile which made her eyes crinkle up, showing off her high cheekbones, and a long supple neck, which set off her delicate shoulders. She also possessed small, beautifully arched feet.

The former imperial ballerina Vera Trefilova was Vyroubova's first real teacher. The young dancer subsequently worked with Olga Preobrazhenska and perfected her technique with Yves Brieux, a brilliant member of the École Française and a former Paris Opéra dancer. Like so many other Russian emigré children, Vyroubova had to help support her family from an early age, and she took on variety engagements at the Chauve-Souris with the ephemeral "Ballets Russes de Paris". Emulating some of her friends, she performed a dance recital at la Salle Pleyel with her partner, the character dancer Vladimir Ignatoff. This lacklustre and ill-conceived evening passed almost unnoticed. In December 1944, after the liberation of Paris, however, Vyroubova was recognized for the first time as a promising ballerina. Irène Lidova presented her at the Sarah Bernhardt Theatre where the so-called "Soirées", or "Vendredis de la danse" were held in order to reveal the miraculous post-war generation of dancers to the Paris population. Vyroubova danced extracts from *Giselle* with Roland Petit, and some Chopin pieces.

Christian Bérard, the famous designer, and Boris Kochno, the librettist and ex-Diaghilev assistant, "discovered" Vyroubova, and in 1945 she was the first to perform the Kochno–Petit ballet *Les Forains*, to music by Henri Sauget, which was the starting-point of the Ballets des Champs-Elysées. In 1946 Vyroubova danced the title role in Victor Gsovsky's version of *La Sylphide* with the same company. This was her definitive step to stardom, and a great Romantic ballerina was born. She set off to conquer London, where the press adored her. Finally, in 1949, Serge Lifar invited the ballerina to join the Paris Opéra.

Vyroubova's ascent was like a ballerina's dream come true. Her début in *Les Mirages* was dazzling. She appeared in *Giselle*, which had become her great role, and new ballets subsequently appeared: *Blanche-Neige*, *Fourberies*, *The Firebird* with Youly Algaroff, and in 1955, *Les Noces fantastiques*, an essentially romantic ballet by Lifar where fantasy and reality are presented side by side. After a misunderstanding with the management of the Paris Opéra, Vyroubova left to pursue her career in the Marquis de Cuevas's ballet company, partnered by Serge Golovine. Her lyrical and romantic qualities did not stifle her talent as a character dancer, and her lively, fiery Slav temperament was also put to good use. In 1960 she was one of the Princesses Aurora in Raymundo de Larrain's outstanding production of *The Sleeping Beauty*, and then she was one of the first Western ballerinas to dance with Rudolf Nureyev, who was taken on by the Marquis after his defection from the Kirov Ballet.

After the de Cuevas company was disbanded, Vyroubova went freelance. Under producer Dominique Delouche, she filmed two short pieces, *Le Spectre de la danse* (1960) and *Adage* (1965), in which her fascinating poetry of movement is immortalized. Afterwards she dedicated herself to teaching, opening a school at the Salle Pleyel and taking on pupils from the Paris Opéra.

In search of a stable life and financial security, however, Vyroubova left Paris for the provinces, settling in Troyes where she taught at the town conservatory for several years, until 1988. Distanced from the capital, she no longer takes part in the choreographic activities of Paris, and little by little her name is fading from memory. However, those who knew her years of glory class her among the greatest ballerinas of our time.

—Irène Lidova

WALL, David

British dancer and teacher. Born in Chiswick, 15 March 1946. Studied in Windsor and at the Royal Ballet School, London. Married dancer Alfreda Thorogood, 1967: one son, one daughter. Dancer, Royal Ballet Touring Company, from 1963, becoming soloist, from 1964, and principal dancer, from 1956; principal dancer, Royal Ballet (at Covent Garden), 1970–84; teacher, including for Yorkshire Ballet seminars, 1980s, and West Street School, London; associate director, Royal Academy of Dancing, London, 1984–87, becoming director, 1987–90. Recipient: *Evening Standard* Award, 1977.

ROLES

1963   Soloist (cr) in *Motus* (Zolan), Royal Ballet School Performance, London
        Principal dancer in *Napoli Divertissement* (Bournonville), Royal Ballet Touring Company
        Florestan Pas de trois in *The Sleeping Beauty* (Petipa; staged Sergeyev, de Valois, Ashton), Royal Ballet Touring Company

1964   The Cousin in *The Invitation* (MacMillan), Royal Ballet Touring Company
        Principal dancer in *Quintet* (Wright), Royal Ballet Touring Company, Oxford
        The Young Man in *The Two Pigeons* (Ashton), Royal Ballet Touring Company

1965   The Stranger (cr) in *The Tribute* (Morrice), Royal Ballet Touring Company, Stratford
        The Rake in *The Rake's Progress* (de Valois), Royal Ballet Touring Company, Cambridge
        Colas in *La Fille mal gardée* (Ashton), Royal Ballet Touring Company, London
        Captain Adoncino in *The Lady and the Fool* (Cranko), Royal Ballet Touring Company, London
        Prince Siegfried in *Swan Lake* (Petipa, Ivanov; staged Sergeyev, Ashton), Royal Ballet Touring Company, British tour
        Albrecht in *Giselle* (Ashton), Royal Ballet Touring Company

1966   Franz in *Coppélia* (Petipa, Cecchetti; staged Sergeyev), Royal Ballet Touring Company
        Oberon in *The Dream* (Ashton), Royal Ballet Touring Company, Oxford
        Jean de Brienne in *Raymonda*, Act III (Nureyev after Petipa), Royal Ballet Touring Company, foreign tour

1967   First Movement in *Concerto* (MacMillan), Royal Ballet Touring Company, London
        Elegy (cr) in *Sinfonietta* (Ashton), Royal Ballet Touring Company, London

Bluebird in *The Sleeping Beauty* (Petipa; staged Sergeyev, de Valois, Ashton), Royal Ballet Touring Company
Prince Florimund in *The Sleeping Beauty* (Petipa; staged Sergeyev, de Valois, Ashton), Royal Ballet Touring Company
The Boy in *House of Birds* (MacMillan), Royal Ballet Touring Company

1968   Drosselmeyer/Prince in *The Nutcracker* (Nureyev), Royal Ballet, London
        The Caricaturist in *Mam'zelle Angot* (Massine), Royal Ballet Touring Company
        Principal dancer (Trois Gnossiennes) in *Monotones* (Ashton), Royal Ballet Touring Company, Wiesbaden

1969   Principal dancer (Adam) (cr) in *In the Beginning* (Cauley), Royal Ballet Touring Company, London
        Chevalier d'amour in *Knight Errant* (Tudor), Royal Ballet Touring Company

1970   Solor in "Kingdom of the Shades" from *La Bayadère* (Nureyev after Petipa), Royal Ballet, London
        Principal dancer in *Dances at a Gathering* (Robbins), Royal Ballet, London
        Romeo in *Romeo and Juliet* (MacMillan), Royal Ballet, London
        The Creature in *The Creatures of Prometheus* (Ashton), Royal Ballet Touring Company, foreign tour

1971   Mathilde Kschessinska's partner in *Anastasia* (MacMillan), Royal Ballet, London
        Principal dancer in *Serenade* (Balanchine), Royal Ballet, London
        First song in *Song of the Earth* (MacMillan), Royal Ballet, London

1972   Principal dancer in *Afternoon of a Faun* (Robbins), Royal Ballet, London
        Principal male dancer (pas de deux) in *Birthday Offering* (Ashton), Royal Ballet, London
        The Prince in *Cinderella* (Ashton), Royal Ballet, London
        Ivan Tsarevich in *Firebird* (Fokine), Royal Ballet, London
        Principal dancer (cr) in *Laborintus* (Tetley), Royal Ballet, London
        The Boy in *Triad* (MacMillan), Royal Ballet, London
        Principal dancer (cr) in *Walk to the Paradise Garden* (Ashton), Royal Ballet gala, London
        Memories in *Poème de l'extase* (Cranko), Royal Ballet, London

1973   Pas de deux in *Agon* (Balanchine), Royal Ballet, London
        Daphnis in *Daphnis and Chloe* (Ashton), Royal Ballet, London
        Principal dancer in *In The Night* (Robbins), Royal Ballet, London

David Wall in *Afternoon of a Faun*, **London, c.1972**

Mazurka in *Les Sylphides* (Fokine), Royal Ballet, London

Principal dancer in *Symphonic Variations* (Ashton), Royal Ballet, London

1974 Golden Hours (cr) in *Elite Syncopations* (MacMillan), Royal Ballet, London

Lescaut (cr) in *Manon* (MacMillan), Royal Ballet, London

1975 Principal dancer in *The Concert* (Robbins), Royal Ballet, London

Summer (cr) in *The Four Seasons* (MacMillan), Royal Ballet, London

Principal dancer (cr) in *Scène dansant* (Ashton), Artists of the Royal Ballet, Aldeburgh

O Homen Blanco (cr) in *Pas de deux* (*Amazon Forest*; Ashton), Gala, Teatro Colón, Buenos Aires

Puppet (cr) in *Rituals* (MacMillan), Royal Ballet, London

Mercutio in *Romeo and Juliet* (MacMillan), Royal Ballet, London

1976 Chanson dansée (An "Athlete") in *Les Biches* (Nijinska), Royal Ballet, London

Beethoven Waltz in *Elite Syncopations* (MacMillan), Royal Ballet, London

Autumn in *The Four Seasons* (MacMillan), Royal Ballet, London

Des Grieux in *Manon* (MacMillan), Royal Ballet, London

Principal dancer in *Symphony* (MacMillan), Royal Ballet, London

Principal dancer in *Voluntaries* (Tetley), Royal Ballet, London

Principal dancer (cr) in *Adagio Hammerklavier* (van Manen), Royal Ballet, London

1977 Principal dancer (cr) in *The Fourth Symphony* (Neumeier), Royal Ballet, London

The Husband in *The Invitation* (MacMillan), Royal Ballet, London

Petruchio in *The Taming of the Shrew* (Cranko), Royal Ballet, London

1978 Friday in *Jazz Calendar* (Ashton), Royal Ballet, London

Crown Price Rudolf (cr) in *Mayerling* (MacMillan), Royal Ballet, London

1980 Principal dancer in *Troy Game* (North), Royal Ballet, London

Pas de deux (cr) in *Adieu* (Bintley), Royal Ballet, London

1981 Gordon Craig in *Isadora* (MacMillan), Royal Ballet, London

Principal dancer in *Napoli* (excerpts; Beck after Bournonville), Royal Ballet, London

1982 Dancer (cr) in *Pas de deux: Villa d'este* (Deane), Royal Ballet, Manchester

Caliban (cr) in *The Tempest* (Nureyev), Royal Ballet, London

Principal dancer (cr) in *Impromptu* (Deane), Royal Ballet gala, London

1983   Georgio's Father (cr) in *Valley of Shadows* (MacMillan), Royal Ballet, London

Principal dancer (cr) in *Chanson* (Deane), Royal Ballet, London

1984   Principal dancer (cr) in *Fleeting Figures* (Deane), Royal Ballet, London

Other roles include: Beliaev in *A Month in the Country* (Ashton), principal dancer in *Scènes de ballet* (Ashton), pas de deux from *Don Quixote* (Nureyev after Petipa), title role in *Prodigal Son* (Balanchine), principal dancer in *Fin du jour* (MacMillan), principal dancer in *Gloria* (MacMillan), Bridegroom in *Blood Wedding* (Rodrigues), principal dancer in *Laborintus* (Tetley), title role in *Apollo* (Balanchine).

PUBLICATIONS

By Wall:
Interview in "A Star by Encouragement", *Dance and Dancers* (London), November 1976
Interview in Newman, Barbara, *Striking a Balance: Dancers Talk About Dancing* (Boston), 1982

About Wall:
Buckley, Peter, "A Royal Pair: Doreen Wells and David Wall", *Dance Magazine* (New York), March 1971
Niehaus, Max, *Ballett Faszination* (Munich), 1972
Goodman, Saul, "Brief Biographies: David Wall", *Dance Magazine* (New York), October 1972
Maynard, Olga, "David Wall", *Dance Magazine* (New York), August 1974
Dougill, David, "David Wall", in *The Royal Ballet: A Souvenir*, London, 1978
Percival, John, "A Whole Dancer", *Dance and Dancers* (London), August 1984
Clarke, Mary, "David Wall: A Tribute", *Dancing Times* (London), October 1984
Woodcock, Sarah, *The Sadler's Wells Royal Ballet*, London, 1991

*   *   *

David Wall's initial appearance at Covent Garden took place in 1961 during the Royal Ballet School's annual performance, amongst ten boys in a gymnastic display. Two years after this, in the year of his graduation, the youngster had progressed to a pas de deux in Miro Zolan's specially created *Motus*, when onlookers had a chance to note a sense of presentation, with an "outwardness" unusual in one so young. He had a neat, shapely physique and good features set off by a sharp jawline, which gave his carriage a natural distinction. Amongst his teachers at the School, Errol Addison had a particular influence on this student who always showed careful placing, clear phrasing, and a ballon maintained by strength. When Wall was taken into the Touring Company, Earling Sunde continued to develop these aspects. In David Wall's case, the movement always showed motivation and there was a marked care with enchaînement.

By the time he had been given a chance in the role of the cousin in *The Invitation*, a keen sense of theatre had been noted in the youngster, and this "thinking" quality was developed while Christopher Gable was still around as an exemplar. It was as a matter of course that Wall was also launched in the

Gable role in *The Two Pigeons*, but when he was pitched into the feverishly dramatic central role in *The Rake's Progress*, he all but panicked at the very thought; he was quite convinced it was an advancement too early by years. None the less, Henry Legerton coached him painstakingly, and the result was fine. In no time he was entrusted with Prince Siegfried, and Colas in Ashton's *La Fille mal gardée*. It was almost unprecedented that a junior dancer should be advanced in so headlong a manner, but his command of the various requirements of leading male roles proved absolutely secure, and among the princes, he was given the role of Albrecht in the same year.

His success in *Swan Lake* was such that he completed over sixty performances in under five years—a considerable milestone in a company with such a wide repertoire—but he was barely nineteen when he was offered his first *Swan Lake* with Fonteyn, during the company's tour of the British provinces. In the event, a rapturous reception immediately cemented a long-lasting and harmonious pairing that was eventually seen worldwide. In the 1969 film *Margot Fonteyn*, Wall can be seen rehearsing *Swan Lake* with the assoluta, and also as the principal cavalier to Fonteyn in the Rose Adagio. He partnered her throughout her farewell tour to the U.K. provinces, and also accompanied her on tours to Brazil, Australia, and the west coast of America. Sir Frederick Ashton created a pas de deux, *Amazon Forest*, for Fonteyn and Wall (to film-score music by Villa-Lobos) which was first seen at a Rio gala in 1975; and the same choreographer had previously used Delius's *Walk to the Paradise Garden* for what was, in effect, an extended pas de deux (somewhat in the Bolshoi manner, with an effusion of lifts) for Wall and Merle Park in 1972.

Jerome Robbins used Wall in his Royal Ballet revivals of *Dances at a Gathering*, and also the less frequently seen *In the Night*, in which Wall was again paired with Park; and for a special evening, Robbins plundered the latter ballet for an adaptation that pitted Baryshnikov against Wall in a comic competition. (This work was subsequently transmogrified into *Other Dances*.) It was Antony Tudor who had first exploited Wall's natural charm to achieve a slightly insidious effect, when he adapted the theme of "Les Liaisons Dangereuses" for a new ballet, *Knight Errant*, in 1968. By this time, Wall had become the principal work-horse prince for the Touring Company, a weight of work which provoked a stress fracture. This was still undiagnosed when Wall had to pass up the premiere of the Tudor ballet, and even when he made belated appearances in *Knight Errant* the following year, the condition was still not diagnosed accurately. But soon enough the dancer was sidelined for an entire year. He spent much of this period in studying his heroes of the theatre, such as Paul Schofield.

In 1970, when he returned to the company (now amalgamated with the London base), it was in support of Lynn Seymour, in *Romeo and Juliet*. It was MacMillan who saw the dramatic possibilities of twisting Wall's basically sunny and ardent stage persona even further than Tudor had done; in his version of *Manon* he made Wall play the debauched and manipulative brother, to sensational effect. This Lescaut glittered scandalously; each half-hidden glance or nonchalant twirl of fine manner set up a frisson of morbid fascination. Later, Wall reverted to innocent rectitude as Des Grieux in the same ballet, just as he had switched from Romeo to Mercutio. He had become adept at these reverses of tone; in *The Invitation* he spanned, uniquely, the roles of the cousin and the seducer husband within six years, yet he was equally capable of switching back again. Finally, MacMillan crammed this gamut into one roller-coaster single role, the undone Crown Prince Rudolf in *Mayerling*, in the process shaping the most exhaustive and exhausting role that has ever been given to a male dancer. Throughout three acts of swirling drama and panoply, Wall held the eye of the storm to remarkable effect, not least because the dramatic dissolution of the character involved ever more disciplined technical partnering in creating its main effects.

Like others before him, Wall found his career with the Royal Ballet marked with a certain curmudgeonliness of attitude from the Covent Garden Board. When Anthony Dowell left to pursue his career with American Ballet Theatre, Wall was left in London sustaining a huge repertory for a demanding audience. But the publicity machine that might have made capital from all this was strangely silent; once more the administration could not muster a flexible policy that would recognize that "star presentation" is dictated by crowds as much as by boardroom. Wall's dance career drifted to a relatively early halt almost by default, and when he made a guest appearance in a tribute performance of *Mayerling* at Covent Garden in the autumn of 1984, it was entirely mysterious that a dancer of such accomplishment should not feel that the stage could offer him more, and he could offer more from that stage. In the event, the idea of passing on his own hard-won lessons, via teaching, claimed his interest, though audiences were left the poorer by that transition.

—Keith Money

WALSH, Christine

Australian dancer. Born Christine Avis Walsh in Sydney, 22 March 1954. Studied with Daphne McDonald and Lorraine Norton, and at Australian Ballet School, pupil of Dame Margaret Scott, 1969–71; later studied with Marika Besobrasova, Monte Carlo. Dancer, corps de ballet, Australian Ballet, 1972–74, becoming soloist, 1975–76; demi-principal, Roland Petit's Ballet National de Marseille, 1977, returning 1980–81; principal dancer, Australian Ballet, 1978–79 and 1983–90, touring with company to United States, Soviet Union, Europe, Japan, China, and Southeast Asia; international guest artist, including as dancer and producer, Ballet Philippines, Manila, 1979 and 1989, and as ballerina, Nantes Opera Ballet, 1982, Nice Dance Theatre, 1983, UNESCO Gala at the Bolshoi Theatre, Moscow, 1986, Central Ballet of China, 1987, Royal Bicentennial Gala for Queen Elizabeth II at Royal Opera House, London, 1988, and Kirov Ballet, Leningrad, 1989; co-founder and director, Onstage Artists, producing tours of "Australian Stars of Ballet", from 1990; also teacher, including master classes for Royal Academy of Dancing in Sydney, Adelaide, and Canberra, for Victorian College of the Arts, and for National Ballet School. Recipient: Green Room Award for Best Performance (as Aurora in *The Sleeping Beauty*), 1984; Order of Australia, 1991.

ROLES

1973   Crystal Fairy in *The Sleeping Beauty* (van Praagh after Petipa), Australian Ballet, Sydney
       One of Florestan's Sisters in *The Sleeping Beauty* (van Praagh after Petipa), Australian Ballet, Sydney
       Lilac Fairy in *The Sleeping Beauty* (van Praagh after Petipa), Australian Ballet, Melbourne
1974   Soloist (cr) in *Perisynthion* (Helpmann), Australian Ballet, Sydney
1975   Principal dancer (Trois Gnossiennes) in *Monotones* (Ashton), Australian Ballet, Adelaide

1977   Title role in *Carmen* (Petit), Ballet National de Marseille, Monte Carlo
1978   Swanilda in *Coppélia* (Petit), Ballet National de Marseille, Naples
       Odette/Odile in *Swan Lake* (Woolliams after Petipa, Ivanov), Australian Ballet, Canberra
       Claudia in *Spartacus* (Seregi), Australian Ballet, Sydney
       Principal dancer in *Afternoon of a Faun* (Robbins), Australian Ballet, Sydney
       Principal dancer (cr) in *Tekton* (Murphy), Australian Ballet, Sydney
1979   Swanilda in *Coppélia* (van Praagh after Petipa, Cecchetti), Australian Ballet, Melbourne
       Kitri in *Don Quixote* (Nureyev after Petipa), Australian Ballet, Israel
       Title role in *Anna Karenina* (Prokovsky), Australian Ballet, Sydney
       Prelude, Pas de deux in *Les Sylphides* (Fokine), Australian Ballet, Sydney
       Elder Sister in *Las Hermanas* (MacMillan), Australian Ballet, Sydney
       The Wife in *The Concert* (Robbins), Australian Ballet, Sydney
       Desdemona in *Othello* (Welch), Australian Ballet, Sydney
       Variation, Adagio of Lovers in *Les Rendezvous* (Ashton), Australian Ballet, Sydney
1980   Clara in *The Nutcracker* (Petit), Ballet National de Marseille, Marseilles
       Bella in *La Chauve-souris* (Petit), Ballet National de Marseille, New York
1982   Principal dancer (cr) in *Avant-Après* (Ariel), Nantes Opera Ballet, Nantes
       Principal dancer (cr) in *Le Concile féerique* (Ariel), Nantes Opera Ballet, Nantes
1983   Title role (cr) in *Cinderella* (Ariel), Nantes Opera Ballet, Nantes
       Title role (cr) in *Anaïs Nin*, Nice Dance Theatre, Nice
       Sugar Plum Fairy in *The Nutcracker* (Welch), Western Australian Ballet, Perth
1984   Princess Aurora in *The Sleeping Beauty* (Gielgud after Petipa), Australian Ballet, Melbourne
       Tatiana in *Onegin* (Cranko), Australian Ballet, Sydney
       Principal dancer in *Voluntaries* (Tetley), Australian Ballet, Sydney
       Lise in *La Fille mal gardée* (Ashton), Australian Ballet, Sydney
       La Flute, Pas de deux in *Suite en blanc* (Lifar), Australian Ballet, Sydney
       The Girl in *Equus* (Reiter-Soffer), Australian Ballet, Sydney
       Pas de deux in *Gaîté Parisienne* (Béjart), Australian Ballet, Sydney
1985   "La Sylphide" in *Graduation Ball* (Lichine), Australian Ballet, Sydney
       Title role in *La Sylphide* (Bruhn after Bournonville), Australian Ballet, Melbourne
       Principal dancer in *In the Night* (Robbins), Australian Ballet, Melbourne
       Principal dancer in *Webern Opus V* (Béjart), Australian Ballet, Sydney
       Principal dancer in *Serenade* (Balanchine), Australian Ballet, Sydney
       The Girl in *Variations on a Nursery Theme* (Seregi), Australian Ballet, Sydney
       Sanguinic in *The Four Temperaments* (Balanchine), Australian Ballet, Sydney

Christine Walsh as Odette in *Swan Lake*

Doreen (cr) in *The Sentimental Bloke* (Ray), Australian Ballet, Sydney

1986 Title role in *Giselle* (Petipa after Coralli, Perrot; staged Gielgud), Australian Ballet, Adelaide

Bianca in *The Taming of the Shrew* (Cranko), Australian Ballet, tour

Principal dancer in *Études* (Lander), Australian Ballet, Sydney

Black Queen in *Checkmate* (de Valois), Australian Ballet, Sydney

Principal dancer (white couple) in *Forgotten Land* (Kylián), Australian Ballet, Sydney

1987 Juliet in *Romeo and Juliet* (Cranko), Australian Ballet, Sydney

Milady in *The Three Musketeers* (Prokovsky), Australian Ballet, Melbourne

Taglioni in *Pas de quatre* (Dolin), Australian Ballet, Melbourne

Nikiya in *La Bayadère* (Petipa; staged Popa), Australian Ballet, Sydney

Eurydice (cr) in *Orpheus* (Tetley), Australian Ballet, Melbourne

Principal dancer in *Song of the Earth* (MacMillan), Australian Ballet, Sydney

The Young Love (cr) in *Beyond Twelve* (Murphy), Australian Ballet, Sydney

1988 Ballerina in *Paquita* (excerpts; Petipa, staged Valukin), Australian Ballet, Sydney

Principal dancer in *Return to the Strange Land* (Kylián), Australian Ballet, Sydney

1989 Principal dancer in *Four Last Songs* (Béjart), Australian Ballet, Sydney

Ballerina in *Birthday Offering* (Ashton), Australian Ballet, Canberra

Ballerina/Mother in *Le Concours* (*The Competition*; Béjart), Australian Ballet, Sydney

Ballerina (cr) in *Airs and Dances* (Shader), Australian Ballet, Manila

1992 La Capricciosa in *The Lady and the Fool* (Cranko), Australian Ballet Dancers Company, Orange, Australia

PUBLICATIONS

Laughlin, Patricia, "Streamlined *Beauty*", *Dance Australia* (Keysborough), April/May 1988

Koch, Peta, "To Russia with Love", *Dance Australia* (Keysborough), October/November 1988

Laughlin, Patricia, "Impressions of Russia", *Dance Australia* (Keysborough), June/July 1989

*   *   *

Christine Walsh perfectly matches the popular image of a ballerina. She is a beautiful woman with long slim legs and arms, a graceful neck, lovely face, and charming smile. When one thinks of her, a picture of Princess Aurora in *The Sleeping Beauty* is immediately conjured up, and indeed she has become very much associated with this role. Despite this association, Walsh has proved herself to be a versatile artist. Her repertoire ranges from the classics—Odette/Odile as well as Aurora—and the romantics—*La Sylphide* and *Giselle*—through Cranko, Balanchine, and Robbins to the contemporary works of Kylián, Tetley, and Béjart.

While an analysis of Walsh's technique reveals features that are less than perfect—her turns are average and her jump poor—she has a pleasing line, mainly due to her physical conformation, and precise musical phrasing. Her strength lies in her personality. There is a quality of daring and self-confidence in her stage presence, and a sense of chic which is almost French. This latter is presumably innate, but undoubtedly would have been developed by the period she spent dancing with Roland Petit's Ballet National de Marseille. In her radiant portrayal of Aurora, all these qualities were put to the service of creating a persona that minimized the technical pitfalls in such a demanding role and accentuated the sheer entertainment value. She has the ability to reduce any technical limitations to irrelevancies as her confidence transmits itself to the audience and convinces them that they are watching the best possible performance.

Walsh is a very good, intelligent actress and develops more each year in this direction. She has given notable performances as Giselle and scored a big personal success in this role when she danced it as a guest with the Kirov Ballet in 1989. She was a moving Juliet in Cranko's version of Shakespeare's famous love story and a charming, if rather shallow, Lise in Ashton's *La Fille mal gardée*. This suspicion of superficiality has prevented some of her interpretations, however well thought-out and detailed, from leaving an emotional impact on the observer. However it proved an asset in *La Sylphide*, as her persona was just right for the poor, beautiful, frivolous, yet doomed sylph, and she will long be remembered in this role. Walsh can also handle comedy and was very funny as the woman with the hats (the "wife") in Jerome Robbins's *The Concert*. Recently she has given some strong and moving performances as Tatiana in Cranko's *Onegin* and it may be that with greater maturity her characterizations will deepen.

For one who is mainly thought of as a classical and romantic ballerina, Walsh has demonstrated an ability to perform outstandingly in a variety of modern styles and techniques. She was striking in Béjart's *Webern Opus V* and again had a big success in Russia when she danced this ballet with David Ashmole at a gala at the Bolshoi Theatre in 1986. Glen Tetley found her style appropriate for his *Voluntaries* and also cast her as Eurydice in his version of *Orpheus*, created for the Australian Ballet in 1987. Her aptitude for contemporary styles has never been fully explored in Australia; whether this is because of Australian Ballet company policy or her own inclination is not known.

Australian dancers tend to retire young and, if Christine Walsh follows this pattern, the greater emotional depth she indicated in *Onegin* may not be followed through and developed in years to come, which would be regrettable.

—Patricia Laughlin

WATTS, Heather

American dancer. Born in Long Beach, California, 27 September 1953. Studied with Sheila Rozann, Chatsworth, California, from 1963, and at School of American Ballet, New York, pupil of Stanley Williams, André Eglevsky, Alexandra Danilova, Summer 1967, and as Ford Foundation Scholar, from 1968; also studied with Natalie Clare, North Hollywood. Dancer, corps de ballet, New York City Ballet, from 1970, becoming soloist, from 1978, and principal dancer, from 1979; also guest performer, with Mikhail Baryshnikov, at the White House, 1979; has appeared on U.S. television, including in Public Broadcasting Service (PBS) "Dance in America" series, and in "Live from Lincoln Center" telecast, PBS, 1988;

Heather Watts in *Calcium Light Night*, New York City Ballet, 1978

director, New York State Summer School of the Arts, Dance Department, Saratoga Springs, New York, from 1982. Recipient: *Dance Magazine* Award, 1985; L'Oreal Shining Star Award, 1985; Lions of the Performing Arts Award from the New York Public Library, 1986.

ROLES

1972/ Concerto in *Episodes II* (Balanchine), New York City
77   Ballet, New York
    Emeralds in *Jewels* (Balanchine), New York City Ballet, New York
    Variations II in *Goldberg Variations* (Robbins), New York City Ballet, New York
    Principal dancer in *Scherzo Fantastique* (Balanchine), New York City Ballet, New York
    Second Movement in *Symphony in C* (Balanchine), New York City Ballet, New York
    Ballerina in *Tchaikovsky Pas de Deux* (Balanchine), New York City Ballet, New York
    Principal dancer in *Ballo della Regina* (Balanchine), New York City Ballet, New York
    Principal dancer in *Piano Concerto No. 2* (Balanchine), New York City Ballet, New York

1977/ The Novice in *The Cage* (Robbins), New York City
78   Ballet, New York
    Gold and Silver Waltz in *Vienna Waltzes* (Balanchine), New York City Ballet, New York

1978 Principal dancer (cr) in *Calcium Light Night* (Martins), New York City Ballet, New York
    Rubies in *Jewels* (Balanchine), New York City Ballet, New York
    Principal dancer (cr) in *Rossini Pas de deux* (Martins) in *A Sketch Book* (works in progress), New York City Ballet, New York

1979 Dewdrop Fairy in *The Nutcracker* (Balanchine), New York City Ballet, New York
    Leader of the Bacchantes in *Orpheus* (Balanchine), New York City Ballet, New York
    Terpsichore in *Apollo* (Balanchine), New York City Ballet, New York
    Principal dancer in *Dances at a Gathering* (Robbins), New York City Ballet, New York
    Andante in *Brahms–Schoenberg Quartet* (Balanchine), New York City Ballet, New York
    Principal dancer in *Stars and Stripes* (Balanchine), New York City Ballet, New York
    Winter (cr) in *The Four Seasons* (Robbins), New York City Ballet, New York
    Principal dancer (cr) in *Sonate di Scarlatti* (Martins), New York City Ballet, New York

1979/ Variation from *La Ventana* (Bournonville), in *Bournon-*
80   *ville Divertissements* (staged Williams), New York City Ballet, New York
    Principal dancer in *In the Night* (Robbins), New York City Ballet, New York
    Principal dancer in *Divertimento No. 15* (Balanchine), New York City Ballet, New York
    Principal dancer in *Symphony in Three Movements* (Balanchine), New York City Ballet, New York
    Principal dancer in *Union Jack* (Balanchine), New York City Ballet, New York
    Principal dancer in *Chaconne* (Balanchine), New York City Ballet, New York
    Principal dancer in *Afternoon of a Faun* (Robbins), New York City Ballet, New York

1980 Solo (cr) in *Walpurgisnacht Ballet* (Balanchine), New York City Ballet, New York
    Divertissement (cr) in *Le Bourgeois Gentilhomme* (Balanchine), New York City Ballet, New York
    Principal dancer (third couple) (cr) in *Robert Schumann's Davidsbündlertänze* (Balanchine), New York City Ballet, New York
    Principal dancer (cr) in *Lille Suite* (Martins), New York City Ballet, New York
    Ballerina in *Theme and Variations* (Balanchine), New York City Ballet, New York
    Sugar Plum Fairy in *The Nutcracker* (Balanchine), New York City Ballet, New York

1981 Principal dancer (cr) in *Piano Pieces* (Robbins), New York City Ballet, New York
    Principal dancer (cr) in *Suite from Histoire du Soldat* (Martins), New York City Ballet, New York

1982 Ragtime (cr) in *Four Chamber Works* (Robbins), New York City Ballet, New York
    Principal dancer (cr) in *Concerto for Two Solo Pianos* (Martins), New York City Ballet, New York
    Principal dancer (cr) in *Delibes Divertissement* (Martins), New York City Ballet, New York
    Principal dancer in *Donizetti Variations* (Balanchine), New York City Ballet, New York
    "Voices of Spring" Waltz in *Vienna Waltzes* (Balanchine), New York City Ballet, New York
    Principal dancer in *Stravinsky Violin Concerto* (Balanchine), New York City Ballet, New York
    Principal dancer in *Tchaikovsky Suite No. 3* (Balanchine), New York City Ballet, New York
    Principal dancer in *In G Major* (Robbins), New York City Ballet, New York
    Principal dancer in *Opus 19* (Robbins), New York City Ballet, New York

1983 Principal dancer (cr) in *Tango* (Robbins), New York City Ballet, New York
    Principal dancer (cr) in *I'm Old Fashioned* (Robbins), New York City Ballet, New York

1984 Principal dancer (cr) in *A Schubertiad* (Martins), New York City Ballet, New York
    Principal dancer in *Bugaku* (Balanchine), New York City Ballet, New York
    Principal dancer in *Liebeslieder Walzer* (Balanchine), New York City Ballet, New York

1986 Principal dancer (cr) in *Songs of the Auvergne* (Martins), New York City Ballet, New York

1987 Principal dancer (cr) in *Ecstatic Orange* (Martins), New York City Ballet, New York

1988 Principal dancer (cr) in *Black & White* (Martins), New York City Ballet, New York
    Principal dancer (cr) in *A Fool for You* (Martins), New York City Ballet, New York
    Principal dancer (cr) in *Sonatas and Interludes* (Richard Tanner), New York City Ballet, New York
    Principal dancer (cr) in *Space* (Dean), New York City Ballet, New York

1990 Pas de deux (cr) in *Prague Symphony* (Tanner), New York City Ballet, New York
    Principal dancer (cr) in *Fearful Symmetries* (Martins), New York City Ballet, New York
    Principal dancer in *Movements for Piano and Orchestra* (Balanchine), New York City Ballet, New York

1991 Principal dancer (cr) in *A Musical Offering* (Martins), New York City Ballet, New York

1992 Principal dancer (cr) in *Ancient Airs and Dances* (Tanner), New York City Ballet, New York

Other roles include: principal dancer in *Allegro Brillante* (Balanchine), pas de deux in *Agon* (Balanchine), principal dancer in *Concerto Barocco* (Balanchine), principal dancer in *Opus 19/The Dreamer* (Robbins), pas de deux from *The Kermesse in Bruges* (Bournonville) in *Bournonville Divertissement* (Williams after Bournonville), principal dancer in *Western Symphony* (Balanchine).

PUBLICATIONS

By Watts:
Interview in Swift, Edward, "A Conversation with Heather Watts", *Ballet Review* (New York), Spring 1985
Interview in Gruen, John, *People Who Dance*, New York, 1988
"Workshop 25: Those Champion Seasons", *Dance Magazine* (New York), May 1989

About Watts:
Croce, Arlene, *Afterimages*, New York, 1977
Gruen, John, "Heather Watts' Difficult and Successful Rise", *Dance Magazine* (New York), February 1980
Croce, Arlene, *Going to the Dance*, New York, 1982
Martin, John, *A Day in the Life of a Dancer*, Mahwah, New Jersey, 1985
Daniels, Don, "Collaborators: The File on New York City Ballet", *Ballet Review* (New York), Spring 1987
Croce, Arlene, *Sight Lines*, New York, 1987
Croce, Arlene, "Dimming the Lights", *The New Yorker* (New York), 7 March 1988
Stuart, Otis, "That Martins Woman", *Ballet Review* (New York), Spring 1989

* * *

In 1970, Heather Watts entered New York City Ballet's corps de ballet under unique circumstances, her début introducing the twin constants that would characterize her subsequent association with New York City Ballet—talent and tension. After two years as a student at the School of American Ballet, City Ballet's affiliate academy, Watts's personal individuality and signature independence had led to a final threat of expulsion, an order countermanded by the direct intervention of George Balanchine, the founder of both institutions. According to Balanchine's successor as director of New York City Ballet, Peter Martins, Balanchine took Watts into his company "because he would not let such a talent disappear". He also launched one of the most controversial, precedent-setting careers in contemporary ballet.

Heather Watts was born in suburban Los Angeles, the daughter of an aerospace engineer and a British-born journalist. She began her ballet training locally with Sheila Rozann and reached the School of American Ballet on a Ford Foundation scholarship after two of New York City Ballet's ranking ballerinas, Diana Adams and Violette Verdy, spotted her in Rozann's classes. The student's unique physical presence and capacities (Verdy described her as a "natural dancer") identified Watts as a blossoming ballerina candidate, just as her independence and fiery intelligence established her as a singular offstage personality.

Watts spent nearly eight years in the City Ballet corps, developing a wide-ranging repertory. Balanchine's first two assignments were from opposite worlds of his vast repertory, the elegiac "Emeralds" section of *Jewels* and the angular extremity of *Episodes* to the music of Webern. Watts's Balanchine repertory grew to include some of the most demanding roles in twentieth-century ballet, such as the

ballerina leads in *Piano Concerto No. 2*, *Symphony in C*, *Tchaikovsky Pas de Deux*, and *Ballo della Regina*. Balanchine made Watts a soloist in 1978 and a principal dancer the following year, by which time she had also become a favored subject of Jerome Robbins and the central figure in the first ballets choreographed by Peter Martins.

Watts belongs to the select society of ballerinas who have introduced a new stage prototype. Her initial impression was made in two areas of the Balanchine repertory. Her exceptional elevation was captured in Balanchine's first original creation for her, the bounding soloist figure in *Walpurgisnacht Ballet*, and her jump was a central feature in her most celebrated role, the Dewdrop Fairy in Balanchine's *Nutcracker*. But Balanchine's second creation for Watts, one of the four ballerina roles in *Robert Schumann's "Davidsbündlertänze"*, emphasized the natural dramatic intensity that became her special trademark in Balanchine ballets such as *Agon* and *Bugaku*, as well as in the ballets of Jerome Robbins and Peter Martins. In Martins ballets such as *Calcium Light Night*, *Concerto for Two Solo Pianos*, and *Ecstatic Orange*, Watts introduced what can be called the "new wave" ballerina of the 1980s, a unique combination of emotional complexity, realized sexuality, and blazing intelligence which was a natural successor to the liberated heroines of Balanchine's Stravinsky repertory. Watts's pioneering work in this area, aligning contemporary ballet with the social, sexual, and cultural colors of its era, has made her New York City Ballet's most consistently controversial ballerina of the 1980s and 1990s.

—Otis Stuart

WEAVER, John
English dancer, choreographer, teacher, and theoretician. Born in or near Shrewsbury, son of dancing master; baptismal date 21 July 1673. Educated at Shrewsbury School from c.1683; studied dance as apprentice to dancing master, probably with Edward Dyer, Shrewsbury. Married (1) Catherine Weaver, c.1696–1702; (2) Susanna Weaver, c. 1716. Dancing master in Shrewsbury, from 1695; dancer in London, performing in theatres at Drury Lane, Lincoln's Inn Fields, and York Buildings, Villiers Street; choreographer, staging first work, *The Tavern Bilkers*, at Drury Lane, 1702/3; also performer in own works, including as Vulcan in *The Loves of Mars and Venus* (1717) and as Orpheus in *Orpheus and Eurydice* (1718); also notator, publishing collection of court dances, 1706, and translation of Feuillet's *Chorégraphie* (published as *Orchesography*, 1706); also published descriptions of own stage works and theoretical works on dance. Died in Shrewsbury, 24 September 1760.

WORKS

1702/ *The Tavern Bilkers*, Drury Lane Theatre, London
03
1717 *The Loves of Mars and Venus* (mus. Symonds, Fairbanks), Drury Lane Theatre, London
The Shipwreck; or, Perseus and Andromeda, Drury Lane Theatre, London
Harlequin Turned Judge, Drury Lane Theatre, London
1718 *Orpheus and Eurydice* (mus. Fairbanks), Drury Lane Theatre, London
1719 *Cupid and Bacchus*, Drury Lane Theatre, London

1728　*Perseus and Andromeda: With the Rape of Columbine; or, The Flying Lovers* (with Roger; mus. Pepusch), Drury Lane Theatre, London

1733　*The Judgement of Paris* (after masque by Congreve; new mus. Seedo), Drury Lane Theatre, London

WORKS (attributed to Weaver)

1728　*Acis and Galatea; or, The Country Wedding*, Drury Lane Theatre, London

PUBLICATIONS

By Weaver:
Orchesography; Or, The Art of Dancing, by Characters and Demonstrative Figures (translation of Raoul-Auger Feuillet's *Chorégraphie*, second edition, Paris, 1701), London, 1706; reprinted Farnborough and New York, 1971

A Small Treatise of Time and Cadence in Dancing, London, 1706; reprinted Farnborough and New York, 1971

An Essay towards an History of Dancing, London, 1712

The Loves of Mars and Venus: A Dramatic Entertainment Attempted in Imitation of the Pantomime of the Ancient Greeks and Romans, London, 1717; second edition, 1724

The Fable of Orpheus and Eurydice, with a Dramatick Entertainment in Dancing thereupon, London, 1718

Anatomical and Mechanical Lectures upon Dancing, London, 1721

The History of the Mimes and Pantomimes, London, 1728

The Judgement of Paris, a Dramatick Entertainment in Dancing and Singing, after the Manner of the Ancient Greeks and Romans, London, 1733

Dances Notated by Weaver:
A Collection of Ball-Dances Perform'd at Court, London, 1706

The Union: a New Dance Compos'd by Mr. Isaac, London, 1707

About Weaver:
Avery, Emmet, "Dancing and Pantomime on the English Stage 1700–1737", *Studies in Philology* (Chapel Hill), vol. 31, no. 3, 1934

Cohen, Selma Jeanne, "The Modern Dance and John Weaver", *Dance Observer* (New York), February 1955

Fletcher, Ifan, et al., *Famed for Dance: Essays on the Theory and Practice of Theatrical Dancing in England 1660–1740*, New York, 1960

Lawson, Joan, "John Weaver", *Dancing Times* (London), September 1960

Chatwin, Amina, and Richardson, Philip, "The Father of English Ballet: John Weaver", *Ballet Annual* (London), vol. 15, 1961

Brinson, Peter, and van Praagh, Peggy, *The Choreographic Art*, London, 1963

Brinson, Peter, *A Background to European Ballet*, Leyden, 1966

Kirstein, Lincoln, *Movement and Metaphor: Four Centuries of Ballet*, New York, 1970

Cohen, Selma Jeanne (ed.), *Dance as Theatre Art: Source Readings in Dance History*, New York, 1974

Winter, Marian Hannah, *The Pre-Romantic Ballet*, London, 1974

Dorris, George, "Music for the Ballets of John Weaver", *Dance Chronicle* (New York), vol. 3, no. 1, 1979

Ralph, Richard, *The Life and Works of John Weaver*, London, 1985

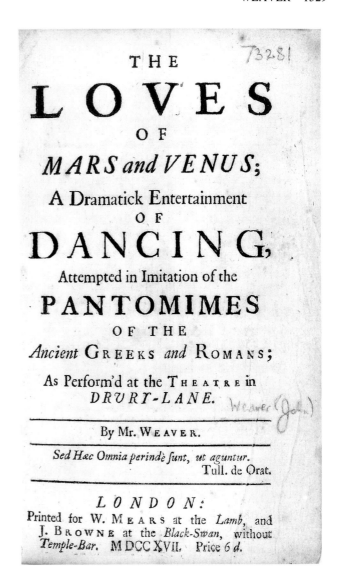

Frontispiece from John Weaver's *The Loves of Mars and Venus*, London, 1717

Foster, Susan Leigh, *Reading Dancing*, Berkeley, California, 1986

*　　*　　*

In 1759 Thomas Wilkes wrote of the achievements of his 86-year-old contemporary: "Weaver, the dancing master, whose character is too well known to need illustration, endeavoured to revive the manner of the ancient mimes, which expressed, by dumb-shew and dancing, a variety of actions and passions; and to his various characters he gave the foreign names by which they are now distinguished." Although befuddled (he makes no distinction between Weaver's serious dance theatre modelled upon "the ancient mimes" and his *commedia dell'arte*-inspired pantomimes), Wilkes quite rightly credits Weaver with having introduced not only Italian pantomime to the English stage (and thus the characters with "foreign names"), but also the *ballet d'action* itself. John Weaver, dance theorist, apologist, teacher, performer, choreographer, and the first English dance historian, devoted his life to the conviction that "by dumb-shew and dancing" alone a performer could not only express passions, but also tell stories. The fact that commercial pressures, professional rivalries, and contemporary tastes constrained the development of his art and the sphere of its influence should not blind us to his genius.

Weaver was a dancing master in the English tradition of Josias Priest, whose capacities for what Weaver would later call "serious" ballet can be seen, for example, in his elaborate choreography for Purcell's *Dido and Aeneas*, commissioned in 1689 for his fashionable girls' boarding school. Weaver, too, ran a boarding school in his native Shrewsbury, and ardently championed the primacy of English dancing masters and the English stage. With true nationalist fervour he inveighed against French virtuosos like Ballon, who "pretended to nothing more than a graceful motion". Weaver was a key figure in the anglicization of the seventeenth-century French tradition of court ballet, both in his publications on dance (his *Orchesography*, an intelligent revision and translation of an early edition of Feuillet's *Chorégraphie*, was published by 1706) and in his serious choreography.

But equally important for Weaver's art was a tradition of popular dancing, a mixture of stage folk-dance (theatre bills of the day advertised pieces like "The Dutch Skipper" or "The Highland Lilt") and fairground *commedia dell'arte* entertainments (imported to England by French performers). Weaver referred to this type of dancing as "grotesque" (from the Italian "grotteschi"); his first attempt to present a full-length piece of unadulterated dance theatre was done in this genre (*The Tavern Bilkers*), and although he complained of its limitations, he never deserted it—partly because of his intense rivalry with one of the genre's great artists, John Rich, during his Drury Lane years, and partly, it appears, because he really enjoyed its vigour.

However, unlike Rich, whose formative years were spent entirely backstage, Weaver had been genteelly educated, and he shared his age's fascination with antique culture. In 1712, he contributed a letter to the most highly regarded cultural journal of his day, *The Spectator*, in which he lamented, "Why should Dancing, an Art celebrated by the Ancients in so extraordinary a manner, be totally neglected by the Moderns, and left destitute of any Pen to recommend its various Excellencies . . . The low Ebb to which Dancing is now fallen, is altogether owing to this silence. The Art is esteem'd only as an amusing Trifle." In the same year he published his *Essay towards an History of Dancing*, the first English apologist treatise on dance, in which he set forth his ideal of narrative ballet, which he called "scenical dancing". Now extant only as "a faint Imitation of the Roman Pantomimes, [it] differs from the Grotesque, in that the last only represents Persons, Passions and Manners; and the former explains whole Stories by Action . . . the Ruins of which remain still in Italy; but sunk and degenerated into Pleasantry, and merry conceited Representations of Harlequin, Scaramouch, . . . etc.". Weaver was already meditating an experiment in serious scenical dance in an effort to restore it to its antique grandeur, when personal tragedy struck: his young wife died in childbirth and it would be five years before he was able to put his ideals into practice, with the production at Drury Lane in 1717 of his *Loves of Mars and Venus*.

Conscious of the ballet's experimental nature, he published a libretto, explaining the nature of ancient mime and the difficulties of reviving the form with untrained dancers and uninitiated audiences. It documents a remarkable moment in dance history, the introduction of a *ballet d'action* decades before Noverre. Weaver wished to give the impression that the experiment was based on his literary archaeology among Ancient writers, with his extensive quotation from Lucian, Aristotle, and Homer; but his notion of the dramatic possibilities of dance is as much indebted to his professional

theatrical experience of Italian pantomime and English stage tradition as to fashionable literary admiration for classical culture. Like all cultural thinkers of his day, he held up the ideal of "Nature" as the yardstick against which all performances were to be measured. By faithful imitation of Nature, the skilled performer can dance, he says, echoing the literary language of Dryden, so that "without the help of an Interpreter, a Spectator shall at a distance, by the lively Representation of a just Character, be capable of understanding" the story and the passions it conveys. Weaver's choreography was a passionate plea for mimesis in an age which understood dance only as entertainment between the acts or brief outbursts of uncomplicated feeling.

The same month that Drury Lane presented *Loves*, John Rich took up his post at the rival theatre, Lincoln's Inn Fields, and commercial pressures began to mount against Weaver's experimentation. Rich burlesqued Weaver's first success in *The Cheats; or, The Tavern Bilkers* and, more seriously, his *Loves*, with flair and sophistication. Nevertheless, in 1718, Weaver presented his second serious scenical work, *Orpheus and Eurydice*, a larger and grander production than *Loves*, published with a libretto full of learned quotation from Dryden's Virgil, but little in the way of dance exposition. Now more self-confident about both his public and his dancers (seven of the cast of sixteen had danced in *Loves*), Weaver created *Orpheus* as an ambitious piece of dance theatre, virtually Noverrian in design and conception. Even so, there are hints of commercial pressure: Weaver resorted to song to convey the complexities of the negotiations for Eurydice's release from Hell, and he gave the piece an untraditionally bleak and flagrantly sensational ending, with Orpheus's murder and dismembering at the hands of the Bacchae. While the bleakness of the ending may have been personally motivated (he had no doubt been attracted to the theme by his own tragic loss), there can be little doubt that the sensational element was a sop to box office concerns. However, *Orpheus* was not the success that *Loves* had been, and Weaver was to spend most of the rest of his intermittent choreographic career at Drury Lane doing comic pantomime.

By the time Weaver mounted *The Judgement of Paris* in 1733, his last serious effort at "scenical dance", the climate which had encouraged, or at least tolerated, his serious mime had changed. His early purist ideals of wordless naturalism had been adulterated with songs and personifications, used to convey what in the early days he would have left to mime. However, *Judgement* still bears the stamp of Weaver's genius: his Paris (danced by Desnoyer, who had returned from Poland to do the role) is restricted entirely to dance and mime, and must convey at times complexities of emotion like those Weaver had demanded of his leading dancers in early productions. Weaver also strengthened the story by creating a special role (Helen) for his longtime principal dancer, the much-loved Hester Santlow (Mrs. Booth).

The question of Weaver's influence upon the combination of historical events which finally established the primacy of the *ballet d'action* later in the eighteenth century has vexed dance historians for years; the names of various dancers and colleagues (Dupré, Sallé, Roger, and others) have been put forward as key figures in the transmission of Weaver's ideas to later choreographers, notably Noverre. However, the important point, as Marian Winter has said, is that it is impossible to write the history of the action ballet "without accepting the interaction of the Italian–French–English exchanges which lasted until about 1760". No single figure was more prominent in the English dance world of the period than Weaver, and by 1759, when Wilkes says that Weaver's character was too well known to require introduction, Noverre had already been to

Drury Lane at Garrick's invitation. It is hard to believe that Weaver's great pioneering efforts passed unmentioned.

—Kathryn Kerby-Fulton

A WEDDING BOUQUET

Choreography: Frederick Ashton
Music: Lord Berners
Design: Lord Berners (scenery and costumes)
Libretto: Gertrude Stein, *They Must. Be Wedded. To Their Wife.* (selections from text originally sung by chorus; later read aloud by onstage narrator)
First Production: Vic-Wells Ballet, Sadler's Wells Theatre, London, 27 April 1937
Principal Dancers: Mary Honer (Bride), Robert Helpmann (Bridegroom), Margot Fonteyn (Julia), June Brae (Josephine), Julia Farron (Pepe), Ninette de Valois (Webster)

Other productions include: Royal Ballet Touring Company, with Marion Tait (Bride), Alain Dubreuil (Bridegroom), Margaret Barbieri (Julia), Vyvyan Lorrayne (Josephine); London, 14 May 1974. Joffrey Ballet (staged Christopher Newton); New York, 18 October 1979.

PUBLICATIONS

Haskell, Arnold, "Balletomane's Logbook", *Dancing Times* (London), June 1937
Coton, A.V., *A Prejudice for Ballet*, London, 1938
Barnes, Clive, "*A Wedding Bouquet*", *Dance and Dancers* (London), April 1959
Stein, Gertrude, "*A Wedding Bouquet*", *About the House* (London), Christmas 1964
Monahan, James, "Dividends of Nostalgia", *Dancing Times* (London), January 1965
Clarke, Mary, and Harris, Dale, "The Royal Ballet of Today and Yesterday, and the First *Wedding Bouquet*", *Dancing Times* (London), November 1969
Balanchine, George, with Mason, Francis, *Balanchine's Com-*

A Wedding Bouquet, with (from left to right) Bryony Brind, Anthony Dowell, and Lesley Collier, Royal Ballet, London

plete Stories of the Great Ballets, Garden City, N.Y., 1977
Vaughan, David, *Frederick Ashton and his Ballets*, London, 1977

*   *   *

Ideas for ballets come from many sources, and *A Wedding Bouquet* originated with the composer Lord Berners, who planned to write a choral work to accompany a selection of words by Gertrude Stein. Stein had collaborated in 1928 with Virgil Thomson in the experimental opera *Four Saints in Three Acts*, which had been staged in New York with choreography by Frederick Ashton. Berners varied the approach, however, by basing his music on a selection of words from Stein's play *They Must. Be Wedded. To Their Wife*. At this point he began discussing with Constant Lambert and Frederick Ashton the possibility of making it into a ballet instead.

The resulting work is an impressionistic, surreal comedy in which a diversity of elements combine to produce delectable entertainment. It is extremely tricky to perform and is easily ruined by unsatisfactory casting or production. Ashton's choreography is delicate, subtle, and rewarding, turning lightly from classical parody to waltz and tango and a top-hat-and-cane solo for the Bridegroom. The text, originally sung by a chorus but infinitely more telling when declaimed by the right narrator, is cunningly related to music and dance, a perfect blending of sense and nonsense. The narrator—Lambert was the first, choosing to sit on stage at a festive table with a champagne bottle and glass—has an immensely difficult task, as the speech must ideally not only follow the cues given by music and choreography but be perfectly paced to link with the score. Technically it is unusually demanding, and not surprisingly, the definitive performance has been by Robert Helpmann (as a dancer, the first and irreplaceable Bridegroom), who could bring to the task his own experience of both drama and ballet.

A Wedding Bouquet is about a French provincial wedding in the 1900s. Servants, supervised by the housekeeper Webster (created by Ninette de Valois), prepare for the reception and guests begin to arrive, in small groups. Flirtatious Josephine, who will later become scandalously tipsy, comes with Paul and John; Violet strongly pursues the reluctant Ernest, and on rejection turns tragically to Thérèse, while the narrator declaims: "Thérèse, I am older than a boat, and there can be no folly in owning it!" Guy, a mystery man, dances on his own, while the exuberant Arthur talks to four simpering young ladies with parasols. The demented Julia (a role for which no one has matched the fey, wild quality of the originator, Margot Fonteyn), reluctantly discarded by the Bridegroom, is accompanied by her Mexican terrier. Embarrassments ensue, small squabbles occur, and eventually the Bridegroom and Bride leave for what will obviously be a miserable marriage. Julia, desolate, has the final curtain with her dog, as the narrator repeats, "Bitterness is entertained by all . . . bitterness . . . bitterness . . .".

A Wedding Bouquet was revived several times by the Sadler's Wells (later the Royal) Ballet, from the 1940s through to the late 1970s, when Jennifer Penney danced Josephine, and Lesley Collier and Michael Coleman danced the Bride and Bridegroom. The ballet was also taken into the repertories of the Royal Ballet Touring Company and the Joffrey Ballet in New York.

—Kathrine Sorley Walker

———

WELCH, Garth

Australian dancer, choreographer, and ballet director. Born in Brisbane, 14 April 1936. Studied with Phyllis Danaher in Brisbane, Victor Gsovsky in Paris, Anna Northcote in London, and Peggy van Praagh and Leon Kellaway in Australia; studied modern dance (on Harkness Foundation grant) with Martha Graham, New York, 1966–67. Married dancer Marilyn Jones: two sons. Dancer in stage musical, *Call Me Madam* (mus. Berlin), 1953–54; dancer, Borovansky Ballet, Australia, 1954–58; soloist, Western Ballet Theatre, Britain, 1958–59, returning to Borovansky Ballet, 1960–61; soloist, becoming leading dancer, Grand Ballet du Marquis de Cuevas, France, 1961–62; principal dancer, Australian Ballet, 1962–73; choreographer, staging own ballets for Australian Ballet from 1964; also choreographer for Australian Ballet School, West Australian Ballet, Ballet Victoria, Queensland Ballet, and Ballet Philippines; associate artistic director, Ballet Victoria, 1974–76; associate artistic director, 1979, becoming artistic director, West Australian Ballet, 1980–82; acting director, Dance North Queensland, from 1989; also teacher: director of dance department, Victorian College of the Arts (incorporating the defunct Ballet Victoria School), from 1977; co-founder and teacher, Marilyn Jones/Garth Welch Ballet School, Sydney, 1983–88; interim dean of dance, Victorian College of the Arts, 1987. Recipient: Order of Australia, 1981.

ROLES

1955   Sailor in *Pineapple Poll* (Cranko), Borovansky Ballet, Sydney

1956   Florestan in *Carnaval* (Fokine), Borovansky Ballet, Melbourne

1959   Prince Désiré in *The Sleeping Princess* (Borovansky after Petipa), Borovansky Ballet, Sydney

1960   Albrecht in *Giselle* (Petipa after Coralli, Perrot; staged Borovansky), Borovansky Ballet, Sydney

Romeo in *The Eternal Lovers* (Grinwis), Borovansky Ballet, Sydney

Variation, Adagio of Lovers in *Les Rendezvous* (Ashton; staged van Praagh), Borovansky Ballet, Melbourne

1961   The Prince in *The Nutcracker* (Lichine), Borovansky Ballet, Melbourne

Principal dancer (cr) in *Sylvia* (Martyn), Australian television

1962   Prince Siegfried in *Swan Lake* (after Petipa, Ivanov), Australian Ballet, Sydney

The Jackaroo (cr) in *Melbourne Cup* (Reid), Australian Ballet, Sydney

Moondog in *The Lady and the Fool* (Cranko), Australian Ballet, Sydney

1964   The Outsider (cr) in *The Display* (Helpmann), Australian Ballet, Adelaide

Red (cr) in *Jazz Spectrum* (Pounder), Australian Ballet, Adelaide Festival of the Arts, Adelaide

Pas de deux from *Flower Festival at Genzano* (Gnatt after Bournonville), Australian Ballet, Sydney

1965   The Fisherman (cr) in *Yugen* (Helpmann), Australian Ballet, Adelaide

Albrecht in *Giselle* (new production; van Praagh after Petipa, Coralli, Perrot), Australian Ballet, Birmingham, England

1966   Jean de Brienne in *Raymonda* (Nureyev after Petipa), Australian Ballet, Adelaide

1968   Principal dancer in *Ballet Imperial* (Balanchine), Australian Ballet, Sydney

The Instigator (cr) in *Threshold* (Butler), Australian Ballet, Sydney

1969 The Friend in *Pillar of Fire* (Tudor), Australian Ballet, Melbourne

1970 The Moor in *Petrushka* (Fokine), Australian Ballet, Sydney

Pas de deux from *Gayané* (mus. Khachaturian), Australian Ballet, Sydney

Title role in *Othello* (also chor.), Australian Ballet, Adelaide

1974 Hilarion in *Giselle* (after Petipa, Coralli, Perrot), Ballet Victoria, Adelaide

1979 Karenin (cr) in *Anna Karenina* (Prokovsky), Australian Ballet, Melbourne

1984 Von Aschenbach (cr) in *After Venice* (Murphy), Sydney Dance Company, Sydney

WORKS

1964 *Variations on a Theme* (mus. Arensky), Australian Ballet, Sydney

1966 *Illyria* (mus. Tarhoudin), Australian Ballet, Adelaide

1968 *Othello* (mus. Goldsmith), Australian Ballet School, Sydney (staged Australian Ballet, 1970)

Jeunesse (mus. Prokofiev), Australian Ballet, Sydney

1972 *The Firebird* (mus. Stravinsky), Australian Ballet, Sydney

Woman of Andros (mus. Badings), West Australian Ballet, Perth

1974 *Images* (mus. Rachmaninov), Ballet Victoria, Leongatha

1975 *Ritual*, Ballet Victoria, Melbourne

The Puppet, Ballet Philippines, Manila

1977 *The Visitor* (mus. Tchaikovsky), Queensland Ballet, tour

Five Spanish Dances (mus. Moskovsky), West Australia Ballet, Perth

1979 *Sur le Balcon* (mus. Chopin), West Australian Ballet, Perth

KAL (mus. Williams), West Australian Ballet, Perth

1980/ *Cinderella* (mus. Prokofiev), West Australian Ballet
82 *The Nutcracker* (mus. Tchaikovsky), West Australian Ballet

Peter Pan, West Australian Ballet

The Tempest, West Australian Ballet

1983 *Love Sonnet*, Royal New Zealand Ballet

Janiculum, Sydney Dance Company

1987 *Love Songs in Absence*, West Australian Ballet

1988 *Voyage Within* (mus. Koehne), West Australian Ballet

Bicentenary Programme, West Australian Ballet

1989 *As Shadows Lengthen*, Queensland Ballet

Also staged:

1964 *Namouna Pas de deux* (after Lifar's *Suite en blanc*; mus. Lalo), Australian Ballet

1965 *La Esmeralda Pas de deux* (after Petipa; mus. Pugni), Australian Ballet, Adelaide

1969 *Giselle* (after Petipa, Coralli, Perrot; mus. Adam), Queensland Ballet, Brisbane

Other works include: dances in *Aida* (opera; mus. Verdi).

PUBLICATIONS

Stoop, Norman McLain, "Up on Top from Down Under: Garth Welch", *Dance Magazine* (New York), January 1971

Laughlin, Patricia, *Marilyn Jones*, Melbourne, 1978

Salter, Frank, *Borovansky: The Man who Made Australian Ballet*, Sydney, 1980

Pask, Edward, *Ballet in Australia: The Second Act*, Melbourne, 1982

Brownbill, Vicki, "Garth Welch: A Life of Dance", *Dance Australia* (Keysborough), no. 24

*   *   *

Garth Welch is best known as one of Australia's finest classical dancers, but in a long and illustrious career he has also gained a considerable reputation as a choreographer and teacher, and perhaps most importantly, as a powerful and original dramatic dancer.

Like so many of his generation who learned their art before the advent of tertiary training courses, Welch learned in the theatre. It was while he was on tour with *Call Me Madam* that Edouard Borovansky, founder of the first Australian ballet company, asked him to join his company. It was not long before he was dancing the entire repetoire.

Garth Welch brought to his roles in the major classical ballets, *Swan Lake*, *Raymonda*, *The Sleeping Beauty*, an air of nobility and elegance that seemed unstrained and quite effortless. A handsome figure on stage, he was an unobtrusive and generous partner for his ballerinas. Very early in his career as a classical dancer, Welch formed a partnership with Marilyn Jones that was to last until he retired from the Australian Ballet in 1973. They were an exciting couple to see dancing together. They brought fresh meaning to whatever they danced and the entire ballet would take on a special lustre on the strength of their performances. In Australia their partnership has become legendary.

As with many male dancers of his generation, Garth Welch's contribution to classical ballet in Australia was, to some degree, overshadowed by the arrival of Nureyev in the West. The dazzling virtuosity and raw masculine energy of the Russian dancer was a far cry from the restrained elegance of most Western male classical dancers at that time. To make matters worse, Australia was still suffering a good deal from "cultural cringe". Too often the country's own artists were relegated to supporting roles while imported guest artists danced the leads. The Australian Ballet was a young company and its dancers probably suffered more than most from this.

For Garth Welch, however, there was compensation in the reputation he gained as an exponent of strong dramatic roles. He has often been quoted as saying, "It is the theatre I am interested in, not just dance", and this has been borne out by the roles which, over the years, he has made his own—roles such as Moondog in John Cranko's *The Lady and the Fool*, the Outsider in Robert Helpmann's *The Display*, and the Fisherman in Helpmann's *Yugen*. Welch approaches a role in the same way an actor develops a character. Every gesture, every step unfolds from a thought or emotion, each one placed carefully within the context of the whole character; no movement is made simply for the sake of movement. The bedrock of Welch's interpretation is complete truth; there are no conventional or superficial balletic interpretations; even fairytale princes suffer and feel remorse, anger, and joy in ways that are instantly recognizable as human.

Welch was a noble, arrogant Albrecht who ultimately suffered a terrible remorse for his betrayal of Giselle. His Hilarion, on the other hand, was a man filled with coarse rage, an ugly and desperate man who was yet so naïve and vulnerable that one was saddened by his plight. In *The Display*, Welch brought a sense of menace and a brooding sexuality that quivered below the surface of what seemed to be a perfectly ordinary bush picnic. In *The Lady and the Fool*, on the other hand, his gentle, innocent Moondog evoked such a sense of joy and wonder when La Capricciosa removed her mask and began to dance with him that it was almost palpable.

The culmination of Welch's career as a dramatic dancer came with his creation of the role of Von Aschenbach in Graeme Murphy's *After Venice*. He literally became the aged Aschenbach, a faded and tired man, who, falling in love with a beautiful young boy, sees in the object of his affection his own lost youth and innocence, the thickened body struggling to recall its old powers yet weighted down by memories and disillusionment.

Garth Welch began choreographing in earnest after his return from America where, with the help of a Harkness Fellowship, he attended the Martha Graham school and studied the technique of Lester Horton. After all his years of classical training, this exposure to the central forces of American contemporary dance came as a revelation to him. The first ballet that he created after his return to Australia, *Othello*, is derivative of everything he learned during this time. Its highly expressionist style makes it very much a product of its time (the 1960s) and of Graham's own work in particular. Yet at the same time, it so potently captures the emotional heart of Shakespeare's story that it has never dated, and to this day is one of Welch's best-loved works.

One of Welch's great strengths as a choreographer is his ability to make the most of his dancers, whatever their degree of experience. In ballets such as *The Visitor*, he has elicited fine performances from relatively inexperienced dancers. Larger works like *KAL*, *Peter Pan*, and *The Tempest*—created when Welch was artistic director of the West Australian Ballet Company—deliberately set out to appeal to family audiences. Welch's early experiences in non-subsidized theatre always made him very conscious of the need for a regional ballet company, operating in a relatively small community, to reach a wider type of audience.

Welch's choreography has its roots in classical technique. The pas de deux which are often the focus of his ballets have long, flowing, lyrical movements and feature sweeping, romantic lifts. Yet Welch will readily break the flowing line, with bodies contracting and limbs flexing in a way that is very contemporary (though he could never go so far as to make a deliberately ugly movement). Steps are used sparingly, and have a clarity and restraint that demands that the dancers fill out every phrase. Welch's inspiration frequently comes from a specific piece of music, and his dancers need a feeling for music in order fully to respond to his choreography.

In the past few years, Welch has begun to choreograph more abstract works, such as *Love Songs in Absence*, *As Shadows Lengthen*, and *Voyage Within*. They are about the recollection of things past and recall the central themes of *After Venice* and Aschenbach's yearning for lost youth and innocence. Garth Welch's ballets are becoming increasingly personal statements, focusing on loss, parting, and the nature of fate. They are the meditations of a mature artist who knows that the deepest and most important truths can only be expressed in the simplest way.

—Vicki Fairfax

WELLS, Doreen

British dancer. Born Doreen Patricia Wells in Walthamstow, England, 25 June 1937. Studied at Bush-Davies School, and Sadler's Wells Ballet School, London. Married the Marquis of Londonderry, 1972: two sons. Dancer in pantomime, London, 1952–53; dancer, Sadler's Wells Theatre Ballet, 1955, and Sadler's Wells Ballet (becoming the Royal Ballet), from 1956; principal dancer, Royal Ballet Touring Company (performing as Royal Ballet New Group, from 1970), 1960–74, also performing with the main company at Covent Garden; retired from the Royal Ballet, 1974, though continuing to make occasional guest appearances; guest artist, Ballet of Rio de Janeiro, Brazil, 1975; also appeared in stage musicals and occasionally as actress, including in *On Your Toes*, London; also appeared frequently on television. Recipient: Adeline Genée Gold Medal, Royal Academy of Dancing, 1954.

ROLES

1956 Hypnotist's Assistant in *Noctambules* (MacMillan), Royal Ballet, London
1959 Pas de deux in *Danses Concertantes* (Balanchine), Royal Ballet, London
 Columbine in *Harlequin in April* (Cranko), Royal Ballet, London
 Title role in *Pineapple Poll* (Cranko), Royal Ballet, tour
1960 Princess Aurora in *The Sleeping Beauty* (Petipa; staged Sergeyev, de Valois, Ashton), Royal Ballet Touring Company, tour
 Odette/Odile in *Swan Lake* (Petipa, Ivanov; staged Sergeyev, de Valois, Ashton), Royal Ballet Touring Company, tour
 Swanilda in *Coppélia* (Petipa, Cecchetti; staged Sergeyev, de Valois), Royal Ballet Touring Company
1961 The Girl in *The Invitation* (MacMillan), Royal Ballet Touring Company
 Adagio, Variation in *Les Rendezvous* (Ashton), Royal Ballet Touring Company
 The Girl in *Solitaire* (MacMillan), Royal Ballet Touring Company
 Young Girl in *The Two Pigeons* (Ashton), Royal Ballet Touring Company
1962 Lise in *La Fille mal gardée* (Ashton), Royal Ballet Touring Company
 The Bride in *Blood Wedding* (Rodrigues), Royal Ballet Touring Company
 Principal dancer in *Napoli Divertissement* (Bournonville), Royal Ballet Touring Company, tour
 Fugue (cr) in *Toccata* (A. Carter), Royal Ballet Touring Company, Newcastle
1963 Title role in *Giselle* (Petipa after Coralli, Perrot; staged Sergeyev), Royal Ballet Touring Company, London
 Title role in *Sylvia* (Ashton), Royal Ballet, London
 The Girl in *House of Birds* (MacMillan), Royal Ballet Touring Company
1964 Eve (cr) in *La Création du monde* (MacMillan), Royal Ballet Touring Company, London
 Ghost (cr) in *Summer's Night* (Wright), Royal Ballet Touring Company, Oxford
 Title role in *Raymonda* (Nureyev after Petipa), Royal Ballet, Spoleto, Italy
1966 Titania in *The Dream* (Ashton), Royal Ballet Touring Company, Oxford
1967 Second Movement in *Concerto* (MacMillan), Royal Ballet Touring Company
 Elegy (cr) in *Sinfonietta* (Ashton), Royal Ballet Touring Company, London
1968 Clara in *The Nutcracker* (Nureyev), Royal Ballet, London

Doreen Wells in *The Two Pigeons*

Can-Can dancer in *La Boutique fantasque* (Massine), Royal Ballet Touring Company, tour

Principal dancer (Trois Gnossiennes) in *Monotones* (Ashton), Royal Ballet Touring Company, Wiesbaden

1970   Juliet in *Romeo and Juliet* (MacMillan), Royal Ballet, London

A Creature (cr) in *The Creatures of Prometheus* (Ashton), Royal Ballet Touring Company, Bonn

1971   Mathilde Kschessinska in *Anastasia* (MacMillan), Royal Ballet, London

Mary Pickford (cr) in *The Grand Tour* (Layton), Royal Ballet New Group, Norwich

Principal dancer (cr) in *Ante Room* (Cauley), Royal Ballet New Group, London

1973   Principal dancer in *Ballet Imperial* (*Piano Concerto No. 2*; Balanchine), Royal Ballet, London

Pas de deux in *Les Patineurs* (Ashton), Royal Ballet, London

PUBLICATIONS

"Dancer You Will Know", *Dance and Dancers* (London), January 1957

Clarke, Mary, "Doreen Wells", *Dancing Times* (London), March 1961

"Doreen Wells: Profile", *Dancing Times* (London), October 1963

Buckley, Peter, "Doreen Wells as Aurora", *Dance Magazine* (New York), February 1967

Herf, Estelle, "Doreen Wells of the Royal Ballet", *Ballet Today*, (London), May–June 1969

Buckley, Peter, "A Royal Pair: Doreen Wells and David Wall", *Dance Magazine* (New York), March 1971

Woodcock, Sarah, *The Sadler's Wells Royal Ballet*, London, 1991

* * *

Doreen Wells belonged to the golden era of Royal Ballet ballerinas, being of the same generation as Merle Park and the slightly younger Lynn Seymour and Antoinette Sibley. She began her career with the Sadler's Wells Theatre Ballet, but, after only a few weeks, she moved to the Sadler's Wells Ballet at Covent Garden, where her purity of line soon attracted attention in solo roles. However, the very abundance of talent at that time meant that she became frustrated by the lack of opportunities and she transferred to the Royal Ballet Touring Company in 1960. Over the next decade, she became the darling of the English provinces, epitomizing for them the ideal ballerina. When paired with the equally good-looking and talented David Wall, she was even more appealing: the combination was irresistible, and the Wells–Wall partnership in the late 1960s was as popular as that of Sibley and Dowell in London. Outside London they were unrivalled.

Wells combined a sparkling personality with inborn elegance. She was perfectly proportioned, with an almost too perfect line—she was a beautiful stylist, serene, with lyrical breadth of movement and a strong, but not aggressive, technique. Her very perfection could make her seem cool and remote, but her natural glamour ensured her a devoted following.

A notable exponent of the classics, Wells was a lyrical Odette, although the inherent evil of Odile was beyond her range; similarly, as Giselle, she missed the tragedy of the first act and the poignancy of Act II. However, as Princess Aurora, she developed from a radiant girl in Act I to a natural princess with authority in Act III. Like many classical stylists, she was a delightful Swanilda, able to encompass the mischievous girl of the first act and the mature ballerina of the last act of *Coppélia*. As her Swanilda hinted, she had a wider range than her natural classical style might have suggested. The formal classicism hid a personality with a natural zaniness and fun, which made her an enchanting Lise in *La Fille mal gardée*; it could also be seen in the first act of *The Two Pigeons*, where in the final pas de deux she could also achieve a heart-rending intensity. Her sense of comedy also ensured her success as Pineapple Poll, of which she was one of the best exponents, letting the comedy arise naturally from the choreography rather than from conscious interpretation.

Wells retired from the Royal Ballet in 1974, but returned occasionally for guest appearances. Two years before her official retirement she married the Marquis of Londonderry, and eventually family commitments overtook those of the stage.

—Sarah C. Woodcock

––––––––

THE WHIMS OF CUPID AND THE BALLET MASTER
(original Danish title: *Amors og Balletmesterens Luner*)

Choreography: Vincenzo Galeotti
Music: Jens Lolle
Libretto: Vincenzo Galeotti
First Production: Royal Danish Ballet, Copenhagen, 31 October 1786

Other productions include: Paris Opéra Ballet (staged Harald Lander after Galeotti, design Roger Chapelain-Midy), as *Les Caprices de Cupidon*; Paris, 27 February 1952.

PUBLICATIONS

Beaumont, Cyril, *Ballets Past and Present*, London, 1955
Kragh-Jacobsen, Svend, *The Royal Danish Ballet*, Copenhagen, 1955
Aschengreen, Erik, *Balletbogen*, Copenhagen, 1982

* * *

The Whims of Cupid and the Ballet Master by Vincenzo Galeotti is the oldest surviving ballet, with its original choreography still preserved in the Danish and international repertory. It is a humorous ballet about a series of couples coming to Cupid's temple to get married. Cupid insists that they be blindfolded and then marries them to different partners from those they arrived with. As long as each is blindfolded, everybody is in marital bliss, but as soon as blindfolds are removed, chaos breaks out and the ballet ends in the utmost confusion. The ballet consists of eight entrées, apart from Cupid's and his five helping priests, and the couples are as follows: a German, a Quaker, a Greek, a Norwegian, an elderly couple, a French, a Danish, and three Negro couples, all of whom present themselves through a dance showing their national characteristics.

The ballet has literally been handed down through the generations from dancer to dancer since its creation in 1786. It has never been out of the repertory of the Royal Danish Ballet for a long period of time; there has always been an older dancer who could show the steps to a younger one. The choreography was eventually written down by Bournonville's successor, ballet master Hans Beck, and the dancer and teacher Valborg Borchsenius at the beginning of this century. The original score is lost; only a transcript for a violin exists. But by comparing the contemporary performance with Galeotti's description of the ballet, it becomes evident that changes in the structure are only minor.

Originally the spectacle took place in Cupid's temple; now its setting is outdoors. Galeotti mentions nine different nationalities, but in the present version only eight appear. Initially the couples remained on stage when they had finished their pas de deux, to watch the successive couples, whereas now they are taken out after their dance. In old notes two boys with torches are mentioned; they are left out today. Until 1915 the finale was improvised, but today this part of the choreography has been written down as well. The whole ballet was revised by ballet master Harald Lander in the 1940s. As there are no pictures from the original ballet, it is not known what the costumes looked like, but Allan Fridericia, the Danish dance scholar, has pointed out that many in the present version are borrowed from various Bournonville ballets.

Galeotti had the idea for the ballet from a discussion with a patron of the arts, who argued that it was not possible to create a ballet consisting of many solos and pas de deux immediately following one another, and to let people remain on stage without either dancing or having any relation to the successive dance or action. He maintained that the rules of art dictated that anybody not being necessary to the action leave the stage. Although Galeotti agreed, the statement intrigued him, and he undertook successfully to prove it wrong.

In his time, Galeotti was most famous for his grand *ballets d'action*, many of which were based on popular contemporary plays and novels. He was a strong proponent of the theory that dance in ballet should follow as a natural consequence of the action and never appear in isolation. This was a reaction against the loose structure of the court ballets, in which dance was generally "divertissement". It is therefore ironic that it is this more insignificant ballet that has survived, out of the 49 ballets Galeotti created. *The Whims of Cupid and the Ballet Master* is not at all representative of the works created by the choreographer who laid down the traditions of the Royal Danish Ballet, and who during his 41 years as ballet master made ballet popular for the first time in Denmark. But the rest of his repertoire was successfully wiped out by his successor, the famous August Bournonville.

Allan Fridericia maintains that *The Whims of Cupid and the Ballet Master* actually has the same structure as the court ballet with its loosely connected entrées, and the dances alternating between the national, grotesque, and serieux. He even calls it a bourgeois court ballet, because of its chaotic ending. This ending would not occur in a court ballet but, says Fridericia, in Galeotti's ballet it reflects the values and morals of the time. Fridericia also claims that the Negro pas de six originally was not humorous but serieux. He argues that at that time foreign natives usually were not depicted as funny or entertaining, but as noble. This, however, needs to be further researched.

The ballet is still very popular, and both Danish dancers and audiences love it. This is not only because the ballet, with its exaggerated caricatures, is quite amusing, but because its authenticity makes it a charming reminder of an earlier era in the history of ballet.

—Jeannette Andersen

The Whims of Cupid and the Ballet Master: Gerda Karstens as the Quaker Lady, Royal Danish Ballet, 1954

WILDE, Patricia

Canadian/American dancer, teacher, and ballet director. Born Patricia Lorrain-Ann White in Ottawa, 16 July 1928. Studied with Gwendoline Osborne, Ontario, with Dorothy and Catherine Littlefield, and at the School of American Ballet, New York; also studied with Olga Preobrazhenska, Paris. Married George Bardyguine, 1954: two children. Dancer, American Concert Ballet, New York, 1943–44, (Marquis de Cuevas's) Ballet International, New York, 1944–45, Ballet Russe de Monte Carlo, 1945–49; guest soloist, Roland Petit's Ballets de Paris, 1949–50, and Metropolitan Ballet, England, 1949; principal dancer, New York City Ballet, New York, 1950–65; director, Harkness Ballet School, New York, 1965–67; teacher, New York City Ballet, Joffrey Scholarship Programme, American Ballet Theatre Scholarship Program, New York, 1968–69; director, Geneva Ballet School, Geneva, 1969–70; also teacher for Dance Theatre of Harlem and Metropolitan Opera Ballet, New York; ballet mistress, American Ballet Theatre, New York, 1970–77; director, American Ballet Theatre School, New York, 1977–82; artistic director, Pittsburgh Ballet Theatre, from 1982; has served as adviser, New York State Council on the Arts. Recipient: Dance Educators of America Award, 1957; Woman of the Year, Y.W.C.A. Pittsburgh, 1990.

ROLES

1945   Soloist in *Danses Concertantes* (Balanchine), Ballet Russe de Monte Carlo, New York
       Principal dancer in *Concerto Barocco* (Balanchine), Ballet Russe de Monte Carlo, New York

1945/ Dancer in *Serenade* (Balanchine), Ballet Russe de
49   Monte Carlo
        Ensemble in *Mozartiana* (Balanchine), Ballet Russe de
        Monte Carlo
        Ensemble in *Le Baiser de la fée* (Balanchine), Ballet
        Russe de Monte Carlo
        Dancer in *Seventh Symphony* (Massine), Ballet Russe de
        Monte Carlo
        Soloist in *Raymonda* (Balanchine, Danilova after Pe-
        tipa), Ballet Russe de Monte Carlo
        The Cowgirl in *Rodeo* (de Mille), Ballet Russe de Monte
        Carlo
        Pas de sept in *Le Bourgeois Gentilhomme* (Balanchine),
        Ballet Russe de Monte Carlo
        Can-Can dancer in *Gaîté Parisienne* (Massine), Ballet
        Russe de Monte Carlo
1949 Principal dancer in *Designs with Strings* (Taras),
        Metropolitan Ballet, tour
        Odette/Odile in *Swan Lake* (after Petipa, Ivanov),
        Metropolitan Ballet, tour
1950 Friend in *The Fairy's Kiss* (revival of *Le Baiser de la feé*;
        Balanchine), New York City Ballet, New York
1951 Third Waltz (cr) in *La Valse* (Balanchine), New York
        City Ballet, New York
        Freebee Leader and Wild Pony (cr) in *Cakewalk* (R.
        Boris), New York City Ballet, New York
        Pas de trois (cr) in *Swan Lake* (one-act version;
        Balanchine after Ivanov), New York City Ballet,
        New York
        Queen of Diamonds in *The Card Game* (revival of *The
        Card Party*; Balanchine), New York City Ballet, New
        York
1952 Principal dancer (cr) in *Caracole* (Balanchine), New
        York City Ballet, New York
        Principal dancer ("Scotch Lass"; cr) in *Scotch Sympho-
        ny* (Balanchine), New York City Ballet, New York
        Principal dancer (cr) in *Kaleidoscope* (R. Boris), New
        York City Ballet, New York
1953 Riches (cr) in *The Five Gifts* (Dollar), New York City
        Ballet, New York
        Principal dancer in *Valse Fantaisie* (Balanchine), New
        York City Ballet, New York
        Captain of the Amazons in *Con Amore* (L. Christensen),
        New York City Ballet, New York
1954 "First Time" (cr) in *Opus 34* (Balanchine), New York
        City Ballet, New York
        First Movement (cr) in *Quartet* (Robbins), New York
        City Ballet, New York
        Sugar Plum Fairy in *The Nutcracker* (Balanchine), New
        York City Ballet, New York
        Dewdrop Fairy in *The Nutcracker* (Balanchine), New
        York City Ballet, New York
        The Marzipan Shepherdess in *The Nutcracker* (Balan-
        chine), New York City Ballet, New York
        Scherzo (cr) in *Western Symphony* (Balanchine), New
        York City Ballet, New York
        "Hallowe'en" (cr) in *Ivesiana* (Balanchine), New York
        City Ballet, New York
1955 Principal dancer (cr) in (*Glinka*) *Pas de trois* (Balan-
        chine), New York City Ballet, New York
        Principal dancer in *Pas de dix* (Balanchine), New York
        City Ballet, New York
1956 Principal dancer in *Allegro Brillante* (Balanchine), New
        York City Ballet, New York
        Principal dancer (cr) in *Divertimento No. 15* (Balan-
        chine), New York City Ballet, Stratford, Connecticut
1957 Principal dancer (cr) in *Square Dance* (Balanchine),

New York City Ballet, New York
1958 Principal dancer (cr) in *Waltz-Scherzo* (Balanchine),
        New York City Ballet, New York
1959 Principal dancer (cr) in *Native Dancers* (Balanchine),
        New York City Ballet, New York
        Odette in *Swan Lake* (one-act version; Balanchine after
        Ivanov), New York City Ballet, New York
1960 Principal dancer (cr) in *Preludios para percussion*
        (*Colombia*; Balanchine) and *Variaciones Concertantes*
        (*Argentina*; Taras) in *Panamerica* (Balanchine, Con-
        treras, Moncion, Taras, d'Amboise), New York City
        Ballet, New York
1961 Principal dancer (cr) in *Valses et Variations* (later called
        Raymonda Variations; Balanchine), New York City
        Ballet, New York
1962 Divertissement in *A Midsummer Night's Dream* (Balan-
        chine), New York City Ballet, New York

Other roles include: Polyhymnia in *Apollo* (Balanchine),
Sanguinic in *The Four Temperaments* (Balanchine), First,
Third, and Fourth Movements in *Symphony in C* (Balanchine),
title role in *Firebird* (Balanchine), Bourrée Fantasque and Fête
Polonaise in *Bourrée Fantasque* (Balanchine), principal dancer
(Clorinda) in *The Duel* (*Le Combat*; Dollar), principal dancer in
Sylvia: Pas de deux (Balanchine), principal dancer in (*Minkus*)
Pas de trois (Balanchine), principal dancer in *Gounod Symphony*
(Balanchine), Ricercata in *Episodes* II (Balanchine), principal
dancer in *Donizetti Variations* (Balanchine), Fourth Campaign
in *Stars and Stripes* (Balanchine), principal dancer in *Modern
Jazz: Variants* (Balanchine).

WORKS

1964 *Palio—A Festival in Siena* (mus. Britten after Rossini),
        New York Philharmonic "Promenade Concert",
        New York
1965 *At the Ball* (mus. Tchaikovsky), New York Philhar-
        monic "Promenade Concert", New York
1966 *Viennese Evening* (mus. Mozart), New York Philhar-
        monic "Promenade Concert", New York
1967 *Petite Suite* (mus. Shostakovich), Alabama State Ballet

PUBLICATIONS

"Ballet Girls on Tour", *Life* (New York), 3 December 1945
Tobias, Tobi, "Patricia Wilde: A Full Life", *Dance Magazine*
    (New York), September 1971
Kirstein, Lincoln, *The New York City Ballet*, New York, 1973
Reynolds, Nancy, *Repertory in Review*, New York, 1977
Terry, Walter, *I Was There: Selected Dance Reviews and
    Articles*, New York, 1978
Anderson, Jack, *The One and Only: The Ballet Russe de Monte
    Carlo*, New York, 1981
Gruen, John, "Balanchine Remembered", *Dance Magazine*
    (New York), July 1983
Reasner, Pamela, "Satin and Steel", *Ballet News* (New York),
    October 1984
Denby, Edwin, *Dance Writings*, edited by Robert Cornfield and
    William Mackay, New York, 1986
Dacko, Karen, "Full Steam Ahead for PBT", *Dance Magazine*
    (New York), August 1986
Dacko, Karen, "Dancing on the Wilde Side", *Dance Magazine*
    (New York), August 1986
Crimboli, J., "Patricia Wilde on George Balanchine", *Tribune
    Review* (Greensburg), 12 November 1989

* * *

Patricia Wilde is most closely associated with the developmental years of the late George Balanchine's New York City Ballet. Under his tutelage, Wilde honed her talents and reached the peak of her technical powers as a ballerina. Applying the knowledge gleaned from Balanchine and from numerous other professional experiences as a dancer, she has since enjoyed international recognition as a superb ballet instructor, and in the third phase of an expansive dance career, she now channels her energies into artistic direction.

Unsurpassed in her technical virtuosity, Wilde in her prime was admired for her incomparable speed, her swift, sharp footwork and brilliant batterie, and for her superb allegro and remarkable elevation, exemplified by her performances in Balanchine's *Square Dance* and *Scotch Symphony*. Vibrant and energetic, she commanded and held the audience's attention with her authority and enthusiasm. Her secure attack, clarity, and carefully calculated precision imbued her movements with lasting visual impact. Reportedly, Wilde maintained aesthetic correctness when observed from any angle. Her innate technical comprehension and sensitivity to the surrounding space, combined with her musicality and impeccable phrasing, were the keys to her artistry.

Wilde was phenomenally strong and athletic, and was supported by a variety of New York City Ballet's danseurs, proving to be a fair competitor to, rather than a partner for, the company's male contingent. Capable of overshadowing her partner with her independent power, she excelled in exhilarating, buoyant duets, receiving accolades for the third movement of Balanchine's *Western Symphony* which she danced with André Eglevsky, and for the pas de deux in *Square Dance*, performed with Nicholas Magallanes.

Though typecast by Balanchine as a technician, with limited opportunities to explore her dramatic potential, Wilde slowly incorporated emotional depth into her performances. She was a dancer with neither temperament nor ethereality, and, overcoming a forced "ballerina" persona, she matured from a technically competent but underdeveloped *Firebird* into one of richer characterization, capable of deeply expressive moments. As Odette in Balanchine's *Swan Lake*, Wilde stretched the perimeter of her dramatic range, and gave a moving performance which was lauded for its "pensive nobility."

As a teacher and company director, Patricia Wilde has shown much of the strength and independence of spirit that characterized her dancing. Wilde, whose tenure at American Ballet Theatre as ballet mistress prepared her for a role in company leadership, made her directorial début with the Pittsburgh Ballet Theatre, as the troupe's fourth artistic director, in 1982. Although Wilde respects her New York City Ballet heritage and acknowledges some American Ballet Theatre influence, she has an independent artistic vision, and a predilection for contemporary eclecticism that is reflected in her preference for mixed repertory programming, which she feels affords the dancers greater challenges.

Wilde's most admirable policy is her eagerness to take choreographic risks on world premiere works, commissioned especially for the company from both young and established choreographers. Although these experiments have not always produced artistically significant ballets or critical successes, the works have been invented in an encouraging, creative atmosphere supplied by Wilde, who enjoys providing opportunities for choreographers.

Not a dance-maker herself, Wilde devised three programmes in the mid-1960s for the New York Philharmonic Orchestra's "Promenade Concerts", which tested her choreographic potential. Although her creative talents proved unequal to her performing prowess, her efforts produced adequate, pleasant choreography, performed innocuously by her small ensemble. Lacking inventive compulsion, Wilde shifted her focus to other artistic areas with greater success.

On par with her performing ability is her gift for teaching. Wilde's technique classes are traditional in content, logically structured with demanding but not frustrating combinations of varied and changeable intricacy. She formulates a succession of danceable exercises, which, though stressing technique, are not rigidly academic. Although she absorbed Balanchine's approach to technique, she derives her teaching style from the many instructors who contributed to her dance education. Agreeing with Balanchine's expansion of the technical vocabulary and his emphasis on speed, extension, and breadth of movement, Wilde concentrates on legs and feet, on technical purity, on unembellished, clean lines, and on correct placement and precision.

A perfectionist who realizes human limitations, Wilde draws from her innate comprehension of movement mechanics and her acquired dance skill, and can scrutinize and evaluate to provide insights into technical malfunctions, faults, and inadequacies. A born teacher, Wilde is unselfishly willing to share all of her knowledge.

Patricia's Wilde's importance to American ballet history throughout her many years as performer, teacher, and director cannot be underestimated. Working with Balanchine during the New York City Ballet's crucial and formative years, Wilde played an important role in the evolution of the Balanchine ballet and in the crystallization of the Balanchine style. Each dancer, unique to the young company, provided the prolific choreographer with different raw materials to test, reshape, and refine. Although Wilde's solid build and firm, muscular legs did not conform to those of the Balanchine body-type, and though she was not one of his primary creative instruments, she was his technical prototype. Offering Balanchine her inherent balletic gifts—speed, technical clarity, musicality, strength, and brilliance, Wilde outlined the qualities which hallmark Balanchine's distinctive style.

—Karen Dacko

WILLIAMS, E. Virginia
American teacher, choreographer, and ballet director. Born Ellen Virginia Williams in Salem, Massachusetts, 12 March 1914. Married (1) Carl Nelson: one daughter; (2) Herbert Hobbs. Studied with Geraldine Cragin, Dana Sieveling, and Miriam Winslow (of Denishawn); also studied with George Balanchine, New York. Dancer, San Carlo Opera Company; ballet teacher and founder of numerous schools, including in Melrose, Stoneham, and Malden, Massachusetts, and finally, the E. Virginia Williams School of Ballet, Boston, from 1940; founder and artistic director, New England Civic Ballet, from 1958, becoming the professional Boston Ballet, 1964: artistic director, 1964–80, co-director, with Violette Verdy, 1980–83, and artistic adviser, 1983–84; also artistic adviser, Lyric Opera of Chicago, 1971–73; choreographer, staging works for companies including Joffrey Ballet, Boston Ballet, Dayton Ballet, Pennsylvania Ballet, Opera Company of Boston, and New England Conservatory of Music. Recipient: Title of Outstanding Woman of Massachusetts from the International Woman's Year, 1975; *Dance Magazine* Award, 1976; title of Distinguished Bostonian, 1980. Died in Boston, 8 May 1984.

PUBLICATIONS

By Williams:
"What Makes a Great Teacher of Classical Ballet?", *Dance Magazine* (New York), August 1963

About Williams:
Hering, Doris, "New England Civic Ballet", *Dance Magazine* (New York), April 1960
Fanger, Iris, "The Fearsome First Ten Years: Boston Ballet", *Dance Magazine* (New York), October 1973
Tobias, Tobi, "E. Virginia Williams and the Boston Ballet", *Dance Magazine* (New York), June 1976
Fanger, Iris, "E. Virginia Williams", *Dance Magazine* (New York), July 1984

*   *   *

E. Virginia Williams was an American original, the founder and director of an American ballet company at a time when ballet in the United States was generally the province of Russian-born artists. In her own independent way, she created a ballet company that reflected her personality and her New England heritage of grit, loyalty, and a ferocious courage that overcame every obstacle.

To look at Williams—short, unprepossessing, dressed in sack-type clothing, and carrying her papers in a shopping bag—you would have supposed that a suburban housewife was out for a day's errands rather than for an 18-hour stint at the ballet studio. Her voice and mannerisms echoed her appearance—plain, down-to-earth, and sensible—yet this lady not only dreamed of creating an artistic medium for dance in her native city, but managed to make a ballet company flourish where one had never existed.

Williams was born in Salem, Massachusetts, and moved with her family to the town of Melrose when she was very young. Her family roots on her mother's side reached back to forebears who came on the ship that followed the Mayflower across the ocean. Her father traced his ancestry to Roger Williams, founder of Rhode Island.

When Virginia Williams was still a toddler, her parents took her to the vaudeville shows at the old B.F. Keith's theatre, where she remembered seeing dancers Maria Gambarelli, Theodore Koslov, Mme. Svoboda, and Irene Castle. She began ballet and "fancy dancing" lessons at age eight with Geraldine Cragin, who had performed with Harriet Hoctor, and then studied with Dana Sieveling, a product of studies with the British Cone sisters, and modern dancer Miriam Winslow. By age twelve, Williams was performing with small groups. For a proper daughter of New England, however, a professional career was out of the question. "Nice girls—ladies—did not go on the stage. It was forbidden. The subject was brought up just once. And never again," she said in a 1976 interview in *Dance Magazine*.

At age sixteen, Williams began to take over classes for her own teacher, eventually opening her first dance school in Melrose, then Stoneham and Malden, suburbs north of Boston. In 1940 she opened her first school in Boston. Among the hundreds of students she trained were Eleanor D'Antuono of American Ballet Theatre, Sarah Leland and Damien Woetzel of New York City Ballet, Joyce Cuocco of Stuttgart Ballet, and Laura Young, who became a principal dancer with the Boston Ballet.

In 1958, as an outgrowth of the elaborate end-of-year school recitals she produced annually, Williams formed the New England Civic Ballet. Five years later, on George Balanchine's recommendation, she received the first of a ten-year series of grants from the Ford Foundation to found a professional company in Boston. The company gave its first performances in the summer of 1964, followed by the official premiere in January 1965. She had able assistance from Balanchine, who gave her advice, ballets for the repertory, and guest stars to attract audiences.

Williams was a choreographer before administrative and teaching responsibilities prevented her from taking time out to make works. Among her choreographic credits were dance sequences for the Arundel Opera Company in Maine and Sarah Caldwell's Opera Company of Boston productions, a piece set to Stephen Foster's songs, two pas de deux—*Sea Alliance* and *Sospiri*—and *Patterns*, created for the Joffrey Ballet's Russian tour. She mounted *The Green Season* and *Chausson Symphony*, first on her own company and then on the fledgling Pennsylvania Ballet. She also designed and sewed many of the costumes in the early seasons before the company could afford to hire professional costume assistants.

Modern dance choreographers were invited to create works for the Boston Ballet long before the trend became popular, including Talley Beatty, Louis Falco, Pearl Lang, Anna Sokolow, Joyce Trisler, and Merce Cunningham, who set his *Summerspace* and *Winterbranch* on the company, provoking a near riot in the audience at their premieres. Williams also brought many guest artists to perform with the company— Margot Fonteyn, Carla Fracci, Natalia Makarova in her American début, Rudolf Nureyev, Edward Villella, and Violette Verdy. In 1980, Verdy became the co-director of the Boston Ballet with Williams. Verdy assumed the title of director in 1983. Williams was named "founder and artistic advisor" but continued to consider the company her own.

Williams was one of a small group of American leaders, including the Christensen brothers and Barbara Weisberger, who fostered the growth of the regional dance movement in the United States. The fact that Williams was able to establish a dance company that has sustained itself in Boston despite the city's often Puritan attitude towards dancers is testament to her Yankee ingenuity and love of dance.

The E. Virginia Williams collection of materials, including her annotated notebooks of works in the Boston Ballet repertory is held at the Harvard Theatre Collection, along with the company archives.

—Iris M. Fanger

WILSON, Sallie

American dancer, choreographer, and teacher. Born in Fort Worth, Texas, 18 April 1932. Studied with Dorothy Colter Edwards, Fort Worth, from 1945, and with Margaret Craske, Antony Tudor, and Edward Caton, New York, from 1948. Married Ali Pourfarrokh, 1960 (div.). Dancer, Ballet Theatre (later American Ballet Theatre), New York, 1949, and Metropolitan Opera Ballet, New York, 1950–55, also performing at Jacob's Pillow Dance Festival, seasons 1951, 1952, 1953; returned to Ballet Theatre, 1955, becoming soloist from 1957, first soloist from 1960, and ballerina, from 1962; also performed with New York City Ballet, 1958–60; guest ballerina, including for Jacob's Pillow Dance Festival, St. Louis Municipal Light Opera, Spoleto Festival, and Carla Fracci's Compagnia Italiano di Balletto; retired from American Ballet Theatre in 1980; guest teacher and producer of ballets, authorized to teach and revive the works of Antony Tudor from 1976, including for American Ballet Theatre (also rehearsal director), Zurich Ballet, Les Grands Ballets Canadiens, Cleveland Ballet, Paris Opéra Ballet, and Australian Ballet; has also staged works by Mikhail Fokine and Agnes de Mille, as well as the nineteenth-century classics; also choreographer, staging original works for companies including Arlington Dance Theatre, 1978, Omaha Ballet, 1981, Fort Worth Ballet, 1983, Milwaukee Ballet, 1984.

ROLES

1951 First song in *Dark Elegies* (Tudor), Resident Company, Jacob's Pillow Dance Festival, Massachusetts
Fortune-teller (cr) in *Les Mains gauches* (Tudor), Resident Company, Jacob's Pillow Dance Festival, Massachusetts
Actress (cr) in *La Ronde du printemps* (Tudor), Resident Company, Jacob's Pillow Dance Festival, Massachusetts

1952 Principal dancer in *Medusa* (D. Noble), Jacob's Pillow Dance Festival, Massachusetts

1953 Principal dancer (cr) in *A Shropshire Lad* (G. Reed), Jacob's Pillow Dance Festival, Massachusetts

1955 A Lover-in-Experience in *Pillar of Fire* (Tudor), Ballet Theatre
Rosaline in *Romeo and Juliet* (Tudor), Ballet Theatre
Lilac Fairy in *Princess Aurora* (suite of divertissements from *The Sleeping Beauty*; Dolin after Petipa), Ballet Theatre

1957 Principal dancer (cr) in *Paean* (Ross), Ballet Theatre Previews, New York
Principal dancer (cr) in *Festa* (Bruhn), Ballet Theatre Previews, New York
Kristin, the Cook in *Miss Julie* (Cullberg), American Ballet Theatre, New York

1958 Waltz, Mazurka in *Les Sylphides* (Fokine), Ballet Theatre
Myrtha in *Giselle* (Petipa after Coralli, Perrot; staged Romanoff), Ballet Theatre
Juno in *The Judgment of Paris* (Tudor), Ballet Theatre
Io and the Cloud (cr) in *Ovid Metamorphoses* (Ross), Ballet Theatre Workshop, New York

1958/ Queen in *The Cage* (Robbins), New York City Ballet,
60 New York
Third Movement in *Symphony in C* (Balanchine), New York City Ballet, New York
Third Movement in *Western Symphony* (Balanchine), New York City Ballet, New York
Third Campaign in *Stars and Stripes* (Balanchine), New York City Ballet, New York
Profane Love in *Illuminations* (Ashton), New York City Ballet, New York
The Coquette in *La Sonnambula* (Balanchine), New York City Ballet, New York
Harp in *Fanfare* (Robbins), New York City Ballet, New York

1959 Elizabeth, Queen of England (cr) in *Episodes* (Part I; Graham), New York City Ballet, New York

1960/ Boulotte in *Bluebeard* (Fokine), American Ballet
61 Theatre
Ballerina in *Theme and Variations* (Balanchine), American Ballet Theatre

1961 Other Woman (cr) in *Points on Jazz* (Krupska), American Ballet Theatre, Hartford
Young Mother in *Fall River Legend* (de Mille), American Ballet Theatre

1961/ Principal dancer in *Caprichos* (Ross), American Ballet
62 Theatre
"La Reine de la danse" from Moscow in *Gala Performance* (Tudor), American Ballet Theatre
Soloist in *Grand Pas Glazunov* (Balanchine), American Ballet Theatre
Odette in *Swan Lake*, Act II (Dolin after Ivanov), American Ballet Theatre

1962 Dancer (cr) in *The Taming* (pas de deux; Sanders), American Ballet Theatre, Madison, Wisconsin

1963 Clytemnestra (cr) in *Electra* (Martinez), American Ballet Theatre, Washington, D.C.
Lucille Grahn in *Pas de quatre* (Lester), American Ballet Theatre
Aili in *Moon Reindeer* (Cullberg), American Ballet Theatre

1964 Principal dancer (cr) in *Le Passage Enchanté* (Sequoio), Ballet Theatre Workshop, New York
Majas in *Caprichos* (Ross), American Ballet Theatre

1965 Groom's Mother (cr) in *Les Noces* (Robbins), American Ballet Theatre, New York
Principal dancer in *Sargasso* (Tetley), American Ballet Theatre, New York
The Accused in *Fall River Legend* (de Mille), American Ballet Theatre, New York
A Lady in *The Frail Quarry* (revival of *Tally-Ho!*; de Mille), American Ballet Theatre

1966 Caroline in *Jardin aux lilas* (Tudor), American Ballet Theatre
Hagar in *Pillar of Fire* (Tudor), American Ballet Theatre

1967 Principal dancer in *Concerto* (MacMillan), American Ballet Theatre

1968 Menuetto and Allegro Assai (cr) in *Gartenfest* (Smuin), American Ballet Theatre, Brooklyn, New York

1970 His Friend's Wife in *The Moor's Pavane* (Limón), American Ballet Theatre, New York
Chief Nursemaid in *Petrushka* (Romanoff, Lazovsky after Fokine), American Ballet Theatre, New York
Two Cities (cr) in *The River* (Ailey), American Ballet Theatre, New York
Principal dancer (cr) in *Times Past* (Lee), American Ballet Theatre, New York
Miss Emily in *A Rose for Miss Emily* (de Mille), American Ballet Theatre, New York

1971 Principal dancer in *Schubertiade* (Smuin), American Ballet Theatre, New York
Whore (cr) in *A Soldier's Tale* (Feld), American Ballet Theatre, Washington, D.C.

1972 Principal dancer (cr) in *Sea Change* (Ailey), American Ballet Theatre, Washington, D.C.

1973 Herodias (cr) in *La Tragedia di Salome* (Gai), (Carla Fracci's) Compagnia Italiano di Balletto, Maggio Musicale, Florence

1975 Emilia in *The Moor's Pavane* (Limón), (Carla Fracci's) Compagnia Italiano di Balletto, Milan

1976 Mrs. Stahlbaum (cr) in *The Nutcracker* (Baryshnikov), American Ballet Theatre, New York

1978 Principal dancer (cr) in *The Fiddler's Child* (Reed), Spoleto U.S.A. Festival, Charleston, Virginia

1979 Gertrude (cr) in *Hamlet* (Gai), (Carla Fracci's) Compagnia Italiano di Balletto, tour
Principal dancer (cr) in *First Solo* (Regnier), Rush Dance Company, New York
Bellaspina (cr) in *Il Principe delle Pagode* (*Prince of the Pagodas*; also chor., with Fracci and company), (Carla Fracci's) Compagnia Italiano di Balletto, Genoa

Sallie Wilson as Hagar in Tudor's *Pillar of Fire*

1988   Madame La Fourmi (cr) in *Mlle Cigale* (Gai), (Carla
        Fracci's) Compagnia Italiano di Balletto, Treviso
1989   Lady Capulet in *Romeo and Juliet* (Gai), (Carla Fracci's)
        Compagnia Italiano di Balletto, Palermo

Other roles include: as guest artist—pas de deux from *Paquita*
(after Petipa), Peasant Pas de deux from *Giselle* (after Petipa,
Coralli).

WORKS

1978   *Liederspiel* (mus. R. Schumann), Arlington Dance
        Theatre, Arlington
1979   *Fête* (mus. Ibert), Arlington Dance Theatre, Arlington
        Il Principe delle Pagode (*The Prince of the Pagodas*, with
        Carla Fracci and company; mus. Britten), Compag-
        nia Italiano di Balletto, Genoa
1981   *Chéri* (mus. Elgar), Omaha Ballet, Omaha
        Double Wedding (mus. Vaughan Williams), SUNY
        (State University of New York) Dance Corps,
        Purchase, New York
1982   *Piazza San Marco* (mus. Mahler), Poughkeepsie Ballet
        Theatre, New York
1983   *The Idol* (mus. Roussel), Fort Worth Ballet, Forth
        Worth, Texas
1984   *Argomento: In the Garden* (mus. Vaughan Williams),
        Milwaukee Ballet, Milwaukee
1986   *Idyll* (mus. Janáček), Riverside Festival, New York

Also staged:
1976   *Giselle* (after Petipa, Coralli, Perrot; mus. Adam),
        Iranian National Ballet, Tehran
        Jardin aux lilas (chor. Tudor; mus. Chausson), Zurich
        Opera Ballet, Zurich (also staged American Ballet
        Theatre, from 1978; Aterballetto, 1980; Les Grands
        Ballets Canadiens, 1980; Ballet Nacional Clasico,
        Madrid, 1983; Cleveland Ballet, 1984; Royal Swedish
        Ballet, 1985; Lyon Opéra Ballet, 1985; Paris Opéra
        Ballet, 1985; Houston Ballet, 1987; Oakland Ballet,
        1988; Boston Ballet, 1988)
1980   *Fall River Legend* (chor. de Mille; mus. Gould), Royal
        Winnipeg Ballet, Winnipeg (also staged Milwaukee
        Ballet, 1983; Dance Theatre of Harlem, 1983;
        American Ballet Theatre, 1990)
1981   *Les Sylphides* (after Fokine; mus. Chopin), Milwaukee
        Ballet, Milwaukee (also staged Houston Ballet, 1987)
1982   *Pillar of Fire* (chor. Tudor; mus. Schoenberg), Austra-
        lian Ballet, Melbourne (also staged American Ballet
        Theatre, 1987; Les Grands Ballets Canadiens, 1991;
        Star Dancers Ballet, Tokyo, 1992)
1985   *Dark Elegies* (chor. Tudor; mus. Mahler), Paris Opéra
        Ballet, Paris (also staged American Ballet Theatre,
        from 1986; Pacific Northwest Ballet, 1986; Houston
        Ballet, 1987; San Francisco Ballet, 1991)
1988   *Gala Performance* (chor. Tudor; mus. Prokofiev),
        American Ballet Theatre, Orange County, California
        (also staged Australian Ballet, 1990; Ballets de Monte
        Carlo, 1990; Norwegian Ballet, 1990; Les Grands
        Ballets Canadiens, 1992)
1992   *Undertow* (chor. Tudor; mus. W. Schumann), American
        Ballet Theatre, San Francisco

PUBLICATIONS

By Wilson:
Interview in Gruen, John, *The Private World of Ballet*, New
York, 1975

About Wilson:
Goodman, Saul, "Brief Biographies: Sallie Wilson", *Dance
Magazine* (New York), May 1961
de Mille, Agnes, *Lizzie Borden: A Dance of Death*, Boston, 1968
Gruen, John, "Close-up: Sallie Wilson", *Dance Magazine*
(New York), March 1975
Payne, Charles, *American Ballet Theatre*, New York, 1977
Wechsler, Bert, "Survivor: Sallie Wilson", *Ballet News* (New
York), April 1982
Szmyd, Linda, "Anthony Tudor: Ballet Theatre Years",
Choreography and Dance vol. 1, pt. 2, 1989

* * *

During the principal years of her tenure as artistic director
(with Oliver Smith) of American Ballet Theatre, Lucia Chase
was flanked by a quartet of ballerinas who were effective in
classically based ballets as well as in dramatic ones. They were
Alicia Alonso, Nora Kaye, Ruth Ann Koesun, and Sallie
Wilson. Remembering Wilson's dancing with the company,
one can visualize with equal clarity the powerful trajectory of
her grands jetés as Myrtha in *Giselle* or the fine-spun stream of
her bourrées in *Les Sylphides*. At the same time, one recalls her
hollow look of despair as Lizzie Borden in *Fall River Legend* or
her stalwart portrayal of the groom's mother in *Les Noces*.

Some dancers favor or are favored by one style over the
other. But for Sallie Wilson, the clarity and musicality of her

purely technical statements was absolutely equal in stature to her dance-acting. As it should, the technique came first. She was trained in her native Texas city of Fort Worth by Dorothy Colter Edwards, who, like Edith James in Dallas or Mary Ann Wells in Seattle, knew how to give her students a sound classical base and also knew when to pass them on to more advanced teachers. In Sallie Wilson's case, that teacher was Margaret Craske, the British-born exponent of Enrico Cecchetti's method.

Wilson also studied extensively with Edward Caton and more important, with Antony Tudor, who saw in her the ideal interpreter of his ballets. The linkage with Tudor was a profound one. There were times when he even formed his classes around her needs or around the next stage in her development. When she joined American Ballet Theatre in 1955 (she had previously spent a year with the company in 1949) she quickly took on the principal roles in Tudor's *Pillar of Fire*, *Jardin aux Lilas*, *Gala Performance*, and *Dark Elegies*. When Wilson left American Ballet Theatre for good in 1980, Tudor asked her to continue to set his works. Since his death, she has assumed even more of this mission.

Characterized by keen intelligence and an unflagging love for dance, Sallie Wilson has often had new roles set on her. The most challenging proved to be that of Queen Elizabeth I in Martha Graham's *Episodes*. In 1959 Graham shared the creation of the ballet with George Balanchine. She was responsible for the dramatic first portion while Balanchine created the abstract second half. At that time Wilson was performing briefly with the New York City Ballet, which had commissioned the work. Graham selected Wilson to be the antagonist to her own portrayal of Mary of Scotland. The choreographer at first set purely balletic passages for Wilson, but when she realized that Wilson had taken the trouble to master the essentials of her style, Graham revised the role. The result was a searing interpretation, especially when the two queens engaged in a grim game of shuttlecock accompanied by the ominous gongs in Anton Webern's score.

Some years after Sallie Wilson had returned to American Ballet Theatre, Alvin Ailey created *Sea Change* for her. She also portrayed Clytemnestra in Enrique Martinez's *Electra*, and Job Sanders set *The Taming* on her with John Kriza as her partner. Subsequently, Agnes de Mille sought her out for the principal role in *A Rose for Miss Emily*, and Eliot Feld selected her for *A Soldier's Tale*. Oddly, all of these works were removed from the repertory before Wilson could make a lasting impression in them. And so it was in the Tudor works, as well as in José Limón's *Moor's Pavane*, that Sallie Wilson was best known.

Despite her impeccable classical technique, Wilson never performed Giselle or Odette/Odile in *Swan Lake* with the company. Since her withdrawal from American Ballet Theatre, Sallie Wilson has also staged her own ballets on companies like the Omaha Ballet, the Milwaukee Ballet, and the Arlington Dance Theatre. She also created a version of *The Prince of the Pagodas* for Carla Fracci to perform in Genoa and Venice.

—Doris Hering

WOIZIKOWSKY, Léon

Polish dancer and choreographer. Born Leon Wójcikowski (Woidzikowsky, or Woizikovsky) in Warsaw, 20 February 1899. Studied at the Imperial Theatre School, Warsaw, pupil of Enrico Cecchetti. Dancer, Diaghilev's Ballets Russes, becoming leading character dancer, 1915–29, performing also with Léonide Massine's company, London, 1922, and Anna Pavlova's company, 1929–30; guest artist and ballet master, Ballet Club (later Ballet Rambert), London, 1930–31; guest artist, Ballet de l'Opéra Russe à Paris, 1931; principal dancer, Les Ballets Russes de Monte Carlo (becoming de Basil's Ballets Russes), 1932–34, with special success in U.S. tour, 1934; performed with Théâtre de la danse à l'Opéra, Paris, 1934; founder and director, Les Ballets de Léon Woizikowsky, performing Paris, London, and on European tour, 1935–36; principal dancer, de Basil's Ballets Russes, 1936–45, directing "second" company (originally under name of Ballets Russes de Léon Woizikowsky), Australian tour, 1936–37, and European tour, 1937–38; ballet master, Polish Opera Ballet, European tour, 1938, and New York, 1939; returned to Poland: principal dancer and ballet master, Opera Ballet School, and New Theatre, Warsaw, from 1945; returned to stage to perform with Massine's company, Ballet Europeo, Nervi, 1960; ballet master, London Festival Ballet, 1961; also choreographer, creating several works for own company, 1935, and staging other choreographers' works, including for Ballet de l'Opéra Russe à Paris, 1931, London Festival Ballet, 1958, 1960, 1961, Ballet of Cologne, and Royal Flemish Ballet; teacher, Cologne Institute for Theatre Dance, early 1960s; also served on dance faculty, Bonn University; returned again to Warsaw, 1974. Died in Warsaw, 23 February 1975.

ROLES

1916   Principal dancer (cr) in *Las Meninas* (Massine), Diaghilev's Ballets Russes, San Sebastián
1917   Dance Prelude (cr) in *Contes Russes* (Massine), Diaghilev's Ballets Russes, Paris
         Niccolo (cr) in *Les Femmes de bonne humeur* (Massine), Diaghilev's Ballets Russes, Rome
         The Manager in Evening Dress (cr) in *Parade* (Massine), Diaghilev's Ballets Russes, Paris
1919   Tarantella (cr) in *La Boutique fantasque* (Massine), Diaghilev's Ballets Russes, London
         The Corregidor (cr) in *Le Tricorne* (Massine), Diaghilev's Ballets Russes, London
1920   Tarantella (cr) in *Le Astuzie femminili* (opera-ballet; Massine), Diaghilev's Ballets Russes, Paris
         Fourbo (cr) in *Pulcinella* (Massine), Diaghilev's Ballets Russes, Paris
         Pierrot in *Papillons* (Fokine), Diaghilev's Ballets Russes
1921   Amoun in *Cléopâtre* (Fokine), Diaghilev's Ballets Russes, Lyons
         The Miller in *Le Tricorne* (Massine), Diaghilev's Ballets Russes, Madrid
         Title role in *Petrushka* (Fokine), Diaghilev's Ballets Russes
         Can-Can dancer in *La Boutique fantasque* (Massine), Diaghilev's Ballets Russes
         The Prince in *Thamar* (Fokine), Diaghilev's Ballets Russes
         Title role in *Pulcinella* (Massine), Diaghilev's Ballets Russes
         Page to Cherry Blossom Fairy, Indian Prince, Ivan (cr) in *The Sleeping Princess* (Petipa; staged Sergeyev, with additional dances Nijinska), Diaghilev's Ballets Russes, London
1922   Dancer (cr) in *The Fanatics of Pleasure* (Massine), Massine's Company at Covent Garden, London
         Dancer (cr) in *Phi-Phi* (Sokolova; uncredited), Pavilion, London

Léon Woizikowsky, with Lubov Tchernicheva and Felia Doubrovska, in *The Gods Go a-Begging*, Diaghilev's Ballets Russes, 1928

Her Husband (cr) in *The Masquerade* (Bowen), Lopokova's Company at the Coliseum, London

1923 Señor de la Cueva (cr) in "Arizona" (Massine), *You'd Be Surprised* (revue), Covent Garden, London

Villager (leading Wedding Guest; cr) in *Les Noces* (Nijinska), Diaghilev's Ballets Russes, Paris

1924 Shepherd (cr) in *Les Tentations de la bergère; ou, L'Amour vainqueur* (Nijinska), Diaghilev's Ballets Russes, Monte Carlo

Chanson dansée (An "Athlete") (cr) in *Les Biches* (Nijinska), Diaghilev's Ballets Russes, Monte Carlo

Golfer (cr) in *Le Train bleu* (Nijinska), Diaghilev's Ballets Russes, Paris

1925 Lezginka (cr) in *Le Démon* (opera; mus. Rubinstein, chor. Balanchine), Diaghilev's Ballets Russes, Monte

Carlo (also performed as part of "Suite de danses", *L'Assemblée*, Monte Carlo, 1925)

Sailor (cr) in *Les Matelots* (Massine), Diaghilev's Ballets Russes, Paris

Title role (cr) in *Barabau* (Balanchine), Diaghilev's Ballets Russes, London

1926 Régisseur (cr) in *Pastorale* (Balanchine), Diaghilev's Ballets Russes, Paris

Principal dancer (cr) in *Hamlet* (*La Fête du Printemps de Hamlet*; from the opera by Thomas; Balanchine), Diaghilev's Ballets Russes, Monte Carlo

Pierre, Servant to Capulet (cr) in *Romeo and Juliet* (Nijinska), Diaghilev's Ballets Russes, Monte Carlo

A Harlequin (cr) in *The Triumph of Neptune* (Balanchine), Diaghilev's Ballets Russes, London

1927 Dancer (cr) in *Le Pas d'acier* (Massine), Diaghilev's Ballets Russes, Paris

Mechanical Nightingale in *Le Chant du rossignol* (Massine), Diaghilev's Ballets Russes, London

1928 The Shepherd (cr) in *The Gods Go a-Begging* (Balanchine), Diaghilev's Ballets Russes, London

Favourite Slave in *Cléopâtre* (Fokine), Diaghilev's Ballets Russes, English tour

1929 Spanish entrance (cr) in *Le Bal* (Balanchine), Diaghilev's Ballets Russes, Monte Carlo

Fox (cr) in *Le Renard* (Lifar), Diaghilev's Ballets Russes, Paris

Confidant of the Prodigal Son (cr) in *Le Fils prodigue* (Balanchine), Diaghilev's Ballets Russes, Paris

1930 Friend in *Polish Wedding* (Pianowski), Anna Pavlova's Company, tour

Principal dancer in *Spanish Dance* (Nijinska), Anna Pavlova's Company, tour

The Count in *Amarilla* (Clustine), Anna Pavlova's Company, tour

A Negro in *The Fairy Doll* (Clustine after N. and S. Legat), Anna Pavlova's Company, tour

Principal dancer in *Invitation to the Dance* (Zuilich), Anna Pavlova's Company, tour

1931 Title role in *Petrushka* (also chor., after Fokine), Ballet de l'Opéra Russe à Paris, London

Officer (cr) in *Waterloo and Crimea* (Salaman), Ballet Club (Marie Rambert's Dancers, later Ballet Rambert), London

1932 Master of Ceremonies, "Le Jardin des Plaisirs", in *Cotillon* (Balanchine), Ballets Russes de Monte Carlo, Monte Carlo

Vagabond (cr) in *La Concurrence* (Balanchine), Ballets Russes de Monte Carlo, Monte Carlo

Sportsman (cr) in *Jeux d'enfants* (Massine), Ballets Russes de Monte Carlo, Monte Carlo

Jota Aragonesa, Komarinskaya (cr) in *Suites de danse* (Balanchine), Ballets Russes de Monte Carlo, Monte Carlo

1933 Fate (cr) in *Les Présages* (Massine), Ballets Russes de Monte Carlo, Monte Carlo

A Sailor (cr) in *Beach* (Massine), Ballets Russes de Monte Carlo, Monte Carlo

Rigadon (cr) in *Scuola di ballo* (Massine), Ballets Russes de Monte Carlo, Monte Carlo

Principal dancer (cr) in *Choreartium* (Massine), Ballets Russes de Monte Carlo, London

1934 Leader of the "Incroyables" in *Variations* (Nijinska), de Basil's Ballets Russes, Monte Carlo

Pedrolino in *Les Comédiens jaloux* (Nijinska), de Basil's Ballets Russes, Monte Carlo

Principal dancer in *Bolero* (Nijinska), de Basil's Ballets Russes, Monte Carlo

The Polygon (cr) in *Les Imaginaires* (Lichine), de Basil's Ballets Russes, Paris

1935 Polichinelle (cr) in *Les Deux Polichinelles* (also chor.), Les Ballets de Léon Woizikowsky, London

The Captain (cr) in *Port Saïd* (also chor.), Les Ballets de Léon Woizikowsky, European tour

The Bridegroom (cr) in *L'Amour sorcier* (also chor.), Les Ballets de Léon Woizikowsky, European tour

Black Hussar (cr) in *Valse Strauss* (also chor.), Les Ballets de Léon Woizikowsky, European tour

1938 The Bridegroom in *Country Wedding* (Zajlich), Polish Opera Ballet, tour

Kobold (cr) in *Eine Kleine Nachthmusik* (also chor.), Polish Opera Ballet, tour

1950 Till (cr) in *Till Eulenspiegel* (also chor.), Polish Opera Ballet, Warsaw

1951 Dr. Coppélius in *Coppélia* (also chor., after Petipa), Polish Opera Ballet, Warsaw

1960 Calandrino (cr) in *La Commedia umana* (Massine), Ballet Europeo, Nervi Festival, Nervi

Chief Eunuch in *Schéhérazade* (Fokine), Ballet Europeo, Nervi Festival, Nervi

Other roles include: for Diaghilev's Ballets Russes—Florestan and Harlequin in *Le Carnaval* (Fokine), Fish in *Sadko* (Bolm), Prelude and Dragon's Funeral in *Contes Russes* (Massine), Groom in *Petrushka* (Fokine), a Greek in *Narcisse* (Fokine), Chief Warrior in *Polovtsian Dances from Prince Igor* (Fokine), Bobyl and title role in *Le Soleil de nuit* (*Midnight Sun*; Massine), Warrior in *Le Chant du rossignol* (Massine), Chinese Conjurer in *Parade* (Massine), Faun in *L'Après-midi d'un faune* (Nijinsky), Dorante in *Les Fâcheux* (Massine); dances (chor. Balanchine) in operas *Turandot* (mus. Puccini), *Ivan the Terrible* (mus. Gunsbourg), *Venise* (mus. Gunsbourg), *La Gioconda* (mus. Ponchielli), *Martha* (mus. von Flotow), *The Tales of Hoffman* (mus. Offenbach), *The Prophet* (mus. Meyerbeer), *Une Nuit à Venise* (mus. Strauss), *Patrie* (mus. Paladilhe), *Manon* (mus. Massenet); for Ballet Club—Bluebird pas de deux in *Aurora's Wedding* (from *The Sleeping Beauty*; Petipa); for de Basil's Ballets Russes—principal dancer ("The Poet") in *Les Sylphides* (Fokine).

WORKS

1935 *Les Deux Polichinelles* (version of *Pulcinella*; mus. Stravinsky), Les Ballets de Léon Woizikowsky, London

Port Saïd (mus. Konstantinov), Les Ballets de Léon Woizikowsky, European tour

L'Amour sorcier (mus. de Falla), Les Ballets de Léon Woizikowsky, European tour

Valse Strauss (mus. Strauss), Les Ballets de Léon Woizikowsky, European tour

1938 *Eine Kleine Nachtmusik* (mus. Mozart), Polish Opera Ballet, tour

1939 *El Amor Brujo* (probably a new version of *L'Amour sorcier*), Polish Opera Ballet, New York

1950 *The Seasons* (mus. Tchaikovsky), Polish Opera Ballet, Warsaw

Till Eulenspiegel (mus. Strauss), Polish Opera Ballet, Warsaw

Suite Espagnol (mus. Granados), Polish Opera Ballet, Warsaw

1952 *Night on the Bald Mountain* (mus. Mussorgsky), Polish Opera Ballet, Warsaw

The Sorcerer's Apprentice (mus. Dukas), Polish Opera Ballet, Warsaw

Also staged:

1930 *Le Carnaval* (with Karsavina, after Fokine; mus. Schumann and others), Marie Rambert Dancers, London

1931 *L'Après-midi d'un faune* (with Sokolova, after Nijinsky; mus. Debussy), Ballet Club (later Ballet Rambert), London

Petrushka (after Fokine; mus. Stravinsky), Ballet de l'Opéra Russe à Paris, London (also staged for Les Ballets de Léon Woizikowsky, and for the Polish Opera Ballet)

1933 *Le Carnaval* (after Fokine; mus. Schumann and others), Ballets Russes de Monte Carlo, London

1935 *Le Spectre de la rose* (after Fokine; mus. Weber), Les Ballets de Léon Woizikowsky, European tour

Les Sylphides (after Fokine; mus. Chopin), Les Ballets de Léon Woizikowsky, European tour

Polovtsian Dances from Prince Igor (after Fokine; mus. Borodin), Les Ballets de Léon Woizikowsky, European tour (also staged for Polish Opera Ballet, and London Festival Ballet, 1951)

1951 *Swantewit* (revival; mus. Perkowski), Polish Opera Ballet, Warsaw

1951 *Coppélia* (two-act version; mus. Delibes), Polish Opera Ballet, Warsaw

1958 *Petrushka* (new production, after Fokine; mus. Stravinsky), London Festival Ballet, London

1960 *Schéhérazade* (after Fokine; mus. Rimsky-Korsakov), London Festival Ballet, London

PUBLICATIONS

Beaumont, Cyril, *The Diaghilev Ballet in London*, third edition, 1951

Grigoriev, Serge, *The Diaghilev Ballet*, translated by Vera Bowen, London 1953

Iwaszkiewicz, J., Turska, I., and Szyfmaw, A., *Leon Wójcikowski*, Warsaw, 1958

Hall, Fernau, "Men in Ballet: Leon Woizikowksy", *Ballet Today* (London), October 1958

Sokolova, Lydia, *Dancing for Diaghilev*, London, 1960

"Personality of the Month: Leon Woizikowksy", *Dance and Dancers* (London), December 1960

Gockel, Eberhard, "Leon Woizikowsky", *Ballet Today* (London), July/August 1969

Sorley Walker, Kathrine, *De Basil's Ballets Russes*, London, 1982

* * *

Léon Woizikowsky was one of the great character dancers of the twentieth century. Born and trained in Warsaw, he continued the line of popular and talented Polish male dancers (including Vaslav Nijinsky and Stanislas Idzikowski) who made their mark touring internationally. Within the scope of character and demi-caractère work he danced a wide range of parts. He could be both grotesque, as in his created role of the Corregidor in *Le Tricorne* (*The Three-Cornered Hat*), and heroic, as the Polovtsian Chief in *Prince Igor*. A compact and supple dancer of precision and vitality, he possessed an unerring sense of rhythm which stood him in good stead when he came to create the role of the leading Wedding Guest in *Les Noces*.

Woizikowsky brought a virile athleticism to many of his roles, which was appropriate when dancing as the Polovtsian Chief or leading the Three Ivans in *The Sleeping Princess*, but more questionable in his interpretation of the title role in *Petrushka*. Among his memorable creations were the sinister bat-like figure of Fate in *Les Présages* (a role that seems unfortunately comic when performed by a lesser artist), and the Vagabond who is transformed into a dandy when he acquires a new suit in *Le Concurrence*. His movement here was dictated by the idea that his new shoes were too tight for comfort.

Lydia Sokolova, Woizikowsky's partner in the late 1910s and the 1920s, has recorded that his sense of character came entirely through movement rather than acting. He was, nevertheless, a skilled mime and his creation of the waiter Niccolo in *Les Femmes de bonne humeur* (*The Good-Humoured Ladies*) allowed him to describe in clear visual terms all the dishes on the menu before he served the meal.

Niccolo was one of the first major roles Woizikowsky created for Léonide Massine, who choreographed many of the dancer's best roles. Indeed, Woizikowsky was lucky to join Diaghilev's company just as Massine was emerging as the chief choreographer; and Massine found in the Polish character dancer one of his most skilled interpreters. They frequently worked together, both within the Ballets Russes and elsewhere, and they shared a common interest in folk dance, stylization, and development of character through dance. Their collaboration lasted on and off until 1960, when Massine created a last role, Calandrino, in *La Commedia umana* (based on Boccaccio's *Decameron*) for Woizikowsky.

When Massine was dismissed from Diaghilev's Ballets Russes in 1920, Woizikowsky inherited most of his roles, including the Can-Can dancer in *La Boutique fantasque*, the Miller in *Le Tricorne*, and the title role in *Pulcinella*. In the 1920s, when Massine returned as a guest, they alternated in these roles—but in the Ballets Russes of the 1930s Woizikowsky felt badly disadvantaged, as Massine danced them at all important performances. This was ostensibly why he left to establish his own company, Les Ballets de Léon Woizikowsky.

Woizikowsky also gave impressive performances in many of Mikhail Fokine's ballets and performed a number of roles created for Nijinsky but, as with Petrushka, he gave them a personal, energetic interpretation. His Golden Slave in *Schéhérazade* seems to have introduced the twist on the head (as in break-dancing) prior to the slave's death, which became a feature of 1930s performances and which was continued by his compatriot Yurek Shabelevsky. Similarly, his interpretation of Nijinsky's Faun (as has been handed down to subsequent performers) was less lyrical than when performed by the choreographer.

Although his interpretations were individual, Woizikowsky did have a sympathetic understanding of the Ballets Russes style of production, which enabled him to stage works originally created for Diaghilev for subsequent companies. These included not only the direct successors to Diaghilev's company but also Marie Rambert's incipient Ballet Club in 1930–31, and two decades later, London Festival Ballet.

Woizikowsky had a retentive memory and his clear recall of specific roles and complete ballets kept them alive. Cyril Beaumont described Woizikowsky as "a collector of steps", as he could be found backstage practising and mastering a wide range of new movements and complete enchainements. These he subsequently used in his own productions, which drew heavily on the work of his predecessors. His *Valse Strauss* was stopped after a few performances because of its plagiarism of Massine's *Le Beau Danube*.

Although his choreography was derivative rather than original, Woizikowsky successfully led several companies—his own, the second de Basil Company, and the Polish Ballet which he took to the World's Fair in New York in 1939. He also played a significant role in keeping ballet alive in Poland during and after the Second World War as a teacher, leader of companies (which first toured and then settled in the rebuilt theatres), and choreographer. He was a generous and considerate ballet master, popular with dancers, and he appears to have been less able only when dealing with administrators and administration.

—Jane Pritchard

THE WOODEN PRINCE
(original Hungarian title: *A Fából Faragott Királyfi*; also
known as *The Woodcut Prince*)

Choreography: Ottó Zöbisch and Ede Brada
Music: Béla Bartók
Design: Miklós Bánffy (scenery and costumes)
Libretto: Béla Balász and Béla Bartók (based on an old
    Hungarian fairy tale)
First Production: Kiralyi Operahaz, Budapest, 12 May 1917
Principal Dancers: Anna Palley (The Prince), Emilia Nirschy
    Ede Brada, Boriska Hormat

Other productions include: Hungarian State Opera Ballet (new
version; chor. Jan Cieplinski, design Gusztav Olah, Zoltan
Fülop); Budapest, 1935. Hungarian State Opera Ballet (new
version; chor. Gyula Harangozó, design Olah); Budapest, 10
November 1939 (revised version, restaged Harangozó; Budapest, 18 June 1958). Hamburg Staatsoper (new version; chor.
Dore Hoyer); Hamburg, 1945. Teatro La Fenice (new version;
chor. Aurel Milloss); Venice, September 1950 (restaged as *Il
Principe di Legno*, design Felice Casorati; Milan, 1951).
Hungarian State Opera Ballet (new version; chor. Erno
Vashegyi); Budapest, 15 March 1952. Frankfurt Ballet (new
version; chor. Herbert Freund); Frankfurt-am-Main, 1 April
1956. Zurich Ballet (new version; chor. Hans Macke); Zurich,
1958. Wuppertal Ballet (new version; chor. Erich Walter);
Wuppertal, 21 January 1962. Ballet Sopianae (new version;
chor. Imre Eck); Szeged, 25 July 1965. Hungarian State Opera
Ballet (new version; chor. László Seregi, design Gabor Forray,
Tivadar Márk); Budapest, 26 September 1970. Bavarian State
Opera Ballet (new version; chor. László Seregi, design Pet
Halman); Munich, 30 December 1973. German Opera Ballet
(restaged Seregi, design Gabor Ferrai); Berlin, 20 January
1974. Wiesbaden Staatstheater (new version; chor. Clara Gora,
scenery Wolf Wanninger); Wiesbaden, 6 December 1978.
Bolshoi Ballet (new version; chor. Andrei Petrov, design
Stanislav Benediktov); Moscow, 26 March 1981. London
Festival Ballet (new version; chor. Geoffrey Cauley, design
Philip Prowse); London, 10 April 1981.

PUBLICATIONS

Sabin, R., "Béla Bartók and the Dance", *Dance Magazine*
    (New York), April 1961
Barnes, Clive, "Bartók Country", *Dance and Dancers* (London),
    October 1963
Körtvélyes, Géza, and Lörincz, György, *The Budapest Ballet* (in
    English) Budapest, 1971
Regner, Otto Friedrich, *Reclams Ballettfuhrer*, Stuttgart, 1972
"Ballets de Bartók", *L'Avant Scene: Ballet/Danse* (Paris),
    May/September 1981
Griffiths, Paul, *Bartók*, London, 1984

*   *   *

The Wooden Prince, a ballet in one act and seven scenes, was the
first of Bartók's three closely related stage works, and was
originally considered by the composer as part of a double bill
with his one-act opera *Bluebeard's Castle* (1918). There are a
number of precedents for such a coupling, most notably
Tchaikovsky's *The Nutcracker* and *Iolanta*. The two Bartók
works share a libretto by Béla Balász, characterized by a
metaphysical symbolic air in which isolation of the individual
can be read as the dominant theme. However, after the
completion of his dance "pantomime", *The Miraculous*

Mandarin (1919), Bartók is said to have wanted them linked as
a triple bill; and although production difficulties prevented this
during his lifetime, it is the context in which they are now most
frequently given in his native country, where two of the most
important productions of both ballets have been mounted.

Though *The Wooden Prince* was initially a tremendous
musical success for Bartók and was his first significant triumph
with the public, it has not since maintained widespread favour.
Bartók himself credited much of its early reception to the
conducting of Egisto Tango, rather than to the slight
choreography of Ottó Zöbisch (which has not survived). At the
time, much praise was also given to the décor of Count Banffy
and the dancing of Anna Palley (en travesti as the Prince),
Emilia Nirschy, Ede Brada, and Boriska Hormat. Diaghilev,
who was not generally well-disposed towards Bartók's music,
made plans to incorporate it in his 1923 Paris season, though
this eventually came to nothing.

Many commentators have attributed the work's subsequent
lack of popularity on stage to a superficiality, or even
emptiness, in Balász's fairy-tale scenario which, if treated
purely as a mechanism, has several difficult twists and turns to
substantiate.

The curtain rises on a fairy-tale landscape to reveal two
kingdoms, each with a castle, facing each other across the
stage. Throughout the ballet all flora and fauna are represented
by the corps de ballet. A princess is seen in the wood around one
of the castles, though she appears to be watched over by a veiled
and enigmatic fairy. A handsome prince comes out of the other
castle, sees the princess and at once falls in love with her. He
attempts to attract her attention and, failing in this, tries to
cross over to her domain to prevent her leaving. The fairy,
however, enchants the forest—causing it to come alive and
block his way. At first he breaks through and attempts to cross
the stream in front of the Princess's castle, but the stream also
comes to life and wrecks the bridge.

Increasingly frustrated, the Prince becomes despondent, but
decides to throw his cloak over a staff and waves it to gain the
princess's attention. By cutting off his golden hair and adding
his crown he finally does so, but the Princess falls in love with
this Wooden Prince instead. The fairy enchants the staff and it
comes to life, gaining access to the Princess, who at first dances
ecstatically with it. The fairy now goes to comfort the Prince
and calls forth the flowers and trees again, this time to pay him
homage and restore his hair, crown, and mantle. When the
Princess at last tires of her wooden doll she begins to find the
real Prince quite attractive, but it is now his turn to rebuff her.
Not until she cuts off all her hair and casts aside her finery does
he take her in his arms and the forest return to its original form.

Most choreographers, including Harangozó and Seregi
(whose version has been most frequently seen outside Hungary), have treated the story as a simple fable but have
encountered difficulties in sections where Bartók has over-
provided music for the pas d'action. But from his correspondence Balász seems to have regarded the story quite seriously as
a symbolic account of the life of an artist, in which the
ambiguous role of the Fairy should be seen as making the
Prince aware of how he may be loved for his art or for himself,
but not both. In this sense *The Wooden Prince* becomes,
surprisingly, a human tragedy rather than a fairy-tale with a
happy ending; and Bartók allows for this in the rather hollow
echo of the opening which he reintroduces in the closing music.

But from the changes he made himself to Balász's original
outline (as well as from the content of the following two stage
works he associated it with), it seems that Bartók's primary
interest in the story lay in its possibilities for an allegorical
treatment of sexual attraction, and the internal dynamics of
unequal relationships. Though entirely in keeping with

Bartók's Freudian preoccupations, the ballet has apparently failed to register on the public as having such a modern edge. While its fairy-tale manner may have meant that it escaped the criticisms subsequently directed at *The Miraculous Mandarin* and *Bluebeard* for their uncompromising depiction of different aspects of sexual violence, *The Wooden Prince* has yet to find a choreographer to give real voice to the delicate, Colette-like ambivalence of its inner motivations.

—Geoffrey Baskerville

WRIGHT, Peter

English dancer, choreographer, and ballet director. Born Peter Robert Wright in London, 25 November 1926. Studied with Kurt Jooss, Vera Volkova, and Peggy van Praagh. Married Sonya Hana, 1954: two children. Dancer, Ballets Jooss, 1945–47, 1951–52, Metropolitan Ballet, 1947–49, and St. James' Ballet, 1948; soloist, Sadler's Wells Theatre Ballet, 1949–51, 1952–56; assistant dance director, Edinburgh International Ballet, 1958; assistant ballet master, Sadler's Wells Theatre Ballet, 1957–59; ballet master (choreographer) and associate director, Stuttgart Ballet, 1961–63; choreographer and producer of ballets for British Broadcasting Corporation (BBC) television, 1963–65; associate to the director, and head of the New Group, Royal Ballet, from 1970; associate director, Royal Ballet, 1970–77; director, Sadler's Wells Royal Ballet, becoming the Birmingham Royal Ballet, from 1977; also governor, Royal Ballet School, from 1976, and Sadler's Wells Theatre, from 1987; special professor, School of Performance Studies, Birmingham University, from October 1990. Recipient: *Evening Standard* Award, 1981; Commander of the Order of the British Empire, 1985; John Newson Award, awarded by Friends of Sadler's Wells Theatre, 1989; Honorary Doctorate of Music, London University, 1990; Queen Elizabeth II Coronation Award, Royal Academy of Dancing, 1990; Fellow of the Birmingham Conservatoire, 1991; Digital Premier Award 1991.

ROLES

1945/   Standard Bearer in *The Green Table* (Jooss), Ballets
47   Jooss, Cambridge
         Tango in *The Big City* (Jooss), Ballets Jooss, Norwich
         Ensemble in *Prodigal Son* (Jooss), Ballets Jooss, Norwich
         Captain's Son in *Sailors Fancy* (Jooss), Ballets Jooss, Wimbledon
1948   Admirer in *Caprice Viennoise* (Littlewood), Metropolitan Ballet, Eastbourne
         Troubadour in *The Merchant's Tale* (Littlewood), Metropolitan Ballet, Eastbourne
         Benno in *Swan Lake*, Act II (after Ivanov), Metropolitan Ballet, Eastbourne
         Artist in *Pygmalian* (V. Gsovsky), Metropolitan Ballet, Eastbourne
         Czardas in *Dances of Galanta* (V. Gsovsky), Metropolitan Ballet, Eastbourne
1949   Young Brother in *The Catch* (A. Carter), St. James' Ballet
         The Lover in *School for Nightingales* (Cranko), St. James' Ballet

1950   Beast and Prince in *Beauty and the Beast* (Cranko), Sadler's Wells Theatre Ballet, London
         Duet in *Jota Toledana* (Andes), Sadler's Wells Theatre Ballet, London
         Bather and leading role in *Summer Interlude* (Somes), Sadler's Wells Theatre Ballet, Oxford
1951   Captain Belaye in *Pineapple Poll* (Cranko), Sadler's Wells Theatre Ballet, Cardiff
         Damien in *Pastorale* (Cranko), Sadler's Wells Theatre Ballet, London
         Pavane in *Capriol Suite* (Ashton), Sadler's Wells Theatre Ballet, London
1951/   Ensemble in *Weg in Nebel* (Jooss), Ballets Jooss, Essen
52   Dandy in *Columbinade* (Jooss), Ballets Jooss, Essen
1953   Bridegroom in *La Fête étrange* (Howard), Sadler's Wells Theatre Ballet, London
1954   Leonardo in *Blood Wedding* (Rodrigues), Sadler's Wells Theatre Ballet
         Captain Adoncino in *The Lady and the Fool* (Cranko), Sadler's Wells Theatre Ballet, Oxford
         Moondog in *The Lady and the Fool* (Cranko), Sadler's Wells Theatre Ballet, Oxford
         Skipper in *Sea Change* (Cranko), Sadler's Wells Theatre Ballet
1955   Pas de deux in *Les Patineurs* (Ashton), Sadler's Wells Theatre Ballet
1959   Pas de six in *Prince of the Pagodas* (Cranko), Stuttgart Ballet, Stuttgart
         Oriental Prince in *Prince of the Pagodas* (Cranko), Stuttgart Ballet, Stuttgart
1960/   Creon in *Antigone* (Cranko), Stuttgart Ballet, Stuttgart
63   Pas de deux in *Solitare* (MacMillan), Stuttgart Ballet, Stuttgart

Other roles include: for Sadler's Wells Theatre Ballet—Danse Arabe (Ashton) in *The Nutcracker* (Ashton after Ivanov), Sevillian boy and leading role in *El Destino* (Andes), principal dancer in *Valses nobles et sentimentales* (Ashton), the Bravo and the Man with a Rope in *The Rake's Progress* (de Valois); for Sadler's Wells Opera—dances in operas *The Bartered Bride* (mus. Smetana), *Eugene Onegin* (mus. Tchaikovsky), *Faust* (mus. Gounod), *Die Fledermaus* (mus. Strauss), *Don Giovanni* (Mozart).

WORKS

1957   *A Blue Rose* (mus. Barber), Royal Ballet Touring Company, London
1958   *The Great Peacock* (mus. Searle), Edinburgh International Ballet, Edinburgh
1959   *Musical Chairs* (mus. Prokofiev), Western Theatre Ballet
1961   *A Ballet to this Music* (mus. Haydn), Western Theatre Ballet
1962   *The Mirror Walkers* (mus. Tchaikovsky), Stuttgart Ballet, Stuttgart
         Quintet (mus. Satie), Stuttgart Ballet, Stuttgart
1963   *Designs for Dancers* (mus. Bartók), Stuttgart Ballet, Stuttgart
         Namouna (mus. Lalo), Stuttgart Ballet, Stuttgart
1964   *Summer's Night* (mus. Poulenc), Royal Ballet Touring Company, Oxford
1965   *Concerto* (mus. Haydn), Bat-Dor Company, Israel
         Corporal Jan (mus. ApIvor), British television
         Peter and the Wolf (mus. Prokofiev), British television

Peter Wright rehearsing *Swan Lake*, **1981**

1968   *Danse Macabre* (mus. McCabe), Western Theatre
         Ballet, London
1974   *Arpège* (mus. Boildieu), Royal Ballet Touring Company,
         London
1975   *El Amor Brujo* (mus. de Falla), Royal Ballet Touring
         Company, Edinburgh
1976   *Summertide* (mus. Mendelssohn), Royal Ballet Touring
         Company, London

Also staged:
1965   *Giselle* (after Petipa, Coralli, Perrot; mus. Adam),
         Stuttgart Ballet, Stuttgart (also staged Cologne Ballet,
         1967; Royal Ballet Touring Company, 1968; National
         Ballet of Canada, 1970; Royal Ballet, 1971; Munich,
         1974; Dutch National Ballet, 1977; Frankfurt Ballet,
         1980; Royal Winnipeg Ballet, 1982; Rio de Janeiro,
         1982; Houston Ballet, 1985; Star Dancers Ballet,
         Japan, 1989)
1968   *The Sleeping Beauty* (after Petipa; mus. Tchaikovsky),
         Cologne (staged Royal Ballet, 1968; Munich State
         Opera Ballet, 1974; Dutch National Ballet, 1977;
         Sadler's Wells Royal Ballet, 1984)
1976   *Coppélia* (after Petipa, Cecchetti; mus. Delibes), Sad-

         ler's Wells Royal Ballet, London (also staged Scottish
         Ballet, 1992)
1981   *Swan Lake* (after Petipa, Ivanov; mus. Tchaikovsky),
         Sadler's Wells Royal Ballet, Manchester (also staged
         Bavarian State Opera Ballet, Munich, 1983)
1987   *Giselle* (new production; after Petipa, Coralli, Perrot;
         mus. Adam), Royal Ballet, London

PUBLICATIONS

By Wright:
"*Quintet* and *Summer's Night*: Peter Wright Talks about his
   Ballets", *About the House* (London), Christmas 1964
Interview in Newman, Barbara, "Speaking of Dance: Peter
   Wright CBE", *Dancing Times* (London), March 1986
Interview in Meisner, Nadine, "No Strings", *Dance and
   Dancers* (London), November 1990

About Wright:
Crisp, Clement, "Peter Wright", *About the House* (London),
   Christmas 1970

Thorpe, Edward, *"Peter Wright"*, *Dance Gazette* (London), March 1985

Crisp, Clement, *"Royal and Ready"*, *Ballet News* (New York), February 1986

Woodcock, Sarah, *The Sadler's Wells Royal Ballet*, London, 1991

*   *   *

Peter Wright is one of the most distinguished figures in British ballet today. His main achievement is his work as director of the Birmingham Royal Ballet (until 1990 the Sadler's Wells Royal Ballet), but he also has a notable record as dancer, teacher, choreographer (for revue and musical as well as the ballet stage), producer, television director, and, by no means least, as organizer of some of the most memorable gala programmes. Peter Wright is a man of many talents, much respected and much loved.

Wright trained as a dancer with Kurt Jooss, Vera Volkova, and Peggy van Praagh; and he danced successively with Ballets Jooss, Metropolitan Ballet, and St. James Ballet. He joined Sadler's Wells Theatre Ballet, returned to Ballets Jooss, and then rejoined SWTB, of which he became assistant ballet master. As a dancer his repertoire included leading roles in works by John Cranko, including Captain Belaye in *Pineapple Poll*, the Beast in *Beauty and the Beast*, and Moondog in *The Lady and the Fool*. Wright taught at the Royal Ballet School and was assistant dance director for van Praagh's short-lived Edinburgh International Ballet.

Wright had already made his first choreography—for SWTB, Edinburgh International Ballet, and Western Theatre Ballet—when, after a spell as ballet master to the Sadler's Wells Opera, he became ballet master and associate director with the Stuttgart Ballet, where John Cranko had recently been appointed director. Wright's choreography for the Stuttgart company included *The Mirror Walkers* and the two-act *Namouna* to Lalo's beautiful score. For five years Wright was joint proprietor with David Hepburn of the Wright Hepburn Gallery, the first in London to be devoted to theatre design.

Wright next joined the BBC as ballet master for its televised ballet productions, which included three works by Cranko as well as two of his own devising. What distinguished Wright's television productions was his careful use of the camera to reveal and enhance the choreography; in Clement Crisp's words, there were "none of those zooming close-ups of a ballerina in mid-fouetté, no changes of camera-angle to madden us in the middle of an enchaînement".

Wright's administrative career with the Royal Ballet began when he was appointed associate director. Seven years later he became director of its touring company, which had taken the name Sadler's Wells Royal Ballet in 1976. He had continued to choreograph—his lyrical *Summertide* received considerable praise—but soon Wright was making a reputation for himself as a producer of the classics. *Giselle* for the Stuttgart Ballet was his first major success (subsequently reproduced for both Royal Ballet companies as well as companies in Europe and North and South America). He has also produced *The Sleeping Beauty* (for both Royal Ballet companies and three in Europe), *Coppélia*, *Swan Lake*, and *The Nutcracker* (for both Royal companies).

What characterizes Wright's productions of the classics is an unmusty respect for period combined with a vivid sense of theatrical momentum; and something of the same feel for tradition allied with a care for individual talents makes him an excellent director and administrator. He gave the second Royal company the clear identity it needed in the mid-1970s; and he has since spotted and brought out the qualities of numerous dancers, and allowed young choreographers to experiment and develop (David Bintley is a notable case in point). Wright's sense of the Royal Ballet's rich inheritance has ensured that, for example, the Ashton repertory is better maintained by his company on tour than it is by the resident company at the Royal Opera House. Wright is a showman of genius and his programming is always inventive and rewarding, for both dancers and audiences alike. His CBE for services to ballet was unquestionably well deserved.

—Martin Wright

YAKOBSON, Leonid

Russian/Soviet dancer, choreographer, and ballet director. Born Leonid Veniaminovich Yakobson in St. Petersburg, 15 January (2 January old style) 1904. Studied privately with Aleksandr Chekrygin, then at the Petrograd, later Leningrad Choreographic School, first in the evening courses and then in the regular school, pupil of Vladimir Ponomarev, and Vladimir Semenov; graduated in 1926. Married dancer Irina Pevsner: one son, Nikolai (Nicholas), b. 1953. Dancer, specializing in character and grotesque roles, State Academic Theatre for Opera and Ballet (GATOB, later the Kirov), Leningrad, 1926–33, and later, 1942–50, 1956–70; first choreography while still a student, creating concert pieces before 1926; collaborator in first production of *The Golden Age*, 1930; choreographer and dancer, Bolshoi Ballet, Moscow, 1933–42, and Kirov Ballet, Leningrad, 1942–69; also choreographer for the Isadora Duncan Studio, Moscow, 1948; founder, choreographer, and director, Choreographic Miniatures Company, Leningrad, from 1970, touring at times as the Yakobson Ballet, and becoming the State Ballet of Leningrad after Yakobson's death. Recipient: State Prize of the USSR (for *Ali-Batyr*), 1951; title of Honoured Arts Worker of the Russian Federation, 1957. Died in Moscow, 17 October 1975.

WORKS

1930 *The Golden Age* (with Vainonen, Kaplan, Chesnakov; mus. Shostakovich), State Academic Theatre for Opera and Ballet (GATOB, later the Kirov), Leningrad

1932 *Chavdarcho* (*The Young Pioneers*; musical pantomime), Leningrad Choreographic School, Leningrad

1933 *Till Eulenspiegel* (dance pantomime; mus. Strauss), Leningrad Choreographic School, Leningrad

1936 *Lost Illusions* (mus. Asafiev), Sverdlovsk Theatre for Opera and Ballet, Sverdlovsk

1941 *Shurale* (mus. Yarullin), Kazan Theatre for Opera and Ballet, Kazan (never performed)

1944 *Romeo and Juliet* (mus. Tchaikovsky), Leningrad Choreographic School, Leningrad

Spanish Capriccio (mus. Rimsky-Korsakov), Leningrad Choreographic School, Leningrad (staged Maly Theatre for Opera and Ballet, Leningrad, 1952)

1946 *The Stone Guest* (mus. Glinka, Asafiev), Leningrad Choreographic School, Leningrad

Dances in *The Orleans Virgin* (opera; mus. Tchaikovsky), Kirov Theatre, Leningrad

Dances in *In Winter Night*, (opera; mus. J. Dzerzhinsky), Leningrad Musical Comedy Theatre, Leningrad

1947 *The Dragon Fly* (mus. Efinova), Leningrad Choreographic School, Leningrad

1950 *Ali-Batyr* (later *Shurale*; mus. Yarullin), Kirov Ballet, Leningrad

1951 Dances in *The Noise of the Mediterranean* (opera; mus. Feltsman), Leningrad Musical Comedy Theatre, Leningrad

1952 *Solveig* (mus. Grieg, Asafiev), Maly Theatre for Opera and Ballet, Leningrad

1955 *Shurale* (new version of *Ali-Batyr*; mus. Yarullin), Bolshoi Ballet, Moscow

1956 *Spartacus* (mus. Khachaturian), Kirov Ballet, Leningrad

1962 *The Bedbug* (mus. Otkazov, Firtich), Kirov Ballet, Leningrad

Spartacus (new version; mus. Khachaturian), Bolshoi Ballet, Moscow

1963 *Love Novellas* (mus. Ravel), Kirov Ballet, Leningrad

1964 *The Twelve* (mus. Tishchenko), Kirov Ballet, Leningrad

1967 *The Land of Miracles* (mus. Shvarts), Kirov Ballet, Leningrad

Miniatures:

1925 *Waltz* (mus. Chopin), Leningrad Choreographic School, Leningrad

I Love You (mus. Grieg), Leningrad Choreographic School, Leningrad

1926 *Pupsiki* (mus. Drigo), Leningrad Choreographic School, Leningrad

Fantasy (mus. Chopin), Leningrad Choreographic School, Leningrad

Norwegian Dance (mus. Grieg), Leningrad Choreographic School, Leningrad

Turkish March (mus. Beethoven), Leningrad Choreographic School, Leningrad

They About Us (no music), Leningrad Choreographic School, Leningrad

1927 *Sport Étude* (mus. Grieg), Leningrad Choreographic School, Leningrad

Sports March (mus. Lobachyov), Leningrad Choreographic School, Leningrad

Butterfly (mus. Grieg), Leningrad Choreographic School, Leningrad

1928 *Waltz* (mus. Ilya Satz), Leningrad Choreographic School, Leningrad

Brazilian Dances (mus. Miyo), Kirov Ballet, Leningrad

1929 *Spring* (mus. Grieg), Leningrad Choreographic School, Leningrad

Waltz (mus. Liszt), Leningrad Choreographic School, Leningrad

1930   *Waltz* (mus. Moskovsky), Leningrad Choreographic
School, Leningrad

Impromptu (mus. Arensky), Leningrad Choreographic
School, Leningrad

1931   *The Sea Suite* (mus. folk melodies), The Kronstadt Fleet
Folk Ensemble, Experimental Studio of the House of
Arts, Leningrad

Skriabiniana (mus. Skriabin), Experimental Studio of
the House of Arts, Leningrad

Adagio (mus. Grieg), Leningrad Choreographic School,
Leningrad

Oriental Dance (mus. Shvarts), Leningrad Choreographic School, Leningrad

Prelude (mus. Arensky), Leningrad Choreographic
School, Leningrad

Physical Exercise (mus. Shostakovich), Leningrad
Choreographic School, Leningrad

May March (mus. Voloskinov), Leningrad Choreographic School, Leningrad

Chaplin (mus. Gerbert), Leningrad Choreographic
School, Leningrad

1932   *Disarmament Conference* (mus. Glinka), Leningrad
Choreographic School, Leningrad

1934   *Waltz* (mus. Strauss), Moscow Choreographic School,
Moscow

The First Polka (mus. Glinka), Moscow Choreographic
School, Moscow

1936   *The Cock, the Hen, and the Chicken* (mus. Mussorgsky),
Sverdlovsk Choreographic School, Sverdlovsk

Eight Girls and Me Alone (mus. Dargonmyzhsky),
Sverdlovsk Choreographic School, Sverdlovsk

Kittens (mus. Tchaikovsky), Sverdlovsk Choreographic
School, Sverdlovsk

Three Bears (mus. Shostakovich), Sverdlovsk Choreographic School, Sverdlovsk

Three Little Pigs, Sverdlovsk Choreographic School,
Sverdlovsk

Russian Dolls (mus. Kaksella), Sverdlovsk Choreographic School, Sverdlovsk

Max and Moritz, Sverdlovsk Choreographic School,
Sverdlovsk

Russian Dance (mus. Pugni), Sverdlovsk Choreographic
School, Sverdlovsk

Skipping Rope (mus. Kazella), Sverdlovsk Choreographic School, Sverdlovsk

Quartet (mus. Strauss), Sverdlovsk Choreographic
School, Sverdlovsk

Soviet Toys, Sverdlovsk Choreographic School,
Sverdlovsk

Pioneers' March, Sverdlovsk Choreographic School,
Sverdlovsk

Jota, Moscow Choreographic School, Moscow

1938   *Russian Pioneer's Dance* (mus. folk melodies), Moscow
Choreographic School, Moscow

Waltz (mus. Ravel), Moscow Choreographic School,
Moscow

Waltz (mus. Debussy), Moscow Choreographic School,
Moscow

Impromptu: The Nymph and the Two .... (mus.
Tchaikovsky), Moscow Choreographic School,
Moscow

Meditations (mus. Tchaikovsky), Moscow Choreographic School, Moscow

Dream (mus. Grieg), Moscow Choreographic School,
Moscow

Tsar-Frog (mus. Hall), Moscow Music Hall, Moscow

1939   *Russian Folk Games and Dances, Nanai Games* (mus. folk

melodies) Moscow Choreographic School, Moscow

Yurochka (mus. folk music), Moscow Choreographic
School, Moscow

Two Naughty Boys, Moscow Choreographic School,
Moscow

Foreigner, Moscow Choreographic School, Moscow

Baba-Yaga, Monument, Artek Theatre, Artek

1940   *Gypsies* (mus. Rachmaninov), Bolshoi Ballet, Moscow

The Bird and the Hunter (mus. Grieg), Moscow
Choreographic School, Moscow

Fantasia (mus. Taneyev), Bolshoi Ballet, Moscow

Turkmen Djigites Dances (mus. folk melodies), Ashkhabad Theatre, Ashkabad

Ak-Shikly (mus. folk melodies), Ashkhabad Theatre,
Ashkabad

1941   The Concert of Political Cartoons:

Twins (mus. Masolov), *Back and Forth* (mus. Petunin),
World Class Football Players (mus. Enke), *Friendship
Hitler Style* (mus. Enke), *Four G* (mus. Petunin), *Two
Napoleons*, Bolshoi Ballet, Moscow

Clown Dances, Moscow Choreographic School, Moscow

Seven Cavaliers Serenade (mus. Enke), Bolshoi Ballet,
Moscow

The Blind Girl (mus. Pons-Heifitz), Bolshoi Ballet,
Moscow

Spanish Dance (mus. Albeniz), Bolshoi Ballet, Moscow

Navarra (mus. Albeniz), Bolshoi Ballet, Moscow

1942   *Waltz* (mus. Strauss), Kirov Ballet, Leningrad

Creole Dance (mus. Granados), Kirov Ballet, Leningrad

Choreographic Étude (mus. Ravel), Kirov Ballet,
Leningrad

1943   *Devil's Dance* (mus. Yarullin), Kirov Ballet, Leningrad

Poem of Ecstasy (mus. Skriabin), Kirov Ballet,
Leningrad

Barkarolla, Kirov Ballet, Leningrad

Russian Folk Dance, Leningrad Choreographic School,
Leningrad

1944   *Hungarian Gypsy Dance* (mus. Brahms), Kirov Ballet,
Leningrad

1945   *Waltz* (mus. Strauss), Kirov Ballet, Leningrad

1946   *Little Spanish Boys*, Leningrad Choreographic School,
Leningrad

Antigue Legend (mus. Liszt), Bolshoi Ballet, Moscow

1947   *Pulcinella* (mus. Rachmaninov), Kirov Ballet,
Leningrad

Sentimental Waltz (mus. Tchaikovsky), Kirov Ballet,
Leningrad

A Shoe (mus. Paderevsky), Bolshoi Ballet, Moscow

1948   *Waltz* (mus. Tchaikovsky), Moscow Choreographic
School, Moscow

Sports Suite, Moscow Choreographic School, Moscow

Heroic Deed (mus. Chopin), Isadora Duncan Studio,
Moscow

Diamond Waltz (mus. Chopin), Isadora Duncan Studio,
Moscow

Étude (mus. Skriabin), Isadora Duncan Studio, Moscow

Horumy (mus. folk music), Leningrad Choregraphic
School, Leningrad

1949   *Polonaise and Mazurka*, Labour Reserve, Leningrad

Youth (mus. Tchaikovsky), Leningrad Choreographic
School, Leningrad

Mazurka (mus. Chopin), Moscow Choreographic
School, Moscow

Joke (mus. Tchaikovsky), Moscow Choreographic
School, Moscow

The Gossips (mus. Aranov), Kishinyov Dance Ensemble

Jewish Dance (mus. folk music), Kishinyov Dance

Ensemble
Wedding Dance (mus. folk music) Kishinyov Dance Ensemble

1950 *Two Spanish Girls* (mus. Ravel), Kirov Ballet, Leningrad
Bacchanalia (mus. Liszt), Leningrad Concert Organization, Leningrad
Youth Suite (mus. Tchaikovsky), Labour Reserve, Leningrad

1951 *Dream* (mus. Liszt), Leningrad Choreographic School, Leningrad
Czardas (mus. Brahms), Leningrad Choreographic School, Leningrad
Krakoviak (mus. Polish folk music), Leningrad Choreographic School, Leningrad

1953 *Sports Suite* (mus. Petrov), Leningrad Choreographic School, Leningrad
Alborada (mus. Ravel), Kirov Ballet, Leningrad
Mexican Dance, Leningrad Concert Organization, Leningrad
Russian Dance Suite, Labour Reserve, Leningrad

1954 *Vienna Waltz* (mus. Strauss), Kirov Ballet, Leningrad
1955 *Vagrant* (mus. Debussy), Kirov Ballet, Leningrad
1957 *Riksha* (no music), Kirov Ballet, Leningrad
The Dying Gaul (no music), Kirov Ballet, Leningrad
Two Comrades (mus. Sitovich), Kirov Ballet, Leningrad

1958 *Acrobatic Étude*, Leningrad Concert Organization, Leningrad
Programme of Choreographic Miniatures including: *The Bird and the Hunter* (1940; mus. Grieg), *Meditations* (1938; mus. Tchaikovsky), *The Blind Girl* (1941; mus. Pons-Heifitz), *The Gossips* (1949; mus. Aranov), *Vienna Waltz* (1954; mus. Strauss), *Last Song* (mus. Ravel), *Skaters* (mus. Kravchenko), *Troika* (mus. Stravinsky), *Encounter* (mus. Kravchenko), *Stronger than Death* (mus. Shvarto), *Prometheus* (mus. Tsitovich), *Mother* (mus. Skriabin), *Polishenel* (mus. Rachmaninov), *Toad Eater* (mus. Tsitovich), *Snow Maiden* (mus. Prokofiev), *The Lovers* (mus. Kagan), *Rodin Triptich* (mus. Debussy)—*Eternal Spring, The Kiss, Eternal Idol*, Kirov Ballet, Leningrad

1959 *The Absent Lover* (mus. Shostakovich), Kirov Ballet, Leningrad
Vagabonds (mus. Karavagchuck), Kirov Ballet, Leningrad

1960 *The Flying Vaults* (mus. Shostakovich), Kirov Ballet, Leningrad

1963 *Waltzes* (mus. Ravel), Kirov Ballet, Leningrad
1964 *Choreographic Picture on the Motives of the Bidstroop Cartoon* (mus. Bakervich), Leningrad Choreographic School, Leningrad
Firebird (mus. Stravinsky), Leningrad Concert Organization, Leningrad
Jester and Merchant (mus. Prokofiev), *Minotaur* (mus. Slonimsky), *Despair* (mus. Prokofiev), Kirov Ballet, Leningrad

1965 *Baba-Yaga* (mus. Mussorgsky), *The Carters' Dance* (mus. Shostakovich), *Naughty Women* (mus. Schedrin), Kirov Ballet, Leningrad

1967 *The Passing Beauty* (mus. Slonimsky), Kirov Ballet, Leningrad
Confessing Magdalene (mus. Knayfel), Kirov Ballet, Leningrad

1969 *Vestris* (solo, created for Baryshnikov; mus. Banschikov), International Ballet Competition, Moscow

1970/ *Ebony Concerto* (mus. Stravinsky), *Travelling Circus*
71 (mus. Stravinsky), *Jewish Wedding* (mus. Shostakovich), *Rodin Sculptures, Despair, Paolo and Francesca*

(mus. Berg), *Crumpled Lily, Minotaur and Nymph* (mus. Berg), *Classicism-Romanticism, Pas de trois* (mus. Rossini), *Medieval Dance with Kisses* (mus. Prokofiev), *Pas de quatre* (mus. Bellini), *Cachucha* (mus. Sarasate), *Pas de deux* (mus. Mozart), *Taglioni's Flight* (mus. Mozart), Choreographic Miniatures Company, Leningrad

1972 *The City, Symphony of Eternity, Exercise XX, The Swan, Brilliant Divertissement*, Choreographic Miniatures Company, Leningrad

1973 *Mozartiana, Pas de deux* (mus. Donizetti, Rossini, Legar, Chopin, Britten, and others), Choreographic Miniatures Company, Leningrad

1974 *The Bedbug* (mus. Shostakovich), Choreographic Miniatures Company, Leningrad

1975 *The Cowboys* (mus. Kogan), Kirov Ballet, Leningrad

PUBLICATIONS

By Yakobson:
"The New Ballet Association", *Zhizn Iskusstva* (Moscow), no. 43, 1928
"For a New Generation in Choreography", *Rabochy i Teatr* (Leningrad), no. 39, 1929
"The Roads of Soviet Choreography", *Rabochy i Teatr* (Leningrad), no. 26, 1931
"The Secret of the Artist's Power", in *Marius Petipa: Documents, Reminiscences, Articles*, Leningrad, 1971
"Leonid Yakobson: 'My Work with *Shurale*'", *Sovetskaya Muzyka* (Moscow), 2 parts: no. 9, 1989; no. 6, 1991

About Yakobson:
Leonid Yakobson (collection of essays), Leningrad and Moscow, 1965
Lopukhov, Fedor, *Sixty Years in Ballet*, Moscow, 1966
Roslavleva, Natalia, *Era of the Russian Ballet*, London, 1966
Krasovskaya, Vera, *Essays on Ballet*, Leningrad, 1967
Swift, Mary Grace, *The Art of Dance in the USSR*, Notre Dame, Indiana, 1968
Dobrovolskaya, G., *Choreographer Leonid Yakobson*, Leningrad, 1968
France, Charles, (ed.), *Baryshnikov at Work*, New York, 1976
Demidov, Alexander, *The Russian Ballet Past and Present*, translated by Guy Daniels, London, 1978
Makarova, Natalia, *A Dance Autobiography*, New York, 1979
Ross, Janice, "A Survivor's Story", *Dance Magazine* (New York), April 1988
Koegler, Horst, "Guests from Leningrad: Leonid Jakobson and his 'Choreographic Miniatures'", *Ballett International* (Cologne), December 1989

*   *   *

Leonid Veniaminovich Yakobson is best known as the leading iconoclastic Soviet choreographer of the twentieth century, although he was also an accomplished character dancer and ballet master. His 130 ballets, while enjoying popular success, angered Soviet cultural authorities, who disliked Yakobson's refusal to create works in the officially sanctioned "Socialist Realist" style of contemporary Russian ballet.

A Jew as well as an innovator, Yakobson was a persistent thorn in the side of Soviet authorities, who objected to his stylistic innovations and his use of music and designs by such artists as Claude Debussy, Alban Berg, Auguste Rodin, and Marc Chagall. Over the 50 years of his creative life, beginning with his first major work, *The Golden Age*, choreographed for the Kirov Ballet in 1930, Yakobson never relinquished his quest for artistic and creative freedom, despite frequent censure by the authorities. *The Golden Age* inaugurated not only Yakobson's career as an artistic rebel but also his lifelong friendship with the man who was to become his companion in artistic exile, the composer of *The Golden Age*, Dmitri Shostakovich. One of the most talked-about inventions of *The Golden Age* was a difficult and almost acrobatic pas de cinq for Galina Ulanova and four cavaliers, an experimentation with classical form that was to become a trademark of Yakobson's work.

Throughout his career Yakobson was to stretch the dynamic and dramatic range of many leading Russian dancers in the Kirov and Bolshoi Ballets. His solo, *Vestris*, was the specially tailored vehicle with which Mikhail Baryshnikov won the International Ballet Competition in Moscow in 1969. A series of taxing mime and virtuoso dance vignettes, *Vestris* reveals the dancer as much as the character of August Vestris, the eighteenth-century danseur who is the ballet's subject. Another young Kirov dancer, Natalia Makarova, was singled out by Yakobson to dance the lead in his *The Bedbug* (1962), a satire of Soviet life during the new economic policy introduced by Lenin, as depicted in a play by Vladimir Mayakovsky. Makarova credits her work with Yakobson as having initiated her understanding of dramatic portrayals in dance.

Yakobson, who was orphaned as a young boy, came to dance at the comparatively late age of sixteen, when he entered a special evening course for "older" dancers at the Petrograd Ballet, or Choreographic, School (later the Leningrad Choreographic School). By 1925, his second year, Yakobson had progressed so rapidly that his teacher Aleksandr Chekrygin arranged for him to be transferred to day-time classes. He graduated the following year with another talented classmate, George Balanchine. Upon graduation, Yakobson immediately joined the State Theatre of Opera and Ballet, which became the Kirov in 1935. Although from the start Yakobson was acclaimed as a "grotesque" and character dancer, he was always more interested in choreographing than in performing.

Rather than full-evening works, Yakobson's principal métier was short ballets, or "choreographic miniatures", the name he later gave to a suite of dances as well as to the company he finally secured in 1970, after a twenty-year battle trying to gain permission from the authorities. At various points in his career Yakobson was forbidden to leave Leningrad, his work censored or banned, and his name not permitted to appear in newspapers; and for six years he was forbidden to work at all. Yet he persisted in making works as diverse as the neo-classically cool and plotless *Exercise XX*, to the Robbinsesque portrait of "schtel" life based on a Marc Chagall painting, *The Jewish Wedding*.

A cornerstone of Yakobson's approach to choreography was his belief that every piece of music inspired a distinctive manner of moving, and that the classical ballet vocabulary was a start, not an end point, in fashioning movement that expressed the sentiment the choreographer wanted. A restless and imaginative thinker, Yakobson worked as choreographer of the Bolshoi Ballet during the 1930s, and for the Kirov Ballet from 1942. In the 1940s Yakobson's interest in pushing beyond the boundaries of classical technique led him to choreograph several dances for the Isadora Duncan Studio in Moscow. His 1956 work for the Kirov, *Spartacus*, the first production of Aram Khachaturian's score, rejected both classical dance and a strictly developed plot, treating the dance instead like an enormous canvas come to life. Yakobson's *Spartacus* used deliberately turned-in positions, eliminating pointe work in favor of naturalistic poses drawn from antique bas-reliefs.

The Russian classical ballet world was unprepared for the radical and relentless nature of Yakobson's departure from these cardinal rules of ballet. Two years later, in 1958, Yakobson created the miniature *Rodin*, begun as a triptych to music by Claude Debussy and inspired by Rodin sculptures Yakobson had seen hidden away in a room at the Hermitage Museum. The *Rodin Triptych* was extended in 1970, with two more sections set to music by Alban Berg. Emblematic of Yakobson's re-thinking of the classical vocabulary, *Rodin* eliminated pointe shoes, used parallel rather than turned-out positions, and conveyed the sense that every movement started from an impulse in the torso that radiated out to the limbs.

After Yakobson's death in 1975, at the age of 71, the Choreographic Miniatures company he had fought all his life to obtain passed to one of his former dancers, Askold Markarov, who later renamed it The State Ballet of Leningrad. In 1982, Yakobson's widow, the former Kirov dancer Irina Pevsner, emigrated with their son Nicholas to San Francisco. Here, as a master teacher for San Francisco Ballet, she oversaw the company's 1990 premiere of *Rodin*, the first Yakobson ballet to feature in the repertoire of an American company.

—Janice Ross

YAROSLAVNA

Choreography: Oleg Vinogradov
Music: Boris Tishchenko
Design: Oleg Vinogradov (scenery and costumes), Yuri Lyubimov (scenic adviser)
Libretto: Oleg Vinogradov (after twelfth-century epic, *The Lay of Igor's Campaign*)
First Production: Maly Theatre Ballet, Leningrad, 30 June 1974
Principal Dancers: Nikita Dolgushin (Igor), Tatyana Fesenko (Yaroslavna)

PUBLICATIONS

Karp, Poel, "Flaming Arrows Fly", *Smena* (Leningrad), 1 November 1974
Melkumyan, M., "Yaroslavna", *Teatr* (Moscow), no. 8, 1979
Degen, Arsen, *The Leningrad Maly Ballet Company*, Leningrad, 1979

* * *

Oleg Vinogradov's choreographic reflections in three acts on motifs from *The Lay of Igor's Campaign* were based on music composed by Boris Tishchenko, with libretto and design also by Vinogradov. The director was Yuri Lyubimov. The premiere took place at the Maly Theatre on 30 June 1974, with Nikita Dolgushin as Igor, and Tatyana Fesenko as Yaroslavna.

The foundation of the ballet is *The Lay of Igor's Campaign*, the ancient twelfth-century Russian literary manuscript. The nameless author was describing a real historical event: the campaign of the Novgorod-Sever prince, Igor, against the Polovtsians, who at the time were attacking Russian princedoms in an attempt to conquer Russian lands. In spite of wise Prince Svyatoslav's warning not to go alone against the Polovtsians, and to unite instead with the other princes, Igor led his army against the Polovtsians and was vanquished, and the Polovtsians penetrated the Russian land even further. The most important episodes of the ballet are: "Summons to

Yaroslavna, **performed by the Maly Theatre Ballet, Leningrad, 1974**

March", "Russian Wives", "Attack", "Eclipse", "Surrounded", "Second Battle", "Captivity", "Yaroslavna's Lament", "Flight", and "Summons to Unification". The ballet takes a new direction in being named after Igor's faithful wife, Yaroslavna, but the story is a familiar one. In the nineteenth century Borodin used the story of the *Lay* in his opera *Prince Igor*, and the "Polovtsian Dances" from this opera, as choreographed by Fokine and others, are well known in the world of ballet.

Oleg Vinogradov staged *Yaroslavna* when he was the artistic director of the Maly Theatre in Leningrad. This ballet is unusual in every respect, both for the choreographer and for Russian ballet in general. First of all, the music of Tishchenko (a pupil of Shostakovich) is not typical, especially for its time: it is polyphonic and ranges from the lamenting sounds of the flute to the most expressive extremes of the idiom of contemporary music. The music of the ballet incorporates a chorus that sings the text of the *Lay*. It is what today might be called a "multi-media" spectacle, a powerful epic and tragic work, in which the "chorus" plays a huge role, as if engendering in dance the soloists and the heroes of the ballet. Through his choreography, scenography, music, and lighting technique, Vinogradov succeeded in creating an immensely emotional spectacle.

The choreographic language of the ballet, too, is unusual for Vinogradov, who is sometimes called a "modern classicist" in view of the fact that the basis of his choreographic creations is, more often than not, classical ballet technique. The choreographic innovations and the visual motifs for the Russian heroes of

Yaroslavna more readily evoked "modern" dance of the West (which, at the time, Vinogradov had not seen): knees turned inwards, free plasticity of arm movement, dancers' bodies emancipated in motion, and women dancing in soft shoes. Interestingly, the classical dances are given to the Polovtsians, the enemies of the Russian people. The virtually characterless Polovtsian cavalry is danced on pointe by the corps de ballet. Slender feminine arms and slender arrows descend on the Russian retinue like a web. The subtle, smug "Polovtses", with their sleek heads, are even visually opposed to the Russian retinue, who are dressed in brightly-coloured shirts and trousers.

The malleable language of the Russian heroes, the costumes, and the laconic set design (the rear of the stage and the curtains are covered with the text of the *Lay*) are fraught with the symbolism of ancient Russian art and recall antique Russian icons. An example of this is the image of the "mourner"—a young woman in a long Slavic blouse who, from time to time, comes out on stage, right up to the footlights, carrying a peculiarly Russian type of bucket by a pole through its handles. She puts the bucket down, dips a piece of cloth in the water and wrings the water out, washing the dead soldiers of the retinue. Her appearance on each occasion underscores the demise of the Russian combatants. She appears for the last time when the whole retinue has perished and Igor is in captivity. And this time she wrings not water but blood out of the rags.

Yaroslavna illustrates many of Vinogradov's discoveries in the world of stage direction and choreography, especially in the composition of the climactic scenes. An example is the scene of the march, where the overhead lights grow strong and the dancers make great leaps in the air towards the audience as if imitating a race. The chorus sings: "Oh, great Russian land! It is already too late for you!" In this way the image of the strenuous haste and thoughtless bravado of the retinue is created. Next comes the scene of the eclipse of the sun. The overhead lights go out and only the sidelights shine from behind the curtain. The dancers form a group reminiscent of a flock of birds ready for flight. In front stands Igor, half kneeling, and behind him stands the army with arms spread out like wings. The group dies, as though covered with the shadow of some terrible omen.

The tragic dénouement of the ballet is magnificent. Following the mass scene of the women lamenting their dead husbands, and after Yaroslavna chides Igor for the senseless deaths of the retinue, the performers leave the stage and the lights go out. On stage, in virtual darkness at the footlights, only Yaroslavna and Igor remain. Embracing Igor's motionless body, a body frozen in the pose of a man crucified, Yaroslavna rocks her beloved, attempting to comfort her grieving husband. The chorus sings a prayer (an innovation which was very bold at the time in Russia). The rear of the stage, blood-red like fire, chars, turns black, and dies out as the music dies down. The Polovtsians now come forward from the rear of the stage. In complete darkness, row by row, the female corps-de-ballet moves towards the footlights. The soles of the women's ballet shoes pound the floor rhythmically: under cover of night the Polovtsian cavalry advances on Russia.

Thus, in *Yaroslavna*, as in *Battleship Potemkin* and *Petrushka* later, Vinogradov appealed, with great artistic force, to the viewer's sense of morality, forcing the members of the audience to think about the eternal themes of love, mercy, and their own responsibility for everything that happens everywhere.

The ballet is still a part of the repertoire of the theatre.

—Nina Alovert

YERMOLAEV, Aleksei

Russian/Soviet dancer, choreographer, and teacher. Born Aleksei Nikolaevich Ermolaev (Yermolaev) in St. Petersburg, 23 February (10 February old style) 1910. Studied at the Petrograd State Theatre School (later the Leningrad Choreographic School); graduated in 1926. Leading dancer, State Academic Theatre for Opera and Ballet (GATOB, later the Kirov Ballet), Leningrad, 1926–30, Bolshoi Ballet, Moscow, 1930–58; also appeared in films, including as Tybalt in film *Romeo and Juliet* (1954); also choreographer, with first major choreography in 1939, and author of numerous ballet librettos; teacher and répétiteur (rehearsal director), Bolshoi Ballet, 1960–75; teacher and artistic director, Moscow Choreographic School, 1968–72: students include Vladimir Vasiliev, Mikhail Lavrovsky, Maris Liepa. Recipient: titles of Honoured Artist of the Russian Federation, 1940, 1951, and People's Artist of the USSR, 1970; State Prize of the USSR, 1944, 1947, 1949. Died in Moscow, 12 December 1975.

ROLES

1926   God of the Wind in *The Talisman* (Petipa), State Academic Theatre for Opera and Ballet (GATOB), Leningrad

Bluebird in *The Sleeping Beauty* (Petipa), GATOB, Leningrad

Genie of the Waters in *The Little Humpbacked Horse* (Petipa after Saint-Léon), GATOB, Leningrad

1927   Basil in *Don Quixote* (Gorsky after Petipa), GATOB, Leningrad

Merchant in *Le Corsaire* (Petipa), GATOB, Leningrad

Winter Bird (cr) in *The Ice Maiden* (Lopukhov), GATOB, Leningrad

1928   Prince Siegfried in *Swan Lake* (Petipa, Ivanov), GATOB, Leningrad

1929   Acrobat and Idol (cr) in *The Red Poppy* (Lopukhov, Ponomarev, Leontiev), GATOB, Leningrad

1931   Frondoso in *The Comedians* (Chekrygin), Bolshoi Ballet, Moscow

1933   Jerome (cr) in *The Flames of Paris* (Moscow version; Vainonen), Bolshoi Ballet, Moscow

1934   Albrecht in *Giselle* (Petipa after Coralli, Perrot), Bolshoi Ballet, Moscow

1935   Tibul in *Three Fat Men* (Moiseyev), Bolshoi Ballet, Moscow

Actor in *The Bright Stream* (Lopukhov), Bolshoi Ballet, Moscow

1939   Title role in *The Nutcracker* (Vainonen), Bolshoi Ballet, Moscow

1945   Abderakhman in *Raymonda* (new version; Lavrovksy after Petipa), Bolshoi Ballet, Moscow

1946   Tybalt (cr) in *Romeo and Juliet* (Moscow version; Lavrovsky), Bolshoi Ballet, Moscow

1949   Li Shan-fu in *The Red Poppy* (Lavrovsky), Bolshoi Ballet, Moscow

Yevgeny (cr) in *The Bronze Horseman* (Zakharov), Bolshoi Ballet, Moscow

Ripafrata (cr) in *Mirandolina* (Vainonen), Bolshoi Ballet, Moscow

1954   Severyan (cr) in *The Story of the Stone Flower* (Lavrovsky), Bolshoi Ballet, Moscow

Girei in *The Fountain of Bakhchisarai* (Zakharov), Bolshoi Ballet, Moscow

1956   Hans in *Giselle* (Petipa after Coralli, Perrot), Bolshoi Ballet, Moscow

WORKS

1928   Creative Evening for "Young Ballet", including *Mariners' Dance*, *Ekspromt*, *Poem*, Press House, Leningrad

1939   *Nightingale* (with Lopukhov; mus. M. Kroshner), Bylorussian Theatre of Opera and Ballet, Minsk

1952   *Peace Will Triumph over War* (mus. various), Bolshoi Filial Theatre, Moscow

1955   *Burning Hearts* (mus. V. Zolotaryov), Bylorussian Theatre of Opera and Ballet, Minsk

PUBLICATIONS

Morley, Iris, *The Soviet Ballet*, London, 1945
Slonimsky, Yuri, *Soviet Ballet*, Moscow and Leningrad, 1950
Roslavleva, Natalia, *Era of the Russian Ballet*, London, 1966
Churova, Marina (ed.), *Aleksei Yermolayev*, Moscow, 1974
Aleksei Yermolayev (various authors), Moscow, 1982
Smakov, Gennady, *The Great Russian Dancers*, New York, 1984

*   *   *

Aleksei Yermolaev was undoubtedly the brightest representative of the Russian ballet school of the 1920s to the 1940s who, for various reasons, has not received the same recognition as either his more fortunate rivals or those who have come after him. Nevertheless, Yermolaev surpassed his contemporaries both in his artistic talent and in the richness of his personality, not to mention his mastery of the demands of classical technique.

Yermolaev has played a historic role in the life of Soviet ballet. It is Yermolaev who went further than anyone else in destroying the solid stereotype—formed in the days of the Imperial Theatre—of the attentive and gallant dancer-cavalier. He appeared instead in the guise of the bold rebel, the passionate, honour-loving, and generously talented common man. His interpretations of the classical repertoire were unexpectedly sharp and deep, and his very manner of dancing was unusually expressive. It was Yermolaev himself who changed many ideas and attitudes with regard to the possibilities in male dance, and in several areas (turns en l'air and pirouettes, large jumps, and above all, speed of movement), he led ballet technique for men to a new level of virtuosity—one which became established as the norm for dancers of the following generations (especially those dancers who were his own pupils). In addition, it is worth mentioning that several of Yermolaev's achievements, such as triple tours in the air, or the double rivoltade, are hardly ever repeated, even today.

Yermolayev single-handedly engineered a virtual revolution in male dance or, at the very least, an undoubted transformation of it. He had all the gifts necessary for such a task: the insatiable fanaticism of the experimenter along with sharp, cool intellect; fearlessness and determination; the desperate readiness to undertake any risk; and, finally, the purely physical inexhaustibility. But as with all revolutionaries, Yermolayev's rise did not last long—little more than ten years. Unsustainable burdens on the muscles eventually took their toll, and in 1937 Yermolaev suffered an irreversible injury to his leg. But perhaps the more important factor was the change in artistic atmosphere which came about, favouring a style of execution that called for a more noble, "worthy" presentation of character. Yermolaev's rebelliousness and common touch began to seem defiant and inappropriate. In addition, the so-called "dram-ballet", a mime-orientated form of ballet theatre, began to dominate the stage, and Yermolaev's unique dancing gift had no application, appearing more and more to leading choreographers to be an encumbrance rather than an asset.

Returning to the stage of the Bolshoi Theatre after a two-year break, Yermolaev continued to dance leading roles (without, in fact, attaining his previous heights) but recast himself anew in the mould of the best pantomime artist. He demonstrated picturesque external form and effective and expressive "plastique" in gesture; but above all he revealed a depth and sharpness of internal experience unusual for the ballet theatre. In this, Yermolaev can be compared with the most eminent dramatic actors for the sheer force of his effect on the audience.

At this same time—the end of the 1930s—Yermolaev began to try his hand at choreography. He produced two ballets in Minsk: *Nightingale* (together with Fedor Lopukhov) and *Burning Hearts*, and he also produced a solo concert in which he performed all the numbers. However Yermolaev's choreographic efforts notwithstanding, the expressiveness and artistic daring of his productions failed to take shape, the reason being that Yermolaev, a born choreographer, was an unsuccessful librettist—particularly when he found himself constrained by the vulgar sociological plots frequently demanded by "Soviet" art. It was a strange and offensive situation for an artistic rebel and a man with so sharp an intelligence to find himself in, but such was the case—and Yermolaev's work was not the only

example of this kind of artistic blindness and absurd drama.

Less dramatic but very much more fruitful was Yermolaev's activity as a teacher. But his character was not disposed towards bearing patiently the routine of daily school teaching, and he did not head the Moscow Choreographic School for long—altogether for about four years. After that he conducted the Class of Perfection at the Bolshoi Theatre for fifteen years with great absorption and success, occupying himself only with the talented and giving all the force of his spirit to stars. Such teaching also has its place in ballet history, and at least Vladimir Vasiliev, Maris Liepa, and Aleksandr Gudunov owe Yermolaev a great deal.

—Vadim Gaevsky

YOUSKEVITCH, Igor

Russian/American dancer and teacher. Born in Piryatin, Ukraine, 13 March 1912. Educated (in engineering) at Belgrade University, 1930–32; early training as a gymnast, then studied ballet with Elena Poliakova, Belgrade, from 1932, and Olga Preobrazhenska, Paris; later perfected technique with Anatole Vilzak and Alexandra Fedorova, New York. Married dancer Anna Scarpova, 1938: daughter, dancer Maria Youskevitch, b.1945. Served in the U.S. Navy, 1944–45. Stage début as partner of dancer Xenia Grunt, 1932; dancer, soon becoming soloist, Ballets Russes de Paris, 1934–35; principal dancer, Les Ballets de Léon Woizikowsky, 1935–36, becoming incorporated into de Basil's Ballets Russes (second company), touring Australia, 1936–37, and Europe, 1937–38; principal dancer, Denham's Ballet Russe de Monte Carlo (previously Les Ballets de Monte Carlo), 1938–44; principal dancer (on return from war service), Massine's Ballet Russe Highlights, 1946; principal dancer, Ballet Theatre (later American Ballet Theatre), 1946–55, and later guest artist, also appearing as principal guest artist, Ballet Alicia Alonso (becoming Ballet Nacional de Cuba), various seasons, 1948–60; principal dancer and artistic adviser, Ballet Russe de Monte Carlo, 1955–57, returning various seasons 1958–60; founder, choreographer, and dancer for touring company performing as Ballet Romantique, from 1963; also appeared on television and in films, including in *Invitation to the Dance* (dir. Kelly, 1956); teacher, co-founding, with wife Anna Scarpova, own school in New York, 1962–80; head of dance, University of Texas, Austin, 1971–82. Recipient: *Dance Magazine* Award, 1959; Capezio Dance Award, 1991.

ROLES

1935   Dancer in *Le Danube au printemps* (Fortunato), Les Ballets Russes de Paris, Paris
        The Poet in *Les Sylphides* (Fokine), Les Ballets Russes de Paris, Paris
        Grand pas de deux from *The Sleeping Beauty* (after Petipa), Les Ballets Russes de Paris
        Title role in *Le Spectre de la rose* (Fokine), Les Ballets de Léon Woizikowsky
1936   Harlequin in *Carnaval* (Fokine), de Basil's Ballets Russes, tour
        The Hero in *Les Présages* (Massine), de Basil's Ballets Russes, tour
        The Prince in *Les Cent Baisers* (Nijinska), de Basil's Ballets Russes, tour

Igor Youskevitch in *Theme and Variations*

The Faun in *L'Après-midi d'un faune* (Nijinsky), de Basil's Ballets Russes, tour

Bluebird in *Aurora's Wedding* (after Petipa), de Basil's Ballets Russes, tour

The Prince in *Aurora's Wedding* (after Petipa), de Basil's Ballets Russes, tour

The Prince in *Swan Lake*, Act II (after Ivanov), de Basil's Ballets Russes, tour

Ivan Tsarevich in *The Firebird* (Fokine), de Basil's Ballets Russes, tour

1938 Officer (cr) in *Gaîté Parisienne* (Massine), Ballet Russe de Monte Carlo, Monte Carlo

A God (cr) in *Seventh Symphony* (Massine), Ballet Russe de Monte Carlo, Monte Carlo

Alyosha (cr) in *Bogatyri* (Massine), Ballet Russe de Monte Carlo, New York

Albrecht in *Giselle* (Petipa after Coralli, Perrot; staged Lifar), Ballet Russe de Monte Carlo, London

Principal dancer in *Les Elfes* (Fokine), Ballet Russe de Monte Carlo

Principal dancer in *Les Éléments* (Fokine), Ballet Russe de Monte Carlo

1939 Franz in *Coppélia* (Zverev after Petipa, Cecchetti), Ballet Russe de Monte Carlo

The Hussar in *Le Beau Danube* (Massine), Ballet Russe de Monte Carlo

The Man (cr) in *Rouge et noir* (Massine), Ballet Russe de Monte Carlo, Monte Carlo

The Lover in *Devil's Holiday* (Ashton), Ballet Russe de Monte Carlo

1940 Jack of Hearts in *Poker Game* (*Jeu de cartes*; Balanchine), Ballet Russe de Monte Carlo, New York

The Prince in *The Nutcracker* (Fedorova after Ivanov), Ballet Russe de Monte Carlo

A Secretary (cr) in *Vienna—1814* (Massine), Ballet Russe de Monte Carlo, New York

Principal dancer in *Serenade* (Balanchine), Ballet Russe de Monte Carlo, New York

A Boy Friend (cr) in *The New Yorker* (Massine), Ballet Russe de Monte Carlo, New York

1941 Prince Siegfried in *The Magic Swan* (*Swan Lake*, Act III; Fedorova after Petipa), Ballet Russe de Monte Carlo, New York

Theseus in *Labyrinth* (Massine), Ballet Russe de Monte Carlo, New York

1942 Principal dancer in *Chopin Concerto* (Nijinska), Ballet Russe de Monte Carlo, New York

Lell, a Shepherd (cr) in *The Snow Maiden* (Nijinska), Ballet Russe de Monte Carlo, New York

1943 Ribbon dancer (cr) in *The Red Poppy* (Schwezoff), Ballet Russe de Monte Carlo, Cleveland

Russian Prince (cr) in *Ancient Russia* (Nijinska), Ballet Russe de Monte Carlo, Cleveland

1946 Albrecht in *Giselle* (new production; Romanoff after Petipa, Coralli, Perrot), Ballet Theatre, New York

Title role in *Apollo* (Balanchine), Ballet Theatre

Pas de deux from *Don Quixote* (Obukhov after Petipa), Ballet Theatre, New York

1947 Principal dancer, lead couple (cr) in *Theme and Variations* (Balanchine), Ballet Theatre, New York

Title role in *Aleko* (Massine), Ballet Theatre, tour

Paris in *Helen of Troy* (Lichine), Ballet Theatre, tour

1948 Principal dancer (cr) in *Shadow of the Wind* (Tudor), Ballet Theatre, New York

Principal dancer (cr) in *Concerto* (Albert Alonso), Ballet Alicia Alonso, Havana

Principal dancer (cr) in *La Valse* (Albert Alonso), Ballet Alicia Alonso, Havana

1949 Colin in *La Fille mal gardée* (Nijinska after Petipa; staged Romanoff), Ballet Theatre, New York

Bluebird in *Princess Aurora* (selections from *Sleeping Beauty*; Balanchine after Petipa), Ballet Theatre, Chicago

1950 Principal dancer (cr) in *Jeux* (Dollar), Ballet Theatre, New York

Romeo in *Romeo and Juliet* (Tudor), Ballet Theatre, European tour

1951 Principal dancer in *Concerto* (also called *Constantia*; Dollar), Ballet Theatre, New York

Principal dancer (cr) in *Tropical Pas de deux* (Martinez), Ballet Theatre, New York

Principal dancer (cr) in *Schumann Concerto* (Nijinska), Ballet Theatre, New York

1954 Stanley in *A Streetcar Named Desire* (Bettis), Ballet Theatre, Princeton, New Jersey

1955 Knight in *La Dame à la Licorne* (H. Rosen), Ballet Russe de Monte Carlo, Toronto

Oedipus in *The Sphinx* (Lichine), Ballet Theatre, New York

1956 Harlequin (cr) in *Harlequinade* (Romanoff), Ballet Russe de Monte Carlo, Chicago

Romeo (cr) in *Romeo and Juliet* (Albert Alonso), Ballet Nacional de Cuba, Havana

Prince Siegfried in *Swan Lake* (four acts; Alberto and Alicia Alonso after Petipa, Ivanov), Ballet Nacional de Cuba, Havana

1958 Principal dancer in *Ballet Imperial* (Balanchine), Ballet Russe de Monte Carlo

Romeo (cr) in *Romeo and Juliet Pas de deux* (Alberto Alonso), Ballet Russe de Monte Carlo, Chicago

Principal dancer in *Delirium* (Parés), Ballet Nacional de Cuba, Havana

1960 Prince Siegfried in *Swan Lake* (Acts II, III, IV; Novak, Vilzak after Petipa, Ivanov), Ballet Russe de Monte Carlo, Los Angeles

1963 Tybalt (cr) in *Romeo and Juliet* (also chor.), Ballet Romantique, New York

Principal dancer (cr) in *Trance-formation* (also chor.), Ballet Romantique, New York

1965 Principal dancer (cr) in *Pas de trois Khachaturian* (also chor.), Ballet Romantique, New York

1966 Iskander (cr) in *La Péri* (also chor., with Heller), New Orleans Opera Ballet, New Orleans

WORKS

1963 *Romeo and Juliet* (mus. Tchaikovsky), Ballet Romantique, New York

Trance-formation (mus. Messager), Ballet Romantique, New York

1965 *Pas de trois Khachaturian* (mus. Khachaturian), Ballet Romantique, New York

La Péri (with Heller), New Orleans Opera Ballet, New Orleans

Also staged:
1967 *Giselle* (after Petipa, Coralli, Perrot; mus. Adam), Houston Ballet Foundation, Houston

Other works include: for University of Texas—*Lamento e Trionfo* (mus. Lizst), *Divertissement* (mus. Ibert); for Berkshire Ballet at Jacob's Pillow—*Coppélia* (after Petipa, Cecchetti;

mus. Delibes); for Richmond Ballet—*La Fille mal gardée* (mus. various).

PUBLICATIONS

By Youskevitch:
"Ballet is a Theatre Art", *Dance News* (New York), June 1945
Contributor to *The Male Image* (Dance Perspectives no. 40), New York, 1969
"Generation Gap in Ballet", *Dancescope* (New York), Spring 1971
"Masculinity in Dance", *Ballet Review* (Brooklyn, N.Y.), Fall 1981
Interview in Newman, Barbara, *Striking a Balance: Dancers Talk about Dancing*, Boston, 1982
"Busing Les Ballets", *Ballet Review* (New York), Fall 1983
"The Ways of Ballet", *Ballett International* (Cologne), June/July 1984

About Youskevitch:
Everett, Walter, "Igor Youskevitch", *Dance Magazine* (New York), September 1943
Denby, Edwin, *Looking at the Dance*, New York, 1949
Cohen, Selma Jeanne, "Prince Igor", *Dance Magazine*, May 1953; reprinted in *25 Years of American Dance*, New York, 1954
Williams, Peter, "Igor Youskevitch", *Dance and Dancers* (London), September 1953
Payne, Charles, *American Ballet Theatre*, New York, 1978
Anderson, Jack, *The One and Only: The Ballet Russe de Monte Carlo*, London, 1981
Gruen, John, "Igor Youskevitch", *Dance Magazine* (New York), 2 parts: March, May 1982
Hunt, Marilyn, "Danseur Noble: Igor Youskevitch", *Ballet News* (New York), March 1982
Terry, Walter, "Indestructables", *Dance Magazine* (New York), June 1982
Hunt, Marilyn, "Igor Youskevitch Dancing", *Ballet Review* (New York), Fall 1983
Barker, Barbara, "Celebrating Youskevitch", *Ballet Review* (New York), Fall 1983
Denby, Edwin, *Dance Writings*, edited by Robert Cornfield and William Mackay, New York, 1986

*   *   *

A great danseur noble noted for his masculinity, romanticism, and meticulous classical style and technique, Igor Youskevitch combined Russian training and elegance with American forthrightness. After an early career in Europe and, for the better part of a year, touring Australia, he made his principal reputation in the United States with both the Ballet Russe de Monte Carlo and Ballet Theatre. In addition, his long-remembered appearances with Alicia Alonso's fledgling company in Cuba were important in providing a model of the male classical dancer for Cuban dancers and audiences.

Most of his formal training was with the Maryinsky expatriate teacher Olga Preobrazhenska in Paris. But because he began ballet classes at the late age of twenty, his success also owed something to the mature analytical approach he brought to his training, as well as to his innate nobility of movement and early conditioning in gymnastics. He was also fortunate to come under the guidance of the veteran Diaghilev dancer, Léon Woizikowsky, in whose company he developed his artistry and technique.

Within four years of beginning his training, Youskevitch had earned a reputation for masculine lyricism, especially in Fokine's *Le Spectre de la rose*, which he was invited to dance under the eye of Fokine himself as a guest with René Blum's Les Ballets de Monte Carlo in London in 1936. He danced *Spectre* on early British television with Tamara Toumanova in 1938. In the early days of Blum's and Denham's Ballet Russe de Monte Carlo, he partnered all the leading ballerinas, especially Alicia Markova, and he created noble, classical roles in Massine's *Seventh Symphony* and *Rouge et noir*—both with Markova—as well as a number of demi-caractère roles.

With World War II, Youskevitch's career became based in the United States. He had great influence there in gaining acceptance for the "danseur noble" and for the ballet classics (especially *Giselle*) with both audiences and dancers. Many young people became interested in ballet careers after seeing him perform on tours all over the country. For example, Erik Bruhn said that he only became interested in the role of Albrecht after seeing Youskevitch dance it. Youskevitch's approach to such narrative roles was to stress a differentiation between classicism in dancing and naturalness in acting. He was interested in bringing logical motivation to everything he did on stage.

He and Alonso formed one of the most popular of all partnerships, based on contrast of masculine and feminine qualities and on their close rapport, which was called "supernatural" by some. Such rapport resulted partly from a mutual interest in working out new details and new approaches: every step should have something to say, they felt. An element of Youskevitch's charm was his concentration on his partner; his admiration for her, presentation of her, and romantic pursuit of her were important elements in his deportment in even the most abstract pas de deux. At the same time, his elegant presence always kept him on an equal footing with the ballerina in the audience's eyes.

For all his innate acting ability, Youskevitch was also known for pure dance works, especially the Black Swan Pas de deux and *Theme and Variations*, which Ballet Theatre commissioned George Balanchine to choreograph for him. His technique was so well centred that many parts of the ballet (such as a series of pirouettes and tours en l'air centre stage) still offer challenges to male dancers.

One aspect of Youskevitch's silky combination of ease and vigour was evoked by the American critic Edwin Denby. "The changing shape of the dancing body is vigorously defined", wrote Denby. ". . . In his leaps, for instance, the noble arm positions, the tilt of the head sideways or forward, make you watch with interest a whole man who leaps; you don't watch, as with most dancers, only the lively legs of one." Ever the thinking dancer, Youskevitch himself explained,

> You take the cue from what type of steps the choreographer gives you. That is a certain indication that you're lyrical or dramatic or whatever. Then of course the music gives you a certain feel. Taking the steps, the feel of the music, and then your relationship to people onstage, what you are supposed to do when, and what they are doing while you are doing it, you can build up your own story. I usually created a story for myself, not necessarily a down-to-earth story, but a story of what kind of spirit I was. Just to make sense of things helped me a lot.

—Marilyn Hunt

Z

ZAKHAROV, Rostislav

Russian/Soviet dancer, choreographer, ballet director, and teacher. Born Rostislav Vladimirovich Zakharov in Astrakhan, 7 September (25 August old style) 1907. Studied at the Petrograd State Ballet School (later the Leningrad Choreographic School), pupil of Vladimir Ponomarev; graduated in 1926; also completed a course in stage direction under Vladimir Soloviev, Sergei Radlov, Leningrad Theatre Institute, 1928–32. Married the dancer Maria Smirnova. Dancer, Kiev Theatre for Opera and Ballet, 1926–29; choreographer, staging first works for amateur stage, from 1926, and for students of School for Circus and Variety Actors; dancer and choreographer, State Academic Theatre for Opera and Ballet (GATOB, later the Kirov), Leningrad, 1934–36; choreographer and opera director, Bolshoi Theatre, Moscow, 1936–56; artistic director of the Moscow Choreographic School, 1945–47; Head of the Choreography Department, State (Lunarsky) Institute for Theatrical Art (GITIS), Moscow, 1946–75, becoming Professor from 1951. Recipient: title of People's Artist of the USSR, 1969. Died in Moscow, 15 January 1975.

WORKS

1932 Dances in *At the Paris Checkpost* (*The Water-Carrier*, opera; mus. Cherubini), Bolshoi Theatre, Moscow
1934 *The Fountain of Bakhchisarai* (mus. Asafiev), State Academic Theatre for Opera and Ballet (GATOB), Leningrad (staged Bolshoi Ballet, Moscow, 1936)
1935 Dances in *The Huguenots* (opera; mus. Meyerbeer), Kirov Theatre, Leningrad
1936 *Lost Illusions* (mus. Asafiev), Kirov Ballet, Leningrad
1937 Dances in *Fallow Land Upturned* (opera; mus. Dzerzhinsky), Kirov Theatre, Leningrad
1938 *The Prisoner of the Caucasus* (mus. Asafiev), Bolshoi Ballet, Moscow
1939 Dances in *Ivan Susanin* (*A Life for the Tsar*, opera; mus. Glinka), Bolshoi Theatre, Moscow (restaged 1945)
1940 *Don Quixote* (mus. Minkus), Bolshoi Ballet, Moscow
1941 *Taras Bulba* (mus. Soloviev-Sedoi), Bolshoi Ballet, Moscow
1944 Dances in *The Barber of Seville* (opera; mus. Rossini), Bolshoi Theatre, Moscow
1945 *Cinderella* (mus. Prokofiev), Bolshoi Ballet, Moscow
1946 *Mistress into Maid* (mus. Asafiev), Bolshoi Ballet, Moscow
1947 *The Daughter of the People* (mus. Kreyn), Kirov Ballet, Leningrad
     The Bronze Horseman (mus. Glière), Kirov Ballet, Leningrad
1951 Dances in *Aida* (opera; mus. Verdi), Bolshoi Theatre, Moscow

1952 Dances in *The Fair at Sorochinsky* (opera; mus. Mussorgsky), Bolshoi Theatre, Moscow
     Under Italian Skies (with S. Sergeyev; mus. Yurovsky), Kiev Theatre for Opera and Ballet, Kiev
1953 Dances in *Carmen* (opera; mus. Bizet), Bolshoi Theatre, Moscow
1959 Dances in *War and Peace* (opera; mus. Prokofiev), Bolshoi Theatre, Moscow
1964 *Into the Port Came "Russia"* (mus. Soloviev-Sedoi), Kirov Ballet, Leningrad

Also staged (as stage director):
1937 *Ruslan and Lyudmila* (opera; mus. Glinka), Bolshoi Theatre, Moscow (restaged in 1948)
1942 *William Tell* (opera; mus. Rossini), Bolshoi Opera, Moscow
1953 *Carmen* (opera; mus. Bizet), Bolshoi Opera, Moscow

PUBLICATIONS

By Zakharov:
"Dramaturgy and the Ballet", reprinted from *Literaturnaya Gazeta* (Moscow), *Dance Magazine* (New York), June 1953
The Art of the Choreographer, Moscow, 1954
Ulanova, Moiseyev and Zakharov on Soviet Ballet (in Russian), edited by Peter Brinson, London, 1954
Talks about Dancing, Moscow, 1963
Choreographer's Work with the Dancers, Moscow, 1967
Notes of a Choreographer, Moscow, 1976
On Dancing, Moscow, 1977

About Zakharov:
Souritz, Elizabeth, "News from the USSR", *Dance Magazine* (New York), January 1965
Roslavleva, Natalia, "Stanislavsky and the Ballet", *Dance Perspectives* (New York), no. 23, 1965
Roslavleva, Natalia, *Era of the Russian Ballet*, London, 1966
Krasovskaya, Vera, "New Thoughts in the USSR", *Dance Magazine* (New York), February 1966
Ivashev, V., and Ilyina, K., "Rostislav Zakharov: Living and Breathing Dance", *Sovetskaya Rossiya* (Moscow), 1982
McMahon, Deirdre, "Corridor to the Muses", *Ballet Review* (New York), Spring 1984

*   *   *

Rostislav Zakharov was one of the most prominent choreographers of the pre-war years, and a leader of the trend known as "dram-ballet".

After graduating from the Leningrad Choreographic School in 1926, Zakharov made his first attempts to stage ballets at

Rostislav Zakharov's *Cinderella*, with Ekaterina Maximova in the title role, Bolshoi Ballet, 1977

amateur theatres. His revival of *Harlequinade*, along with several small productions of his own, drew extensively on the more worn-out patterns of classical ballet, and were not particularly noteworthy.

But at that time a frequent topic in disputes on ballet was how to make choreography more dramatic, and an opinion which was often voiced was that ballet ought to be apprenticed to drama. It was probably under the influence of these ideas that Zakharov decided to get a grasp of theatrical directing. In 1928 he became a student of the Leningrad Theatre Institute, joining the directing course under Vladimir Soloviev. At the same time he continued to work as a choreographer, staging sketches (mostly based on grotesque and political satire) for the students of the School for Circus and Variety Actors.

It was then that Zakharov started working together with the well-known director, Sergei Radlov. Radlov invited him to collaborate in some of his drama productions and also, being at the time the artistic director of the Leningrad Opera and Ballet Theatre, commissioned him to stage dances in a few operas. When the company began to look for a choreographer to stage the new ballet *The Fountain of Bakhchisarai* (after Aleksandr Pushkin's narrative poem of the same title), Radlov supervised the production, making Zakharov responsible for the choreography.

This first independent work brought Zakharov such success that it actually became the "capital" on which he could live for the rest of his life. At the preparatory stage, Zakharov made good use of what he was taught to do as a director of drama: he

collected a lot of illustrative materials in museums and libraries, consulted Pushkin scholars, and spent a long time talking with the dancers about the characters they would be performing.

The concept of *The Fountain of Bakhchisarai* as a "dramatic play in dance" is obvious in Nikolai Volkov's libretto and in Boris Asafiev's music. The plot in Volkov's scenario develops with a logical consistency typical of classical drama; some elements in Pushkin's plot have been further developed and "clarified", and further, several subsidiary elements have been added to the plot to make the environment in which the characters live more vivid. Zakharov used this plan of dramatic development as a guide for his own choreography, splitting the ballet into several sections and working out a special solution for each of them. Many scenes and episodes were staged in an innovative way; particularly impressive were the final episodes of each act.

When working on the parts of individual characters, Zakharov used the approach which he later called "dancing through the personality" ("tanets v obraze"). According to him, dancing as such, when it is not connected with any literary plot, is devoid of content. Every movement should stand for a concrete action, mood, or emotion of the character. Understandably, the main means of choreographic expression should now be mime acting—mime combined with dancing and dancing permeated with acting. Zakharov used predominantly the techniques of classical dance, but even from these he carefully selected the ones which were the easiest to "dramatize".

The Fountain of Bakhchisarai was an ideal "dram-ballet" production. Among its achievements are its enormous accessibility, a plot which any spectator can understand, clear-cut characters, and action in which all events are presented in a moving and dramatic way, without any melodramatic extremes. The authors of the production reached an ideal proportion of the component parts, due to the concerted effort of all the participants.

The ballet was extremely popular with the public and unanimously praised by the critics. After two years it was reproduced on the stage of the Moscow Bolshoi Theatre. In later years *The Fountain of Bakhchisarai* was performed by virtually all the ballet companies in the USSR, as well as in many other countries where Soviet choreographers and ballet teachers worked.

The success of *The Fountain of Bakhchisarai* suggested to Zakharov the possibility of producing more ballets in the same dramatic style, based on other literary works. His collaborators were, in most cases, composer Boris Asafiev and librettist Nikolai Volkov. The productions created then included *Lost Illusions* (after Balzac), *The Prisoner of the Caucasus* and *Mistress into Maid* (after Pushkin), and *Taras Bulba* (after Gogol). However, very soon it became clear that Zakharov's new method was far from being universally applicable. *Lost Illusions* was a failure largely due to the fact that gestures and mime acting, although sufficient for telling a story, were by no means capable of conveying the message of Balzac's novel. Even when the very first productions of "dram-ballet" appeared, the secondary role allocated in them to dancing had caused some concern. *The Fountain of Bakhchisarai*, at least, preserves the general tone of Pushkin's poem; in the later ballets, the literary "background" was often chosen arbitrarily, with both dancing and mime acting turned into nothing more than rather imperfect illustrations of the plot.

Choreographers at the time seemed to find a way out of this plight in the extensive use of pageantry, melodramatic episode, and divertissement which had no direct connection with the actual story. But this, of course, was a distortion of the basic principles of "dram-ballet". So in *Taras Bulba*, there was the scene of Ostap's execution and an even more impressive episode in which Bulba himself was burnt alive, while *The Bronze Horseman* was probably created solely for the sake of the Flood episode, in which the whole Bolshoi stage seemed to be filled with billowing water, carrying and tossing boats, barrels, and even a dog-kennel. All these spectacular details attracted more attention than the theme of Pushkin's poem: the clash between absolute power and the destiny of the single, unimportant individual. The most successful post-war production was *Cinderella*, in which pageantry was justified by the plot, and in which the use of spectacle—given the ballet's creation in the year 1945—could be regarded as a celebration of victory and the end of the war, rather like a display of fireworks.

In the 1950s, Zakharov's method and his productions met with increasingly sharp criticism. He, in his turn, attacked his critics, proclaiming "dram-ballet" to be the only correct type of ballet production, and other forms of balletic experiment a deviation from socialist realism. In this conflict he was supported by party leaders and ministry officials; and the fact that he held a number of important positions (for example, Head of the Choreography Department of the State Institute for Theatrical Art) proved to be of great use to him. Using these advantages, he had his articles published regularly and produced several books in which all people who disagreed with him were condemned as political dissidents, all Western art was proclaimed to be decadent, and its influence upon the Soviet culture was declared pernicious, with anyone who had interest in it deemed to be politically suspect. Particularly ferocious were Zakharov's attacks on the young choreographers like Yuri Grigorovich and Igor Belsky, who emerged in the late 1950s, as well as his criticisms of the Western companies which started to give performances in the USSR in the early 1960s—not to mention the journalists who dared praise them.

Still, despite Zakharov's aggressive manner and the substantial official backing that he had, he was steadily losing power in the ballet world. His production *Into the Port Entered "Russia"* (1964) was a complete failure. However, he remained at the head of the Choreography Department of the State Institute for Theatrical Art, where young choreographers were trained under him until his last day.

—Elizabeth Souritz

ZAKLINSKY, Konstantin

Russian/Soviet dancer. Born Konstantin Yevgenevich Zaklinsky in Leningrad, 28 May 1955. Married Kirov ballerina Altynai Asylmuratova. Studied at the Leningrad Choreographic Academy (Vaganova School), pupil of Abdurakhman Kumysnikov; graduated in 1974. Dancer, Kirov Ballet, from 1974, becoming principal dancer from 1980; also international guest artist, including for Royal Ballet, London, 1989–90, and for German Opera Ballet, Berlin, 1991; has also appeared in films, including *Tristan and Isolde* (1976), *Cowboys* (1976), *Galatea* (1978), *Fouetté* (1986), *Chapliniana* (1988), and on ballet video-films, including *Children of Theatre Street* (1977), *The Magic of the Kirov* (1989). Recipient: Bronze Medal, International Ballet Competition, Moscow, 1981; Gold Medal, International Ballet Competition, Tokyo, 1984; title of Honoured Artist of the Russian Federation, 1983.

ROLES

1975 Troubador in *Raymonda* (Petipa, staged Sergeyev), Kirov Ballet, Leningrad
Prince Siegfried in *Swan Lake* (Petipa, Ivanov; staged Sergeyev), Kirov Ballet, Leningrad
Solo Dancer (cr) in *The Cowboys* (Yakobson), Kirov Ballet, Leningrad

1976 Soloist in *Paquita* (Petipa; staged Gusev), Kirov Ballet, Leningrad
Bluebird in *The Sleeping Beauty* (Petipa; staged Sergeyev), Kirov Ballet, Leningrad

1977 Principal dancer (cr) in *An Old Photograph*, from *Choreographic Novellas* (Bryantsev), Kirov Ballet, Leningrad

1978 Phoebus in *Notre-Dame de Paris* (Petit), Kirov Ballet, Leningrad
Jean de Brienne in *Raymonda* (Petipa; staged Sergeyev), Kirov Ballet, Leningrad
God in *The Creation of the World* (Kasatkina, Vasiliev), Kirov Ballet, Leningrad
Albrecht in *Giselle* (Petipa after Coralli, Perrot), Kirov Ballet, Leningrad

1979 Dantes (cr) in *Pushkin* (Kasatkina, Vasiliev), Kirov Ballet, Leningrad
Prince Désiré in *The Sleeping Beauty* (Petipa; staged Sergeyev), Kirov Ballet, Leningrad

Konstantin Zaklinsky as Albrecht in *Giselle*, **Kirov Ballet, 1990**

Solor in *La Bayadère* (Petipa, Ponomarev, Chabukiani), Kirov Ballet, Leningrad

1980 Andres (cr) in *The Fairy of the Rond Mountains* (Vinogradov), Kirov Ballet, Leningrad

1982 Golfo in *Napoli* (Bournonville; staged von Rosen), Kirov Ballet, Leningrad

Basil in *Don Quixote* (Gorsky after Petipa), Kirov Ballet, Leningrad

The Youth in *Leningrad Symphony* (Belsky), Kirov Ballet, Leningrad

1984 Osman in *Asiyat* (Vinogradov), Kirov Ballet, Leningrad

1985 Tariel (cr) in *The Knight in Tigerskin* (Vinogradov), Kirov Ballet, Leningrad

Title role in *Spartacus* (Yakobson), Kirov Ballet, Leningrad

1987 Lanchedem (cr) in *Le Corsaire* (new production; Gusev after Petipa), Kirov Ballet, Leningrad

Conrad in *Le Corsaire* (Gusev after Petipa), Kirov Ballet, Leningrad

1988 Judas (cr) in *A Rehearsal* (Fodor), Kirov Ballet, Leningrad

1989 Principal dancer in *Theme and Variations* (Balanchine; staged F. Russell), Kirov Ballet, Leningrad

1991 Title role in *Apollo* (Balanchine), German Opera Ballet, Berlin

PUBLICATIONS

Parry, Jan, "Dancing Differently", *Dance and Dancers* (London), September 1982

Rozanova, O., "On the Threshold of Maturity", *Smena* (Leningrad), 6 April 1983

Stupnikov, Igor, "A Theme for Four Variations", *Leningradskaya Pravda* (Leningrad), 10 October 1984

Stupnikov Igor, "The Duo", *Teatralnaya Zhizn* (Moscow), no. 6, 1985

Stupnikov Igor, "A Legend of Modern Life", *Sovetskaya Kultura* (Moscow), 13 August 1988

Willis, Margaret, "Kiroviana: The Glastnost Difference", *Dance Magazine* (New York), August 1989

* * *

Konstantin Zaklinsky has been, in a sense, favoured by the gods. He began immediately in the Kirov Ballet with Prince Siegfried (*Swan Lake*), and he has performed all of the leading male roles in the classical repertoire ever since. An unusually tall, but well-proportioned dancer, Zaklinsky has the natural bearing and stance of the classical ballet Prince, and has become a modern version of the "danseur noble" for the Kirov Ballet. At the same time, he is a man of some wit, and in lighter roles has shown his talent for the ironic and the purely comic.

Zaklinsky is now established as one of the leading dancers of the company, and he is also quite well-known outside the Soviet Union. After his graduation performance at the Leningrad Choreographic School, he immediately won a leading position with the Kirov Ballet. He soon proved himself a sound and reliable classical dancer with a special talent for characterization, which shows in such roles as Judas, Lanchedem, the Suitor in *The Sleeping Beauty* (in which he looks like a Dumas père character), and Quasimodo (a concert piece). He also created a number of comic roles in television films, like Father Doolittle (*Galatea*) or the reckless and brave Cowboy in *The Cowboys*. British audiences in particular appreciated Zaklinsky's sense of humour during the Kirov's 1990 tour, when the dancer performed the role of the slave trader in *Le Corsaire*, and

invested each mimed gesture and movement with his own witticisms; he demonstrated, as the critic Mary Clarke (in *Dancing Times*) wrote, ". . . that he is not only a magnificent dancer but one blessed with irresistible humour."

Zaklinsky's work, be it a leading role in a ballet or just a classical variation in class, is always placed within the context of music and determined by its laws. His weightless leaps and diagonal tours are full of joyful energy, the energy of music itself, which makes classical dance in his interpretation brighten with new tones and colours. Zaklinsky is a dancer who subjects himself to strict professional discipline; his attitude to art is highly moral, but at the same time coldness and indifference are alien to his approach. This is the motivating force behind his continuing artistic development.

Zaklinsky is married to one of the leading young ballerinas of the Kirov Ballet, Altynai Asylmuratova. Together they make a wonderful partnership, and they have danced together in many ballets of the Kirov repertoire. A particularly difficult, but rewarding, challenge for them was to dance in George Balanchine's ballet, *Theme and Variations* (acquired by the Kirov Ballet in 1989, and staged by Francia Russell). In this Balanchine classic, the two young dancers had to acquire a new manner of dancing—sparkling, detached, and extremely intricate in technique. Judging by the reviews of Western critics, both dancers have proven equal to this task.

Zaklinsky is also known for his reliable and strong partnering, a less showy but absolutely crucial aspect of his dancing gift. Zaklinsky was the dancer who partnered Natalia Makarova in her famed reunion performance with the Kirov Ballet in 1988, when she danced the "White Swan Pas de Deux" (Act II, *Swan Lake*) on the stage of the Royal Opera House in London. Here, as in all of his performances, Zaklinsky showed himself to be a sensitive partner, attuned to the ballerina's every movement and as supportive in delicate pauses as in lifts and pirouettes. He was without a doubt a good representative of the Kirov tradition, and a worthy partner to one of the world's greatest ballerinas.

—Igor Stupnikov

ZAMBELLI, Carlotta

Italian dancer and teacher. Born Carolina Celia Luigia in Milan, 4 November 1875. Studied at the Imperial Academy (School of La Scala), Milan, pupil of Adelaide Viganò and Cesare Coppini, from 1884; later studied at the School of the Paris Opéra, pupil of Rosita Mauri. Dancer, while still a student, La Scala, Milan; début at Paris Opéra, 1894, becoming étoile, 1898–1930; guest ballerina, Maryinsky Theatre, St. Petersburg, 1901, also performing in Monte Carlo, from 1904; engaged by Diaghilev to perform in Russia, 1912 (cancelled when Narodny Dom burned down); appeared in London, 1912; toured extensively, performing for the troops at various "Théâtres des armées", World War I; last performance as étoile, 1930, returning to the stage occasionally for gala performances; teacher at own private studio and for class of perfection (succeeding Rosita Mauri), Paris Opéra, 1920–55: pupils include Odette Joyeux, Paulette Dynalix, Renée Jeanmaire, Liane Daydé, Lycette Darsonval, Christiane Vaussard, and Claire Motte. Recipient: Palmes académiques, 1906; Médaille de la reconnaissance française, 1920; titles of Chevalier de la légion d'honneur, 1926, Officier de la légion d'honneur, 1956. Died in Milan, 28 January 1968.

Carlotta Zambelli

ROLES

1894   Courtesan in *Faust* (after Perrot), Opéra, Paris
        Hélène in *Faust* (after Perrot), Opéra, Paris
1895   Fairy of the Snows in *La Maladetta* (Hansen), Opéra, Paris
1896   Divertissement in *La Favorita* (opera; mus. Donizetti), Opéra, Paris
        Salomé (cr) in *Hellé* (opera; mus. Duvernoy), Opéra, Paris
1897   Queen in *Ballet of the Legend of Gold* in *Messidor* (opera; mus. Bruneau), Opéra, Paris
        Zénaïde in *L'Étoile* (Hansen), Opéra, Paris
1898   Variation (cr; chor. Hansen) in *Thaïs* (opera; mus. Massenet), Opéra, Paris
1899   Tyrolienne in *Guillaume Tell* (opera; mus. Rossini), Opéra, Paris
        Yvonnette in *La Korrigane* (Mérante), Opéra, Paris
1900   Divertissement in *Le Cid* (opera; mus. Massenet), Opéra, Paris
1901   Swanilda in *Coppélia* (Petipa, Cecchetti after Saint-Léon), Maryinsky Theatre, St. Petersburg
        Title role in *Giselle* (Petipa after Coralli, Perrot), Maryinsky Theatre, St. Petersburg
        Title role in *Paquita* (Petipa), Maryinsky Theatre, St. Petersburg

1902   Erigone (cr) in *Bacchus* (Hansen), Opéra, Paris
1904   Divertissement in *Les Contes de Hoffmann* (opera; mus. Offenbach, chor. Gedda), Monte Carlo
        Divertissement in *Le Fils de l'étoile* (opera; mus. Erlanger), Opéra, Paris
        Divertissement in *Le Trouvère* (opera; mus. Verdi), Opéra, Paris
1905   Divertissement in *Armide* (opera; mus. Gluck), Opéra, Paris
        Oriel (cr) in *La Ronde des saisons* (Hansen), Opéra, Paris
1906   Divertissement in *Le Roi de Lahore* (opera; mus. Massenet), Monte Carlo
        Tisiphone (cr) in *Ariane* (opera; mus. Massenet), Opéra, Paris
1907   Fiametta-Circé in *Le Timbre d'argent* (opera; mus. Saint-Saëns), Opéra, Paris
        Divertissement in *La Catalane* (opera; mus. Le Borne), Opéra, Paris
        Lulla (cr) in *Le Lac des Aulnes* (Hansen, Vanara), Opéra, Paris
1908   Swanilda in *Coppélia* (Saint-Léon), Opéra, Paris
        Title role (cr) in *Namouna* (Staats after L. Petipa), Opéra, Paris
1909   Title role (cr) in *Javotte* (Staats), Opéra, Paris
        Divertissement in *Henry VIII* (opera; mus. Saint-Saëns), Opéra, Paris
        Bacchante (cr) in *Bacchus* (opera; mus. Massenet, chor. Staats), Opéra, Paris
1910   Mimi Pinson (cr) in *La Fête chez Thérèse* (Stichel, Mauri), Opéra, Paris
1911   Principal dancer (cr) in *España* (Staats, Mauri), Opéra, Paris
        Principal dancer (cr) in *La Roussalka* (Clustine), Opéra, Paris
1912   Gourouli in *Les Deux Pigeons* (Mérante), Opéra, Paris
        Pas de trois from *Le Pavillon d'Armide* (Fokine), Ritz Hotel, London
        Myrrhina (cr) in *Les Bacchantes* (Clustine), Opéra, Paris
1913   Principal dancer (cr) in *Suite de danses* (Clustine), Opéra, Paris
1914   Terpsichore in *Les Fêtes d'Hébé* (opera; mus. Rameau, chor. Bolm), Monte Carlo
        Title role (cr) in *Philotis* (Clustine), Opéra, Paris
        Suzel (cr) in *Hansli le bossu* (Clustine), Opéra, Paris
1917   Queen Bee (cr) in *Les Abeilles* (Staats), Opéra, Paris
1919   Title role (cr) in *Sylvia* (Staats after Mérante), Opéra, Paris
1920   Marie Taglioni (cr) in *Taglioni chez Musette* (Staats), Opéra, Paris
1921   Chloé in *Daphnis et Chloé* (Fokine), Opéra, Paris
1923   Cydalise (cr) in *Cydalise et le chèvre-pied* (Staats), Opéra, Paris
        Gourouli in *Les Deux Pigeons* (new production; Aveline after Mérante), Opéra, Paris
        Variation (cr) in *La Nuit ensorcelée* (Staats), Opéra, Paris
1927   Principal dancer (cr) in *Impressions de music-hall* (Nijinska), Opéra, Paris

PUBLICATIONS

Beaumont, Cyril, *Complete Book of Ballets*, revised edition, London, 1951

Tugal, Pierre, "Carlotta Zambelli", *Dancing Times* (London), May 1953

Guest, Ivor, "Carlotta Zambelli: La Grand Mademoiselle de la danse française", *Ballet Annual* (London), vol. 12, 1957

Guest, Ivor, *Carlotta Zambelli*, Paris, 1969

Guest, Ivor, "Carlotta Zambelli in Russia", *Dancing Times* (London), October 1970

Guest, Ivor, "Carlotta Zambelli", *Dance Magazine* (New York), 2 parts: February, March 1974

Percival, John, "Coppélia Returns to the Source", *Dance and Dancers* (London), March 1974

*   *   *

Carlotta Zambelli's remarkable career as a ballerina and teacher spanned over 60 years, from before World War I, la belle époque, to the mid-1950s, when she retired from her teaching post at the Paris Opéra. Zambelli was a product of La Scala in Milan, then considered the finest ballet school in Europe. Its curriculum had been devised by the great ballet master and theoretician, Carlo Blasis, and the principles established by him were still followed by its ballet masters in Zambelli's era. Her main teacher was the revered ballet master, Cesare Coppini, who instilled in her the finest qualities of the Italian School with its strong emphasis on clean technique, virtuosity, and pointe work, but he was careful not to dampen her natural lively spirit and expressivity. Even before graduation, Zambelli attracted considerable attention, and upon graduating, she was offered contracts at both La Scala and the Paris Opéra. She chose Paris, and thus began a long and distinguished career that was instrumental in reviving the popularity of ballet in France.

When Zambelli arrived in Paris, in 1894, ballet was the poor cousin to opera. There were few ballets in the repertory, no new dance works were being created, and the dancers appeared mostly in short divertissements in the opera. French dancers had also lost the stature they had held during the Romantic era. The current crop of dancers were poorly trained and undisciplined, and the Opéra had taken to hiring mostly Italian and Spanish ballerinas for leading roles.

Although Zambelli was hired as a corps member, she was quickly given solo parts that won her instantaneous approval. In 1896, she cemented her reputation by astounding audiences with a dazzling display of fifteen fouettés—the first seen in Paris—in the divertissement *La Favorita*. Dancer Cléo de Mérode remembered her from those early days at the Opéra: "Her work was admirable for its strength and assurance . . . She performed the miracle of maintaining her style and control even in the most brilliant display. Without disturbing a single hair, without her smile leaving her lips, she would throw herself into dazzling feats of virtuosity, and finish on her pointe, facing the public with her arms in a graceful curve, her radiant features showing no trace of effort." Although Zambelli was clearly destined for stardom, Opéra heirarchy decreed that she wait until the retirement of the two senior ballerinas, the Spanish Rosita Mauri and the Parisienne Julia Subra. By 1900 Carlotta Zambelli reigned supreme.

In 1901 she received an invitation to appear as guest artist at the Maryinsky Theatre in St. Petersburg. The visit secured her reputation, and it also gave her the opportunity to learn and perform *Giselle*, which had not been presented in Paris since 1868. Although the Russian critics were divided on their assessment, most agreed that "The charming, slender Italian, with the beautiful expressive eyes has two qualities which set her apart from the other Italian ballerinas—youth and elegance." Sadly, Zambelli was the last of the Italian stars to appear in Russia. Although she was invited back for the following year, she declined, choosing to remain at the Paris Opéra throughout her career, making only rare guest appearances elsewhere.

The next several years marked the peak of her career, as dance regained its popularity in Paris. New ballets were choreographed for her, especially by her frequent partner, Léo Staats. Classical ballets, including *Coppélia* and *Les Deux Pigeons*, were revived, but her greatest role was in the ballet *Sylvia* which she first danced with her favourite partner, Albert Aveline, in 1919. The critic Maurice Brillant wrote: "It was one of her greatest triumps . . . and her interpretation has remained 'legendary'. No one who saw her will forget the radiant entrance at the head of the nymphs, nor the ethereal poetry of her valse lente, matched by music of exquisite delicacy, nor, later, her celebrated pizzicato, danced with sparkling pointe work, like an exquisite piece of embroidery . . . nor that dazzling adage, absolute in its perfection, danced with Aveline . . . Mlle. Zambelli's range is well known, as also is the ease and harmony with which she undertakes all styles, from the most delicate vivacity to the noblest and purest poetry."

While still continuing her performance career, Zambelli took over the class of perfection from Rosita Mauri and proved to be a gifted teacher. Upon retiring from the stage, in 1930, she taught for many years at the Paris Opéra School and in her own private studio. Almost singlehandedly she raised the technical standards at the Opéra through her exacting teaching methods and emphasis on interpretative qualities. She believed wholeheartedly that "The classical dance is a unity with its basic rules, the fruit of a centuries-old tradition which yet does not exclude improvements. The classical dance can be enriched only if steps and figures remain in accordance with its principles. It is obvious that seeking after excess, lack of symmetry and athleticism cannot satisfy a refined art." She stayed loyal to these tenets, even as the Paris Opéra moved on to a period of experimentation and novelty under Serge Lifar. Zambelli's concentration on tradition, however, helped to preserve the best of the Italian School and to infuse it with both French and Russian style for future generations.

—Mary Jane Warner

ZORINA, Vera

German/American dancer and actress. Born Eva Brigitta Hartwig in Berlin, 2 January 1917. Studied with Eugenia Eduardova, Tatjana and Victor Gsovsky, Berlin; later studied with Nikolai Legat, Paris and London, and Marie Rambert, London. Married (1) choreographer George Balanchine, 1938 (div. 1946); (2) producer Goddard Lieberson, 1946: 2 sons. Stage début as fairy in *A Midsummer Night's Dream* (dir. Reinhardt), Berlin, 1930; dancer in Offenbach's opera *The Tales of Hoffmann* (dir. Reinhardt, chor. Nijinska), Berlin, 1931; dancer, Dayelma Ballet, touring music halls in Europe, c. 1932, also appearing in concert performances staged by Tatjana and Victor Gsovsky, 1932/33; performed with Serge Lifar, Venice, 1933; dancer, partnered by Anton Dolin, in *Ballerina* (play by Lady Eleanor Smith; chor. Dolin), London, 1933; soloist, de Basil's Ballets Russes (also performing as Monte Carlo Ballet Russe, eventually to become the Original Ballet Russe), 1934–36; leading dancer/actress (in starring role) in *On Your Toes* (London production), 1937, moving to New York to star in *I Married an Angel*, 1938; guest ballerina, Ballet Theatre (later American Ballet Theatre), New York, 1943; also dancer/actress in films, including in *Goldwyn Follies* (dir. Marshall, chor. Balanchine, 1938), *On Your Toes* (film

Vera Zorina

version of musical; dir. Enright, chor. Balanchine, 1939), *I Was an Adventuress* (dir. Ratoff; chor. Balanchine, 1940), *Louisiana Purchase* (dir. Cummings, 1941), *Star Spangled Rhythm* (dir. Marshall, chor. Balanchine, Dare, and Durham, 1942), *Follow the Boys* (dir. Sutherland, 1944), *Lover Come Back* (dir. Seiter, 1946); also stage actress, including as Ariel in *The Tempest* (play by Shakespeare; dir. Webster, 1945); narrator/performer, from 1948, with speaking parts in *Jeanne d'Arc au bûcher* (mus. Honegger; 1948), *Perséphone* (mus. Stravinsky; 1955), *Le Martyre de Saint-Sébastien* (mus. Debussy); also opera director, including for Santa Fé Opera and New York City Opera.

ROLES

1933   Leading dancer (cr) in *Ballerina* (play by Lady Eleanor Smith; chor. Dolin), Gaiety Theatre, London

1934   Lead Can-Can dancer in *La Boutique fantasque* (Massine), de Basil's Ballets Russes, London

      Street Dancer in *Le Beau Danube* (Massine), de Basil's Ballets Russes, Mexico City

1934/   Pas de trois in *Aurora's Wedding* (divertissements from
36   *The Sleeping Beauty*; Petipa, Nijinska), de Basil's Ballets Russes

      First Movement in *Les Présages* (Massine), de Basil's Ballets Russes

      Mexican Dancer in *Union Pacific* (Massine), de Basil's Ballets Russes

      Dancer in *Cotillon* (Balanchine), de Basil's Ballets Russes

1935   "The Vision" (cr) in *Jardin public* (Massine), Monte

Carlo Ballet Russe (de Basil's Ballets Russes), Chicago

      A Maid of Honour (cr) in *Les Cents Baisirs* (Nijinksa), de Basil's Ballets Russes, London

      Dancer in *Les Femmes de bonne humeur* (Massine), de Basil's Ballets Russes

1936   "Reverie" in First Movement, A Witch in Fifth Movement (cr) in *Symphonie fantastique* (Massine), de Basil's Ballets Russes, London

      Wedding Guest in *Les Noces* (Nijinska), de Basil's Ballets Russes, New York

1937   Vera Barnova in *On Your Toes* (musical; mus. Rodgers, chor. after Balanchine), Palace Theatre, London

1938   Angel (cr) in *I Married an Angel* (musical; mus. Rodgers, chor. Balanchine), Schubert Theatre, New York

1940   Marina van Linden (cr) in *Louisiana Purchase* (musical; mus. Berlin, ballets chor. Balanchine), Imperial Theatre, New York

      Dancer (cr) in *Pas de deux—Blues* (Balanchine), "All Star Dance Gala", Winter Garden, New York

1943   Ballerina in *Petrushka* (Fokine), Ballet Theatre, New York

      Terpsichore in *Apollo* (Balanchine), Ballet Theatre, New York

      Principal dancer in *The Wanderer* (*Errante*; Balanchine), Ballet Theatre, New York

      Title role in *Helen of Troy* (Lichine, revised Balanchine), Ballet Theatre, New York

1944   Dinah, Schéhérazade (cr) in *Dream with Music* (musical; mus. arranged Warnick, chor. Balanchine), Majestic Theatre, New York

1945   Ariel (cr) in *The Tempest* (new production of play by Shakespeare; dir. Webster, movement by Balanchine), Alvin Theatre, New York

PUBLICATIONS

By Zorina:

Interview in "Vera Zorina Talks for the Camera", *Dance* (East Stroudsburg, Pennsylvania), August 1938

"Triple Play", *Dance* (East Stroudsburg, Pennsylvania), August 1940

"The Inward and the Outward Eye", *Dance Magazine* (New York), December 1959

Interview in Gruen, John, *The Private World of Ballet*, New York, 1975

"Viewpoint: Vera Zorina Talks about the Diaghilev Heritage", *Dance and Dancers* (London), August 1982

Zorina (autobiography), New York, 1986

About Zorina:

Pierre, Dorathi, "American Ballet in Hollywood", *The American Dancer* (Los Angeles), December 1937

Newnham, John, "Hollywood's Latest Dance Star", *Dancing Times* (London), February 1942

Newnham, John, "Filmland's 'Unseen' Dancers", *Dancing Times* (London), September 1942

Newnham, John, "Zorina's Film Future", *Dance Magazine* (New York), December 1942

Chaffée, George, "The Ballettophile", *Dance Magazine* (New York), March 1945

Gruen, John, "Soundings on Dance", *Dance Magazine* (New York), March 1980

Taper, Bernard, *George Balanchine*, revised edition, New York, 1980

*   *   *

Born in 1917 of Norwegian and German descent, Brigitta Hartwig—later known as Vera Zorina—spent her early childhood in Kristiansund. The family returned to Berlin when Brigitta was six, at which time her parents separated. Brigitta was raised by her mother, her father having drowned in 1928. The lonely isolated girl found that ballet could fill a void in her life, and early influential teachers included Eugenia Eduardova, Nikolai Legat, and Victor Gsovsky.

The list of influential men appearing at regular intervals in the life of Vera Zorina is somewhat daunting—and it includes Max Reinhardt, Anton Dolin, Léonide Massine, Colonel de Basil, Sol Hurok, George Balanchine (her first husband), Samuel Goldwyn, and Goddard Lieberson, whom she finally married in 1946. A review of her career development reveals very little, perhaps, of the kind of single-minded ambition most often associated with ballet, and shows it full instead of liaisons with interesting men who played an important role in her professional life. Zorina's life reads like a novel (her autobiography, Zorina, was published in 1986), with the young Brigitta being discovered at each step along her career and offered opportunities that she had not herself engineered. For example, while travelling in Italy with Karl Vollmoeller, she had a chance meeting with Serge Lifar, which led to a performance with him in Venice. Her performance in Ballerina, partnered by Dolin, led to her being invited to join the Ballets Russes de Monte Carlo in 1934, at the age of seventeen.

The stage name Vera Zorina dates from this time, and came from a list of choices presented by Colonel de Basil, in keeping with the Ballets Russes image. "Zorina" was a product of the early post-Diaghilev period, when there was tremendous vitality in European ballet. Perhaps if she had not become embroiled in an affair with artistic director Léonide Massine, this dancer's ballet training and career would have equalled her later accomplishments in film and on Broadway. She was not often described as a technically gifted performer, although it appears that her technique was more than adequate for the many roles she was given. Zorina had mostly minor parts in the major Russian repertory of the era, with perhaps her most notable performance in Massine's Symphonie fantastique. It was her stage quality and beauty that eventually brought her premieres and new works; however, while still a young dancer, Vera Zorina remained in the shadow of stronger ballet personalities. While the touring may have furthered her exposure and developed her strength as a dancer, then, the years with the Ballets Russes were not an especially happy time for Zorina. She was eventually accepted by the "baby ballerinas" and befriended by Sono Osato and Kyra Nijinsky, but her status in the company did not develop beyond that of soloist.

Zorina's natural inclination was that of a more general performer/entertainer of considerable skill. Her childhood performances in Germany included saloon shows and revues, where she encountered her first acrobatic dance. If she had been raised in America, her talents might have found her in vaudeville, not ballet. The dancer's appearance in the London production of On Your Toes, while a box office failure, was critically acclaimed; it launched her career in the United States and signalled her final separation from the Ballets Russes.

Brigitta Hartwig was the second Mrs. George Balanchine, and the relationship between the two runs parallel to interesting events in the history of American ballet prior to the domination of Balanchine. There was no great love affair with Russian choreographers in the 1930s, and while Balanchine was forced to find choreographic opportunities outside the realm of a traditional ballet company, Zorina was finding national prominence as dancer on stage and screen. Balanchine was often the genius behind her performances, setting ingenious dances for Goldwyn Follies, On Your Toes, I Was an Adventuress, and I Married an Angel.

It is for this pioneering work in film that Zorina will be most remembered. Her performances eclipsed even the master choreographer George Balanchine. Her appearances in these early film musicals did much to popularize dance, and to bring ballet in particular to audiences who would never otherwise have encountered it. It was also during this phase in the development of the Hollywood musical that Vera Zorina and Balanchine, joining together to survive the politics and artistic frustrations of the Goldwyn enterprise, were linked romantically. They were married in 1938. However, conflicting work engagements often kept them apart, and their marriage ended in divorce in 1946.

After an unsuccessful return to professional ballet dancing for Ballet Theatre in 1943, Zorina left the dance world. She was never taken back into the ballet family, and remained on the fringe of that world until her formal departure from the dance stage with her marriage to Goddard Lieberson.

—Susan Lee

ZUCCHI, Virginia

Italian dancer. Born Virginia Eurosia Teresa Zucchi in Parma, 10 February 1849. Studied under Pasquale Corbetta, Guiseppa Ramaccini, and Lodovico Montani in Milan; later studied under Blasis and Lepri, School of La Scala, Milan. Two daughters: Rosina, by Emmanuel Albert, Count of Mirafiori, b. 1870; Marie, by painter Adolphe Henri David Jourdan, b. 1879. Début in Varese, 1864; prima ballerina, Teatro Reggio Emilia, and Teatro di Borgognissanti, Florence, 1865, performing in Piacenza and Bologna, 1866, Florence and Turin, 1867–68, Verona, 1869, Messina, 1871–72, Palermo, 1872, 1873, and Teatro Nuovo, Padua (under Hippolyte Monplaisir), 1873; La Scala début, Autumn 1874, returning to work under Manzotti, 1876–77; prima ballerina, Royal Opera Berlin, 1876–78; London début, with Royal Italian Opera, Covent Garden, 1878, returning to Italy to perform in Rome, 1880 and 1881, Naples, 1880–81, Milan, 1881–82; prima ballerina assoluta, La Scala, Milan 1882–83; Paris début, 1883; St. Petersburg début, 1885, performing for the Imperial Theatres 1886–87, 1887–88; danced in Moscow, under ballet master José (Joseph) Mendez, 1888, returning to St. Petersburg, 1889 and 1892; performed in Nice, 1889, 1890, at Bayreuth Festival, producing dances for Wagner's Tannhäuser, 1891, and Paris Opéra, 1895; final stage appearance in 1898; also teacher, for own dancing school, Monte Carlo. Died in Nice, 9 October 1930.

ROLES

1864   Dancer in Nisa; ossia, Lo Spirito danzante (Razzini), Varese

1865   Dancer in Gabriella di Nancy (Magri), Teatro Contavelli, Bologna

Dancer in Jankee (Pedroni), Teatro Borgognissanti, Florence

1866   "Ballet of the Nuns", Divertissement in Roberto il Diavolo (opera; mus. Meyerbeer), Teatro Contaveli, Bologna

1866/ Polka in Flik e Flok (after P. Taglioni), Teatro
67   Communale, Trieste

Virginia Zucchi, 1884

Dancer in *Benvenuto Cellini* (Palladino), Teatro Communale, Trieste

Dancer in *Leonilda* (after P. Taglioni), Teatro Communale, Trieste

1867 Scottish dance in *Vasco di Gama* (Vianello), Zara

Leading role in *Bedra la Maliarda* (Coluzzi), Teatro Nazionale, Florence

Dancer in *La Grotto d'Adelberga* (Pallerini), Teatro Regio, Turin

Dancer in *Zelia* (Pallerini), Teatro Regio, Turin

Dancer in *Nyssa e Saib* (Pallerini), Teatro Regio, Turin

1868 Dancer in *I Quattro Caratteri* (Pratesi), Teatro Balbo, Turin

Dancer in *Lionilla* (Pratesi), Teatro Balbo, Turin

Dancer in *Un Patto infernale* (Pratesi), Teatro Balbo, Turin

Dancer in *Un Casino all'incante* (Provinciali), Teatro Verdi, Busseto

1869 Pas de deux in *Rolla* (Manzotti), Politeama Fiorentino, Florence

Dancer in *La Contessa d'Egmont* (Bini after G. Rota), Teatro Vittorio Emmanuele, Turin

Dancer in *Lo Spirito maligno* (Bini after Rota), Teatro Vittorio Emmanuele, Turin

Dancer in *Fiamma d'amore* (Bini after Saint-Léon), Teatro Vittorio Emmanuele, Turin

Title role in *Esmeralda* (Bini after Saint-Léon), Teatro Vittorio Emmanuele, Turin

1870 Title role in *Ondina*, Teatro La Pergola, Florence

1871/ Dancer in *Kamil* (Pulini), Messina
72

1873 Padmana in *Brahma* (Monplaisir), Teatro Nuovo, Padua

Principal dancer in *La Semiramide del Nord* (Monplaisir), Spoleto

Principal dancer in *Idea* (Borri), Teatro Apollo, Rome

1873/ Principal dancer in *La Dea del Valhalla* (Borri), Teatro
74 Carlo Felice, Genoa

Principal dancer in *Lionna* (Borri), Teatro Carlo Felice, Genoa

1874 Title role in *Estella* (Monplaisir), La Scala, Milan

1875 Elvira in *Rolla* (new production; Manzotti), La Scala, Milan

Dancer in *La Sorgente* (after *La Source*; Saint-Léon), La Scala, Milan

1876 Leading role in *Il Figliuolo prodigo* (Borri), La Scala, Milan

Principal dancer in *Dance of the Hours* (Divertissement) in *La Gioconda* (opera; mus. Ponchielli), La Scala, Milan

Lise in *La Fille mal gardée* (P. Taglioni after Dauberval), Hofoper, Berlin

Dancer in *Sardanapal* (P. Taglioni), Hofoper, Berlin

Title role in *Madeleine* (P. Taglioni), Hofoper, Berlin

Topaze in *Flik und Flock* (P. Taglioni), Hofoper, Berlin

Title role in *Santanella* (P. Taglioni), Hofoper, Berlin

Zobeida (cr) in *Lamea* (P. Taglioni), Hofoper, Berlin

1878 Divertissement in *Le Prophète* (opera; mus. Meyerbeer), Royal Italian Opera, London

Divertissement in *Hamlet* (opera; mus. A. Thomas), Royal Italian Opera, London

Divertissement in *Le Roi de Lahore* (opera; mus. Massenet), Royal Italian Opera, London

1880 Naïla in *La Sorgente* (Marzagora after Saint-Léon), Teatro San Carlo, Naples

1881/ Dancer in *La Giocoliera* (Borri), Dal Verme, Milan
82

1883 Even in *L'Astro degli Afghan* (Smeraldi after Pratesi), La Scala, Milan

Civilization in *Excelsior* (Manzotti), La Scala, Milan

Title role in *Sieba* (Manzotti), Théâtre Eden, Paris

1884/ Title role in *Rodope* (Grassi), Teatro Regio, Turin
85 Swanilda in *Coppélia* (Saint-Léon), Teatro Regio, Turin

1885 Principal dancer in *Ballet of the Stars, Ballet of the Swallows and Snow*, (divertissements) in *Le Voyage dans la lune* (opera; mus. Offenbach, chor. Hansen), Kin Grust, St. Petersburg

Divertissement in *Les Pommes d'or* (operetta; mus. Audran), Kin Grust, St. Petersburg

Aspicia in *Pharaoh's Daughter* (Petipa), Bolshoi Theatre, St. Petersburg

Lise in *Vain Precautions* (*La Fille mal gardée*; Petipa after Dauberval), Bolshoi Theatre, St. Petersburg

1886 Pepita (cr) in *The King's Command* (Petipa), Bolshoi Theatre, St. Petersburg

Title role in *Paquita* (Petipa), Maryinsky Theatre, St. Petersburg

Title role in *Esmeralda* (new production; Petipa), Maryinsky Theatre, St. Petersburg

1887 Title role in *Fenella* (*La Muette de Portici*; opera; mus. Auber), Maryinsky Theatre, St. Petersburg

1888 Title role in *Catarina* (Mendez after Perrot), Rodon Theatre, Moscow

1889 Title role in *Sieba* (own staging, after Manzotti), Arcadia Theatre, St. Petersburg

1890 Principal dancer in *A Life for the Tsar* (opera; mus. Glinka), Grand Theatre, Nice

1890/ Maria in *Pietro Micca* (Manzotti), Anfiteatro Mangano,
91 Palermo

1891 One of the Three Graces (cr) in *Tannhäuser* (opera; mus. Wagner, chor. Zambelli), Festspielhaus, Bayreuth

1893 Marguerite in Dream Scene, *La Damnation de Faust* (opera; mus. Berlioz, mime staged Zambelli), Théâtre de Monte Carlo, Monte Carlo

Dancer in *Robinson Crusoe* (Pantomime; chor. D'Auban), Drury Lane Theatre, London

1894 Winter in "Coming of the Spring", Divertissement in *Hulda* (opera; mus. Franck), Théâtre de Monte Carlo, Monte Carlo

Lady of the Lake (in masque) in *Amy Robsart* (opera; mus. de Lara), Théâtre de Monte Carlo, Monte Carlo

WORKS

1891 Dances in *Tannhäuser* (opera; mus. Wagner), Festspielhaus, Bayreuth (also staged La Scala, Milan, 1891; Paris Opéra, 1895)

1893 Dream Scene in *La Damnation de Faust* (opera; mus. Berlioz), Théâtre de Monte Carlo, Monte Carlo

Also staged:
1889 *Sieba* (after Manzotti), Arcadia Theatre, St. Petersburg

PUBLICATIONS

Pleshcheev, Aleksandr, *Our Ballet*, St. Petersburg, 1899

Svetlov, Valerian, *Contemporary Ballet*, St. Petersburg, 1911

Svetlov, Valerian, "Virginia Zucchi", *Dancing Times* (London), December 1930

Benois, Alexandre, *Reminiscences of the Russian Ballet*, London, 1941

Lifar, Serge, *L'Histoire du ballet russe*, Paris, 1950

Guest, Ivor, *La Fille mal gardée*, London, 1960

Krasovskaya, Vera, *Russian Ballet Theatre of the Second Half of the Nineteenth Century*, Leningrad and Moscow, 1963

Roslavleva, Natalia, *Stanislavsky and the Ballet*, New York, 1965

Roslavleva, Natalia, *Era of the Russian Ballet*, London, 1966

Guest, Ivor, "The 'Divine' Inspiration of Russian Ballet", *Dancing Times* (London), February 1977

Guest, Ivor, *The Divine Virginia*, New York, 1977

Lo Iacono, Concetta, *Virginia Zucchi e il teatro di danza del secondo ottocento* (dissertation), Rome, 1981

*   *   *

The "Divine" Virginia was not only one of the most outstanding Italian dancers of the last quarter of the nineteenth century, but also a fine actress, with a special command of the art of pantomime. Her career in Italy was long and rewarding, although her retirement was perhaps delayed far too long. In Europe and especially in Russia, Virginia Zucchi at the height of her career represented a new trend in ballet, and inspired many ballerinas—among them Kshesinskaya—who were then to establish the fame of the Russian ballet. Other observers affected by Zucchi's influence were Alexandre Benois, who played an important role in the birth of the Ballets Russes, and Konstantin Stanislavsky, who studied her almost childlike absorption in what she was doing, and noted the softness of her muscles during the highly dramatic moments of her performances.

After her studies in Milan (not at La Scala, but with some of the teachers who crowded the then-thriving Italian ballet industry), Zucchi had successive débuts in Turin, Florence, and Rome, the three Italian capital cities. Afterwards, she danced in all the political, theatrical, and fashionable centres of turn-of-the century Europe, from Paris, the queen of the *belle époque*, to the mythical St. Petersburg of the last tsars, while Monte Carlo, paradise of fading stars, was her final residence.

After her arrival in St. Petersburg, Virginia Zucchi roused such wild enthusiasm among the public responding to the intensity of her acting that Russia became the best and most satisfying place to develop her talent. In response to the overwhelming pressure of balletomanes and critics, the directors of the Imperial Theatres invited Zucchi for the season, soon awakening even greater interest in ballet. The stern atmosphere of the Maryinsky Theatre was upset by the arrival of the passionate Italian dancer who, though not satisfying the requirements of the strict French-Russian school, amazed the public with her *terre à terre* technique and led the invasion of the Italian ballerinas in the last decades of the century.

Only a few years after her Russian début, inevitable comparisons with Zucchi's younger colleagues increased the opposition to her style, which had never met with full praise from either Tchaikovsky or Petipa. In fact, she never was the ideal interpreter of Petipa roles, but thanks to her dramatic talent she succeeded in making the choreographer accept such whims as the wearing of shorter skirts, or the introduction of acrobatic lifts, and new steps in his choreography.

Everywhere Zucchi danced, from Imperial or provincial opera houses to private stages or halls, she performed a wide repertoire of roles, be they renowned classical variations or parts in Christmas pantomimes. Dancing in revivals of famous earlier works by Perrot or Saint-Léon, or participating in new productions by Grassi and Manzotti, she renewed the classical ideal of dance and drama united, thereby actually travelling along the same path that Stanislavsky was later to follow. As a complete and utterly committed performer, Zucchi offered with much ingenuousness a sensual image of woman rather than the diaphanous shadow of a sylph.

She was radiant and unaffected in *La Fille mal gardée*, *Paquita*, or *Coppélia*, thoroughly convincing in popular national dances (which she studied in every country she visited), and profoundly moving in the tragic roles of Esmeralda, Fenella, and Padmana, bringing her audiences to tears and inviting comparisons with Ristori, Rachel, Bernhardt, and Duse.

Zucchi's temperament was particularly suited to portraying women in love, like the courtesans Rodope or Manon who eventually redeem themselves through an ultimate sacrifice; but she also showed devilish fury and clever determination in the roles which portrayed women of spirit and daring, as in *Santanella* and *Catarina*. Blessed with a voluptuous body which corresponded to the ideal of feminine beauty of the time, Zucchi offered a style which spoke of the triumph of the senses without descending into lack of style or taste: her exoticism was her own artistic and magnetic personal appeal.

Although she was friendly and sincere in private life, Virginia Zucchi none the less elicited as much bitter criticism as she excited rapturous praise; newspapers were filled with the stories of her escape with the tenor Julián Gayarre, or of her love affairs with Russian and Italian royalty. Her natural beauty was undisputed, as several paintings and drawings (including by Léon Bakst) bear witness; faded old photographs of Zucchi remind one of images of the great silent screen actresses.

Virginia Zucchi is, then, a dancer who exists on a sort of border-line: a ballerina who danced in romantic ballets without actually being romantic, a classical dancer whose outstanding technique was almost overshadowed by her great acting ability, and whose own innovations might seem marginal by comparison to those great artists who changed ballet at the beginning of the century. But her definitive contribution in the context of ballet history, as is now recognized, was her deep insight into the character and motivation of the leading female classical roles, which was a starting-point for subsequent innovations on the Russian ballet scene; she was, as Svetlov said, "the first to show that ballet was not merely dancing, but drama as well".

—Concetta Lo Iacono

COUNTRY INDEX

Entrants are listed below under their country of birth and, where appropriate, the country/ies with which their careers have been most closely associated. Also included are companies, which are listed by country with relevant cross-references.

Argentina
Bocca, Julio (1967–)
Donn, Jorge Itovitch
(1947–1992)
Romanov, Boris (1891–1957)

Australia
Australian Ballet, The
Borovansky, Edouard
(Eduard) (1902–1959)
Heathcote, Steven (1964–)
Helpmann, Robert
(1909–1986)
Horsman, Greg (1963–)
Jones, Marilyn (1940–)
Pavane, Lisa (1961–)
Screcek, Eduard Josef
see Borovansky, Edouard
(Eduard)
Walsh, Christine (1954–)
Welch, Garth (1936–)

Austria
Elssler, Fanny (1810–1884)
Elssler, Franziska see Elssler,
Fanny
Hanka, Erika (1905–1958)
Hilverding (van Wewen),
Franz (1710–1768)
Lanner, Katharina Josefa see
Lanner, Katti
Lanner, Katti (1829–1908)
Minkus, Léon (1826–1917)
Nureyev, Rudolf (1938–1993)

Belgium
Béjart, Maurice (1927–)
Donn, Jorge Itovitch
(1947–1992)

Brazil
Haydée, Marcia (1939–)
Pereira da Silva, Marcia
Haydée Salaverry see
Haydée, Marcia

Canada
Ballets Chiriaeff, Les see
Grands Ballets Canadiens,
Les
Bruhn, Erik (1928–1986)
Chiriaeff, Ludmilla (1923–)

Eagling, Wayne (1950–)
Franca, Celia (1921–)
Grands Ballets Canadiens,
Les
Grant, Alexander (1925–)
Hart, Evelyn (1956–)
Hayden, Melissa (1923–)
Herman, Mildred see
Hayden, Melissa
Kain, Karen (1951–)
Kudelka, James (1955–)
Macdonald, Brian (1928–)
National Ballet of Canada
Penney, Jennifer (1946–)
Royal Winnipeg Ballet
Samsova, Galina (1937–)
Seymour, Lynn (1939–)
Springbett, Berta Lynn see
Seymour, Lynn
Tennant, Veronica (1947–)
White, Patricia Lorrain-Ann
see Wilde, Patricia
Wilde, Patricia (1928–)
Winnipeg Ballet see Royal
Winnipeg Ballet

Chile
De Cuevas, Marquis George
(1885–1961)
Piedrablanca de Guana de
Cuevas, Eighth Marquis de
see De Cuevas, Marquis
George

China
Central Ballet of China
National Ballet of China see
Central Ballet of China

Cuba
Alonso, Alicia (1921–)
Ballet Alicia Alonso see
Ballet Nacional de Cuba
Ballet Nacional de Cuba
Caridad del Cobre Martinez y
del Hoyo, Alicia Ernestina
de la see Alonso, Alicia
National Ballet of Cuba see
Ballet Nacional de Cuba

Czechoslovakia
Borovansky, Edouard
(Eduard) (1902–1959)
Kylián, Jiří (1947–)
Screcek, Eduard Josef see
Borovansky, Edouard
(Eduard)

Denmark
Andersen, Frank (1953–)
Andersen, Ib (1954–)
Beck, Hans (1861–1952)
Bjørnsson, Fredbjørn (1926–)
Bournonville, August
(1805–1879)
Brenaa, Hans (1910–1988)
Bruhn, Erik (1928–1986)
Evers, Belton see Bruhn, Erik
Flindt, Flemming (1936–)
Florentz-Gerhardt, Margot
see Lander, Margot
Gad, Rose (1968–)
Galeotti, Vincenzo
(1733–1816)
Genée, Adeline (1878–1970)
Gnatt, Kirsten Laura see
Ralov, Kirsten
Grahn, Lucile (1819–1907)
Hübbe, Nikolaj (1967–)
Jensen, Anna Kristina
Margarete Petra see Genée,
Adeline
Jeppesen, Lis (1956–)
Kehlet, Niels (1938–)
Kølpin, Alexander (1965–)
Kronstam, Henning (1934–)
Laerkesen, Anna (1942–)
Lander, Harald (1905–1971)
Lander, Margot (1910–1961)
Lander, Toni (1931–1985)
Larsen, Niels Bjørn
(1913–1992)
Madsen, Egon (1942–)
Martins, Peter (1946–)
Pedersen, Hans see Brenaa,
Hans
Petersen, Toni Pihl see
Lander, Toni
Ralov, Kirsten (1922–)
Royal Danish Ballet, The
Ryom, Heidi (1955–)
Sand, Inge (1928–1974)

Schanne, Margrethe (1921–)
Schaufuss, Peter (1949–)
Simone, Kirsten (1934–)
Sørensen, Inge Sand see
Sand, Inge
Stevnsborg, Alfred Bernhardt
see Lander, Harald
Tomasselli, Vincenzo see
Galeotti, Vincenzo
Vangsaae, Mona (1920–1983)
Volkova, Vera (1904–1975)

Dominican Republic
Moncion, Francisco (1922–)

France
Adam, Adolphe (1803–1856)
Albert, Monsieur
(1787–1865)
Allard, Marie (1742–1802)
Arbeau, Thoinot (1520–1595)
Atanassoff, Cyril (1941–)
Aumer, Jean-Louis
(1774–1833)
Babilée, Jean (1923–)
Ballets Russes de Serge
Diaghilev, Les
Ballon (Balon), Claude
(1671–1744)
Ballon (Balon), Jean see
Ballon (Balon), Claude
Beauchamps (Beauchamp),
Charles-Louis see
Beauchamps (Beauchamp),
Pierre
Beauchamps (Beauchamp),
Pierre (1631–1705)
Beaugrand, Léontine
(1842–1925)
Beaujoyeulx (Beaujoyeux),
Balthasar de (1535–1587)
Béjart, Maurice (1927–)
Bérard, Christian
(1902–1949)
Bercher, Jean see Dauberval,
Jean
Bessy, Claude (1932–)
Blondy, Michel (1675–1739)
Blum, René (1878–1942)
Bonnachon, Louis Stanislas
Xavier Henri see Henry,
Louis

Börlin, Jean (1893–1930)
Cahusac, Louis de
  (1706–1759)
Camargo, Marie-Anne
  (1710–1770)
Charrat, Janine (1924–)
Chauviré, Yvette (1917–)
Cocteau, Jean (1889–1963)
Coralli, Jean (1779–1854)
Crespé (Crespi or Crépé),
  Marie-Madeleine de see
  Théodore, Mlle.
Darsonval, Lycette (1912–)
Dauberval, Jean (1742–1806)
Dauberval, Mme. see
  Théodore, Mlle.
Daydé, Liane (1932–)
De Beaumont, Comte
  Etienne (1883–1956)
Debussy, Claude
  (1862–1918)
Decombe, Françoise see
  Albert, Monsieur
De Cuevas, Marquis George
  (1885–1961)
De Cupis, Marie-Anne see
  Camargo, Marie-Anne
De la Fontaine,
  Mademoiselle see La
  Fontaine , Mademoiselle
Delibes, Léo (1836–1891)
De Maré, Rolf (1888–1964)
Denard, Michaël (1944–)
Derain, Andre (1880–1954)
Deshayes,
  André-Jean-Jacques
  (1777–1846)
Diaghilev's Ballets Russes
  see Ballets Russes de Serge
  Diaghilev, Les
Didelot, Charles-Louis
  (1767–1837)
Dupond, Patrick (1959–)
Duport, Louis-Antoine
  (1781–1853)
Dupré, Louis (1697–1774)
Duraud, Claude see Bessy,
  Claude
Emarot, Emma-Marie see
  Livry, Emma
Feuillet, Raoul Auger
  (1660–1710)
Fokine, Mikhail (Michel)
  (1880–1942)
Gardel, Maximilien
  (1741–1787)
Gardel, Pierre (1758–1840)
Gautier, Théophile
  (1811–1872)
Golovine, Serge (1935–)
Gontcharova, Nathalie
  (Natalia) (1881–1962)
Gsovsky, Victor (1902–1974)
Guillem, Sylvie (1965–)
Guillerm, Nelly see Verdy,
  Violette

Guimard, Marie-Madeleine
  (1743–1816)
Henry, Louis (1784–1836)
Hilaire, Laurent (1963–)
Jeanmaire, Zizi (Renée)
  (1924–)
Kniaseff (Kniasev), Boris
  (1900–1975)
Kochno, Boris (1904–1991)
L'Académie royale de danse
  see Paris Opéra Ballet
L'Académie royale de
  l'Opéra see Paris Opéra
  Ballet
Lacotte, Pierre (1932–)
La Fontaine (also de la
  Fontaine), Mademoiselle
  (1655–1738)
Lander, Harald (1905–1971)
Lepicq (also Le Picq, Lepic),
  Charles (1744–1806)
Lifar, Serge (1905–1986)
Livry, Emma (1842–1863)
Lulli, Giovanni Battista see
  Lully, Jean-Baptiste
Lully, Jean-Baptiste
  (1632–1687)
Matisse, Henri (1869–1954)
Mazarini, Giulio see
  Mazilier, Joseph
Mazilier, Joseph (1797–1868)
Mérante, Louis (1828–1887)
Michel, Charles-Victor-
  Arthur see Saint-Léon,
  Arthur
Milhaud, Darius (1892–1974)
Miskovitch, Milorad (1928–)
Noverre, Jean-Georges
  (1727–1810)
Nureyev, Rudolf (1938–1993)
Paris Opéra Ballet
Pécour, Guillaume-Louis
  (1653–1729)
Peretti, Serge (1910–)
Perron, Alice see Darsonval,
  Lycette
Perrot, Jules (1810–1892)
Petipa, Marius (1818–1910)
Petit, Roland (1924–)
Platel, Elisabeth (1959–)
Pontois, Noëlla (1943–)
Poulenc, Francis (1899–1963)
Poupard, Jean-Pierre see
  Sauget, Henri
Prévost, Françoise
  (1681–1741)
Prokovsky, André (1939–)
Rameau, Jean-Philippe
  (1683–1763)
Ravel, Maurice (1875–1937)
Renault, Michel (1927–1993)
Rubinstein, Ida (1885–1960)
Saint-Léon, Arthur
  (1821–1870)
Sallé, Marie (1707–1756)

Satie, Erik (Eric)
  (1866–1925)
Sauget, Henri (1901–1989)
Schwarz, Solange (1910–)
Skouratoff, Vladimir (1925–)
Staats, Léo (1877–1952)
Stevnsborg, Alfred Bernhardt
  see Lander, Harald
Stravinksy, Igor (1882–1971)
Subligny, Marie-Thérèse
  (1666–1735)
Tabourot, Jehan see Arbeau,
  Thoinot
Tchemerzina, Monika
  (Monique) Avenirova see
  Tcherina, Ludmila
Tcherina, Ludmila (1924–)
Théodore, Mlle. (1760–1796)
Verdy, Violette (1933–)
Vestris, Auguste (1760–1842)
Vestris, Gaetano (Gaétan)
  (1729–1808)
Volinine, (Volinin)
  Alexandre (1882–1955)
Vyroubova, Nina (1921–)

Germany
Clauss, Heinz (1935–)
Cragun, Richard (1944–)
Cranko, John (1927–1973)
Forsythe, William (1949–)
Georgi, Yvonne (1903–1975)
Gsovsky, Victor (1902–1974)
Gsovsky (Gsovska), Tatjana
  (1901–)
Hamburg Ballet
Hartwig, Eva Brigitta see
  Zorina, Vera
Haydée, Marcia (1939–)
Heinel, Anne (Anna)
  (1753–1808)
Henze, Hans Werner (1926–)
Hindemith, Paul (1895–1963)
Issatchenko, Tatyana see
  Gsovsky (Gsovska), Tatjana
Keil, Birgit (1944–)
Madsen, Egon (1942–)
Neumeier, John (1942–)
Reinholm, Gert (1926–)
Schaufuss, Peter (1949–)
Schmidt, Gerhard see
  Reinholm, Gert
Stuttgart Ballet
Taglioni, Paul (Paolo)
  (1808–1884)
Von Aroldingen, Karin
  (1941–)
Zorina, Vera (1917–)

Hungary
Bartók, Béla (1881–1945)
Budapest Ballet see
  Hungarian State Opera
  Ballet
Eck, Imre (1930–)

Harangozó, Gyula
  (1908–1974)
Hungarian National Ballet
  see Hungarian State Opera
  Ballet (BudapestBallet)
Hungarian State Opera Ballet
  (Budapest Ballet)
Kun, Zsuzsa (1934–)
Miholy, Urel de see Milloss,
  Aurel (von)
Milloss, Aurel (von)
  (1906–1988)
Nádasi, Ferenc (1893–1966)
Róna, Victor (1936–)
Seregi, László (1929–)

Iceland
Tomasson, Helgi (1942–)

Ireland
De Valois, Ninette (1898–)
Stannus, Edris see De Valois,
  Ninette

Israel
Panov, Valery (1938–)
Shulman, Valery Matyevich
  see Panov, Valery

Italy
Angiolini, Gaspero
  (1731–1803)
Baccelli, Giovanna
  (1753–1801)
Barberina, La (1721–1799)
Beaujoyeulx (Beaujoyeux),
  Balthasar de (1535–1587)
Belgiojoso, Baldassare de see
  Beaujoyeulx (Beaujoyeux),
  Balthasar de
Blasis, Carlo (1795–1878)
Bortoluzzi, Paolo (1938–)
Bozzacchi, Giuseppina
  (1853–1870)
Brambilla, Maria see Fuoco,
  Sofia
Brianza, Carlotta
  (1867–1935)
Campanini, Barbara see
  Barberina, La
Caroso, Fabritio (1526–1605)
Cecchetti, Enrico
  (1850–1928)
Cerrito, Fanny (1817–1909)
Chirico, Giorgio de
  (1888–1978)
Coralli, Jean (1779–1854)
Cornazano, Antonio
  (1430–1484)
Da Ferrara, Domenico see
  Domenico De Piacena
Domenico De Piacena
  (1425–1465)
Durante, Viviana (1967–)
Ferri, Alessandra (1963–)
Fornaroli, Cia (1888–1954)

Fracci, Carla (1936–)
Fuoco, Sofia (1830–1916)
Galeotti, Vincenzo
  (1733–1816)
Galletti, Carolina *see* Rosati,
  Carolina
Gasparini, Domenico Maria
  Angiolo *see* Angiolini,
  Gaspero
Grisi, Carlotta (1819–1899)
Guglielmo Ebreo
  (1420–1481)
Guillaume le Juif *see*
  Guglielmo Ebreo
Legnani, Pierina (1863–1923)
Luigia, Carolina Celia *see*
  Zambelli, Carlotta
Lulli, Giovanni Battista *see*
  Lully, Jean-Baptiste
Lully, Jean-Baptiste
  (1632–1687)
Miholy, Urel de *see* Milloss,
  Aurel (von)
Milloss, Aurel (von)
  (1906–1988)
Negri, Cesare (1536–1604)
Peracini, Giovanni Coralli
  see Coralli, Jean
Pugni, Cesare (1802–1870)
Raffaela, Francesca Teresa
  Guiseppa *see* Cerrito, Fanny
Rosati, Carolina (1826–1905)
Scala Ballet, La
Taglioni, Filippo (1777–1871)
Taglioni, Marie (1804–1884)
Taglioni, Salvatore
  (1789–1868)
Terabust, Elisabetta (1946–)
Tomasselli, Vincenzo *see*
  Galeotti, Vincenzo
Vestris, Gaetano (Gaétan)
  (1729–1808)
Viganò, Salvatore
  (1769–1821)
William the Jew of Pesaro
  see Guglielmo Ebreo
Zambelli, Carlotta
  (1875–1968)
Zanerini, Giovanna
  Francesca Antonia
  Guiseppe *see* Baccelli,
  Giovanna
Zucchi, Virginia (1849–1930)

Japan
Matsuyama Ballet
Morishita, Yoko (1948–)
Shimizu, Yoko *see* Morishita,
  Yoko
Tokyo Ballet, The

Latvia
Chiriaeff, Ludmilla (1923–)

Lithuania
Beriosova, Svetlana (1932–)

Beriozoff (Beriosoff),
  Nicholas (1906–)
Gaskell, Sonia (1904–1974)

Mexico
Magallanes, Nicholas
  (1922–1977)

Monte Carlo
Ballet Russe de Monte Carlo
Ballets Russes de Colonel
  Wassily de Basil *see* Ballets
  Russes de Monte Carlo, Les
Ballets Russes de Monte
  Carlo, Les
Ballets Russes de Serge
  Diaghilev, Les
Covent Garden Russian
  Ballet *see* Ballets Russes de
  Monte Carlo, Les
Diaghilev's Ballets Russes
  see Ballets Russes de Serge
  Diaghilev, Les
Original Ballet Russe *see*
  Ballets Russes de Monte
  Carlo, Les

Netherlands
Dutch National Ballet
Gaskell, Sonia (1904–1974)
Georgi, Yvonne (1903–1975)
Het Nationale Ballet *see*
  Dutch National Ballet
Kylián, Jiří (1947–)
Nederlands Dans Theater 2
  (NDT2) *see* Netherlands
  Dance Theatre
Netherlands Dance Theatre
Snoek, Hans (1910–)
Snoek, Johanna *see* Snoek,
  Hans
Van Dantzig, Rudi (1933–)
Van Hamel, Martine (1945–)
Van Manen, Hans (1932–)
Van Schayk, Toer (1936–)

New Zealand
Grant, Alexander (1925–)

Poland
Idzikowski, Stanislas
  (1894–1977)
Ikowski *see* Idzikowski,
  Stanislas
Rambam, Cyvia *see* Rambert,
  Marie
Ramberg (Rambach),
  Myriam *see* Rambert, Marie
Rambert, Marie (1888–1982)
Shabelevsky, Yurek (1911–)
Szabelevski, Jerzy *see*
  Shabelevsky, Yurek
Woizikowsky, Léon
  (1899–1975)
Wójcikowski, Léon *see*
  Woizikowsky, Léon

Russia/former USSR
Ananiashvili, Nina (1964–)
Andreyanova, Elena
  (1819–1857)
Anisimova, Nina
  (1909–1979)
Asylmuratova, Altynai
  (1961–)
Ayupova, Zhanna (1966–)
Bakst, Léon (1866–1924)
Balanchine, George
  (1904–1983)
Balanchivadze, Georgi
  Melitonovich *see*
  Balanchine, George
Baronova, Irina (1919–)
Baryshnikov, Mikhail
  (1948–)
Belsky, Igor (1925–)
Benois, Alexandre
  (1870–1960)
Benua, Aleksandr
  Nikolaevich *see* Benois,
  Alexandre
Bessmertnova, Natalia
  (1941–)
Bogdanova, Nadezhda
  (1836–1897)
Bolm, Adolph (1884–1951)
Bolshoi Ballet
Burmeister, Vladimir
  (1904–1971)
Cecchetti, Enrico
  (1850–1928)
Chabukiani, Vakhtang
  (1910–1992)
Chaikovsky, Petr Ilyich *see*
  Tchaikovsky, Petr
Chernitseva, Lyubov
  Pavlovna *see* Tchernicheva,
  Lubov
Danilova, Aleksandra
  Dionisievna *see* Danilova,
  Alexandra
Danilova, Alexandra (1903–)
De Basil, Colonel Wassily
  (1888–1951)
Diaghilev, Serge (1872–1929)
Didelot, Charles-Louis
  (1767–1837)
Dluzhnevska, Felzata *see*
  Doubrovska, Felia
Dolgushin, Nikita (1938–)
Doubrovska, Felia
  (1896–1981)
Dudinskaya, Natalia (1912–)
Eglevsky, André (1917–1977)
Egorova, Lyubov (Lubov)
  (1880–1972)
Eifman, Boris (1946–)
Elvin, Violetta (1925–)
Ermolaev, Aleksei
  Nikolaevich *see*
  Yermolaev, Aleksei
Fadeyechev, Nikolai (1933–)

Fedorova, Sophia (Sofia)
  (1879–1963)
Fedorovitch, Sophie
  (1893–1953)
Fokine, Mikhail (Michel)
  (1880–1942)
Froman, Margarita
  (1890–1970)
Gabovich, Mikhail
  (1905–1965)
Geltser, Ekaterina
  (1876–1962)
Gerdt, Elisaveta (1891–1975)
Gerdt, Pavel (1844–1917)
Glazunov, Aleksandr
  (1865–1936)
Glushkovsky, Adam
  Pavlovich (1793–1870)
Goleizovsky, Kasyan
  (1892–1970)
Gontcharova, Nathalie
  (Natalia) (1881–1962)
Gorsky, Aleksandr
  (1871–1924)
Grigoriev, Serge (1883–1968)
Grigorovich, Yuri (1927–)
Gsovsky, Victor (1902–1974)
Gsovsky (Gsovska), Tatjana
  (1901–)
Gusev, Petr (1904–1987)
Issatchenko, Tatyana *see*
  Gsovsky (Gsovska), Tatjana
Istomina, Avdotia
  (1799–1848)
Ivanov, Leonid Mikhailovich
  see Lavrovsky, Leonid
Ivanov, Lev (1834–1901)
Johansson, (Per) Christian
  (1817–1903)
Karinska, Barbara
  (1886–1983)
Karsavina, Tamara
  (1885–1978)
Khachaturian, Aram
  (1903–1978)
Kirov Ballet
Kniaseff (Kniasev), Boris
  (1900–1975)
Kochno, Boris (1904–1991)
Kolpakova, Irina (1933–)
Kriger (Krieger), Viktorina
  (1893–1978)
Kshesinskaya (Kschesinska),
  Matilda (1872–1971)
Kyasht, Lydia (1885–1959)
Larionov, Mikhail
  (1881–1964)
Lavrovsky, Leonid
  (1905–1967)
Lavrovsky, Mikhail (1941–)
Legat, Nikolai (Nicholas)
  (1869–1937)
Legnani, Pierina (1863–1923)
Leningrad Maly Ballet *see*
  Maly (Mussorgsky) Theatre
  Ballet

Lepeshinskaya, Olga (1916–)
Lessogorov, Ivan *see*
  Valbergh (Valberkh), Ivan
Lichine, David (1910–1972)
Lichtenstein, David (Deivid)
  see Lichine, David
Liepa, Andris (1962–)
Liepa, Maris (1936–1989)
Lifar, Serge (1905–1986)
Lopokova, Lydia
  (1891–1981)
Lopukhov, Fedor
  (1886–1973)
Lopukhova (Lopokova),
  Lidiya (Lydia) Vasilievna
  see Lopokova, Lydia
Lukom, Elena (1891–1968)
Makarova, Natalia (1940–)
Makhalina, Yulia (1968–)
Maksimova, Ekaterina
  Sergeevna *see* Maximova,
  Ekaterina
Maly (Mussorgsky) Theatre
  Ballet
Massine, Léonide (Leonid)
  (1895–1979)
Maximova, Ekaterina
  (1939–)
Messerer, Asaf (1903–1992)
Mezentseva, Galina (1952–)
Minkus, Léon (1826–1917)
Moiseev, Igor
  Aleksandrovich *see*
  Moiseyev, Igor
Moiseyev, Igor (1906–)
Mordkin, Mikhail
  (1880–1944)
Mukhamedov, Irek (1960–)
Mussorgsky Theatre of
  Opera and Ballet, The *see*
  Maly (Mussorgsky)
  Theatre Ballet
Myasin, Leonid Fedorovich
  see Massine, Léonide
  (Leonid)
Nemchinova (Nemtchinova),
  Vera (1899–1984)
Nijinska, Bronislava
  (1891–1972)
Nijinsky, Vaslav (1889–1950)
Nikitina, Alice (1904–1978)
Nikolaev, Petr Nikolaevich
  see Vladimirov, Pierre
Nizhinskaya, Bronislava
  Fominichna *see* Nijinska,
  Bronislava
Nureyev, Rudolf (1938–1993)
Obukhov (Oboukhoff),
  Anatole (1896–1962)
Osipenko, Alla (1932–)
Panov, Valery (1938–)
Pavlova, Anna (1881–1931)
Pavlova, Nadezhda (1955–)
Plisetskaya, Maya (1925–)
Ponomarev, Vladimir
  (1892–1951)

Preobrazhenskaya
  (Preobrajenska), Olga
  (1871–1962)
Prokhorova, Violetta *see*
  Elvin, Violetta
Prokofiev, Sergei
  (1891–1953)
Pugni, Cesare (1802–1870)
Pushkin, Aleksandr
  (1907–1970)
Radunsky, Aleksandr
  (1912–)
Riabouchinska, Tatiana
  (1917–)
Romanov, Boris (1891–1957)
Rosenberg, Lev Samoilovich
  see Bakst, Leon
Rubinstein, Ida (1885–1960)
Ruzimatov, Farukh (1963–)
Ryabushinskaya, Tatyana *see*
  Riabouchinska, Tatiana
Samsova, Galina (1937–)
Schollar, Ludmila
  (1888–1978)
Schwezoff, Igor (1904–1982)
Semenova, Marina (1908–)
Semenyaka, Ludmila (1952–)
Sergeev, Konstantin
  Mikhailovich *see* Sergeyev,
  Konstantin
Sergeev (Sergeyev or
  Sergueff), Nikolai
  (Grigorevich) *see* Sergeyev,
  Nicholas (Nikolai)
Sergeyev, Konstantin
  (1910–1992)
Sergeyev, Nicholas (Nikolai)
  (1876–1951)
Shelest, Alla (1919–)
Shollar, Lyudmila Frantsevna
  see Schollar, Ludmila
Shostakovich, Dmitri
  (1906–1975)
Shulman, Valery Matyevich
  see Panov, Valery
Sizova, Alla (1939–)
Skibin, Yuril Borisovich *see*
  Skibine, George
Skibine, George (1920–1981)
Sokolova, Evgenia (Eugenia)
  (1850–1925)
Soloviev, Yuri (1940–1977)
Spessivtseva (Spessiva),
  Olga (1895–1991)
Stravinksy, Igor (1882–1971)
Struchkova, Raisa (1925–)
Tchaikovsky, Petr
  (1840–1893)
Tchelitchev (Tchelitchew)
  Pavel (1898–1957)
Tchernicheva, Lubov
  (1890–1976)
Tikhomirov, Vasily
  (1876–1956)

Timofeeva, Nina
  Vladimirovna *see*
  Timofeyeva, Nina
Timofeyeva, Nina (1935–)
Toumanova, Tamara (1919–)
Trefilova, Vera (1875–1943)
Tumanova, Tamara
  Vladimirovna *see*
  Toumanova, Tamara
Ulanova, Galina (1910–)
Vaganova, Agrippina
  (1879–1951)
Vainonen, Vasily
  (1901–1964)
Valbergh (Valberkh), Ivan
  (1766–1819)
Vasiliev, Vladimir (1940–)
Vasiliev, Vladimir (1940–)
Vazem, Ekaterina
  (1848–1937)
Vecheslova, Tatyana
  (1910–1991)
Vilzak, Anatole (1896–)
Vinogradov, Oleg (1937–)
Virsaladze, Simon (1909–)
Vladimirov, Pierre
  (1893–1970)
Volinine, (Volinin)
  Alexandre (1882–1955)
Volkova, Vera (1904–1975)
Voskresensky, Vasily
  Grigorievich *see* De Basil,
  Colonel Wassily
Vyroubova, Nina (1921–)
Yakobson, Leonid
  (1904–1975)
Yermolaev, Aleksei
  (1910–1975)
Youskevitch, Igor (1912–)
Zakharov, Rostislav
  (1907–1975)
Zaklinsky, Konstantin
  (1955–)
Zhmoudska, Varvara *see*
  Karinska, Barbara

South Africa
Argyle, Pearl (1910–1947)
Cranko, John (1927–1973)
Judd, Nadia *see* Nerina,
  Nadina
Nerina, Nadia (1927–   )
Staff, Frank (1918–1971)

Spain
Picasso, Pablo (1881–1973)

Sweden
Ballets Suédois, Les
Börlin, Jean (1893–1930)
Cramér, Ivo (1921–)
Cramér, Martin Ivo Frederick
  Carl *see* Cramér, Ivo
Cullberg, Birgit (1908–)
De Maré, Rolf (1888–1964)

Johansson, (Per) Christian
  (1817–1903)
Royal Swedish Ballet, The
Von Rosen, Elsa Marianne
  (1924–)

Switzerland
Béjart, Maurice (1927–)
Honegger, Arthur
  (1892–1955)
Spoerli, Heinz (1941–)

United Kingdom
Argyle, Pearl (1910–1947)
Ashton, Frederick
  (1904–1988)
Baccelli, Giovanna
  (1753–1801)
Ballet Rambert *see* Rambert
  Dance Company
Barberina, La (1721–1799)
Baronova, Irina (1919–)
Baylis, Lilian (1874–1937)
Bedells, Phyllis (1893–1985)
Beriosova, Svetlana (1932–)
Beriozoff (Beriosoff),
  Nicholas (1906–)
Bintley, David (1957–)
Birmingham Royal Ballet
Blair, David (1932–1976)
Bliss, Arthur (1891–1975)
Bruce, Christopher (1945–)
Bussell, Darcey (1969–)
Butterfield, David *see* Blair,
  David
Carter, Alan (1920–)
Carter, Jack (1923–)
Chadwick, Fiona (1960–)
Chappell, William (1908–)
Chernitseva, Lyubov
  Pavlovna *see* Tchernicheva,
  Lubov
Collier, Lesley (1947–)
Cook, William (1909–1987)
  see Tudor, Antony
Corbett, Antoinette Sibley
  see Sibley, Antoinette
Cranko, John (1927–1973)
Craske, Margaret
  (1892–1990)
Darrell, Peter (1929–1987)
De Valois, Ninette (1898–)
Dolin, Anton (1904–1983)
Dowell, Anthony (1943–)
Durante, Viviana (1967–)
Eagling, Wayne (1950–)
Edwards, Leslie (1916–)
Elvin, Violetta (1925–)
ENB *see* English National
  Ballet
English National Ballet
Farron, Joyce *see* Farron,
  Julia
Farron, Julia (1922–)
Fedorovitch, Sophie
  (1893–1953)

Ferri, Alessandra (1963–)
Field, John (1921–1991)
Fonteyn, Margot (1919–1991)
Franca, Celia (1921–)
Franklin, Frederic (1914–)
Gable, Christopher (1940–)
Genée, Adeline (1878–1970)
Gielgud, Maina (1945–)
Gilmour, Sally (1921–)
Gilpin, John (1930–1983)
Gore, Walter (1910–1979)
Grant, Alexander (1925–)
Greenfield, John see Field,
  John
Grey, Beryl (1927–)
Groom, Beryl see Grey, Beryl
Hart, John (1921–)
Healey-Kay, Sydney Francis
  Patrick Chippendall see
  Dolin, Anton
Helpmann, Robert
  (1909–1986)
Hens, Ronald see Hynd,
  Ronald
Hookham, Peggy see
  Fonteyn, Margot
Howard, Andrée (1910–1968)
Hynd, Ronald (1931–)
Idzikowski, Stanislas
  (1894–1977)
Jefferies, Stephen (1951–)
Jensen, Anna Kristina
  Margarete Petra see Genée,
  Adeline
Karsavina, Tamara
  (1885–1978)
Kyasht, Lydia (1885–1959)
Laing, Hugh (1911–1988)
Lambert, Constant
  (1905–1951)
Lanner, Katti (1829–1908)
Laverty, Ashley John see
  Page, Ashley
Lester, Keith (1904–)
London Festival Ballet see
  English National Ballet
Lopokova, Lydia
  (1891–1981)
Lopukhova (Lopokova),
  Lidiya (Lydia) Vasilievna
  see Lopokova, Lydia
MacLeary, Donald (1937–)
MacMillan, Kenneth
  (1929–1992)
Mallandaine, William see
  Ashton, Frederick
Markova, Alicia (1910–)
Marks, Lillian Alicia see
  Markova, Alicia
May, Pamela (1917–)
McDonald, Elaine (1943–)
Messel, Oliver (1905–1978)
Morrice, Norman (1931–)
Mukhamedov, Irek (1960–)
Munnings, Hilda see
  Sokolova, Lydia

Nerina, Nadia (1927–)
Nureyev, Rudolf (1938–1993)
Page, Ashley (1956–)
Park, Merle (1937–)
Pavlova, Anna (1881–1931)
Penney, Jennifer (1946–)
Prokhorova, Violetta see
  Elvin, Violetta
Rambert, Marie (1888–1982)
Rambert Dance Company
Royal Ballet, The
Sadler's Wells Opera Ballet
  see Birmingham Royal
  Ballet
Sadler's Wells Royal Ballet
  see Birmingham Royal
  Ballet
Sadler's Wells Theatre Ballet
  see Birmingham Royal
  Ballet
Samsova, Galina (1937–)
Schaufuss, Peter (1949–)
Scottish Ballet
Sergeev (Sergeyev or
  Sergueff), Nikolai
  (Grigorevich) see Sergeyev,
Nicholas (Nikolai)
Seymour, Lynn (1939–)
Shearer, Moira (1926–   )
Sibley, Antoinette (1939–)
Skeaping, Mary (1902–1984)
Skinner, Hugh see Laing,
  Hugh
Skinner, Peter see Darrell,
  Peter
Sokolova, Lydia (1896–1974)
Somes, Michael (1917–)
Staff, Frank (1918–1971)
Stannus, Edris see De Valois,
  Ninette
Taylor, Frederick Robert see
  Gore, Walter
Tchernicheva, Lubov
  (1890–1976)
Tudor, Antony (1909–1987)
Turner, Harold (1909–1962)
Van Praagh, Peggy
  (1910–1990)
Volkova, Vera (1904–1975)
Wall, David (1946–)
Weaver, John (1673–1760)
Wells, Doreen (1937–)
Western Ballet see Scottish
  Ballet
Wright, Peter (1926–)

United States
ABT see American Ballet
  Theatre
Adams, Diana (1926–1993)
Ahearn, Joseph Jacques see
  D'Amboise, Jacques
Alonso, Alicia (1921–)
American Ballet Theatre
Andersen, Frank (1953–)
Andersen, Ib (1954–)

Arpino, Gennaro Peter see
  Arpino, Gerald
Arpino, Gerald (1925–)
Ashley, Merrill (1950–)
Balanchine, George
  (1904–1983)
Balanchivadze, Georgi
  Melitonovich see
  Balanchine, George
Ballet Russe de Monte Carlo
Ballet Theatre (ABT) see
  American Ballet Theatre
Baryshnikov, Mikhail
  (1948–)
Bernstein, Leonard
  (1918–1990)
Bissell, Patrick (1957–1987)
Bissell, Walter Patrick see
  Bissell, Patrick
Bocca, Julio (1967–)
Bolender, Todd (1914–)
Bolm, Adolph (1884–1951)
Browne, Leslie (1958–)
Bujones, Fernando (1955–)
Butler, John (1920–)
Calegari, Maria (1957–)
Chase, Lucia (1907–1986)
Christensen, Lew
  (1908–1984)
Christensen, Willam (1902–)
City Center Joffrey Ballet see
  Joffrey Ballet
Copland, Aaron (1900–1990)
Čorak, Mia see Slavenska,
  Mia
Cragun, Richard (1944–)
Cunningham, Merce (1919–)
Cunningham, Mercier see
  Cunningham, Merce
D'Amboise, Jacques (1934–)
Dance Theatre of Harlem
Danielian, Leon (1920–)
Danilova, Aleksandra
  Dionisievna see Danilova,
  Alexandra
Danilova, Alexandra (1903–)
De Cuevas, Marquis George
  (1885–1961)
De Mille, Agnes (1905–)
Dluzhnevska, Felzata see
  Doubrovska, Felia
Dodson, Robert see North,
  Robert
Dollar, William (1907–1986)
Doubrovska, Felia
  (1896–1981)
DTH see Dance Theatre of
  Harlem
Eglevsky, André (1917–1977)
Evdokimova, Eva (1948–)
Farrell, Suzanne (1945–)
Feld, Eliot (1942–)
Ferri, Alessandra (1963–)
Ficker, Roberta Sue see
  Farrell, Suzanne
Flindt, Flemming (1936–)

Fokine, Mikhail (Michel)
  (1880–1942)
Forsythe, William (1949–)
Franklin, Frederic (1914–)
Greenwald, Milton see Kidd,
  Michael
Gregory, Cynthia (1946–)
Harkarvy, Benjamin (1930–)
Hartwig, Eva Brigitta see
  Zorina, Vera
Harvey, Cynthia (1957–)
Hayden, Melissa (1923–)
Herman, Mildred see
  Hayden, Melissa
Hightower, Rosella (1920–)
Hindemith, Paul (1895–1963)
Houston Ballet
Jaffe, Susan (1962–)
Joffrey, Anver see Joffrey,
  Robert
Joffrey, Robert (1930–1988)
Joffrey Ballet
Johnson, Virginia (1950–)
Karinska, Barbara
  (1886–1983)
Kaye, Nora (1920–1987)
Kent, Allegra (1938–)
Kerpestein, LeRoy see
  Loring, Eugene
Khan, Abdullah Jaffa Anver
  Bey see Joffrey, Robert
Kidd, Michael (1920–)
Kirkland, Gelsey (1952–   )
Kirstein, Lincoln (1907–)
Kistler, Darci (1964–)
Koreff, Nora see Kaye, Nora
Kriza, John (1919–1975)
Lander, Toni (1931–1985)
LeClercq, Tanaquil (1929–)
Lee, Mary Ann (1824–1899)
Lichine, David (1910–1972)
Lichtenstein, David (Deivid)
  see Lichine, David
Littlefield, Catherine
  (1905–1951)
Loring, Eugene (1911–1982)
Magallanes, Nicholas
  (1922–1977)
Makarova, Natalia (1940–)
Martins, Peter (1946–)
Massine, Léonide (Leonid)
  (1895–1979)
Maywood, Augusta
  (1825–1876)
Mazzo, Kay (1946–)
McBride, Patricia (1942–)
McKenzie, Kevin (1954–)
Merrill, Linda Michelle see
  Ashley, Merrill
Mitchell, Arthur (1934–)
Moncion, Francisco (1922–)
Mordkin, Mikhail
  (1880–1944)
Morris, Mark (1956–)

Myasin, Leonid Fedorovich
see Massine, Léonide
(Leonid)
Neary, Patricia (1942–)
Nemchinova (Nemtchinova),
Vera (1899–1984)
Neumeier, John (1942–)
New York City Ballet
Nichols, Kyra (1959–)
Nijinska, Bronislava
(1891–1972)
Nikolaev, Petr Nikolaevich
see Vladimirov, Pierre
Nizhinskaya, Bronislava
Fominichna *see* Nijinska,
Bronislava
North, Robert (1945–1983)
Osato, Sono (1919–)
Page, Ruth (1899–1991)
Piedrablanca de Guana de
Cuevas, Eighth Marquis de
see De Cuevas, Marquis
George
Reed, Janet (1916–)

Riabouchinska, Tatiana
(1917–)
Robbins, Jerome (1918–)
Robert Joffrey Ballet *see*
Joffrey Ballet
Robert Joffrey Ballet Concert
see Joffrey Ballet
Robert Joffrey Theatre Ballet
see Joffrey Ballet
Romanov, Boris (1891–1957)
Ryabushinskaya, Tatyana *see*
Riabouchinska, Tatiana
San Francisco Ballet
Schollar, Ludmila
(1888–1978)
Schwezoff, Igor (1904–1982)
Shabelevsky, Yurek (1911–)
Shollar, Lyudmila Frantsevna
see Schollar, Ludmila
Skibin, Yuril Borisovich *see*
Skibine, George
Skibine, George (1920–1981)
Slavenska, Mia (1916–)
Smith, George Washington
(1820–1899)

Smith, Oliver (1918–)
Stravinksy, Igor (1882–1971)
Szabelevski, Jerzy *see*
Shabelevsky, Yurek
Tallchief, Maria (1925–)
Tallchief, Marjorie (1926–)
Taras, John (1919–)
Taylor, Paul (1930–)
Tchelitchev (Tchelitchew)
Pavel (1898–1957)
Tcherkassky, Marianna
(1952–)
Tetley, Glen (1926–)
Tetley, Glenford Andrew Jr.
see Tetley, Glen
Tharp, Twyla (1941–)
Tomasson, Helgi (1942–)
Toumanova, Tamara (1919–)
Tumanova, Tamara
Vladimirovna *see*
Toumanova, Tamara
Van Hamel, Martine (1945–)
Verdy, Violette (1933–)
Villella, Edward (1936–)
Vilzak, Anatole (1896–)

Vladimirov, Pierre
(1893–1970)
Von Aroldingen, Karin
(1941–)
Watts, Heather (1953–)
White, Patricia Lorrain-Ann
see Wilde, Patricia
Wilde, Patricia (1928–)
Williams, Augusta *see*
Maywood, Augusta
Williams, E. Virginia
(1914–1984)
Wilson, Sallie (1932–)
Youskevitch, Igor (1912–)
Zhmoudska, Varvara *see*
Karinska, Barbara
Zorina, Vera (1917–)

Yugoslavia
Čorak, Mia *see* Slavenska,
Mia
Froman, Margarita
(1890–1970)
Miskovitch, Milorad (1928–)
Slavenska, Mia (1916–)

PROFESSIONS AND INSTITUTIONS INDEX

The index below lists entries by profession or institution. Those with more than one role are listed under the appropriate categories.

Arts patrons

De Beaumont, Comte Etienne (1883–1956)
De Cuevas, Marquis George (1885–1961)
De Maré, Rolf (1888–1964)
Piedrablanca de Guana de Cuevas, Eighth Marquis de *see* De Cuevas, Marquis George

Ballet companies

ABT *see* American Ballet Theatre
American Ballet Theatre
Australian Ballet, The
Ballet Alicia Alonso *see* Ballet Nacional de Cuba
Ballet Nacional de Cuba
Ballet Rambert *see* Rambert Dance Company
Ballet Russe de Monte Carlo
Ballets Chiriaeff, Les *see* Grands Ballets Canadiens, Les
Ballets Russes de Colonel Wassily de Basil *see* Ballets Russes de Monte Carlo, Les
Ballets Russes de Monte Carlo, Les
Ballets Russes de Serge Diaghilev, Les
Ballets Suédois, Les
Ballet Theatre (ABT) *see* American Ballet Theatre
Birmingham Royal Ballet
Bolshoi Ballet
Budapest Ballet *see* Hungarian State Opera Ballet
Central Ballet of China
City Center Joffrey Ballet *see* Joffrey Ballet
Covent Garden Russian Ballet *see* Ballets Russes de Monte Carlo, Les
Dance Theatre of Harlem
Diaghilev's Ballets Russes *see* Ballets Russes de Serge Diaghilev, Les
DTH *see* Dance Theatre of Harlem
Dutch National Ballet

ENB *see* English National Ballet
English National Ballet
Grands Ballets Canadiens, Les
Hamburg Ballet
Het Nationale Ballet *see* Dutch National Ballet
Houston Ballet
Hungarian National Ballet *see* Hungarian State Opera Ballet (Budapes allet)
Hungarian State Opera Ballet (Budapest Ballet)
Joffrey Ballet
Kirov Ballet
L'Académie royale de danse *see* Paris Opéra Ballet
L'Académie royale de l'Opéra *see* Paris Opéra Ballet
Leningrad Maly Ballet *see* Maly (Mussorgsky) Theatre Ballet
London Festival Ballet *see* English National Ballet
Maly (Mussorgsky) Theatre Ballet
Matsuyama Ballet
Mussorgsky Theatre of Opera and Ballet, The *see* Maly (Mussorgsky) Theatre Ballet
National Ballet of Canada
National Ballet of China *see* Central Ballet of China
National Ballet of Cuba *see* Ballet Nacional de Cuba
Nederlands Dans Theater 2 (NDT2) *see* Netherlands Dance Theatre
Netherlands Dance Theatre
New York City Ballet
Original Ballet Russe *see* Ballets Russes de Monte Carlo, Les
Paris Opéra Ballet
Rambert Dance Company
Robert Joffrey Ballet *see* Joffrey Ballet
Robert Joffrey Ballet Concert *see* Joffrey Ballet

Robert Joffrey Theatre Ballet *see* Joffrey Ballet
Royal Ballet, The
Royal Danish Ballet, The
Royal Swedish Ballet, The
Royal Winnipeg Ballet
Sadler's Wells Opera Ballet *see* Birmingham Royal Ballet
Sadler's Wells Royal Ballet *see* Birmingham Royal Ballet
Sadler's Wells Theatre Ballet *see* Birmingham Royal Ballet
San Francisco Ballet
Scala Ballet, La
Scottish Ballet
Stuttgart Ballet
Tokyo Ballet, The
Western Ballet *see* Scottish Ballet
Winnipeg Ballet *see* Royal Winnipeg Ballet

Ballet/Company Directors

Alonso, Alicia (1921–)
Andersen, Frank (1953–)
Arpino, Gennaro Peter *see* Arpino, Gerald
Arpino, Gerald (1925–)
Ashton, Frederick (1904–1988)
Balanchine, George (1904–1983)
Balanchivadze, Georgi Melitonovich *see* Balanchine, George
Baryshnikov, Mikhail (1948–)
Baylis, Lilian (1874–1937)
Béjart, Maurice (1927–)
Belsky, Igor (1925–)
Beriozoff (Beriosoff), Nicholas (1906–)
Blair, David (1932–1976)
Bolender, Todd (1914–)
Borovansky, Edouard (Eduard) (1902–1959)
Bortoluzzi, Paolo (1938–)
Bournonville, August (1805–1879)
Bruhn, Erik (1928–1986)

Butler, John (1920–)
Butterfield, David *see* Blair, David
Carter, Alan (1920–)
Chabukiani, Vakhtang (1910–1992)
Charrat, Janine (1924–)
Chase, Lucia (1907–1986)
Chiriaeff, Ludmilla (1923–)
Christensen, Lew (1908–1984)
Christensen, Willam (1902–)
Čorak, Mia *see* Slavenska, Mia
Cramér, Ivo (1921–)
Cramér, Martin Ivo Frederick Carl *see* Cramér, Ivo
Cranko, John (1927–1973)
Cullberg, Birgit (1908–)
Cunningham, Merce (1919–)
Cunningham, Mercier *see* Cunningham, Merce
Darrell, Peter (1929–1987)
Darsonval, Lycette (1912–)
De Basil, Colonel Wassily (1888–1951)
De Cuevas, Marquis George (1885–1961)
Denard, Michaël (1944–)
De Valois, Ninette (1898–)
Dodson, Robert *see* North, Robert
Dolin, Anton (1904–1983)
Dollar, William (1907–1986)
Donn, Jorge Itovitch (1947–1992)
Dowell, Anthony (1943–)
Dupond, Patrick (1959–)
Duport, Louis-Antoine (1781–1853)
Eck, Imre (1930–)
Edwards, Leslie (1916–)
Eifman, Boris (1946–)
Evers, Belton *see* Bruhn, Erik
Feld, Eliot (1942–)
Field, John (1921–1991)
Flindt, Flemming (1936–)
Fokine, Mikhail (Michel) (1880 1942)
Forsythe, William (1949–)
Franca, Celia (1921–)
Franklin, Frederic (1914–)
Gable, Christopher (1940–)

Gaskell, Sonia (1904–1974)
Georgi, Yvonne (1903–1975)
Gielgud, Maina (1945–)
Gilpin, John (1930–1983)
Gnatt, Kirsten Laura see
  Ralov, Kirsten
Grant, Alexander (1925–)
Greenfield, John see Field,
  John
Greenwald, Milton see Kidd,
  Michael
Grey, Beryl (1927–)
Grigoriev, Serge (1883–1968)
Grigorovich, Yuri (1927–)
Groom, Beryl see Grey, Beryl
Gsovsky (Gsovska), Tatjana
  (1901–)
Guillerm, Nelly see Verdy,
  Violette
Hanka, Erika (1905–1958)
Harangozó, Gyula
  (1908–1974)
Harkarvy, Benjamin (1930–)
Hart, John (1921–)
Haydée, Marcia (1939–)
Hayden, Melissa (1923–)
Healey-Kay, Sydney Francis
  Patrick Chippendall see
  Dolin, Anton
Helpmann, Robert
  (1909–1986)
Hens, Ronald see Hynd,
  Ronald
Herman, Mildred see
  Hayden, Melissa
Hightower, Rosella (1920–)
Hynd, Ronald (1931–)
Issatchenko, Tatyana see
  Gsovsky (Gsovska), Tatjana
Ivanov, Leonid Mikhailovich
  see Lavrovsky, Leonid
Joffrey, Anver see Joffrey,
  Robert
Joffrey, Robert (1930–1988)
Jones, Marilyn (1940–)
Kaye, Nora (1920–1987)
Khan, Abdullah Jaffa Anver
  Bey see Joffrey, Robert
Kidd, Michael (1920–)
Kirstein, Lincoln (1907–)
Koreff, Nora see Kaye, Nora
Kronstam, Henning (1934–)
Kylián, Jiří (1947–)
Lacotte, Pierre (1932–)
Lander, Harald (1905–1971)
Lanner, Katharina Josefa see
  Lanner, Katti
Lanner, Katti (1829–1908)
Larsen, Niels Bjørn
  (1913–1992)
Lavrovsky, Leonid
  (1905–1967)
Lavrovsky, Mikhail (1941–)
Lifar, Serge (1905–1986)
Littlefield, Catherine
  (1905–1951)

Lopukhov, Fedor
  (1886–1973)
Macdonald, Brian (1928–)
MacMillan, Kenneth
  (1929–1992)
Madsen, Egon (1942–)
Mallandaine, William see
  Ashton, Frederick
Markova, Alicia (1910–)
Marks, Lillian Alicia see
  Markova, Alicia
Martins, Peter (1946–)
Massine, Léonide (Leonid)
  (1895–1979)
McKenzie, Kevin (1954–)
Miholy, Urel de see Milloss,
  Aurel (von)
Milloss, Aurel (von)
  (1906–1988)
Mitchell, Arthur (1934–)
Moiseev, Igor
  Aleksandrovich see
  Moiseyev, Igor
Moiseyev, Igor (1906–)
Mordkin, Mikhail
  (1880–1944)
Morrice, Norman (1931–)
Morris, Mark (1956–)
Myasin, Leonid Fedorovich
  see Massine, Léonide
  (Leonid)
Neary, Patricia (1942–)
Neumeier, John (1942–)
Nijinska, Bronislava
  (1891–1972)
Nizhinskaya, Bronislava
  Fominichna see Nijinska,
  Bronislava
North, Robert (1945–1983)
Noverre, Jean-Georges
  (1727–1810)
Nureyev, Rudolf (1938–1993)
Page, Ruth (1899–1991)
Pereira da Silva, Marcia
  Haydée Salaverry see
  Haydée, Marcia
Perron, Alice see Darsonval,
  Lycette
Piedrablanca de Guana de
  Cuevas, Eighth Marquis de
  see De Cuevas, Marquis
  George
Plisetskaya, Maya (1925–)
Prokovsky, André (1939–)
Ralov, Kirsten (1922–)
Rambam, Cyvia see
  Rambert, Marie
Ramberg (Rambach),
  Myriam see Rambert, Marie
Rambert, Marie (1888–1982)
Reinholm, Gert (1926–)
Robbins, Jerome (1918–)
Romanov, Boris (1891–1957)
Róna, Victor (1936–)
Rubinstein, Ida (1885–1960)
Samsova, Galina (1937–)

Sand, Inge (1928–1974)
Schaufuss, Peter (1949–)
Schmidt, Gerhard see
  Reinholm, Gert
Screcek, Eduard Josef see
  Borovansky, Edouard
  (Eduard)
Seregi, László (1929–)
Sergeev (Sergeyev or
  Sergueff), Nikolai
  (Grigorevich) see Sergeyev,
  Nicholas (Nikolai)
Sergeyev, Nicholas (Nikolai)
  (1876–1951)
Seymour, Lynn (1939–)
Shabelevsky, Yurek (1911–)
Skeaping, Mary (1902–1984)
Skibin, Yuril Borisovich see
  Skibine, George
Skibine, George (1920–1981)
Skinner, Peter see Darrell,
  Peter
Slavenska, Mia (1916–)
Smith, Oliver (1918–)
Snoek, Hans (1910–)
Snoek, Johanna see Snoek,
  Hans
Somes, Michael (1917–)
Sørensen, Inge Sand see
  Sand, Inge
Springbett, Berta Lynn see
  Seymour, Lynn
Staats, Léo (1877–1952)
Staff, Frank (1918–1971)
Stannus, Edris see De Valois,
  Ninette
Stevnsborg, Alfred Bernhardt
  see Lander, Harald
Szabelevski, Jerzy see
  Shabelevsky, Yurek
Tallchief, Maria (1925–)
Tallchief, Marjorie (1926–)
Taras, John (1919–)
Taylor, Paul (1930–)
Tetley, Glen (1926–)
Tetley, Glenford Andrew Jr.
  see Tetley, Glen
Tharp, Twyla (1941–)
Vaganova, Agrippina
  (1879–1951)
Van Dantzig, Rudi (1933–)
Van Hamel, Martine (1945–)
Van Manen, Hans (1932–)
Van Praagh, Peggy
  (1910–1990)
Vasiliev, Vladimir (1940–)
Verdy, Violette (1933–)
Vinogradov, Oleg (1937–)
Von Rosen, Elsa Marianne
  (1924–)
Voskresensky, Vasily
  Grigorievich see De Basil,
  Colonel Wassily
Welch, Garth (1936–)
White, Patricia Lorrain–Ann
  see Wilde, Patricia

Wilde, Patricia (1928–)
Williams, E. Virginia
  (1914–1984)
Wright, Peter (1926–)
Yakobson, Leonid
  (1904–1975)
Zakharov, Rostislav
  (1907–1975)

Choreographers
Ahearn, Joseph Jacques see
  D'Amboise, Jacques
Albert, Monsieur
  (1787–1865)
Alonso, Alicia (1921–)
Andersen, Ib (1954–)
Angiolini, Gaspero
  (1731–1803)
Anisimova, Nina
  (1909–1979)
Arpino, Gennaro Peter see
  Arpino, Gerald
Arpino, Gerald (1925–)
Ashton, Frederick
  (1904–1988)
Aumer, Jean-Louis
  (1774–1833)
Babilée, Jean (1923–)
Balanchine, George
  (1904–1983)
Balanchivadze, Georgi
  Melitonovich see
  Balanchine, George
Ballon (Balon), Claude
  (1671–1744)
Baryshnikov, Mikhail
  (1948–)
Beauchamps (Beauchamp),
  Charles-Louis see
  Beauchamps (Beauchamp),
  Pierre
Beauchamps (Beauchamp),
  Pierre (1631–1705)
Beaujoyeulx (Beaujoyeux),
  Balthasar de (1535–1587)
Beck, Hans (1861–1952)
Béjart, Maurice (1927–)
Belgiojoso, Baldassare de see
  Beaujoyeulx (Beaujoyeux),
  Balthasar de
Belsky, Igor (1925–)
Bercher, Jean see Dauberval,
  Jean
Beriozoff (Beriosoff),
  Nicholas (1906–)
Bessy, Claude (1932–)
Bintley, David (1957–)
Bjørnsson, Fredbjørn
  (1926–)
Blasis, Carlo (1795–1878)
Blondy, Michel (1675–1739)
Bolender, Todd (1914–)
Bolm, Adolph (1884–1951)
Bonnachon, Louis Stanislas
  Xavier Henri see Henry,
  Louis

Börlin, Jean (1893–1930)
Borovansky, Edouard
  (Eduard) (1902–1959)
Bournonville, August
  (1805–1879)
Bruce, Christopher (1945–)
Bruhn, Erik (1928–1986)
Bujones, Fernando (1955–)
Burmeister, Vladimir
  (1904–1971)
Butler, John (1920–)
Camargo, Marie-Anne
  (1710–1770)
Caroso, Fabritio (1526–1605)
Carter, Alan (1920–)
Carter, Jack (1923–)
Cecchetti, Enrico
  (1850–1928)
Cerrito, Fanny (1817–1909)
Chabukiani, Vakhtang
  (1910–1992)
Charrat, Janine (1924–)
Chiriaeff, Ludmilla (1923–)
Christensen, Lew
  (1908–1984)
Cook, William (1909–1987)
  see Tudor, Antony
Čorak, Mia see Slavenska,
  Mia
Coralli, Jean (1779–1854)
Cramér, Ivo (1921–)
Cramér, Martin Ivo Frederick
  Carl see Cramér, Ivo
Cranko, John (1927–1973)
Cullberg, Birgit (1908–)
Cunningham, Merce (1919–)
Cunningham, Mercier see
  Cunningham, Merce
D'Amboise, Jacques (1934–)
Danielian, Leon (1920–)
Danilova, Aleksandra
  Dionisievna see Danilova,
  Alexandra
Danilova, Alexandra (1903–)
Darrell, Peter (1929–1987)
Darsonval, Lycette (1912–)
Dauberval, Jean (1742–1806)
Decombe, Françoise see
  Albert, Monsieur
De Cupis, Marie-Anne see
  Camargo, Marie-Anne
De Mille, Agnes (1905–)
Deshayes, André-Jean-
  Jacques (1777–1846)
De Valois, Ninette (1898–)
Didelot, Charles-Louis
  (1767–1837)
Dodson, Robert see North,
  Robert
Dolgushin, Nikita (1938–)
Dolin, Anton (1904–1983)
Dollar, William (1907–1986)
Duport, Louis-Antoine
  (1781–1853)
Dupré, Louis (1697–1774)

Duraud, Claude see Bessy,
  Claude
Eck, Imre (1930–)
Eifman, Boris (1946–)
Elssler, Fanny (1810–1884)
Elssler, Franziska see Elssler,
  Fanny
Ermolaev, Aleksei
  Nikolaevich see
  Yermolaev, Aleksei
Evers, Belton see Bruhn, Erik
Feld, Eliot (1942–)
Feuillet, Raoul Auger
  (1660–1710)
Flindt, Flemming (1936–)
Fokine, Mikhail (Michel)
  (1880–1942)
Forsythe, William (1949–)
Franca, Celia (1921–)
Franklin, Frederic (1914–)
Froman, Margarita
  (1890–1970)
Galeotti, Vincenzo
  (1733–1816)
Gardel, Maximilien
  (1741–1787)
Gardel, Pierre (1758–1840)
Gaskell, Sonia (1904–1974)
Gasparini, Domenico Maria
  Angiolo see Angiolini,
  Gaspero
Georgi, Yvonne (1903–1975)
Gerdt, Pavel (1844–1917)
Gielgud, Maina (1945–)
Glushkovsky, Adam
  Pavlovich (1793–1870)
Gnatt, Kirsten Laura see
  Ralov, Kirsten
Goleizovsky, Kasyan
  (1892–1970)
Gore, Walter (1910–1979)
Gorsky, Aleksandr
  (1871–1924)
Grahn, Lucile (1819–1907)
Greenwald, Milton see Kidd,
  Michael
Grigorovich, Yuri (1927–)
Gsovsky, Victor (1902–1974)
Gsovsky (Gsovska), Tatjana
  (1901–)
Guglielmo Ebreo
  (1420–1481)
Guillaume le Juif see
  Guglielmo Ebreo
Gusev, Petr (1904–1987)
Hanka, Erika (1905–1958)
Harangozó, Gyula
  (1908–1974)
Harkarvy, Benjamin (1930–)
Healey-Kay, Sydney Francis
  Patrick Chippendall see
  Dolin, Anton
Helpmann, Robert
  (1909–1986)
Henry, Louis (1784–1836)

Hens, Ronald see Hynd,
  Ronald
Hilverding (van Wewen),
  Franz (1710–1768)
Howard, Andrée (1910–1968)
Hynd, Ronald (1931–)
Issatchenko, Tatyana see
  Gsovsky (Gsovska), Tatjana
Ivanov, Leonid Mikhailovich
  see Lavrovsky, Leonid
Ivanov, Lev (1834–1901)
Joffrey, Anver see Joffrey,
  Robert
Joffrey, Robert (1930–1988)
Jones, Marilyn (1940–)
Kerpestein, LeRoy see
  Loring, Eugene
Khan, Abdullah Jaffa Anver
  Bey see Joffrey, Robert
Kidd, Michael (1920–)
Kniaseff (Kniasev), Boris
  (1900–1975)
Kudelka, James (1955–)
Kyasht, Lydia (1885–1959)
Kylián, Jiří (1947–)
Lacotte, Pierre (1932–)
Laerkesen, Anna (1942–)
Lander, Harald (1905–1971)
Lanner, Katharina Josefa see
  Lanner, Katti
Lanner, Katti (1829–1908)
Larsen, Niels Bjørn
  (1913–1992)
Laverty, Ashley John see
  Page, Ashley
Lavrovsky, Leonid
  (1905–1967)
Lavrovsky, Mikhail (1941–)
Legat, Nikolai (Nicholas)
  (1869–1937)
Lepicq (also Le Picq, Lepic),
  Charles (1744–1806)
Lessogorov, Ivan see
  Valbergh (Valberkh), Ivan
Lester, Keith (1904–)
Lichine, David (1910–1972)
Lichtenstein, David (Deivid)
  see Lichine, David
Lifar, Serge (1905–1986)
Littlefield, Catherine
  (1905–1951)
Lopukhov, Fedor
  (1886–1973)
Loring, Eugene (1911–1982)
Macdonald, Brian (1928–)
MacMillan, Kenneth
  (1929–1992)
Mallandaine, William see
  Ashton, Frederick
Martins, Peter (1946–)
Massine, Léonide (Leonid)
  (1895–1979)
Mazarini, Giulio see
  Mazilier, Joseph
Mazilier, Joseph (1797–1868)
McKenzie, Kevin (1954–)

Mérante, Louis (1828–1887)
Messerer, Asaf (1903–1992)
Michel, Charles-Victor-
  Arthur see Saint-Léon,
  Arthur
Miholy, Urel de see Milloss,
  Aurel (von)
Milloss, Aurel (von)
  (1906–1988)
Mitchell, Arthur (1934–)
Moiseev, Igor
  Aleksandrovich see
  Moiseyev, Igor
Moiseyev, Igor (1906–)
Moncion, Francisco (1922–)
Mordkin, Mikhail
  (1880–1944)
Morrice, Norman (1931–)
Morris, Mark (1956–)
Myasin, Leonid Fedorovich
  see Massine, Léonide
  (Leonid)
Nádasi, Ferenc (1893–1966)
Negri, Cesare (1536–1604)
Neumeier, John (1942–)
Nijinska, Bronislava
  (1891–1972)
Nijinsky, Vaslav (1889–1950)
Nizhinskaya, Bronislava
  Fominichna see Nijinska,
  Bronislava
North, Robert (1945–1983)
Noverre, Jean-Georges
  (1727–1810)
Nureyev, Rudolf (1938–1993)
Page, Ashley (1956–)
Page, Ruth (1899–1991)
Pavlova, Anna (1881–1931)
Pécour, Guillaume-Louis
  (1653–1729)
Peracini, Giovanni Coralli
  see Coralli, Jean
Perron, Alice see Darsonval,
  Lycette
Perrot, Jules (1810–1892)
Petipa, Marius (1818–1910)
Petit, Roland (1924–)
Plisetskaya, Maya (1925–)
Ponomarev, Vladimir
  (1892–1951)
Prokovsky, André (1939–)
Radunsky, Aleksandr (1912–
)
Raffaela, Francesca Teresa
  Guisepppa see Cerrito, Fanny
Ralov, Kirsten (1922–)
Rambam, Cyvia see Rambert,
  Marie
Ramberg (Rambach),
  Myriam see Rambert, Marie
Rambert, Marie (1888–1982)
Robbins, Jerome (1918–)
Romanov, Boris (1891–1957)
Róna, Victor (1936–)
Saint-Léon, Arthur
  (1821–1870)

Sallé, Marie (1707–1756)
Sand, Inge (1928–1974)
Schaufuss, Peter (1949–)
Schwezoff, Igor (1904–1982)
Screcek, Eduard Josef *see*
 Borovansky, Edouard
 (Eduard)
Seregi, László (1929–)
Sergeev, Konstantin
 Mikhailovich *see* Sergeyev,
 Konstantin
Sergeyev, Konstantin
 (1910–1992)
Seymour, Lynn (1939–)
Simone, Kirsten (1934–)
Skeaping, Mary (1902–1984)
Skibin, Yuril Borisovich *see*
 Skibine, George
Skibine, George (1920–1981)
Skinner, Peter *see* Darrell,
 Peter
Slavenska, Mia (1916–)
Snoek, Hans (1910–)
Snoek, Johanna *see* Snoek,
 Hans
Sørensen, Inge Sand *see*
 Sand, Inge
Spoerli, Heinz (1941–)
Springbett, Berta Lynn *see*
 Seymour, Lynn
Staats, Léo (1877–1952)
Staff, Frank (1918–1971)
Stannus, Edris *see* De Valois,
 Ninette
Stevnsborg, Alfred Bernhardt
 see Lander, Harald
Taglioni, Filippo
 (1777–1871)
Taglioni, Salvatore
 (1789–1868)
Taras, John (1919–)
Taylor, Frederick Robert *see*
 Gore, Walter
Taylor, Paul (1930–)
Tetley, Glen (1926–)
Tetley, Glenford Andrew Jr.
 see Tetley, Glen
Tharp, Twyla (1941–)
Tikhomirov, Vasily
 (1876–1956)
Tomasselli, Vincenzo *see*
 Galeotti, Vincenzo
Tudor, Antony (1909–1987)
Turner, Harold (1909–1962)
Vainonen, Vasily
 (1901–1964)
Valbergh (Valberkh), Ivan
 (1766–1819)
Van Dantzig, Rudi (1933–)
Vangsaae, Mona (1920–1983)
Van Hamel, Martine (1945–)
Van Manen, Hans (1932–)
Van Schayk, Toer (1936–)
Vasiliev, Vladimir (1940–)
Vestris, Gaetano (Gaétan)
 (1729–1808)

Viganò, Salvatore
 (1769–1821)
Vinogradov, Oleg (1937–)
Volkova, Vera (1904–1975)
Von Rosen, Elsa Marianne
 (1924–)
Weaver, John (1673–1760)
Welch, Garth (1936–)
William the Jew of Pesaro
 see Guglielmo Ebreo
Wilson, Sallie (1932–)
Woizikowsky, Léon
 (1899–1975)
Wójcikowski, Léon *see*
 Woizikowsky, Léon
Wright, Peter (1926–)
Yakobson, Leonid
 (1904–1975)
Yermolaev, Aleksei
 (1910–1975)
Zakharov, Rostislav
 (1907–1975)

Clerics
Arbeau, Thoinot (1520–1595)
Tabourot, Jehan *see* Arbeau,
 Thoinot

Composers
Adam, Adolphe (1803–1856)
Angiolini, Gaspero
 (1731–1803)
Bartók, Béla (1881–1945)
Beauchamps (Beauchamp),
 Charles-Louis *see*
 Beauchamps (Beauchamp),
 Pierre
Beauchamps (Beauchamp),
 Pierre (1631–1705)
Beaujoyeulx (Beaujoyeux),
 Balthasar de (1535–1587)
Belgiojoso, Baldassare de *see*
 Beaujoyeulx (Beaujoyeux),
 Balthasar de
Bernstein, Leonard
 (1918–1990)
Bliss, Arthur (1891–1975)
Chaikovsky, Petr Ilyich *see*
 Tchaikovsky, Petr
Copland, Aaron (1900–1990)
Debussy, Claude
 (1862–1918)
Delibes, Léo (1836–1891)
Gasparini, Domenico Maria
 Angiolo *see* Angiolini,
 Gaspero
Glazunov, Aleksandr
 (1865–1936)
Henze, Hans Werner (1926–)
Hindemith, Paul (1895–1963)
Honegger, Arthur
 (1892–1955)
Khachaturian, Aram
 (1903–1978)
Lambert, Constant
 (1905–1951)

Lulli, Giovanni Battista *see*
 Lully, Jean-Baptiste
Lully, Jean-Baptiste
 (1632–1687)
Michel, Charles-Victor-
 Arthur *see* Saint-Léon,
 Arthur
Milhaud, Darius (1892–1974)
Minkus, Léon (1826–1917)
Poulenc, Francis (1899–1963)
Poupard, Jean-Pierre *see*
 Sauget, Henri
Prokofiev, Sergei
 (1891–1953)
Pugni, Cesare (1802–1870)
Rameau, Jean-Philippe
 (1683–1763)
Ravel, Maurice (1875–1937)
Saint-Léon, Arthur
 (1821–1870)
Satie, Erik (Eric)
 (1866–1925)
Sauget, Henri (1901–1989)
Shostakovich, Dmitri
 (1906–1975)
Stravinksy, Igor (1882–1971)
Tchaikovsky, Petr
 (1840–1893)

Dancers
Adams, Diana (1926–1993)
Ahearn, Joseph Jacques *see*
 D'Amboise, Jacques
Albert, Monsieur
 (1787–1865)
Allard, Marie (1742–1802)
Alonso, Alicia (1921–)
Ananiashvili, Nina (1964–)
Andersen, Frank (1953–)
Andersen, Ib (1954–)
Andreyanova, Elena
 (1819–1857)
Angiolini, Gaspero
 (1731–1803)
Anisimova, Nina
 (1909–1979)
Argyle, Pearl (1910–1947)
Arpino, Gennaro Peter *see*
 Arpino, Gerald
Arpino, Gerald (1925–)
Ashley, Merrill (1950–)
Ashton, Frederick
 (1904–1988)
Asylmuratova, Altynai
 (1961–)
Atanassoff, Cyril (1941–)
Aumer, Jean-Louis
 (1774–1833)
Ayupova, Zhanna (1966–)
Babilée, Jean (1923–)
Baccelli, Giovanna
 (1753–1801)
Balanchine, George
 (1904–1983)

Balanchivadze, Georgi
 Melitonovich *see*
 Balanchine, George
Ballon (Balon), Claude
 (1671–1744)
Ballon (Balon), Jean *see*
 Ballon (Balon), Claude
Barberina, La (1721–1799)
Baronova, Irina (1919–)
Baryshnikov, Mikhail
 (1948–)
Beauchamps (Beauchamp),
 Charles-Louis *see*
 Beauchamps (Beauchamp),
 Pierre
Beauchamps (Beauchamp),
 Pierre (1631–1705)
Beaugrand, Léontine
 (1842–1925)
Beck, Hans (1861–1952)
Bedells, Phyllis (1893–1985)
Béjart, Maurice (1927–)
Belsky, Igor (1925–)
Bercher, Jean *see* Dauberval,
 Jean
Beriosova, Svetlana (1932–)
Beriozoff (Beriosoff),
 Nicholas (1906–)
Bessmertnova, Natalia
 (1941–)
Bessy, Claude (1932–)
Bintley, David (1957–)
Bissell, Patrick (1957–1987)
Bissell, Walter Patrick *see*
 Bissell, Patrick
Bjørnsson, Fredbjørn
 (1926–)
Blair, David (1932–1976)
Blasis, Carlo (1795–1878)
Blondy, Michel (1675–1739)
Bocca, Julio (1967–)
Bogdanova, Nadezhda
 (1836–1897)
Bolender, Todd (1914–)
Bolm, Adolph (1884–1951)
Bonnachon, Louis Stanislas
 Xavier Henri *see* Henry,
 Louis
Börlin, Jean (1893–1930)
Borovansky, Edouard
 (Eduard) (1902–1959)
Bortoluzzi, Paolo (1938–)
Bournonville, August
 (1805–1879)
Bozzacchi, Giuseppina
 (1853–1870)
Brambilla, Maria *see* Fuoco,
 Sofia
Brenaa, Hans (1910–1988)
Brianza, Carlotta
 (1867–1935)
Browne, Leslie (1958–)
Bruce, Christopher (1945–)
Bruhn, Erik (1928–1986)
Bujones, Fernando (1955–)

Burmeister, Vladimir
(1904–1971)
Bussell, Darcey (1969–)
Butler, John (1920–)
Butterfield, David see Blair,
David
Calegari, Maria (1957–)
Camargo, Marie-Anne
(1710–1770)
Campanini, Barbara see
Barberina, La
Caridad del Cobre Martinez y
del Hoyo, Alicia Ernestina
de la see Alonso, Alicia
Carter, Alan (1920–)
Carter, Jack (1923–)
Cecchetti, Enrico
(1850–1928)
Cerrito, Fanny (1817–1909)
Chabukiani, Vakhtang
(1910–1992)
Chadwick, Fiona (1960–)
Chappell, William (1908–)
Charrat, Janine (1924–)
Chase, Lucia (1907–1986)
Chauviré, Yvette (1917–)
Chernitseva, Lyubov
Pavlovna see Tchernicheva,
Lubov
Chiriaeff, Ludmilla (1923–)
Christensen, Lew
(1908–1984)
Christensen, Willam (1902–)
Clauss, Heinz (1935–)
Collier, Lesley (1947–)
Cook, William (1909–1987)
see Tudor, Antony
Čorak, Mia see Slavenska,
Mia
Coralli, Jean (1779–1854)
Corbett, Antoinette Sibley
see Sibley, Antoinette
Cragun, Richard (1944–)
Cramér, Ivo (1921–)
Cramér, Martin Ivo Frederick
Carl see Cramér, Ivo
Cranko, John (1927–1973)
Craske, Margaret
(1892–1990)
Crespé (Crespi or Crépé),
Marie-Madeleine de see
Théodore, Mlle.
Cullberg, Birgit (1908–)
Cunningham, Merce (1919–)
Cunningham, Mercier see
Cunningham, Merce
D'Amboise, Jacques (1934–)
Da Ferrara, Domenico see
Domenico De Piacena
Danielian, Leon (1920–)
Danilova, Aleksandra
Dionisievna see Danilova,
Alexandra
Danilova, Alexandra (1903–)
Darrell, Peter (1929–1987)
Darsonval, Lycette (1912–)

Dauberval, Jean (1742–1806)
Dauberval, Mme. see
Théodore, Mlle.
Daydé, Liane (1932–)
Decombe, Françoise see
Albert, Monsieur
De Cupis, Marie-Anne see
Camargo, Marie-Anne
De la Fontaine,
Mademoiselle see La
Fontaine, Madamoiselle
De Mille, Agnes (1905–)
Denard, Michaël (1944–)
Deshayes,
André-Jean-Jacques
(1777–1846)
De Valois, Ninette (1898–)
Didelot, Charles-Louis
(1767–1837)
Dluzhnevska, Felzata see
Doubrovska, Felia
Dodson, Robert see North,
Robert
Dolgushin, Nikita (1938–)
Dolin, Anton (1904–1983)
Dollar, William (1907–1986)
Domenico De Piacena
(1425–1465)
Donn, Jorge Itovitch
(1947–1992)
Doubrovska, Felia
(1896–1981)
Dowell, Anthony (1943–)
Dudinskaya, Natalia (1912–)
Dupond, Patrick (1959–)
Duport, Louis-Antoine
(1781–1853)
Dupré, Louis (1697–1774)
Durante, Viviana (1967–)
Duraud, Claude see Bessy,
Claude
Eagling, Wayne (1950–)
Eck, Imre (1930–)
Edwards, Leslie (1916–)
Eglevsky, André (1917–1977)
Egorova, Lyubov (Lubov)
(1880–1972)
Elssler, Fanny (1810–1884)
Elssler, Franziska see Elssler,
Fanny
Elvin, Violetta (1925–)
Emarot, Emma-Marie see
Livry, Emma
Ermolaev, Aleksei
Nikolaevich see
Yermolaev, Aleksei
Evdokimova, Eva (1948–)
Evers, Belton see Bruhn, Erik
Fadeyechev, Nikolai (1933–)
Farrell, Suzanne (1945–)
Farron, Joyce see Farron,
Julia
Farron, Julia (1922–)
Fedorova, Sophia (Sofia)
(1879–1963)
Feld, Eliot (1942–)

Ferri, Alessandra (1963–)
Ficker, Roberta Sue see
Farrell, Suzanne
Field, John (1921–1991)
Flindt, Flemming (1936–)
Florentz-Gerhardt, Margot
see Lander, Margot
Fokine, Mikhail (Michel)
(1880–1942)
Fonteyn, Margot (1919–1991)
Fornaroli, Cia (1888–1954)
Forsythe, William (1949–)
Fracci, Carla (1936–)
Franca, Celia (1921–)
Franklin, Frederic (1914–)
Froman, Margarita
(1890–1970)
Fuoco, Sofia (1830–1916)
Gable, Christopher (1940–)
Gabovich, Mikhail
(1905–1965)
Gad, Rose (1968–)
Galeotti, Vincenzo
(1733–1816)
Galletti, Carolina see Rosati,
Carolina
Gardel, Maximilien
(1741–1787)
Gardel, Pierre (1758–1840)
Gaskell, Sonia (1904–1974)
Gasparini, Domenico Maria
Angiolo see Angiolini,
Gaspero
Geltser, Ekaterina
(1876–1962)
Genée, Adeline (1878–1970)
Georgi, Yvonne (1903–1975)
Gerdt, Elisaveta (1891–1975)
Gerdt, Pavel (1844–1917)
Gielgud, Maina (1945–)
Gilmour, Sally (1921–)
Gilpin, John (1930–1983)
Glushkovsky, Adam
Pavlovich (1793–1870)
Goleizovsky, Kasyan
(1892–1970)
Golovine, Serge (1935–)
Gore, Walter (1910–1979)
Gorsky, Aleksandr
(1871–1924)
Grahn, Lucile (1819–1907)
Grant, Alexander (1925–)
Greenfield, John see Field,
John
Greenwald, Milton see Kidd,
Michael
Gregory, Cynthia (1946–)
Grey, Beryl (1927–)
Grigoriev, Serge (1883–1968)
Grigorovich, Yuri (1927–)
Grisi, Carlotta (1819–1899)
Groom, Beryl see Grey, Beryl
Gsovsky, Victor (1902–1974)
Guillem, Sylvie (1965–)
Guillerm, Nelly see Verdy,
Violette

Guimard, Marie-Madeleine
(1743–1816)
Gusev, Petr (1904–1987)
Hanka, Erika (1905–1958)
Harangozó, Gyula
(1908–1974)
Hart, Evelyn (1956–)
Hart, John (1921–)
Hartwig, Eva Brigitta see
Zorina, Vera
Harvey, Cynthia (1957–)
Haydée, Marcia (1939–)
Hayden, Melissa (1923–)
Healey-Kay, Sydney Francis
Patrick Chippendall see
Dolin, Anton
Heathcote, Steven (1964–)
Heinel, Anne (Anna)
(1753–1808)
Helpmann, Robert
(1909–1986)
Henry, Louis (1784–1836)
Hens, Ronald see Hynd,
Ronald
Herman, Mildred see
Hayden, Melissa
Hightower, Rosella (1920–)
Hilaire, Laurent (1963–)
Hilverding (van Wewen),
Franz (1710–1768)
Hookham, Peggy see
Fonteyn, Margot
Horsman, Greg (1963–)
Howard, Andrée (1910–1968)
Hübbe, Nikolaj (1967–)
Hynd, Ronald (1931–)
Idzikowski, Stanislas
(1894–1977)
Ikowski see Idzikowski,
Stanislas
Istomina, Avdotia
(1799–1848)
Ivanov, Leonid Mikhailovich
see Lavrovsky, Leonid
Ivanov, Lev (1834–1901)
Jaffe, Susan (1962–)
Jeanmaire, Zizi (Renée)
(1924–)
Jefferies, Stephen (1951–)
Jensen, Anna Kristina
Margarete Petra see Genée,
Adeline
Jeppesen, Lis (1956–)
Joffrey, Anver see Joffrey,
Robert
Joffrey, Robert (1930–1988)
Johansson, (Per) Christian
(1817–1903)
Johnson, Virginia (1950–)
Jones, Marilyn (1940–)
Judd, Nadia see Nerina,
Nadina
Kain, Karen (1951–)
Karsavina, Tamara
(1885–1978)
Kaye, Nora (1920–1987)

Kehlet, Niels (1938–)
Keil, Birgit (1944–)
Kent, Allegra (1938–)
Kerpestein, LeRoy see
Loring, Eugene
Khan, Abdullah Jaffa Anver
Bey see Joffrey, Robert
Kidd, Michael (1920–)
Kirkland, Gelsey (1952–)
Kistler, Darci (1964–)
Kniaseff (Kniasev), Boris
(1900–1975)
Kolpakova, Irina (1933–)
Kølpin, Alexander (1965–)
Koreff, Nora see Kaye, Nora
Kriger (Krieger), Viktorina
(1893–1978)
Kriza, John (1919–1975)
Kronstam, Henning (1934–)
Kshesinskaya (Kschesinska),
Matilda (1872–1971)
Kudelka, James (1955–)
Kun, Zsuzsa (1934–)
Kyasht, Lydia (1885–1959)
Kylián, Jiří (1947–)
Lacotte, Pierre (1932–)
Laerkesen, Anna (1942–)
La Fontaine (also de la
Fontaine), Mademoiselle
(1655–1738)
Laing, Hugh (1911–1988)
Lander, Harald (1905–1971)
Lander, Margot (1910–1961)
Lander, Toni (1931–1985)
Lanner, Katharina Josefa see
Lanner, Katti
Lanner, Katti (1829–1908)
Larsen, Niels Bjørn
(1913–1992)
Laverty, Ashley John see
Page, Ashley
Lavrovsky, Leonid
(1905–1967)
Lavrovsky, Mikhail (1941–)
LeClercq, Tanaquil (1929–)
Lee, Mary Ann (1824–1899)
Legat, Nikolai (Nicholas)
(1869–1937)
Legnani, Pierina (1863–1923)
Lepeshinskaya, Olga (1916–)
Lepicq (also Le Picq, Lepic),
Charles (1744–1806)
Lessogorov, Ivan see
Valbergh (Valberkh), Ivan
Lester, Keith (1904–)
Lichine, David (1910–1972)
Lichtenstein, David (Deivid)
see Lichine, David
Liepa, Andris (1962–)
Liepa, Maris (1936–1989)
Lifar, Serge (1905–1986)
Littlefield, Catherine
(1905–1951)
Livry, Emma (1842–1863)
Lopokova, Lydia
(1891–1981)

Lopukhov, Fedor
(1886–1973)
Lopukhova (Lopokova),
Lidiya (Lydia) Vasilievna
see Lopokova, Lydia
Loring, Eugene (1911–1982)
Luigia, Carolina Celia see
Zambelli, Carlotta
Lukom, Elena (1891–1968)
Lulli, Giovanni Battista see
Lully, Jean-Baptiste
Lully, Jean-Baptiste
(1632–1687)
Macdonald, Brian (1928–)
MacLeary, Donald (1937–)
MacMillan, Kenneth
(1929–1992)
Madsen, Egon (1942–)
Magallanes, Nicholas
(1922–1977)
Makarova, Natalia (1940–)
Makhalina, Yulia (1968–)
Maksimova, Ekaterina
Sergeevna see Maximova,
Ekaterina
Mallandaine, William see
Ashton, Frederick
Markova, Alicia (1910–)
Marks, Lillian Alicia see
Markova, Alicia
Martins, Peter (1946–)
Maximova, Ekaterina
(1939–)
May, Pamela (1917–)
Maywood, Augusta
(1825–1876)
Mazarini, Giulio see
Mazilier, Joseph
Mazilier, Joseph (1797–1868)
Mazzo, Kay (1946–)
McBride, Patricia (1942–)
McDonald, Elaine (1943–)
McKenzie, Kevin (1954–)
Mérante, Louis (1828–1887)
Merrill, Linda Michelle see
Ashley, Merrill
Messerer, Asaf (1903–1992)
Mezentseva, Galina (1952–)
Michel, Charles-Victor-
Arthur see Saint-Léon,
Arthur
Miholy, Urel de see Milloss,
Aurel (von)
Milloss, Aurel (von)
(1906–1988)
Miskovitch, Milorad (1928–)
Mitchell, Arthur (1934–)
Moiseev, Igor
Aleksandrovich see
Moiseyev, Igor
Moiseyev, Igor (1906–)
Moncion, Francisco (1922–)
Mordkin, Mikhail
(1880–1944)
Morishita, Yoko (1948–)
Morrice, Norman (1931–)

Morris, Mark (1956–)
Mukhamedov, Irek (1960–)
Munnings, Hilda see
Sokolova, Lydia
Nádasi, Ferenc (1893–1966)
Neary, Patricia (1942–)
Negri, Cesare (1536–1604)
Nemchinova (Nemtchinova),
Vera (1899–1984)
Nerina, Nadia (1927–)
Neumeier, John (1942–)
Nichols, Kyra (1959–)
Nijinska, Bronislava
(1891–1972)
Nijinsky, Vaslav (1889–1950)
Nikitina, Alice (1904–1978)
Nikolaev, Petr Nikolaevich
see Vladimirov, Pierre
Nizhinskaya, Bronislava
Fominichna see Nijinska,
Bronislava
North, Robert (1945–1983)
Noverre, Jean-Georges
(1727–1810)
Nureyev, Rudolf (1938–1993)
Obukhov (Oboukhoff),
Anatole (1896–1962)
Osato, Sono (1919–)
Osipenko, Alla (1932–)
Page, Ashley (1956–)
Page, Ruth (1899–1991)
Panov, Valery (1938–)
Park, Merle (1937–)
Pavane, Lisa (1961–)
Pavlova, Anna (1881–1931)
Pavlova, Nadezhda (1955–)
Pécour, Guillaume-Louis
(1653–1729)
Pedersen, Hans see Brenaa,
Hans
Penney, Jennifer (1946–)
Peracini, Giovanni Coralli
see Coralli, Jean
Pereira da Silva, Marcia
Haydée Salaverry see
Haydée, Marcia
Peretti, Serge (1910–)
Perron, Alice see Darsonval,
Lycette
Perrot, Jules (1810–1892)
Petersen, Toni Pihl see
Lander, Toni
Petipa, Marius (1818–1910)
Petit, Roland (1924–)
Platel, Elisabeth (1959–)
Plisetskaya, Maya (1925–)
Ponomarev, Vladimir
(1892–1951)
Pontois, Noëlla (1943–)
Preobrazhenskaya
(Preobrajenska), Olga
(1871–1962)
Prévost, Françoise
(1681–1741)
Prokhorova, Violetta see
Elvin, Violetta

Prokovsky, André (1939–)
Pushkin, Aleksandr
(1907–1970)
Radunsky, Aleksandr
(1912–)
Raffaela, Francesca Teresa
Guiseppa see Cerrito, Fanny
Rambam, Cyvia see
Rambert, Marie
Ramberg (Rambach),
Myriam see Rambert, Marie
Rambert, Marie (1888–1982)
Reed, Janet (1916–)
Reinholm, Gert (1926–)
Renault, Michel (1927–1993)
Riabouchinska, Tatiana
(1917–)
Robbins, Jerome (1918–)
Romanov, Boris (1891–1957)
Róna, Victor (1936–)
Rosati, Carolina (1826–1905)
Rubinstein, Ida (1885–1960)
Ruzimatov, Farukh (1963–)
Ryabushinskaya, Tatyana see
Riabouchinska, Tatiana
Ryom, Heidi (1955–)
Saint-Léon, Arthur
(1821–1870)
Sallé, Marie (1707–1756)
Samsova, Galina (1937–)
Sand, Inge (1928–1974)
Schanne, Margrethe (1921–)
Schaufuss, Peter (1949–)
Schmidt, Gerhard see
Reinholm, Gert
Schollar, Ludmila
(1888–1978)
Schwarz, Solange (1910–)
Schwezoff, Igor (1904–1982)
Screcek, Eduard Josef see
Borovansky, Edouard
(Eduard)
Semenova, Marina (1908–)
Semenyaka, Ludmila (1952–)
Seregi, László (1929–)
Sergeev, Konstantin
Mikhailovich see Sergeyev,
Konstantin
Sergeev (Sergeyev or
Sergueff), Nikolai
(Grigorevich) see Sergeyev,
Nicholas (Nikolai)
Sergeyev, Konstantin
(1910–1992)
Sergeyev, Nicholas (Nikolai)
(1876–1951)
Seymour, Lynn (1939–)
Shabelevsky, Yurek (1911–)
Shearer, Moira (1926–)
Shelest, Alla (1919–)
Shimizu, Yoko see
Morishita, Yoko
Shollar, Lyudmila Frantsevna
see Schollar, Ludmila
Shulman, Valery Matyevich
see Panov, Valery

Sibley, Antoinette (1939–)
Simone, Kirsten (1934–)
Sizova, Alla (1939–)
Skeaping, Mary (1902–1984)
Skibin, Yuril Borisovich see
   Skibine, George
Skibine, George (1920–1981)
Skinner, Hugh see Laing,
   Hugh
Skinner, Peter see Darrell,
   Peter
Skouratoff, Vladimir (1925–)
Slavenska, Mia (1916–)
Smith, George Washington
   (1820–1899)
Snoek, Hans (1910–)
Snoek, Johanna see Snoek,
   Hans
Sokolova, Evgenia (Eugenia)
   (1850–1925)
Sokolova, Lydia (1896–1974)
Soloviev, Yuri (1940–1977)
Somes, Michael (1917–)
Sørensen, Inge Sand see
   Sand, Inge
Spessivtseva (Spessiva), Olga
   (1895–1991)
Spoerli, Heinz (1941–)
Springbett, Berta Lynn see
   Seymour, Lynn
Staats, Léo (1877–1952)
Staff, Frank (1918–1971)
Stannus, Edris see De Valois,
   Ninette
Struchkova, Raisa (1925–)
Subligny, Marie-Thérèse
   (1666–1735)
Szabelevski, Jerzy see
   Shabelevsky, Yurek
Taglioni, Filippo (1777–1871)
Taglioni, Marie (1804–1884)
Taglioni, Paul (Paolo)
   (1808–1884)
Taglioni, Salvatore
   (1789–1868)
Tallchief, Maria (1925–)
Tallchief, Marjorie (1926–)
Taras, John (1919–)
Taylor, Frederick Robert see
   Gore, Walter
Taylor, Paul (1930–)
Tchemerzina, Monika
   (Monique) Avenirova see
   Tcherina, Ludmila
Tcherina, Ludmila (1924–)
Tcherkassky, Marianna
   (1952–)
Tchernicheva, Lubov
   (1890–1976)
Tennant, Veronica (1947–)
Terabust, Elisabetta (1946–)
Tetley, Glen (1926–)
Tetley, Glenford Andrew Jr.
   see Tetley, Glen
Tharp, Twyla (1941–)
Théodore, Mlle. (1760–1796)

Tikhomirov, Vasily
   (1876–1956)
Timofeeva, Nina
   Vladimirovna see
   Timofeyeva, Nina
Timofeyeva, Nina (1935–)
Tomasselli, Vincenzo see
   Galeotti, Vincenzo
Tomasson, Helgi (1942–)
Toumanova, Tamara (1919–)
Trefilova, Vera (1875–1943)
Tudor, Antony (1909–1987)
Tumanova, Tamara
   Vladimirovna see
   Toumanova, Tamara
Turner, Harold (1909–1962)
Ulanova, Galina (1910–)
Vainonen, Vasily
   (1901–1964)
Valbergh (Valberkh), Ivan
   (1766–1819)
Van Dantzig, Rudi (1933–)
Vangsaae, Mona (1920–1983)
Van Hamel, Martine (1945–)
Van Manen, Hans (1932–)
Van Praagh, Peggy
   (1910–1990)
Van Schayk, Toer (1936–)
Vasiliev, Vladimir (1940–)
Vazem, Ekaterina
   (1848–1937)
Vecheslova, Tatyana
   (1910–1991)
Verdy, Violette (1933–)
Vestris, Auguste (1760–1842)
Vestris, Gaetano (Gaétan)
   (1729–1808)
Viganò, Salvatore
   (1769–1821)
Villella, Edward (1936–)
Vilzak, Anatole (1896–)
Vladimirov, Pierre
   (1893–1970)
Volinine, (Volinin)
   Alexandre (1882–1955)
Volkova, Vera (1904–1975)
Von Aroldingen, Karin
   (1941–)
Von Rosen, Elsa Marianne
   (1924–)
Vyroubova, Nina (1921–)
Wall, David (1946–)
Walsh, Christine (1954–)
Watts, Heather (1953–)
Weaver, John (1673–1760)
Welch, Garth (1936–)
Wells, Doreen (1937–)
White, Patricia Lorrain-Ann
   see Wilde, Patricia
Wilde, Patricia (1928–)
Williams, Augusta see
   Maywood, Augusta
Wilson, Sallie (1932–)
Woizikowsky, Léon
   (1899–1975)

Wójcikowski, Léon see
   Woizikowsky, Léon
Wright, Peter (1926–)
Yakobson, Leonid
   (1904–1975)
Yermolaev, Aleksei
   (1910–1975)
Youskevitch, Igor (1912–)
Zakharov, Rostislav
   (1907–1975)
Zaklinsky, Konstantin
   (1955–)
Zambelli, Carlotta
   (1875–1968)
Zanerini, Giovanna
   Francesca Antonia
   Guiseppe see Baccelli,
   Giovanna
Zorina, Vera (1917–)
Zucchi, Virginia (1849–1930)

Designers
Bakst, Léon (1866–1924)
Benois, Alexandre
   (1870–1960)
Benua, Aleksandr
   Nikolaevich see Benois,
   Alexandre
Bérard, Christian
   (1902–1949)
Chappell, William (1908–)
Chirico, Giorgio de
   (1888–1978)
Cocteau, Jean (1889–1963)
De Beaumont, Comte
   Etienne (1883–1956)
Derain, Andre (1880–1954)
Fedorovitch, Sophie
   (1893–1953)
Gontcharova, Nathalie
   (Natalia) (1881–1962)
Howard, Andrée (1910–1968)
Karinska, Barbara
   (1886–1983)
Larionov, Mikhail
   (1881–1964)
Matisse, Henri (1869–1954)
Messel, Oliver (1905–1978)
Picasso, Pablo (1881–1973)
Rosenberg, Lev Samoilovich
   see Bakst, Leon
Smith, Oliver (1918–)
Tchelitchev (Tchelitchew)
   Pavel (1898–1957)
Van Schayk, Toer (1936–)
Virsaladze, Simon (1909–)
Zhmoudska, Varvara see
   Karinska, Barbara

Impresarios
Blum, René (1878–1942)
De Maré, Rolf (1888–1964)
Diaghilev, Serge (1872–1929)

Librettists
Cahusac, Louis de
   (1706–1759)
Cocteau, Jean (1889–1963)
De Beaumont, Comte
   Etienne (1883–1956)
Gautier, Théophile
   (1811–1872)
Kochno, Boris (1904–1991)

Poets
Cocteau, Jean (1889–1963)
Cornazano, Antonio
   (1430–1484)
Gautier, Théophile
   (1811–1872)

Teachers
Adams, Diana (1926–1993)
Ahearn, Joseph Jacques see
   D'Amboise, Jacques
Andersen, Frank (1953–)
Angiolini, Gaspero
   (1731–1803)
Arpino, Gennaro Peter see
   Arpino, Gerald
Arpino, Gerald (1925–)
Ballon (Balon), Claude
   (1671–1744)
Beauchamps (Beauchamp),
   Charles-Louis see
   Beauchamps (Beauchamp),
   Pierre
Beauchamps (Beauchamp),
   Pierre (1631–1705)
Beaujoyeulx (Beaujoyeux),
   Balthasar de (1535–1587)
Beck, Hans (1861–1952)
Bedells, Phyllis (1893–1985)
Belgiojoso, Baldassare de see
   Beaujoyeulx (Beaujoyeux),
   Balthasar de
Beriozoff (Beriosoff),
   Nicholas (1906–)
Bessy, Claude (1932–)
Bjørnsson, Fredbjørn (1926–)
Blair, David (1932–1976)
Blasis, Carlo (1795–1878)
Blondy, Michel (1675–1739)
Bolm, Adolph (1884–1951)
Borovansky, Edouard
   (Eduard) (1902–1959)
Bournonville, August
   (1805–1879)
Brenaa, Hans (1910–1988)
Brianza, Carlotta
   (1867–1935)
Butterfield, David see Blair,
   David
Caroso, Fabritio (1526–1605)
Cecchetti, Enrico
   (1850–1928)
Chabukiani, Vakhtang
   (1910–1992)
Charrat, Janine (1924–)
Chauviré, Yvette (1917–)

Chernitseva, Lyubov Pavlovna *see* Tchernicheva, Lubov
Christensen, Lew (1908–1984)
Christensen, Willam (1902–)
Cook, William (1909–1987) *see* Tudor, Antony
Čorak, Mia *see* Slavenska, Mia
Cornazano, Antonio (1430–1484)
Craske, Margaret (1892–1990)
D'Amboise, Jacques (1934–)
Da Ferrara, Domenico *see* Domenico De Piacena
Danielian, Leon (1920–)
Danilova, Aleksandra Dionisievna *see* Danilova, Alexandra
Danilova, Alexandra (1903–)
De Valois, Ninette (1898–)
Didelot, Charles-Louis (1767–1837)
Dluzhnevska, Felzata *see* Doubrovska, Felia
Dodson, Robert *see* North, Robert
Dolgushin, Nikita (1938–)
Dollar, William (1907–1986)
Domenico De Piacena (1425–1465)
Doubrovska, Felia (1896–1981)
Dudinskaya, Natalia (1912–)
Dupré, Louis (1697–1774)
Duraud, Claude *see* Bessy, Claude
Edwards, Leslie (1916–)
Eglevsky, André (1917–1977)
Ermolaev, Aleksei Nikolaevich *see* Yermolaev, Aleksei
Fadeyechev, Nikolai (1933–)
Farron, Joyce *see* Farron, Julia
Farron, Julia (1922–)
Feuillet, Raoul Auger (1660–1710)
Fokine, Mikhail (Michel) (1880–1942)
Fornaroli, Cia (1888–1954)
Franklin, Frederic (1914–)
Froman, Margarita (1890–1970)
Galeotti, Vincenzo (1733–1816)
Gardel, Maximilien (1741–1787)
Gardel, Pierre (1758–1840)
Gaskell, Sonia (1904–1974)
Gasparini, Domenico Maria Angiolo *see* Angiolini, Gaspero
Georgi, Yvonne (1903–1975)

Gerdt, Elisaveta (1891–1975)
Gerdt, Pavel (1844–1917)
Gielgud, Maina (1945–)
Gilpin, John (1930–1983)
Glushkovsky, Adam Pavlovich (1793–1870)
Gnatt, Kirsten Laura *see* Ralov, Kirsten
Golovine, Serge (1935–)
Gorsky, Aleksandr (1871–1924)
Grigoriev, Serge (1883–1968)
Gsovsky, Victor (1902–1974)
Gsovsky (Gsovska), Tatjana (1901–)
Guglielmo Ebreo (1420–1481)
Guillaume le Juif *see* Guglielmo Ebreo
Gusev, Petr (1904–1987)
Harkarvy, Benjamin (1930–)
Hayden, Melissa (1923–)
Herman, Mildred *see* Hayden, Melissa
Hightower, Rosella (1920–)
Hilverding (van Wewen), Franz (1710–1768)
Idzikowski, Stanislas (1894–1977)
Ikowski *see* Idzikowski, Stanislas
Issatchenko, Tatyana *see* Gsovsky (Gsovska), Tatjana
Ivanov, Leonid Mikhailovich *see* Lavrovsky, Leonid
Ivanov, Lev (1834–1901)
Joffrey, Anver *see* Joffrey, Robert
Joffrey, Robert (1930–1988)
Johansson, (Per) Christian (1817–1903)
Jones, Marilyn (1940–)
Karsavina, Tamara (1885–1978)
Kerpestein, LeRoy *see* Loring, Eugene
Khan, Abdullah Jaffa Anver Bey *see* Joffrey, Robert
Kirkland, Gelsey (1952–)
Kniaseff (Kniasev), Boris (1900–1975)
Kolpakova, Irina (1933–)
Kronstam, Henning (1934–)
Kshesinskaya (Kschesinska), Matilda (1872–1971)
Kun, Zsuzsa (1934–)
Kyasht, Lydia (1885–1959)
Lacotte, Pierre (1932–)
Lander, Harald (1905–1971)
Lander, Toni (1931–1985)
Lanner, Katharina Josefa *see* Lanner, Katti
Lanner, Katti (1829–1908)
Larsen, Niels Bjørn (1913–1992)

Lavrovsky, Leonid (1905–1967)
LeClercq, Tanaquil (1929–)
Lee, Mary Ann (1824–1899)
Legat, Nikolai (Nicholas) (1869–1937)
Lessogorov, Ivan *see* Valbergh (Valberkh), Ivan
Lester, Keith (1904–)
Lichine, David (1910–1972)
Lichtenstein, David (Deivid) *see* Lichine, David
Loring, Eugene (1911–1982)
Luigia, Carolina Celia *see* Zambelli, Carlotta
Lukom, Elena (1891–1968)
MacLeary, Donald (1937–)
Madsen, Egon (1942–)
Markova, Alicia (1910–)
Marks, Lillian Alicia *see* Markova, Alicia
Martins, Peter (1946–)
Massine, Léonide (Leonid) (1895–1979)
May, Pamela (1917–)
Mazzo, Kay (1946–)
Mérante, Louis (1828–1887)
Messerer, Asaf (1903–1992)
Michel, Charles-Victor-Arthur *see* Saint-Léon, Arthur
Miskovitch, Milorad (1928–)
Mitchell, Arthur (1934–)
Mordkin, Mikhail (1880–1944)
Morrice, Norman (1931–)
Myasin, Leonid Fedorovich *see* Massine, Léonide (Leonid)
Nádasi, Ferenc (1893–1966)
Neary, Patricia (1942–)
Negri, Cesare (1536–1604)
Nemchinova (Nemtchinova), Vera (1899–1984)
Nijinska, Bronislava (1891–1972)
Nikitina, Alice (1904–1978)
Nizhinskaya, Bronislava Fominichna *see* Nijinska, Bronislava
North, Robert (1945–1983)
Noverre, Jean-Georges (1727–1810)
Obukhov (Oboukhoff), Anatole (1896–1962)
Osipenko, Alla (1932–)
Park, Merle (1937–)
Pavlova, Anna (1881–1931)
Pécour, Guillaume-Louis (1653–1729)
Pedersen, Hans *see* Brenaa, Hans
Peretti, Serge (1910–)
Perrot, Jules (1810–1892)
Petersen, Toni Pihl *see* Lander, Toni

Petipa, Marius (1818–1910)
Petit, Roland (1924–)
Ponomarev, Vladimir (1892–1951)
Pontois, Noëlla (1943–)
Preobrazhenskaya (Preobrajenska), Olga (1871–1962)
Prévost, Françoise (1681–1741)
Pushkin, Aleksandr (1907–1970)
Radunsky, Aleksandr (1912–)
Ralov, Kirsten (1922–)
Rambam, Cyvia *see* Rambert, Marie
Ramberg (Rambach), Myriam *see* Rambert, Marie
Rambert, Marie (1888–1982)
Reed, Janet (1916–)
Reinholm, Gert (1926–)
Riabouchinska, Tatiana (1917–)
Ryabushinskaya, Tatyana *see* Riabouchinska, Tatiana
Saint-Léon, Arthur (1821–1870)
Schmidt, Gerhard *see* Reinholm, Gert
Schollar, Ludmila (1888–1978)
Schwarz, Solange (1910–)
Schwezoff, Igor (1904–1982)
Screcek, Eduard Josef *see* Borovansky, Edouard (Eduard)
Semenova, Marina (1908–)
Sergeev (Sergeyev or Sergueff), Nikolai (Grigorevich) *see* Sergeyev, Nicholas (Nikolai)
Sergeyev, Nicholas (Nikolai) (1876–1951)
Shelest, Alla (1919–)
Shollar, Lyudmila Frantsevna *see* Schollar, Ludmila
Simone, Kirsten (1934–)
Skeaping, Mary (1902–1984)
Skouratoff, Vladimir (1925–)
Slavenska, Mia (1916–)
Smith, George Washington (1820–1899)
Sokolova, Evgenia (Eugenia) (1850–1925)
Spoerli, Heinz (1941–)
Staats, Léo (1877–1952)
Stannus, Edris *see* De Valois, Ninette
Stevnsborg, Alfred Bernhardt *see* Lander, Harald
Struchkova, Raisa (1925–)
Taglioni, Paul (Paolo) (1808–1884)
Taglioni, Salvatore (1789–1868)

Tallchief, Maria (1925–)
Taras, John (1919–)
Tchernicheva, Lubov
 (1890–1976)
Tikhomirov, Vasily
 (1876–1956)
Tomasselli, Vincenzo *see*
 Galeotti, Vincenzo
Trefilova, Vera (1875–1943)
Tudor, Antony (1909–1987)
Turner, Harold (1909–1962)
Ulanova, Galina (1910–)
Vaganova, Agrippina
 (1879–1951)
Valbergh (Valberkh), Ivan
 (1766–1819)
Vangsaae, Mona (1920–1983)
Van Praagh, Peggy
 (1910–1990)
Vazem, Ekaterina
 (1848–1937)

Vecheslova, Tatyana
 (1910–1991)
Vestris, Auguste (1760–1842)
Vestris, Gaetano (Gaétan)
 (1729–1808)
Viganò, Salvatore
 (1769–1821)
Vilzak, Anatole (1896–)
Volinine, (Volinin)
 Alexandre (1882–1955)
Volkova, Vera (1904–1975)
Von Rosen, Elsa Marianne
 (1924–)
Vyroubova, Nina (1921–)
Wall, David (1946–)
Weaver, John (1673–1760)
White, Patricia Lorrain-Ann
 see Wilde, Patricia
Wilde, Patricia (1928–)
Williams, E. Virginia
 (1914–1984)

William the Jew of Pesaro
 see Guglielmo Ebreo
Wilson, Sallie (1932–)
Yermolaev, Aleksei
 (1910–1975)
Youskevitch, Igor (1912–)
Zakharov, Rostislav
 (1907–1975)
Zambelli, Carlotta
 (1875–1968)

Writers
Arbeau, Thoinot (1520–1595)
Cahusac, Louis de
 (1706–1759)
Caroso, Fabritio (1526–1605)
Cocteau, Jean (1889–1963)
Cornazano, Antonio
 (1430–1484)
Feuillet, Raoul Auger
 (1660–1710)

Gautier, Théophile
 (1811–1872)
Guglielmo Ebreo
 (1420–1481)
Guillaume le Juif *see*
 Guglielmo Ebreo
Kirstein, Lincoln (1907–)
Kochno, Boris (1904–1991)
Kriger (Krieger), Viktorina
 (1893–1978)
Lifar, Serge (1905–1986)
Negri, Cesare (1536–1604)
Noverre, Jean-Georges
 (1727–1810)
Struchkova, Raisa (1925–)
Tabourot, Jehan *see* Arbeau,
 Thoinot
Weaver, John (1673–1760)
William the Jew of Pesaro
 see Guglielmo Ebreo

NOTES ON CONTRIBUTORS

ADAMA, Richard. Ex-dancer, choreographer, and ballet director, including in Bremen, Munich, Hanover, and Vienna. **Essays:** Yvonne Georgi; Patricia Neary.

ALOFF, Mindy. Freelance writer. Has contributed to *The Atlantic, The New Yorker*, and *The New Republic*. **Essays:** Suzanne Farrell; New York City Ballet.

ALOVERT, Nina. Freelance photographer and journalist, Russia and the U.S.; contributing editor, *Dance Magazine*. Author of *Baryshnikov in Russia* (1985) and for several years writer of dance programmes for "Voice of America" radio. **Essays**: Zhanna Ayupova; Boris Eifman; *Fountain of Bakhchisarai*; Yuri Grigorovich; *Laurencia*; Maris Liepa; Natalia Makarova; Yulia Makhalina; Maly Theatre Ballet; *Othello*; *Romeo and Juliet* (Lavrovsky); Alla Shelest; Oleg Vinogradov; Simon Virsaladze; *Yaroslavna*.

ANAWALT, Sasha. Freelance dance writer. Has published articles in *Dance Magazine* and *The New York Times*. Essays: Gerald Arpino; Joffrey Ballet; *Trinity*.

ANDERSON, Jack. Co-editor, *Dance Chronicle*, New York; also contributing editor, *Ballet Review*, associate dance critic, *The New York Times*, and New York correspondent, *Dancing Times*. Author of *Dance* (1974), *The Nutcracker Ballet* (1979), and *The One and Only: The Ballet Russe de Monte Carlo* (1981). **Essay:** Ballet Russe de Monte Carlo.

ANDERSON, Jeanette. Freelance dance writer and cultural correspondent for the Danish daily newspapers *Berlingske Tidende* and *Jyllands Posten,* and U.S. editor for the Danish theatre magazine *Teater Et*. **Essays:** Flemming Flindt; Lucile Grahn; Lis Jeppesen; Harald Lander; Toni Lander; *Napoli*; Kirsten Simone; *The Whims of Cupid and the Ballet Master*.

ARAH, Jessica. Freelance writer. **Essays:** Lucia Chase; Ludmilla Chiriaeff; *Elite Syncopations*; *Études*; *A Folk Tale*; Natalia Gontcharova; Les Grands Ballets Canadiens; Barbara Karinska; Boris Kochno.

ASCHENGREEN, Erik. Professor of History and Aesthetics of Dance at the University of Copenhagen. Contributing editor of *Perspektiv på Bournonville* (1980); author of *Jean Cocteau and the Dance* (1986). Member of the advisory boards of *Dance Chronicle* and *Dance Research*. Has also contributed articles to *Dance Perspectives*, *Les Saisons de la danse, Dance Magazine*, and *Balletto*. Adviser to *The International Dictionary of Ballet*. **Essays:** August Bournonville; Henning Kronstam; Margot Lander; Royal Danish Ballet.

ASTIER, Régine. Choreographer, dancer, and Baroque dance historian. Has published articles in *Dancescope, Dance Chronicle, York Dance Review, Dance Research, La Recherche en danse, Les Goûts réunis,* and *Dance and Ancient Greece*. **Essays:** Claude Ballon; Marie-Anne Camargo. **Roles research:** Claude Ballon; Pierre Beauchamps; Marie-Anne Camargo; Raoul Feuillet; Mlle. La Fontaine; Françoise Prevost; Pierre Rameau.

BABSKY, Monique. Freelance dance critic, researcher, and historian. Formerly Librarian, Centre international de documentation pour la danse. Regular contributor to *Les Saisons de la danse*; has also published articles in *L'Avant- scène: Ballet/Danse*. Contributor to *Pipers Enzyklopädie des Musiktheaters*. **Essays:** Laurent Hilaire; Elisabeth Platel. **Roles research:** Twentieth-century French ballet.

BAER, Nancy van Norman. Curator, Theatre and Dance Department of the Fine Arts Museum, San Francisco. Author of *Bronislava Nijinska: A Dancer's Legacy* (1986), *The Art of Enchantment: Diaghilev's Ballets Russes 1909-1929* (1988), and *Theatre in Revolution: Russian Avant-Garde Stage Design* (1991). **Essay:** *Le Chant du rossignol.*

BARZEL, Anne. Dance critic, *Chicago Skyline*, and Senior Editor, *Dance Magazine*. Has published articles in *Dance Index, Ballet Review, Dance Magazine, The New York Times* and others; also contributor to *Barnes Dance Encyclopedia, Scribners Dance Encyclopedia*, and the London *Ballet Annual*. Author of *European Dance Teachers in the U.S.* (1942). Adviser to *The International Dictionary of Ballet*. **Essays:** Adolph Bolm; Catherine Littlefield; Ruth Page.

BASKERVILLE, Geoffrey. Dance critic, British Broadcasting Corporation (BBC); formerly writer for *The Scotsman*. **Essays:** *Cléopâtre*; Aleksandr Glazunov; Hans Werner Henze; Aram Khachaturian; Leonid Lavrovsky; Elaine McDonald; *The Miraculous Mandarin; Requiem;* Scottish Ballet; Dmitri Shostakovich; *Voluntaries;* The Wooden Prince.

BASSETT, Peter. Librarian, Laban Centre for Movement and Dance, London. Author of *Building a Resource for Research into Dance* (Laban Centre Working Papers); also Administrative Secretary, Society for Dance Research. **Essays:** *Carmen* (Petit); *Les Demoiselles de la nuit; Les Forains; Le Jeune Homme et la mort;* Roland Petit. **Roles research:** Twentieth-century French and German ballet.

BECKWITH, Kristin. Faculty Member, Boston Ballet School, and freelance dance writer. **Essays:** *Flore et Zéphire*; Nikolai Legat; *The Little Humpbacked Horse*; Agrippina Vaganova.

BERRY, Irmgard E. Freelance writer and researcher. Formerly Librarian, Institute of Choreology (now The Benesh Institute), London. **Essay:** Mary Skeaping.

BINDIG, Susan F. Freelance writer and dance historian. Has published articles in *Dance Chronicle*. **Essays:** Raoul Feuillet; Guillaume-Louis Pécourt.

BRAINARD, Ingrid. Dance historian and writer. **Essay:** Gaspero Angiolini.

BREMSER, Martha. Editor of *The International Dictionary of Ballet*. **Essays:** Altynai Asylmuratova; Darcey Bussell; Dance Theatre of Harlem.

BRISSENDEN, Alan. Reader in English, University of Adelaide, Australia, and dance critic for *Dance Australia* and *The Australian*. Author of *Shakespeare and the Dance*, 1981. **Essay:** Robert Helpmann.

BROOKS, Lynn Matluck. Director of Dance and Associate Professor of Drama, Franklin and Marshall College, Pennsylvania. Author of *The Dances of the Processions of Seville in Spain's Golden Age*; has also published work in *Dance Chronicle*, *Dance Research Journal*, and *The Journal of Aesthetic Education*. **Essays:** Mary Ann Lee; George Washington Smith.

BURNS, Judith. Dance historian and co-editor of journal, *Women & Performance*; has also taught at Brooklyn College. **Essay:** Paul Taylor.

CARTER, Françoise. Professor of Euro-American Culture in the Faculty of Law and Literature at Ehime University, Japan. Formerly lecturer in Dance History, London School of Contemporary Dance and Department of External Studies, Oxford University. Has contributed articles to *Dance Research* and *Guglielmo Ebreo da Pesaro e la Danza Nelle Corti Italiano del XV Secolo (Milan, 1990)*. Adviser to *The International Dictionary of Ballet*. **Essays:** *Ballet Comique de la Reine*; Balthasar de Beaujoyeulx; *Ballet de la Nuit*; *Les Fâcheux*; *Le Bourgeois Gentilhomme*; Guglielmo Ebreo; Paris Opéra Ballet.

CHALMERS, Kenneth. Composer and freelance writer on music. Regular translator for *Opera* magazine. **Essays:** Leonard Bernstein; Paul Hindemith.

CHAPMAN, John. Director, Division of Dance, University of California, Santa Barbara. Editor of *Studies in Dance History*. **Essays:** Monsieur Albert; Jean-Pierre Aumer; Jean Coralli; *Dansomanie*; Louis Antoine Duport; *Les Elements*; *La Fille mal gardée* (Dauberval); Maximilien Gardel; Pierre Gardel; *La Gipsy; Giselle*; Louis Henry; *Le Jugement de Pâris*; Joseph Mazilier; *Paquita*; *La Péri*; Jules Perrot; *Les Quatre Saisons; La Sylphide*; *La Tarentule*; Auguste Vestris; *La Vivandière*.

CHAZIN-BENNAHUM, Judith. Assistant Professor of Theatre and Dance, College of Fine Arts, University of New Mexico. **Essays:** *Echoing of Trumpets*; Benjamin Harkarvy; *The Leaves are Fading*; *Pillar of Fire*; *Romeo and Juliet* (Tudor); *Shadowplay*; *Undertow*.

CHISNELL, Amanda. Freelance writer. **Essays:** *Le Baiser de la fée*; Victor Gsovsky; *Raymonda*.

CHRISTIAN, Virginia. Dance critic and freelance writer. **Essays:** Leslie Browne; *Daphnis et Chloé*; *The Magic Flute*; Kevin McKenzie; *Push Comes to Shove*; Igor Schwezoff; Marjorie Tallchief; Martine van Hamel.

CHRISTOUDIA, Melanie Trifona. Curatorial Assistant, Theatre Museum, Victoria and Albert Museum, London. **Essays:** Carlotta Brianza; *Le Diable boîteux*; *Don Juan*; Michel Renault; Ludmila Schollar; Pavel Tchelitchev.

CHRISTOUT, Marie-Françoise. Librarian and Specialist, Départment des arts du spectacle, Bibliothèque national, Paris. Author of *Le Merveilleux et le Théâtre du Silence* (1965), *Le Ballet de cour de Louis XIV* (1967), *Maurice Béjart* (1972), *Histoire du ballet* (1975). **Essays:** Cyril Atanasoff; Michael Denard; Arthur Honegger; *Icare*; Serge Lifar.

COREY, Mary E. Assistant Professor of Dance, University of California at Irvine. Notator of several ballets and modern dances; reconstruction credits include *Loring's Billy the Kid* for the University of California. Labanotator for Daniel Lewis's *The Illustrated Dance Techniques of José Limón* (1984); has also contributed to *Ballet Review*. **Essays:** *Billy the Kid*; Eugene Loring.

COSTONIS, Mary Needham. Assistant Professor of Dance History, Blair School of Music, Vanderbilt University, Tennessee. Advisor and chief contributor on dance for *Groves New Dictionary of Opera* (1992); editor and chief contributor for *Therapy in Motion* (1978). Has published articles in *Bulletin of Research in the Humanities*, *Dance Chronicle*, and *American Music*. **Essays:** Pierre Beauchamps; Jean Dauberval; Marie-Madeleine Guimard; Mlle La Fontaine; Jean-Georges Noverre; Gaetano Vestris. **Roles research:** Gaetano Vestris.

COURNAND, Gilberte. Dance critic for *Le Parisien* and contributor of articles on dance for numerous other French publications. **Essays:** Lycette Darsonval; Serge Peretti; Solange Schwarz.

CRABB, Michael F. Producer (Radio Arts) for the Canadian Broadcasting Corporation, and freelance dance critic for the *Toronto Star*. Canadian correspondent, *Dance Magazine*. Author (with photographer Andrew Oxenham) of *Dance Today in Canada* (1977), and editor of *Visions: Ballet and its Future* (1979). **Essays:** Karen Kain; James Kudelka; Brian Macdonald; Royal Winnipeg Ballet; Veronica Tennant.

CRAINE, Debra. Assistant Arts Editor and regular dance critic for *The Times*, London. Adviser to *The International Dictionary of Ballet*. **Essays:** Sylvie Guillem; Jennifer Penney.

DACKO, Karen. National critic for *Dance Magazine*, and news correspondent in Pittsburgh, Philadelphia. **Essays:** Léontine Beaugrand; Giuseppina Bozzacchi; *Coppélia*; Frederic Franklin; *Pas de quatre*; Arthur Saint-Léon; *La Source*; Patricia Wilde.

DEAN, Beth. Australian correspondent for *Dance Magazine* and dance writer for *Australasian Dance* and *Sydney Morning Herald*. Author of *Dust for the Dancers* (1955), *The Many Worlds of Dance* (1964), *Pacific Islands Arts and Dance* (1972), *Some Great Moments in Ballet* (1969), *Three Dances of Oceania* (1976), and *South Pacific Dance* (1978). **Essay:** The Australian Ballet.

DEGEN, Arsen. Ballet critic, Leningrad/St. Petersburg. Author of *Master Dancers, 1917-1973* (1974); *Leningrad Maly Ballet Company* (1979); *Leningrad Ballet 1917-1987* (1988). **Essays:** Elena Andreyanova; Nadezhda Bogdanova; *Don Quixote*; Lubov Egorova; Sophia Fedorova; *Heart of the Hills*; Anatole Obukhov; *Paquita*; Olga Preobrazhenskaya; Olga Spessivtseva; *The Stone Flower*; Vasily Vainonen.

DEVEREUX, Tony. Freelance dance writer. Has contributed articles to *Dancing Times* and *Soviet Ballet*. **Essays:** Lev Ivanov; Fedor Lopukhhov; Marius Petipa; *Shurale; Swan Lake*.

DIXON, Mike. Dance critic, *Dance Australia*, and freelance writer. Served as advisor to the London Festival Ballet Education Unit. **Essays:** *Dances at a Gathering*; Eva Evdokimova; Niels Kehlet; *Suite en blanc*.

DORRIS, George. Co-editor, *Dance Chronicle*, New York.

Author of *Paoli Rolli and the Italian Circle in London 1715-1744* (1967). Has also contributed regularly to *Ballet Review* and *Dance Chronicle*, as well as to *Proceedings of the Society of Dance History Scholars*. **Essays:** Robert Joffrey; Vaslav Nijinsky.

DORVANE, Jeanne. Dance critic, *Les Saisons de la danse*, Paris. Member of the Dance Perspective Foundation, New York. **Essay:** Jorge Donn.

EGAN, Carol. Dance critic and historian. **Essays:** Ballets Russes de Serge Diaghilev; Fanny Cerrito; Serge Diaghilev; Fanny Elssler; Carlotta Grisi; Tamara Karsavina; Augusta Maywood.

FAIRFAX, Vicki. Dance critic for the *Sunday Herald*, Melbourne, and contributor to *Dance Australia*. Author of *Garth Welch: A Life of Dance* (1986). **Essays:** Garth Welch.

FANGER, Iris. Drama critic (formerly dance critic), *Boston Herald*, and contributing editor, *Dance Magazine*. Also director, Harvard Summer School. Has published articles in *World Monitor*; also dance editor, *Columbia University Encyclopedia*. Adviser to *The International Dictionary of Ballet*. **Essays:** Ida Rubinstein; E. Virginia Williams.

FARK, William E. Freelance writer. **Essays:** John Butler; Eliot Feld; John Kriza; Mikhail Lavrovsky.

FINKEL, Anita. Editor, *New Dance Review*, and freelance writer. **Essays:** American Ballet Theatre; *Bourrée Fantasque*.

FISHER, Jennifer. Freelance writer. **Essay:** *The Dying Swan*.

FISHER-STITT, Norma Sue. Sessional assistant professor, York University, Canada, and writer on dance. **Essays:** Christian Johansson; Evgenia Sokolova; Ekaterina Vazem.

FLEMING, Bruce E. Assistant Professor of English, United States Naval Academy, Annapolis, Maryland, and writer on dance. Has contributed to, among others, *Philosophy and Literature, Southwest Review, Washington Dance View, Dutch Quarterly Review, and Essays in Literature*. **Essays:** *Agon; Birthday Offering; The Concert; Davidsbündlertänze; The Four Temperaments; The Prodigal Son; Serenade*.

GAEVSKY, Vadim. Dance and theatre critic and historian, Moscow. Author of *Divertissement* (1981) and *Flute of Hamlet* (1990). Has published articles in, among others, *Teatr*. **Essays:** Natalia Bessmertnova; Olga Lepeshinskaya; Ekaterina Maximova; Asaf Messerer; Marina Semenova; Aleksei Yermolayev.

GALE, Joseph. Dance critic for the Independent Press. Author of *Lust of Jade* (1936), *Wine Without Dregs* (1938), *A Critical Catalogue of Recorded Jewish Music* (1943), *Behind Barres: The Mystique of Masterly Teaching* (1980), *I Sang for Diaghilev: The Merry Life of Michel Pavloff* (1982), and *Pugni and Minkus: The Gold Dust Twins*. **Essays:** Agnes de Mille; *Fall River Legend; Rodeo*.

GARCIÁ-MÁRQUEZ, Vincente. Cultural Historian. Author of *Les Ballets Russes* (1990) and *Léonide Massine: A Biography* (forthcoming). **Essays:** Tatiana Riabouchinska; Tamara Toumanova.

GAYE, Pamela. Freelance writer and lecturer in dance history;

has also been contributing editor for *Dance Scope* and *Canadian Dance News*. Author of *In Search of Béjart* (1975) and *Katherine Dunham: A Biography* (1978). Has contributed articles to *The Dial, The New York Times, San Francisco Ballet Program*, and *Dance Magazine*. **Essays:** Maurice Béjart; Rosella Hightower; *Les Indes galantes; Nijinsky, Clown de dieu*.

GEORGE, Rosaline. Freelance writer and dance critic. Has published articles in *The Performing Arts Magazine, Senior Life Magazine*, and *La West Magazine*. **Essays:** *Jeux*; Lydia Sokolova.

GLASSTONE, Richard. Dance teacher and writer. Examiner and Fellow, Cecchetti Society, London; formerly Director, Cecchetti Centre; also Member of the Executive Committee, Society for Dance Research. **Essays:** Carlo Blasis; Enrico Cecchetti; *La Fête étrange*; Andrée Howard; Nadia Nerina; *Pineapple Poll; Prince of the Pagodas*; Peggy van Praagh.

GOODWIN, Noël. Freelance critic and editor, *Dance and Dancers*, London. Author of *A Ballet for Scotland* (1979). Has contributed to *Encyclopedia Britannica* (1976), *Britannica Books of the Year, The Concise Oxford Dictionary of Ballet* (1977, 1987), *New Grove Dictionary of Music and Musicians* (1980), *Cambridge Encyclopedia of Russia and the Soviet Union* (1982), *New Oxford Companion to Music* (1983), *and Pipers Enzyklopädie des Musiktheaters* (1988-91). **Essays:** Charles Adolf Adam; Béla Bartók; Arthur Bliss; *Concerto*; Claude Debussy; Léo Delibes; *Las Hermanas*; Léon Minkus; Francis Poulenc; Sergei Prokofiev; Cesare Pugni; Maurice Ravel; *Song of the Earth*; Igor Stravinsky; Petr Ilyich Tchaikovsky.

GRADINGER, Malve. Freelance dance and theatre writer. Regular contributor to *Münchner Merkur, Applaus, Ballett Journal, Ballett International, Tanz Aktuell*, and *Tanz Affiche*. **Essays:** William Forsythe; Marcia Haydée; *Lady of the Camellias*; Stuttgart Ballet.

GREEN, Harris. Contributing editor, *Dance Magazine*, New York. Has published articles in *The New Republic, Ballet Review, The New York Times, Opera News, Commonweal*, and *The New Leader*. **Essays:** *Afternoon of a Faun; Fancy Free*; Susan Jaffe.

GREGORY, John. Artist and writer. Author of *Understanding Ballet, Heritage of a Ballet Master: Nicolas Legat, Giselle Immortal, The Varna Ballet Olympiad, Les Sylphides — Chopiana* (1989), *Brangwen — The Poet and the Dancer* (1989), *and The Legat Saga* (1992); has also published articles in *The Dancing Times*. **Essay:** *Les Sylphides*.

GRESKOVIC, Robert. Associate Editor, *The New Dance Review*, New York. Also freelance critic for, among others, *Ballet Review, The New Dance Review*, and *Dance Theatre Journal*. Adviser to *The International Dictionary of Ballet*. **Essays:** George Balanchine; Mikhail Baryshnikov; Patrick Bissell; *Divertimento No.15*; Nikita Dolgushin; *Drink To Me Only With Thine Eyes; Harlequinade; Jewels; Vienna Waltzes*.

GRIFFIN, Jessica. Dance historian and writer. **Essays:** Giovanna Baccelli; La Barberina; Paul Taglioni.

GRUZDEVA, Irina. Librarian, Moscow Theatre Library, and writer on dance. **Essays:** Vladimir Burmeister; Mikhail Gabovich; Victorina Kriger; Nadezhda Pavlova; Nina Timofeyeva; Raisa Struchkova.

HELPERN, Alice. Administrator, Merce Cunningham Studio, New York. Author of *The Evolution of Martha Graham's Dance Technique* (1981). Has also published articles in *American Dance* and *Ballet Review*; board member, Society of Dance History Scholars, 1987-89. **Essay:** Leon Danielian.

HERING, Doris. Senior Editor, *Dance Magazine*, New York. Ballet critic for numerous journals; chief critic and associate editor of *Dance Magazine*, 1950-70. Author and editor of *25 Years of American Dance* (1950), *Wild Grass: The Memoirs of Rudolf Orthwine*, and *Dance in America*. Contributor to *Encyclopedia of Dance and Ballet* (1977). **Essays:** Todd Bolender; *The Cage*; Jacques d'Amboise; William Dollar; Cynthia Gregory; Melissa Hayden; Houston Ballet; Lincoln Kirstein; Tanaquil LeClercq; Nicholas Magallanes; Mikhail Mordkin; Jerome Robbins; Oliver Smith; Galina Ulanova; Mona Vangsaae; Violette Verdy; Sallie Wilson.

HETHERINGTON, Monica. Lecturer in Dance Studies, University of Surrey. Editor, with Janet Adshead, *Directory of Dance Courses in Higher Education* (1987); contributor to *Choreography: Principles and Practice* (1987). **Essay:** David Bintley.

HORWITZ, Dawn Lille. Associate Professor at City College, City University of New York. Author of *Michel Fokine* (1985). Editor of *Dance Notation Journal: Balanchine Issue* (1988-89); Has also published articles in *Ballet Review*, *Choreography and Dance*, *Dance News*, and *Dance Chronicle*. **Essays:** Marie Allard; René Blum; *Le Carnaval*; *L'Epreuve d'amour*; *Paganini*; *Petrushka*.

HUDSON, Elizabeth. Dance critic and freelance writer. **Essays:** Margarita Froman; Sofia Fuoco; *Mayerling*; Boris Romanov; Salvatore Taglioni; Mlle. Théodore; Pierre Vladimirov.

HUNT, Marilyn. Associate Editor and former London Correspondent, *Dance Magazine*; was President of the Society of Dance History Scholars. Has contributed articles to *Dance Chronicle*, *Dance Magazine*, *Ballet Review*, and *Ballet News*. **Essays:** Alexandra Danilova; *Liebslieder Walzer*; *Mozartiana*; Kyra Nichols; *Orpheus*; *Symphony in C*; *Theme and Variations*; *Violin Concerto*; Igor Youskevitch.

INGLEHEARN, Madeleine. Professor of Early Dance, Guildhall School of Music and Drama, London, and Tutor in Period Dance and Movement at the Academy of Live and Recorded Arts. Author of *Fifteenth-Century Dances from Burgundy and Italy* (1981) and *Ten Dances from Sixteenth-Century Italy* (1983); translator of Antonio Cornazano's *The Book of the Art of Dancing* (1981). Has published articles in *The Music Review* and *Early Music*. **Essays:** Michel Blondy; Antonio Cornazano; Domenico da Ferrara; Jean-Baptiste Lully; Pierre Rameau; Marie Sallé.

JACKSON, George. Dance writer for *The Washington Post*, *Dance Magazine*, and *Dance View*. Member of Advisory Board, *Ballet Review*. Contributor to *The Dance Has Many Faces* (ed. Walter Sorell, 1992) and also to *Bounonvilleana* (ed. M. Hallar and A. Scavenius, 1992). **Essays:** *Die Puppenfee*; Mia Slavenska.

JOHANSEN, Birthe. Dance writer and researcher, Copenhagen. **Essays:** Frank Andersen. **Roles research:** Twentieth-century Danish ballet.

JOHNSON, Robert. Associate editor, *Dance Magazine*, and writer on dance. **Essay:** Léon Bakst.

JONES, Susan. Ex-soloist, Scottish Ballet; dance teacher, writer, and doctoral candidate at the University of Oxford. **Essays:** Harald Lander; Egon Madsen; Kirsten Ralov; *Triumph of Death*.

JORDAN, Stephanie. Lecturer in Dance Studies, University of Surrey, and dance critic for *The Listener*. Author of several books and articles on dance. **Essay:** Ashley Page.

JOWITT, Penelope. Dance teacher, writer, and doctoral candidate at the University of Oxford. Adviser to *The International Dictionary of Ballet*. **Essays:** Adam Glushkovsky; Mathilde Kshesinskaya; *L'Oiseau de feu*; *Les Rendezvous*; *Romeo and Juliet* (Ashton).

KANE, Angela. Senior Lecturer in Dance, Roehampton Institute of Higher Education, London, and freelance dance critic and historian. Has published articles in *World Ballet and Dance*, *Dancing Times*, *Dance Theatre Journal*, *Dance Gazette*, and *Dance Research*. **Essays:** *Anastasia*; *Aureole*; Viviana Durante; *La Fille mal gardée* (Ashton); *Giselle*; *Manon*; Rambert Dance Company; *Romeo and Juliet* (MacMillan); Glen Tetley.

KAPLAN, Larry. Freelance dance writer. Co-author of *Dancing for Balanchine* (with Merrill Ashley, 1984), and *Prodigal Son* (with Edward Villella, 1992). Has published ballet reviews in numerous journals. **Essays:** Merrill Ashley; Darci Kistler; Patricia McBride; *Square Dance*.

KELLY, Deirdre. Dance critic, *The Globe and Mail*, Toronto. **Essays:** *L'Après-midi d'un faune*; Erik Bruhn; Fernando Bujones; Evelyn Hart; *Le Papillon*; *La Ventana*.

KEMP, C. Sandra. Lecturer in English Literature, University of Glasgow, and writer on dance. Adviser to *The International Dictionary of Ballet*. **Essay:** Robert North.

KENDALL, Yvonne G. Assistant Professor of Music, Davidson College, North Carolina. Translator and author of introduction, Cesare Negri's *Le Gratie d'amore* (1985); has published articles in *Dance Research*. **Essays:** Cesare Negri.

KERBY-FULTON, Kathryn. Associate Professor of English, University of Victoria, Canada. Author of *Piers Plowman and Reformist Apocalypticism*; also freelance writer on dance. **Essays:** Franz Hilverding; Charles LePicq; *The Loves of Mars and Venus*; *Les Petits Riens*; *Song of a Wayfarer*; Marie-Thérèse Subligny; *The Taming of the Shrew*; John Weaver.

KERSLEY, Leo. Ex-dancer, Ballet Rambert, Sadler's Wells Ballet, Anglo-Polish Ballet, and Sadler's Wells Theatre Ballet, and freelance dance writer. Co-author of *A Dictionary of Ballet Terms* (with Janet Sinclair, 1952); has also published articles in *The Dancing Times*, *Dance and Dancers*, *Opera*, *The Stage*, *The Daily Telegraph*, *Music and Musicians*, and *Nieuwe Rotterdamse Courant*. **Essays:** *Le Beau Danube*; William Chappell; *Designs with Strings*; Stanislas Idzikowski; Lydia Lopokova; *Les Patineurs*; *Prince Igor (Polovtsian Dances from)*; *Spectre de la rose*; Frank Staff; Harold Turner.

KING, Jane. Dance critic for the *Morning Star*. Contributor to *World Ballet and Dance* (1989); occasional contributor to *Soviet*

Ballet and *Tanecni Listy* (Prague) and reviewer for *Cuba en el Ballet* (Havana). **Essays:** Alicia Alonso; Christopher Bruce; Ballet Nacional de Cuba.

KING, Kate. Administrative Assistant, National Resource Centre for Dance, University of Surrey. Author of *Waterless Method of Swimming Instruction* (1974), and editor of *What's Afoot* (newsletter of the National Resource for Dance), 1988-90; has also contributed to *Pipers Enzyklopädie des Musiktheaters* (1988-90). **Essays:** *Job*; Netherlands Dance Theatre; Hans van Manen.

KJØLBYE, Marie-Louise. Dance critic at *Information* (Copenhagen). Has contributed many articles to *Kanonhallen*, *World Ballet and Dance*, *Teater Et*, *Musik og Teater*, and others. Also contributor to the *Danish National Encyclopedia*. Author of *Separation* (1993); co-editor (with Anne McClymont) of *Between Dance and Dream* (1993). **Essays:** Hans Beck; Rose Gad; Nikolaj Hübbe; Margrethe Schanne.

KLOOS, Helma. Freelance journalist and teacher, and Dutch correspondent for *Dance Magazine*. **Essays:** Jiří Kylián; *Sinfonietta*; *Soldiers' Mass*.

KOKICH, Kim. Dance critic for *Ballet Review*, and dance reporter for National Public Radio (NPR), Washington, D.C. **Essays:** *Bugaku*; Felia Doubrovska; Alessandra Ferri; Maya Plisetskaya; Edward Villella; Karin von Aroldingen.

KÖRTVÉLYES, Géza. Dance historian and critic; teacher at the Hungarian Dance College, Budapest. Author of *The Miraculous Mandarin at the State Opera* (1961), *Following the Road of Modern Dance* (1970), *Budapest Ballet* I and II (1979 and 1981), *The Art of Hungarian Ballet at the State Opera 1919-1984* (1983 and 1985) and *The Arts and Dance* (1990). Has also published articles in *Muzsika*, the daily *Magyar Nemzet*, and the daily *Nèpszabadsag*. **Essay:** Imre Eck.

KRASSOVSKAYA, Vera. Dance historian and writer, Leningrad/St. Petersburg. Author of *Vakhtang Chabukiani* (1960), *Russian Ballet Theatre from the Beginning to the Middle of the Nineteenth Century* (1958), *Leningrad Ballet* (1961), *Russian Ballet Theatre in the Second Half of the Nineteenth Century* (1963), *Anna Pavlova* (1965), *Russian Ballet Theatre at the Beginning of the Twentieth Century* (1972), *Nijinsky* (1974), *European Ballet Theatre* (volumes 1-3; 1979, 1981, and 1983). **Essays:** Elisaveta Gerdt; Pavel Gerdt; Avdotia Istomina; Vera Trefilova; Ivan Valbergh.

LAUGHLIN, Patricia. Freelance dance writer. Author of *Marilyn Jones* (1978). Senior feature writer for *Dance Australia*; has also published articles in *Dance Magazine*, *Ballett International*, and *Vandance*. **Essays:** Edouard Borovansky; Stephen Heathcote; Greg Horsman; Marilyn Jones; Lisa Pavane; Christine Walsh.

LAWSON, Joan. Dance critic, writer, and teacher. Author of *European Folk Dance* (1953), *Mime* (1955), *Classical Ballet: Its Style and Technique* (1960), *A History of Ballet and its Makers* (1964), *The Teaching of Classical Ballet* (1973), *Teaching Young Dancers* (1975). Has also contributed to the *Encyclopaedia Britannica* and *Oxford Children's Encyclopaedia*; has published numerous articles in *The Dancing Times*. Adviser to *The International Dictionary of Ballet*. **Essays:** *Le Coq d'or*; Mikhail Fokine; *Le Pavillon d'Armide*.

LEADER, Jody. Dance critic, *Los Angeles Daily News*. Has also published articles in *The Chicago Tribune*, *The San Francisco Examiner*, *The Detroit Free Press*, *The Cleveland Plain Dealer*, and *Dallas Morning News*. **Essays:** *Apollo*; Aaron Copland; *Le Sacre du printemps*.

LEE, Susan. Chair of Theatre and Director of Dance, Northwestern University, Evanston, Illinois. Founding Editor of *American Dance*; author of *Dance: The Last 100 Years* (1986). Has published articles in *Medical Problems of Performing Artists* and *Dance: Current Selected Research* (volume 1). **Essays:** Sono Osato; Maria Tallchief; Vera Zorina.

LIDOVA, Irène. Critic and dance writer. Author of *17 Visages de la danse franáaise* (1953), *Roland Petit* (1954), *and Ma Vie avec la danse* (1992). Regular critic, *Les Saisons de la danse*, and French correspondent for *Ballet Annual*, *Dance News*, *Balletto Oggi* and *Ballet 2000*. **Essays:** Claude Bessy; Janine Charrat; Liane Daydé; Marquis George de Cuevas; Serge Golovine; Boris Kniaseff; George Skibine; Vladimir Skouratoff; Ludmila Tcherina; Nina Vyroubova.

LO IACONO, Concetta. Teacher of Dance History, Academy of Dance, Rome. Has publised articles in *La Danza Italiana*, *Nuova Rivista Musicale Italiana*, and *Cenerentola*. **Essays:** Cia Fornaroli; *Pharaoh's Daughter*; Virginia Zucchi.

LOURDEAUX, Lee. Freelance writer. **Essays:** Julio Bocca; Helgi Tomasson.

MACAULAY, Alastair. Dance critic and writer. Regular contributor to *Dancing Times* and *The New Yorker*. Adviser to *The International Dictionary of Ballet*. **Essay:** Frederick Ashton.

MAIER, Eric. Freelance writer. **Essay:** Alexander Kølpin.

MANNING, Emma. London Editor, *Dance Australia*, and freelance dance critic. **Essays:** Fiona Chadwick; Maina Gielgud; *Graduation Ball*; André Prokovsky.

MARINARI, Sylvia. Choreographer and freelance writer. Has published articles in *Danza & Danza* (Milan). **Essay:** *The Green Table*.

MATHESON, Katy. Freelance dance critic. Formerly Associate Editor and Assistant to the Editor-in-Chief, *Dance Magazine*, New York. **Essays:** Ib Andersen; Maria Calegari; Peter Martins.

MATTHEW, Alanna. Freelance writer. Has published articles in *Vandance*, *Dance in Canada*, and *Dance Chronicle*. **Essays:** Tatjana Gsovsky; Inge Sand.

MAZO, Joseph. Contributing Editor, *Dance Magazine*, New York, and writer on dance. **Essays:** *A Midsummer Night's Dream*; Arthur Mitchell.

McCLYMONT, Anne. Freelance writer, Denmark. Co-editor (with Marie-Louise Kjølby) of *Between Dance and Dream* (1993). **Essays:** Anna Laerkesen; Heidi Ryom.

McDONAGH, Don. Managing Editor, *Ballet Review*, New York. Author of *Martha Graham* (1973), *The Complete Guide to Modern Dance* (1976), How to Enjoy Ballet (1978), *George Balanchine* (1983), *Dance: A Very Social History* (1986), and *The Rise and Fall and Rise of Modern Dance* (1990). **Essays:** Diana Adams; *Concerto Barocco*; *Interplay*; John Taras.

McLEAN, Adrienne L. Dance historian and writer, and doctoral candidate at Emory University, Atlanta, Georgia. Has published articles in *Dance Chronicle* and *Dancing Times*, among others. **Essays:** John Hart; Moira Shearer.

MEINERTZ, Alexander. Freelance dance writer. **Essay:** Vera Volkova.

MONEY, Keith. Writer, painter, and photographer. Author of *The Art of the Royal Ballet* (1964), *The Art of Margot Fonteyn* (1965), *The Royal Ballet Today* (1968), *Fonteyn: The Making of a Legend* (1973), and *Anna Pavlova: Her Life and Art* (1982). Also producer and director, full-length documentary film *Margot Fonteyn*, 1969. Adviser to *The International Dictionary of Ballet*. **Essays:** Margot Fonteyn; Christopher Gable; Anna Pavlova; David Wall.

MORRIS, Gay. Freelance writer and San Francisco correspondent, *Art in America*. Has published articles in *The New York Times*, *The Christian Science Monitor*, *Dance Magazine*, and *Dance and Dancers*. Editor of *DCA*, the quarterly publication of the Dance Critics Association. **Essays:** *Ode*; *Pulcinella*; San Francisco Ballet.

NÁDASI, Mia. Freelance dance and theatre writer. Has published articles in *Plays International*, and numerous pieces on Hungarian theatre. **Essays:** Hungarian National Ballet; Ferenc Nádasi.

NÄSLUND, Erik. Director, Dance Museum, Stockholm. Founding editor, *Dans*, and critic, *Dagens Nyheter*, *Svenska Dagbladet*; has been Swedish correspondent for *Dance News* and *Les Saisons de la danse*. Author of *Birgit Cullberg: A Biography* (1978), *Carina Ari: A Biography* (1984), *Nils Dardel: Biography of a Painter* (1988), and *Carl Milles: Biography of a Sculptor* (1991). Adviser to *The International Dictionary of Ballet*. **Essay:** Birgit Cullberg.

NEUFELD, James E. Professor of English, Trent University, Peterborough, Ontario. Regular reviewer for *Dance in Canada* and *The Journal of Canadian Studies*. Author of *History of National Ballet of Canada* (forthcoming). **Essays:** Celia Franca; National Ballet of Canada.

NICHOLAS, Larraine. Assistant Editor, *The International Dictionary of Ballet*. **Essays:** Les Ballets Russes de Monte Carlo; Phyllis Bedells; Ivo Cramér; *Miss Julie;* Royal Swedish Ballet; Elsa Marianne von Rosen.

NØRLYNG, Ole. Arts correspondent, *Berlingske Tidende*, Copenhagen, and writer on dance. **Essay:** *The Kermesse in Bruges*.

OBERZAUCHER, Alfred. Co-editor, *Tanzblätter*, Vienna, 1976-82, and dance writer and historian. **Essay:** Erika Hanka.

OU JIAN-PING. Director, Dance Research Institute, China National Arts Academy, Beijing. Member of the U.S. Dance Critics Association; has published articles in *American Dance Festival*, *Dance Magazine*, and *World Ballet and Dance Yearbook*. **Essays:** Central Ballet of China; *The Red Detachment of Women*.

PERLMUTTER, Donna. Los Angeles correspondent for *Dance Magazine*. Has published articles in *The Los Angeles Times*; was chief dance critic, *Los Angeles Herald Examiner*.

Author of *Shadowplay: The Life of Antony Tudor* (1991). **Essays:** Nora Kaye; Hugh Laing; Antony Tudor.

PIERSON, Rosalind M. Associate Professor, Department of Dance, Ohio State University, Columbus, Ohio. **Essay:** Vera Nemchinova.

PITT, Freda. Freelance critic and dance writer. Italian correspondent, *Dancing Times*; contributor to *Decca Book of Ballet*, *The Encyclopedia of Dance and Ballet* (1977), and *World Ballet and Dance* (1990 and 1991). **Essays:** Paolo Bortoluzzi; Patrick Dupond; *Excelsior*; Carla Fracci; Renée (Zizi) Jeanmaire; Aurel (von) Milloss; La Scala Ballet; Elisabetta Terabust.

POTTER, Michelle. President of ACT Branch, Australian Association for Dance Education, and teacher of dance and movement. Contributor to *A Companion to Theatre in Australia* and *Entertaining Australia*; has published articles in *Dance Chronicle*. **Essays:** Alexandre Benois; Giorgio de Chirico; Michel Larionov; Henri Matisse; Pablo Picasso.

PRITCHARD, Jane. Archivist, Rambert Dance Company, London, and English National Ballet, London. Member of Executive Committee of the Society for Dance Research. Author of *English National Ballet 1950-1990* (pamphlet, 1990) and contributor to *Les Ballets 1933* (1987); has published articles in *Dancing Times*, *Dance Research*, and others. **Essays:** Pearl Argyle; *La Bayadère*; *Le Corsaire*; Comte Etienne de Beaumont; André Derain; English National Ballet; Sophie Fedorovitch; Ekaterina Geltser; Sally Gilmour; John Gilpin; Marie Rambert; Galina Samsova; Peter Schaufuss; Nikolai Sergeyev; *La Valse*; Alexandre Volinine; Léon Woizikovsky.

RICHARDSON, Rachel S. Lecturer in Dance, Roehampton Institute of Higher Education, London. **Essays:** *Dark Elegies*; *Gala Performance*; *Jardin aux lilas*; *The Judgment of Paris*; *Konservatoriet*; *The Lady and the Fool*.

RIES, Frank W.D. Professor, Division of Dance, University of California, Santa Barbara. Has published numerous articles in *Dance Scope*, *Dance Chronicle*, *Dance Magazine*, *Ballet Review*, and *Dance Research Journal*. Author of *The Dance Theatre of Jean Cocteau* (1986), and contributor to *Lydia Lopokova* (ed. Milo Keynes, 1983). **Essays:** Jean Cocteau; Bronislava Nijinska; *Phèdre*; *Le Train bleu*.

RIETSTAP, Ine. Critic for *NRC Handelsblad*; editor of *Dansjaarboek*, Amsterdam, 1983-84 and 1984-85. Has published articles in *Septenrion* and *Revue de Culture Neerlandaise*. Author of *Alexandra Radius* (1982). **Essays:** Dutch National Ballet; Sonia Gaskell; *Monument for a Dead Boy*; Rudi van Dantzig; Toer van Schayk.

ROBERTSON, Allen. Dance Editor, *Time Out*, London, and dance correspondent for *The Daily Mail*. Author of *The Dance Handbook* (1988). **Essay:** Twyla Tharp.

ROBOZ, Agnes. Character dance teacher, choreographer, and writer. Co-author of *Dances of Eastern Europe* (with Maria Szentpàl, 1954). Has published articles in *Dansimperium Nederland*, *Das Tanz Journal*, *Das Tanzarchiv*, and *Tàncmüvészet*. Also editor of Hungarian transalations of *Russian Folk Dance Suite* (Moiseyev, 1952) and *Russian Folk Dances* (Okuneyeva, 1949). **Essays:** Zsuzsa Kun; Viktor Róna.

ROGERS, Amelia E. Composer and recording producer. **Essays:** Darius Milhaud; Erik Satie.

ROSS, Janice. Dance writer and historian. Faculty member, Dance Division, Stanford University, California. Has published articles in *Dance Magazine, The New York Times, Los Angeles Times, Horizon Magazine.* Author of *Dancing in the West* (1980), *Anna Halprin* (forthcoming); editor of *Why a Swan?* (1989), *On the Edge: Challenges to American Dance* (1990); contributor to *Androgyny Revisited* (edited by S. Matteo and M. Yalom, 1994). **Essay:** Leonid Yakobson.

RUTLEDGE, Richard W. Dance writer and teacher, New York. Has contributed to New York City Ballet *Newsletter*; also contributing editor for *National Horseman Magazine.* **Essays:** *Ballet Imperial; Danses Concertantes; In the Night*; Virginia Johnson; Allegra Kent; Francisco Moncion; Janet Reed; *La Sonnambula*; Léo Staats; Marianna Tcherkassky.

SAYERS, Lesley-Anne. Freelance writer and researcher. Has published articles in *Dance Theatre Journal, World Ballet and Dance, Dancing Times*, and the *Laban Papers*, volume I (1987). **Essays:** *Les Biches*; André Eglevsky; Théophile Gautier; Adeline Genée; *The Invitation*; Emma Livry; Alicia Markova; Norman Morrice; *Les Noces; Parade.*

SCHOLL, Tim. Assistant Professor, Department of Russian Studies, Mount Holyoke College, South Hadley, Massachusetts. Author of *Rebuilding the Academy: Twentieth Century Classicism and the Modernization of Russian Ballet* (dissertation, Yale University, 1991); and *From Petipa to Balanchine* (forthcoming). **Essay:** *The Sleeping Beauty.*

SCHØNBERG, Bent. Founding Editor, World Ballet and Dance, London. Author of *Harald Lander i Paris* (1952), *The First Steps* (1957), *Hans Brenaa: Multimenneske* (1989), *Hans Brenaa: Danish Balletmaster* (1990), and *Sylfiden: La Sylphide* (1990). Adviser to *The International Dictionary of Ballet.* **Essay:** Hans Brenaa.

SHUCART, Laura H. Assistant to the Curator, Harvard Theatre Collection. Has published articles in *The Newton Graphic*; contributor to *The Encyclopedia of World Biography.* **Essay:** *Schéhérazade.*

SIMONSEN, Majbritt. Freelance dance critic and cultural correspondent, including for *The Christian Daily*, Denmark. **Essays:** Frebjørn Bjørnsson; Niels Bjørn Larsen.

SIMPSON, Herbert M. Associate Professor, State University College, Geneseo, New York. Freelance theatre and dance critic; New York correspondent for *Dance Magazine* since 1974. Choreographer of the Geneseo Dance Ensemble; member of Board of Directors, Dance Critics Association, 1982-85. Has published articles in *Ballet News, Northwest Arts, Dance Connection, Theater Week, High Performance*, and *Soviet Ballet.* **Essay:** *Romeo and Juliet* (Cranko).

SINCLAIR, Janet. Freelance dance writer. Co-editor of *Ballet Today*, 1951-52, editor of *Ballet Jaarboek*, Holland, 1957-58. Co-author of *A Dictionary of Ballet Terms* (with Leo Kersley, 1952). Has published regular articles in *Dancing Times* and *Dance and Dancers*; also contributor to *The Encyclopedia of Dance and Ballet* (1977). **Essays:** *Apparitions; La Boutique fantasque*; Jack Carter; *Checkmate; Choreartium*; Julia Farron; *Les Femmes de bonne humeur; Gaîté Parisienne*; Beryl Grey;

Ronald Hynd; *Jeux d'enfants; The Lesson; Mam'zelle Angot;* Léonide Massine; Pamela May; *Les Presages; The Rake's Progress; Symphonie fantastique; Le Tricorne.*

SORLEY WALKER, Kathrine. Dance critic, historian, and writer. Ballet critic, *The Daily Telegraph*, London; has also published articles in *Dancing Times* and *The Stage.* Author of *Brief for Ballet* (1948), *Robert Helpmann* (1957), *Eyes on Mime* (1969), *Dance and its Creators* (1972), *De Basil's Ballets Russes* (1983), *Ninette de Valois: Idealist without Illusions* (1987); co-author of *The Royal Ballet: A Picture History* (with Sarah C. Woodcock, 1981); has also contributed to *Encyclopedia Britannica, Enciclopedia dello Spettacolo*, and *The Encyclopedia of Dance and Ballet* (1977). Adviser to *The International Dictionary of Ballet.* **Essays:** Jean Babilée; Alan Carter; Yvette Chauviré; Peter Darrell; Colonel Wassily de Basil; *The Dream*; John Field; Walter Gore; *Hamlet* (Helpmann); Constant Lambert; Keith Lester; David Lichine; *A Month in the Country*; Rudolf Nureyev; Filippo Taglioni; Marie Taglioni; *A Wedding Bouquet.*

SOURITZ, Elizabeth. Chief researcher and Head of Dance Division, Moscow Institute of History of the Arts. Author of *Vse o Balete* (All About Ballet; Russian ballet dictionary, 1966), and *The Art of Choreography in the 1920s* (1979), translated as *Soviet Choreographers in the 1920s* (1990); also contributor to *The Influence of Constructivism in the Soviet Union* (1980). Has published articles regularly in *Teatr* magazine; also contributor to *Balet Entsiklopedia* (1981). Adviser to *The International Dictionary of Ballet.* **Essays:** The Bolshoi Ballet; Kasyan Goleizovsky; Petr Gusev; Aleksandr Gorsky; *The Ice Maiden; Joseph the Beautiful; The Red Poppy*; Vasily Tikhomirov; Rostislav Zakharov.

SOWELL, Debra H. Adjunct Professor, Department of Dance, Brigham Young University. Has published articles in *Performance Magazine, Dance Chronicle*, and *Dance Critics Association Newsletter.* **Essays:** Willam Christensen; Lew Christensen.

STEIN, Louise. Freelance writer and researcher. Has contributed to *The Opera Guide* and *The International Dictionary of Opera*; also reviews for *Opera Now* magazine. **Essays:** *La Korrigane*; Louis Mérante; Jean-Philippe Rameau; Carolina Rosati; Henri Sauget; *Sylvia: ou, La Nymph de Diane.*

STONE, Claudia B. Freelance writer on dance. Author of *Gertrude Hoffman: Artist or Charlatan* (Masters thesis, 1987). **Essays:** Jean Börlin; Rolf de Maré; Les Ballets Suédois.

STUART, Otis. Freelance writer. Associate editor, *Dance Magazine*, 1985-89; editor, *New York Native*, 1985-87, and *Ballett International*, 1983-84. Has published articles in *Ballet Review, Ballet News, Boston Globe, International Herald and Tribune*, and *The New York Times.* **Essays:** Pierre Lacotte; Noëlla Pontois; Heather Watts.

STUPNIKOV, Igor. Professor, Leningrad University, and historian, Kirov/St. Petersburg Ballet. Author of *Young Dancers of the Leningrad Ballet* (1968), *Master Dancers 1917- 1973* (1974), *The World of Dance* (1982), *Oleg Vinogradov* (1984), *Leningrad Kirov Ballet* (1965 and 1976), and *Leningrad Ballet 1917-1987* (1988). **Essays:** Nina Anisimova; Igor Belsky; *The Bronze Horseman*; Vakhtang Chabukiani; Natalia Dudinskaya; *The Flames of Paris; Gayané*; Kirov Ballet; Irina Kolpakova; *The Legend of Love*; Elena Lukom; Galina Mezentseva; Alla

Osipenko; Vladimir Ponomarev; Aleksander Pushkin; Farukh Ruzimatov; Konstantin Sergeyev; Alla Sizova; Tatiana Vecheslova; Konstantin Zaklinsky.

SUTTON, Julia. Chairman, Deparment of Music History and Musicology, New England Conservatory. Editor of Arbeau's *Orchesography* (translated by Mary Stewart Evans, 1966); translator and editor of Fabritio Caroso's *Nobiltà di dame* (1988). **Essay:** Fabritio Caroso.

SWAN, Anna. Freelance writer. Regular contributor to *The Peak Magazine*, *The Music Magazine*, *Film Review*, and *Satellite Times*. **Essays:** Lesley Collier; Wayne Eagling.

SWIFT, Mary Grace. Professor, Loyola University, New Orleans. Author of *The Art of Dance in the USSR* (1968) and *A Loftier Flight: The Life and Accomplishments of Charles-Louis Didelot, Balletmaster* (1974). **Essay:** Charles-Louis Didelot.

TEMIN, Christine. Senior dance critic and visual arts critic, *The Boston Globe*. Has published articles in numerous journals, including *Ballet Review* and *Dance Magazine*. Adviser to *The International Dictionary of Ballet*. **Essay:** Mark Morris.

TÉRI, Evelyn. Professor of Dance at the Conservatoire, Vienna. Has published articles in *Dance Magazine*, *Ballet Journal*, and *Tanzarchiv*. **Essay:** Gyula Harangozò.

TERZIAN, Elizabeth. Early Dance historian and writer. Contributing Speaker, Annual Conference of Dance History Scholars, 1987. **Essays:** Louis de Cahusac; *The Creatures of Prometheus*; Salvatore Viganò.

THOM, Rose Anne. Professor of Dance, Sarah Lawrence College, Bronxville, New York. Regular contributor to *Dance Magazine*. **Essays:** *As Time Goes By*; Gelsey Kirkland; Kay Mazzo.

THORPE, Edward. Dance critic, *Evening Standard*, London. Author of *Creating a Ballet: MacMillan's Isadora* (1981), *Kenneth MacMillan: the Man and the Ballets* (1985), *Ballet Genius* (with Gillian Freeman, 1988). Adviser to *The International Dictionary of Ballet*. **Essays:** Anton Dolin; Anthony Dowell; Kenneth MacMillan; Merle Park; Lynn Seymour; Antoinette Sibley.

USUI, Kenji. Director of the Soviet Ballet Institute, Tokyo. Author of *The Nutcracker* (1950) and *The Sleeping Beauty* (1986); also translator of Arnold Haskell's *Ballet* (1950). **Essays:** Matsuyama Ballet; Yoko Morishita; Tokyo Ballet.

VAUGHAN, David. Archivist, Cunningham Dance Foundation, New York. Author of *Frederick Ashton and his Ballets* (1977) and co-editor (with Mary Clarke) of *The Encyclopedia of Dance* (1977). Also Associate Editor of *Ballet Review* and *The International Encyclopedia of Dance*. Adviser to *The International Dictionary of Ballet*. **Essays:** Merce Cunningham; Cynthia Harvey.

VELDUIS, Jenny. Freelance dance writer, publicist, and teacher. Co-author of *Ballet, Wat, Waar en Hoe* for the Dutch Ministry of Education (1984); has also published articles on ballet and training in various journals. **Essay:** Hans Snoek.

VOLLMER, Horst. Freelance dance critic. Author of *Auf die Spitze Getrieben-Tänzer Werden, Aber Wiez* (1988). Has published articles in *Stuttgarter Zeitung*, *Tagesspiegel*, and *Ballett International*. **Essays:** *Carmen* (Cranko); Richard Cragun; John Cranko; Hamburg Ballet; Birgit Keil; John Neumeier; Heinz Spoerli.

WARNER, Mary Jane. Associate Professor and Chair, Department of Dance, York University, Toronto. Founder of historical dance group Entreé à danse, 1971-73. Author of *Laban Notation Scores: An International Bibliography*, volumes I and II (1984 and 1988); also fellow, International Council of Kinetography Laban, and consultant, *Dictionary of Canadian Biography*. **Essays:** André Jean-Jacques Deshayes; Vincenzo Galeotti; Anna Heinel; Katti Lanner; Carlotta Zambelli.

WHITLEY-BAUGESS, Paige. Visiting Artist, Craven Community College, New Bern, North Carolina. Has contributed to the *Dance Notation Journal* and the Society of Dance Scholars Proceedings, 11th Annual Conference in 1988. **Essay and roles research:** Louis Dupré.

WHYTE, Sally. Assistant Editor of *Dance and Dancers* and Chairman of the Committee for the Dance of Israel, Europe Division. International Arts Correspondent for various publications including *Dance and Dancers*, *Music and Musicians*, *Arts Review*, and *Dance Magazine*. **Essays:** Alexander Grant; Milorad Miskovitch; Valeri Panov; Gert Reinholm; László Seregi.

WILLIS, Margaret. Freelance writer for dance publications in Europe, Australia and The Soviet Union. Contributing Editor to *Dance Magazine* and author of *Russian Ballet on Tour* (1989). **Essays:** Nina Ananiashvili; *The Golden Age*; *Ivan the Terrible*; Andris Liepa; Ekaterina Maximova; Igor Moiseyev; Irek Mukhamedov; Ludmila Semenyaka; *Spartacus*; Vladimir Vasiliev.

WINDREICH, Leland. Staff writer for *Vandance* and also a freelance writer. Edited *Dancing for de Basil: Letters to her Parents by Rosemary Deveson* (1989) and has contributed to the *Dance Chronicle*. **Essays:** Nicholas Beriozoff; Michael Kidd.

WOHLFAHRT, Hans Theodor. Editor, writer, and broadcaster on dance and music. Regular contributor to *Ballettjournal*, *Tanzarchiv*, *FonoForum*, *Neue Musikzeitung*, and many other international publications. **Essay:** Heinz Clauss.

WOODCOCK, Sarah C. Subject Specialist (Dance), responsible for Photographs and Costumes, Theatre Museum, Victoria andAlbert Museum, London. Co-author of *The Royal Ballet: A Picture History* (with Katherine Sorley Walker, 1981); author of the *Birmingham Royal Ballet* (1991). Has also contributed to *Dance Research* and *The Royal Ballet: The First 50 Years* by Alexander Bland. **Essays:** *Alma; ou, La Fille du feu*; Irina Baronova; Lilian Baylis; Christian Bérard; Svetlana Beriosova; Birmingham Royal Ballet; David Blair; *Cotillon*; Ninette de Valois; *Le Diable à Quatre*; Leslie Edwards; Violetta Elvin; *La Esmeralda*; Serge Grigoriev; Stephen Jefferies; Lydia Kyasht; Donald MacLeary; Oliver Messel; Alice Nikitina; *Ondine: ou, La Naïade*; Yurek Shabelevsky; Michael Somes; Lubov Tchernicheva; Doreen Wells.

WRIGHT, Martin. Lecturer in English, University of Warwick, and writer on dance. **Essays:** *Cinderella*; *Les Deux Pigeons*; *Enigma Variations*; *Facade*; *Illuminations*; *Marguerite and Armand*; *Monotones*; *The Nutcracker*; *Ondine (Ashton)*; *Onegin*; *Scènes de ballet*; *Symphonic Variations*; *The Two Pigeons*; Peter Wright.

PICTURE ACKNOWLEDGEMENTS

Nina Alovert, New York: Ananiashvili, Ayupova, Baryshnikov, Bujones, Dolgushin, Fadeyechev, Grigorovich, Gusev, Leningrad Maly Ballet, Andris Liepa, Osipenko, *Othello*, Ruzimatov, Konstantin Sergeyev, Shelest, *The Sleeping Beauty* (Kirov Ballet), Vecheslova, Vinogradov, *Yaroslavna*

Australian Ballet: Horsman, Pavane

Stichting Fotoarchief Maria Austria/Particam, Amsterdam: Gaskell

Bibliothèque Nationale, Paris: Allard, Beaugrand, Bozzacchi, Gardel, Nijinsky (*Le Pavillon d'Armide*), Noverre, *Parade*, *Le Pavillon d'Armide*, *Les Petits riens*, Picasso

University of Bristol Theatre Collection: Ballon, Lully, *L'Oiseau de feu* (Bakst)

British Library (by permission), London: Arbeau, Caroso, Delibes, *Les Fâcheux*, Feuillet, *La Source*, Tchaikovsky, Weaver

Judy Cameron, Los Angeles: Bruhn, Chabukiani, *Cinderella*, Denard, Dudinskaya, *La Fille mal gardée*, Fracci, *Gayané*, Kehlet, Mikhail Lavrovsky, Maris Liepa, *The Little Humpbacked Horse*, *The Miraculous Mandarin*, Nadezhda Pavlova, Plisetskaya, Sizova, Tennant, Timofeyeva, Zakharov

Castle Howard Costume Galleries, York: *Le Chant du rossignol*

Deutsches Theatermuseum, Munich: La Barbarina, Hilverding

Zoë Dominic, London: *La Baiser de la fée*, Blair, Evdokimova, *Marguerite et Armand*, Minkus, *Romeo and Juliet* (MacMillan)

English National Ballet, London: Carter (photograph Studio Lemaire, Amsterdam), Dolin, Gilpin, Grey, Lander, Markova

Harvard Theatre Collection, Harvard College Library: Fuoco, Guimard, Lee, Maywood

Het Nationale Ballet, Amsterdam: *Monument for a Dead Boy*, van Dantzig, van Schayk (photographs by Jorge Fatauros)

Hulton-Deutsch Collection, London: *Apparitions*, *Bourrée fantasque*, *The Cage*, *Carmen*, Chauviré, *Checkmate*, *Concerto Barocco*, Cranko, Daydé, Elvin, *Études*, Fonteyn, *Gaîté Parisienne*, *Interplay*, Jeanmaire, *Le Jeune homme et la mort*, *Job*, Kidd, Kriza, Laing, Lambert, Leonid Lavrovsky, LeClercq, Petit, Schanne, Vyroubova, *Symphonic Variations*, *Le Tricorne*, *Undertow*, *The Whims of Cupid* (photographs by Baron); Baronova, *Le Beau Danube*, de Chirico, *Choreartium*, Danilova, *Les Femmes de bonne humeur*, The

Green Table, Lichine, Nemchinova, Riabouchinska, Sokolova, Toumanova, Zorina (photographs by Sasha); Bedells, *Le Carnaval*, Cinderella, Dauberval, Field, Gautier, Grahn, *Hamlet*, *Jeux*, Kniaseff, Mordkin, *L'Oiseau de feu* (Fonteyn), *Paquita* (Mazilier), Pavlova (Dragonfly), *Les Quatre saisons*, *The Rake's Progress*, Rubinstein, Slavenska, Zambelli, Zucchi

Humberstone Collection, London: Turner

Joffrey Ballet, New York: Joffrey

Ilya B. Koltun, St. Petersburg: Asylmuratova, Kolpakova

Matsuyama Ballet Foundation: Matsuyama Ballet Company (photograph by A. Iijima)

Keith Money, Thetford, Norfolk: Gable, MacLeary, Nijinska, Nureyev, *Ondine* (Fonteyn), Sibley, Somes, *Sylvia*, *The Two Pigeons*, Wells

Musée des Beaux-Arts, Tours (Photographie Giraudon, Paris): Prévost

National Ballet of Canada: Kain, National Ballet of Canada

Netherlands Dance Theatre, The Hague: Harkarvy, Netherlands Dance Theatre, *Sinfonietta*, *Soldiers' Mass*

New York Public Library for the Performing Arts, Astor, Lenox and Tilden Foundations (Dance Collection): Adams (photograph by Walter E. Owen), *Agon*, Alonso, Andersen, Arpino, Ashley, Babilée, Béjart, Bernstein, *Billy The Kid*, Bjørnsson, Blum, Börlin, Bortoluzzi, Cecchetti, Chase, Copland, de Cuevas, de Maré, de Mille, *Les Demoiselles de la nuit*, Dollar, Eglevsky, *Fall River Legend*, *Fancy Free*, Fornaroli, Froman, Georgi, Golovine, Grigoriev, *Harlequinade*, Hayden, *Illuminations*, Kaye, Littlefield, Miskovitch, Moncion, Osato, Page, *Pillar of Fire*, Smith, Tallchief, Taylor, *Trinity*, Tudor, Villella, Wilson, Youskevitch

Novosti Photo Library, London: Ivanov

Pritchard Collection, London: Fedorova, Geltser, Genée, Idzikowski, Kshesinskaya, Kyasht, Lopokova, Lukom, Obukhov, Preobrazhenskaya, Trefilova, Volinine

Rambert Dance Company, London: Argyle, Chappell, *Dark Elegies*, Franca (photograph by Gilbert Adams), *Gala Performance*, Gilmour (photograph by Gilbert Adams), Gore, Howard, *Le Jardin aux lilas*, Rambert, Staff, Tetley, van Praagh

Réunion des musées nationaux, Paris / © DACS 1993: *Pulcinella*

Roger-Viollet, Paris: Bessy, Charrat, Cocteau, *Icare*, Pontois

Royal Library, Copenhagen: Beck, Bournonville, Margot Lander, *Napoli, La Ventana*

Royal Theatre Archives and Library, Copenhagen: *A Folk Tale, Kermesse in Bruges*

Royal Theatre, Copenhagen: Hübbe, Jeppesen, Kirsten Ralov, Royal Danish Ballet

Royal Winnipeg Ballet: Hart, Royal Winnipeg Ballet

San Francisco Ballet: Bolm, Christensen, Gregory, Reed, San Francisco Ballet, Tomasson

Society for Cultural Relations with the USSR, London: Bessmertnova, *The Fountain of Bakhchisarai*, Messerer, Nerina, *The Red Poppy, Romeo and Juliet* (Lavrovsky), Struchkova, Ulanova

Elizabeth Souritz, Moscow: *The Flames of Paris*, Gabovich, Goleizovsky, Gorsky, *The Heart of the Hills, The Ice Maiden*, Lopukhov, Maximova (photograph by Alexander Trubitzyn), Semenova, Vasiliev (photograph by Alexander Trubitzyn)

Leslie E. Spatt, London: *Afternoon of A Faun, Anastasia, Apollo*, Ashton, Beriosova, Beriozoff, Bintley, *Birthday Offering*, Bussell, Chadwick, Collier, *The Concert, Concerto, Coppélia, Le Coq d'or, Le Corsaire*, Cragun, Dance Theatre of Harlem, *Don Quixote*, Donn, Dowell, *The Dream*, Dupont, Durante, Eagling, Edwards, *Elite Syncopations*, English National Ballet, *Enigma Variations, Facade*, Farron, Ferri, *La Fête étrange*, Forsythe, *The Four Temperaments*, Gielgud, *Giselle* (Royal Ballet), *The Golden Age, Graduation Ball*, Grant, Guillem, Haydée, *Las Hermanas*, Hightower, Hynd, *The Invitation, Ivan The Terrible*, Johnson, Keil, Kirkland, *Konservatoriet*, Kylián, Lacotte, *Lady of the Camellias, The Lady and the Fool, Laurencia, Legend of Love*, Lepeshinskaya, MacMillan, Madsen, Makarova, *Mam'zelle Angot, Manon, Mayerling*, Mezentseva, *Monotones, A Month in the Country*, Morishita, Mukhamedov, Neary, *Les Noces, Onegin*, Page, *Paquita*, Park, *Les Patineurs, Pineapple Poll*, Platel, Poulenc, *Prince Igor, The Prince of the Pagodas, The Prodigal Son*, Prokovsky, Raymonda, *Requiem, Romeo and Juliet* (Ashton), Samsova, *Scènes de ballet*, Schaufuss, Semenyaka, Semizorova, Seymour, *Shadowplay, The Sleeping Beauty* (Royal Ballet), *Song of the Earth, Song of a Wayfarer*, *Spartacus, Le Spectre de la rose*, Spoerli, *Square Dance, Suite en blanc, Swan Lake, Les Sylphides* (Birmingham Royal Ballet), *Symphony in C, The Taming of the Shrew*, Terabust, *Theme and Variations, La Valse*, van Manen, Vangsaae, *Voluntaries*, Wall, *A Wedding Bouquet*, Wright, Zaklinsky

Martha Swope Photography Inc., New York: *Aureole*, Balanchine, *Ballet Imperial, La Bayadère*, Bocca, Bolender, *Bugaku*, Butler, Calegari, Chryst, Cunningham, d'Amboise, *Dances at a Gathering, Danses Concertantes, Davidsbündlertänze, Drink To Me Only*, Farrell, Feld, Harvey, *Jewels*, Kent, Kirstein, *The Leaves Are Fading, Liebeslieder Walzer*, Magallanes, Martins, Mazzo, McBride, *A Midsummer Night's Dream, Miss Julie*, Mitchell, Morris, *Mozartiana, The Nutcracker, Orpheus, Pierrot lunaire, Push Comes To Shove*, Robbins, *La Sonnambula*, Stravinsky, *La Sylphide* (ABT), Taras, Tcherkassky, Tharp, van Hamel, Verdy, *Vienna Waltzes, Violin Concerto*, Vladimirov, von Aroldingen, Watts

Theatre Museum, Victoria and Albert Museum, London: *L'Après-midi d'un faune*, Baccelli, *Ballet de la nuit, Ballet Comique de la Reine*, Ballets Russes de Monte Carlo, Beaujoyeulx, *Les Biches*, Blasis, *La Boutique fantasque*, Bruce (photograph by Anthony Crickmay), Camargo, *Cléopâtre, Cotillon, Daphnis et Chloé*, de Valois, Diaghilev, *The Dying Swan*, Elssler, *La Esmeralda*, Fedorovitch, *Flore et Zéphire*, Fokine, Franklin, *Giselle* (Carlotta Grisi), Gontcharova, Helpmann, *Jeux d'enfants*, Karsavina, Larionov, Legnani, Lifar, Livry, Massine, May, Mazilier, Mérante, Messel (photograph by Houston Rogers), Nijinsky (*Le Dieu bleu*), Nikitina, *Ode, Pas de Quatre*, Pavlova (*Chopiniana*), Pécourt, *La Peri*, Perrot, *Les Présages*, Rameau, Ravel, *Les Rendezvous*, Royal Ballet, *Le Sacre du printemps*, Sallé, Schollar, Nicholas Sergeyev, Subligny, *La Sylphide* (Taglioni), *Les Sylphides* (1911), Tchernicheva, Auguste and Gaetano Vestris, Vilzak

Thyssen-Bornemisza Collection , Lugano: *Schéhérazade*

Beryl Towbin, New York: *Serenade*

Wadsworth Atheneum, Hartford. The Ella Gallup Sumner and Mary Catlin Sumner Collection: Bakst, Benois, Bérard, Derain, *Petrushka*, Tchelitchev

Sally Whyte, London: Panov